ENCYCLOPAEDIA JUDAICA

ENCYCLOPAEDIA JUDAICA

SECOND EDITION

VOLUME 12
Kat–Lie

Fred Skolnik, *Editor in Chief*
Michael Berenbaum, *Executive Editor*

MACMILLAN REFERENCE USA
An imprint of Thomson Gale, a part of The Thomson Corporation

IN ASSOCIATION WITH
KETER PUBLISHING HOUSE LTD., JERUSALEM

THOMSON
GALE

Detroit • New York • San Francisco • New Haven, Conn. • Waterville, Maine • London

THOMSON
GALE

ENCYCLOPAEDIA JUDAICA, Second Edition

For more information, contact
Macmillan Reference USA
An imprint of Thomson Gale
27500 Drake Rd.
Farmington Hills, MI 48331-3535
Or you can visit our internet site at
http://www.gale.com

LIBRARY OF CONGRESS CATALOGING-IN-PUBLICATION DATA

Encyclopaedia Judaica / Fred Skolnik, editor-in-chief ; Michael Berenbaum, executive editor. -- 2nd ed.
v. cm.
Includes bibliographical references and index.
Contents: v.1. Aa-Alp.
ISBN 0-02-865928-7 (set hardcover : alk. paper) -- ISBN 0-02-865929-5 (vol. 1 hardcover : alk. paper) -- ISBN 0-02-865930-9 (vol. 2 hardcover : alk. paper) -- ISBN 0-02-865931-7 (vol. 3 hardcover : alk. paper) -- ISBN 0-02-865932-5 (vol. 4 hardcover : alk. paper) -- ISBN 0-02-865933-3 (vol. 5 hardcover : alk. paper) -- ISBN 0-02-865934-1 (vol. 6 hardcover : alk. paper) -- ISBN 0-02-865935-X (vol. 7 hardcover : alk. paper) -- ISBN 0-02-865936-8 (vol. 8 hardcover : alk. paper) -- ISBN 0-02-865937-6 (vol. 9 hardcover : alk. paper) -- ISBN 0-02-865938-4 (vol. 10 hardcover : alk. paper) -- ISBN 0-02-865939-2 (vol. 11 hardcover : alk. paper) -- ISBN 0-02-865940-6 (vol. 12 hardcover : alk. paper) -- ISBN 0-02-865941-4 (vol. 13 hardcover : alk. paper) -- ISBN 0-02-865942-2 (vol. 14 hardcover : alk. paper) -- ISBN 0-02-865943-0 (vol. 15: alk. paper) -- ISBN 0-02-865944-9 (vol. 16: alk. paper) -- ISBN 0-02-865945-7 (vol. 17: alk. paper) -- ISBN 0-02-865946-5 (vol. 18: alk. paper) -- ISBN 0-02-865947-3 (vol. 19: alk. paper) -- ISBN 0-02-865948-1 (vol. 20: alk. paper) -- ISBN 0-02-865949-X (vol. 21: alk. paper) -- ISBN 0-02-865950-3 (vol. 22: alk. paper)
1. Jews -- Encyclopedias. I. Skolnik, Fred. II. Berenbaum, Michael, 1945-
DS102.8.E496 2007
909'.04924 -- dc22

2006020426

ISBN-13:

978-0-02-865928-2 (set)
978-0-02-865929-9 (vol. 1)
978-0-02-865930-5 (vol. 2)
978-0-02-865931-2 (vol. 3)
978-0-02-865932-9 (vol. 4)
978-0-02-865933-6 (vol. 5)
978-0-02-865934-3 (vol. 6)
978-0-02-865935-0 (vol. 7)
978-0-02-865936-7 (vol. 8)
978-0-02-865937-4 (vol. 9)
978-0-02-865938-1 (vol. 10)
978-0-02-865939-8 (vol. 11)
978-0-02-865940-4 (vol. 12)
978-0-02-865941-1 (vol. 13)
978-0-02-865942-8 (vol. 14)
978-0-02-865943-5 (vol. 15)
978-0-02-865944-2 (vol. 16)
978-0-02-865945-9 (vol. 17)
978-0-02-865946-6 (vol. 18)
978-0-02-865947-3 (vol. 19)
978-0-02-865948-0 (vol. 20)
978-0-02-865949-7 (vol. 21)
978-0-02-865950-3 (vol. 22)

This title is also available as an e-book
ISBN-10: 0-02-866097-8
ISBN-13: 978-0-02-866097-4
Contact your Thomson Gale representative for ordering information.
Printed in the United States of America

10 9 8 7 6 5 4 3 2

TABLE OF CONTENTS

Initial letter "K" for Karolus (Charlemagne), from the opening of Book 25 of Vincent of Beauvais, Speculum Historiale, *Metten, S. Germany, 1332. Munich Bayerische Staatsbibliothek, Cod. lat. 8201c, fol. 9v.*

KAT-KZ

KATCHEN, JULIUS (1926–1969), pianist. Born in New Jersey, Katchen studied with David Saperton in New York. He made his first public appearance at the age of ten and his debut with the Philadelphia Orchestra in 1937. He played with the New York Philharmonic and at the age of 12 gave his first New York recital. Katchen gave up his promising career to study philosophy and English literature at Haverford College. Subsequently awarded a French government fellowship (1945), he settled in Paris, which became his home for the rest of his life. He became a major figure on the international music scene, noted for his powerful musical intelligence and a virtuoso technique, and toured as a soloist, recitalist, and chamber music artist. He was well known for his chamber music collaborations with violinist Joseph Suk and cellist Janos Starker. Katchen maintained a broad repertoire extending from the Classical era to contemporary music, but was most closely associated with Brahms. His death from cancer at the age of 42 robbed the world of a pianist who could convey the feeling that music is the richest and most inclusive reflection of human experience.

BIBLIOGRAPHY: Grove online; MGG[2]; *Baker's Biographical Dictionary* (1997); N. Rorem. *Critical Affairs – A Composer's Journal* (1970); C. Meher-Homji, "A Life on the Edge (Julius Katchen)," in: *International Piano Quarterly,* 3 (Autumn 1999), 38–42.

[Naama Ramot (2nd ed.)]

°**KATKOV, MIKHAIL NIKIFOROVICH** (1818–1887), journalist, publicist, and editor of the influential newspaper *Moskovskiya Vedomosti.* In his youth, Katkov was associated with the revolutionary circles of Herzen and Bakunin. From the 1840s, he was attracted by the ideas of British liberalism, but after the Polish revolt (1863), he joined the camp of the extremist Conservatives. He nevertheless remained faithful to his liberal principles with respect to the Jewish problem. At the height of the anti-Jewish riots (1881–82), he condemned the "sudden mobilization against the Jews" which was due to "malicious devisers of evil" who deliberately sought to confuse the consciousness of the nation and encourage it to solve the Jewish problem, not by reasoning and enquiry, but with the assistance of "upraised fists."

BIBLIOGRAPHY: *Nedelnaya Khronika Voskhoda*, no. 30 (1887).

[Yehuda Slutsky]

KATOWICE (Ger. **Kattowitz**), capital of Katowice province Silesia, part of Prussia until 1921. Information regarding Jewish communities in the vicinity of Katowice goes back to 1733. At the end of the 18th century certain Jews leased the iron foundries in the suburb in Bogucice (Ger. Bogutschuetz). The Jews were expelled from the nearby localities in 1781, but they were permitted to return in 1787. In 1840 there were 12 Jews in the city. Following the industrial development of the city, Jews played an increasing role in its economic life. The Jewish population numbered 102 in 1855, and in 1867, when Katowice was declared a city, 624; it numbered 2,216 in 1899, 2,979 in 1910, and 9,000 in 1932. The non-Jewish population grew at a much faster rate, rising from 14,000 in 1888 to 130,645 in 1930.

An independent community was organized in 1866. From 1850 religious services were held in prayer-houses. The first synagogue was built in 1862 (expanded in 1880) and a new one was built in 1900. A cemetery was opened in 1868, and the first community rabbi was appointed in 1872. Communal activities expanded as the community grew. The Ḥovevei Zion conference was held in Katowice in 1884 (see *Kattowitz Conference). The Jewish communal organization developed considerably after World War I when Bruno Altmann headed the community from 1919. A new community building was inaugurated in 1937 which served as a center for cultural and organizational activities. The community paid much attention to Jewish education, maintaining a school, named after Berek *Joselewicz, and a Hebrew school, established in 1935.

Antisemitic agitation in Katowice increased during the 1930s. In 1937 there were pogroms, and bombs were thrown into shops owned by Jews. As most of the Jews there were tradesmen, their economic position suffered severely as a result of the anti-Jewish *boycott. The Polish artisans' organizations introduced "Aryan" articles into their regulations, and the Jewish artisans were expelled: the barbers' association introduced an Aryan article in 1937, and the tailors' association and others introduced similar articles in 1938. As a result of antisemitism many Jews left Katowice, and by 1939, 8,587 remained (6.3% of the total population). Rabbis Kalman Chameides and Mordechai Vogelmann served the community from 1928 until just before the Holocaust. In 1937 Rabbi Chameides was appointed adviser on Jewish affairs at the municipal law courts.

[Shimshon Leib Kirshenboim]

Holocaust Period and Modern Period

The Germans entered the city on September 3, 1939, and found a refugee-swelled Jewish population of 11,000–12,000 there. With many fleeing, 3,500 remained in October. Further flight and expulsions left 900 at the end of the year. These were expelled to other localities in May-June 1940, mostly to Chrzanow, and shared the fate of the local Jews

After World War II about 1,500 Jews (almost all of whom were from other parts of Poland and had spent the war years in the Soviet Union) settled in Katowice, and a Jewish Commitee for Upper Silesia was established there. A chapter of the Communist-led Jewish Cultural and Social Society was active until 1967, when the Polish authorities launched their antisemitic campaign. As a result of official hostility, almost all the Jews in Katowice left Poland.

[Stefan Krakowski]

BIBLIOGRAPHY: J. Cohn, *Geschichte der Synagogen-Gemeinde Kattowitz…* (1900); A. Szefer, *Miejsca stracen Ludnscicywilnej wojewodztwa katowickiego, 1939–1945* (1969); Yad Vashem Archives. **ADD. BIBLIOGRAPHY:** P. Maser et al., *Juden in Oberschlesien I* (1992), 107–21; W. Majowski (ed.), *100 Jahre Stadt Kattowitz 1865–1965*.

KATSH (Katz), ABRAHAM ISAAC (1908–1998), U.S. educator, author, and archivist. Katsh was born in Indura (Amdur), Poland, and immigrated to the United States in 1925. He received a B.S. from New York University in mathematics in 1931 and a J.D. from the law school in 1936. In 1933, he persuaded NYU to allow him to offer a course in modern Hebrew, the first such course at a U.S. university. There, he founded the Jewish Culture Foundation, the Department of Hebrew Language and Education, and the Institute of Hebrew Studies. A chair in his name was established at NYU's Hebrew studies department in 1957. Katsh received a Ph.D. from *Dropsie College in 1942 and, in 1967, was elected president of Dropsie College (later University).

Katsh was a wide-ranging scholar. As a student, he translated Einstein's theory of relativity into Hebrew. In 1954 he published *Judaism in Islam*, an analysis of biblical and talmudic backgrounds of the Koran and its commentaries. During a visit to the Soviet Union and Hungary in 1956, Katsh discovered what he called a "bibliophile's paradise," many thousands of Hebrew manuscripts that were being stored in various libraries. He arranged for the microfilming of several thousand manuscripts that had been hidden from Western view since the Russian Revolution of 1917. One of the collections contained medieval manuscripts on all aspects of Judaica, including biblical commentaries, law, poetry, and liturgy. Another collection consisted of a quarter of a million pages and scraps of paper from the Cairo *Genizah*. Among them were 427 fragments of Talmud manuscripts – dating from the 7th through the 11th centuries – that corrected some inaccurate interpretations of talmudic material. During trips in the late 1950s and 1960s, during the height of the Cold War, he persuaded the Soviet authorities to microfilm additional manuscripts in libraries in Moscow and Leningrad, on the basis of which he published *Catalogue of Hebrew Manuscripts Preserved… (On Microfilm) in the U.S.S.R.* (2 vols., 1957–58); *The Antonin Genizah in Leningrad* (1963); *Ginze Mishnah* (1971), a study of 149 *Genizah* fragments dating from the 9th to the 12th centuries; *Ginze Talmud Bavli*, a companion volume of 178 fragments from the Antonin Collection (1975, 1979). He also published a collection of 50 Hebrew poems of the Spanish period. For his works on the *Genizah*, Katsh was awarded the Rabbi Kaniel Prize of the Municipality of Haifa in June 1979.

In 1963, Katsh learned of a diary written by a Hebrew school principal, Chaim Aron *Kaplan in the Warsaw ghetto that had been smuggled out of the ghetto and had been hidden for more than two decades. Katsh translated the diary, obtained missing volumes, and published it as *Scroll of Agony: The Warsaw Diary of Chaim A. Kaplan* (1965).

Katsh published a number of essays on Hebrew and Jewish studies in U.S. universities. In 1957 he founded the National Association of Professors of Hebrew in American Universities. In addition to the books listed above, Katsh edited an anthology, *Bar Mitzvah, Illustrated* (1955), and *Biblical Heritage of American Democracy* was published in 1979. He retired from his posts at Dropsie and NYU in 1976.

BIBLIOGRAPHY: T. Naamani et al. (eds.), *Dōrōn; Hebraic Studies (Essays in Honor of Abraham I. Katsh*; 1965); Y. Ben-Josef (ed.), *Sefer Avraham Yiẓḥak Katsh* (1969); J. Komlosh, in: *Bitzaron*, 60 (1969), 158–64.

[Ethan Katsch (2nd ed.)]

KATTAN, NAÏM (1928–), writer and critic. Naïm Kattan was born into a low-income family in *Baghdad, Iraq. He studied at a Jewish elementary school and then at a Muslim secondary school. His mother tongue was Arabic, and his first literary efforts were in that language. He also learned Hebrew, English, and French. In 1946, he left for Paris, where he enrolled in literature courses at the Sorbonne. In 1954, he moved to Montreal ("My third 'birthplace'… a city that contains all the others, where all nationalities, religions, and languages exist, but which needs a common tongue – French – for people to communicate with each other.") French then became his main vehicle of literary expression. Kattan published numerous books: essays, novels, plays, and short-story collections. *Adieu, Babylone* (1975), *Les Fruits arrachés* (1977), and *La Fiancée promise* (1983) are transposed autobiographical novels centered, respectively, in each of Kattan's three "birthplaces." In the first, he uses the name "Babylone" to designate the ancient state where Jews, originally captives, lived for more than 2,000 years, but from which virtually all eventually left. Kattan's writing is concerned with explaining differences between Oriental and Occidental societies, inter-ethnic relations, migration, and integration. He believes that the various components of his own hetero-cultural identity all have validity and importance. Kattan quickly became part of the majority Francophone cultural milieu after moving to Montreal a half-century ago. He founded the *Bulletin du Cercle juif*, the first French-language Jewish publication in Quebec. He was a book reviewer for the Montreal daily, *Le Devoir*, for many decades, often discussing books on Arabic culture. In 1967, he was named first director of the literature section of the Canada Council for the Arts. After leaving that post in 1991, he became associate professor at the Université du Québec à Montréal. Kattan won many distinctions. He is a member of the Order of Canada, of the Académie des lettres du Québec and a fellow of the Royal Society of Canada. He won the Prix Québec Paris for *Le Réel et le théâtral* (1971). In 1989, he was named Officier de l'Ordre des arts et lettres de France, and in 1990, Chevalier national du Québec. In 2004, Kattan was given Quebec's highest literary honor, the Prix Athanase-David, for the corpus of his work. From 1994, he presided over the jury of Le Grand Prix de la Ville de Montréal.

BIBLIOGRAPHY: *Voix et images* (Montréal) 41:1 (Fall 1985), 7–54.

[Ben-Zion Shek (2nd ed.)]

KATTINA, JACOB (second half of 19th century), rabbi and author. Kattina served as *dayyan* in Huszt, Carpathian Russia, in the *bet din* of Moses *Schick (1849–79). Kattina wrote two works which he published anonymously. The first, *Raḥamei ha-Av*, was first published in Czernowitz in 1865 and has been frequently reprinted. In 1936 it was published in Marghita, Transylvania, with the notes of Solomon Zalman Ehrenreich (2nd ed. Jerusalem, 1950 and 1958), and in 1939, in Djerba, with the Judeo-Arabic translation of Ḥayyim Houri. The work has 58 chapters on moral improvement and in the introduction, the author says: "I called this booklet *Raḥamei ha-Av* ["Mercy of the Father"] for it is true mercy for a man to chasten his child to lead him in the ways of God, this being the sole purpose of man." The second work, *Korban he-Ani*, homilies on the Pentateuch in a kabbalistic and ḥasidic vein, was published in Lemberg in 1872 and 1882.

BIBLIOGRAPHY: J.J.(L.) Greenwald (Grunwald), *Zikkaron la-Rishonim* (1909), 19; J. Cohen, in: KS, 33 (1957/58), 136.

[Naphtali Ben-Menahem]

KATTOWITZ CONFERENCE, a convention of *Ḥibbat Zion societies from various countries held in Kattowitz (i.e. *Katowice, then in Germany) in 1884. With the activation of the movement to settle Ereẓ Israel in the early 1880s and the establishment of Ḥibbat Zion societies in various countries, the need to create a unifying and coordinating center for the early Zionist activities was expressed. The only country in which a central committee functioned was Romania. An attempt to found a central committee for Russia, made at a small conference in Bialystok in 1883, produced no results; other attempts also failed. In the end L. *Pinsker, M.L. *Lilienblum, H. Ẓ. *Schapira, M. *Mandelstamm, and others took the initiative to convene a conference. Following the suggestion of David *Gordon, Kattowitz was selected as the site for the conference. Its date was fixed for Oct. 27, 1884, the 100th anniversary of the birth of Moses *Montefiore, at the suggestion of the Warsaw society. The conference was intended primarily for the Ḥibbat Zion societies in Russia, as the movement in Romania had greatly weakened and there were very few Ḥibbat Zion societies in other countries. As delegates from Russia encountered difficulties in arriving at the appointed time, the opening of the conference was postponed until November 6.

Twenty-two delegates came to the conference from Russia and ten from other countries (one from France, one from Romania, two from England, and the rest from Germany). At the request of the Warsaw society, many other groups submitted proposals for organization and action. Schapira, who could not attend, sent a telegram to point out the importance of establishing financial institutions, including a general Jewish fund, whose primary task would be to redeem land in Ereẓ Israel. In his newspaper, *Ha-Ẓefirah*, N. *Sokolow published concrete proposals for activities and stressed the necessity to develop not only agriculture, but commerce, the trades, and industry in Ereẓ Israel. Pinsker was elected chairman of the conference; S. *Mohilewer, honorary chairman; A. *Zederbaum, the editor of *Ha-Meliẓ*, deputy chairman; S.P. *Rabbinowitz, Hebrew secretary.

In his opening address, Pinsker stressed the necessity for the Jews to return to work on the land, but he did not mention the striving for national renascence and political independence, with a view to winning over the Jews of Western Europe, who opposed the concept of Jewish nationalism. At the proposal of Pinsker the conference established an institution named Agudat Montefiore to promote farming among the Jews and support Jewish settlement in Ereẓ Israel. A decision was reached to send immediately 10,000 francs to *Petaḥ Tikvah and 2,000 rubles for *Yesud ha-Ma'alah. It was also decided to send a reliable emissary to Ereẓ Israel to investigate the standing of the colonies there. Nineteen members were elected to the central committee, including Pinsker, Mohilewer, K.Z. *Wissotzky, J.L. *Kalischer (the son of Ẓevi Hirsch *Kalischer), M. Mandelstamm, Ch. Wollrauch, and others. At the first meeting of the central committee, which took place at the time of the conference, it was decided that two committees, one in Odessa and the other in Warsaw, should temporarily manage the affairs of the organization. The central committee, to be headed by Pinsker, was to reside temporarily in Odessa, and a subcommittee was to be established in Warsaw, subject to the authority of Pinsker. Kalischer announced his presentation of land acquired by his father near Rachel's Tomb to the central committee.

Incomplete versions of the proceedings were published in German and in Hebrew. S.P. Rabbinowitz, who was responsible for the Hebrew text, permitted himself to add from memory or to alter the text out of his desire to bestow a nationalistic flavor on the proceedings. The press that was opposed to the movement found discrepancies between the two sessions and Pinsker made Rabbinowitz publish an apology in *Ha-Meliẓ* (no. 13, 1885). The Kattowitz Conference laid the foundations for the organization of the Ḥibbat Zion societies, especially in Russia. The few Ḥibbat Zion societies outside Russia, especially in Serbia, London, Germany, Paris, and New York, considered the leadership chosen in Kattowitz the center of the movement and maintained steady contact with it.

BIBLIOGRAPHY: *Road to Freedom, Writings and Addresses by Leo Pinsker* (1944); N. Sokolow, *Hibbath Zion* (Eng., 1935), index; A. Druyanow, *Ketavim le-Toledot Ḥibbat Ẓiyyon ve-Yishuv Ereẓ Yisrael*, 1 (1919), 269–318; L. Taubes, *Asefat Kattowitz* (1920); J.L. Apel, *Be-Tokh Reshit ha-Teḥiyyah* (1936), 171–95; I. Klausner, *Be-Hitorer Am* (1962), index; M. Yoeli (ed.), *J.L. Pinsker Mevasser ha-Teḥiyyah ha-Le'ummit* (1960), 107–12.

[Israel Klausner]

KATZ, ALBERT (Heb. pseudonym א"ך איש הרוח); (1858–1923), writer, journalist, and Zionist. Katz, who was born in Lodz, served as teacher and preacher at Fuerstenwalde, near Berlin (1883–86). Katz and W. *Bambus founded the periodical *Serubabel* (1886–88), which advocated colonization in Ereẓ Israel. In 1890 Katz joined the editorial staff of the **Allgemeine Zeitung des Judentums* and eventually succeeded G. Karpeles and L. Geiger as chief editor. He was co-founder and secretary of the Verband der Vereine fuer Juedische Geschichte und Literatur and edited its *Jahrbuch* (JJGL) with Karpeles. Katz's published books include: *Der Jude und das Land seiner Vaeter* (also published in Hebrew; 1883); *Der Wahre Talmudjude* (against *Rohling, 1893, 1928[4]); *Die Juden im Kaukasus* (1894); *Die Juden in China* (1900); and *Christen und Juden als Foerderer der hebraeischen Sprache* (1907). He also wrote some short stories and translated I.B. *Levinsohn's *Efes Damim* (against the blood *libel) into German as *Die Blutluege* (1892).

[Nathan Michael Gelber]

KATZ, ALEPH (pseudonym of **Morris Abraham Katz**; 1898–1969), Yiddish poet. Born in Mlyniv (Mlinov, Volhynia), Katz attended a Russian school before immigrating to the U.S. in 1913. He worked at various jobs while attending City College (New York). His first poems were in Hebrew, but in 1917 he published his first Yiddish poem in *Der Groyser Kundes*. Encouraged by Jacob *Glatstein, he published his Yiddish lyrics in organs of the *In-Zikh movement and in the journal, *Zangen*, which he founded and edited in 1920, as well as in dozens of other journals. His first two volumes, *A Mayse fun Yam* ("A Tale of the Sea," 1925) and *Akertsayt* ("Plowing Time," 1929), were influenced by the American Imagists and the Yiddish Inzikhists. Following his first pamphlet, *Dos Telerl fun Himl* ("Heavenly Saucer," 1934), he found his own original tone in the lyrics of *Amol Iz Geven a Mayse* ("Once There Was a Story," 1944), written under the impact of the Holocaust, and in his play *Gut Morgn Alef* ("Good Morning, Aleph," 1950), which had as its *dramatis personae* the scattered but indestructible letters of the Hebrew alphabet. Katz reaffirmed his links with the Jewish people by writing for the children of Yiddish schools. Under the influence of *Naḥman of Bratslav's narrative approach, Katz often hints at a reality beyond observed phenomena, at a mystic realm which can be best expressed in allegorical symbols. His works also include *Di Emese Khasene* ("The True Wedding," 1967), *Der Morgnshtern* ("The Morning Star," 1975), and children's books such as *Kholem Aleykhem* ("Dreams Be with You," 1958). Katz was also a Yiddish editor of the Jewish Telegraphic Agency for more than forty years.

BIBLIOGRAPHY: LNYL, 4 (1961), 344–7; B. Rivkin, *Yidishe Dikhter in Amerike* (1959), 295–302; J. Glatstein, *In Tokh Genumen* (1960), 335–9; S. Bickel, *Shrayber fun Mayn Dor* (1965), 95–9.

[Sol Liptzin / Jerold C. Frakes (2nd ed.)]

KATZ, ALEX (1927–), U.S. painter, sculptor, and printmaker. Katz primarily painted in the traditional mode of portraiture, often eschewing perspective and the psychological interpretation of his models, while flattening bright colors. Born in Brooklyn to newly immigrated parents from Eastern Europe, Katz joined the Navy a month before the end of World War II. After a year in the Pacific he returned home and began his art studies, initially at the Cooper Union Art School (1946–49) training to be a commercial artist. This early exposure to the style of billboards, magazine advertisements, and comic strips would affect his later artistic production. Katz decided to focus on the fine arts in his last year, at which time he studied with, among others, the Jewish painter Morris Kantor. He also took summer art classes at the Skowhegan School of Painting and Sculpture in Maine (1949, 1950), honing his skills and his interest in working from nature. During 1950–51 Katz painted many landscapes in a loose, sketchy style encouraged by Jackson Pollock's allover canvases.

In the late 1950s Katz began painting his wife, Ada, as he started to develop his mature style and to discover his overriding interest in portraiture. The following year he also made his first cut-outs – freestanding, double-sided figures painted on aluminum or wood. By the early 1960s Katz's canonical style of large-scale, cropped portraits painted with sharp, crisp contours and employing strident colors began to evolve (e.g., *The Red Smile*, 1963, Whitney Museum of American Art). Painted with thinned-out oil paint, Katz explored form and color much as the Fauvist Henri Matisse did in the earlier part of the century. Unlike social realist painters of a generation earlier – including Raphael, Moses, and Isaac *Soyer – who emphasized their humanist intentions, Katz repeatedly asserts that these works and others are more about style than content.

While continuing to paint portraits, Katz also made a series of enlarged flower paintings that press to the front of the picture plane, filling up the canvas (1966–67). Beginning in 1960, Katz designed sets and costumes for choreographer Paul Taylor's dance performances in addition to sets for other productions. His set for Kenneth Koch's off-Broadway play *George Washington Crossing the Delaware* incorporated around 20 almost life-size wood cutouts, including Washington in his rowboat, army officers, and props such as a cherry tree all rendered in Katz's straightforward style. Starting in 1965, Katz began making prints, some of which were executed as illustrations for published books of poetry by leading writers such as John Ashbery.

Over the years Katz experimented with including background details omitted in earlier canvas portraits, painting group portraits often of family and friends in social situations, and landscapes.

BIBLIOGRAPHY: N.P. Maravell, *Alex Katz: The Complete Prints* (1983); R. Marshall, *Alex Katz* (1986); S. Hunter, *Alex Katz* (1992); I. Sandler, *Alex Katz: A Retrospective* (1998).

[Samantha Baskind (2nd ed.)]

KATZ, BENZION (1875–1958), Hebrew journalist and writer. Born in Daugi (Vilna district), Katz began to contribute to *Ha-Ẓefirah* at an early age. At the invitation of Baron David *Guenzburg, he went to St. Petersburg in order to engage in talmudic research, the results of which he later published in the journal *Ha-Shilo'aḥ*. He also conducted much research in the history of Polish and Russian Jewry, in light of halakhic and responsa literature; part of this work was published under the title *Le-Korot ha-Yehudim be-Rusyah u-Polin ve-Lita ba-Me'ot ha-Shesh-Esreh ve-ha-Sheva-Esreh* ("History of the Jews in Russia, Poland, and Lithuania in the 16th and 17th centuries," 1898). Katz's contributions to the Hebrew press inspired him to publish his own periodicals, and in 1903 in St. Petersburg he founded a newspaper and a quarterly, both under the name *Ha-Zeman*; a monthly, bearing the same name, was also published by him in Vilna (1905–06). At the end of 1916 Katz began to publish a Hebrew weekly, *Ha-Am*, in Moscow, which became a daily at the outbreak of the 1917 Revolution. The newspaper was critical of the Communist Revolution and was closed down in 1918. In 1920 he left Russia and after a short stay in Kovno, moved to Berlin, residing there until he settled in Ereẓ Israel in 1931. He was a regular contributor to *Haaretz* and *Ha-Boker*, and for a few years, also resumed publication of an independent daily, *Ha-Zeman*. Toward the end of his life Katz published chapters of his memoirs, afterward collected in *Zikhronot* (1963). In 1953 he founded *He-Avar*, a journal devoted to Russian Jewish history. The results of his historical researches appear in his books *Perushim, Ẓedukim, Kanna'im, Noẓerim* ("Pharisees, Sadducees, Zealots, Christians," 1948) and *Rabbanut, Ḥasidut, Haskalah* ("Rabbinism, Ḥasidism, Enlightenment," 1956–59).

BIBLIOGRAPHY: Rejzen, Leksikon, 2 (1927), 17–20; LNYL, 4 (1961), 348–51; *He-Avar*, 6 (1958), 3–24.

[Getzel Kressel and Yehuda Slutsky]

KATZ (Benshalom), BENZION (1907–1968), Hebrew translator, literary critic, and educator. He was the brother of Juliusz *Katz-Suchy. Born in Sanok, Galicia, he studied at the University of Cracow, taught Hebrew language there (1929–39), and lectured at the Warsaw Institute of Jewish Studies (1937–39). In 1940 he immigrated to Palestine, and from 1941 to 1963 was director of the Jewish Agency's Youth and He-Ḥalutz Department. He also lectured on classical literature at the Tel Aviv University, where he was appointed rector in 1964. Katz's books include *Mishkalav shel Ḥ.N. Bialik* ("Metrics in Bialik's Poetry," 1942); *Ha-Sifrut ha-Ivrit Bein Shetei Milḥamot Olam* (1943; *Hebrew Literature between the Two World Wars*, 1953); *Sheki'ot Yerushalayim* ("Jerusalem Sunsets," poems, 1965); and *Orḥot Yeẓirah* ("Creative Paths," literary essays, 1966). He translated into Hebrew selections from the Persian epic *Shahnama* by Firdausi and the *Rubáiyát* of Omar Khayyam, as well as several classical Greek works.

[Getzel Kressel]

KATZ, SIR BERNARD (1911–2003), British physiologist and Nobel Prize laureate. Katz was born in Leipzig, Germany. He studied medicine at the University of Leipzig, 1929–34; he received the Siegfried Garten Prize for physiological research in 1933 and obtained his M.D. in 1934. He left Germany in 1935 and finished his education in London, where he settled. He received a Ph.D. from London University in 1938 and in 1942, he was awarded the degree of Doctor of Science. In 1939 Katz joined J.C. Eccles' laboratory at Sydney Hospital, Australia, as a Carnegie Research Fellow. He collaborated with J.C. Eccles and S.W. Kuffler in neuromuscular research. In 1942, after naturalization in 1941, he joined the Royal Australian Air Force, and served as a radar officer in the Southwest Pacific until the end of the war. In 1946, he returned from Australia to University College, London. In 1952 he became professor and head of the biophysics department at University College, a position he held until his death. He received many awards and was made a fellow of the Royal Society of which, in 1965, he was elected vice president, and a fellow of the American Academy of Arts and Sciences in 1969. He was knighted in 1969. He was a member of the Agricultural Research Council from 1967 and the Biological Secretary of the Royal Society from 1968. In 1970 he was awarded the Nobel Prize in medicine. Katz demonstrated the relationship between neural transmission and acetylcholine release in quantitative terms, and clarified the action of calcium in the propagation of the nerve impulse. His main research was in the field of the nature of both the nerve impulse and nerve-muscle connections. He wrote *Electric Excitation of Nerve* (1939) and *Nerve, Muscle, and Synapse* (1966).

BIBLIOGRAPHY: Lex pris Nobel/Nobel Lectures.

[George H. Fried / Ruth Rossing (2nd ed.)]

KATZ, DANIEL (1903–1998), U.S. psychologist. Born in Trenton, New Jersey, Katz was the world's first recipient of a doctorate in a formal program of study in social psychology, which he received from Syracuse University in 1928. Conducting some of the earliest empirical research on stereotyping, his studies at Princeton with Kenneth Braly on the nature of ethnic stereotypes eventually became models for subsequent generations of research on prejudice. He was appointed instructor at Princeton in 1924 and in 1940 became associate professor. In 1943 he became chair of Brooklyn College's newly formed department of psychology.

Katz joined the Office of War Information in 1943 as a research director. After the war, he joined the staff of the University of Michigan's Survey Research Center, which subsequently became a branch of the Institute for Social Research. Katz was later appointed to the university's psychology department as well. Katz served as president of the Society for the Psychological Study of Social Issues and earned a number of career awards for his contributions to social psychology.

A leader in social psychology and public-opinion research, Katz served on the editorial boards of many journals in his field. He co-authored *Social Psychology* (with R.L. Schanck, 1938), *Research Methods in the Behavioral Sciences* (with L. Festinger, 1953), *The Social Psychology of Organizations* (with R. Kahn, 1966), *Bureaucratic Encounters* (with the University of Michigan, 1975), and *The Study of Organizations* (with R. Kahn and J. Adams, 1980).

[Ruth Beloff (2nd ed.)]

KATZ, DAVID (1884–1953), German psychologist. Born in Kassel, Katz studied at various universities including Goettingen, where he worked under Georg Elias Mueller and taught until the outbreak of World War I, when he served in the army. In 1919 Katz was appointed to the newly established chair of psychology and pedagogy at the University of Rostock which, under his direction, became one of the leading centers for psychological research in Germany. In 1933 he was dismissed by the Nazis, and for four years he was supported as a refugee scientist in England, first in Manchester and then in London. In 1937 he was appointed to the chair of psychology and pedagogy in Stockholm, where he developed a productive psychological laboratory.

He was one of the pioneers in experimental phenomenology. As Katz presented it, it was an attempt to bring under experimental control all the phenomena of experience. He is best known for the distinction he made between surface colors and film colors, and his work on touch paralleled his work on color. His interests ranged widely and he is also remembered for his contributions to animal psychology, child psychology, the psychology of thinking, and psychological instrumentation. Among his many publications, the most important are *Der Aufbau der Farbwelt* (1930; *The World of Colour*, 1935), originally published in 1911 in: *Zeitschrift fuer Psychologie und Physiologie*, as "Die Erscheinungsweisen der Farben"; *Der Aufbau des Tastwelt* (1925); together with Rosa Katz, *Gespraeche mit Kindern* (1928; *Conversations with Children*, 1936); *Animals and Men* (1937, 1953[2]); and *Gestaltpsychologie* (1944; *Gestalt Psychology*, 1950).

BIBLIOGRAPHY: R.B. MacLeod, in: IESS, 8 (1968), 352–4, includes bibliography; S. Kaznelson (ed.), *Juden im deutschen Kulturbereich* (1962[3]), 286, 289; *History of Psychology in Autobiography*, 4 (1952), 189–211. **ADD. BIBLIOGRAPHY:** NDB, vol. 11 (1977), 332f.

[Robert B. MacLeod]

KATZ, DAVID S. (1953–), Israeli historian of British Jewry. Educated at Columbia University and at Oxford, Katz became professor of English history at the University of Tel Aviv. He is considered one of the foremost authorities on the Anglo-Jewish community in the early modern period. His work *The Jews in the History of England, 1485–1850* (1994) is regarded as one of the most sophisticated treatments of a period previously examined by relatively few academic historians. He also wrote *Philo-Semitism and the Readmission of the Jews to England, 1603–1655* (1982) and is the author or editor of many other works.

[William D. Rubinstein (2nd ed.)]

KATZ, DOVID (**Heershadovid Menkes**; 1956–), Yiddish linguist, author, and educator. Born in New York, son of Menke *Katz, he developed, while studying at Columbia University (1974–78), the idea of direct links between the Aramaic and Yiddish periods of Jewish linguistic history; at the University of London he specialized in historical phonology and dialectology (Ph.D. 1982). He founded and directed Yiddish Studies at Oxford University (1978–96), at the Oxford Centre for Postgraduate Hebrew Studies (1978–94), and was fellow at St. Antony's College (1986–97), founding the *Winter Studies in Yiddish* series (4 vols. 1987–91), and the *Oksforder Yidish* series (3 vols. 1990–95), initiating and editing the literary monthly *Yiddish Pen* (1994–96). He founded the Oxford Summer Programme in Yiddish Language and Literature (1982), which he later moved to Vilnius, Lithuania (from 1998). Following a visiting professorship at Yale University (1998–99), he took up a new chair in Yiddish at Vilnius University. After directing the new Center for Stateless Cultures (1999–2001), he helped establish the university's Vilnius Yiddish Institute (2001). He initiated Yiddish teachers' courses at Oxford (1996) and in Vilnius (2005), publishing *Grammar of the Yiddish Language* (1987) and *Tikney Takones: Fragn fun Yidisher Stilistik* ("Amended Amendments: Issues in Yiddish Stylistics," 1993). He became known for his ardently descriptivist stance, challenging the "purist" school that developed in postwar New York; he also championed the more traditionalist version of modern Yiddish orthography in *Klal-takones fun Yidishn Oysleyg* ("Code of Yiddish Spelling," 1992). As Heershadovid Menkes he published three volumes of fiction: *Eldra Don* (1992), *Der Flakher Shpits* ("The Flat Peak," 1993) and *Misnagdishe Mayses fun Vilner Gubernye* ("Tales of the Misnagdim of Vilna Province," 1996). After experimenting with modern settings, he settled on pre-WWI Lithuanian Jewish settings, which earned critical acclaim. He became a regular contributor to *Yidishe Kultur*, *Forverts* and the *Algemeyner Zhurnal*. From 1990, he carried out expeditions to record the last native Yiddish in Lithuania, Latvia, northeastern Poland, and especially Belarus, collecting materials for a future atlas of Northeastern Yiddish. His *Lithuanian Jewish Culture* (2004) traces the cultural history of Lithuanian Jewry from its origins to the present. He co-edited the collected translations of his father's works (*Menke: The Complete Yiddish Works in English Translation*, 2005). A prolific scholar and writer, Katz published numerous studies on the historical sociology of Yiddish, the structure of Ashkenazi Hebrew and Aramaic, medieval rabbinic history, the history of Yiddish studies, and methodology in historical linguistics, with emphasis throughout on the history of ideas. For a more general readership, he published *Words on Fire: The Unfinished Story of Yiddish* (2004). Katz was awarded the 1979 Marshak Award in Yiddish Literature (Montreal), the 1995 Chaim Grade Award in Yiddish Culture (New York), the 1996 Zhitlovsky Prize in Yiddish Literature (New York), the 1997 Manger Prize in Yiddish Literature (Tel Aviv) and a Guggenheim Fellowship (2001–2).

BIBLIOGRAPHY: B.Z. Goldberg, *Algemeyner Zhurnal* (Sept. 1, 1972), 18; P. Slobodjans'kyj, *Language*, 64:4 (1988), 761–6; 67:1 (1991), 114; R.F. Shepard, *New York Times* (Apr. 6, 1991), 17; A. Karpinovich, *Letste Nayes* (Aug. 21, 1992), 8–14; *ibid.* (Aug. 6, 1993), 5; *Lebns-fragn*, 525–6 (1996), 16; S. Vorzoger, *Letste Nayes* (Nov. 13, 1992), 8; *ibid.* (May 7, 1993), 8–14; *Tsukunft*, 100/1 (1996), 19–22; L. Prager, *Mendele Review*, 08.010/149 (Oct. 29, 2004); J. Sherman, *Times Literary Supplement* (May 27, 2005), 22–3. **WEBSITE**: www.dovidkatz.net (bibl.).

[Dov-Ber Kerler (2nd ed.)]

KATZ, ELIHU (1926–), professor of sociology and communications. Born in New York, Katz received his doctorate from Colombia University in 1956. In 1963 he immigrated to Israel and joined the Guttman Institute for Applied Social Research of the Hebrew University of Jerusalem. During the 1960s he took time out from his academic career and headed the task force charged with the introduction of television broadcasting in Israel. He founded the Communications Institute at the Hebrew University in 1966, heading it until 1980. In the mid-1970s he and Daniel Dayan initiated a series of live broadcasts of recreated historic events inspired by the peace process with Egypt. He was a professor of sociology and communications at the Hebrew University until 1991, when he retired. He also served as professor at the Annenberg School of Communication at the University of Southern California. With his colleagues in Jerusalem and California he published 10 books and over 90 articles, among them: *Personal Influence: The Part Played by People in the Flow of Mass Communications* (with Lazarsfeld, 1955); *Medical Innovation: A Diffusion Study* (with Coleman and Menzel, 1966); *The Secularization of Leisure: Culture and Communication in Israel* (with Gurevitch, 1976); *The Export of Meaning: Cross-Cultural Readings of "Dallas"* (with Liebes, 1990); *Media Events: The Live Broadcasting of History* (with Dayan, 1992); and *Canonic Texts in Media Research: Are There Any? Should There Be? How About These?* (with Peters, Liebes, and Orloff, eds., 2003). In 1989 he was awarded the Israel Prize for social sciences. He also received the UNESCO-CANADA McLuhan Prize and Burda Prize (in media research).

WEBSITE: www.asc.upenn.edu/ascfaculty/facultyBioDetails.asp?txtUserID=ekatz#research.

[Fern Lee Seckbach / Shaked Gilboa (2nd ed.)]

KATZ, HANNS LUDWIG (1892–1940), German painter and graphic artist. Katz was born in Karlsruhe. After leaving school he made a short sojourn in Paris at the atelier of Henri Matisse. From 1913 to 1918 Katz studied painting, history of art, and architecture in Karlsruhe, Heidelberg, and Munich. He married the pianist Franziska Ehrenreich and they moved to Frankfurt-on-the-Main in 1920, after he had published a series of expressionist lithographs entitled *Danse macabre* which alluded to the revolution in 1919. In Frankfurt, Katz became known as a painter of portraits, cityscapes, and still lifes, which revealed the influence of Max Beckmann and the Neue Sachlichkeit. But despite the success and the support of the art critic Max Osborn, he had to become a partner in a whitewashing company in 1923 in order to make a living. One of his portraits in the style of the Neue Sachlichkeit shows the artist at work. After getting his master craftman's certificate, he worked in the business until 1936. After the Nazi takeover in 1933, Katz took an active part in the Frankfurt section of the Juedischer Kulturbund, and in 1935, one year after his wife died, he planned to establish a semiautonomous Jewish settlement in Yugoslavia. After his endeavors failed he immigrated to South Africa in 1936. Before leaving Frankfurt, Katz married

Ruth Wolf, who followed him into exile. Thus he was able to escape before one of his best expressionist portraits, of Gustav Landauer (1919–20, private collection, Kapstadt), was publicly denounced in *Degenerate Art* in 1938. Despite becoming deeply involved in painting the landscapes of his new homeland, Katz was unable to make headway in the South African art scene and died in Johannesburg.

BIBLIOGRAPHY: Heuberger, H. Krohn (ed.), *Hanns Ludwig Katz* (1992).

[Philipp Zschommler (2nd ed.)]

KATZ, ISRAEL (1917–2003), U.S. aeronautical engineer. Katz was born in New York and graduated from the Boston Trade School. He earned a B.S. in mechanical engineering from Northeastern University, Boston (1941); a naval architecture and marine engineering degree from the Massachusetts Institute of Technology, a degree sponsored by the U.S. Navy (1942); and a master's degree in mechanical engineering from Cornell University (1944). He was a staff member of Cornell (1944–57) where he became associate professor and was head of the aircraft power unit. He worked in the advanced electronic center of the General Electric Company in Ithaca, N.Y. (1957–63) but returned to Northeastern University (1967–88), where he became professor of mechanical engineering and held senior academic appointments, including dean of the Center for Continuing Education, before retiring as emeritus professor. Katz worked on submarine and aircraft propulsion and submarine launched missile systems. He was a consultant for the U.S. Department of Defense and the Pratt and Whitney Aircraft Company. He was an outstanding teacher of basic and advanced teaching courses in engineering, and his books on aircraft propulsion and mechanical engineering in industry became standard texts. He received the New England Award in engineering (1993). He was an active supporter of Temple Beth El and Temple Ohabei Shalom in Boston.

[Michael Denman (2nd ed.)]

KATZ, ISRAEL (1927–), Israeli social scientist and politician. Katz was born in Vienna and came to Ereẓ Israel under the *Youth Aliyah scheme in 1937. He studied physics and chemistry at The Hebrew University and, after completing his military service, studied social work at Columbia University, New York. Returning to Israel in 1953, he was appointed director of a home for emotionally disturbed children and from 1955 to 1959 was educational supervisor of Youth Aliyah. He returned to the United States to continue his studies and received his doctorate in social work administration from the Western Reserve University, Cleveland, Ohio. On his return to Israel he was appointed director of the Paul Baerwald School of Social Work of The Hebrew University, also serving as director-general of the National Insurance Institute and director of the Brookdale Gerontological Institute. In 1982 he received a Ph.D. from The Hebrew University of Jerusalem and subsequently became a senior lecturer in the department of sociology and anthropology.

He joined the Democratic Movement for Change in 1977 and, when his party joined the coalition in October 1977, was appointed minister of labor and social betterment, serving until August 1981.

KATZ, ISRAEL (**Joseph**; 1930–), U.S. ethnomusicologist. Katz graduated from UCLA (B.A., 1956) and later spent two years (1959–61) in Jerusalem, where he studied privately with Edith *Gerson-Kiwi and undertook field research among the Sephardic communities of Israel. He returned to UCLA and took his doctorate in 1967 with a dissertation on Judeo-Spanish ballads, comparing the stylistic features of traditional ballads from Jerusalem with those preserved among the Sephardim of Turkey, Greece, and Morocco. Among other places, he taught at McGill University (Montreal, 1968–74); Columbia University (1974–75); York College (CUNY), chairing the Department of Fine and Performing Arts; and Hebrew Union College as a visiting lecturer. He conducted research in Spain on a Guggenheim Fellowship (1975–76) and again as a Fulbright scholar (1985–86). In 1982, he became associated with the University of California, Santa Cruz (1982–89) and Davis (1989–2004), collaborating as an associate researcher with the renowned hispanists Samuel G. Armistead and Joseph H. Silverman (d. 1989) on the series *Folk Literature of the Sephardic Jews*. Katz served as editor of *Ethnomusicology* (1970–72); for the *Yearbook of the International Folk Music Council*, he was editor (1977–70), coeditor (with Albert Weisser, 1976–82), editor (1983–88), and coeditor with Arbie Orenstein (2001–). He was a founding member of the American Society for Jewish Music (1974) and served as chairman of the board (until 1988).

Katz concentrated his studies on the Sephardic and Oriental Jewish communities of the Mediterranean region, and on the traditional folk music of Spain, with special studies on the 13th-century *Cantigas de Santa Maria*. He collected traditional ballads in Morocco (summer 1961), Spain (summer 1978) and Portugal (summer 1988), where he followed the footsteps of Kurt *Schindler. Transcription and analytical techniques as well as comparative tune scholarship are basic to his researches. He wrote the books *Judeo-Spanish Traditional Ballads from Jerusalem: An Ethnomusicological Study* (1972–1975) and, with S.G. Armistead and J.H. Silverman, the six-volume *Judeo-Spanish Ballads from Oral Tradition* (1986–2005). He was also editor of many important studies and wrote numerous articles.

[Amnon Shiloah (2nd ed.)]

KATZ, JACOB (1904–1998), Israeli historian. Born in Magyargencs, Hungary, Katz studied at various yeshivot and at the university of Frankfurt. From 1936 to 1950 he taught at religious schools and the Mizrachi Teachers' Seminary in Jerusalem. From 1950 he taught at the Hebrew University, becoming professor of Jewish social and educational history in 1962. In 1969 he was appointed rector of the Hebrew University. Katz's published works include *Toledot Yisrael ve-he-Ammim* ("Israel and the Nations," several editions, 1941–62); *Maso-*

ret u-Mashber (1958; *Tradition and Crisis*, 1961); *Exclusiveness and Tolerance* (1961); *Freemasons and Jews* (1970); *Emancipation and Assimilation: Studies in Modern Jewish History* (1972); *Out of the Ghetto: The Social Background of Jewish Emancipation, 1770–1870* (1973); *Toward Modernity: The European Jewish Models* (1987). His work is significant for the understanding of the intricate relationships between Jews and gentiles and offers insights into Jewish sociology in medieval and modern times. For his studies he utilized rabbinical sources which had been usually unexplored for historical-sociological research. In 1980 he was awarded the Israel Prize for studies in Jewish history.

BIBLIOGRAPHY: J.M. Harris, *The Pride of Jacob: Essays on Jacob Katz and His Work* (2002).

KATZ, JOSEPH BEN ELIJAH (17th century), writer of ethical works. Little is known about his life, except that he was *av bet din* in Zaslavl in the beginning of the 17th century. Joseph wrote *Rekhev Eliyahu* (Cracow, 1638). The book, which follows the order of Mishnah *Avot*, uses the Mishnah as a starting point for discussing ethical subjects such as reward and punishment, ethical behavior in commerce, and *teshuvah* (see *Repentance). Joseph draws upon various subjects from the Kabbalah and he mentions some kabbalistic and ethical works, such as *Sefer Ḥasidim, Sefer ha-Zohar, Tola'at Ya'akov* (by R. Meir ibn Gabbai), *Tomer Devorah* (R. Moses ben Jacob Cordovero), *Reshit Ḥokhmah* (Elijah ben Moses De-Vidas), *Beit Ha-Shem* (R. Solomon Alkabez), and also cites R. Isaac Luria Ashkenazi (Ha-Ari).

[Esty Eisenmann (2nd ed.)]

KATZ, LABEL A. (1918–1975), U.S. attorney, realtor, and community leader. Katz, who was born in New Orleans, Louisiana, practiced law but concentrated on the home-construction industry and investment, and from 1951 was president of Label A. Katz Investment Co., Inc. He was president of the Communal Hebrew School of New Orleans (1943–48), and served in various district and national offices of the B'nai B'rith Hillel Foundation. He served as president of B'nai B'rith International for two terms (1959–65). At the age of 41, he had the distinction of being the youngest international president in the history of the organization. Katz was particularly concerned with Jewish education and with international affairs, notably the position of Soviet Jewry; in 1964 he helped organize the American Jewish Conference on Soviet Jewry, which encompassed 24 organizations. He also served as chairman of the Presidents' Conference of Major American Jewish Organizations (1960–61). In Louisiana he served on the New Orleans Mayor's Citizens' Committee on Housing Improvement (1953), as vice president of the Urban League of Greater New Orleans, and as chairman of the board of Sophie Newcomb College of Tulane University.

In his honor, B'nai B'rith International established the Label Katz Young Leadership Award, which honors members under the age of 40 who display distinguished leadership skills.

BIBLIOGRAPHY: E.E. Grusd, *B'nai B'rith, Story of a Covenant* (1966), index.

KATZ (Wannfried), MENAHEM, also known as **Menahem Prossnitz** (c. 1800–1891), Hungarian rabbi. The name Wannfried indicates his family's origin in Hesse-Nassau. Born in Prostejov (Prossnitz), Moravia, Katz was one of the outstanding disciples of R. Moses *Sofer. He was head of the yeshivah in his native town. Elected rabbi of Rajka (Ragendorf), Hungary, he was later appointed rabbi of *Deutschkreutz (Ẓelem), one of the "Seven Communities" of *Burgenland, where he served for over 50 years. Here too, he headed an important yeshivah. Katz is best known for his activity on behalf of the Orthodox faction at the Congress of Hungarian Jewry (1868). After the schism in Hungarian Jewry, he was a member of the delegation of rabbis which obtained independent rights for the Orthodox organization from Emperor *Francis Joseph I. In 1870 he also convened a meeting of Orthodox rabbis which served as the basis for the separate organization.

BIBLIOGRAPHY: S. Sofer, in: *Iggerot Soferim* (1929), 9; J.J.(L.) Greenwald (Grunwald), *Li-Felagot Yisrael be-Hungaryah* (1929), 78.

[Baruch Yaron]

KATZ, MENKE (1906–1991), Yiddish and English poet. Known as Menke (*Méyn-keh*) in Yiddish literature, he was born in Svintsyan (now Švenčionys, Lithuania) and spent World War I in Micháleshik (Michalishki, Belarus) before immigrating to New York in 1920. He made his poetic debut with "Bowery" in the avant-garde *Sparták*, coedited by A. *Pomerantz and Russian poet V. Mayakovsky, and joined the leftist writers' group that coalesced into Proletpen, from which he was expelled (1932) for publishing his first book, *Dray Shvester* ("Three Sisters"), a mystical and erotic poetic drama in four acts. His two-volume World War I epic, *Brenendik Shtetl* ("Burning Village," 1938) brought a new storm for its longing, lyrical descriptions of *shtetl* life and its failure to indulge socialist realism. Katz replied with "Der Braver Pakhdn" ("The Brave Coward"), a manifesto for a Yiddish poetry free of the shackles of politics, including the line "I will not lead by poem into battle." His book, *S'hot dos Vort mayn Bobe Moyne* ("Grandmother Mona Takes the Floor," 1939), is written in the voice of his *shtetl* grandmother who mercilessly takes on the New York Yiddish literary-political establishment. In 1944, he coedited the literary journal *Mir*. In midlife he turned to universal themes, particularly in the book *Inmitn Tog* ("Midday," 1954). Due to political squabbling in the Yiddish literary establishment, he turned to writing English as well, and made his debut with "A Patched Window" (*Commentary*, Feb. 1956), and soon began to publish in the *Atlantic, The New York Times, Midwest Quarterly, Poet Lore*, and other English outlets. His first English book, *Land of Manna* (1965), synthesized motifs from the Lithuanian *shtetl* and the American metropolis. In English he became known for his opposition to rhyme and his experimentation with novel forms, including the twin narrative chant royal; the unrhymed unrefrained chant royal; and most famously, the "Menke Sonnet," whose increasing or decreasing number of syllables per line forms graphic triangles.

Major works in English include *Rockrose* (1970), *Burning Village* (1972; not a translation of the 1938 text), *A Chair for Elijah* (1985), and *Nearby Eden* (1990). In all, he published 18 books of verse, nine in each language. His "World of Old Abe" won the 1974 Stephen Vincent Benet Award and he was nominated for a Pulitzer Prize for *Burning Village*. He edited the poetry magazine *Bitterroot* (1962–91), which became known for seeking out unknown talent and inspiring poetic experimentation. His collection of folktales from Micháleshik, *Forever and Ever and a Wednesday*, appeared in 1980. Translations of his work have appeared in book form in French (1972), Greek (1968), Hebrew (1973), Italian (1972), Japanese (1967), Kannada (1968) and Lithuanian (2006). A compendium of translations in 21 languages of "On the Death of a Day Old Child" appeared in 1973. A near-complete collection of his Yiddish works in English translation by Benjamin and Barbara *Harshav appeared in 2005. He worked as a Yiddish teacher for much of his life. In 1985 he completed a collection of Yiddish folksongs, including many unknown variants from his native Lithuanian villages (unpublished, as is his 1951–2 diary to his brother Yeiske). He is the father of Dovid Katz and Troim Katz Handler.

BIBLIOGRAPHY: B.Z. Goldberg, *Tog* (April 29, 1932); A. Reisen, *Feder Zamlbukh* (1936); I. Bashevis [Singer], *Tsukunft* (March 1940); M. Shtarkman, *Hemshekh Antologye* (1945), 259–68; H. Leivik, *Tog* (Nov. 14, 1953); Y. Varshavski [I. Bashevis [Singer]], *Forverts* (Dec. 9, 1956); M. Ravitsh, *Mayn Leksikon*, 3 (1958), 360–1; J. Glatstein, *Tsukunft* (Feb. 1963); LNYL, 8 (1981), 110–11; A. Evory and L. Metzger, *Contemporary Authors*, 11 (1984), 285–8; 110–11; B. Kagan, *Leksikon fun Yidish Shraybers* (1986), 551–2; M. Zadrozny (ed), *Contemporary Authors*, 9 (1989), 49–71 (autobiography); D. Katz, *Di Goldene Keyt*, 132 (1991), 98–123; B. Harshav, *Jerusalem Review*, 1 (1997), 137–9; H. Smith and D. Katz, *Menke: The Complete Yiddish Poems of Menke Katz* (2005), v–cxxxv. **WEBSITE:** www.dovidkatz.net > Menke Katz.

[Dovid Katz (2nd ed.)]

KATZ, MICKEY (1909–1985), U.S. musician, comic. Known for his unusual blend of *klezmer* music and Borscht Belt humor, Katz began playing the clarinet as a young child in his hometown of Cleveland, Ohio. He was performing with local bands by the time he was in high school. After he began to incorporate comic routines into his musical act, he gained the attention of Spike Jones, who invited Katz to become a member of his City Slickers band in 1946. Katz can be heard on a number of classic Spike Jones recordings including "Hawaiian War Chant," in which he provides the "glug-glug-glug" sound effect. It wasn't long before Katz pitched his own solo act to Spike Jones' label RCA and got a record deal of his own, performing popular American tunes with a Yiddish interpretation, adding Yiddish lyrics and instrumentation to the well-known songs as well as a comically exaggerated Jewish accent. After his RCA singles met with success, Katz went on the road, doing a tour he called the "Borscht Capades." Katz's son, later to be known in his own right as actor Joel *Grey, was included in the cast of Katz's road show. Katz eventually left RCA for Capital Records, where he remained until his retirement in the 1960s. However, this was not to be the last that the American public heard from Mickey Katz, who went on to publish his autobiography, *Papa Play for Me*, in 1977. Katz's legacy received another boost with the 1993 release of *Don Byron plays the Music of Mickey Katz* by the noted African-American jazz artist. In addition to being the father of Joel *Grey, Katz is the grandfather of *Dirty Dancing* dynamo Jennifer Grey.

[Casey Schwartz (2nd ed.)]

KATZ, MINDRU (1925–1978), Romanian-born Israeli pianist. Born in Bucharest and recognized as a child prodigy by **George Enescu**, Katz was recommended to Floria Musicescu, with whom he studied at the Royal Academy of Music in Bucharest. Katz made his debut with the Bucharest Philharmonic Orchestra (1947), won prizes at international competitions, and the state prize, first class, of the Romanian Republic (1954). Between 1947 and 1959 he went on concert tours in Eastern Europe, and made his debuts in Paris (1957) and in London (1958). In 1959 he gave his first Festival Hall recital, recorded Khachaturian's concerto and Prokofiev's First Piano Concerto, and settled in Israel. He first played with the Israel Philharmonic under Martinon and continued to make extensive tours in Western Europe, Africa, the Far East, and the Americas. He performed with leading orchestras and illustrious conductors such as Sir John Barbirolli, Antal Dorati, and Joseph Krips. Katz was appointed lecturer at the Rubin Academy of Music at Tel Aviv University and a professor in 1972. He had great impact on the level of piano culture in Israel. His piano playing managed to be both technically brilliant and full of poetry. His repertoire ranged from Bach to Prokofiev but he was most acclaimed in Beethoven, Chopin, and Brahms. He died during a recital.

ADD. BIBLIOGRAPHY: *New Grove Dictionary* (1980).

[Naama Ramot (2nd ed.)]

KATZ, MOSES (1885–1960), Yiddish journalist. Born near Minsk, he received a traditional Jewish and secular education. He was arrested in 1903 for participating in an illegal Zionist education group. After the Kishinev pogrom he joined the Socialist-Zionists and took part in self-defense activities. After a two-year stay in Palestine (1908–10), he returned to Russia and then went to the U.S. in 1913. Katz started his career as a writer in Russian in 1904, but from 1905 contributed to Yiddish journals. In the U.S. he joined Chaim *Zhitlowsky's journal *Dos Naye Lebn* and served as a correspondent for foreign publications in Yiddish and Russian. He returned to Russia in 1917 after the February Revolution. Between 1917 and 1920 Katz held various editorial posts in Russia, helped to found the Ukrainian *Kultur-Lige*, and managed the Jewish Division of the State Publishing House in Kiev. After his return to America in 1922, he worked on the Yiddish Communist daily *Frayhayt* (later *Morgn Frayhayt*) and also contributed to many leftist journals. He wrote numerous articles on travel as well as popular discussions of history and of Marxism, often using pseudonyms. He translated Ivan Franko, Heine, and Kipling into Yiddish and edited a six-volume edition of Lenin in Yiddish (Moscow, 1933). Among his works are *Nikolay Lenin* (1920), *Di Ershte Yidishe Oytonomye* ("The First Jewish Autonomy," 1934), and *A Dor Vos Hot Farloyrn di Moyre* ("A Generation that Lost its Fear," 1956).

BIBLIOGRAPHY: LNYL, 4 (1961), 358–62. **ADD. BIBLIOGRAPHY:** P. Novick (ed.), *Moyshe Kats Bukh* (1963), 9–24; B. Kohen, *Leksikon fun Yidish-Shraybers* (1986), 311.

[Henry J. Tobias]

KATZ, NAPHTALI BEN ISAAC (Ha-Kohen; 1645–1719), rabbi and kabbalist. Katz was born in Stepan (Volhynia), where his father was rabbi. In his youth he was taken captive by the Tatars but managed to escape. He succeeded his father as *av bet din* of Stepan and then served as rabbi of Ostrow (1680–89), Posen (1690–1704), and Frankfurt on the Main (1704–11). In the latter year a fire broke out in his house, destroying the whole Jewish quarter of Frankfurt. After he had been maliciously charged with preventing the extinguishing of the fire because he wanted to test his amulets – in the use of which he was expert – he was imprisoned and compelled to resign his post. He went to Prague, staying in the house of David *Oppenheim, where he met Nehemiah *Ḥayon and even gave approbation to his book *Oz le-Elohim* (also called *Meheimnuta de-Kalla*; Berlin, 1713). From 1713 to 1715 he lived in Breslau, where together with Ẓevi Hirsch *Ashkenazi he excommunicated Ḥayon after realizing his true character. In 1715, after King Augustus of Poland had rejected his application to be restored to his post as rabbi of Posen, he returned to Ostrow where his son Bezalel was rabbi. While journeying to Ereẓ Israel he was taken ill in Constantinople and died there.

Among his works are *Pi Yesharim* (Frankfurt, 1702), kabbalistic comments to the word *bereshit* ("in the beginning"); *Birkat ha-Shem* (2 pts., *ibid.*, 1704–06), including *Semikhat Ḥakhamim*, consisting of *hadranim* (see *Hadran) and *Kedushah u-Verakhah*, novellae to the tractate *Berakhot*; and *Sha'ar Naftali*, poems and *piyyutim* (Bruenn, 1757). Several works are still in manuscript. Katz was one of the important halakhic authorities of his generation and one of the greatest kabbalists of Poland. His image persisted in the memory of the people, and many legends and wondrous tales about him circulated for many generations. He conducted his rabbinate high-handedly and as a result met much opposition from the leaders of the communities, which was apparently the cause of his frequent wanderings. Despite this he had a sensitive soul which found expression in his poems, *piyyutim*, and prayers which have been published in various places. His well-known ethical will (1729?) contains profound thoughts and moral instruction and some see in it one of the first sparks of practical *Ḥasidism.

BIBLIOGRAPHY: Perles, in: MGWJ, 14 (1865), 92f.; M. Horovitz, *Frankfurter Rabbinen*, (1969), 98–114; Horodezky, in: *Ha-Goren*, 1 (1898), 100–2; Kaufmann, in: REJ, 36 (1898), 256–86; 37 (1898), 274–83; idem, in: JJGL, 2 (1899), 123–47; M.M. Biber, *Mazkeret li-Gedolei Ostraha* (1907), 63–69; Lewin, in: HHY, 6 (1922), 261–63; M.E. Rapoport-Hartstein, *Shalshelet Zahav* (1931); Davidson, Oẓar, 4 (1931), 453; Narkis, in: KS, 15 (1938–39), 370–2; Halpern, Pinkas, 206ff., 601; Peli, in: *Sinai*, 39 (1956), 242–60; A. Yaari, *Meḥkerei Sefer* (1958), 55ff.

[Yehoshua Horowitz]

KATZ, REUVEN (1880–1963), talmudist. After studying in various yeshivot, Katz went to Vilna to study under Ḥayyim Ozer *Grodzinski. He became known as the *Illui* ("prodigy") of Olshany. He married the daughter of Abraham *Maskileison. After holding appointments in a number of towns, including Minsk in 1905, Indura in 1909, and Stawiski in 1923, he joined a delegation visiting the United States and remained there as rabbi of Bayonne, New Jersey. In 1932 he was appointed chief rabbi of Petaḥ Tikvah where he also headed the Lomza Yeshivah, founded by the heads of the Lithuanian yeshivah of the same name. Katz headed a variety of communal organizations, including the aid committee for Grodno Jewry and the Aguddat ha-Rabbanim of Poland. He was vice president of Aguddat ha-Rabbanim of America and in Israel he was president of Aguddat Rabbanei Yehudah ve-ha-Sharon and an associate of the Council of the Chief Rabbinate and of the Va'ad ha-Yeshivot. Among his published works are the responsa *Degel Re'uven* (3 pts., 1923–49); *Duda'ei Re'uven* (1928; 2nd ed. 2 pts., 1954) on the Pentateuch; and *Sha'ar Re'uven* (1952), a collection of essays on topical and practical problems. Of his sons, Aaron succeeded him as *rosh yeshivah* in Petaḥ Tikvah, Simeon served on the *bet din* there, Michael and Leon taught at Yeshiva *University, while a fifth son, Abraham *Katsh, became president of Dropsie University.

BIBLIOGRAPHY: Harkavy, in: R. Katz, *Sha'ar Re'uven* (1952), 5–11 (introd.); Bergstein, in: *Shanah be-Shanah* (1965), 447–52; Raphael, in: *Sinai*, 56 (1965), 183f.; A. Shurin, *Keshet Gibborim* (1964), 141–6; Tidhar, 3 (1949), 1490f.

[Itzhak Alfassi]

KATZ, RUTH (1927–) Israeli musicologist. Born in Germany, Katz emigrated to Palestine in 1934. She studied piano with E. Rudiakoff and music theory with P. *Ben-Haim in Tel Aviv, and earned her Ph.D. in 1963 at Columbia University. She joined the newly established department of musicology at the Hebrew University of Jerusalem in 1965 where she became professor of musicology in 1984 and emeritus since 1995. Ruth Katz was head of the School of Graduate Studies (1983–86) at the Hebrew University and fellow at the Institute of Advanced Studies in Berlin (1986–87).

Her fields of interest encompass a wide scope of research: aesthetics, philosophy and sociology of music, historical musicology, study of non-western traditions, musicological and ethnomusicological methods, and cognitive science of music. She distinguished herself with her broad interdisciplinary approach and methodological creativity.

In 1957 Katz developed, together with D. Cohen, the melograph – an instrument for the continuous graphic representation of melody (or any monophonic vocal expression with definite pitch). The melograph is used for analyzing melodic elements that cannot be expressed exactly in traditional Western notation, e.g., those based on other intonation systems, microtonal intervals, contours of glissandi, attack and decay of notes, vibrato, or the relation of pitch to loudness. This method has been applied to studies on the music of the Samaritans:

"Explorations in the Music of the Samaritans: An Illustration of the Utility of Graphic Notation" (with D. Cohen), *Ethnomusicology*, 4 (1960), and also to the music of Syrian (Aleppo) Jews, Palestinian Arabs (secular and sacred), and Israeli folksongs. Unlike similar *apparati* developed independently at the same time (in Los Angeles and Norway), the Katz-Cohen melograph set the basic methodology and interpretative approach still used today. Other ethnomusicological interests concern latent vs. manifest theory (with D. Cohen) and historical continuity vs. change in oral traditions.

Her research on Western tradition includes the history and theory of notation; the origins of opera as collective problem-solving, analogous to science; eighteenth-century music and aesthetic theory; the relationship of language to music (her work on this subject was an example of the "cognitive turn" in epistemology and was an early contribution to cognitive science); music in philosophical writings (with C. Dahlhaus); and the relationship among stylistic change, aesthetic judgment, and historical process, examined through the case of the institutionalization and diffusion of opera (early 17th c.). Among her major books are *Divining the Powers of Music: Aesthetic Theory and the Origins of Opera* (1986); *Contemplating Music: Source Readings in the Aesthetics of Music* (4 vols.; with C. Dahlhaus, 1988–1992); *Tuning the Mind: Connecting Aesthetics to Cognitive Science* (with R. Ha-Cohen, 2003); *The Lachmann Problem: An Unsung Chapter in Comparative Musicology* (2003); and *Palestinian Arab Music: A Maqam Tradition in Practice* (with D. Cohen, 2005).

[Elisheva Rigbi (2nd ed.)]

KATZ, SHMUEL (1914–), Israeli publicist. Katz was born in South Africa and came to Eretz Israel in 1936 as secretary to the Honorary South African Consul, Michael Haskel. He was active in the *Irgun Ẓeva'i Leummi, then under the leadership of David *Raziel. At the request of Ze'ev Jabotinsky he came to London in 1940, where he launched and edited a weekly Revisionist magazine. On his return in 1946 he resumed his activity in the Irgun and was a member of its High Command until it dissolved. He then took over the responsibility for the branch of the Irgun which remained in Jerusalem during the final phase of fighting in the War of Independence.

Katz was elected to the First Knesset, but left public life in 1951 and set up a publishing house. After the Six-Day War he became active in the Land of Israel Movement, carrying on propaganda on its behalf in the United States. After the victory of the Likud in March 1977, Menaḥem Begin appointed him adviser on information abroad, but he resigned in January 1978 as he found himself in disagreement with the policy of the prime minister and joined the Ḥerut group which opposed Begin's peace negotiations. Later on, he retired from Ḥerut politics.

Katz published five books, *Days of Fire*, *Battleground: Fact and Fantasy in Palestine*, *No Courage, No Splendor*, *Zabo*, and *The Wild East*. In addition, he translated works of Jabotinsky, and Menaḥem Begin's *Revolt*, into English.

KATZ, SHOLOM (1919–1982), *ḥazzan*. Born in Oradea, Romania, Katz studied voice in Budapest and Vienna and was *ḥazzan* in Kishinev, Bessarabia, until he was deported in 1941. At the Bralow, Ukraine, concentration camp, he was taken out to be shot but requested permission to sing the prayer for the dead. The officer in charge was so impressed by his voice that he spared him and allowed him to escape. In 1947 he emigrated to the U.S. and became *ḥazzan* of the Beth Sholom Congregation in Washington, D.C. A powerful tenor with an extensive range and exceptional voice control, Katz developed an individualistic, unhurried and dramatic style.

KATZ, SOLOMON (1909–1990), U.S. historian. Born in Buffalo, New York, Katz was hired in 1936 as an instructor by the history department of the University of Washington, where he remained for 53 years. In 1950 he was appointed professor of history. Katz's main scholarly interest was the period of the decline of the Roman Empire and the emergence of the medieval world. His doctoral dissertation, "The Jews in the Visigothic and Frankish Kingdoms of Spain and Gaul" (1937), combined Jewish sources with Roman and Germanic sources to illustrate the status and organization of the Jews. Katz developed such an interest in the history of the late Roman Empire, or Byzantine history, that he began to offer courses in the subject in 1940, making the UW one of the few institutions to offer such classes at the time. He served in the U.S. Army Air Force (1942–46). During his tenure at the university, Katz also served as chair of the history department, dean of the College of Arts and Sciences, provost, and vice president for academic affairs.

His book *The Decline of Rome and the Rise of Medieval Europe* (1955) is a brief popular survey. He also published in Jewish and general scholarly journals. Katz was a member of the Commission on Academic Affairs of the American Council on Education (1967); president of the Pacific Coast Branch of the American Historical Association (1967–68); and a member of the Commission on Students and Faculty of the Association of American Colleges (1969). An avid supporter of the arts and humanities in the Northwest, he served as a member of numerous arts, civic, and educational boards as well, including the Seattle Repertory Theater, the Seattle Art Museum, the Seattle Symphony, and Lakeside School. In 1978 he received the Seattle Mayor's Public Service Award in the Arts. That year, the UW established the Solomon Katz Distinguished Lectureship Series in the Humanities and, later on, an endowed professorship was created in his honor. In addition, the Solomon Katz Distinguished Lectures in the Humanities Series was established by private donors to recognize distinguished scholars in the humanities. In 1983 Katz was presented with the University of Washington's Outstanding Public Service Award.

[Irwin L. Merker / Ruth Beloff (2nd ed.)]

KATZ, STEVEN T. (1944–), U.S. scholar and philosopher. Katz was born in Jersey City, New Jersey. He earned his B.A. degree from Rutgers University (1966), his M.A. degree from

New York University (1967), and his Ph.D. from Cambridge University (1972). He served on the faculties of Cambridge University (1971–72); Dartmouth College (1972–84); and Cornell University (1984–96). In 1995 he was named as director of the United States Holocaust Memorial Museum but when a controversy developed, he resigned without serving. He served as director of the Elie Wiesel Center for Judaic Studies and professor of religion, comparative mysticism, and Judaica (Holocaust) at Boston University (from 1996).

Katz published articles and books on Shoah history and theology, including *Post-Holocaust Dialogues: Critical Studies in Modern Jewish Thought* (1983) and *Historicism, the Holocaust, and Zionism: Critical Studies in Modern Jewish Thought and History* (1992). His stellar contribution on the singularity of the Shoah evolved in 1979 when Katz proposed his agenda on why the Shoah is unmatched in history. He expanded on the topic in *The Holocaust in Historical Context. Volume 1: The Holocaust and Mass Death Before the Modern Age* (1994) in which he discusses other horrific events deemed parallel to the Shoah. With dedicated persistence, he tackles a plethora of literature and scholarship and maintains that the issue at hand is not essentially a problem of economics, history, politics, religion, sociology, or theology but one of intentionality, that is Nazism's *Weltanschaung*, the total genocidal intent against the Jewish people for being and becoming. A similar point is made in his essay "Children in Auschwitz and the Gulag: Alternative Realities" (in R.L. Millen, ed., *New Perspectives on the Holocaust: A Guide for Teachers and Scholars* (1996)), which documents that only in the brutal environment of Auschwitz *all* children were marked for extermination by the fiat of Nazi racial ideology. His edited volume, *The Impact of the Holocaust on Jewish Theology* (2005), brings together an array of international scholars who wrestle with profound post-Shoah religious and theological problems, including, how our belief in a providential all-good Creator has changed in the wake of the Holocaust.

Katz contributed and edited several acclaimed works on mysticism: *Mysticism and Philosophical Analysis* (1978), *Mysticism and Religious Traditions* (1983), *Mysticism and Language* (1992), *Mysticism and Sacred Scriptures* (2000), and *Comparative Mysticism: An Anthology of Original Sources* (2005), which argue against others that the mediated experience is not peripheral but highly philosophical and historical to religious traditions. His scholarly works in the field of Judaica include *Jewish Philosophers: A History* (1975), *Jewish Ideas and Concepts* (1977), *Antisemitism in Times of Crises* (1991 with Sandor L. Gillman), *Jacob Agus, American Rabbi* (1997), and *The Essential Agus* (1997). For B'nai B'rith Books, he edited two volumes of original essays, *Frontiers of Modern Jewish Thought* (1992) and *Interpreters of Judaism in the Late Twentieth Century* (1993).

Katz served as general editor of several series: *Jewish Philosophy, Mysticism, and the History of Ideas: Classics of Continental Thought* (1979–80, 65 volumes); *Judaica Festschrift zu Hermann Cohens Siebzigstem Geburtstage* (1979, a reprint series); Judaica Series, and *Modern Jewish Masters* (periodic monograph series, New York University Press). Finally, Katz founded and continued to serve as the editor of the award-winning journal, *Modern Judaism* (from 1981).

[Zev Garber (2nd ed.)]

KATZAV, MOSHE (1945–), eighth president of the State of Israel, member of the Ninth to Fifteenth Knessets. Katzav was born in Yazd in Iran. At the age of one Katzav's family moved to Teheran, and five years later the family immigrated to Israel; after a short sojourn in the Sha'ar ha-Aliyah immigration center in Haifa, the family was sent to the Kastina *ma'barah* near Be'er Toviyyah – today Kiryat Malakhi. In the floods of 1951 Katzav was moved to Kefar Bilu, without his family's knowledge. The family's housing conditions gradually improved from a tent to a hut, and finally to a small apartment. As a boy Katzav visited the residence of President Yitzhak *Ben-Zvi, together with other children from *ma'barot* who excelled in reading.

Katzav studied at the youth village of Ben-Shemen and later went to high school at Be'er Toviyyah.

During his military service in the Communications Corps, he helped support his family in construction jobs. After completing his military service he worked as a clerk in Bank Hapoalim, and as an assistant in the Vulcani Institute for Agricultural Research. At the same time he started to work as a reporter for *Yedioth Aḥaronoth* and served as president of B'nai B'rith Youth.

He was the first student from Kiryat Malakhi at the Hebrew University in Jerusalem, where he started to study in 1968, after saving money to finance his studies. At the university he was head of the *Gaḥal students cell. He received his B.A. in economics and history in 1971. While still a student he began teaching history and mathematics at high school, and in 1969, at the age of 24, was elected head of the local council of Kiryat Malakhi, at the head of a coalition that included Gaḥal and the *National Religious Party. However, after several months repeat elections were held, and he lost his majority in the Council. He was reelected head of the local council on behalf of the Likud and served in this position in the 1976–81 term – in the first two years on the basis of a rotation agreement with the Alignment.

Katzav served as a reservist in both the Six-Day War and the Yom Kippur War.

In 1977 he was elected to the Ninth Knesset on behalf of the Likud, and served in the Knesset until he was elected president of the State in 2003. In the course of the Ninth Knesset, before the rise of the Ayatollah Homeini to power, he was sent twice on missions on behalf of Prime Minister Menaḥem *Begin to Iran, to encourage the Jews to immigrate to Israel. In the Tenth Knesset he served as deputy minister of construction and housing, responsible on behalf of the government for *Project Renewal. In the National Unity Government of 1984–88 he served as minister of labor and welfare, and in 1988–92 as minister of transportation. In the opposition in 1992–96 he served as chairman of the Likud parliamentary group, and in the government formed by Binyamin *Netanyahu he served as deputy prime minister and minister of tourism in 1996–99.

Among the various public posts he filled over the years was chairman of the roof organization of the immigrants from Iran, chairman of the Committee to Determine Salaries in Institutions for Higher Education, and member of the Board of Trustees of Ben-Gurion University. After Ezer *Weizman resigned as president in 2000, Katzav contended for the position opposite Shimon *Peres, and against all odds was elected as Israel's eighth president. He was the second Sephardi to be elected to the post (Itzhak *Navon had been the first), and the first president to have been born in a Muslim state.

As president, Katzav did his best to serve as a moderating and unifying figure, and unlike his predecessor avoided provocative statements. He has paid numerous state visits abroad and received several honorary doctorates.

BIBLIOGRAPHY: M, Michaelson, *Moshe Katzav – Mima'aberet Kastina le-Kiryat ha-Memshalah* (1992).

[Susan Hattis Rolef (2nd ed.)]

KATZBURG, DAVID ẒEVI (1856–1937), talmudic scholar, author, and editor. Katzburg was born in Vác near Budapest to a rabbinic family originating in Moravia. He studied under the most distinguished rabbis of Hungary, including Hezekiah Feivel Plaut of Surány and Simḥah Bunim Sofer of Pressburg. After completing his studies he engaged in business for a short time and also served as rabbi in several communities. In 1892 he returned to Vác, and that same year he began the publication of *Tel Talpiot*, the first rabbinical periodical in Hungary. It was devoted chiefly to *halakhah*, both theoretical and practical, and among other things it clarified halakhic problems that had arisen because of contemporary conditions, such as the use of electricity on the Sabbath, machine baking of matzah, civil marriages, and problems of religion during World War I. These discussions had considerable repercussions in the rabbinical world. *Tel Talpiot* also included articles on homiletics, *aggadah*, and exegesis, as well as on communal problems. Of considerable historical importance are the discussions on Zionism among the Orthodox that arose as a result of the emergence of political Zionism in 1896 and with the first world congress of the Mizrachi in 1904. Katzburg took up a positive attitude to settlement in Ereẓ Israel. The contributors to *Tel Talpiot* were mostly from Hungary but also included scholars from Russia, Germany, Holland, and the United States. It appeared at first as a biweekly and after World War I as a monthly. An index to the first 45 volumes appeared in 1967.

Katzburg was the author of: *Zer Ẓedek* (1878), sermons on and expositions of the Bible and rabbinic dicta; *Mevasser Ẓedek* (1911), on *Avot; Mevasser Ẓedek* (1922), sermons; *Iggeret Ẓedek Olamim* (1918), on socialism in the light of Torah and Judaism; *Yalkut ha-Meliẓot*, 2 vols. (1931–36), homilies on the Pentateuch; *Raz Hadek* (1938), religious philosophy; *Pirḥei Kehunnah* (1940), talmudic novellae; and *Sheloshah Sefarim Niftaḥim* (1942), on *halakhah* and on Zionist topics.

BIBLIOGRAPHY: A. Katzburg (ed.), *Temunat ha-Gedolim* (1925); H. Brody, *Festschrift… Misrachi* (1927); N. Ben-Menaḥem, *Sefer ha-Mizraḥi* (1946); idem, *Sinai*, 24 (1949); N. Katzburg, *Aresheth*, 1 (1958), 279–98; Ẓ. Zehavi, *Toledot ha-Ẓiyyonut be-Hungaryah*, 1 (1966).

KATZENBERG, JEFFREY (1950–), U.S. film industry executive. Born and raised in Manhattan, Katzenberg volunteered to work on John V. Lindsay's New York City mayoral campaign in 1964, when just 14. He worked for the mayor for the next seven years, until he attained the position of controller of Lindsay's Democratic presidential nomination campaign. By 1977 he had moved to California to be vice president of programming at Paramount television. Senior vice president of production in the company's movie division from 1980 to 1982, Katzenberg became president of production for motion pictures and television in 1982, a position he held until 1984.

When Paramount president Michael Eisner became company chairman at Disney Films in 1984, he took Katzenberg with him; the latter, as chairman of Walt Disney Studios, helped mastermind the strategy of diversification and increased production that saw Disney move from least successful to first place among Hollywood's nine major distributors. Under Katzenberg's guidance, Disney's animated features were highly successful, with movies such as *Beauty and the Beast* (1991), *Aladdin* (1992), and *The Lion King* (1994) netting record grosses at the box office. By 1994, Disney was the most profitable studio in the world.

In that year, however, Katzenberg was involved in a rancorous split from Disney after Eisner denied him the promotion to company president. In October 1994 Katzenberg, Steven *Spielberg, and David *Geffen announced the formation of DreamWorks, the first major new studio to be launched since Disney's own creation 60 years previously. Its program was live-action films overseen by Spielberg, animated features handled by Katzenberg, record albums produced by Geffen, and multimedia products in cooperation with Microsoft's Bill Gates.

Under Katzenberg's leadership, the company's animation division developed into a high-quality computer-generated animation studio with production locations on several continents. As an executive producer, Katzenberg brought to the screen such popular animated feature films as *The Prince of Egypt* (1998), *The Road to El Dorado* (2000), *Chicken Run* (2000), *Joseph: King of Dreams* (2000), *Shrek* (producer, 2001), *Spirit* (producer, 2002), *Shrek 4-D* (producer, 2003), *Sinbad* (producer, 2003), *Shrek 2* (2004), and *Shark Tale* (2004).

In 2002, *Shrek* won the Academy Award for Best Animated Feature, making it the first full-length animated film in history to win an Oscar. In 2004 Katzenberg published *Animation Art: From Pencil to Pixel*, which he co-authored with Jerry Beck and Bill Plympton.

BIBLIOGRAPHY: K. Masters, *The Keys to the Kingdom: How Michael Eisner Lost His Grip* (2000); R. Grover, *The Disney Touch* (1991).

[Rohan Saxena / Ruth Beloff (2nd ed.)]

KATZENELENBOGEN, URIAH (1885–1980), Yiddish writer, journalist, and translator. Born in Vilna (Vilnius), Lithuania, he early became a member of the *Bund. His play *Kraft un Libe* ("Power and Love," 1904) was one of the first examples of Yiddish literary modernism in Vilna. In 1913 he organized a group of the Jewish intelligentsia that stood for closer Jewish political and cultural contacts with other national groups in Lithuania. He edited the Yiddish cultural almanac *Lite* (1914–22) and the Russian weekly *Nash Kraj* (1914), where he advocated the multicultural coexistence of Lithuanian Jews and non-Jews. He left Europe in 1927 and taught in Yiddish schools in various cities in North America. He translated numerous works of Lithuanian, Belorussian, and Latvian literature into Yiddish. His major work was a unique collection of 600 Baltic folksongs in Yiddish translation, *Daynes: Litvishe and Letishe Folkslider* ("Daynes: Lithuanian and Latvian Folksongs," 1930, 1936²). He edited the massive *yizkor*-book of Lithuania, *Lite* (1951).

BIBLIOGRAPHY: Kh.M. Kayzerman-Vital, *Yidishe Dikhter in Kanade* (1934), 149–52; LNYL, 8 (1981), 124–5.

[Mindaugas Kvietkauskas (2nd ed.)]

KATZENELLENBOGEN, family widely dispersed throughout Eastern and Central Europe. It originated in the town of Katzenelnbogen in Hesse, the birthplace of Meir ben Isaac *Katzenellenbogen (1473–1565), head of the Padua yeshivah. His son, SAMUEL JUDAH (1521–1597), inherited his father's position; Samuel Judah's son was Saul *Wahl (c. 1541–1617), the Polish Court Jew and legendary "king for a day." Saul had six sons and five daughters, who married into the leading families of East European Jewry. Such was the fame of the family that men who married women members took their wives' family name, as did R. Joel Ashkenazi who married R. Samuel's daughter. There are at least 12 variant Hebrew spellings of the name as well as derivative forms such as Ellenbogen, Elbogen, Bogen, and Katzenelson. One of Saul's sons, MEYER, an influential member of the *Councils of the Lands, was recorded as Kaẓin Elin Bogen (Heb. *kaẓin*, "officer," "leader"). The family was widely dispersed, but its unity was maintained through meticulously kept family records. Members of the family intermarried with other prominent Jewish families (Te'omim, Heilprin, *Fraenkel, etc.) and produced many rabbis. Especially notable were David Tevel *Katzenellenbogen, rabbi of St. Petersburg, and Ẓevi Hirsch Katzenellenbogen, Vilna communal leader. Ezekiel ben Abraham Katzenellenbogen was rabbi of Hamburg, Altona, and Wandsbeck (1714–49); his grandson, ABRAHAM BEN DAVID, rabbi in Slutsk and Brest-Litovsk, was an opponent of Ḥasidism who conducted polemics with *Levi Isaac of Berdichev. Gabriel *Riesser, leader of German Jewry's struggle for emancipation, was a descendant of the family through his father, ELIEZER (LAZARUS RIESSER). NAPHTALI HIRSCH BEN MOSES KATZENELLENBOGEN (c. 1715–1800), *Landrabbiner* of the Palatinate (1763), was the first to head the famous Mannheim *Klaus* (1768). His namesake, NAPHTALI HIRSCH BEN ELIEZER KATZENELLENBOGEN (d. 1823), rabbi of Bamberg and Haguenau, participated in Napoleon's *Sanhedrin.

BIBLIOGRAPHY: M. Ellenbogen, *Ḥevel ha-Kesef: Record of the Kacenelenbogen Family...* (Heb. and Eng., 1937); M. Wollsteiner, *Genealogische Uebersicht ueber einige Zweige der Nachkommenschaft des Rabbi Meir Katzenelenbogen von Padua* (1898); J.B. Samuel, *Records of the Samuel Family Including the Katzenelenbogen...* (1912); Graetz, Hist, 5 (1949), 238–41 (on Ezekiel); N. Rosenstein, *These are the Generations* (1967).

[Reuven Michael]

KATZENELLENBOGEN, DAVID TEVEL (1850–1930), rabbi and talmudic scholar in Russia. Born in Taurage, Lithuania, he was appointed rabbi in Virbalis, Lithuania, in 1876, serving there until 1908, when he became rabbi of St. Petersburg, where he remained until his death. He gained the respect of the czarist authorities and was able to have the ban on *sheḥitah* in force in Finland canceled. In 1915 he headed the religious committee for the supply of *kasher* food to the Jewish soldiers in the Russian army. On his initiative a fund was established in the U.S. for the support of Russian refugees. Katzenellenbogen, whose notes to the Jerusalem Talmud first appeared in the Krotoschin edition of 1871, was the author of *Ma'yan Mei Nefto'aḥ* (1923) and *Divrei David* (1927).

BIBLIOGRAPHY: S.N. Gottlieb, *Oholei Shem* (1912), 369.

KATZENELLENBOGEN, MEIR BEN ISAAC (known as **Maharam** (acronym of **M**orenu **Ha-R**av **M**eir) **of Padua**; 1473–1565), one of the greatest Italian rabbis and halakhists of his time. Meir's father was the son-in-law of Jehiel *Luria, the first rabbi of Brest-Litovsk (Brisk). Meir was born in Prague where together with Shalom *Shakhna he studied under Jacob *Pollak. From Prague he went to Padua, where he studied under Judah b. Eliezer ha-Levi *Minz, marrying his granddaughter, Hannah, daughter of Abraham b. Judah ha-Levi *Minz. In 1525, after his father-in-law's death, he was appointed rabbi of the Ashkenazi synagogue of Padua, serving there until his death. Meir was also head of the council of regional rabbis in Venice and he took an active part in their meetings despite his many other responsibilities. Many rabbis, including Moses *Isserles, addressed him in their responsa as the "*av bet din* of the republic of Venice." He also represented the Padua region at Venice meetings in matters of a general nature, not only in religious affairs. On June 21, 1554 the heads of seven Italian communities (Venice, Rome, Bologna, Ferrara, Mantua, Reggio, and Modena) assembled in Ferrara and enacted *takkanot* for the benefit of the population. Katzenellenbogen presided and headed the list of signatories in the capacity of "delegate of representations of the republic of Venice." He was renowned for his modesty, his benign disposition, and the fatherly interest he took in the students in his yeshivah of Padua, to which aspiring scholars streamed from near and far. The great esteem in which he was held by his contemporaries found expression in a tablet affixed to his seat in the Ashkenazi synagogue which read, "No man [has] sat there till this day," as testified by Isaac Ḥayyim

Kohen, a cantor who saw the tablet 120 years after Meir's death. In 1555 Joshua *Soncino of Constantinople appealed to him to intervene against the boycott by the Jews of the port of *Ancona, a boycott supported by Don Joseph *Nasi, his mother-in-law Gracia Mendes *Nasi, and the greatest rabbis of Turkey. It is not known, however, whether Meir took any action. In 1558 he signed two bans against the study of Kabbalah. The great scholars of the generation, including Samuel di *Modena, Isaac *Foa, Joseph *Katz, Solomon *Luria, Moses Isserles, Obadiah *Sforno, and Moses *Alashkar, were in halakhic correspondence with him.

His son Samuel Judah succeeded him after his death. Katzenellenbogen published the responsa of Mahari Mintz and Maharam Padua (Venice, 1553), including 16 responsa of Judah Minz salvaged from his writings, followed by the *Seder Gittin va-Ḥaliẓah* of Abraham Minz, completed by Katzenellenbogen, and finally 90 of his own responsa, and Maimonides' *Mishneh Torah* (Venice, 1550–51), with his own glosses and novellae. The publication of the *Mishneh Torah*, with an abridgment of Katzenellenbogen's commentary and without Katzenellenbogen's knowledge, by Marcantonio Justinian, rival of Katzenellenbogen's co-publisher, the non-Jewish printer Bragadin, gave rise to a quarrel and recriminations and led finally to the burning of the Talmud in 1554 by order of the pope. Moses Isserles placed a ban on Justinian's *Mishneh Torah*. In 1563 Katzenellenbogen, together with his partner, Ezra b. Isaac of Fano, published in Mantua the *Midrash Tanḥuma*. In 1546 he published in Heddernheim, Germany, *seliḥot* (penitential prayers) with omissions and changes dictated by censorship. S.I. Mulder (see bibliography) claims that the first portrait to be painted of a Jew was that of Katzenellenbogen, which was made without his knowledge.

BIBLIOGRAPHY: Ghirondi, in: *Kerem Ḥemed*, 3 (1838), 91–96; S.I. Mulder, *Eene zeldzame medaille* (1859), 3; Zunz, Gesch, 255f.; Zunz, Ritus, 148; I. Eisenstadt and S. Wiener, *Da'at Kedoshim* (1897–98), 82–84; S. Assaf, *Mekorot u-Meḥkarim* (1946), 240–6; M. Straschun, *Mivḥar Ketavim* (1969), 168–86; Schwarzfuchs, in: *Scritti in Memoria di Leone Carpi* (Italian pt.; 1967), 112–32; Siev, in: *Hadorom*, 28 (1968), 160–95; Tishby, in: *Perakim*, 1 (1967/68), 131–82; I.S. Lange, in: *Miscellanea di Studi in Memoria di D. Disigni* (1969), 49–76 (Heb. pt.).

[Shlomo Tal]

KATZENELLENBOGEN, ẒEVI HIRSH (Naphtali; 1796–1868), one of the early *maskilim* in Vilna, Hebrew author, and educator. In his youth, he wrote *Netivot Olam*, a commentary on the *Baraita of the 32 Rules* (Vilna, 1822). He also wrote poetry and eulogies, among them a eulogy of R. Ḥayyim of *Volozhin, "*Naḥal Dimah*" ("A Stream of Tears," 1821). He was popular both with the old generation in Vilna and with the *maskilim*, and contributed to the periodicals *Pirḥei Ẓafon* and *Ha-Karmel*. When the government rabbinical school was founded in Vilna in 1847, he became director of Hebrew studies despite the opposition of the Orthodox, and served for 18 years. Upon his retirement his son Ḥayyim succeeded him.

BIBLIOGRAPHY: H.N. Maggid, *Ir Vilna* (1900), 232–48; S. Ginzburg, *Historishe Shriftn*, 2 (1937), 91–116.

[Yehuda Slutsky]

KATZENELSON, BARUCH (1900–1968), Hebrew and Yiddish poet. Born in Slutsk, Belorussia, Katzenelson moved in 1922 to the U.S., where he studied and taught Hebrew. In 1934 he settled in Israel, where he lived in Kefar Sava and taught high school from 1939 to 1965. From the age of 13, he wrote in both Yiddish and Hebrew. Between 1919 and 1926 Katzenelson published poetry and literary criticism in Yiddish. From 1925 on his Hebrew poetry again appeared, and was published in most of the literary forums in the United States and Israel. His books of poetry are: *Le-Or ha-Ner* (1930), *Be-Kur Demamah* (1948), and *Mi-Lev el Lev* (1954). Yehudah Ereẓ and Avraham M. Koler edited his letters in two volumes (1970).

BIBLIOGRAPHY: Rejzen, Leksikon, 3 (1929), 536; N. Hinitz, in: *Hadoar*, 47 (1968), 593–4.

[Getzel Kressel]

KATZENELSON, ITZHAK (1886–1944), poet and dramatist in Hebrew and in Yiddish. Born in Korelichi, near Novogrudok, in Russia, he received his early education from his father, the Hebrew writer Jacob Benjamin Katzenelson. He later lived in Lodz, where he opened a Hebrew secular school of which he was principal until the outbreak of World War II. During this period he visited Palestine a number of times but did not realize his dream of settling there. During the early years of the war he was in the Warsaw ghetto where he witnessed the methodic annihilation of the Jewish community of Warsaw, including his wife and two of his sons, and where he joined the Jewish partisan organization Deror. In possession of a Honduran passport, he was transferred to the Vittel concentration camp in France, in May 1943. In April 1944, however, he was deported to Auschwitz, where he and his surviving son perished on May 3, 1944.

Katzenelson began his literary career in 1904, writing in Yiddish for Mordecai *Spector's *Yidishe Folkstsaytung* and *Peretz' *Yidishe Bibliotek*, and in Hebrew for *Frischmann's *Ha-Dor*. During the Holocaust he wrote prolifically in both Hebrew and Yiddish, and kept a Hebrew diary which is a moving eyewitness account of the period. His poem, *Dos Lid fun Oysgehargetn Yidishn Folk* ("Poem of the Murdered Jewish People," 1945) which he began in October 1943 and completed at Vittel in 1944, is one of the greatest literary expressions of the tragedy of the Holocaust. Written after he witnessed the extermination of the Jews, this poem gives a shattering account of what he saw and expresses his horror and grief, his protest and helplessness. While Katzenelson's songs and poems for children and his light verse gained him a reputation as a poet who wrote about youth and the joy of life, he also wrote sad, ironic, and sentimental songs about tragic aspects of life. He was greatly influenced by Heine, whose poems he translated into Hebrew. His poems, with their original style and rhythm, combine lightness with a deep elegiac tone.

Many of Katzenelson's poems were set to music and became favorite children's songs and Israeli folk songs. These include: *Mah Yafim ha-Leylot bi-Khena'an; Raḥel Amdah al ha-Ayin; Ḥad Gadya; Heidad, Heidad; Ginnah Ketannah; Gillu ha-Gelilim; Ḥamesh Shanim al Mikha'el*; and the Ḥanukkah play song *Antiochus*. In his Hebrew prose poem *"Bi-Gevulot Lita"* ("In Lithuania's Borders," 1909), he writes with depth and emotion about both the spiritual and the earthly. The major problem and purpose of existence is treated by Katzenelson in his dramatic poem *"Ha-Navi"* ("The Prophet," 1922), which he considered his greatest work. A number of Katzenelson's plays have been produced. His Hebrew works appeared in three volumes (1938); *Ketavim Aḥaronim* ("Final Works," 1947) was published posthumously. In 1950, an institute for research of the Holocaust, which bears his name, was established at Kibbutz Loḥamei ha-Getta'ot in Israel. Katzenelson's biblical play *Al Neharot Bavel* was published in 1995. An English translation of his Vittel Diary (May 1943–September 1943) was published in 1964. A translation of *Dos Lid fun Oysgehargetn Yidishn Folk* appeared as *The Song of the Murdered Jewish People* in 1980. Katzenelson's *Ketavim* appeared in 1982, followed by Yeḥiel Szeintuch's edition of *Ketavim she-Niẓlu mi-Geto Varshah* (1990).

BIBLIOGRAPHY: A. Ben-Or, *Toledot ha-Sifrut ha-Ivrit ha-Ḥadashah*, 3 (1950), 120–9; Ẓ. Katzenelson-Nachumov, *Yitzḥak Katzenelson* (Yid., 1948); J.J. Trunk, *Poyln* (1951), 145–66; Rejzen, Leksikon, 3 (1929), 539–46; Kressel, Leksikon, 2 (1967), 791–2; S. Even-Shoshan (ed.), *Yesh li Shir le-Yaldei Yisrael* (1954), 122, 125–34, 137–49. **ADD. BIBLIOGRAPHY:** S. Even-Shoshan, *Y. Katzenelson Mekonen ha-Sho'ah* (1964); N.H. Rosenbloom, "The Threnodist of the Holocaust," in: *Judaism*, 26 (1977), 232–47; Y. Szeintuch, "The Work of Y. Katzenelson in the Warsaw Ghetto," in: *Jerusalem Quarterly*, 26 (1983), 46–61; Y. Szeintuch, "Y. Katzenelson and His 'Vittel Diary,'" in: *Jewish Book Annual*, 42 (1984), 199–207; E. Shmueli, *"Al Shirat Y. Katzenelson,"* in: *Mi-Bifenim*, 46:3 (1984), 339–50; E. Lahad, Y. Szeintuch, and Z. Shaner (eds.), *Ha-Yeẓirah ha-Sifrutit be-Yiddish u-ve-Ivrit ba-Geto* (1984).

[Elias Schulman]

KATZENELSON, JUDAH LEIB BENJAMIN (pseudonym **Buki ben Yogli**; 1846–1917), physician, writer, and scholar. Born in Chernigov, he studied at the yeshivot of Bobruisk but became attracted to the Haskalah, and attended the government rabbinical seminary at Zhitomir. He later studied medicine at the Military Medical Academy at St. Petersburg, where he practiced medicine. Katzenelson wrote both in Hebrew and in Russian and from 1879 to 1884 he was a correspondent for the Russian-Jewish newspaper, *Russki Yevrey*, using it as a means through which he called on the Russian-Jewish intelligentsia to help their persecuted brethren. Katzenelson believed that the Haskalah with its particular emphasis on trades and agricultural work would solve the problems of Russian Jewry. In 1891 he published a series of articles in *Ha-Meliẓ* in which he called for a return to the soil. He became a member of the Central Committee of the *Jewish Colonization Association, which was established for this purpose. Katzenelson was also active in Ḥevrat Mefiẓei ha-Haskalah ("The Society for the Dissemination of Enlightenment") and was chairman of Agudat Ḥovevei Sefat Ever ("Society of Friends of the Hebrew Language") in Russia. A lecturer at the Institute of Jewish Studies established by Baron David *Guenzburg in St. Petersburg, he headed the school after the death of its founder. In 1909 Katzenelson visited Palestine and returned to Russia full of enthusiasm for Jewish agriculture and the renaissance of the Hebrew language.

In 1905, the first and only volume of *Kol Kitvei J.L. Katzenelson*, entitled *Ḥezyonot ve-Hirhurim*, was published. His studies on early Jewish history were mostly written in Russian; he was also one of the editors of the Jewish-Russian encyclopedia *Yevreyskaya Entsiklopediya*. Among his literary endeavors, his best-known work is *Shirat ha-Zamir* ("The Song of the Nightingale," 1895), a novel whose protagonist is a rabbinical student yearning for agricultural life. The motif recurs in *Adnei ha-Sadeh*, an allegorical legend in which a wanderer comes upon a race of men who are tied to the soil by a living cord. His envy and longing also to be bound to the land echoes that of the student in *Shirat ha-Zamir*. A collection of Katzenelson's legends and stories were published posthumously in 1918, and in 1944 Jacob *Fichmann edited an anthology of his stories entitled *Shirat ha-Zamir* (the main work included in it), to which he wrote an introduction on the life of the author.

[Yehuda Slutsky]

Since he was well versed in rabbinical and general literature as well as in medicine, Katzenelson was able to make significant contributions to the study of ancient Hebrew medicine. His medical historical articles, first published in the Hebrew journal *Ha-Yom* and later in book form under the title *Remaḥ Evarim* (St. Petersburg, 1888), considerably enriched the medical terminology of the Hebrew language. His chief work, *Ha-Talmud ve-Ḥokhmat ha-Refu'ah* ("Talmud and Medicine"), published posthumously in Berlin (1928), includes studies on talmudic osteology, pathologic anatomy, and hemophilia. His other medical historical contributions concern nomenclature of skin diseases in the Bible, ritual cleanliness in the Bible and Talmud, and anatomy in the Talmud.

[Suessmann Muntner]

BIBLIOGRAPHY: D. Frishman, *Parẓufim* (1931), 54–61; M. Ribolow, *Sefer ha-Massot* (1928), 72–77; Z. Shazar, *Or Ishim*, 1 (1964), 154–62; S.R. Kagan, *Jewish Medicine* (1952), 555; Waxman, Literature, 4 (1960^2), 154ff., 702ff.; Rejzen, Leksikon, 3 (1929), 536–9; Kressel, Leksikon, 2 (1967), 790–1; P. Lachower, *Meḥkarim ve-Nisyonot*, 1 (1925), 135–41; J. Klausner, *Yoẓerim u-Vonim*, 1 (1943^2), 293–7; B. Katz, in: J.L. Katzenelson, *Mah she-Ra'u Einai ve-Shame'u Oznai* (1947), 169–277.

KATZENELSON, NISSAN (1862–1923), Russian Zionist. Born in Bobruisk, Belorussia, he completed his studies in physics in Berlin. He settled in Libau (Liepaja), where he worked in his father's timber business. Joining the Zionist movement at its inception, at the Third Congress (1899) he was elected a director of the *Jewish Colonial Trust. He was one of *Herzl's close aides and made the preparations for his Russian journey, on which he accompanied him (1903). Herzl appointed Katzenelson as his personal representative in all negotiations with the Russian authorities. In 1905 he was elected chairman of the board of the Jewish Colonial Trust. He participated in the activities of the League for Equal Rights for Jews in Russia. Elected to the First Duma (1906), Katzenelson joined the Russian liberal Kadet party, and as its spokesman took part in the work of the Duma finance committee. When the First Duma was dissolved, he was among the signatories of the manifesto calling for civil disobedience and the nonpayment of taxes ("The Vyborg Manifesto"), for which he was sentenced to six months' imprisonment. After his release, he concentrated on local communal work and was chairman of the committee for Jewish emigration in Libau, one of the chief Baltic ports of Jewish emigration from Russia. In World War I he moved to Petrograd and helped in relief work for Jewish refugees, returning to Libau in 1918.

BIBLIOGRAPHY: S.L. Zitron, *Leksikon Ẓiyyoni* (1924), 594–5; *Yevreyskaya Letopis*, 3 (1924), 230–1; J. Slutzky, in: *Bobruisk*, 2 (Heb. and Yid., 1967), 518–9 and index.

[Yehuda Slutsky]

KATZENELSON, YOSEF (1896–1940), *Revisionist leader. Born in Bobruisk, Belorussia, Katzenelson went to Palestine in 1924. He was active in the Revisionist movement in Palestine and the *Irgun Ẓeva'i Le'ummi. In 1938 he was sent on a mission to Europe where he headed the "illegal" immigration operations of the New Zionist Organization until the outbreak of World War II. In January 1940, he fell ill and died in Nazi-occupied Warsaw. His remains were brought to Jerusalem in 1957.

BIBLIOGRAPHY: Tidhar, 1 (1947), 235–6; D. Niv, *Ma'arekhot ha-Irgun ha-Ẓeva'i ha-Le'ummi*, 2 (1965), 3 (1967), index; H. Lazar-Litai, *Af-Al-Pi* (1959), index; *Bobruisk – Sefer Zikkaron*, 2 (1967), 559–62.

[David Niv]

KATZIR (Katchalski), AHARON (1913–1972), Israeli biochemist and biophysicist. Born in Kiev, Russia, he immigrated to Ereẓ Israel in 1925 with his family, which included his brother Ephraim, who later became the fourth president of the State of Israel (see *Katzir, Ephraim). He studied biology and chemistry at the Hebrew University in Jerusalem and completed his doctorate with honors. To complement his studies in life sciences he also studied mathematics and philosophy and began working at the university as an assistant in the Department of Theoretical Organic and Macromolecular Chemistry. At the invitation of Prof. Chaim *Weizmann he joined the Weizmann Institute of Science in 1948, where he established and chaired the Department of Polymer Research until his death. To strengthen the ties between basic and industrial research he also established the institute's Department of Plastics. In his scientific research Katzir sought to understand the molecular basis of the processes of life. His discoveries in the study of polyelectrolytes led to a new field of study of energy exchange, known as mechanochemistry. The contemporary developments in the field of nanotechnology, such as molecular robots, are based on mechanochemistry. His interest in thermodynamics led him to develop a mathematical approach to exact research on the permeability of biological membranes. His mathematical theory, summarized in his *Non-Equilibrium Thermodynamics in Biophysics*, was accepted and applied by scientists worldwide. As a result of this research he was awarded the Israel Prize in natural science together with Ora *Kedem in 1961 and many more important prizes. Katzir was instrumental in founding the Israel Academy of Sciences in 1959 and was its vice president from 1960 to 1962 and president from 1962 to 1968. Among his many other activities, he played an active role in founding Ben-Gurion University of the Negev. Katzir was involved in military defense, both as a member of the *Haganah and as one of the founders of Hemed, the scientific corps of the Israel Defense Forces. He was also an extraordinarily gifted lecturer and was considered one of the fathers of popular science in Israel. Over the years he published numerous popular articles and books such as *The Crucible of Scientific Revolution* (1971), and lectured in nonscientific forums. He was committed to humanity in general and to Israeli society in particular, and was very much involved in day-to-day affairs such as education, community action, and defense. On May 30, 1972, Aharon Katzir was murdered while waiting for his luggage during a terrorist attack at Ben-Gurion Airport.

[Bracha Rager (2nd ed.)]

KATZIR (Katchalski), EPHRAIM (1916–), fourth president of the State of Israel (1973–78); biochemist and biophysicist. Born in Kiev, Russia, Katchalski was taken to Ereẓ Israel in 1925. He studied life sciences at the Hebrew University of Jerusalem and completed his doctorate under the supervision of Prof. Max Frankel, head of the Department of Theoretical and Macromolecular Chemistry at the University (1941–45). He joined the Weizmann Institute of Science, Rehovot, Israel (1948), and served as head of the Department of Biophysics (1949–73). He was chief scientist of the Ministry of Defense (1966–68), and was instrumental in establishing the office of Chief Scientist in the major government ministries as well as in the promotion of high-tech industry and the establishment of the biotechnology industry in Israel. He was influential in advancing education in the country. His research dealt mainly with the synthesis and study of the physicochemical and biological properties of polyamino acids as protein models and the synthetic polyamino acids synthesized, such as polyglycine, polylysine, polyglutamic acid, and polyproline.

Katchalski wrote extensively on proteins and natural products such as nucleic acids. He was a member of many national and international societies and in 1966 was the first Israeli to be elected to the U.S. National Academy of Sciences. Katchalski was a brother of Aharon *Katzir, the polymer chemist. In the early days of the State of Israel, together with his brother and Prof E.D. *Bergmann, he was among the founders of the research, development, and production of novel weapons for the Israeli army.

Upon assuming the presidency, Katchalski adopted the name Katzir, which had previously been adopted by his brother Aharon, who was murdered at Ben-Gurion Airport in 1972 by a Japanese terrorist in the service of the Palestinians. As president he hosted President *Sadat of Egypt during his historic 1977 visit to Jerusalem.

[Bracha Rager (2nd ed.)]

KATZIR, JUDITH (1963–), Israeli writer. Katzir was born in Haifa. She studied general literature and cinema at Tel Aviv University and began publishing her stories in the Israeli press in the 1980s. Her first book, *Sogrim et ha-Yam* ("Closing the Sea," 1992), a collection of four novellas, appeared in 1990. The opening story, "Schlafstunde," recounts the first love experience of the narrator and her cousin, and interweaves moments of sexual excitement with the story of death in the family. It is already in this novella that Katzir's rich language and powerful, sensual descriptions are evident. Another story, "Fellini's Shoes," tells of a hotel waitress who dreams of becoming a movie star with the help of a failed film director who apparently had once met Fellini. "Disneyel" is a moving monologue of a daughter to her unconscious mother, and "Closing the Sea" recounts a disillusioned friendship. Katzir's first novel, *Le-Matisse Yesh et ha-Shemesh ba-Beten* ("Matisse Has the Sun in his Belly," 1995), is the story of a passionate liaison between a young woman and an older man, ending when the woman emancipates herself and goes her own way. Three novellas make up Katzir's collection *Migdalorim shel Yabasha* ("Inland Lighthouses," 1999) and all three have in common the sense of resignation and the acceptance of a stable life in lieu of passionate intensity.

In her second novel, *Hineh Ani Mathilah* ("Here I Begin," 2003), Katzir tells the story of Rivi, an imaginative and talented schoolgirl and her intense, erotic relationship with Michaela, her teacher of literature. The story oscillates between past experiences recorded by Rivi as a girl who is writing diary-letters to Anne Frank, and her new role as wife and mother, who nonetheless remains in touch with the teacher in New York. Friendship and physical attraction of women open a window on a subject rarely touched upon in Hebrew literature. Katzir also wrote books for children and a play about the writer Devorah *Baron. She occasionally taught courses in creative writing and worked as editor for Hakibbutz Hameuchad Publishing House. All her books were bestsellers, and she received the Platinum and the Golden Book Prizes. In 1996 she was awarded the Prime Minister's Prize for literature. Her books were translated into a number of languages (including German, Dutch, and French). "Schlafstunde" is included in G. Abramson (ed.), *The Oxford Book of Hebrew Short Stories* (1996). Further information concerning translations are available at the ITHL website at www.ithl.org.il.

BIBLIOGRAPHY: H. Herzig, "*Efsharuyot Aḥerot be-Sogrim et ha-Yam*," in: *Siman Keriah*, 21 (1990), 293–299; R. Kritz, "*J. Katzir, Bibliografiyah*," in: *Erev Rav* (1990), 360–362; Y. Oren, "*Azah mi-Mavet ha-Ahavah*," in: *Apiryon*, 41 (1996), 21–33; S. Schifman, "*Ha-Im Ani Nimẓet: Sippur ha-Ḥanikhah ha-Nashi eẓel Z. Shalev ve-J. Katzir*," in: *Mikan*, 2 (2001), 125–141; Y. Ben-Mordechai, "*Kevod ha-Adam ve-Ḥeruto shel ha-Maḥazai: Al 'Devorah Baron' shel J. Katzir*," in: *Bamah*, 162 (2001), 5–11; M. Muchnik, "Sentence Length in two Novellas by Y. Katzir," in: *Hebrew Studies*, 43 (2002), 7–20; E. Adivi-Shoshan, in: *Iton 77*, 285 (2003), 20–25; E. Carandina, "Il sabra 'senza qualità' in un racconto di Y. Katzir," in: *Annali di Ca'Foscari*, 43:3 (2004), 43–58.

[Anat Feinberg (2nd ed.)]

KATZMAN, SAM (1901–1973), U.S. motion picture producer. Born in New York, Katzman entered the film industry as a prop boy at age 13 and worked his way up, learning virtually every aspect of film production before becoming a producer himself. A prolific producer, his more than 230 films (between 1934 and 1974) ran the gamut as well, starting with action/adventure serials and proceeding to cover such genres as westerns, science fiction, teenage musicals, and hippie/biker films. Many of his serials were based on comic strip and radio characters.

Chiefly a producer for low-budget films, Katzman's movies include the *Jungle Jim* series; *Brenda Starr, Reporter* (1945); the first live-action *Superman* (1948); *Batman and Robin* (1949); *Captain Video* (1951); *The Lost Planet* (1953); *Drums of Tahiti* (1954); *The Gun That Won the West* (1955); *Rock around the Clock* (1956); *The Werewolf* (1956); *Escape from San Quentin* (1957); *Let's Twist Again* (1962); *Kissin' Cousins* (1964); *When the Boys Meet the Girls* (1965); *Get Yourself a College Girl* (1965); *The Fastest Guitar Alive* (1967); *The Young Runaways* (1968); and *The Loners* (1972).

[Ruth Beloff (2nd ed.)]

°KATZMANN, FRIEDRICH (**Fritz**; 1906–1957), Nazi official, SS and police leader in the Radom district of the General Government from 1939 to 1941 (see *Poland, Holocaust Period). He joined the party in 1928 and the SS in 1930. In 1941 he was appointed SS and Police Leader in the newly occupied district of Galicia. In this capacity Katzmann brutally and ruthlessly organized the destruction of its local Jewry. According to Katzmann's report (Nuremberg document L-18), 434,329 Jews were deported (*ausgesiedelt*) by June 30, 1943, and 21,156 were placed in 21 labor camps, but this number was being steadily "reduced." After the war Katzmann lived under the assumed name of Bruno Albrecht but confessed his true identity before his death in Darmstadt.

BIBLIOGRAPHY: R. Henkys, *Die nationalsozialistischen Gewaltverbrechen* (1964), index; IMT, *Trial of the Major War Criminals*, 24 (1949), index; G. Reitlinger, *Final Solution* (1968), index; R. Hilberg, *Destruction of the European Jews* (1961), index.

[Yehuda Reshef]

KATZNELSON, BERL (**Beeri**; 1887–1944), central figure of the Second Aliyah, a leader of the Zionist Labor movement, educator, and writer. Born in Bobruisk, Belorussia, son of a merchant, *maskil*, and a member of Ḥovevei Zion, Katznelson was a frail child. He attended *ḥeder* irregularly and was taught by private tutors, with his father's well-stocked Hebrew, Yiddish, and Russian library serving as a constant source of instruction and knowledge. A passionate reader with an exceptional memory and keen interest in current problems, he mastered Hebrew literature and Russian revolutionary and scientific writing, took the requisite state examinations, and served for some time as tutor in a rural family.

In 1902, as an usher at the Russian Zionist Conference in Minsk, Katznelson was deeply impressed by Ḥ.D. *Horowitz's lecture on the abnormality of the Jewish economic structure. While still young, he had already developed a reputation as an acute and independent-minded debater on theoretical problems of nationalism and socialism. In his own neighborhood, as well as in Kiev and Odessa, he took part in public discussions with leaders of the various movements, including Ber *Borochov. Although he first joined *Po'alei Zion, Katznelson shifted his allegiance to the *Zionist-Socialists, whose leaders, Naḥman *Syrkin, Jacob *Lestschinsky, and Nahum *Shtif, were convinced by their study of contemporary Jewish life that the future of the Diaspora would be dark and uncertain. For a short time Katznelson joined the ranks of Ha-Teḥiyyah, attracted by its national spirit, revolutionary anti-Czarist ardor, and devotion to Jewish self-defense, including such terrorist acts as the attempted assassination of Krushevan, the organizer of the Kishinev pogrom. He was repelled, however, by its lack of interest in actual settlement in Ereẓ Israel, as well as its negative attitude toward the revival of Hebrew.

In Bobruisk, Katznelson took a post in a school for poor girls, subsidized by the Jewish Society for the Propagation of Enlightenment (Mefiẓei Haskalah), where he taught Hebrew literature and Jewish history, both in Yiddish, and sent to the society's headquarters reports that were published in its monthly pedagogic journal. He also served as librarian in the Hebrew-Yiddish public library that had been established in Bobruisk to counter the municipality's Russian library. Beloved by the young people who came to him for books, he became their guide and teacher.

In 1908, Katznelson wrote in one of his letters: "What I want is to go to Ereẓ Israel, to do something worthwhile, to light a little spark. I am drawn to the stubborn, hard-working few who have abandoned everything they had here to begin a new life and free themselves of Exile." This had been his goal since childhood. In order to achieve it and to be able to bring his family after him, he decided to learn a trade. At first he worked for a tinsmith; then went to the "Trud" Trade School in Odessa, where he was an iron engraver; and finally he became a laborer in a Bobruisk foundry. Lacking dexterity, he found these efforts enormously difficult and became deeply depressed. In the fall of 1908, after having been rejected for military service and suffering from a severe illness, he was able to sail from Odessa with his pay from the Hebrew library and a prize from the Society for the Propagation of Enlightenment.

Katznelson felt that the Zionist movement had begun by summoning the Jewish people to greatness, but only a decade later its leaders were lost in trifles, playing with superficial nationalism and elections to parliaments in the countries of the Diaspora. Even Labor Zionism, initially inspired by messianic hopes for the Jewish people and the world, had become the "servant of alien revolutions." His own comrades were opposed to his *aliyah*, and he kept his departure a secret from virtually all of them. Though he met disillusioned young people returning to Europe from Ereẓ Israel both in Odessa and in Jaffa, he was undismayed by their scorn for Zionism and for the "naive newcomers misled by Zionist propagandists." When he landed at Jaffa, making his way among the crowds of Arabs on the shore, he felt certain that this was his "final destination" and that he had broken completely with the past. His only friend in Ereẓ Israel, whom he knew from home, was the poet David Shimonovitz (*Shimoni), who had left a few months before Katznelson and had become a watchman in the vineyards of Judea.

Katznelson found work at Bahria, about an hour by foot from *Petaḥ Tikvah. He shared a room in *Ein Gannim with A.D. *Gordon and Joseph Ḥayyim *Brenner, who quickly became his closest friends. As he was employed only intermittently, he spent much time wandering about the country. His observations led him to question the value of "the conquest of labor" in the Jewish villages, although this was then the principal goal of the labor movement. He was depressed by the poverty and dependence of the workers in those villages; by the Jewish overseers armed with whips; and by the farmers' eagerness to employ Arabs. He envisaged instead free settlement of self-employed workers on the nationally owned land of the *Jewish National Fund (JNF). His devotion to the principles of the JNF led him to conceive the idea of the smallholders' cooperative (later called *moshav ovedim), while his pursuit of equality in work and life led him to the concept of the kevuẓah. When the Kinneret Farm was established by the *Palestine Office of the Zionist Organization, Katznelson made his way there. Along with the other workers, he was in a constant state of conflict with the administration. When the head of the Palestine Office, Arthur *Ruppin, was finally asked to come to Kinneret to settle matters, Katznelson was chosen to present the workers' case, demanding that the workers themselves be allowed to manage their affairs.

Katznelson became secretary of the Council of Galilean Farm Workers, which was founded during his stay at Kinneret. A year later, when he returned to Petaḥ Tikvah, the first workers' conference in Judea (1911) elected him secretary of the Council of Judean Farm Workers. His first essay, "*Mi-Bifnim*" ("From Within"), published in *Ha-Po'el ha-Ẓa'ir* (Autumn 1911) described his disillusionment with the Zionist and even the Ẓe'irei Zion and Po'alei Zion movements for trying to influence life in Ereẓ Israel though their members remained in the Diaspora: "We workers here are not simply a small fraction of the Jewish working class, but a completely unique group – self-reliant, self-supporting – something whole.… If ever we, as an organized group, enter into connection with a movement abroad, it will have to be a movement not merely 'interested' in Ereẓ Israel, but dedicated to the ideal of personal *aliyah*, to a life of labor and liberation of the personality."

Returning to Kinneret in the World War I period of hunger and want, Katznelson, together with Meir Rotberg, proposed the establishment of consumer cooperatives, to which he gave the name "Hamashbir" (see *Hamashbir Hamerkazi). To meet the health problems of the workers, almost all of whom were unmarried and without families or homes, he helped initiate Kuppat Ḥolim (the Sick Fund). He also began to develop a network of cultural activities – lectures, libraries, adult education, translations of world classics, and book publishing. When news of *He-Ḥalutz reached Katznelson during World War I, he wrote a memorable epistle to the *ḥalutz* movement (1917), setting forth a program of agricultural and cultural training to be followed by its members until it became possible for them to come to Ereẓ Israel. In "Toward the Future," an address delivered at the seventh conference of agricultural workers on Purim, 1918 – when only a small number of Jews had managed to remain in Judea, and Galilee was cut off entirely – Katznelson called on the labor parties to unite in order to establish a self-reliant working community. Influenced by reading this address, David *Ben-Gurion, then in the ranks of the *Jewish Legion (with which he had returned to Palestine), enthusiastically agreed with the call for labor unity. Katznelson joined the Jewish Legion as a volunteer in 1918, serving until 1920. In the Legion Ben-Gurion met Katznelson, whom he had hardly known before. The two addressed an assembly of legionnaires in the Tell-al-Kabīr Camp, and from that moment on the movement for labor unity began to gain adherents. A committee was established representing Po'alei Zion, Ha-Po'el ha-Ẓa'ir and nonpartisans. In the three centers of the Agricultural Workers' Union – Judea, Samaria, and Galilee – a committee was elected to work toward the unification of the three area councils and to investigate the feasibility of a general union of workers.

Katznelson was asked to compose and publish a program for working-class unity in Ereẓ Israel ("*Aḥdut ha-Avodah"), which was to be affiliated with the Zionist movement and the world socialist movement. Through large-scale immigration, the program was to recreate Jewish national life in Ereẓ Israel in the form of a labor society, based on freedom and equality, self-reliance, control over its property, and self-determination in matters of economy and culture. The means toward this end would be national ownership of the soil and of natural resources; public-owned capital; a pioneering *aliyah*; and dissemination of the Hebrew language and culture among all Jews.

In the spring of 1919, the conference of agricultural workers convened at Petaḥ Tikvah to vote on the issue of labor unity. The lecturer on this issue was Katznelson, and his program was adopted, with Ha-Po'el ha-Ẓa'ir abstaining. The conference defined the aim of Zionism as the establishment of a free Jewish state in Ereẓ Israel. Katznelson was chosen to edit *Kunteres*, the newly created weekly that voiced Aḥdut ha-Avodah's ideas. Labor unity was still incomplete, with the majority of Ha-Po'el ha-Ẓa'ir remaining outside the new framework. In 1920, in accordance with the proposal made by Joseph *Trumpeldor, a General Federation of Jewish Labor (the *Histadrut) was established at a conference in Haifa. Ha-Po'el ha-Ẓa'ir and Aḥdut ha-Avodah still continued to exist independently, and Katznelson and his colleagues on *Kunteres* continued to urge that the two merge, first in Ereẓ Israel and then abroad. The union was eventually achieved in 1930, when a united labor party – *Mapai – was founded.

A decision to found a labor daily followed the establishment of the Histadrut. Katznelson insisted that the editor be elected by the national conference of the Histadrut and thus derive his authority directly from it, as did the members of the Histadrut Executive. In addition, the editor was to be free to choose the members of his staff. After protracted discussion and debate, the first edition of *Davar* was published in 1925 according to Katznelson's terms. He was selected as the editor and chose a staff of five. His moral authority and the influence he exercised over his colleagues attracted many attentive readers to the paper, even outside its own movement, and made it a spiritual guide for the labor class and many of the intelligentsia. Katznelson was a member of the delegation sent to the United States in 1921 to muster support among American Jewish workers for the Workers' Bank (Bank ha-Po'alim), established by the Histadrut. This journey marked the beginning of the close relationship between labor in Ereẓ Israel and the American Jewish trade unions, which had been far removed from Zionism up to that time. Thereafter, annual delegations from the Histadrut came to America to work with the *Gewerkschaften* (Trade Union) Campaign for the Histadrut and brought "Labor Palestine" close to masses of Jews in the United States and Canada.

Katznelson believed that the JNF was the most important Zionist factor in the building of a labor society. He was appointed a director of the Fund by the Zionist Organization and was devoted to it until his death; however, he refused to join either the Zionist executive or the executive of the Va'ad Le'ummi. In order to understand the attitudes of the younger generation, he would sometimes visit groups abroad anonymously, and he invested all his ardor and talent in youth seminars at Reḥovot, on the Carmel, and at Ben Shemen. A large part of the 12 volumes of his collected works consists of his lectures at seminars and conferences which he reworked into essays.

All his life Katznelson was acutely aware of the importance of fostering the relationship between the *yishuv* and the Diaspora; viewing Labor Zionism as the Jewish revolution, equal to the revolutions of other nations; maintaining the influence of eternal Jewish values and of Hebrew literature in the movement; and thoroughly imbuing the younger generation with the age-old culture of the Jewish people. He would never compromise with his principles, even when he stood virtually alone. His was one of the few voices in labor circles to press for observance of the Sabbath and festivals, dietary laws in Histadrut kitchens, and circumcision in the kibbutzim. He showed special concern for the religiously observant members of the Histadrut and the attitude of educational institutions toward the hallowed traditions of Judaism. He was convinced that not compulsion, but the inculcation of affection and understanding for tradition, would bring young people to respect and appreciate the Jewish religious heritage.

Katznelson differed from Weizmann and Ben-Gurion in his opposition to the partition of Palestine into a Jewish state and an Arab state, as proposed by the Peel Commission in 1939. When Great Britain became increasingly hostile, he urged active struggle against the Mandatory power. Both at Zionist Congresses and within the *yishuv*, he pressed for "illegal" immigration, stating: "From now on, not the pioneer but the refugee will lead us." Under his guidance, his disciples parachuted into Nazi-held territory to try to aid Jewish survivors.

At the very beginning of World War II, Katznelson prophesied that the Jews would have to emerge from the war with a Jewish state. Ultimately he reluctantly accepted the idea of partition for the sake of free Jewish immigration, which otherwise would not have been feasible. The last stage of his activity before his death was the establishment and successful direction of the Histadrut's publishing house, Am Oved, as editor in chief. On Aug. 15, 1944, Berl Katznelson died in Jerusalem. He was buried in the cemetery of Kevuẓat Kinneret. Bet Berl at Ẓofit, Oholo on Lake Kinneret, and Kibbutz *Be'eri are all monuments to his memory.

BIBLIOGRAPHY: M. Shnir (ed.), *Al Berl Katznelson, Zikhronot ve-Divrei Ha'arakhah* (1952); Z. Goldberg, *Perakim be-Mishnato ha-Ḥevratit shel Berl Katznelson* (1964); D. Shimoni, *Pirkei Zikhronot* (1953), 235–44; Z. Shazar, *Or Ishim* (1963), 108–34; Gilboa, in: *Ot*, nos. 3–4 (1968), 120–4; M. Sharett, *Orot she-Kavu* (1969), 39–55; *Iggerot B. Katznelson*, 1900–1914, ed. by J. Sharett (1961); 1919–1922, ed. by Y. Ereẓ and A.M. Koller (1970).

[Shneur Zalman Shazar]

KATZNELSON (Shazar), RAḤEL (1888–1975), leader of the working women's movement in Ereẓ Israel, Hebrew writer, editor, and wife of the third president of the State of Israel, Zalman *Shazar. Born in Bobruisk, Belorussia, she studied in Russia and Germany and was active in Jewish working women's circles. She settled in Ereẓ Israel in 1912 and worked in agriculture in the Jezreel Valley and Galilee. Raḥel Shazar was active in the women's labor movement during the Second Aliyah and was the principal speaker during the first women workers' conventions. With the establishment of *Aḥdut ha-Avodah (A), she became the cultural coordinator of the movement and fulfilled the same post in the Histadrut from its establishment in 1920. In 1920 she married Zalman Shazar. Throughout her life she was active in the women workers' movement and carried out various missions abroad on its behalf and for the Histadrut. She edited the central journal of the women's movement, *Devar ha-Po'elet* (1934–59), and an anthology on its 25th anniversary, *Im Pa'amei ha-Dor*, 2 vols. (1964). After her husband's inauguration as president of the state, she shared his work in participating in the various study circles that met in their home. Raḥel Shazar published her first essays in 1918 and from then contributed to the labor press in Ereẓ Israel. Her articles were collected in two works, *Massot u-Reshimot* ("Essays and Articles," 1946) and *Al Admat ha-Ivrit* ("On the Soil of Hebrew," 1966). She also published *Tenu'at ha-Po'elet, Mifaleha u-She'ifoteha* ("The Projects and Aspirations of the Women Workers' Movement," 1941) and *She-Livvuni ve-Einan*, essays on women active in public life (1969).

BIBLIOGRAPHY: Z. Katznelson, in: *La-Merḥav* (May 20, 1968); I. Harari, *Ishah va-Em be-Yisrael* (1959), 358–60; D. Sadan, *Bein Din le-Ḥeshbon* (1963), 364–9; Kressel, Leksikon, 2 (1967), 904–5.

[Getzel Kressel]

KATZNELSON, REUBEN (1890–1977), Ereẓ Israel pioneer in medical services, brother of Raḥel (Shazar) *Katznelson. Born in Bobruisk, Belorussia, Katznelson was wounded in 1905 in a pogrom while on duty in the Jewish self-defense organization. In 1906 he was a member of the territorialist movement called the "Zionist Socialists (SS)" and later joined the Zionist student society He-Ḥaver in Kiev. At the outbreak of World War I he was in Ereẓ Israel and worked in Tel Aviv in building and as an agricultural laborer in Reḥovot, where he served as chairman of the workers' council. Deported by the Turks at the beginning of World War I he went to Alexandria, where he joined Joseph *Trumpeldor in the Zion Mule Corps; at the time the corps was disbanded, he had achieved the rank of sergeant major. In 1920 Katznelson was appointed director of the department of statistics of the Hadassah Medical Organization and in 1922–30 served as assistant director of Hadassah. In 1931 he established a medical organization for the Jewish villages (moshavot) in Palestine and became the director of Kuppat Ḥolim Ammamit (see State of Israel: *Health Services). In the same year he joined the General Zionists, later serving as a member of its national council. He was also the chairman of the Organization of Demobilized Soldiers. His son SHMUEL *TAMIR (1923–1987) was an Israeli politician and lawyer.

BIBLIOGRAPHY: Tidhar, 1 (1947), 305–6.

KATZNELSON, SHULAMIT (1919–1999), Ulpan founder and director. Katznelson was born in Geneva, Switzerland, and at the age of two came to Eretz Israel. Her father, Dr. Shmuel Katznelson, was a pioneer of public health care and social work in Israel. Her mother, Batsheva Katznelson, was an educator and member of the Second Knesset. Katznelson studied social work and received her master's degree from the University of Michigan in Ann Arbor. In 1951 she founded one of the first three *ulpanim* (intensive Hebrew-language courses) in Israel. As founder and director of Ulpan Akiva in Netanyah, she was cited as an outstanding example of Hebrew humanism in adult education. Katznelson managed Ulpan Akiva until 1996. From the outset, Ulpan Akiva was open not only to Jewish immigrants (*ollim*) but to the non-Jewish population as well. Subsequently, Ulpan Akiva included the teaching of spoken Arabic. In 1983 Katznelson was awarded the Knesset's Speaker's Prize for quality of life. In 1986 she was awarded the Israel Prize for her pioneering work in adult education and in the teaching of spoken Hebrew and Arabic. Katznelson was nominated for the Nobel Prize twice, in 1992 and 1993.

KATZ-SUCHY, JULIUSZ (1912–1971), Polish statesman. Born in Warsaw, Katz-Suchy joined the illegal Polish Communist Party and was the editor of several socialist publications between 1934 and 1938. He was forced to leave Poland in 1938 and made his way via Czechoslovakia to England. Katz-Suchy was the representative of the Polish Press Agency in London from 1940 to 1945 and after the war became press attaché at the Polish embassy there. Later he became department director of the Polish Foreign Ministry. From 1946 to 1951 and from 1953 to 1954 he was Poland's delegate to the United Nations. Subsequently he was Poland's representative to the European Economic Commission, representative to the International Conference of Atomic Energy (1955), and ambassador to India (1957–62). He was also director of the Polish Institute for International Affairs, and after his return from India, professor of international law at the University of Warsaw. During the antisemitic campaign in Poland following the *Six-Day War of 1967 he was removed from that position. In 1970 he went to Denmark to teach at the University of Aarhus. His brother was Benzion *Katz, rector of Tel Aviv University.

[Abraham Wein]

KAUDER, SAMUEL JUDAH BEN DAVID (Shmuel Loeb Kauders; 1766–1838), Bohemian rabbi. Born in *Bechyne, Bohemia, Kauder studied in the yeshivah of Eleazar Kallir in Kolin (where he made the acquaintance of Bezalel *Ranschburg, his lifelong friend and correspondent), and in Prague under Michael Bachrach. He settled in Prague where he officiated in the Altschul, and took an active part in the affairs of the *ḥevra kaddisha* and other communal institutions. In 1817 he was appointed to the rabbinate of the district of Budweis and Tabor with his seat in Kalladay. In 1834 he succeeded Samuel *Landau in the post of *Oberjurist* (*av bet din*; chief rabbi de facto, but not in name) of Prague. He was the last native Bohemian to hold this position, and was succeeded by the Galician *maskil* S.L. *Rapoport. His son Moses succeeded him as rabbi of the Altschul. His published works are: *Olat Shemu'el*, consisting of 111 responsa to *Oraḥ Ḥayyim* (Prague, 1823); *Ahavat Emet* (part 1, 1828), 18 homilies and sermons; and appended to it *Pe'ullat Emet*, seven halakhic discourses; and *Zikkaron ba-Sefer* (1937), a short commentary on tractate *Megillah*.

BIBLIOGRAPHY: AZDJ, 2:72 (1838), 291f.; S.L. Kauder, *Zikkaron ba-Sefer* (1937), introduction by S.Z. Lieben; R. Kestenberg-Gladstein, *Neuere Geschichte der Juden in den boehmischen Laendern*, 1 (1969), index.

[Abraham Schischa]

KAUFFMANN, ISAAC (1805–1884), founder of the Kauffmann Jewish publishing house in Germany. Kauffmann, who was born in Bouxwiller, Alsace, in 1832 went to Frankfurt where he set up a bookshop. In 1850 he established the publishing house J. Kauffmann. The first book published by the firm was *Buch vom rechten Lebenswandel* (1850), his own translation of the ethical treatise of Zerahiah ha-Yevani *Sefer ha-Yashar.* Kauffmann published the works of S.R. *Hirsch, among others.

Isaac's son IGNATZ KAUFFMANN (1849–1913) succeeded to the direction of the firm; under his aegis it published for the first time works by adherents of the *Wissenschaft des Judentums, including Moritz *Steinschneider, Leopold *Zunz, Abraham *Geiger, Abraham *Berliner, and David *Kaufmann. In 1900 Ignatz Kauffmann took over the printing house of M. Lehrberger and Co., successor to Wolf *Heidenheim's Hebrew publishing house.

From 1909 to 1936 Ignatz' son FELIX KAUFFMANN (d. 1953) directed the firm; in 1913 he became sole owner. He continued to publish works in all fields of modern Jewish scholarship, textbooks, juvenile literature, and books on Jewish art and music. Among important writers and scholars published in this later period were Hermann *Cohen, Leo *Baeck, and Franz *Rosenzweig. The 1936 catalog, the last of nearly 100 issued, contained close to 1,000 items published by the firm. Felix Kauffmann remained active in the book trade after his emigration to the United States in the Nazi era.

BIBLIOGRAPHY: *Neue Juedische Monatshefte*, 4 (1919), 69–77. **ADD. BIBLIOGRAPHY:** NDB, vol. 22 (2005), 68*.

KAUFMAN, ANDY (1949–1984), U.S. comic actor. Andrew Geoffrey Kaufman was born in New York and grew up in suburban Long Island. He graduated in 1971 from the now defunct Grahm Junior College in Boston, where he studied television. Kaufman lived in a hazy borderland between comedy and performance art. After appearing on the inaugural telecast of *Saturday Night Live* in 1975, he became famous as a comedian who provoked nervous laughter, if any at all. He was believed to be the first person to publicly, and repeatedly, perform in the garb and persona of Elvis Presley, and his impersonation was believed to be a Presley favorite. His comedy act often caused his audience to become rowdy or to simply walk out in the middle of his show. He would read *The Great Gatsby* to the audience in its entirety, sing all verses of "100 Bottles of Beer on the Wall," or impersonate a fictitious Las Vegas lounge singer named Tony Clifton. In 1978, Kaufman began playing the part of Latka Gravas on the ABC television network show *Taxi*. Latka was an immigrant auto mechanic in the taxi garage who spoke in a high-pitched accent that Kaufman concocted, and indulged in a bewildering array of personality changes. On *Saturday Night Live*, he affected what he called a Puerto Rican accent, recited nonsensical verse, and got the audience to imitate barnyard animals while he sang "Old MacDonald Had a Farm." Kaufman outraged feminists with a character he called the Intergender World Wrestling Champion, in which guise Kaufman offered $1,000 to any woman who could pin him in a match. More than 60 women accepted the challenge, and Kaufman claimed that he never lost, although he fought some to a draw. Kaufman suffered neck and back injuries in a bout with a professional male wrestler, Jerry Lawler, who was reportedly angered by Kaufman's disparaging on-air remarks about "professional" wrestling, and challenged him. Kaufman died of lung cancer, although he was not a smoker, and countless fans doubted his death, thinking he had staged it as the ultimate Andy Kaufman stunt. In 1992 the actor Jim Carrey starred in a film about Kaufman, *Man on the Moon.*

[Stewart Kampel (2nd ed.)]

KAUFMAN, AVRAHAM YOSIFOVICH (1885–1971), Jewish public figure, head of Jewish communities in the Far East. He was born in Mglin, Chernigov province, into a family of Ḥasidim and, on his mother's side, he was great grandson of the founder of this movement, *Shneur Zalman of Lyady. In 1903 Kaufman graduated from high school in Perm where he became an enthusiastic Zionist. From 1904 to 1908, he studied medicine at Berne University in Switzerland where he was vice chairman of the Union of Jewish Students. In 1908 Kaufman returned to Russia where, at the initiative of Jehiel *Tschlenow, he visited the cities of the Volga and Ural regions to disseminate Zionism. He was a delegate to three Zionist Congresses.

In 1912 Kaufman moved to *Harbin in Manchuria where he became involved in communal and Zionist activity. In late 1918 he was elected vice chairman of the National Council of Jews of Siberia and the Urals (the chairman was Moshe *Novomeysky). From 1919 to 1931 and 1933 to 1945 Kaufman was chairman of the Harbin Jewish community. During that period he was representative in China of the *Jewish National Fund and *Keren Hayesod, and official representative of the *World Zionist Organization and the *Jewish Agency, chairman of the Zionist Organization of China and head of almost all the cultural and social institutions of the Jews of Harbin. From 1921 to 1943 he was editor of the Russian language weekly *Yevreyskaya zhizn* ("Jewish Life"). At the same time he worked as chief physician at the Jewish hospital in Harbin which he had founded. From 1937 he was chairman of the National Council of Jews of East Asia (i.e., the Far East).

Kaufman was a brilliant orator and publicist and was very knowledgeable about Judaism. He devoted considerable efforts to Jewish education. Recognized as the spiritual leader of Chinese Jewry, he staunchly opposed antisemitic tendencies among the Russian emigrés in Harbin which became particularly strong after the Japanese occupation of Manchuria in 1931. Due to his indefatigable energy and personal charm, he was able to establish direct contact with the Japanese authorities in Tokyo and succeeded in having countermanded the orders issued at Hitler's urging for concentrating the Jews of China under Japanese occupation into camps specially established for that purpose.

When the Soviet Army occupied Harbin in August 1945, Kaufman was among the many arrested and taken to the Soviet Union. He was accused of spying and Zionist activities and sentenced to 25 years' imprisonment. He spent 11 years in confinement (three years in a solitary cell in Moscow and eight years in prison camp). He was released in 1956 with his criminal record erased and sent to Karaganda in Kazakhstan. During his five-year stay there he endeavored to reach Israel and succeeded in 1961. For the rest of his life he worked as a physician in an ambulatory care clinic in Ramat Gan. He also wrote his memoirs as well as a history of the Jewish communities in the Far East. He vividly described his life in the Soviet Union in his book *Lagerniy vrach* ("Camp Physician," Hebrew, 1971; Russian, Tel Aviv, 1973).

[The Shorter Jewish Encyclopaedia in Russian (2nd ed.)]

KAUFMAN, BEL (1911–), U.S. author. Born in Berlin, Kaufman was the granddaughter of the Yiddish writer *Shalom Aleichem. *Up the Down Staircase* (1965), an amusing book based on her experiences as a teacher in New York City, was made into a motion picture. She also wrote short stories and published translations from the Russian.

KAUFMAN, BORIS (1906–1980), motion picture cameraman. Kaufman was born in Bialystok, Poland. He immigrated to France in 1927, where he became the cameraman on all of Jean Vigo's films, such as *L'Atalante* (1934), as well as those of other French directors. After serving in the French army, he went to New York in 1942. He worked for American war propaganda productions and became one of America's foremost cameramen. Renowned for his exquisite black-and-white photography, Kaufman won an Academy Award and a Golden Globe in 1955 for Best Black/White Cinematography for *On the Waterfront.* Other films he worked on include *Baby Doll* (Oscar nomination for Best Cinematography, 1956), *Twelve Angry Men* (1957), *The Fugitive Kind* (1959), *Splendor in the Grass* (1961), *Long Day's Journey into Night* (1962), *The Pawnbroker* (1964), *The World of Henry Orient* (1964), *The Group* (1966), *Bye Bye Braverman* (1968), *The Brotherhood* (1969), and *Tell Me That You Love Me, Junie Moon* (1970).

Kaufman was the brother of Soviet directors Dziga Vertov (1896–1954) and Mikhail Kaufman (1897–1980).

[Ruth Beloff (2nd ed.)]

KAUFMAN, GEORGE SIMON (1889–1961), U.S. playwright and stage director. Born in Pittsburgh, Kaufman began his career as a journalist, but in 1918 turned to writing for the stage. His name is linked with over 30 hits, almost all his plays having been written in collaboration with others, such as Marc Connelly, Edna Ferber, Morrie Ryskind, and Moss Hart. For each year from 1921 to 1941, Kaufman, as either writer or director, had at least one hit Broadway show. He was an acknowledged master of stage technique and comedy, and plays such as *Once in a Lifetime* (1930), *You Can't Take it With You* (1937, Pulitzer Prize), and *The Man Who Came to Dinner* (1939) have found their way into many anthologies. In 1946 he wrote his dramatic version of *The Late George Apley*, the novel by J.P. Marquand, an admirable example of his skill in adapting from one artistic medium to another. Kaufman's versatility was shown in the musicals *The Coconuts* (1925) and *Animal Crackers* (1928), written for the Marx Brothers; *Strike up the Band* (1930); *The Band Wagon* (1931); and *Of Thee I Sing* (1932, Pulitzer Prize). Perhaps his most serious play, inspired by the prejudices and hatreds of the Hitler era, was *The American Way* (1939). Other successes by Kaufman include *Dinner at Eight* (1932), *Stage Door* (1936), *George Washington Slept Here* (1940), and *The Solid Gold Cadillac* (1951). He directed such stage hits as *Front Page* (1928), *Of Mice and Men* (1937), and *Guys and Dolls* (1950). Kaufman's early experience as a columnist and as a dramatic critic on New York newspapers developed his sensitivity to language and the demands of the theater. His plays made exciting entertainment and his satirical flashes poked fun at weaknesses in American life.

BIBLIOGRAPHY: J.M. Brown, *Broadway in Review* (1940), 88–94, 169–76; idem, *Seeing Things* (1946), 205–11; E.M. Gagey, *Revolution in American Drama* (1947), 217–20; J. Mersand, *Traditions in American Literature* (1939), 14–24; A.H. Quinn, *History of the American Drama*, 2 (1937), 220–5. **ADD. BIBLIOGRAPHY:** S. Meredith, *George S. Kaufman and His Friends* (1975).

[Joseph Mersand / Robert L. DelBane (2nd ed.)]

KAUFMAN, SIR GERALD (1930–), British politician. Originally a journalist, Kaufman served as a staff writer for the London *Daily Mirror* (1955–64) and the *New Statesman* (1964–65) as well as parliamentary press officer for the Labour Party (1965–70) before becoming a Labour Member of Parliament for a Manchester seat in 1970. He held junior ministerial posts in Labour's 1974–79 government. During Labour's long period in opposition (1979–97) Kaufman held senior posts in the shadow cabinet and was shadow home secretary (1983–87) and shadow foreign secretary (1987–92). Originally on the left of the party, in the 1980s he was increasingly attacked by Labour's militant extreme left. In latter years Kaufman was outspokenly critical of Israel's policies toward the Palestinians, especially after the fall of the Barak government, for which he was heavily criticized by the Manchester Jewish community. Kaufman was also one of the leading critics of the "dumbing down" of the BBC, and is the author or editor of several books. A backbench member of Parliament since Labour's return to power in 1997, he was recognized as a respected elder statesman and received a knighthood in 2004.

[William D. Rubinstein (2nd ed.)]

KAUFMAN, IRVING R. (1910–1992), U.S. judge who presided over the trial of Ethel and Julius Rosenberg. Born in New York City, Kaufman was educated at Fordham University, graduating from Fordham Law School in 1931 at the age of 20. He worked in the law offices of Louis Rosenberg (who was not related to Julius Rosenberg), and afterward as an assistant United States attorney. In 1949 he was appointed a judge of the U.S. District Court for the Southern District of New York; President John F. Kennedy appointed him to the U.S. Court of Appeals for the Second Circuit in 1961. Kaufman was chief judge of the Manhattan circuit court for seven years, from 1973 to 1980. Formally retiring in 1987, he was designated a senior judge and remained active on the court until the illness that preceded his death in 1992.

Much to Kaufman's frustration, his reputation was forever linked to the trial of Julius and Ethel Rosenberg in 1951. The Rosenbergs, charged with espionage for conspiring to deliver nuclear secrets to the Soviet Union, were found guilty. Kaufman sentenced them to death in the electric chair, calling their crime "worse than murder." Despite a worldwide campaign on their behalf, seven appeals of the verdict were denied, and two pleas for executive clemency (first to President Harry S. Truman in 1952 and then to President Dwight D. Eisenhower in 1953) were dismissed. On June 19, 1953, the Rosenbergs became the first American civilians to be put to death for espionage in the United States. Even after their death, debate about the case continued. Some contended that the conviction and sentence were influenced by the wave of anti-Communism fostered by Senator Joseph McCarthy and the House Un-American Activities Committee. Federal Bureau of Investigation (FBI) documents released in the 1970s disclosed that Judge Kaufman had conducted private discussions about the sentence with the prosecution and that he had called the FBI to request that the executions be expedited. Though discussions with one side in a case under trial are usually considered a violation of judicial ethics, a subcommittee of the American Bar Association exonerated Kaufman, reporting that the FBI memos did not cast doubt on the propriety of the proceedings or the judge's conduct.

Kaufman's subsequent judicial career was marked by liberal rulings. Kaufman issued the first judicial order to desegregate an elementary school in the North in *Taylor v. Board of Education* (1961). In 1971 he was the lone dissenter in the case of *United States v. The New York Times*, when the court ruled not to allow publication of the Pentagon Papers; the Supreme Court later overturned that ruling. Many of his decisions involved First Amendment rights, including *Edwards v. The National Audubon Society* (1977), *Herbert v. Lando* (1977), and *Reeves v. ABC* (1983). His widely cited decision in *Berkey v. Kodak* (1979) is considered a landmark in antitrust law.

In 1983 Kaufman was appointed chairman of the President's Commission on Organized Crime, and he received the Presidential Medal of Freedom in 1987.

[Dorothy Bauhoff (2nd ed.)]

KAUFMAN, JOYCE JACOBSON (1929–), U.S. chemist. Born in New York City but raised and educated in Baltimore, Maryland, Kaufman earned her B.S. with honors in chemistry from Johns Hopkins University in 1949, soon after her marriage to Stanley Kaufman, an engineer. After graduation, she worked as a technical librarian and then a research chemist at the Army Chemical Center before returning to Johns Hopkins in 1952 as a researcher in the physical chemistry lab of her former professor, Walter S. Koski, who was later to become her second husband. With Koski as her advisor and mentor, she received her M.A. in 1959 and then her Ph.D. in physical chemistry in 1960. In 1962, accompanied by her mother and her young daughter, she went to Paris, where she became a visiting scientist, receiving a doctoral degree in theoretical physics from the Sorbonne the following year.

After working in industry as a staff scientist and later as leader of the quantum chemistry group at the Research Institute for Advanced Studies of the Martin Marietta Company, Kaufman rejoined Koski's research group at Johns Hopkins as a principal research scientist, a position which she held until her retirement. She also held a joint appointment in the Johns Hopkins School of Medicine as associate professor of anesthesiology and later of plastic surgery, but she never received tenure or promotion to full professor, perhaps due to discrimination against her as a woman. In addition to working with doctoral students, postdoctoral associates, and visiting scientists, she also served as mentor to many undergraduates.

The author of more than 300 scientific publications, Kaufman conducted groundbreaking research in a variety of fields, including pharmacology, drug design, theoretical quantum chemistry, experimental physical chemistry, chemical physics of energetic compounds, biochemical research, and superconductors. She served on numerous editorial advisory boards for scientific books and journals and as consultant to many scientific organizations. In 1965 Kaufman was elected fellow of the American Institute of Chemists and, the following year, of the American Physical Society; in 1969, she was named Dame Chevalière de France; in 1973, she received the Garvan Medical Award of the American Chemical Society; and in 1981, she was elected corresponding member of the European Academy of Science, Arts, and Letters. In 1974, the Jewish National Fund honored her with a Woman of Achievement Award as one of the ten outstanding women in Maryland. Her daughter, JAN CARYL KAUFMAN (1955–), was one of the first three women admitted to the Conservative rabbinate.

BIBLIOGRAPHY: P.E. Hyman and D.D. Moore (eds.), *Jewish Women in America, 1* (1997), 729–30; W.S. Koski, "Joyce Jacobson Kaufman (1929–)," in: L.S. Grinstein et al. (eds.), *Women in Chemistry and Physics: A Biobibliographic Sourcebook* (1993), 299–313; B.F. Shearer and B.S. Shearer (eds.), *Notable Women in the Physical Sciences: A Biographical Dictionary* (1997), 223–27.

[Harriet Pass Freidenreich (2nd ed.)]

KAUFMAN, PHILIP (1936–), U.S. director-screenwriter. Born in Chicago, Ill., Kaufman graduated from the University of Chicago in 1958 with honors and returned a year later after leaving Harvard Law School to complete a master's degree in history. Kaufman married screenwriter Rose Fisher in 1959. In 1960, he moved to San Francisco and then to Europe, where he taught in Greece and Italy, and then to work on an Israeli kibbutz while attempting to write a novel. In 1962, Kaufman and his family returned to Chicago, where his unpublished novel, with the help of Benjamin Manaster, became the film *Goldstein* (1965), loosely based on one of Martin Buber's *Tales of the Hassidim*. For it, Goldstein shared the Prix de La Nouvelle Critique at the Cannes Film Festival. *Fearless Frank* (1967), which he wrote and directed, failed to find a distributor until its star, Jon Voight, became an overnight success with *Midnight Cowboy* (1969), earning Kaufman an invitation to the Universal Studios Young Directors Program. His first film for Universal was *The Great Northfield Minnesota Raid*, (1972), followed by an adaptation of the James Houston novel, *The White Dawn* (1974) for Paramount. Kaufman co-wrote the script for and agreed to direct Clint Eastwood in *The Outlaw Josey Wales* (1976), but two weeks into the film Eastwood took over the direction. Kaufman's remake of *Invasion of the Body Snatchers* (1978), however, became a huge hit. He followed this up with a successful adaptation of Richard Price's *The Wanderers* (1979), a writing credit for *Raiders of the Lost Ark* (1983), and a major critical success in adapting and directing Tom Wolfe's bestselling book about the U.S. space program, *The Right Stuff* (1983). In 1988, Kaufman received an adapted screenplay Oscar nomination for his work on Milan Kundera's *The Unbearable Lightness of Being*. His next film, *Henry and June* (1990), a film about the erotic relationship of Anaïs Nin and Henry Miller, was the first film to earn the MPAA's NC-17 rating. Kaufman's later work included an adaptation of the Michael Crichton book *Rising Sun* (1993); *Quills* (2000), a tale about the notorious French writer Marquis de Sade; and *Twisted* (2004), a police thriller set in San Francisco.

[Adam Wills (2nd ed.)]

KAUFMANN, DAVID (1852–1899), Austrian scholar. Kaufmann was born in Kojetein, Moravia, and received his first instruction in Talmud from Jakob *Bruell. From 1867 to 1877 he attended the rabbinical seminary in Breslau and also studied at the university there. In 1874 he received his doctorate at Leipzig, for a dissertation concerning Sa'adiah's philosophy of religion, which he subsequently published as a part of his *Attributenlehre* (1877; repr. 1967, 1982). He began teaching Jewish history, religious philosophy, and homiletics at the new rabbinical seminary in Budapest, where he remained until his death.

Kaufmann was a scholar of unusually wide and thorough knowledge and produced an astonishingly large number of works in his short life – almost 30 books and over 500 smaller essays and book reviews. His work was distinguished also for its literary style. A complete bibliography was compiled by M. Brann, in *Gedenkbuch zur Erinnerung an David Kaufmann* (ed. M. Brann and F. Rosenthal, 1900; repr. 1980). Though Kaufmann dealt with every area of Jewish scholarship, he contributed especially to history, medieval Jewish philosophy, history of religion, and the history of Jewish art. His most important works are: "Die Theologie des Bachia Ibn Pakuda" (in *Sitzungsberichte der Wiener Akademie der Wissenschaften*, 1874); *Geschichte der Attributenlehre in der juedischen Religionsphilosophie des Mittelalters von Sa'adja bis Maimuni* (1877; repr. 1967, 1982), Kaufmann's major work; *Jehuda Halevy. Versuch einer Charakteristik* (1877); and *Die Spuren al-Bat-*

lajusi's in der juedischen Religionsphilosophie (in *Jahresbericht der Landes-Rabbinerschule in Budapest*, 3, 1880; also in Hungarian; repr. 1967). Kaufmann's comprehensive schooling in the natural sciences and philology is attested by his study *Die Sinne; Beitraege zur Geschichte der Physiologie und Psychologie im Mittelalter aus hebraeischen und arabischen Quellen (ibid.*, 7, 1884; repr. 1972, 1980). To the last year of his life belongs his *Studien ueber Salomon Ibn Gabirol* (1899; repr. 1972, 1980).

His historical and genealogical monographs include *Samson Wertheimer, der Oberhoffaktor und Landesrabbiner 1658–1724 und seine Kinder* (1888), *Urkundliches aus dem Leben Samson Wertheimers* (1891), and *R. Jair Chajjim Bacharach (1638–1702) und seine Ahnen* (1894). *Die letzte Vertreibung der Juden aus Wien und Niederoesterreich, ihre Vorgeschichte (1625 bis 1670) und ihre Opfer* (1889), and *Die Erstuermung Ofens und ihre Vorgeschichte nach dem Berichte Isaak Schulhofs (1650–1732)* (1895), together with *Megillat Ofen*, deal with the history of the Jews in the Austrian and Hungarian capitals. The history of the Italian Jews is dealt with, among others, in *Dr. Israel Conegliano und seine Verdienste um die Republik Venedig bis nach dem Frieden von Carlowitz* (1895) and *Die Chronik des Achimaaz von Oria* (1896). David Kaufmann edited the autobiography (*zikhronot*) of Glueckel von Hameln in its original Yiddish version (1896), which is considered one of the most valuable sources for the history of the Jews in Early Modern Times. In the last years of his life, Kaufmann turned to investigations in the history of Jewish art, in which field he was a pioneer. He co-founded the Gesellschaft fuer Sammlung und Konservierung von Kunst- und historischen Denkmaelern des Judentums in Wien.

Kaufmann took an active stand against attacks on the Jewish community and the Jewish religion. To this category of writings belong *Paul de Lagarde's juedische Gelehrsamkeit; eine Erwiderung* (1887), in which Kaufmann indicates Lagarde's gross errors in the field of Jewish studies, and particularly rejects the derogatory manner in which this German Orientalist had spoken of the accomplishments of Zunz and other Jewish scholars, and *Ein Wort im Vertrauen an Herrn Hofprediger Stoecker* (1880). On the other hand, Kaufmann wrote an enthusiastic review of *Daniel Deronda* by George Eliot, in which the concept of national Judaism is extolled (in MGWJ, 26, 1877) In association with M. Brann, Kaufmann published the new series of the *Monatsschrift fuer Geschichte und Wissenschaft des Judentums* (1892–99) and cooperated on this and many other Jewish scholarly and Oriental publications. M. Brann published a selection of Kaufmann's essays and shorter writings in three volumes, *David Kaufmann, Gesammelte Schriften* (1908–15; repr. 1980). A collection of his essays appeared in Hebrew translation, *Meḥkarim ba-Sifrut ha-Ivrit shel Yemei ha-Beinayim* (1962). Kaufmann's rich library (cataloged by M. Weisz, 1906), which contained many valuable manuscripts, incunabula, and *genizah* fragments, is now owned by the Hungarian Academy of Sciences (see *Microcard Catalogue of the Rare Hebrew Codices… in the Kaufmann Collection* (1959), with an introduction by Ignaz *Goldziher).

BIBLIOGRAPHY: F. Rosenthal, in: M. Brann and F. Rosenthal (eds.), *Gedenkbuch… David Kaufmann* (1900), i–lxxxvii, biography and bibl.; M. Klein, *ibid.*, 667–74; M. Brann, in: *D. Kaufmann, Gesammelte Schriften* (1908), ix–xii; S. Krauss, *David Kaufmann* (Ger., 1901); R. Brainin, in: *Sefer ha-Shanah*, 1 (1900), 186–96; S.A. Horodezky, in: *Ha-Goren*, 2 (1900), 119–20; D.H. Mueller, in: JJGL, 3 (1900), 196–206; *Jahresbericht der Landes-Rabbinerschule in Budapest*, 22 (1899); *Révai Nagy Lexikona*, 11 (1914), 365; *Magyar Zsidó Lexikon* (1929), 456; A. Scheiber, *The Kaufmann Haggadah* (1957); S. Loewinger and A. Scheiber (eds.), *Genizah Publications in Memory of Prof. Dr. David Kaufmann*, 1 (1949), Eng. and Heb. **ADD. BIBLIOGRAPHY:** M. Carmilly-Weinberger (ed.), *The Rabbinical Seminary of Budapest 1877–1977* (1986), Eng. and Heb.

[Moshe Nahum Zobel]

KAUFMANN, FELIX (1895–1949), philosopher and methodologist. Kaufmann, who was born in Vienna, immigrated to the U.S. when the Nazis took over Austria in 1938. From then until his death he was a member of the graduate faculty at the New School for Social Research in New York City. Although Kaufmann was greatly influenced by Moritz Schlick, and was himself involved in the early discussions of the Vienna Circle, he never rigidly adopted the main principles of logical positivism. This was perhaps more a matter of interest than ideology, his main concerns being to discriminate between the methodology of the social sciences, and the methodology of the physical sciences. His view was that the rules which social scientists adopt differ both in their purposes and in their applications from those found in the physical sciences, especially being directed toward the clarification of knowledge rather than its acquisition. His most important book in this connection is *Methodenlehre der Sozialwissenschaften* (1936), translated in 1944 into English as *Methodology of the Social Sciences.*

[Avrum Stroll]

KAUFMANN, FRITZ (1891–1958), philosopher. He was born in Leipzig, became *Husserl's assistant at Freiburg, remaining there until 1936, when he joined the Hochschule fuer die Wissenschaft des Judentums in Berlin. He left Nazi Germany for America, where he taught at Northwestern University and the University of Buffalo. He was a leading exponent of Husserl's phenomenology, which he helped to make known in the United States, and wrote extensively on phenomenology, aesthetics, and literary themes. His major works are *Die Philosophie des Grafen Paul Yorck von Wartenburg* (1928); a posthumous volume, *Das Reich des Schoenen – Bausteine zu einer Philosophie der Kunst* (1960); and articles on Buber, Cassirer, Thomas Mann, Nietzsche, Rilke, Goethe, Flaubert, and Husserl.

[Richard H. Popkin]

KAUFMANN, FRITZ MORDECAI (1888–1921), German essayist and writer on Yiddish culture. Born in Eschweiler, Kaufmann studied medicine and history in Geneva, Munich and Leipzig. He joined a Zionist student group in Leipzig and came into contact with East European Jews. Their culture fascinated him and he began to study Yiddish. Here, he also came to know Nathan *Birnbaum, and was profoundly influenced by the latter's zeal for the organic culture of unassimilated Jewry, however much more with its socialistic aspects than Birnbaum's new-Orthodox tendency. Kaufmann's first essays appeared in the *Juedische Rundschau* in 1912. In the following year, moving to Berlin, he founded his own periodical, *Die Freistatt* (1913–14), which he symbolically subtitled *Alljuedische Revue*, thus affirming his faith in Jewish national unity, however, herein following Birnbaum, not in his Zionist sense. Although he accepted Jewish nationalism, Kaufmann opposed Zionism's emphasis on Palestine and its negation of the Diaspora. He believed in *Alljudentum*, the strengthening of Jewish culture everywhere, especially in the Yiddish-speaking communities. There, in his opinion, Jewish life had not degenerated as it had among the Central and Western European intellectuals who had lost their Jewish roots. Kaufmann sought particularly to instill in his Western-Jewish readers a love for the Eastern-Jewish culture, i.e. Yiddish language, literature, folklore, and customs. After having served as an officer in the war and being disabled by typhus in 1915, he resumed writing for the Jewish press in 1916, specifying this position. Some of his essays were published after the war in *Vier Essais ueber ostjuedische Dichtung und Kultur* (1919) and in the collection *Die Einwanderung der Ostjuden* (1920). He also published the pamphlet *Das juedische Volkslied* (1919) and the anthology *Die schoensten Lieder der Ostjuden* (1920) while working as secretary general of the *Arbeiterfürsorgeamt der jüdischen Organisationen Deutschlands.* He also began a German translation of the Yiddish works of Mendele Mokher Seforim, but committed suicide before it was completed.

BIBLIOGRAPHY: F.M. Kaufmann, *Gesammelte Schriften*, ed. by L. Strauss (1923), 7–20 (incl. bibl.). **ADD. BIBLIOGRAPHY:** M. Flohr, *Fritz Mordechai Kaufmann und 'Die Freistatt'* (2006).

[Sol Liptzin / Andreas Kilcher (2nd ed.)]

KAUFMANN, HANNE (1926–1997), Danish author. Born in Frankfurt, she was taken by her family to Denmark in 1933 and ten years later found temporary refuge in Sweden as a result of Danish rescue operations. Her works, which reflect her experience of these events, include *Kathedral* (1964), on the Holocaust, and *Hvorfor er denne nat anderledes end alle andre naetter?* ("Why is this Night Different from All Other Nights?," 1968), on the flight to Sweden. In 1970 she wrote her book *Alle disse skæbner* about the Polish refugees who fled to Denmark during this period.

KAUFMANN, ISIDOR (1853–1921), Hungarian painter. He was born in Arad, Hungary. At 14 he started to work and in the evening he drew, decorating his room with his own pictures. A head of Moses, displayed in his uncle's store, attracted the attention of connoisseurs who arranged for the young man to study art, first in Budapest, and then in Vienna. Kaufmann's earliest works – historical paintings – are of no real importance. He achieved originality and strength only after discovering the *shtetl*. He traveled in Galicia, Poland, and the Ukraine from one village to another, making sketches. He had a meteoric career. Emperor Franz Josef bought *The Rabbi's Visit* and presented it to Vienna's Museum of Fine Art. Honors were bestowed upon the artist by the German emperor, and even the Russian czar. After his death his reputation declined. Kaufmann did not intend to open up new avenues of aesthetic perception; rather he wanted to tell stories or illustrate subjects of everyday Jewish life. His small genre paintings have definite charm, and his numerous portraits were executed with taste and skill. At the same time, his pictures are of considerable historical value, as they document the folkloristic aspects of the *shtetl*, and the *shtibl* (small synagogue) with ritual objects. Beyond this, he can be appreciated as a cultured observer who, with his sensitive brush, sought to reproduce every nuance of the people and objects he portrayed. His son PHILIP KAUFMANN (1888–1969), who emigrated from Vienna to England in 1938, also achieved a reputation as a painter.

BIBLIOGRAPHY: Kunta, in: *Ost und West*, 3 (1903), 590–603, includes plates; H. Menkes, *Isidor Kaufmann; A Painter of Jewish Life* (1925); A. Wiener in: *Jewish Chronicle Literary Supplement*, Dec. 4, 1970.

[Alfred Werner]

KAUFMANN, OSKAR (1873–1956), German theatrical architect, born in Neu St. Anna/Pancota, now Romania. He studied music in Budapest and architecture in Karlsruhe. In 1900 he settled in Berlin and built the Hebbel Theater (1907), the Stadttheater and Museum, Bremerhaven (1909), the Volksbuehne (1914), the Kroll Opera (1923), the Komoedie Theater (1924), and the Renaissance theaters (1927). Kaufmann played an important part in creating the design of the modern theater. He believed that a theater should reflect the social status of its users. Thus the proletarian Volksbuehne was decorated with wood paneling, while the fashionable Komoedie has delicately colored frescoes. He immigrated in 1933 to Palestine and built the Hebrew theater Habimah.

BIBLIOGRAPHY: A. Hansen, "The Theatre Architect Oskar Kaufmann," in: *Assaph*, Section B (Studies in Art History), 8 (2003), 149–70.

[Bjoern Siegel (2d ed.)]

KAUFMANN, RICHARD (1877–1958), Israeli architect. Kaufmann was born in Frankfurt and studied in Munich. He worked as an architect and town planner in Germany and Norway before settling in Palestine in 1920. There he entered the service of the Zionist Executive. A large proportion of the agricultural settlements established from the early 1920s were built according to his plans, and he laid down the general design of cooperative agricultural settlements (moshavim). In Nahalal, he created an architectural model for the *moshav ovedim. Kaufmann also designed many urban settlements and neighborhoods, including Afulah, Kiryat Ḥayyim near Haifa, and Reḥavyah, Talpiot, and Bet ha-Kerem in Jerusalem. He built many apartment houses in Jerusalem and Tel Aviv, and also at the Dead Sea Works and in the Jordan Valley. These last two undertakings were noteworthy for their efficient solutions to cooling problems in the difficult climate of these areas. He was one of the first modern architects in Palestine, and in his buildings achieved the new aims of European architecture of the 1920s.

BIBLIOGRAPHY: Roth, Art, 741.

[Abraham Erlik]

KAUFMANN, WALTER (1921–1980), U.S. philosopher. Born in Freiburg, Germany, Kaufmann was raised as a Lutheran but returned to Judaism. He went to the U.S. in 1939 and studied at Williams College and Harvard University, where he received his B.A. from the former (1941) and his Ph.D. from the latter (1947). From 1944 to 1946, he served in the United States Army Air Forces and Military Intelligence Service.

Kaufmann began teaching philosophy at Princeton in 1947 and became a full professor in 1962. He remained at Princeton throughout his career. His main interests were philosophy of religion, social philosophy, and the history of ideas since the 19th century. Kaufmann was a vigorous opponent of arguments for religion. He made an attack on theology of all kinds and favored a naturalistic, humanistic approach.

His best-known writings include *Nietzsche: Philosopher, Psychologist, Anti-Christ* (1950), *Critique of Religion and Philosophy* (1958), *The Owl and the Nightingale: From Shakespeare to Existentialism* (1959), *The Faith of a Heretic* (1961), *Hegel: Reinterpretation, Texts and Commentary* (1965), *Tragedy and Philosophy* (1968), *Religions in Four Dimensions* (1976), *Man's Lot* (3 vols., 1979), and *Discovering the Mind* (Trilogy, 1980). He translated (with R.J. Hollingdale) Nietzsche's *Will to Power* (1967), as well as several of his other works. He also translated Goethe's *Faust* and Martin Buber's *I and Thou*. His *Existentialism from Dostoyevsky to Sartre* (1956), a selection of texts which he edited and introduced, helped popularize existentialist philosophy in the United States.

[Richard H. Popkin / Ruth Beloff (2nd ed.)]

KAUFMANN, YEḤEZKEL (1889–1963), biblical scholar, thinker, and essayist. Born in the Podolia region of the Ukraine, Kaufmann studied in the modern yeshivah of Ch. *Tchernowitz (Rav Ẓa'ir) in Odessa and at the advanced courses of Baron David Guenzburg in Petrograd (Leningrad). He received a Ph.D. from the University of Berne in 1918. After World War I he lived in Berlin, where he began to work on his scholarly writings. In 1928 he migrated to Ereẓ Israel and taught in the Re'ali School in Haifa. In 1949 he was appointed professor of Bible at the Hebrew University, a post he held until his death. Of his many writings, two monumental works stand out: *Golah ve-Nekhar*, "Exile and the Alien Land" (4 vols. in 2, 1929–30), a sociological study on the fate of the Jewish people from ancient times to the modern period; and *Toledot ha-Emunah ha-Yisre'elit*, "The History of Israelite Faith" (8 vols. in 4, 1937–57), a history of Israelite religion from ancient times to the end of the Second Temple. The first seven volumes were condensed and translated into English by M. Greenberg under the title *The Religion of Israel* (1960). The beginning of volume 8 was translated into English by C.W. Efroymson under the title *The Babylonian Captivity and Deutero-Isaiah* (1970). His other works include: *Ha-Sippur ha-Mikra'i al Kibbush ha-Areẓ* (1956), of which an English version had been published previously (*The Biblical Account of the Conquest of Palestine*, 1953); *Be-Ḥevlei ha-Zeman* (1936), "In Troubled Times," a collection of articles and studies on contemporary problems; commentaries on the Book of Joshua (1959) and the Book of Judges (1962); and *Mi-Kivshonah shel ha-Yeẓirah ha-Mikra'it* (1966), "From the Crucible of Biblical Creativity," a posthumous collection of studies on the Bible. His essay on "The Biblical Age" appeared in *Great Ages and Ideas of the Jewish People* (edited by L.W. Schwarz, 1956).

Biblical Period

Kaufmann's main contribution to the study of biblical religion was his thesis that Israel's monotheism was not a gradual evolutionary development from paganism but an entirely new beginning, *sui generis*, in religious history. From its beginnings, Kaufmann asserted, the Israelite monotheistic structure was devoid of any element of polytheistic mythology. Kaufmann claimed that nowhere in the Bible is there any trace of mythical elements – no battles among gods or birth of gods – and that theogony is totally absent. He suggested that this is due to the fact that the battle with myth had been waged and won long before the Bible was compiled. Israelite monotheism for Kaufmann began with Moses.

To bridge the gap between the concept of the one God of all humankind, on the one hand, and on the other, the fact that God's grace and works were known for 1,000 years only to Israel, Kaufmann developed the principle of theoretical (or ideational) universalism. So long as Israel was in its native land, this was expressed in the wish that all nations would some day acknowledge the one God, just as, according to Genesis, all humankind in the beginning knew only one God. In the exilic period, Israel began to move the monotheistic teaching beyond its territorial borders.

On Kaufmann's reading, the Bible was so fundamentally the product of a monotheistic world view that it claimed that all humans were originally monotheistic; it was human rebelliousness that produced the religious retrogression of paganism. Kaufmann went so far as to argue that Israelites of the biblical period had no understanding of polytheism. Ancient Israelites did not even know how to worship gods other than Yahweh and assumed that their neighbors worshipped fetishes of wood and stone. Most Bible scholars, in the main Protestant, tended to paraphrase the biblical accounts of Israelite idolatry, and conclude that there was a vast difference between the official religion, which was either monolatrous or monotheistic, and the popular religion, which was polytheistic. In contrast, Kaufmann maintained that there was no fundamental difference between "popular" and "official" religion with regard to monotheism. The prophetic denunciations of Israelite "idolatry" were the rhetoric of zealots who equated low-level superstition with full-blown apostasy from Yahweh. Much of the prophetic critique, argued Kaufmann, was due to the demands of theodicy; the prophets needed to account for Israel's frequent reversals. What were in reality minor superstitious lapses were transformed by the prophets into apostasy.

Kaufmann's general approach to the Bible was conservative. Although he accepted the Documentary Hypothesis of the sources of the Penateuch and the multiple authorship of Isaiah and Hosea, he resisted the tendency to analyze books into increasingly smaller units. In a similar vein, he maintained that the Book of Joshua provides an accurate account of the conquest of the land. The banishment of the Canaanites was not a nationalist necessity but a religious one, whose purpose was the purification of the land that was to serve as the locale for Israel's monotheism. For Kaufmann, Isaiah is a watershed in the prophetic tradition. He is the creator of visionary universalism, which envisages the end of paganism and the establishment of eternal peace. According to Isaiah, Israel's "chosenness" as the bearer of monotheism will then disappear and God's name will be acknowledged by all. Jeremiah brought this concept to its logical conclusion by stressing that idolatry was a sin for nations as well as for individuals. Whereas Isaiah prophesied that "a man" would cast away his gold and silver idols (Isa. 2:20), Jeremiah said that "the nations shall come from the ends of the earth" to worship the one God (Jer. 16:19). With the preaching of Deutero-Isaiah monotheism came to the gentiles.

Because Kaufmann wrote in *Ivrit* (Modern Israeli Hebrew) at a time when few gentile scholars were competent in the language, Kaufmann's influence was largely confined to Israelis and Jewish religious moderates. (He was too radical for Jewish fundamentalists.) One reason for Kaufmann's popularity in these circles was his early dating of the Priestly Code (P). In the classic scheme of *Graf and *Wellhausen, the post-exilic P had encased monotheism in a legalism leading finally to a Pharisaic notion of salvation through works, so stifling that it required no less a figure than Jesus to overturn it. Naturally, most Jews regarded this analysis as Christian suppressionism in scholarly garb. Tacitly accepting the Wellhausenian claim that earlier was better, Kaufmann attempted to demonstrate that P was pre-exilic in origin, rather than the product of later debased Jewish legalism. Another reason for Kaufmann's popularity among Jewish religious moderates was that although Kaufmann was a secularist, his argument that monotheism was an original Israelite institution that had originated with Moses could be read as an empirical validation of the theological assertion of divine revelation. Through the efforts of H.L.*Ginsberg and Moshe *Greenberg, Kaufmann's work was very influential at the Jewish Theological Seminary of America (JTS) in New York City, a religiously moderate institution, at which several generations of Jewish Bible scholars were introduced to the serious study of the Bible. Oddly, Kaufmann was never invited to teach or lecture there (Schorsch).

[Emanuel Green / S. David Sperling (2nd ed.)]

Post-Biblical Period

About the time of the Hasmonean era Judaism created a proselytization ceremony that was unique in the ancient world. It was a revolutionary innovation that obliterated all racial distinctions and converted the foreigner as if he were born a Jew in every respect. Religious conversion is one of the great revelations of Judaism as a universal, supra-racial religion. The movement for conversion was especially strengthened during the Hasmonean period, when the monotheistic nation attained statehood and served as a powerful instrument of Jewish religious propaganda. During that era Judaism spread by means of religious conversion to all parts of the known world to which Jews came.

Kaufmann says that had Israel succeeded in maintaining a large state, its faith would have spread among many peoples, to such an extent that the Jewish people would have later become absorbed among the Judaized masses. Its subsequent political weakness and decadence, the destruction of Jerusalem and the Temple, and the exile, prevented this from happening. The other nations were unable to accept the faith of a subjugated people. After cutting themselves off from Judaism, Christianity and Islam continued the Jewish mission of eradicating idolatry.

Kaufmann regarded Christianity as a monotheistic religion in which a revolutionary change occurred, in contrast to the Eastern mystery religions and Hellenistic paganism. Judaism rejected the new sacred symbols of Christianity concerning the status of Jesus as a redeemer, messiah, and son of God. Jesus and Muhammad were rejected as bearers of divine revelation, and with them everything connected with their name. "The quarrel between Judaism and Christianity and Islam is a quarrel of covenants" (*"Golah ve-Nekhar,"* pt. I, 322).

Israel persisted in its national religious stance and alone preserved the inherited religion of its ancestors. Kaufmann saw Judaism as the enemy of Greek paganism and science; the war of Judaism with idolatry was also a war against intellectual idolatry, against the belief that intellectual knowledge will redeem man. Man will be redeemed only by moral goodness and not by intellectual power. Judaism believes that man holds the key of his redemption in his own hands. The prophetic answer has not become dated. The hope of man lies in the prophetic pathos and the light of Isaiah's vision.

Kaufmann's basic conception is that individual Israelites can become assimilated, but that the fundamental conclusion to be drawn from the whole of Jewish history is that the Jewish people will continue to exist. "The battle of the exile will not cease," however, "and in consequence the Jewish nation cannot achieve redemption from its exile by assimilation among other peoples. The end of being an alien and of the battle of the exile can only come through national redemption, by the conquest of the national heritage" (*ibid.* II, 264). Kaufmann stressed that the Jewish people always preferred to live in ghettos in the midst of existing towns and countries and did not, in the course of its history, seek to obtain a national territory. Kaufmann, who wrote his book in Berlin, in the 1920s, believed that, in addition to rebuilding Ereẓ Israel, its ancient birthplace, the Jewish people should establish for itself additional territory in one of the empty spaces of the world. Research into the problem of the exile and the alien condition of Israel, coupled with analysis of problems of the past and the present, gave Kaufmann the status of an outstanding researcher in the sociology and thought of Judaism. In his effort to prove his outlook on the history of Israel as a monotheistic people, with its beginning in the time of Moses, Kaufmann shed light upon all the sectors and accomplishments of the book of the Bible.

[Haim M.I. Gevaryahu]

BIBLIOGRAPHY: *Y. Kaufmann Jubilee Volume* (Eng. and Heb., 1960), incl. bibl., 1–6 (Heb. sect.); M. Haran, in: *Moznayim*, 24 (1964), 52–55; idem, *Biblical Research in Hebrew* (1970), 21–22, 25–28; Z. Woislavsky, *Yeḥidim bi-Reshut ha-Rabbim* (1956), 265–88; Potok, in: *Conservative Judaism*, 18 no. 2 (Winter, 1964), 1–9; S. Talmon, in: *ibidum* 25 no. 2 (Winter, 1971), 20–28. **ADD. BIBLIOGRAPHY:** J. Levenson, in: *Conservative Judaism*, 36 (1982), 36–43; T. Krapf, *Yehezkel Kaufmann: Ein Lebens – und Erkenntnisweg zur Theologie der hebraeischen Bibel* (1990); idem, *Die Priesterschaft und die vorexilische Zeit: Yehezkel Kaufmanns vernachlaessigte Beitrag zur Geschichte der biblischen Religion* (1992); M. Greenberg, in: idem (ed.), *Studies on the Bible and Jewish Thought* (1995), 175–88; J. Hayes, in: DBI, 2:16–17; S.D. Sperling, in: D. Snell (ed.), A *Companion to the Ancient Near East* (2005), 408–20; I. Schorsch, *Conservative Judaism*, 59 (2005), 3–22.

KAULLA, family of German Court Jews and bankers. The family became prominent with CHAILA (CAROLINE) RAPHAEL KAULLA (1739–1809) who, as "Madame Kaulla," was one of the few woman court agents in German principalities. Born in Buchau, Wuerttemberg, she married Akiba Auerbach in 1757, a Jewish scholar who left business activities to his wife. She served the princes of Donaueschingen, Hechingen, and Wuerttemberg, as well as the Imperial Court in Vienna, as a banker, jeweler, and army contractor. Her brother, JACOB RAPHAEL KAULLA (c. 1750–1810), who was also born in Buchau, a court banker, was among the members of the Kaulla family who were granted citizenship rights in Wuerttemberg by King Frederick for their services to the country in critical periods. The family later settled in Stuttgart. During the first decade of the 19th century the Kaullas were said to be financially stronger than most contemporary German-Jewish banking houses. Their most significant achievement was the 1802 establishment, in cooperation with the Duke of Wuerttemberg, of the Wuerttembergische Hofbank which, until the arrival of modern corporate banking, was the country's leading credit institution; it was eventually absorbed by the Deutsche Bank. The family contributed generously to Jewish and general community projects. JOSEPH WOLF KAULLA (1805–1876), Madame Kaulla's grandson, was ennobled in 1841 by the prince of Hechingen after the king of Wuerttemberg had refused a request to that effect. Among the Kaullas were a number of high-ranking economic and financial officials; many of them left the Jewish faith. ALFRED VON KAULLA (1833–1899), manager of the Wuerttembergische Vereinsbank, another Kaulla affiliation, counted among its clients the Mauser rifle factory, a leading German arms manufacturer. When negotiating contracts for the Ottoman army he became interested in Turkish railway projects including the Baghdad railway and was successful in securing the participation of the Deutsche Bank in that famous plan.

BIBLIOGRAPHY: H. Schnee, *Die Hoffinanz und der moderne Staat*, 4 (1963), 148–78. **ADD. BIBLIOGRAPHY:** K. Hebell, in: *Hofjuden* (2002), 332–48.

[Joachim O. Ronall]

KAUNAS (Pol. **Kowno**; Rus. **Kovno**; Ger. under Nazi occupation, **Kauen**), city in Lithuania situated at the confluence of the rivers Viliya and Neman. Formerly in Poland-Lithuania, it passed to Russia in 1795, was occupied by Germany in World War I (1915–18), and became capital of the independent Lithuanian Republic from 1920 to 1939. In World War II it was under Soviet rule from June 1940 to June 1941 and subsequently under Nazi occupation to July 1944. Jews took part in the trade between Kaunas and Danzig in the 16th century. Their competition aroused opposition from the Christian merchants, and through their influence Jews were prohibited from Kaunas on numerous occasions. However, the ban was not strictly enforced, and gradually a small group of Jews settled in Kaunas. The ban was renewed in 1682, and Jews were not permitted to settle in Kaunas and engage in trade until the 18th century when they were permitted to reside in two streets. In 1753 they were expelled from land belonging to the municipality. The Jews were again expelled in 1761, when there were anti-Jewish riots. They found refuge in the suburb of *Slobodka (Vilijampole) on the other side of the River Viliya, where a Jewish settlement had existed long before that of Kaunas. In 1782 the expelled Jews were permitted to return to Kaunas.

After the partition of Poland in 1795 Kaunas became part of Russia. In 1797 the Christians in Kaunas again demanded the expulsion of the Jews, but the authorities in 1798 ordered that they should be left alone, and not be prevented from engaging in commerce and crafts. Restrictions on Jewish settlement there were again introduced in 1845 but abolished in 1858. The Jewish population increased as the town expanded. There were 2,013 Jews living in Kovno (Kaunas) and Slobodka in 1847; 16,540 in 1864; 25,441 in 1897 (30% of the total population); and 32,628 in 1908 (40%).

From the second half of the 19th century, Kovno became a center of Jewish cultural activity in Lithuania. Prominent there were Isaac Elhanan *Spektor (the "Kovner Rav,"; officiated 1864–96), Abraham *Mapu, one of the first modern Hebrew writers, and the literary critic *Ba'al Makhshoves (Israel Isidor Elyashev). The yeshivot of Slobodka became celebrated, in particular the Or Ḥayyim yeshivah, founded by Ẓevi Levitan about 1863, which attracted students from other countries. It was headed by noted scholars. Nathan Ẓevi *Finkel introduced **musar* ideals there; from 1881 it was known as the Slobodka yeshivah. Subsequently there was opposition among the students to the *musar* method, and in 1897 the yeshivah was divided into two: the followers of *musar* established the Keneset Israel yeshivah, named after Israel *Lipkin (Salanter), while its opponents founded the Keneset Bet Yiẓḥak yeshivah, named after Isaac Elhanan Spektor. In May 1869 a conference was convened at Kovno to help Jewish refugees from northwestern Russia where the failure of the crops had led to famine and an outbreak of typhus. Another was held in November 1909 to work out a proposal for a law to establish Jewish community councils in Russia. The Kovno community maintained numerous *ḥadarim*, schools, and libraries. It returned Jewish deputies to the first and second *Duma (L. *Bramson and Sh. *Abramson). The Jews in Kovno underwent many vicissitudes during World War I. In May 1915 an edict was issued by the czarist government expelling the Jews from the entire province. When later the city was occupied by the Germans, about 9,000 Jews returned, and communal life was revived with the help of Jews in Germany. Many who had been expelled to the Russian interior returned after the 1917 Revolution.

After Kaunas became capital of independent Lithuania its community grew in importance. There were 25,044 Jews living in Kaunas according to the census of 1923 (over 25% of the total population) and 38,000 in 1933 (30%). The most important Jewish commercial and industrial enterprises in independent Lithuania were in the capital. Other Jewish institutions included a central Jewish cooperative bank, part of the share capital being held by the Jewish people's banks, which numbered 81 in 1930, and were directed from Kaunas. During the period when Jewish national cultural autonomy was authorized in Lithuania, at the beginning of the 1920s, Kaunas was the seat of the Ministry for Jewish Affairs, the Jewish National Council, and other central Lithuanian Jewish institutions and organizations. At the beginning of the 1930s five Jewish daily newspapers were published in Kaunas, the oldest being the Zionist daily *Yidishe Shtime*, founded in 1919. The network of Hebrew schools included kindergartens, elementary and high schools, and teachers' seminaries. There were also schools where the language of instruction was Yiddish. Many of the youth belonged to the Zionist associations and *He-Ḥalutz. Under Soviet rule from June 1940 to June 1941, the Jewish institutions were closed down. A Yiddish newspaper *Kovner Emes* was published.

Holocaust Period

During World War II, after the outbreak of the German-Soviet war and even before the Germans occupied the city (June 24, 1941), Jews were killed in Kaunas by Lithuanian Fascists. Immediately after the German occupation, large-scale anti-Jewish pogroms took place affecting some 35,000 Jews. At the instigation of Einsatzgruppe A, Lithuanian "partisans" carried out a pogrom in Slobodka (Vilijampole), in which 800 Jews were killed. Jews were also arrested in various parts of the city and taken to the Seventh Fort, a part of the old fortress, where between 6,000 and 7,000 of them were murdered in the beginning of July. An order issued on July 11, 1941, stipulated that between July 15 and August 15 all the Jews in the city and its suburbs were to move into a ghetto to be set up in Slobodka. This was followed by other anti-Jewish measures. On Aug. 7, 1941, 1,200 Jewish men were picked up in the streets and about 1,000 put to death. In these pogroms, as in the later persecution and *Aktionen*, the Lithuanians again took a very active part.

The Slobodka ghetto contained 29,760 people. Following an *Aktion* there, 9,200 Jews were killed at the Ninth Fort situated near Slobodka on October 29, 1941. Another 20,000 with their belongings were sent there from Germany, Austria, France, and other European countries – for "resettlement in the East" – and murdered. Another 4,000 ghetto residents were murdered in various other *Aktionen* between August and December 1941. Two "resettlement actions" took place in 1942 in which Jews from Kaunas ghetto were transferred to *Riga. On Oct. 26, 1943, approximately 3,000 Jews were deported to concentration camps in Estonia. The ghetto was then turned into "concentration camp Kauen." At this time the united Jewish underground, which had been operating in the ghetto from the end of 1941 and had 800 members, began sending people to the Augustova forests (74 mi. (120 km.) south of Kaunas) to join the partisan resistance against the Germans. Through lack of experience and the hostility of the local population many of the members of the underground were killed or captured. A group of them, who were employed by the *Gestapo in burning the corpses of the victims in the Ninth Fort, managed to escape on Christmas Eve of 1943. They were then sent by the ghetto underground to the forests of Rudnicka (about 90 mi. (150 km.) east of Kaunas) and were absorbed into the Soviet partisan units, which comprised various national groups. From the fall of 1943 to the spring of 1944, the underground, aided by members of the *Aeltestenrat* (see *Judenrat), especially its chairman, Elhanan *Elkes, and the Jewish ghetto police, managed to send about 250 armed fighters to Rudnicka and other forests, where more than one-third were killed in action against the Germans. The leader of the underground, Chaim Yelin, was captured and killed by the Gestapo. A group of Jewish partisans died in a clash with Gestapo forces on the outskirts of Kaunas in April 1944. On March 27–28, 1944, another special *Aktion* took place in which 2,000 children, elderly and sick persons were hunted down. When the Soviet attack began in July 1944, the Germans liquidated the Kaunas ghetto and concentration camps in the area, using grenades and explosives, to kill the Jews hiding in the bunkers. In this *Aktion* about 8,000 Jews and others were sent to Germany. The men were sent to *Dachau and the women to *Stutthof, and over 80% of them died in these camps before liberation. Kaunas was taken by Soviet forces on Aug. 1, 1944. Most of the Jewish survivors did not return to Lithuania, but chose to remain in the *Displaced Persons' camps, where they were later joined by other Jews from Kaunas who had left Lithuania after its liberation.

Contemporary Period

Most of the survivors from Kaunas eventually settled in Israel. Jews settled there from other places, however. The Jewish population numbered 4,792 (2.24% of the total) in 1959. There was a synagogue. In 1961 a Jewish amateur theater troupe (Yidisher Selbsttetigkeyt Kolektiv), consisting of a drama group, choir, orchestra, and dance group, was organized in Kaunas, holding public performances from time to time. In 1963 the Jewish cemetery was plowed up and Jews were ordered to bury their dead in the general cemetery. However, at their request, they were permitted a separate Jewish section. Several incidents in which Jews were beaten up in the streets were reported in 1968. In independent Lithuania (from 1991), the Kaunas Jewish community made efforts to reconstitute itself, renovating the synagogue and opening a museum. Around 500 Jews remained there.

BIBLIOGRAPHY: S.A. Bershadski, *Litovskiye Yevrei 1388–1569* (1883); D.M. Lipman, *Le-Toldot ha-Yehudim be-Kovno u-ve-Slobodka* (1931), 82–233; M. Sundarsky et al. (eds.), *Lite*, 1 (1951), index; 2 (1965), 641–72; *Yahadut Lita*, 1 (1959), index; 3 (1967), 273–83; J. Gar; *Umkum fon der Yidisher Kovne* (1948); *In Geloyf fun Khoreve Heymen* (1952); *Algemeyne Entsiklopedye; Yidn*, 6 (1969), index; L. Garfunkel, *Kovne ha-Yehudit be-Ḥurbanah* (1959); Z.A. Brown and D. Levin, *Toledoteha shel Maḥterer* (1962), with bibl. pp. 402–9; *Edut Ḥayyah: Getto Kovna bi-Temunot* (1958).

[Joseph Gar]

KAUSHANY (Rom. **Căuşani**), small town in Bessarabia, S.E. Moldova. A number of tombstones in the ancient Jewish cemetery in Kaushany, thought to date from the 16th century, indicate that there may have been Jews living in the place in this period. However, it is certain that there was a Jewish settlement in Kaushany by the beginning of the 18th century, when it was the center of the Tatar rule in southern Bessarabia. By 1817 it numbered 53 Jewish families. The community increased with the large Jewish immigration into Bessarabia in the 19th century, and in 1897 numbered 1,675 persons (45% of the total population). In 1853 over 80 families of Jewish farmers in Kaushany were granted landholdings by the state, and were reclassified as "state farmers." Due to difficult economic conditions, they were permitted to return in 1864 to the category of townsmen. A number of Jews in Kaushany continued in agricultural occupations, however, among whom there were large cattle and sheep farmers: in 1849 two Jewish farmers owned between them approximately one thousand head of cattle and three thousand sheep and goats. The Jews in Kaushany numbered 1,872 in 1930 (35.1% of the total population).

[Eliyahu Feldman]

Holocaust Period

After Kaushany passed to Soviet control in 1940, the new authorities immediately arrested the Zionist leaders and exiled them to Siberia, where they all perished. All but one of the synagogues in the town were closed down. When war broke out in the summer of 1941, the Soviet authorities lent their help to all who wanted to escape. Some Jews went to Odessa on foot and continued from there into the interior of the U.S.S.R. Others were handed over to the Germans by local collaborators. All those who remained, as well as those who had been caught while attempting to escape, were taken to the cemetery. The Germans, after removing their gold teeth and rings, poured petrol over them and burned them to death. Local Romanians and Ukrainians assisted in the massacre.

Only three families returned to Kaushany after the war. All the Jewish houses were in ruins and the Jewish cemetery had been desecrated and destroyed. The community was not revived after the war.

[Jean Ancel]

°**KAUTZSCH, EMIL FRIEDRICH** (1841–1910), German Protestant Bible critic and Semitist who as editor of a number of works on Bible and Semitic philology helped educate a generation of German theologians and biblicists. Born in Plauen, Saxony, he taught in Leipzig (until 1872), Basle (1872–80), Tuebingen (1880–88), and Halle (from 1888). Kautsch visited Ottoman Palestine in 1876 and 1904, which led him in 1877 to participate in founding the Deutscher Palästina Verein. From 1888 he was one of the editors of the influential *Theologische Studien und Kritiken*. In the area of Bible studies Kautzsch published a translation and commentary on the Book of Psalms (1893) and a dissertation on biblical poetry (1902). In collaboration with other scholars he wrote about the sources of Genesis (1888, with A. Solchin), the books of the Bible (1894), and Proverbs in the Polychrome Bible (1901, with A. Mueller). He helped edit *Die Apokryphen und Pseudepigraphen des Alten Testaments...* (1899) and *Textbibel des Alten und Neuen Testaments* (1900, 1911³). On the subject of Hebrew and Aramaic philology he edited the second to eighth editions of H. Scholz' *Abriss der hebraeischen Laut-und Formenlehre* (1874–99), and the 22nd to 28th editions of *Gesenius' *Hebrew Grammar* (1878–1908), and a valuable grammar of biblical Aramaic in 1902, based on a similar work of 1888. Kautzsch's literary activity also includes a study on the apostle Paul (1869), a history of the Moabites (1876, with A. Solchin), and the editorship of the tenth and 11th editions of K.R. Hagenbach's *Encyklopädie und Methodologie* (1880–84). Kautzsch was an involved church member who attempted to bring the results of biblical scholarship to the wider German Protestant community.

BIBLIOGRAPHY: *The New Schaff-Herzog Encylopedia of Religious Knowledge*, 6 (1953), 302 (incl. bibl.); Gesenius, *Hebrew Grammar* (1910), preface by Cowley includes bibliography. **ADD. BIBLIOGRAPHY:** C. Begg, in: DBI II, 17.

[Zev Garber]

KAUVAR, CHARLES ELIEZER HILLEL (1879–1971), U.S. rabbi, communal leader, and educator. Few rabbis leave an imprint on a community as did Kauvar during the 69 years he served in *Denver, Colorado, from 1902 to 1971, as active rabbi at the Beth HaMedrosh Hagadol Congregation for 50 years and as rabbi emeritus for 19 years. Born in Vilna, Lithuania, he came to New York in 1881 at the age of two, received a B.A. from City College of New York and was ordained at the Jewish Theological Seminary in 1902, where he also earned a D.H.L. in 1909.

Kauvar brought Conservative Judaism to Denver at a time when it was predominantly Reform on the East Side of the city, with an Orthodox enclave growing on the West Side. He became an active communal leader, helping to found the Jewish Consumptive Relief Society in 1904 to aid traditional Jews who came to Denver for a cure of their tuberculosis. He was president of the Central Jewish Council from 1912 to 1920 and aided in the establishment of the *Intermountain Jewish News*. He was a life-long Zionist, a founder of Mizrachi in Denver, and has a colored stained glass window dedicated in his honor in the Beit Medrash of the Heichal Shlomo in Jerusalem.

Although Kauvar helped found the United Synagogue of America (Conservative), serving as its first vice president from 1912 to 1914, and becoming the first president of the Midwest Region of the Rabbinical Assembly (Conservative) in 1923, he felt that by the 1950s the Conservative movement had lost its traditional moorings, and he was instrumental in having his congregation disaffiliate with the movement in 1955. In 1956, the BMH Congregation, as it was known, elected its first Orthodox rabbi to the pulpit, and it became a member of the Union of Orthodox Jewish Congregations in 1972. Kauvar was one of the earliest professors of Judaic studies at universities in the United States, having joined the faculty at the University of Denver, a private institution established by the Methodist Church, in 1920, where he taught until 1966. An endowed Charles Eliezer Hillel Kauvar Publications Fund was established at the later formed university's Center for Judaic Studies in his honor in recognition of his intellectual contributions to the University and community.

Among his published works are *Pirkei Aboth Comments* (1929), *What Is Judaism?* (1933), *Religion, the Hope of the World* (1949) and *Torah Comments* (1952).

[Stanley M. Wagner (2nd ed.)]

KAVALLA, city in Macedonia, Greece. After the capture of Budapest by the Turks in 1526 Hungarian Jews were brought first to Sofia, and in 1529 to Kavalla. Eventually both Sephardi and Ashkenazi Jews settled there. Eventually, the Sephardi community influenced the Ashkenazim in matters of *halakhah*, and they assimilated into the general Sephardi community. In the 16th century, there were four synagogues and a total of 500 Jews in the community. In 1676 the Jews comprised a third of the general population. By 1740 the Jewish population had dwindled to barely enough families for a *minyan*. The city developed in the first half of the 19th century due to the presence of local relatives of Mohammed Ali, who was born in Kavalla and as Egypt's ruler contributed greatly to local growth. In the mid-19th century, as the port developed, several affluent Jewish families from Salonika moved to Kavalla. In 1880, the Jewish community numbered only 24 families, half of them from Salonika and Serres. The city's synagogue, Beth El, was built in 1885. In the 19th century the Jewish community was augmented by an influx of tobacco merchants. A Jewish boys' school was founded in 1889 and in 1905 a coed Alliance Israélite Universelle school was established. Blood libel accusations circulated against local Jews in 1894, 1900, and even 1926 under Greek rule. In the latter incident, the Jews were falsely blamed for the murder of a girl, and Greek-Orthodox rioters destroyed Jewish property in the ensuing riots.

By 1900, the local Jewish community had grown to 230 families, comprising 1,000 to 1,300 people. About half the Jews worked in the tobacco industry and most of the others were storekeepers. There was also a group of poor Jews. In 1913 the Jewish population numbered 2,500, 3,200 in 1923, and 2,200 in 1940. Many Jews worked in the tobacco warehouses. As the Jewish community grew, so did Jewish poverty. In 1900, the Jewish community had several welfare societies: Ozer Dalim, Ezra be-Ẓarrot, Ahavat Re'im, and a soup kitchen for children called Melo ha-Peh Leḥem.

In the First Balkan War, in November 1912, Bulgaria captured the city, and seven prominent Jews were arrested on suspicion of collaborating with the Turks. The Jews suffered, like the rest of the population, from neglect, and in the winter 120 families received food and coal for heating from the Chief Rabbinate of Bulgaria, the Alliance Israélite Universelle in Paris, and donors from among Hungarian Jewry. The Greeks took over the city on July 6, 1913, and brought relief to the residents of the city. In 1916, the Bulgarians recaptured the city, and the Jews, like the other residents of the city, suffered from starvation. Many were affected by the bombings. Many were recruited for forced labor by the Bulgarians, and again suspicions of treason circulated. Greek rule returned on October 19, 1918. That same month, 120 Jews and Muslims were mobilized for forced labor to repair war damages. Jews also had to do such menial work as cleaning the streets and Greek-Orthodox homes. The Jewish community complained to the French government via the Alliance Israélite Universelle and after six days the Jews were relieved from this burden.

In 1913 the local Zionist Or Zion society was established. Judah Ḥayyim Perahia edited its weekly Judeo-Spanish newspaper, *Ha-Ẓiyyonut*.

In the 1920s, two-thirds of the Jews worked in the tobacco industry and a hundred were shopkeepers or worked for merchants. As early as 1921, there were accounts of the Greek government forcing Jews to work on the Sabbath and taking Sunday as their day of rest. In Kavalla, as opposed to many other cities where the Jews protested, many Jews opened their businesses, including the president of the Jewish community himself. The community suffered greatly from the worldwide depression in the 1930s. In 1931, there were 200 unemployed Jewish tobacco workers. Throughout the 1930s, the local Jews received financial assistance from the Salonikan Jewish community.

In 1941 Kavalla came under Bulgarian occupation. The Jews were pressured to assist the Bulgarians against the Greeks but they resisted. In retaliation the Bulgarians, guided by the Nazis, applied the racial laws in 1942 (see *Bulgaria, Holocaust). In the summer of 1942 many hundreds of Jews were put to forced labor in Kavalla and a few months later in early 1943 another group was sent to Bulgaria to work. On March

3, 1943, 1,800 Jews were arrested and later deported to the Treblinka death camp in Poland. Part of the Kavallan Jewish community was on the *Karageorge* when the Bulgarians shot passengers on the Danube River. The Jewish population in 1948 numbered 42; according to the 1967 census there were 47 Jews living in Kavalla. By the beginning of the 21st century, the last elders of the three remaining families had passed away and no more Jews resided in the city. There still remains a Jewish cemetery intact.

BIBLIOGRAPHY: J.B. Angel, in: *Almanak Izraelit* (1923), 72–75 (Ladino). **ADD. BIBLIOGRAPHY:** B. Rivlin, "Kavalla," in *Pinkas Kehillot Yavan* (1999), 327–39; Y. Kerem, "New Finds on Greek Jews in the Sobibor and Treblinka Death Camps in the Holocaust," in: I. Hassiotis (ed.), *The Jewish Communities of Southeastern Europe from the Fifteenth Century to the End of World War Two* (1997), 249–62; Central Zionist Archives, Jerusalem, S25/10746 and Karageorge photo file; Yad Vashem Archives, Jerusalem, TR 10/641, Beckerle Trial.

[Simon Marcus / Yitzchak Kerem (2nd ed.)]

KAVERIN, BENJAMIN ALEKSANDROVICH (pseudonym of **Benjamin A. Zilberg**; 1902–1990), Soviet Russian author. The son of a musician, Kaverin was born in Pskov. His training as a historian and specialist in Oriental languages left a strong imprint on his choice of literary themes. Several of his books have foreign settings, both eastern and western. Thus the plot of *The Great Game* (1926) involves both Englishmen and Ethiopians. Others deal with historical subjects, such as *Baron Brambeus* (1929), a scholarly biography of Osip Senkovski, one of the most picturesque figures in 19th-century Russian literature. At the same time Kaverin was one of the few Russian detective-story writers, and some of his stories – especially those published in the permissive atmosphere of the 1920s – make good use of many of the devices of the genre. One of the most notable is *Konets khazy* ("The End of the Gang," 1926), a captivating account of the Leningrad underworld.

Kaverin's most significant novel, *Khudozhnik neizvesten* (1931; *The Unknown Artist*, 1947), was a plea for the maintenance of the dignity of the individual in a collectivist society and for the preservation of beauty in a utilitarian age. *Ispolneniye zhelaniy* (1935; *The Larger View*, 1938) dealt with the problems of adjustment facing an intellectual in Soviet society. His long novel *Dva kapitana* (1946; *Two Captains*, 1957) was a great favorite with Russian youngsters when it was originally serialized between 1938 and 1944. He received the Stalin Prize for it in 1946. Aside from introducing Jewish allusions in some of his works, he wrote, for the *Jewish Antifascist Committee, a biography of Hero of the Soviet Union Fisanovich, and "The Uprising in Sobibor" together with P. Antokolski. In post-Stalinist Russia Kaverin was among the leading exponents of liberalization, frequently incurring the wrath of the Stalinist establishment. His later works include *Sem par nechistykh* ("Seven Pairs of the Unclean," 1962), which describes inmates of a Soviet concentration camp fighting for the right to defend their homeland in the ranks of the Soviet army, and speeches published by Samizdat in 1967.

BIBLIOGRAPHY: G. Struve, *Soviet Russian Literature 1917–50* (1951), 107–11, 275f., 360; M. Slonim, *Modern Russian Literature* (1953), 294f., 297; M. Friedberg and R.A. Maguire (eds.), *A Bilingual Collection of Russian Short Stories*, 2 (1965), 89–211.

[Maurice Friedberg]

KAVNER, JULIE (1951–), U.S. actress. Born in Los Angeles, California, Kavner is best known for her roles as Rhoda's sister, Brenda Morgenstern, on the television show *Rhoda* – one of the first television shows to feature an openly Jewish lead character – and as the voice of Marge Simpson on the animated show *The Simpsons*. On *The Simpsons*, Kavner also provided the voices for Patty, Selma, Jacqueline, and Gladys Bouvier. Kavner's most notable on-screen film role was her portrayal of a divorced Jewish woman struggling to reconcile her aspirations as a stand-up comedian with her responsibilities to her children in Nora Ephron's *This Is My Life* (1992). In addition to appearing as Treva in *New York Stories* (1989), Eleanor Costello in *Awakenings* (1990), and Lucy in *Forget Paris* (1995), Kavner worked extensively with Woody Allen, appearing in a number of his films, including the role of Allen's mother in the comedy *Radio Days* (1987), Alma in *Shadows and Fog* (1992), Nan Muhanney in *I'll Do Anything* and Grace in *Deconstructing Harry* (1997).

[Walter Driver (2nd ed.)]

KAVVANAH (Heb. כַּוָּנָה; lit. "directed intention"), the phrase used in rabbinic literature to denote a state of mental concentration and devotion at prayer and during the performance of *mitzvot*. Although the demand for *kavvanah* as an obligatory component of religious prayer and action is not explicitly mentioned in the Pentateuch, it is clearly referred to by the prophets. Isaiah, for instance, condemns those who "with their mouth and with their lips do honor Me, but have removed their heart far from Me" (Isa. 29:13).

Kavvanah in Prayer

The Talmud attaches considerable importance to *kavvanah* in prayer. The Mishnah quotes R. Simeon's dictum: "Do not regard your prayer as a fixed mechanical device, but as an appeal for mercy and grace before the All-Present" (Avot 2:13). It is, furthermore, related that the early *ḥasidim* used to wait an hour before and after prayer to achieve a state of *kavvanah* and emerge from it (Ber. 5:1). However, from the discussion in the Mishnah and the *Gemara* (Ber. 32b), it is clear that the rabbis, keenly aware of the "problem" of prayer were by no means unanimous in their interpretation of what proper *kavvanah* should be. Later medieval authors distinguished between the preparation for *kavvanah* which precedes prayer and the achievement of *kavvanah* during prayer itself (e.g., Kuzari, 3:5 and 17), while repeatedly stressing the importance of both. Maimonides ruled as a matter of *halakhah* (which was not, however, agreed with by later codifiers) that "since prayer without *kavvanah* is no prayer at all, if one has prayed without *kavvanah* he has to pray again with *kavvanah*. Should one feel preoccupied or overburdened, or should one have just returned from a voyage, one must delay one's prayer until one can once again pray with *kavvanah*… True *kavvanah* implies freedom from all strange thoughts, and complete awareness of the fact that one stands before the Divine Presence" (Yad, Tefillah, 4:15, 16). The Shulḥan Arukh states "better a little supplication with *kavvanah*, than a lot without it" (OH 1:4).

Many talmudic decisions relating to *kavvanah* were modified in the course of time. Thus, although the Mishnah (Ber. 2:5) states that a bridegroom is not required to read the *Shema* on his wedding night (because he would not be able to achieve a proper degree of concentration), it was later ruled that "since nowadays we do not pray with proper attention in any case" he must do so (Sh. Ar., OH 60:3). Similarly, "even if one did not recite the *Amidah* with *kavvanah*, it is not necessary to repeat it," since it is assumed that the *kavvanah* of the repetition would be no better (*ibid.*, 101:1, and see Isserles, ad loc.).

In the Kabbalah *kavvanot* (the plural of *kavvanah*) denotes the special thoughts one should have at the recitation of key words in prayer. Very often these thoughts are divorced from the contextual meaning of the words and are of a mystical, esoteric nature. Some kabbalists were thus known as *mekhavvenim* (i.e., those who have *kavvanot*) and guides to *kavvanot* were written (cf. Emmanuel Ḥai Ricchi's *Mafte'aḥ ha-Kavvanot*, Amsterdam, 1740).

Kavvanah in Mitzvot

This is defined as the intention of the person performing the action to do so with the explicit intention of fulfilling the religious injunction which commands the action. One example of a lack of *kavvanah* quoted in the Mishnah (Ber. 2:1) is the case of one who reads the *Shema* during the morning (or evening), for the purpose of study and not fulfillment of the *mitzvah*; another is the case of one who hears the *shofar* on Rosh Ha-Shanah accidentally and thus does not have *kavvanah* for the *mitzvah* (RH 3:7). All authorities agree that due *kavvanah* to perform such *mitzvot* is desirable. There is, however, a difference of opinion as to whether *mitzvot* performed without *kavvanah* are valid, or whether they must be repeated (cf. Ber. 13a; RH 28a; Sh. Ar., OH 60:4).

BIBLIOGRAPHY: Enelow, in: *Studies… K. Kohler* (1913), 82–107; Scholem, in: MGWJ, 78 (1934), 492–518; Weiss, in: JJS, 9 (1958), 163–92; A.J. Heschel, *Torah min ha-Shamayim be-Aspaklaryah shel ha-Dorot*, 1 (1962), 168–9.

[H. Elchanan Blumenthal]

KAWKABĀN, important mountain stronghold during the Ottoman occupation of the lower regions of *Yemen, northwest of San'a. Kawkabān is about one hour's walk from Shibām. Although the exact date of the city's origin is not precisely known, the existing ruins and artifacts of the city give us a clue to its ancient existence from the Himyari period. Recorded history goes back 950 years and speaks of Kawkabān as a depository for grain. Kawkabān is known from the description of Jacob *Saphir, who stayed in these places in 1858 during his travels. The Jewish quarter of Kawkabān, in which some 60 families lived during the last generation before the emigration from there to Israel, was considerably distant from the Arab town; one had to descend into a wadi and climb a slope on the opposite side in order to reach the Jewish section. There was one synagogue. Most of the Jews made their living in pottery; others were shoemakers and tailors, especially of leather jackets.

BIBLIOGRAPHY: J. Saphir, *Even Sappir* (1864), 77–8; C. Rathjens and H. Wissmann, *Landeskundliche Ergebnisse* (1934), 94, 134; C. Rathjens, *Jewish Domestic Architecture in Sana, Yemen* (1957), 64–7.

[Yosef Tobi (2nd ed.)]

KAY, BARRY (1932–1985), stage designer. Kay was born in Melbourne, Australia, but studied in Switzerland and at the Académie Julien, Paris. He moved to London in 1956 and began designing for the Western Theater Ballet and the Aldeburgh and Edinburgh Festivals. His first complete production was for Shakespeare's *Measure for Measure* at the Old Vic Theatre in 1957. He designed productions for the Théatre de la Monnaie, Brussels, the Royal Shakespeare Company, England, the Royal Ballet Company, Covent Garden, the Staatsoper, Berlin, and the Stuttgart Ballet. His principal work was for ballet, notably in association with the choreographer Kenneth Macmillan for the ballets *The Sleeping Beauty* and *Anastasia*. Kay designed a number of ballets for Rudolph Nureyev including *Raymonda* and *Don Quixote*, which was also filmed with the Australian Ballet Company. His work is noted for brilliant decorative invention as well as remarkable psychological interpretation of the themes and subjects involved. He held a number of exhibitions of his stage designs in London, Berlin, Australia, and New York. Kay was noted for his pioneering use of three-dimensional sets in the 1960s. His work is in important museum collections, including the Victoria and Albert Museum, London, the National Gallery of Western Australia, and the National-Bibliothek, Vienna.

[Charles Samuel Spencer (2nd ed.)]

KAYE, DANNY (**David Daniel Kaminsky**; 1913–1987), U.S. actor and entertainer. The son of a tailor, Kaye was born and brought up in Brooklyn, New York. He turned to entertaining after a brief career as an insurance agent and, starting in the Catskill Mountains, was a great success on the "Borscht Circuit." In 1939 he played ten weeks on Broadway in *The Straw Hat Revue*, a show partly devised by Sylvia Fine, whom he married and who continued to write material for him. His spectacular rise to stardom began in 1941, when Moss *Hart saw him at a New York night club and decided to write a part for him in the musical *Lady in the Dark*, in which Kaye scored an immediate success. His other Broadway performances were in *Let's Face It* (1941–43); *Danny Kaye Revue* (Tony Award, 1953 and 1963); and, later in his career, *Two by Two* (1970).

He became a favorite on both sides of the Atlantic, with appearances on stage and screen. His versatile gifts were fully displayed in the film version of James Thurber's short story *The Secret Life of Walter Mitty* (1947). His other films include

The Kid from Brooklyn (1946), *A Song Is Born* (1948), *The Inspector General* (1949), *On the Riviera* (Golden Globe for Best Actor, 1951), *Hans Christian Andersen* (1952), *White Christmas* (1954), *The Court Jester* (1956), *Merry Andrew* (1958), *Me and the Colonel* (Golden Globe for Best Actor, 1958), *The Five Pennies* (1959), *On the Double* (1961), and *The Madwoman of Chaillot* (1969).

Kaye developed a highly individual style that relied on mime, song, irony, and a sunny personality. His specialty was reciting tongue-twisting songs and monologues. Those powers were perhaps seen at their best in the theater, where he could hold an audience with an hour-long act of song and patter.

In 1960, he began doing specials on television, which led to his own TV series, *The Danny Kaye Show* (1963 to 1967). He won an Emmy for his variety show in 1964. In 1955 he won an honorary Academy Award for his unique talents, and in 1982 he was honored with the Jean Hersholt Humanitarian Award.

He retired from show business in 1967, serving as ambassador-at-large for the United Nations International Children's Fund (UNICEF) and conducting symphony orchestras in fund-raising concerts. He was a frequent visitor to Israel and wrote *Around the World Story Book* (1960).

BIBLIOGRAPHY: M. Gottfried, *Nobody's Fool: The Lives of Danny Kaye* (1994); M. Freedland, *The Secret Life of Danny Kaye* (1985).

[Jo Ranson / Ruth Beloff (2nd ed.)]

KAYE, SIR EMMANUEL (1914–1999), British industrialist. Born in Russia, Emmanuel Kaye came to England as a small child and was educated at Twickenham Technical College. In 1940, he founded J.E. Shay Ltd., precision gauge tool and instrument makers; in 1943 he took over Lansing Bagnall, making it the largest manufacturers of electric fork lift trucks in Europe. He supplied the Royal Household and won the Queen's Award for exports and for technological innovation. Kaye served as chairman of the Kaye Organization and of Lansing Bagnall, and allied companies in Switzerland and Germany, and of many other companies. At its peak in the 1970s, Lansing Bagnall employed 3,500 people and was the largest manufacturer of fork lift equipment in Europe. His public activities included the Confederation of British Industry and membership of the Reviewing Committee on the Export of Works of Art. He was a trustee of the Glyndebourne Opera from 1979 to 1984. He was knighted in 1974. Kaye left a fortune of £46.3 million at his death.

ADD. BIBLIOGRAPHY: *ODNB online*; L.T.C. Rolt, *Lansing Bagnall: The First Twenty-One Years at Basingstoke* (1970).

[Vivian David Lipman / Willian D. Rubinstein (2nd ed.)]

KAYE, JUDITH S. (1938–), first woman to serve as chief judge of the State of New York . Kaye was born in Monticello, N.Y., to Lena and Benjamin Smith. She attended Barnard College (B.A., 1958) and New York Law School (LL.B., 1962) and married attorney Stephen Rackow Kaye. Kaye and her family were long-time members of Sephardi Congregation Shearith Israel in New York City. Her meteoric career began as a litigation associate at the New York law firm of Olwine, Connelly, Chase, O'Donnell, and Weyher (1969–83), where she became the firm's first woman partner. Recognizing Kaye's accomplishments as a trial lawyer and her efforts on behalf of the Bar Association, and looking to diversify the court system, Governor Mario Cuomo appointed her as the first female associate judge of the New York State Court of Appeals in 1983, and chief judge in 1993, a position that makes her head of the state judiciary as well as of the Court of Appeals. As chief judge she promoted jury reform and streamlined the court system by creating special courts throughout the state to deal with drug abuse, domestic violence, and family dysfunction. Her reanalysis of traditional legal roles and partnering of specialized courts with outside agencies led to improved results and more public trust and became a model for other U.S. states. Kaye was also active in improving the status of women and children and in addressing domestic violence; in 1993, she convened the state's first Matrimonial Commission to reform New York's divorce custody system, and in 2004 she created a new 32-member panel State Matrimonial Commission to examine excessive costs in child custody divorce battles. She was a founding member and honorary chair of the Judges and Lawyers Breast Cancer Alert, co-chair of the Permanent Judicial Commission on Justice for Children, and a member of the American Bar Association Commission on Domestic Violence. Her publications address domestic issues and legal process, state constitutional law, women in law, professional ethics, and problem solving. Kaye's many honors include the American Bar Association Commission on Women in the Profession's Margaret Brent Women Lawyers of Achievement Award, the National Center for State Courts' William H. Rehnquist Award for Judicial Excellence, New York University Law School's Vanderbilt Medal, and the Barnard Medal of Distinction.

BIBLIOGRAPHY: J.F. Rosen, "Kaye, Judith S.," in: *Jewish Women in American: An Historical Encyclopedia* (P.E. Hyman and D.D. Moore, eds.), Vol. 1 (1997), 733–34.

[Judith Friedman Rosen (2nd ed.)]

KAYE, NORA (1920–1987), U.S. dramatic ballerina. She began her ballet training when she was eight, and at 15 joined the corps of the Metropolitan Opera Ballet. When Ballet Theater was founded in 1939, she entered the corps de ballet and quickly rose to prima ballerina status. She starred in classical repertory and in many contemporary ballets, but she was primarily identified with the English choreographer, Antony Tudor. Her characterization of Hagar in *Pillar of Fire* (1942) was regarded as a great example of tragic acting. Others of Tudor's works in which she appeared were *Lilac Garden*, *Dark Elegies*, and *Dim Lustre*. In 1951 Nora Kaye left Ballet Theater for the New York City Ballet, where she created the role of the novice in Jerome Robbins' *The Cage*. Returning to Ballet Theater in 1954, she danced in the works of Herbert Ross, whom she married in 1959. After a brief tour with a company organized by herself and Ross, Ballets of Two Worlds, she retired from dancing in 1960.

[Marcia B. Siegel]

KAYFETZ, BEN (1916–2002), Canadian Jewish public servant, journalist, broadcaster, human rights activist, Yiddishist. Kayfetz was born in Toronto's immigrant community. In 1939 he graduated from the University of Toronto with a B.A. in modern languages and, after a short stint as a high school teacher, he worked for the Canadian Wartime Information Board, then for the Canadian Control Commission in postwar Germany. After visiting Holocaust survivors in Displaced Person's Camps and attending the 1946 Zionist Conference in Basle, Kayfetz returned to Canada as director of public relations for the Canadian Jewish Congress (CJC). He worked in the Central Region CJC for the next 37 years, becoming director of the Joint Community Relations Committee in 1955 and executive director of the CJC Central Region in 1973. During that time he was involved with numerous issues, including international affairs, Soviet Jewry, Yiddish, *kashrut* and Israel advocacy. He retired in 1985, but continued to advise CJC leadership until his death in 2002.

Kayfetz is remembered for his important work advancing human rights in postwar Canada. He was instrumental in organizing successful campaigns for passage of legislation banning discrimination in employment and housing, removing nonsectarian teaching from Ontario public schools, and enactment of federal anti-hate legislation and legislation dealing with war crimes. He remained a backbone of the Canadian Jewish community's struggle against antisemites, Holocaust deniers, and racists, often organizing the secret infiltration of hate groups.

While Kayfetz insisted that he was not a professional historian, he had an encyclopedic knowledge of the Canadian Jewish community and the Toronto community in particular. He published many popular and scholarly articles on the Canadian Jewish community and freely shared his knowledge with scholars and students alike. Kayfetz was a founder and president of the Toronto Jewish Historical Society; he wrote *Toronto Jewry 60 Years Ago* and edited Canadian content entries in the first edition of *Encyclopaedia Judaica*. He was also a frequent contributor to the *Globe and Mail*, the Canadian *Jewish Standard* (under the pseudonym of Gershon B. Newman), *The American Jewish Yearbook*, *The Jewish Chronicle* of London, and the Jewish Telegraphic Agency. In his last years, he was a radio commentator in Toronto.

In 1985 Kayfetz was honored with membership in the Order of Canada in 1985 in recognition of his efforts in securing human rights.

[Frank Bialystok (2nd ed.)]

KAYSER, RUDOLF (1889–1964), German author and literary journalist. After studying in Berlin, Munich, and Wuerzburg, Kayser was for several years a teacher in Berlin. In 1919 he joined the editorial staff of the S. Fischer publishing house and became editor in chief of the literary periodical *Die Neue Rundschau* in 1924. Kayser was dismissed from these posts by the Nazis in 1933, settled in the U.S. two years later, and held the chair of German and European literatures at Brandeis University from 1951 to 1957. His Jewish interests found expression in the essays and reviews that he contributed to Jewish periodicals, which included the *Neue Juedische Monatshefte, Der Jude*, and *Historia Judaica*, and in books such as *Moses Tod. Legende* (1921), *Spinoza, Bildnis eines geistigen Helden* (1932), and *The Life and Time of Jehuda Halevi* (1949). His biographical studies also include *Stendhal, oder das Leben eines Egotisten* (1928), and *Kant* (1934). In his biographies he was less interested in discovering new facts about his subjects than in revealing their mental outlook and their *Weltanschauung*. He was especially influential in pre-Nazi Germany, discovering and encouraging literary talent not only through *Verkuendigung* (1921), his anthology of young lyricists, but also as editor of the *Neue Rundschau*, one of the most authoritative literary organs of the era.

BIBLIOGRAPHY: Kuerschner, in: *Literatur-Kalender* (1931), s.v. **ADD. BIBLIOGRAPHY:** P. de Mendelssohn, *S. Fischer und sein Verlag* (1970); T.S. Hansen, "Rudolf Kayser," in: *Deutschsprachige Exilliteratur seit 1933*, J.M. Spalek and J.P. Strelka (eds.), 2 (1989), 421–32; C. Foucart, "André Gide, Rudolf Kayser et Die Neue Rundschau," in: *Bulletin des Amis d'André Gide*, 31/37 (2003), 67–79.

[Sol Liptzin]

KAYSERLING, MEYER (**Moritz**; 1829–1905), German rabbi and historian. Kayserling, born in Hanover, studied with S.R. Hirsch in Nikolsburg, S.J. Rapoport in Prague, and S.B. Bamberger in Wuerzburg and at Halle University. From 1861 to 1870 he was rabbi at Endingen, Switzerland, where he fought strenuously for Jewish rights; thereafter he was rabbi and preacher in Budapest.

Kayserling published a large number of works on various aspects of Jewish history, literature, and religion, mostly in German, which were very popular in their day, including *Moses Mendelssohn: sein Leben und seine Werke* (1862, 1888^2); *Bibliothek juedischer Kanzelredner* (2 vols., 1870–72); *Die juedischen Frauen in der Geschichte…* (1879); and a popular Jewish history, *Lehrbuch der juedischen Geschichte und Literatur* (1874); which ultimately went through ten editions. He also contributed the section on modern Jewish literature to Winter and Wuensche's handbook on post-biblical Jewish literature, *Juedische Literatur seit dem Abschluss des Kanons…* (vol. 3, 1896).

But Kayserling's reputation rests on his long series of pioneering publications on the history of Spanish Jewry and the Marranos, based to a great degree on original and, in some cases manuscript, sources. His *Geschichte der Juden in Spanien und Portugal*, which in fact covered mainly Navarre and the Balearic Islands (vol. 1, 1861) and Portugal (vol. 2, 1867), was the first work in which Hebrew sources were consistently used. His works on Marrano history and literature put the study on a new footing and were the basis of all subsequent treatments. They include *Sephardim: Romanische Poesien der Juden in Spanien* (1859); *Menasseh ben Israel* (1861); *Christoph Columbus und der Anteil der Juden an den spanischen und portugiesischen Entdeckungen* (1894; *Christopher Columbus and the Participation of the Jews in the Spanish and Portuguese Discoveries*, 1894, repr. 1968), written at the request of the Spanish government on the occasion of the 400th anniversary of the discovery of America; and his great bibliography of Marrano literature *Bibliotheca española-portugueza-judaica* (Fr., 1890, repr. 1962 and 1971). In addition, the articles he contributed to the *Jewish Encyclopedia* on these subjects have retained their importance. Many of his works were translated into English and some into Hebrew. More than 100 of his articles on Jewish history and literature published before 1900 are listed in M. Schwab's *Répertoire des articles relatifs à l'histoire et à la littérature juives…* (1914–23).

BIBLIOGRAPHY: L. Philippson, *Biography of Meyer Kayserling* (1898); W.A. Meisel, *Ein Lebens-und Zeitbild…* (1891); M. Weisz, *Bibliographie der Schriften Dr. M. Kayserlings* (1929); E. Neumann, *Kayserling* (Hg., 1906).

[Cecil Roth]

KAZAKEVICH, EMMANUIL GENRIKHOVICH (1913–1962), Soviet Russian author. Born in the Ukrainian town of Kremenchug, Kazakevich grew up in a Yiddish-speaking milieu. As a young man he went to *Birobidzhan, capital of the autonomous Jewish region in the Soviet Far East, where he worked in a variety of jobs: managing a collective farm, directing a theater, and writing for a Yiddish newspaper. From 1938 he lived in Moscow. In the 1930s Kazakevich was considered one of the most promising young poets in Soviet Yiddish literature. Much of his original Yiddish verse is to be found in the antholoy *Di Groyse Velt* ("The Great World," 1939). He was also known for his Yiddish translations of prerevolutionary and Soviet Russian writers, including Pushkin, Lermontov, and Mayakovsky.

During World War II Kazakevich served in the Red Army and was wounded four times. He rose from ordinary scout to the rank of deputy commander of an army reconnaissance unit. Most of his later writings were inspired by his wartime experiences. After the war he began to write exclusively in Russian. Indeed, his former career as a Yiddish poet appears to have caused him some embarrassment. His first Russian novel, *Zvezda* (1947; *The Star*, 1950), was followed by *Dvoye v stepi* ("Two on a Steppe," 1948) and *Vesna na Odere* (1949; *The Spring on the Oder*, 1953). He was severely criticized for these works, because he emphasized the problems of honor and free choice. Although Kazakevich, twice a Stalin prize-winner, escaped the tragic fate of many Soviet Jewish intellectuals during the virulently antisemitic purges of Stalin's last years, he was undoubtedly aware of the constant danger to his life during that period. This may explain his novel *Dom na ploshchadi* (1956; *The House on the Square*, 1960), published at the height of the post-Stalin "thaw." The book describes the atmosphere of morbid suspicion prevalent in the Soviet army during the early postwar years. The 1962 novella *Vragi* ("The Enemies"), a thinly veiled appeal for tolerance, even toward political dissenters, depicted Lenin's magnanimity to his Menshevik opponents. The work was severely criticized as politically dangerous. Some of his works remained unpublished, such as "The Call for Help," about a ghetto seen through the eyes of a Russian officer. In the 1950s he went back to writing in Yiddish, and his articles were published in the Yiddish press in Warsaw, Poland.

BIBLIOGRAPHY: A. Bocharov, *Emanuil Kazakevich* (Rus., 1965); O.D. Galubeva et al., *Russkiye Sovetskiye Pisateli*, 2 (1964), 264–73.

[Maurice Friedberg]

KAZAKHSTAN, former Soviet republic in Central Asia, and from 1991 an independent republic of the CIS. It numbered 19,240 Jews (0.3% of the total) in 1939. In 1979 its Jewish population totaled 23,500 and in 1989, 19,900. By the early 2000s the figure had dropped to around 4,000 after the mass emigrations of the 1990s.

The Jewish community is very assimilated. In 1987 47.2% of children born to Jewish mothers had non-Jewish fathers. Nonetheless a Jewish educational system and synagogue were operating in Alma-Ata in 2006 under Rabbi Menachem Gershovich and a rabbi was also installed in Kavaganda.

[Michael Beizer (2nd ed.)]

KAZAN, capital of Tatarstan autonomous republic, in the Russian Federation, an important commercial and industrial center, mainly of the oil industry. Until the 1917 Revolution, Kazan was outside the Jewish *Pale of Settlement. In 1861, 184 Jews lived in the city, most of them veterans of the army of Nicholas I. By 1897, their numbers had increased to 1,467 (1.1% of the total population). Pogroms broke out in the city in October 1905. During World War I many exiles from the battle areas and from Lithuania arrived in Kazan. In 1926, there were 4,156 Jews in the city (2.3% of the population), which grew to 5,278 (1.33% of the total) in 1939. During the subsequent years, under the Soviet regime there was no possibility of developing any Jewish communal life. During WWII many refugees reached the city and remained there after the war. The Jewish population of Kazan was estimated at about 8,000 in 1970. One synagogue existed until 1962, when it was closed down by the authorities. Jews prayed in private houses (*minyanim*), even though this was prohibited. The Jewish cemetery was still in use in 1970.

[Yehuda Slutsky / Shmuel Spector (2nd ed.)]

KAZAN, LAINIE (**Levine**; 1940–), U.S. singer, actress. A Brooklyn native, Kazan has achieved considerable success as an actress in film, television, and the stage and as a singer in both musicals and nightclub acts. Her big break came as Barbra *Streisand's understudy in the Broadway production of *Funny Girl*, replacing Streisand for two shows and earning rave reviews. Kazan began starring in nightclub acts and musicals before making the jump into film and television. In 1982, she received a Golden Globe nomination for her portrayal of Jewish mother Belle Carroca in *My Favorite Year* (1982). She would later receive a Tony award nomination for her reprisal of the same role in the Broadway musical adaptation. Kazan's other notable film credits include a role in fellow Hofstra alumnus Francis Ford Coppola's *One From the Heart* (1982) and such films as *Lust in the Dust* (1985), *Harry and the Hendersons* (1987), *Beaches* (1988), *The Cemetery Club* (1993), *My Big Fat Greek Wedding* (2002), and *Gigli* (2003). Kazan has made many television appearances over a period of four decades, receiving an Emmy nomination for her guest role on *St. Elsewhere*, appearing in repeat roles on *The Nanny, Veronica's Closet, Beverly Hills 90210*, and *My Big Fat Greek Life* as well as making guest appearances on shows such as *The Paper Chase, Touched By An Angel*, and *Will and Grace*.

[Walter Driver (2nd ed.)]

KAZARNOVSKI, ISAAC ABRAMOVICH (1890–?), Russian inorganic chemist. Kazarnovski studied in Switzerland and received his doctorate in Zurich in 1914 and in 1922 he joined the Karpov Physico-chemical Institute of the University of Moscow. He became a corresponding member of the U.S.S.R. Academy of Sciences in 1939 and was awarded the Stalin Prize in 1941. Kazarnovski wrote on chlorides and peroxides of metals, the production of anhydrous aluminum chloride from clays, and of sodium peroxide, and methods for regenerating air. He discovered sodium dioxide $Na\text{-}O_2$ and potassium ozonide KO_3.

[Samuel Aaron Miller]

KAZATIN, city in Vinnitsa district, Ukraine, an important railroad junction. A Jewish community developed in the late 19th century, numbering 1,731 (20% of the total population) in 1897. During the civil war (1917–20) the Jews suffered greatly at the hands of the various armies passing through the town. In 1926 the Jewish population reached 3,012 (20%). During the Soviet period many Jews worked in a sugar refinery, on the railroad, and in two Jewish kolkhozes. Most of the children studied in a Yiddish school. In 1939 there were 2,648 Jews (15.8% of the total). The Germans entered Kazatin on July 14, 1941. They set up a ghetto. On June 4, 1942, they killed 508 Jews and another 250 in early July. In August they murdered 183, and the last 30 in December 1942. Jews returned after the war but their last synagogue was closed by the authorities in 1960. In 1970 the Jewish population was estimated at about 300 families. Most left in the emigration of the 1990s

[Yehuda Slutsky / Shmuel Spector (2nd ed.)]

KAZAZ, ELIJAH BEN ELIJAH (1832–1912), important Karaite public figure and pedagogue, a member of the Haskalah. Born in Armyansk, Crimea, he studied there in a *bet midrash*, moved to Evpatoria, and became the disciple of Abraham ben Yosef *Lutski (Aben Yashar). He started writing poems in Hebrew at an early age. He lived for a while in Kherson, where he studied secular subjects with a priest and was on friendly terms with Yekuti'el Berman, a member of the Haskalah, who introduced him to the world of modern Jewish literature. He studied at St. Petersburg University, at the faculty of Oriental Studies. After graduating, he founded in 1859 a Karaite school in Odessa. In the 1860s he taught general history and Latin in Simferopol. In 1886 he became director of the Tatar pedagogical college in Simferopol. In 1895, when the officials, after his endeavors, opened the Alexander III School for Karaite teachers and *ḥazzanim*, Kazaz became its director, holding the position until 1908.

He published numerous poems in Hebrew periodicals. The collections of poems appearing in book form, *Shirim Aḥadim* (1857) and *Yeled Sha'ashu'im* (1910, Ashdod 2002), are among the few Karaite contributions to secular Hebrew literature. Later, influenced by the teachings advocated by Abraham *Firkovich, he tried to sever all connection between the *Karaites and the mainstream of Jewry. He asserted that the Karaites were not Semites, but a Tatar or *Khazar tribe which had become converted to the Jewish faith. His works include a Hebrew textbook in Tatar, *Le-Regel ha-Yeladim* (1868–69), intended for the Karaite youth speaking the Tatar language; *Torat ha-Adam* (1889), an adaptation of *Eléments de morale* by P. Janet (1870); *Kivshono shel Olam* (1889), after *La religion naturelle* by J. Simon (1856); *Emet me-Ereẓ* (1908), a shortened version of F. Vigouroux's *La Bible et les découvertes modernes en Palestine…* (1879); *Cicero, Ẓiyyur Biografi* (a biographical sketch; 1908). He also translated the Karaite prayer book entitled *Ketoret Tamid* into Russian (1905). The Russian authorities regarded him as the official Karaite representative.

BIBLIOGRAPHY: B. Elyashevich, *Materialy k serii narody i kultury XIV*, kn. 2 (1993), 79–82; S. Poznański, in: ZHB, 13 (1909), 117–8, 146, 148; 14 (1910), 114; *Reshumot*, 1 (1925), 476–83; R. Fahn, *Sefer ha-Kara'im* (1929), 138ff., MGWJ, 74 (1930), 141–4.

[Isaak Dov Ber Markon / Golda Akhiezer (2nd ed.)]

KAZDAN, ḤAYYIM SOLOMON (**Shlomo**; 1883–1979), Yiddish educator, editor, and essayist. A teacher in Yiddish schools in Eastern Europe, Kazdan began his career in 1902 as a teacher in the Girls' Professional School in his native Kherson (Ukraine). As contributor to pedagogical journals, textbook writer, supervisor of schools and classroom teacher, he advanced the teaching of Yiddish language and literature. Kazdan was active in Jewish Socialist circles in Kherson, Kiev, and Warsaw. In the 1930s, he was the director of C.Y.S.O. (Central Yiddish School Organization) in Warsaw. He was a key figure among those educators who believed that Yiddish was not only an educational means but also an end in itself. Fleeing the Nazis, Kazdan arrived in the U.S. in 1941, where for more than a decade he was instructor at the Workmen's Circle high school ("mitlshul"), and from 1955 professor of Yiddish language and literature at the Jewish Teachers Seminary.

The author of many books and monographs, his major works are: *In di Teg fun Revolutsye* ("In the Days of the Revolution," 1928); *In Eyner a Shtot* ("Once in a City," 1928); *Di Geshikhte fun Yidishn Shulvezn in Umophengikn Poyln* ("The History of the Jewish School System in Independent Poland," 1947); and *Fun Kheyder un Shkoles biz Tṣisho* ("From Kheyder and Shkoles to Tsisho," 1956).

BIBLIOGRAPHY: Rejzen, Leksikon, 3 (1929), 413–7. **ADD. BIBLIOGRAPHY:** LNYL, 8 (1981), 36–38.

[Judah Pilch]

KAZIMIERZ (Kuzhmir), ḥasidic dynasty, especially known for their development of ḥasidic melody. Its founder, EZEKIEL BEN ẒEVI-HIRSCH TAUB OF KAZIMIERZ (d. 1856), was the disciple of *Jacob Isaac ha-Ḥozeh of Lublin and of other ḥasidic leaders. He began as a merchant in his home town of Plonsk, and eventually settled in Kazimierz, where he established himself as a *ẓaddik*. He became celebrated for his musical gifts, and composed numerous ḥasidic melodies characterized by joyful lyricism. He used to say: "I do not feel the delight of Sabbath without a new melody." His sermons were collected in *Neḥmad mi-Zahav* (1909).

DAVID ẒEVI OF NEUSTADT (d. 1882) Ezekiel's eldest son, and one of the outstanding disciples of Menahem Mendel Morgenstern of Kotsk, founded the ḥasidic dynasty of Yablonov. His sermons are collected in *Ḥemdat Dodo* (1930). His grandson EZEKIEL OF YABLONOV founded the Naḥalat Ya'akov society in 1924, and in the following year settled in Ereẓ Israel at the head of a group of Ḥasidim. They established an agricultural settlement, Naḥalat Ya'akov, at the western approaches to the Jezreel Valley (later part of *Kefar Ḥasidim).

SAMUEL ELIJAH TAUB OF ZWOLEN (d. 1888), also a son of Ezekiel, like his father had musical gifts, but as a *ẓaddik* suppressed this bent and led the prayers only on rare occasions. He said: "In every melody there is a soul, and a spirit is breathed into it by the singer-creator; within the melody there is both youth and old age; it is like a living being, and therefore whoever subtracts a note from or adds to it is as though he harms, as it were, the 248 organs of the human body." His son, MOSES AARON TAUB OF NOWY DWOR (d. 1918), succeeded his father, first at Zwolen and later at Nowy Dwor near Warsaw. ḤAYYIM JERAHMEEL TAUB (d. 1942), son of Moses Aaron, lived in Zwolen, Mlawa, and finally Warsaw; he headed a ḥasidic community and composed ḥasidic melodies. He perished in *Treblinka. ELEAZAR SOLOMON BEN EPHRAIM TAUB (d. 1938), of Wolomin, the grandson of the first Ezekiel, moved to Warsaw during World War I. He also possessed musical gifts.

BIBLIOGRAPHY: M.S. Geshuri, *Neginah ve-Ḥasidut* (1952).

[Avraham Rubinstein]

KAZIN, ALFRED (1915–1998), U.S. author, critic, and editor. Born to immigrants and educated in New York, Kazin pointed out that he was temperamentally drawn to the idea of revolution and social transformation. Kazin first made his reputation as a book reviewer for the *New York Herald Tribune* and as an editor for *The New Republic* and other newspapers and periodicals. His first and best-known work, *On Native Grounds* (1942), was an explication of modern American literature, studying the estrangement of the American writer from American culture. His critical articles and reviews have been collected in a number of books, including *Contemporaries* (1962). His autobiographical reflections can be found in *A Walker in the City* (1951), *Starting Out in the Thirties* (1965), and *New York Jew* (1978). They are also descriptions of the generation which grew up in the depression years and matured under the impact of the Spanish Civil War and Nazism. *A Lifetime Burning Every Moment* (1996) consists of selections from his journals. In his *Writing Was Everything* (1995), Kazin reflected on his literary heritage and life. Kazin also edited works by William Blake (1946), and others on Dreiser and Emerson. Together with A. Birstein he edited *The Works of Anne Frank* (1959).

ADD. BIBLIOGRAPHY: T. Solotaroff (ed.), *Alfred Kazin's America: Critical and Personal Writings* (2003).

[Milton Henry Hindus / Lewis Fried (2nd ed.)]

KAẒIN, JUDAH BEN YOM TOV (1708–1783), rabbi and halakhic authority of *Aleppo, whose rabbinical office he filled for many years. Kaẓin was involved in the controversy which broke out among the rabbis of Aleppo over the imposition of the authority of the local rabbis on the "Francos" (Jewish merchants of Western European origin who arrived in Aleppo during the late 17th century). The chief rabbi Raphael Solomon *Laniado demanded that the local customs be imposed on them, while the rabbis of Aleppo, led by Kaẓin, were opposed to this. During his last years he wrote *Maḥaneh Yehudah* (Leghorn, 1803), which includes his arguments concerning this controversy and the approbations of the rabbis of Aleppo and *Jerusalem. It appears that with the deaths of Laniado and Kaẓin at the end of the 18th century the dispute subsided. Kaẓin also wrote responsa, which form the first part of the work *Ro'ei Yisrael* (1904), and sermons, *Ve-Zot li-Yhudah* (still in Ms.).

BIBLIOGRAPHY: M.D. Gaon, *Yehudei ha-Mizraḥ be-Ereẓ Yisrael*, 2 (1937), 630; D.Z. Laniado, *Li-Kedoshim Asher ba-Areẓ*, 1 (1952), 32; A. Lutzky, in: *Zion*, 6 (1940/41), 73–79.

[Abraham David]

KAẒIN, RAPHAEL BEN ELIJAH (1818–1871), rabbi of Baghdad. Kaẓin was born in Aleppo. On the death of his father he left his birthplace, visiting Ereẓ Israel and Persia, and in 1846 went to Baghdad as a "self-appointed emissary." He was an outstanding scholar and accomplished speaker. At that time the *av bet din* in Baghdad was Elijah Obadiah b. Abraham ha-Levi, who had come from Ereẓ Israel. With the arrival of Kaẓin a violent controversy arose which split the community. Most of the wealthy men sought to depose Obadiah and appoint Kaẓin in his place, while most of the rabbis supported Obadiah. So deep-seated was the animosity that was engendered between the rival factions that for many years they did not even intermarry. Finally the supporters of Obadiah triumphed and in 1847 Kaẓin left Baghdad. He went to Constantinople where he succeeded in obtaining a firman from the sultan appointing him *ḥakham bashi* ("chief rabbi") of Baghdad, an office that previously did not exist. He filled this office from 1849 to 1852, and according to *Benjamin II he exercised his authority with firmness. Four soldiers were stationed as guards at the entrance of his house and when he went out he was preceded by five Jews in uniform carrying scepters in their hands, as was the custom for nobles at that time. In 1852 the "Obadiah faction" rose to power and Kaẓin was compelled to return to Aleppo. There is no information available on the activities of Kaẓin after his return to Aleppo. Three of his seven works have been published: *Iggeret Maggid Meẓarim* (1837), an appeal to the Jews of Europe to come to the aid of the Jews of Persia, and two polemics against Christianity, *Derekh ha-Ḥayyim* (1848) and *Likkutei Amarim* (second ed. 1855, with a Ladino translation). His other works, including a third polemic on Christianity, *Derekh Emet*, are in manuscript.

BIBLIOGRAPHY: A. Ben-Jacob, *Yehudei Bavel* (1965), 156–61.

[Abraham Ben-Yaacob]

KAẒIR ḤARISH (Heb. קָצִיר חָרִישׁ), urban community in northern Israel. Kaẓir Ḥarish is located in the eastern hills of Wadi ʿArra, and is an amalgamation of two settlements, with an area of 2.3 sq. mi. (6 sq. km.). Kaẓir was established as a community in 1982 by a group *Hitaḥdut ha-Ikkarim (Farmers Association) settlers, with assistance from the *Jewish Agency. Ḥarish was established as a kibbutz by Ha-Kibbutz ha-Artzi, also with the assistance of the Jewish Agency, southwest of Kaẓir. Neither settlement succeeded in expanding as expected. In the beginning of the 1990s, Kaẓir numbered just 30 families, while Ḥarish was abandoned by its founders in 1993. But with the mass immigration of the 1990s, Kaẓir and Ḥarish were selected to be included in the "star plan" aimed at populating settlements bordering on Judea and Samaria. In 1992 the government decided to unite the two settlements in a single municipal council. In 2002 its population was 3,500. The majority of the residents work outside the settlement, mainly in Ḥaderah, Haifa, and Tel Aviv.

WEBSITE: www.cityindex.co.il.

[Shaked Gilboa (2nd ed.)]

KAZNELSON, SIEGMUND (1893–1959), publisher and editor. Born in Warsaw, Kaznelson completed his studies at the German University in Prague. During his student days, he began publication of articles on Jewish and Zionist subjects in *Die Welt* and *Selbstwehr*, the Zionist periodical of Prague which he edited during World War I. After the war, he moved to Berlin, where he first worked on the editorial staff of M. *Buber's monthly, *Der Jude*. From 1920 he managed the Juedischer Verlag publishing house, which he developed into the largest publishing house of German Jewry. Under his management it published Herzl's diary, Dubnow's history, the *Juedisches Lexikon*, the works of Aḥad ha-Am, and other important Jewish works. In 1937 Kaznelson immigrated to Ereẓ Israel and took up residence in Jerusalem. While still in Germany he began his scientific-literary project on the role of the Jews in German culture. Part of this work was published during his lifetime; the rest was published posthumously as *Juden im deutschen Kulturbereich* (1962^3), *Beethovens ferne und unsterbliche Geliebte* (1954); *Juedisches Schicksal in deutschen Geschichten* (anthology, 1959); *The Palestine Problem and its Solution* (1946); and *Zionismus und Voelkerbund* (1922).

BIBLIOGRAPHY: F. Weltsch, in: *Haaretz* (April 3, 1959); idem, in: MB (Mar. 26, 1954); Juedischer Verlag, *Almanach: 1902–1964* (1964).

[Getzel Kressel]

KAẒRIN (Heb. קַצְרִין), urban community in the *Golan Heights. Kaẓrin was established in 1977 following the government's decision to settle and populate the Golan Heights. In 1979 the town received municipal status. It was planned as an urban center that would provide a variety of services to the rural communities and military bases scattered throughout the Golan. At the end of 2002 the population of Kaẓrin was 6,280, among them 30% immigrants from the former Soviet Union. The town has an area of 4.7 sq. mi. (12.2 sq. km.). Its industrial area includes the Golan Heights Wineries and the Eden natural mineral water bottling plants, making it "the city of water and wine." In addition, Kaẓrin's industries include dairy, plastic, and electronics factories. The town has an academic center, which includes the Ohalo Teachers Training College, a branch of Haifa University, and a branch of the Open University. The Museum of Golan Antiquities exhibits archeological finds. The town's name is derived from the ancient talmudic village of Qasrin, which was destroyed in an earthquake 1,300 years ago. The remains of the ancient synagogue and other buildings are open to the public.

WEBSITE: www.qatzrin.muni.il.

[Shaked Gilboa (2nd ed.)]

KAZVIN, a town situated between *Teheran and the Caspian Sea. The name of the town is probably related to the word "Caspian." *Benjamin of Tudela (1167) mentions the existence of Jews in mountains and areas adjacent to Kazvin. The local tradition relates that in the "Imām mosque" in Kazvin are buried the biblical friends of the prophet Daniel, namely Hananiah, Mishael, and Azariah. Kazvin for some time was the capital city of the first Safavids. Later, Shah *Abbās I made *Isfahan the capital (1588). However, Jews continued to live in Kazvin, and it is known that around 1746 Nāder Shah transferred many Jews from the city and its neighborhood to the northeast of *Iran. According to Levy at the beginning of the 19th century there were 6,000 Jews in Kazvin. According to Neumark some Jewish families of Kabul in *Afghanistan originated from Kazvin. He avers that there were no Jews living in Kazvin in his time (1884). According to the unpublished memoirs of Solayman Cohen-Sedeq, a prominent Iranian Jew, reported by Levy (p. 1029), there were in 1876 in Kazvin 11 Jewish families who had two synagogues. Most of them were immigrants from *Kashan and *Hamadan. Israeli contracting firms were active in Iran, particularly in reconstruction and development works in the area of Kazvin, which suffered heavily from an earthquake in 1962. It has been reported that Kazvin ceased to be a dwelling place of Jewish families some time during the 20th century.

BIBLIOGRAPHY: M.D. Adler (ed.), *The Itinerary of Benjamin of Tudela* (1907); H. Levy, *History of the Jews of Iran*, 3 (1960); E. Neumark, *Massa be-Ereẓ ha-Kedem*, ed. by A. Ya'ari, 1947.

[Amnon Netzer (2nd ed.)]

KAZYONNY RAVVIN (Rus. "an official rabbi"; Heb. expression, *rav mi-ta'am*), title of the officials elected by the communities of Russia between 1857 and 1917 in accordance with the instructions of the government. Their official function was "to supervise public prayers and religious ceremonies so that the permanent regulations be respected; to regularize the laws of the Jews and clarify the problems connected with them; to educate them in the true spirit of the law." In practice the "official rabbis" represented their communities before the authorities. They delivered patriotic speeches, mostly in Russian, on festivals and on the birthdays of the czars. They supervised Jewish government schools, administered the oath to those who had been enlisted into the Russian army, and kept the records of births, marriages, and deaths in their communities. The institution of *kazyonny ravvin* was linked with the attempts of the Russian government to influence and control Jewish communal activities. As early as in the "Jewish constitution" of 1804 it was stated that, as from 1812, only those who could read and write Russian, Polish, or German would be authorized to officiate as rabbis. In the "Jewish legislation" of 1835, the rabbis' functions were defined as "to guide the Jews in the fulfillment of their moral duties, the observance of the state's laws, and obedience to the authorities." The rabbi was to officiate at circumcision, marriage, and burial ceremonies, and keep the records of births and deaths. In 1836, when the government decided to censor the books of the Jews, the task was imposed on the rabbis of the large communities, to whom books were presented for inspection by their owners.

With the growth of the Haskalah movement, the *maskilim* began to call for the appointment of rabbis who had a general education also. Projects were advanced for the establishment of a body of official rabbis after the example of the *Consistory in France. It soon became evident, however, that there were no men suitable for such positions among the Russian Jews. The suggestion of inviting "enlightened" rabbis from Western Europe was rejected on political grounds. As an exception, the election of "enlightened" rabbis was approved for Riga (Abraham Neumann, 1854) and Odessa (Simeon Aryeh *Schwabacher, 1860). In 1847 two government seminaries for the training of rabbis in the spirit of Haskalah were established in Vilna and Zhitomir, financed from the revenues of the *candle tax. In 1857, on the occasion of the graduation of the first classes of these institutions, a law was passed which declared that henceforward the Jewish communities were only to "appoint such rabbis who had completed their studies in the government seminaries, and the government Jewish schools of the second grade, the general schools, high, secondary, or district schools."

The application of the law encountered opposition from the communities. Poor salaries were granted to the rabbis thus appointed, and since they were dependent on reelection by their communities every few years their influence was insignificant. The *maskilim* called on the government to impose the election of such rabbis on the communities or to appoint them itself and pay their salaries so that they should be independent of their congregants. These demands, which were at times supported by the local authorities, were rejected by the central government with the argument that they contradicted the fundamental right of the Jewish communities to elect their own rabbis. The government rabbinical seminaries did not achieve their objective, and in 1873 were closed down and converted into government schools for Jewish teachers. In practice, every Jew who had completed six, or even four classes of a Russian secondary school could present his candidature for the post of *kazyonny ravvin*.

The Jewish communities generally regarded the institution of official rabbis with hostility and endeavored to restrict their activities as far as possible. On many occasions, men without any knowledge of Judaism and its contents were appointed to this position, which they merely considered a sinecure. At times, even the moral conduct of the incumbents of this office was doubtful. The true religious influence within the communities continued to be wielded by the rabbis of the traditional style whom the Russian government recognized, though not officially, under the title of "spiritual rabbis." Jewish folklore abounds in descriptions of the official rabbi as covetous, an ignoramus, and one who despises the values of the Jewish religion. Their connections with the authorities, and at times even with secret police, occasionally led them to be suspected as informers. At the same time, the official rabbinate became a source of livelihood for many Jewish *maskilim*, some of whom elevated this function to the level of a valuable public service (Z.S. Minor, in Minsk and later in Moscow; A.A. Pumpianski, in Riga; J.L. *Kantor, in Libava (Liepaja), Vilna, and Riga; J. *Mazeh, in Moscow; H.Y. Katzenelson, in Oriol; I.B. *Levner, in Lugansk; S.Z. Luria, in Kiev; and also *Shalom Aleichem, in Lubny, 1880–83).

With the growth of nationalism and Zionism, Zionist circles, with the slogan "Conquest of the Communities," attempted to convert the function of *kazyonny ravvin* into a channel for nationalist influence, and in many communities leaders and activists of the movement were elected to this office through the influence of the Zionists. They attempted to influence their communities in a nationalist direction, to strengthen Jewish education, and to educate the youth and bring it nearer to Judaism. This was a thankless function, however, and its incumbents were compelled to tread a tightrope between the czarist authorities and their nationalist conscience. Rabbis of this category included Vladimir *Tiomkin (Yekaterinoslav), Shemariah *Levin (Grodno, Yekaterinoslav), Menahem *Sheinkin (Balta, 1901–05), Y.N. Vilenski (Nikolayev, 1903–05), and Mordecai Rabinsohn (Bobruisk). J. Mazeh, Shemariah Levin, Y.N. Vilenski, A.I. Freudenberg (Kremenchug), and Isaac *Schneersohn (Chernigov) described their public activities as official rabbis in their memoirs.

BIBLIOGRAPHY: A. Margulis, *Voprosy, yevreyskoy zhizni* (1889), 168–92; Yu. Hessen, in: YE, 13 (c. 1910), 226–31.

[Yehuda Slutsky]

KECSKEMET (Hung. **Kecskemét**), city in central Hungary. The first Jews arrived there when the area was under Turkish domination in the 16th to 17th centuries. Subsequently the city came under Austrian rule. In 1715 the municipal council was requested to order the Jews attending the fairs there to do their business separately from the other merchants. In 1746 four Jewish families from Obuda (Alt-Ofen) settled in the city. At first the Jews mainly engaged in the trade of hides and feathers. Later, they organized the internationally celebrated trade of the region in cattle, poultry, preserves, alcoholic liquor, and wine.

A community was established in 1801, and in 1814 the Jews were authorized to use a house which they had purchased as a synagogue. The Jews in Kecskemet were attacked during the revolution of 1848 and their shops were looted. The community was declared neologist (see *Neology) in 1868. A magnificent synagogue was erected in 1871; it was destroyed by an earthquake in 1911 but was rebuilt in 1913. A separate Orthodox community was founded in 1917. After the end of World War I, following the collapse of the brief Communist regime, the White Terror fomented pogroms in the town and eight Jewish victims lost their lives.

Rabbis of Kecskemet included Simeon Fischmann, Armin Perls, later rabbi of *Pecs, Joseph Bárány, Joseph Borsodi (1916–42), and Joseph Schindler (1942–50) who, after his return from the concentration camps, continued to hold rabbinical office in the city. There was a Jewish school in the city from 1844 to 1870.

In the wake of the growing antisemitism after 1930 there was an increase in Zionist activity, particularly after 1939. The Jewish population numbered 47 in 1785, 441 in 1840, 1,514 in 1869, 1,984 in 1900, 1,860 in 1920, 1,567 in 1930, and 1,346 in 1941.

Holocaust Period

In May 1944, after the German invasion of Hungary (March 19, 1944), the Jews in Kecskemet were rounded up and treated with exceptional brutality by members of the SS from among the Hungarian Volksdeutsche. Their suffering was so great that 70 of them committed suicide by taking poison; 13 people were smuggled out at the last minute with the aid of forged documents. At the end of June, the 940 remaining Jews in the ghetto were sent to Auschwitz, from which only 150 returned.

Between 1945 and 1947, there were 410 Jews living in Kecskemet, including refugees from the siege in Budapest. The Jewish population numbered 221 in 1949, 84 in 1954, and 40 in 1970.

BIBLIOGRAPHY: J. Bárány, in: IMIT, 9 (1899), 102–26; M. Sandberg, *Shanah le-Ein Kez* (1966).

[Alexander Scheiber]

KECSKEMÉTI, ÁRMIN (1874–1944), Hungarian rabbi and scholar. Kecskeméti was born in Kecskemet, Hungary. He studied in Budapest at the rabbinical seminary and the university. He served as rabbi in Mako, Hungary, from 1898 to 1944 and also lectured on Jewish history at Szeged University. He died in the Strasshof concentration camp. For his studies Kecskeméti was able to use the rich library of Immanuel *Loew. Kecskeméti's works, which were mainly popular, include *A zsidó irodalom története* ("History of Jewish Literature," 2 vols., 1908–09); *Azsidók egyetemes története* ("Universal History of the Jews," 2 vols., 1927); *Izrael története a bibliai korban* ("History of Israel in Biblical Times," 1942); and *A csanádmegyei zsidók története* ("History of the Jews in the District of Csanád," 1929), which discusses his own community, Mako.

[Alexander Scheiber]

KECSKEMÉTI, GYŐRGY (1901–1944), Hungarian journalist, born in Makó, the son of Rabbi A. Kecskeméti. From 1929 to 1936 Kecskeméti taught at the Jewish secondary school of Budapest and in 1931 joined the staff of the government's German newspaper *Pester Lloyd*. From 1936 he was editor in chief, and held the position in spite of anti-Jewish legislation until the Nazi occupation. He wrote a book of poems *Változatok hat témára* ("Variations on Six Themes"), and contributed to periodicals. When the Germans occupied Hungary, he was among the journalists deported to Auschwitz, where he died. He left several manuscripts.

KECSKEMÉTI, LIPÓT (1865–1936), Hungarian rabbi and scholar. Kecskeméti was born in Kecskemét. He studied at the rabbinical seminary and the University of Budapest and at the Lehranstalt fuer die Wissenschaft des Judentums in Berlin. He served as rabbi of Nagyvárad from 1890 to his death. Kecskeméti, a magnificent orator and a highly respected leader, was a convinced anti-Zionist and assimilationist and a Hungarian patriot, courageously resisting attempts to Romanianize Nagyvárad and the other Hungarian regions transferred to Romania after World War I. He founded a Jewish high school there. Among his published works are *Zsidó költőkből* ("By Jewish Poets," 1887), an anthology of medieval Jewish poetry; his Ph.D. thesis, *A pokol a középkori zsidó költészetben* ("Hell in Medieval Jewish Poetry," 1888); *Egy zsidó vallás van-e, több-e?* ("Is There One Jewish Religion or More?" 1913); *Az* *izraelita vallás története* ("History of Jewish Religion," 4 vols., 1932); *Jeremiás próféta és kora* ("The Prophet Jeremiah and His Age," 3 vols., 1932); *Ezsajás* ("Isaiah," 3 vols., 1935); and many articles in Hungarian-Jewish periodicals. He also translated the Prophets for a Hungarian edition of the Bible.

BIBLIOGRAPHY: F. Fischer, *Das Buch von Dr. L. Kecskeméti "Gibt es blos eine juedische Religion oder mehrere"* (1934); *Emlékkönyv Dr. Kecskeméti Lipót* (1936).

[Alexander Scheiber]

KEDAINIAI (Rus. **Keidany**; Yid. **Kaidan**), town in central Lithuania, founded during the 14th century. From 1490 the locality was ruled by the Kishkis family, which invited Jewish merchants to settle there. The town became a Calvinist center in 1560 under the rule of the princes Radziwill, and the Jews were granted civic rights and religious freedom. Jews there engaged in the import and export trades, winemaking, and moneylending. Jewish craftsmen, ritual slaughterers, butchers, and cattle dealers were organized in guilds. The community played an important economic and social role in the Council of Lithuania (see *Councils of the Lands). There were 501 Jewish poll-tax payers in the town in 1766. The rabbis of the *Katzenellenbogen family made Kedainiai a center of Jewish learning. After Kedainiai passed to Russia in 1795, the Jews there lost their specific rights. The community, which numbered 4,987 in 1847, decreased by emigration during the 1880s, and by 1897 numbered 3,733 (64% of the population). During World War I, in May 1915, the Jews were expelled from Kedainiai to the interior of Russia, but some returned after the war. There were 2,500 Jews living in Kedainiai in 1923 (33% of the population), of whom approximately 15% were engaged in the cultivation and marketing of vegetables and agricultural exports. In 1939 Jewish refugees from Poland including the scholars of the yeshivah of *Mir settled in Kedainiai. On June 24, 1941, the Germans occupied the town, executing around 325 Jews in the forests by July, and on Aug. 28, 1941, with the cooperation of the Lithuanians, the rest of the Jewish population – including 1,000 from surrounding towns – was massacred at the Smilaga Creek. Senior *Sachs and M.L. *Lilienblum were born in Kedainiai.

BIBLIOGRAPHY: B.H. Kasel, *Kaidan* (1930).

[Dov Levin]

KEDAR (Heb. קֵדָר), a nomadic tribe or league of tribes in the Arabian Desert. Kedar is mentioned in Genesis 25:3 and I Chronicles 1:29 among "the sons of Ishmael," the latter being tribes of Arabs known from the eighth century B.C.E. onward in the desert tracts surrounding Palestine (see *Ishmaelites). The mode of life of the Kedarites, as reflected in the Bible, was associated with the rearing of sheep and camels (Isa. 60:7; Jer. 49:28–29, 32; Ezek. 27:21), and with dwelling in tents (Jer. 49:29; Ps. 120:5; Song 1:5) and in unfortified villages and camps (Isa. 42:11; Jer. 49:31).

Biblical information on their locality and history is extremely scant, but many details about these are known from other sources, in particular from inscriptions of Assyrian kings. The earliest document which refers to the Kedarites is the inscription of Tiglath-Pileser III found in Iran (unpublished). In it they are mentioned together with other nations in the west of the Fertile Crescent who surrendered to the Assyrian king and whose rulers paid him tribute in 738 B.C.E. From parallel inscriptions of Ashurbanipal it is evident that Hazail, king of the Arabs, against whom Senacherib's army fought between 691 and 689 B.C.E. in the region of Duma (Jawf) in Wadi Sirḥān, and who surrendered to Esarhaddon, was the king of Kedar. Close to 652 B.C.E. the Kedarites under Uate᾽ the son of Hazail, who broke his oath of allegiance to Ashurbanipal, raided the frontier regions on the western border of the Assyrian empire, but were repulsed and defeated by King Kamashtalta of Moab and by units of the Assyrian army stationed along the border from the Valley of Lebanon to Edom.

Another leader who took part in these raids and is likewise described as "king of Kedar" in the inscriptions of Ashurbanipal was Ammuladi(n). Following the defeat of Uate᾽ the leadership of the Kedarites passed to Abiate᾽ the son of Te᾽ri, who in 652 B.C.E. sent soldiers to Babylon to help Shamash-shum-ukin king of Babylonia in his war against his brother Ashurbanipal. In the period of the intensive military operations of the Assyrian army in Babylonia and Elam (652–646 B.C.E.), the Kedarites under Abiate᾽ and Aamu sons of Te᾽ri were among other units of nomads that exerted pressure on the inhabited area along the frontier of the desert, from the region of Jebel Bishrī to the vicinity of Damascus. The grave situation resulting from the pressure of the nomads compelled the king of Assyria to launch an extensive campaign against them mostly in the desert and under difficult conditions (Ashurbanipal's ninth campaign). The information in Jeremiah 49:28ff. combined with that in the Babylonian Chronicle (BM 21946 rev. 9–10) shows that in 599 B.C.E. units of Nebuchadnezzar's army raided the encampments of the Kedarites in the western region of the Syrian desert.

With the ending of the political existence of the Transjordanian kingdoms in the first half of the sixth century B.C.E., the Kedarites together with other units of "the children of the east" penetrated to the settled country whose borders were breached. The dimensions of their expansion and the area of their operations in the west are attested by the votive inscription "זי קרב קיני בר גשם מלך קדר להנאלת" on a silver bowl originating from the temple of the Arab goddess Han-Ilat at Tell al-Maskhūṭa (in the neighborhood of Ismailia) at the eastern approach of Egypt. On the basis of paleographical and archaeological considerations, the bowl and the inscription have been dated to the fifth century B.C.E. Accordingly, some hold that Geshem king of Kedar is the Arab Geshem, Nehemiah's enemy (Neh. 2:19; 6:1ff.). However the data for this identification are inconclusive.

Later references to the Kedarites occur not only in inscriptions dating from the centuries close to the Common Era and found in a temple at Ma᾽īn in southern Arabia but also in

Pliny (*Historia Naturalis*, 5:65), who mentions them among the peoples of northern Arabia, alongside the Nabateans.

The wide dispersion of the Kedarites, extending as it did from the region of Duma (Jawf) in Wadi Sirḥān to Palmyrene and to the eastern port of the Nile Delta, lends probability to their having been a union of various sub-units. Evidence of the existence of such a social organization occurs in the inscriptions of Ashurbanipal, according to which Uate' son of Hazail and Ammuladi(n) flourished at the same time and in which both are referred to as "king of Kedar." Similarly Ezekiel 27:21 refers to "Arabia, and all the princes of Kedar."

BIBLIOGRAPHY: A. Musil, *Arabia Deserta* (1927), 490–91; K. Mlaker, *Die Hierodulenisten von Maˣin* (1943), 40; J. Rabinowitz, in: JNES, 15 (1956), 1–9.

[Israel Eph'al]

KEDEM, ORA (1924–), physical chemist. Kedem was born in Vienna and immigrated to Ereẓ Israel in 1940 as an "illegal" immigrant on the ill-fated *Patria*. She graduated from the Hebrew University and received her doctorate from the Weizmann Institute in 1953. Together with Prof. Aharon *Katzir she initiated the analysis of biomembrane processes in terms of nonequilibrium thermodynamics, defining the energy conversion in active transport and muscle action. In the 1960s and early 1970s she helped to found Ben-Gurion University (the University of the Negev). She founded and chaired the Department of Membrane Research at the Weizmann Institute and was scientific director of membrane products there and then of RPR). She contributed to the understanding and development of membrane processes for desalination and other separation technologies. In 1965 she was appointed associate professor in the Department of Polymer Research at the Institute and full professor in 1970. She was awarded the Israel Prize for science in 1961.

[Bracha Rager (2nd ed.)]

KEDEMITES OR EASTERNERS (Heb. בְּנֵי קֶדֶם (*benei kedem, bene qedem*), adjective *qadmoni*, קַדְמֹנִי; Gen. 15:19) is a general designation for the peoples living on the eastern border of Syria and Palestine, from as far north as Haran (Gen. 29:1–4) to as far south as the northern end of the Red Sea (Gen. 25:1–6). In Israelite ethnology, all these peoples, and the Ishmaelites as well, who ranged from the border of Egypt to Assyria (i.e., the Middle Euphrates), and who included the inhabitants of Tema and Dumah (Gen. 25:12–18), were all related. Their center of dispersion was the Middle Euphrates region – called Aram-Naharaim (Gen. 24:10; Deut. 23:5), Paddan-Aram (Gen. 28:2, 5, 6, 7; 31:18 (or Paddan, Gen. 48:7)), "the country Aram" (Hos. 12:13), or simply Aram (Num. 23:7). From here Abraham and Lot moved to Canaan (Gen. 12:5). Lot eventually moved to Transjordan and became the ancestor of Moab and Ammon (Gen. 19:30ff.), while Abraham became the ancestor of all the other Kedemites, including the Ishmaelites, and of the Israelites as well. His son Isaac and the latter's son Jacob-Israel married wives from Abraham's original homeland, where Jacob even lived for 20 years. Hence the confession, "My father was a wandering/ fugitive Aramean who migrated to Egypt" (Deut. 26:5). The Israelites acknowledged all those peoples as their kin in contrast to the Canaanites. The Kedemites enjoyed among the Israelites a great reputation for wisdom. Not only does David quote a Kedemite proverb which he characterizes as such, but the wisdom of the Kedemites is rated only lower than Solomon's though higher than that of the Egyptians (I Kings 5:10), and Isaiah represents the Egyptian king's wise men as seeking to impress him by claiming descent from sages of Kedem (this, not "of old," is the meaning of *qedem* in Isa. 19:11). A wise instruction by the mother of a Kedemite king, *Lemuel, to her royal son is preserved, according to the superscription, in Proverbs 31:1–9; for Massa is the name of an Ishmaelite tribe (Gen. 25:14; on the Aramaizing diction, see *Job). *Agur son of Jakeh was doubtless of the same nationality as Lemuel, according to Proverbs 30:1, where *ha-massa'i*, "the Massaite," is to be read. The reputed wisdom of the Edomites (included among the Kedemites in Isa. 11:14) is alluded to in Jeremiah 49:7; Obadiah 7 end, 8.

ADD. BIBLIOGRAPHY: M. Cogan, I *Kings* (AB; 2000), 220.

[Harold Louis Ginsberg]

KEDEMOTH (Heb. קְדֵמֹת, קְדֵמוֹת), city and desert E. of the Jordan. It was from the wilderness of Kedemoth that Moses sent messengers to Sihon, the Amorite king of Heshbon, asking for peaceful passage through his lands, and was refused. The city of Kedemoth is mentioned among the cities of the tribe of Reuben together with Jahaz and Mephaath (Josh. 13:18); "Kedemoth with the open land about it" was a levitical city of the tribe (I Chron. 6:64).

The identification proposed for the wilderness of Kedemoth is the desert east of the settled area of Moab where the Arnon River begins. The city of Kedemoth has been identified with one of the tells in the adjoining cultivated area, either Qaṣr al-Zaʿfarān or Khirbat al-Rumayl. Both mounds have upper Nabatean levels followed by Early Iron Age strata; Khirbat al-Rumayl also contains the remains of a large Moabite fortress.

BIBLIOGRAPHY: Glueck, in: BASOR, 65 (1937), 27; Press, Ereẓ, s.v.; Aharoni, Land, index.

[Michael Avi-Yonah]

KEDUSHAH (Heb. קְדֻשָּׁה). The biblical term for holiness is *kodesh*; mishnaic Hebrew, *kedushah*, and that which is regarded as holy is called *kadosh*. Jewish exegetes, following early rabbinic interpretation (*Sifra*) of Leviticus 19:2: "You shall be holy, for I the Lord your God am holy," have consistently taken the verb *kadesh* to mean "distinguished, set apart." The *Sifra* paraphrases the command with the words "You shall be set apart" (Heb. *perushim*). The traditional interpretation coincides with the findings of modern phenomenologists of religion who describe the holy as "the wholly other" and as that which is suffused with a numinous quality. The latter is both majestic and fearsome (*The Idea of the Holy*, Rudolph Otto, 1923, ch. 8) or to use the term Otto popularized, "the mysterium tremendum."

General Considerations

The concept of holiness, because of its centrality in the Bible, affords an excellent illustration of how the biblical authors, under the dominance of the monotheistic idea, radically refashioned, in whole or part, notions of the sacred in the religions of the Near East. In primitive Semitic religions, as in primitive religions generally, the holy is considered an intrinsic, impersonal, neutral quality inherent in objects, persons, rites, and sites, a power charged with contagious efficacy and, therefore, taboo. Seldom is the quality of holiness ascribed to the deity. In biblical religion, on the contrary, holiness expresses the very nature of God and it is He who is its ultimate source and is denominated the Holy One. Objects, persons, sites, and activities that are employed in the service of God derive their sacred character from that relationship. The extrinsic character of the holy is reflected in the fact that by consecrating objects, sites, and persons to God, man renders them holy. Further, since holiness is conceived as the very essence of God, biblical religion, in both the priestly and prophetic writings, incorporates moral perfection as an essential aspect of holiness, though by no means its total content. Therefore, unlike contemporary ancient Near East religions, biblical Judaism does not confine the sacred to the sphere of the cult. God's moral perfection and purpose is not in static terms alone but in its redemptive acts in history. Indeed, holiness, since it is derived from God, is related to the realm of nature, history, human experience and conduct as well as to the election of Israel and the covenant. "The energy with which from the time of Moses onward the person of the divine Lord concentrates all religious thought and activity upon himself gives even the statements about holiness an essentially different background from that which they possess in the rest of the Near East" (*Theology of the Old Testament*, Walther Eichrodt, 1961, vol. 1, p. 271). Finally, since pagan religions regard holiness as a mysterious intrinsic power with which certain things, persons, locales, and acts are charged, the division between the realms of the holy and the profane are permanently, unalterably fixed. In fact, the latter represents an ever-present danger to the former. By contrast, biblical religion looks forward to the universal extension of the realm of the holy in the end of days so as to embrace the totality of things and persons.

While biblical religion recognizes an area of the profane ("impure") as capable of defiling and polluting the sacred, nowhere does it regard the former as possessing a threatening dangerous potency. The following elements of the concept of holiness are, however, held by the Bible in common with other ancient Near Eastern religions:

(1) the concept of the mortal danger involved in unauthorized approach to or contact with the sacred;

(2) the notion of various degrees of holiness; and

(3) the contagious, communicable character of the sacred. In the words of Eichrodt: "The whole system of taboo is pressed into the service of a loftier idea of God" (*ibid.*, p. 274).

The following sections offer specific and varied biblical illustrations of the general considerations set forth above.

The Holiness of God

Seeking to express the ineffable holiness of God, an ultimate category, the biblical authors drew on a vast and varied series of predicates. With the single exception of God's moral perfection and action, they all fall within the scope of the "mysterium tremendum." The most frequent is "fearsome," "awesome," (Heb. *nora*; Ps. 89:7, 8; 99:3; 111:9). A site at which a theophany has been experienced is described as "awesome" and induces in the visioner a state of fear (Gen. 28:17). God's works are called "fearful" (Ex. 15:11; 34:10; Ps. 66:3, 5). This aspect of the divine holiness and man's attitude toward it are perhaps best summed up in the verse (I Sam. 6:20), "Who is able to stand before the Lord, the Holy God?" In several passages, e.g., Joshua 24:19, God's fearful, unapproachable holiness is equated with His jealousy, His unrelenting demand for exclusive virtue.

The fearful aspect of the divine holiness is reflected in the warning to keep one's distance from the outward manifestation of the divine presence (Ex. 3:5; 19:12, 13, 23; Num. 18:3; Josh. 5:15). To gaze directly upon the divine manifestation or even upon the sacred vessels when the latter are not in actual use may cause death (Ex. 33:20; Num. 4:20; 18:13; Judg. 13:22; I Kings 19:13). God is "glorious in holiness" (Ex. 15:11); His holiness is unique (I Sam. 2:2); His "way" is that of holiness (Ps. 77:14).

Preeminently, it is the divine name which is characterized as holy since the name of God expresses His essence (Lev. 20:3; 22:2, 32; Ps. 103:1; 105:3; 145:21; I Chron. 16:10). Noteworthy is Ezekiel's repeated use of the phrase "My Holy Name." To Isaiah, we owe the appellation of God as the "Holy One of Israel" (Isa. 1:4; 5:19, 24; 10:20; 12:6; 17:7; 29:23; 30:12, 15; 31:1; 37:23). The term is employed even more consistently by Deutero-Isaiah (Isa. 41:14; 43:3, 14; 45:11; 47:4; 48:15; 49:7; 54:5; 60:14). It appears once in Jeremiah (50:29) and in Psalms (71:22). Isaiah's tendency to characterize God as the "Holy One of Israel" may be assumed to derive from the divine call to the prophet (ch. 6) in which he hears the dramatic thrice-repeated proclamation of the seraphim (the trisagion) of "Holy, holy, holy, the Lord of Hosts, the whole earth is full of His glory" (6:3). In this encounter, in the presence of the absolute holiness of God – the apparent intention of the dramatic repetition – the prophet is overcome by an acute sense of his own sinfulness and that of the people among whom he dwells (v. 5). The passage clearly implies, and indeed emphasizes, the moral aspect of God's holiness.

However, it is erroneous to assert, as is frequently done, that the interpretation of the divine holiness as essentially an expression of God's moral perfection is the unique contribution of the prophets. Distinctly priestly writers associate God's holiness with moral qualities. This is to be seen in the so-called Holiness Code (Lev. 17–26). In priestly law (Lev. 19) the purely ritualistic aspects of holiness are combined with distinctly moral injunctions. Priestly liturgy (Ps. 15; 24:3–6) stresses that only he who "has clean hands and a pure heart" can stand on God's holy mountain (Ps. 24:3, 4). The prophets deepen and broaden the moral dimension of the divine holiness. For Amos (2:7) oppression of the poor and sexual profligacy are tantamount to the profanation of God's holy name. For Hosea, divine compassion constitutes a basic element in God's holiness (Hos. 11:8 f.), and the prophet insists on purity of heart and a radical break with moral offense as preconditions for any intimacy with the holy God. For Isaiah, it is righteousness that sanctifies the holy God (5:16). Deutero-Isaiah conceives of God's holiness as active in the realm of history as a redemptive power. The "Holy One of Israel" is the redeemer of Israel (Isa. 41:14; 43:3, 14; 47:4; 48:17; 49:7; 54:15). Divine holiness is thus conceived less as a state of being than as an expression of the fulfillment of divine purpose. It manifests itself in divine judgment and destruction (Isa. 1:4–9; 5:13, 16; 30:8–14; Ezek. 28:22; 36:20–32) as well as in divine mercy and salvation (Isa. 10:20–23; 12:6; 17:7–9; 29:19–21). For Ezekiel, God manifests His holiness in the sight of the nations (20:31; 28:25; 36:23; 38:23), when He vindicates Himself as supreme Lord of the world.

Fire as Symbol of God's Holiness

Perhaps the ambivalent effects of fire, at once warming and creative yet consuming and destructive, suggested it as an apt symbol of the divine holiness, itself conceived as essentially polar in effect (see below). Whatever the origin of fire as a symbol for the sacred, its employment in the Bible is as vast as it is varied. Only some of the passages in which it is associated with holiness can be cited here (Ex. 3:2, 3; 19:18; 24:17; Deut. 4:12, 24; 5:22–27; 9:3; Ezek. 1:4–28; Hab. 3:3, 4). Repeatedly in the laws and practices of the cult, fire imagery is used in those passages that emphasize holiness (Lev. 2:3, 9, 10; 6:16–18; 7:3–5).

The Transitive Effects of God's Holiness

As stated above, whatever or whoever is engaged in the service of God and therefore stands in intimate relationship with Him becomes endowed with holiness. Essentially, that which brings man or things or locales into the realm of the holy is God's own activity or express command. The nation is sanctified and commanded to be holy since it has entered into a covenant relationship with the holy God (Ex. 19:6; Lev. 11:44 ff.; 19:2; 20:7; Deut. 7:6; 26:19). The *Ark of the Covenant is holy since it is regarded as the throne of the invisible God. Though the phrase "Holy Ark" (Heb. *Aron Kodesh*) is not found in the Bible, numerous contexts indicate that it was regarded as sacred as were all the vessels employed in the *tabernacle, as well, of course, as the sanctuary itself. The prophet, having been summoned and consecrated to God's service, is looked upon as a holy man (II Kings 4:9). Initially, it is God who ordains the holy seasons and places – "And God blessed the seventh day and declared it holy" (Gen. 2:3). But the Sabbath, having been declared holy, must be sanctified by Israel (Ex. 20:8; Deut. 5:12; Jer. 17:22; Neh. 13:22). In the case of the *festivals, the divine declaration is joined with the injunction that they should be proclaimed: "These are my fixed times, the fixed time of the Lord, which you shall proclaim as sacred occasions" (Lev. 23:21). Likewise, it is God who sanctifies the Tent of Meeting, the altar, Aaron and his sons (Ex. 29:43) but each of these undergoes rites of consecration performed by humans (see Ex. 29 for the description of the elaborate rites of consecration of Aaron and his sons).

War, since it is carried out under the aegis of God as "Man of War" (Ex. 13:3), is service rendered to Him. In his martial activity, the warrior enters the sphere of the holy and becomes subject to the particular prohibitions incumbent upon those directly involved in that sphere (I Sam. 21:5–7; II Sam. 11:11). This concept serves as the basis for the verbal usage "to consecrate war" (Heb. *kiddesh milḥamah*; Micah 3:5; Jer. 6:4). Frequently, the enemy's goods and chattels are declared banned (Heb. *ḥerem*); that is to say, banned from human use. For the priestly biblical authors, the concept of holiness, as might be expected, finds its focus in the realm of the cult and everything involved in it. Accordingly, there is mention of "holy garments" (Ex. 28:2, 4; 29:21; 31:10); "holy offerings" (Ex. 28:36; Lev. 19:8); the "holy priestly crown" (Ex. 29:6; 39:30); "holy flesh" (Ex. 29:37); "holy anointing oil" (Ex. 30:31–37); the "holy tabernacle" and its furnishings (Ex. 40:9); "holy fruit" (Lev. 19:24); and "holy food" (Lev. 22:14).

The Polarity of Holiness

As has been noted, the concept of God's holiness is rooted in a basic polarity; the quality of holiness is majestic and hence attractive, and yet it remains fearsome. It is, therefore, no cause for wonder that this polarity finds expression in both the rituals and objects of holiness. In the law of the "red heifer," whereby the ashes of the sacrificial victim are used in a rite to purify one who has become defiled through contact with a corpse, the priest who ministers the rite becomes defiled (Num. 19:8–10; Lev. 16:26–28). This polarity is to be discerned in several biblical episodes describing an improper entrance into the inner precincts of the sanctuary. Here, in the holy of holies, the ritual of expiation is carried out. Yet, when *Nadab and *Abihu, the sons of Aaron, bring "strange fire" into the inner sanctuary, they are consumed by divine fire (Lev. 10:1–11; cf. Num. 16–17; II Sam. 6:6; cf. the warning in Ex. 19:10 ff.).

The idea that holiness can be conveyed by mere touch or intimate approach is illustrated in various biblical passages. Those, for instance, who come in physical contact with the altar automatically become holy (Ex. 29:37; 30:29; Lev. 6:11, 20). The notion is likewise reflected in the divine command that the vessels used by *Korah and his company were to be added to the altar as an outer covering because, once having been brought "into God's presence," they had become holy (Num. 17:2).

Holiness and Glory

Glory (Heb. *kavod*) is intimately associated with God's holiness and signifies the self-manifesting presence of God, whereas holiness (Heb. *kodesh*) is expressive of God's transcendence (Ex. 14:4 f.; Lev. 10:3; Num. 20:13; Ezek. 20:41), though the polar concepts of holiness and glory are strikingly joined by Isaiah – "Holy, holy, holy, the Lord of Hosts, His glory fills the whole earth" (6:3). The hope that the divine glory will fill the whole earth takes on a messianic tinge in Numbers 14:21. The latter is conceptually linked with Zechariah 14:20, 21. There, in a messianic prophecy, Zechariah anticipates the day when even the bells of the horses will be engraved with the legend "Holy unto the Lord" as well as every pot in Jerusalem and Judah. The ultimate extension of the sphere of the holy so that it will embrace even the mundane and profane underscores the biblical concept of holiness not as a natural, inherent quality, but rather as a quality conferred both by God and man. This aspect of holiness in the messianic age is reflected in the prophet Joel's promise that prophecy – an endowment of holiness – will become a gift possessed by young and old, by servants and handmaids (3:1,2).

[Theodore Friedman]

Comparative Considerations

The derivation of the common Semitic root *q-d-š* is still uncertain. It has been suggested that it means "pure, brilliant, dazzling," or the like, but this is questionable, tempting though it is, and no theory as to the character of holiness may legitimately be based on this alleged meaning. More important than etymology, is the actual history of the terms "holiness," and "holy." The comparative evidence suggests that nominal and adjectival forms of the root *q-d-š* were first used in professional titles given to various types of priests and priestesses. Usage was subsequently expanded to apply to divine beings, holy persons, sacred places, cultic objects, and to rites and celebrations. Finite verbal forms were used to convey the process of consecration by which holiness could be attributed; especially *kiddesh* (*qiddesh*), "to consecrate," and its derivatives, in biblical Hebrew.

Beginning in the Old Babylonian period the title *qadištu* (Heb. *kedeshah* (*qedeshah*)) designates a class of priestesses. It should be noted, however, that the same term, both in Akkadian and in Hebrew, can mean "prostitute, harlot," in contexts where no cultic associations are overtly evident (cf. Gen. 38:16, 21–22, where *kedeshah* (*qedeshah*) alternates with *zonah*, "harlot"). This connotation probably relates to the institution of temple prostitution, or at least to the orgiastic rites often associated with fertility cults. In Deuteronomy 23:18 and Hosea 4:14 the term *kedeshah* (*qedeshah*) is clearly related to the cult.

The masculine plural *qdšm*, "priests, cultic servitors," occurs in Ugaritic administrative lists, so that there are precursors to both *kadesh* (*qadesh*), the masculine, as well as *kedeshah* (*qedeshah*), the feminine, in biblical Hebrew. Ugaritic yields additional relevant evidence: the Ugaritic *mqdšt* parallels the Hebrew *mikdash* (*miqdash*, "temple, sanctuary"), and the Ugaritic *qdš*, like the Hebrew *kodesh* (*qodesh*), means "holiness; sanctuary." There can be little doubt, therefore, that the biblical *kadesh* (*qadesh, qedeshim*) designates a cultic function, as the biblical evidence itself strongly indicates (cf. Deut. 23:18; I Kings 14:24; 15:12; 22:47; II Kings 23:7). Another line of comparative inquiry relates to the Ugaritic designation *bn qdš* ("son (s) of holiness," i.e., "deities, divine beings"), which occurs in parallelism with *ilm* ("gods"). In this connection Aramaic yields *qdšm*, "gods," and *bʿl qdšn*, "chief of the gods." The connotation "deity, divine being" is preserved in usages of the Hebrew *kadosh* (*qadosh*) which, in addition to serving as an adjective, may be a substantive. Thus in Hosea 11:9, *kadosh* (*qadosh*) is parallel to *eʾl* ("deity"), and Job 5:1 reads: "Pray – call out! Is there any who answers you? And, to whom of the divine beings (Heb. *kedoshim* (*qedoshim*)) may you turn?" (cf. Isa. 10:17; 43:15, Ezek. 39:7; Hab. 1:12(?); 3:3; Ps. 16:3; Job 15:15, according to the *keri*, and possibly Deut. 33:3, a cryptic passage). It is this connotation which underlies the frequent epithet *Kedosh Yisrael* (*Qedosh Yisrael*), "the holy one (deity) of Israel" (frequently in Isaiah, in II Kings 19:22; Jer. 51:5; Ps. 71:22, et al.). All of this is in addition to the adjective *kadosh* (*qadosh*) that designates an attribute of God, of holy persons, places, objects, etc. Isaiah 6:3 contains the well-known liturgy proclaiming God's holiness in the dramatic repetition: *Kadosh, Kadosh, Kadosh* (*Qadosh, Qadosh, Qadosh*).

Mention should be made of the Syrian goddess *Qudšu*, who is known in Ugaritic literature, and whose cult was imported into Egypt during the New Kingdom, along with those of other Syrian and Canaanite deities. From literary references and graphic representations of *Qudšu* it appears that this goddess was at times known as "the queen of heaven, mistress of all the gods," and that she was identified with the Egyptian goddess Hathor. It is difficult to ascertain exactly how the evidence concerning *Qudšu* relates to the Semitic root *q-d-š* and its associated phenomena. It would be unwarranted to conclude that the priests and priestesses known as *kadesh* (*qadesh*) and *kedeshah* (*qedeshah*) were so called because they were devoted to the cult of *Qudšu*, although this might have been true in certain cases. It is more likely that such priestly functionaries were devoted to various goddesses of fertility, one of whom was probably *Qudšu*. Biblical traditions are consistent in their abhorrence of such cultic servitors, and it may be deduced from various allusions that the objection was at least partially based on their sexual practices, characteristic of idolatrous cults (cf. Deut. 23:19; Jer. 2:20; Micah 1:7, et al.; and probably the use of the verb *zanah* "to commit harlotry" as a way of characterizing idolatry, as in Hos. 9:1, et al.). It is not certain, however, whether the particular vocalizations of *kadesh* (*qadesh*) and *kedeshah* (*qedeshah*) represent a tendentious change from the model of *kadosh* (*qadosh*), so as to express abhorrence, or whether these vocalizations actually reflect earlier vocalizations in Semitic, such as *qadištu* in Akkadian, and the probable *qadišūma* in Ugaritic (cf. contemporary *qadîšîm/în* in Aramaic).

[Baruch A. Levine]

In Rabbinic Literature

In rabbinic theology, holiness is repeatedly defined as separateness. The Sifra (Lev. 19:2) paraphrases the verse (Lev. 19:2) "Ye shall be holy" by "You shall be separated." While separation

(Heb. *perishut*) is frequently equated with abstinence from illegitimate sexual relations as well as from lewdness generally and he who abstains from such practices is called holy (TJ, Yev. 2:4, 3; cf. Lev. R. 24:6; Ber. 10b), the concept of holiness is by no means restricted to the connotation of sexual purity despite the emphasis placed on the latter meaning. An examination of a variety of contexts in which "separateness" (equated with holiness) appears yields the following distinct meanings:

(1) Strict abstention from all practices even remotely related to idolatry, e.g., attending circuses or cutting one's hair in the heathen fashion (Sifra, Kedoshim, Perek 9:2, Aḥarei, Perek 13:9; Sif. Deut. 85). Separation from the nations and their "abominations" (idolatrous practices) is tantamount to holiness. Accordingly, R. Nahum b. Simai is called a holy man because he never looked at the figure of the emperor engraved on a coin (TJ, Av. Zar. 3:1, 42c). (Presumably, his refusal to do so was based on emperor worship prevalent in his time.)

(2) Separation from everything that is impure and thus defiling. This is suggested by the context of the verse (Lev. 11:44), one among several, on the basis of which the Sifra equates separateness with holiness.

(3) Abstention from meat and wine (BB 60b; Tosef. Sot. 15:11. See also Ta'an. 11a where the biblical designation of the Nazirite as holy is attributed to the latter's abstention from wine).

(4) Moderation or complete abstention from marital intercourse (Sot. 3:4; Shah. 87a; Gen. R. 35:1).

The connotation of sexual modesty and restraint is reflected in the reason given (Shab. 118b) for the appellation of R. Judah ha-Nasi as "Our Holy Master" (Heb. *Rabbenu ha-Kadosh*). It is probably the latter meaning of holiness that R. Phinehas b. Jair had in mind when he described some of the rungs of the ladder of virtue as "separateness leads to purity, purity leads to holiness" (Mid. Tannaim to Deut. 23:15; Av. Zar. 20b; TJ, Shek. 3:4, 47c). However, in the case of other *tannaim* who earned the epithet holy (R. Meir-TJ, Ber. 2:75b; Gen. R. 100:7 and R. Ḥiyya Gen. R. 33:3), the respective contexts indicate that the epithet bears no particular or especial reference to sexual matters. In this connection, it may be noted that in keeping with rabbinic thought, the human body too could be regarded as holy since sin defiles the body as well the soul. The rabbis state (Gen. R. 45:3) that Sarah declared to Hagar: "Happy art thou, that thou clingest to a holy body" (i.e., that of Abraham).

Holiness is considered God's very essence and the "Holy One, Blessed be He" (Heb. *Ha-Kadosh Barukh Hu*) is the most frequent name of God found in rabbinic literature. God's holiness is incommensurate with that of man and is permanently beyond human attainment (Gen. R. 90:2). "For God is holy in all manner of holiness" (Tanḥ. B. Kedoshim 3). Even though the divine holiness is absolute, Israel sanctifies God (Ex. R. 15:24) just as God sanctifies Israel (*ibid.*), "As much as to say, if you make yourselves holy, I impute it to you as though you hallowed Me; and if you do not make yourselves holy, I impute it to you as though you did not hallow Me. Can the meaning be, if you make Me holy, I am holy, and if not, I am not made holy? Scripture, however, teaches: 'For I am holy.' I abide in My holiness whether you hallow Me or not." (Sifra Kedoshim Parashah 1:1.) Unlike God's holiness, that of Israel is not inherent. It is contingent upon its sanctification through the performance of the commandments. Their fulfillment lends holiness to Israel. The latter concept originated with the *tannaim*. Preeminent among the commandments whose observance sanctifies Israel are the Sabbath (Mekh. Shabbat 1) and the ritual fringes (Sif. Num. 115). This notion is expressed in the formula of the traditional benediction "… who has sanctified us by His commandments," the benediction recited on the performance of a commandment. It has been suggested that in this way rabbinic thought sought to strip the material objects involved in the performance of various commandments of any inherent holiness magico-mythical thought ascribed to them. Clearly implied is the notion that the observance of a commandment endows the observer with sanctity and that the object is merely a means thereto (Heb. *tashmish kedushah*). Material objects such as a Scroll of the Torah, phylacteries, and *mezuzah* possess sanctity only if they have been prepared by someone who is legally bound to perform the commandment involved and for the purpose for which they were originally intended (Git. 45b). The Mishnah (Kel. 1:6–9) enumerates ten ascending degrees of holiness beginning with the Land of Israel and concluding with the Holy of Holies. The notion of ascending degrees of holiness is reflected in the halakhic principle that sacred objects or, more precisely, objects that serve a sacred purpose should only be sold or exchanged for objects that possess a higher sanctity (Meg. 9b).

The epithet holy as applied to man is used sparingly in rabbinic literature. The angels, the Midrash declares, upon seeing Adam at the time of his creation wanted to sing and praise him as a holy being. But when God cast sleep upon him, they realized that he was a mere mortal and they refrained (Gen. R. 8:10). The Patriarchs, according to the Midrash (Yalkut Job 907), were not called holy until after their death. But here, as elsewhere in rabbinic thought, there is no dogmatic consistency. Thus, the Talmud declares (Yev. 20a) that he who fulfills the words of the sages is called holy. Man has it in his power to sanctify himself and, if he does so, even in small measure, he is greatly sanctified from above (Yoma 39a). Man is bidden to sanctify himself by voluntarily refraining from those things permitted to him by the Law (Yev. 20a). Nor is it abstemiousness alone that wins sanctity for man. When men fulfill the requirements of justice and thus exalt God, God causes His holiness to dwell among them (Deut. R; 5:6). The sanctity of man's deeds invokes God's aid (Lev. R. 24:4). An extraordinary act of charity is deemed a sanctification of the name of God (PdRK 146b). It is supremely hallowed when men are prepared to lay down their lives rather than abandon their religion or violate the law of God. Such an act is known as "sanctification of the Name" (Heb. **kiddush ha-Shem*). It may fairly be said to embody the highest ideal of rabbinic Judaism (Ber. 61b). Solomon Schechter wrote "Holiness is the highest achievement of the Law and its deepest experience as well as the realization of righteousness. It is a composite of various aspects not easily definable, and, at times, seemingly contradictory" (*Some Aspects of Rabbinic Theology*, 199).

In Jewish Philosophy

Medieval Jewish philosophers rarely use the term "holiness" as a technical term. When they do use this term, it appears, as a rule, in connection with quotations from Scripture or from the sages, and its explication derives from these sources. Thus, "holiness" describes the distinction between spirit and flesh, between the eternal and temporal, and between the absolute and changing. God is holy, for He has been "hallowed [distinguished] from any like Him" and He is "aloof and above all change." The people of Israel is holy, because it separated itself from worldly pursuits and turned to the worship of God. The Sabbath is holy, since it is devoted to spiritual matters rather than worldly affairs (Abraham b. Ḥiyya, *Meditation of the Sad Soul*, passim). There is, therefore, a close connection between the notions of "holiness" and "uniqueness" in the sphere of theology, and "holiness" and "separation" in the sphere of ethics, though the term "holiness," in its primary meaning refers to the realm of ritual.

Maimonides

*Maimonides associates holiness with the idea of distinction and uniqueness, giving it an extreme intellectual interpretation. God is holy for He is absolutely different from creation. He is not similar to it in any of His attributes, and is independent from its being (Yad, Yesodei ha-Torah, 1:3). The angels are holy, for they are separate from any body (*ibid.*, 4:12), and the heavenly spheres are holy, for their body can neither be destroyed nor changed (*ibid.*, 3:9). Sanctification, therefore, means separation from the body. A place, name, or object are holy only insofar as they have been set aside from the outset to divine worship (*ibid.*, 6 passim). Sanctification through the precepts of the Torah also implies uniqueness and separation. There are three ways, according to Maimonides, of sanctification through the precepts (*Guide of the Perplexed*, 3:47):

(1) sanctification by virtue, i.e., the restraint of physical desires and their satisfaction only up to the limits of necessity, in order to devote oneself wholly to God;

(2) the fulfillment of those precepts which remove man from concern with this world and its errors, and prepare him for the attainment of truth;

(3) the holiness of worship, which means observance of the laws of pollution and purity, which are not of primary importance in the doctrine of Maimonides.

A man who has attained the highest degree of sanctification, as did the Patriarchs or Moses, is freed from his dependence upon his flesh, and thus he imitates God, for he too acts without being involved in creation (*ibid.*, 3:33).

Judah Halevi

*Judah Halevi also states that God is holy because He is of the spirit, aloof from the defects which inhere in matter, and governs creation without being dependent on it (*Kuzari*, 4:3). Nevertheless, Halevi is far from the intellectual and distinctive conception of Maimonides. Holiness, according to Judah Halevi, is a power that engulfs the soul which unfolds toward it. This is a living spiritual power flowing from God and present in everybody who worships Him (*ibid.*; see also 1:103). The people of Israel is called holy, for such a power, manifested mainly in prophecy, inspires the people, the Hebrew language, in the Land of Israel, and the Temple. There is some notion of separation in Judah Halevi's conception of holiness. The prophet and the worshiper must purify themselves from sin, from negative emotions, from sorrow and weariness, exactly as they have to be pure from vice and wicked acts; but this does not mean separation from the world. Nor is the purpose of purification the attainment of truth; it is rather a preparation for the proper performance of the commandments and rituals prescribed by the Torah. The consecrating person has to separate himself from the polluted, but not from the living flesh; he has to overcome dullness, tiredness, frustration and stupidity, but not to remove himself from the life of the senses and emotions.

Nachman Krochmal

The discussion of the term "holiness" in modern Jewish philosophy is associated with medieval ideas, but has undergone changes under the influence of various secular systems. Nachman *Krochmal, influenced by *Hegel, defines the holy as a static and lasting spiritual attribute, whose opposite is profane, which is dynamic and variable (*Moreh Nevukhei ha-Zeman* (1824), ch. 6). The holy is a symbol of the spiritual, i.e., it arouses spiritual thoughts. The precepts sanctify, for their fulfillment reflects perception and enforces it. Objects are pure insofar as the idea embodied in them can be perceived clearly, i.e., they are capable of receiving holiness, while the polluted is the body which is impenetrable to reason, i.e., a barrier to holiness (*ibid.*). This appears to be an integration of elements from both Maimonides and Judah Halevi, but actually, contrary to them, Krochmal conceived the spiritual as innate in nature and history, identifying it with reason. Sanctification, therefore, is not withdrawal from the world, but the self-realization of reason within existence itself.

Moritz Lazarus

Under the influence of neo-Kantianism, a change took place. Moritz *Lazarus identified the holy with conduct, according to the pure moral postulates of reason, which is free from causal necessity existing in nature. According to this system, God is identified with the idea of moral conduct. He has no reality beyond this ideal and only in this respect is He holy. Divine worship is, therefore, identical with ethics (the ritual is only a symbol of pure ethics). Thus, one is holy through moral conduct, and society is sanctified by subordinating it to the categorical imperative (*Ethik des Judentums*, 1 (1904), 311ff.), although, according to Lazarus, this can never be achieved.

Hermann Cohen

Hermann *Cohen, similarly, defines the holy as the sphere of ethical activity, the meeting place between human and divine reason. God is holy because the ideal of ethics is inherent in Him; but only man can accomplish this ideal, with God's help, thus consecrating himself and society by his conduct (*Religion der Vernunft* (1929), 116–29). Thus, according to him, holiness is the sphere where the human and the divine meet to perfect each other.

Franz Rosenzweig

A diametrically opposite view is to be found in the existentialist doctrine of Franz *Rozenzweig. He returns to the emphasis of the "otherness" or separation contained in holiness. God is placed opposite the world. He is holy, for He is eternal and, therefore, exists beyond the world. The world attains holiness only through revelation, which is the grace of God granted to man. Facing God, man is freed from the temporal and transient, and becomes associated with the eternal. This is the function of the biblical commandments, which consecrate the life of the Jew within the framework of his community (*Der Stern der Erloesung*, 3 (1954), passim). It should be pointed out that new trends have emerged, which derive directly from the *Kabbalah philosophy of the Middle Ages. Outstanding among them is the doctrine of R. Abraham I. *Kook, who interpreted holiness, in the spirit of the Kabbalah, as the all-embracing existence of the divine in its absolute unity.

[Eliezer Schweid]

BIBLIOGRAPHY: G. van der Leuw, *Religion in Essence and Manifestation* (1938); A.L. Oppenheim, *Ancient Mesopotamia* (1964), 171–205; C.H. Gordon, *Ugaritic Textbook* (1965), glossary, no. 2210, s.v. *qdš*; C.F. Jean and J. Hoftijzer, *Dictionnaire des Inscriptions Sémitiques de l'Ouest* (1965), 253–4, s.v. *qdš* I, II, II, esp. III, 1; Pritchard, Texts, 428; J. Milgrom, *Studies in Levitical Terminology*, 1 (1970); B.A. Levine, in: JAOS, 85 (1965), 307–18; idem, in: *Religions in Antiquity*, ed. by J. Neusner (1967), 71–87; idem, in: *Eretz Israel*, 9 (1969), 88–96; idem, in: *Leshonenu*, 30 (1965–66), 3–4; M. Haran, in: HUCA, 36 (1965), 191–226; J. Pedersen, *Israel, its Life and Culture*, 1–2 (1926), 187–212, 244–59; 3–4 (1940), 150–534; Kaufmann Y., Toledot, vols. 1 and 2, index, s.v. *Kedushah*, esp. vol. 1, 537–59; J. Liver, in: EM, 5 (1968), 507–8, 526–31; R. Otto, *The Idea of the Holy* (19433), 30–41, 52–84; M.D. Cassuto, in: EM, 2 (1954), 354–8; J. Reenger, in: *Zeitschrift fuer Assyriologie*, 58 (1967), 110–88; R. Stadelmann, *Syrisch-Palaestinensische Gottheiten in Aegypten* (1962), 110–23; de Vaux, Anc Isr 221–9, 345–57, 406–13. IN RABBINIC LITERATURE: S. Schechter, *Some Aspects of Rabbinic Theology* (1909), index s.v. *holiness*; G.F. Moore, *Judaism* (1927), index, s.v. *holiness*; A. Buechler, *Types of Jewish-Palestinian Piety* (1922); M. Kadushin, *The Rabbinic Mind* (1952), 167–88; E.E. Urbach, *Ḥazal, Pirkei Emunot ve-De'ot* (1969), index s.v. *Kadosh, Kedushah*; Montefiore and Loewe, *Rabbinic Anthology* (1960^2), index s.v. *holiness*.

KEDUSHAH (Heb. קְדֻשָּׁה; lit. "holiness"), the third blessing of the *Amidah. The blessing's full appellation is *Kedushat ha-Shem* (Sanctification of the Name) to distinguish it from *Kedushat ha-Yom* (Sanctification of the Day), the central blessing of the Sabbath and festival *Amidah* (RH 32a). Popularly, however, the term *Kedushah* refers to the additions and responses recited by the cantor and congregation in the third benediction during the repetition of the *Amidah*. The word *kadosh* (קָדוֹשׁ, "holy") is the main theme of this doxology, hence the name *Kedushah*.

During public worship, the *Kedushah* is inserted at the start of the third benediction when the reader repeats the *Amidah*. It is recited only when a quorum of ten men (**minyan*) is present, since it is written: "I will be hallowed among the children of Israel" (Lev. 22:32), which is interpreted to infer that at least ten children of Israel must be present (Bet. 21). The nucleus of the different forms of the *Kedushah* consists of the following three biblical passages: "Holy, holy, holy, is the Lord of hosts; The whole earth is full of His glory" (Isa. 6:3); "Blessed be the glory of the Lord from His place" (Ezek. 3:12); "The Lord will reign for ever, Thy God, O Zion, unto all generations, Halleluyah" (Ps. 146:10).

To these sentences various additions were made during the first millennium C.E. Some of the changes were adopted in all liturgies, while others remained solely part of one or two local rites. The actual text of the basic *Kedushah* is not cited in the Talmud, although the prayer is mentioned (Ber. 21; Sot. 49a). It may be that the essential *Kedushah* text was already standardized during the tannaitic period, if not earlier. *Natronai Gaon (second half of the ninth century) opposed any change in the *Kedushah* text because "We do not change our usage from that which the scholars of the Talmud taught" (*Seder Rabbi Amram*, ed. by D. Hedegård, 1 (1951), no. 57; J. Heinemann, *Ha-Tefillah bi-Tekufat ha-Tanna'im ve-ha-Amora'im* (1966^2), 23, 141).

The following is the most common form of the short *Kedushah*, incorporating the three basic texts, and recited daily during the morning and afternoon services and during the afternoon service on Sabbath and festivals:

> Reader – We will sanctify Thy Name in the world even as they sanctify it in the highest heavens, as it is written by the hand of thy prophet:
>
> And they called one unto the other and said,
>
> Cong. – Holy, Holy, Holy is the Lord of Hosts: the whole earth is full of His glory.
>
> Reader – Those over against them say, Blessed –
>
> Cong. – Blessed be the glory of the Lord from his place.
>
> Reader – And in Thy Holy Words it is written, saying
>
> Cong. – The Lord shall reign for ever, thy God, O Zion, unto all generations, Praise ye the Lord (Hertz, Prayer, 135–7).

There are three different introductions to the *Kedushah* which are preserved in the various rituals and recited on different occasions: (1) *Na'ariẓkha ve-Nakdishkha* – "We will reverence and sanctify thee according to the mystic utterance of the holy Seraphim, who sanctify thy Name in holiness, as it is written by the hand of thy prophet…" (Sof. 16:72). This introduction is retained in the Sephardi, the later Italian, the Persian, and the Yemenite rituals. It is based on Isaiah 29:23 and is utilized by these rituals for weekday, Sabbath, and festival **Shaḥarit* and **Minḥah Kedushot*. The Ashkenazi and Egyptian rituals use this introduction for the *Kedushah*. (2) *Keter yittenu lekha* –

"Unto Thee, O Lord our God, shall the heavenly angels above, with Thy people Israel assembled beneath, ascribe a crown; all shall repeat thrice with one accord the holy praise unto Thee, according to the word spoken by Thy prophets..." (see Ḥul 91b). The Sephardi, Italian (originally also for *Shaḥarit*), Romanian, Yemenite, and most ḥasidic rituals (following *Nusaḥ Ari*) have this introduction for the *Musaf Kedushah*. (3) *Nekaddesh* – "We will sanctify Thy Name in the world...," introduces the *Kedushot* in Ashkenazi rite in both the *Shaḥarit* and *Minḥah* services on weekdays, Sabbaths, and festivals.

Additional changes in the body of the various daily, Sabbath, and festival *Kedushot* have been inserted. The most important of these insertions is the *Shema* –"Hear, O Israel" (Deut. 6:4) in the *Musaf Kedushah* – which dates from the sixth century C.E., when the Jewish communities of the Byzantine Empire attempted to circumvent a prohibition against its recitation in the synagogue. The Jews thought that its presence in the *Kedushah* of the *Musaf* service would not be suspected by the authorities (Baer, Seder, 237). *Saadiah and *Maimonides later abrogated the recitation of the *Shema* during the *Musaf* service, and as a result the Yemenite and Persian rituals do not retain the insertion. All other rituals continue the tradition of reciting the *Shema*.

The *Kedushah* recited during the repetition of the *Amidah* is called *Kedushah de-Amidah* (*Kedushah* recited while standing), since it may be recited only when standing. An abridged form of the *Kedushah*, called *Kedushah de-yeshivah* (*Kedushah* recited while seated), is recited after **Barekhu* during the *Shaḥarit* service. It is permissible to recite this *Kedushah* when seated since it is essentially descriptive of the angels' acknowledgment of God's sovereignty as related in Isaiah 6:3 and Ezekiel 3:12. A third *Kedushah, Kedushah de-Sidra* (*Kedushah* recited at the conclusion of study), is also recited daily toward the end of the morning service for those who missed the previously recited *Kedushah* during the repetition of the *Amidah*. The collection of verses composing this *Kedushah* begin with "And a redeemer shall come to Zion" (Hertz, Prayer, 202), and also includes the passages from Isaiah 6:3 and Ezekiel 3:12, and their Aramaic translations. The *Kedushah de-Sidra* probably derives its name from the Babylonian custom of having rabbinical discourses after the morning service. Along with a prayer for the observance of the Torah, this *Kedushah* would be recited upon the conclusion of the lecture. The *Kedushah de-Sidra* is also recited before the reading of the Torah during the *Minḥah* services on Sabbath and festivals, and after reading Psalm 91 at the conclusion of the Sabbath. "The world is maintained by the *Kedushah*" (Sot. 49a) refers to the *Kedushah de-Sidra*.

Musical Rendition

The *Kedushah* has no standard melodic pattern of its own. In the East European Ashkenazi tradition there is a tendency to render the first *Kedushah* in a minor and the second in a major key, and on the High Holidays it follows the intonation of the *Shema Israel and *Ve-ha-kohanim*. In general, the *Kedushah* is considered a vehicle for the *ḥazzan* or synagogal composer to give it a suitably brilliant yet solemn rendition. The early cantorial manuals contain many examples of especially ornate settings of *Na'ariẓkha* (such as the "more than forty" settings in the so-called "Hanoverian Compendium" of 1744 described by Nadel). Solomon de *Rossi's *Kedushah* for four voices, in his *Ha-Shirim asher li-Shelomo* (Venice 1622/23, no. 7), follows the Sephardi version (*Keter*). However, S. *Naumbourg, in his 1877 edition of the *Shirim*, substituted for this the Ashkenazi version (*Na'ariẓkha*). Because of the mystical connotations of the *Kedushah*, controversies arose in the 17th century about the repetitions of the Divine name and the word *keter* in artistic compositions, since these were thought to contain the dangerous implication of "two authorities" (*shetei rashuyyot*), i.e., a negation of the unity of God.

BIBLIOGRAPHY: E. Levy, *Yesodot ha-Tefillah* (1952^{2}), 164–7; Elbogen, Gottesdienst, 61–67; J. Heinemann, *Ha-Tefillah bi-Tekufat ha-Tanna'im ve-ha-Amora'im* (1966^{2}), index; Werner, in: HUCA, 19 (1945–46), 292–307; Idelsohn, Liturgy, 94–98; Abrahams, Companion, lx–lxi, cxlv–cxlvi, clxv–clxvi.

[Bathja Bayer]

KEFAR AKKO (Heb. כְּפַר עַכּוֹ), village mentioned in the Tosefta as the seat of R. Judah b. Agra (Kil. 1:12) and in the Babylonian Talmud as a place from which 1,500 people made a pilgrimage to Jerusalem (Ta'an. 21a). Some scholars have identified it with the Caphareccho appearing in one version of Josephus' writings (Wars, 2:573). If, however, the location of Kefar Akko at Tell al-Fukhkār outside Acre is accepted, it cannot correspond to the locality mentioned by Josephus since the latter is included in the list of his fortifications and Josephus would hardly have fortified a suburb of Acre, the headquarters of his enemy Vespasian.

BIBLIOGRAPHY: Saarisalo, in: JPOS, 9 (1929), 27ff.; Avi-Yonah, in: IEJ, 3 (1953), 96–97.

[Michael Avi-Yonah]

KEFAR AZAR (Heb. כְּפַר אַזַ"ר), moshav in central Israel, about 6 mi. (10 km.) E. of Tel Aviv, affiliated to Tenu'at ha-Moshavim, and founded in 1932 by veteran agricultural laborers of the Second and Third Aliyah. Engaged in suburban truck farming from the outset, Kefar Azar principally raised vegetables, dairy cattle, and poultry. In the largely urbanized surrounding area, the moshav preserved to an extent its character of a rural "island." Kefar Azar is named after the writer Alexander Siskind *Rabinovitz (abbr. "Azar"). In 1968 its population was 330, rising to 460 in the mid-1990s and 539 inhabitants in 2002 after expansion.

[Efraim Orni / Shaked Gilboa (2nd ed.)]

KEFAR BARAM (Heb. כְּפַר בַּרְעָם), locality in Upper Galilee, 7 mi. (11 km.) N.W. of Safed. Its Jewish settlement is mentioned only in the Middle Ages (by R. Samuel b. Samson, 1210, and R. Jacob, mid-13th century). Later travelers (including R. Moses Basola, 1522) mention two synagogues there. In 1762 Kefar Baram was destroyed; Maronites resettled the village in the

19th century. The remains of a synagogue from the third century C.E. were found, built on the highest point of the village. It measures 59 ft. (18 m.) by 43 ft. (13 m.). In front of the main building stands a porch with a row of six columns, of which one has survived *in situ*. The building, entered through three ornate doorways, contains two rows of columns joined by one transverse row. Traces of stairs leading to an upper (women's) gallery have been found in the northwestern corner. The lintels of the doors and the window pediments are elaborately decorated with floral ornaments; two angels holding a wreath above the main entrance have been hammered away. An inscription below a window mentions the builder as Eleazar b. Judan. The synagogue has been partly restored by the Israel Department of Antiquities. Kibbutz Baram, affiliated to Ha-Kibbutz ha-Me'uḥad, was founded near the ruins of Kefar Baram in 1949 by former members of the *Palmaḥ. The main farming branches included fruit orchards, poultry, dairy cattle, and field crops. The kibbutz owns a plastics factory producing medical equipment. Its tourist attractions include a spa and alternative medicine center. A small museum with a Judaica collection is located in the kibbutz. In 2002 the population of Kibbutz Baram was 488.

BIBLIOGRAPHY: H. Kohl and C. Watzinger, *Antike Synagogen in Galilaea* (1916), 89ff. **WEBSITE:** www.galil-elion.org.il.

[Michael Avi-Yonah / Shaked Gilboa (2nd ed.)]

KEFAR BARUKH (Heb. כְּפַר בָּרוּךְ), moshav near the Kishon reservoir of the National Water Carrier in the Jezreel Valley, Israel, affiliated to Tenu'at ha-Moshavim. It was founded in 1926 by settlers from Kurdistan, Iraq, Romania, Poland, Germany, and also "Mountain Jews" from the Caucasus. In its initial years, Kefar Barukh suffered from a lack of water and difficulty of access (although it was a station on the then-existing Jezreel Valley narrow-gauge railway). Its field crops, dairy cattle, and fruit orchards constituted prominent farming branches. Later on, other farming branches such as flowers, poultry, fishery, and goose fattening were added. The moshav is named after Baruch Kahana of Ploesti, Romania, who dedicated his wealth to the *Jewish National Fund. In 1968 its population was 202; in 2002, 261.

[Efraim Orni / Shaked Gilboa (2nd ed.)]

KEFAR BIALIK (Heb. כְּפַר בְּיַאלִיק), moshav in Haifa Bay, Israel, affiliated to Ha-Iḥud ha-Ḥakla'i, and founded in 1934 by immigrants from Germany who were later joined by settlers of different origin. Kefar Bialik, separate from the nearby Kiryat Bialik suburb, preserved its agricultural character and moshav form. Nevertheless, in the late 1960s housing estates were built within its confines. Kefar Bialik, named after the poet Ḥ.N. *Bialik, had 610 inhabitants in 1968. The population maintained its size through the-mid-1990s and rose to 768 in 2002.

[Efraim Orni]

KEFAR BILU (Heb. כְּפַר בִּיל״וּ), moshav in the Coastal Plain of Israel, near Reḥovot. Affiliated to Tenu'at ha-Moshavim, it was founded in 1932 in the framework of the "Thousand Families Settlement Scheme." The village was partly based on intensive farming, but due to the limited farm area at the village's disposal, many settlers held jobs in Reḥovot or in the Tel Aviv area. The village is named after the *Bilu movement. In 1968 its population was 370, rising to 450 in the mid-1990s and 978 in 2002 after residential expansion.

[Efraim Orni / Shaked Gilboa (2nd ed.)]

KEFAR BLUM (Heb. כְּפַר בְּלוּם), kibbutz in the Ḥuleh Valley, Israel, affiliated to Iḥud ha-Kevuẓot ve-ha-Kibbutzim. It was founded in 1943 on the edge of the malarial swamps existing at the time, by the so-called "Anglo-Baltic" kibbutz, composed of pioneers from the Baltic countries and the first group of the *Iḥud Habonim movement of England. The settlers endeavored to make their kibbutz a focal point for pioneers from English-speaking countries. The kibbutz engaged in intensive farming, including field crops, orchards, poultry, and dairy cattle, and has developed several industrial enterprises, with factories manufacturing automatic irrigation equipment and electric grids. The kibbutz has a large guesthouse, kayaking, and a cultural center. In 2002 its population was 527. The American Nationaler Arbeter Farband (Farband Labor Zionist Order) contributed toward the establishment of Kefar Blum and named it in honor of the French Jewish statesman and socialist leader Leon *Blum.

[Efraim Orni / Shaked Gilboa (2nd ed.)]

KEFAR DAROM (Heb. כְּפַר דָּרוֹם), locality in the southern coastal plain of Philistia. It is first mentioned in the Talmud as the seat of R. Eleazar b. Isaac (Sot. 20b). It was captured by the Arabs in 634 and in Crusader times it was a fortress called Dārūm. Taken by Saladin in 1188, it was destroyed in 1192 by Richard the Lionhearted and later rebuilt by the Ayyubids. Arab writers describe it as one hour distant from Gaza (whose southern gate was known as Bāb al-Dārūm) on the border of the desert in an area famous for its vines. It is generally identified with the village of Dayr al-Balaḥ, 10 mi. (16 km.) south of Gaza. The village contains an ancient mound and the ruins of an old mosque. Kefar Darom was also the name of a modern kibbutz founded in 1946 which fell to the Egyptians in the Israel War of Independence (1948–49). Settlers from Kefar Darom then moved to a new site which they called Benei *Darom. In 1970 a *Naḥal group moved back to the original site of kibbutz Kefar Darom, making it the first settlement in the *Gush Katif area. In 1973 it became a civilian settlement and served as a training farm for *Gush Emunim settlers. A few years later, it was abandoned, until 1989, when new inhabitants settled there. From the 1990s, Kefar Darom came under terror attacks. In the mid-1990s the population was approximately 150 and at the end of 2002 the population of Kefar Darom increased to 324 residents. In August 2005 Kefar Darom was evacuated along with the other settlements of Gush Katif as part of the government's disengagement plan. Resistance was particularly strong, with settlers barricading themselves inside the synagogue and on its roof before being forcibly removed by the police and army.

BIBLIOGRAPHY: Abel, in: RB, 49 (1940), 67ff.

[Michael Avi-Yonah /Shaked Gilboa (2nd ed.)]

KEFAR EZYON (Heb. כְּפַר עֶצְיוֹן), kibbutz in the Hebron Hills about 14 mi. (23 km.) S. of Jerusalem, affiliated to *Ha Kibbutz ha-Dati. A first attempt at settlement there was made by religious Jews from Iraq who established Migdal Eder (1926/27; the place is not identical with the biblical site of that name). The site was abandoned in the 1929 Arab riots. In 1935, a Jewish citrus grove owner, S.Z. Holzmann, acquired the land, prepared it for setting up a mountain village and country resort, and named it Kefar Ezyon, a translation of his own name. His work was brought to a standstill by the 1936–39 Arab rebellion. In 1943, Kevuzat Avraham of Ha-Kibbutz ha-Dati, whose members hailed from Poland, founded Kefar Ezyon, the first of the four villages constituting the Ezyon Bloc (the others were *Massu'ot Yizhak, *Ein Zurim, and *Revadim). The kibbutz members worked in afforestation and developed farm branches. From the end of 1947 the kibbutz repelled frequent Arab attacks. It also improved its strategic position and harassed Arab communications sent to reinforce Arab forces on the Jerusalem front. A unit of 35 men (remembered in Hebrew as "Ha-Lamed-He") of *Palmah and *Haganah members from Jerusalem making its way on foot from Hartuv to reinforce the Ezyon Bloc was intercepted by Arabs and all its members killed (Jan. 16, 1948). A relief convoy suffered severe losses on March 27. On May 12, the Arab Legion and vast numbers of Arab irregulars mounted the final assault on the Bloc, which two days later succumbed against overwhelming odds. Most of the defenders of Kefar Ezyon, men and women, were massacred by an Arab mob after having capitulated to the Arab Legion. The Arabs totally obliterated all traces of the Jewish villages and an Arab Legion camp was set up on the site. The Bloc area, together with the Hebron Hills, was taken by the Israel Army in the *Six-Day War on June 7, 1967. In September 1967, kibbutz Kefar Ezyon was renewed by a group of Ha-Kibbutz ha-Dati which included children of the original settlers massacred in 1948. The new kibbutz set up industrial branches along with farming. Its farming was based on poultry, turkeys, and orchards. Industry included the Mofet ballistic armor plant. Kefar Ezyon operates a guest house and has a nature preserve. In 2002 its population was 408.

WEBSITE: www.kfar-etzion.co.il.

[Efraim Orni]

KEFAR GAMALA (Heb. כְּפַר גַּמְלָא), ancient village in the territory of Jerusalem. It is mentioned in Byzantine sources as the place where the tomb of R. *Gamaliel, the grandson of Hillel the Elder, the teacher of the apostle *Paul, was discovered following a dream by Lucian the local priest (PL 41:807, 809). Interred together with the Jewish sage were the remains of his two sons and of St. Stephen the deacon, the first Christian martyr. The distance of Kefar Gamala from Jerusalem is given as 20 miles. After the discovery of the tomb, the body of the saint was exposed in Jerusalem and then transferred to Constantinople in 415. Kefar Gamala is generally placed at Jammāla, a ruin 7 mi. (11 km.) west of Ramallah and this identification is supported by the fact that Kefar Gamala is mentioned in the sources together with Arimathea (Rantis) and Selemia (Khirbat Salamiyya) in the vicinity. From 1851 it was proposed to identify it with Beit Jimāl, 16 mi. (26 km.) southwest of Jerusalem, but this village was outside the territory of Jerusalem in Byzantine times.

BIBLIOGRAPHY: Abel, in: RB, 33 (1924), 235ff. 306; Beyer, in: ZDPV, 51 (1931), 225–6; A. Sacchetti, *Studi Stephaniani* (1934).

[Michael Avi-Yonah]

KEFAR GIDEON (Heb. כְּפַר גִּדְעוֹן), moshav in the Jezreel Valley, Israel, 1.2 mi. (3 km.) N. of Afulah, affiliated to *Agudat Israel, and founded in 1923 by religious Jews from Romania. An insufficient water supply at first deterred the moshav's progress, but in the 1940s ample groundwater reserves were discovered. After 1948, new immigrants were absorbed into the moshav, which engaged mainly in field crops and dairy cattle. The moshav is named after the biblical figure of Gideon. In 1968 its population was 140; in 2002, 198.

[Efraim Orni]

KEFAR GILADI (Heb. כְּפַר גִּלְעָדִי), kibbutz in N. Israel, on the N.W. rim of the Huleh Valley, affiliated to Ihud ha-Kevuzot ve-ha-Kibbutzim. Founded in 1916 on *Jewish Colonization Association (ICA) land, Kefar Giladi was established by *Ha-Shomer (Guardsmen Association) to guard outlying Jewish land in the area during World War I and to increase the food supply to the starving *yishuv*. By 1919 two more small outposts, one of them *Tel Hai, were established in the vicinity. When the area was marked for inclusion in the French Mandate territory of Syria, Arabs revolting against the French in 1920 attacked these Jewish settlements. Kefar Giladi had to be temporarily abandoned, but the settlers returned 10 months later. In 1926 the settlements of Kefar Giladi and Tel Hai merged. During World War II (1941), Kefar Giladi, together with *Metullah, guarded the country's northern border against an invasion of Vichy French troops. In 1946 Kefar Giladi suffered casualties when British forces besieged and searched the kibbutz, known for its assistance in organizing "illegal" Jewish immigration across the nearby border. In 1952 Kefar Giladi decided to join Ihud ha-Kevuzot ve-ha-Kibbutzim after the split in Ha-Kibbutz ha-Me'uhad movement. In 1968 the kibbutz had 680 inhabitants, in the mid-1990s the population was approximately 710, but by 2002 it had dropped to 559. Its economy is based mainly on irrigated field crops, deciduous fruit orchards, dairy cattle, and fishery. Kefar Giladi also runs a quarry, plant nursery, and rest home. The kibbutz is named after Israel *Giladi, one of the founders of Ha-Shomer.

[Efraim Orni]

KEFAR GLICKSON (Heb. כְּפַר גְּלִיקְסוֹן), kibbutz in the N. Sharon, Israel, on the rim of the Manasseh Hills, affiliated to Ha-Oved ha-Ẓiyyoni. It was founded in 1939 on *Palestine Jewish Colonization Association (PICA) land. The founding settlers, from Romania, erected a permanent village only in 1945. In 1969 Kefar Glickson's economy was based on intensive farming and on a factory processing lime. Later on it set up guest rooms and a youth hostel. The kibbutz was linked to a neighboring youth village, *Allonei Yiẓḥak, and is named after the journalist and General Zionist leader Moshe *Gluecksohn (Glickson). Its population in 1968 was 250; in 2002, 284.

WEBSITE: www.glikson.co.il.

[Efraim Orni]

KEFAR ḤABAD (Heb. כְּפַר חַבַּ"ד), village in central Israel near the Lydda–Tel Aviv railway, established by Ḥabad Ḥasidim in 1949. Founded on the initiative of the Lubavitch rabbi Joseph Isaac Shneersohn, Kefar Ḥabad was initially intended for Ḥabad immigrants from Russia. The original settlers were later augmented by families from North Africa. At the end of 1969, it had 1,540 inhabitants, in the mid-1990s the population was approximately 3,460, and in 2002 it was 4,220. It became a center for Ḥabad Ḥasidim in Israel and the location of many religious and educational institutions. In addition to its yeshivot and a teachers' seminary for girls, Kefar Ḥabad also sponsored institutions for vocational education including a printing school dedicated in memory of the five children and their teacher murdered in the village in 1955 by *fedayeen* raiders while at evening prayers. Kefar Ḥabad is the focal point for Ḥabad celebrations, such as Yod-Tet Kislev, the anniversary of the release of the founder of Ḥabad, Rabbi *Shneur Zalman of Lyady, from a Czarist prison in 1798. A community center known as the "House of the President," in honor of President Zalman *Shazar, serves as a meeting place for the youth of Kefar Ḥabad and its neighboring settlements. In 1970, an absorption center for new immigrants was opened there. Many of the settlers engage in farming of field crops, poultry, and dairy cattle.

BIBLIOGRAPHY: *Challenge: An Encounter with Lubavitch-Chabad* (1970), 136–50.

[Aaron Rothkoff]

KEFAR HA-ḤORESH (Heb. כְּפַר הַחוֹרֶשׁ; "Woodland Village"), kibbutz in Lower Galilee, Israel, W. of Nazareth, affiliated to Iḥud ha-Kevuẓot ve-ha-Kibbutzim. It was founded in 1933 by a group from the *Gordonia youth movement in Poland. In the initial years, the settlers were employed in planting forests in the neighborhood, notably the King George V Forest. Citrus groves, poultry, and field crops constituted prominent farming branches. The kibbutz also operated a margarine factory. In 1969 Kefar ha-Ḥoresh had 244 inhabitants. In 2002 its population was 421.

[Efraim Orni / Shaked Gilboa (2nd ed.)]

KEFAR HA-MACCABI (Heb. כְּפַר הַמַּכַּבִּי), kibbutz in the Haifa Bay area, Israel, affiliated to Iḥud ha-Kevuẓot ve-ha-Kibbutzim. It was founded in 1936 by pioneers from Austria, Czechoslovakia, and Germany, who were members of the *Maccabi Sports Organization and the Maccabi ha-Ẓa'ir youth movement. Some of them had come to participate in the *Maccabiah which took place in the country that year, and stayed on "illegally" (see *Immigration, "Illegal"). The kibbutz developed intensive, irrigated farming based on field crops, avocado orchards, dairy cattle, poultry, and fishery; it also went into partnership in a food factory with the neighboring kibbutz, *Ramat Yoḥanan. In 1969 it had 310 inhabitants; in 2002, 291. Kefar ha-Maccabi is named after the Maccabi Organization which contributed funds toward the purchase of its land.

[Efraim Orni / Shaked Gilboa (2nd ed.)]

KEFAR ḤANANYAH (Heb. כְּפַר חֲנַנְיָה), ancient Jewish village, situated, according to the Mishnah, on the border between Upper and Lower Galilee (Shev. 9:2). It was known as a village of potters, who utilized the black (Tosef., BM 6:3) or white soil (BM 74a) found there. Vessels of special forms produced in the potters' workshops of Kefar Ḥananyah are mentioned in the Jerusalem Talmud (Pe'ah 7:4, 20a) and the Midrash (Lam. Zuta 1:5). Hawkers living there visited four or five villages in the vicinity, returning home to sleep (TJ, Ma'as. 2:3, 49d). At least one rabbi, Abba Ḥalafta, lived there (BM 94a). Cattle and goats were raised in the vicinity.

Kefar Ḥananyah is usually identified with Kafr ʿAnān, 6 mi. (c. 9½ km.) southwest of Safed. In 1522, according to R. Moses Basola, there were 50 priestly Jewish families and a synagogue in Kafr ʿAnān. This community is also mentioned in the middle of the 16th century by R. Samuel b. Judah and it seems to have endured until the end of the 17th century. Remains of an ancient synagogue and tomb caves of talmudic times have been found on the site.

BIBLIOGRAPHY: Braslavski, in: BJPES, 1 (1933), 18ff.

[Michael Avi-Yonah]

KEFAR HA-NASI (Heb. כְּפַר הַנָּשִׂיא), kibbutz in Upper Galilee, Israel, S. of the Ḥuleh Valley, affiliated to Iḥud ha-Kevuẓot ve-ha-Kibbutzim. It was founded on July 2, 1948, during the Israeli War of Independence, just when the Syrians established their bridgehead at nearby *Mishmar ha-Yarden in an attempt to cut off the whole of Upper Galilee. When fighting was renewed a week later to contain and reduce the bridgehead, the kibbutz found itself in the middle of battle. The settlers were graduates of the *Iḥud Habonim youth movement of England, Australia, and other English-speaking countries. Its economy was based on intensive farming (orchards, citrus groves, field crops, a plant nursery, and poultry), a factory producing industrial valves, a small hydroelectric plant, and guest rooms. The communal system was gradually phased out, with members receiving salaries or working outside the kibbutz and covering their own expenses. In 2002 the population of Kefar ha-Nasi was 489. Its name (President's Village) commemorates Chaim *Weizmann.

WEBSITE: www.villageinn.co.il.

[Efraim Orni / Shaked Gilboa (2nd ed.)]

KEFAR HA-RO'EH (Heb. כְּפַר הָרֹא"ה), moshav in the Ḥefer Plain, Israel, affiliated to Ha-Po'el ha-Mizrachi Moshavim Association, founded in 1934 by pioneers from Eastern Europe. It became a spiritual center for the religious moshavim in the country. In 1968, Kefar ha-Ro'eh had 860 inhabitants including the students in its yeshivah, which was the study institute of the *Bnei Akiva youth movement. Its population rose to approximately 1,050 in the mid-1990s and 1,430 in 2002. Its economy was based on intensive farming, such as poultry, dairy cattle, citrus (mainly citrons), and flowers. The moshav's name is composed of the initials of Rabbi Avraham ha-Kohen *Kook.

[Efraim Orni / Shaked Gilboa (2nd ed.)]

KEFAR ḤASIDIM (Heb. כְּפַר חֲסִידִים), moshav and suburban area in the Zebulun Valley, 7½ mi. (12 km.) S.E. of Haifa, Israel. The moshav, affiliated to Ha-Po'el ha-Mizrachi Moshavim Association, was founded in 1924 by two groups of Ḥasidim from Poland who, together with their leaders, the rabbis of Kozienice and Yablonov, initially settled on two sites further east, on the Jezreel Valley border. In 1927 they together established a permanent village at Kefar Ḥasidim and with great dedication drained the malarial swamps and developed farming there. In 1937 an agricultural school, Kefar ha-No'ar ha-Dati, was established near the moshav.

In 1950 a second religious village, Kefar Ḥasidim Bet, was set up (unaffiliated to a country-wide organization). Simultaneously, two large *ma'barot* (transitory immigrant camps) were established nearby, whose inhabitants were later gradually transferred to the suburban religious community of Rekhasim whose construction began in 1951. In 1968 Rekhasim had 2,540 inhabitants, while Kefar Ḥasidim and Kefar Ḥasidim Bet together had 675, and Kefar ha-No'ar ha-Dati, 590. In the mid-1990s Kefar Ḥasidim and Kefar Ḥasidim Bet together had approximately 650 residents, and Kefar ha-No'ar ha-Dati dropped to approximately 484. At the end of 2002 the population of Kefar Ḥasidim was 508 residents and the population of Kefar Ḥasidim Bet was 188, while Rekhasim's population was 7,750.

[Efraim Orni / Shaked Gilboa (2nd ed.)]

KEFAR ḤATTIN, Hittaya (Heb. כְּפַר חַטַּיָא), village in Galilee, the seat of R. Jacob (Ḥag. 5b) and R. Azariah (PdRK 54). It had a synagogue (Gen. R. 65:16) and served as a refuge for R. Simeon b. Lakish, who escaped from the wrath of the patriarch Judah II (TJ, Sanh. 2:1, 19d). According to the Jerusalem Talmud (Meg. 1:1, 70a), it was identified with the Ziddim-Zer of Joshua 19:35. The name of the village ("Grain Village") indicates its fertile surroundings. It is identified with the Arab village of Ḥiṭṭīn or Ḥaṭṭīn al-Qadīm ("ancient Ḥattin"), which gave its name to the Horns of Hittin, where the Crusaders were defeated by Saladin in 1187. In this village, the Druze venerate the tomb of al-Nabī Shuʿayb, who is identified with Jethro, Moses' father-in-law, and hold an annual festival. Building remains and ancient tombs have been found there.

BIBLIOGRAPHY: S. Klein (ed.), *Sefer ha-Yishuv* (1939), s.v.; G. Dalman, *Sacred Sites and Ways* (1935), index, s.v. *Ḥaṭṭin*.

[Michael Avi-Yonah]

KEFAR ḤAYYIM (Heb. כְּפַר חַיִּים), moshav in the Ḥefer Plain, central Israel, affiliated to Tenu'at ha-Moshavim. Kefar Ḥayyim was one of the first settlements established in the region (1933), founded by two groups of veteran pioneers – Third Aliyah immigrants from Russia, of which one had attempted settlement in the Negev as early as the 1920s and had defended *Ḥuldah in the 1929 riots. Citrus groves and dairy cattle were prominent farming branches. The kibbutz name commemorates Chaim *Arlosoroff. In 1968 its population was 360, increasing to 468 in 2002.

[Efraim Orni]

KEFAR HESS (Heb. כְּפַר הֶס), moshav in the southern Sharon, Israel, affiliated to Tenu'at ha-Moshavim, founded in 1933 by settlers from Eastern Europe. After 1948, the moshav was enlarged by newcomers from Hungary. Its economy was based on intensive farming: citrus groves, field crops, poultry, flowers, and beehives. In 1967 its population was 410, rising to around 650 in the mid-1990s and 971 in 2002 after additional expansion. Kefar Hess is named after Moses *Hess.

[Efraim Orni / Shaked Gilboa (2nd ed.)]

KEFAR ḤITTIM (Heb. כְּפַר חִטִּים), moshav shittufi northwest of Tiberias. After earlier attempts at settlement failed, the settlement was renewed in 1924 by a Ha-Po'el ha-Mizrachi moshav group, which was replaced in 1932 by a group of Sephardi Jews who left two years later. In 1936 the immigrant group "Ha-Koẓer" from Bulgaria permanently established the first moshav shittufi in the country there. Farming was based on field and garden crops, deciduous and other fruit trees, dairy cattle, and poultry. In the mid-1990s the population was approximately 290, rising to 330 in 2002.

[Efraim Orni]

KEFAR JAWITZ (Heb. כְּפַר יַעְבֵּץ; **Kefar Ya'bez**), moshav in the southern Sharon, Israel, near Tel Mond, affiliated to Ha-Po'el ha-Mizrachi moshavim association. First founded as a moshav in 1932, it suffered from insufficient cultivable land and, situated on what was then the eastern rim of the Jewish settlement zone, it came under frequent attacks in the 1936–39 Arab riots. In the 1948 *War of Independence, Kefar Jawitz was in the line of battle. That year, it was taken over by kibbutz Neẓer Yissakhar, which later became a moshav shittufi but eventually dispersed. In 1953, a moshav of immigrants from Yemen was established and developed intensive farming (citrus groves, cattle, poultry, flowers, and vegetables). In 1969 there were 360 inhabitants, rising to 496 in 2002 due to expansion. The village is named after the historian Zeev *Jawitz.

[Efraim Orni]

KEFAR KANNA (**Kenna**; Ar. **Kafr Kanna**), a village in Galilee, 4 mi. (6½ km.) N.E. of Nazareth. Owing to its convenient position on the main Nazareth-Tiberias road, it has been identified since Byzantine times with the *Kanah of the Gospels. A mosaic inscription found in the present church of the village indicates that it stands on the ruins of a Byzantine synagogue whose mosaic pavement, according to the inscription, was made by Yose, the son of Tanḥum, and his sons. A Jewish settlement existed in Kefar Kanna in the 15th–16th centuries; in 1481 there were 80 families there and in 1522, 40 families (as attested by the travelers Obadiah of *Bertinoro and Moses b. Mordecai *Basola). Since its identification with the Kana of the Gospels was firmly established by Quaresmius in the 17th century, several churches were erected in the village and it has been included in the itineraries of pilgrims. It has recently been proposed to identify it with Garis (Jos., Wars, 3:129; 5:474; Life, 395, 412). In 1968, the village numbered 4,550 inhabitants, the majority Christian (Greek-Orthodox, Roman, and Greek Catholic), and the rest Muslim. Over the years, the ratio between Christians and Muslims has been reversed, so that by the end of 2002 the majority of Kefar Kanna's population (16,100 residents) were Muslims. The population growth rate is a high 2.7% per year. Income in 2000 was about half the national average. In 1968 Kefar Kanna received municipal council status. Its jurisdiction extends over 4.1 sq. mi. (10.7 sq. km.). In the vicinity of Kefar Kanna there is a large industrial area employing workers from all over the region and including cinder block and tire factories.

BIBLIOGRAPHY: Clermont-Ganneau, in: PEFQS, 43 (1901), 374ff.; P.D. Baldi, *Enchiridien Locorum Sanctorum* (1955), 205ff.; Abel, Geog, 2 (1938), 291–2.

[Michael Avi-Yonah]

KEFAR KISCH (Heb. כְּפַר קִישׁ), moshav in eastern Lower Galilee, Israel, about 2½ mi. (4 km.) E. of Kefar Tavor, affiliated to Tenu'at ha-Moshavim. It was founded in 1946 by demobilized soldiers who in World War II served with the Royal Engineer Corps and other units. The original settlers established a moshav shittufi, but most of them left in the ensuing years, and in 1953, Kefar Kisch was renewed, this time as a moshav, by immigrants from Poland, Romania, and Hungary. Its principal farming branches were field crops, fruit orchards, and dairy cattle. In 1969 there were 189 inhabitants in Kefar Kisch and in 2002 around 300. The moshav is named after Frederick H. *Kisch.

[Efraim Orni]

KEFAR MALAL (Heb. כְּפַר מַלַ"ל), moshav in the southern Sharon, Israel, affiliated to Tenu'at ha-Moshavim, first founded on privately owned land in 1911 and named Ein Ḥai. It was destroyed in the battles of World War I. Renewed by a laborers' group after the war, it was again destroyed in the 1921 Arab riots, but was rebuilt as a moshav in 1922, when the land became *Jewish National Fund property. In the 1929 Arab riots, Kefar Malal successfully repelled several attacks. Its settlers hail from Eastern Europe. Citrus groves and dairy cattle constituted the principal farming branches. Kefar Malal's name is composed of the initials of Moses *Lilienblum. In 1967 its population was 270, rising to 443 in 2002.

[Efraim Orni]

KEFAR MANDI (Heb. כְּפַר מַנְדִּי), village in Galilee, the seat of R. Issachar (TJ, RH 1: 3, 57a). A document found in the Cairo *Genizah* indicates that in 1065 Jews lived there, in particular one Abraham b. David al-Kafrmandi. Later travelers located the tombs of *Akavyah b. Mahalalel, and Rabban *Simeon b. Gamaliel, in the village. Arab sources, confusing Mandi with Midian, located there the tomb of Ṣaffūra (*Zipporah), the wife of Moses, and the well from which he rolled the stone, which was shown to travelers. The tombs of Athīr (*Asher) and *Naphtali, sons of Jacob, were also placed there. The present-day Arab village Kafr Mandā, with an area of 4.1 sq. mi. (10.7 sq. km.), is situated between Tiberias and Acre, 8 mi. (c. 13 km.) north of Nazareth. In 1964 it received municipal council status. In 1968, it had 3,180 inhabitants, increasing to 13,800 in 2002. Olive and other fruit trees, field crops, sheep, and cattle have constituted its principal farming branches.

BIBLIOGRAPHY: Assaf, in: *Tarbiz*, 9 (1937/38), 201; A.-S. Mannardji, *Textes Géographiques Arabes…* (1951), 175–6.

[Michael Avi-Yonah]

KEFAR MASARYK (Heb. כְּפַר מַסָרִיק), kibbutz in the Haifa Bay area, Israel, S. of Acre, affiliated to Kibbutz Arẓi ha-Shomer ha-Ẓa'ir. It was founded as a *stockade and tower settlement in 1938 by pioneers from Czechoslovakia. The partly brackish swamps near the Na'aman Stream mouth required, in the first years of the settlement, concentrated reclamation and drainage work. Beside intensive farming branches (field crops, orchards, fishery, dairy cattle, and poultry), the kibbutz has also developed industrial enterprises such as a plant producing printed cartons, a company servicing satellite equipment, and an R&D plant for electronic devices. Its population was 480 in 1967 and 592 in 2002. It is named after Tomáš G. Masaryk, first president of Czechoslovakia.

WEBSITE: www.kfar-masaryk.org.il.

[Efraim Orni / Shaked Gilboa (2nd ed.)]

KEFAR MENAḤEM (Heb. כְּפַר מְנַחֵם), kibbutz in the southern Coastal Plain of Israel, about 9 mi. (14 km.) S.E. of Gederah, affiliated to Kibbutz Arẓi Ha-Shomer ha-Ẓa'ir. The original settlers set up a moshav on the site in 1936, but the local soil and security conditions were inimical to the smallholder type of settlement, and the moshav group moved west to found *Kefar Warburg. In 1937, the village was refounded as a kibbutz by a group composed of pioneers from North America, Germany, and Poland. The kibbutz developed intensive farming (field crops, poultry, and dairy cattle) and industrial enterprises (a quarry, ceramics plant, and metal plant). In 1968, it had 555 inhabitants, rising to 600 in the mid-1990s but then dropping to 460 in 2002. The kibbutz is named after Menaḥem Mendel *Ussishkin.

WEBSITE: www.kfar-menachem.org.il.

[Efraim Orni / Shaked Gilboa (2nd ed.)]

KEFAR MONASH (Heb. כְּפַר מוֹנַשׁ), moshav in the central Sharon (Ḥefer Plain), Israel, affiliated to Tenu'at ha-Moshavim, founded in 1946 by demobilized soldiers who had served with the British Royal Engineer Corps in World War II. They were later joined by settlers from South Africa and other countries. Kefar Monash was initially a moshav shittufi and engaged in farming and maintained a photolithographic printing plant. Later it became a moshav based exclusively on farming. The main farming branches included citrus groves, flowers, and turkeys. The moshav is named after the Australian Sir John *Monash. The land on which the moshav was founded is part of Wadi Kabani in the eastern *Ḥefer Plain, acquired through contributions of Australian Jewry. In 1967 it had 320 inhabitants. In the mid-1990s the population was approximately 450, further increasing to 690 in 2002 after expansion.

[Efraim Orni / Shaked Gilboa (2nd ed.)]

KEFAR MORDEKHAI (Heb. כְּפַר מָרְדְּכַי), moshav in the Coastal Plain of Israel, W. of Gederah, affiliated to Ha-Iḥud ha-Ḥakla'i (middle-class settlers' association), founded in 1950 by pioneers from England. It was later joined by newcomers from Australia and other English-speaking countries, and by Israeli-born settlers. Citrus groves and dairy cattle constituted its principal farming branches. Kefar Mordekhai is named after Mordecai *Eliash, Israel's first minister in Great Britain. Its population in 1968 was 230 rising to 305 in the mid-1990s and 476 in 2002.

[Efraim Orni]

KEFAR NEBURAYA (**Nibborayya**; Heb. כְּפַר נְבוֹרַיָה), village in Upper Galilee, the home of Jacob of Kefar Neburaya, a popular preacher of the third century C.E., who was often in conflict with the rabbinical authorities and was suspected of heresy (TJ, Yev. 2:5). It has been identified with Khirbat al-Nabratayn, a ruin 2.5 mi. (4 km.) north of Safed. Here were found the remains of an ancient synagogue measuring 55 by 39 ft. (17 × 12 m.) whose facade is oriented toward Jerusalem. Inside are two rows of four columns. The limestone lintel is decorated with a laurel garland and a menorah within a wreath. An inscription added to the lintel in 564 C.E. records the reconstruction of the building by Ḥanina son of Lezer (Eliezer) and Luliana (Julianos) son of Judah. A sculptured figure of a lion was also found there.

BIBLIOGRAPHY: H. Kohl and C. Watzinger, *Antike Synagogen in Galilaea* (1916), 101ff.; Alt, in: PJB, 21 (1925), 37; Avigad, in: BRF, 3 (1960), 49ff.

[Michael Avi-Yonah]

KEFAR NETTER (Heb. כְּפַר נֶטֶר), moshav in the southern Sharon, Israel, about 4 mi. (7 km.) S. of Netanyah, initially a member of Tenu'at ha-Moshavim, but later unaffiliated. It was founded in 1939 by graduates of the *Mikveh Israel agricultural school. After 1948, Kefar Netter was enlarged when new immigrants from Poland settled there. Its farming was highly intensive, but subsequently only citrus groves and avocado plantations have remained. In 1967 the population was around 420; in 2002, 510. The moshav is named after the founder of Mikveh Israel, Charles *Netter.

WEBSITE: www.kfar-neter.co.il.

[Efraim Orni / Shaked Gilboa (2nd ed.)]

KEFAR OTNAY (**Otnai**; Heb. כְּפַר עוֹתְנָאי), ancient village, 24 Roman mi. from Caesarea, 24 from Scythopolis (Beth-Shean), and 16 from Sepphoris. It is defined in talmudic sources as the farthest limit of Galilee in the direction of Judah and anyone passing it was considered to have left Galilee (Git. 7:7). It was the hometown of R. Shemaiah, a pupil of R. Johanan b. Zakkai, and the patriarch Gamaliel occasionally visited there. Samaritans living in the vicinity (Git. 1:5) cultivated vegetables on the land of the village (Tosef., Dem. 5:23). In the time of Hadrian, Kefar Otnay (Gr. Caparcotnei – Καπαρκοτνεί) was chosen as the camp of the sixth legion and renamed *Legio. Previously proposed identifications with Kafr Dān or Kafr Qūd are no longer accepted.

BIBLIOGRAPHY: Ramsay, in: JRS, 6 (1916), 129; Alt, in: ZDPV, 68 (1951), 57ff.

[Michael Avi-Yonah]

KEFAR PINES (Heb. כְּפַר פִּינֶס), moshav in the northern Sharon, Israel, affiliated to Ha-Po'el ha-Mizrachi moshavim association. The settlers, from Poland, Germany, and other countries, founded Kefar Pines in 1933. Citrus orchards, dairy cattle, and poultry constituted its principal farm branches. The moshav is named after Yehiel Michael *Pines. In 1967 its population was 400, increasing to 730 in the mid-1990s and 972 in 2002 after expansion.

[Efraim Orni]

KEFAR ROSH HA-NIKRAH (Heb. כְּפַר רֹאשׁ הַנִּקְרָה), kibbutz in the Acre Plain, Israel, near the Lebanese border, on the slope of the Rosh ha-Nikrah-Ḥanitah ridge, affiliated to Iḥud ha-Kevuẓot ve-ha-Kibbutzim. It was founded in 1949 by a group of Israeli-born youth. In addition to highly intensive farming (field crops, bananas, avocado orchards, citrus groves, poultry, dairy cattle, fruit trees) the kibbutz operated a cafe on top of the Rosh ha-Nikrah Cape (which forms part of Sullam Ẓor, the Ladder of *Tyre separating the Acre and Tyre plains), near the police frontier post, and a cable car leading down to the sea grottoes of the cape. In addition, the kibbutz had a holiday village with a spa. Below Rosh ha-Nikrah Cape, to the south, was the Israel Police Force rest resort. In 1969 Kefar Rosh ha-Nikrah had 318 inhabitants. In the mid-1990s the population was approximately 560, while in 2002 it decreased to 491. The name Rosh ha-Nikrah ("Headland of the Cleft") is derived from the Arabic name for the spot Ra's al-Nāqūra.

WEBSITE: www.kfar-rosh-hanikra.co.il.

[Efraim Orni / Shaked Gilboa (2nd ed.)]

KEFAR RUPPIN (Heb. כְּפַר רוּפִּין), kibbutz in the Beth-Shean Valley, near the Jordan River; founded in 1938 as a *stockade and watchtower settlement by pioneers from Germany, Czechoslovakia, and Hungary, later joined by immigrants from other countries. From 1967, Kefar Ruppin, situated within close firing range of the Jordanian positions beyond the river, endured frequent shelling and sniping. The kibbutz engaged in intensive farming, including branches adapted to the local hot climate, e.g., date palms, which withstand soil salinity, and field crops, fishery and ornamental fish, poultry, and dairy cattle. In addition, the kibbutz operated the Palkar Co. for fencing and storage facilities. For a time, the kibbutz was a center for nutria fur production. An international birdwatching center is located in the kibbutz. Its population rose from 310 in 1967 to 448 in 2002, with families becoming economically independent. The kibbutz is named after Arthur *Ruppin.

WEBSITE: www.kfar-ruppin.org.il.

[Efraim Orni / Shaked Gilboa (2nd ed.)]

KEFAR SAVA (Heb. כְּפַר סָבָא), town in central Israel, in the southern Sharon, near the Arab village Kafr Sābā. Ḥibbat Zion bought the holdings in 1892, but settlement began in 1896 when the land was taken over by Baron Edmond de *Rothschild, who invested considerable sums in an abortive experiment to raise plants for perfume. In 1903 part of the land was bought by *Petaḥ Tikvah farmers for farmsteads for their sons, and almond orchards became the principal farming branch. The Turkish authorities, however, did not issue permits to build houses, so the place remained largely empty until 1912, when permits were finally granted. A eucalyptus grove was planted in the place where about 1,000 inhabitants of Tel Aviv set up camp in 1917 after the Turks expelled them from their homes; the following year, several hundred died there in a typhus epidemic. In September 1918 Kefar Sava, which lay in the front line of battle between the Turko-German and Allied armies, was entirely destroyed. The settlers soon returned and rebuilt their houses, but Kefar Sava was again laid waste in the 1921 Arab riots. In the following years, local abundant groundwater resources were discovered and the developing citrus branch attracted investors and provided a solid foundation for Kefar Sava's economy. From the end of the 1920s, the struggle for Jewish labor on Jewish farms focused on Kefar Sava and became more violent in the 1930s when a number of kibbutzim set up their temporary camps there prior to their permanent settlement in other parts of the country. The number of Kefar Sava's inhabitants grew from 450 in 1927 to 3,500 in 1941. From the end of the 1930s, immigrant housing quarters were built and partly provided with auxiliary farms. During World War II industrial plants were established, primarily for citrus preserves, as fresh fruit could not be exported at the time. In the Israeli *War of Independence (1948) Kefar Sava lay again in the front line facing the "Arab triangle" of Samaria; fighting died down only after the neighboring Arab village Kafr Sābā was taken by Jewish forces and abandoned by its inhabitants. After 1948 Kefar Sava's population rapidly grew, approaching 20,000 when it received city status in 1962. In 1969 Kefar Sava had 23,000 inhabitants. By the mid-1990s the population had risen to approximately 65,800, and in 2002 it was 77,800. The municipal area is 5.8 sq. mi. (15 sq. km.). Kefar Sava serves as an administrative, commercial, and health-service center for the south Sharon region. The large Me'ir Hospital (which, in its initial years, specialized in lung diseases) and Bet Berl, a teachers college, seminary, and study center, are located there. The city also has a large industrial area.

WEBSITE: www.kfar-saba.muni.il.

[Efraim Orni / Shaked Gilboa (2nd ed.)]

KEFAR SHEMARYAHU (Heb. כְּפַר שְׁמַרְיָהוּ), semi-rural Israeli settlement with municipal council status in the southern Sharon. Kefar Shemaryahu is named after Shemaryahu *Levin. Founded in 1937 as a middle-class moshav by immigrants from Germany, from the outset it was based on intensive farm branches, primarily poultry breeding, with its farmers belonging to the Ha-Mo'aẓah ha-Ḥakla'it association. From the 1950s, its proximity to the *Herzliyyah beach and the extension of the Tel Aviv conurbation caused its gradual transformation into a middle-class garden suburb, which has also developed as a recreation and entertainment center. A writers' and artists' house was opened there. Besides smaller industrial enterprises, it housed the Tene-Nogah central dairy. In 1969, the village numbered 1,260 inhabitants, becoming an upscale community. In 2002 its population was 1,790 residents, occupying a square mile (2.5 sq. km.)

WEBSITE: www.kfar.org.il

[Efraim Orni / Shaked Gilboa (2nd ed.)]

KEFAR SHIḤLAYIM (Heb. כְּפַר שִׁיחְלַיִים), village in Idumea, probably identical with the Sallis in which the Jewish general Niger took refuge after an unsuccessful assault on Ashkelon (Jos., Wars, 3:20). According to talmudic sources, Kefar Shiḥlayim was a large village, which was destroyed either in the First Jewish War against Rome or in the war of Bar Kokhba (Lam. R. 2:2, no. 4). The inhabitants of the village grew cress (*shiḥlah*). A man from the village appeared before R. Tarfon in the early second century (TJ, Jer. 16:5, 15d). The location of the village of Saleim, mentioned by Eusebius (Onom. 160:9–10) as lying seven Roman miles west of Eleutheropolis (Bet Guvrin), seems to correspond to that of Kefar Shiḥlayim. This would place the ancient site of Khirbat Shaḥla, 2 mi. (3.2 km.) east of ʿIrāq al-Manshiyya. The suggested identification with the biblical Shilhim (Josh. 15:32) is doubtful.

BIBLIOGRAPHY: Loew, Flora, 1 (1924), 50 ff.; P. Romanoff, *Onomasticon of Palestine* (1937), 215 ff.

[Michael Avi-Yonah]

KEFAR SYRKIN (Heb. כְּפַר סִירְקִין), moshav in the Coastal Plain of Israel, E. of Petaḥ Tikvah; affiliated to Tenu'at ha-Moshavim; founded in 1936 by veteran agricultural laborers, who were soon joined by immigrants from Germany and other countries. In 1968, Kefar Syrkin had 570 inhabitants, rising to 931 in 2002. The settlers engaged in various farming branches, such as fruit orchards, poultry, and the operation of a horse ranch. The moshav is named after the Zionist labor leader Nachman *Syrkin.

[Efraim Orni]

KEFAR SZOLD (Heb. כְּפַר סאלְד), kibbutz on the eastern outskirts of the Ḥuleh Valley, Israel, affiliated to Ha-Kibbutz ha-Me'uḥad. It was founded in 1942 by pioneers from Hungary, Austria, and Germany, later joined by new members from South America and other countries. Until the *Six-Day War (June 1967) Kefar Szold was a constant target for the Syrian artillery position on the Golan slopes. Its farming was intensive, based on field crops, apple orchards, citrus groves, poultry, and cattle. The kibbutz also operated a factory producing batteries and rented guest rooms. In 2002 its population was 455. The kibbutz is named after Henrietta *Szold.

[Efraim Orni]

KEFAR TAVOR (Heb. כְּפַר תָּבוֹר; initially better known by its Arab name **Meshah**), moshavah at the foot of Mt. Tabor, Israel, 10½ mi. (17 km.) N.E. of Afulah, founded in 1901 by the *Jewish Colonization Association as one of the villages based on the settlers' own labor, with grain cultivation as a principal branch. Until World War I, Kefar Tavor was a center for the activity of *Ha-Shomer, the first armed Jewish defense organization in Ereẓ Israel. Lack of water impeded the village's economic progress for many years. Later field and fruit crops have constituted its main farming branches. In 1968 its population was 315. In the mid-1990s the population was approximately 1,140 and by the end of 2002 it had doubled to 2,290 owing to the expansion of the moshavah, with the majority of residents no longer farmers and income well above the national average. The village extends over an area of 4 sq. mi. (10.6 sq. km.).

[Efraim Orni / Shaked Gilboa (2nd ed.)]

KEFAR TRUMAN (Heb. כְּפַר טְרוּמָן), moshav in the Coastal Plain of Israel, N.E. of Lydda, affiliated to Tenu'at ha-Moshavim, founded in 1949 by immigrants from Poland. Its economy was based on intensive farming. It is named after the former U.S. president Harry S. Truman. In 1968 its population was 251, rising to about 330 in the mid-1990s and 483 in 2002.

[Efraim Orni]

KEFAR URIYYAH (Heb. כְּפַר אוּרִיָּה), moshav in the Judean Foothills, Israel, 6 mi. (10 km.) N.E. of Bet-Shemesh, affiliated to Tenu'at ha-Moshavim. The land at Kefar Uriyyah was purchased by individuals in 1909, and a workers' group established a farm there in 1912. After World War I, some of the proprietors went to settle, but progress was slow, due to lack of water and difficulty of access. In the 1929 Arab riots, the village was abandoned. A group of Kurdish Jews, who had previously worked as stonecutters in Jerusalem, settled there in 1943. The isolated village came under frequent attacks from its Arab neighbors in the War of Independence and had to be evacuated (1948). In 1949, a moshav was set up there by immigrants from Bulgaria when the new road connecting Tel Aviv and Jerusalem provided access to the site. The initial difficulties confronting the moshav resulted in a frequent turnover of settlers. In the 1950s, ample groundwater resources were discovered and these eventually supplied the bulk of Jerusalem's water needs. The name is based on the Arabic Kafrūriyya, which may have its root in an ancient Hebrew name, perhaps Kefar Aryeh – "Lion's Village" (a nearby site was called in Arabic Khirbat al-Asad – "Lion's Ruin"). Remnants of ancient buildings and tombs were found there. Its population in 1968 was 255, rising to 315 in the mid-1990s and 416 in 2002.

[Efraim Orni]

KEFAR VERADIM (Heb. כְּפַר וְרָדִים), town in northern Israel. Kefar Veradim lies on the northern slopes of Mt. Eshkar in western *Galilee, 2,100 ft. (641 m.) above sea level, 11 mi. (18 km.) east of *Nahariyyah. The municipal area extends over 1.8 sq. mi (4.7 sq. km.). The settlement was founded in 1982 on the initiative of the industrialist Steff *Wertheimer. The establishment of the settlement was part of a plan to develop the region industrially and attract new settlers by creating an attractive upscale urban setting. In 1993 Kefar Veradim received municipal council status. By the end of 2002 the population had reached 5,030 inhabitants, with a high annual growth rate of 3.1%.

WEBSITE: www.kvol.co.il.

[Shaked Gilboa (2nd ed.)]

KEFAR VITKIN (Heb. כְּפַר וִיתְקִין), moshav in the central Sharon (Ḥefer Plain), Israel, affiliated to Tenu'at ha-Moshavim. It was founded in 1933 by a group of veteran agricultural workers who were the first to come to the Ḥefer Plain (early 1930) and reclaim its wastes. Kefar Vitkin became the largest moshav in the country with over 1,100 inhabitants in the late 1940s and 845 in 1968. Orange groves, dairy cattle, poultry, orchards, and flowers were the mainstays of its intensive farming. By 2002 the moshav's population had risen to 1,480 due to expansion. Several central regional institutions were situated in Kefar Vitkin, which is named after Joseph *Vitkin.

[Efraim Orni]

KEFAR WARBURG (Heb. כְּפַר וַרְבּוּרְג), moshav in the southern Coastal Plain of Israel, near Be'er Toviyyah, affiliated to Tenu'at ha-Moshavim. It was founded in 1939 by a group of experienced agricultural laborers, joined by immigrants from different countries. They had previously settled at *Kefar Menaḥem and defended it in the 1936–39 Arab riots, but moved to the present site which appeared better suited to the moshav type of settlement. Its farming is highly intensive. In 1968 Kefar Warburg had 500 inhabitants, rising to 745 in 2002. The moshav is named after Felix *Warburg.

[Efraim Orni]

KEFAR YASIF (Heb. כְּפַר יָסִיף), a large village at the foot of the mountains of Upper Galilee, about 7 mi. (10 km.) N.E. of Acre. The antiquity of the name Kefar Yasif is alluded to in the Septuagint, which instead of "Hosah," the portion of Asher (Josh. 19:29), reads ʾΙασιφ. The Jewish antiquity of the locality is evident from the stone door of a burial cave which is preserved at the Louvre in Paris. On it appear reliefs of a candelabrum and an ark. A stone tablet which is affixed over the door of one of the houses of the village bears reliefs of a candelabrum, a *shofar* (ram's horn), and a *lulav* (palm branch). In Crusader times it was a village called Cafersi in the territory of *Acre. As a result of the revival of Acre at the beginning of the 16th century, the Jewish settlement of Kefar Yasif was also renewed. It is reflected in the responsa of the rabbis of Safed and in the tax lists of the Ottoman archives of Istanbul. As one of the ten 16th-century Jewish village settlements in Galilee, its inhabitants also engaged in agriculture. Taxes were paid from the cotton crops.

With the renewed impetus of Jewish settlement in Acre during the first half of the 18th century, a new Jewish settlement was created in Kefar Yasif. This settlement also engaged in agriculture and observed the laws applicable to the Land of Israel. The community left in 1707 as a result of an attack of locusts, but was renewed by the kabbalist R. Solomon Abbadi in 1747 who sought, under the protection of Sheikh Dhaher el-ʾAmr, the ruler of Galilee, to establish a Torah center. The last settlement ceased to exist at the end of the first half of the 19th century (1841). The number of Jewish settlers fluctuated from 10 families in 1702, to 20 in 1764, to 15 in 1827. The present inhabitants of the village point to a "Jewish quarter." With the revival of the Jewish settlement in Kefar Yasif during the 18th century, the village became the burial site for the Jews of Acre (and not during the 13th–14th centuries as generally thought) because, according to the *halakhah*, it is doubtful whether Acre forms part of Ereẓ Israel or not. Upon their death, the wealthy of Acre were borne to Kefar Yasif on the shoulders of their pallbearers. Others preferred to be buried near the sacred tomb of "*Hushai the Archite" in the Druze village of Yirkah (3 mi. (5 km.) to the east of Kefar Yasif). The poor were buried on the eastern side of the walls of Acre. The custom of burial in Kefar Yasif was abolished either after the riots of 1929 or those of 1936.

[Joseph Braslavi (Braslavski)]

Kefar Yasif is now an Arab village with 7,820 inhabitants in 2002 (up from 3,470 in 1968), the majority Greek Catholic and Greek Orthodox and the rest Muslim (57% Christians, 43% Muslims). Kefar Yasif has been governed by a municipal council since 1925. Its jurisdiction extends over an area of 2.6 mi. (6.7 sq. km.), with the village economy historically based on olive plantations, tobacco, and livestock as well as some intensive mixed farming, workshops, and small factories. In 2000 income was about half the national average.

[Efraim Orni]

BIBLIOGRAPHY: R. Dussaud, *Les Monuments Palestiniens et Judaïques* (1912), 88; R. Gottheil and W.H. Worrell, *Fragments from the Cairo Genizah* (University of Michigan Studies, 13, 1927), 263; Rivkind, in: *Reshumot*, 4 (1925), 332–44; B. Lewis, *Notes and Documents from the Turkish Archives* (1952), 9, 16, 18, 20–21; Braslavi, *Le-Ḥeker Arẓenu* (1954), 123–8; idem, in *Ma'aravo shel ha-Galil* (1961), 179–98; idem, in *Ma'aravo shel Galil ve-Ḥof ha-Galil* (1965), 147–52; I. Ben Zvi, *She'ar Yashuv* (1965), 132–47.

KEFAR YEḤEZKEL (Heb. כְּפַר יְחֶזְקֵאל), moshav in the Harod Valley, Israel, N.W. of *En-Harod, affiliated to Tenu'at ha-Moshavim. It was founded in 1921 as one of the first settlements in the valleys of Jezreel and Harod, by a group of pioneers of the Second and Third Aliyah. Farming at Kefar Yeḥezkel was intensive, diversified, and fully irrigated. The moshav operates a tourist center that features a robotic dairy. The moshav is named after Yeḥezkel *Sassoon, whose contribution aided the Jewish National Fund in financing the purchase of the Jezreel and Harod valley lands. In 1968 it had a population of 440. In the mid-1990s the population was approximately 591; in 2002, 610, with expansion underway.

WEBSITE: www.kfar-y.co.il.

[Efraim Orni / Shaked Gilboa (2nd ed.)]

KEFAR YEHOSHU'A (Heb. כְּפַר יְהוֹשֻׁעַ), moshav in the western Jezreel Valley, Israel, affiliated to Tenu'at ha-Moshavim. It was founded in 1927 by a pioneer group, mostly from Russia, many of whom had been members of *Gedud ha-Avodah. In 1968 Kefar Yehoshu'a had 645 inhabitants; in 2002, 674. Like its neighbor *Nahalal, it was laid out in a circular pattern on the architect Richard *Kaufmann's blueprints. A mosaic in honor of Kaufmann is located in the center of the moshav. The moshav has a regional museum principally displaying the history of settlement in the Jezreel Valley. At the entrance to the moshav is a reconstruction of the historic Ha-Emek train station on the line that once linked Haifa to Damascus. It is named after Yehoshua *Hankin, who was instrumental in purchasing the Jezreel Valley lands.

[Efraim Orni / Shaked Gilboa (2nd ed.)]

KEFAR YONAH (Heb. כְּפַר יוֹנָה), rural settlement, possessing municipal council status, in central Israel, about 4 mi. (7 km.) E. of Netanyah, founded in 1932 by veteran farm workers from Nes Ẓiyyonah, followed soon afterwards by other settlers. The village's establishment was aided by the Belgian Zionist Jean Fischer Fund. Based mainly on citriculture, the village expanded and introduced small industrial enterprises during World War II to take the place of citrus which no longer had export outlets. With the mass immigration to Israel beginning in 1948, Kefar Yonah grew considerably when a large immigrant camp (*ma'barah) in the vicinity, Shevut Am (Bet Lid), later transferred part of its inhabitants to permanent housing in Kefar Yonah. In 1968, the settlement had 2,650 inhabitants. In the mid-1990s the population was approximately 5,650, and by the end of 2002 it had nearly doubled to 10,900, attracting city dwellers seeking a rural environment. The settlement's area is about 5 sq. mi. (12.7 sq. km.). Its name commemorates Jean (Yonah) *Fischer.

[Ephraim Orni / Shaked Gilboa (2nd ed.)]

KEHIMKAR, ḤAYIM SAMUEL (1830–1909), historian of the *Bene Israel community in Bombay (Mumbai). Born in Alibag on the Konkan coast like many in his community he became a civil servant in Bombay. In 1853 he founded the Bombay Bene Israel Benevolent Society. In 1875 he and his two brothers opened a school in Bombay which taught both Marathi and Hebrew. He was the editor of the periodical *Israel*, which appeared until 1885, and his work *Sketch of the History of the Beni-Israel and an Appeal for Their Education* was published in 1892. On his death, he left in manuscript his "History of the Bene-Israel of India," a mine of information on the history and customs of the Bene Israel community, which was published in Tel Aviv in 1937 on the initiative of Immanuel *Olsvanger.

BIBLIOGRAPHY: H.S. Kehimkar, History of the Bene-Israel of India (1937), iii–viii. **ADD. BIBLIOGRAPHY:** S.B. Isenberg, *India's Bene Israel: A Comprehensive Inquiry and Sourcebook* (1988); J.G. Roland, *Jews in British India: Identity in a Colonial Era* (1989).

[Walter Joseph Fischel]

°**KEIL, KARL FRIEDRICH** (1807–1888), German Bible critic, born in Lauterbach, Saxony. Keil was appointed to the theological faculty of Dorpat in Estonia where he taught Bible, New Testament exegesis, and Oriental languages. In 1859 he was called to serve the Lutheran church in Leipzig. In 1887 he moved to Rödletz, where he died. Keil was a conservative critic who reacted strongly against the scientific biblical criticism of his day. He strongly supported Mosaic authorship of the Pentateuch. He maintained the validity of the historico-critical investigation of the Bible only if it proved the existence of New Testament revelation in the Scriptures. To this aim he edited (with Franz *Delitzsch) his principal work, a commentary on the Bible, *Biblischer Kommentar über das Alte Testament* (5 vols., 1866–82; *Biblical Commentary on the Old Testament*, 5 vols., 1872–77). The work remains his most enduring contribution to biblical studies. He also published commentaries on Maccabees and New Testament literature.

ADD. BIBLIOGRAPHY: A. Siedlecki, in: DBI, 2:18–19.

[Zev Garber]

KEILAH (Heb. קְעִילָה), city of Judah, in the fourth district of the kingdom, together with Achzib and Mareshah (Josh. 15:44; cf. I Chron. 4:19). It is first mentioned in the *el-Amarna letters, in connection with disputes between the king of Jerusalem and the kings of the Shephelah (nos. 279, 280, 287, 289, 290). In I Samuel 23:7 it is described as a town with gates and bars, threshing floors, and cattle. Attacked by the Philistines, it was defended by David, then a fugitive outlaw. When, after the defeat of the enemy, Saul approached the town intending to capture David with the help of the inhabitants, who were ready to betray him, David escaped into the desert. In post-Exilic times, Keilah served as the headquarters of a district divided into two parts (Neh. 3:17, 18). The Keilah whose fig-cakes are mentioned in talmudic literature (TJ, Bik. 3:3, 65c) may be another place on the other side of the Jordan River. Eusebius refers to Keilah as a village 8 mi. (12¾ km.) from Eleutheropolis (Bet Guvrin) on the way to Hebron (Onom. 114:15ff.). A tomb of Habakkuk is located near the village in *Onomasticon* 88:27 and by Sozomenus (*Historia Ecclesiastica* 7:2). Keilah is identified with Khirbat Qīlā, 10 mi. (16 km.) northwest of Hebron.

BIBLIOGRAPHY: Alt, in: PJB, 21 (1925), 21–22; 24 (1928), 26–27; Albright, in: BASOR, 15 (1924), 4; Beyer, in: ZDPU, 54 (1931), 222, n. 5; Aharoni, Land, index.

[Michael Avi-Yonah]

KEITEL, HARVEY (1939–), U.S. actor, producer. The son of a Polish mother and Romanian father, Keitel was born and raised in Brooklyn, New York. He enlisted in the U.S. Marine Corps at the age of 16 and served in Lebanon. Following his return to the U.S., he worked as a court reporter before being accepted at the New York Actors Studio, where he studied under legendary teachers such as Lee *Strasberg, Stella *Adler, and Frank Corsaro. In 1967, Keitel began his long relationship with director Martin Scorcese, as the two made their respective feature film debuts in *Who's That Knocking at My Door.* Five years later, Keitel and Scorcese made their breakthrough with *Mean Streets* (1973). Keitel's relationship with Scorcese continued throughout his career in acclaimed films such as *Taxi Driver* (1976), *Alice Doesn't Live Here Anymore* (1974), and *The Last Temptation of Christ* (1988). Keitel continued to work with distinctive directors on such breakthough films as Ridley Scott's *The Duellists* (1977), James Toback's *Fingers* (1978), Paul Schrader's *Blue Collar* (1978), and Betrand Tavernier's *La Mort en direct* (1980). Keitel's stature as an actor grew with his 1991 portrayal of gangster Mickey Cohen in *Bugsy*, for which he was nominated for an Oscar, and continued with his role as a detective in *Thelma and Louise* (1991). In 1992, Keitel's performance as Mr. White in Quentin Tarantino's *Reservoir Dogs* sustained his successful run, followed by important roles in such films as Abel Ferrara's *The Bad Lieutenant* (1992) and Jane Campion's *The Piano* (1993). Later work includes *Smoke* (1995), *From Dusk Till Dawn* (1996), *U-571* (2000), *Little Nicky* (2000), *Red Dragon* (2002), and *National Treasure* (2004).

[Walter Driver (2nd ed.)]

KELAL YISRAEL (Heb. כְּלָל יִשְׂרָאֵל; "Jewish community as a whole"), a term employed when discussing the common responsibility, destiny, and kinship of all members of the Jewish community. The rabbis declared that "all Israel are sureties one for another" (Shevu. 39a); and sinners must be rebuked because the entire community is ultimately responsible for their wrongdoings. Nevertheless, the rabbis recognized that a community will always possess some sinners and the Midrash interpreted the *Four Species as symbolizing four categories of Jews ranging from those who possess both Torah and good works to those who possess neither (Lev. R. 30:12). The unity of the Jewish nation was considered an historic and spiritual concept, in addition to being a social reality. All subsequent generations of Jews (including proselytes) were viewed as having been present at Mount Sinai and sharing in the responsibilities of the covenant with God (Shevu. 39a). Likewise, the righteous of all generations will be reunited at the time of the resurrection of the dead during the messianic period (Maim., Commentary to Mishnah, Sanh. 10:1). This concept of community and shared fate is a more concrete version of the aggadic notion, often found in the Midrash, of *keneset Yisrael*, i.e., "the community of Israel" as a spiritual and even mystical entity. The term *keneset Yisrael* is often used in aggadic literature as a personification of Israel in its dialogue with God and its faithfulness to Him. It praises the Almighty who in turn praises *keneset Yisrael* (Tanḥ., Ki-Tissa 18). The latter is also described as the mother of every Jew; the father is the Almighty Himself (Ber. 35b). *Keneset Yisrael* also boasts that "never did it enter the theaters and circuses of the heathen peoples to make merry and rejoice" (Lam. R., introd., p. 6). In the Zohar, God and *keneset Yisrael* are one when together in Ereẓ Israel. The community of Israel in exile is not united with God until it emerges from captivity and returns to its land (Zohar, Lev. 93b).

In modern times the concept of *kelal Yisrael* was further developed and utilized by Solomon *Schechter in defining change and development within Jewish law. Schechter held that the collective conscience of "catholic" Israel as embodied in the "universal synagogue" was the only true guide for determining contemporary *halakhah*. His viewpoint was an elaboration upon the talmudic principle "Go forth and see how the public is accustomed to act" (Ber. 45a).

BIBLIOGRAPHY: S. Schechter, *Studies in Judaism*, 1 (1896), xviiiff.

KELEN, IMRE (Emery or Emerich; 1895–), cartoonist. Kelen, who was born in Győr and won the Hungarian Military Cross in World War I, made his name with his caricatures of the statesmen at the Paris Peace Conference in 1919. Not long afterward he went to live in Switzerland, where in 1922 he began his collaboration with another Hungarian Jew, Aloysius Derso (1888–1964). Together the two men attended the League of Nations and major international conferences, and the Kelen-Derso cartoons appeared in many European newspapers over the next 15 years. In 1938 they emigrated to the United States, where they continued their collaboration until 1950. Collections of their work include *Guignol and Lausanne* (1922), *Indian Round Table Conference* (1930), *Le Testament de Genève* (1931), *Pages Glorieuses* (1932), *The League at Lunch* (1936), and *Peace in Their Time* (1963). Kelen also wrote children's books. From 1948 to 1957 he was adviser to and then director of the United Nations Television Service in New York, and in 1966 published a biography of the former secretary-general of the UN, Dag Hammarskjöld.

KELETI, AGNES (Klein; 1921–), Hungarian gymnast, the most successful Jewish female Olympian in history, winner of 11 medals including five gold, four silver, and two bronze, member of the International Gymnastics Hall of Fame and the Hungarian Sports Hall of Fame. Keleti began to study gymnastics at the age of four in Budapest, winning her first national title at 16, the first of 10 national titles in her career. She began focusing on the 1940 Olympics, but World War II caused the cancellation of the Games. At the beginning of the war Keleti's father was sent to Auschwitz, while her mother and sister were saved by Swedish diplomat Raoul *Wallenberg. Keleti purchased the papers of a Christian girl and escaped to a small Hungarian village, where she worked as a maid. After the war, she learned that her mother and sister had survived the concentration camps, but that her father and all her other relatives had been murdered at Auschwitz.

Keleti made the 1948 Hungarian gymnastic team, but an injury caused her to miss Olympic competition. She was nonetheless awarded a silver medal when Hungary finished second in team competition. At the 1952 Helsinki Olympics, Keleti – by now an "old" 31 – won a gold medal in the Floor Exercises, silver in the Combined Team competition, and a bronze in both Team Hand Apparatus and Uneven Parallel Bars. She also finished fourth in the Balance Beam, and sixth in the Individual All-Around.

In 1954, Keleti captured the World Championship in Uneven Bars, and her Hungarian team won the silver medal in Team Exercises (portable apparatus). She also took the bronze medal in the Balance Beam, and finished fourth in the Floor Exercise. Keleti won the All-Around Hungarian Championships 10 straight times from 1947 to 1956.

At the 1956 Melbourne Olympics, Keleti – now at the advanced age of 35 – won gold medals in the Free-Standing Exercise, Balance Beam, Parallel Bars, and Team Combined Exercise (portable apparatus), and silver medals in the individual all-around and team all-around competitions.

Four weeks before the opening of the Games the Hungarian Revolution began, with the Soviet Union sending troops into Hungary to quash a revolution aimed at ending the country's Communist domination. Two weeks after the revolt, Keleti and the rest of the Hungarian team left for the Melbourne Olympics and, once there, Keleti refused to return home, defecting to the West. She was able to get her mother and sister out of Hungary, and in 1957 they settled in Israel, where Keleti became an instructor in physical education at the *Wingate Institute, where she developed a number of national gymnastic teams.

Keleti's total of 10 Olympic medals ranks third all-time among women athletes, and her five gold medals rank fourth all-time for individual winner of Olympic gold medals. Keleti was inducted into the Hungarian Sports Hall of Fame in 1991 and the International Gymnastics Hall of Fame in 2002.

[Elli Wohlgelernter (2nd ed.)]

KELIM (Heb. כֵּלִים; "vessels"), first tractate of the Mishnah order of *Tohorot*. Including vessels of all kinds, the term also embraces clothing, furniture, and weapons – indeed any artifact, utensil, or implement. This tractate deals in 30 chapters with the law of ritual purity affecting the different kinds of *kelim*: the scriptural basis is in Leviticus 11:29–35; 15:4–6, 9–12, 19–27; Numbers 19:14–16, 31:19–24. Being the first, the longest, and the most important tractate of the order *Tohorot*, this tractate was itself sometimes referred to as *Tohorot* (e.g., in the commentary to *Tohorot* ascribed to Rav Hai Gaon, ed. Epstein). Because of its inordinate length this tractate was divided into three parts, of ten chapters each, respectively designated *Bava Kamma*, *Bava Meẓia*, and *Bava Batra* (the first, middle, and last gate), but this nomenclature survived only in the Tosefta.

The first chapter, which is a kind of introduction, sets out the various degrees of impurity and sanctity. Chapters 2–10 deal with earthen vessels, including ovens (Lev. 11:35), and vessels with a close-bond covering (Num. 19:15). Chapters 11–14 cover metal vessels, 15–19 vessels of wood, leather, bone, etc. Chapter 20 discusses the problem of *midras*, indicated in Leviticus 15:26. Chapters 21–25 deal with artifacts composed of various parts and pieces, e.g., plow, saw, table, riding equipment, etc., and chapters 26–28 deal with leatherware and garments, etc. Chapter 29 deals with the incidental parts of garments and vessels, like cords, handles, etc., and chapter 30 deals with glassware. The last halakhic statement in the tractate is that an *afarkas* of glass (*clepsydra*, or waterclock) does not receive impurity; it thus ends on a note of cleanness, which makes R. Yose exclaim: "Blessed art thou, O *Kelim*, for thou didst enter in uncleanness, but art gone forth in cleanness." This shows that an early version of this tractate, with the same name, existed prior to the Mishnah of Judah ha-Nasi. There is in addition some evidence that many anonymous parts of the tractate are according to him. Certain other characteristics of *Kelim* are also in accordance with Yose's usages. Rich in valuable detail on daily life, *Kelim* contributes much to knowledge of the material culture of the tannaitic period. It has also preserved many Greek, Latin, and other words, which were then in popular use. Though there is no Talmud to *Kelim*, all the sayings concerning it which can be found in various Babylonian tractates were collected and arranged in the form of the usual *Gemara* by R. Gershon Ḥanokh Leiner, and printed by him, with his commentaries in *Sidrei Tohorah* (1873), a work of cardinal importance to the understanding of this complicated tractate. J.N. Epstein has written a short but important commentary on *Kelim* which sheds much light for the modern student (Tanna'im, 479–94). Mishnah *Kelim* was translated into English by H. Danby (*The Mishnah*, 1933), and J. Neusner published a translation of both the Mishnah (1991) and the Tosefta (2002) of *Tohorot*.

BIBLIOGRAPHY: Epstein, Tanna'im, 459–94; 71ff.; J. Brand, *Kelei ha-Ḥeres be-Sifrut ha-Talmud* (1953). Epstein, *The Gaonic Commentary on the Order Toharot (Hebrew)*, (1982); idem, *Kelei Zekhukhit be-Sifrut ha-Talmud* (1978); S. Lieberman, *Tosefet Rishonim*, vol. 3 (1939); J. Neusner, *A History of the Mishnaic Laws of Purities* (1974–77), vols. 1–3; D. Sperber, *Material Culture in Eretz-Israel* (Hebrew) (1993); *Mishnayot Da'at Eliahu, Kelim* (chs. 11–14), (2005).

[Arnost Zvi Ehrman]

KELLER, MORTON (1929–), U.S. historian. Born in New York, Keller received his B.A. from the University of Rochester (1950) and his M.A. (1952) and his Ph.D. from Harvard University (1953). He taught at the North Carolina and Pennsylvania universities, and in 1964 became chairman of the history department at Brandeis University. Specializing in late 19th- and 20th-century American history, he lectured at Harvard and at the University of Sussex, England. After retiring from teaching, Keller became the Spector Professor of History emeritus at Brandeis and a visiting fellow at the Hoover Institution. In 1999 he was named resident scholar at Rockefeller Center at Bellagio and librarian of the American Academy of Arts and Sciences.

He is the author of *In Defense of Yesterday: James M. Beck and the Politics of Conservatism, 1861–1936* (1958), *The Life Insurance Enterprises, 1885–1910* (1963), *The Art and Politics of Thomas Nast* (1968), *Affairs of State* (1977), *Regulating a New Society* (1990), *Regulating a New Economy* (1990), and *Making Harvard Modern* (with P. Keller, 2001). He edited *The New Deal: What Was It?* (1963) and *Theodore Roosevelt* (1967); and co-edited *Taking Stock: American Government in the 20th Century* (1999).

[Ruth Beloff (2nd ed.)]

KELLERMAN, FAYE (1952–), U.S. mystery writer. Born in St. Louis, Mo., Kellerman grew up in Los Angeles. She earned a bachelor's degree in mathematics and a D.D.S., both from the University of California at Los Angeles. She never practiced dentistry, however, and was a full-time mother of four before publishing her first novel, *The Ritual Bath* (1986), in which she introduced a series with a Los Angeles police officer, Sgt. Peter Decker, and Rina Lazarus. In the book, Decker is called to investigate a rape charge in an isolated Orthodox Jewish community. Lazarus, a young widow who found the victim, guides Decker through her suspicious community as all the signs point to the rapist's first crime not being his last. Kellerman's writing frequently deals with Jewish themes and characters, incorporating them into the framework of the traditional mystery. Her debut novel won the 1987 Macavity Award for best first mystery. Since then, she has published more than 15 mysteries, with titles like *Milk and Honey*, *Day of Atonement*, *False Prophet*, *Grievous Sin*, *Sanctuary*, *Prayers for the Dead*, and *The Stone Kiss*. Kellerman is a practicing Orthodox Jew, as is her husband, the novelist Jonathan *Kellerman. They are believed to be the only married couple ever to appear on the *New York Times* bestseller list simultaneously (for two different books). "Religion is a major factor in my life," Faye Kellerman said in an interview in 1999. "I consider myself a modern Orthodox Jewish woman with attachments to my synagogue, my children's religious school, and the community at large." In another interview, she explained: "The religion in the books comes from personal experience. I have a great deal of love for my religion. I felt that maybe I could transmit some of that feeling and emotion. Also, I felt that people would enjoy learning about the rites and rituals of Orthodox Jewry the same way I enjoy learning about other cultures and religions."

[Stewart Kampel (2nd ed.)]

KELLERMAN, JONATHAN (1949–), U.S. mystery writer, psychologist. Kellerman, who was born in New York City and grew up in Los Angeles, received a bachelor's degree in psychology from the University of California at Los Angeles and a doctorate in psychology from the University of Southern California, where he became clinical professor of pediatrics at the School of Medicine. His internship and postdoctoral fellowship were at the Children's Hospital/School of Medicine, where he became founding director of the Psychosocial Program, Division of Hematology-Oncology. He is the author of numerous articles in the scientific and popular press, three books on psychology, including *Psychological Aspects of Childhood Cancer* and *Helping the Fearful Child*, two children's books, *Daddy, Daddy, Can You Touch the Sky?* and *Jonathan Kellerman's ABC of Weird Creatures*, which he also illustrated, and about 20 consecutive bestselling novels. After a decade of nonsuccess in his writing career, his first published work, *When the Bough Breaks* (1985), sold more than a million copies and kick-started his career. He has continued at a rate of about one a year since. Most of the books feature a pair of friends, Dr. Alex Delaware, a sensitive child psychologist, and the more macho Milo Sturgis of the Los Angeles Police Department, who happens to be a homosexual. Some of his novels, like *Dr. Death*, about a self-styled euthanasia champion, seem to have been inspired by people in the news or by then-current news events. All are considered fast-paced, intense, and edgy. Like his wife, Faye *Kellerman, he is a practicing Orthodox Jew.

[Stewart Kampel (2nd ed.)]

KELLERMANN, BENZION (1869–1923), rabbi and author. Born in Gerolzhofen, Bavaria, he served as instructor in religion in Berlin, Frankfurt, and Konitz, and in 1917 was appointed rabbi of the Berlin community. A disciple of Hermann *Cohen, he based his religious philosophy and his rational concept of Judaism as ethical monotheism on the teachings of that German-Jewish philosopher. Kellermann was the author of the following works: *Kritische Beitraege zur Enstehungsgeschichte des Christentums* (1906); *Liberales Judentum* (1907); *Der wissenschaftliche Idealismus und die Religion* (1908); *Der ethische Monotheismus der Propheten und seine soziologische Wuerdigung* (1917); *Das Ideal im System der Kantischen Philosophie* (1920); and *Die Ethik Spinozas, ueber Gott und Geist* (1922). He also translated the major part of the medieval philosophical work *Milḥamot Adonai (Die Kaempfe Gottes)* by *Levi b. Gershom (introduction and four tractates, with extensive commentary 1914–16). There was much controversy over the translation, due to the fact that some passages contain an inaccurate rendering of the thoughts expressed in the original text (see S. Rubin, in: MGWJ, 63 (1919), 71–74).

BIBLIOGRAPHY: I. Husik, in: JQR, 7 (1916/17), 553–94; 8 (1917/18), 113–56, 231–68; L. Baeck, in: *Juedisches Gemeindeblatt* (Berlin, July 6, 1923); Liebert, in: *Kant-Studien*, 28 (1923), 486–90.

[Bernard Suler]

KELLNER, LEON (1859–1928), professor of English literature and one of Herzl's early friends and advisers. Teaching in various schools, and after a scholarship at the British Museum in London (1887), he became a lecturer in English literature at the University of Vienna in 1890. Besides his employment at a high school in Vienna he continued his lectures at the University in 1894–1904. From 1904 to 1914 he was a professor at the University of Czernowitz, where he was active in public life as a representative of the Jewish-national list to the *Landtag* (local parliament). When World War I broke out, Kellner flew to Vienna. After the war he served as an English expert in the office of the president of the Austrian Republic (Praesidentenkanzlei). He gave lectures at the Technical University and at the adult college in Vienna. From the publication of his first article (1884), he was active in scholarly writing, mainly in the research of English literature. He published critical editions of English texts, grammar books, an English-German, German-English dictionary, a dictionary of Shakespeare, and a history of English and American literature. His works were highly successful and were published in several editions because of their attractive style, even in purely academic subjects. He also published articles, stories, and feuilletons in newspapers and periodicals in English and German.

In 1896 he made the acquaintance of Herzl and was invited by him to edit the Zionist organ *Die *Welt*, but did not accept. He contributed to *Die Welt* from its first issue (at first under his own signature and later under the signature Leo Rafaels), and in 1900 edited the paper. Kellner assisted Herzl by opening many locked doors in England and was one of his closest associates. Herzl wrote of him in his diary: "Kellner, my best and dearest friend, whose visits are rays of light in the murk of all these worries" (March 26, 1898), "he knows more than anybody about my intentions" (May 27, 1898); Herzl even requested that Kellner publish his diary. Kellner fulfilled his request by publishing a selection of Herzl's writings in two volumes (*Theodor Herzl's Zionistische Schriften*, 1908), by aiding the publication of the diaries, and beginning to write a comprehensive biography of Herzl, of which only the first part *Theodor Herzl's Lehrjahre* was published (1920).

BIBLIOGRAPHY: A. Kellner, *Leon Kellner* (Ger., 1936); P. Arnold, in: *Herzl Yearbook*, 2 (1959), 171–83; idem, in: B. Dinur and I. Halperin (eds.), *Shivat Ẓiyyon*, 4 (1956), 114–60; idem, *Zikhronot be-Ahavah* (1968). **ADD. BIBLIOGRAPHY:** H. Arnold, in: *Neue Deutsche Biographie*, 11 (1977), 477–78; *Lexikon deutsch-juedischer Autoren*, vol. 13 (2005), 348–57.

[Getzel Kressel / Archiv Bibliographia Judaica (2nd ed.)]

KELMAN, WOLFE (1923–1990), U.S. rabbi and administrator. Born in Vienna, the scion of a Ḥasidic dynasty, Kelman's family moved to Toronto, Ontario, where he was educated in the public schools. He served in the Royal Canadian Air Force during World War II and earned a B.A. from the University of Toronto in 1946 and then entered the Jewish Theological Seminary, from which he was ordained in 1950.

At the urging of Chancellor Louis Finkelstein, Kelman became the director of the Rabbinical Assembly in 1951, a position that was variously called executive secretary, executive director, and finally as executive vice president. The titles changed but not the job. Under his leadership the Rabbinical Assembly grew from 300 rabbis to 1,200 in 12 countries. For the first 15 years of his tenure he served as the head of the Joint Placement Commission during a time of the most rapid expansion of the Conservative Movement, and thus became a matchmaker between rabbis and their congregations. He facilitated the placement of non-seminary graduates from Yeshiva University and even Torah Vadaat along with the seminary graduates. In total, he placed more than 1,500 rabbis in their positions.

Kelman's greatest contribution to the rabbinate was to ensure rabbis were paid a professional salary and that they and their families were treated with dignity. In one instance, Kelman threatened to stage a march of one hundred rabbis for the media if a particular congregation dared to cast a widow and her children out of the parish home without providing for them.

Kelman was a confidante of his teacher Abraham Joshua *Heschel throughout Heschel's and Rabbi Joseph Baer *Soloveitchik's negotiations with the Vatican and Pope Paul VI regarding *Nostra Aetate*. He also marched with Heschel in Montgomery and pleaded with him to make major addresses to White House Conferences on Education and Aging. Kelman mentored Elie *Wiesel when he was a young and relatively unknown rabbi.

Colleagues in other movements praised Kelman. The Hebrew Union College-Jewish Institute of Religion awarded him an honorary doctorate shortly before his death. Under his leadership the Rabbinical Assembly became economically viable, most especially from its publishing division. Toward the end of his career, he led the admission of women into the hitherto all male rabbinate.

From 1986 he served as the chairman of the American section of the World Jewish Congress. He was also the director of the Louis Finkelstein Institute for Religious and Social Studies. The son of an Orthodox rabbi and the son-in-law of a Reform rabbi, Kelman was an early believer in religious pluralism. His own son Levi led a neo-Ḥasidic Reform Congregation in Jerusalem.

[Michael Berenbaum (2nd ed.)]

KELME (Lithuanian **Kelmė**; Rus. **Kelmy**; Yid. **Kelm**), town in W. central Lithuania. It became known as a center of the *musar movement in Lithuania. The Jewish community there may have been in existence for several hundred years; its synagogue was said to be 300 years old, and there was a tradition that its reconstruction had been financed by a Polish landlord, Graszewsky. The Jewish population numbered 759 in 1847, and 2,710 (69% of the total) in 1897. The town became associated with the "Kelmer Maggid" Moses Isaac Darshan. According to the 1923 census there were 1,599 Jews living in Kelme. Most were occupied as small shopkeepers and artisans, but there were also grain and timber merchants, and owners of brush factories and tanneries. Communal institutions included two Jewish elementary schools (*Tarbut and Yavneh), a Jewish preparatory school, and a bank, among others. A number of prominent scholars served as rabbis in the town, among them Eliezer *Gordon, later rabbi of Telsiai. A *musar* yeshivah in Kelme was established by Simḥah Zissel *Broida, which also attracted students from other places; it existed until World War II.

During World War II, Kelme was occupied by the Germans shortly after the outbreak of the war between Germany and Soviet Russia. Most of the Jews were murdered in July and August 1941.

BIBLIOGRAPHY: H. Karlinski, in: *Lite*, 1 (1951), 1438–51; M. Karnovich, *ibid.*, 1 (1951), 1846–50; *Yahadut Lita*, 1 (1959), index; 3 (1967), 350–2.

[Joseph Gar]

KELSEN, HANS (1881–1973), jurist, whose "pure theory of law" made him one of the most famous legal theoreticians of the 20th century. Born in Prague, Kelsen was taken to Vienna when he was 14. He studied at the universities of Vienna, Heidelberg, and Berlin, and was professor of constitutional and administrative law and of legal philosophy at the University of Vienna from 1919 to 1929. In 1920 he drafted the constitution of the Austrian Republic and was a judge of the supreme court of Austria from 1920 to 1929. Kelsen was professor of law at Cologne University from 1929 until 1933, when, although baptized, he was compelled to resign his post. He taught at the Institut des Hautes Etudes Internationales in Geneva until 1940 and at the University of Prague before he immigrated to the United States. He became professor of political science at the University of California in 1944.

The breakdown of the Austro-Hungarian Empire, and the interwar tragedy of frustrated democracy in Austria, led him to a theory of law transcending nations and states. While he was professor of law at Vienna University, Kelsen founded the so-called Vienna school of jurisprudence, which preached the "pure theory of law." Originally developed 20 years earlier in his *Hauptprobleme der Staatsrechtslehre* (1911), the "pure theory" is a logical analysis of the law considered as a system of norms. A "basic norm" (*Grundnorm*) stands at the head of the system: this gives validity to the whole of the legal order and all the legal rules in the order may be ultimately referred to it. The "pure theory of law" was the result of a vigorous campaign by Kelsen to treat law as a science free from sociological and political elements, even though he recognized that each country's legal system must be determined by the state. This approach brought him into open conflict with communist doctrines, which subjected law to the political structure of the state, and with sociological jurisprudence, which regarded law as reflecting the society in which it existed. The climax of Kelsen's theory was a vision of the unification of legal systems within a framework of international law which would establish a universal legal order. Although his "pure theory of law" has been subject to widespread criticism and rejected by most schools of jurisprudence, Kelsen has greatly influenced legal thinking in the 20th century. Kelsen was a prolific writer and his works have been translated into almost every European language (Russian being a noteworthy exception).

BIBLIOGRAPHY: G.A. Lipsky (ed.), *Law and Politics in the World Community; Essays on Hans Kelsen's Pure Theory...* (1953); S. Engels (ed.), *Law, State, and International Legal Order* (1964). **ADD. BIBLIOGRAPHY:** R. Walter, "Hans Kelsen," in: H. Erler, E.L. Ehrlich, and L. Heid (eds.), *Meinetwegen ist die Welt erschaffen*, (1997), 333–38; D. Diner, *Hans Kelsen and Carl Schmitt – A Juxtaposition* (1997); I. Englard, "Nazi Criticism Against the Normativist Theory of Hans Kelsen," in: *Israel Law Review*, 32:2 (1998), 183–249; K. Bruckschwaiger, *Die Rolle von Philosophie und Politik bei Hans Kelsen* (2002); S.L. Paulson, *Hans Kelsen – Staatsrechtslehrer und Rechtstheoretiker des 20. Jahrhundert* (2005); G.N. Dias, *Rechtspositivismus und Rechtstheorie – Das Verhaeltnis beider im Werke von Hans Kelsen* (2005); R.C. van Ooyen, *Der Staat der Moderne – Hans Kelsens Pluralismustheorie* (2003); P. Hack, *La philosophie de Kelsen* (2003).

[Josef J. Lador-Lederer]

°**KEMAL MUSTAFA** (**Ataturk**; 1881–1938), Turkish general and statesman, founder of the Republic of Turkey and its first president (1923–38). Endowed with far-sighted vision and boundless energy, he was responsible, after the defeat of the *Ottoman Empire in World War I and its dismemberment, in leading the remnants of the Ottoman army to victory. No less significantly, he shaped Turkey into a state with institutions modeled on West-European patterns, aiming to achieve a modern society. What was noteworthy in his reforms was the comprehensiveness of his approach and his drive to institute change in practically all walks of life, from the roots up. His most important reforms in modernization and secularization (he limited, intentionally, the influence of *Islam) were the following:

The creation of a modern republican state structure with a constitution (proclaimed in 1924), a freely elected parliament (for which women could vote), the founding of a political party (as an agent of modernization), recruitment of a modern bureaucracy, building a new capital in Ankara, disestablishment of religion by secularizing education and the courts, emancipation of women both politically (by giving them the right to vote) and socially (by instituting monogamy and discouraging the veil), adoption of the Latin instead of the Arabic alphabet, and reformation of the Turkish language.

Mustafa Kemal set out to change the mentality of his people in order to induce them to adopt and support his reforms. He never tired of lecturing them on their proud past (and insisted on a patriotic school curriculum in history as well as on historical research at the universities). He insisted on symbols that would enhance love for the fatherland and increase national solidarity for nation-building. The single party he headed was mobilized for these ends and for promoting the reforms within parliament and outside it. While Turkey's economy did not improve visibly, other aspects covered by the reforms did, largely carried out due to his impressive charisma.

Jews and other religious groups were freed from all limitations imposed by the late Ottoman Empire and considered equal citizens. Of course, equality had some drawbacks such as the laws instituting Turkish as the language of instruction (instead of minority languages) in the entire school system. However, Mustafa Kemal should be remembered, also, for his magnanimous and far-sighted decision to invite about 300 professors, physicians, and lawyers, most of them Jewish, from Germany, during the 1930s (along with their extended families), thus rescuing them from Nazi persecution (and worse) and raising the level of teaching and research in Turkey's universities, where many were offered academic appointments.

BIBLIOGRAPHY: The best bibliography on Mustafa Kemal is still the 3-vol. compilation of Mozaffer Gökman, *Atatürk ve devrimleri bibliyografyasi* (1963–1977). See also: R. Mantran, "Atatürk," in: EIS², 1 (1960), 734–35; Lord Kinross, *Atatürk: The Rebirth of a Nation* (1964²); A. Kazancigil and E. Özbudun, *Atatürk: Founder of a Modern Nation* (1981); J.M. Landau, "New Books about Atatürk," in: *Wiener Zeitschrift für die Kunde des Morgenlandes*, 75 (1983), 183–92; idem, *Tekinalp: Turkish Patriot* (1984); idem (ed.) *Atatürk: Founder of a Modern Nation* (1984); L. Macfie, *Atatürk* (1994); E.J. Zürcher, *Turkey: A Modern History* (1997); A. Mango, *Atatürk* (1999); F. Tachau, "German Jewish Emigrés in Turkey," in: A. Levy (ed.), *Jews, Turks, Ottomans* (2002), 233–45; G.E. Gruen, "Turkey," in: R.S. Simon a.o. (eds.), *The Jews of the Middle East and North Africa in Modern Times* (2003), 303–15.

[Jacob M. Landau (2nd ed.)]

KEMELMAN, HARRY (1908–1996), U.S. author. Kemelman wrote entertaining novels of detective fiction in which the hero is a rabbi-sleuth, David Small. They include *Friday the Rabbi Slept Late* (1964), *Saturday the Rabbi Went Hungry* (1966), and *Sunday the Rabbi Stayed Home* (1969). He also published *The Nine Mile Walk* (1967), a collection of stories originally published in *Ellery Queen's Magazine*.

KEMÉNY, SIMON (1882–1945), Hungarian poet and editor. In his emotional impressionist poetry, he overcame his tendency to religiosity. Kemény, a converted Jew, was murdered during the last days of the siege of Budapest by Hungarian Nazis. His main work is *Lamentàciok* ("Lamentations," 1909).

KEMPEN, town in the Rhineland, Germany. The first settlement of Jews in Kempen must have taken place sometime before 1288, when persecutions claimed 17 victims, among whom was a Torah scribe, Isaac, and a young boy, Abraham, who was burned to death. In the 14th century Jews originating from Kempen are found in *Cologne. Kempen Jews were allowed to deal in meat, and to slaughter both for themselves and for non-Jews, but they had to use the public scales and pay a fee to the weight master. In 1330, in return for a loan of 8,000 marks, the archbishop of Kempen granted the Jews of Kempen protection and citizenship. However, in 1347 another persecution drove a number of Jews from the town, and this was followed soon after by the *Black Death persecutions in which Jews also suffered. In 1385 Jews are recorded as living in a *Judengasse* northeast of the market. There are no further traces of permanent Jewish settlement in the city until 1807, when under French rule there were 32 Jews in Kempen under the authority of the Krefeld consistory. A synagogue was consecrated in 1849; in 1854 there were 125 Jewish families affiliated to it, 26 of them (92 persons) living in the town of Kempen. From 1854 to 1922 the community had its own elementary school. In 1895 the number of Jews in the city of Kempen was 103 (1.5%), in 1925; 80 with another 500 or so living in the county. At the beginning of the 1930s there were 150 Jewish families in the county, and 23 of them (70 persons) dwelling in the town. The synagogue was destroyed in 1938. On July 25, 1942, about 200 Jews were deported from Kempen, mainly to *Theresienstadt.

BIBLIOGRAPHY: A. Kober,… *Aus der Geschichte der Juden im Rheinland…* (1931); Germ Jud, 2 (1968), 395–6.

KEMPF, FRANZ MOSHE (1926–), Australian artist and printmaker. Born in Melbourne, Kempf studied different subjects, among them art at the National Gallery School in Australia. In 1956 he went to Italy and studied with Oskar Kokoschka in Salzburg in 1957. He focused not only on art but also on illustration and technological design and became a lecturer in printmaking. As president of the Contemporary Art Society of South Australia, he lectured in graphic art at the South Australian School of Art, becoming head of the department in 1969. During the same time he was also chairman of the Australian Jewish Art Group. Kempf, from an absolutely assimilated background, turned to the ḥasidic path of Chabad and became a strictly observant Jew. His work reflects his deep involvement with Judaism. Both his paintings and his prints contain biblical and ḥasidic themes, ranging from the *shtetl* to the messianic portrayal.

Kempf's style tends towards the semiabstract, but his statements are definite. His painting unites profundity of theme with subtlety of expression. *The End of Days* (by S. Gorr, 1968) was illustrated by Kempf with four original etchings composed specially for the text. His works have been acquired by the city galleries of all the Australian state capitals, by the National Gallery in Canberra, and others in the U.K. and Israel. He has also had exhibitions in the U.K., U.S., Europe, and Israel. Kempf's publications are "Art in Israel," in *Broadsheet* (Contemporary Art Society, 1965); "Polish Printmakers 1972," in *Art and Australia* (1973); "Sculpture in South Australia," in *Art and Australia* (1974); and *Contemporary Australian Printmakers* (1976).

ADD. BIBLIOGRAPHY: D. Peters, *Franz Kempf and Karin Schepers*, Museum of Modern Art and Design (1964); R. Brooks, *Franz Kempf* (1991).

KEMPINSKY, AHARON (1939–1994), Israeli archaeologist. Brought up in Nahariyyah, Kempinsky participated as a teenager in 1952–53 in P. *Delougaz's excavations at Bet Yeraḥ. His academic studies were undertaken at the Hebrew University and it was there that he acquired his M.A. and eventually his Ph.D. In time he became a professor of archaeology at the Institute of Archaeology, Tel Aviv University, and taught at Ben-Gurion University in Beersheba as well. As a student at the Hebrew University, Kempinsky worked as Professor Nahman *Avigad's assistant at Makhmish. Many archaeological excavations followed, some of which he directed, at Palmaḥim (1961), Hazor (1965–66), Megiddo (1965), and Bet ha-Emek (1973). In 1972–75, and again in 1979, Kempinsky (with V. Fritz) uncovered an important early Iron Age village at Tel Masos, not far from Beersheba. In 1975 Kempinsky made a short excavation at Tel Kabri, which was followed by an intensive project there (conducted together with W.D. Niemeyer) from 1986 to 1993. At Kabri a Middle Bronze Age building (perhaps a palace) was exposed, with wall and floor paintings resembling those from Thera (Santorini). Kempinsky was an insatiable reader with an encyclopedic mind; he also traveled all over the world and was a visiting scholar at various universities and colleges, notably at Tuebingen University in 1975. Kempinsky was a prolific writer and wrote many research papers on a diverse number of subjects. Important publications include *The Architecture of Ancient Israel from the Prehistoric to the Persian Periods*, which he co-edited with Ronny Reich, and the final reports on the Tel Masos and Kabri excavations. Kempinsky was a mentor for many of the younger generation of archaeologists in Israel.

BIBLIOGRAPHY: C. Dauphin, "Aharon Kempinsky (1939–1994), Friend and Colleague: An Evocation," in: *Bulletin of the Anglo-Israel Archaeological Society*, 13 (1993–94), 63–66.

[Shimon Gibson (2nd ed.)]

KEMPNER, AVIVA (1946–), U.S. director-writer. Kempner was born in Berlin, Germany, to Chaim Kempner and Helen (née Ciesla). Kempner's Lithuanian father, an immigrant to the United States who served in the U.S. Army during World War II, met Kempner's Polish mother after liberation. Kempner's family moved to Detroit, Mich., in 1950. She graduated from the University of Michigan in 1969 with a bachelor's degree in psychology and in 1971 earned her master's in urban planning. In 1976, she earned her law degree from the Antioch School of Law. Inspired by her own family's Holocaust legacy, Kempner turned to Josh Waletzky for help in writing and directing *Partisans of Vilna* (1986), a film about Jewish resistance against the Nazis which was produced by The Ciesla Foundation, a nonprofit organization that Kempner established in 1981 to produce and distribute films about social and public interest issues. Kempner wrote the narration for *Promises to Keep* (1988), an Oscar-nominated documentary about homelessness. A resident of Washington, D.C., Kempner started the Washington Jewish Film Festival in 1989. In 1998, she wrote and directed *The Life and Times of Hank Greenberg*, a documentary about the Jewish baseball star that won the George Peabody Award. In 2002, she released *Today I Vote for My Joey*, a comic short inspired by the 2000 election and the candidacy for vice president of Sen. Joseph *Lieberman, which she wrote for AFI's Directing Workshop for Women. Kempner then went on to work on *Gertrude Berg: America's Molly Goldberg*, about the creator, writer, and star of *The Goldbergs*, a popular 1930s radio show about a Jewish family that went on to become a television series. Kempner reviewed films for *The Boston Globe, The Forward, Washington Jewish Week*, and *The Washington Post*, among others, and contributed chapters to the books *Daughters of Absence* and *What Israel Means to Me*.

[Adam Wills (2nd ed.)]

KEMPNER, HARRIS (1837–1894), U.S. financier. Kempner, who was born in Russia, emigrated to the United States at the age of 17. He worked for two years in New York City and then moved to Cold Springs, Texas (1856), where he opened a general store. After fighting for the Confederacy during the Civil War, Kempner returned to his Texas store. He moved to Galveston in 1870 and opened a wholesale grocery business that soon became the largest in the South. This business provided Kempner with the initial capital to move into the railroad, commodities, and banking fields. He provided funds for the building of the Gulf, Colorado, and Santa Fe Railroad, and led the fight that resulted in the line's subsequent merger with the Topeka and Santa Fe Railroad. In 1885 Kempner became president of the Island City (Texas) Savings Bank. He soon became a major figure in Texas banking, controlling several big Texas banks. The cotton brokerage firm which Kempner founded in Galveston in 1886, with offices in major European capitals, soon became one of the biggest in the South.

His eldest son, ISAAC HERBERT KEMPNER (1873–1967), was a businessman, banker, and public servant. An early advocate of the commission form of city government, Kempner served as Galveston city treasurer (1899), city finance commissioner (1901–15), and mayor (1917–19).

KEMPNER, ROBERT MAX WASILII (1899–1993), lawyer and historian. Born in Freiburg, Germany, Kempner became an assistant to the state attorney in Berlin (1926) and later a judge. From 1926 to 1933 he was a senior government adviser in the Prussian Ministry of Interior in Berlin. In this period he demanded that Hitler be tried for perjury and treason. He also officially called for disbanding the Nazi Party and Hitler's deportation as an undesirable alien. Removed from office on Hitler's rise to power, he was arrested by the Gestapo, and after his release went to Italy, where he taught until 1939. From there he immigrated to the U.S., where he became a research associate at the University of Pennsylvania and, among other government appointments, worked on President Roosevelt's Manhattan Project. From 1945 to 1946 he was a U.S. prosecutor and from 1946 until 1949 chief prosecutor of Nazi political leaders at the Nuremberg Trials. From 1949 he engaged in special research on the Nazi Holocaust of European Jewry. As a consultant to the Israel government, he helped assemble evidence for the *Eichmann trial (1960–61). Subsequently he fought against the Statute of Limitations in West Germany. Kempner practiced law in Frankfurt on the Main in the 1960s. He then moved back to Philadelphia.

He wrote numerous books and articles on the Nazi era and related post-war topics, notably *Eichmann und Komplizen* (1961), containing a description of Eichmann's activities based on original documents; *SS im Kreuzverhoer* (1964), based on protocols of war-crime trials; and *Edith Stein und Anne Frank, Zwei von Hunderttausend* (1968). Kempner's wife, Ruth Lydia, assembled archives of documents and other materials on Nazi crimes against the churches throughout Europe.

[B. Mordechai Ansbacher]

KENAANI, DAVID (1912–1982), Hebrew essayist and editor. Born in Warsaw, Kenaani was an active member of Ha-Shomer ha-Ẓa'ir. He settled in Ereẓ Israel in 1934 and joined kibbutz Merḥavyah. He began his literary career in the journal *Ha-Shomer ha-Ẓa'ir* in Warsaw in 1932, and wrote extensively on social and literary subjects in the Israel press from a left socialist-Zionist point of view. His books include: *Le-Nogah Eẓ Rakav*, an examination of U.Z. Greenberg's poetry (1950); *Beinam le-Vein Zemannam*, essays on modern Hebrew literature (1955); and *Battei Middot*, essays on communal life (1960). He edited, among other publications, a historical atlas (1954); an anthology of Hebrew and Yiddish literature in the past 100 years (1954); an anthology on Soviet Jewry (with A. Shimri, 1957), and the Hebrew edition of *Zinberg's *History of Jewish Literature* (6 vols., 1955–60). He was principal editor of an encyclopedia of the social sciences *Enẓiklopedyah le-Madda'ei ha-Ḥevrah* (5 vols., 1962–70).

BIBLIOGRAPHY: Kressel, Leksikon, 2 (1967), 142.

[Getzel Kressel]

KENAN, AMOS (1927–), Hebrew writer. Kenan was born in Tel Aviv. He was a member of the anti-British military underground movement, and he became known during the 1950s as the author of the satirical column *"Uzi ve-Shut"* in the daily *Haaretz*. During the following decade he wrote a number of plays which were close in spirit and expression to the Theater of the Absurd, much in vogue in those days, and published his first novella *Ba-Taḥanah* ("At the Station") in 1963. Eschewing realistic narrative, Kenan's stories resist the familiar pattern of plot and character in favor of an episodic texture which evokes a particular atmosphere and communicates sharp images. Kenan, who voiced "dovish" political views soon after the War of Independence and was co-founder of the Israeli-Palestinian Council in the 1970s, vented subversive political ideas in both his fiction and essay writing. *Ha-*

Derekh le-Ein Ḥarod (1984; *The Road to Ein Harod*, 1988) is a fantastic, historiosophical novel, a wild dystopia, the story of an Israeli who, having killed someone, flees for his life towards Ein Ḥarod in the Jezreel Valley. On the way he meets the Arab Mahmud, who becomes a friend on a bizarre voyage which ends with the realization that the ideas of freedom and decency are no longer to be found in that exemplary kibbutz. The collection *Block 23 / Mikhtavim mi-Nes Ẓiyyonah* (1996) contains two apocalyptic novellas which portray a grim picture of future Israel. "Block 23" depicts Tel Aviv after a disastrous war, with its inhabitants living in camps, overshadowed by daily executions and spreading leprosy. Satire and parody are fused with poetic, lyrical descriptions. *Shoshanat Yeriḥo* ("The Rose of Jericho," 1998) is a collection of essays describing landscapes and places in Ereẓ Israel, nature, sounds and flavors, while recollecting biblical episodes and confronting history and shattered dreams. Kenan, known also as painter, sculptor, and Tel Aviv bon vivant, published among others *Ha-Delet ha-Keḥulah* ("The Blue Door," 1972), *Et Waheb be-Sufah* ("Waheb in Sufah," 1988), and the poems collected under *Keẓ Idan ha-Zoḥalim* ("End of Reptile Era," 1999). For translation see the ITHL website at www.ithl.org.il.

BIBLIOGRAPHY: A. Zehavi, in: *Yedioth Aharonoth* (November 23, 1979); G. Shaked, *"Namer-ha-Bayit shel Ereẓ Yisrael,"* in: *Haaretz* (March 1, 1985); A. Inbari, *"Keriah le-Diyyun Sifruti be-Amos Kenan,"* in: *Prozah*, 101–102 (1988), 25–30; G. Shaked, *Ha-Sipporet ha-Ivrit*, 5 (1998), 138–144; Y. Kaniuk, *"Sefer im Re'aḥ,"* in: *Yedioth Aharonoth* (December 18, 1998); Y. Reshet, in: *Haaretz* (January 8, 1999); A. Giladi, in: *Haaretz* (November 21, 2003).

[Anat Feinberg (2nd ed.)]

KENATH (Heb. קְנָת), ancient city of the *Hauran. Kenath is possibly the city mentioned as Qen in the Egyptian Execration texts (19th/18th centuries B.C.E.), Qanu in the list of cities conquered by Thutmosis III (c. 1469 B.C.E.), and Qana in the el-Amarna Letters (no. 204). It was captured by the tribe of Manasseh and named after its leader Nobah; the Arameans later took it from Israel (Num. 32:42; I Chron. 2:23). It was probably taken by Tiglath-Pileser III during his expedition in 733/2 B.C.E. and appears in his inscriptions as [Qa-]ni-te on the border of Aram-Damascus. Kenath, called Canatha in Hellenistic-Roman times, was the site of a battle between Herod and the Nabatean Arabs and in 23 B.C.E. it was given to Herod by the emperor Augustus (Jos., Ant., 15:112; Wars, 1:366). It was a city of the Decapolis (Pliny, *Historia Naturalis* 5:18; Ptolemeus, 5:14, 18) and apparently the earliest urban unit in the Hauran. Its founding by Pompey is commemorated in its date (64 B.C.E.); its name Gabiniana recalls its building by Gabinius. In the time of Claudius coins were struck there with the images of Tyche, Athena, and Zeus. Septimus Severus made it a colony called Septimia Canotha. It continued to be an episcopal see into Byzantine times (Hierocles, *Synecdemus* 723:4; Georgius Cyprius 1075). It is the present-day Druze town of al-Qanawāt in Syria.

BIBLIOGRAPHY: Schuerer, Gesch, 2 (1907²), 166; R. Dussaud, *Topographie Historique de la Syrie* (1927), 362ff.; Dunand, in: *Syria*, 11 (1930), 272ff. (Fr.); Tadmor, in: *Kol Ereẓ Naftali*, ed. by H.Z. Hirshberg (1967), 65.

[Michael Avi-Yonah]

KENAZ, YEHOSHUA (1937–), Hebrew prose writer. Kenaz was born in Petaḥ Tikvah. He studied philosophy and Romance languages at the Hebrew University and French Literature at the Sorbonne. Kenaz worked for many years on the editorial staff of the daily *Haaretz*, and is known also for his masterly translations of French literature into Hebrew. One of Israel's most prominent prose writers, Kenaz published his first novel, *Aḥarei ha-Ḥagim* ("After the Holidays," 1987), in 1964, the story of the Weiss family in Petaḥ Tikvah of the Mandate period. Avoiding sentimentality and nostalgia, Kenaz portrays the tense, neurotic relationships between the parents and their two daughters in a dilapidated house which is indeed a metonymy for the disintegration of the family. Hatred, envy, and madness mark the atmosphere in this narrative about the first moshavah in Ereẓ Israel, with strange people, Jews and Arabs alike, frustrated passions, and unfulfilled dreams. Kenaz debunks the idealized and idealistic Zionist project, yet avoids addressing directly the traditional central themes of Hebrew writing. Neither warriors nor kibbutz members are his concern. Instead, he depicts the life of individuals against a prosaic, desolate urban setting, oscillating between the pathetic and the grotesque. Indeed, the unpoetic and the mundane fuel his poetic world. At the heart of his prose is not the heroic, successful, or thriving Israeli, but old, deranged people, losers of sorts, frustrated lovers. The "*condition humaine*" in a nutshell, set in an urban apartment house, a pattern recurring in Kenaz's prose, appears for the first time in his second novel *Ha-Ishah ha-Gedolah min ha-Ḥalomot* ("The Great Woman of the Dreams," 1973): The story of the sado-masochistic marriage of Shmulik and Malka and the unhappy relationship of Levanah and Zion is interwoven with the fates of a childless German-Jewish couple, a lonely Hungarian bachelor, and the blind, hypersensitive, and sensual Rosa. Similar in approach are *Ha-Derekh el ha-Ḥatulim* (1991; *The Way to the Cats*, 1994) and *Maḥzir Ahavot Kodmot* (1997; *Returning Lost Loves*, 2001). *The Way to the Cats* focuses on bodily decrepitude and mental deterioration as well as the loneliness of old people, primarily Yolanda Moskovich, who leaves an old age home and returns to her flat, yet cannot get rid of her paranoia and anxieties. The tragic and the comic, empathy and resentment mark the changing tone in *Returning Lost Loves*, in which, once again, several plots run in parallel. The central plot revolves around the liaison between a woman past her prime and a married man and is closely related to the story of unrequited love, rape, and murder taking place in the same building. Other episodes unfold the tortuous relationship between a father and his son, an army deserter. In 1980 *Moment Musikali* (*Musical Moment*, 1995) appeared, four stories which delineate the end of innocence and rites of manhood. Suffused with sensuality and passion, Kenaz depicts the painful process of maturing and self-awareness. Two novellas entitled *Nof im*

Sheloshah Eẓim ("Landscape with Three Trees") appeared in 2000. Undoubtedly one of Kenaz's finest accomplishments is his novel *Hitganvut Yeḥidim* (1986; *Infiltration*, 2003), the story of a platoon of recruits with minor physical disabilities during their basic training at an army camp sometime in the 1950s. Kenaz offers an impressive Israeli polyphony representing various ethnic and social groups and at the same time a rich texture of unique personal fates. This microcosmos of Israeli life reveals in an imposing, albeit disconcerting, manner the changes which have taken place in Israeli society, and in particular the shifting attitudes to the extolled paradigm of the Sabra, to politics, and to army life. Kenaz was awarded many literary prizes, including the Agnon Prize (1993) and the Bialik Prize (1995). His books have been translated into many languages, and information about translations is available at the ITHL website under www.ithl.org.il.

BIBLIOGRAPHY: G. Shaked, "*Lehit'orer min ha-Ḥalom*," in: *Siman Keriah*, 11 (1980), 119–24; Z. Shamir, in: *Maariv* (August 8, 1980); A. Balaban, "*Bein ha-Kinor la-Palmaḥ*," in: *Moznayim*, 55:4–5 (1982), 52–56; Y. Oren, "*Deyukano shel ha-Amman ke-Tiron Ẓava*," in: *Moznayim*, 60, 7 (1987), 76–78; M. Shaked, in: *Hadoar*, 66:2 (1987), 18–21; N. Amit, "*Lehitbager zeh Livgod ba-Ḥalom*," in: *Mibifnim*, 49:2 (1987), 146–55; A. Zemach, "*Bi-Shlosha Rashim*," in: *Prozah*, 103–104 (1988), 25–30; Y. Oren, "*Mi-Ymei Ẓiklag le-Hitgannevut Yeḥidim*," in: *Moznayim*, 62:5–6 (1988), 117–20; N. Calderon, "*Avner Gabai, Kazanovah*," in: *Siman Keriah*, 20 (1990), 389–93; O. Bartana, "*Ma Yadu'a Lahem she-Lo Yadu'a Lanu?*," in: *Moznayim*, 66:2 (1993), 26–30; N. Ben-Dov, "*Separtah ve-Yeladeha ha-Avudim*," in: *Alei Siaḥ*, 33 (1993), 113–19; N. Levy, *Ha-Sipporet shel Y. Kenaz* (1994); H. Herzig, *Ha-Shem ha-Perati* (1994); Y. Laor, *Ha-Heterogeniyyut Hi ha-Gehenom*," in: *Anu Kotevim Otakh Moledet* (1995), 13–49; L. Haber, "Dread and Joy in Y. Kenaz," in: *Midstream*, 42:1 (1996), 43–45; N. Levy, *Me-Reḥov ha-Even el ha-Ḥatulim: Iyyunim ba-Sipporet shel Y. Kenaz* (1997); G. Shaked, *Ha-Sipporet ha-Ivrit*, 5 (1998), 273–303; Y. Oren, "*Ha-Tofet ve-ha-Eden*," in: *Moznayim*, 75:3 (2001), 43–47; H. Shacham, "*Le-Hitpakkeaḥ mi-Ḥalom, le-Hippared mi-Ḥazon*," in: *Meḥkarei Yerushalayim be-Sifrut Ivrit*, 18 (2001), 321–39; K. Alon, in: *Alpayim*, 26 (2004), 203–12; D. Grossberg, "Y. Kenaz's Army Novel: a Time for Celebration," in: *Midstream*, 50:2 (2004), 38–39.

[Anat Feinberg (2nd ed.)]

KENESET YISRAEL (Heb. כְּנֶסֶת יִשְׂרָאֵל; "the community of Israel"), a phrase found frequently in rabbinic literature referring to the totality of the Jewish community. Largely identical with **kelal Yisrael*, it is used as the personification of the Jewish community in its dialogue with the Almighty. In modern times this title was adopted by the official Jewish community in Ereẓ Israel when it was organized as a corporate entity in 1927 (see *Israel, State of: History 1880–1948). *Keneset Yisrael* was also the name of a literary and historical annual which appeared in Warsaw, 1886–88.

KENITE (Heb. קֵינִי), a large group of nomadic clans engaged chiefly in metal working. The root *qyn* has the same meaning in cognate Semitic languages, e.g., in Arabic *qayna*, "tinsmith," "craftsman"; in Syriac and Aramaic *qyn'h*, *qyny*, "metalsmith." In the Bible the word *kayin* (*qayin*) also means a weapon made of metal, probably a spear (II Sam. 21:16); and the proper noun "Tubal-Cain, who forged all the implements of copper and iron" (Gen. 4:22) is a compound name in which the second noun indicates the trade. There is a connection between this trade and the story of *Cain who wandered from place to place and was protected by a special sign: "Therefore, if anyone kills Cain, sevenfold vengeance shall be taken on him" (Gen. 4:15). Among primitive tribes to the present day there are clans of coppersmiths and tinsmiths whom it is considered a grave offense to harm.

The Kenites came from the south: Midian, Edom, and the Arabah. Hobab (*Jethro), son of Reuel the Midianite, who aided the Israelites in the desert and served as their pathfinder (Num. 10:29–32), was also known as the Kenite (Judg. 1:16; 4:11). Enoch, son of Cain (Gen. 4:17), is also mentioned among the Midianites (Gen. 25:4; I Chron. 1:33). Balaam's prophecy about the Kenites, "Though your abode be secure, and your nest be set among cliffs" (Num. 24:21) appears to be a reference to the mountains of Midian and Edom (cf. Obad. 3–4), and Sela ("cliffs") designates perhaps the Edomite mountain-fortress Sela (today al-Saʿl near Baṣrah) around which rich copper deposits were located. The house of Rechab, which had preserved traditions of the time of the Exodus, was related to the Kenites (I Chron. 2:55), and apparently also to Ir-Nahash and Ge-Harashim (I Chron. 4:12–14), modern Khirbet Naḥās ("copper ruin," or "ruin of the copper city") in the Arabah, a copper mining center.

The Kenites were enumerated among the early peoples of Canaan, together with the Kenizzites and the Kadmonites (Gen. 15:19). Relations between the Israelites and the Kenites were good, but B. Stade and others argued for Kenite influence on Moses and the religion of Israel. This "Kenite hypothesis" (updated by Halpern and by van der Toorn) holds that YHWH was not originally the God of the Hebrews and was not even known to the Hebrews. He was originally a Kenite tribal god who became known to Moses through his Kenite father-in-law, Jethro. Moses then made YHWH known to the Hebrews, who accepted Him as their God. As observed by van der Toorn, the Kenite hypothesis nicely accounts for the absence of Yahweh from earlier pantheons, Yahweh's link with Edom (Deut. 33:2), the Kenite connection of Moses, and the Bible's positive attitude to Kenites. The major problem comes from the current scholarly view that the majority of Israelites originated in Canaan and did not trek through the desert encountering Kenites all the way as the Bible would have it. The historical role of Moses is likewise problematic. Nonetheless, the important role of the Kenites in early Israelite worship has been emphasized by the discovery of an Israelite sanctuary at *Arad. This explains the note of Judges 1:16 about the Kenite family related to Moses (according to the Septuagint descendants, this venerated family served as priests in the sanctuary). They entered the region from the "city of palm trees," which cannot here indicate Jericho, but more likely refers to Zoar or Tamar in the northern part of the Arabah. Also, Heber, the Kenite husband or clan of Jael, who was at the time of the Deborah battle in northern Ereẓ Israel near Mount Tabor belonged to the Hobab family (Judg. 4:11). It is hardly incidental that they pitched their tent at the oak (Heb. *e'lon*) in Zaanaim or Zaananim, evidently a holy tree. Their connection with early Yahwistic worship does not exclude the assumption that for a good part they made their livelihood as metal craftsmen (Judg. 5:26).

Other Kenite families evidently occupied the region in the south, centering around Arad. This is the Negev of the Kenites and the cities of the Kenites referred to in the stories from the time of David (I Sam. 27:10; 30:29). These settlements apparently included Kinah near Arad (Josh. 15:22), and possibly Kain on the border of the wilderness of Judah (15:57). In the same region were also found the Amalekites, who wandered in Edom, Sinai, and the Negev, and among whom the Kenites lived. According to the Septuagint, Judges 1:16 should read "and dwelt among the Amalekites" (MT, "among the people (*'am*)"). In view of the kindness the Kenites had shown to Israel during the Exodus (I Sam. 15:6), Saul gave them friendly warning before attacking the Amalekites.

BIBLIOGRAPHY: Abel, Geog, 1 (1933), 273; W.J.T. Phythian-Adams, *Israel in the Araba* (1934); Th. J. Meek, *Hebrew Origins* (1936), 93ff; S. Abramsky, in: *Eretz Israel*, 3 (1954), 116–24; W.F. Albright, in: CBQ, 25 (1963), 3–9 (incl. bibl.); idem, *Yahweh and the Gods of Canaan* (1968), 33–37; Aharoni, in: Land, 185, 198, 259, 298; B. Mazar, in: JNES, 24 (1965), 297–303; R. De Vaux, in: *Ereẓ Israel*, 9 (1969), 28ff. **ADD. BIBLIOGRAPHY:** B. Halpern, in: ABD, 4:17–22; K. van der Toorn, DDD, 910–19.

[Yohanan Aharoni / S.D. Sperling (2nd ed.)]

°KENNEDY, JOHN FITZGERALD (1917–1963), 35th president of the United States. John F. Kennedy's grandfathers were both sons of Irish immigrants who rose to success in Boston Democratic politics. His father, Joseph Patrick Kennedy, was a multimillionaire businessman and an early supporter of President Franklin D. Roosevelt, who in 1937 appointed him ambassador to England. Joseph Kennedy was rumored to have expressed antisemitic views, but this was untrue. In any case, his son repudiated all such opinions.

After outstanding service in the Navy during World War II, he served the U.S. House of Representatives as a Democrat for the 11th Congressional District in Massachusetts (1946–52). In 1952 Kennedy was elected to the U.S. Senate from Massachusetts and was reelected in 1958. In 1957 Kennedy proposed two bills affecting Jewish immigration, one that included the admission of Middle Eastern Jews to the United States and the other with a clause insuring nonquota status to about 10,000 Jewish refugees from the United Arab Republic. In the pamphlet *A Nation of Immigrants* (1959) he reviews the role of immigration in U.S. history.

In 1960, when he was elected president, Kennedy had the support of an estimated 80 percent of Jewish voters. As president he demonstrated friendship for Israel by tripling the amount of American financial assistance to Israel and by selling the country ground-to-air Hawk missiles in 1962 for protection against air attack. He alerted the U.S. Sixth Fleet in the Mediterranean when subversion in Jordan by the United Arab Republic threatened to undermine the stability of the entire area. He increased the shipments of military supplies when Soviet weapons sent to the Arab states appeared to be giving them arms superiority. He promised United States assistance in the development of a desalination plant to expand Israel's water and power resources.

President Kennedy launched two unsuccessful initiatives aimed at bringing peace to the Middle East. First, he sent personal letters to the heads of all the Arab governments offering the services of the United States government as an "honest broker" in bringing them together with Israel "to find an honorable and humanitarian solution to the disputes, which waste precious energies in the Middle East countries and defer the economic progress which all free peoples truly want to enjoy." He also sent emissaries to seek a solution to one of the key obstacles to peace, the refugee problem. Some of his speeches and statements on foreign policy are collected in Allan Nevins (ed.), *Strategy of Peace* (1960); J.W. Gardner (ed.) *To Turn the Tide* (1962); and E.E. Barbarash (compiler), *John F. Kennedy on Israel, Zionism, and Jewish Issues* (1965).

BIBLIOGRAPHY: A.M. Schlesinger, Jr., *A Thousand Days* (1965); T.C. Sorensen, *Kennedy* (1965); J.M. Burns, *John Kennedy: A Political Profile* (1960).

[Myer Feldman]

KENT, ALLEGRA (1938–), U.S. dancer. Kent was born in Santa Monica, California. Her mother, born in Wisznice, Poland, steered the family toward Christian Science and changed their last name from Cohen to Kent. Inspired by George Balanchine's *Night Shadow*, Kent studied with Bronislava and Irina Nijinska, and with Carmelita Maracci, and at the School of American Ballet. She joined the New York City Ballet in 1953 and was promoted to principal dancer in 1957, creating roles in such Balanchine ballets as *Ivesiana* (1954), *Agon* (1957), *Bugaku* (1963), and *Brahms-Schoenberg Quartet* (1966), as well as in *Dances at a Gathering* (1969) and *Dumbarton Oaks* (1972) for Jerome *Robbins. In 1962 she made a highly successful tour in the U.S.S.R., dancing in the Kremlin. During her nearly 30 years with the New York City Ballet, she interrupted her career three times to have children. She retired in 1981 to work as a teacher. In 1997 she published her autobiography, *Once a Dancer*.

BIBLIOGRAPHY: N. Abrahami, in: P.E. Hyman and D.D. Moore, *Jewish Women in America: An Historical Encyclopedia*, vol.1 (1997), 735–37.

KENT, ROMAN R. (1925–), Holocaust survivor and activist. Born in Lodz, Kent was the son of a textile manufacturer. He was confined to the Lodz ghetto with his family in 1939, deported to Auschwitz, transferred to Gross-Rosen and its satellite camps and Flossenberg, and liberated by the Third Army while on a death march. He immigrated to the United States in 1946, under the Orphaned Children's Quota, as a ward of the U.S. government.

Kent and his younger brother, Leon, were sent to live in Atlanta, Georgia, where Kent graduated from Henry Grady High School with honors and went on to take liberal arts courses at Emory University. He began his successful business as a merchant from the trunk of his car to sharecropper families in the boondocks. He eventually expanded his business and moved to the Empire State Building in New York City and sold houseware on the QVC Network.

An active and important leader of the Holocaust survivor movement, Kent worked on a number of major survivor events, including the *American Gathering of Jewish Holocaust Survivors in Washington, D.C., in 1983. Kent also produced a movie called *Children of the Holocaust* in 1980, which won the International Film Festival Award in New York City. The film was narrated by Academy Award-winning actress Liv Ullman.

Kent also served as a negotiator for the *Conference on Material Claims Against Germany (the Claims Conference), where he was also the treasurer and a member of the executive board. He was also chairman of the American Gathering of Jewish Holocaust Survivors, Inc., the umbrella organization for survivors in North America. He was vice president of the Jewish Foundation for the Righteous, an organization that supports non-Jews who helped save Jewish lives during the Holocaust.

As a member of the Claims Conference, Kent was one of 12 commissioners of the International Commission on Holocaust Era Insurance Claims created by President Bill Clinton. The commission is chaired by former Secretary of State Lawrence Eagleburger.

Kent was also a member of the Presidential Advisory Commission on Holocaust Assets in the United States that settled the claims of the Hungarian Gold Train suit filed by survivors against the United States government.

Kent was always known for his outspoken criticism of those who do not understand the urgent needs of impoverished Holocaust survivors living in the United States, Israel, and the rest of the world. He is concerned about monies being misdirected at a time when survivors, he says, "Need to die with dignity." He has also been a vocal and visible advocate of Holocaust and tolerance education around the world and a supporter of humanitarian causes for all.

He wrote a memoir called *Strictly Business: Ruminations from Auschwitz to Atlanta, New York and Berlin* and a children's book called *Lala: The True Story of a Boy and His Dog during the Holocaust.*

[Jeanette Friedman (2nd ed.)]

KENTNER, LOUIS (Lajos Philip, 1905–1987), British pianist and composer of Hungarian birth. Born in Karwin, Kentner entered the Budapest Royal Academy of Music at the age of six. He studied piano under Szekely and Leo *Weiner, and composition with Kodaly. After his concert debut in 1918, he started a tour throughout Europe. Kentner settled in England in 1935 and was naturalized in 1946. In 1956, he made his U.S. debut in New York. Kentner was notable for his pianistic elegance, bel canto phrasing, and comprehensive technical mastery. He was praised for his interpretation of works by Mozart, Beethoven, and Chopin. An admired exponent of Liszt, he founded the British Liszt Society and performed his works with authority, eloquence, and color. Kentner also specialized in playing Kodaly and Bartók. He gave the first Hungarian performance of Bartók's Second Piano Concerto (Budapest, 1933), the European performance of his Third in London (1945), and the British première of the Scherzo, Op. 2 in 1962. As regards British contemporary music, he played the first performances of works by Tippett, Walton, Bliss, and others. As a chamber musician, his long partnership with his brother-in-law Yehudi *Menuhin was noteworthy. His compositions include works for piano as well as songs and orchestral and chamber music. Kentner was made a Commander of the Order of the British Empire in 1978. He is the author of *Piano* (2nd ed., 1991), and a tribute to him by students and admirers (*Kentner: A Symposium*) was published in 1987.

BIBLIOGRAPHY: *Grove online*; V. Harrison, *Baker's Biographical Dictionary* (1997).

[Max Loppert / Naama Ramot (2nd ed.)]

KENTRIDGE, MORRIS (1881–1964), South African lawyer and politician. Born in Lithuania, he was the son of W. Kantrovich, minister of the Vryheid Hebrew Congregation. He joined the South African Labour Party, was elected to Parliament, and from 1920 until his retirement in 1958 represented a Johannesburg division. Kentridge boldly championed the workers' cause in the strikes of 1922 and spent some time under detention in consequence. He remained a leading representative of the Labour Party until it lost its influence after the pact with the Nationalists. In 1932 he joined Smuts' United Party and while on the government front bench helped to frame a considerable volume of progressive industrial legislation. One of the leading Jewish spokesmen in Parliament, he opposed Hertzog's anti-Jewish immigration laws of the 1930s. During the Hitler period he fought the activities of the South African pro-Nazi agitators. His memoirs, *I Recall*, were published in 1959.

[Lewis Sowden]

KENTRIDGE, SIR SYDNEY (1922–), South African and British lawyer who won international fame for his work in the human rights field. Born in Johannesburg, he was admitted to the Johannesburg Bar in 1949 and in 1965 was appointed senior counsel. He was called to the English Bar in 1977 and appointed queen's counsel in 1984. From 1981 to 1986, he served as judge of appeal in Botswana and from 1988 to 1982 he was judge of appeal of Jersey and Guernsey. In his early days at the Bar in South Africa, Kentridge appeared in a number of cases of historical and political significance, during which he represented opponents of South Africa's race laws that helped entrench white minority rule. He was a leading member of the defense team that successfully defended 30 leading political activists, including future President Nelson Mandela, against charges of treason in the 1958–61 Treason Trial. He subsequently appeared as counsel for the local community and the bishop of Johannesburg, Ambrose Reeves, at the inquiry into the shooting at Sharpeville, 1961, and for the family of Steve Biko at the inquest into his death in 1977. Further afield, he appeared for Stella Madzimabuto in both the then Rhodesia and the Privy Council in her challenge to the legality of the white minority regime of Ian Smith in Rhodesia. Widely regarded as one of the world's most eminent advocates, he was knighted in 1999 for his international human rights work over the years. Kentridge's father, Morris *Kentridge, was a long-serving Member of Parliament in the Union of South Africa, representing first the Labour Party, and after 1934 the United Party. His son is the artist William Kentridge.

[David Saks (2nd ed.)]

KENTUCKY, state in the south central United States. A receipt with a Yiddish notation surviving from 1781 reveals that the firm of Cohen and Isaacs in Richmond, Virginia, paid Daniel Boone for surveying land on its behalf in Kentucky, and other evidence of early Jewish involvement in the area exists as well. The first Jewish settlers in Kentucky arrived at the very beginning of the 19th century, but they were unable to maintain a Jewish life on the frontier. The Baltimore-born John Jacob was apparently resident near Louisville as early as 1802, and Benjamin *Gratz, scion of the famous Philadelphia merchant family, settled in Lexington in 1819; both married gentile women not once, but twice.

Jewish communal life began in Kentucky in the 1830s, first in *Louisville and a little later elsewhere. Communal organizations appeared in Owensboro and Paducah, both on the Ohio River, in the late 1850s, and in Lexington just after the Civil War. By the 1870s there were lodges of B'nai B'rith in Louisville, Owensboro, Paducah, and Lexington. In 1880, four synagogue buildings stood in Louisville, one in Owensboro, one in Paducah, and one in Henderson, and the Jewish population of Kentucky was reported to be 3,600, with 2,500 Jews in Louisville, 213 in Owensboro, 203 in Paducah, 140 in Lexington, and the rest in other small towns. By the turn of the 19th century, aside from Congregation Adas Israel in Henderson, Congregation Adath Israel in Owensboro, Temple Israel in Paducah, and a variety of Jewish institutions in Louisville, there was a multi-purpose Spinoza Society in Lexington (founded 1873) as well as Jewish social clubs in Henderson (the Harmony club, founded 1873), Owensboro (the Standard Club, founded 1889), Shelbyville (the Jewish Literary and Social Club, founded 1895), and Paducah (the Standard Club, founded 1903).

East European Jews arriving in Kentucky around the turn of the 19th century reinforced existing communities and also established additional Jewish centers. These immigrants founded Congregation Agudath Achim in Ashland in 1896, the United Hebrew Congregation in Newport in 1897, and congregations in Covington, Hopkinsville, and Harlan in the early

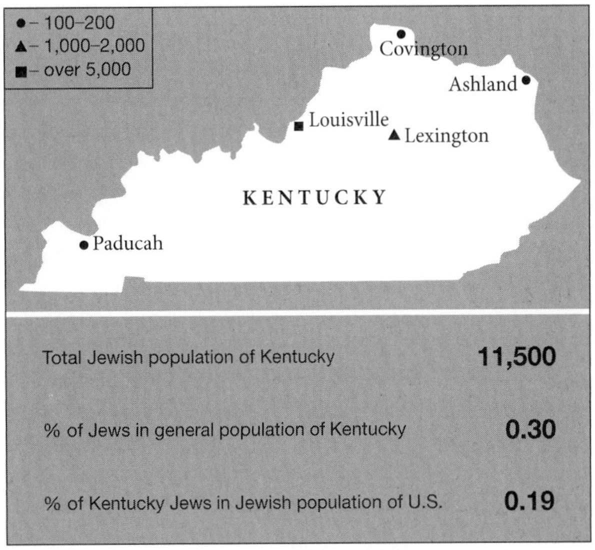

Jewish communities in Kentucky. Population figures for 2001.

part of the 20th century. By the time of World War I, Lexington had two congregations: the Reform Adath Israel (founded 1904) and the Orthodox Ohavay Zion (founded 1912).

Immigrants established new ethnic and cultural institutions in several small towns as well. In Newport, for example, the Jewish community had created a Free Hebrew School offering programs for both children and adults as early as 1907. By that year, Newport's Jews also were supporting a branch of the Zionist Po'alei Zion and a Jewish Protective League, demanding better police protection for their community. In Lexington, the poet Israel Jacob *Schwartz (1885–1971) completed his epic Yiddish poem cycle *Kentucky* in 1922. In 1927, Kentucky's Jewish population was reported to be 19,500, with 12,500 Jews in Louisville and triple-digit communities in Ashland, Covington, Lexington, Newport, and Paducah. Henderson, Hopkinsville, Owensboro, and the area around Harlan each was home to between 65 and 90 Jewish individuals.

Throughout the 19th century and into the 20th, Jews were involved in civic affairs not only in Louisville, but also elsewhere. For example, Abraham *Jonas (1801–1864), brother of Joseph *Jonas, settled in Williamstown in 1827 and was elected several times to the state legislature. Meyer Weil (1830–91) served as mayor of Paducah between 1871 and 1881, and at about the same time the presiding officers of both chambers of the Lexington town council were Jews. Morris Weintraub of Newport (1909–96) was speaker of the Kentucky House of Representatives in the 1950s.

In the second half of the 20th century, Kentucky's Jewish population declined and, as elsewhere in the U.S., many small-town Jewish communities deteriorated. By the end of the century, fully functioning congregations and communal institutions could be found only in Louisville and Lexington, although tiny congregations holding occasional services still existed in Owensboro and Paducah. Kentucky's Jewish population was reported as 11,000 in 1960, 13,000 in 1984, and 11,500 at the turn of the 20th century.

BIBLIOGRAPHY: L.S. Weissbach, *The Synagogues of Kentucky: Architecture and History* (1995); idem, "Kentucky's Jewish History in National Perspective: The Era of Mass Migration," in: *The Filson Club Quarterly*, 69 (July 1995), 255–74; idem, "Stability and Mobility in the Small Jewish Community: Examples from Kentucky History," in: *American Jewish History*, 79 (Spring 1990), 358–60; L.N. Dembitz, "Jewish Beginnings in Kentucky" in *Publications of the American Jewish Historical Society*, 1 (1898), 99–100.

[Lee Shai Weissbach (2nd ed.)]

KENYA. Jewish settlement in East Africa started at the turn of the 20th century, when the first Jewish families settled in Nairobi, then a labor camp and minor administrative center of the Uganda Railways. The area proposed to Herzl for Jewish settlement by the British colonial secretary Joseph Chamberlain in 1903 (the "*Uganda Scheme") is in present-day Kenya. By 1913 there were 20 Jewish families in Nairobi and the first synagogue was built. World War II brought in its wake an influx of Jewish immigrants from Europe, many of them former inmates of Nazi camps. By 1945 the Jewish community in Kenya numbered about 150 families, the majority settling in Nairobi. Most Jews engaged in commerce or the free professions, and some were absorbed in the colonial administration. A landmark in the community's history was the arrival from Palestine in March 1947 of a trainload of detainees, members of the *Irgun Ẓeva'i Le'ummi and *Loḥamei Ḥerut Israel, who were placed in a detention camp in Gilgil. The Jewish community greatly assisted in improving their conditions. The new synagogue of the community, consecrated in 1955, is located in downtown Nairobi. By 1957 the community had reached a peak membership of 165 families. The president of the Board of Kenya Jewry, Israel Somen, was elected Nairobi's mayor. From 1957 the community decreased steadily and in 1968 totaled 113 families. The Nairobi congregation maintained a full-time rabbi who was also responsible for Jewish education. In 1968 the community maintained a Hebrew Aid Society and the *ḥevra kaddisha* ("burial society"). It had a Zionist organization from 1909, and a WIZO branch from 1944. In the early 21st century the community numbered around 400, with a Chabad rabbi officiating at the Nairobi synagogue.

[Ze'ev Levin]

Relations with Israel

From its independence, at the end of 1963, the government of Kenya and its leader Jomo Kenyatta displayed a friendly attitude toward Israel. Full diplomatic relations were established between the two countries. Israel maintains an embassy in Nairobi, while Kenya's diplomatic mission in Israel is handled by a nonresident ambassador. In 1966 the two countries signed an agreement for technical and scientific cooperation. Israel extended aid in the establishment, direction, and teaching of the Machakos School for Social Workers up to the stage at which the Kenyan government could take it over. Kenyan trainees participated in courses in Israel on agriculture, labor and cooperation, community development, and training of military officers and air cadets. In 1969 Israel exported $2,947,000 to Kenya and imported $793,000 worth of goods. Israel corporations expended $14,800,000 on highways, water-supply projects, housing, and office buildings through 1969. They also invested in small-scale industry, and El Al was a partner in the Hilton Hotel in Nairobi. Kenya has acted as a moderating factor in Israel issues within African forums.

Though Kenya broke off relations with Israel after the Yom Kippur War of 1973, trainees continued arriving, and during the Entebbe rescue operation in 1976, the Kenyan government allowed Israeli planes to refuel in its territory. Relations were resumed in 1988. In 2002 terrorists bombed the Israeli-owned Paradise Hotel in Kikambala, killing 15, and then fired rockets at an El-Al plane taking off from Mombassa International Airport. The hotel was reopened in 2004 after a joint Kenyan-Israeli cleanup effort

[Yoav Biran]

BIBLIOGRAPHY: J. Carlebach, *The Jews of Nairobi 1903–1962* (1962), incl. bibl. See also bibliography on *Uganda Scheme.

°**KENYON, DAME KATHLEEN MARY** (1906–1978), British archaeologist; daughter of biblical scholar and director of the British Museum, Sir Frederic Kenyon. Early in her career she took part in excavations at Zimbabwe (1929), St Albans/Verulamium (1930–35), and Samaria (1931–34). From 1935 to 1951 she directed excavations at various Roman sites in England and at Sabratha, Tripolitania (1948–49, 1951). At the University of London Institute of Archaeology Kathleen Kenyon served as secretary (1935–48), acting director (1942–46), and lecturer in Palestinian archaeology (1948–62). While acting as director of the British School of Archaeology in Jerusalem (1951–66), she conducted excavations at Jericho (1952–58) and Jerusalem (1961–67). W.G. Dever summed up her character as follows: "her gruff manner often obscured her gentler personal qualities, and she showed obvious impatience with excavators who did not possess an immediate and intuitive grasp of stratigraphical complexities, in which she reveled and excelled." From 1962 she was principal of St. Hugh's College, Oxford. Her publications include *Beginning in Archaeology* (2nd rev. ed. 1953); *Digging up Jericho* (1957); *Samaria-Sebaste*, 3 vols. (with J.W. and G.M. Crowfoot; 1942–57); *Excavations at Jericho*, 1 (1960); *Archaeology in the Holy Land* (1965²); *Jerusalem. Excavating 3000 Years of History* (1967); and *Digging up Jerusalem* (1974). Her major excavations remained largely unpublished until after her death, with the work being undertaken by T. Holland, A.D. Tushingham, H. Franken, M. Steiner, K. Prag, and others.

ADD. BIBLIOGRAPHY: P.R.S. Moorey, "Kathleen Kenyon and Palestinian Archaeology," in: PEQ, 111 (1979), 3–10; P.R.S. Moorey and P.J. Parr (eds.), *Archaeology in the Levant: Essays for Kathleen Kenyon* (1985); G.I. Davies, "British Archaeologists," in: *Benchmarks in Time and Culture: An Introduction to Palestinian Archaeology* (1988), 37–62; S. Gibson, "British Archaeological Institutions in Mandatory Palestine, 1917–1948," in: PEQ, 131 (1999), 115–43, esp. note 25; W.G. Dever, "Kathleen Kenyon (1906–1978)," in G.M. Cohen and M.S.

Joukowsky (eds.), *Breaking Ground: Pioneering Women Archaeologists* (2004), 525–53.

[Michael Avi-Yonah / Shimon Gibson (2nd ed.)]

KERAK or **CHARAX**, the place to which the Jews under Judah Maccabee in his expedition to Gilead advanced after their victory at Caspin (II Macc. 12ff. as Charax). It was located 750 stadia (c. 100 mi.) from Caspin and while inhabited by the Jews was known as Tubieni (II Macc. 12:17). A land called Tob appears in the list of cities conquered by Thutmosis III and in the Bible in connection with Jephthah (Judg. 11:3, 5) and as allies of the Ammonites (II Sam. 10:6, 8). It is identified with the region around al-Ṭayyiba, between Bostra and Edrain in the Bashan in northern Transjordan. In the vicinity is the village of al-Karak, a name which corresponds to the Greek name Charax (meaning "fortification"). The distance from Kerak to Caspin is only half the distance mentioned in II Maccabees, but the text does not necessarily refer to a straight line.

BIBLIOGRAPHY: F.M. Abel, *Les Livres des Maccabées* (1948), index, s.v. *Charax*.

[Michael Avi-Yonah]

KERCH (in antiquity, **Panticapaeum**), port at the eastern extremity of Crimea, Ukraine. A Jewish settlement appears to have existed on this spot during the period of the independent kingdom of Bosphorus (fifth century B.C.E.) but the earliest extant evidence dates from the time that the town was under the dominion of the Roman Empire. A Greek inscription of 81 C.E. concerning the liberation of a Jewish slave reveals that a Jewish community existed in the town at that period and that there was also a synagogue. Non-Jewish inscriptions belonging to the first centuries of the Christian era bear numerous Jewish symbols. During the second half of the ninth century the patriarch Photius wrote to Archbishop Antony of Kerch thanking him for his efforts to convert the Jews of the city. In his letter to *Ḥisdai ibn Shaprut the *Khazar king Joseph mentions Kark (Kerch) among the cities of his kingdom, and it may be assumed that the Jewish community flourished there during the eighth and ninth centuries under the Khazar kings, who became converts to Judaism. As a result of the wars between the Khazars and the Russians during the second half of the tenth century and the wars between the Russians and the Greeks at the close of the 11th century, the Jews abandoned Kerch, so that when *Pethahiah of Regensburg visited the city in 1175 he found a community of *Karaites only.

During the 17th century the Turks built a fortress in the city and a site was granted to the Karaites for a cemetery. After the city had been captured by the Russians in 1771, a new community of local and Russian Jews was established but it was destroyed during the Crimean War (1854–56). After a number of years, the Jewish settlement was reconstituted, and in 1897 numbered 4,774 persons (14% of the city's population), including *Krimchaks and Karaites. Most of them earned their livelihood in the dried fish and salt industries and in the oil refineries, but also in petty trade and crafts. There were several synagogues in Kerch, including one built in the 1830s, another in 1875, a separate Krimchak synagogue, and a Karaite one. In 1859 the *talmud torah* had 160 pupils, and there were schools for boys and girls, and a number of charitable institutions. On July 31, 1905, several Kerch Jews were killed in a pogrom; the Jews there organized *self-defense. There were 3,067 Jews in Kerch (8.9% of the city's population) in 1926, and their numbers had risen by 1939 to 5,573 (total population 104,443), including about 500 Krimchaks. A few Jewish schools were probably opened in the 1920s. The Germans occupied Kerch on November 16, 1941. On December 1–3 they killed about 2,500 Jews, and the rest of them were murdered by the end of the month. On December 30, 1941, the town was taken by the Soviet army, but by May 23, 1942, it was retaken by the Germans, who killed the few remaining Jews, mostly Krimchaks. Together some 7,000 Jews from Kerch and surroundings were murdered. The city was liberated on April 11, 1944. In 1970 the Jewish population of Kerch was estimated at about 5,000, but there was no organized religious life. Most left in the mass emigration of the 1990s.

BIBLIOGRAPHY: A. Tcherikower, *Ha-Yehudim ve-ha-Yevanim ba-Tekufah ha-Hellenistit* (1963), 271, 281; B. Dinur, *Yisrael ba-Golah*, 1 (1962), index; D.M. Dunlop, *History of the Jewish Khazars* (1967), index; I. Ben-Zvi, *The Exiled and the Redeemed* (1967), 109–111; S.M. Schwarz, *The Jews in the Soviet Union* (1951), index; M. Osherovich, *Shtet un Shtetlekh in Ukraine*, 1 (1948), 241–51.

[Shmuel Spector (2nd ed.)]

KEREM ḤEMED (Heb. כֶּרֶם חֶמֶד; "vineyard of delight"), Hebrew annual of the Galician *Haskalah. Published in Vienna, Prague, and Berlin from 1833 to 1856, *Kerem Ḥemed* served as a central forum for Eastern and Western Jewish scholars and authors. The publisher and nominal editor, Samuel Leib *Goldenberg, was a prominent Galician *maskil* who founded it to take the place of **Bikkurei ha-Ittim*, which ceased publication in 1831. *Kerem Ḥemed* differed from its predecessor in that it did not print *belles lettres* and was concerned mainly with scholarly research in Judaism and Jewish literature. In accordance with a literary convention in 18th-century Italy and Germany, the studies were published in the form of letters exchanged by scholars in Eastern Europe (mainly Galicia) and those in the West (first Italy and then other countries). In addition to the talmudic and medieval literary studies, editions of ancient manuscripts and treatises were published with notes and prefaces. The annual reflected Jewish preoccupations during the first half of the 19th century, namely the various facets of the Haskalah: humanistic and scientific studies, revival of the Hebrew language, and opposition to Ḥasidism and to mystical movements generally. *Kerem Ḥemed* also published Samuel David *Luzzatto's criticism of medieval Jewish rationalism (Maimonides, Abraham ibn Ezra) and his commendation of Rashi's conservative and traditional approach.

Kerem Ḥemed published the first works of the philosopher Nachman *Krochmal (mostly unsigned or under a pseudonym), the anti-ḥasidic essays of Josef *Perl and Isaac

*Erter, and the controversy between Tobias *Feder and Jakob Samuel *Bick regarding the use of Yiddish, the first such controversy to be carried on in Hebrew. The acting editor of the third and subsequent volumes was Solomon Judah *Rapoport, who, in addition to his studies and commentaries, annotated the works of others. The number of contributors grew from year to year and included writers from Russia, Germany, Hungary and in the last annuals, such figures as L. Zunz, A. Geiger, and the astronomers H.Z. Slonimsky and H.M. Pineles. After Goldenberg's death publication of the annuals ceased until it was revived by Senior Sachs who published the last two annuals in a style similar to their predecessors. Altogether nine volumes appeared, seven edited by Goldenberg and Rapoport, and two by Sachs. An index to all the volumes appears in the first part of *Die hebraische Publizistik in Wien* (1930), compiled by B. Wachstein whose preface to the index includes an extensive monograph on *Kerem Ḥemed.*

BIBLIOGRAPHY: Klausner, Sifrut, 2 (1952^2), 37f.

[Getzel Kressel]

KEREN HAYESOD (Palestine Foundation Fund), the financial arm of the *World Zionist Organization, founded at the Zionist conference held in London in July 1920. Two basic views were expressed on the problem of how the World Zionist Organization should finance its work in Palestine after the important political gains made at the end of World War I. One group favored the establishment of a company run on banking lines to promote undertakings solely on a business basis. The other emphasized the need to preserve the pioneering character of the Zionist effort by mobilizing national capital through donations from the Jewish masses. There was also a proposal, which won little support, to float a national loan. The conference adopted a compromise combining the first and second proposals. The Keren Hayesod was to appeal to Zionists and non-Zionists alike for funds to finance on a nonprofit basis immigration and colonization in Palestine in order to lay the foundations of the Jewish National Home, as well as to encourage business enterprise in close cooperation with private capital. Contributions were to constitute an annual voluntary tax, with a certain minimum level.

Keren Hayesod was registered on March 23, 1921, as a British limited company. Its members (limited to no more than 50), together with the chairman of the board of directors, were chosen by the executive of the Zionist Organization. The head office was in London until 1926 when it was transferred to Jerusalem. When the enlarged *Jewish Agency for Palestine was founded in 1929, with equal representation for non-Zionists, Keren Hayesod continued to be the main instrument for financing the Zionist budget. From 1925, the fund operated in the United States as the United Palestine Appeal (which was a partnership of Keren Hayesod and the Jewish National Fund) which combined in 1939 with the American Jewish *Joint Distribution Committee and the National Refugee Service to form the *United Jewish Appeal. The UJA operates in the United States, while the Keren Hayesod head office in Jerusalem coordinates operations in other countries including the State of Israel, where it is a joint fund of the Keren Hayesod and JNF The Keren Hayesod has cooperated with the *Jewish National Fund, *Youth Aliyah, constructive funds associated with Zionist parties, and other officially Zionist-connected institutions. In 1956 it was incorporated in Israel under the Keren Hayesod Law adopted by the *Knesset.

Keren Hayesod and the United Jewish Appeal in the United States are based mainly on the work of volunteers. In almost every country with a Jewish population there is a central committee to collect contributions. There is also a committee in each city with a large Jewish community, as well as divisions for business, trade, professional, and women's groups. In Belgium and Switzerland there are central committees for each language section of the population. The chairman of Keren Hayesod is responsible for its operations in all countries except the United States. There are departments for Latin America, the English speaking countries, and Europe, as well as for special projects in Israel, wills and legacies, information, reception of guests, administration and finance.

The emergency campaign initiated just before the Six-Day War, 1967, increased twelvefold Keren Hayesod's normal annual income from countries other than the United States. This was achieved by an increase in both the size of individual contributions and the number of donors, which rose from 200,000 to 400,000. The income rose from $15m in 1966 to $150m in 1967. A second emergency campaign in 1968 raised $42,300,000 in cash and $13,200,000 in additional pledges.(See Table: Keren Hayesod.)

Among the founders of Keren Hayesod were Chaim *Weizmann, Aharon Barth, and Isaac *Naidich. The first directors were Berthold *Feiwel (also managing director), George Halpern, Vladimir *Jabotinsky (also director of propaganda), Shelomoh *Kaplansky, Shemaryahu *Levin, Isaac Naidich, Israel M. *Sieff (later Lord Sieff) and Hillel Zlatapolsky. When the head office of Keren Hayesod was moved to Jerusalem in 1926 the managing directors were Arthur *Hantke and Leib *Jaffe (who was killed in March 1948 by a bomb explosion in the Jewish Agency courtyard), Kurt *Blumenfeld joined them in 1934. Since the establishment of the State of Israel, the following served as chairmen: Arthur Hantke, Zvi Hermann, Eliahu *Dobkin, Israel *Goldstein and Ezra *Shapiro. Administrative heads were Leo *Hermann, as secretary-general, who was succeeded by Yehudah *Yaari. M. Ussoskin, and Shimshon Y. Kreutner (from 1968) were directors-general. Treasurers included Abraham Ulitzer and Moshe Ussoskin.

Funds collected through the Keren Hayesod United Israel Appeal (the second half of the name was adopted in 1948 to cover united operations of primary Zionist funds) have helped to establish and develop 820 villages and towns in Israel since 1921, and to help finance such important enterprises as the General Mortgage Bank, Israel Land Development Corporation, Mekorot Water Company, Rassco (Rural and Suburban Settlement Company), Solel Boneh (the Histadrut's building and contracting company), the Palestine (Israel) Electric

Corporation, the Palestine Potash Works (Dead Sea Works), the Anglo-Palestine Bank (now Bank Leumi), Amidar Housing Corporation, Zim Navigation Company, El Al Airlines, and many others.

[Israel Goldstein]

Later Developments

In the early 1990s Keren Hayesod achieved unprecedented results from its fund-raising campaigns in 47 countries (and 90 cities) on five continents. With no increase in staff, and citing both the Exodus of Russian Jews to Israel and above all the Gulf War and Scud attacks on Israel, it was able to raise in 1990/91 some quarter of a billion dollars of which 201 million were transferred to the Jewish Agency, mainly for immigration and absorption purposes. The massive flow of Russian Jews to Israel, coupled with the dramatic rescue of Ethiopian Jews in Operation Solomon (May 1991), captured the imagination of the contributors and their leaders were able to capitalize on tens of thousands of volunteers, recruited and trained over the years by Keren Hayesod staff from Jerusalem, and its many emissaries overseas.

But the great euphoria of 1990–1991 soon waned and the campaign results showed a drop in income. The reasons for this were not hard to discern. From 1993, and mainly after the signing of the Oslo Agreement between Israel and the PLO, and the Israel-Jordan Peace Treaty, the impression was created that Israel was now launched on the road to peace, and there was less need for Jewish contributions. As Israel's economy showed signs of healthy growth, and highly positive and praising articles appeared in the world's media, more contributors wondered if the time had not come to deal with the plight of their own communities.

As the process of assimilation and intermarriage continued unabated, stronger voices were heard in the Diaspora communities calling for the need to retain more funds at home for local needs, mainly in the area of education and welfare, rather than to send them to Israel, some of whose leaders were openly saying there was no longer need for them. A debate erupted in Israel in 1993 between Deputy Foreign Minister Yossi Beilin, who called on Jews to strengthen their communities and Prime Minister Rabin who rejected this approach calling on Jews to continue to help Israel deal with the massive immigration.

The drama of the immigration also waned, when the

Keren Hayesod United Israel Appeal, 1920–1970

	1920–1948	1948–1970
Immigration and Absorption	487,000 immigrants, including 28,700 children brought to Palestine by Youth Aliyah, settled and absorbed in the country.	1,400,000 immigrants, including 95,800 children brought to Israel by Youth Aliyah. (Many of the children came with parents and Youth Aliyah accepted them as its wards.)
Agricultural Settlement. Development Towns and Housing	257 agricultural settlements were established with a population of 90,000 working some 700,000 dunams (175,000 acres) of land.	525 new agricultural settlements and 27 development towns built; 175,000 new housing units provided permanent homes for nearly 1,400,000 new immigrants
Total Funds Raised	$ 143,000,000 – 70% from the United States through United Jewish Appeal. – 30% from other countries through Keren Hayesod.	$ 1,990,000,000 – 65% from the United States through United Jewish Appeal – 35% from 71 other countries through Keren Hayesod.
Total expenditures of the Jewish Agency 1948–1970	Immigration and Absorption	$573,900,000
	Health Services	$77,100,000
	Education	$74,600,000
	Youth Aliyah	$156,200,000
	Immigrant Housing	$432,500,000
	Agricultural Settlement	$945,800,000
	Educational Activities	$294,200,000
	Overseas Operations	$160,500,000
	Various Activities	$301,000,000
	Total	$3,015,800,000
Grand Total Funds Raised	1920–1948	$143,000,000
	1948–1970	$1,990,000,000
	Total	$2,133,000,000[1]

1. The balance of the expenditures not covered by the income of Keren Hayesod United Israel Appeal and the United Jewish Appeal came from additional sources, such as German reparations and heirless property, collections on account of the repayment of loans from Jewish Agency-Keren Hayesod funds; the realization of property; special Youth Aliyah campaigns; participation by the Government of Israel in agricultural settlement and long and medium term loans.

numbers settled into 65,000–75,000 a year. It was difficult to keep the momentum and the interest alive. By 1991 the funds Keren Hayesod transferred to Jerusalem were 185 million dollars. A year later it dropped to 150 and by 1995, 115 million dollars.

Keren Heyesod began to focus attention on new sources of income, focusing mainly on wills and bequests, which yielded a growing income. One such bequest in Europe was worth over 100 million German marks. Efforts were also directed at retaining the coming generation and maintaining a high level of educational, motivational, and inspirational programs centering on visits to Israel and to Jewish communities in the former Soviet Union. In the countries where it operates, Keren Hayesod continues to be a major link between Israel and the Diaspora.

By the turn of the century, in addition to helping create over 800 settlements in Israel, Keren Hayesod had helped to rehabilitate 90 disadvantaged neighborhoods and developments towns through *Project Renewal, to educate 300,000 youngsters in Youth Aliyah, and to bring 175,000 young people to Israel in "Israel Experience" programs.

[Meron Medzini (2nd ed.)]

BIBLIOGRAPHY: Keren Hayesod, *Memorandum and Articles of Association* (1921), *Constitution and Palestine Work* (1922), *Jewish Fund* (1921), *Keren Hayesod Book* (1921), *Reports to the Zionist Congresses* (1921–), *Facts and Figures on Israel Population and Economy* (1950), *A Decade of Freedom* (1958); I. Klinov, *Will and Fulfilment: Keren Hayesod Twenty-Five Years Old* (1946); A. Ulitzur, *Foundations: A Survey of 25 Years of Activity of the Palestine Foundation Fund Keren Hayesod* (1947); M.M. Berman, *The Bridge to Life: A Saga of Keren Hayesod 1920–1970* (1971).

KERET, ETGAR (1967–), Israeli author. Keret, often referred to as Israel's hippest young artist, is one of the most popular writers among Israeli youth. Critic Nissim Calderon wrote that Keret is "the Amos Oz of his generation." Keret's books have all been bestsellers and each of them was awarded the Platinum Prize for selling more than 40,000 copies. Born in Tel Aviv, Keret published his first collection of 56 short stories, *Ẓinorot* ("Pipelines"), in 1992, followed two years later by *Ga'aguai le-Kissinger*, which was enthusiastically received by critics and readers alike. The mini-narratives, often only two or three pages long, are compact stories, postmodernistic texts in the fashion of video-clips, depicting an episode, portraying a certain situation, opening thereby a window on a surreal world and on strange inner lives. As in the work of the American writer Raymond Carver, an important influence on many young writers in Israel, the unexpected often springs from what seems to be the common and everyday. In the spirit of postmodernism, there is no dichotomy between low and high, pop and classic culture, real and imaginary; comic moments coalesce with melancholy ones, sentimental episodes with serious reflections and the grotesque. Having been deserted by his girlfriend, Meir meets four dwarfs who try to help him overcome his sorrow; a young man has to prove to his girlfriend that he really loves her by literally tearing his heart out; Israeli soldiers discover that the terrorists who attacked them were just a bunch of Hebrew-speaking rabbits. Nonsense conceals biting criticism. Indeed, the argument that Keret is one of the seminal voices of a "private generation" in Hebrew literature is misleading: Politics come in through the back door, as it were, between the lines, or, as in the case of "Cocked and Locked" (included in E. Ben Ezer's English anthology *Sleepwalkers*, 1999) with a cynical twist. Like Orly *Castel-Bloom, Keret too plays with language, probes metaphors and clichés, underlines the inadequacy of words and at times creates his own vocabulary. In 1996 Keret published his first "Comics" (with Rutu Modan) entitled *Lo Banu Lehenot*, followed a year later by *Simte'ot ha-Za'am* ("Streets of Rage"; with illustrator Asaf Hanuka). *Ha-Kaytana shel Kneller* ("Kneller's Happy Campers") appeared in 1998, containing a novella and stories. Ḥayyim, the anti-hero of the novella, commits suicide and lives on in a world remarkably similar to the real one, with one major difference: the ability to perform miracles. In the surreal world, he meets his beloved Desirée as well as the Messiah, and although the dream of happiness is soon shattered, he remains optimistic. *Anihu*, a collection of stories, followed in 2004, and the same year also saw the publication of *Pizzeria Kamikaze*, a comics version (with illustrations by Asaf Hanuka) of Keret's bestselling novella *Kneller's Happy Campers*. Keret's creative output does not restrict itself to comics and prose, it includes newspaper columns, a book for children, films and comedy. Keret, whose movie *Skin Deep* won the Israeli Oscar as well as first prize at several international film festivals, lectures at Tel Aviv University Film School and was invited to Berlin in winter 2003 as Samuel Fischer Guest Professor. He received the Prime Minister's Prize for literature and the Ministry of Culture Cinema Prize. His works have been translated into many languages. Available in English translation are *Selected Stories* (1998); *How to Make a Good Script Great* (1996); *Jetlag* (1998); *Kneller's Happy Campers* (2001); *Anihu* (2004); as well as the collection *Gaza Blues* with Palestinian author Samir el-Youssef (2004), and the children's book *Dad Runs Away with the Circus* (2004). For further information about translations see the ITHL website at www.ithl.org.il.

BIBLIOGRAPHY: N. Govrin, "*Ha-Shoah ba-Sifrut ha-Ivrit shel ha-Dor ha-Ẓa'ir*," in: *Ẓafon*, 3 (1995), 151–160; L. Chudnovski, "*Ha-Im Kayyamim Ḥorim Sheḥorim*," in: *Iton* 77:222–223 (1998), 24–29; A. Mendelson-Maoz, "*Situaẓiyot Kiẓoniyyot be-Yeẓirotehem shel Castel-Bloom ve-Keret*," in: *Dappim le-Meḥkar be-Sifrut*, 11 (1998), 269–295; I. Zivoni, "*Ki mi-Komiks Bata ve-el Komiks Tashuv*," in: *Iton* 77:234–235 (1999), 24–26; M. Shilgi, *Keri'at Etgar* (2002); H. Navon, "*Iyyun Teologi be-Sippur shel Etgar Keret*," in: *Alon Shevut*, 19 (2004), 79–92.

[Anat Feinberg (2nd ed.)]

KERI'AH (Heb. קְרִיעָה), rending of the garments as a sign of grief. *Keri'ah* is a traditional Jewish mourning custom, based on Genesis 37:34 and Job 1:20. At the death of one of the seven relatives for whom mourning is decreed (father, mother, children (at least 30 days old), brother (a half-brother), sister (a half-sister), husband, wife), a rent, at least four inches long, is made in the lapel of an outer garment prior to the funeral. For parents, the *keri'ah* is made in all clothes, save the undershirt. For parents, the *keri'ah* is made on the left side; for other relatives, on the right. A member of the **ḥevra kaddisha* usually makes the incision with a knife and the mourner tears it to the required length and pronounces the blessing: "Blessed be Thou, O Lord, the righteous Judge." According to the Talmud (MK 25a) *keri'ah* should be done at the moment of death. Present practice is to defer *keri'ah* until just before the funeral service or prior to interment. It should be performed in a standing position. The *keri'ah* is exposed during the whole mourning period. It may, however, be roughly stitched together after the "seven-day mourning period" and completely sewn up after 30 days. When mourning for parents, it may be stitched only after 30 days and may never be sewn up. Women may stitch it together immediately. During *ḥol ha-mo'ed* (intermediate festival days) the *keri'ah* rite is delayed and is performed after the festival, except in many communities in the case of mourning for parents. The custom is also practiced on seeing a Torah Scroll destroyed by fire. In talmudic times, it was customary to express grief by *keri'ah* at the death of the **nasi* (president of the Sanhedrin), or of a great scholar (MK 22b), or upon seeing Jerusalem and the temple mount in ruins. In the U.S. Conservative and Reform practice a torn black ribbon can be worn on the lapel for 30 days. Some Orthodox Jews follow this custom, others tear a tie, and some adhere to the tradition as above.

BIBLIOGRAPHY: Sh. Ar., YD 340; Maim. Yad, Evel, 8–90; Eisenstein, Dinim, 376; H. Rabinowicz, *Guide to Life* (1964), 34–37.

KERITOT (Heb. כְּרִיתוֹת), tractate of the order *Kodashim* in the Mishnah, Tosefta, and Babylonian Talmud, which derives its name from the 36 sins for which the Torah gives the punishment of **karet*. The Mishnah consists of six chapters dealing with the conditions that necessitate the bringing of the sin-offering (*ḥattat*) or a guilt offering (*asham*, or *asham talui*) to be brought only in case of the inadvertent or doubtful commission of sins which if committed intentionally would entail *karet*. After enumerating these sins in its first Mishnah, the rest of the first chapter deals with the unusual "sin offering" required of women after childbirth (Lev. 12:6). The second chapter lays down the rules stating exactly who is obliged to bring the respective offerings, and specifies if one or more offerings must be brought when there has been manifold transgression. The third chapter gives the rules applicable to the inadvertent commission of a sin requiring a sin offering. The fourth chapter deals in detail with cases of doubtful commission of a sin requiring a guilt offering. The fifth chapter first defines and classifies the types of forbidden blood which if consumed require a sin offering, and then discusses the doubtful commission of sacrilege. The sixth chapter deals with the question of what is to happen to the animal designated as a sacrifice if, before or after it has been slaughtered, it becomes clear that no sin was committed. The tractate ends with a discussion as to who has priority of honor, father or mother, and concludes that the honor due to one's teacher has priority over that to one's father.

The statement that *Keritot* is according to the opinion of R. Akiva (Ker. 3b: but see Sanh. 65a) does not apply to the entire tractate (Albeck, *Mavo la-Mishnah* (1959) 87), as various strata can be discerned there, but refers to the fact that it contains the rulings of R. Akiva, as recorded by his disciple Meir (Epstein, *Tanna'im*, 82). Thus Albeck claims that Mishnah 2:6 is a gloss to Mishnah 2:4 taken from other tannaitic sources and placed at the end of the chapter. Mishnah 6:2, 3 was taken from the *mishnayot* of Judah b. Ilai. The order of the paragraphs in the Tosefta does not correspond fully to that in the Mishnah. Chapter 3 contains a group of laws each of which begins with the word *ḥatikhah* ("a piece"). An interesting passage debates the role of the *asham talui* (a sacrifice for uncertain sins) which some rabbis call *asham ḥasidim* ("guilt offering of the pious"), holding that its purpose is to atone for every unknown sin. As an extreme example the Tosefta cites the case of Bava b. Buta who offered this sacrifice every day. Other rabbis, however, limit it to a certain category of grave sins. The Tosefta concludes with an aggadic saying to the effect that the patriarchs were equal to one another, as was Aaron to Moses and Joshua to Caleb.

The language of *Keritot* in terminology, style, and grammar resembles that of **Nedarim*,**Nazir*, **Temurah*, and **Me'ilah*, their language representing a dialect different from the rest of the Talmud and close to the language of the Targum (J.N. Epstein, *Dikduk Aramit Bavlit* (1960), 14–16). *Keritot* did not pass through the stages of development of the other tractates since it was not (like the other above-mentioned tractates) taught in the academies of the *geonim* (see *Halakhot Pesukot* Mss. Adler no. 2639; A. Marmorstein, in: MGWJ, 67 (1923), 134f.). Despite this, it resembles other tractates in content, in names of its *amoraim*, and in its internal construction (see A. Weiss, *Hithavvut ha-Talmud bi-Shelemuto* (1943), 57f.). The Babylonian *Gemara* gives the ingredients of the incense in the Temple (6a; see *Pittum ha-Ketoret*). Among aggadic passages of interest in *Keritot* are a number which deal with education. The Mishnah and Talmud were translated into English in the Soncino edition by I. Porush (1948).

BIBLIOGRAPHY: Ḥ. Albeck, *Shishah Sidrei Mishnah, Seder Kodashim* (1959), 243–5.

[Arnost Zvi Ehrman]

KERLER, DOV-BER (1958–), Yiddish scholar and poet. Kerler was born in Moscow (son of the Yiddish dissident poet Josef Kerler). Raised in an environment steeped in Yiddish culture that included summers spent among traditionally religious communities in the Carpathian Mountains of western Ukraine, he immigrated with his parents to Jerusalem in 1971. After completing his B.A. in Yiddish literature and Indo-European linguistics in Jerusalem (1983), he became Oxford

University's first doctoral candidate in Yiddish Studies in 1984, teaching there from 1984, as fellow at Lincoln College 1989–2000. His doctoral thesis on the origins of modern (East European-based) literary Yiddish (1988) moved the accepted dating back to the 18th century, forming the basis of his *Origins of Modern Literary Yiddish* (1999). He edited *The History of Yiddish Studies* (1991), *The Politics of Yiddish* (1998), and became editor-in-chief of *Yerusholaymer Almanakh* in 2003 (after serving as co-editor from 1993). Also an accomplished Yiddish poet, publishing under the pen name Boris Karloff, his books of verse include *Vu mit an Alef* ("Vu with an Aleph," 1996), and a collection of his and his father's works, *Shpigl Ksav* ("Mirror Writing," 1996). Relocated to the U.S. in 2000 to take up the chair in Yiddish Studies at Indiana University, from 2002 he led the Yiddish Ethnographic Project (YEP) to film expeditions to elderly Yiddish speakers in the Ukraine and other parts of Eastern Europe. He created and edits a number of major Yiddish culture websites (http://www.geocities.com/berkale/index.html; http://members.aol.com/_ht_a/kerlerdovber/myhomepage/business.html?mtbrand=ol_us; http://elabrek.blogspot.com). Kerler was awarded the Hofstein Prize for Yiddish literature (1997), the Modern Language Association's Leviant Prize for Yiddish scholarship (2004), and a National Endowment for the Humanities grant for ethnographic expeditions to Eastern Europe (2005–6).

BIBLIOGRAPHY: E. Podriatchik, in: *Yidishe Kultur,* 6 (1990), 36–8; M. Hoffman, in: *Forverts* (June 15, 1990), 18; D. Wolpe, in: *Forverts* (Dec. 18 1998), 14; J. Baumgarten, in: *Histoire épistémologie langage,* 21:2 (1999), 172–4; D. Katz, in: *Forverts* (Oct. 1 and 15, 1999), 13:13; A. Brumberg, in: *Jewish Quarterly* (Winter 1999–2000), 82–5; A. Goldschläger, in: *Literary Research* (2000), 191–2; J. Fishman, in: *Journal of Multilingual and Multicultural Development,* 21 (2000), 353–4; J. Frakes, in: *Journal of English and Germanic Philology* 100 (2001), 303–5; M. Isaacs, in: *Journal of Sociolinguistics* 5 (2001), 97–100; L. Lubarski, *Letste Nayes* (Dec. 18, 2003).

[Dovid Katz (2nd ed.)]

KERLER, YOYSEF (1918–2000), Yiddish poet and editor. Kerler was born in Haysin (Gaisin, Ukraine). When he was seven his family moved to a Jewish kolkhoz (Mayfeld, Crimea). He studied at a Yiddish technical school in Odessa (1934–37), began to study Yiddish literature, and debuted with a poem in the *Odeser Arbeter* (1935). He studied at the Yiddish Drama School of the Moscow State Yiddish Theater (GOSET, 1937–41). At the outbreak of World War II he enlisted in the Red Army and was wounded three times. His war poems constituted his first book, *Far Mayn Erd* ("Fighting for My Earth," 1944). Further poems and articles appeared in *Der Emes, Eynikayt, Heymland, Shtern* (Kiev), and *Folks-Shtime* (Warsaw). In 1947 he moved to Birobidjan, worked for *Birobidzhaner Shtern,* and openly protested the official policy to stop teaching Yiddish in schools. After returning to Moscow, he was arrested (April 1950) and sentenced to 10 years for "anti-Soviet nationalistic activity." In the Vorkuta Gulag, he wrote and later smuggled out several poem cycles, some of which were included under the guise of "songs of the [Nazi] ghetto" in his second book, appearing in authorized Russian translation only (*Vinogradnik Moego Otsa* / "My Father's Vineyard," 1957), and a few also in his third book *Khochu byt' dobrym* ("I'd Love to be Good-Natured," 1965). During the continued lack of Yiddish publishing in the early post-Stalinist period, he collaborated with many Yiddish performers as lyricist, author of short plays, and artistic consultant. Many of his poems were arranged and set to music, several of which became popular, some even acquiring the status of "folksongs" ("A Glezele Yash," "Der Tam-Ganeydevdiker Nign," "Am Yisroel Khay"). Many of his gulag and protest poems appeared in the *Forverts* (1969) and *Di Goldene Keyt* (1970). Together with his wife, Anya Kerler, he became one of the first long-term *refuseniks and open campaigners for free Jewish emigration. After a six-year struggle with the Soviet authorities, he was finally permitted to immigrate to Israel with his family, settling in Jerusalem (1971). Just before his arrival there he was awarded the honorary Itzik Manger Prize, followed in ensuing years by numerous other literary prizes in Israel and abroad. In addition to publications in periodicals throughout the world, six volumes of his poetry appeared in Israel: *Dos Gezang Tsvishn Tseyn* ("The Song through Clenched Teeth," 1971; Heb. tr. *Zemer ben ha-Shinayim,* 2000); *Zet Ir Dokh* ("Despite All Odds," 1972); *Di Ershte Zibn Yor* ("The First Seven Years," 1986); *Himlshaft* ("Heaven Above," 1986); *Abi Gezunt* ("For Health's Sake," 1993); *Shpigl-Ksav* ("Words in the Mirror," 1996), and two prose collections: *12 Oygust 1952* ("12 August 1952," 1977) and *Geklibene Proze* ("Selected Prose," 1991). He was instrumental in organizing the Jerusalem branch of the Israeli Yiddish Writers and Journalists Association, campaigned to institute perennial public commemoration of the Yiddish writers, actors, and intellectuals murdered by the Stalinist regime in 1937 and 1952, edited a number of collections, and founded the acclaimed organ for Yiddish literature and culture, *Yerusholaymer Almanakh* (26 vols., 1973–98). His poems have been widely translated and anthologized.

BIBLIOGRAPHY: Y. Druker, in: *Folks-Shtime* (April 1961); D. Sadan, in: *Heymishe Ksovim* (1972), 157–85; Y. Mark, in: *Jewish Book Annual,* 30 (1973), 40–2; D. Sfard, *Mit Zikh un mit Andere* (1984), 447–55; M. Tsanin, in: *Di Goldene Keyt,* 132 (1991), 192–7; Y. Shargel, in: *Yerusholaymer Almanakh,* 27 (2003), 41–4; M. Wolf, in: *Forverts* (Jan. 6, 2004).

[Dov-Ber Kerler (2nd ed.)]

KERMAN, city located in the province with the same name in the southeast of *Iran. A popular Kermani saying considers Kerman "the heart of the world," a great exaggeration. The origin of Kerman itself goes back to the Sasanian period, but, as far as we know, the Jewish community there is relatively new. Oral tradition indicates that because of severe famine in Yazd/Yezd about 150 years ago, several Jews of that city immigrated southward and eventually settled in Kerman. Historically this may be true, because the Jews of Kerman are not mentioned in the two Jewish chronicles, that of *Bābāi ben Lutf (17th century) – except for a mention of "ignorant

Yezdi-Kermani people" who extracted money from the Jews of Yezd – and that of *Bābāi ben Farhād (about 1730), nor are they referred to in other Jewish and non-Jewish travelogues from the first half of the 19th century. The Yezdi origin of the Jews of Kerman is attested by a linguistic investigation of their Jewish dialects. Neumark, who did not visit Kerman, said in 1884: "Not far from there (Yezd) there is the city of Kerman where a number of 30 Jews live".

One does not know of any important Jewish event, significant literary productions, or personalities concerning the Jewish community of Kerman. Like Yezd, Kerman too is a dwelling place of a substantial numbers of Zoroastrians. Several disastrous events befell the city of Kerman, culminating in 1794, when for the support given to the Zand monarch by the Kermanis, his foe, Muhammad Khan of Qajar, wreaked a terrible revenge on the Kermanis by allowing his men to pillage the town for three months, selling 20,000 of the inhabitants into slavery and blinding the same number of its men. With its population decimated and most of its buildings in ruins, it is hard to believe that Kerman attracted any Jews to settle there. Kerman did not regain its prosperity until after 1860 and most probably this is the time when Jews of Yezd found it appropriate to immigrate to Kerman and settle there. Neumark in the above-mentioned report confirms this assumption. At the beginning of the 20th century it was reported that 2,000 Jews were living in Kerman In course of time many immigrated to *Teheran and to Israel. Just before the Islamic Revolution 500 Jews were in Kerman. They had one elementary school and one synagogue. By the end of the 20th century fewer than 10 Jewish families remained in Kerman.

BIBLIOGRAPHY: BAIU (*Bulletin de l'Alliance Israélite Universelle*), Paris; G. Lazard, "Le dialecte des Juifs de Kerman," in: Les *Hommages et opera minora*, 7 (1981), 333–46; H. Levy, *History of the Jews of Iran*, 3 (1960); L. Lockhart, *Famous Cities of Iran* (1939); E. Neumark, "Massa' be-Ereẓ ha-Kedem," ed. A. Ya'ari (1947); E. Yarshater, "The Jewish Communities of Persia and Their Dialects," in: Ph. Ginoux and A. Tafazzoli (eds.), *Mémorial Jean de Menasce* (1974), 453–66.

[Amnon Netzer (2nd ed.)]

KERMANSHAH (called **Qirmisin** by Arab geographers), city located in the west of *Iran close to the border of *Iraq, on a commercial route between the two countries. The earliest mention of the city as a dwelling place of the Jews occurs in *Nathan ha-Bavli's report from the 10th century. Surprisingly, the Jewish community of Kermanshah is not mentioned in the chronicle of *Bābāi ben Lutf though it is almost certain that Jews lived in the city during the Safavid period (1501–1736). Rabbi *David de-Beth Hillel (around 1827) reports that there were 300 Jewish families living among 80,000 Muslim inhabitants. Most of the Jews were poor. *Benjamin II (about 1850) counted 40 Jewish families in Kermanshah. Rabbi Castleman reported in 1860 that there were few Jews in Kermanshah, and that "they are not God fearing people." According to Neumark, in 1884 there were 250 Jewish families. He says, "Muslims hate the Jews." Several Jewish families in Kermanshah embraced the Christian or Bahai faith in the last half of the 19th and the first half of the 20th centuries. In March 1909 there was a terrible pogrom against the Jews which resulted in killing, wounding, and looting of their property.

An important figure of Kermanshah was Shmuel Haim (1891?–1931), who became editor in chief of a Judeo-Persian weekly paper, *Ha-Ḥaim* (established in June 1922) and was president of the Iranian Zionist Organization and the Jewish representative in the Majles (1923–26). In 1926 he was accused of having joined a group of officers to overthrow the Shah (Reza Shah). He was tried in a military court and put to death on December 15, 1931, although the charge against him was never proved. In 1948 the Jews of Kermanshah numbered 2,864 persons, including a few Jewish families from Iraq, living among 80,000 Muslims They had five synagogues, one bath-house, and one school (Alliance) that had opened in 1904 and went up to ninth grade. According to a report, at the end of the 20th century about 20 Jewish families lived in Kermanshah.

BIBLIOGRAPHY: *Bulletin de l'Alliance Israélite Universelle*, Paris; J.J. Benjamin II, *Eight Years in Asia and Africa from 1846 to 1855* (1863); A. Ben-Jacob, *Yehudei Bavel* (1965), index; Y.F. Castleman, *Massa'ot Shali'aḥ Ẓefat be-Arẓot ha-Mizraḥ* (1942); A. Cohen, *Ha-Kehillah ha-Yehudit be-Kermanshah* (1992); David d'Beth Hillel, *Unknown Jews in Unknown Lands (1824–1832)*, ed. by W.J. Fischel (1973); H. Levy, *History of the Jews of Iran*, 3 (1960); A. Netzer, "Yahudiyānei Iran dar avāset-e qarn-e bistom," in: *Shofar*, a Jewish monthly in Persian published in Long Island; E. Neumark, *Massa be-Ereẓ ha-Kedem*, ed. by A. Ya'ari (1947).

[Amnon Netzer (2nd ed.)]

KERN, JEROME DAVID (1885–1945), U.S. composer of popular music. Born in New York, Kern published his first song, "At the Casino," in 1902. In 1903, while working in London, he had his first real success – a political song "Mr. Chamberlain" with lyrics by P.G. Wodehouse, who later contributed lyrics to many of Kern's musicals. Returning to the U.S., he wrote songs that were used in musical productions, particularly in operettas coming from Europe, such as *La Belle Paree* (1911) and *The Red Petticoat* (1912), which was followed by *Oh I Say* (1913). From then on, his musicals appeared regularly on Broadway, the most important being *Very Good, Eddie* (1915), *Oh Boy!* (1917), *Oh Lady, Lady* (1918), *Sally* (1920), and *Sunny* (1925). His greatest success was *Show Boat* (1927) with libretto and lyrics by Oscar *Hammerstein. It was followed by *Sweet Adeline* (1929), *The Cat and the Fiddle* (1931), and *Roberta* (1933). In later years, Kern lived in Beverly Hills, California, and wrote scores for a great number of films, many of them adaptations of his most successful musicals. In all he wrote more than 1,000 songs, for 104 stage shows and films, and many of them proved to have a lasting popularity (e.g., "Ol' Man River," "Smoke Gets in Your Eyes"). In 1946 his life story was filmed under the title *Till the Clouds Roll By*.

BIBLIOGRAPHY: D. Ewen, *World of Jerome Kern* (1960), incl. bibl.; K. List, in: *Commentary*, 3 (1947), 433–41; G. Saleski, *Famous Musicians of Jewish Origin* (1949), 85–86.

KEROVAH (Heb. קרובא), name for various types of *piyyutim* in the *Amidah prayer. The reader who chanted the prayer was called *karova* (Aram. קרובא; in Hebrew it would be *karov* קרוב). The *kerovah* intended for the *Amidah* in which *Kedushah was recited, i.e., for the *Shaḥarit Amidah*, according to the early usage of Ereẓ Israel, was designated *kedushta* while that for the *Musaf Amidah, where it was not customary to recite a *Kedushah*, was called *shivata* or *shivah*. The subject matter of the *kedushta* is fixed, being pertinent to the day on which it is recited, i.e., the weekly portion of the Torah, the *haftarah*, or the theme of a festival. But the *shivata* allowed for varied topics open to the choice and discretion of the *paytan*. The *kedushta* contains *piyyutim* for the first three blessings of the *Amidah*, those for the third blessing being numerous. The *shivata* contains seven equal sections corresponding to the number of blessings in the *Amidah*, except on festivals when the fourth blessing containing "the sanctity of the day" is made longer.

The following are the sections of the early *kedushta*: (1) *Magen*, generally speaking a *piyyut* with an acrostic from *alef* to *lamed*, ending with an allusion to the first blessing of the *Amidah*, *Magen Avraham* (Shield of Abraham); (2) *Meḥayyeh*, a continuation of the previous acrostic with the conclusion alluding to the second blessing, *Meḥayyeh ha-metim* ("Who revives the dead"); (3) a *piyyut* with an acrostic of the author's name; (4) a *piyyut* without an acrostic that ends with the word *kadosh* (holy); (5) a *piyyut* whose acrostic is from *alef* to *yod*, which in early manuscripts was called *asiriyyah* (group of ten); (6) an alphabetical acrostic based on the theme or subject of the day, its parts being connected with one another by the pertinent scriptural verses; (7) various *piyyutim* of an unfixed nature; (8) *silluk*, a long *piyyut* without an acrostic, containing a description of the importance of the subject matter of the day according to the midrashim. Just as it concluded the arrangement of the day's *piyyutim*, so it also served as a kind of preliminary to the *Kedushah*; (9) *Kedushah*, which is a hymn to God.

Among the sections of the *kerovah* were intertwined, as has been mentioned, scriptural verses appropriate to the topic; but beginning in the 16th century the verses no longer appeared in the prayer books. The *kerovot* for the *Amidah* of 18 blessings are similar in structure to the *shivata*, but their *piyyutim* are in general shorter and they are interwoven in all the blessings. Many of the *kerovot* also have *reshut* (prelude) which leads into the *kerovah* itself. In the course of time, slight changes were introduced into the early *kerovah*, but its essence was preserved. The *kerovot* for Rosh Ha-Shanah and the Day of Atonement received various additions, such as the *teki'ot* and the **Avodah*. In the *kerovot*, there is no scope for individuality of composition, although there are *kerovot* for bridegrooms, for the death of important men, and for various events. The earliest known author of *piyyutim* to write *kerovot* was *Yannai, followed by Eleazar *Kallir, *Joshua, and *Phinehas b. Jacob ha-Kohen (Kafra). These *paytanim*, who lived and worked in Ereẓ Israel, influenced the writers of Babylon, Spain, Italy, France, and Germany.

BIBLIOGRAPHY: Elbogen, Gottesdienst, 212ff., 309; M. Zulay, *Piyyutei Yannai*; (1938), 13–16; A.D. Goldschmidt, *Mavo le-Maḥzor Rosh Ha-Shanah* (1970), 32–42.

[Abraham Meir Habermann]

KERR, ALFRED (pen name of **Alfred Kempner**; 1867–1948), German literary and theater critic and author. Kerr was born in Breslau and studied there and in Berlin. He became drama critic for the Berlin newspaper *Der Tag* and later for the *Berliner Tageblatt*. Together with Paul Cassirer and Wilhelm Herzog, Kerr founded the theater magazine *Pan*, which was published from 1900 until World War I. Because of his public warning against national socialism, he immediately had to leave Germany in February 1933. Together with his second wife and his two children he fled to Prague, and subsequently to Switzerland, Paris, and London, where the family settled and lived in poverty. He worked for various newspapers and the BBC and became correspondent of the Munich newspaper *Neue Zeitung* in 1945. During his first visit to Germany after World War II he became severely ill and put an end to his life soon afterwards. Perhaps the leading impressionistic critic in modern German literature, Kerr considered criticism an art, and based his judgments on personal impressions. He believed that criticism should aim to "illuminate" a literary work, its author, and the author's attitude to life. He wished to be considered an interpreter rather than a literary "lawgiver." He was especially prominent as a champion of Hauptmann and Ibsen.

Kerr's *Gesammelte Schriften* fill seven volumes. The first five, *Die Welt im Drama*, appeared in 1917; the last two were published as *Die Welt im Licht* in 1920. A new edition in eight volumes was published from 1989 to 2001, *Werke in Einzelbänden*, as well as a collection of early letters, *Wo liegt Berlin? Briefe aus der Reichshauptstadt 1895–1900* (1998). His travels included a journey to Palestine in 1903, which he recorded with poetic enthusiasm in "Jeruschalajim," one of the chapters in *Die Welt im Licht*. Kerr devoted one of his studies to the ill-fated German-Jewish statesman Walter *Rathenau (1935). Some of Kerr's poems were set to music by Richard Strauss and a posthumous volume of his verse appeared in 1955. Though inclining to mannerism in his later years, Kerr had an incomparable literary style. His choice of language shows the influence of Heine and Nietzsche.

BIBLIOGRAPHY: J. Chapiro, *Fuer Alfred Kerr…* (1928); Luft, in: *A. Kerr, Die Welt im Licht* (1961), 435–42. **ADD. BIBLIOGRAPHY:** H. Schneider: *Alfred Kerr als Theaterkritiker* (2 vol., 1984); D. Vietor-Engländer, in: B. Wolfgang Benz and M. Neiss (eds.), *Deutsch-juedisches Exil; das Ende der Assimilation? Identitätsprobleme deutscher Juden in der Emigration*, (1994), 67–77. L. Schoene, *Neuigkeiten vom Mittelpunkt der Welt. Der Kampf ums Theater in der Weimarer Republik* (1995).

[Rudolf Kayser / Mirjam Triendl (2nd ed.)]

KERSH, GERALD (1911–1968), English author and journalist of the "tough" school. Kersh was born in Teddington, near London, and began to write stories as a child. He was a war correspondent for the Sunday newspaper *The People*, and an

MGM screenwriter. His works, notable for their fantasy and bohemianism, include the controversial *Jews Without Jehovah* (1934); *They Die with Their Boots Clean* (1941); *The Thousand Deaths of Mr. Small* (1950), a novel of Anglo-Jewish Life; and *The Best of Gerald Kersh* (1960). His novels about Soho's low-life, like *Harry Fabian: Night and the City* (1938) still have a cult following. In his last years he lived in upstate New York.

KERTESZ, ANDRE (1894–1985), photographer. One of the most influential photographers of the 20th century, Kertesz was born in Budapest, Hungary. He attended the Academy of Commerce there but had little interest in business. He served in World War I and was wounded. At 18 he bought his first camera, one that made 4.5 × 6-centimeter glass negatives. This early work, prints not much bigger than a postage stamp, included cityscapes, landscapes, portraits, and outdoor studies of the artist's brother capering about nude. In 1925 Kertesz moved to Paris, changed his given name from Andor to Andre, and met and photographed some of the most glamorous personalities of the time, including Chagall, Colette, Sergei Eisenstein, and Mondrian. One black and white photograph, which became his most famous, shows the austerely luminous image of the door and vestibule of Mondrian's studio, but the work, *Chez Mondrian*, became better known for its subject than for its creator. Kertesz's work, praised by critics, appeared in the most fashionable magazines of the day. Many of his pictures capture the incongruities of time and space. In *Meudon*, from 1928, the view down a narrow street opens up to a high aqueduct, across which charges a locomotive belching smoke. In the foreground, a man in a dark suit with eyes shadowed by his low hat brim approaches, carrying a large flat package. Buoyed by his success in Paris, Kertesz took a job as a fashion photographer in New York and he and his wife sailed to America in 1936. The new job did not work out and his efforts were not warmly embraced. He made a living making pictures of celebrity homes for *House & Garden* magazine but others, including his fellow Hungarian Brassai and Henri Cartier-Bresson, became famous. Kertesz felt that those photographers had appropriated his innovations. But in his late sixties, Kertesz, a pioneer in the use of small, 35-mm. cameras, began to receive recognition. He was included in exhibitions at the Museum of Modern Art and a new generation of photographers began rediscovering him, and he continued photographing into his nineties.

[Stewart Kampel (2nd ed.)]

KERTÉSZ, IMRE (1929–), Hungarian novelist and translator. Kertész was born in Budapest and deported to Auschwitz in 1944, and from there to Buchenwald, where he was liberated in 1945. In postwar Budapest he worked as a journalist and translator, publishing his first novel in 1975. *Sorstalanság* (*Fateless*, 1992), deals with his experience as a teenager in Auschwitz, as does his *Kaddis a meg nem született gyermekért* (1990; *Kaddish for a Child not Born*, 1997), which shares much of Primo Levi's pessimism regarding the human condition and explores the dubious blessing of survival and the price paid for that survival. In 2003 he published *Felszámolás* (*Liquidation*, 2004), a novel about a Holocaust survivor with echoes of Kafka and Beckett. His collected lectures and essays include *A holocaust mint kultúra* ("The Holocaust as Culture," 1993).

In 2002, Kertész was awarded the Nobel Prize for literature "for writing that upholds the fragile experience of the individual against the barbaric arbitrariness of history." The citation read: "In his writing Imre Kertész explores the possibility of continuing to live and think as an individual in an era in which the subjection of human beings to social forces has become increasingly complete.... For him Auschwitz is not an exceptional occurrence that like an alien body subsists outside the normal history of Western Europe. It is the ultimate truth about human degradation in modern existence."

KERTESZ, ISTVAN (1929–1973), conductor. Born in Budapest, Kertesz studied the violin at the Liszt Academy, whose student orchestra he later conducted, and in Rome. After becoming a conductor at Györ (1953–55), he was appointed junior conductor at the Budapest Opera, but left Hungary during the 1956 uprising. From 1958 he was music director at the Augsburg Opera and from 1964 until his death, at the Cologne Opera. From 1965 to 1968 he was principal conductor of the London Symphony Orchestra, with which he made many recordings. A leading conductor of the younger generation, he was admired for his conducting of the works of Schubert, Dvorák, Bruckner, Bartok, and – his greatest love – Mozart. Kertesz made frequent guest appearances at leading opera houses and with important orchestras, notably the Vienna Philharmonic and the Israel Philharmonic with which he was engaged at the time of his death. He died by drowning, while swimming off the coast of Herzliyyah.

[Max Loppert (2nd ed.)]

KESHET, YESHURUN (**Koplewitz, Jacob**; 1893–1977), Hebrew poet, literary critic, and translator. Born in Minsk Mazowiecki, near Warsaw, he first went to Palestine in 1911. He left in 1920 to study in Europe, and also taught in Marijampole, Lithuania. In 1926 he returned to Palestine, and after a short period of teaching devoted himself to writing and translation work. His first poems were published in *Ha-Aḥdut* and *Revivim* (1913), and he then contributed poetry, essays, and literary criticism to most Hebrew newspapers and periodicals. His volumes of poetry include *Ha-Helekh ba-Areẓ* (1932), *Elegyot* (1944), and *Ha-Ḥayyim ha-Genuzim* (1959). Keshet's poems are deeply influenced by European, particularly French, decadent poetry. Their lyricism converts what might have been the poet's despair and *Angst* into an elegiac melancholy. His tendency to use more traditional forms also mitigates their harshness. Many of his poems reflect preoccupation with aesthetic and philosophical problems. His monograph on *Berdyczewski (1958) is a significant contribution to Hebrew literary criticism. His prose works include *Ha-Derekh ha-Ne'elamah* (1941); diary (1919–39); *Be-Doro shel Bialik* (1943);

Be-Dor Oleh (1950); *Maskiyyot* (1953), literary criticism; *Shirat ha-Mikra* (1945); *Ruḥot ha-Ma'arav* (1960), on European writers; *Havdalot* (1962); *Keren Ḥazut* (1966), essays in national self-criticism; *Maḥarozot* (1967); *Bein ha-Armon ve-ha-Li-lakh* (1967), an autobiography; and *Rashuyyot* (1968), essays of evaluation on Israel writers. He also translated numerous books into Hebrew, many of which were classics of European literature. His collected poems, entitled *Ha-Oẓar ha-Avud*, were published in 1996. A list of his books and translations appears in his *Keren Ḥazut* (1966), 381f.

BIBLIOGRAPHY: A. Cohen, *Soferim Ivriyyim Benei Zemannenu* (1964), 179–85; M. Mevorakh, *Anshei Ru'aḥ be-Yisrael: Deyokena'ot Soferim* (1956), 183–5; Kressel, Leksikon, 2 (1967), 805f. **ADD. BIBLIOGRAPHY:** S. Kremer, *"Deyukano ha-Aẓmi shel Sofer,"* in: *Moznayim*, 38 (1974), 138–46; M. Avishai, in: *Al Hamishmar* (March 4, 1977); A.H. Elhanani, *"Ha-Otobiografyah shel Y. Keshet,"* in: *Al Hamishmar* (Nov. 28, 1980); E. Ben Ezer, in: *Haaretz* (Jan. 30, 1981).

[Getzel Kressel]

KESSAR, ISRAEL (1931–), Israeli political and union leader, member of the Eleventh to Thirteenth Knessets. Born in San'a, Yemen, Kessar was brought to Israel at the age of two. He went to school in Jerusalem. Before and after the War of Independence he studied and worked at the Youth Center for New Immigrants. In 1956 he received a B.A. in sociology and economics at the Hebrew University of Jerusalem. In 1960–61 he was employed as assistant and advisor to the minister of labor, Giora Josephtal, and in 1961–66 he served as head of the Department for Rehabilitation and Professional Direction in the Ministry of Labor. In 1966 he began his career in the *Histadrut, serving until 1971 as chairman of the Youth and Sports Department. In this period he was also appointed chairman of the Manpower Department of the Histadrut. He resumed his studies, and in 1972 completed an M.A. in Labor Studies at Tel Aviv University. In 1972–77 Kessar served as treasurer of the Histadrut, and in the latter year joined the Labor Party Secretariat. In the years 1977–84 he headed the Trade Union Section, and served as deputy secretary general of the Histadrut, under Yeruham Meshel. In 1984 he was elected on behalf of the Labor Party as secretary general of the Histadrut, and was elected to the Eleventh Knesset on the Alignment list. He supported the government economic stabilization plan when Shimon *Peres served as prime minister, and Yitzhak *Modai as minister of finance, but struggled to prevent a steep fall in real wages and an increase in unemployment.

Kessar participated in the contest for the Labor Party leadership in 1992 against Yitzhak *Rabin, Peres and Ora *Namir, receiving close to 20% of the votes. Peres' supporters argued that had Kessar withdrawn from the leadership contest, Peres, who received 34% of the vote, might have beaten Rabin, who received just over 40%. In the Labor government of 1992–96 Kessar served as minister of transportation. He did not run in the elections to the Fourteenth Knesset owing to his wife's poor health.

[Susan Hattis Rolef (2nd ed.)]

KESSEL, BARNEY (1923–2004), U.S. guitarist. Kessel grew up on the same Oklahoma plains that nurtured Charlie Christian, the first great electric guitarist, and it was to Christian that Kessel first looked as an influence. Kessel bought his first guitar at age 12 with money he had saved from his paper route and taught himself to play by listening to radio broadcasts and imitating what he heard. Within two years, he was playing in a local band, the only white musician in an all-black unit. In 1938 he spent a long weekend playing and jamming with Christian and his musical style was changed forever. Ironically, it was playing with Christian in a jam session that led him to pursue his own style. He told The *New York Times*, "I realized that I had been methodically lifting his ideas from records. What was I going to play? All I knew was his stuff.... I knew I had to find myself." With Christian's encouragement, Kessel moved to Los Angeles and in 1942 took a job with Chico Marx's band. He rapidly made a name for himself as a talented and versatile guitarist, playing with Benny *Goodman, Artie *Shaw, and Charlie Barnet. He became a mainstay of Norman *Granz's Jazz at the Philharmonic troupe, appearing in the acclaimed 1944 short film *Jammin' the Blues*, and finally hooking up with the Oscar Peterson Trio in the early 1950s. It was this last gig that earned him his most significant reputation as a jazz guitarist, but he also began spending a lot of time playing studio jobs for the movies, television, and commercials, as well as on records. Kessel can be heard on an astonishing range of recordings from the 1950s and 1960s, from Liberace to the Beach Boys, Frank Sinatra to Gene Autry. He continued to play jazz too, joining with fellow guitarists Herb Ellis and Charlie Byrd in the 1970s to form the group Great Guitars. Kessel was silenced in 1992 by a stroke from which he never recovered and died of brain cancer.

BIBLIOGRAPHY: P. Keepnews, "Barney Kessel, 80, a Guitarist with Legends of Jazz, Dies," in: *New York Times* (May 8, 2004); "Barney Kessel," in: Music Web Encyclopaedia of Popular Music, at: www.musicweb.uk.net; "Barney Kessel," in: *Times of London* (May 13, 2004); "Musicians Gather to Perform at Benefit for Legendary Jazz Guitarist Barney Kessel," in: *Down Beat* (June, 19, 2002).

[George Robinson (2nd ed.)]

KESSEL, JOSEPH (1898–1979), French author. Kessel was born in Clara, one of the Jewish agricultural settlements in Argentina, where his father was physician. The family returned to Russia and, when Joseph was ten years old, settled in France. By 1915 he was already writing for the *Journal des Débats*, and he also began training as an actor. The following year, however, he volunteered for war service and became an officer in the air force. Between the two world wars Kessel built up a considerable reputation as a novelist, journalist, and writer of screenplays. When World War II broke out he became a war correspondent. After the fall of France he escaped to England and spent the rest of the war in a Free French air force squadron, flying special missions to occupied France. He received French, British, and American decorations.

Two of Kessel's earliest books were *La Steppe rouge* (1922), a collection of travel sketches, and *L'Equipage* (1923), the first novel about French aviation, based on his experiences in World War I. Three other novels of this period were *Nuits de princes* (1927; *Princes of the Night*, 1928), a story with a Russian background; *Belle de jour* (1928), translated into English in 1962 and later filmed; and *Vent de sable* (1929). During the late 1920s and throughout the 1930s Kessel traveled extensively in the U.S. and in the Near and Far East. His lively reaction to people and events made him a compelling storyteller, and his books were easily adapted to the screen. His World War II story, *Le bataillon du ciel* (1947), was an aviation epic. *Les mains du miracle* (1960; *The Magic Touch*, 1961) is a biography of Felix Kersten, *Himmler's Finnish physiotherapist, who saved many Jews from the Nazis. Kessel's prize-winning book, *Les coeurs purs* (1927; *The Pure in Heart*, 1928), contained the story *"Makhno et sa juive,"* while *Terre d'amour* (1927) examined the Zionist experiment, but he was remote from Jewish life. The birth of the State of Israel, however, fired his imagination and *Terre de feu*, first published in 1948 and revised and enlarged many years later under the title *Terre d'amour et de feu; Israël 1925–1948–1961* (1965), attests to his belief that Israel is one of the noblest enterprises of the 20th century. In his address upon his acceptance into the Académie Française in 1964 he spoke about his pride in being a Jew.

Kessel's works include a collection of essays, *L'armée des ombres* (1944; *Army of Shadows*, 1944), and the autobiographical *Témoin parmi les hommes* (1956). Among his novels are *Le Tour du malheur* (1950), *Le Lion* (1958; *The Lion*, 1959), *Avec les alcooliques anonymes* (1960; *The Enemy in the Mouth*, Brit. ed. 1961; *The Road Back*, U.S. ed. 1962); *Le Coup de grâce* (1953) and *Les cavaliers* (1967; *The Horsemen*, 1968).

BIBLIOGRAPHY: Vailland et al., in: *Livres de France*, 10 (October 1959), 2–12.

[Moshe Catane]

KESSLER, DAVID (1860–1920), Yiddish actor. He was one of the leading actor-managers of the New York Yiddish theater during its heyday early in the twentieth century. Born in Kishinev, at the age of 20 he joined the troupe of Judel Goldfaden (brother of Abraham Goldfaden) and together they toured the towns of south Russia. When Yiddish theater was prohibited by the czar in 1883, he toured with S. *Mogulesco in Romania, went to London in 1886, and to New York in 1890. There he acted under Jacob *Adler in Jacob Gordin's first play *Siberia* (1891), and soon made his name. He subsequently appeared in other plays by Gordin, enjoying great success in *God, Man, and Devil.* Others of his outstanding roles were in Sholem Asch's *God of Vengeance*, David Pinski's *Yankel the Smith*, and Leon Kobrin's *Yankel Boile*. In 1913 he established the David Kessler Theater, which ranked with Adler's and Thomashefsky's theaters, and produced many plays by the leading Yiddish writers.

[Joseph Leftwich]

KESSLER, LEOPOLD (1864–1944), engineer and one of Herzl's early aides. Born in Tarnowice, Upper Silesia, Kessler completed his studies and went to South Africa, where he was a consulting mining engineer. He was influenced by Zionism when Herzl's *Der Judenstaat* was published, and from the Second Zionist Congress was one of Herzl's loyal aides and a member of the Zionist General Council. He headed the scientific delegation to *El-Arish in 1903 and submitted its report on March 26. Later he was chairman of the Jewish National Fund in England. During World War I he became a member of the committee that helped Chaim Weizmann during the negotiations with the British government which led to the *Balfour Declaration. He also was chairman of the Zionist Federation of England (1922). From 1907 he served as a director of the *Jewish Chronicle*, assumed controlling editorship, and became its chairman in 1932. From 1939 Kessler lived in the United States, where he was active in the Freeland League, a territorialist association (see *Territorialism). His son, DAVID FRANCIS KESSLER (b. Pretoria, 1906), became managing director of the *Jewish Chronicle* in 1936 and chairman in 1958.

BIBLIOGRAPHY: C. Roth *The Jewish Chronicle* (1949), index; R. Patai, in: *Herzl Year-Book*, 1 (1958), 107–44.

[Getzel Kressel]

KESTEN, HERMANN (1900–1996), German novelist. In 1927 Kesten became literary adviser to the Berlin publishing house of Kiepenheuer. He had to leave Germany in 1933 and was active in European refugee circles, but fled to the U.S.A. after the outbreak of World War II. He lived in New York for several years, but after the collapse of Fascism in Italy made his home in Rome. Kesten's first novel, *Josef sucht die Freiheit* (1927), was translated into seven languages. *Glueckliche Menschen* (1931) and *Der Scharlatan* (1932) both deal with life in Berlin. During his exile, Kesten completed *Ferdinand und Isabella* (1936; U.S. ed. 1946; U.K. ed. *Spanish Fire*, 1946), a historical novel which recreates the period of the Jewish expulsion from Spain; and *Koenig Philipp der Zweite* (1938), which deals with Ferdinand and Isabella's successor on the Spanish throne.

Die Kinder von Gernika (1939) was written under the impact of the Spanish Civil War and portrays the tragic history of the Basques. *Die fremden Goetter* (1949) portrays the return to Judaism of a father and daughter during the Hitler era. Kesten's many other works included biographies of Copernicus (1945; *Copernicus and His World*, 1946) and Casanova (1952), and various plays and essays. His writing is remarkable for its good-natured humor alternating with sardonic irony in a manner reminiscent of Heine. Although he depicts man's inhumanity, Kesten also reveals his own faith in man and his love of freedom is combined with a sense of responsibility and duty.

[Sol Liptzin]

KESTENBERG, LEO (1882–1962), pianist and music educator. Born in Rózsahegy (Rosenberg), Hungary, the son of a *ḥazzan*, Kestenberg studied the piano in Berlin with

G. Albrecht, F. Kullak, and Ferruccio Busoni whose personality exercised a lasting influence on his career. Attaining early fame as a concert pianist, he at the same time joined the young Social-Democratic movement, and began to work toward his major ideal, the social integration of musical life. From 1905, Kestenberg organized the performances of the Freie Volksbuehne (Popular Theater) – folk choirs, concerts, and meetings. Especially after his appointment in 1918 as the music adviser, and in 1927, as the music counselor, at the Prussian Ministry of Culture, he turned to the thorough reform of musical education known today as the "Kestenberg-Reform." His yearly educational decrees extended to music teachers in academies, seminaries, conservatories, schools, and kindergartens. In 1933, Kestenberg fled to Prague where he founded, under the sponsorship of the Czech Ministry of Education, the International Society for Music Education, which held three major international congresses. Arriving in Ereẓ Israel in 1938, he became the general manager of the Palestine Orchestra (later the Israel Philharmonic Orchestra). In 1945 Kestenberg founded the Music Teachers' Training College in Tel Aviv, which he headed for over 15 years and regarded it as the fulfillment of his musical mission. At the college he realized for a third time his ideas on the role of music in the life of a nation. As professor at the Tel Aviv Academy of Music, he educated a number of well-known Israeli pianists. Among his publications are: *Musikerziehung und Musikpflege* (1921); *Jahrbuch der deutschen Musikorganisation* (1929); *Kunst und Technik* (1930); *Bewegte Zeiten* (autobiography, 1961); and he was the editor of *Musikpaedagogische Bibliothek.*

BIBLIOGRAPHY: G. Braun, *Die Schulmusikerziehung in Preussen. Von den Falkschen Bestimmungen bis zur Kestenberg-Reform* (1957); E. Gerson-Kiwi, in: *Acta Musicologica*, 30 (1958), 17–26 (Eng.); idem, in: *Gesher*, 5:3 (1959), 110–1; idem, in: *Haaretz*, 25 (Nov. 30, 1942), 2; MGG, incl. bibl.; Grove, Dict; Baker, Biog Dict, incl. bibl.; Riemann-Gurlitt, incl. bibl.

[Edith Gerson-Kiwi]

KESTLEMAN, MORRIS (often spelled **Kestelman**; 1905–1998), painter. Born in the East End of London, he became head of the Fine Art Department of the Central School of Art. He was influenced by his teacher Bernard *Meninsky, and also by Van Gogh and Gauguin. Two Anglo-Jewish artists also influenced his career, the painter and illustrator Barnett *Freedman and the print-maker Michael Rothenstein. He developed an interest in theater design and made a distinguished contribution in this field. He became a member, and secretary, of the London Group, was later vice chairman of the United Kingdom branch of the International Association of Art, and was a fellow of the Royal Academy. His mature work was influenced by Matisse, Braque, and Picasso, and his emotional character was thus tempered by controlled and elegant design; the English critic Bryan Robertson once remarked, "Kestleman cannot be judged as an English painter; he is a Continental artist who happens to reside here." He belonged to the "second generation" of Anglo-Jewish artists, following the major figures of David *Bomberg, Mark *Gertler, etc. His daughter Sarah Kestelman is a well-known actress, painter, and poet in London.

[Charles Samuel Spencer]

KESZI (Kramer), IMRE (1910–1974), author and literary and music critic. A pupil of the composer Zoltán Kodály, Keszi wrote on Jewish themes and his World War II experiences. Among his books are *A várakozók lakomája* ("The Feast of Those Waiting," 1944[1]; 1969[2]), stories and meditations on the Passover Seder; and two works on the Holocaust, *Elysium* (1958) and *Szőlőből bor* ("Wine from the Grape," 1961).

KETER PUBLISHING HOUSE, Israeli publisher. Keter operates its own independent book marketing and distribution network and is also a key provider of print services and book production for the Israeli market and export through its industrial division.

Keter has been the most prominent publisher of contemporary Hebrew literature in Israel for many years, and its publishing activities cover a wide range of genres, including translated fiction and non-fiction, albums, guides and general trade books, children's books, and multi-volume encyclopedias. Among the many contemporary Israeli writers Keter publishes are Aharon *Appelfeld, Amos *Oz, Alona Kimhi, Sayed Kashua, Savyon *Liebrecht, Uri *Orlev, and Zeruya *Shalev. Keter has published many translated works, including those of Douglas Adams, Paul Auster, Paolo Coelho, Sandor Marai, Haruki Murakami, Boris Pasternak, Philip Pulman, Salman Rushdie, W.G. Sebald, Susan Sontag, Donna Tartt, and Mario Vargas-Llosa. Keter is the publisher of the first edition of the *Encyclopedia Judaica* and is a co-publisher of the *Junior Britannica.*

Operating from Jerusalem, the company was first established and owned by the Israeli government under the auspices of the Prime Minister's Office in 1959 at the initiative of Teddy *Kollek, Jerusalem's mayor (1965–93). Originally named The Israel Program for Scientific Translations (IPST), the company engaged in the translation and publishing of scientific and technical manuscripts from Russian into English, primarily for the National Science Foundation of the United States. During the 1960s the company began to diversify its publishing activities in English under the Israel Universities Press (IUP) and Keter Books imprints. The company was purchased from the government by Meniv Israel Investment Company in 1966 and subsequently sold to Clal Israel in 1969. At this time the company name was changed to Keter Publishing House, with key objectives to expand the publishing of titles concerned with Judaica and Israel for export, to publish the recently acquired *Encyclopedia Judaica* (published in 1972), and to establish an independent printing and bindery division (Keterpress Enterprises). During the late 1970s Keter consolidated its position as a leading publisher in Hebrew in all categories.

Keter has been a public company since 1987. Controlling interest in the company was briefly held by Robert *Maxwell, through Macmillan, at the beginning of the 1990s, and thereafter by Arledan, a Jerusalem based investment company. Keter has provided the managerial infrastructure for Sifriat Maariv, the *Maariv* daily newspaper's imprint, since 2003. In 2005 Keter and the Steimatzky Group joined forces to form a new publishing and distribution partnership "Keter-Books" for titles published in Hebrew. The second edition of the *Encyclopedia Judaica* is now published by Thomson Gale, under license from Keter.

KETI'A BAR SHALOM (first century C.E.), Roman councillor or senator who sacrificed his life to save the Jews of the Roman Empire from extermination (or persecution), probably toward the end of *Domitian's reign (c. 96 C.E.). According to the main source (Av. Zar. 10b), an emperor who hated the Jews – presumably Domitian – consulted his councillors as to whether a sore on the foot should be cut away, i.e., whether the Jews should be exterminated, or be left alone to cause pain. The councillors favored "radical" treatment, but Keti'a b. Shalom pointed out that the Jews, scattered as they were all over the world, could not be exterminated anyway; that the world could not exist without Israel; and that the empire would be crippled without the Jews. The emperor agreed with the soundness of Keti'a's reasoning, but nevertheless ordered him to be put to death. Advised by a Roman matron who exclaimed, "Pity the ship that sails without paying the tax," Keti'a circumcised himself, so that he should enter paradise as a Jew. Just before his execution he willed all his property to R. Akiva (cf. Ned. 50b) and his colleagues who were in Rome at the time.

In a similar story told in *Deuteronomy Rabbah* 2:24, an unnamed senator commits suicide (after having himself circumcised) in order to annul a Senate decree to exterminate the Jews within 30 days. Graetz plausibly identifies Keti'a with Flavius *Clemens, Domitian's nephew, who was executed for "atheism," i.e., for Judaizing tendencies. Keti'a b. Shalom is a fictitious name meaning "through circumcision he obtained salvation" (so J.Z. Lauterbach, quoted by Braude) or, more probably, "the circumcised one, may he rest in peace."

BIBLIOGRAPHY: Graetz, Gesch, 4 (1908[4]), 109–11, 402f.; idem, in: MGWJ, 1 (1852), 192–202; J. Kobak, in: *Jeshurun*, 8 (1871/72), Heb. pt. 161–70; B.J. Bamberger, *Proselytism in the Talmudic Period* (1939; repr. 1968), 235–8, 279, 282f.; W.G. Braude, *Jewish Proselyting* (1940), 75; Alon, Toledot[3], 1 (1959), 74f.

[Moses Aberbach]

KETUBBAH (Heb. כְּתֻבָּה), a document recording the financial obligations which the husband undertakes toward his wife in respect of, and consequent to, their marriage, obligations which in principle are imposed on him by law. For the *ketubbah* of a betrothed woman (*arusah*) see *Marriage.

The Concept

In talmudic times in certain places it was customary to dispense with the writing of a *ketubbah* deed, relying on the fact that the said obligations are in any event imposed by law (Ket. 16b), but the *halakhah* was decided to the effect that a *ketubbah* deed must always be written, since it is forbidden for the bridegroom to cohabit with his bride until he has written and delivered the *ketubbah* to her (Maim. Yad, Ishut 10:7; Sh. Ar., EH 66:1). On the other hand, they are allowed to cohabit only when they are married, and so the *ketubbah* deed must be ready for delivery to the bride when the betrothal blessings (*berakhot ha-erusin*) are recited and before the recital of the marriage blessings (*berakhot ha-nissu'in*; see *Marriage). Since in modern times it is customary in practically all communities to celebrate the *kiddushin* and *nissu'in* at the same time, the deed must be ready at the commencement of the recital of the *berakhot ha-erusin*. At the present time a standard form of *ketubbah* deed is normally used, which is read before the bridegroom and the witnesses and signed by them (for a standard *ketubbah* deed, see A.A. Rodner, *Mishpetei Ishut*, 179f.).

The *ketubbah* was instituted for the purpose of protecting the woman, "so that he shall not regard it as easy to divorce her" (Ket. 11a; Yev. 89a; Maim. loc. cit.), i.e., in order to render it difficult for the husband to divorce his wife by obliging him to pay her, in the event of a *divorce, the sum mentioned in the *ketubbah*, which generally exceeded the sum due to her according to law. As this is the object of the *ketubbah*, some scholars are of the opinion that since the *ḥerem* of Rabbenu *Gershom, which prohibited the divorce of a wife against her will, the same object is achieved in any event; it is therefore argued – on the analogy of *Ketubbot* 54a concerning the ravished woman who is thereafter married by her ravisher and, according to pentateuchal law, cannot be divorced – that there is no longer any need for a *ketubbah* to be written. However it has remained the *halakhah* that a *ketubbah* is to be written (*Rema* EH 66:3, concl.).

The amounts specified in the *ketubbah* deed are those of the "main" *ketubbah* and its increment (*ikkar ketubbah* and *tosefet ketubbah*) and those of the *dowry and its increment, which amounts the wife is entitled to receive upon divorce or the death of her husband (Sh. Ar., EH 93:1).

The "Main" Ketubbah and its Increment

The "main" *ketubbah* specifies the amount determined by law as the minimum that the wife is entitled to receive from her husband or his estate on the dissolution of the marriage (Sh. Ar., loc. cit.). According to some scholars the liability to pay the main *ketubbah* is pentateuchal law (Ex. 22:15–16 and Rashi thereto; Mekh. Nezikin 17; Ket. 10a and Rashi thereto), but the *halakhah* is that the *ketubbah* is rabbinical law (Ket. loc. cit; Yad, Ishut 10:7; *Ḥelkat Meḥokek* 66, n. 26). The minimum amount, as laid down in the Talmud, is 200 *zuz* in the case of a virgin and 100 *zuz* in all other cases (Ket. 10b; Sh. Ar., EH 66:6). Since in all matters concerning the *ketubbah* local custom is followed, the equivalent of the main *ketubbah* is fixed in accordance with custom and with the kind and value of the currency prevailing at the respective place (Ket. 66b; Yad, Ishut 23:12; Sh. Ar., EH 66:6, *Rema* EH 66:11). The said minimum amount is an obligation imposed on the husband by virtue of a rabbinical regulation (*takkanat bet din*), i.e., he is liable to pay this even when a lesser amount has been fixed in the *ketubbah* or no deed at all has been written (Ket. 51a). The authorities were at pains to safeguard the woman's rights in this respect, condemning cohabitation as tantamount to prostitution if the amount fixed as the main *ketubbah* is less than the said legal minimum (R. Meir, Ket. 54b; Sh. Ar., EH 66:9). The only circumstances in which the husband is exempted from meeting his obligations under the *ketubbah* are those in which the wife forfeits her *ketubbah* according to law (see *Divorce).

If the husband so wishes, he may add to the minimum amount of the *ketubbah*, an increment known as the *tosefet ketubbah*. Here, too, local custom prevails: i.e., if by virtue of local custom or rabbinical regulation it is customary for an increment to be made, the husband will be bound by this and cannot stipulate less (Sh. Ar., EH 66:9–11). The general custom at the present time is to grant the increment, and this is also reflected in the standard form of the *ketubbah* deed. It is not required that the two amounts be separately stated in the deed; they may be fixed as an aggregate amount, provided that this is not less than the minimum locally determined for the main *ketubbah* (*Rema* EH 66:7). In 1953 it was laid down by the chief rabbinate of the State of Israel that the minimum amount of the *ketubbah* – i.e., for the main *ketubbah* and its increment – must not be less than IL200 for a virgin and IL100 for a widow or divorcee. The law regarding the increment is generally the same as that regarding the main *ketubbah*, unless the *halakhah* expressly stipulates otherwise (Maim. Yad, Ishut 10:7; Sh. Ar., EH 66:7).

Dowry (Aram. נְדוּנְיָא, *nedunya*)

In addition to the above-mentioned amounts, there is also fixed in the *ketubbah* deed the amount which the husband – of his own free will and by virtue of his undertaking under the *ketubbah* deed – renders himself liable to return to his wife, when he pays her the *ketubbah*, as the equivalent of her dowry (within the restricted meaning of term). This amount is called *nedunya*, and the husband's liability to return it becomes a monetary debt and a charge upon his estate (*Rema* EH 66:11). The question of whether, in the event of a fluctuation in currency values, the wife is entitled to recover the dowry to the amount specified in the *ketubbah* deed or according to its equivalent at the time of the recovery is greatly influenced by local law and custom concerning the repayment of a regular debt in such circumstances (Resp. *Ḥatam Sofer*, EH 1:126). Since the husband is permitted by law to trade with the dowry, it is the accepted custom for him to undertake liability for an increment to the dowry, i.e., to pay his wife an additional amount over and above the amount specified as the dowry; this is known as the dowry increment (*tosefet nedunya*), and all laws of the dowry are applicable to it. The usual custom, from early times, is to fix this increment at one-half of the sum specified as the dowry. As in all matters concerning the *ketubbah*, local custom is followed, this custom has become obligatory on the bridegroom; thus he undertakes in the *ketubbah* deed to pay the main *ketubbah* and the dowry, together with their increments (Sh. Ar., EH 66:11).

The Custom Concerning Consolidation of all the Ketubbah Amounts

As it is not required that the component amounts of the *ketubbah* be stated separately, an aggregate amount may be fixed, but it is also customary in some countries to enumerate them first separately and then state the aggregate amount (for the custom in Israel, see Rodner op. cit.). If, therefore, separate amounts for the component portions are not expressly stated, they are deemed to be included in the aggregate amount specified in the deed (*Rema* EH 66:7, concl.). Since, generally speaking, the possibility of divorcing a wife without her consent is precluded by the *ḥerem* of Rabbenu Gershom, and in practice she may make her consent conditional on the satisfaction of her pecuniary claims, it is customary in many countries of the Diaspora to specify a nominal amount only for each or all of the *ketubbah* components (e.g., 200 *zekukim kesef ẓaruf*: see *Baḥ* EH 66). If, however, the wife is able to establish that the amount was written as a mere formality and not with the intention of limiting her rights, and that in fact the value of the property brought by her to the marriage exceeded the amount specified in the *ketubbah* deed, there is no legal obstacle to her obtaining satisfaction of her claims as far as she may prove them due to her. In the State of Israel it is the custom to specify in the *ketubbah* a realistic amount according to the specific respective facts.

In cases where the wife "forfeits" her *ketubbah*, the effect, in general, is that the husband is released from his liability to pay her those portions of the *ketubbah* which had to come out of his own pocket, i.e., the main *ketubbah* and its increment; in the absence of any express halakhic rule to the contrary, the wife does not forfeit the dowry or its equivalent, which is regarded as her own property, even when she is obliged to accept a bill of divorce with forfeiture of her *ketubbah* (see, e.g., Sh. Ar., EH 115:5).

The Ketubbah Conditions (Heb. תְּנָאֵי כְּתֻבָּה)

The financial obligations imposed on the husband by law (see *Husband and Wife) and specified in the *ketubbah* – in addition to the amount the wife is entitled to receive on divorce or the death of her husband – are called the "*ketubbah* conditions" (Maim. Yad, Ishut 12:2). The rule is that "the *ketubbah* conditions follow the law applying to the *ketubbah* itself" (Yev. 89a); i.e., insofar as the wife is entitled to the main *ketubbah*, she is also entitled to the rights due to her under the *ketubbah* conditions. On the other hand, her forfeiture of the right to the main *ketubbah* also carries with it the loss of her rights under the *ketubbah* conditions, such as her maintenance (Yev. loc. cit.; Rashi and Asheri thereto; see also Sh. Ar., EH 115:5).

Loss of the Ketubbah Deed

Just as the bridegroom is forbidden to cohabit with his bride after marriage unless he has written and delivered the *ketub*-

bah to her, so the husband is forbidden to live with his wife for even one hour if she has no main *ketubbah* deed. Therefore, in the case of loss or destruction of the deed, the husband is obliged to write a new one, and, since the loss of the original deed does not relieve the husband of his obligations under it, the new deed must ensure the rights that the wife was entitled to under the original one (Sh. Ar., EH 66:3; *Ḥelkat Meḥokek* 66, no. 14; for an example of such a deed (כתבה דאירכסא) see Tur, EH after 66). For the same reason, the wife's waiver of her *ketubbah* is of no effect in respect to the main *ketubbah,* and in such an event the husband is also obliged to write a new deed for her, but here only in respect of the main *ketubbah* (Sh. Ar., loc. cit.; for an example of such a *ketubbah*, see Tur, loc. cit.).

For recovery of the *ketubbah*, see *Divorce, *Widow, and *Limitation of Actions.

In the State of Israel

The wife's rights under the *ketubbah* are unaffected by the laws of the State of Israel. However, according to the Succession Law 5725/1965, whatever she receives on the strength of her *ketubbah* must be taken into account against her rights of inheritance or of maintenance from the estate of her deceased husband (sec. 11 (c); 59).

[Ben-Zion (Benno) Schereschewsky]

Status of the Ketubbah in Modern Times

POLICY OF THE RABBINICAL COURTS. In general, when a divorce suit reaches the rabbinical courts, the court recommends to the couple that they arrive at a consensual agreement regarding the division of their joint property, and only afterwards does the court transact their *get* (bill of divorcement). In most cases, division of property involves, inter alia, the wife foregoing all rights entailed in the *ketubbah* deed. The courts tend not to enforce the commitments included in the *ketubbah* owing to their concern that enforcing the additional debts included in the *ketubbah*'s increment (*tosefet ketubbah*) would trigger additional disputes between the husband and wife. As a result, the husband might find himself in the position of being forced to give the *get*, and the *get* would thus become a *get me'useh*, a coerced *get*. Moreover, the reason for the *ketubbah*'s enactment – "so that he shall not regard it as easy to divorce her" (Ket. 39b) – has lost much of its significance, given that Rabbenu Gershom's enactment prohibits a man divorcing his wife against her will. In most cases, therefore, the parties come to an agreement on monetary matters before the divorce, in order to expedite their agreement on the divorce *per se*.

THE KETUBBAH'S PRACTICAL RELEVANCE. In some, albeit not many, cases, a *ketubbah* has practical legal relevance, and the rabbinical courts, and even the civil courts, do obligate the husband to pay the *ketubbah*. Alternatively, they may impose a different obligation, while relying on the sum recorded in the *ketubbah*. It should be noted that Israeli law recognizes the *ketubbah* as a binding document (Section 17 of the Monetary Relations (Spouses) Law 1973; as well as in various sections of the Succession Law, 1965).

For this reason, in recent years prominent halakhic authorities have exhorted the public not to ridicule the sum recorded in the *ketubbah*, not to fix exaggerated sums for the *ketubbah* and the increment, and not to treat it as a purely ceremonial document (Resp. Iggerot Moshe, EH 4:92). This is the legal situation in the State of Israel.

By contrast, in civil courts in the United States, the *ketubbah* is related to as a purely ceremonial document, with no legal force attaching to it. The commitment of civil courts in Israel to the *ketubbah* and its laws is similarly limited. Inter alia, this matter finds expression with respect to imposing a lien on the property to secure the *ketubbah*. In a recent case, a husband transferred title on his apartment to his father's name before his own death. The rabbinical court ruled that, as there was no other property from which to collect on the *ketubbah*, the wife was entitled to collect from the apartment that had been transferred to her father-in-law's name. Yet the Supreme Court annulled this ruling, since the rabbinical courts lacked the authority to adjudicate the case between the wife and her late husband's father, who did not consent to the rabbinical court's adjudication of the case (HC 2621, *Levi v. Rabbinical Court*, 54 (3) PD 809).

Recently, a number of halakhic authorities have related to the *ketubbah* as a document designed to provide a woman with minimum sustenance during the initial period following divorce. The background to this is as follows: the Sages fixed the sum of the *ketubbah* as an amount that in their times was considered sufficient to support a person for a year, even if this was not the main purpose underlying its institution. Therefore, today, in wake of our above comments, we should view this as its primary purpose. Accordingly, rabbinical courts occasionally rule that the debt owed by force of the *ketubbah* be treated as a debt for the non-payment of alimony, i.e., *mezonot* after the *get*. In terms of Israeli law, the significance of this distinction is that, in execution proceedings, a debt for *mezonot* has priority over all other debt, and in contradistinction to a regular debt, the debtor can even be imprisoned for failure to pay a *mezonot* debt. In this manner the *ketubbah* can be utilized for collecting payments from a husband who attempts to evade payment.

The *ketubbah* may also be resorted to in cases of recalcitrant husbands who refuse to give a *get*. When the rabbinical court rules that the man is obligated to give a *get*, he can be compelled to pay the *ketubbah* and to return the dowry even before the giving of the *get*. If the ground for divorce is the husband's behavior, then even the *ketubbah*'s increment can be included in this sum. These means can also serve to pressure a recalcitrant husband into giving the *get* (Resp. Ketav Sofer, EH 100; Resp. Even Yekarah no. 53). The Rabbinical Court of Appeals recently ruled that payment of both the *ketubbah* and its increment may be imposed independent of the completion of the divorce proceedings. (See *Divorce).

THE SUM OF THE KETUBBAH. In the regulations enacted by the Chief Rabbinate of Ereẓ Israel in 1944, a minimum sum was fixed for the *ketubbah*. In today's terms, that sum sufficed to fulfill the Sages' intent of preventing the husband from viewing divorce lightly. This sum was increased in regulations enacted in 1953. Obviously today, after so many years, and extensive inflation, these sums are meaningless, and each couple decides on a generic amount when the *ketubbah* is written.

In some cases, pressure exerted by family members, or the couple's excitement over their approaching wedding, leads to the stipulation of exaggerated sums in the *ketubbah*. In such cases, rabbinic authorities and *dayyanim* are divided over whether these sums are binding. One view is that, so long as the groom does not swear to the amount of the sum when signing the *ketubbah*, it should not be given binding force. Rather, the husband should be obligated to pay the primary sum of the *ketubbah* (*ikkar ha-kettubah*) without the increment, i.e., the value of two hundred zuz. This view regards the original undertaking solely as an *asmakhta* (see *Asmakhta), i.e., the person assumed an obligation without really intending to be bound thereby, but was only exaggerating, or operated on the belief that the obligation would never actually take effect.

Another view is that, in principle, even a large sum binds the husband, in accordance with the ruling of *Keẓot ha-Hoshen* (264:4) that a person cannot claim "I was only joking with you," provided that he either swears or shakes hands on the agreement (see *Undertaking), and also because the undertakings included in the *ketubbah* are considered as essential preconditions for marital life.

Nevertheless, when a manifestly "astronomical" sum is involved, to the extent that it is obvious that neither party ever contemplated the possibility of the sum being binding, the husband cannot be compelled to pay it. In such a case, even according to the second view, the husband should be required to pay a *ketubbah* and increment "in accordance with accepted practice and the family's social level, whatever is accepted amongst families of that ethnic community in our day."

A third opinion is that, fundamentally, the husband is obligated by any amount he undertook, even if exorbitant. The mere fact of his having undertaken to pay that amount is tantamount to an acknowledgment that he has the sum at his disposal and, accordingly, the law of *asmakhta* does not apply to the sum of his *ketubbah*. In a ruling by the Rabbinical Court of Appeals (2128/48 PDR 15, 211), the majority of *dayyanim* ruled in accordance with the second opinion.

In 2000, the Chief Rabbinate issued a proclamation that there is no minimum sum for the *ketubbah*, but that the maximum sum of the *ketubbah*'s increment is NIS 1,000,000.

Furthermore, when the sum stipulated in the *ketubbah* is only an expression of respect for the proceedings, or symbolic in some other way, the question of *asmakhta* also arises. Regarding cases in which the sum is not exorbitant, the Rabbinical Court of Appeals rejected the husband's claim that the sum has no binding significance, ruling that it is legally binding.

The husband's argument that he did not understand the *ketubbah*'s wording, or the implications of specifying such a large sum when he signed it, is unacceptable. After all, there is also the testimony of the witnesses who are signed on the *ketubbah*, and "for it is presumed that they did not sign without their first having orally testified (i.e., orally explained the document they were signing) in his presence, for without this presumption, there would be no possibility of obliging the ignorant … to comply with their obligation under the *kettubah* … for they would all raise this claim" (Resp. Rashba 1:629; Rema, Sh. Ar. EH 66:13).

REVALUATING THE KETUBBAH AMOUNT. When the *bet din* or the court rules on the husband's obligation to pay the *ketubbah*, the question arises as to how to revaluate the *ketubbah*. This is particularly relevant during inflationary periods, when there is liable to be an immense discrepancy between its value at the time it was signed and its value at the time of divorce or the husband's death. The Israeli rabbinical courts have adopted various methods for revaluating the *ketubbah*. The *ketubbah* cannot be reassessed unless it explicitly states how it should be reassessed. The possibilities for revaluation include linking it to the American dollar; linking it to the consumer price index; leaving the original sum but obligating the husband in accordance with the currency used at the time of payment; arbitration (*Takkanat Ra'anaḥ* – i.e., the Enactment of Rabbi Eliyahu ben Ḥayyim; see Resp. Maharit EH 2); linkage to the silver standard; reevaluation of the sum so that it does not fall below the amount needed to support the wife for a year.

PRENUPTIAL AGREEMENTS. Given that in most instances the *ketubbah* does not actually fulfill its purpose of regulating the couple's financial relationship at the time of the divorce, in recent years there has been a growing tendency to use prenuptial financial agreements between the couple for that purpose. Besides serving a monetary role similar to that of the *ketubbah*, these agreements also assist in preventing refusal to grant a *get*, as within the framework of these agreements both parties undertake a legal or financial commitment which spurs them into giving a *get* in the event of the marriage failing and one of the parties desiring to terminate it. These agreements raise a number of problems in the context of the laws of divorce, such as the risk of a "coerced *get*" (*get me'useh*), questions with which halakhic authorities have dealt extensively in recent years (see Bibliography; see *Divorce).

DIVORCE COMPENSATION. In addition to the wife's *ketubbah* rights, the rabbinical court sometimes rules that the husband must pay her compensation. The roots of this compensation award are found in a number of responsa from the last few hundred years, and in the mid-20th century the matter became a binding *minhag*, conferring on the wife a right to receive part of the joint property. This compensation, which can be viewed as a quasi "equitable right," is similar in purpose and source to the joint property presumption (see *Matrimonial Property).

It serves to provide the woman with part of the property created during the years of marriage, through the couple's joint efforts. In addition, it provides the wife with economic stability during the period following the divorce.

Originally, the Israel Supreme Court distinguished between divorce compensation and the joint property rule, explaining that the latter is based on the legal presumption that, when the couple wed, their intent was that their property be shared between them equally. By contrast, the law of divorce compensation does not derive from any presumption. Rather, "its source lies in the principle of justice and fairness, for it is fitting for the wife to be compensated in accordance with her efforts in raising and nurturing the family unit … in order to enable her reasonable subsistence after the divorce" (CA 630/70, *Lieberman v. Lieberman*, PD 35(4), 373, per Justice Menachem Elon). However, in recent years the Supreme Court's justification for the joint property rule has changed, and it is now similarly regarded as deriving from principles of justice and fairness, and a number of halakhic authorities have noted the similarity of the logic behind the presumption regarding joint property and the logic guiding a Rabbinical court to award divorce compensation. (For an elaboration on this point, see *Matrimonial Property).

Some halakhic authorities, however, oppose giving the wife divorce compensation, because it has no halakhic basis. In their view, such compensation can only be awarded as a means of effecting a divorce when a problem arises in attaining the wife's consent.

In recent years, in accordance with the decision of the Supreme Court, even rabbinical courts are obligated to divide the property up equally in accordance with the joint property rule (regarding the way the *halakhah* relates to this, see **Dina de-Malkhuta Dina*). This division of property does not apply to obligations deriving from the *ketubbah*. Hence, the Rabbinic courts need to proceed with caution, lest a situation be created in which a woman receives double rights.

[Menachem Elon (2nd ed.)]

Conservative and Reform

To meet and resolve the problem presented in Jewish law by the **Agunah*, the Rabbinical Assembly of America (Conservative) in 1953 adopted a *takkanah* ("enactment") proposed by Saul *Lieberman. The enactment went into effect in 1954 and the modified form of the *ketubbah* into which it was incorporated is currently widely used by Conservative Rabbis. The additional clause in both the Aramaic and English versions of the *ketubbah* provides that both bride and bridegroom "agree to recognize the Beth Din of the Rabbinical Assembly and the Jewish Theological Seminary of America … as having authority … to summon either party at the request of the other in order to enable the party so requesting to live in accordance with the laws of Jewish marriage …." By mutual agreement, the "Beth Din" is authorized to impose such terms of compensation as it may see fit for failure to respond to its summons or to carry out its decision. The clause is aimed to compel a recalcitrant husband or wife divorced by civil law to agree to the writing and acceptance of the traditional *get*. At the time of marriage, the *ketubbah* is filled out in duplicate by the officiating rabbi and the copy is forwarded for filing at the marriage registry established by the Rabbinical Assembly.

Reform Judaism has dropped the use of the traditional *ketubbah*. Instead, most Reform rabbis issue a marriage certificate drawn up by the Central Conference of American Rabbis (Reform). The certificate makes no reference to the halakhic formulations of the traditional *ketubbah*.

[Theodore Friedman]

Illuminated Ketubbot

Most Jewish communities have followed the custom of decorating the *ketubbah*. An Ashkenazi *ketubbah* from Krems. Austria, dated 1392, shows that illumination was usual among Ashkenazi communities during the Middle Ages. However, the best-known illuminated *ketubbot*, which date from the 16th century onward, were from Italy, certain Sephardi communities, and from Near and Far Eastern Jewry.

EUROPEAN KETUBBOT. Richly illuminated *ketubbot*, which date from the 17th and 18th centuries, are from Italy, Corfu, the Balkans, and Gibraltar. They are written on parchment and the text is usually bordered by an illuminated frame, depicting a variety of decorative themes in many bright colors. The frame, which is sometimes divided into a diptych, is often illustrated with biblical or mythological motifs, portraits of the bride and groom in contemporary costume, family coats of arms, symbols representing conjugal bliss, and even nude figures. Typical Jewish symbols were used, such as the hands forming the priestly blessing, a sign that the groom was from a family of *kohanim*, or a ewer and basin indicating a levite. Sometimes, the biblical figures represented in the *ketubbah* symbolize the bride or groom's name; thus a scene from the life of Joseph might mean that the groom's name was Joseph, a scene from the Book of Ruth that the bride's name was Ruth.

Dutch Sephardi *ketubbot* of the same period are distinguished by their delicate ornamental engraving. They were mainly executed on parchment and are in the best Dutch copper-engraving tradition. An outstanding example is a 1658 Rotterdam *ketubbah*, executed by Shalom Italia, a copper engraver from Mantua who emigrated to Holland. This *ketubbah* is rich in biblical motifs. Another famous copper-engraved *ketubbah*, dating from the late 17th century, is decorated with flowers and allegorical figures in the typical Dutch-Jewish contemporary manner. The border contains the date 1693, commemorating the year of the death of the renowned Amsterdam rabbi, Isaac *Aboab de Fonseca.

EASTERN KETUBBOT. *Ketubbot* from the Near East and countries bordering Israel are decorated in a manner different from the European ones. They are mostly on paper and are decorated with plant motifs, mainly flowers, or geometric patterns similar to carpet patterns. The best-known examples are from the Persian community of *Isfahan, which also feature the national emblems of Persia, the lion, a half-sun with a face, and sometimes a sword. Other noteworthy Persian *ketubbot* are from Hamadan. The decorations of these *ketubbot* sometimes include wood-block prints. The *ketubbot* from the Teheran community were made in the form of small booklets. Their pages are illuminated in typical Persian style. Other interesting Persian *ketubbot* are from *Meshed. In 1839, the Jews of Meshed were forcibly converted to Islam. They thus prepared two *ketubbot* for the marriage ceremony: one in Arabic and Persian in order to prove that the couple were Muslim, and an "illegal" one in Hebrew and Aramaic, in the Jewish form. These *ketubbot* were decorated with an abundance of colored flowers. *Ketubbot* from the *Herat community in Afghanistan are noteworthy for the delicate composition of garlands and wreaths of colored flowers surmounting the text. One interesting feature of Persian and Afghan *ketubbot* is that the signature of the illuminator sometimes appears on the bottom margin.

Although the Yemenite *ketubbot* were mostly undecorated, an occasional gaily-colored example is to be found. Human forms, as well as flower motifs, appear in the *Sanʿa ketubbah* of 1793 in the Israel Museum. *Ketubbot* from North Africa are illuminated with multicolored decorations, but are mainly distinguished by the exquisitely written text. Sometimes the frame is decorated with black-white arabesques. Indian *ketubbot*, from Calcutta and Bombay, are written on parchment and decorated with colored ornamentation. These *ketubbot* are heavily influenced by Indian art motifs, such as gateways and animals. Those from *Cochin bore above the text a circle with verses of good omen, the whole in a floral border. The typical 19th-century Jerusalem *ketubbah*, although belonging geographically to the Arab countries, shows no evidence of this in its decorative style. The most commonly used ornamentation is a garland of flowers over the text, with palm or cypress trees on either side.

[David Davidovitch]

BIBLIOGRAPHY: A. Buechler, in: *Festschrift ... Lewy* (1911), 118, 122–9; J.S. Zuri, *Mishpat ha-Talmud*, 2 (1921), 57–93; Gulak, Yesodei, 3 (1922), 35f., 46f., 60–63; idem, Oẓar, 28–30, 41–67, 93–109, 167–70; idem, in: *Tarbiz*, 3 (1932), 249–57; S. Zeitlin, in: JQR, 24 (1933–34), 1–7; L.M. Epstein, *The Jewish Marriage Contract* (1927); Ḥ. Albeck, in: *Kovez Madda'i le-Zekher Moshe Schorr* (1945), 12–24; ET, 2 (1949), 18, 183f.; N. Lamm, in: *Tradition*, 2 (1959/60), 93–113; S. Goren, in: *Maḥanayim*, no. 83 (1963), 5–14; B. and H. Goodman, *The Jewish Marriage Anthology* (1965); Elon, Mafte'aḥ, 114–20. ILLUMINATED: D. Davidovitz, *Ha-Ketubbah ki-Khetav-Yad Ommanuti* (1963); idem, *Ketuba: Jewish Marriage Contracts through the Ages* (Eng. and Heb., 1968); M. Gaster, *Ketubah* (1923); Roth, Art, index; Meyer, Art, index; F. Landsberger, *A History of Jewish Art* (1946); Narkiss, in: *Tarbiz*, 25 (1955/56), 441–51; 26 (1956/57), 87–101; Yoel, in: KS, 38 (1962), 122–32. **ADD. BIBLIOGRAPHY:** M. Elon, *Ha-Mishpat ha-Ivri* (1988), 1:112f, 116, 188, 190f., 205, 336, 351–56, 362, 373f., 403f., 449f., 458f., 470f., 483, 485f., 531, 540f., 543, 577, 633, 637, 640, 651, 653, 663, 672, 682f., 773f., 775, 794f.; 2:887, 1233, 1339; 3:1473; idem, *Jewish Law* (1994), 1:126f, 130, 211, 213f., 231, 403, 424–30, 437, 452f., 491f., 547f., 559f., 573f., 588, 590f., 646, 658f., 661, 711, 783, 789, 792, 805, 808, 820, 830, 841f., 951f., 953, 974f.; 3:1070, 1476, 1599; 4:1573; M. Elon, *Ma'amad ha-Ishah* (2005), 233ff., 259–62, 266, 278 ff., 285; idem, *Ḥakikah Datit* (1968), 165–67; M. Elon and B. Lifshitz, *Mafte'aḥ ha-She'elot ve-ha-Teshuvot shel Ḥakhmei Sefarad u-Ẓefon Afrikah* (legal digest) (1986), 1:195–201; B. Lifshitz and E. Shochetman, *Mafte'aḥ ha-She'elot ve-ha-Teshuvot shel Ḥakhmei Ashkenaz, Ẓarefat ve-Italyah* (legal digest) (1977), 143–47; A. Bar Shalom, *Mishpat ha-Ketubbah*, 1–2 (1995); Z. Boblil, "*Ketubbah Mufrezet u-Piẓu'ei Gerushin*," in: *Teḥumin*, 25 (2005), 204–15; M. Broid, Y. Reis, and Z. Boblil, "*Erkah shel Ketubbah*," in: *Teḥumin* 25 (2005), 180–94; S. Dikhovsky, "*Heskemei Mammon Kedam-Nissu'in*," in: *Teḥumin* 21 (2001), 279–87; idem, "*Ḥiyyuvei Haẓmadah be-Batei Din Rabbaniyyim*," in: *Dinei Yisrael*, 12–13 (1984–85), 103–18; G. Gorman, "*Shi'arukh ha-Ketubbah*," in: *Teḥumin*, 25 (2005), 195–203; D. Mikhelov, "*Heskemim Kedam-Nissuin*," in: *Dinei Yisrael*, 12–13 (1984–85), 324–39; P. Shiffman, *Dinei ha-Mishpaḥa be-Yisrael* (1995); B. Schereschewsky, *Dinei ha-Mishpaḥah* (1993[4]), 89–95.

KETUBBOT (Heb. כְּתֻבּוֹת; "Marriage Contracts"), second tractate in the order *Nashim*, dealing with rights and duties arising out of the contract of marriage. *Ketubbah*, literally, "that which is written," denotes in this tractate not so much the marriage document itself (see **Ketubbah*) as the obligations statutorily contained in it. In fact, according to Mishnah 4:7–12, the usual terms of a *ketubbah* are binding upon husband and wife even if no document has been drawn up. The word *ketubbah* came to be identified with the most important provision in the marriage contract from the point of view of the *halakhah*, namely the sum of money due to the wife if she is divorced or widowed. Thus, throughout this tractate, phrases like "the *ketubbah* is so-and-so many zuzim," or "she is entitled to the *ketubbah*" refer to the amount due to the wife according to the *ketubbah*. The *ketubbah* of a virgin was fixed at 200 zuzim while that of a non-virgin, by rabbinical enactment, at 100 zuzim. This distinction between virgin and non-virgin as it relates to the amount of the *ketubbah* takes up much of the first two chapters of this tractate. In this context the proof of *virginity is widely discussed, with digressions, for most of the second chapter, into general questions of trustworthiness and evidence. Chapter 3 deals with fines payable in cases of rape and seduction (Ex. 22:15; Deut. 22:29). Chapter 4, after stating that fines for seduction to a girl go to her father, mentions other rights of the father vis-à-vis his daughter; the chapter also includes duties incumbent upon the husband even if not written in the *ketubbah*. Chapters 5–6 deal mostly with the mutual rights and duties of husband and wife in marital and material respects, and also touches on the question of a daughter's dowry.

Chapter 7 deals with circumstances in which a woman can demand divorce and receive her statutory *ketubbah* money, and gives instances in which a man can divorce a woman without being liable to pay the *ketubbah*. Chapters 8–9 deal with the rights of the woman to her own property and with her claims upon her husband's property after his death. Chapter 10, in the context of polygamy, deals with the problem of adjudicating the conflicting claims of several wives. Chapters 11 and 12 deal with the rights of the widow and the duties of heirs toward her (whether she is their mother or stepmother), and the position of the stepdaughter. Chapter 13 has a distinctive character, quoting various *halakhot* of earlier authorities (Adom and Hanan). The last Mishnah speaks of the great merit of living in the land of Israel (especially in Jerusalem), with the halakhic consequence that if a man wishes to go to live in Israel and a woman refuses to go with him, he can divorce her without payment of the *ketubbah*, and if she wishes to do so and he refuses, she is entitled to divorce with *ketubbah*.

According to Epstein (*Tanna'im*, passim), Mishnah 10:4 belongs to the Mishnah of R. Nathan (Ket. 93a), while 3:1; 7:10; 8:3, 7 belong to that of R. Meir, and 1:5 to that of R. Judah b. Ilai. The Tosefta has 12 chapters. Interesting differences between the marriage customs of Judea and Galilee are mentioned in 1:4. There are several independent passages of ancient origin, one of which, 4:1–3, contrasts the respective rights of the father, husband, and levir of a woman. Another, 4:9–14, lists a series of laws each beginning with the phrase, "Rabbi [so and so] expounded." A. Weiss discerned three major strata in the Babylonian Talmud to *Ketubbot*: The most ancient contains the opinions of Rav and Samuel and the teachings of the academy of *Pumbedita. The second stratum is that of Abbaye and Rava, who also lived in Pumbedita, but part of Rava's sayings originate from other academies. The third stratum is Papa's, and hails from his academy in Naresh. These three strata do not receive equal representation in the *Gemara*. Thus, although chapter 7 is replete with the opinion of Samuel on almost every Mishnah (cf. 77a, where R. Assi testified to Samuel's having delved deeply into the chapter), chapter 3 contains almost no material of this stratum and is dominated by the viewpoints of rabbis of the second and third strata. This pattern of chapter 3 is also seen in chapters 5, 9, 10, 11, 12, and 13 (*Hithavvut ha-Talmud bi-Shelemuto* (1943), 6–27).

Both the Jerusalem and the Babylonian Talmuds maintain that the Roman governor insisted on the *jus primae noctis*. According to the Jerusalem Talmud, in order to prevent this it became customary for the groom to have intercourse with his bride while she was still in her father's house, a custom which remained in effect even after the decree was no longer enforced (1:5; 25c). Another saying is that God valued the *mitzvah* of procreation over that of the construction of the Temple (5:7; 30a,b). The entire passage of 12:3, 35a–b is devoted to aggadic discussion, and contains biographical details about Judah ha-Nasi and his nephew Ḥiyya, and, like the Babylonian Talmud, expatiates on the virtues of Ereẓ Israel. In the Babylonian Talmud the discussions of *miggo* which play a significant role in the Jewish law of *evidence (chapter 2) are of particular halakhic interest, as are the references to the *takkanot* of Usha (49b–50a). Some of the aggadic passages to the Babylonian *Gemara* are of great beauty. They include accounts of rabbis dancing and singing at wedding festivities in fulfillment of the precept of gladdening bride and bridegroom (16b–17a; see also Ber. 6b); of the romance of R. Akiva (then a shepherd) with the daughter of Kalba Savua (62b–63a); Rabban Gamaliel's example of simplicity in burial (8b); and the description of Judah ha-Nasi's death and burial (103b–104a). Taking up the last Mishnah's allusion to the superiority of Ereẓ Israel, the concluding portion of the tractate is dedicated to praise of that land. The aggadic portion starts with the saying (110b) that one should live in Israel, even in a town with a heathen majority, rather than in the Diaspora, even if it be a place abounding with Jews; its concluding sentence expounds Joel 2:22, stating that in Israel even the barren trees will bear fruit.

BIBLIOGRAPHY: Epstein, Tanna'im index; Ḥ. Albeck, *Shishah Sidrei Mishnah, Seder Nashim* (1954), 77–87; A. Weiss, *Hithavvut ha-Talmud bi-Shelemuto* (1943), index.

[Arnost Zvi Ehrman]

KETURAH (Heb. קְטוּרָה), a wife (Gen. 25:1) or concubine of Abraham (cf. 25:6; I Chron. 1:32). She bore him six sons (Gen. 25:2; I Chron. 1:32), the most prominent of these being *Midian. All these names are eponyms of peoples and locales. These children complete the fulfillment of the promise that Abraham would be the father of many nations (Gen. 17:5). Abraham is said to have given them gifts and to have sent them away from his son Isaac eastward, to the land of the East (Gen. 25:6). The text emphasizes that Abraham was still living when he sent Keturah's sons away in order to show that they had no claims to rival Isaac. The peoples and locales Sheba, Dedan, Ephah, Midian, and Medan are mentioned in connection with ancient international trade, especially in spices, gold, and precious stones which were brought from southern Arabia (Isa. 60:6; Ezek. 27:15, 20, 22; cf. Gen. 37:25, 28, 36). Given that these locales were on the incense route, it is probable that the writer of the account named Abraham's wife Keturah to connect her with the word *ketoret* (*qeṭoret*, קְטֹרֶת, "incense"), of which a by-form *ketorah* (*qeṭorah*, קְטוֹרָה) occurs in Deuteronomy 33:10.

[Israel Eph'al / S. David Sperling (2nd ed.)]

In the Aggadah

Keturah is identified with Hagar. The connection with incense (see above) is that her good deeds gave off a fragrance like incense; or that she combined (*kitrah*) in herself piety and nobility (Gen. R. 61:4). She was a daughter of Japheth (Yal. Reub. Gen. 26:2, 36c).

BIBLIOGRAPHY: E. Meyer, *Die Israeliten und ihre Nachbarstämme* (1906), 312–22; J.A. Montgomery, *Arabia and the Bible* (1934), 42–45. IN THE AGGADAH: Ginzberg, Legends, index; I. Ḥasida, *Ishei ha-Tanakh* (1964), 375. **ADD. BIBLIOGRAPHY:** N. Sarna, *JPS Torah Commentary Genesis* (1989), 171–73; E. Knauf, in: ABD, 4:31.

KEVER AVOT (Heb. קֶבֶר אָבוֹת; "grave of the fathers"), the custom of visiting the graveside of parents or close relatives and praying there. The theme of the prayers is peaceful eternal rest for the departed and an invocation for God's aid to the living on the basis of the pious deeds of the dead performed in their lifetime.

Judaism did not encourage "praying to the dead" and the custom of *kever avot* was, therefore, limited to special occasions; the day of the *Yahrzeit, the eve of Rosh Ḥodesh especially that of the month of Elul, and in various Ashkenazi communities also the Ninth of *Av in the afternoon (Isserles to Sh. Ar., OḤ 459:10 and 481:4).

It was also customary to visit the graveside of pious individuals so that "the departed will intercede for mercy on behalf of the living" (Ta'an. 16a). It was related that Caleb visited Hebron and prostrated himself upon the graves of the patriarchs, saying to them, "My fathers, pray on my behalf that I may be delivered from the plan of the spies" (Sot. 34b). According to the Midrash, Jacob buried Rachel on the way to Ephrath near Bethlehem so that she could later pray for her children as they passed by her grave on the way to the Babylonian exile (Gen. 35:19; Jer. 31:15).

This practice was particularly stressed by the Ḥasidim who considered the earth above the final resting places of their rabbis as holy as the Land of Israel. Rooms known as *ohalim* were constructed above their graves, and Ḥasidim gathered there to pray on the *Yahrzeit* or whenever they desired the heavenly intervention of the departed rabbis. Those who opposed the Ḥasidim, however, discouraged these practices. It was related that R. *Elijah b. Solomon of Vilna even regretted the one time he visited his mother's grave. R. Ḥayyim *Volozhin reportedly left instructions that his disciples were not to visit his final resting place. Likewise, R. Ḥayyim *Soloveichik of Brest-Litovsk never visited the graves of his parents.

See: *Av the Ninth, *Cemetery, **Hillula*, *Holy Places, *Lag ba-Omer, *Mourning Customs.

BIBLIOGRAPHY: Aaron Wertheim, *Hilkhot va-Halikhot ba-Ḥasidut*, 226f.; Harry Rabinowicz, *A Guide to Life*, 99f.

KEYSERLING, LEON H. (1908–1987), U.S. economist. Born in Charleston (South Carolina), after a short period of teaching at Columbia University Keyserling became, in 1933, Legislative Assistant to Senator Robert F. Wagner. He then served as a consultant to numerous Senate committees on banking, taxation, monetary policy, public works, housing, labor relations, social security, and employment. Under the Truman administration he was chairman of the President's Council of Economic Advisers. He was frequently consulted by Israel government agencies. Keyserling's main economic interests were the fields of employment and production, and his numerous publications included *The Federal Budget and the General Welfare* (1959); *Food and Freedom* (1960); *Poverty and Deprivation in the United States* (1962); *Progress and Poverty* (1964); and *Role of Wages in a Great Society* (1966). His wife, MARY DUBLIN KEYSERLING (1900–1997), who was born in New York City, was a professional economist, connected with federal agencies in the United States.

[Joachim O. Ronall]

KEẒAẒAH (Heb. קְצָצָה; "a severing of connections," lit. "cutting-off"), a technical term used in the Talmud for a ceremony, whereby a family severs its connection with one of its members who marries a person beneath his social rank (Ket. 28b), or when one sells part of his estate (TJ, Kid. 1:5, 60c). In both of these instances the *keẓaẓah* acts as a kind of publicity for the act done. It would seem from the Jerusalem Talmud that the *keẓaẓah* was at one time a form of *kinyan* ("act of possession"), but even in early times it fell, as such, into disuse. The Talmud gives the following description of the *keẓaẓah*. "How is the *keẓaẓah* performed? If one of the brothers married a woman unsuitable for him, members of the family come and bring a barrel filled with fruit and break it in the town square, saying, 'O brethren of the House of Israel, give ear, our brother so-and-so has married an unsuitable woman and we are afraid lest his seed mingle with our seed. Come and take yourselves a sign for the generations [which are to come], that his seed mingle not with our seed'" (Ket. 28b). A similar *keẓaẓah* took place when the renegade divorced his unsuitable mate, or when the estate which had been sold was repurchased (TJ, *ibid.*).

BIBLIOGRAPHY: Freund, in: *Festschrift A. Schwarz* (1917), 179f.; Krauss, Tal Arch, 2 (1911), 33; 3 (1912), 188.

[Abraham Hirsch Rabinowitz]

KHALAẒ, JUDAH BEN ABRAHAM (d. before 1537), rabbi and kabbalist from Castile, Spain. In 1477 Judah fled from anti-Jewish excesses in his native town and went to Granada, where he remained for five years, acting as a teacher. From there he proceeded to Malaga, where he spent another four years in a similar capacity. In 1486 he arrived in Honain, from where he proceeded to Tlemcen, Algeria, where he was resident tutor to the son of the wealthy Joseph b. Sidon. There he wrote *Mesi'aḥ Illemim*, on Rashi's Bible commentary and *Sefer ha-Musar* (also called *Sefer ha-Mefo'ar*, Constantinople, 1537), an ethical work with both rational and kabbalistic expositions, which is essentially an adaptation of the *Menorat ha-Ma'or* of Israel *Al-Nakawa. In his work, Judah interprets kabbalistic explanations of the commandments and prayers by his relative Moses b. Eleazar Khalaẓ. Judah is probably the author of *Maggid Mishneh* (a commentary on the laws of *sheḥitah* of *Maimonides) published in *Zevaḥim Shelamim* by Abraham Ankawa (Leghorn, 1858). He also wrote an introduction to the Talmud, containing 58 rules of talmudic methodology (published by M. Herschler, in: *Sinai*, 55 (1964), 25–36). A work on the Exodus, *Pi Yehudah*, is still in manuscript. JUDAH BEN ABRAHAM HA-KOHEN KHALAZ, who lived in the 16th–17th century, was a member of the same family and according to some the grandson of Judah. He studied under Solomon b. Ẓemah Duran II, to whom he dedicated a laudatory poem published in Duran's *Ḥeshek Shelomo* (Venice, 1623).

BIBLIOGRAPHY: A. Neubauer, in: REJ, 5 (1882), 47–52; M. Steinschneider, in: JQR, 11 (1899), 125; Israel al-Nakawa, *Menorat ha-Ma'or* ed. by H.G. Enelow, 3 (1931), 56 (introd.); S. Wiener, *Kohelet Moshe* (1893–1918), 405, no. 3377.

[Abraham David]

KHALYASTRE (Yid. "The Gang"), post-World War I Warsaw group of Yiddish expressionist and futurist poets. It received its title from Hillel *Zeitlin, editor of the influential Warsaw daily *Moment*, who used the term in a derogatory sense because the slogans and practices of the group's members outraged public opinion in their struggle against realism in art. These writers were led by Peretz *Markish, Uri Zvi *Greenberg, and Melech *Ravitch. Accepting Zeitlin's designation as a badge of honor, they termed their short-lived literary review *Khalyastre*. The first issue appeared in Warsaw in 1922 under the editorship of Markish and I.J. *Singer. The second, final, issue appeared in Paris two years later, under the editorship of Markish and O. *Warszawski, with illustrations by Marc *Chagall. Contributors also included D. *Hofstein, I. *Kipnis, M. Khashchevatsky, and Israel Stern. Not all of these writers were in sympathy with the flamboyant futurism of the *Khalyastre*, but they were impressed by the irrepressible vitality of the lyric triumvirate. Ravitch's *Nakete Lider* ("Naked Songs," 1921), Greenberg's *Mefisto* (1922), and Markish's *Di Kupe* ("The Mound," 1922) were among the best products of the *Khalyastre*. The climax of the group's striving was reached in the issues of *Albatros* (edited by Greenberg in Warsaw, 1922, and in Berlin, 1923), a periodical which proclaimed itself as the organ of extreme individualism in poetry. It advocated exaltation, renovation, and revolution of the spirit. It set out to fragment the language of the classical masters and to rebuild Yiddish anew. It preferred rhythmic tautness and explosiveness to rounded, melodious verses. *Khalyastre* came to an end with the dispersal of many of its leading figures: Markish to Soviet Russia, Greenberg to Ereẓ Israel in 1925, and Ravitch to Australia. The journal was endowed with a kind of second life with the publication of a French translation of its two issues, including the original illustrations and an exhaustive critical apparatus: Rachel Ertel, *Khaliastra: La Bande* (1989).

[Sol Liptzin / Alan Astro (2nd ed.)]

KHANAQIN (Khaniqin, Khanikin), town in Diyāla province of E. Iraq; on the ancient Baghdad-Hamadan road, N.E. of Baghdad. In the middle of the 19th century there were about 20 Jewish families residing in Khanaqin; a century later the Jewish community numbered 700 people, most of whom were Arabic-speaking – about a quarter of them spoke Mountain Aramaic. The Jews were cloth and iron merchants, shopkeepers, itinerant money changers, innkeepers, etc. In 1911 the *Alliance Israélite Universelle established a coeducational school in the town which had an attendance of 181 pupils. In the 1920s Zionist activities were introduced. In August 1949, the police arrested the head of the community, accusing him of organizing an illegal Zionist organization; many other Jews were arrested at the same time. In the early 1950s the community left Khanaqin for Israel.

BIBLIOGRAPHY: A. Ben-Jacob, *Yehudei Bavel* (1965), 317.

[Abraham Haim]

KHĀN YŪNIS, town 14 mi. (23 km.) S.W. of Gaza. This may be the town ʾΙήνυσος which Herodotus lists among the Philistine towns (3:5). During the period of *Mamluk rule, Khān Yūnis served as an important market for the caravan trade between Ereẓ Israel and *Egypt. At that time the sultan Barqūq ordered an inn (*khān*) to be built there. There are remnants of this inn with Arabic transcriptions and architectural fragments. Almost all the population was Muslim, except for 316 Christians. The 1931 census indicated 3,811 inhabitants in Khān Yūnis (and another 3,440 then living in its vicinity); among these were three Jews and 40 Christians. In 1944, the population figure stood at 11,220. Before 1948, Jewish institutions and private persons repeatedly attempted to buy holdings, particularly *Jiftlik* (i.e., lands in public ownership), but legal difficulties precluded the final transfer. In 1948, the town was in the Gaza Strip, which remained under Egyptian rule. It was briefly in Israeli hands after the Sinai Campaign in 1956 and again from the Six-Day War of 1967. In 1994 it was transferred to the jurisdiction of the *Palestinian Authority. Its economy was based almost exclusively on farming (citrus groves, date palms, other fruits, vegetables, and irrigated and unirrigated field crops). In 1967 its population was 52,997 inhabitants, nearly half (23,475) living in refugee camps. By 1997 its population had reached 123,056, nearly two-thirds of whom were refugees. A stronghold of the Hamas terrorist organization, Khān Yūnis was hit by Israeli forces during the al-Aqsa Intifada (see *Israel, State of: Historical Survey) and buildings have been razed after providing cover for terrorists firing at Israeli settlements in *Gush Katif.

[Efraim Orni]

KHARĀJ AND JIZYA, Arabic-Turkish for tribute or remuneration in general which later came to mean land tax and poll tax, respectively. According to the constitution of the Muslim state, as conceived by the legislators, the payment of the poll tax by the non-Muslim gives him the right to live within the state. Many times the *jizya* is named *jilya* or *aljavali*. Although the *jizya* is mentioned in the *Koran (Sura 9:29), the poll tax probably was a continuation of the policies of the Persian and Byzantine empires. In Sassanid *Persia all subjects, with the exception of the aristocracy, had to pay a poll tax according to their wealth. The poll tax in the various provinces of the Byzantine empire was not collected in the same way and when the Arabs conquered the lands of the Fertile Crescent, they concluded treaties with certain towns and districts, determining lump sums to be paid to them and to be collected by local notables. Therefore, the sources of the early period of Muslim rule reveal a bewildering confusion. *Kharāj* (Sura 23:74) and *jizya* were apparently used interchangeably in various regions, reflecting the lack of uniform fiscal systems. Under the later *Umayyads, from Omar II (717–720), the authorities began to distinguish between the *kharāj*, the land tax to be paid by most landholders, and the *jizya*, the poll tax to be paid by non-Muslims. Under the first *Abbasids, at the end of the eighth century, the Muslim lawyers fixed the rules of the *jizya*. According to the precepts of Abū Ḥanīfa, which were taken over by most jurists, the poor had to pay one dinar per year; the middle class, two; and the rich, four. Women, children, old men, the sick, the mentally ill, and those without any income were to be exempt. They also established that the tax should be paid at the beginning of the lunar (Muslim) year. The majority of the Muslim jurists thought jizya as a punishment, a means to degrade the non-Muslims.

Both Arabic reports referring to the period of the Umayyad and Abbasid caliphs, and Judeo-Arabic documents from the 11th century show that the authorities used very harsh methods in collecting the *jizya*, imposing it even on those exempt from paying by virtue of the *sharīʿa* (the canon law of Islam). Under the first caliphs the punishment of those who had not paid the *jizya* consisted of pouring oil on their heads and exposing them to the sun. Many extant **Genizah* letters state that the collectors imposed the tax on children and demanded it for the dead. As the family was held responsible for the payment of the *jizya* by all its members, it sometimes became a burden and many went into hiding in order to escape imprisonment. For example there is a *Responsum* by *Maimonides from another document, written in 1095, about a father paying the *jizya* for his two sons, 13 and 17 years old. From another document, written around 1095, it seems that the tax was due from the age of nine. Even foreigners and transients were compelled to pay the poll tax; hence, nobody dared travel without a certificate of payment (*barāʾa*). Everyone paid where he was registered as resident. These documents also prove that the non-Muslims had to pay the *jizya* in advance (i.e., some time before the beginning of the Muslim year). The Jews in the Muslim territories did not try to ask exemption from the *jizya*, because they wanted to be protected. The stability of this tax gave the Jews stable security. There is a famous legend from the tenth century about the Jewish banker *Natira, who objected to the idea of an Abbasid caliph to exempt the Jews from paying *jizya*. The leaders of Egypt in the *Fatimid period were requested many times by poor people to help them out of difficulties incurred with the Muslim *jizya* collectors. Since the payment of the *jizya* was considered a sign of humiliation, Muslim lawyers insisted that it be paid in person. Such was the practice in 12th- and 13th-century Iraq and in Fatimid and *Ayyubid *Egypt. Sometimes the authorities made agreements with local communities, fixing a lump sum to be paid regardless of the number of taxpayers. Several extant *Genizah* letters point to the fact that the Jews in *Jerusalem in the 11th century paid the *jizya* as a fixed sum; the Italian rabbi Obadiah di *Bertinoro presents a similar situation in Jerusalem in the second half of the 15th century. In Ottoman Turkey the method of collecting the *jizya* (called *kharāj*) underwent several changes. At the end of the 15th century it was paid individually, but in later agreements, communities apparently would pay a lump sum (*maḳṭūʿ*). A letter written c. 1500 points out that the Jews of *Aleppo were arrested by the *Mamluk ruler because they could not pay the high *jizya* following a very difficult winter in which their economic life had declined.

In the second half of the 16th century the Jews of Jerusalem, like the local Christians, paid personal *jizya* through the community. The community had to pay the Ottoman authorities a sum of money for *jizya* according to a list of Jews which was prepared during the censuses. That list was the basis for the annual *jizya* payment, and everyone paid it for the male members of his family (*hane*). A law promulgated in 1691 provided for the reestablishment of the old system of individual payment. The new law was acted upon in Ereẓ Israel. In any case, it is clear that the leaders of Jewish communities in various Muslim lands (or in the confederations of the communities) were not responsible for the payment of the *jizya*. The rates of the *jizya* varied throughout and usually did not correspond to those fixed by the *sharīʿa* law. Generally, Jews from poor communities paid a low rate of *jizya*. In Egypt during the reign of the caliphs, all non-Muslims paid two dinars per year. Ibn Mammātī stated that under the *Ayyubids the **dhimmīs* paid according to three rates; the rich paid 4.16 dinar; the middle class, 2.08; and the poor, 1.59. At the beginning of *Mamluk rule the rate of the poll tax was doubled. At the end of the 14th century, however, the highest rate amounted to one dinar and the lowest to 0.4 dinar. In 1412 the Egyptian government once more decided to levy the poll tax according to the rates fixed in the *sharīʿa* law, i.e., 1, 2, and 4 dinars. The accounts of Italian Jews who visited or settled in Ereẓ Israel in the late 15th century indicate a lower rate. According to their reports the (uniform) rate of the *jizya* would have been between one and two ducats. In Ottoman Turkey the rate was relatively low, in comparison with the rates fixed in the *sharīʿa*. In most provinces during the 17th century it was collected at a uniform rate, from 25 to 50 *akçe*, whereas in the provinces conquered from the Mamluks it reached up to 80 *akçe* (60–70 *akçe* equaled the value of one silver piece). In addition to these rates, all non-Muslims had to pay a collection fee. In the 18th century the Jews continued to pay *jizya* individually. In the *Ottoman Empire men paid the *jizya* until they were 60 or 65 years old. In the list of *jizya* taxpayers in Ruschuk in the year 1831, many children 12 years old and even younger were included. After the conquest of *Istanbul in 1453 the Ottomans determined a total assessment for the Jewish community as a whole and submitted it to the community representative. In the 16th century the secular leaders of every congregation apportioned its share among its individual members. In the second half of the 16th century all Jews paid the *jizya* according to the lowest rate: 80–90 akçe. The tax was sent to the Central Treasury in Istanbul, but the *jizya* of 85 Jews was sent to the Wakf of the Dome of the Rock. Throughout this century the government explored the *jizya* lists and requested the *Jerusalem community to pay the real *jizya*. The Jews often complained about these lists, especially in times when the community was in steep decline. They also complained frequently about the authorities oppressing them and forcing them to pay a high rate of the poll tax. In addition, there were many complaints about forcing the Jewish pilgrims to pay this tax. The Grand Vezir Sinan Pasha issued an order in 1586/7 to examine the subject of the *jizya* of the Jews and to bring him a list of Jews who had to pay this tax. A special official was sent from Istanbul to make enquiries about the Jews evading the *Jizya*. In the Muslim court of Jerusalem and in the responsa literature many documents deal with these difficulties. Few lists of poll tax taxpayers in Jerusalem and *Hebron have survived. These together cover the course of 400 years. For example, we can point to a list of 400 Jerusalem Jews who paid the *jizya* during 1760–1763. In the year 1762 only 31 persons paid the high rate (*evla*) of *jizya*, 123 persons paid the medium rate (*evsat*), and 195 persons paid the low rate (*edna*). Women were exempted from this tax, but rich widows who had inherited land from their husbands were listed and paid the *jizya*. In the 18th century Rabbi Raphael Shelomo Laniado of Aleppo wrote a halakhic decision that persons who could not pay the *jizya* could pay it from their charity money (*maʿaser kesafim*), "because it is like a ransom *mitzvah*." He meant that everyone who did not pay the poll tax was arrested by the Ottoman authorities. Until the 19th century this tax in Aleppo was personal, but it was the duty of the community to collect the money from its members, and the leaders of the community were responsible for the sum of the requested tax. In 1672, 380 Jewish residents of Aleppo paid *jizya*. Under the Safavid government in *Persia the *nasi* of *Isfahan was responsible for collecting the *jizya* and delivering it to the local officials. Under *Reza Shah this tax was cancelled. In Ruschuk the *jizya* was collective. In 1831/2, 15 Jews paid a total of 420 grossos, 53 paid 1,272 grossos and 36 paid together 432 grossos. Under the reign of Sultan Bayezid II in 1510–1511 the Ottomans used the monies raised by the poll tax in *Salonika and its environs for the purchase of textiles to outfit the Janissary corps. The Ottoman registry books from the reign of *Suleiman the Magnificent indicate tax payments according to the congregations of the community. But the tax total shown in the registry books was a tally for all the Jews of Salonika, without an itemization by congregation. Rabbi Moses Almosnino wrote in 1568 that he had succeeded in his mission to Istanbul in modifying the poll-tax procedures for the Jews of Salonika.

Undoubtedly the poll tax was a burden to the poor for more than one thousand years. Therefore, the Jewish communities collectively raised money to pay the tax, the poor contributing only a small amount. Many documents referring to these drives are extant in the Cairo *Genizah*. These drives helped prevent the compulsory payment of the poll tax from becoming a reason for conversion to *Islam, as it had been for Christians. In urgent cases the local leaders of the communities regarded the payment of the *jizya* for the poor as a holy obligation and a pious deed. For example, there are letters given by the *nagid* Abraham Maimonides dealing with the payments in place of the poor living in Fustat. The poll tax continued to be levied in the Ottoman Empire until the *hatti-sherif* (the order of the Sultan) in 1856, when the *jizya* was abolished by law and non-Muslims were required to pay a tax exempting them from military service (*bedel i-askeri*). This tax continued to be levied until the Young Turk Revolution, when military service was imposed upon non-Muslims (1909). In Egypt the *jizya* was abolished by the Napoleonic regime that briefly ruled in Egypt and later in 1855 by Saʿid Pasha. During the Ottoman era it was stipulated that the communities must guarantee the *jizya* payment for merchants away from the town. In many Jewish communities the family (*hane*) paid the *jizya*. There are numerous censuses from the Ottoman period which give the number of the families and the number of bachelors who paid this tax in many communities. The *jizya* taxpayers were males aged 15–60. We have many documents from the Ottoman period dealing with disputes between rich and poor, in the communities where the *jizya* was collective. In other communities the *jizya* was personal. The community of Istanbul in 1771/2 had a list of taxes paid by it to the state; it suggests that the community had to pay the *jizya* for 1,200 impoverished taxpayers who could not meet their tax obligations to the government. In Ottoman Egypt the government demanded the *jizya* from the Jewish community collectively and the Jewish leaders collected the money from the taxpayers according to their economic status, It is possible that in the later years of the 17th century Egyptian communities changed this system and adopted a new *jizya* that was personal and not collective. In the 18th century the rich Jews in Egypt paid 440 para every year, the middle class community members paid 220 para, and the poor paid 110 para. Other documents give other rates of *jizya*: 420, 270 and 100 paras, respectively. In Ottoman Egypt the *jizya* money was sent by the Ottoman government to the Ulema and other pious Muslims in Egypt. In some cities, such as Hebron, the revenues of the *jizya* were earmarked for Muslim religious institutions. The 17th-century historian Joseph *Sambari writes that "…in the time of Mehmed Gazi Pasha the Oriental Jews, named al-Masharika, began to pay the *kharāj* to the Sherif Ali Savis, because [until that time] they had an old order from the Sultan of that time exempting them and their descendants from *kharāj*, and that *minhag has been cancelled*."

The Jews did not object to the *jizya*, but there were certain Jews under Islam who were granted exemption from the *jizya*. A few such cases occur in **Genizah* letters related to Egypt, and there are documents about Jewish communities that paid the tax burden for their scholarly officials. This was an internal arrangement. There seem to have been special arrangements in the Ottoman communities exempting Torah scholars holding recognized positions from all tax obligations, including the *jizya*. The communities undertook these payments. Scholars who had no recognized positions were obliged to make *jizya* payments during most of the 16th century, in spite of the regulation of the **nagid* R. Issac Hacohen Solal in Jerusalem at the beginning of that century, which was also adopted in *Safed. But from 1535 until the end of the 16th century the scholars in Safed paid it gradually. While in Jerusalem during the 16th century the payments were fixed and uniform, in Safed they were progressive until the mid-1560s, a fact which caused many Jews to settle in Safed, and from then on they were apparently made in full. About 1560 Rabbi David Ibn Zimra (Radbaz) decided to demand *jizya* from the community scholars of Jerusalem. At the end of the 16th century Rabbi Moshe Alshekh urged the establishment of yearly support from the communities of *Venice and Istanbul for paying the *jizya* of 25 Safed Jewish residents.

In Egypt Rabbi Mordechai Halevi and the other spiritual leaders of Cairo in the 17th century issued a regulation exempting scholars who did not work but rather studied Torah all day from paying *jizya*. The Jewish communities in the Ottoman Empire tried to prevent new *jizya* censuses as well as government inquiries about this tax. Many Jews left the city and hid when Ottoman officials came to write new lists of *jizya* taxpayers. Generally, the number of persons in the *jizya* lists is incorrect and probably the real number of community members was higher. Many communities arranged special *jizya* record books. Sometimes there were congregations (synagogues, *kehalim*) in the community that paid the Ottoman authorities the *jizya* of their members by themselves and were listed in the Ottoman records as independent communities. Such registration existed in 16th century in Salonika and Safed. The *francos* active especially in the great communities of the Ottoman empire were exempted from *jizya*, but there were *francos* who had been settled in the Ottoman Empire for 10 years and were compelled to pay the *jizya* according to the Ottoman law.

In Africa, especially in Arab sources, the term *jāliya* (plur: *jawālī*) is used many times in place of the term *jizya*. The meaning of *jaliya* is exile. We know nothing concerning its collection, but we may suppose that it was collected by the Jewish authorities together with other taxes and charges to which the members of the community were liable, the amounts due to the government being set apart from the general collection. The Tunisian constitution of 1857 contains a reference to the *jizya*. Exemption from personal taxes is mentioned in the *capitulations concluded in the second half of the 19th century between *Morocco and European countries; therefore, the poll tax must have remained in force there. In the emirate of *Bukhara the *jizya* was collected from the Jews, but not from the Russian Christians. This and other forms of discrimination continued even after Bukhara had become a Russian protectorate. Complaints about the existence of a poll tax do not occur but at times the collection methods were a source of hardship to the non-Muslim populations. The Jews of *Tripoli (Libya) paid the *bedeli-askari* until the year 1901.

BIBLIOGRAPHY: Løkkegaard, *Islamic Taxation* (1950), chapter 6; D.C. Dennett, *Conversion and the Poll-Tax in Early Islam* (1950); A. Fattal, *Statut légal des non-musulmans en pays d'Islam* (1958), chapter 7; S.D. Goitein, in: *Journal of the Economic and Social History of the Orient*, 6 (1963), 278–95; Ashtor, Toledot, 2 (1951), 259–316; 3 (1970), 11–12, 85, 102, 121; P.K. Hitti, *History of the Arabs* (19679), 171. **ADD. BIBLIOGRAPHY:** H. Inalcik, "Djizya," in: EIS², 3 (1965), 146–48; M. Gil, *Documents of the Jewish Pious Foundations from the Cairo Geniza* (1970), index; A. Cohen, *Palestine in the 18th Century* (1973), 249–56; S.D. Goitein, *Mediterranean Society, The Jewish Communities of the Arab World as Portrayed in the Documents of the Cairo Geniza*, 1–3 (1967, 1971, 1978), index; A. Shochet, in: *Sefunot*, 11 (1971–1978). 301–8; S.J. Shaw, *History of the Ottoman Empire and Modern Turkey*, (1977), 1, 84, 95, 96, 97, 100, 104, 128; M. Benayahu, in: *Sefunot*, 14 (1971–78), 92; H.Z. Hirschberg, *A History of the Jews in North Africa*, 1 (1974), 117, 120, 132, 207, 288, 199, 267–69; A. Cohen and B. Lewis, *Population and Revenue in the Towns of Palestine in the Sixteenth Century* (1978), 28–75, 155–69; A. Schochet, in: *Cathedra*, 13 (1979), 6–9, 15, 30–37; M.R. Cohen, *The Jewish Self-Government in Medieval Egypt:* (1980), 217, 260, 320; M.A. Epstein, *The Ottoman Jewish Communities and their Role in the Fifteenth and Sixteenth Centuries* (1980), 62, 66, 72, 90, 111, 122, 134f, 178. 184f., 191, 195; M. Kunt, in: B. Braude and B. Lewis (eds.), *Christians and Jews in the Ottoman Empire*, 1 (1982), 58; J.R. Hacker, in: *ibid.* (1982), 117–26; F. Ahmad, in: *ibid.*, 398, 447; H. Gerber, *Yehudei ha-Imperya ha-Otmanit ba-Me'ot ha-Shesh Esre ve-ha-Sheva-Esre, Ḥevrah ve-Kalkalah* (1983), 27, 36–37, 122–26, 130–31; 40–43, 48, 105, 109, 117–19, A. Cohen, *Jewish Life Under Islam* (1984), index; A. Shmuelevitz, *The Jews of the Ottoman Empire in the Late Fifteenth and Sixteenth Centuries* (1984); J. Hacker, in: *Shalem*, 4 (1984), 63–117; M. Rozen, *Ha-Kehillah ha-Yehudit bi-Yrushalayim ba-Me'ah ha-Sheva-Esre* (1985), index. S. Bar Asher, in: S. Ettinger (ed.), *Toledot ha-Yehudim be-Arẓot ha-Islam*, 1 (1981), 145; 2 (1986), 333–39; L. Bornstein-Makovetsky, in: Jacob M. Landau (ed.), *Toledot Yehudei Mitzrayim ba-Tekufah ha-Otmanit (1517–1914)* (1988), 131, 181–182, 188; M. Winter, *ibid.*, 387, 390–92, 404; Rozan, *ibid.*, 423–25, 443, 458–59; M. Zand, in: *Pe'amim*, 35 (1988), 57–59; B. Masters, *The Origins of Western Economic Dominance in the Middle East: Mercantalism and the Islamic Economy in Aleppo*, 1600–1750 (1988), 38, 89, 107 no. 49, 127; A. Marcus, *The Middle East on the Eve of Modernity: Aleppo in the Eighteenth Century*, (1989), 148, 338; M. Gil, *A History of Palestine 634–1099* (1992), 242, 245, 262, 761; A. Levy, *The Sephardim in the Ottoman Empire* (1992), 15, 59, 92, 144; A. Cohen, *Yehudim be-Veit ha-Mishpat ha-Muslemi* (1993), 37–52, 70–84; M. Rozen, in: A. Levy (ed.), *The Jews of the Ottoman Empire* (1994), 254–62; Y. Barnai, in: Cathedra, 72 (1994), 135–68; M.R. Cohen, *Under Crescent and Cross, The Jews in the Middle Ages* (1994), index; M. Ben- Sasson, *Ẓemiḥat ha-Kehillah ha-Yehudit be-Arẓot ha-Islam* (1996), 354, 386–88, 398; N. Gruenhaus, *Ha-Misuy ba-Kehillah ha-Yehudit be-Izmir ba-Me'ot ha-Sheva-Esre ve-ha-Shemone-Esre* (1997), 57–59; I. Abramski-Bligh (ed.), *Pinkas ha-Kehillot: Libya,Tunisia* (1997); Y. Avrahami, *Pinkas ha-Kehillah ha-Yehudit Portugezit be-Tunis* (1997), 27–28; B. Rivlin (ed.), *Pinkas ha-Kehillot: Yavan* (1999); A. David, *To Come to the Land: Immigration and Settlement in the 16th Century Eretz Israel* (1999), index; J.R. Hacker, in: *Shalem*, 7 (2002), 133–50; Y. Barnai, *ibid.* (2002), 199–205; M. Rozen, *A History of the Jewish Community in Istanbul: The Formative Years, 1453–1566* (2002), 26–27; D. Schroeter, in: A. Levy (ed.), *Jews, Turks, Ottomans* (2002), 90, 92, 99; Y. Harel, *Bi-Sefinot shel Esh La-Ma'arav, Temurot Be-Yahadut Surya bi-Tekufat ha-Reformot ha-Otmaniyyot 1840–1880* (2003), 103, 173–74; M. Gil, *The Jews in Islamic Countries in the Middle Ages* (2004), 166, 172, 173, 252, 268, 307, 324, 326, 353, 363; A. Levy (ed.), *Jews, Turks, Ottomans* (2002), 6, 90–92, 99, 109; E. Alshech, in: *Islamic Law and Society*, 10 (2003), 348–75; Z. Keren, *Kehillat Yehudei Ruschuk*, 1788–1878 (2005), 56, 77, 84, 95–96, 102, 106, 130–32, 134, 143–44.

[Eliyahu Ashtor / Leah Bornstein-Makovetsky (2nd ed.)]

KHARASCH, MORRIS SELIG (1895–1957), organic chemist. Kharasch was born in Kremenets, Ukraine, and educated in the U.S. He was professor at the University of Maryland (1922–28) and at the University of Chicago from 1930; he was also a consultant to the U.S. Department of Agriculture from 1926. His field of research included the electronic structure and physical properties of organic compounds, free radicals, chain reactions, hydro-peroxides, and ergot.

KHARIK, IZI (Yitskhok; 1898–1937), Soviet Yiddish poet. Born in Zembin, Belorussia, he began publishing Yiddish poetry in 1920. His talent and dedication to building socialism earned him an invitation to Moscow to study the arts. His literary career skyrocketed after he published his *shtetl* poems in the literary magazine *Shtrom* and his epic poem, "*Minsker Blotes*" ("Minsk Swamps"), which appeared in *Nayerd* (1925) and portrays the transformation of a *shtetl* during the Revolution. It was heralded as one of the first Yiddish works to depict Jewish life, as opposed to death, during the Civil War. After returning to Belorussia, Kharik published his first major collection of poems, *Af der erd* ("On the Land," 1926), marking him as the Yiddish poet who best expressed the ambiguous relationship between Jewish tradition and modernity, between memory and imagination. He also began editing for the Minsk newspaper, *Oktober*. His most important contribution to Soviet Jewish literature, the pessimistic narrative poem "*Mit Layb un Lebn*" ("With Body and Soul," 1928), portrays the life of the Soviet Jewish intelligentsia through the eyes of a young Jewish teacher whose grand hopes for rebuilding the *shtetl* are ultimately dashed. Reviewers nonetheless lauded Kharik for portraying "real Soviet life" and showing the remaking of Soviet society. In the 1930s, he became a member of the prestigious Belorussian Academy of Sciences, and his colleagues celebrated him in poetry readings, special book dedications, and other rites that conferred importance on Soviet writers. He became editor of the Minsk literary journal *Shtern* and, in 1932, put out his third important collection of poetry, *Kaylekhdike Vokhn* ("Week After Week"). In June 1937, at the peak of his career, he was arrested, and killed later that year, as part of the Great Purges that decimated the Soviet cultural elite. His work was not republished until the late 1950s after his rehabilitation following Stalin's death.

BIBLIOGRAPHY: LNYL, 4 (1961), 382–6; E.H. Jeshurin, *Dovid Hofshteyn, Izi Kharik, Itsik Fefer: Bibliografye* (1962). **ADD. BIBLIOGRAPHY:** I. Howe and E. Greenberg (eds.), *Ashes Out of Hope: Fiction by Soviet-Yiddish Writers* (1977); Sh. Rozhansky (ed.), *Dovid Hofshteyn, Izi Kharik, Itsik Fefer: Oysgeklibene Shriftn* (1962); D. Shneer, *Yiddish and the Creation of Soviet Jewish Culture, 1918–1930* (2004).

[Elias Schulman / David Shneer (2nd ed.)]

KHARKOV, city in Ukraine. It was built as a fortress against the invasions of Crimean Tartars in the 16th century, and it was the headquarters of a Cossack brigade in the 18th. Kharkov was outside the *Pale of Settlement. Jewish merchants often attended the large fairs held there from the second half of the 18th century, however, and individual Jews even settled there without hindrance. In 1821 the authorities forbade Jews to enter the town, but, on the complaint of the local authorities that the order was harmful to the business of the fairs, Jewish merchants were again admitted in 1835. From 1859 Jews who were allowed to live outside the Pale of Settlement began to settle in Kharkov. In 1868 they were permitted to build a synagogue and nominate a community council. There were then 35 families of merchants and craftsmen. In that period there were 26 Jewish pupils studying at the local secondary school and university and 68 Jewish soldiers. By 1878 Jews numbered 2,625 (total population 83,507). When the fairs were held, some 3,000 Jews would visit the town. In the mid-1800s there was a Karaite community of 525 persons with a synagogue and cemetery. They dealt mostly in tobacco.

Toward the end of the 19th century, many Jewish youths from the provinces of the Pale began to attend the University of Kharkov, and in 1886 the 414 Jewish students formed 28.3% of the student body. A *Bilu society was founded among the Jewish students there. The community numbered 11,013 (6.3% of the total population) in 1897. At that time there were three large Jewish banks, and many wholesale businesses with many trade connections abroad. Others lived from petty trade and crafts. The community opened a hospital and a soup kitchen for the needy. In 1880 the Goldfaden theatrical group performed there for a month. During World War I and the Civil War (1918–20) many Jews, expelled from their places of residence or escaping from the fighting zone or pogroms, took refuge in Kharkov. The pedagogic seminary of *Grodno and its teachers and pupils were transferred to Kharkov in this period. Kharkov became an important Jewish center. A Hebrew secondary school and popular Jewish university were established, and books and newspapers in Yiddish and Hebrew were published there. The conferences of He-Ḥalutz (1920, 1922), the Socialist-Zionist Party (1920), and Ha-Shomer ha-Ẓa'ir (1923) were held in the town. A group of Hebrew writers was also active there. The consolidation of the Soviet regime marked the end of organized Jewish life, but the choice of Kharkov as capital of Ukraine from 1919 to 1934 and its general development resulted in a rapid increase in the Jewish population, which numbered 65,007 (17.2% of the total) in 1923, 81,138 in 1926, 115,811 in 1935, and 130,250 (total population 832,913) in 1939. The town was the center of the *Yevsektsiya's activities in Ukraine. Several Yiddish Communist newspapers, including the daily *Der Shtern* (1925–41), and the journals *Di Roite Welt* ("The Red World") and *Sovetishe Literatur* were published there. In 1925 the All-Ukrainian Jewish State Theater was opened, performing there until it was moved with the capital to Kiev in 1934. The Jewish State Theatre, Kharkov took its place. In the 1920s there existed Jewish sections in the court of law, the militia sectors, and the municipality. At the end of the 1920s there were four Yiddish schools with about 1,900 pupils, a teachers' college, a vocational school for machine production (over 400 pupils), and a Jewish section at the journalism school.

Holocaust and Modern Periods

The Germans occupied Kharkov on October 24, 1941. Most of the city's Jews succeeded in evacuating or fleeing the town. The commander of the 6th Army (quartered there and led by General von Paulus) ordered hostages taken, most of them Jews, and they were shot for every breach of martial law. In mid-November buildings in which German headquarters and organizations were housed were blown up, and 1,000 hostages, mostly Jews, were taken and executed. On December 14, 1941, the Jews were ordered to move in two days to barracks that housed workers of a machine and tractor factory in the city's district 10. The barracks were without windows and doors and had no heating. No food was allowed and water only during limited hours. Many died of diseases and starvation. At the end of December 100 were killed. Between January 2 and 8 the ghetto was liquidated, and the Jews were murdered nearby in the Drobitski Yar (about 8 km. from town) – according to the Soviet Commission to Investigate Nazi Crimes, about 15,000 persons. Together with the hostages and Jews from hospitals and old-age homes, the number of victims was 21,685 Jews, according to German sources. Kharkov was liberated on August 23, 1943. Jewish settlement was renewed in Kharkov, and the Jewish population numbered 81,500 (9% of the total) in 1959, dropping to 62,800 in 1970. The last synagogue was closed down by the authorities in 1948–49. All subsequent attempts to obtain permission to organize a synagogue were unsuccessful, and the former synagogue was converted into a sports gymnasium. In 1957, 1958, and 1959 private prayer groups were dispersed on the High Holidays (*New York Times*, May 21, 1959). Several Torah scrolls were confiscated. In 1960 the *minyanim* were again dispersed and Jews were arrested for baking *maẓẓah*. In 1967 Jews attending private services on the High Holidays were beaten by the militia. The old cemetery was converted into a park. In 1970 Jews had their own section in the general cemetery, and *kasher* poultry was available. In the 1990s many Jews immigrated to Israel and the West.

BIBLIOGRAPHY: M. Osherowitch, *Shtet un Shtetlekh in Ukraine*, 2 (1948), 24–34; *Dokumenty obviniayut'*, 2 (1945), 307–12.

[Yehuda Slutsky / Shmuel Spector (2nd ed.)]

KHARKOV CONFERENCE, a consultation of the leading Zionists from the various parts of Russia convened at the beginning of November 1903 in order to organize the opposition to the *Uganda Scheme. When the Sixth Zionist Congress adopted *Herzl's proposal to send a commission to investigate whether Uganda was suitable for Jewish settlement, a storm of protest was aroused in the Zionist Movement, especially among the Russian Zionists – the overwhelming majority of those who voted "no." Menahem *Ussishkin, who did not attend the Congress because he was in Ereẓ Israel at the time, was the head of the opposition movement. Upon his return to Russia, he published a sharp open letter in the Zionist press against the Congress' decision and the "diplomacy and exaggerated politization" of the Zionist Movement, stressing that the Congress had no right to adopt a resolution that constituted the abandonment of Zion. In reaction to this letter, Herzl accused Ussishkin (in the official Zionist *Die *Welt*, Oct. 30, 1903) of a breach of discipline and severely criticized his activities in Ereẓ Israel.

At the beginning of November of that year, the Russian members of the Zionist General Council and their deputies (together numbering 15) met in Kharkov on the initiative of Ussishkin, who was the moving force at the conference, and demanded a condemnation of Herzl. The conference decided to oppose the Uganda scheme as a contradiction of the *Basle Program and to present Herzl with an ultimatum under which he was to commit himself in writing to the following demands: not to propose in the future any territorial programs other than the settlement of Syria and Ereẓ Israel; to withdraw and dissolve the Uganda Scheme entirely by no later than the Seventh Congress, and to convene a special session of the General Council to discuss the matter prior to the dispatch of the commission to Uganda; and to embark immediately on practical settlement work in Ereẓ Israel.

Should Herzl reject the ultimatum, another consultation would be convened to devise measures of opposition to the Zionist leadership, including withholding contributions to the Zionist Executive in Vienna, a publicity campaign, the dispatch of opposition propagandists to all Zionist centers in Europe and America, a convention of the opposition prior to the Seventh Zionist Congress, establishing an independent Zionist organization, appealing to world public opinion and before a British court against the rights of the "East African majority" (supporters of the Uganda Scheme) to the finances of the Zionist Organization-the *Jewish Colonial Trust and the *Jewish National Fund. *Z. Belkowsky, *V. Tiomkin, and *S. Rosenbaum were chosen as members of the delegation to present the ultimatum to Herzl with *J. Bernstein-Kogan as an alternate member. It was also decided that the transfer of funds to the Zionist treasury in Vienna should be suspended until the conclusion of negotiations with Herzl and that the money should be kept temporarily in Russia.

The delegation arrived in Vienna on Dec. 31, 1903, but Herzl, who was gravely offended by the aggressive tone of the Kharkov resolutions, refused to receive it officially. He agreed, however, to meet with each of its members privately and invited them to attend the meeting of the Executive as guests after they had declared for the record that they did not come as emissaries and that they did not intend to deliver any ultimatum. In the meantime, the British government, under pressure from the English settlers in Uganda, withdrew its offer to the Zionist movement. As a result, a reconciliation took place between Herzl and the Russian Zionists on April 11, 1904.

BIBLIOGRAPHY: A. Bein, *Theodor Herzl* (Heb., 1962[7]), 453–503; Th. Herzl, *Complete Diaries*, 5 (1960), index s.v. *Kharkov*; S. Schwarz, *Ussishkin be-Iggerotav* (1949), 79–87; J. Klausner, *Ha-Oppozizyah le-Herzl* (1960), 231–49; M. Heymann, *The Uganda Controversy*, 1 (1970).

[Yitzhak Maor]

KHAYBAR, the largest Jewish settlement in *Arabia in the time of *Muhammad, approximately 60 mi. (97 km.) from Medina. Khaybar is located on a very high mountainous plateau entirely composed of lava deposits, containing very fertile valleys that are, however, covered by malarial swamps; the Jews of Khaybar were thus forced toward the mountains, only going down into the valleys (during the day) in order to work their lands. They cultivated dates, grapes, vegetables, and grain, and raised sheep, cattle, camels, horses, and donkeys. They also engaged in spinning, weaving, and the manufacture of silk clothing, garments which were well-known in the entire Hejaz, and benefited from the caravan trade between Arabia, *Syria, and *Iraq and traded with Syria. The Arabs were not at that time capable of producing for themselves the tools, the weapons, the textiles, and the jewelry which they needed or coveted, and the Jews, being skillful artisans and drawn towards commerce, were in a position to supply these objects because they understood the art of manufacturing them or the means of importing them. The Jews provided the capital for commercial activities while the Arabs acted as intermediaries between them and the tribes of the interior. The Jews of Khaybar were well known for their diligence, wealth, and hospitality. During the night they would place beacons in the towers of their castles, guiding those who were lost to their houses, which remained open all night. The Jewish Banū *Naḍīr of *Medina, who claimed to be descendants of Aaron the priest, owned lands in Khaybar and had castles, fortresses, and their own weapons there. After Muhammad expelled them from Medina in 625, their leaders moved to their estates in Khaybar in order to prepare for war against Muhammad and to recruit the aid of Arab tribes. In fact, they led those who fought against Muhammad, and the men of Khaybar, who had intermarried with them, treated them with respect and obeyed them. The settlements of Khaybar were concentrated around three centers – Naṭāt, Shiqq, and Katība – scattered over a wide area. The settlers engaged in the manufacture of metal implements for work and weapons such as battering rams and catapults, which they stored in their castles and even lent to Arab tribes. According to the sources, most of them written by Arabic chroniclers, they had 10,000 warriors but this number is probably very exaggerated.

Muhammad's war against the Jews of Khaybar (628) was very harsh. At first he sent disguised guests to the homes of the leaders of Banū Naḍīr who then killed their hosts. Muhammad's victory over the Jews of Khaybar, some of whom were held in esteem by the enemy, was also aided by the distance of the settlements and their castles from one another, the absence of coordination between the fighting forces, the death of the leader Sallām ibn Mishkam, and the treachery of a Jew who showed the Muslims the secret entrances to one of the fortresses. The castles of Khaybar had tunnels and passages which in wartime enabled the besieged to reach water sources outside the castles. Muhammad treated the Jews of Khaybar with cruelty, murdering Ḥuyayy ibn Akhṭab, head of Banū Naḍīr, in Medina. He ordered the son of the leader and the husband of his daughter Ṣafiyya killed in Khaybar. He married Ṣafiyya, who herself was taken captive, on the way from Khaybar to Medina. The sources emphasize her beauty, her faithfulness to Muhammad, and her privileges, which included the inheritance of her property by a relative and his uncle in Khaybar.

Concerned that Khaybar would remain desolate and would not continue supplying its agricultural produce to the Hejaz, Muhammad and the Jews signed an agreement which allowed many of its inhabitants to remain on their lands, even though the payment of half their crops to the conquerors undermined the economic position of the Jews of Khaybar. From a legal point of view the pact was defective, since it did not define the situation of the Jews and did not say whether they were to remain the owners of the soil which they were to cultivate. In later years Muslim jurists defined this settlement as land tenure with rent paid in produce. One version of this agreement was copied by Joseph *Sambari in the 17th century. According to Muslim sources, Muhammad returned to the Jews copies of the Torah seized during the siege, since he opposed desecrating them. After captives of war and slaves from other countries were brought to Khaybar and the people of Hejaz became more accustomed to agriculture, the caliph *Omar decided to expel the Jews of Khaybar in 642 under the pretense that before his death Muhammad had commanded that two religions could not exist simultaneously in the Hejaz. Contrary to the statements of Graetz, Dubnow, and others, however, not all the Jews of Khaybar were expelled by Omar. Those who had made special treaties and covenants with Muhammad, especially the members of the family of his wife Ṣafiyya, were allowed to remain. Graetz's theory about the wanderings of the Jews of Khaybar to Kufa on the Euphrates, where they influenced the center of the gaonate in Babylonia and served as an ethnic background for the growth of Karaism there, is basically incorrect. Some of the Jews of Khaybar settled in Wadi al-Qurā and *Tayma, but most of them settled in *Jericho. Among those exiled to Jericho was the son of the chief warrior of Khaybar, Ḥārith, who was the father of Zaynab, the woman credited with the attempt to poison Muhammad in revenge for the slaughter of her people. The Jews of Khaybar apparently spread out from Jericho along the Jordan Valley, reaching the Sānūr Valley in northern Samaria. This is indicated by the names Tell-Khaybar and Khirbat-Khaybar in that valley and an ancient Arab tradition about a Jewish king and princess who lived in these places. An Arabic source published by I. *Goldziher (REJ, 28 (1894), 83) quotes an Arabic account in which the Muslims express their astonishment that the Jewish women of Khaybar put on their most beautiful jewelry on the Day of Atonement.

The Jews of Khaybar, like Jews in other parts of the Hejaz, are mentioned hundreds of years after the expulsion of some of them by Omar. At the end of the 11th century they still had possessions, lands, fields, and castles in the region of Katība, which was a region of Banū Naḍīr in the time of Muhammad. The Jews of Wadi al-Qurā addressed questions about the cultivation of dates to R. Sherira and Hai Gaon in Babylonia. *Benjamin of Tudela (12th century) heard rumors, which are exaggerated, about the power of the Jews of Khaybar and Tayma, who were still addressing questions to the exilarchs in *Baghdad. He noted that the Jews of Khaybar were descendants of the Re'uben, Gad, and Menashe tribes and that they numbered 50,000, including scholars and war heroes who fought against their enemies. In the 11th and 12th centuries the Jews of Khaybar are mentioned in Egypt and Babylonia. In a letter from the *gaon* Solomon b. Judah written in Jerusalem around 1020, a certain Isaac from Wadi al-Qura is mentioned. This man deserted his family for four years, traveled to Egypt and returned "to his land," that is, to Wadi al-Qura. Two *Genizah documents attest the settlement of Khaybar Jews in Tiberias during that period. According to Muslim tradition, the Jews of Khyabar were expelled in the days of Omar. They claimed in Tiberias to be Khayberis, and therefore exempt from tax,

Great attention has been devoted by scholars to a letter from the Cairo *Genizah*, written in Arabic in Hebrew letters, to "Ḥanina (or Ḥabiba) and the people of Khaybar and Maqnā," showering numerous privileges on them and promising their safety from harm by the Muslims for the sake of their cousin Ṣafiyya; the letter, which is written on paper, is probably copied from one which had been written on leather, as was the case with the letters and treaties of Muhammad. Arabic sources attest that correspondence to Jews in the time of Muhammad was in Arabic in Hebrew letters. The letter, however, has been recognized by most scholars as a forgery, although there is disagreement as to whether its details are drawn from authentic treaties and historical facts and are copies of these sources. In any event, the letter was composed at the time of the caliph Al-Ḥākim bi-Amr Allah (ca. 1010) as a defense against persecutions, expropriation of property, and coercion to accept the Muslim faith in his time, not only in Egypt but in other parts of his rule and including Khaybar itself. An Arabic source explicitly states that "Khaybar Jews" are exempt from the decrees. A *Genizah* letter tells about the poet Yakhin who fled from *al-Mahalla (Egypt) when he was requested to pay the poll tax. The letter supposes that Yakhin was entitled to tax exemption because he was a Khayberi. In other *Genizah* letters from the 11th century there are references to persons called Ibn al-Khayberi. It seems to *Goitein that a distinction should be made between Jews who really emigrated from north Arabia and were called Hizajis, and the Khaybaris, who probably came to the West via Iraq and had no real connection with Khaibar. Gil also doubts whether those Jews claiming exemption and special status were in fact Khayberis.

From the 16th century onward, when European travelers began to visit Arabia, rumors were spread about the presence of the Jews of Khaybar in the Hejaz, their bravery, their control of the roads to Mecca, and their collection of road taxes from pilgrims. Varthema, who traveled in Arabia during the early years of the 16th century, noted that in a locality between *Damascus and *Medina there lived between 4,000 and 5,000 Jews, but the orientalist Pirenne doubts this. David Hareuveni claimed in 1524 in Italy that he was the army general of the king Solomon from Habur (Khaybar) desert. During the 19th century these rumors encouraged some hardy, imaginative Jews to go out into the wilderness of Arabia in search of the "Sons of Rehab" (Khaybar) and the "Sons of Moses, Dan, and Asher." Some of them died on the way and were not heard of again. Pirenne writes that in the mid-19th century, the Jews were in considerable numbers in that area. According to rumors, a few Khaybar Jews arrived in Palestine and appeared in synagogues. Of special interest is the Muḥamara family in the village of Yutah in the mountains south of Hebron, which traces its lineage to the Jews of Khaybar, as well as the family of the head of the deserted village of Hūj, near kibbutz Dorot, who was related to the descendants from Khaybar in Yutah. The old father of the Muḥamara family settled in Yutah in the second half of the 18th century. G.M. Kressel wrote (in 2001) about the symbolic meaning amongst the Negev Bedouin population of Muhammad's war against the Jews of Khaybar.

BIBLIOGRAPHY: I. Ben-Ze'ev, *Ha-Yehudim ba-Arav* (1957²), index; H.Z. Hirschberg, *Yisrael ba-Arav* (1946), index; I. Ben Zvi, in: *Keneset*, 5 (1940), 281–302; J. Braslavsky, *Le-Ḥeker Arẓenu* (1954), 3–52 (English summaries: 3–4, English section); S.D. Goitein, in: KS, 9 (1932/33), 507–21; Caetani, in: *Annali dell' Islam*, 2 (1905), 8–41; R. Leszynsky, *Juden in Arabien zur Zeit Mohammeds* (1910). **ADD BIBLIOGRAPHY:** J. Pirenne, *A la découverte de l'Arabie* (1958), 33, 76, 215 ff.; Ashtor (Strauss), Toledot, 2 (1953), 298–309; I. Ben-Zvi, *She'ar Yashuv* (1966), 370, 380, 415–23; B.Z. Dinur *Israel ba-Golah*, 2:2 (1959), 26–27, 169–170; 2:3 (1968), 424–25; M.A. Shaban, *Islamic History, A New Interpretation (600–750)* (1971), 10, 13; EIS² (1978), 1137–43; Goitein, *A Mediterranean Society*, 2 (1971), 386, 611; 5 (1988), 603; M. Lecker, in: *Jerusalem Studies in Arabic and Islam*, 5 (1984), 1–11; N. Dana, in: *Moreshet Yisrael*, 1 (2005), 88–99; M.R. Cohen, *Under Crescent and Cross, The Jews in the Middle Ages* (1994), index; M. Gil, *A History of Palestine, 634–1099* (1992), index; M. Lecker, in: *Pe'amim*, 61 (1994), 6–15; S. Shtuber, *Sefer Divrei Yosef le-Rabbi Yosef be-Rabbi Yiẓhak Sambari* (1994), 97, 293, 313; G.M. Kressel, in: *Israel as Center Stage* (2001), 165–87; M. Gil, *The Jews in Islamic Countries in the Middle Ages* (2004), 3–45.

[Joseph Braslavi (Braslavski) /
Leah Bornstein-Makovetsky (2nd ed.)]

KHAZARS, a national group of general Turkic type, independent and sovereign in Eastern Europe between the seventh and tenth centuries C.E. During part of this time the leading Khazars professed Judaism. The name is frequently pronounced with an a-vowel, as in the Greek Χάζαροι and Arabic Khazar (*Ḥazar*), but there are traces of a different pronunciation in Hebrew (*Kuzari*, pl. *Kuzarim*), Greek (Χότζιροι), and Chinese (*K'o-sa*). The name has been explained as having derived from Turkish *qazmak* ("to wander," "nomadize (?)"), or from *quz* ("side of mountain exposed to the north"). The latter etymology would account for the o/u-vowel in some forms of the name, for which no satisfactory explanation has been given.

The Origin of the Khazars

The Khazars, of Turkic stock, originally nomadic, reached the Volga-Caucasus region from farther east at some time not easily determinable. They may have belonged to the empire of the Huns (fifth century C.E.) as the Akatzirs, mentioned by Priscus. This name is said to be equivalent to Aq-Khazar, i.e., White Khazars, as opposed to the Qara-Khazar or Black Khazars mentioned by al-Iṣṭakhrī (see below). The Khazars probably belonged to the West Turkish Empire (from 552 C.E.), and they may have marched with Sinjibū (Istämi), the first khāqān of the West Turks, against the Sassanid (Persian) fortress of Ṣul or Darband.

In the time of Procopius (sixth century) the region immediately north of the Caucasus was held by the Sabirs, who are referred to by Jordanes as one of the two great branches of the Huns (*Getica*, ed. Mommsen, 63). Masʿūdī (tenth century C.E.) says that the Khazars are called in Turkish, Sabīr (*Tanbīh*, ed. Cairo, 1938, 72).

In 627 (Theophanes, *Chronographia*, ed. De Boor, 1 (1883), 315) "the Turks from the East whom they call Khazars" under their chief, Ziebel, passed the Caspian Gates (Darband) and joined Heraclius at the siege of Tiflis. In view of what is known of a dual kingship among the Khazars (see below), it would be natural to assume that Ziebel, described by Theophanes as "second in rank to the khāqān," was the subordinate Khazar king or beg. However, there are grounds for thinking that Ziebel stands for *yabgu*, a Turkish title – in the parallel Armenian account (Moses of Kalankatuk, trans. Dowsett, 87) he is called Jebu Khāqān – and that he is T'ung-ye-hu, Ye-hu Khagan of the Chinese sources, i.e., T'ung Yabgu, Yabgu Khāqān, the paramount ruler of the West Turks, who is represented as second in rank to "the King of the North, the lord of the whole world," i.e., the supreme khāqān of the Turks. In the narratives of Theophanes and Moses of Kalankatuk respectively, the Khazars are also called Turks and Huns. From 681 C.E., we hear much in the latter author of the Huns of Varachʿan (Warathān), north of Darband, who evidently formed part of a Khazar confederation or empire. Their prince Alp Ilutver was often in attendance on the Khazar khāqān and was converted to Christianity by an Albanian bishop.

It will be seen that the question of the precise racial affinities of the Khazars is not readily solved (see also below). There appears to be insufficient evidence to warrant the conclusion of K. Czeglédy that the Khazars were of Sabīr origin and distinct from the Caucasian Huns and West Turks ("Bemerkungen zur Geschichte der Chazaren," *Acta Orientalia... Hungariae*, 13 (1961), 245), since it is not known how far these ethnic names mean the same thing.

Consolidation of the Khazar State

According to Theophanes (*ibid.*, 358), the ruler of the Bulgars in the region of the Kuban River (West Caucasus) died c. 650 C.E., leaving five sons of whom only the eldest remained in his inheritance, while the others moved further west, as far as the Danube. On this, the Khazars, described as a "great nation ... from the interior of Berzilia in the First Sarmatia," emerged and took possession of the territory as far as the Black Sea. The change of position was completed by 679, when one of the brothers crossed the Danube and conquered present-day Bulgaria. Earlier than this, in 576 C.E., a West Turkish force had been present at the siege of Bosporus (Kerch) in the Crimea (Menander Protector, ed. Bonn, 404), but hitherto there is no mention of the Khazars as such so far to the west. The advance of the Khazars to the Black Sea and Crimea area appears to be mentioned also in the Reply of Joseph (see below, Khazar Correspondence), where a great Khazar victory over the W-n-nt-r is referred to. A people north of the Khazars called W-n-nd-r is mentioned in the *Ḥudūd al-ʿĀlam* (*Regions of the World*, trans. by V. Minorsky (1937), 162). Both names are best explained as corresponding to Onogundur, an old name in Greek sources for the Bulgars. The advent of the Khazars on the Black Sea was clearly of great consequence for the future, for they now came within the sphere of Greek political and cultural influence. By 700 C.E. or earlier there were Khazar officials in Bosporus and Phanagoria. Henceforth the Crimea, as well as the Volga and the Caucasus, came to be specially associated with the Khazars, and a further way westward was opened for them toward both Kiev and the Slav lands via the Dnieper (see below).

Arabs and Khazars had already been in conflict on the line of the Caucasus (first Arab-Khazar war, 642–52 C.E.). *Bāb al-Abwāb at the eastern end of the range was occupied by the Arabs in 22 A.H. (643). In the same year the caliph Omar sent instructions to advance northward. Though the Arabs attacked *Balanjar repeatedly, they were unable to take it. The defeat and death of the Arab general at Balanjar in 32 A.H. (653) practically marks the end of the war and the close of the first phase of Arab-Khazar relations. According to Musʿūdī, the Khazar capital was at this time moved from *Samandar to *Atil, but he says elsewhere that Balanjar was the former capital.

Further Relations with Byzantium and the Arabs

After the exile of Justinian II to the Crimea in 695, the Khazars on several occasions played an important, even determining, part in Byzantine politics. Toward 704 the khāqān helped the emperor at a crucial moment and gave him his sister Theodora in marriage. Justinian returned to Constantinople to reign a second time. His successor Bardanes (711–13) was likewise indebted to the khāqān. In 732 the emperor Leo the Isaurian married his son, the future Constantine V, to a Khazar princess called in the sources Irene. The child of this marriage was Leo IV, the Khazar (775–80). It is to be understood that Irene and Theodora above are baptismal, i.e., not Khazar, names.

The second Arab-Khazar war began in 722 or earlier, and ended in 737 with the defeat of the Khazars by Marwān b. Muhammad (later Marwān II). The Khazar khāqān is said at this time to have professed Islam. If so, we hear no more about it. Later the khāqān was a Jew, as we know from the Arabic geographers Ibn Rustah (c. 290/903), Iṣṭakhrī (c. 320/932), Ibn Ḥauqal (367/977), etc., and it is implied in the Reply of Joseph that the beginnings of Khazar Judaism dated as far back as 112/730, when the Khazars defeated the Arabs south of the Caucasus, and from the spoils consecrated a tabernacle on the Mosaic model. The conversion of the leading Khazars to Judaism perhaps took place toward 740 C.E. (see below). It seems at all events certain that the Khazars successfully resisted the Arabs for several decades, and that they were reduced only with difficulty and at a time when the internal situation of the caliphate prevented the Arabs from exploiting their victory: Marwān was called away to become the last *Umayyad Caliph (744) and to struggle against ever-growing opposition, until

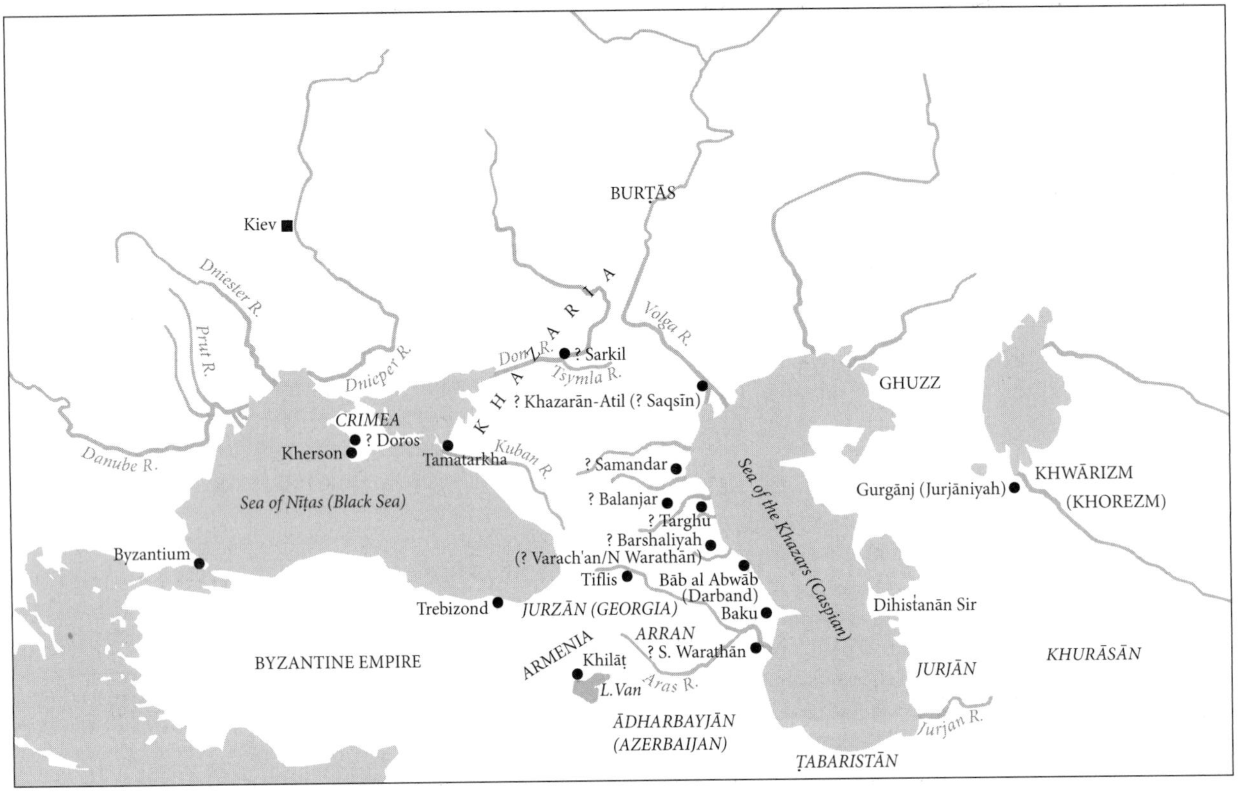

The Khazar kingdom, c. seventh–tenth century. From D.M. Dunlop, History of the Jewish Khazars, *New York, 1967.*

his death in 750 at the hands of *Abbasid soldiers in Egypt. The dynastic crisis probably saved Khazaria. At the same time the situation had wider implications, for if Marwān had been able to hold the Khazar territory permanently, the history of Eastern Europe might have been very different.

The Khazar Double Kingship

This was a phenomenon found among other Turkic peoples, e.g., the Qara-Khanids, and not unknown elsewhere; compare the double kingship at Sparta in antiquity, and the shogun and mikado of medieval Japan. How far back the institution goes among the Khazars cannot be exactly determined. Yaʿqūbī (ninth century) speaks of the Khazar khāqān and his representative (*khalīfa*) apparently in the sixth century (*Historiae*, ed. by M.T. Houtsma, 1 (1883), 203; cf. above for Ziebel Jebu Khāqān in 627). Arab accounts, in Ṭabarī, Ibn al-Athīr, etc., of the Arab-Khazar wars (see above) afford no precise evidence of the dual kingship, yet the Arab geographers regularly mention it. The account of al-Iṣṭakhrī, written c. 320/932, is as follows (*Viae regnorum*, ed. by M.J. De Goeje (1927), 223ff.): "As to their politics and system of government, their chief is called khāqān of the Khazars. He is greater than the king of the Khazars [elsewhere called by al-Iṣṭakhrī the *bak* or *bāk*, i.e., beg], except that the king of the Khazars appoints him. When they wish to appoint this khāqān, they bring him and throttle him with a piece of silk, till, when his breath is nearly cut off, they say to him, 'How long do you wish to reign?' and he says, 'So-and-so many years.' If he dies short of them, well and good. If not, he is killed when he reaches that year. The khaqanate is valid among them only in a house of notables. He possesses no right of command nor of veto but he is honored, and people prostrate themselves when they enter his presence.... The khaqanate is in a group of notables who possess neither sovereignty nor riches. When the chief place comes to one of them, they appoint him, and do not consider his condition. I have been informed by a reliable person that he had seen a young man selling bread in one of the *sūqs*. People said that when their khāqān died, there was none more deserving of the khaqanate than he, except that he was a Muslim, and the khaqanate is not conferred on any but a Jew."

A remarkable parallel to the inauguration ceremony described by Iṣṭakhrī is found in a Chinese source on the Turks in the sixth century C.E., the Chou Shu (trans. by Liu Mau-Tsai, *Die chinesischen Nachrichten zur Geschichte der Ost-Tuerken*, 1 (1958), 8). Recently the theory of A. Alföldi that the double kingship among nomadic peoples corresponds to leadership of the two wings of the horde ("Türklerde çift krallik," *Ikinci Türk Tarih Kongresi*, Istanbul, 1943, 507–19) has won wide acceptance, but does not apply particularly well to the Khazars. Masʿūdī had already suspected that the Khazar khāqān represented a dynasty which had been superseded (*Murūj al-Dhahab*, ed. by B. de Maynard and P. de Courteille, 2 (1878), 13). K. Czeglédy (op. cit.) has suggested that the khāqān was the representative at the Khazar capital, Atil, of the West Turks, whom he thinks of as in control of Khazaria. This is not likely to have been the situation except for a very short time, since the Khazar capital was not transferred to Atil before the time of the first Arab-Khazar war (642–52) and the destruction of the West Turkish power took place in 652–57. Yet the Khazar khāqān may in fact have represented the West Turk ruling dynasty. This seems to be the view of the tenth-century Persian work, *Ḥudūd al-ʿĀlam* (trans. Minorsky, 162), according to which the khāqān of the Khazars was "of the descendants of Ansā," apparently corresponding to Asnā, or Achena, well-known as the ruling family among the Turks. *Ko-sa* (different from *Kʿo-sa* above), the name in Chinese of a subtribe of the Uigurs, is often taken as the equivalent of Khazars. We know that the destruction of the West Turks was brought about by a coalition of which the Uigurs formed part. It may therefore be that the convulsions which attended the breakup of the West Turkish Empire brought forward this section of the Uigurs, so that, while the khāqān represented the old ruling family, the Khazar beg, i.e., the effective king, was their representative.

Date of the Khazar Conversion to Judaism

This has already been referred to above (see *Būlān and below Khazar Correspondence). The date c. 740 C.E. is suggested by converging considerations, namely, the circumstances of the reported conversion to Islam in 737 and the dating given by *Judah Halevi in the *Kūzari* (*Cosri*). The absence of distinct references to the Judaism of the Khazars in the biographies of St. Abo of Tiflis, who was in Khazaria c. 780 C.E. and of Constantine (Cyril), who was there c. 860, should not be pressed as proof that the conversion to Judaism took place only later (cf. also M.I. Artamonov, *Istoriya Khazar*, 332–3). Masʿūdī states positively that the king of the Khazars became a Jew in the caliphate of Hārūn al-Rashīd (786–809 C.E.). This may well refer to the reformation c. 800 under *Obadiah of which the Reply of Joseph speaks. S.P. Tolstov has sought to explain the Khazar conversion to Judaism as a result of the conquest of Khwārizm (*Khorezm) by the Arab general Muslim ibn Qutayba in 712.

The Khazar Empire

The extent of the territory ruled by the Khazars has been variously estimated. Thus B.A. Ribakov ("K voprosu o roli khazarskogo kaganata v istorii Rusi," *Sovetskaya Arkheologiya*, 18 (1953), 128–50) makes Khazaria a small territory on the lower courses of the Volga and Don, to include Sarkil (see below) and the Khazar capital (assigning separate localities to Atil, Khamlīj, and al-Bayḍā', usually taken to be the same place). This is based principally on the data in the world map of Idrīsī, which offers a somewhat misleading picture of Khazaria (see K. Miller, *Mappae Arabicae*, 1 (1926), Heft 2). On the other hand, S.P. Tolstov envisages a Khazaria united with Khwārizm under one ruler to form a single state, a view for which the evidence is slight.

It must be allowed, however, that at one time Khazar rule extended westward a long way beyond the Crimea-Caucasus-Volga region which for the Greek and Arabic sources is Khazaria. *The Russian Primary Chronicle* ((1953), 58–59; Chronicle of Nestor, *Povest vremennykh let*) reports that at an unspecified date the Polians south of the Middle Dnieper paid tribute to the Khazars of a sword per hearth, and that in 859 C.E. the Polians, Severians, and Viatichians paid them a white squirrel skin per hearth (trans. Cross and Sherbowitz-Wetzor, 58, 59). Later these payments in kind ceased to be made, being evidently replaced by money payments; e.g., the Radimichians paid the Khazars a shilling or dirham apiece until 885 C.E., according to the Chronicle (61), and the Viatichians until 964, the same per plowshare (*ibid.*, 84). All these peoples were exposed to attack by any strong forces coming up the valleys of the Don and Donets from the Khazar territory. Kiev itself was occupied by the Khazars for some period before 862, but presumably was not built by or for them (*ibid.*, 60, cf. 54), unlike Sarkel or *Sarkil on the Don, which on the application of the khāqān and beg to Emperor Theophilus was constructed by Byzantine workmen in 833 C.E. All of these territories were to be taken from the Khazars, some already in the ninth century, by the advancing Russians.

East of the Volga, in the direction of Khwārizm, the situation is obscure. Al-Iṣṭakhrī tells of caravans passing between Khwārizm and Khazaria, mentioning specifically Slav, Khazar, and Turkish slaves and all kinds of furs among the principal merchandise of Khwārizm. On the other hand, he says that Khwārizm has the nomad Turks (Ghuzz) on its northern and western frontier, not the Khazars. According to Tolstov, a "royal road" led from Khorezm to the Volga, traces of which may be seen from the air, and he finds in it an indication of the emergence of a great Khorezmian-Khazar state in the tenth and beginning of the 11th century (cf. above).

The Extent of Khazar Judaism

While the Khazars were generally known to their neighbors as Jews (cf. notably the narrative of Ibn Faḍlān), they seem to have had little or no contact with the central Jewish organization in Iraq, and they tend to be mentioned less by Rabbanite than by Karaite authors. This is not to say that the Khazars were Karaites, a view which has not lacked defenders, at least since the time of A. *Firkovich. Yet such contemporary or nearly contemporary documents as we possess offer no evidence of the Karaism of the Khazars. On the other hand, it would seem that the lack of interest in the Khazars on the part of the Jewish authorities, as reflected in the literary works at our disposal, was due at least partly to their imperfect adherence to Judaism. This is illustrated notably in their retention of a number of pagan (shamanist) customs, dating back to their Turkic past, which are duly noted by the Arab geographers.

We may here consider the position of H. Baratz that in the oldest Russian writings of a legal character there are Hebrew, mostly biblical-talmudic, elements, and that these go back to Khazar times. Thus the fact that early Russian codes, including the *Zakon sudni liudem* ("Law for the Judging of the People"), contain traces of Mosaic and talmudic legislation, is due not to contact with the Catholic West, as has also been maintained, but to the influence of the Jewish Khazars. This view has been characterized by a Russian academician (I.V. Yagich) as "a scarlet thread for everyone to walk by." Yet the chance of Khazar influence on Russian codes, in the form of the introduction of Mosaic and talmudic elements, clearly becomes less if it is demonstrable, as seems to be the case, that Khazar Judaism was never very strong. (For Baratz's view see his *Collection of Works on the Question of Hebrew Elements in Ancient Russian Literature* – in Russian – Vol. I, Paris, 1926–27, Vol. II, Berlin, 1924; also Léon Baratz, *Sur les origines étrangères de la plupart des lois civiles russes*, Publications de l'Institut de Droit Comparé de l'Université de Paris (lère Série), 52, Appendice.)

The Downfall of Khazaria

The Reply of Joseph mentions that the Khazars guarded the mouth of the Volga before 961 C.E. and prevented the Russians from reaching the Caspian. On several occasions, notably c. 913 and again in 943, the Russians made raids down the Volga, passing through Atil. Later, apparently in 965, Khazaria was the object of a great Russian attack, which was aimed at the Khazar capital and reached as far as Samandar, as we know from Ibn Ḥawqal. From this disaster the Khazars appear to have recovered only partially. Again at this time (cf. above) we hear of a Khazar khāqān adopting Islam. His motive is said to have been to secure the help of the people of Khwārizm (Miskawayh, ed. Amedroz, II, 209; Ibn al-Athīr, VIII, 196).

After 965 the Khazars are still mentioned occasionally, but scarcely for long as an independent people. We cannot use the Cairo *Genizah* document published by J. Mann, concerning a messianic movement supposedly in Khazaria in the time of al-Afḍal, the great Fatimid vizier who ruled 1094–1121 (REJ, 71 (1920), 89–93; 89 (1930), 257–8), as proof of continued Khazar existence until this time, since it has been shown that the movement in question took place in Kurdistan (see S.D. Goitein, "Obadyah, a Norman Proselyte," in JJS, 4 (1953), 74ff.). Furthermore, Oleg, the same who, according to the Russian Chronicle, established himself in Tmutorokan in 1083, is called in a seal of the 11th–12th century "archon of all Khazaria" (N. Bănescu in *Bulletin of the Romanian Academy*, Hist. Sect. 22 (1941), cited by A.V. Soloviev, *For Roman Jakobson* (1956), 478). Whatever is precisely indicated here by "Khazaria" – e.g., the Khazar country in the Crimea – such a claim could not have been made prior to 965. We must therefore see the Khazar state as having subsisted until the second half of the tenth century, or the 11th century at the latest. By the 12th century the Qipchaqs or Cumans (identified also with the Polovtsi) appeared in the steppes once ruled by the Khazars. At the time of the Mongol invasions in the 13th century, it was they, not the Khazars, who were in possession.

The Khazar Correspondence

This name is usually given to what appears as an interchange of letters in Hebrew between *Ḥisdai ibn Shaprut, a well-known personality of Muslim Spain in the tenth century, and *Joseph, king of the Khazars. M.I. Artamonov (*Istoriya Khazar*, 12) includes the Cambridge Document as well as the Letter of Ḥisdai and the Reply of Joseph in the Khazar Correspondence, but this would seem to be contrary to general usage. The Reply is available in a Long Version and a Short Version (LV and SV). The Correspondence involves serious critical difficulties, and its authenticity has been much debated.

The Letter of Ḥisdai begins with a *piyyut* containing an acrostic which gives his own name and that of Menaḥem b. Saruq, the latter presumably acting as Ḥisdai's secretary and being the author of the *piyyut*. The prose part, after compliments, refers to the geographical situation of al-Andalus and Khazaria and describes the natural wealth of al-Andalus and Ḥisdai's own position there. It seems that his interest has been aroused by his having heard repeatedly that the Khazars are Jews. The Letter mentions attempts made by Ḥisdai to get in touch with the Khazar king. He was finally successful through the instrumentality of two Jews, Mar Saul and Mar Joseph, who accompanied an embassy which arrived at Cordoba from the "king of the G-b-līm, who are the Ṣaqlab" (see below). The Letter of Ḥisdai was conveyed to the East by their means, i.e., overland, and eventually was put into the hands of the Khazar king, according to the Reply, by a certain Jacob or (LV) Isaac b. Eliezer, a Central European Jew. The tone of the Letter of Ḥisdai is mostly one of enquiry, and it invites an answer to questions which range over a variety of topics: Is there a Jewish kingdom anywhere on earth? How did the Jews come to Khazaria? In what way did the conversion of the Khazars take place? Where does the king live? To what tribe does he belong? What is his method of procession to his place of worship? Does war abrogate the Sabbath? Has the Khazar king any information about the possible end of the world? Ḥisdai mentions that ʿAbd al-Raḥmān III al-Nāṣir is the reigning king of al-Andalus. This gives 961 as the *terminus ad quem* for the Letter, with 953–55 as a possible *terminus a quo*, for in those years Cordoba was visited by John of Gorz, as envoy of the German emperor Otto I, who may be the "king of the G-b-līm, who are the Ṣaqlab" already referred to.

The Reply of Joseph begins by referring to the principal contents of the Letter and recapitulates a number of its questions. It then relates the early history of the Khazars, and proceeds to deal at length with the conversion to Judaism under Būlān. The conversion is initiated by a dream of Būlān, which he communicates to a certain general among them (LV), apparently the beg. From the spoils of a Khazar attack on Ardabil, south of the Caucasus, for which we have the synchronism 730 in the Arabic sources, a tabernacle on the biblical model is set up. A religious debate between representatives of Judaism, Christianity, and Islam is held, after which Būlān and the principal Khazars accept the religion of Israel. Under a later king, Obadiah, there was a reform of religion. Synagogues and schools were built, and the Khazars became familiar with Torah, Mishnah, Talmud, and the liturgy, i.e., rabbinic Judaism was introduced. Joseph then traces his descent from Obadiah and gives a description of his country and capital. He refers to Ḥisdai's question concerning the end of the age in a somewhat noncommittal fashion, and finally expresses his desire that Ḥisdai may come to Khazaria, which, if a notice in a map of Ibn Ḥawqal can be trusted, he actually did.

The correspondence has been available since the appearance of the work *Kol Mevasser* of Isaac Akrish in or after 1577, and more generally since the two letters were published by the younger *Buxtorf in his edition of the book *Cosri* (*Kūzārī*) of Judah Halevi in 1660. It is not known what manuscript source was used by Isaac Akrish; Buxtorf depended on *Kol Mevasser*. The only known manuscript of the Correspondence as a whole, containing the Letter of Ḥisdai and the Reply of Joseph (SV), is in the library of Christ Church, Oxford. This manuscript is very similar to the printed text, which, it has been suggested, is a transcript. There appear to be no special grounds for this opinion, though the manuscript, which is undated, has no claims to great antiquity. Nothing is sure about its provenance, but it is thought to have belonged originally to the celebrated Dr. Fell (1625–1686).

A longer version of the Reply of Joseph was published by A. *Harkavy in 1874, from a manuscript of the Second Firkovich Collection in the Leningrad Public Library. The Long Version bears no indication of any alterations or additions, and is supposed to date from the 13th century. Harkavy, in spite of his very critical attitude to Firkovich, regarded it as the undoubted original of the Short Version.

It appears impossible to suppose that the Khazar Correspondence is a fabrication of the 16th century in view of a reference to it, with the citation of part of the Reply of Joseph, agreeing in general with the Long Version, in the *Sefer ha-Ittim* of Judah b. Barzillai al-Bargeloni, dated between 1090 and 1105, and a similar reference in the *Sefer ha-Kabbalah* of Abraham *Ibn Daud in the 12th century. It cannot be admitted that these works were interpolated in the 16th century or later, to support the authenticity. Nor does it appear at all plausible that the letters forming the Khazar Correspondence were forgeries of the tenth century, composed with a view to informing the Jews about the Khazars. It is demonstrable that the literary style of the Letter of Ḥisdai differs from that of the Reply of Joseph in a marked manner. The classical Hebrew construction of *vav* conversive with the imperfect to express the past tense is freely used in the Letter of Ḥisdai, actually 48 times as against 14 times when the past tense is rendered by simple *vav* with the perfect. In the Reply (LV), on the other hand, *vav* conversive with the imperfect occurs not more than once or twice, while the past is expressed by the perfect and simple *vav* nearly 100 times. Further, in the Short Version of the Reply the *vav* conversive with the imperfect to express the past, instead of simple *vav* with the perfect, occurs in a number of passages where the wording is different from the Long Version. There is a new proportion of *vav* conversive with the imperfect to simple *vav* with the perfect: 37 to 50. It may therefore be affirmed that there is a separate authorship for the Letter and the Reply, and assumed that the Long Version of the Reply, or something very like it, has been worked over by a third hand to produce the Short Version. There are grounds for thinking that the Reply originally was written in a non-Arabic-speaking environment. Most people would agree with Kokovtsov's cautious statement that as basis for both versions there is the same original text, in general better preserved in the Long Version. B.A. Ribakov supposed that an authentic letter of King Joseph was worked over in Tmutorokan toward the end of the 11th century ("about 1083"), which resulted in the Long Version, and that some time afterward the text of the Long Version was modified by Jews of Barcelona to produce the Short Version of the Reply.

[Douglas Morton Dunlop]

Khazar Jews After the Fall of the Kingdom
The artifacts of the Khazars appear to be scant. A number of sites have been excavated, and though details of the archaeological activity in Russia are difficult to obtain (the Russians hold a monopoly on digs in ancient Khazaria), it appears that there have not been any sensational discoveries to date. No royal burial sites have been unearthed – hardly surprising since, according to Ibn Faḍlān, the khāqāns were buried under a stream – and no inscriptions, public or private.

Prior to 1914 archaeological excavations were conducted in successive years, especially at Verkhniĭ Saltov on the Donets. Since then, scholars have been divided on whether or not Saltov is a Khazar site. Additional work has been done at Bulghār and at the neighboring town of Suwār, which was mentioned in al-Iṣṭakhrī. A tenth-century two-storied palace, in which many coins were found, was discovered at the latter site, but this, the only building of a public character which has come to light, might possibly be Bulgar rather than Khazar.

Belaya (Bela) Vezha, the ancient Sarkil, near the village of Tsimlyanskaya on the left bank of the lower Don, has been the site which has attracted the most interest in recent years. Though not the Khazar capital, as had been erroneously attested, it was an important settlement. Nothing specifically Jewish has been found there. Nevertheless, discoveries analogous to the culture of Saltov and Mayatskoe Gorodishche, both at least presumed Khazar sites, were unearthed, as well as ceramics engraved with markings of the type found in the Don inscriptions. No traces of the fortress constructed by the Greeks for the Khazars have been found.

In spite of the negligible information of an archaeological nature, the presence of Jewish groups and the impact of Jewish ideas in Eastern Europe are considerable during the Middle Ages. Groups have been mentioned as migrating to Central Europe from the East or have been referred to as Khazars, thus making it impossible to overlook the possibility that they originated from within the former Khazar Empire. Even though the 12th-century traveler Benjamin of Tudela did not mention Khazaria as such he did refer to Khazars in Constantinople and Alexandria. Aside from the Kabars (Khazars) who migrated earlier to Hungary, the Hungarian duke Taksony (tenth century) is said to have invited the Khazars to settle in his lands. In about 1117 Khazars appear to have come to Vladimir Monomakh, Prince of Kiev, after fleeing from the Cumans, building a town they named Bela Vezha (near Chernigov). If this assumption is correct, these Khazars previously lived in Bela Vezha (Sarkil) and then settled near Chernigov. Prior to this time Jews who were possibly Khazars were introduced by Svyatopolk into Kiev. The Khalisioi in the 12th century, who were mentioned as fighting against Manuel I Comnenus, retained, according to John Cinnamus, "the Mosaic laws but not in their pure form" (see bibl.). As late as 1309 a council of the Hungarian clergy (at Pressburg) forbade Catholics to marry those people who were at that time described as Khazars; papal confirmation of this decision was given in 1346.

Both the Mountain Jews and the Karachais seem to be connected with the Khazars of the Caucasus region. It is also possible that there were Khazar Jews in the Crimea, which was known to the Italians in the late Middle Ages and perhaps still later as Gazaria. The Turkish-speaking Karaites of the Crimea, Poland, and elsewhere have affirmed a connection with the Khazars, which is perhaps confirmed by evidence from folklore and anthropology as well as language. There seems to be a considerable amount of evidence attesting to the continued presence in Europe of descendants of the Khazars.

The story of the conversion of the Khazar king to Judaism formed the basis for Judah Halevi's famous philosophical dialogue, *Kūzārī* (see *Judah Halevi).

BIBLIOGRAPHY: D.M. Dunlop, *History of the Jewish Khazars* (1954, p. b. 1967), includes extensive bibliography; idem, in: Roth, Dark Ages, ch. 8, and index; M.I. Artamonov, *Istoriya Khazar* (1962), especially valuable for the archaeology; V. Minorsky, in: *Oriens*, 11 (1958), 122–45 (review of Dunlop's *History*...); G. Moravcsik, *Byzantinoturcica*, 2 (1958), 334–6 (refers to Greek sources); A. Zajączkowski, in: *Acta Orientalia Hungaricae*, 12 (1961), 299–307 (regards the Karaites as successors of the Khazars); Szyszman, in: *Revue de l'Histoire des Religions*, 152 (1957), 174–221 (an original short treatment from the Karaite standpoint); A.N. Poliak, *Kazariyyah* (Heb., 1951[3]); A. Yarmolinsky, in: *Bulletin of the New York Public Library*, 42 (1938), 695–710; 63 (1959), 237–41 (bibliographies); B.D. Weinryb, in: *Studies in Bibliography and Booklore*, 6 (1963), 111–29 (updates Yarmolinsky's bibliographies); B.A. Ribakov, in: *Sovetskaya Arkheologiya*, 18 (1953), 128–50.

KHERSON, city in Nikolayev district, Ukraine. The town was founded in 1778 and Jews began to settle there a few years later. In 1799 there were 39 Jewish merchants in Kherson and 180 Jewish townsmen. A Jewish hospital was built in 1827. Like other communities in New Russia, that of Kherson grew rapidly during the 19th century, as a result of the settlement of the whole area by Jewish emigrants who left the northwestern provinces of the *Pale of Settlement for the southern provinces which were developing in this period. The number of Jews increased from 3,832 in 1847 to 17,755 (30% of the total) in 1897. Jews played an important role in the development of the town, and in 1862 the governor of Kherson province even recommended that one of the Jewish merchants be elected mayor, claiming that there were no suitable Christian candidates. He added that since many of the Jewish merchants owned properties and were educated, the election of one of them to the mayoralty would result in tangible benefits to the town. Although also supported by the governor-general of New Russia, this recommendation was not approved. In 1884, of 150 merchants, 73 were Jews; 8 factories out of 53 and 55 shops out of 123 belonged to them. At the end of the 19th century, Kherson became an active center of Zionism: the Biluists Ya'akov Shertok and Ze'ev Smilansky were then active. When Eliezer Paper was appointed director of the *talmud torah* in 1896, he introduced the "*Ivrit-be-Ivrit*" method, teaching Hebrew through the medium of Hebrew. Jewish pupils constituted a majority in the secondary schools. From the beginning of the 20th century there operated a mutual fund bank for petty merchants and artisans. In 1909 it had 1,093 members and a capital of 13,880 rubles. The Jews of Kherson suffered during the pogroms which swept the Ukraine in 1905 and during the civil war. *Denikin's soldiers carried out pogroms in April 1919. In the beginning of the Soviet regime, in the years 1921–22, there was great hunger, and many died of starvation (in December 1921, 39; in February 1922, 189). In the 1920s there was a court of law in which proceedings were held in Yiddish, and a Jewish elementary school with an enrollment of 220 in 1925, out of 1,200 children of school age. There were also an industrial school and Jewish departments in the local university. An underground Chabad yeshivah existed at the beginning of the 1930s. Early in the 1930s many Jews worked in factories, and in the biggest – the Petrovski plant – there were 1,500 Jews out of 4,500 workers. There were 14,837 Jews (19% of the total population) in the town in 1926, and 16,145 (of a total population of 96,988) in 1939. The Germans occupied Kherson on August 19, 1941. On August 29 they killed 100 Jews and in early September, 110. On September 7, a ghetto was established, and a Judenrat and Jewish police were organized. On September 24–25 *Einsatzkommando* 11a murdered 8,000 Jews. Later Jews found hiding were executed, and in February 1942 some 400 children of mixed marriages were killed. In 1959, there were 9,500 Jews (6% of the total population) living in Kherson. The last synagogue was closed by the authorities in 1959 but was returned to the community in 1991 as Jewish life revived despite the emigration of most of the Jews.

Province of Kherson

The province (gubernia) of Kherson was until the 1917 Revolution among the provinces of New Russia, and during the 19th century one of the main areas attracting Jews from other parts of Russia. The number of Jews in the province grew from 11,870 in 1818 to 339,910 in 1897, one of the highest rates of increase in the Pale of Settlement. The majority of the Jews lived in the towns: 70.89% in 1897, as against 10.18% in the townlets and 18.93% in the villages. A considerable part of the Jewish population was concentrated in the large urban centers, especially *Odessa. Other large communities at the end of the 19th century were Yelizavetgrad (*Kirovograd), *Nikolayev, and Kherson. The province of Kherson was the principal center for government-sponsored Jewish agricultural settlement in Russia, and the largest relative concentration of Jewish farmers in the country was found there (7.15% of the Jewish population of the province in 1897). From the economic point of view, the Jews of the Kherson province were among the wealthiest and most stable in the Pale of Settlement. Like the Jews of the other southern provinces of Russia, those of Kherson were mainly engaged in commerce (41.36% in 1897), particularly trading in grain and other agricultural products; 20.52% of the Jews of the region earned their livelihood from this trade in 1897. General education and modification in the traditional way of life made greater progress among the Jews of Kherson province than in the other regions of the Pale of Settlement; 45.1% of the Jewish men and 24.6% of the Jewish women in the province were able to read Russian in 1897. After the 1917 Revolution, the province was divided up into several separate administrative units.

BIBLIOGRAPHY: *Ḥakla'im Yehudim be-Arvot Rusyah* (1965); M. Golinkin, *Me-Heikhalei Yefet le-Oholei Shem* (1948), 15, passim.

[Yehuda Slutsky]

KHMELNIK (Humielnik, Khmelnik until 1772), town in the Vinnitsa district, Ukraine. A Jewish community is mentioned there as early as 1565; it possessed five houses. In 1606 the local Christian merchants and artisans complained about Jewish competition. It can be assumed that the community suffered during the *Chmielnicki massacres, but it slowly recovered, mainly during the Turkish occupation, 1672–99. In the first half of the 18th century the Jews suffered from the *Haidamacks' attacks. In 1789 there were 38 Jewish shopkeepers, 53 innkeepers, and 43 artisans, most of them tailors. From 1,417 persons in 1765 (in Khmelnik and environs), the number of Jews had risen to 3,137 in 1847, and to 5,977 in 1897 (of a total population of 11,657). On the eve of World War I most of the shops – in some trades, all of them – belonged to Jews. On May 5, 1919, Jewish *self-defense in Khmelnik was organized. It fought successfully for three months against the bands of Ataman Shepil and Volyniets, killing many of them and taking their arms. In 1926 Khmelnik had 6,011 Jews (of a total population of 10,792), their number dropping to 4,793 (of 7,513) in 1939. In the 1920s artisans' cooperatives were organized, and in 1927 an agricultural cooperative of former merchants, which numbered 100 Jewish families in 1935, had 60 *desyatines*, a large number of livestock, and agricultural machines. In the 1920s there was a local Jewish council that conducted its deliberations in Yiddish. In 1934 the Jewish school had 600 pupils (most of the children of the town). The German forces occupied the town on July 17, 1941, and most of the Jews stayed, because the local Party boss was against evacuation. The Jews were ordered to establish a Judenrat of four, to wear a white armband with a blue *Magen David*, to do slave labor, and to turn over all radios, sewing machines, bicycles, etc. On August 12, 1941 *Einsatzkommando* 5 murdered 387 men. On January 5, 1942, a ghetto was established, swelled by refugees. On January 9, 5,800 Jews were killed, leaving skilled workers with families and the many who hid. Another 1,240 were gathered and executed on January 18. On June 12 Ukrainian policemen along with Hungarian soldiers killed 360 Jews. On March 3, 1943, the ghetto was liquidated and 1,300 were murdered. Another 132 were executed on June 26, 1943, while 85 Jews escaped. The last 14 escaped in December 1943. Some of them joined Soviet partisan units. Khmelnik was liberated on March 18, 1944. In 1959 over 1,000 Jews (8.5%) lived there. In 1979 they numbered about 500. Most of them left for Israel and the West in the 1990s.

BIBLIOGRAPHY: *Reshummot*, 3 (1923), 393; B. West (ed.), *Naftulei Dor*, 2 (1955), 142–59 (Eng., *Struggle of a Generation*, 1959); idem, *Be-Ḥevlei Kelayah* (1963), 94–98; *Vyestnik Zapadnoy Rossii* (1869).

[Shmuel Spector (2nd ed.)]

KHODASEVICH, VLADISLAV FELITSIANOVICH (1886–1939), Russian poet, son of a Russified Pole and of the daughter of J. *Brafman. Khodasevich began to publish verse in 1905, and his first anthology appeared in 1908. Born in Moscow, he emigrated from the U.S.S.R. in 1922 and settled in Paris, where he lived destitute and in poor health. A highly gifted lyric poet in his own right, Khodasevich is also remembered as a translator of Polish, Armenian, and modern Hebrew verse. His appreciation of *Bialik (1934) is probably the best brief essay on the Hebrew poet ever written in Russian. Khodasevich translated many Hebrew poets, most notably Saul *Tchernichowsky, and he published a volume of these translations, *Iz yevreyskikh poetov* (1921, 1923²). He was also coeditor, with L.B. Jaffe, of *Yevreyskaya antologiya*, an anthology of Hebrew writing brought out in Russia in 1918 by the Safrut publishing house. The foremost Russian émigré poet, Khodasevich remained unknown in the U.S.S.R., where none of his books or translations was allowed to appear or to circulate in the U.S.S.R. after his departure for the West. *Literaturnye stati i vospominaniya*, a volume of essays and recollections, appeared in New York in 1954, and a modern edition of his poetry in 1961.

BIBLIOGRAPHY: N.N. Berberova, *The Italics Are Mine* (1969); idem, in: *Russian Review*, 11:2 (1952), 78–85; V.V. Veidle, *Poeziya Khodasevicha* (1928).

[Maurice Friedberg]

KHODORKOVSKY, MIKHAIL BORISOVICH (1963–), Russian "oligarch." Born in Moscow to a Jewish father who was a factory worker, Khodorkovsky graduated from the Mendeleev Institute of Chemical Technology, where he studied economics, and served as deputy head of the Communist Youth League, the Komsomol. With several partners from the Komsomol he opened a private coffee house in 1986, expanding to import and sell such goods as brandy and computers. By 1988 he had built up an import-export business that brought in $10 million a year. In 1989 he and his partners opened Bank Menatep, one of Russia's first privately owned banks. Highly successful, Menatep was the first Russian enterprise to issue stocks to the public since the Russian Revolution (1917). Its clients included many government services and ministries. Meanwhile, Khodorkovsky continued to expand his import-export empire. In 1995 Menatep won the bid to acquire a controlling interest in the state-owned oil company Yukos.

When the ruble collapsed in 1998 Menatep went under as well, losing its banking license and its shares in Yukos. By 2000 Khodorkovsky was back on his feet, and back in control of Menatep and Yukos. In 2003 Yukos merged with the Sibneft oil company. With 19.5 billion barrels of oil and gas, the corporation owned the second-largest oil and gas reserves in the world, after Exxon Mobil. That year, Khodorkovsky ranked #26 on the list of the World's Richest People and #1 as the wealthiest man in Russia.

On October 23, 2003, the billionaire Khodorkovsky was arrested on charges of fraud and tax evasion. His dramatic arrest was carried out by 15 masked federal operatives and dozens of armed agents. In May 2005 he was sentenced to nine years' imprisonment. In October 2005, he was sent to a labor camp.

The Russian crackdown on the economic crimes of the so-called oligarchs – a few dozen Jews and non-Jews controlling a quarter of Russia's national product and worth over $100 billion – has been perceived by many as tinged with antisemitism.

[Ruth Beloff (2nd ed.)]

°**KHOMEINI, AYATOLLAH** (1902–1989), Iranian religious leader. He was born in the small town of Khomein situated in the central part of *Iran and died in *Teheran. He lost his father when he was an infant and later his mother when he was 15. He studied Islamic theology in Arāk, a town in central Iran, and years later completed his studies in the holy city of Qomm.

In 1961 and 1963 Khomeini showed strong opposition to Mohammad Reza Shah's reforms, leading demonstrations and riots against the Shah. He consistently blamed the U.S. and Israel for all the corruption and backwardness in Iran. On June 3, 1963, he gave a provocative speech mainly against what he called the dependence of the Shah's regime upon the U.S. and Israel. Two days later he was arrested, which resulted in anti-Shah demonstrations in Qomm and in other cities of Iran. The slogan "Death to the Shah, Death to America, and Death to Israel" was seen and heard almost everywhere. The demonstrations were crushed by the Shah's troops; many were killed or wounded. On November 4, 1963, Khomeini was sent into exile, first to *Turkey and then to *Iraq where he resided in the Shi'i holy city of Najaf.

Anti-regime demonstrations motivated by Khomeini's speeches, recorded on cassettes and pamphlets in Najaf, continued however to arrive in Iran. The unrest and commotions culminated in 1977/78. The shah requested the Iraqi Government to expel Khomeini from Iraq. Khomeini chose to go to France (October 5, 1978). His frequent speeches from there, too, agitated the people against the Shah, the U.S. and Israel. The future of the Jewish community in Iran was in jeopardy. Several thousand Jews in Teheran, headed by some well-known social and religious personalities were "advised" to take part in demonstrations, which they did (December 11, 1978). Finally the Shah left Iran on January 16, 1979, and two weeks later Khomeini entered the country, being welcomed by millions of people; the Jews of Teheran once again were "advised" to join the demonstration to welcome Khomeini's arrival (February 13, 1979). Soon afterwards, an Islamic Republic was formed with a new Islamic constitution. Though it contained many discriminatory provisions against non-Muslims, it still granted second-class citizenship rights to Jews and other religious minorities, as protected non-Muslim monotheists – with the exception of the Bahais who were persecuted and over 200 of them were massacred all over Iran. The treatment of the Jews was ambivalent.

In the first two to three years of the Islamic Republic of Iran (IRI), about one-third of Iran's 80,000 Jews left for Israel, Europe, and the U.S. IRI broke its relations with Israel. The regime adapted a pro-Palestinian policy declaring that Israel and Zionism must be destroyed. IRI also encouraged the foundation of Hizbollah in Lebanon by supporting it with money, arms, and military advisers. Any tie with Israel was considered war against Islam. Though upon his return from Paris Khomeini met with the heads of the Jewish community, declaring that Jews were to be protected by Islamic law, some 200 Jews were arrested and jailed. During his rule, about 20 Jews were executed by the Revolutionary Courts, among them the former head of the Jewish Organization, the industrialist millionaire Habib Elghanaian (May 9, 1979). Many were deprived of their administrative, university, and high business positions. Jewish property on a large scale, amounting to more than one billion dollars, was confiscated by the regime. In recent years the IRI has tried to demonstrate some "friendly relations" with the remaining Jews of Iran who were led by the former Tudeh Party member, Parviz (Haroon) Yeshayai, the head of the Jewish Central Organization in Teheran. Nevertheless, events, such the arrest of 13 Jews in the last decade of the 20th century, allegedly spying for Israel, show the true face of these relations. As long as the hatred against Israel and Zionism and the support of terrorist organizations such as Hizbollah continue to fuel the foreign policy of Iran, the situation of Jews in IRI will remain precarious.

BIBLIOGRAPHY: Sh. Bakhash, *The Reign of the Ayatollas: Iran and the Islamic Revolution* (1984); A. Netzer, "*Be'ayot ha-Integrazyah ha-Tarbutit, ha-Ḥevratit ve-ha-Politit shel Yehudei Iran*," in: *Gesher*, 25:1–2 (1979), 69–83; idem, "Yehudei Iran, Yisrael, ve-ha-Republikah ha-Islamit shel Iran," *ibid.*, 26:1–2 (1980), 45–57; idem, "Iran ve-Yehudeha be-Parashat Derakhim Historit," *ibid.*, 1:10 (1982), 96–111; R.K. Ramazani, *Revolutionary Iran* (1986), 282–85; B. Souresrafil, *Khomeini and Israel* (1988).

[Amnon Netzer (2nd ed.)]

KHOREZM (Ar. **Khwarizm**), formerly also called Khīva, district in N.W. Uzbekistan, on the lower course of the Amu Darya River (Oxus), S. of the Aral Sea. From references in the Chronicles of the Arab historian al-Ṭabarī (838–923) to the Arab conquest of Khorezm, and from related passages in the Cambridge Document (see *Khazars), S.P. Tolstov concluded that the religion of the people of Khorezm before the Arab conquest was a peculiar syncretistic form of Judaism and that this was imported to Khazaria by survivors from the Judaizing circles from Khorezm (i.e., around 712 C.E.). The refugees were responsible not only for the Khazar conversion to Judaism but also, through setting aside the original Khazar khāqān and making their chief, *Būlān, the real ruler of Khazaria, responsible for the establishment of the Khazar dual kingship. However, no firm evidence exists for these conclusions and some of Tolstov's details are manifestly incorrect: e.g., that R. Isaac Sangari, traditionally credited with playing an important part in the Khazars' conversion to Judaism, should be identified with Khāmjird (presumed = Khangiri, a name found on some Khorezmian coins), who is mentioned by al-Ṭabarī. Yet in al-Ṭabarī's account Khāmjird is evidently the name of a region and not of a person. Tolstov further held that at one time, apparently in the eighth century, Khazaria and Khorezm formed a single state. However, his evidence, based largely on coins, is again far from conclusive. Similarly doubtful is his projected second union between Khazaria and Khorezm in the 10th and 11th centuries.

Nevertheless it is clear that some relations existed between Khorezm and Khazaria. Caravans passed between the two countries, and a corps of some thousands of men who had originally come "from the neighborhood of Khwārizm" were stationed at the Khazar capital, *Atil, in the tenth century (according to the contemporary Arab historian, al-Masʿūdī).

BIBLIOGRAPHY: M. ibn J. al-Ṭabarī, *Annales: Tarīkh al-Rusul wal-Mulūk*… ed. by M.J. de Goeje, ser. 1 pt. 5 (repr., 1964), 2903; ser. 2 pt. 2 (repr., 1964), 1142–43, 1236–41; cf. Fr. tr. by M.H. Zotenberg, 3 (1871), 573; 4 (1874), 177; Abu-Raiḥān al-Bīrūnī, *The Chronology of Ancient Nations*, tr. and ed. by C.E. Sachau (1879), 42; D.M. Dunlop, *History of the Jewish Khazars* (1954), index S.V. *Khwārism*; A.N. Poliak, *Kazariyyah* (1951), index; Baron, Social², 3 (1954), 326; S. Szyszman, in: RHR, 152 (1957), 186–90; S.P. Tolstov, *Po sledam drevnekharezmiyskoy tsivilizatsii* (1948: *Auf den Spuren der altchoresmischen Kultur*, 1953), esp. chs. 9–10; idem, in: *Sovetskaya etnografiya* (1946), 94–104; M.I. Artamonov, *Istoriya Khazar* (1962), 283–7 and index; F. Altheim and R. Stiehl, in: *Anales de historia antigua y medieval*, 8 (1955), 56–61; idem, *Finanzgeschichte der Spaetantike* (1957), 264–72.

KHOROL, city in Poltava district, Ukraine. Jews first settled in Khorol in the early 19th century; from only 78 in 1847 their number grew to 2,056 (25% of the total population) in 1897. The Jews of Khorol constituted a typical community of *Chabad Ḥasidim, described by B. *Dinur, a native of Khorol, in his memoirs *Be-Olam she-Shaka* (1958). Dinur's grandfather, Abraham Madeyevski, was rabbi of Khorol in the second half of the 19th century. There were schools for boys and girls as well as *ḥadarim*. In October 1905 a pogrom occurred, and in 1919 another pogrom was organized by soldiers of General Denikin. In 1926 the Jewish population numbered 2,089 (19.7%), but dropped to 701 (6.4% of the total population) in 1939. The Germans occupied Khorol on September 13, 1941, and in October they murdered the 460 remaining Jews.

[Yehuda Slutsky]

KHOTIN (**Hotin** in Romanian; **Khocim** in Polish), town in Bessarabia, today Moldova. Jewish merchants traveling from Constantinople to Lvov in the 15th and 16th centuries used to pass through Khotin, then an important customs station on the Polish-Moldavian border on the commercial route between Turkey and Poland. Similarly, Jewish merchants from Poland used to visit Khotin for the fairs held there, evidence for which dates from 1541. However, the residence of Jews in Khotin is first mentioned in documents in 1741. When the Frankist movement arose in nearby Podolia in the 18th century (see Jacob *Frank and Frankists), Khotin, then under direct Turkish rule, served as a refuge for Frank and his followers when they were forced to leave Poland. In this period it also served as a refuge for *Judaizers who fled from Russia, and the community even sent emissaries to Germany to collect contributions for their maintenance. The Jews of Khotin then maintained a flourishing trade with the Ukraine and other regions of Bessarabia, and they also leased the management of estates and various branches of the farm economy. There were 340 Jewish families in 1808.

After the incorporation of Bessarabia into Russia in 1812 the community grew as a result of the large Jewish immigration into the region. The community numbered 6,342 in 1864 and 9,227 (50.2% of the total population) in 1897. A Jewish government school was established in 1847 which encouraged the growth of Haskalah; a private school for girls was opened in 1857. The Jews in Khotin were subject to the restrictions on Jewish residence in the border zones, and suffered, mainly at the end of the 19th century, from persecution by the authorities, who expelled them from Khotin on the grounds that they had no rights of residence in the city. In the first half of the 19th century, Isaiah Schorr, one of the most important rabbis in Bessarabia in the period, officiated in Khotin. After Bessarabia was incorporated into Romania in 1918 the community led an active cultural and communal life. Before World War II its institutions included a hospital (founded in 1865), an old-age home, a soup kitchen, a *talmud torah*, and a *Tarbut elementary school. It numbered 5,786 (37.7% of the total population) in 1930.

[Eliyahu Feldman]

Holocaust Period

In 1940, after Khotin was incorporated into Soviet Russia, it had a Jewish population of 15,000, including some Russian Jews who had settled there. When war broke out with Germany a number of Jews managed to escape to other parts of the Soviet Union. The city was captured by German-Romanian forces on July 7, 1941. The Jews were ordered to stay indoors, and detachments of soldiers, commanded by SS officers, went from house to house and arrested some 2,000 of them who were taken to the city square and shot. A few days later the remaining Jewish population was ordered to assemble in the Jewish school, and all those found hiding were shot on the spot. At night the soldiers removed women and girls from the school and assaulted them, sometimes killing them afterward. After a few days spent without food or water, hundreds of Jews died, especially the sick, the old, and the very young. On the fifth day German troops, commanded by an SS officer, picked out Rabbi Twersky and 57 professional men among the detainees (lawyers, doctors, and teachers), took them to the outskirts, and killed them all. Meanwhile, the Jewish houses were looted by the local population. On August 1, the surviving Jews were taken to the village of Barnova, east of the town, where some of them were forced by the Romanian soldiers to dig their own graves, in which they were buried alive. The rest were sent to the concentration camp at Secureni (Sekiryany). The 3,800 Jews now left in the city of Khotin were marched to *Ataki, where many succumbed to an epidemic that broke out there. The survivors were sent back to Secureni, where hundreds more died of typhus and other diseases. Finally, the rest were deported to *Transnistria, from which only a few returned. Of the prewar Jewish community, only 500 Jews were left in 1945.

In 1970 the Jewish population was estimated at about 1,000. The Jews had their own cemetery, but there was no synagogue.

[Jean Ancel]

BIBLIOGRAPHY: M. Carp, *Cartea Neagră*, 3 (1947), 81; Herz-Kahn, in: *Eynikeyt* (Sept. 22, 1945).

KHOURI, MAKRAM (1945–), Israeli actor. Khouri, an Israeli Arab, was born in Jerusalem and raised in Acre. He performed with the Cameri Theater and then with the Haifa Municipal Theater. He appeared frequently on Arabic and Hebrew general Israeli television as well as on educational television and played in films. In 1987 he was awarded the Israel Prize for theater, cinema, and television arts. In addition, Khouri was awarded the Moshe ha-Levi prize and the Kinnor David as the theater actor of the year in 1984. He was also awarded the Israeli Oscar as a film actor. Among his films are *Wedding in Galilee* (1987) and *The Syrian Bride* (2005). In 2004 he was selected to play the Palestinian president in the TV series *West Wing*.

[Shaked Gilboa (2nd ed.)

KHOUSHI (Schneller), ABBA (1898–1969), Israeli labor leader and mayor of Haifa. Born in Turka, Eastern Galicia, he was active in *He-Ḥalutz and Ha-Shomer ha-Ẓa'ir in Galicia. He settled in Palestine in 1920 and participated in the founding conference of the *Histadrut. In his first years in the country he worked in road construction, and also in the drainage of swamps in Nahalal and the Jezreel Valley. He was one of the founders of kibbutz Beit Alfa, where he engaged in agriculture. Khoushi gained a proficient knowledge of Arabic, and had numerous Arab acquaintances. In 1927 he settled in Haifa, where he organized dock workers in a trade union within the framework of the Histadrut, and helped to bring 500 Jewish dock workers to Palestine from Salonika. In 1931–51 Khoushi was the secretary of the Haifa Labor Council. On "Black Saturday," June 29, 1946, he managed to avoid detention. He was a member of Aḥdut ha-Avodah, and later of Mapai. He was elected to the First Knesset on the Mapai list, but resigned in 1951 to be elected mayor of Haifa, against the background of the violent seamen's strike that had broken out in Zim ships. Though Mapai objected to the seamen's strike that was supported by Mapam and the Communists, and the police in Haifa participated in the efforts to break up the strike, Khoushi was known for his support of the workers in their industrial struggles, frequently demonstrating his contempt for the "bourgeoisie" of Mount Carmel. As mayor he invested great efforts in developing Haifa, which remained the only city in Israel in which there is public transportation on Saturday, and constructed an underground funicular – the Carmelit – that connected Mount Carmel with the downtown area. He also promoted the creation of parks and places of recreation in the city, and was instrumental in helping establish the University of Haifa. He actively promoted good neighborly relations with the Arab residents of Haifa, and with the Druze settlements of Usfiyya and Dāliyat al-Karmil on the outskirts of Haifa.

He wrote *Be-Veit Po'alei Ereẓ Yisrael* ("In the Home of the Workers in Ereẓ Yisrael," 1943).

[Benjamin Jaffe / Susan Hattis Rolef (2nd ed.)]

KHURASAN (also **Khorasan**), province of N.E. *Persia. The earliest mention of Jews living in Khurasan in the early fourth century appears in the Babylonian Talmud (Avodah Zarah 31b), where the present city of Merv is written in its older form MRGW'N. The Tang-e Azao inscription written in Hebrew script indicates the date 1064 Seleucid era/753–4 C.E. It was found in the Gur region in eastern Khurasan. In the same period a commercial note, also written in Hebrew script, was also found in eastern Khurasan in the place called Dandan Uiliq. In the Middle Ages Khurasan also included *Afghanistan, Turkestan, and Transoxiana. Jewish history has a long association with Khurasan, which in some Hebrew sources was believed to be the dwelling place of the *Ten Lost Tribes. Reliable rabbinical, *Karaite, and Muslim sources testify to a widely spread Jewish settlement in Khurasan. The caliph Omar II (717–720) ordered his governor in the province "not to destroy any synagogues, but also not to allow new ones to be erected." Muslim sources also speak of Jewish jewelers and poets from Khurasan in the period of the *Abbasid caliphate (750–1258). An interesting Jewish figure from the ninth century known as *Hiwi al-Balkhi was the resident of the city of Balkh situated in the far eastern part of then Khurasan. The Arab geographer al-Maqdisī (985) stated, "There are in Khurasan many Jews and only a few Christians." The Hebrew chronicle of *Nathan b. Isaac ha-Kohen ha-Bavli (10th century) and the parallel version of *Seder Olam Zuta* deal with a dispute between the head of the academy in *Pumbedita and the exilarch *Ukba concerning jurisdiction over the Jews in Khurasan. The Jewish authorities in *Baghdad used Khurasan as a place of exile for undesirables. Geonic literature speaks of a special Khurasan custom in matters of the calendar, marriage laws, and other halakhic subjects, but the Jews of Khurasan were enjoined by the Jewish authorities in Babylonia to comply with the Babylonian *minhag*. According to *Benjamin of Tudela in the 12th century the authority of the Exilarch in Baghdad extended over the communities of Khurasan. The Jews lived in the cities of Sistan, *Nishapur, *Merv, Kabul, Kandahar, Ghazni (see *Afghanistan), *Balkh, and the region east of *Herat. During the 16th century, Jews from Khurasan arrived in *India. They settled mainly in Old Delhi, Lahore, Kashmir, Agra, and Fatehpur. Many Jewish communities in Afghanistan and Turkestan were later augmented by Jews from *Meshed fleeing after the forced conversion of 1839.

BIBLIOGRAPHY: Neubauer, Chronicles, 2 (1895), 78ff.; W.J. Fischel, in: HJ, 7 (1945), 29–50. **ADD. BIBLIOGRAPHY:** M. Zand, "Bukhara," in: *Encyclopaedia Iranica*, ed. by E. Yarshater (1989), 532ff.

[Walter Joseph Fischel / Amnon Netzer (2nd ed.)]

KHUST (Czech **Chust** or **Husté**; Hung. **Huszt**), city in Subcarpathian Ruthenia (Transcarpathian district), Ukraine. The Jewish community established in the middle of the 18th century numbered 14 families in 1792. Jacob of Zhidachov was appointed as the first rabbi in 1812. In the mid-19th century, the community became one of the largest and most important in northern Hungary, mainly through the authority of the Orthodox leader, Moses *Schick, rabbi of Khust from 1861 to 1879. Most of the Orthodox rabbis in Hungary were trained in his yeshivah, which had some 400 students. His successors, Amram *Blum and Moses *Grunwald (1893–1912), prevented the development of Ḥasidism in the community. Under Czechoslovakian rule (1920–38), Khust had an active Jewish life: five town councillors represented a United Jewish Party in 1923. The rabbi of the city from 1921 to 1933 was Joseph *Duschinsky, later rabbi of the separatist Orthodox community of Jerusalem. The number of Jews living in the town was 3,391 in 1921, 4,821 in 1930, and 6,023 (of a total population of 21,118) in 1941. Most of the businesses and artisan shops in the town belonged to Jews, among them three banks, factories, and flour mills. Among professionals were seven doctors, three pharmacists, and officials. The Jews of Khust were among the first to suffer when the area came under Hungarian rule in March 1939. Jewish men of military service age were forced into the labor battalions, some were sent to the Eastern front, where they perished. Hundreds without Hungarian citizenship were deported to Ukraine, and were murdered there. In 1942 there were approximately 100–130 yeshivah students in Khust. In March 1944 there were 5,351 Jews in Khust, and a ghetto and a Judenrat were set up. Another 5,000 Jews from the area were brought into the ghetto. In late May and early June, all ghetto inhabitants were deported in four transports to Auschwitz, where most of them were sent to gas chambers. In June 1944 the town was declared "**judenrein*." A few dozen Jews volunteered for the Czechoslovakian army, which fought together with the Soviet army. After World War II the community was revived. In the late 1960s the authorities permitted a synagogue to open in Khust, the only one in the district, and the community had a *shoḥet*. At the time the number of Jewish families in the town was estimated at 400.

BIBLIOGRAPHY: J.J.(L.) Greenwald (Grunwald), *Maẓẓevat Kodesh* (1952), 45–53; Y. Ereẓ (ed.), *Karpatorus* (1959), passim; S. Rozman, *Zikhron Kedoshim li-Yhudei Karpatorus-Marmorosh* (1968, Yid.), 274–5, 322–7, 458–61, and passim.

[Meir Lamed]

KIBBUTZ FESTIVALS. Kibbutz celebrations originated in the 1920s and 1930s as an attempt to recapture the "ancient Hebrew" – mainly the agricultural – character of Jewish holidays. (See Table: List of Published Texts of Kibbutz Festivals and Special Occasions.) Over the years they acquired a tradition of their own, as nearly two generations of kibbutz children grew up celebrating them. When the first kindergarten and school were established in each kibbutz, the settlers became aware of a need for festive occasions, both as an educational experience for the children and to relieve the monotony of daily life. The traditional Jewish festivals thus served as the basis for a revival enriched by biblical and mishnaic sources.

Passover

Passover (*Pesaḥ*) was the first festival to be revived in its seasonal context, as it is both the Spring Festival and the Festival of Freedom. The kibbutz **Haggadah* – the *Haggadah* compiled at kibbutz Yagur was the prototype – was based on the theme of the Exodus from Egypt, but included events of a similar nature pertinent to modern Jewish history and kibbutz life, as well as appropriate passages from modern Hebrew literature. The **seder* was held in public and became an elaborate function, with music and dancing, for members, children, and guests. The 1985 *Haggadah* of the Kibbutz ha-Me'uḥad movement reflected a tendency to return to traditional materials.

The Counting of the Omer

The counting of the Omer (*Sefirat ha-Omer*). An **omer* festival based on biblical and mishnaic sources was inaugurated, symbolizing the harvesting of the first ripe grain. On the eve of the first day of Passover, kibbutz members and their children formed a procession and went singing and dancing to the fields. A number of ears of grain were ceremonially cut, to be placed in the communal dining hall as part of the Passover decorations.

The Festival of the First Fruits

The Festival of the First Fruits (*Ḥagigat ha-Bikkurim*) takes place during the Feast of Weeks (Shavuot) and marks the peak of the first grain harvest and the first ripe fruits. The seven species mentioned in the Bible (wheat, barley, vines, pomegranates, olive trees, fig trees, and honey; Deut. 8:8) are represented graphically and through song and dance. There were also mass rallies to bring offerings of first fruits to the *Jewish National Fund.

The Sheepshearing Festival

The Sheepshearing Festival (*Ḥagigat ha-Gez*) originated in the 1920s in the Valley of Jezreel, and is based on biblical sources. It was celebrated only in kibbutzim that own flocks, and symbolizes the joy of the shepherd when the shearing is finished. The last sheep is ceremonially sheared to the accompaniment of singing and dancing. Short plays are performed, usually on the theme of 1 Samuel 25 (the story of Abigail and Nabal), and displays of woolen goods and art on pastoral themes are held.

The Festival of the Vineyards
The Festival of the Vineyards (*Ḥagigat ha-Keramim*). Several attempts were made to revive this festival, mentioned in the Mishnah (Ta'an. 4:8) and held on the 15th of Av. Festivities combined music, choreography, poetry, and love songs.

The Harvest Festival
The Harvest Festival (*Ḥagigat ha-Asif*), which was added in the 1950s to Tabernacles (Sukkot), has as its themes the gathering of the second grain crop and the autumn fruit, the start of the agricultural year, and the first rains. Based on the Water-Drawing (*Bet ha-Sho'evah*) Festival (Mish. Suk. 5:1–4), it is celebrated in some kibbutzim at night around the swimming pool.

Anniversaries of events important in the history of a particular kibbutz inspire many pageants, acted by the members and their children. Marriage and bar mitzvah ceremonies are celebrated, as are Children's Day, and the day on which the young people of the kibbutz become members. Martyrs and Heroes Day on the anniversary of the Warsaw Ghetto Uprising (the 27th of Nisan) commemorates the victims of the Holocaust and is marked by memorial ceremonies and dramas on the subject of the Warsaw Ghetto and other Jewish resistance. Other festivals, such as the 15th of Shevat, Hanukkah, and Israel Independence Day (the 5th of Iyyar) are celebrated, but they do not take a form peculiar to the kibbutz. Kibbutz festivals symbolize the new life and farming background of the settlers, and are a rich treasure of Jewish folklore and culture. Providing outlets for the talents of those kibbutz members who are artists, poets, composers, producers, and choreographers, the festivals are a distinct contribution to Israel culture. An archive housed in Kibbutz Beit ha-Shitah contains extensive information about kibbutz festivals and cultural life.

List of Published Texts of Kibbutz Festivals and Special Occasions

Name of Work	Author	Composer	Publisher
Yagur Haggadah (for Passover)	Yehudah Sharett (ed.)	Yehudah Sharett	The Center for Education and Culture of the Histadrut
Zikhron Hava'at ha-Omer (Omer Celebration)		Shalom Postolsky	*Mo'adim* series, "Pesah," (5.3.1946) JNF and *Ommanut* magazine (M. Lipson, ed.)
Hava'at ha-Omer (Omer Celebration)	Matityahu Shelem	Matityahu Shelem	The Center for Education and Culture of the Histadrut
Massekhet ha-Omer (Omer Celebration)	Anadad Eldan	Avraham Daus	Reprint, Kibbutz Hefẓibah
Bi-Sedeh Koẓerim (pageant for the First Fruits Festival)	Ḥanan Shadmi	Yekutiel Shor	The Center for Education and Culture of the Histadrut
Koveẓ Ḥag ha-Gez (Sheepshearing Festival)	Matityahu Shelem (ed.)	Matityahu Shelem	Aguddat ha-Nokedim be-Israel
Shirim le-Tu be-Av (15 of Av)	Dov Shay	Yiẓhar Yaron	in Y. Yaron, *Rinnot*, the Center for Education and Culture of the Histadrut
Shirim u-Meḥolot le-Tu be-Av (pageant) (15 of Av)	Efrayim ben Ḥayyim		Reprint, Kibbutz Kiryat Anavim
Simḥat Beit ha-Sho'evah u-Mo'adei ha-Mayim (Water Festival)		Yehudah Sharett	*Onot*, no. 4, Ha-Kibbutz ha-Me'uḥad
Simḥat Beit ha-Sho'evah (pageant for Water Festival)	Yiẓḥak Asher	Karel Salmon	Kibbutz ha-Dati (1958)
Tekes Ḥag ha-Asif (Harvest Festival)	Anadad Eldan	David Zahavi	The Center for Education and Culture of the Histadrut
Yalkut Bar Mitzvah (bar mitzvah ceremony, anthology)	Yehudah Sharett	Yehudah Sharett	Aryeh Ben-Gurion (ed.), Va'adat ha-Ḥaggim ha-Bein-kibbutzit
Massekhet ha-Sho'ah ve-ha-Gevurah (anthology for Holocaust Memorial Day)			Va'adat ha-Ḥaggim ha-Bein-kibbutzit
Kovez "B" le-Yom ha-Zikkaron, "Ha-Sho'ah ve-ha-Mered" (Holocaust Memorial Day)	Ẓevi Shua, Israel Guttman		Va'adat ha-Ḥaggim ha-Bein-kibbutzit and *Moreshet* (1968)
"Kelulot" (for kibbutz weddings)	Matityahu Shelem		Ha-Va'adah ha-Bein-kibbutzit le-Havvai u-Mo'ed (1968)
Kibbutz festivals for Israel's 20th anniversary:			
"Yerushalayim" (choreographic play)	Leah Yisre'eli	David Ori	Ha-Musikah ha-Yisra'elit, Ltd. (1968)
"La-Ḥag Mizmor" (Cantata for choir and orchestra)	Yehudah Engel	Yehudah Engel	Ha-Merkaz le-Tarbut u-le-Ḥinnukh (1968)
Songs for Miscellaneous Festivals			The Music Committee of Kibbutz Arẓi – ha-Shomer ha-Ẓa'ir
Anniversary celebrations (playlets)			Various kibbutzim

[Matityahu Shelem]

WEBSITE: www.chagim.org.il

KIBBUTZ MOVEMENT. The kibbutz, or kevuẓah (plural: kibbutzim, kevuẓot) is a voluntary collective community, mainly agricultural, in which there is no private wealth and which is responsible for all the needs of the members and their families. The kibbutz movement in Israel in 1969 numbered 93,000 people in 231 kibbutzim and kevuẓot organized in several federations according to social, political, and religious outlook. Since that time the kibbutz has undergone enormous changes, distancing itself from the classic model (see below) and becoming what its founders never dreamed it would become.

The first kevuẓah was founded in 1909 at *Deganyah by a group of pioneers, who, after working at first as employees of the Palestine Land Development Company, undertook collective responsibility for the working of the farm. Another group, which started work at *Kinneret in the same year, became an independent kevuẓah in 1913. By 1914 there were 11 kevuẓot established on Jewish National Fund land under the responsibility of the Zionist Organization, and the number grew to 29 by the end of 1918. The early kevuẓot had small memberships based upon the idea that the community should be small enough to constitute a kind of enlarged family. During the Third Aliyah, after World War I, when larger numbers of pioneering settlers (*ḥalutzim*) arrived, Shelomo *Lavi and others proposed the establishment of large, self-sufficient villages, combining agriculture with industry, for which the name "kibbutz" was used. The first of this type was *En Harod, founded in 1921, and many others followed. Later, however, the distinction between the two terms almost disappeared. The kibbutzim and kevuẓot combined to establish federations in accordance with their social character, political affiliations, or religious outlook: Ḥever ha-Kevuẓot, founded in 1925 (later merged in Iḥud ha-Kevuẓot ve-ha-Kibbutzim); Ha-Kibbutz ha-Arẓi ha-Shomer ha-Ẓa'ir, and Ha-Kibbutz ha-Me'uḥad, both founded in 1927; and Ha-Kibbutz ha-Dati, founded in 1935. In 1979 the two kibbutz organizations, Kibbutz Ha-Meuḥad and Iḥud Ha-Kevutzot ve-ha-Kibbutzim reunited after 28 years of separation to form the Ha-Tenuah ha-Kibbuẓit ha-Meuḥedet (TaKaM). (For separate accounts, see below.)

The kibbutzim received their manpower mainly from the pioneering youth movements abroad and, in their turn, provided the movements with a practical ideal of pioneering settlement on the land in order to make a major contribution to the building of the Jewish National Home and create a model and a basis for the socialist society of the future. They played an important part in expanding the map of Jewish settlement and safeguarding the growing community. In the late 1930s many were set up overnight on the *Tower and Stockade plan so as to forestall official obstruction and Arab attack. The kibbutzim served as bases for the *Haganah defense force and later the *Palmaḥ, its commando section. Most of the new villages established under emergency conditions during and immediately after World War II, especially in the Negev, were kibbutzim. By the establishment of independence, they numbered 149 out of the 291 Jewish villages in the country.

In 1948 and 1949 the momentum of kibbutz expansion continued: out of 175 new villages founded during the two years, 79 were kibbutzim. The Jews from Muslim countries and survivors of the Holocaust who arrived in enormous numbers during the early years of the state were not favorably disposed to the kibbutz idea, however, and most of them preferred to settle in *moshavim. Youngsters born or brought up in Israel, including the second or third generation from older kibbutzim and graduates of *Youth Aliyah and Israel youth movements, became more prominent among the founders of new kibbutzim, especially in the Negev and, after the Six-Day War (1967), in the Golan Heights.

The Original Character of the Kibbutz

The kibbutz was a unique product of the Zionist labor movement and the Jewish national revival. It was not conceived theoretically as an escapist or utopian project; it was developed by Jewish workers inspired by ideas of social justice as an integral part of the Zionist effort to resettle the homeland. From its inception, the kibbutz movement played a pioneering role in the economic, political, cultural, and security activities required to carry out that purpose. The movement was composed of people from different countries and backgrounds, and of varying political beliefs. Some communities were inspired by A.D. *Gordon's ethical Jewish identification with nature and of physical labor as the supreme human value. Others cherished the tradition of the *Gedud ha-Avodah of the early 1920s, which regarded itself as a militant constructive task force. Others, again, do not regard themselves as a part of the socialist movement, while a number of kibbutzim (mostly organized in Ha-Kibbutz ha-Dati) have been established by religious Jews and combine communal life with the fulfillment of the laws of the Torah.

In the early 1950s differences of opinion over Marxist theory and support for pro-Soviet policies led to a split in Ha-Kibbutz ha-Me'uḥad, and one section joined with Ḥever ha-Kevuẓot to form Iḥud ha-Kevuẓot ve-ha-Kibbutzim. Ha-Kibbutz ha-Arẓi Ha-Shomer ha-Ẓa'ir, believing that the kibbutz as an economic unit could not be divorced from its political ideals, regarded itself as a political unit as well. Over the years, each of the federations was associated to a greater or lesser degree with one of the Israel parties. With the passage of time, many of the initial differences between one type of kibbutz and another disappeared. Most of the small, purely agricultural ones grew and established industries, and the differences between the small kevuẓah and the large kibbutz vanished. With the intensification of Soviet hostility to Israel, the attitude to the U.S.S.R. ceased, to all intents and purposes, to be a dividing factor, especially since the Six-Day War. There was an increasing trend toward inter-kibbutz activity and cooperation in all spheres, ranging from education to the economy.

The movement was supported from its inception by Zionist and Israel government agencies with long-term leases of national land, technical advice, development projects, and long-term financing. Through a special corps, *Naḥal, composed of youth movement graduates, the Israel Defense Forces trained nuclei of future kibbutzim and helped in their establishment. Sites for new kibbutzim were chosen in the light of national settlement and defense policy, often at the expense of economic viability. Many of them were in border areas and played an important part in the regional defense system.

Organization

In the classic model, the basis of kibbutz administration was a weekly general meeting of the membership, which formulated policy, elected officers, and superviseed the overall working of the community. Candidates for membership were usually accepted after a year's probation. Kibbutzim were incorporated cooperative enterprises, and generally speaking members transferred all assets, other than personal effects, to the kibbutz. If a member decided to leave he was entitled to his personal effects and, in line with a later decision of the movement, to a cash grant proportional to the time he had been in the kibbutz. Uniform national bylaws governing individual rights in the kibbutz were approved.

Affairs of the kibbutz were conducted by elected committees, the principal one being the secretariat, which usually consisted of a secretary, treasurer, chairmen of some of the key committees, the production manager, and others. There were committees in charge of education, cultural activities, questions of principle and personal problems of members, economic planning, coordination of work, and nominations. Elective positions, including managerial ones, were rotated every year or two.

The kibbutz federations provided financial assistance to their member villages through independent loan funds and national negotiation with financial and governmental institutions. They offered technical advisory services ranging from economic analysis to the planning of communal kitchens and laundries. Central purchasing and marketing services cut costs for individual kibbutzim and a special department dealt with kibbutz-based industry. They operated their own psychological clinics for children (including a school for disturbed children) and, in cooperation with institutions of higher learning, offered courses in specific branches of technology, agriculture, and kibbutz management. Cultural activities ranged from movement-wide choirs and amateur orchestras to regional schools for adult education on a non-university and university level. The kibbutz federations were joined together in Berit ha-Tenu'ah ha-Kibbutzit ("Kibbutz Movement Alliance"), which coordinated their activities in the many areas in which they cooperated. The three major ones jointly operated Israel's largest teachers' training college – Seminar ha-Kibbutzim.

Each federation operated an ideological center, where seminars were conducted, and published bulletins and journals of letters and opinion. Berit ha-Tenu'ah ha-Kibbutzit established a company for the production of television material on kibbutz topics. Each federation negotiated with its kibbutzim for manpower for general movement activity, not only within the movement itself but in the Zionist and labor movements and in government service. There was an increasing degree of regional cooperation cutting across federation boundaries. This included regional secondary schools, youth and cultural activity, and large regional economic and industrial complexes – including plants for canning, poultry slaughtering and dressing, packing and fodder preparation, cotton gins and large silos, trucking and hauling cooperatives, and large regional garages.

Social and Educational Aspects

The kibbutz movement believed in personal labor and placed equal value on all kinds of work. In the course of time people took up more or less permanent jobs, but there was a great deal of work mobility. With economic expansion and the increasing technical complexity of the kibbutz economy, it became necessary in many instances to hire outside labor in contradiction to the movement's socialist principles. It was hoped to solve this problem in the course of time with increased population and efficiency. Another problem which the movement tried to solve was the absorption of the increasing proportion of members who pursued academic or professional careers, often outside the kibbutz, while retaining their membership.

The kibbutz provided a complete spectrum of services to its members, ranging from razor blades to housing and from honeymoons to financial aid for dependents living outside, with complete medical coverage. Each kibbutz had a communal dining hall, laundry, and tailor shop. With the rise in the standard of living, increasing allowance was made for individual tastes and for spending in accordance with personal inclination on clothing, furnishings, cultural activities, hobbies, vacations, and so forth.

Up to 1970, in all but some dozen kibbutzim children lived in children's houses, which included sleeping quarters and play and study rooms, where community living was taught from the very earliest age. They were part of an organized children's community, living, eating, and studying together; in some ways they constituted a miniature kibbutz, conducting their own affairs, with the advice of teachers and group leaders, and in many kibbutzim operating their own small farms. Children "graduated" from one house to another as they advanced in age. Mothers – especially, of course, when nursing – visited their children frequently during the day, and after work the children were with their parents. People working with children were trained in kibbutz-sponsored courses, ranging from intensive three-month seminars to full-fledged kindergarten and teacher training. The kibbutz school differed from the city school in its emphasis on agriculture and on work as an integral part of the curriculum. It was considered an extension of the children's society, so that the teacher-pupil relationship was close and informal. All kibbutz children continued through secondary school; the increasing number who intended to go on to higher education were prepared for the matriculation examinations. A number of kibbutzim, principally among those belonging to the Iḥud, changed the system to provide for children sleeping in the homes of their parents.

Advocates of the change believed that it enhanced the psychological security of the child, as well as improving the position of the woman and the family in the kibbutz. The effect of the kibbutz and its educational system on its children has been extensively studied. Research has not shown significant indications of maternal deprivation, though some psychologists have found some signs of this at the younger ages. They feel, however, that this was overcome at a later age by the powerful supporting environment.

There were some kibbutzim in which the third, and in a few even the fourth, generation had reached maturity, and a goodly number in which the kibbutz-born had become the dominant group. Through 1970 over 75% of the latter remained in the kibbutz, despite the attraction of the cities. Though only 4% of the total population of Israel, their percentage among army officers was three or four times as high. A quarter of all the casualties in the Six-Day War were soldiers from kibbutzim. More direct and practical than their parents, and less given to hairsplitting ideology, it was the young people who were the principal force pushing toward the ultimate unification of the movement.

Some sociological studies have shown that although there was no material basis for social stratification, elements of such stratification did exist on the basis of social prestige or kinds of work. There were some differences in personal possessions as well, due to outside sources of income such as gifts, reparations from Germany, or inheritances, which were not always handed in to the kibbutz in their entirety, though very large sums of money received by beneficiaries of reparations were handed over to the kibbutzim. Women were disappointed at times in their relationship with the kibbutz community. The idea of freeing women from household chores so that they could work at other tasks was one of the prime aims of the movement, but this became increasingly difficult as a kibbutz grew older and pressure was generated for increased work in child care and household services. Kibbutzim attempted to improve the personal and family status of women by improving physical conditions of work in the services, by raising the work level of a profession through training and study, and, in some cases, by reducing working hours for women with families.

The kibbutz movement was a major factor in the activities of the Zionist movement and the State of Israel. Its influence was both moral and practical, ranging from settlement and security functions (including settling new areas after the Six-Day War), to the absorption of immigrants and Youth Aliyah children, and the provision of leading personnel for Zionist and government service. The number of kibbutz members in the Knesset and among army officers was far beyond their proportion in the population. This influence is indicated by such diverse statistics as the fact that in 1970 its production accounted for 12% of Israel's gross national product, and that more than 20 members of the Knesset were kibbutz members. In the late 1960s the movement was increasing in size at the rate of about 2–3% a year. Although it had become an established institution, it was still demonstrating a capacity for changing with the times.

Iḥud ha-Kevuzot ve-ha-Kibbutzim

Iḥud ha-Kevutzot ve-ha- Kibbutzim (Heb. "Union of Collective Settlements") was founded in 1951 through the unification of Ḥever ha-Kevuẓot and Iḥud ha-Kibbutzim, which had split off from Ha-Kibbutz ha-Me'uḥad (see below). In 1969 it comprised 81 communities, with a total population of about 30,000. Ḥever ha-Kevuẓot was the federation of the smaller, purely agricultural collective settlements, many of whose members believed in the ethical socialist concepts of A.D. *Gordon, and most of whom belonged to *Mapai, the Israel Labor Party; it included such long-established villages as *Deganyah and *Geva. The Iḥud ha-Kibbutzim settlements also leaned toward Mapai. The Iḥud was considered the most liberal of the three major kibbutz federations, allowing for more diversity and imposing less social or political discipline. In 1970, for example, children slept in the parents' homes in more than a dozen of its villages, though most of the other kibbutzim regard the dormitory system as a part of the movement's educational methods. A number of Iḥud kibbutzim also allowed for more latitude in the spending of personal funds. In 1953, the non-socialist kibbutzim of *Ha-No'ar ha-Ẓiyyoni, associated with the Independent Liberal Party, joined the Iḥud on condition of educational and political autonomy.

Each kibbutz elected its representatives to the national executive, and the national secretariat consisted of members drafted from the kibbutzim. The movement operated a loan fund, purchasing services, and departments for economic planning and assistance, social and ideological problems, education, youth work, military security, manpower, and immigrant absorption. It delegated members for work in youth movements both in Israel and abroad, in Zionist and political affairs, in the labor movement, and in government service. It conducted a variety of seminars and courses in cultural and technical subjects. It cooperated with the other kibbutz federations in operating Seminar ha-Kibbutzim for training teachers, and at its convention in 1969 it decided actively to encourage university education for members. The kibbutzim conducted their own elementary schools and regional secondary schools, attended in some areas by children from moshavim and Kibbutz ha-Me'uḥad communities as well.

The movement published a weekly bulletin, *Iggeret la-Ḥaverim* (from 1951); a quarterly journal, *Niv ha-Kevuẓah* (from 1930); a bimonthly journal of opinion, *Shedemot* (from 1948); and a periodical for educators, *Iggeret le-Ḥinnukh* (from 1952). It organized regional and national cultural activities, such as discussion circles and the federation's choir. The youth of the movement was affiliated as a group to *Ha-No'ar ha-Oved, the Histadrut's youth section. The Iḥud had a special relationship with a number of youth movements in Israel and abroad, sending youth workers to them and receiving reinforcements from them. Among these are Ha-No'ar ha-Oved, Ha-Ẓofim (see *Scouts), *Iḥud ha-Bonim, and La-Merḥav.

[Moshe Kerem]

Ha-Kibbutz ha-Arzi-ha-Shomer ha-Za'ir

Founded in 1927, comprised 73 kibbutzim and two *Naḥal outposts in 1969. Its ideological basis was a belief in the kibbutz as an instrument for fulfilling the Zionist ideal, furthering the class struggle, and building a Socialist society. Its founding members, who belonged to the *Ha-Shomer ha-Ẓa'ir ("Young Guard") youth movement, came from Poland and Galicia in 1919, and in 1920 established the movement's first kibbutz, which settled at *Bet Alfa in 1922. By 1927 there were six Ha-Shomer ha-Ẓa'ir kibbutzim, four of which founded Ha-Kibbutz ha-Arẓi. In the 40 years that followed, the population of its villages grew from 249 members and 19 children to over 31,000 persons, of whom some 16,000 were members and 10,000 children.

Ha-Kibbutz ha-Arẓi ("The National Kibbutz [Movement]") regarded the kibbutz as an autonomous unit of social life, comprehending all spheres of economic, social, cultural, political, and educational activity, which were developed on principles laid down by the movement as a whole – both as an instrument for the realization of Zionism, the class struggle and the building of Socialism, and as an end in itself: the archetype of the Socialist society. Through continual democracy in all fields, the movement strove to develop a common outlook on life that united all its members (the so-called "ideological collectivism"). Its ideology was founded on pioneering Zionism paving the way for mass *aliyah*, the kibbutz way of life, integration of settlement work with political activity, Jewish political independence combined with Jewish-Arab cooperation, and the defense of Israel's security coupled with unremitting efforts to achieve peace.

From the start, Ha-Kibbutz ha-Arẓi favored a union of all workers, including those in the cities, based on Zionist pioneering and Socialist principles. Since such a union failed to materialize, a Socialist League was formed in 1936 as its political partner. In 1946 they combined to form the Ha-Shomer ha-Ẓa'ir party, which, in turn, joined with two other groups in 1948 to found *Mapam, the United Workers' Party, of which Ha-Kibbutz ha-Arẓi with its constituent kibbutzim was an integral part.

Members of Ha-Kibbutz ha-Arẓi played a prominent part in the struggle for Jewish independence. They formed the first Tower and Stockade settlement, Tel Amal (Nir David) in 1936; many of them joined the supernumerary police, the Jewish units in the British army, and the Jewish Brigade; and they made an important contribution to Aliyah Bet (*"illegal immigration") and the founding of the *Palmaḥ.

Ha-Kibbutz ha-Arẓi regarded the education of its members' children as a matter of central importance. It trained them for active and creative participation in collective life, employing youth movement traditions and progressive educational methods. There were independent children's communities, covering the first six years of schooling, in almost every kibbutz, as well as 25 schools serving the kibbutzim, with youth communities covering the 7th–12th school years,and a teachers' training seminar at Givat Ḥavivah. The aim of the movement's educational institutions was to inculcate a general philosophy of life, and not mere booklearning. Some 4,800 of their alumni became kibbutz members and in 1967 the first group aiming at the formation of a new kibbutz was founded. Members of the older kibbutzim served an additional year in newer kibbutzim after completing their army service.

Although Ha-Kibbutz ha-Arẓi had as its primary objective the development of agriculture, most kibbutzim started up industrial plants. In 1968, the movement's agricultural output was valued at IL 168,000,000 ($48,000,000), or 9.9% of agricultural output in the country, and the industrial output at IL 98,500,000 ($28,000,000). Ha-Kibbutz ha-Arẓi published various periodicals for its members. It maintained a publishing house, Sifriat ha-Poalim, founded in 1931, which had issued about 1,000 books by 1970, and the Moreshet Institute for research on the Holocaust, established in 1962. The highest authority in Ha-Kibbutz ha-Arẓi was the triennial convention, which had committees that meet annually. The convention chose an executive council, which appointed a secretariat. Younger members had their own sectional organization.

[Yaakov Arie Hazan]

Ha-Kibbutz ha-Me'uhad

Founded in 1927, Ha-Kibbutz ha-Me'uḥad ("The United Kibbutz [Movement]") was a national organization of kibbutzim united by a common concept of the kibbutz and a common approach to the building of a labor society in the Land of Israel. The ideology of the movement was based on the following principles: the kibbutz should be a large settlement, with no predetermined limit to the number of members; it should be open to all comers and should not restrict itself to the graduates of any particular youth movement; it should engage in all forms of essential production, both agricultural and industrial; it should play a role in the integration of newcomers to the country by aiming at a membership representing a wide range of geographic origin. The first kibbutz with these aims was En Harod (founded in 1921 by *Gedud ha-Avodah, "the Labor Legion") and when the Kibbutz Me'uḥad movement was founded, at a conference in Petaḥ Tikvah in 1927, it was based on En Harod, groups of newcomers, and local youth from the moshavot. Other kibbutzim joined in 1929, and a second conference, held at Yagur in 1936, further elaborated the movement's principles. It exercises authority over the kibbutzim of the movement in matters of ideology, each kibbutz being autonomous in administration and finance. From its foundation, it regarded Yiẓḥak *Tabenkin of En Harod as its spiritual and ideological leader. During the Mandatory regime Ha-Kibbutz ha-Me'uḥad played a large part in the defense of the *yishuv*, the organization of "illegal" immigration, and the struggle for independence, with a special role in the creation and maintenance of the Palmaḥ. The movement's kibbutzim were scattered all over Israel, and it prided itself that their location had always been determined by the country's pioneering needs. Thus the first Jewish settlement to be established on the Golan Heights after the Six-Day War was founded by Ha-Kibbutz ha-Me'uḥad, conforming to the principle, adopted at the 1955 conference held at Givat Brenner, that "the natural borders of Ereẓ Israel are those of the historic homeland of the Jewish people, and this is the area for *aliyah*, settlement, and the realization of the Zionist program."

Most of the movement's members belonged in the 1940s to the left-wing faction of Mapai. When the latter split in 1944, Ha-Kibbutz ha-Me'uḥad was the nucleus of the newly formed Si'ah Bet (B Faction), later *Aḥdut ha-Avodah, which joined with Ha-Shomer ha-Ẓa'ir in 1945 to form Mapam, though a minority remained in Mapai. Owing to the fact that its members came from a variety of youth movements, there was never a dearth of internal political and social controversy in the movement and its kibbutzim. Differences came to a head as a result of the growing intensity of the struggle between Mapai and Mapam and the decision of the Mapai minority to set up its own cultural and educational institutions. At a meeting of the movement's council, held at Na'an in 1951, kibbutzim with a Mapai majority seceded and formed Iḥud ha-Kibbutzim, which joined with Ḥever ha-Kevuẓot to form Iḥud ha-Kibbutzim ve-ha Kevuẓot. Four kibbutzim (one of them En Harod itself), which were evenly divided between Mapai and Mapam, were each split into two separate settlements.

Members of Ha-Kibbutz ha-Me'uḥad have figured prominently among the founders and leaders of the Israel labor movement and the Haganah, officers in the Israel forces in the War of Independence, authors and artists, Knesset members and cabinet ministers. Always a strong advocate of the unification of the labor movement, it supported the formation of the Israel Labor Party, which was joined by practically all its members. Ha-Kibbutz ha-Me'uḥad had a chain of economic enterprises and cultural and social institutions: Keren ha-Kibbutz and Mishkei ha-Kibbutz, its major financial and economic instruments; Efal, a center for higher education and leadership training; *Mi-Bifnim* ("From Within"), an ideological quarterly; and *Ba-Kibbutz*, a weekly. It also published periodicals for youth and others dealing with education, culture, etc. Ha-Kibbutz ha-Me'uḥad publishing house issued 700 original works up to 1968. The movement maintained a museum and research center for the study of the history of the Holocaust, Beit Yiẓḥak Katznelson, at Kibbutz *Loḥamei ha-Getta'ot, and an art museum, Ha-Mishkan le-Ommanut, at En Harod.

In 1968 it comprised 58 settlements, with a population of some 25,000. One of these, Givat Brenner (population 1,604), was the largest kibbutz in the country. In the 1960s the population of the settlements grew by an average of 3.5% per year. The area under cultivation was 12,500 acres (50,000 dunams), and the number of industrial enterprises was 45, with a turnover of about IL50,000,000.

[Shlomo Derech]

Ha-Kibbutz ha-Dati

Ha-Kibbutz ha-Dati (Heb. "The Religious Kibbutz"), the union of *Ha-Po'el ha-Mizrachi kibbutzim, was established in 1935 by four religious pioneer groups consisting of members of Baḥad (see *Mizrachi)-Ha-Po'el Ha-Mizrachi from Germany and the Mizrachi Pioneers from Poland. Most of its development took place before Israel's independence. Seven pioneer groups were founded before 1940 and another nine before 1948. Ten groups were able to establish kibbutzim: three in the Beth-Shean valley (Tirat Ẓevi, Sedeh Eliyahu, En ha-Naẓiv), three in the Hebron hills (Gush Eẓyon), three in the neighborhood of Gaza (Be'erot Yiẓḥak, Sa'ad and Kefar Darom), and Yavneh. Two more were founded in 1948 – Sheluḥot in the Beth-Shean Valley and Lavi in Lower Galilee. Six of the villages, which were situated at the edge of the Jewish area in a completely Arab district, were totally destroyed during the War of Independence and many of the adult population were killed. They were reestablished later, three of them as *moshavim shittufiyyim. After a lengthy period of stagnation, most of the religious kibbutzim recovered in the 1960s and numbered among the most flourishing in the country. One new kibbutz, Alummim, was founded in 1966, and at the end of 1967 Ha-Kibbutz ha-Dati had 11 member settlements with a total population of 4,000, including Naḥal outposts on Mount Gilboa and at Kefar Eẓyon.

PRINCIPLES. Ha-Kibbutz ha-Dati was based, from the beginning, on the idea of combining religious practice with labor – *Torah va-Avodah*. Its founders believed that the best means to this end is the communal group, within the framework of which the community can carry out religious precepts in daily life; this attitude was in contrast to the general view of Ha-Poel Ha-Mizrachi of the time. While implementing the general kibbutz principles of communal production and consumption, equality, self-labor, and pioneering, it also emphasized the importance of Jewish religious tradition. Its religious socialism was founded on prophetic concepts of social justice and talmudic principles of human relations and good government; as regards their attitude to contemporary problems, its way was that of religious socialism. It regarded democracy as a basic value of the kibbutz, and not merely as a corollary of equality. In its view, communal ownership was important not only for economic reasons but as an expression of religious and human attitudes.

PUBLIC ACTIVITIES. Ha-Kibbutz ha-Dati aimed at establishing a self-contained religious society as a major instrument for bringing about religious renewal under present conditions of national renascence and the resettlement of Ereẓ Israel. It developed an approach of its own to the celebration of Independence Day, army service for girls, public prayer, *shemittah*, and so forth. It aimed at establishing groups of kibbutzim in the same area, with a view to developing regional activities in education and economy in accordance with its principles.

Ha-Kibbutz ha-Dati influenced public life in Israel in various ways: it was among the founders of *Youth Aliyah and of various religious youth villages, yeshivot, and other educational institutions, and it provided help and guidance for the *Bnei Akiva youth movement. Politically, it expressed its independent view within the frameworks of Ha-Po'el ha-Mizrachi and the *National Religious Party, having been instrumental in the establishment of La-Mifneh, the left-wing faction in these movements. The association published a journal, *Ammudim* (called *Alonim* 1938–49, *Yedi'ot ha-Kibbutz ha-Dati* 1951–56), which appeared monthly and was devoted to questions of the religious public and the state, apart from purely internal affairs.

[Moshe Unna]

The Beginnings of Change

The period commencing in 1977 was particularly significant because of a series of events that had unusual importance for the kibbutz movement. The first event was the political upheaval of 1977, in which the Labor Alignment – to which the decisive majority of kibbutzim belonged – lost control of the government, which it had held in various coalitions since the establishment of the state. The change in the political conditions had far-reaching effects in many areas of the kibbutz: these were felt only several years later. In an apparent paradox, the years of the Likud government, 1977–1984, were a period of rapid economic growth and development in the kibbutz movement. However, at the end of this period an economic crisis began, with social consequences within the kibbutzim themselves. According to some analyses, the sources of their subsequent problems are to be found in the long-term consequences of the economic policies carried out by the Likud government. The political changes also sped up the processes of change in the structure of the kibbutz movement, which culminated in the unification of the Iḥud ha-Kibbutzim and the Kibbutz ha-Me'uḥad movements in the United Kibbutz Movement (UKM *Takam* in Hebrew). One of the main justifications for the unification was the necessity for the creation of a large and united kibbutz body which would aid in renewing the labor movement and in influencing the general Israeli society.

As a basis for understanding these events, three structural developments, which had previously taken place within the kibbutzim, must be noted:

(1) The kibbutzim were no longer small, rural, communal farms, but were now large settlements, with a varied economic base, with several generations born and living there, plus new members from all over the world.

(2) There was a transformation from almost complete dependence on agriculture as a source of income to a complex economic formation, integrating agriculture, industries of many kinds, educational and service systems, and connections to large and powerful local and national economic and financial institutions, both in and outside of the kibbutz movement itself.

(3) A noticeable rise occurred in the standard of living in the kibbutzim, which made possible the meeting of more varied material and personal needs, even as it raised expectations in those areas.

More than in the past, this period posed the question of whether and how it was possible to realize the communal and egalitarian values upheld by the kibbutz in the conditions of a large and complex society which had become increasingly heterogeneous and more similar to the surrounding nonkibbutz society.

GROWTH PATTERNS. During this period there was relatively fast growth in the kibbutz population. Between 1976 and 1986, it grew from 98,800 to 126,700 people. This was an increase of 28.2%, which was much greater than the rate of growth during other periods after the establishment of the state (from 1950–1960 the growth was 16.4%; between 1960 and 1970, 7.7%; and from 1970 to 1976, 7.9%). The rate of growth of the kibbutz population in this period was greater than that of the rate of growth of the Israeli population as a whole (21.1%), and even more so when compared to the rate of the Jewish population (17.9%). This was a change from the pattern which had existed from after the establishment of the state, where the rate of growth of the Jewish population was much greater than that of the kibbutzim. This change was mainly a result of the large waves of immigration in the 1950s and 1960s, which caused the share of the kibbutz within the total Jewish population to fall from its height of 7.4% in 1947 to only 3.3% in 1970. The turnaround of this tendency in the 1980s was reflected in the small, but significant rise in the kibbutz share of the Jewish population to 3.6%.

The rate of growth of the kibbutz population was also much faster during this period than that of the moshavim, which grew only by 10%. The moshavim – the second major form of cooperative settlement – grew much more quickly than the kibbutz after the establishment of the state, because the vast majority of the mass immigrations which were sent to agricultural settlements were directed to them. The moshav has been traditionally based largely on individual agricultural holdings worked by a single family as its source of income, while maintaining some limited forms of communal, social, and economic cooperation. This form of settlement was considered more suitable for absorbing the waves of immigrants who came from North Africa and the Middle East in the 1950s.

The growth of the kibbutz population slowed in 1986. Apparently this was connected with the economic crisis that had overtaken the kibbutz movement and whose effects were especially felt at the end of the period.

The vast majority of the kibbutz population (more than 85%) were members of the kibbutzim and their children. In addition there were children from outside and youth groups who were being educated in the kibbutz; groups of young people receiving training prior to their joining the kibbutz or setting up a new one; students at special schools for learning Hebrew and groups of young men and women from abroad working in the kibbutz in order to learn about its way of life.

The sources for the growth in membership of the kibbutzim have changed during the different stages of development of the kibbutz movement. Before the 1960s few of the children of the kibbutz had reached the age at which they might join the kibbutz as members – this would be in their early twenties, after finishing their army service. Most of the members of the kibbutzim were immigrants, mostly from Europe, and a few who were born in Israel or had come from North or South Africa or from Middle Eastern countries. From the 1960s the proportion of kibbutz-born children rose significantly among those joining the kibbutz. Among those coming from outside the kibbutz, from the 1970s an increase occurred in the proportion of young people who applied for membership without having gone through the traditional path of the youth groups connected to the kibbutz movements. These youth movements originally developed independently, principally in Eastern Europe, and continued with the guidance and help of the kibbutz movements, which saw in them a major source for growth.

According to figures from one kibbutz movement (Kibbutz Arẓi), during the decade of 1970–1980, kibbutz-born individuals made up 38% of those joining the kibbutz, and young people who came out of the youth movement or who were educated in the kibbutz made up 26%, while those who came from outside the kibbutz, but were not in the youth movement, were the largest source of growth comprising 44%. Statistics from the other kibbutz movements were not available. However, there is reason to believe that the situation was similar.

The proportionate weight of different groups in the growth of the kibbutz was dependent not only on their weight among the joiners, but also on the rate of those now leaving the kibbutz. Each of the groups had a different rate of leaving the kibbutz. The highest relative leaving rate was that of people coming out of the youth movement, particularly the Israeli branch. As a consequence the proportion of the three different groups in the net growth of the kibbutz in this decade was as follows: children born in the kibbutz – 43%; graduates of the youth movement – 13%; and absorbees without movement background – 44%.

The group of absorbees without movement background was not homogeneous in its make-up or motivation for joining. They joined in large part through marriage to people born in the kibbutz, and they were thereby connected indirectly with internal sources of growth of the kibbutz. (Boys and girls from the same kibbutz tended not to marry among themselves; the majority of marriages were with people from outside the kibbutz movement.) Another group of those without movement background were graduates of the ulpanim for learning Hebrew or volunteers from abroad. There were also young families from the city who chose the kibbutz way of life. Unlike the past, the kibbutz movements made special efforts in the 1980s to encourage absorption from among the latter element by means of advertisements in the mass media or by special programs aimed at certain communities.

Evidence of the rise in the importance of internal growth may be seen from a comparison between the natural growth and the "migration balance" (the ratio between those staying and leaving among those who came from outside the kibbutz) as factors in the increase in the total kibbutz population. During the entire period from 1950 until 1975, natural increase was the only source of growth, while the migration balance was negative; the number of those who left was greater than those who joined the kibbutz from the general society. Of course, some of the kibbutz children left and some of the absorbees stayed on, but the latter were so few as to be unable to account for any significant part of the population growth. The relatively low percentage of absorbees staying reflects the process of selection and choice involved in joining a cooperative society whose way of life is essentially different from that on the outside.

Starting in 1975 this pattern changed, and, in most years through the 1980s, the number of those joining from the outside was greater than that of those leaving. However, in this period, too, natural increase remained the main source of growth. This was despite the higher rate of death in these years due to the relative aging of the kibbutz population. The large share of internal sources in the growth of the kibbutz stems also from the relatively higher rate of birth in the kibbutz compared to other sectors of the Jewish-Israeli society, which will be dealt with below.

The kibbutz population was originally younger than the general population, since it was established by homogeneous groups of young people. Within this decade, in the older kibbutzim which were founded in the 1920s and 1930s, large groups of the founders passed the age of 70, or even of 80 and 90. In some of these kibbutzim the members over 65 make up a quarter or more of the population. However, in the total population of the kibbutzim the percent of this stratum reached only 9.2%, and this was slightly lower than that of the Jewish population in Israel, 10.1%. The percent of the kibbutz population in the younger age groups was also greater than is found in the general Jewish population (in the age group from 0–14, it is 30.3% in the kibbutz vs. 19.9% in the city; and for the age group 15–24, it is 19.1% vs. 16%, respectively). In general, then, the kibbutz population was younger than that of surrounding Jewish society. There was, nevertheless, importance in the age distribution in the individual kibbutz. In some kibbutzim the existence of a large group of aged created problems that demanded new solutions.

When the first members in the older kibbutzim reached the age of retirement, they came to a decision, which was later taken in all the kibbutz movements, that these older members would not stop working at this fixed age. Later on, a decision was reached that specified a gradual reduction in the daily norm of work hours (the standard was eight hours per day), starting at the age of 50 for women and at 55 for men – down to four hours a day, at the age of 60 for women and 65 for men. Most of the oldsters worked until a very old age, and research findings show that there was a positive influence on their mental health from the continuing activity. The kibbutz took care to develop suitable places of work, appropriate for the skills and capacities of the older members, yet many continued to work in their previous work places. In general the work of the older people made an economic contribution of real significance.

The extended family, with children and grandchildren in the same community, was an important supporting element in the process of aging, along with the development of welfare institutions and services which dealt with health and rehabilitation problems (cases of members being sent to old people's homes were very rare). These conditions led to a much longer life expectancy in the kibbutz than in other societies. At the age of 50 life expectancy for men in Israel was an additional 25.7 years, while in the kibbutz 28.3 and for women in Israel 27.9 and in the kibbutz 31. The average in 64 other countries in 1980 was 23.5 for men and 27.3 for women. It seems that in addition to the social support within the family a major factor was the contribution of the communal framework. Furthermore, it has been noted that in the kibbutz there is no difference in the death-rates for married and unmarried people, while in other societies there is a higher death rate for unmarried people.

Different age-structures as found among various kibbutzim was only one of the many differences among them in the area of demographic characteristics. One crucial difference between kibbutzim resulted from the different sizes of their population, connected in many cases with when they were established.

While in 39 kibbutzim, most of them young, the number of members was less than 100, in the 16 largest kibbutzim the number of members was over 500. However, in only four of these large kibbutzim were there more than 700 members, and in only one did the number approach 1,000. The total population in a single kibbutz community that includes in addition to adult members also children and temporary groups varies between less than 100 and more than 1,500.

Patterns of growth occurred in almost all the kibbutzim in this decade, but the rate of growth was higher in the younger settlements than in the older kibbutzim. In the older kibbutzim the internal growth was augmented by absorbees from the outside, who did not come from a movement background. In contrast the growth of the younger kibbutzim was based more on graduates from the youth movement and to a certain degree also on young people who had left the older kibbutzim where they had been born.

From 1967 to the late 1980s, around 50 new kibbutzim were set up, mostly in the Galilee and Negev areas, continuing the traditional trend of settlement distant from the metropolitan center (51% of kibbutzim were concentrated in the north and 20% in the south of Israel).

As a result of government policy that favored settlement in the West Bank over that in other areas, the settlement activity of the kibbutz movement ran into difficulties during the decade and had to be partly financed by the movements themselves. Some of the newer settlements did not achieve social stability. Up to this period almost all the new settlements had been set up by graduates from the youth movements who went to them immediately after their army service.

CHANGES IN THE ROLE OF THE FAMILY. During the period under discussion the process of the strengthening of the family continued within the social structure of the kibbutz. In addition, there were other tendencies that appeared. The beginnings of the process of enhanced importance of the family date back to the 1950s and 1960s. and found expression in the kibbutz's demographic patterns: a rise in the birth rate, low rates of divorce, and a low marriage age.

There were also effects in the social and institutional areas. At the social level there appeared the extended family of several generations: in the same community would be found, besides the parents of the older stratum, the families of their children, and in the senior kibbutzim, the families of their grandchildren. In the oldest kibbutz therefore, four generations of the same family might be living together in the same community. This phenomenon was in contrast to the pattern outside the kibbutz of intergenerational mobility, geographic, occupational, and social.

In the institutional area, expression of the strengthening of the family took the form of demands which arose in different kibbutzim for a transfer of authority in both the educational and consumption fields from the kibbutz institutions to the individual families. The most obvious example was the demand that the children spend the night in their parents' homes, and not in the children's houses as was standard in the past. This issue raised stormy arguments in many kibbutzim before the final decision was taken.

Until the early 1970s only one kibbutz movement (the former "Iḥud") gave legitimacy to this change. However, during the 1980s, the changeover was completed in almost all of the kibbutzim of the United Kibbutz Movement. The demand to have the children sleep in their parents' homes also came up in the kibbutz movement which had always opposed this move. As a result of pressure from members/parents, approximately one-quarter of this movement's kibbutzim were already in different stages of the changeover during the 1980s.

The process of the changeover to having children sleeping at home developed in parallel with other symptoms of the strengthened status of the family, mainly in the area of consumption. At the same time efforts were made to strengthen the cohesion of other groups (work groups, age groups) besides the extended family.

The growing importance of the family in the kibbutz contradicted prevailing tendencies within Western society to weaken its status. On the other hand patterns similar to the more general direction began to appear in some areas of kibbutz demography.

With larger groups of kibbutz-born children reaching the stage of parenthood in the 1960s, there appeared a significant rise in the rate of birth in the kibbutzim and for the first time they surpassed the rates prevalent in the general Jewish population. During the period from 1965 to 1975, the birthrate of the kibbutzim was 26.8 per thousand, compared to 23.4 per thousand for the total Jewish population. From 1974 onwards a sharp change appeared in this pattern, and the birthrate went down from 28.6 to 22% in 1984, which was only slightly higher than that of the general Jewish population (21.6 per thousand).

A movement in the opposite direction appeared in regard to the divorce rate. From 1965 until 1975, there were lower rates of divorce in the kibbutz than in the past, and they were similar to those in the general Jewish society (less than one percent). From 1975 the rate went up from less than one percent to 1.4, which was greater than that prevailing in the society at large. There was also a rise in the age of marriage. While in the early 1970s many young adults married close to the end of their military service, it now became more popular to marry after a long trip abroad or after studies.

In any event, the family continued to play a more central role in the area of social relationships and this despite the fact that it had no economic function and its educational authority was relatively limited, even after the children began to sleep at home. The family did not have a defined formal status in the kibbutz since kibbutz membership was individual. The strengthening of the family resulted from the weakening of the overall social bonds in the kibbutz, with the growth and differentiation of the population. Furthermore, the family provided a kind of personal refuge from the intense communal life. These familial tendencies also expressed a desire for privacy and, sometimes, individualistic tendencies. On the other hand it would seem that the family appeared also as a framework bound up with obligations that might limit the freedom of the individual. This was evidently the significance of the rise in the divorce rate and the delaying of the marriage age.

CHANGES IN THE ECONOMIC AND OCCUPATIONAL STRUCTURE. The economy of the kibbutz went through many rapid changes in the 1980s. The process of industrialization, which began to accelerate in the 1960s, continued at a fast pace, and in most of the kibbutzim industrial operations employed more workers than agriculture and the income from industry was greater than that from agriculture. In 1986, 25.5% of the kibbutz's active population worked in agriculture versus 5.2% of Israel's active population; 22.7% versus 24.6% worked in industry. Nevertheless, the agricultural output continued to rise during this period, but at a rate slower than the growth of the industrial output. The agricultural output of the kibbutz movement grew by 30.8% and in 1986 accounted for 39.7% of the Israeli total, while the industrial output grew by 73.4% and made up 6.8% of the total Israeli product.

The relative increase in the role of kibbutz agriculture in overall Israeli output took place during a period in which many crises hit the agricultural sector. Besides a deterioration in the export conditions and for various agricultural products, such as cotton, flowers, and citrus fruits, the change in the government's policy had a negative effect on Israeli agriculture as a whole. In some periods the agricultural planning was drastically curtailed and surpluses were formed, causing a fall in prices which badly hurt many farmers and certain branches of agriculture. The conditions under which credit and loans were given were made more difficult, with extremely high interest rates, far above the norm in the West, and research and development activities were limited.

Kibbutz agriculture was affected relatively less than other sectors of agriculture partly due to professional and organizational advantages which accrued to the large kibbutz farming operation and partly due to capacity to balance the damage to agricultural income by means of the income from other branches, particularly industry. The data from the agricultural census of 1981 give evidence of the more efficient use of labor and capital in the kibbutz, especially as compared to the moshav.

Kibbutz agriculture continued to concentrate on those crops which demanded less manual labor and progressed in its process of modernization by introducing computers in different areas, for example, control of the field crop's irrigation and of the nutrition of dairy cows. Those branches in which the majority of production was in the hands of the kibbutzim were cotton, apples and bananas, fish ponds, potatoes, and the raising of cattle for meat and milk.

However, the principal economic efforts concentrated on the development of kibbutz industry. In contrast to their dominant position in agriculture, the kibbutz enterprises made up a relatively small sector within Israeli industry in the mid-1980s: 5.8% of the workers, 4.8% of the plants, and 6.8% of the production. From this it can be seen that the average number of workers per plant was greater in the kibbutz. However, about half of those employed in Israeli industry worked in plants with more than 300 workers, while in the kibbutzim, most workers were concentrated in plants with fewer than 100 workers.

The smaller size of kibbutz plants stemmed from the tendency to base operation principally on kibbutz members alone. In the early stages of kibbutz industrialization, it was thought that, in order to succeed in the competition of the larger market, the number of workers could not be limited to just those who were available from the kibbutz workforce, and some kibbutz industries hired a relatively large number of workers from the outside. Most kibbutzim opposed this tendency and decided to avoid setting up plants which were labor-intensive; they specialized in plants that were relatively capital-intensive and with a high level of modern technology. An example of this type of operation was the plastics branch of the kibbutz industries, whose production made up 45% of the total Israeli output. Other areas in which the kibbutz sector constituted more than the average of kibbuṭz industries were wood and furniture (18.3%) and metalworking (10.6%). The avoidance of hired labor and the focus on industrial branches based on high technology became the general direction of kibbutz industry in the 1980s, in which a relatively large number of new plants were set up (73 of the 335 total). At the same time, there was a constant decline in the proportion of hired workers within the kibbutz industry workforce from 43% in 1975 to 28% in 1986.

In the 1980s the introduction of advanced technology became a rapid process, including the use of computerized numerical control (CNC) and the use of industrial robots. It seems that the introduction of advanced technology in kibbutz industry was significantly faster than was the case in similar industries in the general Israeli society. This is supported by the fact that 60% of all the industrial robots in Israel were to be found in kibbutz enterprises.

The capital and technological intensity of the kibbutz industries and its special organization and social structure seem able to explain the difference in the accomplishments in various areas between kibbutz industry and the other sectors of Israeli industry. For example, between 1976 and 1986 the index of exports grew in the kibbutz industries from a base of 100 to 364 in contrast to the growth of Israeli industry as a whole to an index level of 224. The index of sales per worker was 20% more for the kibbutz than in the general industrial sector, and, in the plastics branch, this index was 25% higher than in Israeli plastics industry overall. The capital investment per worker was also higher in the kibbutz industries, and, with the advent of the economic difficulties that appeared after 1983, criticisms were voiced asserting that the investments in industry were too high given their decreasing rate of return.

There were other problems in regard to the direction of the development of kibbutz industry which arose with the economic crisis. Some critics asserted that the relatively small size of the kibbutz plants limited their capacities for research and development and for proper marketing operations and that there was a lack of the necessary experts in the technological professions.

Efforts were made to build up systems of research and development and those for marketing to be shared by kibbutz industrial plants in the same production branch, and steps was taken to improve and encourage technological education and training.

Throughout the decade there was a remarkable rise in the level of education of kibbutz members, especially the younger ones. In 1972, only 20.4% of kibbutz members had post-secondary education, while in 1985, the rate had risen to 32.3% of the kibbutz members. This was considerably higher than the level of the general Jewish population in Israel, which stood at 24.4%. There was an important difference in the distribution of the level of higher education, however. In the kibbutz there were fewer people with higher degrees, while the percentage of people with post-secondary training in the fields of education, technology, and social services was much higher than that of the overall Jewish population of Israel. The difference in regard to holders of higher university degrees (i.e., M.A. and doctorate) stemmed from the fact that only in the 1970s did the kibbutz movement free itself of ideological opposition to the acquisition of university degrees and begin to encourage academic studies. Thus in the 1980s the proportion of holders of academic degrees grew at the same time that the representation of kibbutz members on the teaching and research faculties of the institutions of higher learning also increased.

Along with the contribution made by people with academic degrees to the economic and social capacities of the kibbutz, problems caused by the unsuitability of the kibbutz work structure, based on work in agriculture, industry, and the services, to the academic qualifications of its members arose. Most of the jobs simply did not demand the high level of education acquired by college graduates, and this created conflicts with their expectations and desires for professional advancement.

A labor market did not exist in the kibbutz because there were neither the wages nor economic incentives or sanctions which operate in the general society to direct people into the different occupations in some relation to supply and demand. This made the coordination between the changing needs of kibbutz society and economy and, on the other hand, the professional and academic aspirations of the members more complicated than ever before. Decisions about the economic structure were made democratically at the general assemblies and in the committees and were thereby influenced by the preferences of the members. The other side of this relationship was that the professional plans of the members were themselves influenced by the present and/or expected occupational structure, although increasing numbers of young and old members chose courses of academic studies which seem to have no direct connection to the kibbutz's expressed economic and educational needs.

The 1980s saw changes as a result of the rising level of education and of the rapid technological advances, but the economic crisis of the kibbutz movement also had very important effects in this period. Different factors contributed to the development of the crisis, expressed principally by the formation of a large debt accompanied by high interest payments, which weighed heavily on ongoing economic activities. This occurred despite the successes in the fields of both industry and agriculture. The major cause of the crisis was the lack of economic stability that characterized the Begin years and was most obviously reflected in the rates of hyperinflation which ran rampant from the late 1970s until the mid-1980s. From 1978 to 1984, the rate of inflation jumped from 51% a year to 445%! As a result of the government's economic program in the mid-1980s, there was a sharp drop to an approximately 20% rate of inflation per year, which was accompanied by an even steeper rise in the cost of money, i.e., the interest rate, which rose from 11.8% in 1983 to 89% in 1985.

Besides these outside factors, financial mistakes were made by the kibbutz movements and by individual kibbutzim, which invested in unsuccessful business ventures, in speculative stocks, or in consumption projects. The economic crisis was especially damaging to those kibbutzim that had not been successful in their attempt to balance the decline in the profitability of agriculture with an increase in their industrial activity. This had the added effect of exacerbating the inequality among the kibbutzim. For example, in the United Kibbutz

Movement, the group of 19 kibbutzim in the most difficulties had to use 38% of their yearly income just to pay the interest on their debt, while another group of 38 kibbutzim had to earmark 25% of their income for interest payments; the majority of the kibbutzim, 83 in number, had to earmark only 6.6% of their yearly income for interest payments.

In an attempt to overcome the crisis and to make possible the continuation of production operations, the United Kibbutz Movement asked the government for help, not for grants but to restructure its loan repayment schedules. This request made the issue of help to the kibbutzim the focus of a political debate, where representatives of the Likud took advantage of this situation to criticize the kibbutz movement while putting pressure on the Labor party, to which the UKM is affiliated.

Kibbutz ha-Arẓi, which also was in need of additional sources of funding, preferred to mobilize capital on a commercial basis, essentially without government intervention, by means of bonds issues, which avoided dependence on the political system. The requests of the UKM for aid were only approved in part, after many delays and after a public political campaign by the kibbutz and moshav movements. Even before the public aid could come, the kibbutzim strengthened their apparatus of mutual support. The kibbutzim which were economically stronger were helping the weaker ones both by giving them loans from the movement's trust funds, which were funded by means of a progressive tax on the kibbutzim, and by providing guarantees for loans taken out by the weaker kibbutzim.

At the same time all the kibbutzim decided to lower their standard of living, regardless of their economic situation. This took various forms, such as not allowing trips abroad or kibbutz-financed vacations, lower spending on food in the communal dining room, and reducing the number of members sent to study, etc. All of these cutbacks were even more harsh in those kibbutzim in the worst shape, where even their autonomy in day-to-day expenses was severely curtailed. Parallel to these moves, cutbacks in capital spending, particularly in such area as apartments and public buildings, were made.

EQUALITY AND DEMOCRACY. The cutbacks in spending, including the member's personal yearly budget, gave rise to demands in some kibbutzim for a larger share of the kibbutz's total budget to be given to the individual member and his/her family (such as clothing, shoes, furniture, and vacation allowances). This would have entailed a corresponding cutback in public spending, such as for communal dining, education, health, etc. For the first time suggestions were made to allow members to increase their budgetary income by working extra hours in branches that suffered from a manpower shortage.

In a similar vein, a far-reaching demand was made by a new settlement group, Si'on, which had recently joined the UKM and was heading for Kibbutz Bet Oren, which was on the verge of dissolution after passing through an extended social crisis. The group proposed that they would work five days a week in the framework of the kibbutz work regimen, but that on the sixth day each member would decide whether to work and make extra money which could be used as one pleased or to take the day off. All proposals linking extra work to additional income had met with firm opposition by the movement's institutions, and this was the fate of Si'on's proposal: they were told that they would have to give up their plan as a condition for being accepted into the kibbutz federation. The reason for such severe opposition to these kinds of proposals was the principle of separation between the obligation of the kibbutz to satisfy the needs of each member and the amount and quality of the work done by that member. It is precisely this principle which distinguishes the kibbutz from other forms of communal living.

The absence of a link between the function a member fulfills in work or public activity and his or her standard of living and opportunities made it possible to prevent or, at least, to limit the processes of social stratification and polarization. These processes had occurred all too often in egalitarian organizations and had caused the dissolution of cooperative communities in the past.

The simultaneous processes of industrial development, economic expansion, differentiation in levels of education and administration, and the increased importance of the family in the kibbutz social structure created conditions that would appear to encourage stratification. Various studies had shown the existence of differences among members in regard to their influence on kibbutz life and in regard to the esteem in which they were held within the community. At the material level, some members had access to private sources of income from outside the kibbutz, as a result of inheritances, presents from family, and so forth. Nevertheless, one could not point to the crystallization of groups benefiting from special rights or privileges in contrast to other groups who were relatively discriminated against or disadvantaged as a unit. Another important factor in minimizing stratification was the maintenance of the pattern of rotation of leadership and management functions among the membership of the kibbutz and the movement as a whole. The continued operation of the rotation principle was aided by the fact that, although those holding managerial positions have greater power to influence issues during their term, they do not achieve a higher standard of living. In addition they must deal with many difficulties in fulfilling the responsibilities of their positions, due to which they were generally unwilling to continue in their demanding jobs for long periods of time.

In addition there were many members active on the various committees which were responsible for the organization of diverse areas of kibbutz life. In most kibbutzim there was a general assembly every week, although in some cases it was held every two weeks. There were great differences between the kibbutzim in regard to the number of people participating in kibbutz discussions. There seemed to be more participation in those kibbutzim with a higher level of social cohesion and in which the democratic idea was more highly regarded. However, even in kibbutzim where the general assembly was not so highly esteemed as an institution, proposals to replace it with some form of elected council were met with opposition.

In one kibbutz it was actually decided to stop convening the kibbutz assembly, but after a year and a half its meetings were reinstituted. The reason for this is probably that, in a society in which so many of the vital issues in one's private life, such as educational opportunities, personal consumption, and living arrangements, were determined by the community, members were unwilling to give up their right to participate in making such decisions, even if they do not often make use of this right. The kibbutz assembly still had the supreme authority in determining policy in the kibbutz, even though many specific decisions were reached in the committees and only brought before the assembly for ratification. However, the assembly had the authority to overturn any decision of a committee, and each member had the right to bring up any issue for discussion in the assembly. Some aspects of the running of the assembly had changed, and certain issues, especially regarding individuals and families, were voted upon by secret ballot, and in the larger kibbutzim, referenda were conducted outside the kibbutz assembly.

The existence of participatory democracy in all areas of life, together with the maintenance of cooperative consumption, which made possible the separation of the needs of members from their contribution at work or in other activities, had forestalled the emergence of elite social strata. Nevertheless, this was not enough to prevent the continued existence of a certain degree of gender inequality, whose roots were in the division of labor according to sex. Most of those working in the productive branches are men, while in the services and in education mostly women are employed. This inequality exists despite the fact that there is complete economic equality, and membership in the kibbutz is on an individual basis, not familial, as is the case in the moshav. In the past this inequality had expressed itself by the fact that the productive branches had a higher status than the service branches, which were discriminated against from the point of view of budgets and manpower. Later the inequality took the form of the more limited opportunities for women to choose the work that they prefer, which stems from an assumption that work in the services and in education is the main responsibility of women.

Women's lack of experience in economic management, which was usually acquired in those productive branches from which women were largely excluded, was a factor in their low level of representation in managerial positions, such as economic manager, treasurer, or industrial plant manager, all of which are positions with much authority in the running of the kibbutz. In the 1980s, the awareness of women of the existing inequality was heightened, although in earlier periods inequality was also considered a deviation from the values of the kibbutz. In both Kibbutz ha-Arẓi and in the United Kibbutz Movement departments for "Sexual Equality" were set up and worked to increase awareness of the issue, to encourage women to enter professions commonly defined as "for men only," and, conversely, to encourage men to go into those areas of education and services traditionally the domain of women. Overall, there was some progress in the proportion of women fulfilling public positions like secretary of the kibbutz or head of a committee, and the number of women working in industry rose, but there was no meaningful improvement in other areas, particularly those having to do with economic management.

CHANGES IN KIBBUTZ EDUCATION. The greater importance of the family in the kibbutz, the increased involvement in the system of higher education, and the changes in technology and occupational structure caused fundamental changes in the kibbutz educational system.

The greatest change, which was accompanied by much debate, was the changeover to having children sleep at home instead of the children's houses. A few kibbutzim made this change in the 1950s and the 1960s, and it became a legitimate way of life in the former Iḥud ha-Kibbutzim movement. However, only in the 1980s did most of the kibbutzim of the United Kibbutz Movement (which includes the above Iḥud with the former Kibbutz ha-Meuḥad) adopt the new system, while in Kibbutz ha-Arẓi it was given only limited and conditional legitimacy. In the past sleeping in the children's houses was seen as an integral part of the education, where the children's house served as an all-encompassing center for the child, while the parents' home had only a supplementary function. Gradually awareness of the crucial role played by the parents in the educational process grew, and the proponents of home sleeping arrangements saw the changeover as another step in this direction, which, first and foremost, expressed the desire of parents.

In contrast to this approach, those who opposed having the children sleep in their parents' homes asserted that the change in sleeping arrangements would affect the all-embracing character of kibbutz education, which would turn the children's house into merely a "day care center" and would curtail the responsibility of the educators. Other justifications for maintaining the old system were voiced: The change would exacerbate sexual inequality because additional burdens and responsibilities would be placed on mothers. This would in turn have a negative effect on their kibbutz jobs, limit their opportunities for further study, and especially limit their participation in community activities, whether administrative or social.

The growing number of kibbutz-educated children applying for higher academic studies raised the issue of changing the policy of the kibbutz movements, which had previously opposed the high school matriculation tests necessary for entry into Israeli universities. The opposition to these tests was directed at the achievement orientation and competitive factor of the tests, and, in some kibbutzim, the opposition was connected to an unwillingness to introduce graded tests. The opposing view wanted to keep the emphasis on the development of internal motivation to study, on supportive peer opinion as a source of motivation, and on the development of the capacity for independent study in each child.

At first an arrangement was reached with the universities in which a graduate of a kibbutz high school would have to do a preparatory course, usually about a year long, before entering the university. However, due to the difficulties involved in this arrangement, which was only designed to be a temporary solution, almost all the kibbutz schools started to prepare their students for the matriculation certificate, if the students wanted one. In conjunction with the change, efforts were made to preserve the special social foundations of the kibbutz high school by means of an increased emphasis on values and socialization.

Almost all the kibbutz high schools were regional institutions, taking in students from several kibbutzim and sometimes from moshavim and also other children sent there for various reasons. In Kibbutz ha-Arẓi the high schools were also boarding schools (several days of the week) in order to achieve an all-embracing secondary school framework. On the other hand, the primary schools were, until the mid 1980s, based in each individual kibbutz, integrated into the life of the community. However, due to the relatively small size of these schools and as part of the policy of the Ministry of Education, a process began of joining together the primary schools of neighboring kibbutzim and making one area day school. The establishment of the area schools, both primary and especially secondary levels, raised anew the question of the integration of the kibbutz schools with those of the surroundings, the development towns and the moshavim.

Despite the desire of the kibbutzim to maintain their independent framework, which was needed in their opinion in order to educate their children to their special values and way of life, some move in the direction of inter-community integration occurred. A number of schools were set up with the participation of moshavim, arrangements for cooperation with schools in development towns were made, and the absorption of youth groups, often from deprived backgrounds, within the kibbutz schools, continued and were even expanded. Nevertheless, the argument continued between those who favored greater integration to break down the barriers between kibbutz children and other sectors of the population and those who demanded the maintenance of the independent kibbutz framework.

As part of the effort to strengthen the commitment to education for kibbutz and movement values of both youth and adults, the 1980s saw an energetic expansion and utilization of the kibbutz institutions for higher education, which were intended for high school students and for academic studies and research. In the first centers, Efal and Givat Ḥavivah, the range of courses of study were broadened, and research departments were established. The Ruppin Institute, for the training of agricultural and industrial workers and managers, and Oranim, the school for training teachers, and the Kibbutz Seminar in Tel Aviv reached various forms of academic recognition. At the University of Haifa, there was the Institute for Research on the Kibbutz and the Cooperative Idea, which also ran a large number of courses in kibbutz studies in coordination with the Sociology and Anthropology departments. In some areas, at the initiative of the kibbutzim, local colleges were set up to provide academic level studies for the members of the surrounding kibbutzim and moshavim. These were usually connected to universities and the course credits went towards earning a college degree.

THE KIBBUTZ AND ISRAELI SOCIETY. The question of regional cooperation and integration in the field of education was only one aspect of the complex relationships between the kibbutzim and the surrounding settlements, mainly developmental towns and moshavim. The major issue in these relations was their economic connections where the kibbutz-owned regional enterprises had an important function in the area's pattern of employment. These plants whose major task was to process the agricultural produce of the local kibbutzim, employed many hired workers from among the area residents. However, most of the administrative and managerial posts were held by members of kibbutzim. In most areas the moshavim had their own separate regional enterprises. The speed of the development of the area enterprises can be seen from the growth of the number of employees from 5,000 in 1977 to 7,300 in 1982. Afterwards, the rate of growth slowed, partially because of the crisis that hit agriculture all over Israel and also due to a decline in investments, which had already begun during the first period of fast development.

In some areas, e.g., Bet Shean and Kiryat Shemonah, the regional plants became a focus for tensions between some of the hired laborers from the development towns and the kibbutzim, which were exploited for political purposes. Particularly during election campaigns, fierce attacks on the kibbutz movement appeared in the local and national media, which in turn produced widespread effects and responses in Israeli society. Subsequently, all the sides involved made efforts to improve their relations. The local residents were interested in the continued activity and development of the area enterprises as a source of employment, whose importance increased as unemployment rose. From the point of view of the kibbutzim, steps were taken to improve labor relations, to expand the possibilities for advancement for the hired workers, and to push for their participation in profits and in management. Through the initiative of the Histadrut, a program for regional cooperation was developed, which included the encouragement of social and personal connections and joint cultural activities among all the residents of the area.

The relations between the kibbutz and development towns were only one part of the striking changes in the status of the kibbutz within Israeli society as a whole in the 1980s. The most significant change was in the political sphere, when the Likud won the elections for the first time in 1977, and the Alignment (the Labor Party and Mapam), to whom the kibbutz movements were tied, entered the opposition. The quantitative expression of the decline of the political status of the kibbutz movements was in the sharp fall in the number of kibbutz members elected to the Knesset, who usually got there via the

Alignment. Their number dropped from 20 in the First Knesset, to 16 in the Eighth Knesset, which was elected in 1973, and down to eight in the elections of 1977, which brought the great change in Israeli politics. This situation did not change in the Tenth Knesset, despite the improvement in the Alignment's number of seats, and in the Eleventh Knesset there were nine kibbutz members, three from Mapam, four from the Labor party, one in the Citizens' Rights Movement, and one in the Teḥiyyah party on the right.

The decline in status of the kibbutz representatives in the Knesset, as part of the general weakening of the workers' parties, was also reflected in the makeup of the government. Until the upheaval of 1977, there were always a number of ministers who were members of kibbutzim, some of them in central positions, like Yigal Allon and Yisrael Galili, Haim Gvati and Shlomo Rosen. There were no kibbutz members in the Likud governments and only one in the National Unity government. This decline in the power and representation of the kibbutz movement was to be found also in other national frameworks. However, the proportion of kibbutz members in certain areas of national leadership, such as the higher levels of command in the army, in leadership of the Histadrut, and in its Ḥevrat Ovedim economic operations, was still much higher than their proportion of the general Jewish Israeli population.

The kibbutz movement also had an influence in various social and cultural areas beyond its numerical weight. The major youth movements, such as Ha-No'ar ha-Oved ve-ha-Lomed, the Scouts, Ha-Shomer ha-Ẓair, etc., were all connected to and supported by the kibbutz movements. There were also various cultural projects, like the Tzavta clubs and various publishing enterprises which were aimed at the general public of the cities and towns.

Despite these achievements there was a definite decline in the status and prestige of the kibbutz in the eyes of the general Israeli public and a corresponding lowered self-image on the part of kibbutz members in regard to the kibbutz's contribution and role on the national level. It seemed that, in contrast to the clearly high status of the kibbutz before the establishment of the state and in its first years, there arose a lack of consensus about the role which the kibbutz was to fulfill in Israeli society and the state. In the beginning the kibbutz was seen as a pioneering body which fulfilled central tasks in the building up of the people and of the state, such as settlement, defense, and the organization and absorption of immigration, both legal and "illegal." The first changes in this role occurred with the establishment of the State of Israel when many functions previously undertaken by the kibbutzim were transferred to the responsibility of government bodies. In the period after the war of 1967, there seemed to be renewed importance in the kibbutz movement's settlement role, but, after the ascendancy of the Likud, there was an increasing tension between the Likud government's policy of almost exclusive priority to settlements in areas of Judea and Samaria with a dense Arab population and the policy of the kibbutz movements which preferred settlement within the pre-1967 area of Israel.

Certain pronouncements and actions of the Begin-led Likud governments contributed to the creation of an image for the kibbutz movement as just another special-interest group seeking to preserve and strengthen its economic and social positions. The right-wing of Israeli politics sought to minimize the defense, settlement, and social functions which the kibbutzim continued to fulfill. This negative image was reinforced as a result of the kibbutz movement's financial speculations and failures and the economic crisis which caused the United Kibbutz Movement to apply for government aid in restructuring its debts.

In addition, within the kibbutz movement itself tendencies towards isolation were pronounced in regard to activities and relations with the surrounding society, at both the regional and national level. In regard to relations with the neighboring communities, this was the response to the sometimes virulent attacks made during the elections. In the face of a weakened self-image as a pioneering leader of society and the growing perception of the kibbutz as an element that first and foremost takes care of its own needs and interests, a third direction began to take shape.

The new direction placed its emphasis on the continuing connection between the kibbutz and other sectors of Israeli society in order to strengthen the influence of egalitarian and cooperative principles which the kibbutz upheld. Some examples were the following projects, initiated and/or supported by the kibbutz movement: the establishment of "urban kibbutzim," the plan to set up a cooperative city in the Negev, efforts to reform the producer and consumer cooperatives in the city, and the attempt to support the Histadrut's program for participation of workers in the management of its industrial and commercial plants and firms. Only some of these projects bore fruit, but they were an indication of an ongoing commitment of the kibbutz to be involved in Israeli society in ways which were compatible and supportive of its own values. The "urban kibbutzim," in cities and development towns, aimed to taking part in the educational and cultural activities of the residents. The first of these attempts, Kibbutz Reshit ("Beginning") was located in the Bukhara neighborhood of Jerusalem, and its members were active in various aspects of their community's life. There were also two more urban communes, in Bet Shemesh and in Sederot.

The changes in society's view of the kibbutz and the lack of consensus about both its public and self-image were reflected in opinion polls. Between 1978 and 1983 the percent of those polled who expressed a positive attitude towards the kibbutz declined from 62% to 52%. This was not matched by a rise in those who opposed the kibbutz movement, which remained stable at 8% of those polled, but it reflected a rise in those who were indifferent to it. There was a more positive view of the kibbutz among those born in Europe or America, among the more educated and those who were older. The more those polled knew about the kibbutz, the more positive were their attitudes: however, only 44% said that they were well acquainted with the kibbutz, while 40% had never visited a kibbutz even once.

These figures demonstrated the gap between the kibbutz and large segments of the public whose views were largely based on what was said about the kibbutz in the mass media, rather than on first-hand experience. In later, unpublished polls, it seemed that positive attitudes towards the kibbutz were influenced more by people's attitudes towards the egalitarian and cooperative values embodied by the kibbutz than by the demographic characteristics described above. The changes in the attitude of Israeli society towards the kibbutz as well as the changes in the political system influenced the kibbutz movement's actions and policies.

THE KIBBUTZ MOVEMENTS. From the beginning of the kibbutz movement there have been many splits and amalgamations in the movement's organizational forms. Before the establishment of the state, the reasons for the existence of separate movements were mainly the different ideological, social, and economic positions regarding the desired structure of the kibbutz. With the sharpening of the political struggles over the shaping of the state's character after its establishment, the exacerbation of the political debate within the kibbutz movement caused a bitter and painful split in the largest movement at that time, Kibbutz ha-Me'uḥad. A substantial minority of members and kibbutzim split off from Kibbutz ha-Me'uḥad and formed, with another movement, Ḥever ha-Kevuẓot, a new movement, Iḥud ha-Kibbutzim. This split occurred in 1951, and it involved in some cases the physical splitting up into two separate kibbutzim where there had previously been one large settlement. The two separate movements also were connected to different political parties until the parties' unification and the two kibbutz movements formally became united in 1979 as the United Kibbutz Movement (UKM).

The UKM contained within it 167 kibbutzim as of 1987, with a population of 76,560. For the first time in the history of the movement there were only two large kibbutz movements, the second one being Kibbutz ha-Arẓi – Hashomer ha-Ẓa'ir. Kibbutz ha-Arẓi had 83 kibbutzim with a population of 41,500. The smaller religious kibbutz movement, Ha-kibbutz ha-Dati, had 17 kibbutzim and a population of 7,300.

In general the differences that separated the kibbutz movements in the past were decreasing, although there was still some importance attached to traditions of the past. Despite this tendency, Kibbutz ha-Arẓi maintained its own identity and organization. This was due in part to the fact that this movement went through very few splits in the first 50 years of its existence and was relatively more homogeneous. The movement's connection to its political party, the United Workers' Party (Mapam), is collective, and not personal, as in the UKM. Further, Kibbutz ha-Arẓi placed more emphasis on what it saw as the preservation of the original kibbutz values and ways of life. It more strictly opposed hired labor in the kibbutzim, resisted the transfer of various responsibilities from the kibbutz institutions to the family and upheld special educational approaches, e.g., a regional boarding school during the stage of high school education. Kibbutz ha-Arẓi invested more efforts in internal and external, i.e., ideological, activity, and officially supported the *Peace Now extra-parliamentary movement. This movement also maintained a tighter framework for mutual aid, through a "movement tax" among its kibbutzim and for direction of the individual kibbutz's activities by the movement. Although some of the differences became less marked during the 1980s, there did not seem to be any tendencies towards the surrendering of the independent existence of Kibbutz ha-Arẓi. This was reinforced by the breakup of the 20-year-old Alignment between the Labor Party and Mapam after the formation of the 1984 National Unity government, as a result of which Mapam tried to reestablish itself as an independent party in the opposition.

The two large kibbutz movements, along with the smaller religious kibbutz movement, maintained close cooperation in the framework of the Confederation of the Kibbutz Movements, which represented the kibbutz movement as a whole to outside authorities. There were also national and regional frameworks within which joint activities, economic and cultural, took place. This strengthening of cooperation among the kibbutz movements should have contributed to weakening the separate organizational movement frameworks. But with the onset of the economic crisis in the 1980s, the influence of the national movements was greatly strengthened because they were the link between the external financial sources, whether private or governmental, and the individual kibbutzim. The national movements were the means by which most funds were transferred, and, even when an individual kibbutz arranged some of its own financing, it was the financial guarantees of the movement that induced private institutions to give these loans. Finally, it was by means of the national movements that mutual aid was carried out, whereby the weaker and debt-ridden kibbutzim received help from the better-off kibbutzim or from the debt-restructuring program.

It would seem that at this stage inter-movement cooperation based more on ideological and political issues was more significant than regional inter-movement cooperation based more on pragmatic, lower-level economic and social issues.

In the 1980s there was widespread interest in the kibbutz experiment on the part of people and institutions outside of Israel. The beginning of this interest started with the rise of new forms of cooperative and communal living and work in various countries around the world in the late 1960s and the 1970s. This interest was expressed in the convening in Israel of conferences representing cooperative communities and enterprises from around the world, the exchange of delegations between the kibbutz and these different groups. There was cooperation in research on egalitarian communities in Israel and abroad, as well as on cooperative, worker-owned industrial or agricultural enterprises. A special project was established for the study of the kibbutz under the auspices of Harvard University in the U.S. There were attempts to learn from the experience of the kibbutz in its response to the challenges of the technological revolution as it might be applied in smaller productive frameworks while maintaining a priority on the quality of the working life and on environmental protection, along with participatory democracy.

The interest in the kibbutz experience from the viewpoint of its Jewish significance became another focus of interest. On the one hand the kibbutz had created a value-oriented Jewish way of life which was essentially non-religious and, on the other hand, it formed a bridge between Jewish youth in the Diaspora and Israel. Research has shown that the time spent by young people in a kibbutz contributes more to their connection to Israel than their experiences with other aspects of Israeli society. Based on these findings, new forms of short-term programs on kibbutzim for young Jews from abroad were developed, in addition to existing kibbutz ulpanim for the study of Hebrew, visits by youth groups for short periods, or programs of study in kibbutz high schools for Jewish teenagers from Europe and the Americas.

In sum, the 1980s were a period of many changes in the development of the kibbutz movement. Beginning with an accelerated growth of population and economic progress, a crisis arose in the political and economic situation facing the kibbutzim, which now found themselves in serious economic straits, which had a negative effect on many other areas of the communities' way of life.

[Menahem Rosner]

The New Kibbutz

The severe economic crisis faced by the kibbutzim continued into the 1990s. The reasons for the crisis were many: some linked it to changes in Israeli society and the shift from collectivism to individualism; others pointed to internal problems, such as inefficiency and old-fashioned industries and farming techniques, segregation from the wider population, and demographic decline. However, the visible mark of the crisis was the difficulty individual kibbutzim and the kibbutz organizations had in paying their debts. As a consequence, money owed to the banks increased significantly, especially after the government raised interest rates to curb inflation. Despite the government's agreement to restructure the debt, many kibbutzim faced difficulties that led to a momentous change in their way of life.

Many of the kibbutzim instituted changes that distanced them from the traditional kibbutz model but helped them survive the crisis. Among those changes was the separation of industry from the kibbutz, provision of services to the non-kibbutz population (such as swimming pool facilities, apartments to let, etc.), encouraging members to find work outside the kibbutz, hiring nonkibbutz workers, differential salaries among kibbutz members, privatization of services (utilities, food, rent, etc.), new neighborhoods for nonmembers built by private contractors on kibbutz land, and less centralized administration. All these changes moved the kibbutzim from the traditional model to something resembling ordinary community life. Almost all the kibbutzim adopted some of these changes. Today there are three categories of kibbutzim: the collective kibbutz including around 30 kibbutzim that chose to preserve the traditional model; the community kibbutz including kibbutzim that instituted differential salaries; and a third group including kibbutzim still undergoing change.

The economic and social changes in many of the secular kibbutzim, which blurred political differences between the movements, led to the reunification of the United Kibbutz Movement (*UKM*) and Ha-Kibbutz ha-Arẓi ha-Shomer ha-Ẓa'ir into the Kibbutz Movement in 2000. The new Kibbutz Movement represents 260 kibbutzim. Its aims include protecting the rights of the kibbutzim, assisting kibbutzim under change, and remaining involved in the larger Israeli society.

DEMOGRAPHIC PATTERNS. During the 1990s the kibbutzim faced for the first time a decline in population. In 2002 the kibbutz population comprised 1.5 percent of the overall population in Israel. From 1997 to 2002 population figures declined by 2 percent. The permanent population declined by 9%, but this figure was compensated for by temporary residents who rent apartments in the kibbutzim. This decline was reversed in 2003, when for the first time after 19 years the kibbutz population began to grow again. This growth is related to the new way of life in the kibbutzim today, which is more private and less collective. Other reasons relate to the fact that many Israelis prefer to live in a rural community with good educational facilities, so that the new kibbutz neighborhoods are an attractive option.

The decline in population was also due to the aging of the kibbutz population and a sharp decline in birth rates. From 1998 to 2002 there was drop in the number of kibbutz children from 28,606 to 24,055. While in 1998 there were 1,142 births in the kibbutzim, the figure dropped to only 730 in 2002. A major reason for this can be found in the fact that many kibbutz youngsters had left the kibbutz after their army service. Another reason has to do with the general trend toward smaller families out of economic and social considerations, enabling parents to give their children more attention and material benefits.

The decline in the child population directs attention to the main problem of the kibbutzim, namely the aging of the population. The average age of the adult kibbutz population was 55 in 2003 (it was calculated as the mean from 30 up, since most of the population under 30 are temporary residents), compared to the national average of 52. The 25–45 age group in the kibbutzim is proportionately smaller than in the overall population, while the 45+ group is proportionately higher. This means that a small group of working people is responsible for a larger group of older people. This situation is a cause of concern in the kibbutz movement and the kibbutzim invest much effort to attract younger people, e.g., by building the new neighborhood for non-members who wish to live in rural settlements.

The average kibbutz varies from 300 to 400 residents. There have been voices calling for the creation of larger communities of 1,000 to 1,500 residents. These communities will come about by uniting neighboring kibbutzim or by the absorption of newcomers.

ECONOMIC ACTIVITY. Kibbutz agriculture is based on field crops, fruit plantations, dairy cattle, poultry, and fishery. The revenue from agriculture was quite stable between 1997 and 2002, amounting to IS 5 billion in 2002, representing about a third of national farm revenue. Kibbutz agriculture accounted for 70 percent of field crops, 40 percent of livestock, and 20 percent of plantations.

Kibbutz industry includes the following: rubber and plastics; food; metal and machinery; textiles and leather; printing, paper and cardboard; electronics and electricity; construction materials; wood and furniture; and other branches. Kibbutz industry had a 7.5 percent share of the country's industry in 2002, five times its share in the population. The contribution of kibbutz industry to the GDP was 6.5 percent in 2002. The kibbutz plastics industry had a 51% share of the industry as a whole.

Industrial revenues constituted 70 percent of total kibbutz income. In 2002, kibbutz industry operated 333 factories, employing 27,600 workers and recording sales of IS 17.344 billion, up 7.7% 21101. In 1997 gross profit was IS 690 million, dropping to IS 434 million in 1999 but rising to IS 900 million in 2002.

A new source of income, in addition to agriculture and industry, was salaried work outside the kibbutz, with individuals bringing in about IS 1 million in 1997 and IS 1.5 million in 2002.

In 2002 75 kibbutzim earned more than IS 100 million compared with 108 kibbutzim earning less than IS 50 million. Thus, 30% of the kibbutzim were responsible for 47% of total kibbutz income. This demonstrates the differences between kibbutzim, some being quite wealthy while others face bankruptcy.

Figures for the last decade indicate an improvement in the economic situation of the kibbutzim. The total debt decreased from IS 28 billion in 1996 to IS 17 billion in 2002. The improvement can be attributed to the write-off of part of the debt by the government and the economic and social changes that many kibbutzim underwent. Nonetheless, kibbutz per capita income remained lower than the national average.

A CHANGING WAY OF LIFE. Since the 1990s the kibbutzim have undergone vast changes in their way of life. The main cause of the changes was the enormous debt of the kibbutzim to the banks. The changes can be summarized under four heads: changes in the personal budgets of kibbutz members; separation of the sources of livelihood from the community; professional management; external committees.

DIFFERENTIAL SALARIES. Many kibbutzim adopted a system of differential salaries in place of equal budgets for its members. The new system gives each member a salary based on hours worked, education, experience, etc. The majority of the kibbutzim adopted the "security" model, in which pensioners and the elderly receive fixed salaries from the kibbutz, while the working population is responsible for making its own living. A different system, "the combined model," is based on quasi-differential distribution that takes into account number of years in the kibbutz and hours worked. The latter system seeks to distribute income in a more equal way. It is worth noting that 93 kibbutzim chose to maintain the traditional model, in which members receive an equal budget.

SEPARATION BETWEEN SOURCES OF LIVELIHOOD AND THE COMMUNITY. In this system kibbutz members become shareholders in kibbutz businesses, which are managed outside the community framework, like private enterprises anywhere.

PROFESSIONAL MANAGEMENT. Until the 1990s the kibbutzim were managed by an elected secretariat composed of kibbutz members. In recent years this has changed. Many kibbutzim failed to find suitable candidates from among their members and hired professionals from outside the kibbutz. The manager's job is to lead the kibbutz into a new era and successfully implement changes. Two-thirds of the kibbutzim were already operating under such management in the first years of the 21st century.

EXTERNAL COMMITTEES. A small group of kibbutzim (28) were managed by external committees, given authority to manage the kibbutz when it faced severe crises. The external committee manages the kibbutz for up to a year in order to enable kibbutz members to assume responsibility again.

[Shaked Gilboa (2nd ed.)]

Into the 21st Century

The kibbutz at the outset of the 21st century, which had once represented for many the essence of Israel, was thus far removed from what it had once been, just as Israeli society was. Stripped of ideology, losing its special qualities, it was rapidly becoming another habitat in an environment geared to satisfy personal ambition. Its place, however, in the history of Zionist settlement was assured. Not only did it contribute the sheer muscle power that reclaimed the land, it had also created the ethos that sustained the nation. Without it the Zionist enterprise could hardly have succeeded.

BIBLIOGRAPHY: GENERAL: A. Bein, *The Return to the Soil* (1952); Y. Baratz, *A Village by the Jordan* (1954); M. Weingarten, *Life in a Kibbutz* (1955); M.E. Spiro, *Kibbutz, Venture in Utopia* (1956); idem, *Children of the Kibbutz* (1958); H. Darin-Drabkin, *The Other Society* (1962); B. Bettelheim, *Children of the Dream* (1969); J. Blasi, *The Communal Future – The Kibbutz and the Utopian Dilemma* (1987); K. Bartolke, Th. Bergmann, L. Liegle (eds.), *Integrated Cooperatives in the Industrial Society: The Example of the Kibbutz* (1980); K. Bartolke, W. Eshwieler, D. Flechsenberg, M. Palgi, M. Rosner, *Participation and Control* (1985); A. Cherns (ed.), *Quality of Working Life and the Kibbutz Experience* (1980); M. Gherson, *Family, Women and Socialization in the Kibbutz* (1978): J. Gorni, Y. Oved, J. Paz (eds.), *Communal Life* (1987); E. Krausz, (ed.), *The Sociology of the Kibbutz* (1983); U. Leviatan, M. Rosner, *Work and Organization in Kibbutz Industry* (1980); Amia Lieblich, *Kibbutz Makom* (1981); Sh. Lilker, *Kibbutz Judaism* (1982); St. Maron, *The Communal Household* (1987); D. Mittelberg, *Strangers in the Paradise* (1988); M. Palgi, J. Blasi, M. Rosner, M. Safir (eds.), *Sexual Equality – the Israeli Kibbutz Tests the Theories* (1986); A. Rabin, B. Bettelheim, *Twenty Years Later: Kibbutz Children* (1981); P. Rayman, *The Kibbutz Community and Nation Building* (1981); M. Rosner, *Democracy Equality and Change: The Kibbutz* *and Social Theory* (1982); I. Shepher, *The Kibbutz, an anthropological study* (1983); B. Shenker, *Intentional Communities* (1986); Sh. Shur, B. Beit-Hallahmi, J. Blasi, A. Rabin (eds.), *The Kibbutz: A Bibliography of Scientific and Professional Publications in English* (1981); A. Tannenbaum, B. Kavcic, M. Rosner, M. Vianello, G. Wieser, *Hierarchy in Organizations* (1974); L. Tiger, J. Shepher, *Women in the Kibbutz* (1975); A. Zamir, *Mothers and Daughters – Interviews with Kibbutz Women* (1986). PERIODICAL ENGLISH PUBLICATIONS. *Kibbutz Studies; Kibbutz Currents* (formerly *Shdemot*); English publications series of the Institute for Research on the Kibbutz and the Cooperative Idea, University of Haifa. KIBBUTZ ARẒI: D. Leon, *The Kibbutz* (1964); E.H. Samuel, *The Children's Community of the Hashomer Hatzair at Mishmar Haemek* (1962); L. Dror et al. (ed.), *Sefer ha-Shomer ha-Ẓa'ir*, 3 vols. (1956–64), passim. KIBBUTZ DATI: M. Unna, *Shutafut shel Emet* (1965); M. Krone, *From Rodges to Yavne* (1945); A. Fishman, *The Religious Kibbutz Movement* (1957); Bnei Akiva, *The Religious Kvuẓah* (1960); J. Walk, in: YLBI (1961), 236–56. **ADD. BIBLIOGRAPHY:** *Kibbutz Movement Yearbook* (Heb., 2003); H. Biur, "For the First Time in 19 Years: Growth in the Kibbutzim Population," in: *Haaretz* (July 23, 2004). **WEBSITE:** www.kibbutz.org.il.

KIBEL, WOLF (1903–1938), South African painter. Son of a cantor of Godzisk near Warsaw, Kibel was orphaned in boyhood but his artistic talent attracted the attention of a visiting artist who befriended him. In 1926 he went to Vienna, lived in poverty, but was helped by patrons to obtain some formal training and enabled to go to Palestine where he came under the influence of modern expressionism. In 1929 he emigrated to Cape Town, South Africa. There the strength and individuality of his style and his artistic integrity received quick recognition from fellow artists, but it was only toward the end of his life that his paintings in various media began to find their way into public galleries and private collections. Tinged with the melancholy of his own suffering and the tragedy of his people, Kibel's work was also marked by a sensitive humanity and joy in the common things of life. His life was a constant struggle against poverty and ill health, and he died in Cape Town of tuberculosis brought on by years of malnutrition.

BIBLIOGRAPHY: F. Kibel, *Wolf Kibel…* (1968).

[Louis Hotz]

KI-BUKH ("Book of Cows"), anonymous 16th-century Yiddish fable collection. First mentioned in the *Mayse-Bukh (1602) as a morally corrupting book, the collection comprises 35 tales (each accompanied by an explicitly framed "moral of the story"), deriving from two fable traditions: the Aesopic (the sources of which were *Berechiah ben Natronai ha-Nakdan's late 12th- or early 13th-century Hebrew *Mishlei Shu'alim* and Ulrich Boner's *Edelstein* (1461)) and the Arabic *maqama*. Most of the fables in the *Ki-Bukh* are longer than their sources and tend toward humor, earthiness, and an interest in the details of Jewish daily life of the time, while emanating the comparatively liberal tonality characteristic of 16th-century Yiddish literature composed in Northern Italy. The collection provides corroborative evidence of the persistent popularity of didactic fable in the Jewish literary tradition during the period. The condemnation of the book as morally corrupting so soon after its initial publication indicates its great popularity. While the date of the first edition remains unclear (1555?), the first extant edition is Verona 1595. The number of woodcuts included in the book is little less than astonishing: 83 in 67 folios. With some relatively minor omissions and (anti-liberal) revisions, Moses b. Menassah Eliezer b. Moses Wallich's *Seyfer Mesholim* (1697) is a reprint of the *Ki-Bukh*.

BIBLIOGRAPHY: M.N. Rosenfeld (ed.), *The Book of Cows: A Facsimile Edition of the Famed Kuhbuch, Verona 1595* (1984); E. Katz (ed.), *Book of Fables: The Yiddish Fable Collection of Reb Moshe Wallich, Frankfurt am Main, 1697* (1994); J.C. Frakes (ed.), *Early Yiddish Texts: 1100–1750* (2004), 415–20, 750–72; J. Baumgarten, *Introduction to Old Yiddish Literature* (2005), 321–26.

[Jerold C. Frakes (2nd ed.)]

KIDD, MICHAEL (born **Milton Greenwald**) (1919–), U.S. dancer and stage and film choreographer. Kidd studied at the school of the American Ballet in New York. His debut as dancer was in *The Eternal Road* (1937). He was a member of the American Ballet and toured with Lincoln *Kirstein's Ballet Caravan and as a soloist and assistant director of Dance Players before joining Ballet Theater in 1942. He was noted for comic and character roles in Eugene Loring's *Billy the Kid* and Jerome Robbins' *Fancy Free*. He choreographed his first ballet, *On Stage!*, in 1945. Over five decades Kidd created winsome and imaginative dances for the Broadway stage and Hollywood musicals. He also choreographed for television, including the television special *Baryshnikov in Hollywood* (1982). For the movies Kidd choreographed *Where's Charley* (1949), *Seven Brides for Seven Brothers* (1954), and *Hello, Dolly* (1969).

As he approached his sixtieth birthday Kidd capped a vital career in the theater with superb performances as a comic actor.

Kidd received Antoinette Perry Awards for the choreography in the musicals *Finian's Rainbow* (1947), *Guys and Dolls* (1951), *Can-Can* (1953), *Li'l Abner* (1956), and *Destry Rides Again* (1959).

[Amnon Shiloah (2nd ed.)]

KIDDUSH (Heb. קִדּוּשׁ, lit. "sanctification," derived from *kaddesh* (קַדֵּשׁ; lit. "to sanctify")), prayer recited over a cup of wine in the home and the synagogue to consecrate the Sabbath or festival in fulfillment of the biblical commandment to "Remember the Sabbath day, to keep it holy" (Ex. 20:8; Pes. 106a). Although women are exempt from performing positive precepts whose execution is bound to a specific time, they are obliged to observe the sanctification of the Sabbath because the Talmud maintains that the phrases "Remember the Sabbath" (Ex. 20:8) and "Observe the Sabbath" (Deut. 5:12) include women. "Whoever has to 'observe' has to 'remember'; and since the women have to 'observe' [by performing no work] they also have to 'remember'" (Ber. 20b). The primary *Kiddush* is recited on the eve of the Sabbath or festival before the start of the meal, since it is forbidden to eat on these occasions until *Kiddush* has been recited (Pes. 105a).

The text of the current Sabbath *Kiddush* consists of an introductory paragraph from Genesis 1:31 and 2:1–3; the blessing over wine; and the blessing for the sanctification of the day which concludes with "Blessed art Thou, O Lord, Who hallowest the Sabbath" (Hertz, Prayer, 409). The introductory scriptural passage is omitted on festivals and only the blessings over wine and over the sanctification of the day are recited. The blessing sanctifying the day for a festival concludes with "Blessed art Thou, O Lord, Who hallowest Israel and the festive seasons" (Hertz, Prayer, 811). The schools of Shammai and Hillel differed as to whether the benediction over the sanctity of the day or that over the wine is recited first (Ber. 8:1). On all full festivals, except for the last days of Passover, the *She-Heḥeyanu* blessing, thanking God for having "kept us in life… and enabling us to reach this season" is recited at the conclusion of the *Kiddush*. When a festival immediately follows the Sabbath, a special benediction celebrating the termination of the Sabbath (**Havdalah*) is added. While it is preferable to chant the evening *Kiddush* over wine (Pes. 107a), two loaves of bread may be used where wine is not obtainable (Sh. Ar., OḤ 272:9).

Although there can be no proper recitation of the *Kiddush* except prior to the meal and at the place the meal will be eaten, the custom of also reciting the prayer at the conclusion of the Sabbath evening services in the synagogue gradually evolved. Despite the opposition of some rabbis, the practice was defended on the ground that at one time travelers were housed and fed in a room adjoining the synagogue. The travelers therefore discharged their obligation to sanctify the Sabbath through the public recitation of the *Kiddush* (Pes. 101a). Reciting the *Kiddush* in the synagogue has been retained only in the Ashkenazi ritual, except in Israel where the *Kiddush* is no longer recited as part of any synagogal rite.

Along with the principal evening *Kiddush*, the rabbis instituted a minor *Kiddush*, euphemistically called the "Great *Kiddush*" (Pes. 106a), to be recited on the morning of the Sabbath or festival before the first meal. This *Kiddush* consists of the recitation of some biblical verses referring to the Sabbath or festival, followed by the benediction over wine (Hertz, Prayer, 565). When no beverage is available, the prayer is recited over two loaves of bread (Sh. Ar., OḤ 289:1–2 and *Magen Avraham* ad loc.). Strong drink other than wine also may be used for the morning *Kiddush*, as may any beverage which is considered *ḥemer ha-medinah* ("national beverage").

For the development of the *Kiddush* text during the talmudic period see J. Heinemann, *Ha-Tefillah bi-Tekufat ha-Tanna'im ve-ha-Amora'im*, 37ff., 62.

The *Kiddush* ceremony, an integral part of Orthodox and Conservative practice, has also been retained by Reform Judaism. The Saturday morning *Kiddush* has often assumed new importance in the modern synagogue since it is often sponsored by the congregation and also serves as a communal social hour.

BIBLIOGRAPHY: Abrahams, Companion, 139–41, 169f., 194; Idelsohn, Liturgy, 132f., 154; Eisenstein, Dinim, 355f.

[Aaron Rothkoff]

KIDDUSH HA-ḤAYYIM ("sanctification of life"), term first attributed to Rabbi Isaac *Nissenbaum, a Zionist rabbi in the Warsaw ghetto, which sought to differentiate between the classical response of Jewish martyrdom, **kiddush ha-Shem*, the sanctification of the Divine Name, and the imperative of the hour, to spiritually resist the Nazis and their intention of annihilating the Jewish people by remaining alive. Nissenbaum wrote: "In the past our enemies demanded our soul and the Jew sacrificed his body in sanctifying God's name. Now the enemy demands the body of the Jew. That makes it imperative for the Jew to defend it and protect it."

Primo *Levi, the great Italian Jewish writer and survivor of Auschwitz, argued that had the lagers lasted longer they would have had to invent a vocabulary of their own, new words to describe an unprecedented situation. "Our language lacks words to express this offense, the demolition of a man." That was true not only for life inside the camps but for the unprecedented circumstances of Jews in German-occupied Europe during the time when the "Final Solution" was the operative German policy. Literary students of the Holocaust Lawrence Langer and Terrence Des Pres invented new words to describe what the perpetrators did to their victims. For Langer, the term was "choiceless choices" and for Des Pres "excremental assault." These were the circumstances in which Jews were placed by the killers. But how were Jews to respond?

Two such concepts developed by which the Jews described their own behavior, their own choice of response. *Iberleben*, the determination to outlive the enemy, to survive and to endure and to deny the Nazis the victory of one more Jew's demise. For Nissenbaum, the language he chose was religious. He understood that the circumstances were unprecedented and therefore the response required was also unprecedented. It demanded a language all its own. Other rabbis pushed for the same response, but saw it in continuity with the previous tradition of *kiddush ha-Shem*. Thus, Rabbi Abraham Isaac Goldberg of Zelichowo admonished his Jews: "every Jew that remains alive sanctifies the name of God among many [*ba-rabbim*]." Nissenbaum chose a new language, in part to stress the uniqueness of the Nazi's murderous intention. They did not want the conversion of the Jews nor their expulsion, but their annihilation and thus life itself was a form of defiance of their ultimate wish. Israeli Holocaust scholar Shaul Esh termed this "The Dignity of the Destroyed" in an article of that title.

BIBLIOGRAPHY: S. Esh, "The Dignity of the Destroyed: Toward a Definition of the Period of the Holocaust," in: *Judaism* (Spring 1962); J. Rudavsky, *To Live with Hope, to Die with Dignity* (1987); P. Schindler, "Kiddush ha-Hayyim," in: Y. Gutman (ed.), *Encyclopedia of the Holocaust* (1990).

[Michael Berenbaum (2nd ed.)]

KIDDUSH HA-SHEM AND ḤILLUL HA-SHEM (Heb. קִדּוּשׁ הַשֵּׁם וְחִלּוּל הַשֵּׁם). The antithetical terms *kiddush ha-Shem* ("sanctification of the [Divine] Name") and *ḥillul ha-Shem* ("defamation of the [Divine] Name") are complementary antonyms and denote the two aspects of one of the most significant concepts in Judaism. They imply, respectively, the glorification of the God of Israel and the diminution of His honor. The specific terms are rabbinic; the concepts themselves, however, are biblical in origin and are included among the 613 commandments: "Ye shall keep My commandments and do them: I am the Lord. Ye shall not profane My holy Name; but I will be hallowed among the children of Israel; I am the Lord who hallow you" (Lev. 22:31, 32). The entire people was subject to these principles, although the priests were especially cautioned to avoid *ḥillul ha-Shem* (Lev. 21:6; 22:2).

In the Bible

Two patterns of thought are discernible in the biblical conception of *kiddush ha-Shem* and *ḥillul ha-Shem*. One considers God as the primary actor, while Israel remains passive; the other regards the Israelites as the initiators of either the sanctification or the desecration of God's Name. The first is fully crystallized in Ezekiel (chs. 20, 36, 39), for whom the sanctification of the Name is essentially an act of the Lord bestowed upon Israel before the onlooking nations of the world. The Name is sanctified when God wondrously redeems Israel and the gentiles behold the vindication of the divine promise and are moved to worship Him. Inversely, if the Lord visits privation or exile upon Israel, or suffers the people to remain in captivity, the nations question God's strength or faithfulness, and the Name is thus defamed. This general rubric holds true for Ezekiel (with the exception of 20:39) and for most instances of *kiddush ha-Shem* in the Pentateuch.

According to the second view, man is responsible for God's honor in the eyes of the world. Moses and Aaron were punished because of their failure to sanctify God's Name (Num. 20:12; Deut. 32:51). God's Name must be sanctified not only before the gentiles but in the eyes of Israel as well (*ibid.*, and Lev. 22:32). Jeremiah accuses his countrymen of profaning God's Name when they circumvent the law and emancipate their slaves only to capture and enslave them again (34:16). Amos condemned extortion from the poor and immorality as *ḥillul ha-Shem* (2.7).

Rabbinic Literature

The rabbinic tradition laid more emphasis on the personal-ethical than on the national-redemptive significance of the concept. It developed especially the second view of the biblical theme: human initiative, and a wider designation so as to include Jews as well as non-Jews. It could even be performed in private with no one present, as in the case of Joseph who, by restraining himself in the face of temptation, fulfilled the sanctification of God's Name (Sot. 36b). This does not mean that the rabbis entirely ignored *kiddush ha-Shem* and *ḥillul ha-Shem* as divine acts. When God decided to visit destruction indiscriminately on both the righteous and the wicked of Sodom, Abraham protested that this would be *ḥillul ha-Shem* (Gen. R. 49:9). Were God to have permitted Absalom to slay his father David, His Name would have been publicly profaned (Sanh. 107a). The punishment of the righteous for their sins, relative to their own high standards, is divine *kiddush ha-Shem* (Sifra to Shemini 45d; Zev. 115b).

The sanctification of God's Name before gentiles was always a potent element in the folk understanding of the concept. The rabbis, however, for the most part, concerned themselves with the active role of man in the drama of bestowing glory upon, or detracting from, the honor of God. This human initiative in *kiddush ha-Shem* could be consummated in three different ways: martyrdom, exemplary ethical conduct, and prayer.

MARTYRDOM. The readiness to sanctify God's Name has its most dramatic expression in the willingness to die a martyr, and since tannaitic times the term *kiddush ha-Shem* also denotes martyrdom (see below Historical Aspects). When a person willingly suffers death rather than violate one of three specific commandments (see below) he achieves *kiddush ha-Shem*; if he fails to do so in these cases, or in other instances where the *halakhah* demands martyrdom, he is guilty of *ḥillul ha-Shem* (Av. Zar. 27b; Sanh. 74a, b). On the verses, "Ye shall not profane My holy Name,… I am the Lord who hallow you, brought you out of the land of Egypt, to be your God: I am the Lord" (Lev. 22:32, 33), the rabbis taught: "On this condition did I bring you out of the land of Egypt that you submit yourselves to sanctify My Name, that I be your God even by force; I the Lord am faithful to grant you your reward" (Sifra, Emor, Perek 9). Since the second century, "to die for the sanctification of the Name" has been the accepted idiom for dying a martyr's death. A martyr was, appropriately, called a *kadosh*, one who is holy. In time, this honorific was extended and applied as well to those who died solely because they were Jewish even without their consciously offering up their lives for religious purposes (Moshe Lamm, *Darkah shel ha-Yahadut be-Mavet u-ve-Avelut* (2005), 221–222.) A child, growing up in the Jewish tradition, was exposed to the concept of martyrdom as an ideal. From his earliest youth he was taught stories about martyrs, e.g., *Hannah and her seven sons, R. *Akiva and the other of the *ten martyrs; the latter in the form of a lamentation is part of the synagogue service on the *Day of Atonement and on the Ninth of *Av. Hananiah, Mishael, and Azariah (Dan. 3) are held up by the rabbis as models of conduct in the sanctification of the Name (Pes. 53b).

At the famous rabbinical council in *Lydda (second century), the laws of martyrdom were formulated. *Kiddush ha-Shem* was declared obligatory in the case of three commandments and a person had to suffer death rather than violate them: idolatry, unchastity (*gillui arayot*: including incest, adultery, and, under certain circumstances, any infraction of the code of sexual morality), and murder (Sanh. 74a). One should violate all other commandments rather than suffer death. Should a Jew, however, in the presence of ten other Jews, be coerced into transgressing these other laws in order to demonstrate his apostasy, he must sanctify God's Name and choose death. If ten Jews are not present, he should transgress rather than be killed. These rules hold for "normal" times. In times of religious persecution of the entire community, however, one must choose to die for *kiddush ha-Shem* even if no other Israelites are present, and one must not violate any commandment, including minor customs which are distinctively Jewish (Maim. Yad, Yesodei ha-Torah, 5:3). Martyrdom rather than violation, when transgression is permissible, became a point of discussion; the *halakhah* had to decide between two opposing principles – that of sanctifying God's Name versus that of preserving life ("and he shall live by them" (Lev. 18:5), i.e., the commandments). According to Maimonides, a person who chose *kiddush ha-Shem* where the law decides for life is culpable (Maim. *ibid.*, 5:1); others consider such voluntary martyrdom praiseworthy (Tos. Av. Zar. 27b). The Ashkenazi talmudists were instinctual rather than rationalistic in their attitude to martyrdom – an attitude characteristic of most of medieval German Jewry. The tosafists reacted negatively to the problem as it is viewed in the *halakhah*. They recoiled – "Heaven forbid!" – from such formal halakhic reasoning that does not require martyrdom of a person forced to worship an idol in private, and they demanded obligatory *kiddush ha-Shem* (Tos. Av. Zar. 54a).

Among modern halakhic authorities, the question whether an individual should sacrifice his life in order to save the entire community is a point of contention. Rabbi A.I. Kook considered it obligatory as an emergency measure (*Mishpat Kohen* (1966[2]), no. 143). Others regarded such action as meritorious but not mandatory (J.J. Weinberg, *Seridei Esh*, 1 (1961), 303–16). The problem arose often during the Holocaust in Europe. In one typical responsum of this period, the question was asked whether (considering the danger to the emissary who might be imprisoned and killed) a particular rabbi should accept his mission of approaching the Lithuanian henchmen of the Nazi authorities in Kovno in 1941 in order to release certain Jews. The answer was that he may not be ordered to accept the mission but he should do so as an act of piety; he did, and subsequently survived (E. Oshry, *Mi-Ma'amakim*, 2 (1963), responsum no. 1). The same work also includes a discussion on a contemporaneous practical problem: the wording of the blessing to be recited upon being martyred for the sanctification of God's Name (*ibid.*, no. 4). The question was first raised by R. Isaiah ha-Levi *Horowitz (16th–17th centuries) who initially was reluctant to sanction a blessing over the *mitzvah* of martyrdom because one should not seek out a situation which would require him to surrender his life. Later, however, he agreed to the blessing over *kiddush ha-Shem*.

The sages of the Talmud were divided in their opinions as to whether gentiles are required to sanctify God's Name. *Abbaye held that a non-Jew who is forced to violate one of the seven Noachide laws is not obligated to suffer *kiddush ha-Shem*; *Rava maintained that he is (Sanh. 74b). The accepted ruling is that non-Jews are not required to sanctify the Name (TJ, Shev. 4:3, 35b; Maim. Yad, Melakhim, 10:2). According to some authorities, however, a gentile must perform *kiddush ha-Shem* rather than be forced to commit murder (*Mishneh le-Melekh*, to Yad, *ibid.*).

ETHICAL CONDUCT. The ideal of man's initiative in sanctifying God's Name beyond the strict requirements of the law was developed by rabbinic tradition in the area of ethical conduct. When *Simeon b. *Shetaḥ bought an ass from an Arab and his servants were delighted at finding a jewel hanging from its neck, he at once returned the gem to its owner, who cried out, "Blessed be the God of the Jews Who renders His people so scrupulous in their dealings with other men" (TJ, BM., 2:5, 8c). His supererogatory conduct is considered *kiddush ha-Shem*. Joshua kept his oath to the Gibeonites, though they exacted it from him by fraud (Git. 46a). Moral acts such as Joseph's restraint in the face of temptation and Judah's public confession of his relations with Tamar are also considered *kiddush ha-Shem* (Sot. 10b).

The designation of an unethical act as *ḥillul ha-Shem* proved a powerful deterrent. The punishment for such is immediate, even if the sin was unintentional (Shab. 33a); it is the most heinous of all sins (TJ, Ned. 3:14, 38b) and only death can atone for it (Yoma 86a). According to R. Akiva, there is no forgiveness at all for it (ARN[1] 39).

In the Talmud, the concepts of *kiddush ha-Shem* and *ḥillul ha-Shem* are discussed with reference to stealing from a non-Jew (BK 113a–b). According to R. Akiva, the law itself prohibits this, and thus protects all property, whether of a Jew or non-Jew. R. Ishmael, however, holds that biblical law applies formally only to the relation of Jews with fellow Jews. The protection of non-Jews, therefore, requires a supplementary principle, that of *kiddush ha-Shem*. Hence, ethical perfection beyond the minimum standards of the law itself becomes law, that of sanctifying the Name: reflecting honor upon God and the Torah by striving for moral excellence. Although medieval talmudists almost unanimously decided in favor of R. Akiva, they had to use the themes of *kiddush ha-Shem* and *ḥillul ha-Shem* to plug occasional loopholes in the formal law. They often cited the Tosefta (BK 10:15) that stealing from a non-Jew is a worse crime than stealing from a Jew, since the former includes *ḥillul ha-Shem* as well as "ye shall not steal."

Kiddush ha-Shem imposes special and exacting standards of conduct on the scholar. He must, for instance, pay his debts promptly, never cause embarrassment to his colleagues, not walk four cubits without *tallit* or *tefillin*, and not overindulge in merrymaking (Yoma 86a; Av. Zar. 28a; Maim. Yad, Yesodei ha-Torah, 5:11).

While the ethical moment is quite strong in *kiddush ha-Shem*, the latter should not be interpreted exclusively as moral behavior toward others. *Kiddush ha-Shem* includes martyrdom for any of a number of reasons: refusing to worship an idol, under certain conditions circumcising one's son or studying Torah or abiding by the dietary laws. In all these cases, it is not necessarily a question of performance in the presence of non-Jews. The *halakhah* considers any consciously rebellious act against God as *ḥillul ha-Shem* (Maim. *ibid.*, 5:10). The principal motif of *kiddush ha-Shem* is religious and this includes the ethical dimension; the aim of the latter is not so much to teach the world morality as to increase the respect of the world for the morality of Judaism (H.G. Friedman, see bibliography). Principally, *kiddush ha-Shem* seeks to demonstrate to Jew and non-Jew alike the power of the Jewish commitment to God and to Torah.

PRAYER. *Kiddush ha-Shem* also found expression in prayer. This took two forms. One was in a liturgical declaration of readiness to accept martyrdom if necessary: "'Nay, but for Thy sake are we killed all the day; we are accounted as sheep for the slaughter' (Ps. 44:23). Is it then possible to be 'killed all the day?' When one takes upon himself to sanctify His great Name every day, he is accounted as 'sheep for the slaughter'" (Sif. Deut. 6:5). Similarly, when reciting the **Shema*, a person must spiritually intend the readiness to offer himself for *kiddush ha-Shem* (Zohar, Num. 195b). Second, the recital of the prayer is itself regarded as an act of sanctification of God's Name. A number of such liturgical expressions of *kiddush ha-Shem* have been found in the Merkabah literature (G. Scholem, *Jewish Gnosticism, Merkabah Mysticism, and Talmudic Tradition* (1965^2), Appendix C).

Two formal prayers stand out in this respect: the **Kedushah* and the **Kaddish*. The *Kedushah* is based on the Song of the Seraphim in Isaiah 6:1–3. The more esoteric *Kedushah*, recited before the *Shema*, refers to the praise of God by the angels, while the *Kedushah* of the **Amidah* prayer speaks of Israel sanctifying God's Name. The more esoteric *Kedushah*, recited before the *Shema*, refers to the praise of God by the angels, while the *Kedushah* of the Amidah prayer speaks of Israel sanctifying God's Name. The latter is parallel to and perhaps surpasses the *Kedushah* of the angels, adding a cosmic element to the theme of *kiddush ha-Shem*. The Zohar (Lev. 93a) considers the key verse "I will be hallowed among the children of Israel" (Lev. 22:32) as the source and warrant for the *Kedushah*.

In the *Kaddish*, the key parts refer quite literally to the "sanctification" of the "Name." At a comparatively early period, the *Kaddish* was already ascribed to the biblical source of *kiddush ha-Shem* (Zedekiah b. Abraham ha-Rofe, *Shibbolei ha-Leket*, ed. S.K. Mirsky (1966), 149–50). The absence of any specific Divine Name in this prayer, and the emphasis on the "Name" as such, has been thought by some scholars to have been deliberate, in order to emphasize its idiomatic affinity to the biblical "*kiddush ha-Shem.*" It has been suggested that the *Kaddish* was originally recited by martyrs who, at the threshold of death, declared the sanctification of God's Name and consoled the bereaved onlookers by speaking of the redemption and the Messiah "in your lifetime and in your days" (J. Kaufman, *Midreshei Ge'ullah* (1954^2), 58 n. 12, quoting Ḥ.N. Bialik). S.Y. Agnon's interpretation carries the impact of poetic truth, if not historic accuracy: the orphan's recitation of the *Kaddish* (*Samukh ve-Nireh, "Petiḥah le-Kaddish"*), is a kind of consolation to God who sustained a double *ḥillul ha-Shem* – His Name both diminished and desecrated by the loss of even a single soldier (who as a human being is irreplaceable) in the legions of the Almighty; hence, the prayer that the injured Name be *magnified* and *sanctified*. R. Joseph B. *Soloveitchik writes movingly that "through the *Kaddish* we hurl defiance at death and its fiendish conspiracy against man. [The mourner] declares more or less the following: no matter how powerful death is … no matter how black one's despair is … we declare and profess publicly and solemnly that we are not giving up, that we are not surrendering, that we will carry on the work of our ancestors as if nothing had happened, that we will be satisfied with nothing less than the full realization of the ultimate goal – the establishment of God's kingdom ("Aninut and Avelut," in: David Shatz, B. Wolowelsky, and Reuven Ziegler (eds.),*Out of the Whirlwind: Essays on Morality, Suffering, and the Human Condition* (2003), p. 5).

[Norman Lamm]

Kiddush Hashem: Historical Aspects

The concept of *kiddush ha-Shem* has thus always been implicit in the Judaic faith and view of life. Its first explicit expression occurred during the confrontation of Judaism with *Hellenism, the first pagan culture with "missionary" and synthesizing tendencies. The Book of Daniel tells about the three "Jewish men" – Shadrach, Meshach, and Abed-Nego – who disobeyed a royal command to worship an idol and endangered their lives. Under *Antiochus Epiphanes Hellenization employed violent and coercive methods in regard to Jews. After the victorious revolt of the Hasmoneans, a Jew in the Hellenistic Diaspora recorded the martyrdom of an old man, little children, and their mother who had died for their faith:

> Eleazar, one of the principal scribes,… of a noble countenance, was compelled to eat swine's flesh … Now those in charge of that forbidden sacrificial feast took the man aside, for the sake of old acquaintance, and privately urged him to bring some flesh of his own providing, such as he was lawfully allowed to use, and to pretend he was really eating of the sacrifice which the king had ordered, so that in this way he might escape death and be kindly treated for the sake of their old friendship. But he with a high resolve, worthy of his years and of the dignity of his descent … and, still more, of the holy laws divinely ordained, spoke his mind accordingly:… "It ill becomes our years to dissemble," said he, "and thus lead many younger persons to imagine that Eleazar in his ninetieth year has gone over to a heathenish religion … for the mere sake of enjoying this brief and momentary life … Even were I for the moment to evade the punishment of men, I should not escape the hands of the Almighty in life or in death … I will … leave behind me a noble example to the young how to die willingly and nobly on behalf of our reverend and holy laws." With these words he stepped forward at once to the instrument of torture, while those who a moment before had been friendly turned against him, deeming his language to be that of a sheer madman…. Under the strokes of torture, he groaned out: "The Lord who has holy knowledge understandeth that, although I might have been freed from death, I endure cruel pains in my body from scourging and suffer this gladly in my soul, because I fear Him" (II Macc. 6:18–30; Charles, Apocrypha, 140).

The basic ideals motivating *kiddush ha-Shem* are thus set out at this early stage: personal nobility and courage, a categorical refusal to employ any form of dissimulation or live an undercover existence, and readiness to undergo bodily and spiritual torture in the full knowledge that this behavior may appear sheer madness to those who inflict it. Hannah, "the mother of the Maccabees" according to Christian tradition, exhorts her seven sons in a similar way not to be afraid of either hangmen or death. These figures became the prototypes for and symbols of martyrdom and martyrs in both Judaism and Christianity. The Fourth Book of Maccabees is almost entirely a philosophical sermon on the meaning and glory of *kiddush ha-Shem* in Hellenistic times.

Whereas in the Christian and Muslim interpretation the Jewish *kiddush ha-Shem* became an act of mainly individual martyrdom, the lot of saints chosen by God for their individual path of suffering – and (in Christianity) their participation in the mystery of Crucifixion, the martyred saints following Christ on the cross – in Judaism *kiddush ha-Shem* remained a task set for each and every Jew to fulfill if the appropriate moment came. It found logical expression in the readiness to die as a son of the Chosen People. In the war against Rome of 66–70/73, whole communities committed suicide as a culmination of their fight against alien power. Thus, in the many trials of revolt and war in which Jews were tested, from the wars of liberation of the Maccabees up to the failure of the revolts against the Romans both in Ereẓ Israel and the Diaspora, *kiddush ha-Shem* acted as a motivating force giving meaning to the struggle of the Jewish warriors, strength of endurance under cruel torture by victors, and offering suicide as a way out of submission and slavery. The famous mass suicide at *Masada was inspired more by the conception of *kiddush ha-Shem* as a commandment, and a proud refusal to submit to the Roman enemy, than by the philosophical argumentations that Josephus, an arch enemy of the self-sacrificing *Zealots, put in the mouths of the defenders of Masada.

As if referring to an everyday, ordinary incident, one of the *tannaim* describes "those who dwell in the land of Israel and risk their lives for the sake of the commandments: 'Why are you being led out to be decapitated?' 'Because I circumcised my son to be an Israelite.' 'Why are you being led out to be burned?' 'Because I read the Torah.' 'Why are you being led out to be crucified?' 'Because I ate the unleavened bread.' 'Why are you getting a hundred lashes?' 'Because I performed the ceremony of the *lulav*.' These wounds caused me to be beloved of my Father in heaven" (Mekh. Ba-Ḥodesh, 6). They were conscious that this behavior appeared strange to the gentiles who asked the Jews: What is the nature of your God that "you are so ready to die for Him, and so ready to let yourselves be killed for Him … you are handsome, you are mighty, come and intermingle with us" (Mekh. Shirata, 3). *Samaritans also chose the Jewish path of *kiddush ha-Shem* in the course of their revolts and sufferings for the Torah and its truth as they conceived it.

MIDDLE AGES. The ideology of *kiddush ha-Shem* and devotion to it as crystallized in antiquity continued and strengthened in the Middle Ages. Christian persecution and the humiliation meted out to Jews intensified the underlying wish to safeguard individuality, and fortified the ethic of *kiddush ha-Shem* in the struggle to preserve their national identity and freedom to profess their faith. For Jews living in the lands of their enemies *kiddush ha-Shem* became the only convincing way of asserting when faced with Christian missionary coercion that if they were not to be permitted to live openly as Jews they chose not to live at all. Surrounded by feudal warriors and the feudal mode of fighting, torn from their country and appearing as aliens everywhere, for Jews *suicide as *kiddush ha-Shem* was in many cases the only way in which they could exemplify and give expression to human courage. When confronted by brute force, Jews tried to defend themselves wherever and however they could; however, since they often failed, as was inevitable in the case of a small minority, readiness to die was the only way of maintaining a lofty exemplar for Jewish existence. Where Christian knights ruled through their warrior techniques and conformed to their specific knightly scale of values, Jews, influenced involuntarily by this spirit, could hold their own – both in point of physical survival and more importantly from the spiritual and psychological aspect – only through ultimate readiness to face the supreme sacrifice.

In the 11th century the conception of holy war became predominant in Western Christian thought. Popular religious feeling in the West became more fanatical and was often connected with social unrest. Even before the beginning of the *crusades, cases of suicide to avoid forced conversion to Christianity are recorded. The suicide of Jews in the tenth century in southern Italy for the sake of their faith is described by contemporaries as "pure total burnt offering" (*olah temimah*). In the spring of 1096 many of the participants in the First Crusade conceived that their armed pilgrimage to free the sepulcher of Jesus logically demanded either the extinction of the Jewish religion in Christian countries or the annihilation of those Jews who would not accept Christianity. In the atmosphere of holy war many Jews believed that the glory of the Lord and the honor of their Law would be debased if they did not bear witness for them by open and public proclamation of their abiding truth in a chivalrous manner. Thus, through the curious workings of historic irony the Christian crusading venture and Jewish martyrdom by *kiddush ha-Shem* each became in its own particular way expressions of a holy war waged for the glory of God.

During the crusading onslaught on them in 1096 the communities of the Rhine district sacrificed themselves for their faith in this spirit. Those who remained alive related the sacrifices of the martyrs in the same spirit. Thousands of Jews lost their lives in the course of those terrible months; a few of the victims fell in direct battle, and the majority perished through suicides of whole families. In the chronicles of the massacres of the First Crusade and the threnodies composed on the martyrs the ideology of *kiddush ha-Shem* is reformulated. A mother in Mainz is related as having said that she killed her children as sacrifices to God to fulfill His commandment to be "whole with him" (*liheyot temimim immo*) (A.M. Habermann (ed.), *Sefer Gezerot Ashkenaz ve-Ẓarefat* (1945), 34), thus tacitly framing a condemnation of forced converts leading a halfhearted underground existence as **anusim*. The writings about these acts employ the ancient symbols of aggadic literature – **Akedah*, *Abraham's bosom, and the divine light which will be vouchsafed to the martyrs, and stress the open challenge offered to the crusaders by the Jews who proclaimed the superiority of their faith over Christianity. The silence of the sources sometimes bears eloquent testimony to the conception of *kiddush ha-Shem* as the Jewish way of waging the holy war: the pillage and robbery, loss of property and homes that accompanied the attacks are only hinted at, while the motives of the crusaders are formulated in a way that conveys their Christian religious determinants only (see *ibid.*, pp. 24, 26, 27, 72, 93, 94). Wherever possible, in these attacks Jews tried to fight off their assailants at the gates and at the entrances to houses (*ibid.*, pp. 30–31a, 33, 97, 99–100), but when their endeavors at defense failed they killed themselves and took special care to slay their children first to prevent them from being carried off and brought up as Christians. Such sources describe these events for future generations not as acts committed out of desperation but from the feeling that these Jews had chosen to die in this way so that the remnant of the nation should be able to continue its existence with pride. The community of *Xanten is remembered for having added to their last communal benediction after food, just before the mass suicide, the following prayer: "The merciful One will avenge in the days of those who will remain after us, before their eyes the blood shed by your servants and the blood that is to be shed" (*ibid.*, p. 49).

After the wholesale burning of Jews at the stake in *Blois in 1171 a Jewish sage signing his name "Ovadiah" summed up something like a set of rules for Jewish behavior under enemy sovereignty, speaking as if from the mouths of the martyred: "For the saints have proclaimed … if the rulers decree … as to taxation … it is permissible … to plead to ease the burden … but … when they take it into their evil hearts … to blandish, to terrorize, to make them impure [through apostasy] … the chosen ones shall answer … we shall pay no heed to your lies … we shall remain true" [to the Jewish faith] (see S. Spiegel, in: *Sefer ha-Yovel… Mordekhai Menaḥem Kaplan* (1953), 286). This steadfastness continued to fortify Jews throughout the tribulations, libels, and massacres to which they were subjected in these centuries. When the Nordhausen community was led to be burned on the pyre during the *Black Death massacres in 1349 they obtained permission to hire musicians, and went singing and dancing to their deaths. Medieval Jewish prayer books include, in addition to the benedictions for bread and drink, a benediction to be recited by a Jew before killing himself and his children. Special memorial lists were compiled to preserve the memory of those who had sacrificed themselves for *kiddush ha-Shem* (see **Memorbuch*). As the victims of the blood *libel, Host *desecration libel, and other calumnies were subjected to continuous torture intended to extort "confessions," endurance under excruciating pain or suicide to avoid making a false confession came to be considered a true manifestation of *kiddush ha-Shem.*

Among the Jews of Christian Spain *kiddush ha-Shem* was recognized both as a phenomenon distinguishing Ashkenazi Jewry and a problem to be reckoned with in their own existence, as the writings of Judah Halevi and Naḥmanides show for the 12th and 13th centuries. From the end of the 14th century *kiddush ha-Shem* became part of the fate and sufferings of Spanish Jewry, whether upheld through massacres, persecutions, or libels as Jews openly professing their faith, or under the fire and torture of the *Inquisition chambers and tribunals as *anusim*. *Abraham b. Eliezer ha-Levi applied the ancient Maccabean tradition and theory of *kiddush ha-Shem* to the victim of the torture chambers and at the auto-da-fé:

> Whoever firmly resolves to devote himself to the honor of His name … such a man, being exposed to cruel tortures and sorely tormented, as was the case with the holy martyrs in the Land, those marvelous young men, the sons of saintly Hannah, in the days when the priests could come near the Presence of God; they were the heroes who fought God's battles – if such a man will but concentrate and put between his eyes the "awe-inspiring and great Name," resolve to undergo martyrdom, and his eyes will incline towards the Holy One of Israel … then he may be sure that he will withstand the test … nor feel any pain, blows or torments … And these things are worthy to be made known to His people Israel for the generation is one of religious persecution, and no Israelite should go in ignorance of this principle … And it may well be that it was to such a saintly person, who, albeit his soul is given over completely to God and rejoices in His love, is yet buried together with the wicked and consumed by fire, the wise Solomon alluded when he said (Song 8:5), "Who is that coming up from the wilderness, Leaning upon her beloved?" For the promise of the Lord proves true: she [the soul] leans and falls, limb by limb and piece by piece; but of such a saintly soul the righteous who dwell in the innermost mansion of the King, where joy resides, expound: Who is that coming up from the terrestrial world, which is like unto a wilderness?… Out of love for her beloved her body falls part by part; because of the trials she undergoes, her flesh pierced by tongs or cut to pieces by the sword; and the King, to Whom all peace belongs, for Whose love she suffers so, looks down from His abode and proclaims as she ascends to Him: "Behold thou are upright and pure, today have I begotten thee" (Ps. 2:7), and "under the apple tree I awakened thee" (Song. 8:5) (as quoted in Baer, Spain, 2 (1966), 430–1).

In this early 16th-century summation the wheel has turned full circle: the motives which inspired individuals to choose the path of *kiddush ha-Shem* at the time of the clash with Hellenism merge with the sufferings of the tortured body of the individual Jew in his pain and fire-wracked isolation looking from his physical breakdown to his meeting with the loving God in heaven.

MODERN TIMES. In early modern times the general trends of enlightenment and abatement of medieval religious pressures were accompanied by growing secularization in

Jewish life and thought, leanings toward assimilation, and striving for emancipation, all factors which both separately and in combination conduced to disintegration in Jewish society and abandonment of specifically Jewish values. Thus, while the necessity to uphold *kiddush ha-Shem* diminished in fact, the concept also lost actuality and significance.

With the awakening of Jewish national feeling in later modern times, as expressed by the formation of political parties like the *Bund, the organization of *self-defense against pogroms, and Zionism, the principle of *kiddush ha-Shem* reasserted its influence, consciously or subconsciously, manifested in new ideological frames for the defense of Jewish dignity and in modes of response by Jews to social and spiritual challenge. Jewish revolutionary attitudes bear its imprint in the courage and readiness to struggle and self-sacrifice for the sake of humanity even when there is no immediate prospect of victory on the horizon. In the same way, the fight and death of the rebels in the Nazi ghettos was ultimately inspired by this ancient Jewish tradition.

Kiddush ha-Shem is an original contribution by the Jewish faith and culture to the whole monotheistic world. Through it was expressed for the first time in human history the readiness of simple people to die for their faith and opinions. It is an ultimate prop of individual expression when all other physical supports have been withdrawn.

Kiddush ha-Shem has played a central and formative role in Jewish history, both through the reality of the sacrifices made to uphold it as well as through the spiritual images and attitudes by which it has been activated. It is a powerful and valid expression of human courage and readiness for supreme sacrifice. In a large measure due to the principle of *kiddush ha-Shem* Jews have escaped spiritual degradation throughout the long **galut* ("Diaspora"), thus failing to justify the hopes and views of their enemies and detractors. Through it courage and the spirit to resist have been continuously kept alive in Jewish hearts and transmitted to posterity from the days of Daniel to the present. Individual exemplary behavior and collective enthusiasm have sustained it in changing situations and forms.

The valor and heroism shown in defense of the State of Israel in the 20th century can be seen as the direct inheritance of chivalrous courage which Jews from generation to generation have transmitted in upholding the principle of *kiddush ha-Shem.*

[Haim Hillel Ben-Sasson]

BIBLIOGRAPHY: H.G. Friedman, in: HUCA (1904), 193–214; I. Gruenwald, in: *Molad*, 1 (1967/68), 476–84; A. Holz, in: *Judaism*, 10 (1961), 360–7; J. Katz, *Exclusiveness and Tolerance* (1961), ch. 7 and passim. HISTORICAL ASPECTS: Roth, Marranos; Baer, Spain; idem, in: *Sefer Assaf* (1953), 126–40; Baron, Social², index, s.v. *Martyrs*; S. Spiegel, in: *Sefer ha-Yovel… Mordekhai Menaḥem Kaplan* (1953), 267–87; Ha-Ḥevrah ha-Historit ha-Yisre'elit, *Milḥemet Kodesh u-Martirologyah* (1968); H.H. Ben-Sasson, in: idem, *Historiyyonim ve-Askolot Historiyyot* (1962), 29–40; idem (ed.), *Toledot Am Yisrael*, 3 vols. (1969).

KIDDUSHIN (Heb. קִדּוּשִׁין), the last tractate in the order *Nashim* in the Mishnah, Tosefta, and both Talmuds. It deals with matrimonial matters. Its position at the end of the order is due to the fact that the order of the tractates is determined by their size and *Kiddushin* has only four chapters, less than all other tractates of *Nashim*. There is no corresponding word for *kiddushin* in English. It is more than an "engagement" in the current sense, as it can be dissolved only by divorce, and moreover the law of adultery, carrying the biblical death penalty, applies from the moment of *kiddushin*. On the other hand *kiddushin* is like "betrothal" in the sense that it represents a formal stage preliminary to marriage proper (*nissu'in*), the latter term referring to the induction of the wife into the husband's house, symbolized by the *ḥuppah*. Chapter 1, applying to *kiddushin* the term acquisition (*kinyan*), opens with the modes of *kiddushin*: by money, by writ, and by intercourse. The rest of the chapter deals with the acquisition of slaves and animals, of land and chattels, and with other extraneous matters. The chapter concludes with aggadic sayings. Chapter 2 deals mainly with *kiddushin* by proxy. Chapter 3 examines "*kiddushin* on condition" and "doubtful *kiddushin*," leading up to the problem of blemished descent. Chapter 4 deals mainly with questions of genealogy and bastardy. As usual, the tractate ends with homiletic material, on education, and after deliberating at length which craft to teach one's sons, reaches the conclusion that Torah study is the best vocation. In the Tosefta, this tractate is divided into five chapters.

Important masoretic observations are made in the Babylonian Talmud. It states that the scribes were called *soferim* because they counted (*safar*) the letters of the Torah; exact indications are then given as to the number of letters, words, and verses in the Pentateuch and in other parts of the Bible, and as to which letter, word, or verse mark the middle of the Pentateuch, the Psalms, or the Chronicles respectively (30a). Interesting is the characterization of various nations: Rome is credited with welfare, Persia with courage, Babylon is said to be poor and ignorant, and Arabia immoral. Elam is characterized by hypocrisy and arrogance (49b). Historically important is the account of the struggle between the Pharisees and John Hyrcanus (66a). According to the letter of R. Sherira Gaon, a considerable section of the beginning of the *Gemara* text (up to "*Ve-ein davar aḥer kortah*"; 3b) is of savoraic origin.

The first chapter of tractate *Kiddushin* belongs to an ancient collection of *mishnayot*. The manner in which the halakhic material is arranged in this chapter suggests that it might originally have been a separate tractate, on *kinyanim*, later perhaps prefixed to the tractate *Kiddushin* because it happened to start with the "acquisition" of the wife. In fact, in the Babylonian Talmud this chapter comprises half of the tractate. Its language is slightly archaic, and the conclusion of the first chapter: "whoever performs a single precept is well rewarded, his days are prolonged, and he inherits the land" similarly testifies to an early date. To the same category belong also the end of the third and the fourth chapter of the tractate, which contain early *halakhot* on forbidden marriages (cf. the end of ch.

1 of Mishnah *Ḥagigah*). The influence of Pumbedita is clearly perceptible in the editing of the Talmud of *Kiddushin*, even though it is possible to discern the large share of Ravina and R. Ashi in its final editing. In the Soncino Talmud, *Kiddushin* was translated into English by H. Freedman (1936).

BIBLIOGRAPHY: Epstein, Tanna'im, 52–54, 414–6; idem, Amora'im, 95–102; Ḥ. Albeck, *Shishah Sidrei Mishnah*, 3 (1954), 307ff.

[Arnost Zvi Ehrman]

KIDRON (Heb. קִדְרוֹן), valley to the N. and E. of Jerusalem, separating the city from the Mount of Olives. The name derived from the root *kdr* ("dark," "shady"), refers to its depth. The valley begins near the Sanhedria saddle, northwest of Jerusalem, at a height of 2,585 ft. (788 m.), close to the watershed. It continues eastward for about 1½ mi. (2½ km.) as Naḥal Egozim (Wadi Jauz). At a height of 2,346 ft. (715 m.) the valley turns south. Several valleys converge with the Kidron as it runs southward: the Bethzeita Valley, which traverses the northeast corner of the Old City, at 2,260 ft. (686 m.) from the west; the Tyropoeon Valley, which bisects the Old City, at 2,035 ft. (617 m.); the Ben-Hinnom Valley, which passes the Old City on the west, at 2,000 ft. (606 m.). The Kidron then continues in a southeasterly direction, the banks becoming steeper and more craggy. It passes the monastery of Mar Saba and issues into the Dead Sea 2 mi. (c. 3 km.) south of Ra's al-Fashkha.

The great importance of the Kidron for Jerusalem lies in the fact that it and its confluents determined the orographical shape of the area on which the city was built. The valley protected the City of David and its northern continuation, the Temple Mount, on the east. The Gihon, Jerusalem's only spring, issued from its west slope. Only toward the end of the Second Temple period, when Agrippa I built the Third Wall there, was the westward bend of the Kidron utilized for protection of the city. Situated on the leeward side of the city and presenting rock surfaces suitable for the cutting of tomb caves, the valley served from early times as a necropolis of Jerusalem, the early tombs culminating in the magnificent rock-cut monuments along the eastern slope.

The first biblical reference to the "brook" Kidron occurs in connection with David's flight before Absalom (II Sam. 15:23). In the time of the divided monarchy, the reforming kings of Judah, Asa, Hezekiah, and Josiah, cast away and burnt the various idols which defiled Jerusalem there (I Kings 15:13; II Kings 23:4, 6, 12; II Chron. 15:16; 29:16). Jeremiah included the Kidron within the area holy to the Lord (31:39–40). In later times the central part of the valley was called the Valley of Jehoshaphat and was assumed to be the place where the dead were resurrected. In this legend, as adapted by the Muslims, all men had to cross the valley on a sword suspended over it.

BIBLIOGRAPHY: Abel, Geog, 1 (1933), 400–1; N. Avigad, *Mazzevot Kedumot be-Naḥal Kidron* (1954); M. Avi-Yonah (ed.), *Sefer Yerushalayim* (1956), passim. **ADD. BIBLIOGRAPHY:** Y. Tsafrir, L. Di Segni, and J. Green, *Tabula Imperii Romani. Iudaea – Palaestina. Maps and Gazetteer.* (1994), 102, s.v. Cedron Torrens.

[Michael Avi-Yonah]

KIEL, city in *Schleswig-Holstein, Germany. In the 17th century, Jews went to Kiel for the annual fair (*Kieler Umschlag*). Permission to settle in the city was given in 1690 to the Sephardi Court Jew Jacob Musaphia, followed in 1728 by Samson Lewin, another Court Jew. Together they laid the foundations for the small Jewish community. In 1766 Kiel had six Jewish families engaged in small businesses and moneylending. Although Schleswig-Holstein was annexed by Denmark in 1733, the legal status of the Jews in the duchy was not ameliorated. The community had a prayer hall and buried their dead at Rendsburg. In 1803 Jewish students were admitted to the University of Kiel. There were then 29 Jews in the city; the numbers grew to 75 in 1845 and 156 in 1855. A cemetery was consecrated in 1852; the community was officially organized in 1867 and two years later a synagogue was erected, to be replaced by a new one in 1910. In 1900 the community numbered 338 persons, 526 in 1910, 600 in 1925, and 522 in 1933. Kiel rabbis included Emil *Cohn (1907–12) and A. Posner (1912–33). On the Nazi rise to power, the community was exposed to severe repression and persecution: Jewish professors were dismissed from the university and the works of 28 Jewish authors – mainly lecturers in Kiel University – were removed from the library of the university. Anti-Jewish boycott meetings were held all over the city. As all Jewish children were removed from the city's public school system, the community opened its own grade school. A total of 586 Jews left the city during the Nazi era. Of those who remained 85 were deportees and 12 committed suicide. On Nov. 10, 1938, the synagogue was burned down and Jewish homes and stores were looted. After the war 11 Jews returned to Kiel; the bombed Jewish cemetery was later restored.

BIBLIOGRAPHY: M. Stern, *Die israelitische Bevoelkerung der deutschen Staedte*, 2 (1892); W. Victor, *Die Emanzipation der Juden in Schleswig-Holstein* (1913); A. Posner, in: MGWJ, 72 (1928), 287–91; 76 (1932), 229–39; *Fuehrer durch die juedische Gemeindeverwaltung* (1932–33), 122; H. Kellenbenz, *Sephardim an der unteren Elbe* (1958), index; EJ, 9. S.V.

[Chasia Turtel]

KIEL, YEHUDA (1917–), Israel educationist. Born in Petrograd, as a child he lived in Lithuania and Latvia. Arriving in Palestine in 1935, he helped develop the state religious education system and was its national supervisor of elementary and secondary education. In 1992 he was awarded the Israel Prize for Jewish studies in recognition of his commentary on books of the Bible, particularly his wide-ranging ones on First and Second Chronicles.

KIELCE, capital of Kielce province, S.E. Poland. Jews were excluded from Kielce by a royal "privilege" granted to the city in 1535. Kielce belonged to the estates of the bishops of Cracow until 1818, and thus the prohibition on Jewish settlement remained in force. In 1833 a small number of Jews settled in Kielce. They were expelled in 1847 but returned shortly afterward. In 1852 there were 101 Jews in Kielce and the congregation was affiliated to the neighboring community at Checiny.

It became a separate community in 1868, and a cemetery was established. The Jewish population increased from 974 in 1873 to 2,659 in 1882, 6,399 in 1897, and 11,206 in 1909, mainly by immigration from the adjacent small towns. A pogrom in 1918 did not prevent the growth of the community, which by 1921 numbered 15,530 (37.6% of the total population), and by 1931, 18,083. Jews pioneered in exploiting the natural resources of the region and developed industries, commerce, and crafts; among enterprises established by Jews were several banks. Jewish organizations included associations of Jewish merchants and artisans, an old-age home, and an orphanage, as well as a library, a high school, and a number of religious and secular Jewish schools. A Yiddish weekly was published jointly for the Kielce and *Radom communities.

[William Glicksman]

Holocaust Period

In 1939 about 25,000 Jews lived in Kielce. The German army entered the city on Sept. 4, 1939, and the Jews became the subject of terror and persecution. During the first months of 1940 about 3,000 Jews from Cracow as well as Jews from Lodz and Lalisz and its vicinity were deported to Kielce, whose Jewish population swelled to about 28,000. On March 31, 1941, after 7,500 Jews arrived from Vienna, a decree was issued to establish a ghetto. On the eve of Passover the ghetto was sealed off from the outside world. A *Judenrat was appointed, chaired by Moshe Pelc, who was eventually arrested and deported to *Auschwitz for resisting German orders. His place was filled by Herman Levi, who tended toward collaboration with the Germans. The situation of the population in the ghetto rapidly deteriorated. About 4,000 people died during a typhus epidemic in 1941. In the course of three days (Aug. 20–24, 1942), about 21,000 Jews were deported to *Treblinka and exterminated. The ghetto was virtually liquidated. The remaining 2,000 Jews were concentrated in a newly established slave labor camp. Preparations in the camp for an armed rising, conducted by an underground organization headed by David Barwiner and Gershon Levkowicz, did not succeed. In 1943 a number of deportations from the labor camp took place of about 1,000 people for slave labor camps in *Skarzysko-Kamienna, Blizyna, and Pionki, where only a handful survived. The last deportation took place in August 1944, when all the remaining Jewish prisoners were sent to Auschwitz and Buchenwald. Kielce became officially *judenrein*. Leon Rodal of Kielce was one of the commanders of the *Warsaw Ghetto uprising.

Postwar Period

After the war about 200 Jews went to Kielce; some were survivors of Nazi camps, or had hidden in the district, and others had come back from the interior of the U.S.S.R. Their reconstruction of the former organized Jewish community aroused anger among Polish antisemites, who opened a vituperous campaign against the existence of a renewed Jewish community in Kielce. The campaign culminated in an armed pogrom against the Jews – mostly by Polish nationalists and including a few Communists (July 4, 1946). The Jews had no adequate means for self-defense since the police had confiscated the few pistols among them just one day previously. In this pogrom, the largest attack on Jews following the Nazi era, 60–70 Jews were murdered, including children and pregnant women, and around 100 were injured. The pogrom gave impetus to the Jews in Kielce and to the other Jewish survivors of the *Holocaust in Poland, including those who had returned from the Soviet Union, to leave Poland en masse for the West. They reached the *displaced persons camps and joined the massive **Beriḥah* movement to Ereẓ Israel. A monument was erected in the Kielce Jewish cemetery to perpetuate the memory of the victims of the Kielce pogrom. Organizations of former Kielce residents exist in Israel, the U.S., Canada, Argentina, and France.

[Stefan Krakowski]

BIBLIOGRAPHY: J. Lestschinsky, *Dos Yidishe Folk in Tsifern* (1922), 77–78; *Concise Statistical Yearbook of Poland*, 13 (1963), Eisenbach, in: *Bleter far Geshikhte*, 3:2–3 (1950), 3–62, and index; Rutkowski, in: BZIH, 15–16 (1955), 75–182; 17–18 (1956), 108–28; P. Meyer et al., *Jews in the Soviet Satellites* (1953), index; S. Mikołajczyk, *The Rape of Poland* (1948); A memorial book, *Sefer Kielts*, was published in 1957 (Heb., partly Yid.). **ADD. BIBLIOGRAPHY:** B. Szaynok, *Pogrom Zydow w Kielcach, 4 lipca 1946* (1992); D. Engel, *Bein Shiḥrur le-Beriḥah* (1996). Index; PK.

KIERA (also **Kyra**, **Kira**, **Chiera**), a Greek title meaning "lady," given to women who handled the relations of the wives in the Ottoman sultan's royal harem in various external matters. In general these women were Jewish. They acted as commercial intermediaries between the women in the harem and the world beyond it and thereby gained the former's trust. It appears that there were at least two women with the name of Esther who held this position. One was mentioned during the first half of the 16th century, as confidant of the mother of Selim II. Information is available on the activities of three kieras, and probably there are other Jewish women who filled the same position, but did not receive the title. The first known kiera was Strongilah (after her conversion her name was changed to Fatma (Fatima)) Kadin, who was apparently a Karaite from the Crimea. She was a daughter of Eliyah Gibor. She rendered various services to the ladies of the harem and became very close to Hafsa Sultan, the mother of *Suleiman the Magnificent, and died in 1548 after adopting Islam. When Suleiman ascended to the throne his mother managed to obtain for Strongilah and her descendants an exemption from taxes and permission to own non-Muslim slaves, The exemption, originally given in 1520/21, was reconfirmed in 1612, 1624/25, 1691/92, 1791/92, 1839/40 and 1867/68. Some of her children remained Jewish and appeared as a separate group in the poll tax registers with the designation "sons of Kurd" (one of her grandchildren).

The second kiera was Esther, the wife of the Jewish merchant Elijah *Handali, probably a Sephardi; she supplied jewelry to the women of the harem and rapidly became the confidant of Nur Banu, the favorite concubine of *Selim II and the mother of Murad III (1574–95), and died in about 1590.

She was certainly active before 1566. She exerted a decisive influence in court and state affairs during the second half of the 16th century. She attained powerful influence and special status. Her activity reached its climax with the settlement of a diplomatic conflict between the Ottomans and the Venetians during the 1580s and in the arrangement which granted several commercial privileges to the Venetians. In appreciation of this the Venetian government authorized her to organize a lottery in the city. In internal affairs of state, Esther assisted several individuals in purchasing honorific titles and positions – a trend which began to develop toward the close of the 16th century. She thus gained many friends for herself in the upper Ottoman circles, but also some enemies. In the Jewish community she was renowned for her generosity and extensive support of scholars and authors (e.g., the physician Samuel Sullam and R. Isaac *Akrish); she assisted Jewish merchants when the government sought to conspire against them; she even intervened in order to prevent the enforcement of Sultan Murad III's decree to destroy the Jewish community throughout the empire. After the great fire of 1569, she gave shelter and aid for a long period to many of the survivors. Samuel Sullam, who published a book she sponsored, wrote in the introduction that she had spent her entire fortune on charity. Through their mother her sons also amassed great wealth and obtained special privileges, mainly in the form of exemptions from taxes. The eldest leased the customs duties of the capital, *Istanbul, and enjoyed a special status among both the Jewish and foreign merchants.

The third kiera was Esperanza *Malchi (or Malkhi), who served as agent for Safiye, the consort of Murad III and the mother of Mehmed III (1595–1603). She played some part in a correspondence between Safiye and Queen Elizabeth I of England. She addressed at least one letter, in Italian, to Elizabeth in 1599, in which she identified herself as a Jewess. In this letter she dealt with the exchange of gifts between the two queens and suggested that in the future Elizabeth should not send jewels but rather cosmetics and fine cloths of silk and wool and advised Elizabeth to deliver these items for the Queen Mother only by her own hand. It is difficult to distinguish Handali from Malki except in a few documents in which their full names appear. It seems that the kiera was murdered on April 1, 1600, at the hands of rebellious, sword-wielding soldiers on the staircase of the house of Halil Pasha, the *kaimakam* of Istanbul. Enormous wealth was confiscated from Malki's estate after her death. Her fall occurred suddenly in 1600, and according to various testimonies it made a depressing impact on the Jewish community of Istanbul. It was due to several simultaneous factors: the rapid devaluation of the Ottoman currency which, among other things, was the cause of great discontent within the army; the extensive wealth of the family which attracted the attention of Sultan Mehmet III, who was in need of money; and the desire in various army and government circles to undermine the influence of the sultan's mother. The immediate cause of Malki's downfall was her intervention in a military appointment – she proposed a candidate of her own for a position which had been promised to someone else. The sipahis (cavalry) of the sultan, who sought to undermine the influence of the sultan's mother, rebelled on this occasion and demanded that Malki be handed over to them. The sultan gave his consent. The sipahis subsequently seized Esther and her eldest son and executed them. The second son disappeared and the third converted to Islam. All of the family's property was confiscated by the sultan's treasury.

Jewish kieras must have continued to serve the ladies of the imperial harem in the 17th century. In 1622, an unnamed Jewish woman with connections to the sister of Sultan Osman II (1618–22) was mentioned as having been involved in promoting the candidacy of Locadello to the office of governor of Moldavia. In 1709, another unnamed woman was believed to have helped the Jewish physician Daniel de *Fonseca pass on information to the mother of Sultan Ahmed III (1703–30) in order to bring about an Ottoman-Swedish alliance against Russia.

BIBLIOGRAPHY: Rosanes, Togarmah, 3 (1938), 65–66, 280–4; 4 (1934), 188–89; A. Galanté, *Esther Kyra d'après des nouveaux documents* (1926); J.H. Mordtmann, in: *Mitteilungen des Seminars fuer Orientalische Sprachen*, 32:2 (1929), 1–38; W. Foster (ed.), *Travels of John Sanderson in the Levant 1584–1602* (1931), 85–86, 185, 188, 201–4; C. Roth, *House of Nasi, Doña Gracia* (1947), 105–6, 202; idem, *Duke of Naxos* (1948), 200–2, 347; **ADD BIBLIOGRAPHY:** S.A. Skilliter, in: S.M. Stern (ed), *Oriental Studies*, 3. *Documents from Islamic Chanceries*, First Series (1965), 119–157; S.W. Baron, *Social and Religious History*, 18:145–146; A. Levy, in: A. Levy (ed), *The Jews of the Ottoman Empire* (1994), 29–30; L. Bornstein, *Ha-Hanhaga shel ha-Kehillah ha-Yehudit ba-Mizrah ha-Karov* (1978), 29, 391–92.; M.A. Epstein, *The Ottoman Jewish Communities and their Role in the Fifteenth and Sixteenth Centuries* (1980), 185; M. Rozen, in: *Michael*, 7 (1982), 195; idem, *A History of the Jewish Community in Istanbul, The Formative Years, 1453–1566* (2002). 204–205, 207, 262, 280; L.P. Pierce, *The Imperial Harem: Women and Sovereignty in the Ottoman Empire* (1993), 18, 40, 59–63, 78–79, 121, 126, 223, 225–226, 230, 277.

[Cecil Roth and Aryeh Shmuelevitz /
Leah Bornstein-Makovetsky (2nd ed.)]

KIESLER, FREDERICK JOHN (1896–1965), U.S. architect and scenic designer. Born in Vienna, Kiesler worked first as an architect, but by the mid-1920s had gained a European reputation as an avant-garde stage designer, promoting such innovations as theater in the round. He settled in New York in 1926 and from 1933 to 1957 was scenic director for the Juilliard School of Music. His revolutionary method of hanging pictures in the Museum of Modern Art (1942) gave rise to the term "environmental sculpture." Kiesler was joint designer of the "Shrine of the Book" at the Israel Museum, Jerusalem, to house the Dead Sea Scrolls.

KIEV (**Kiov**), capital of Ukraine.

The Jewish Community before 1667

Kiev's central position on the River Dnieper at the commercial crossroads of Western Europe and the Orient attracted Jewish settlers (*Rabbanites and *Karaites) from the foundation of the town in the eighth century C.E. At first most of them were transient merchants from both east and west. According to letters dated 930 from the Cairo *Genizah there were Jews in Kiev at this time. Ancient Russian chronicles relate that some Jews from *Khazaria visited Vladimir, the prince of Kiev, to try to convert him to Judaism (986). About that time a Jewish community already existed in the city. Jewish merchants from the West (Radanites) took part in the trade of the city, and were called in Hebrew sources "goers to Russia." The abbot of Kiev, Theodosius the Blessed (11th century), is said to have visited Jewish homes at night and to have held disputations with the householders. There were two Jewish suburbs of Kiev, Kozary and Zhidove. A "Gate of the Jews" is mentioned at the time of the riots which broke out on the death of Prince Svyatopolk (1113), when the populace also attacked Jewish houses and burned them. *Benjamin of Tudela mentions "Kiov, the great city," and *Pethahiah of Regensburg visited the town on his way to the Orient (12th century). At the end of the 12th century two Jews, Ephraim son of Moses and Anabel Jasin, served in the court of the prince Andrey Bogoliubski. During the same century *Moses of Kiev lived in the town. He corresponded with Jacob b. Meir *Tam in the west and the *gaon* *Samuel b. Ali in Baghdad. Under Tatar rule (1240–1320) the Jews had been protected, earning them the hatred of the Christian population. With the annexation of Kiev to the principality of Lithuania (1320), the Jews were granted certain rights ensuring the safety of their lives and property. Several of them (such as Simkha, Riabichka, Danilovich, and Shan in 1488) leased the collection of taxes and amassed fortunes. As the Jewish community increased in numbers so did the number of scholars, although the statement found in several sources, "from Kiev emanate Torah and light," is an exaggeration. During the 15th century *Moses (b. Jacob Ashkenazi the Exile) of Kiev II wrote commentaries on the *Sefer Yeẓirah*, on the Pentateuch commentaries of Abraham *Ibn Ezra and others, and held disputations with the Karaites. In the Tatar raid on Kiev (1482) many Jews were taken captive. In 1470 Zekharia, whom Russian sources link to the beginning of the Zhidovstvuyushchiye movement (Jewish heresy), left Kiev for Novgorod.

Like the rest of the Jews in the principality of Lithuania, the Kiev community was expelled in 1495. When the decree was revoked (1503), the community was reestablished. However, in 1619 the Christian merchants obtained from King Sigismund III a prohibition on permanent settlement of Jews or their acquisition of real estate in the town. They were allowed to come into Kiev for trading purposes alone and might remain one day only in an inn assigned to them. In spite of this, many Jews continued to live in the town under the protection of the Vojevoda (district governor) and noblemen in their properties in town (who saw them as a source of income). Russian sources relate that Jews were killed in Kiev during the *Chmielnicki massacres (1648). On the demand of the citizens, John II Casimir of Poland and Czar Alexis renewed the prohibition on Jewish settlement (1654). This became final with the annexation of Kiev to Russia (1667). The Russian Orthodox academy there fomented hatred of the Jews and its students attacked any Jew they found trading in the town.

From 1793

After a break of about 150 years the community of Kiev was reestablished in 1793, after the second partition of Poland. In 1798 the community acquired land for a cemetery. The earlier conflict between the Christian citizens and the Jews began once more. While the Jews struggled for settlement in Kiev, the economic and commercial center of the southwestern region of Russia, the citizens persistently endeavored to expel them, basing their claim on the status quo since Sigismund III and adding that "holy" Kiev was "profaned" by the presence of the Jews.

In spite of this in 1809 there were 452 Jews in Kiev (of about 20,000 total population), and their numbers rose by 1815 to about 1,500 (not including transients), with two synagogues and other communal institutions. The citizens proceeded with the demand to expel the Jews but owing to the negative stand of the governor, Czar Alexander I ordered them to leave the city. Eventually Czar *Nicholas I acceded to the demands of the citizens and at the end of 1827 residence in Kiev was forbidden to Jews. In part due to representations by state officials, who pointed out that the expulsion would worsen economic conditions in the town, the execution of the decree was twice deferred. In 1835, however, on the expiry of the last postponement, the Jews left the town, and the Jewish community facilities ceased to function. Despite this, they still played an important part in its economic life, for Jewish merchants came in their hundreds to the large annual fairs held from 1797 in Kiev in January. With their assistants and servants, they made up 50–60% of the fairs' participants. In 1843 Jewish temporary visitors were officially permitted, provided that they resided and bought food in two specially appointed inns. These were leased by the municipality to Christian agents, who were empowered to deliver to the police any Jew who did not stay in them. At the beginning of the reign of Alexander II these inns were abolished (1858), and instead a special payment to the municipality was levied upon the Jews as compensation for the losses caused by the abolishment of the inns. In 1861 two suburbs, Lyebed and Podol, were assigned to those Jews entitled to reside in Kiev (wealthy merchants and industrialists and their employees, members of the free professions, and craftsmen). The number of Jews in Kiev increased to 3,013 (3% of the total population) in 1863 and to 13,803 (11.8%) in 1872.

In May 1881 a pogrom raged in the streets of the city, supported and encouraged by the governor-general, General Drenteln. Jewish houses and shops were looted, and many people were injured; 762 families were completely ruined. The damage caused was evaluated at 1,750,000 roubles. From that date the authorities began sporadically to investigate the residence rights of the Jews in Kiev. Until 1917 the city became notorious for the police "*oblavy*" ("hunt attacks") for Jews without residence rights. For example, expelled in 1883 were 1,179 persons, in 1884 1,254, in 1885 1,368, and in the first half of 1886 2,076. The night searches and expulsions continued almost until WWI. In 1891 the authorities ordered that a considerable portion of the income of the Jewish community be allotted to the police to cover the cost of their measures to prevent Jews' entering the town. In spite of all these persecutions, the number of Jews in Kiev continued to increase. From 31,801 (12.8%) in 1897, it rose to 50,792 (10.8%) in 1910 and 81,256 (13%) at the end of 1913. In fact the number of Jews was greater, since a large number evaded the census. Many Jews also lived in the suburbs and townlets around Kiev and only came into the city daily on business. There were some wealthy Jewish families in Kiev, who included many of the magnates of the southwestern Russian sugar industry (the *Brodsky and Zaitsev families). Many Jews were employed in their factories in the town and the vicinity. There was a very active branch of the Society for Enlightenment of Russian Jews, which maintained 21 Jewish schools in the town and the district, as well as a library of 6,500 books. The city also had many Jewish physicians, lawyers, and other members of the liberal professions. Kiev University attracted Jewish youth; in 1886 Jewish students numbered 236 and in 1911, 888 (17% of the total number of students), the largest concentration of Jewish students in a Russian university. In Kiev were born Golda Meir (Mabovich), who became prime minister of Israel, the writer Ilya *Ehrenburg, and some Hebrew writers, notably J. Kaminer, J.L. *Levin (Yehalel), M. Kamionski, I.J. Weissberg, E. *Schulman, and A.A. Friedman. *Shalom Aleichem, who lived in Kiev for some time, described the town in his account of life in Yehupets. According to the 1897 census, 29,937 Jews (out of 31,801) declared Yiddish as their mother language. There were 12,317 who earned incomes, divided into three main groups: artisans (42%), merchants (24%), and army service (10%). The artisans were mainly occupied as follows: the clothing industry (54%), metal works (11%), woodworking (9%), and printing (6%). The main occupations of traders were in farm products (34%), textiles and clothing (16%), and building materials (7%). The Jewish merchants constituted 44% of all the merchants in Kiev.

In the wake of Jewish revolutionary activity, a large-scale pogrom occurred on Oct. 18, 1905. Neither army nor police controlled the rioters, who ran amok unhindered for three days. Indeed, soldiers protected the hooligans from the Jewish *self-defense organization. The rioters attacked the houses of the wealthy, but their attacks were mainly directed against the poor suburbs. However, the pogrom did not interrupt the development of the community, which became one of the wealthiest in Russia as well as one of the most diversified socially. In 1910 there were 4,896 Jewish merchants in the town, 42% of all the merchants there, but nevertheless 25% of the community had to apply for Passover alms during that same year. The community was officially recognized in 1906 as the "Jewish Representation for Charity Affairs at the Municipal Council." Its income from the meat tax (see **korobka*) and other sources amounted to 300,000 rubles annually. A Jewish hospital for the poor which served the whole of Ukraine was opened in 1862, followed by a hospital specializing in surgery, a clinic for eye diseases (under the direction of M. *Mandelstamm), and other welfare institutions. In 1898 a magnificent central synagogue was built by means of a donation from L. *Brodsky. From 1906 to 1921 S. *Aronson was rabbi of Kiev; notable as **kazyonny ravvin* ("government-appointed rabbi") were Joshua Zuckerman, the first to be appointed to this office, and S.Z. Luria. Between 1911 and 1913 Kiev was the site of the notorious *Beilis blood libel trial and the town was then racked by the agitation of the members of the *Union of Russian People ("Black Hundreds"). In 1911, after the assassination of prime minister Stolypin by a Jew in Kiev, severe pogroms were on the point of breaking out there, but the authorities decided to restrain the rioters.

During World War I, residence restrictions in the town were lifted for Jewish refugees from the battle areas. The years 1917–20 were years of upheaval for the Jews of Kiev. With the February 1917 Revolution, all the residence restrictions were abolished and Jews at once began to stream into the town. In the census at the end of 1917, 87,246 Jews (19% of the total population) were registered. A democratic community was established, led by the Zionist Moses Nahum *Syrkin. Meetings and congresses of Russian and Ukrainian Jews were held in Kiev, the central institutions of Ukrainian Jewry were set up there, and Jewish writers and communal workers of every shade of opinion and party became active in the town. Books and newspapers were published and cultural institutions, led by the Hebrew *Tarbut and the Yiddish Kultur Lige, engaged in a variety of activities. In the spring of 1919, the number of Jews had grown to 114,524 (21%).

With the first conquest of the town by the Red Army, which lasted from February to August 1919, Kiev became a haven for refugees from the pogroms sweeping the provincial towns of Ukraine. The running of the Jewish community was handed over to the *Yevsektsiya, and the systematic destruction of communal institutions, traditional Jewish culture, and national parties began. With the retreat of the Red Army, an attempt was made to form a Jewish self-defense unit. When *Petlyura's forces entered the city they arrested the members of the self-defense unit and 36 of them were executed. A month after Kiev was occupied by *Denikin's "Volunteer Army," thugs initiated a period of pillage, rape, and murder of the Jews which lasted until the "Volunteers" were driven out by the Red Army (December 1919). The Jews in Kiev suffered heavily during the famine and typhus outbreak of 1920. In the August 1920 census they constituted one third of the town's population. In 1923 Kiev had 128,041 Jews (32%), 140,256 (27.3%) in 1926, and in 1939, 224,236 (of a total population of 845,726).

In the years 1920–22 the famine and typhus epidemic ravaged Kiev and took a heavy toll on the Jewish population. OZE, the JDC, and other relief organizations from abroad organized food and medical help. The Jews went through a process of proletarianization, engaging in physical labor or crafts; later in the second half of the 1920s half of them were government employees. In 1926, 16,690 Jews were members of trade unions (out of 77,257). The number of Jews in heavy industry grew to 4,080 in 1932. In 1931 they constituted 80% of the 3,300 workers of the shoe factory.

During the first 20 years of the Soviet regime, Kiev became a major center of the officially fostered Yiddish culture, with a school system catering to many thousands of pupils and students, culminating in institutes of higher education and learning, such as the department for Jewish culture at the Ukrainian Academy of Sciences (1926) which in 1930 became the "Institute of Proletarian Jewish Culture" under the direction of Joseph Liberberg. This state-sponsored activity attracted even Jewish writers and scholars from the west, such as Meir *Wiener and others. Some valuable research works on Yiddish language and literature were published there. Many Yiddish poets and writers, among them David *Hofstein and Itzik *Feffer, lived and wrote in Kiev. There were also the All-Ukrainian Jewish State Theater, a Yiddish children's theater, Yiddish newspapers, journals, and publishing houses. In the early 1930s Liberberg and some of his associates headed a group of Yiddish intellectuals who went to the newly established Jewish autonomous region in *Birobidzhan to organize Jewish educational and cultural work there in conjunction with the Jewish academic institute in Kiev. Several years later, with the forcible liquidation of all Jewish institutions, including libraries and archives in Kiev, one of the most important centers of Soviet Yiddish culture ceased to exist.

[Yehuda Slutsky]

Holocaust Period

The fall of the city to the Germans on Sept. 19, 1941 marked the end of Kiev Jewry. A considerable part of the Jews living in Kiev in 1939 were among the 335,000 evacuees; some managed to flee eastward to central Russia, just before the Nazi occupation. Between September 20–24 buildings in the Khreshchatik area where headquarters of German military units were housed blew up, and many German soldiers and officers were killed. Thousands of hostages, among them many Jews, were taken and executed. On September 26 the city commander convened a meeting in which participated Friedrich Jaeckeln, commander of police and SS on the Southern Front; Dr. Otto Rash, head of *Einsatzgruppe* C; and SS Colonel Paul Blobel, commander of *Einsatzkommando* 4a. It was decided to annihilate all the Jews of Kiev. Blobel was in charge of the execution, with the help of units of the German Police and Ukrainian Auxiliary Police. On September 28 (Tishri 7) 2,000 notices in German, Ukrainian, and Russian were posted in Kiev, announcing that "All the Zhids (Jews) of Kiev and the suburbs are to appear on Monday, September 29, 1941, at 8:00 A.M. on the corner of Melnikovskaya and Decktiarovska streets [near the cemeteries]. They are to bring their documents, money, other valuables and warm clothes, linen, etc. Any Zhid found disobeying these orders will be shot. Citizens breaking into flats left by the Jews and taking possession of their belongings will be shot." (For Jew the derogatory word "*zhid*" was used and not the usual *evrei*.) Since the location was near the Petrovski goods railway station, and owing to the rumors about evacuation of the Jews to other towns or camps, nobody suspected what was coming. On the morning of September 29, tens of thousands of Jews concentrated there were led through Melnik Street to the Jewish cemetery in the Babi Yar ravine, stripped naked, and led in groups to the edge of the ravine, where they were machine-gunned, their bodies falling into the ravine. At the end of the day heaps of earth were thrown over the bodies, burying both dead and wounded. According to the official report of the S.S. unit in charge of the mass extermination, 33,771 Jews were murdered in Babi Yar on Sept. 29–30, 1941. A later report said that about 36,000 Jews were killed then.

Babi Yar continued to be a mass execution ground throughout the German occupation. On October 1–3 *Einsatzkommando* 5 murdered in Babi Yar 2,500–3,000 Jews, including 308 mentally ill. All the time Jewish prisoners of war, mostly from Darnitsa camp, were executed. Hiding in the city were many Jews, some in mixed marriages. Many of them were denounced by local Ukrainians, caught, and shot. From spring 1942, Jews who were caught were sent to labor camps in the city, such as that on Kerosinnaya Street (5,000 prisoners of war and 3,000 Jews), Pecherskaya Street, and Institutskaya Street. The number of inmates diminished due to selections, starvation, and daily killings. In May 1942 the Syretsk camp (near Babi Yar) was opened, and in December it housed 2,000 inmates, more than a third of them Jews. The regime was very cruel – prisoners were shot for the smallest infraction or for not being able to work. On August 18, 1943, 100 prisoners from Syretsk were taken to Babi Yar, and soon the group was enlarged to 321 inmates. Their task was to eradicate any sign of the mass graves in the ravine. A bonfire was made from railway ties, and excavators opened the graves. The prisoners, whose legs were in chains, took the bodies, searched them for valuables and gold teeth and fillings, and threw them into the bonfire; any bones remaining were ground, and the ashes spread around and leveled. A garden was planted on the site. The prisoners lived in two bunkers dug into the wall of the ravine, kept closed by an iron grate that was shut for the night; opposite them was a machine gun position. The Russian Fedor Yershov, a senior KGB officer, organized an escape group. They managed to find a key to the grates, a wire cutter to cut the chains, and a few knives. On September 28, 1943, they learned through the interpreter (a Jewish prisoner) Yakov Steyuk (Stein) that their work was finished and that the following day they were to be shot and cremated. At about 3 A.M. on September 29, they cut the chains, opened the grates, and escaped under the cover of fog. Many were machine-gunned, among them the leader Yershov, and only 15 succeeded in remaining alive until the liberation of Kiev on November 6, 1943 – among them nine Jews. The State Commission to Investigate Nazi Crimes in Kiev could not locate graves to exhume in Babi Yar, so they set the approximate number at 100,0000. According to Steyuk, who reported daily to the Germans on the numbers of burned bodies, an estimated 45,000 belonged to Jews. To this number we may add figures attained from other exhumed mass graves, such as Syretsk, Darnitsa, and reach an approximate number of 60,000 Jewish victims. Jews were active in the city's underground, including Shimon Bruz, one of the underground city party committee who died in a fight with the Gestapo, and Tania Markus, who carried out various sabotage acts and was caught and executed in summer 1942.

In the struggle against *antisemitism in the Soviet Union, Babi Yar became a symbol of pro-Jewish support, crystallized in the poem *Babi Yar* by Yevgenii *Yevtushenko. Despite recurring requests by Soviet intellectuals, including Yevtushenko and Viktor Nekrasov, the Soviet authorities refused to erect a monument to those massacred there. Jewish survivors made attempts to hold a memorial day each year, circumspectly choosing the eve of the Day of Atonement. When in early 1959 the ravine was filled with earth, and Babi Yar was turned into a new residential area, there were protests from Jews and non-Jews alike. In 1961 a flood swept away the earth and destroyed the houses; many people were drowned. At the end of the 1960s, the ravine of Babi Yar remained a desolate wasteland. "In Babi Yar there is neither monument nor memorial" (Yevtushenko). It was only in 1976 that a stone with an inscription was put there, but it mentioned Soviet citizens, not Jews.

[Benjamin West / Shmuel Spector (2nd ed.)]

After World War II

At the end of World War II, when thousands of Jews began to return to liberated Kiev, they often encountered a hostile attitude on the part of the Ukrainian population, many of whom had been given, or had taken, the dwellings and jobs of the absent Jews. There were even isolated physical clashes between Jews and Ukrainians. In the 1959 census, their number was 154,000 (13.9% of the total population). Nearly 15% of them declared Yiddish to be their mother tongue. Out of about 14,000 Jews living in the smaller towns of the Kiev district, around 33% declared Yiddish to be their mother tongue. In 1979 there were 132,000 Jews in the city.

The only synagogue in Kiev, with room for about 1,000 persons, was situated downtown in the Podol quarter. On holidays, particularly on the Day of Atonement, also the memorial day of the Babi Yar massacre, several thousands attended the service, overflowing into the courtyard and the street. A number of services (**minyanim*) were held in private homes, but when their existence was discovered, they were closed and the owners severely punished. A *mikveh*, a place for the ritual slaughtering of poultry, and a *maẓẓah* bakery were attached to the synagogue. From 1960 until 1966 the baking of *maẓẓah* was prohibited and several Jews were punished for baking them illegally in their homes. The last rabbi to officiate in Kiev was Rabbi Panets, who retired in 1960 and died in 1968; a new rabbi was not appointed. Until 1960 the synagogue board's chairman was Bardakh; the atmosphere was relatively relaxed, and visitors from abroad, who arrived in increasing numbers from the late 1950s, were cordially received. The situation changed abruptly in 1961, when a new board, headed by Gendelman, was appointed. Gendelman, in an aggressive manner, implemented meticulously the instructions of the Soviet authorities, harassed members of the congregation, and prevented any contact between them and foreign visitors. He was eventually forced to resign in 1967 because of the growing tension between him and the congregation.

In 1959, on the 100th anniversary of the birth of *Shalom Aleichem, a plaque was affixed to the house where he lived before World War I, bearing the text: "Here lived the famous Jewish writer Shalom Aleichem (Rabinovich)." Shortly afterward the plaque was replaced by a new one on which the words "famous Jewish" and "Rabinovich" were omitted. In May 1966 a group of Kiev Jews went to Moscow and submitted a petition to Mikhailova of the Central Committee of the Communist Party, about the establishment of a Yiddish theater in Kiev. The petition stressed the fact that 82 Jewish actors were ready to participate. M. Goldblat, one of the survivors of the Yiddish theater in the U.S.S.R. and the last director of the Yiddish theater in Kiev, declared his readiness to organize the new Yiddish theater. The petition also included a list of plays by Jewish Soviet and classic writers for the repertoire. The petition was rejected.

In 1957 four elderly Jews were sentenced in Kiev to several years of imprisonment for "Zionist activity." One of them was Baruch Mordekhai Weissman, whose Hebrew written diary about the "black years" was smuggled out and published anonymously in Israel, under the title "To my Brother in the State of Israel" (1957). At the trial Weissman was not accused of smuggling out his manuscript, but of keeping Hebrew newspapers and participating in a "Zionist circle."

In 1959 the Kiev municipality opened a new Jewish cemetery and decided to close the old one at Lukyanovka, near Babi Yar, which had been desecrated and partly destroyed during the Nazi occupation. Local and foreign Jews were allowed to transfer the remains of their relatives to the new cemetery if they defrayed the expenses involved. American rabbis arranged for the transfer of the remains of the ḥasidic rabbis of the Twersky family, and the president of Israel, Iẓhak Ben-Zvi, received permission from the Soviet head of state to transfer to Israel the remains and the tombstone of his friend Ber *Borochov (1963).

Kiev continued to be a center of Yiddish writers, many of whom had served terms of imprisonment under Stalin. Among them were Itzik Kipnis, Hirsh Polyanker, Nathan Zbara, Eli Schechtman, and Yehiel Falikman. Several books in Yiddish and translations in Russian and Ukrainian were published between 1960 and 1970. The Ukrainian authorities usually prevented Jewish cultural events from being held in the city.

During the campaigns against "economic crimes" two Jews, B. Mirski and Shtifzin, who worked in a Kiev publishing house for art books, were sentenced to death (1962). At that time the local Ukrainian press indulged in almost undisguised antisemitic incitement. This campaign culminated in the publication of T. Kichko's notorious "Judaism without Embellishment" by the Academy of Sciences of the Ukrainian Republic (1963). Though the book was later censured by the ideological commission of the Central Committee of the Soviet Communist Party in Moscow, Kichko reappeared in 1968 with a new anti-Jewish book, "Judaism and Zionism," and was rewarded by the authorities for his achievements in "anti-religious education."

The refusal of the municipal authorities to erect a memorial in Babi Yar, after an exhibition of models for such a memorial was officially arranged in 1965, was ascribed to the popular antisemitic atmosphere prevailing in the city. Protests against this omission were voiced by Russian and Ukrainian writers (e.g., Y. Yevtushenko, V. Nekrasov, Ivan Dzyuba, and others).

When an international poultry exhibition took place in Kiev in 1966, and Israel was represented by a stand equipped with exhibits and explanatory literature, tens of thousands of Jews from Kiev and all over the Ukraine streamed there. After the Six-Day War (1967), Jewish national feeling reemerged publicly in Kiev. The anniversary of Babi Yar became a rallying day for Jews, most of them young, who came not only to recite *Kaddish* but also to express their Jewish identification. Wreaths bearing inscriptions in Yiddish and Hebrew were laid and there were occasional attempts to make speeches, but on every such occasion the police intervened to remove the wreaths and silence the speakers. After one such gathering a young Jewish engineer, Boris Kochubiyevski, was arrested in 1968 on the charge of "spreading slander against the Soviet regime," after he and his non-Jewish wife Larissa had applied for an exit permit to Israel. In May 1969 he was sentenced to three years' imprisonment with hard labor. At his trial Kochubiyevski made a passionate speech, declaring his Zionist credo. In summer 1970 an open letter was published abroad, addressed to the prime minister of Israel, Golda Meir, to UN Secretary General U Thant, and to various international institutions, signed by ten Jews from Kiev who claimed the right to settle in Israel. In August 1970 the same ten persons wrote a second letter to President Shazar, making it known that, after having been refused exit permits, they had renounced their Soviet citizenship and asked to become citizens of Israel.

Though most of Kiev's Jews emigrated in the 1990s, Jewish life revived at the community level as the city became the seat of the Ukrainian chief rabbinate and a Jewish day school was opened.

[Zvi Ofer]

BIBLIOGRAPHY: A. Harkavy, *Ḥadashim gam Yeshanim* (1886–1912), no. 1, 6–12; no. 2, 13–17; I.N. Darevsky, *Le-Korot ha-Yehudim be-Kiev* (1902); Ettinger, in: *Zion*, 21 (1956), 107–42; idem, in: Roth, Dark Ages, index; Gurevich, in: *Shriftn far Ekonomik un Statistik*, 1 (1928), 104–5; J. Lestschinsky, in: *Bleter far Yidishe Demografye, Statistik un Ekonomik*, 5 (1925), 149–67; A. Druyanow, in: *Reshummot*, 3 (1923), 221–36; A.A. Friedman, *Sefer ha-Zikhronot* (1926), 195–227, 315–97; A. Golomb, *A Halber Yorhundert Yidishe Dertsiung* (1957), 95–114; B. Dinur, *Bi-Ymei Milḥamah u-Mahpekhah* (1960), 311–420; A. Pomeranz, *Di sovietishe Harugei Malkhus* (1962), 44–60, passim; *Die Judenpogrome in Russland*, 2 (1909), 339–406; G. Reitlinger, *Final Solution* (1953), 233–5; M. Malishevski, *Yevrei v yuzhoy Rossii i v Kiyeve v x–xii vekakh* (1878); I. Zinberg, in: *Yevreyskaya Starina*, 11 (1924), 93–109; M. Kulisher, *ibid.*, 6 (1913), 351–66; Y. Galant, *ibid.*, 264–78; idem, in: *Zbirnyk prats Zhydivskoyi istorychno-arkheografichnoyi komisii*, 1 (1928), 149–97; Rybynsky, in: *Yubileyny zbirnyk D.I. Bagalya* (1927), 938–55; E. Turats, *K istorii kiyevskogo pogroma* (1906); P.T. Neyshtube, *Kiyevskaya yevreyskaya bolnitsa 1862–1912* (1912); Badanes, in: *Vestnik yevreyskoy obshchiny*, 2 (1914), 49–54; 3 (1914), 33–37; Polyakov, in: *Yevreyskaya Letopis*, 2 (1923), 17–36; 3 (1924), 60–70.

KIEVAL, HAYYIM (**Herman**) (1920–1991), Conservative rabbi and scholar of Jewish liturgy. Kieval was born and raised in Baltimore where he studied with Dr. Louis *Kaplan at Baltimore Hebrew College and with Prof. William F. *Albright at Johns Hopkins. He received an M.H.L. and was ordained as a rabbi by the *Jewish Theological Seminary (JTS) in 1942.

Kieval served as a congregational rabbi for over 40 years, including 31 years at Temple Israel in Albany, New York. The congregation created its own day school as well as a Hebrew-speaking day camp called Camp Givah. It also produced scholars of international renown such as Robert Alter and Robert Chazin as well as numerous rabbis. He was heavily involved in ecumenical work, teaching at Notre Dame University, Princeton Theological Seminary, and Siena College, where he founded and directed the Institute for Jewish-Christian Studies.

Kieval's main academic interest was Jewish liturgy. From 1958 to 1980 he served as visiting associate professor of liturgy in the Cantorial School of the Jewish Theological Seminary. He also served as committee member or advisor for Conservative prayer books (1961–85) and published a series of scholarly articles about Jewish liturgy. His *magnum opus* is *The High Holy Days: A Commentary on the Prayerbook of Rosh Hashanah and Yom Kippur.* Book One on Rosh Hashanah was published in 1959. It was republished together with Book Two: *Kol Nidre Night* in 2004. The text is aimed at laypeople while the footnotes are intended for rabbis and scholars. It is considered by many to be the best English-language commentary on the High Holiday Mahzor.

[David Golinkin (2nd ed.)]

KIKOINE, MICHEL (1891–1968), French painter, born in Gomel, Russia, and a member of the School of Paris. As a Jew he was not permitted to study art at the Royal Academy in St. Petersburg, and therefore moved to Paris in 1912 where he joined the Académie des Beaux Arts and associated with his fellow Russian Jews, *Soutine and Kremègne. Kikoine visited Israel in 1950 and 1953. In 1956 he executed a series of colored lithographs titled *Children of Israel*.

Primarily a colorist, Kikoine claimed to be influenced by Courbet, with his feeling for the organic life of nature. His paintings of figures and landscape are subtle and poetic, making a slow impact.

BIBLIOGRAPHY: *Catalogue of Exhibition at the Redfern Gallery, London* (1955), introduction; George, in: Roth, Art, 660–1.

KILAYIM (Heb. כִּלְאַיִם), the name of a tractate in the Mishnah, Tosefta and Jerusalem Talmud dealing with several biblical prohibitions of mixed species.

The Torah (Lev. 19:19; Deut. 22:9–11) lists a number of different examples of mixtures that are prohibited as mixed species. The *halakhah* reflected in the Mishnah and related works classifies the prohibitions under at least five categories: (1) interbreeding of animals (Ch. 8); (2) planting mixed seeds (Chs. 2 and 3), understood to include the grafting of trees (1:4, 7–8); (3) *sha'atnez*: mixing wool and linen in garments (Ch. 9); (4) planting grain or greens in a vineyard (Chs. 4–7); (5) ploughing or doing other work with two different species of animal (8:2–4). In its ten chapters, the Mishnah *Kilayim* deals with the regulations governing all five. In contrast to the assumption of the rabbinic *halakhah*, mixed seeds was not accepted as a separate biblical prohibition by some early traditions, who applied the relevant scriptural expression to the prohibition of grain in a vineyard. Although the *kil'a'im* laws themselves were derived from a relatively straightforward reading of the Torah, the details discussed in the tractate were deduced through the exercise of logic, analogies with other areas of law, or by application of the general rules to specific objects and situations. Jewish thinkers through the ages have speculated about the rationale for this prohibition, or have classified it as an unexplained or mysterious ordinance; however, the Mishnah and talmudic works deal with the technicalities of deriving and applying the law and not with its purpose.

Because the prohibitions only apply to the mixing of distinct species, but not to variants of a single species, Mishnah 1:1–6 deals with the botanical or biological classifications of seeds, trees or animals with a view to determining which are or are not separate species. There is evidence that the earlier stratum of *halakhah*, as represented by Beit Shammai, held to a stricter position that forbade even the mixing of sub-species (see Tosefta and Jerusalem Talmud 1:4). The rabbis' interpretations can be better understood when compared with ancient naturalists, as well as with the agricultural realia of Israel. Important contributions to the elucidation of *kilayim* from those perspectives have been made by I.E. Loew, S. Lieberman, and J. Feliks. On the whole, the halakhic classifications seem to owe more to popular usage and terminology than to scientific biology.

Questions dealt with in the Mishnah include the amount or proportion of the prohibited species that renders the field prohibited; separation of different species by visible barriers or distances (Ch. 3); procedures for changing a field over from one crop to another without leaving forbidden traces of the previous crop (3:6–7). Suggestions are offered on how to grow several species of greens of legumes in a small patch by separating them into distinct geometric patterns (3:1 etc.).

The prohibition of *kilayim* in the vineyard is spelled out very clearly in the Torah, along with the explicit penalty "lest the fruit of your seed which you have sown, and the fruit of your vineyard, be defiled"; hence it is treated more stringently, and the produce of such a mixture does not become permitted after the fact, as would occur in the case of mixed seeds.

The sages cited in the Mishnah *Kilayim* cover all the generations of tannaitic activity, from the days of the Temple (Eliezer ben Jacob) through to the scholars of Jabneh, Rabbi Akiva and his principal disciples. The Jerusalem Talmud, in addition to its commentary on the laws of the Mishnah and Tosefta, contains an aggadic digression (9:3, 32b) with biographical and hagiographical stories about Rabbi *Judah ha-Nasi and his contemporaries, material that was reworked in a less authentic version in TB, BM 83bff.).

BIBLIOGRAPHY: J. Feliks, *Ha-Ḥakla'ut be-Ereẓ Yisrael bi-Tekufat ha-Mishnah ve-ha-Talmud.* (1963); idem, *Kilei Zera'im ve-Harkavah: Masekhet Kilayim* (1967); S. Friedman, "*La-Aggadah ha-Historit ba-Talmud ha-Bavli*," in: S. Friedman (ed.), *S. Lieberman Memorial Volume* (1993), 335, 11p.; I. Loew, *Die Flore der Juden* (1967); I. Mandelbaum, *A History of the Mishnaic Law of Agriculture: Kilayim* (1982); I. Mandelbaum, *The Talmud of the Land of Israel: A Preliminary Translation and Explanation: Kilayim.* Chicago Studies in the History of Judaism, eds. J. Neusner, W.S. Green, and C. Goldscheider (1990).

[Stephen G. Wald (2nd ed.)]

KILIYA (Rom. **Chilia-Nouǎ**), city in Izmail district, Bessarabia, today Moldova. Jews are first mentioned there in 1545. In the latter part of the century Jewish merchants from Constantinople used to pass through Kiliya on their way to Lvov. Information on a Jewish community is available only from the early 18th century (1713; 1715). There were 27 Jewish families (out of a total of 478) in 1808, and 249 persons in 1827. The community grew as a result of Jewish immigration into Bessarabia during the 19th century, and numbered 2,153 (18.5% of the total) in 1897. In 1930 there were 1,969 Jews (11.3% of the total). Before World War II the communal institutions included two old-age homes and a *Tarbut school and kindergarten. In 1940 it was annexed by the Soviet Union and incorporated in the Moldavian SSR. The Jews were transferred to Bolgrad and killed there by the German and Romanian armies when they entered Bessarabia in July 1941.

[Eliyahu Feldman]

KIMBERLEY, city in the Western Province of the Cape Province, South Africa, center of the South African diamond industry. Jews flocked to Kimberley on the discovery of diamonds there in 1870, and as early as 1871 a congregation, named the Griqualand West Hebrew Congregation, was formed, and the first synagogue was built in 1876. Among the early settlers were Barney *Barnato, his brother Harry, and his cousin David (later Sir David) *Harris. The first temporary minister was the Rev. Joel *Rabinowitz who returned to South Africa from England after his retirement. The first permanent minister was Meyer Mendelsohn. Until the founding of Johannesburg in 1886, Kimberley was home to the second largest Jewish community in South Africa, numbering over 2,000 souls at its peak. No fewer than five Jews have served as mayors of Kimberley: William Sagar (1906–08), Ernest (later Sir Ernest)

Oppenheimer (1913–15), Bernard Cohen (1931–32), Gustave Haberfeld (1953–55, 1966–67), Lionel Jawno (1959–61), and C. Sussman (1964–65). Sir David Harris, who also commanded the Kimberley Town Guard during the famous Boer siege of the town in the Anglo-Boer War, was MP for Kimberley and Griqualand West from 1897–1929. The discovery of gold on the Rand drew many Jews from Kimberley to Johannesburg. By 1970, the Jewish population of Kimberley had dropped to about 600 and by 2005, fewer than 50 Jews remained.

[Louis Isaac Rabinowitz / David Saks (2nd ed.)]

KIMCHE, JON (1909–1994), British editor and author. Born in Switzerland, he was educated in England where he took up journalism and specialized in Middle East affairs. From 1942 to 1946 he was editor of the Labour weekly *Tribune*. Kimche was a close friend of George Orwell, whom he first met in 1934 when they both worked as assistants in a bookshop in Hampstead, London. Kimche edited the *Jewish Observer and Middle East Review*, published by the British Zionist Federation, from 1952 to 1967. From 1968 he edited the monthly *New Middle East*. He wrote several books on the Middle East, including *Both Sides of the Hill* (1960), an account of the Israeli War of Liberation, written with his brother David Kimche; *Seven Fallen Pillars* (1953); and *The Unromantics* (1968), dealing with the Balfour Declaration.

ADD. BIBLIOGRAPHY: S. Wadhams (ed.), *Remembering Orwell* (1984).

KIMḤI, DAVID (known as **Radak** from the acronym of **R**abbi **D**avid **K**imḥi; **Maistre Petit**; 1160?–1235?), grammarian and exegete of Narbonne, Provence. The son of Joseph *Kimḥi and brother and pupil of Moses *Kimḥi, David was a teacher in his native town and was active in public causes. He is known to have participated in the judgment (between 1205 and 1218) of several contentious persons from Barcelona who dishonored the memory of Rashi. During the Maimonidean controversy of 1232, he undertook a journey to Toledo to gain the support of Judah *Ibn Alfakhar for the Maimonideans. He was prevented from reaching his destination because of illness but his strong defense of Maimonides and the latter's followers together with Ibn Alfakhar's critique of Kimḥi have been preserved in the correspondence between them (in *Kovez Teshuvot ha-Rambam*, Leipzig, 1859, pt. 3).

Philology

Kimḥi's first work was his philological treatise, the *Mikhlol*, written in two sections; the grammatical portion (*Ḥelek ha-Dikduk*) which itself came to be known as the *Mikhlol* (Constantinople, 1532), and the lexicon (*Ḥelek ha-Inyan*) known independently as the *Sefer ha-Shorashim* (before 1480). Kimḥi's purpose in composing the *Mikhlol* was to provide a middle ground between the lengthy and detailed treatises of Jonah *Ibn Janaḥ and Judah b. David *Ḥayyuj and the extreme brevity and concision of Abraham *Ibn Ezra and the elder Kimḥis. His chief contribution in grammar lies in the arrangement of the material and the popularization of the innovations of his father and brother. These include the division of the vowels into five long and five short, the treatment of the *nifal* as the passive of the *kal*, the recognition of the *dagesh lene*, etc. Seeing himself only as a "gleaner after the reapers," Kimḥi nevertheless made some original contributions, including his distinguishing of the *vav* consecutive (*vav ha-sherut*) from the *vav* conjunctive and his concern for the continued development of the language through the recognition of the legitimacy of post-biblical forms. In point of fact, Kimḥi was criticized for being highly unconventional as a grammarian by such figures as Joseph ibn *Kaspi, Profiat *Duran, David b. Solomon *Ibn Yaḥya, and Abraham de *Balmes. He found advocates, however, in the *Magen David* of Abraham b. Elisha b. Mattathias, the *Mikhlol Yofi* of Solomon ibn Melekh, and the writings of Elijah *Levita, and it was due to the *Mikhlol* and the *Shorashim* that most of the works of his predecessors sank into oblivion. In Jewish circles, the phrase "If there is no flour [*kemaḥ*, etymon of Kimḥi], there is no Torah" (Avot 3:17) was applied to him, while his influence on the Christian Hebraists of the Renaissance was profound. *Reuchlin's *Rudimenta Linguae Hebraicae* and *Lexicon Hebraicum* (1506) and Santes Pagninus' *Institutiones* (1520) and *Thesaurus* (1529) are basically reworkings of Kimḥi, while Sebastian *Muenster's writings betray his influence heavily.

Masorah

Much of the material in the *Mikhlol* was abridged in the *Et Sofer* (Lyck, 1864), a manual for copyists of the Bible, necessitated by widespread ignorance among scribes and the proliferation of biblical manuscript traditions in the 12th century. In it he treats in detail such problems as the *keri* and the *ketiv* and the accents. His interest in masorah was not limited to this treatise, for numerous observations in this area are recorded in the commentaries. Especially noteworthy is his theory that the *keri* and the *ketiv* developed out of a confusion of readings in the time of the men of the *Great Synagogue who, according to him, established the text ("Introduction to Joshua"). His concern for the establishment of the correct text is attested to by his travels in pursuit of old manuscripts.

Exegesis

Kimḥi began his exegetical activity with a commentary to the Book of Chronicles (in Rabbinic Bible, Venice, 1548) written in response to the request of a student of his father's for an exegesis of that book in accordance with the plain sense or *derekh ha-peshat* in contrast to the homiletic commentaries which were then prevalent. This was followed by commentaries to Genesis (ed. by R.L. Kirchheim, 1842), all the prophetic books (Guadalajara, 1482), and Psalms (1477). In all of these, Kimḥi endeavored to utilize the methodology of Ibn Ezra and the elder Kimḥis, stressing scientific philological analysis and de-emphasizing homiletical digression. Unlike these predecessors, however, Kimḥi relied heavily on rabbinic literature, distinguishing between *perush* or interpretation which conformed to his standards of *peshat*, and purely homiletical interpretations or *derashot*, many of which he included nonetheless for added interest. In his exegesis too, Kimḥi strove for clarity and readibility in an attempt to depart from the compression and obscurity of his predecessors.

Philosophical Interests

Kimḥi read widely in philosophic and scientific literature and was strongly influenced by the rationalism of Ibn Ezra and Maimonides. He frequently alluded to philosophical matters as an aid to exegesis on the one hand and in an attempt to popularize such studies on the other. He was no original philosopher and his theories are adaptations of those of his predecessors. Thus his theory of prophecy parallels that of Maimonides in the discussion of the prerequisites for and the levels of prophecy, although Kimḥi goes farther in recognizing the possibility of the prophethood of a gentile. He follows Maimonides too on the problem of providence in saying that individual providence is subject to intellectual attainment, although he expresses the somewhat independent view that animals may be subject to individual providence in the event that their actions benefit or harm a human being. Kimḥi generally attempted to explain miracles naturalistically or to underplay them. There is considerable discussion of the classification of the commandments with reliance principally on pre-Maimonidean terminology and conceptions, but there is little actual analysis of the "reasons for the commandments" (*ta'amei ha-mitzvot*) since he did not write on the legal portions of the Pentateuch. Using the material in Maimonides' *Guide of the Perplexed* as a model, Kimḥi wrote two very detailed "esoteric" (*nistar*) commentaries to Genesis 2:7–5:1 (see bibliography) and to the first chapter of Ezekiel (in the Rabbinical Bible, Warsaw, 1902).

Kimḥi's dissemination of philosophic material in the commentaries, intended to whet the appetite of the general reader, came under severe censure from a number of authorities, including Judah ibn Alfakhar, Jacob *Emden, and *David b. Solomon ibn Abi Zimra, despite the fact that, with the exception of the two philosophical commentaries, his rationalistic material was cited with considerable discretion. Ironically, Kimḥi's commentaries were considered deficient in their rationalism by *Immanuel b. Solomon of Rome who himself was given to allegorical interpretation.

Polemics

The commentaries contain a considerable amount of polemical material, much of it based on the *Sefer ha-Berit* of Joseph Kimḥi. He attacks a number of christological interpretations by demonstrating Christian "corruption" of the text (Isa. 2:22; Ps. 22:17; 110:1, etc.) or the inapplicability (Isa. 7:14; Ezra 44:2) or irrationality (Ps. 87, end; 110, end, etc.) of the interpretation. He inveighs frequently against the allegorical mode of the Christian interpreters (Ps. 19:10; 119 passim, etc.). Certain basic questions in the Jewish-Christian controversy, chief among which is the identity of the "true Israel," were frequently raised. Kimḥi wards off the attempt of Christian theologians to claim the name of Israel or other biblical names of the Jewish people for the Church and lays great stress on the superior morality and religiosity of the Jews. He defends the taking of interest from a gentile "for in general they hate Israel" but discourages exacting it from a righteous gentile (Ps. 22:23). Although very much aware of Israel's tribulations in exile, Kimḥi believed in a special providence for the Jewish people which paralleled the special providence of the sage, in that Israel is a nation of sages "who meditated on My deeds and confessed My unity" (Isa. 43:7). Never explaining how this providence is manifested, he limited himself to frequent references to the future redemption in the messianic age. The polemic material in the Psalms commentary was collected and printed separately as *Teshuvot la-Noẓerim* in the Altdorf (1644) edition of Lipmann Muehlhausen's *Sefer ha-Niẓẓaḥon*. The so-called "*Vikku'aḥ ha-RaDaK*," printed in the *Milḥemet Ḥovah* (Constantinople, 1710), has been shown to be falsely attributed to Kimḥi.

Spurious Writings

Several other works have been wrongly ascribed to Kimḥi, including a commentary to *Ethics of the Fathers* (Turin *Siddur*, 1525); the commentaries on part of the *Guide* and the creed of Maimonides; the commentary on *Pittum ha-Ketoret (Koveẓ Devarim Neḥmadim*, 1902); the *Perush Sheḥitah* (H.B. Levy, *Mikdash Me'at*, Ms. 152, 4); a commentary on Ruth (published by J. Mercier, Paris, 1563). There are several medieval testimonies to commentaries on the remaining four books of the Pentateuch and on Proverbs but these, like the Job commentary in I. Schwartz's *Tikvat Enosh* (1868), may have been culled from his philological writings.

BIBLIOGRAPHY: A. Geiger, in: *Oẓar Neḥmad*, 2 (1857), 157ff.; L. Finkelstein (ed.), *The Commentary... on Isaiah* (1926), includes the esoteric commentary to Genesis; H. Cohen (ed.), *The Commentary... on Hosea* (1929). Other critical editions are: S.M. Schiller-Szinessy (ed.), *The First Book of the Psalms...* (1883); J. Bosniak (ed.), *Commentary... Fifth Book of Psalms* (1954); S.I. Esterson (ed.), *The Commentary on Psalms* (42–72), in: HUCA, 10 (1935). The *Mikhlol* was edited and translated by W. Chomsky (1952[2]). Best edition of *Shorashim* is by F. Lebrecht and J.H.R. Biesenthal (1847). The extensive bibliography in EJ, 9 (1932), 1239 should be supplemented by Melamed, in: *Aresheth*, 2 (1960), 35–95; Talmage, in: HTR, 60 (1967), 323–48; idem, in: HUCA, 38 (1967), 213–35; 39 (1968), 177–218.

[Frank Talmage]

KIMḤI, DOV (originally **Meller, Berish**; 1889–1961), Hebrew author, translator, and editor. Born in Jaslo, Galicia, Kimḥi became an ardent Zionist in his youth and immigrated to Palestine in 1908. He settled in Jerusalem, and from 1912 until his retirement taught at the Reḥaviah Gymnasium, Jerusalem. He made his literary debut in the journal *Ha-Mizpeh* in 1905, under his original name Berish Meller. After his arrival in Jerusalem he began writing novels, short stories, and essays, and also engaged extensively in translation work. His fiction covers a wide range of settings from his native Galicia, through Western Europe, to Ereẓ Israel. In addition to several works on the Bible, two collections of essays, and numerous translations, he published anthologies of world literature and of Israel stories. His other works include *Ma'barot* (1923); *Sefer ha-Ki-*

lyonot (1926); *Ha-Kufsah ha-Keḥullah* (1926); *Emesh* (1927); and *Ẓiyyurim me-Olam Nishkaḥ* (1943). His novel *Beit Ḥefeẓ* (1951), a "European novel" (Menahem Peri) of love intrigues and betrayals set against the background of Jerusalem on the eve of World War I, gained much attention upon its "rediscovery" and publication by Peri in 1993.

BIBLIOGRAPHY: M. Rabinson, *Deyokenaʾot mi-Soferei ha-Dor* (1932), 49–52; M. Carmon, *Dor le-Dor* (1956), 150–3; Kressel, Leksikon, 2 (1967), 774–6. **ADD. BIBLIOGRAPHY:** G. Shaked, *Ha-Mesapper Dov Kimhi*, in: *Yerushalayim*, 9–10 (1975), 239–250; J. Amoial, in: *Beit Ḥefeẓ* (1993), 225–236; A. Lipsker, "*Ẓamarot shel Hazayah*," in: *Bikkoret u-Farshanut*, 29 (1993), 121–142; I. Rikin, in: *Maariv* (March 19, 1993); B. Gur, in: *Haaretz* (March 19, 1993); N. Govrin, "*Mi-Ganenet Yerushalmit le-Eshet ha-Olam ha-Gadol*" (on Kimhi's *Al Shivah Yamim*), in: *Yerushalayim*, 20–21 (2004), 241–257.

[Getzel Kressel (2nd ed.)]

KIMḤI, JACOB BEN SAMUEL (c. 1720–1800), talmudist and author in London. Jacob Kimḥi was born in Constantinople where his father Samuel, whose responsa are mentioned in the *Masat Moshe* of Moses *Israel (ḤM nos. 50–51; Constantinople, 1734), was rabbi. At an early age Kimḥi undertook journeys through Europe, finally arriving in London, where he remained until his death. There he engaged in business but became well known through his extensive knowledge of Talmud. Ḥ.J.D. *Azulai made his acquaintance in London and describes him as "an acute and erudite" scholar. He was the author of *Shoshannat Yaʿakov* (Sulzbach, 1748), novellae to tractates *Beẓah* and *Taʿanit*. He states that his aim was "to avoid casuistry and hairsplitting and establish the plain meaning of the Talmud in order to arrive at the law"; he sought to answer difficulties raised against the statements of Rashi and the tosafists. His *Sheʾelah u-Teshuvah be-Inyan Bedikat ha-Reʾah ve-ha-Sheḥitah u-Vedikah be-London* ("A Responsum on the Subject of the Slaughtering of Cattle and the Examination of their Lungs in London"; Altona, 1760) was occasioned by a dispute that broke out in London between 1755 and 1766 in connection with *sheḥitah*, which led to a schism between the Ashkenazi and Sephardi communities, in consequence of the accusations of the Sephardi *shoḥet* Ḥayyim Albahali (1755) that the slaughterers did not sufficiently supervise the examination of the meat after *sheḥitah*. Kimḥi published his work, in which he supported the view of Albahali, when the dispute was at its height.

BIBLIOGRAPHY: Azulai, 1 (1852), 177 no. 149; idem, *Maʿgal Tov ha-Shalem*, ed. by A. Freimann (1934), 31f.; C. Duschinsky, in: JHSET, 7 (1915), 272–90; idem, *The Rabbinate of the Great Synagogue* (1921), 7 n. 1, 279, 282.

[Yehoshua Horowitz]

KIMḤI, JOSEPH (also known as **Maistre Petit**; **Rikam**, from the acronym of **R**abbi **J**oseph **Kimḥi**; c. 1105–c. 1170), grammarian, exegete, translator, and polemist. Kimḥi migrated from Spain in the wake of the Almohad persecutions and settled permanently in Narbonne. Overshadowed by his more prominent sons, Moses and David *Kimḥi, he nevertheless performed a major function as a pioneer scholar by helping to introduce the learning and methodology of Spanish Jewry into Christian Europe. In this respect, his activities paralleled those of Abraham Ibn Ezra, whom Kimḥi probably knew personally and who cited him in his writings. He had several disciples, including his son Moses, Menahem b. Simeon of Posquières, R. Solomon b. Isaac ha-Nesiah, and Joseph ibn Zabara. He composed works for the benefit of his countrymen who could not read the grammars written in Arabic, especially those of *Ḥayyuj and *Ibn Janaḥ, whom he generally followed. In the *Sefer ha-Zikkaron* (published by W. Bacher, 1888), he introduced the concept of five long and five short vowels, presented the *piʿel* and the *hofal* as distinct conjugations, and provided a list of nominal forms. In addition to its influence on the grammars written by his sons, the *Zikkaron* was used by Elijah Levita and Abraham de Balmes. His second grammatical treatise, the *Sefer ha-Galui* (published by H.J. Mathews, 1887), consists of two parts; a critique of R. Jacob *Tam's *Hakhraʾot* on the *Maḥberet* of *Menahem b. Jacob ibn Saruq and a compilation of Kimḥi's own critical remarks on points in the *Maḥberet* left untouched by Tam. A defense of the latter by Benjamin of Canterbury has been incorporated into the text of the *Sefer ha-Galui.*

As an exegete, Kimḥi stressed the "plain sense" or *peshat* of Scripture in contrast to the homiletical school of exegesis prevalent in the Provence of his day. In addition to the exegetical material in his grammars, he composed the following commentaries: *Sefer ha-Torah* on the Pentateuch (published by H. Gad, in *Ḥamishah Meʾorot Gedolim*, 1953); *Sefer ha-Miknah* on the Prophets (no longer extant); on Proverbs (entitled *Sefer Ḥikkah* by the publisher, 1868); on Job (published incompletely by I. Schwarz in *Tikvat Enosh*, 1868); on Song of Songs (in Ms.). An unknown commentary *Ḥibbur ha-Leket* was ascribed to him by his son David. Much of Kimḥi's exegesis influenced and was cited in the commentaries of his sons, of Menahem b. Simeon, and of Jacob b. Asher. Kimḥi prepared a translation of Baḥya ibn Paquda's *Ḥovot ha-Levavot* (fragment published in the I.A. Benjacob edition (1846) of Ibn Tibbon's translation). He was the author too of the *Shekel ha-Kodesh*, extant in two recensions (one of which was published by H. Gollancz in 1919), a rhymed collection of gnomic sayings based upon the *Mivḥar ha-Peninim* of Solomon ibn *Gabirol. Kimḥi himself composed a number of liturgical works which found their way into the prayer books of several communities. His polemical treatise, the *Sefer ha-Berit* (Constantinople, 1710), vies with Jacob b. Reuben's *Milḥamot ha-Shem* for the honor of being the first anti-Christian polemical work written in Europe. Cast as a dialogue between the "believer" (*maʾamin*) and the "heretic" (*min*), the work attacks certain basic christological interpretations of scriptural passages, in addition to such doctrines as original sin, the incarnation, and the relative morality of Jews and Christians including the question of lending money on interest. The *Sefer ha-Berit* especially influenced the polemics of Kimḥi's son David and of Naḥmanides.

BIBLIOGRAPHY: Blueth, in: MWJ, 18 (1891), 1ff.; 19 (1892), 89ff.; Eppenstein, in: MGWJ, 40 (1896), 173ff.; 41 (1897), 83ff.; Geiger, in: *Oẓar Neḥmad*, 1 (1856), 97–119; 2 (1857), 98f.; 3 (1860), 114f.; Marx, in: HUCA, 4 (1927), 433–48; Newman, in: *Jewish Studies in Memory of I. Abrahams* (1927), 365–72.

[Frank Talmage]

KIMḤI, MORDECAI (second half of 13th century), a Provençal rabbi and halakhic authority of Carpentras, grandson of David *Kimḥi. Urbach's opinion that he was the maternal grandfather of *Perez b. Elijah cannot be accepted since Mordecai was an older contemporary of Solomon b. Abraham *Adret, and around 1305 wrote a moderate and tolerant responsum in reply to *Abba Mari b. Moses' request for his opinion on the ban on the study of philosophy (Abba Mari b. Moses, *Minḥat Kena'ot*, no. 9), whereas Perez had died some 10 years earlier. Various collections of his responsa are extant, one of which was published by A. Sofer in *Teshuvot Ḥakhmei Provinẓyah* (1967). His son, ISAAC (or Maistre Petit de Nions, as he was known in French), also a well-known scholar, appears to have lived in Narbonne, and it is possible that he married there into the family of *David b. Levi, author of *Sefer ha-Mikhtam*, since he refers to him as "my relation." Isaac was in close correspondence with Solomon b. Abraham Adret, many of whose responsa are addressed to him. A collection of his responsa was published together with those of his father in the above-mentioned work. Isaac also wrote commentaries, novellae, and halakhic rulings on most of the Talmud and on other branches of scholarship (Isaac de Lattes, *Sha'arei Ẓiyyon*, ed. by S. Buber (1885), 47), and one of his responsa was published with those of Isaac de Lattes (1860). Six of his *azharot* for the afternoon service of the Feast of Shavuot appear in the *Maḥzor Carpentras* (ed. Amsterdam, 1759).

BIBLIOGRAPHY: Gross, Gal Jud, 607–8, no. 3; Landshuth, Ammudei, 124; A. Sofer (ed.), *Teshuvot Ḥakhmei Provinẓyah* (1967), xxiv (introd.); Neubauer, in: REJ, 12 (1886), 80–91; I. Lévi, *ibid.*, 38 (1899), 103–22; 39 (1899), 76–84, 226–41; Poznański, *ibid.*, 40 (1900), 91–94; Davidson, Oẓar, 4 (1933), 423, index, s.v. *Yizḥak Kimḥi (ben Mordekhai)*; Urbach, Tosafot, 451; Zunz, Lit Poesie, 505; Zunz, Gesch, 466; L. Zunz, in: AWJD, 3 (1839), 679ff.; Frankl, in: MGWJ, 33 (1884), 556–7.

[Israel Moses Ta-Shma]

KIMḤI, MOSES (known by the acronym **Remak,** i.e., **R**abbi **M**oses **K**imḥi; d. c. 1190), grammarian and exegete of Narbonne, Provence; son of Joseph *Kimḥi and brother of David *Kimḥi. As a grammarian, he generally followed his father, although his work shows traces of the influence of Abraham *Ibn Ezra, especially in terminology. He was little concerned with phonology and stressed the morphology of the verb. In the *Mahalakh Shevilei ha-Da'at* (Pesaro, 1508), Moses introduced the use of the root *pkd* (פקד) in paradigms and, considering *nifal* the passive of *kal*, arranged the conjugations in the order: *kal, nifal, pi'el, pu'al, hifil, hofal, po'el, hitpa'el*. These innovations became common in later grammars. The *Mahalakh* was glossed both by Elijah Levita and Shabbetai b. Isaac of Przemysl and was translated into Latin by Sebastian Muenster under the title *Liber viarum linguae sacrae* (Paris, 1520). Moses also wrote *Sekhel Tov* (published by D. Castelli, in REJ, 28 (1894), 212–27; 29 (1894), 100–10), a brief supplementary treatise dealing principally with the theoretical classification of nouns, particles, and verbs. A *Sefer Taḥboshet*, apparently dealing with anomalous grammatical forms, is no longer extant.

In his exegesis, Moses followed the method of literal interpretation employed by his father and Ibn Ezra. Preferring to comment on generally neglected books of the Bible, he composed commentaries on Proverbs, Ezra, and Nehemiah – which have been printed in rabbinic Bibles but ascribed to Abraham Ibn Ezra – and a commentary on Job (published by I. Schwarz in *Tikvat Enosh*, 1868). *Ta'anug Nefesh*, an ethical work, has also been attributed to him. Moses Kimḥi exercised considerable influence on his brother David, who referred to him as "my brother, my teacher." Through Muenster's translation, his *Mahalakh* became one of the most popular grammars used by the 16th-century Christian Hebraists and was reprinted many times.

BIBLIOGRAPHY: Geiger, in: *Oẓar Neḥmad*, 1 (1856), 118; 2 (1857), 18–24; F.J. Ortuta y Murgoito, *Moisés Kimchi y su obra Sekel Tob* (1920); Bacher, in: REJ, 21 (1890), 281–5; J.B. Sermoneta, in: *Seritti in Memoria di L. Carpi* (1968), 59–100.

[Frank Talmage]

KIMḤI, RAPHAEL ISRAEL BEN JOSEPH (first half of 18th century), emissary of Safed. Kimḥi was born in Constantinople where he studied under Ḥayyim b. Isaac Raphael *Alfandari. When his teacher moved to Ereẓ Israel in 1713 he followed him and settled in Safed, where he studied under Jacob Vilna Ashkenazi. In 1728 he traveled to Italy as an emissary of the Safed community and was in Mantua in 1729. In Padua he was a guest of the father of Moses Ḥayyim *Luzzatto, where he immersed himself in Luzzatto's works and in the polemic (of 1730) which raged about them, justifying Luzzatto's views. A responsum written by him to Raphael *Meldola during this visit – in Venice 1730 – on the laws of writing a **Sefer Torah* is included in *Mayim Rabbim* (1737). From Venice, Kimḥi sent a letter to Corfu (1730) in which he complained of discrimination against Safed in the matter of contributions assigned to Ereẓ Israel. In his letter he stresses the critical situation of the Safed community and demands greater interest in the lot of his town as against the other "holy towns." Kimḥi was requested by the Safed community to go to Corfu, but the Venetian rabbis persuaded him to delay this journey because of the state of his health and promised to undertake the task themselves in Corfu. He died during his mission, apparently before 1737. In that year his brother Abraham published from his literary remains the *Avodat Yisrael* on the order of the Temple service on the Day of Atonement. Comments on this work are to be found in the *Shifat Revivim* (1788) of David *Pardo, who also mentions it in his *Shoshannim le-David* (1752). Besides this Kimḥi left a commentary in manuscript called *Einei Yisrael* on the *Sefer Mitzvot Katan* which was seen by Ḥ.J.D. Azulai.

BIBLIOGRAPHY: Rosanes, Togarmah, 5 (1937–38), 291–2; Yaari, Sheluḥei, 433–5; I. Ben-Zvi, in: *Sinai*, 27 (1950), 80–86; idem, in: *Sinai Sefer Yovel* (1958), 13–26.

[Yehoshua Horowitz]

KIMḤI, SOLOMON BEN NISSIM JOSEPH DAVID (mid-19th century), talmudist of Constantinople. Solomon's father, who died in 1836, was rabbi in Constantinople; Solomon himself was at the height of his activity in 1861 and was still alive in 1870. He wrote *Melekhet Shelomo* (1862) consisting of responsa, novellae to various tractates, and sermons; *Yakhil Shelomo* (1865), novellae to the four parts of Jacob b. Asher's Tur; *Yemei Shelomo* (1874), novellae to Maimonides' *Mishneh Torah*. The *Melekhet Shelomo* (YD no. 4, p. 8b) includes his interesting reply to the question whether a Jew may teach the Oral Law to Karaites. He takes up a consistent and extreme attitude, insisting that Karaites of his day are to be regarded as non-Jews and that, as their intention is undoubtedly merely to embarrass Jewish scholars, such teaching is forbidden. This ruling gave rise to considerable controversy and the Karaites reacted strongly in an article in the *Journal Israélite* (no. 513/14, December 1866) demanding that Yakir Gheron, the chief rabbi of Constantinople, intervene in the matter. The latter in fact ordered the burning of all copies of the book that could be found and severely censured the author. In accordance with his view of the status of the Karaites, Kimḥi laid down that one may use milk drawn by a Karaite on a day which is a Jewish festival but not according to the Karaite calendar (*Yakhil Shelomo*, 35:b).

BIBLIOGRAPHY: Frankl, in: MGWJ, 33 (1884), 553f., 557f.; A. Galante, *Histoire des Juifs d'Istanbul*, 1 (1941), 133.

[Yehoshua Horowitz]

KIMḤIT, high priestly family in the last years of the Second Temple. Although the Talmud states: "Kimḥit had seven sons, each of whom served as high priest" (TJ, Meg. 1:12, 72a; Yoma 47a), the only members of the family known as such were: SIMEON son of Kimḥit, high priest in 17–18 C.E., also known as Ishmael. He was appointed by the procurator Valerius Gratus and deposed after a year when the high priesthood was given to Joseph *Caiaphas (Jos., Ant., 18:34). The Talmud relates that on the Day of Atonement he fell into conversation with an Arab ruler and inadvertently became unclean. His brother Yeshovav was substituted for him so that their mother saw both her sons high priests on the same day. JOSEPH son of Kimḥit, high priest 44–47 C.E., probably brother of the above. After the emperor Claudius granted *Herod, king of Chalcis, the right to appoint high priests the latter removed Elionaeus (or Cantheras; see Jos., Ant., 20:16n.) and appointed Joseph to the post. JOSEPH son of Simeon, high priest 61–62 C.E., appointed by Agrippa II in succession to *Ishmael b. Phiabi. He was among the group of priests who escaped to the Roman camp in 70 C.E., after the fall of the fortress *Antonia. Josephus refers to him as "Joseph, son of the high priest Simeon, called Kabi" (Ant., 20:196). This has led some scholars to believe that he was a member of the Boethus family, but it is more probable that he was a member of the Kimḥit family (see Schuerer, Gesch, 2:275). The Talmud praises the members of this family: "all flour [*kemaḥim*] is good but the flour of Kimḥit is of the best [*solet*]" (TJ, Meg. 1:12, 72a).

BIBLIOGRAPHY: Klausner, Bayit Sheni, 4 (1950^2), 304; 5 (1951^2), 22, 26.

[Edna Elazary]

KIMMEL, SIDNEY (1928–), U.S. businessman, philanthropist. The son of a Philadelphia cab driver, Kimmel, a self-made man, became not only a leading apparel manufacturer but possibly the biggest individual donor to cancer research in the U.S. Although he had virtually no religious education as a child, he became committed to Jewish causes and was a bar mitzvah at the age of 73. A college dropout from Temple University between two tours of duty in the U.S. Army, Kimmel was born and raised in Philadelphia. His first job, setting up pins in a bowling alley, paid $2 a day. He started working in a knitting mill in the 1950s, then was hired by Villager, a Philadelphia sportswear company. Kimmel supervised the knitwear line, Villager's fastest-growing unit, becoming the company's president in 1968. The following year, he left to run the Jones apparel division of the conglomerate W.R. Grace. He was joined by designer Rena Rowan, who remained with him for the next 33 years. With a new label, Jones New York, the company produced modestly priced sportswear and suits with a designer look. Kimmel and a partner bought the Jones New York name from Grace in 1975, and Kimmel became chairman. In the 1980s, overexpansion and a problematic licensing deal almost bankrupted him. In 1989, Jones returned to profitability and in 1991 Kimmel took the company public. It became one of the world's top designers and marketers of branded apparel, footwear, and accessories, boasting such global brands as Jones New York, Lauren by Ralph Lauren, Polo Jeans, Nine West, Evan-Picone, and Gloria Vanderbilt. In 2002, Kimmel stepped down as chief executive officer of Jones Apparel Group, but remained chairman. His other business interests included the Miami Heat basketball team, the Harry Cipriani international restaurant chain, and a movie company, Sidney Kimmel Entertainment. In 1993, Kimmel, who married late in life and has no children, created the Sidney Kimmel Foundation and its subsidiary, the Sidney Kimmel Foundation for Cancer Research. He funded Kimmel Cancer Centers in San Diego, Calif., at Thomas Jefferson University Hospital in Philadelphia, at Baltimore's Johns Hopkins University, and at New York's Memorial Sloan-Kettering. His Kimmel Scholars program provides grants to promising young cancer researchers, and he was the top individual donor to the Kimmel Center for the Performing Arts in Philadelphia. Kimmel, together with Rowan, gave $5 million in 1995 for a special exhibitions hall at the U.S. Holocaust Memorial Museum in Washington, D.C. In 2001, he pledged two $20 million endowments, one to the Jewish Federation of Greater Philadelphia, the other to the Raymond and Ruth Perelman Jewish Day School, to be given after his death. He said he would give both institutions $1 million each every year for the rest of his life. He also pledged $25 million to the National Museum for American Jewish History's new building being planned for Philadelphia. Among his many honors are the American Jewish Committee's National Human Relations Award, the Award for Excellence in Corporate Leadership from the Society of Memorial Sloan-Kettering Cancer Center, the American Cancer Society's Humanitarian Award, and Temple University's Musser Award for Excellence in Leadership.

[Mort Sheinman (2nd ed.)]

KINAH (Heb. קִינָה; pl. קִינוֹת, *kinot*), poem expressing mourning, pain, and sorrow. One of the earliest poetic forms, it is also termed **hesped* (lamentation), from which developed, in the course of time, the customary prose eulogy over the dead (called *martiyyah* in the Spanish-Arabic communities). Spoken first over important dead of the family or nation (e.g., Gen. 23:2, Jer. 22:18; Zech. 12:10), *kinot* were subsequently recited over calamities which befell the nation or the country, as well as over oppressive edicts decreed upon the community or upon the people. Professional female (Heb. *mekonenot*, see Jer. 9:16 and 19) and male mourners (Heb. *sofedim*, Eccl. 12:5) recited the *kinot*, some of which they composed themselves. Several ancient *kinot* are recorded in the Bible, such as David's *kinah* over Saul and Jonathan (II Sam. 1:19–27), and the Book of Lamentations – also called "the scroll [or book] of *kinot*" – a collection of *kinot* in alphabetical order on the destruction of Jerusalem and the Exile of Israel. The Talmud preserves a number of whole *kinot* and fragments of *kinot* (MK 25b). In the Middle Ages, many *kinot* were composed for various calamities, such as the earthquake in the Sabbatical year (*ra'ash shevi'i*) in Tiberias and other cities of Israel (YMHSI, 3 (1936), 153–63), the *kinah* of Solomon ibn *Gabirol on the death of *Jekuthiel (Davidson, Oẓar, 2 (1929), 23 no. 525); and the *kinah* of *Eleazar b. Judah, author of *Sefer ha-Roke'aḥ*, on the murder of his wife and two daughters (A.M. Habermann (ed.), *Gezerot Ashkenaz ve-Ẓarefat* (1946), 165–7). Those composed over the restrictive edicts of the Middle Ages were usually appended to the *kinot* recited on the Ninth of *Av (*Megillat Eikhah* and the *kinot* of Eleazar ha-Kallir), and other fast days.

In popular parlance the term *kinot* is generally used for those recited on the Ninth of Av. Many *kinot* written for that day start with the word Zion and are thus known as Zionides (see Jerusalem in **Piyyut*).

Some *kinot* are without any acrostic; others have an alphabetical acrostic, or one indicating the name of the author, or both; some are also rhymed. Since the first publication of the group of *kinot* according to the Ashkenazi rite (Cracow, 1585), hundreds of editions have appeared, both with and without commentaries. A scientific edition was published by D. Goldschmidt (1968). The *kinot* of the Sephardi Jews were published in *Seder Arba Ta'aniyyot* (Venice, 1590). Many of the *kinot* of the Middle Ages, however, have not yet been published.

BIBLIOGRAPHY: Elbogen, Gottesdienst, 229–31; Davidson, Oẓar, 4 (1933), 494–6.

[Abraham Meir Habermann]

KINDERFREUND, ARYEH LEIB (1788–1837), Galician Haskalah poet. Born in Zamosc (Poland), the son of a well-to-do family, he received a broad Jewish and secular education. His family's fortunes declined, and he moved to Galicia and became a teacher. For a time he taught in Tarnopol, in the Hebrew school established by J. *Perl; later he moved to Jaroslaw, and finally to Brody. He published one collection of poems, *Shirim Shonim* (Lemberg, 1834), which includes occasional lyric poems and pastoral odes. He left in manuscript form a study of the Hebrew language (he attempted to prove that it is the mother of all tongues), in which he also deals with tonal poetic meter in Hebrew, in which he was a pioneer, using examples from his own works.

BIBLIOGRAPHY: Waxman, Literature, 3 (1960²), 197f.; Kressel, Leksikon, 2 (1967), 754.

[Getzel Kressel]

KINDERTRANSPORT, the movement of German and Austrian Jewish children to England in advance of World War II. On November 15, 1938, a few days after **Kristallnacht*, a delegation of British Jewish leaders appealed in person to British Prime Minister Neville Chamberlain. Among other measures, they requested that the British government permit the temporary admission of children and teenagers, who would later re-emigrate. The Jewish community promised to put up guarantees for the refugee children.

The next day, the British cabinet debated the issue. The home secretary, Sir Samuel Hoare, said that the country could not admit more refugees without provoking a backlash, but the foreign secretary, Lord Halifax, suggested that an act of generosity might have the benefit of prompting the United States to accept additional immigrants. The cabinet committee on refugees subsequently decided that the nation would accept unaccompanied children ranging from infants to teenagers under the age of 17. No limit to the number of refugees was ever publicly announced.

The home secretary announced the program to the assembled members of Parliament at the House of Commons, who broadly welcomed the initiative that would come to be known as the *Kindertransport*.

Within a very short time, the Movement for the Care of Children from Germany, later known as the Refugee Children's Movement (RCM), sent representatives to Germany and Austria to establish the systems for choosing, organizing, and transporting the children. On November 25, British citizens heard an appeal for foster homes on the BBC Home Service radio program. Soon there were 500 offers. They did not insist that prospective homes for Jewish children should be Jewish homes. Nor did they probe too carefully into the motives and character of the families: it was sufficient for the houses to look clean and the families to seem respectable.

In Germany, a network of organizers was established, and these volunteers worked around the clock to make priority lists of those most imperiled: teenagers who were in concentration camps or in danger of arrest, Polish children or teenagers threatened with deportation, children in Jewish orphanages, those whose parents were too impoverished to keep them, or those with parents in a concentration camp.

The first *Kindertransport* from Berlin departed on December 1, 1938, the first from Vienna on December 10. For the first three months, the children came mainly from Germany, and then the emphasis shifted to Austria. In March 1939, after the German army entered Czechoslovakia, transports from Prague were hastily organized. Trains of Polish Jewish children were also arranged in February and August 1939.

The last group of children from Germany departed on September 1, 1939, the day the German army invaded Poland and provoked Great Britain, France, and other countries to declare war. The last known transport of *Kinder* from the Netherlands left on May 14, 1940, the day the Dutch army surrendered to Germany. Tragically, hundreds of *Kinder* were caught in Belgium and the Netherlands during the German invasion, making them subject once more to the Nazi regime and its collaborators.

Upon arrival at port in Great Britain, *Kinder* without prearranged foster families were sheltered at temporary holding centers located at summer holiday camps on the cold windy coast of East Anglia – Dovercourt near Harwich – and, for a short period, Pakefield near Lowestoft. Finding foster families was not always easy, and being chosen for a home was not necessarily the end of discomfort or distress. Some families took in teenage girls as a way of acquiring a maidservant. There was little sensitivity toward the cultural and religious needs of the children, and, for some, their heritage was all but erased. A few, mainly the youngest, were given new names, new identities, and even a new religion. In the end, many of the children for whom no home could be found were placed on farms or in hostels run by the RCM.

From the moment of their arrival, the children struggled to maintain contact with their parents. At first, letters between parents and children flowed fairly easily, and many were filled with hopes and plans for reunion. The beginning of the war in 1939 meant the end of this dream. In addition, the German government restricted the delivery of mail to and from Jews, forcing parents and children to rely on intermediaries or the Red Cross. In 1942 many stopped receiving letters for reasons they could not understand until later.

Older children suffered a different hardship when, in 1940, the British government ordered the internment of 16- to 70-year-old refugees from enemy countries – so-called "enemy aliens." Approximately 1,000 of the *Kinder* were held in makeshift internment camps, and around 400 were transported overseas to Canada and Australia. Those shipped to Australia on the *HMT Dunera* were mistreated during the long voyage, and a scandal that followed revelations about the mishandling of internment led to a program of releases in late 1940. Men in particular were offered the chance to do war work or to enter the Alien Pioneer Corps. About 1,000 German and Austrian teenagers served in the British armed forces, including combat units. Several dozen joined elite formations such as the Special Forces where their language skills could be put to good use.

Most of the *Kinder* survived the war, and some were reunited with parents who had either spent the war in hiding or endured the Nazi camps. Reunions were not always happy as children had grown and changed and their parents were also changed by what they had undergone. The majority of children, however, had to face the reality that home and family were lost forever.

In all, the *Kindertransport* rescue operation brought approximately 10,000 children to the relative safety of Great Britain – a large-scale act of mercy unique in a tragic historical period marked by brutality and widespread indifference.

[Deborah Oppenheimer, Scott Chamberlin, Gretchen Skidmore, and David Cesarani (2nd ed.)]

°KINDĪ, ABU YŪSUF YAʿQŪB IBN ISḤAQ AL- (805–873), most notable "philosopher of the Arabs." Al-Kindī is known to have written more than 270 works. His writings, many of them short treatises, deal with arithmetic, geometry, astronomy, astrology, pharmacology, meteorology, chemistry, medicine, optics, divination, music, and polemics. Through condensed writing, redundant passages, and repetitive arguments, Al-Kindī developed ideas and terminology from the philosophical works originally written in Greek and Syriac, and dressed the classical philosophic ideas in a popular style. For this purpose Al-Kindī oversaw the work of important early translators, such as Ustath, translator of Aristotle's *Metaphysics*; Yaḥya b. al-Biṭrīq, translator of Aristotle's *De Caelo*; and Ibn Naʿīma al-Ḥimsī, who translated logical works of Aristotle and parts of the *Enneads* of Plotinus known as the *Theology of Aristotle*. He was also involved in the translation of Proclus' *Elements of Theology*, named in Arabic *Book on the Pure Good* and called in Latin *Liber de Causis*.

Al-Kindī's works on philosophical topics are his treatise *On First Philosophy* (*Fī al-Falsafa al-Ūlā*) and the treatise *On the Definitions of Things and Their Descriptions* (*Fī Ḥudūd al-Aʾshyāʾ wa-Rusūmihā*); his treatise on the unity of God, *On the Oneness of God and the Limitation of the Body of the World* (*Fī Waḥdaniyat Allah wa-Tunahiy Jirm al-ʾAlām*); and a scientific work, dealing with *The Quantity of the Books of Aristotle and What Is Required for the Acquisition of Philosophy* (*Fi Kammiyat Kutub Aristutalis wa ma Yaḥtāj ilahi fi Taḥsīl al-Falsafa*). Among his ethical writings the best known is the treatise *On the Art of Averting Sorrows* (*Risālah fī al-hīlah li-Dafʿ al-Aḥzān*). Almost all of his works in Arabic, aside from translations into Hebrew and Latin, were lost until the mid-20th century, when 24 works of different size and varying importance were published in Cairo (1950, 1953) from an Istanbul manuscript.

Al-Kindī was born in *Kufa and served the *Abbasid caliphs al-Maʾmūn and al-Muʿaṣṣim. He fell from favor in the time of the caliph al-Mutawakkil. His status under the patronage of the Muʿtazilah-oriented Abbasid caliphs has naturally connected Al-Kindī with Mu'tazilite ideology, but in spite of external similarities (such as perceiving the unity of God as involving no attributes, predicates, or characteristics), Al-Kindī avoids characteristic Muʿazilite themes (such as God's unity and justice) and typical Muʿtazilite argumentation (such as the proofs for the creation of the world, and the supremacy of the revealed truth to all knowledge).

Al-Kindī based his philosophical views on an incomplete acquaintance with the teachings of Plato and Aristotle and other popular late Greek and Hellenistic authors. He contributed greatly to the formation of the philosophical-theological body of knowledge, enthusiastically embraced by Arabic philosophers who came after him. Much of the philosophical and scientific information reached Al-Kindī through oral transmission of paraphrases and commentaries and through secondary sources, such as encyclopedias and doxographies. Al-Kindī was the first to use systematically the science of philosophy to support faith. He deserves to be called the "First Arabic Philosopher," not only because of his ethnic origin but also because of his courageous and pioneering stand in favor of the superiority of philosophy to Arabic sciences and traditional Koranic studies. His distinction between logical, demonstrative information, and revealed, spontaneous knowledge is correlative to the distinction between objective nature and subjective self and between particulars and universals.

His unawareness of systematical differences between Aristotelianism and Neoplatonism is especially remarkable in Al-Kindī's perception of God as the True One in relation to the world and in his perception of the divine intellect as reflected in the human soul. While Aristotle bases the notion of the True One on its simplicity, uniqueness, and self-containment, in Neoplatonism these qualities are considered as deriving from the exaltedness of God. In his treatise on the soul, Al-Kindī also combines Platonic moral philosophy and the Platonic trichotomy of the soul with Aristotelian philosophy. He mentions the four platonic cardinal virtues but recommends observance of the Aristotelian golden mean. In his remarks on the intellect, Al-Kindī anticipates later mature theories of intellection, which explain the working of the human intellect as a minimized and imperfect imitation of the universal intellect. He alludes to the existence of a divine cosmic intellect, which is always in actuality in comparison to human intellect, which must overcome its state of potentiality in order to acquire knowledge. The status of the individual soul and its enduring life is still embryonic in Al-Kindī's full concept of the human soul, but here too Al-Kindī prefers to talk about interior serenity in current life rather than discuss eschatological topics common to theological literature, such as the resurrection of the dead, the end of days, the final judgment, and the nature of reward in the hereafter.

When describing the universe as composite and corruptible while arguing for its createdness, Al-Kindī follows John Philoponus' proofs of creation based on the impossibility of an infinite number, by using them as proofs for the finiteness of time and bodies.

Influence on Jewish Philosophy

Al-Kindī was one of the two main sources used by Isaac *Israeli (855–c. 955), the first Jewish Neoplatonist, in his philosophic writings. Whether Israeli read Al-Kindī's works, or acquired his knowledge through personal contact with Al-Kindī's disciples, is not known.

*Saadiah Gaon (882–942), in his *Book of Doctrines and Beliefs*, makes extensive use of arguments posited by Al-Kindī in his *On First Philosophy* and other treatises in favor of the finiteness of the world.

*Kalonymus b. Kalonymus translated three of Al-Kindī's minor treatises on astronomy and meteorology into Hebrew. Al-Kindī was mostly known in Hebrew literature as an astrologer, and *Abraham Ibn Ezra quotes him in this connection.

BIBLIOGRAPHY: PRIMARY SOURCES: Al-Kindī, *Rasa'il Al-Kindī al-Falsafiyya (Philosophical Treatises of al-Kindī)*, ed. M.A. Abu Ridah (1950–1953; 1999); Al-Kindī, *Fi al-Falsafa al-Ūlā (On First Philosophy: Al-Kindī's Metaphysics)*, ed. and trans. A.L. Ivry (1974). SECONDARY SOURCES: P. Adamson, "Al-Kindī and the Reception of Greek Philosophy," in: P. Adamson and R.C. Taylor (eds.), *The Cambridge Companion to Arabic Philosophy* (2005), 32–51; G.N. Atiyeh, *Al-Kindī: The Philosopher of the Arabs* (1966); G. Endress, "The Circle of al-Kindi: Early Arabic Translations from the Greek and the Rise of Islamic Philosophy," in: G. Endress and R. Kruk (eds.), *The Ancient Tradition in Christian and Islamic Hellenism: Studies in the Transmission of Greek Philosophy and Sciences* (1997), 43–76; A. Ivry, "Al-Kindi as Philosopher: The Aristotelian and Neoplatonic Dimension," in: S.M. Stern, G. Hourani, and V. Brown (eds.), *Islamic Philosophy and the Classical Tradition: Essays Presented to Richard Walzer* (1972), 39–117; J. Jolivet, *L'Intellect selon Kindi* (1971); F. Klein-Franke, "Al-Kindi," in: S.H. Nasr and O. Leaman (eds.), *History of Islamic Philosophy* (1996), 77–165; R. Rashed and J. Jolivet, *Oeuvres Philosophiques & Scientifiques d'al-Kindi*, 1–2 (1997–8): S.M. Stern, "Notes on Al-Kindī's Treatise on Definitions," in: *Journal of the Royal Asiatic Society*, 1–2 (1959), 32–43. INFLUENCE ON JEWISH PHILOSOPHY: A. Altmann and S.M. Stern, *Isaac Israeli* (1958); R. Walzer, *Greek into Arabic* (1963), 175–205; H.A. Davidson, *Proofs for Eternity, Creation and the Existence of God in Medieval Islamic Jewish Philosophy* (1987), 106–116.

[Amira Eran (2nd ed.)]

KING, ALAN (**Irwin Alan Kniberg**; 1927–2004), comedian, actor, producer, author. Born in Brooklyn to poor Russian-immigrant parents, King parlayed a borscht-belt sense of humor into a varied show business career that spanned over half a century, including countless appearances on national television shows. His political activism on behalf of civil rights (he marched with the Rev. Dr. Martin Luther King Jr.), his campaigning for John F. Kennedy and Robert F. Kennedy, and his philanthropic contributions to Jewish causes in the United States and Israel (he founded the Alan King Diagnostic Medical Center in Jerusalem) made him one of the best-known figures in entertainment.

An unabashed wisecracking New Yorker, King honed his skills in the Jewish hotels of the Catskill Mountains after being expelled from high school at the age of 17. He got his first big break in 1949 when he headlined at New York's Paramount Theater. Seven years later he opened for Judy Garland at the Palace, and he accompanied the actress-singer when she performed in London. From there his career took off, leading to comedy, television, movies, theater and film production and five best-selling books. He took on the persona of a swaggering crank – part impatient executive, part put-upon husband and father – complete with elegant haberdashery, a fine cigar, and a sour expression

On stage, he mocked life in suburbia and criticized everything from airline food to marriage. He also appeared in almost 30 films (often as a rabbi, an agent, or a gangster), including *Bonfire of the Vanities*, *Bye, Bye Braverman*, and *Enemies, a Love Story*. As a Broadway producer, his credits included *The Impossible Years*, in which he also starred, *The Lion in Winter*, and Tyrone Guthrie's revival of *Dinner at Eight*.

In Israel, he also established a nonsectarian scholarship fund for American students at the Hebrew University and an Albert Einstein scholarship fund. He conducted fundraising efforts for the Nassau (L.I.) Center for Emotionally Disturbed Children and established a chair in dramatic arts at Brandeis University. He was a member of the board of the North Shore Medical Center.

His books include his autobiography, *Name Dropping: The Life and Lies of Alan King*, *Anyone Who Owns His Own Home Deserves It*, *Help! I'm a Prisoner in a Chinese Bakery*, *Is Salami and Eggs Better Than Sex?*, and *The Alan King Great Jewish Joke Book*.

In 1998, the National Foundation for Jewish Culture bestowed on King its first award for American Jewish humor. After that, the award carried King's name. On the New York stage in 2002, he portrayed the film tycoon Samuel *Goldwyn as a man of chutzpah and brass very much like himself, the *New York Times* said.

[Stewart Kampel (2nd ed.)]

KING, CAROLE (**Carole Klein**; 1942–), U.S. singer and songwriter. Born in Brooklyn, New York, King entered into a songwriting partnership with her husband Gerry Goffin (from whom she was divorced in 1968), and became part of one of the most successful songwriting teams of pop music of the early 1960s. They wrote such hit songs as "Will You Still Love Me Tomorrow?" (1960) for the Shirelles, "He's a Rebel" (1960) for the Chiffons, "The Locomotion" (1961) for Little Eva, "Go Away, Little Girl" (1962) for Steve Lawrence, "Up on the Roof" (1962) for the Drifters, "Take Good Care of My Baby" (1963) for Bobby Vee, "I'm into Something Good" (1964) for Herman's Hermits, "Natural Woman" (1965) for Aretha Franklin, and "Pleasant Valley Sunday" (1967) for the Monkees. She herself had a top-twenty hit during this period as well, "It Might As Well Rain until September" (1961), also co-written with Goffin.

Soon after her divorce, King started a solo career as a recording artist. Her album *Tapestry* (1970) was one of the biggest-selling albums in pop music annals, with recorded worldwide sales of 20,000,000. It won a Grammy as Album of the Year, while one of its tracks, "It's Too Late," was voted Record of the Year; and another, "You've Got a Friend," was named Song of the Year; and she won the Grammy for Best Pop Vocal Performance – Female. King was the only woman to win all four awards. She went on to write and record such hit songs as "I Feel the Earth Move" (1971), "So Far Away" (1971), and "One Fine Day" (1980).

King recorded more than 20 albums, as well as songs for such films as *Head* (1968), *Pocket Money* (1972), *Murphy's Romance* (1985), and *A League of Their Own* (Grammy nomination for Best Song, "Now and Forever," 1992). For television, she wrote the music for the TV special *Really Rosie* (1975); the theme for the series *The Trials of Rosie O'Neill* (1990–92); the title song for the TV movie *Freedom Song* (Emmy nomination for Outstanding Music and Lyrics, 2000); and she sang her song "Where You Lead," the opening theme of the series *Gilmore Girls* (2000). On Broadway, three original musical revues have featured her songs: *Rock 'n Roll! The First 5,000 Years* (1982); *Andre De Shield's Haarlem Nocturne* (1984); and *Uptown… It's Hot!* (1986). She also performed in the musical *Blood Brothers* (1993).

In 1990, King (with Gerry Goffin) was elected to the Rock and Roll Hall of Fame. In 2001 she was one of three recipients of the New York chapter of the Recording Academy's New York Heroes Award. And in 2004, King and Goffin were awarded the Grammy's Trustees Award for their contributions to the music industry.

BIBLIOGRAPHY: J. Perone, *Carole King: A Bio-bibliography* (1999); M. Cohen and G. Shaw, *Carole King: A Biography in Words and Pictures* (1976); P. Taylor, *Carole King* (1976).

[Ruth Beloff (2nd ed.)]

KING, KINGSHIP (Heb. מֶלֶךְ, מַלְכוּת).

In the Bible

The term "king" in the biblical frame of reference and that of the Ancient Near East generally designates a governor and ruler, usually the sole authority over his subjects. This term is used to designate the rulers of great empires such as Egypt, Assyria, and Persia; rulers of nation-kingdoms such as Moab, Edom, and Israel; and the rulers of city-states, such as Tyre, Hazor, and Jericho. Occasionally the term "king" is used to designate a tribal chief, or the chief of a group of tribes, e.g., "The kings of Midian" (Num. 31:8), and "the king of Kedar," mentioned in an Aramaic inscription of the Persian era.

Concept of Monarchy

The status of the monarchy and the concept of monarchy are not identical in the various cultures of the Ancient Near East. The distinctions in the concept of monarchy are sometimes the differences between the ruler of a vast empire, and a city-state king who is in effect a vassal, and sometimes the differences among the cultures. The status of monarchy in Egypt is not the same as in Mesopotamia, and it differs again from its status in the Hittite and the Canaanite cultural spheres. Nevertheless, the general notions of the nature of monarchy and of the figure of the king in the various cultures of the Ancient Near East have much in common. All shared the view that there was a direct relationship between the king and the deity – whether the king was actually considered divine or son of a god, or the god's representative on earth who makes known the god's will, or as the god's chosen servant. The king's power over his subjects – which was usually supreme and absolute – was not regarded as arbitrarily arrogated but as an embodiment of the god's will and as a gracious gift of the god to humanity. In many of the Ancient Near Eastern cultures the monarch was seen as part of the eternal order. In Egypt the monarchy was regarded as an essential element in the order of creation. The monarchy was divine, as the natural order of things is divine. In Mesopotamia, in the view that finds expression in the Sumerian kings list, the monarchy was introduced from heaven, although the Sumerian kings themselves were generally not divine. There are few sources concerning the character of monarchy in Canaan and the immediate vicinity, but there too it appears to have been considered elemental.

Origins of Kingship in Israel

The kingdom of Israel, both in the features it shared with other Ancient Near Eastern cultures and in its unique features, was affected by the circumstances in which the monarchy was established. Unlike the situation in Mesopotamia and Egypt, we have no royal inscriptions or surviving royal annals from ancient Israel or Judah. Much of our information must be gleaned from the Bible. The Torah, which reached its final form in the post-exilic period, ignores the king almost entirely, referring to him in only two passages; the law of the king in Deuteronomy 17:14–20 and the mention of the king going into exile along with the people who set him on the throne in the curses section of Deuteronomy 28 (v. 36). The law of the king treats kingship as an initiative of the people motivated by the desire to act "like all the nations" (*ke-kol ha-goyim*; Deut. 17:14), a term with distinctly negative overtones (cf. I Sam. 8:5–6, 20). The law says nothing about the obligation of the people to obey the king in contrast to the laws about obeying the priests and judges immediately preceding (Deut. 17: 8–13), or the laws about obeying the prophet (Deut. 18:15, 19). Instead, the law emphasizes the king's limitations. He is to be chosen by God, i.e., a priest or prophet, and he must not be a foreigner, e.g., the leader of a military coup, or an adventurer (Tigay, 167). He should not have too many horses or wives or silver and gold. He is commanded to write, or have written for him, a copy of the Torah, which he is to read all the days of his life so that he may be pious, god-fearing, and humble. Within the biblical narrative, the monarchy was not regarded as a fixed feature of creation but rather as a later development in the history of the nation. In Israelite tradition the earliest era of the people's history, namely, the period of the desert wanderings, and the conquest of Canaan, was regarded as the period of a superior social order and of the Lord's rule through his servants Moses and Joshua. The Book of Judges vests authority in the non-dynastic leaders upon whom God calls to rescue his people in times of trouble. Indeed, the clan and tribal society persisted in Israel for a long time after the rise of the nation, in contrast to the biblical account that the kindred peoples Edom, Moab, and Ammon had established monarchies shortly after settling in their lands (Gen. 36:31ff.; Num. 21:26 et al.). The persistence of the tribal order in Israel was no doubt due to an opposition to the idea of a monarchy, which was part of the tribal tradition and had assumed a religious significance. (Among modern scholars, Mendenhall goes so far as to characterize the monarchy as a reversion "to the Old Bronze age paganism.") In practical terms, the Israelite tribal system was not sufficiently strong to withstand the growing strength of the national kingdoms of Moab and Ammon, and the increasing pressure of these and of the cities of the Philistine league of city-states, with its feudal-military organization. And, indeed, in the beginning an Israelite monarchy originated as a conferral of hereditary authority upon a judge who had successfully delivered the people from their enemies. Such was the case of *Gideon (Judg. 8:22), and his son *Abimelech, and according to the tradition recounted in II Samuel, Saul was made king under similar conditions.

In the biblical stories regarding the early attempts made in the age of Gideon and his son Abimelech to establish hereditary rule, and in the stories about the crowning of Saul, there is evidence that the establishment of a monarchy was regarded by some as a contradiction of the idea of the direct rule of the Lord over His people (Judg. 8:22–23; I Sam. 8:7 et al.). These references appear to represent an actual opposition to monarchy on the part of segments who were particularly attached to the traditions of the tribal society. Needless to say, within the tribal society those who advocated direct divine rule would have been those who claimed direct access to the divine ruler, among them judges, prophets, and priests at local or tribal shrines. This opposition has left some traces in the later Israelite attitude toward the monarchy (Machinist). Monarchy in Israel combined the tribal tradition with the influence of the general political environment. Israel adopted not merely the royal trappings, the institutions of authority, of its Canaanite environment, but also certain of the traits of the Canaanite monarchy which, in turn, reflected the influence of the great civilizations of Egypt and Mesopotamia. As can be seen from I Samuel 8, the Israelites acquired their conception of monarchy from their neighbors in Canaan. The rule of the king, as described in this text, closely resembles the forms of rule in Canaan, and Ugarit in Syria, in the period prior to the settlement. This close resemblance suggests that this description of monarchical rule was well established and was based on a reality with which the Israelites had been acquainted before the establishment of their own monarchy. Royal rule involved the sacrifice of certain personal freedoms, military service, and taxation. Nevertheless, Saul's kingdom and, to some extent, subsequent royal rule in Israel, were based on the Covenant of the Kingship (see below), with the king in the position of national leader, and not upon the hereditary rights of an absolute monarch. In any event, the acceptance of monarchy entailed the transfer of much tribal authority, especially in regard to military decision making, into the hands of the king. Even in Saul's day, there were already certain appurtenances of kingship, with an officialdom owing personal loyalty to the king, but it was only David and Solomon who adopted all the appurtenances of monarchy and established a ramified administrative apparatus.

CORONATION OF THE KING. The status and the trappings of monarchy and all that they entailed were clearly expressed in the coronation ceremonies which were customary in Israel. Detailed descriptions of two such ceremonies are given in the Bible. The descriptions of the coronations of King *Solomon (I Kings 1:33–48) and of *Joash (II Kings 11:10–20) were given because of the unusual circumstances surrounding them, but nevertheless they do provide a picture of the ceremony; it seems reasonable to assume that the description of the coronation of Joash reflects the established custom in Judah. The two principal features of the coronation were the anointing of the king with oil by a priest in the Temple, and his seating himself on the throne in the royal palace. The ceremony began in the Temple and was conducted with great pomp, with the royal guard standing around. During this ceremony the future king was given the insignia of the monarchy, i.e., the crown and the *edut* (II Kings 11:12). The crown was the symbol of the kingdom and is one of the commonest of royal symbols (II Sam. 1:10; Ps. 89:40; 132:18). The word *edut* is used in the Bible to denote covenant, law, and statute (see Ex. 31:18; II Kings 17:15; Ps. 19:8; 132:12 et al.).Some scholars translate *edut* as "testimony," which they then posit was a document that listed the conditions of the royal covenant, and by which the king had to abide during his reign. According to Von Rad, the testimony was not a written covenant, but a species of divine authorization, in which were listed the titles of the king as God's son and His anointed, his appointment to be ruler of his people, his royal name, etc. (see below); in effect, a kind of Egyptian *nhb.t*, namely, the document which listed all of Pharaoh's names and titles. However, it is doubtful if there is much substance to Von Rad's theory of a document of divine authorization of the king. It is possible though that in the course of the coronation the king was handed the covenant of the kingdom, or "the book of the manner of the kingdom" which was kept in the Temple (see I Sam. 10:25). Another possibility is that *edut* is related to *ʿdh*, "bedeck," and refers to royal garb (Kimḥi a.l.) or jewels associated with the royal office (Cogan and Tadmor, 128). After this the king was anointed with oil by a priest and/or a prophet and thereby became the reigning monarch, YHWH's Anointed (*Meshiʾaḥ YHWH*). The anointment, which represented the change in status as well as the sanctification and appointment to the post, was a sacral act, not confined to kings. The anointing of kings is mentioned in the descriptions of the coronations of Solomon and Joash, as well as David (II Sam. 5:1ff.) and Jehoahaz (II Kings 23:30). The sacral character of the anointment is seen in the stories of the secret anointing of the future kings Saul (I Sam. 9:1ff.) and David (I Sam. 16:13). They were, according to these stories, secretly anointed by Samuel and were immediately inspired by the spirit of God. Something of that nature is also related in the story about Jehu (II Kings 9:1ff.). The anointment bestowed upon the king the status "YHWH's anointed," the ruler chosen by YHWH.

At present there is only indirect evidence regarding this custom in coronation ceremonies in the Ancient Near East. A Hittite account of a mock coronation, which seems to be a close imitation of a real induction ceremony, lists the following features: anointment with the royal oil, bestowal of a royal name, and investment with the royal robes and crown. In Assyria the king would place anointing oil before the deity in the course of the ceremony. In Egypt anointment was an important part of the ritual, and it is known that vassal kings were anointed. It appears, therefore, that this was not specifically an Israelite custom, but was prevalent in the Ancient Near East. It is possible that the Israelites adopted this custom along with other ceremonies of king inductions from their neighbors. Indeed, *Jotham's fable, which is apparently based on Canaanite custom, opens with the words: "The trees went forth on a time to anoint a king over them…" (Judg. 9:8). Once the king was anointed the people present shouted "Long live the king!" (I Sam. 10:24; II Sam. 15:10; I Kings 1:39; II Kings 9:13, 11:12). This acclamation was part of the ceremony and expressed the recognition of the new monarch and the acceptance of his rule (cf. II Sam. 16:16). In the description of the induction of Joash there is also a mention of a covenant between God, the king, and the people (II Kings 11:17); but there is no way of determining whether such a covenant was made every time a new king was crowned, or whether this was a renewal of the covenant because of the special circumstances of Joash's induction. After the anointing of the king before God, he was led ceremoniously to the royal palace, followed by the people, and there he sat on the throne (I Kings 1:45–46; II Kings 11:19), which was the symbol of kingly authority. The words of Pharaoh to Joseph in Genesis express the import of this concept: "Only in the throne will I be greater than you" (Gen. 41:40). Phrases such as "as soon as he sat on his throne" (I Kings 16:11) mean, when he became king (cf. II Sam. 3:10; I Kings 2:4; Ps. 132:12 et al.). The Book of Psalms contains much more material about royalty than does the Torah. Many scholars accept Gunkel's theory that Psalms 20, 101, and 110 are hymns which were traditionally sung at the investiture of the king, and some scholars have even attempted to learn something about the nature of the ceremony of induction from these texts. But in all probability these and other hymns, such as Psalms 18, 72, 89, and 132 were royal hymns which were sung at various ceremonies on various royal occasions. It is not possible to isolate with any degree of certainty those hymns which were sung at the induction, much less learn about the nature of that ceremony from cryptic references in the hymns. It is known that in Egypt there was a practice of giving a royal name to the new monarch, and by indirect evidence (see above) also in the Hittite kingdom. In Israel the changing of a monarch's name on his accession is attested only toward the end of the kingdom of Judah (II Kings 23:34; 24:17), and there under special circumstances; but some writers believe it was the regular practice in Judah. Also, although it is not recorded that any other kings were given new names when they were crowned, there were kings who apparently had two names: Abijam (I Kings 15:1) was also known as Abijah (I Chron. 3:10); Jehoahaz (II Kings 23:30) was also called Shallum (Jer. 22:11), etc.; possibly this also accounts for the two names of Solomon-Jedidiah (II Sam. 12:24–25). But these few cases are not sufficient evidence that it was customary to change the king's name upon his accession, certainly not as a matter of practice.

SUCCESSION OF KINGS. The Israelite monarchy was, from its inception, hereditary in principle.

In the Northern Kingdom there were frequent changes of dynasty, brought about by rebellion. In Judah, in contrast, the monarchy remained in the House of David, and although there were frequent regicides, when a monarch was killed his heir ascended the throne (see II Kings 11:4ff.; 12:21ff.; 14:5–6; 21:23ff.). Some scholars have theorized that there was, to begin with, an element of election in transferring authority from king to king, and that he was elected who was considered favored by God. Indeed, Saul was elected before God at Mizpah (I Sam. 10:17ff.). The elders of Israel accepted David's reign in Hebron (II Sam. 5:1–3) and even Rehoboam went to Shechem in order to be crowned by all of Israel (I Kings 12:1ff.). A. Alt maintained that the principle of the divine choice of kings persisted in the Northern Kingdom and accounts for the frequent changes of dynasty; but this theory presents problems. The monarchy throughout the Ancient Near East was based on the hereditary principle: in Egypt, Babylon, Assyria, the Hittite kingdom, at Ugarit in Phoenicia, the Aramean kingdom in Syria, and even southern Arabia. All these kingdoms experienced revolts and changes in succession, but the general concept remained hereditary. It is therefore unlikely that the dynastic principle was not accepted in Israel, when the very concept of monarchical rule is that of hereditary rule. During Saul's reign his son Jonathan was regarded as the heir to the throne (I Sam. 20:30–31). After Solomon's death the people did not question Rehoboam's right to reign, but wished to be rid of his tyranny. In the Kingdom of Israel, too, the monarchy passed from father to son, unless there was a revolt which brought about a change of dynasty. The confirmation of the king in his kingship was an act of religious significance and did not imply a renewed popular election. In Mesopotamia, Canaan, and the Aramean kingdoms the hereditary principle of the monarchy was highly regarded. (Compare Kulamūwa (Kilamuwa in earlier publications) inscription (COS II, 147–48); Bar- Rakib inscription (COS II, 160–61).) Nevertheless, a king could boast of having attained the throne by his own efforts – not by hereditary privilege, but by divine grace. This was especially the case if the king was a usurper, or of non-royal lineage. Thus Zakkur, king of Hamath and Lʿsh, boasted that he was a poor man but the god Baalshamain loved him and made him king (Inscription of Zakkur (COS II, 155), lines 2–3). The situation in Israel was similar. On the one hand there was the principle of legitimacy, i.e., a monarch occupying his father's throne (see I Kings 2:12; II Kings 10:3; Isa. 9:6; et al.), and on the other hand, the kingship was by God's choice. This view also manifested itself in dynastic changes in the kingdom of Israel (I Kings 16:1ff.; II Kings 9:1ff.), and as a general principle of all monarchies, including non-Israelite ones (Hazael – II Kings 8:7ff.; Cyrus – Isa. 45:1ff.). The succession in Israel was generally from father to son, but sometimes special circumstances such as the death of a king who left no sons, or the intervention of a foreign ruler, a brother of the king (e.g., Jehoram son of Ahab; Jehoiakim) or his uncle (Zedekiah) succeeded him. The daughters of a king did not succeed him. Athaliah, the dowager queen who reigned in Judah after her son Ahaziah's death, seized the throne by force. Normally the eldest son was expected to succeed, but the king had the right to choose his heir. Solomon was crowned by his father David in preference to his elder brothers, and Abijah was chosen by Rehoboam to succeed him, although he had older sons (II Chron. 11:18ff.). Similarly, one finds that in Assyria in the seventh century B.C.E. neither Esarhaddon nor Asurbanipal were eldest sons, but were both chosen by their fathers to be king. The passing of a king and the transfer of power to his son always entailed danger to the dynasty. In Egypt at certain periods the succession was assured by co-regency, namely, the heir to the throne shared the rule and the regal status with his father. The same method was regularly used in the kingdoms of Sheba and Maan in southern Arabia. In Assyria and the kingdom of the Chaldeans in Babylon, the continuity of the dynasty was assured by giving the heir a special status and his own palace – *bît riduti*. In the Hittite kingdom, too, the heir to the throne had a special status. This concern for the continuity of the succession was also expressed in a special clause which was introduced into international agreements, in which it was stated that members of the pact, or the vassal, were obliged to come to the aid of the heir in the event of revolt. Such clauses were incorporated into Hittite pacts with Egypt and with vassal states, and at a later period also in an Aramean pact and in Esarhaddon's treaties with vassal kings.

In Israel the heir to the throne seems to have held a special position among his brothers. Rehoboam made Abijah "the chief, to be ruler among his brethren, for he thought to make him king" (II Chron. 11:22). Jotham ruled in his father's lifetime (II Kings 15:5); the regal trappings displayed by Absalom and Adonijah (II Sam. 15:1ff.; I Kings 1:5–6) were, no doubt, privileges of the heir to the throne, even though they behaved in this manner without David's consent. Solomon was anointed in his father's lifetime in order to ensure his succession. It can be assumed that the method of co-regency was also used by other kings of Judah, as becomes evident from a study of the figures for the lengths of the reigns; they cannot be made to tally unless it is assumed that the reigns of some kings overlapped those of their predecessors, namely, that they ruled as co-regents (see *Chronology).

BIBLICAL VIEWS OF KING AND KINGSHIP. As has been seen, the biblical concept of the monarchy was based upon the monarchical concept of the Ancient Near East, which was the cultural environment in which Israel developed from a tribal society into a kingdom. Nevertheless, in view of the fact that the monarchy was established in Israel in historical times, kingship was not in itself regarded as a gift of God to humankind, and was not regarded as a permanent feature of human life (this is especially noticeable in the books of the early prophets and in the "King Law," Deut. 17:14ff, above). Nevertheless, the monarchy was not entirely an earthly institution. The king was the Lord's chosen and anointed and carried a certain sanctity in virtue of this status. The concept of divine choice was expressed even when the attitude toward monarchy was reserved, e.g., in Deuteronomy (17:15) and in the story of Saul's ascension. The king, the Lord's "prince over His inheritance" (I Sam. 10:1), was chosen to be prince over Israel (II Sam. 7:8); he is the shepherd (II Sam. 5:2; Ezek. 34:23; Micah 5:3; Ps. 78:71). The title "The Shepherd" or "The Faithful Shepherd" is one of the commonest titles of the sovereigns of Mesopotamia. The king is God's anointed, and God's spirit is upon him, and he is therefore sanctified, so that whoever harms him shall be punished (I Sam. 24:7; II Sam. 7:14; 19:20–25 et al.). This status of the king as the Lord's anointed is evidenced also in the oath sworn "before the Lord, and before His anointed" (I Sam. 12:3). The idea that the king, the Lord's Anointed, protects the people and that their fate is part of his fate, is expressed in Lamentations 4:20, which transfers the ancient Egyptian concept that the breath of the Pharaoh is life-giving (EA 147) as well as that of the Mesopotamian notion of the protective shadow of the king (Oppenheim) to the king of Judah: "The breath of our nostrils, the anointed of the Lord,… of whom we said: 'Under his shadow we shall live among the nations…'" Whereas the anointing of kings was an accepted practice among the Ancient Near Eastern civilizations, there seems to be no other culture in which the term *mashi'aḥ* ("anointed," "Messiah") is used to describe the king, with all the implications of the term, except in Israel.

One of the chief traits of the king in the biblical view is his capacity to judge justly. The list of David's ministers opens with the words "… and David executed justice and righteousness unto all his people" (II Sam. 8:15). And Solomon asks God to "Give Thy servant… an understanding heart to judge Thy people…" (I Kings 3:9). The idea that the king was endowed with the ability to do justice is common to all Ancient Near Eastern cultures. In Mesopotamia the king was regarded as the judge who convicts the evildoers and protects the weak (see Code of Hammurapi, prologue, 1, lines 27ff.; 5, line 15ff.). In Canaan the good king is the just and honest one, who does justice unto the widows and the orphans (Kirta [Keret in earlier publications], Tablet 2, lines 39–54 (COS I, 342); and acts as father and mother to all (Kulamuwa lines 10–13 (COS II, 148)). And indeed, in the story of the beginning of the monarchy in Israel, the people ask Samuel to "make us a king to judge us like all the nations" (I Sam. 8:5). This is clearly an essential element of the monarchical concept. The king is the supreme judge in the land, and the people come to him in search of justice (see II Sam. 15:2, etc.). At the same time, the Bible does not view the king as the source of the law, and law and justice are not regarded as royal edicts. The source of the law is the Law of the Lord, which was given to Moses. The "King Law" of Deuteronomy 17 does not entitle the king to pass new laws; on the contrary the kingship obligates the king to observe the laws and rules of the Lord.

In Ancient Near Eastern kingdoms the kings were usually also priests of the deities. In Egypt the king was "the priest," and all the priests served in the king's name. In the Hittite kingdom the sovereign was the "high priest." In Mesopotamia the kings referred to themselves as priests from the earliest days of the monarchy, and in theory were supposed to perform various priestly duties. A priestly dynasty ruled in Sidon. And, in a story set in the days of Abraham, the Bible mentions a king of Jerusalem in the era prior to the settlement who was "Priest of God the Most High" (Gen. 14:18). In Psalms 110:4 it says, "Thou art a priest for ever, after the manner of Melchizedek"; this early hymn probably refers to the tradition of the sovereign-priest of Jerusalem, the psalmist associating the kingdom of David in Jerusalem with the tradition of Melchizedek king of Shalem, priest of God the Most High. The king had certain sacral privileges in the Temple and in the ritual, and often played various priestly roles. David "offered burnt offerings" dressed in a linen ephod, which was a priestly garment, when the Ark was brought up to Jerusalem (II Sam. 6:14–18). David's sons were priests (II Sam. 8:18). Solomon offered burnt offerings and burned incense before God when worship began in the Temple (I Kings 9:25 et al.). The king blessed the people both in the tent and in the Temple (David – II Sam. 6:18; Solomon – I Kings 8:55ff.), a function which, according to Numbers 6:23–27, is reserved for Aaron and his sons. There is no protest against this royal custom of offering sacrifices, burning incense, and blessing the people in the books of the prophets, which antedate the Aaronide priestly legislation of the Torah. The temples in Jerusalem and Beth-El (and apparently also the temple in Dan), in the Northern Kingdom, were considered to be royal temples. The Torah's depiction of a priesthood that was well defined and completely apart from the monarchy is a product of the post-exilic period.

The relationship between the king and the deity is expressed in various biblical texts as that of father and son. In Nathan's vision concerning David and his dynasty, the prophet, speaking in the name of the Lord, says about each of the future kings of David's line, "I will be to him for a father, and he shall be to me for a son" (II Sam. 7:14; and similarly in Psalms 89:27–28, and in other texts based on Nathan's vision). This idea is expressed with great clarity in Psalms 2:7–8: "Thou art my son, this day have I begotten thee," etc. In line with this are Psalms 110:1, "The Lord saith unto my Lord, Sit thou at My right hand," and Psalms 45:7, "Thy throne, O God, is forever and ever; a scepter of equity is the scepter of thy kingdom." It is on the basis of these texts that scholars of the myth and ritual school maintain that the religious concept in biblical Israel regarded the king as a son of God, as a divine figure; and some have gone so far as to state that the king participated in ritual acts which reflected his divine status.

These scholars base their theory upon a "cultic pattern" of this type, which allegedly prevailed in the Ancient Near East, and of which biblical literature deliberately suppressed all evidence. But this assumption rests on false premises. In Egypt the monarch had divine status and in the Hittite kingdom the king became a god after his death. But in Mesopotamia the kings were not regarded as divine beings, and only at a certain period (particularly that of the Eridu dynasty and the Ur III dynasty) did they add divine epithets to their names, and this was an isolated phenomenon and was not constant, even in this period. In an Ugaritic text Kirta/Keret is indeed described as son of El, but he is nevertheless a mortal. There is nothing in Babylonian ritual or the Ugarit texts, upon which these scholars have attempted to base their cultic pattern of the divinity of the monarch, to substantiate this theory; all attempts to prove the divine status of the king and the existence of such ritual are based upon an improper interpretation of the texts. Accordingly, the concept of the divinity of kings is absent not only from the Bible, but from the Canaanite and the Mesopotamian cultural spheres. Even the few texts in which the king is called son of God, etc., do not prove the king's supposed divinity, but rather the courtly style of hyperbolizing the sovereign's glory, which the Israelite poet shared with his cultural environment. Thus, the poet's words in Psalms 45:7 are no more than a concise simile to suggest "Your throne is like that of God" (compare I Chron. 29:23), meaning, a throne founded upon law and justice (see Ps. 89:15; and others). Even the poetic image of the king as God's son does not imply more than God's protection of the king, and the particular relationship between monarch and God. This poetic image can be found in Mesopotamia and in the Ugaritic texts, and here, too, the king is not viewed as a divinity, but as a mortal. It is possible that this term suggests that God adopts the king on the day of his anointing and crowning, as suggested by Gunkel, and that the phrase in Psalms 2:7 "Thou art My son, this day have I begotten thee" was a formula for adoption.

A detailed description of the king's prerogatives over his subjects is given in Samuel's speech concerning the "manner of the King" (I Sam. 8:11–17). These are based essentially upon the general practice of monarchy in Canaan, and were no doubt also accepted in Israel.

In the story of the choosing of Saul for the kingship before God, it is stated that Samuel wrote "the manner of the kingdom" in a book and deposited it before the Lord (I Sam. 10:25). This "manner of the kingdom" is perhaps not equivalent to the "manner of the king" presented in I Samuel 8:11ff. Instead, Samuel's "manner of the kingdom" may have embodied certain limitations concerning the king's privileges, and in particular, stressed the king's duty to follow the Lord and obey His laws, as the Lord's chosen and anointed and as prince of His people.

THE COVENANT OF MONARCHY. An important element in the concept of monarchy in Israel was the covenant of monarchy. One learns about the covenant between the king and the people, who accept the king's authority, in the account of David being made king of Israel. A pact between the elders of Israel and David before the Lord preceded the anointing of David as king over all Israel (II Sam. 5:3). A more detailed description of the covenant of the kingship is found in the story of the proclamation of Joash as king of Judah. The covenant was made "between the Lord (on the one hand) and the king and the people (on the other); and also between the king and the people." This covenant does not represent an election of the king, nor a limitation of his rule by the elders and captains of the people. It is essentially a religious covenant, and the limitation of the king's authority consists of the king's duty to observe the Law of the Lord (Deut. 17:19ff.; cf. I Kings 3:14, etc.). The king is not responsible to the people and does not have to account for his actions – he is responsible only to God. Only God can punish for breaking the covenant, by removing the king from his favor and by ending the dynasty, though not necessarily the rule of the king himself (I Sam. 13:13; I Kings 14:7ff., etc.).

The concept of a covenant of kingship is clearly expressed in Psalms 132: "The Lord swore unto David in truth; He will not turn back from it: 'Of the fruit of thy body will I set upon thy throne. If thy children keep My covenant and My testimony that I shall teach them, their children also forever shall sit upon thy throne'" (Ps. 132:11–12). This is an eternal covenant which is undoubtedly based on Nathan's vision in II Samuel 7:8–9, which is in the nature of a promise that the kingship will remain in the House of David forever. And indeed the monarchy in Israel is essentially a dynastic one, and the divine choice lay in appointing the king and his descendants to sit on God's throne in Israel (I Chron. 28:5; 29:23; II Chron. 9:8). The concept of a commitment to a dynasty is not exclusive to Judah and the House of David. Only circumstances caused the fall of the House of Saul and the change in succession (cf. the commitment to Jeroboam in I Kings 11:38: "… if thou wilt hearken unto all that I command thee… and do that which is right in Mine eyes, to keep My statutes and My commandments… that I will be with thee and will build a sure house…"). This principle was kept in practice in Judah, where the throne remained in the House of David until the end of the kingdom. Prophecies of the future declare that "in the last days" it will again be a descendant of David who will reign (Isa. 11:1ff.; Jer. 23:5; Ezek. 37:24, etc.). This stems from the association between the image of the future king and the concept and symbols which prevailed during the monarchy of the First Temple era, namely, the House of David. These prophecies describe the ideal future king as a shepherd whom God will send to lead Israel (Micah 5:3; Jer. 23:4; Ezek. 37:24;

cf. II Sam. 5:2). The future king or the ideal ruler, as seen in biblical writings, would be a king of justice, a suppressor of iniquity (Isa. 9:6; 11:3–5; Jer. 23:5); "His dominion shall be from sea to sea, and from the river to the ends of the earth" (Zech. 9:10). This simile is also a regular element in the description of the ideal king (Ps. 72:8ff. et al.), as well as the peace and abundance of the future kingdom (Isa. 9:5–6; Zech. 9:10; cf. I Kings 5:5; Ps. 72:2ff. et al.).

[Jacob Liver / S. David Sperling (2nd ed.)]

In Rabbinic Literature

Two problems faced the talmudic sages with regard to the institution of monarchy. The first was the apparent contradiction between the positive command to establish the monarchy (Deut. 17:14–20) and the opposition by Samuel to the demand of the people to appoint a king (I Sam. 8:4–22). The second was the legitimacy of the kings of the seceded Northern Kingdom of Israel. On the one hand the monarchy was regarded as belonging solely to the House of David and on the other many of the kings of the Northern Kingdom were appointed by a prophet (cf. the appointment of Jeroboam by Ahijah the Shilonite: I Kings 11:29–39). Since the restoration of Jewish monarchy – which in Jewish tradition will apply only to the Davidic dynasty – is regarded as belonging to the "messianic age," the laws appertaining to the monarchy are not found in the majority of the codes, since they limit themselves to laws which had a practical application in their times. The only exception is Maimonides, whose code embraces the whole of Jewish law, and the pertinent laws are fully detailed there (see bibl.). The following details are substantially taken from it.

It is a positive divine commandment to appoint a king; the opposition of Samuel was due to the fact that the people asked for it "in a querulous spirit" and their main purpose was to rid themselves of the authority of Samuel. The monarchy was to be hereditary in the House of David, and it was confined to males. Even where the possibility of a king of non-Davidic descent was envisaged (e.g., the Hasmonean kings) he had to be of pure Jewish descent. The greatest respect had to be shown to the king, and it was forbidden to marry his widow or divorced wife. He had the power of inflicting the death penalty, of confiscating the property of rebellious subjects which accrued to his estate, of imposing taxes, of conscripting for the army, and of imposing forced labor both on men and women, providing he paid them their wages. He had the power to declare a "religious war" (*milḥemet mitzvah*), which Maimonides defines as "the war against the seven nations, that against Amalek, and a war to deliver Israel from the enemy atacking him" (Yad, Melakhim 5:1) without obtaining the previous sanction of the Sanhedrin. For an optional war, however ("to extend the borders of Israel and to enhance his glory and prestige," *ibid.*), the decision of the Great Sanhedrin of 71 was necessary.

The kings of non-Davidic descent were deemed legitimate monarchs provided they were appointed by a prophet, fought the battles of the land, and conducted themselves in accordance with the precepts of the Torah. Whereas kings of Davidic descent were anointed (where their right to succession was in dispute) with olive oil, the others were *anointed with balsam oil, and there are various other distinctions. The extensive and almost standard parables based upon the difference between the mortal "king of flesh and blood" and the "Supreme King of Kings, the Holy One blessed be He," with which the Talmud, and especially the Midrash are replete (cf. especially Ber. 28b where Johanan b. Zakkai appears to refer to the feelings which filled him when he appeared before Vespasian), as well as such injunctions as that "to pray for the welfare of the monarchy" (Avot 3:2) are in the main directed against Roman rule, and to this certainly belongs the phrase *shi'bud malkhut* ("subjection to monarchy"), the removal of which the *amora* Samuel declares as marking the advent of the messianic age (Sanh. 91b).

The constant emphasis in the liturgy and in Jewish thought on the restoration of the Davidic dynasty (see *David in Liturgy) and the conception of God as king, which is central to that liturgy, has resulted in a strong monarchical tradition in Judaism, and in both talmudic and medieval literature the institution and legitimacy of the monarchy is generally accepted as a halakhic norm. However, there is also an ongoing uneasiness among medieval scholars concerning monarchy, which echoed Rav Nehorai's saying that monarchy is a disgrace to Israel. This tendency can be found in *Saadiah Gaon, *Samuel ben Hophni, *Samuel ben Ali, *Rashi, *Baḥya ben Asher, Joseph ibn *Kaspi, and others. It culminated with Isaac *Abrabanel, who although, or because, he spent his life in royal service, came out strongly in favor of republicanism, both for the Jewish people and for other nations. Abrabanel was influenced here by his experience with some republican city-states of the Italian Renaissance. Mostly, however, he viewed human monarchy as a revolt against the kingdom of heaven.

[Louis Isaac Rabinowitz / Avraham Melamed (2nd ed.)]

BIBLIOGRAPHY: Y. Kaufmann, Toledot, 2 (1947), 178ff., 214ff.; S. Talmon, in: *Sefer Biram* (1956), 45–56; J. Liver, *Toledot Beit David* (1959), 51–77, 95–116; S. Yeivin, *Meḥkarim be-Toledot Yisrael ve-Arẓo* (1960), 196–207, 227–31, 250–5; M. Buber, *Darko shel Mikra* (1964), 164–269; idem, *Königtum Gottes*, 2 (1937), passim; C.J. Gadd, *Ideas of Divine Rule in the Ancient East* (1948); W. Beyerlin, in: ZAW, 73 (1961), 186–201; K.H. Bernhardt, in: VTS, 8 (1961); G. von Rad, in: *Theologische Literaturzeitung*, 72 (1947), 211–6; Alt, Kl Schr, 2 (1953), 1–65, 116–34; de Vaux, Anc Isr, 1 (1958), 91–132 (incl. bibl.). IN RABBINIC LITERATURE: L. Rabinowitz, in: *Isaac Abravanel, Six Lectures* (1937), 88f.; A.M. Hershman (tr.), *Code of Maimonides*, 14 (1949), 205–43; B.Z. Netanyahu, *Don Isaac Abravanel* (Eng., 1968), 178–80. **ADD. BIBLIOGRAPHY:** A.L. Oppenheim, in: JNES, 54 (1947), 7–11; H. Frankfort, *Kingship and the Gods* (1948); G. Mendenhall, in: *Interpretation*, 29 (1975), 155–70; G. Gerbrandt, *Kingship According to the Deuteronomistic History* (1986); M. Cogan and H. Tadmor, *II Kings* (AB; 1988); H.Cazelles, in: ABD, 5:863–66, incl. bibl.; D. Goodblatt, *The Monarchic Principle* (1994); J. Tigay, *JPS Torah Commentary* (1996); J. Roberts, *The Bible and the Ancient Near East* (2002), 313–89; P. Machinist, in: *Constituting the Community Studies …McBride* (2005), 153–81. IN RABBINIC LITERATURE: J. Blidstein, "The Monarchic Imperative in Rabbinic Literature," in: *AJS Review*, 7–8 (1982–83), 15–39.

KING, LARRY (Lawrence Zeiger; 1933–), U.S. radio and television talk-show host. Born in Brooklyn, New York, the son of Russian immigrants to the U.S., King began in radio as a disc jockey on WAHR-Radio in Miami, Florida. He moved on to host shows on a number of Miami radio stations and wrote newspaper columns for the *Miami Herald*, the *Miami News*, and the *Miami Beach Sun-Reporter.* But his career suffered a setback in 1971 when he faced grand larceny charges because of his alleged misappropriation of funds given into his keeping. The charges were dropped with the expiry of the statute of limitations, and from 1972 to 1975 King worked as a sportscaster and freelance writer.

In 1975 King returned to WIOD-Radio, Miami. *The Larry King Show* was launched in 1978 on the Mutual Broadcasting System, Arlington, Virginia, and by the early 1980s the show was syndicated to some 250 radio stations in all 50 states. His television talk show, *Larry King Live*, on Cable News Network (CNN), started in 1985, became a leading talk show combining in-depth interviews with public figures and media personalities with viewers' telephone calls. King thus became the first American talk show host to have a worldwide audience. The program reached more than 200 countries, with a potential audience of 150 million.

Said to have interviewed more than 30,000 people during his career, King was listed in the 1989 *Guinness Book of World Records* as having logged more hours on national radio than any other talk show personality in history. Among his many honors and awards, King received the Peabody Award in 1982; the National Association of Broadcasters' Radio award; and the Jack Anderson Investigative Reporting award in 1985. He was named Broadcaster of the Year by the International Radio and TV Society in 1989; was named the American Heart Association's Man of the Year in 1992; and was inducted into the Radio Hall of Fame in 1989 and the Broadcaster's Hall of Fame in 1992.

As a result of his bout with heart disease, King established the Larry King Cardiac Foundation, whose aim is to provide funding for life-saving cardiac procedures for individuals who cannot afford to pay for such treatment on their own.

From 1982 to 2001 King had a regular column in the magazine *USA Today.* He also wrote *Larry King* (1982), *Mr. King, You're Having a Heart Attack* (1989), *Tell It to the King* (with P. Occhiofrosso, 1989), *Tell Me More* (1990), *How to Talk to Anyone, Anytime, Anywhere* (1994), *Daddy Day, Daughter Day* (with C. King, 1997), *Powerful Prayers* (with Rabbi I. Katsof, 1998), *Future Talk* (with P. Piper, 1998), and *Anything Goes* (2000).

[Rohan Saxena / Ruth Beloff (2nd ed.)]

KINGS, BOOK OF, biblical book divided into two roughly equal parts, beginning with an account of the end of *David's reign, Solomon's succession and reign, and the disruption of the kingdom at his death, and continuing with the parallel histories of the kingdoms of Judah and Israel until the end of the latter in 723 B.C.E. and of the former in 586 B.C.E. The last event mentioned is the alleviation of the lot of King *Jehoiachin on the accession of *Evil-Merodach to the throne in Babylon in 561 B.C.E. (See Table: Book of Kings- Contents.) Kings is the fourth part of the Former Prophets, its connection with the preceding book – that of Samuel – being indicated by the fact that I Kings 1–2 brings the life of David to a close. The Jewish classification of Joshua, Judges, Samuel, and Kings as "the Former Prophets" accurately indicates that the work, though using historical sources, is not secular or objective history but a theological interpretation of Israel's past. Since M. Noth's *Ueberlieferungsgeschichtliche Studien* (1943, 1957²), it has been designated "the Deuteronomistic History." For fuller details of the period see *History.

First Part

The account of Solomon's accession (I Kings 1–2:46) bridges the reigns of David and Solomon. David had risen to the throne through talent and cunning. He was aided by the convenient deaths of Saul, Jonathan, Abner, and *Ish-Bosheth. Solomon was aided by the talent and cunning of his mother and the prophet *Nathan (Cogan). On his own he brought about, the demotion of *Abiathar (2:26–27), the elimination of Joab (2:28–35) and Shimei (2:36–46a), and the death of *Adonijah (2:13–25).

The account of Solomon's reign (3:1–11:43) is composed of miscellaneous matter from the public archives, royal annals, and possibly a Solomon saga. A source explicitly cited is "the Acts of Solomon" (11:41), but it is not known whether this refers to annals or a saga.

The section begins (3:1–15) with the account of Solomon's dream at *Gibeon, in which God offered him a gift, and his choice of wisdom (*ḥokhmah*), probably meaning primarily practical administrative ability. This is to emphasize Solomon's special endowment, to rule according to the tradition of charismatic authority in Israel, thus supplementing the tradition of the Davidic covenant in authenticating dynastic succession. The authentication of novel measures by a dream-oracle at a shrine is attested in Egypt (so S. Hermann, in: *Wissenschaftliche Zeitschrift der Karl Marx Universitaet Leipzig*, 3 (1953–54), 51–62). This may have been incorporated in a Solomon saga, particularly since wealth and political preeminence were associated with wisdom (3:13), in what may be a secondary development of the original tradition of 3:1–15, like the story of the judgment of Solomon between the two harlots (3:16–28). The popular character of this story is indicated by Gressmann's citation of 22 versions of the same theme from various parts of the world.

The account of Solomon's reign in 4:1–10:29 amplifies the theme of the wisdom of the king. The nature of the subject matter and the sources drawn upon varies according to the interpretation of Solomon's "wisdom" as administrative or academic, some sections interpreting it as the former, others as the latter.

The greatness of Solomon's administration is described

BOOK OF KINGS – CONTENTS

I Kings	**1:1–11:43**	**The Monarchy under David and Solomon.**
	1:1–2:46	The end of David's reign and Solomon's accession.
	3:1–10:29	The reign of Solomon.
	11:1–43	The troubles of Solomon's reign and its end.
I Kings	**12:1–II Kings 17:41**	**The Divided Kingdom.**
	12:1–24	The disruption of the Kingdom.
	12.25–32	Significant events of the reign of Jeroboam I of Israel.
	12:33–14:18	A prophetic tradition of the reign of Jeroboam.
	14:19–16:34	Synchronistic history of Israel and Judah.
	17:1–II Kings 10:31	The reign of Ahab and the fall of the House of Omri.
	10:32–17:41	Synchronistic history of Israel and Judah.
II Kings	**18:1–25:21**	**Judah alone.**
	18:1–20:21	The reign of Hezekiah.
	21:1–26	The reigns of Manasseh and Amon.
	22:1–23:30	The reign and reformation of Josiah.
	23:31–35	The reign and removal of Jehoahaz.
	23:36–25:21	The end of the Kingdom of Judah.
II Kings	**25:22–30**	**Appendixes.**
	25:22–26	The Mizpah incident.
	25:27–30	The captive King Jehoiachin.

as a consequence of his administrative wisdom in the lists of ministers of state (4:1–6) and of fiscal officials and their districts (4:7–19) and the note on the provisions they supplied for the palace (5:7–8 [4:27–28]), which significantly follows 4:19 in the Septuagint. The fact that the aim of these passages is to illustrate the greatness of his administrative wisdom, suggests that 4:20–5:6, describing Solomon's realm "beyond the river" (i.e., west of the *Euphrates), from Tiphsah, the ford of the Euphrates, to Gaza (5:4), together with the specification of the quantities of daily provisions for the palace (5:2–3 [4:22–23]) and the obviously exaggerated note of 40,000 horses (5:6 [4:26], cf. 12,000 in 10:26 and the much more realistic 4,000 in II Chron. 9:25) are less reliable accretions. The note of his agreement with *Hiram of Tyre (in 9:11–14, excluding the popular etymology of Cabul in verses 12–13), and the explanation of Solomon's corvée (9:15a, 20–23) and the public works in the kingdom and in Jerusalem for which it was levied (9:15b–19) also belong to the account of Solomon's administration. This material was probably derived from archives, but was freely composed in retrospect. The note on the occupation of the palace which Solomon had built for Pharaoh's daughter and the building of the *millo*ʾ (Millo; 9:24), possibly the terrace- and buttress-work on the steep east slope of Jerusalem (so K.M. Kenyon), and the statement concerning the naval enterprises from Ezion-Geber (9:26–28) also derive from state archives.

The incident of the Queen of *Sheba is part of the legend of Solomon's academic wisdom and his magnificence (10:1b, 3–13). To this source, possibly a Solomon saga, may be assigned 5:9–14 [4:29–32], which states that Solomon's wisdom surpassed that of all the men of the East and of Egypt, and was expressed in 3,000 proverbs and 1,005 songs (5:12 [4:32]) and a mass of encyclopedic lore or sayings concerning natural phenomena (5:13 [4:33]). This is not strange inasmuch as ancient Near Eastern kings prided themselves on their wisdom. *Hammurapi claims to have mastered all wisdom as does Ashurbanipal a millennium later.

The theme that occupies the bulk of the account of Solomon's reign is the building of the *Temple, which also marks a period in the Deuteronomistic history as a whole, signifying the culmination of God's grace to Israel and of his confirmation of the Davidic dynasty, foreshadowed in the elaboration of *Nathan's oracle on the Davidic covenant in II Samuel 7:4ff. Together with the account of the building of the Temple (I Kings 6) and its furnishings (7:13ff.) there are notes on the construction of the palace and public buildings that were connected with it (7:1–12). The marked contrast between the detail in which the Temple and its fittings are described and the vagueness regarding the palace complex suggests that the writer was more familiar with, or more interested in, the Temple, and was probably a priest. Noting that the focus of attention is on measurements (6:2, 3, 6a, 10a, 16a, 17a, 20a, 23b, 24–26), materials (6:7, 9b, 10b, 15, 16a, 20b, 21b, 23a, 31a, 32a, 33, 34a, 35b, 36), and technique (7:9b, 10b, 29a, 32b, 35b, 36), rather than on the more generally interesting and important details concerning the site, orientation, foundations, thickness of walls, method of roofing, and general appearance, and noting also that this material is largely arranged according to materials used, Noth (*Koenige, Biblischer Kommentar,* 1964–) suggests that the account of the Temple in I Kings 6 was based on the oral tradition of instructions to the various craftsmen, which was eventually included in the annals of Solomon's reign in the general form in which the Deuteronomistic historian has included it in I Kings 6 and 7. This suggestion would account for the obviously incomplete source-material and the many technical terms that, it is conjectured, have been often misunderstood by the compiler and later glossators, and would account for the fact that the statement concerning the foundation and actual building of the Temple comes at the end (6:37–38), after which 6:1 has been adapted by the compiler as an introduction. The account of the furnishing of the Temple (7:13–50) shows a similar construction. The source which we have assumed for this material may have been incorporated in a priestly history of the Temple, which included notes, rather out of proportion to the context, concerning matters intimately touching the Temple, i.e., war indemnities from the Temple treasure by Rehoboam (14:26–28), Asa (15:18), Jehoash (II Kings 12:19 [18]), Amaziah (II Kings 14:14), and Hezekiah (II Kings 18:15) and the spoilation of the Temple by the Babylonians (II Kings 24:13; 25:13–17). The special notice given to Joash's reform of Temple finance (II Kings

12:4–16) and the cultic innovations of *Ahaz (II Kings 16:10–18) may belong to such a Temple history. The obscurity of much information in the source and the interest in the Temple may have occasioned later accretions.

The compiler has concentrated Solomon's troubles in the end of his account of his reign, though actually the insubordination of Edom (I Kings 11:21) and Damascus (11:25) was earlier. This arrangement exemplifies his theme of the operation of the word of God in the history of Israel through blessing and curse (cf. Deuteronomy 28:1–14 and 15ff.). Thus Solomon's marriages with alien women and his toleration of alien cults are noted with censure, and his political troubles, external and internal (11:14–40), are described as a consequence of this behavior. In this section verses 1–13 are the compiler's resumé, while verses 14–40, the account of the escape and insurrection of Hadad of Edom (14–22; 25b, reading *Edom* for MT Aram after LXX and Pesh.) and of the rise of Rezon of Damascus (23–25a), are quite free from Deuteronomistic language and comment and were evidently based upon a reliable historical source which was not modified. There is apparently a conflation of two accounts of Hadad's rising, one of which briefly records his refuge in Egypt and his eventual return with Egyptian support, and the other, his refuge with supporters in Midian (al-Ḥismā) in the early days of his exile. The latter might have been drawn from Edomite annals available to a Judean writer during the reign of Jehoshaphat (co-regent, 870–867 B.C.E., king, 867–846 B.C.E.), when Edom was subject to Judah (22:48). The account of the aborted revolt of Jeroboam (11:26–40), prefaced by a note on his origins, probably comes ultimately from the annals of Israel. However, the digression on the role of *Ahijah the prophet of Shiloh in support of Jeroboam (29–32) may be from a prophetic legend, like the story of Ahijah's encounter with Jeroboam's wife (14:1–18). Then follows the compiler's expansion of Ahijah's oracle, elaborating on the defection of the northern tribes as retribution for Solomon's religious laxity (11:33–9). Since the permanence of the Davidic house is assumed in this section (36), it must be part of the compilation in its first stage before the collapse of the monarchy in 586 B.C.E.

The section ends with the standard editorial obituary (41–43), with which the compiler punctuates his work. The decisive phase in the history of Israel signalized by the building and dedication of the Temple complex (8:1–21, 62–66) is marked, like all such crises in the Deuteronomic history, by a formal address, here the prayer of Solomon (8:22–61), which is both retrospective and anticipatory. The main lines along which the tradition of the dedication at the great autumn festival is described are doubtless reliable. This section possibly stems from a priestly history in somewhat free narrative. The prayer of Solomon, however, exhibits traces of the pre-Exilic compiler in its phraseology, in the characteristic theological notions of the divine presence in "the Name" (e.g., 16, 18, 19, 20, 29), of God's transcendence (e.g., 27, 30, 32, 34, 36, 39, 43, 45, 49), and the somewhat mechanical doctrine of sin and retribution (e.g., 34, 46, 47). In references to exile there are probably also evidences of the hand which finished the work after 586 B.C.E. until the definitive redaction around 550 B.C.E.

Second Part

In the second part of Kings (I Kings 12:1–II Kings 17:41), the compiler is mainly concerned with the calamities of the Northern Kingdom as an illustration of the operation of the word of God in the curse which was a consequence of the tolerance of the ancient calf cult and various deviations from the sole worship of Yahweh. He consistently refers to this in his obituaries and particularly in his lengthy treatment of the reign of Ahab and his house (I Kings 16:29–II Kings 10:31). This matter is kept in historical perspective in the synchronistic history of Israel and Judah, especially in I Kings 14:19–16:34 and II Kings 10:32–17:41, with its notices of the accession and death of the various kings with synchronistic chronology. The compiler has drawn this matter selectively from the annalistic sources, the chronicles of the kings of Israel and Judah, to which he repeatedly refers for fuller information on secular history, a sure indication that the nature of his work is a theological interpretation of the history.

The disruption of the kingdom is communicated in a self-contained narrative concerning the rejection of Rehoboam at Shechem (I Kings 12:1, 3b–19 and possibly 20), with practically no editorial comment except verse 15, which connects the event with the prophecy of Ahijah (11:30ff.). The sequel, after an editorial accretion on the suspension of civil war between Rehoboam and the Northern tribes (21–24) and an annalistic note on Jeroboam's fortifications (25), continues with a resume of his organization and staffing of the cult at Beth-El (26–32), followed by a prophetic denunciation of the Beth-El cult in 12:33–13:10. Significant differences in detail in 13:2–3a; 43 and 12:24 between the Masoretic Text and the Septuagint are important for an understanding of the details of Jeroboam's return from Egypt, where Septuagint may have preserved the genuine Israelite tradition.

The account of the reign of Jeroboam in 12:33–14:18 rests on prophetic traditions of varying worth. The denunciation of the cult at Beth-El by a prophet from Judah (12:33–13:10), in which the reference to Josiah's reformation in 13:2 is a later insertion, is part of an ancient prophetic legend, which forms a unity with the story of the death of that prophet because of his unintentional disobedience to his prophetic commission (11–32; so Fichtner, Klopfenstein, Noth). This passage has secondary elements both in the embellishment of prophetic legend by the miraculous (e.g., 4ff.) and in the editorial comment (e.g., 2, 32). The denunciation of Jeroboam and his house (14:1–18), occasioned by his wife's enquiry of Ahijah about their sick son, is an important source for the history of Israel being part of the prophetic adaptation of generally historical narratives (e.g., 16:1–4; 20:1–43; 21:1–19; 22:1–38, II Kings 9:1–10:28) to express severe criticism of the monarchy in Israel. (It is likely that Ahijah as a Shilonite would have hoped, mistakenly, that in Jeroboam he had found a leader who would restore Shiloh to its ancient cultic prominence.) In I Kings 20:1–43 and 22:1–38 it was probably this prophetic reworking of historical data which introduced Ahab as the king of Israel, the account of whose violent death in verse 37 is apparently contradicted by Ahab's obituary in 22:40.

The rule of the dynasty of Omri from Ahab's succession in Jehu's revolt (I Kings 17:1–II Kings 10:31) is treated at disproportionate length because of the prophetic traditions of *Elijah and *Elisha and their relevance to the criticism of the liberal religious policy of this dynasty, which probably reflected a contemporary crisis, on which the Deuteronomistic compiler animadverts at length in pursuance of his general theme, the operation of the word of God in the history of Israel. The material is of various character and historical worth.

Certain passages, e.g., I Kings 18 (the ordeal on Carmel), 19 (Elijah at Horeb), 21 (Naboth's vineyard), II Kings 8:7–15 (Elisha and the coup d'état of Hazael) and 9:1ff. (Elisha and the coup d'état of Jehu), show a sound sense of history and are generally reliable, their critical attitude to the monarchy indicating prophetic authority. The traditions of this type concerning Elijah may rest on the authority of Elisha at the beginning of the eighth century B.C.E., while those concerning Elisha and possibly II Kings 6:24–7:20 (Elisha in the siege of Samaria) and 13:14–19 (Elisha's encouragement of the king on his deathbed) may rest on the authority of a responsible prophetic circle associated with Elisha, probably in Samaria.

Of less historical value are traditions of Elijah and Elisha of a more personal nature that are not primarily related to historical crises, in which miracles abound, e.g., I Kings 17 (Elijah fed in famine), II Kings 1 (Elijah calls down fire upon the emissaries of Ahaziah), II Kings 2:19–22 (Elisha and the water of Jericho); 2:23–25 (Elisha and the rude boys of Beth-El); 4:1–7 (Elisha and the widow's oil); 4:8–37 (Elisha and the Shunammite's son); 4:38–41 (death in the pot); 4:42–44 (Elisha and the multiplication of food); 6:1–7 (Elisha and the floating axe); 6:8–23 (Elisha and the blinding of the Syrians); and perhaps 5 (the healing of Naaman). This matter may owe its inclusion in the Deuteronomistic history to its popularity and its association with Elijah and Elisha; but the compiler, having decided to draw on it, may have used it to emphasize the control over nature exerted by the prophet of YHWH in opposition to the prophet of Baal, as in the ordeal on Carmel in I Kings 18 (so L. Bronnen, *The Stories of Elijah and Elisha*, 1968).

In the sections devoted to the reign of Ahab and his successors there are rather full historical narratives, e.g., I Kings 20 (the Syrian attack on Samaria with a prophetic anecdote) and 22 (the death of the King of Israel at *Ramoth-Gilead), II Kings 3:4ff. (the Moabite campaign of Jehoram), II Kings 6:24–7:20 (the famine in Samaria and the defeat of Benhadad), II Kings 9:1–10:27 (*Jehu's coup d'état) and II Kings 13:14–19 (the last meeting of Elisha and King Joash). In these sections the prophet is the central figure, except in the passages concerning the revolt of Jehu, although even this section is introduced by the anointing of Jehu by an emissary of Elisha as the agent of the doom that was proclaimed by Elijah on the house of Ahab. The critical attitude of the prophet to the house of Omri and the phraseology of the oracle of doom on Ahab recalls the prophet Jehu's oracle against Baasha (I Kings 16:1–4), and may belong to the same prophetic adaptation of historical narrative (so Noth, *Könige*). This source accorded so well with the theme of the Deuteronomic compiler that it needed little adaptation.

In the synchronistic history the general annalistic style, which reflects archival sources, is varied by fuller historical narrative dealing with Athaliah's usurpation of the throne and her suppression of the rise of Joash (II Kings 11) and Joash's reform of Temple finance (II Kings 12:4–16). Certain discrepancies in the former in form and substance suggest a compilation of two sources, a priestly tradition (11:1–12, 18b–20) and a popular one (13–18a). The treatment reflects the compiler's interest in the Temple and his sense of the political and religious crisis precipitated by Athaliah. The excursus on Ahaz' innovations in the Temple (II Kings 16:10–18) reflects the same interest in the Temple on the part of the compiler. With the fall of Samaria in 723 B.C.E. (II Kings 17) the synchronistic history of Israel and Judah comes to an end. The account of the end of the Kingdom of Israel is based on both Israelite and Judean annals, with comment by the compiler in verses 18 and 21–23, and by the redactor in 7–17 and 19–20, emphasizing the principle of sin and retribution in the history of Israel, familiar in the Deuteronomistic history. There is also an addendum on the Assyrian resettlement of Beth-El (24–28) with expansion on the religion of the province of Samaria (29–33; 34–40 and 41).

Third Part

The third part of Kings, concerning Judah alone, is much more full and detailed, but still limited by the theological nature of the compilation. Thus, despite the significant role played by *Hezekiah in stimulating resistance to Assyria for most of the first 14 years of his reign, the compiler proceeds, after a statement concerning his religious reforms (II Kings 18:3–6), almost directly to the Assyrian campaign in his 14th year (18:13–19:37). Here, after a short statement on the beginning and end of the campaign (18:13–16), the narrative suddenly expands, describing embassies from *Sennacherib's field headquarters to demand Hezekiah's surrender (19:1–5, 14–19), the encouraging oracles of Isaiah (19:6–7, 20–34; verses 21–31 being secondary), and the fulfillment of the oracle in 19:6–7, in 19:35–37. This is followed by passages from prophetic tradition concerning Isaiah's relations with Hezekiah during the period of his illness (20:1–11) and the Babylonian delegation (20:12–19). Here 18:13, 17–20:19 is closely, if not completely, parallel to Isaiah 36:39. II Kings 18:17–19:37 evidently consists of two parallel versions of the same incident, 18:17–19:9a, 36–37 and 19:9b–35. These, unlike the annalistic note in 18:13–16, cannot be categorized as history, but are rather popular anecdotal traditions centering on the prophet Isaiah and "the good king Hezekiah" and the theme of God's vindication of his honor and inviolability of his seat on Zion. The prophetic story is probably from the periphery of the tradition of Isaiah, though the actual oracles (19:20, 21–28, 29–31, 32–33, 34) may well be genuine. Assyrian documents concerning the siege of Babylon around 731 B.C.E. support the historicity of the account of the approach of the Assyrian delegation in 18:17–19:7, 36 (so B.S. Childs, *Isaiah and the Assyrian Crisis*, 1967). The second version (19:9b–35), which summarizes the arguments of the Assyrian envoys in 18:17–19:36 from a theological standpoint and emphasizes Hezekiah's piety in prayer (19:15–19) and Isaiah's assurance that he has been heard, in support of which oracles are cited (21–28, 29–31, 32–33, 34), is an edifying tale concerning the good king Hezekiah. The episode closes with a midrash concerning the oracles (35) and a historical comment on the oracle dealing with Sennacherib's withdrawal and violent death in his homeland (37).

Hezekiah's traditional piety is further dealt with by the compiler in the two oracles of Isaiah delivered during the period of the king's sickness, 20:1–11, composed of verses 1–7, with the simple reassuring oracle (5–6), and the sign of the receding shadow (9–11), which may be a secondary development in prophetic tradition of some saying or token which was more rationally intelligible.

The account of Hezekiah's reign closes with Isaiah's rebuking him for his too cordial welcome of the Babylonian delegates (20:12–19). This may be from an account based on a historical tradition. The incident owes its prominence and perhaps its position, probably out of its real chronological context, to the forthcoming Babylonian Exile. The reigns of Manasseh and Amon (21:1–26) are largely summarized in narrative style by the compiler and the redactor in anticipation of the decline and fall of Judah.

The account of Josiah's reign and reformation (22:1–23:30) comes within 25 years of what we believe to be the completion of the first stage of the compilation of the Deuteronomistic history, so that this may well be a free narrative from the compiler himself of matters in which he had been personally involved or which he might have heard from eyewitnesses. This section is composed of historical narrative from the compiler describing the finding of the lawbook, the covenant and the great Passover (22:3–23:3, 21–25), and the reforms of Josiah (23:4–20), which is based on the annals of Judah. Both have received redactional supplements in the response of the prophetess Huldah (22:16–20), in the elaboration of the incident of the desecration of Bethel (23:16–20), and in the note on the rejection of Jerusalem (23:16–27).

From the death of Josiah until the revolt against Babylon in the reign of Jehoiakim (23:30–24:1) the compiler used the annals of Judah which he freely glossed, the whole being further glossed by the later redactor, who continued in the style and tenor of the pre-Exilic compiler until the fall of Jerusalem in 586 and the deportation under *Nebuchadnezzar (25:21), the work ending with two appendices in historical narrative. The appendix concerning the Mizpah incident and its sequel (25:22–26) is the summary of a fuller historical account in Jeremiah 40:7–41:18, and the one concerning the alleviation of the lot of the captive Jehoiachin (25:27–30) seems to betray the hand of the redactor in Babylon, since it reveals intimate knowledge of local conditions there, illustrated by fiscal dockets from the palace of Nebuchadnezzar concerning rations to Jehoiachin.

Compilation and Redaction

The extant Books of Kings must postdate the accession of Evil-Merodach to the throne of Babylon in 561 B.C.E. (II Kings 25:27–30). Hoelscher (*Gunkel-Eucharisterion*, 1 (1923), 158ff.) proposed a date around 500, but it is unlikely that there would have been no mention of the fall of Babylon in 539 B.C.E. and the new prospect for the Jews under Cyrus the Great. Traces of a later hand after this date detected by Noth and Jepsen (*Die Quellen des Koenigsbuches*, 1953) are associated with the Priestly interest, as in the final compilation of the Pentateuch. It is to be questioned, however, if this amounted to a full-scale redaction of the Deuteronomistic history. At any rate, the Priestly element is certainly at a minimum in Kings. There remains the probability that the main redaction was made around 550 B.C.E. and it has been held (e.g., by M. Noth) that the whole compilation dates from then. There is a certain amount of evidence, however, for a pre-Exilic compilation before this definite Exilic redaction. This is indicated by the persistence throughout Kings of the promise of the permanence of the Davidic dynasty according to the divine covenant with David and by the fact that such references to the final disaster and Exile as do occur (e.g., I Kings 9:6–9; II Kings 17:19–20; 23:26–27) are obvious intrusions in the context.

Among the views concerning the compilation and subsequent redaction of Kings, Jepsen (op. cit.) contends for a compilation written by a Priestly compiler about the end of the Kingdom of Judah based on the synchronistic chronicle of Israel and Judah to which were added excerpts from the annals of both kingdoms and an Exilic redaction, incorporating especially prophetic traditions together with traditions from Solomon's reign and the Davidic succession story (I Kings 1–2). This according to Jepsen was the definitive Deuteronomistic redaction, the theology of which was normative for the whole work. Like Noth, Jepsen maintains that there were later adjustments, which he terms "the levitical redaction," which we have seen reason to limit. Contending for the first stage of the main compilation before the Exile and a subsequent continuation of the work till a final redaction around 550, Fohrer (*Introduction to the Old Testament* (1968), 248) marks the break before the death of King Josiah in 609, since II Kings 23:30 is apparently contrary to the report of the prophecy of Huldah that Josiah will be gathered to his grave "in peace." This, however, may refer to the state of the kingdom rather than to the personal circumstances of Josiah's death. Evidence of a break in the compilation might be detected in the confused and scanty notice of the end of Jehoiakim's reign in 598 (II Kings 23:36–37) and in the revolt against Babylon (24:1–7), and of the short reign of Jehoiachin in the Babylonian siege in 597 (24:8, 10–12; 24:15). The work could have been continued, perhaps by different hands though in the same style, until a final redaction of the whole soon after 561, which inserted references to the Exile into the earlier compilation. Some scholars have argued for an initial redaction as early as Hezekiah. F. Cross and R. Nelson argue that under Josiah a first pre-exilic Deuteronomistic edition of Kings was produced, which then underwent an exilic/post-exilic redaction. The question has not yet been resolved.

Aims and Purposes

Appreciation of the purpose of Kings depends upon the recognition that it belongs to the Deuteronomistic history as an illustration of the operation of the word of God in the history of Israel, adumbrated in *Deuteronomy 28. After the collapse of the Northern Kingdom and the subsequent deportation, with a similar fate imminent in Judah and realized after 586, doubts of God's purpose for Israel according to the Covenant assurances must have been current. Those are fairly rebutted in the Deuteronomistic history by recalling the consequences of Israel's endorsement of the covenantal obligations under solemn adjuration (Deut. 27:15–26), which are amplified in the final harangue to the assembly of the Covenant community in Deuteronomy 28. For the author of the Deuteronomistic history, as for Deutero-Isaiah, the great disasters, which seemed to some to dissolve the Covenant-association, far from impugning the purpose of God, betokened the consistency and firmness of His purpose. Moreover, in the framework of Judges and in Solomon's prayer at the dedication of the Temple the renewal of God's grace to the contrite is emphasized, and from His consistency in grace as well as in judgment new hope is drawn. To construe the national disasters as consistent with the positive purpose of God as declared in the sacrament of the Covenant, to rally the people in contrition to fidelity to the fundamental religious and ethical demands of the Covenant, and to quicken a sober hope on the basis of the traditional experience of renewed grace was the purpose of the Deuteronomistic historian.

BIBLIOGRAPHY: R. Kittel, *Die Buecher der Koenige* (1900); C.F. Burney, *Notes on the Hebrew Text of the Books of Kings* (1903); A. Sanda, *Die Buecher der Koenige* (1911–12); H. Gressmann, *Koenige* (1921); O. Eissfeldt, *Koenige*, ed. by E. Kautzsch (1922–234); I.W. Slotki, *Kings I and II* (Soncino Bible; 1950); J.A. Montgomery, *Kings* (ICC, 1951); D.N. Freedman and F.M.Cross, in: JNES, 12 (1953), 56–58; A. Malamat, in: VT, 5 (1955), 1ff.; A. Jepsen, *Die Quellen des Koenigsbuches* (19562); M. Noth, *Ueberlieferungsgeschichtliche Studien* (1957²); idem, *Koenige* (1964); H.W. Wolff, in: ZAW, 63 (1961), 171–86; J. Mauchline, *I and II Kings* (1962; Peake's Commentary on the Bible), 338–56; G. Fohrer, *Elia* (Ger., 1968²); J. Gray, *I and II Kings: a Commentary* (1970²); Kaufmann Y., Toledot, 2 (1960), 335–62. **ADD. BIBLIOGRAPHY:** F. Cross, *Canaanite Myth and Hebrew Epic* (1973); R. Nelson, *The Double Redaction of the Deuteronomistic History* (1981); idem, *First and Second Kings* (1987); L. Rost, *The Succession to the Throne of David* (1982; translation of 1926 German original); M. Cogan and H. Tadmor, *II Kings* (AB; 1988); S. Holloway, in: ABD, 4:69–83; G. Keys, *The Wages of Sin: The Reappraisal of the "Succession Narrative"* (1996); C. Begg, in: DBI, 2:25–28; M. Cogan, *I Kings* (AB; 2000).

[John Gray]

KINGSLEY (originally **Kirschner**), **SIDNEY** (1906–1995), U.S. playwright. His first success was *Men in White* (produced by the Group Theater in 1933), a play with a background of hospital life which won a Pulitzer Prize in 1934, and was made into a motion picture. A meticulous researcher, always careful to preserve authentic detail, Kingsley gained a reputation as a "tough" writer, specializing in dramas dealing with social tensions. Slum life in his native New York inspired the theme of *Dead End*, first staged in 1935 and also filmed. His other plays include *Ten Million Ghosts* (1936); *The World We Make* (1939); the farce *Lunatics and Lovers* (1955); and *Night Life* (1962), a play about racketeering. *The Patriots* (1942), a study of early American democracy based on the conflict between Jefferson and Hamilton, was written in collaboration with his wife, Madge Evans. *Detective Story* (1949) was a "documentary" set in a police station. His dramatization of Arthur *Koestler's novel, *Darkness at Noon* (1951), won various awards.

BIBLIOGRAPHY: S.J. Kunitz and H. Haycraft, *Twentieth Century Authors* (1942), s.v. and first supplement (1955).

[Samuel L. Sumberg]

KING'S LYNN (or **Lynn**), port on the east coast of Norfolk, England. It had a Jewish community in the 12th century. As the result of the massacre in February 1189, the whole community was exterminated. Jews later resettled there and in 1238 were ordered to maintain one of the royal crossbow-men. A diminutive community was established in 1747 which survived approximately a century. At the outset of the 21st century, it had no organized Jewish community.

BIBLIOGRAPHY: J. Jacobs, *Jews of Angevin England* (1893), 113–5, 348, 351; Roth, England, index; C. Roth, *Rise of Provincial Jewry* (1950), 77–81.

[Cecil Roth]

KINNAROT, VALLEY OF (Heb. בִּקְעַת כִּנֲּרוֹת), the level plain surrounding the Sea of Galilee (Lake *Kinneret) on all sides. The Valley of Kinnarot includes the Plain of Ginnosar northwest of the sea; the Buṭayḥa Valley at the Jordan's outlet into the sea in the north; the Jordan Valley south of the sea called the Negev ("south") Kinnarot; and the narrow coastal strip surrounding the sea on its other sides. The valley forms part of the Jordan rift which is itself part of the great Syrian-African Rift. The unusual feature of the valley is that it encompasses the Sea of Galilee inside the rift.

The valley was settled in very early prehistoric times; remains of early man have been discovered on the lands of ʿUbaydiyya near kibbutz Afikim. Much later prehistoric remains have been found in the caves in Naḥal Ammud which is drained by the Gennesareth Plain and the Sea of Galilee, as well as along the eastern shore of the sea near Ein Gev, and on the banks of the Yarmuk near Sha'ar ha-Golan. The area reached a peak of prosperity in the early historical periods (Canaanite and Israelite) when large cities were established there: Bet Yeraḥ (in the early Canaanite period) in the south; Kinneret (Tell ʿUrayma) in the north in the late Canaanite and

Israelite periods, and others. The valley also flourished in the Hellenistic-Roman, Byzantine, and early Arab periods. Great new cities were built on the shore of the sea (Tiberias, Migdal Taricheae, etc.) and the old cities returned to their former prosperity (Bet Yeraḥ, etc.). The valley began to decline during the Crusader wars, when Tiberias and many other settlements were destroyed (the famous battle between Saladin and the combined Christian armies took place nearby at Hattin). It deteriorated further with the Mongolian invasion and reached its lowest point in the last centuries of the Middle Ages when it was overrun by Bedouin tribes from the Arabian peninsula. The revival of Jewish settlement in the valley in the early 20th century brought with it a new wave of prosperity.

The valley, situated about 660 ft. (c. 200 m.) below sea level and surrounded by mountains, contains an abundance of water (Sea of Galilee, Jordan River, and Yarmuk River) and its unique climate is characterized by high temperatures and rapid rises in temperature as winter turns into summer. The area is intensively cultivated today. The combination of abundant water and hot climate makes it especially suitable for growing bananas and other crops which require the early ripening found in this area.

[Yehoshoua Ben-Arieh]

KINNERET (Heb. כִּנֶּרֶת), second oldest kibbutz in Israel, just S.E. of Lake Kinneret, affiliated to Iḥud ha-Kevuẓot ve-ha-Kibbutzim. Its land (Dalayqā-Umm Jūnī) was among the first holdings acquired in the country by the *Jewish National Fund. In 1908, Arthur *Ruppin, director of the Zionist Organization's Palestine Office, decided not to renew the temporary lease to Arab tenants, and set up a training farm there for Jewish laborers. Tensions arose as the farm administrator, M. Bermann, was inclined to regard the Jewish workers, who were Second Aliyah pioneers from Russia, as wage earners rather than trainees and preferred the cheaper, more experienced, and more pliable Arab laborers. After a strike broke out, Ruppin suggested allocating to a group of seven workers the Umm Jūnī lands east of the Jordan, where they then founded *Deganyah. A second strike, led by Berl *Katznelson, ended in a change of both the administrator and the workers. In May 1912, a girls' agricultural-training farm was added to Kinneret, directed by Hannah Maisel-Shoḥat. That month, Jewish pioneers from America, members of Ha-Ikkar ha-Ẓa'ir, came to Kinneret under Eliezer *Joffe's leadership. He worked out the idea of the *moshav form of settlement, and among the majority of the Kinneret laborers, the idea of the "large kevuẓah" (later called kibbutz) was developed (as opposed to the "small kevuẓah" on the Deganyah model). Outstanding leaders of the *yishuv* and labor movement, e.g., David *Ben-Gurion, Shelomo *Lavi, Yiẓḥak *Tabenkin, Shemuel *Dayan, and Ben Zion *Yisreeli all worked at Kinneret prior to and during World War I. The kibbutz cemetery is known for the famous figures buried there: Berl *Katznelson, Naḥman Sirkin, Moses *Hess, Ber *Borochov, Avraham *Harzfeld, and others. The grave of the young poet *Rachel is in Kinneret, where she lived; a date palm grove, which first served to propagate the date species in Israel, was planted nearby and named "Gan Raḥel." Naomi *Shemer, who was born in the kibbutz, was buried there in 2004.

After the war, Kinneret absorbed pioneer immigrants of the Third Aliyah, and also served as a camp for members of *Gedud ha-Avodah (labor legion) employed in the construction of the Ẓemaḥ-Tiberias road. The Ha-Kibbutz ha-Me'uḥad movement crystallized at Kinneret. The settlement developed exemplary, fully irrigated, mixed and highly intensive farming. It served as one of the spiritual centers of the *Ha-Po'el ha-Ẓa'ir movement and *Mapai. With the split in Ha-Kibbutz ha-Me'uḥad, in 1951, Kinneret joined Iḥud ha-Kevuẓot ve-ha-Kibbutzim. In 1968, it had 700 inhabitants, dropping to 612 in 2002. The main economic branches are farming (field crops, orchards, citrus groves, and dairy cattle), tourism, industry, and a quarry.

The *Bet Yeraḥ excavations and the seminary and convention buildings of Oholo lie within Kinneret's boundaries. A mound near the northwest corner of the lake was identified as the site of biblical Kinneret (*Chinnereth).

BIBLIOGRAPHY: A. Ruppin, *Three Decades of Palestine* (1936), index; A. Bein, *Return to the Soil* (1952), 67, 79–90, 202, 248–51; S. Dayan, *Al Gedot Yarden ve-Kinneret* (1959), passim; J. Baratz, *Deganyah Alef* (1948), 7–12.

[Efraim Orni / Shaked Gilboa (2nd ed.)]

KINNERET (Heb. כִּנֶּרֶת), moshavah in northern Israel, near the S.W. corner of Lake Kinneret, founded on Jewish Colonization Association (ICA) land in 1909 by settlers from Eastern Europe. The village developed at a slow pace, as the settlers frequently differed with the ICA (later *PICA) administration. The land was transferred to the settlers only in 1944. After that their progress accelerated somewhat. In 1959 the moshavah received municipal council status. In 1968 it numbered 195 inhabitants, rising to 335 in the mid-1990s and 497 in 2002. In addition to intensive farming (mainly orchards), Kinneret set up a small hotel, a restaurant, and other tourist enterprises. The first experiments in lake fishing were made by Jewish fishermen on the shore by the moshavah. In the nearby "Kinneret Courtyard," where the *kevuẓah* *Kinneret was founded previously, several nuclei of kibbutz settlements had their temporary camp before establishing their own villages in the region, e.g., *Afikim, *Ein Gev, and Ma'agan. In the moshavah's graveyard, shared with nearby Kibbutz Kinneret, lie the remains of Berl *Katznelson, Naḥman Sirkin, Moses *Hess, Ber *Borochov, Avraham *Harzfeld, the poet *Rachel, and Naomi *Shemer.

[Efraim Orni]

KINNERET, LAKE (Heb. יָם כִּנֶּרֶת, **Yam Kinneret**, or יָם כִּנְּרוֹת, **Yam Kinnerot**), freshwater lake in N.E. Israel. The Jordan enters it from the north and flows out from the south. Several names have been applied to the lake in the past, including "Sea of Chinneroth" or "Chinnereth" (Josh. 13:27; 12:3), "Water of

Gennesar" (I Macc. 11:67), and "Lake of Gennesareth" (Jos., Wars, 3:506), while in the New Testament it is called "the Sea of Galilee" or simply "the Sea" (Matt. 4:18; 17:27; John 6:1; etc.), and sometimes "the sea of Gennesareth" or "the sea of Tiberias" (Luke 5:1; John 6:1; 21:1). In talmudic sources it is usually called *yammah shel Teveryah* ("sea of Tiberias," Tosef. Suk. 3:9, etc.). The Arabs also called it Baḥr al-Ṭabariya. In Israel the biblical name *Yam Kinneret* has been revived.

Physical Data

The lake occupies a section of the central Jordan Rift Valley. It covers an area of 64 sq. mi. (165 sq. km.). The level of the water surface, which varies considerably with the shift from rainy to drought years, averages 696 ft. (213 m.) below Mediterranean sea level. The water is deepest, 144 ft. (44 m.) on the average, northeast of the lake's center.

The region of Lake Kinneret has a seismic character, borne out by hot mineral springs on its bottom and on its circumference. The lake was created in its present form when, in the recent geologic past, its bottom subsided more strongly than the area south of it, where diagonally posed young rock strata testify to an uplift which created a sill preventing the drainage of Jordan and other waters coming in from the north. Whereas the lake is thought to have originally been more or less rectangular, streams entering it, in addition to the Jordan itself, deposited alluvial material thus creating the Ginnesar Valley in the northwest and the Bethsaida (Buṭayḥa) Valley in the northeast and rounding off the north shore. At the same time, erosion at the Jordan's outflow in the south contributed to give the lake its present pear-like shape, with a north-south length of 15 mi. (23 km.) and a maximum east-west width of 10 mi. (16 km.). Alluvium deposited by the Yarmuk River in the south blocked the inflow of this watercourse into the lake and displaced the Jordan outflow to the southwest corner of the lake.

Although the waters entering the lake are fresh, brackish springs at the lake bottom and near its shore raise its water salinity; strong evaporation in the region's hot climate further increases the water's salt content. Measurements taken in the 1950s and 1960s show oscillations in salinity ranging from 250 to 400 mm/liter chlorine content, again to be attributed to the varying amount of water entering the lake; the more water fills the lake, the better the saline bottom springs are plugged by its weight, causing a further reduction in salinity.

History

Owing to its abundant water supply, warm climate, the fertile land in its vicinity, and the numerous fish in the lake, Lake Kinneret has attracted man since prehistoric times; in fact, the most ancient human remains and artifacts found in Ereẓ Israel come from ʿUbaydiyya not far from its shores. In Neolithic times the inhabitants of the Yarmuk valley adjoining the lake engaged in agricultural activities ("hoe" agriculture). In the Early Bronze Age some of the largest cities in Canaan were founded there, in particular, *Bet Yeraḥ, a site of some 60 acres (250 dunams). The *Via Maris* (Maritime Route) which passed its shores contributed to the wealth of the riparian cities. Egyptian documents (Papyrus Anastasi I) mention the hot springs on its shores and their beneficent effects. In the Bible, Kinneret serves as a prominent boundary mark: it was the border of Sihon king of the Amorites (Deut. 3:17); its western shores were in the possession of Naphtali, whose cities of Hammath, Rakkath, and *Chinnereth were situated along its banks; most of the eastern shore belonged to Manasseh, and the tribe of Gad extended up to its southern end (Josh. 12:3; 13:27). In the time of David, Geshur held part of its northeastern coastline, and after the division of the monarchy the kings of Israel had to engage in combat with Aram for control of its eastern shore; in this the Omrid dynasty was most successful. In 732 B.C.E. Tiglath-Pileser III captured the area from Israel and assigned the western shore to the Assyrian province of Megiddo and the eastern to Karnaim (II Kings 15:29). The lands west of the lake were a royal estate in the Persian and Hellenistic periods. The Ptolemies established one of their administrative centers (Philoteria) along its shore. Part of the territory of the city of Susitha (Hippus) bordered on its eastern shore. Under the Hasmoneans the entire area was Jewish. In 30 B.C.E. Herod received Hippus and in 20 B.C.E. the Gaulan. His sons Antipas and Philip founded the cities of *Tiberias and Julias (*Bethsaida) on the seashore. In the time of Herod Antipas the area around the sea was a main center of *Jesus' activities. Under Roman rule the western shore (Tiberias) and part of the eastern (Gaulan) were Jewish while the rest was gentile. The entire lake was later included in the province of Palaestina Secunda; in Byzantine times many churches were built on its shores (e.g., Heptapegon, Capernaum, etc.). After the Arab conquest it remained in the same province which was renamed Jund al-Urdun (Jordan). The crusaders kept a firm hold on the western shore and fought repeatedly to gain control of the eastern (the Terre de Sueth). The Mamluks included the lake in the *mamlaka* (province) of Safed, and the Turks in the pashalik of Acre.

Beginning from the first decade of the 20th century, Jewish settlements were founded on and near the lake's west and south shore (*Migdal, *Kinneret, *Deganyah, etc.). The frontier drawn between the British Mandate over Palestine and the French Mandate over Syria included the entire lake in the former territory, together with a 1.1–2.2 mi. (1.8–3.5 km.) broad strip on the southern half of the east coast and a tiny 32.8 ft. (10 m.) broad strip along the Bethsaida Valley in the northeast. Under the Mandate, the settlement chain was strengthened in the west and south, and the kibbutz *Ein Gev set up in the east. It engaged, together with two other kibbutzim, in lake fishing and the development of pleasure-boat trips and tourism on the lake and in the area. After the 1948 War of Independence, the Israel-Syrian border remained unchanged, although the Ein Gev strip was declared a demilitarized area. More Jewish settlements (Ma'agan, *Ha-On, *Tel Kaẓir in the south and east, *Almagor in the north) were added in the statehood period. Lake Kinneret was chosen as the National Water Carrier's principal reservoir, completed in 1964; the water was lifted from the lake by the huge Eshed Kinnarot pumping station in its northwest corner. As the main source of water in Israel, the Kinneret's levels are of public interest. Its low level is 698 ft. (213 m.) below sea level, while its high level is 685 ft. (208.9 m.) below sea level. In dry years, when the low level is reached, pumping is stopped. In contrast, in rainy years, when the high level is reached the Deganyah dam is opened. After years of relative drought the abundant rains of 2003/2004 again brought the level to the high-water mark.

Growing Syrian aggressiveness (attempts at setting up military positions on Israel territory near Ein Gev and in the Chorazin area, harassing of Israel fishermen, etc.) became one of the sources of friction building up the tension which led to the Six-Day War. The occupation of the dominating *Golan Heights by Israel in this war moved the border with Syria away from Lake Kinneret, which became an inland lake of Israel. The settlements around the Kinneret are mainly rural, while Tiberias serves as the urban center of the region. In 2003 the population of the Kinneret region was 96,000.

BIBLIOGRAPHY: Abel, Geog, 1 (1933), 163, 494–8; Picard, in: ZDPV, 55 (1932), 169ff.; Neumann, in: IEJ, 3 (1953), 246ff.; M. Schmorak, *Atlas Yisrael* (1961), V map 3; S. Yeivin and H. Hirschberg (eds.), *Ereẓ Kinnerot* (1950); EM, 4 (1962), 204–8.

[Michael Avi-Yonah and Efraim Orni / Shaked Gilboa (2nd ed.)]

KINNIM (Heb. קִנִּים), the 11th and last tractate in the *Mishnah order of *Kodashim*. The term means "nest" or "birds in a nest," and it designates the pair of sacrificial "birds," "two turtledoves" or "two young pigeons," which were obligatory offerings in certain cases and voluntary in others (Lev. 1:14–16; 5:1–10; 12; see Shek. 6:5). In the case of "obligatory offerings" one of the two birds is a burnt offering and the other is a sin offering, while in the case of "voluntary offerings" both are burnt offerings. This distinction plays a significant role in the discussions of this tractate. Equally important is the distinction between *ken meforeshet*, meaning that the offerer has decided which of the two birds is to be the burnt offering and which the sin offering, and *ken setumah*, where no such decision has been taken and the designation is left to the priest. *Kinnim* is not concerned with the laws of bird sacrifices in general (dealt with in Zev. 6:4ff.) but with the special problem of "confusion of birds"; e.g., birds assigned as sin offerings mixed up with those assigned as burnt offerings. The problem arising in such a case is indicated in the opening paragraph of the first chapter. The blood of a sin offering is sprinkled on the lower part of the altar (under the "red line"), while that of a burnt offering on the upper part; if the actions were performed in the reverse fashion the sacrifice would be invalid. Subtle differences arise if the confused birds belong to one or to several persons, and the confusion of birds of the same sacrificial species belonging to one person also has some consequence.

The second chapter elaborates on the distinction between *ken meforeshet* and *ken setumah*. It mentions incidentally that a turtledove and young pigeon do not constitute a *ken*, and concludes, somewhat out of context, with the qualified ruling on the duty of an heir to supply the sin offering for a woman who died in childbirth. The third chapter enlarges on points already discussed in the two previous chapters and ends with the adage that the stupidity of an ignoramus, like the wisdom of a scholar, increases with age. English versions are to be found in the Mishnah translation of Danby (1933) and Blackman (1951).

BIBLIOGRAPHY: Ḥ. Albeck, *Shishah Sidrei Mishnah, Kodashim* (1959), 337–8.

[Arnost Zvi Ehrman]

KINROSS, ALBERT (1870–1929), British journalist and author. Born in Russia, he became London correspondent of the Boston *Evening Transcript* (1896–98) and dramatic critic of the *Morning Post* (1901–03). In 1904 he returned to Russia as special correspondent during the Russo-Japanese War and the Russian Revolution of 1905. He served throughout World War I in the British army, started the *Balkan News* for British Salonica Force and for several months edited the *Palestine News*. He left journalism in 1907 to become a full-time writer of short stories, which were published in leading magazines in Britain and America, returning to journalism during World War I.

ADD. BIBLIOGRAPHY: D. Griffiths (ed.), *Encyclopedia of the British Press, 1422–1992* (1992), 352.

KINSKY, GEORG LUDWIG (1882–1951), musicologist. Born in Marienwerder, Kinsky, who was entirely self-taught in musicology, became curator and director of the Heyer Museum of Musical History in Cologne (1909–26) and lecturer at the University of Cologne (1921–32), where he obtained his doctorate in 1925. After 1933 he was able for some time to pursue his research privately and to lecture in the *Kulturbund, but in 1942 he was deported and worked as a slave laborer until 1945. His last years were spent in near destitution in Berlin. In his fields of research – music bibliography and the study of musical instruments – Kinsky made several major contributions to modern musicology. He prepared a bibliographical index to Beethoven's works, *Das Werk Beethovens* (completed by A. Halm and published 1955). His other publications include *Geschichte der Musik in Bildern* (1929, and several subsequent editions in German and English), an unfinished series of catalogs of the Heyer collection, and about 150 studies in periodicals.

KIPEN, ALEKSANDR ABRAMOVICH (1870–1938), Russian writer. In 1894 he graduated from the National School of Agriculture in Montpellier, France. In the 1910s he taught agriculture in St. Petersburg and in 1920 became a professor at the Odessa Agricultural Institute. He wrote a number of scientific works on viticulture, mainly on vine growing in the southern areas of the Ukraine. Kipen's literary activity began in 1903. He mainly published in collections and journals of Marxist and populist orientation but also in Russian-Jewish periodicals. He depicted the life of the working classes of southern Russia, and was interested in events connected with the Revolution of 1905. He is familiar with the internal and external aspects of Jewish life. His documentary tale *V octyabre* ("In October [1905]," in the collection *Znanie*, no. 11, 1906) is an impassioned eye-witness account of an outbreak during a pogrom in Odessa, including the brutal murder of women and children who were flung from their balconies; Cossacks shooting unarmed civilians, Jewish self-defense, soldiers aiming machine-guns and cannons at Jewish homes, Zionists defending the honor of their people, and the moral vacuousness of Jewish apostates. The hero of the story "Liverant" (published in *Evreyskiy mir* in 1910) rejects the idea of converting to Christianity as an escape from frustration of Jewish lack of rights. In his story "Gangrena" ("Gangrene") Kipen suggests that the solution to the Jewish problem should be the overthrow of autocracy and the elimination of all limitations of rights throughout the Russian empire.

Kipen conveyed in a masterful way the nuance of southern Russian folk speech, including the hybrid Russian-Jewish way of speaking which to some degree characterized the language of the Odessa school of Russian literature.

His brother GRIGORIY ABRAMOVICH KIPEN (1881–?), was an economist and active member of the Russian revolutionary movement. After February 1917 he was deputy chairman of the Moscow Soviet of Workers' and Soldiers' Deputies and co-editor of the newspaper *Izvestia* of the Moscow Soviet. From late 1917 until 1920 he was secretary of the Moscow Menshevik organization. In the 1920s he taught at higher educational institutions in Moscow. From 1930 to 1933 he was kept in political isolation in the town of Verkhneuralsk. Subsequently he was sent to Tomsk where he presumably perished.

[Mark Kipnis / *The Shorter Jewish Encyclopaedia in Russian*]

KIPNIS, ALEXANDER (1891–1978), bass-baritone. Born in Zhitomir, Kipnis began his career in Germany, and was a member of the Berlin State Opera until the Nazis came to power. He performed at Bayreuth and Salzburg, at Covent Garden and Glyndebourne in England, and at the Metropolitan Opera, New York. A singer of great range and flexibility, he excelled in lieder as well as in opera and oratorio. His son Igor (1930–) was a well-known harpsichord player.

KIPNIS, ITZIK (1896–1974), Yiddish novelist. Born in Volhynia into a maskilic family, Kipnis worked as a tanner before being sent by his union to Kiev to study (1920). There he befriended David *Hofstein, associated with the Kiev Group, and debuted in the Kiev children's monthly *Freyd* (1922), becoming one of the finest Yiddish children's writers. He published a book of poetry, *Oksn* ("Oxen," 1923), but soon found prose to be his medium. His narrative *Khadoshim un Teg* ("Months and Days," 1926), depicting the pogroms of 1919–21 and idealizing his native *shtetl*, won acclaim from readers and critics. S. *Niger and David *Bergelson hailed him as a successor to *Sholem Aleichem, but Soviet critics, while recognizing his great narrative talent, attacked him for the apolitical and petit bourgeois character of his lyricism and idyllic melancholy. He was expelled several times from the Soviet Writers' Union for resisting Party pressure. Evacuated from Kiev during World War II, he returned in 1944 and penned his moving sketch *Babi-Yar,* commemorating the German massacre of Kiev's Jews (1941) and calling for Jewish revival. In 1948, he was arrested as a Jewish nationalist and imprisoned in a remote labor camp. His rehabilitation following Stalin's death did not permit residence in a large city, so he lived in Boyarka, famed as Sholem Aleichem's Boiberik. In 1958 he returned to Kiev and published in the sole (revived) Soviet Yiddish literary periodical, *Sovetish Heymland*; a volume of his stories, *Tsum Lebn* ("To Life") was published in Moscow in 1969. In his works, published in Israel in the 1970s, he instructed the editors to restore his texts crippled by Soviet censorship.

BIBLIOGRAPHY: Meisel, in: I. Kipnis, *Untervegns* (1960), 7–23, (introd.); S. Bickel, *Shrayber fun Mayn Dor,* 2 (1965), 341–7; E. Rosenthal, in: *Goldene Keyt*, 61 (1967), 123–68. **ADD. BIBLIOGRAPHY:** LNYL, 8 (1981), 191–5; B. Kagan, *Leksikon fun Yidish Shraybers* (1986), 483–7.

[Sol Liptzin / Eugene V. Orenstein (2nd ed.)]

KIPNIS, LEVIN (1894–1990), author of children's Hebrew literature. Born in Ushomir, Volhynia, he went to Ereẓ Israel in 1913, studied at the Bezalel School of Arts, and taught in a kindergarten. After a period of study in Germany in 1923 he joined the staff of the Lewinsky Teachers' Seminary in Tel Aviv. One of the first children's authors in Ereẓ Israel, his numerous storybooks included *Pa'am Aḥat* (1931), *Yeladim ba-Maḥteret* (1946), *Ḥaggai* (1949), *Alef* (1955), *Bet* (1956), *Gimmel* (1957), *Ẓivonim* (1967), and *Ḥidon ha-Torah li-Yladim* (1968). Later he also wrote children's stories in Yiddish and published, in 1961, *Untern Taytelboym*. He also edited the journals for kindergarten teachers, *Gannenu* (1919–20) and *Hed ha-Gan* (1938–59). In 1978 he was the recipient of the Israel Prize for children's literature. A collection of essays examining the influence of Kipnis on Hebrew children's literature was published under *Iyyunim bi-Yẓirat Levin Kipnis* in 1982. A list of his works translated into English appears in Goell, Bibliography, 105 (index).

BIBLIOGRAPHY: Tidhar, 5 (1952), 2103–05, incl. bibl.; Ẓ. Scharfstein, *Yoẓerei Sifrut ha-Yeladim Shellanu* (1947), 111–6; Kressel, Leksikon, 2 (1967), 754–5. **ADD. BIBLIOGRAPHY:** H. Nesher, "*Al L. Kipnis,*" in: *Sifrut Yeladim va-Noar* 7:2–3 (1981), 44–48; S. Mashiah, "*Mishirei Misḥak le-Dramah: Levin Kipnis,*" in: *Bamah,* 116 (1989), 43–50; G. Almog, "*Sheloshah Parparim ve-Gezer,*" in: *Olam Katan*, 1 (2000), 243–51.

[Getzel Kressel]

KIPNIS, MENAHEM (1878–1942), singer, folklore collector, and writer. Born in Ushomir, Ukraine, Kipnis came from a family of ḥasidic rabbis and *ḥazzanim*. As a boy he sang in the choirs of Nissan *Spivak ("Nissi Belzer") and Jacob Samuel *Morogowsky ("Zeidel Rovner"). In 1901 he went to Warsaw where he completed his musical education, sang in the chorus of the opera, and began to publish articles on various aspects of Jewish music in the major Hebrew and Yiddish newspapers. From 1912 to 1932 he toured Poland, Germany, and France, appearing in concert with his wife and former pupil, Zimra Seligsfeld, in combined lecture-performances of the Jewish folk songs which he had collected and studied. These he published successively in 1918 (*60 Folkslider*), 1923 (*80 Folkslider*), and a combined edition in 1931 (*140 Folkslider*), with a parallel edition of 25 tunes with piano accompaniment which appeared between 1924 and 1926. He also published three collections of songs for children, and was active in the Polish cantors organization.

BIBLIOGRAPHY: Sendrey, indices; Rejzen, Leksikon; P. Szerman, in: *Di Khazzonim Velt* (Jan. 1934), 2–4; J. Mastbaum, *Warsaw 1939* (Heb., 1944), 174–5; M. Ravitch, *Mayn Leksikon*, 1 (1945), 230, 232; H. Zeidman, *Yoman Getto Varshah* (1957).

[Haim Bar-Dayan]

KIPPER (Heb. כִּפֶּר).

Etymology

The customary rendering of *kipper* is "to atone for," or "expiate" but in most cases this is, at best, imprecise. In poetry its parallel synonym is *maḥah* ("to wipe away"; Jer. 18:23), or *hesir* ("to remove"; Isa. 27:9, cf. the passive, *ibid.* 6:7), suggesting that *kipper* means "to purge." Also, ritual texts regularly couple *kipper* with *ṭiher* ("to purify"), and *ḥiṭṭe'* ("to decontaminate"; Lev. 14:48, 52, 53). However, other poetic passages use in parallel *kissah* ("to cover"; Neh.3:37; cf. Jer. 18:23), as if *kipper* connotes smearing on a new substance rather than effacing an existent one. Linguists have been divided as to which is the basic meaning since evidence from Semitic cognates can be cited in support of both, mainly from the Arabic for "to cover" and from the Akkadian for "to wipe." But perhaps both these meanings go back to an original common notion of rubbing. Since a substance may either be "rubbed on" or "rubbed off," the derived meanings "to wipe" and "to cover" may be complementary rather than contradictory. This is especially clear in Akkadian where both usages are attested in medical/ritual texts and where "the step between 'rubbing off' and 'rubbing on' is so short that one cannot distinguish between cleaning and treatment" (B. Landsberger). Akkadian *kuppuru* includes within its semantic range the purification of temples and other ritual cleansing (CAD K, 179).

Ritual Kipper as "Cover"

It must be admitted, however, that while there can be no doubt that blood is "rubbed onto" the evidence of the house as an apotropaic in the *Pesaḥ* ritual (cf. the verb *pasaḥ*, "protect," in Exodus 12:23 (I will *pasaḥ* over the entrance and will not let the destroyer into your house), 27; Isa. 31:5), the evidence that *kipper* can have this connotation is confined to Numbers 17:11, where it is not decisive.

Ritual Kipper as "Purge"

In Israel, however, it is important to note that the meaning "to rub off" predominates in the ritual texts, whereas that of "to cover" probably never occurs. This is best illustrated by the blood of the *ḥaṭṭa't*, the purification offering (see *Sacrifice). Its use is restricted to the sanctuary: it is never used on a person. The rites for the healed leper and for the consecration of the priest call for a *ḥaṭṭa't*, but the blood daubed on them does not come from the *ḥaṭṭa't* but from other animal sacrifices. Moreover, a study of the syntax of the *kipper* prepositions is decisive. It reveals that: (1) A non-human object of *kipper* is either direct or indirect through one preposition, *'al* or *be*, the direct object being that which is purged and the prepositional object that "on" which or "in" which purgation takes place and (2) a human object is never governed by *kipper* directly but only through either *'al* or *be'ad*, both signifying "in behalf of." This means that a human is not only the object but the beneficiary of the rite which is performed for him by a priest. There is an object, but it is the object that is sprinkled or smeared with the *ḥaṭṭa't* blood, and this is done not to the human beneficiary, but to the sanctuary and its sancta. By placing the blood upon the altar horns or bringing it inside the sanctuary (e.g., Lev. 16:14–19) the priest thereby purges the most sacred areas in behalf of the person(s) who caused their contamination either by physical impurity (Lev. 12–15) or by inadvertent misdemeanor against God (Lev. 4). Deliberate sins and impurities, however, cannot be purged by the offender's own *ḥaṭṭa't* (Num. 15:30–31) but must await the annual rite of purgation for the sanctuary and the nation (*Day of Atonement). *Kipper* undergoes further qualification in the context of the sacrificial system.

The Theology

The net result of these deductions from the function of sacrificial *kipper* is that there is sufficient evidence to reconstruct the missing priestly doctrine of theodicy. It presumes that sin is a miasma which wherever committed is attracted to the sanctuary. There it adheres and accumulates until God will no longer abide in it. Hence, it is forever incumbent upon Israel, through the indispensable medium of its priesthood, to purge the sanctuary regularly of its impurities lest God abandon it and the people to their doom. Thus, evil is never unheeded by God, even when the individual evildoer is not immediately punished, but accumulates in the sanctuary until the point of no return: the sum of individual sin leads inexorably to the destruction of the community.

This priestly theology of *kipper* is easily traceable to older non-Israelite analogues, for the ancient Near East shared a common obsession with temple purification. Impurity is inherently dangerous to divinities and humans. The *kipper* rite effectively removes that danger.

Remaining Kipper Cases

The agents of ritual *kipper*, exclusive of the *ḥaṭṭa't* blood, which have not yet been discussed are: the scapegoat (Lev. 16:10, 21–22); the broken-necked heifer (Deut. 21:1–9); the money for the military census (Ex. 30:16); the levites (Num. 8:19); the human deaths by plague for people's idolatry (Num. 25:1–15); the priest whose death frees the homicide from exile (Num. 35:32–33); and finally, the blood of sacrifices other than *ḥaṭṭaʾt*. Their elucidation will establish a new meaning for *kipper*.

Kipper as "To Represent" or "To Transfer"

It has been noticed in Mesopotamian magic that "the dirt called *kupirtu* or *takpirtu* is absorbed by a medium, mostly dough which is thrown away, buried or carried away" (B. Landsberger). This leads to the phenomenon of "the representative," "carrier," or "transfer agent," the substance to which the evil is transferred and thereupon eliminated.

This notion of *kipper*-carrier is clearly represented in the Bible by the rituals of the scapegoat (*Azazel) and the heifer whose neck is broken, as shown by extra-biblical parallels (see *Day of Atonement). Though such evidence is not available for the remaining cases, the representative principle is nonetheless operative. The common denominator of all these cases is their avowed goal: to avert the wrath of God from the entire community (cf. respectively: Ex. 30:16; Num. 8:19; Num. 25:13; II Sam. 21:1,3). This *kipper* must be sharply distinguished from that of the sanctuary. In the latter case, the impurities are purged lest they cause the indwelling God to leave; in this instance, however, *kipper* has the immediate goal of preventing the divine anger from incinerating innocent and guilty alike. Furthermore, in the case of the census money, *lekhapper ʿal nafshoteikhem* is related to *kofer nafsho* (Ex. 30:12, 15–16); the same combination is again found in the homicide law (Num. 35:31–33). The verb *kipper* is thus tied by the context to its *kal* (*qal*) noun *kofer* whose meaning is undisputed (i.e., "ransom"; Ex. 21:30). Therefore, there exists a strong possibility that all texts which assign to *kipper* the function of averting God's wrath have *kofer* in mind: innocent lives spared by their substitution by the guilty parties or their representative (already noted by Ibn Ezra for the levites of Num. 18:9). Thus, the above-mentioned cases are elucidated as follows: though no substitute is allowed for a deliberate murder, the accidental homicide is ransomed by the natural death of the high priest; similarly, the census money ransoms each counted soldier; and the levite guards supplant the Israelites when one of the latter encroaches upon the sancta (Num. 1:53; 8:19; 18:22–23).

Kipper as "To Expiate"

The final stage in the evolution of the root *kipper* yields the abstract, figurative notion, "expiate." Having begun as an action which eliminates dangerous impurity by absorbing it through direct contact (rubbing) or indirect (transference), it eventuates into the process of expiation in general. Thus, the *kipper* role of all other sacrifices – whose blood is not daubed on the altar's horns like the *ḥaṭṭaʾt* but is dashed on its sides – is to expiate sin. This is one of the functions of the *ʿolah* (Lev. 1:4) and the *minḥah* (Lev. 14:20), and the sole function of the *aʾsham* (Lev. 5:16, 18, 26; for details, see *Sacrifice). So with the *kapporet* placed over the Tabernacle Ark (Ex. 25:17–22); being a feminine abstract noun from *kipper*, it probably means "that which expiates" or "the expiatory." And since it also designates the place where Moses "would hear the Voice addressing him" (Num. 7:89), it is the expiatory, par excellence.

Kipper Blood

One more ritual *kipper* remains: the crux of Leviticus 17:11. This verse states explicitly that the function of the altar blood is "to expiate for your lives," and it has been construed as a generalization defining the purpose of all sacrificial blood. But *shelamim* have nothing to do with sin and neither have votive and thanksgiving offerings (Lev. 22:17ff.; Ps. 116:17–18). The key to the nature of the "expiation" of Leviticus 17:11 is the context. Leviticus chapter 17 concentrates on the prohibition of ingesting blood, and therefore deals nearly exclusively with the *shelamim*. For the *shelamim* (of which the thanksgiving offering is a special variety) is the one sacrifice whose flesh is permitted to the laic and the consuming of flesh itself requires expiation. That is why Leviticus 17:4 makes the killing of sacrificeable animals except at the sanctuary tantamount to murder. The sanctuary altar, in the priestly code, legitimates animal slaughter by being the divinely appointed instrument which restores the life of the animal, symbolized by the blood, to God. Thus Leviticus 17:11 is to be translated: "And I have assigned it [the *shelamim* blood] to you upon the altar, to expiate for your lives; for it is the blood, as life, that can expiate." Of course Leviticus 17:3ff. is not unique in forbidding the consumption of blood (cf. Gen. 9:3–4; Lev. 3:17; 7:20–21 – all P), whereby animal flesh is conceded by God on condition that the blood is not consumed. It is not even the only source that requires slaughter at an altar for domestic cattle (I Samuel 14:32–35), though it is the only one that requires a sacrifice. (For the Deuteronomic change see Deut. 12:13–28.)

Ritual Atonement without Kipper

Whenever a sacrifice concludes the purification ritual for physical impurity it is always a *ḥaṭṭaʾt*, and its purpose is to *kipper* or purge the contaminated sanctuary. It is of interest that when a prophet or a psalmist resorts to a ritualistic metaphor in his call for moral purification, he never uses the term *kipper* but one which signifies lustration with water (e.g., Isa. 1:16; Ezek. 36:25; Zech. 13:1; Ps. 51:4,9).

Of the sources just cited, Isaiah 1 (cf. in addition to v. 16, vs. 19–20, and v. 27 ("Those in Zion who repent")) demands repentance as the proper atonement for moral wrongdoing, and so do many other non-ritual passages (see below). But the indispensability of repentance is a stipulation of the ritual texts as well. To begin with, the possibility of sacrificial atonement is explicitly denied to the individual who presumptuously violates God's law (Num. 15:30–31). This, however, does not mean, as many critics aver, that sacrificial atonement is possible only for involuntary wrongdoers. To cite but one exception, the *asham* offering is prescribed for that premeditated crime called by the rabbis *asham gezelot* (Lev. 5:20ff.; Num. 5:5–8). A more correct assertion, then, would be that the priestly system prohibits sacrificial atonement to the unrepentant sinner, for the one who "acts defiantly… it is the Lord he reviles" (Num. 15:30). This is an explicit postulate of post-biblical literature: "the *ḥaṭṭaʾt*, the *ʾasham*, and death do not atone except with repentance" (Tosef., Yoma 5:9; cf. Yoma

8:8). That it is also explicitly demanded by the ritual texts of the Bible can only be sketchily demonstrated here as follows: The phrase *ve(we)-ʾashem*, the leitmotiv of the two exclusive expiatory sacrifices, the *ḥaṭṭaʾt* and the *ʾasham* (Lev. 4:13, 22, 27; 5:2, 3, 4, 17, 23), can be shown to mean: "when he feels guilty" or "when he is guilt-stricken." Contrition, therefore, is an explicit *sine qua non* for expiation by sacrifice. Furthermore, it is precisely when the sin is deliberate, not accidental, that another penitential requirement is added, namely that the contrition must be openly declared; it must be supplemented by confession (*we-hitwaddah*; Lev. 5:5; Num. 5:7; cf. Lev. 16:21; 26:40). Even the annual purification rite for the sanctuary and nation requires that the high priest confess the deliberate sins of the Israelites (Lev. 16:21), while the latter demonstrate their penitence, not by coming to the Temple – from which deliberate sinners are barred – but by fasting and other acts of self-denial (Lev. 16:29; 23:27–32; Num. 29:7). Thus, contrition for involuntary sin and confession for deliberate sin are indispensable to the atonement produced by the sacrificial system, and they differ in no way from the call to repentance formulated by the prophets. Finally, the prescriptions of the *asham* offering ordained for cases of calculable loss to the deity stipulate that restitution must be made to the wronged party (man or sanctuary) before atonement by sacrifice is permitted. Indeed, the prophetic insistence that repentance is not an end in itself, but must lead to rectification of the wrongdoing (e.g., Isa. 1:13–17; 58:6–12; Micah 6:6–8), is only the articulation of a basic postulate of the sacrificial system.

Non-Ritual Kipper for Sin

Outside the sanctuary, *kipper* undergoes a vast change that is at once made apparent by its new grammatical syntax. Whereas in ritual, the subject of *kipper* is invariably a priest, and the direct object is a contaminated thing, in the non-ritual literature, usually the subject is the deity and the direct object is a sin (e.g., Jer. 18:8; Ezek. 16:63; Ps. 65:4; 78:38; 79:9). Actually, this represents no rupture with ritual *kipper*; on the contrary, it gives voice to its implicit meaning. As for the object, though the cult concentrates on the purging mainly of sanctuary impurity, it, too, recognizes that its source is human sin. The subject implies even less change: though the priest performs the rituals, it is only due to the grace of God that the ritual is efficacious. Thus, non-ritual exhortations, requiring no priestly mediation, uncompromisingly turn to God, the sole dispenser of expiation. True, there are a few *kipper* passages with man as subject (e.g., II Sam. 21:3; Isa. 47:11; Prov. 16:14), but all these exceptions are explicable by the representative *kipper*, i.e., man is required to provide the necessary ransom. The exceptional *akhapperah panav* (Gen. 32:20) is capable of similar interpretation, but the unique object "face" may go back to another facet of the Akkadian cognate, meaning "polish" (an aspect of "rub on"), hence "polish the face" or "propitiate," "appease." If rituals stipulate repentance as a precondition for atonement, moral exhortation will place a greater value upon repentance – and its vehicle, prayer – than upon ritual and sacrifice (e.g., Lev. 26: 40–41; Deut. 4:29; I Kings 8:28–30, 33, 35, 47–48; Ps. 51:19; 141:2; see also *Prayer).

Forgiveness

It has been maintained that early Israel knew no forgiveness of sin because both *kipper* and *salaḥ* ("forgive") are mainly found in post-Exilic texts and because the pre-Exilic literature speaks exclusively of *ve-niḥam al ha-raʿah* and *avar le*, implying that "God overlooks mild sins but does not obliterate them" (K. Koch). At once, a statistical objection should be raised against the arbitrary assignment of all cultic passages (where *kipper* would chiefly occur) and all consolatory prophetic passages (where *salaḥ* would predominate) to the post-Exilic period. Moreover, this view suffers from a more serious fault: it blurs the distinction between two stages in the process of divine pardoning common to all the biblical sources. The first, involving the above-mentioned idioms, never occurs when God is just contemplating punishment but only when He has actually decided upon it. The consequence is that before the guilty can implore God for forgiveness, they must prevail on Him to revoke His decree. This fundamental distinction is the touchstone that splits the story of Moses' intercession for the Israelites when they sinned with the golden calf (Ex. 32–34) into plausible divisions. His initial plea (32:11–13) fulfills the first stage: "God renounced the punishment He had declared He would bring upon His people" (32:14). Moses, however, is not content with the cancelation of the divine decree. After slaying many, presumably the most guilty, he presses for the complete obliteration of Israel's sin (32:30–32). This God does not grant (32:33–34), but when He reveals to Moses that His mercy can supersede His justice (34:6–7a), whenever He desires (33:19b), an opening is provided Moses whereby he can explicitly ask for forgiveness (*salaḥ*, 34:9).

That the renunciation of punishment must be distinguished from forgiveness of sin is also clear from another instance of prophetic intercession (Amos 7:1–8; 8:1–2). Amos wants forgiveness (7:2); God only concedes the cancellation of punishment (7:3, 6). Even this He will not do more than twice (7:8), and finally Israel's sins drive Him to declare "the end has come" (8:2). With Amos as with Moses, the language is crucial: God concedes partially to the prophet's plea; he suspends punishment but does not grant the complete remission of sin.

Finally, it should be noted that the idiom *nasaʾ ḥetʾ ʿavon* (*ʿawon*) *peshʿa* can have the meaning "remove sin," implying forgiveness. Moreover, it is used synonymously with *maḥah* and *kipper*, *heʿevir ʿawon* (Job 7:21), and *salaḥ* itself (Num. 14:18–19). So many early sources illustrate this usage (e.g., Ex. 34:7; I Sam. 15:25; Isa. 33:24; Hos. 14:3; Micah 7:18; Ps. 32:5) that it cannot be denied that the consciousness and absolution of sin were moral realities in all periods of Israel's history.

NON-RITUAL KIPPER FOR THE LAND. The holiness of the sanctuary is complemented in the Priestly Source by the notion of the holiness of the Land of Israel. Correspondingly, the land too is capable of defilement (e.g., Lev. 18:25, 28, for sexual misconduct; Num. 35:33–34, for murder; cf. also Ezek. 36:17 and Deut. 21:23), and just as the sanctuary needs *kipper* so does the land (expressly, Num. 35:33). Furthermore, the implications are likewise identical: defilement of the land will vomit out Israel as it vomited out its previous inhabitants (Lev. 18:28; 20:22) for God can no longer abide in it (Sif. Num. 161). In this case, however, the parallels end, for there is no ceremony by which the land is purged; *kipper*, therefore, is not used ritually, but refers to general moral expiation. Atonement for the land becomes a more important concept in post-biblical times (e.g., LXX, Deut. 32:43; Jub. 6:2ff., where it is sacrificial!). The Dead Sea sectarians believed that their consecrated life was an atonement not just for themselves but also for the entire land (1QS 8:6, 10; 9:4).

KIPPER-INTERCESSION. Another postulate of the biblical doctrine of atonement is that God will spare the community by virtue of the merit of its just, e.g., Abraham's intervention on behalf of Sodom and Gomorrah (Gen. 18:16–33). However, intercession is chiefly the vocation of the prophet. The Psalmist eulogizes Moses for interceding on behalf of the worshipers of the golden calf (see Ex. 32:9–10) in these words: "He said He would destroy them had not Moses, His chosen one, stood in the breach before Him" (Ps. 106:23). To intercede at the risk of one's life is to "stand in the breach." (It should be recalled that though there are gentile analogues to the prophet as the deity's messenger to humans (see *Mari, *Prophets), there is still none which demonstrates that the prophet is also man's intercessor to the deity.)

It has been thought that Ezekiel refutes this doctrine of the atonement by the righteous, for he does say repeatedly and forcefully that the righteous will not save his generation, but that each man will be judged according to his sins (Ezek. 18:3–4). This is not so. Ezekiel, a priest as well as a prophet, is expatiating on a corollary of the priestly theology of the Temple (above). The reason why God abandons His sanctuary is that the level of impurity rises to a point beyond toleration. Beyond this point, God will neither seek man's repentance nor allow the prophet to intercede for him: the decree of doom becomes irrevocable. This postulate is found beyond the confines of the Priestly Source; it informs all biblical teaching on evil: the hardening of Pharaoh's heart (Ex. 7:3, 14; 8:11, 15, 28, etc.); Isaiah's harsh commission (Isa. 6:10); and the prohibition placed on the prophet to intercede (Jer. 14:11; 15:1–2). This latter Jeremian passage illuminates Ezekiel's message as well, for both prophets experienced the destruction of Judah, and both had taught that their generation was doomed. However, Ezekiel never abandoned his belief in the efficacy of prophetic intercession, as demonstrated by his wistful comment on the Psalmist's allusion to Moses' self-sacrifice: "I sought a man who would plug up the wall and *stand in the breach before Me* on behalf of the land that I should not destroy it; but I found none" (22:30).

The concept of atonement developed among the Dead Sea sectarians takes a unique turn. Without the Temple, they were forced to concentrate upon non-sacrificial expiation (e.g., 1QS 9:4–5), and they developed a lofty spiritual doctrine which taught that purity of thought and deed were necessary preconditions of all ritual acts and that the virtuous life of the individual effects atonement for others. However, the circle of the latter was restricted to members of the sect (perhaps also the like-minded, 1QS 5:5–7), and the rest of Israel was uniformly excluded. This insularity is not surprising in view of the teaching of Jeremiah and Ezekiel. Like these prophets, the sect also felt that universal doom was at hand, from which the righteous would save only themselves. This will also help explain the sectarians' insistence that their atonement also extended to the land (see above). Since they envisaged for themselves no additional exile (1QM 1:2f.; CD 4:2f.; 7:13f.) – as did the prophets – the Land of Israel was therefore in need of atonement so that the righteous survivors of the impending cataclysm could settle on it immediately (1QSa 1:3).

The atoning power of the righteous reaches out not only horizontally to the community but also vertically to posterity. This principle undergirds all of God's covenants with Israel: with the Fathers for offspring and the Promised Land (Gen. 15; 17:1–8; 22:17–18; 25:23; 35:9–12; Ex. 32:13); with Phinehas for a priestly line (Num. 25:13); and with David for a royal dynasty (II Sam. 7:12–16).

In the wisdom literature the suffering of the righteous is rationalized into a theological postulate: suffering is a test whereby God enables the righteous to merit an even greater reward (e.g., Ps. 66:9–12; Job 5:17–18; 33:9–12; 36:8–10). This idea also informs the narratives of the Wilderness (Ex. 16:4; Deut. 8:2, 16) and of the Fathers (e.g., Gen. 22:1, 16–18). A logical extension of this theodicy is that suffering can serve as an atonement for society. However, it is not an explicit biblical doctrine, for nowhere do the innocent suffer to atone for the guilty. It may be adumbrated by the final Servant poems (Isa. 50:4ff.; 53), but its unfolding is realized in post-biblical times (see Deutero-Isaiah in *Isaiah).

BIBLIOGRAPHY: Médebielle, in: DBI, *Supplément*, 4 (1938), 48–81; H.H. Rowley, *Worship in Ancient Israel* (1967); Landsberger, in: AFO, 17 (1967), 30–34; L. Moraldi, *Espiazione sacrificiale e riti espiatori nell' ambiente biblico* (1956), 109–81; R. de Vaux, *Studies in Old Testament Sacrifice* (1964), 91–112; J. Milgrom, *Studies in Levitical Terminology*, 1 (1969), §28; idem, in: JQR, 58 (1967/68), 115–25; Extreme opposing positions are taken by: A. Buechler, *Studies in Sin and Atonement* (1928), and K. Koch, in: *Evangelische Theologie*, 26 (1966), 217–39. **ADD. BIBLIOGRAPHY:** B. Levine, in: *ErIsr*, 9 (1969), 88–95; idem, *JPS Torah Commentary Leviticus* (1989); J. Milgrom, *Leviticus 1–16* (AB; 1991); idem, *Leviticus 17–22* (AB; 2000); idem, *Leviticus 23–27* (AB; 2001).

[Jacob Milgrom]

KIRBY, JACK (**Jacob Kurtzberg**; 1917–1994), U.S. comic book creator. Kirby was born in New York City and began work in the comics industry in the 1930s. By 1940 he had teamed with Joe Simon, his partner for the next 15 years. They created the character Captain America in 1941 and it instantly became an American icon and the country's morale-boosting anti-Nazi hero. The following year they produced the Boy Commandos comics, stories about young soldiers, which sold a million copies an issue. After World War II the team created popular-romance comics. In 1958 Kirby went to work for Marvel Comics, where he collaborated with the dialogue writer and editor Stan *Lee. They created such characters as Mighty Thor and the Incredible Hulk, among many superheroes with human characteristics. In a 50-year career, Kirby produced many of the comics' most successful concepts and was considered responsible for more comic book sales than any other artist, writer, or editor.

[Stewart Kampel (2nd ed.)]

KIRCHHEIM, RAPHAEL (1804–1889), German scholar and author. Kirchheim was born in Frankfurt. He served as *shoḥet* in Frankfurt and later became a partner in a banking house, which allowed him to devote most of his time to scholarly pursuits. He was at first an opponent of Reform and severely criticized the radicalism of the 1845 rabbinical assemblies of Brunswick and Frankfurt, as in his edition of S.J. Rapoport, *Tokhaḥat Megullah* (Heb. and Ger., 1845) and his open letter to A.J. Adler of Worms (1845). Under the influence of Abraham *Geiger, however, he became a proponent of Reform. Kirchheim edited Geiger's Hebrew writings under the title *Kevuẓat Ma'amarim* (1877). Among Kirchheim's published works are the annotations to the section "*Va'ad la-Ḥakhamim*" and a biography of Ḥ.J.D. *Azulai in the annotated edition of Azulai's biobibliographical lexicon *Shem ha-Gedolim* prepared by Kirchheim in association with A. Fuld and others (1847); *Karmei Shomron* (1851), a study of the history, religion, and literature of the Samaritans; an edition with commentary of the seven minor Palestinian tractates, *Sheva Massekhtot Ketannot Yerushalmiyyot* (1851, repr. 1966); an edition of Eliezer Ashkenazi's *Ta'am Zekenim* (1854); an edition of *Perush al Divrei ha-Yamim*, a tenth-century commentary on Chronicles (1874); the introduction to B. Goldberg's 1856 edition of Ibn Janaḥ's *Sefer ha-Rikmah*; and a number of other introductions. In his *Neue Exegetenschule* (1867) he severely criticized S.R. Hirsch's Pentateuch commentary, particularly his extravagant etymologies. Kirchheim's library passed to the Religious School of the Frankfurt community and later to the National and University Library, Jerusalem.

BIBLIOGRAPHY: S. Unna, in: JJLG, 12 (1918), 318ff.; 20 (1929), 19ff.; B.Z. Dinur, in: KS, 1 (1924), 150ff., 318ff.; 4 (1927), 67ff., 166ff., 328ff.; J. Unna, in: BLBI, 4 (1961), 221–31.

KIRCHHEIMER, OTTO (1905–1965), political scientist. Born in Germany, Kirchheimer was admitted to the German bar and was active in the social democratic movement. He lectured at German trade union schools and published a number of essays on the political and legal problems of the Weimar Republic. After the advent of Nazism, he went first to Paris and in 1937 to the U.S. From 1944 to 1951 Kirchheimer worked in the Office of Strategic Services and later in the State Department. He taught at various universities and from 1960 to his death was professor of political science at Columbia University in New York. In his major work, *Political Justice* (1961), he pointed out how the misuse of justice can lead to the destruction of democracy.

[Edwin Emanuel Gutmann]

KIRCHNER, LEON (1919–), U.S. composer, and pianist. Born in Brooklyn, Kirchner studied piano and began to compose at an early age. When he was nine, the family moved to Los Angeles, where he studied under Ernst *Toch, and later Arnold *Schoenberg. In 1938–39 he studied at Berkeley with Elkus and Strickland. After a year of graduate work at the University of California in Los Angeles, he returned to Berkeley, where he came under the influence of Ernest *Bloch. In 1942 he studied with Roger Sessions in New York and was awarded the George Ladd Prix de Paris. After his military service (1943–46), he was appointed lecturer in music at Berkeley. In 1954 he became professor of music at Mills College in Oakland and in 1961 was appointed to the Walter Bigelow Rosen Chair of Music at Harvard (until 1989). Kirchner was a distinguished pianist who gave the first performances of many of his own works, notably the *First Piano Concerto* in 1953, when it won the Naumberg Foundation Award. Other prize-winning works include the *First and Second String Quartets* (New York Music Critics' Circle Award for Chamber Music), the *Third String Quartet* (Pulitzer Prize, 1967), and *Music for Cello and Orchestra* (the Friedheim Award, 1992). He received awards from institutions such as the Guggenheim Foundation, the American Academy of Arts and Letters (1962), the American Academy of Arts and Sciences (1963), and the Center for Advanced Study of Behavioral Sciences (1974). His music, complex in idiom, is nevertheless strongly passionate, even romantic, in feeling and always crafted with masterly technical skill. His other works include, *Sinfonia* for orchestra (1951); *Toccata* for strings, wind, and percussion (1955); the *Second Piano Concerto* (first performance 1963, soloist Leon *Fleisher); *Music for Orchestra* (1969); *Piano Sonata* (1948); *Little Suite* for piano (1949); the opera *Lily* (1973–76); *Music for Flute and Orchestra* (1978); *5 Pieces for Piano* (1984); *Music for Orchestra II* (1989); *Trio* for violin, cello, and piano (1993); *Of Things Exactly as They Are*, for soprano, bass, chorus and orchestra (1997); *Interlude II* for piano (2003).

ADD. BIBLIOGRAPHY: Grove online; MGG^2.

[Max Loppert / Israela Stein (2nd ed.)]

KIR-HARESETH (Heb., קִיר־מוֹאָב, קִיר־חֶרֶשׂ, קִיר־חֲרֶשֶׂת, Kir Heres; Kir of Moab), ancient capital of *Moab situated on the high plateau east of the Dead Sea and south of the Arnon River. In the days of *Mesha, king of Moab in the mid-ninth century B.C.E., Kir-Hareseth was besieged by Jehoram of Israel and Jehoshaphat of Judah; their failure to capture the city ended in a disastrous retreat for their armies (II Kings 3). It is mentioned as a Moabite city in the "burdens of Moab" which foretell its destruction (Isa. 15:1; 16:7,11; Jer. 48:31,36). In postbiblical times it was known as Charachmoba, a city striking coins under Heliogabalus (Ptolemaeus, 5:16, 4). Impressions of seals of municipal authorities with zodiac signs and the names of Nabatean months (in Greek) were discovered at Maurpsis. It was the seat of a bishop in Byzantine times (Hierocles, *Synecdemus*, 721:5). The Greek *Charach*, "palisade," corresponds to *Kir* in Hebrew. On the Madaba Map it is represented as a walled fortress with a gate flanked by towers on the south. Within the walls are colonnaded streets and two churches. Kir-Hareseth is now known as Karak, a name which is mentioned by Arab geographers in about 1225. In Crusader times Payen le Bouteiller transferred his residence to Karak in 1140 and built a famous fortress there. Held from 1177 to 1187 by Renauld de Chatillon, it was the principal stronghold of this baron; from there he attacked Muslim caravans. Saladin failed to take Karak in 1183; it fell only in 1188 after a year-long siege. The fortress is c. 800 m. (2,600 ft.) long and 100 m. (330 ft.) wide, with a fosse 30 m. (100 ft.) deep. It was later held by al-Malik al-Ayubi. It was the scene of revolts against Turkish rule in 1893 and 1910. Karak in 1970 was a district town in Jordan, with about 15,000 inhabitants.

BIBLIOGRAPHY: A. Musil, *Arabia Petraea*, 1 (1907), 45ff., 359ff.; Glueck, in: AASOR, 15 (1935), 4; M. Avi-Yonah, *Madaba Mosaic Map* (1954), 41–42; Aharoni, Land, index; A. Negev, in: IEJ, 19 (1969), 89.

[Michael Avi-Yonah]

KIRIATH-JEARIM (Heb. קִרְיַת יְעָרִים), city of the Hivites belonging to the Gibeonite confederation (Josh. 9:17). Its original name was Kiriath-Ba'al or Baalah. Kiriath-Jearim was situated on the border of Judah and Benjamin (Josh. 15:9, 60; 18:14, 15) and was connected with the family of *Caleb (I Chron. 2:50, 52, 53). The tribe of Dan camped in its vicinity for some time (Judg. 18:12). When the Ark was rescued from the Philistines, it was placed in the house of Abinadab in Kiriath-Jearim (I Sam. 6:21; 7:1, 2) until eventually brought by David to Jerusalem (II Sam. 6:2ff.; I Chron. 13:5, 6; II Chron. 1:4). It was the home town of *Uriah, the son of the prophet Shemaiah, who fled to Egypt and was caught and executed by the king Jehoiakim (Jer. 26:20). The inhabitants of Kiriath-Jearim were among those who returned from Babylonian exile (Ezra 2:25; Neh. 7:29). According to Eusebius, the place was a station 9 or 10 mi. from Jerusalem on the road to Diospolis (Lod; Onom. 48:22; 114:23). The identification of Kiriath-Jearim with Tell/Deir (Dayr) al-ʿAzār about 8 mi. (13 km.) west of Jerusalem in the village of *Abu Ghosh is generally accepted. The Crusaders considered this site to be the ancient Emmaus, also calling it Fontenoid because of the springs below the tell.

BIBLIOGRAPHY: Abel, in: RB, 34 (1925), 580; 43 (1934), 351; M. Noth, *Das Buch Josua* (1938), 61–62, 81; EM, s.v. *Ba'alah* (includes bibliography); Aharoni, Land, index; Avi-Yonah, Geog, index.

[Michael Avi-Yonah]

KIRIMI, ABRAHAM (14th century), Crimean rabbi and Bible commentator. One of the first Jewish scholars in the Crimea, Abraham was named Kirimi after the town of Eski-Krym (Solkhat). He wrote a commentary to the Pentateuch entitled *Sefat Emet*. In a poem which precedes the introduction he mentions the year 1358, but it is not clear whether he is referring to the date of his birth or to the composition of the work. In the introduction he gives as his reasons for compiling the work the urging of his contemporaries, particularly his "friend and pupil," Hezekiah b. Elchanan "Ish Kara'i," a phrase apparently meaning "the Karaite." Deinard's opinion, however, is that Hezekiah was not a Karaite and that the words mean "versed in the bible," as it seems incredible that Abraham was urged by a Karaite to write an anti-Karaite work. It is nevertheless possible that Hezekiah asked Abraham for a Bible commentary, and the latter wrote one in keeping with his outlook. Apparently Abraham was a pupil of the biblical exegete *Shemariah b. Elijah Ikriti, whom he quotes in numerous passages in the *Sefat Emet*, and who exercised great influence over him. The book reveals Abraham as a literal commentator who explains the text according to the plain meaning of the words and the rules of grammar. In accordance with this approach, he on one occasion criticizes Rashi despite the great respect in which he held him, and praises Abraham Ibn Ezra and, above all, Maimonides. The spirit of the *Guide of the Perplexed* infuses the whole of the *Sefat Emet*, but occasionally Abraham even goes beyond the rationalism of Maimonides. He attempts to give a rational interpretation to the miracles of the Bible. He explains the visit of the three angels to Abraham and the burning bush of Moses as dream visions, and in explaining the paschal lamb he mentions the Egyptian cult of the bull. Despite these views he was highly regarded among the Jews of the Crimea, and in their memorial prayers he is mentioned immediately after Abraham Ibn Ezra. It is possible that the high regard in which he was held was the result of his opposition to Karaite Bible exegesis and his support of the traditional view.

BIBLIOGRAPHY: M. Steinschneider, in: HB, 11 (1871), 38f.; A. Firkovich, in: *Ha-Karmel*, 3 (1863), 53f.; Fuenn, Keneset, 62f.; Y. Zinberg, in: *Yevreyskaya Starina*, 11 (1924), 97–101; Zinberg, *Sifrut*, 3 (1958), 157–61, 353; E. Deinard, *Massa Krim* (1878), 178–80.

[Isaak Dov Ber Markon]

KIRJATH SEPHER, Hebrew bibliographical quarterly. *Kirjath Sepher* was founded in 1924 as a publication of the Jewish National and University Library in Jerusalem. The bibliographical section consists of three major divisions: Israel publications; Hebraica and Judaica (published outside of Israel); and periodical articles on Judaica and Hebraica. The last served as basis for the publication of index volumes of articles on Jewish studies, *Reshimat ha-Ma'amarim be-Madda'ei ha-Yahadut* (ed. by I. Joel, 1–2 [1966–67]). A special section is devoted to articles on Jewish, particularly bibliographical, subjects. These include, apart from bibliographies of the works of individual authors and of special subjects, an annual bibliography of medieval Hebrew poetry (ed., H. Schirmann) and studies on the history of Hebrew printing in places to which previously little attention had been paid. An important section of *Kirjath Sepher* is reserved for book reviews; Hebrew University faculty and others contribute detailed criticisms of current Jewish literature. From time to time larger studies appear as special supplements (cf. "Index to Volumes 1–40" [supplement to vol. 41, 1966/67], 105). The first editors of *Kirjath Sepher* were S.H. *Bergmann and H. *Pick, in association with S. *Assaf, B. *Dinur, A. Tauber, L.A. *Mayer, and G. *Scholem. From 1927 to 1968 the editor was I. Joel who was succeeded by G.Y. Ormann.

[Baruch Yaron]

KIRKISĀNĪ, JACOB AL- (**Abu Yusuf Yaqub ibn Ishaq ibn Samʿawayh al-Qirqisani**; first half of tenth century), Karaite scholar. His surname has been variously derived from Qirqīsīyā, the ancient Circesium, in the Midrash (Lam. R. 1:18, no. 53), Kirkesyon, in Upper Mesopotamia, and from Qarqasān, a small town in the vicinity of Baghdad. The sequence of his names implies that he was called Jacob, his father Isaac, and his son Joseph, reproducing the sequence of the biblical patriarchs. Later Karaite authors thought erroneously that his forename was Joseph and confused him with the Karaite scholar Joseph b. Abraham ha-Ro'eh (Yūsuf *al-Baṣīr) who lived a century later.

Nothing is known of al-Kirkisānī's personal life beyond what may be inferred from his own works. He was thoroughly acquainted with the contemporary Arabic theological, philosophical, and scientific literature, and had a substantial knowledge of the Mishnah, the *Gemara*, some midrashic works, and the *Rabbanite liturgy. He also read the New Testament and the Koran, and perhaps some of the Christian patristic literature. Of his non-Karaite associates he mentions the Rabbanite scholar *Jacob b. Ephraim and the Christian "bishop," or rather deacon, Yasʿu Sekhā, with both of whom he was on terms of personal friendship. Unlike some Karaite fanatics, he avoided personal vituperation in his anti-Rabbanite polemics. Al-Kirkisānī let the logic of his thought and the range of his learning speak for themselves, so that he was by far the most formidable champion of Karaism of his age. Since he was a firm believer in the use of reason and intelligence in theology and jurisprudence, his views in this field are characterized by common sense and moderation, although he did not hesitate to ally himself with the partisans of such rigoristic laws as the catenary (*rikkuv*) theory of forbidden marriages.

Al-Kirkisānī's principal work is divided into two parts, of which the first, entitled *Kitāb al-Anwār wa-al-Marāqib* ("Book of Lights and Watch-Towers"), is a systematic code of Karaite law, while the second part, entitled *Kitāb al-Riyāḍ wa-al-Ḥadā'iq* ("Book of Gardens and Parks"), is a commentary on the nonlegal parts of the Torah, prefaced by a detailed discourse on the methods of biblical exegesis. The "Book of Lights" is divided into 13 discourses:

(1) history of the Jewish sects;

(2) on the validity of the application of rational investigation to theology and jurisprudence;

(3) refutation of the doctrines of the various sects, including Christianity and Islam;

(4) treatise on the methods of interpretation of the law;

(5) on circumcision and Sabbath;

(6) on commandments, other than the Sabbath, including a detailed treatise on the liturgy;

(7) on new moons;

(8) on the Feast of Weeks;

(9) on the remaining holy days;

(10) on cleanness and uncleanness;

(11) on incest;

(12) on dietary law;

(13) on inheritance.

Throughout Kirkisānī makes constant reference to the views of other Karaite jurists, particularly Anan and Benjamin b. Moses *Nahawendi, as well as those of the Rabbanites. Its erudition, detail, and excursuses on various subjects (e.g., on dialectics, witchcraft, the psychopathology of sleep and dreams, suicide, the varying pronunciation of Hebrew words) give the "Book of Lights" permanent importance as a source book.

Several smaller works of al-Kirkisānī, now untraceable, are cited in the "Book of Lights." They include (1) extensive philosophic-exegetical commentaries on Genesis, Job, and Ecclesiastes; (2) a tract in refutation of Muhammad's claim to prophecy *Kitāb fī Ifsād Nubūwat Muḥammad*; (3) an essay on the art of interpretation, *Al-Qawl ʿalā al-Tafīr wa-Sharḥ al-Maʿānī*; (4) an essay on the art of translation, *Al-Qawl ʿalā al-Tarjamah*; (5) a treatise on the principles of faith (literally, "on the oneness of God") *Kitāb al Tawḥīd*, perhaps intended as a Karaite reply to Saadiah's *Emunot ve-De'ot*.

The *Kitāb al-Anwār* is the only work of Kirkisānī which has been published in its entirety (by L. Nemoy, 5 vols., 1939–43). The first discourse was translated into English by L. Nemoy (HUCA, (1930), 317ff.), who also translated several chapters from other discourses (for example in JBL, 57 (1938), 411ff.; 59 (1940), 159ff.). An abridgement of it (*Mukhtaṣar al-Anwār*) is extant in manuscript. The introduction to the *Kitāb al-Riyāḍ* was published by H. Hirschfeld (*Qirqisānī Studies*, 1918). A revised translation of part of the first discourse and of Hirschfeld's text is found in L. Nemoy, *Karaite Anthology* (1952), 42ff.

BIBLIOGRAPHY: G. Vajda, in: REJ, 106 (1941–45), 87–123, 137–40; 107 (1946–47), 52–98; 108 (1948), 63–91; 120 (1961), 211–57; 122 (1963), 7–74; Mann, Texts, index; Z. Ankori, *Karaites in Byzantium* (1959), index, s.v. *Jacob [al] Kirkisani*; Steinschneider, Arab Lit, 79ff.; S. Poznański, *Karaite Literary Opponents of Saadiah Gaon* (1908), 8ff.

[Leon Nemoy]

°**KIRKPATRICK, ALEXANDER FRANCIS** (1849–1940), English Bible critic who as general editor of the Bible and Apocrypha sections of the semi-popular *Cambridge Bible for Schools and Colleges* championed a series of commentaries which attempted to show how textual, linguistic, historical, and higher criticism compel readers to reverse many of their traditional ideas in regard to the Bible. Kirkpatrick taught at Cambridge and in 1882 at the early age of 33 was appointed Regius Professor of Hebrew and canon of Ely. He later served as master of Selwyn College, Cambridge (1898–1927), and dean of Ely (1906–36). Kirkpatrick was a popular lecturer and administrator who helped educate a conservative English clergy and laity to the merits of biblical criticism, which seeks to confirm, correct, and supplement the history and narrative of Holy Scriptures. The most important of his books are: *The Divine Library of the Old Testament*... (1891), *The Doctrine of the Prophets* (1892, 1958²), and commentaries on Psalms (1902), and Samuel (1930). These last two were published in the Cambridge Bible series.

ADD. BIBLIOGRAPHY: R. Clements, in: DBI, 2:28–29.

[Zev Garber]

KIRKUK, town in N. Iraq. The first known Jewish settlement in Kirkuk dates from the 17th century. There is information available on local Jews who traded mainly with Baghdad during the 18th century. Various travelers – Jewish and non-Jewish – of the 19th and early 20th centuries report on the existence of a Jewish community numbering about 200 families which lived in a separate quarter in the town. In May 1918 the town was captured by the British with the assistance of its Christian and Jewish inhabitants. After two weeks the town was retaken by the Turks, who persecuted the Jews who had not succeeded in leaving. After the war the number of Jews in Kirkuk increased, especially after it became a center of the petroleum industry. In 1947, 2,350 Jews were counted in a census. The Jews engaged in commerce, hawking, and handicrafts. In 1913 an elementary school was opened by the Alliance Israélite Universelle, but it closed with the outbreak of World War I. It was only in 1934 that a Jewish school was founded in the town by the philanthropist Ellis *Kadoorie. Social progress was slow, and it was only during the 1940s that some of the youth who graduated from the government secondary school acquired an academic education. Some individuals now left the closed quarter in order to build houses outside it. The attitude toward the Jews by the population, which was mostly Turkish, was generally hostile. In 1888 a Jewish child was abducted by a maidservant and taken to a mosque, the Muslims refusing to return him. There were, however, no anti-Jewish riots as elsewhere in *Iraq, not even in 1941. All the Jews of the town immigrated to Israel in 1950–51.

BIBLIOGRAPHY: A. Ben-Jacob, *Kehillot Yehudei Kurdistan* (1967), 117–22.

[Haim J. Cohen]

KIROVOGRAD (until 1924 **Yelizavetgrad**, from 1924 to 1936 **Zinovyevsk**, and from 1936 to 1939 **Kirovo**), district capital in Ukraine. Jews began to settle in Kirovograd in 1769 together with other nationalities. In 1799 they numbered 398 persons (out of 4,327 total population), and in 1803 there were 574 Jews listed in the municipal register. The Jewish population of Kirovograd increased rapidly during the 19th century as a result of the settlement of the New Russia provinces by Jewish emigrants from the northern provinces of the *Pale of Settlement. In 1861 there were 8,073 Jews in the city, while in 1897 their numbers had increased to 23,967 (39% of the total population). In 1879 there were 120 large-scale Jewish merchants among 160; 650 petty traders among the 900; 280 Jewish craftsmen and 368 Christians; and 46 Jewish landowners. From the mid-19th century there were an old-age home for 25 people, about 50 *ḥadarim*, two first-level state Jewish schools, two *talmudei torah*, and 17 private schools, mostly for girls. In 1882 a Reform anti-talmudic society called the Bible Brotherhood (*Bibleitzy*) was founded by Jacob *Gordin. Severe riots broke out in Kirovograd on April 15–17, 1881, marking the beginning of the spate of pogroms which struck the Jews of southern Russia during the 1880s. The damage from robbery and destruction of shops and houses was estimated at 1.9 million rubles. In 1887 there were 12 Jewish city council members out of 67. At the end of the 19th century there were signs of powerful tendencies toward assimilation and russification among the Jews of Kirovograd, but at the same time the nationalist and Zionist movement under the leadership of V. *Tiomkin also gained adherents. The Jews played an important role in the town. The majority of the flour mills and the spirit and tobacco factories were under their control, and the commerce in grain was also concentrated in their hands. On October 18–19, 1905, a state-sponsored pogrom occurred, 11 Jews were murdered, 150 wounded, and the police forbade the mutual Christian-Jewish self-defense to intervene. In the course of World War I about 3,000 deported Jews reached Kirovograd. Among them was the Lida yeshivah with 96 pupils. During the Civil War there were three pogroms in 1919: the first, on February 4–5, claimed the lives of 13 Jewish self-defenders; the second, on May 15–17, resulted in 1,926 killed; and the third, on August 11, claimed about 1,000 victims. The last two pogroms were staged by the Grigoryev gang. With the establishment of the Soviet regime, Jewish institutions were closed down and Jewish communal life was suppressed. In 1926, 18,358 Jews (27.6% of the total population) lived in Kirovograd, with the number dropping to 14,641 (14.6%) by 1939. During the 1920s trade was liquidated, and some Jewish merchants went to work in factories, while 142 families settled on land. In 1925 there were 2,500 Jewish artisans, and they composed the vast majority in some trade unions, such as 99% in the tailors' union and 75% in the printers' union. In 1929 most of the workers in the textile industry were Jews, and among 6,000 workers of the farm machinery factory – 900 were Jews. In the 1920s there were several Yiddish schools, but due to the pressure of the authorities and the russified parents most of them closed in the 1930s. The Germans occupied the town on August 14, 1941. The registration by nationality showed a bit more than 5,000 Jews in town. On August 23 and in mid-September *Einsatzkommando* 4b murdered a few hundred Jews. Several hundreds of men were taken to a camp and killed after a while. On September 30, 1941, all Jews were gathered together, taken to anti-tank ditches about 3 km. from town, and murdered there. Anyone hiding who was caught was executed in prison. Only about ten Jews survived. In 1970 the Jewish population was estimated at about 10,000. The synagogue was closed by the authorities in 1957 but returned to the community in 1991 as Jewish life revived despite large-scale emigration.

BIBLIOGRAPHY: *Die Judenpogrome in Russland*, 2 (1909), 138–43; E. Heifetz, *The Slaughter of the Jews in the Ukraine in 1919* (1921), 243–8; Rosenthal, in: *Reshumot*, 3 (1923), 413–14; E. Tcherikower, *Di Ukrainer Pogromen in Yor 1919* (1965), index.

[Yehuda Slutsky / Shmuel Spector (2nd ed.)]

KIRSANOV, SEMYON ISAAKOVICH (1906–1972), Russian poet. Kirsanov was born in Odessa as the son of a tailor and graduated there from the philological faculty in 1925. He became a disciple of the Soviet writer Vladimir Mayakovsky. He continued that poet's tradition of brash, masculine verse with unconventional imagery and metrics and unexpected verbal acrobatics. Kirsanov was one of the very few Soviet poets to build on the foundations laid by the futurist movement. He favored social and political subjects. Much of his poetry is declamatory in form and propagandistic in content. Though outwardly similar to much of mediocre Soviet verse, it is redeemed by its hyperbolic quality which imparts to it a myth-like quality. Among his more noteworthy collections are *Stikhi v stroyu* ("Verses in Military Formation," 1932), and *Mys zhelaniya* ("The Cape of Desire," 1938). The best of his longer poems include *Tovarishch Marks* ("Comrade Marx," 1933), *Poema o robote* ("A Poem About the Automaton," 1935), and *Noch pod Novy vek* ("New Century's Eve," 1937). During World War II Kirsanov wrote much anti-Nazi verse. He also produced rhymed ditties for propaganda posters, and was the creator of *Zavetnoye slovo Fomy Smyslova* ("Mark the Words of Foma Smyslov"), an anti-Nazi comic strip serialized in Soviet army newspapers. His marked fondness for biblical imagery may be connected with memories of childhood in the intensely Jewish milieu of Odessa. Thus, a poem written in the late 1940s is entitled *Edem* ("Paradise") – an unusual instance of a biblical word used as a title for a Russian poem. Kirsanov's best-known post-Stalin poetic work – and one of the most important of the "thaw" – was *Sem dney nedeli* ("Seven Days of the Week," 1957). This long narrative poem, modeled after the account of the creation in Genesis, states that the Soviet system has been successful in creating material objects, but that real man, free of cowardice and greed, is yet to be created. The poem was violently denounced as anti-Soviet slander, but Kirsanov succeeded in weathering the storm.

[Maurice Friedberg]

KIRSCHBAUM, ELIEZER SINAI (1798–1870), physician and author; leader of the *Haskalah in Galicia; born in Sieniawa, Poland. In 1816 he went to Berlin to study medicine and later practiced in Cracow, where he distinguished himself during the cholera epidemic in 1831. In appreciation, the senate of the Republic of Cracow awarded him a building plot. As ownership of land was forbidden to Jews, Kirschbaum took out a certificate of baptism, but he nevertheless remained faithful to Judaism. From his student days he was in contact with David *Friedlaender and Leopold *Zunz. He was a member of the *Verein fuer Kultur und Wissenschaft des Judentums and in 1821 presented it with a memorandum in which he adopted a positive attitude toward the idea of a Jewish state, identified himself with the program of Mordecai Manuel *Noah, but advocated Ethiopia instead of the United States as the transitional territory to Ereẓ Israel. His works include *Leket Shirim u-Meliẓot* (1820, Heb. and Ger.), a collection of poems and proverbs; *Hilkhot Yemot ha-Mashi'aḥ* (1822), in which he interpreted messianism as the political, non-miraculous redemption of the Jewish people; *Maimonides Specimen Diacteticum* (1822); *Vorschlaege betreffend einige gesellschaftliche Institutionen* (1842), lectures on social institutions; *Aufsaetze im Gebiete der Religion und des sozialen Lebens* (1843), essays relating to religion and socialism; and *Es ist noch heute oder Der Familie Apotheose* (1858).

BIBLIOGRAPHY: A. Ginzig, in: *Oẓar ha-Sifrut*, 3 (part 4, 1890), 9–10; *Sefer Kraka* (1959), 81–83; N.M. Gelber, *Toledot ha-Tenu'ah ha-Ẓiyyonit be-Galiẓyah*, 1 (1958), 24–29.

[Moshe Landau]

KIRSCHBRAUN, ELIJAH (1882–1931), leader of *Agudat Israel in Poland. Kirschbraun, who was born in Warsaw into a religious family and was a notable scholar, formed an independent religious organization in Warsaw in 1911, and in 1912 took part in the founding convention of Agudat Israel in Katowice. After World War I, when the Jewish communities were constituted in independent Poland, he was elected chairman of the Jewish community council in Warsaw and representative of religious Jewry on the Warsaw municipal council. Between 1922 and 1931 Kirschbraun was member of the Polish parliament (Sejm) and member of its security committee. He was chairman of the Agudat Israel faction in parliament, and vice president of the "Jewish club" ("Koło") in 1926. His personal integrity and efforts for the benefit of the public won appreciation among all sectors of Jewry and Polish government circles. In the 1922 elections he recommended that his party join the *minority bloc led by Y. *Gruenbaum, but after Pilsudski's coup (May 1926) he abandoned Gruenbaum's policy and supported the *Sanacja* regime. His last act, on his deathbed, was to send a letter to Pilsudski, which both the Jewish public and Polish leaders regarded as a testament, urging full and just rights for the Jews in independent Poland.

ADD. BIBLIOGRAPHY: J. Majchrowski et al. (eds.), *Kto byl kim w drugiej Rzeczypospolitej* (1994), 316.

[Yitzchak Arad]

KIRSCHENBAUM, MORDECHAI (**Motti**; 1939–), Israeli television producer and broadcaster. A graduate of the University of California in theater, cinema, and television, Kirschenbaum was among the founders of Israeli television. Producer in the 1970s of a hugely popular weekly satirical show called

Niku'i Rosh ("Cleaning the Head"), in 1976 he won the Israel Prize for radio, film, and television arts. The program was not without its critics and was subject to political pressure. Kirschenbaum's tenure as head of Hebrew programming at Israel Television, including the drama department, was not renewed in 1979 by Tommy *Lapid, the Likud-appointed Broadcasting Authority director-general. In 1993 he was appointed the Authority's director-general by Shulamit *Aloni, the Meretz communications minister. Kirschenbaum's period as director-general, until 1998, was characterized by strict impartiality in editorial decision-making, despite his generally leftist outlook, as well as protection of broadcasters from political pressure. Yet he failed in financial management, and the Broadcasting Authority ran into a heavy deficit. Moreover, ratings dropped with the creation of a second, privately run and more commercially oriented second channel (Channel 2). In 2001 Kirschenbaum headed the television production company that won the tender for Channel 10 television, another commercial station. Subsequently he also co-hosted Channel 10's popular and free-wheeling *London and Kirschenbaum* talk show with Yaron London.

[Yoel Cohen (2nd ed.)]

KIRSCHNER, EMANUEL (1857–1938), German *ḥazzan* and composer. Born in Upper Silesia, Kirschner became a music student at the Jewish Teachers' Training College, Berlin, in 1874. In 1877 he taught in the Berlin Jewish community's school and was appointed assistant *ḥazzan* in its new synagogue. Four years later he was appointed chief cantor at the Great Synagogue of Munich and teacher in the synagogue school. His principal work *Tehillot le-El Elyon* ("Praises to the Almighty," 1896) for cantor, choir, and organ, written in four parts, gave prominence to traditional melodies. Kirschner also published studies on various aspects of synagogue music. He died shortly after the destruction of his synagogue by the Nazis.

BIBLIOGRAPHY: Sendrey, Music, indexes; A. Friedmann, *Dem Andenken Eduard Birnbaums*, 1 (1922), 78; E. Zaludkowski, *Kultur-Treger fun der Yidisher Liturgye* (1930), 199; J. Hohenemser, in: *Proceedings of the Third Annual Conference-Convention of the Cantors Assembly of America* (1950), 11–15.

[Joshua Leib Ne'eman]

KIRSCHSTEIN, MORITZ (1826–1900), pedagogue, active in Reform Judaism. Born in Chodziez (Poznan), he received his talmudic education in Glogau and, under the guidance of Israel b. Gedaliah *Lipschuetz, in Danzig (Gdansk). After studying philosophy in Berlin, where he also studied under L. *Zunz, he taught religion at the Jewish community's boys' school, and from 1866 he was director of the first Jewish religious school in Berlin. He was a member of the commission that compiled the Reform prayer book for the Berlin community and was entrusted by Abraham *Geiger with editing the German text of the prayers. Kirschstein published *Der Unterricht in der Religion und im Hebraeischen* (1863), on teaching religion and Hebrew; and *Der Unterricht in der biblischen Geschichte* (1871), on the teaching of biblical history. A collection of scientific treatises, lectures, speeches, and sermons, among them *Avnei Zikkaron* (*Predigten*; 1902), was published after his death.

BIBLIOGRAPHY: *Festschrift zur Feier des hundertjaehrigen Bestehens der Knabenschule der juedischen Gemeinden in Berlin* (1926), 107; A. Kober, in: LBYB, 2 (1957), 111.

[*Encyclopaedia Judaica* (Germany)]

KIRSCHSTEIN, SALLI (1869–1935), German writer and art collector. Kirschstein, who was born in Kolmar, Poland, became a prominent merchant in Berlin. He was active in Jewish affairs and as director of the Juedischer Volksverein did much to help foreign Jews living in Germany during World War I. Kirschstein was an expert on Jewish art and wrote articles on the subject for many publications. His main work in this field was a study of Jewish engravers, *Juedische Graphiker aus der Zeit von 1625–1825* (1918). He amassed an important collection of Jewish art and cult objects, the catalog of which appeared as *Die Judaica Sammlung* (1932). Most of his collection was bequeathed to the Hebrew Union College, Cincinnati. By collecting Judaica, Kirschstein wished to emphasize that Judaism had its own cultural traditions. Like his contemporaries Max Grunwald and Heinrich Frauberger, Kirschstein created a concept of presenting Jewish art as based on tradition and history.

ADD. BIBLIOGRAPHY: J. Gutmann, "The Kirschstein Museum of Berlin," in: *Jewish Art*, 16–17 (1991), 172–76; M. Osborn, "Eine Sammlung juedischer Kunstdenkmäler. Das Museum Kirschstein in Nikolassee bei Berlin," in: *Der Schild* (March 15, 1926).

KIRSHBLUM, MORDECAI (1910–1993), rabbi and Zionist leader. One of the most prominent leaders of religious Zionism in the United States during the 20th century, Kirshblum was born in Bialistok, Poland, and immigrated to America at the age of 13. He received his Orthodox rabbinic ordination in 1931 at the Isaac Elchanan Theological Seminary, which was a division of what later became the Yeshiva University. He accepted a pulpit at the Jewish Community House in 1944, one of the only institutions associated with the Jewish Center Movement in the United States that also housed a synagogue. He held this position for more than 20 years, serving the Bensonhurst Jewish community in Brooklyn, New York. Because of his extraordinary oratorical skills in English, Yiddish, and Hebrew, he addressed many other audiences throughout the city. When he became president of the Mizrachi Organization of America in 1952, he traveled throughout the country on its behalf, forging it into a powerful force within American Zionism, during the five years he held the office. As a member of the Jewish Agency Executive, to which he was appointed in 1956, he served as director of the Agency's Torah Education and Culture Department and of the Aliyah Department of the American Section. In 1968, Kirshblum settled in Israel and became head of the Agency's Aliyah and Absorption

Department in Jerusalem. His fervent advocacy of religious Zionism attracted many disciples who ultimately served the movement both in the United States and Israel. His brother I. Usher Kirshblum was for many years the rabbi of the Conservative Kew Gardens Hills Jewish Center.

[Stanley M. Wagner (2nd ed.)]

KIRSHON, VLADIMIR MIKHAILOVICH (1902–1938), Soviet playwright. Kirshon was trained by the Communist Party as a lecturer and propagandist, and in 1925 became secretary of the Association of Proletarian Writers in Moscow. During the Stalinist purges he was expelled from the Communist Party 1937, arrested, and executed for "bureaucratic attitudes" and "Trotskyism". His writings were banned until 1956, when he was "rehabilitated." In 1962 the Soviet Union took official note of the 60th anniversary of his birth.

Kirshon's plays generally deal with contemporary Communist themes, and are strongly propagandist. His first play was "Red Dust," about the degeneration of a revolutionary during the years of the New Economic Policy. Then came *Konstantin Terekhin* (1926), written in collaboration with A. Uspenski, that deals with the moral dissolution of a young Communist and the reaction of loyal Communist youth. *Relsy gudyat* ("The Rails Are Humming," 1928) portrays the clash between a Soviet Communist factory administrator and the engineering experts of the old regime, still employed in Soviet industry. The play "Bread" (1930) dealt with the accumulation of private property in the kolkhozes. His last play, *Bolshoy den* ("The Great Day," 1936) predicted the outbreak of war between the U.S.S.R. and Nazi Germany. Kirshon's work has been translated into many languages.

BIBLIOGRAPHY: E.J. Brown, *The Proletarian Episode in Russian Literature, 1928–1932* (1953), 229ff., 265; L. Tamashin, *Vladimir Kirshon* (Rus., 1965).

[Yitzhak Maor]

KIRSTEIN, LINCOLN (1907–1996), U.S. impresario, arts patron, and dance historian. Born in Rochester, New York, he became interested in dance while at Harvard and soon emerged as one of the creative personalities in modern American ballet. He persuaded Russian-born choreographer George Balanchine, whom he met in London in 1933, to go to the United States, where the great master's artistic vision would evolve in freedom for almost 50 years. In 1934, with Balanchine and Edward Warburg, Kirstein cofounded the American Ballet, which acted as the official ballet of the Metropolitan Opera from 1935 to 1938. In 1936 Kirstein founded Ballet Caravan to present American works. Among its productions was Eugene Loring's *Billy the Kid*, for which Kirstein wrote the libretto. Ballet Caravan and the American Ballet merged and disbanded in 1941. Kirstein, after serving with the U.S. Army during World War II, formed a new company, Ballet Society. In 1948 this group, with Kirstein as general director and Balanchine as artistic director, was invited to become the resident company of the New York City Center of Music and Drama, and changed its name to the New York City Ballet. Kirstein was also the sponsor of Japanese theater in the U.S., including Gagaku (dancers and musicians) and Kabuki (classic dramatic theatre). Kirstein did considerable research and was a leading dance historian. He founded and edited the scholarly periodical *Dance Index* (1942–48) and published books on Fokine (New York, 1935); Nijinsky (New York, 1974); and the New York City Ballet (New York, 1973). Among his awards are the Order of the Sacred Treasure (Japanese government, 1960); the Benjamin Franklin Medal of the Royal Society of the Arts (1981), and the National Medal of Arts (1985).

BIBLIOGRAPHY: IED, 4:26–30

[Marcia B. Siegel / Amnon Shiloah (2nd ed.)]

KIRSTEIN, LOUIS EDWARD (1867–1942), U.S. department store executive and public worker. Kirstein was born in Rochester, New York. Leaving home at 16, he spent seven years as a traveling salesman. In 1912 he joined Filenes, the Boston department store, as vice president, subsequently becoming a director of the other stores in the Federated Group. Kirstein did much to develop Filenes and to advance employee relationships. He played an important part in the public life of Boston, serving as president of the public library and chairman of the port authority. Within the Jewish community his most significant contribution was as president of the Federation of Jewish Charities, where he first assumed leadership in 1919, enlarging its activities and encouraging it to cope with the responsibilities of the depression period. He was also president of the Beth Israel Hospital and chairman of the General Committee of the American Jewish Committee.

[Sefton D. Temkin]

KIRSZENBAUM, JESEKIEL DAVID (1900–1954), painter, draftsman, and etcher. His work is a synthesis of abstract and representational painting. Kirszenbaum was born in Staszow, Poland, and began his career by painting signs for the local tradesmen. At the age of 17 he went to Germany, where he studied for a short period at the Bauhaus in Weimar. Later he moved to Berlin where he worked for newspapers as an illustrator and cartoonist under the pseudonym Duvdevani. In 1933 he settled in Paris. His paintings of this period include biblical themes. During the German occupation he went into hiding; his studio was looted and his wife deported and murdered. After World War II he returned to Paris. His work is characterized by its nostalgic evocation of the past, particularly of the world of his childhood. This is especially true of his postwar paintings. On a journey to Brazil in 1948 he witnessed the carnival at Rio de Janeiro with its fantastic figures. His paintings of this subject, which evoke the Jewish festivities he had known as a child, express an element of East European mysticism.

[Elisheva Cohen]

KIRSZENSTEIN-SZEWINSKA, IRENA (1946–), Polish track and field athlete, winner of seven Olympic medals and

10 European Championship medals; member of the International Women's Sports Hall of Fame. Kirszenstein-Szewinska was born in Leningrad (now St. Petersburg), Russia, but her parents soon moved the family back to their native Poland, for which Kirszenstein-Szewinska made her Olympic debut as an 18-year-old at the 1964 Tokyo Olympics. There she won a gold medal as a member of Poland's world record-setting 4 × 100m. relay team (43.6) and silver medals in the long jump with a leap of 21′ 7¾″, as well as the 200 m., with her mark of 23.1 setting the European event record. Four years later at the Mexico City Olympics, Kirszenstein-Szewinska won the 200 m. event in 22.5, breaking her own world record set three years earlier, and won a bronze medal in the 100 m. event (11.19).

At the 1971 European Championships, Kirszenstein-Szewinska won a bronze medal in the 200 m. sprint, and then won the bronze in the same event the following year at the 1972 Olympics (22.74). In 1973, Kirszenstein-Szewinska switched to the 400 m. event, and the following year became the first woman to break 50 seconds at that distance. At the 1976 Olympics in Montreal two years later, she set a world record (49.29) in winning the 400 m. gold medal. Kirszenstein-Szewinska participated in the Moscow Olympics in 1980, but pulled a muscle in the semifinals of the 400 m. and was eliminated.

Overall, Kirszenstein-Szewinska won three Olympic gold medals, two silver, and two bronze – tying the record for most medals won by a woman in Olympic athletic competition – and five gold, one silver and four bronze medals in the European Championships. Between 1973 and 1975 she won 38 consecutive 200 m. races, and between 1973 and 1978 she won 36 straight 400 m. races – both being the longest winning streaks in these events in history. Other highlights of her career include tying the 100 m. world record in 1965 (11.1); being the first woman to hold world records in the 100 m., 200 m., and 400 m. at the same time; lowering her own world record in the 200 m. (22.0) in 1974; and lowering her 400 m. world mark (49.0) at the World Championships in Duesseldorf in 1977.

Kirszenstein-Szewinska was named Poland's Athlete of the Year in 1965 as well as Outstanding Woman Athlete in the World by Tass, the official Soviet press agency. In 1966 she was named *World Sport Magazine's* Sportswoman of the Year, and in 1974 United Press International's (UPI) Sportswoman of the Year and *Track & Field News* Woman Athlete of the Year. She was elected to the International Women's Sports Hall of Fame in 1992 and was named a member of the International Olympic Committee in 1998.

[Elli Wohlgelernter (2nd ed.)]

KIRYAS JOEL, an incorporated ḥasidic village 60 miles (90 km.) northwest of New York City, just outside the village of Monroe. It was settled in 1974 on property purchased by Kahel Yatev Lev, a Brooklyn-based congregation, representing the Satmar ḥasidic group.

The village was the fulfillment of a long standing aspiration of the Satmar Rebbe, Rabbi Joel *Teitelbaum (1888–1979). The *rebbe*, a Holocaust survivor, arrived in New York in 1947 and settled in the Williamsburg section of Brooklyn. He was a prominent Orthodox leader in Hungary of the 1930s and gathered a large following of Ḥasidic Jews throughout his first decades in America. He stressed ultra-Orthodox religious standards and showed fierce opposition to Zionism and the State of Israel.

Teitelbaum often spoke of his desire to fulfill the Maimodean imperative (Yad, De'ot 6:8) to "forsake the cities of evil doers." He further emphasized that he desired a settlement free of any Zionist influences. However, provided prospective villagers adhered to these standards, he did not seek to limit their ranks to his own followers. In addition, he wanted the village to be close enough to sources of livelihood.

Despite the opposition of some influential Satmar communal leaders, who feared fragmentation of the group, the *rebbe* promised that he would divide his time between the proposed village and those Ḥasidim remaining in Williamsburg. Over two decades beginning in the early 1960s, assorted plans to purchase properties in Staten Island, northern New Jersey, Congers, New York, and other sites came to naught.

It was in the early 1970s, when the *rebbe* appointed Leibush Lefkowitz, the president of Congregation Yatev Lev and a wealthy businessman, to the task of seeing the project to fruition that matters moved towards a conclusion.

In the fall of 1974 the first families settled in Kiryas Joel. Among Teitelbaum's stated demands of the village's residents was that women dress modestly, secular literature be avoided, and, in keeping with his anti-Zionist stance, no Hebrew be spoken.

In 1977 the community's large synagogue was opened. Eventually the village, which incorporated in 1977, would feature over 50 prayer groups in assorted synagogues. This was reflective of the village's rapid growth and tolerance of differing orientations within ultra-Orthodoxy. The 2005 population was estimated at over 15,000.

After the *rebbe*'s passing in 1979 and the succession of his nephew Rabbi Moshe Teitelbaum (1915–2006), the community was plagued by a series of controversies. In the late 1980s a dissident group, who opposed the appointment of Moshe's son Aaron to various rabbinic positions in Kiryas Joel, founded a rival congregation, Bnei Yoel. This group would eventually establish its own synagogues and educational network in the village.

A further split took place in recent years with Moshe in ill health, as followers of Aaron and his brother, Zalmen Leib, battled for communal leadership. In struggles that have at times become violent and have also been played out in the courts, the two factions have largely established rival congregations, each claiming be the legitimate representative of the community. Their rival viewpoints are represented in competing Yiddish newspapers with *Der Yid* speaking for Zalmen Leib's contingent and *Der Blatt* for Aaron's.

In the 1990s the village established a public school for its developmentally disabled children This move was challenged in the courts as a violation of church-state separation and was still pending in 2006.

Interestingly, right-wing dissidents, in Kiryas Joel and throughout the ultra-Orthodox world, also criticized the school, which they viewed as conforming to religiously prohibited standards of secularization.

BIBLIOGRAPHY: S.S. Teller, *Divrei ha-Yamim* (n.d.); M.A. Zabel, *Ha-Kehillah be-Tifarto* (n.d.); S.Y. Gelbman, *Rezon Zaddik* (1998).

KIRYAT ANAVIM (Heb. קִרְיַת עֲנָבִים; "Vineyard City"), kibbutz in the Judean Hills, 8 mi. (12 km.) W. of Jerusalem, affiliated with Iḥud ha-Kevuẓot ve-ha-Kibbutzim, founded in 1920 by Third Aliyah agricultural workers from Eastern Europe, who were later joined by immigrants from other countries. The initiative for founding a kibbutz at this spot came from Akiva *Ettinger, who wished to work out methods for modern hill farming, land reclamation, and afforestation. As the Zionist institutions had insufficient means to aid the settlers, who in the initial years suffered severe hardships, they proposed transferring the kibbutz to a better site in the Jezreel Valley, but the settlers insisted on staying on until their hill farm would become established. The development of deciduous fruit orchards, vineyards, and dairy cattle made Kiryat Anavim an important supplier to the population of Jerusalem. In the *Israeli War of Independence (1948), the kibbutz defended a highly endangered position and served as a base for Operations Naḥshon and Makkabi – the first steps in opening the Jerusalem Corridor. In addition to field crops, the kibbutz operated factories manufacturing insulation and silicone products and ran a resort for which the woodland in the vicinity formed a suitable setting. Its population was 301 in 1968 and 314 in 2002.

WEBSITE: www.kiryatanavim.homestead.com.

[Efraim Orni]

KIRYAT ATA (Heb. קִרְיַת אָתָא), town with municipal council status in northern Israel, 9 mi. (14 km.) N.E. of Haifa. It was founded in 1925 as a rural settlement. Abandoned after the 1929 Arab riots, it was renewed in 1934 when one of the country's largest textile plants was erected there. In 1948, the town had 2,300 inhabitants and expanded quickly after the Israeli *War of Independence (1948), when the immigrant camp (*ma'barah*) Gilam was included in the municipal area and its inhabitants transferred to permanent dwellings. In 1967 Kiryat Ata received municipal status. The population steadily grew to 25,000 in 1969, 41,800 in the mid-1990s, and 48,800 in 2002. The municipal area is about 8 sq. mi. (20 sq. km.). Residents earn their living in local industry, commerce, and services or commute to work. The Ata textile plant closed down in 1985.

The name Kiryat Ata, originally Kefar Ata, is based on the Arabic denomination of the site (Kufrattā), which in turn is assumed to have its origin in Aramaic. Remnants of buildings, mosaic floors, and tombs of the late Roman and early Muslim period have been found.

[Efraim Orni / Shaked Gilboa (2nd ed.)]

KIRYAT BIALIK (Heb. קִרְיַת בְּיַאלִיק; named after Ḥayyim Naḥman Bialik), urban community with municipal council status (since 1950) in northern Israel, in the Haifa Bay area, founded in 1934 as part of the residential zone north of the industrial Bay area. The first settlers, 160 families, originated from Germany. In the ensuing years they were joined by immigrants from European, African, and Asian countries. Kiryat Bialik had 900 inhabitants in 1944 and grew to 13,100 by 1969. In 1976 Kiryat Bialik received city status. In the mid-1990s the population was approximately 35,300, and at the end of 2002 the population of Kiryat Bialik was 37,100 residents.

Until the early 1950s, "Ahavah," a Youth *Aliyah center for children with educational problems, was located at Kiryat Bialik. Initially a purely residential quarter with one- and two-family houses with gardens, Kiryat Bialik's municipal area was enlarged northward on the east side of the Haifa-Acre highway, multistory houses were built, public gardens planted, and a new industrial area developed in the northernmost part, including one of the country's important textile factories. Today the city's area consists of 7,200 dunams, with a large immigrant population, including Russians, Ethiopians, and Latin Americans.

[Efraim Orni / Shaked Gilboa (2nd ed.)]

KIRYAT EKRON (Heb. קִרְיַת עֶקְרוֹן), semi-urban community, with municipal council status (since 1963), in the Coastal Plain of Israel, 2 mi. (3 km.) S.E. of Reḥovot. The town's area is 0.8 sq. mi. (2.2 sq. km.). Immigrants from Bulgaria and Iraq were housed soon after the Israeli *War of Independence (1948) in the former Arab village of ʿAqir, abandoned in 1948. The site grew into a modern agglomeration which in 1969 had 4,100 inhabitants, some of whom worked in local plants (e.g., a cotton gin), in farm work, and various enterprises in Reḥovot and elsewhere. In the mid-1990s the population was approximately 5,350, increasing to 9,600 in 2002, with four new neighborhoods created in the expanding community.

[Efraim Orni / Shaked Gilboa (2nd ed.)]

KIRYAT GAT (Heb. קִרְיַת גַּת), town with municipal status (from 1972) in the southern Coastal Plain of Israel. Kiryat Gat was founded in 1955 near the tell then held to be the site of Philistine *Gath. West of the present municipal area lay the village Fālūja, which was abandoned in 1948. It was destroyed after the "Ten Plagues" Operation in the *War of Independence, when Israeli forces laid siege to a large contingent of Egyptian forces there. Kiryat Gat, planned to serve as the urban center of the *Lachish Development Region, expanded quickly, rising from 4,400 inhabitants in 1958, to 17,000 in 1969. Of the adult population (1968), about 50% were immigrants from Mediterranean countries, mainly North Africa, 20% from Eastern Europe, mainly Romania, and 15% from Western Europe and North and South America, while the rest were Israeli-born or veteran Israelis. In the mid-1990s the population was approximately 38,300, increasing to 48,200 in 2002, with a municipal area of around 4 sq. mi. (10 sq. km.).

The development of the town's economy began with services rendered to the Lachish Region's rural settlements and with industries based on farming produce, e.g., cotton ginneries. These were soon followed by large cotton and wool spinning and weaving plants, clothes factories, and a sugar factory. In the later 1960s other enterprises developed. The local labor demand made it necessary to attract additional population by stepping up apartment building. The industrial area, to the southwest of the town, was twice enlarged to make room for new enterprises, while the commercial region in the center was replanned and a municipal park laid out. At the end of the 1990s Intel Industries opened a microprocessor factory in Kiryat Gat. The plant employed 3,700 workers. Another 400 workers were employed in nearby factories servicing the Intel plant. Average income in the city was considerably below the national average.

[Efraim Orni / Shaked Gilboa (2nd ed.)]

KIRYAT ḤAROSHET (Heb. קִרְיַת חֲרֹשֶׁת), village in northern Israel, between Mount Carmel and the Tivon Hills, founded in 1935 by workers from the Haifa industrial zone. It became the object of frequent attacks during the 1936–39 Arab riots and some of its first settlers were murdered. Although planned as an urban community, Kiryat Ḥaroshet remained a small hamlet (with 217 inhabitants in 1969), as it was overshadowed by nearby *Kiryat Tivon and other centers. The name, literally translated as "City of Industry," is in fact an allusion to biblical Harosheth-Goiim mentioned in the report of Deborah's victory over the Canaanites (Judges 4) and assumed to have been located near this site. In 1979 Kiryat Ḥaroshet was united with *Kiryat Tivon.

[Efraim Orni / Shaked Gilboa (2nd ed.)]

KIRYAT MALAKHI (Heb. קִרְיַת מַלְאָכִי), development town in southern Israel, 12 mi. (20 km.) N.E. of Ashkelon. Its name is the Hebrew for Los Angeles, whose Jews financed its first housing scheme.

Kiryat Malakhi was founded in 1950 as a **ma'barah* (immigrant transit camp). It gradually became a center based on the variegated produce of the quickly developing agricultural hinterland. In 1965 Kiryat Malakhi received municipal council status and in 1998 city status. Its area is around 2 sq. mi. (5 sq. km.). In 1968 it had 7,500 inhabitants, 50% of whom were from Asian and African countries, 35% were Israeli-born or veteran Israelis, and 15% from Eastern Europe. A large poultry slaughterhouse and packing plant, an ice-cream factory, and factories for textiles, cardboard, plastics, leatherwear, and metal were located in the town. In 2002 the population was 19,100, including about 3,000 Ethiopian Jews, with income about half the national average. Israel's president, Moshe *Katzav, was a former mayor of the town.

[Efraim Orni / Shaked Gilboa (2nd ed.)]

KIRYAT MOTZKIN (Heb. קִרְיַת מוֹצְקִין), urban community in the Haifa Bay area in Israel, founded in 1934 as part of the residential zone north of the Bay area allocated for industry. Its name commemorates Leo *Motzkin.

The first settlers, the majority of whom came from Eastern Europe, lived in one- and two-family houses with gardens. Kiryat Motzkin's layout was gradually superseded by large apartment houses as the population grew from a few hundred at the end of the 1930s to 3,700 in 1948, reaching 13,800 in 1969. In 1976 Kiryat Motzkin received city status; its area was expanded to 1.2 sq. mi. (3.1 sq. km.). In the mid-1990s the population was approximately 33,400, increasing to 39,400 in 2002. Kiryat Motzkin is the commercial center of the "Kerayot" area.

WEBSITE: www.kiriat-motzkin.muni.il.

[Efraim Orni / Shaked Gilboa (2nd ed.)]

KIRYAT ONO (Heb. קִרְיַת אוֹנוֹ), an urban settlement in central Israel, 5 mi. (8 km.) east of Tel Aviv. Founded in 1939 as a moshav by immigrants from European countries, Kiryat Ono (originally Kefar Ono) is named after the ancient site of *Ono, which is assumed to have been a few kilometers further south. The 40 founder families initially lived together with Arab Bedouins. The settlement, which numbered 377 inhabitants in 1948, expanded quickly when new immigrants, many of whom had entered the country on "illegal" ships, were housed in it. There were 6,530 inhabitants in 1951, 8,363 in 1961, and 14,200 in 1969. In 1992 Kiryat Ono received city status with an area of about 2 sq. mi. (5 sq. km.). In 2002 the population was 23,900. Kiryat Ono is principally a residential area on the border of the Tel Aviv conurbation, and economically dependent on the large city.

[Shlomo Hasson / Shaked Gilboa (2nd ed.)]

KIRYAT SHEMONAH (Heb. קִרְיַת שְׁמוֹנָה; "City of Eight"), town in northern Israel, in the Ḥuleh Valley, founded in 1950 when a local camp for new immigrants (**ma'barah*) was transformed into a permanent residential area. In 1953 it received municipal council status and in 1974 it become a city, with an area of about 4 sq. mi. (10 sq. km.). The name Kiryat Shemonah commemorates Joseph *Trumpeldor and seven others who fell in 1920 in the defense of neighboring Tel Ḥai (*Kefar Giladi) against an attack led by notables of Khāliṣa village, which stood until 1948 on the site of what would later become Kiryat Shemonah. The town grew from 3,300 inhabitants in 1954 to 6,000 in 1956 and 10,000 in 1959, although the lack of solid economic foundations caused a much larger turnover of population in that period. The population then reached 15,300 in 1969 and stabilized somewhat. The oldest part of the town, in the valley between the narrow basalt ridge (the "Snake Head"), had small houses with adjoining auxiliary farms. Later, the main part of the town developed with multistory houses on the mountain slope to the west. In the mid-1990s the population was approximately 19,000, and by the end of 2002 it had risen slightly to 21,600, of whom 18% were new immigrants; 30% of the city's population was younger than 17. In 1969 local industry began to develop, e.g., a spinning mill (the largest enterprise), a fruit-packing plant and other plants based on the region's farming produce, and textile factories. Some of the enterprises were initiated by the Upper Galilee (i.e., Ḥuleh Valley) Regional Council, which has its seat at Kiryat Shemonah. In the initial years most of Kiryat Shemonah's workers were employed as hired farm laborers in the vicinity. This type of employment diminished in the 1960s, although the Ḥuleh Valley settlements, including kibbutz factories, were still important sources of employment for Kiryat Shemonah inhabitants. The beginning of settlement of the *Golan after the *Six-Day War furthered the town's development, though the city continued to suffer from severe economic problems, with income considerably below the national average. The city served as an urban center for the rural settlements around it.

From 1968 Kiryat Shemonah became the object of repeated shelling from beyond the nearby Lebanese frontier. The escalation of attacks on the city at the end of the 1970s and the beginning of the 1980s led to the *Lebanon War. During these years the economic situation worsened and many residents left the city. The shelling – mainly by the Hizballah organization – continued after the end of the war, but to a lesser extent. Up to May 2000, when Israel withdrew its troops from Lebanon, the city was hit by 4,000 shells, causing 24 casualties and wrecking nearly 7,000 apartments and 250 cars. Since the withdrawal the Upper Galilee area, including Kiryat Shemonah, has enjoyed relative quiet.

BIBLIOGRAPHY: Levenberg, *Pirkei Kiryat Shemonah* (1964); E. Spiegel, *New Towns in Israel* (1966). **WEBSITE:** www.k-8.co.il.

[Efraim Orni / Shaked Gilboa (2nd ed.)]

KIRYAT TIVON (Heb. קִרְיַת טִבְעוֹן), town with municipal council status (since 1958) in northern Israel, between the Jezreel and Zebulun valleys. A workers' suburb, Kiryat Amal ("City of Toil"), was founded there during the Arab riots in 1937 and expanded after World War II. Its inhabitants were employed partly in Haifa and partly in auxiliary and full-fledged farms. In 1947, "Keret," an investment company formed by British Zionists, established a second suburb, Tivon, north of Kiryat Amal, which after the Israeli *War of Independence (1948) became an important holiday resort. In 1957, Tivon, which had 4,850 inhabitants, and Kiryat Amal with about 4,000 merged into Kiryat Tivon together with El-Ro'i, a moshavah founded in 1935 by immigrants from Kurdistan. In 1969 it had a population of 9,700, rising to 13,300 in 2002, including the population of *Kiryat Ḥaroshet, which merged with Kiryat Tivon in 1979. The municipal area is 3.5 sq. mi. (9 sq. km.).The foremost economic branch continued to be the recreation and tourist trade, but by the beginning of the 21st century, Kiryat Tivon was no longer a tourist center. The town's residents mostly commuted to work in nearby Haifa, Jokneam, and Afulah.

Large natural oak and pine forests are located in the vicinity, and the *Bet She'arim antiquities lie within Kiryat Tivon's muncipal area. The home of *shomer* (guardsman) Alexander *Zeid has been transformed into a youth hostel. Basmat Tab'ūn, a Bedouin housing project, adjoins Kiryat Tivon in the northwest. The Oranim academic college, with 5,500 students, founded by the kibbutzim movement, is located in the town.

[Efraim Orni / Shaked Gilboa (2nd ed.)]

KIRYAT YAM (Heb. קִרְיַת יָם; "City of the Sea"), urban community in northern Israel, in the Kerayot residential zone near the Haifa Bay shore. Kiryat Yam was founded in 1946, after beginnings in construction had already been made in 1939 but were interrupted with the outbreak of World War II. The settlement, with 650 inhabitants in 1948, expanded rapidly, reaching 16,000 in 1969 and 38,700 residents in 2002, with a municipal area of 2.7 sq. mi. (7 sq. km.). One- and two-family homes were gradually superseded by apartment houses. Inside the municipal area there was little industry, with most of the inhabitants employed in Haifa. Income was considerably below the national average.

[Efraim Orni / Shaked Gilboa (2nd ed.)]

KIRZHNITZ, ABRAHAM (1888–?), Soviet bibliographer. Kirzhnitz, who was born in Bobruisk, was among the directors of the well-known Jewish library there, and published articles on the problem of founding Jewish popular libraries. A member of the *Bund until 1920, he, like most of the members of his party, then joined the Communist Party. He was the author of *Di Yidishe Prese in der Gevezener Ruslendisher Imperye 1823–1916* (1930); *Di Yidishe Prese in Ratnfarband 1917–1927* (1928), and *Di Yidishe Prese in Vaysrusland* (1925), pioneering works on the Jewish press in Eastern Europe. He edited the collection *Der Yidisher Arbeter* (4 vols., 1925–28), and a collection of documents (in Russian) on Jewish participation in the 1905 Revolution (1928). Containing valuable material on the history of the Jewish workers' movement in Russia, these collections stress the central role of the Bund. Kirzhnitz disappeared at the end of the 1930s at the time of the great purges.

BIBLIOGRAPHY: Kh. Shmeruk, *Pirsumim Yehudiyyim bi-Verit ha-Mo'aẓot, 1917–1960* (1961), index; M. Altshuler (ed.), *Pirsumim Rusiyyim bi-Verit ha-Mo'aẓot al Yehudim ve-Yahadut, 1917–1967* (1970), index; Y. Slutsky (ed.), *Sefer Bobruisk* (1967), index; Rejzen, Leksikon, 3 (1929), 652–9.

[Yehuda Slutsky]

KIŠ, DANILO (1935–1989), Yugoslav author and translator. Born in Subotica, Kis survived the Holocaust and after the war completed high school in Cetinje, Montenegro. He received his B.A. from the Faculty of Philosophy at the University of Belgrade. He was a freelance writer, dramaturge in the Belgrade Atelier 212 Theater, and lecturer on Serbo-Croat at various French universities. Kis wrote short stories, novels, essays, dramas, and television screenplays, translated poetry from French and Hungarian. He published *The Mansard, Psalm 44* (1962), but made his name with the meditative novel *Garden, Ashes* (1965 and 1978) in which the fascinating image of his

Jewish father who was killed in Auschwitz in 1944 appears for the first time. He went on to publish *Early Griefs* (1968) and *Hourglass* (1969) for which he was awarded the 1972 Belgrade NIN magazine prize for the best novel in Yugoslavia.

A master of style, modern in expression, and an outstanding talent, Kis was attacked for his anti-Stalinist book, *A Tomb for Boris Davidovich* (1976), by a group of Belgrade writers and journalists. His reply was the polemic treatise *The Anatomy Lesson* (1978). He lived in isolation in Paris, away from public life, but surrounded by friends. In Paris he wrote *The Encyclopedia of the Dead* (1983). In 1984 he was awarded the Ivo Andrić Prize in Belgrade and in 1989 received the Bruno Schulz Prize in New York. He was a member of the Serbian Academy of Sciences and Arts and a Chevalier des arts et lettres (Paris, 1986). His works have been translated into English, French, German, Russian, Hungarian, Hebrew, and other languages.

His mother was Montenegrine of the Orthodox faith. When he was five, his mother had him baptized in a Serbian Orthodox Church. His writings are deeply influenced by the Holocaust and his own family's struggle for survival. Despite his use of dialect, his personal inclinations are decidedly cosmopolitan. He visited Israel and was impressed by it, but resented having apparently been described by someone as a non-Jew.

In accordance with his will, he was buried ceremoniously in Saborna Crkva, the primary Serbian Orthodox Church of Belgrade.

[Eugen Werber / Zvi Loker (2nd ed.)]

KISCH, prominent family in Prague. The name derived from the village of Chyse (Chiesch) in western Bohemia, from where the family came in the 17th century. For about 200 years it held the license for the only pharmacy in the Jewish quarter of Prague. One of its members was the physician ABRAHAM KISCH (1725–1803), the first Prague Jew to receive a doctorate in medicine (at Halle University in 1749). The founder of the Jewish hospital in Breslau (Wroclaw), he was head of the Prague community's hospital. Abraham Kisch taught Latin to Moses *Mendelssohn and championed the admission of Jewish students to the universities. JOSEPH KISCH opened the first modern private school in the Jewish quarter. His son ENOCH HEINRICH (1841–1918), a physician, specialized in balneology and was active in the development of the Bohemian spas, especially Marienbad, where he also directed the Jewish hospice. His memoirs, *Erlebtes und Erstrebtes* (1914), are an important source for the history of Jewish Prague after the 1848 Revolution. When the Jews were expelled from Prague by Maria Theresa (1744), members of the family went to Holland and from there to England, where they founded other branches of the family (see *Kisch (British family)).

BIBLIOGRAPHY: G. Kisch, *Die Prager Universitaet und die Juden* (1935, repr. 1969), 27ff., 128–38; R. Kestenberg-Gladstein, *Neuere Geschichte der Juden in den boehmischen Laendern*, 1 (1969), index; EJ, 10 (1934), 18–22, incl. bibl.; UJE, 6 (1942), 400–3, incl. bibl.; L. Fuks, in: *Studia Rosenthaliana*, 3 (1969), 193–201.

[Meir Lamed]

KISCH, family of British government officials descended from the *Kisch family of Prague. HERMANN MICHAEL KISCH (1850–1942) entered the Indian civil service in 1873 and rose to become a deputy secretary to the government of India, postmaster-general of Bengal, and director-general of the Indian post office and represented India at four international postal congresses. He returned to England in 1904 and was active in Jewish affairs. His letters, *A Young Victorian in India*, were edited by his daughter Ethel A. Waley Cohen and published in 1957. Both of Kisch's sons followed their father into government service. Frederick Hermann *Kisch was a British delegate to the Versailles peace conference. His elder brother, SIR CECIL KISCH (1884–1961), joined the Indian civil service in 1909 and in 1917 went to India with Edwin *Montagu, the secretary of state for India, as his private secretary. In 1921 he became secretary of the Indian finance department and promoted numerous monetary reforms including the establishment of the Reserve Bank of India. Kisch represented India at the monetary conference at Geneva in 1933 and later served on the supervisory finance committee of the League of Nations. From 1933 to 1942 he was assistant under-secretary of state for India and from 1942 to 1943 deputy under-secretary. A man of wide-ranging interests, Kisch translated Russian poetry into English, published a standard work (with W.W.A. Elkin) on central banking, *Central Banks – a Study of the Constitution of Banks of Issue* (1928, 1932[4]), and wrote *The Portuguese Bank Note Case* (1932), the story of a famous fraud of the 1920s. He was knighted in 1932. Another member of the family, DANIEL MONTAGU KISCH (1840–1898), English traveler, voyaged to Australia and from there went to Mauritius and South Africa, where he settled. He became manager of a Natal sugar estate and later joined an expedition to Matabeleland where he was chief adviser to King Lobengula. From 1874 Kisch lived in Pretoria and was auditor-general of the Transvaal during the British annexation from 1877 to 1881. He campaigned for civic equality for the Jews in Transvaal.

[Joachim O. Ronall]

KISCH, ALEXANDER (1848–1917), Austrian rabbi and scholar. Born in Prague, Kisch studied at the Breslau Jewish theological seminary, and at various universities. In Paris he became a tutor in Baron Horace *Guenzburg's house. He served as rabbi in Bruex (Most), Bohemia (1874–77); in Zurich, Switzerland (1877–81); in Jungbunzlau (Mlada Beleslav), Bohemia (1881–86); and at the Meisels Synagogue in Prague (1886–1917). While serving in Zurich, Kisch founded and published (1878–80) the first Swiss-Jewish weekly, *Neue Israelitische Zeitung*. In 1899, Franz Joseph I awarded Kisch a gold medal for 25 years' service as a military chaplain; at the audience, Kisch persuaded the monarch to strongly condemn antisemitism, which was then assuming alarming proportions after the *Hilsner trial for ritual murder. Kisch was the first and only rabbi in Austria to be appointed a government professor of religion (1900) and an inspector of religious education (1909). Among Kisch's published works are: *Papst Gregor* *des Neunten Anklageartikel gegen den Talmud* (1847), *Hillel der Alte* (1889), *Das Testament Mardochai Meysels mitgetheilt und … beleuchtet: Festschrift zum 300-jaehrigen Jubilaeum der Meyselssynagogue* (1893), *Das mosaisch-talmudische Eherecht von R. Ezechiel Landau* (1900), and *Versuch einer neuen Erklaerung der in der Alkuinhandschrift Nr. 795 der Hofbibliothek Wien enthaltenen gotischen Fragmente* (1902).

Bruno *Kisch and Guido *Kisch were his sons.

BIBLIOGRAPHY: G. Kisch, *Alexander Kisch 1848–1917* (Ger., 1934); G. Kisch (ed.), *Breslau Seminary* (1963), 423 (incl. bibl.)

[Oskar K. Rabinowicz]

KISCH, BRUNO ZECHARIAS (1890–1966), medical authority and Jewish scholar. Kisch was born in Prague, the son of Alexander *Kisch and brother of Guido *Kisch. He was one of the founders of the Juedisches Lehrhaus in Cologne and taught experimental medicine, physiology, and biochemistry at the university there until 1936, when he was forced to leave Nazi Germany. During that time, he made particular studies on reflexes and discovered the law of irradiation of autonomic reflex, proving that each reflex in the field of autonomic nerves influences the tone of the entire autonomic nervous system. Subsequently, he taught at Yale and Yeshiva universities in the United States.

Kisch combined interests in several fields. He published several books on the relationship of religion and science, including *Naturwissenschaft und Weltanschauung* (1931), *Wege zum Glauben* (1935), and *Gottesglaube und Naturerkenntnis* (1936). He was a well-known authority on medical science, his special fields being biochemistry, cardiology, and electron microscopy. He was a founder and president of the American College of Cardiology and contributed a great deal to the progress of medicine. He made significant contributions to the study of biochemistry and the study of enzymes and described the presence of procain-esterase in blood and tissues, and of the enzyme aminodehydrase in certain parts of the kidney. He also introduced a test for toxic goiter. Among his works on medicine is *Electron Microscopy of the Cardiovascular System* (1960). Kisch was also interested in Jewish numismatics, publishing "Shekel Medals and False Shekels" (in *Historia Judaica*, 3 (1941), 67–101) and *Scales and Weights* (1965). He wrote an autobiography, *Wanderungen und Wandlungen* (1966).

BIBLIOGRAPHY: Reichert, in: *American Journal of Cardiology*, 18 (1966), 967; Proggendorf, *Biographisch-Literarisches Handwoerterbuchs*, 6 (1923–31), 1323; S.R. Kagan, *Jewish Medicine* (1952), 178.

[Alexander Tobias / Suessmann Muntner]

KISCH, EGON ERWIN (1885–1948), German author and journalist. He was born in Prague, where he was active in Czech-Jewish literary circles. Kisch joined the staff of the *Berliner Tageblatt* in 1913 and had an adventurous career as a leftist writer and politician. In 1918, Kisch led the Communist "Red Guard" in Vienna and a year later was sentenced to three months' imprisonment and expelled from Austria. He returned to Berlin and, after the Reichstag Fire in 1933, was arrested and deported to Czechoslovakia. Refused admission to Australia as an "undesirable alien" in 1934, Kisch caused a sensation by throwing himself overboard in Perth harbor. He was sentenced to six months' imprisonment and was deported. Kisch fought in the Spanish Republican Army in 1937–38, emigrated to New York in 1939, and eventually settled in Mexico. He returned to Prague in 1946, and became honorary president of the Prague Jewish community. His books reflect the times in which he lived and his own tumultuous journeys through many different lands (including the U.S.S.R. and China) and cultures. Always an exponent of the ideals of the "good European," he opposed all forms of nationalism. His most successful book was *Der rasende Reporter* ("The Rushing Reporter," 1924). After the Communist coup d'etat of February 1948 Kisch was appointed by the authorities to the "Action Committee," which supervised the activity of the Council of Jewish Religious Congregations in Bohemia and Moravia. His works include books about Prague and World War I, the anthology *Klassischer Journalismus* (1923), *Hetzjagd durch die Zeit* (1925), *Zaren, Popen, Bolschewiken* (1927), and *Paradies Amerika* (1930). He also wrote *Prager Pitaval* (1931), an account of Czech scandals, lawsuits, and the Prague underworld; books on Prague Jewish life, such as *Geschichten aus sieben Ghettos* (1934; *Tales from Seven Ghettos*, 1948); and the autobiographical *Marktplatz der Sensationen* (1945; originally published as *Sensation Fair*, 1941). Collections of Kisch's writing appeared in Czech (3 vols., 1947–49) and in German (8 vols., from 1960). A last book appeared in Czech as *Karel Marx v Karlových Varech* ("Karl Marx in Karlsbad," 1949).

BIBLIOGRAPHY: E. Utitz, *Egon Erwin Kisch* (Ger., 1956); D. Schlenstedt, *Deutsche Reportage bei Egon Erwin Kisch* (1959); *Věstnik židovské náboženské obce v Praze*, 10 (1948), 165–7; 11 (1949), 136–8, 164, 230, 304–5; 12 (1950), 149; D. Hamšík and A. Kusák, *O zuřivém reportéru E.E. Kischovi* (1962; includes bibliography).

[Rudolf Kayser]

KISCH, FREDERICK HERMANN (1888–1943), military engineer and Zionist leader. Born in Darjeeling, India, where his father, Hermann, was in the Indian Civil Service, Kisch finished in second place at the Royal Military Academy, Woolwich, joined the Indian Army, and was posted to Baluchistan in World War I. He was wounded in France and again in Mesopotamia; the second wound prevented further active service. He was then appointed to the Directorate of Military Intelligence at the War Office in the section covering Russia, Persia, China, and Japan. He was a member of the British delegation at the Paris Peace Conference (1919–21), and headed the military intelligence section. Although he was a lieutenant colonel by that time, he nevertheless failed to obtain a nomination to the Staff College. He resigned from the army and in 1923 accepted *Weizmann's invitation to become a member of the Zionist Executive in Jerusalem and head of its Political Department. Later he became chairman of the Jerusalem Executive, where his main task was to interpret the Jews to the Mandatory government and vice versa. Kisch's problems were compounded by his inevitable English orientation, so that while he and the British understood but did not agree with one another, he and the Jews agreed but did not understand one another. Anxious to find common ground with the Arabs, he met King Hussein of Hejaz (1924 and 1931), the emir Abdullah of Transjordan in Amman (1924), and Egyptian leaders in Cairo. He left the *Jewish Agency Executive in 1931 and engaged in private business in Haifa, at the same time advising the *yishuv* on security matters. His experiences are recounted in his book, *Palestine Diary* (1938).

On the outbreak of World War II he returned to active service in the British Army and was sent to Egypt, where by 1941 he was chief engineer, Eighth Army, with rank of brigadier. He was responsible throughout all North Africa for maintaining the water supply lines for military construction during the advances and demolition during the retreats, and for designing mine fields and devising anti-mine measures. Almost at the end of the fighting he was killed while inspecting a German mine field and was buried in Tunisia. He was decorated by the British and French governments. Kefar Kisch and the Kisch Memorial Forest in Lower Galilee are named after him.

BIBLIOGRAPHY: N. Bentwich and M. Kisch, *Brigadier Frederick Kisch, Soldier and Zionist* (1966).

[Semah Cecil Hyman]

KISCH, GUIDO (1889–1986), historian of law and of the legal status of Jews. Kisch, the son of Alexander *Kisch, was born in Prague. He was educated in Prague and taught the theory and history of law at Leipzig, Koenigsberg, Halle, and Prague universities. Dismissed by the Nazis in 1933, for a time he taught Jewish history at the Breslau *Juedisch-Theologisches Seminar. In 1935 he immigrated to the United States and taught history at the Jewish Institute of Religion in New York. In 1949 he served as visiting professor at the University of Lund in Sweden. In 1953 he began to teach at the University of Basel, and settled in Switzerland in 1962. His main interest was the investigation of the legal position of the Jews as reflected in non-Jewish legal sources.

Apart from many publications on medieval German law, Kisch wrote *Juedische Aerzte im alten Prag* (1934), *Die Prager Universitaet und die Juden 1348–1848* (1935), *Jewry-Law in Medieval Germany* (1941), *Sachsenspiegel and Bible* (1941), *In Search of Freedom, a History of American Jews from Czechoslovakia* (1949), *Jews in Medieval Germany* (1949), *Forschungen zur Rechts-und Sozialgeschichte der Juden in Deutschland waehrend des Mittelalters* (1955), *Recht und Gerechtigkeit in der Medaillenkunst* (1955), *Gestalten und Probleme aus Humanismus und Jurisprudenz* (1969), *An Innovator of Hagaddah Illustration – Cyril Kutlik* (1971), *Studies in Medallic History* (1975), and his autobiography, *Der Lebensweg eines Rechtshistorikers: Erinnerungen* (1975). He also prepared a new edition of Pseudo-Philo's *Liber Antiquitatum Biblicarum* (1949; cf. HJ, 12 (1950), 153ff.; and HUCA, 23 (1950/51), pt. 2, 81ff.). Kisch was the founder and editor of the periodical *Historia Judaica* (1938–61), amalgamated in 1962 with the *Revue des Etudes Juives*; and continued as associate editor with the *Revue*. He edited the volume memorializing the Breslau seminary (1963).

BIBLIOGRAPHY: *Jews of Czechoslovakia*, 1 (1968), index; *Festschrift Guido Kisch* (1955); HJ, 23 (1961), 31, 159–63; G. Kisch (ed.), *Das Breslauer Seminar* (1963), 397–8; K. Froelich, in: *Zeitschrift der Savigny-Stiftung fuer Rechtsgeschichte*, 67 (1950), 450–9 (Ger. sec.); *ibid.*, 68 (1951), 476–84.

KISH (Heb. קִישׁ), Benjaminite from Gibeah, father of King Saul. He is variously described as the son of Abiel (I Sam. 9:1), Jeiel (I Chron. 9:35), and Ner (I Chron. 8:33; 9:39). In I Chronicles 9:35 Jeiel is the *keri* for the *ketiv* Jeuel, the latter having the same vowel points as Abiel, indicating either Jeiel or Abiel. The correct reading is probably Abiel (cf. I Sam. 9:1). According to I Samuel 14:50–51, Ner is not the father of Kish but his brother, which agrees with I Chronicles 9:36 where Kish is mentioned before Ner, implying that Kish was the older brother of Ner. The Bible does not say very much about Kish, except that he was a man of wealth, possessing servants and asses (I Sam. 9:1–3). Saul is mentioned as "the son of Kish" in I Samuel 10:11, among other places. The sepulcher of Kish was at Zela, in the country of Benjamin (II Sam. 21:14), which was probably the landed property of his family. Both Saul and his son Jonathan were to be buried at this place (II Sam. 21:14).

The Akkadian adjective *qīšu*, "given as a present," "granted" (derived from the verb *qâšu*, "to deed," "grant") is attested in Akkadian personal names and provides a good etymology for the biblical name.

ADD. BIBLIOGRAPHY: CAD K, 280; D. Edelman, in: ABD, 4:85–87.

KISHINEV (Rom. **Chişinău**), capital of Moldova, formerly within Bessarabia. A Jewish cemetery is known to have existed in a village near Kishinev during the 18th century. In 1774, a *ḥevra kaddisha* was founded in the town with a membership of 144. When Kishinev became the capital of Bessarabia under Russian rule (1818) it developed rapidly, becoming a commercial and industrial center, and many Jews moved there from other places in Russia. The first rabbi of Kishinev was Zalman b. Mordecai Shargorodski. In 1816, R. *Ḥayyim b. Solomon Tyrer of Czernowitz laid the foundation stone of the Great Synagogue and in 1838, in the wake of the authorities' efforts to hasten the assimilation of the Jews, the first Jewish secular school was opened. In time two other government schools were opened. The poet J. *Eichenbaum and the scholar J. *Goldenthal taught there. The *Haskalah movement won few adherents among the Jews of Kishinev.

From 10,509 (12.2% of the total population) in 1847, the numbers of Jews in the city grew to 18,327 (21.8%) in 1867 and 50,237 (46%) in 1897. At the close of the 19th century most of the Jews were engaged in commerce, handicrafts, and industry. About 20,000 Jews were in miscellaneous occupations, in particular in the garment and timber industries and in the manufacture and trade of agricultural products, for which the region was noted. Jews owned many flour mills and plants for curing tobacco and drying fruit, and wine cellars. In 1898, 29 of the 38 factories of all kinds in Kishinev were owned by Jews. Large commercial houses and printing presses were also owned by Jews and employed thousands of Jewish workers. Because of the policy of the Russian authorities, who deliberately fostered antisemitism and passed legislation restricting the sources of livelihood open to Jews, Kishinev had a particularly large number of poor and destitute who were supported by various charitable institutions. In 1898, the separate welfare organizations amalgamated to form the Society in Aid of the Poor of Kishinev. Until World War I, the framework of Jewish life remained unchanged.

Kishinev was the seat of the Bessarabian headquarters of several Jewish institutions, which included the *Jewish Colonization Association (ICA), the *American Jewish Joint Distribution Committee (after World War I), and the American Joint Reconstruction Foundation. Judah Leib *Zirelson, the chief rabbi of Kishinev and Bessarabian Jewry (from 1909), founded a yeshivah here. There were also Jewish schools with instruction in Yiddish and Hebrew, and a *Tarbut school. In 1898 there were 16 Jewish schools in Kishinev with 2,100 pupils; 700 Jewish pupils attended general schools.

Persecutions and Pogroms

The name of Kishinev became known to the world at large as a result of two pogroms. The first, initiated and organized by the local and central authorities, took place during Easter on April 6–7, 1903. Agents of the Ministry of the Interior and high Russian officials of the Bessarabian administration were involved in its preparation, evidently with the backing of the minister of the interior, V. *Plehve. The pogrom was preceded by a poisonous anti-Jewish campaign led by P. *Krushevan, director of the Bessarabian newspaper *Bessarabets*, who incited the population through a constant stream of vicious articles. One of the authors of the most virulent articles was the local police chief, Levendall. In such a heated atmosphere any incident could have dire consequences, and when the body of a Christian child was found, and a young Christian woman patient committed suicide in the Jewish hospital, the mob became violent. A *blood libel, circulated by the *Bessarabets*, spread like wildfire. (It was later proved that the child was murdered by his relatives and that the suicide of the young woman was in no way connected with the Jews.) According to official statistics, 49 Jews lost their lives and more than 500 were injured, some of them seriously; 700 houses were looted and destroyed and 600 businesses and shops were looted. The material loss amounted to 2,500,000 gold rubles, and about 2,000 families were left homeless. Both Russians and Romanians joined in the riots. Russians were sent in from other towns and the students of the theological seminaries and the secondary schools and colleges played a leading role. The garrison of 5,000 soldiers stationed in the city, which could easily have held back the mob, took no action. Public outcry throughout the world was aroused by the incident and protest meetings were organized in London, Paris, and New York. A letter of protest written in the United States was handed over to President Theodore Roosevelt to be delivered to the czar, who refused to accept it. Under the pressure of public opinion, some of the perpetrators of the pogrom were brought to justice but they received very lenient sentences. L.N. Tolstoy expressed his sympathy for the victims, condemning the czarist authorities as responsible for the pogrom. The Russian writer Vladimir *Korolenko described the pogrom in his story "House No. 13" as did Ḥ.N. Bialik in his poem "*Be-Ir ha-Haregah*" ("In the Town of Death").

On Oct. 19–20, 1905, riots broke out once more. They began as a protest demonstration by the "patriots" against the czar's declaration of Aug. 19, 1905, and deteriorated into an attack on the Jewish quarter in which 19 Jews were killed, 56 were injured, and houses and shops were looted and destroyed: damages amounted to 300,000 rubles. On this occasion, some of the Jewish youth organized itself into *self-defense units. The two pogroms had a profound effect on the Jews of Kishinev. Between 1902 and 1905 their numbers dropped from around 60,000 to 53,243, many immigrating to the United States and the Americas, while many more left after the second attack. The economic development of the town was brought to a standstill.

1914–1939

During World War I, when Russian units retreated from the Romanian front in 1917–18, they looted Jewish houses on their homeward journey. When the Romanian army entered the town soon afterward, it proved no less savage in its treatment of the Jews. Romanian rule, which lasted for 22 years (1918–40), made no improvement in the condition of the Jews, who were still harassed by official and unofficial antisemitism. However, their numbers increased through the arrival of waves of refugees from the pogroms in the Ukraine during the Russian Civil War. As in the past, the local agitators were led by students, especially from the theological seminary and the faculty of agriculture. The local press was once more in the fore in propagating antisemitism; most prominent were the official organ *România Nouă* ("New Romania"), *Cuvântul Moldovenesc* ("The Moldavian Word"), and especially the *Scutul Național* ("The National Defender," published from 1921) which declared from the start its aim of fighting "against the Jew-boys, the speculators, the parasites, and the corrupt." There was also an antisemitic periodical, *Gîndul Neamului*. When the authorities deprived many of the Jews of Kishinev (and Bessarabia in general) of their citizenship in 1924, they lost their very means of livelihood. Hardly a year went by without demonstrations, riots, looting, and threats against the Jews. In these activities, members of the antisemitic organization "National and Christian Defense League," headed by A.C. *Cuza, played a leading role; they organized frequent "parades" with the intention of terrorizing the Jews and fomenting riots against them. In addition, the authorities took official measures, such as the closure of Jewish institutions, schools, newspapers, and cultural organizations. Many Jewish youth left for Ereẓ Israel or America. In 1938 the Jews were further hit by the antisemitic laws of the Cuza government, and more of them lost their civic rights.

Many Zionist movements were active in Kishinev, especially under Romanian rule; almost all trends of Zionism were represented, including a strong *He-Ḥalutz movement. Zionists and Yiddishists waged a sharp struggle to determine the character of the Jewish schools. The Yiddishists at first gained the upper hand. For political reasons – in order to weaken the influence of Russian culture – the Romanian authorities at first encouraged the development of independent Jewish education. Education in Hebrew made steady progress; outstanding among the leading Hebrew schools was the Magen David secondary school, founded in 1923. The authorities later tried to restrict Jewish education but it continued until Russian annexation in June 1940. Among the noteworthy achievements was the Hebrew kindergarten (1918) of the Yavneh society, the institute for the training of kindergarten teachers (1921), and the cultural center, which published its own monthly, *Min ha-Ẓad*. Sportsmen from Kishinev participated in the First and Second *Maccabiahs which were held in Ereẓ Israel in 1932 and 1935; many of them remained in the country.

From the close of the 19th century, a large number of Hebrew books were published in the town. Rabbinical works, as well as a variety of textbooks for the Hebrew and Yiddish schools, were also published. In 1912 there was a Russian Zionist weekly, *Yevreyskaya Khronika*. Many Yiddish newspapers appeared but they were shortlived (*Dos Bessaraber Leben*, *Der Morgen*, *Der Yid*, the weekly *Erd und Arbet* (1920–35) of the Ẓe'irei Zion party). *Unzer Tseit*, an important daily, was published between 1922 and 1938, with a few brief interruptions, under the direction of the lawyer Michael Landau.

By German-Russian agreement, in June 1940 Russia annexed Bessarabia. During the year of Russian domination (until July 1941), all Jewish institutions were closed down and the Zionist movement outlawed. In May 1941 the authorities arrested and exiled to Siberia all who were defined as enemies of the regime: these included the activists of the various Jewish movements and the wealthy Jews.

There were 70,000 Jews in the town on the eve of the Holocaust.

[Jean Ancel]

Holocaust Period

On July 17, 1941, Kishinev was occupied by German and Romanian units, who entered it together with units of *Einsatzgruppe* D. The massacre of Kishinev's Jews began immediately under the auspices of the *Einsatzgruppe*, and by the time the concentration of Jews into a ghetto was completed, about 10,000 had been slaughtered. The order to establish a ghetto and to wear the yellow badge was issued by the *Einsatzkommando* unit 11a, which from time to time took a number of people out of the ghetto and killed them. The Romanian gendarmerie acted similarly; German and Romanian reports mention three such operations. On August 1, 411 persons were killed by the Germans. The 39 survivors, who buried the dead, were returned to the ghetto to inform its inhabitants of the deed. On August 7, Unit 11a liquidated 551 Jews on the pretext of their being communist agents. On August 8, Romanian gendarmes removed 500 men and 25 women from the ghetto for forced labor. A week later, 200 of them were returned, as unfit for work, while the rest disappeared. Although documentation is available only on these three operations, it appears from eyewitness accounts that the method was more frequently employed.

On Oct. 4, 1941, deportations began to *Transnistria, the first group containing 1,600 persons. After this, between 700 and 1,000 Jews were deported daily, the last group leaving on October 31. Many of the deportees were robbed and murdered on the way to the Dniester River, while mass murder took place on the banks of the river, carried out by the Romanian gendarmes and German soldiers. In Transnistria Jews were sent to various camps and ghettos, where two-thirds of them died from epidemics, hunger, and exposure. The exact number of dead is not known, but taking into account the proportion of those killed in Bessarabia from the time of the Romanian and German conquest until the deportations to Transnistria on the one hand, and the number of those who died in Transnistria on the other, it may be estimated that of the 65,000 Jewish inhabitants in Kishinev in 1941, 53,000 perished.

Contemporary Period

In 1947 there were 5,500 Jews in Kishinev. In November 1956 Rabbi Greenberg of Kishinev was compelled to sign a government-organized protest against the Sinai Campaign which was published in *Izvestiya*. Restrictive measures were imposed on the Jewish community in the 1960s. The bar-mitzvah ceremony was forbidden in 1961; all synagogues but one were closed in 1964; and *mohalim* were repeatedly warned to cease performing circumcisions; the baking of matzah, however, was permitted in 1965. The Jewish cemetery, halved in area to make room for development, was completely closed in the 1960s and tombstones were damaged and destroyed, although the new cemetery was kept in order. Thirty-one Jews were arrested for "economic crimes" in 1962. In 1967 several Jewish students were expelled from the university when they refused to make a public denunciation of Israel's "aggression." A Jewish dramatic society established in 1966 with about 100 members put on a performance of *Hershele Ostropoler*. The official census of 1959 reported 42,934 Jews in Kishinev; in 1970 the Jewish population was estimated at approximately 60,000; and in 1998 it was put at around 21, 000.

[Theodor Lavi]

BIBLIOGRAPHY: L. Errera, *Les Massacres de Kishinev* (1903); I. Singer, *Russia at the Bar of the American People* (1904); C. Adler, *The Voice of America on Kishineff* (1904); *Die Judenpogrome in Russland*, 1–2 (1910); American Joint Reconstruction Foundation, *Report* *of Activities 1924/26*; B. Dinur, in: *Be-Kishinev bi-Melot 60 shanah* (1963), 243–59; E. Feldman, in: *He-Avar*, 17 (1970), 137–50. HOLOCAUST PERIOD: M. Carp, *Cartea Neagră*, 3 (1947), index; M. Mircu, *Pogromurile din Basarabia* (1947); Broszat, in: *Gutachten des Instituts fuer Zeitgeschichte* (1958), 102–82. **ADD. BIBLIOGRAPHY:** M. Landau, *O Viaţă de luptă* (1971), 73-97; Hebrew version: *Ma'avak Ḥayyay* (1970).

KISHON (Heb. קִישׁוֹן), river which drains the Jezreel Valley. The upper reaches are dry in summer and torrential in winter. Numerous small streams branching out from the hill of Moreh, the Jenin Valley, and elsewhere in the Jezreel Valley converge on the river. In the middle of its course, the Kishon has for the most part been drained. From Sha'ar ha-Amakim, between the Jezreel Valley and the plain of Acre–Haifa, it becomes a perennial river, flowing the last 6 mi. (10 km.) of its total length of 25 mi. (40 km.) along the Carmel and issuing into the Mediterranean approximately 2 mi. (3 km.) northeast of Haifa. Just before it runs into the sea, it reaches a width of 65 ft. (20 m.) Due to its swampy character, the Kishon was a serious obstacle to transport in early times. The irregular flow of the river gave rise to the Arabic name "The Cut River" (Nahr al-Muqattʿa).

The Kishon appears in connection with the defeat of Sisera by Barak and Deborah in the battle of Mt. Tabor (Judg. 4, 5), in which the Canaanite chariots mired in the swamps of the Kishon basin fell prey to the Israelite attack. As a result, the river is praised in the Song of Deborah (Judg. 5:21). The victory is also commemorated in Psalms 83:10. The prophets of Baal, defeated by Elijah on Mt. Carmel, were slaughtered on the banks of the river (1 Kings 18:40). Some scholars ascribe various paraphrases in the Bible to the Kishon: "the brook that is before Jokneam" (Josh. 19:11) and "the waters of Megiddo" (Judg. 5:19). The assumption by some scholars that the biblical Kishon is Wadi al-Bīra, which flows eastward from Mt. Tabor, on the basis of the nearby city of Kishion in the territory of Issachar, is usually rejected. The Kishon is called Pacida by Pliny (*Historia Naturalis* 5:19) and Cyson or Flum de Cayphas ("River of Haifa") by the Crusaders. Arab authors also refer to it as Nahr Hayfā. In the last decade, the issue of the river was deepened and a channel 984 ft. (300 m.) long, 164 ft. (50 m.) wide and 13 ft. (4 m.) deep was excavated to form an auxiliary harbor to Haifa, serving as a fishing harbor and depot.

BIBLIOGRAPHY: Abel, Geog, 1 (1933), 467ff.; I. Garstang, *Joshua-Judges* (1931), 299ff.; Zimbalist (Zori), in: BIES, 13 (1947), 28ff.

[Michael Avi-Yonah]

KISHON, EPHRAIM (formerly **Ferenc-Kishont**; 1924–2005), Israeli satirist, playwright, film writer, and director. Born in Budapest as Ferenc Hoffman, Kishon studied sculpture and painting. After the Nazi invasion of Hungary, he was deported to a concentration camp and managed to escape and survive in hiding in Budapest. "They made a mistake – they left one satirist alive," he wrote in his book "The Scapegoat." Kishon began publishing humorous essays and writing for the stage in post-war Communist Hungary. He immigrated to Israel in 1949 and acquired a mastery of Hebrew with remarkable speed, starting a regular satirical column in the easy-Hebrew daily, *Omer*, after only two years in the country. From 1952, he wrote a column (called "*Ḥad Gadya*") which became one of the most popular in the country. It appeared in the daily *Ma'ariv*, and was devoted largely to political and social satire but included essays of pure humor. His extraordinary inventiveness, both in the use of language and the creation of character, was applied also to the writing of innumerable sketches for theatrical revues. His full-length play, *Ha-Ketubbah*, "The Marriage Contract," had one of the longest runs in the Israeli Theater, while his feature films, *Sallah Shabbati* and *Blaumilch Canal*, which he wrote, directed, and produced, enjoyed international distribution. His sketches and plays have been performed, in translation, on the stages and television networks of several countries. Many titles and various collections of his humorous writings have appeared in Hebrew as well as in translation, the English translations including *Look Back Mrs. Lot* (1960), *Noah's Ark, Tourist Class* (1962), *The Sea-sick Whale* (1965), and two books on the Six-Day War and its aftermath, *So Sorry We Won* (1967), and *Woe to the Victors* (1969). Two collections of his plays have also appeared in Hebrew, *Shemo Holekh Lefanav* (1953) and *Ma'arkhonim* (1959). In many ways, Kishon, an immigrant who never got rid of his Hungarian accent, shaped the notion of "Israeliness." An ardent Israeli patriot, he was one of Israel's best unofficial ambassadors abroad, and spent the last years of his life in Switzerland and Tel Aviv. Kishon published the Hebrew novel "The Bald Truth" in 1998; a collection of articles, "Picasso's Sweet Revenge," in 2002; and many books for children. In 2002 he was awarded the Israel Prize for his lifetime achievement and for his contribution to society and state.

By 2005, 43 million copies of Kishon's books had appeared in translation worldwide, 33 million in Germany alone. In fact, Kishon's books played an important role in shaping the image of Israel and the Israeli in postwar Germany and kindled the interest of many readers and publishers in Israel and its modern literature. In 1978 he was honored with the Aachen "Carnival Society Against Deadly Seriousness" award, the most distinguished award in West Germany for humorous works.

For a list of Kishon's works in English translation, see Goell, Bibliography, and the ITHL website at www.ithl.org.il.

BIBLIOGRAPHY: Kressel, Leksikon, 2 (1967), 756. **ADD. BIBLIOGRAPHY:** R.L. Cargnelli, "L'humour israeliano: E. Kishon," in: *Rassegna Mensile di Israel*, 35 (1969), 454–60; N. Bacharach, "*Olim ve-Koletim bi-Shenot ha-Ḥamishim bi-Re'i Yeẓirato shel E. Kishon*," in: *Alon la-Moreh le-Sifrut*, 16 (1996), 109–22; A. Zanger, "Zionism and the Detective: Imaginary Territories in Israeli Popular Cinema of the 1960s," in: *Journal of Modern Jewish Studies*, 3:3 (2004), 307–17; *Frankfurter Allgemeine Zeitung* (January 31, 2005).

[Getzel Kressel / Anat Feinberg (2nd ed.)]

KISLEV (Heb. כִּסְלֵו), the post-Exilic name of the ninth month of the Jewish year. The name occurs in Assyrian inscriptions, in biblical records (Zech. 7:1; Neh. 1:1), and frequently in the Apocrypha and in rabbinic literature (e.g., *Megillat Ta'anit*) with variants in Assyrian and Palmyrian inscriptions and Greek transcriptions. The etymology of the term has not yet been satisfactorily elucidated. Like *Marḥeshvan, it consists of 29 or 30 days, in either common or *leap years. The 1st of Kislev never falls on the Sabbath. In the 20th century, Kislev, in its earliest occurrence, extended from November 4th to December 3rd (4th), and, in its latest, from December 3rd to 31st (January 1st).

Historic days in Kislev comprise: (1) 1st of Kislev, the announcement of a series of public fasts in Judea in the intercession for rain in years of drought (Ta'an. 1:5); (2) 3rd of Kislev, the anniversary of a Hasmonean victory over the Greeks (Meg. Ta'an. 339); (3) 7th of Kislev, the anniversary of the death of Herod (*ibid.*); (4) 21st of Kislev, "the day of Gerizim," commemorating the decision by Alexander the Great in favor of the Temple of Jerusalem against the rival Samaritan claim for the Temple on Mount *Gerizim (Meg. Ta'an 339–40, with variance of the date in Yoma 69a and parallels); (5) 25th of Kislev to 2nd (3rd) of *Tevet, the festival of *Ḥanukkah.

[Ephraim Jehudah Wiesenberg]

KISLING, MOISE (1891–1953), French painter. Kisling was born in Cracow, where he studied at the Academy of Fine Arts. In 1910 he went to Paris and lived there in poverty until an anonymous benefactor, on the recommendation of the novelist Sholem *Asch, offered him a year's allowance. Influenced by Cézanne, Kisling painted sober, chromatically restrained landscapes of Britanny and the Pyrenees, and by 1914 was selling well. On the outbreak of World War I he enlisted in the French Legion, but after being wounded in action resumed his career in Paris. He became a close friend of *Modigliani, with whom he shared his studio. From 1941 to 1946 Kisling found refuge from the Nazis in the U.S., where he painted many portraits, including one of the pianist Artur Rubinstein. Kisling's serene and calm paintings reveal his character. Their hint of melancholy is a characteristic shared with nearly all the artists of Jewish origin who worked in Paris between the two world wars. Strongly outlined and painted carefully in cool, restrained colors, his figures have much in common with those of Picasso's early "Blue Period," but his work has perhaps a closer affinity to certain works of the New Objectivity school that flourished in the Weimar Republic. Kisling was fully immersed in the centuries-old *belle peinture* of classical France. His paintings, mostly landscapes, flower still lifes, and nudes, are characterized by his particular sensitivity.

BIBLIOGRAPHY: G. Charensol, *Moïse Kisling* (Fr., 1948); A. Salmon, *Kisling* (1928).

[Alfred Werner]

KISS, JÓZSEF (1843–1921), Hungarian poet. Kiss, one of Hungary's greatest literary figures, was born in Mezőcsát. His father was a shopkeeper, his mother the daughter of a Lithuanian cantor. The boy was sent first to the yeshivah of Miskolc and later to other Hungarian yeshivot, but he ran away. When he was 19 his mother died and his father failed in business, and he was compelled to become an itinerant *melammed* (Hebrew tutor). For three years he wandered through the Hungarian provinces – an experience on which he was later to draw for material about Magyar and Jewish peasant life. In 1867 Kiss tried unsuccessfully to persuade the Pest Jewish community to sponsor the publication of his first collection of verse. He, therefore, had it published privately, under the title *Zsidó dalok* ("Jewish Poems," 1868), but it was a failure. He then worked as a proofreader in a printing firm. In 1870 he became editor of the magazine *Képes világ* ("Picture World"), but it ceased publication in 1873. Under the pseudonym "Rudolf Szentesi" he then wrote a series of eight popular detective novels inspired by the works of Eugène Sue and entitled *Budapesti rejtelmek* ("Secrets of Budapest," 1874). From 1875 to 1876 he was an editor of *Zsidó Évkönyv*, Hungarian Jewish Yearbook.

Kiss first made an impact as a poet in 1875, when a public performance of his ballad *Simon Judit* ("Judith Simeon") was given good reviews by Ferenc Toldy and other Hungarian critics. This recognition, however, did nothing to alleviate his financial plight and he accordingly left Budapest for Temesvár, where he became secretary to the Jewish community (1876–82). After his arrival there another volume of his poetry was published, and as a result he was elected a member of the distinguished Petőfi literary society in 1877. By 1882 he had become a celebrity. His *Ünnepnapok* ("Holy Days," 1888) was commissioned by the Pest Jewish community, but repudiated by it because of its unacceptable religious views. He had a job for some time in an insurance company but in 1890, with the backing of some friends, launched a successful literary journal, *A Hét* ("The Week"). As its editor he gained a reputation as the leading figure in Hungarian literature. He reached the pinnacle of his fame with the publication of a bibliophile edition of his collected poems, and on his 70th birthday was honored with election to the exclusive Kisfaludy literary society.

József Kiss's early poems followed the tradition of 19th-century Hungarian verse, although their heroes were Jews on the road to assimilation rather than Hungarian nobles and peasants. The first professing Jew to achieve fame as a Hungarian writer, he broke new ground with poems about social change, moral degeneration, and the breakdown of traditional Jewish family life (*Szép Batoné*, 1877; *Simon Judit*, 1875; *Jehovah*, 1884). In other poems he describes the cruelty of economic life in the city: *Mese a varrógépről* ("Song of the Sewing Machine," 1884), and *De Profundis* (1876). The theme of antisemitism recurs in all his poems. During *Tisza-Eszlar and other blood libels he wrote *Az ár ellen* ("Against the Tide," 1882) and the pogroms in Russia occasioned *Uj Ahasvér* ("The New Ahasuerus," 1875) and *Odessza* (1905). In all these works he expressed a love for the Jew which has no equal among Hungarian Jewish poets. Echoes of the 1905 Russian Revolution and the idea of world revolution found their way into his poems *Knyaz Potemkin* (1906) and *Tüzek* ("Flames"). He commemorated his Lithuanian grandfather in the poem *Legendák* *a nagyapámról* ("Legends of My Grandfather," 1888). His later poems are "pearls" of Hungarian lyrics, examples of which are *Ó mért oly későn* ("Why So Late") and *Borongás* ("Brooding"). Important collections of his verse include *Kiss József összes költeményei* ("Collected Poems of Joseph Kiss," 1930), *Levelek hullása* ("When the Leaves Fall," 1908), *Esteledik, Alkonyodik* ("Nightfall, Twilight," 1920). English translations of his poems appear in W.N. Loew's *Modern Magyar Lyrics* (1926).

BIBLIOGRAPHY: M. Rubinyi, *Kiss József* (Hung., 1926); A. Roth, *Judem im ungarischen Kulturleben in der zweiten Haelfte des 19. Jahrhunderts. Die ersten bedeutenden juedischen Dichter in der ungarischen Literatur* (1934), 15–21; *Kiss József és kerek asztala* (1934); S. Scheiber, *Zsidó néprajzi adatok Kiss József műveiben* (1948); *Magyar Irodalmi Lexikon*, 1 (1963), 645–48; A. Komlós, in: IMIT, 54 (1932), 49–73.

[Baruch Yaron]

KISS AND KISSING. Although frequently mentioned in the Bible, kissing was regarded by the rabbis (Gen. R. 70:12) as obscene except in three instances: as a sign of respect – Samuel kissed Saul after he was anointed king (I Sam. 10:1); as a salutation if meeting after a long interval – Aaron kissed Moses (Ex. 4:27); and in farewell – Orpah kissed her mother-in-law Naomi (Ruth 1:14). R. Tanḥuma stated that kissing is also permissible between close relatives: Jacob kissed Rachel even before their marriage (Gen. 29:11). Kissing on the mouth was regarded as unhygienic and the custom of the Medes to kiss only the hand was praised by R. *Akiva (Ber. 8b).

According to the Talmud (BB 17a) the patriarchs and Aaron, Moses, and Miriam died from a kiss of God (*mitah bi-neshikah*). This was considered the highest privilege and was reserved for the pious (Ber. 8a; Maimonides, *Guide of the Perplexed*, part 3, 51 end).

In later rabbinical literature, it is stated that a man should avoid kissing women because this leads to lewdness. Leviticus 18:6 "None of you shall approach to any that is near of kin to him to uncover their nakedness" is interpreted by Maimonides to refer "not only to sexual relations but to embracing and kissing too" (*Sefer ha-Mitzvot*, Negative Commandment, no. 353). A husband should not kiss his wife during menstruation and after she has given birth (see **Niddah*); these periods last until the termination of the woman's "uncleanness" and her immersion in a *ritual bath. To kiss a woman other than one's mother, wife, daughter, or sister was regarded as indecent and was forbidden.

To kiss religious objects is a sign of reverence and is a traditional custom popularly observed by Orthodox Jews: when putting on the *tallit*, the fringes are kissed; so are the *tefillin*; the *mezuzah* on the doorpost is kissed when leaving or entering a room, as is the Torah scroll when it is carried in a procession in the synagogue. It is also customary to kiss a Bible or prayer book if it falls on the floor. In some communities, children kiss the hand of their father on Friday eve before receiving the parental blessing at the commencement of the Sabbath (**Kabbalat Shabbat*). Ḥasidic Jews kiss the hand of their *rebbe* and pious Jews the stones of the *Western Wall.

BIBLIOGRAPHY: Loew, in: MGWJ, 65 (1921), 253–76, 323–49 (incl. bibl.); L.M. Epstein, *Sex Laws and Customs in Judaism* (1967^2), 105–9.

KISSIN, HARRY, BARON (1912–1997), financier and patron of the arts. Kissin was born in Danzig of Russian-Jewish parents. After living in Switzerland he settled in England in 1933, and devoted himself to finance, becoming executive chairman of the Guinness Peat Group Ltd., merchant bankers, and chairman and director of other city companies. He was appointed chairman of the Institute of Contemporary Arts in 1969, and in 1973 director of the Royal Opera House, Covent Garden, and chairman of the Royal Opera Trust. Kissin was a longtime friend of Harold Wilson, who frequently consulted him on trade matters; in the 1950s, when Wilson's Labour Party was in opposition, Kissin used Wilson as a consultant. In 1974 Kissin was given a life peerage by Wilson. Kissin was a generous supporter of Jewish and Israeli causes and was a governor of the Hebrew University.

ADD. BIBLIOGRAPHY: *ODNB*.

[Michael Wallach / William D. Rubinstein (2nd ed.)]

KISSINGEN (Bad Kissingen), town in Bavaria, Germany. The presence of Jews in Kissingen during the 13th century is attested by Jewish victims of the *Rindfleisch massacres (1298). Nothing more is heard of them until 1650, when local butchers complained that Jews were illegally practicing their trade. Complaints against their growing number were lodged in 1798. In 1801 a cemetery was established; a synagogue was built in 1852 and another in 1902. The community numbered 181 (17% of the total population) in 1816; it then fluctuated between 300 and 350, reaching a temporary peak of 504 in 1925. In 1933 there were 344 (4%) Jews living in Kissingen; their number had been reduced to 63 through emigration by Dec. 17, 1939. Bad Kissingen was an important health resort and the catering and hotel business was largely in Jewish hands. Seckel Bamberger, the district rabbi (1902–32), established a large children's sanatorium in 1905; in 1919 and 1927 wards for women and the aged were added.

On Nov. 10, 1938, the synagogue was burned down, and numerous shops and hotels were looted. The rabbi's sons were bound together, paraded through the town, and forced to dig up sacred objects consigned to the *genizah* in the community's cemetery. In April 1942, 23 of the remaining 43 Jews were transported to *Izbica near *Lublin and others to Theresienstadt. The city possesses the *pinkas kahal* (1770–1820) and maintains the cemetery.

BIBLIOGRAPHY: M. Weinberg, *Die Memorbuecher der juedischen Gemeinden in Bayern*, 2 vols. (1937–38), 109–17; Germ Jud, 2 (1968), 401; FJW, 290; PK; Part of the communal archives (1770–1938) are in the Jewish Historical General Archives in Jerusalem.

KISSINGER, HENRY ALFRED (1923–), U.S. secretary of state, winner of the Nobel Peace Prize. Born into an Orthodox Jewish family in the Bavarian town of Furth, and named

Heinz Alfred, Kissinger immigrated to New York in 1938. He attended high school at night, working during the day at a shaving brush company. He went to the City College of New York at night for a degree in accounting, which was his father's occupation. In 1943 his schooling was interrupted when he was drafted into the Army. While serving at Camp Claiborne, La., Kissinger met and came under the influence of Fritz Kraemer, a German refugee who was 35 and had European doctorates in law and political science. For many years, Kraemer, a conservative of a Central European background, was Kissinger's guide and mentor, and helped forge his fundamental political beliefs. After getting out of the Army, Kissinger, on Kraemer's recommendation, enrolled at Harvard University, where he wrote an appreciative dissertation on the diplomacy of the 19th-century Austrian statesman Prince Metternich, who was famous for his policy of suppressing any movement threatening the existing dynastic order. Kissinger's academic years, in which he helped set up the Harvard International Seminar, provided a base for his career in world politics. The seminar brought aspiring younger leaders to Harvard for a summer of study under his direction and provided him with a network of contacts around the world in years to come. He headed the seminar from 1951 to 1969. He also founded and edited a quarterly magazine on foreign affairs, *Confluence*, which lasted six years.

While still at Harvard, he obtained an appointment as staff director of a study group on nuclear weapons and foreign policy at the Council on Foreign Relations in New York. His first book, *Nuclear Weapons and Foreign Policy*, published in 1957, argued against the doctrine of massive retaliation, which implied full-scale nuclear war, and in favor of a "limited nuclear war" that would not escalate into total destruction. The book became a bestseller. The council received all the royalties, Kissinger all the credit. Kissinger then became the director of a Special Studies Project to define the nation's critical choices. The project was sponsored by Nelson Rockefeller. In the report that emerged from the study, *International Security: The Military Aspect*, in 1958, Kissinger lent his name to the doctrine that it was necessary to develop tactical nuclear weapons in order to prepare to fight a limited nuclear war. Kissinger later backed away from that view, and in 1961, in *The Necessity for Choice*, he declared that a limited nuclear war was untenable in practice, and he supported a doctrine of conventional warfare, with the use of nuclear weapons as a last resort. Kissinger received tenure at Harvard in 1959 and the rank of full professor of government in 1962. Although he was a Democrat, he also served as a part-time consultant to Rockefeller, a Republican, who in 1959 had become governor of New York. Kissinger had a small role in the administration of John F. Kennedy as a part-time consultant, but when Rockefeller sought the Republican presidential nomination in 1964, Kissinger worked as an adviser.

In 1965, Ambassador Henry Cabot Lodge asked him to visit South Vietnam as a consultant. For the United States, the Vietnam War was in an early stage. Although Kissinger came away deeply pessimistic, he supported the war anyway. He believed the United States could not win, but neither could it withdraw. It was necessary, he believed, to negotiate a way out. Kissinger did not say how that was to be accomplished. As the war proceeded, poorly for the United States, Kissinger became increasingly critical, and he called it a "disaster," but he urged only an assessment of the procedures and concepts that had gotten the United States involved. In 1968, the president-elect, Richard M. Nixon, unexpectedly chose Kissinger to be his national security adviser. At the time, the two did not know each other. Kissinger was an ally of Rockefeller, who was disdainful of Nixon. There are several conflicting views, including Kissinger's own account, Nixon's, and those of other biographers, of how the two hooked up. The net result is that Kissinger became knowledgeable in the ways of Washington and soon had complete access to the Oval Office. Lawrence Eagleburger, a long-time close aide to Kissinger and acting secretary of state, told a Kissinger biographer: "Kissinger and Nixon both had degrees of paranoia. It led them to worry about each other, but it also led them to make common cause on perceived mutual enemies. They developed a conspiratorial approach to foreign policy management."

In 1973 Nixon appointed Kissinger secretary of state, the first Jew and the first person not of American birth to get such an appointment. He took the oath of office on a Saturday with his hand on a Christian Bible, a matter to which the Jewish community paid considerable attention. With the conclusion of the Vietnam War, Kissinger played a leading role in trying to solve the thorny problems of the Middle East, especially after the Yom Kippur War. For a period of 72 hours, the fate of Israel during the Yom Kippur War depended on an American president who was pro-Israel but who had frequently expressed antisemitic views, an American secretary of defense, James Schlesinger, who had become a Christian while at Harvard, and the first American secretary of state of Jewish origin, to use a term common then. Kissinger used the incomplete victory of Israel as an opportunity to defuse the Arab-Israeli conflict and establish a countervailing American presence in the Arab world that would serve as a check on, and ultimately a diminution of, Soviet influence in the area. He succeeded in bringing the fighting to a halt by means of a six-point cease-fire plan, face-to-face negotiations between Egypt and Israel, a peace conference in Geneva, and the reestablishment of diplomatic relations between Cairo and Washington.

Kissinger retained Nixon's loyalty, by most accounts, by being obsequious to the president. Kissinger wrote that it was "almost suicidal" to challenge Nixon and that "Nixon's favor depended on the readiness to fall in with the paranoid cult of the tough guy." In his memoirs, Kissinger explained that Nixon had a "powerful tendency to see himself surrounded by a conspiracy reaching even among his Cabinet colleagues." One Kissinger biographer, Walter Isaacson, told of how Nixon and Kissinger conspired to exclude, humiliate, or deceive Secretary of State William Rogers, Secretary of Defense Melvin Laird, and others. Nixon's presidency was pathological,

Isaacson said, and his book shows that Kissinger was part of that pathology. The wiretaps of colleagues and friends that were secretly authorized or abetted by Nixon and Kissinger "ultimately led to the plumbers, which led to Watergate," Isaacson said. And Watergate, the break-in at the Democratic campaign headquarters and the cover-up orchestrated by the White House and top Cabinet officials, led Nixon to resign in 1974 before he would have been impeached. During that crucial period in the White House, Nixon got on his knees to pray, and Kissinger joined him.

Kissinger played a key role in all the foreign policy events of the Nixon administration: the negotiations with North Vietnam in Paris to end the war, the opening of China to the West, the overthrow of the regime of Salvador Allende Gossens in Chile, the invasion and secret bombing of Cambodia, the arms control agreements, and the 1973 Yom Kippur War.

In the early 1970s, Kissinger became involved in negotiations in Paris with Xuan Thuy and Le Duc Tho of North Vietnam to end the war in Vietnam that had dragged on for years. To the North Vietnamese, the goal was to get the United States to withdraw its forces from Vietnam while the North Vietnamese kept their forces in the South. The main achievement of the negotiations was effective capitulation to the North Vietnamese terms. To achieve this deal, Isaacson wrote, it was necessary to engineer the "appalling betrayal" of the South Vietnamese regime. When Nguyen Van Thieu, the South Vietnamese leader, refused to go along with his own political suicide and upset the deal, Kissinger advocated bombing North Vietnam to get amendments to the agreement that would appease the South Vietnamese. As Isaacson wrote: "Hanoi was bombed in order to force changes in a treaty that the U.S. had already seen fit to accept. The modifications for which these lives were lost were so minor that neither Nixon nor Kissinger would adequately remember what they were." The months and years of the negotiations, carried out in secrecy, were Kissinger's way of cutting out the State Department and the rest of the United States government from the negotiations, Isaacson said.

Later, Kissinger declared that the Watergate scandal had so weakened the Nixon presidency that it could not effectively continue the war for as long as he thought might be necessary. In 1973 Kissinger and Tho were awarded the Nobel Peace Prize. The award was so fatuous that Kissinger, in *Years of Upheaval*, the second volume of his memoirs, felt "ill at ease," he wrote, when he learned of it.

After Nixon was driven from office and Gerald Ford took his place, Kissinger urged the United States to become re-engaged in Vietnam, despite a vote in Congress to stop all aid. In 1975, when Ford brought the war to an official end, he concealed his public announcement from Kissinger, then still secretary of state. Nixon and Kissinger also engaged in elaborate secrecy in their negotiations with China. While the foreign ministries of China, Pakistan, Romania, and the Soviet Union all knew about the American initiative, the U.S. State Department did not.

In 1970 Chile elected a leftist, Allende, as president. Kissinger actively participated in plans to prevent him from taking office. Before the election, Kissinger had told the American ambassador "to reinforce with the [Chilean] military the serious consequences of an Allende presidency" and to "reiterate the assurances of continued American military assistance" if the military moved against him. Allende was the victim of a bloody military coup, after which a right-wing dictatorship under Gen. Augusto Pinochet seized power. Kissinger denied any responsibility for the coup on the ground that the Chilean military leaders had not consulted the United States in advance.

Kissinger hoped his cultivation of Soviet and Chinese leaders would pay off in greater success in handling regional crises, but this did not happen. The Communist regimes had no intention of reining in their Third World allies, and their continued aggression gradually undermined Kissinger's credibility. By 1976 he had become an electoral liability for President Ford, who had to fight accusations from both left and right that his secretary of state was pursuing an immoral foreign policy.

Kissinger also had a knack for cultivating the press and frequently granted exclusive or off-the-record interviews to favored journalists and columnists. He appeared on the cover of *Time* magazine 21 times during his heyday. In 1973 he came out first in a Gallup Poll of the most-admired Americans. That same year the contestants in the Miss Universe Pageant voted him "the greatest person in the world today."

After leaving Washington and returning to New York in 1977, Kissinger formed Kissinger Associates and gave advice on foreign policy to private corporations. He and the company undertook diplomatic assignments for clients like American Express, the Chase bank, Coca-Cola, and others and served as a foreign policy adviser to their chairmen. He also served as an eminence-gris for foreign affairs specialists. All of the more than two dozen national security advisers after Kissinger either worked for him or worked directly for someone who did, and by the early years of the 21st century Kissinger's followers had essentially become the modern foreign policy establishment.

BIBLIOGRAPHY: J. Hanhimaki, *The Flawed Architect: Henry Kissinger and American Foreign Policy* (2004); W. Isaacson, *Kissinger: A Biography* (1992); S. Hersh. *The Price of Power: Kissinger in the Nixon White House* (1983).

[Stewart Kampel (2nd ed.)]

KISSUFIM (Heb. כִּסּוּפִים; "Longings"), kibbutz in N.W. Negev, Israel, affiliated to Ha-Kibbutz ha-Me'uḥad, and founded in 1951 by settlers from South America. Later, immigrants from the United States and Canada, together with Israeli-born youth, made up the majority of members. Kissufim's agriculture was based on field crops, citrus groves, avocado plantations, dairy cattle, poultry, and organic farming. It also ran a guest house. Prior to the *Sinai Campaign (1956), and again before the *Six-Day War (1967), Kissufim played an important security role as an outpost opposite the Gaza Strip. In the mid-1990s the population was approximately 350, declining to 202 in 2002.

WEBSITE: www.kissufim.org.il.

[Efraim Orni]

KISTARCSA, transit camp 9 mi. (15 km.) N.W. of *Budapest, where Hungarian Jews were detained during World War II. In the 1930s opponents of Horthy's regime and left-wing political prisoners, including many Jews, were interned there. When Hungary was occupied by the Germans (March 19, 1944), a large number of Jews were immediately arrested and shipped to the *SS-run Kistarcsa camp administered by the Hungarian police. The camp commandant, Istvan Vasdenyei, behaved well and cooperated with Jewish organizations. A trainload of 1,800 Jewish prisoners was dispatched from Kistarcsa to *Auschwitz on April 29, 1944, followed by another 18 trainloads of similar size with Budapest's Jews. Information about the Auschwitz extermination center and the unbearable living conditions of its inmates had reached Hungary during the German invasion. The camp became more particularly known when *Eichmann and his assistants attempted various deceptions after Regent Horthy decided (June 26, 1944) to halt the deportations. Eichmann would not accept the Hungarian order for cessation and on July 14, he made an attempt to ship 1,500 Jews from Kistarcsa. His move was revealed to leaders of the Jewish Council in Budapest, who succeeded in alerting Horthy. On Horthy's intervention, the trainload was turned back before it could cross the border. Eichmann considered this move as a heavy blow to his extermination program and ordered a new transport. It was organized by *SS-Hauptsturmfuehrer* Franz Novak and his men, specially sent to Kistarcsa (July 19, 1944) to order the Hungarian camp commander to round up the 1,500 persons released from the previous transport for reshipment. They contended that "Eichmann will not stand for the flouting of his orders, not even by the Regent." This transport (of 1,200) reached Auschwitz. To prevent the Jewish leaders from again getting Horthy's intervention, Eichmann called them to his office, where his assistants Otto Hunsche and Hermann Krumey detained them all until the train crossed the border. About 1,000 Jews remained in the camp until it was dismantled on September 27, 1944, which coincided with Yom Kippur, and they were then sent to other labor camps. Eichmann's role was raised at his trial in Jerusalem as evidence of Eichmann's intransigence on matters of persecution of the Jews. On Feb. 3, 1965, Krumey and Hunsche were sentenced but released, as it was deemed they had already served sentence through previous custody. On July 11, 1968, Hunsche and Krumey were brought for retrial in Frankfurt. On August 29, 1969, the defendants were found guilty and sentenced: Krumey to life imprisonment with hard labor and Hunsche to 12 years imprisonment.

BIBLIOGRAPHY: G. Hausner, *Justice in Jerusalem* (1967), index; J. Lévai, *Black Book on the Martyrdom of Hungarian Jewry* (1964), passim; E. Landau (ed.), *Der Kastner-Bericht…* (1961), index. **ADD. BIBLIOGRAPHY:** R. Braham, *The Politics of Genocide: The Holocaust in Hungary* (1981).

[Yehouda Marton]

KISTER, MEIR J. (1914–), Israel scholar of Arabic. Born in Mosciska, Poland, Kister received his Ph.D. from the Hebrew University of Jerusalem in 1964, from which year he was senior lecturer there. He became full professor in 1970. His scholarly endeavors dealt with the traditions of the tribes of the pre-Islamic period in the Arab peninsula, the *sira* of Muhammad, and the early *hadith* and its compilations. He was a member of the Israel Academy of Sciences and Humanities. In 1981 he was awarded the Israel Prize in Arabic literature and Oriental studies.

KISVARDA (Hung. **Kisvárda**; Yid. **Kleinwardein**), town in N.E. Hungary. The Jewish community was organized in 1796; at first it was subordinate to the community of Nagykallo, but became independent in 1843 when Isaiah *Banet was appointed to the rabbinate. In the main, the members of the community were leaseholders, petty tradesmen, and peddlers. The synagogue was erected in 1801. The Jewish population rose from 118 in 1784 to 500 in 1840, and to 1,483 in 1860. The first rabbi of Kisvarda was Moses Mikhaelowitz (1818–24), who was succeeded by Moses b. Amram *Grunwald. Also among the rabbis of Kisvarda was Moses Ḥayyim Segal (1896–1942). Kisvarda had many *ḥadarim* and a yeshivah. From 1932 the Zionist movement had an active following. Dov Gruner, a member of the *Irgun Ẓev'ai Le'ummi executed by the Mandatory government in Palestine, was born in Kisvarda. The Jewish population numbered 3,454 in 1920, 3,658 in 1930, and 3,770 in 1941. In the revolution of 1918 the Jewish inhabitants were persecuted. From then on antisemitism increased: an armed mob attacked the Jews in 1938. In 1940 the Jews were enlisted into forced labor gangs and in 1942 they were deported to the front. After the German occupation (Spring 1944), a ghetto was set up and 7,000 Jews from the town and the neighboring villages were concentrated there. On May 25 and 27 the Jews were deported to the gas chambers of Auschwitz. After World War II, the community was reorganized. The Jewish population dwindled from 804 in 1946 to 650 in 1948 and 355 in 1953.

BIBLIOGRAPHY: Y. Komlós, in: BJCE.

[Baruch Yaron]

KITAJ, R.B. (1932–), U.S. painter and printmaker. Born in Cleveland as Ronald Brooks, Kitaj took his surname from his stepfather, a Viennese refugee from the Nazi regime. From 1956 to 1958 he served in the Army as an illustrator, immediately after which he moved to England to study under the G.I. Bill at the Ruskin School of Art (1958–59). Before this time Kitaj received art training at the Cooper Union in New York (1950) and at the Academy of Fine Arts in Vienna (1951–52). In 1959 Kitaj transferred to the Royal College of Art in London. During this early period he experimented with a number of styles, including Surrealism and Abstract Expressionism, while taking life-drawing classes. His work often included collage elements and also a sense of collage through the painted juxtaposition of diverse subjects. In 1963 he had his first one-person exhibition at the Marlborough Gallery in London, the same year he began printmaking.

From the 1970s Kitaj painted highly personal subjects in an expressionistic manner, often of a Jewish nature. The recurrent figure of Joe Singer, the archetypal wandering Jew and a figure with strong autobiographical associations for the artist, appears for the first time in *The Jew, Etc.* (1976–79, collection of the artist). The exilic condition indeed preoccupies Kitaj, who wrote a book on the subject, *The First Diasporist Manifesto.*

In the early 1980s, Kitaj explored visual responses to the Holocaust. Seeking a symbol for the Jews akin to the Christian cross, in 1985 Kitaj began to utilize a chimney in reference to the ovens in which Nazis burned Jews. The eight pictures in the series that explored this iconography bear the overarching title *Passion*. One of the best-known *Passion* images, a picture of a train passenger titled *The Jewish Rider* (1984–85, Astrup Fearnley Museum of Modern Art, Oslo, Norway), plays on Kitaj's knowledge of art history; the canvas is based partly on *The Polish Rider* (c. 1655, Frick Collection, New York), a work once attributed to Rembrandt. Other works by Kitaj that adapt an artistic precedent and explore Jewish identity include *The Jewish School* (*Drawing a Golem*) (1980, private collection, Monte Carlo), a painting derived from a 19th-century antisemitic German engraving titled *Die Judenschule*.

Following scathing reviews of his 1994 retrospective at the Tate Gallery, London, and the death of his wife soon after, Kitaj left England and moved to Los Angeles in 1997. Among Kitaj's many impressive accolades, in 1985 he became the first American since John Singer Sargent to be elected to the Royal Academy in London.

BIBLIOGRAPHY: R.B. Kitaj, *First Diasporist Manifesto* (1989); R. Morphet, *R.B. Kitaj* (1994); M. Livingstone, *R.B. Kitaj* (1999); J. Aulich and J. Lynch (eds.), *Critical Kitaj: Essays on the Work of R.B. Kitaj* (2001).

[Samantha Baskind (2nd ed.)]

KITE (Heb. דָּאָה *da'ah*, דַּיָּה *dayyah*; AV, vulture; JPS "kite"), a bird of prey of the genus *Milvus*, of which two species inhabit Israel: the *M. milvus* which in limited numbers winters in the country, and the dark brown *M. migrans* which is indigenous to Israel. The kite is found in various places in the country, in particular near refuse: it feeds on carcasses, and preys on mice and even hares. The Pentateuch enumerates among the birds prohibited as food the *da'ah, dayyah, ra'ah*, and *ayyah* (Lev. 11:14; Deut. 14:13). On these the Talmud quotes two opinions, the one that all four are synonyms for a single genus of birds, the other that the first two are identical (Ḥul. 63b). The name *dayyah* or *da'ah* refers to the gliding flight of the kite as it searches for prey or a carcass. The Talmud speaks of a *dayyah* that snatched meat from the market or from a person's hands (BM 24b; TJ, Shek. 7:3, 50c). The presence of flocks of kites where there are corpses and refuse is mentioned by Isaiah (34:15).

BIBLIOGRAPHY: Lewysohn, Zool, 167f., no. 196; J. Feliks, *The Animal World of the Bible* (1962), 67.

[Jehuda Feliks]

KITEL (Yid. "gown"), white garment worn in some Ashkenazi rites by worshipers during the prayer service on the High Holidays (*Rosh Ha-Shanah and the *Day of Atonement), and by the *ḥazzan* at the *Musaf* service on *Shemini Aẓeret*, the eighth day of *Sukkot (when the prayer for rain is recited) and the first day of *Passover (when the prayer for dew is recited). It is also worn, in some rites, by the person conducting the *seder on Passover eve and by the groom during the *marriage ceremony. Formerly a white garment was worn every Sabbath and on all solemn occasions (TJ, RH 1:3). The association of the color white with the notion of purity (and hence also forgiveness of sins) and solemn joy contributed to the special use of the *kitel* on all these occasions. The day of marriage is considered a day of atonement for the groom and the bride, and the idea of atonement and penitence is also associated with that of death. The white *kitel* is therefore also part of the raiment in which the dead are clothed for burial. In some communities, the *kitel* is also called *sargenes*, either because it was made of a material called *serge* or *sericum* (see: Rashi to Shab. 77b), or because its origin from the German word *Sarg* (coffin) denotes a garment of death.

BIBLIOGRAPHY: Eisenstein, Dinim, 364.

KITRÓN (Kostrinsky), MOSHE (1909–1972), Argentinean Zionist leader and educator. Kitrón was born in Pinsk, Belarus, and immigrated to Argentina in 1927. There he became a teacher in Jewish schools and was the secretary of the Zionist Po'alei Zion Party, dealing especially with its relations with the Argentinean Socialist Party. Having given up an academic career for ideological reasons, he became an intellectual on the political scene; Kitrón published a large number of articles in party periodicals and in other publications in a number of languages and countries. He also translated David Ben-Gurion's writings into Spanish and contributed to encyclopedias. In 1934 he founded the Zionist pioneer youth movement Dror and was its ideological leader. The members of the movement founded kibbutz Mefallesim in Israel in 1949. In the same year Kitrón made *aliyah* with his family. In Israel, Kitrón was secretary of Mapai in Tel Aviv and an official member of its inner circle, heading its department for Oriental Jews – a highly sensitive position during the 1950s waves of immigration. Kitrón also served as a liaison between immigrants from Latin America and the Israeli milieu. He served as director of the Educational and Cultural Center of the Histadrut ha-Ovedim ha-Kelalit (Workers Union), creating contacts with Latin American worker's organizations. His career declined during the 1960s, as he failed to find his place in Israel as an ideologist and intellectual. His wife, Ruth Gold, was an outstanding teacher and leader in the Jewish schools of Argentina.

[Efraim Zadoff (2nd ed.)]

KITSEE, ISADOR (1845–1931), U.S. inventor. Born in Vienna, Kitsee went to the U.S. in 1867 and became city chemist in Cincinnati, Ohio. In 1886 he moved to Philadelphia. Kitsee's inventions approach 2,000 in number. They include Philadelphia's first trolley streetcar, a refrigerator car, railroad signals, coal breaker, underground telegraph, phonograph disc, color motion pictures, improvements in sulfuric acid manufacture, and methods of extracting gold from its ores. In 1889 he sold a wireless patent to Marconi and in 1912 patented a device for the use of speech with motion pictures.

°**KITTEL, RUDOLF** (1853–1929), German Bible scholar. Kittel taught Bible and theology at the universities of Tübingen (1879–81), Stuttgart (1881–88), Breslau (1888–98), and Leipzig (1898–1924). He was the father of the New Testament scholar Gerhard Kittel (1853–1929). Rudolph Kittel demonstrated antisemitic tendencies in private and popular expression, but these did not affect his scholarship. One of his closest aides in the preparation of *Biblia Hebraica* (see below) was Isser Kahn, an observant Lithuanian Jew. Kittel considered himself a follower of the *Wellhausen School but departed from its teachings in various aspects. In his monographs on biblical history and religion Kittel helped establish the importance of supplementing the results of internal criticism with extra-biblical evidence. In his *Geschichte des Volkes Israel* (3 vols., 1922–28), a second edition of *Geschichte der Hebräer* (2 vols., 1888–92; *A History of the Hebrews*, 2 vols., 1895–96), he stated that Israel's unique religious expression resulted from the tension between a strict Yahweh oriented minority fashioned by Moses and a Yahweh cult assimilated to the Baal worship of the Canaanites and supported by the mass of the people who were unable to grasp the full implications of the Sinaitic covenant. The Mosaic religion was kept alive in certain circles until it became the official national expression through the triumphant teachings of the prophets.

Kittel published commentaries on Kings (1902), Chronicles (1902), Psalms (1929), and Isaiah 1–39 (with A. Dillman, 1898). He wrote on the contributions of the Hellenistic mystery religions to Hebrew wisdom literature (1924), on warfare in biblical times (1918), and on biblical theology (1899). He also edited *Beitraege zur Wissenschaft vom Alten [und Neuen] Testament* from 1908 to 1920. He is remembered as the originator of the *Biblia Hebraica*, a work which presents the Masoretic Text of the Bible along with the variants of the versions and other manuscripts; it has become a classic text book used in seminaries and universities. First and second editions of the *Biblia Hebraica* (1905–06 and 1912) provide the *textus receptus* of *Jacob ben Ḥayyim ibn Adonijah's edition of 1525–26 in the Second Rabbinical Bible. The third edition of *Biblia Hebraica*, published posthumously in 1937 and edited together with P. *Kahle, is based upon the older and more reliable Ben Asher codex of Leningrad. This was followed by the *Biblia Hebraica Stuttgartensia* (1967–77). The *Biblia Hebraica Quinta* has begun to appear under the auspices of the Deutsche Bibelgesellschat (2004ff).

BIBLIOGRAPHY: Hempel, in: ZDMG, 84 (1930), 78–93; T. Fritsch, *Der Streit um Gott und Talmud…* (1922), 27–41; P.E. Kahle, *The Cairo Geniza* (19592), 131–8; H.F. Hahn, *The Old Testament in Modern Research* (1956), 103–9; E. Würthwein, *The Text of the Old Testament* (1957), passim; *Alttestamentliche Studien, Rudolph Kittel zum 60. Geburtstag dargebracht* (1913). **ADD. BIBLIOGRAPHY:** C. Begg, in: DBI, 2:30; H. Wasserman, in: *Modern Judaism*, 22 (2002), 92.

[Zev Garber / S. David Sperling (2nd ed.)]

KITTIM (Heb. כִּתִּים, כִּתִּיִּים, the final *mem* possibly a suffix and not a plural ending), the name of a place and its inhabitants. In the table of nations Kittim is mentioned among the sons of Javan and the brothers of *Elishah (Gen. 10:4). Josephus (Ant. 1:128) identified Kittim with Kition, or Kitti, a Phoenician city on the island of *Cyprus near present-day Larnaca, an identification accepted by most scholars. Many scholars identify Elishah with Cyprus, or with part of it, and in Ezekiel 27:6–7, Elishah is mentioned along with Kittim as a place which traded with Tyre. Kittim is used in connection with Tyre and Sidon in Isaiah 23:1, 12. In these verses Kittim refers not only to a city but also to a land (Isa. 23:1) and to islands (Ezek. 27:6). Jeremiah 2:10 mentions isles of Kittim as the symbol of the western extremity of the world. Apparently the Israelites used the name Kittim to include the islands of the Aegean Sea and even the coastal areas of the Mediterranean Sea (Jos., Ant., 1:128). There is no foundation for the opinion of some scholars that ancient Kittim is in Asia Minor, but various passages in the Bible indicate a connection between Kittim and Assyria. There is an obscure verse in the prophecies of Balaam, which seems to say: "Ships come from the quarter of Kittim; they subject Ashur, subject Eber. They, too, shall perish forever" (Num. 24:24). The proximity of Kittim to Assyria in this verse seems to have been the cause of an alteration in the text of Ezekiel 27:6. The phrase *bat-Ashurim* in the masoretic text of this verse probably originally read *bi-t'ashurim* "with cypress(?) wood" (cf. Isa. 41:19; 60:13), and it is this wood that Ezekiel describes as brought "from the coastlands of Kittim." The very obscure statement of Isaiah 23:12–13 seems to say that Assyria conquered Kittim. In fact, Sargon II of Assyria had a stele erected at Larnaca in Cyprus and received tributes from its kings. (For an interpretation of Isa. 23:12–13 see Duhm in bibl., and the standard commentaries.) It is evident that Daniel's prediction, "But ships of Kittim shall come against him…" (11:30), is based upon a midrash on Baalam's words which identifies the Kittim with the Romans and Assyria with the Seleucid dynasty of Syria. The identification of Kittim with the Romans was accepted by the Jews in later generations (Targ. Onk., Num. 24:24 "Romans") and served as a basis for eschatological thought in succeeding generations. In I Maccabees 1:1, Macedonia is called Kittim (cf. 8:5), and apparently even this appellation is derived from the Midrashim on Balaam's utterances that are mentioned above.

[Amos Hakham]

(1) The War of the Kittim

In a number of Qumran texts the Kittim appear as the last gentile world power to oppress the people of God. In the *Habakkuk Commentary* from Cave 1 the prophet's "Chaldeans" are understood to be the Kittim, sent by God to execute His judgment on the godless rulers in Judea but destined, because of their unconscionable rapacity, to be the objects of His judgment in their turn. In a fragmentary commentary on Isaiah from Cave 4, the advance and downfall of the Assyrians (Isa. 10:22ff.) is interpreted as the "war of the Kittim"; an invader who marches from Acre to the precincts of Jerusalem is probably the leader of the Kittim. The "war of the Kittim" is described in detail in the War Scroll; early in this document the sons of light take the field against "the bands of the Kittim of Asshur and with them as helpers those who deal wickedly against the covenant" (1 QM 1:2) and after dealing with them proceed against "the [king] of the Kittim in Egypt" (1 QM 1:4; see *War Scroll). While the word "king" in this last quotation is the conjectural restoration of a lacuna in the text, the context suggests that this is an interpretation of "the king of the south" of Daniel 11:40. Later in the scroll, in what may be an annex to the main work, the fighting men "encamp against the king of the Kittim and the whole host of Belial" (1 QM 15:2). The "Kittim of Asshur" probably had their base in Syria; but Kittim and Asshur seem to be used interchangeably in the scroll: thus, when the sons of Belial are destroyed, "Asshur shall come to his end; none shall help him [a quotation from Dan. 11:45] and the dominion of the Kittim shall pass away, that wickedness may be brought low with no survivor and that there may be no deliverance for all the sons of darkness" (1 QM. 1:6ff.). In such a passage Asshur (Assyria), as in Isaiah, is probably a term to denote the gentile oppressor of Israel, whereas Kittim indicates more precisely where this oppressor comes from. If the arms and tactics specified in the War Scroll are of Roman type, as Y. Yadin argues, the Kittim would be the Romans, as in Daniel 11:30. Likewise, in the *Nahum Commentary*, Jerusalem remains uncaptured by the kings of Greece "from Antiochus (VII) to the rise of the rulers of the Kittim," who are most probably the Romans.

(2) In the Habakkuk Commentary

The same conclusion is probably indicated by the evidence of the *Habakkuk Commentary*. There the Kittim are a world power, pursuing a career of conquest and empire from the west. In their irresistible advance they overwhelm all who stand in their way and bring them under their own rule. They take possession of many lands and plunder the cities of the earth; they carry on negotiations with other nations in a spirit of cunning and deceit; they lay their subversive plans in advance and tolerate no opposition in carrying them into execution. Their lust for conquest is insatiable; they mock at kings and rulers; fortress after fortress falls before them. Their leaders follow one another in quick succession: "they come one after another to destroy the earth." This rapid replacement happens "by the counsel of a guilty house." They exact tribute so heavy as to improverish the lands which have to pay it; their methods of warfare do not spare men, women, or the tiniest children. The prophet's description of the Chaldeans as catching men like fish and then paying divine honors to their nets is said to denote the Kittim's practice of offering sacrifice to their standards and worshiping their weapons. This last feature of the Kittim is reminiscent of the fact that Roman military standards were treated as sacred objects, particularly the eagle, the legionary standard, which was kept in a special shrine in the camp and was regarded as affording sanctuary. Titus' victorious legionaries in 70 C.E. offered sacrifice to their eagles against the East Gate of the Temple; but this action was not necessarily an innovation. The successors of Alexander the Great may have had a similar practice, but the evidence in their case is scanty and ambiguous as compared with that for the Romans. While features in the commentator's account of the Kittim could describe other imperial conquerors, the overall impression is particularly appropriate to the Romans. This conclusion is the more confirmed when comparing the commentator's description of the Kittim with the anti-Roman propaganda disseminated throughout the Middle East between 88 and 63 B.C.E. by Mithridates VI of Pontus, of which a sample is provided in his letter to Arsaces XII of Parthia preserved in a fragment of Sallust's *Histories*. The relevant section of the *Habakkuk Commentary* is almost an echo of this.

[Frederick Fyvie Bruce]

BIBLIOGRAPHY: Luckenbill, Records, 2 (1927), 100–3; N. Slouschz, *Oẓar ha-Ketovot ha-Finikiyyot* (1942), 66–96; M.H. Segal, in: JBL, 70 (1951), 133ff.; W. Brandenstein, in: *Festschrift A. Debrunner* (1954), 172ff.; R. North, in: *Biblica*, 39 (1958), 84–93; W.F. Albright, in: Wright, Bible, 451–2, 458ff.; B. Duhm, *Das Buch Jesaia* (19224), 170; J.M. Cross, Jr., *The Ancient Library of Qumran and Modern Biblical Studies* (1958), 92–93. A. Dupont-Sommer, *Jewish Sect of Qumran and the Essenes* (1954), 14ff.; Rowley, in: PEFQS, 88 (1956), 92ff.; G.R. Driver, *Judaean Scrolls* (1965), 197ff.

KITTSEE, ḤAYYIM BEN ISAAC (c. 1772–1850), Hungarian rabbi whose family name was originally Schlesinger. He was born in Alt-Ofen (Óbuda) where his father, his main teacher, was head of the *bet din*. He also studied under Moses *Mintz, the local rabbi. He served as a *dayyan* in Veszprém, and from about 1824 as rabbi of Albertirsa, near Budapest. He vigorously opposed the religious reforms which were advocated in his time. He took part in the rabbinical conference at Paks (see *Hungary) in 1844 and was among the signatories to the protest against the Brunswick Conference held in that year. Kittsee was regarded as one of the greatest contemporary Hungarian talmudists and left 60 works in manuscript on all branches of talmudic lore. Of these, *Oẓar Ḥayyim* (pt. 1, 1913; pt. 2, 1962), responsa on Shulḥan Arukh, *Oraḥ Ḥayyim* and *Yoreh De'ah*, and talmudic novellae and expositions have been published.

BIBLIOGRAPHY: N. Ben-Menahem, *Mi-Sifrut Yisrael be-Ungaryah* (1958), 195f.; Schwartz, in: Ḥ. Kittsee, *Oẓar Ḥayyim*, 1 (1913), introd.; 2 (1962), introd.; *Ha-Ohel*, 2 (1956), 48.

[Nathaniel Katzburg]

KITTSEE, JEHIEL MICHAEL BEN SAMUEL (c. 1775–1845), Hungarian talmudic scholar. His family name was originally Figdor, an abbreviation of Avigdor, the name of the founder of the family who lived in the small town of Kittsee near Pressburg, after which he came to be called. He studied under Mordecai *Banet. He was a businessman, well known for his generosity, but spent most of his time in study. His contemporary, Moses *Sofer, described him as "one of the leading notables of our community whom God has greatly blessed and filled with his bounty … despite which his preoccupation all his life has been with the Torah, business being secondary" (quoted in *Shalmei Nedavah*, pt. 1 (1838), 2a). Kittsee is the author of *Shalmei Nedavah*: part 1 (Pressburg, 1838), talmudic novellae; part 2 (*ibid.*, 1842), novellae on the Talmud, on the Shulḥan Arukh, *Yoreh De'ah* and *Even ha-Ezer*, and aggadic sayings. Kittsee married the daughter of Mendel Jacob, known as Kopel Teven, a leader of Hungarian Jewry in the 18th century.

BIBLIOGRAPHY: S. Mayer, *Die Wiener Juden* (1918^2), 136; J.J.(L.) Greenwald (Grunwald), *Ha-Yehudim be-Ungaryah* (1913), 81f.; S. Sofer (Schreiber), *Iggerot Soferim*, pt. 2 (1928), 88, n.2.

[Nathaniel Katzburg]

KITZINGEN, city in Bavaria, Germany. In 1147 the local Jewish community was subordinate to that of *Wuerzburg, but soon after, it attained independent status. Eleven Jews were tortured and killed following a *blood libel in 1243; 15 died during the *Rindfleisch massacres (1298); in 1336 many lost their lives in the *Armleder uprising; the *Black Death persecutions (1349) finally annihilated the community. In 1490, 1529, and 1538, returning Jews were granted letters of protection and a synagogue was built in the 16th century (demolished in a World War II air raid). Expulsion was narrowly averted in 1516 and 1608. In 1641 there were 63 Jews living in Kitzingen, but they were subject to severe restrictions and exactions. A number of renowned scholars and rabbis bore the city's name. Persecutions in 1778 were followed by total expulsion in 1798. After the emancipation (1861) Jewish wine and cattle merchants resettled in the city; the community numbered 57 in 1867, 337 (4.8% of the total population) in 1880, and 478 in 1910. Rabbi E. Adler (1868–1911) was also district rabbi (from 1871). He was followed in office by R. Joseph Wohlgemuth (1914–35). Fourteen social, religious, and cultural organizations were active in the strictly Orthodox community.

On *Kristallnacht* (Nov. 10, 1938), the second synagogue (consecrated in 1883) was desecrated and the scrolls burned; many homes were ransacked. Of the 360 Jews in the city in 1933, 192 emigrated, including 84 to the U.S. and 52 to Palestine, and 111 left for other German cities. Of those in the city in 1942, 76 were deported to *Izbica Lubelska and 19 to *Theresienstadt.

BIBLIOGRAPHY: N. Bamberger, *Geschichte der Juden von Kitzingen…* (1908); Germ Jud, 1 (1963), 505; 2 (1968), 402–3; FJW, 293–4.

KLABIN, Brazilian family. The founder, MAURÍCIO (1860–1923), born in Posvol, Lithuania, established himself in São Paulo in 1887. His brothers and other members of the family (named by marriage Lafer and Kadischevitz) followed later. In 1890 the firm Klabin Irmãos & Cia. was founded. The family began with a small paper factory (1906), followed by Cia. Fabricadora de Papel (1909) and in the paper and cellulose manufacturing line by Indústria Klabin do Paraná de Celulose S/A, in Monte Alegre (1941), the largest newsprint plant in Latin America. A factory specializing in corrugated cardboard opened in 1950, and, as a result of basic research in available raw material, the Papel & Celulose Catarinense plant followed in 1961. The family pioneered in the field of floriculture, planting eucalyptus and American pines, and also raised cattle. A small factory, Manufatura Nacional de Porcelana (acquired 1931), producing china and small insulators, became one of Latin America's largest tile-producing factories. In the synthetic textile field, the group acquired control of Cia. Brasileira de Sintéticos in São Paulo. Members of the family also pioneered in Jewish life. Mauricio was head of the budding Jewish community of São Paulo. Considered the first Zionist in the city, he was also the first Brazilian to sponsor a Jewish National Fund forest in Palestine. Together with his family, he donated the first modern synagogue to the community (Beth El), generally called the "Russian temple" or the "Klabin synagogue," and the first Jewish cemetery in the suburb of Vila Mariana, where the family had extensive land holdings. His wife, BERTA, was a founder of the first Jewish women's organization in São Paulo, Sociedade Beneficente das Damas Israelitas, in 1915. WOLFF KADISCHEVITZ-KLABIN developed many new sectors of the Klabin group and was active in Jewish activities in Rio de Janeiro. MIGUEL LAFER founded the Jewish school and college Renascença.

[Alfred Hirschberg]

KLACZKO, JULIAN (**Judah**; 1825–1906), Polish author, critic, and historian. Klaczko was raised in the atmosphere of the Lithuanian Haskalah and displayed his precocious talent as a poet with *Duda'im…* (1842), a volume of Hebrew poems, mainly translations and pastiches. He also wrote Hebrew versions of two poems by *Mickiewicz, whose correspondence he later edited. In 1840 Klaczko moved to Germany and then settled in Paris, where he contributed to the *Revue des deux mondes* and conducted an increasingly violent anti-Prussian campaign in support of Polish nationalism. By this time Klaczko had converted to Catholicism. He remained in France from 1849 until 1869, when he accepted an official appointment in Vienna, later serving in the Galician and Imperial Austrian parliaments. There he advocated a Franco-Austrian alliance against Prussian expansionism. From 1888 Klaczko lived in Cracow, associating with the conservative writers and politicians. Although he edited the influential émigré periodical *Wiadomości polskie* in Paris (1858–60) and published a collection of his Polish works (1865), Klaczko wrote mainly in French. He is best remembered for three historical studies, *Lex deux chanceliers: Gortschakoff et Bismarck* (1876), *Quatre causeries florentines* (1880), and *Rome et la Renaissance* (1903).

BIBLIOGRAPHY: S. Tarnowski, *Julian Klaczko* (Pol., 1908); R. Brandstaetter, *Tragedja Juliana Klaczki* (1933).

[Moshe Altbauer]

KLAGENFURT, capital of Carinthia, S. Austria. A *Judendorf* now within the bounds of the city was mentioned in 1162, and in 1279 a Jewish quarter outside a city gate was recorded. In 1335, 36 Klagenfurt Jews were listed as taxpayers. When in 1496 the Carinthian estates reimbursed *Maximilian I for the loss of Jewish taxes after the expulsion of the Jews from the region, the city contributed its share. A street was called *Judengasse* until 1829. In 1783 an imperial decree permitted Jews to attend the fairs at Klagenfurt and they resettled in the city in the second half of the 19th century. A **Kultusverein* was founded in 1886 and a *ḥevra kaddisha* in 1888. A Jewish cemetery was consecrated in 1895 (enlarged in 1930) and an existing building was converted into a synagogue in 1905. The congregation was under the jurisdiction of the *Graz community and a separate community was not constituted until 1922. In 1869, 16 Jews lived in the city, increasing to 90 in 1880, 126 in 1899 (0.6% of the total population), 180 in 1934, and after the Anschluss (1938) 116 families. Many then left for Vienna. On *Kristallnacht* (Nov. 10, 1938), the interior of the synagogue and several Jewish homes were destroyed. By this time the Jewish shops had already been "Aryanized." Forty Jews were arrested and sent to *Dachau concentration camp. The Jews remaining in the city were deported to the Nazi extermination camps. The few Jews living in Klagenfurt after World War II (ten in 1968) were affiliated to the Graz community. The synagogue was reopened in 1961. The oldest gravestone in the Danube region, that of Shabbetai ha-Parnas, was placed in the Klagenfurt museum. Joseph Babad, rabbi of the community until the Anschluss, published several historical essays, including one on the history of Carinthian Jewry (in HJ, 7 (1945), 13–28, 193–204).

BIBLIOGRAPHY: S.S. Stoessl, in: J. Fraenkel (ed.), *The Jews of Austria* (1967), 385–94; H.T. Schneider, in: *Klagenfurt*, 18 (Ger., 1968), 83–85, 153–6; W. Neumann, in: *Carinthia*, 152 (Ger., 1962), 92–104, passim; Germ Jud, 2 (1968), 403; PK Germaniyah.

[Meir Lamed]

KLANG, HEINRICH (1875–1954), Austrian judge and jurist. Born in Vienna, Klang was an expert on Austrian civil law and the editor of *Kommentar zum Allgemeinen Buergerlichen Gesetzbuch* (2 vols. in 4, 1931–35), the last complete commentary on the Austrian civil code. He was also the author of works on the laws of landlord and tenant. Following the Anschluss of 1938, Klang was pensioned and in 1942 was deported to Theresienstadt. On his release in 1945 he returned to Vienna where he was chairman of one of the divisions of the supreme court and honorary professor at the University of Vienna.

BIBLIOGRAPHY: *Neue oesterreichische Biographie*, vol. 14, 178–86. **ADD. BIBLIOGRAPHY:** NDB, vol. 11 (1977), 705 f.

[Josef J. Lador-Lederer]

KLAPPER, PAUL (1885–1952), U.S. educator and administrator. Born in Jassy, Romania, he was brought to the United States at the age of seven. From 1907 he taught education at City College of New York, where he rose to the rank of full professor in 1921 and dean of its School of Education, 1921–37. In 1937 Klapper became the first president of Queens College which developed rapidly under his direction. The college library is named for him. Upon his retirement in 1948 he became dean of teacher education of the Board of Higher Education of New York. Klapper's philosophy of education and theories of pedagogy influenced educational practices in schools across the nation. He was widely known as a firm opponent of formal curricula and traditional modes of discipline. He was concerned with raising the economic status of teachers and giving them the dignity that he felt the profession deserved. Klapper's publications include: *College Teaching* (1920); *Principles of Educational Practice* (1912); *Teaching Children to Read* (1946); *Teaching English in Elementary and Junior High Schools* (1925); *Contemporary Education…* (1929); *Childhood Readers* (1939).

BIBLIOGRAPHY: *New York Times*, March 26, 1952, 29; *ibid.* (March 27, 1952), 28; *ibid.* (May 18, 1952), 11.

[Ernest Schwarcz]

KLAR, BENJAMIN MENAḤEM (1901–1948), Israeli Hebrew scholar. Klar, born in Linets, Ukraine, was educated at the university and the Jewish Theological Seminary in Vienna. In 1936 he emigrated to Palestine and taught at the Mizrachi Teachers' Seminary in Jerusalem, and from 1944 he taught Hebrew language and grammar at the Hebrew University. He was among those killed by Arabs in the convoy to Mount Scopus on April 13, 1948.

Klar's main interest was in medieval and modern Hebrew poetry. In 1936 he published a book on Bialik in German, *Bialik, Leben fuer ein Volk*. A volume of studies, *Meḥkarim ve-Iyyunim be-Lashon, be-Safah u-ve-Sifrut* ("Researches and Studies in Language and Literature"), published posthumously in 1954, contained parts of an autobiography. Other works by Klar include editions of the chronicle of *Aḥimaaz, *Megillat Aḥima'az* (1944–45), and early Hebrew poetry in Italy; of Moses b. Isaac's *Sefer ha-Shoham* (1947); and letters and documents relating to Ḥayyim ibn *Attar, *Rabbi Ḥayyim ibn Attar* (1950). Klar completed and issued with an introduction S. Ginzburg's edition of M.Ḥ. Luzzatto's poetry, *Sefer ha-Shirim* (1945); he published Z. Jawitz's letters, *Leket Ketavim li-Ze'ev Jawitz* (1943), and D. Yellin's history of Hebrew grammar, *Toledot Hitpatteḥut ha-Dikduk ha-Ivri* (1945). He also translated selected poems of Goethe, *Mi-Shirei Goethe*, and the commentary on Genesis from J.H. Hertz's English edition of the Pentateuch, *Targum Perusho ha-Angli shel R. Yosef Ẓevi Hertz* (1942).

BIBLIOGRAPHY: M. Zulay, in: KS, 24 (1947/48), 243ff. (bibliography); R. Avinoam (ed.), *Gevilei Esh*, 2 (1958), 178ff., 634; Kressel, Leksikon, 2 (1967), 756f.

KLARMAN, YOSEF (1909–1985), Zionist leader. Klarman was born in Busko Zdroj, Russian Poland, and was active in the Revisionist movement from his youth. In 1934 he was elected to its Executive and was secretary-general and editor of its journal *Unzer Welt*.

Settling in Ereẓ Israel in 1940, he was appointed Revisionist representative on the Presidium of the Jewish Agency's Rescue Committee for European Jews, and was active in Turkey in 1943–44. In 1947 he helped to organize the departure from Romania of the ships *Pan York* and *Pan Crescent*.

He was for many years chairman of the World Executive of Ḥerut ha-Ẓohar. In 1965 he was appointed a member of the Executive of the Jewish Agency and in 1968, head of its Youth Aliyah Department, holding the position until 1977.

°**KLARSFELD, BEATE AUGUSTE** (née **Kunzel**; 1939–), anti-Nazi, Nazi hunter responsible for bringing Klaus *Barbie to justice, pro-Israel activist. Beate Klarsfeld was born in Berlin to a Protestant family, her father had served in the Wehrmacht. She began her working career as a secretary. In 1960 she went to Paris, where in 1963 she married a Jewish lawyer, Serge *Klarsfeld, a Holocaust survivor.

Beate Klarsfeld took a deep interest in the Holocaust and into the efforts necessary to locate Nazi war criminals and bring them to justice. Together with her husband she wrote in 1967 a series of articles in the newspaper *Combat* in which they attacked Chancellor Kurt Kiesinger of Germany for his Nazi past. For this series Beate was dismissed by the French-German Youth Office.

In November 1968, at a Christian Democrat party rally, she went to the podium and slapped the chancellor, calling him a "Nazi criminal." For this act Mrs. Klarsfeld was sentenced to one year in prison. She successfully fought against the appointment of a former Nazi diplomat, Ernst Aschenbach, to the Commission of the European Economic Community as representative of the German Federal Republic and led a four-year campaign in which she succeeded in having the Bundestag ratify the Franco-German judicial convention of 1971, authorizing the trial in Germany of directors of the Nazi police system who had been active in France. Beate Klarsfeld devoted other efforts toward the bringing to justice of Kurt Lischka, one of the persons responsible for the deportation of the Jews of France; he was convicted in 1980 and sentenced to a long prison term.

As a Nazi hunter she had three tasks: to locate the war criminal, to convince the country in which he resided to deport him, and to convince the appropriate country to try them. Beate Klarsfeld carried her endeavors to South America, where she worked undauntedly even in the face of dictatorships: in 1972 in Bolivia, where she located Klaus Barbie; in 1977 in Argentina and Uruguay, where she protested repressive measures and the use of torture; and in 1984 in Chile and 1985 in Paraguay. In 1986 she campaigned vociferously against Kurt Waldheim's candidacy for president of Austria because of his Nazi past. She was arrested in Warsaw in 1970 and in Prague in 1971 for protesting against antisemitism and repression.

Klarsfeld also held personal protests in Middle Eastern countries. She went to Damascus after the Six-Day War to obtain a list of the Israeli prisoners held by the Syrians and to protest the conditions of the Syrian Jews, and in 1974 was arrested in Rabat at the October summit meeting of the Arab countries for distributing tracts calling for peace between Israel and the Arab states. In early 1986 she spent a month in west Beirut, offering to substitute herself for the Lebanese Jewish hostages held by terrorists.

Beate and Serge Klarsfeld were the targets of a much publicized car bombing at their home in France on July 9, 1979. No one was in the car when the bomb went off and no one was injured in the blast. The ODESSA organization took credit for the attack and demanded that they stop pursuing Nazis.

The Klarsfelds' anti-Nazi campaign was dramatized in a 1986 film titled *Nazi Hunter: The Beate Klarsfeld Story* starring Farrah Fawcett as Beate and Tom Conti as Serge. She and her husband have been the recipients of numerous prestigious awards in recognition of the importance of their activities.

BIBLIOGRAPHY: B. Karsfeld: *A Portrait in the First Person* (video recording, 1994).

KLARSFELD, SERGE (1932–), lawyer, historian, Nazi-hunter, and documenter of the Holocaust. Klarsfeld was born in Bucharest and moved with his family to France as a child. While he, his mother, and sister remained in hiding in Nice, his father Arno allowed himself to be discovered so his family, which was hiding behind a wall, would not be found. Arrested there in 1943, he was deported to Auschwitz where he died. His son never forgot cowering behind a wall, unable to defend himself, defend his family, or protect his father. Klarsfeld has a varied academic background with a degree in history from the Sorbonne, a law degree from the Paris Faculty of Law, and a diploma from the Institute of Political Science in Paris. While a student he met his wife, Beate *Klarsfeld.

In the middle part of his career Klarsfeld devoted himself to seeking out Nazi criminals who were successful in evading punishment and seeing that they were brought to justice. Working as a team, he and his wife, a German non-Jew whose father had served in the Wehrmacht, focused on Kurt Lischka, Klaus *Barbie, and several others. He located Alois *Brunner in Syria and traveled there to seek Brunner's extradition; in this instance, he was not successful.

The Klarsfelds were instrumental in locating Klaus Barbie in Bolivia in 1972 and continued their struggle to have him brought to trial in France for more than ten years. At the

1987 trial, Serge Klarsfeld was the first of many private prosecution lawyers testifying against Barbie, who was ultimately sentenced to life imprisonment.

Klarsfeld published a number of works, including *Vichy – Auschwitz – The Role of Vichy in the Final Solution to the Jewish Question in France* (1983); *Memorial to the Jews Deported from France, 1942–1944* (1978), which includes the names and vital statistics of the 75,721 Jews deported from France to extermination camps in Eastern Europe; and *The Holocaust and the Neo-Nazi Mythomania* (1978). He commissioned an important work on the gas chambers by Jean Claude Presaac to deny any intellectual legitimacy to the challenges of Holocaust deniers. He presented Lili Jacob's *Auschwitz Album* in France and David Olere's testimony as a **Sonderkommando.* He also wrote of the *Children of Izieu.*

Klarsfeld protested the execution of Jewish community leaders in Teheran in 1979 by going there to intercede on behalf of those members of the community still in prison, and in February 1986 he went to Beirut to express his condemnation of the execution of Lebanese Jews who had been taken hostage. He protested against Karazdic and Mladic in the Serb Republic of Bosnia in 1996. Serge Klarsfeld was president of the Association of Sons and Daughters of the Jews Deported from France. He led and initiated the Bousquet, Leguay, Papon, and Touvier cases. He revealed to the French public the crimes of Vichy and is seen as the inspiration of President Jacques Chirac's declaration that officially recognizes the responsibility of France during World War II. Klarsfeld has been vehement in his defense of Israel and his condemnation of antisemitism is France. Both his supporters and his adversaries regard him as formidable and a man to be reckoned with.

[Michael Berenbaum (2nd ed.)]

KLARWEIN, JOSEPH (1893–1970), Israeli architect. Klarwein, who was born in Warsaw, worked in Hamburg, Germany, until 1933, when he immigrated to Palestine. He became architectural adviser on official buildings to the Israel government, his best-known building being the Knesset (Parliament) in Jerusalem (1967). His other works in Jerusalem include the memorial to Theodor Herzl at Mount Herzl, the stadium and law faculty at the Hebrew University, and the *kiryah* (government compound). He also designed the town center in Nahariyyah and the Dagon silo and Bet ha-Keranot in Haifa.

KLATOVY (Ger. **Klattau**), town in S.W. Bohemia, Czech Republic. One Jewess is mentioned in Klatovy in the early 14th century; although no further documentary evidence exists, it is assumed that there was a community there until the 16th century. In the 18th century the seat of the Klatovy district rabbinate was in *Pobezovice (Ronsperg). After 1867, Jews mainly from nearby Strazov, Janovice, and Svihov established a congregation in Klatovy, opened a cemetery, and dedicated a synagogue in 1873. There were 1,345 Jews living in the district in 1869 and 1,305 in 1881. In the town itself the community numbered 724 (108 families) in 1893, with Jews in 14 villages affiliated to it. At the end of the 19th century Jews established more than three-quarters of the town's factories. Antisemitic riots occurred on three occasions: in connection with the *Hilsner blood-libel trial in 1899; when a Jewish youth was accused of defiling the statue of a saint; and later in 1919. Between the world wars Klatovy's Jewish population fluctuated; while the town continued to attract Jews from the countryside, many others moved to the larger cities. In 1930 the community numbered 344 (2.4% of the total population). At the time of the Sudeten crisis (Fall 1938), many Jews from the southwestern Bohemian border found refuge in Klatovy. The synagogue was plundered by Czech Fascists on July 15, 1941. The mayor had the attackers arrested and intended to bring them to trial, but they were released as a result of German pressure. The synagogue building was put at the disposal of the local museum. In the fall of 1942 the Germans deported all Jews from Klatovy and district to the extermination camps and none returned. The synagogue equipment was sent to the Central Jewish Museum in Prague. Both the cemetery and synagogue existed in the early 1970s. The Czech-language author František *Gottlieb originated from Klatovy. The chief rabbi of Bohemia-Moravia, Gustav Sicher (1880–1960), was born there, as was the Czech-Jewish poet Karel Fleischmann (1897–1944) who perished in Birkenau. A memorial for Nazi victims was dedicated in the cemetery in 1989.

BIBLIOGRAPHY: M. Steiner, in: YIVOA, 12 (1958/59), 247–58; Germ Jud, 2 (1968), 403. **ADD. BIBLIOGRAPHY:** J. Fiedler, *Jewish Sights of Bohemia and Moravia* (1991), 175.

[Jan Herman]

KLATZKIN, ELIJAH BEN NAPHTALI HERZ (1852–1932), rabbi and author. Klatzkin's father (1823–1894) was rabbi of Ushpol (1851–58), where Elijah was born, and later of Schoemberg (Courland). Elijah was known in his childhood as the *Shklover Illui* ("child prodigy of Shklov"). He is said to have mastered the Talmud at the age of 12, and when he was only 23, R. Meir *Malbim pronounced him without equal in his generation. He also acquired a profound knowledge of medicine, pharmacology, chemistry, history, geography, and mathematics, and was acquainted with a number of European languages. Elijah served as rabbi of several communities, being appointed in 1881 to Bereza Kartuskaya in the province of Grodno, in 1884 to Mariampol in the province of Suwalki, and in 1910 to the famous community of Lublin, hence his title the "Lubliner Rav." In 1928 he settled in Ereẓ Israel where he spent his remaining years. He was an outstanding talmudic authority and queries were directed to him from distant places. He was well known for his tendency to leniency in questions of ritual law. Most famous for his efforts on behalf of *agunot*, he even proposed a formula that would (in most cases) annul these marriages retroactively. Elijah's works are *Even ha-Roshah* (1887), *Imrei Shefer* (1896), *Even Pinnah* (1930^2), *Devar Eliyahu* (1915), *Devar Halakhah* (1921) and its complement *Millu'im* (1923), *Millu'ei Even* (1925), *Ḥibbat ha-Kodesh* (1926), and *Devarim Aḥadim* (1929). Also by Elijah is a collection of lectures and papers in Russian. Some of his responsa were published in the *Sedei Ḥemed* (1896–1911) by Ḥayyim Hezekiah *Medini.

Elijah had an elder brother ISRAEL ISSAR (1844–1921), many of whose responsa and novellae appear in *Devar Eliyahu* and in *Ammudei Shesh* published by Moses Ẓevi Hirsch Klatzkin (as appendix to *Ayyalah Sheluḥah*, 1912). *Devar Eliyahu* also contains novellae by Israel's son JOSHUA MORDECAI (1862–1925), who was head of a yeshivah in Slobodka and later rabbi of Libau (Libawa), where he died. Elijah was the father of Jacob *Klatzkin.

BIBLIOGRAPHY: J. Klatzkin, in: L. Jung (ed.), *Jewish Leaders* (1953), 317–41; *Yahadut Lita*, 3 (1967), 84f.

[Shlomo Eidelberg]

KLATZKIN, JACOB (1882–1948), author, philosopher, and Zionist. Klatzkin was born in Bereza Kartuska, Brest-Litovsk district, today Belarus. The son of Elijah *Klatzkin, a prominent rabbinical scholar, who gave him a thorough education in all branches of traditional Jewish studies. At the age of 18, Klatzkin went to Germany, first to Frankfurt on the Main and then to Marburg, where he studied philosophy under Hermann *Cohen. He received his doctorate from the University of Berne in 1912. In the following years Klatzkin was active in Germany as a writer for Hebrew periodicals, including *Ha-Zeman*, *Ha-Shilo'aḥ*, and *Ha-Tekufah*, and as editor of *Die *Welt*, the organ of the Zionist Organization (1909–11), and later in Heidelberg, of the *Freie Zionistische Blaetter*. From 1912 to 1915 he was director of the Jewish National Fund in Cologne. From 1915 to 1919 he edited the Swiss *Bulletin Juif*, which covered world events of special relevance to Jews during World War I and established the publishing firm Al ha-Mishmar, which issued a series of books on Jewish problems in French and German. In Berlin Klatzkin founded another publishing house, Eshkol, and continued writing for the Jewish press. In 1924 he and his lifelong friend Nahum *Goldmann initiated the *Encyclopaedia Judaica*, of which ten volumes (to the article "Lyra") appeared between 1928 and 1934. Two volumes of a parallel Hebrew edition, *Enẓiklopedyah Yisre'elit*, were issued in 1929–32. Klatzkin acted as editor in chief in cooperation with leading Jewish scholars. Although the advent of Hitler prevented the publication of the remaining volumes, what was published continues to be an important reference work. After the curtailment of the publication of the encyclopedia, Klatzkin took refuge first in Switzerland and then in the U.S., where he lectured at the College of Jewish Studies in Chicago. In 1947, after a further period in New York, he returned to Switzerland.

Klatzkin was a student of philosophy as well as a brilliant Hebrew essayist. In philosophy Klatzkin opposed his teacher Cohen, whose philosophy and interpretation of Judaism he submitted to searching criticism in the monograph *Hermann Cohen* (1921^2; Heb., 1923). He also devoted a critical study to Spinoza, *Baruch Spinoza* (Heb., 1923, 1954^3), in which he stressed the Jewish influences in his intellectual background and style; he translated Spinoza's *Ethics* from the Latin to Hebrew as *Torat ha-Middot* (1924; last reprinted, 1967). Klatzkin developed his own philosophy, which may be described as vitalistic, emphasizing the biological, instinctive aspect of life rather than the intellectual one, in *Sheki'at ha-Ḥayyim* ("Decline of Life," 1925), and in *Der Erkenntnistrieb als Lebens und Todesprinzip* (1935). It comprises epistemology, ethics, aesthetics, and a "metaphysic of human impulses." According to Klatzkin, the constantly increasing cognitive impulse leads to the weakening of man's vitality. Spirit, the culture-creating force in man, tends to change from a life-creating to a life-negating process. History is the arena in which this conflict develops, and self-preservation demands a reaction against the over-intellectualization of life. Within this framework culture, religion, and art are expressions and functions of the life process. Klatzkin's philosophical system is not "pure" philosophy but is, rather, a philosophy of culture and art; and as such, to his distress, it was ignored by academic philosophers. His Jewish-nationalist ideology was based on his general philosophy and is presented in *Probleme des modernen Judentums* (1918; second edition, *Krisis und Entscheidung im Judentum*, 1921). In his view the impulse of self-preservation among Jews in modern times created a revolutionary situation, in which the Jewish people turned away from over-intellectualization and spiritualization to the resumption of national life in its own country, with its own language. A country and a language, according to Klatzkin, determine the life of a nation, not abstract religious or cultural ideas. This nationalistic and secularist theory was as much opposed to Hermann Cohen's assimilationist concept of the messianic role of the Jews in the Diaspora as to the spiritual nationalism of *Aḥad Ha-Am, who advocated Ereẓ Israel merely as a spiritual center. Klatzkin's miscellaneous writings were published in a number of collections of essays: *Kera'im* (1924), *Zutot* (1925), *Teḥumim* (1928), and the posthumously published *Ketavim* (1953), and *Yalkut Massot* (1965; ed. by J. Schachter with introduction, notes, bibliography, 1965). A volume in English, *In Praise of Wisdom*, appeared in 1943. A major contribution to Jewish scholarship as well as to Hebrew revival was his and M. Zobel's edition of *Thesaurus Philosophicus Linguae Hebraicae*, which includes a dictionary of Jewish philosophical writers; *Antologyah shel ha-Pilosofyah ha-Ivrit* (1926); and a philosophical dictionary, *Oẓar ha-munnaḥim ha-Pilosofiyyim* (4 vols., 1928–33), which contains the terminology of medieval religious philosophers. Klatzkin also published a Hebrew anthology of aphorisms and fragments from classical philosophy, *Mishnat Rishonim* (1925) and *Mishnat Aḥaronim* (posthumous, 1952), the latter covering the period from Montaigne to modern times. A first installment of an autobiography, *Zikhronot* (*1899–1901*), appeared in 1902. Despite his unusual talents and achievements in several areas, Klatzkin was not accepted as a scholar by academicians and, to his great disappointment, was not invited to teach philosophy at the Hebrew University.

BIBLIOGRAPHY: J. Klausner, in: *Moznayim*, 4:4–5 (1932–33); M. Waxman, in: *Festschrift… Hadoar* (1927), 106–10; J. Rosenheim, *Beitraege zur Orientierung im juedischen Geistesleben der Gegenwart*

(1920); I. Zollschan, *Revision des juedischen Nationalismus* (1919); M. Meisels, in: *Hadoar* (Nov. 11, 1932); E. Ginzberg, *Keeper of the Law* (1966), 270–2; T. Ben-Mosheh, in: S. Federbush (ed.), *Ḥokhmat Yisrael be-Ma'arav Eiropa*, 1 (1958), 433–44; J. Klausner, *Pilosofim ve-Hogei De'ot* (1956), 235–55; Z. Woyslowski, *Yeḥidim bi-Reshut ha-Rabbim* (1956), 248–64; I. Cohen, *Sha'ar ha-Soferim* (1962), 227–49; M.Z. Sole (ed.), *Le-Mahutah shel ha-Yahadut* (1969), 121–39; Kressel, Leksikon, 2 (1967), 771–3 (with additional bibliography).

[Moshe Zeev Sole and Samuel Scheps]

KLATZKO (Melzer), MORDECAI BEN ASHER (1797–1883), Lithuanian rabbi and author. Klatzko was born in Vilna where he studied under *Ḥayyim of Volozhin. He married the daughter of R. Loeb Malzer (Melzer), later adopting his surname. In 1840 he was appointed head of the R. Meilis yeshivah in Vilna, succeeding Israel *Salanter who had headed it for a short period. From 1865 Klatzko served as rabbi in Lida until his death. At an advanced age he became a follower of the ḥasidic movement and led an ascetic life, devoting much attention to the needs of his fellow men. Some of his responsa and talmudic novellae were published by his pupil Abba Joseph Triwusch, together with a biographical introduction, under the title *Tekhelet Mordekhai* (1889).

BIBLIOGRAPHY: Ḥ.N. Maggid-Steinschneider, *Ir Vilna* (1900), 122–7; idem, in: *Oẓar ha-Sifrut*, 4 (1892), 531–41; S.M. Chones, *Toledot ha-Posekim* (1910), 598–600; D. Katz, *Tenu'at ha-Musar*, 1 (1958), 148f.; 4 (1963), 153f.; *Yahadut Lita*, 3 (1967), 84.

[Samuel Abba Horodezky]

KLAUSNER, ABRAHAM (d. 1407/8), Austrian talmudist. Klausner was a pupil of Moses of Znaim. In 1380 he was living in Vienna where he served as rabbi together with Meir Halevy, by whom he was apparently ordained with the title "*morenu*." He was a brother-in-law of the martyr, *Aaron of Neustadt (Blumlein), one of the great scholars of Austria and the uncle and teacher of Israel *Isserlein. Jacob *Moellin (the *Maharil*) studied under him and he was the main teacher of Isaac *Tyrnau. Klausner's responsa are mentioned in the responsa of Isserlein and Israel *Bruna. His main reputation, however, rests upon his *Sefer ha-Minhagim* (Riva di Trento, 1558). This was already known to his contemporaries and is mentioned by Moellin and by Isserlein. It is the first extant work in the field of local religious customs (see *Minhagim Books), to which insufficient attention was paid by the **posekim* until his time. Klausner adapted the **minhagim* of Ḥayyim Paltiel, a contemporary of Meir of Rothenburg (part of which has been published by D. Goldschmidt from a manuscript of 1305 (see bibl.)), adding explanations in the margins, which were incorporated by the printer in the text and made to appear as one work. The customs in the printed edition are dealt with at greater length than in the manuscript and arranged differently. It was printed with errors, omissions, and repetitions. A new edition based upon the Riva di Trento edition with introduction, notes, and sources was published by C.J. Ehrenreich in 1929.

BIBLIOGRAPHY: Carmoly, in: *Ben Chananja*, 8 (1865), 737; J. Freimann (ed.), *Leket Yosher*, 2 (1904), XVIIIf. (introd.); C.J. Ehrenreich (ed.), *Sefer ha-Minhagim le-R. Avraham Klausner* (1929), III–VII (introd.); J. Kaufman, *R. Yom Tov Lippmann Muehlhausen* (Heb. 1927), 3f.; Goldschmidt, in: KS, 23 (1946/47), 324–30; 24 (1947/48), 73–83.

[David Tamar]

KLAUSNER, ABRAHAM J. (1915–), U.S. rabbi and activist. Born in Memphis, TN, raised in Denver, CO, Klausner received an M.A. from the University of Denver in 1938 and a Master of Hebrew Letters and ordination from Hebrew Union College in 1943. In June 1944 he volunteered as a chaplain in the U.S. Army.

Klausner arrived in Europe in late 1944 and in mid-1945 was assigned to the 116th Evacuation Hospital, a mobile unit. He arrived in Dachau within three weeks of its April 29, 1945, liberation. Klausner's responsibility was to American Jewish troops, not the survivors, but he felt duty bound as a rabbi and as a Jew to come to the aid of Jews. He worked on creating separate DP camps for Jews; evacuated Jewish patients from outlying areas and consolidated them in hospitals where they could be treated by Jewish, not German, doctors; and played a key role in the establishment of the Central Committee of Liberated Jews in Bavaria – so that the Jews could assume responsibility for their own fate.

His unauthorized June 24, 1945, report "A Detailed Report on the Liberated Jew As He Now Suffers His Period of Liberation" was sent to the leadership of the American Jewish community.

Klausner's – and other – contemporaneous reports prompted Earl G. Harrison, former U.S. Commissioner of Immigration and U.S. representative on the Intergovernmental Committee, to go on a fact-finding mission as the representative of President Harry S. Truman. His mandate was to determine whether or not Holocaust survivors' needs were being met by military, government, and private organizations. Harrison's trip was pre-arranged by the Army to cover areas that were less than problematic.

Col. Milton Richmond, a Jewish officer who headed a special military unit out of Dachau, saw the schedule and asked Klausner to intervene. Klausner met with Harrison and as a result, Harrison's itinerary was changed, and Klausner was asked to accompany him on his inspection tour of the camps.

Harrison's report resulted in the creation of a post for an advisor on Jewish affairs who would report on issues affecting Jewish Displaced Persons (DPs) to the commanding general in the European theater of operations.

Klausner was honorably discharged in 1946. With the help of Robert A. Taft, the senator from Ohio, he returned to Germany in 1947 to work with the DPs.

When Klausner returned to the U.S. in 1948, he accepted the position of senior rabbi of Temple Israel in Boston, MA, until 1953. In 1954 he became the rabbi of Temple Emanu-El in Yonkers, New York, where he served for more than 35 years, retiring in 1989. He subsequently wrote his autobiography, *A Letter to My Children from the Edge of the Holocaust* (2002).

BIBLIOGRAPHY: A. Grobman, *Rekindling The Flame: American Jewish Chaplains and the Survivors of European Jewry, 1944–1948* (1993); AJYB, 47 (1945–1946); Archives of Temple Emanu-El, Yonkers, New York.

[Alex Grobman (2nd ed.)]

KLAUSNER, ISRAEL (1905–1981), Hebrew writer and historian. Born in Troki (Lithuania), Klausner, a cousin of Joseph *Klausner, settled in Palestine in 1936. He joined the staff of the Zionist Archives in Jerusalem, where he served as assistant director from 1956. His writings on the history of the Jews in Vilna include *Korot Beit ha-Almin ha-Yashan be-Vilna* (1935), and *Toledot ha-Kehillah ha-Ivrit be-Vilna* (1938). Among his works on Zionist history are *Ḥibbat Ẓiyyon be-Romanyah* (1958), *Oppoziẓyah le-Herzl* (1960), and *Mi-Katoviẓ ad Basel* (2 vols., 1965).

BIBLIOGRAPHY: Kressel, Leksikon, 2 (1967), 764.

[Getzel Kressel]

KLAUSNER, JOSEPH GEDALIAH (1874–1958), literary critic, historian, and Zionist. Klausner was born in Olkienik, near Vilna, but in 1885 his family moved to Odessa where he attended a Hebrew day school. Already in his earliest years he evinced a passion for the Hebrew language, which was to be one of the main interests of his life. He was the youngest member of the *Sefatenu Ittanu*, a society for the revival of Hebrew as a spoken language, established in Odessa in 1891 and with his friends, who included Nahum *Slouschz and Saul *Tchernichowsky, he spoke only Hebrew. In 1897 he proceeded to Germany, where he studied Semitic and modern languages, history, and philosophy at Heidelberg. In the same year he participated in the discussion in the Jewish press in Russia with regard to the forthcoming Zionist Congress to be convened in Basle, strongly urging participation, and he attended this First Congress. At the age of 28 he moved to Warsaw to succeed Aḥad Ha-Am as editor of *Ha-Shiloʾaḥ* a position he held for 23 years (together with H.N. *Bialik for volumes 13–21 and with Jacob Fichman for volumes 45–46). In Warsaw he became friendly with I.L. *Peretz and up-and-coming writers such as Z. Shneour, Itzhak Katzenelson, Jacob Steinberg, and Y.D. Berkowitz, who would meet regularly in his home on Saturdays, and to whom he extended every encouragement and guidance. *Ha-Shiloʾaḥ*, which had ceased publication in 1904 was revived in Odessa in 1907 and Klausner moved there. He lectured on Jewish history at the modern yeshivah in Odessa. After the Revolution in February 1917, he was invited to lecture at Odessa University, but following the Bolshevik Revolution in October he immigrated to Palestine, settling in Jerusalem in 1919. He took an active part in the Vaʾad ha-Lashon, the *Academy of the Hebrew Language, first as scientific secretary, then as editor of its proceedings, and later as president. He continued to act as editor of *Ha-Shiloʾaḥ* when it was revived in Ereẓ Israel, from 1921–26. When the Hebrew University was established, to his disappointment he was not appointed to the chair of Jewish history, as his views were considered too secular, but was appointed to the chair of Hebrew literature. It was only in 1944, at the age of 70, that he was appointed to the chair of the History of the Second Temple, endowed by his friends and admirers. From 1950 until shortly before his death he acted as editor in chief of the *Encyclopaedia Hebraica* and was responsible for volumes 2–5 and 7–8. He published his autobiography in 1946 (enlarged edition 1955). Klausner was active as a literary critic and philologist, as a historian, and as a Zionist.

Literary Criticism and Philology

Klausner's essays on criticism, appearing first in 1894, took the form of literary exegesis of contemporary works in which he also discussed the tasks of Hebrew literature in the age of national renaissance. He supported the expansion of the Hebrew language and its use as a living language, both by reviving words from the ancient sources and by coining new words, but he took a moderate stand vis-à-vis both radical innovators and purists. Many of the new words coined by Klausner were criticized by the latter. Klausner insisted on the significance of the Haskalah which he enunciated in the detailed work, *Ruḥot Menashevot* (1896), by stressing its strong links with the national movement, indicating that, notwithstanding the essential difference between the two movements, the national movement and its literature derived from the Haskalah. His essays on Aḥad Ha-Am, Bialik, Tchernichowsky, Shneour, Yaʾakov Cahan, David Shimoni, Shalom Yankev *Abramovitsh (Mendele Mokher Seforim), and Peretz, published in various periodicals, were collected in his three-volume *Yoẓerim u-Vonim* (1925–28). They reveal an even-handed treatment of diverse authors, and a high regard for detail and biographical data. He believed that Hebrew culture should be open to the influences of European literature. In this respect he represented the moderate line that advocated the synthesis of Judaism and humanism. Klausner believed that poetry was a spiritual force whose influence on the Jewish people should be increased. At the same time he continuously stressed the need for a synthesis between national and universal ideas in the intellectual and literary spheres. He believed that it was not enough for Hebrew literature to reflect and depict reality; it was a fundamental and essential part of the movement of national revival and that it therefore must also take an active part in molding the young generation and in guiding Jewish society. While defending the need for the freedom and autonomy of literature, he also insisted that authors must be alert to public affairs and committed to the national idea. This approach was combined with his militant partisanship on behalf of the Hebrew language and literature as expressed during the debate over whether Hebrew or Yiddish should be considered the national language of Russian Jewry. *Ha-Shiloʾaḥ*, under Klausner, published the best poetry, fiction, and criticism of the early 20th century, including works by Mendele Mokher Seforim, Bialik, Tchernichowsky, and Brenner.

In Ereẓ Israel, too, he argued that authors must strive to create a literature which would help determine the new existence, stressing that Jewish spiritual trends had always been influenced by the contemporary Hebrew literature. Often he used the work under discussion to advance his own ideological and emotional views. His strength in criticism resides in emphasizing a work's conceptual framework, while his evaluation of its aesthetic, poetic, and formal qualities are only of a general nature.

Literary History

Many of the above characteristics also mark his work as a historian of modern Hebrew literature. As early as 1907 he revealed his dream of writing a comprehensive history of modern Hebrew literature. He had published a short history of modern Hebrew literature in Russian in 1900 and in Hebrew in 1920 (*Toledot ha-Sifrut ha-Ivrit ha-Ḥadashah*). His principal scholarly achievement in this field, based on his university lectures, is the important *Historyah shel ha-Sifrut ha-Ivrit ha-Ḥadashah* (6 vols., 1930–50; second revised edition 1952–59; translated by H. Danby as *History of Modern Hebrew Literature*, 1932; 1972). His earlier evaluations of Haskalah authors, e.g., Mapu, A.D. Lebensohn, and Mendele, are here almost fully preserved. The *History* also evinces Klausner's interest in such contemporary considerations as the writer's contribution to the revival and expansion of the Hebrew language, to the idea of Jewish nationalism, and to the love of Ereẓ Israel before the Zionist period. He also stresses the relationship between Hebrew literature and the general trends in world literature. Klausner adheres strictly to the historical-biographical method to advance his didactic-explanatory approach.

The *History* consists of separate monographs connected by general surveys. Striving toward a chronological and objective historical perspective, he only brought his study up to 1880 (from 1784) to avoid dealing with contemporary literature in which he was subjectively involved. Klausner devoted much attention to the discussion of periodization. He rejected the view that the history of modern Hebrew literature began with Moses Ḥayyim *Luzzatto, since his writings were neither modern nor secular, regarding it as having begun with the Haskalah literature in Germany in 1787. Klausner saw the starting point of the new period in the political and cultural development of German and Austrian Jewry. Taking into consideration the interrelationship of secular and religious trends, he divided literary history into three periods: the first – a defensive war of Haskalah against religion (Germany, end of 18th century); the second – reconciliation of Haskalah and religion (Galicia and Italy, first half of 19th century); and the third – the attack of Haskalah against religion (Russia and Poland, mainly from 1860 to 1870). Klausner restricted his concept of Hebrew literature to the secular genres, intentionally disregarding traditional and ḥasidic literature, although they were reflected in his discussion of the satiric works of Haskalah authors. On the other hand he dealt extensively with literary genres, discussing not only belles lettres, but also Jewish studies and essays on philosophy, history, ethics, and science. He virtually ignored important Yiddish works because of his active involvement in the "language controversy" between Hebrew and Yiddish. As a result he did not fully understand the complexity of bilingual phenomena in the works of authors such as M. *Levin, J. *Perl, A. *Gottlober, and Mendele Mokher Seforim.

Some of Klausner's observations regarding the impact of world literature are useful as a starting point for the comparative study of modern Hebrew literature. His approach to literary research is based on methods that were current among 19th-century positivist literary scholars such as Taine – who stressed the influence of time, place, and national character on the spiritual and artistic life – and Georg *Brandes who gave primacy to the writer's biography as the effective and even determining factor in shaping his creative personality. In assessing an author Klausner used social-national criteria, which were standards also current in 19th-century Russian criticism. Despite his own methodological deficiencies and the fact that great progress has since been made in methods of literary criticism, Klausner's work remains a notable landmark in modern Hebrew literary criticism. His works in this field also include: *Be'ayot shel Sifrut u-Madda* (1956); *Yoẓerei Tekufah u-Mamshikhei Tekufah* (1956); *Meshorerei Dorenu* (1956); *Mi-Gedolei ha-Sifrut ha-Olamit* (1954).

[Samuel Werses]

Revival of Hebrew

Klausner's research in the Hebrew language was not merely an abstract diversion, but rather an activity with the practical goal of transforming Hebrew into a spoken tongue capable of meeting all the linguistic demands of modern life. He believed this undertaking, which he called "practical philology" as distinguished from "scientific philology," would aid in the national rebirth of the people. To achieve his goal, Klausner saw the necessity for studying the development of post-biblical Hebrew and, equally important, other semitic languages in regard to vocabulary, morphology, style, and syntax. Consequently he analyzed lexical material from the Book of Ben Sira, the Mishnah, and the Talmud, and published his major findings and opinions in *Sefat Ever Safah Ḥayyah* (Cracow 1914–15; rev. ed., *Ha-Lashon ha-Ivrit Lashon Ḥayyah*, Jerusalem 1948–49). Here and in articles collected in the anthology, *Ha-Ivrit ha-Ḥadashah u-Ve'ayoteha* (Tel Aviv, 1952), Klausner expressed his preference for mishnaic and talmudic usage over biblical usage on the grounds that modern Hebrew must continue the process of linguistic development, even at the expense of foregoing biblical forms. Similarly, he opposed the use of Aramaisms, contending that the vocabulary should be enlarged by creating new words based on Hebrew morphological constructions, by borrowing from related languages, and by adopting words of Greek or Roman origin that have attained international currency. These opinions aroused criticism and opposition among purists. In the style of expression, Klausner advocated clarity and simplicity rather than the traditional rhetorical forms. For practical reasons he deemed it necessary to standardize orthography (*ketiv male*) and to adopt a system of punctuation.

[Meir Medan]

History of Christianity

Of special importance are Klausner's studies of *Jesus and the beginnings of Christianity. These works represent the first comprehensive books on these subjects written in Hebrew by a modern Jewish scholar in Ereẓ Israel. His *Yeshu ha-Noẓeri, Zemanno, Ḥayyav ve-Torato* was published in Jerusalem in 1922 and has been translated into many European languages (Eng. transl. by H. Danby, *Jesus of Nazareth*, 1925). Klausner had first-hand knowledge of the Jewish sources, especially the rabbinic literature, which enabled him to portray Jesus as he lived among his contemporaries. In contrast to Klausner's Jewish predecessors who had written about Jesus from the liberal point of view, he described the background of Jesus' life and activity in rediscovering the original meaning of many of Jesus' sayings. He stresses the Jewishness of Jesus, claiming that he was a proud Jew and never abandoned Judaism, and that he regarded himself as the Jewish messiah. Klausner holds that Jesus' humanistic message, though sometimes more extreme and impracticable than similar contemporary Jewish doctrines, fitted the Judaism of the time. Nevertheless, certain of Jesus' utopian and individualistic doctrines are seen as extending beyond the frame of Judaism and in tragic opposition to Judaism's strong sense of national unity. The work, based on extensive Jewish learning, was welcomed by Christian scholars and readers as a Jewish witness of a new positive evaluation of Jesus and has contributed to a better understanding of Jesus as a wholly Jewish figure. He also shows that Jesus was not executed by Jews but by Pilate the Roman.

In his other book on Christianity, *Mi-Yeshu ad Paulus* (1939; Eng. transl. by W.F. Stinespring, *From Jesus to Paul*, 1943), he traces the development of Christianity from Jesus to Paul. He began collecting the material as early as 1907. The work deals mainly with Paul who is depicted in the light of his Jewish and Hellenistic background. He stressed that had there been no Jesus there would have been no Paul and no Christians; but it was due to Paul that Christianity became a world religion.

[David Flusser]

As a Historian

A period of 40 years separates Klausner's two historical works. In 1909 he published *Historyah Yisre'elit*, consisting of the lectures which he gave in Odessa, covering the period from the conquest of Canaan to the Maccabean period. In 1949 his historical magnum opus *Ha-Historyah shel ha-Bayit ha-Sheni* appeared in five volumes, covering the period from the destruction of the First Temple to the destruction of the Second. It was based on the lectures he delivered at the Hebrew University. Its exhaustive treatment of all the available sources, and his essentially Jewish approach makes it a major contribution to the subject. A fervent nationalist, however, Klausner makes no secret of the fact that his approach is a subjective one. In his introduction (which appears in the fifth volume) he states frankly, "It is permitted – and even a duty imposed on us… to compare the past with the present no less than the present with the past. Only he who sees the important incidents of his time as part of the universal historical process and views them *sub specie historitatis* is permitted to write the history of the past… there is no question but that he who writes the history of the past writes at the same time the history of his own time, evaluating the past in the light of the values of the present… the revolutionary events of the last 50 years have disclosed historical causes and factors which operated in previous generations as they do in this."

In an appendix to the third edition (1952) he added an appendix on the Dead Sea Scrolls and the Qumran sect, in which he was the first to suggest that these sectarians were Zealots (a view which was adopted by Cecil Roth and Sir Godfrey Driver).

As a Zionist

Klausner was an active Zionist and a fervent nationalist throughout his life, and his Zionist views color all his work. A delegate to the First Congress, he was greatly influenced by the political ideas of Herzl, although his cultural approach remained that of the Ḥovevei Zion and Aḥad Ha-Am. He attended nearly every subsequent Congress until the eleventh, contributing surveys on them to *Ha-Shilo'aḥ*. From 1930 he began to identify himself more and more with the policy of Jabotinsky and was regarded by the Revisionist Party, and later by its successor, Ḥerut, as the ideologist of the movement. He edited the monthly *Beitar* (together with B. Netanyahu) from 1932–33 and came out vigorously, both in speech and in writing, in support of the ideals of the right-wing nationalists. In 1949 they put his name forward as their candidate for the first president of the State of Israel in opposition to Chaim Weizmann. Amos Oz describes Joseph Klausner, who was the brother of his grandfather, in the autobiographical novel *Sippur al Ahavah ve-Ḥoshekh* (2002; *A Tale of Love and Darkness*, 2004).

BIBLIOGRAPHY: *Sefer Klausner, Me'assef le-Madda u-le-Sifrut Yafah* (1937); J. Klausner, *Darki likrat ha-Teḥiyyah ve-ha-Ge'ullah*, 2 vols. (1946–55); Y. Beker and H. Toren, *Yosef Klausner, ha-Ish u-Fo'olo* (1947); S. Werses, in: *Molad*, 16 (1958), no. 124; B. Shohetman and B. Eliẓedek, *Kitvei Yosef Klausner* (1937), a bibliography; I. Barzilai, in: KS, 41 (1966), 107–16, (bibliography); Waxman, Literature, 4 (1960), 377–82, 451–2, 751–6, 822–5; A. Broides, *"Pegishot ve-Siḥot im Y. Klausner,"* in: *Moznayim*, 28 (1969), 116–19; S. Kling, *Joseph Klausner* (1970, including bibliography). **ADD. BIBLIOGRAPHY:** Y. Barzilai, *"Ketavav ha-Publiẓistiyyim shel Y. Klausner,"* in: *Ha-Ẓiyyonut*, 11 (1986), 413–31; I. Parush, *Kanon Sifruti ve-Ideologyah Le'ummit: Bikkoret ha-Sifrut shel Frischmann be-Hashva'ah le-Bikkoret ha-Sifrut shel Klauzner u-Vrenner* (1992); S. Werses, *"Y. Klausner ve-Reshit ha-Hora'ah ve-ha-Meḥkar shel ha-Sifrut ha-Ivrit ha-Ḥadashah ba-Universitah ha-Ivrit,"* in: *Toledot ha-Universitah ha-Ivrit bi-Yrushalayim* (1997), 487–515; V. Pilovski, *"Y. Klausner, Avi ha-Ideologyah shel ha-Yamin ba-Ẓiyyonut u-me-Rasheha,"* in: *Galei Iyyun u-Meḥkar*, 9 (2000), 25–31; D.F. Sandmel, *Into the Fray: Joseph Klausner's Approach to Judaism and Christianity in the Greco-Roman World* (2002).

KLAUSNER, ẒEVI HIRSCH (1802–1887), rabbi and author. Klausner received his education from his father, ZE'EV WOLF OF RAWICZ (1761–1861), a scholar, who from 1804 to 1811 was rabbi of Oborniki, and from 1811 until his death, of Exin (Kcynia), where he was head of a yeshivah. One of four children, Ẓevi Hirsch suffered greatly during his lifetime, wandering from place to place. After the successive deaths of two wives, he married a third time and settled in the small town of Mechisko. There, isolated from all intellectual contact, he published his works. *Raẓ le-Mishnah* (1857), on the commentators to the Mishnah, attempts in particular to resolve the well-known difficulties in the Mishnah raised by Akiva Eger, and has a moving introduction by Klausner to explain his "impertinence." He added supplements to this work, one entitled *Ta ha-Raẓim* (1864), and two poems by his brothers, MORDECAI ISAAC and JACOB. The books received approbations, particularly from the rabbis of Germany.

BIBLIOGRAPHY: A. Heppner and J. Herzberg, *Aus der Vergangenheit und Gegenwart der Juden und der juedischen Gemeinden in den Posener Landen* (1909), 377f., 628f.

[Itzhak Alfassi]

KLAVAN, ISRAEL (1915–1980), U.S. Orthodox rabbi. Klavan, who was born in Zazkevich, Lithuania, was raised in Burlington, Vermont, where his father was a rabbi. He was ordained at Yeshiva University (1940). Klavan served as rabbi of congregations in Fitchburg, Massachusetts (1940–42), Williamsport, Pennsylvania (1942–46), and Mount Vernon, New York (1946–53). He became executive secretary of the Rabbinical Council of America in 1950 and later executive vice president.

[Louis Bernstein]

KLEE, ALFRED (1875–1943), Zionist leader in Germany. He practiced law in his native Berlin, acting notably in cases defending Jewish honor (such as the case against **The Protocols of the Elders of Zion*, etc.). With Herzl's appearance he became a foremost propagandist for Zionism in Germany. He was especially active in "the conquest of the communities," and after World War I he established the Juedische Volkspartei, a coalition of Zionist parties in Berlin; similar parties were also established in other cities. Representatives of the party "conquered" Jewish communities that until that time, and especially from 1926 to 1930, had been in the hands of the anti-Zionist liberals. At the party's initiative a Jewish national educational network was established, social work was improved, and the cultural institutions in Palestine were assisted. Klee served briefly as chairman of the Zionist Federation in Germany and represented the German Jewish community in the management of the *Jewish Colonization Association. With the rise of the Nazis he was active in representing German Jewry before the authorities. In 1938 he left for Holland, where he continued his activities until his internment in Westerbork concentration camp where he died in 1943. He was the father-in-law of Hans *Gosslar and Simon *Rawidowicz.

BIBLIOGRAPHY: R. Lichtheim, *Toledot ha-Ẓiyyonut* (1951), index; E.G. Lowenthal, *Bewaehrung im Untergang* (1965), 9497; J. Meisel, in: *Meẓudah*, 4 (1945), 426–8. **ADD. BIBLIOGRAPHY:** M. Brenner, in: YBLBI 35 (1990), 219–43; *Biographisches Handbuch der deutschsprachigen Emigration nach 1933*, vol. 1 (1999), 368.

[Getzel Kressel]

KLEEREKOPER, ASSER BENJAMIN (1880–1943), Dutch journalist and politician, first a Zionist, then a Socialist. He was a grandson of the well-known Rabbi Isaiah Kleerekoper of Amsterdam. Being one of the first Zionists and modern Hebraists in Holland, he translated *"*Ha-Tikvah*" into Dutch and was an early editor of the Dutch Zionist periodical *De Joodsche Wachter*. In 1907 he delivered the welcoming speech at the Eighth Zionist World Congress in the Hague, and recorded his impressions of the congress in his *Zionistisch Schetsboek*. However, Kleerekoper became increasingly critical of social inequality and an advocate of the proletariat. This brought him into conflict with the Dutch Zionist establishment. In 1909 he exchanged his Zionist mantle for Socialist commitment and placed his highly developed oratorical and propagandistic talents in the service of the Sociaal-Democratische Arbeiders Partij (SDAP), the Dutch Labor Party. Kleerekoper became a prominent Socialist, serving as a member of the Amsterdam municipal council and of the Second Chamber of Parliament, 1914–32. He never went back to the Zionists, but his Socialism was colored by Jewish solidarity. He spoke out in favor of a large-scale settlement in Palestine for the Jewish East European masses: "It is not a question of Capital looking for expansion, but of Labor looking for bread." In his "Oproerige Krabbels," a widely read column in the socialist daily *Het Volk* appearing almost daily between 1915 and 1940, he lambasted national-socialism and antisemitism as few others did. After a long period of illness Kleerekoper was buried in April 1943 in an Amsterdam from which most Jews had been already deported.

BIBLIOGRAPHY: S. Bloemgarten, *Henri Polak sociaal-democraat, 1868–1943* (1993); E. Gans, in: *Dutch Jewish History*, vol. 3 (1993), 321–39; idem, *De kleine verschillen die het leven uitmaken. Een historische studie naar joodse sociaal-democraten en socialistisch-zionisten in Nederland* (1999); L. Giebels, *De zionistische beweging in Nederland 1899–1941* (1975); E.H. de Levita, in: *Ons Amsterdam*, 40:4 (1988), 106–10; idem, *ABK "oproerige krabbels." Hoekstukjes van A.B. Kleerekoper* (1994); P. van Praag, in: *Bulletin Nederlandse Arbeidersbeweging*, 15 (1987), 44–54; idem, *Biografisch Woordenboek van het Socialisme en de Arbeidersbeweging in Nederland*, at: www.iisg.nl/bwsa/bios/kleerekoper.html.

[Evelien Gans (2nd ed.)]

KLEIN, ABRAHAM MOSES (1909–1972), poet, novelist, journalist. Klein was the first Canadian Jewish writer to gain wide influence in English. Conversant in Hebrew and Yiddish, he brought the influence of these languages into his poetry, fiction, and journalism. A remarkable aspect of Klein's career was his willingness to assert himself in a wide array of fields. Trained as a lawyer at the Université de Montréal, he was a practicing lawyer; as editor of the English-language *Cana-*

dian Jewish Chronicle between 1938 and 1955 he played a major journalistic role in Montreal; running unsuccessfully for the left-leaning CCF party he presented himself as a would-be progressive politician; and, in his strangest role, Klein wrote a variety of public speeches and ephemeral material for the liquor baron and community leader Samuel *Bronfman. The latter role caused Klein private embarrassment, and his willingness to stretch himself across such broad professional boundaries may suggest the precariousness of literary life in Canada in the 1940s and 1950s, as well as Klein's own middle-class aspirations.

Klein's initial literary forays took place when he was an undergraduate at Montreal's McGill University. He became an influential member of the city's nascent modernist small press and magazine culture, acting as a model and mentor to younger poets. His first published poems appeared in important American journals, and he was associated with such key early Canadian magazines as *Preview* and *First Statement*. From the earliest stages of his output, Klein mused about the precarious role of the poet in modern society while making subtle plays on Jewish types, street life, history, and ritual. Unlike younger poets, who would either abandon or view the old Jewish world with impatience, Klein's poetry is dedicated to a detailed, often nostalgic portrayal of what he viewed as the pathos and intimacy of Jewish family and communal life.

Alongside Klein's Jewish-themed work are a substantial number of poems devoted to marrying the English and French spirit of Montreal. In a 1948 chapbook, Klein writes of his effort to create in his work "un 'langage bilingue'" – a poetic language built of French and English words in such a way that it could be enjoyed by native speakers of either language. The best example of this effort can be found in "Parade of St. Jean Baptiste": "Bannered, and ranked, and at its stances fixed/the enfilade and vestment colors the air./Roll now the batons of the tambours round/ruminant with commencement …." Klein's love of Montreal's Frenchness, his willingness to embrace it and convey the city's multilinguality, reveal the existence of his multicultural tendencies long before Canadians were conscious of the possibility of describing their country in these terms.

Klein's lone novel, *The Second Scroll* (1951), was published in the United States to critical acclaim, but the book did not receive the readership Klein had hoped for. A difficult modernist narrative built of disparate pieces of prose, poetry, drama, and liturgical writing, it is an early effort to come to terms with the Holocaust in a literary context. Klein's meditation on 20th-century evil leads him to a consideration of messianism, mysticism, and the meaning of national regeneration in the newly established State of Israel. The book reveals a dividedness, which Klein also expressed in his private journals, over the status of diasporic Jewish culture in light of the new state. Ultimately, Klein was deeply rooted in and loved diaspora Jewishness, though he recognized the value of a Jewish state in the wake of the Holocaust.

In his final years, Klein withdrew from public and literary life. In recent years, his status as a role model for younger Jewish writers has gained greater prominence in Canada. His literary output has been well documented by the University of Toronto press, which has published the *Complete Poems*, including his translations (2 vols, ed. Z. Pollock, 1990); a selection of his essays and editorials *Beyond Sambation* (ed. M.W. Steinberg and U. Caplan, 1982); *Short Stories* (ed. M.W. Steinberg); and *Notebooks: Selections from the A.M. Klein Papers* (ed. Z. Pollock and U. Caplan).

BIBLIOGRAPHY: U. Caplan, *Like One That Dreamed: A Portrait of A.M. Klein* (1982); Z. Pollock, *A.M. Klein: The Story of the Poet* (1994).

[Norman Ravvin (2nd ed.)]

KLEIN, ALBERTO (1897–1983), Argentinian engineer. Klein was born and educated in the Argentine. He was professor of mechanics at the National University of Technology at Buenos Aires from 1923 to 1960. He was prominent in Jewish communal work. Klein wrote several books, among them *Technical Rules for Metallic Structures and Reinforced Concrete* (1935) and *Elements of Mechanics* (1944–60), and he was coauthor of *Building Code for the City of Buenos Aires* (1944, 1949, 1959).

KLEIN, ANNE (1923–1974), U.S. fashion designer. Born Hannah Golofsky in Brooklyn, the daughter of Russian immigrants, Klein became one of the most influential fashion designers in the U.S. Known for clothing that was casual, but elegant and feminine, she was acknowledged to be ahead of her time. "Clothes aren't going to change the world," she said in 1969, just as the women's movement was getting under way. "The women who wear them will." She was also the mentor of Donna *Karan, who was hired by Klein right out of school and became an internationally renowned designer. While in high school, studying fine arts and design, Klein won a scholarship to Traphagen School of Fashion in New York City and, at 15, began her career as a freelance sketcher. Her first regular job was at Varden Petites. She married a garment manufacturer named Ben Klein and in 1948 they launched Junior Sophisticates, a highly successful company that applied a youthful spirit to traditional apparel. She divorced Klein in the early 1960s but continued working with him until 1965. By that time, she had remarried and, in 1968, she and her second husband, Matthew "Chip" Rubinstein, formed Anne Klein & Co. The first collection under her own name revolutionized American fashion: a mix-and-match wardrobe of jackets, pants, and related pieces for working women that was equally appropriate at the office, at night, and on weekends. A short while later, Saks Fifth Avenue gave Klein her own in-store boutique, the start of a new approach to retailing. She became the first designer to win two Neiman Marcus awards for fashion leadership, in 1959 and 1969. She also won two Coty Awards and was named to the Coty American Fashion Awards Hall of Fame in 1971. Two years later, she became an international presence by taking on new investors, Takihyo Co. Ltd. of Japan.

In 1973, she was one of five U.S. designers selected to participate, along with five French houses, in a landmark fashion show at Versailles.

[Mort Sheinman (2nd ed.)]

KLEIN, CALVIN RICHARD (1942–), U.S. fashion designer. Born and reared in a middle-class Bronx community of first- and second-generation American Jews, Calvin Klein – the son of a Hungarian immigrant who owned a neighborhood grocery store – became one of the world's best-known designers. The Calvin Klein label became familiar from Broadway to Beijing and Klein himself made headlines, some of them scandalous, with his provocative advertising campaigns as well as an unconventional lifestyle. His name appeared on everything from jeans to jewelry, from evening gowns to eyewear, and his Eternity and Obsession fragrances are among the world's most popular. By the time he sold his privately owned company in 2003, his products were generating retail sales of $5 billion a year. As a designer, Klein created a particularly American style that was accepted everywhere. Its components: clean, spare sportswear in luxurious fabrics; soft, sensuous evening clothes; layering; and multiple uses for jackets and sweaters.

Displaying a passion for fashion that was evident when he was still a boy, Klein was raised in the same neighborhood that nurtured Ralph *Lauren, the designer who would become his fiercest rival. Klein attended the High School of Industrial Art in New York City, then majored in apparel design at the Fashion Institute of Technology. For the next few years, he took various jobs in the garment industry, including a four-month stint as a copy boy at *Women's Wear Daily*, the trade newspaper that would write about him for decades to come. In 1968, when Klein was 26, he wanted to open his own business. He went to Barry Schwartz, whom he had known since the age of five, and asked for a loan of $10,000. Schwartz, six months older than Klein, was working at his family's supermarket in Harlem. He loaned Klein the money and two months later, following the assassination of Martin Luther King Jr. and the ensuing Harlem riots, Schwartz walked away from the food business and became Klein's partner. Almost immediately, Klein was championed by Bonwit Teller, one of the country's most prestigious department stores. At first, Klein's firm made only coats and dresses, but in 1973 expanded into sportswear. By then, his designs had begun making regular appearances in the major fashion magazines, but it was around that time that Klein really took off with that most basic item of the American wardrobe: jeans. Calvin Klein jeans, snug-fitting and with the designer's name emblazoned on the back pocket, created an international sensation. Promoted by a now legendary series of television commercials, they were made by Puritan Fashions Corporation, headed by Carl *Rosen. In 1983, Klein acquired Puritan for $68 million, but also inherited a mountain of debt. During the 1980s, Klein expanded his business to include the first successful designer underwear for men and women, and entered the fragrance market with Obsession and Eternity. In 1992, facing serious financial difficulties, Klein was rescued by his friend David Geffen, who purchased all the company's outstanding debt securities. Klein also added a less expensive line of casual apparel and accessories under the CK brand and moved into the home decor and cosmetics markets.

In 1994, he sold the jeans business for $50 million and his underwear business for $64 million, but retained royalty rights in each. He also opened a business in Japan. In 2000, he became embroiled in a contentious trademark infringement suit against The Warnaco Group, the company then licensed to make Calvin Klein jeans. Klein said Warnaco was damaging his reputation and his brand by changing his designs, exercising poor quality control, and selling the jeans to cheap discount stores. A settlement was reached. In 2003, Klein and Schwartz, who had remained his partner since the day the company was born, sold their business to the publicly owned Phillips-Van Heusen Corp. for $430 million, plus other considerations, including a 4.4 percent stake in PVH for both men. Klein agreed to stay on as a creative consultant.

Twice divorced and treated for substance abuse, Klein was frequently fodder for the tabloids. In 1978, his daughter, Marci – then 11 – was kidnapped and held for $100,000 ransom before being released unharmed the following day. And his ad campaigns, from the teenage Brooke Shields provocatively purring, "Nothing comes between me and my Calvins," to his overtly suggestive underwear billboards, to the sexual ambiguity of his fragrance commercials, have achieved their own notoriety. At the same time, he has been lauded by the industry. In 1973, he became the youngest designer to win a Coty Award. He won two more in 1974 and 1975. He garnered awards for his men's and women's fashions from the Council of Fashion Designers of America in 1982, 1983, and 1986, and in 1993 the CFDA picked him as Designer of the Year.

[Mort Sheinman (2nd ed.)]

KLEIN, EDWARD E. (1913–1985), U.S. Reform rabbi. Klein was born in Newark, New Jersey. Upon ordination from the Jewish Institute of Religion in New York in 1940, Klein served as assistant rabbi and director of education at the Free Synagogue, New York, for two years. He was director of the B'nai B'rith Hillel Foundation at the University of California at Berkeley. Upon the death of Stephen S. Wise in 1949, Klein succeeded him as rabbi of the Free Synagogue. Noted for involvement in community action, Klein supported causes for peace, civil liberties, civil rights, and civic reform as well as the security of the State of Israel. In 1962 he became a member of New York City's Fair Housing Practices Panel. He was chairman of the Church-State Committee of the Central Conference of American Rabbis, and the Social Action Committee of the New York Board of Rabbis. Klein was a fellow of the National Council on Religion in Higher Education (1970).

[Myron E. Schoen]

KLEIN, GEORGE (1925–), Swedish medical research scientist. Klein was born in Budapest, Hungary where he started his university education before immigrating to Sweden (1947) and earning his M.D. degree from the Karolinska Institute in Stockholm (1951). He was on the staff of that institute from 1947, initially as a research fellow and then progressing to professor and head of the Department of Tumor Biology (1957–93) and research group leader in the Microbiology and Tumor Biology Center from 1993. He was visiting professor at the Hebrew University of Jerusalem (1973–93). His research interests concerned the biology and clinical problems of cancer, and he made outstanding original contributions to defining and investigating many key issues, notably the role of anti-tumor immunity, the contribution of viral infections and in particular herpes virus infections to human cancer, and the influence of genetic abnormalities on the growth of malignant cells. These observations have had a major influence on our understanding of cancer and its control. Many of his influential scientific papers were written with his scientist wife, Eva Klein, and with collaborators in the Hebrew University. His many honors including the Harvey Prize from the Haifa Technion (1975), the Gairdner Award (1976), honorary doctorates from the Hebrew University of Jerusalem (1989) and Tel Aviv University (1994), membership in the Royal Swedish Academy of Sciences, election as foreign associate of the U.S. National Academy of Sciences, and the Robert Koch Gold Medal (1998). He was a noted thinker on broader aspects of science, memorably set out in his books *The Atheist and the Holy City* (1994), *Pieta* (1992), and *Holy City* (1994).

[Michael Denman (2nd ed.)]

KLEIN, GERDA WEISSMANN (1924–) and **KURT** (1920–2002). Holocaust survivor Gerda Klein, author, speaker, and humanitarian, is a testament to the power of hope. She and her husband, Kurt Klein, took tragedy and turned it into triumph – along the way inspiring millions of people to overcome their own personal battles.

Gerda Weissmann was only 15 years old in 1939 when Germans took over her hometown of Bielsko, Poland. She, along with her parents and brother, Artur, had led a happy and comfortable life. It was not long before the Nazis took Artur away. In 1942, Gerda was separated from her parents and sent to work in slave labor camps for three years. Her parents, brother, and entire extended family died in the Holocaust. Gerda was subject to starvation and torture, yet she never stopped praying that liberation day would come. On May 7, 1945, after a five-month death march through Eastern Europe, U.S. Army soldiers liberated Gerda Weissmann and a handful of other survivors. The first soldier on the scene was Lt. Kurt Klein.

Kurt Klein was born and raised in Waldorf, Germany. When Hitler ascended to power, Klein's parents realized Jewish people had no future in Germany. They sent 17-year-old Kurt and their other children to safety in the United States. During the *Kristallnacht* attacks on German Jews, the Kleins' home was vandalized and Kurt's parents were deported to Eastern Europe. They ultimately perished at Auschwitz. Kurt Klein was drafted in 1942 and served in the U.S. Army as an intelligence officer. In May 1945, he stumbled upon an abandoned factory in Volary, Czechoslovakia, where about 120 girls, all victims of Nazi concentration camps, were near death. One of the girls guided Lt. Klein to her fellow prisoners, most of whom lay sick and dying on the ground. With her hand, she made a sweeping gesture and quoted the German poet Goethe: "Noble be man, merciful, and good." Perhaps it was her irony – or her composure – or her compassion amidst the tragedy that struck Kurt Klein. Whatever it was, a great love affair began.

Gerda and Kurt Klein married in Paris on June 18, 1946, and settled in Buffalo, New York. He started a business in printing and editing. She wrote her autobiography, *All But My Life*, in 1957. They raised three children. But their collective experiences during their early lives motivated them to educate others about the dangers of intolerance and hatred. They traveled the world together speaking to diverse groups about the power of the human spirit and the importance of addressing the needs of the hungry.

Gerda was the subject of the Emmy- and Oscar-winning HBO documentary, *One Survivor Remembers*, based on *All But My Life*, which is now in its 57th printing. Both Kleins are part of the Testimony film, which is shown as a permanent exhibit at the U.S. Holocaust Memorial Museum in Washington, D.C. Gerda Klein appeared on *The Oprah Winfrey Show*, *CBS Sunday Morning*, and *60 Minutes*. She was also the subject of a *Nightline* broadcast that highlighted her work with Columbine High School students following the 1999 massacre at the school. Gerda and Kurt Klein helped survivors at the school cope with their feelings and empowered them to begin the healing process. The story of Kurt's indefatigable but ultimately unsuccessful efforts to save his parents was chronicled in the award-winning PBS program *America and the Holocaust: Deceit and Indifference*, part of The American Experience series.

In 2000, the Kleins wrote a book together called *The Hours After: Letters of Love and Longing*. It is a compilation of Gerda and Kurt's loving exchange of letters during their one-year separation after the Holocaust. Over the years Gerda also wrote *Promise of a New Spring*, *The Blue Rose*, *Peregrinations*, *A Passion for Sharing*, and, most recently, *A Boring Evening At Home*.

Because of the war, Gerda's formal education stopped at age 15. But her humanitarian work has earned her numerous honorary doctorates. In 2001, Gerda and Kurt received joint doctorates from Chapman University for their collective work fighting racism and intolerance.

[Julie Simon Loftsgaarden (2nd ed.)]

KLEIN, GOTTLIEB (1852–1914), rabbi and historian of religion. Klein was born in Homonna, Slovakia (then in Hungary), and received a traditional Jewish education, although he later adopted Reform Judaism. He studied at several universities, the Berlin rabbinical seminary, and later the Hochschule fuer die Wissenschaft des Judentums. After serving as rabbi at Schuettenhofen (Bohemia) and Elbing (East Prussia), in 1883 Klein became chief rabbi of Stockholm, a position he held until his death. He was an outstanding preacher, lecturer, and scholar, and his influence extended far beyond his congregation to leading liberal Swedish theologians, with many of whom he enjoyed close friendships. He also delivered discourses before King Oscar II.

Klein's main scholarly interest was early Christianity in the light of biblical and talmudic sources. Some of his works in this field are *Fader Var* (1905, "The Lord's Prayer"), *Den foersta kristna katekesen* (1908, Ger. 1910, "First Christian Catechism"), and *Studien ueber Paulus* (edited by Archbishop Nathan Soederblom, 1918). Klein also wrote "Ueber das Buch Judith" (in: *Transactions of the Eighth International Congress of Orientalists*, 1889), and *Steht die Moral des Alten Testaments wirklich auf der Stufe der Barbaren?* (1892).

BIBLIOGRAPHY: *Svensko maen och kvinnor*, 4 (1948); *Foersamlingsblad foer Mosaisko foersomlingen i Stockholm*, 13:1 (1952); L. Geiger, in AZDJ, 76 (1912), 76–77.

[Hugo Mauritz Valentin]

KLEIN, HYMAN (1908–1958), English talmudic scholar. Klein was born in London, where he attended the Etz Chaim yeshivah and Cambridge University, where he received honors in mathematics. He was principal of Aria College, Southsea, 1938–44, and headed the Liverpool Talmudical College, 1944–50. Thereafter he was in London for a short period and spent his last years in Jerusalem. Klein wrote many papers on the literary composition of the Babylonian Talmud, which were published from 1933 onwards (in: JQR, 23 (1932/33), 211–31; 28 (1937/38), 189–216). They constitute an important contribution to the analysis of the talmudic *sugya* (cf. JQR, 38 (1947/48), 67–91; 43 (1952/53), 341–63; 50 (1959/60), 124–46; *Journal of Semitic Studies*, 3 (1958), 363–72; *Tarbiz*, 31 (1961/62), 23–42). Among his other works are annotated editions of the Mishnah *Rosh Ha-Shanah* (1938), *Berakhot* (1948), and *Megillah* (1952); a Talmud correspondence course; *Introduction to the Aramaic of the Babylonian Talmud* (1943); and translations into English of Maimonides, *The Code of Maimonides, Book Eleven: Book of Torts* (1954) and of Kasher's *Encyclopaedia of Biblical Interpretation* (vol. 4, 1958). He edited and co-translated with A. Black *Maimonides' Laws of Inheritance* (1950) and revised Gandz's translation of *The Code of Maimonides, Book Three: The Book of Seasons* (1961). He was also co-translator of tractate *Nazir* (Soncino, 1936).

KLEIN, ISAAC (1905–1979), Conservative rabbi, leader, and *posek* (halakhic authority). Klein was born and raised in the town of Palanka in Ruthenia, Hungary. In 1921, he and his family immigrated to New York to join his father, who had moved there before World War I. Klein received a B.A. from City College in 1931. He began to study at *Yeshiva University, but transferred to the *Jewish Theological Seminary (JTS) where he was ordained in 1934. After ordination, he continued to study Talmud and Codes. In 1948, Klein received a Ph.D. from Harvard University.

During the 45 years of his rabbinate, Rabbi Klein served as a pulpit rabbi, army chaplain, and visiting professor at two rabbinical schools. His pulpits were in Springfield, Mass. (1934–53) and Buffalo, N.Y. (1953–72). Klein also served as a U.S. Army chaplain during World War II (1942–46) and as President *Truman's adviser on Jewish Religious Affairs to the U.S. High Commissioner of Germany (1949–50), helping to resettle displaced persons and reorganize Jewish communities in Germany after the *Shoah*.

Beginning in 1959, Klein served as visiting associate professor of Jewish Law at JTS, where he taught Practical *Halakhah* (Jewish Law). When he retired from the pulpit in 1972, he wintered in Los Angeles where he taught Jewish Law at the University of Judaism.

Klein was also a leader of the Conservative Movement, serving as president of the *Rabbinical Assembly (1958–60). He was an active member of the Committee on Jewish Law and Standards (1935–79) and served on the Joint *Bet Din* of the Conservative Movement.

Klein published a total of nine books, which can conveniently be divided into three categories: translations of three of the fourteen volumes of the Yale Judaica Series; three books relating his experiences as an army chaplain and pulpit rabbi; and three halakhic works. The third of these is his magnum opus, *A Guide to Jewish Religious Practice* (1979), which is based on the course he taught for many years at JTS. It combines a survey of most aspects of practical *halakhah* together with introductions explaining *ta'amei ha-mitzvot*, the reasons for the commandments, based on a wide range of rabbinic, medieval, and modern sources.

At the end of his 1968 article on "The *Shulḥan Arukh* after 400 Years," Rabbi Klein explains that there is a need to update the Shulḥan Arukh "at least for the Conservative Movement, and hopes that it will be helpful to *kelal Yisrael* (the collective Jewish People)." He goes on to say that the person who writes such a code must possess scholarship, saintliness, humility, and a deep awareness of and sympathy for the needs of the Jewish community. Rabbi Klein was such a person and that is why his *Guide* has become a veritable *Kiẓẓur Shulḥan Arukh* for Conservative Jews.

BIBLIOGRAPHY: H. Dicker, *Piety and Perseverance: Jews from the Carpathian Mountains* (1981), 33, 122–24; M. Lockshin, *Tradition*, 18:2 (Summer 1980), 227–30; P. Nadell, *Conservative Judaism: A Biographical Dictionary and Sourcebook* (1988), 159–61.

[David Golinkin (2nd ed.)]

KLEIN, JULIUS (1901–1984), U.S. soldier and leader of the Jewish War Veterans. Born in Chicago, Klein served in World War I as a war correspondent and a spy in Germany. He then returned to journalism and public relations. He worked as a criminal reporter for the *State Herald* in Chicago and initiated the first German-language radio broadcasts in the United States. In 1933 he joined the Illinois National Guard, becoming a lieutenant colonel in 1941. That year, he formulated a military plan called Combat Public Relations, which encompassed such techniques as propaganda and psychological warfare. During World War II he served in the Philippines and the South Pacific, where he heroically saved many lives during an explosion in New Caledonia. Klein was in charge of public relations for Generals Douglas MacArthur and Robert Richardson. In that capacity, he originated the South Pacific edition of the *Stars and Stripes* military newspaper. In 1946 he was appointed special assistant to the secretary of war. Klein was given command of the 109th Anti-Aircraft Artillery Brigade. After the war, he lent his expertise to the attempt to improve relations between Germany and the United States, and Germany and Israel. In 1954 he ran for the US Senate.

Klein retired in 1961 with the rank of major general. He was one of the leaders of the Jewish War Veterans of the U.S. and its national commander from 1947 to 1948. Under his leadership, the war veterans played an important part in the fight against antisemitism and in other Jewish activities. For example, on April 4, 1948, he staged an impressive show of support for the establishment of the State of Israel by organizing a Jewish War Veterans parade down New York's Fifth Avenue.

To honor Klein's military achievements, a permanent exhibition entitled "Major General Julius Klein: His Life and Work" has been installed at the National Museum of Jewish Military History in Washington, D.C.

[Mordechai Kaplan / Ruth Beloff (2nd ed.)]

KLEIN, JULIUS LEOPOLD (1810–1876), playwright and literary historian who wrote in German. Born in Miskolc, Hungary, Klein took a medical degree at Berlin University, but never practiced his profession. He edited *Baltische Blaetter* at Wismar (1838), and then settled in Berlin, where he became a member of the circle of K.A. Varnhagen von Ense. There he began his career as a dramatist with the publication of his tragedy *Concini* (1841), the title of which was later changed to *Maria von Medici*. Klein's later tragedy *Kavalier und Arbeiter* (1850), inspired by the revolt of the Silesian Weavers in 1844, was the first serious attempt in German drama to portray the proletariat and the new problems created by the Industrial Revolution. Like his other plays, it has a complicated plot, lacks unity, and tends to pile horror upon horror. Klein's real claim to fame is based on his monumental *Geschichte des Dramas* (1865–76), a history of drama up to Shakespeare, of which 13 volumes were completed, but not including the history of German drama. His letters were published as *Briefe von Klein an Varnhagen von Ense*, ed. J. Trostler, in: *Ungarische Rundschau* (1914).

BIBLIOGRAPHY: M. Glatzel, *Julius Leopold Klein als Dramatiker* (1914); S. Liptzin, *Weavers in German Literature* (1926), ch. 4. **ADD. BIBLIOGRAPHY:** H.H. Houben, *Jungdeutscher Sturm und Drang. Ergebnisse und Studien* (1911).

[Sol Liptzin]

KLEIN, LAWRENCE ROBERT (1920–), U.S. economist, Nobel Prize laureate. Klein was born in Omaha, Nebraska, and received his doctorate from MIT in 1944. He served on the faculties of the University of Chicago (1944–47) and the University of Michigan (1949–54). During those periods, he was research associate at the National Bureau of Economic Research (1948–50) and the Survey Research Center (1949–54). From 1954 to 1958 he was a member of the Oxford Institute of Statistics. In 1958 he was appointed professor at the University of Pennsylvania. In 1968 he began to serve as a professor of economics and finance at the university's Wharton School. There he built the Wharton model of the U.S. economy, which contains more than a thousand simultaneous equations that are solved by computers. From 1963 to 1972 he was principal investigator for the econometric model project at the Brookings Institute. In 1977 he served as president of the American Economic Association. Klein lectured at the Hebrew University in Jerusalem and was a board member of the Falk Institute for Research in Economics.

Klein received the Nobel Prize in economics in 1980 for "the creation of economic models and their application to the analysis of economic fluctuations and economic policies." After retiring from teaching, he was named Benjamin Franklin Professor Emeritus of Economics at the University of Pennsylvania.

Among his works are *The Keynesian Revolution* (1947), *Textbook of Econometrics* (1953), *An Econometric Forecasting Model* (1967), *Essay on the Theory of Economic Production* (1968), *A Textbook of Econometrics* (1974), *The Brookings Model* (with G. Fromm, 1975), *An Introduction to Econometric Forecasting Models* (with R. Young, 1980), *The Economics of Supply and Demand* (1983), *Economics in Theory and Practice* (1990), *A Quest for a More Stable World Economic System* (1993), and *Modeling Global Change* (with F. Lo, 1995).

BIBLIOGRAPHY: M. Dutta, *Economics, Econometrics, and the Link: Essays in Honor of Lawrence R. Klein* (1995); B. Hickman (ed.), *Global Econometrics: Essays in Honor of Lawrence Klein* (1983).

[Ruth Beloff (2nd ed.)]

KLEIN, MANNIE (Emmanuel; 1908–1994), U.S. trumpeter. One of the most prolific freelance musicians of the Broadway, big-band, and Hollywood studio era, the New York-born Klein began playing trumpet as a child. Three of his brothers (trumpeter Dave, violinist Sol, and bassist Merrill) were professional musicians, and he eagerly followed their path, performing with B.F. Keith's Boys' Band and the New York Police Junior Band before turning pro in his late teens. A list of the groups with whom he worked is a veritable Who's Who of the era: Red Nichols, Roger Wolfe Kahn, Benny *Goodman, Matty Malneck, the Dorsey Brothers, Lionel Hampton. He dubbed trumpet parts for Montgomery Clift in *From Here to Eternity* and an ailing Ziggy *Elman in *The Benny Goodman Story*. In the 1950s he was a mainstay of Mickey Katz's comic klezmer band.

BIBLIOGRAPHY: J. Chilton, "Manny Klein," in: *Who's Who of Jazz: Storyville to Swing Street* (1978). M. Katz, *Papa, Play for Me: The Autobiography of Mickey Katz* (2002).

[George Robinson (2nd ed.)]

KLEIN, MELANIE REIZES (1882–1960), British psychoanalyst. Born Melanie Reizes in Vienna, she settled in Budapest after her marriage to businessman Arthur Klein. There she became interested in psychoanalysis and was analyzed by Sándor Ferenzi. In 1919 she read her first paper on child development before the Budapest Psychoanalytical Society, and was subsequently invited by Karl *Abraham to practice in Berlin. Melanie Klein then began the therapy of children, interpreting their play as symbolic of fantasies and feelings of anxiety and guilt, in a manner similar to Sigmund *Freud's interpretation of dreams. On the invitation of Ernest Jones, in 1926 she moved to London, where she developed the technique of play analysis, and from 1930 began to analyze adults. Her findings aroused much controversy, but drew the support of a group of the British Psychoanalytical Society known as the "Kleinians." She expounded her main ideas in *Die Psychoanalyse des Kindes* (1932; *The Psychoanalysis of Children*, 1932, 1950^{3}), which dealt with the child's love-hate relationship with the mother and with introjection. Her monograph, *Love, Guilt and Reparation* (in *Love, Hate and Reparation*, written with Joan Riviere, 1937), stressed that the instinctual urges of the child are experienced as unconscious fantasy. Her study of these processes was an important contribution to the understanding of infantile development. Melanie Klein remains one of the best-known psychoanalysts of her time; her theories remain both influential and controversial.

BIBLIOGRAPHY: H. Segal, *Introduction to the Work of Melanie Klein* (1964), includes bibliographies; J.A. Lindon, in: F.G. Alexander et al. (eds.), *Psychoanalytic Pioneers* (1966), 360–72. **ADD. BIBLIOGRAPHY:** ODNB online; P. Grosskuth, *Melanie Klein: Her Life and Work* (1986); J. Segal, *Melanie Klein* (1992); O. Weininger, *Melanie Klein: From Theory to Reality* (1992).

[Louis Miller]

KLEIN, MORITZ (1842–1915), Hungarian rabbi and scholar. Klein, born in Miskolc, was a pupil of S.J. *Rapoport in Prague and studied at the university there. He served in Miskolc, Ungvar, Papa, and Nagybecskerek as a Liberal preacher and rabbi. In addition to publishing many sermons in Hungarian and German, he published a Hungarian translation of Maimonides' *Guide of the Perplexed, A tévelygők útmutatója* (3 vols., 1878–91), and a version in Hungarian of Jedaiah Bedersi's *Beḥinat Olam, A lélek tragédiája* (1901). A translation into Hungarian of Judah Halevi's *Kuzari* remained unfinished.

KLEIN, MORTON (1947–), president of *Zionist Organization of America. Klein revived a moribund Zionist Organization of America (ZOA) in the 1990s and made it one of the most outspoken – and often controversial – organizations on the American Jewish scene. Klein has periodically angered governments in Israel because of his vehement opposition to their policies and upset the pro-Israel lobby groups he has challenged with his own aggressive lobbying on Capitol Hill. However, he has also made ZOA one of the most visible Jewish organizations in the United States; his crusade to focus U.S. policy on American victims of Palestinian terrorism was widely credited as a success.

Klein was born in Gunzberg, Germany, in a displaced persons camp; his family immigrated to the U.S. in 1950 and settled in Philadelphia. Klein received an undergraduate degree and an M.B.A. from Temple University. In a varied career, he worked as a high school math teacher, a government economist on health policy issues, and a biostatistician for the Linus Pauling Institute of Science and Medicine.

Klein became active in Jewish life in 1990, first as an activist with the local chapter of CAMERA, a pro-Israel media watchdog group. In 1992, he was elected president of the Philadelphia chapter of ZOA and in 1993 as national president. In the campaign, Klein, an opponent of the Oslo peace agreement signed earlier that year, argued that the group should not refrain from criticizing the policies of the government of Prime Minister Yitzhak Rabin; longstanding ZOA policy discouraged criticism of Israeli governments.

In 1994, Klein organized opposition to the appointment of former *Time* magazine columnist Strobe Talbott as deputy secretary of state because of what the new ZOA leader claimed were the anti-Israel views expressed in some Talbott columns. Two years later Klein led an opposition to scholar John K. Roth as first director of the Center for Advanced Holocaust Studies for very similar reasons.

Early in his tenure, Klein also challenged the dominance of the *American Israel Public Affairs Committee (AIPAC) in lobbying Congress for pro-Israel causes, objecting to AIPAC's support for the Oslo agreement. The issue of lobbying against Israeli government policies was a factor in the decision by several local ZOA chapters, including Baltimore and Pittsburgh, to disaffiliate from the national group. In 1994, Klein created a Peace Accord Monitoring Group in Congress to focus on Yasser Arafat's violations of the Oslo Accords.

Klein was particularly effective in highlighting the issue of Americans killed by Palestinian terrorists, pressing for a more active State Department role in investigating and prosecuting such crimes and legislation spotlighting the issue.

After President George W. Bush put U.S. policy behind creation of a Palestinian state in 2002, Klein's ZOA began a vigorous campaign of documenting Yasser Arafat's violations of the conditions the president had set for statehood.

While most major Jewish and pro-Israel groups supported Israel's withdrawal from Gaza under Prime Minister Ariel Sharon, Klein and ZOA waged an extensive campaign against the unilateral action in Israel and in the United States.

Under Klein's presidency, ZOA president term length limits were removed. Also ZOA opened a Washington office in 1996 and a division for campus activities in 2001. The group also created a Center for Law and Justice, which uses the courts to force implementation of pro-Israel provisions in the law.

[James D. Besser (2nd ed.)]

KLEIN, PHILIP (1849–1926), U.S. Orthodox rabbi. Klein, who was born in Baracs, Hungary, was ordained by the Hildesheimer Rabbinical Seminary of Berlin in 1871. Klein served as rabbi in Kiev (1874–80) and Libau, Latvia (1880–91). Russian antisemitism, exacerbated by the policies of Alexander III, caused Klein to leave Russia for the U.S. in 1891. He served as rabbi of the First Hungarian Congregation Ohab Zedek, New York City, from 1891 until 1926, was a leader of the war-relief drive (1914) in the U.S., and was serving as president of the U.S. Agudat Israel movement at the time of his death. Extremely active in New York City's Orthodox religious life, Klein was one of the very few such rabbis with middle-class acculturated congregations.

KLEIN, PHILIP (1890–), U.S. social worker. Klein was born in Hungary and immigrated to the United States in 1902. After receiving his training in social sciences in New York City, he directed many large-scale research projects, including a national survey of unemployment (1921–22) and a social study of Pittsburgh, Pennsylvania (1938). From 1923 to 1926 he served as the executive director of the American Association of Social Workers, and from 1927 to 1953 he was first director of research and later professor of research, New York School of Social Work. He was research director, White House Conference on Children in a Democracy (1939–40). Klein served as consultant to the American Jewish Joint Distribution Committee in planning the Paul Baerwald School of Social Work, Versailles, France (1948–50), and on social work manpower needs in Israel (1954–56). He was a United Nations expert assigned to the Israel Ministry of Social Welfare in 1959. Later he was a consultant to the Department of Welfare of the State of Pennsylvania. During the 1930s and 1940s he led a minority group of social work educators who favored greater emphasis on the social action functions of social workers rather than the clinical or treatment emphasis. Klein proposed broad governmental social welfare programs and wrote widely on the subject.

His works include *Prison Methods in New York State* (1920); *The Burden of Unemployment* (1923); articles in the *Encyclopaedia of Social Sciences* (1930–35); *A Social Study of Pittsburgh* (1938); *Next Steps in Dealing with Delinquency* (1945); and *From Philanthropy to Social Welfare* (1968).

ADD. BIBLIOGRAPHY: C. Kasius (ed.), *New Directions in Social Work* (1954).

[Jacob Neusner]

KLEIN, RALPH (1931–), Israeli basketball coach. Klein was the first coach to lead an Israeli basketball team, Macabbi Tel Aviv, to a European championship. Klein, a German-born Holocaust survivor, arrived in Israel after the end of the war. During the 1960s he played for Maccabi Tel Aviv under Coach Yehoshua *Rosen. After his retirement, he became Rosen's assistant coach and then head coach in 1969. He took the team to 11 national championships and 10 national cups. The summit of his career came in 1977, when Maccabi Tel Aviv won the European championship, defeating Italy's Mobil Girgi 78–77 in the final. On the way there Maccabi also defeated CSKA Moskow in a historic match played on a neutral court in view of the Soviet Union's break with Israel after the Six-Day War. Klein led the team to another three European finals. As coach of Israel's national team as well, he took it to a second-place finish in the European championships of 1979. In 1984, as coach of the German national team, he appeared at the Olympic Games in Los Angeles. From 1973 he taught basketball coaching at the Wingate Institute. On Israel's 50th anniversary he was awarded the Jubilee Prize for his achievements, and in 2004 was selected as a torch bearer on Independence Day. Although in his seventies and fighting cancer, he coached a girls team that won a school championship in 2004. In 2006 he received the Israel Prize.

WEBSITES: www.most.gov.il; www.tzahevet.co.il.

[Shaked Gilboa (2nd ed.)]

KLEIN, SALOMON WOLF (1814–1867), French rabbi. Born in Bischheim near Strasbourg into a family of chiropodists, he began his secular studies at the age of 18 and, in a few years, he acquired an extensive knowledge which included Latin and Greek. He then graduated from the rabbinical seminary of Metz (1839), and served as rabbi successively at Bischheim, Durmenach, and Rixheim (Haut-Rhin). Klein distinguished himself by numerous publications and by his indefatigable struggle against every attempt at reform. He became the leader of French Orthodoxy, but was unsuccessful in his candidacy for the office of chief rabbi of Paris. In 1850 Klein was appointed chief rabbi of the consistory of the Haut-Rhin department at Colmar, and for a long time was also its president. Here he came under attack following a change in composition of the consistory through the accession of liberal elements. His main works are *Nouvelle grammaire hébraïque raisonnée et comparée* (1846), *Guide du traducteur du Pentateuque* (2 vols. 1852–53), *Le Judaïsme ou la Vérité sur le Talmud* (1859), *Recueil de lettres pastorales et de discours d'inauguration* (1863). He also published some pamphlets in Hebrew, among them *Ma'aneh Rakh al Ḥazut Kashah* (1846), *Mi-Penei Koshet* against Zacharias *Frankel (1861), and *Ha-Emet ve-ha-Shalom Ehavu* (1861), on the position of S.J. *Rapoport vis-à-vis Frankel.

BIBLIOGRAPHY: P. Klein, in: *Bulletin de nos Communautés*, 10 (1954), nos. 10–12.

[Moshe Catane]

KLEIN, SAMUEL (1886–1940), historian and geographer of Ereẓ Israel. Born in Szilas Balhas, Hungary, Klein studied at the Berlin Rabbinical Seminary, where Hirsch *Hildesheimer aroused his interest in the geography of Ereẓ Israel, and at German universities. From 1909 to 1913 he served as rabbi in Dolnja Tuzla, Bosnia, and 1913–28 at Ersekujvar (Nove Zamky, Slovakia), serving as a military chaplain in World War I. His first visit to Palestine took place in 1908 with the aid of a grant from the Gesellschaft zur Foerderung der Wissenschaft des Judentums, and in 1924 he was appointed lecturer at the Institute of Jewish Studies in Jerusalem (incorporated in the Hebrew

University in 1925), while continuing until 1928 his rabbinical work in his community, and even lecturing at the Vienna Seminary. From 1929 Klein was professor of historical topography of Ereẓ Israel at the Hebrew University. For eight years he was president of the Jewish Palestine Exploration Society and was active in the Va'ad ha-Lashon as well as many other educational ventures.

Klein's great contribution to the study of the history and geography of Ereẓ Israel was his research into Talmud and Midrash as a primary source for the country's topography and the history of its settlement ("*Siedlungsgeschichte*"). He branched out into biblical and apocryphal geography, using also Hellenistic (Josephus) and patristic (Eusebius, etc.) sources, and making important contributions to Jewish epigraphy. Apart from numerous articles in the leading learned periodicals and his thesis (*Beitraege zur Geographie und Geschichte Galilaeas*, 1909), his major works include *Juedisch-palaestinisches Corpus Inscriptionum* (1920); *Ever ha-Yarden ha-Yehudi* (1925); *Toledot ha-Yishuv ha-Yehudi be-Ereẓ Yisrael*... (1935); *Toledot Ḥakirat Ereẓ Yisrael*... (1937); *Ereẓ Yehudah* (1939); and *Ereẓ ha-Galil* (1946). Klein also edited *Sefer ha-Yishuv* (vol. 1, 1939), and contributed most of the articles on Ereẓ Israel in the German *Encyclopaedia Judaica* and the *Juedisches Lexikon*.

BIBLIOGRAPHY: Z. Harkavy, in: *Yavneh*, 1 (1939), 1–3; I. Werfel, *ibid.*, 4–44 (bibl.); BJPES, 7:3–4 (1940), dedicated to the memory of S. Klein (incl. bibl.); B.M., *ibid.*, 4:1–4 (1937), 83–94 (a bibliography); S.D. Loewinger, in: S. Federbush (ed.), *Ḥokhmat Yisrael be-Ma'arav Eiropah*, 2 (1963), 240–8.

[Michael Avi-Yonah]

KLEIN, SAMUEL SHMELKA (d. 1875), Hungarian rabbi. Klein was a disciple of Shalom Ulman Ḥarif of Lakenbach. After serving in Balkany, he was appointed rabbi of Huszt (Mármaros region), a large city which had authority over half the district. There he founded a great yeshivah. In 1860 he moved to Szöllős, although it was a much smaller town. In Szöllős Klein became very well known, many Hungarian rabbis turning to him with their difficulties. Because he inclined to Ḥasidism, his admirers began to relate extraordinary stories about him. He was the author of *Ẓeror ha-Ḥayyim* (1876), novellae on the Talmud. His sons were Jacob, rabbi of Técső and Bilke; Moses, rabbi of Csev; Shalom, rabbi of Halmi; and Phinehas Ḥayyim who succeeded him in Szöllős.

BIBLIOGRAPHY: S.Z. Klein, *Rabbi Shmelka* (Heb., 1956).

[Itzhak Alfassi]

KLEIN, THEODORE (**Theo**; 1920–), French lawyer and Jewish communal leader, Klein was born in Paris and completed his studies in law and political science there. He was actively involved in the Jewish Resistance during WWII. A successful business lawyer, he worked in France, Africa, and Israel (as a member of the Israel Lawyers' Association since 1970). Both a French and Israeli citizen, he was also extremely active in Jewish communal affairs: he was president of CRIF, the political representative body of French Jewish institutions (1983–89), and president of the European Jewish Congress, (1986–91), which he helped found and headed in critical periods, such as the first visit of Arafat in Paris. His term as leader of the French Jewish community coincided with an increase in the influence of the community during the tenure of President Mitterrand, who was a personal friend of Klein. Klein is also close to the leaders of the French Socialist Party and the Israeli Labor Party. He took a leading role in the negotiations to remove the Carmelite convent from Auschwitz (*L'affaire du carmel d'Auschwitz*, 1991). Among his books are *Libérez la Torah, Moïse, l'homme et la loi: une relecture* (2001), where he calls upon the Jews to go directly to the text of the Bible and to free themselves from centuries of commentary. He was also president of the *Musée d'Art et d'Histoire du Judaïsme in Paris from 2001.

[Gideon Kouts / Nelly Hansson (2nd ed.)]

KLEIN, WILHELM (1850–1924), classical archaeologist. Born in Karansebes, Hungary, Klein taught at the German University of Prague. He made field trips to Greece and Italy on behalf of the Austrian government primarily to study Greek vase painting. He published a book on Euphronios (1879) who was one of the outstanding Attic red-figure vase painters active between 515 and 500 B.C.E. It was the first comprehensive study of the Athenian ceramists and their great potters' workshops. In 1898–99 he published two books on Praxiteles. Here he tried to reconstruct from existing Roman copies the work of the leading sculptors of the Greek classical period whose work had been lost or destroyed. In his last publication, *Vom antiken Rokoko* (1921), Klein distinguishes between two stylistic trends, the baroque and the rococo, within the development of Hellenistic sculpture.

[Penuel P. Kahane]

KLEIN, YVES (1928–1962), painter and judo expert. Klein was born in Nice. He first became a jazz musician and then went to Paris to study judo in which he became an expert. In Paris he met the French artists Arman and Pascal, and as a result began experimenting with painting and collage techniques. He traveled extensively, became a teacher at the National Spanish Judo Federation, Madrid, and opened his own judo school in Paris in 1955. By this time Klein was established as one of the most eclectic and daring younger European artists. In 1956 he figured in the "Festival of Avant-Garde Art" in Marseilles alongside Agam, Soto, and Tinguely. The following year he inaugurated his famous "blue period," in which both paintings and sculptures were only in this color. Klein was one of the most brilliant and influential members of the post-war school of "anti-art" protagonists. His ideas and philosophy stemmed directly from the informality and gestural "magic" which originated with Marcel Duchamp. He sought to bring back excitement and freedom into art, and at the same time to make it more "real," and more meaningful to ordinary people. In addition to his preference for monochrome canvases, he used live nude figures, daubed with paint, to make impressions on a flat space; he also introduced photographic conceptualism and everyday objects in the art statement. He was one of the founders of the "New Realism" movement which included artists like Arman, Rauschenberg, Tinguely. Since his death Klein has been rediscovered and reclaimed as one of the major artists of the century.

[Charles Samuel Spencer]

KLEINMANN, MOSHE (1870–1948), Hebrew and Yiddish author and editor. Born in Holptchinitz, Podolia, Kleinmann was an active Zionist from a young age, and at the end of the 1890s he published his own and other writers' popular pamphlets in Yiddish on Jewish history, the Jewish people, and Zionism. He began his career in journalism in *Ha-Shiloʾaḥ* in 1896 with criticisms of *Aḥad Ha-Am's ideology. After the February Revolution in 1917 in Russia, he was one of the editors of the short-lived Hebrew daily *Ha-Am*. In 1921 he settled in Berlin, and became a member of the editorial board of the central organ of the Zionist organization, *Ha-Olam, and from 1923 until his last days he was its editor in chief. Along with the paper, he moved to London in 1924 and then to Jerusalem in 1936. A selection of his journalism was gathered in three books: *Be-Hitorer Am* (1943), *Leʾom ba-Nekhar* (1944), and *Bein Lehavot* (1944). Other of his works are *Demuyyot ve-Komot* (essays on Hebrew literature, 1928), monographs on Theodor Herzl (1944), on Chaim Weizmann (1945), on Ḥibbat Zion (1940), and the General Zionists (1945). He edited a Hebrew Zionist Encyclopedia *(Enẓiklopedyah le-Ẓiyyonut)*, but succeeded in publishing only one volume before his death (1947).

BIBLIOGRAPHY: Rejzen, Leksikon, 3 (1929), 682–6; Kressel, Leksikon, 2 (1967), 767.

[Getzel Kressel]

KLEMPERER, GUTMANN (Gumpel; 1815–1884), Bohemian rabbi and historian. A member of an old Prague family formerly named Klopper, he attended the yeshivot of Nehemiah *Trebitsch in Prague and Moses *Sofer in Pressburg. While studying at Prague University, he was also a pupil of Solomon Judah *Rapoport. From 1843 until his death, Klemperer was rabbi of *Tabor, and in 1868 took charge of the district rabbinate formerly located in *Koloděje (Kaladei). His moderately reformed divine service influenced other Bohemian communities. In 1858 he published *Ḥayyei Yehonatan*, a biography of Jonathan *Eybeschuetz and an apologia of the latter's stand in his controversy with Jacob Emden. From 1861 until his death, 16 of his articles on talmudic subjects appeared in *Pascheles' almanac. His articles on *Judah b. Bezalel and other Prague rabbis, which appeared from 1873 until 1884, were published in an English translation by Guido Kisch in *Historia Judaica* (vol. 12, 1950). Klemperer also published a series of articles on the Kabbalah (1875–79) and planned to write a history of Bohemian Jewry. Excerpts from parts of his German translation of David *Gans' *Ẓemaḥ David* were published after his death by Moritz Gruenwald (1890). Fifty-two letters to his friend Simon *Hock, expressing his optimistic views on the Jewry of his time, are preserved in the Jewish State Museum in Prague.

BIBLIOGRAPHY: G. Klemperer, in: *Zeitschrift fuer die Geschichte der Juden in der Tschechoslowakei*, 4 (1934), 25–27; L. Klemperer, *ibid.*, 3 (1933), 203–9; S. Poper, in: *Vèstnik židovské náboženské obce v Praze*, 11 (1949), no. 9, 28; G. Kisch, in: HJ, 12 (1950), 33; D. Muneles, in: *Judaica Bohemiae*, 1 (1965), 69–74.

[Meir Lamed]

KLEMPERER, OTTO (1885–1973), conductor and composer. Born in Breslau, Klemperer studied in Frankfurt and Berlin. In 1905 he met *Mahler, who exercised a decisive influence on his career. On Mahler's recommendation he was appointed chorus master and conductor in Prague (1907) and then in Hamburg (1910–12). His next appointments were in Cologne (1917–24) and Wiesbaden (1924–27). He conducted a wide range of contemporary music and offered a less overtly emotional interpretation of the classics than had been common among older conductors. His period as conductor of the Kroll Opera in Berlin (1927–31) was of crucial importance in the development of opera in the first half of the 20th century. He introduced new works by Janaček, *Schoenberg, Stravinsky, and Hindemith. From 1931 he conducted in Berlin, but in 1933 was compelled to immigrate to the U.S. Klemperer became director of the Los Angeles Philharmonic, reorganized the Pittsburgh Symphony Orchestra, and undertook tours to various countries. Illness and accidents interrupted his career, but he returned to the podium in spite of increasing physical handicaps. His next engagements were at the Hungarian State Opera (1947–50) and the newly formed Philharmonia Orchestra in London. In 1970 he conducted in Jerusalem and accepted Israeli citizenship. Klemperer was considered the last of the great conductors in the grand German tradition. His performances were notable above all for their heroic dimensions and his architectural grasp. He was admired for his interpretations of Bruckner, Beethoven, and Mahler. Klemperer studied composition with Schoenberg in the mid-1930s. His output includes several operas, about 100 lieder, string quartets, and symphonies. Among his publications are *Erinnerungen an Gustav Mahler* (1960) and *Klemperer on Music* (ed. M. Andersen, 1986).

ADD. BIBLIOGRAPHY: Grove online; MGG; P. Heyworth. *Otto Klemperer: His Life and Times* (1983–96).

[Uri (Erich) Toeplitz / Naama Ramot (2nd ed.)]

KLEMPERER, PAUL (1887–1964), U.S. pathologist. Born in Vienna, Klemperer studied law but transferred to medicine. In 1923 he went to the New York Postgraduate School of Medicine and three years later was appointed pathologist to New York's Mount Sinai Hospital. Klemperer's careful research into microscopic patterns led to the understanding of several diseases. His research was in lymphomas and the structure of the spleen. With co-workers, he described the pathology of malignant nephrosclerosis and a variety of newly recognized diseases of blood vessels, alimentary tract, and the hematopoietic system. The culmination of his research was the recognition of the significance of altered intermediate substances in systemic connective tissue disease.

[Fred Rosner]

KLEMPERER, VICTOR (1881–1960), German professor of Romance languages and literature. Klemperer was born in Landsberg (Warthe) as the ninth child in his family. He was the son of a Reform rabbi, and a cousin of the famous conductor Otto *Klemperer and brother of the surgeon Georg Klemperer, who was a physician to Lenin. Klemperer moved to Berlin at the age of nine and studied German, French literature, and theater in Munich, Geneva, Paris, and Berlin. In 1906 he married Eva Schlemmer and converted to Protestantism. In 1913 he was awarded a Ph.D. for his dissertation on *Die Zeitromane Friedrich Spielhagens und ihre Wurzeln* (1913). He then specialized in French literature and wrote his professorial dissertation on *Montesquieu* (2 vols. 1914/15). He held his first chair of French literature and history of literature at the University of Dresden. During his tenure at the university he published various academic articles and monographs; among them his *Idealistische Literaturgeschichte* (1929) in which he expressed his notion of the symbiosis between language and cultural history.

When the Nazis came to power in 1933 Klemperer was deprived of his academic position and isolated. Nonetheless, he continued to express his feelings as a German patriot. He survived with the help of his non-Jewish wife and fled Dresden for the last few months of the war. Klemperer returned to Dresden after the war and joined the Communist Party in 1945 but distanced himself from its ideas. Living in the former GDR, Klemperer was allowed by the party to pursue his career ambitiously. His most important book, *LTI. Notizbuch eines Philologen* (1947), focused on the speech and language of Nazism. The LTI stood for Lingua Tertii Imperii, the language of the Third Reich with its barrage of abbreviations and euphemisms and its exploitation of humanity. Klemperer became a significant cultural figure in East Germany, teaching at the universities of Greifswald and Halle. He even became a delegate of the Cultural Union in the GDR parliament. However, he despaired of the political situation and called the prevailing language of the Communists during the Cold War Lingua Quartii Imperii. This language in Klemperer's opinion closely resembled the LTI but he himself also used it when polemicizing against West Germany. Klemperer's desire for recognition was not satisfied. Obtaining a chair at the famous Humboldt University and the national award of the former GDR seemed not to be honorable enough.

In West Germany Klemperer remained unknown until his diaries written during the Nazi persecution were published in the 1990s. They became a national bestseller and the basis of a TV series. His first diary, covering the years 1918 to 1933, was published under the title *Leben sammeln, nicht fragen wozu und warum* (1996). His personal notes from 1933 to 1945, *Ich will Zeugnis ablegen bis zum letzten* (1995), became a means to cope with his desolate situation and were meant to be a cultural history of the time and a testimony of daily tyranny. It was followed by the publication of his diaries from June through December 1945, *Und alles ist so schwankend* (1996). His ambivalence between official political assimilation and his personal liberal thinking during that time can be retraced in his publication of personal notes between 1945 and 1959, *So sitze ich zwischen den Stuehlen* (1999).

BIBLIOGRAPHY: J.W. Young, "From LTI to LQI: Victor Klemperer on Totalitarian Language," in: *German Studies Review*, 28 (2005), 45–64; S. Landt, *Faschismuskritik aus dem Geist des Nationalismus: Victor Klemperers antifaschistische Sprachkritik* (2002); S.E. Aschheim, *Scholem, Arendt, Klemperer: intimate chronicles in turbulent times.* (2001); K. Fischer-Hupe, *Victor Klemperers "LTI. Notizbuch eines Philologen": ein Kommentar* (2001).

[Ann-Kristin Koch (2nd ed.)]

KLENICKI, LEON (1930–), rabbi and interfaith leader. Klenicki was born in Buenos Aires, Argentina, and attended the University of Buenos Aires. He received his B.A. from the University of Cincinnati in 1963 and his M.H.L. and ordination from the *Hebrew Union College in 1967. In 1992, HUC-JIR awarded him an honorary Ph.D. Immediately after ordination, he returned to Buenos Aires to serve as director of the Latin American Office of the *World Union for Progressive Judaism. In 1969, he was appointed rabbi of Congregation Emanu-El in Buenos Aires. While in Argentina, Klenicki edited and published Spanish and Hebrew versions of a new Reform **siddur*, a Passover **Haggadah* and (together with Roberto Graetz) a High Holiday **mahzor*. He also launched a life-long career in interfaith relations when he addressed the first Latin American meeting of Jews and Catholics in Bogotá, Colombia. This historic conclave, organized by the *Anti-Defamation League and CELAM (Latin American Episcopal Conference) and held during the visit of Pope Paul VI to the continent, paved the way for future dialogue and interreligious work. Klenicki was authorized by CELAM and the Argentine Council of Jews and Christians to undertake a study of catechisms and Catholic religious texts, the first of its kind to be done in South America. His final recommendations were presented to the Bishops Conference in Argentina for a revision of the depiction of Jews and Judaism in Catholic texts. He traveled to Rome on behalf of the Council of Jews and Christians for study sessions at the Vatican. He also served as an advisor on interfaith affairs for the DAIA, the central Jewish organization in Argentina.

In 1973, Klenicki moved to the national headquarters of the Anti-Defamation League in New York City as head of its Jewish-Catholic Relations Department. In 1984, he became director of ADL's Department of Interfaith Affairs and the organization's co-representative to the Vatican, holding both these positions until his retirement in 2001 and his elevation to director emeritus, Interfaith Affairs. While at ADL he initiated programs with Christian organizations, seminaries and churches to revise and improve the depiction of Jews in their teaching, publications, preaching and liturgy, and lectured throughout the world. He also advised ADL on programs and activities involving Jewish-Christian relations in Latin America. Publications he initiated and edited during his tenure at ADL include: *The Passover Celebration*, a Passover *Haggadah* for an interfaith service published by ADL and the Archdiocese of Chicago, the text of which has been translated into Portuguese and Spanish; *Face to Face: An Interreligious Bulletin*; *Du'Siach*, a rabbinical interreligious bulletin; *In Dialogue, Interfaith Focus*; and *Nuestro Encuentro*, a Spanish-language bulletin directed at the Hispanic community in the United States.

In 2002, Klenicki was appointed the first Hugo Gryn Fellow at The Centre for Jewish-Christian Relations, Cambridge University, England, where he lectured and taught. Concurrently, he was selected as a scholar-at-large at the Graymoor Ecumenical & Interreligious Institute and was a visiting professor of Jewish Theology at Leuven Catholic University in Belgium. He has also taught at Immaculate Conception Seminary, Huntington, N.Y., and was appointed by the government of Argentina as a member scholar of CEANA, the Ministry of Foreign Affairs Commission that investigated Nazi activities in Argentina from 1933 to 1945. He was a founding member of the Interfaith Theological Forum, established at the Pope John Paul II Center in Washington D.C. in 2004. In 2001, the International Catholic-Jewish Liaison Committee honored him for his "outstanding contributions to the work of reconciliation between the Catholic Church and the Jewish people."

Klenicki has written or edited many published works on Jewish religious thought and interreligious dialogue. Among the most notable are *A Dictionary of the Christian-Jewish Dialogue* (co-edited with Geoffrey Wigoder, 2004); *In Our Time: The Flowering of Jewish-Catholic Dialogue* (with Dr. Eugene J. Fisher, National Conference of Catholic Bishops, 1990); *A Challenge Long Delayed: The Diplomatic Exchange Between the Holy See and the State of Israel* (1996, documenting the Vatican's historic recognition of Israel); *Believing Today: Jew and Christian in Conversation* (with Rev. Richard John Neuhaus and Father Peter Stravinskas, 1989); and *Toward a Theological Encounter: Jewish Understandings of Christianity* (1991).

[Bezalel Gordon]

KLEPFISH, SAMUEL ZANVIL (1820–1902), Polish rabbi. Born in Nemirov, Klepfish studied under Moses Judah Leib, *av bet din* of Kutno, who in his old age immigrated to Ereẓ Israel, and who implanted in Klepfish the love of Ereẓ Israel. Klepfish, who belonged to the family of Motele the Ḥasid, one of the first *dayyanim* of Warsaw, was already as a youth appointed to decide halakhic questions in Warsaw. With Jacob *Gesundheit's resignation from the position of rabbi of Warsaw, the post was abolished and Klepfish was appointed (1875) to succeed him, but given the title of *av bet din* only. Regarded as one of the outstanding halakhic authorities of his time, he received queries from all over the world. In 1888 Klepfish investigated the problem of the sabbatical year in connection with the new agricultural settlements in Ereẓ Israel. A consultation of Polish rabbis took place in his house and, with his colleagues Samuel *Mohilever and Joshua Kutner, he issued the permission to work during the sabbatical year 1889, upon which the present-day permission is based. Well known as a communal worker and interested in all Jewish problems, both in Poland and abroad, he was in contact with communal leaders in Kovno, St. Petersburg, and London. Despite the fact that he was a *Mitnagged* of the school of *Ḥayyim b. Isaac of Volozhin, Klepfish was highly respected and esteemed by the Ḥasidim of Warsaw who submitted to him all matters of *halakhah*, and he was equally accepted by the *maskilim*, who were influential in Warsaw. His son, Motele, and sons-in-law Samuel David Kahana and Ḥayyim Leib Yadkovski, were appointed rabbis of Warsaw during his lifetime and sat together with him at the consultations of rabbis of the community. His third son-in-law, Alba Ḥayyim Miklishansky, served as preacher in the large Nozik synagogue of Warsaw. Another son-in-law, Ḥayyim Fein, was rabbi of Radzyn.

BIBLIOGRAPHY: Flinker, in: EG, 1 (Warsaw, 1953), 299.

KLEPFISZ, IRENA (1941–), U.S. poet, essayist, Yiddishist, and political activist. Born in the Warsaw ghetto, Klepfisz is the daughter of Michal Klepfisz, a ghetto hero who died early in the uprising, and Rose Perczykow Klepfisz, who survived the Holocaust by passing as a Pole. Klepfisz spent the war in a Polish orphanage and was reunited with her mother after liberation. After a short stay in Sweden, they entered the United States in 1949, where Klepfisz learned English and also studied Yiddish at Workmen's Circle Yiddish schools. She earned her B.A. at the City College of New York and her Ph.D. at the University of Chicago.

Self-described as a Jew, a survivor of the Holocaust, a lesbian, a poet, a teacher, and an activist, Klepfisz's poems and essays reflected her commitment to socialist secular Judaism and to the challenge of living Jewishly as a lesbian feminist. As in her signature poem, "Bashert," her work often blended Yiddish with English. Klepfisz founded a feminist magazine, *Conditions*, co-edited *A Tribe of Dina: A Jewish Woman's Anthology* (1986), and *A Jewish Woman's Call for Peace: A Handbook for Jewish Women on the Israeli/Palestinian Conflict* (1990). Her collections of poetry include *Periods of Stress* (1977); *Keeper of Accounts* (1982); *A Few Words in the Mother Tongue: Poems Selected and New (1971–1990)* (1991); and *Dreams of an Insomniac: Jewish Feminist Essays, Speeches, and Diatribes* (1990), which also contains prose pieces.

BIBLIOGRAPHY: E. Torten Beck, Introduction to *Dreams of an Insomniac* (1990); A. Rich, Introduction to *A Few Words in the Mother Tongue* (1991).

[Myrna Goldenberg (2nd ed.)]

KLETSK (Pol. **Kleck**), town in Minsk district, Belarus, formerly within Poland. A document of 1529 confirms the existence of a community in the town. At that time, Isaac *Jozefowicz of Brest held various leases in Kletsk. In 1552 living there were four Jewish families, who owned their houses and land outside town. Tax assessments of 1556 and 1563 indicate that the community was regarded as one of the most important in Lithuania. According to the regulations of the *Council of Lithuania of 1623, the Kletsk community was under the jurisdiction of the Pinsk community.

The old synagogue (*bet ha-midrash*) of the community was built during the late 17th century, and several years later a Jewish cemetery was opened. Construction of the Great Synagogue was completed in 1796, by the town owner, Count Radziwill. There were 29 Jewish poll tax payers in 1766. Noted rabbis of Kletsk during the 18th century were Michael Eisenstadt and his son Moses. The philosopher Solomon *Maimon lived in the neighborhood of Kletsk for several years. R. Meir Berlin (Bar-Ilan; 1880–1949), who was the leader of the Mizrachi movement, was born and raised there. In 1811 there were 662 Jewish male inhabitants in Kletsk and its surroundings, of whom 65 were craftsmen (33 tailors) and 40 lived in the villages. The community numbered 2,138 persons in 1847. In 1885 a considerable part of the town was destroyed by fire. In the 19th and 20th centuries Jews lived mainly from trade in farm products, though some dealt in crafts. The economic crisis which ensued compelled many Jews to emigrate from the town. The authors Yehoshua *Barzillai and Benzion *Eisenstadt lived in Kletsk. Jews from Kletsk also immigrated to Ereẓ Israel during the Second and Third Aliyah. In 1897 there were 3,415 Jews (73% of the total population) living in Kletsk.

In the first democratic elections to the municipality of Kletsk, held in 1918, 17 of the 24 delegates elected to the municipal council were Jews, one of whom was appointed vice-mayor. In 1932, when the Jewish delegates opposed the arbitrary limitation of their number in the municipal council, the authorities made an abortive attempt to accuse them of having violated the regulations concerning foreign currency and the trade in gold. In 1921 there were 4,190 Jews (74%) in Kletsk, of whom 40% were occupied in crafts and 30% in shopkeeping; the wealthiest engaged in the horse and cattle trade and the lease of orchards. In 1921, the Slutsk yeshivah in Kletsk was headed by Aaron *Kotler, who was one of the leading yeshivah heads of his time. There were also a reformed *ḥeder* (founded in 1903), a Hebrew *Tarbut school (from 1924), and a Beth Jacob school in Kletsk. The Zionist parties, particularly the *He-Ḥalutz organization, were strong in the community.

[Arthur Cygielman]

1939–1941

In the fall of 1939 Kletsk came under Soviet rule and Jews from the western parts of Poland found refuge there. Under the Soviet regime, large apartments and enterprises were nationalized, and the yeshivah building was requisitioned for a municipal club (the Jewish population declined at first to attend). The three Jewish high schools were merged into one school. The language of instruction was Yiddish until 1940–41, when the school became Russian.

Under the Nazis

On June 25, 1941, Kletsk fell to German troops. A Belorussian police force was set up and began attacking the Jewish population. On Oct. 24, 1941, 35 Jews were arrested on charges of Communism and were shot and buried near the Catholic cemetery. A Judenrat was set up by the German authorities, headed by Itzhak Czerkowicz. On Oct. 30, 1941, the Jews were ordered to assemble in the marketplace, where they were surrounded by Germans and Lithuanians. They were divided into two separate groups. About 1,400 persons were led to the Great Synagogue and kept alive; the second group of 3,880 were murdered near the Catholic cemetery. The *Aktion* was commanded by *Einsatzkommando* 8. On July 21, 1942, the Germans came to liquidate the ghetto. Upon a sign from the underground headed by Moshe Fish, its members set fire to the ghetto houses. Some were burned alive, others shot, and about 400 tried to escape, but only a few dozen succeeded in reaching the forests. Some of them were the founders of the Jewish partisan unit which operated under the command of Lyova Gilchik in the Kopil woods. In summer of 1944, after Kletsk was liberated, some 25 survivors, most of them partisans, returned to the town but soon left for the West.

[Aharon Weiss / Shmuel Spector (2nd ed.)]

BIBLIOGRAPHY: S. Dubnow (ed.), *Pinkas ha-Medinah* (1925), nos. 44, 89; A.L. Feinstein, *Ir Tehillah* (1886), 57, 111; S. Ginzburg, *Ketavim Historiyyim: Ha-Malshin Binyamin Goldberg (Brafman)* (1944); *Pinkas Kletsk* (Heb. and Yid., 1959).

KLETZKI, PAUL (1900–1973), conductor. Born in Lodz, Poland, Kletzki was a violinist in the Lodz Philharmonic Orchestra, took up conducting in Berlin, and in 1931 was invited by Wilhelm Furtwaengler to conduct the Berlin Philharmonic Orchestra. Compelled to leave Germany in 1933, he settled in Switzerland. After World War II, he conducted in various countries, shared the Israel Philharmonic Orchestra's 1955 European tour with Paul Paray, and in 1958 was appointed conductor of the Dallas Symphony Orchestra in Texas. In 1967, Kletzki was appointed conductor of the Suisse Romande Orchestra of Geneva. He excelled in romantic music, but also promoted contemporary works.

KLEY, EDUARD (**Israel**; 1789–1867), German pedagogue and Reform preacher. Orphaned at an early age, Kley studied Talmud at Breslau and then became tutor to the Beer family of Berlin. There he preached in Israel *Jacobson's private temple and associated with L. *Zunz, Auerbach, and other reformers. In 1817–18 he and C.S. Ginsburg published in Berlin *Die deutsche Synagoge*, which proposed a complete liturgy in German. Moving to *Hamburg as director of the Jewish free school there, Kley preached in the Hamburg Temple, delivering sermons on Sunday and introducing the organ and a choir. He composed numerous hymns imbued with prevalent Romantic themes. Considered one of the leading preachers of his day, Kley published many collections of his hymns and sermons, which were indebted to F. *Schleiermacher and other Protestant preachers. His catechism, published in 1814, influenced Isaac *Leeser, the American reformer. Kley stressed the devotional aspect of religion in his sermons and held that the essence of Judaism was exemplified in the three fundamental principles of Joseph *Albo – belief in the existence of God, belief in revelation, and belief in divine retribution.

BIBLIOGRAPHY: H. Jonas, *Lebensskizze des Herrn Doctor Eduard Kley...* (1859); A. Altmann (ed.), *Studies in Nineteenth Century Jewish Intellectual History* (1964), index; D. Philipson, *The Reform Movement in Judaism* (1931), 23, 30, 227; M. Eliav, *Ha-Ḥinnukh ha-Yehudi be-Germanyah bi-Ymei ha-Haskalah ve-ha-Emanẓipaẓyah* (1960), index; B. Mevorach, in: *Zion*, 34 (1969), 196ff.

KLIGLER, ISRAEL JACOB (1889–1944), bacteriologist. Kligler was born in Kamenets-Podolski, Ukraine, and was taken to the U.S. in 1901. He went to Ereẓ Israel in 1920 and worked with the *Hadassah Medical Organization. In 1921–22 he undertook a year's experimental fieldwork on malaria on the basis of a special grant he received from Justice Louis D. *Brandeis. From 1923 to 1926 he was director of the malaria research unit financed by the American Joint Distribution Committee, and from 1926 until his death was director of the department of hygiene at the Hebrew University of Jerusalem.

Kligler was a leading personality in public health, preventive medicine and malaria control in the mandatory era in Palestine. He was chairman of the health department of the Va'ad Le'ummi, adviser on malaria to the *Jewish National Fund, and consultant to the Hadassah Medical Organization. He founded the Microbiological Society and the Malaria Research Station at Rosh Pinnah. Kligler's scientific papers covered bacteriology, virology, immunology, hygiene, nutrition, epidemiology, and the control of infectious diseases. His main interest, however, was malaria, and his *Epidemiology and Control of Malaria in Palestine* (1930) dealt with the disease as it existed in the country at that time, giving a detailed epidemiology, prophylaxis, treatment, and control of the disease, and a description of the biology and bionomy of the local anopheline vectors. He published over 100 scientific studies.

[Zvi Saliternik]

KLÍMA, IVAN (1931–), Czech writer, playwright, and publicist. Born in Prague, Klima spent three and a half years in the Theresienstadt concentration camp. After finishing his studies at the Faculty of Philosophy at Charles University in Prague (Czech language and literary criticism), he worked as an editor in a publishing house and in many literary magazines until they were banned by the Communist regime. After his return in 1970 from a year's teaching in the U.S. at the University of Michigan, he was expelled from all literary organizations, lost his job, and the publication of his books was prohibited. Until 1990, his works appeared only abroad or in *samizdat*. He served as president of the Czech Pen Club (1989–1993) and, from 1993, as its vice president. He was a member of the Club of Rome. Klíma lived in Prague.

Klíma's novels, short stories, plays, and essays have been translated into 29 languages. His published work includes the novels *An Hour of Silence* (1963); *The Ship Named Hope* (1970); *The Summer Affair* (1987); *Judge on Trial* (1991); *Waiting for the Dark, Waiting for the Light* (1994); *Love and Garbage* (1990); *The Ultimate Intimacy* (1998); *Neither Saints nor Angels* (2001); and the plays *The Castle* (1964); *The Master* (1967); *Sweetshop Miriam* (1968); and *The Jury* (1968), *Franz and Felice* (1985), *America* (the dramatization of a novel [with P. Kohout]) – all three inspired by Franz *Kafka.

Klíma's Jewish origin, his experience in Theresienstadt, feelings of responsibility of an individual for the collective, the loss of trust in God, problems of injustice, alienation and feeling like a social outcast are reflected in his literary characters. He was awarded the Egon Hostovský Prize and the Franz Kafka Prize.

BIBLIOGRAPHY: J. Čulík, *Knihy za ohradou. Česká literatura v exilových nakladatelstvích* 1971–1989 (s. d.); P. Kubínová, *Čeští spisovatelé – Czech Writers* (1999); J. Lehár et al., *Česká literatura od počátků k dnešku* (1998); V. Menclová et al., *Slovník českých spisovatelů* (2000); A. Mikulášek et al., *Literatura s hvězdou Davidovou*, vol. 1 (1998); *Slovník českých spisovatelů* (1982).

[Milos Pojar (2nd ed.)]

KLINE, FRANZ (1910–1962), U.S. painter. Kline was born in Wilkes-Barre, PA., but grew up in Philadelphia, and attended the School of Fine and Applied Arts at Boston University from 1931 to 1935 and Heatherly's Art School, London (1937–38). He settled in New York in 1938, by which time his later colleagues in the Abstract-Expressionist movement were already installed in the city, moving toward the distinctly American form of art. Until the late 1940s Kline concentrated on urban landscapes, influenced by the great overwhelming structures of the metropolis, notably the linear skeletons of railways and bridges. Gradually, however, the nature of his brush-strokes took over so that huge drawings in black enamel, a quick-drying house paint, became abstract ideograms. As in the case of his contemporary, Mark Tobey, these seem to have their origin in Oriental calligraphy. Kline's work became increasingly abstract, although always with a strong representational background, so that one is tempted to "read" his work. The restriction to black and white was one of the characteristics of the newly emergent American school, but Kline's work was best suited to the monochrome limitation. Even at its most abstract, the great sweeps of the brushstroke across the canvas and the conglomeration of linear intersections seem to describe heavy, industrial cityscapes. Later Kline introduced color, so that the explosive energy and vitality of his brush strokes were allied with denser, more closed, definitions of space. Kline had considerable influence on a number of distinguished younger painters, among them Philip *Guston, Jack *Tworkov, and Milton Resnick. Kline's first one-man exhibition was at the Egan Gallery, New York, in 1950; his work has since been exhibited in most parts of the world and is represented in major American exhibitions and important collections of modern art in Europe.

[Charles Samuel Spencer]

KLINE, NATHAN S. (1916–1982), U.S. psychiatrist and psychopharmacologist. Kline was born in Philadelphia. He graduated in medicine from New York College of Medicine in 1943 and founded the Rockland Psychiatric Center in 1952, which became the Rockland Research Institute in 1975 and was later named after him following his death. By utilizing serendipitous clinical observations, Kline pioneered the introduction of anti-psychotic and anti-depressant drugs in psychiatric practice. He discovered the anti-psychotic effects of reserpine and was the first to use the monoamine-oxidase inhibitor iproniazid to treat severe depression. The Rockland Institute's work introduced psychopharmacology to psychiatric practice and collated data on clinical trials and drug safety, including the application of new computer systems. Kline assisted in establishing mental health clinics worldwide. He was deeply involved in lay education on mental diseases and founded and directed the International Committee against Mental Illness. He was twice awarded the Lasker Prize for clinical medical research (1957 and 1964).

[Michael Denman (2nd ed.)]

KLINTSY, city in Oriol district, Russian Federation. Jews settled there at the turn of the 18th century. Before the 1917 Revolution, Klintsy belonged to Chernigov province and was included in the *Pale of Settlement. In 1897 the Jewish community numbered 2,605 (21% of the total population). In pogroms instigated by local government officials in October 1905 two Jews were killed and Jewish homes looted. The Jewish population numbered 5,248 (23.4%) in 1926, and grew to 6,505 (16% of the total) by 1939. There was a Yiddish elementary school and an evening school for adults. The Germans occupied the town on August 20, 1941, and they set up a ghetto. Some 150 skilled workers were taken to an unknown destination and were probably killed. In early December 1941, the Germans murdered the remaining 3,000 Jews. Jews returned after World War II and one synagogue still existed in 1970.

BIBLIOGRAPHY: *Die Judenpogrome in Russland*, 2 (1910), 275.

[Yehuda Slutsky / Shmuel Spector (2nd ed.)]

KLODAWA (Pol. **Kłodawa**), town in Poznan province, central Poland. A Jewish settlement existed there in 1487, when the Jewish poll tax was levied by Jan Chelmski. At the beginning of the 19th century, it was argued that Jewish residence in Klodawa had been excluded by a privilege *de non tolerandis Judaeis* dated 1647, allegedly granted to the town by "King Augustus." However in privileges issued to the town of 1720 and 1739, confirming those granted by kings Ladislas Jagello (1386–1434) and Sigismund II Augustus (1548–72), there is no mention of a prohibition on Jewish residence in Klodawa. This was first forbidden in 1755 and is also mentioned in a privilege given to the guilds by King Michael Wisnowiecki (1660–73). All these restrictions were abolished at the end of the 18th century. According to a 1789 census, a number of Jews in Klodawa engaged in crafts. Under Prussian rule the growing Jewish population was assigned to a special residential quarter (Dziadowice); they numbered 221 (22% of the total population) in 1808. After 1815 the town was within Congress Poland. In 1860 the old wooden synagogue, located in the Dziadowice quarter, was replaced by a stone building. The community numbered 443 in 1827, 585 in 1857, 874 in 1897, 1,148 (29.4%) in 1921, and 1,350 in 1939.

[*Encyclopaedia Judaica* (Germany)]

Holocaust Period

Before World War II about 1,350 Jews lived in Klodawa. Under the German occupation Klodawa came within the Hohensalza district. In December 1940 there were 1,186 Jews, including 108 refugees from localities in the region. Nearly 300 Jews must have fled from Klodawa or were deported by the Nazis to the General Government in the first two years of the occupation (1939–40). On Jan. 2–4, 1942, 46 Jews from Klodawa were killed in the Kazimierzow forest near the town of Zagorow. From Jan. 9–12, 1942, the remainder were deported to the nearby *Chelmno death camp.

[Danuta Dombrowska]

BIBLIOGRAPHY: M. Rawita-Witanowski, *Kłodawa* (1904); Warsaw, Archiwum Główne, no. 485; Warsaw, Archiwum Akt Dawnych, Akty Komisji do spraw wewnętrznych, no. 186; I. Schiper, *Studya nad stosunkami gospodarczymi Żydów Polsce podczas Średniowiecza* (1911), index; B. Wasiutyśnki, *Ludność żydowska w Polsce w XIX i XX wiekach* (1930), 25; D. Dabrowskad, in: BŻIH, no. 13–14 (1955), passim.

KLOSTERNEUBURG, town in Lower Austria (until 1298 combined with Neuburg rechts der Donau). In 1187 a nobleman granted his annual income from a Jew to the monastery in Klosterneuberg, but it is not known if the Jew was living in the town. One of the monastery's vineyards was pawned to a Jewess in 1275, and from 1295 the sources mention other Jews functioning as moneylenders. A community is first mentioned in accounts of persecutions in 1302, 1334, 1338, and 1341. Several Jews owned houses in the town in 1339, among them David *Steuss. The community had a richly adorned synagogue, first mentioned in 1371. A member of the city council who was **iudex Judaeorum* is recorded in 1330, and records of numerous moneylending activities exist. The Klosterneuburg community, which had close ties with that of Vienna, ceased to exist in 1420 after the **Wiener Gesera* expulsions.

In 1845 a Jewish peddler who had been plying his trade in the neighboring villages was allowed to settle in the town after reporting a theft from a church. A congregation, consisting of 16 families, was established in 1852 and a cemetery was consecrated in 1874 (enlarged in 1906). The community, in which the congregation of Tulln was included, was recognized in 1892 and in 1900 numbered 280 persons. Approximately 60 Jewish families lived in Klosterneuburg in 1938. The interior of the new synagogue (erected in 1914) was wrecked on *Kristallnacht*, Nov. 10, 1938. Emigration, largely to Vienna, emptied the town of its Jewish inhabitants. After the war the synagogue building was used as a municipal storehouse.

BIBLIOGRAPHY: L. Moses, *Die Juden in Niederoesterreich* (1935), 134; H. Erber, in: *Juedisches Archiv*, 1:6 (1927/28), 14–16; Ružička, *ibid.*, 2:1–2 (1928), 23; S. Krauss, *Die Wiener Geserah* (1920), index; Germ Jud, 1 (1963), 143–4; 2 (1968), 405–7.

[Henry Wasserman]

KLOTZ, LOUIS-LUCIEN (1868–1930), French politician and journalist. Born in Paris, Klotz, who was trained as a lawyer, began his journalistic career at the age of 20 by founding the illustrated journal, *Vie Franco-Russe*. He became editor of the *Voltaire* in 1892, and in 1895 founded the *Français Quotidien*. He served in various municipal and other offices, and in 1898 was elected to the Chamber of Deputies for the Somme department as a Radical Socialist. He remained a member of the chamber for 30 years, and between 1910 and 1920 was minister of finance in six administrations and once minister of the interior. In 1919 he was one of the French delegates to the Versailles Peace Conference and was a signatory of the Treaty. In 1928 Klotz was appointed to the Senate, but at the end of that year he was charged with fraud and sentenced to two years' imprisonment. Because of illness, however, he was released after serving only two months. Klotz was much interested in military and defense affairs, and his writings include *De la guerre à la paix* (1906) and *L'armée en 1906* (1906).

[Shulamith Catane]

KLUG, AARON (1926–), British biochemist and Nobel laureate. Born in Lithuania, Klug was taken by his parents to South Africa at the age of two. As a youngster, he was a member of the Habonim Zionist youth movement. In 1949, after attending the University of Witwatersrand and the University of Cape Town, he moved to Cambridge, England. He began as a medical student, transferred to science, earning his Ph.D. at the Cavendish laboratory and Trinity College, Cambridge University. From 1954 to 1958 he pursued his academic career with Rosalind Franklin, at Birkbeck College of the University of London studying the structure of the tobacco mosaic virus, and in 1958 he became director of the Virus Structure Research Group there. In 1962 he joined the Medical Research Council Laboratory of Molecular Biology in Cambridge, became joint head of the Structural Studies Division in 1978, and he was director of the Laboratory from 1986 to 1996.

Klug was awarded the Nobel Prize in chemistry in 1982 for his contribution to the advancement of science through his study of the three-dimensional structure of the combinations of nucleic acids and proteins. He developed techniques which enabled the study of both crystalline and non-crystalline material and led to "crystallographic electron microscopy." He demonstrated that a combination of a series of electron micrographs taken at different angles can provide a three-dimensional image of particles, a method which is of use in studying protein complexes and viruses. His work later formed the basis of X-ray CT scanner. His subsequent research was on the structure of DNA and RNA binding proteins which regulate gene expression and in particular on the interaction with the zinc finger family of transcription factors which he discovered.

Klug was president of the Royal Society (1995–2000), a member of the Order of Merit, a foreign associate of the U.S. National Academy of Sciences and the French Academy of Sciences, and received many honorary degrees. He also made important contributions in biotechnology and was involved in the creation of the Sanger Center in Cambridge, which was responsible for sequencing one-third of the human genome. Klug was a very active supporter of Ben-Gurion University in Israel and from 2004 was the chairman of its Institute of Biotechnology.

[Michael Denman (2nd ed.)]

KLUGER, SOLOMON BEN JUDAH AARON (1785–1869), talmudist and halakhist. Kluger became known as the *Maggid* of Brody and as **MaHaRSHaK** (**M**orenu **ha**-**R**av **Sh**elomo **K**luger). He received his early education from his father, the rabbi of Komarov, who died during Solomon's boyhood. At 13 he went to Zamosc where he studied under Mordecai Reuben and Jacob *Kranz, the famous *maggid* of Dubno. He soon became known as an *illui* ("prodigy"). For a time he lived in Rava where he became a shopkeeper, but failed. He was then prevailed upon to accept the post of rabbi at Kolki; from there he went to Josefov and in 1820 to Brody, where he remained for about 50 years.

Kluger had a great reputation which still endures. A prolific writer, he wrote hundreds of responsa. He is said to have written 375 books, the numerical equivalent of his name Solomon; the list of his known works comprises no less then 174, of which 15 were published during his life and 15 posthumously. Kluger was an extremist in his orthodoxy, vehemently opposing the *maskilim*, whose influence was already making itself felt in Brody, and fighting against every endeavor to change the least important of religious customs prevalent in Eastern Europe. He led the opposition to the use of machine-baked unleavened bread for Passover, but in this he was motivated mainly by social considerations, claiming that it would rob many poor people of a much needed source of income on Passover. He was succeeded in Brody by his son, Abraham Benjamin.

BIBLIOGRAPHY: O. Feuchtwanger, *Righteous Lives* (1965), 82–85; D. Halaḥmi, *Ḥakhmei Yisrael* (1958), 307f.; J.A. Kluger, *Toledot Shelomo* (1888).

[Mordechai Hacohen]

KLUGMAN, JACK (1922–), U.S. actor. Born in South Philadelphia, Klugman rose from a working-class background to become a fixture in American television during the 1970s. He is perhaps best known for his portrayal of disheveled sportswriter Oscar Madison in the television series *The Odd Couple*, based on Neil Simon's play of the same title, a role which earned him two Emmy Awards. Following his years on *The Odd Couple* from 1970 to 1975, Klugman continued his success on the small-screen during a seven-year stint as the crime-solving medical examiner Dr. R. Quincy on the television show *Quincy* (1976–83). Klugman was trained as an actor at Carnegie Mellon University and then at New York's American Theater Wing. He gained respect as an actor in "the golden age" of live television drama, performing in programs for the U.S. Steel Hour, Kraft Television Theater, Studio One, and Playhouse 90, most notably in Reginald Rose's *Twelve Angry Men* (1957) and Rod Serling's *Velvet Alley* (1959). Klugman also appeared in four episodes of Rod Serling's *Twilight Zone* as well as in many films, including *Cry Terror* (1958), *Days of Wine and Roses* (1962), *Act One* (1963), *The Detective* (1968), *Goodbye, Columbus* (1969), and *Two Minute Warning* (1976). Klugman has battled oral cancer since 1974, a condition that necessitated the removal of one of his vocal chords in 1989 and threatened to permanently keep him from speaking, yet Klugman has continued to perform and received the American Speech and Hearing Association's International Media Award in recognition of his struggle to regain his speech.

[Walter Driver (2nd ed.)]

KLUMEL, MEIR (1875–1936), Zionist leader in Poland. Born in Widze (now Vidzy) near Vilna, Klumel completed his studies in Semitic linguistics at the University of Strasbourg in 1902 with the publication of a scientific edition of a Samaritan commentary on Exodus 22 written in Arabic by Yaʿqūb al-Sāmirī. He lived in Warsaw and became active in the Zionist movement, serving as chairman of the Zionist Organization in Poland from 1917 to 1924, in "*Tarbut," *Keren Hayesod, various economic institutions, etc. In 1932 he moved to Palestine and until his last days was active in the association of Polish immigrants, the Berit Ivrit Olamit, and other organizations.

BIBLIOGRAPHY: *Beit Kevarot ha-Yashan be-Tel Aviv* (1940), 306–7; Tidhar, 3 (1949), 1436–37. **ADD BIBLIOGRAPHY:** "Dr. Meir Klumel," in: Y. Gruenbaum, *Penei ha-Dor* 1 (1958), 250–54.

[Getzel Kressel]

KLUTZNICK, PHILIP MORRIS (1907–1999), U.S. community planner, diplomat, and communal leader. Klutznick was born in Kansas City, Missouri. While in high school, he was vice president of the local YMCA's Hi-Y Boys Club; but, as a Jew, he was not permitted to become president. This prompted him to establish the second chapter of the Aleph Zadik Aleph (AZA) youth branch of B'nai B'rith.

Klutznick received his law degree from Creighton University law school in Omaha, Nebraska. He was admitted to the bar (1930) and, as assistant corporation counsel for the city of Omaha, brought a federal housing development to that city. His success as a community planner in the posts of special assistant on housing to the U.S. attorney general (1935–36) and general counsel for the Omaha Housing Authority, which he was instrumental in creating (1938–41), led to his appointment as federal housing commissioner (1944–46) by presidents Roosevelt and Truman. He also served as assistant administrator of the National Housing Agency. Among his many innovative actions, he arranged for hundreds of houses to be dismantled in some parts of the country and shipped to other parts to be rebuilt for defense factory workers who needed them.

As board chairman of American Community Builders, Inc., Klutznick developed the model middle-income community of 30,000 of Park Forest (1947). A satellite city located 27 miles out of Chicago, it was designed for returning war veterans. Klutznick served as board chairman and director of banking, insurance, and utilities corporations, and was senior partner of Klutznick Enterprises. He extended his pioneering efforts in community development to Israel as co-founder of the modern seaport of *Ashdod. He was appointed to the U.S. delegation to the United Nations in 1957 by President Eisenhower. In 1961–63 he served as ambassador to the United Nations Economic and Social Council.

Klutznick was one of the foremost figures in postwar American Jewish life. He was international president of B'nai B'rith (1953–59), general chairman of the United Jewish Appeal, president of the American Friends of the Hebrew University, vice president of the Jewish Welfare Board, a board member of the *Conference on Jewish Material Claims Against Germany, and helped to establish the *Conference of Presidents of Major American Jewish Organizations. In 1956 he went to Morocco to secure the release of 8,500 Moroccan Jews. In these capacities he spoke out against religious and cultural genocide and for the observance of human and civil rights. In his *No Easy Answers* (1961), he was critical of disunity among Jewish religious groups.

In 1974 he undertook the development of the 74-story Water Tower Place complex in Chicago. In 1975, President Ford appointed him to serve on an advisory committee that facilitated resettlement of Vietnamese and Cambodians in the United States.

[Maurice Bisgyer]

Klutznick received the 1976 Liberty Award of the United States and was elected president of the *World Jewish Congress in November 1977, in succession to Nahum *Goldmann. In November 1979 he was nominated as secretary of commerce by President Carter and received the unanimous approval of the U.S. Senate; at age 72, he became the oldest member of Carter's cabinet. He oversaw the 1980 U.S. Census and established the Office for Productivity, Technology, and Innovation. He served until the Carter administration ended in January 1981 and returned to Chicago.

In 1986, he and his wife established the Philip M. and Ethel Klutznick Chair in Jewish Civilization at the College of Arts and Sciences at Chicago's Northwestern University. In the following year they established the Klutznick Endowed Chair in Jewish Civilization at Creighton University.

The B'nai B'rith Klutznick National Museum is located in Washington, D.C. and Creighton University's law library also bears his name. Klutznick's *Angles of Vision: A Memoir of My Lives* (with S. Hyman) was published in 1991.

[Ruth Beloff (2nd ed.)]

ADD. BIBLIOGRAPHY: M. Berger, *They Built Chicago: Entrepreneurs Who Shaped a Great City's Architecture* (1992); M. Baer, *Dealing in Futures: The Story of a Jewish Youth Movement* (1983).

KNEFLER, FREDERICK (1833–1901), U.S. army officer. Born in Hungary, Knefler immigrated to the United States in 1859 and volunteered for the Union army in 1861 on the outbreak of the Civil War. He rose from the rank of private to captain in the 11th Indiana regiment within a year and from captain to colonel in the 79th Indiana within another year. He fought in all the great battles in the west, taking part in the assault on Missionary Ridge at Chattanooga and Sherman's Atlanta campaign, and was promoted to brevet brigadier general in 1865 shortly before the end of the war. In the late 1870s he was appointed by President Hayes to head the Pension Bureau.

KNESSET (Heb. כְּנֶסֶת; "Assembly"), the parliament and legislature of the State of Israel. The name of the assembly and the number of its members were both adopted from *the Knesset ha-Gedolah* – the Great Assembly of the fifth century B.C.E.

The Knesset is unicameral, and consists of 120 members. Its basic functions are to legislate, supervise the government, represent the various points of view prevalent in the society regarding the main issues on the national agenda, and elect the president of the State and the state comptroller. The government cannot operate without the confidence of the Knesset, which means that it requires the support of at least 61 members of the Knesset.

Basic Laws passed by the Knesset

Law	Date of enactment	Knesset	Current status
Basic Law: The Knesset	February 12, 1958	Third	In force
Basic Law: Lands of Israel	July 25, 1960	Fourth	In force
Basic Law: The President of the State	June 16, 1964	Fifth	In force
Basic Law: The Government (first version)	August 13, 1968	Sixth	Replaced
Basic Law: The State Economy	July 21, 1971	Seventh	In force
Basic Law: The Military	March 31, 1976	Eighth	In force
Basic Law: Jerusalem the Capital of Israel	December 13, 1980	Ninth	In force
Basic Law: The Judiciary	February 28, 1984	Tenth	In force
Basic Law: The State Comptroller	February 15, 1988	Eleventh	In force
Basic Law: Freedom of Occupation (first version)	March 12, 1992	Twelfth	Replaced
Basic Law: Human Dignity and Freedom	March 17, 1992	Twelfth	In force
Basic Law: The Government (second version)	March 18, 1992*	Twelfth	Replaced
Basic Law: Freedom of Occupation (second version)	March 9, 1994	Thirteenth	In force
Basic Law: The Government (third version)	March 7, 2001**	Fifteenth	In force

* Went into force toward the elections to the Fourteenth Knesset in 1996.
** Went into force toward the elections to the Sixteenth Knesset in 2002.

The Provisional State Council, which exercised legislative authority in the State of Israel after the Proclamation of Independence, adopted, on November 18, 1948, an ordinance providing for the election of a Constituent Assembly, to which general elections were held two months later. Soon after its election the Constituent Assembly changed its name to "Knesset" and adopted basic constitutional arrangements for the running of the country. However, it was unable to adopt a full constitution, due to political constraints, and in June 1950, decided that the preparation of a constitution would take the form of Basic Laws, each dealing with another element in the system of government. The idea was that after being enacted, all the Basic Laws together would constitute the State's Constitution. The first basic law, Basic Law: the Knesset, was passed on February 12, 1958. By the beginning of the 21st century, the task had not yet been completed.

The main laws governing the Knesset and its work are (in chronological order): The Knesset Members Immunity Law, 1951; Basic Law: the Knesset (passed in 1958); The Knesset Building and Compound Law, 1968; The Knesset Law, 1994 (which deals with certain issues not dealt with in Basic Law: the Knesset). All these laws have been amended since being passed.

Elections

The rules by which Israel's electoral system operates are stipulated in the Election Law, 1969. The Central Elections Committee is responsible for its implementation.

Elections to the Knesset are general, national, direct, equal, secret, and proportional. Every citizen from the age of 18 who is in Israel at the time of election, unless he is on a diplomatic mission abroad or a seaman at sea, is eligible to vote, regardless of sex, race, or religion. Candidates for election must be at least 21 years of age. Civil servants, judges, army officers in active service, rabbis paid from state funds, and holders of certain other state offices are not eligible as candidates. As a rule, elections are held every four years, but early elections may be called at the request of the prime minister, or upon a resolution of the Knesset to dissolve itself. The Knesset may serve for over four years if elected in early elections, or should the Knesset resolve to delay the date of elections (as occurred on the occasion of the *Yom Kippur War in 1973).

The contestants in the elections are lists, where each list must consist of at least one party, registered with the Party Registrar on the basis of the Parties Law, 1992. A list may consist of more than one registered party, and in practice can include bodies that are not registered parties, though this was more prevalent in the past than it is today.

Each list that gets elected receives a number of seats proportional to the valid votes it received. Originally there was a 1% qualifying threshold, which was raised to 1.5% towards the elections to the Thirteenth Knesset. In May 2004 the qualifying threshold was raised to 2%. The reason for raising

Knesset elections and date of first sitting

Knesset	Date of election	Date of first sitting	Length of term
First	January 25, 1949	February 14, 1949	2 years and 6 months
Second	July 30, 1951	September 20, 1951	4 years
Third	July 6, 1955	August 15, 1955	4 years and 4 months
Fourth	November 3, 1959	November 30, 1959	1 year and 9 months
Fifth	August 15, 1961	September 9, 1961	4 years and 2 months
Sixth	November 2, 1965	November 22, 1965	4 years
Seventh	October 28, 1969	November 17, 1969	4 years and 2 months
Eighth	December 31, 1973	January 21, 1974	3 years and 5 months
Ninth	May 17, 1977	June 13, 1977	4 years and 1 month
Tenth	June 30, 1981	July 20, 1981	3 years and 1 month
Eleventh	July 23, 1984	August 13, 1984	4 years and 3 months
Twelfth	November 1, 1988	November 21, 1988	3 years and 8 months
Thirteenth	June 23, 1992	July 13, 1992	3 years and 11 months
Fourteenth	May 29, 1996	June 17, 1996	3 years
Fifteenth	May 17, 1999	June 7, 1999	3 years and 8 months
Sixteenth	January 28, 2003	February 17, 2003	3 years and 2 months
Seventeenth	March 28, 2006	April 17, 2006	

the qualifying threshold has been to prevent one- and even two-person lists from being elected. Nevertheless, the basic concept is that all parts of Israel's heterogeneous population should have the opportunity to be represented to the Knesset. The relatively extreme application of the proportional representation system has resulted in ten to fifteen lists being elected to each Knesset.

All efforts over the years to reform the electoral system to a mixed system, whereby half the members would be elected in multi-member constituencies, and the other half on the basis of proportional representation, failed. The only major change in the electoral system that was adopted introduced the direct election of the prime minister side by side with the election of the Knesset. This change was adopted through the amendment of Basic Law: the Government, and accompanying laws, in March 1992. It was canceled nine years later because it had led to greater political fragmentation, did not strengthen the status of the prime minister, and weakened the two major political parties.

Members of the Knesset and Parliamentary Groups

As noted above, members of the Knesset are not elected directly, but as members of lists. Each party has its own method of putting together its list. In the past "arrangement committees" were customary, where the leaders of the party were those who decided who should run on the party's list. Some, like the *Israel Labor Party since the elections to the Thirteenth Knesset, hold closed primaries among the registered party members, in which representatives from national lists and district lists are elected. In others, like the *Likud in recent elections, it is the party Central Committee that elects the representatives to the list. In the *haredi* (ultra-Orthodox religious) parties it is the spiritual leaders who decide who will be on the list.

The candidates on the lists who pass the qualifying threshold enter the Knesset according to the order in which their names appear on the list. Should a party receive 12 seats, it is the first 12 persons whose names appear on the list who enter the Knesset. After entering the Knesset, the lists are referred to as "parliamentary groups," and in the course of each Knesset parliamentary groups are able to split or merge, or the number of their seats might change due to individual Knesset members, or groups of members, moving from one parliamentary group to another. Except for the Third Knesset, the number of parliamentary groups at the end of the term of each Knesset has been larger than at its start. No list has ever won a majority of the Knesset seats. The most any list ever received was the 56 seats received by the Alignment (Labor-*Mapam coalition) in the elections to the Seventh Knesset. All of Israel's governments have been coalitions, made up of at least three parliamentary groups, but usually more.

Though the members of the outgoing Knesset continue to serve until the first sitting of the new Knesset, the newly elected members enjoy parliamentary immunity, and start receiving a salary as members, from the moment the results of the elections are announced. In the past it was customary to consider someone a member of the Knesset only from the moment that he or she declared his or her allegiance to the Knesset. However, today the rule is that newly elected members are considered full members from the first sitting of the new Knesset, while in the event of a member's passing away or resigning from the Knesset in mid-term, the next person on the list becomes a member immediately upon the death or resignation.

Though there is a law that describes the legal obligations and immunities of members of the Knesset, and the Rules of Procedure *inter alia* deal with issues of discipline and the Rules of Ethics with ethical questions, there is no document that describes the official duties of a member. However, as representatives of the constituencies that elected them, members are expected to attend the House regularly, fulfill any specific post to which they have been elected within the Knesset, participate in the sittings of the plenum, attend the meetings of the committees of which they are members, propose bills, table motions, ask questions, and take part in debates. In important votes the coalition and the parliamentary groups impose discipline, though voting discipline has greatly weakened since the early 1990s. Members of the Knesset are expected to conduct themselves with dignity and represent it with honor.

It should be noted that Israel has a parliamentary system; since the establishment of the state, between 12 to 29 members of the Knesset have simultaneously also served as ministers in the Government, and additional members as deputy ministers.

The Knesset is entitled to lift the immunity of a member of the Knesset against whom there are criminal charges. It is the state attorney who requests that the immunity be lifted, and should the House Committee decide to comply with the request, the plenum must approve the decision as well.

For many years the number of women elected to the Knesset was relatively small, running from seven in the Twelfth Knesset to 12 in the Third. However, since the Fifteenth Knesset the numbers have risen, and in the Sixteenth Knesset 17 were elected. Since the First Knesset the number of members born in Israel has risen from a mere 17 in the First Knesset (of whom three were members of minorities) to an overwhelming majority in the Sixteenth Knesset. The number of Arabs and Druze in the Knesset has also risen significantly since the First Knesset.

Work of the Knesset

The work of the Knesset is divided into parliamentary work, performed by the members of the Knesset with the help of the Knesset staff, and administrative and maintenance work, performed by the Knesset employees and contract workers. The speaker, usually elected at the first sitting of each new Knesset, or soon thereafter, is the head of the parliamentary hierarchy, while the secretary general of the Knesset – appointed by the speaker – is head of the administration. The speaker, assisted by his deputies, runs the sittings of the plenum.

The Knesset's annual session is divided into a winter session and a summer session. When the Knesset is in session, it usually sits in plenum on Monday and Tuesday afternoons and evenings, and on Wednesday morning. The rest of the time on Mondays, Tuesdays, and Wednesdays, and frequently Sundays and Thursdays, is devoted to committee meetings.

The Knesset's agenda is determined by the speaker and his deputies. Mondays and Tuesdays are usually devoted to government business, while Wednesdays are devoted to members' motions for the agenda and private members' bills.

The work of the Knesset is divided between the plenum and the committees. The most important activities in the plenum are the debating and passing of bills, the debating and approval or rejection of motions for the agenda and motions of no-confidence in the government, questions to ministers, general debates, one-minute speeches, and the election of the president of the State and the state comptroller. On occasion, visiting foreign heads of state or of international organizations are invited to speak before the Knesset plenum.

Since 1989 the plenum has had an electronic voting system. Before the electronic voting most votes were taken by show of hands. On important issues votes are taken by roll call, and on some issues, such as the election of the president of the State and the state comptroller, the vote is by secret ballot.

Speakers of the Knesset

	Name and party affiliation of speaker	Date of election	End of term
1.	Yosef Sprinzak (Mapai)	February 14, 1949	January 28, 1959
2.	Naḥum Nir (Aḥdut ha-Avodah)	March 2, 1959	November 30, 1959
3.	Kaddish Luz (Mapai, Alignment)	November 30, 1959	November 17, 1969
4.	Reuven Barkatt (Alignment)	November 17, 1969	April 5, 1972
5.	Israel Yeshayahu (Alignment)	May 9, 1972	June 13, 1977
6.	Yitzḥak Shamir (Likud)	June 13, 1977	March 10, 1980
7.	Yitzḥak Berman (Likud)	March 12, 1980	July 20, 1981
8.	Menaḥem Savidor (Likud)	July 20, 1981	August 13, 1984
9.	Shelomo Hillel (Alignment)	September 11, 1984	November 20, 1988
10.	Dov Shilansky (Likud)	November 21, 1988	July 13, 1992
11.	Shevaḥ Weiss (Labor Party)	July 13, 1992	June 24, 1996
12.	Dan Tikhon (Likud)	June 24, 1996	June 7, 1999
13.	Avraham Burg (Labor Party)	July 6, 1999	February 17, 2003
14.	Reuven Rivlin (Likud)	February 19, 2003	May 4, 2006
15.	Dalia Itzik (Kadimah)	May 4, 2006	

Most of the work of preparing bills, before they turn into law, is performed in the committees, each of which has its own staff, a legal advisor, help from research assistants provided by the Knesset's Research and Information Center (established in 2000), and the occasional assistance of external experts.

However, it is the plenum that approves the bills. Government bills and committee bills go through first, second, and third readings. Private members' bills must also go through preliminary reading. Since the Twelfth Knesset many thousands of bills have been proposed by private members, but most of them never pass preliminary reading. Nevertheless, the majority of bills passed into law by the Knesset are private members' bills, a phenomenon unique in Western democracies.

There are 12 permanent (statutory) committees with specific terms of reference, and the Knesset is entitled to appoint additional temporary committees on specific issues. The 12 permanent committees are:

The Constitution, Law, and Justice Committee
The Economics Committee
The Education and Culture Committee
The Finance Committee
The Foreign Affairs and Security Committee

The House Committee
The Immigration, Absorption, and Dispersions Committee
The Internal Affairs and Environment Committee
The Labor, Welfare, and Health Committee
The Science and Technology Committee
The State Control Committee
The Committee on the Status of Women

Many of the Committees have subcommittees, and there are several joint committees.

The permanent committees and the committees on specific issues do not only deal with bills. They also deliberate motions for the agenda passed on to them by the plenum, and raise issues for deliberation. Occasionally they venture out of the House for tours, in connection with the issues they are dealing with. Committees are entitled to call upon ministers, civil servants, and members of the armed forces to appear before them and provide information, and usually invite specialists, experts, and representatives of interest groups to participate in their meetings. There are numerous lobbies and lobbyists operating in the Knesset corridors, in an attempt to influence legislation and Knesset resolutions. The Knesset may also appoint parliamentary committees of inquiry, to investigate specific issues or events.

Each Knesset selects an Ethics Committee and an Interpretations Committee (in the event of differences of opinion regarding the Rules of Procedure).

There is a special Knesset TV channel that is funded by the Knesset. The TV channel broadcasts all the meetings of the plenum, important committee meetings, interviews and talk shows with current and past members of the Knesset, programs about parliaments in other countries, etc. In addition all the various branches of the media in Israel have reporters in the Knesset, and on occasion the foreign media are also present.

The agendas and the minutes of the plenum are published in print and on the Knesset's website. The minutes of committee meetings that are not secret are also published on the website. The website, which includes a good deal of information on the history of the Knesset, its work, the laws it passes, background papers and studies prepared for the committees and individual members by the Research and Information Center, etc., includes sections in English and Arabic.

On the basis of the Freedom of Information Law, the Knesset provides the public with information about the Knesset and its work.

The Knesset's Relations with the Government and the Judiciary

The relations between the Knesset and the government is complex, and a strict separation of powers does not exist. Most of the ministers and all the deputy ministers are members of the Knesset, and have the right to vote in the plenum. Ministers and deputy ministers cannot be members of committees, though they appear before them as representatives of the Executive.

No government can start to function unless it is approved by the Knesset, and if new ministers are added to the government, their appointment must be approved by the Knesset as well. A government can be brought down by a vote of no-confidence. In the past an ordinary majority of the members could bring a government down, but today a government can only be brought down if at least 61 members of the Knesset vote for a motion of no-confidence, and propose the name of an alternative prime minister.

One of the tasks of the Knesset is to supervise the government. It does this by having the last word on all government bills, by means of motions for the agenda and questions. The ministers are also called upon to report to the Knesset on the activities of their ministries. Another means of supervision is by means of deliberations in the State Control Committee on the annual and occasional reports of the state comptroller, who reviews the functioning of the ministries and other government bodies that are under his supervision.

Most of the important laws passed by the Knesset are initiated by the government, and the government is obliged to act in accordance with the laws that the Knesset passes. However, due to the inflation of private legislation, it was necessary to place limitations on the passing of private members' bills involving expenditure. The inflation of private legislation has also resulted in many laws not being implemented, either partially or in full, frequently due to the technical inability of the government to implement them.

The government has found a way of amending laws without close Knesset supervision, by means of the Arrangements Law (*ḥok ha-hesderim*), which is attached to the annual Budget Law.

The relationship between the Knesset and the judiciary is also complicated. The judiciary judges on the basis of the laws passed by the Knesset, and the deliberations of the Knesset on bills – whether in the plenum or in the Committee – constitute part of the evidence concerning "the intention of the legislator." Members of the Knesset are appointed to the various committees that elect judges, both for the secular and the various religious courts. In the absence of a constitution, the Supreme Court, sitting as the High Court of Justice, is frequently called upon to decide on constitutional matters, and has on occasion declared a certain law, or part of a law, to be unconstitutional because it is in conflict with a Basic Law. This phenomenon has caused great tension between the Knesset and the Court. Some Knesset members who are dissatisfied with the activism of the Supreme Court, especially after Chief Justice Aharon Barak became its president in 1995, have called for the establishment of an independent Constitutional Court. It should be noted that among those petitioning the High Court of Justice there have been many members of the Knesset.

The Knesset Building and Compound

After its first sitting in the Jewish Agency building in Jerusalem on February 14, 1949 (*Tu bi-Shevat* of the Jewish year

5719), for 10 months the Knesset held its sittings in various locations in Tel Aviv before moving back to Jerusalem. Until its new building was inaugurated on August 30, 1966, the Knesset met in the Arazi-Frumin building on King George Street, which had originally been planned as a bank. In 1956 a competition was held for the construction of the permanent building. The winner of the competition was the architect Joseph Klarwein, but several other senior and junior architects – including Shimon Powsner, Ze'ev Rabina, Yohanan *Ratner, Dov *Karmi and his son Ram *Karmi, the British William Gillitt, and the Swiss Hans Ruegg – were involved in the deliberations about the building, its planning and construction.

The building that finally emerged – in Late International Style, with much use of bare concrete and some reddish stone from Galilee to comply with the municipal laws of Jerusalem – hardly resembles the one originally planned by Klarwein. The exterior of the building, which is a square structure, with ten rectangular pillars on each side, and an overhanging roof, resembles the U.S. Embassy in Athens, planned by Walter Gropius and completed in 1961.

The interior of the Knesset building was done by the interior decorator Dora *Gad, who made much use of wooden panels and soft pastel colors. Some elements in the internal architecture resemble the work of Finnish architect Alvar Alto. The building is adorned by numerous works of art made especially for the Knesset. Among these are the iron gates to the Knesset compound, created by the sculptor David *Palombo, the stone front wall of the plenary hall, created by sculptor Danny *Karavan, three tapestries, 12 floor mosaics and one wall mosaic created by the artist Marc*Chagall for the State Hall (commonly known as the Chagall Hall), two paintings by artist Reuven *Rubin, which hang in the Government meeting room and the Speaker's bureau, and a bronze relief created by sculptor Buki *Shwartz. Outside the gates of the Knesset is a large seven-branched **menorah* depicting scenes from Jewish history. The *menorah* was created by the German-born British sculptor Benno *Elkan, and presented to the Knesset by the British Parliament in 1956.

Most of the cost of the original building was covered by money bequeathed by James de *Rothschild in his will.

A new wing, including 48 rooms for members of the Knesset, an auditorium, several committee rooms, a gym, and storage rooms, was constructed in 1991. Due to the growing number of staff and visitors regularly present in the building, the construction of a major addition to the building was begun in 2002.

The foreground to the Knesset building is occasionally used for official ceremonies, with the participation of the Knesset Guard, which was established in 1959. At the front of the Knesset building there is an eternal flame to commemorate all those who fell in defense of the country.

The immunity of the Knesset building and its compound is protected by a special law, which lays down that the writ of the ordinary police does not apply. Within this area, no demonstration or assembly may take place without the speaker's permission, no person can be arrested without his leave, and no person may bear arms unless licensed by him. The Knesset Guard, headed by the serjeant-at-arms who is directly responsible to the speaker, is in charge of maintaining peace and order in and around the building.

See also *Israel, State of: Governance; Political Life and Parties.

WEBSITE: www.knesset.gov.il.

[Susan Hattis Rolef (2nd ed.)]

KNIEŽA, EMIL (originally **Fuerst**; 1920–1990), Slovak writer and publicist. Knieža was born in Nacina Ves, Slovakia. A partisan fighter during World War II, he later described the horrors of the Nazi occupation in his novels and stories, *Šiestý prápor na stráž!* ("The Sixth Battalion on Guard!," 1964), *Kóšer rota* ("The Kosher Battalion," 1966), and *Mušketieri žltej hviezdy* ("Musketeers of the Yellow Star," 1967), while other works broke new ground with their accounts of Jewish forced labor units under the fascist regime. Knieža left Czechoslovakia for Switzerland after 1968 where he lived until his death. During his exile he visited Israel many times. He also published Slovak translations from the Yiddish (Shalom Aleichem).

[Avigdor Dagan / Milos Pojar (2nd ed.)]

KNOPF, ALFRED A. (**Abraham**; 1892–1984), U.S. book publisher. Born in New York City, Knopf graduated from Columbia College in 1912. He started his own publishing firm in 1915 after working for Doubleday, Page Publishing, and Mitchell Kennerley. Owner of a Russian wolfhound, he labeled his publications Borzoi Books. His insistence on excellent design and craftsmanship helped to raise book production standards in the United States and to attract many new authors to his ever-expanding list. His wife, Blanche Wolf *Knopf (1894–1966), active in the firm from the beginning, discovered many talented European writers. Alfred A. Knopf Inc. published translations of these works and specialized in producing books that were distinctive in their high-quality printing, binding, and design. Knopf paid close attention to the content of the books as well, tending to publish books with subject matter that interested him, such as history, sociology, and music. In addition to the foreign authors, Knopf published the works of many modern American writers, including James Baldwin, Dashiell Hammett, and Langston Hughes. Over time, 26 of Knopf's authors – including Willa Cather, John Updike, John Cheever, Wallace Stevens, and Richard Hofstadter – won Pulitzer Prizes, more than any other American publishing house. The company also boasted 16 Nobel laureates, among them Thomas Mann and T.S. Eliot. For about a decade from 1924, Knopf published the monthly *American Mercury*, edited by H.L. Mencken and George Jean Nathan. By 1965 his firm had issued more than 5,000 titles.

In 1959 his only son, Alfred A. Knopf, Jr., who had been with the firm for many years, became a founder-partner of Atheneum Publishers. In 1960 Knopf sold the company to

Random House, which was owned by his friend and Columbia schoolmate Bennett Cerf.

[Israel Soifer / Ruth Beloff (2nd ed.)]

KNOPF, BLANCHE WOLF (1894–1966), U.S. publisher known for discovering and nurturing literary excellence. Knopf was born in New York City. Her education at the Gardner School was supplemented by tutors in French and German. She met her husband, Alfred A. *Knopf, in 1911 and, as their relationship grew closer, encouraged his dream of starting a publishing house, which he did a year before their 1916 marriage.

Blanche Wolf Knopf began her career in publishing with her husband at a time when neither women nor Jews were welcome as leaders in the field. She skillfully used her natural and acquired assets to make a lasting contribution to both American and world letters. Not the least of her contributions was the selection of the *borzoi* or Russian wolfhound as the Knopf logo. She became vice president of Alfred A. Knopf Inc. in 1921, and its president in 1957, when her husband became chairman of the company.

Blanche Knopf's fluency in French and German, bolstered by her intellectual interests and social sensibilities, helped persuade European authors, such as de Beauvoir, Shokolov, and Freud to join Knopf's list. Her reach extended beyond Europe to Latin America and the Far East, while including American writers such as Fannie Hurst and H.L. Mencken. In recognition of her support and dissemination of French literature, the French government named her a Chevalier in the Legion of Honor (1949) and awarded her the Cross of Officer (1960). An elegant figure dedicated to music, Knopf maintained a busy social life while being actively involved in the affairs of Alfred A. Knopf Publishing. Shortly after the Knopfs' only child, Alfred A. Knopf, Jr., decided to leave his parents' firm and venture out to found his own publishing house (Athaneum Publishers) in 1959, they sold their business to Random House while continuing to run it as a Random House division.

[Anne Lapidus Lerner (2nd ed.)]

KNOPFLER, MARK (1949–), British singer, songwriter, and producer. Knopfler was born in Glasgow, Scotland. After working as a journalist, he formed the rock group Dire Straits, which established itself as a serious force to be reckoned with in the late 1970s. The song "Sultans of Swing" from the album *Dire Straits* (1978) was critically lionized and shot out of nowhere to the top of the charts. Knopfler followed this smash debut with four more hit Dire Straits albums, *Communiqué* (1979), *Making Movies* (1980), *Love over Gold* (1982), which included the single "Private Investigations," and *Alchemy-Live* (1984). During this time Knopfler also became recognized as an outstanding guitarist. In 1985, he released Dire Straits' *Brothers in Arms*, which dwarfed every other record in its wake and became one of the biggest-selling albums in the history of the music industry. The album included the U.S. No. 1 single "Money for Nothing." Knopfler was then acknowledged (with Paul McCartney and David Bowie) as one of the three richest recording artists in the U.K. Knopfler waited six years before issuing a sixth Dire Straits album, *On Every Street* (1991), which became an instant No. 1 on the album charts, but only briefly. The band's last album was the live recording *On the Night*. He also produced high-quality albums for Bob *Dylan (*Infidels*, 1983) and Randi *Newman (*Land of Dreams*, 1988). Knopfler had another band, the Notting Hillbillies.

Knopfler wrote the soundtracks for a number of films as well, such as *Local Hero* (1983), *Cal* (1984), *Comfort and Joy* (1984), *The Princess Bride* (1987), *Last Exit to Brooklyn* (1989), *Tishina* (1991), *Wag the Dog* (1997), and *A Shot at Glory* (2000).

In 1999 he was named an Officer of the Order of British Empire (O.B.E.) by Queen Elizabeth. In 2002 he released the solo album *The Ragpicker's Dream*, and in 2004 he released *Shangri-la*.

[Jonathan Licht / Ruth Beloff (2nd ed.)]

°**KNORR VON ROSENROTH, CHRISTIAN** (1636–1689), Protestant theosophist and Kabbalah scholar. The son of a Protestant minister in Silesia, he traveled around Western Europe for several years. During his travels he came in contact with circles interested in mysticism, and was deeply influenced by the writings of Jacob Boehme. On his return, he settled in Sulzbach, in northern Bavaria, and from 1668 until his death was a close adviser and senior official in the service of Prince Christian August, who shared his mystical leanings. Knorr became known as an inspired poet, some of his poems being regarded among the finest in German religious poetry. While in Holland, he acquired an interest in Kabbalah, becoming engrossed in the study of the source material in the original. For some time he studied with rabbis such as Meir Stern in Amsterdam, and acquired manuscript copies of the writings of Isaac *Luria, coupling these inquiries with his interest in Christian mysticism. He was in close touch with the Cambridge philosopher Henry More and the Belgian mystic Franciscus (Frans) Mercurius van Helmont, who were likewise interested in Kabbalah as a theosophical system of great significance to philosophy and theology alike. In his lifetime Knorr was reputed to be the most profound Christian scholar of Kabbalah. His studies were summarized in the two bulky volumes of his main work, *Kabbala Denudata*: "The Kabbalah Uncovered, or, The Transcendental, Metaphysical, and Theological Teachings of the Jews" (Sulzbach, Latin, 1677–84). This work, which had a widespread influence, was superior to anything that had been published on Kabbalah in a language other than Hebrew. It gave non-Jewish readers a broad view of the first sources to be translated into Latin, and these were accompanied by explanatory notes. Here, too, appeared long disquisitions by More and Van Helmont on kabbalistic subjects (some of them anonymously), with Knorr's replies to them. In his translations Knorr aimed at precision, sometimes to the extent that the meaning is obscure to those not familiar with the original. Although the book contains many errors and mistranslations, particularly of difficult Zoharic passages, there is no justification for the contemporary Jewish claims that the author misrepresented the Kabbalah.

His book, which served as the principal source for all non-Jewish literature on Kabbalah until the end of the 19th century, opens with a "Key to the Divine Names of the Kabbalah," an extensive glossary of kabbalistic symbolism according to the *Zohar, *Sha'arey Orah, Pardes Rimmonim*, and some of the writings of Isaac Luria. He also made use of an Italian work on *alchemy and Kabbalah, *Esh ha-Meẓaref*, whose Hebrew original is no longer extant and is preserved only in the extracts translated by Knorr. This was followed by translations of some of Luria's writings, of the chapter on the soul in *Cordovero's *Pardes Rimmonim*, and selections from Naphtali *Bacharach's *Emek ha-Melekh*, an abridged translation of *Sha'ar ha-Shamayim* by Abraham Kohen de *Herrera, and a detailed explanation of the kabbalistic "Tree" according to the teachings of Luria, after the manner of Israel *Sarug. The "Tree" itself (which he possessed in manuscript form) he printed separately in 16 pages. To this were added several disquisitions by Henry More. The first part of the second volume opens with a translation of *Mareh Kohen* by *Issachar Berman b. Naphtali ha-Kohen (Amsterdam, 1673), followed by a translation of the first 25 leaves of *Emek ha-Melekh*, on the doctrine of *ẓimẓum* and the primordial world of chaos *(tohu)*, as "an introduction to a better understanding of the Zohar." The second part includes translations of the *Idrot* of the Zohar, *Sifra di-Ẓeni'uta* and the commentary on it by Ḥayyim *Vital taken from a manuscript, the chapters on angelology and demonology from *Beit Elohim* of Abraham Kohen de Herrera, and a translation of *Sefer ha-Gilgulim* from a manuscript "of the writings of Isaac Luria." This manuscript includes precisely what was published in the same year, 1684, by David Gruenhaut in Frankfurt on the Main. The volume closes with a separate work – *Adumbratio Kabbalae Christianae* – a summary of Christian Kabbalah; although it was published anonymously, the author was Van Helmont. Apart from the translation from *Beit Elohim*, all the texts in the second part of the second volume have been translated into English or French: the *Idrot* and *Sifra di-Ẓeni'uta* by S.L.M. Mathers (*The Kabbalah Unveiled*, 1887, 5th repr. 1962), *Sefer ha-Gilgulim* by E. Jégut (Paris, 1905), and the *Adumbratio* by Gilly de Givry (Paris, 1899). Knorr's major anthology to a great extent determined the image of Kabbalah in the eyes of historians of philosophy until the close of the 19th century. The philosopher Leibnitz, impressed by Knorr's publication, visited him in 1687 and discussed kabbalistic subjects with him.

Late in life Knorr worked on a major book on the childhood of *Jesus, based on rabbinical and kabbalistic sources. The manuscript reached his friend Van Helmont, who promised to have it published in Amsterdam; the project, however, was not realized, and this lengthy work, *Messias Puer*, was lost. During his lifetime Knorr helped to establish a Hebrew publishing house at Sulzbach, and he had a hand in the edition of the Zohar that appeared in 1684. It includes a Latin dedication to Prince Christian August, the anonymous author of which was doubtless Knorr. He likewise played a role in the publication of *Ḥesed le-Avraham* by Abraham *Azulai (Amsterdam, 1685) which is mainly a summary of the Kabbalah of Cordovero.

BIBLIOGRAPHY: Wolf, Bibliotheca, 1 (1715), 1140–43; 2 (1721), 1232–35; 3 (1727), 677–8; K. Salecker, *Christian Knorr von Rosenroth* (Ger., 1931); Scholem, *Bibliographia Kabbalistica* (1927), 86–88; F. Kemp, in: *Neue Zuercher Zeitung* (May 9, 1971), 51–52.

[Gershom Scholem]

KNUT, DOVID (pseudonym of **David Mironovich Fichman** 1900–1955), Russian poet. Knut was born in Kishinev into a merchant family and made his literary debut in the Kishinev press: in 1918 he edited the *Journal Molodaya mysl'* ("Young Thought"). In 1920 he emigrated to Paris where he participated in circles of Russian-language poets, and organized the group of poets "Palata poetov" ("Palace of Poets"). He published in emigré journals and edited *Noviy dom* (1925–27), the Russian-language Jewish newspaper **Razsvet*, and other publications. In 1925 he published *Moikh tysyacheletiy* ("My Millennia") which included many poems infused with biblical motifs and allusions, and with consideration of the historical fate of the Jewish people. In subsequent collections, *Vtoraya kniga stikhov* ("Second Book of Verses," 1928); *Parizhskie nochi* ("Parisian Nights," 1932); *Nasushchnaya lyubov'* ("True Love," 1938) the predominant themes are love, loneliness, death, rejection of the city, the oppression of life, and unrealizability of hopes. Knut dedicated a cycle of poems to his visit to Palestine in the mid-1930s; this was called "Prarodina" ("Original Homeland," published in periodicals from 1938 to 1948 and partially included in *Izbrannyestikhi* ("Selected Poetry," 1949)). Initially Knut's poetry was close to that of the Acmeists. His outstanding talents as a publicist were demonstrated in his essays (*"Al'bom puteshestvennika"* in *Zh. Russkiye Zapiski*, 1938).

In August 1940 Knut joined the Jewish resistance movement (L'Armée juive) in France whose activity he described in "Contribution to the History of the Jewish Resistance in France, 1940–1944" (in French, 1947). In 1949 he moved to Israel and settled in Tel Aviv, where he continued his literary activity and began to write poems in Hebrew.

Knut's wife, ARIADNA (Sarah after her conversion to Judaism; 1905–44), daughter of the composer Scriabin, was a Russian poet. Her book *Stikhi* ("Poem S," 1924) contains a poem on the biblical Joshua. While an active participant in the Jewish Combat Organization she transported a group of Jewish refugees to Switzerland. Killed in July 1944 in Toulouse in a clash with policemen collaborating with the Nazis, she was posthumously awarded the first French "military cross" and "medal of resistance."

[Mark Kipnis / *The Shorter Jewish Encyclopaedia in Russian* (2nd ed.)]

°**KOBAYASHI, MASAYUKI** (1906–?), Japanese specialist on Jewish and modern European history. Born in Iida, Japan, he taught at Waseda University from 1945. In the course of his studies on modern European history, especially into the problems of minorities, he developed a lasting interest in Jewish affairs. In the late 1930s he published "Frederick the Great's Policy Toward the Jews" and "Problems of the Jews during the French Revolution," pioneering studies in Japanese historical scholarship. After World War II he was a prime mover in Japan for the promotion of scholarship and education on Jewish history and culture and in fostering understanding of the reborn State of Israel. Kobayashi translated into Japanese Norman Bentwich's *Israel* (1960) and Harry Orlinsky's *Ancient Israel* (1961).

[Hyman Kublin]

KOBE, port on Osaka Bay, Japan. Before World War I a small number of Jews, mainly from the Middle East and Europe, carried on their business activities in Kobe; the Jewish community increased slightly with the advent of refugees from the Bolshevik Revolution. The Sephardi and Ashkenazi congregations in Kobe maintained synagogues and a community center. With the rise of Nazism in Europe, and particularly after the outbreak of World War II, hundreds of Jews from Eastern Europe fled across Siberia to Japan, which served as a transit point for their journeys to more or less permanent homes elsewhere. Many of them made their way to Kobe in 1940–41 where they were given emergency assistance by the local Jewish community, Jewish international relief organizations, and some sympathetic Japanese. Notable among the refugees who passed through Kobe at this time were teachers and students from the famous *Mir yeshivah in Lithuania who, lacking the necessary visas, were sent on to Shanghai. After World War II, a small Jewish community, augmented at times by American and European businessmen and professionals, continued to live in Kobe.

BIBLIOGRAPHY: A. Kotsuji, *From Tokyo to Jerusalem* (1964), 159–67.

[Hyman Kublin]

KOBER, ADOLF (1879–1958), Reform rabbi and historian. Kober was born in Beuthen, Upper Silesia, and he studied at the Jewish Theological Seminary and the University of Breslau. He served as rabbi at Wiesbaden (1908–18) and Cologne (1906–08, 1918–39). As historian of Rhenish Jewry, he organized the Jewish section for the exhibition celebrating the Rhineland's 1,000-year association with the German Reich in Cologne in 1925. With Bruno *Kisch, Kober was responsible for establishing the Juedisches Lehrhaus in Cologne in 1928; he also lectured on Jewish history at the Volkshochschule ("People's University") and the University of Cologne. In 1939 he emigrated to the United States, where in New York he formed a congregation of emigrants from Germany in association with the B'nai Jeshurun synagogue. Kober specialized in German-Jewish history and, in particular, the history of the Rhenish and Cologne Jews, basing his research on the scrupulous study of archival material. He wrote numerous studies on the history of the Jews in the Rhineland, among them *Grundbuch des Koelner Judenviertels* (1920) and *Cologne* (Eng. trans. by S. Grayzel, 1940). He also published many articles in this field. In the U.S. he worked as a research fellow of the American Academy of Jewish Research.

BIBLIOGRAPHY: Z. Asaria (ed.), *Juden in Koeln* (1959), index; G. Kisch, in: HJ, 21 (1959), 149–50; G. Kisch (ed.), *Das Breslauer Seminar* (1963), 413f. (incl. bibl.).

KOBER, ARTHUR (1900– 1975), U.S. humorist and playwright. Born in Brody, Galicia, Kober was raised in New York, which forms the scene of his amusing books about Jewish life, including *Thunder over the Bronx* (1935), *My Dear Bella* (1941; published in England as *Parm Me*, 1945), *Bella, Bella, Kissed a Fella* (1951), and *Ooh, What You Said!* (1958). He wrote the comedy *Having a Wonderful Time* (1937), and collaborated on *Wish You Were Here* (1952) and *A Mighty Man Is He* (1960). Kober also wrote screenplays and sketches of Hollywood life.

°**KOBIELSKI, FRANCISZEK ANTONI** (1679–1755), Polish priest. In 1735 he became the confessor and chancellor to Queen Maria Josephine, the wife of Augustus III; in 1736 he was appointed bishop of Kamenets-Podolski, and in 1739 bishop of Lutsk. He was zealous in missionary activities among the Jews of Podolia, sometimes preaching in the synagogues, as well as engaging in a disputation with the rabbis of Brody (1742–43). Upon its conclusion, he instructed the local clergy to pursue their missionary activities with more energy, and in 1746 he published a collection of sermons, *Światło na oświecenie narodu niewiernego* ("Light on the Enlightenment of the Infidel People"). At the same time Bishop Kobielski imposed various anti-Jewish restrictions. These included a restriction prohibiting Christian servants to sleep in the houses of their Jewish employers; public masquerades on Purim; and the lighting of synagogues at night was also prohibited. At the Sejm (diet) of Warsaw, in 1748, he sought to reduce the taxes levied upon the Jews and accused the rabbis of exploiting the poorer classes of the Jewish population. In 1752 he published a circular on the attitude of the clergy toward the Jews, *Wszystkiemu duchowieństwu na zdrowie* ("Greetings to All the Clergy"), and an essay, *Proces tykający Żydów* ("A Trial Concerning the Jews").

BIBLIOGRAPHY: N.M. Gelber, in: MGWJ, 68 (1924), 232–3; W. Smoleński, *Stan i sprawa Żydów polskich w XVIII wieku* (1876), 24 (= *Pisma historyczne*, 2 (1901), 240); *Polski Słownik Biograficzny*, 13 (1967–68), 146–8; A. Kitowicz, *Opis obyczajów w Polsce wostatnich latach panowania Augusta III*, ed. R. Pollak (1951); M. Balaban, *Le-Toledot ha-Tenu'ah ha-Frankit* (1934), 200–12.

[Arthur Cygielman]

KOBLENZ, city in Germany. Jews are first mentioned in a customs toll of 1104; an individual Jew, Vives of Koblenz, is noted as living in Cologne about 1135; the community is mentioned in *Benjamin of Tudela's *Itinerary* (c. 1172). A 1209 toll register set a discriminatory fee for Jews but the Mainz Nuremberg **Memorbuch* credits "Isaac and his wife Bela" with its removal. The Jew Suesskind granted a loan against the security of a mortgage on a house to Archbishop Theodore of *Trier, which the latter had redeemed by 1238. In 1265 Archbishop Henry granted the Jews a privilege of protection, yet on April 2, 1265, some 20 Jews were slain. A father who had martyred his wife and four sons but was himself saved from committing suicide by gentiles asked *Meir of Rothenburg if he had to do penance and was given a lenient reply, referring to earlier such events.

Archbishop Henry's peace treaty with the city, signed in 1285, after a revolt, stipulated that violation of Jewish life and property should be punished. In 1307 the Jewish community (*universitas Judeorum*), headed by a magistrate, received the rights of joint citizenship from the municipality. Jewish houses and properties are mentioned in sources dating from 1275 to 1333, the Jews' gate in 1282, the cemetery in 1303, and the nursing home in 1356. The main Jewish quarter was near the Old Town. R. *Asher b. Jehiel moved to Koblenz (c. 1282) and his older brother Ḥayyim functioned there as rabbi. The scribe Eliezer b. Samuel ha-Levi wrote a parchment Bible in 1344. The names of three Jews who died as martyrs in 1287 or 1288 have been preserved. From 1279 to 1346 Jews appear as moneylenders to the city council, the archbishop of Trier, and the local nobility: the Moselle bridge tolls were frequently farmed to them. The Jews were persecuted again in 1337, and most severely during the *Black Death in 1348–49. Their property was sold by Archbishop Boemund, but they were again living in Koblenz from 1351 on under the archbishop's protection. The city law, codified some time before 1424, excluded Jews, along with clerics and servants, from jury service in the courts. Added sections concluded in 1515 contain a Jewish oath formula with threatening clauses in case of perjury characteristic of the 15th century and later. The Jews were expelled from Koblenz in 1418.

Almost 100 years later (1512–18) a new community came into being with the admission of five families, who obtained a charter. The Trier bishopric issued successive Jewry regulations from 1555 to 1771, restricting the Jews to pawnbrokerage and certain kinds of trade. In 1723 they were ordered to live on a Jews' street (renamed Mint Street in 1886), and to refrain from wearing bright, costly clothes. The rabbinical synods of the Trier bishopric frequently met in Koblenz, concerning themselves with education and communal welfare. The authority of the local rabbi extended over the entire region. A welfare organization was founded in 1772. The *Memorbuch* begun in 1610 (continued until 1850) lists the names of the community leaders, many of whom were talmudic scholars and physicians, foremost among them the *Wallich family.

In 1794 the Jews' gate was broken down and emancipation came to Koblenz in 1797. The Rhine and Moselle district Jewish assembly was held in Koblenz in 1808. In 1811 the bank of Leopold Seligmann was founded, and in 1815 that of R.J. Goldschmidt. Antisemitic Hep! *Hep! riots occurred in 1819. A synagogue was built in 1826 and a new one in 1851. Mutual aid and welfare agencies were founded (1827–30) and a school in 1840. In 1808, 342 Jews lived in Koblenz; the number fell to 242 in 1836, but rose to 400 in 1849, 558 in 1880, 709 (1.8% of the total population) in 1925, 800 in 1929, and dropped to 669 in 1933; in May 1939 there were only 308. The figures reflect the restrictive laws in the early 19th century, their later removal, and emigration from 1933 on. Beginning in 1933 the Nazi boycott of Jewish stores began and Jews were harassed in other ways. The synagogue was burned in November 1938. From 1942 to 1943, 177 Jews were deported to the East, and 544 from the Bendorf-Sain-Koblenz district, where a Jewish mental hospital was located. Twenty-two Koblenz Jews survived the Holocaust. The city erected a memorial to the Jewish victims. In 1948 the burial hall was converted into a synagogue, also used by Jews of nearby towns. The Jewish population of the whole area was 68 in 1945/46, 78 in 1948, and 94 in 1963, and in Koblenz itself it was 35 in 1961 and around 100 in 1987.

BIBLIOGRAPHY: K. Schilling (ed.), *Monumenta Judaica-Handbuch* (1963), index; Germ Jud, 1 (1963²), 141–7; 2 (1968), 407–14; EJ, 6 (Berlin, 1934), 145–50, with bibliography; G. Engelbert, in: E. Keyser (ed.), *Staedtebuch fuer Rheinland-Pfalz und Saarland* (1964), 211f.; M.N. Adler, *The Itinerary of Benjamin of Tudela* (1901), 1, 80; 71 (Hebr.); I.A. Agus, *Rabbi Meir of Rothenburg* (1947), no. 784; S. Neumann, *Statistik der Juden in Preussen* (1884), 48; *Die Originallisten der Gestapo mit den Namen der Deportierten des Kreises Koblens* (n.d.) passim.

[Toni Oelsner]

KOBLER, FRANZ (1882–1965), lawyer, pacifist, and writer. Kobler, who was born in Vienna, edited *Der Strahl*, the Austrian pacifist publication in Vienna, wrote extensively on legal problems and pacifism (*Gewalt und Gewaltlosigkeit*, 1928), and practiced law there from 1914 to 1938. In 1938 Kobler left Austria and subsequently took refuge in Switzerland, England, and finally in the U.S. Kobler's contribution to Jewish scholarship consisted of his pioneering anthologies of Jewish letters: *Juden und Judentum in deutschen Briefen…* (1935); *Juedische Geschichte in Briefen… aus Ost und West* (1938); and the two-volume *Letters of Jews Through the Ages* (1952; published in the U.S. as *A Treasury of Jewish Letters*, 1953). Kobler also contributed to Jewish periodicals, and published Napoleon Bonaparte's 1799 proclamation to the Jews, which he had discovered (*New Judaea*, 16 (1939/40), 189–90; 17 (1940/41), 18–19; 36–37; 69–70).

KÓBOR, TAMÁS (originally **Adolf Bermann**; 1867–1942), Hungarian author and journalist. Kóbor was born in Pressburg and raised amid the poverty of its ghetto district. He worked in a bank and began to write for the Budapest daily press and for *A Hét*, the literary periodical edited by his brother-in-law József Kiss. For several years he helped to edit the liberal newspaper *Az Újság* for which he himself wrote articles on topical and political issues, including Jewish rights. Having grown up at a time when the drift from Judaism was already under way, Kóbor had no hesitation in advocating assimilation, although he remained sentimentally attached to Jewish culture. His concern with the problem of maintaining Jewish loyalties while supporting the Hungarian national cause is the central issue in the novel *Ki a gettóból* ("Out of the Ghetto," 1911). His many novels and short stories include *Budapest* (1901), *A Halál* ("Death," 1918), *Pók Ádám hetvenhét élete* ("The Seventy-Seven Lives of Adam Pók," 1923), and *Hamlet az irodában* ("A Hamlet in the Office," 1934).

BIBLIOGRAPHY: L. Steiner, in: IMIT (1942), 423; *Magyar Zsidó Lexikon* (1929), 92; B. Halmi, *Kóbor Tamás, az iró és az ember* (1935).

[Baruch Yaron]

KOBRIN (Pol. **Kobryń**), city in Brest district, Belarus, formerly in Poland. The earliest information on the Jewish community there is found in a document of 1511 in which King Sigismund I, among others, ratified its privileges. In the 1563 census the names of 23 Jews are mentioned as holding 25 houses, as well as about 20 orchards and vegetable gardens, and a synagogue. In 1589, when Kobrin received rights of a town, the Jews were accorded equal rights with the other inhabitants. In the frame of the Council of Lithuania Land, the Kobrin community was under jurisdiction of the Brest-Litovsk community. The Jews of Kobrin mainly earned their livelihood from local and interurban trade with Lublin, the leasing of inns, and the collection of custom duties. During the *Chmielnicki massacres of 1648–49, some Jews suffered from the Cossacks, and a number of Jews from the Ukraine took refuge in Kobrin. In the first half of the 18th century, owing to the wars with the Swedes, plagues, and fires, the city became impoverished, the economic situation of the Jews also deteriorated, and the community incurred considerable debts. Most of the local Jews in this period were engaged in peddling and various crafts, while a wealthy minority continued to trade in salt, cereals, and timber. In 1766 there were 946 Jews in Kobrin and the surrounding villages who paid a poll tax. Spiritual leaders of Kobrin included *Bezalel b. Solomon of Kobryn (d. 1678), and Jacob b. David Shapira (d. 1718), author of *Ohel Ya'akov* (Frankfurt on the Oder, 1729), *av bet din* of Kobrin, who founded a yeshivah.

In the beginning of Russian rule, the town was granted by the czar to the famous army commander Suvorov, and also proclaimed as a county capital. All these helped the development of the town, and the Jewish population of Kobrin and the surrounding townlets increased. There were 4,184 (total population 6,500) Jews living in Kobrin in 1847. In 1882 Jews were prohibited from leasing farms and rural buildings. The introduction of the government monopoly on liquor distilling in 1897 severely affected Jewish economic activity in Kobrin. Many emigrated, especially to America. The Jewish population numbered 6,687 in 1897 (69% of the total). During the 19th century, Ḥasidism, led by the dynasty of *Kobrin, founded by R. Moshe Rabinovich, was influential in the community, and lasted until the Holocaust. One of his grandchildren was the poet Yehuda Leib Lilenblum (YHL"L). Ḥayyim Berlin (the son of Naphtali Ẓevi Judah *Berlin) served as rabbi there. Zionism at first encountered violent opposition from the local Orthodox circles. After the revolution of 1905 Jewish workers, mainly organized in the *Bund and later the *Po'alei Zion, took an active part in the struggle for political, social, and cultural rights. The community had modernized *ḥadarim*, as well as a religious school, a *Tarbut school, a Yiddish school of the Central Yiddish School Organization (CYSHO), and a yeshivah. The community numbered 5,431 (c. 66% of the total) in 1921, and 5,617 in 1931. Most of them were employed in construction, linen manufacture, embroidering, porterage, haulage, shopkeeping, and retail trade in agricultural produce.

[Arthur Cygielman]

Holocaust Period

Soon after the outbreak of World War II, on Sept. 20, 1939, the Soviets took the city. The Zionist youth there tried to reach Vilna which was then in independent Lithuania, whence many of them continued on to Palestine. Many refugees from western Poland arrived in Kobrin, and by 1941 the Jewish population reached 8,000. On June 23, 1941, the Germans occupied Kobrin. Soon after the occupation, they established a Judenrat, instituted forced labor, and murdered about 170 Jews not far from the village of Patryki. In August 1941 the Germans imposed a fine of 6 kg of gold and 12 kg of silver on the Jews. In November 1941 a ghetto was set up, into which about 8,000 Jews were crowded. It was divided into two sections: part A for skilled workers and families, and part B for the others. Jews from the neighboring towns of Hajnówka and Bialowieza were also brought to the ghetto, which was greatly overcrowded. On July 27, 1942, ghetto B was surrounded, and about 3,000 Jews were shipped to Brona Gora, and murdered there. The youth organized and began to collect ammunition. On Oct. 14, 1942, another *Aktion* took place about 2.5 mi. (4 km.) from Kobrin on the road to Dywin. The Jews attempted active self-defense, the Germans were attacked, and attempts were made to take their arms. A group of about 500 persons managed to escape, but only 100 reached the forests and joined the partisans. They were active in the Voroshilov and Suvorov partisan units. A group of Jewish craftsmen was held in Kobrin until the summer of 1943 and then murdered in the prison courtyard. After the war, the community was not revived. A few survivors left Kobrin for Poland and then continued to Israel or other countries.

[Aharon Weiss]

BIBLIOGRAPHY: *Dokumenty i regesty k istorici litovskikh yevreyev*, 1 (1882), no. 62; *Russko-yevreyskiy arkhiv*, 2 (1882), nos. 179, 180, 185; S. Dubnow (ed.), *Pinkas ha-Medinah* (1925), index; B. Wasiutyński, *Ludność żydowska w Polsce…* (1930), 80, 83, 88, 192, 202, 211; B. Schwarz and I.H. Biletzky (eds.), *Sefer Kobrin, Megillat Ḥayyim ve-Ḥurban* (1951).

KOBRIN, LEON (1872–1946), Yiddish dramatist and novelist. Kobrin was born in Vitebsk, Russia, where he began writing in Russian. Only after immigrating to Philadelphia in 1892 did he develop an interest in Yiddish literature. After translating stories from Russian into Yiddish, his first original story was "*A Merder Oys Libe*" ("A Murderer for Love," 1894) in the *Filadelfyer Shtot-Tsaytung*. Further sketches published in the *Ovntblat* won him a permanent position on the newspaper and he moved to New York. His writing was strongly influenced by Jacob *Gordin and Russian and French realism. The majority of his plays and stories depict the social and emotional problems of adaptation to life in urban sweatshops and tenements. Occasionally, with varying degrees of nostalgia, he returned to an East European setting, as in *Yankl Boyle* (1898) a story in which he portrays the tragic love of a Jewish fisherman for a peasant girl. In this and other works, the innovative presentation of raw eroticism invites comparison with David *Pinski's *Yankl der Shmid* ("Yankl the Smith," 1906). Kobrin's dramatized version of *Yankl Boyle* was successfully performed in 1913 in both the U.S. and Europe, and was revived in New York in 1963. His debut as a playwright had come with *Mine* (1899), which was controversially rewritten and staged by Gordin, the original text appearing, however, later the same year. Kobrin wrote several novels and more than 30 plays, not all of which were published, but most were staged. They deal predominantly with problems of nationalism, assimilation, and inter-generational conflict in the U.S. He also translated and adapted for the stage *Shakespeare's *Hamlet*, *Goethe's *Faust*, and Israel *Zangwill's *Children of the Ghetto*, as well as plays by Tolstoy and Chirikov. Among his major works are *Di Imigrantn* ("The Immigrants," 1909), *Di Dervakhung* ("The Awakening," 1920), and *Ore di Bord* ("Ore the Beard," 1918), a novel dealing with the life of a religious Jew during a real estate boom in New York. His memoirs appeared as *Derinerungen fun a Yidishn Dramaturg* ("Memories of a Yiddish Playwright," 1925) and *Mayne Fuftsik Yor in Amerike* ("My Fifty Years in America," 1955, 1966). A collection of short stories, *A Lithuanian Village* (1928), appeared in English, and further translations have appeared in a number of anthologies. Together with his wife, Pauline Segal, Kobrin translated into Yiddish from Artsibashev, Chekhov, Turgenev, and Zola, as well as the collected works of du Maupassant.

BIBLIOGRAPHY: S. Liptzin, *The Flowering of Yiddish Literature* (1963), 154–5; E. Schulman, *Geshikhte fun der Yidisher Literatur in Amerike* (1943), 129–33; Rejzen, Leksikon 3 (1929), 359–70; Z. Zilbercweig, *Leksikon fun Yidishn Teater* 4 (1963), 2962–3044; Waxman, *Literature* 4:2 (1960^2), 1000–1.

[Elias Schulman / Hugh Denman (2nd ed.)]

KOBRIN, MOSES BEN ISRAEL POLIER OF (1784–1858), ḥasidic rabbi. He was a disciple of the *ẓaddikim* Mordecai and Noah of *Lachowicze (Lyakhovichi); on the latter's death he became rabbi of the ḥasidic community in *Kobrin and its vicinity. Moses was particularly known for his virtues of truthfulness, humility, and the bearing of suffering with love. He did not insist on fasts and ascetic practices. His sayings were short and to the point, and he influenced and educated his congregation of Ḥasidim by proverbs and examples. He placed great importance on the personal link between the Ḥasid and the *ẓaddik*, who is "like a branch to a tree," but "the *ẓaddik* will be answerable for every single step that the ḥasid makes in his direction." He wrote his Ḥasidim letters of encouragement when they were in distress. He had adherents in Ereẓ Israel among the Ḥasidim of *kolel* Lyakhovichi. His sayings are collected in *Amarot Tehorot* (1910).

His successor in Kobrin was his grandson NOAH NAPHTALI (d. 1889); his sayings and maxims entitled *Ma'amarim Tehorim* are published with the sayings of his grandfather in *Amarot Tehorot* (1910). Kobrin Ḥasidism declined in his day owing to competition from the growing adherence to *Slonim Ḥasidim. Noah Naphtali was succeeded by his sons DAVID SOLOMON (d. 1918), who remained ḥasidic rabbi in Kobrin, and AARON (d. 1907), who settled in the townlet Domachevo. The son of David Solomon, MOSES AARON, led the Ḥasidim of Kobrin until the Holocaust, in which he perished in 1942. David Solomon's son-in-law, BARUCH JOSEPH ZAK (d. 1949), the last to hold the title of "Rabbi of Kobrin," led a group of Kobrin Ḥasidim who emigrated to the United States.

BIBLIOGRAPHY: B. Schwarz and I.H. Biletzky (ed.), *Sefer Kobrin* (1951); W. Rabinowitsch, *Lithuanian Ḥasidism* (1970); M. Buber, *Tales of the Hasidim*, 2 (1966), 159–73.

[Wolf Zeev Rabinowitsch]

KOBRIN, SOLOMON (1910–1996), U.S. criminologist. Born in Chicago, Kobrin received his bachelor's and master's degrees from the University of Chicago and a Ph.D. from the University of Southern California (USC). He pioneered ecological studies of juvenile delinquency at the Chicago Institute for Juvenile Research and contributed significantly to the development of modern theories on delinquency and rehabilitation. His research focused on the sociology of street gangs; the study of deviant behavior; and methods to evaluate programs for crime control, delinquency prevention, and juvenile justice.

During the 1940s he helped to organize an innovative project at the Illinois Institute for Juvenile Research that worked to mobilize community residents to provide recreational and other constructive activities for youths in Chicago neighborhoods with high delinquency rates. Kobrin headed the institute's Division of Social Systems Analysis. He later served as a member of the President's Committee on Law Enforcement and the Administration of Justice (1955–56).

In 1967 he joined the sociology faculty of USC's College of Letters, Arts, and Sciences. He also worked as a senior research associate at USC's Social Science Research Institute. In the 1970s he was a consultant to the U.S. Department of Health, Education, and Welfare. He served on an advisory board to evaluate addict-treatment centers for the U.S. Office of Economic Opportunity (1971); was a consultant to the California Council on Criminal Justice (1972); and chaired the HEW Task Force on Youth Development and Delinquency Prevention Administration (1973).

After he retired from teaching and received emeritus status in 1975, he continued his research activities at the institute. In 1977, he received the American Society of Criminology's Edwin H. Sutherland Award for his outstanding research achievements.

He was president of the Illinois Academy of Criminology (1958) and the California Association for Criminal Justice Research (1975).

Kobrin wrote several influential books on delinquency prevention and crime control, including *Interaction between Neighborhood Change and Criminal Activity* (with L. Schuerman, 1988) and *Community Treatment of Juvenile Offenders* (with M. Klein, 1983).

[Ruth Beloff (2nd ed.)]

KOCH, ADELHEID LUCY (1896–1980), first psychoanalyst recognized by the International Psychoanalytic Association (IPA) in Brazil and founder of Sociedade Brasileira de Psicanálise de São Paulo, the first official Brazilian psychoanalytic society. Born in Germany, Adelheid graduated in medicine from the University of Berlin in 1924. She was psychoanalyzed by Otto Fenichel and became a member of Berlin's Psychoanalytic Society in 1935. As a refugee from the Nazi regime, Adelheid and her husband Ernst immigrated to Brazil in 1936, settled in São Paulo and took part in the foundation of the Congregação Israelita Paulista (1936), which was created by Jewish refugees from Germany. Adelheid worked as a volunteer in the Congregação's youth programs (and Ernst was the president of the organization between 1956 and 1967). After she settled down in São Paulo, Adelheid was officially recognized by Ernest Jones, president of IPA, and became the first authorized "training analyst" in Brazil. She was mentor (with Durval Marcondes) of the founding group of Grupo Psicanalítico de São Paulo (1944), which later became the Sociedade Brasileira de Psicanálise de São Paulo (1951). From then on, psychoanalytic treatments and concepts developed considerably in Brazil (as well as in Argentina). There was an important presence of Jewish professionals and intellectuals among the Brazilian psychoanalysts in the early 21st century.

BIBLIOGRAPHY: Documentation of Arquivo Histórico Judaico Brasileiro; *Álbum de Família da Sociedade Brasileira de Psicanálise de São Paulo: Imagens, Fontes e Idéias da Psicanálise em São Paulo* (1994); R.Y. Sagawa, *Os Inconscientes no Divã da História* (1989); A.I. Hirschberg. *Desafio e Reposta. A História da Congregação Israelita Paulista* (1976).

[Roney Cytrynowicz (2nd ed.)]

KOCH, EDWARD IRVING (1924–), U.S. politician. Born in the Bronx, New York, Koch attended the City College of New York from 1941 to 1943. In his last year of college, he was drafted into the army, where he served with the 104th Infantry Division. He received two battle stars and was honorably discharged in 1946 with the rank of sergeant. He graduated from New York University School of Law in 1948 and began to practice law. Deeply committed to the service of his native city, he entered public life in 1963, when he replaced Carmine de Sapio, the long-time Tammany Hall district leader in Greenwich Village. He was reelected in the following two years. Koch was elected to the New York City Council in 1966 and was the first Democrat to represent his district in more than 30 years. Two years later he was elected to Congress, where he served for nine years. He led the fight for urban-orientation and was instrumental in having the mass transit operating subsidy bill passed in 1974. He has strongly supported measures aimed at furthering equal opportunity, human rights, health care, and the arts. In 1976 he was voted "the most effective Congressman from New York" by his congressional colleagues from New York City.

In November 1977 he was elected the 105th mayor of New York, assuming office on January 1, 1978, and was overwhelmingly reelected in 1981. His rallying cry "How'm I doing?" was best answered by the fact that he held the position for three terms, until 1989. Among his many achievements as mayor, Koch succeeded in restoring financial stability to New York City and placed the Big Apple on a balanced budget. He ran for a fourth term but was defeated in the Democratic primary.

Koch then became a partner in the law firm of Robinson, Silverman, Pearce, Aronsohn & Berman. He also wrote political columns; was a commentator for Bloomberg Television; hosted a radio talk show; and wrote movie, book, and restaurant reviews, as well as a weekly column for *Newsday*.

Among Koch's books are *How'm I Doing? The Wit and Wisdom of Ed Koch* (with M. Shestack and R. Sayre, 1981), *Mayor* (1984), *Politics* (1985), *His Eminence and Hizzoner* (1989), *All The Best: Letters from a Feisty Mayor* (1990), *Citizen Koch* (1992), *Ed Koch on Everything* (1994), *Giuliani: Nasty Man* (1999), and *I'm Not Done Yet: Remaining Relevant* (with D. Paisner, 2000).

BIBLIOGRAPHY: J. Mollenkopf, *A Phoenix in the Ashes: The Rise and Fall of the Koch Coalition in New York City Politics* (1992); J. Newfield and W. Barrett, *City for Sale* (1989); M. Goodwin, et al. *I, Koch: A Decidedly Unauthorized Biography of the Mayor of New York City* (1985).

[Rohan Saxen and Ruth Beloff (2nd ed.)]

KOCH, KENNETH (1925–2002), U.S. poet. Koch was born in Cincinnati, Ohio, and as a young man, fought in the U.S. Army in the Pacific during World War II. He later studied at Harvard, and one of his teachers was the poet Delmore Schwartz. He received an M.A. from Columbia University as well as a Ph.D. Along with Frank O'Hara and John Ashbery, he was one of the major figures of the "New York School" of poetry. He was also part of a group that included the painter Larry Rivers. His own poetry, which makes free and exuberant use of the absurd, the non sequitur, and the juxtaposition of incongruous images, exerted wide influence among younger poets. Among his published volumes are *Ko, or A Season on Earth* (1959), *Thank You, and Other Poems* (1962), *The Art of Love* (1975) and *The Duplications* (1977). Koch taught poetry at Columbia University beginning in 1959. Koch also became well-known for teaching poetry to school children as well as to the elderly. His *Rose, Where Did You Get That Red? Teaching Great Poetry to Children* (1973) is considered one of the landmarks in teaching creative writing. *The Collected Fiction of Kenneth Koch* and his *Collected Poems* were published in 2005.

[Lewis Fried (2nd ed.)]

KOCHAN, LIONEL (1922–), British historian. Kochan was educated at Cambridge and London Universities and was Bearsted reader in Jewish History at Warwick and East Anglia Universities. He wrote widely on modern Russian and modern German history as well as on modern Jewish history. Kochan was the editor of *The Jews in Soviet Russia since 1917* (1970; rev. ed. 1978), *The Jew in His History* (1977), *Jewish Idols and Messiahs – The Challenge From History* (1990), and many other works. With his wife, Miriam, he contributed for many years the annual survey of Jewish life in Great Britain to *The American Jewish Year Book.*

[William D. Rubinstein (2nd ed.)]

KOCHI (formerly known as **Cochin**, "the Queen of the Arabian Sea"), port city on the southwest coast of India, famous for its excellent natural harbor. Its population is 1,600,000 (2005) and it is regarded as the commercial and industrial capital of Kerala, one of the most prosperous and literate states in India. The municipality was created in 1967 out of Fort Kochi, Mattanchery, Ernakulam, Willingdon Island, and a number of nearby villages.

Kochi is also the name of the princely state that was absorbed into the Union of India upon independence in 1947. Prior to that time, the State of Cochin was ruled by a rajah and enjoyed at least nominal independence despite domination by Portuguese (1498–1663), Dutch (1663–1795), and British (1797–1947) colonial powers. In 1957, the former princely states of Cochin, Travancore, and Malabar were merged into the State of Kerala.

Kochi attained dominance as southwest India's premier port after a flood silted up the harbor at nearby Kodugallur (known to the British as Cranganore, to the Romans as Muziris, and to the Jews as Shingly) and simultaneously created Kochi's harbor. The local royal family, along with its leading families and institutions, migrated 20 miles (30 km.) south and reestablished themselves at Kochi.

The Origin of Kochiís Jews

Kochi is home to the oldest Jewish community east of Persia. According to local historical traditions, when the Romans destroyed Jerusalem in 70 C.E., a number of Jews set sail on recently discovered monsoon shipping lanes. They reached Shingly, which was known to them as the source of spices and other luxury items since the time of King Solomon. They were welcomed by the local king, who gave them land for synagogues and for coconut estates. Another king, called Cheraman Perumal, had two copper plates inscribed with a charter for the community, granting the Jews material rights and the symbolic trappings of royalty, which he presented to the Jewish leader, Joseph Rabban. Thereafter, Cheraman Perumal and Joseph Rabban became archetypes of the cordial lord-vassal relationship between Hindus and Jews in Kochi. The copper plates are stored in the ark of the Cochin Synagogue.

Communal discord foreshadowed the 1341 flood that led to the migration of the Jews from Cranganore to Kochi, where another rajah welcomed them and granted them land immediately adjacent to his palace and personal Hindu temple for their synagogue and their settlement at Mattanchery, which came to be known as Jew Town. In 1568 they built the beautiful Paradesi, or Foreignersí, synagogue, in use to this day.

Shingly and the Early Jewish Settlements

That Shingly and its Jewish prince remain for Kochi Jews the paramount symbols of their pleasant life in India is clear. What is less clear is the history of the settlements, migration patterns, or even reliable accounts of daily life in Shingly. Indigenous historians and medieval travelers report Jewish settlements in the area at Paalur, Mount Deli, Chendamangalam, Parur, Calicut, Cannanore, Quilon, and elsewhere; Shingly does not necessarily seem to be preeminent, even if it was the oldest. Jews came from ancient Israel, Yemen, Persia, the Middle East, and even Europe.

In Shingly, Jews were a substantial minority, a privileged and respected community, close to the king and enjoying religious liberty. They built synagogues and composed liturgical songs in Hebrew and Malayalam, the local language. They evolved a unique *minhag* that bears evidence of waves of immigration as well as indigenous, Indian influences. Recently discovered documents confirm that many of the traditions of Kochi have their origin in Shingly. It is believed that the great medieval religious figures *Judah Halevi and Abraham *Ibn Ezra, visited Shingly, and some believe that the latter is buried there.

In pluralistic Shingly, Jews were merchants, petty traders, agriculturalists, and soldiers, but they are best known as international spice merchants, especially in the lucrative pepper trade.

Migration to Kochi and the Arrival of the Portuguese

A combination of factors – internal strife, a rivalry with Muslim competitors that was exacerbated by the arrival of the Portuguese, and the 1341 flood – prompted a migration from Shingly to Kochi, where the Jews built their first synagogue in 1344. Satellite communities sprung up in Malah, Cranganore, Parur, Ernakulam, and Chendamangalam.

Whatever battles the Jews may have had with their Muslim, Christian, and even Hindu neighbors, their greatest tormentors were, without doubt, the Portuguese. Vasco da Gama, the Portuguese adventurer and explorer, landed in Kochi in 1498, and in 1503 built the first Catholic church in India and in the same year the first European fortress, located at today's Fort Kochi.

The Portuguese injected themselves into the rivalry between the Muslim Zamorin of Calicut and the Hindu Rajah of Kochi, first taking one side, then the other. Through the

Portuguese, Kochi rose in importance as a seaport and her Jews were placed in direct contact with their co-religionists in Western Europe for the first time. But the Portuguese were as intolerant in India as they had been at home. Not only did they establish an Office of the Inquisition at Goa in 1560, they also burned and sacked Jew Town some years later. The Rajah of Kochi refused demands from the King of Portugal to collaborate in the persecution of his Jewish subjects, an expression of sympathy that earned him the contempt of the Portuguese, who derisively called him the King of the Jews.

The Dutch Era

During Portuguese rule, the Jews suffered many persecutions, but the era had its achievements as well. It was under Portuguese rule that the Jews managed to establish themselves at Kochi, when they built most of their beautiful synagogues, and they began a novel system of self-government known at the mudaliar system.

The leaders of the Jewish community came to be known by the Tamil/ Malayalam term mudaliar, meaning simple "headman." First appointed by the Rajah of Kochi, the mudaliars had the authority to enforce punishments and impose and collect fines and taxes, but deferred to the rajah in capital cases. Not only that, the mudaliars became the rajah's closest and most trusted advisors, and one, Ezekiel *Rahabi, became prime minister to the rajah. The institution lasted until British rule during the 19th century.

The Dutch became involved in Kochi due in part to native dissatisfaction with the Portuguese. An expeditionary force in 1662 was repelled by the Portuguese garrison, who blamed the Jews and carried out ferocious reprisals. They burned the synagogue, including all of the Torah scrolls, holy books, and historical records, and sacked Jew Town. The Jews fled to the hills, where they remained for the better part of a year until the Dutch finally defeated the Portuguese and established their rule in 1663.

Under the tolerant, commercially minded Dutch, the Jews experienced a flowering of commerce and culture to rival the glory days at Shingly. Not only did their economic fortunes rise sharply, but the Kochi Jews were put into contact with Jews from Holland and throughout the Dutch empire, from Indonesia to New York. On November 21, 1686, they received a delegation from Amsterdam led by the Portuguese reconverso Moses Pereyra de Paiva. De Paiva arranged for the Kochi Jews to obtain replacements for their Torah scrolls and holy books, and the Jews arranged to have their own traditions enshrined in *maḥzorim* (festival prayer books) published by Proops, the well-known Dutch Hebrew press. The Jews also narrated their history to de Paiva, who published their account in Portuguese.

The most famous family of Kochi was the Rahabis. Their fame was due, in part, to their prominence in trade and diplomacy, and also to the many authors and scholars in the family. David Rahabi was the head of the family at the time of de Paiva's visit, and was very influential with the royal family. He was able to smooth over a festering succession dispute, earning the family an even more intimate role in the affairs of state. David's son, Ezekiel, assumed his father's role as "Joods Koopman," or Jewish agent for the Dutch East India Company, and at the same time accepted the role of prime minister to the rajah.

Ezekiel towered over the Malabarí pepper trade. His home became a salon for the high and mighty of Kochi and beyond, and he was considered one of the best-informed people of his day, with a wealth of information about commodity prices, currency fluctuations, troop and naval movements, and the lines of succession in Europe's royal families. He undertook a number of diplomatic missions on behalf of both the rajah and the Dutch, negotiating peace accords among rival states. He was a philanthropist, supporting an impoverished local Christian community, and building a church at Cranganore and a Carmelite center in Travancore. He commanded a fleet of sailing ships that plied the waters from the Red Sea to the South China Sea, mainsails emblazoned with Stars of David. He was also considered a military genius, all the while adhering strictly to Jewish law.

Ezekiel's son, David, also achieved his share of success. He was able to effect the release from Sultan Haidar Ali's prison of Samuel Ezekiel Divekar, a *Bene Israel soldier who later built Mumbai's first synagogue, inspired by the fine edifice in Kochi. David also visited Bene Israel villages in the Konkan, spurring their "first awakening" of Jewish identity. David was also an author of note, best known for his "Letter of 1798" in which he detailed the historical traditions of Kochi's Jews.

The Dutch "second golden age" saw a flourishing of literature and mysticism. It was during this secure and prosperous time that many lovely Hebrew songs and poems were composed in Jew Town by such poets as Eliahu Adeni, the kabbalist Nehemiah Mota, Levi Belilah, Ephraim Saala, Solomon B. Nissim, and Joseph Zakkai. Their songs became part of the unique Cochini *minhag* and were anthologized in later liturgical books, along with the songs of such Sephardi liturgists as Judah Halevi, Moses ibn Ezra, Solomon ibn Gabirol, and Israel Najara.

British Raj

The first British ships visited Malabar in 1615, but it was not until 1797 that they replaced the Dutch as overlords of Kochi. Never, however, was Kochi placed directly under the British Crown. The British raj extended to the northern half of Malabar, but Kochi and Travancore remained autonomous "princely states," nominally ruled by the rajah with the guidance of the British resident, or dewan.

The retention of Kochi's autonomy in the face of the economic, military, and political juggernaut that was the British Empire, which had consumed most of India, had positive and negative effects for the Jews. On the positive side, they continued to receive the rajah's protection and privileges, to which they had become accustomed. On the negative side, however, was British neglect of Kochi, leading to the deterioration of its economy. At first they favored Calicut, which was within the boundary of British Malabar, as a trading center, and eventually Mumbai emerged as the supreme west Indian port.

Four 19th century Jewish travelers – Rabbi David DeBeth Hillel during the 1820s, I.J. Benjamin around 1850, Shlomo Reinman during the 1850s, and Jacob Sapir during the 1860s – wrote about their visits to Kochi, from which an accurate and detailed composite portrait of life in Jew Town during the British era may be culled. These visitors recorded many of the unique religious observances of Kochi, and mentioned the very high level of Hebrew and Jewish learning in the community. Their magnificent synagogue, spacious houses, and tasty cuisine, as well as the modesty, hospitality, and erudition of their women, were lavishly praised.

The Kochi Minhag

Drawing as it does from the many cultures from which Jews migrated to Kochi – ancient Israel, Syria, Turkey, Iraq, Yemen, Persia, Afghanistan, as well as Italy and Poland – and influenced by local Indian culture, the system of observant Judaism, or *minhag*, in Kochi is both rich and unique.

In the most general terms, Kochi's Jews were able to adopt certain Indian cultural patterns in their religious life while remaining faithful to normative Judaic observance as codified in *halakhah*. Living in a culture in which antisemitism was unknown, Kochi's Jews felt no defensiveness about their religious practices. By the norms of Indian society, religiousness per se is valued, so the Jews there were entirely free to celebrate their religion.

Indian culture has two sources of power and prestige: the royal and the priestly-ascetic. Jewish observance in Kochi reflected these two poles.

For example, Simḥat Torah is considered Kochi's most distinctive festival. Circumambulations (*hakkafot*) are added during the afternoon service, accompanied by unique Hebrew songs. Torah scrolls are displayed on a temporary ark especially constructed in front of the *aron ka-kodesh*, the scrolls are carried out of the synagogue and into the street, and the temporary ark is ritually demolished at the conclusion of the festival. All of these activities are attributable to rites found in nearby Hindu temples. All reflect the symbols of Hindu royalty. But none of these practices is in violation of any halakhic principle. Similarly, Kochi's elaborate wedding rites parallel those of their Hindu neighbors, which also embody the symbols of royalty, but with no compromise of *halakhah*.

The ascetical tendencies inherent in the Hindu priestly ideal find expression, for example, in the community's fastidious Passover preparations. Avoidance of gentiles mirrors avoidance of low-born Hindus; annual repainting of houses parallels Hindu practice; and activities and jokes pertaining to the festival's stringent dietary concerns resonates well in a culture in which hierarchy is closely connected with diet.

Social Structure

Jews in Kerala occupied a high rung on India's strict hierarchy known as the caste system. Furthermore, Jews divided themselves into subcastes, which is typical of Indian castes, and now that their numbers have been so severely reduced, these subcastes have been amalgamated in group behavior also found among attenuated Hindu groups.

The Kochi Jews evolved a pattern of social organization that reflected Indian values. Some of the Kochi Jews joined a liberal rabbi from South Africa in contemptuously describing this social system as "Jewish Apartheid," after the system of racial oppression in South Africa.

From as early as the beginning of the 16th century and perhaps before then, a rivalry emerged within the Jewish community based on who had attestable Jewish descent (*yiḥus*, those with *yiḥus* being known as *meyuḥasim*) and who did not (the *meshuḥrarim*, those in possession of a *shiḥrur*, a bill of manumission from slavery). In other words, one group of Kochi Jews considered themselves to descend from Israel, and they considered their rival group to be descendants of slaves. As early as 1520, Kochi Jews sought rabbinical adjudication of their rivalry and, when the response was not to their liking, ignored it.

The arrival of the Portuguese injected race into the equation, and the newly arrived Sephardi Jews, together with some of the *meyuḥasim*, were considered "white," while those of longer residence in Malabar were considered "black," and descendents of the white slaves were labeled "brown." To further complicate the picture, among the Malabari Jews, the *meshuḥrarim* were known by the Malayalam word, "orumakers." Depending on how one counts, the Jews proliferated three or four subcastes, and over time they refused to marry outside their group, would not count one another for the prayer quorum, and would not eat meat slaughtered in the rival community. In all of these features, their behavior reflected Hindu caste behavior. It also contravened *halakhah*.

Predictably, members of the less-favored group tried to redress their grievances. There was a 19th-century rebellion led by one Avo, who led a breakaway faction in establishing their own prayer hall in Fort Kochi. The rebellion ended unceremoniously in a cholera epidemic.

Avo's grandson, A.B. Salem, the first Kochi Jew to attend law school and a disciple of Mahatma *Gandhi, led his faction in a series of civil disobedience exercises in the synagogue, and lobbied so articulately on their behalf that he eventually prevailed, and religious rights were gradually restored to the *meshuḥrarim*.

Women's Malayalam Songs

Kochi's Jewish women are strikingly well educated in Hebrew and generally exhibit autonomy and freedom beyond what might be expected in a traditional Jewish community. This cultural theme reflects the values of the local Hindu culture, in which the matrilineal Nayar caste is dominant.

Another avenue for women's participation in religious life is through their Malayalam-language folk songs. These songs, copied into notebooks and passed on from generation to generation, often narrate biblical themes in a richly tropical setting, replete with elephants, parrots, and palanquins. Other songs praise the archetype of Hindu-Jewish amity, Cheraman Perumal and Joseph Rabban. These songs are sung on festivals and at circumcisions, weddings, and other joyous occasions. They have become identity markers for Cochinim resettled in Israel, where groups of women gather monthly to sing and transmit these songs to the next generation.

The 20th Century

The 20th century in Jew Town was marked by four unprecedented events. The first was Indian Independence in 1947, enthusiastically welcomed by the Jews. Second was the establishment of the State of Israel in 1948, cause of another joyous celebration in Jew Town. Third was the gala celebration of the 400th anniversary of the Cochin Synagogue, as the Paradesi Synagogue has come to be known. The fourth event was painful: one Sabbath during July 1987, for the first time in its glorious history, there were no formal prayers in the synagogue; the prayer quorum could no longer be mustered, symbolically noting the death of communal life in Kochi.

BIBLIOGRAPHY: N. Katz and E.S. Goldberg, *The Last Jews of Cochin: Jewish Identity in Hindu India* (1993); A.M. Lesley, "Shingly in Cochin Jewish Memory and in Eyewitness Accounts," in: *Journal of Indo-Judaic Studies*, 3 (2000), 7–21; B.C. Johnson, *Oh, Lovely Parrot! Jewish Women's Songs from Kerala* (2004).

[Nathan Katz (2nd ed.)]

KOCK (Kotsk), town in the province of Lublin, E. Poland. Jews first settled in Kock at the beginning of the 17th century; an organized community existed from the middle of the century. One of the sons of Moses b. Isaac Judah *Lima (author of *Ḥelkat Meḥokek*) served as rabbi in Kock from 1670. In 1699 the Jews were granted unrestricted rights to settle by the owner of the town. According to the census of 1765, there were 793 Jews in the community and the surrounding villages, 489 of them in the town itself. Of the 108 Jewish families of Kock, 62 owned the houses that they occupied. By 1827 the number of Jews in the town had risen to 645 (36% of the total population), by 1857 to 1,480 (56%), and by 1897 to 3,014 (64%). About half of the Jews earned their livelihood from tailoring, hat-making, and shoemaking. Others were tanners, carpenters, potmakers, and locksmiths. In 1809 Berek *Joselewicz fell in a battle which was fought on the outskirts of the town. He was buried there.

When the "court" of the *ẓaddik* Menahem Mendel of *Kotsk was established in 1829, Kock became an important center of *Ḥasidism. In 1913 a yeshivah was founded in the town. The Jewish workers of Kock began to organize themselves into labor unions from 1905. Zionist organizations, particularly the *General Zionists and *Po'alei Zion, were active in Kock, as were the *Bund and *Agudat Israel. In 1926 nine of the 12 members of the municipal council were Jews. According to the 1921 census, the Jewish population of the town numbered 2,092 (54%); in 1927 there were 2,529 (68%). The last rabbi of Kock (from 1924) was R. Joseph Morgenstern, a *ẓaddik* from 1929; he perished in the Holocaust. The Ḥasidim of Kock are described by J. *Opatoshu in his book *In Polish Woods* (1938). About 3,000 Jews were in Kock after the German occupation in September 1939 and the arrival of refugees. In August 1942 around 100 Jewish families were deported to Parczew en route to Treblinka. Others were sent to Treblinka via Lukow. No Jews returned to the town after World War II.

BIBLIOGRAPHY: R. Mahler, *Yidn in Amolikn Poyln in Likht fun Tsifern* (1958), index; B. Wasiutyński, *Ludność żydowska w Polsce…* (1930), 35; M. Balaban, in: *Studja historyczne* (1927); *Sefer Kock* (Heb. and Yid., 1961).

[Arthur Cygielman]

KODASHIM (Heb. קָדָשִׁים), the fifth of the six orders of the Mishnah. The title *Kodashim* ("sacred things") is apparently an abbreviation of *Sheḥitat Kodashim* ("the slaughter of sacred animals") since its main subject is sacrifices. It has been suggested that since **Zevaḥim*, the first tractate of the order, had also once been called *Sheḥitat Kodashim*, the name was applied to the order as a whole, as is the case with the order **Nezikin*. However, the subjects dealt with in the order are chiefly the sacrifices of animals, birds, and meal offerings and also the laws of those obligated to bring a sacrifice, such as the sin offering and the guilt offering, and the laws of misappropriation of sacred property. In addition it contains a description of the Second Temple (tractate *Middot*) and of the morning service in the Temple until the completion of the offering of the daily sacrifice (*Tamid*). As well as the tractates discussing sacred things, the order includes the tractate *Sheḥitat Ḥullin* (in short, **Ḥullin*) which deals not only with the slaughter of animals for human consumption, but other germane dietary laws applying to meat and animal products. The order contains 11 tractates, arranged, like most of the orders of the Mishnah, in descending sequence according to the number of chapters. They are: (1) *Zevaḥim*, 14 chapters; (2) *Menaḥot*, 13; (3) *Ḥullin*, 12; (4) *Bekhorot*, 9; (5) *Arakhin*, 9; (6) *Temurah*, 7; (7) *Keritot*, 6; (8) *Me'ilah*, 6; (9) *Tamid*, 6 (this was the number originally); (10) *Middot*, 5; and (11) *Kinnim*, 3–90 chapters in all. In the *Tosefta, *Zevaḥim* has 12 chapters, *Ḥullin* 10, *Menaḥot* 13, *Bekhorot* 7, *Arakhin* 5, *Temurah* 4, *Me'ilah* 3, and *Keritot* 4, while for *Tamid, Middot*, and *Kinnim* there is no Tosefta. There is no Jerusalem Talmud on any of *Kodashim* and in the Babylonian Talmud there is no *Gemara* to *Middot* and *Kinnim*.

The study of the order *Kodashim* was neglected for many generations, and even talmudic scholars, with a few outstanding exceptions, ignored it. In the time of Maimonides many justified this neglect by claiming that the laws appertaining to the sacrifices were of no practical benefit. Maimonides disagreed and in his commentary on the Mishnah, at the end of tractate *Menaḥot*, he states: "This is the law of the burnt offering, of the meal offering [Lev. 7:37]… everyone occupying himself with the law is as if he had offered a burnt offering, and a meal offering, and a sin offering. And the sages said: 'Scholars who occupy themselves with the *halakhot* of the Temple service are regarded by Scripture as if the Temple had been rebuilt in their time.' Consequently it is proper for a person to occupy himself with matters concerning the sacrifices and to discuss them." In recent years, largely under the influence of the Ḥafeẓ Ḥayyim, there has been a considerable revival of interest in the study of this order, and in many *kolelim it is the particular subject of study. This revival is partly connected with the hope that the Temple will be rebuilt.

BIBLIOGRAPHY: Epstein, Mishnah, 980ff.; Ḥ. Albeck, *Shishah Sidrei Mishnah, Kodashim* (1959), 3–4.

[Abraham Arzi]

KODER, SAMUEL SHABDAI (1869–1941), merchant and leader of the community of White Jews in Cochin (*Kochi). From 1903 until his death, he was a warden of the Pardesi synagogue. He was the first Jewish councilor on the municipal council of Cochin and its chairman from 1920 to 1924. He organized the water supply from Alwaye to the town of Mattancheri, and was managing director of the ferry and transport service of the port conservancy and the Cochin electricity company. Deeply concerned with the welfare of his people, he made generous contributions to Jewish and other charities, and through his efforts Jewish students were granted exemption from sitting for examinations on the Sabbath and Jewish holidays. He was the recipient of many honors in recognition of his public services. After his death, his son, Shabdai Samuel *Koder (1907–1994), became the leader of the Jewish communities in southern India.

BIBLIOGRAPHY: Fischel, in: Herzl Yearbook, 4 (1961/62), 318–9. **ADD. BIBLIOGRAPHY:** N. Katz and E.S. Goldberg, *The Last Jews of Cochin: Jewish Identity in Hindu India* (1993).

[Walter Joseph Fischel]

KODER, SHABDAI SAMUEL (1907–1994), Jewish communal leader in Cochin (*Kochi). He was educated in Cochin and at Madras University, after which he entered the family business. For 12 years he represented the Jews of Cochin in the Cochin Legislative Assembly. He was honorary consul for the Netherlands and on his retirement received a knighthood of the Order of Nassau. Koder held high office in Rotary International and the Freemasons. In 1968 he presided at the 400th anniversary of Cochin's famous Paradeis synagogue, which was attended by Indian Prime Minister Indira Gandhi. Koder was the author of a number of articles on the history of Cochin Jewry. He succeeded his father, Samuel Shabdai *Koder, as leader of the community and president of the South India Jewish Association.

ADD. BIBLIOGRAPHY: N. Katz and E.S. Goldberg, *The Last Jews of Cochin: Jewish Identity in Hindu India* (1993).

[Percy S. Gourgey / Tudor Parfitt (2nd ed.)]

KOEBNER, RICHARD (1885–1958), historian. Koebner was born in Breslau and studied at the universities of Berlin, Breslau, and Geneva between 1903 and 1910. In 1920 he began teaching at Breslau University and in 1924 he was appointed professor of medieval and modern history. His primary interest at this time was urban development and German expansion eastward. His books in these fields included his dissertation *Die Eheauffassung des ausgehenden deutschen Mittelalters* (1911); *Venantius Fortunatus, seine Persoenlichkeit und Stellung in der geistigen Kultur des Merowinger-Reiches* (1915); *Die Anfaenge des Gemeinwesens der Stadt Koeln* (1922); and *Staatsbildung und Staedtewesen im deutschen Osten* (1931).

Removed from his post by the Nazis, Koebner settled in Jerusalem in 1934 and was appointed professor of modern history at the recently founded Hebrew University, where he established, together with Victor *Tcherikover and Yitzhak *Baer, the History Department. From then until his retirement in 1955 he influenced the character of the department and set its guidelines. During those years his research concentrated, among other subjects, on the changing concepts of "empire" and "imperialism." His *Empire* (1961) dealt with the evolution of the meaning of the term from Roman to Napoleonic times. Koebner's voluminous notes were used by one of his former students, H.D. Schmidt, for a book published in their joint names, *Imperialism, The Story and Significance of a Political World, 1840–1960* (1965). In 1990 a collection of studies from Koebner's archive was compiled and published under the title *Geschichte, Geschichtsbewusstsein und Zeitwende.*

ADD. BIBLIOGRAPHY: H.D. Schmidt, in: *Geschichte, Geschichtsbewußtsein und Zeitwende* (1990), 11–21; J. Arieli, in: *Geschichte, Geschichtsbewußtsein und Zeitwende* (1990), 22–48; idem, in: *Toldot ha-Universita ha-Ivrit be-Yerushalaim: Shorashim ve-Hatchalot* (2000), 541–574.

[Oscar Isaiah Janowsky / Noam Zadoff (2nd ed.)]

KOENIG, GHISHA (1922–1993), English sculptor, born in London, the daughter of the Yiddish writer and art critic Leo *Koenig. She studied under Henry Moore, and became a gifted portraitist, especially of children. Living in an industrial area, she visited local factories to study men and women at work. She then made bronze or terracotta bas-reliefs of the subject. These are characterized by a humanist sense of involvement and a classical feeling in the modeling and grouping. She and her husband, Dr. Manny Tuckman, were left-wing political activists, her political beliefs being reflected in some of her work.

ADD. BIBLIOGRAPHY: ODNB online.

KOENIG, LEO (pseudonym of **Arye-Leyb Yaffe**; 1889–1970), Yiddish critic and journalist. Raised in Odessa, Koenig published his first story at age 16: "Der Ekstern" ("The Extern") in *Der Veg*. He studied art in Jerusalem (at the Bezalel School, 1907–10), where he also wrote stories under the name Arye Yaffe, and in Munich (1910–12) and Paris (1912–14), where he was close to Marc *Chagall and, under the name Leo Koenig, wrote art criticism for leading Yiddish periodicals – the first serious work of this kind in Yiddish. From 1914 to 1952, in which year he settled in Haifa, Koenig lived in London, working for the Yiddish press in England and abroad. In 1920 he edited Anglo-Yiddish literary journals. In Israel he was a frequent contributor to the newspaper *Davar*. Only a fraction of his writing has appeared in book form: *Shrayber un Verk* ("Writers and Works," 1929); *Vu Haltn Mir in der Velt* ("Where Are We in the World," 1933); *A Vokh nokhn Lebn* (*A Week After Life*, trans. Joseph Leftwich, 1934); *Geto oder Melukhe* ("Ghetto or State," 1939); *Folk un Literatur* ("Folk and Literature," 1947); and *Dos Bukh fun Lesterungen* ("The Book of Blasphemies," 1948).

BIBLIOGRAPHY: Rejzen, Leksikon, 3 (1929), 710–4; A. Shaanan, *Millon ha-Sifrut ha-ḥadashah ve-ha-Kelalit* (1959), 726. **ADD. BIBLIOGRAPHY:** LNYL, 8 (1981), 230–32; J. Glatstein, *In Tokh Genumen*, 2 (1960), 105–11.

[Leonard Prager]

KOENIGSBERG (Rus. **Kaliningrad**), former capital of East Prussia, now an outpost of Russia. Two Jewish physicians lived in Koenigsberg in 1540, but sizable Jewish settlement did not begin until the latter half of the 17th century when Jewish merchants from Lithuania and Poland began attending the Koenigsberg fairs and in 1680 were allowed to open a prayer room for the duration of the fairs. A *ḥevra kaddisha* was founded and a cemetery consecrated in 1704; a rabbi was appointed three years later. By 1716 there were 38 Jewish families in Koenigsberg; the first synagogue was constructed in 1756, when the community numbered around 300 persons. A steady stream of immigrants from Russia gradually swelled this figure to 1,027 in 1817, 5,082 (3.6% of the total) in 1880, and 4,049 in 1925, later declining to 3,200 persons (1%) by 1933.

Along with *Berlin, Koenigsberg became the center of Jewish Enlightenment. Here, too, affluent Jewish families gained access to Christian society, the most prominent being the family of H.J. Friedlaender, textile entrepreneurs, to which David *Friedlaender belonged. Jews began attending the university, mainly as students of medicine, in 1712; one of them was Marcus *Herz. Among *Kant's pupils were a number of Jews. In 1783 Isaac Abraham *Euchel and Menahem Mendel Breslau, influenced by the ideas of Mendelssohn, founded an association "for the fostering of the Hebrew language," and began to publish a Hebrew periodical, *Ha-Me'assef*, which first appeared in Koenigsberg. A number of Hebrew printers were active in Koenigsberg in the 18th and 19th centuries. For a number of reasons, among which may have been import and censorship difficulties, some works printed in Koenigsberg bear a different imprint or no imprint at all.

The community had no school until 1820, when Isaac Asher Francolm came as religious teacher and preacher. A follower of the Reform movement, he set about establishing a school for religious instruction. However, his efforts failed when the Orthodox majority of the community, resenting his holding a confirmation ceremony for boys and girls, protested to the authorities who, already suspicious of all innovation, prohibited the opening of his institution. When Francolm settled in Breslau, Joseph Lewin *Saalschuetz continued his work. In 1847 Saalschuetz taught archaeology of the Hebrews at Koenigsberg University, publishing several important treatises in this field, although, as a Jew, he could not be appointed to a professorship. Also active in the community at this time was the radical politician, Johann *Jacoby, who published a memorandum (1847) in defense of Jewish emancipation. Jacob Z. Mecklenburg was rabbi at Koenigsberg from 1830 to 1865, succeeded by Isaac Bamberger (1865–96). Orthodox circles established their own congregation in 1870, which later rejoined the communal union. Significant for the community were the years from 1897 to 1920, when Hermann *Vogelstein served as its spiritual leader. He was one of the most important leaders of liberal Jewry in Germany. Felix *Perles, his contemporary, was rewarded for his scientific research in Bible and linguistics by his appointment in 1924 as honorary professor of modern Hebrew and Aramaic literature at the university. The 20th century also saw Jews playing a significant role in the faculty of medicine, among them Ludwig Lichtheim, Julius Schreiber, Max Jaffe, and Alfred Ellinger. In 1925 there were five different synagogues in the city as well as a variety of social and welfare institutions.

The Jewish population was 3,170 in 1933. The onset of Nazism drove Jewish professors from the university, many seeking asylum in the United States and Ereẓ Israel (including Willy Wolflein and Frieda Reichmann). After the prohibition against Jewish children attending the public schools, a successful Jewish school was founded in 1935. By October 1938, after emigration and flight, 2,036 remained. On Nov. 10, 1938, the main synagogue was burned down. The ḥasidic, Polish, and Orthodox ones were similarly destroyed. The inhabitants of the orphanage and the home for the aged were thrown out on the streets. The men were arrested, mistreated, and imprisoned for two and a half months. A year later only 1,585 Jews remained. Mass deportations to Minsk and Theresienstadt in 1942 claimed at least 1,000 Jewish lives, leaving around 45 families in mixed marriages in the city. From 1943 Polish Jews were brought to the city for forced labor. About 3,700 participated in the death march to the Palmicken near the Baltic in January 1945. The Jews who remained in Koenigsberg after the war were expelled by the Russians in 1948 together with the Germans.

BIBLIOGRAPHY: J.L. Saalschuetz, in: MGWJ, 7 (1858), 163–78, 203–17, 397–407; 8 (1859), 81–100; 11 (1862), 209–22; H. Jolowicz, *Geschichte der Juden in Koenigsberg* (1867); H. Vogelstein, *Beitraege zur Geschichte des Unterrichtswesen in der juedischen Gemeinde zu Koenigsberg* (1903); J. Rosenthal, *Die gottesdienstlichen Einrichtungen in der juedischen Gemeinde zu Koenigsberg i. Pr.* (1921); FJW, 17–19; D.F. Kaelter, in: BLBI, 4 (1961), 145–66; S. Rosenbaum, *ibid.*, 6 (1963), 92–97; H.J. Kruger, *Die Judenschaft von Koenigsberg in Preussen, 1700–1812* (1966); BJCE; PK Germani'ah; S. Stern, *Der preussische Staat und die Juden*, 1 (1962), Akten, no. 444–528; 2 (1962), Akten, no. 169–97; Part of the communal records (1769–1929) are in the Jewish Historical General Archives, Jerusalem; the necrology is in the Jewish National and University Library, Jerusalem.

[Reuven Michael]

KOENIGSBERG, DAVID (1889/1891? –1942?), Yiddish poet. One of the earliest Yiddish sonneteers, Koenigsberg was born in Busk (Galicia). His first book was *Lider* ("Poems," 1912), followed by his sonnets, *Soneten* (1913), and *Hundert Soneten* ("One Hundred Sonnets," 1921), which abound in romantic imagery of damsels, knights, and nightingales. While translating Heine into Yiddish, he was captivated by that poet's sentimental *Weltschmerz*; but he lost a sense of immediacy and intimacy by forcing his feelings into the artificial form of sonnets. He was at his best when he wrote of Jewish nationalism. He felt that the Balfour Declaration would enable Jews to escape their age-old woe by returning to Zion. He spoke of himself as a bridge over which others could cross into the Promised Land. When the Russians marched into Lvov (Lemberg) in 1939, he was put at the head of the Yiddish Authors' Society, and when the Nazis ousted the Russians, he was taken to the Yanove extermination camp and killed.

BIBLIOGRAPHY: Rejzen, Leksikon, 3 (1929), 714–17; M. Ravitch, *Mayn Leksikon* (1945), 236–38; M. Neugroeschel, *Fun Noenten Over* (1955), 305–12; S. Liptzin, *Maturing of Yiddish Literature* (1970), 134–36. **ADD. BIBLIOGRAPHY:** LNYL, 8 (1981), 232–33; S. Liptzin, *A History of Yiddish Literature* (1972), 238–41; Y. Papernikov, *Heymishe un Noente* (1958), 256–57.

[Sol Liptzin]

KOENIGSBERG, MOSES (1878–1945), U.S. editor and publisher. He organized the King Features syndicate as well as other news and feature services. Koenigsberg was born in New Orleans and at the age of thirteen he became a reporter for the *San Antonio* (Texas) *Times*. By 1903, he was managing editor of the *Chicago American* and in 1908 publisher of the *Boston American*. He formed King Features in 1916 and was also president of the International News Service and Universal Service. His books include *Southern Martyrs* (1898), *The Elk and the Elephant* (1899), and an autobiography, *King News* (1941).

[Lawrence H. Feigenbaum]

KOENIGSBERGER, BERNHARD (**Barukh**; 1866–1927), rabbi and scholar. Koenigsberger, who was born in Kattowitz, Upper Silesia, studied with B.H. *Auerbach in Halberstadt and at the Berlin Rabbinical Seminary. From 1895 he served as rabbi in Pasewalk, Pomerania; from 1898 in Pleschen (Pleszew), Poznania, and from 1912 in Berlin. He edited the *Monatsblaetter fuer die Vergangenheit und Gegenwart des Judentums* (4 vols., 1890–91), and the weekly *Jeschurun* (1901–04). Apart from numerous contributions to Jewish and general periodicals, Koenigsberger's publications include *Quellen der Halachah* (1890); *Hiobstudien* (1896); *Fremdsprachliche Glossen bei juedischen Commentatoren* (1896); a Passover *Haggadah* with German translation (1916); *R. Ismael b. R. Jose* (1902); and *Oneg Shabbat* (1913), notes on Bible and Talmud in Hebrew; he edited *Sifrei Zuta* (1894).

BIBLIOGRAPHY: W. Bacher, in: JQR, 8 (1896), 329–33; *Israelitisches Familienblatt* (June 9, 1927), 3; *Der Israelit*, 68 (June 16, 1927), 13.

[Joseph Elijah Heller]

KOENIGSWARTER, family of European bankers and philanthropists. The founder of the family, JONAS HIRSCH KOENIGSWARTER (d. 1805), was born in Kynzvart (Koenigswart), Bohemia, and moved to the German city of Fuerth, where he opened a successful banking house. His eldest son, SIMON KOENIGSWARTER (d. 1854), carried on his father's business. Simon was succeeded by his son, KARL WILHELM KOENIGSWARTER (1809–1887), who became an honorary freeman of Fuerth. He distinguished himself by his philanthropies for charitable institutions in Fuerth and in Merano, Italy, where he spent the latter part of his life. Jonas Hirsch's son MARCUS KOENIGSWARTER (1770–1854) settled in Frankfurt and established a bank there. A third son, MORITZ KOENIGSWARTER (1780–1829), opened a bank in Vienna. He received legal privileges from the government, and played an important role in Viennese Jewish communal life. Marcus' son JONAS FREIHERR VON KOENIGSWARTER (1807–1871) went to Vienna, where he married his uncle Moritz's daughter Josephine, and eventually succeeded him as head of the bank. He formed the Vienna banking firm of Koenigswarter and Todasco, and in 1850 became a director of the Austrian National Bank. He was associated with the *Rothschilds in establishing Austria's largest bank, the Creditanstalt, in 1855. He helped to develop the Austrian railroads, was active in the affairs of the Jewish community and was its president from 1868 to 1871. He was ennobled by Franz Joseph I and appointed to the Upper House (1870). Jonas Freiherr von Koenigswarter's son MORITZ BARON VON KOENIGSWARTER (1837–1893) was one of the most important banking and financial figures in Vienna, and continued his father's expansion of the Austrian railroad system. In 1879 he was appointed to Austria's upper legislative house as a Liberal, and there in 1890 represented the united Jewish community in negotiations to secure a law regulating the community's external relations. He founded Vienna's Institute for the Jewish Blind and was a co-founder and director of the Israelitisch-Theologische Lehranstalt. Jonas' son HERMANN FREIHERR VON KOENIGSWARTER (d. 1915) converted to Christianity and gave to charity the million gulder specified in his father's will as a penalty for any male descendant leaving the Jewish faith. He maintained racing stables but died destitute.

A fourth son of the original Jonas Hirsch Koenigswater went to Holland and founded a bank in Amsterdam. His sons settled in Paris. The elder, LOUIS JEAN KOENIGSWARTER (1814–1878), became a legal historian. In 1851 he was named a member of the Académie des Sciences Morales et Politiques. He was the author of several books on French legal history and established the Koenigswarter prize for the best work in this field. He was also active in Jewish affairs and was president of the council of the *Alliance Israélite Universelle (1860–63). His brother, MAXIMILIAN KOENIGSWARTER (1817–1878), became a banker in Paris. In 1851 he was elected to the French parliament and supported Napoleon III, but their warm relations cooled when in 1859 Koenigswarter opposed the war against Austria. The two were reconciled in 1861, but Koenigswarter lost his deputy's seat in 1863 to a republican candidate. In that year Napoleon made him a baron. Other distinguished members of the Koenigswarter family, both grandsons of Jonas Hirsch, were LEOPOLD KOENIGSWARTER, another Paris banker, who played an important part in the construction of railroads in Holland and Belgium; and HEINRICH KOENIGSWARTER, who was the resident minister of Coburg-Gotha in Paris, and was created a baron in 1870.

BIBLIOGRAPHY: H. Tietze, *Die Juden Wiens* (1933), index; A. Taenzer, *Geschichte der Koenigswarter Stiftung in Meran* (1907); L. Bamberger, *Erinnerungen* (1899); K. Grunwald, in: YLBI, 12 (1967), 198–200.

[Joachim O. Ronall]

KOERNER, MOSES BEN ELIEZER PHOEBUS (1766–1836), rabbi and author. He was rabbi at Rendsburg (Schleswig), Shklov, and Grodno. In his later years he traveled extensively in Europe soliciting aid for the publication of his works. Koerner subsequently settled in Breslau where he died. His published works are: *Torat Moshe* (Nowy Dwor, 1786), containing homilies on obscure passages in Bible and Midrash, and also novellae, partly by Ẓevi Hirsch b. Abraham, of Posen; *Zera Kodesh* (Berlin, 1798), a commentary on the **Sifra* with homiletic discourses; *Ke-Or Nogah* (Breslau, 1816), an attempt to synthesize Kabbalah and Jewish philosophy, the **Zohar* and Maimonides' *Guide of the Perplexed; Iggeret Rishfei Keshet* (Hanover, 1831), an account of his wanderings and tribulations, including a rebuttal of his detractors; *Megillat Eivah* (Breslau, 1837), the autobiography of his ancestor Yom Tov Lipmann *Heller, with Koerner's notes and a German translation by Miro; and *Birkat Moshe* (Berlin, 1834).

BIBLIOGRAPHY: Zeitlin, Bibliotheca, 183f.; Lewin, in: MGWJ, 76 (1932), 2 n.3.

[Jacob Hirsch Haberman]

KOESTLER, ARTHUR (1905–1983), author. Born in Budapest and educated in Austria and Germany, Koestler was probably the most cosmopolitan of 20th-century European writers, changing his language from Hungarian to German at the age of 17, and from German to English at the age of 35. In 1926 Koestler went to Palestine, where for three years he was correspondent for a German publisher and a foreign correspondent for German newspapers. He then returned to Europe and in 1931 was the only journalist on board the "Graf Zeppelin" during its Arctic expedition. He joined the Communist Party in the same year and visited the U.S.S.R. during 1932–33, but abandoned the party at the height of the Stalinist purges of 1936–38. This disillusionment was described in a contribution to *The God That Failed* (1949).

Koestler's revulsion against the inhuman judicial processes of the age was expressed in the novel *Darkness at Noon* (1940), generally regarded as his best work and as one of the great political novels of the 20th century; it was later adapted for the stage. It tells the story of an old Bolshevik, Rubashov, who is arrested by the Soviet secret police and forced to confess to crimes which he did not commit. The strange psychological inversion which causes the victim to accept and acknowledge the justice of the charges leveled against him, while knowing that the evidence produced is false, provides the core of the novel's interest. During the Spanish Civil War Koestler was in Spain, and in 1937, while reporting the war for the London *News Chronicle*, he was captured and his *Spanish Testament* (1937) describes his hundred days in Franco's jails and the commutation of his death sentence to a term of imprisonment. In 1940 he volunteered for the French army and, after the collapse of France, escaped to England and fought with the British.

An interest in the problems of the Jews in Mandatory Palestine was a natural outcome of Koestler's years there during the 1920s. His novel *Thieves in the Night* (1946) documents the Arab-Jewish conflict during the period before the British withdrawal, when the Jewish underground movements incurred official wrath for their involvement in "illegal immigration" and "terrorism." Though obviously sympathetic to the Zionist cause, Koestler directs a streak of irony at the mixture of religious mysticism and practical socialism which, to his mind, animated the settlers in the kibbutzim. Koestler returned to Ereẓ Israel for a brief visit during the War of Independence in 1948, and his *Promise and Fulfillment: Palestine, 1917–49* (1949) surveys the era of the Mandate and the emergence of the State of Israel. After the establishment of the State, Koestler maintained that the Jews in the Diaspora were left with two choices: immigration to Israel, or total assimilation. He himself opted for the latter.

Koestler's works range from novels on political and ethical problems to polemical essays and autobiography. His rejection of various ideologies, the outcome of a disappointed idealism, led him to probe the workings of modern society and the rise of totalitarian movements, which enslaved men, repressed their individualism, and threatened to destroy the striving for a nobler social and metaphysical order. His books include: the novel *Arrival and Departure* (1943); *The Yogi and the Commissar* (1945), a volume of essays; *The Age of Longing* (1951), a political novel; two volumes of autobiography entitled *Arrow in the Blue* (1952) and *The Invisible Writing* (1954); *The Sleepwalkers* (1959), a history of man's changing vision of the universe; *The Lotus and the Robot* (1960); *The Act of Creation* (1964) and a philosophical work, *The Ghost in the Machine* (1967), both of which constituted a philosophical attack upon the theory of determinism; and *Scum of the Earth* (1968). In *The Thirteenth Tribe* (1976), he suggested that European Jewry was largely descended from the *Khazars.

Koestler and his wife committed suicide together.

BIBLIOGRAPHY: J.A. Atkins, *Arthur Koestler* (Eng., 1956); J. Nedava, *Arthur Koestler* (Eng., 1948); J. Strachey, *The Strangled Cry* (1960), 1–7 (an *Encounter* pamphlet).

[Harold Harel Fisch]

KOF (**Qof**; Heb. ק; קוֹף), the nineteenth letter of the Hebrew alphabet; its numerical value is 100. In the Proto-Sinaitic inscriptions its form was 8, which later, in the linear Phoenician script turned into . In the eighth and seventh centuries B.C.E. the *kof* developed as follows: the circle was opened , it turned into two half-circles , and then the left one was drawn with the downstroke without lifting the pen . The last form was preserved in the Hebrew script, while in other scripts the head of the *kof* formed an S, as in Phoenician ( ), Samaritan ( ), and Aramaic ( ). The later Aramaic and Jewish *kof* reduced the left curve of its head . The Nabatean script went further and the letter was written as follows: . This developed into , until it became similar to the *pe* ( ). In the Arabic script it was necessary to add diacritic marks in order to distinguish between *pe* ( ) and *kof* ( ). See *Alphabet, Hebrew.

[Joseph Naveh]

KOFFKA, KURT (1886–1941), U.S. psychologist; one of the founders of Gestalt psychology. He was born and educated in Berlin. Working as an assistant at Frankfurt, he came under the influence of Max *Wertheimer and served as a subject in the first studies of apparent movement that became the starting point of the Gestalt school of psychology. Gestalt theory rejected the notion that consciousness is built up of separate elements and substituted the view that experience was organized in whole patterns (i.e., *Gestalten*). Appointed in 1911 to Giessen, Koffka tried to deal with the problem of development, publishing *Growth of the Mind* (1925). With the aid of his "convergence theory," similar to the views of William *Stern, he tried to show that every capacity is the result of the convergence of inner capacities and outer conditions of development. Goals are seen as an attempt to bring about closure. Insight replaces trial and error learning. In 1921 he founded the journal *Psychologische Forschung*, together with Wertheimer, Koehler, Goldstein, and Gruhle, to publish the results of the new school, to which most American psychologists were introduced by his article: "Perception: An Introduction to the Gestalt-Theory" in *Psychological Bulletin*, 19 (1922), 531–85. Unfortunately this article had the effect of making Gestalt psychology appear to be only a perceptual theory. Koffka went to the United States in 1924, and in 1927 took up permanent residence as professor at Smith College. In 1932 he joined an expedition to Uzbekistan in Central Asia. In his own words, "the official task of the expedition was to study the dependence of the mental functions of a people upon the historico-economic conditions of their country."

On his return he embarked on his monumental *Principles of Gestalt Psychology* (1935). In this work Koffka attempted a comprehensive Gestalt theory covering learning, memory, emotion, and personality. He introduced the concept of the organismic field, the total field of interacting forces governing behavior. He distinguished the environment as it appears to an individual, the "behavioral environment," from the real environment. The Gestalt principles of organization explain why the behavioral environment corresponds as well as it does to the real environment.

BIBLIOGRAPHY: S.H. MacColl, *Comparative Study of the Systems of Lewin and Koffka…* (1939).

KOFFLER, MURRAY (1924–), Canadian pharmacist, entrepreneur, philanthropist. Koffler was born in Toronto. His Romanian-born parents married in Toronto in 1921 where his father, Leon, eventually operated two pharmacies, one in the downtown Jewish neighborhood. Murray Koffler inherited the stores after his father's death and in 1946 graduated from the Ontario College of Pharmacy at the University of Toronto. With a keen business sense, he recognized the opportunities offered in meeting the drugstore needs of expanding suburban communities and the drawing power of an inviting self-service shopping format. The Shopper's Drug Mart chain took shape. By the time he sold his interest in Shopper's Drug Mart, Koffler had overseen a public company of more than 500 licensed and franchised drugstores across Canada. Koffler's business interests also extended beyond drugstores. In addition, he was a founding partner in the successful up-market Four Seasons Hotel chain.

Together with his wife Marvelle, Koffler shared his success with the Jewish and larger community. A member or director of many charitable organizations, he remained a strong supporter of the arts, education, and medicine, the founder of the annual Toronto Outdoor Art Exhibition, and a moving force behind incorporation of the Koffler Centre for the Arts into the large Toronto Jewish Community Centre complex. His generous contributions to the University of Toronto include the Koffler Student Centre and the Institute for the Study of Pharmacy Management. Active in the Toronto Jewish community, he was a major contributor to the Mount Sinai Hospital in Toronto and the Baycrest Centre Jewish Home for the Aged. A champion of Israel, Koffler was a patron of the Weizmann Institute for Science, where his financial initiatives enabled construction of the Koffler Accelerator Tower, the centerpiece of the Institute's Canada Centre for Nuclear Physics.

Murray Koffler was honored with the Order of Canada and in 1997 Murray and Marvelle Koffler were named Outstanding Philanthropists by the National Society of Fund Raising Executives.

BIBLIOGRAPHY: F. Rasky, *Just a Simple Pharmacist: The Story of Murray Koffler* (1988).

[Harold Troper (2nd ed.)]

KOGAN, ABRAHAM (1921–), Israeli physicist. Kogan was born in Kishinev in the former U.S.S.R. (now Chisinau, Moldova). He received his M.Sc. from the Hebrew University of Jerusalem (1950) and Ph.D. from Princeton University (1956). From 1952 he was a member of the aeronautics faculty of the Haifa Technion where he became professor (1963). Since 1989 he has been emeritus professor at the Technion and visiting scientist at the Weizmann Institute. His main research interest was fluid mechanics and its application to efficient systems for desalinizing seawater. More recently he analyzed the effects of solar heat on water and the practical implications for utilizing solar power. His achievements were recognized by many honors including the Rothschild Prize (1966) and election to the Israel Academy of Sciences.

[Michael Denman (2nd ed.)]

KOGAN, LEONID BORISSOVICH (1924–1982), Russian violinist. Kogan, who was born in Dniepropetrovsk, played the violin from the age of seven. He achieved great technical mastery, winning the first prize at the international competitions in Prague in 1947 and the Queen Elizabeth competitions in Brussels in 1951. His foreign tours included appearances with orchestras in the U.S.A. With the pianist Emil *Gilels and the cellist Rostropovich, Kogan organized a concert trio, and also gave recitals with his wife, the violinist, Elizabeth (née Gilels). Later he appeared with his son, Pavel. The Soviet composers A. Khachaturian, T. Khrennikov, and M. Weinberg wrote violin works for him. He was awarded the Lenin Prize in 1965.

BIBLIOGRAPHY: M. Zazovski, *L. Kogan* (Russ., 1958); L. Raaben, *Zhizn zamechatel nykh skripachey* (1957), 279–89; Baker, Biog Dict.

[Michael Goldstein]

KOGAN, MOYSE (1879–1942), sculptor. Born in Bessarabia, he became a chemist, but went to Munich in 1903 to devote himself to art, although he had had no previous training. To maintain himself, he designed embroideries and other objects, and also created medallions. As a member of the New Artists' Association in Munich, he participated in the group's exhibitions in 1910 and 1911. In 1910 he moved to Paris where he received encouragement from Maillol, whose work greatly influenced him. In 1925 Kogan was elected vice president of the Salon d'Automne, an unusual honor for one who was not a Frenchman. When France was overrun by the Germans, he was arrested, deported, and killed. His best works are terracotta figurines and delicate heads, carved in limestone, marble, or wood. He was also a master of print in wood and linoleum cuts as well as lithographs.

[Alfred Werner]

KOGEN, (Chaim) DAVID (1919–2005), teacher and administrator in the Conservative movement. Born in Rutki, Poland, Kogen came to the United States in 1928 at the age of nine and was raised in Cleveland, Ohio. After earning his bachelor's degree at the University of Chicago in 1942, he was ordained a rabbi at the Jewish Theological Seminary in 1946.

Although Kogen spent the bulk of his career in education and administration, the beginning of his career was in the rabbinate serving as a congregational leader. He moved to Vancouver, British Columbia, upon receiving his rabbinical ordination. There, he founded and directed the B'nai Brith Hillel Foundation at the University of British Columbia while simultaneously serving as the spiritual leader of Congregation Beth Israel. After returning to New York City in 1956, Kogen served as the visiting rabbi at the Park Avenue Synagogue until 1957, temporarily replacing the recently deceased Milton *Steinberg, after which he spent one year at Temple Ansche Chesed.

He devoted the first 10 years of his rabbinical career to Jewish and general community leadership in Canada. He was involved in many local community service organizations, including the Jewish Family Welfare Bureau and the Institute for Church and Social Service Workers.

After spending 12 years as a congregational rabbi, Kogen directed his energies towards leadership of the Conservative movement itself. In the United Synagogue of America, Kogen served as a member of the Committee on Congregational Standards and as director of community activities. In the Rabbinical Assembly, he served temporarily as executive vice president during Rabbi Wolfe Kelman's sabbatical. He was also a member of the RA's Executive Council and the Membership Committee.

In 1958, Kogen joined the faculty of Jewish Theological Seminary. He was assistant to the vice chancellor until 1966, after which time he became the administrative vice chancellor himself. He was a director and teacher of liturgy in the Cantors Institute-Seminary College of Jewish Music. He also taught a practical rabbinics class on the ritual and administrative skills of congregational life. He was chairman of the department of professional skills, and director of the Graduate School of Humanities.

[Aaron Shub (2nd ed.)]

KOHATH (Heb. קְהָת) **AND KOHATHITES**. Kohath was the second son of Levi and grandfather of *Moses, *Aaron, and *Miriam (Num. 26:58–59). Few personal details about him are recorded. He is invariably listed between his brothers Gershon and Merari (Gen. 46:11; Ex. 6:16; Num. 3:17; I Chron. 5:27). He lived for 133 years and had four sons: Amram, Izhar, Hebron, and Uzziel (Ex. 6:18). The information about his descendants is more detailed, since the Kohathites were among the most important levitical clans. Their story is interwoven with four periods in biblical history – the Wilderness Wanderings, the Settlement, the Monarchy, and the Return to Zion. In the census taken in the wilderness the Kohathites numbered 8,600 males (LXX, 8,300) aged above one month, including 2,750 males between 30 and 50 years old (Num. 3:28; 4:1–3, 34–37). They were subject to service for work relating to the Tent of Meeting. They camped along the south side of the Tabernacle and were in charge of the most sacred objects, the Ark, the table, the lampstand, the altars, the sacred utensils, and the screen, all of which they carried on their shoulders. The sons of Kohath were granted a privilege greater than that awarded to the other clans of the Levites, the Gershonites and the Merarites, in that they bore their burden on staves, unlike others who carried them on ox wagons (Num. 3:29, 31; 4:2, 7:8–9). Another episode which relates to the wilderness period was the rebellion by *Koraḥ, grandson of Kohath, against the leadership of Moses and Aaron (Num. 16:1ff.). The details about the allotted settlements of the Kohathites are given in Joshua (21:4–5, 9–26) and I Chronicles (6:39–46). Those descended from Aaron received 13 towns within the tribal territories of Judah, Simon, and Benjamin. The remaining Kohathites received ten additional towns from the tribes of Ephraim, Dan, and half of Manasseh. Their allotted lands were thus mainly in the southern and central parts of the country. In the Chronicler's reconstruction of the period of the monarchy the Kohathites are mentioned in connection with the four kings – David, Hezekiah, Jehoshaphat, and Josiah, always in relation to service in the Tabernacle or the Temple. According to Chronicles, it was during David's reign, that the family of Heman the Kohathite was among the levites assigned to direct the singing in the Tabernacle (I Chron. 6:16–23; cf. Ps. 88:1). Led by Uriel "the Chief," 120 Kohathites participated in the installation of the Ark in Jerusalem (I Chron. 15:5), and the family is again listed in the census of levites and their organization in divisions is undertaken by David (I Chron. 23:1–6, 12). Another tradition in Chronicles reports that in the days of King Jehoshaphat, during the invasion of Judah by the Moabites and Ammonites, it was the Kohathites who led the congregation in praise of God at the service of intercession (II Chron. 20:19). They also participated in the cleansing of the Temple in the time of Hezekiah (II Chron. 29:12), and two of their men supervised the work of renovating the Temple undertaken by King Josiah (II Chron. 34:12). In the era of the return to Zion, the time of Ezra and Nehemiah, when functions were determined in the Temple, several of the sons of Kohath were put in charge of the changing of the showbread (I Chron. 9:32).

[Nili Shupak]

In the Aggadah

Kohath was one of the seven righteous men who helped bring the *Shekhinah*, the Divine Presence, back to earth, after it had ascended to heaven because of the sins of previous generations (PdRK, I, 22). Because of the superiority of the family of Kohath among the families of the tribe of Levi they were given the privilege of carrying the Ark in the wilderness. The diminution in numbers which this caused the family of Kohath (cf. Num. 4:18–19) was due to the fact that a fire emerged from the Ark, which occasionally destroyed those who carried it, and from the deaths which occurred as a result of the frantic desire of members of the family to be granted the privilege (Gen. R. 5:1). Their humility is praised. "Although the family of Kohath were aristocrats, when they came to carry the ark, they assumed the demeanor of ordinary slaves"; they carried the ark on their shoulders, while walking backward, as a sign of respect (*ibid.* 5:8).

BIBLIOGRAPHY: Ginzberg, Legends, 2, 260; 3, 229–30, 287; 5, 396; I. Ḥasida, *Ishei ha-Tanakh* (1964), 37 (1964), 375. **ADD. BIBLIOGRAPHY:** S. Japhet, *I & II Chronicles* (1993), 143–62; B. Levine, *Numbers 1–20* (AB; 1993), 171–75; W. Propp, ABD, 4:95–97.

KOHELETH MUSSAR (Heb. "The Moral Ecclesiastes"), a collection of moralistic Hebrew literature published in Berlin by Moses *Mendelssohn and Tobias Bock sometime during the 1750s. Considered by many to be the first modern Hebrew periodical, *Koheleth Mussar* was the publication in which Mendelssohn's lucid, biblically influenced Hebrew style first appeared. Mendelssohn composed descriptions of nature as well as didactic exhortations to a moral way of life, and praises of the neglected Hebrew tongue. Citing the example of other peoples who had begun to revive and develop their languages, Mendelssohn asked, "Why are we dreaming and inert; why do we not apply their example to our language which is most eminent and ancient?" Only two issues appeared, each four pages in length and comprising six chapters. Precise data about the author(s), publishers, place, and year of publication are lacking. There have been many conjectures as to the year of publication, which range from 1750 to 1758. Until World War I three copies of the first issue were known to be extant (one in the British Museum), and only one copy of the second issue (Leipzig University Library). It was reprinted with a preface by J. Edelstein in the *Festschrift zum 50 jaehrigen Bestehen der Franz-Josef-Landesrabbinerschule in Budapest* ((1927), Heb. pt. (55–76)) and in an amended version in volume 14 of the complete works of Moses Mendelssohn, edited by Borodianski (Bar-Dayyan (d. 1978); Berlin, 1939, the last Hebrew book printed in Nazi Germany; the only extant copy is preserved by the editor in Jerusalem).

BIBLIOGRAPHY: J. Toury, in: KS, 43 (1967/68), 279–84; idem, in: BLBI, 10 (1967), 93–110; H.M.Z. Meyer, *ibid.*, 11 (1968), 48–60; J. Toury, *ibid.*, 60–65.

[Getzel Kressel]

KOHEN, first major family of Hebrew printers in Prague and all of Central Europe. Hebrew printing began in Prague – before anywhere else in Central or Eastern Europe – no later than 1512, when four craftsmen and two backers produced a prayer book. By 1514 the group had been joined by GERSHOM BEN SOLOMON KOHEN (d. 1544), who was evidently a man of means and destined to dominate the group, and two others. From then until 1522 they issued four works of prayers and a handsome Pentateuch.

Kohen's importance and dominance in the group is indicated by two facts: in all these works, the colophons list him first; and an ornamental border on the opening page of the Pentateuch, used again in the 1522 *maḥzor*, shows a pair of hands held in position for the priestly blessing – a symbol for him, since he was a *kohen*. He was to use this as his printer's mark in later works also, with his name added.

After 1522 the group broke up in order to open several Hebrew printing shops in Prague. Together with his brother GRONEM KOHEN, Gershom produced a Passover *Haggadah* (1526). Set in large, handsome type and lavishly illustrated with over 60 woodcuts (mostly by Hayyim Shahor, a fellow printer), this earliest printed, illustrated *Haggadah* is a masterpiece. Each double page has a harmonious unity and balance of its own. A facsimile edition appeared in Berlin in 1926 (but by error the order of facing pages was not kept), and two others in the latter 1960s – one (Shulsinger, New York) a faithful, splendid replica, the other (Universitas, Jerusalem) in colors.

In 1526 Ferdinand I became king of Bohemia, and Kohen applied to him for a *privilegium* (royal decree), to make him the exclusive Hebrew printer in Bohemia. This was granted him in 1527 and his competitors had to close their shops. He engaged Meir Michtam, the typographer of the original group of printers of 1512, as his assistant to instruct his sons in the craft. With his sons SOLOMON and MORDECAI (d. 1592) Kohen produced a steady stream of prayer books and Pentateuchs, as well as learned and talmudic works. In time his sons MOSES (d. 1549) and JUDAH (d. 1593) also joined the firm. Printing more volumes than the Prague community could absorb, the Kohen family appointed the *Halicz brothers of Cracow as its agents in Poland; in 1535 Mordecai Kohen, the strongest and most talented businessman among Kohen's sons, went to the Frankfurt trade fair to arrange for distribution there.

The 1540s was an unsettled time for Prague's Jews. An edict of expulsion left only 15 families in the city, until the decree was lifted in 1543. In 1544 the resulting economic difficulties forced Mordecai Kohen to travel about in an attempt to sell some of the stock. Toward the end of the year Gershom Kohen died, and shortly afterward his son Moses Kohen applied to Ferdinand I for the same *privilegium* that his father had enjoyed. In 1545 his request was granted. In the 1550s, however, life for all Prague Jewry was unusually difficult. Fire ravaged the ghetto and expulsion threatened. Beset in any case by competition from Hebrew works imported from Italy, Mordecai Kohen left printing and devoted himself to the communal welfare, acting as *shtadlan*. His brother Moses Kohen died, and for years no volumes were issued from the Kohen family press, except for a small prayer book (afternoon and evening services) printed by Judah Kohen. In 1566, however, Mordecai Kohen resumed the craft with his five sons. Yet conditions brought another interruption of activity for seven years (1571–77), after which Mordecai's sons continued, while he himself remained immersed in communal affairs until his death. The firm was then named in his memory. In 1589 Kohen's son Bezalel died. In 1590 his son Solomon requested, and received, yet another royal *privilegium*, enabling the Kohen firm to remain the sole Hebrew printers in Prague until the very early 1600s.

From 1592 the firm was managed by Solomon Kohen and his son MOSES (d. 1659). Afterward, Moses continued alone for over 50 years, personally supervising proofreading and corrections. The Thirty-Years' War, however, brought the press to a standstill when Moses was already old; when he died, his grandsons ISRAEL and MOSES continued under the firm name of "the Grandsons of Moses Katz" (= *kohen ẓedek*, "the righteous *kohen*"). They were succeeded in time by this latter Kohen's son AARON (d. 1701), who managed the press until his death. After 1701 Aaron Kohen's son DAVID carried on, until 1735, under the firm name of "the descendants of Moses Katz." The press continued sporadically thereafter, until economic conditions moved the Kohen family to merge with the *Bak firm in 1784, thus bringing its long course of independent printing to an end.

BIBLIOGRAPHY: S.H. Lieben, in: B'nai B'rith, *Die Juden in Prag* (1927); J. Volf, *Geschichte des Buchdrucks in Boehmen und Maehren bis 1848* (1928), includes bibliography; B. Friedberg, *Toledot ha-Defus ha-Ivri… be-Eiropah ha-Tikhonah* (1935); A. Freimann, in: ZHB, 21 (1918), 30ff.; A. Yaari, *Diglei ha-Madpisim ha-Ivriyyim* (1943), index; C. Wengrov, *Haggadah and Woodcut* (1967), index.

[Charles Wengrov]

KOHEN, ALBERT (1885–1949), Turkish journalist, educator, community leader. Born in *Istanbul, Kohen studied at the Alliance Israélite school. At the age of 18 he became involved in community affairs in Hasköy and then established the Hinukh Yeladim school, where he taught the children Hebrew, Jewish history, and culture. Starting in 1910, he became the president of the Jewish community of Sirkeci. From 1940 he was a member of the Secular Council of the Chief Rabbinate and also a member of the board of the Or Ahayim Jewish Hospital. He began publishing in 1922 in *El Telegrafo* and then in *La Boz de Oriente*. In 1939 he founded *La Boz de Türkiye*, a biweekly journal published in Turkish, French, and Ladino. He was Turkey's correspondent of the *Jewish Telegraphic Agency until his death. As his journalistic activities did not bring in material remuneration, he worked in the Banque de Salonique until 1947. His published works include *Maimonides Su Vida Y Sus Obras* (1935); *La Evolución de la Mujer y el Rolo de La Mujer Judia en la Historia de Israel* (1936); *La Signification de Kippour* (1936); *La Vertud de Kippour* (1937); *Abraham Elmaleh Quelques Traits de Sa Vie: Publié à l'Occasion du 60ème Anniversaire de sa Naissance* (1945).

BIBLIOGRAPHY: *"Ishiyuto shel Albert Kohen,"* in: *Hed ha-Mizraḥ* (Sept. 1949), 10.

[Rifat Bali (2nd ed.)]

KOHEN, ELEAZAR BEN ZE'EV WOLF (d. 1883), Polish rabbi and author. Kohen was the son-in-law of Jacob *Lorbeerbaum. He served as rabbi in Makow, Pultusk, Plock, and finally in Sochaczew. Among his pupils were Aaron *Walden, author of *Shem ha-Gedolim he-Ḥadash* (1864), to which he gave an approbation. Kohen wrote *Zikhron Nifla'ot*, a commentary on the Passover *Haggadah* (1880) and a commentary on *Avot* (1889). His novellae on the Shulḥan Arukh, the Talmud, and Maimonides were published by his son Joshua under the title *Ḥiddushei Maharakh* (2 vols., 1897–1913). He published a number of eulogies on contemporary rabbis, among them *Zekher Ẓaddik Yesod Olam* (1866) on Isaac Meir Alter.

BIBLIOGRAPHY: L. Lewin, *Geschichte der Juden in Lissa* (1904), 223; *Eẓ Avot*, bound with Eleazar Kohen, *Ḥiddushei Maharakh*, 2 (1913, repr. 1969).

[Samuel Abba Horodezky]

KOHEN, RAPHAEL BEN JEKUTHIEL SUESSKIND (1722–1803), rabbi and author. Raphael was born in Livonia and in his youth studied in Minsk at the yeshivah of his relative, Aryeh b. Asher *Gunzberg, author of the *Sha'agat Aryeh*. In 1742 Raphael was appointed head of the yeshivah, and between 1745 and 1776 he served successively as rabbi of the communities of Minsk, Rakov, Wilkomir, and Pinsk. In 1771, while he was in Berlin in connection with the printing of his *Torat Yekuti'el*, he was received by the scholars of the city with enthusiasm and was offered the rabbinate, but he refused and returned to Pinsk. From 1773 he served as rabbi of Posen and in 1776 was appointed to the combined communities of Altona, Hamburg, and Wandsbeck. In 1799 he planned to settle in Ereẓ Israel but did not succeed in fulfilling that desire because of the war in Europe, where he remained until his death. He did, however, resign from the rabbinate in 1799 and became a private citizen. The king of Denmark, in whose territory the communities were, sent him a letter of appreciation for the services he had rendered to the community. Kohen strongly opposed the Haskalah and Mendelssohn's German translation of the Pentateuch. When Kohen published his *Torat Yekutiel* (Berlin, 1772), glosses on the first three chapters of the Shulḥan Arukh, *Yoreh De'ah*, Saul *Berlin criticized it mercilessly in his *Mizpeh Yokte'el* (*ibid.*, 1789), charging that the work contained mistakes and errors, forgeries and plagiarisms. A stormy controversy ensued. Kohen's colleagues on the *bet din* of Altona decided to excommunicate Berlin. Various rabbis – among them Mordecai *Banet – intervened in the quarrel and protested against Berlin's accusations. His other works include *Ve-Shav ha-Kohen* (Altona, 1792), 101 responsa; *She'elat ha-Kohanim Torah* (*ibid.*, 1792), novellae and expositions on seven tractates of the order *Kodashim; Marpe Lashon* (*ibid.*, 1790), divided into six "pillars," containing expositions of rabbinic *aggadot* and ethics; and *Da'at Kedoshim* (*ibid.*, 1797), 12 sermons in *halakhah* and *aggadah*. The last two sermons he delivered in 1799 were published in the *Zekher Ẓaddik* (*ibid.*, 1805) of his son-in-law Eliezer Leiser Katzenellenbogen-Reiser, which also includes a biography of Kohen entitled *Ma'alelei Ish* and the eulogies delivered on him. According to his son-in-law, Kohen sought to determine the plain sense of the Talmud and the language of the early halakhic authorities in order to trace every *halakhah* back to its source. He was opposed to those who relied almost entirely on the Codes for halakhic decisions without examining the early authorities, and he insisted on the need to delve into the origin and source of each law. He rejected the "casuistic method which does not accord with the *halakhah*"; he frequently emphasized his trepidation and hesitation in laying down the law, referring to himself as *mi-yirei hora'ah* ("one who fears to state the *halakhah*"), a pun on *moreh halakhah* ("a teacher of *halakhah*"). In a problem concerning the permission of an *agunah* to remarry, he states that if "two more renowned halakhic authorities will agree with me, then I too will join them, but if not, then my words are null and void and I do not wish my decision to be relied upon" (responsa 3 in the appendix to *Torat Yekutiel*). Kohen cites Torah novellae of his son, Ẓevi Hirsch, the *av bet din* of Krotoschin (Krotoszyn), and of his father-in-law, Ẓevi Hirsch b. Abraham, the *av bet din* of Posen and Fuerth.

BIBLIOGRAPHY: Graetz, Gesch, 11 (1900^2), index; J. Perles, in: MGWJ, 14 (1865), 261; E.L. Landshuth, *Toledot Anshei ha-Shem u-Fe'ulatam ba-Adat Berlin* (1884), 85–89; E. Duckesz, *Iwoh Lemoschaw* (1903), 63–74; S.M. Chones, *Toledot ha-Posekim* (1910), 417f.; Y. Wolfsberg, in: *Arim ve-Immahot be-Yisrael*, 2 (1948), 32f.; B. Katz, *Rabbanut, Ḥasidut, Haskalah* (1956), 220; Zinberg, Sifrut, 5 (1959), 124–7; O. Wolfsberg-Aviad, *Die Drei-Gemeinde* (1960), 65f.; M. Samet, in: KS, 43 (1968), 430f.; idem, in: *Meḥkarim … le-Zekher Z. Avneri* (1970), 246–8.

[Yehoshua Horowitz]

KOHEN, SAMI (1928–), Turkish journalist. Born in Istanbul, the son of journalist and community leader Albert *Kohen, Sami Kohen's first articles were published in his father's journal, *La Boz de Türkiye*. After his father's death he published a weekly newspaper in Turkish, *Türkiyenin Sesi*, between November 1949 and May 1950. He attended Istanbul University's School of Journalism and was also trained in the U.S. He started his own career in 1950 in the newspaper *Yeni Istanbul* and two years later moved to *Istanbul Ekspres*, working in the foreign news department. In 1954 he joined *Milliyet* as foreign news editor. In 1982 he started writing a regular daily column on international affairs and Turkey's foreign policy which was highly regarded in Turkey and abroad. As a senior editor with more than 40 years of service, he is considered the dean of Turkish journalists specializing in foreign affairs. He is an active correspondent for *Newsweek* and *Christian Science Monitor*. Between 1950 and 2002 he was the Turkish correspondent for *Maariv* and from 1949 the Turkish correspondent for *The Jewish Chronicle*. His published works are *Bugünkü Japonya* (1982) and *Değişen Çin* (1982).

BIBLIOGRAPHY: A. Galante, "*Veinte y cinco asnios de periodismo. La actividad jurnalistica de senior Albert Cohen*," in: *La Boz de Türkiye* (Feb. 15, 1948), 231; M. Asayas and Y. Barokas, "*Hep Aynı Çizgiyi Korumuş Bir Gazeteci Sami Kohen*," in: *Şalom*, 20 (Nov. 20, 1996).

[Rifat Bali (2nd ed.)]

KOHEN-ZEDEK, JOSEPH (1827–1903), Hebrew poet, writer, and publicist. Kohen-Zedek, who was born in Lvov, studied rabbinics with Solomon *Kluger in Brody and S.J. Nathanson in Lvov. He first engaged – unsuccessfully – in business and then turned to literature and journalism. He published a number of collections of his patriotic poetry in honor of the Austro-Hungarian emperor – from whom he received a gold medal for art and science in 1851 – and an anthology of contemporary poetry dedicated to Moses Montefiore, *Neveh Kehillah* (1864). Kohen-Zedek edited a number of more or less short-lived Hebrew periodicals: *Meged Yeraḥim* (4 issues, 1855–59), *Oẓar Ḥokhmah* (3 issues, 1859–65), *Ha-Yehudi ha-Nizḥi* (4 issues, 1866), and *Or Torah* (4 issues, 1874). His weekly *Ha-Mevasser*, which included a literary supplement, *Ha-Nesher*, was the first Hebrew paper in Galicia (1861–66); some of the best Hebrew writers and scholars contributed to it. He himself wrote in a lively and original *meliẓah* style. Following a dispute with one of his associates which led to a denunciation, Kohen-Zedek had to leave Austria in 1868. He went first to Frankfurt on the Main, and in 1875 to London, where he served as preacher to immigrant congregations. In London he wrote a number of mainly homiletic works, including *Elef Alfin*, a thousand-word eulogy on Chief Rabbi Nathan Adler, each word beginning with *alef*. Of some scholarly importance are his *Sefat Emet* (1879), a polemic against Michael *Rodkinson; *Ohole Shem: Tents of Shem, Being an Account of the Trial of Jacob and Isaac of the City of Madrid in the Year 5202* (1883), on blood libels; *Divrei ha-Yamim le-Mal-*

khei Ẓarefat (1859), an edition of *Joseph ha-Kohen's chronicle with Kohen-Zedek's introduction; and *Even Boḥan* (1865), an annotated edition of Kalonymus b. Kalonymus' satirical work. His *Biographical Sketches of Eminent Jewish Families* (1897) is in English. Kohen-Zedek maintained a lively correspondence with the leading rabbis and scholars of his time. He has been called "the last publicist of the Galician Haskalah."

BIBLIOGRAPHY: G. Bader, *Medinah va-Ḥakhamehah* (1934), 119–21; N. Sokolow, *Ishim* (1958[2]), 205–13.

[Getzel Kressel]

KOHEN-ẒEDEK BAR IVOMAI (or **Ikhumai**; 9th century), *gaon* of Sura from 838–48, succeeding R. Mesharshiya (or Moshe) Kahana after an interregnum of two years. Kohen-Ẓedek's responsa, usually in Hebrew (rather than the Aramaic common to most of the *geonim* before him) and couched in succinct terms, encompass all aspects of *halakhah*, particularly laws of blessings and texts of the liturgy. He apparently devoted a whole work to the Passover *seder.* It is assumed that Kohen-Ẓedek was the first (even before *Natronai b. Hilai) to compose a prayer book. He was very careful not to force upon communities who turned to him for advice the customs which prevailed in the Babylonian academies.

BIBLIOGRAPHY: Abramson, Merkazim, 14; H. Tykoczynski, *Takanot Ha-Geonim* (1959), passim; M. Havazelet, *Ha-Rambam ve-ha-Geonim* (1967), 162; Baron, Social[2], 5 (1957), 30; 6 (1958), 446; Weiss, Dor, 4 (1904[4]), 38.

[Meir Havazelet]

KOHEN ẒEDEK OF PUMBEDITA (10th century), *gaon* of Pumbedita from 917 to 936. Kohen Ẓedek was active in raising the spiritual and material status of his academy, striving to make it the equal of *Sura. Before his time Pumbedita received only a third of the donations collected for the academies and Sura two-thirds. As a result of his efforts they were divided equally. His appointment as head of the academy was fraught with controversy. After the death of Judah b. Samuel in 917, the scholars of the yeshivah, with the support of the court banker Aaron b. Amram, chose Mevasser Kahana b. Kimoi as head of the academy, while the exilarch David b. Zakkai selected Kohen Ẓedek. After their reconciliation and until the death of Mevasser in 922 or 925, both scholars served as *geonim* of Pumbedita, each in a separate academy. Kohen Ẓedek then served as the sole head of the yeshivah until his death. *Saadiah ben Joseph (Gaon), a member of his academy, received the title **alluf* from Kohen Ẓedek. No responsa of Kohen Ẓedek are extant and nothing is known of his teachings.

BIBLIOGRAPHY: B.M. Levin (ed.), *Iggeret Sherira Ga'on* (1921), 119–20; Neubauer, Chronicles, 2 (1895), 78–80; L. Ginzberg, *Geonica*, 1 (1909), 35, 38–66; H. Malter, *Saadia Gaon* (Eng. 1921), 104; Mann, in: *Tarbiz*, 5 (1933/34), 148–61.

[Eliezer Bashan (Sternberg)]

KOHL, HERBERT (1935–), U.S. senator and owner of Milwaukee Bucks basketball team. Kohl was born in Milwaukee, Wisconsin, to Max and Mary, both immigrants (Max from Poland, Mary from Russia). He graduated from the University of Wisconsin and was president of his Jewish fraternity Phi Lambda Phi, then earned an MBA at Harvard Business School. He served in the United States Army Reserves from 1958 to 1964.

Kohl, the third of four children, watched his father keep an exhausting schedule at the family's small grocery. His parents instilled a pride and emphasis on education in the children as well as the importance of charity and helping others, both driving factors in the senator's life. His parents also hired an Orthodox rabbi to come to the family home daily for nearly ten years to instruct the children in the Torah and the Hebrew language. His Jewish background and culture remain an inspiration for much of his work for charity and in the Senate.

Kohl got his start in business with his family's retail operation, which he watched grow from his father's small grocery on Milwaukee's south side to larger department stores and entire shopping centers. In 1972 the family sold 80 percent of the company's stock to a British retailer, though Herb ran Kohl Corporation until 1979 when the remaining stock was sold. He purchased the Milwaukee Bucks after the sale of Kohl Corporation and began to support more philanthropic pursuits.

A respected businessman, Kohl ventured into politics in the 1970s when he became chairman of the Wisconsin State Democratic Party from 1975 to 1977. In 1988, he spent nearly $7 million of his own funds running for the U.S. Senate seat vacated by retiring William Proxmire.

In the Senate, Kohl was known for his attention to children's issues, supporting issues relating to working parents and child nutrition. Kohl worked to pass the Child Care Infrastructure Act, a law signed in 2001 that encourages private companies to create child care options for their employees by way of on-site or near-site day care centers. Other causes to which Kohl was dedicated are Wisconsin farming, anti-crime legislation, and particularly laws that protect children from criminal acts.

Senator Kohl served on three committees. His Senate Appropriations Committee appointment allowed him to work on several subcommittees, including those that benefited education and human services initiatives in his home state. His work on the Special Committee on Aging included introducing a Nursing Home Safety Bill that would hold caregivers accountable in the case of abuse of a resident. On the Senate Judiciary Committee, Kohl's focus was on crime prevention programs, consumer protection issues, and confirmation of the most qualified federal judges.

It is estimated that Kohl has donated more than $1 million each year, often with no recognition, and his own fortunes fund the Herb Kohl Foundation, which awards educational scholarships and grants.

[Lisa Deshantz-Cook (2nd ed.)]

KOHLBACH, BERTALAN (1866–1944), Hungarian Liberal rabbi and scholar of Jewish-Hungarian folklore. Kohlbach was born in Liptoszentmiklos, Hungary, into a family of rabbis. In 1890, he became rabbi of the Conservative community of Temesvar. Six years later, he resigned as a result of opposition to his Reform views, and he taught secondary school in various Hungarian cities. Kohlbach was one of the pioneers in folklore research in Hungary. Of his writings on Jewish folklore, only extracts were published in German and Hebrew periodicals. He also wrote on the Jewish archaeological material in the Hungarian Museum; he described the Hasmonean coins of the Jewish Museum of Budapest, of which he was a founder; and he wrote on classical philology, archaeology, and general education.

BIBLIOGRAPHY: A. Scheiber, in: *Az Országos Rabbi Egyesület Értesitője* (Dec. 1948), 15–19.

[Baruch Yaron]

KOHLER, KAUFMANN (1843–1926), U.S. Reform rabbi and president of Hebrew Union College. Kaufmann Kohler was born in Fuerth, Bavaria, long known as a center of rabbinic learning, and was himself descended from rabbinic stock. He pursued rabbinical studies from an early age and in 1862 entered the gymnasium at Frankfurt. While in that city he came under the influence of Samson Raphael *Hirsch, champion of Neo-Orthodoxy, and, though later diverging sharply from his viewpoint, never ceased to pay tribute to his influence. Kohler pursued his university studies at Berlin and Erlangen, receiving a doctorate in 1867. His university studies had shattered Kohler's Orthodoxy and his doctoral thesis, *Der Segen Jacobs* (1867), took such a radical viewpoint that no rabbinic position was open to him. For a time he continued his studies at Leipzig with a view to entering the academic world, but, warmly recommended by the German Reform leader Abraham *Geiger, Kohler accepted the office of rabbi of Congregation Beth El, Detroit (1869). In 1871 he moved to Sinai Congregation, Chicago (where he introduced Sunday services in 1874), and in 1879 he succeeded his father-in-law, David *Einhorn, at Temple Beth El, New York.

Kohler emerged as a national champion of Reform Judaism in 1885 when, replying to attacks by Alexander *Kohut, he published a series of sermons entitled *Backward or Forward* (1885). The outcome was his convening of the Pittsburgh Conference of Reform Rabbis and its adoption of a radical program on the basis of Kohler's draft. In 1903 Kohler was appointed president of *Hebrew Union College and set about immediately to improve the curriculum and to bring fresh talent to the faculty. His dealings were not always diplomatic, and he was soon involved in a clash with several members of the faculty on the subject of Zionism, which he opposed. He became the chief spokesman for classical Reform. His major theological work was *Jewish Theology Systematically and Historically Considered* (1918; repub. 1968), which traces Jewish thought from the perspective of 19th-century Reform Judaism. He revamped the curriculum, introduced biblical criticism and reduced the time spent on Talmud, but also held daily services and taught reverence through study. Under his presidency the College moved to a new, spacious setting. Upon his retirement, Kohler received the title of president emeritus (1921) and returned to New York.

Throughout his career Kohler showed wide scholarly interests and prodigious industry as a researcher and writer. When *Studies in Jewish Literature Issued in Honor of Professor Kaufmann Kohler on the Occasion of his 70th Birthday* was published in 1913, 801 of his articles were listed in the bibliography. He was editor of the department of philosophy and theology of the *Jewish Encyclopedia*, to which he contributed 300 articles, and a member of the board of editors of the JPS English translation of the Bible. His *Studies, Addresses and Personal Papers* (1931) was published posthumously.

Kohler was an active member of the Central Conference of American Rabbis and his learning and position enabled him to exercise a significant influence on the trend of American Reform Judaism in his day. He was an unusual combination of rationalist and believer. The evolutionary theory of Charles Darwin exercised an important influence on his thinking. Man, Kohler declared in 1874 "… is driven by the creative forces farther and farther away from his root, away from his natural origin, toward the higher, the infinite; away from the transient shell towards the eternal … everything that stamps man as man … our entire culture has grown from rude beginnings into ever higher perfection." With this he combined a strong belief that the task of the Jew was to lead the world to a universal religion and that the Messianic era was approaching in his own day.

BIBLIOGRAPHY: Philipson, in: AJHSP, 31 (1928), 268–71; idem, in: CCARY, 36 (1926), 170–7; Enelow, in: AJYB, 28 (1926–27), 235–60; R.J. Marx, *Kaufmann Kohler as Reformer* (1951); J.L. Blau, in: K. Kohler, *Jewish Theology* (1968), xi–xii. **ADD. BIBLIOGRAPHY:** K.M. Olitzky, L.J. Sussman and M.H. Stern, *Reform Judaism: A Biogrpahical Dictionary and Sourcebook* (1993).

[Sefton D. Temkin / Michael Berenbaum (2nd ed.)]

KOHLER, MAX JAMES (1871–1934), U.S. attorney, specialist in immigration and naturalization law, and communal leader. Kohler, the son of Kaufmann *Kohler, was born in Detroit. He served as assistant U.S. district attorney in the southern district of New York from 1894 to 1898. He then entered private law practice as defender of the legal and public rights of immigrants, naturalized citizens, and aliens, taking up test cases and hardship cases particularly and arguing them in appeals to the highest courts, including the U.S. Supreme Court. In his quest to define and extend these rights and to clarify the law, he represented various national Jewish organizations at legislative and executive agency hearings on issues in naturalization and immigration law, and publicized the problems of new citizens and aliens in pamphlets and educational articles for the press. In these tasks he was associated with Oscar S. *Straus, Louis *Marshall, and Simon *Wolf.

Kohler was concomitantly a dedicated student of history and contributed articles to the *Jewish Encyclopedia* and *Publications of the American Jewish Historical Society* on early American Jewish history and the struggle for Jewish emancipation, particularly as carried on at postwar congresses in Europe in the 19th and early 20th centuries. His *Immigration and Aliens in the United States: Studies of American Immigration Laws and the Legal Status of Aliens in the United States* was published in 1936. Kohler served on the commission on Ellis Island and Immigrant Relief in 1933. He was a member of and held office in many Jewish organizations, including the American Jewish Historical Society (to which he bequeathed his unpublished writings, his library, and his law briefs).

BIBLIOGRAPHY: I. Lehman, in; AJYB, 37 (1935), 21–25; E.D. Coleman, in: AJHSP, 34 (1937), 165–263 (bibl.).

[Isidore S. Meyer]

KOHN, ABRAHAM (1807–1848), Austrian rabbi and *maskil*. Born in Zálužany, Bohemia, he became a disciple of Naphtali Herz *Homberg in Prague. After serving as rabbi in Hohenems, in 1844 he became a preacher in Lemberg (Lvov), where he was known as an extremist *maskil* in his conduct and religious outlook. Appointed district rabbi, Kohn headed the *Reform movement and propagated its ideas throughout Galicia. Kohn also attempted to influence the authorities to prohibit Jews from wearing their traditional dress and observing traditional customs, and, in particular, to act against the existence of the *ḥadarim*. He founded a modern Jewish school in Lvov modeled on German Haskalah lines. In 1846, he founded a Reform temple, thus aggravating the dissension of the Orthodox sector whose representatives opposed him unremittingly. Kohn gave the impetus to press for abolition of the *kasher* meat tax and *candle tax, in connection with which he traveled with a special delegation to Vienna in order to submit a petition to the emperor. His leading opponent, Jacob Naphtali Herz *Bernstein, tried to obtain Kohn's dismissal from the office of district rabbi. A number of attempts were made to humiliate him and also to assault him. After Kohn and his son died from food poisoning, murder was suspected. An investigation was ordered by the authorities, and the leaders of the Orthodox sector, Bernstein and Hirsh Orenstein, were arrested. After a time, both were released for lack of evidence. Kohn published textbooks; his sermons were published by his son Jacob (in *Jeshurun*, 1856).

BIBLIOGRAPHY: J. Kohn, *Leben und Wirken Abr. Kohn* (1885); N.M. Gelber, in: EG, 4 (Sefer Lwow, 1956), 231, 235ff.; J.L. Tenenbaum, *Galitsye Mayn Alte Heym* (1952).

[Moshe Landau]

KOHN, EUGENE (1887–1977), U.S. Reconstructionist rabbi and editor. Kohn, who was born in Newark, New Jersey, earned his B.A. from New York University (1907) and was ordained by the Jewish Theological Seminary in 1912. He occupied pulpits, perhaps not quite successfully, in Baltimore, Maryland (1912–18); Perth Amboy, New Jersey (1921–23); Milwaukee, Wisconsin (1923–26); Youngstown, Ohio (1926–29); Bayonne, New Jersey (1929–34); and St. Albans, New York (1936–39); and served on the staff of Young Judea. Associated with the Reconstructionist movement from its inception, he played an important role in its development as the first managing editor of its magazine *Reconstructionist* from 1938 until his retirement in 1963. During the 1930s and 1940s, *The Resonstructionist* attracted some of the leading religious thinkers of the era; it was provocative, stimulating, and quite controversial. Kohn also edited the Reconstructionist Press, as resident administrator and ideologist. He edited *Shir Ḥadash* (1939), a book of readings and prayers; *The New Haggadah* (1941); *The Reconstructionist Prayer Book* (1948; with M.M. Kaplan and I. Eisenstein); *Faith of America* (1951), a book of readings for the celebration of American holidays (with M. M. Kaplan and Paul Williams); *American Jewry – The Tercentennary and After* (1955); and co-edited *Mordecai M. Kaplan: An Evaluation* (1952). Kohn wrote: *A Manual for Teaching Biblical History* (1917); *The Future of Judaism in America* (1934); *Religion and Humanity* (1953); and *Good to be a Jew* (1959). He also wrote *The Future of Judaism in America* (1934) and *Religious Humanism* (1953), which was a staunch defense of Reconstructionism.

[Jack Reimer / Michael Berenbaum (2nd ed.)]

KOHN, HANS (1891–1971), U.S. historian and political scientist. Born in Prague, Kohn was an active member of *Bar Kochba, the Zionist student group led by Hugo (Shemu'el) *Bergmann. He joined the Austrian army at the outbreak of World War I and was taken prisoner by the Russians in 1915. He remained in captivity in Samarkand and later in Siberia, and returned to Prague in 1920. Kohn was secretary to the Comité des Délégations Juives at the Paris Peace Conference in 1920–21 and from 1921 to 1925 lived mainly in London, working for the *Keren Hayesod. He was in Jerusalem from 1925 to 1929 when he returned to Europe, and in 1931 went to the U.S.A. From 1934 to 1949 he was professor of history at Smith College, and from 1949 to 1962 at the City College of New York. Kohn was a prolific writer with more than 30 books to his credit. He was one of the major scholars of modern nationalism to which he was first drawn in the last years of the Austrian Empire and also by the Zionist movement, but later he differed on the Arab question. His major work is *The Idea of Nationalism* (1944), later continued by *The Age of Nationalism* (1962), and *Prelude to Nation-States* (1967), and he wrote on modern history and historiography. Kohn was the author of works on Martin Buber, Heinrich Heine, and Zionist ideology and politics; he edited writings by Aḥad Ha-Am (*Nationalism and the Jewish Ethic*, 1962). In 1921 Kohn translated the second edition of J. Klausner's *History of Modern Hebrew Literature* into German. His autobiography (*Living in a World Revolution*) was published in 1964. It contains a list of his publications (pp. 357–60).

BIBLIOGRAPHY: *Orbis*, 10 (winter 1967), special issue dedicated to Hans Kohn, incl. bibl.; S.J. Kunitz (ed.), *Twentieth Century Authors* (1955), first suppl.; *Times Literary Supplement* (London, Oct. 19, 1946).

[Edwin Emanuel Gutmann]

KOHN, JACOB (1881–1968), U.S. Conservative rabbi, scholar, and educator. Kohn was born in Newark, New Jersey, and was ordained at the Jewish Theological Seminary (1907). He earned a doctor of Hebrew letters at the Seminary in 1917. After leading the Adath Jeshurun Congregation in Syracuse, New York (1908), Rabbi Kohn served Ansche Chesed Congregation in Manhattan, New York (1911–31). Located on the West Side, his congregation introduced decorum, mixed seating, and a choir. Many a student at the Jewish Theological Seminary would attend these services as part of their rabbinic experience, contrasting Kohn with Mordecai *Kaplan. Among those, whose career in the rabbinate Kohn guided, was Milton *Steinberg. In 1931 he moved to Los Angeles, which was then growing into a Jewish community of substance, to begin at the ripe age of 50 a long career as rabbi of Sinai Temple. Learned and scholarly, Kohn became associated with the newly founded *University of Judaism (1947), where he was dean of the graduate school and professor of theology until his death. He was president of the Alumni Association of the Jewish Theological Seminary, the precursor of the Rabbinical Assembly. He helped edit the Conservative Movement's *Festival Prayer Book* and was a member of the commission that prepared its *Sabbath and Festival Prayerbook* in 1946. Kohn wrote *Modern Problems of Jewish Parents* (1932), and later in his career he wrote *Moral Life of Man – Its Philosophical Foundations* (1956) and *Evolution as Revelation* (1963). Kohn also contributed many articles to philosophical journals and to periodicals dealing with Jewish life and thought. In addition to his scholarly interests, he was active in the affairs of the Jewish community, serving on the Overseas Committee of the Jewish Welfare Board in leadership positions during World War I, and in the Rabbinical Assembly, the Los Angeles Zionist District, and the Jewish Community Council and its affiliated organizations. He was a leading voice of Conservative Judaism in Los Angeles when the modern day Los Angeles Jewish community was being formed in the prewar and immediate postwar years.

[Max Vorspan / Michael Berenbaum (2nd ed.)]

KOHN, JINDŘICH (1874–1935), Czech political writer and philosopher. A lawyer by profession, Kohn was the author of scores of essays and articles on political, sociological, historical, and philosophical subjects. Only a few of his studies, such as *Politika a právo* ("Politics and Law," 1910) and *Co jest a co není právo sebeurčení* ("What is and what is not the Right of Self-determination," 1919), were published in book form during his lifetime. The originality of his thought and breadth of his interests became fully appreciated only when his essays and lectures were collected and published posthumously in 1936 as *Asimilace a věky* ("Assimilation and the Ages"). Kohn developed a philosophy of assimilation as a permanent process of progressive adaptation of man to changing conditions. Adapting his philosophy to the Jewish question, Kohn became the leading ideologist of Jewish assimilation in Czechoslovakia without ever becoming a militant opponent of Zionism. He gave a summary of his assimilationist historiography in JGGJČ, 2 (1930), 1–16 ("*Soziologische Einfuehrungsskizzae in die Geschichtsschreibung des Judentums in der čechoslovakischen Republik*").

BIBLIOGRAPHY: O. Donath: *Židé a židovství v české literatuře 19. a 20. století*, 2 vols. (1923–30); Hostovský, in: *Jews in Czechoslovakia*, 1 (1968), 444; F. Thieberger, in: *Czechoslovakian Jewry, Past and Future* (1943), 24–27.

[Avigdor Dagan]

KOHN, LEO (Yehudah Pinḥas; 1894–1961), Israeli scholar and diplomat. Born in Frankfurt, Germany, Kohn settled in Palestine in 1921. For 27 years he was at the center of Zionist and Israeli diplomatic activity. In 1932 he went to Dublin where he wrote a study of the constitution of the Irish Free State. From 1934 he was political secretary of the Jewish Agency and from 1948 to 1952 political adviser to Chaim Weizmann. From the establishment of the State (1948) until his death, Kohn served as political adviser to the Ministry for Foreign Affairs. In recognition of his services he was given the personal rank of ambassador in 1958. From 1953 he also held the chair of international relations at the Hebrew University. His draft constitution for Israel was adopted as the basis for the deliberations of the Constitution Commission of the State Council in 1948. Kohn's draft constitution stipulated Israel's historical claim to Ereẓ Israel, followed Jewish teachings on the sanctity of human life and the dignity of man, and rejected the death penalty and all forms of degrading punishment. However, the *Knesset decided to legislate a series of Basic Laws that would eventually be consolidated into a written constitution.

BIBLIOGRAPHY: J.G. Mc-Donald, *My Mission in Israel* (1951); D. Horowitz, *State in the Making* (1953); M. Davis (ed.), *Israel, its Role in Civilization* (1955); M. Sharett, *Yoman Medini 1936* (1968).

[Shmuel Bendor]

KOHN, MAIER (1802–1875), German cantor and teacher. Born in Schwabach, Bavaria, Kohn opened a school for Jewish girls in Munich in 1825 and in 1832 was a member of a committee organizing a choir "for improving the standard of the divine service." He became assistant cantor in Munich, and in 1839 the choir committee of the Munich synagogue published his book, *Vollstaendiger Jahrgang von Terzett- und Chorgesaengen der Synagoge in Muenchen*, containing his own compositions and others for a choir of three or four voices. This was the first modern collection of synagogue melodies and included many traditional songs. Kohn also left a manuscript dated 1870, *Der Vorbeter in der Synagoge von Muenchen*, dealing with weekday, Sabbath, and festival prayers in which he expressed his intention of collecting ancient forms of *ḥazzanut* without modernizing them. Both his published work and his

1870 manuscript were used by *Idelsohn as source material for volume seven of his *Melodienschatz.*

BIBLIOGRAPHY: Idelsohn, Melodien, vol. 7; id., *Music*, index; Friedmann, Lebensbilder, 2 (1921), 43–48; Sendrey, Music, index; *Di Geshikhte fun Khazones* (1924), 209.

[Joshua Leib Ne'eman]

KOHN, PINCHAS (1867–1942), Orthodox leader. A pupil of Azriel *Hildesheimer, Kohn served as district rabbi at Ansbach, Bavaria, from 1896 to 1916. During World War I he became an adviser on Jewish affairs to the military government established by Germany in occupied Poland. When working in Warsaw under Ludwig *Haas, Kohn was largely responsible for instituting the Polish Jewish community statutes which remained in force until 1939. His activities were violently opposed by Zionists in Poland and Germany. From 1919 to 1938 Kohn directed the office of the *Agudat Israel World Organization in Vienna, subsequently settling in Jerusalem. Apart from contributing regularly to the Orthodox press, Kohn was, from 1913 to 1920, coeditor with S. *Breuer of the Orthodox *Juedische Monatshefte* (דוֹרֵשׁ טוֹב לְעַמּוֹ), and wrote two novels, *Joël Gern; der Werdegang eines juedischen Mannes* (1912; under the pseudonym Kopi), and *Kosbi Salonaë* (1932; under the pseudonym Sanon). He also published a volume of memoirs.

BIBLIOGRAPHY: J. Rosenheim, *Zikhronot* (1955), 87, 216–20; A. Carlebach, *Adass Yeshurun of Cologne* (1964), 55ff.; idem, in: LBYB, 6 (1961), 60–121; H. Schwab, *Chachme Ashkenaz* (Eng., 1964), 86.

KOHN, SALOMON (1825–1904), Prague German-language novelist. Despite their illogical plots, his books were avidly read, frequently reprinted, and translated into many languages. As he signed his books S.K. only, he later had difficulty in establishing his copyright. His first short story, *Kaddisch vor Kol Nidre*, was published in Wolf *Pascheles' *Sippurim* in 1847. His most famous work was the novel *Gabriel* (1854[1]), set in the period of the Thirty-Years War. His *Prager Ghettobilder* (1884[1]) and *Neue Ghettobilder* (1886[1]) are valuable documents on Jewish life in 18th- and 19th-century Prague. A strictly observant Jew, he was a member of the board of the Prague community for 40 years.

BIBLIOGRAPHY: A. Kohut, *Beruehmte israelitische Maenner und Frauen*, 2 (1901), 29–31; V. Marcus, in: *Kalendář česko-židovský*, 52 (1932/33), 162–5; *Věstník židovské náboženské obce v Praze*, 27:1 (1965), 9; *Oesterreichisches biographisches Lexikon*, 4 (1969), 66–67 (with bibliography).

KOHN, SAMUEL (1841–1920), Hungarian rabbi and scholar. Kohn, born in Baja, Hungary, was the grandson of Eliakim *Goetz-Schwerin. He studied at A. *Hildesheimer's yeshivah in Eisenstadt and later at the Jewish Theological Seminary of Breslau and at the University of Breslau. He served as rabbi in Budapest from 1866 to 1905, when he was appointed chief rabbi. As an influential member of the 1868–69 Jewish Congress of Hungary, he was one of those responsible for the establishment of the Jewish Theological Seminary in Budapest. In his research Kohn dealt first with the Samaritans, but his major and lasting contribution was his work on the history of Jews in Hungary, *Héber kútforrások és adatok Magyarország történetéhez* ("Hebrew Sources and Data Relating to the History of Hungary," 1881) and, especially, *A zsidók története Magyarországon…* ("History of the Jews in Hungary," 1884). Kohn prepared material for a second volume treating the period after 1526, but this remained unpublished. Kohn also cataloged the Hebrew manuscripts in the Hungarian National Library (see MWJ, 4 (1877), 76–104; also in *Magyar Könyvszemle*; repr. separately in both Ger. and Hung.) and wrote an important study, *Mordechai ben Hillel, sein Leben und seine Schriften* (1878), on the life of the 13th-century codifier and martyr. He was one of the first rabbis in Budapest to give sermons in Hungarian. He edited a collection of sermons entitled *Zsinagógai szónoklatok* (1875).

BIBLIOGRAPHY: *Emlékkönyv néhai Dr. Kohn Samuel…* (1941); Z. Grossmann, in: *Magyar Zsidó Szemle*, 37 (1920), 1–5; M. Weisz, *ibid.*, 5–11; M. Brann, *Geschichte des Juedisch-Theologischen Seminars, Breslau* (1904), 173ff.

[Alexander Scheiber]

KOHN, THEODOR (1845–1915), prince-archbishop of *Olomouc (1892–1904). Kohn's father, a peasant in a Moravian village, had been baptized at the age of three. Entering the priesthood in 1871, Kohn subsequently became a professor of canon law, publishing many articles in his field. From 1883 he was chancellor of the bishopric of Olomouc and in 1892 became prince-archbishop. In 1893, commenting on blood libels at Holesov and Kojetin, he called antisemitism a "sickly condition that only time can heal." After anonymous attacks on him in a Czech newspaper (1903), he was accused of trying to discover the identity of the author by violating the secrecy of the confessional. Kohn, who himself had expressed the anti-Jewish views then prevalent in the Catholic Church, became the object of an unrestrained campaign of racial antisemitism and his palace was raided. As a result he was forced to retire. He willed his fortune to the newly founded Czech university in Brno. Anecdotes featuring Kohn were very popular in the Hapsburg lands.

BIBLIOGRAPHY: A. Frankl-Gruen, *Geschichte der Juden in Kremsier*, 2 (1898), 102–8; B. Muenz, in: *Liberales Judentum*, 8 (1916), 113–4; J.S. Bloch, *Reminiscences* (1923), 166–77; *Oesterreichisches Biographisches Lexikon*, s.v.; F. Engel-Janosi, *Oesterreich und der Vatikan 1846–1918*, 2 (1960), 56–78; J.S. Máchar, *Arcibiskup Theodor Kohn* (1927).

[Meir Lamed]

KOHN, WALTER (1923–), U.S. physicist and Nobel laureate. Kohn was born in Vienna where he attended the Akademische Gymnasium. He moved to the Jewish Chajes Gymnasium where he received exceptional teaching in mathematics from Dr. Victor Sabbath and in physics from Dr. Emil Nohel, both of whom perished in the Holocaust. After the Nazi annexation of Austria, he reached England on the **Kindertransport* in August 1939 but left for Canada in July 1940. After periods of internment in both countries of refuge he graduated and next received his master's degree in mathematics and physics at the University of Toronto in shortened courses interrupted by service in the Canadian Army (1941–46). He gained his Ph.D. from Harvard University for work on variational principles under the guidance of Julian Schwinger (1948). He was a fellow in Schwinger's department (1948–50) followed by an initial period at the Carnegie Institute of Technology in Pittsburgh (1949–51) before he went as a visiting research worker to Niels Bohr's laboratory at the Institute of Experimental Physics in Copenhagen on a National Research Council Fellowship (1951–52). He returned as professor to the Carnegie and regular collaboration with Bell Laboratories (1952–60) before moving to the University of California at San Diego (1960–79). He then moved to the University of California at Santa Barbara, initially to direct the National Science Foundation's Institute for Theoretical Physics (1979–84) and subsequently as professor of physics (1984–91), where he became emeritus research professor. Kohn developed mathematical models and computational techniques for applying quantum mechanics to chemistry. His density functional theory based on electrons' spatial distribution made it possible to describe the bonding of atoms and thereby to study the structure and function of complex molecules. These principles are now used universally. He remained active in that field. He was awarded the Nobel Prize for chemistry (1998) jointly with John Pople. His other honors include the National Medal of Science (1988), the UNESCO Gold Medal (1998), fellowship of the U.S. Academy of Sciences, and foreign membership of the Royal Society of London. He was a visiting professor at the Hebrew University of Jerusalem (1970) and a member of the Board of Governors of the Weizmann Institute from 1996. He also had a sustained interest in the Pugwash organization and in other world issues such as population pressure on resources. The father of his second wife, Mara, was Roman Vishniac, the noted photographer of Eastern Europe.

[Michael Denman (2nd ed.)]

KOHS, SAMUEL CALMIN (1890–1984), U.S. social worker and psychologist. Kohs was born in New York City. He began his career as a psychologist with the Portland, Oregon, Court of Domestic Relations (1919–24). In 1925 he founded the Oakland, California, Placement and Guidance Service. He taught at a number of colleges, including Reed College (1918–22) and the University of Oregon extension division (1919–22) and in 1929 returned to New York to serve as chairman of the Department of Social Technology at the Graduate School of Jewish Social Work, a post he held for ten years. In 1929 Kohs also became editor of the *Jewish Social Service Quarterly*. He served as chairman of the board of directors of *YIVO in 1937–40, and from 1938 to 1940 he was director of the Resettlement Division of the National Refugee Service in New York City. In 1940 Kohs was appointed director of the Refugee Service Committee in Los Angeles, where he also did war statistical work for the Jewish Welfare Board. He was the administrative field secretary of its western states section (1941–56), evolving the "distinctive Jewish names" method of identifying Jewish populations for his *Jewish War Records of World War II* (1946). Kohs was active in Jewish charity work on the East and West coasts, serving as director of the Jewish Welfare Federation of Oakland, California (1924–26), initiating the first national Jewish welfare fund in 1926, and serving as director of the Federation of Jewish Charities in Brooklyn, New York (1928–33). From 1956 on he served as a consultant in psychological and social services. Kohs' authoritative work ranges over the philosophy of social work, ethnic differentials and value systems, the non-verbal measurement of intelligence and non-verbal manifestations of mental development, and the psychology and education of mentally retarded and physically handicapped children. His Block Design Test, which he introduced in 1918, is incorporated into the Wechsler-Bellevue, one of the most widely used U.S. tests of intelligence, and is employed in testing the blind and determining brain injury. The term "Kohs blocks" has been coined to denote the set of small colored blocks that are used to form test patterns in psychodiagnostic examinations. In 1923 his book *Intelligence Measurement: A Psychological and Statistical Study Based Upon the Block-Design Tests* was published. Kohs also designed the IQ Slide Rule, a device that eliminates the arithmetic computation of the intelligence quotient from chronological and mental age scales.

His *Roots of Social Work* (1966) emphasizes "the deficiencies of an exclusively secular approach" to social work and suggests that, as the group is the source of values, sectarian differences in approach may contribute to the practice of casework.

KOHUT, Hungarian-American family. ALEXANDER KOHUT (1842–1894) was a rabbi and scholar. He was born in Felegyhaza (Kiskunfelegyhaza, Hungary). He earned his doctorate in Oriental languages at the University of Leipzig in 1865, and was ordained at the Breslau Seminary in 1867. After graduation he served as rabbi in Stuhlweissenburg (Szekesfehervar, Hungary). While there he was county superintendent of schools, the first Jew to hold this position. At Budapest in 1868, the Congress of Jewish Notables elected Kohut secretary. In 1872 he became chief rabbi of Fuenfkirchen (Pecs, Hungary), where he remained for eight years. He was appointed to the Hungarian parliament by the prime minister as representative of the Jews, but shortly thereafter (1885) he left for the United States to serve as rabbi of Congregation Ahabath Chesed in New York.

Kohut's reputation as rabbi and scholar had preceded him and he was warmly welcomed. He became involved in the struggle between the traditionalists and Reform. Out of this controversy came his *Ethics of the Fathers* (1885, 1920[2]), which established the traditionalists' position. Kohut played a major role in the establishment of the Jewish Theological Seminary and taught Midrash and talmudic methodology there. He was one of the first scholars to write about the Yemenite Midrashim, in his *Notes on…Commentary to the Pentateuch…by Aboo Manzûr al-Dhamâri…* (1892).

His greatest work was the *Arukh ha-Shalem* (8 vols., 1878–92), a lexicon of talmudic terms which Solomon *Schechter called "the greatest and finest specimen of Hebrew learning ever produced by a Jew on this continent." In form it is a new scholarly edition of the *Arukh* of *Nathan b. Jehiel of Rome, but in fact it is a path-finding contribution to talmudic philology in which Kohut offers etymologies and additional sources which exhibit his wide knowledge of Oriental and classical languages. In his introduction he investigated the sources of the *Arukh*, the biographies of its author's teachers, and the quotations therefrom mentioned in the works of early and late commentators. With every entry in the *Arukh ha-Shalem*, there is a German translation of the title, as well as an etymological explanation of the words. This was followed by proofs and a discussion on the different versions found in the manuscripts. Kohut shows a special preference for Persian and he enlarges on the etymological presentations from that language. A volume of supplementary comments, *Tosefet Arukh ha-Shalem* (1937), was prepared by Samuel Krauss, Bernhard Geiger, Louis Ginzberg, Immanuel Loew, and Benjamin Murmelstein. In the *Tosefet Arukh ha-Shalem*, some of the exaggerated presentations of the *Arukh ha-Shalem* were corrected by B. Geiger (for example, in the entry *anbag*, which Kohut derives from the Persian, Geiger notes that this is etymologically inadmissible). The derivations from the Greek were also corrected in many cases by the editors of the *Tosefet*…. In arranging the entries, Kohut did not show a consistency in the spelling of words, and this is at times a source of difficulty in finding required entries. His etymological work in another field consisted of a critical discussion on the translation of the Torah into Persian by Jacob b. Joseph Tavus (Leipzig, 1871).

Alexander's second wife, REBECCA (1864–1951), was an educator, vocational expert, and community leader. Born in Kaschau (Kosice, Slovakia), she was the daughter of Rabbi Albert *Bettelheim. Rebecca was taken by her family to the United States in 1867. In 1887 she married Alexander, who had recently lost his first wife and had eight children to care for. When Alexander died seven years later, she undertook to support the family by giving a series of lectures on Jewish topics, held at the home of Mrs. Jacob H. *Schiff. In 1899 she founded the short-lived Kohut School for Girls; later she became a director of the Columbia Grammar School. She was president of the New York Council of Jewish Women from 1897 to 1901, and in 1914 headed the Young Women's Hebrew Association's employment bureau. Recognized for special competence in the problems of the unemployed, she was appointed to the Federal Employment Clearing House in 1917, and in 1931 to the New York State Employment Service Advisory Commission. She served in 1932 on the State Joint Legislative Commission on Unemployment. In 1942 she became president of the World Congress of Jewish Women; she also played a leading role in the American Women's Association, the Vocational Service for Juniors, and the Bureau of Jewish Social Research. Her books include the autobiographical *My Portion* (1925) and *More Yesterdays* (1950), and *George Alexander Kohut: His Memoir* (1936).

GEORGE ALEXANDER (1874–1933), one of Alexander's sons, was also an educator. He was born at Szekesfehervar and went to New York with his father in 1885. When his father died he returned to Europe for three years to study at the Hochschule fuer die Wissenschaft des Judentums and at the university in Berlin. He was ordained in the United States in 1897 by Bernard *Felsenthal and served as rabbi for three years in Dallas, Texas. Desiring a broader role as an educator, Kohut left for New York City, where he was a teacher and for a time assistant librarian at the Jewish Theological Seminary. From 1902 to 1912 he served as school principal at Temple Emanu-El. He founded the Kohut School for Boys and was its head in 1909–18; he also headed Camp Kohut (1907–26), the Children's University School and the Dalton High School (1924–26), and the Columbia Grammar School (1920–33).

Kohut sought to encourage Jewish scholarship in a number of ways. Through the Alexander Kohut Memorial Foundation, which he set up in 1915, he helped sponsor the publication of important works. In 1919 he presented the 8,000-volume Alexander Kohut Memorial Collection to Yale University library. His own 4,000-volume library was bequeathed to the American Jewish Historical Society, the Kohut Memorial Collection at Yale, and the Jewish Institute of Religion, where he was a trustee. He compiled the Italian index to his father's *Arukh ha-Shalem*, edited *Semitic Studies in Memory of Alexander Kohut* (1897), and published *Morituri: A Reminiscence of My Father* (1907). His many scholarly and popular essays reflect his interest in the prose and poetry of Hebrew, Hungarian, English, French, German, and Spanish, and in the bibliography and history of Jewish life and literature and Hebrew learning in the Americas.

Alexander's brother ADOLF (1848–1917) was a journalist, author, and biographer. He was born in Mindszent (Hungary). He studied briefly at the Jewish Theological Seminary in Breslau and wrote critically of his experiences in his *Memoiren eines juedischen Seminaristen* (1870). Kohut was the editor of several important German papers. In 1884, when he was the editor of *Berliner Zeitung*, he was expelled from Prussia for writing articles attacking Chancellor Bismarck; five years later Kohut was pardoned. He was a prolific writer, producing several hundred articles, monographs, and books on subjects ranging from studies of Heine, Herder, Feuerbach, Van Humboldt, and Frederick the Great to music and theater reviews, to the history of the Jews in Germany, including *Moses Mendelssohn und seine Familie* (1886), *Geschichte des deutschen Juden* (1899), and *Beruehmte israelitische Maenner und Frauen* (2 vols., 1901). He married the prima donna of the Dresden opera, Elizabeth Manstein. In 1892 he was knighted by Emperor Francis Joseph for contributions to literature.

BIBLIOGRAPHY: ON ALEXANDER: J. Fischer, *Dr. Alexander Kohut; ein Lebensbild* (1927); G.A. Kohut, *Concerning Alexander Ko-*

hut: A Tentative Bibliography (1927); idem, in: *Semitic Studies in Memory of Alexander Kohut* (1897), 17–35 (introd.); I. Elbogen, in: AJYB, 44 (1942), 73–80; *Tributes to the Memory of Rev. Dr. Alexander Kohut* (1894); M. Davis, *Emergence of Conservative Judaism* (1963), index. ON GEORGE ALEXANDER: J. Bloch, in: AJHSP, 34 (1937), 303–7; E.D. Coleman, in: *Jewish Studies in Memory of George Alexander Kohut 1874–1933*, ed. by S.W. Baron and A. Marx (1935), introd.; A. Marx, in: AJYB, 36 (1934), 55–64.

[Jack Reimer and Menahem Zevi Kaddari]

KOI or **Kevi** (Heb. כֹּוִי ,כּוֹי), an animal referred to in the Talmud. The Mishnah, *Bikkurim* 2:8 states: "The *koi* is in some ways like a wild animal (*ḥayyah*); in some ways like both wild animals and cattle; and in some ways like neither wild animals nor cattle." The *mishnayot* which follow give the details. This enigmatic creature is further discussed in *Ḥullin* 79b–80a where there occurs a controversy between *tannaim* on its nature and status: "A *koi* is a wild goat. Others are of the opinion that it is a cross between a goat and a gazelle. R. Yose states: 'A *koi* is a distinct species and the rabbis did not decide whether it belongs to the genus of cattle or of wild animals'" (cf. TJ, Bik. 2:8, 65b). Rabban Simeon b. Gamaliel states that it is of the genus of cattle, and adds that Bet Dushai (or Reshai) used to raise them in herds. Thus already in early tannaitic times it was not clearly known what a *koi* was, nor its halakhic status. Several attempts have been made to identify the *koi* in modern times. The commonest view is that it is some kind of bearded deer or antelope (Jastrow, Dict. 1 (1950), 618f., s.v.; Levy, Woerterbuch, 2 (1924), 303, s.v.), perhaps identical with the Greek *tragelaphos*, "a goat-stag, a fantastic animal, represented on eastern carpets and the like" (H.G. Liddell and R. Scott, *Greek-English Lexicon*, 2 (1940[9]), 1809a, s.v.).

BIBLIOGRAPHY: Lewysohn, Zool, 115–8, no. 149; Kohut, Arukh, 4 (1926[2]), 205f., s.v.; S. Krauss, *Tosefot he-Arukh ha-Shalem* (1937), 218.

[Daniel Sperber]

KOIDANOV (Koidanovo), ḥasidic dynasty in *Koidanovo. Koidanov Ḥasidism was a branch of the *Karlin trend of Ḥasidism and the continuation of *Lachowicze Ḥasidism. Its founder was SOLOMON ḤAYYIM (Perlow) OF KOIDANOV (1797–1862), grandson of the *ẓaddikim* Asher of *Stolin and Mordecai of Lachowicze (Lyakhovichi); he was educated in the former's home. Solomon Ḥayyim apparently first served as a rabbi in Stolin and Turov in Polesye province. On the death of his uncle the *ẓaddik* Noah of Lachowicze in 1832, Solomon Ḥayyim was chosen by many of Noah's followers as *admor* and took up residence in Koidanovo. His influence spread to the northern part of Polesye and beyond into Belorussia (Minsk). He left no written works. The Koidanov prayer book *Or ha-Yashar*, published after his death (1877; 1903[2], 1928[3]), contains a special supplement relating the customs of Solomon Ḥayyim and details about his life. During his life the *kolel* Koidanov was founded in Ereẓ Israel, in Tiberias.

His son and successor, BARUCH MORDECAI (1818–1870), was active on behalf of the *kolel*. Another son, Noah (d. 1904), was *admor* in Gorodishche near Novogrudok. The third son was ABRAHAM AARON OF PUKHOVICHI (Marina Gorka). The dynasty was continued by AARON (d. 1897), son of Baruch Mordecai, whose personality and wide knowledge of Kabbalah and Ḥasidism helped to strengthen Koidanov Ḥasidism. In 1866 he appealed to the Koidanov Ḥasidim to support the *kolel*. He published *Or Ne'erav* by Moses *Cordovero, to which he added a supplement *Nireh Or* (Vilna, 1899), and *Sefat Emet* by Moses *Hagiz with a collection of teachings on the value of Ereẓ Israel in kabbalistic and ḥasidic works (1876). On the title page of the Koidanov prayer book he added eight principles to be observed in order to achieve perfection.

His brother SHALOM (1850–1925) served as rabbi in Bragin and edited and published the teachings of the Koidanov rabbis and genealogical details on the dynasty. His most important works are *Divrei Shalom* (1882), and *Mishmeret Shalom* (1912, 1959?). The successor in the dynasty was Aaron's son JOSEPH (1854–1915), a scholar who founded a yeshivah which became an important educational institution in the Koidanovo area. In 1890 he wrote an introduction to the Koidanov prayer book. During his lifetime Koidanovo remained a center of Ḥasidism. The Koidanov Ḥasidim had synagogues also in Vilna, and the United States. NEHEMIAH (1860–1927), the brother of Joseph, headed the Ḥasidim remaining in Poland and lived in Baranovichi. His son and successor in Baranovichi, SHALOM ALTER (b. 1906), perished in Vilna in 1941 during the Holocaust.

BIBLIOGRAPHY: S.E. Stamm, *Zekher Ẓaddik* (1905); W.Z. Rabinowitsch, *Ha-Ḥasidut ha-Lita'it* (1961), 120–7; M. Buber, *Tales of the Hasidim*, 2 (19663), 153–8. W.Z. Rabinowitsch, *Lithuanian Hasidism* (1970), 161–9.

[Wolf Zeev Rabinowitsch]

KOIDANOVO (or **Kaidanovo**; from 1935 **Dzerzhinsk**), town in Minsk district, Belarus. There were 560 Jews paying poll tax in 1765. From 1833 it became a ḥasidic center. The community numbered 2,497 in 1847 and 3,156 in 1897 (67% of the total population); many Jews were occupied in the bristle industry. During World War I the town suffered severely. On July 10–12, 1920 it was set on fire during the retreat of the Polish army and there was general looting of Jewish property. The Jewish population numbered 1,788 in 1926 (32.5% of the total), and 1,314 (15% of the total population) in 1939. In 1924 a Yiddish school was opened and named after the locally born poet Avraham *Reisen. About 150 Jews worked in agriculture. The Germans occupied the town on June 26, 1941, and murdered 1,000 Jews on October 20 or 21, 1941. In March 1942, 1,300 Jews – probably from Minsk – were killed at the local railway station. Jewish partisan units which had joined the general partisan movement were active in forests in the vicinity. The 1959 census contained no data on the Jewish population. The U.S. trade unionist Joseph *Schlossberg was born in Koidanovo.

BIBLIOGRAPHY: *Pogromy v Belorussii* (1922), 31–38; A. Reisen, *Epizodn fun mayn Lebn*, 1 (1929), 5–95; *Sefer Kaidanovo* (1955); *Sefer* *ha-Partizanim ha-Yehudim*, 1 (1958), index; W.Z. Rabinowitsch, *Ha-Ḥasidut ha-Lita'it* (1961), 120–7.

[Yehuda Slutsky / Shmuel Spector (2nd ed.)]

KOIDONOVER (Kaidanover), AARON SAMUEL BEN ISRAEL (c. 1614–1676), talmudic scholar and preacher. Koidonover took his name from Koidanovo near Minsk, where he was born. He was known also by the abbreviation *Maharshak* (**M**orenu **H**a-**R**av **Sh**emu'el **K**aidanover). In his youth he studied in Brest-Litovsk under R. Jacob and his son Joshua Heschel of Lublin. Following the Chmielnicki pogroms of 1648 he fled to Vilna where he became a member of the *bet din* of Moses Lima, author of the *Ḥelkat Meḥokek*, the other members being *Shabbetai b. Meir ha-Kohen (the *Shakh*), and Ephraim Katz, author of the *Sha'ar Efrayim*. In 1656 during the war between Russia and Sweden in Poland he took refuge in Kurow near Lublin, where he served as rabbi, and there his two daughters were killed by Cossacks. He went to Austria, where he became a rabbi in a small town, and from there to Moravia where he became rabbi of Nikolsburg. Subsequently he was rabbi and *av bet din* of important communities, including Fuerth, Reischer, Brest-Litovsk, and Frankfurt. He stayed some six months in the sister communities of Altona, Hamburg, and Wandsbeck in 1669 where he enacted many *takkanot* which were included in the regulations of Altona. Toward the end of his life he returned to Poland and was appointed *av bet din* of Cracow. He died in Chmielnik.

Koidonover wrote many important halakhic and homiletical works. In his learning he sought to return to the primary sources of the *halakhah* and refrained from relying upon the *aḥaronim*. He also wrote responsa, largely on the permissibility of **agunot* to remarry, which had become an urgent question as a result of the massacres. His sermons contain in popular form the ideas of the kabbalists of Safed and Poland. His main work is the *Birkat ha-Zevaḥ* (Amsterdam, 1669), novellae and glosses to most of the order of *Kodashim*, with an autobiographical introduction. Three more of his works were published by his son Ẓevi Hirsch: *Birkat Shemu'el* (Frankfurt, 1682), sermons partially kabbalistic in content; *Emunat Shemu'el* (*ibid.*, 1683), responsa; and *Tiferet Shemu'el* (*ibid.*, 1696), novellae on the Talmud, glosses and novellae to the *Piskei ha-Rosh* of Asher b. Jehiel, to the *Turim* and *Beit Yosef*, and **hassagot* on the novellae of Samuel Edels. Koidonover also compiled a book on the procedure to be followed in executing divorces and *ḥaliẓah*, which is in manuscript in the Bodleian Library, Oxford.

BIBLIOGRAPHY: M. Horovitz, *Frankfurter Rabbinen*, ed by J. Unna (1969), 87–90; L. Loewenstein, in: JJLG, 6 (1908), 158–63; *Beit Yisrael be-Polin*, 2 (1953), 22, 39; I. Markon, in: *Studies in Jewish Bibliography in Memory of A.S. Freidus* (1929), 374–5.

[David Tamar]

KOIDONOVER (Kaidanover), ẒEVI HIRSCH (d. 1712), rabbi and ethical writer (his name derived from Koidanovo, a town near Minsk). Koidonover was born in Vilna and spent his childhood in Kurow near Lublin until 1658 when his father's house was pillaged and his two sisters killed. The rest of the family escaped to Austria, and subsequently settled in Nikolsburg, where his father, Aaron Samuel, was appointed rabbi. Koidonover received his religious education from his father and from Joseph b. Judah, rabbi of Minsk and Dubnow, author of the moralistic treatise, *Yesod Yosef.*

In Frankfurt, where his father became rabbi in 1667, Koidonover married the daughter of Isaac Ganz. A few years later he returned to Vilna, where he prospered in business and achieved prominence in the community. He was imprisoned, however, on a false charge, and on his release, returned with his family to Frankfurt. There he published *Kav ha-Yashar* (1705), a work he had written in Vilna (*Kav* equivalent to 102, the number of chapters in the book, *ha-Yashar* an acrostic of Hirsch). *Kav ha-Yashar* holds the torments of hell over the heads of those who do not mend their ways and fulfill God's commandments. The book is replete with wondrous tales (incidentally of great folkloric value) depicting the punishment of the evil and the reward of the righteous. The book reflects the suffering and persecution of European Jewry, and the despair wrought by the Shabbatean disillusionment. It also reveals aspects of the communal life of this time – the economic struggle, oppression by leaders of the community, and disregard of religious rituals by Jewish tax collectors whose business brought them into contact with Christian government officials and noblemen. Most of Koidonover's ideas were borrowed from *Yesod Yosef*; his main contribution lies in his engaging style, which made the *Kav ha-Yashar* popular with the masses, and rapidly gained a reputation for it among European Jewry. It has been frequently reprinted (see Friedberg, Eked, 3, 882). Koidonover prepared a popular Yiddish translation (Frankfurt, 1709), and a Ladino translation appeared in Constantinople (1724). Koidonover also published the halakhic work of his father.

BIBLIOGRAPHY: L. Loewenstien, in: JJLG, 6 (1908), 159–60; E. Tcherikover, in: *Jiwobleter*, 4 (1932), 159–67.

[Shlomo Eidelberg]

KOIGEN, DAVID (1879–1933), philosopher and sociologist. He was born in Wachniaki, Ukraine, and studied in European universities. He lived in Germany until 1912, then returned to Russia, and in 1921 was appointed professor of philosophy and sociology at the Ukrainian University in Kiev. He wrote an autobiographical work, *Der apokalyptische Reiter* (1925), about these years in Russia. He returned to Germany, working mainly on Jewish problems and cultural sociology. From 1925 to 1927 he edited the quarterly *Ethos*. His first writings were on socialism, beginning with his thesis on the Young Hegelians (1901), followed by *Die Kulturanschauung des Sozialismus* (1903). He further developed his cultural-sociological approach in *Ideen zur Philosophic der Kultur* (1910) and *Die Kultur der Demokratie* (1912). In 1922 he published *Der moralische Gott*, a study of the relationship of religion and culture, and in 1929 his main work on sociology, *Der Aufbau der sozi-*

alen Welt im Zeitalter der Wissenschaft. After his death, some of his Jewish writings appeared, entitled *Heimat Israels* (1939). Koigen tried to delineate the peculiarity of Jewish experience in history and culture, pointing to the difficulty the Jew has in gaining normal historical experience. Using methods like Max *Weber's, he attempted to specify the elements involved in Jewish existence in historical processes.

[Richard H. Popkin]

KOILA (or **Kales**; Turk. **Kilye**), Byzantine city in the Gallipoli Peninsula. There was a Jewish quarter there in the 12th century. In 1136 the revenues of whole markets (*emporia*) of the Jewish quarter in Koila and the tithe on the wines were assigned to the Monastery of Christ Pantokrator in Istanbul. *Benjamin of Tudela, who visited the city as it was on his way back home after Gallipoli, speaks of 50 Jews, with R. Jacob and R. Judah at their head. There remain no traces of this community.

BIBLIOGRAPHY: J. Thomas et al. (eds.), *Byzantine Monastic Foundation Documents: A Complete Translation of the Surviving Founders' Typika and Testaments*, 2 (2000), 725, 770; *The Itinerary of Benjamin of Tudela, Critical Text, Translation and Commentary*, ed. M.N. Adler (1907), 25; S. Bowman, *The Jews of Byzantium 1204–1453* (1985), 335.

[M. Mustafa Kulu (2nd ed.)]

KOJETIN (Czech **Kojetín**; Ger. **Kojetein**; Heb. גויט״ן, גוט״ן), town in central Moravia, Czech Republic. Jews apparently lived in Kojetin from the 13th century, but their first documented mention dates from 1566, when 52 families lived in the *Judengasse*. The consecration of a cemetery is recorded in 1574. The synagogue, then seating 300, was renovated in 1614 (and restored again in 1718). In 1657 only 16 houses were owned by Jews, but the community absorbed many refugees from the *Chmielnicki massacres (1648) and some of those expelled from Vienna (1670). The *Minhag Polin*, the Polish prayer rite, was introduced in Kojetin in 1648. When the Jews were segregated in a special sector of the town in 1727, 500 of them lived in 40 houses. Kojetin was then in the possession of the Prague archbishop, who treated the Jewish community fairly. There was a scandal in Kojetin, echoed in rabbinical literature of the period, when a *Frankist was accused of making the sign of the cross when blessing the community. The *Familiants Law allotted 76 Jewish families to Kojetin in 1798. In 1829 there were 443 Jews in the town, living in 45 houses. The community flourished in the 19th century but began to decline after 1860 when many of its members were attracted to the larger cities. It numbered 162 in 1869.

Only 72 Jews (1.1% of the total population), 30 of them of declared Jewish nationality, were left in the town in 1930. The remnant of the community was deported to Nazi extermination camps in 1942 and the synagogue equipment transferred to the Central Jewish Museum in Prague. A small congregation, affiliated with *Olomouc, was established after World War II. The burial hall in the cemetery was still standing in 1970.

Among the rabbis who officiated in Kojetin were Eleazer *Fleckeles (1779–83), Jacob *Bruell (1843–89), and Richard *Feder (1903–06). Several Jewish families – Goitein, Guttein, Kojeteiner, etc. – took their names from the town. The scholar David *Kaufmann was a native of Kojetin.

BIBLIOGRAPHY: Steiner, in: H. Gold (ed.), *Juden und Judengemeinden Maehrens* (1929), 279–87.

[Meir Lamed]

KOJÈVE, ALEXANDRE (1902–1968), philosopher. Born in Russia, after the 1917 Revolution he studied in Berlin, and in the early 1930s moved to Paris. From 1933 to 1939 he taught at the École Pratique des Hautes Études. Kojève is best known for his book, *Introduction à la lecture de Hegel* (1962[2]), which consists of the notes from his course compiled by the novelist Raymond Queneau, one of his students. It is considered one of the best studies of Hegel's phenomenology. Kojève is also the author of *Tyrannie et Sagesse* (1954), part of a debate on tyranny with Leo *Strauss, the political theorist. From shortly after the end of World War II, Kojève worked in the French Ministry of Economic Affairs and was one of the chief planners for the European Common Market.

[Myriam M. Malinovich]

KOKAND, city in Fergana district, Uzbekistan; before the 1917 Revolution, a county town in the Fergana province. There were a few Jews living in the town, which was formerly capital of the Kokand khanate, before its capture by the Russians in 1876. They engaged in dyeing and petty trade, and, as unbelievers, suffered from oppression by the Muslim rulers. After the Russian conquest, many Jews migrated from the emirate of *Bukhara to Kokand. They contributed to the development of the town and engaged in the cotton, wool, and silk trade. The community numbered 1,029 in 1897 (1.25% of the total population), and 2,000 before the outbreak of World War I. During the civil war in Russian Central Asia (1918), the rebel Uzbeks and Kazakhs rioted in Kokand, destroyed the community, and looted Jewish property. By 1926, only 746 Bukharan Jews remained in Kokand; their number reached 3,196 (4% of the total population) in 1939. In 1970 the Jewish population was estimated at about 1,500. Most left in the 1990s. One synagogue existed and the Jewish cemetery was well kept.

BIBLIOGRAPHY: Z.L. Amitin-Shapiro, *Ocherki sotsialisticheskogo stroitelstva sredi sredne-aziatskikh yevreyev* (1933).

[Yehuda Slutsky]

KOKESCH, OZER (1860–1905), Austrian Zionist and Herzl's aide. Born in Brody, Galicia, Kokesch practiced law in Vienna. From the early 1880s he was active in the Jewish national movement and was one of the founders of the Jewish students' association *Kadimah. When Herzl appeared on the Zionist scene, Kokesch joined him, becoming the secretary of the committee that made preparations for the First Zionist Congress (he was unable to participate because of an accident). He became a member of the Zionist Executive and laid the foundation for the World and the Austrian Zionist Organizations' structure. Kokesch opposed the *Uganda Scheme and was an active supporter of agricultural settlement in Ereẓ Israel.

BIBLIOGRAPHY: A. Bein, *Theodore Herzl* (Eng., 1962²), index; T. Herzl, *Complete Diaries*, ed. by R. Patai, 5 vols. (1960), index.

[Getzel Kressel]

KOKHAVI (Estella), DAVID BEN SAMUEL (c. 1300), Provençal talmudist, active in Avignon. No biographical details are known of him. His signature occurs on two responsa included in the responsa of Isaac di Lattes (Vienna, 1860) in connection with an incident which occurred in 1305. He wrote many works, of which, however, only fragments have been published. His main work, *Sefer ha-Battim*, also called *Kiryat Sefer*, consists of halakhic rulings. It is based upon, and follows, Maimonides' *Mishneh Torah*, with regard to arrangement and style, but gives additional rulings, clarification of halakhic problems, and decides between conflicting views. A fragment of the introduction was published by Neubauer and additional fragments by M. Herschler (Moriah 1 and 2 (1969), *Sinai*, 62, 1968, 199–228). The whole work is extant in various libraries in manuscript (Oxford, Escorial (Spain), and elsewhere). There is also extant a manuscript of his, *Migdal David*, which deals with philosophical topics. It is likewise based on Maimonides (Mss. Moscow, Guenzburg Collection, no. 234).

BIBLIOGRAPHY: Neubauer, in: REJ, 9 (1884), 214–28; Neubauer, Chronicles, 2 (1895), 239f.; Gross, Gal Jud, 54; Renan, *Ecrivains*, 471–7; Shatzmiller, in: *Sefunot*, 10 (1966), 20f., 36; Isaac de Lattes, *Sha'arei Zion* (ed. S. Buber; 1881); Albeck (ed.), in: Abraham b. Isaac of Narbonne, *Sefer ha-Eshkol* (1935), 25.

[Shlomoh Zalman Havlin]

KOKHAV YAIR (Heb. כוכב יאיר), urban community in central Israel, east of *Kefar Sava. In 1981, 15 families settled in temporary houses, and two years later the first permanent foundations were laid. Between 1986 and 1996, about 800 families joined the settlement. In 2002 its population was 4,840, occupying an area of 0.65 sq. mi. (1.7 sq. km.). The settlement's population is mixed, secular and religious, Israeli-born and new immigrants. Among them are 100 immigrant families from South Africa. In 2003 the local council of Kokhav Yair was united with that of *Ẓur Yigal. The settlement is named after Avraham *Stern (known as "Ya'ir"), the Lehi underground leader.

WEBSITE: www.kyair.org.il.

[Shaked Gilboa (2nd ed.)]

°**KOKOVTSOV, PAUL KONSTANTINOVICH** (1861–1942), Russian Orientalist. Kokovtsov, who was born in Pavlovsk, near Leningrad, came from a noble family of distinguished engineers. In his school days he developed a deep interest in Hebrew which widened in his university studies at St. Petersburg (completed in 1884) into mastery of the various branches of Semitics and included Turkic and Sanskrit philology and Near Eastern history and literature. His thesis, a capital work of great and meticulous learning, was devoted to Ibn Barun's 11th–12th century Arabic work comparing Hebrew with Arabic; published as *Kniga sravneniya yevreyskogo yazyka s arabskim* ("Book of Comparison of Hebrew with Arabic," 1893), it formed the first volume of a series on the history of medieval Hebrew philology and Judeo-Arabic literature. Kokovtsov's *Novye materialy dlya kharakteristiki Iekhūdy Khayūdzha, Samuila Nagida i nekotorykh drugikh predstaviteley yevreyskoy filologicheskoy nauki v x, xi i xii veke* ("New Materials for the Characterization of Judah Ḥayyuj, Samuel Nagid and Other Representatives of Jewish Philological Scholarship in the 10th–12th Centuries," 1916) was published as the second volume in the same series.

Kokovtsov succeeded his own teacher, Daniel *Chwolson, as professor of Hebrew at St. Petersburg University in 1894. His influence as a teacher was enormous; most Russian Semitists during his tenure of about 50 years were his disciples. He began publishing in 1885, and most of his publications, scattered in journals and collections, deal with Aramaic, Syriac, Turkic, and Ethiopic manuscripts and epigraphic material. Kokovtsov worked on Moses Ibn Ezra's Arabic book on Hebrew poetry (in *Vostochnye Zametki*, 1895); the commentary of Tanḥūm on Jonah (in *Sbornik statey uchenikov… V.R. Rosena*, 1897); Hebrew volumes in the Imperial Academy of Sciences' Asiatic Museum (*Notitia codicum hebraicarum…*, 1905), and on Baḥya's lifetime (in Eng., in *Livre d'hommage à… S. Poznański*, 1927). His edition of the 10th-century Jewish Khazar correspondence (*Yevreysko-khazarskaya perepiska v X veke*, 1932) is outstanding. Kokovtsov was elected a full member of the Academy of Sciences in 1909. In 1913, as expert in the blood-libel trial of Mendel *Beilis, Kokovtsov helped to expose the ignorance of the prosecution. This gave him deep satisfaction; he annually reread the proceedings of the trial.

BIBLIOGRAPHY: N.V. Pigulevskaya, in: *Vestnik Leningradskogo Universiteta*, 2 (1947), 106–18; I. Yu. Krachkovski, *Izbrannye sochineniya*, 5 (1958), 416–27; idem (I.J. Kratschkowski), *Die russische Arabistik* (1957), passim; *Palestinskiy sbornik*, 74 (1964), 170–81 (incl. bibl.).

[Moshe Perlmann]

KOL (Kolodny), MOSHE (1911–1989), Israeli politician, member of the Second and Fourth to Eighth Knessets. Born in Pinsk, Russia, he was a leader of the Zionist youth movement Ha-No'ar ha-Ẓiyyoni in Poland, and settled in Palestine in 1932. He became the representative of his movement's workers faction (which later assumed the name Ha-Oved ha-Ẓiyyoni) in the *Histadrut Executive. He was elected a deputy member of the *Jewish Agency Executive in 1946, and became a full member in 1948, when he was appointed head of the *Youth Aliyah Department, a post he held until 1964. In 1948, after the establishment of the State of Israel, he was one of the founders and leaders of the Progressive Party and served on the Provisional State Council in 1948. He was first elected to the Second Knesset in 1951. In the years 1961–65 the Progressive Party formed part of the *Israel Liberal Party, but in 1965 broke away from the Liberal Party when the latter joined Gaḥal, assuming the name "the Independent Liberal Party," of which Kol became the leader. In 1966–69 he served as minister of tourism and development and in 1969–77 as minister of tourism. In the Second Knesset, and again in the Sixth, Seventh, and Eighth Knessets, from which he soon resigned to enable the next in line on his party list to enter the Knesset.

Among his writings are *Masekhet Aliyyat ha-No'ar* (1961) and *Aliyyat ha-No'ar* (1966), both on Youth Aliyah; *Morim ve-Ḥaverim* ("Teachers and Friends," 1968); and *Ba-Ma'avak le-Shittuf Yehudi-Aravi be-Yisrael* ("On the Struggle for Jewish-Arab Cooperation in Israel," 1979).

BIBLIOGRAPHY: Nafatali Zahar, *Moshe Kol le-Yom Huladeto ha-75; Me'at Mikhtavim mi-Ymei Meẓukah ve-Tikvah* (1986).

[Susan Hattis Rolef (2nd ed.)]

KOLAROVGRAD (since 1956, **Shumen**), town in eastern Bulgaria. Jews first settled in Kolarovgrad in the 18th century, in what became a special Jewish quarter. The first school to be established by the Alliance Israélite Universelle in Bulgaria (1869), a girls' school, was situated at Kolarovgrad. In 1878 there was a Jewish population of 1,100, in 1910 of 1,200. In 1943 the Jews were threatened with deportation, but the 1943 decree of expulsion from Bulgaria was not carried out. In 2004 there was a small community of around 40 Jews affiliated to the local branch of the nationwide Shalom organization.

BIBLIOGRAPHY: S. Mézan, *Les Juifs espagnols en Bulgarie* (1925), passim.

[Simon Marcus / Emil Kalo (2nd ed.)]

KOLATCH, ALFRED JACOB (1916–), U.S. rabbi, author, and publisher. Kolatch was born in Seattle, Washington, and received his B.A. from Yeshiva College in 1937 and his ordination from the Jewish Theological Seminary in 1941. After two years as rabbi of the House of Peace (later Beth Sholom) Congregation in Columbia, South Carolina (1941–43), he enlisted as a chaplain in the U.S. Army and was discharged in 1946 with the rank of captain. From 1946 to 1948, he served as rabbi of the Kew Gardens Jewish Center in Queens, New York.

In 1948, Kolatch and his wife, Thelma, founded Jonathan David Co., named for their two sons, and Jonathan David Publishers, specializing in Judaica book publishing and distribution. After decades of growth at several Manhattan locations, the company relocated to expanded quarters in Middle Village, New York, where Kolatch continued to serve as its president and editor-in-chief. Over the years, some 700 Judaica titles have appeared under the Jonathan David imprint, including such classics as *The Jewish Way in Death and Mourning* by Maurice Lamm; *God, Man and History* by Eliezer Berkovits; *The Encyclopedia of Jewish Humor*, by Henry D. Spalding; and the *Great Jews* volumes by Robert and Elinor Slater and Darryl Lyman.

Kolatch himself is the author of more than 50 books, most notably the *Jewish Book of Why* series, comprising *The Jewish Book of Why* (1981); *The Second Jewish Book of Why* (2004); *The Jewish Child's First Book of Why* (1995); *The Jewish Book of Why: The Torah* (2004) and *The Jewish Mourner's Book of Why* (1993). These titles alone have cumulatively sold more than 1.5 million copies in English, French, Spanish, German, and Portuguese. Recognized as one of the world's leading authorities on Hebrew and English nomenclature, Kolatch also wrote *These Are the Names* (1948), *The Name Dictionary* (1967); *The Jonathan David Dictionary of First Names* (1980); *The New Name Dictionary* (1989); *Best Baby Names for Jewish Children* (1986); *The Complete Dictionary of English and Hebrew First Names* (1984), and *The Comprehensive Dictionary of English and Hebrew First Names* (2005). Other works by Kolatch include *Who's Who in the Talmud* (1964); *Masters of the Talmud: Their Lives and Views* (2003); *Our Religion: The Torah* (1951); *The Family Seder* and *The Concise Family Seder* (1987); *A Child's First Book of Jewish Holidays* (1997); *Great Jewish Quotations: By Jews and About Jews* (1996, 1998); *A Handbook for the Jewish Home* (2005); *The Presidents of the United States and the Jews* (with David Dalin, 2000); and *What Jews Say About God* (1999).

In the 1960s, Kolatch served as president of the Association of Jewish Chaplains of the Armed Forces and as vice president of the interdenominational Military Chaplains Association of the United States. In 1966, he was awarded a Doctor of Divinity degree, *honoris causa*, by the Jewish Theological Seminary.

[Bezalel Gordon (2nd ed.)]

KOLB, LEON (1890–1977), physician, art collector, and bibliophile. Kolb was born in Czernowitz, Austria. A physician by profession, he was awarded the Iron Cross and the Order of Franz Josef I during World War I, and after settling in the United States was appointed associate clinical professor of pharmacology and therapeutics at Stanford University Medical School in 1954.

Kolb began to collect rare books and art in 1908 in Vienna, specializing in graphics. He immigrated to Palestine in 1935 and moved to the U.S. in 1937, settling in San Francisco. After his retirement he devoted himself entirely to art. He presented parts of his large collection to various American and Israeli institutions. The majority of the rare books, Bibles, and art objects were given to the Hebrew University; the music collection to the Haifa Music Museum; and other gifts to Stanford and Brandeis universities and to local institutions in California.

Kolb established a Jewish Museum at Temple Emanuel in San Francisco in 1957 and gave his Jewish library, with Israeli art and archaeological artifacts from Israel, to the Kolb Library in Congregation Rodef Shalom of San Rafael, California.

Among his published works are the novel *Moses, The Near Easterner* (1956), *The Vienna Jewish Museum*, and *The Sabbath Princess*. He also edited *The Woodcuts of Jacob Steinhardt* (1959).

His main literary and historical interest, however, was in *Berenice, on whom he published a trilogy of novels: *Berenice,*

Princess of Judea (1959), *Mission to Claudius* (1963), and *The Sage, Father of Generations to Come* (1965).

He married Chanah, the daughter of Max *Grunwald and granddaughter of Samuel Joseph Bloch.

KOLBERG (Pol. **Kołobrzeg**), city in Pomerania, Poland. The first evidence of Jews in Kolberg dates from 1261. After the expulsion of 1492/93 some Jews who converted to Christianity remained in the town. Jewish wool merchants were again to be found in Kolberg in the 17th century. In 1702 Hirschel Salomon and Aaron Moses were refused permission to settle there after protests by Christian merchants. In 1785–88 three *Schutzjuden* ("protected Jews") were contractors for obtaining amber. After 1812 Jews were legally allowed to reside in Kolberg, and in that year a cemetery was consecrated. There were 40 persons in the community in 1816 and 440 in 1895. A convalescent home was dedicated in 1899 by Salomon Goldschmidt, who served as rabbi until 1925. In 1933, 197 Jews remained, maintaining a school, cemetery, synagogue, and teacher who was also cantor. The community came to an end in World War II and was not subsequently reconstituted.

BIBLIOGRAPHY: U. Grotefend, *Geschichte und rechtliche Stellung der Juden in Pommern von den Aufaengen bis zum Tode Friedrichs des Grossen* (1931 = *Baltische Studien*, vol. 32, 1930); PK Germanyah; FJW (1932–33), 77.

KOL BO (Heb. כָּל בּוֹ; "everything within"), an anonymous work containing both halakhic rulings as well as, at times, explanations of *halakhot*, arranged in accordance with the subject matter. The book was written at the end of the 13th or the beginning of the 14th century. The identity of its author and its relation to the *Orḥot Ḥayyim* (on OḤ, Florence, 1750–51; on YD, ed. by M. Schlesinger, 1899–1902) of *Aaron b. Jacob ha-Kohen of Lunel are very complicated problems that have not yet been resolved. The fact that both books cover the same material but that the *Orḥot Ḥayyim* contains additional and more abundant halakhic material than the *Kol Bo* has given rise to the view that the *Kol Bo* is a later abridgment of the *Orḥot Ḥayyim* (thus Joseph Caro, Ḥ.J.D. Azulai, and others). However, the arrangement of the material in the two books does not support this view. The *Orḥot Ḥayyim* is much more systematic than the *Kol Bo* and it is difficult to explain the latter's arrangements in its present form; nor can any reasonable explanation be given for the manner of its abridgment, if it is indeed such. M. Schlesinger, who edited the second part of the *Orḥot Ḥayyim*, also subscribed to the above view (see his introduction) and added nothing new to previous arguments. An attempt has been made to identify the author with Shemariah b. Simḥah, the grandson of Samuel Schlettstadt (see his pamphlet published in I.A. Benjacob's *Devarim Attikin*, 2 (1846), which Zunz followed), but for this opinion, too, there is no basis, and the author remains unknown. The view of Benjacob and S.D. Luzzatto appears to be close to the truth, namely, that the *Kol Bo* is the first edition of the *Orḥot Ḥayyim* and is by the same author, Aaron b. Jacob ha-Kohen. In any event, the *Kol Bo* in the extant text undoubtedly preceded the *Orḥot Ḥayyim*. It is probable that it represents the first stages of the text of the *Orḥot Ḥayyim* and is earlier than the versions in the three known manuscripts of the *Orḥot Ḥayyim* (the Ms. from which Part II was published, Jews' College, London, and Ms. Moscow, Guenzburg).

Kol Bo contains 148 sections embracing the following subjects: blessings, prayer, the synagogue, the meal, Sabbath and festivals, marriage, monetary matters, **niddah*, vows and oaths, *halakhot* relevant to Ereẓ Israel, forbidden foods and **issur ve-hetter, mezuzah*, the redemption of the first-born son and the firstborn of an ass, visiting the sick, mourning, the *takkanot* of R. *Gershom and others. Included in this anthology were also collections of laws from various works such as the *Even ha-Roshah* of *Eliezer b. Nathan; laws from the *Tashbeẓ* of Simeon b. Ẓemaḥ *Duran; from the *Sefer Mitzvot Katan* of *Isaac b. Joseph of Corbeil; from *Perez b. Elijah of Corbeil; Isaac, author of the *Sefer ha-Menahel*; *Baruch b. Isaac of Worms, author of the *Sefer ha-Terumah*; and various responsa. The book is chiefly based upon *Maimonides' *Mishneh Torah*, combined with and having additions from the rulings of the scholars of Germany, France, and Provence. Few of the rulings of Spanish scholars are cited (as against the *Orḥot Ḥayyim* which adds many statements of such Spanish scholars as *Naḥmanides, Solomon b. Abraham *Adret, Yom Tov b. Abraham *Ishbili, and others). The anthology contains much material from various books, not all of which are extant today. With the discovery and publication of the *Sefer ha-Mikhtam* (ed. by A. Sofer, 1959) of *David b. Levi of Narbonne, the *Sefer ha-Maḥkim* (ed. by J. Freimann in *Ha-Eshkol*, 6 (1909)) of Nathan b. Judah, and the *Sefer ha-Minhagot* (in S. Assaf, *Sifram shel Rishonim* (1935)) of *Asher b. Saul of Lunel, it has become evident that a large part of the *Kol Bo* was taken from them, even though this fact is not indicated there. It is possible to conjecture that the original material in the *Kol Bo* is negligible, and that almost all of it was taken from various sources. It was first printed in Naples in 1490–91. The one known manuscript of it in the Guenzburg Collection, Moscow, may well be a copy of the printed edition.

BIBLIOGRAPHY: Azulai, 1 (1852), 9:130; 2 (1852), 33:14; Benjacob, Oẓar, 51:984, 239:118; S.D. Luzzatto, in: *Meged Yeraḥim*, 1 (1855), 5–10; idem, *Iggerot Shadal*, 8 (1892), 1232:562; Zunz, Ritus, 31f., 179f.; H. Gross, in: MGWJ, 18 (1869), 433–50, 531–41; Gross, Gal Jud, 290, 420; S.M. Chones, *Toledot ha-Posekim* (1910), 23, 303; Aaron ha-Kohen of Lunel, *Orḥot Ḥayyim*, pt. 2, ed. by M. Schlesinger, 1 (1902), introd.; J. Freimann, in: *Ha-Eshkol*, 6 (1909), 107–9.

[Shlomoh Zalman Havlin]

KOLDYCHEVO CAMP (**Koldyczewo**), forced labor camp in Belorussia, located 11 miles from Baranovichi, established by the Germans in late 1941. In November 1942 a crematorium was constructed in which some 600 people were incinerated. It later became an extermination camp in which Russians and Polish underground members were interned along with the Jews transferred from the surrounding ghettos of Baranovichi,

*Nowogrodek, *Slonim, and others. Jews were separated from the other prisoners and the camp in the stables of what had once been a farm. Prior to the camp's liquidation on June 29, 1944, more than 22,000 inmates were murdered and buried in 38 mass graves in and around the camp. A prisoner, Dr. Zelik Levinbrook, supplied medicine to the partisans with the help of a former patient. An active Jewish resistance, headed by Shlomo Kushnir, a former shoemaker, existed in Koldychevo. Its arms supply was meager: two guns, four grenades, and some acid. On the night of March 17, 1944, it succeeded in leading almost all the Jewish inmates out of the camp after killing ten Nazi guards and poisoning the guard dogs. Kushnir committed suicide when he was caught with 25 others. Seventy five prisoners survived. The rest joined the partisans in the forest.

BIBLIOGRAPHY: Foxman, in: Y. Suhl (ed.), *They Fought Back* (1967), 172–5; *Ha-Partizanim ha-Yehudim*, 1 (1958), 453. **ADD. BIBLIOGRAPHY:** *Barnowicze Memorial Book* (1953); S. Cholawski, "Koldichevo," in: Y. Gutman (ed.), *The Holocaust Encyclopedia* (1990).

[Joseph M. Foxman / Michael Berenbaum (2nd ed.)]

KOLEL (Heb. כּוֹלֵל; literally "comprehensive," "embracing all"), a word used in comparatively recent times to describe two entirely different groups. (1) It refers to a group of Ashkenazi Jews in Ereẓ Israel all originally from one country or from one district, the members of which received allocations from the funds collected in their countries of origin for their support. From a passage in the *Megillat Sefer* of Jacob *Emden (pp. 14–15) it would appear that the word originally referred to the organization in the country which collected the funds, and only later was applied to those who received them (for details see *Ḥalukkah*). (2) The word *kolel* was subsequently also applied to institutions for advanced talmudic studies which were for married students, since the yeshivot were confined to unmarried students. This name was coined by R. Israel *Lipkin (Salanter). In 1878 he persuaded a wealthy donor in Berlin (who insisted on anonymity, but whose name was later revealed as Lachman) to devote a large sum of money to establish a yeshivah for young married men, to which he gave the name *kolel perushim, perushim* ("separatists") referring to those who separated themselves in order to devote themselves to study. In his stirring appeal to the Jewish communities for further support (*Eẓ Peri*, Vilna 1881), however, he does not use this name. The *kolel*, which continued to exist for a long time after his death, concentrated on the study of Lipkin's doctrine of *musar. In later years, however, and particularly in the State of Israel, it was applied to all institutions of higher talmudic studies for married students. The members of the *kolel* receive a monthly stipend sufficient for bare livelihood. In recent years the number of *kolelim* in Israel has grown to a considerable extent.

BIBLIOGRAPHY: L. Ginzberg, *Students, Scholars and Saints* (1928), 161–3.

KOLIN (Czech **Kolín**; Ger. **Kolin**, in older sources **Neukollin**), city in central Bohemia, Czech Republic. Its Jewish community was one of the four communities known by the abbreviation Karban (Heb. קרב"ן), Kolin, Roudnice, Bumsla, Nachod), second in importance only to Prague. Town records of 1376–1401 mention 16 Jewish households; a gravestone from 1492 was preserved; a synagogue is mentioned as being old in 1512. Expelled in 1541, the Jews returned in 1557, to be expelled once more in 1561 and return again in 1564. The community numbered 33 families in 1574. There were 37 Jewish houses in Kolin in 1623. A synagogue with an ark donated by Samuel *Oppenheimer was dedicated in 1696. In a fire in 1796, 43 Jewish houses, housing 205 families, were burned down. In 1848, 30 Jews were members of a unit of the national guard sent to aid the revolution in Prague, but later they were forced out of the national guard. Kolin was known for its yeshivah, which in the 19th century became modernized and was called "Beth Hamidrash-Anstalt" (i.e., institution). Moses *Montefiore was impressed by it during his visit in 1855 and endowed a foundation for students there. In 1913 a young Roman Catholic priest, Hrachovsky, tried to implicate the Jews in a *blood libel charge following the death of a girl who had committed suicide because she was pregnant by him.

Between the two world wars Kolin was a stronghold of the Czecho-Jewish movement (see *Čechů-židů, Svaz). In October 1938 many refugees from Sudetenland sought refuge in Kolin. From March 1939 *kasher* meat for Prague was supplied from the town. About 600 Jews organized themselves for collective emigration and were offered the support of the French government in establishing a settlement in New Caledonia, but with the outbreak of World War II the project could not be realized. In January 1940 Jewish shops were confiscated, three months sooner than in the rest of the German protectorate of Bohemia and Moravia. Jewish women were forced to work in a local soap factory. The cemetery was damaged by aircraft bombardment during World War II. From June 10, 1942, 2,202 Jews from Kolin and other places were deported in three transports from Kolin to *Theresienstadt and 2,098 died in Nazi extermination camps. Of these, 475 were members of the Kolin community. The synagogue equipment was sent to the Prague Central Jewish Museum. A small community was reestablished in 1945 and a memorial to the Nazi victims erected in 1950.

Among the noted rabbis who officiated in Kolin were Jacob *Illowy (1746–81), Eleazar b. Eleazar *Kallir (1781–1802), and Daniel Frank (1839–60). The last rabbi was Richard *Feder. The town was the birthplace of the Viennese philosopher, Joseph *Popper-Lynkeus; the Jewish national politician, Ludwig Singer; the Czech poet and literary critic, Otakar *Fischer; and the economists, Isidor, Julius, and Ignaz *Petschek.

From 1,347 Jews (16.1% of the total population) in Kolin in 1857, the number declined to 1,148 in 1881 (9.8%), and 430 in 1930 (2.3%). Most of the Jews were sent to Theresienstadt on June 13, 1942, and from there to the death camps of Poland. In 1948 there were 98 members of the community and 118 nonconfessing Jews living in the town. The congregation in Kolin in 1969 was affiliated with the Prague community. Two cemeteries (one dating from the 15th century and the other from 1887) were still in existence. The synagogue was used occasionally. Virtually no Jews lived there by the end of the century.

BIBLIOGRAPHY: S. Back, in: MGWJ, 26 (1877), 410–20; M. Popper, *ibid.*, 38 (1894), 219–36; R. Feder, *Zidovská tragedie* (1947), passim; idem, in: *Česko-židovsky kalendář*, 47 (1927/28), 197; idem, in: H. Gold (ed.), *Juden und Judengemeinden Boehmens* (1934), 277–98; T. Jacobovits, in: JGGJČ, 1 (1929), 332–68; M. Zobel, in: *Almanach des Schocken Verlags* (1936/37), 132–40; G. Stein, *Die Familie Schudlow* (1925); J. Toury, Mehumah u-Mevukhah be-Mahpekhat 1848 (1968), 60–61; Germ Jud, 2 (1968), 415.

[Jan Herman and Meir Lamed]

KOLIN (Kelin), SAMUEL BEN NATHAN HA-LEVI (1720–1806), rabbi and *posek*. Kolin took his name from his birthplace, Kolin, in Bohemia, where he received his talmudic education, and was considered a child prodigy. After his marriage he settled in Boskovice and his material needs were provided by his wife, who managed a wool business, leaving him free for study. Although he never held an official rabbinic appointment, for over 60 years he conducted a yeshivah which attracted many pupils. Kolin achieved fame through his comprehensive work, *Maḥazit ha-Shekel*, a commentary on the Shulḥan Arukh, *Oraḥ Ḥayyim* and *Yoreh De'ah*. The section on *Oraḥ Ḥayyim* (Vienna, 1807–08) is in fact a supercommentary on the *Magen Avraham* of A.A. *Gombiner. Its main purpose is to give the actual wording of the sources to which Gombiner alludes, or which he abbreviates, and to simplify his rather difficult language. Only portions of the commentary to the *Yoreh De'ah*, part 1, and on the laws of *niddah* were published (1858-60). The *Maḥazit ha-Shekel* achieved wide popularity among scholars who depended on it in arriving at halakhic decisions. It was published separately a number of times, and in later editions together with the text of the Shulḥan Arukh. Kolin's sermons (1906) and his commentaries to *Bava Batra* and *Avodah Zarah* (1958) were also published under the same title.

BIBLIOGRAPHY: I. Reich, *Die Geschichte der Chewra Kadischa zu Boskovice* (1931), 41–48; A. Stern, *Melitsey Esh al Ḥodshei Adar* (1938), 71a–72a; H. Gold (ed.), *Die Juden und Judengemeinden Maehrens in Vergangenheit und Gegenwart* (1929), index; S. Knoebil, *Toledot Gedolei Hora'ah* (1970^2), 164f.; C. Tchernowitz, *Toledot ha-Posekim*, 3 (1947), 201–6.

KOLISCH, IGNAZ VON (1837–1889), Austrian chess player. Von Kolisch drew a match with Louis Paulsen (1861). He won several tournaments, notably at Cambridge (1860) and Paris (1867) ahead of Wilhelm *Steinitz. Kolisch became a successful banker with the aid of the Vienna Rothschilds and was later made a baron. He then became patron of many players and organizers of tournaments and owned the *Wiener Allgemeine Zeitung* in Vienna (until 1888).

ADD. BIBLIGRAPHY: *Oesterreichisches Biographisches Lexikon*, vol. 4, 82.

KOLISCH, RUDOLF (1896–1978), violinist. Born in Klamm, Austria, Kolisch studied at Vienna with Otakar Ševčik (violin) and Arnold *Schoenberg (composition), and in 1922 founded the Kolisch String Quartet, which existed until 1939 and was the first such group to perform from memory. He promoted the works of modern composers, particularly those of Schoenberg and his circle. Kolisch emigrated to the United States in 1940 and in 1942 became the leader of the Pro Arte Quartet. He was one of the few left-handed concert violinists. His sister Gertrud was Schoenberg's second wife.

KOLISCHER, HEINRICH (1853–1932), politician in Galicia and a leading spokesman of its assimilationist and anti-Zionist groups. Born in Lemberg, Kolischer studied medicine at Goettingen and agriculture at the University of Vienna. He also acquired a wide knowledge of economics. From 1907 to 1918 Kolischer was a member of the Austrian parliament, and one of the most prominent members of its "Polish Club" as an economic expert. His paper mill was the largest of its kind in Galicia. In his support of Polish national orientation, Kolischer firmly opposed the establishment of an independent Jewish "curia" (electoral body) in Bukovina. His lack of contact with the Jewish masses made it difficult for Kolischer to compete with the Zionist candidates. On the dissolution of the Hapsburg Empire after World War I, Kolischer automatically became a member of the Polish Sejm of 1918–22. During this period he joined the conservative faction, known as the "Club for Drafting the Constitution," *Klub Pracy Konstytucyjnej*, in which he was prominent as an expert on financial matters. His advocacy of assimilation created a rift between him and the Jewish national delegates who were fighting to ensure the vital interests of Polish Jewry in its struggle for survival. After a time he returned to Vienna.

BIBLIOGRAPHY: J.L. Tenenbaum, *Galitsye mayn Alte Heym* (1952), index; N.M. Gelber, *Toledot Yehudei Brody* (1955), 303, 318, 319; idem, *Toledot ha-Tenu'ah ha-Ẓiyyonit be-Galizyah*, 2 vols. (1958), index. **ADD. BIBLIOGRAPHY:** J. Majchrowski et al. (eds.), *Kto byl kim w drugiej Rzeczypospolitej* (1994), 321.

[Joseph Kaplan]

KOLLEK, TEDDY (**Theodore**, 1911–2007), Israeli public figure, mayor of Jerusalem 1965–93. Kollek was born in Vienna, and as a youth was a member of the Blau-Weiss Zionist youth movement. In 1931–34 he was active in the Ḥalutz movement in Czechoslovakia, Germany, and Great Britain. He settled in Palestine in 1934, and was one of the founders of kibbutz Ein-Gev in 1936. In 1938–39 he was involved in Europe in Zionist educational activities, and in 1939 met with Adolf *Eichmann to negotiate the release of 3,000 Jewish youths from concentration camps and arrange their transfer to Great Britain for agricultural training. From 1940 to 1947 he served in the Jewish Agency Political Department and was stationed in its Istanbul office as a contact with the Jewish underground in Europe, trying to rescue Jews, acting as a liaison with British and U.S. intelligence in Cairo. After World War II he was involved in the organization of *"illegal" immigration to Palestine. In 1947–48 he represented the *Haganah in the United States, and was inter alia involved in illicit purchases of military equipment. In 1947–48 Kollek was Israel's minister plenipotentiary in Washington. Upon his return to Israel he was appointed director general of the Prime Minister's Office, a job that he held until 1964. In that period he was one of Prime Minister David Ben-Gurion's confidants. In this capacity he initiated the Government Tourist Corporation, of which he was chairman in 1956–65, and various cultural activities, such as the Israel Festival. He assisted in raising the funds for the *Israel Museum in Jerusalem, and served as the museum's chairman from 1964 until being elected mayor of Jerusalem the following year. Kollek left Mapai, of which he had been a member since arriving in the country, together with Ben-Gurion, and was one of the founding members of *Rafi. He was elected mayor with the support of Rafi. After the 1967 Six-Day War Kollek, now representing the *Israel Labor Party, was responsible for the actual reunification of Jerusalem, and he came to personify the united Jerusalem. During his 28 years as mayor he managed to raise a great deal of money to develop the city, and he established the Jerusalem Fund for this purpose. However, despite his liberal policy toward the Arabs of East Jerusalem, many of whom supported him in the early years after the Six-Day War, he was not successful in bringing about a real integration and the services in the Arab part of the city never reached the standard of those in the Jewish part.

Even though Kollek had considered not to run in the municipal elections in 1993, he was finally convinced to run and was defeated by the Likud candidate Ehud *Olmert, despite the Labor victory in the general elections the previous year. He nevertheless continued to raise funds for the city. In 1988 he was awarded the Israel Prize for exemplary lifelong service to society and the State.

His writings focus on Jerusalem: *Yerushalayim Aḥat: Sippur Ḥayyim* (1979) and with Dov Goldstein, *Yerushalayim Shel Teddy* (1994).

Biographies on him have been published: R. Kolodany-Baki, *Zehu Teddy: Biografyah mi-Pi Ḥaverim* (1995) and B. Amikam (ed.), *Kenes Hitpatteḥut Yerushalayim bi-Tekufat Teddy Kollek 1965–1993* (2001).

[Susan Hattis Rolef (2nd ed.)]

KOLLER, CARL (1857–1944), ophthalmologist. Koller, who was born in Bohemia, settled in New York in 1888 as a practicing oculist. He was ophthalmic surgeon in Mount Sinai and other New York hospitals. His most significant contribution to medicine was his introduction of cocaine as a local anesthetic in the treatment and surgery of eye afflictions. This method was later applied to various other branches of medicine and surgery. He also invented the system of lighting used in the electric ophthalmoscope. He wrote various treatises on biology and ophthalmology, especially on astigmatism and on the origin of the mesoderma.

BIBLIOGRAPHY: S.R. Kagan, *Jewish Medicine* (1952), 521.

[Suessmann Muntner]

°KOLLONITSCH, LEOPOLD (1631–1707), Austrian bishop, moving spirit behind the expulsion of the *Vienna community in 1670. Until 1659 he was with the Knights of Malta. When bishop of Wiener Neustadt, he gained a strong influence over *Leopold I, whom he incited to expel the Jews from Vienna. As a member of the commission of inquiry into the dubious financial activities of Meyer Hirschel, he was instrumental in turning this into a commission preparing the expulsion of the Viennese community. The dedication of the church installed in the Viennese synagogue after the expulsion was delayed because of a conflict on precedence between Kollonitsch and the bishop of Vienna. In his sermon on that occasion he compared the emperor with Abraham, who expelled Hagar and Ishmael, i.e., the synagogue and her children. Kollonitsch became head of the imperial treasury in 1692, and in that capacity he had frequent contact with Samuel *Oppenheimer, Leopold's agent. After first attempting, without success, to oust Oppenheimer, he played a leading role in the agent's imprisonment; among the charges against Oppenheimer was that he was trying to take Kollonitsch's place as president of the court chamber. Kollonitsch is still venerated in Austria today (his statue stands in front of the town hall in Vienna) for his activities during the Turkish siege of Vienna (1683).

BIBLIOGRAPHY: D. Kaufmann, *Die letzte Vertreibung der Juden aus Wien* (1889), 114, 142, 152, 155; H. Tietze, *Die Juden aus Wien* (1935), index; M. Grunwald, *Samuel Oppenheimer* (1913), index; C. Wurzbach, *Biographisches Lexikon*, 12 (1861), 361–2; M. Grunwald, *Vienna* (1936), index.

[Meir Lamed]

KOLMAN, ARNOŠT (Ernest; 1892–1979), Czech philosopher and mathematician. Born in Prague, he studied mathematics and electrical engineering, and in 1913 began working as computing assistant at the observatory in Prague. In World War I, he fought in the Austrian Army, was taken prisoner by the Russians, was arrested for socialist propaganda and liberated after the October Revolution. In 1918 he joined the Communist Party. From 1918 to 1920 he fought on many fronts in the Red Army. Among his party activities was illegal work in Germany (1921–22, 1926), work at the Marx-Engels Institute and the Communist Academy in Moscow, and editorial work on the periodical *Pod znamenem marksizma* (1929–43). From 1939 to 1945 he was in the department for dialectical materialism at the Philosophical Institute of the Academy of Sciences of the U.S.S.R. During World War II he was in the political department of the General Staff of the Soviet armies. From 1945 to 1948 he taught at the University of Prague. Imprisoned from 1948 to 1952, he returned fully rehabilitated. He was then professor of mathematics at the Institute for the History of Science and Technology in Moscow (1952–59). Back in Prague, he was director of the Institute of Philosophy of the Czechoslovakian Academy of Sciences (1959–62).

Among his many writings are *N.I. Lobachevski* (Rus., 1958^2), *Bernard Bolzano* (Rus., 1955; Ger., 1963); *Istoriya matematiki v drevnosti* (1961); and *Zanimatelnaya logika* (with O. Zich, 1966).

[Dirk Jan Struik]

KOLMAR, GERTRUD (pseudonym of **Gertrud Chodziesner**; 1894–1943), German poet. The daughter of an assimilated lawyer and the cousin of Walter Benjamin, Kolmar was for some years a translator and interpreter attached to the German Foreign Office and later taught handicapped children. Her first book of verse, *Gedichte* (1917), attracted little attention. However, in 1930 some of her poems were published in the *Insel-Almanach*. A gentle, self-effacing writer, Gertrud Kolmar devoted many of her poems (e.g., "Die Juedin," "Wir Juden," and "Judith") to Jewish themes; in others, she delved into history, art, and animal lore. Her poetry is serious, conservative, and disciplined, yet visionary, rich in imagery, and linguistically beautiful. In 1930/31 she wrote the novel *Eine jüdische Mutter*, which was not published until 1965, then again in 1999; she also wrote some plays in the 1930s. After Hitler's rise to power, Kolmar chose to remain in Germany with her aged father. Her *Preussische Wappen* (1934, written in 1927/28), a poetic attempt to distill the history and genius of Germany from the Prussian coats of arms, had especial poignancy in its time. Her last volume to appear was *Die Frau und die Tiere*, which was produced in 1938 by the Jewish publishing house Erwin Loewe and destroyed soon afterward. After the outbreak of World War II, she was conscripted for forced labor in a cardboard factory, while she continued writing poetry (the poems *Welten*, written in 1937, published in 1947) and the novel *Susanna* (written in 1939/40 and published in 1959). In her last years she studied Hebrew and even wrote some Hebrew verse. After her father's death in Theresienstadt in February 1943, she was sent to an East European extermination camp (probably Auschwitz), where she is believed to have perished. Her work was discovered and published after the war first through the efforts of Elisabeth Langgaesser and Hermann Kasack. Her complete poetry was published in 2003 (*Das lyrische Werk*), her plays in 2005 (*Dramen*) by Regina Nörtemann.

BIBLIOGRAPHY: H. Kasack, *Mosaik-Steine: Beitraege zu Literatur und Kunst…* (1956); J. Picard, in: *Jewish Frontier* (March 1960), 12–15; B. Eichmann-Leutenegger, *Gertrud Kolmar*, (1993); B.R. Erdle, *Antlitz – Mord – Gesetz* (1994); J. Woltmann, *Gertrud Kolmar* (1995); K. Lindemann, *Widerstehen im Wort* (1996); K. Zarnegin, *Tierische Träume* (1998).

[Harry Zohn / Andreas Kilcher (2nd ed.)]

KOL MEVASSER ("The Voice which Brings Tidings"; cf. Isa. 52:7), pioneering Yiddish periodical founded in Odessa in 1862 by Alexander *Zederbaum as a supplement of the Hebrew weekly *Ha-Meliz*, and issued from 1869 to 1872 as a separate publication. It was first edited by Zederbaum and his son-in-law Aaron Isaac Goldenblum (1827–1912), who was later joined by Moses Leib *Lilienblum and M. *Beilinson. While Ḥasidim opposed the journal on the grounds that it furthered unbelief and weakened Orthodoxy, *maskilim* attacked it on the grounds that it furthered Jewish separatism in Russia and hindered the Russification of Jews. Throughout the paper's life, Zederbaum's objective was to fight ignorance, superstition, and the mismanagement of Jewish public institutions, and to strengthen Jewishness against the fanatical extremists of both Ḥasidism and Haskalah. This first modern Yiddish journal helped to raise the prestige of the folk vernacular then despised as "jargon." It began the process of standardizing Yiddish spelling, and enriched Yiddish vocabulary with many neologisms. Reporting on Jewish life in communities throughout the world, but especially in Eastern Europe, it also surveyed the contemporary scene from the Jewish viewpoint, with articles on science, education, history, and literature. By bringing to public attention earlier Yiddish writers, such as Solomon *Ettinger, Israel *Axenfeld, and Abraham *Gottlober, and introducing new writers, such as the lexicographer S.M. Lifshitz, I.J. *Linetzky, Abraham *Goldfaden, and Sholem Yankev *Abramovitsh, *Kol Mevasser* may be said to have paved the way for the Yiddish classical renaissance, and the advent of modern Yiddish journalism.

BIBLIOGRAPHY: Malachi, in: JBA, 20 (1962), 84–94; M. Mandelman, *Der Onzoger fun der Yidish-Veltlikher Kultur* (1963).

[Sol Liptzin / Jack S. Berger (2nd ed.)]

KOL NIDREI (Aram. כָּל נִדְרֵי; "All Vows"), a declaration of annulment of *vows with which the evening service of the *Day of Atonement commences. The worshipers proclaim that all personal vows, oaths, etc., that they made unwittingly, rashly, or unknowingly (and that, consequently, cannot be fulfilled) during the year should be considered null and void. The recitation must begin while it is still daylight and must be prolonged until sunset. It is the custom to repeat *Kol Nidrei* three times in order to accommodate latecomers. In *Kol Nidrei* only vows affecting the self, i.e., vows made between man and God (*Tosafot*, R. Nissim and R. Asher b. Jehiel to Ned. 23b; Sh. Ar., YD 211:4) are comprehended. Not formally a prayer, *Kol Nidrei* nevertheless became the most beloved ritual of the Day of Atonement. It alleviated anxiety which was especially intense in the *Rosh Ha-Shanah season because of possible violation of the sanctity of pledges (cf. Deut. 23:22–24). Sensitive to inherent juridical and ethical difficulties, the rabbis set definite conditions and restrictions on the annulment procedure. Vows could only be abrogated by a *bet din* or by an expert scholar, after careful investigation of their nature and bearing (Bek. 36b; Tur, YD 228:1). The Mishnah (Naz. 5:3; Ned. 3:1; cf. Ned. 23b) permits the nullification of the vows of an individual; its extension to an entire community, however, taxed the ingenuity of later authorities and aroused bitter controversy.

The origins of *Kol Nidrei* are unknown; none of the many theories is conclusive. The first reference to *Kol Nidrei* as a collective declaration is found in the responsa of the Babylonian *geonim* (beginning in the eighth century). It is stated that *Kol Nidrei* was familiar to them from "other lands"; but the *geonim* (especially of Sura) sharply condemned it for many generations. The "other lands" are not identified. An obvious possibility is Palestine, yet none of the extant sources of the old

Palestinian liturgy has *Kol Nidrei*. The scholars S. Poznański, S. Krauss, and J. Mann nevertheless contended that congregational recitation of *Kol Nidrei* originated in Palestine, as a reaction to *Karaite attacks on the *Rabbanite practice. S. Baron suggested that the *geonim* opposed *Kol Nidrei* because of possible innovations by mystical circles for whom it assuaged a magic fear of vows that might have been unwittingly broken. C.H. Gordon, citing parallel Aramaic formulas found inscribed on incantation bowls from the time of talmudic Babylonia, proposed that the original function of *Kol Nidrei* had been "the annulment of curses or oaths... that touch off evil forces in the community."

The *geonim* of Pumbedita were more lenient than those of Sura, probably in response to popular demand. About the time of Hai Gaon (c. 1000 C.E.), general acceptance had been gained for a *Kol Nidrei* formula; it invoked divine "pardon, forgiveness, and atonement" for the sin of failing to keep a solemn vow (or, possibly, for having vowed at all). The period envisioned was "from the previous Day of Atonement until this Day of Atonement." The tosafists of 12th-century France and Germany, notably R. Meir b. Samuel and his son Jacob (known as Rabbenu Tam), did not accept the geonic version but reworded *Kol Nidrei* as an annulment of vows which may possibly be made "from this Day of Atonement until the next Day of Atonement." Rabbenu Tam's (Aramaic) version has remained standard for *Ashkenazim. The geonic (Hebrew) version was adopted by the Romanian and Italian rites. Western *Sephardim recite only the geonic text referring to vows of the past year, while Oriental Sephardim and Yemenites add Rabbenu Tam's version.

Antisemites have frequently taken *Kol Nidrei* as evidence that the oath of a Jew is worthless. In the Disputation in Paris in 1240 it was attacked by Nicholas Donin and defended by R. Jehiel b. Joseph. Suspicion about the effects of *Kol Nidrei* on testimony given by Jews influenced the wording of the *more judaico*. It appeared too in the attacks of antisemitic writers such as *Eisenmenger, *Buxtorf, and *Wagenseil. To counteract these accusations, Jewish apologists have cited the severe limitations that the *halakhah* has imposed on *Kol Nidrei*. In 1860 a Hebrew introduction to *Kol Nidrei* was included in prayer books in Russia on the recommendation of a rabbinic commission. It explained that *Kol Nidrei* was not meant to apply to oaths taken before courts of law. In Germany in 1844, a synod of the Reform movement recommended that *Kol Nidrei* be expunged from the liturgy; later Reformers, however, offered substitute versions. The 1961 edition of the Reform Union Prayer Book (U.S.) restored the full Aramaic text. *Kol Nidrei*'s persistent popularity is partly attributed to emotional factors, especially its association with Jewish martyrdom. In 1917, Joseph S. Bloch propounded a dramatic, though unsubstantiated, theory that *Kol Nidrei* arose as a reaction to forced Jewish conversions to Christianity by the Visigoths in seventh-century Spain, to persecutions in the Byzantine Empire (700–850), and in Spain to persecutions by the Inquisition (1391–1492).

[Herman Kieval]

Musical Rendition

The standard Ashkenazi melody for *Kol Nidrei* is deservedly famous as a superior example of the musical tradition of the Diaspora, and, with much justification, of "Jewish music" as such. It is not a melody in the conventional sense, but an artistic concatenation of motives, stylistically related to the general melodic conventions of the High Holy Days. The motives alternate between solemn syllabic "proclamations" as in the opening, intensely devotional wave-like phrases, and virtuoso vocal runs. It may even be asked whether the musical rendition of *Kol Nidrei* was shaped by the solemnity of the liturgical and ideological status of the prayer, or whether the latter did not come about in a great measure, at least during the last two centuries, through the extraordinary effect of the melody.

Eastern Ashkenazi version of Kol Nidrei, *with its introduction,* Al da'at ha-Makom. *From Idelsohn,* Melodien 8, *1932.*

The source of the melody is still a subject of research, and the frequent attempts to relate it to Sephardi traditions (because of the presumed connections of the text with the Spanish *Marranos) are highly hypothetical. In the Sephardi traditions *Kol Nidrei* is rendered by the entire congregation, which alternates with the *ḥazzan*, and the rendition is, therefore, more syllabic in character; there seems to be no standard melody common to the entire Sephardi Diaspora. In the *Carpentras (Provençal rite) the *Kol Nidrei* is said in a whisper and therefore has no melody.

The Ashkenazi version of *Kol Nidrei* was arranged in 1880 by the non-Jewish composer Max Bruch for cello and orchestra, on commission from the Jewish community of Liverpool, and it became his most popular work. Arnold *Schoenberg's *Kol Nidrei* for speaker, chorus, and orchestra, opus 39 (1938) is based on a text by Jacob Sonderling, and some of the traditional motives are reworked there in Schoenberg's twelve-tone technique. The text itself, written in close collaboration with the composer, is a personal philosophic reinterpretation of the prayer.

[Bathja Bayer]

BIBLIOGRAPHY: Davidson, Oẓar, 2 (1929), 480; idem, in: AJYB, 25 (1923/24), 192–4 (incl. bibl.); Baron, Social, 7 (19582), 78–79, 252; H. Leshem, *Shabbat u-Mo'adei Yisrael*, 1 (1965), 161–6; C.H. Gordon, in: *Biblical Motifs* (1966), 6–7; J.J. Petuchowski, *Prayerbook Reform in Europe* (1968), 334–47; H. Kieval, in: *Commentary* 46 (Oct. 1968), 53–8.

KOLNIK, ARTHUR (1890–1972), French painter and printmaker. Kolnik was a native of Stanislavov, Galicia, and studied at the School of Fine Arts in Cracow. He fought as an officer in the Austro-Hungarian Army in World War I, and was wounded. After the war, he went to Czernowitz (then Romania), where he took part in the intellectual life of the city, and became a close friend of the Yiddish poet, Itzik *Manger. In 1921, with Reuven *Rubin, he went to the United States where they had a joint exhibition under the sponsorship of Prince Bibesco, the Romanian minister. Kolnik returned to Czernowitz, where he made woodcuts. Among the books he illustrated was one of fables by Eliezer Steinbarg. In 1931 he settled in Paris. As a printmaker and painter, Kolnik depicted the ghetto dwellers of Eastern Europe. He presented them with sympathy and understanding, the human forms being very sharply outlined and the whole space freely divided into patterns of geometric planes.

[Alfred Werner]

KOLO (Pol. **Koło**; Yid. **Koil**), town in Poznan district, central Poland, near the River Varta; passed to Prussia in 1793, and restored to Poland in 1919. Jews were living there in the 15th century, and in 1564 they received the right of residence from King Sigismund II Augustus. In 1611 there were 24 Jewish-owned houses in Kolo. A synagogue was built in 1763–65. During the 19th century, Jews played an important role in the economic development of the town. They owned factories for colored cloths, bricks, porcelain ware, agricultural machinery, and oil, as well as various workshops. In 1897, 52% of the Jews of the town were engaged in commerce. The community numbered 1,184 (37.2% of the total population) in 1827; 4,013 (42.8%) in 1897; 5,154 (45%) in 1921; approximately 6,000 (44%) in 1931; and 5,000 (41.6%) in 1939. Between the two world wars, the Jews continued active in economic life, and, in 1938 37.7% of the workshops in the town were Jewish-owned. Antisemitism in the economic sphere during the 1930s forced them out of several occupations. There were eight Jews among the 24 members elected to the municipal council in 1924 and ten in 1929. The Jewish community administration elected in 1931 consisted of three members for the General Zionists, five for Poalei Zion-Right, four for Poalei Zion-Left, and one for Agudat Israel. Its last chairman was Joseph Schwarz, and the last rabbi of Kolo was Hayyim David Zilber Margalioth (d. 1941), who officiated there for about 50 years.

[Shimshon Leib Kirshenboim]

Holocaust Period

The town was occupied by the Germans on Sept. 15, 1939 (the second day of Rosh Ha-Shanah). On the following day a German raid was made on Jewish homes, and all the men were forced to assemble in the market place. The men were sent to do repair work on the Warta River bridges which had been blown up by the Polish army when hostilities began. The Germans set fire to the synagogue, accused the Jews of arson, and extorted a large sum of money from them. The Jewish intelligentsia was arrested and anyone caught hiding executed. Two hostages were taken every day. In December 1939, 1,139 Jews were forced out of their homes and kept starving and freezing for weeks in barracks. They were eventually deported to the *Lublin district. Their homes were then turned over to Volksdeutsche brought there from the Baltic regions. Almost a year later 150 Jewish families were expelled from Kolo, and a ghetto was established for the remainder of the Jewish population. Contacts and trade with the non-Jewish side continued, and helped to alleviate the ghetto conditions. Its inhabitants were decimated by a typhoid epidemic and the conscription of able-bodied persons for slave labor. In June 1941 all the Jewish males were deported to the labor camp near *Poznan. In August about 100 girls were sent to a labor camp in Breslau. The final liquidation of the Kolo ghetto took place early in December 1941 when the remaining 2,300 Jews were assembled in front of the Judenrat building, placed on trucks, and sent to the death camp at *Chelmno.

[Danuta Dombrowska]

BIBLIOGRAPHY: *Sefer Kolo* (1958; Heb. and Yid.); Trunk in: *Bleter far Geshikhte* 2:1–4 (1949), 64–166 (passim); W. Bednarz, *Obóz straceń Chełmna nad Nerem* (1946); Dabrowska in: BZIH, no. 13–14 (1955).

KOLODEJE NAD LUZICI (Czech **Koloděje nad Lužicí**; Ger. **Kaladei**; **Kalladay**), village in S. Bohemia, Czech Republic. Its Jewish community, known as ק״ק׳, was founded by Jews expelled from nearby Tyn nad Vltavou (Moldautein) in 1681 because it was alleged that they had spread the plague. The local lord built a synagogue (dedicated in 1697) and ten dwelling houses for them. The members of the community were mainly peddlers, some of them trading in Upper Austria, where they remained for months. The seat of the district rabbi for the district of Ceske Budejovice and Tabor was in Kolodeje. R. Samuel *Kauder officiated there (1817–34) before becoming chief rabbi of Prague. In 1721 the community numbered 154 persons; in 1869 there were 258 tax-paying members and 40 children attending the Jewish elementary school. From 153 in 1886, it shrank to 35 in 1904 and eight in 1932, coming to an end soon after. The smaller community in nearby Nezdášov (104 members in 1869) had a similar origin and history; its synagogue collapsed in the late 1920s.

BIBLIOGRAPHY: Fried, in: *Juedisches Archiv*, 2 (1929), no. 3–4, 39–43; no. 5–7, 50–51; no. 8–9, 61–64; Sakař, in: H. Gold (ed.), *Die Juden und Judengemeinden Boehmens* (1934), 240–5.

[Meir Lamed]

KOLODIN, IRVING (1908–1988), U.S. music critic. Born in New York City, Kolodin was raised in Newark, New Jersey, where he began to study music at an early age. From 1927 to 1931 he attended the Institute of Musical Art in New York. Beginning his career as assistant music critic to W.J. Henderson at the New York *Sun*, he eventually became the newspaper's chief critic, leaving there in 1950. He was also a critic of recordings and published a number of books of record reviews: *A Guide to Recorded Music* (1941), *Mozart on Records* (1942), *The Saturday Review Home Book of Recorded Music and Sound Reproduction* (1952; revised 1956), and *Orchestral Music* (1955). In 1970 he chose the classical music that was included in the first official White House music library. He taught criticism at the Juilliard School from 1968 to 1986.

Kolodin was well known as a historian of the New York Metropolitan Opera, publishing *The Metropolitan Opera: 1883–1935* (1936); a second edition, *The Story of the Metropolitan Opera, 1883–1950*, appeared in 1953 and was again updated in 1966.

Among his other works are *The Interior Beethoven* (1975), *The Opera Omnibus* (1976), and *In Quest of Music* (1980).

KOLOMYYA (Pol. **Kołomyja**; Ger. **Kolomea**), city on the Prut River in the Ukraine; under Polish rule until 1772, Austrian rule until the end of World War I, and then again under Poland until 1939, and then annexed to the Ukrainian S.S.R. There was a flourishing Jewish community in Kolomyya as early as the 16th century. They paid two-thirds of the city taxes and received various trading rights; they were allowed to take part in the election of the mayor and other city officials. During the *Chmielnicki massacres (1648/49) the community was destroyed and some 300 Jews murdered; however, it soon recovered. After 1772 it shared the fate and status of all Polish communities under Austrian rule (see *Austria-Hungary, *Galicia, *Joseph II). The Jews of Kolomyya engaged in a wide range of economic activities, including the retail trade, the leasing of forests, and the wholesale trade in wood; they benefited from Kolomyya's new ties with Walachia and Moldavia, which became even more profitable when Kolomyya became an important railway junction on the Lvov-Chernovtsy-Jassy line. In the beginning of the 18th century there was some influence of the *Shabbetai Ẓevi movement in the city and its environs; preachers such as Ḥayyim Malakh, Moses Meir from Zholkiev, and Elisha Shor from Rohatyn visited there. Besides the many *ḥadarim*, a Jewish elementary school was established by the government in 1788 (see Naphtali Herz *Homberg). The number of Jews in the town rose from 1,057 in 1765 to 2,033 in 1812; 8,232 (almost 50% of the total population) in 1869; 12,002 in 1880; and 16,568 (again almost 50%) in 1900. From the beginning of the movement Ḥasidism gained adherents in the town, becoming predominant in the community and thus ensuring its extreme Orthodox character until the second half of the 19th century. In 1886 a Jewish elementary school was founded by the *Israelitische Allianz zu Wien. During the elections to the town council in 1878, Jews obtained the majority of seats and a Jew, Dr. Maximilian Trachtenberg, was elected mayor. In 1873 a Jew, Dr. Oscar Henigsman, was elected to represent Kolomyya in the Austrian parliament. Hillel *Lichtenstein, rabbi from 1863 to 1891, strengthened Orthodoxy in the community. At the end of the 19th century almost all craftsmen were Jews, and Jewish industrialists owned most of the clothing factories and some of the oil refineries; there was a factory for prayer shawls. All transportation by carts was in Jewish hands.

From 1918 Kolomyya suffered economically as a result of the loss of the Moldavian and Walachian markets and the Jews were further hit by the anti-Jewish economic policies of modern Poland. The number of Jews in the town began to decline, from 18,930 in 1919 to 14,544 (total population 31,708) in 1921, and 14,332 in 1931. In 1921, 499 industrial premises (mostly small ones) belonged to Jews, and they employed 1,362 Jewish workers (90% of all employed), 557 of them in textile and clothing production. In 1930 they suffered from aggressive competition from Polish and Ukrainian cooperatives, which led to economic decline and the need for the community to organize relief for many of the local Jews. The social and cultural life in the Jewish community was marked by the activities of the different parties. Especially active among the Zionist organizations were the Ha-Shomer Ha-Ẓa'ir youth groups, the Hitaḥadut, and the *He-Ḥalutz. The first group of *ḥalutzim* left Kolomyya for Ereẓ Israel in 1920. *Hakhsharah* groups, which prepared their members for life in Ereẓ Israel, operated in the town. *Betar organized a group called "the national soldier" which led paramilitary activities. Two Zionist newspapers appeared in Kolomyya: the *Nasz Glos* in Polish and the *Unser Shtime* in Yiddish. In 1930 a coalition of *Agudat Israel and *Mizrachi parties elected the politically active Joseph Lau as rabbi.

[Shimshon Leib Kirshenboim / Shmuel Spector (2nd ed.)]

Holocaust Period

After the Soviet occupation of the town on Sept. 17, 1939, all organized Jewish life ceased. Jewish economic life was affected by the nationalization of factories and wholesale and petty trade. A sizable number of Jewish pupils studied in government schools where Yiddish was the language of instruction. When the Soviet-German war broke out in June 1941, Kolomyya Jews were drafted into the Soviet army. Many young Jews volunteered, as did Jewish doctors and nurses. On July 4 the city was captured by the German-allied Hungarian army. On August 18 the Ukrainians dragged out some 2,000 Jews in the nearby forest to be killed, but the Hungarian governor intervened and prevented their execution. During the following weeks Jewish refugees from Hungary who did not have Hungarian citizenship were sheltered by the Jewish community in Kolomyya. In September 1941 the town came under direct German administration, resulting in mass murder, extortion of large sums of money, and the kidnapping of Jews for slave labor. The head of the *Judenrat, Mordecai Horowitz, committed suicide in November 1942.

The Jewish community of Kolomyya was liquidated in the following *Aktions*: Nov. 15, 1941 – 500 Jews were murdered on the excuse that a Jewish leader who had been active during the Soviet occupation was hiding on their street; Jan. 24, 1942 – attacks were directed against the Jewish intelligentsia; March 24, 1942 – three separate ghettos were established, each surrounded with barbed wire; April 2, 1942 – 1,000 Jews were sent to *Belzec; Sept. 7, 1942 – 8,700 Jews were sent to Belzec; Oct. 3, 1942 – 4,500–5,000 Jews were sent to Belzec. All the remaining Jews, some 1,500 in number, were concentrated in one ghetto and were subsequently taken to Szeparowce forest nearby and executed (February 1943). When the Soviet army liberated Kolomyya in early August 1944, only a handful of Jews remained alive. They were joined by another small group of Jews who returned from the Soviet Union. They stayed in the town for a short period to mark out and enclose the sites of the Jewish mass graves, and soon left for Poland and for overseas. Kolomyya societies exist in Israel and New York. A memorial book, *Pinkas Kolomei*, was published in 1957. The Jewish population in Kolomyya in 1957 was estimated at about 200 families and at about 350 persons (70 families) in 1969.

[Aharon Weiss]

BIBLIOGRAPHY: *Pinkas Kolomei* (1957), incl. bibl.

KOLTANOWSKI, GEORGE (1903–2000), U.S. chess master. Born in Antwerp, Belgium, Koltanowski won the Belgian championship six times and prizes in international tournaments. Endowed with a magnificent memory, he concentrated on simultaneous blindfold play, sharing supremacy with Miguel *Najdorf. In 1937 in Edinburgh he set the world record for blindfold chess, where the player commits the game to memory and does not look at the board or touch the pieces while opponents play in the normal way. Koltanowski played 34 opponents simultaneously while blindfolded without losing a game, making headlines around the world. His record still stands in the *Guinness Book of Records*.

When World War II broke out, he was in Guatemala on a chess tour of South America, so he remained there. In 1940, the United States consul in Cuba saw him giving a chess exhibition in Havana and granted him a U.S. visa. In 1947 Koltanowski moved to San Francisco, where in 1948 he became the chess columnist for the *San Francisco Chronicle*. It carried his syndicated chess column every day for the next 52 years. Publishing an estimated total of 19,000 columns, Koltanowski wrote the only daily newspaper chess column in the world and the longest-running daily chess column in history.

In 1950, in San Francisco, he played 50 games in an event lasting nine hours, winning 43, drawing five, and losing two. He turned most of his attention to touring, teaching chess, writing books and articles, and directing tournaments. Although he played in at least 25 international tournaments, Koltanowski became better known for touring and giving simultaneous exhibitions and blindfold displays. In 1960 in San Francisco he set another world record when he played 56 opponents consecutively while blindfolded and did not lose a single game. He also gave hundreds of charitable performances worldwide, particularly for schoolchildren. In the 1960s, he hosted *Koltanowski on Chess*, a series of half-hour broadcasts about chess, aired nationally on public television. It was the first such program of its kind. In the 1970s he seized upon the chess mania inspired by Bobby *Fischer and established chess clubs in countless schools, community centers, and at San Quentin Prison.

He served as president of the United States Chess Federation 1975–78 and was awarded the title of International Master in 1950 on the basis of his prewar results; in 1960 he was awarded the title of International Arbiter; and in 1988 he was given an honorary Grand Master title by the FIDE (World Chess Federation). He was one of the three original inductees into the U.S. Chess Hall of Fame (1986).

Koltanowski spoke eight languages. The books he wrote in English include *Practical Chess* (1947), *Adventures of a Chess Master* (1955), *TV Chess* (1968), *With the Chess Masters* (1972), *Checkmate* (with M. Finkelstein, 1978), and *Chessnicdotes* (1978). He also wrote books in Flemish, French, and Spanish.

[Ruth Beloff (2nd ed.)]

KOLTHOFF, IZAAK MAURITS (1894–1993), chemist. Kolthoff was born in Almelo in the Netherlands, graduated in pharmacy in 1915, and obtained his Ph.D. in chemistry at the University of Utrecht. In 1927 he started a one-year appointment as professor and head of the Analytical Division of the School of Chemistry of the University of Minnesota, where he remained for the rest of his career. Kolthoff's main achievement was to apply the principles of physical chemistry and biochemistry to analytical chemistry, thereby transforming it from a largely pragmatic and descriptive branch of science into an intellectually rigorous discipline. His insights led him to explore a diverse range of basic and applied problems. One important practical application in World War II concerned the production of synthetic rubber. His continuous output of 944 truly original papers as well as monographs between 1915 and 1993 was prodigious, and his co-edited *Treatise on Analytical Chemistry* is a majestic testimony to his preeminence in this field. His many honors included election to the U.S. Academy of Sciences in 1958. He was greatly concerned with social issues and highly influential in relocating victims of Nazi persecution in the U.S. in the 1930s.

[Michael Denman (2nd ed.)]

KOL'TSOV, MIKHAIL (pseudonym of **Mikhail Yefimovich Fridland**; 1898–1940), Soviet publicist and social activist. Kol'tsov was born in Kiev and in 1915 he entered the Petrograd Psychoneurological Institute. He took part in the February and October Revolutions in Petrograd (1917) and in the Civil War, the subject of a series of sketches in his books *Petlyurovshcina* ("The Petlyura Terror," 1922), *Sotvrorenie mia* ("Creation of the World," 1928), and others. In 1920 he began working in Moscow in the press department of the People's Commissariat of Foreign Affairs. From 1922 he worked for *Pravda*, publishing almost daily a topical feuilleton on domestic and foreign policy. His keen observation, inexhaustible humor, and biting sarcasm, as well as the ability to manipulate facts, together with a keen political sensitivity allowed Kol'tsov to follow every fluctuation of Soviet policy, thanks to which he became one of the most authoritative and popular Soviet journalists of the 1920s and 1930s. Enjoying the confidence and support of the "authorities," he was editor of the journal *Ogoniok*, which he founded in 1923, editor of the satirical journals *Chudak* (1928–30) and *Krokodil* (1934–38), co-editor (with Maxim Gorky) of the journal *Za rubezhom* (1932–38); member of the editorial board of *Pravda*; he headed the cooperative publishing house of the *Ogoniok* society (1926–31), the journal and newspaper association (1931–38), the foreign commission of the Union of Writers (1934–38), and represented the Soviet Union at international congresses of writers (Paris, 1935; Madrid and Valencia, 1937, when he headed the Soviet delegation).

In 1936, when the Spanish Civil War broke out, Kol'tsov became not only *Pravda* correspondent there (his articles were included in his book *Ispanskiy dnevnik* ("Spanish Diary," 1938)), but also political adviser – with a direct link to Stalin – to the Central Committee of the Communist Party of Spain and the Republican government. In the latter role Kol'tsov is depicted under the name Karkov in Ernest Hemingway's novel *For Whom the Bell Tolls* (1940). In November 1937 he was called back to Moscow and awarded the Order of the Red Banner. In 1938 he was elected a corresponding member of the Academy of Sciences of the U.S.S.R. and deputy of the Supreme Soviet of the Russian Federation (RSFSR), but in December of the same year he was arrested. He was shot to death in Lefortovo prison in Moscow in 1940, and was rehabilitated in 1954.

Jointly with A. Barginym, Kol'tsov wrote the propaganda brochure *Sud'ba evreyskikh mass v Sovetskom soyuze* ("The Fate of the Jewish Masses in the Soviet Union," 1924). From 1927 to 1937 he was a member of the editorial board of the monthly of the OZET society, *Tribuna evreyskoy sovetskoy obshchestvennosti*.

Kol'tsov's brother, BORIS EFIMOVICH EFIMOV (1900–), caricaturist, corresponding member of the Academy of Arts of the U.S.S.R. (1954), People's Artist of the U.S.S.R. (1967). In 1922 he began working for *Pravda* and *Izvestia*, and the magazine *Krokodil*. In 1966 he became editor-in-chief of the Agitplakat organization. He was awarded the Stalin Prize (1950, 1951) and the State Prize (1972). He created cartoons on international themes (often with considerable satirical commentary and explanatory captions). In depicting Jewish political figures out of favor with the Soviet rulers or in cartoons critical of Israel and Zionism, he grotesquely exaggerated so-called Jewish national features.

[Mark Kipnis / *The Shorter Jewish Encyclopaedia in Russian*]

KOMARNO (Slovak **Komárno**; Hung. **Komárom**; Ger. **Komorn**), fortress town in S. Slovakia. Until 1992 Czechoslovak Republic, since 1993 Slovak Republic. The Trianon peace treaty (1920) divided Komárno between Czechoslovakia and Hungary. The Jewish community of Komárno was considered one of the oldest in the Danube region, as traditionally there were Jews in the town at the Magyar conquest (end of the ninth century). In 1440 and 1583 Jews worked as Ottoman agents; in 1600 they were moneylenders. In 1788 there was a case of blood libel. In 1791 there were 250 Jews, who were permitted to form a congregation. In 1803 the first synagogue was built. In 1851 Jewish entrepreneurship was liberalized, thanks to a royal order permitting Jews to join guilds.

During the Hungarian revolution of 1848/49, many Jews joined the Magyar army. A subsequent cholera epidemic claimed many lives. In 1848, a fire destroyed the Jewish communal buildings, including the archive. In an effort to rebuild, the community created a cemetery in 1858 and built a synagogue in 1863. In 1890 there were 1,925 Jews; in 1900, there were 2,296. In 1895 the community built an edifice for social activities. There was a matzah bakery, a *ḥevra kaddisha*, a women's club, Bikkur Ḥolim organizations to help the sick, an Ahavat Achim social circle, and a youth club.

The community split following the Jewish Congress of 1868, the majority choosing the *Neolog path. In 1889 an Orthodox congregation was established; it built a synagogue in 1907. Another small synagogue was built in 1896, together with a building for orphans and the needy. This synagogue served the congregation into the 21st century. During World War I, many enlisted in the army. The riots and looting that characterized the end of the war in Slovakia did not take place in Komárno; however, the city was a battleground for the Hungarian Commune of 1919. Following the Trianon treaty, the southern part of the Danube coast became Hungarian, and in it some 25 Jewish families. (During the Hungarian conquest of 1938–1945, Komárno and its congregation were united.) The Czechoslovak period was quiet. Several Zionist movements were active in the city, including Hashomer (later Ha-Shomer ha-Ẓa'ir), Maccabee ha-Ẓa'ir, a Zionist branch, and Young Agudat Israel. In 1930 the community built a house for social institutions. The Orthodox congregation had a small yeshivah.

In November 1938 southern Slovakia came under Hungarian rule, including Komárno. The anti-Jewish legislation, already in existence in Hungary, was applied to the conquered territory as well. In Komárno, Jews were forced to leave certain streets; in January 1942, they were forbidden to work.

On March 19, 1944, German troops entered Hungary. Along with them were local collaborators, the infamous gendarmerie, and a unit of Nyilas (*Arrow Cross Fascist party) from Szabolcs. A part of Komárno was made into a ghetto, where the Jews were forced to live. On June 12–16, the inhabitants of the ghetto, as well as neighboring Jews, were deported. The director of the Komárno city museum, witnessing the desecration of the three synagogues, gathered 12 Torah scrolls and other ritual items and hid them in the museum. After the war, he returned the sacred items to the Jewish congregation. On October 15, 1944, the Nyilas party took Hungary by force. In Komárno the Szabolcs unit was responsible for many outrages. After the war, some were caught and put on trial. On September 26, 1945, some 114 Nyilas victims were buried in a mass grave in the Jewish cemetery. In 1947 there were 314 Jews in Komárno.

The community tried to rebuild its religious life and the public buildings. In March 1948, a memorial to the victims of the Holocaust was erected. In 1949–50, 343 Jews immigrated, most to Israel. Those who were left, and those who moved to Komárno, preserved religious life. The depleted community was forced to sell its land. In 1972 a large part of the cemetery was expropriated to build a highway. In 1990 there were 45 Jews in the city. The tombstones and memorials of defunct neighboring villages and congregations were deposited in the local cemetery.

BIBLIOGRAPHY: MHJ, indices, s.v. *Comoronium*; A. Schnitzer, *Juedische Kulturbilder* (1904), 172–224; *Magyar Zsidó Lexikon* (1929), 498; R. Iltis (ed.), *Die aussaeen unter Traenen…* (1959), 152–6; M. Lányi and B.H. Propperné, *Szlovenszkói zsidó hitközségek története* (1933), 280–1. **ADD. BIBLIOGRAPHY:** E. Bàrkàny-L. Dojč, *Židovské náboženské obce na Slovensku* (1991), 167–71; F. Raab, A komáromi zsidoság krónikája (1989).

[Meir Lamed / Yeshayahu Jelinek (2nd ed.)]

KOMARNO, town in Lvov district, Ukraine. When the town was granted municipal status in 1555, Jews settled there. Construction of the synagogue was begun in 1620, and the cemetery was established in 1644. During the 1648 Cossack uprising of *Chmielnicki, the Jews of Komarno and the townspeople together successfully defended the town against them. The rabbi in 1666 was Isaiah Segal, the son of the author of *Turei Zahav*. In 1686, Eliakim b. Jacob Melammed of Komarno published a Hebrew grammar, *Leshon Limmudim*. During the rabbinate of Saul Margalioth (1754–73), the influence of Ḥasidism was felt in the community. In 1765 there were 686 poll-tax paying Jews in the town and 844 in the neighboring villages. Their main sources of livelihood were tailoring, shopkeeping, trade in livestock and wood, the leasing of estates, and brandy distillation. Toward the end of the 18th century, a second synagogue was erected. At the beginning of the 19th century, the "court" of the *ẓaddik* R. Alexander, a disciple of *Jacob Isaac Horowitz ha-Ḥozeh of Lublin, was established in Komarno. The dynasty of *ẓaddikim* of the *Safrin family remained in the town until the Holocaust (the last *ẓaddik*, R. Baruch Safrin, perished in the Holocaust). As a result of the development of crafts and the trade in agricultural produce, the Jewish population of Komarno increased in the 19th century; in 1880 it numbered 2,161 (40% of the total population) and in 1910, 2,716 (44%). During World War I the Russian invasion brought sufferings; 17 Jews were murdered, and 50 were taken hostage. After 1918 and for a number of years, the municipal council was headed by a Jew. According to the Polish census of 1921, there were 2,004 Jews (25% of the population) in the town, and 2,387 in 1931. In the interwar years, Zionist organizations were active and Jewish educational and cultural institutions functioned in the town. The U.S. Yiddish writer, Kalman Heisler, was born in Komarno.

[Aharon Weiss]

Holocaust Period

Before the outbreak of World War II there were 2,500 Jews in Komarno. The German army entered the town on Sept. 17, 1939, but, according to the German-Soviet agreement, it withdrew after two weeks when the Red Army entered. With the Soviet regime, all Jewish communal life stopped, and shops and industrial premises were nationalized. The town was again captured by the Germans on June 30, 1941, and a ghetto and a Judenrat were established there. The first *Aktion* took place on Oct. 24, 1941, when hundreds of prominent Jews were killed. During the winter of 1941/1942 about 400 Jews died of hunger. The second *Aktion* took place on Nov. 6, 1942, when about a thousand Jews were deported to the *Belzec death camp. The remaining few hundred were crowded into a few small houses, and in December 1942 deported to Rudki ghetto, and were killed there, together with the Jews of Rudki, on April 9, 1943. After the war, the Jewish community of Komarno was not reconstituted.

BIBLIOGRAPHY: Wroclaw, Zakład im. Ossolińskich, 2494/II (= CAHJP, ḤM 661); Cracow, Wojewódzkie archiwum państwowe, *Zbiory Czartoryskich*, no. 519 (= CAHJP, ḤM 2747); M. Berensohn, *Dyplomataryusz dotyczący Żydów w Polsce* (1910), no. 53; Halpern, Pinkas, index; N.N. Hannover, *Yeven Meẓulah* (1949), 63; B. Wasiutyński, *Ludność żydowska w Polsce w wiekach XIX i XX* (1930), 117; M. Balaban, *Toledot ha-Tenu'ah ha-Frankit*, 1 (1934), 29; I. Schiper, *Dzieje handlu żydowskiego na ziemiach polskich* (1937), index; B. Yashar (Schluehter), *Beit Komarno: Korot ha-Ir ve-Toledoteha me-Hivvasedah ve-ad Ḥurbanah* (1965).

°**KOMÁROMI CSIPKÉS, GYÖRGY** (1628–1678), Calvinist Bible translator, born in Komárom (Komarno), Hungary.

After studying at Utrecht and other places, Komáromi was professor of Hebrew at the reformed academy in Debrecen, Hungary. He published an *Oratio Hebraea* (Utrecht, 1653) and a Hebrew grammar (1654), but his main significance is as reviser of the translation of the Bible into Hungarian. He completed this version in 1675, although it was not published earlier than 1718. His *Catalogus operum...Comoronii* (Claudiopolis (Ger. Klausenburg; Hung. Kolozsvár), 1677), gives a list of his own works.

BIBLIOGRAPHY: J. Illési, in: *Magyar Könyvszemle*, 14 (1889), 138–46; L. Földvári, in: *Protestáns Szemle* (1891), 315–35, 515–31; L. Muzsnai, in: *Károlyi Gáspár Emlékkönyv* (1940), 141–57; L. Szimonidesz, in: *Egyháztörténet* (1945), 65–91.

[Robert Dan]

KOMAROVSKY, MIRRA (1905–1999), U.S. sociologist. Born in Akkerman, Russia, Komarovsky fled to the U.S. with her family in 1921. She was a professor of sociology at Barnard College of Columbia University in New York and specialized in the sociology of the family.

When she majored in economics and sociology at Barnard College as an undergraduate, one of her professors, sociologist William Ogburn, warned her that her goal of teaching sociology was unrealistic, saying: "You are a woman, foreign born, and Jewish. I would recommend some other occupation." Undeterred, she was granted a one-year graduate fellowship, was elected to Phi Beta Kappa, graduated in 1926, and earned an M.A. in 1927 under Ogburn's direction.

In 1935 Komarovsky joined New York's Institute for Social Research. In 1940 she wrote *The Unemployed Man and His Family.* Through her research and theoretical views, she contributed to an understanding of the part played by women in modern society. In her 1946 paper "Cultural Contradictions and Sex Roles," she sees the role conflict in women as a result of cultural contradictions. Feminine roles traceable to traditional views contradict the modern roles that stem from equalitarian expectations. Her paper "Functional Analysis of Sex Roles" (1950) provides a general analysis of the social factors that define women's roles.

In 1948 she was promoted from instructor at Barnard to associate professor; in 1954 she became a full professor. Komarovsky urged that all students be prepared for careers, that good nursery schools be made universally available, and that men accept their fair share of domestic work.

In 1970 Komarovsky retired from Barnard and was named professor emeritus, continuing to teach part time until 1992. In 1973, in recognition of her pioneering challenge to the functionalist approach in sociology, the American Sociological Association elected her president, an honor previously accorded only one other woman: Dorothy S. Thomas. In 1978–79 she served as chair of the newly created Women's Studies program at Barnard. In 1991 she received the Distinguished Career Award from the American Sociological Association.

Other books by Komarovsky include *Women in the Modern World* (1953), *Common Frontiers of the Social Sciences* (1957), *Blue-Collar Marriage* (with J.H. Philips, 1964), *Sociology and Public Policy* (1975), *Dilemmas of Masculinity* (1976), *Common Frontiers of the Social Sciences* (1978), and *Women in College* (1985).

[Louis Miller / Ruth Beloff (2nd ed.)]

KOMLÓS (originally **Kredens**), **ALADÁR** (1892–1980), Hungarian poet, author, and literary scholar. Komlós was born at Alsósztregova. After the 1918–19 revolution he went to Vienna and for a time was on the editorial boards of the radical newspapers *Bécsi Magyar Ujság* and *Jövő*. Between the world wars, Komlós taught at the Jewish high school in Budapest. In World War II he was saved from arrest by the Gestapo by joining the group associated with Rudolf *Kasztner. He was in the Bergen-Belsen concentration camp, from where he was sent to Switzerland, and then returned to Hungary. After the war he became a lecturer at Budapest University, but was removed from his post in 1950. The university later appointed him a professor, and he was also chairman of the Hungarian Literary Society. Komlós' first book of verse was *Voltam poéta én is* ("I too was a poet," 1921), and this was followed by two other volumes, *A néma őrült arca* ("The Face of the Silent Madman," 1931) and *Himnusz a mosolyhoz* ("Hymn to the Smile," 1941). He was mainly distinguished, however, as a literary scholar and critic, particularly as the author of a monumental work on modern poetry, *Az új magyar lira* ("The New Hungarian Lyrics," 1928). His essays, which appeared in important periodicals, are delicate and systematic analyses of contemporary works, and masterpieces of scholarship. Most noteworthy are his books *Irók és elvek* ("Authors and Principles," 1937) and *Táguló irodalom* ("Expanding Literature," 1967). In addition to his work as a scholar, Komlós continued to write prose. He published two novels of an exceptionally high standard: *Római kaland* ("Adventure in Rome," 1933), and *Néro és a VII*[a] ("Nero and the Seventh Grade," 1935). Komlós never concealed his opinions on general and Jewish matters. During the Hungarian "White Terror," his book *Zsidók a válaszuton* ("Jews at the Crossroads," 1920) attacked assimilationist Jewish leaders. In his essays, Komlós analyzes with keen perception the works and attitude to Judaism of Jewish authors such as Sándor *Bródy, M. Földi, and Béla *Zsolt. In his penetrating and logical investigation of the Jewish soul, *A zsidó lélek* (1927) – or the Jewish joke – *A zsidó vicc* (1934) – he claimed that the Jew must equate himself with the world and his surroundings, but foremost with himself. Several of his poems are on Jewish themes. He also edited an anthology of Jewish poetry and the Hungarian Jewish yearbook, *Ararat* (1939–44). He began writing a history of Hungarian-Jewish literature, but only excerpts have been published.

[Baruch Yaron]

KOMOLY (originally **Kohn**), **OTTÓ** (1892–1945), Hungarian Zionist leader. Born in Budapest, he studied engineering. He was wounded in World War I and received military awards. Afterward a member in the reserves, he rose to the rank of captain, an unusual achievement for a Jew at that time. He published two books on Zionist matters: under the name Kohn, O., *A zsidó nép jövője* ("The Future of the Jewish People," 1919) and under Komoly, O., *Cionista életszemlélet* ("Zionist View of Life," 1942). He also wrote a book dealing with problems in construction engineering. In 1940, Komoly was elected deputy chairman of the Zionist federation of Hungary, becoming its chairman in 1941.

In 1943 he was elected chairman of the underground Relief and Rescue Committee. His deputy was Rezső (Israel) *Kasztner. Komoly attempted to rouse the progressive and humanitarian individuals in Hungarian society to protest against the Nazi extermination program against the Jews. For this purpose he formed ties with church leaders, diplomats, members of parliament, and even with the regent Miklós Horthy's son, who passed information on to his father. Komoly helped organize the rescue train which led 1,686 Jews to safety outside Hungary. When Ferenc *Szálasi took over rule, Komoly continued his work under the auspices of the International Red Cross, which made him their representative in Hungary. However, *Arrow Cross leaders abducted him, and killed him. After the liberation, Komoly was posthumously awarded Hungary's highest distinction – the "Hungarian Freedom Order." In Israel, Komoly's Hebrew name was given to moshav Yad Natan in the Adullam Region.

BIBLIOGRAPHY: J. Lévai, *Black Book on the Martyrdom of Hungarian Jewry* (1948), passim; E. Landau (ed.), *Der Kastner-Bericht…* (1961), index; A. Biss, *Der Stopp der Endloesung* (1966), index; A. Weissberg, *Desperate Mission* (1958), index; L. Fürst-Komoly, in: G.E. Galili (ed.), *Tanúk vagyunk* (1970), 292–4; *Nathan Otto Komoly* (Heb., 1970).

[Yehouda Marton]

KOMOR, ANDRAS (1898–1944), Hungarian poet and author. Komor's verse collections, notably *Allomás* ("Station," 1925) and *Jane and Johnny* (1928), dealt with the self-doubting intellectual and were influenced by Claudel. His stories, such as *Fischmann S. utódai* ("The heirs of S. Fischmann," 1929) and *A varázsló* ("The Magician," 1927), dealt either with Jewish middle-class life or with the world of children. He committed suicide when threatened with deportation to a Nazi labor camp.

KOMPERT, LEOPOLD (1822–1886), Austrian writer, celebrated in his days mainly for Bohemian Ghetto-Tales. A native of Muenchengraetz (Mnichovo Hradiště, Bohemia), he moved in 1837 to Prague and in 1839 to Vienna to study philosophy and medicine but had to interrupt his studies to earn his living as a private tutor (Hofmeister). In 1840 he traveled through Hungary, and then stayed in Pressburg as a journalist, publishing in *Pressburger Zeitung* and the German-language literary periodical *Pannonia*, in which he published his first articles on Hungarian life (*Reisebilder aus Ungarn*, 1841). In 1843 he returned to Hungary as a tutor and published his novel *Roman der Puszta*. Ludwig August *Frankl asked him to write for the Vienna *Sonntagsblaetter*, in which he published his first picture of Jewish life, "Die Schnorrer," 1846. His first collection of Ghetto-Tales, *Aus dem Ghetto*, was published in 1848 and became a big success (1850^2, 1859^3). Joining the *Oesterreichisches Central-Organ für Glaubensfreiheit, Cultur, Geschichte und Literatur der Juden* in 1848, he campaigned for "right, not rights" *(Recht, nicht Rechte)* for the Jews, particularly the poor and uneducated ones. Although Kompert acclaimed its democratic and social aims, he was deeply disappointed by the anti-Jewish riots in Prague (from April until June 1848) which accompanied the revolution there; therefore he wrote an article urging the suppressed and plundered Jews to emigrate to the United States (*Österr. Central-Organ*, May 6, 1848, reprinted by Kisch, AJHSP 38:98–201).

In 1848 Kompert settled in Vienna as a journalist (*Oesterreichischer Lloyd*, 1848–52); in the following years he published a number of collections of Ghetto-Tales, such as *Boehmische Juden* (1851), *Neue Geschichten aus dem Ghetto* (2 vols., 1860), and *Geschichten einer Gasse* (2 vols., 1865), which established his international reputation. Some of them were translated into English, *Scenes from the Ghetto* (1882), *The Silent Woman* (1890), and *Christian and Leah: Other Ghetto Stories* (1895). His stories were based on personal observation, childhood memories, and incidents related by his elders. In a romantic vein, they were intended for the assimilated Western Jewish but also gentile readers; some of them are nostalgic, some deal with the confrontation of Jews and gentiles. In many of them Kompert deals with mixed marriage, which is the central problem of his novel *Zwischen Ruinen* (3 vols., 1875). His novel *Am Pflug* (2 vols., 1855) intended to encourage the Jews to take up agriculture and made a strong impression on Jewish youth in Eastern Europe at the time of the Second and Third Aliyah (in the first two decades of the 20th century) in the original and the Hebrew translation. His last work, the novel *Franzi und Heini: Geschichte zweier Wiener Kinder* (2 vols., 1881), deals with non-Jewish schoolchildren, but a Jewish woman peddler is a major figure. Kompert was coeditor of the *Jahrbuch fuer Israeliten* (1859–65). He also co-edited the **Neuzeit* with Simon Szánto. In his later years he was active in Jewish affairs and in Viennese civic life, taking an especial interest in education and the welfare of orphans. Two editions of his collected writings were published, in 1882–83, reprinted in 1887 and in 1906. New editions in German are *Ghetto-Geschichten* (1988); *Der Dorfgeher* (1997); and *Die Kinder des Randars* (1998).

BIBLIOGRAPHY: S. Hock, in: L. Kompert, *Saemtliche Werke*, 1 (1906), v–viii; K.E. Franzos, in: *Jahrbuch f. jüd. Geschichte und Literatur* (1906), 147–60; G. Kisch, *In Search of Freedom* (1949), index; idem, in: AJHSP, 38 (1948/49), 185–234; S.W. Baron, in: PAAJR, 20 (1951), 26–27; O. Wittner, *Moritz Hartmanns Gesammelte Werke*, 1 (1906–07), index; J. Shatzky, in: *Freedom and Reason*, Morris Raphael Cohen Memorial Volume (1951), 413–37 passim; *Jews of Czechoslovakia*, 1 (1968), index; M. Grunwald, *Vienna* (1936), index; R. Michael, in: YLBI, 9 (1964), 102–7 (Ger.); H. Bergmann, in: *Czechoslovak Jewry, Past and Future* (1943), 22–24. **ADD. BIBLIOGRAPHY:** Th. Winkelbauer, "L. Kompert und die boehmischen Landjuden," in: B. Horch, *Conditio Judaica* (1989), 190–217; G. v. Glasenapp, *Aus der Judengasse*

(1996), 102–21; F. Krobb, Nachwort, in: *Der Dorfgeher*, 1997 (with bibliography and literature); M. Th. Wittemann, *Draußen vor dem Ghetto: L. Kompert und die "Schilderung juedischen Volkslebens" in Boehmen und Maehren* (1998); *Lexikon deutsch-juedischer Autoren*, 14 (2006).

[Sol Liptzin / Archiv Bibliographia Judaica (2nd ed.)]

KOMROFF, MANUEL (1890–1974), U.S. journalist, editor, and author. He enjoyed a varied career in the arts and journalism, writing musical scores for motion pictures and working for the China Press in Shanghai. Among his works are a volume of short stories, *A Grace of Lambs* (1925), a volume entitled *Oriental Romances* (1930), and the novel *Coronet* (1929). He also published his autobiographical reminiscences, *Big City, Little Boy* (1953).

KOMZET, committee for the agricultural settlement of Jews under the auspices of the Presidium of the Nationality Council, of the Central Executive Committee of the U.S.S.R. (VTSIK). Komzet was established on August 29, 1924, with the aim of productivizing the Jewish population primarily by engaging it in agricultural labor. This followed the massive impoverishment of the Soviet Jewish population which had been hard hit by pogroms, government requisitioning of property during the Military Communism period (beginning of the 1920s), the general economic disaster in the country, and the heavy burden of taxes. Among the Jews the number of persons classified as "without definite occupation," such as merchants, religious functionaries, etc., deprived of voting and other civil rights, such as state schooling, or state medical help (*lishentsy*), reached massive proportions, amounting in 1926–27 to 30% (reaching 40% in the *shtetls*) of the recognized laboring population among the Jews of the Ukraine.

The Komzet was empowered to organize Jewish settlement and regions, recruit Jewish settlers, and care for them on their journeys and until they became established in their new locations. Komzet had departments with a special recruiting office attached to the central executive committees of the Soviet Union's republics. It received significant assistance from Jewish philanthropic organizations abroad such as Agro-Joint (see *American Jewish Joint Distribution Committee), the Jewish Colonization Association, and *ORT.

As early as 1924 Komzet began establishing new Jewish villages in the Ukraine. Poor *shtetl* Jews were resettled on uncultivated land while the allocation of land was intended to unite the previously Jewish agricultural settlements destroyed in the Civil War into a compact area populated by Jews. Thus in the late 1920s three Jewish national regions were established in the Ukraine: *Kalinindorf, *Novo-Zlatopol, and *Stalindorf. By 1936 Jewish collective farms occupied 175,000 hectares in the Ukraine.

In the mid-1920s Komzet proposed large-scale Jewish agricultural settlement as the only way to solve the Jewish problem in the Soviet Union and as an alternative to Zionism. The area initially allocated for this purpose was the uninhabited and agriculturally quite inappropriate northern and northwestern steppe region of the Crimea. Komzet hoped to cover the preliminary expenses for preparing the land by receiving funds and farm machinery from abroad. Of the 22.5 million rubles expended before 1929 on settling Jews on the land in the U.S.S.R., 16.7 million rubles (74.2%) came from abroad. In the Crimea the Jewish settlers were allocated 342,000 hectares mainly in the Yevpatoria and Dzhankoysk regions of which, in 1930, 240,000 were allocated to the (Fraydorf) Jewish National Region. In 1927 a plan was proposed for massive Jewish settlement in one of the Amur regions; due to the tensions in this area, close to the Chinese border, it was considered of paramount political and strategic importance and its settlement was of top priority for the Soviet government. In the spring of 1927 Komzet decided to send to the *Birsko-Bidzhan of the Far Eastern Territory a scientific expedition to explore the possibilities for resettling large numbers of people there. Despite the less than enthusiastic report of the expedition and the objections of some of the leaders of the *Yevsektsiya (the Jewish section of the Communist Party), the presidium of the Central Executive Committee of the U.S.S.R. on March 28, 1928, resolved to charge Komzet with responsibility for settling the Birobidzhan region, and in the event of favorable results, to have the possibility of establishing a national administrative-territorial region. From that time all of Komzet's activity was basically connected with the Birobidzhan project. On January 10 and 26, 1928, the Central Executive Committee of the U.S.S.R. lifted the deprivations of rights for the Jews who settled in the framework of the Komzet.

Komzet also operated, on a smaller scale, in Belorussia (where the Jewish population was allocated 22,000 hectares), in the Smolensk area, and also among the Soviet Asian Jewish communities. In the last context, ten collective farms of Bukharan Jews were established in Uzbekistan, 15 collective farms of Georgian Jews were established in Georgia, and collective farms of Mountain Jews were established in Daghestan, Azarbaijan, the northern Caucasus, and in the Crimea.

In 1928 Komzet drew up a five-year plan for the restructuring of the social composition of the Jewish population of the U.S.S.R. The plan projected that by 1933, 250,000 Jews (compared with 100,000 in 1927–28) would be employed in agriculture, that 70,000 scholarship students (vs. 30,000 in 1929/30) would be sent to technical schools, and that artisans cooperatives would be formed which would number only 200,000 (vs. 293,000 in 1929/30). A long-range plan of Komzet envisaged half a million Jews in agricultural labor but this was never realized. In 1936 there were slightly more than 200,000 Jewish agricultural workers farming approximately 250,000 hectares. The heads of the Komzet were non-Jews, P. Smodovich (1924–35) and S. Chutskayev (1935–38), and their deputies were Jewish Yevsektsiya activists, A. Merezhin and B. Troitski. During the period of mass repression in the mid-1930s the activities of Komzet were practically halted. In the summer of 1938, it was liquidated.

[Mark Kipnis / *The Shorter Jewish Encyclopaedia in Russian*]

KON, FELIKS (1864–1941), Communist politician and journalist. Born in Warsaw, Kon was arrested in 1884 and sentenced to 11 years' hard labor as a revolutionary. In Siberia he conducted ethnographic and anthropological research, and met Russian revolutionary leaders, including Lenin. Returning to Warsaw in 1904, Kon became a leader of the Polish Socialist Party's left wing. Arrested again in 1906, he was exiled to Galicia (then in Austria), where he published *Historja ruchu rewolucyjnego w Rosji* ("History of the Revolutionary Movement in Russia," 1908) and *Sądy wojenne w Królestwie Polskim* ("Military Courts in Congress Poland," 1909). After the February Revolution (1917) he went to Russia and was active in Polish affairs there. He joined the Communist Party, serving as a member of its Polish bureau. Kon was also a member of the Provisional Polish Revolutionary Committee established in Bialystok during the Russo-Polish War of 1920–21. His writings include *Sovremennaya Polsha* ("Contemporary Poland," 1924) and *Natsionalny vopros v Polshe* ("The National Question in Poland," 1927). He also published a biography of F. Dzierżyński (1936), and a bio-bibliographical dictionary of leading revolutionaries entitled *Deyateli revolyutsionnogo dvizheniya* (5 vols., 1927–33). He was a leading political journalist in the U.S.S.R., editing *Krasnaya Zvezda* (1925–28), *Rabochaya Gazeta* (1928–30), and *Nasha Strana* (1937–41). During the Stalinist "purges" he fell into disfavor, but on the outbreak of war between Germany and the U.S.S.R. (1941), he participated in Polish broadcasts from Moscow. His memoirs, *Za pyatdesyat let*, appeared in four volumes in 1932–34.

BIBLIOGRAPHY: A. Żarnowska, *Geneza rozłamu w Polskiej Partii Socjalistycznej, 1904–1906* (1965); *Polski Słownik Biograficzny*, 13 (1967–68), 439–44. **ADD. BIBLIOGRAPHY:** Cz. Kozlowski, *Zarys dziejow Polskiego Ruchu robotniczego do 1948* (1980), index.

KONFINO, ŽAK (1892–1975), physician and author. Konfino, who was born in Leskovac (Serbia), practiced as a physician until World War II and only began to write at the age of 40. Two of his early works were books of short stories: *Moji opštinari* ("Members of My Community," 1934) and *Lica i naliičja* ("Heads and Tails," 1936). Serving in the Yugoslav army in the war, he was captured by the Italians in 1941 and sent to a POW camp, from which he managed to escape to Switzerland. He returned to Belgrade in 1944 and became a full-time writer, coming to be regarded as one of Yugoslavia's outstanding satirists. Two themes are especially important in his works: the day-to-day life of Sephardi Jews in Serbia and the psychological relationship between doctor and patient. His books include the novel *Moje jedinče* ("My Only Child," 1952) and two collections of short stories: *Lekareve priče* ("The Doctor's Tales," 1953) and *Nove humoreske* ("New Humoristic Tales," 1960). His plays for stage, radio, and television include the comedies, *Siroto moje pametno dete* ("My Poor, Clever Child," 1957) and *Eksperiment* (1962). The latter was staged in Warsaw, and his works appeared in translation in many countries. He translated *Shalom Aleichem's *Marienbad* into Serbo-Croat. He also wrote the novel *Jesi li Ti razapeo Hrista* ("Did You Crucify Jesus?" 1968).

In the post-World War II era, he was member of the Board of the Jewish Federation. In a letter to his colleagues on the Board dated June 29, 1946, he stressed the special character and near totality of Jewish losses in the Holocaust. Only two of his short stories appeared in Hebrew translation.

ADD. BIBLIOGRAPHY: D. Katan Ben-Zion, "Presence and Disappearance – Jews and Judaism in Former Yugoslavia in the Mirror of Literature" (Hebrew, 2002), 75–76.

[Zdenko Lowenthal]

KONIG, LEA, Israeli actress. Born in Poland, Konig moved to Romania after World War II. She studied acting at the Romanian Academy of Art in Bucharest and from the age of 17 appeared with the National Jewish Theater. After immigrating to Israel in 1961 she studied Hebrew and continued her acting career. In 1987 she was awarded the Israel Prize for theater, cinema, and television arts. In 1997 she was awarded the Rosenblum Prize for theater. She has appeared in more than 50 roles, ranging from the classical repertoire to the modern and has always maintained her connection to Yiddish theater. At an advanced age, she continued performing in various plays at the Habimah Theater.

KONIN, town in the province of Poznan, central Poland. The Jewish settlement there was among the first 12 to be established in Poland. The earliest information on the Jews of Konin dates from 1397. At the close of the 15th century approximately 150 Jews lived in the town, inhabiting 12 wooden houses, and engaged in moneylending, commerce, and crafts. After a great fire there, the number of Jews decreased considerably. During the early years of the 18th century the Jewish settlement again began to grow. According to the census of 1765, 30 Jewish families, comprising 133 individuals who were liable to poll tax, lived in Konin. Between 1580 and 1764 the local Jews were affiliated with the community of *Kalisz. A magnificent synagogue was erected in Konin (1763–66), later (1829) decorated by the Jewish artist Zanvel Barash of Kepno.

After Konin passed to Russia (in 1815, becoming part of Congress Poland), it became an important center for trade with Germany, and the Jewish population increased. It numbered 369 in 1807, 872 (24% of the total) in 1827, 2,006 (39%) in 1857, 2,502 in 1897. Wealthy Jews engaged in the wholesale trade of salt and timber and established flour mills and a textile industry. From 1810 to 1849, the rabbi of Konin was Ẓevi Amsterdam. He was succeeded by Ẓevi Auerbach of Leszno. The last rabbi of Konin, Jacob Lipshitz, officiated from 1906 until the annihilation of the community in 1941.

During World War I, Jewish political organizations became active. A Zionist society was formed, consisting of about 200 members in 1915. The *Bund and *Po'alei Zion were also active, and a *Maccabi sports group was established. A Jewish wine merchant, Bernard Danziger, was appointed mayor of the town. According to the Polish census of 1921, there were

2,902 Jews in Konin (29% of the total population). Between 1920 and 1929, a Jewish secondary school functioned which was attended by 200 pupils. Its directors included the physicist Leopold *Infeld. A Jewish library was opened in 1902. In 1933, a training kibbutz of *He-Ḥalutz was organized.

[Arthur Cygielman]

Holocaust Period

There were approximately 3,000 Jews living in Konin in 1939. After the occupation of Konin by the Germans they took Jewish hostages, some of whom were executed in the market place on the Day of Atonement. On the following day the rabbi of Konin and other Jewish leaders were forced to clean the streets and to perform other humiliating tasks. A few days later many Jewish families were forced to evacuate their homes within ten minutes, and 1,100 evicted Jews were deported to the Kielce district. In the middle of July 1940 the Jewish community of Konin was liquidated when the local Jews with Jewish refugees who had arrived there were expelled to ghettos in central Poland and the rest were murdered in the forests. A small Jewish labor camp with about 1,000 persons existed near Konin until August 1943.

[Danuta Dombrowska]

BIBLIOGRAPHY: M. Gelbart (ed.), *Kehillat Konin bi-Ferihatah u-ve-Ḥurbanah* (1968); B. Wasiutyński, *Ludność żydowska w Polsce w wieku XIX i XX* (1930), 26; I. Trunk, in: *Bleter far Geshikhte*, 1 (1948), 114–69; D. Dąbrowska, in: BŻIH, no. 13–14 (1955).

KONITZ (Pol. **Chojnice**), town in Poland, until 1918 in Germany, scene of a 20th-century *blood libel. Although a few Jews probably lived and traded in Konitz from the middle of the 15th century, the first Jewish resident is mentioned in 1767. After *Hardenberg's decree of 1812, a steady stream of Jewish emigrants came to the town (80 attained citizenship in 1813–50), and in 1856 the Jewish population totaled 429. On March 15, 1900, the dismembered body of Ernst Winter, aged 19, was found in the river. The police charged a number of Jews on flimsy and insubstantial grounds. The first defendant, Israelski, was acquitted, but the crime was defined as ritual murder. Antisemites accused the authorities of shielding Jewish suspects and anti-Jewish riots broke out; the synagogue was attacked, and widespread agitation and unrest shocked the world. Adolf Lewy and his son Moritz, butchers, were accused of the ritual murder of Winter on the prefabricated evidence of a petty thief, B. Masloff. Moritz was acquitted of the murder charge but sentenced to four years' imprisonment for denying that he was acquainted with the victim. The jury awarded Masloff the minimal sentence, one year, for perjury, and petitioned for his pardon. However, William II granted a pardon to Moritz but refused to give one to Masloff. The Jewish population of Konitz subsequently declined (many were economically ruined) to 257 in 1913. After World War I, when the town was annexed to Poland, the number of Jews declined further, to 110 in 1920. Jews have not lived there since World War II.

BIBLIOGRAPHY: *Mitteilungen aus dem Verein zur Abwehr des Anti-Semitismus*, 10 (1900), index s.v. *Konitz, Mord in; Der Prozess gegen Massloff und Genossen* (1900); G. Sutor, *Der Konitzer Mord und seine Folgen* (1900); R. Kleinpaul, *Menschenopfer und Ritual-Morde* (1900); G. Zimmer, *Der Mord in Konitz am 11 Maerz 1900* (1900); F. Spaet, *Die Gutachten der Sachverstaendigen ueber den Konitzer Mord* (1903); W. Zeller, *Wer hat Ernst Winter ermordet?* (1904).

KONITZ, LEE (1927–), U.S. alto and soprano saxophonist. With his coolly geometric lines and lightly breathy tone with just the faintest hint of vibrato, Konitz's playing is instantly recognizable; his creativity and longevity have allowed him to bestride post-World War II jazz like a colossus. Konitz was the first major voice on alto to emerge after Charlie Parker, a disciple of pianist-composer Lennie Tristano whose improvisations reflected his mentor's cerebral approach to the music. Born in Chicago and originally trained as a clarinetist, Konitz played locally before joining Jerry Wald and then Claude Thornhill. While in Thornhill's band, he met arranger Gil Evans, which led to Konitz's participation in the pivotal Miles Davis "Birth of the Cool" sessions in 1949–50. After a stint in the Stan Kenton Orchestra, he joined forces with Tristano, being paired with tenor player Warne Marsh, with whom he would play frequently over the next five decades. After leaving Tristano towards the end of the 1950s, Konitz would experiment with a wide range of jazz contexts, a practice he continued throughout his career. Konitz has said, "The concentration involved and the ability to play spontaneously and with other people, that's an extreme challenge that I welcome every time." His openness to that challenge and to new developments in the music resulted in a fruitful and prolific discography totaling well over a hundred recordings. He was awarded the Jazzpar Prize for career achievement in 1992.

BIBLIOGRAPHY: B. Case, Brian and S. Britt, "Lee Konitz," in: *The Illustrated Encyclopedia of Jazz* (1978); R.J. DeLuke, "The Constantly Creative Lee Konitz," in: *All About Jazz* (March 3, 2003); at http://www.allaboutjazz.com; E. Holley, "Lee Konitz," in: *Downbeat* (Dec. 1985).

[George Robinson (2nd ed.)]

KONOTOP, Sumy district in Ukraine. At the beginning of the 19th century, only about 80 Jews lived in Konotop, but by 1847 the number had grown to 521. Jewish life in the town during the 19th century is described in her memoirs by Pauline *Wengeroff, who lived there for some years. The numbers increased considerably during the second half of the 19th century as a result of the movement of Jews from the northwestern provinces of the *Pale of Settlement to the southeastern ones, reaching 4,426 (23.5% of the total population) in 1897. On April 29, 1881, the Jews of Konotop suffered from a pogrom which left one dead, and many destroyed houses. They were again attacked during the Civil War by the volunteer army of General *Denikin on September 19, 1919; six were killed, ten injured, women were raped, and houses robbed. With the establishment of the Soviet regime, about 500 artisans were organized in cooperatives and had a savings and loan fund. Komzet sent 83 Jewish families from Konotop to farm in the Kherson Jewish colonies. In 1926 there were 5,763 Jews (17.2% of the population) in Konotop, dropping to 3,941 (8.6% of the total population) in 1939. The Germans occupied the town on September 9, 1941; in the first few days they killed 123 Jews. Later registration showed 1,000 Jews in Konotop, and they were ordered to wear the yellow badge and report for forced labor. In early November they were concentrated mostly in the local prison, and shortly thereafter all were murdered. Jews returned there after the war. In 1959 there were 1,900 Jews, and in 1970 their number was estimated at about 250 (50 families).

BIBLIOGRAPHY: P. Wengeroff, *Memoiren einer Grossmutter*, 2 (1910), 64–115.

[Yehuda Slutsky / Shmuel Spector (2nd ed.)]

KONRÁD, GYÖRGY (1933–), Hungarian author and sociologist. Konrad's first novel, *A látogató* (1969; Eng., *The Case Worker*, 1987), and a later one, *A városalapító* (1977; Eng., *The City Builder*, 1987), caused considerable outcry in official circles, and – until 1987 – publication of most of his works was prohibited in Hungary.

[Eva Kondor]

KONSKIE (Pol. **Końskie**; Rus. **Konsk**), town in the province of Kielce, E. central Poland. In 1588 the Jews of Konskie were granted a privilege by King Sigismund III Vasa allowing them to buy without hindrance food and other goods in all the cities, towns, and villages of the kingdom. In 1635 King Ladislas IV ratified these rights, also granting the Jews permission to build houses in Konskie and to engage in trade. After 1748, when Konskie was granted the status of a town, the number of Jews increased; in 1796 there were 2,534 Jews (62% of the total population). The town developed in the 19th century and 4,450 Jews (54.7% of the total population) lived there in 1897. By 1921 the number had risen to 5,037 (61.2%). In independent Poland after World War I, the Jews in Konskie had an active communal life. The main Jewish parties were represented in the municipality, headed by the *Bund. In an effort to increase its influence on the community administration in 1931, *Agudat Israel used its prerogative to deny right of election to nonreligious Jews. With the increasing antisemitism in Poland in the 1930s, attempts were made to oust the Jews from economic life; there were anti-Jewish attacks in 1931, and in 1937 pogroms accompanied by an economic boycott.

[Shimshon Leib Kirshenboim]

Holocaust Period

In 1939, 6,500 Jews lived in Konskie. The German army entered the town on Sept. 6, 1939. In February 1941 about 1,200 Jews from *Plock were expelled to Konskie. The following month a ghetto, consisting of two sections, was established in the town. On Dec. 10, 1941, a decree was issued carrying the death penalty for anyone crossing the ghetto boundary. During the summer of 1942 about 1,500 Jews from the smaller towns nearby were deported to Konskie, and the ghetto population swelled to about 9,000. On November 3–9, 1942, the Germans carried out an *Aktion* in which almost the entire Jewish population was deported to the *Treblinka death camp via *Szydlowiec. On January 13, 1943, the remaining Jews were also sent to Trebkinka. After the war the Jewish community in Konskie was not rebuilt.

[Stefan Krakowski]

BIBLIOGRAPHY: BŻIH, no. 15–16 (1955), 84. **ADD. BIBLIOGRAPHY:** *Haynt* (Feb. 14, 1918; May 5, 1939); *Nasz Przeglad* (July 14, 1937; Sept. 3, 1937).

KONSKOWOLA (Pol. **Końskawola**), small town near Pulawy, Lublin province, Poland. In 1712 the lady of the manor, Helena Czartoryska, permitted Jews to settle and to acquire real estate. In 1765 the Jewish community numbered 643 poll tax payers, 569 in the township and 74 in 11 villages. In 1776, during the census of Jewish books, 519 books were taxed in Konskowola. In 1816, 40 Jewish families applied to Prince Czartoryski requesting agricultural land for settlement. The Jewish population numbered 872 (44% of the total) in 1827, 1,536 (59%) in 1857, 1,453 (52%) in 1897, and 876 (53.6%) in 1921. Before the outbreak of World War II there were about 1,100 Jews in Konskowola. At the end of 1940 a ghetto was established there. On May 8, 1942, 1,600 of the 2,000 Jews in the ghetto (including refugees) were sent to Sobibor, to be replaced by about 3,000 Jews from Slovakia and additional refugees. Around 3,000 of them were sent to labor camps and in October 1942, 1,000 "unproductive" Jews, including women and children, were executed outside the town. The labor camps were liquidated in May 1943. No Jewish community was subsequently reconstituted in Konskowola.

BIBLIOGRAPHY: *Gazeta narodowa i obca* (June 20, 1793); *Słownik geograficzny Królestwa Polskiego*, s.v.; B. Wasiutyński, *Ludność żydowska w Polsce w XIX i XX wiekach* (1930), 63; R. Mahler, *Yidn in Amolikn Poyln in Likht fun Tsifern* (1958), index; *Bleter far Geshikhte*, 3:1 (1950), table no. 9; Yad Vashem Archives.

[Stefan Krakowski]

KONVITZ, JOSEPH (1878–1944), Ereẓ Israel and U.S. rabbi. Konvitz was born in Kaisiadorys, Kovno province, Lithuania. He joined the Kneset Israel Yeshivah in Slobodka at the age of 12, and was already recognized for his scholarly ability when he was 19. He was one of the ten students at the yeshivah selected to form the nucleus of the new yeshivah at Slutsk founded by Rabbi Jacob David *Willowski (the Ridbaz), whose daughter he subsequently married. After serving as rabbi of Shadov (Seduva) from 1902 to 1903 and of Kowarsk from 1903, both in the province of Kovno, he immigrated to Ereẓ Israel in 1906, settling in Safed, where the Ridbaz had established a yeshivah, and serving as *rosh yeshivah* and rabbi there until 1914. In that year he was visiting the United States on behalf of the Safed yeshivah when the outbreak of World War I made it impossible for him to return to his home. He settled in the United States and was appointed rabbi of the united Orthodox congregations of Elizabeth, N.J. (1915–19), Trenton, N.J. (1919–24), and several leading congregations in Newark, N.J. (1924–44). Konvitz was soon recognized as a leading Orthodox rabbi, both on account of his scholarship and of his ability to mediate and settle communal disputes. He was president of the Union of Orthodox Rabbis of the United States and Canada (Agudat Harabbonim) from 1933 to 1939, and honorary president until his death. He was closely identified with Orthodox institutions in Jerusalem and with the rescue of rabbis and scholars from Europe and the transfer of yeshivot from Europe to Israel during World War II. In addition to his halakhic contributions to rabbinical periodicals, his selected responsa, novellae, and sermons, *Divrei Yosef*, have been published (vol. 1, 1947, vol. 2, 1948). After his death, the Yeshivah Rabbi Joseph Konvitz, an all-day modern Orthodox school on New York's East Side, was established in his memory.

BIBLIOGRAPHY: J. Konvitz, *Divrei Yosef*, ed. Ch. Karlinsky (1947).

KONVITZ, MILTON RIDVAS (1908–2003), U.S. legal scholar. His father and maternal grandfather were distinguished rabbis. He was born in Safed in Ereẓ Israel and taken to the United States in 1915. He received his B.A. (1929) and law degree (1930) from New York University and his Ph.D. in philosophy from Cornell University (1933). He practiced law for a number of years in New Jersey as general counsel for the Newark and New Jersey housing authorities; he was also staff counsel of the American Civil Liberties Union, and assistant counsel of the National Association for the Advancement of Colored People (NAACP). After teaching law and public administration at New York University, he joined the Cornell faculty in 1946 as an associate professor in the New York State School of Industrial and Labor Relations, was made full professor in 1949, and was appointed professor in the law school in 1956. He retired from Cornell in 1973 and was named professor emeritus.

At Cornell, Konvitz was a founder of the university's Department of Near Eastern Studies and Program of Jewish Studies. He also helped to initiate Young Israel House, where Orthodox Jewish students could reside, have kosher meals, conduct daily prayer services, and study religious texts. Konvitz was renowned for his two-semester American Ideals course, which introduced students to the great thinkers and philosophers throughout history whose writings had shaped those ideals. In teaching the course to more than 8,000 students during his career, he is said to never have delivered the same lecture twice.

His article "Judaism and the Democratic Ideal" appeared in *The Jews: Their History, Culture, and Religion* (ed. by L. Finkelstein (1960^3), 1430–51). In the article he points out that although Judaism has often had to accommodate itself to the accidents of time and place, the spirit and energy of democracy are at the very heart of Judaism; the Torah is its constitution; and, as elaborated in the Bible and by the rabbis, Judaism has as one of its fundamental precepts the equality of all men before God.

Konvitz was director of the project that drew up the official body of statutory law now used in Liberia. In 1959 he went there to advise the government on new labor legislation. The Liberian government honored him with the Grand Band of the Order of the Star of Africa, the highest award given to foreigners. In 1998 Cornell established the Milton R. Konvitz Professorship of Jewish and Near Eastern Studies in the university's Jewish Studies program.

Konvitz wrote a number of articles and books dealing with civil rights. He was co-founder of the periodicals *Midstream, Judaism,* and *Journal of Law and Religion.* He also served as the *Encyclopaedia Judaica* departmental editor (first edition) on law and on socialism in the United States. Among his books are *The Constitution and Civil Rights* (1947), *Fundamental Liberties of a Free People* (1957), *A Century of Civil Rights* (1961), *Expanding Liberties* (1966), *Religious Liberty and Conscience* (1968), *A Century of Civil Rights* (1983), *Torah and Constitution* (1998), and *Judaism and Human Rights* (2001^2). He also edited *Bill of Rights Reader* (1968^4), *First Amendment Freedoms* (1963), and *Aspects of Liberty* (with C. Rossiter, 1958).

BIBLIOGRAPHY: *Contemporary Authors*, 1–4 (1967), 549.

[Charles Reznikoff / Ruth Beloff (2nd ed.)]

KOOK (Kuk), ABRAHAM ISAAC (1865–1935), rabbinical authority and thinker; first Ashkenazi chief rabbi of modern Ereẓ Israel. Born in Greiva (now Griva), Latvia, Kook received the type of Jewish education that was customary in 19th-century Eastern Europe. At a very early age he showed independence of mind and far-reaching curiosity. Desirous to supplement his traditional education which was restricted to the study of Talmud, he undertook the study of the Bible, Hebrew language, Jewish and general philosophy, and mysticism. In 1888 he was appointed rabbi of Zaumel, and in 1895 became rabbi of Bausk (now Bauska). In 1904 he immigrated to Ereẓ Israel, where he served as rabbi of Jaffa and the surrounding towns. There he fostered close ties with people of all shades of opinion and belief. He identified with the Zionist movement, thus antagonizing the rabbinical establishment, and at the same time, engaged in a vigorous debate with the irreligious pioneers and laid the foundations for a Religious Zionism that did not settle for the political pragmatism of the *Mizrachi (the Religious Zionist Movement) or that of Binyamin Ze'ev Theodor *Herzl, the founder of the Zionist Movement, but sought to view Zionism as a process of redemption, of repentance, and of an overall Jewish renaissance. Rabbi Kook was a man of complexity whose persona unified opposing spiritual worlds: the Lithuanian Torah scholarship with the ḥasidic spiritual experience, a commitment to *halakhah* and Jewish tradition with a modern worldview and Western culture and philosophy, a tendency towards spirituality and mysticism with full involvement in the practical matters of rabbinic and public leadership. In his effort to urge traditional Jews to fulfill the Zionist ideal, he traveled to Europe in 1914 to participate in a conference of *Agudat Israel. Unable to return to Ereẓ Israel because of the outbreak of World War I, Kook spent the war years 1914–18 in Switzerland and accepted a temporary position as the rabbi of the Maḥzikei ha-Dat congregation in London, where he was very active in trying to influence the Jews of England to back Zionist political activity. Upon returning to Palestine after the war, Kook was appointed chief rabbi of Jerusalem, and with the formation of the chief rabbinate in 1921 he was elected the first Ashkenazi chief rabbi of Palestine.

Kook developed his own views on the role of *Zionism in Jewish history. He held that the return to Ereẓ Israel marked the beginning of divine redemption (*atḥalta di-ge'ullah*), and that the *Balfour Declaration of 1917 had ushered in a new era in the renewal of the Jewish people. However, in his view, the existing Zionist movement was incomplete insofar as it had taken up only the revival of the secular and material needs of the Jewish people. In the beginning of 1918 he published an open letter, in which he called upon Jews the world over to help in setting up the Degel Yerushalayim movement, which was to emphasize the spiritual aspects of the national revival. For a short while Kook's movement created some interest. However, this interest soon spent itself, and before long, the movement was entirely forgotten.

Kook was often misunderstood by the irreligious and despised by religious extremists. His relations with the religious Zionist party, *Mizrachi, were ambivalent. He made it clear that, while he was glad of its existence, he viewed it as a political party which was out to safeguard purely practical religious interests. He was also continually at odds with the rabbis. While Kook thought of the chief rabbinate in Palestine as the first step toward the revival of the Sanhedrin, the majority of the rabbis were concerned with the preservation of the traditional patterns of rabbinical authority.

Kook also formulated a new program for yeshivah education. Critical of the yeshivot of his time for excluding secular subjects from the curriculum, Kook dreamed of establishing a yeshivah which would present to the student an integrated program of higher Jewish education. Students would be chosen not only on the basis of proficiency in Talmud but also on the basis of their knowledge of Bible. Emphasis would be placed on the development of a lucid style in both writing and speaking, for Kook hoped that the graduates would become teachers and spiritual leaders in their communities. While this ambitious program was never put into practice, Kook did, in 1924, set up a yeshivah in Jerusalem which was unique among yeshivot in its religious philosophy and its positive attitude to Zionism. This yeshivah became known as Merkaz ha-Rav.

In the last years of his life, Kook took up an extremely unpopular stance in defense of Stavsky, who was accused of the murder of *Arlosoroff, placing himself in the painful position of fighting the Zionist Labor movement. At the same time the *Neturei Karta zealots kept up their unrelenting campaign of vilification against him. Through out all this, Kook never gave up his love for the whole of the Jewish people, and not surprisingly, this love has been requited by the Jewish masses.

Mysticism

Kook is an example of a rare 20th-century phenomenon – the deeply religious mystic who takes an active interest in human affairs. Rabbi Kook's thought is based on a mystical intuition and on a radically monistic perception. He views reality as an absolute unity whose source is the divine infinity and is expressed in all dimensions of existence: in the cosmic, natural, and physical dimension, in the historical-political and in the cultural dimension. All reality is a revelation or manifestation of the divine. This view led, in turn, to his tolerant and pluralistic outlook, according to which all cultures, each worldview and every ideology, are partial expressions of the divine truth. Despite Kook's basic assumption that no single philosophical or kabbalistic theory can contain the multiple dimensions of existence, and that, therefore, each theory is partial and relative, he nonetheless usually formulated his ideas within a Neoplatonic mystical framework, using concepts borrowed sometimes from the Kabbalah and sometimes from the idealistic European philosophy of the 19th century. He did not regard the Kabbalah simply as an ancient tradition, but also as a discipline of free thought and creativity, which springs from the depths of a person's spirit, and deciphers the secrets of Torah. His contemplative works were, for the most part, not written in a systematic fashion; his writing was automatic and spontaneous, and in general he did not later edit and arrange these writings in book form. His student and friend Rabbi David Cohen ("Ha-Nazir"), who edited a large portion of his works, arranged them in the book called "Lights of Holiness" according to the major topics of philosophical inquiry: epistemology, ontology, and anthropology (including ethics and morality). His nationalist thought is mostly to be found in several essays which were collected in the book "Lights," which was edited by his son, Rabbi Ẓevi Yehudah *Kook.

There existed in Kook's personality a harmonious blending of mystical speculation and practical activities, which led to a synthesis of these two elements in his thought. Most mystical systems insist that man divest himself of the restraints of physical life in order to enable his soul to unite with the ineffable, i.e., to achieve the *unio mystica*. In Kook's system, however, the mystical urge for unity was meant to combine the communicable with the ineffable – to infuse the physical life of man with a religious purpose. There was no stress on self-abnegation in his mysticism.

Kook's personal religious experience moved him to be deeply concerned about the contemporary opposition to religion, and throughout his life he carried on a relentless search for the meaning of religion in the modern world. While identifying with the Zionist movement, he felt that it was a great tragedy that Zionism had sprung up toward the end of the 19th century, at a time when there was a general decline of all religions, including Judaism. Zionism, in his view, was a movement of rebellion, which attracted many of the young Jewish intellectuals who had shaken off their religious faith. He believed that the movement of return to the national homeland should be an essentially religious movement, for it was only in the Land of Israel that the Jewish people could work out its full religious life.

Modern Challenges to Religion

In Jewish life the beginning of the 20th century witnessed the most corroding assimilation and the most exhilarating national revival. Kook, who thoroughly understood his age, characterized his generation in dialectical terms as consisting of clashing opposites: "Ours is a wonderful generation… It consists of opposites, darkness and light exist in confusion."

Kook was convinced that in spite of the decline of religion, humanity had moved to a higher stage in cultural growth. The tragedy of modern man was that he had made tremendous progress in everything but religion, so that religion appeared to have stood still. In Kook's eyes, the secular Zionist undertaking was to be neither ignored nor discounted; it mandated confrontation with the attitudes and philosophical methods pervading contemporary literature and setting the wheels of that generation's social and scientific revolution in motion. Kook could not but remark the progress, the blessing, and the promise brought by these events. In his eyes, the sincerity, search for truth and hatred of fraud expressed in the great rebellion of his era were commendable, and he shared the sense of freedom that characterized it. He felt compelled to find religious meaning for the central processes and spiritual cultural phenomena that deemed religion, at the very least, to be superfluous and completely irrelevant.

Against this background, Kook's thought is revolutionary as well in the realm of Jewish religious thought, as a general philosophy seeking to propose an alternative to all existing systems by reinterpreting reality, human nature, and religion itself. Historical and social reality yields no direct revelation of the religious meaning it contains, and even the classical sources of religious literature do not speak in a language disclosing their "true" meaning in modern concepts. Both reality and religion, therefore, must be interpreted if they are to be understood, enabling one to respond to the divine summons issuing from them. If the most virulent contention of Nietzsche's thought consists in his biting criticism of morality, with its hypocrisy and falsehood, in order to build a new morality on its ruins, we can say that Kook sought to wage war against the religiosity of his age, against the hypocrisy and lies infecting it, not to create a new religion but rather to develop renewed understanding of the meaning of religion. Only through a reinterpretation of religion could one engage in combat on the battlefield of general culture and theology and emerge victorious. What is mandated is by no means a mere apologetics but rather an essential reorientation. His message was addressed first and foremost to observant Jews and to the Jewish people as a whole, and only afterward was it meant to spread further.

Social Philosophy

While criticizing social ideologies that limit their interest to material conditions, Kook at the same time criticized religious people who were not interested in social questions, lashing out against "any ideology that ignores the need of improving the state of the world… and instead hovers in a rarefied atmosphere and boasts of the perfection of the soul."

It is interesting, in this context, to note the surprising resemblance between Kook's reaction to European cogitation and that of another philosopher and theologian of his time, propelled as well by profound religious and moral motives, whose theological formation was also greatly influenced by 19th century philosophy. The man in question is Albert Schweitzer, whose thought is also characterized as "ethical mysticism" and in it a concept of self-perfection is central as well.

The similarity, in other aspects, between Kook and Leonard Ragaz and Teilhard de Chardin has already been pointed out. For Schweitzer and Ragaz, as for Kook, the interest of freedom is primordial. In Ragaz's view, the church and theology would like to imprison God within the narrow confines of ecclesiastical thought, while the holy spirit in fact finds true expression out in the wide word. The kingdom of heaven, which is in effect the kingdom of justice, freedom, and social equality, comes into being wherever God's will is realized in human freedom. These views resemble those expressed by Kook. He addressed the subject directly in one of his letters. "We would not regret it if some quality of cultural justice could be built without any spark or mention of God, for we know that the very aspiration to justice, in any light, is itself the more luminous divine influence" (*Iggerot Rayah*, vol. 1, p. 45).

The Sacred and the Profane

Regarding the idea of holiness, in accordance with his harmonistic view of man and of the world, Kook refused to see a sharp dichotomy between the sacred and the profane, maintaining that all that was essential to human life was potentially sacred. All the advances that men achieved in science were part of the intellectual growth of mankind, and if these advances appeared to undermine religion, this was no reason to suspect their intrinsic value. What was wrong, Kook argued, was not the progress of science but the fact that religious thinking did not progress intellectually at an equal rate.

The physical concerns of man are inseparable from his spiritual aspirations. Kook wrote: "The sacred and the profane together influence the spirit of man and he becomes enriched through absorbing from each of them whatever is suitable." In order for holiness to be achieved, the sacred and profane must be synthesized. The activation of the intellect is a prerequisite for the attainment of holiness, and only the man who is physically healthy can activate his intellect. Using the metaphor of ascending a ladder to describe the process of attaining holiness, Kook compared the physical needs of man to the lowest rungs of the ladder. Just as the lower rungs of the ladder must be climbed before the higher rungs can be reached, so man must satisfy his physical needs before he can attain spiritual perfection.

The interpretation of holiness as being in continuous relation to the profane is "the natural view of holiness." The opposite view of holiness as a state of pure spirituality was criticized by Kook for its one-sidedness and lack of balance. He maintained that this view of holiness became prevalent among the Jewish people in the course of their dispersion, when they were cut off from a normal existence in their homeland and, therefore, called this "the holiness of the exile." The renaissance of a normal Jewish life in the national homeland should bring about the return to the ideal of "normal" holiness.

Science

In an address delivered at the opening ceremony of the Hebrew University in Jerusalem in 1925, Kook advocated the synthesis of religious and secular studies. He maintained that the study of the secular sciences should be complementary to the study of Torah, but warned that the exclusive preoccupation with scientific research would alienate man from ultimate religious values.

Kook was critical of the modern predilection for pure scientific research that deliberately ignores ultimate objectives and consequences. Although pure science can explain much about the things that exist, it cannot "create" their meaning and significance, nor can it give shape and direction to man's life. Contrasting the biblical account of man's origin with the Darwinian theory of the origin of the species, Kook wrote: "It is absolutely immaterial to us whether there was in fact in antiquity a golden age when man enjoyed an abundance of material and spiritual wealth, or whether life began from the bottom and rose from the lowest rung of existence toward a higher, and that it continues upwards. What we must recognize is that it is distinctly possible that man, even after he has risen high, can forfeit everything by wickedness, and that he is likely to harm himself and generations to come. This is what we should learn from the story of Adam in paradise." Rejecting the literal exegesis of the second chapter of Genesis, he maintained that the creation chapters required a profound mystical interpretation. While many people regarded the concept of evolution as a threat to religion, Kook considered evolution congenial to the deeper insights of Jewish mysticism which has always viewed the world as continuously evolving toward the goal of ultimate perfection. Unlike Bergson, who regarded evolution as the product of a blind and undirected *élan vital*, Kook maintained that there was a passionate purpose and direction in evolution – the overwhelming longing of man to cleave to God, which can be attained only through the progressive effort of generations, each moving closer to the goal of holiness.

Universalism and Nationalism

Kook believed that the world is continually evolving toward universalism, which is at present only an ideal toward which man must be educated within individual national units. Nationality is, accordingly, an essential step in the divine scheme of evolution toward universalism. In this scheme Jewish nationality is marked by the concept of "chosenness": the Jews are a people who were designated to "work and toil with the utmost devotion" to further the divine goal of human perfection and universalism. According to Kook, God imposed a divine task upon the Jewish nation, but it is up to the Jews to accept upon themselves and carry out this divine task. Kook's approach to the Zionist Movement was based both on his "historiosophical" religious and metaphysical worldview and on his personal experiences of direct contact with the pioneers of the Second Aliyah. In his eyes, Zionism was an opportunity for an overall Jewish renaissance, and he yearned to witness a far-reaching renewal, not only of the Hebrew language and the Jewish settlement in Israel, but also of Jewish literature, Torah scholarship, and the creative arts, as well as an expansion of the meaning of the Torah itself. All of these changes, he believed, would bring about the establishment of the State of Israel in the Land of Israel, an ideal state that would actualize in all dimensions of its existence the noble ideals of Judaism and thus reveal the kingship of God in the world. He valued the Zionist movement as a practical-political instrument whose function was to realize this vision. He also admired and loved the pioneers, in whom he saw unadulterated idealism and innate moral values. However, he also voiced harsh criticism of both wings of the Zionist Movement, the religious and the secular for their narrow understanding of their role. Kook was actively involved in the Zionist public life and the British Mandate related to him as one of the representatives of the Zionist leadership.

Works

Kook was a prolific writer, who, according to his students, wrote out of the constant urge to create. He never attempted to construct a comprehensive system, and his style mirrors the quality of his personal insights and mystical reflections. Kook's extensive writings traverse a wide range of literary styles and forms. He wrote contemplative compositions, halakhic books, ideological articles and essays, a commentary to the Talmud, poetry, and many letters. His language and style reflect the complex nature of his spiritual world. The unique synthesis found in his writings between mystical concepts and kabbalistic ideas on the one hand, and philosophical thought and his bold and novel interpretation of the meaning of Judaism on the other, as well as the personal and original nature of his thought, required the creation of a new mystical language.

Kook's speculative writings are contained in the following works: *Orot ha-Kodesh*, 4 vols. (1963–64^2); *Iggerot ha-Re'ayah*, 3 vols. (1962–65^2); *Orot* (1961^2); *Orot ha-Teshuvah* (1955^2), translated into English as *Rabbi Kook's Philosophy of Repentance* (1968); *Ereẓ Ḥefeẓ* (1930); *Eder ha-Yekar ve-Ikvei ha-Ẓon* (1967^2); and E. Kalmanson (ed.), *Ha-Maḥashavah ha-Yisre'elit* (1920). The following are among his halahkhic works: *Shabbat ha-Areẓ* (1937^2); *Da'at Kohen* (1942); and *Mishpat Kohen* (1966^2).

BIBLIOGRAPHY: S.H. Bergman, *Faith and Reason* (1961), 121–41; L.J. Kaplan & D. Shatz (eds.), *Rabbi Abraham Isaac Kook and Jewish Spirituality* (1994); N. Rotenstreich, *Jewish Philosophy in Modern Times* (1968), 219–38; J.B. Agus, *Banner of Jerusalem* (1946); I. Epstein, *Abraham Yitzhak Hacohen Kook; His Life and Times* (1951); B. Efrati, *Ḥazon ha-Ge'ullah be-Mishnat ha-Rav Kook* (1956); idem, *Ha-Sanegoryah be-Mishnat ha-Rav Kook* (1959); S. Avidor, *Ha-Ish Neged ha-Zerem* (1962); *Azkarah... A.I. Kook*, 3 vols. (1937); L. Jung (ed.), *Guardians of our Heritage* (1958), 489–509. **ADD. BIBLIOGRAPHY:** B. Ish-Shalom, *Rav Avraham Itzhak HaCohen Kook: Between Rationalism and Mysticism* (1993); idem, "Tolerance and its Theoretical Basis in the Teaching of Rav Kook," in: L. Kaplan and D. Shatz (eds.), *Abraham Isaac Kook and Jewish Spirituality* (1995), 178–204; E. Goldman, "Rav Kook's Relation to European Thought," in: B. Ish-Shalom and S. Rosenberg (eds.), *The World of Rav Kook's Thought*, tr. from Heb. Y. Orot (1991), 115–22; T. Ross, "Rav Kook's Concept of the Divine," part 1, in: *Daat* (Winter 1982),109–28; part 2, *ibid.* (Summer 1982), 39–70 (Heb.); D. Schwartz, *Challenge and Crisis in Rav Kook's Circle* (Heb., 2001).

[Zvi Zinger (Yaron) / Benjamin Ish-Shalom (2nd ed.)]

KOOK, HILLEL (1915–2001), political activist in World War II. As a teenager in British Mandatory Palestine in the 1930s, Kook became active in the *Irgun Ẓeva'i Le'ummi, the Jewish underground militia associated with Revisionist Zionist leader Vladimir Ze'ev *Jabotinsky. The Irgun sent Kook to Poland in 1937 to help organize Jewish immigration to Palestine. In 1940, Jabotinsky dispatched Kook and other Irgun emissaries to the United States for fundraising and political activity.

After Jabotinsky's death that year, Kook – using the pseudonym Peter Bergson – and several colleagues created the Committee for a Jewish Army of Stateless and Palestinian Jews, which campaigned for the establishment of a Jewish armed force to fight the Nazis. Their rallies and newspaper advertisements attracted the support of celebrities, intellectuals, and many representatives of Congress. This public pressure, supplemented by the quiet lobbying efforts of major Jewish organizations, ultimately persuaded the British to create the Jewish Brigade.

When news of the Nazi genocide was confirmed by the Allies in late 1942, Bergson shifted his focus and established a new group, the Emergency Committee to Save the Jewish People of Europe. It lobbied Congress, sponsored more than 200 newspaper advertisements, and organized public rallies, including a march of 400 rabbis in Washington. Bergson's campaign culminated in the introduction of a Congressional resolution urging creation of a government agency to rescue Jewish refugees. The Congressional hearings on the resolution, combined with pressure from Treasury Secretary Henry Morgenthau, Jr., convinced President Roosevelt to establish the *War Refugee Board. The Board played a major role in the rescue of more than 200,000 Jews from Hitler.

In 1943–44, Bergson established the American League for Free Palestine, to rally American public support for Jewish statehood, and the Hebrew Committee of National Liberation, to serve as a government-in-exile for the future Jewish state. Through newspaper ads, Congressional lobbying, and theatrical productions, they sought to increase the pressure on the British to withdraw from Palestine.

Bergson's efforts were opposed by some mainstream Jewish leaders, who feared his unorthodox tactics would provoke antisemitism or usurp their positions of leadership in the community. The clashes between the Bergson group and Jewish leaders undermined both sides' political effectiveness.

Reassuming his real name, Kook moved to the newly established State of Israel in 1948, and served a term in the Knesset as a representative of Menaḥem Begin's *Ḥerut Party.

BIBLIOGRAPHY: R. Medoff, *Militant Zionism in America: The Rise and Impact of the Jabotinsky Movement in the United States* (2002); D.S. Wyman and R. Medoff, *A Race Against Death* (2002); P. Bergson, *America and the Holocaust* (2002).

[Rafael Medoff (2nd ed.)]

KOOK, SAUL ḤONE BEN SOLOMON ZALMAN (1879–1955), Israeli Hebrew writer and scholar. Kook, who was born in Grajewe (Poland), was a younger brother of Rabbi Abraham Isaac *Kook. He studied in yeshivot and with his brother, whom he followed, settled first in Jaffa in 1904, and later in Tel Aviv. Here he engaged in business, and was active in the city's various cultural and educational organizations and institutions. At the same time, he contributed many valuable studies to various journals and periodicals relating to all fields of Jewish scholarship, including Bible, Hebrew linguistics, apocryphal, midrashic and talmudic, geonic and rabbinic literature, folklore, the history of the Jewish settlement in Ereẓ Israel, Hebrew liturgy, and other subjects. His studies were collected and published posthumously in two volumes as *Iyyunim u-Meḥkarim* (1959–63).

BIBLIOGRAPHY: Tidhar, 1 (1947), 345–6; A.Z. Ben-Yishai, in: *Sinai*, 38 (1955/56), 184–91.

KOOK, ẒEVI JUDAH BEN ABRAHAM ISAAC HA-KOHEN (1891–1982), Israeli *rosh yeshivah*. Born in Zimel, Kovno region, Ẓevi Judah was the only son of A.I. *Kook. In 1904 he settled in Ereẓ Israel with his parents and studied in the yeshivah Eẓ Ḥayyim in Jerusalem. He helped his father with the administration of the central yeshivah of Israel, Yeshivat Merkaz ha-Rav, and after his father's death in 1935, succeeded him as its head, together with his brother-in-law, Shalom Nathan-Ra'anan (d. 1972). Continuing his father's thought and method in education, he succeeded in educating thousands of pupils from all sections of the population. His positive attitude toward the State of Israel influenced the yeshivah. He published innumerable articles, mainly dealing with the halakhic attitude to topical events, and some were collected in the work *Li-Netivot Yisrael* (1967). He also devoted himself to editing and publishing his father's writings with source references and notes.

Following the Six-Day War the aged Rabbi Kook achieved considerable prominence as the spiritual father of Gush Emunim, and generally adopted an extreme nationalistic view, strenuously advocating the right of the Jews to the whole of Ereẓ Israel and opposing any withdrawal.

KOPELMAN, ARIE LEONARD (1938–), U.S. businessman. Born in Brookline, Mass., and brought up in Boston, Kopelman spent the first part of his professional life as a highly accomplished advertising executive, then achieved even greater success at Chanel, the Paris-based fashion and fragrance house. Although he was nominally in charge of Chanel's U.S. business, Kopelman's influence was international. He majored in art history at Johns Hopkins University before graduating in 1960, then earned an M.B.A. at Columbia Business School in 1962. He began his career at Procter & Gamble, marketing Ivory soap, and in 1965 he joined the advertising agency Doyle Dane Bernbach, becoming vice chairman and general manager. His work on the Chanel account led to a friendship with Chanel chairman Alain Wertheimer, who hired him in 1985 as vice chairman and chief operating officer of the company's U.S. subsidiary. Within a few years, Kopelman was president. He remained at Chanel Inc. for 19 years, retiring in 2004 after leading the company to $2.2 billion in worldwide sales. "If you have the right product, you can have a very good business," he once said, "but if you have the right product backed by the right marketing, you can have a great business." When Kopelman arrived, Chanel was just beginning to open its own stores. When he stepped down, Chanel had 16 of its own stores in the U.S., eight fine jewelry boutiques, and more than 90 retail accounts. He is credited with building strong relationships with retailers and magazine publishers; maintaining Chanel's reputation for sophistication, taste, and elegance; and broadening its product range. A philanthropist and supporter of the arts, he served on the boards of many organizations, including the U.S. Holocaust Memorial Museum. He became a fixture as chairman of the Winter Antiques Show in New York and was a director of the Municipal Art Society, the New York City Ballet, and the Nantucket Historical Society. He was also a director of the Heinz Awards, named for the late U.S. Senator John Heinz, with whom he developed a close friendship.

[Mort Sheinman (2nd ed.)]

KOPELOWITZ, LIONEL (1926–), British communal leader. Kopelowitz was born in Newcastle-upon-Tyne and lived there much of his life. He was educated at Clifton and Cambridge and practiced as a physician, serving on the council of the British Medical Association. From the 1970s he held numerous senior positions in Anglo-Jewish life. He was president of the Board of Deputies of British Jews in 1985–91 and was also president of the National Council for Soviet Jewry in the same period.

[William D. Rubinstein (2nd ed.)]

KOPELSON, ẒEMAḤ (pseudonyms: **Timofey**; **Timoshin**; **Grishin**; **Polyakevich**; 1869–1933), leading pioneer of the *Bund. Born in a merchant family in Vilna, while still a student in high school in Panevezys (Ponevezh) he formed a socialist youth study circle. In 1887 he belonged to the Narodnaya Volya (Populist) circle in Vilna which also included L. Axelrod and Charles *Rappoport. He then turned to Marxism, and with L. *Jogiches began to organize Social Democratic groups of workers and intelligentsia in Vilna, in 1889–90 serving as their chief instructor. Subsequently Kopelson studied dentistry in Warsaw. Imprisoned for a time for political activities, on his return to Vilna he made use of the experience he had gained in the struggle of the Polish workers' movement. In 1895 he left the country and lived in Switzerland and Berlin. Kopelson was active on behalf of the Bund in the "Union of Russian Social Democrats Abroad" and acted as its secretary. In it he became involved in the ideological controversy between the "youth" and the "economists" with Plekhanov and P. *Axelrod, and later with the "Iskra" (Lenin; *Martov), being more in sympathy with the former. At the fifth congress of the Bund (1903) he dissented from its national Jewish program. He was a member of the "Committee Abroad" of the Bund until 1905, when he returned to Russia secretly and took charge of the Bund publishing house Die Velt. In 1908 he immigrated to the United States. He contributed to the Yiddish and Russian socialist press, and also served on the executive of the Jewish Socialist Federation of America. After the 1917 Revolution he returned to Russia and joined the Communist party, although he was not active in public affairs. His important memoirs of the period preceding the founding of the Bund were published in the *Arbeter Luekh* ("Workers' Calendar," 1922), and in greater detail in the collection *Revolyutsionnoye dvizheniye sredi yevreyev*, edited by S. Dimanstein (1930). He died in a road accident in Moscow.

BIBLIOGRAPHY: Rejzen, Leksikon, 3 (1929), 518–20; D. Mil, *Pionern in Bund*, 2 vols. (1946–49), index.

[Moshe Mishkinsky]

KOPF, MAXIM (1892–1958), painter. Born in Vienna, he studied art in Prague and Dresden. During World War I, he served in the Austrian army and was severely wounded. In 1922 he had his first exhibition, showing the painting *Pilgrims* (1920). In 1927 he married his partner Mary Durasová but divorced her in 1933. He became the leader of a group of followers of German expressionism, known under the name "Prager Sezession." Like other artists of his time, Kopf flirted with esotericism and mysticism which became obvious in his works with crystalline elements (*Budha*, 1920; *Varieté*, 1920). Akin to Gauguin spiritually and artistically, Kopf traveled through the Pacific Islands in 1925, creating a large number of canvases, especially of Tahiti. The artistic harvest of this trip was shown in a highly successful exhibition in 1927. Later Kopf settled in Paris, and after the fall of France he moved to New York. He married the American journalist and political writer Dorothy Thompson and built his reputation as an artist through many exhibitions. At his death his last painting, a monumental crucifixion, was left unfinished.

ADD. BIBLIOGRAPHY: *Gesamtausstellung von Maxim Kopf. Krasoumná jednota prozechy* (1923); I. Habán (ed.), *Maxim Kopf 1892–1958, Ausst. Kat. Galerie der bildenden Kunst in Cheb* (2002).

[Avigdor Dagan / Sonja Beyer (2nd ed.)]

KOPIT, ARTHUR (1937–), U.S. playwright. Arthur Lee Koenig (his mother, Maxine, was divorced when Arthur was young and married George Kopit, a jewelry salesman) was born in New York City but grew up in an affluent Long Island suburb.

He became excited by theater when he took a modern drama workshop at Harvard and began writing short plays with outlandish titles. In 1959, the summer he graduated with a degree in engineering, he entered a playwriting contest. In five days he wrote a wacky one-act tragicomedy about an elegantly monstrous woman who keeps her husband's coffin at her bedside and her grown son attached to her apron strings at all times. He finished the play, *Oh Dad, Poor Dad, Mamma's Hung You in the Closet and I'm Feelin' So Bad*, while he was in Europe, where he was traveling on a fellowship. He won the $250 first prize and a production of the play at Harvard. *Oh Dad* was staged Off Broadway by Jerome *Robbins in 1960, ran for more than a year, toured for 11 weeks, and ended with a six-week run on Broadway. Kopit received awards for best new play of 1962. His next play, *Indians*, a depiction of American hypocrisy and violence during the 19th century, had scenes from the lives of Sitting Bull and Buffalo Bill Cody juxtaposed in a scathing, symbolic attack on American genocide. It was first produced by the Royal Shakespeare Company in London in 1968. Next came *Wings* (1979), a drama about the recovery of a stroke victim, with innovative staging techniques used to replicate the healing process. In 1984, Kopit's *End of the World* explored the corrupting forces in American life. A playwright becomes a private investigator and exposes the parties responsible for nuclear proliferation. Kopit used black humor to explore this troubling subject and showed how easily even his good characters can be caught up in the momentum toward destruction.

[Stewart Kampel (2nd ed.)]

KOPLIK, HENRY (1858–1927), U.S. pediatrician. Koplik, who was born in New York, became assistant professor of pediatrics at Bellevue Medical College as well as consulting physician to other New York hospitals. Koplik is known as the discoverer of the diagnostic spots of measles, known as "Koplik's spots," which are bluish-white spots surrounded by red areas found inside the mouth. He founded the first milk depot in the United States which supplied pasteurized milk free of charge to the needy. He wrote *Diseases of Infancy and Childhood* (1902) and was the author of several other publications on pediatrics.

BIBLIOGRAPHY: S.R. Kagan, *Jewish Medicine* (1952), 361.

[Suessmann Muntner]

KOPPEL, HEINZ (1919–1980), painter. Koppel was born in Berlin, and went to London at the age of 16. He studied under the painter Martin *Bloch, who remained the principal influence in his work. After working intermittently in Czechoslovakia, Italy, and Belgium, he taught in art schools in England and in Wales, where he lived from 1944 to 1956 and again later in his life. His depictions of the Welsh landscape have a strongly mystical note, bordering on fantasy. German expressionism played its part in Koppel's art but his work, notably portraiture, is marked by great delicacy. His recent work includes experiments with different material, such as fiber glass and resin. He died in Dyfed.

[Charles Samuel Spencer]

KOPPEL, TED (1940–), U.S. television journalist. Koppel was born in Lancashire, England, where his parents fled to escape from the Nazis. His father, Erwin Koppel, was the owner of a major tire factory in Germany and immigrated to England in 1936. His mother followed two years later. Koppel spent his first 13 years in England, where he attended boarding school. He and his family moved to the United States and he graduated from Syracuse University with a bachelor's degree and from Stanford University with a master's in mass communications research and political science. Koppel started working in journalism at a New York City radio station and joined the American Broadcasting Company news division as a full-time general assignment correspondent at the age of 23. In a four-decade career at ABC, Koppel had a major reporting role in every presidential campaign beginning in 1964. In 1968 he became Miami bureau chief, where his assignments included covering Latin America. From 1969 to 1971, as Hong Kong bureau chief, he covered stories from Vietnam to Australia. He served as ABC's chief diplomatic correspondent from 1971 to 1980, a period that included traveling more than a quarter of a million miles for coverage of Secretary of State Henry A. *Kissinger's "shuttle diplomacy." During the time he was on the State Department beat, Koppel co-wrote the bestseller *In the National Interest*, with his friend and colleague, Marvin *Kalb, then with CBS News.

Koppel came to national prominence with the seizure by Iranians of the American Embassy in Teheran in 1979. Four days after the takeover, ABC News aired a program called *The Iran Crisis: America Held Hostage*. The president of the network decided that the program would continue until the hostage crisis was over, and that it would eventually become a regular late-night newscast. After about five months, *The Iran Crisis* became *Nightline*, and Koppel, who had anchored the show several times, became the permanent anchor. From 1980 onward, it was difficult to separate Koppel from the show. It was television's first late-night network news program, and Koppel was also the program's managing editor. On the air, Koppel interviewed key political figures and others who were working to free the hostages, and broadcast biographies of those in custody in Iran. Over the years, Koppel won every major broadcasting award, including 37 Emmy awards, six George Foster Peabody awards, ten duPont-Columbia awards, nine Overseas Press Club awards and others. A member of the Broadcasting Hall of Fame, Koppel in 1994 was named a Chevalier de l'Ordre des Arts et des Lettres by the Republic of France. He speaks fluent German, Russian, and French. In 2003 Koppel was embedded with the U.S. Army's 3d Infantry Division as it marched toward Baghdad during the U.S. invasion of Iraq. Koppel, a feisty interviewer, made news with occasionally blunt comments delivered off the air. *Nightline* earned its highest ratings for a broadcast in 1987 featuring the scandalized television evangelist Jim Bakker and his wife Tammy Faye Bakker. In 1988 Koppel went to the Middle East to report on Arab-Israeli problems and held a town meeting attended by hundreds of Israeli and Arab citizens. Koppel is also the author, with Kyle Gibson, of *Nightline: History in the Making and the Making of Television* (1996). According to one website, he considers his family Torah his most prized possession. His daughter Andrea is a reporter with CNN.

[Stewart Kampel (2nd ed.)]

KOPPELMAN, JACOB BEN SAMUEL BUNIM (1555–1594), talmudic scholar distinguished for his broad erudition and interest in secular sciences. Jacob was born in Freiburg and studied under Mordecai *Jaffe. Early in his life he embarked upon mathematical and astronomical studies, in addition to intensive occupation with traditional Jewish learning. He is the author of *Omek Halakhah* (Cracow, 1593). In it he elucidates the laws appertaining to *Kilayim, Eruvin*, etc., with the aid of diagrams and models; discusses the talmudic references to mathematics, botany, engineering, and geography; establishes the various weights and measures of the Talmud; and draws the site of the Temple, the candelabrum, the table of showbread, revealing considerable knowledge in all of these fields. On the title page of *Ohel Ya'akov* (Freiburg, 1584), a commentary on Joseph *Albo's *Ikkarim* dealing with the elucidation of difficult passages compiled by Jacob in Frankfurt in 1583, he is described as "the encyclopedic scholar and divine philosopher." Jacob also translated into rhymed Yiddish the Targum of the five scrolls, the *Targum Sheni* to Esther (Freiburg, c. 1584), and the *Mishlei Shu'alim* of *Berechiah ha-Nakdan (*ibid.*, 1588; Vilna, 1825).

BIBLIOGRAPHY: Ḥ.N. Dembitzer, *Kelilat Yofi*, 2 (1893), 87b; Fuenn, Keneset, 540; E. Schulmann, *Sefat Yehudit-Ashkenazit ve-Sifrutah* (1903), 31–34.

[Abram Juda Goldrat]

KOPPETT, LEONARD (Kopeliovitch; 1923–2003), U.S. sportswriter; only writer elected to both the baseball and basketball halls of fame. Born in Moscow, Koppett moved to New York at age five, living a block from Yankee Stadium. The family then moved to Brooklyn, where Koppett went to high school at Poly Prep, and then to Columbia College, where he wrote for the undergraduate *Columbia Spectator*. Through his job at the university's publicity office, Koppett eventually became the campus sports correspondent for *The New York Times* and the *New York Herald Tribune*. After graduating in 1944 and serving in the Army, Koppett landed his first full-time job with the *Tribune*, where he worked from 1948 to 1954, and subsequently at the *New York Post* from 1954 to 1963 and *The New York Times* beginning in 1963, covering the Yankees, the Giants, the Dodgers, the Knicks, and the Mets. In 1973, he became the *Times*' first West Coast sports correspondent, but tired of traveling, he quit in 1978. A year later, he was hired by *The Peninsula Times Tribune* of Palo Alto, California, serving as sports editor, editor in chief, and editor emeritus until the paper folded in 1993. He also wrote a general-interest column, which fed perfectly into his encyclopedic knowledge of astronomy, history, literature, music, art, theater, language, geography, culture as well as sports. Koppett, or "Koppy" as he was known, freelanced extensively, writing a column for *The Sporting News* from 1965 to 1984 as well as for *The Oakland Tribune, San Francisco Chronicle, San Mateo County Times*, and later *The Seattle Post-Intelligencer*. He also wrote for numerous national magazines, such as *Sports Illustrated*, the *Saturday Evening Post, Penthouse*, and several specialty sports and airline magazines. Koppett was acknowledged for his analytical approach to sports that went beyond the frenzy of the moment, and for exploring issues that were not confined to events on the field. Koppett was the author of 16 books, most notably *The Thinking Man's Guide to Baseball* (1967), a benchmark work that introduced to the general public the basic concepts of looking at baseball performance in a new way. He also authored *24 Seconds to Shoot: An Informal History of the National Basketball Association*, (1968), *The New York Times Guide to Spectator Sports* (1971), *The Essence of the Game Is Deception: Thinking About Basketball* (1973), *Sports Illusion, Sports Reality: A Reporter's View of Sports, Journalism, and Society* (1981), *The Man in the Dugout: Baseball's Top Managers and How They Got That Way* (1993), *Koppett's Concise History of Major League Baseball* (1998), and *The Rise and Fall of the Press Box* (2003). Koppett was elected to the writers' wing of the Baseball Hall of Fame in 1992 and the Basketball Hall of Fame in 1994.

[Elli Wohlgelernter (2nd ed.)]

KOPPLE, BARBARA (1946–), U.S. director-producer. Born in New York City and raised in Scarsdale, New York, Kopple graduated with a degree in psychology from Northeastern University. She began her career by working for documentary filmmakers Albert and David Maysles as an assistant editor. She then co-directed *Winter Soldier* (1972), a documentary about U.S. soldiers in Vietnam. Her first solo project, *Harlan County, U.S.A.* (1976), which documented a 1973 coal miners' strike against the Eastover Mining Company in Harlan County, Kentucky, earned Kopple an Academy Award for a feature-length documentary. In 1981, she directed the made-for-television film *Keeping On*, a fictional story built around a labor dispute in a Southern town. Kopple's *American Dream* (1991), the story of the Hormel Food strike in the mid-1980s, earned her a second Academy Award and a Directors Guild of America award for outstanding directorial achievement in documentaries. In 1993, she received her second Directors Guild of America award for *Fallen Champ: The Untold Story of Mike Tyson*. For *Wild Man Blues* (1997), Kopple followed Woody *Allen around Europe as he toured with his jazz band. In 1998, she released *Woodstock '94* and followed up with *My Generation* (2000), a documentary that explored the differences and similarities of the youth cultures present at the different Woodstock concerts. In 2005, Kopple's *Bearing Witness* looked at female journalists working in combat zones.

[Adam Wills (2nd ed.)]

KOPPLEMANN, HERMAN PAUL (1880–1957), U.S. politician and civic leader. Kopplemann, who was born in Odessa,

Russia, was brought to Hartford, Connecticut, by his parents at the age of two. He established the H.P. Kopplemann Agency for the distribution of newspapers and magazines, which subsequently became the largest in the state. In 1904 Kopplemann was elected to the Hartford City Council where he served four consecutive terms. He was elected to the Connecticut House of Representatives in 1913 and to the Connecticut Senate in 1917. From 1929 to 1957 he served as a member of the Metropolitan District Commission. In 1932 Kopplemann became the first Jew to be elected to Congress from Connecticut. He served four terms and consistently supported the New Deal. Kopplemann was also extremely active in Jewish affairs, and his posts included chairman of the United Jewish Appeal; vice president of the United Synagogue of America; and secretary of the Board of Overseers of the Jewish Theological Seminary of America.

[Morris Silverman]

KOPS, BERNARD (1926–), English playwright, born in the East End of London. His searingly frank autobiography, *The World Is a Wedding* (1963), portrays his early home life. After World War II, he held a succession of menial jobs in factories and hotels and made first, tentative attempts at acting and writing songs and verse. Under the influence of the postwar Bohemian society of Soho, he finally began his literary career. He received an award from the Arts Council for his first notable play, *The Hamlet of Stepney Green* (1959). Often grouped with the "angry young men" in English literature after World War II, Kops had a special lyrical pathos of his own, as in his portrayal of the dying fathers who are the central characters in two of his best-known works, *Hamlet*... and *Yes from No-Man's Land* (1965). In the latter, a novel describing a London Jewish family with East End roots, virtually the entire gamut of modern Jewish experience is touched upon, from memories of the Holocaust and personal involvement with Israel, to intermarriage and alienation. His *By the Waters of Whitechapel* (1969) had its setting in the residual Jewish community of London's East End. Kops was resident dramatist at the Old Vic in 1958. His plays include *The Dream of Peter Mann* (1960) and *Enter Solly Gold* (1961). Both his style and his social philosophy are reminiscent of Berthold Brecht, and like him, he is given to fantasy and extravagance. Kops's poetry includes the volume *Erica, Let Me Read You Something* (1967). In addition to *The World Is a Wedding,* he wrote several other volumes of autobiography, including *Shalom Bomb* (2000).

[Shulamit Nardi]

KOPYTMAN, MARK RUVIMOVICH (1929–), Israeli composer, teacher and musicologist. Kopytman was born in Kamenets-Podolski, U.S.S.R. He graduated from the Chernovtsy Music School in piano in 1950 and from the Lvov Conservatory in composition and music theory in 1955. He received a Ph.D. from the Moscow Conservatory (where he studied from 1956 to 1958 in the class of Professor S. Bogatyrev) and also graduated from the Chernovtsy Medical Institute in 1952. He taught composition and music theory at the Alma Ata Conservatory from 1958 to 1963 and the Kishinev Institute of Arts from 1963 to 1972. In 1972 he immigrated to Israel and became a professor at the Rubin Academy of Music and the Hebrew University, both in Jerusalem. His master classes, as well as his participation in composers' competition juries, are highly esteemed all over the world. His honors include the Koussevitsky International Record Critics Award (1986) and the ACUM lifetime achievement award from Israel (1992).

Kopytman's early works show the influence of Prokofiev and Bartok (his symphony of 1956; his choral cycle *Distance beyond Distance* based on the poem by Tvardovsky, 1960; his vocal cycle based on the poems of S. Kaputikyan (*Songs of Anguished Love*, 1964)). Kopytman's interest in the folklore of various peoples was reflected in his first quartet of 1962, where he used themes from Kazakh folklore, while Moldavian folklore and traditional images of Moldavia are reflected in his 1965 *Songs of the Woods* oratorio with text by V. Teleuke, and his opera *Casa Mare* (1966), based on the play by I. Drutze. Kopytman's second quartet (1966) and the re-orchestration for cello and string orchestra (1981) which he entitled *Kaddish* can be considered in some ways close to the "Jewish line" in the work of Shostakovich.

From the late 1960s Kopytman began to use contemporary avant-garde means of composition (aleatory music, sonoristics, etc.), employing them creatively and sometimes combining them with traditional elements (the long development of melodic lines, polytonality, with free use of Eastern, including Jewish, folklore). Kopytman's works from the 1970s on were characterized by the use of heterophony, a blending of some simultaneously sounding layers, which are the variants of the same melodic line. Such musical textures characterize Kopytman's *October Sun* (1974) for mezzo-soprano, piano, flute, and percussion with text by the Israeli poet Yehuda *Amichai about the tragedy and heroism of the Yom Kippur War; *Rotations*, a piece for mezzo-soprano and orchestra (1979); *Cantus II* (1980) for string trio; *Memory* (1982) for singer and orchestra; *Letters of Creation* (1986) for voice and string orchestra, and so on. In many of his works since the 1980s, the deeply imbued stratum of Jewish historical memory is present. His chamber opera *Susskind von Trimberg* (1982–83), with libretto by Recha *Freier (premiered in Jerusalem in 1983), is based on the tragic story a of Jewish musician in medieval Germany. Usually, Kopytman preferred to avoid citations while revealing the national nature of a piece first of all through its melodic atmosphere. However, in *Memory*, Kopytman introduced a Yemenite Jewish melody, being inspired by the voice and performance of the authentic Yemenite singer Gila Bachari. In his recent vocal cycle *If There Are Seven Heavens* (2001, on the metaphoric text of E. Jabes), the composer touched on the subject of the Holocaust. Among Kopytman's works on music theory are *Muzykal'nye formy i zhanry* ("Musical Forms and Genres," 1959); O *polifonii* ("On Polyphony," 1961); and *Khorovoe pis' mo* ("Choral Composition," 1971).

ADD. BIBLIOGRAPHY: NG[2]; MGG[2]; Y. Kreinin (ed.), *Mark Kopytman: Voices of Memories,* Essays and Dialogues (2004).

[Yaakov Soroker / *The Shorter Jewish Encylopaedia in Russian* / Yulia Kreinin (2nd ed.)]

KORAH (Heb. קֹרַח), son of Izhar, son of Kohath, son of Levi. Korah is the central figure in the story of the revolt against the authority and status of Moses at the time of the wanderings in the wilderness (Num. 16). According to the story in its present form, *Dathan and Abiram of the tribe of Reuben, together with 250 chieftains of the community, also took part in this revolt. Behind the uprising were Korah's complaint against the religious authority of Moses and Aaron, and the complaint of Dathan and Abiram against the leadership of Moses in general, charging that he had brought Israel out of Egypt to lord it over them and to have them die in the wilderness. In punishment for their rebellion, Korah, together with Dathan and Abiram and their people, was swallowed up by the earth, while the 250 chieftains, whose complaint against Moses and Aaron was in the domain of holy privileges, were consumed by the fire of the Lord after they had offered incense before him.

The story is referred to with minor or major variations in other passages (Num. 26:9–10; 27:3; Deut. 11:6; Ps. 106:16–18). Our present text offers what Levine calls "braided" accounts of strife in the wilderness. At the very least we can distinguish two literary strata, each with its own theme. The JE account did not involve Levites at all, but told of a rebellion against Moses led by the Reubenites Dathan and Abiram. The P(riestly) writers, who had access to JE, added the element of a protest led by the Levite Korah against the exclusive right of the Levite line of Aaron to the priesthood (Levine). As is true of most of the Torah's narratives, the stories here are given a fictitious setting in the desert prior to the rise of Israel in its own land. However, the actual historical circumstances that underlie them are to be sought in later periods. The Reubenite element in the story is probably related to territorial disputes in Transjordan in the pre-monarchic or early monarchic period. The other element is the quarrel of Korah the Levite with the sacral status of Moses and Aaron the priest. The background would be the consolidation of the temple hierarchy during the period of the Second Temple. According to the Torah (Ex. 28:1; P), Aaron and his descendants were first chosen for the priesthood during the wanderings in the wilderness. Yet scholars have long observed that Aaron is never identified as a priest in the prophetic literature of the pre-exilic period. Ezekiel, a priest and prophet of the sixth century, devotes much attention to priestly conduct and ritual. Yet he does not mention Aaron, but considers the legitimate priestly line to run through Zadok (Ezek. 44:15–16). Outside of the Torah, it is only in the books Ezra-Nehemiah and Chronicles, universally dated to the Persian period (539–331), that the Aaronide priesthood is depicted as the only legitimate priestly line. This is in harmony with the excavations at Arad, which unearthed a mention of *bny qrḥ*, "sons of Korah," who were apparently cultic personnel by the eighth century B.C.E., if not earlier. It is to these "sons of Korah" that many biblical Psalms (below) are ascribed. During the first half of the first millennium B.C.E. the existence of two distinct Israelite states with numerous shrines in each meant that no single family or clan had a monopoly on the priesthood. In contrast, the temple rebuilt in Yehud, the former Judah, in the late sixth century adhered to the principle of centralization associated with the reform of *Josiah in being the single sacrificial temple in the land. The result was that far fewer people could become priests. The restriction of the priesthood to the "sons of Aaron" must have resulted from a compromise among many competing factions. One of the factions unhappy with the compromise was the "sons of Korah," who were being demoted to "performing the sanctuary's labor" (Num. 16:9–10). The Torah's story of their unsuccessful challenge to Aaron, which resulted in their being swallowed up without a trace (Num. 16: 31–5), was meant to illustrate the fate in store for all who would challenge the new order (Num. 17:5).

The Bible provides other notices about the status of the sons of Korah as a levitical family in the census list of Numbers 26:58, and in the detailed genealogies in, e.g., Exodus 6:24. That the Korahites, or part of them, functioned as choristers in the Temple, is clear from the heading "For the sons of Korah" found at the beginning of many Psalms (42–49; 84–85; 87–88). According to the genealogical list of the levites in I Chronicles 6, the chorister Heman, too, is connected with Korah (6:18–23). With this must be associated the report of II Chronicles 20:19 concerning levitical *Kohathite families and the Korahites who rose to praise the Lord, i.e., who acted as choristers. At the same time, Chronicles numbers the Korahites among the families of gatekeepers (I Chron. 9:19ff.; 26:1ff.). According to I Chronicles 9 they were also in charge of the treasures and vessels, of making the flat cakes, and of carrying out other similar functions. Although the simplest reading of Numbers 16:31–4 indicates that Korah left no survivors, the author of Numbers 26:11 wrote that "the sons of Korah did not die," apparently to account for the Psalms of the sons of Korah, and other cultic traditions about them.

[Jacob Liver / S. David Sperling (2nd ed.)]

In the Aggadah

Many reasons are given for Korah's opposition to Moses and Aaron. In Egypt, Korah had been Pharoah's treasurer, and he amassed so much wealth that 300 mules were required to carry the keys of his treasures; his pride in his wealth brought about his subsequent downfall (Pes. 119a). He resented Moses for appointing his cousin (Elizaphan b. Uzziel; Num. 3:30) as head of the levite division of Kohathites, maintaining that this office belonged to him (Num. R. 18:2). He did not doubt the ultimate success of his challenge since he foresaw that Samuel, whose importance would equal that of Moses and Aaron (cf. Ps. 99:6), would descend from him, and felt that God would not permit the forefather of such a man to perish (Num. R. 18:8). Korah's wife also encouraged him in his insurrection (Num. R. 18:4). Korah is regarded as the arch-detractor of the Torah.

He negated its laws and sought to demonstrate the injustice of the laws instituted by Moses by telling the following tale to the masses: A widow, the mother of two young daughters, started to plow her solitary field whose yield was just sufficient to keep body and soul together. Moses told her that it was forbidden to plow with an ox and an ass together (Deut. 22:10). When she began to sow, Moses told her not to sow with diverse seeds (Lev. 19:19). When the first fruits appeared, Moses demanded that she give them to the priests (Deut. 26:2), and when she began to harvest the field, Moses reminded her to leave the gleanings and the corner of the field for the poor (Lev. 23:22). When she was about to thresh the grain, Moses demanded the separations for the priests and levites (Num. 18:8, 21). Unable to maintain herself from the field under such conditions, she sold it and purchased ewes. Once again, she knew no peace. When the firstling of the sheep was born, Aaron demanded it for the priests (Num. 18:15). When she began to shear the sheep, Aaron claimed the initial shearings (Deut. 18:4). The widow thereupon decided to slaughter the sheep. This time Aaron came for the priestly portions (Deut. 18:3). The widow then vehemently cried out: "If you persist in your demands, I consecrate the flesh to the Lord." "If so," Aaron replied, "the whole belongs to me" (Num. 18:14). Aaron then took away all the meat, leaving the widow and her two daughters entirely unprovided for (Mid. Ps. to 1:15).

Korah tried to make Moses appear ridiculous in the eyes of the people. He appeared with his 250 followers, all dressed in garments of *tekhelet*, requesting a ruling from Moses on whether they were obliged to attach fringes to such garments. On Moses' affirmative response, Korah mocked him by declaring, "If one fringe of blue suffices to fulfill this commandment when the garment is entirely white, should not a garment which is entirely blue meet the requirements of this commandment even without the addition of fringes." Likewise, they asked Moses about the necessity of affixing a *mezuzah* to the entrance of a house filled with sacred scrolls. Once again they decried Moses' answer that such a doorpost also needed a *mezuzah* despite the fact that its passages are included in the scrolls (TJ, Sanh. 10:1, 27d–28a). In this and similar *aggadot*, Korah is presented as the prototype of the opponents of the Torah and of the authority of the rabbis.

Moses desperately attempted to appease Korah and his followers, but they insisted on opposing him (Num. R. 18:4). Finally, Moses had to make a public stand against them, realizing that the integrity of the Torah was at stake when they proclaimed that "the Torah was not given by God, Moses is not a prophet, and Aaron is not the high priest" (TJ, Sanh. 10:1, 28a). At the time of Korah's engulfment, the earth became like a funnel, and everything that belonged to him, even clothes at the laundry and needles borrowed by neighbors, rolled until they fell into the gap (Num. R. 18:13). Korah himself suffered the double punishment of being burned and swallowed up alive by the earth (Num. R. 18:19), while his repentant sons were spared and became the progenitors of Samuel (Num. R. 18:8). Later, a place was set aside for them in the netherworld, where they sit and sing praises to God (Sanh. 110a). Rabbah b. Bar Ḥuna related that he saw the place of Korah's engulfment and heard voices crying, "Moses and his Torah are true, and we are liars" (BB 74a).

[Aaron Rothkoff]

In Islam

One of the world's wealthiest men, he prided himself on his wealth and, therefore, the earth swallowed him up (Sura 28:76–82). Along with Firʿawn (*Pharaoh) and *Hāmān, Qārūn (Korah) ranks among the proud (29:38), and with them he proposed the counsel to kill all the sons born to the people of Israel (40:25). Muslim legend emphasized the familial relationship between Qārūn and Moses (Ar. Mūsā). The jealousy of the former increased as the greatness of Moses grew. One of the explanations of the source of his treasures is that his wife was the sister of Moses, who taught her the art of "alchemy," and that Qārūn, in turn, learned the method of making and amassing gold from her. Qārūn built one house after another and constructed the walls of his palace from silver and gold (see bibl. Thaʿlabī, Kisāʾī). These and similar tales come from Jewish legends which spoke of the fabulous "treasures of Korah." The stories of the haughtiness of Qārūn and his associates also are derived from Jewish sources.

[Haïm Z'ew Hirschberg]

BIBLIOGRAPHY: J.W. Rothstein and J. Hänel, *Kommentar zum ersten Buch der Chronik* (1927), 174ff., 462ff.; K. Möhlenbrink, in: ZAW, 52 (1934), 188ff., 191ff.; H.S. Nyberg, in: *Svensk Exegetisk Årsbok*, 12 (1947), 214–36; M.Z. Segal, *Masoret u-Vikkoret* (1957), 92–95; J. Liver, in: *Scripta Hierosolymitana*, 8 (1961), 189–217; idem, *Perakim be-Toledot ha-Kehunnah ve-ha-Leviyyah* (1968); S. Lehming, in: ZAW, 74 (1962), 291–321; S. Mowinckel, *The Psalms in Israel's Worship*, 2 (1962), 82, 95ff. IN THE AGGADAH: Ginzberg, Legends, 3 (1947[3]), 286–303; 6 (1946[3]), 99–105. IN ISLAM: Tabari, *Taʾrīkh*, 1 (1357 A.H.), 312–9; idem, *Tafsīr*, 20 (1328 A.H.), 67; Thaʿlabī, *Qiṣaṣ* (1356 A.H.), 179–82; Kisāʾī, *Qiṣaṣ* (1356 A.H.), 229–30; H. Speyer, *Die biblischen Erzaehlungen im Qoran* (1931 repr. 1961), 342–4. **ADD. BIBLIOGRAPHY:** R. Hutton, in: ABD, 4:100–1; B. Levine, *Numbers 1–20* (AB; 1993), 405–32; idem, *Numbers 21–26* (AB; 2000), 318; S. Japhet, *I & II Chronicles* (1993), 151–56; S.D. Sperling, *The Original Torah* (1998), 112–19. IN ISLAM: "Kārūn," in: EIS[2] 4 (1978), 673, incl. bibl.

KORAḤ, AMRAM BEN YIḤYE (1871–1953), writer and leader of Yemenite Jewry. Born in *Sanʿa, he immigrated to Israel in 1950 and died in Jerusalem. His father, R. Yiḥye *Koraḥ (1840–1881), was – although a kabbalist – the first enlightened Jewish scholar in *Yemen whose works took into account rationalist considerations. They reflect on one hand the wish to improve the social and spiritual conditions of the Jewish community in Yemen, and on the other hand the encounter with modern rabbinical and scholarly works in order to prove the correctness and genuineness of Yemenite traditions. On his death, the young son Amram was maintained by R. Yiḥye Qāfiḥ, his father's student and young colleague. His education by R. Qāfiḥ is well documented in his works, strongly colored with the latter's enlightened attitude toward Jewish studies, both religious and secular. However, when the Jewish community was thrown into a bitter disagreement about *Kabbalah, he sided with R. Yiḥye Yiẓḥak, the leader of the followers of the Kabbalah and the main opponent of R. Qāfiḥ. Owing to his excellent knowledge of Arabic, an indispensable component in the education of R. Qāfiḥ's students, he acted as secretary to the *bet din* of San'a and took care of inheritances, community funds, taxes, and charitable trusts, as well as accounts of private firms and businessmen, and functioned as the community scribe in the correspondence with Muslim authorities. From 1905 he was part of the communal leadership of the Jewish community of Sanʿa and after the death of R. Yiḥye Abyaḍ (1939?) he was nominated as chief rabbi of the Jews of Yemen, a position he held until his immigration to the State of Israel. His best-known work is *Saʿarat Teman* ("The Tempest of Yemen," 1954), the first to bring a comprehensive history and description of the ways of life of the Jews of Yemen, based on both Jewish and Muslim sources (books and documents). In this book he included a zealous Zionist manifesto expressing the ultimate hope of the State of Israel to be the National Home of the Jewish people. Another significant work of his is *Alamot Shir* (1964), the first scholarly compilation of the Yemenite *Diwān* including some 200 poems, mostly by Yosef ben Israel and Shalom Shabazī, accompanied with outstanding brief and simple exegesis. In addition, he wrote *Neveh Shalom*, establishing and explaining the correct version of *Saadiah Gaon's *Tafsīr* ("exegesis") to the Bible.

BIBLIOGRAPHY: A. Qoraḥ, *Saʿarat Teiman* (1954); Y. Tobi, in: *Ha-Ivrit ve-Aḥyoteha*, 2–3 (2002/3), 205–22; N. Ilan, in: TEMA, 8 (2004), 131–48.

[Yosef Tobi (2nd ed.)]

KORAḤ, ḤAYYIM BEN JOSEPH (1824–1914), Yemenite scholar, preacher, and kabbalist, born in *Sanʿa. Many of the Yemenite scholars were among the disciples of his *bet ha-midrash*. Queries in the fields of Torah and *halakhah* were addressed to him from all parts of Yemen. His sermons – a combination of Torah and *halakhah*, Midrash, and Kabbalah – enthralled the masses. He was deeply involved in mystical studies, and acts and miracles wrought by practical Kabbalah are attributed to him. He left three works extant in manuscript, one of which is a collection of responsa arranged according to the order of the Shulḥan Arukh.

BIBLIOGRAPHY: J. Kafaḥ, in: *Ha-Mesillah*, 2 (1957), 3–5; A. Koraḥ, *Sa'arat Teiman* (1954), 45f.

[Yehuda Ratzaby]

KORAḤ, SHALOM BEN YIḤYE (1873–1953), author and educator, from *Sanʿa, *Yemen. By profession Koraḥ was a copyist of books and a talented teacher who taught many pupils. An active participant in the communal life of Sanʿa and respected by the community, he acted as the community secretary and drafted the texts of many letters in its name, many of them kept in public archives in Israel, such as the Central Zionist Archives, as well as in private collections and which are a very helpful source for the 20th century history of the Jews of Yemen. He was considered the spokesman and writer of the Dor Deʿah movement, with two of which most distinguished leaders he studied: R. Yiḥye Qāfiḥ and R. Yiḥye Abyaḍ. In latter years he himself became a prominent leader of this movement. One of his works, *Iggeret Bokhim* (1963), is a monograph on R. Yiḥye Qāfiḥ and the eulogies which were delivered upon his death. Another book reflecting his tendency to historical documentation of his Jewish Yemenite community is *Rogez Teman*, separate chapters on the modern history of the Jews of Yemen, most of them published after his death. One of his most important works is *Tiklāl Qadmonim* (The Prayer Book of the First Generation), in which he documented the ancient version of the Yemenite rite in liturgy and everything connected to it in an annual and life cycles. He wrote the book in 1938, when still in Yemen, responding to a request of Yosef Ḥubārah, a Yemenite activist who had already immigrated to the Holy Land. This *Tiklāl*, published in a facsimile edition with introductory articles by some scholars (1964), is based on ancient copies of the Yemenite *Tiklāls* and constitutes trustworthy evidence for the old liturgical and halakhic Yemenite traditions. The remainder of his works, including many poems, is extant in manuscript and part of it has been recently published by his grandson R. Pinḥas Qorah. Near the end of his life he went to Israel in the mass immigration from Yemen. His son R. Yosef (1913–1990), who was counted with the leaders of the Jewish Sanʿani community in the 1940s, was a teacher in the modern girls' school in Sanʿa and took part in the organization of the mass *aliyah* to the State of Israel. R. Yosef continued his activity in Israel in education, especially to transmit the original Yemenite traditions to the young Yemenite generation, as well as his literary work.

BIBLIOGRAPHY: Y. Qāfih, *Ketavim*, 2 (1989), 1007–14; Moshe Gavra, *Encyclopedia of the Scholars of Yemenite Jewry* (Heb., 2001), 566–67; J.L. Naḥum, *Mi-Sefunot Yehudei Teman* (1962), 251.

[Yosef Tobi (2nd ed.)]

KORAḤ, YIḤYE (Yaḥya) BEN SHALOM (1840–1881), scholar and kabbalist, in *San'a, *Yemen. Koraḥ's works are concerned with *masorah*, the Targum Onkelos, grammar, explanations on the Pentateuch, and exegesis on Yemenite poetry. In two fields, those of Targum Onkelos and Yemenite poetry, he was a pioneer researcher in Yemen. His works are distinguished by their sharp-wittedness and originality. The most important of them is *Marpe Lashon*, a linguistic and textual study on the Targum Onkelos of the Pentateuch, which is based on ancient Yemenite manuscripts (published in *Keter Torah*, 1960). An essay entitled *"Berit ha-Lashon"* ("Covenant of the Tongue") precedes the work and deals with the Yemenite Jewish pronunciation and the principles of the upper (Babylonian) vocalization. His work on the Pentateuch, *Maskil Doresh* (1964), consists of new commentaries (*ḥiddushim*), explanations of words in the way of *notarikon* and mystic style.

BIBLIOGRAPHY: S. Koraḥ, in Y. Koraḥ, *Maskil Doresh* (1964), 7–19; Ratzaby, in: KS, 28 (1952–53), 266, 401, 404.

KORAN (Ar. **Qur'ān**), the holy scripture of the Muslims. The name signifies "recital," "recitation." Islamic tradition holds that the Koran was sent down to *Muhammad with the angel Gabriel. Gabriel revealed the book to Muhammad in an ongoing process which lasted 20 years: It began in Mecca when Muhammad was 40, and went on for 10 years till Muhammad's emigration to *Medina, where Gabriel continued the process of revelation till Muhammad's death at the age of 60.

Chronology of Revelation

Muslim tradition is able to tell when each passage of the Koran was revealed, and in present day printed copies of the Koran one finds at the heading of each chapter (in Arabic: *sūra*) details telling whether the chapter was revealed in Mecca (before the *hijra*) or in Medina. However, in many "Meccan" chapters, "Medinan" verses are singled out, and vice versa. The overall framework was nevertheless adopted by modern scholars who reconstructed the history of revelation according to Islamic tradition (especially Th. Nöldeke and many of his followers). There have been also more skeptical scholars who rejected the traditional views concerning the authenticity of the Koran as a collection of Muhammad's own prophecies. They were not even sure that the Koran originated in *Arabia and not in *Syria. Some of them suggested that the Koran was created decades after Muhammad, while others held that this scripture contains passages which predate Muhammad (for details see G. Böwering s.v. "Chronology and the Koran," *The Encyclopaedia of the Koran* (2001). Muslim tradition tells us also how the Koran was written down by companions of the prophet and how the entire canon was compiled decades after Muhammad's death from the different fragments preserved by the companions. Tradition also contains reports about variant readings (in Arabic: *qirā'āt*) of the Koran prevalent in the different regions of the Islamic world. The standard version today is based on the reading of Ḥafṣ from 'Āṣim (d. 745).

The collection is not arranged according to contents or literary forms, nor according to the time in which the separate parts were revealed. It rather consists of 114 chapters which generally follow one another according to the principle of decreasing length, but with many exceptions to the rule. The whole book is composed in rhymed prose.

The Koran as Scripture among Scriptures

According to koranic terminology, revelation took place in a process of sending down (Arabic: *anzala*) messages. The sending down of the *kitāb*, i.e., its revelation, is described as part of a universal process that has included the revelation of other scriptures, namely "the Torah and the Gospel" (Koran 3:3–4). This implies that all monotheistic scriptures are perceived as representing the same divine revelation. All revealed scriptures originate in the pre-existent divine Book in which the pre-ordained Law of God has been recorded. This is, at any rate, how Muslim exegetes explain the locution "Book of God" in Koran 33:6 (also Koran 30:56), which, they hold, is identical with the "Guarded Tablet" (*lawḥ maḥfūẓ*) mentioned in Koran 85:22. The Koran is said to have formed part of this Tablet (Koran 85:21), so that this revealed scripture is actually a reflection of a celestial universal text. The original celestial version of all scriptures is *umm al-kitāb* ("mother of the Book") mentioned in Koran 43:4. Because all books come from the same celestial origin, they share the same message, and therefore Muhammad's own revealed scripture (= the Koran) is perceived as "verifying" (*muṣaddiq*) what was revealed before it (e.g., Koran 3:3–4).

One substantial difference between Muhammad's *kitāb* and previous ones is the language. Since Muhammad's audience is Arabian, the language of his *kitāb* must be Arabic, but it remains nonetheless "verifying" with respect to the previous *kitābs* (Koran 46:12).

Monotheism

The main purpose of Muhammad's prophetic mission is to spread monotheism among the polytheists (Arabic: *mushrikūn*). The Arab polytheists are accused of worshipping idols whom they consider God's partners, or even His offspring, as is the case with the three Goddesses, Allāt, Manāt, and al-'Uzzā (Koran 53:19–20). The one God is Allāh who is also named *rabb* ("Lord"), or *raḥmān* ("compassionate"). Koranic polemics against polytheism include not only Arabs worshipping idols but also Jews who believe that 'Uzayr (Ezra) was the son of God and Christians who believe that Jesus was His son (Koran 9:30).

The Prophets

Just as the Koran sees itself as a scripture among scriptures, the prophet Muhammad is seen as the final link in the universal line of prophethood ("Seal of the Prophets" (Koran 33:40)). God started sending prophets after humankind became separated, when the initial state of righteousness was replaced by moral corruption. This is at least how the exegetes explain Koran 2:213 in which it is stated: "The people were (united in) one nation (*umma wāḥida*), then (they became divided, and) God sent the prophets to bear good tidings and to warn...." The prophets represent a divinely chosen pedigree (Koran 3:33–34), and their divine election provides them with abilities not shared by ordinary humans. They possess knowledge of the unseen (Koran 72:26–27; 3:179), and are immune to misbehavior of any kind (3:161). Some prophets possess unique traits that mark their singular status among the rest of the prophets. *Abraham is described in Koran 4:125 as one whom God took as a friend (*khalīl*). *Moses is described as pure (*mukhlaṣ*) (Koran 19:51), and as one whom God brought near in communion (*najiyyan*) (Koran 19:52), and with whom God spoke (*kallama*) (Koran 4:164). The prophets are sent each to his own nation (Koran 10:47; 16:36), preaching to them in their own language (Koran 14:4). This is an appropriate precedent for Muhammad, the Arabian prophet who has brought to his nation an Arabic Koran (e.g., Koran 12:2). But unlike the previous prophets, Muhammad appears in some other passages as a universal prophet whose mission goes beyond ethnic boundaries and encompasses all humankind (Koran 4:79;

21:107) as well as the jinn (Koran 46:30). Apart from general declarations about the prophets, the Koran provides stories about individual ones. Many of the stories draw on biblical themes. Some stories appear in a condensed form, other stories, such as those of Abraham, Moses, and Jesus, are given in elaborate detail and even with subtle revisions of the biblical accounts. Elements unknown in the Bible appear mainly in the Punishment Stories. The Koran itself is aware of the affinity between the stories about the prophets and the biblical literature, for which reason the Jews and the Christians are called upon to confirm the truth of the koranic allusions to the previous prophets. This is at least how Muslim exegetes explain the meaning of Koran 16:43 (see also Koran 21:7) which says: "And We did not send before you any but humans to whom We sent revelation, so ask the People of the Reminder if you do not know." The exegetes say that the "People of the Reminder" (*ahl al-dhikr*) are scholars well versed in the Torah and the Gospel, which means that they know best about the history of the prophets from their own scriptures. Narratives about the prophets are related to Muhammad "to strengthen your heart therewith" (Koran 11:120), as well as to teach the audience the bitter lesson of disobedience which already led ancient towns to destruction (Koran 7:101; 9:70). But the listeners are not responsive as expected, and they discard the koranic message as "tales of the ancients" (Koran 16:24). The nations to whom prophets have been sent were expected to receive them with consent and obedience, but the prophets were received with anything but obedience. They were mocked (Koran 15:11, etc.) and called liars (e.g., Koran 3:184; 22:42; 23:44; 35:25, etc.), and their message was denied (Koran 11:59), and denounced as "medleys of dreams" (Koran 21:5). The prophets were rejected mainly on account of their being ordinary human beings (*bashar*) (e.g., Koran 14:10; 17:94; 36:15; 64:6), and were accused of being mere poets, magicians (*sāḥir*) and madmen (*majnūn*) (e.g., Koran 21:5; 51:52). Some of them were received with skeptical questions (Koran 2:108), and above all, their audience expressed devotion to the pagan tradition of the ancestors (Koran 43:23). The prophets have also suffered actual persecution, such as the threat of expulsion (e.g., Koran 14:13), and also death at the hand of their own peoples, as was the fate of the Israelite prophets (e.g., Koran 2:61, 91, etc.). Rejection is met with retribution, which is the direct result of the fact that God has promised to protect the prophets (Koran 14:47), and is defined as God's *sunna* with respect to those who persecute the prophets (Koran 17:76–77). Destruction is never arbitrary or unjust, and is only inflicted on towns that have been warned in advance by their prophets (Koran 17:15; 28:59). The prophets and their close entourage are always saved from the collective disaster (Koran 10:103, etc.). Apart from warnings from the past, the Koran elaborates on the reward awaiting believers and unbelievers in the world to come. Many passages insist on the idea of resurrection which was denied by the infidels, and describe the last Judgment and the fate of believers and unbelievers in paradise and hell, respectively.

Jews and Judaism

The Koran expects the Jews to believe in the concrete Islamic message as represented in the Koran. While a minority of them did believe in Muhammad, most of them rejected him, and the koranic attack on them is shaped according to models encountered in the New Testament. Already in the latter, the Jews are accused of having persecuted and murdered their own prophets (Matthew 5:12, 23:30–1; Luke 11:47). These are said to have foretold the coming of Jesus (Acts 7:52), and the Jews are said to have persecuted Jesus himself, plotting to kill him (John 7:1; 18:12; Acts 9:29). They are also described as stirring up the Gentiles against Jesus' apostles, and as conspiring to kill them too (Acts, 13:50; 14: 2; 20:3; 26:2). The Jews are also accused of not keeping the laws of the Torah which had been given to them (Acts 7:53). The conviction of the Jews that they were God's chosen people is also refuted, and it is stressed that God is not only of the Jews but also of the Gentiles (Romans 3:29). On the other hand, a group of Jews who have believed in the message of the apostles is also mentioned (Acts 14:1). All these elements recur in the koranic attack on the Jews. To begin with, the Jewish arrogance stemming from the conviction that the people of Israel were God's chosen nation is reproved in various ways. In Koran 2:111, the Jews, as well as the Christians, are challenged to prove their claim that they alone will enter paradise. In Koran 5:18 the koranic prophet is requested to refute the idea that the Jews and the Christians were no less than "the sons of God and His beloved ones." The koranic prophet is requested to tell them that if this were so, God would not have punished them as He did. The arrogant Jews seem also to be referred to in Koran 4:49, which speaks about people who consider themselves pure, while only God decides whom to purify. Elsewhere (Koran 62:6) it is maintained that if the Jews are really God's favorites, to the exclusion of other people, they had better die soon. This is a sarcastic response to their unfounded conviction that Paradise is in store for them (see also Koran 2:94).The Jews have lost their right to be considered a chosen people mainly because of their insubordination and disbelief. The Koran imputes to them the blame of persecuting and killing their own prophets (Koran 3:181, 183), a sin that is usually mentioned with reference to the Children of Israel (Koran 2:61, 87, 91; 4:155; 5:70). The Christians too share some of the blame, because they have rejected the prophets sent to the Jews. This is implied in Koran 2:113 where the Jews and the Christians reject each other's religion as a false one. This they do in spite of the fact that they read "the Book" which testifies to the relevance of all the prophets sent by God. Likewise, the Koran condemns in Koran 4:150–1 unbelievers (*kāfirin*) who have only believed in some prophets while rejecting the others. It seems that the rift between Jews and Christians is also referred to in Koran 23:53 (cf. Koran 15:90–1) which condemns those who cut off their religion into sects (*zubur*).

Apart from persecuting the prophets, the Jews are blamed for failing to keep the laws of their own Torah. In Koran 62:5, those who have been given the Torah but do not carry it out are likened to an ass carrying books. The Torah, it is said elsewhere, contains guidance and light by which the prophets and the rabbis judged the Jews, but those who do not judge by what God has revealed are unbelievers (Koran 5:44). Elsewhere they are said to have believed only in parts of the Book and to have disbelieved in its other parts (Koran 2:85). The Christians too are suspect of ignoring their own law, as is implied in Koran 5:68, in which the People of the Book are warned against failing to observe the Torah and the Gospel (*Injīl*). In fact, a party of the People of the Book is accused of deliberate rejection of the scriptures given to them by their prophets. They have cast them behind their backs, yet they expect to be praised for their assumed devotion to the Torah (Koran 2:101; 3:187–8). The Koran is also aware of the wrath of God, which resulted in various hardships that the Jews suffered in the course of their history. Their rigid dietary laws, for example, which the Koran adopts in a passage mentioned above, are interpreted elsewhere in the Koran as a punishment from God inflicted on the Jews for oppressing the poor and for taking usury (Koran 4:160–1; 6:146; 16:118). The Koran further claims that these restrictions were not yet prescribed in the Torah, in which all kinds of food were still permitted except for that which Jacob prohibited (Koran 3:93). Apart from the dietary restrictions, the state of internal friction and discord which divided the Jews into sects was also seen as the sign of God's vengeance (Koran 5:64). God has also punished some Jews who have violated the Sabbath by transforming them into apes (Koran 2:65; 7:163–66). The sins committed by the Jews with respect to their own scriptures have continued into Islamic times, and bear serious anti-Islamic implications. These come out in passages imputing to the Jews the distortion (*taḥrīf*) of the original text of their own sacred scriptures (Koran 4:46; 5:13, 41–3. Cf. Koran 2:75). This seems to be dealt with indirectly also in Koran 2:79, which denounces those "who write the Book with their own hands claiming that it is of God, in order to sell it at a small price…." It is probably implied here that the Jews sold to the believers forged copies of their scriptures. In one verse (Koran 3:78), the act of forging is oral. It is performed by people who "twist" the Book with their tongues, claiming that this is the true form of the Book, although it is not. In this context, the Jews are also accused of playing with (Hebrew?) words that bear a mischievous sense (Koran 4:46. Cf. Koran 2:104). All this is designed to mislead and offend the Muslims and their prophet.

The distortion of the Torah goes hand in hand with the Jewish sin of rejecting those rulings of the koranic prophet which corresponded to their own laws. They refused to follow his verdict, after having made him a judge, and the Koran blames them for preferring the legal advice of others (Koran 5:41–3). The Jews are also said to have plotted to conceal from the Muslim believers what God has revealed to them, so as not to give the believers arguments which they might use against them (Koran 2:76. Cf. Koran 4:37; 2:42). The sin of concealment is imputed mainly to the People of the Book (Koran 2:146; 3:71). They are said to have made their scriptures into separate writings (*qarāṭīs*) of which they concealed much (Koran 6:91). The message of the koranic prophet is said to have reintroduced those parts of the previous scriptures, which the People of the Book attempted to conceal (Koran 5:15). The Koran promises the sinners guilty of concealment a severe curse from God (Koran 2:159), which is the fire of hell (Koran 2:174). It seems that when accusing the Jews of concealing the Torah, the Koran refers to those parts in their scriptures which foretold the emergence of Muhammad. This is supported by koranic verses asserting that the description of the Islamic prophet was recorded in the Torah and the Gospel as the "Gentile" (*ummī*) Prophet (Koran 7:157), and that Jesus knew him as Aḥmad (Koran 61:6). The Jews, or rather the People of the Book, are also accused of rejecting the authenticity of the Koran as the true Word of God. On one occasion, they demand that the Prophet produce a book from heaven (Koran 4:153), and they seem to have in mind the written Torah of Moses. Their demand seems to be designed to annoy the Prophet who only receives sporadic oral revelations. It implies that the People of the Book do not believe he is a true prophet. This goes hand in hand with the accusation that Muhammad learned the Koran from a non-Arab (Koran 16:103). The gravest aspect of the Jewish anti-Islamic sin is the hostility towards the Muslim believers. In this respect, the Koran differentiates between them and the Christians. This comes out in Koran 5:82, which states that the Jews as well as the polytheists bear the strongest enmity against the believers, while the Christian priests and hermits are the closest in love to the believers. In some passages the Koran offers a concrete substitute for the Jewish evil ways, namely, the religion of Abraham (e.g., Koran 2:135). The latter is said to have been a *ḥanīf*, i.e., a non-Jewish and a non-Christian monotheist. The particularistic insistence on Abraham's non-Jewish and non-Christian identity comes out in explicit statements, as, for example, in Koran 2:140, where Abraham, as well as Ishmael, Jacob and the Tribes (i.e., Jacob's sons) are said to have been neither Jews nor Christians (Koran 2:140). But elsewhere the non-Jewish/Christian identity is stated concerning Abraham in particular, with the assertion that the Torah and the Gospel were only revealed after his time (Q 3:65). This statement is addressed to the People of the Book, probably with the intention of refuting their own aspirations concerning Abraham, whose religious heritage they were probably claiming to have preserved. In other words, the image of Abraham has been appropriated from the Jews and the Christians and was turned into the prototype of the non-Jewish and non-Christian model of Islam. This is also the context of Koran 3:67–8, which asserts that the people nearest to Abraham are the Muslim believers. Some passages refer to military clashes between Muhammad and the Jews. In one passage (Koran 5:64) it is stated that whenever the Jews light the fire of war, God puts it out. But in other passages, the Jews are the party that comes under the Islamic military pressure, and their military weaknesses are exposed. In Koran 59:14, for example, it is observed that the People of the Book never fight the believers in one solid formation, but only in sporadic groups, hiding behind the walls of their fortresses. They are divided among themselves and fight each other vehemently. The People of the Book have suffered actual defeat, which is mentioned in Koran 59:1–4. Here they are driven out of their houses, although they thought that their fortresses would defend them against God. Apart from the military defeat of the People of the Book, the Koran also refers very briefly to their social status under Islamic domination. They must be killed unless they pay the tribute called **jizya*, but even then, they remain socially inferior to the believers (Koran 9:29).

Pillars of Islam and the Koran

SHAHĀDA. The declaration that there is no God but Allāh and that Muhammad is His messenger does not appear in the Koran as an independent unit, but separate elements of it are found in several passages. The declaration about God is found, for example, in Koran 40:65, and the one about Muḥammad is found in Koran 48:29.

PRAYER. Prayer is a basic element of Islamic ritual, and the believers are urged to pray day and night, although the exact times are not specified. Perhaps the most specific formulation is provided in Koran 30:17–18: "Therefore glory be to God when you enter upon the time of the evening and when you enter upon the time of the morning, and to Him belongs praise in the heavens and the earth, and at nightfall and when you are at midday." Muslim exegetes have read into this passage the idea of the five daily prayers. The direction of prayer (*qibla*) is the sacred Mosque (in Mecca) (Koran 2:144), but Islamic tradition knows of an earlier direction which was abandoned: Jerusalem. Ritual ablution before prayer is prescribed in Koran 5:6.

Friday prayer is prescribed in Koran 62:9–10.

ZAKĀT (ALMS GIVING). In many verses, prayer goes hand in hand with alms giving (e.g., Koran 2:43. etc.). The collection of the latter is prescribed in Koran 9:103, and the criteria for its distribution among the needy are provided in Koran 9:60.

FASTING. Fasting during the month of Ramaḍān is prescribed in Koran 2:183–87 and replaces previous rulings (according to the exegetes: Jewish ones) of fasting during a few days only. Ramaḍān is said in these verses to have been the month during which the Koran started to be sent down from heaven, and some exegetes say that Laylat al-Qadr, which according to another verse marked the beginning of the koranic revelation (Koran 97:1), occurred in Ramaḍān.

PILGRIMAGE. The koranic duty of pilgrimage is closely associated with Abraham. According to Koran 22:27, God commanded Abraham to proclaim the duty of pilgrimage to Mecca. It was Abraham and Ishmael who have raised the foundations of the "house," i.e., the Ka'ba (Koran 2: 127), and they purified it for the pilgrims (Koran 2:125). The obligation to keep the sanctity of the sacred months during which pilgrimage takes place is ordained in Koran 5:2. The lesser pilgrimage, i.e., the *u'umra*, is mentioned in Koran 2:196.

HOLY WAR (*JIHĀD). Holy war was regarded by some scholars as the sixth pillar of Islam. In the Koran (9:5) it is called by the exegetes: "the sword verse," and it declares total war against the infidels. Many exegetes hold that this verse repeals any other verse implying tolerance towards the unbelievers.

AMONG THE RITUAL COMMANDMENTS, THOSE PERTAINING TO DRINKING OF WINE ARE SAID TO HAVE BEEN GIVEN BY DEGREES. While the most explicit condemnation of wine drinking is given in Koran 5:90 (together with gambling and other pagan activities), other verses give the impression that intoxication is still not entirely prohibited (Koran 16:67; 4:43). Eating of carrion, blood, flesh of swine, and that which was sacrificed to idols, is prohibited in Koran 2:173. Regulations of marriage, divorce and inheritance are provided in various chapters, especially in Sura 2 and 4. Moral commandments, such as prohibition of extramarital sexual intercourse, the commandment to honor one's parents, the condemnation of bribery, false measurements, damaging lies, are provided in various chapters.

Hebrew Translations of the Koran

Early Hebrew translations of the Koran have been preserved in unpublished manuscripts. One in Oxford (Bodleian, MS Michael 113 [Ol. 50]), from the 17th century, and the other in the British Library (Or. 6636), probably written in India in the 18th century. They both contain a translation done in the 17th century by Jacob b. Israel Halevi. He used an Italian translation of the Koran published in Venice in 1547. The latter was done from a Latin version. A third manuscript is found in the Library of Congress, based on a Dutch version of the Koran (see Myron M. Weinstein, "A Hebrew Qur'ān Manuscript," in Thomas A. Timberg, *Jews in India* (1986), 205–47). Hebrew translations of the Koran done directly from the Arabic are by Z.H. Reckendorf (1857), J.J. Rivlin (1933–36), A. Ben Shemesh (1971), and U. Rubin (2005).

BIBLIOGRAPHY: J. Horovitz, "Das koranische Paradies," in: *Scripta Universitatis atque Bibliothecae Hierosolymitanarum* (1923), 53–73; R. Paret, "Der Koran als Geschichtsquelle," in: *Der Islam*, 37 (1961), 24–42; H. Speyer, *Die biblischen Erzählungen im Qoran* (repr. 1961); A.J. Arberry, *The Koran Interpreted* (1964); K. Wagtendonk, *Fasting in the Koran* (1968); J. Wansbrough, *Quranic Studies* (1977); W. Madelung, "The Origins of the Controversy Concerning the Creation of the Koran," in: *Orientalia Hispanica sive studia F.M. Pareja octogenario dicata*, ed. J.M. Barral, vol. 1:1 (1974), 504–25; M.S Seale. *Qur'an and Bible: Studies in Interpretation and Dialogue* (1978); R. Firestone. "Abraham's Son as the Intended Sacrifice (al-Dhabīḥ, Qur'ān 37:99–113): Issues in Qur'ānic Exegesis," in: *Journal of Semitic Studies*, 34 (1989), 95–131; idem, "Conceptions of Holy War in Biblical and Qur'ānic Tradition," in: *The Journal of Religious Ethics*, 24 (1996), 99–123; Ibn Warraq (ed.), *The Origins of the Koran: Classic Essays on Islam's Holy Book* (1998); H.C. Graf Von Bothmer, Karl-Heinz Ohlig, and Gerd-Rüdiger Puin, "Neue Wege der Koranforschung," in: *Magazin Forschung*, 1 (1999), 33–46; *Encyclopaedia of the Qur'ān* (2001); R. Tottoli, *Biblical Prophets in the Qur'ān and Muslim Literature* (2002).

[Uri Rubin (2nd ed.)]

KORCHNOY, VIKTOR (1931–), Russian chess master. Korchnoy was one of the top prizewinners in international tournaments and was three-time champion of U.S.S.R. In 1970 he defected to the United States, after he lost a match to Anatoly Karpov. He claimed that he was forced to lose by pressure of the Soviets, because Karpov was their favorite, and because he was a Jew. In 2001 he settled in Switzerland, was awarded citizenship, and represented the country in international chess tournaments.

KORCZAK, JANUSZ (**Henryk Goldszmidt**; 1878 or 1879–1942), Polish author, educator, and social worker. Korczak, who was born into a wealthy and assimilated Warsaw family, qualified as a physician and soon became interested in the poor, working as a volunteer in summer camps for underprivileged children. His social concern was first revealed in *Dzieci ulicy* ("Children of the Street," 1901), which described the horrifying plight of homeless orphans in the cities, living on their wits and stealing to survive, yet retaining their sense of right and wrong. *Dziecko salonu* ("A Child of the Salon," 1906) painted a contrasting picture of a pampered middle-class boy whose existence depends on the dictatorship of money. Both books aroused discussion and controversy, especially among the reactionary elements subjected to Korczak's incisive criticism. In 1911 the writer became the head of a new Jewish orphanage in Warsaw and retained the post for the rest of his life, apart from his World War I service as a Polish medical officer. Korczak's educational approach, revolutionary in its time, gave children a system of self-government and the opportunity of producing their own newspaper, *Mały Przegląd* ("Little Journal"), which appeared as a weekly supplement to the Zionist daily *Nasz Przegląd* (1920–39). His success prompted the authorities to secure his aid in establishing a parallel non-Jewish orphanage near Warsaw. Korczak also became a probation officer, a lecturer at the Free Polish University and the Jewish teachers' institute, and a frequent broadcaster on topics relating to children and adults.

On the basis of his experiences Korczak published theoretical works, such as *Jak kochać dziecko* ("How to Love a Child," 1920–21) and *Prawo dziecka do szacunku* ("The Child's Right to Respect," 1929). Two early children's books were *Mośki, Jośki, Srule* (1910), the story of three Jewish boys, and *Józki, Jaśki, and Franki* (1911). In later years, in his small bare room in the Jewish orphanage, Korczak wrote many others, including *Sam na sam z Bogiem* ("Alone with God," 1922), on prayer; *Kiedy znów będę mały* ("When I Am Small Again," 1925); *Król Maciuś Pierwszy* ("Matthew the Young King," 1928); and *Kajtuś czarodziej* ("Kajtuś the Magician," 1934). These were translated into several languages, including Hebrew, and later became especially popular in Israel. His last works include *Uparty chłopiec* ("A Stubborn Boy," 1937) about Pasteur; *Ludzie są dobrzy* ("People as Good," 1938); and *Refleksje* ("Reflections," 1938).

With the rise of Hitler and the spread of antisemitism Korczak's Jewish consciousness deepened and he became Poland's non-Zionist representative on the Jewish Agency. In 1934 and again in 1936 he visited Palestine, where he met many of his old pupils who had become *ḥaluẓim*, spending some time at kibbutz Ein Ḥarod. The educational and social philosophy of the kibbutz movement greatly impressed Korczak, who would undoubtedly have settled in Ereẓ Israel, had this not meant deserting his orphans in Warsaw. After the Nazi invasion of Poland, he strove to protect the orphanage in the Warsaw Ghetto, to which it had been transferred in 1940, and rescued many other hapless youngsters. When the Nazi deportation order was served in 1942, Korczak, suppressing the truth, told his children that they were going on a picnic in the country. When he, his assistant, and some 200 orphans at last reached the cattle trucks waiting to ship them to Treblinka, Korczak refused a last-minute offer of his freedom in return for abandoning his charges and went with them to his death. Korczak's heroism and martyrdom created a legend and invested him with the glory of a saint. His achievements have inspired various studies and Erwin Sylvanus' German drama *Korczak und die Kinder* (1958; *Dr. Korczak and the Children*, 1958). Commemorative postage stamps were issued on the 20th anniversary of his death in both Poland and Israel.

Korczak committees have been formed in Poland, Israel and West Germany. The Warsaw Committee was established in 1946, but because of the Stalinist regime in Poland at the time it did not become active until 1956, when it undertook the publication of his works, the assembly of archives, lectures on his works, etc. Much of its activity was related to the fact that many of its members – including for a time the chairman – were Jews. After the Six-Day War, however, the Jewish members were gradually weeded out and a Pole, who was prepared to suppress Korczak's Jewish origin and his positive approach to Ereẓ Israel, was appointed chairman.

The Israel Committee was established in 1957 and the West German Korczak Society in 1977.

In 1972 the Warsaw Committee was awarded the annual Frankfurt Book Fair Peace Prize by the German Booksellers' and Publishers' Association. The citation, however, referred to Korczak only as "a Pole [who] from 1917 directed a Jewish orphanage in Warsaw [and] lived and died with the children entrusted to him in the Warsaw Ghetto on the death march in Treblinka." The Israel Korczak Committee protested against the failure to mention that Korczak was a Jew, and against giving the prize to Poland, on the grounds that it was an antisemitic country. As a result of these protests the West German government agreed to grant an equal amount to the Israel Korczak Committee, but the committee decided not to accept it unless it received an official prize in the same way as the Polish Committee had.

In 1972 there appeared *Min ha-Getto*, which includes Korczak's ghetto diary, documents, and a chapter on his life and activities in the ghetto. The first volume of the collected works of Korczak *Im ha-Yeled* ("With the Child") consisting of three works published before the end of World War I, translated into Hebrew from the original Polish by Ẓevi Arad, appeared in 1974. In 1976 there appeared a volume of his writings translated into Hebrew under the title *Yaldut shel Kavod*, and in 1978 another similar volume *Dat ha-Yeled*.

The centenary of the birth of Korczak was widely celebrated, and the Polish Government took the initiative in having 1978 proclaimed the Janusz Korczak Celebration Year. In Israel an International Conference was held under the auspices of UNESCO, from April 12–17, with sessions held in Jerusalem, Haifa and Tel Aviv, where a permanent Janusz Korczak Exhibition was opened and a special medallion struck by the Bet Loḥamei Ha-Getta'ot. In Jerusalem a school was named in his honor. An official representative of the Polish government attended the celebration.

A monument by a Russian immigrant sculptor, Baruch Saktsier, showing Korczak with a protective hand round some of his wards at the Warsaw Jewish orphanage, was unveiled in the Memorial Garden in Yad Vashem dedicated to Jewish children who perished in the Holocaust.

The Polish celebration, to which Israeli representatives were officially invited, took place in Warsaw in October. The original date fixed for the celebration, October 11, was postponed to the following day at the request of the Israel Committee since the original date fell on Yom Kippur.

No less than 70 schools have been named after him in Poland.

I. Perlis has revealed the Jewish background of Korczak and his positive attitude to Israel.

BIBLIOGRAPHY: H. Olczak, *Mister Doctor* (1965); J. Hyams, *A Field of Buttercups* (1969); P. Apenszlak, *Una luz en las Tinieblas* (1961); J. Frost, in: *Jewish Education*, 33:3 (1963), 89–96; Z.E. Kurzweil, *Modern Trends in Jewish Education* (1964), 171–97; E. Dauzenroth, *Janusz Korczak der Pestalozzi aus Warschau* (1978); I. Perlis, in: *Mi-Befenim* 40 (1978), 368–374. **ADD. BIBLIOGRAPHY:** M. Shereshevski, *Shetei ha-Moladot* (1990), incl. bibl.; I. Perlis, *Ish Yehudi mi-Polin* (1986).

KORCZAK-MARLA, ROZKA (1921–1988), Zionist youth movement and underground leader, partisan. Korczak-Marla grew up in Plock, Poland, and was a member of the Zionist youth movement Ha-Shomer ha-Ẓa'ir. With the start of World War II she fled to Vilna, then under Soviet control, and became a leader of the local Ha-Shomer ha-Ẓa'ir group. At the time of the German invasion in the summer of 1941, she remained in the Vilna area where within six months the Einsatzgruppen along with Lithuanian collaborators killed about 40,000 Jews. At a meeting of Ha-Shomer ha-Ẓa'ir activists in a convent just outside of Vilna to discuss the Jewish response, Abba *Kovner proposed that the remaining Jews of Vilna should ready themselves to resist the occupiers with arms. Korczak-Marla published the minutes of the ensuing discussion in her memoir of the period, *Lehavot ba-Efer* ("Flames in the Ashes," 1964). The protocol of the discussion is an important source for understanding the concerns and motivations of Zionist youth at the time.

Korczak-Marla was a member of the Fareinkte Partizaner Organizatsie (FPO; United Partisan Organization), which was created as a result of the meeting. She escaped from the ghetto to the Rudninkai Forest shortly after the suicide of the FPO leader Yiẓḥak Wittenberg, in July 1943. In the forest she took part in the establishment of Jewish partisan units. In July 1944, after the liberation of Vilna, Korczak-Marla returned to the city. At the end of 1944 she left for Palestine, where she joined kibbutz Eilon. After a while she moved to kibbutz Ein-Ḥoresh, along with other former partisans, including Abba Kovner. Korczak-Marla took part in the creation of Moreshet, the museum Bet Loḥamei ha-Getta'ot, the Givat Ḥavivah Holocaust study center, and the museum and study center at Yad Mordekhai.

[Robert Rozette]

KORDA, SIR ALEXANDER (1893–1956), film producer. Born Sandor Laszlo Kellner in Hungary, Korda worked for Hungarian newspapers, but in 1915 became a stagehand in a Budapest film studio and went on to writing and directing. After World War I he moved to Vienna, Rome, the UFA studios in Berlin, and then to Hollywood. Korda settled in London in 1929 and sprang to fame when he made *The Private Life of Henry VIII* in 1933, an enormously successful film that introduced Charles Laughton and Merle Oberon (who became Korda's second wife). He founded London Film Productions Ltd. in 1932, became a director of United Artists in 1935, and founded Alexander Korda Film Productions in 1939. During the 1930s, he produced a number of memorable movies including *Catherine the Great* (1934), *The Scarlet Pimpernel* (1935), and *Rembrandt* (1936). In 1942 he sold his interest in United Artists and became manager of Metro-Goldwyn-Mayer's London operators. Later films include *The Thief of Baghdad* (1940); *The Third Man* (1950), perhaps his most famous film; and *Richard III* (1955). Korda produced 112 films. He was knighted for his services to the British film industry in 1942. Korda was one of the most famous of British film producers during British cinema's "golden age," and probably the one most like the legendary producers of Hollywood.

BIBLIOGRAPHY: P. Tabori, *Alexander Korda* (Eng., 1959); I. Dalrymple, in: *Quarterly of Film, Radio, TV*, II (Spring 1957), 294–309; *Current Biography Yearbook 1956* (1957), 346; *New York Times* (Jan. 24, 1956), 31 (obituary). **ADD. BIBLIOGRAPHY:** ODNB online; DBB, III, 624–27; K. Kulik, *Alexander Korda: The Man Who Could Work Miracles* (1990).

[Mark Perlgut]

KOREFF, DAVID FERDINAND (1783–1851), German author and physician. Koreff was the son of a physician in Breslau and became known for his use of unorthodox medical techniques (mesmerism) and the treatment of mental cases. He cured scores of patients after other physicians had abandoned hope of their recovery.

He was a member of the *Nordsternbund*, a circle of young romantic poets (Varnhagen v. Ense, A. v. Chamisso, W. Neumann, L. Robert) in Berlin and displayed considerable literary ability, translating Hippocrates, Plautus, and Tibullus, and composing several original romantic poems. In Prussia his friends were Rahel Levin (*Varnhagen), L.Tieck, J.E. Hitzig, E.T.A. Hoffmann, F. de la Motte Fouqué, and H. v. Pueckler-Muskau. From 1807 to 1811 he lived in Paris and combined the practice of medicine with a literary career. His patients included the family of Emperor Napoleon and a number of diplomats. In 1814 he served as a physician in the Prussian army and participated in the last battle against Napoleon for which he received the decoration "Eisernes Kreuz." After being appointed after 1815 as physician in ordinary of the Prussian king, Frederick William III, and the Prussian chancellor, Prince von Hardenberg, he received a full professorship at Berlin, but as a Jew he had no right to occupy such a post and the chancellor immediately ensured that he underwent baptism in the Lutheran Church (Aug. 13, 1816, in Meissen). His main literary work was *Lyrische Gedichte* (1815). He also wrote the text for *Aucassin und Nicolette*, an opera performed in Berlin in 1822, and was instrumental in founding the University of Bonn in 1818. In 1822, after the death of Hardenberg, he moved to Paris again, where he resumed his practice of medicine. Koreff's circle in the French capital included the painter Delacroix, the philosopher Victor Cousin, and such writers as Stendhal, Mérimée, Musset, Hugo, and Dumas; he also befriended Heine (whom he treated) and Meyerbeer. As an intermediary between the leading French and German literary groups, Koreff was a personality of considerable significance.

BIBLIOGRAPHY: M. Martin, *Le docteur Koreff* (1920); F. von Oppeln-Bronikowski, *David Ferdinand Koreff* (Ger., 1928). **ADD. BIBLIOGRAPHY:** Aus dem Nachlaß v. Varnhagen's v. Ense (1871), 1–58; G. Jaeckel, *Die Charité* (1986), 186–95; *Lexikon deutsch-juedischer Autoren*, vol. 14 (2006).

[Sol Liptzin / Archiv Bibliographia Judaica (2nd ed.)]

KORÈNE, VERA (1901–1996), French actress. Born in Paris, Vera Korène starred in Marcel Pagnol's play *Topaz* (1928) and joined the Comédie Française, playing mostly classical roles in Racine, Molière, and Shakespeare. She also appeared in films from 1933. In 1940 the Vichy government deprived her of French citizenship and she had to flee the country. She returned to the Comédie Française as actress and director after the war and retired in 1956.

KORETS (Pol. **Korzec**), town in Rovno district, Ukraine. The community in Korets was one of the oldest in Poland. Jews were living there in the 16th century. During the *Chmielnicki massacres in 1648/49 the community was almost annihilated, and only ten Jewish houses were left. The community recovered soon afterward to become the largest and most influential in the Council of Volhynia Land. A textile factory established by Joseph Czartoryski in Korets in 1786 employed 60 Jewish workers, and another textile factory founded in 1787 by Pinkhas Israel employed only Jews. In 1765, 937 Jews lived there but the number dropped in 1787 to 364 persons. Between 1766 and 1819 there were four Hebrew printing presses in Korets, some of them associated with those in Shklov, Nowy Dwor, and Ostrog. They printed nearly 100 books, mostly works of Kabbalah and Ḥasidism, which contributed considerably to the spread of Ḥasidism in Poland and adjoining countries. Works by *Jacob Joseph of Polonnoye and *Dov Baer of Mezhirech were first printed there. Korets was a center of Ḥasidism. Dov Baer the Maggid of Mezhirech and Phinehas Shapiro were active there. The Jewish population grew in the 19th century, to 3,832 in 1847 and 4,608 (76% of the total population) in 1897. Additional factories were founded, such as tanneries and a large sugar refinery, all owned by Jews. In the beginning of the 20th century a modern *talmud torah*, a private Hebrew school, and a large library existed in Korets. During World War I and the Civil War, pogroms were averted due to the intervention of the Ukrainian town mayor and the self-defense unit, and only two Jews were killed. The Jewish population diminished during World War I, and amounted to 3,888 (83%) in 1921, increasing to 4,695 in December 1937. The first democratic elections to the community administration were held in 1917. Elections were held again, under Polish rule, in 1927, and Nehemiah Herschengon (d. 1923) was rabbi of the community for 67 years. In 1924 many Jews were elected to the City Council. One of them served as a vice-mayor. Apart from the *talmud torah*, there were a Hebrew Tarbut school and a Yiddish school, and in 1920 the Zvihil yeshivah from Novograd-Volynsk, headed by R. Joel Shurin (the Poltava *Illui* ("prodigy")), moved to Korets.

Holocaust Period

Soviet forces entered Korets on Sept. 17, 1939. Jewish institutions and political parties were disbanded, and Jews whose means of livelihood had been taken away attempted to settle into new occupations. Cooperatives for artisans and craftsmen were set up. The Tarbut school was closed, and the communal charitable bodies were forced to stop their activities, although they managed to continue some operations, especially in aiding Jewish refugees. Religious life as such was not disturbed. When war broke out between Germany and the Soviet Union on June 22, 1941, over 500 Jews managed to escape from Korets to Russia. German troops entered on July 2, 1941. On Aug. 8, 1941, Jewish men were called up for forced labor. The 112 who appeared were murdered on the outskirts of the city. On Aug. 20, 1941, another 350 Jewish men were murdered there, and on August 25 a fine of 100,000 marks (a million rubles) was levied against the Jews. In the winter that followed, the community suffered from hunger and epidemics, and many were conscripted for labor camps. On May 21, 1942, 2,200 Jews were killed near the village of Kozak. The survivors in the community, about 1,000, were subsequently concentrated in a ghetto. A Judenrat was established under Moshe Krasnostawski. The Judenrat maintained contacts with the Jewish underground headed by Misha Gildenman and his son Simkha, and a resistance group of 20 members was formed in the ghetto, armed with one pistol and knives. On September 25, 1942, when the final liquidation of Korets Jews came, Krasnostawski set fire to the ghetto houses (he died in the flames), and under the cover of fire and smoke many escaped, among them 11 persons, led by Gildenman to the forests north of the town. Gildenman built up a partisan unit, connected later with the partisan division of General Saburov, and became one of the outstanding partisan leaders of the region. About 500 survivors returned there after the liberation on January 13, 1944, but most left for Israel and the West. The Jewish population in 1970 was estimated to be only a few families. During Passover 1959 a *minyan* conducting services in private was dispersed by militia.

BIBLIOGRAPHY: A. Tauber, in: KS, 1 (1924/25), 222 ff., 302 ff.; 2 (1925/26), 54 ff., 215 ff., 274 ff.; 3 (1926/27), 281 ff.; Rivkind, *ibid.*, 58 ff.; Ḥ.D. Friedberg, *Toledot ha-Defus ha-Ivri be-Polanyah* (1950²), 74 f.; E. Leoni (ed.), *Sefer Korez* (Heb. and Yid., 1959).

[Aharon Weiss / Shmuel Spector (2nd ed.)]

KORETS, PHINEHAS BEN ABRAHAM ABBA SHAPIRO OF (1726–1791), ḥasidic rabbi. Born in Shklov, he later lived in Korets, but because of differences of opinion with the followers of Dov *Baer, the Maggid of Mezhirech, he left the town around 1770. He moved to Ostrog, later settling in Shepetovka where he died. His plans to emigrate to Ereẓ Israel were never fulfilled.

Having studied Maimonides' *Guide of the Perplexed* as a young man, Phinehas later gave primacy to the study of the *Zohar which he considered a means of strengthening faith. He was active in small circles, and his disciples included *Jacob Samson of Shepetovka, *Ze'ev Wolf of Zhitomir, *Aaron Samuel b. Naphtali Hertz ha-Kohen, and *Raphael of Bershad. His sermons were published in various collections: *Midrash Pinḥas* (Bilgoray, 1931), *Pe'er la-Yesharim* (Jerusalem, 1921), *Nofet Ẓufim* (Lemberg, 1864), *Ge'ullat Yisrael* (Lemberg, 1864), and *Likkutei Shoshannim* (Czernowitz, 1857). They appeared also in the works of his disciples: *Benei Yissakhar* (Zolkiew, 1850), *Ve-Ẓivvah ha-Kohen* (Belaya Tserkov, 1823), and *Kodesh Hillulim* (1864). Extant manuscripts of his works are preserved in Jerusalem, Cincinnati, and in private collections. A great number of his sayings are given in brief, in the original Yiddish.

Although Phinehas met *Israel b. Eliezer, the Ba'al Shem Tov, he should not be considered his disciple in the full sense of the word. He opposed many teachings of the Maggid of Mezhirech, mainly on the question of *devekut* ("devotion"). Phinehas, who represents the enthusiastic trend in Ḥasidism, prayed with particular *devekut.* He emphasized the special value of prayer and its influence on the upper worlds. Unlike other Ḥasidim, Phinehas held that the *mitzvot* should be performed for their own sake, believing that when a man observes a *mitzvah*, he raises the world to its highest point of origin, i.e., he abolishes its material presence. Expressing a measure of opposition to praying according to the prayer book of the "Ari" (Isaac *Luria) with *kavvanot* ("meditations"), he stated that this evades the main issue: "To unite the heart to God in truth." Thus Phinehas opposed contemplative prayer, stating that man should pray explicitly for human needs, believing that God would fulfill his request. He thus opposed the custom of delaying the time of prayer, which had become widespread among the Ḥasidim. It is related that Phinehas praised highly the writings of *Jacob Joseph of Polonnoye. He advised his followers not to take part in disputes with the **Mitnaggedim*.

In Phinehas' thought, the substance of the world derives from the life force which God continuously renews and causes to flow into its midst, but we must be wary of interpreting his words as expressing pantheistic ideas. On the face of it, it is possible that this conception negates the existence of the world, but it does not render it identical with God. The Sabbath in particular is considered a day of elevating the wordly sphere, to the extent that man does not see the need to eat on that day. Because of this it is also impossible to make special preparations for the Sabbath, because "it comes from Heaven and no one knows how and what is given to it." He also emphasized the use of melodies as a means of religious expression. In matters of morals, Phinehas emphasized the importance of truth and modesty. He advocated fasting as a way to overcome evil impulses.

BIBLIOGRAPHY: M. Biber, *Mazkeret li-Gedolei Ostraha* (1907), para. 171; Dubnow, Ḥasidut (1960), 104–6; A.J. Heschel, in: *YIVO Bleter*, 33 (1949), 9–48; 36 (1952), 124–5; idem, in: *Alei Ayin* (1952), 213–44; R. Schatz, *Ha-Ḥasidut ke-Mistikah* (1968), index.

[Moshe Hallamish]

KORETZ, ZVI (1894–1945), rabbi in Greece. Koretz was born in Galicia. He studied in a yeshivah and after World War I went to Vienna to study in the university. After receiving his doctorate, he went to the Vienna Rabbinical Seminary, the Hamburg Institute for Oriental Sciences, and the Berlin Hochschule fuer die Wissenschaft des Judentums.

In 1933 he was appointed chief rabbi of Salonika. After three months he delivered his first sermons in Greek and Judeo-Spanish.

Shortly after the beginning of the German invasion of Greece on April 15, 1941, Koretz and the community president, Dr. Halevi, were arrested by the Germans in Athens. Koretz was exiled to a prison in Vienna on the pretext that he had cabled the Jewish communities of Palestine, Egypt, England, and the United States, protesting the Italian air bombing of the Saint Sophia church in Salonika.

In February 1942 he was freed from imprisonment in Vienna, but was imprisoned again in June 1942 in Salonika. He was the sole Jew taken, along with 600 Greek Orthodox. On August 2, 1942, he was freed, along with the other prisoners.

He was then forced by the Germans to fill several positions which affected his image among the Jews. Koretz was installed as liaison with the Germans. In the course of the next few months, as a member of the Jewish Community Committee, Koretz had an active and leading role in negotiating with the German Command for the ransom of thousands of Jews sent to forced labor. When the German commander of Salonika, Max Merten, changed the ransom fee from an agreed two billion drachmas to three and a half billion drachmas, the Committee had great difficulties in raising the money. As one of the Committee members the rabbi was present when they were compelled to hand over the 500-year-old cemetery for its desecration in exchange for the deduction of one billion drachmas from the ransom fee. Koretz endured great difficulties in raising money from the wealthier members of the community. This was one of several factors in the community's failure in contributing the necessary funds.

On December 11, 1942, Koretz was appointed president of the Jewish community. He made his acceptance conditional upon the agreement that six members of the committee and he would bear collective responsibility to the German authorities.

As head of the community, Koretz bore much of the brunt of complying with the orders issued by Eichmann's representatives, Alois *Brunner and Dieter *Wisliceny, who instigated a constant state of terror. The preliminary steps taken to prepare the expulsion of the Jews were the establishment of ghettos, curfews, and the collection of money in a special account. Koretz had the responsibility of transmitting these and other harsh German orders to the members of the Jewish community.

On March 10, 1943, five days before the first transport, Koretz tried to defer the deportations by offering the Germans one half of the property of the Jews in the form of real estate. The high command in Berlin refused the offer. Koretz arranged a meeting with Greek Prime Minister Rallis on April 9, 1942. He requested that the latter mediate with the Germans to prevent the expulsion of the ancient Jewish community of Salonika. Rallis replied evasively. Koretz was imprisoned, and sent to a camp and then deported, with his family, to Bergen-Belsen. In the camp Koretz was forced to do hard labor and eventually caught typhus after he was transferred to Theresienstadt. Three months after the liberation by the Russians he died in the small town of Trebitz, 45 miles (70 km.) from Dresden.

[Yitzhak Kerem]

KORIAT, ASHER (1939–), Israeli cognitive psychologist. Born in Morocco, Koriat immigrated to Israel in 1949. In 1965 he received his M.A. degree in psychology from the Hebrew University of Jerusalem and in 1970 he received his Ph.D. from University of California, Berkeley. From 1970 until 1976 he taught in the department of psychology at the Hebrew University. From 1976 he lectured at Haifa University and from 1981 until 1984 he was the head of the department of psychology there. In 1990 he became a professor. He was also a visiting professor in universities and research centers in the U.S., Canada, and Germany. He was head of the Center for Decision Making and Information Processing and the Minerva Center for Cognitive Processes and Human Performances as well as a member of various boards and societies. Among his research interests are memory organization; psychology of reading; spatial representation and transformation; metacognition; monitoring and control processes in learning and remembering; subjective experience; and memory accuracy and distortion. In 2002 he was awarded the Israel Prize for psychology.

[Shaked Gilboa (2nd ed.)]

KORINE, EZRA (1906–1976), Israeli physician. Born in Iraq where he was active in Jewish and Zionist educational institutions, he graduated from the Medical School in Beirut, after which he immigrated to Israel in 1951. He served as a specialist in ear, nose and throat diseases at the Tel ha-Shomer Hospital, and he devoted himself particularly to the rehabilitation of deaf children and to the advancement of children from Iraq. He also undertook research into the history of the Jewish community of Iraq. He was awarded the Israel Prize in 1976 for special contributions in social and national fields.

KORKIS, ABRAHAM ADOLF (1865–1921), Polish Zionist. Born in Kamionka Strumiłowa, Galicia, Korkis studied law at the University of Lemberg, and was the chief clerk of the government Commerce and Industry Office for the province of Galicia. He began his Jewish Zionist activity as a student. When the first organization uniting all the nationalist associations and groups for settlement in Ereẓ Israel was established in Galicia (1892) and the first national organ in Polish, *Przyszłość* ("The Future") was founded, Korkis became head of the organization (intermittently until 1903) and editor of *Przyszlosc*. He participated in the First Zionist Congress and was elected to the Zionist General Council. He also published studies on economic matters. In 1918 he was among the founders of the Polish Zionist daily *Chwila*, published in Lwow.

BIBLIOGRAPHY: L. Jaffe (ed.), *Sefer ha-Congress* (1950²), 352–3; *Haolam* (April 23, 1942), 239. **ADD. BIBLIOGRAPHY:** N.M. Gelber, *Toledot ha-Tenu'ah ha-Ẓiyyonit,* 2 vols. (1958), index.

[Getzel Kressel]

KORMAN, EDWARD R. (1942–), U.S. District Court judge. Born in New York City, Korman received a bachelor's degree from Brooklyn College in 1963, an LL.B. degree from Brooklyn Law School in 1966, and an LL.M. from New York University in 1971. He served as law clerk to Judge Kenneth B. Keating of the New York Court of Appeals from 1966 to 1968 and was an associate in the firm of Paul, Weiss, Rifkind, Wharton, and Garrison from 1968 to 1970. Korman served as assistant U.S. attorney for the Eastern District of New York from 1970 to 1972 and as assistant to the solicitor general of the United States from 1972 to 1974. He returned to the U.S. attorney's office for the Eastern District, serving as chief assistant U.S. attorney from 1974 to 1978 and as U.S. attorney from 1978 to 1982. He joined the law firm of Stroock and Stroock and Lavan as partner from 1982 to 1984 and as counsel from 1984 to 1985.

A professor of law at Brooklyn Law School from 1984 to 1985, Korman also served as a member of the Temporary Commission of Investigation of the State of New York and was chairman of the Mayor's Committee on New York City Marshals from 1983 to 1985. In 1985 he was appointed U.S. District Judge for the Eastern District of New York.

Judge Korman authored several significant opinions. In 1989 he ordered the extradition of a member of the Abu Nidal organization to Israel to stand trial for a terrorist attack on a bus traveling between the West Bank and Tel Aviv, rejecting the argument that "any atrocity, if politically motivated," falls under the political offense exception to extradition. He ruled in 1996 that the New York State Republican Party's presidential primary election ballot access rules imposed an unconstitutional burden on the right to vote, ordering that the party put Steve Forbes and other candidates on the primary presidential ballot statewide.

Perhaps the most noteworthy case to come before him was the class-action lawsuit on behalf of more than half a million plaintiffs against Swiss banks. The suit was filed by Holocaust victims who had deposited money in Swiss banks but were unable to claim it after the war. The plaintiffs claimed that, among other obstacles, some bankers demanded the death certificates of people who had been killed in Nazi concentration camps – obviously impossible to obtain. Korman approved a $1.25 billion settlement between the banks and the plaintiffs in 2000, and later approved a distribution plan for the settlement. Elan Steinberg, executive director of the World Jewish Congress, praised Korman's ruling as a "belated victory" that achieved a measure of justice "for the victims of the greatest crime of the century." Though the distribution plan, which placed emphasis on compensating needy Holocaust victims in the former Soviet Union, was challenged, Judge Jose Cabranes of the Second U.S. Circuit Court of Appeals upheld Judge Korman's decision, stating that Korman approached every step of the litigation with "thoughtful analysis and scrupulous fairness."

[Dorothy Bauhoff (2nd ed.)]

KÖRMENDI, FERENC (1900–1972), Hungarian novelist. Born and educated in Budapest, Körmendi became a journalist and music critic. In 1932 he rose to sudden fame with the publication of *Budapesti kaland*, a novel that won an international publishers' competition and was translated into many languages (*Escape to Life*, 1933). The books that followed reflect the situation of bourgeois Budapest between the world wars, and of the doubts and sense of isolation of Hungarian Jewish intellectuals. These popular novels included *Ind. 715 Via Bodenbach* (1932; *Via Bodenbach*, 1935); *A boldog emberöltő* (1934; *The Happy Generation*, 1945); *Bűnösök* (1935; *The Sinners*, 1948), and *Találkozás és búcsú* ("To Meet and Say Goodbye," 1937). In 1938 Körmendi fled to London, where he joined the Hungarian section of the BBC. Except for a few years in South America, he continued to live in England. His principal work of Jewish interest is the novel *Júniusi hétköznap* (1943; *Weekday in June*, 1946). Based on fact, this tells the tragic story of an assimilated Hungarian Jew who, on the eve of emigration, is killed when a local Nazi throws a bomb in front of a synagogue.

BIBLIOGRAPHY: *Magyar Irodalmi Lexikon*, 1 (1963); M. Szabolcsi, *A magyar irodalom története (1919–töl napjainkig)*, 6 (1966), 185–6.

[Baruch Yaron]

KORMIS, FRED (1897–1986), sculptor. Kormis was born in Frankfurt on the Main, served in the Austrian army during World War I, and was a prisoner-of-war in Siberia from 1915 to 1920. He lived in Germany until 1933 and then moved to Paris before settling in England in 1934. He studied sculpture in Germany and exhibited in Europe before his regular exhibitions in London, including a group of his medals acquired by the British Museum. His public commissions include works for various local authorities in Britain. In later years he created a large group dedicated "To Those who Died in Captivity," at Gladstone Park, London, in memory of "Prisoners of War and Victims of Concentration Camps 1914–1945." It includes five large bronze figures, of which a number of maquettes are in the Imperial War Museum, London.

[Charles Samuel Spencer]

KORN, ARTHUR (1870–1945), electrophysicist and inventor. Born in Breslau, Korn lectured at the Technische Hochschule in Munich (1895–1914) and in Berlin (1914–35). He fled to the U.S. and in 1940 joined the Institute of Technology, Hoboken, New Jersey. Korn specialized in radio photography, and his system for transmitting photographs electrically was first used by a French magazine in 1906. In 1928 his wireless method was used for transmitting pictures from Italy to the U.S. and by the German police. In America he elaborated a method for transmitting maps from aircraft to the ground and another for reproducing textile designs on cloth. His books include: *Elektrische Fernphotographie* (1904) and *Bildtelegraphie* (1923).

KORN, BERTRAM WALLACE (1918–1979), U.S. Reform rabbi, author, and historian. Korn, who was born in Philadelphia, was educated at the University of Pennsylvania and Cornell, earning his degree at the University of Cincinnati in 1939. He was ordained at Hebrew Union College in 1943. He earned his DDL in American Jewish History at HUC in 1949. He was a leading U.S. Jewish historian, particularly in the area of 19th-century studies. He served as a rabbi in Mobile, Alabama (1943–44) before entering the Chaplaincy and serving in China. He then went to Mansfield, Ohio (1946–48) while he pursued his doctorate at HUC. Having completed his doctorate he assumed the pulpit of Keneseth Israel, Philadelphia, in 1949. Each summer he continued his work as a navy chaplain. He was promoted to rear-admiral, the first Jewish chaplain to achieve this rank. He retired in 1978. He served as chairman of the Jewish Welfare Board's Chaplaincy Commission. Korn was an active scholar and teacher, a visiting professor at HUC-JIR in New York and at Dropsie College in Philadelphia.

Korn chaired the Central Conference of American Rabbis' Commission on History (1953–57), and was president of the American Jewish Historical Society (1959–61) and earned its Lee M. Friedman Gold Medal. He also edited the Yearbooks of the Central Conference of American Rabbis for many years. His books include: *The American Reaction to the Mortara Case* (1957); *American Jewry and the Civil War* (1951,

19612); *The Early Jews of New Orleans* (1969); and *The Middle Year of American Jewish History* (Heb., 1970).

BIBLIOGRAPHY: K.M. Olitzsky, L.J. Sussman and M.H. Stern, *Reform Judaism in America: A Biographical Dictionary and Sourcebook* (1993).

KORN, RACHEL HÄRING (1898–1982), Yiddish poet. Korn was born on the farming estate of "Sucha Gora" (Dry Mountain) near Podliski, East Galicia, the eldest of three children and an only daughter. Her family on both sides had owned and managed farmland for several generations. Growing up on an isolated farm in an area with very few Jewish families, she peopled her world with the living things around her and began to write poetry. Her elementary education was mainly in Polish, the language of her household. When World War I broke out, her family fled to Vienna. They returned to live in Przemysl from 1918 to 1941.

Korn's first publications were in Polish in 1918, in *Nowy Dziennik*, a Zionist newspaper, and in *Glos Przemyski*, a socialist journal, but she switched to Yiddish in the wake of pogroms in Poland after the war. She had been taught to speak, read, and write Yiddish by her husband, Hersh Korn, a Left Labor Zionist. In 1919 she published her first Yiddish poem in the *Lemberger Tageblatt* and was a steady contributor to Yiddish literary journals and newspapers over the next two decades. With the publication of her early volumes of poetry, *Dorf* ("Village," 1928) and *Royter mon* ("Red Poppies," 1937), and her first collection of stories, *Erd* ("Land," 1936), she was recognized as an accomplished and original writer. The profusion and directness of her nature imagery, the dramatic confrontations of village life as she pictured it, and the intensity of her love poetry were all new to Yiddish literature.

When the Germans invaded eastern Galicia in June 1941, Korn and her daughter escaped into the Soviet Union. Korn's husband, her mother, her brothers and their families all perished in the war. Korn fled to Uzbekistan, then until the war ended lived in Moscow, where the leading figures in the world of Soviet Yiddish culture (Bergelson, Markish, Mikhoels, Der Nister) welcomed her as a colleague. Korn and her daughter returned to postwar Poland in 1946, but took refuge in Sweden and in 1948 immigrated to Canada and settled in Montreal.

The dislocation, loss, and anguish of those years are evident in her first postwar collection of poems, *Heym un heymlozikayt* ("Home and Homelessness," 1948). In her earlier work she spoke for the helpless and neglected. She now saw herself as an eternal debtor, with the obligation to speak for the Jewish people who perished in the war. In later volumes, like *Fun Yener Zayt Lid* ("On the Other Side of the Poem," 1962), she wrote of a new dependence on the "the word," on the poem itself, which supplanted the home she lost. She also moved on from narrative to a tighter, meditative lyric. This change in style enabled her to generalize her own experience of loss, to use it as a symbol of Jewish experience.

In all, Korn published eight volumes of poetry and two collections of fiction. She was awarded numerous prizes, among them the Manger Prize of the State of Israel (1974). Some of her work is available in translation, in I. Howe, R. Wisse, Kh. Shmeruk, *The Penguin Book of Modern Yiddish Verse*; S. Levitan, *Paper Roses*; S. Mayne and R. Augenfeld, *Generations*; S. Meltzer, *Shirim ve-Adamah*.

BIBLIOGRAPHY: LYNL, 8 (1981), 140–42; Z. Reyzn, *Leksikon fun der Yidisher Literatur, Prese un Filologie*, 3 (1929), 569–70; R. Oyerbakh, in: *Di Tsukunft*, 84, no. 1 (Jan. 1978), 20–22; Y.Glatshteyn, in: *In Tokh Genumen* (1956), 315–22; E. Orenstein, in: *The Canadian Jewish Mosaic* (1981), 293–313; S. Levitan, in: *Identifications: Ethnicity and the Writer in Canada* (1982), 116–34.

[Seymour Levitan (2nd ed.)]

KORNBERG, ARTHUR (1918–), U.S. biochemist and Nobel laureate. Born in Brooklyn, N.Y., Kornberg received his B.Sc. at City College, New York, in 1937 and his M.D. at the University of Rochester in 1937. After medical posts including an appointment with the U.S. Coast Guard, he started his scientific career in the Nutrition Section of the National Institutes of Health at Bethesda, followed by appointments at New York University with Prof. Severo Ochoa, Washington School of Medicine with Prof. Carl and Gerty Cori, and the University of California with Prof. H.A. Barker before becoming chief of the Enzyme and Metabolism Section at NIH. In 1953–59 he was head of the Department of Microbiology at Washington University School of Medicine, St Louis, Missouri, and subsequently head of the Department of Biochemistry at Stanford University School of Medicine, Palo Alto, California. He had a major career interest in enzymes, substances which increase the rate of biochemical reactions, and nucleic acid control of heredity. Crick and Watson's work strongly indicated that DNA contains the genetic blueprint which is copied in newly formed, complementary DNA sequences through the process of base pairing. Kornberg and his colleagues verified this concept experimentally and discovered the first of the enzymes, polymerase I, which controls the process of DNA copying. These enzymes play a crucial role in modern biotechnology. For this work he received the Nobel Prize for medicine in 1959 with Severo Ochoa. Later he investigated the role of inorganic polyphosphates and their contribution to the evolution of life forms. His many honors include membership in the U.S. National Academy of Sciences and fellowship in the Royal Society. He had a profound interest in training scientists and in the application of science to medicine.

[Michael Denman (2nd ed.)]

KORNBERG, SIR HANS LEO (1928–), U.K. biochemist. Kornberg was born in Herford, Germany, and came to England as a refugee from the Nazis (1939). Encouraged by Hans Krebs, after working initially as a laboratory assistant, he gained his B.Sc. (1949) and Ph.D. (1953) from the University of Sheffield before joining Efraim Racker at Yale University and at the Public Health Institute, New York, as a Commonwealth Fund Fellow (1953–55). He returned to the U.K. to join the scientific staff of Sir Hans Krebs' Medical Research Council Cell

Metabolism Research Unit at Oxford University (1955–60). He was appointed the first professor and head of the University of Leicester's new biochemistry department (1960–75) before becoming Sir William Dunn Professor of Biochemistry (1975–95) and Master of Christ's College (1982–95) at the University of Cambridge. After statutory retirement, he took up an appointment as professor of biology at Boston University. Kornberg's research focuses on microbial metabolism, mainly on elucidating the "anaplerotic" pathways that enable single cell organisms to derive both energy and the precursors of cell constituents from defined nutrients. Later his research concerned identifying the proteins which span the cell membrane and enable nutrients to be taken up by the cell. His findings have helped to understand how cells respond to chemical signals and have important implications for understanding the regulation of vital processes in health and disease. His honors include election to the Royal Society of London (1965) and to numerous worldwide scientific academies and societies, and a knighthood (1978).

[Michael Denman (2nd ed.)]

KORNEUBURG, town in Lower Austria. According to 15th-century legends, Korneuburg was the capital of *Judaesaptan in pre-Christian times. Though the earliest documentary evidence for the presence of Jews dates from the beginning of the 14th century, a Jewish settlement already existed in the 13th century. On the Day of Atonement, 1297 or 1298, it was alleged that a bleeding Host was found near the home of a Jew; ten members of the community, men and women, were subsequently burned at the stake (see Desecration of the *Host). The Host was interred in the church, where it reputedly performed a number of miracles. When the bishop of Passau ordered an investigation to be opened in 1305, it was discovered that the affair was the result of gross deceptions, but in spite of this the story was popularized in paintings and engravings.

The Jews were expelled from Korneuburg in 1420. The synagogue that had been built in the 14th century was given to the city by Frederick III in 1460. In the 17th century Jews were allowed to frequent the annual fairs but not the weekly ones. A number of complaints were lodged against Jewish peddlers and merchants. Only in 1848 did Jews settle again in Korneuburg. In 1869 there were 819 Jews in the district of Korneuburg (63 in the town itself), and 1,118 in 1880. In 1933 the ancient synagogue was still standing. There were 80 Jews in the town and there was a small congregation that held services in a prayer room. The dead were buried in a part of the municipal cemetery. After the *Anschluss* (1938), Korneuburg Jews moved to Vienna.

BIBLIOGRAPHY: *Dr. Bloch's Wochenschrift*, 26 (1909), 770–1; Strakosch-Grassmann, in: *Juedisches Archiv*, 2:1–2 (1928), 14–20; L. Moses, *Die Juden in Niederoesterreich* (1935), 134–5; 203; *Germ Jud*, 1 (1963), 143; 2 (1968), 450–1.

KORNFELD, AARON BEN MORDECAI BAER (1795–1881), last *rosh yeshivah* of Bohemia. Kornfeld's father, Mordecai Baer, turned an old distillery in *Golcuv Jenikov into a modern factory, and his uncle Salman supplied potash to glass factories and founded a tannery. The wealth they thus gained was used for the upkeep of a yeshivah, headed first by Mordecai Baer and, on his death, by Aaron, who was then only 18 years old. Becoming renowned throughout the Jewish world as Aaron Jennikau, Kornfeld was strictly Orthodox in his teaching, yet he conceded the necessity for secular studies. Up to 80 students attended his yeshivah, among them Ignaz *Kuranda and Simon *Szanto. On his return from his intervention in the *Damascus Affair, Moses *Montefiore stopped at Golcuv Jenikov to make Kornfeld's acquaintance. Kornfeld published in 1847 a dialogue between an Orthodox father and a Liberal son in the *Shomer Ẓiyyon ha-Ne'eman*, and in 1865 *Ẓiyyunim le-Divrei ha-Kabbalah*, a collection of judgments alluded to through **gematria*. These he compiled from memory while preparing to undergo an eye operation. With Aaron's death, his yeshivah, the last in Bohemia, was closed. Kornfeld's brother-in-law, MEIR ALTAR HA-LEVI (1812–after 1865), was an early protagonist of *Haskalah in Bohemia and contributed to **Bikkurei ha-Ittim*. Among his works was a translation of the Psalms into Greek. In 1850 Kornfeld and Altar were members of a committee formulating a curriculum for a rabbinical seminary to be established in Prague. Members of the same family include SIGMUND KORNFELD, the Vienna psychiatrist and philosopher, a friend of Theodor *Herzl, Joseph *Popper-Lynkeus, and Zsigmond *Kornfeld, the Budapest banker. The German expressionist writer Paul *Kornfeld was Aaron's great-grandson.

BIBLIOGRAPHY: M.B. May, *Isaac Mayer Wise … a Biography* (1916), 28–29; J. Maximovič in: H. Gold (ed.), *Juden und Judengemeinden Boehmens* (1934), 165–6; R. Kestenberg-Gladstein, *Neuere Geschichte der Juden in den boehmischen Laendern*, 1 (1969), 322–4; I.H. Weiss, *Zikhronotai* (1895), 76–77; M.H. Friedlaender, *Leben und Wirken der hervorragendsten rabbinischen Autoritaeten Prags* (1892), 51–59; A. Stein, *Geschichte der Juden in Boehmen* (1904), 139–43.

[Meir Lamed]

KORNFELD, JOSEPH SAUL (1876–1943), U.S. rabbi and diplomat. Born in Austria-Hungary, Kornfeld went to the United States as a child and received his rabbinical ordination at Hebrew Union College in 1899. After serving congregations in Pine Bluff, Arkansas, and Montreal, Canada, he was appointed to Temple B'nai Israel, Columbus, Ohio, in 1907. In Columbus he became active in civic affairs, being elected to the Charter Commission (1913) and the Board of Education (1914–19). He was on friendly terms with the leading Ohio politicians and campaigned for Warren G. Harding in the 1920 presidential election. In 1921 Harding appointed him U.S. ambassador to Persia, where he was called upon at various times to intervene at the court of the Shah in favor of his coreligionists. His presence in Teheran had a beneficial effect on the Jews. Kornfeld returned to the United States in 1925 and became rabbi of the Collingwood Avenue Temple, Toledo, Ohio, remaining there until 1934. Thereafter he devoted himself to lecturing. At the time of his death he was acting rabbi of Holy Blossom Temple, Toronto, Canada.

[Walter Joseph Fischel]

KORNFELD, PAUL (1889–1942), German playwright and novelist. Born and raised in Prague in the circle of the young Franz *Werfel, Ernst Deutsch, Willy *Haas, Franz *Kafka and Max *Brod, Kornfeld moved to Frankfurt in 1914 working as a drama adviser while publishing his first tragedy, *Die Verführung* (1916), which won him a reputation as an important expressionist playwright. Kornfeld's technique may be described as symbolic realism. His aim was to avoid any imitation of physical reality, and he urged the actors in his plays to refrain from any suggestion of realism. Soon he became known for the stories "Legende" (1917) and "Die Begegnung" (1917) as well as for the important programmatic expressionist essay "Der beseelte und der psychologische Mensch" (1918), a fundamental critique of psychology and at the same time the foundation of his anti-mimetic program of acting. After the less successful tragedy *Himmel und Hölle* (1919) Kornfeld turned towards comedy in the 1920s, writing *Der ewige Traum* (1922), *Palme oder Der Gekraenkte* (1924), *Kilian oder Die gelbe Rose* (1926), *Smither kauft Europa* (1930) and, after moving to Berlin in 1928, the important historical drama *Jud Suess* (1930), dealing with the problem of assimilation and antisemitism. In Berlin, Kornfeld also wrote essays and criticism for Leopold Schwarzschild's *Das Tage-Buch*. In 1932, he returned to his native Prague, was captured by the Nazis in 1941, and deported to the Lodz ghetto, where he died soon after. In his last years he wrote the novel *Blanche oder Das Atelier im Garten*, a comédie humaine far removed from expressionism, which was published posthumously in 1957 and ever since has been considered his most important work.

BIBLIOGRAPHY: Sborowitz, in: G. Krojanker (ed.), *Juden in der deutschen Literatur* (1922), 219–30; M. Maren-Grisebach, *Weltanschauung und Kunstform im Fruehwerk Paul Kornfelds* (Thesis, Hamburg, 1960). **ADD. BIBLIOGRAPHY:** S. Nugy, *Paul Kornfeld, Jud Süss* (1995); W. Haumann, *Paul Kornfeld* (1996).

[Rudolf Kayser / Andreas Kilcher (2nd ed.)]

KORNFELD, ZSIGMOND (1852–1909), banker and politician; born in Golcuv Jenikov, Bohemia. He joined the Hungarian General Credit Bank in Budapest, becoming its general director in 1900. As such, he had a considerable influence on Hungarian financial policy and the encouragement of private enterprises. He successfully effected the conversion of shares for the strengthening of state credit, and promoted the 1894 currency reform. In 1902 Kornfeld was decorated by the king, and became a member of the Chamber of Magnates of the Hungarian Parliament. His activities included the founding of the Hungarian River and Maritime Navigation Company, and presidency of the Budapest Stock Exchange (from 1899). He was created a baron in 1909.

When, on the eve of the Russo-Japanese War he represented the Austro-Hungarian government in negotiating an extensive loan for the czarist empire, he refused the decoration offered him by the Russians. He told the czar's ambassador that in his capacity as a banker he had conducted the negotiations at the request of his government, but being a Jew, he could not accept favors from a country where Jews were persecuted and even massacred. He refused to accept remuneration for his part in the transaction. He took part in Jewish community life, and in 1893 became deputy president of the *kehillah* of Budapest.

BIBLIOGRAPHY: J. Radnóti, *Kornfeld Zsigmond* (1931); N. Katzburg, *Antishemiyyut be-Hungaryah 1867–1914* (1969), 45–46.

[Jeno Zsoldos]

KORNGOLD, ERICH WOLFGANG (1897–1957), composer. Born in Brno, Czechoslovakia, Korngold was the son of the Viennese music critic Julius Korngold (1860–1945), who was also his first music teacher. Hailed as a child prodigy when his first large-scale work, *Der Schneemann*, a pantomime, was performed in 1908, he went from success to success with instrumental and operatic works. His short operas *Violanta* and *Der Ring des Polykrates* were performed when he was only 19 and his best-known opera, *Die Tote Stadt*, had its premiere in 1920. In 1934 Korngold settled in Hollywood, where he arranged Mendelssohn's *Midsummer Night's Dream* music for Max *Reinhardt's film version of the play. His music was that of a conservative modernist, being colorful, melodious, and sensuous. Korngold's instrumental works include symphonic overtures, a sinfonietta, chamber music, a piano concerto for left hand, and a violin concerto. His later operas, *Das Wunder der Heliane* (1927), *Kathrin* (1939), and *Die stumme Serenade* (1954), did not attain the success of the earlier *Die Tote Stadt*.

BIBLIOGRAPHY: R.S. Hoffmann, *Erich Wolfgang Korngold* (Ger., 1923); Grove, Dict; *Current Biography Yearbook 1958*, 234; MMG; Riemann-Gurlitt.

[Peter Emanuel Gradenwitz]

KORNHEISER, TONY (Anthony Irwin; 1948–), U.S. sportswriter, radio talk show host, newspaper columnist. Kornheiser grew up in Lynbrook, N.Y., on Long Island. He celebrated his bar mitzvah in a Conservative synagogue, and the Kornheisers celebrated the Jewish holidays. Kornheiser graduated from Harpur College in upstate New York, now part of SUNY-Binghamton, in 1970, and taught elementary school for a year. He then went to work as a feature writer for *New York Newsday*, covering general-interest stories and writing a weekly column on rock music. In 1976, he left *Newsday* to join the sports section of *The New York Times* and was hired by *The Washington Post* in 1979, becoming a sports columnist there in 1984. Kornheiser hosted a radio show on WTEM-AM in Washington, D.C., beginning in 1992, and joined ESPN Radio in November 1997 as host of *The Tony Kornheiser Show*, which premiered January 5, 1998. Kornheiser then began working at ESPN television, co-hosting the popular *Pardon the Interruption* (PTI) show, which debuted on September 22, 2001. His Satellite Radio show debuted on February 28, 2005, on XM

Channel 152. Kornheiser is the author of a non-sports book, *The Baby Chase* (1983), about infertility and adopting a child, and three compilations of his newspaper columns: *Pumping Irony: Working Out the Angst of a Lifetime* (1995), *Bald As I Wanna Be* (1997), and *I'm Back for More Cash: A Tony Kornheiser Collection (Because You Can't Take Two Hundred Newspapers into the Bathroom)* (2003).

[Elli Wohlgelernter (2nd ed.)]

KORNIK (Pol. **Kórnik**; Ger. **Kurnik**), town in Poznan province, W. Poland. Documentary evidence points to the presence of Jews in the town from 1618. In 1687 and 1713 the *Great Poland Council convened in Kornik. A privilege granted by the local nobleman allowed the Jews permanent residence and the right to trade in cloth, livestock, etc. against payment of special taxes. Communal records, beginning from the early 18th century, existed until World War II and included the special statutes of the tailors' guild, which was founded in 1754 with 44 members and still had 51 members in 1853. A small wooden synagogue was erected in 1736, and a larger one in 1767. According to the 1765 census, there were 367 Jews in Kornik, some of whom owned houses outside the Jewish quarter. After the Prussian occupation a provincial assembly met in Kornik in 1817 with the aim of submitting to the government suggestions for improving the lot of Poznan Jewry. Among Kornik rabbis was R. Israel Moses b. Aryeh *Loeb who served from 1781. A schoolhouse was built in 1846. During the 1848 revolution the Jews were attacked by the rebels. In 1808 the Jewish community numbered 566 (36% of the total population), increasing to 1,170 (43%) in 1840. From then on their number continually diminished due to migration to larger cities, falling to 399 (15%) in 1871, 220 (9%) in 1895, 111 (4.4%) in 1905, 92 (3.6%) in 1910, 57 (2.6%) in 1921, and only 36 in 1939. They were expelled by the Germans to Lodz and Kalisz in December 1939, sharing the fate of the local Jews.

BIBLIOGRAPHY: R. Mahler, *Yidn in Amolikn Poyln in Likht fun Tsifern* (1958), index; B. Wasiutyirski, *Ludność żydowska w Polsce w XIX i XX wiekach* (1930), 167; G. Loukomsky, *Jewish Art in European Synagogues* (1947), 37, 64; A. Warschaur, *Die staedtliche Archive in der Provinz Posen* (1901), 118; AZDJ, 63 (1899), 521; *Mitteilungen der Gesamtarchive der deutschen Juden*, 4 (1913), 110; A. Grotte, *Deutsche, boehmische und polnische Synagogentypen* (1915), 14, 17, 39, 41, 51–60; *Deutsche wissenschaftliche Zeitschrift fuer Polen*, 13 (1929), 139ff.; *Mitteilungen zur juedischen Volkskunde*, 3 (1907), 67f.; E. Callier, *Powiat pyzdrski w XVI stuleciu* (1888–91), 141; L. Lewin, *Die Landessynode der grosspolnischen Judenschaft* (1926), 33, 46, 98, 104ff.; A. Heppner and I. Herzberg, *Aus Vergangenheit und Gegenwart der Juden und der juedischen Gemeinden in den Posener Landen* (1909), 585–90; M.K. Piechotkowie, *Bóżnice drzewniane* (1957), illustrations nos. 100, 101.

[*Encyclopaedia Judaica* (Germany)]

KORNIK (Kurnik), MEIR BEN MOSES (d. 1826), rabbi. Kornik was born in Glogau (Silesia), where he later served as rabbi. He wrote the following books: *Ezrat ha-Sofer* (Amsterdam, 1796), the Book of Esther, with the masoretic rules for writing this scroll; *Hadrei Kodesh* (Dyrhenfurth, 1817), commentary on parts of *Sefer Yeẓirah* and on parts of the Zohar which are included in *Tikkun Leil Shavuot* and in *Tikkun Hoshana Rabba; Davar be-Itto* (Breslau, 1817), on the Jewish calendar with a refutation of Lazarus Bendavid's *Zur Berechnung und Geschichte des juedischen Kalenders* and some glosses by M.B. Friedenthal; and *System der Zeitrechnung in chronologischen Tabellen* (Berlin, 1825), a complete guide to the Julian, Gregorian, Jewish, and Muslim calendars. Kornik corresponded with R. Moses Sofer and R. Akiva Eger on Jewish calendar problems.

[Salomon Wolf]

KORNITZER, LEON (1875–1947), *ḥazzan* and composer. Born in Vienna, the son and grandson of *ḥazzanim*, Kornitzer served the communities of Klattau, Saaz, and Prague before being called to the Hamburg Tempelverein in 1913. His imaginative and skillful compositions, published in *Romemot El* (1928), are in the tradition of *Sulzer and *Lewandowski, but they also evince the influence of Emanuel *Kirschner's 19th-century German romantic style. Kornitzer was the editor of *Der Juedische Kantor* for ten years from its inception in 1927 and edited a collection of liturgical songs and instrumental compositions, *Juedische Klaenge* (1933). After his emigration to Ereẓ Israel in 1939 he continued to compose and was conductor of the choir at the Central Synagogue in Haifa.

BIBLIOGRAPHY: Idelsohn, Music, 241, 510–11; A.M. Rothmueller, *Music of the Jews* (1967²), 136–7.

[David M.L. Olivestone]

KOROBKA (deriving from Rus. basket, "box"; Yid. *takse*), a tax imposed on consumption items, mainly on *kasher* meat. It was introduced among the communities of *Poland-Lithuania in the 17th century to assist individual communities in paying their debts, as well as a means of achieving the independence of the individual community from the hegemony of the *Councils of the Lands. In Russia, from the end of the 18th century, one of the aims of the *korobka* also was to help cover the taxation quota which the Jewish communities had to pay in continuation of the collective debt of the Councils of the Lands. In the 19th century, the *korobka* mainly served to pay for the salaries of rabbis and other religious officials and the support of educational and charitable institutions in the individual communities.

The Russian government, however, turned the *korobka* into an instrument for additional exaction of money from the Jews. It was generally leased for collection for a period of four years to individual Jews, who paid fixed sums to the regional government treasuries. The sums were apportioned according to a list submitted by the municipal council (on which the Jews were seldom consulted). Surpluses were deposited with the State Treasury. Regulations for the *korobka* were drawn up in 1839. They restricted the tax to meat alone and it became a compulsory tax levied upon all the Jewish communities in the *Pale of Settlement, with the exception of the provinces of Russian Poland. In 1844, when the Jewish **kahal* autonomy was officially abolished, new regulations were issued concerning the meat tax. In them, the *korobka* was allocated for the Jewish communal requirements, in the first place to assure payment of the government taxation quota and of the debts of the community, and the remainder for the maintenance of Jewish schools, the support of Jewish agricultural settlement, and the requirements of charitable enterprises. The apportionment of the taxation tariff, the methods of its collection, and supervision over the funds was assigned to the non-Jewish municipal administration, in consultation with "wealthy Jews and permanent residents." Authority was granted to the tax lessees to prevent the ritual slaughter of animals without paying the tax, and the police were called upon to assist them in this task. Soldiers and graduates of high schools were exempted from the payment of this tax.

In the provinces of Russian Poland, a tax on *kasher* meat, which was directly transferred to the State Treasury, was introduced in 1809, in addition to the tax on meat for the requirements of the community. The Jews derived no benefit from it; this tax was abolished in 1863.

The system of leasing the meat tax encouraged exploitation and corruption by the lessees, who raised the price of *kasher* meat in order to increase their incomes. The *maskilim* condemned such practices in their periodicals and writings, and the *ba'al-takse*, as the lessee was called, became a frequent target of their attacks. (The comedy by Mendele Mokher Seforim, *Di Takse* (1869), is based on such incidents in the community of Berdichev.) The *korobka* system also gave rise to illegal *sheḥitah* to evade its payment and make possible cheaper prices for *kasher* meat.

The meat tax was sharply criticized by governmental as well as Jewish circles. Its opponents argued that it was unjust to impose a tax based on the necessity of carrying out a religious observance (*kashrut*) and this was a typical indirect tax whose brunt fell on the poorer classes. The exemption of the Jewish intelligentsia from its payment, and the fact that with the spread of Haskalah many Jews (especially in the provinces of southern Russia) did not observe *kashrut*, only aggravated the burden on the observant Jewish masses. While poverty and dearth were felt throughout the Jewish communities, millions of surplus rubles from the *korobka* funds were being deposited in the government bank (in January 1887, these surpluses totaled over 3,000,000 rubles, and in the year 1905, for the provinces of Kiev, Podolia, and Volhynia alone, there were reserves of over 1,500,000 rubles). It was only in exceptional cases, such as fire or flood, or to support the establishment of a large institution (a hospital, a school, or the like), that allocations were granted for the communities from these "surpluses." On the other hand, many allocations were granted for state purposes, such as the construction of general schools, to which the admission of Jews was restricted, payments to the special police of various towns, for street paving, road construction, and sanitation purposes. The Jews, who shared the burden of general tax payment, were thus compelled in addition to contribute a special Jewish tax. For continuation of the *korobka* system, it was argued that the tax was easily collected and that its abolition would remove the financial basis of the Jewish community budgets.

The first public debate in a Jewish forum took place at the conference of Jewish community leaders held at Kovno in 1909. The expert on the *korobka*, H.B. *Sliozberg considered it a fine for the observance of a religious precept and called for its conversion into a progressive income tax which the government should recognize as compulsory.

The scope of the *korobka* system is indicated by the annual payments made by the lessees shortly before World War I. The annual payment for the lease then amounted to 370,000 rubles in Odessa, 147,000 in Vilna, 100,000 in Riga, over 50,000 in Berdichev, 42,000 in Dvinsk, 325,000 rubles in the whole of the province of Volhynia, and 108,000 rubles in the whole of the province of Kovno. During this period, several communities introduced a community-sponsored collection of the tax, without the intermediary of lessees. In Vilna, for example, its collection was delegated to a special commission appointed by the community and all profits were handed over to the charitable institutions of the town.

After the outbreak of World War I, when restrictions were introduced against the consumption of meat ("meatless days," etc.) and the price of meat rose, the decline in *korobka* revenues fell sharply, and the financial resources of many communities collapsed. In a large number of communities, the meat tax was then replaced by a progressively assessed tax which was determined by a variety of data (amount of rent paid, size of living quarters, etc.). Following the 1917 Revolution, the meat tax was abolished with the rest of the anti-Jewish legislation.

BIBLIOGRAPHY: M. Morgulis, *Voprosy yevreyskoy zhizni* (1903); S. Levin, *O korobochnom i svechnom sbore* (1910); Yu. Hessen, *K istorii korobochnago sbora v Rossii* (1912); M. Gordon, *Opyt izucheniya yevreyskogo finansovogo khozyaystva v Rossii* (1918), incl. bibl.

[Yehuda Slutsky]

°**KOROLENKO, VLADIMIR GALAKTIONOVICH** (1853–1921), Russian writer. One of the most illustrious representatives of the liberal Russian intelligentsia of the turn of the century, Korolenko was very active in many humanitarian causes, and was also among the most vocal opponents of antisemitism in Russia. He began by publicly condemning the pogroms of 1881–82. In his *Skazaniye o flore, Agrippe i Menakheme, syn Yegudy* ("Tale of Florius, Agrippa and Menahem ben Judah" (1886), in: *Ocherki i Razskazy* (vol. 3, 1894[2])) he not only condemns persecution of the Jews, but has his Jewish protagonist voice the view that the Jews will achieve equality through armed struggle, and only then will human brotherhood prevail. Antisemitic prejudice is mocked in gentle tones in *Sudny den* ("The Day of Atonement"), in *Ocherki i Razskazy*, 1888–94[2] (Brit. ed. *The Murmuring Forest*; 1916) and in *Makar's Dream*, a fantastic tale in the Gogolian tradition, while *Dom Nomer 13* ("House No. 13," 1903) is an angry denunciation of the murderous pogrom in *Kishinev. Korolenko's prolific journalistic writings include numerous articles about the notorious blood-libel trial of Mendel *Beilis in 1913.

BIBLIOGRAPHY: F. Haeusler, in: *Wissenschaftliche Zeitschrift der Martin-Luther Universitaet, Halle-Wittenberg*, 10:1 (1961), 237–48; YE, 9 (c. 1910), 771.

[Maurice Friedberg]

KORONE (Coron), town and port located on the southwest Peloponnesus, Greece. The 12th-century traveler Benjamin of Tudela found 300 Jews in Korone. After the expulsion from Spain a number of Jews settled in Korone. During the 14th and 15th centuries the Jews were engaged in maritime commerce. Under Venetian rule they suffered oppression and degradation. When Andrea Dorea attacked Turkish-held Greece in 1532, Jewish property was plundered, and some of the Jews taken captive. During the Venetian assault on Korone in 1646 Jews were carried off to Malta as slaves. With the conquest of Korone in 1685 by Venice the Jewish community dispersed. It was not reorganized after the Peloponnesus peninsula again became a part of the Ottoman Empire in 1715.

BIBLIOGRAPHY: AZDJ, 54 (1890), 3–4; Roth, JHSET, 12 (1931), 217, 241; J. Starr, *Romania* (1949), 63–72.

[Simon Marcus]

KOROSTEN (or **Iskorost**), Zhitomir district, Ukraine. Although a Jewish leaseholder is mentioned in 1618, the Jewish community began to develop only in the 19th century with the increase of traffic through the railroad junction. The 331 Jews in Korosten in 1847 had grown to 1,299 (49% of the population) in 1897. When convoys of troops passed through the town in 1919, the Jews suffered severely and in that same year they were the victims of a pogrom perpetrated by the forces of Simon *Petlyura in February 1919, and by the Red Army on March 13, 1919. In 1926, 6,089 Jews (50.7% of the population) lived in Korosten. In October 1926 a gathering of 90 Ukrainian rabbis and 1,500 guests was held there, headed by R. Shlomo Zevin (later a well-known rabbi in Jerusalem). Jewish workers were employed in an iron foundry, and furniture and porcelain factories. They also worked on the railroad and in nine artisan cooperatives. There were two Yiddish schools with an enrollment of 1,000 in 1934. In 1939 Jews numbered 10,991 (35.7% of the total population). The Germans occupied the town on August 8, 1941. Most of the Jews were evacuated or fled. The Germans murdered 770 Jews in September 1941 and about 1,000 in March 1942. After the war, when the town was rebuilt and enlarged, many Jews took up residence there and in 1959 they numbered 6,800 (17.9% of the population). Most left in the 1990s, but a yeshivah and day school were active.

[Yehuda Slutsky / Shmuel Spector (2nd ed.)]

KORSUN-SHEVCHENKOVSKI, city in Kiev district, Ukraine. A Jewish community existed in Korsun from the 17th century. When the Cossack armies defeated the Polish army near Korsun in May 1648 this sparked off the revolt throughout Ukraine which resulted in the destruction of Ukrainian Jewry (see *Chmielnicki massacres). In 1702 the town suffered heavily in an attack by the *Haidamacks and only a quarter of them survived. In 1734 the Haidamacks killed 27 Jews and stole much Jewish property. The number of poll-tax paying Jews in Korsun in 1785 was 187. With the Russian annexation (1793), the community increased in number, growing from 1,456 Jews in 1847 to 3,800 (46.3% of the total population) in 1897. In 1881 a yeshivah was opened, where Russian and arithmetic were also taught. On March 1, 1918, Bolsheviks murdered several community leaders, including the rabbi, in a riot. In the summer of 1919 the Cossacks of *Denikin's army rioted in Korsun, killed 16, with the result that many Jews left the town. There were 2,449 Jews (50.1% of the population) living there in 1926, and the number dropped to 1,329 (14.2% of the total population) in 1939. A Jewish council was active in the 1920s. The Germans occupied the city on July 30, 1941. In September they killed 226 Jews, and probably the rest of them in November.

[Yehuda Slutsky / Shmuel Spector (2nd ed.)]

KORTNER, FRITZ (1892–1970), Austrian actor. Born in Vienna, he made his debut in 1910 in Mannheim and performed in Vienna, Dresden, and Hamburg before working with Leopold *Jessner at the Staatstheater Berlin (in 1919–23 and 1926–30) as the leading actor of Jessner´s highly influential theatrical style. With his stentorian voice and his physical power he excelled in the classical repertoire (as Richard III, Othello, Hamlet, Macbeth) as well as in modern roles. Against the background of the increasing antisemitic spirit of Nazism in Germany he often played Jewish characters threatened by their surroundings, such as Shylock and Professor Bernhardi (A. Schnitzler). He fled Germany in 1933 and settled first in London and later in the United States (1938). He returned to Germany in 1947 and developed a second career as a controversial but soon highly esteemed director. His autobiography, *Aller Tage Abend* (1959), is a brilliant and fascinating book.

BIBLIOGRAPHY: M. Brand, *Fritz Kortner in der Weimarer Republik* (1981); K. Voelker, *Fritz Kortner. Schauspieler und Regisseur* (1987); P. Schuetze, *Fritz Kortner* (1994).

[Jens Malte Fischer (2nd ed.)]

KOS (Cos), the second largest of the Greek Dodecanese Islands in the Aegean Sea off the shores of Asia Minor. Despite the absence of any direct reference to Jewish settlement, it is assumed that Jews lived there during the Second Temple period. Josephus (Ant., 14:111–3) quotes Strabo to the effect that the Jews deposited 800 talents of silver on Kos for security, for fear of its being seized by King Mithridates, who, however, succeeded in taking the money. Kos is also mentioned in an obscure passage in I Maccabees 15:16–23. Herod bestowed some gifts on the islanders (Jos., Wars, 1:423) and his family maintained relations with the local population after his death, and Jewish emissaries were said to have passed through the island (Jos., Ant., 14:233). Romaniot Greek-speaking Jews lived on the island during the rule of the Knights of St. John (1315–1523) and according to one source they numbered 1,500. The Jews were exiled to Nice (1502) by the Grand Master of the Order of St. John at Rhodes. When the island was captured by the Turks in 1522, Jews again settled on it. In the 16th century, several noted Italian Jewish families, such as Romano, Finzi, and Capeluto, resided on the island. The first known rabbi was Isaac Katan, who headed the community in 1700. A small synagogue was built in 1747. In 1850 a *blood libel was perpetrated on the island, but the instigators were punished. In 1861, The small community of Kos was subordinate to the community at Rhodes until 1870. In the second half of the 19th century, 40 Jewish families lived on Kos, but there were only 20 in 1880, ten in 1901, and three or four families in 1910. The Italians captured the island in 1912 and annexed it in 1923 under the Lausanne Treaty. During World War I and the Greco-Turkish wars (1918–23), there was an influx of Jews from Anatolia and Rhodes, and the community reached 160 persons. The old cemetery was at Cape Sable but disappeared by the early 20th century, and a newer cemetery was used. About 100 Jews were buried there between the two world wars and the oldest grave dated from 1715. The Baron Edmond de Rothschild visited the community in 1903 and financed a wall for the cemetery. The earthquake of 1933 killed five Jews and destroyed the synagogue, which had stood on a hill for centuries. In 1934 a new synagogue, Kahal Shalom, was built near the port and the Italian government financed half of the construction expenses. The Jews exported raisins and grapes to Egypt and Europe and traded in cloth, iron, and other goods. The 1938 Italian anti-Jewish racial laws were imposed on the Jews of the island. On the eve of the Holocaust, the community numbered 20 families. After the Germans captured the island on October 3, 1943, eight families succeeded in fleeing to Turkey. Following the German occupation of the Dodecanese in World War II, about 100 Jews from Kos were deported to Auschwitz, together with those from Rhodes (July, 1944). Twelve of the Jews deported survived the death camps. Four Jews were exempt due to their neutral Turkish citizenship and survived. In the 1960s only one Jewish family remained on Kos. After the last local Jew, Michel Menashe, died in 1995, the synagogue closed and became a cultural center and library.

BIBLIOGRAPHY: A. Galanté, *Histoire des Juifs de Rhodes. Chio, Cos…* (1935), 161–7; idem, *Appendice à l'Histoire des Juifs de Rhodes, Chio, Cos, etc.* (1948), 75–76; Schuerer, Gesch, 1 (1901[4]), 432n.; 3 (1909), 4n. 2, 56. **ADD. BIBLIOGRAPHY:** L.P. Fargion, *Il Libro della Memoria – Gli Ebrei deportati dall'Italia (1943–1945)* (1991); B. Rivlin, "Kos," in: *Pinkas Kehillot Yavan* (1999), 347–50.

[Uriel Rappaport /Simon Marcus / Yitzchak Kerem (2nd ed.)]

°**KOŚCIUSZKO, TADEUSZ** (1746–1817), Polish military commander and freedom fighter. In 1775 he left Poland for America, where he joined the army of George Washington (1776), distinguishing himself at the siege of Saratoga, where he was impressed by the Jewish volunteers who participated in the fighting. Returning to Poland in 1784, he was attracted by the movement for political reforms there, and after a period of voluntary exile returned in 1794 to organize armed resistance against Russia and Prussia, then menacing the independence of Poland. In the official *Gazeta Rządowa* (Sept. 17, 1794) he declared that the liberation of Poland from foreign yoke would also improve the status of the Jews in the country. He praised the initiative of Berek *Joselewicz and others in organizing a cavalry regiment for the war against Poland's enemies. Even at the beginning of the rebellion many Jewish craftsmen in Warsaw took part in fighting the Russian units stationed in the town. Kościuszko was eventually wounded in 1794 and imprisoned in St. Petersburg. After two years he was set free and in 1798 arrived in Paris. He spent the last years of his life in Switzerland.

BIBLIOGRAPHY: J. Szacki (Shatzky), *Kościuszko a Żydzi* (1917); E. Ringelblum, *Żydzi w powstaniu kościuszkowskim* (1938); P. Wiernik, *History of the Jews in America* (1912), 95–98. **ADD. BIBLIOGRAPHY:** M. Balaban, *Historja i literatura Zydowska*, vol. 3 (1925), 429–31; J. Tomaszewski et al., *Zydzi w Polsce … Leksykon* (2001), 564–65.

[Arthur Cygielman]

KOSHETZ, NINA (1894–1965), soprano singer. Born in Kiev, Koshetz entered the Moscow Conservatory to study piano at the age of 11 and singing at 16. She toured Russia with the conductor *Koussevitzky and also gave many concerts with Rakhmaninov, of whose songs she was a famous interpreter. In 1921, she made her American debut, following which she appeared with many American and European orchestras. She also gave numerous recitals featuring Russian songs. In 1941, she settled in Hollywood, where she taught singing until her death.

[Max Loppert (2nd ed.)]

KOSICE (Slovak **Košice**; Hung. **Kassa**; Ger. **Kaschau**), city in S.E. Slovakia. Until 1992 Czechoslovak Republic, since 1993 Slovak Republic. Documentation testifies to Jewish appearances in Kosice in 1484 and 1524, but they were not permitted to live in the city or to belong to the guilds. In 1765 Jews doing business in Kosice settled in the nearby village of Rozhanovce (Hung. Roygony, Yiddish Rozdewisz) and Velka Ida (Hung. Nafty Ida). Municipal and professional institutions fought against Jewish activity in the city. In 1840 the Hungarian parliament allowed Jews to settle freely in Hungary, including Kosice. Jewish inhabitants of Rozhanovce moved there in 1840–42. The next year 17 families were permitted to live there; in 1844 some 40 families were registered. In 1851 there were 721 Jews; in 1853 there were 752; and in 1857 about 1,500. In 1865 there were 2,178; in 1880 there were 2, 846; in 1890 they numbered 4,988; in 1910 there were 6,723 Jews. At the first Czechoslovak census of 1921 there were 8,762 Jews in Kosice. In 1938 the community numbered 11,420.

When Rozhanovce Jewry settled in Kosice, they developed community life. The *ḥevra kaddisha* was founded in 1844, and a cemetery was sanctified. The congregation erected an imposing synagogue, had a *mikveh*, kosher slaughterhouse, and other Jewish institutions. After the 1868 Congress of Hungarian Jewry, the congregation chose the *Neolog path, and the Orthodox founded its own congregation. Both had their own *ḥevra kaddisha*, women's clubs, and social institutions.

Poor Jews from Carpathian Ruthenia and Galicia settled in several streets of Kosice, giving them a particular Jewish character. Several ḥasidic *admors* kept their court in these streets. When World War I started, several hundred Kosice Jews enlisted in the army. In 1918 the war ended, the Austro-Hungarian Empire collapsed, and the returning soldiers and POWs were fired by revolutionary zeal. Leftist Jewish leaders gained prominence. In 1919, the Magyar commune was created, soon engulfing Kosice. Many leaders of the commune were Jewish. After the retreat of the Bolsheviks and the defeat of the commune, many Jewish Communists remained in Kosice.

The new Czechoslovak republic imposed its rule over Kosice, which augured well for the Jews. The end of the fighting left many Jews impoverished. Kosice became the eastern Slovakian center of the *American Joint Distribution Committee. One of its main undertakings was an orphanage. Vocational schools were added, and a bank providing small loans to rebuild businesses. Irene Matzner, a local resident, was the leading figure in the resurrection effort.

The Zionist movement existed in Kosice before the war. After the war, its influence expanded. The Ha-Shomer ha-Ẓa'ir, Bnei Akiva, and Betar youth movements had strong branches in the city, and Kosice served as their temporary Slovakian headquarters.

Jews participated in political life outside of Jewish parties. Assimilationist Jews supported parties for Magyar independence. The Social Democrats and the Communists also found Jewish support. Many members of the community were wealthy industrialists, landowners, and prosperous lawyers and physicians.

In November 1938 Kosice was annexed to Hungary, following the Viennese arbitration of November 2, 1938. Soon the antisemitic laws of Hungary were imposed on the conquered territories. Jews lacking Hungarian citizenship were imprisoned, and some sent to the no man's land on the Slovakian-Hungarian borders. Slovakia proclaimed autonomy in October 1938, and Jews lacking Slovakian citizenship were sent to the Slovakian-Hungarian borders.

Antisemitic legislation hit the Jewish community hard. Jews were deprived of jobs and their property. On January 1, 1940, Jewish males were sent into forced military service. In 1941 the Hungarian authorities deported thousands of Jews for alleged lack of citizenship to the region of Kamenets-Podolski and other places, where they were killed. In 1942 deportation of Jews to Poland started, and hundreds tried to find safety by illegally crossing the Hungarian border. The Kosice community summoned its inner resources to assist the refugees.

Persecution in Hungary and Kosice increased, even against those Jews who had been active in patriotic Magyar organizations. They lost income and property and were denied civil and human rights.

On March 19, 1944, German forces occupied Hungary. Wealthy Jews were imprisoned by the Magyar agencies and tortured to reveal where their property and possessions were. On April 27, 1944, all Jews were ordered to assemble in the three major synagogues; from there they were transferred to two brickwork factories on the outskirts of the city. Jews who escaped from Slovakia made strenuous efforts to return, along with some Hungarian Jews. Kosice was one of the centers of escape. There were 10,590 Jews in the brickworks, and several hundred in a ghetto in the city. On April 30, 1944, there were 13,253 Jews in Kosice; about 3,000 were not inhabitants of Kosice proper. On May 16, 1944, the deportation of the interned Jews to Auschwitz began. Some 15,707 Jews were deported. On October 15, 1944, the Nylas (Arrow Cross) fascist party took over the government in Hungary and established a reign of terror.

Shortly after the liberation, a Jewish committee to assist the returning Jews was organized in Kosice, supported by UNRAA and later the Joint. A committee to manage the congregation's affairs was also organized. This committee, with a few Orthodox on its staff, was criticized severely. The attempt to stamp the entire congregation Orthodox caused tension. For the High Holydays of 1945, an Orthodox and a Neolog synagogue were restored for prayer. A new *ḥevra kaddisha* was established and other Jewish institutions resurrected. Communal Jewish life was restored, and Kosice became the center of Jewish life for eastern Slovakia.

In 1947 there were 2,542 Jews in Kosice. Zionist youth movements were revived, and Ha-Shomer ha-Ẓa'ir established a home for future immigrants to Palestine. With the proclamation of the State of Israel on May 14, 1948, the community began to feverishly collect money for Israel and recruit volunteers for the Israeli army.

Between 1949 and 1950, more than 1,000 Jews left for Israel, and others emigrated overseas; consequently, the congregation was largely depleted. Other waves of emigration took place in 1964, 1968–1970, and after the Velvet Revolution of 1989. Following the Communist takeover of Czechoslovakia and the first wave of emigration, the Kosice community had to adjust to the new conditions. The yeshivah, founded in late 1940, was closed. The major tasks of the community were to preserve the prayers in the synagogue, to supply kosher meat, and to provide children with basic Jewish education. A council existed, which had to be approved by the Communist authorities. The municipal authorities tried to stop the ritual slaughter and to interfere with the activity of the kosher restaurant. Jewish informers plagued patrons of the restaurant and participants in the prayers. Occasionally tensions rose between the Federation of Jewish Religious Congregations, located in Bratislava, and the Kosice council. However, schooling continued, Hanukkah and Purim parties for the children were held, and the Kosice congregation supplied at least minimal services for Jews of eastern Slovakia, where congregations no longer existed. For most of 1949–1989, a rabbi or a qualified replacement resided in Kosice.

The Jewish community was revitalized after 1989. It pulsed with social and cultural activity, the Zionist movement returned to the city, and it established close ties with Jewish organizations and with Israel.

In 2005 there were 240 members in the congregation. There was a kosher restaurant. The congregation has published several books devoted to the Holocaust and the story of the congregation. A group of Israeli students study veterinary medicine at the local university.

[Erich Kulka / Yeshayahu Jelinek (2nd ed.)]

BIBLIOGRAPHY: E. Enlen, in: *Zeitschrift fuer die Geschichte der Juden in der Tschechoslowakei*, 2 (1931/32), 279–91; 3 (1932/33), 47–60; M. Lányi and H. Proppern, *Szlovenskoi zsidó hitközssegek története* (1933), 11–90; *Pinkas ha-Kehillot* (1963), 26–30; J. Lévai, *Abscheu und Grauen vor dem Genocid in der ganzen Welt* (1968), 355–6 and passim; R. Iltis (ed.), *Die aussaeen unter Traenen mit Jubel werden sie ernten* (1959), 157–61. **ADD. BIBLIOGRAPHY:** E. Bárkány and L. Dojc, *Zidovské nábozenské obce na Slovensku* (1991), 371–382; Y. Schlanger, *The Story of the Jewish Community of Kosice* (1991); A. Jurov and P. Salamon, *Kosice a deportacie Zidov v roku 1944* (1994).

KOSICE, GYULA (**Fernando Falik**; 1924–), Argentine sculptor. Born in Kosice, Czechoslovakia, he was taken to Buenos Aires in 1928 and became an Argentine citizen. Kosice published many works on the plastic arts. He was cofounder of the revues *Arturo* in 1944 and *Invention* in 1945. Kosice was one of the early promotors of abstract constructivism and kinetic art in Latin America. In 1946 he founded the group "Art Madi." From this time Kosice began to work in Plexiglas and to create sculpture in which light and movement became essential elements. In 1957, Kosice went to Paris where he had the first exhibition of hydraulic sculpture. In 1963 he organized the exhibition "L'Art Argentin Actuel" at the Museum of Modern Art in Paris, where an entire room was devoted to kinetic art.

[Gunter Bohm]

KOSINSKI, JERZY (1933–1991), U.S. novelist. Born the son of Mieczyslaw and Elzbieta Lewinkopf in Lodz, Poland, Kosinski's early years were shaped under Hitler's regime. The only full biography (*Jerzy Kosinski* by James Park Sloan, 1996) reports that the Jewish family survived as Catholic "Kosinskis," avoiding the camps. Postwar schooling resulted in two master's degrees (social science and history) and notoriety as a photographer before Kosinski emigrated to the U.S. in 1957 as a doctoral student.

There, Kosinski soon attained success as a writer. Under the pseudonym Joseph Novak, he completed *The Future Is Ours, Comrade* (1960) and *No Third Path* (1962). After these non-fictional works, Kosinski coined the term "autofiction," blurring the boundary between autobiography and literature, and confusing critics and interviewers. He wrote nine novels, two of which were revised and reissued. *The Painted Bird* (1965), banned in Poland, earned the Prix du Meilleur Livre Etranger in France and received public and critical acclaim. Often claiming that portions were autobiographical, Kosinski also insisted that *The Painted Bird* was a work of fiction. It remains a classic of Holocaust literature, combining historical realities – not his own experience – with myth and fairy tales. Thereafter, Kosinski considered enduring themes: identity, technology, consumerism, sexuality, politics, and violence. His experiments with stylistic and narrative structures garnered both acclaim and criticism. *Steps* (1968) received the National Book Award and *Being There* (1970) was adapted by the author for a film, starring Peter Sellers (1979), which won the British Film Critics Award and an American Oscar. Other novels include *The Devil Tree* (1973, rev. ed. 1981), *Cockpit* (1975), *Blind Date* (1977), *Passion Play* (1979), *Pinball* (1982), and *The Hermit of 69th Street* (1988, rev. ed. 1991). A collection of his essays, *Passing By* (1992), was published after his death.

As a writer and performer (as Zinoviev in Warren Beatty's film *Reds* (1981), the voice of Chaim Rumkowski in the documentary *The Lodz Ghetto* (1989), and a guest on TV talk shows), Kosinski continued to interest both European and American scholars/artists. Kosinski was president of the American chapter of PEN (poets, playwrights, publishers, essayists, and novelists), from 1973 to 1975, and served on United Nations committees. He received the B'rith Shalom Humanitarian Freedom Award for his efforts in behalf of jailed writers. Kosinski also obtained a Guggenheim Fellowship (1967) and taught writing at Princeton, Wesleyan, and Yale. Charges launched by the *Village Voice* in 1982 that Kosinski relied heavily on collaborators/ghost writers have been largely dismissed by scholars, but the damage to his reputation was significant. He committed suicide in New York City, his home since 1957, in 1991.

BIBLIOGRAPHY: B.T. Lupack (ed.), *Critical Essays on Jerzy Kosinski* (1998); J.P. Sloan, *Jerzy Kosinski: A Biography* (1996); W. Everman, *Jerzy Kosinski: The Literature of Violation* (1991).

[Mary Lazar (2nd ed.)]

KOSMIN, BARRY (1946–), British sociologist and demographer. One of the best-known contemporary Jewish sociologists and demographers, Kosmin was born in London and served as executive director of the Research Unit of the Board of Deputies of British Jews from 1974 to 1986. He then became a professor (1986–96) at the City University of New York before becoming executive director of Jewish Policy Research, the successor body to the Institute of Jewish Affairs, which conducts research and undertakes policy studies about contemporary Jewish life. Kosmin was director of the well-known 1990 U.S. National Jewish Policy Survey and wrote extensively on Jewish demography, contemporary religious identity, and antisemitism.

[William D. Rubinstein (2nd ed.)]

KOSNER, EDWARD A. (1937–), U.S. editor. New York-born and bred, Kosner graduated from the City College of New York, where he had also served as the campus correspondent of the *New York Times*. After graduation in 1958, Kosner became a reporter for the *New York Post*, and later worked as a series writer and assistant city editor. In 1963 he joined *Newsweek* magazine as a national affairs writer, and over the next 16 years held all the top editorial positions, serving as editor from 1975 to 1979. During his tenure, Kosner wrote more than 20 cover stories on politics and urban affairs, and produced major projects, including "The Negro in America: What Must Be Done," "Poverty in America," and "Justice on Trial," which won the Robert F. Kennedy Journalism award and the American Bar Association's Silver Gavel award. Kosner also directed *Newsweek*'s award-winning coverage of the Watergate scandal, which resulted in more than 40 cover stories. In 1980, Kosner became editor of *New York* magazine, and later held the titles of editor and publisher and editor and president. During 13 years at *New York*, the magazine set records in advertising and circulation and won four National Magazine Association awards. From 1993 to 1997 he was editor in chief of *Esquire* magazine, but the magazine's circulation and advertising faltered during a weak economic period. He served as president of the American Society of Magazine Editors and was a long-time member of its board of directors. In November 1998, Kosner joined the staff of the *Daily News* of New York as Sunday editor and set about revamping that edition. In March 2000 Kosner became editor in chief of the paper, which became involved in a nasty fight for circulation and advertising revenue with New York City's other principal tabloid, the *New York Post*. During Kosner's tenure the paper gave extensive coverage to the attack of September 11, the New York Mets-New York Yankees subway World Series, and published many exclusive investigative stories. The *News* was twice a finalist for the Pulitzer Prize. Kosner announced in July 2003 that he would be retiring when his contract with the *News* ended in March 2004, but he left the paper several months early.

[Stewart Kampel (2nd ed.)]

KOSOV (Pol. **Kosów**), town in Ivano-Frankovsk (formerly Stanislavov) district, Ukraine; within Poland until 1772 when it passed to Austria; reverted to Poland between 1919 and 1939. Although Jews are mentioned in 1635, the organized community formed at the beginning of the 18th century. During the 1730s *Israel b. Eliezer, the Ba'al Shem Tov, stayed in the vicinity of Kosov with his family. During the middle and the second half of the 18th century, *Naḥman of Kosov, a disciple of the Ba'al Shem Tov, and *Baruch b. Abraham of Kosov (d. 1795) were active there. A branch of the ḥasidic dynasty of the Hager family was founded there during the last decade of the 18th century. The descendants of R. Jacob Koppel Ḥasid (d. 1787) served as rabbis of the town for 150 years: his son Menahem Mendel between 1790 and 1827; his son Ḥayyim, until 1854; Jacob Samson until 1880; his son Moses, until 1925; and Ḥayyim, who perished in the Holocaust in 1942. According to the census of 1764, the community of Kosov (including villagers from the surrounding area) numbered 343 families. They earned their livelihood in small trade, forestry, crafts, transportation, tailoring, and the leasing of inns. During the 19th century the Jews of Kosov also traded in cereals (particularly from Bukovina) and livestock, and were occupied in crafts such as carpentry, locksmithery, wood-carving, and carpet weaving. In 1847 Ḥasidim from Kosov built a synagogue in Safed. The community numbered 2,179 persons (78% of the total population) in 1880, 2,563 (82%) in 1900, 2,950 (53%) in 1910, and 2,166 (51%) in 1921. A vocational school was established in the town in 1898 with the assistance of the fund of Baron Maurice de *Hirsch. The local Agudat Zion, organized in 1898, established the Safah Berurah Hebrew school in 1909. In 1928, 40 carpet weavers formed a cooperative. A Jewish cooperative bank was founded in the town in 1929. All Zionist parties were active in the interwar period. A fortnightly newspaper, *Kosover Shtime*, was published there between 1934 and 1936. Half of the members of the municipal council elected in 1928 were Jews. In 1929 Jacob Gertner was elected as mayor. He resigned in 1934 as a result of government pressure. A railway that reached the town added tourism (Carpathian foothills) to the Jewish livehoods.

After the outbreak of World War II many Jews from western Poland took refuge in Kosov, and the Jewish population had increased to 4,000 by 1941. Under Soviet rule (1939–41) the community institutions and political parties were disbanded. The widely known local carpet industry largely ceased.

[Arthur Cygielman]

Holocaust Period

When the war between Germany and the Soviet Union broke out in June 1941, small groups of young Jews joined the retreating Soviet army and later fought against the Germans. Kosov was captured by the Hungarian Axis forces in early July. A local Jewish emergency committee was set up comprising the community leaders who had been active before September 1939. Acting under and in conjunction with the Hungarian military administration, it prevented groups of Ukrainian nationalists from attacking Jews and Jewish property. Jewish refugees from Subcarpathian Ruthenia, recently annexed by Hungary, who were not recognized as Hungarian citizens, sought shelter in Kosov, and the committee, with the cooperation of the local Jews, gave them assistance and medical care. In September 1941 the Germans took over the town's administration. In an *Aktion* on Oct. 16–17, 2,200 Jews, about half of the community, were taken to the hill behind the Moskalowka bridge and murdered. That winter the Jews struggled against starvation and epidemics. The Judenrat established soup kitchens and other aid. On April 24, 1942, 600 Jews without working papers were sent to Kolomyya. As the extermination campaign heightened, more attempts were made by Jews to cross the border to Romania. In early May 1942 a ghetto was established. On Sept. 7, 1942, another *Aktion* was carried out. The Jews were rounded up in the square and the German and Ukrainian police searched the houses and killed about 150 persons who had disobeyed the order to assemble. About 600 Jews were marched to Kolomyya and from there sent to *Belzec death camp. A number of able-bodied men were sent to the Janowska Street camp in Lvov. Only a few persons managed to go into hiding. On Sept. 28, 1942, the Germans announced that persons in hiding could now come out and remain, but all those who appeared were killed. On Nov. 4, 1942, the last suvivors of the Kosov community were sent to Kolomyya and the city was declared *judenrein*. In the following months the Germans and Ukrainians continued to track down and murder Jews who had taken refuge in the forests and in the city.

[Aharon Weiss]

BIBLIOGRAPHY: G. Kressel and L. Olitsky (eds.), *Sefer Kosov* (1964); B. Wasiutyński, *Ludność żydowska w Polsce w wiekach XIX i XX* (1930), 101, 122, 148, 154, 157; I. Alfasi, *Tiferet she-ba-Malkhut* (*Beit Kosov-Vizhnitz*; 1961).

KOSOVÁ HORA (Ger. **Amschelberg**), small town in central Bohemia. In 1570 two Jews were mentioned in Kosová Hora. By 1724 there were 22 families there, who were increased to 44 by the *Familiants Law of 1726. Twenty-one Jewish houses were recorded in 1781. The community comprised half of the town in 1870, when it numbered almost 400 persons. The number fell from 268 (31% of the total population) in 1876 to only 32 (4%) in 1931. In the 19th century Kosová was a prosperous community, and many of its members were leaseholders in the surrounding district. In the stories of Vojtech *Rakous, Kosová Hora represents the affluent society, in contrast to his heroes, who were mainly poor village Jews. However, during the 19th century the Jews were increasingly attracted to the large cities. Consequently the Jewish congregation was abolished c. 1893, and its members joined the nearby Sedlcany religious congregation. The synagogue, built in 1741 after a fire, and the cemetery, containing gravestones from the same date, were in existence in 1970. Many Jewish families named Amschelberg, after this community, changed their names to the German surnames Amman, Ahrens, etc. Under Nazi occupation the community was annihilated. A few Jews lived in the town after the war.

BIBLIOGRAPHY: J. Rokycana, in: *česko-Židovský kalendař*, 51 (1932/33), 91, 105; R. Rosenzweig, in: *Zeitschrift fuer die Geschichte der Juden in der Tschechoslowakei*, 3 (1933), 61–71; M. Loewy, *Amschelberger Jugenderinnerungen* (1909). **ADD. BIBLIOGRAPHY:** J. Fiedler, *Jewish Sights of Bohemia and Moravia* (1991), 98–99.

[Jan Herman]

KOSSOFF, DAVID (1919–2005), British actor. Kossoff started as an interior designer and studied for the stage privately. He performed in shows in the London shelters and for the troops during World War II. His first professional appearance was at the Unity Theater, London. Kossoff then became a film actor, typically playing stage Central Europeans, such as Professor Kokinitz in *The Mouse That Roared* (1959). He subsequently gained a reputation for his manner of telling, with modern emphasis, Bible stories for children on radio and television. He played in *The Bespoke Overcoat* (1953), *Tobias and the Angel* (1953), and *The World of Sholem Aleichem* (1955). Kossoff became a well-known anti-drug campaigner after a son died of drug abuse.

[William D. Rubinstein (2nd ed.)]

KOSSOFF, LEON (1926–), English painter. Born in London, Kossoff studied art under David Bomberg. Kossoff taught at the Royal College of Art, London, and St. Martin's School of Art. His portraits are treated with a deeply sympathetic point of view. His style is clearly expressionistic and emotional. His work has attracted much interest and he has been the subject of several studies.

ADD. BIBLIOGRAPHY: P. Moorehouse (ed.), *Leon Kossoff* (1996); *Leon Kossoff: Paintings From a Decade, 1970–1980* (1981).

KOSSOVSKI, VLADIMIR (pseudonym of **Nahum Mendel Levinsohn**; 1867–1941), most outstanding theorist and publicist among the early leaders of the *Bund, born in Dvinsk (Daugavpils), Latvia. His father, a wealthy and educated businessman, came from a rabbinical family. While a student at the secondary school in Kovno, Kossovski joined a revolutionary circle influenced by the Narodnaya Volya, the Russian terrorist organization. While being hunted by the police, he wandered through various cities. From about 1895 he was in Vilna and active in the group of Jewish Social Democrats, supporting himself by tutoring. Kossovski subsequently participated in founding the Bund (September 1897) and was elected a member of its first central committee. For several years he edited its principal organs (*Arbeiter Shtime*), and wrote a number of its publications. Imprisoned for a time for revolutionary activities, he escaped from Russia in 1900. He subsequently served as a member of the Committee Abroad of the Bund. Kossovski played a decisive part in publicizing the Bund's right to exist, opposing the Polish Socialist Party (PPS) and the Iskra group in the Russian Social Democratic Party by challenging their demands for Jewish assimilation. A leading proponent of the Bund's program of national-cultural autonomy, Kossovski opposed the idea of "neutralism," then predominating in Bundist circles, concerning the future of the Jewish people. In 1905 he returned to Russia and was editor-in-chief of the Bunds' organ, *Folkstsaytung*. In 1911 he became associated with *Zukunft*, the socialist periodical in New York, and continued to write in the Bundist and international socialist publications. From 1920 he lived in Switzerland, later moving to Berlin. In 1930 he settled in Warsaw and again worked for the *Folkstsaytung*. During World War II he managed to evade the German invasion of Warsaw in 1939, and imprisonment by the Soviets, and in 1941 reached New York, where he soon passed away.

BIBLIOGRAPHY: *Doyres Bundistn*, 1 (1956), 66–67.

[Moshe Mishkinsky]

°**KOSSUTH, LAJOS** (1802–1894), Hungarian statesman and patriot who headed the struggle for Hungarian independence from Austria. After the outbreak of the 1848 Revolution he became minister of finance in the revolutionary government and president of the committee of national defense. Subsequently he was elected regent.

Kossuth favored the cause of Jewish emancipation in Hungary, although he held that the Jews were not yet ready for equality. With the outbreak of the Revolution, the question of Jewish equality came up for discussion in the national assembly, but Kossuth declared the times inopportune. In reference to the anti-Jewish riots which had broken out in several places, he declared that "legislation on the Jewish question now would be equivalent to delivering many of them up to the wrath of their enemies." Only with the final collapse of the struggle, and the withdrawal of the revolutionary government to Szeged, was the proposed legislation granting equality to the Jews passed, strongly influenced by the part taken by Jews in the struggle and the heroism they had displayed. After the Hapsburg reversal Kossuth left Hungary never to return.

While in exile Kossuth made two important declarations regarding Jewish matters. During the *Tisza-Eszlar blood libel in 1882 he came out strongly against the nonsensical accusations, and during the struggle for legislation conferring religious equality on the Jews, he influenced the opposition Hungarian Independence Party in favor of supporting the proposed law.

BIBLIOGRAPHY: H. Marczali, in: IMIT, 55 (1933), 89–97; B. Bernstein, *A negyvennyolcas magyar szabadságharc és a zsidók* (19392), 30–31, 70, 120; I. Einhorn, *Die Revolution und die Juden in Ungarn* (1851).

KOSTELANETZ, ANDRÉ (1901–1980), conductor, pianist, and composer. Born in St. Petersburg, Russia, Kostelanetz gave his first piano recital at the age of five. In 1920 he became assistant conductor and choirmaster of the Petrograd Grand Opera. He left Russia for the United States in 1922, and served as an operatic coach and accompanist. Later, Kostelanetz entered commercial broadcasting, and from 1931 became renowned for his arrangements of light classical and popular compositions, performed by his own orchestra. He married the soprano Lily Pons.

°KOSTOMAROV, NIKOLAI IVANOVICH (1817–1885), historian, writer, and one of the founders of Ukrainian nationalism. Professor of Russian history in Kiev and St. Petersburg, he edited the monthly *Osnova* (1861–62), in which he discussed the national problems of the Ukraine, including the Jewish problem. Although in favor of granting civic rights to the Jews, he attacked their attitude of separatism toward the Christians and their supposed domination of entire branches of the economy and public services, concluding "rights should be granted to the Jews, but the Christians should be encouraged in their economic struggle so that they will be capable of regaining those positions which the Jews have seized." In his research on Ukrainian history, and in particular on the *Chmielnicki revolt (1648), Kostomarov emphasized the role of the Jews, alleging that they had not only leased the estates of the Polish landowners but also the Orthodox churches, imposed taxes on the baptism of children, etc., thus arousing the anger of the Ukrainian masses. He appeared as an "expert" at the blood libel trial of *Saratov (1853), and in his historical articles he left open the question of the truth of such accusations. Kostomarov's works had a great influence on the development of the Ukrainian nationalist movement and its attitude toward the Jews.

BIBLIOGRAPHY: *Ukrayinski Pismennyky*, 2 (1963), 464–89 (extensive bibliography); L.K. Polukhin, *Formuvannya istorychnykh poglyadiv M.I. Kostomarova* (1959); YE, 9 (c. 1910), 788–9.

[Yehuda Slutsky]

KÖSZEG (Ger. **Guens**), town in W. Hungary, near the Austrian border. In 1395 King Sigismund authorized the owner of the castle in Köszeg to admit Jews to the town. During the battle against the Turks in 1532, the Jews were apparently compelled to flee from Köszeg. At the time of the revolt of Count Rákóczi in the 17th century, the whole town was destroyed by fire and Jews did not return to the rebuilt town until early in the 18th century. The first to attempt to settle was M. Schlesinger (1735–37). When endeavors by the townspeople were made to expel him, he appealed to the king, who issued a decision in his favor. A descendant of this family was Akiva *Eger, who added the name of the town – Guens – to his name. Previously under the jurisdiction of the Rechnitz (Rohonc) community, the Köszeg community became independent in 1821. Jews contributed to the development of the town, especially the philanthropist, Philipp Schey, who financed the building of the synagogue in 1860. There was a yeshivah in Köszeg from 1835 to 1881. Prominent rabbis were Jacob Gruenwald (until 1862), Markus Wiener (1892–1915), and the last rabbi, Isaac Linksz (1923–44), who was deported with the members of his community in the Holocaust. The Jewish population numbered 50 in 1789, 91 in 1840 (1.4% of the total), 266 in 1910 (3.2%), 131 in 1930 (1.5%), and 109 in 1941 (1.1%).

Holocaust Period

From 1940 the Jewish men were conscripted into forced labor groups. After the German occupation (March 19, 1944), the Jews were first confined in a narrow ghetto (May 14, 1944), and later were forced to lodge in an open barn. On June 18 all were transported to the central ghetto of the region, in the town of *Szombathely. There they were tortured to induce them to hand over their property. The 117 Jews from Köszeg were deported to *Auschwitz on July 4, 1944; only 15 returned. Under the regime of the Fascist *Arrow Cross Party, a labor camp was set up outside the town in which 5,000 Jews, including women who had been brought there on a death march, were imprisoned. By March 1945 some 3,000 Jews had died of hunger, disease, or torture, or had been executed. The survivors were then marched to *Mauthausen and Wells; those who were unable to walk were either gassed or shot.

BIBLIOGRAPHY: PK; MHJ, 8 (1965); 10 (1968); 12 (1969), index locorum; *Magyar Zsidó Lexikon* (1929); *ÚJ Élet*, 24:15 (1969); S. Scheiber, *Héber kodexmaradványok magyarországi kötéstáblákban* (1969), 80–84, incl. bibl. notes; J. Házi, in: *Vasi Szemle*, 24 (1970).

[Laszlo Harsanyi]

KOTARBIŃSKA, JANINA (b. **Dina Sztejnbarg**; 1901–1997), Polish philosopher. Kotarbińska was born in Warsaw, and at Warsaw University became the closest pupil of the foremost Polish philosopher, Tadeusz Kotarbiński, whom she married after World War II. In prewar Poland she was one of the few Jewish scholars to obtain even a modest academic post; in 1934 she received the status of a privatdocent and worked as a senior assistant in the philosophy department at Warsaw University. Her prewar work was devoted to the methodology of empirical sciences, her main published study dealing with the problem of indeterminism in physics, biology, and the humanities (1932–33). She survived both the German prison in Warsaw and Auschwitz. Immediately after the war she was appointed associate – and eventually full – professor of logic and methodology of science at Warsaw. Her later work was devoted mainly to the theory of definition, especially ostensive definition, and to semantics, in which she made an extensive study of the concept of sign. During the 1960s she served as dean of the Faculty of Humanities and chairman of the Department of Logic at Warsaw University.

[Edward I.J. Poznanski]

KOTIK, YEKHESKL (**Ezekiel**; 1847–1921), Yiddish author. Born in Kamieniec Litewski (Kamenets-Litovsk), near Grodno, Belorussia, of a prosperous ḥasidic family, Kotik settled in Kiev in his late twenties and fled to Warsaw after the 1881 pogroms. There he founded a *kheyder* (**ḥeder*) and later opened a coffeehouse which became a rendezvous of Jewish writers and labor activists. A lifelong communal worker, Kotik founded numerous welfare societies. In the Haskalah tradition, he published brochures in Hebrew and Yiddish, among them a plan whereby tenants could become home owners (*Di Lokatoren mit di Virtslayt* ("The Tenants and the Landlords," 1909). Kotik's fame rests on his two-volume memoirs, *Mayne Zikhroynes* ("My Memories," Warsaw 1913–14; Berlin 1922), in which he describes numerous facets of 19th-century Russian Jewish daily life (mainly in and around Kamieniec, but in the second volume also in Kiev and Moscow). These are important not only as social history (his descriptions of ḥasidic life are especially noteworthy), but as a significant contribution to Yiddish letters. Kotik's impact on *Sholem Aleichem may be seen not only in that writer's letters to Kotik but in his use of Kotik as a character in the last series of *Menakhm Mendl*.

BIBLIOGRAPHY: *Filologishe Shriftn*, 3 (1929), 152–71 [Sholem Aleykhem's letters to Kotik]; Reyzn, Leksikon, 3 (1929), 424–6; Ch. Shmeruk, in: *Di Goldene Keyt*, 56 (1966), 22–55. **ADD. BIBLIOGRAPHY:** LNYL, 8 (1981), 44; D. Assaf (ed.), *Journey to a Nineteenth-Century Shtetl* (2002) (= *Mayne Zikhroynes*, vol. 1); D. Assaf (ed.), *Ma she-Ra'iti* (1999) and *Na ve-Nad* (2005) [= *Mayne Zikhroynes*, vols. 1–2]

[Leonard Prager]

KOTLER, AARON (1892–1962), prominent yeshivah head. A descendant of renowned rabbis, he received his early education from his father R. Shneur Zalman Pines, the rabbi of Sislowitz, and from R. Zalman Sender Shapiro of Krinik, to whose yeshivah he was admitted before he reached the age of 13 since he possessed exceptional talents. At 14 he entered the Slobodka yeshivah and soon gained prominence as one of its most outstanding students. He married the daughter of R. Isser Zalman *Meltzer, head of the yeshivah Eẓ Ḥayyim in Slutsk, and became his assistant (1914). After the yeshivah's forced transfer to Kletsk (1921) and his father-in-law's immigration to Ereẓ Israel, Kotler directed the yeshivah for 20 years. Kotler's original teaching methods attracted many students from all over the world. He also distinguished himself as a forceful communal leader, particularly in the sphere of Jewish education, becoming one of the pillars of *Agudat Israel in this area. On a visit to the U.S. on behalf of his yeshivah, he established an institute of higher rabbinical learning at Spring Valley, New York. During World War II Kotler fled with a number of his students from country to country, finally reaching Japan. Kotler went to the U.S., where he established the Va'ad Haẓẓalah (Rescue Committee) of the Agudat ha-Rabbanim in aid of the war refugees. Kotler established in Lakewood, New Jersey, the Beth Medrash Govoha, a school for advanced, nonprofessional talmudic study, with an enrollment of ten students, which grew to 250 students at his death. Its name was changed to the Rabbi Aaron Kotler Institute for Advanced Studies in 1964. Kotler became president of the Supreme Council of Agudat Israel in 1954 and held this post until his death. He was the leader of the right-wing, yeshivah-based American independent Orthodoxy, a member of the presidium of the Union of Orthodox Rabbis, and a founder of Israel's independent Orthodox (Ḥinnukh Aẓma'i) educational system. On his father-in-law's death, Kotler was nominally appointed his successor as head of the Eẓ Ḥayyim yeshivah in Jerusalem. His responsibilities in the United States, however, permitted him to pay only occasional visits there which became major events for the scholars of Jerusalem. Kotler died in the United States and was buried in Jerusalem. He was succeeded at Lakewood by his son Shneur.

BIBLIOGRAPHY: O.Z. Rand, *Toledot Anshei Shem* (1950), 109; O. Feuchtwanger, *Righteous Lives* (1965), 122ff.; J.D. Kamzon (ed.), *Yahadut Lita* (1959), 235.

[Mordechai Hacohen]

KOTOVSKOYE, Russian rural settlement, Odessa district. It was founded as a Jewish colony in the early 1920s and had 100 farms and 485 persons in 1929. There was a Yiddish school. The few Jews who remained under German occupation in August 1941 were probably killed.

KOTOVSKOYE (Rom. **Hâncești**; until 1944 called in Russian **Gancheshty**), a small town 18 mi. (36 km.) S.W. of Kishinev (Chișinău), in Bessarabia, Moldova. Kotovskoye developed from a village into a town during the first half of the 19th century as a result of the settlement of the Jews who then came in large numbers to Bessarabia. In 1847, 372 Jews were registered in Kotovskoye, and in 1897 the Jewish population numbered 2,228 (44% of the total). The Jews were mainly merchants but also engaged in crafts and some in agriculture. Of the 390 members registered in the local loan society in 1925, 203 were merchants, 94 artisans, and 21 farmers. There were 1,521 Jews living in Kotovskoye (24% of the total) in 1930.

[Eliyahu Feldman]

Holocaust Period

When the war broke out in June 1941, German and Romanian forces advanced toward Kishinev along two axes, one passing through Sculeni (Skulyany) and the other through Kotovskoye. In both places the Jewish population was slaughtered and not a single Jew appears to have escaped.

[Jean Ancel]

BIBLIOGRAPHY: M. Carp, *Cartea Neagră*, 3 (1947), 36.

KOTSK, MENAHEM MENDEL (Morgenstern) OF (1787–1859), one of the outstanding and most original leaders of the ḥasidic movement. Menahem Mendel was born in Bilgoraj, Poland, to a rabbinic family. After his marriage he was exposed to Ḥasidism and traveled to Lublin to see R. *Jacob Isaac ha-Ḥozeh but only when he met R. Jacob Isaac ("The Holy Jew") of *Przysucha (Pshishka), did he know that he had found himself a *rebbe*. After R. Jacob Isaac's death in 1814, he followed R. *Simḥah Bunem of Przysucha until his death (1827). An elite group of R. Simḥah Bunem's ḥasidim accepted R. Menahem Mendel as a *rebbe*. He moved to Tomaszow with his followers, who left their families to live in a commune, led by him in the search for perfection in his extreme, intensive way. His contempt for conventions, social or religious, was more radical than his teachers' and it showed itself bluntly in the behavior of his *ḥasidim*. The hostility toward him grew and so too the number of those who where attracted to him. After two years he moved to Kotsk, gradually becoming more and more saturnine and remote from his disciples. Disagreeing with R. Menahem Mendel's approach, his disciple and old friend R. Mordecai Joseph of Izbica left Kotsk to establish an alternative leadership as the dispute between them broke out dramatically on Simḥat Torah 1839. R. Mordecai Joseph, who taught the complexity of the God's demands, and who was supportive in his relations with his disciples, challenged R. Menahem Mendel's absolute truth and his harshness toward his followers. Soon after, he closeted himself in a room next to the *bet midrash*, rarely leaving it for the last 20 years of his life. Only his family and a small number of disciples were allowed to enter. When he did enter the *bet midrash* he terrified those who saw him by his mere appearance. Before his death he made sure that all of his writings had been destroyed.

His prominent disciples, who faithfully followed him until his death, were R. Isaac Meir Alter, his brother-in-law, who became the *rebbe* of Gur after his death, his son-in-law R. Abraham Bornstein, who was to become the *rebbe* of *Sochaczew, and R. *Ḥanokh of Aleksandrow, who succeeded R. Isaac Meir Alter after his death.

Teachings

R. Menahem Mendel's originality as well as his influence and legendary place in the ḥasidic tradition should be attributed to his singular personality and to the way Pshishka's heritage was refracted through the prism of his unique character. In his intense life he expressed his great teachers' ideas as he carried them to extremes. He exemplified the well-known phenomenon of religious innovation embodied more in the very life of the person behind it than in the originality of his thought.

He had a strong, charismatic personality which was feared yet admired by his disciples. The main idea of his religiosity was the sincere quest for truth. This idea was well founded in the teachings of "the Holy Jew" and R. Simḥah Bunem, but R. Menahem Mendel gave it a different shade. The demands on the individual became total. He searched for the source of religiosity, striving persistently for the pure origins of the religious movement before its contamination by social conventions and the petty interests of everyday life. His laconic style is strongly connected to a striving for depth rooted in simplicity.

A dark skeptical tone characterizes his search for truth. For a short period, when he began leading his disciples in Tomaszow, he was more optimistic, but as time passed he recognized his loneliness, as there were very few who could bear the burden he demanded. His pessimistic approach is of one who is aware of the infinite chasm between godly demands and human abilities, but at the same time had deep-seated beliefs that created a strong sense of tragic duty to overcome what cannot be overcome. Recognizing how little human beings can achieve, and understanding the effort demanded in any true achievement, he understood that the value of one's deeds is related to one's effort and not to one's spiritual level. He believed that by the very performance of the *mitzvot* one could elevate oneself far beyond one's spiritual level. The sincere person should see himself as one who did not achieve anything, making the pretentious person despicable. Thus, R. Menahem Mendel's profound seriousness went hand in hand with disregard for himself, and for others.

The burdensome duty of bridging the chasm between man and God is above all a human responsibility. The way to God is not to be found in mystical speculation but rather in purifying one's intentions so that they bear no false echoes. Menahem Mendel's frame of reference was mainly the talmudic literature, as its prosaic nature suited the task that he had set for himself, seeing in the study of Torah the primary vehicle for getting closer to God. Unlike "the Holy Jew," his ascetic nature was not a mystical ecstatic one. His asceticism derived from the demand to give up anything that keeps a person from being attuned to his true self, which was the reason for his condemnation of social institutions, especially money and status.

God's way is hard and involves effort and suffering. Accordingly R. Menahem Mendel understood that the role of the *rebbe* is to help his followers meet the challenge, mercilessly exposing any hint of falsehood. The ultimate demand cannot be alleviated since there is no possible compromise with the truth.

BIBLIOGRAPHY: Y.K.K. Rakatz, *Si'aḥ Sarfei Kodesh* (1913–32); E.Z. Ẓigelman, *Ohel Torah* (1919); M. Arten, *Emet ve-Emunah* (1940); A. Marcus, *Ha-Ḥasidut* (1980), index; J. Weiss, *"Antologyah Koẓka'it,"* in: *Haaretz* (Aug. 10, 1945); A.Z. Eshcoly, *Ha-Ḥasidut be-Polin* (2000), 89–106; R. Mahler, *Ha-Ḥasidut ve-ha-Haskalah* (1961), index; M. Orian, *Seneh Bo'er be-Kotsk* (1962); M. Buber, *Or ha-Ganuz* (1965), 56–59, 428–44; A.J. Heschel, *Kotsk* (1973); Ya'akov Levinger, in: *Tarbiz*, 55 (1986), 109–35, 413–31; M.M. Faierstein, *All Is in the Hands of Heaven* (1989), 89–98.

[Yehuda Ben-Dor (2nd ed.)]

KOTSUJI, SETSUZO (Abraham; 1899–1973), Japanese Hebraist. Kotsuji was born in Kyoto, Japan, into a family claiming descent from a long line of Shinto priests. Converted to Christianity when a youngster, he attended the American Presbyterian College in Tokyo from 1916 to 1923. After serving as a minister for several years, he went to the United States in 1927 and studied at Auburn Theological Seminary in New York and then at the Pacific School of Religion in Berkeley, California. There he received his B.D. degree in 1931. His thesis, "The Origin and Evolution of the Semitic Alphabet," was published several years later in Tokyo. Returning to his homeland, he taught the Old Testament and Hebrew at the Theological Seminary of Aoyama Gakuin University. In 1937 he wrote a Hebrew grammar and for a brief while struggled to organize the Institute of Biblical Research in Tokyo. Shortly before Japan's involvement in World War II, Kotsuji exerted himself in assisting numerous East European Jews who found temporary haven in Kobe. In his volume, *Yudaya-jin no Sugata* (1943), he sought to familiarize his countrymen with the history and life of the Jewish people. Kotsuji continued his Hebraic and biblical studies in the postwar period, and in 1959 journeyed to Israel where taking the name Abraham, he formally became a Jew. In the next few years he lectured before Jewish audiences in the United States. In his autobiography, *From Tokyo to Jerusalem* (New York, 1964), Kotsuji recounted the central theme of his life – the quest for spiritual satisfaction, which he ultimately found in Judaism.

[Hyman Kublin]

KOTTLER, MOSES (c. 1892–1977), South African sculptor. Born in Joniskis, Lithuania, probably in 1892 but possibly up to four years later, Kottler went to South Africa in 1912 and except for a period of study in Europe and Jerusalem after World War I, spent the rest of his life there. Kottler's qualities, among them a vein of poetic simplicity, were apparent in his early portraiture and modeling. His life-size wood carving, *Meidjie*, a portrayal of girlhood, marked the beginning of his reputation. His bronze group of Sir Quentin Brand and Sir Pierre van Ryneveld, commemorating their flight from London to Cape Town in 1920, is at the Johannesburg airport. His architectural figures for the Johannesburg Public Library aroused controversy but won acceptance for their monumental strength. Still more acute controversy followed the installation of his nude group at the Population Register Building in Pretoria and led to its removal. Kottler was also commissioned to provide ornamental sculpture for Johannesburg mining houses and in 1967 to do a war memorial for the University of the Witwatersrand, Johannesburg. Kottler's many portraits include busts of Smuts and the shah of Persia. He was often inspired by biblical subjects, such as Jacob and the Angel, and David and the Shunammite.

ADD. BIBLIOGRAPHY: E. Berman, *Arts and Artists of South Africa* (1993).

[Lewis Sowden]

KOUCHNER, BERNARD (1939–), French humanitarian. Born in Avignon, the son of a doctor, Kouchner qualified as a physician and specialized in digestive endoscopy. From 1968, he was sent on specialized missions to many parts of the Third World. In 1971, he founded the organization "Doctors without Frontiers" which he headed until 1979 and which sent doctors and nurses to disaster areas throughout the world, and in 1980 founded "Doctors of the World" which he headed until 1988. He also originated the "Boat for Vietnam" project which brought succor and hospitalization to thousands of refugees in the China Seas area. Other projects in which he was involved included "A plane for Salvadorian refugees" and "International Committee against Piracy."

He was secretary of state in the Ministry of Social Affairs and Employment in the first government of Michel Rocard; in 1988 he was appointed secretary of state for humanitarian action in the Prime Minister's Office; in 1991, secretary of state in the Foreign Ministry; and in 1992–93 was minister of health and humanitarian action in the Socialist government. As a minister, he was personally involved in the operations to aid the victims of the wars in Yugoslavia (flying into besieged Dubrovnik to negotiate the cessation of its destruction), Somalia, and Kurdistan. He achieved an international reputation for his bold initiatives, and his view of "the right of intervention" of the international community in humanitarian matters was approved by a UN decision.

Kouchner is the author of many books, among them *Le devoir d'ingérence* and *Le Malheur des Autres*, and has received many awards including the Prix Europa for his activities on behalf of human rights.

[Gideon Kouts]

KOUFAX, SANDY (Sanford Braun; 1935–), U.S. baseball player, one of the greatest pitchers in its history, and with

Hank *Greenberg one of only two Jewish players elected to the Baseball Hall of Fame. Koufax was born in the Borough Park section of Brooklyn to Jack Braun, a salesman, and Evelyn (Lichtenstein), a CPA. His parents divorced when he was three. When he was nine, his mother married Irving Koufax, a neighborhood lawyer, and though Irving never legally adopted Koufax, his stepson always referred to Irving as his father, and took his last name. After graduating Lafayette High School, Koufax accepted a basketball scholarship to the University of Cincinnati in the fall of 1953, and averaged 9.7 points on the 12–2 freshman team. Koufax then joined the varsity baseball team, and on December 14, 1954, two weeks before his 19th birthday, signed with his hometown Brooklyn Dodgers as a $14,000 bonus baby.

Koufax made his debut on June 24, 1955, and played with the Dodgers from 1955 to 1966, first in Brooklyn and then Los Angeles. His first seven years were ordinary, with a wild fastball resulting in a 54–53 record. In 1961, Koufax went 18–13 and led the NL in strikeouts with 269, breaking by two the 58-year-old NL record in a remarkable 255 innings.

But beginning in 1962, when the team moved to spacious Dodger Stadium, Koufax put together what some consider the most dominant five-year stretch in history: a 111–34 record while leading the National League in ERA all five years. Along the way, Koufax tied the then-ML record by striking out 18 players in nine innings on April 24, 1962; pitched a no-hitter each season from 1962 to 1965, the first major leaguer to pitch more than three no-hitters, with the last one a 1–0 perfect game against the Cubs on September 9, 1965; struck out 382 batters in 1965 to set a ML record, as well as going 26–8 with a 2.04 ERA, eight shutouts, 27 complete games, and setting the ML record for most innings pitched (323) without hitting a batter; and led the Dodgers to pennants in 1963, 1965, and 1966, winning the NL Cy Young Award each of the years as well as the MVP in 1963 following his 25–5 season. Koufax led the league in wins three times, strikeouts four times, shutouts three times, and in 57 innings in eight World Series games he posted a 0.95 ERA. He won the first game of the 1963 World Series while striking out 15 Yankees, then the World Series record, and won the fourth game as well, earning him the World Series MVP.

In 1965, the first game of the World Series fell on Yom Kippur, a day on which Koufax never pitched. As *Greenberg had done 31 years before, Koufax instead went to synagogue, emerging as the Jewish sports icon. "By refusing to pitch, Koufax defined himself as a man of principle who placed faith above craft," Jane Leavy wrote in her biography of Koufax. "He became inextricably linked with the American Jewish experience. As John Goodman put it in the movie *The Big Lebowski*: "Three thousand years of beautiful tradition – from Moses to Sandy Koufax." Koufax pitched the next day and lost, but he shut out the Minnesota Twins in Games 5 and 7 – the last game on two days' rest – giving the Dodgers the Series and Koufax his second World Series MVP.

Arthritis forced Koufax into premature retirement at the end of the 1966 season while still at his peak. In a 12-season career, Koufax compiled a 165–87 record with a 2.76 ERA, 2,396 strikeouts in 2,324⅓ innings, 167 complete games, 40 shutouts, was selected to seven All-Star teams, and is fifth all-time in strikeouts per nine innings pitched (9.28). In 1972 at age 36, Koufax became the youngest player voted into the Hall of Fame. He wrote his autobiography *Koufax* (1966) with Ed Linn, and is the subject of *Sandy Koufax: Strikeout King* (1964) by Arnold Hano, *The Baseball Life of Sandy Koufax* (1968) by George Vecsey, *Koufax* (2000) by Ed Gruver, and the bestselling *Sandy Koufax, A Lefty's Legacy* (2002) by Jane Leavy.

[Elli Wohlgelernter (2nd ed.)]

KOUSSEVITZKY (frequently spelled **Kusevitsky**), **MOSHE** (1899–1966), *ḥazzan*. Born in Smorgon, near Vilna, Koussevitzky became *ḥazzan* in the Great Synagogue of Vilna in 1924. He succeeded Gershon *Sirota at the Tlomackie Street synagogue in Warsaw in 1927. At the outbreak of World War II he escaped to Russia where he sang in Russian, Polish, and Yiddish and appeared in opera. He emigrated to the U.S. in 1947, toured widely in America, South Africa, and Israel and in 1952 became *ḥazzan* in Temple Beth El, Brooklyn. His public appearances in synagogues and concert halls and his recordings brought him renown as a graceful and powerful lyric tenor with a particularly fine upper register. Koussevitzky was popularly regarded as the greatest *ḥazzan* of his time. He died in the U.S. but his body was taken to Jerusalem for burial. His three brothers were all notable *ḥazzanim*: JACOB (1903–1959) held positions in Lvov, London, Winnipeg, and New York; SIMCHA (1905–1998) officiated in Rovno, Glasgow, London, Johannesburg and, from 1952, in Cape Town; DAVID (1911–1985) was *ḥazzan* in Rovno, London where he also lectured in *ḥazzanut* at Jews' College, and, from 1949, in Temple Emanu-El, Boro Park, Brooklyn, New York. Moshe's only son, ALEXANDER (1927–), also became a *ḥazzan*.

BIBLIOGRAPHY: E. Zaludkowski, *Kultur Treger fun der Yidisher Liturgie* (1930), 337–9; Jewish Ministers Cantors' Association of America, *50 Yoriger Yoyvl Zhurnal* (1947), s.v.; G. Saleski, *Famous Musicians of Jewish Origin* (1949), 596–7; N. Stolnitz, *Negine in Yidishen Lebn* (1957), 43–57; *Yedi'ot ha-Makhon ha-Yisre'eli le-Musikah Datit*, 8 (1966), 264–89.

[Joshua Leib Ne'eman]

KOUSSEVITZKY, SERGE (1874–1951), conductor. Born in Tver, Russia, he went to Moscow at the age of 17 and entered the double-bass class at the Conservatory because instruction in this instrument was free. He became a virtuoso player, arranged classical works, and wrote solos to augment the double-bass repertoire. After his marriage into a rich family, he went to Berlin, and in 1908 made his first public appearance as a conductor. In 1909 he established the publishing firm of Editions Russes de Musique, which became the pioneer publisher of modern Russian composers, whose works, especially those of Scriabin, he championed in his concerts. Koussevitzky organized an orchestra, gave concerts in Moscow and St. Petersburg, and made summer tours on the Volga River in a specially chartered steamer. After the war he settled in Paris, founded the Concerts Koussevitzky which gave the first performances of many important works, including the orchestration of Moussorgsky's *Pictures at an Exhibition* (1922) which he had commissioned from Ravel. Koussevitzky attained his greatest fame when he went to the U.S. to become musical director of the Boston Symphony Orchestra in 1925. During the ensuing 25 years of his directorship he made the orchestra one of the great orchestras of the world. It became a focus for new music, European and American, overriding the objections of his hitherto conservative subscribers. From 1935 the orchestra gave summer concerts at Tanglewood, Massachusetts, augmented from 1940 by a permanent institution of summer courses, the Berkshire Music Center, of which Koussevitzky was president and which became an important center of American musical life.

In 1950 Koussevitzky was persuaded by his pupil, Leonard Bernstein, to go to Israel and conduct the *Israel Philharmonic Orchestra in a series of concerts. With Bernstein he also became director of the Israeli orchestra's first American tour in 1950/51. The Koussevitzky Music Foundation was established in 1943 in memory of his first wife, Natalie, to commission new works by composers of all nationalities. It was later directed by her niece Olga who became Koussevitzky's second wife. Among the works commissioned by the foundation were: Bartók's *Concerto for Orchestra* and Stravinsky's *Symphony of Psalms*.

Koussevitzky's conducting style was distinguished by its nobility and emotional power, especially in works of the late 19th and 20th centuries; his interpretations of the classical masters were sometimes criticized for what could be described as "personal intervention." He donated his large library of musical scores to the Koussevitzky Collection, which was established at the Hebrew University, Jerusalem.

BIBLIOGRAPHY: A. Lourie, *Sergei Koussevitzky and his Epoch* (1931); M. Smith, *Koussevitzky* (Eng., 1947); H. Leichtentritt, *Serge Koussevitzky, the Boston Symphony Orchestra and the New American Music* (1946); MGG; Baker, Biog Dict.

[Uri (Erich) Toeplitz]

KOVADLOFF, SANTIAGO (1942–), Argentine poet, essayist, and cultural critic. Born in Buenos Aires, he received a degree in philosophy from the University of Buenos Aires. Kovadloff was also an accomplished translator of Brazilian and Portuguese literature into Spanish. He was the author of numerous volumes of poetry, including *Zonas e indagaciones* (1978), *Canto abierto* (1979), *Ben David* (1988), *La vida es siempre más o menos* (1994), and *Hombre en la tarde* (1997). *Ben David* is the collection that most overtly undertakes an examination of identity. In addition to his poetry, Kovadloff published short stories in *Mundo menor* (1986). While a skillful poet, he was most recognized for his insightful and keenly critical essays. Along with Marcos Aguinis, Kovadloff was one of the most visible and widely respected cultural critics in Argentina. He contributed regularly to newspapers and periodicals in Argentina and abroad. Kovadloff published several volumes of influential essays on a wide variety of subjects. His early volumes – *Una cultura de catacumbas* (1982), *Argentina, oscuro país* (1983), *Por un futuro imperfecto* (1987) – dealt almost exclusively with the political violence and repression that seized Argentina during the military dictatorship (1976–1983). Essays from these volumes, in addition to new ones, were gathered in *La nueva ignorancia* (1992). Many of Kovadloff's essays specifically address Jewish issues within the context of Argentine society. A constant theme in his essays is the need for greater cultural pluralism in Argentina. In more recent volumes, Kovadloff takes on topics as diverse as the multiple meanings of silence in *El silencio primordial* (1993), Moses and Judaism in *Lo irremediable: Moisés y el espíritu trágico del judaísmo* (1996), the difficulty of everyday life in *Sentido y riesgo de la vida cotidiana* (1998), and the search for personal spirituality in *Ensayos de intimidad* (2002). In 1992, Kovadloff received the National Literary Award for his essays. In 1998 he became a member of the Argentine Academy of Letters and in 2000 he was awarded first prize for poetry from the city of Buenos Aires.

[Darrell B. Lockhart (2nd ed.)]

KOVEL, town in Volhynia district, Ukraine; within Poland until the end of the 18th century, passed to Russia until 1918, and within Poland again until 1939. A Jewish community is known to have existed there from 1536, when Kovel received Magdeburgian rights (city rights). In 1540, representatives of Kovel Jews, together with other Volhynian Jews, participated in a delegation to King Sigismund I, to respond to the accusation of kidnapping or buying Christian children, converting them to Judaism, and smuggling them to Turkey. The owner of the town, Queen Bona, usually made the rights of the Jews there equal to those of other citiziens. In 1609 Jews took part in fortifying the town and defending it against invaders. Kovel suffered severely during the *Chmielnicki massacres of 1648–49 when most of the poor Jews there, as well as Christians, were murdered; some were drowned in the river. The community was reconstituted in Kovel under the protection of King John II Casimir in 1650. Around the 1680s the Kovel community became a main community in the Volhynian Land. From the end of the century a Kovel representative was elected to the Four Lands Council, and even represented this body.

In 1765 the Jews of Kovel numbered 827. Under Russian rule in 1799 there were 11 merchants, all Jews, and 811 Jewish citizens, as against 1,308 Christians. The Russian authorities permitted the Jews of Kovel to select the deputy mayor. Kovel became a commercial center during the 19th century. The Jewish population numbered 2,647 and grew to 8,521 in 1897 (48%). In 1857 a fire destroyed many Jewish houses and most of the synagogues, but the town was quickly restored. Among others, the Russian soldiers stationed in Kovel were an important source of livelihood. At the end of World War I, the Jews suffered severely at the hands of *Haller's Polish army which killed two Jews. In 1921 there were 12,758 Jews (61.2%)

in Kovel. They predominated in light industry, in the production of such commodities as beer and leather, in building construction, and ownership of workshops. They were also active in the wholesale and retail trade. Half of the members of the municipal council were Jews. There was a Hebrew high school, and two primary Hebrew schools with Hebrew kindergartens, all affiliated to *Tarbut. There was also a Yiddish CYSHO-affiliated primary school.

Among the rabbis of Kovel in the 17th century was Judah Idl, son of Moses Idl, a descendant of *Judah Loew b. Bezalel. Its last rabbi, Nahum *Twersky, perished in the Holocaust. Between the two world wars, the *Bund organized trade unions and had a significant influence on Jewish life in Kovel. Among the Zionist parties, the Ereẓ Israel Workers' Front gained the majority during the elections held in Kovel in 1939 for the 21st Zionist Congress. In the municipality elections in 1939 the Jews obtained ten seats (eight Zionists, and two members of the Bund). The Yiddish periodicals *Di Kovler Shtime* and *Unzer Lebn* were published in Kovel in the 1930s. A dramatic circle was also a focus of literary activities. The Jewish population in 1939 numbered approximately 17,000 (out of 33,000).

[Shimshon Leib Kirshenboim / Shmuel Spector (2nd ed.)]

Holocaust and Postwar Periods

Soon after the Soviet occupation of Kovel in September 1939, organized Jewish public life was discontinued. Factories were nationalized, private commerce almost ceased to exist, and craftsmen were organized into cooperatives. However, the Jewish high school, elementary schools, and four kindergartens, whose language of instruction was Yiddish, continued to function, and the teachers clandestinely continued to give a Jewish national character to their educational work.

Kovel was occupied by the Germans on June 28, 1941, on which day 60 to 80 Jews belonging to the intelligentsia were shot. During the first month of occupation some 1,000 Jews were executed. A few weeks later the Germans collected some 200 Torah scrolls from all the synagogues and burned them. Under most difficult conditions the Judenrat endeavored to assuage the suffering of the Jewish population. By the end of 1941, thousands of Jews had been murdered in the nearby forest of Czerewacha. By German order the ghetto was established on May 25, 1942, in two sections: one within the city limits and the other in the suburb of Piaski. The Germans separated the able-bodied (about 8,000) from the elderly, the sick, and the children (about 6,000), and the latter were earmarked for immediate annihilation. The Jewish population in both ghettos numbered approximately 24,000, including refugees from the neighboring small towns and villages. On June 2, 1942 the city section of the disabled was liquidated, and the inhabitants were taken to the Bykhava quarries and killed there. On August 19, 1942, the liquidation of the ghetto of the able-bodied began in the Bykhava village. About 1,000 Jews tried to escape, but most of them were captured and kept in the Great Synagogue, whence they were taken to their death. Many of them wrote their names and wills on the walls calling to be avenged. The inscriptions were found after the liberation and were copied, but later were painted over. The liquidation lasted until October 6, 1942. In May 1942 the Kovel ghetto was visited by two messengers of the Jewish resistance in Warsaw – Frumka Plotnicka and Temi Shneiderman. Kovel Jews belonged to partisan units which were active in the Cuman forests, most of them in the Linkov division, and helped carry out acts of sabotage and retaliation against the Nazis and their collaborators among the local population. The Soviet army reentered Kovel on July 6, 1944, and in the following months about 40 Jewish survivors returned to the city. Jewish life there was not reestablished and the survivors soon left for Israel and other countries. In 1959 plans were announced to convert the Jewish cemetery into a site for an industrial plant. In 1970 the Jewish population was estimated at about 250 (50 families).

[Aharon Weiss / Shmuel Spector (2nd ed.)]

BIBLIOGRAPHY: S. Leoni-Cuperfein (ed.), *Kovel, Sefer Edut ve-Zikkaron* (1957).

KOVNER, ABBA (1918–1987), Lithuanian resistance fighter and Israeli Hebrew poet. Born in Sevastopol, Russia, Kovner grew up in Vilna. He was active in the *Ha-Shomer ha-Ẓa'ir movement and prepared to immigrate to Ereẓ Israel but the outbreak of World War II prevented him from doing so. During the German occupation of Vilna, he remained in the city, first under the protection of nuns in a convent, and later in the ghetto. Kovner, one of the commanders of the Vilna ghetto, helped to organize the armed revolt and issued a manifesto urging Jews not to go like sheep to the slaughter. He continued to fight the Germans as leader of Jewish partisan groups in the Vilna forests. After the war Kovner was among the organizers of the **Beriḥah*, responsible for bringing hundreds of thousands of Jews to Ereẓ Israel. In 1945 he went to Ereẓ Israel; but when he attempted to return to Europe to continue Jewish rescue work he was caught by the British secret police and imprisoned in Egypt. During his imprisonment he wrote the poem "*Ad Lo Or*" ("Until There is no More Light," 1947). After his return from Egypt he joined kibbutz Ein ha-Ḥoresh. At the beginning of the War of Independence, he enlisted in the Givati Brigade and wrote a daily *Battle Sheet* which brought news of the war to the troops.

Early in World War II, Kovner's first poems, both in Hebrew and Yiddish, were published in Vilna in the organs of the Ha-Shomer ha-Ẓa'ir, including *Ma'amakim*. In 1943 his Hebrew poetry was published for the first time in Ereẓ Israel. The poem, which was signed Uri, was printed in the newspaper *Haaretz* after having been transmitted by the partisan post. His books of poetry include *Ad Lo Or* (1947); *Preidah me-ha-Darom* (1949); *Admat ha-Ḥol* (1961); and *Mi-Kol ha-Ahavot* (1965), which includes the poem "*Ha-Mafte'aḥ Ẓalal.*" first printed in *Yevul* (1950). Kovner's poetry, unique in its rhythm, oscillates in theme between the horrors of the Holocaust and the struggles in Ereẓ Israel. His poems also treat of a religious experience in Brazil, encountered in 1955 while he was on a mission in Latin America. Experiences during the War of Independence gave rise in 1953–55 to his prose trilogy *Panim el Panim*, *She'at ha-Efes* (1954), and *Ha-Ẓomet* (1955). The trilogy, with its diverse characters, both sabras and former partisans, is a monument to the Givati Brigade. In 1972 Kovner's poem *Lahakat ha-Keẓev Mofi'ah al Har Gerizim* ("The Pop Orchestra Appears on Mt. Gerizim") was published. Dan Miron edited *Kol Shirei Abba Kovner* (The Collected Poems) 1996–2003, and volume five includes an index and comments by R. Frenkel. In 1973 a selection of his poems, translated into English by Shirley Kaufman and others, was published by Pittsburgh University under the title *A Canopy in the Desert*. It includes an introductory essay on Kovner by the translator. His *Scrolls of Fire* appeared in 1981. The English collection *My Little Sister and Selected Poems* was published in 1986, followed in 2001 by *Scrolls of Testimony* in 2001 and *Sloan Kettering: Poems* (2002).

In 1970 he was awarded the Israel Prize and in the same year he was elected chairman of the Hebrew Writers' Association of Israel. Kovner was responsible for the scheme adopted for the Beth Hatefutsoth.

BIBLIOGRAPHY: R. Gurfein, *Mi-Karov u-me-Raḥok* (1964), 117–21, 224–7; A. Kohen, *Soferim Ivriyyim Benei Zemannenu* (1964), 242f.; Y. Bauer, *Flight and Rescue: Beriḥah* (1970), index. **ADD. BIBLIOGRAPHY:** E. Alexander, "Abba Kovner: Poet of Holocaust and Rebirth," in: *Midstream*, 23:8 (1977), 50–59; E. Sharoni, "Abba Kovner's 'Observations,'" in: *Modern Hebrew Literature*, 4:1 (1978), 35–39; R. Shoham, *Ha-Mareh ve-ha-Kolot: Kri'ah Kashuvah be-"Preidah me-ha-Darom" le-Abba Kovner* (1994); Z. Ben-Yosef Ginor, *Ad Keẓ ha-Bedayah: Iyyun be-Shirat A. Kovner* (1995); Z. Ginor, "The *'Sheliah Zibur'* as a Poetic Persona: A. Kovner's Self-Portrayal," in: *Prooftexts*, 15:3 (1995), 227–247; R. Shoham, "Intertextual Relations and Their Rhetorical Significance in A. Kovner's *Daf Kravi*," in: *Hebrew Studies, 37* (1996), 99–118; E. Porat, *"Bein ha-Shir ha-Liri la-Po'emah ha-Epit,"* in: *Ru'aḥ Aḥeret* 3 (1998), 75–80; S. Luria, *"Po'emah min ha-Genizah,"* in: *Ẓafon*, 5 (1998), 117–129; N. Barzel, *Ad Kelot u-mi-Negged: ha-Mifgash bein Manhigei Mered ha-Getta'ot le-vein ha-Ḥevrah ha-Yisra'elit* (1998); Z. Ginor, "'Meteor Yid': A. Kovner's Poetic Confrontation with Jewish History," in: *Judaism*, 48:1 (1999), 35–48; D. Porat, *Me'ever la-Gashmi: Parashat Ḥayyav shel Abba Kovner* (2000); D. Porat, *"Mahapekhanut be-tokh Konzensus: Parshanuto shel A. Kovner la-Historiyyah ha-Yehudit,"* in: *Yalkut Moreshet*, 71 (2001), 151–161; N. Barzel, "Testimony as Literature and Literature as Testimony: A. Kovner and Amir Guttfreund," in: *Jewish Studies Quarterly*, 9:2 (2002), 160–172; U.S. Cohen, *"Ha-Or ha-Nora she-Metil et Ẓilo ad Aḥron ha-Shirim,"* in: *Ereẓ Aḥeret*, 20 (2004), 72–75; L. Yudkin, "Poet and Activist: Aba Kovner," in: *Literature in the Wake of the Holocaust* (2003), 65–84.

[Getzel Kressel]

KOVNER, ABRAHAM URI (1842–1909), Hebrew writer and pioneer of modern Hebrew literary criticism. Born in Vilna, Kovner studied at various yeshivot in Lithuania and was ultimately attracted to secular studies. He was married at the age of 18, but left his wife in order to pursue his studies of Russian and the sciences. He was influenced in particular by the Russian radical writers. In 1862 he began publishing articles in the Hebrew press, and two essays, *"Davar el Soferei Yisrael"* and *"Lo Shalom ve-Lo Emet"* on Hebrew literature, appeared in *Ha-Meliẓ*. In these he takes the Hebrew authors of his day to task for writing inconsequential poetry and calls on them to write novels and works dealing with science and history. In 1865 he published a collection of essays, *Ḥeker Davar*, in which he attacked the narrow, romantic confines of the Haskalah literature. Kovner contends that the Haskalah Hebrew literature is devoid of any contact with contemporary life, has no readers, and deals with irrelevancies of the ancient past or with meaningless phraseology. Translations of scientific works are made, he avers, by men who are ignorant of science or of the language in which the work was written. Belles lettres and literary criticism, which are the mainstays of other literatures, are completely lacking in Hebrew. A small number of writers are exceptions to the rule, such as I.B. *Levinsohn, I.S. *Reggio, H.S. *Slonimski, and A. *Mapu whose novel *Ayit Ẓavu'a* (1857) depicts contemporary life. Unaware that J. *Perl is the author of *Megalleh Temirin* (1819) and *Boḥen Ẓaddik* (1838), he nevertheless praises these anti-ḥasidic satires. In the final essay he attacks the Hebrew press for concentrating on antiquities and ignoring contemporary life. His sharpest criticism comes at the end of the book, where he declares that all of Hebrew and Yiddish literature is merely a transitional phase and that in Russia, as in the West, Jewish literature "will be written in the language of the country and will flourish in it."

Ḥeker Davar aroused bitter controversy, and A.B. *Gottlober, *Mendele Mokher Seforim, and others took issue with Kovner. They did not enter into a substantive debate but simply called him a "nihilist" and accused him of sacrilege. Kovner reacted with great vehemence, and denounced *Ha-Meliẓ* to the Russian authorities, charging that it supported the Ḥasidim and plotted to buy Palestine in order to establish a monarchy under the House of Rothschild. In subsequent articles, which he published in *Ha-Meliẓ* and *Ha-Karmel*, Kovner became increasingly extremist, predicting the imminent demise of Hebrew literature. His last Hebrew work, *Ẓeror Peraḥim*, appeared in 1868, and then he began writing in Russian. He published articles in the Odessa Jewish weekly *Den* between 1869 and 1871, in which he urged the closing down of yeshivot and replacing them with a modern rabbinical college, and repeated many of the views expressed in his Hebrew writings. He contends that the Jewish problem is essentially economic and will disappear as the general condition of society is improved. His last comment on Hebrew literature was in an article on contemporary Hebrew literature which he wrote for the yearbook *Yevreyskaya Biblioteka* (vol. 4, 1873) and in which, among other things, he examines P. *Smolenskin's *Ha-To'eh be-Darkhei ha-Ḥayyim* and J.L. *Gordon's *Olam ke-Minhago*.

In 1871 Kovner moved to St. Petersburg, where he worked as a minor bank official and wrote for the Russian press. In 1875 he was arrested on charges of forging a check for a large sum of money and was sentenced to four years of hard labor in Siberia. After his release he settled in Siberia, converted to Christianity, and married a gentile woman. Later he was permitted to return to the European part of Russia and he settled in Lomza, where he worked as a government official. He continued to take an interest in Jewish affairs, carried on a correspondence with some of the leading Russian writers, including Dostoevski and Tolstoi, on the subject of the Jewish problem, and in 1908 he published anonymously a pamphlet on the self-isolation of the Jews. In 1903 he published his memoirs in the St. Petersburg journal *Istoricheskiy Vestnik*. An edition of his collected writings (incomplete) appeared in Tel Aviv (1947).

While Kovner's basic thesis predicting the inevitable decline of Hebrew literature proved to be entirely unfounded, through his unsparing attacks on the writers of his day he forged the first genuine literary criticism in the Hebrew language, and thus had a profound effect on the future development of modern Hebrew literature.

BIBLIOGRAPHY: Klausner, Sifrut, 4 (1953), 139–75 (incl. bibl.); Breiman, in: *Mezudah*, 7 (1954), 416–57; Auerbach, in: *Orlogin*, 4 (1951), 21–32; 9 (1953), 166–87; 11 (1955), 94–122; S. Ginzburg, *Meshumodim in Tsarishn Rusland* (1946), 157–93; I. Zinberg, *Di Geshikhte un der Literatur bay Yidn*, 9 (1966), 208–38; M. Weinreich, *Fun Beyde Zayten Ployt* (1955); Waxman, Literature, 3 (1960^2), 319–22, 338, 341.

[Yehuda Slutsky]

KOWALSKI, MAX (1882–1956), composer. Born in Poland, but in his infancy the family emigrated to Germany. By profession, he was a lawyer in Frankfurt, but he studied voice and composition, the latter under Bernard Sekles. His early songs, published in 1913, included the *Pierrot Lunaire Lieder:* he continued writing songs until 1934 and his works were sung by many famous singers. Sent to Buchenwald concentration camp in 1938, he was released in March 1939 and settled in London, where he continued composing songs for voice and piano. Seventeen of his works have been published, while many have remained in manuscript. He died in London.

KOWALSKY, JUDAH LEIB (1862–1925), rabbi and Mizrachi leader in Poland. Born in a suburb of Warsaw, Kowalsky was an ordained rabbi who also acquired a general education. He served in the rabbinate in Grabow, Chorzele, and Wloclawek. He joined the Zionist movement as a youth and preached on its behalf in synagogues and meetings, in spite of the opposition of other rabbis. Kowalsky participated in the conference that established the Mizrachi movement in Vilna and worked on behalf of the movement throughout Poland. In 1919 he was elected president of Mizrachi in Poland and did much to develop the network of religious education there. He visited Palestine during the 1921 riots, and on his return he called on Diaspora Jewry to aid the *yishuv* and went on tours on behalf of the Zionist funds. From 1923 he was a member of the Polish senate. As a leader of the association of rabbis in Poland, he participated in consultations and decisions in halakhic matters. Kowalsky left many volumes of responsa on *halakhah* which were lost in the Holocaust. He published articles in the Yiddish and Hebrew press in Poland. He died in Breslau and was buried in Wloclawek.

BIBLIOGRAPHY: Y. Gur Aryeh, *Ha-Rav Y.L. Kowalsky* (1926); *Sefer Włocławek ve-ha-Sevivah* (1967), 143–76, 547–50, 649–54.

[Yitzchak Raphael]

KOZAKOV, MIKHAIL EMMANUILOVICH (1897–1954), Soviet Russian author. Born in the Ukraine, Kozakov studied medicine and law. His most ambitious work was the novel *Krusheniye imperii* ("The Fall of the Empire," 1956), a much enlarged version of his *Devyat tochek* ("Nine Points," 4 brochures, 1931–39; serialized from 1929). It deals with the last years of Imperial Russia and with the Revolution, and portrays numerous historical figures. Some of Kozakov's early tales, such as *Abram Nashatyr* (1927), depict life in a Jewish shtetl of the old Pale of Settlement, similar to the one Kozakov remembered from his own childhood. He wrote the novella *Chelovek, padayushchiy nits* ("The Man Who Prostrates Himself"), one of the very few frank portrayals of antisemitism under Soviet conditions to appear in the U.S.S.R. (1929, 1932).

BIBLIOGRAPHY: *Russkiye Sovetskiye Pisateli Prozaiki*, 2 (1964), index.

[Maurice Friedberg]

KOZER, JOSÉ (1940–), Cuban poet, essayist, and translator, born in La Havana of Jewish East European parents. He left Cuba in 1960, lived in the U.S. and Spain, and ultimately settled in Florida. He taught Spanish and Latin American literatures for 32 years at Queens College, N.Y. His poetry centers on his existential condition as a Jew and an exile, from which he strives towards a universal spiritual unity for the individual and mankind as a whole. It includes references to his ancestors and Jewish tradition as well as Christian and Oriental religious imagery. Kozer's poetry has been translated into English, Portuguese, French, Italian, German, Hebrew, and Greek and has been widely anthologized. Among his books are *La rueca de los semblantes* ("The Spinning Wheel of Faces," 1980); *Bajo este cien* ("Under This One-Hundred," 1983); *La garza sin sombras* ("The Shadeless Heron," 1985); *Carece de causa* ("Lacking a Cause," 1988); *De donde oscilan los seres en sus proporciones* ("From Where Beings Oscillate in Their Proportions," 1990); *et mutabile* ("and mutating," 1995); *Dípticos* ("Diptychs," 1998); *Farándula* ("Show Business," 1999); *Mezcla para dos tiempos* ("Mixture for Two Times," prose, 1999); *No buscan reflejarse* ("They Do Not Try To Be Reflected," 2001); *Ánima* ("Soul," 2002).

BIBLIOGRAPHY: R. DiAntonio and N. Glickman, *Tradition and Innovation: Reflections on Latin American Jewish Writing* (1993); D.B. Lockhart, *Jewish Writers of Latin America. A Dictionary* (1997); G. Pérez Firmat, *Life on the Hyphen: The Cuban-American Way* (1994); J. Sefamí, *La voracidad grafómana: José Kozer. Crítica, entrevistas y documentos* (2002).

[Florinda F. Goldberg (2nd ed.)]

KOZIENICE (Rus. **Kozenitsy**), town in Kielce province, E. central Poland. In 1661 the Jews of Kozienice referred to a privilege dated 1616, which probably was the oldest granted to the community. In 1661 five Jewish house owners lived in Kozienice, while ten other families resided in rented dwellings. In 1722 the Jews paid a poll tax of 354 zlotys; this was increased to 630 zlotys in 1726. In the 1780s, through Jewish initiative, a soap factory was established in the town. From 1791 the Jews of Kozienice also engaged in the production of stockings. At the beginning of the 19th century the *Maggid* Israel b. Shabbetai Hapstein, one of the most influential *ẓaddikim*, lived in Kozienice (see *Kozienice, Israel, below). The community numbered 1,365 in 1765, 1,185 (59% of the total population) in 1827, 1,980 (65%) in 1857, 3,764 (59%) in 1897, 3,811 (55%) in 1921, and 4,780 in 1939. Between the world wars the Jews were shopkeepers and artisans and the town remained a ḥasidic center. The Germans entered the city on September 9, 1939, and burned the synagogue. A ghetto was sealed off in late 1940, its population doubling with the arrival of refugees. On September 2, 1942, around 8,000 Jews were deported to Treblinka.

BIBLIOGRAPHY: B. Wasiutyński, *Ludność żydowska w Polsce…* (1930), 32, 58, 71, 76; Halpern, Pinkas, index; I. Schiper, *Dzieje handlu żydowskigo na ziemiach polskich* (1937), index; E. Heller, *Żydowskie predsiebiorstwa memystowe w Polsce…*, 4 (1923). **ADD. BIBLIOGRAPHY:** B. Kaplinski (ed.), *Sefer Kozienits* (1969); S. Spector (ed.), *Encyclopedia of Jewish Life Before and During the Holocaust* (2001), s.v.

[*Encyclopaedia Judaica* (Germany)]

KOZIENICE, ISRAEL BEN SHABBETAI HAPSTEIN (1733–1814), ḥasidic *ẓaddik* and preacher, born in Apta; one of the first propagators of Ḥasidism in Congress Poland. His teachers were Samuel Shmelke *Horowitz of Nikolsburg, *Dov Baer the Maggid of Mezhirech, *Elimelech of Lyzhansk, and *Levi Isaac of Berdichev, with whom he was on friendly terms. In his early years, Israel withdrew from society and became an ascetic. After the death of his father, a poor bookbinder, he moved to Przysucha where he earned his living as a teacher (*melammed*). He then settled in Kozienice where his eloquent preaching gained him the appellation the "*Maggid* of Kozienice." Israel's homilies were notable for their elegant structure and lucid exposition, even though they included much kabbalistic symbolism, and had a great impact on his listeners. He would admonish them "with pleasing and sweet persuasion and not with hard words" (*Avodat Yisrael, Avot*). On the role of the preacher he taught: "He who reproves people and teaches them the Law and the word of God must have insight into the heart of every single one of them, even of the very wicked."

However, Israel became noted mainly for his activity as a *ẓaddik*. Many followed him because of his whole-hearted approach to the worship of God and his ecstatic mode of prayer through **Devekut*.

According to Israel, the principal duty of the *ẓaddik* was to give spiritual guidance to his followers and assist them in divine worship. The devotion to God by the *ẓaddik* is a dynamic action through which those under his protection also attain devotion to God. Thus the *ẓaddik* elevates the spirit of the average man and brings him nearer to the Creator, which is the aim of Ḥasidism. However, the simple man will never attain the heights which the *ẓaddik* himself reaches. As a "practical *ẓaddik*" Israel gained great popularity, actively assisting his followers apart from his duties of spiritual guidance. He thus cared for the welfare, children, and livelihood of his Ḥasidim and even distributed remedies and amulets. The *Mitnaggedim* sharply criticized him for this activity while the Ḥasidim justified it, explaining that the amulets contained his name only. Israel's fame also reached high-ranking Poles, and he apparently had connections with the family of the Polish prince Czariorski. He was alive to public affairs and during the period of the grand duchy of Warsaw was to have participated in a convention of delegates of the Polish communities convening in Warsaw mainly to discuss the heavy taxes imposed on the Jews. Israel took steps against the opponents of Ḥasidism and tried, unsuccessfully, to prevent the printing of anti-ḥasidic works appearing in Warsaw in the late 18th century. A man of the people, he spiced his discourse with proverbs. With his friend *Jacob Isaac ha-Ḥozeh of Lublin he was among the principal disseminators of Ḥasidism of the school of *Israel b. Eliezer Ba'al Shem Tov in the interior of Poland. He had a profound knowledge of both traditional and esoteric learning, and participated with the greatest scholars of his time in a halakhic discussion on the question of the *agunah*. His principal halakhic work is *Beit Yisrael* (Warsaw, 1864). His tractates on the Kabbalah testify to his great esoteric knowledge. A ḥasidic story relates "that before he traveled to the Maggid of Mezhirech he studied 800 books on Kabbalah and after all that when he came to the holy Maggid of blessed memory he realized that he had not yet learned anything" (*Toledot Adam le-Shabbat Ḥanukkah*); however, his writings on Kabbalah (*Or Yisrael*, Czernowitz, 1862; *Ner Yisrael*, Vilna, 1822; and others) do not contain original interpretations of his own. His principal work on Ḥasidism is *Avodat Yisrael* (Yozepof, 1842).

BIBLIOGRAPHY: Dubnow, Ḥasidut (1960²), 215–9, 288, 328–32, 481–3; A.I. Bromberg, *Mi-Gedolei ha-Torah ve-ha-Ḥasidut*, 18 (1961); H.Z. Halberstam, *Toledot ha-Maggid mi-Kozniz* (1966); Z.M. Rabinowicz, *Ha-Maggid mi-Kozniz* (1947); I. Berger, *Sefer Zekhut Yisrael ha-Nikra Eser Orot* (1907), 68–83; A. Rubinstein, in: *Tarbiz*, 32 (1963), 80–97; M. Wilensky, *Ḥasidim u-Mitnaggedim* (1970), index; M. Buber, *Gog u-Magog* (1967²), 64–67, 135–8, 147–9, 150–6, 185–7, 193–7, 200–5, 215–22; idem, *Tales of the Ḥasidim*, 1 (1968⁴), 286–99; 2 (1968⁴), 177, 178–81; L.I. Newman, *Ḥasidic Anthology* (1963), index s.v. *Koznitzer*.

[Aaron Rothkoff]

KOZINKSI, ALEX (1950–), U.S. Court of Appeals judge. Born in Bucharest, Romania, Kozinski immigrated to the United States in 1962 with his parents, both Holocaust survivors. He attended public schools and received his bachelor's degree from the University of California, Los Angeles (UCLA), in 1972. He graduated from UCLA Law School in 1975 and was admitted to the California bar that year. From 1975 to 1976 Kozinski served as clerk for Anthony Kennedy, a judge on the Ninth Circuit of the U.S. Court of Appeals, who later became a Supreme Court justice. In 1976 Kozinski clerked for Chief Justice Warren Burger, then in 1977 he entered private practice in Los Angeles. In 1978 he was admitted to the District of Columbia bar, and in 1979 he joined the firm of Covington and Burling as an associate. He was named deputy counsel to the office of president-elect Ronald Reagan in 1980; after Reagan took office in January 1981, Kozinski became assistant counsel in the Office of Counsel to the President. He was appointed special counsel of the Merit Systems Protection Board later that year. In 1982 he was named chief judge on the U.S. Court of Claims. In 1985 President Reagan appointed Kozinski to the Ninth Circuit of the U.S. Court of Appeals.

Though considered a conservative jurist, Kozinski gained attention in 2001 for his stand against electronic surveillance in the workplace. The Administrative Office (AO) of the federal judiciary had installed a monitoring system designed to identify federal court workers who were engaging in unauthorized use of the Internet; Kozinski and some of his colleagues protested its use in the Ninth Circuit. In an interview with *Newsweek*, Kozinski stated that he considered such a surveillance system a violation of court employee's civil rights.

In addition to workplace privacy, Kozinski was involved in other issues, including commercial speech. In a 1990 article, coauthored by law professor Stuart Banner, in the *Virginia Law Review*, he argued against allowing commercial speech a lower level of protection, warning that existing doctrine "gives government a powerful weapon to suppress or control speech by classifying it as merely commercial."

[Dorothy Bauhoff (2nd ed.)]

KOZLE (**Kosel**; **Cosel**), town in Silesia, Poland. Jews lived in Kozle long before the first documentary evidence of their presence in 1373. In 1563 Emperor *Ferdinand I decreed, on the urging of the municipality, that none might reside there any longer. According to an imperial decree of 1713, Jewish merchants were prohibited from even entering the town, although in 1750 two merchants were recorded as living there. The number of Jews in the town increased from 30 in 1766 to 112 in 1782. In 1820 a community was organized and a school opened, and five years later a private home was converted into a synagogue. A new synagogue was consecrated in 1884 when the community numbered 236 persons (4.7% of the total population). The community subsequently declined to 119 in 1910 and 80 in 1932. By 1939 only 24 remained. The community was destroyed during World War II and not reestablished since.

BIBLIOGRAPHY: M. Bronn, *Geschichte der Juden in Schlesien* (1896–1917), passim; FGW, 103–4.

KRACAUER, ISIDOR (1852–1923), gymnasium teacher, historian of Frankfurt Jewry. Kracauer was born in Sagan, Germany, studied philology and history at the University of Breslau, receiving a doctorate, and from 1876 taught at the Philanthropin school at Frankfurt on the Main as a teacher of history. He published numerous studies on the history of Frankfurt Jews. His chief works are *Urkundenbuch zur Geschichte der Juden in Frankfurt am Main von 1150–1400*, (1914); the two-volume *Geschichte der Juden in Frankfurt a. M., 1150–1824* (1925–27), and (with A. Freimann) *Frankfurt* (translated from the German ms. by Bertha Szold Levin, Philadelphia 1929). For a list of his works see M. Brann, *Geschichte des Juedisch-theologischen Seminars… in Breslau* (1904), 175.

BIBLIOGRAPHY: H.O. Schembs, *Bibliographie zur Geschichte der Frankfurter Juden 1781–1945* (1978), 514; *Lexikon deutsch-juedischer Autoren*, vol. 14 (2006).

[Archiv Bibliographia Judaica (2nd ed.)]

KRACAUER, SIEGFRIED (1889–1966), sociologist, philosopher, film critic, and novelist. Born in Frankfurt, the sole son in a Jewish family, he studied architecture (1911–14) and in 1921 became an editor of Germany's leading liberal newspaper, the *Frankfurter Zeitung*. As head of the Berlin feuilleton section (1930–33), he tried to raise public awareness of the encroaching Third Reich by observing and describing cultural and social symptoms of change. In March 1933 he emigrated to France, settled in Paris and had henceforth to make his living as a freelance journalist and author. Encouraged by the success of his novel *Ginster* (1928) and his sociological study *Die Angestellten* (1930), he wrote another novel, *Georg* (1934, unpublished until 1973), and portrayed French society of the mid-19th century in *Jacques Offenbach and the Paris of His Time* (1937). After being temporarily interned, he managed in spring 1941 to flee from Marseille via Lisbon to New York. He started to work on the impact of mass media propaganda and drafted a study on "Propaganda and the Nazi War Film" (1942), on behalf of the Film Library at the Museum of Modern Art. Further essays, such as "National Types as Hollywood Presents Them" (*Public Opinion Quarterly*, 1949) and "The Challenge of Qualitative Content Analysis" (*Public Opinion Quarterly*, 1952–53), followed. Support from the Rockefeller Foundation and the Simon Guggenheim Memorial Foundation enabled him to complete his renowned book, *From Caligari to Hitler: A Psychological History of the German Film*, published in 1947. After 20 years of writing and rewriting, he managed in 1959 to finish his second film book, *Theory of Film: The Redemption of Physical Reality* (published in 1960). In the early 1950s Kracauer began to win international recognition: he became research director at Columbia University's Bureau of Applied Social Research and an adviser to the Bollington Foundation. He edited a compilation of his articles written for the *Frankfurter Zeitung* and republished them as *Das Ornament der Masse* (1963) and *Strassen in Berlin und anderswo* (1964). Kracauer died before completing his work on *History: The Last Things before the Last*. The book was published in 1969, edited by the historian Paul Oskar Kristeller in cooperation with Kracauer's widow, Lili.

BIBLIOGRAPHY: Stalder, *Siegfried Kracauer: Das journalistische Werk in der 'Frankfurter Zeitung' 1921–1933* (2003); H. Bratu, "Introduction," in: Siegfried Kracauer, *Theory of Film*, Princeton 1997, vii–xlv; Koch, *Kracauer zur Einführung* (1996); Barnouw, *Critical Realism: History, Photography and the World of Siegfried Kracauer* (1994); Anderson (ed.), *Special Issue on Siegfried Kracauer*, of the *New*

German Critique: An Interdisciplinary Journal of German Studies, 54 (1991); Levin, *Siegfried Kracauer: Eine Bibliographie seiner Schriften*, (1989); Belke and Renz, *Siegfried Kracauer 1889–1966* (1988); Frisby, *Fragments of Modernity* (1985); I. Muelder, *Siegfried Kracauer – Grenzgänger zwischen Theorie und Literatur: seine fruehen Schriften 1913–1933* (1985).

[Werner J. Cahnman / MirjamWenzel (2nd ed.)]

KRAFT, LOUIS (1891–1975), U.S. social worker. Kraft, who was born in Moscow, Russia, was educated in New York. From 1914 to 1917 he served as executive director of the Bronx YM & YWHA. He served as executive director of the *National Jewish Welfare Board (1917–20) and consultant on community organization in Europe for the American Jewish Joint Distribution Committee and the Conference on Jewish Material Claims Against Germany. As secretary of the World Federation of YMHAS and Jewish Community Centers, he established the YM & YWHA in Jerusalem in 1948. Kraft was president of the National Conference of Jewish Communal Service (1943) and honorary president of the National Association of Jewish Center Workers (1947). A founder of the United Service Organizations (USO), he was on its executive committee in World War II. From 1961 until 1974, Kraft served as voluntary executive secretary of the Association of Jewish Center Workers.

Kraft wrote *Century of the Jewish Community Center Movement (1854–1954)* (1953); *Social Agency Administration* (1967); and *The Development of the Jewish Community Center* (1968); he co-authored *Change and Challenge: A History of 50 Years of JWB* (1966) and edited, with C.S. Bernheimer, *Aspects of the Jewish Community Center* (1954). Recognized as "the architect of the Jewish community center movement," he received many academic and professional honors.

In 2002, the World Confederation of Jewish Community Centers established the Louis Kraft Memorial Lecture and the Louis Kraft Maor Award, given to exemplary Jewish community centers in the former Soviet Union.

[Philip Goodman / Ruth Beloff (2nd ed.)]

KRAFT, ROBERT K. (1942–), owner of the National Football League's New England Patriots as well as Major League Soccer's New England Revolution. Kraft, who grew up in Brookline, Mass., graduated from Columbia College in 1963, and received his MBA from Harvard Business School in 1965. Kraft began his business career with the Rand-Whitney Group, Inc. of Worcester, Mass., a company he later acquired. In 1972, he founded International Forest Products, a trader of paper commodities that does business in more than 80 countries. Rand-Whitney and International Forest Products comprise one of the largest privately owned paper and packaging companies in the United States. In 1998, he founded the Kraft Group to serve as the holding company for the family's varied business interests, including the Rand-Whitney Group, Rand-Whitney Containerboard, International Forest Products, the New England Revolution, as well as a portfolio of more than 30 private equity investments.

In 1985, Kraft took out a 10-year option on the 300 acres surrounding Foxboro Stadium, where the New England Patriots played, which gave him access to all stadium parking. By 1988 he had bought the stadium, and then six years later he purchased the team for $172 million, then the highest price for a sports franchise in history. He built a new stadium to replace Foxboro, with $325 million of his own money invested in the state-of-the-art Gillette Stadium. Kraft was heavily criticized for offering a first-round draft choice to acquire head coach Bill Belichick in 2000, but he was vindicated with three Super Bowl Championships in the ensuing four years. Since taking ownership in 1994, no NFL team has won as many conference championships or more Super Bowl championships than the Patriots.

Kraft is also heavily involved in numerous philanthropic endeavors, both in the United States and Israel. He and his wife, Myra, are ardent supporters of Jewish education in the Boston area, and also donated the $11 million to build the Kraft Center for Jewish Student Life at Columbia University. They also created the Kraft-Hiatt Fund, a joint endowment fund through which gifts to Holy Cross and Brandeis University are used to encourage greater understanding between Christians and Jews.

Kraft is the primary shareholder of the $40-million Carmel Container Systems in Caesarea, Israel, the largest export packaging plant in the country. In 1999, he built the Kraft Family Stadium in Jerusalem, which became home field for American Flag Football in Israel.

[Elli Wohlgelernter (2nd ed.)]

KRAFT, WERNER (1896–1991), Israeli author writing in German. Kraft was born in Brunswick, and worked in the Leipzig and Hanover State Libraries. He maintained his deep involvement with the classical and humanist German traditions, even after making his home in Ereẓ Israel in 1934. He was profoundly influenced by Karl Kraus, Franz Kafka, and Rudolf Borchardt (all three of Jewish origin), particularly in his uncompromising attitude toward the moral obligations of a writer and his language. He wrote major works on all three authors, including two books on Kraus: *Karl Kraus – Beitraege zum Verstaendnis seines Werks* (1956) and *Das Ja des Neinsagers* (1974).

Kraft also wrote important essays on Friedrich Hoelderlin, J.G. Seume, and the otherwise completely forgotten Carl Gustav Jochmann. He edited a volume of previously unknown writings by Else *Lasker-Schueler, which were found after her death in Jerusalem in 1945. He published two volumes of his own lyrical poems in German and a novel, *Der Wirrwarr*, which refers to the fate of Jewish youngsters seeking their identity in the years of distress after 1933.

Kraft's memoirs, *Spiegelung der Jugend* (1973), deal with his life before his arrival in Jerusalem. In Jerusalem he was in close contact with Martin *Buber and published an account of his discussions with him after the philosopher's death in 1965.

BIBLIOGRAPHY: E. Simon, in: *Neue Zuercher Zeitung* (May 5, 1966); J. Drews, in: W. Kraft, *Spiegelung der Jugend* (1973), 154ff. **ADD. BIBLIOGRAPHY:** U. Breden, *Von Hannover nach Jerusalem – Werner Kraft 1896–1991* (1996); J. Drews, *Werner Kraft 1896–1991* (1996); U. Pörksen, *Der Wünschelrutengänger – Erinnerungen an Werner Kraft* (1997); U. Breden, *Werner Kraft – Bibliothekar und Schriftsteller* (1992).

[Erich Gottgetreu]

KRAKAUER, LEOPOLD (1890–1954), Israel architect and designer. Krakauer was born in Vienna, where he studied architecture and engineering. In 1920–21 he helped to design the parliament building in Belgrade, Yugoslavia. He immigrated to Palestine in 1924, and settled in Jerusalem. Krakauer was primarily an architect, and it was only later that he concentrated on drawing. He designed several public buildings and private houses, which, with their harmonious, simple lines, often close to Bauhaus ideas, remain among the best examples of the second phase of Palestinian architecture. They include kibbutz dining halls at Bet Alfa (1930) and Tel Yosef (1933), and the Megiddo Hotel, Haifa (1935). From 1948 he concentrated on town planning, and designed the Katamon Gimmel quarter of Jerusalem (1952) and several new immigrant villages. His charcoal and brown-wash drawings are detailed studies of the countryside round Jerusalem. After World War I, his work was expressionist, but his vision became more and more objective, and his line stronger and more precise. His work conveyed the subtleties and stark harmonies of the mountains, terraces, and lone cypresses. His unadorned, sober style is exceptional in Israel art.

His wife, GRETE KRAKAUER-WOLF (d. 1970), was born in Vienna, where she also studied. An abstract painter in her youth, she painted landscapes and portraits after settling in Ereẓ Israel, and in later years imaginative compositions featuring rocks, plants, and fossils.

[Yona Fischer]

KRAMER, JACOB (1892–1962), British painter. Kramer was born at Klintsy, in the Ukraine. His father, Max Kramer (d. 1915), was a painter and his uncle Sion was a court painter who exhibited at the Chicago Exhibition of 1893. The Kramer family immigrated to England in 1900 and settled in Leeds, where Jacob lived most of his life. At school the eight-year-old Jacob was recognized as being artistically talented and in 1907 entered the Leeds School of Art. With the assistance of the Jewish Education Aid Society he studied at the Slade School of Art in London in 1912. A gifted and sensitive draughtsman, Kramer never quite lived up to his early promise. His masterpiece is undoubtedly the powerful *The Day of Atonement* (1919) now in the Leeds City Art Gallery, together with the equally impressive *Hear Our Voice, O Lord Our God* (1919). Kramer illustrated Israel Cohen's *A Ghetto Gallery* (1931). He spent most of his life in Leeds and taught at the Leeds and Bradford colleges of art.

ADD. BIBLIOGRAPHY: ODNB online; M. Kramer (ed.), *Jacob Kramer: A Memorial Volume* (1969); *Jacob Kramer Reassessed* (Ben Uri Art Society, London) 1984.

[Charles Samuel Spencer]

KRAMER, LARRY (1935–), U.S. writer and social activist. Born in Bridgeport, Conn., Kramer earned a B.A. degree from Yale University in 1957. Entering British films, he produced and wrote dialogue for *Here We Go Round the Mulberrry Bush* in 1967. Three years later he adapted the D.H. Lawrence novel *Women in Love* and produced the Ken Russell film. His adaptation won four Oscar nominations, including best screenplay. He also wrote the screenplay for the 1973 remake of *Lost Horizon*, which Kramer called "the only thing in life I am ashamed of." Nevertheless, the film was a financial success for him. In 1978 his sexually audacious novel *Faggots* appeared, and it remained in print for more than 20 years. The book was an indictment of a homosexual lifestyle on Fire Island, N.Y., that equated promiscuity with liberation. His 1985 play about AIDS, *The Normal Heart*, had more than 600 productions worldwide.

Kramer was among the early public figures to identify and publicize the disease AIDS and became one of the leaders in the decades-long history of AIDS advocacy in the United States. He responded to the spread of the disease among homosexual men by founding the Gay Men's Health Crisis in New York City, the first and largest AIDS service organization in the world, and later, frustrated by what he saw as the medical community's inadequate response to the epidemic, he founded ACT UP, the international AIDS advocacy and protest organization. The latter organization used guerrilla-style protests and extensive negotiations to accelerate the development of treatments for the disease. He caused scenes on several television programs, identifying homosexuals who were hiding their sexual identity, in an effort to call attention and jolt public action into finding a cure for a disease that had been a scourge since its identification in 1981. He himself contracted HIV and hepatitis B some time in the 1970s, he said, but the treatments for the disease damaged his liver. In 2001, after a change in policy by several transplant centers, Kramer received a new liver. He then began agitating for changes in the organ-donor system to make more organs available.

He published a collection of essays, *Reports From the Holocaust: The Making of an AIDS Activist* (1989); a short play, *Just Say No* (1988); and *The Furniture of Home* (1989). *The Destiny of Me,* which had its premiere in 1993, continued the story of the main character in *The Normal Heart*.

In 2001 Kramer donated his papers to Yale for the creation of a Larry Kramer Initiative for Lesbian and Gay Studies. Kramer's brother, Arthur, also a Yale graduate, gave $1 million to set up the study program.

[Stewart Kampel (2nd ed.)]

KRAMER, MOSES BEN DAVID, OF VILNA (d. 1688), talmudist and rabbinic leader. Kramer was born in Cracow. He was called Kramer (shopkeeper) because he obtained his livelihood from a shop managed by his wife, refusing to accept a salary from the community. After serving for a time as *dayyan* in Brest-Litovsk, he was appointed as head of the Vilna *bet din* in 1673. He was regarded as one of the main Jewish spokesmen of his time and participated in the meetings of the *Council of Four Lands. His name appears among the signatories to the resolutions adopted at the "assembly of Selts," at the "assembly of Leaders," and, together with other Lithuanian rabbis, at the "assembly of Khomsk." Kramer was an erudite scholar but no works written by him are known. However his son-in-law, Joseph b. Jacob of Pinczow, included some of his statements in his *Rosh Yosef* (Amsterdam, 1707). In the introduction he states, "I have included many things which I myself heard from my father-in-law, Moses. As is well known he excelled in many directions, both in the revealed law and in esoteric lore. He would almost seem to have been divinely inspired and wondrous deeds were accomplished by him.... He directed great yeshivot." His extant statements indeed reveal brilliance and profundity. Many of his novellae are quoted in the *Derash Shemu'el* of Samuel Feibush (Duerenfurth, 1694). Many great scholars and leaders of Vilna were descended from him, including Elijah of Vilna.

BIBLIOGRAPHY: S.J. Fuenn, *Kiryah Ne'emanah* (1915²), 102–3; Ḥ.N. Dembitzer, *Kelilat Yofi*, 1 (1888), 71; H.N. Maggid-Steinschneider, *Ir Vilna* (1900), 9–11.

[Abram Juda Goldrat]

KRAMER, SAMUEL NOAH (1897–1990), U.S. Sumerologist. Born in Russia, Kramer was taken to the United States in 1906. His early years were spent in Philadelphia. He first embarked on a career in education. He then studied at Dropsie College (1926–27) and the University of Pennsylvania in 1929, writing his doctoral dissertation on an aspect of the then newly discovered *Nuzi texts (cf. Kramer, in: AASOR, 11 (1929–30), 62–119). In 1930–31 he was in the field in Iraq and excavated at Tell Billah, Tepe Gawra, and Fara (cf. Kramer, in JAOS, 52 (1932), 110–32). From 1932 to 1942 he was on the staff of the Oriental Institute, University of Chicago, specializing in the Sumerian language. His publications during this period include *The Sumerian Prefix Forms be-and bi-in the Time of the Earlier Princes of Lagash* (1936), *Gilgamesh and the Ḥuluppu Tree* (1938), and *Lamentation over the Destruction of Ur* (1940). In 1937–38 he copied Sumerian literary tablets in Istanbul, which were published in *Sumerian Literary Texts from Nippur in the Museum of the Ancient Orient at Istanbul* (1944). Kramer returned to study the Istanbul collection in 1946–47 and 1951–52. From 1942 to 1968 he was associated with the University of Pennsylvania, as research associate in the Babylonian collection of the University Museum in 1942–43, associate curator of the tablet collection from 1943 to 1947, and curator of the tablet collection and Clark Research Professor of Assyriology from 1948 to 1968. In 1968–69 Kramer was at the University of Indiana where he gave the Patton Lectures (cf. *The Sacred Marriage Rite*, 1969). In 1970 he was appointed to the department of religious sciences at the Ecole Pratique des Hautes Etudes in Paris. Kramer's research and extensive travels in search of Sumerian literary texts have been fundamental in the reconstruction of Sumerian literature. Kramer continued working intensively after his official retirement in 1968 until the time of his death at the age of 93. A member of the American Oriental Society, the Society of Biblical Literature, and the American Philosophical Society, he also received several honorary degrees. When the University Museum marked his ninetieth birthday with a public symposium, "History Begins at Sumer," in his honor, most of the world's Sumerian scholars attended. His basic research has resulted in several volumes of texts, some edited by Kramer himself and some in collaboration with other scholars who were able to benefit from his experience. He is also the author of numerous studies, including works on comparative aspects of Sumerian literature, society, and religion; editions of Sumerian compositions of various types; as well as several more popular works, *Sumerian Mythology* (1961); *From the Tablets of Sumer* (1956), revised as *History Begins at Sumer* (1958, 1961²); and *The Sumerians* (1963). In his work Kramer made numerous comparisons between Sumerian literature and the Bible.

ADD. BIBLIOGRAPHY: S. Kramer, in: JAOS, 103 (1983), 337–53 (personal reflections).

[Aaron Shaeffer / Rohan Saxena (2nd ed.)]

KRAMER, STANLEY E. (1913–2001), U.S. film producer and director. Born in Manhattan, New York, Kramer graduated from New York University and set off for Hollywood at the age of 19. He became known for his handling of sensitive and controversial subjects. He worked in Hollywood from 1933 as a writer and film editor, but in 1949 won wide attention as a producer with *Home of the Brave*, a pioneering film on racial prejudice in the army. He handled racial themes again in *The Defiant Ones* (1958), which dealt with two escaped convicts, one white and one black, chained together (Oscar nomination for Best Picture); and in *Guess Who's Coming to Dinner* (Oscar nomination for Best Picture, 1967), a story about interracial marriage.

Kramer's *On the Beach* (1959), about survival in the atomic age, provoked controversy in U.S. government circles, where it was felt that the movie alarmed the public unduly. In 1961, Kramer produced and directed *Judgement at Nuremberg*, dealing with the trial of German judges for war crimes (Oscar nomination for Best Picture and Best Director). His other major pictures include *Champion* (1949), *The Men* (1950), *Cyrano de Bergerac* (1950), *Death of a Salesman* (1951), *The Caine Mutiny* (Oscar nomination for Best Picture, 1954), *The Wild One* (1954), *Not as a Stranger* (1955), *Inherit the Wind* (1960), *It's a Mad, Mad, Mad, Mad World* (1963), and *Ship of Fools* (Oscar nomination for Best Picture, 1965).

In 1962 the Academy of Motion Picture Arts and Sciences honored Kramer with the Irving G. Thalberg Memorial Award, which is presented to a creative producer who has been responsible for a consistently high quality of motion picture production.

After a string of less successful films, such as *The Secret of Santa Vittoria* (1969) and *Bless the Beast and the Children* (1971), Kramer retired in 1980 and moved to Seattle, where he taught and wrote a newspaper column.

Kramer wrote *Dining In – Seattle* (with E. Lotzkar and R. Abbott, 1980), and his autobiographical *A Mad, Mad, Mad, Mad World: A Life in Hollywood* (with T. Coffey, 1997).

BIBLIOGRAPHY: R. Newquist, *A Special Kind of Magic* (1967), 19–55. **ADD. BIBLIOGRAPHY:** D. Spoto, *Stanley Kramer: Film Maker* (1978).

[Paul Freireich / Ruth Beloff (2nd ed.)]

KRAMER, THEODOR (1897–1958), Austrian poet. Kramer was born in Niederhollabrunn, Lower Austria. After being seriously wounded in World War I he tried his hand at various trades before devoting himself to poetry. Much of his verse has a clinical frankness derived from his memories as the son of a country doctor and from his own hospital experience. Kramer wished to be the voice of the underprivileged outcasts of society – tramps, cripples, alcoholics, prostitutes, beggars, and peasants – and his poetry is notable for a realism bordering on coarseness. His collection *Die Gaunerzinke* (1929) was awarded the City of Vienna's poetry prize. Later volumes include *Kalendarium* (1930); *Wir lagen in Wolhynien im Morast* (1931), inspired by war experiences; and *Mit der Ziehharmonika* (1936). After the *Anschluss*, Kramer sought refuge in England and, after a period of internment, worked as a librarian at the Guildford Technical College. The collections of verse he wrote in exile were the haunting *Verbannt aus Oesterreich, Neue Gedichte* (1943); *Die untere Schenke* (1946); *Wien 1938* (1946); *Die gruenen Kader* (1946); and *Lob der Verzweiflung* (1946), much of which remained unpublished. *Vom schwarzen Wein* (1956) was the last collection published in Kramer's lifetime. Despite the recognition accorded him in later years, Kramer could not bear his joyless exile and became a hypochondriac. He died within six months of his return to Vienna.

BIBLIOGRAPHY: E. Lissauer, in: *Die Literatur*, 31 (1929), 451–3; M. Guttenbrunner, in: *Frankfurter Hefte* (June, 1953); H. Zohn, in: *Books Abroad*, 29 (1955); idem, *Wiener Juden in der deutschen Literatur* (1964), 73–82; E. Chvojka, *Einer bezeugt es* (1960). **ADD. BIBLIOGRAPHY:** D. Strigl, *"Wo niemand zuhaus ist, dort bin ich zuhaus" Theodor Kramer – Heimatdichter und Sozialdemokrat zwischen den Fronten*, (1993); W. Schmidt-Dengler, *Verlockerungen österreichische Avantgarde im 20. Jahrhundert. Studien zu Walter Serner, Theodor Kramer, H.C. Artmann, Konrad Bayer, Peter Handke und Elfriede Jelinek. Ergebnisse eines Symposions*, Stanford, May 1991 (1994); K. Kaiser, "Theodor Kramer. Exil in Großbritannien," in: S. Bolbecher (ed.), *Literatur und Kultur des Exils in Großbritannien* (1995), 281–297; S. Schlenstedt, "'So gibt es eine Anzahl ganz kleiner Chancen': Material zu Theodor Kramer in den dreißiger Jahren," in: *ibid.* (1995), 267–280; E. Chvojka and K. Kaiser, *Vielleicht hab ich es leicht, weil schwer, gehabt. Theodor Kramer 1897–1958. Eine Lebenschronik* (1997); H. Staud, *Chronist seiner Zeit – Theodor Kramer* (2000); S. Bolbecher, "Das Potential der Exilliteratur. Am Beispiel der Theodor Kramer Gesellschaft," in: E. Adunka (ed.), *Die Rezeption des Exils. Geschichte und Perspektiven der österreichischen Exilforschung*, (2003), 111–120.

[Harry Zohn]

KRAMM, JOSEPH (1907–1991), U.S. playwright. Beginning his career as an actor on Broadway and in London, Kramm turned to writing and directing. He won the Pulitzer Prize for *The Shrike* (1952), a drama about an unhappy marriage, and also wrote *Giants, Son of Giants* (1962).

KRANTZ, JUDITH (1928–), U.S. novelist. After growing up in New York City, and graduating from Wellesley College, Judith Tarcher Krantz raised two sons with her husband, a film and television producer. In 1976, after her husband took flying lessons, she decided to face her fear of flying and took lessons as well. When she overcame that fear, she supposedly looked for other fears to conquer, and so decided to write fiction. Nine months later, she produced her first novel, *Scruples*, about the lives and steamy loves of people who work and shop in a Beverly Hills, Calif., boutique named Scruples. It was published in 1978, the year she turned 50, and reached No. 1 on the *New York Times* bestseller list. Her byline was familiar to readers of women's magazines such as *Good Housekeeping* and *Cosmopolitan* before she turned to fiction, but in the romance genre she produced bestseller after bestseller, more than ten of them, including *Princess Daisy*, set in the splendor of St. Petersburg and Venice; *I'll Take Manhattan*, a drama of power, sexual obsession, betrayal, and true love played out in the arena of magazine publishing; *Mistral's Daughter*, the story of an artist, Julien Mistral, and his relationship with three raven-haired women; and *Lovers*, the sequel to *Scruples* and *Scruples Two*, a tale of love, money, talent, ambition, and passion. All the books display a scrupulous knowledge of the fashion business and often the art, antiques, and jewelry trades, with intricate plots jammed with industry details while providing an inside look at high-octane glamour. A Judith Krantz heroine, according to an article in the *Times*, is "beautiful (of course) but also smart, smart, smart." Her books sold more than 100 million copies in 52 languages and some of her books were made into television series. Her memoir *Sex and Shopping: The Confessions of a Nice Jewish Girl* appeared in 2000.

[Stewart Kampel (2nd ed.)]

KRANTZ, PHILIP (pseudonym of **Jacob Barukhovitsh Rombro**; 1858–1922), Yiddish journalist. Born in Rodok (Ukraine), Krantz developed early ties to revolutionary causes, and fled to Paris and later England because of his connections with the assassins of Alexander II. In 1889 he was a delegate to the first congress of the Socialist Second International. He first contributed to Russian-Jewish periodicals but became a major Yiddish journalist in England during the 1880s. In 1890 he immigrated to the U.S., where he edited and contributed theoretical articles on socialism and translations of popular fiction to the *Arbeter Tsaytung*. In 1892, he edited *Di *Tsukunft*, and, from 1894 to 1899, *Dos Abend Blatt*, the first U.S. socialist Yiddish daily. In Poland in 1906–8 he edited *Di Proletarishe Velt* for the Polish Socialist Party. In the course of his long career he contributed as correspondent, editor, and organizer of dozens of primarily socialist and anarchist newspapers and periodicals in several countries, also publishing dozens of popularizing books on history, biography, science, and politics.

BIBLIOGRAPHY: Rejzen, Leksikon, 3 (1929), 728–40; L. Kobrin, *Mayne Fuftsik Yor in Amerike* (1966), 90–102; M. Starkman, in: *Filologishe Shriftn*, 3 (1929), 57–82. **ADD. BIBLIOGRAPHY:** LNYL, 8 (1981), 243–9; M. Shtarkman, *Geklibene Shriftn*, 1 (1979), 128–34; 2 (1980), 63–70, 130–3; G.G. Branover (ed.), *Rossiĭskaia evreĭskaia entsiklopediia*, 2 (1995), 83.

[Henry J. Tobias / Jerold C. Frakes (2nd ed.)]

KRANZ, JACOB BEN WOLF (known as the **Maggid of Dubno**; 1741–1804), preacher. Born in Zietil, in the province of Vilna, Kranz demonstrated his homiletical skill at an early age and was known as preacher to his fellow yeshivah students especially in Mezhirech, where he received his halakhic, and probably his kabbalistic, education. He was barely 20 years old when he became **Darshan* in his city. From there he wandered through several other cities, holding the post of preacher in Zilkiew, Wlodawa near Lublin, Kalisz, and Zamosc. But he achieved his fame as preacher in Dubno, where he served for 18 years. As his reputation spread, he came into contact with some of the most prominent rabbis of his time, such as *Elijah b. Solomon Zalman (the Gaon of Vilna). It is told that when Elijah was too ill to study, he asked Kranz to visit his bedside and read him his homiletical interpretations, stories, and parables.

All of Kranz's works were printed posthumously by his son, Isaac, and his pupil, Baer Plahm. His major homiletical work, *Ohel Ya'akov* ("The Tent of Jacob"), was printed in four parts (Genesis, Yosepov, 1830; Exodus, Zolkiew, 1837; the third and fourth parts in Vienna, 1859–63). In addition, his homilies on the five scrolls, *Kol Ya'akov* ("The Voice of Jacob"), were printed in Warsaw in 1819. Among his other published homiletical works are an exegesis of the Passover *Haggadah* (Zolkiew, 1836) and a collection of homilies called *Haftarot* (Warsaw, 1872).

Baer Plahm edited Kranz's *Sefer ha-Middot* ("The Book of Ethics," Vilna, 1860), a work consciously modeled after the 11th-century *Ḥovot ha-Levavot* by Baḥya ibn Paquda. In describing the attitude required of the Jew in his spiritual relationship with God, as well as the observances required in his practical relationship, Kranz discusses such subjects as the fear of God, love of God, knowledge of God, and prayer.

Although he made use of the vast treasure of Jewish ethical, homiletical, halakhic, and kabbalistic material, Kranz succeeded in composing homilies which the Jewish layman could readily understand. The inclusion of many parables, fables, stories, and epigrams captivated the hearts of less scholarly listeners. Yet the homilies are not simplistic, but represent the highest achievement of Hebrew homiletical art at that time. That Kranz integrated folkloristic material into his homilies without vulgarizing them was a significant achievement. His parables were culled from his works and printed separately as *Mishlei Ya'akov* ("The Parables of Jacob," Cracow, 1886). However, taken out of their homiletical context, the parables lose most of their artistic effect.

BIBLIOGRAPHY: H.A. Glatt, *He Spoke in Parables* (1957); I. Bettan, in: HUCA, 23 (1950–51), pt. 2, 267–93; A.B. Plahm, introduction to: I. Kranz, *Sefer ha-Middot* (1860); I. Avigur, in: *Yahadut Lita* (1960), 346–52; J.L. Maimon, *Sefer ha-Gra* (1954), 160–75; Zinberg, Sifrut, 3 (1957), 299–303.

KRASLAVA (Rus. **Kreslavka**), town in Latgale district, Latvia. The Jewish community was established in 1764 by families from Vilna, and numbered 733 in 1772 when the Russians annexed the town. It grew rapidly from 1,483 persons in 1847 to 4,051 Jews living in Kraslava (51% of the total population) in 1897. Kraslava became noted in the history of the Jewish labor movement in Russia through the events connected with the bristle factories there, whose owners and most of the workers were Jews, 200 in the factory and 300 in the home bristlemaking industry. As a result of the harsh working conditions and low wages, the workers organized the *Bund, and also *Po'alei Zion and the *Independent Jewish Workers' Party; there were a number of strikes which had widespread publicity and influence. It earned them better conditions in the 1890s, mainly an eight-hour working day. After the Kishinev pogrom (1903) the Bund and Po'alei Zion formed a defense group of 250 members. During World War I, in 1915, the Jews were expelled from the town by the Russian army, only some of them returning after the war. Because of the end of trade with the hinterland in Russia and Poland, the bristle industry did not reopen. The Jews in Kraslava numbered 1,446 (40.5%) in 1920, 1,550 (36.19%) in 1930, and 1,444 (33.77%) in 1935. Until 1934 Jews served as the town's mayors. The Jewish economy improved in the 1930s, and 183 trade establishments out of 372 belonged to Jews. In 1927, 230 pupils attended the Jewish municipal school. The Jews in Kraslava were mainly occupied in commerce and crafts and trade in agricultural products of the area; they also figured considerably in the professions there. Naum *Aronson, the sculptor, and Abel *Pann, the painter, were born in Kraslava.

Holocaust Period

During World War II, shortly after the outbreak of war between Germany and Soviet Russia, 200 Jews left with the Soviets. Kraslava was occupied by the German army in late June 1941. During the first half of July dozens of Jews were killed by the Latvians. On July 29, 1941, they were brought to the Daugavpils (Dvinsk) ghetto, and were shortly thereafter murdered in the Pogulianka forest with Jews from other towns. Some 30 families were left in Kraslava and were executed in September 1941. After the war 40 Jewish families lived there, but they left for Riga in the 1950s and for Israel in the 1970s.

BIBLIOGRAPHY: M. Bobé, in: *He-Avar*, 17 (1970), 247–51; M. Kaufmann, *Die Vernichtung der Juden Lettlands* (1947), 286–94; J. Gar, in: *Algemeyne Entsiklopedie*, 6 (1963), 376–90. **ADD. BIBLIOGRAPHY:** Jewish Life, s.v.

[Joseph Gar / Shmuel Spector (2nd ed.)]

KRASNA, NORMAN (1909–1984), U.S. film producer and playwright. Born in Queens, New York, Krasna attended New York University, Columbia University, and Brooklyn Law

School. He started as a clerk, worked as a film and theater critic in New York, and ultimately rose to earn $100,000 for writing and directing a single motion picture in Hollywood.

Among his Broadway plays were *Louder, Please* (1931), *Small Miracle* (1934), *Dear Ruth* (1944), *John Loves Mary* (1947), *Time for Elizabeth* (1948, which he co-wrote with Groucho Marx), *Kind Sir* (1953), *Who Was That Lady I Saw with You?* (1958), *Sunday in New York* (1961), *Love in E Flat* (1967), and *We Interrupt This Program* (1975).

In the film industry, Krasna was known as the master of the wisecrack, peppering his comedies with crisp dialogue and sharp one-liners. His dramatic films were very well scripted as well. The many screenplays that Krasna wrote – or contributed to – include *Hollywood Speaks* (1932); *That's My Boy* (1932); *Bombshell* (1933); *The Richest Girl in the World* (Oscar nomination for Best Story, 1934); *Four Hours to Kill* (1935); *Hands Across the Table* (1935); *Wife vs. Secretary* (1936); *Fury* (Oscar nomination for Best Story, 1936); *The King and the Chorus Girl* (1937); *Bachelor Mother* (1939); *It's a Date* (1940); *Mr. and Mrs. Smith* (1941); *It Started with Eve* (1941); *The Devil and Miss Jones* (Oscar nomination for Best Screenplay, 1941), which he also directed; *Practically Yours* (1944); *White Christmas* (1954); *Princess O'Rourke* (Academy Award for Best Screenplay, 1943), which he also directed; *Bundle of Joy* (1956); *The Ambassador's Daughter* (1956), which he also directed; *Indiscreet* (1958); *Who Was That Lady?* (1960); *Let's Make Love* (1960); *Sunday in New York* (1961); *My Geisha* (1962); and *I'd Rather Be Rich* (1964).

In 1960, Krasna received the Laurel Award from the Writers Guild of America for Writing Achievement.

[Ruth Beloff (2nd ed.)]

KRASNER, LEE (1908–1984), U.S. painter. Born Lena Krassner in Brooklyn, New York, to Orthodox, Russian immigrant parents, early on she studied art at the Women's Art School at Cooper Union (1922–25), Art Students League (1928), and National Academy of Design in New York (1929–32). Beginning in 1935 she worked as a Works Progress Administration artist. Although she designed one mural, for the WNYC radio station building, which was never executed, Krasner did work as an assistant to the muralist Max Spivak. During the 1930s she experimented with various styles and forms, including Social Realism and Giorgio de Chirico's mysterious perspectives.

Resuming her art studies in 1937 with the avant-garde, German expatriate Hans Hofmann, Krasner absorbed aspects of Pablo Picasso's Cubism and Henri Matisse's color. She showed her Cubist inspired still-lifes, semi-abstracted from nature, in the annual group exhibitions of the American Abstract Artists from 1940 to 1943.

In 1941 Krasner met Jackson Pollock, soon to be recognized as the pioneer abstract expressionist, when the pair were asked to show their work in a group exhibition. She and Pollock married in 1945. Throughout their relationship, Krasner and Pollock engaged in an aesthetic dialogue as Krasner schooled Pollock in European modernism while she adopted Pollock's synthesis of abstraction and automatism. Her Little Image paintings (1946–49) employed and reinterpreted Pollock's allover technique. The Hieroglyphs, one of the three cycles of Little Image paintings, have been interpreted by some scholars as influenced by Hebrew script.

Throughout the years Krasner engaged collage techniques, sometimes on a large scale. In *Black and White Collage* (1953, Hans Namuth Estate, New York), Krasner utilized her own cut up drawings rearranged in the new, abstract work. In the mid-1950s she also cut up several of Pollock's discarded canvases and used them in collages. Her collage paintings first showed at New York's Stable Gallery in 1955 to acclaim.

After Pollock's death in a car accident in 1956 Krasner began her Earth Green series (1957–59), a colorful and rhythmic group of images exploring growth and nature; and the gloomier Night Journey series (1959–62; also known as the Umber series), the latter promoted by her turbulent state and also bouts of insomnia. In these paintings she reduced her palette to gradations of blacks, whites, and browns so that the artificial light she was working in would not undermine her color choices. Throughout her career, Krasner continued to reinvent herself and her style. She consistently reacted to the current trends in the art world, absorbing and modifying the work of artists such as Morris *Louis, Philip *Guston, and Frank Stella, much as she had done with Pollock's example. Indeed, in the 1970s Krasner eschewed her spontaneous working method, instead creating hard edge paintings in the vein of Stella.

BIBLIOGRAPHY: B. Rose, *Lee Krasner: A Retrospective* (1983); R. Hobbs, *Lee Krasner* (1993); E.G. Landau, *Lee Krasner: A Catalogue Raisonné* (1995); R. Hobbs, *Lee Krasner* (1999).

[Samantha Baskind (2nd ed.)]

KRASNIK (Pol. **Kraśnik**), town in Lublin province, E. Poland. Jews are first mentioned in 1531 as merchants trading with *Gdansk and visiting the Lublin fairs. In 1587 they were granted the right of residence by the ruler of the town, Prince Alexander Slucki. The steady increase in the Jewish population caused the lord of the manor to decree in 1654 that Jews were to reside only in the street where the synagogue was being built. In the 18th century the Krasnik community always provided one of the three elders for the *councils of the Lublin province. The community numbered 1,353 persons in 1765 (921 in the town itself). The majority of the Jewish artisans were tailors. The Krasnik community numbered 1,778 (55% of the total population) in 1857, 3,261 (49%) in 1897, and 4,200 (51%) in 1921.

Holocaust Period

Over 5,000 Jews lived in Krasnik before the outbreak of World War II. The German army entered the town in September 1939 and established a ghetto in August 1940. On April 12, 1942, around 2,000 Jews were deported to Belzec. The next deportations to Belzec took place on November 1, when another 2,700 were sent to Belzec. Others were employed in local labor camps. A few hundred fled into the forests, but most of them were shot by Germans. In the vicinity of Krasnik, a few Jewish guerilla units were organized, including the unit under the command of Abraham Braun ("Adolf") and the unit called "Berek Joselewicz" under the command of Eduard Forst.

BIBLIOGRAPHY: Halpern, Pinkas, index; R. Mahler, *Yidn in Amolikn Poyln in Likht fun Tsifern* (1958), index; B. Wasiutyáski, *Ludność żydowska w Polsce…* (1930), 33; I. Schiper, *Dzieje handlu żydowskiego na ziemiach polskich* (1937), index; *Słownik geograficzny Królestwa Polskiego*, s.v.; R. Przegaliński, *Opowiadania o Kraśniku* (1927); T. Wierzbowski, *Matricularum Regni Poloniae Summaria*, 4 (1910–17), no. 16175; Warsaw, Archiwum Głóne Akt Dawnych, *Dyspartymenta pogłónego zydowskiego*, no. 2; T. Brustiń-Bernstein, in: *Bleter far Geshikhte*, 3:1–2 (1950), 51–78, passim. **ADD. BIBLIOGRAPHY:** *Sefer Krasnik* (1973); J. Bartys, *O zydowskim osadnictwie rolniczym w Ordynacji Zamojskiej w pierwszej polowie 19w.* BŻIH, 15–16 (1955).

[Stefan Krakowski]

KRASNODAR (formerly **Yekaterinodar**), capital of Krasnodar Territory (N. Caucasus), Russia. Until 1917 the city was outside the *Pale of Settlement, and only demobilized soldiers, professionals, highly skilled artisans, and wealthy merchants were allowed to settle in the city, so in 1897 only 562 Jews (0.8% of the total population) lived there. By 1926 their numbers had increased to 1,740 (1.1%), and by 1939 to about 5,818 persons in the entire territory except for the Adygei Autonomous District. Probably most of them lived in Krasnodar. Apparently the majority of the Jews succeeded in escaping before the town was occupied by the Germans on August 12, 1942. Those remaining, about 500 persons, were executed on August 21–22, 1942, at a kolkhoz outside the city. The Jewish population was estimated at 1,500 (300 families) in 1970. The only synagogue was closed by the authorities in the 1950s and there was no Jewish cemetery.

BIBLIOGRAPHY: Special Committee for Documentation and Research of German-Fascist Crimes…, *Dokumenty obvinyayut* (1945).

[Yehuda Slutsky / Shmuel Spector (2nd ed.)]

KRASNOYE, village in Vinnitsa district, Ukraine. Jews are first mentioned in 1648, when the uprising Cossacks of Chmielnicki neared the town; the Jews fled to Bar and were massacred there. The community was renewed, and numbered 466 in 1765, and it grew after the Russian annexation to 1,747 in 1847, and 2,590 (92% of the total population) in 1897. Most of the shops in town and most of the craftsmen were Jewish. In 1926 there were 2,002 (96%) Jews, though their number dropped to only hundreds on the eve of World War II. Between the wars a Jewish town council and a Yiddish school operated there. Krasnoye was occupied by Germans on July 19, 1941. After it was annexed to Romanian Transnistria, a ghetto was established for the few hundred local Jews and about 1,000 deportees from Bessarabia and Bukovina. The Jews who lived in the ghetto were compelled to do forced labor. With the assistance of the Jewish aid committee in Bucharest a hospital run single-handedly by a physician who had been deported to Krasnoye was established. When Krasnoye was liberated on March 30, 1944, a few hundred Jews remained there.

BIBLIOGRAPHY: H. Cohen, in: *Nedelnaya Khronika Voskhoda*, 15 (1895), 1350–51; PK Romanyah, 1 (1970), 507.

[Yehuda Slutsky / Shmuel Spector (2nd ed.)]

KRASNYSTAW (Rus. **Krasnostav**), town in Lublin province, E. Poland. The customs records of the town for 1548 show that Jews were living in Krasnystaw then. In 1554 Jews were prohibited from owning dwelling houses in the town and suburbs, and in 1584 they were allowed to reside in the suburbs only. In 1761 three Jews from Wojslawice and one from Czarnoloz were convicted in a *blood libel trial in Krasnystaw; another accused, the rabbi of Wojslawice, committed suicide in prison. In the first half of the 19th century there was a bitter struggle between the Jews and the townsmen, who wished to keep their privilege of *de non tolerandis Judaeis*. In 1824, Jews were permitted to reside temporarily in several villages near the town, but the last restrictions on Jewish residence in Krasnystaw were not abolished until 1862. From 11 Jews residing in the suburbs in 1827, the community grew to 151 (4% of the total population) in 1857, and 1,176 (25% of the total) in 1897. At that time four-fifths of the local trade was in Jewish hands. In 1921 the 1,754 Jews still constituted 20% of the town's population. In the whole district, including the town, there were 10,494 Jews (9% of the total population). The old synagogue, which still stood at the beginning of the 20th century, retained 14th- and 15th-century architectural features (probably relics of a building which had formerly served another purpose). The Germans set up a ghetto for around 2,000 Jews including refugees in August 1942. All were deported to Izbica and from there mostly to the *Belzec death camp.

BIBLIOGRAPHY: Warsaw, Archiwum Akt Dawnych, *Akty Komisji spraw wewnętrznych*, nos. 97, 107, 185, 188; Halpern, Pinkas, index; B. Wasiutyński, *Ludność żydowska w Polsce w XIX i XX wiekach* (1930), 33, 61, 76; I. Schiper, *Dzieje handlu żydowskiego na ziemiach polskich* (1937), index; A. Strunzeiger (ed.), *Yisker tsum Ondenk fun di Kdoyshi Krasnystaw* (1948); *Sefer Turbin* (1967), 74–79.

KRASUCKI, HENRI (1924–2003), French labor leader. Krasucki was born in a suburb of Warsaw to a family of textile workers who were members of the Communist Party. In 1926 the family settled in Paris, where Krasucki joined the Jewish Communist Youth movement at the age of 14. In 1940 he became a leader of this group in the underground and in 1941 also became a leader of a Resistance group made up of foreign Communist workers. In 1943 his father was arrested and deported to Auschwitz, where he was murdered. He was arrested along with his mother and sent to Auschwitz; from there he was transferred to Buchenwald. After the Liberation he returned to France and started working in the Renault auto works, advancing at the same time within the Communist Party. In 1960 he became the publisher of *La Vie Ouvrière*, the weekly of the CGT, the Communist-affiliated trade union, and in 1961 he joined the latter's Bureau. In 1964 he was elected to the Political Bureau of the Communist Party. Krasucki was secretary-general of the CGT between 1982 and 1992, in a period during which leftist governments had to deal with the consequences of the economic crisis for the working class. He wrote *Syndicats et lutte de classe* (1969), *Syndicats et socialisme* (1972), and *Syndicats et unité* (1980)

[Gideon Kouts / René Sirat (2nd ed.)]

KRAUS, ADOLF (1850–1928), U.S. lawyer, and civic and communal leader. Born in Bohemia, Kraus emigrated to the United States in 1865 and worked as a clerk in small-town Ohio stores for several years. In 1871 he went to Chicago, studied law, and was admitted to the bar (1877). Highly successful in his legal practice, Kraus became involved in civic affairs and local politics. He served in Chicago as a member (1881–87) and president (1884–86) of the Board of Education, as corporation counsel (1893), and as president of the Civil Service Commission (1897–98). He was also, briefly, publisher and editor of the *Chicago Times* (1894). Active in Jewish affairs, Kraus was international president of B'nai B'rith from 1905 to 1925 and helped establish its Anti-Defamation League. He was a staunch conservative and a leading member of the dominant Jewish elite during the early decades of the 20th century.

BIBLIOGRAPHY: E. Grusd, *B'nai B'rith: The Story of a Covenant* (1966), index.

[Morton Rosenstock]

KRAUS, FRANTIŠEK R. (1903–1967), Czech novelist, publicist, and radio editor. Born in Prague, Kraus started to work very early in Bohemia and contributed to the newspapers *Prager Tagblatt*, *Prager Presse*, and *Tribuna*. His tutor and friend was Egon Erwin *Kisch, who introduced him to writers and journalists from the Prague Circle, such as Franz *Kafka, Max *Brod, Franz *Werfel, Otto *Pick, and Johannes *Urzidil. At *Tribuna* he met Karel *Poláček, and Karel and Josef Čapek. By the end of the 1920s Kraus had become an editor at *Mluven· noviny* and for Czech Radio. In his radio reports, he warned the Czech public of growing Nazism in the Sudetenland's German minority. He survived the Holocaust, having escaped from the Theresienstadt, Auschwitz, Glivic, and Blechhammer concentration camps. He lost his job at Czech Radio in 1952, where he had been working since 1945. He freelanced until his death.

Kraus' work is either connected with Holocaust themes or with the problems of Czech's frontier regions. Just after the war he published one of the first testimonies about Auschwitz *Plyn, plyn… pak oheň* ("Gas, Gas… and Then Fire," 1945), followed by an autobiographical report "And Bring Back Our Dispersed" (1946) about the reasons for and consequences of the Jewish tragedy. His first novel was to be dedicated to Jan Masaryk and was titled "Shemarjahu Looks for God." It was published as "David Shall Live" (1949) after changes forced by the publisher. It is the story of a Jewish physician from Theresienstadt and Auschwitz. In his next novel *Proměněn země* ("The Changed Country," 1957), Kraus returned to the problems of his beloved north Bohemia. A classic work of postwar Czech literature, *Kat beze stenu* ("Hangman without Shadow") appeared semi-legally in 1984 and then in 2000. Two novels and a short story for children remain unpublished.

BIBLIOGRAPHY: A. Lustig and F. Cinger, *Frantisek Robert Kraus*, Přísně taj (2002); A. Mikulšek et al., *Literatura s hvězdou Davidovou*, vol. 1 (1998); "O autorovi," in: F.R. Kraus, *Kat beze stnu* (2000).

[Avigdor Dagan / Milos Pojar (2nd ed.)

KRAUS, GERTRUD (1901–1977), dancer, pianist, and choreographer. Kraus was born in Vienna, where she studied the piano and also worked as a pianist. She became a dancer and choreographer in the 1920s known for expressionist dances such as *The Town Is Waiting* and *Dream of a Musician*. Kraus performed in Europe and created a dance school in Vienna. In 1930 she established a dance company that performed at the Munich International Congress. In 1935 she settled in Tel Aviv, where she performed as a soloist in a program comprising six of her dances and worked at the Opera (1941–47) and at the Habimah and Ohel theaters. Despite her success as a dancer she did not succeed in creating a new dance company, so she opened a private ballet school and created, with her students, works in close cooperation with composer Mark Lavri but they did not receive favorable public reception. During the 1940s she created works for the Israel Philharmonic called "Tune and Dance." In 1948 she was invited to the U.S. and was exposed to the modern dance of the time. Her meeting with Agnes de Mille, Martha Graham, and Anthony Tudor influenced her immensely. In her previous works, her style had been experimental and abstract, emphasizing personal movement and body language. In the new phase she became more aware of the importance of technique. In the 1950s she created for the musical theater and the Israeli Ballet Theater, and from the 1960s on she concentrated on sculpture, painting, and teaching in her studio, at the Rubin Music Academy, and at the Israeli Ballet and Kibbutz Dance Company. In 1968 she was awarded the Israel Prize.

BIBLIOGRAPHY: G. Manor, *The Life and Dance of Gertrud Kraus* (1978)

[Bina Shiloah (2nd ed.)]

KRAUS, IVAN (1939–), Czech writer. Kraus was born in Prague into a Czech-Jewish family. His father, Oto Kraus (see *Kulka, Erich), survived Auschwitz. Kraus studied at the School of International Economic Relations. As an actor he performed in many Czech plays and lived in exile in France and Germany from 1971. In his literary works he worked in the tradition of Czech and Anglo-American humor, focusing on family relations with rich comedy and irony, often displaying the absurdity of socialist life. His stories were published abroad until 1990 as well as by the exiled Czech publishing house Konfrontace in Zurich. He lived in Baden Baden and Paris.

After 1990 his works include *To na tobě doschne* ("It Will Get Dry on You," 1991); *Prosím tě, neblázni* ("I Beg You, Don't Be Crazy," 1992); *Číslo do nebe* ("Number to the Heaven," 1994); these appeared together in Prague as *Má rodina a jiná zemětřesení* ("My Family and Other Earthquakes," 1998). He also published *Rodinný sjezd* ("The Family Reunion," 1996, 2000); *Muž za vlastním rohem* ("The Man behind the Corner," 1999); and *Medová léta* ("Honey Years," 2001).

[Milos Pojar (2nd ed.)]

KRAUS, KARL (1874–1936), Austrian satirist and poet. Born in Bohemia as the last of nine children to Jacob Kraus, a paper manufacturer, and his wife Ernestine née Kantor, Kraus was one of the greatest stylists in the German language and a vitriolic critic of the liberal culture of pre-Nazi Austria. In 1877 the family moved to Vienna; in 1892 Kraus enrolled in the university there to study law, philosophy, and German literature but never completed a degree. Though at first associated with the well-known *Jung-Wien* circle of writers, which included Arthur Schnitzler, Hugo von Hofmannsthal, and Stefan Zweig, he distanced himself from them in 1897 with the publication of *Die demolierte Literatur*, a political satire of the groups' activities. In 1899 he founded *Die Fackel*, an aggressively satirical magazine, which he wrote single-handedly beginning in 1911 and edited until his death. At times Kraus was a conservative moralist who tirelessly attacked hypocrisy and the permissive intellectual atmosphere fostered by Austrian liberalism; however, he also advocated more liberal attitudes toward sex in Viennese society. He yearned for a return to the aristocratic government of an earlier, more disciplined era. His greatest venom and most pungent wit were, however, reserved for corrupters of the language. Kraus, who left the Jewish religious community in 1899, was baptized in 1911, and then left the Catholic Church in 1922, had few kind things to say about Judaism. He blamed Jews themselves and the "Jewish press" (particularly the *Neue Freie Press*) for the existence of antisemitism. His pamphlet *Eine Krone fuer Zion* (1898) mocks Zionism, while *Heine und die Folgen* (1910) gives a disparaging estimate of the German-Jewish poet. Kraus' many essays were collected in six volumes (1908–37) and four volumes of epigrams and aphorisms appeared between 1909 and 1927. His most important drama is the lengthy *Die letzten Tage der Menschheit* (1919). This play, which if performed in its entirety would take ten evenings, is a massive diatribe on the collapse of civilization in World War I, consisting largely of verbatim extracts from the newspapers of the period. Kraus' *Untergang der Welt durch schwarze Magie* was published in 1922. His lyric poetry, in which he displays a scrupulous form, appeared between 1916 and 1930 in nine volumes titled *Worte in Versen*. It was not until Hitler turned his attention to Austria that Kraus brought his satire to bear on the evils of Nazism, but to the last day his battles were fought mainly against the Viennese liberal and socialist press. *Auswahl aus dem Werk*, containing selections from 11 of Kraus's works, was published in 1961.

BIBLIOGRAPHY: O. Kerry, *Karl Kraus Bibliographie* (1954); L. Liegler, *Karl Kraus und sein Werk* (1920); E. Bin-Gorion, *Der Fackel-Reiter* (1932); R. Schaukal, *Karl Kraus* (1933); E. Heller, *The Disinherited Mind* (1952); W. Kraft, *Karl Kraus* (1956); Grunberger, in: JC (Dec. 24, 1965), Literary Supplement; C. Kohn, *Karl Kraus le polémiste et l'écrivain…* (1962); F. Field, *The Last Days of Mankind: Karl Kraus and his Vienna* (1967); H. Zohn, *Wiener Library Bulletin*, 24 (1970), no. 2, n.s. no. 19, 22–260. **ADD. BIBLIOGRAPHY:** W. Benjamin, *Karl Kraus* (1931); G. Carr and E. Timms (eds.), *Reading Karl Kraus: Essays on the Reception of Die Fackel* (2001); K. Krolop, *Refexionen der Fackel: neue Studien ueber Karl Kraus* (1994); L. Lensing, "Karl Kraus Writes 'He's a Jew After All'," in: *Yale Companion to Jewish Writing and Thought in German Culture, 1096–1996* (1997), 313–21; P. Reitter, "The Soul of Form: Karl Kraus, Essayism and Jewish Identity in Fin-de-Siecle Vienna" (diss. 1999); "Karl Kraus and the Jewish Self-Hatred Question," in: *Jewish Social Studies*, 10:1 (2003), 78–116; F. Rothe, *Karl Kraus, die Biographie* (2003); E. Timms, *Karl Kraus: Apocalyptic Satirist* (1986); idem, *Karl Kraus: Apocalyptic Satirist, Volume 2: The Postwar Crisis and the Rise of the Swastika* (2005); N. Wagner, *Geist und Geschlecht: Karl Kraus und die Erotik der Wiener Moderne* (1987); H. Zohn, *Karl Kraus and the Critics* (1997); idem, "Karl Kraus: 'Juedischer Selbsthasser' oder 'Erzjude'," in: *Modern Austrian Literature*, 8 (1975), 1–19; idem, *Karl Kraus* (1971).

[Harry Zohn / Lisa Silverman (2nd ed.)]

KRAUS, LILI (1903–1986), pianist born in Budapest. She was admitted as a talented child to the Royal Academy of Music and studied with Kodály and Bartók. After graduating in 1922, she studied at the Vienna conservatory with Steuermann and was appointed a full professor there (1925–31). She also studied with *Schnabel in Berlin. During the 1930s she lived in Italy and embarked on a world concert tour and rapidly established herself as a successful soloist. From 1935 to 1940 she toured with the violinist Szymon *Goldberg, with whom she made the first recording of Mozart's piano and violin sonatas (1939). At the start of another tour (1942) she was taken prisoner by the Japanese in Java, and for three years was interned with her family. After the war she toured Australia and New Zealand, and for her "unrelenting efforts in the aid of countries in need" was granted New Zealand citizenship. She resumed her international career touring widely, giving recitals and playing with leading orchestras. Kraus played all the Mozart piano concertos in a single series (New York, 1966–7); and the next season the complete Mozart sonatas. In 1967 she made her home in America and served as artist-in-residence at Texas Christian University (1968–83). Kraus was one of the most extraordinary musicians of the 20th century. Nobility, grace, refinement, and virtuosity distinguished her playing. A sophisticated champion of the Viennese classics, she was esteemed for her interpretations of Mozart and Schubert and for her valuable recordings of Haydn and Beethoven. She published "Master Class" in *Clavier*, 19:7 (1980), 26–29.

BIBLIOGRAPHY: Grove Music Online; *Baker's Biographical Dictionary* (1997); J.W. Newcomer, *Lili Kraus and the Van Cliburn International Piano Competition* (1997); S. Roberson, *Lili Kraus: Hungarian Pianist, Texas Teacher, and Personality Extraordinaire* (2000).

[Naama Ramot (2nd ed.)]

KRAUS, MICHAEL (1901–?), U.S. historian. Born in New York, Kraus taught at City College from 1925. His main area was intellectual history, with emphasis on the cultural interplay between Europe and America. He explored the common culture of the Atlantic world in his seminal works, which include *The Atlantic Civilization: Eighteenth-Century Origins* (1949). After he retired from teaching, he was named professor emeritus of history at City College, City University of New York. Kraus made significant contributions to American historiography, notably in *A History of American History* (1937), *The Writing of American History* (1953), *The United States to 1865* (1959), *Family Album for Americans* (with V. Edelstadt, 1961), and *Immigration, the American Mosaic* (1966).

[Ruth Beloff (2nd ed.)]

KRAUS, MOSHE (1923–), *ḥazzan*. Kraus is a native of Ungvar in Czechoslovakia. He learned cantorial liturgy from his ḥassidic father, and together they sang in the synagogue. He studied in yeshivot, was ordained as rabbi, and went to Vienna to study under the well-known cantor Yehuda Leib Miller. Kraus served as cantor in Marmoresh, Szeged, and Budapest. During the Holocaust he was imprisoned in extermination camps, but miraculously survived. He joined Tito's partisans and after the war went to Bucharest where he was appointed cantor to the Malbim synagogue. From 1946 to 1949 he served as cantor and rabbi in Germany and in 1949 moved to Israel, joining the Israel Defense Forces, where he became the first chief cantor. He appeared in concerts and led prayers in the main Jewish centers of Europe. He served as cantor in the Oxford Street synagogue in Johannesburg, South Africa, and also officiated in Mexico, Venezuela, and Canada, finally making Ottawa his residence. He made records of cantorial liturgy and ḥasidic tunes and also composed prayer-tunes and ḥassidic melodies.

[Akiva Zimmerman]

KRAUS, OSKAR (1872–1942), author and philosopher. Kraus was born in Prague, where he became a student of the philosopher Anton Maurus Marty. In 1902 he joined the faculty of the German University at Prague, and later became professor of philosophy. Kraus coedited his mentor's *Gesammelte Schriften* (2 vols., 1916–20), and *Raum und Zeit* (1916), a treatment of time and space. In addition, Kraus undertook an evaluation of Marty's impact in his book, *Anton Marty; sein Leben und seine Werke* (1916). The personality of Albert Schweitzer had a strong attraction for Kraus, and the two men corresponded. In 1926 Kraus published a character study of Schweitzer which described him as an ethical personality and philosophic mystic. This work appeared posthumously in English and was entitled *Albert Schweitzer, his Work and his Philosophy* (1944). Another personality compelling Kraus' attention was Franz Clemens Brentano. Five of Brentano's philosophic works edited by Kraus were published between 1926 and 1930. Previously Kraus had written *Franz Brentano, zur Kenntnis seines Lebens und seiner Lehre* (1919). Kraus' own philosophy was early characterized by a satirical pessimism, which he elaborated in *Wege und Abwege der Philosophie* (1934) and *Werttheorien; Geschichte und Kritik* (1937). He ventured into disciplines beyond the realm of technical philosophy, studying the general implications of Albert Einstein's theory of relativity. These ideas on the relativity theory appear in his letters to Einstein, *Offene Briefe an Albert Einstein und Max V. Laue ueber die gedanklichen Grundlagen der speziellen und allgemeinen Relativitaetstheorie* (1925). In a foray into the principles of international law, Kraus edited *Jeremy Benthams Grundsaetze fuer ein kuenftiges Voelkerrecht um einen dauernden Frieden* (1915). About 1938 Kraus was detained in a concentration camp. Paradoxically, the harsh new realities of camp life turned him from his critical pessimistic outlook toward a positivistic mysticism. During the period of his confinement he devoted himself to a consideration of Brentano's proof for the existence of God, a proof in which Kraus had early detected a flaw, and which he was now moved to improving. Before the outbreak of the war he was released and managed to escape to England. Kraus settled in Cambridge, and became active as a public lecturer.

KRAUS, OTA B. (1921–2000), Czech writer. Born in Prague, Kraus spent World War II in the concentration camps of Theresienstadt, Auschwitz, and Schwarzheide. After 1945 he started his studies of philosophy and literature at Charles University. In 1949 he immigrated to Israel and lived on a kibbutz. His first novel, *Země bez boha* ("Land without God,"1948, 1992), was published in Czechoslovakia. It describes life in the Auschwitz-Birkenau concentration camp, as does his novel *The Diary* published as *Můj bratr dým* (1993) in the Czech Republic. His other works, *Dream Merchant and other Galilean Stories* (1991) and a best-selling novel *Vítr z hor* ("Mountain Wind," 1991), reflect kibbutz life.

[Milos Pojar (2nd ed.)]

KRAUS, PAUL ELIEZER (1904–1944), Orientalist and historian of science. Born in Prague, Kraus went in 1922 to Ereẓ Israel. After a time on a kibbutz, he studied at the newly founded School of Oriental Studies of the Hebrew University. In 1927 he went to Berlin University and obtained a doctorate for an edition of *Altbabylonische Briefe aus der vorderasiatischen Abteilung der Preussischen Staatsmuseen zu Berlin (Mitteilungen der vorderasiatischaegyptischen Gesellschaft*, 35–36, 1931–32). At the same time he published "Ausgrabungen und Funde" in the German *Encyclopaedia Judaica* (vol. 3 (1929), 701–34). Appointed assistant to the Forschungsinstitut fuer Geschichte der Naturwissenschaften in Berlin in 1929, he made the major discovery that the corpus of writings attributed to the Arab alchemist Jābir ibn Ḥayyān (eighth century) was in fact the work of a group of Isma'ili sectarians of the tenth century who supported the rise of the *Fatimid dynasty of Egypt. In 1933 Kraus went to Paris and cooperated with L. Massignon in the latter's research into the mystic martyr al-Ḥallāj (executed 922). In 1935 he published a collection of Jābir texts in Arabic. The following year he accepted a post in Cairo, though a lectureship at the Hebrew University was simultaneously offered to him. In Cairo he published two volumes of his magnum opus: *Jābir ibn Ḥayyān, contribution à l'histoire des idées scientifiques dans l'Islam* (*Mémoires de l'Institut d'Egypte*, 44–45, 1942–43); the third volume, which was to deal with the place of Jābir in Islamic religious thought, remained unwritten, owing to the author's death by suicide. Kraus's work caused a revolution not only in the history of alchemy, but in that of Islamic science in general. Other works of his were: *Abū Bakr ar-Rāzī, Opera philosophica*, 1 (1939); *Das Kitāb az-Zumurrud des Ibn ar-Rāwendī (Rivista degli Studi Orientali*, 14, 1934); *Galenus; Compendium Timaei Platonis* (with R. Walzer, 1951); *Galenus, kitāb al-akhlāq (de moribus)*, 1939; *Epître de Bērūnī contenant le répertoire des ouvrages de Muḥammad b. Zakarīyā al-Rāzī* (1936).

BIBLIOGRAPHY: H.J. Lewy, in: *Moznayim*, 5 (1945); Ch. Kuentz, in: *Bulletin de l'Institut d'Egypte*, 27 (1946), 431–41 (with bibl.).

KRAUSE, ELIYAHU (1876–1962), agronomist and pioneer in Ereẓ Israel. Born in Berdyansk, Russia, Krause in 1892 went to the *Mikveh Israel Agricultural School in Ereẓ Israel. After further study at the Ecole Supérieure Agricole in France, he was employed by the *Jewish Colonization Association (ICA) and founded the Or Yehudah Agricultural School in Smyrna, Turkey. When ICA took over the management of the Jewish settlements in Ereẓ Israel from Baron Edmond de *Rothschild, it founded the *Sejera farm in Galilee for the training of settlers, and Krause was appointed farm manager (1901). At Sejera he met members of the Second Aliyah for the first time. His brother-in-law, Yehoshua *Hankin, persuaded him to accept Mania *Wilbushewitch-Shochat's proposal to hand over the farming of the land in Sejera for a year to a group of workers on their collective responsibility. This was the first step of collective agricultural labor in Ereẓ Israel. Early in 1914 he was appointed director of the Mikveh Israel Agricultural School. Many of these workers, in addition to the students, received agricultural training at Mikveh Israel and some of them went on to found moshavim and kibbutzim. In World War I Krause carefully protected the interests of his school. Subsequently he introduced Hebrew (instead of French) as the language of instruction and introduced Jewish labor and watch duty throughout the farm. From the 1930s Mikveh Israel was a center for training Youth Aliyah wards. His daughter, Judith (1907–1936), archaeologist, was born at Sejera. She took part in *Garstang's excavations at Jericho and from 1933 to 1935 directed the excavations at et-Tell (*Ai). Her description, *Les Fouilles de Ay, 1933–1935*, was published posthumously in 1949.

BIBLIOGRAPHY: Mikveh Israel, *Ish ha-Adamah* (1939); R. Yanait-Ben Zvi, *Eliyahu Krause* (Heb., 1963).

[Israel Klausner]

KRAUSKOPF, JOSEPH (1858–1923), U.S. Reform rabbi. Krauskopf was born in Ostrowo, Prussia. He settled in the U.S. in 1872. He emigrated to join his brother who was killed on the day before his arrival. He only learned of Hebrew Union College by reading a book from a library, ostensibly to improve his English, and enrolled in 1875 in the first class of Hebrew Union College, receiving his ordination in 1883. At the College he wrote a periodical for Jewish youth entitled the Sabbath Visitor and three textbooks for religious education. After serving a congregation in Kansas City, Missouri, in 1887 Krauskopf became rabbi of the Reform Congregation Kenesseth Israel, Philadelphia, which he served for the remainder of his life. Krauskopf became a leader of radical Reform, introducing Sunday services and compiling a *Service Ritual* (1888, 1902[4]). A leading figure in the national organizations of Reform Judaism, he served as a vice president of the conference which adopted the Pittsburgh Platform in 1885, the conference which he first proposed to Kohler, and president of the Central Conference of American Rabbis (1903–05). He was active in work for the poor, arguing for increased sanitation and better living conditions. He proposed a program of direct contact between successful and poor Jews, an unsuccessful forerunner of Big Brother programs. A man of forceful energy, he paid attention to the need for Jewish literature, and the outcome was the foundation in 1888 of the Jewish Publication Society of America, of which he was the first honorary secretary. Impressed during a visit to Russia in 1894 by the zeal with which Jews engaged in agriculture where the Russian government allowed, he established the National Farm School at Doylestown, Pennsylvania, in 1896 "as one of the best means of securing safety and happiness to the sorely afflicted of our people." In 1917 he was appointed to direct food conservation among Jews for the U.S. Food Administration. At first an anti-Zionist, Krauskopf modified his attitude as a result of the labors of Jewish agriculturalists in Palestine. There too he was impressed with their agricultural work and soon found himself a defender of Zionism against anti-Zionists.

BIBLIOGRAPHY: Feldman, in: AJYB, 26 (1924), 420–47; Pool, in: DAB, 10 (1933), 500–1. **ADD. BIBLIOGRAPHY:** K.M. Olitzsky, L.H. Sussman, and M.H. Stern, *Reform Judaism in America: A Biographical Dictionary and Sourcebook* (1993).

[Sefton D. Temkin]

KRAUSS, FRIEDRICH SALAMO (pseudonym, **Suljo Serhatlya**; 1859–1938), Austrian ethnographer and folklorist. Born at Pozega, Slavonia, Krauss studied classical philology but soon turned his attention to ethnography and folklore. He specialized in the southern Slavs, being the first to make a scientific investigation of these groups. A commission from the archduke Rudolph to study the folklore of the various Slavic provinces of the then Austro-Hungarian Empire – Bosnia, Herzegovina, Slavonia, Croatia, and Dalmatia – led to the writing of *Sagen und Maerchen der Suedslaven* (1883–84), *Sitte und Brauch der Suedslaven* (1885), and others. At the same time he discovered much Slavic and Moslem folk music and popular poetry, including the epic poem of the Bosnian Muslims,

Smailagić Meho, which he published in 1886. A German translation appeared in 1890 under the title *Mehmeds Brautfahrt*. Krauss edited the monthly folklore journal *Der Urquell*, and wrote many important works on folklore, some of which have become classics. One of these was *Allgemeine Methodik der Volkskunde* (jointly with Lucien Scherman). Krauss developed a special interest in human sexuality as reflected in folkways, beliefs, and law, and in the evolution of sexual morality (*Das Geschlechtsleben im Glauben, Sitte, Brauch und Gewohnheitsrecht der Japaner*, 1911). He also did some creative writing, in particular a popular play, *Kuenstlerblut*. He was active in Jewish communal affairs in Vienna, and was for some years secretary of the Israelitische Allianz.

ADD. BIBLIOGRAPHY: C. Daxelmueller, "Friedrich Salomo Krauss 1859–1938," in: W. Jacobeit, *Voelkische Wissenschaft* (1994), 463–76; R.L. Burt, *F.S. Krauss 1859–1938* (1990).

[Ezra Fleischer]

KRAUSS, JUDAH HA-KOHEN (1858–1939), Hungarian rabbi, halakhist, and preacher. Krauss was ordained by his teacher Moses *Schick and by Moses Pollak, the *av bet din* of Bonyhád and by Eliezer Susman of Paks. In 1885 he was appointed rabbi of Lackenbach where he served for 50 years. The community was one of the seven oldest in Hungary and had a long tradition of learning. Here Krauss founded a yeshivah which attracted many students, and his fame spread. He was an outstanding preacher. At the request of Moses Schick, he published homiletical and aggadic works in German written in Hebrew characters. He also published and edited in six volumes *Davar be-Itto* (1909–13), a religious homiletical journal which became a source book for preachers and lecturers in German-speaking countries. Krauss paid especial attention to the education of youth. In 1935 he immigrated to Jerusalem where he devoted himself to study.

BIBLIOGRAPHY: *Magyar Zsidó Lexikon* (1929), 514; S.N. Gottlieb, *Oholei Shem* (1912), 249; P.Z. Schwartz, *Shem ha-Gedolim me-Ereẓ Hagar*, 1 (1913), 54b no. 297.

[Adonijahu Krauss]

KRAUSS, SAMUEL (1866–1948), historian, philologist, and talmudic scholar. Born in Ukk, Hungary, Krauss studied at Papa Yeshivah and at the Budapest rabbinical seminary and university. From 1894 to 1906 Krauss taught Bible and Hebrew at the Jewish teachers' seminary in Budapest. In 1906 he began to teach Bible, history, and liturgy at the *Israelitisch-Theologische Lehranstalt in Vienna. It was due to his efforts that the college did not succumb to financial difficulties after World War I. He traveled widely for his archaeological and historical research. Krauss was appointed head of the seminary in 1932 and rector in 1937. Krauss founded the Vienna Verein fuer juedische Geschichte und Literatur, and was active in many communal institutions. During the *Kristallnacht* in November 1938, the Nazis destroyed his valuable library and papers, and he fled to England, joining his daughter in Cambridge, where he remained until his death.

Works

Krauss wrote over 1,300 articles and monographs, many of them major works, ranging widely in Judaica, philology, history, Bible, Talmud, Christianity, and medieval Hebrew literature. In philology, one of Krauss's early works, *Griechische und lateinische Lehnwoerter im Talmud, Midrasch und Targum* (2 vols., 1898–99; repr. 1964), was of major importance. The first volume of this standard work deals with the problems of phonetics, grammar, and transcription; the second is a dictionary of loan words. Scholars have found much to criticize in this work, particularly the "proclivity to find Latin and Greek in words indisputably Semitic" (M. Jastrow), and Immanuel *Loew made many corrections in Krauss's notes, which the author willingly incorporated. He also prepared a volume of additions and corrections to A. Kohut's *Arukh* titled *Tosefot ha-Arukh ha-Shalem* (1936, repr. 1955). Among Krauss's historical studies was *Antoninus und Rabbi* (1910), in which he offered his solution to the problem of the identity of the talmudic *Antoninus, the friend of Judah ha-Nasi. According to Krauss, he was Avidius Lassius, the Roman legate in Syria (164 C.E.) who in 175 usurped the title of emperor. On the then little-known Byzantine period in Jewish history, Krauss contributed "Studien zur byzantinisch-juedischen Geschichte" (in *Jahresbericht der Israelitisch-Theologischen Lehranstalt*, vol. 21, 1914). He also explored the *aliyah* of the Polish Ḥasidim in the 18th century (in *Abhandlungen… Chajes* (1933, 51–95), and Viennese and Austrian Jewish history in *Die Wiener Geserah vom Jahre 1421* (1920), in *Geschichte der israelitischen Armenanstalt* (1922), and in *Joachim Edler von Popper* (1926). His *Vier Jahrtausende juedischen Palaestinas* (1922) is a popular survey of the history of Ereẓ Israel, Zionist in inspiration, demonstrating the unbroken record of a Jewish presence in the Holy Land. Krauss contributed to A. Kahana's edition of the Hebrew Bible a modern commentary of Isaiah (1905). He also cooperated in the Hungarian Bible translation edited by Bacher and Bánóczi, *Szentirás* (1898–1907). Krauss's greatest work is his *Talmudische Archaeologie* (3 vols, 1910–12; repr. 1966, 1979), a classic description of every aspect of life reflected in talmudic and midrashic literature. Despite its shortcomings, it is still a rich source on the daily life and economic and social conditions of the period. A similar work in Hebrew (not a translation) is his unfinished *Kadmoniyyot ha-Talmud* (2 vols., 1914–23). The history of the synagogue is described in his *Synagogale Altertuemer* (1922, repr. 1966). His last work, *Korot Battei ha-Tefillah be-Yisrael*, ed. by A.R. Malachi (1955), was an extension and continuation of this work. His "Griechen und Roemer" (in *Monumenta hebraica: Monumenta Talmudica*, 5 pt. 1, 1914) and *Paras ve-Romi ba-Talmud u-va-Midrashim* (1948) also deal with the talmudic period. Krauss contributed the German translation and commentary on *Sanhedrin* and *Makkot* to the Beer-Holzmann edition of the Mishnah (1933), and prepared an English translation of *Sanhedrin* with introduction and notes (1909), as well as a popular description of the Mishnah, *Die Mischna* (1913), and a Hungarian translation of the minor talmudic tractate *Derekh Ereẓ*. Though most Jewish scholars shied away from the subject of Christianity, Krauss tackled it with his usual vigor in his *Das Leben Jesu nach juedischen Quellen* (1902) and in several articles. He also wrote a series of articles titled "Jews in the Works of the Church Fathers" (in JQR, vols. 5–6, 1892–94). Krauss deals with the geonic period in a number of articles. His interest in Hebrew poetry of the Spanish period is reflected in his *Givat Sha'ul* (1923), his edition of the commentaries of Saul Abdallah *Joseph of Hong Kong on Judah Halevi; and in his *Mishbeẓet ha-Tarshish* (1926), on Moses Ibn Ezra. His *Geschichte der juedischen Aerzte* (1930) is a description of the work and status of Jewish physicians of the Middle Ages. Krauss turned to the contemporary problem of the use of the organ in the synagogue in *Zur Orgelfrage* (1919), in which he adopts a Conservative stance. He contributed articles and book reviews to newspapers and learned periodicals in half a dozen languages, hundreds of articles to the *Jewish Encyclopedia*, the *Encyclopaedia Judaica* (German), and the *Juedisches Lexikon*, and wrote for or edited many *Festschriften*. He wrote biographies of his teachers Wilhelm *Bacher, David *Kaufmann, and Alexander *Kohut.

BIBLIOGRAPHY: J. Klausner, in: *Sefer ha-Yovel li-Shemu'el Krauss* (1936), ix–xxiii; E. Ashtor (Strauss), *Bibliographie der Schriften Samuel Krauss, 1887–1937* (1937); idem, in: *Sefer ha-Zikkaron le-Veit ha-Midrash le-Rabbanim be-Vinah* (1946), 60–63; N. Ben-Menahem, in: S. Federbush (ed.), *Ḥokhmat Yisrael be-Ma'arav Eiropah*, 1 (1958), 445–50; E.R. Malachi, in: S. Krauss, *Korot Battei ha-Tefillah be-Yisrael* (1955), 324–32 (incl. bibl. for 1937–55, and bibl. on Krauss in Heb.); *Magyar Zsidó Lexikon* (1929), 514. **ADD. BIBLIOGRAPHY:** P. Landesmann, *Rabbiner aus Wien*, (1997), 256–259.

KRAUSZ, ZSIGMOND (1815–1874), journalist and Orthodox communal worker. Born in Györ, Hungary, he later settled in Körösladany. From his youth he was a spokesman for the Orthodox community, and in 1867 was among the founders of the Shomer Hadas, the nucleus of the national Orthodox organization of Hungary. He was a delegate at the general congress of the Jews of Hungary held in Budapest (1868–69). After the schism in Hungarian Jewry, he demanded complete autonomy for the communities without any form of centralism. On the establishment of the national Orthodox organization, he was made a member of the executive. Krausz was editor of the Hungarian-language weekly, *Magyar Zsidó* (1868–69). As well as polemics against antisemites, he published a series of articles (in 1857) on the Jewish religion and the Talmud in the largest Hungarian daily, *Pesti Napló*. He maintained a lively correspondence on Jewish subjects and halakhic questions with leading contemporary personalities and did much to foster the friendly attitude of some Hungarian statesmen toward Orthodox aspirations for independence.

BIBLIOGRAPHY: I. Reich, *Beth-El*, 2 (1868^2), 163ff.; R. Schwartz, *Shem ha-Gedolim me-Ereẓ Hagar*, 1 (1913), 183; L. Venetianer, *A magyar zsidóság története* (1922), 288, 292–3.

[Baruch Yaron]

KRAVIS, HENRY R. (1944–), U.S. financier. Born in Tulsa, Okla., the son of an oil engineer and a former oil-business partner of Joseph P. Kennedy, Kravis went to Claremont College in California and earned a master's degree in business from Columbia University in 1969. That year he joined Bear Stearns, the Wall Street firm, along with his cousin, George R. Roberts. Both worked under Jerome Kohlberg Jr., the corporate finance manager. Kohlberg sought out undervalued small companies, or undervalued operations within larger companies, and helped the management of these companies borrow the capital to buy the businesses themselves. In 1976, when Bear Stearns would not appropriate the funds for these projects, Kohlberg resigned and took his two young associates with him. Together they founded the investment banking concern Kohlberg Kravis Roberts & Co. For the next six years, KKR created a series of limited partnerships to acquire companies, reorganize them, sell off some assets or subsidiaries, and resell the company. Typically, KKR put up 10 percent of the buyout price and borrowed the rest from investors by issuing so-called "junk bonds." In the 1980s these bonds were usually underwritten by the investment bank Drexel Burnham Lambert, led by Michael *Milken. These so-called leveraged buyouts in the late 1970s and early 1980s were wildly successful for KKR. Houdaille Industries was the first major company listed on the New York Stock Exchange to be taken over in a leveraged buyout. In those years, KKR averaged $50 million a year for itself and earned a 36 percent return on investment for its limited partners.

In 1984 KKR pulled off its first billion-dollar buy-out: Wometco Enterprises. In the same year the firm introduced the public tender offer. The firm and its partners paid $465 for the sugar refiner Amstar and sold it in 1986 for $700 million. In 1987, after other well-publicized takeover attempts, Kohlberg resigned from the firm and Kravis succeeded him as senior partner. The following year the firm won a five-week bidding war to control RJR Nabisco, the 19th largest corporation in the United States. This giant food and tobacco conglomerate owned such familiar brands as Camel, Winston and Salem cigarettes, Wheat Thins and Ritz Crackers, Oreo and Fig Newton, Del Monte vegetables, Planter's Peanuts and LifeSavers. Kravis and his group bought the company for $25 billion, nearly double the previous record sale price of a commercial enterprise. Since its inception, KKR has spent more than $73 billion, acquiring more than 45 companies. It divested its holdings in RJR Nabisco in 1995.

The publicity surrounding the RJR Nabisco deal led to the story being dramatized in a book and film, *Barbarians at the Gate*. Kravis was the model for the lead male character, Edward Lewis, in the 1990 romantic comedy film *Pretty Woman*, a love story about two people from opposite ends of the social spectrum who meet and fall in love. Julia Roberts, played a prostitute opposite Richard Gere, portraying a wealthy and ruthless businessman who makes a living as a corporate takeover specialist.

In addition to his business activities, Kravis contributed more than $10 million to New York's Mount Sinai Hospital and the Metropolitan Museum of Art. He served on the board of trustees of the Metropolitan and of the New York City Ballet and was chairman of the board of New York City's public television station. A supporter of right-wing politics, Kravis joined with Edgar *Bronfman Sr. and Lewis Eisenberg to establish the Republican Leadership Council. Kravis was New York State co-chairman of the failed presidential re-election campaign of George H.W. Bush in 1992. Kravis funded the Henry Kravis Leadership Institute at his alma mater, Claremont McKenna College, and the Henry Kravis Internships for Teachers of Color. As trustees of Mount Sinai Medical Center, Kravis and his wife donated $15 million to establish the Center for Cardiovascular Health and financed a professorship.

[Stewart Kampel (2nd ed.)]

KRAVITCH, PHYLLIS (1920–), senior judge on the U.S. Court of Appeals. Born in Savannah, Georgia, Kravitch received her bachelor's degree from Goucher College in 1941 and her LL.B. degree from the University of Pennsylvania Law School, where she served on the editorial board of the Law Review, in 1943. Though she graduated near the top of her class, she was unable to obtain a federal clerkship – or even an interview for a position with a law firm – because of her gender. She returned to Savannah to practice law with her father, Aaron Kravitch, at a time when there were very few female lawyers.

Kravitch engaged in a general trial practice from 1944 to 1976 and was active in civil rights litigation. As a member of the Chatham County Board of Education from 1949 to 1955, she fought to eradicate sex- and race-based salary inequalities and the use of substandard buildings for minority schools. She helped establish the Savannah Area Family Emergency Shelter for battered women and the Savannah Rape Crisis Center. She served on the selection committees for Rhodes Scholars, White House Fellows, and Truman Scholars.

In 1975 Kravitch was elected the first female president of the Savannah Bar Association. In 1976 she was the first woman to be elected a superior court judge in the state of Georgia. When President Jimmy Carter appointed her to the U.S. Court of Appeals for the Fifth Circuit in 1979, she became the first woman to be appointed to the federal bench in the Southeast and the third woman in the nation to be appointed to the U.S. Court of Appeals. In 1981 the Eleventh Circuit was created from the Fifth Circuit; Kravitch, one of the 12 original judges of the Eleventh Circuit, was designated a senior judge in 1996 at the age of 76, having remained on active status long after she was eligible for senior status.

Kravitch authored many noteworthy rulings, including the decision in *Sparks v. Pilot Freight Carriers* (1987) that a sexual harassment plaintiff in a Title VII action was not required to demonstrate an employer's liability for a supervisor's actions. She ruled in *United States v. Evans* (1990) that passive acceptance of a benefit by a public official would be sufficient to form the basis of a Hobbs Act violation if the official knew that he was being offered payment in exchange for an exercise of official power.

Considered a pioneer in a judiciary long dominated by men, Kravitch received many honors, including the National Council of Jewish Women's Hannah G. Solomon Award in 1978, the American Bar Association's Margaret Brent Women Lawyers of Achievement Award in 1991, the James Wilson Award from the University of Pennsylvania Law School in 1992, and an honorary degree from Emory University in 1998.

[Dorothy Bauhoff (2nd ed.)]

KRAYN, HUGO (1885–1919), German painter. He was born in Berlin, where he studied print making and book design. Success came to him early. His health was delicate and, after a long period of overwork, he sought recuperation in Davos, Switzerland, where he painted many landscapes. On his return to Berlin, he received wide recognition. In 1915 he became a member of the Berlin *Sezession*. He died in the 1919 influenza epidemic. He was a post-impressionist, bordering on expressionism. Much of his work concentrates on rendering, powerfully and unmercifully, the hard life of the industrial workers, and the drab atmosphere of the slums in the German capital.

BIBLIOGRAPHY: K. Schwarz, *Hugo Krayn* (1919).

[Alfred Werner]

KRAYZELBURG, LENNY (1975–), U.S. swimmer, winner of four Olympic gold medals. Krayzelburg was born in Odessa, Russia, to Oleg, who owned a coffee shop, and Yelena, an accountant. He started swimming at age five, and by 10 had won the silver medal in his age group in the All-Soviet championships. But Krayzelburg's parents felt there would be limited opportunities for their Jewish family, and were also afraid their son would be drafted into the army, so Krayzelburg immigrated to the U.S. with his parents and sister in 1989, settling in Los Angeles. Krayzelburg joined the swimming team at the Westside Jewish Community Center, learning English while also working there as a lifeguard. After graduating from Fairfax High School in 1993, Krayzelburg attended Santa Monica City College for one year, winning the 1994 junior college state title in the 200 m. backstroke in 1:47.91. Krayzelburg then transferred to USC, where he began to win national and world titles. After becoming a U.S. citizen in 1995, Krayzelburg burst onto the national scene at the Olympic trials in 1996, where he had the second-best time in the heats of the 200 m. backstroke, but missed making the team when he finished fifth in the final race.

Krayzelburg won gold medals in the 100 m. and 200 m. backstroke at the 1998 World Championships, and then broke an unprecedented three world records in the 50 m. (24:99), 100 m. (53:60), and 200 m. (1:55:87) backstroke while winning three gold medals at the Pan American Pacific Championships in August 1999. Krayzelburg was subsequently voted U.S. Swimmer of the Year.

At the Sydney Olympics in 2000, Krayzelburg won a gold medal in the 100 m. backstroke, while smashing the Olympic record with a time of 53.72. Krayzelburg then broke the Olympic record in the 200 m. backstroke in the semifinals with a time of 1:57.27. In the finals of the 200 m. backstroke he took another gold medal, again breaking the Olympic record with a mark of 1:56.76. Krayzelburg won his third gold medal in the 4x100-meter medley relay by swimming the opening (backstroke) leg in 53.87. The American team, following his pace, set the world record with a time of 3:33.73. He was again named U.S. Swimmer of the Year as well as one of *People* magazine's 50 Most Beautiful People.

In the summer of 2001, Krayzelburg decided not to compete at the World Championships, opting instead to participate at the Maccabiah Games, where he shattered the Maccabiah record in the 100 m. backstroke with a time of 55.24 (the old record was 58.08). He injured his shoulder and was unable to compete in either the 100 m. freestyle or 200 m. backstroke, and was sidelined the rest of the year. His decision to forgo the World Championships earned Krayzelburg the honor of being named captain of the U.S. Maccabiah team for the 2005 Maccabiah.

Krayzelburg returned to form in 2002 and by the end of the year was ranked No. 2 in the U.S. in the 200 m. backstroke (1:58.67) and No. 3 in the 100 m. backstroke (54.48). In 2003, he won the 100 m. backstroke at the U.S. Open Swimming Championships, and finished second in the 200 m.

At the 2004 Athens Olympics, Krayzelburg missed a medal in the 100 m. backstroke final by 2/100ths of a second, finishing fourth in 54.38. He swam the opening leg in the men's 4 × 100 medley relay team heat, and though he did not swim in the final, he was awarded a gold medal as the U.S. took first place and smashed the world record.

Krayzelburg formed the Lenny Krayzelburg Foundation to support swimming in the inner city, and in June 2005 donated $100,000 to renovate the facility at his first swimming home, the Westside Jewish Community Center.

[Elli Wohlgelernter (2nd ed.)]

KREBS, SIR HANS ADOLF (1900–1981), British biochemist and Nobel Prize winner. Krebs was born in Hildesheim, Germany, and pursued research with Otto Heinrich *Warburg at the Kaiser Wilhelm Institute for Biology in Berlin for four years, subsequently working at Professor Thannhauser's clinic at Freiburg. He worked out the cyclic process for urea synthesis in the liver. Forced to leave Germany with the advent of Hitler, Krebs became a research fellow in the department of biochemistry at Cambridge. In 1935 he joined Sheffield University, where he became professor of biochemistry in 1945. In 1954 he was appointed professor of biochemistry at Oxford University. In 1953 Krebs received the Nobel Prize for medicine and physiology (which he shared with Fritz *Lipmann) for his discovery of the citric acid cycle. This is the sequence of processes by which foodstuffs are converted in the living cell into carbon dioxide, water, and energy. The "Krebs cycle" was first elucidated for pigeon-breast muscle, but is known to apply to most living cells of aerobic organisms. Krebs was elected a Fellow of the Royal Society in 1947 and was knighted in 1958.

BIBLIOGRAPHY: T.N. Levitan, *The Laureates: Jewish Winners of the Nobel Prize* (1960), 169–72.

[Samuel Aaron Miller]

KREFELD, city in N. Rhine-Westphalia, Germany. The first Jew living in Krefeld was mentioned in 1617, and in 1728 there were five Jewish families settled in the town. By Prussian royal decree (1743), the city council refused admittance to Jews, except for those who received special permission. Nevertheless, by 1756 the number of Jewish families in Krefeld had increased to ten.

A community was organized in 1764 and a cemetery consecrated. After 1795, under French rule, the community began to expand, numbering 160 persons in 1806. On March 17, 1808, a Napoleonic decree introduced the consistorial system; the consistory of Roerdepartement, comprising 20 Jewish communities extending from Cologne to Brussels, had its seat in Krefeld. In March 1809, a conference of 25 notables representing 12 communities elected Judah Loeb Carlburg (Karlsburg; d. 1835) as chief rabbi of Krefeld Consistory. When the Rhine province was incorporated into Prussia in 1814, the consistorial system was retained. Chief rabbi in Krefeld from 1836 until 1843 was Leo Ullmann, who translated the Koran into German. In 1847, during the term of office of his successor, Loeb Bodenheimer (1844–68), the consistorial system was abolished. Successive rabbis were Jacob Horowitz (1868–1904), Joseph Levi (retired 1927), and Arthur Bluhm.

During the 19th century most of the community's cultural, social, and benevolent institutions came into being. A synagogue was built in 1851. From the first quarter of the 19th century the community developed rapidly from 308 in 1840 to 1,088 in 1875, and 2,000 (1.9% of the population) in 1895; it subsequently declined to 1,626 in 1925.

In the years after World War I the community was beset by severe antisemitism. The Jews were vilified in the local press; in 1927 the cemetery was desecrated; in 1928 windows of the synagogue were smashed and the main entrance defiled with swastikas. Posters urging townspeople not to patronize Jewish business establishments were displayed prominently in 1930. When the Nazis seized power in 1933, there were 1,481 Jews in Krefeld. On the night of February 5/6 of that year the synagogue windows were smashed again. Nevertheless the community's elementary school continued to function. Efforts to emigrate were intensified and by 1937 about 500 had left the town. The economic boycott by the Nazis resulted in all Jewish firms being taken over by gentiles. During *Kristallnacht*, SS men broke into the synagogue, removing the scrolls and burning it to the ground. Two other communal buildings were also burned down. Emigration was now speeded up and by May 17, 1939, 800 Jews remained in the city, many of them newcomers from the countryside. Between 1939 and 1945, 67 were killed and 11 committed suicide. Of the 1,374 Jews deported from Krefeld to the East, the majority to *Theresienstadt, 626 were natives of Krefeld. Fifty-six Jews were living in Krefeld in 1946 and 111 in 1964 when a community center and synagogue were opened.

BIBLIOGRAPHY: A. Kober, *Cologne* (Eng., 1940), index; JC (Feb. 17, 1933), 26; (May 4, 1934), 19; (July 19, 1935), 17; (July 30, 1937), 17; S. Andorn, in: AZDJ, 72 (Nov. 27, 1908), 573–4; 74 (Aug. 19, 1910), 393–4; Rheinische Rabbiner-Konferenz, *ibid.*, 74 (Oct. 7, 1910), 473; FJW (1932/33), 234f.; L. Bodenheimer, *Predigt, zur Einweihungs-Feier der Neuen Synagoge zu Crefeld am 17. Juni 1853* (1853); *Der Israelit*, 10 (Aug. 4, 1869), 608–10; A. Wedell, *Geschichte der juedischen Gemeinde Duesseldorfs* (1888), 30–33, 37, 82–83; *Aus alter und neuer Zeit* (Dec. 20, 1928), 262.

[Chasia Turtel]

KREIN, ALEXANDER ABRAMOVICH (1883–1951), composer. After Krein completed his studies at the Moscow Conservatory in 1908 (cello and composition), he was named professor at the same institution (1912–17). He was also secretary of the Russian Board of Education (1918–20), and member of the board of the State Publishing Department (1918–27). He became one of the leaders of the Jewish musical movement and was an active member of the Moscow branch of the *Society for Jewish Folk Music. His very lyrical music is in an impressionistic style mingled with Jewish traditional folk motifs, creating a strongly personal Jewish style. His brother GRIGORI (1880–1955), composer and violinist, studied in Moscow with Hrimaly, Juon, and Glière, and later in Leipzig with Reger (1905–08). He also lived in Paris (1926–34) and in Tashkent (1941–43). His modern music is intellectual and occasionally has Jewish content. Grigori's son JULIAN (1913–1996), composer and pianist, studied at the Ecole Normale de Musique in Paris with Dukas (1926–33). He wrote technically brilliant music and occasionally employed Jewish motifs.

BIBLIOGRAPHY: Grove, Dict; MGG; Baker, Biog Dict; Rieman-Gurlitt; L. Sabaneev, *Alexander Krein* (Rus. and Ger., Moscow, 1928); A. Weisser, *The Modern Renaissance of Jewish Music* (1954), with bibl. of Krein's works; Sendrey, Music, index; M. Gorali, in: *Taẓlil*, 9 (1969), 170–3.

[Claude Abravanel]

KREININ, MEIR (1866–1939), civic leader, born in Bykhov, Belorussia. In 1905 he was a member of the central committee of the League for Equal Rights for Jews in Russia. Together with S. *Dubnow, in 1907 he founded the Jewish *Folkspartei in Russia. From 1914 he acted as vice chairman for the *Society for the Promotion of Culture among Jews of Russia (OPE). Vice chairman of the Jewish communities in Russia from 1918, he was active in relief work on behalf of the Jewish population. Leaving Russia in 1921, he went first to Berlin and in 1927 to Paris. He was chairman of Emigdirect (United Committee for Jewish Emigration) and from 1927 one of the three directors of HICEM. In 1934 he settled in Palestine and died in Jerusalem.

BIBLIOGRAPHY: B. Dinur, *Benei Dori* (1963), 207–8.

KREISEL, HENRY (1922–1991), Canadian author. Kreisel is among the few influential Jewish Canadian writers whose working life was spent in the country's western provinces. Born in Vienna, he escaped with his parents to London shortly before World War II. He and his father were arrested by the British as "enemy aliens," and interned, through 1940 and 1941, near Fredericton, New Brunswick. There, Kreisel was influenced by numerous compatriots who would go on to become important Canadian musicians, philosophers, and academics after the war. An important contribution to our understanding of wartime Canada is his little-known "Diary of an Internment," written during 1940 and 1941. In Kreisel's view the internees were treated reasonably, and when they did work, the Canadian landscape presented them with respite. The diary provides us with a prelude to the appearance of one of the first Jewish voices in mainstream Canadian fiction.

Kreisel attended the University of Toronto upon his release from internment, (B.A., 1946; M.A., 1947) and began work on his first novel, *The Rich Man*, which appeared in 1948. It is among the first major works by a Jewish writer on Jewish themes to appear from a mainstream Canadian publisher. *The Rich Man*'s action begins in the College and Spadina neighborhood where Kreisel lived upon settling in Toronto. It portrays the Spadina-area streetscapes and sweatshop work, and paints a rather downbeat portrait of the Jewish immigrant experience. The novel's startling narrative leap takes shape as the novel's main character – an immigrant from Vienna who works in a local factory – decides to make a return trip, at great cost, to see his family. The bulk of the novel then captures the creeping state of dread and helplessness experienced by Viennese Jews shortly before the war. The returnee from the *goldene medine* is mistaken for a rich man, and awkwardly allows his European relatives to believe he has made a great success of himself in Canada.

Kreisel did not publish another novel until the 1964 appearance of *The Betrayal*, which again takes up themes of doubled lives created by the challenge of immigration and exile. By then, he had earned a Ph.D. from the University of London in 1954. He devoted much of his energy to a long and productive scholarly and administrative career at the University of Alberta, which began in 1947. He was founder of the University of Alberta's pioneering Canadian literature program, and retired from university work in 1987.

As an Edmontonian, Kreisel's writing embraced the particularity of the prairie landscape, though prewar Europe and the Holocaust continued to haunt his fiction and memoiristic writing. Kreisel's short stories were collected in *The Almost Meeting* (1981).

BIBLIOGRAPHY: S. Neuman (ed.), *Another Country: Writings by and about Henry Kreisel* (1985)

[Norman Ravvin (2nd ed.)]

KREISER, JACOB GRIGORYEVICH (1905–1969), Jewish general in the Soviet army and one of the most famous Jewish fighters in the Russian campaign against Nazi Germany in

World War II. Born in Voroniezh, the son of a former *Cantonist and a small merchant, he joined the Red Army in 1921. In 1923 he graduated from the Voronezh Infantry Officers' School, and in 1931 he finished the Higher Officers' School. From 1923 to 1941 he served in the Moscow Proletarian Division, where he was promoted from company commander to commander of the division. In 1941 he graduated from courses at the Frunze War Academy. When war broke out he commanded the Moscow Proletarian Infantry Division, distinguishing himself in the defense of the approaches to Moscow, for which he was made a Hero of the Soviet Union. Shortly after, Kreiser was appointed commander of the Third Army, responsible for directing operations on the Kalinin front (1941). Later he commanded the Third Army on the Yelets front; he was appointed commander of the Second Army, and then of the 51st, which fought fiercely on the Rostov and Donbass fronts. He took part in the Melitopol campaign and helped to destroy German forces in western Ukraine and later to liberate Crimea and the Baltic States. During the war he was a member of the Jewish Anti-fascist Committee. In 1953 he refused, like *Ehrenburg and the singer Reisen, to sign a petition inspired by the authorities asking to execute the accused in the Doctors' Trials. In July 1945 Kreiser was promoted to the rank of colonel-general and in April 1962 to the rank of general of the army. In 1962 he was elected deputy to the U.S.S.R. Supreme Soviet and continued to serve in the army, becoming commander of several military districts, among them the Far East region with headquarters at Vladivostok, and from May 15, 1969, he served as supervisor and adviser in the Defense Ministry. He died in Moscow on November 29, 1969.

BIBLIOGRAPHY: *Istoriya Velikoy Otechestvennoy Voyny Sovetskogo Soyuza, 1941–1945*, 2 (1961), 39, 281; 3 (1961), 318; 5 (1962), 89, 191, 358; *Who's Who in the U.S.S.R.* (1966), 446; Bagramian, in: *Voyenny Vestnik*, 10 (1964).

[Mordechai Kaplan / Shmuel Spector (2nd ed.)]

KREISKY, BRUNO (1911–1990), Austrian statesman and the first Jew to become chancellor of Austria. Born in Vienna, Kreisky was the son of a rich textile manufacturer. He joined the Socialist Workers Youth Association at the age of 15 and became head of its education department. After the Fascist seizure of power in 1934, Kreisky was active in the clandestine Socialist Party and was arrested in 1935. He spent nearly two years in prison and after the Nazi Anschluss in 1938, immigrated to Sweden.

Kreisky returned to Austria in 1946 and joined the diplomatic service. He was personal assistant to the Socialist president of Austria, Theodor Koerner, and in 1953 became undersecretary for foreign affairs in the coalition government of the People's Party and Socialist Party. He participated in the negotiations with the Soviet Union which led to the Austrian Treaty of 1955 and from 1959 to 1966 was foreign minister of Austria. Following the Socialist defeat in the 1966 elections, Kreisky was made leader of the Socialist Party. He succeeded in creating a new image for the party by the formulation of new economic, social, and cultural policies and with the Socialist victory in the general election of 1970 – with a relative majority – he became chancellor of Austria. In 1971 – after early elections – the Socialist Party achieved an absolute majority. In 1975 and 1979 these victories were repeated. After the next elections in 1983, when the party failed to get a majority, Kreisky resigned as chancellor and as head of the Socialist Party.

Contrary to frequent assertions Kreisky never denied his Jewish origin. But he came from an assimilated background and left the Jewish community in his youth. He never committed himself (until the 1980s) to the unsatisfactory restitution of Austria's Jews.

In 1970 Simon *Wiesenthal informed the German magazine *Der Spiegel* that Kreisky's government included no fewer than four former members of the Nazi Party. Kreisky defended his cabinet members and reacted furiously against Wiesenthal. The secretary of the Socialist Party Leopold Gratz called Wiesenthal's work private policing which operated outside the law and asked whether Austria needed this organization.

But in 1975 the conflict between Kreisky and Wiesenthal became much more bitter. In that year, Wiesenthal discovered that Friedrich Peter, the head of the Freedom Party, Kreisky's intended coalition partner, had been a member of an SS brigade, whose explicit duty was the killing of civilians. Peter declared that he was never personally involved in atrocities and Kreisky said he believed him. Accordingly, he attacked Wiesenthal for his "mafia-like" methods, hinted that he was a collaborator of the Gestapo, and said that he wanted to stop Wiesenthal's work in Austria. The end of the affair was a compromise. Because of Kreisky's parliamentary immunity Wiesenthal withdrew his legal action; the Socialist Party's threat of a parliamentary inquiry committee was withdrawn. Kreisky said in Parliament that he never accused Wiesenthal of collaboration with the Nazis. Later, after Kreisky was no longer legally immune as a parliamentarian, Wiesenthal took legal action against Kreisky, who in 1989 was required to pay a fine of 270,000 ATS. During this trial Kreisky hinted at alleged intelligence reports from Communist countries at Wiesenthal, which were never revealed, and he tried in vain to get the former Nazi and later federal German politician Theodor Oberländer to appear as a court witness.

Kreisky's vicious attacks on Wiesenthal caused antisemitic comments in the Austrian press.

During the 1970s Austria became the most important transit point for 270,000 Jews from Russia. In 1973 two Arab terrorists took three Russian Jewish hostages on a train in Austria. They demanded the closing of the transit camp in the castle of Schoenau. Kreisky negotiated with the terrorists, who released the hostages, and closed the castle. Israel's Prime Minister Golda *Meir flew to Austria and asked Kreisky in vain to change his decision. With the help of the Red Cross other transit camps were opened and the emigration process through Austria continued. In her memoirs Golda Meir conceded that

Kreisky's decision "was not altogether unreasonable" and that Schoenau "had become far too well known."

Chancellor Kreisky consistently adopted a pro-Arab and anti-Israel position. However, he arranged two meetings in 1978 between Shimon *Peres, Israel Labor Party leader, and President *Sadat, under the auspices of the Socialist International, of which he then was a vice president as well as chairman of its permanent fact-finding mission for the Middle East. The first took place in Salzburg in February and the second in Vienna in July, which led to a statement to the effect that there was a "negotiating potential" between Israel and Egypt.

In September 1978, in an interview which he gave to the Dutch daily *Trouv*, Kreisky made an unprecedented vitriolic attack upon Israel and Menaḥem *Begin, referring to him in the most abusive terms, calling him a small political peddler. It roused a storm of protest, and caused the resignations of Leopold Gottesmann, honorary consul general of Austria in Israel, Elimelech Rimalt, co-chairman of the Israel-Austria friendship league, and Otto Probst, a veteran member of the Socialist Party and co-chairman of the Israel-Austria friendship league. A few days later Kreisky stated that he was "prepared to apologize," but he did not do so. After the signing of the Camp David agreement, however, in congratulating all three leaders for their efforts, he formally apologized to Begin, still maintaining, however, that there would be no peace without a solution of the Palestinian problem and without an agreement with Syria.

In July 1979 Kreisky officially received Yasser *Arafat in Vienna, and in November, during what was ostensibly a private visit to the United States in connection with the U.S. tour of the Vienna Opera, he appealed to the United States to recognize the PLO as the sole legitimate representative of the Arabs and made a similar plea in his address to the General Assembly of the United Nations, proposing that as a first step toward peace, Israel should likewise accept the PLO.

Kreisky's complex personality and his efforts to advance the Middle East peace process were recognized by his Israeli friends. Shimon Peres wrote in his memoirs: "Judged by his political pronouncements, he was Israel's most implacable adversary among European leaders. And yet, when judged by actions rather than words, he was one of our staunchest friends."

BIBLIOGRAPHY: E. Adunka, *Die vierte Gemeinde* (2000), 384–451; M. van Amerongen, *Kreisky und seine unbewältigte Gegenwart (1977)*; G. Bischof and A. Pelinka (eds.), *The Kreisky Era in Austria* (1993); I. Etzersdorfer, *Kreiskys große Liebe* (1987); E. Horvath, *Aera oder Episode: Das Phaenomen Bruno Kreisky* (1989); J. Kunz (ed.), *Die Aera Kreisky* (1975); P. Lendvai and K. Ritschel, *Kreisky* (1972); W. Perger and W. Petritsch, *Bruno Kreisky: Gegen die Zeit* (1995); *W. Petritsch, Bruno Kreisky* (2000); A. Pittler, *Bruno Kreisky* (1996); V. Reimann, *Bruno Kreisky* (1972); F.R. Reiter (ed.), *Wer war Bruno Kreisky?* (2000); P. Secher, *Bruno Kreisky. Chancellor of Austria* (1993).

[Evelyn Adunka (2nd ed.)]

KREISLER, FRITZ (1875–1962), violinist and composer. Born in Vienna and a child prodigy, Kreisler gained admission to the Musikverein Konservatorium at the age of seven. His principal teachers were Hellmesberger (violin) and Bruckner (theory). He first performed when he was nine and was awarded the Konservatorium's gold medal at ten. Later he studied at the Paris Conservatoire with Massart and Delibes. Kreisler's rise to fame was interrupted by medical and art studies and a period of military service. His debut with the Berlin Philharmonic (1899) launched his international career. He was presented with the Philharmonic Society's gold medal (1904) and gave the premiere of Elgar's *Violin Concerto*, a work dedicated to him (1910). At the outbreak of World War I he joined his former regiment, but upon being quickly wounded he was discharged and went to the U.S. He returned to Europe in 1924, living first in Berlin, then in France. In 1939 he settled permanently in the U.S., becoming a citizen in 1943. Kreisler was one of the greatest masters of the violin. His remarkable sweet and expressive tone, graceful phrasing, and vitality of rhythm match his brilliant technique. He developed personal methods of bowing, fingering, and vibrato. Among the works he wrote as a gifted composer are a string quartet, operettas, short compositions (such as *Caprice viennois*, *Liebeslied*, and *Liebesfreud*), and a series of pieces he attributed to lesser known 18th-century composers but which were in fact his own. He also prepared cadenzas for the Beethoven and Brahms violin concertos and published music arrangements.

BIBLIOGRAPHY: Grove Music Online; MGG[2]; *Baker's Biographical Dictionary* (1997); Amy Biancolli, *Fritz Kreisler: Love's Sorrow, Love's Joy* (1998); C.R. Scheidemantle, "The Violin of Fritz Kreisler: An Analysis and Performance Guide" (doctoral diss., 1999);

[Naama Ramot (2nd ed.)]

KREITMAN, BENJAMIN ZVI (1920–), U.S. Conservative rabbi and organization executive. Kreitman was born in Warsaw, Poland, and immigrated to the United States in 1924. He received his B.A. from *Yeshiva University in 1940 and ordination from the *Jewish Theological Seminary in 1942, as the seminary accelerated ordination of rabbinical candidates in order to meet the wartime need for chaplains. Kreitman enlisted immediately and served as a chaplain in the United States Navy until 1946, when he became assistant rabbi of Kehillath Israel in Brookline, Massachusetts. His next pulpit was Beth El Synagogue in New London, Connecticut (1948–52), followed by 16 years at Brooklyn Jewish Center, where he worked with Rabbi Israel *Levinthal. Kreitman developed innovative adult education programs for this very large Conservative urban synagogue center, including the Mishnah Fellowship, Great Books Seminar, and Great Jewish Books Seminar. In 1968, he became rabbi of Congregation Shaare Torah in Flatbush (Brooklyn), where he was elected rabbi emeritus in 1976.

During his nearly three decades as a congregational rabbi in Brooklyn, Kreitman served as president of the Brooklyn Jewish Community Council (1970–73), chairman of the Brooklyn Borough Human Rights Commission (1960–67) and as the only non-medical member of the New York City Board of Health. He also lectured at Brooklyn College (1974) and the Jewish Theological Seminary (1975). In addition, he was chairman of the Brooklyn Region of the *Rabbinical Assembly and vice chairman of the Metropolitan Region of the RA. More influentially, as chairman of the organization's Committee on Jewish Law and Standards (1966–72), Kreitman – who believed that Jewish law "must concern itself with and accommodate itself to the needs of the day" – took bold leadership positions that shaped key halakhic rulings of the Conservative movement in the areas of *kashrut* and freeing the *agunah* (a married woman denied a divorce by a missing or recalcitrant husband). His committee also sanctioned the abolition of the widely ignored second day of festivals outside of Israel.

In 1976, Kreitman left the practicing rabbinate to become executive vice president of the *United Synagogue, succeeding Rabbi Bernard *Segal. He spearheaded the development of new programs and publications for a Conservative movement that was now catering to multi-generational member families. He was also instrumental in strengthening the movement's relationship with Israel, leading a reorganization of the World Council of Synagogues that paved the way for its joining the *World Zionist Organization and establishing *aliyah* and absorption desks in New York and Israel to encourage Conservative Jews to immigrate to Israel.

BIBLIOGRAPHY: P.S. Nadell, *Conservative Judaism in America: A Biographical Dictionary and Sourcebook*, 1988.

[Bezalel Gordon (2nd ed.)]

KRÉMÈGNE, PINCHAS (1890–1981), sculptor and painter. Krémègne was born in Vilna, and went in 1912 to Paris, with Chaim *Soutine, in the movement of East-European Jewish artists that evolved into the *Paris School of Art. He first exhibited as a sculptor, but from 1915 onward only painted. At first influenced by Matisse and Fauvism, Krémègne developed a more relaxed style in which masterly composition is matched by delightful color. He painted a considerable number of still lifes, studio interiors and portraits, but in addition a considerable group of landscapes of France, Corsica, Sweden, and Israel. Highly considered in Paris, Krémègne's work was described by the critic Maximilien Gauthier as "Judaic disenchantment." This unusual phrase possibly suggests the detachment in Krémègne's oeuvre, in contrast to the paintings of Chagall and Soutine. There is, in fact, far less "Jewish" content to his work, except for the warm humanity of his subject matter and treatment. Krémègne's work is represented in leading French museums and also in the Tretyakov Gallery, Moscow.

[Charles Samuel Spencer]

KREMENCHUG, Poltava district, in Ukraine. The earliest information on Jewish settlement in Kremenchug dates from 1782; 454 Jews were registered as poll-tax payers in the district of Kremenchug in 1801. In accordance with the policy "of directing the Jews toward productive professions," the Russian government opened a weaving mill in the city in 1809, designed to teach this craft to Jews who lacked a profession. The number of Jews employed in the mill in 1810, together with the members of their families, amounted to 232. After this date the Jews began to leave the mill because of the difficult conditions there, and in 1817 it closed down. Later in the 19th century, the Jewish population increased rapidly, as a result of emigration from the northwestern provinces of Russia to the southeastern ones. In 1847 there were 3,475 Jews registered in the community of Kremenchug, while by 1897 there was a large Jewish population of 29,869 persons (47% of the total population). The Jews played a most important role in the economic development of the town, especially in the grain and timber trades and the manufacture of tobacco. They owned ten sawmills and several tobacco factories. Early in the 19th century a Jewish hospital was opened, and in 1844 a Chabad yeshivah was established. By the end of the century, there were two *talmudei torah*, one with carpentry and metalworking classes, and Jewish private schools for boys and girls. During World War I, the yeshivot of *Lubavich and *Slobodka (from Kovno) were transferred to Kremenchug. Pogroms were staged in October 1905, in April 1918 by armed bands of Grigoryev, and in August 1919 by the soldiers of the "Volunteer Army" of General *Denikin. In the 1920s the Jews made up 50% of the workers in the factories, and about 75% in tobacco production, shoes, and carpentry. In the 1930s there were two Jewish schools and an electro-mechanical college. In 1926 there were 28,969 Jews (49.2% of the total) living in the town, with the number dropping by 1939 to 19,880 (22% of the total population). The Germans occupied Kremenchug on September 9, 1941, and they soon – together with the Ukrainian police – pillaged the Jews, ordered them to wear the yellow star, and forbade them to buy food in the stores. On September 27, 1941, they were ordered to register and to move into ghetto barracks in the Novo-Ivanovka suburb; all their belongings were taken from them. From September 27 to November 7 about 8,000 Jews were murdered by the Germans. The small group of professionals, such as doctors and nurses, who were left were killed in January 1942. Hundreds of Jewish soldiers from the Soviet army, from the local prisoner of war camp, were also murdered. In 1959 the Jewish population numbered about 5,200 (6% of the total) and in 1970 it was estimated at about 1,000. Of the 60 synagogues in 1917, only one remained open in 1959, only to be closed down in the early 1960s. The old "Great" synagogue, destroyed by the Nazis, was still standing, roofless. Most Jews left in the 1990s but community life revived, with both educational and religious services being offered. Natives of Kremenchug included the Zionist leader J. *Tschlenow and the painter Mané *Katz. The poet A. *Shlonsky was born in Kryukov, a suburb of Kremenchug, as was the Jewish Soviet army officer Alexander Pecherski who headed the uprising in the Sobibor death camp in 1943.

BIBLIOGRAPHY: A. Litai, in: *Reshumot*, 3 (1923), 237–63; A.I. Freidenberg, *Zikhroynes fun a Tsionististishn Soldat* (1938), 220–60; M. Osherowitch, *Shtet un Shtetlekh in Ukraine*, 2 (1948), 35–46; *Die Judenpogrome in Russland*, 2 (1910), 250–5; J.B. Schechtman, *Pogromy dobrovolcheskoy armii na Ukraine* (1932), 312–6; I. Juditski, *Yidishe*

Burzhuazye un Yidisher Proletariat in Ershter Helft 19 Yarhundert (1930), 14–19; B. Weinryb, *Neueste Wirtschaftsgeschichte der Juden in Russland und Polen*, 1 (1934), 106–7.

[Yehuda Slutsky / Shmuel Spector (2nd ed.)]

KREMENETS (Pol. **Krzemieniec**), town in Tarnopol district, Ukraine, from 1344; under Lithuania until 1569; Poland-Lithuania until 1793; Russia until 1918; and again under Poland until 1939. Jews are first mentioned there in 1438, when they were granted a charter by the Lithuanian grand duke Svidrigailo. They were expelled in 1495 along with all other Jews in Lithuania, returning in 1503. The number of Jews in the town rose from 240 (10.6% of the total population) in 1552 to 500 in 1578 and 845 (15% of the total) in 1629. The community developed and prospered in the 16th and 17th centuries, up to 1648. It was a center of **Arenda* activity and the related trade. Among the rabbis of that period were Mordecai b. Abraham Jaffe and Samson b. Bezalel, brother of Judah Loew b. Bezalel of Prague. The representatives of the community participated in the work of the Volhynian Council, and in the work of the Council of Four Lands. Outstanding among the scholars of the yeshivah at the beginning of the 17th century was *Joseph b. Moses of Kremenets. In the *Chmielnicki massacres (1648–49) and the Russian and Swedish wars soon after, many Jews were savagely murdered and many others fled. Subsequently the community was unable to regain its former importance. In 1765 only 649 Jews lived there. The Jews were prohibited from rebuilding the houses burned down in the frequent fires that broke out in the town. At the beginning of Russian rule Kremenets was an impoverished community of petty traders and craftsmen.

Kremenets was within the range of 50 versts from the Russian border, which was prohibited to Jews, but the authorities did not apply this prohibition to the town. The number of Jews increased from 3,791 in 1847 to 6,539 (37% of the total population) in 1897. At the end of the 19th century they played an important role in the economy of the town, in particular the paper industry, and the Jewish carpenters and cobblers of Kremenets exported their goods to other towns in Poland and Russia. There was an active cultural life in the community with the Haskalah and Ḥasidism competing for influence. The Haskalah writer Isaac Baer *Levinsohn lived there, as did the Ḥasid R. Mordecai, father-in-law of Nahum Twersky of Chernobyl. In 1918–20 Kremenets suffered from the attacks of marauding bands in the Ukraine. In 1921, 6,619 Jews lived there, and 7,256 in 1931. In modern Poland the Jews faced both the need for reorganization of their markets, as they were cut off from Russia, and the anti-Jewish policies of Polish society and state. Cultural life continued, influenced mostly by Zionism. Two periodicals in Yiddish, which appeared at the beginning of the 1930s, merged in 1933 into one weekly newspaper, *Kremenitser Lebn*. Until 1939 there operated in town a Hebrew Tarbut school, as well as a Hebrew nursery, a *talmud torah*, and an ORT vocational school. A local drama circle and a string orchestra gave public performances. The violonist Isaac *Stern took his first steps in music there.

[Shimshon Leib Kirshenboim]

Holocaust Period

The Soviet authorities took over the town on Sept. 22, 1939. In the spring of 1940 the refugees from western Poland were obliged to register with the authorities and to declare whether they wished to take up Soviet citizenship or return to their former homes, now under German occupation. For family reasons, many refugees declared that they preferred to return; that summer they were exiled to the Soviet interior. All Jewish communal life was forbidden, and Zionist leaders moved to other cities to keep their past activities from the knowledge of the authorities. By 1941 the Jewish population had increased to over 10,000, including about 4,000 refugees.

Kremenets was occupied by the Germans on July 1, 1941. Hundreds of young Jews managed to flee to the Soviet Union. A pogrom broke out on July 2, 1941, when Ukrainian police, aided by Germans, concentrated 800 Jewish men, women, and children, made them open graves of Ukrainian prisoners – killed by the Soviet NKVD before retreating – and accused the Jews of being to blame, and murdered all of them. In the beginning of August 1941 the *Gestapo ordered all Jews with academic status to report for registration. All those who did so were murdered, and thus the Jewish community's leadership was destroyed. That month the Germans bombed the main synagogue and exacted a fine of 11 kg. of gold from the community. They also imposed a *Judenrat, headed by Benjamin Katz, but he was murdered for his refusal to collaborate with the Nazis. Eventually the Judenrat consisted of a number of people whose influence was detrimental. On March 1, 1942, a ghetto was imposed and 9,340 Jews were crowded there. The inmates endured great hardship, such as starvation and diseases, and there was a serious shortage of water. Each day 10–12 persons died. On Aug. 10, 1942, the Germans initiated an *Aktion* to annihilate the inmates. Fifteen hundred able-bodied persons were dispatched to slave labor in Bialokrynica, where they met their death on August 18, 1942. The vast majority of the ghetto inhabitants rounded up in the *Aktion* were taken in groups and murdered over trenches dug near the railway station, near a former army camp. The local Zionist leader Benjamin Landsberg committed suicide at this time. There existed a Jewish underground in the ghetto, which acquired arms and false Aryan documents with the help of Poles. The *Aktion* surprised them while they were still organizing themselves. They initiated sporadic fighting, inflicting some casualties on the enemy, and also set fire to ghetto houses. Only 14 of the Kremenets community survived the Holocaust.

[Aharon Weiss / Shmuel Spector (2nd ed.)]

BIBLIOGRAPHY: A. Stein (ed.), *Pinkas Kremenets: Sefer Zikkaron* (Heb. and Yid., 1954).

KREMENETZKY, JOHANN (1850–1934), engineer and industrialist; first head of the *Jewish National Fund (JNF). Born in Odessa, Kremenetzky settled in Vienna in 1880 and built the first factory in Austria for electric bulbs, which soon grew into one of the largest enterprises in Europe. In 1920 he built a factory for electric appliances and, together with Boris *Goldberg, the "Silikat" factory in Tel Aviv. Kremenetzky joined Herzl after the publication of *Der Judenstaat* (1896) and became one of his close friends and admirers. He was elected to the Zionist Executive at the First Zionist Congress and remained a member until 1905. At the subsequent Congresses (1905–13) he was elected to the Zionist General Council. On the basis of a memorandum drafted by Kremenetzky and read in his absence to the Fifth Zionist Congress (1901) by Isidor *Schalit, the JNF was officially established. He became head of the JNF until its headquarters were moved to Cologne from Vienna in 1907, and his activities laid the foundations for this popular Zionist institution. Herzl nominated him as one of the executors of his will. Together with M. Reichenfeld he founded the Herzl Archive. He was made an honorary citizen of Vienna (1930).

BIBLIOGRAPHY: L. Jaffe (ed.), *Sefer ha-Congress* (1950²), 353–4. **ADD. BIBLIOGRAPHY:** M. Hoff, *Johann Kremenetzky und die Gründung des KKL* (1986); *Oesterreichisches Biographisches Lexikon*, vol. 4, 252.

[Oskar K. Rabinowicz]

KREMER, ARKADI (**Aaron**, "**Alexander**"; 1865–1935), central figure in the Jewish labor movement in Russia in the 1890s, described as "the father of the *Bund." The son of an enlightened Hebrew teacher in Svencionys (Sventsyany) in the province of Vilna, Kremer received little traditional Jewish education. His persuasive and unifying influence as a propagandist and an organizer made him the moving spirit in the Jewish Social Democratic Group in Vilna between 1891 and 1897. His pamphlet *Ob agitatsü* ("On Agitation," 1893/94) influenced the transition of the labor movement in Vilna, and many other cities in Russia, from closed circles of socialist propaganda to action among the masses adapted to their actual economic requirements. Kremer was among the founders of the Bund in the fall of 1897, and of the Russian Social Democratic Labor Party in 1898, and a member of their central committees. After a term in prison for revolutionary activities he escaped abroad in 1900. There, and from 1905 again in Russia, he continued his activities in the Bund. In 1908 he abandoned political life, studied and worked from 1912 to 1921 as an electrical engineer in France. He later returned to Vilna and taught there. In 1928 he resumed his activities in the local branch of the Bund, but was a moral and political authority of the Bund in Poland. His wife, "PATI" KREMER (Matla Srednicki; 1867–1943), a dentist, was also a Bundist, and one of the few leaders of the Jewish Social Democrats in Vilna in the 1890s capable of writing Yiddish. She died in the Vilna ghetto.

BIBLIOGRAPHY: *Arkadi: Zamlbukh tsum Ondenk…* (1942); Pinson, in: JSOS, 7 (1945), 233–64; Rejzen, Leksikon, 3 (1929), 779–85; V. Medem, *Fun Mayn Lebn*, 2 (1923), 11–14.

[Moshe Mishkinsky]

KREMER, ISA (1887–1956), international balladist, possibly the first woman to bring Yiddish song to the concert stage. Born in Beltz, Bessarabia, Kremer started her career at 15 by writing revolutionary poetry which was published in an Odessa newspaper. After meeting Isa, the newspaper's editor, Israel Heifetz, helped send her to Milan to study singing with Polonia Ronzi. She had her operatic debut in 1902 in *La Bohème*. When she returned to Odessa, Kremer and Heifetz married. Their daughter, Toussia, was born in 1917.

Kremer joined a group of intellectuals that included Mark *Warshawski, *Sholom Aleichem, and Sholem Yankev *Abramovitsh (Mendele Moykher Sforim), who introduced her to the Hebrew poet Ḥayyim Naḥman *Bialik. She credited Bialik with challenging her to give voice to her own people and to sing in Yiddish. Kremer continued touring with opera companies, performing in *Madam Butterfly, Eugene Onegin*, and *Manon* to great acclaim. She also began collecting Yiddish folk songs with the hope of performing them as art songs on the concert stage. During the Russian Revolution, her husband was jailed while she was on tour in Constantinople. In 1919, she managed to get her child and finally her husband out of Russia and they settled in Paris. In 1922, on tour in Poland, Kremer, who was scheduled to sing Jewish songs in Warsaw, was the object of an antisemitic riot. This led the family to relocate to America, where her reputation preceded her. Represented by Sol *Hurok, Kremer made her American debut at Carnegie Hall in 1922. Kremer brought glamour and charisma to the stage, singing artistically arranged folk songs in Yiddish, Russian, Italian, Polish, French, German, and English. She began singing on the Orpheum vaudeville circuit in 1927 with tremendous success, reaching a weekly audience of 35,000.

Touring Argentina in the late 1930s, Kremer met Gregorio Bermann, a psychiatrist. They were together for years, although they never married. During WWII, Kremer's husband was arrested and died in a concentration camp. In 1943, Bermann was arrested in Argentina, where the couple was living. Kremer was blacklisted and went into bankruptcy. In 1946, Kremer visited Palestine, and sang there in Yiddish, although many were opposed to her use of the language. She told the crowd, "I sang in Yiddish in Nazi Germany, I'll sing in Yiddish in Israel." Even as late as 1951, Isa still concertized for loyal fans in European cities, but by 1956 she was ill with stomach cancer; she died in Córdoba, Argentina, in 1956. Her papers were donated to the Jewish Center in Buenos Aires, where they survived the terrorist attack of 1994.

[Judith S. Pinnolis (2nd ed.)]

KREMNITZER, JOHANAN BEN MEIR (17th century), Polish talmudist. Kremnitzer came from Kalisz. He was a *dayyan* in Mezhirech and subsequently proofreader for the Talmud edition of Frankfurt on the Oder, where he stayed for three years (1697–99) at the expense of Issachar Bermann (see Behrend *Lehmann). He was responsible for the *Ein Mishpat* to the tractate *Nedarim*, which gives the references to the *halakhah* in the standard code. Kremnitzer was the author of *Oraḥ Mishor* (Sulzbach, 1692), a supercommentary on the *Darkhei Moshe* to *Yoreh De'ah* by Moses Isserles. Despite Kremnitzer's scholarship his commentary did not achieve great popularity. He also wrote *Oraḥ Mishor* (Berlin, 1723–24) to the tractate

Nazir and Hilkhot Nazir in Maimonides' *Mishneh Torah*, appended to which were supplements and additions to his commentary on the *Darkhei Moshe*. This was republished in the 1884 edition of the Romm-Vilna Talmud; to it he appended a reply to the criticism of Simeon b. Jacob Reischer incited by Kremnitzer's critical remarks on the *Minḥat Ya'akov* of Simeon's father. Kremnitzer's *Zer Zahav*, mentioned in his *Oraḥ Mishor*, remained unpublished.

BIBLIOGRAPHY: R.N.N. Rabbinovicz, *Ma'amar al Hadpasat ha-Talmud*, ed. by A.M. Habermann (1952), 98f.; Fuenn, Keneset, 437; Lewin, in: *Festschrift … A. Harkavy* (1908), 169f.; idem, in: JJLG, 5 (1907), 152f.; Goldrath, in: *Tagim*, 1 (1969), 27–30.

[Samuel Abba Horodezky]

KREMS, city in Lower Austria. Jews are first mentioned in Krems in 1136 when "Ernustus Judeus" witnessed a legal transaction. In 1293 two Jews were broken on the wheel following a *blood libel; the rest of the community was forced to pay the local nobility for their protection. In the 13th and 14th centuries the Krems community was one of the most important in Austria. The Jews were moneylenders and they were not restricted to dwellings in any one quarter of the city. Persecutions occurred in 1337 and 1347. On Sept. 29, 1349, inflamed by rumors that the Jews had caused the *Black Death, the populace of Krems and the nearby villages massacred most of the Jews and plundered their homes. A few escaped to the fortress. Duke Albrecht V ordered his soldiers to punish the attackers, laid penalties on the city, and sentenced three of the ringleaders to death. In 1355 Jews are recorded as living in Krems, owning houses all over the city, but in 1422 a Jewish street is mentioned. There was a local Jewish oath, recorded in 1416. The gravestone of a rabbi, Naḥlifa or Nehemiah, forms part of the outer wall of the 15th-century parish church. Other personages of note from Krems include R. Israel (great-grandfather of R. Israel *Isserlein) who may have been appointed chief rabbi of the Jews in all the German communities, and R. Aaron Blumlein, a colleague of R. Jacob *Moellin (Maharil), who died a martyr in Vienna. The Vienna archives preserve a *ketubbah* of 1391/92 from Krems, and the Krems municipal archives contain fragments of a *Megillat Esther* used in the cover of a tithe book of 1431.

In 1421 the Jews were expelled from Krems. Individual Jewish hide, fur, and feather merchants did business in the local markets in the 17th century. In 1638, every Jew visiting the market paid one reichsthaler. By 1652 there were 12 Jewish families in Krems. R. Samuel Koidonover wrote his *Naftali Ẓevi* there in 1656–59. In reprisal for a sentence passed against a Jew accused of theft, Moldavian Jews boycotted the Krems market in 1701. The community was reestablished in the middle of the 19th century. A cemetery was opened in 1853, another in 1880. A synagogue was consecrated in 1894. The community numbered 179 in 1869, 595 in 1880, and about 200 in 1932. In September 1938 the synagogue was seized, ostensibly to serve as a shelter for Sudeten refugees. Doors and windows were smashed on *Kristallnacht* (Nov. 10, 1938) and the 92 remaining Jews fled to Vienna soon after. The synagogue building still existed in 1970 but was no longer in use.

The neighboring locality of Langenlois had a Jewish settlement in 1245, a synagogue and a Jewish street, and in nearby Spitz and Stein an der Donau there were also important medieval communities.

BIBLIOGRAPHY: Germ Jud, 1 (1937), 149–50, 2 (1968), 453–5; L. Moses, *Juden in Niederoesterreich* (1935), 203; idem, in: *Juedisches Archiv* (Nov. 1927), 9–17; (Mar. 1928), 18; (June–Aug. 1928), 3–8; (Jan.–Feb. 1929), 52–3; H. Ebner, in: *Mitteilungen des Kremser Stadtarchives* (1965), 73f.; O. Brunner (ed.), *Rechtsquellen der Staedte Krems und Stein* (1953), 56, 80, 99, 112; H. von Voltelini, in: *Mitteilungen des Vereins fuer die Geschichte d. Stadt Wien*, 12 (1932), 64–70; A. Engel (ed.), idem, in: *Gedenkbuch Kuratoriums* (1936), 90–101.

KRENGEL, MENAHEM MENDEL (1847–1930), Polish rabbinical author and bibliographer. Krengel was a pupil of Simon Schreiber-*Sofer of Cracow. His important contribution to Jewish scholarship is his edition of Ḥ.J.D. *Azulai's dictionary of scholars and their works, *Shem ha-Gedolim ha-Shalem*, which he enlarged and provided with a biography of the author, a bibliography of his works, and extensive annotations (vol. 1, 1905; vol. 2, 1930; new ed., 3 vols., 1958); among other additions are the names of Cracow scholars that Azulai had omitted. Krengel also published commentaries on the Song of Songs, *Tirat Kesef* (1897), the Pentateuch, *Devash ve-Ḥalav* (1911), and the *Haggadah* (1896), to which he also appended the commentary of *Isaiah di Trani, the Elder, *Sha'arei Ge'ullah*, his own commentary being entitled *Zekher le-Fesaḥ*. His account of the heated controversy with H.A. Horowitz, Cracow's rabbi, over the latter's *eruv* arrangements in the town appears in *Torat Eruvim* (1888).

[Itzhak Alfassi]

KRESSEL, GETZEL (1911–1986), bibliographer and Hebrew writer. Born in Zabłotów, eastern Galicia, Kressel settled in Ereẓ Israel in 1930. From 1945 to 1951 he was one of the editors of *Davar* and of the Am Oved publications. He founded Genazim, the Biobibliographical Institute of the Association of Israel Writers, and was its director (1951–60), enriching its collection of manuscripts and letters. A methodical researcher, his most important work is *Leksikon ha-Sifrut ha-Ivrit ba-Dorot ha-Aḥaronim* ("Lexicon of Hebrew Literature in Recent Times," 1965–67). He also published *Toledot ha-Ittonut ha-Ivrit be-Ereẓ Yisrael* (1964), a history of journalism in Ereẓ Israel; various works on Zionism and on the history of the *Yishuv*, including *Ereẓ Yisrael ve-Toledoteha* (1943); and *Em ha-Moshavot – Petaḥ Tikvah* (1954). He was editor of the Zionism division of the *Encyclopaedia Judaica* (first edition).

BIBLIOGRAPHY: Tolkes, in: *Bitzaron*, 44 (1961), 109–12; idem, *Sifrei G. Kressel* (1968), bibliography; Orlan, in: *Hadoar*, 45 (1966), 153.

[Shimon Oren]

KRESSYN, MIRIAM (1911–1996), actress in Yiddish theater and film, singer and songwriter, radio personality, and historian of the Yiddish theater; known as the "First Lady of Yiddish Theater." Born in Bialystok, Poland, the seventh child of Mashe and Yankev Kressyn, she immigrated to Boston in 1923. A voice student at the New England Conservatory of Music, she eventually joined a Yiddish theater troupe and began a successful career on the Yiddish stage. She toured in North and South America and throughout Europe. In 1937 she starred in *Der Purimshpiler*, produced in Warsaw, her only film role. With her husband, Seymour Rexsite, Kressyn recorded numerous albums; for more than 40 years she and her husband broadcast their radio program, *Memories of the Yiddish Theater*, on New York's WEVD radio. From the late 1980s until her death, Kressyn was a professor of drama at Queens College in New York City.

BIBLIOGRAPHY: M. Rosenfeld. "Kressyn, Miriam," in: P.E. Hyman and D.D. Moore (eds.), *Jewish Women in America*, vol. 1 (1998), 760–61; N. Sandrow. *Vagabond Stars: A World History of Yiddish Theater* (1977).

[Judith R. Baskin (2nd ed.)]

KRESTIN, LAZAR (1868–1938), Austrian painter. Born in Kovno, Krestin studied in Vienna and Munich. He specialized in landscape paintings, reflecting the style of the great French impressionists. His work also contains many portraits and genre scenes of East European Jewish life. His subjects were similar to those of Isidor *Kaufmann, but Krestin did not attain a similar level of success.

From 1904 he was a member of the Wiener Kuenstlerhaus, the association of Austrian artists founded in 1861.

BIBLIOGRAPHY: Juedisches Museum Wien / G.T. Natter, G. Tobias, *Rabbiner, Bocher, Talmudschüler. Bilder des Wiener Malers Isidor Kaufmann*, exhibition catalogue Vienna (1995).

[Jihan Radjai-Ordoubadi (2nd ed.)]

KRETINGA (Ger. **Krottingen**), town in W. Lithuania, 13 mi. (20 km.) N.E. of Memel (Klaipeda). Jews first settled there during the 17th century. The Jewish leader in the Polish uprising of 1794, Berek *Joselewicz, was born and brought up in Kretinga. The community numbered 1,738 in 1847, 1,203 (35% of the total population) in 1897, approximately 1,000 in 1921, and approximately 800 in 1939. The Jews mainly derived their livelihood from commerce with East Prussia, the manufacture of amber jewelry, and the provision of services to vacationers at the nearby Baltic resort of Palanga (Ger. Polangen). During the period under independent Lithuania (1918–40) the community institutions included a *Tarbut school, a Bikkur Ḥolim society, a benevolent society, and a people's bank (with 233 members in 1932). The youth was organized in Zionist societies and the "Tiferet Baḥurim" society. The last rabbi, Benjamin Perski, was murdered along with the rest of the community after the town was occupied by the Germans on June 22, 1941.

[Dov Levin]

KREUZNACH (**Bad Kreuznach**), city in Germany. Some Jews lived in the city from the second half of the 13th century. Under unknown circumstances a Jew was martyred on March 31, 1283. Individual Jewish moneylenders are mentioned at the beginning of the 14th century; an organized community is known only from 1336. The Jews were victims of the *Black Death persecutions of 1348–49, but Jewish life revived not long after. In 1414 a local Jew, named Gottschalk of Kreuznach, was taken under the protection of Elector Rupert III of the Palatinate. In 1464 and 1466 two other Jews were granted privileges for a ten-year period of residence in Kreuznach. A special decree of 1525 regulated Jewish business activities, and permitted the consecration of a cemetery. In 1548 these regulations were renewed with additional provision for a schoolmaster. A Rabbi Liebman of Creutzonach is mentioned in 1554–55. Until 1739, when a synagogue was erected, services were held in a private home. The number of Jewish families in Kreuznach increased from 17 in 1715 to 22 in 1722. From the first decade of the 19th century the community developed steadily, from 286 persons in 1808 to 461 in 1840 and 601 in 1880. At the turn of the century there were 657 Jews in Kreuznach. In 1920 a sanatorium for children was established which had 600 beds in 1928. In 1933, Kreuznach's Jewish community of 713 persons had a synagogue, cemetery, four charitable and benevolent institutions, and three sociocultural societies. For over 40 years Rabbi Tawrogi (1857–1929) was spiritual head of the community and chief rabbi of the entire district. Two hundred Jews left almost immediately, and by May 1939 the number of Jews in Kreuznach had dwindled to 199 under the impact of Nazi persecution and the resulting organized emigration. Those remaining in 1942 were deported to the East. There is no record of Jews returning to Kreuznach after World War II; the cemetery was cared for by the city council.

BIBLIOGRAPHY: AZDJ, 74 (Oct. 7, 1910), 2–3; FJW (1932/33), 221–2; JC (July 21, 1933; Sept. 6, 1935); JSOS, 9 (1947), 207; L. Loewenstein, *Geschichte der Juden in der Kurpfalz* (1895), index; idem, in: JJLG, 6 (1908), 189; K.A. Schaab, *Diplomatische Geschichte der Juden zu Mainz und dessen Umgebung* (1855), 83–4; Salfeld, Martyrol, index; Germ Jud, 2 (1968²), 456.

[Chasia Turtel]

KREYMBORG, ALFRED (1883–1966), U.S. poet and playwright. Kreymborg's verse collections include *Mushrooms* (1916), *Manhattan Men* (1929), *Prologue in Hell* (1930), *The Little World, 1914 and After* (1932), and *No More War* (1950). As editor of the experimental periodicals *Globe* and *Broom*, he stimulated young poets, but reached a wider public with *Lyric America* (1930) and *American Caravan* (1927–36), an anthology of experimental writing of which he was coeditor. In the late 1930s he wrote verse plays for radio, including *The Planets* (1938), a pacifist allegory. His other works include the novel *I'm No Hero* (1933).

KRICHEV, town in Mogilev district, Belarus. Jews are mentioned in 1494 as having leased the customs dues of Krichev. In 1667 the Jew Eliash Issakovich leased the town from its owner, Duke Radziwill, and contributed to the towns' economy. During the Voschilo persecutions (1743–44), rebels drove the Jews out of the town and their property was stolen and destroyed. In 1766 there were 424 poll-tax paying Jews in Krichev and the vicinity. The number of Jews rose to 1,255 in 1847, and 2,566 (39% of the total population) in 1897, but had decreased to 1,546 (24.5%) by 1926. In 1928 a Jewish kolkhoz with 18 families began to operate and many Jews also worked in the local cement factory. There was a Yiddish elementary school. The number of Jews in 1939 was 1,362 (8.5% of the total population). The Germans occupied Krichev on July 17, 1941, and most of the Jews fled from town. In October they were confined to a ghetto and taken to do forced labor. Two months later they were taken to the vicinity of the cement factory and killed there. The number of Jews among the 19,000 inhabitants registered in the 1959 census is unknown.

BIBLIOGRAPHY: S. Dubnow, in: *He-Avar*, 1 (1918), 63–65; I. Halpern, in: *Zion*, 22 (1957), 56–57.

[Yehuda Slutsky / Shmuel Spector (2nd ed.)]

KRIEGEL, ANNIE (1926–1995), French sociologist and historian of communism, socialism, and workers' movements. Kriegel was born in Paris. From 1944, she was a leader of the underground Jewish Communist Youth in the region of Grenoble and after the war she was an official of the French Communist Party active among Parisian intellectuals until her break with the party in 1956. She was professor and head of the department of sociology at the University of Paris X-Nanterre. She made her name with her writings on the history of communism, socialism, and workers' movements. She also studied the situation of Judaism and the Jews in the modern period, and published a number of pro-Zionist essays ideologically oriented to the right. She was an eminent figure in the French academic world and journalism and served as senior commentator for *Le Figaro*, as a columnist for the Jewish monthly *L'Arche*, and as editor of the journals *Communisme* and *Pardes*, and was a member of the editorial board of *Commentaire* and *Mouvement Social*. In 1981 she undertook the presidency of the central group for Zionist thinking in France, sponsored by the World Zionist Organization. Among her many works are *Les internationales ouvrières* (1964, 1983^3; *Les juifs et le monde moderne* (1977), *Israel est-il coupable?* (1982), *Le systeme communiste mondial* (1984), *Reflexion sur les questions juives* (1984), and an autobiography, *Ce que j'ai cru comprendre* (1991).

[Gideon Kouts (2nd ed.)]

KRIEGEL-VALRIMONT, MAURICE (1914–), French Communist politician. Born in Strasbourg, he became in World War II, under the assumed name of Valrimont, one of the three members of the Action Committee of the French Resistance. After the liberation of France, he was a member of the Communist Party's Central Committee. He sat in the National Assembly from 1944 to 1958, when he was expelled from the party as a revisionist. His wife, Annie Besse *Kriegel, at one time an active Communist, later wrote several books criticizing the evolution of Marxism.

KRIEGER, LEONARD (1918–1990), U.S. historian. Born in Newark, New Jersey, Krieger was educated at Rutgers and Yale University, where he did graduate research for the Office of Strategic Services on the German system of domination in Eastern Europe. He joined the Yale history department, and was appointed professor in 1961. The following year he moved to the University of Chicago. As a historian, his overall objective was to bring historical experience to light through the individual's own intellectual process and to explore how ideas – including those of the historian – have a role in shaping history. For Krieger, intellectual history meant connecting the dots between ideas and events rather than merely collating and recounting facts and historical episodes.

Krieger's main works are *The German Idea of Freedom: History of a Political Tradition* (1957) and *Politics of Discretion: Pufendorf and the Acceptance of Natural Law* (1965), which examined the problem of a "trimmer." He also wrote *Kings and Philosophers, 1689–1789* (1970), *The German Revolutions* (with F. Engels, 1970), *Ranke: The Meaning of History* (1977), and *Time's Reasons* (1989). He was co-author of *History* (1965), and co-editor of *Responsibility of Power* (1968).

BIBLIOGRAPHY: M. Brick (ed.), *Ideas and Events: Professing History* (1992).

[Ruth Beloff (2nd ed.)]

KRIM, MATHILDE (1926–), U.S. medical researcher and philanthropist. Born in Italy to an Austrian Catholic mother and a Swiss Calvinist father, Mathilde Gallard was raised and educated in Geneva, Switzerland, and received her Ph.D. in biology from the University of Geneva in 1953 for her research in electron micrography. A convert to Judaism, in 1948 she married a Jewish medical student, David Danon, and together they worked on behalf of the *Irgun. After the couple moved to Israel with their daughter in 1953, Mathilde Danon became a research assistant at the Weizmann Institute in Reḥovot. She was soon promoted to junior scientist and then research associate, co-authoring several research papers, including "The Diagnosis of Sex Before Birth Using Cells from the Amniotic Fluid" (*Bulletin of the Research Council of Israel* 5B, 1955), which paved the way for the prenatal diagnostic technique known as amniocentesis. In 1958, after marrying a wealthy American, Arthur Krim, who was president of United Artists and also a prominent fundraiser for the Democratic Party, she moved to New York, where she became a researcher in virology, first at Cornell University Medical School and, after 1962, at Sloan-Kettering. Mathilde Krim's research and publications focused first on cancer-inducing agents, then on interferon, and finally on AIDS. From 1975 to 1985, she served as research scientist and director of the interferon laboratory at the Sloan-Kettering Institute for Cancer Research in New York. Thereafter, she held an adjunct position as associate research scientist in the Columbia University School of Public Health, but devoted most of her energy to AIDS-related fundraising, supervisory, and lobbying activities.

Beginning in the early 1980s, Mathilde Krim was extremely active in the fight against AIDS. In 1983, she founded the AIDS Medical Foundation (AMF), which merged in 1985 with another California-based group to form the American Foundation for AIDS Research (amFAR), the preeminent national nonprofit AIDS research and advocacy organization. Krim chaired amFAR's Board of Directors from its founding. She was also an active board member of the American Committee for the Weizmann Institute, the National Biomedical Research Foundation, the Committee of 100 for National Health Insurance, the Federation of Parents and Friends of Lesbians and Gays, and the African-American Institute.

In recognition of her research contributions and her highly successful lobbying and fundraising efforts over the years, Krim received 13 honorary degrees and numerous other honors and distinctions. She served on the President's Committee on Mental Retardation (1966–69), the congressional advisory commission on the war against cancer (1970–71), and the President's Commission for the Study of Ethical Problems in Medicine and Biomedical and Behavioral Research (1979–81). In August 2000, Mathilde Krim was awarded the Presidential Medal of Freedom, the highest civilian honor in the United States, in recognition of her "extraordinary compassion and commitment."

BIBLIOGRAPHY: Paula E. Hyman and D. Dash Moore (eds.), *Jewish Women in America*, I (1997), 761–63; *New York Times*, Section 1 (Nov. 3, 1984), 48; Section 6 (Feb. 14, 1988), 30.

[Harriet Pass Freidenreich (2nd ed.)]

KRIMCHAK LANGUAGE (or dialect). The spoken and written language of the Krimchaks, which is close to the Crimean-Tatar language or basically a variant of the latter. However, it is today considered an independent language belonging to the Kipchak group of Turkic languages.

Of the total population of approximately 2,000 Krimchaks today, several members of the older generation still know the Krimchak language.

A distinguishing feature of the language is a broad lexical stratum of Hebrew-Aramaic origin, e.g. *adoni* – sir, *hodesh* – month, *mazon* – food, *nes* – miracle.

In the Krimchak language, written in the Hebrew script, Hebrew words undergo phonetic adaption; the letter *ṣade* (צ) is pronounced "ch" (e.g., *rachon* – wish, will), the Hebrew *tav* without a *dagesh* (ת) as "s" as in Yiddish and Ashkenazi pronunciation (e.g., *akosev*, from *ha-Kotev*, the writer). Krimchak appears in two variations: the spoken language, and the literary language (the language of the Bible translation). Almost all printed works in Krimchak consist of religious literature translated from Hebrew published in the early 20th century in Russia and in Ereẓ Israel. A number of these translations contain Hebrew-Krimchak glossaries. Transcriptions of the rich Krimchak folklore has partially been published in scientific editions. The Krimchak language also had a connection to Yiddish as well as to Ladino, or Judeo-Spanish (for example, the word *pastel*, a kind of pastry, in all likelihood derives from Judeo-Spanish).

[Wolf Moskovitz / *The Shorter Jewish Encylopaedia in Russian*]

KRIMCHAKS (inhabitants of the *Crimea), Jewish ethnic and linguistic community. Prior to World War II Krimchaks lived mainly in the Crimean peninsula. Before the Russian invasion of 1783 they called themselves *Yehudi* (Jew) or *srel balalary* (sons of Israel). Only at a relatively late period – in the end of the 19th–beginning of the 20th century – did they begin to call themselves *Kirymchakh* from the Russian *Krymchak*. The name *Krimchaks* (the Crimean Jews) first appeared in official Russian sources in 1859. Evidently the term was coined to distinguish the Rabbanite Jews in the Crimea from the *Karaites who lived in the same region, and also from the *Ashkenazi Jews who had moved there. In the documents issued by the Crimean rulers before the peninsula was captured by Russia the members of the community were called *yehudiler*, i.e., the Jews, which was the name also given to the Karaites. Neither the documents of the European colonies in the Crimea nor the writing of European travelers visiting the region in the Middle Ages differentiated between the two. The Crimean Tatars called the Krimchaks colloquially *zuluflu chufutlar* (Jews with earlocks), while they called the Karaites *zulufsuz chufutlar* (Jews without earlocks). The Krimchak language is akin to the Crimean-Tatar languages.

Demography

In the 14th–16th centuries the Rabbanite Jews had their main center in the town of Kaffa, now Feodosiya. However, already by the end of the 18th century, the majority of Jews lived in Karasu-Bazar, now Belogorsk, which remained the main center of the Krimchaks up to the middle of the 1920s when the majority of them moved to Simferopol.

According to the census conducted by the Turks during the rule of Sultan Suleiman I (1520–66), 92 Jewish families and one single Jew lived in Kaffa, which according to the demographic notions of the time denoted a total of about 460 people. The total number of Krimchaks at the time was 500–700 people.

In 1847 the population of Rabbanite Jews in the Crimea numbered 2,837, the majority of them being Krimchaks. The census of 1897 listed 3,345 Krimchaks in the Crimea.

From the end of the 19th century Krimchaks who had previously lived in Karasu-Bazar began to move to the other towns in the Crimea. A small number might have moved to Ereẓ Israel in the late 19th century or early 20th century.

By 1912 the number of Krimchaks had reached 7,500; 2,487 of them lived in Karasu-Bazar, about the same number in Simferopol, 750 in Feodosiya, 500 in Kerch, 400 in Sevastopol, while the rest were scattered among 28 other towns of the Crimea and the Caucasus.

The Soviet census of 1926 showed a decrease in the number throughout the country: the total was now 6,383 Krimchaks among 42,000 Jews (without the Karaites). The number of Jews in Crimea rose in 1939 to 47,387 (8% of the total population) and it can be assumed that the number of the Krimchaks increased only slightly. The drop in the Krimchak population was due to the Civil War and the famine of 1921–22 which led to the death of 700 members of the community; about 200 members immigrated to Palestine, and 400 to the U.S. According to the 1926 census, 98.4 percent of the Krimchaks lived in towns, and 74.1 percent declared the Krimchak language their mother tongue. Simferopol was now their main center, where about 2,500 persons lived.

Prior to the German attack on the U.S.S.R. in 1941, the Krimchaks numbered about 9,000. The majority perished during the Nazi occupation of their regions in 1941–42. In 1948 in the whole Crimea only 700–750 Krimchaks could be found. After World War II not more than 1,000–1,500 remained alive throughout the Soviet Union. The Nazis destroyed about 75 percent of the community; about 1,000 lived in Palestine and in the U.S.

According to the Soviet census of 1959, only 189 of the 1,500 Krimchaks declared *Krimchak* their native tongue. In the 1970s–1980s the number of the Krimchaks, according to available data, dropped not less than 15 percent, decreasing to 900. However other estimates put their number at about 2,000 in 1982. Nevertheless the remnants of the community were rapidly assimilating among the surrounding Russian and Ukrainian population.

At the end of the 19th and the beginning of the 20th centuries, those Krimchaks in Ereẓ Israel adopted the Sephardi prayer rite. A Krimchak synagogue existed in Tel Aviv up to 1981. In Israel the Krimchak population intermingled with other Jewish settlers, and did not found a separate community. Those who immigrated to the U.S. assimilated with the Ashkenazi Jews and did not retain a separate identity.

Although already in the 13th century some of the Crimean Jews spoke Turkish, and the final crystallization of the Krimchaks into a separate ethnic and linguistic group occurred in the 14th–16th centuries, a number of historians – Simon *Dubnow included – thought that the Krimchak community descended from the ancient Jewry of the Crimea.

History

BOSPHORUS PERIOD. The appearance of the Jews in the Crimea was connected with the Greek colonization of the shores of the Black Sea in the second–first centuries B.C.E. although it is possible that they had reached the Crimea from the Caucasus through the Taman peninsula already at the time of the Assyrian and Babylonian invasions (seventh–sixth centuries B.C.E.).

The first mention of the Crimean Jews is from the 1st century C.E. They are found in documents concerning the liberation of the slaves by their Jewish owners and epitaphs discovered mainly in the southeastern part of the Crimea and on the Taman peninsula.

The documents concerning the slaves refer to the obligations imposed on them to visit regularly the synagogue under the supervision of the Jewish community. Thus, the Hellenized Jewish communities of the Bosphorus Kingdom, never having suffered from persecutions or limitations of any kind, grew – thanks to the conversion of the liberated slaves to Judaism. Moreover, the so-called *Sebomenoi*, non-Jews partially observing Jewish law, also tended to join the Jewish communities. A fourth-century inscription has been found on the construction of the synagogue in Panthikapei, now Kerch.

Little is known about the occupations of the Crimean Jews of the period. They must have dealt mostly in trades and crafts. The Jews also occupied state positions and served in the army, as evidenced by a first-century tombstone found in Taman. The tombstones of the third and fourth centuries preserve, besides Greek inscriptions, a Hebrew inscription, as well as Hebrew names and symbols.

In the second and third centuries, the Jews moved along the southern coast of the Crimea. In 300, the Jews are mentioned in Kherson, in southwestern Crimea, in connection with the rebellion of the local population protesting the introduction of Christianity.

In the late fourth century, *Jerome wrote about Jews in the Bosphorus Kingdom. Traditionally they included descendants of families who had been exiled by the Assyrians and the Babylonians as well as of imprisoned warriors of Bar Kokhba.

The invasion of Huns in the 370s destroyed the Bosphorus Kingdom, and another state rose on its ruins – the Alan-Hun, which ceased to exist in the early sixth century. Those events contributed to the further dehellenization of the Crimean Jews, evidenced by the tombstones of the period, usually without inscriptions of names but with Jewish symbols such as the seven-branched candelabrum.

At the beginning of the sixth century the territory was invaded by the Byzantine Empire, and Byzantine chroniclers mention Jews in the area. In the Taman region, Jewish tombstones of the sixth–eighth centuries have been excavated.

THE KHAZAR PERIOD. In the middle of the seventh century *Khazars occupied most of the Crimean territory.

The Jewish population might have played a decisive role in the process of establishing Judaism among the Khazars, who adopted Judaism as their religion in the late eighth–early ninth century.

The Jewish population also grew as a result of the influx of Jewish refugees coming mostly from the Byzantine Empire where Jews were periodically persecuted (843, 873–874, and 943). Judaism in the Crimea was greatly influenced by the Jewish refugees from the Byzantine Empire and by constant contacts with Byzantine Jewry. Under this influence the so-called Crimean Rite was elaborated. The most ancient of all known synagogues on Russian territory was built in 909 in Kaffa (Feodosiya). Several sources mention authors of religious hymns (*piyyutim) in the region, such as Abraham ben Simḥah ha-Sefaradi (died 1027). Silk processing, fabric-dyeing, and trade were the main occupations of the Jews.

From the mid-ninth century the power of the Khazars in the Crimea weakened as a result of invasions and also because of renewed wars with the Byzantine Empire. In 940–41 the Kiev princedom at the instigation of the Byzantines, waged war against the Khazar state, resulting in the victory of the Khazars who recaptured the southern and southwestern parts of the Crimea up to Kherson. Attempts by the Byzantine Church to convert the Crimean Jews to Christianity failed.

The Khazar ruler Joseph wrote to *Ḥisdai ibn Shaprut, in approximately 960, stating that he ruled over many other areas besides the 12 settlements in the Crimea and in Taman. The most numerous Jewish communities existing at the time were in the towns of Samkush or Samkersh (Tmutarakan), Mangup (Doros), and Sudak. Large Jewish communities were known in the towns of Solkhat (presently Stariy Kryn), Kaffa (presently Feodosiya), and Kherson, where already in 861 Cyril, a preacher of Christianity, found a Jewish community of long standing including Khazars converted to Judaism. The decline of the Khazar kingdom began after Prince Svyatoslav defeated the Khazars in 965.

In 1096 the Byzantine emperor Alexei I ordered that all Jews should be driven from Kherson and their property confiscated. The exiles from Kherson must have settled in those regions of the Crimea where the Byzantines did not reach. However 60 to 70 years later the Jews were still living in the Byzantine part too as *Benjamin of Tudela in the 1160s reported on the existence of a community of Rabbanite Jews in the town of Sogdia (presently Sudak), which was a significant Crimean port. At that time the Jews of the Crimea comprised a provincial part of the Romaniot community, whose members spoke Greek.

Khazars observing Judaism must have assimilated among the Jewish population of the Crimea. Some of the immigrant Jews were Karaites. In approximately 1175, the traveler Pethahiah of Regensburg confirmed the existence of Jewish groups in the region of the Azov Sea, whose customs were identical to those of the Karaites. The Jews of the Crimea continued to maintain contact with the Jews of the Byzantine Empire and of Islamic countries.

THE TATAR PERIOD. In 1239 the steppe area of the Crimea was occupied by the Tatars and Mongols. Along the southern coast, the colonies of Genoa entrenched themselves. Thanks to the Genoese colonies, the Crimea became an important trading center attracting numerous Jewish emigrants from the eastern countries (Persia, Asia Minor, Egypt) as well as from the West (Italy, and later, Spain).

The economic flourishing of the Jewish communities contributed to their cultural development. *Se at Emet* ("Language of Truth"), a rationalistic commentary on the Pentateuch by Avraham Kirimi (i.e., of Crimea), written in 1315, is the first known original work by a Crimean Jew. Several sources point to the town of Solkhat (where Kirimi was born and lived), as an important center of Jewish rationalism at the time.

From the 14th century on, the Karaite communities were centered in Chufut-Kale and in Mangup. Most Rabbanite Jews settled in Solkhat, and later in Karasu-Bazar. However Kaffa was the largest Jewish community in the Crimea with both Rabbanite and Karaite Jews.

The Genoese authorities endeavored to calm the tensions between various ethnic and religious groups in their colonies related, in particular, to the forced conversions of the Jews to Christianity and the plunder of property. In 1449 they issued a decree for the Black Sea colonies, which included a confirmation of the rights of all peoples and groups including the Jews to observe their own religion. Later decrees from the Genoese ordered that the Jews be free from interference in their affairs, so that the Jews enjoyed freedom until the conquest of Kaffa by the Turkish troops in 1475.

Already prior to 1475, some Jews living in Kaffa had established contacts with the court of the Crimean Khans in Solkhat. One of these Jews, Khozya Kokos, a merchant, mediated in 1472–86 the negotiations between the Grand Duke of Moscow, Ivan III, and the Crimean Khan, Mengly-Girei, a part of the correspondence being written in Hebrew.

Centuries of Tatar rule resulted in a considerable Orientalization of the Crimean Jews: to a great extent they adopted the language, customs, and mores of the Moslem Tatars. Already in the 13th century some of the Crimean Jews spoke Turkish. The Bible was translated into Krimchak. The decline of trade led to the increased share of crafts and agriculture in the occupations of the Crimean Jews. Many Jews in Mangup and Chufut-Kale engaged in leather tanning, mountain vegetable gardening, and viticulture. The Jewish merchants obtained credentials from the ruler to protect themselves and their property from the encroachment of local feudal lords.

Throughout their history the Krimchaks absorbed Jews coming from other communities: the Byzantine Empire, Babylonia and the Khazar kingdom, Italy, and the Caucasus, as well as Ashkenazi Jews brought to the Crimea as prisoners of the Tatars, or those who fled from pogroms and later moved to the Crimea for economic reasons.

Prior to the conquest of the Crimea by Russia, all Rabbanite Jews in the Crimea merged with the Krimchak community, and it was only in the 19th–early 20th century that a separate Ashkenazi community emerged. The merger of the various communities resulted in a special prayer rite incorporating elements of different communities (*minhag Kaffa*). Various trends of Jewish mysticism made their impact on Krimchak tradition: *Ḥasidei Ashkenaz, the Kabbalah of the Zohar, Isaac *Luria, and especially, practical Kabbalah. Rabbi Moses ben Jacob, who went to the Crimea from Kiev, reconciled the different traditions and elaborated the single rite compiling the prayer book *Maḥzor Minhag Kaffa*; he also established rules for guiding community life.

THE RUSSIAN PERIOD. The successful struggle of Karaites to be exempted from the anti-Jewish laws of the Russian Empire and their move from the dilapidated town-fortresses to other regions of the Crimea for economic reasons led to a complete break in relations between the Karaites and the Krimchaks.

From 1866 to 1899 Ḥayyim Hezekiah *Medini (born in Jerusalem in 1832, and died in 1904) was chief rabbi of Karasu-Bazar. He raised the spiritual and cultural level of the Krimchaks, increasing the Sephardi influence. He introduced changes in the community's customs, and founded several schools, and a yeshivah.

In his monumental multi-volume *Sedei Hemed* Medini described at length Krimchak traditions and elaborated his own regulations (**takkanot*). In 1899 Medini returned to Ereẓ Israel to publish religious literature with translations into Krimchak.

Polygamy among the Krimchaks disappeared early in the 19th century. Girls married at an early age, and marriages between close relatives, such as an uncle and his niece, were permitted. Widows could never remarry because a husband and wife were considered inseparable also after death.

The everyday life of the Krimchaks was influenced by that of the Crimean Tatars. The patriarchal nature of the family was preserved up to the end of the 19th century. The practice of good deeds was regarded to be of great significance. They carried out charity extensively, caring for widows and orphans; no beggars were found in their midst, and the poor received firewood, flour, and candles at the community's expense.

In the 19th century the Krimchaks lived in small poor communities almost untouched by the European enlightenment. Most of them were craftsmen, and the minority was engaged in agriculture, gardening, and vine-growing, with only a few in trade.

In 1840 the Krimchaks founded an agricultural settlement, Rogatlikoy, with 140 members. However, in 1859 the Krimchak peasants received the status of middle-class citizens of the town of Karasu-Bazar, and their lands were transferred to Russian Christian settlers. Count A. Stroganov, governor-general of Novorossijsk, interceded for the Jews who wanted to acquire property in the Crimea and as a result the transfer decree failed to be ratified by the czarist government in 1861. The attitude of the Russian authorities to the "Talmudic Jews" in the Crimea was relatively favorable: the community enjoyed several privileges in the fields of taxation and conscription.

The Krimchaks created a rich folklore: collections of legends, songs, riddles, and proverbs, written by hand in Hebrew letters and passed from one generation to another. Samples of their folklore were published in the original with translations into Russian, Yiddish, and Hebrew. Literature in Krimchak consisted, apart from folklore, mainly in translations of religious texts.

Drawn into Russian culture from the beginning of the 20th century, some of the Krimchaks participated in revolutionary movements and a considerable part of them joined Zionist organizations.

After the Revolution of 1917, the Krimchaks were subject to the same social and demographic processes as all the other Jewish ethnic and linguistic groups. The considerable increase in their educational level led to a decline in everyday traditional life. Many Krimchaks who had received professional education as physicians, engineers, and teachers severed contacts with their native community.

The German occupation of Crimea started with the city of Perekop on October 30, 1941, and was finalized on November 16 with the conquering of Kerch. Sevastopol was under German siege until July 3, 1942. Although 50% of Crimean Jews succeeded in evacuating themselves, it can be assumed that the escape of the Krimchaks was less. *Einsatzgruppe* D established its headquarters in Simferopol on November 12, 1941, having previously asked for guidance from the Main Reichs' Security Office in Berlin on how to treat the Krimchaks. The reply was to include them like all Jews in the "Final Solution." That is, they should be destroyed with the rest of the Jewish population.

During the main period of killings by subunits of the *Einsatzgruppe* D, November 16 to December 15, 1941, they reported the murder of 17,645 Jews and 2,504 Krimchaks. These numbers are not final, because those in hiding were hunted and many were caught and executed. The Krimchaks who spoke the same language as the native Tatars tried to hide among them. But since the Tatars cooperated with the Germans, the Jews were denounced and turned over to the killers. Some 1,500 Krimchaks from Simferopol were executed on December 9 near the village of Mazanka. The Krimchaks of Feodosiya were among the 1,052 Jews who met their death on December 15, the 7,000 Jews of Kerch, including the Krimchaks, were murdered on December 1–3, 1941, and the Krimchaks of Karasu-Bazar met their death on November 15; the 90 Krimchaks of Bakhchisarai were killed on December 13, 1941, and about 1,052 Jews, among them Krimchaks, from Feodosiya were murdered on November 17, 1941, in gas vans. Krimchaks fought in the Soviet army and in partisan detachments. Many perished, including the poet Ya. I. Chapichev (1909–1945), who received the posthumous title of Hero of the Soviet Union.

After the war there were about 1,500 Krimchaks, with fewer than 500 living in Simferopol. At present, any remaining Krimchaks are being rapidly assimilated, and their culture inadequately preserved. In the post-war period, they were officially defined in the Soviet Union as a special nationality of mixed ethnic origin, mostly non-Jewish. In the 1990s most of them left for Israel.

[Michael Zand / Dan Kharuv / *The Shorter Jewish Encyclopaedia in Russian* / Shmuel Spector (2nd ed.)]

KRINITZI, AVRAHAM (1886–1969), Israeli public figure. Born in Grodno, Krinitzi began working as a carpenter from his youth. Krinitzi went to Ereẓ Israel in 1905, but returned to Russia to serve in the army. In 1908 he settled in Ereẓ Israel, establishing a furniture factory in Jaffa which was the first in the country to use modern machinery. Active in *yishuv* defense, he was arrested several times. He was one of the founders of the Naḥalat Binyamin quarter of Tel Aviv and headed a Tel Aviv watchmen's committee. During World War I, the Turkish authorities placed him in charge of fuel supplies for the railways in Palestine and Syria, and he later ran a factory for repairing cannons in Damascus. In 1947 Krinitzi was arrested by the Mandatory authorities together with other public figures, and imprisoned in Latrun.

From 1926 he headed Ramat Gan's local government, first as chairman of its local council and from 1950 as its mayor. In his term of office, Ramat Gan was transformed from its small beginnings, with 750 inhabitants, to a town of over 100,000 citizens. From the 1920s he was a leading member of the General Zionist (later the *Liberal) Party. His autobiography is entitled *Be-Khoah ha-Ma'aseh* (1961[4]; *Going My Own Way*, 1963, tr. I.M. Lask).

BIBLIOGRAPHY: A. Remba, *Deyokano shel Ish Rav-Pe'alim* (1968).

[Abraham Aharoni]

KRIPKE, SAUL AARON (1940–), U.S. philosopher interested in metaphysics, philosophy of language, epistemology, philosophy of mind, and philosophy of logic and mathematics. Kripke helped advance understanding in modal logic, intuitionistic logic, and set theory. Formerly the McCosh Professor of Philosophy at Princeton University (where he became professor emeritus) and professor of philosophy at CUNY Graduate Center, Kripke was the winner of the 2001 Schock Prize in Logic and Philosophy, and author of several seminal works, including *Naming and Necessity* (1980), based on a series of lectures he delivered at Princeton in 1970; a never-published but much circulated tome, based on lectures at Oxford in 1973, called *Reference and Existence*; and a controversial study called *Wittgenstein on Rules and Private Language*.

Kripke was born in Bay Shore, New York, one of three children of a rabbi, Myer Kripke, and Dorothy Kripke, a teacher and writer of Jewish educational books for children. The family moved to Omaha, Nebraska, where Rabbi Kripke stewarded the Beth El synagogue, the city's only Conservative congregation. After graduating from Omaha Central High School in 1958, Kripke demonstrated an early and precocious interest in philosophy – at 15, he developed a semantics for quantified modal logic that would debut in *The Journal of Symbolic Logic* during his freshman year at Harvard. There, Kripke shared a dormitory room with constitutional law scholar Laurence *Tribe and, briefly, with Theodore Kaczynski, who would gain notoriety as "The Unabomber." After receiving a B.A. in mathematics in 1962, Kripke was appointed to the Harvard Society of Fellows.

Kripke began his academic career lecturing at Princeton and Harvard before joining the philosophy department at Rockefeller University in New York City, where he remained as professor of philosophy until leaving for Princeton in 1977. He was the youngest person ever to be asked to present the John Locke lectures at Oxford. Kripke married and subsequently divorced Margaret Gilbert, sister of British historian Martin *Gilbert.

Kripke devoted his earliest professional attention to the problems of naming, identity and possible (or counterfactual) worlds, arguing that identity is the necessary function of a relationship between a thing and itself, and never between a thing and something else. This argument, which he presented at his Princeton lectures and collected in *Naming and Necessity*, caused great consternation when published, standing analytic philosophy, according to the London Review of Books, "on its ears" and, according to others, making "metaphysics respectable again." In *Reference and Existence*, which circulates in *Samizdat* form and whose own existence may not, per Kripke's instructions, be referenced or quoted without permission, he addressed issues related to fictional names and perceptions. Kripke's analysis of the later Wittgenstein, presented in *Wittgenstein on Rules and Private Language: An Elementary Exposition* (1982) proved no less controversial than his other works, not least for arguments purportedly at variance with positions on meaning held by the historical Wittgenstein.

[Sheldon Teitelbaum (2nd ed.)]

KRIPS, JOSEF (1902–1974), conductor. Born in Vienna, Krips studied at the Vienna Academy with E. Mandyczewski and Weingartner and made his opera debut in 1921. He joined the Vienna Volksoper as chorus master and répétiteur and in 1924 was appointed head of the opera department at Aussig/Elbe. From 1925 to 1926 he was at Dortmund and then at Karlsruhe as music director (1926–33). Between 1933 and 1938 he conducted at the Vienna State Opera, losing his position after the Nazi annexation of Austria. During the war his musical activities were suspended; from 1945, he conducted at the Salzburg Festival and in various European countries. A visit to England in 1947 to conduct Mozart operas at Covent Garden led to his appointment as chief conductor of the London Symphony Orchestra in 1950. Later he moved to the United States and was a guest conductor at the Chicago Lyric Opera from 1959, the Metropolitan from 1967, and the Deutsche Oper, Berlin, from 1970.

BIBLIOGRAPHY: Grove online; MGG[2].

[Israela Stein (2nd ed.)]

KRIS, ERNST (1900–1957), art historian and psychoanalyst. Kris was a junior keeper at the Kunsthistorisches Museum in his native Vienna when in 1924 he met *Freud, who sought his help with his collection of intaglios, and by 1927 had become an associate member of the Vienna Institute of Psychoanalysis. In 1933, at Freud's request, he gave up his medical studies and assumed the editorship of the journal *Imago*. In 1929 he wrote the standard work on the art of stone cutting. After the Austrian *Anschluss* in 1938, Kris and his wife Marianne (née Rie; 1900–1980), also a psychoanalyst, followed Freud to England. Shortly after the outbreak of World War II he organized a government department for the analysis of enemy broadcasts. He was sent to Canada and then to the United States to perform a similar task. In America his interest in psychoanalysis predominated over his profession of art history which, however, continued to influence his work.

Kris's first important analytic writing, "A Psychotic Sculptor of the Eighteenth Century" (1933), was the beginning of a series of papers applying analysis to art. He pioneered group research in psychoanalysis and made many contributions together with Heinz *Hartmann and Rudolph *Loewenstein. The work in which the three men collaborated, which included *Comments on the Formation of Psychic Structure* (1946) and *Some Psychoanalytic Comments on Culture and Personality* (1951), extended and integrated the newer developments of psychoanalytic theory. In 1950 Kris formulated some of the ideas underlying the interdisciplinary child study project at Yale University in which he participated under the aegis of Milton Senn.

In 1952 he collected his papers in *Psychoanalytic Explorations in Art*. In these essays he stressed the contribution of the study of the creative process to psychoanalytic psychology, to communication, and to the understanding of the ego development of the child.

BIBLIOGRAPHY: S. Ritvo and L. Ritvo, in: F.G. Alexander et al. (eds.), *Psychoanalytic Pioneers* (1966), 484–500; A. Grinstein, *Index of Psychoanalytic Writings*, 2 (1957), 1130–34.

[Louis Miller]

KRISPIN (Krespin), JOSHUA ABRAHAM (d. 1855), rabbi of Smyrna. Krispin was the author of *Avraham ba-Maḥazeh* (1869), sermons and eulogies delivered between 1793 and 1851; *Va-Yeshev Avraham* (1893), responsa, and novellae on tractates of the Talmud in alphabetical order. This was published by his son ISAAC who included it in his own *Shemo Yiẓḥak*, consisting of 27 sermons and eulogies. Another son, AARON, was the author of *Beit Aharon* (1863) on the Shulḥan ʿArukh, *Oraḥ Ḥayyim, Yoreh De'ah* and *Even ha-ʿEzer,* arranged in alphabetical order, and on the writing of names in bills of divorce.

BIBLIOGRAPHY: A. Freimann, *Inyanei Shabbetai Ẓevi* (1912), 149:185; A. Galante, *Les Juifs d'Izmir (Histoire des juifs d'Anatolie, 1)* (1937), 58; M.D. Gaon, *Yehudei ha-Mizraḥ be-Ereẓ Yisrael*, (1937), 632 n. 1,749.

[Simon Marcus]

KRISS, GRIGORI (1940–), Soviet fencer, winner of four Olympic medals. Born in Kiev, Kriss represented the Soviet Union at three Olympics: At the Tokyo Games in 1964 he won the gold in Team Epée and finished fourth in individual epée; in Mexico City in 1968 he won the silver in Individual Epée, losing to Gyozo Kulcsar of Hungary, and silver in team competition; and he won a bronze in Team Epée in Munich in 1972. Kriss also won the silver medal in 1967 and the gold medal in 1971 in the individual epée at the World Championships, and bronze in 1965, silver in 1966, gold in 1967 and 1969, and silver in 1971 in Team Epée at those World Championships. He subsequently coached the Ukrainian Olympic fencing team, which won four gold medals at the 1996 Atlanta Olympics.

[Elli Wohlgelernter (2nd ed.)]

KRISTALLNACHT (Ger. "Night of the Broken Glass"), known in Germany and elsewhere as the November pogroms. Nazi anti-Jewish pogroms throughout the country committed on November 9–10, 1938. The events of the November pogroms were ostensibly provoked by the assassination of Ernst vom Rath, third secretary of the German embassy in Paris, by Herschel *Grynszpan, the son of Polish-Jewish parents living in Germany until their deportation to the Polish-German frontier in Zbaszyn in October 1938. Grynszpan received a postcard from his distraught sister and wanted revenge. On November 7 he went to German embassy in Paris, where he shot vom Rath, who died in the afternoon of November 9. In the meantime, attempts were made to persuade the British government to use its influence with the German government to suspend apparently imminent measures of retaliation against German Jewry. Thus, amid the Germans' deliberately engineered atmosphere of tension, widespread attacks on Jews, Jewish-owned property, and synagogues were made throughout Germany and Austria, which had been part of the Reich since March 1938, on the night of November 9–10.

Just before midnight on November 9, Gestapo Chief Heinrich Mueller sent a telegram to all police units telling them that "in shortest order, actions against Jews and especially their synagogues will take place in all Germany. These are not to be interfered with." Rather, the police were to arrest the victims. Fire companies stood by synagogues in flames with explicit instructions to let the buildings burn. They were to intervene only if a fire threatened adjacent Aryan properties. Thus, synagogues that were part of larger structures were spared in order not to damage those structures.

Within 48 hours, more than 1,000 synagogues were burned, along with their Torah scrolls, Bibles, and prayer books. Around 7,500 Jewish business establishments were trashed and looted, 91 Jews were killed, and Jewish cemeteries, hospitals, schools, and homes were destroyed. Often, the attackers were not strangers but neighbors. Around 30,000 Jewish men age 16–60 were arrested. To accommodate so many new prisoners, the concentration camps of *Dachau, *Buchenwald, and *Sachsenhausen were expanded and now contained a majority of Jews, often for the first time.

When the fury subsided, the pogrom was given a fancy name: *Kristallnacht* – crystal night, or night of broken glass. It came to stand for the final shattering of Jewish existence in Germany. In the aftermath of *Kristallnacht*, the regime made sure that Jews could no longer survive in the country.

The cost of the broken glass alone came to 5 million marks, the equivalent of well over $2 million. Any compensation claims paid to Jews by insurance companies were confiscated by the Reich. The rubble of ruined synagogues had to be cleared by the Jewish community. Jews of German nationality, unlike Jewish-owned corporations from abroad, could not file for damages. A fine of one billion Reichmarks ($400 million) was imposed collectively on the Jewish community. After assessing the fine, Goering, who had assumed control in the aftermath from Goebbels, said: "I would not like to be a Jew in Germany." Harsher decrees followed immediately thereafter.

On November 15, Jews were barred from schools. Two weeks later, local authorities were given the right to impose a curfew, and by December Jews were denied access to most public places. All remaining Jewish businesses were "Aryanized."

The November pogrom shattered all Jewish illusions. Life in the Reich was no longer possible. There was another wave of suicides. Most tried desperately to leave. It shattered some German illusions as well. Violence thereafter in Germany would be planned and executed with precision and aforethought.

The events had occurred in public and thus the world could see what had happened. The U.S. recalled its ambassador in protest, but diplomatic ties were not broken.

BIBLIOGRAPHY: L. Kochan, *Pogrom, November 10, 1938* (1957); Tenenbaum, in: *Yad Vashem Studies*, 2 (1958) 49–78; K.Y. Ball-Kaduri, *ibid.*, 3 (1959), 261–82; H. Graml, *Der 9 November 1938 "Reichskristallnacht"* (1958[6]); Rosenkranz, in: *Yad Vashem Bulletin*, no. 14 (March, 1964); F.K. Kaul, *Der Fall des Herschel Grynszpan* (1965). **ADD. BIBLIOGRAPHY:** A. Read and D. Fisher, *Kristallnacht: The Unleashing of the Holocaust* (1990).

[Lionel Kochan / Michael Berenbaum (2nd ed.)]

KRISTELLER, PAUL OSKAR (1905–1999), scholar of Renaissance thought. Kristeller was born in Berlin and received his Ph.D. from the University of Heidelberg (1928). In 1934 he left Germany for Italy, where he taught in Florence and Pisa. When the antisemitic laws were passed, Kristeller fled to the U.S., and taught at Columbia (from 1939; professor, 1956–76). He served as president of the Renaissance Society of America and of the Medieval Academy of America. After he retired from teaching, he continued his scholarly endeavors as Columbia University's F.J.E. Woodbridge Professor of Philosophy Emeritus.

Regarded by many as the foremost authority on Renaissance thought and philosophy, Kristeller did his major work in the study and interpretation of Italian humanistic thought of the Renaissance, and in locating and cataloging the available published and manuscript sources of the period. He played an important role in encouraging and directing basic research into Renaissance thought. His own studies have been of great significance in reinterpreting the thinkers and movements of the time. His bibliographical work on the source materials is invaluable. On Jewish subjects, Kristeller wrote on *Steinschneider, on *Pico della Mirandola's Jewish interests, and was concerned with questions about Judah *Abrabanel.

In 1984, at age 78, he was named a MacArthur Fellow – the second oldest recipient of the award at that time. In 1989, he received the American Historical Association's Award for Scholarly Distinction. In 1995, Columbia commended his lifelong scholarly achievements with the Nicholas Murray Butler Cold Medal, which is given every five years to an individual who has made a distinguished contribution in philosophy or education.

Among Kristeller's important publications are *The Philosophy of Marsilio Ficino* (1943), *Studies in Renaissance Thought and Letters* (1956), *Latin Manuscript Books before 1600* (1960), *Renaissance Thought* (2 vols., 1961–65), *Iter Italicum, A Finding List of Uncatalogued or Incompletely Catalogued Humanistic Manuscripts of the Renaissance in Italian and other Libraries* (2 vols., 1965–67), *History: The Last Things before the Last* (with S. Kracauer, 1969), *Medieval Aspects of Renaissance Learning* (1974), *Renaissance Thought and Its Sources* (1979), *Renaissance Thought and the Arts* (1990), and *Greek Philosophers of the Hellenistic Age* (1993).

[Richard H. Popkin / Ruth Beloff (2nd ed.)]

KRISTELLER, SAMUEL (1820–1900), obstetrician and gynecologist. Kristeller, who was born in Posen, served as medical director of the obstetrical and gynecological departments in the Charité Hospital, Berlin. His main contribution to obstetrics was the introduction of a method to hasten and ease the ejection of the placenta after birth by special located pressure on the abdomen. This technique, called "Kristeller's method," is still used. He also described a new method of grafting mucous membrane.

BIBLIOGRAPHY: S.R. Kagan, *Jewish Medicine* (1952), 478.

[Suessmann Muntner]

KRISTIANPOLLER, family of Polish rabbis. The first of the family to adopt this name was MEIR BEN ẒEVI HIRSH (1740–1815) after he became rabbi of Kristianpol in East Galicia. He studied under his father, who was rabbi of Bialy-Kamien near Brody and later *av bet din* in Lemberg, and subsequently under Samuel ha-Levi *Horowitz of Nikolsburg. The author of *Yad ha-Me'ir* (Warsaw, 1874), novellae on various talmudic tractates, he engaged in halakhic correspondence with the rabbis of his time and R. Ezekiel Landau praised him highly. Ephraim Zalman *Margolioth wrote a lengthy eulogy on him at the end of his work *Beit Efrayim*. He was also eulogized by R. Ẓevi Hirsch *Horowitz of Frankfurt in his *Laḥmei Todah*. He served as rabbi of Brody from 1785 until his death. His son JEHIEL MICHAEL (d. 1863) acted as rabbi of Brody in 1831, but his appointment was not officially recognized by the Austrian government until 1846 because he did not possess the required educational standard. Jehiel Michael was admired in his community, but his relatively liberal rabbinical policy made him the object of sharp attacks from many quarters, especially from R. Solomon *Kluger. On his death Jehiel Michael was succeeded as rabbi of Brody by his son MEIR (1816–1886). Meir's grandson, ALEXANDER (1884–1942), was rabbi of Linz, Austria, and later, 1932–38, professor at the Israelitisch-theologische Lehranstalt, Vienna. He was the editor of *Traum und Traumdeutung im Talmud* (*Monumenta Talmudica* 4, 2 (1922) and *Die hebraeische Publizistik in Wien* (1930). He was deported to the Minsk ghetto in 1942 and died there.

BIBLIOGRAPHY: S. Buber, *Anshei Shem* (1895), 197:492; N.M. Gelber, in: *Arim ve-Immahot be-Yisrael*, 6 (1955), 165, 167, 301 and index.

[Itzhak Alfassi]

KRISTOL, IRVING (1920–), founder of neoconservatism. A gifted polemicist and savvy intellectual operator, Kristol exemplifies the intellectual odyssey from radicalism to liberalism to neoconservatism that took place among a number of New York Jewish intellectuals in the 20th century. As the husband of Gertrude *Himmelfarb, the historian who focused on Victorian morality, and the father of William *Kristol, a prominent second-generation neoconservative and editor of the *Weekly Standard*, he created the milieu in which the neoconservative movement has flourished.

Kristol grew up on New York's Lower East Side. He attended the City College of New York, where he devoted more energy to radical politics than his coursework. Kristol earned his B.A. in 1940 and went on to serve as a staff sergeant in the armored infantry in Europe in World War II.

Kristol shed his belief in radicalism during the war and in 1947 he began to work for a new magazine founded by the American Jewish Committee called *Commentary*. From 1953 to 1958 Kristol lived in London to co-edit the monthly *Encounter*, which was sponsored by the Congress for Cultural Freedom. From 1961 to 1969 he served as executive vice president of Basic Books before becoming a professor of social thought at the New York University Graduate School of Business.

In 1965, disconcerted by the renewed prominence of radical ideas in the United States, Kristol and his childhood friend Daniel *Bell launched a small quarterly called *The Public Interest*, a moderately liberal journal, and focused on social science. But as the Vietnam War further radicalized debates and black radicals attacked Israel's right to exist, Kristol kept moving to the right and by 1972 raised eyebrows in New York's intellectual community by voting for Richard Nixon. The socialist Michael Harrington dubbed Kristol and others "neoconservatives" – a term of opprobrium that Kristol soon embraced.

Neoconservatives such as Kristol did not oppose the welfare state, as did traditional conservatives, but believed that radicals were attempting to expand it into an American version of a socialist state. Kristol was an important advocate of the implementation of supply-side economic policy during the Reagan administration.

In the 1990s Kristol's unwavering support for Israel and concern about morality in the United States itself prompted him to espouse an alliance with Protestant evangelical leaders such as the Reverend Pat Robertson. Kristol and other neoconservatives believed that traditional Jewish apprehensions about evangelicals were grossly exaggerated. In their view, the true threat to the United States and Israel came from American liberals who were equivocal about using U.S. military power and overly eager to reach peace agreements with the Palestinians. Kristol sees the United States as imperiled by liberal impulses and in 1995 defended fundamentalists by noting that "their motivation has been primarily defensive – a reaction against the popular counter-culture, against the doctrinaire secularism of the Supreme Court, and against a government that taxes them heavily while removing all traces of morality and religion from public education…."

With the cessation of the *Public Interest* in 2005, Kristol largely retired from the intellectual battles that he fought for decades. But now that a new generation led by his son William is expanding the neoconservative crusade, Kristol's influence will likely remain undiminished.

[Jacob Heilbrunn (2nd ed.)]

KRISTOL, WILLIAM (1952–), U.S. lobbyist. Kristol, the son of Irving *Kristol and Gertrude *Himmelfarb, was the leader of a new neoconservative generation that focused its efforts on foreign policy. As the editor of the *Weekly Standard* and a commentator for Fox News, Kristol was a shrewd political operative who wielded considerable influence in the Republican Party. Kristol ensured that neoconservatism, whose demise had been predicted after the Soviet Union collapsed, remained a potent intellectual and political force. Where the older generation of neoconservatives focused on writing essays and books, Kristol was the first neoconservative media star.

Kristol, who was born in New York, did not experience the political conversion of his elders from liberalism to neoconservatism. He attended the Collegiate School for Boys in Manhattan before entering Harvard in 1970 where he studied under disciples of the German émigré philosopher Leo *Strauss, who emphasized the enduring wisdom of the ancient philosophers rather than what he viewed as facile doctrines of progress. At Harvard, Kristol drew on Strauss to denounce what he saw as left-wing relativism and passivity in the face of communist totalitarianism in Vietnam and elsewhere. Kristol went on to earn a Ph.D. in political science in 1979 at Harvard.

Upon graduation, Kristol taught at the University of Pennsylvania and Harvard's Kennedy School of Government, but his true love was politics. In 1972, he had organized the Harvard-Radcliffe Students for Senator Henry "Scoop" Jackson's abortive run for the presidency and in 1985 he served as chief of staff to Education Secretary William J. Bennett in the Reagan administration.

Kristol first came to public prominence when he served as vice president Dan Quayle's chief of staff in the first Bush administration and became known as "Quayle's Brain." Never himself a candidate for political office, Kristol was following the Straussian precept of serving as an intellectual advisor to the prince.

Kristol solidified his political base in 1995 when he met with the media mogul Rupert Murdoch, whose holdings include Fox Networks, and persuaded him to fund a magazine called the *Weekly Standard*. The magazine did not hit its stride until it focused on foreign policy. The shift toward foreign affairs began when Kristol and prominent neoconservative Robert Kagan insisted in a controversial 1997 *Foreign Affairs* essay upon a return to Ronald Reagan's aggressive foreign policy in order to achieve a U.S. "benevolent hegemony." It was a theme that would resound in the *Weekly Standard*, which viewed itself as the keeper of the Reagan flame. At the same time, Kristol and Kagan founded the Project for a New American Century (PNAC), which served as the braintrust for George W. Bush's crusading foreign policy doctrine.

Though Kristol had backed Senator John McCain during the 2000 GOP primary, he supported Bush wholeheartedly after the September 11 terrorist attacks. *The Weekly Standard* became the leading neoconservative voice explicitly endorsing the creation of an American empire. In essence, Bush, who had entered office as a cautious realist who shunned nation-building, seemed to espouse this neoconservative view as he launched the war in Iraq.

Whatever the outcome of the war, Kristol's will remain a leading voice in Republican debates about domestic and foreign affairs in coming decades. More than any other neoconservative, he has succeeded in wedding ideas to actual policies and aggressively promoting them in articles and on television.

[Jacob Heilbrunn (2nd ed.)]

KRIVOI-ROG, city in Dnepropetrovsk district, Ukraine. Jews settled there after the status of Krivoi-Rog was changed in 1860 from a village to a town. In the 1870s fine iron ores were found, and by 1900, 79 mines were operative. An iron foundry was built, the largest in Russia, and beside metallurgical industries, there also developed food and other factories. All these attracted many Jews, and they numbered 2,672 persons (17.9% of the population) in the town in 1897. The city was included in the Yekaterinoslav gubernia (region) which was also an important area of Jewish agricultural settlements. There were pogroms in October 1883 and on October 26, 1905, when four Jews lost their lives. By 1889 there was a synagogue, a *talmud torah*, and a school for girls, and in 1910, five Jewish public schools and four private. With the establishment of the Soviet regime, the community institutions were liquidated and Jewish communal life suppressed. In 1926 the Jewish population numbered 5,730 (18.3% of the population), doubling by 1939 to 12,745 (197,546 total population). Again in the 1920s the area served as one of the main regions of Jewish agricultural settlements. In 1929 beside the eight old Jewish colonies, there were 78 new settlements with a population of 28,000 persons and 21 Yiddish schools with 800 pupils. In 1924 there were 350 Jewish artisans, some of whom were organized in cooperatives, such as shoemakers, carpenters, bakers, and others. In the second half of the 1930s many Jews were absorbed as workers and clerks in the city industries. In the 1920s a Yiddish school existed but owing to negligence it was apparently closed. It was opened again in 1933 as a seven-year school, later to become a ten-year high school. In 1935 there were 220 pupils, 75 of them from the farms in the county. The Germans occupied Krivoi-Rog on August 14, 1941; many Jews escaped or were evacuated before then. The Jews were ordered to give up all their valuables and to pay a heavy ransom. At the end of August *Einsatzkommando* 6 killed 105 Jews. In the first 21 days of September another 86 were killed by the same unit. On October 14 about 4,000 Jews and 800 Soviet prisoners of war were gathered, taken to mine number 6, and murdered there, while infants were thrown alive into the mine. This was done by a unit from the 1st SS Infantry Brigade. According to official Soviet sources, 6,419 civilians were murdered. Krivoi-Rog was liberated on February 22–24, 1944. Many Jews returned to the city. The synagogue was closed in 1959. In 1970 the Jewish population was estimated at about 15,000. Most left in the 1990s but Jewish life revived.

[Yehuda Slutsky / Shmuel Spector (2nd ed.)]

KRIVOYE OZERO, in Odessa district, Ukraine. Only nine Jews were found there in 1765, but a Jewish community was established during the first half of the 19th century that numbered 1,116 in 1847 and 5,478 (70% of the total population) in 1897. At this time most of the stores in the town belonged to Jews, and the majority of artisans were also Jewish. Two Jewish colonies were in the vicinity. The Jews of Krivoye Ozero suffered severely in pogroms during the Civil War. On May 24, 1919, the area was attacked by a band of Ukrainians, who killed 300 Jews within several hours. In the same year, the soldiers of the Volunteer Army of General *Denikin struck twice, the first time killing 280 Jews and the second (end of December 1919) a few hundred more. The townlet was then abandoned by the majority of its inhabitants, who returned after the Soviets took the town in 1920. In 1926, there were 3,917 Jews (c. 94% of the population), and in the late 1930s dropped to 1,447. Many Jews worked in cooperatives and in a butter factory. There was a Yiddish school with 300 pupils, and a library with a large Yiddish collection. Instead of the colonies, a Jewish kolkhoz with 180 members operated until World War II. The Germans entered the town on September 2, 1941, and three days later 52 Jews were murdered. After the town was included in Romanian Transnistria, some hundreds of Jews were brought from Bukovina. In December they were confined within a ghetto; 184 Jews were killed in October, and 228 local Jews were murdered in January 1942. In late 1943 there were still 624 Jews in Krivoye-Ozero who probably remained alive until the liberation on March 29, 1944.

BIBLIOGRAPHY: M. Maidanik, in: *Reshumot*, 3 (1923), 264–310; PK *Romanyah*, 1 (1969), 507–8.

[Yehuda Slutsky / Shmuel Spector (2nd ed.)]

KROCH, JACOB LEIB BEN SHEMAIAH (1819–1898), talmudic scholar descended from a distinguished Prague family whose name was Korch. Kroch was born in Rawicz in Prussia (now Poland). In his youth he studied at the local yeshivah under Aaron Joshua Elijah b. Solomon who had been previously rabbi of Glogau and was rabbi of Rawicz from 1814 to 1846. At the age of 15, Kroch proceeded to the yeshivah of Jacob Judah *Falk in Dyernfurth. In 1837 Falk sent him to Akiva *Eger in Posen. The latter was exceptionally friendly to him and on his advice Kroch married Falk's elder daughter. While in his father-in-law's house, Kroch devoted all his time to study and continued to do so even after the latter moved to Breslau, although he used to spend an hour a day on business. In his studies Kroch specialized in particular on the subject of the conflict between *ḥazakah* ("presumption") and *rov* ("following the majority"). Later he went with his son Shemaiah, who had prospered in business, to Leipzig where he died. He was buried in Berlin.

Kroch published nothing during his lifetime. The mass of writing which he left behind was handed by his grandsons to R. Phinehas Jacob Kohn who managed to publish 11 volumes under the title *Ḥazakah Rabbah* (1927–61). The last volume (1963) as well as three volumes of the *Halakhah Rabbah* (1964–67) were published in Jerusalem by A. Krauss. The *Ḥazakah Rabbah* comprises no less than 1,170 *halakhot* on topics of *ḥazakah* and *rov* in the order of the Shulḥan Arukh. Two hundred and sixty principles of *ḥazakah* as well as other talmudic subjects were published in the *Halakhah Rabbah*. The whole series is amazing for its remarkable erudition as well as for its profundity.

BIBLIOGRAPHY: J.L. Kroch, *Ḥazakah Rabbah*, 1 (1927), introduction by P.J. Kohn; J.L. Kroch, *Halakhah Rabbah*, 2 (1966), introduction by A. Krauss.

[Adonijahu Krauss]

KROCHMAL, ABRAHAM (d. 1888), Galician-born scholar and writer. Very little is known of Krochmal's life. His birthdate is put between 1818 and 1823 and his birthplace identified as Brody or Zolkiew. He studied Jewish and rabbinic subjects with his father Nachman *Krochmal, with Solomon *Kluger of Brody, and with Ẓevi Hirsch *Chajes in Zolkiew and received a general education as well. He led a rather unsettled life, living precariously in Lemberg, Brody, Odessa, and finally in Frankfurt on the Main. In Galicia and Odessa he moved in Haskalah circles and was friendly with Peretz *Smolenskin and Moses Leib *Lilienblum.

Krochmal's scholarly interests encompassed Bible, Talmud, and philosophy. He regularly contributed to *He-Ḥalutz, Ha-Meliẓ, Ha-Maggid*, and other Hebrew periodicals; his articles are collected in *Aguddat Ma'amarim* (1885). His *Da'at Elohim ba-Areẓ* (1863) is a philosophy of history showing the influence of his father's writings and of the German idealistic philosophy of the 19th century; *Iyyun Tefillah* (1885) is a historical study on the God-man relationship; *Yerushalayim ha-Benuyah* (1867) contains interpretations of sayings of the Jerusalem Talmud; his *Ha-Ketav ve-ha-Mikhtav* (1873) is a collection of textual conjectures on the Bible, with a German translation; and *Theologie der Zukunft* (1872) is a critical-philosophical tractate on the justification of religious consciousness. Krochmal was a radical and rather unsystematic thinker. Strongly influenced by Spinoza, to whom he devoted his *Even ha-Roshah* (1871), by Kant, and, above all by his father, he saw in Judaism an ethico-cultural idea which had undergone a long historical development. The loss of statehood and diasporal existence was an important element in this development; but fundamental ethical and religious principles, such as the belief in one God, the love of one's neighbor, and the self-perfection of man, were preserved. Krochmal rejected the dogmatism of the medieval religious philosophers but recognized the sanctity of ritual and commandments as a means of moral education. At the same time he pleaded for reform. In his Bible and Talmud studies, too, he adopted a critical stance. He was the first to recognize Spinoza as the fountainhead of textual criticism of the Bible.

BIBLIOGRAPHY: Klausner, Sifrut, 4 (1954), 78–103; Waxman, Literature, 3 (1960²), 573ff.

[Getzel Kressel]

KROCHMAL, MENAHEM MENDEL BEN ABRAHAM (c. 1600–1661), chief rabbi of Moravia. A native of Cracow and pupil of Joel *Sirkes, in his youth he was already the leader of a circle of scholars which included Gershon *Ashkenazi (Uli), who later became his son-in-law and succeeded him as *Landesrabbiner*, and Menahem Mendel *Auerbach. From 1630 he attended the *Council of Four Lands and in 1636 became rabbi of Kromeriz (Kremsier). In 1646 he was in Cracow but became rabbi of Prostejov (Prossnitz) in the same year. Two years later he was elected rabbi of Mikulov (Nikolsburg), and *Landesrabbiner* of Moravia in 1650, an appointment he held until his death. Krochmal presided over several synods of Moravian Jewry and formulated the *Shai Takkanot* which regulated the organization of the Moravian communities until the 1848 revolution. His responsa *Ẓemaḥ Ẓedek* throw light on Jewish suffering during the Thirty Years' War (1618–1648), especially those dealing with **agunot* (nos. 42, 45, 57, 58, 59, 70, 78, 88, 101, 103, 106, 123, 127). Several responsa dealing with organizational problems in the communities (nos. 1, 2, 16, 18, 19, 24, 28, 34, 37, 109) reveal his independent attitude vis-à-vis plutocratic communal leadership and his sympathy with the poorer classes. A commentary on the Pentateuch, *Pi Ẓaddik* (Warsaw, 1884), is attributed to him. His son ARYEH JUDAH LOEB (d. 1684) became rabbi of Trebic (Trebitsch) at an early age in about 1660 and *Landesrabbiner* of Moravia in 1672. He was head of a large yeshivah in Mikulov. Aryeh had his father's responsa printed in Amsterdam in 1675 with his own additions.

BIBLIOGRAPHY: H. Gold, *Juden und Judengemeinden Maehrens* (1929), index; A. Frankl-Gruen, *Geschichte der Juden in Kremsier*, 1 (1896), 87–95; S.A. Horodezky, *Le-Korot ha-Rabbanut* (1910), 32–37; H.H. Ben-Sasson, *Hagut ve-Hanhagah* (1959), index; I. Halpern, *Takkanot Medinat Mehrin* (1952), index; Y.Z. Kahana, in: *Arim ve-Immahot be-Yisrael*, 4 (1950), 265–8.

[Meir Lamed]

KROCHMAL, NACHMAN (ReNaK; 1785–1840), philosopher, historian, one of the founders of the "science of Judaism" (*Wissenschaft des Judentums), and a leader of the *Haskalah movement in Eastern Europe. Krochmal was born in the town of Brody, Galicia. His father Shalom Krochmalnik maintained contact with Haskalah circles in Germany, particularly with

M. *Mendelssohn and D. *Friedlaender, and Krochmal himself attracted the luminaries of the Haskalah – S.J. Rapoport, I. Erter, S. Bloch, H.M. Pineles, J.H. Schorr, M.H. Letteris, and Z.H. Chajes – to the town of Zolkiew in Galicia, where he spent most of his life. He returned to Brody after his wife's death in 1836 and later settled in Tarnopol, where he died after a long illness.

Krochmal acquired his extensive education completely on his own. He devoted himself largely to philosophy and history. His chief inspiration in Jewish thought came from *Maimonides and Abraham *Ibn Ezra, and in general philosophy from Kant, Schelling, and Hegel. His interest in philosophy and history, however, was subservient to the central preoccupation of Krochmal's life, namely, the understanding of Judaism in its historical manifestation. This was summed up in his Hebrew *Moreh Nevukhei ha-Zeman* ("Guide of the Perplexed of the Time"), which was edited by L. Zunz and published posthumously in 1851 (critical edition by S. Rawidowicz, 1924; revised edition, 1961). Krochmal believed that his chief contribution should be made through teaching and discussion. Through verbal communication he exerted a decisive influence on his associates, and it was only at the insistence of his friends that he set down his views in writing.

Philosophy

Krochmal's lifework, *Moreh Nevukhei ha-Zeman*, was only partially devoted to pure philosophic speculation. Consisting of 17 chapters, the work may be divided into four sections: chapters 1–7 deal with issues in philosophy of religion and philosophy of history; chapters 8–11 provide a summary of Jewish history; chapters 12–15 contain an analysis of Hebrew literature by means of the critical-historical method; and chapters 16–17 present the nucleus of Krochmal's philosophy, which was never fully developed. Despite the absence of a systematic philosophical presentation, the direction of Krochmal's thought is evident. He belonged to the school of idealist philosophers (Schelling, Hegel), who regarded philosophic speculation as the proper vehicle for the final understanding of the nature of reality. Following *Hegel, he defined reality in itself as *ha-Ruḥani ha-Muḥlat*, "the Absolute Spirit," which in his opinion, corresponded to the concept of God in religious tradition. Krochmal speaks of the Absolute Being as "a power equal to every latent and potential form within itself," and this being he identifies with God. This definition reflects the tendency of post-Kantian idealistic philosophy to identify the Absolute Being with total acting power, whose essential nature is pure, unqualified cognition. The transition from the Absolute Reality to the generated reality of finite things, which for Krochmal corresponds to the religious concept of the creation of the world out of nothing, is explained by him as an infinite process of God's self-confinement, which must be described as a voluntary contingent act. Krochmal's exposition reflects the kabbalistic notion that the world is created by divine self-confinement, and by identifying the "nothing" out of which the world was created with God, as did the kabbalists, Krochmal draws the conclusion that God created the world out of Himself.

In contrast to the major idealistic philosophers Schelling and Hegel, Krochmal was not content with accounting for the overall derivation of finite reality from the Absolute. He concentrated on determining the relationship of religion and philosophy in respect to their relationship to the Absolute Spirit. Krochmal based his religious philosophy on the premise that the Absolute Spirit is the exclusive subject of human knowledge. Religion by its very nature is knowledge, no less than philosophic knowledge. Therefore, the difference between philosophy and religion is not one of essence but merely of form or degree. Religious belief and philosophic understanding are different degrees of comprehending the Spirit. The first is the level of "ideas of incipient thought," or the understanding of reality by means of images, whereas the second is the level of the "ideas of mind and intellect," or the understanding of reality by means of concepts and ideas. Since the intellectual understanding is more general than that of images, philosophy imparts to religion (religious belief) a greater and more complete value. Krochmal assumed that in presenting philosophy as the higher means of understanding religious truth, he was continuing the view accepted by medieval philosophers, especially Maimonides, that the Torah encourages philosophic speculation, and contains within itself, at least potentially, philosophic truth. All religious faith is based upon the Spirit, and thus there is no essential difference between the various faiths. Nevertheless the biblical faith is unique in its purity and the universality of its imagery.

Philosophy of History

Krochmal's philosophy of history is based on the assumption that history, like all products of human civilization, depends upon its spiritual content. Each nation has its own spiritual principle which is the foundation of its existence, and its life and continuity is determined by the extent to which it directs itself toward that principle. In order to understand the internal, concrete structure of the history of nations, Krochmal turned to the evolutionary method of the philosophy of history of Vico and Herder, according to which the history of every nation can be divided into three periods: growth and development, vigor and enterprise, and decline and annihilation. The various factors – economic, intellectual, and cultural – determining the life of a nation must be analyzed in the light of these periods. However, Krochmal being an idealist, subjects these factors – without adequate clarification – to the metaphysical principle of the Spirit: "The substance of a nation lies not in its being a nation, but in the substance of the Spirit therein."

Krochmal attempted, by thorough historical analysis, to establish as an empirical fact that the history of the people of Israel has the same threefold structure as that of other peoples. The Jewish people differs from all other nations, whose existences are transitory, in being eternal. Krochmal explains that this eternity is caused by a special relation existing between the Jewish people and God, the Absolute Spirit, and that this is lacking in the case of other nations. This relation was at its strongest in the revelation on Mt. Sinai and in Israelite prophecy. In spite of its special character, Krochmal does not believe that the people of Israel transcend history; its eternity is assured by a continuous renewal of national life. With this concept of the earthly and metaphysical elements of Israel and the belief in the necessity of renewing the creative national forces following a period of spiritual stagnation, Krochmal became the forerunner of modern nationalist-Zionist philosophy of history.

Contribution to the "Science of Judaism"

Krochmal was one of the first scholars investigating Judaism to propose the method of historical investigation "for the purpose of recognizing our essence and our nature." With this he helped to lay the foundation of "the science of Judaism." While his method differed from that of the historical school represented by L. Zunz, A. *Geiger, and H. *Graetz, because he maintained that only philosophy can reveal the "ultimate purpose" of history, he also insisted that historical analysis must apply the evolutionary method in studying Judaism.

Halakhah

Krochmal's particular, and perhaps most important, contribution lies in his application of this method to the study of Hebrew literature. Especially noteworthy is his study of *halakhah* (*Moreh*, ch. 13) and *aggadah*. In his study of *halakhah* Krochmal had two basic aims: the interpretation of the Oral Law by establishing its origin in antiquity and the description of its development from its beginnings until its codification and publication by the sages of the Talmud. In reference to the antiquity of the Oral Law, Krochmal's position held that the fact that the Law was given to an entire nation required that its specific laws and customs be expounded only in a general way. The central theme of the evolution of *halakhah* is interpretation, namely, the systematic and logical development of the content of the Written Law. This approach determined Krochmal's position on the overall nature of the *halakhah*. Since only the fundamental laws were given verbally to Moses on Mt. Sinai, there can be no essential difference between the subsequent three phases of *halakhah*, which are the direct transmission of tradition from person to person, the deduction of new laws, and the formulation of ordinances, strictures, and customs (*takkanot, gezerot, minhagim*). But despite the unity of the *halakhah*, it is nonetheless possible to discern the stages of its development. Thus, Krochmal systematically studied the development of the *halakhah* from the *soferim*, who were chiefly concerned with interpreting the written law in response to religious questions, through the *shonei ha-halakhot*, who expanded the Oral Law by means of exegetical rules, to the final phase of the organization and editing of the *halakhah* by the late *tannaim*. While Krochmal owed much to various other scholars, he emerged as the mentor to later talmudic scholars, for example, Z.H. Chajes, A.H. *Weiss, and I. *Halevy.

Aggadah

Krochmal also applied the evolutionary method to his study of *aggadah*, although without the systematic approach of his study of *halakhah*. *Aggadah* grew out of the moral-didactic need to bring biblical ideas to the people. Its chief concern lies in the thought content of the Bible, but it does not attempt to interpret it conceptually. *Aggadah* is popular philosophy, and the parables that deal explicitly with God, the world, man, history, and Israel are its best exponents. The intellectual substructure of *aggadah*, not its stylistic exterior, reveals the essential ideas of Jewish philosophy, which, in turn, are nothing but the conceptual interpretation of the truths contained in the Torah. According to Krochmal, the development of Jewish thought from Philo to Mendelssohn is an integral process, a *philosophia perennis*, subdivided into various periods according to degree of conceptual purity.

BIBLIOGRAPHY: Guttmann, Philosophies, 365–91; N. Rotenstreich, *Jewish Philosophy in Modern Times* (1968), 136–48; S. Schechter, *Studies in Judaism* (1896), 46–72; Rotenstreich, in: *Keneset*, 6 (1941), 333–44; idem, in: *Zion*, 7 (1942), 29–47; Guttmann, in: *Keneset*, 6 (1941), 259–86; P. Lachover, in: *Sefer Bialik* (1934), 74–98; I. Schorsch, in: *Judaism*, 10 (1961), 237–45; J. Taubes, *ibid.*, 12 (1963), 150–64; S. Spiegel, *Hebrew Reborn* (1962), index.

[Moshe Schwarcz]

KROCK, ARTHUR (1886–1974), U.S. journalist and newspaper editor. As a Washington columnist, Krock knew and reported on every president from William Howard Taft to Lyndon Johnson. Born in Glasgow, Kentucky, he first went to Washington in 1909 to report for the *Louisville Times* and the *Louisville Courier-Journal*. In 1915 he became editorial director of both newspapers and served as editor in chief of the former from 1919 to 1923. In 1918–19 his articles on the Versailles Peace Conference were widely syndicated, and he played an important role in persuading the conference to hold meetings in public. In 1927 Krock began a 40-year association with the *New York Times*, first as a member of its board of editors, then from 1932 to 1953 as its Washington correspondent, and from 1953 to 1967 as a Washington commentator. He wrote the column "In the Nation" for 32 years before he retired from the *New York Times* in 1966.

His memoirs, entitled *60 Years on the Firing Line*, were published in 1968. His early recollections, *Myself When Young: Growing Up in the 1890s*, came out in 1973. A keen observer of the national scene, he won two Pulitzer Prizes for outstanding reporting (1935, 1938), a special Pulitzer commendation (1951), and a special Pulitzer citation (1955). Regarded as one of the most influential American journalists of his time, Krock was awarded the Medal of Freedom by President Nixon in 1970, the highest civilian honor in the United States.

Other books by Krock include *In the Nation: 1932–1966* (1966); *Memoirs: Intimate Recollections of Twelve American Presidents from Theodore Roosevelt to Richard Nixon* (1970); and *The Consent of the Governed, and Other Deceits* (1971).

[Irving Rosenthal / Ruth Beloff (2nd ed.)]

KROJANKER, GUSTAV (1891–1945), German author and Zionist editor. Born in Berlin, Krojanker studied economics in the universities of Berlin and Munich. Under the direction of the economist Lujo Brentano he published his dissertation *Die Entwicklung des Koalitionsrechts in England* in 1914. He began his Zionist activity at the age of 18 among Jewish students, editing a collection of essays *Der zionistische Student* (1912) and their paper *Der juedische Wille* (1918–19). After serving in the German army in World War I he was active in the German Zionist movement as a writer, publisher, editor, and translator. Taking a liberal Zionist position, he participated in the controversial debate on the role of the Jews in German culture and literature by editing an important work titled *Juden in der deutschen Literatur* (1922, repr. 1926), including essays on the young generation of German-Jewish writers from Paul *Adler and Albert *Ehrenstein up to Franz *Kafka, Else *Lasker-Schüler and Arnold *Zweig. In 1920 he became the literary director of the Zionist publishing house Welt-Verlag, later also working for the *Juedischer Verlag and co-editing the papers *Der Jude*, *Juedische Rundschau*, and *Juedische Revue*. Krojanker studied Hebrew and began to publish essays on Hebrew literature, first in German and later in Hebrew. He also traveled to Poland to research the problems of East European Jewry. He was among the first to recognize the danger to the Jews and Zionism posed by the post-liberal nationalism, as he argued in his widely discussed essay "Zum Problem des neuen deutschen Nationalismus; eine zionistische Orientierung gegenueber den nationalistischen Stroemungen unserer Zeit" (1932). Krojanker settled in Palestine in 1932; was active in the Aliyah Ḥadashah Party, established by immigrants from Germany; and contributed essays on Hebrew literature to *Haaretz* (particularly on the works of Shemuel Yosef Agnon and Joseph Ḥayyim Brenner) and to the Hebrew newspaper of the Aliyah Ḥadashah *Ammudim*, which he also edited. At the same time he translated Hebrew literature into German (S. Ben Zion, *Die Bilu auf dem Wege* and *Die Bilu am Ziel*, 1935); collected and wrote an introduction to the speeches of Chaim Weizmann from 1901 to 1936, *Reden und Aufsaetze* (1937); and published a number of pamphlets in German and Hebrew on the question of *aliyah* from Germany, *Aliyah ve-Yeridah ba-Yahadut ha-Germanit* (1937), and *Ha'avarah, The Transfer* (1936; capital transfer of immigrants from Nazi Germany to Palestine).

BIBLIOGRAPHY: H. Tramer, in: BLBI, 7 (1964), 264; A. Schenker, *Der juedische Verlag* (2003).

[Getzel Kressel / Andreas Kilcher (2nd ed.)]

KROMERIZ (Czech **Kroměříž**; Ger. **Kremsier**), town in central Moravia, Czech Republic. The Jewish community of Kromeriz was among the oldest in Europe. In 1322 the bishop of *Olomouc (Olmuetz) was permitted to allow one Jew to settle in the town, exempt from servitude to the royal chamber (*servi camerae regis). A community under the protection of the bishop grew up soon after; it remained under the protection of the successive bishops until 1848, and the synagogue and community house displayed the episcopal coat of arms, with a cross and cardinal's hat. In the 1340s a Jew sued a gentile before the town court. In 1546, the Jews moved to another part of the town because of conflicts with their neighbors. In 1642, during the Thirty Years' War, the community was destroyed by the Swedes, an event mourned in several contemporary *seliḥot*. Kromeriz absorbed many refugees from the *Chmielnicki massacres (1648) and eight families expelled from Vienna settled there under the bishop's protection (1670). In 1676, 27 Jewish families lived in the town. In 1689 Kromeriz was considered the most important and most affluent Moravian community after *Mikulov (Nikolsburg) and from then until 1697 it was the seat of the country rabbinate. However, during the 18th century the community became impoverished and many left. After protracted legal proceedings (begun in 1785) the community had to give up the site of its old cemetery in 1882; a new one had been opened in 1850. Following a *blood libel there was unrest in the town in 1889 and again in 1896. In 1910 a new synagogue was dedicated. In Kromeriz, under the *Familiants Law there were 106 families (546 persons) in 1829; 783 Jews lived there in 1880, 611 in 1900, and 390 in 1921. In 1930 the community numbered 382 (12% of the total population). After the Nazi occupation (1939) *sheḥitah* was forbidden. The Czech population paid little attention to the antisemitic laws promulgated in 1940. However, the Nazis attempted to blow up the synagogue; the community was deported in 1942, and the synagogue equipment sent to the Central Jewish Museum in Prague. After the Holocaust a small congregation was reestablished, affiliated to *Kyjov. A total of 268 Jews perished in the Holocaust.

The scholars Joseph Weiss and Emanuel *Baumgarten were natives of Kromeriz. Among rabbis who served there were Menahem Mendel *Krochmal (1636–42), Issachar Berush *Eskeles (1710–19), and the historian Adolf *Frankl-Gruen (1877–1911).

BIBLIOGRAPHY: D. Kaufmann, *Die letzte Vertreibung der Juden aus Wien*... (1889), 181–5; A. Frankl-Gruen, *Geschichte der Juden in Kremsier*, 3 vols. (1896–1901); H. Gold (ed.), *Juden und Judengemeinden Maehrens* (1929), 295–300; I. Halpern, *Takkanot Medinat Mehrin* (1952), 128–35, 148–57; W. Mueller, *Urkundliche Beitraege* (1903), 58–60; PK.

[Meir Lamed]

KRONECKER, HUGO (1839–1914), Swiss physiologist, pioneer in the study of blood pressure. Born in Silesia, Kronecker was a pupil of the famous pathologist Ludwig Traube and the physicist Helmut Helmholtz. This influenced his approach to the field of physiology, in particular his work on reflex action and animal heat. In his studies of the cardiac muscle, Kronecker discovered the coordinating center of the heart and the importance of inorganic salts for the heartbeat. His experiments led him to the invention of appliances for blood transfusion, a perfusion cannula, the phrenograph, the frog-heart manometer, and other equipment. After his conversion to Christianity Kronecker was appointed professor of physiology at the University of Berne, Switzerland, in 1884. His dynamic personality and his keen powers of observation and dissertation justly gave him the reputation of one of the leading physiologists of his time. Among his publications were *Beitraege zur Anatomie und Physiologie* (1874) and *Haller Redivivus* (1902). From 1881 to 1884 he was editor of *Centralblatt fuer die medizinischen Wissenschaften*.

BIBLIOGRAPHY: S.R. Kagan, *Modern Medical World* (1945), 185; R.H. Major, *A History of Medicine*, 2 (1954), 901–2.

[Suessmann Muntner]

KRONECKER, LEOPOLD (1823–1891), German mathematician. He was born in Liegnitz, brother of Hugo *Kronecker. Following the death of his uncle, a successful banker, Kronecker entered the business world. He prospered and was able to retire after eight years and devote the remainder of his life to the study of mathematics. In 1883 he was appointed professor at Berlin. Kronecker insisted that the concept of "continuity" was meaningless and mathematics can only discuss discrete quantities. He is reputed to have said "God made the integers, all the rest is the work of man." Despite his friendship with the famous mathematician K.T.W. Weierstrass, Kronecker attacked him for including the concept of irrationals in his development of analysis. He became imbued with enthusiasm for Christian theology and was converted to Christianity in the last year of his life. Kronecker's main contributions were in number theory, elliptic functions, and algebraic numbers. His theory of algebraic magnitudes made a fundamental contribution to the modern theory of commutative fields. Kronecker's entire work was edited by K. Hensel in five volumes (1895–1931).

BIBLIOGRAPHY: E.T. Bell, *Men of Mathematics* (1937), 519–37.

[Barry Spain]

KRONENBERG, wealthy banking family of Jewish origin in Warsaw. The founder SAMUEL LEIZER (d. 1825), who left Wyszograd for Warsaw when the latter was still under Prussian rule, was at first a successful money changer. In 1822 he founded a bank, managed by his widow after his death. While giving his son a traditional education, he also sent him to a Catholic school for his general education. His son LEOPOLD (Leibel, 1812–1878) was prominent in the assimilationist circle of the Warsaw community. An ambitious man, he sought power both in economic life and in politics. To this end, he first became connected with the Polish "Red" group which supported revolution to bring about the revival of Poland; later, with the intention of becoming reconciled with the Russian authorities, he turned to the moderate "White" group. Although he apostasized in 1846, he did not break off relations with Jewish society and continued to intercede on behalf of the Jews with the authorities, who regarded him as the perfect assimilationist. The scope of his manifold activities was extensive and he succeeded in gathering around him a wide circle of financiers, industrialists, merchants, scholars, and political and public figures, among whom Jews were prominent as his closest advisers. An astute merchant, he succeeded, by granting loans and developing the monopoly of the tobacco industry, in attracting the allegiance of both Jews and Poles, who considered his achievements as steps toward the independence of Poland. The Russian authorities also regarded him as one of their supporters, believing that his practical awareness would prevent him from becoming involved in revolution.

Kronenberg leased government factories and organized the distribution of their goods. He established sugar factories, and developed the glass industry, tube-rolling works, coal mines, and a shipping company. By means of a consortium of Jewish bankers and Polish aristocrats, in 1869 he defeated his rivals and won the concession to extend the existing railroad network between Warsaw and Vienna in the direction of Germany and of Russia. Chairman of the merchants' union and president of the stock exchange commission, in 1870 he participated in the founding of the Commercial Bank of Warsaw. In 1859 he played an active role in the Warsaw affair known as the "Jewish War," the expression of the struggle of antisemitic circles (through the channels of the newspaper *Gazeta Warszawska*) against the influence of assimilationist Jews on Polish culture and art. Kronenberg founded a rival newspaper, *Gazeta Polska*, and he invited the famous Polish author, Kraszewski, an antisemite, to become its editor. Although the new newspaper made no serious contribution to the improvement of the relations between Jews and Poles, it prejudiced the status of the rival antisemitic organ. As a result of his initiative and investments, the Higher School for Commerce was founded in Warsaw in 1875. According to his will, the institution was committed to admitting pupils without any distinction of religion. During his last years, Kronenberg was prominent as an exponent of positivism.

His eldest son STANISLAW (1846–1894) enlisted in the French army during the Franco-Prussian War (1870). He became president of the Commercial Bank and secured the official establishment of the Scientific Fund, the first institution of its kind in Poland. For a while, he published the weekly *Nowiny*, which showed little sympathy toward the Jews. Leopold's second son, Baron JULIUS (1849–1930), was a composer and a member of the Russian Senate, in which he represented the curia of Polish nobility. He liquidated his father's bank. A third son, WLADYSLAW (d. 1892), was an engineer and industrialist.

BIBLIOGRAPHY: *Leopold Kronenberg, monografia zbiorowa* (1922); J. Shatzky, *Geshikhte fun Yidn in Varshe*, 3 vols. (1947–53), indexes; A. Levinson, *Toledot Yehudei Varshah* (1953), index; A. Haftke, in: EG, 1 (1953), 225–8; R. Mahler, *Ha-Ḥasidut ve-ha-Haskalah* (1961), 227–8, 252, 285; S. Lastik, *Z dziejów oświecenia żydowskiego* (1961), index.

[Moshe Landau]

KRONENBERGER, LOUIS (1904–1980), U.S. dramatic and literary critic and author. Kronenberger, who was born and educated in Cincinnati, Ohio, was a relative of Isaac Mayer *Wise, the founder of American Reform Judaism. He first worked in publishing in New York, joined the editorial staff of *Fortune* magazine in the mid-30s, and from 1938 to 1961 was drama critic of *Time* magazine. In 1953 he became professor of theater arts at Brandeis University, where he also served as librarian for a time. Kronenberger's books include *Marlborough's Duchess* (1958); a study of English stage comedy, *The Thread of Laughter* (1952); *The Republic of Letters* (1955); and critical essays on American society, notably *Company Manners* (1954) and *The Cart and the Horse* (1964). He also wrote the novels *The Grand Manner* (1929) and *A Month of Sundays* (1961). He compiled several prose and verse anthologies and edited a number of English classics as well as a series of plays, great letters, and masters of world literature. His best-known work is *Kings and Desperate Men* (1942), a study of life in 18th-century England. Kronenberger's reflections about his career can be found in his *No Whippings, No Gold Watches; The Saga of a Writer and His Jobs* (1970).

BIBLIOGRAPHY: S.J. Kunitz (ed.), *Twentieth Century Authors*, first supplement (1955), incl. bibl; *Contemporary Authors*, first revision (1967), incl. bibl.

[Milton Henry Hindus]

KRONER, RICHARD (1884–1974), German philosopher. He was professor at Dresden, Kiel, and Frankfurt universities. After Hitler's rise to power, he emigrated to the U.S., and became professor at the (Protestant) Union Theological Seminary in New York, and later at the theological school of Temple University. Kroner was editor of the philosophical quarterly *Logos* from 1910 to 1938. He revived interest in Hegel's philosophy, which was unknown and even scorned at the time. His book *Von Kant bis Hegel* (2 vols., 1921–24) was a brilliant analysis of German idealism, which in Kroner's opinion had reached its peak in Hegel. Kroner was the initiator and chairman of the First International Hegel Congress at The Hague in 1931. Kroner's *Die Selbstverwirklichung des Geistes* (1928; *Culture and Faith*, 1951) attempted to explain the structure of human culture in one comprehensive system. He also wrote *The Primacy of Faith* (1943), *How Do We Know God?* (1943), *Selbstbesinnung* (1958), and *Speculation and Revelation in the History of Philosophy*, 3 vols. (1956–61).

BIBLIOGRAPHY: S. Marck, *Die Dialektik in der Philosophie der Gegenwart* (1929), 56ff.; H. Levy, *Die Hegel-Renaissance in der deutschen Philosophie* (1927), 80–84; S.H. Bergman, *Anashim u-Derakhim* (1967); idem, in: *Haaretz* (June 5, 1953).

[Samuel Hugo Bergman]

KRONER, THEODOR (1845–1923), German rabbi and teacher. Kroner, who was born in Dyhernfurth, was rabbi in Muenster (1869); director (1872) of the Jewish Teachers' Seminary at Muenster; *Landesrabbiner* of Saxony-Weimar (1883); rabbi of Erfurt; and rabbi of Stuttgart (1893). He was active in Jewish educational and welfare activities and founded the Verein israelitischer Kultusbeamten Mitteldeutschlands. His publications include *Geschichte der Juden in Erfurt* (1884); *Geschichte der Juden von Esra bis zur Jetztzeit* (1899); *Die Juden in Wuerttemberg* (1899); and *De Abrahami Bedaresii vita et operibus* (1868). He also edited several popular and pedagogical journals. On his 70th birthday, his colleagues published a *Festschrift* in his honor (1917).

BIBLIOGRAPHY: *Israelitisches Familienblatt*, 17:18 (May 6, 1915), 3.

[Jacob Hirsch Haberman]

KRONIK (Kornik, Karnik), MOSES BEN AKIVA (first half of 19th century), rabbi and author. He wrote *Tefillah ve-Todah* (Breslau, 1814), a collection of hymns and prayers for the Jewish community of Glogau, Lower Silesia, to commemorate the lifting of a siege on April 24, 1814. This was published both in Hebrew and in Meyer Neumark's German translation. Kronik's most important book is *Yemin Moshe* (Breslau, 1824), a homiletic work of 17 *she'arim* ("gates," chapters), each of which opens with a poem suggesting the themes to be treated. The themes, ethical and religious, include the love of God, *teshuvah* ("repentance"), and slander. In the concluding chapters Kronik deals with the problem of philosophic and scientific research and faith, holding that the results of such research must be compatible with faith. Moreover, he believed that everything discoverable by research can be found in the Torah. *Evel Yaḥid*, an elegy on the death of Abraham Tiktin, the rabbi of Glogau, appears in the appendix of the work.

BIBLIOGRAPHY: S. Wiener, *Kohelet Moshe*, 15 (1904), 600, no. 4889.

KRONISH, LEON (1917–1996), U.S. Reform rabbi and Zionist leader. Kronish was born in New York and received his B.A. from Brooklyn College in 1936. He studied under Mordecai *Kaplan at the Jewish Theological Seminary (1937–38) and then attended the Jewish Institute of Religion (JIR), where he was ordained by Stephen *Wise in 1942. HUC-JIR awarded him an honorary D.D. degree in 1967. He served as an associate rabbi at Huntington Jewish Center, Long Island, New York (1941–44) before moving to Miami Beach on a self-proclaimed mission to bring a Zionist and Jewish presence to "the American Negev." He realigned a 40-member storefront Conservative congregation, the Beth Sholom Center, with Reform Judaism, renamed it Temple Beth Sholom, and it grew into a leading center of Jewish worship and culture in the South, with a membership exceeding 1,200 families. Kronish actively campaigned to weaken discriminatory practices and change laws throughout south Florida that were antisemitic and racially biased. He also campaigned for the separation of church and state in Miami's public schools and challenged Miami Beach residents, nearly three-quarters Jewish, to adopt a policy of permitting the busing of African-American children from black neighborhoods to Miami Beach schools.

The *Six-Day War was a watershed for Kronish, who expounded his ideas in two articles: "*Yisrael Goralenu*"("Israel is Our Destiny," 1968) and "The Zionist Mitzvot" ("The [Ten] Zionist Commandments," 1977). Under his motto "Bring Israel to America and America to Israel," he became the personality most identified with the "Israelization" of Reform Judaism. Kronish was a founding member of the *Association of Reform Zionists of America (ARZA) in 1977 and was instrumental in creating permanent committees on Israel for the *Central Conference of American Rabbis – which he also chaired – and for the *Union of American Hebrew Congregations (UAHC). He advocated that individual congregations establish Israel committees and supported the launching of Reform kibbutzim. He called on Jews to visit Israel, to link with Israeli families, and respond politically when Israel is in need. He endorsed a policy that required entering rabbinical students to spend their first year in Israel and lobbied for the resolution that the CCAR would host conventions in Israel. In south Florida, Kronish led the effort for El Al to fly to Miami and for the Israeli government to open a consulate there. He initiated a national program for students to study in Israel for a semester and receive American educational credits. All during this time (1970–85), Kronish also served on the Board of Governors of the Hebrew University of Jerusalem.

Through leadership roles in the *Labor Zionist movement and the State of Israel Bonds Organization, Kronish forged close relationships with Israeli leaders Golda Meir, Abba Eban, and Yitzhak Rabin. He assisted in the founding of the Histadrut Foundation of the United States (1965), and served Israel Bonds as chairman of its rabbinic cabinet in the 1970s and national chairman in the early 1980s. In recognition of his fundraising, Kronish was awarded the Prime Minister's Anniversary Medal on the occasion of Israel's silver anniversary in 1973. Kronish Plaza in Miami Beach and the Leon Kronish Memorial Lecture sponsored by HUC-JIR in Jerusalem honor his myriad contributions.

BIBLIOGRAPHY: H.A. Green, *Gesher Vakesher, Bridges and Bonds: The Life of Leon Kronish* (1995).

[Bezalel Gordon (2nd ed.)]

KROOK (Gilead), DOROTHEA (1920–1989), English literary scholar. Krook was born in Riga, Latvia, but immigrated to South Africa with her parents in 1928. After graduating in English literature at Cape Town University, she attended Newnham College, Cambridge, and spent 14 years in Cambridge as a lecturer. Her most famous student was Sylvia Plath, the iconic American-born poet; Plath regarded Krook as one of her most significant role models. In 1960 Krook immigrated to Israel, where she taught at the Hebrew University and was appointed associate professor in 1963. In 1971, she was appointed full professor of English literature at Tel Aviv University. Krook is the author of *The Ordeal of Consciousness in Henry James* (1962), and she is regarded as an authority on the author. In 1969, she published The *Elements of Tragedy* (Hebrew ed. translated by A. Yavin, 1971), in which she portrays the Aristotelian vision of tragedy which she traces in the works of Ibsen and Chekhov, and it is particularly for this work that she was awarded the Israel Prize in 1973, and in 1974 was elected a member of the Israel Academy of Sciences and Humanities. Krook wrote an essay-length introduction to the first Hebrew translation of *The Portrait of a Lady* by Henry James (*Diyuknah shel Geveret*, Mosad Bialik, 1978), entitled *"El P'nei Goral Savukh"* ("Facing a Complex Fate"). Her "Recollections of Sylvia Plath" appeared in *Edward Butscher (ed.), Sylvia Plath: The Woman and Her Work* (1977). In 1968 she married the Hebrew poet Zerubavel *Gilead, and was a member of Kibbutz En-Ḥarod.

KROSHNER, MIKHAIL YEFIMOVICH (1900–1942), composer. Born in Kiev, Kroshner studied piano from 1918 to 1921 in Kiev (with Blumenfeld), Moscow, and Sverdlovsk. From 1931 he studied composition with Zolotaryev, with whom he moved to Minsk in 1933, graduating from the Minsk conservatory in 1937. Kroshner collected Belorussian folklore and used folk tunes in his compositions. His ballet *The Nightingale* (1939) was the first Belorussian national ballet and was successfully staged in Minsk, Moscow, and Odessa. Unable to escape from Minsk before the German occupation in 1941, he perished there a year later. Among his major works are the cantata *The Drowned Man, Symphonic Dances*, a string quartet, songs, and arrangements of Jewish folk songs for voice and piano.

BIBLIOGRAPHY: NGG²; A. Livshits, "Pervyi belorusskiy balet Solovey M. Kroshnera," in: *Sovetskaya muzyka*, 11 (1939), 75–80; D. Zhuravlev: "Kroshner, M.," in: *Belorusskaya entsiklopedia literatury i iskusstva* (1986).

[Marina Rizarev (2nd ed.)]

KROSNO, town in Rzeszow province, S.E. Poland. Jewish presence in Krosno is mentioned before 1434. In spite of the privilege *de non tolerandis Judaeis* granted to the town by King Sigismund II Augustus (1548–72), Jews were allowed to settle there as tenants of taverns, leading to a complaint by the inhabitants to the authorities in 1655. As Jews from the neighboring towns of *Rymanow and Dukla visited the annual fairs of Krosno, disregarding the prevailing prohibition, the municipal council issued an order that the robbing and even the murder of a Rymanow Jew was to go unpunished. The restrictions on Jewish residence in the town were not abolished until 1860. With the development of the oil and petroleum industry, there was increased economic activity in the town and vicinity. In 1880 the Jewish community of Krosno numbered 327 (12% of the total population), while there were 4,612 Jews (6.6%) in the whole district; in 1900 there were 961 (22%) in the town and 5,839 (7.2%) in the district, rising to 1,559 (28%) in the town and 6,253 (7.2%) in the district in 1910, and 1,725 (27%) in the town and 4,861 (6%) in the district in 1921. At that time there were 55 Jewish workshops in Krosno. Between the two world wars Krosno Jews were engaged in petty trade, weaving, tailoring, and shoemaking. During this period antisemitism increased and economic boycotts were common. Before World War II 2,500 Jews lived in Krosno with another 5,870 in nearby smaller places.

Holocaust Period

The Germans arrived on September 9, 1941. In August 1942 they executed the sick and old and then deported 1,000 Jews to the Belzec death camp. Another 300–600 were put in a ghetto and sent to work in the nearby airfield and quarries. On December 4 they were deported to *Rzeszow, where they shared the fate of the local Jews.

BIBLIOGRAPHY: I. Schiper, *Studja nad stosunkani gospodarczymi żydów Polsce podczas Śedniowiecza* (1911), index; idem, *Dzieje handlu żydowskiege na ziemiach polskich* (1937), index; B. Wasiutyński, *Ludność żydowska w Polsce w XIX i XX wiekach* (1930), 96, 107, 115; *Kortshin – Sefer Yizkor* (Yid., 1967); E. Podhorizer-Sandel, in: BŻIH, 30 (1959). **ADD. BIBLIOGRAPHY:** J. Garbacik, *Krosno, Studja z dziejow miasta i regionu* (1975); PK.

[Stefan Krakowski]

KROSS, ANNA (née **Moscowitz**; 1889–1979), U.S. lawyer, penologist, and penal administrator. Born in Nesheves, Russia, she studied law at New York University. As a student, she became interested in prisoners and penal reform, and volunteered for work visiting prisons. In 1933 she was appointed to the bench in New York City as a magistrate, the first woman judge in the city magistrate court. She was reappointed in 1940 and again in 1950. In 1946 she organized and became the first presiding magistrate of the Home Term Court of the Borough of Manhattan, an experimental social court dealing with the problems of troubled families. She initiated the development of psychiatric and guidance services to assist the court in dealing with severely disturbed families. During her 20 years in court, Kross fought the injustice of the bail system, by which suspects, some of them innocent, were kept under arrest because they could not afford bail or the bondsman's fee. In 1954 she was appointed commissioner of correction of the City of New York, serving until her retirement in 1966 at the age of 75. During her 12 years in this office, she endeavored to apply progressive ideas in correctional treatment in the system she administered. She conceived, planned, and established the reception and classification center on Rikers Island. This became the focus of a system designed to rehabilitate offenders by social casework, psychotherapeutic treatment, constructive recreational activities, academic and vocational education, guidance, and aftercare. She founded Friendly Visitors, Inc., a group of volunteers at the New York City House of Detention for Women dedicated to helping released prisoners adjust to life outside prison through vocational and educational programs and to help promote community acceptance of former inmates.

ADD. BIBLIOGRAPHY: M. Wylie, *400 Miles from Harlem: Courts, Crime, and Correction* (1972).

[Zvi Hermon / Ruth Beloff (2nd ed.)]

KROTO, SIR HAROLD WALTER (1939–), U.K. chemist and Nobel laureate. He was born in Wisbech, Cambridgeshire, the son of refugees from Nazi Germany. When he was one year old, his family moved to Bolton, Lancashire, where he was educated at Bolton School. He graduated with a B.Sc. (1961) from the University of Sheffield where he also gained his Ph.D. with a thesis on the spectroscopy of free radicals under the supervision of Richard Dixon (1964). After postdoctoral research with the National Research Council of Canada in Ottawa (1964–66) and Bell Laboratories, Murray Hill, New Jersey (1966–67), he joined the department of chemistry of the University of Sussex where he became professor (1985–91) and Royal Society Research Professor (1991). He later worked in the department of physics, chemistry, and environmental science of the University of Sussex. His main research interest was spectroscopy and its application to the study of carbon molecules in many research areas. He and his colleagues founded the field of fullerene science after their discovery that some carbon molecules (C_{60}) self-assemble spontaneously at high temperatures into spheres resembling the Geodisic Dome designed by Buckminster Fuller. The crucial collaborative work was completed over ten days in 1985. The appearance and symmetrical composition of these macromolecules are aesthetically appealing to organic chemists and laymen alike. His later research involved the rapidly expanding field of fullerenes, radioastronomy, the evolution of carbon-based molecules, and the implications for virology, biological systems, and the origins of life on Earth and possibly elsewhere in the universe. Kroto was awarded the Nobel Prize in chemistry (1996) with Robert Curl and Richard Smalley. Subsequently Kroto and his colleagues established the University of Sussex as a major center in the growing field of nanotechnology that seeks to analyze and simulate the microarchitecture of biological structures. Kroto had a deep interest in science education in schools and universities and was the founding co-chairperson of the Vega Trust, a non-profit organization for producing programs for scientific education. His many honors included election to the Royal Society of London, the Longstaff Medal of the Royal Society of Chemistry (1993), the Royal Society's Copley Medal (2004), and a knighthood. Krota also had a great interest in graphic design and his awards in this field included winner of the *Sunday Times* book jacket design competition (1994) and the Louis Vuitton Science pour l'Art Prize (1994). Krota was a humanist and a strong supporter of human rights and organizations such as Amnesty International.

[Michael Denman (2nd ed.)]

KROTOSZYN (Ger. **Krotoschin**), town in the province of Poznan, Poland. The Jewish community was established in the 14th century, and by virtue of an ancient privilege allowing the Jews to trade, engage in crafts, and build houses, the community prospered. The privilege was reissued in 1638 by the owners of the town, and ratified and extended in 1648 and in 1673. In the course of the wars which ravaged Poland in the 17th century, the Jews suffered severely. Polish troops headed by the hetman *Czarniecky murdered 350 Jewish families out of 400 in Krotoszyn in 1656 during the war against the Swedes. Later the Jewish community recovered and its representatives filled important functions in the *Councils of Four Lands. Especially notable were Avigdor b. Abraham Katz, who in 1671 took part in the negotiations with Cristof Bressler of Breslau concerning the debt owed him by the Polish Jews, and Leibel b. Mordecai, who was one of the representatives of Polish Jewry in 1691. Riots broke out in 1704 and Jewish property was looted. A fire in 1774 destroyed the Jewish quarter, including the 16th-century synagogue, the *bet midrash*, and the library. Before the fire the Jews numbered 1,384 (37.5% of the total population). In the 18th century there were wealthy Jews of the town who traded with Germany and attended the fairs in Breslau, Leipzig, and Frankfurt on the Oder. A permanent representative of Krotoszyn, Leibel b. Baruch, stayed in Breslau at the beginning of the century to manage the business of the Jewish merchants during the fairs. The community regulations were fixed in 1728 by decree of the provincial governor, Potocki. The annexation of Krotoszyn to Prussia on the 1793 partition of Poland had critical results for the town's economy: the large Polish market was lost when the other parts of Poland were annexed to Austria and Russia. However, the Jews managed to thrive until the mid-19th century. A new synagogue was built in 1846. In 1849 the Jewish population numbered 2,327 (about 30% of the total). From then on the numbers of Jews declined and in 1910 only 411 (about 3%) remained. Jews from Krotoszyn settled in other places in Germany. Jewish public life in Krotoszyn ceased completely when the town passed to independent Poland after World War I. The number of Jews diminished to 112 (less than 1%) in 1921 and 50 in 1939.

Krotoszyn was known as a center of Jewish learning and scholarship. Shabbetai *Bass, the rabbis Menahem Mendel b. Meshullam Auerbach, author of *Ateret Zekenim*, Moses Jekutiel Kaufmann, author of *Leḥem ha-Panim*, and Benjamin b. Saul Katzenelbogen were active there. In the 19th century the scholars David *Joel and Eduard *Baneth served as rabbis in Krotoszyn.

[Shimshon Leib Kirshenboim]

Hebrew Printing

In 1833 Dov Baer (Baer Loeb) Monash (1801–1876) set up a press in Krotoszyn which was active until 1901. Monash had learned the trade (and obtained the Hebrew type) from *Dyhernfurth. The most important books printed by him were a five-volume Pentateuch with Onkelos, Rashi, *haftarot*, and German translation by Johlson (1837); a 12-volume Bible with Onkelos, Rashi, and German translation (1839–43); and a *maḥzor* (*Minḥah Ḥadashah*, 1838). The Hebrew press in Krotoszyn was known through its edition of the Jerusalem Talmud which has become standard (1866–67). The most beautiful production of this press was Isaac *Aboab's *Menorat ha-Ma'or*, with German translation by Fuerstenthal and Behrend (1845–48). Here also were printed – though not in Hebrew – 17 volumes of the **Monatsschrift fuer Geschichte und Wissenschaft des Judentums* (1869ff.).

Holocaust Period

Before the outbreak of World War II Krotoszyn had only 17 Jews. Under Nazi occupation, the town belonged to the district of Posen of the Warthegau. On November 21, 1939, the remaining Jews were deported to the Lodz ghetto.

[Danuta Dombrowska]

BIBLIOGRAPHY: L. Lewin, in: MGWJ, 77 (1933), 464ff.; Posner, in: *Aresheth* 1 (1949), 260–78; D.D. Dąbrowska, in: BŻIH, 13–14 (1955). **ADD. BIBLIOGRAPHY:** H. Berger, *Zur Geschichte der Juden in Krotoschin* (1907).

°**KRUG, WILHELM TRAUGOTT** (1770–1842), German philosopher. While professor of philosophy at Leipzig University, Krug supported the complete *emancipation of German Jewry; indeed, the term itself became common through his *Ueber das Verhaeltnis verschiedener Religionsparteien zum Staate und ueber die Emanzipation der Juden* (1828). In his next work, *Die Politik der Christen und die Politik der Juden in mehr als tausendjaehrigem Kampfe* (1832), he demanded that freedom of occupation, mixed marriages, and instruction in common be permitted as a means of ending the eternal feud between Jews and Christians. Krug, who also demanded full equality for Catholics and all sectarians, striving for the fusion of all religions, actively sponsored his proposals in the Saxonian Diet and encouraged Bernhard *Beer and other leaders in their demands for emanicipation.

BIBLIOGRAPHY: V. Eichstaedt, *Bibliographie zur Judenfrage* (1938), index.

KRUGER, BARBARA (1945–), U.S. conceptual artist. Born in Newark, New Jersey, Kruger studied at Syracuse University (1964–65) and the Parsons School of Design (1965–66), where her teachers included the photographer Diane *Arbus and Marvin Israel, a graphic designer and an art director of *Harper's Bazaar* in the early 1960s. After a year Kruger stopped taking classes and began to work as a designer at *Mademoiselle* magazine. Kruger's early forays into the artworld included experimentation with fiber art and then painting large abstract canvases. The mid-1970s were an important period of transition when she became interested in feminist criticism and theoretical writings by such authors as Roland Barthes. She also began writing poetry, reviewing films, and taking photographs. In 1978 Kruger published *Picture/Readings* (1978), a book of photographs of California residential buildings accompanied by narratives describing her imaginings of the inhabitants' thoughts and activities. This interest in photographs and text initiated the works for which she is best known.

Her experience as a graphic designer influences her economy of means and the direct confrontation of her signature style: a format of glossy black and white found photographs, cropped and enlarged, overlaid with catchy phrases and surrounded by a red metal frame. Indeed, through a juxtaposition of text and image Kruger uses photographs to examine, question, and exploit power relations – frequently gender and consumer – in such works as the photo-montage *Untitled (Your Gaze Hits the Side of My Face)* (1981, private collection). The black and white words of the work's title are glued on the left side of this appropriated image of a woman's profile. The terse caption employs an accusatory tone directed at the masculine viewer (Your) who has objectified the woman (My) for centuries. Starting in 1985 Kruger also created lenticular images.

By placing two photographs behind a lenticular lens screen the images shift depending on the viewer's angle, allowing Kruger to make works that employ two messages and to create an illusion of three-dimensionality. Kruger's political messages can be found in traditional gallery spaces as well as in the more general public domain, including postcards, posters, t-shirts, and billboards.

BIBLIOGRAPHY: C. Squiers, "Diversionary (Syn)tactics: Barbara Kruger Has Her Way with Words," in: *ArtNews* (1987), 76–85; B. Kruger, *Barbara Kruger* (1988); K. Linker, *Love for Sale: The Words and Pictures of Barbara Kruger* (1990); B. Kruger, *Barbara Kruger* (1990); B. Kruger, *Barbara Kruger* (1999).

[Samantha Baskind (2nd ed.)]

KRULEWITCH, MELVIN LEVIN (1895–1978), U.S. soldier. Born in New York City, Krulewitch was a sergeant in the U.S. army in France during World War I. After practicing law for several years he returned to the army when the Japanese attacked Pearl Harbor, rejoining the Marine Corps as an officer. During World War II Krulewitch was the first to fly the American flag on Japanese territory. He was decorated for meritorious service at Iwo Jima. He was awarded the Bronze Star with Clusters; the Purple Heart; a Presidential Unit Citation; and the Naval Unit Citation. He also received a Special Commendation Ribbon of the secretary of the Navy.

He was a military observer in Israel in 1948 and in Korea in 1950. He retired in 1956 with the rank of major general, the highest-ranking Jewish officer in the U.S. Marine Corps. He was one of the founders of the World Boxing Council (1963) and served as chairman of the New York State Athletic Commission.

Krulewitch wrote *Now That You Mention It: Memoirs from the Halls of Montezuma to the Madison Square Garden Ring by Way of Old New York and the State of Israel* (1973).

[Ruth Beloff (2nd ed.)]

°**KRUSHEVAN, PAVOLAKI** (1860–1909), Russian journalist who became notorious in connection with the *Kishinev pogroms of April 1903. Krushevan began to publish the newspaper *Bessarabets* in 1897 in Kishinev, the capital of the province of Bessarabia. Though at first liberal, the newspaper soon became the mouthpiece of the province's reactionary circles, the Russian landowners and merchants, and received support from the government. The publication of all other newspapers was prohibited in Bessarabia. The newspaper conducted a violent campaign against the Jews, accusing them of exploiting the Christian masses and encouraging revolution. After the bankruptcy of the *Bessarabets*, Krushevan, assisted by friends, published a new paper *Drug*, which had a similar policy. In February 1903 he headed a group of agitators trying to whip up a *blood libel around the death of a Christian child of *Dubossary who in fact was murdered by a gentile. The bloody pogroms in Kishinev on Passover 1903 broke out as a direct consequence of his inflammatory articles. Continuing his agitation with even greater vehemence, he rapidly became a central figure in antisemitic circles and began to publish the newspaper *Znamya* in St. Petersburg. His series of articles on "The Program for the Conquest of the World by the Jews" formed the nucleus of the Protocols of the Learned *Elders of Zion. In June 1903 Krushevan was stabbed by the Zionist student Pinḥas *Dashewski but was only slightly wounded. Elected to the Second Duma in 1907 as a delegate of the *Union of the Russian People, he had an undistinguished parliamentary career.

[Yehuda Slutsky]

KRUSTPILS (Ger. **Kreuzburg**), town in Latgale district, Latvia; until World War I in the Vitebsk province. The community, which was first in Latgale district, was organized in the late 17th century. There were 2,156 poll-tax payers living in Krustpils and the communities under its jurisdiction in 1765. The Jewish population numbered 1,090 in 1847, 3,164 (76.31% of the total) in 1897. During World War I the town was almost destroyed, and the Jewish population dropped to 1,149 (35.76%) in 1930, and 1,043 (28.52%) in 1935. Most were occupied in commerce and crafts. The "old synagogue" was noted for its mural decoration. In 1925 Jews ceased to be a majority on the city council, and in 1930 lost the position of town mayor. There was a Jewish school, attended by 206 children in 1928. During World War II, shortly after the German attack on the Soviet Union in June 1941, a few hundred Jews succeeded in escaping to the interior of the Soviet Union. The Germans, with the collaboration of Latvian auxiliary police, murdered the Jews in Krustpils and the vicinity during the fall of 1941. In 1966 a monument was erected to the memory of the Jewish martyrs in the Holocaust. The Jewish population was estimated at approximately 100 in 1970.

BIBLIOGRAPHY: *Congress Weekly* (Dec. 4, 1942), 9–13; Gar, in: *Algemeine Entsiklopedie*, 6 (1963), 375–94. **ADD. BIBLIOGRAPHY:** Dov Levin (ed.), *Pinkas Hakehillot, Latvia, Estonia* (1988).

[Joseph Gar / Shmuel Spector (2nd ed.)]

KRYGIER, RIVON (1957–), French rabbi. Born in Brussels, Krygier was active in the Ha-Shomer ha-Ẓa'ir youth movement until his *aliyah* to Jerusalem in 1977. There he was a student at the Hebrew University and at the Ma'ayanot Institute of Jewish Studies led by the nonconformist French rabbi Leon Askenazi. Krygier was the first French-speaking rabbi to graduate from the Schechter Institute, the Jerusalem branch of the Jewish Theological Seminary of America. In 1991 he became the rabbi of the first *masorti* (Conservative) congregation in France, the Adath Shalom synagogue in Paris. With a doctorate from the Sorbonne in religious sciences, he became an important figure in Jewish intellectual debate in France through his lectures and writings, notably in *La loi juive à l'aube du XXIème siècle* (preface by Charles Mopsik, 1995), a collection of responsa published in Hebrew by Conservative rabbis on issues of modern life and translated into French for the first time; *À la limite de Dieu: l'énigme de l'omnniscience divine et du libre-arbitre humain dans la pensée juive* (his doctoral thesis,

1998); *Epitre de l'amour* (an adaptation of Rabbi Eliot Dorff's study of human sexuality as perceived in Jewish sources, 2000), *Epitre de la vie* (an adaptation of Rabbi Jonathan Wittenberg's study of Jewish attitudes towards mourning).

[Philippe Boukara (2nd ed.)]

KRYMOV, YURI (Yuri Solomonovich Beklemishev; 1908–1941), Russian author. The son of a publisher, Krymov was an industrial engineer. His novel *The Tanker "Derbent"* (1938; Eng., 1944), which was set in the Caspian region, was one of the very few successful Soviet works describing labor heroism. Critics praised its ideological message, while ordinary readers welcomed its believable characters and their human foibles. Krymov, who also wrote *Inzhener* ("The Engineer," 1941), was killed in action early in World War II.

KRYNKI (also **Krinki**), town in the province of Bialystok, N.E. Poland. Jews settled in the town during the first half of the 17th century, and by the middle of the century there was already an organized community in Krynki, subordinate to that of Grodno. The royal charter granted to the Jews of Krynki in 1662 authorized them to erect a synagogue, maintain a bathhouse and cemetery, and gave them the right to purchase municipal building plots, houses, and to plow land, own inns, and distill brandy. Such a liberal charter aroused the opposition of the townspeople, but by a compromise of 1669, they agreed to recognize the status of the local Jews, and these documents were confirmed by King Augustus III in 1745. In order to encourage Jewish commerce, the king ordered the market day to be changed from Saturday to Thursday. In 1680 the Jews paid 150 zlotys in poll tax. The Council of the Land of Lithuania convened in Krynki in 1687. The 1765 census recorded 1,285 poll-tax paying Jews in the town and the surrounding villages.

In 1827 Jewish contractors opened a heavy-wool textile factory, which gave employment to many Jewish workers. There were 1,846 Jews living in the town in 1847. As a result of a succession of fires in 1879, 1882, and 1887, many Jews were ruined and compelled to emigrate. In 1864 Jewish contractors opened tanning workshops and in the 1890s expanded their trade to markets in central Russia (also supplying for the army), Poland, and Germany. About 400 tannery workers founded the Po'alei Ẓedek Union, one of the first Jewish labor unions in Russia, in 1894. In 1897 the Jewish population numbered 3,542 (71% of the total). Just before and during the 1905 Revolution, several political parties were active in the town: the *Bund (c. 250 members), the Social Revolutionaries, and the Anarchists, and from 1905 the *Po'alei Zion. A Jewish worker from Krynki, Sikorski, took part in the attempt on the life of the Russian minister of the interior, V.K. von *Plehve. When the disorders of the 1905 Revolution subsided, the Jewish factory owners and merchants of Krynki organized the Aguddat Aḥim, which led the struggle against the local labor movement. From 1903 an Aguddat Zion group was active in the town, and in 1908 a Ẓe'irei Zion circle was established. During the intermediary period which followed the departure of the German military authorities (autumn 1918), a Jewish revolutionary workers' council seized power in the town. In 1921, the Jewish population of Krynki numbered 3,495 (67% of the total population), of whom about 800 workers were employed in local tanning factories. Jewish delegates constituted a majority in the municipal council, one holding the office of deputy mayor. From 1919 a Hebrew *Tarbut school and a CYSHO school functioned in the town, and from 1923 a private Hebrew secondary school, and there were also *Maccabi and *Bar Kochba sports clubs. Between the two world wars, branches of all the Jewish parties were to be found in the town; the most powerful were the Bundist circles, the Po'alei Zion, the *Ha-Shomer ha-Ẓa'ir, and the *Agudat Israel.

[Arthur Cygielman]

Holocaust Period

There were around 4,000 Jews in Krynki in 1939. During the period of Soviet rule (1939–41), Jewish life changed considerably: the community institutions were dispersed and petty trade was severely restricted, although the Jews continued to play an important role in the leather factory that supplied the whole of Soviet Belorussia. Jewish refugees from German-occupied western Poland found refuge in the city, but most of them were deported to the Soviet interior in the summer of 1940. Krynki was captured by the Germans on June 28, 1941, and on the same day about 30 Jews were shot outside the city. On July 1, 1941, the synagogues were set aflame and burned down with the Torah scrolls still inside. A ghetto was established in December, and disease and starvation claimed many lives. In the spring 1,200 Jews arrived from Brzostowica Wielka, causing a second outbreak of typhoid in the overcrowded ghetto. On November 2, 1942, the Jews were transferred to the Kelbasin transit camp and from there to Treblinka. A group of craftsmen was concentrated in a work camp and was deported to *Auschwitz in June 1943. The last rabbi of Krynki, Hezekiah Joseph Myszkinski, who was elected in 1922, perished in the Holocaust.

[Aharon Weiss]

BIBLIOGRAPHY: D. Rabin (ed.), *Pinkas Krinki* (1970); S. Dubnow (ed.), *Pinkas ha-Medinah* (1925), index; A. Margolis, *Geshikhte fun Yidn in Rusland 1772–1861* (1930), 280; E. Ringelblum, *Di Poylishe Yidn in Oyfshtand fun Kaściuszko 1794* (1937), 198; H. Katz-Blum, *Zikhroynes fun a Bundist* (1940), 148–50; B. Wasiutyński, *Ludność żydowska w Polsce w wiekach XIX i XX* (1930), 83; *Ha-Ẓefirah* (April 16, 1912); *Lite*, 1 (1951), 181; *Regesty i nadpisi*, 3 (1913); Yu. Hessen, in: *Yevreyskaya Letopis*, 4 (1926), 46; Kh. Korobkov, in: *Yevreyskaya Starina*, 4 (1911), 555.

KRZEPICE, town in Kielce province, S. Poland. Jewish presence in Krzepice is attested to as early as 1633. In 1730 a synagogue was built. The 1765 census recorded 116 Jewish poll tax payers in Krzepice and vicinity. A separate Jewish quarter, Nowokrzepice (New Krzepice), was founded in 1795 and a synagogue established. Between 1823 and 1862 the Russian authorities restricted Jewish emigration from the interior of the country into Krzepice since the town was located on the Prussian border. The synagogue, which existed until World War II, was built in pseudo-classical style with frontal columns. The community numbered 322 (21% of the total population) in 1808, increasing to 876 (43%) in 1827, and 1,057 (49%) in 1857. In 1897 their number had grown to 1,395 (43%) and in 1921 to 1,772 (43%). Apart from shopkeeping, the Jews made their living as tailors, hatters, carpenters, and locksmiths.

[*Encyclopaedia Judaica* (Germany)]

Holocaust Period

The Germans captured Krzepice on Sept. 1, 1939, and within a few weeks a fine ("contribution") of 20,000 zlotys was imposed upon the Jewish community; the confiscation of Jewish property also began. In March 1940 the transport of Jewish youth to forced-labor camps began and continued at an accelerated rate throughout 1941. In June 1942 the large majority of the Jews were transported to *Auschwitz. Some tried to escape and found temporary refuge in the Czestochowa ghetto. After the deportation of June 1942, only a few families of artisans remained in the city, and they were later transferred to the Sosnowiec ghetto.

[Aharon Weiss]

BIBLIOGRAPHY: K.S. Muznerowski, *Krepice w przszłosci* (1914); M. Baliński and T. Lipiński, *Starożytna Polska*, 2 (1845), index; Lódź, Wojewódzkie Archiwum Państwowe, *Anteriozia piotrkowskiego rządu gubernskiego*, nos. 2517–19; R. Mahler, *Yidn in Amolikn Poyln in Likht fun Tsifern* (1958), index; B. Wasiutyński, *Ludność żydowska w Polsce…* (1930), 30. **ADD. BIBLIOGRAPHY:** "*Tavnit Sefer Zikaron le-Kehilat Kshepitz ve-ha-Sevivah*," in: *Sefer Klobuck* (1960), 222, 264, 266.

KUBA, city in N.E. Azerbaijan. From the 17th century, there was an important community of *Mountain Jews in Kuba. In 1734, during the military expedition of *Nadir Shah from Persia, many communities in the vicinity of Kuba were destroyed and many Jews were compelled to adopt Islam. The rest settled in Kuba where they were under the protection of Gussein, the ruler of the town. Large numbers of Jews fled to Kuba from *Baku when a *blood libel was raised there in 1814. For many years the Jews in Kuba maintained separate communities, constituted according to their towns of origin. Many of the Jews were engaged in agriculture. There were 5,492 Jews in the town in 1837, 6,662 (43.5% of the total population) in 1897, and 5,200 in 1926. During the Civil War (1918–20) in the north Caucasus the Jewish community suffered greatly. It is probable that the greater majority of the 8,357 Jewish inhabitants of Azerbaijan who declared Tat as their mother tongue in the 1959 census were living in Kuba. In 1970 it was estimated that about 10,000 Tat Jews lived in the town. Most left in the 1990s.

BIBLIOGRAPHY: J.J. Chorny, *Sefer ha-Massa'ot* (1884); G. Levi, in: *Voskhod Weekly*, 21:46 (1901), 21–22.

[Yehuda Slutsky]

KUBIE, LAWRENCE (1896–1973), U.S. psychiatrist and psychoanalyst. Kubie graduated from Harvard in 1916 and received his M.D. from Johns Hopkins University in 1921. Later he received a National Council research fellowship in neurology in London. From 1930 to 1959 he practiced psychoanalysis in New York, at the same time serving on the faculties of various institutions, including the College of Physicians and Surgeons, the New York Psychoanalytic Society, Columbia University, the Yale School of Medicine, the Neurological Institute, and Mount Sinai Hospital in New York. At the time of his death he was emeritus lecturer in psychiatry at Johns Hopkins University and a consultant in psychiatric research and training at Sheppard and Enoch Pratt Hospital in Towson.

Kubie's first published work was *Practical and Theoretical Aspects of Psychoanalysis* (1936) and his later studies include *Neurotic Distortion of the Creative Process*. In addition, he served for a period as editor of the *Journal of Nervous and Mental Disorders* and published a large number of papers dealing with the employment of hypnotic trance as a treatment and diagnostic method (with Milton H. Erickson) and (with S.G. Margolin) with psychotherapy aided by sedative drugs. In 1965, he called for a total reversal of the training of psychiatry, which should begin with the study of the child. Kubie was described by his colleagues as an orthodox Freudian analyst who constantly challenged orthodoxies, including his own. It was conceded, nevertheless, that his heterodox views, originally scorned, have now been incorporated into analytic theory. However, he deplored trends in psychiatry that distracted the psychiatrist from direct therapeutic care of the patient.

BIBLIOGRAPHY: O. Fenichel, *The Psychoanalytic Theory of Neurosis* (1945), 609, 633.

[Louis Miller (2nd ed.)]

KUBLIN, HYMAN (1919–), U.S. historian. Born in Boston, Kublin was professor of history at Brooklyn College, N.Y., from 1961, and associate dean of Graduate Studies (1966–69) at the City University of New York. A specialist in Far Eastern history, notably that of modern Japan, Kublin made important contributions to this field. These include *Meiji Rode Undo-shi No Hito-Koma; Takano Fusataro No Shogai to Shiso*, a study of Fusataro Takano, the founder of the Japanese trade-union movement; and *Asian Revolutionary: The Life of Sen Katayama* (1964) on an architect of modern Japan's socialist and communist movements. Kublin was consultant on Asian affairs to various universities, foundations, government agencies, and cultural groups. He was actively identified with Jewish affairs as chairman of the American Student Program to Israel and participation in many other bodies. Kublin served as *Encyclopaedia Judaica* departmental editor for the history of Jews in Japan.

Other books by Kublin include *India: Regional Study* (1973) and *The Middle East (World Regional Studies)* (with D. Peretz, 1989). In the Regional Study series he also wrote about Africa, Russia, China, and Japan. He edited *Jews in Old China: Some Western Views* (1971).

[Oscar Isaiah Janowsky / Ruth Beloff (2nd ed.)]

KUBOVY (Kubowitzki), ARYEH LEON (1896–1966), Zionist leader, Israel diplomat, and writer. Born in Kurshany, Lithuania, Kubovy received a traditional Jewish education in his native town, and a secular education in Belgium, where he settled with his parents in his childhood. He became a prominent lawyer and leader of Belgian Jewry up to the outbreak of World War II. He was a leading figure in the anti-Nazi *boycott movement in the 1930s. When Nazi Germany occupied Belgium in 1940, Kubovy went to the U.S. and from there directed the *World Jewish Congress rescue work for European Jewry, later becoming WJC secretary-general. He submitted rescue plans to the allied governments and to the pope. In 1948 he went to Israel and became its minister to Poland and Czechoslovakia. He served there during the difficult years of the early 1950s, when both countries followed the Soviet antisemitic policy, and was declared *persona non grata* during the *Slansky trial. He was Israel minister (later ambassador) to Argentina and minister to Chile and Paraguay in 1953–58. In 1959 he was elected chairman of the *Yad Vashem Remembrance Authority, the leading institution in research on the Holocaust, and served in this capacity until his death in Jerusalem. Kubovy was the author of several books, among them the history of the World Jewish Congress, *Unity in Dispersion*. A Festschrift in his honor *Im Eshkaḥekh ha-Sho'ah; Ne'umim ve-Harẓa'ot* appeared in 1967.

His wife MIRIAM (née Goldstein; 1898–?) was a writer. She was active in women's organizations and wrote in French and Hebrew.

BIBLIOGRAPHY: A. Weiss, in: *Yad Vashem Bulletin*, no. 19 (1966), 3–7; A. Tartakower, *ibid.*, 8–10; N. Eck, *ibid.*, 11–17.

[Alexander Tobias]

KUBRICK, STANLEY (1928–1999), U.S. film producer and director. Born in the Bronx, New York, Kubrick worked as an apprentice photographer at *Look Magazine* at the age of 17. He made his first feature film, *Fear and Desire*, in 1953, and his first moneymaking film, *The Killing*, in 1956. He aroused much controversy with films such as *Paths of Glory* (1958), on the stupidity of war, and *Spartacus* (1960). In the early 1960s he moved to England, where he led a reclusive life, co-founded the Directors Guild of Great Britain, and made all his subsequent films. These included the provocative film *Lolita* (1962); *Dr. Strangelove* (Oscar nomination for Best Picture, 1963), an anti-military establishment movie; the sci-fi film *2001: A Space Odyssey* (1968), which was widely considered to be a major work; the disturbing and very violent *A Clockwork Orange* (Oscar nomination for Best Picture, 1971); the period piece *Barry Lyndon* (Oscar nomination for Best Picture, 1975); *The Shining* (1980); the Vietnam war film *Full Metal Jacket* (1987); and the erotic thriller *Eyes Wide Shut* (1999). In 1993 Kubrick began work on the futuristic film *Artificial Intelligence: AI* but died before he could complete it. Steven Spielberg finished the film, which was released, ironically, in 2001.

Voted the 23rd Greatest Director of All Time by *Entertainment Weekly*, Kubrick was the least prolific of the lot. However, although he made only 16 films during his 48-year career, his impact on the film industry and on his audiences was profound. Kubrick's films are characterized by a common theme of dehumanization and a demonstration of the dark side of human nature. All his films except his first two (*Fear and Desire* and *Killer's Kiss*, 1955) were adapted from novels. He produced, directed, and wrote the screenplay for the majority of them. Among his countless awards, Kubrick won an Oscar for Best Visual Effects for *2001: A Space Odyssey* and was nominated for 12 other Academy Awards for writing, producing, and/or directing.

BIBLIOGRAPHY: C. Kubrick, *Stanley Kubrick: A Life in Pictures* (2002); M. Herr, *Kubrick* (2000); P. Duncan, *Stanley Kubrick* (1999); F. Raphael, *Eyes Wide Open: A Memoir of Stanley Kubrick* (1999); V. Lobrutto, *Stanley Kubrick: A Biography* (1997); T. Nelson, *Kubrick: Inside a Film Artist's Maze* (1992).

[Ruth Beloff (2nd ed.)]

KUDROW, LISA (1963–), U.S. actress. Born in Encino, Calif., Kudrow graduated from Vassar College with a bachelor of science degree in biology. She began her acting career after studying improvisational comedy beginning in 1987 with a theater company in Los Angeles called the Groundlings. She got small parts on several television series before being cast as an absent-minded, eccentrically silly waitress named Ursula Buffay in the series *Mad About You*. This led to a starring role in 1995 on the television series *Friends* as Phoebe Buffay, Ursula's ditzy twin and bitter rival who was also a waitress and folk singer. Kudrow's was one of several major characters, including one played by David *Schwimmer, in the most successful comedy series of that period. Kudrow, who won an Emmy award for best supporting actress in a comedy series in 1998, has had a number of serious film roles as well as comedic ones. Among her films are *Romy and Michele's High School Reunion* (1997), *The Opposite of Sex* (1998), and *Analyze This* (1999). In addition, in 2005 she was co-creator, executive producer, and writer of *The Comeback*, in which she portrayed Valerie Cherish, a former television star trying to make a comeback.

[Stewart Kampel (2nd ed.)]

KUENEN, ABRAHAM (1828–1891), Netherlands theologian and biblical critic. Although Julius *Wellhausen is generally acclaimed as the chief exponent of the so-called literary-critical school, earliest scientific espousal of its essential theses must be ascribed to Kuenen, along with Karl H. *Graf. Graf's contribution is little known because of his early death. Kuenen's work went unrecognized because most of it remained untranslated from Dutch. The central proposition of the Kuenen-Graf-Wellhausen school is that the religion of the early Hebrews developed along slow evolutionary lines, from patriarchal totemism to prophetic and priestly monotheism. This depends on the documentary hypothesis concerning the composition of the Hexateuch which assigns its material, in respective chronological order, to the Jahwistic (J), Elohistic (E), Deuteronomistic (D), and Priestly (P) documents. Earlier in the nineteenth century, the last of these documents (combined with E) had been held to be the first chronologically; the revolutionary insight of Graf and Kuenen was that P was post-Exilic. Kuenen's work, *De Godsdienst van Israël* (2 vols., 1869–70; *The Religion of Israel to the Fall of the Jewish State*, 1873), was the earliest full-length, scientific exposition of this thesis. Although later biblical critics made improvements and modifications in this scheme, its essential outlines are still widely accepted. Born in Haarlem, Kuenen became professor of New Testament, Ethics, and Old Testament Interpretation at Leiden. Strongly opposed to Calvinist orthodoxy and supernatural revelation, he was one of the influential leaders of the rising modernist movement, whose vigorous anti-traditionalism was strongly motivated by the dominant rationalism and empiricism of the nineteenth century. Kuenen produced an impressive list of scientific articles, monographs, and reviews. In addition to *The Religion of Israel*, his major works were *De Profeten en de Profetie onder Israël* (1875; *Prophets and Prophecy in Israel* 1877), *Volksgodsdienst en wereldgodsdienst* (1882), and *Historisch-kritisch onderzoek naar het ontstaan en de verzameling van de Boeken des Ouden Verbonds* (3 vols., 1861–65; *An Historico-Critical Inquiry into the Origin and Composition of the Hexateuch…*, 1886).

BIBLIOGRAPHY: K. Budde, *Gesammelte Abhandlungen zur biblischen Wissenschaft von Dr. Abraham Kuenen* (1894); S.J. de Vries, *Bible and Theology in the Netherlands* (1968); idem, in: JBL, 82 (1963), 31–57; Toy, in: JQR, 4 (1892), 571–605; H.J. Kraus, *Geschichte der historisch-kritischen Enforschung des Alten Testaments* (1956), 229–35. **ADD. BIBLIOGRAPHY:** S. DeVries, in: DBI, 2:38–39.

[Simon J. De Vries]

KUFA (Al-Kūfa), town on the banks of the Euphrates in central *Iraq, founded by the Muslims in 638. Kufa was at first a military camp, but rapidly became an important Muslim religious and cultural center, especially from the time of the reign of Caliph Alī ibn Abū Ṭālib. From the ninth century onward a decline gradually set in so that only a few ruins remain. During the geonic period there was a large Jewish community, among whose members were the teacher Solomon b. Joseph ha-Kohen and Mūsā ibn Isrā'īl (Moses b. Israel) al-Ṭabīb ("the physician") al-Kūfī. This community is also mentioned in the letters of R. *Samuel b. Ali. Benjamin of Tudela, the 12th-century traveler, found about 7,000 Jews living there. After this time there is no further confirmation of the presence of Jews in the town. According to ancient Jewish traditions, the tomb of King Jehoiachin was situated in Kufa. A large construction stood over the tomb and a synagogue alongside of it.

BIBLIOGRAPHY: A. Ben-Jacob, *Yehudei Bavel* (1965), 51. **ADD BIBLIOGRAPHY:** "al-Kūfa," in: EIS², 5 (1986), 345–51 (includes bibliography).

[Abraham Haim]

KUGEL, ḤAYYIM (1897–1966), Czechoslovakian pioneer of Hebrew education. Born into a *Ḥovevei Zion family in Minsk (Belorussia), Kugel was sent for his secondary education to the Tel Aviv Gymnasium, Herzlia. The outbreak of World War I (1914) prevented his return to Tel Aviv; he continued his studies in Russia and from 1920 at Prague University. In Prague he founded a club called Ivriyyah which later became part of the Tarbut organization, and pioneered the teaching of living Hebrew and founding of Hebrew schools in Czechoslovakia. After completing his studies, he moved to Mukachevo where in 1924 he founded the Hebrew high school Ha-Gimnasyah ha-Ivrit. In 1935 Kugel was elected along with Angelo *Goldstein to the Czechoslovak parliament on behalf of the Židovská strana (Jewish party). He served as the principal of the school until his emigration to Palestine in 1938. In the school he supported a Jewish national and Zionist spirit, and was therefore reviled by Orthodox Jews and the Magyars. He escaped with his family before the arrival of the Hungarian army, and indeed the Hungarian Secret Service began to look for him as soon as the city was occupied. In Palestine he was among the founders of the city of Ḥolon. In 1940 he became head of the Ḥolon town council and from 1950 to his death was its mayor. He was active in organizations of Jews from Czechoslovakia.

BIBLIOGRAPHY: *Jews of Czechoslovakia*, 1 (1968), index; Y. Ereẓ (ed.), *Karpatorus* (Heb., 1959), 533–53 and passim; Tidhar, 4 (1950), 1978; Y.M. Immanuel (ed.), *Yadan Ḥolon* (1961), 65, 84–85. **ADD. BIBLIOGRAPHY:** Y.A. Jelinek, *Exile in the Foothills of the Carpathians. The Jews of Carpatho-Rus and Mukachevo, 1848–1948* (2003), index

[Meir Lamed / Yeshayahu Jelinek (2nd ed.)]

KUGEL, JAMES L. (1945–), U.S. scholar of biblical studies and comparative literature. Kugel was born in New York City. He earned his B.A. degree in European poetry at Yale University in 1968 and his Ph.D. from the City University of New York Graduate Center's Comparative Literature Program in 1977. He worked as translator, journalist, and poetry editor at *Harper's* magazine (1973–75). Following three years as assistant professor of religious studies and comparative literature at Yale University, he joined the faculty at Harvard University (1982–2004). During his tenure, he was Harry Starr Professor of Classical and Modern Jewish and Hebrew Literature, professor of Comparative Literature, director of the Center for Jewish Studies, and a member of the Divinity School. He later became professor of Bible at Bar-Ilan University in Israel.

Kugel's significant contributions to biblical scholarship are his studies on ancient Bible interpretation and its role in shaping text-based religious communities. In *The Idea of Biblical Poetry: Parallelism and its History* (1981, 1998), he coined the term "omnisignificance" to describe rabbinic exegesis of scriptures. The volume offers a new approach to biblical poetry and prose that is less dependent on the Greek model and more in concert with the rabbinic framework of thinking. Kugel also wrote *The Great Poems of the Bible: A Reader's Companion with New Translations* (1999) and *In Potiphar's House: The Interpretive Life of Biblical Texts in Early Judaism and Christianity* (1990; 1994).

Kugel's most important work on the earliest interpretations of the Torah is his *The Bible As It Was: Biblical Traditions of Late Antiquity* (1997), for which he was awarded the prestigious Grawemeyer Award in religion in 2001. Focusing primarily on well-known Torah narratives, he postulates that four basic assumptions governed the earliest exegesis: Scripture requires trained interpreters, the interpretation is harmonious in all its parts and meaningful in all its details, the insights gained are deeply relevant to people's lives, and the interpretive process is divinely inspired. A complementary volume, *Traditions of the Bible: A Guide to the Bible as It Was at the Start of the Common Era* (1998), provides additional interpretive material, more detailed explanation of motifs, and a survey of relevant scholarship for each motif.

Kugel's other books include *The Ladder of Jacob: Biblical Interpretation in the Apocrypha and Pseudepigrapha* (2004), *The Ladder of Jacob: Ancient Interpretations of the Biblical Story of Jacob and His Children* (2006), and several edited volumes that encompass studies in poetry and prophecy. His venture into theology and religion are reflected in *The God of Old: Inside the Lost World of the Bible* (2003), and in *On Being a Jew* (1990, 1998), a self-revealing advocacy for traditionalist Judaism, told in an engaging dialogue between a Syrian Jewish banker and an American graduate school student. *The Idea of Biblical Interpretation: Essays in Honor of James L. Kugel* (2004) honors Kugel's influence and accomplishments to the branch of Bible studies suggested by the title.

[Zev Garber (2nd ed.)]

KUH, ANTON (1890–1941), German journalist and essayist. Coming from a Prague Jewish family of journalists – his grandfather David Kuh was the founder of the *Tagesboten in Boehmen*, his father, Emil Kuh, the chief of the *Neue Wiener Tagblatt* – Kuh began his career as a journalist in 1912. From then on, living in Vienna, Prague, and (after 1925) Berlin, he wrote more than 1,000 critical and satirical articles, essays, and reviews on cultural and political issues for many German papers such as the *Prager Tagblatt* (1912–37), *Der Friede* (1918–19), *Das Tagebuch* (1922–26), *Die Stunde* (1923–26), *Der Querschnitt* (1924–33), *Die Weltbuehne* (1928–32), *Die Neue Weltbühne* (1934–38), and, after emigrating to New York, *Der Aufbau* (1939–41). Some of his articles were collected in the volumes *Von Goethe abwärts* (1922), *Der unsterbliche Oesterreicher* (1931), and *Physiognomik* (1931), and more recently in *Luftlinien* (ed. R.Greuner, 1981), *Zeitgeist im Literatur-Café* (ed. U. Lehner, 1983), and *Sekundentriumph und Katzenjammer* (ed. T. Krischke, 1994). Kuh also made himself known for his controversial contribution to the debate on Judaism in speeches, which he made between 1918 and 1920 in Prague, Bruenn, and Berlin (published under the title *Juden und Deutsche*, 1921). Criticizing at the same time assimilation and Zionism as ultimately non-Jewish concepts, Kuh defended the Diaspora as offering a free, non-bourgeois, and genuinely Jewish mode of existence. He negated the institutions of family, state, and religion, using arguments from the psychoanalyst Otto Gross and the anarchist Krapotkin as well as from Nietzsche and Boerne, a selection of whose writings he edited (*Boerne der Zeitgenosse*, 1922). Already attacked for *Juden und Deutsche* (among others by Max *Brod, Robert *Weltsch, Berthold Viertel, and Johannes Urzidil), Kuh was involved in another debate with Karl *Kraus, whom he criticized in a speech in October 1925 (published under the title *Der Affe Zarathustras*, 1925). In 1933, Kuh returned to Vienna, and in 1938 went to Prague and New York, writing mostly against the Nazi ideology until his death of a heart attack.

BIBLIOGRAPHY: U. Lehner, in: J. Spalek (ed.), *Deutschsprachige Exilliteratur seit 1933*, vol. 4 (1994), 1019–49; A. Kilcher, *Juden und Deutsche* (2003), 7–65.

[Andreas Kilcher (2nd ed.)]

KUH, DAVID (1818–1879), Bohemian politician and journalist. Born in Prague, Kuh studied medicine and law in Vienna and advocated Jewish integration with the Slavs. He argued that the Jews should assist the Slavs in winning their rightful place in Europe and become the middle class in Slav society. Kuh went to Budapest as a journalist and supported the revolutionary forces of Louis *Kossuth in 1848. After the failure of the Hungarian Revolution, he was imprisoned. He was released in 1849 and returned to Prague where he founded the German-language newspapers *Prager Zeitschrift fuer Literatur* and *Tagesbote von Boehmen*. Kuh was elected to the Bohemian Diet in 1862 and in complete contrast to his former beliefs, opposed the Czech nationalists in their conflict with the Germans. His influence on German-language journalism in the Hapsburg dominions was considerable, and he was described by Egon Erwin *Kisch as the "father of the Viennese press."

BIBLIOGRAPHY: Shatsky, in: *Freedom and Reason, essays in memory of Morris Raphael Cohen* (1951), 420–1; AZDJ (1844), 195–7, 207–9, 219–20; F. Mauthner, *Prager Jugendjahre* (1969^2), 180–4 and passim.

KUH, EPHRAIM MOSES (1731–1790), German poet. After a traditional Jewish education, Kuh successfully resisted his father's efforts to prepare him for the rabbinate and left his native Breslau in 1763 to seek his fortune in Berlin with a wealthy relative, Veitel Ephraim, the banker of Frederick the Great. Kuh's interest in literature was stimulated by his acquaintance with Moses *Mendelssohn, Gotthold Ephraim *Lessing, and the Berlin rationalists. Having neglected his business activities and spent his money on books, Kuh spent the years 1768–70 traveling in Europe. He then returned to Breslau, where he suffered six years of mental illness. However, he recovered sufficiently to continue writing poetry. After his death, about 5,000 of his unpublished poems were turned over to his friend and fellow-poet, Karl Wilhelm Ramler, who published a selection, *Hinterlassene Gedichte* (2 vols., 1792), together with a biographical sketch by Moses Hirschel. Kuh's poetical works were strongly influenced by classical writers. He is the hero of Berthold *Auerbach's novel *Dichter und Kaufmann* (1839).

BIBLIOGRAPHY: M. Kayserling, *Der Dichter Ephraim Kuh* (1864); H. Rhotest, *E.M. Kuh* (Ger., 1927).

[Sol Liptzin]

KUḤAYL, SHUKR BEN SĀLIM, two false messiahs with this name who appeared in *Yemen in the 19th century. The first was active between 1859 and 1863 and the other between 1868 and 1870. The first was born in Bayt Radam, a small place not far from *San'a, to where he moved and made his humble living by repairing leather buckets and shoes. He is depicted as a religious erudite, expert in the Bible, Zohar, and Kabbalah; an innocent and humble person, believing himself a messiah. For that reason he divorced his wife, increased his prayers and fasts, refused donations, and in 1859 went through villages and towns, heralding the forthcoming of salvation and redemption and urging the Jews to repent. After two years he settled on Mount Tiyyāl, where he was later killed by the messengers of the Imam. Since he had some Muslim adherents, his story and death were documented by contemporary Muslim chroniclers in Yemen, but almost nothing was reported about him in Jewish sources out of Yemen. Conversely, the second Shukr Kuḥayl was a con man who presented himself as a transfiguration of the former. He is depicted as a conspirator, arrogant and greedy, strongly attracted by worldly, materialistic pleasures. He sent emissaries and letters throughout Yemen and even to *Aden, *Egypt, the Holy Land, and *India, where he acquired many zealous followers. He compelled his local adherents to pay him a tithe of their revenues and established a wide network of fundraising to finance his profligate habits. His fame reached far beyond the boundaries of Yemen, particularly owing to the reports of Jacob *Saphir in the Jewish journal *Ha-Levanon* published in Paris by his son in-law J. Brill. In 1873 Saphir published his *Iggeret Teiman ha-Shenit*, in which he attacked Kuḥayl, but this unintentionally contributed to enhancing his name and influence. Thus, for example, the Italian Hebrew poetess Rachel *Morpurgo wrote a poem about the false messiah. But eventually he got into trouble over money and as a result of the complaint by the heads of the Jewish community of San'a to the Turkish governor he was arrested and sent to Izmir. After some years he returned to San'a where he died in solitude in 1878. It should be noted that, although both religious and temporal leaders of the Jewish community in San'a rejected the false claims of Shukr Kuḥayl the first and the second, the treacherous political and economic situation in Yemen, from which the Jews suffered more than any other segment of the population, brought not a few of them to support him and to follow him. The character of the second false messiah is well represented in the modern novel *Ha-Mashi'aḥ mi-Teiman* by Shalom Medinah (1977).

BIBLIOGRAPHY: A. Yaari, in *Shevut Teiman* (1945), 124–48 (incl. bibl.); A. Qoraḥ, *Sa'arat Teiman* (1954), 36–39; Y. Tobi, *Yehudei Teiman ba-Me'ah ha-Yod Tet* (1976), 62–68; Y. Nini, *The Jews of Yemen 1800–1914* (1991), 136–53; B. Klorman-Eraqi, *The Jews of Yemen in the Nineteenth Century* (1993), 104–58.

[Yosef Tobi (2nd ed.)]

KUHN, THOMAS S. (1922–1996), U.S. historian and philosopher of science. Born in Cincinnati, Ohio, Kuhn was educated at Harvard University, earning his bachelor's degree in 1943, his master's degree in physics in 1946, and his Ph.D. in the history of science in 1949. He remained at Harvard as a junior fellow, becoming an assistant professor of general education and the history of science in 1952. He taught at the University of California at Berkeley from 1956 to 1964, and at Princeton University from 1964 to 1979. Kuhn was named professor of the philosophy and history of science at the Massachusetts Institute of Technology in 1979, becoming professor emeritus in 1984.

Kuhn's first book, *The Copernican Revolution* (1957), was a study of the development of the heliocentric theory of the solar system. His second work, *The Structure of Scientific Revolutions* (1962), has become one of the most influential books in the philosophy of science, the social sciences, and the humanities. In this work, Kuhn argued against the conventional view of science as a gradual acquisition of knowledge, based on experimental data, which develops over time. Instead, Kuhn maintained that scientific theory has been defined by "paradigms," or worldviews, which consist of both theories and experimental methods. The acceptance of a paradigm by scientists influences all subsequent experimental work as scientists seek to refine its theories; the paradigm determines not only the type of experiments performed but also the interpretation of their results. Puzzling results are considered to result from flawed methodology. Eventually, however, an accumulation of difficult results and insoluble problems may cause a crisis that must be resolved by an intellectual revolution – in other words, by the creation of a new paradigm. Though initial reviews of the work were mixed, it was later considered to have revolutionized its field. Its influence has been considerable in areas beyond the history and philosophy of science, as Kuhn's concept of paradigm shifts was extended to political science, sociology, economics, and other fields.

Kuhn received many honors during his lifetime. He was a Guggenheim Fellow in 1954 and a fellow of the Center for Advanced Studies in Behavioral Science from 1958 to 1959. He served as director of the project Sources for the History of Quantum Physics, sponsored by the American Physical Society and the American Philosophical Society, from 1961 to 1964. He was a member of the Institute for Advanced Study at Princeton from 1972 to 1979. He received the Howard T. Behrman Award from Princeton in 1977, the George Sarton Medal from the History of Science Society in 1982, and the Bernal Award from the Society for Social Studies of Science in 1983.

[Dorothy Bauhoff (2nd ed.)]

KUHN-LOEB, U.S. immigrant dry-goods and clothing merchants in Cincinnati, who later became prominent investment bankers in New York. The firm Kuhn, Loeb and Co. was founded in 1867 by the brothers-in-law ABRAHAM KUHN (1819–1892) and SOLOMON LOEB (1828–1913) and included four other members of the family as partners. After Kuhn returned to Germany, Loeb became joint head of the firm with his son-in-law Jacob H. *Schiff. Schiff's business acumen and negotiating ability brought great prosperity to the bank. He persuaded Kuhn, Loeb and Co. to provide financial aid to Japan but refused to lend money to the czarist government because of its treatment of the Jews. His successors followed his example and supported Jewish causes, such as the American Jewish Joint Distribution Committee, the American Jewish Committee and, after World War I, the Jewish Agency. Another of Loeb's sons-in-law, Paul M. *Warburg, entered Kuhn, Loeb and Co. in 1902 to join his brother Felix M. *Warburg, Schiff's son-in-law, who had become a member of the firm five years previously and was later to become senior partner. Although after 1911 Kuhn, Loeb and Co. accepted partners from outside the family, over half a century later the senior partners, John M. Schiff and Frederick M. Warburg, were both grandsons and great-grandsons of Jacob *Schiff and of Solomon Loeb. A fifth-generation member of the firm, David T. Schiff, joined Kuhn, Loeb and Co. in 1967. Other members of the family were Dorothy *Schiff (1903–1989), newspaper publisher; and James P. *Warburg (1896–1969), economist and political analyst. Otto H. *Kahn (1867–1934), who was a member of the firm, became a patron of the arts. Kahn wrote the pamphlet *The War and Business* (1917).

BIBLIOGRAPHY: Kuhn, Loeb and Co., *Investment Banking through Four Generations* (1955).

[Hanns G. Reissner]

KUIBYSHEV (until 1935 and after 1991 **Samara**), city in the Russian Federation. In the czarist period, Kuibyshev was beyond the *Pale of Settlement. During the second half of the 19th century, Jews in the categories authorized to live outside the Pale began to settle in the town. In 1875 there were between 25 and 30 Jewish families there. As a consequence of the railroad which passed through the town, the Jewish population increased during the last quarter of the 19th century. The town's first synagogue was built in 1880, and in 1895 the existence of the local Jewish community was officially confirmed. A great synagogue was erected in 1908. From 1,327 (1.5% of the total population) in 1897, the number of Jews increased considerably during World War I and later so that in 1926 they numbered 6,981 (4% of the total), and 7,722 (2% of the total population) in 1939. During World War II, many refugees from the German-occupied regions arrived in Kuibyshev. The Soviet Government moved there when the Germans neared Moscow. The headquarters of the Jewish *Anti-Fascist Committee was in the town for some time, and from 1942 to 1943, the organ of the committee, **Eynikeyt*, was published there. The community was still in existence in 1970 when there was a rabbi, a *shoḥet*, and an estimated Jewish population of about 25,000. Although a local paper published articles against the synagogue in 1961 and 1962, the synagogue was not closed down.

[Yehuda Slutsky]

KUKIZOW, Karaite family name, originating from the name of the town Kukiziw (Krasny Ostrow), in Galicia. The founder of this dynasty was MORDECHAI BEN NISAN (d. 1709), prominent Karaite scholar, disciple of *Joseph ben Samuel ha-Mashbir from *Halicz and of *Solomon ben Aaron from Troki. Mordechai was born and lived in Troki, but in 1688, upon the order of King Jan III Sobieski, Mordechai and some Karaite families were forced to settle in Kukizow, a private possession of the Sobieskis, where he suffered from isolation and seclusion. In Kukizow he served as *ḥazzan* of the small community. He and his son Nisan were murdered on their way from Eastern Galicia to the Crimea.

Mordechai was the first Karaite author in Eastern Europe who wrote treatises on Karaite historiography and influenced the following generations of authors. However, his works are important mainly for the history of the historiographic genre in Karaite literature, rather than for their historical material. On the instructions of Charles XII of Sweden, several Swedish scholars asked Kukizow for information on the origins of Karaism and the difference between them and the Rabbanites, in the belief that the Karaites were in some ways similar to the Protestants. Kukizow's answer, contained in *Levush Malkhut* completed in 1698, (published by A. Neubauer, *Aus der Peterburger Bibliothek*, Leipzig (1866), 30–66) discusses the antiquity of Karaism and gives a brief description of Karaite doctrine. His most important composition, *Dod Mordechai*, completed in 1699 (Hamburg, 1714, with Latin translation by J.L. Wolf; reprinted without translation, Vienna, 1830; Ramla 1966), was written as responses to questions by the Protestant professor Jacob Trigland of Leiden, Holland, mainly concerning the split between Karaites and Rabbanites. Without any critical approach Mordechai introduces the traditional apologetical Karaite claim that the split between Rabbanism and Karaism began in the Second Temple period. He cited many previous Karaite authors as well as Rabbanite literature, including the Talmud, trying to prove the concept of the early appearance of Karaism and that the Karaites originated from *Judah ben Tabbai, and the Rabbanites – from *Simeon ben Shetaḥ. He also wrote: *Kelalim Yafim* (Bodl. MS Opp. Add. Qu. 117), a grammatical work; *Ma'amar Mordekhai* (several mss. at the St. Petersburg Institute of Oriental Studies of the Russian Academy), a supercommentary on the *Sefer ha-Mivḥar* by the Karaite *Aaron b. Joseph; *Derekh Yam* (several mss. at the St. Petersburg Institute of Oriental Studies of the Russian Academy), commentary on the weekly portion of Noaḥ in *Sefer ha-Mivḥar*; *Imrei Binah* (Bodl., MS Reggio 22), treatise on Kabbalah. He also wrote liturgical poems, incorporated in the Karaite *siddur*.

His grandson, also named MORDECHAI BEN NISAN (the second). He was *ḥakham* of Kukizow's community. He studied Torah with Rabbanite teachers and taught himself astronomy from Latin and Polish books. He wrote a book, *Yad ha-Shem* (St. Petersburg Institute of Oriental Studies of the Russian Academy), in 1774 on Kabbalah.

His son DAVID BEN MORDECAI (1777–1855) was born in Kukizow, served as *ḥazzan* of its community and took the family name Mordkovich. He moved to Evpatoria in 1822 and changed his name to Kukizow. In 1825 was appointed *ḥazzan* and later *shoḥet* in Evpatoria by Joseph ben Solomon *Luzki. He knew German and Polish and was involved in community affairs. He served as a proofreader of Karaite books in the printing press where he also managed publishing and printing works in 1835–45. In 1834 he reprinted the *Adderet Eliyahu* of Elijah *Bashyazi, adding to the section dealing with the new moon two treatises, *Yemot Olam* and *Halikhot Olam*. He also wrote *Kevi'ot Rashei Ḥodashim u-Tekufot ke-Minhag ha-Kara'im* and *Ma'amar be-Kiddush ha-Ḥodesh* (Eupatoria, 1840), on calendation and the calculation of the new moon. His main work *Ẓemaḥ David*, completed in 1848, but published posthumously (St. Petersburg, 1897; Ashdod, 2004), contains essays on the laws concerning Sabbath, abstinence, determination of the new moon, etc., and poems and elegies, as well as annotations to biblical passages, the obligations of a man before God, resurrection of the dead, and so on. Still in Kukizow he learned rabbinic literature and was friendly with Nachman *Krochmal. In 1854 he left the Crimea because of the Crimean War and moved to Nickolaev, where his sons dwelled and spent the rest of his life there. He died in Nickolaev of cholera.

He had five sons, Mordechai, Joseph, Moses, Judah, and Nisan. His most famous son, JUDAH (1840–1917), lived in the Crimea and St. Petersburg. His works include two treatises on calendation; *Binah la-Ittim* (parts 1–2, Odessa, 1878–79), and *Halikhot Olam* (part 1, Odessa, 1880); an edition with Russian translation of the Passover *Haggadah* according to the Karaite rite (Odessa, 1883; St. Petersburg, 1889); and two works in Russian "A Short Sketch of the History of the Karaites" (St. Petersburg, 1900) and "Forty-Four Epitaphs from the Karaite Cemetery at Chufut-Qaleh" (*ibid.*, 1910), where he tried to refute the accusations about *Firkovich's falsifications of the dates on tomb inscriptions. Judah disappeared after he left his house in Petrograd during the events of the Bolshevik revolution in October 1917.

David Kukozow, possibly the grandson of David ben Mordechai, was a member of the Haskalah. He wrote a number of articles in the Karaite journal in Russian "Karaite Life" (*Karaimskaja zhizn*) in 1911–12 about Karaite national identity, the importance of the study of Russian language and secular sciences by Karaite youth, and the importance of modernization of the curriculum in Karaite school.

BIBLIOGRAPHY: MORDECAI B. NISAN: Graetz, Gesch, 10 (1896), 479–81; A. Neubauer, *Aus der Petersburger Bibliothek* (1866), 76–78; Mann, Texts, 2 (1935), index 1570; s.v.: *Mordecai b. Nisan b. Noaḥ, of Kukizow.* DAVID B. MORDECAI: Poznański, in: ZHB, 13 (1909), 111–4, 180; 14 (1910), 57–58. JUDAH: Poznański, in: ZHB, 13 (1909), 115, 144, 147; 14 (1910), 59; Markon, in: *Bulletin de l'Académie des Sciences de Russie* (1923), 161–3; idem, in: *Ha-Goren*, 10 (1928), 153–60; M. Polliack (ed.), *Karaite Judaism: A Guide to Its History and Literary Sources*, (2003), index. **ADD. BIBLIOGRAPHY:** R. Fahn, *Sefer ha-Kr'aim* (1929), 36–8, 81, 85–88; B. Elyashevich, *Materialy k serii narody i kultury* XIV, 2 (1993), 109–10, 112–14.

[Isaak Dov Ber Markon / Golda Akhiezer (2nd ed.)]

KULBAK, MOYSHE (1896–1940), Yiddish poet, novelist, and dramatist. Kulbak was born in Smorgon near Vilna. He wrote first in Hebrew but soon changed to Yiddish and published his first book of poems *Shirim* ("Poems," 1920) while teaching in Vilna's Yiddish schools. His early poetry was under the influence of Neo-Romanticism and Symbolism. He spent the years 1920–23 in Berlin, where he was exposed to the latest literary trends, especially Expressionism, the influences of which were apparent in his poetry, in the messianic drama *Yakov Frank* (1923), and in the grotesque short novel *Meshiekh ben Efroyim* (1924). In 1923 he returned to Vilna, taught modern Yiddish literature at the famous "Real-Gimnazye" and at the Yiddish Teachers' Seminary, and published the long poem "Vilna" (1926) and the apocalyptic novel *Montog* ("Monday," 1926), among other works. A collection of his works in three volumes appeared in 1929 in Vilna. Kulbak was interested in theater and with his students performed Yiddish plays. In 1928, disappointed with the literary atmosphere in Poland, he cast his lot with the Minsk Group of Soviet Yiddish writers. As a modernist, decadent, and pessimistic writer, it was hard for Kulbak to conform to the dictates of socialist-realism and Soviet utopianism. His major work from this period is *Zelmenyaner* (1931; Heb. 1940), a novel that narrates with lively colors and black humor the story of a Soviet-era Jewish family in Minsk. In his comic epic, *Disner Tshayld Harold* (1933; modeled after Lord Byron's work), his satiric barbs were directed against the decadent German bourgeoisie. In 1937, while he was at the height of his popularity and his last play, *Boytre* (1936), was being performed in Moscow, the secret police arrested him, forbidding further performances of his plays and all mention of his books. He was imprisoned as a slave laborer until his death in 1940. He was posthumously rehabilitated in 1956.

BIBLIOGRAPHY: Rejzen, Leksikon, 3 (1960), 600–6; LNYL, 8 (1981), 164–7; M. Ravitch, *Mayn Leksikon* (1945), 227–9. I. Howe and E. Greenberg, *A Treasury of Yiddish Stories* (1953), 342–50. **ADD. BIBLIOGRAPHY:** Ch. Shmeruk et al. (eds.), *A Shpigl oyf a Shteyn* (1964), 515–66; Sh. Rozhanski (ed.), *Oysgeklibene Shriftn* (1976); I Howe et al. (eds.), *The Penguin Book of Modern Yiddish Verse* (1987), 379–411; A. Novershtern, in: *Di Goldene Keyt*, 126 (1989), 181–203; 127 (1989), 151–170; A. Novershtern, in: *Kesem ha-Dimdumim* (2003), 225–52.

[Sol Liptzin / Itay B Zutra (2nd ed)]

KULISHER, family of scholars and communal workers in Russia. Its founder, MOSES KULISHER, went to Russian Volhynia from Galicia at the beginning of the 19th century. An adherent of *Haskalah, he engaged in agriculture.

His son REUBEN (1828–1896) was a physician and communal worker. After completing his studies at the Medico-Surgical Academy of St. Petersburg in 1856, he became an army physician and was sent by the government to Western Europe to specialize in the fields of military hygiene and sanitation, on which he later wrote studies and articles. Reuben was a friend and disciple of I.B. *Levinsohn. He also wrote scientific articles in Hebrew (*"Al ha-Koḥot ha-Po'alim ba-Beri'ah"* (after Helmholtz), in *Ha-Ẓefirah*, 1862, and "*Mah Hi ha-Ẓara'at*" in *Gan Peraḥim*, 1891). His memoirs, *Itogi* (1896), originally published in the Russian Jewish periodical *Voskhod* from 1891 to 1894, contain important material on the history of the education of the Jews in Russia; the author describes "the hopes and expectations of Russian Jewry over the last 50 years, 1838–88."

Moses' grandson MICHAEL (1847–1919), a historian, ethnographer, and communal worker, studied at the rabbinical seminary of Zhitomir and at the law faculty of the University of St. Petersburg. From 1869 to 1871 he was on the editorial board of the Russian Jewish newspaper *Den*. Proceeding to study scientific subjects in Western Europe, he published numerous articles in Russian and German periodicals, as well as several books, including *Das Leben Jesu – Eine Sage* (1876), in which he was one of the first to claim that the stories of the New Testament were only legends. He also attacked the blood libel. Michael Kulisher was a committee member of the *Society for the Promotion of Culture among the Jews of Russia and the *Jewish Colonization Association (ICA) as well as one of the founders of the *Jewish Society for History and Ethnography, in whose quarterly he published several articles. His basic contention in these studies on the Jews in Poland and Russia is that the fate of the Jews in the Diaspora depends on the economic situation of the various host countries. Michael Kulisher was among the founders of the "Jewish Democratic Group," established in 1906 under the leadership of M. *Vinaver, which considered that the future of the Jews was bound up with the establishment of a liberal regime in Russia.

JOSEPH (1878–1934), son of Michael, was a noted economic historian, author of important studies in Russian and German on the economy of Russia and Western Europe. In the field of Jewish history, he wrote on the economic situation of the Jews during the Middle Ages (in *Voskhod*, 21:9 (1901), 30–50; no. 10 (1901), 120–142) and on the Jews in Prussian silk production in the 18th century (in *Yevreyskaya Starina*, 11 (1924), 129–61). Another of Michael's sons, EUGENE (1881–1956), jurist and legal historian, moved to Germany after the Communist Revolution and lectured on Russian law at the University of Berlin. He later moved to France and then to the United States. His works include *Europe on the Move: War and Population Changes 1917–1947* (1948). A third son, ALEXANDER (1890–1942), jurist and sociologist, settled in Paris after the 1917 Revolution. There he became one of the leading contributors to the newspaper of the liberal Russian emigrants, *Posledniya Novosti*. He lost his life in the Holocaust in France.

BIBLIOGRAPHY: *Aḥi'asaf*, 5 (1897), 315–6; S. Ginzburg, *Amolike Peterburg* (1944), 139–51.

[Yehuda Slutsky]

KULKA, ERICH (originally **Schön**; 1922–1995), Czech author, publicist, and historian. Born in Vsetín, Moravia, Kulka spent 1939–1945 in concentration camps; from 1942 he was in Auschwitz. He escaped in January 1945 with his son Otto. In 1968 he immigrated to Israel, where he worked at the Institute of Contemporary History at the Hebrew University of Jerusalem. In his writing, Kulka drew on events from World War II and the Holocaust. He published many articles, studies, and books on these themes in Czechoslovakia, Israel, and many other countries.

His works include *Továrna na smrt* (1946, "The Death Factory") with Otto Kraus; *Noc a mlha* ("Night and Mist," 1958) with Otto Kraus; *Frankfurtský proces* ("The Frankfurt Trial," 1964); *Útěk z tábora smrti* ("Escape from a Death Camp," 1966); *Soudcové, žalobci a obhájci* ("Judges, Prosecutors, Defenders," 1966); *Židé ve Svobodově armádě* ("Jews in the Czechoslovak Svoboda Army," 1979, 1990); *Židé v československém vojsku na Západě* ("Jews in the Czechoslovak Western Army," 1992).

Of his three sons, Otto Dov Kulka is an Israeli historian; Dan Kulka is an Israeli sculptor; Tomáš Kulka is an Israeli-Czech philosopher and esthetician living in Prague.

BIBLIOGRAPHY: *Slovník českých spisovatelů* (1982).

[Milos Pojar (2nd ed.)]

KULTUR-LIGE ("Culture League"), a Yiddish organization, created in Kiev in January 1918, when the Ukraine enjoyed its short-lived independence, with national-personal autonomy declared for the country's Russian, Jewish, and Polish population. The league was conceived as a supraparty body whose aim was to construct and promote a new Jewish culture, based on Yiddish and secular democratic values. Among its founders were the Kiev Yiddish activists Dovid *Bergelson, Yekhezkel *Dobrushin, Moshe *Litvakov, and Nakhman *Mayzel. The league epitomized the idea of Jewish national-cum-cultural survival as an extraterritorial, autonomous Yiddish-speaking nation. The league was headed by its Central Committee and realized its trend-setting projects through the following sections: educational, publishing, library, musical, theatrical, literary, artistic, archival, and statistical. Thanks to scores of its local branches, it monopolized virtually all Yiddish cultural activities in the Ukraine and continued opening its chapters in other countries. In December 1920, the league's Central Committee was liquidated by a decree of the Kiev Province Revolutionary Committee. In its place there was appointed an Executive Committee dominated by communists. In the Soviet environment, the league's numerous successful programs were gradually reduced to activities of a publishing house, which existed until 1931. In December 1921 an attempt was made to reregister the league as an organization with headquarters in Moscow and "chief committees" in Kiev and Minsk. The (aborted) application was signed by Litvakov, Maria *Frumkin (alias Esther), Mikhl Levitan, Aleksei Granovskii, and Josef Bregman. Outside the Soviet Union, culture leagues were opened in such towns as Warsaw, Vilna, Bialystok, Grodno, Paris, Amsterdam, and Berlin, some of which survived as significant Yiddish cultural and educational institutions until the beginning of World War II.

BIBLIOGRAPHY: H. Kazovsky, *The Artists of the Kultur-Lige* (2003); G. Estraikh, *In Harness* (2005), index.

[Gennady Estraikh (2nd ed.)]

KULTUSVEREIN (Ger. "religious union"), an organizational form of Jewish communal life in the Hapsburg *monarchy between 1848 and 1890. The founding of new Jewish communities had been forbidden from 1779, but after 1848, when Jews were allowed to settle in localities previously prohibited to them, they organized their communal life into associations of this kind, although continuing to be members of their communities of origin and bound to pay taxes to them. In 1869 there were 69 such societies in Bohemia and six in Moravia. In time some of these congregations were acknowledged as communities (*Kultusgemeinde*) by the authorities, although old communities, losing their members and their dues, went to any lengths to prevent this (e.g., the *Udlice community tried to prevent recognition of the *Chomutov congregation and the *Kromeriz community tried to take legal action to force its members who had settled in *Brno to continue paying taxes). The problem was solved by the law of March 21, 1890 which set up a new organizational status for Jewish communities.

BIBLIOGRAPHY: C. Ritter d'Elvert, *Zur Geschichte der Juden in Maehren…* (1895), 200–7.

[Meir Lamed]

KUN, BÉLA (1886–1938), communist who was dictator of Hungary for a short period in 1919. Born in Szilagycseh, Kun joined the Social Democratic Party when only 16 and became secretary of the Workers' Sick Fund in Klausenburg. He fought in the Austro-Hungarian army during World War I and was captured by the Russians. He spread revolutionary ideas among his fellow prisoners in Tomsk and in February 1918 became a member of the Tomsk committee of the Bolshevik Party. He was released following the armistice in November 1918. Kun returned to Hungary shortly after the outbreak of the Hungarian revolution. He founded the Communist newspaper *Vörös Ujság* (Red Newspaper) and attempted to overthrow the moderate government in Hungary and replace it by an extreme revolutionary regime as in Russia. Arrested and imprisoned for incitement to violence in February 1919, Kun was released a month later when the government fell and he was made a member of a new cabinet of Socialists and Bolsheviks. Within a short period the moderate elements were removed from the government, Hungary was proclaimed a Soviet republic, and Kun became commissar for foreign affairs and dictator.

Kun was inspired by fanaticism and tremendous energy. His extremism led to growing discontent among the landed classes while he failed to receive the promised Russian aid from Lenin, with whom he was in regular contact. In August 1919, after the failure of the counteroffensive against the Romanian army invading Hungary, Kun fled to Vienna and then to Moscow. He was made political commissar of the Red Army of the South, and after 1920 promoted communism in Germany and Hungary through the Communist International of which he was a member of the executive. In the 1930s *Stalin turned against the supporters of international revolution as advocated by *Trotsky. Kun was discredited and disgraced and was executed on August 29, 1938. The Soviet Communist Party announced that he was tried during the Stalinist purges on charges of being "a Trotskyite conspirator, plotting to undermine the Communist International," and executed several hours after being sentenced to death. He was rehabilitated in 1955. Kun was completely alienated from Judaism.

BIBLIOGRAPHY: R.L. Tőkés, *Béla Kun and the Hungarian Soviet Republic* (1967), incl. bibl.

KUNFI (Kohn), ZSIGMOND (1879–1929), Hungarian socialist. Born in Nagykanizsa, Kunfi joined the radical Sociological Society and wrote for its political organ *Twentieth Century*. His anti-religious views led him to leave his post as secondary school teacher and join the Social Democratic Party, becoming editor of its newspaper *Népszava*.

When the revolution of 1918 overthrew the Hungarian regime, Kunfi was made minister of social welfare and later minister of education. He was commissar of education during the Communist dictatorship of Béla *Kun but resigned soon afterward in protest against Kun's extremist policies. In August 1919, when the counterrevolutionaries seized power in Hungary, he immigrated to Austria. He became editor of the socialist *Arbeiter Zeitung* and also of *Vilagossag*, an emigrant socialist paper in Hungarian. He taught at the People's University of Vienna, where he preached against the danger of Communism and even criticized his own role in the Hungarian revolution.

Kunfi was a brilliant essayist, a convincing orator, and a sociologist of distinction. He translated the works of Marx, Kautsky, *Lassalle, Anatole France, and *Zola into Hungarian and, although he officially left the Jewish community, he wrote a penetrating study of the Jewish problem in Hungary. He committed suicide in 1929.

BIBLIOGRAPHY: UJE, 6 (1942), 488; *Magyar Irodalmi Lexikon*, 1 (1963), 721; E. Fischer, *Erinnerungen und Reflexionen* (1969), index.

[Baruch Yaron]

KUNIN, MADELEINE MAY (1933–), U.S. politician, governor of Vermont. Kunin was born in Zurich, Switzerland. Her mother was Swiss and her father, who died when Kunin was three, was born in Germany. Amid the rising threat of Nazism and fear of a German invasion, Kunin's mother was able to obtain United States visas for her children and herself and the family arrived in New York City in June 1940. Kunin graduated from the University of Massachusetts in 1956 with a B.A. in history and went on to receive an M.S. from the Columbia University School of Journalism. In the 1950s Kunin worked as a journalist in Burlington, Vermont, and as a tour guide at the United States Pavilion at the Brussels World Fair. During the 1960s, Kunin was a homemaker with an active volunteer life in the fields of health, child welfare, and Democratic Party politics. Inspired by the women's movement, Kunin sought public office and was elected to the Vermont House of Representatives in 1972. During a second

House term, Kunin became minority whip, the first woman elected to a legislative leadership position in Vermont. Kunin was elected lieutenant governor in 1978 and became the leader of Vermont's Democrats in 1980; she became Vermont's first female governor in 1984. As governor, Kunin promoted environmental programs, the establishment of a family court, and land-use planning legislation. She strongly supported women's reproductive rights and encouraged young women to enter politics. Kunin always stressed her status as an immigrant and a Jew. In her autobiography, *Living a Political Life*, she wrote, "On some level that I do not yet fully understand, I believe I transformed my sense of the Holocaust into personal political activism. This was the source of my political courage. I could do what the victims could not: oppose evil whenever I recognized it. The United States of America would protect me. I lived in a time and place when it was safe for a Jew to be a political person, to speak, to oppose, to stand up." In 1993, Kunin, who had declined to run for a fourth term as governor, was appointed deputy secretary of education in the first Clinton term. She became United States ambassador to Switzerland, the country of her birth, in 1996. Kunin returned to Vermont in 2000; in 2003 she was named distinguished visiting professor at the University of Vermont. Her books include *The Big Green Book: A Four Season Guide to Vermont* (1976) and *Living a Political Life* (1994).

BIBLIOGRAPHY: *Current Biography Yearbook* (1987); *Who's Who of American Women* (2003); *Working Woman* (July 1986).

[Libby White (2nd ed.)]

KUNITZ, STANLEY JASSPON (1905–), U.S. poet and editor. Born in Worcester, Massachusetts, of Russian parents Kunitz applied himself to mastering the English language while still a child, and the acquisition of new words became his hobby. Educated at Harvard, he taught poetry at the New School for Social Research and at Brandeis and Columbia universities. His first verse collection, *Intellectual Things* (1930) was well received, as was his second, *Passport to the War* (1944). His *Selected Poems 1928–1958* (1958), received the Pulitzer Prize and other awards. Kunitz's *The Poems of Stanley Kunitz 1928–1978* was published in Boston (1979) and was awarded the Leonore Marshall Poetry Prize in 1980.

Of special note are his *A Kind of Order, A Kind of Folly: Essays and Conversations* (1975); *Collected Poems* (2000), and *The Wild Braid: A Poet Reflects on a Century within the Garden* (2005). With Howard Haycraft, Kunitz also gained distinction as the editor of reference works on literature, for some of which he used the pen name "Dilly Tante." Works of this kind include: *Authors Today and Yesterday* (1933); *American Authors 1600–1900* (1938); and *Twentieth Century Authors* (1942; *First Supplement*, 1955).

ADD. BIBLIOGRAPHY: M. Henault, *Stanley Kunitz* (1980); G. Orr, *Stanley Kunitz: An Introduction to his poetry* (1985).

[Milton Henry Hindus / Lewis Fried (2nd ed.)]

KUNSTADT, ISAAC (Ignáz) BEN ELIEZER LIPMAN (1838–1909), Hungarian rabbi. Kunstadt was born in Pressburg and studied under Abraham Samuel Benjamin *Sofer (Schreiber), and afterward proceeded to Vienna. He was rabbi of Nagyabony (Hungary) from 1862 to 1882, and of the "status quo" community (i.e., the moderates who stood between the Orthodox and the Neolog communities) of Nagyvárad (Grosswardein) from 1882 to 1884. In the latter year he was appointed chief rabbi of Radautz (Radauti, in Bukovina). He possessed a good knowledge of German and was a fluent preacher in that language, but his ignorance of Hungarian, which was then rapidly becoming the vernacular of Hungarian Jewry, was a stumbling block. He is the author of *Lu'aḥ Ereẓ* (2 pts., 1885–87), consisting of talmudic novellae and scriptural interpretations; *Lu'aḥ Ereẓ he-Ḥadash*, a second edition with additions, was published in Vienna in 1915. Many of the sermons he preached on special occasions were published as separate pamphlets.

BIBLIOGRAPHY: M. Kunstadt, in: I. Kunstadt, *Lu'aḥ Ereẓ he-Ḥadash* (1915), introd.; C.D. Lippe, *Bibliographishes Lexicon*, 1 (1899), 216f.; S. Sofer (Schreiber), *Iggerot Soferim*, pt. 4 (1928), 94f.; P. Ujvári, *Magyar Zsidó Lexikon* (1929), 518; P. Vajda, *A zsidók tőrténete Abonyban* (1896), 96f., 148.

[Nathaniel Katzburg]

KUNSTLER, WILLIAM (1919–1995), U.S. lawyer. Kunstler was born in New York. He majored in French at Yale University, where he was elected to Phi Beta Kappa, and graduated in 1941. He served with the Army Signal Corps in the Pacific in World War II, rising to the rank of major and earning a Bronze Star. After the war, he attended Columbia Law School, graduating in 1949. In the mid-1950s, Kunstler represented a State Department employee whose passport had been confiscated when he traveled to China as a freelance reporter. By the early 1960s he was doing work with the American Civil Liberties Union and representing the Rev. Dr. Martin Luther King Jr. and his allies in the civil rights cause, and his course was set: he became one of the best-known lawyers in the United States, championing left-of-center clients and unpopular causes. He not only made a career but also a life out of representing people and movements that were often despised. His clients' "popularity" seemed to inspire him, and he earned praise as a brilliant lawyer and a skillful and courageous litigator, but also scorn as a showoff and publicity seeker. He represented Dr. King as he battled segregation in Georgia; Representative Adam Clayton Powell Jr., who contended that his skin color made him unpopular with Congressional colleagues, and Stokely Carmichael, who popularized the "black power" rallying cry. Among his notorious clients was a man who shot six people to death on a Long Island Rail Road train, and he had a role in the defense of suspects in the 1993 bombing of the World Trade Center. One of his notable victories was winning acquittal of El Sayyid Nosair on murder charges in the 1990 death of Rabbi Meir *Kahane, despite eyewitnesses who said they had seen the defendant slay the militant leader of the Jewish Defense League. Nosair was convicted of gun possession and other lesser charges. Perhaps his best-known case involved the so-called Chicago Seven, who were tried on charges that they conspired to incite riots that made a tumult of the Democratic National Convention in 1968 in Chicago. His clients in the trial were people whose names were constantly linked to the turbulence of that era: Jerry Rubin, Tom Hayden, Rennie Davis, David Dellinger, Abbie Hoffman, John R. Froines, and Lee Weiner. Bobby Seale, a member of the militant Black Panther party, was originally included in the group but his case was tried separately. The infamous trial, in which the defendants mocked the judge, ended with the acquittal of all on conspiracy charges, although five were found guilty of crossing state lines with intent to riot. For his many sharp exchanges with the judge, Julius J. Hoffman, Kunstler got a contempt-of-court sentence of 4 years 13 days. But all the convictions in the trial, including Kunstler's, were overturned on appeal. Kunstler wrote several books, including *Beyond a Reasonable Doubt?: The Original Trial of Caryl Chessman*, a 1961 account of a convict in California executed after more than a decade on death row, and *The Case for Courage: The Stories of Ten Famous American Attorneys Who Risked Their Careers in the Cause of Justice*, published in 1962.

[Stewart Kampel (2nd ed.)]

KUNTERES (Heb. קֻנְטְרֵס), a written sheet, a notebook, or (later) a pamphlet. Various suggestions have been put forward as to the derivation of the word. L. Zunz regarded it as an abbreviation, or corruption, of the Latin word *commentarius*. Although in *Yalkut Shimoni* Psalms 749, the reading is "He took a blank *kunteres* and handed it to the judge," the parallel passage in *Midrash Tehillim* to 45:5 reads "he took a קרטס," and on this basis it has been suggested that it is a corruption of the Greek Χάρτης ("a card, or sheet"). Elijah Levita, on the other hand (Tishbi s.v.), connects it with the Latin *quinterno* or *quaterno* ("a notebook"). The essence of the *kunteres* was that it consisted of individual sheets bound together, in contrast to the continuous scroll. Rashi (to Shab. 98b) explains the word *atba* ("a clasp"; Men. 32a; Shab. 98a) to refer to "the clasp which held together the pages of a *kunteres*," and he himself refers to the "*kunteres* of my old teacher" (Git. 82a). It seems certain that these *kunteresim* for talmudic works originated in the geonic period, from the fact that those who received answers to the questions addressed to the *geonim* collected them in bound volumes, arranging them either in accordance with their contents, or in the order of the tractates, or joining together all the responsa emanating from one *Gaon* (see S. Abramson, *Sinai – Sefer Yovel* (1958), 404ff., and especially idem in *Jubilee Volume in Honor of Harry Wolfson* (1965), 1–23). In this respect the *kunteresim* played a significant role in the emergence of the Hebrew book. The most common use of the word, however, is as the common designation used by the tosafists for Rashi's commentary to the Talmud (although Rashi himself as well as his pupils refer to his Bible commentary by this name), probably because it was written on separate sheets and bound together. In later ages, however, authors of rabbinic works used the word *kunteres* for a pamphlet which was usually in the form of an appendix to the main work, and from this the word came to be used for any pamphlet or booklet.

BIBLIOGRAPHY: J. Fuerst, in: MGWJ, 38 (1894), 306; S. Krauss, *Griechische und lateinische Lehnwoerter im Talmud, Midrasch und Targum*, 2 (1899), 509f.; A. Berliner, *Beitraege zur Geschichte der Raschi-Commentare* (1903), index, s.v.

[Louis Isaac Rabinowitz]

KUNZ, JOSEF LAURENZ (1890–1970), international lawyer. Born in Vienna, Kunz lectured in international law at the University of Vienna from 1927–32, when he emigrated to the United States. From 1934, Kunz was professor at the Toledo college of law in Ohio. He lectured at various universities in Europe and America including The Hague Academy of International Law. Kunz wrote numerous books and articles on international law including *Die Voelkerrechtliche Option* (2 vols., 1925–28), *Kriegsrecht und Neutralitaetsrecht* (1935), *The Mexican Expropriations* (1940), and the introduction to *Latin-American Legal Philosophy* (1948). *The Changing Law of Nations* (1968) contains Kunz's principal writings on international law.

[Josef J. Lador-Lederer]

KUPER, JACK (1932–), graphic designer, actor, dramatist, filmmaker, and author. Kuper was born in Poland, and during World War II, at the age of nine, he was separated from his family and then spent four years hiding in the Polish countryside. His mother and brother were murdered in the Sobibor death camp. In 1947, Kuper arrived in Toronto as part of the Canadian-sponsored War Orphans Project which resettled several thousand child Holocaust survivors in Canada. He went to school in Toronto, where he studied commercial art. During the 1950s he worked as a graphic designer and actor with CBC television and began to write and produce radio and television dramas. In 1966 Kuper published an account of his wartime experiences, *Child of the Holocaust*. Widely praised, the book was translated into numerous languages and remains a staple of Holocaust testimony. A second autobiographical volume published in 1994, *After the Smoke Cleared*, chronicles Kuper's postwar life in Canada and his reunification with his father, who survived the war in Siberia. Kuper eventually turned his talents to documentary film. His most controversial documentary, *Who Was Jerzy Kosinski* (1996), examines the enigma of the author of *The Painted Bird*, ostensibly an autobiography, but a fabrication of a story very similar to that of Kuper. Kuper's other notable films include *A Day in the Warsaw Ghetto: A Birthday Trip in Hell* (1991), based on the photos of a Wehrmacht soldier; *Shtetl* (1995), documenting the paintings of folk artist Mayer Kirshenblatt and his memories of prewar Poland; *Children of the Storm* (2000), on the postwar Jewish orphans who found refuge in Canada; and *The Fear of Felix Nussbaum* (2000), about an artist who was killed in Auschwitz.

[Frank Bialystok (2nd ed.)]

KUPER, SIMON MEYER (1906–1963), South African Supreme Court judge. Kuper was appointed King's Counsel in 1946 and raised to the bench in 1955. He was chairman of the South African Jewish Board of Deputies (1944–49) and the South African Zionist Federation (1950–55). He gave evidence on behalf of South African Jewry before the Anglo-American Commission of Inquiry on Palestine (1946). Kuper died of a shot fired through the window of his house by an unknown assassin.

KUPERNIK, ABRAHAM (1821–1892), Russian communal worker and writer. After studying at the yeshivah of Volozhin, he was attracted by the Haskalah movement and studied languages and sciences. From 1851 he was employed as a clerk in J.Y. Guenzburg's brandy-distilling monopolies and was appointed director of the Kiev province monopoly in 1858. Opening a private bank in Kiev, he became one of the wealthiest men in the city and a leader of the Jewish community. He also participated in the general public affairs of the city and was decorated by the Russian government. One of the founders of the *Society for the Promotion of Culture among the Jews of Russia (1863), he also joined the Ḥovevei Ẓion and was one of the contributors to **Ha-Meliẓ*. In his short work, *Le-Korot Benei Yisrael be-Kiev* ("History of the Jews in Kiev," 1891), he reprinted extracts from the register of the *ḥevra kaddisha* of Kiev.

His son LEV (1845–1905), one of the most prominent advocates in Russia, converted in order to marry a Christian woman. Renowned throughout southern Russia as the defender of the ordinary man from the arbitrariness of the law, he contributed to the liberal Russian press, especially the *Zaria* of Kiev, publishing sharp contributions which included attacks on the antisemitic press. Lev Kupernik attained fame among the Jews for his defense of the accused in the blood libel trial of Kutais (1879) and of the members of the Jewish *self-defense in *Gomel (1904).

BIBLIOGRAPHY: *Aḥi'asaf*, 1 (1893), 292–3; *Ha-Asif*, 6 (1893), 160–1; A. Ginsberg, *Meshumodim in Tsarishn Rusland* (1946), 264–78.

[Yehuda Slutsky]

KUPFERMAN, MOSHE (1926–2003), Israeli painter. Kupferman was born in Jaroslav, Poland, and received a Jewish education. On October 10, 1939, the German army entered his town. The Kupferman family was expelled together with the other 10,000 Jews of Jaroslav to a small village in the region of Krasnofimsk. His mother died in 1942 and his father in 1944. He and his sister returned to Poland after the war, but his sister died. In 1948 Kupferman immigrated to Israel. In the spring of 1949 he was one of the founders of Kibbutz Loḥamei ha-Getta'ot, where he lived for the rest of his life.

He studied art in various frameworks – private lessons, art seminars, and a kibbutz class. He was in contact with other kibbutz artists such as Haim Atar and Shimon Avni. In 1961 he traveled to Europe and visited all the famous museums. From 1964 Kupferman worked at his studio in the kibbutz, referring to his painting as one of the kibbutz occupations. Kupferman's art was exhibited in Europe and United States. In 1987, his one-man show, "Paintings, Works on Paper," was held at the Musée national d'Art moderne of the Georges Pompidou Center.

Kupferman's style was Abstract. His artistic language was quite Minimalist and had a repetitive character. The color scale went from gray to smokey purple. His lines were straight, precise, and dense. Much was written about these lines in an attempt to understand them. Some connected them to Holocaust images; others suggested that the lines expressed the influence of his occupation in the first years of the kibbutz as a form maker in the building trade. Kupferman himself did not confirm any of these suppositions.

Kupferman's method of artistic creation was by layers. He would start with one color, usually green, and then layer by layer add other colors, some of which he removed during the process and then, after they were mixed on his palette with other colors, put back on the canvas. This was his special way of creating his unique purple.

Most of Kupferman's paintings are untitled. Nevertheless a few series do have titles: *With Beirut-After Beirut-With Beirut* (1982); *Yitzhak Rabin in Memoriam* (1996) *The Rift in Time – Di Kriye* (1999). Although Kupferman's art was not symbolic, it seems that the term "time" in his art referred to the Holocaust.

Kupferman's art fascinated the Israeli art world. Some writers made a connection between his Abstraction and the abstractness of the Jewish God.

In 2000 Kupferman received the Israel Prize.

BIBLIOGRAPHY: Y. Fischer (ed.), *Moshe Kupferman: Works from 1962 to 2000* (2002).

[Ronit Steinberg (2nd ed.)]

KUPISKIS (Lith. **Kupiškis, Kupiškiai**; Yid. **Kupishok**; Rus. **Kupishki**), town in N.E. Lithuania. Tombstones from the 17th century have been found in the local Jewish cemetery. There were 1,350 Jews living in Kupiskis in 1847 and 2,661 (71% of the population) in 1897. During World War I, in May 1915, the Jews were expelled from Kupiskis, and only part of the Jewish population returned there after the war. The community numbered 1,444 (54%) in 1923, and continued to decrease in the interwar period, many of the youth immigrating to South Africa and Ereẓ Israel. The Jewish people's bank there had 369 members in 1929. As Kupiskis was one of the few towns in Lithuania with a considerable community of Ḥasidim, there were two officiating rabbis. The community had three synagogues, a yeshivah, a *talmud torah*, and three schools (Yavneh, *Tarbut, and a Yiddish school). After the German occupation the community was annihilated. In all, including Jews from the vicinity, around 3,000 were murdered.

[Dov Levin]

KURANDA, IGNAZ (1812–1884), liberal politician and Jewish communal leader in Austria. Born in Prague into a family of second-hand book dealers, Kuranda considered himself of Hussite origin. He studied for a time at Aaron *Kornfeld's yeshivah in Golcuv Jenikov. Moving to Vienna in 1834, he concentrated on writing, and one of his plays was performed. After living in Stuttgart and Paris, he went to Brussels, where he lectured on German literature and became popular with the anti-French Flemish movement, which admired everything German. In 1841 he founded the periodical *Die Grenzboten* in Brussels. It served as an organ of the pre-1848 German liberal opposition which criticized Austrian internal policy while upholding the supremacy of Austria over Germany. An outcome of his Brussels stay was his book *Belgien seit seiner Revolution* (1846). In 1842 he transferred *Die Grenzboten* to Leipzig, where he was once more mainly occupied with Austrian affairs and smuggling his periodical into that country. Jewish writers, including Moritz *Hartmann, were among his collaborators, and Kuranda helped Joseph von *Wertheimer to publish *Die Juden Oesterreichs* (1842). Returning to Vienna at the time of the 1848 revolution, he was elected to the German National Assembly in Frankfurt. Kuranda became the focus of the Czech nationalist hatred of the Jews, whom they identified with the Germans. A popular song advocated sending Kuranda to Frankfurt, urging that all the useless Jews in Bohemia be sent after him. Nevertheless, Kuranda headed the unsuccessful delegation sent by the National Assembly to Prague to persuade Czech politicians to attend the assembly. On the occasion of his wedding in Kolin (Bohemia) in the same year, anti-Jewish rioting broke out and he had to flee the town. In Vienna he established the *Ostdeutsche Post* (discontinued in 1866). After the failure of the 1848 revolution, he was kept under police supervision. After forcing the antisemite S. *Brunner to sue him for libel in 1860, Kuranda was acquitted, thereby gaining popularity among East European Jewry. Kuranda was elected to the Diet of Lower Austria in 1861, retaining his seat for 20 years. An ardent supporter of Centralism and German supremacy in Austria, he opposed the declaration of war against Prussia in 1866. A leader of the German liberal party for 23 years, he represented it on the Vienna city council.

At the same time, he devoted himself to Jewish affairs. From 1860 he was on the board of the Vienna community, serving as its president from 1872. He caused a crisis in the community through his attempt to introduce liturgical reforms, but a split was averted when a compromise was found. A supporter of Jewish studies, he was also vice president of the *Israelitische Allianz. He assisted Joseph *Bloch in his action against August *Rohling. Toward the end of his life, Kuranda's hopes of identifying the Jews with German policy in Austria began to decline. In 1882 he said, "I fear that tomorrow will destroy what has been created today."

His son CAMILLO (1851–1919), a civil servant, was a specialist in classical Roman law, publishing several books in the field, but was never admitted to the deputies' club because he was a Jew. He was also on the board of the Israelitische Allianz.

BIBLIOGRAPHY: L. Wolf, *Essays on Jewish History* (1934), 51–54; Z. Szajkowski, in: JSOS, 19 (1957), 37–38; J.S. Bloch, *Reminiscences* (1923), 136–8 and passim; M. Grunwald, *Vienna* (1936), index; Y. Toury, *Mehumah u-Mevukhah be-Mahpekhat 1848* (1968), index; H. Tietze, *Juden Wiens* (1935), index; G. Franz, *Liberalismus, Die deutschliberale Bewegung in der habsburgischen Monarchie* (1955), index; A. Kohut, in: AZDJ, 76 (1912), 273–5, 282–4, 292–4; ADB, 51 (1906), 445–50; P.G.J. Pulzer, *Rise of Political Anti-Semitism in Germany and Austria* (1964), index.

[Meir Lamed]

KURDISTAN, region in the Middle East, divided among three countries: *Turkey, *Iraq, and *Iran. The majority of the Muslim population of Kurdistan lives in Turkey, another part in Iran, and the smallest part in Iraq. In contrast, the Jews of Kurdistan – until their great exodus in 1950–51 – lived mainly in the Iraqi region (146 communities), some in the Iranian region (19 communities), and only a few in Turkey (11 communities). There were also a few Jews in the Syrian region and other places (11 communities). There are no accurate statistics on the Jews of Kurdistan. It has been estimated that before the establishment of the State of Israel there were between 20,000 and 30,000 Jews living there. Kurdish Jews also lived in the Diyala province of Iraq, especially in the town of *Khanaqin, the number of Jews varying between 1,689 in 1920; 2,252, 1932; and 2,851, 1947. The Jews of Mosul speak Arabic and some also understand Turkish and Kurdish. For this reason, some scholars do not reckon them among the Kurdish Jews, even though they resemble them somewhat in their way of life. They form a separate unit known by the name *Miṣlawim*.

In Iraq

HISTORY. An ancient tradition relates that the Jews of Kurdistan are the descendants of the Ten Tribes from the time of the Assyrian exile. The first to mention this was R. *Benjamin of Tudela, the 12th-century traveler who visited Kurdistan in about 1170 and found more than 100 Jewish communities. In the town of *Amadiya alone, there were 25,000 Jews who spoke the language of the Targum (Aramaic) and whose numbers included scholars. The traveler *Benjamin the Second, who visited Kurdistan in 1848, also mentioned this tradition and added that the Nestorian (Assyrian) tribes were also descendants of the Ten Tribes and that they practiced Jewish customs. According to his assumption, they were descendants of Dan and Naphtali. There is no doubt that Halah and Ḥabor (modern Khabur), the river of Gozan (II Kings 17:6) – the places to which Shalmaneser, the king of Assyria, exiled the tribes – are in the vicinity of Kurdistan. During the Second Temple era the kingdom of *Adiabene was situated in this region; its inhabitants, together with their king, Monobaz, and his mother Helena, converted to Judaism in the middle of the first century. It may be presumed that there are descendants of these proselytes among the Jews of Kurdistan. *Onkelos translated *Harei Ararat* as "the mountains of Kardu" (Gen. 8:4); he also translated *Mamlekhot Ararat* as "the Kingdom of the land of Kardu" (Jer. 51:27). Josephus mentions the "mountains of Kurdukhim" (Ant. 1:93). In the Talmud it is related that "one accepts proselytes from the Kardus" (Yev. 16a).

An ancient popular tradition states that among the Assyrians of northern Iraq there were many families of Jewish origin and these were forcibly converted to Christianity more than 500 years ago. They still observe special Jewish customs, have not assimilated among the Christians, marry among themselves, and are afraid of revealing their origin in front of the Christians. Another popular tradition states that many of the descendants of the Ten Tribes who were exiled to this region by the kings of Assyria converted to Christianity. In 38 villages of Iraqi Kurdistan there were hundreds of Jews who claimed descent from the tribe of Benjamin and who possessed a holy book in Kurdish. They lived in the provinces of Mosul, Kirkuk, and Khanaqin. Some of them emigrated to *Afghanistan and the Caucasus. During the middle of the seventh century – at the time of the Arab conquest – the treaty of conquest was signed in the town of Dabil, on the Armenian border, with the "Magians [Zoroastrians] and the Jews" (according to al-Balādhurī, *Futūḥ al-Buldān* (1318 A.H.), 280; Yāqūt, *Muʿjam*, s.v. Dabīl). From this it is ascertained that there was another Jewish community in addition to that of Mosul and possibly that of Irbil.

During the 12th century two messianic movements arose in the neighborhood of the town of Amadiya: that of Menahem b. Solomon ibn Ruḥi (or Dugi) and that of David *Alroy. Some scholars regard these as one movement. There is no clear information available on the situation of the Jews during the 13th–15th centuries. From the beginning of the 16th century, however, information gradually becomes more available. The statistics provided by various travelers of different periods indicate great fluctuations over short periods of time in the Jewish population of every town and village. At times, the Jewish population increased or decreased by several hundred within four or five years. The cause for this was the instability of their economic and security situation; consequently, they often migrated from the smaller villages to the larger ones and from there to the large towns. Every pogrom caused the local Jews to flee to neighboring communities – for long or short periods – until the danger was past. In the 20th century the use of motor vehicles was an important reason for the removal of commerce from the smaller centers to the larger ones. Since there were no official statistics, the travelers relied solely on estimates.

ECONOMIC CONDITIONS. The economic situation of the Jews was difficult; many of them lived in poverty and distress. The urban Jews were essentially engaged in commerce and crafts. Several of them owned estates with peasants and agricultural laborers. In eastern Kurdistan the number of merchants was greater than that of craftsmen. These tradesmen could be divided into wholesalers, shopkeepers, and peddlers. The craftsmen were weavers, gold- and silversmiths, dyers, carpenters, tanners, cobblers, and unskilled workers. There were no bankers among the Jews, this occupation being in the hands of the feudal lords. The Jewish farmers cultivated mainly wheat, barley, rice, sesame, lentils, and tobacco. They owned orchards, vineyards, flocks of sheep, and herds of cattle. There were also agricultural villages, all of whose inhabitants were Jews (e.g., Sindur). Jewish peasants were found mainly in *Ruwandiz, Tel-Kabar, Barazan, *Dehok, Aqrah, Shandukha, Bitanura, Bashkala, Koi-Sanjaq, Mirawa, Karada, and Girzengal. As a result of droughts, famines broke out in several places (1880, 1888, 1889, etc.) and their inhabitants were compelled to migrate to other places. Many fled to Baghdad, where they found employment in various occupations. The Jews of Kurdistan are known for their strength and sturdiness.

INSTABILITY OF LIVING CONDITIONS. The lives of the Jews of Kurdistan were subject to anarchy. Political and economic factors determined their places of residence and their migrations from one place to another. They were scattered in many villages and lived among various Muslim and Christian sects. Robbery and murder were common occurrences. Because of their isolation from the outside world, no concern was shown for them; their persons and belongings were enslaved to feudal rulers. In order to safeguard their lives, they were compelled to seek the protection of the powerful Agha, to whom they paid a special tax. He was a kind of tribal chief who traveled about accompanied by groups of armed servants. The Jews subordinated themselves to him and fulfilled his orders. Some of the Aghas sold Jews or gave them away as presents; this servitude continued until the beginning of the 20th century. In 1912, 12 Jews were murdered in Kurdistan. For them this was the sign to liquidate their affairs and sell their fields and houses at a low price in order to emigrate to Palestine. The anti-Zionist propaganda which began in Iraq in 1925 adversely affected the position of the Jews of Kurdistan. The persecutions gained in intensity from day to day and reached their height at the time of the revolt of Rashīd ʿĀlī (1941). With establishment of the State of Israel, most of them traveled to Baghdad and from there flew to Israel in the "Operation Ezra and Nehemiah." In 1970 a small number of Kurdish Jews remained in the regions of Iran, Turkey, and Syria.

THE ORGANIZATION OF THE COMMUNITIES AND THEIR SPIRITUAL FOUNDATION. Prior to the 19th century the large communities were headed by *nesi'im* who imposed their authority on the public and collected special taxes. The *nasi* was also called *shoter* ("officer of the law") or *sar* ("minister"). The *ḥakhamim* were also subordinated to them. This position was abolished during the 19th century. From the beginning of the 16th century, there were several rabbis of the Adoni (or *Barazani), Mizraḥi, Duga, and Ḥariri families. Some of them practiced practical Kabbalah and various legends were woven around them. About 30 Kurdish *paytanim* are known from among the inhabitants of Barazan, Mosul, Amadiya, Ḥarīr, Naṣībīn, *Zākho, and other places. They wrote religious and secular poems in Hebrew and in Aramaic; 54 of them were published by Abraham Ben-Jacob in his book *Kehillot Yehudei Kurdistan* (1961). The most important of these poets were R. Samuel b. Nethanel ha-Levi *Barazani, who was also a *rosh yeshivah* in Mosul during the 17th century, and his daughter Asenath; R. Phineas b. R. Isaac Ḥariri and his son R. Ḥayyim; R. Simeon b. Jonah Mizraḥi; R. Gershon b. Raḥamim; R. Simeon b. Benjamin Abidani; R. Moses b. Isaac Bajulnaya; R. Samuel b. Simeon ʿAjamiya; R. Baruch b. Samuel Mizraḥi, the author of *Shirei Zimrah*; and others.

Each community was headed by the *ḥakham*, who was also a *ḥazzan, mohel, shoḥet*, and *bodek* ("examiner of slaughtered animals"), treasurer, teacher, scribe, and writer of amulets. The smaller communities were subordinated to the larger ones; in all religious and legal matters they turned to the rabbis of Baghdad. Religious and spiritual life was centered around the synagogue and the *talmud torah*. In the large communities there were several synagogues, some of which were very old. One was built in 1210 (in Mosul) and a second in 1228 (in Amadiya). The Alliance Israélite Universelle opened schools only in the towns of Mosul (1900 and 1906) and Kirkuk (in 1912).

KURDISH LANGUAGE. The Jews of Kurdistan spoke an Aramaic with insertions of Turkish, Persian, Kurdish, Arabic, and Hebrew words. They called it the "language of the Targum" or *Lishna Yehudiyya* ("language of the Jews"), as well as *Lashon ha-Galut*. The Arabs called it *jabalī*, i.e., "of the mountains," because it was essentially spoken by the inhabitants of the mountains. They called themselves *Anshei Targum* ("People of [the language of] the Targum"). A.J. Maclean found four dialects in the language; J.J. *Rivlin found only three dialects. The Nestorian Christians who live in this region also speak Aramaic, which they refer to as "Syrian." This language is also spoken by the Sabeans, who live along the banks of the Lower Euphrates, around the town of Nāṣiriyya, and along the banks of the Lower Tigris in the region of Amadiya. In about 1930 it was estimated that 9,837 persons spoke *Aramaic in Iraqi Kurdistan; they were to be found in the following provinces (*qaḍā*'): Zakho (1,471), Amadiya (1,821), Zibar (100), Ruwandiz (250), Dehok (843), ʿAqrah (1,000), Irbil (250), Matuk (1,900), Koi-Sanjaq (302), Sulaimaniya (900), Halabja (400), and in others (500). In addition to the above, Aramaic was also spoken in Persian and Turkish Kurdistan and in Israel. It is estimated that between 15,000 and 20,000 people speak Aramaic.

ALIYYOT TO PALESTINE. Dozens of emissaries from Palestine visited Kurdistan; they noted the Jews' sympathy for and contributions to the Holy Land. The *aliyah* to Palestine already began during the 16th century. The first immigrants lived in Safed. Between 1920 and 1926, 1,900 Kurdish Jews emigrated to Palestine. In 1935, 2,500 Jews emigrated. With the establishment of the State of Israel almost all the Jews of Iraqi Kurdistan (see *Iraq, Kurdish Jews), and many from other places, emigrated there. In Israel they formed committees, according to the provinces and towns where they had lived in Kurdistan, and are scattered in many towns and settlements, with a large proportion living in and around Jerusalem.

[Abraham Ben-Yaacob]

In Iran

The Jewish Kurds of Iran have traditionally been living in Iran since 722 B.C., when according to II Kings (17:6; 18: 9–12) they were deported from Samaria and brought to the cities of the Medes, which roughly correspond to the present provinces of *Azerbaijan, Kurdistan, and the western part of *Gilān. Jewish Kurds are mentioned by Benjamin of Tudela. The Jewish Kurds of Iran speak their own language, which linguistically is classified as a Neo-Judeo-Aramaic language. They have produced their own literature in this language. It is close to the present language of the Assyrians (Ashuri). If their language is an indication of their ethnic identity, one may say they do not live only in the province of Kurdistan but also in the cities and villages of Azerbaijan and territories adjacent to Gilān, *Hamadan, *Kermanshah, and their vicinity. As such, it is safe to say that in the 20th century they lived in more than 45 towns and villages in north and northwest Iran.

There are no coherent historical records of their past except some scattered information gathered from Jewish and non-Jewish travelogues. Rabbi David d'Beth Hillel visited the following settlements of the Iranian Jewish Kurds around 1827/28: Bāneh, where ten Jewish families lived together with 1,000 Muslim families; they were poor and possessed one synagogue. Fifteen Jewish families lived in Saqqez which had 1,000 Muslim families. They had one synagogue and some of them were wealthy. Sāvoj-Bulāgh (today called Mahābād) was a large city, having 25 Jewish families and a fine synagogue. They were generally rich and lived among 15,000 Muslim families. R. David mentions a village where 10 Jewish families lived but he does not give its name (most probably the village was Tāzeh-Qal`eh). In Urmiah (name changed to Rezāiyeh) 200 Jewish families lived among 60,000 Muslims who, according to the traveler, were "wicked" and spoke Persian, Turkish, and Kurdish. Jews had three synagogues and most of them lived comfortably. The rabbi of the Jewish community was a rich man. The Christians there were more mistreated than the Jews. The "beautiful city" of Salmās (changed to Shāhpur) had 100 Jewish and 400 Christian families and 10,000 Muslim inhabitants. Most of the Jews were rich. They had one fine synagogue. In the city of Bāsh-Qalʿeh there lived 20 Jewish, 100 Christian, and 2,000 Muslim families. Most of the Jews were rich and they had one small synagogue. In the small town of Miyāndoab there were 15 Jewish families among 4,000 Muslims. The town had no Christians. In 1801 a violent pogrom befell the Jews of the city as a result of a blood libel. The town of Garus had 25 Jewish families living among 3,000 Muslim families. Some of the Jews were rich. There were no Christians in the town. In the big city of Seneh (name changed to Sanandaj) there were 300 Jewish families among 50,000 Muslim families. They had two synagogues and some were rich merchants. In the small town of Qoslān five

Jewish families lived among 1,000 Muslims. No Christians lived there.

There is no doubt that there were several dozen towns and villages where Jewish Kurds lived. Reports about some of them came before their immigration to the State of Israel. In addition to what has been mentioned above, we hear of towns and villages such as Bijār, Bukān, Gahvāreh, Marivān, Naqdeh, Oshnoviyeh, Qorveh, Sardasht, Shāhin-Dez, Soldoz, Takāb, and others. In 1948, the Jewish Agency in Teheran estimated the total number of Jewish Kurds in Iran, Iraq, and Turkey at about 50,000, of which about 15,000 lived in Iran. It is possible that the real figures were higher. Almost all of them were preparing themselves for *aliyah* to the Jewish State. In general, relative to other Jewish communities across Iran, Jewish Kurds had correct relations with the Muslims, particularly with the Sunnis. The Israel-Arab conflict aggravated their fragile relations, however. By the end of the 20th century a small number of Jews were reported to have been living in large cities of Kurdistan such as Sanandaj and Mahābād. In Israel, the Jewish Kurds of Iran separated themselves from those of other countries. They have their separate organizations and even plan their feast on the last day of Passover on different days and under different names: Seyrānah for the Kurds of Iran and Sahrānah for other Jewish Kurds. Their common periodical in Israel is called *Hitḥadshut*.

[Amnon Netzer (2nd ed.)]

Musical Tradition

The style of Jewish music in Kurdistan is conditioned by the multinational and multilingual character of the country which in its long history scarcely ever aimed at a cultural centralization and thus helped to preserve the musical dialects of the Iraqi, Iranian, Syrian, and Turkish regions of the area. The foremost feature of Jewish song in Kurdistan is the unique melodic style of the renditions of Aramaic texts (which is distinct from the general "Oriental Sephardi" style used for Hebrew texts). Connected with liturgical or spiritual texts, this melodic style is basically determined by the speech-melody of the Aramaic language, with a tendency to proceed over long stretches in a litany or parlando style, especially if the text is of a narrative nature (as in the chanting of the biblical books in the local Aramaic version, or the Zohar). If the contents are of a poetical or meditative-kabbalistic nature, the words may be interrupted by long and drawn-out melismatic insertions produced in a slow and deep vibrato, often with a curious change of voice timbre.

A further factor for the formation of Jewish song in Kurdistan is the contact with Arab music, which since the early days of Islam had gradually replaced the older musical idiom of the Mesopotamian area, especially in the sphere of artistic urban music. Equally important for the formation of the Jewish-Kurdish style of synagogue song were the bonds with the major tradition of Jewish music, foremost – cantillation and *ḥazzanut* styles. These were brought in and taught by emissaries from the spiritual centers of Near-Eastern Judaism, in the "Oriental Sephardi" idiom which was in itself already a synthesis, and which is different from the indigenous "mountain" (*jabalī*) idiom. The Kurdish cantors thus tended to be musically bilingual. However, time works against the continuation of the indigenous tradition.

Still another factor is the Kurdish folk song proper, in the Kurmanji language, with its epics, ballads, and dances, which has been widely accepted by the Jews, and synthesized with their other singing styles. The fact that Kurdish Jews lived as free peasants side by side with their Muslim neighbors is a rare instance in the history of Diaspora life, and has doubtlessly contributed to the acceptance of the host culture's lore and song.

Summarizing the distribution of languages and musical structures, which exists even within the boundaries of the one (and main) region of Iraqi Kurdistan, the following divisions become apparent in which the distinction of language is congruent with the distinctiveness of musical style: (1) Hebrew, for the liturgical music of the synagogue; (2) "Targum," i.e., Aramaic, for the religious and paraliturgical music of the *ḥeder*, yeshivah, and some rituals, serving for the study, vernacularization, and paraphrasing of the sacred texts; (3) Arabic, for the secular songs taken over from popular and artistic urban music, serving for purely social gatherings; and (4) Kurdish (*Kurmanji*), for the folk tradition of heroic epics, ballads, and dances of the rural milieu. The Hebrew and Aramaic idioms belong to the cycle of the liturgical year and the religious life cycle, and the Arabic and Kurdish idioms belong to the social folk level functions.

In this abundance of structures some main classes of music deserve particular attention. First is the chanting of the Bible, which has always been the nucleus of all creative imagination in Jewish music and its main contribution to the world's music culture. One of its basic forms is the chanting of the Psalms in a kind of speech-melody oscillating around an (imaginary) tone axis, which closely follows the poetical structure of the two half-verses, marking the main divisive points with definite and distinct melodic turns. The elaborate system of the masoretic accents is not utilized, and it is likely that an earlier version has been preserved here. Similar archaic trends can be observed in the melodic patterns of the cantillation of the biblical prose books, which suggest a pre- or extra-masoretic *jabalī* tradition for the "mode of the Prophets." The most ingenious part of Kurdish-Jewish song tradition is the paraphrasing of biblical stories in epic form, in the Aramaic vernacular. Its melodic frame reveals many common traits with the cantillation of the Pentateuch.

[Edith Gerson-Kiwi]

BIBLIOGRAPHY: IN IRAQ: E. Brauer, *Yehudei Kurdistan* (1947); A. Ben-Jacob, *Kehillot Yehudei Kurdistan* (1961); idem, *Yehudei Bavel* (1965), passim; idem, in: *Maḥanayim*, 119 (1968), 30–35; S. Assaf, in: *Zion Me'assef*, 6 (1934), 85–112; A.J. Brawer, in: *Minḥah le-David Yellin* (1935), 245–51; S. Assaf, *Be-Oholei Ya'akov* (1943), 116–44; J.J. Rivlin, *Shirat Yehudei ha-Targum* (1959); M. Benayahu, in: *Sefunot*, 9 (1964), 21–125; P.J. Magnarella, in: JJSO, 11:1 (1969), 51–58; I. Ben-Zvi, *The Exiled and the Redeemed* (1958), 40–49. IN IRAN: **ADD. BIBLIOGRAPHY:** M.D. Adler (ed.), *The Itinerary of Benjamin of Tudela* (1907);

J. Blau, *Le problème kurde, essai sociologique et historique* (1963); E. Brauer, *The Jews of Kurdistan*, completed and edited by R. Patai (1993); R.W. Cottam, *Nationalism in Iran* (1978); David d'Beth Hillel, *Unknown Jews in Unknown Lands (1824–1832)*, ed. by W.J. Fischel (1973); A.R. Ghassemlou et al., *People Without a Country* (1980); S. Landshut, *Jewish Communities in the Muslim Countries of the Middle East* (1950), 61–66; H. Levy, *History of the Jews of Iran*, vol. 3 (1960), 804ff.; E.E. Lytle, *A Biography of the Kurds, Kurdistan, and the Kurdish Question* (1977); Sh. Marcus, *Yehudei Kurdistan* (1964); Y. Sabar, *The Folk Literature of the Kurdistani Jews, An Anthology* (1982). MUSICAL TRADITION: E. Gerson-Kiwi, in *Studia Musicologica*, 7 (1965), 61–70; Idelsohn, Melodien, 2 (1922), 31, 128–9.

KURREIN, MAX (1878–1966), Israeli engineer. Born in Austria, Kurrein worked in Birmingham (England) and in Duesseldorf, and from 1921 to 1934 was professor at the Technische Hochschule in Berlin. In 1934 he went to Palestine and was professor of industrial engineering at the Technion, Haifa, until 1958. Kurrein wrote many books, including *Cutting Tools for Metal Machining* (with F.C. Lea, 1940, second edition, 1947) and *Plasticity of Metals* (1964).

KURSHEEDT, ISRAEL BAER (1766–1852), U.S. merchant, broker, and communal leader. Kursheedt, who was born in Germany, studied under Rabbi Nathan *Adler in Frankfurt. After finishing his studies, he went into business as a contractor supplying the Prussian Army, an undertaking which proved successful. In 1796 he immigrated to the United States. After a short stay in Boston, Kursheedt settled in New York City, became active in Jewish affairs there, and was eventually chosen president of the Shearith Israel Congregation. During this period, he married the daughter of the Sephardi rabbi Gershom Mendes *Seixas. In 1812 he moved to Richmond, Virginia, where he remained for 12 years and was a member of the city's Beth Shalom synagogue. Upon returning to New York, he joined in founding the B'nai Jeshurun Congregation in 1825. In 1834 he organized the Hebrath Terumath Hakodesh, a charity dedicated to aiding the Jewish community in Palestine. Kursheedt was also president during this period of the Hebrew Mutual Benefit Society. When U.S. Jews organized themselves in protest over the *Damascus Affair (1840), Kursheedt was elected chairman of the action committee. In this capacity, he wrote to President Van Buren requesting that the American consul in Alexandria use his influence to obtain a fair trial for the persecuted Syrian Jews.

BIBLIOGRAPHY: H. Ezekiel et al., *The History of the Jews of Richmond* (1917).

[Leo Hershkowitz]

KURSK, capital of Kursk district, Russian Federation. Before the 1917 Revolution, Kursk was outside the *Pale of Settlement. In 1858 there were 458 Jews in the entire province (gubernia), most of them army veterans. The numbers for the province had risen to 4,355 in 1897, 1,689 of them (2.2% of the total population) in the city itself. The Kursk community was under the jurisdiction of the rabbi of Konotop. A pogrom occurred on October 20, 1905. In 1926, the Jewish population in the city was 4,154 (4.2%) and 4,914 (4.1%) in 1939. A Yiddish school existed from the early 1920s. The Germans occupied Kursk on November 2, 1941, and it seems that most of the town's Jews managed to escape. Nine Jews were killed a week later, 150 by February 1941, and a 100 in June or July 1942. In November 1956, after the *Sinai Campaign, the local Jews were compelled to sign an anti-Israel declaration published in *Izvestiya*. The only synagogue left in Kursk was closed by the authorities in the late 1960s. In 1970 the Jewish population of Kursk was estimated at about 9,000. In the early 2000s fewer than 1,000 remained but Jewish life had revived.

BIBLIOGRAPHY: *Die Judenpogrome in Russland*, 2 (1910), 513.

[Yehuda Slutsky / Shmuel Spector (2nd ed.)]

KURSKY, FRANZ (pseudonym of **Samuel Kahan**; 1874–1950), early Bundist, born in Courland. He was one of a large family which produced many revolutionaries, inspired by the memory of a grandfather in St. Petersburg who had fought against the anti-Jewish legislation. Kursky became a member of the Polish Social Democrats in the 1890s in Warsaw, and in 1899 joined the *Bund. He subsequently went abroad where for many years he directed the Bundist conspiratorial contacts with Russia. From 1906 he supervised the Bund archives in Geneva, later installed in New York and named after him. Kursky represented the Bund in the bureau of the Second Socialist International, and contributed to the international socialist press. After many years of activity in Berlin and Paris, he was, from 1941, active in Bundist groups in New York. His writings on the history of the Jewish labor movement, including his own part in it (see pp. 407–13), are included in his *Gezamlte Shriftn* (1952).

[Moshe Mishkinsky]

KURTH, ERNST (1886–1946), musicologist. Born in Vienna, Kurth studied there and from 1912 taught at the University of Bern. His *Grundlagen des linearen Kontrapunkts; Bach's melodische Polyphonie* (1917) established his reputation. It also influenced the younger generation of composers, and stimulated the study of Bach and the teaching of counterpoint. This work was followed by *Romantische Harmonik und ihre Krise in Wagner's Tristan* (1920), an account of romantic harmony down to Debussy. In his biographical study *Bruckner* (1925) Kurth propounded a theory of musical form. He summarized his conclusions in *Musikpsychologie* (1931).

KURTZ, AARON (1891–1964), Yiddish poet and editor. Born in Vitebsk, he wandered in Russia for five years as a wigmaker's apprentice and immigrated to the United States in 1911. In 1916 he began to publish Yiddish lyrics; at first he was attracted to the *In-Zikh movement and participated in its annuals, but he later joined the Association of Yiddish Proletarian Writers. In his third volume of verse, *Plakatn* ("Placards," 1927), he introduced a new form of poetry, which he called "placard style," which sought to reproduce the kaleidoscopic metropolis. The volumes *Di Goldene Shtot* ("The Golden City," 1935), *¡No Pasaran!* (1938), and *Mark Shagal* (1946) dealt, respectively, with New York, the Spanish republicans, and the painter, whose soul like his own was rooted in Jewish Vitebsk and who continued to seek a world of justice and pure love.

BIBLIOGRAPHY: Rejzen, Leksikon, 3 (1929), 616–18; B. Green, in: *Yidishe Kultur* (November 1964), 35–39. **ADD. BIBLIOGRAPHY:** LNYL, 8 (1981), 177–78; H. Gold, *Unzder Bukh* (1926), 371–73; J. Glatstein, *ibid.*, 53–54; L. Khanukov, *Literarishe Eseyen* (1960), 108–21.

[Sol Liptzin]

KURTZ, VERNON H. (1951–), U.S. Conservative rabbi. Kurtz was born in Toronto, Canada, where he earned his B.A. from York University in 1971. In 1973 he received his M.A. from the *Jewish Theological Seminary, where he was ordained in 1976. He received his doctor of ministry degree from Chicago Theological Seminary in 1981. He served as rabbi of Congregation Rodfei Zedek in Chicago from 1976 to 1988, when he moved to the north suburban synagogue Beth El in Highland Park, Ill. He was also appointed adjunct assistant professor of Rabbinic Literature at the Spertus Institute and adjunct lecturer in Jewish Studies at the Chicago Theological Seminary. In addition, he was a monthly Torah commentator for the *Chicago Jewish News*.

Kurtz served in numerous leadership positions in the areas of Jewish communal and interfaith activities. He was president of the Chicago Board of Rabbis (1995–97), president of the Council of Religious Leaders of Metropolitan Chicago (1997–99), chairman of the *United Jewish Appeal Rabbinic Cabinet (1995–97), and a member of the Board of Trustees and of the Executive Committee of the United Jewish Communities (1998–2004). He was a member of board of The Jewish Federation of Metropolitan Chicago and chairman of its Overseas Committee as well as a member of the board of governors of the *Jewish Agency for Israel.

In 2000 Kurtz was elected president of the *Rabbinical Assembly (RA), in which capacity he established a Women's Task Force, expanded the global focus of the RA with the center being in Israel, and worked to improve lay-professional relations with the drafting of a model rabbinic contract. Following his term of office, Kurtz was elected president of Mercaz USA (in 2002) and Mercaz Olami (in 2005), the American chapter and international arm of the Zionist Organization of the Conservative movement. By virtue of this succession of presidencies, he was a member of the *Presidents' Conference of Major American Jewish Organizations long enough to be appointed its membership chairman. He also returned to the RA's Committee on Jewish Law and Standards and was named to the Leadership Council of Conservative Judaism.

Kurtz received numerous awards from local and national Jewish organizations, including the Council of Jewish Federations and the State of Israel Bonds Organization, culminating in the Rabbi Simon Greenberg Rabbinic Achievement Award bestowed upon him by the Jewish Theological Seminary in 1998. He was awarded an honorary doctorate from JTS in 2003.

[Bezalel Gordon (2nd ed.)]

KURTZER, DANIEL CHARLES (1949–), U.S. diplomat. Kurtzer was born in 1949 and raised as an Orthodox Jew in Elizabeth, New Jersey. He received his B.A. from Yeshiva University and two M.A.s and his Ph.D. in political science from Columbia University. He has remained an Orthodox Jew, embodying the twin values of Torah U-Mada that characterized his alma mater during his generation.

Kurtzer began his career in the Foreign Service in 1976, within the Bureau of International Organizational Affairs where he worked on UN political, economic, humanitarian, and developmental issues. Later, he left the State Department and became the youngest dean of Yeshiva College in New York. In 1979 Kurtzer was re-appointed to the Foreign Service and assigned as second secretary for political affairs at the American Embassy in Cairo. Then in 1982 he was appointed first secretary for political affairs at the American Embassy in Tel Aviv. He returned to Washington in 1986 and served as deputy director of Egyptian affairs and later as a speechwriter and a member of the secretary's policy planning staff. While in Tel Aviv, he won the Director General of the Foreign Service Award for reporting. In 1989 Kurtzer was appointed as deputy assistant secretary for Near Eastern affairs. After this, he served as principal deputy assistant secretary for intelligence and research, and then became acting assistant secretary in May 1997. President Bill Clinton named him U.S. ambassador to Egypt, the first Jew assigned as an American ambassador to an Arab country.

His appointment to Cairo raised considerable discomfort in the Egyptian capital, but over time Kurtzer impressed his Egyptian counterparts with the depth of his knowledge and his sheer professionalism. His appointment as U.S. ambassador to Israel by President George W. Bush was no less controversial. The Zionist Organization attacked his appointment, fearing that Kurtzer would be unduly harsh on the Israelis and unduly partisan toward the Arabs.

An anomaly as an Orthodox Jew working for the American government who negotiated with both Arabs and Israelis, Kurtzer was one of several Jews in the Clinton and the George W. Bush administrations responsible for Middle Eastern policy, along with Dennis *Ross, Martin *Indyk, and Eliot *Abrams. Each had a deep Jewish identity; Ross, Indyk, and Kurtzer were strong supporters of the Israeli peace process, and therefore doubly suspect by the right wing in Israel and the United States.

Kurtzer also faced antisemitism in Israel when Knesset member Zvi Hendel of the right-wing National Union Party attacked Kurtzer, calling him a "*yehudon*" ("little Jew") on the floor of the Knesset and charging Kurtzer with "interfering in [Israel's] internal affairs."

In Israel as well, Kurtzer conducted himself with professionalism and credibility. He was passed over for the presidency of Yeshiva University, where he had served as a dean, because he was too dovish for contemporary Orthodox life, but upon retiring from the Foreign Service in 2005 he returned to academia.

[Michael Berenbaum (2nd ed.)]

KURTZMAN, HARVEY (1924–1993), U.S. comic book creator. A cartoonist, writer, and editor with enormous influence on several generations of cartoonists and readers, Kurtzman was born in New York City and grew up with comic books. He was drawing a regular strip called *Ikey and Mikey* in chalk on neighborhood streets before he was in his teens. He had his first drawing published in 1939 in an issue of *Tip Top Comics.* He broke into the world of the commercial comic book market in 1939. After service in the army, Kurtzman found a job with Stan *Lee at Timely Comics, the precursor of modern-day Marvel. His first work was collected in the 1992 book *Hey Look!*, one-shot comic fillers he wrote, drew, and lettered. In the early 1950s, he created the ground-breaking and fabulously successful *Mad*, first as a wild color comic book, then as a black and white magazine. Under Kurtzman the magazine vigorously and fearlessly lampooned American institutions, including other comic strips and television, a medium then in its infancy. It was a publication aimed at adults. Kurtzman rediscovered and developed the character Alfred E. Neuman, *Mad*'s moronic gap-toothed mascot, created the distinctive logos, drew many early covers, and wrote most of the material for the historic first 28 issues. He left abruptly in a bitter dispute over equity with the magazine's publisher, William M. *Gaines. In 1957 Kutzman created *Trump*, a glossy high-budget satire magazine for Hugh Hefner, publisher of *Playboy*, who ceased publishing the magazine after two issues. In 1957, with other cartoonists, Kurtzman created *Humbug*, an innovative publication that lasted 11 issues. On his own, in 1959 he started his first pocketbook of all-new comics, *Jungle Book*. Its impact was profound but it too was commercially unsuccessful. He then partnered with James Warren to create his final satirical publication, *Help!* There, in the early 1960s, Kurtzman discovered and gave the first national exposure to a number of young cartoonists, including R. *Crumb, who later became integral to the "underground" comix movement. A Kurtzman assistant was Gloria *Steinem, who contributed to the magazine and who later was a founder of the magazine *Ms*. She was replaced by a college dropout, Terry Gilliam, who became one of the founders of Monty Python's Flying Circus. While at *Help!*, which relied a lot on photography (old movie stills were fitted out with new captions and complex and zany scenarios were depicted in a comic-book-like format), Kurtzman created a hilarious Candide-like feature called *Goodman Beaver* with Will *Elder. Kurtzman took the concept to a more financially secure Hugh Hefner, who approved a sex change in the character. The resulting *Little Annie Fanny*, starting in *Playboy* in 1962, was the most lavish comic strip ever created, and it continued as a *Playboy* mainstay until 1988. Such was the respect for Kurtzman and his contribution to the comic medium that the comics industry's oldest and most respected awards, The Harveys, are named for him.

[Stewart Kampel (2nd ed.)]

KURZ, SELMA (1874–1933), soprano singer. Kurz was born in Biala, Galicia, and made her debut in Hamburg as a mezzosoprano in 1895. Four years later, she was engaged by Gustav *Mahler for the Vienna Court Opera, where she appeared as a lyric-dramatic, then a coloratura, soprano, and where she remained on the roster until 1927. Her technique was brilliant enough to arouse, during her London appearances (1904–07), the jealousy of Melba, who subsequently kept her out of Covent Garden until 1927. Notable among her many Viennese successes was the creation of Zerbinetta in the revised version of Richard Strauss's *Ariadne auf Naxos* (1916), which displayed to advantage her gift of coloratura agility and her remarkable trill.

[Max Loppert (2nd ed.)]

KURZWEIL, BARUCH (Benedict; 1907–1972), Israeli literary critic, author, and educator. Born to a family of rabbis in Moravia, Kurzweil received his higher education in Germany and was ordained a rabbi. Immigrating to Palestine in 1939, he taught at Ḥugim High School in Haifa. In 1955 he was appointed professor of Hebrew literature at Bar-Ilan University. Kurzweil represents the New Criticism in modern Hebrew literature with its stress on close reading of the literary text itself and its internal structural and conceptual authenticity. Yet he also formulated a unified ideological framework for modern Hebrew literature, based on the assumption that its secularism breaks with the religious tradition which underlay all previous Jewish literature. As a result, the meaning of Jewish history is ignored, and modern Hebrew literature is in danger of losing its roots and, aesthetically, its depth. Kurzweil's work also opposes the secular concepts of *Aḥad Ha-Am, as well as *Scholem's assumption that the Shabbatean movement marks the beginning of modern Jewish history and paves the way, in part, for modern Hebrew literature. He considered the Shabbatean movement as an unhealthy deviation from normative Judaism.

Kurzweil's studies of *Agnon's writings led to a new and deeper appraisal of this writer's work. He gave a close reading of Agnon's stories, analyzing the symbols and explaining them within the framework of his total achievement. In his view Agnon was a novelist of epic proportions whose work depicts all the problems of a Jewish world that has broken with normative Judaism. He explained *Bialik's achievement along similar lines, believing that Bialik ultimately despaired of the Aḥad Ha-Amist attempt to give a secularist reading of the Jewish past, this despair being reflected in the death motif that dominates Bialik's later poems. In Uri Ẓevi *Greenberg, Kurzweil found a poet who by a leap of faith was able to reassert the mystique of Israel's unique connection with God and the complete "otherness" of the Jewish people.

First and foremost a cultural historian, Kurzweil also dealt with sociological phenomena. He thus analyzed the ideology of the movement and showed how it grew out of certain secular assumptions made by modern Hebrew authors. A contributor to *Haaretz and other Israel periodicals, his style, often polemical, was imbued with irony and wit. While his philosophical and historical views were controversial, Kurzweil was a significant commentator on the great artistic works of Hebrew literature. He also made a great contribution to the understanding in Israel of important European writers, such as Goethe, Kafka, and Thomas Mann.

His main works are *Massekhet ha-Roman* ("On the Novel," 1953), *Sifrutenu ha-Ḥadashah – Hemshekh o Mahpekhah?* ("Our New Literature; Continuation or Revolution?" 1965^2), *Bialik ve-Tchernichovsky* (1961); *Massot al Sippurei S.Y. Agnon* (1966^2); and *Bein Ḥazon le-Vein ha-Absurdi* ("Between the Vision and the Absurd," 1966). The Hebrew works of B. Kurzweil were edited (with a bibliography) by J. Barzilay (1963–65). The correspondence between S.Y. Agnon and B. Kurzweil was edited by L. Dabi-Guri (1987); a collection of essays and satires, *Miḥuẓ la-Teḥum*, appeared in 1998. Essays by Kurzweil in English translations include "Is There Such Thing as Biblical Tragedy?" in: *An Anthology of Hebrew Essays*, ed. by I. Cohen and B. Michali, 1 (1966), 97–116; "Job and the Possibility of Biblical Tragedy," in: *Arguments and Doctrines* (1970), 325–344; and "Notes on Hebrew Literature," in: *What is Jewish Literature?* (1994), 78–87. For other works in English see Goell, p. 88.

ADD. BIBLIOGRAPHY: *Haaretz* (July 28, 1967); H. Barzel, "*Aḥdut ve-Ribbui be-Mishnato shel B. Kurzweil*," in: *Moznayim* 25 (1967), 266–72; A.B. Jaffe, in: *Al ha-Mishmar* (Elul 22, 1972); J.S. Diamond, *The Literary Criticism of B. Kurzweil: A Study in Hebrew-European Literary Relationships* (1978); idem, "B. Kurzweil and Modern Hebrew Literature," in: *Hebrew Annual Review*, 3 (1979), 41–89; A. Oz, in: *Haaretz* (May 23, 1980); J.S. Diamond, "B. Kurzweil: The Sensibility of Weimar Germany in Ramat Gan," in: *Go and Study* (1980), 251–56; J.S. Diamond, *Barukh Kurzweil and Modern Hebrew Literature* (1983); S.L. Nash, "Criticism as a Calling: The Case of B. Kurzweil," in: *Prooftexts*, 5:3 (1985), 281–87; D.N. Myers, "The Scholem-Kurzweil Debate and Modern Jewish Historiography," in: *Modern Judaism*, 6:3 (1986), 261–86; Y. Amir, *Teguvot Ereẓ-Yisra'eliyyot le-Haguto shel Franz Rosenzweig: A.E. Simon, S.H. Bergman, B. Kurzweil, Y.J. Gutman* (1993); Y. Yitzhaki, "*Tarbut Ḥayyah ve-Noshemet: Kurzweil, Y. Dan ve-Dan Miron neged ha-Sifrut ha-Yisra'elit*," in: *Alei Siaḥ*, 9:3 (1997), 47–55; D. Laor, "*Kurzweil ve-ha-Kena'anim*," in: *Keshet* (1998), 32–45.

[Hillel Barzel]

KUSHNER, ALEKSANDER SEMENOVICH (1936–), Russian poet and translator. Kushner was born in Leningrad. In 1959 he graduated from the philological faculty of Leningrad's Herzen Pedagogical Institute and until 1970 worked as an evening school teacher. He began publishing poetry in 1957. His first collections of verse, *Pervoe vpechatlenie* ("First Impression," 1962) and *Nochnoy dozor* ("Night Watch," 1966), reflect to some degree the influence of V. *Khodasevich. Starting with the collection *Primety* ("Omens," 1969), Kushner can be linked with the tradition of the Acmeists (particularly with O. *Mandelshtam). His verse is distinguished, however, by considerable semantic simplicity and restraint in the choice of metaphor, which imparts an electric tension to his poetry. Kushner's poetry is written in classical meter, in strophes with a precise, somewhat subdued, rhythm. Basic motifs in his poetry are the inevitability of death, suffering, and persecution as necessary conditions for happiness; external lack of freedom as the source of internal freedom; solitude; and the metaphysical exile of the individual. His philosophical lyrics are based on rejection of the perceptible reality of daily life, of the urban scene, on precise and concrete observation, and filled with associations, reminiscences, and veiled allusions to the cultural symbols of all times and peoples (excluding, however, allusions to the Hebrew Bible). From the late 1960s, both Kushner and his poetry were criticized, and after an attack by the secretary of the Leningrad Party provincial committee of the Communist Party, he was not published for a while.

He became well known with the publication of his collections *Pis'mo* ("Letter," 1974) and *Pryamaya rech'* ("Direct Speech," 1975). The appearance of his collection *Golos* ("Voice," 1978) coincided with a raging argument, encompassing the Soviet *samizdat* (underground press) and émigré press, about the place and significance of his poetry which some considered the most outstanding in contemporary Russian literature. His book of selected poems *Kanva* ("Canvas," 1981) was succeeded by the collections *Tavricheskiy sad* ("Tauride Garden," 1984) and *Dnevnie sny* ("Day Dreams," 1986). Aleksander Kushner also published books of poems for children: *Zavetnoe zhelanie* ("Secret Wish," 1973), *Gorod v podarok* ("City as Gift," 1976), and *Velosiped* ("Bicycle," 1979).

In Kushner's poetry Jewish motifs appear only in references or allusions. An exception is the poem "Kogda tot pol'skiy pedadog…" ("When That Polish Pedadogue") about the educator and writer Janusz *Korczak. Upholding the principle of not leaving the Soviet Union and of not expressing an attitude about the Soviet regime, Kushner reacted to the mass emigration of other Jews from the Soviet Union with poems such as "The Next Time Too I Want To Live in Russia."

[Yuri Kulker / *The Shorter Jewish Encyclopaedia in Russian*]

KUSHNER, HAROLD S. (1935–), U.S. Conservative rabbi, bestselling author. Kushner was born in Brooklyn, N.Y., and received his B.A. from Columbia University in 1955. He was ordained at the Jewish Theological Seminary in 1960 and earned a Doctor of Hebrew Letters there in 1972. After serving as a U.S. Army chaplain at Fort Sill, Oklahoma (1960–62), he became assistant rabbi to Mordecai *Waxman at Temple Israel in Great Neck, N.Y. (1962–66) and then rabbi of Temple Israel in Natick, Mass., where he was named rabbi laureate in 1991. He also taught at Clark University as well as at the Jewish Theological Seminary. In the Conservative movement, Kushner was president of the New England Region of the Rabbinical Assembly (1972–74), editor of the quarterly *Conservative Judaism* (1980–84), and a member of the editorial committee that compiled the Rabbinical Assembly's prayer books *Likrat Shabbat* and *Mahzor Hadash*.

Kushner gained international fame with the publication of his third book, *When Bad Things Happen to Good People* (1981), a philosophical reflection on the death of his 14-year-old son that became a national bestseller, was translated into a dozen languages, and was named by Book of the Month Club as one of the most influential books of its time. In it he expressed the theology that not everything that happens to people is necessarily part of God's master plan; and when tragedy does strike, religion and faith can serve as sources of strength and comfort for the individual in pain. Kushner's next book, *When All You Ever Wanted Isn't Enough: The Search for a Life That Matters* (1986), was equally well received: his exploration of human aspiration was awarded a Christopher Medal for its "contribution to the exaltation of the human spirit."

Kushner continued to write books that invariably made the bestseller lists, including *Who Needs God* (1989); *To Life!: A Celebration of Jewish Being and Thinking* (1994); and *How Good Do We Have to Be?: A New Understanding of Guilt and Forgiveness* (1996); *Living a Life That Matters: Resolving the Conflict Between Conscience and Success* (2001); *The Lord Is My Shepherd: Healing Wisdom of the Twenty-third Psalm* (2003); and *Overcoming Life's Disappointments* (2006) – all the while serving the pastoral needs of his congregation. Many of Kushner's works – as well as seminars he had given based on his writings – have been recorded as audiobooks.

In 1995, Kushner was honored by the Christophers as one of 50 individuals who made the world a better place in the second half of the 20th century. His earlier books are *When Children Ask About God* (1971) and *Commanded to Live* (1973).

[Bezalel Gordon (2nd ed.)]

KUSHNER, LAWRENCE (1943–), U.S. Reform rabbi, theologian, author. Kushner was born in Detroit, Mich., and earned his B.A. from the University of Cincinnati in 1965. He was ordained at *Hebrew Union College in 1969, whereupon he became rabbinic fellow-in-residence at Congregation SOLEL in Highland Park, Ill. He also taught at Lake Forest College and the University of Kentucky. In 1971, he assumed the pulpit of Congregation Beth El in Sudbury, Mass., where he led his congregants to publish their own Sabbath and Festival Prayerbook, *V'taher Libenu* (*Purify Our Hearts*), the first gender-neutral Jewish liturgy ever written (1979). He also established a Tzedaka Collective, wherein members anonymously contribute 2% of their gross income to a common fund and determine its disbursement. In addition, Kushner was a visiting professor at Hebrew Union College-Jewish Institute of Religion in New York City (1986–2000), where he remained an adjunct member of the faculty. In 2002, Kushner was appointed scholar in residence at the Congregation Emanu-El of San Francisco, where he teaches and writes about institutional and individual spiritual renewal. He also serves as visiting professor of Jewish Spirituality at the Graduate Theological University in Berkeley.

Kushner is credited with originating the concept of synagogue havurot – small family fellowship groups that draw on the resources of the larger congregation – a phenomenon that spread throughout the Reform movement and into Conservative Judaism. As the first rabbinic chairman of the *Union of American Hebrew Congregations-*Central Conference of American Rabbis' Commission on Religious Living (1987–93), he designed the summer *kalla* for Spiritual Renewal and has since conducted numerous adult and family *kalla* weekends for personal religious growth. He also co-directed the Conference on Jewish-Christian Spirituality (1987) and served on the UAHC Board of Trustees.

Widely regarded as one of the most creative religious writers in America, Kushner has been a commentator on National Public Radio (1966–68). His articles have been published in many periodicals, and he has contributed to more than 20 books (including collaborating with Lawrence *Hoffman on *Siddur Ami: My People's Prayerbook*). He has co-authored six books and written 10, translated into six languages. They include *God Was in This Place and I Did Not Know: Finding Self, Spirituality and Ultimate Meaning* (1991); *Sparks Beneath the Surface: A Spiritual Commentary on the Torah* (with Kerry Olitzky, 1993); *The Book of Words: Talking Spiritual Life, Living Spiritual Talk* (1994); *Invisible Lines of Connection: Sacred Stories of the Ordinary* (1996); *The Book of Miracles: A Young Person's Guide to Jewish Spirituality* (1997); *Eyes Remade for Wonder: A Lawrence Kushner Reader* (1998); *Kabbalah: The Way of Light* (1999); *Because Nothing Looks Like God* (with Karen Kushner, 2000); *The Way Into Jewish Mystical Tradition* (2001); *Jewish Spirituality: A Brief Introduction for Christians* (2001); *Five Cities of Refuge: Weekly Reflections on Genesis, Exodus, Leviticus, Numbers and Deuteronomy* (with David Mamet, 2003); *Filling Words With Light: Ḥasidic and Spiritual Refractions of Jewish Prayer* (with Nehemiah Polen, 2004); *In God's Hands* (with Gary Schmidt, 2005); and *Kabbalah: A Love Story* (2006).

[Bezalel Gordon (2nd ed.)]

KUSHNER, TONY (1956–), U.S. playwright. Born in New York City, Kushner grew up in Lake Charles, Louisiana, where his father inherited the family lumber business. He attended Columbia University, where he earned a degree in medieval studies, and New York University, where he completed a master of fine arts degree in 1984. His first plays, starting with *The Age of Assassins* (1982), *Yes, Yes, No, No* (1985), and *A Bright Room Called Day* (1987), about Hitler's rise and contemporary America, attracted little notice. But in 1991 and 1992, his *Angels in America*, a two-part, seven-hour drama about life in the age of AIDS, burst upon the theatrical scene and became one of the most widely admired works of the late 20th century. The play mingles the political, personal, and universal in its treatment of such apparently disparate elements as homosexual and traditional relationships, Mormonism, Roy M. Cohn, Ethel Rosenberg, disease, love, and death. The play follows the lives of two couples and their friends, relatives, and visionary visitors as they struggle to come to terms with the realities of the late 20th century. One character, Prior

Walter, has AIDS. Unable to cope, his lover, Louis, leaves him and begins an affair with Joe, a Mormon lawyer who is about to leave his wife. Abandoned and dying, Prior begins to have visions of an angel. At the same time, Joe is drawn into the orbit of Cohn, an unscrupulous lawyer and political operator who is himself dying of AIDS. Kushner was hailed as a major talent, intelligent, witty, and humane. *Angels in America* won the Pulitzer Prize for drama, the Tony award for best play, best actor, and best direction, among other honors. A television miniseries version, directed by Mike *Nichols in 2003 and starring Al Pacino, Meryl Streep, and Emma Thompson, swept the national television awards, the Emmys, winning 11 prizes. In 1998 London's National Theater selected *Angels in America* as one of the 10 best plays of the 20th century.

Overall, Kushner intends his plays to be part of a greater political movement. His work is concerned with moral responsibility during politically repressive times, and he brought the lofty into the approachable by creating everyday characters who collide both comically and tragically on stage.

Kushner's other works include *Slavs!* (1995) and *Homebody/Kabul*, a play about Afghanistan that opened shortly after the terrorist attacks of September 11, 2001. He also wrote adaptations of Corneille's *The Illusion*, S.Y. Ansky's *The Dybbuk*, and Brecht's *The Person of Sezuan*. *Caroline or Change*, a musical he wrote with the composer Jeanine Tesori, had its debut in 2004. He also wrote an original screenplay for a 2005 film directed by Steven *Spielberg that chronicles the events of the 1972 Munich Olympics, in which 11 members of the Israeli team were murdered, and the plan by the secret Mossad squad to track down and kill the assassins.

His books include *Brundibar* (2003), a book for children with illustrations by Maurice *Sendak, and *Wrestling With Zion: Progressive Jewish-American Responses to the Palestinian-Israeli Conflict* (2003), co-edited with Alisa Solomon. Among his honors were an Arts Award from the American Academy of Arts and Letters, a Spirit of Justice Award from the Gay and Lesbian Advocates and Defenders, and a Cultural Achievement Award from the National Foundation for Jewish Culture.

[Stewart Kampel (2nd ed.)]

KUSHNER, TONY (1960–), British historian. Tony Kushner, Marcus Sieff Professor of Jewish history at Southampton University, wrote widely on antisemitism and the immigrant experience, especially in Britain, and on the Holocaust. His very prolific writings emphasized the ambiguity of the Jewish experience and discerned, often from a left-wing perspective, more antisemitism in British society than some previous historians. Kushner linked this with British liberalism, which often could not accommodate the specific situation of the Jews and had difficulties in imagining the unprecedented evil of the Holocaust. He is the author of *The Persistence of Prejudice: Antisemitism in British Society During the Second World War* (1989) and *The Holocaust and the Liberal Imagination* (1994). He was also the editor or co-editor of more than a dozen collections of original essays, such as *Refugees in an Age of Genocide* (1999).

[William D. Rubinstein (2nd ed.)]

KUSHNIROV, AARON (1890–1949), Soviet Yiddish poet, prose writer, and dramatist. Born near Kiev, Kushnirov published his first poem in 1920, while serving in the Red Army, followed by his first collection of poems, *Vent* ("Walls," 1921). In 1922 he settled in Moscow and joined *Shtrom*, the last independent Yiddish journal in the Soviet Union. He attempted to launch an alternative periodical, *Ekran*, as a forum of proletarian writers. In 1925 he became a leading member of the Yiddish group at the Moscow Association of Proletarian Writers. In a classical style, containing elements of imagism, Kushnirov wrote both about the joy of the Revolution and of his despair at the pogroms in Ukraine. His poem "Azkore" ("In Memoriam," 1923) attracted wide attention. His second collection of poems, *Broyz* ("Rage," 1928), which combines classical and expressionist forms, continues the revolutionary motif. His collection of short stories, *Kinder fun Eyn Folk* ("Children of One People," 1928), was hailed in Russia as a model of good Soviet prose. Kushnirov also composed the verse dramas *Der Urteyl Kumt* ("Judgment Arrives") and *Hirsh Lekert* (1929), the latter of which was successfully staged in Minsk, describing the Bundist worker's attempt to assassinate the governor of Vilna in 1902. Ironically, it was an anti-Bundist play. *Geklibene Werk*, a selection of his works, was published in Moscow in 1947. After serving in World War II, where he was decorated twice for bravery, he was editor of the Moscow bimonthly *Heymland* (1947–1948). He died soon after the disbanding (as part of Stalinist repression of Jewish culture) of the Yiddish section at the Writers' Union.

BIBLIOGRAPHY: Rejzen, Leksikon, 3 (1929), 619–23; S. Niger, *Yidishe Shrayber in Sovyet-Rusland* (1958), 56–61. **ADD. BIBLIOGRAPHY:** Ch. Shmeruk (ed.), *A Shpigl oyf a Shteyn* (1987), 309–34, 745–7; G. Estraikh, *In Harness* (2005), index.

[Elias Schulman / Gennady Estraikh (2nd ed.)]

KUTNO, town in the province of Lodz, central Poland. Jews lived in the town from its beginnings in the 15th century and are mentioned in an official document of 1513. Between 1728 and 1738 the Jews paid 1,500 to 1,800 zlotys in poll tax. In 1753 a fire destroyed the town, and all Jewish documents, including the community minute book (*pinkas*), were burned so that no sources remain which would throw light on Jewish activity there. The extent of the commercial activities of the Jews there may be indicated by the surnames Kutnis or Kutnes found among Jews in the 17th and 18th centuries in western Germany and in Amsterdam. After 1753 the town was soon rebuilt and the Jews reestablished their institutions. The *pinkas* of the *ḥevra kaddisha* contains records from 1755. Various institutions were built only at the beginning of the 19th century, e.g., the *ḥevrah kaddisha* hospital, erected after 1808. Jews from Kutno attended the fairs at Leipzig and Frankfurt on the Oder in 1793. The number of Jews in Kutno increased from 928 in 1765 to 1,376 (70.2% of the total population) in 1800 and 8,978 (63.1%) in 1908, but fell to 6,784 (42.4%) in 1921 and 6,440 (27.5%) in 1931. Kutno was a center of Torah study and Haskalah; the most famous of its rabbis was Israel Joshua *Trunk.

[Shimshon Leib Kirshenboim]

Holocaust and Postwar Periods

In 1939 Kutno had 6,700 Jewish inhabitants out of a total population of 27,000. The Germans took Kutno on Sept. 15, 1939, and immediately rounded up a few score Jewish men and sent them to forced labor camps or *Leczyca and/or Piatek. The synagogue was burned and Jewish property plundered. The head of the Gestapo especially indulged in beating up Jewish women, jailing members of the *Judenrat, and extorting precious gifts. In February 1940 a group of *Volksdeutsche* arrived and took possession of about 70–80% of Jewish property. For a while the Jews were able to engage in "illegal" trade with the areas of the General Government. In June 1940 the Jews were transferred to a ghetto on the site of a destroyed sugar refinery. Close to 7,000 persons were crowded into this small area without fuel, with three lavatories, and one water pump. Typhoid broke out and 280 died. The only medical care was at first provided by a single Polish doctor, who did not even reside in the ghetto, and no medication was available. The Judenrat managed to bring in two Jewish doctors from other localities. Extra provisions were brought into the ghetto by guards. The situation deteriorated in the latter half of 1941 when the ghetto was sealed off because of renewed epidemics. Despite the gravity of the situation, the Judenrat took care of refugees from other localities, arranged a public kitchen, and even provided some educational facilities for the children. At the end of March 1942 the entire Jewish population was rounded up and sent to the *Chelmno death camp.

[Danuta Dombrowska]

BIBLIOGRAPHY: I. Trunk, in: *Bleter far Geshikhte*, 2:1–4 (1949), 64–166; D. Dabrowska, in: BŻIH, 13–14 (1955); *Dos Naye Lebn*, 14 (July, 1946). **ADD. BIBLIOGRAPHY:** J. Trunk, *A Yidishe Kehille in Poylen baym sof fun 18-yorhundert – Kutneh* (1934); *Sefer Kutno veha-Sevivah* (1968).

KUTSCHER, EDWARD YECHEZKEL (1909–1971), Hebraist. Kutscher studied in his native Slovakia, in Frankfurt on the Main, and then in Jerusalem. After teaching for some time in schools in Tel Aviv and Jerusalem, he was appointed secretary of the Hebrew Language Academy (1942), lecturer in Hebrew at the Hebrew University (1949), and professor (1960). From 1958 he also lectured at Bar-Ilan University. Kutscher's published work includes a study of the linguistic background of the Dead Sea Isaiah Scroll (Heb. and Eng., 1959); *Millim ve-Toledoteihen* (1961), with a summary in English; and *Language of the "Genesis Apocryphon"* (1967). He was editor of *Leshonenu* (the organ of the Hebrew Language Academy) from 1965. Kutscher also translated into Hebrew the German text of a number of art books, such as J. Bab's work on Rembrandt (1952), and works by others on V. Van Gogh (1953), and A. Rodin (1948). A collection of Kutscher's research work in Hebrew and Aramaic edited by Ze'ev Ben Ḥayyim, Aharon Dotan, and Gad Ben Ami Zarfaty, was published posthumously in 1977.

BIBLIOGRAPHY: Kressel, Leksikon, 2 (1967), 738.

KUTY (Yid. **Kitev**), town in Ivano-Frankovsk district, Ukraine, formerly in Stanislawów province, Poland. The town was founded by its owner, the Kiev governor Józef Potocki (18th century), and in the founding law the Jews received full town rights and permission to construct a synagogue, which was to be free from taxation in perpetuity. The Jewish population over the age of one year numbered 972 in 1765. In the 19th century the Jews of Kuty engaged in the timber trade, carpet weaving, and petty commerce. The community numbered 2,966 (47% of the total population) in 1880, 3,197 in 1900, and 2,605 (47.5%) in 1921. There was a strong ḥasidic element, and one of them, Rabbi Avraham-Gershon Kitover, was the brother in-law of the Baal-Shem Tov, and is mentioned frequently in the ḥasidic literature. Between the two world wars, the town was connected to the railway, and electricity was installed there. Jewish livelihoods were from trade and crafts, carpet weaving, and summer resort for guests. The girls studied in state schools, and from 1930 also in a Beth Jacob school; the boys learned in a *talmud torah* as well as in a supplementary Hebrew School. Under Soviet rule (September 1939–41) the Jewish community institutions were closed down, and all independent political activity was prohibited. The Hebrew education network was disbanded and active Zionists were arrested.

[*Encyclopaedia Judaica* (Germany) / Shmuel Spector (2nd ed.)]

Holocaust Period

In early July 1941, after the outbreak of the German-Soviet war, Kuty was taken by Romanian and Hungarian Axis forces. The Romanian troops moved on, leaving the city solely under Hungarian control for the next two months. At the end of August 1941 Jews who were expelled from the territories newly annexed to Hungary, on the contention that they were not Hungarian citizens, found refuge in Kuty. The local Jewish community took them in. A *Judenrat was set up, headed by Menashe Mandel, but when he refused to submit to German orders, he was replaced by Zygmund Tilinger. The regional Judenrat in *Kolomyya held authority over that in Kuty. With the annihilation of the Jewish communities in the vicinity, the Jews of Kuty began preparing hideouts. Many of the groups who tried to flee to Romania were caught and killed by Ukrainian peasants on the way. On April 10, 1942, the Germans carried out an *Aktion*, igniting the houses of the Jews to draw them out of hiding. About 950 Jews were killed in this attack. On April 24 an order was given for all the Jews who did not have work certificates to evacuate to the ghetto in Kolomyya. Many of them died in the death march on the way. On September 7, in a second German mass raid, over 800 persons were dispatched to Kolomyya. Of the 18 craftsmen permitted to remain in Kuty, 16 were killed two months later; the two others escaped. The evacuees sent to Kolomyya were dispatched to the *Belzec death camp, but one group of young people was sent to the Janowska Street camp in *Lvov. The hunt for Jews in hiding proceeded over the next months, until liberation on April 2, 1944. The few survivors who returned soon left, and no Jew remained in Kuty.

[Aharon Weiss]

BIBLIOGRAPHY: M. Balaban, *Dzieje Żydów w Galicji i w Rzeczypospolitej Krakowskiej…* (1916), index; B. Wasiutyńiski, *Ludność żydowska w Polsce w XIX i XX wiekach* (1930), 123; R. Mahler, *Yidn in Amolikn Poyln in Likht fun Tsifern* (1958), index; Halpern, Pinkas, index, s.v. *Kutev; Kitever Yizkor Bukh* (1958).

KUWEITI, SALAH (1910–1986), Iraqi Jewish composer, violinist, and singer. He was born in Kuwait, of Iraqi parents who returned to Iraq with him at the age of 17. While in Kuwait he studied music as an autodidact by listening to records. Kuweiti, who rapidly rose to prominence in Baghdad, belonged to the category of artists endowed with a natural disposition for music, combining creative power as composer and a great ability as performer. The many-sidedness of his talent found expression in his ability to modify his musical style, masterfully passing from one type of music to another. He used to sing, to his own accompaniment on the violin, traditional Jewish religious poems and folk songs, as well as the intricate classical repertoire of the Iraqi *maqam* and the songs he himself composed. Among the latter was a widely acclaimed one which had been sung by the celebrated Oriental vocalist, the legendary Umm Kulthum. His songs were included in an anthology of Iraqi songs published in 1933.

In 1936, when the official Iraqi broadcasting station was opened, Salah was summoned to start up the music ensemble, of which his brother Da'ud, a fine *'ud* player and composer, was a member. Salah acted as the director and conductor of the ensemble and composed the music performed by it. The music they played was in the mainstream style, which subsequently had a great influence on the new music in Iraq. He introduced innovative styles and added musical instruments from the West unknown in the Oriental music, such as the cello.

Although he reportedly performed mainstream and other Middle Eastern styles, Salah preferred the Iraqi style. All the members of this ensemble, except one, were Jewish and all of them including the Kuweiti Brothers immigrated to Israel in 1951 and continued their musical activity in the framework of the Israel Broadcasting Authority.

[Amnon Shiloah (2nd ed.)]

KUZKOVSKI, JOSEPH (1902–1970), Russian Jewish artist. Kuzkovski was born in Mogilev, Belorussia. In 1920 he enrolled at the Kiev Academy of Art, where in 1941 he held a one-man exhibition. He was selected as a member of a group of Russian representative artists at an exhibition in Oslo, Norway. During World War II he lived in Uzbekistan, and it was during this period that he began to use Jewish themes and characters in a series of works which were lost. After the war he took up residence in Riga and devoted himself to themes connected with the Holocaust. His greatest work, *The Last Way*, on Jews being led to their death at *Babi Yar, first exhibited in 1964, was acquired by the Knesset, where it is on permanent exhibition.

Kuzkovski and his wife immigrated to Israel in 1969. He was engaged on what he called a sequel to *The Last Way – Masada Shall Not Fall Again* – the theme of which was to be hope instead of despair, but died before it was completed. An album of his works was published in 1971.

KUZNETS, SIMON (1901–1985), U.S. economist, Nobel laureate. Born in Russia, Kuznets was educated in the U.S. He was assistant professor and then full professor of economics at the University of Pennsylvania (1936–54), and in 1960 was appointed professor of economics at Harvard. Kuznets' research in quantitative economics and his contribution to the understanding of modern economic growth encouraged new studies of the economic growth of nations. He sponsored the annual Conference of Research in Income and Wealth, organized from 1935 by the National Bureau of Economic Research, and he was among the founders in 1947 of the International Association for Research in Income and Wealth. From 1954 to 1964 he was chairman of the United States-based advisory committee of the Falk Project for Economic Research in Israel, and from 1964 he was a member of the board of trustees of its successor, the Maurice Falk Institute for Economic Research in Israel.

Kuznets' research may be divided into three periods. Between 1926 and 1930 he concentrated on analyzing economic change, examining movements in production and prices, cyclical fluctuations, and seasonal variations in industry and trade. During the following two decades his work centered on measuring national income with emphasis on capital formation. After 1950 he focused on explaining the comparative economic growth of nations. He was also particularly concerned with the practical application of his research, and during World War II his national account framework served to study the feasibility of the war production program and to control it. Kuznets stressed the link between the social and economic framework of society that is apparent not only in the history of nations but also in minority groups like the Jews. In the Diaspora they congregated in urban areas where they entered the professions or specialized in finance and trade. Their frequent displacements affected their economic development. Jews have been conditioned to accept economic change and to enter occupations and industries with growth potential where there have been opportunities for economic advancement. This significantly influenced the level of income and wealth of Jewish minorities as compared with their gentile surroundings.

Kuznets retired from Harvard in 1971 and was given the title of George F. Baker Professor Emeritus of Economics. In 1971 he was awarded the Nobel Prize in economics for his "empirically founded interpretation of economic growth which has led to new and deepened insight into economic and social structure and process of development."

Kuznets' publications include *National Income and its Composition 1919–1938* (1941), *Shares of Upper Income Groups in Income and Savings* (1953), *Capital in the American Economy: Its Formation and Financing* (1961), and *Modern Economic Growth* (1966), *Economic Growth of Nations* (1971), *Quantitative Economic Research* (1972), *Population, Capital, and Growth* (1973), *National Income* (1975), and *Commodity Flow and Capital Formation* (1975).

ADD. BIBLIOGRAPHY: M. Feldstein et al., *American Economy in Transition* (1980).

[Rachel Floersheim / Ruth Beloff (2nd ed.)]

KVITKO, LEIB (1890–1952), Yiddish poet and novelist. Born in the Ukraine, he was orphaned while very young and had to earn his living from the age of ten, working in various Ukrainian cities as a dyer, shoemaker, porter, and stevedore. Along with David *Hofstein and Peretz *Markish, he made up the Ukrainian lyric triumvirate. His first poems, published in 1918 in the group's almanac, *Eygns*, edited by David *Bergelson, won him immediate recognition. His first two books, *Trit* ("Steps," 1919) and *Royter Shturm* ("Red Storm," 1919), are full of pathos and enthusiasm for the Revolution. In 1920 Kvitko settled in Germany and joined the Communist Party. In 1922 he published *Grin Groz* ("Green Grass") and *1919*, the latter lamenting the 1919 Ukrainian pogroms. His narrative *Riogrander Fel* ("Rio Grande Furs," 1928) was based on his experiences among Hamburg dock workers. In 1925 Kvitko returned to the Soviet Union, living in Kharkov (until 1933), Kiev, and Moscow. He edited journals and wrote poems and stories, becoming one of the greatest masters of Soviet children's verse, widely known as Lev Kvitko. Kvitko's works were translated into many of the languages of the Soviet Union, and millions of copies were printed. In 1939 he was awarded the Order of Red Banner for Labor. Arrested in the Stalinist purges early in 1949, Kvitko was murdered on August 12, 1952, among a group of leading members of the Jewish Antifascist Committee.

BIBLIOGRAPHY: Rejzen, Leksikon, 3 (1929), 581–6; LNYL, s.v.; S. Niger, *Yidishe Shrayber in Sovyet-Rusland* (1958), 41–9; Ch. Shmeruk et al. (eds.), *A Shpigl oyf a Shteyn* (1964), 335–71, 748–51, 781–3; I. Yanasovich, *Mit Yidishe Shrayber in Rusland* (1959), 133–212. **ADD. BIBLIOGRAPHY:** D. Bechtel, in: *Le Yiddish: langue, culture, société* (1999), 247–71; J. Rubenstein and V.P. Naumov (eds.), *Stalin's Secret Pogrom: The Postwar Inquisition of the Jewish Anti-Fascist Committee* (2001); G. Estraikh, in: *East European Jewish Affairs*, 2 (2002), 70–88.

[Elias Schulman]

KWARTIN, ZAVEL (**Zevulun**; 1874–1953), *ḥazzan* and composer. Born in Novoarkhangelsk, Ukraine, Kwartin worked in his father's business while studying music and singing in a synagogue choir. He first officiated as a *ḥazzan* in 1896, on the Sabbath preceding his marriage in Yelizavetgrad. After spending some time in Odessa and studying the *ḥazzanut* of *Sulzer in Vienna, he was *ḥazzan* at synagogues in Vienna and St. Petersburg, and for ten years at the Tabak Temple in Budapest. In 1919 Kwartin emigrated to the United States and was appointed *ḥazzan* at Temple Emanuel of Borough Park, Brooklyn. There he became known for the richness and fervor of his lyric baritone, and he made many recordings. In 1926 he moved to Ereẓ Israel, where he conducted services and gave concerts, acquiring property near Safed. Eleven years later, in 1937, Kwartin returned to the U.S. and accepted a position as cantor in Newark, New Jersey. His compositions, recorded as traditional improvisations, were transcribed and published as *Zemirot Zevulun* (2 vols., 1928). A supplementary volume, *Tefillot Zevulun* (1938), appeared with an autobiographical introduction. He also published his memoirs, *Mayn Lebn* (1952).

BIBLIOGRAPHY: Cantors' Association of the U.S. and Canada, *Di Geshikhte fun Khazones* (1924), 173–4; E. Zaludkovski, *Kultur Treger fun di Yidishe Liturgie* (1930), 331; A. Holde, *Jews in Music* (1959), index; Sendrey, Music, index.

[Joshua Leib Ne'eman]

KYBARTAI (Pol. and Rus. **Kibarty**; in Jewish sources, קיבארט), town in S. Lithuania; on the German border until 1941. Through its position on the Kovno-Koenigsberg railroad, opposite the German town of Eydtkuhnen, Kybartai developed into an important commercial center in the 19th century. There were 533 Jews living in the town in 1897 (approximately half of the total population). The town was destroyed during the retreat of the Russian army in 1914 and rebuilt after the war. The community numbered 1,253 (20%) in 1923. For many years the Kybartai community remained linked with the nearby community in Wirballen (Virbalis), being under its rabbinical jurisdiction, and using the same cemetery. Kybartai was the birthplace of the painter, Isaac *Levitan. Around 350 Jews remained when the Germans arrived in June 1941. The men were executed in July, the others in the Verbalis ghetto in September.

BIBLIOGRAPHY: *Yahadut Lita*, 3 (1967), 345.

[Yehuda Slutsky]

KYJOV (Ger. **Gaya**; Heb. גאיי, גא"י), town in S. Moravia, Czech Republic, the only one of the royal cities in which Jews were allowed to dwell. The rights of the Jews were protected by a charter of 1613. The community had existed long before then, the ancient synagogue (demolished in 1851) having been built in 1506. Jews remained in Kyjov in 1650 when all communities which had not been in existence before 1618 were expelled. There were 12 Jewish houses in Kyjov in 1688. The burghers petitioned several times for their expulsion, but the royal charter was adhered to. In 1651 a compromise was signed, which included a clause permitting the Jews to distill spirits. In 1727 the Jews were segregated. After 1848 the Jewish quarter remained a *politische Gemeinde* until 1918. The number of Jewish families permitted by the *Familiants Law was 74. The community grew from 427 in 1830 to 510 in 1848, and 884 in 1869, and declined to 820 in 1890 and 620 in 1900. In 1930 the community numbered 319 (7% of the total population). During World War I a large refugee camp near Kyjov was administered by the community. After the end of the war, the Czechoslovak central authorities prevented the local authorities from expelling its inhabitants. In 1938 the camp was reopened for 670 refugees from the Sudeten area and for refugees from Vienna. The Nazis used the camp to assemble all the Jews from the town and the surrounding district; early in 1943, 2,852 persons were deported in three transports from this camp to *Theresienstadt, and from there to Auschwitz later in the year. The synagogue equipment was sent to the Central Jewish Museum in Prague. After the Holocaust Kyjov became the central community for the region, with jurisdiction over the congregations of Hodonin, Holesov, Kromeriz, Uhersky Brod, and Vsetin, which all together numbered about 300 individuals in 1959. In 1956 a memorial to the victims of the Holocaust was dedicated in the cemetery. The community of Kyjov also cared for the community of Bzenec and opened a prayer room there in 1956.

BIBLIOGRAPHY: Ehrlich, Hayek, in: H. Gold (ed.), *Juden und Judengemeinden Maehrens…* (1929), 199–203; H. Flesch, *ibid.*, 31–44; idem, in: MGWJ, 73 (1929), 119–30; I. Halpern, *Takkanot Medinat Mehrin* (1952), 1–102; R. Iltis (ed.), *Die aussaeen unter Traenen…* (1959), 58–60.

[Meir Lamed]

KYRGYZSTAN (formerly **Kirghizia**), a member of the Commonwealth of Independent States, bordered on the north and northwest by Kazakhstan, to the southwest by Uzbekistan, and on the south by Tadzhikistan, with a population of some 4,500,000 people. In 1939 there lived in Kirgizian S.S.S.R. 1,578 Jews (0.58% of the total population), most of them, 1,031 (1.1%), in the capital Frunze. In the beginning of World War II many Jews were evacuated there. In 1979 Kirghizia had a Jewish population of 6,900, with 5,700 living in the capital Frunze which in 1991 was renamed Bishkek. In 1989 the Jewish population of the republic was 6,000 (with 5,200 in the capital); 178 Jews emigrated in 1989. In 1990, 1,170 Jews from Kyrgyzstan immigrated to Israel, 1,111 of them from Frunze. In 1991, the year the republic gained independence, the corresponding figures were 696 and 629.

One Jew was elected to the Supreme Soviet of the republic in 1990. The government of the republic expressed its opposition to Islamic fundamentalism. In 1992 Kyrgyzstan passed a law making knowledge of the Kirghiz language a prerequisite for high government positions. This latter condition effectively barred most Jews from holding high government offices.

[Michael Beizer]

There were an estimated 3,300 Jews in Kyrgyzstan at the end of 1993. In 1992, 250 people left Kyrgyzstan for Israel, and 449 in 1993. Around 800 remained in the early 2000s.

Three summer camps for the young were opened in the Kyrgyz highland in 1993: in Tioplyie Kliuchi, 60 km. from Bishkek (Orthodox, sponsored by Jewish organizations of Belgium); another one, run by Bnei Akiva – 30 km. from Bishkek; and a third, on the shore of Issyk-Kul lake. The camps were intended for Jewish children and teenagers from the whole C.I.S.

Anti-Jewish articles appeared in some newspapers in 1993–94. The Russian-language newspaper *Svobodnyie gory* ("Free Mountains") in February 1994 condemned the immigration to Israel and blamed Jews for the problems of the country.

[Daniel Romanowski (2nd ed.)]

BIBLIOGRAPHY: U. Schmelz and S. DellaPergola in: AJYB (1995), 478; *Supplement to the Monthly Bulletin of Statistics*, 2 (1995), Jerusalem; *Antisemitism World Report (1995)*, London: Institute of Jewish Affairs, 61; *Mezhdunarodnaia Evreiskaia Gazeta* (MEG) (1993).

KYUSTENDIL, town in W. Bulgaria. In the 16th century this town had a small Jewish community. In 1878 when Bulgaria gained its independence, the community numbered 853 and grew steadily. They were artisans, merchants, porters, etc. The merchants among them dealt in plums, wool, butter, and tobacco. The local synagogue was built in 1863. In 1874 a *blood libel against the Jews spread, when a Christian child was missing; there were also anti-Jewish riots in 1901 for the same reason. The 1935 census gave the number of Jews as 853, while the 1943 census listed 980 Jews. The community did not suffer severely during World War II. The 1943 expulsion decree from Bulgaria was not carried out. In 2004 there was a community of around 90 Jews affiliated with the local branch of the nationwide Shalom organization.

BIBLIOGRAPHY: S. Mézan, *Les juifs espagnols en Bulgarie* (1925), passim.

[Simon Marcus / Emil Kalo (2nd ed.)]

K. ZETNIK (pseudonym of **Jehiel Dinur**, originally **Feiner**; 1917?–2001), author. Much about the life of Jehiel Dinur is shrouded in mystery. He seems to have wanted it that way. An Israeli scholar claims that Dinur was born eight years earlier than his announced date of birth. Born into a ḥasidic family in Sosnowiec, Poland, he was active in the Orthodox youth movement of the Agudat Israel in Poland. He first published his poems in Yiddish in the Agudat Israel newspapers. At the age of 22, just before the outbreak of World War II, he published a book of Yiddish poems entitled *Tsvai un tsvantsik* (1931; "Twenty-Two Years – Twenty Two Poems"). Suffering all the torments and tortures of the Holocaust, he was one of the few survivors of Zagłembia, Poland. He was an inmate of Auschwitz, arriving with the last transports from Sosnowiew in August 1943 and incarcerated there for a year and a half. In 1945 he immigrated to Ereẓ Israel and settled in Tel Aviv.

A writer whose themes relate to the Holocaust, K. Zetnik held that he had survived for the sole purpose of telling future generations the horrors of the Holocaust and to be the spokesman for its millions of victims. When testifying at the Eichmann trial in 1961, he collapsed after saying "If today I can stand before your honors, the judges, and relate the events of the 'planet' called Auschwitz, then it is for the sake of 'its inhabitants' whom I now see and they are looking at me…." When asked in court why he called himself "K. Zetnik" (a term referring to a concentration camp inmate), he replied: "This is not a literary name. I must continue with it as long as the nation has not aroused itself following the crucifixion of the nation to erase this evil." His work belongs to the first generation of Holocaust survivor writing, stressing the cruelty of the perpetrators and the anguish of their Jewish victims. Like several other survivors, he referred to Auschwitz as "planet Auschwitz," echoing the sense that the world of the *Lager* was not our world. He described the evil of the perpetrator without regard to the sensibilities of his readers and touched on issues such as forced sexual enslavement that others would have preferred be forgotten. His style was terse, almost clinical, leaving it to the readers to impose their harsh judgment. His works, dealing with different aspects of the horrors of the Holocaust, written in Yiddish and Hebrew, include: *Salamandra* (1946), *Bet ha-Bubbot* (1953; *House of Dolls*, 1956) about Nazi degradation of Jewish women; *Ha-Sha'on asher me'al ha-Rosh* (1960), stories about the Holocaust; *Kare'u Lo Pipel* (1961; *Piepel*, 1961), a story about the terror of Auschwitz, especially relating to children; *Kokhav ha-Efer (Star of Ashes*, in Hebrew, English, and Yiddish, 1967); and *Ḥol me-Efer* (1966; *Phoenix over the Galilee*, 1969), a novel containing autobiographical material, describing a Holocaust refugee's painful integration into life in Israel. His books have been translated into more than 20 languages. In keeping with the mystery of his life, he instructed his children not to make public his death.

[Getzel Kressel / Michael Berenbaum (2nd ed.)]

Initial letter "L" for Librum, *showing Haman being hanged, from the beginning of the Book of Esther in the* Moulins Bible, *a 12th-century Latin manuscript from France. Moulins, Bibliothèque Nationale, Ms. 1, fol. 284. Courtesy Bibliothèque Nationale, Paris.*

LA'AZ, a foreign-language gloss in Hebrew transliteration. *La'az* (plural *le'azim*) originally meant a foreign language into which a Hebrew text, especially a sacred text, was translated (Meg. 2:1; Tosef., Meg. 2:6; Ber. 18a; Sot. 49b; TJ, Sot. 7:1). Somehow, *la'az* became identified with Latin and its meaning was later restricted to liturgical translations in any of the Romance languages into which Latin evolved. Thus, the biblical *lo'ez* (Ps. 114:1) is rendered in the medieval Jewish translations by *latinar* (Italy), *ladinar* (Provence), *ladinar* or *romançar* (Spain), and *aromancer* (northern France). Italian Jews were known as *Lo'azim*. When the French *roman* came to signify "a novel," the Jews called it *la'az*.

Medieval rabbinical texts written in Romance-speaking countries were interspersed with vernacular words to clinch an argument or specify an object. More often than not, these glosses were preceded by the formula *be-La'az* ("in Romance"), even when they did not refer to the biblical translation. The overwhelming ascendancy of *Rashi's commentaries, with their 1,300 glosses on the Bible and 3,500 on the Talmud, further restricted the meaning of *la'az* to "a gloss in Old French." Like any other grammatical term in Jewish manuscripts, בְּלעז was superscribed by a circumflex; בלעֿז was, therefore, later mistaken for an abbreviation of בִּלְשׁוֹן עַם זָר ("in a foreign tongue").

A distinction must be made between the *le'azim* in biblical commentaries and those in other rabbinical writings. The latter are valuable because they often carry Old Romance words, whose meaning is circumscribed by the Hebrew context, while they are seldom found in literary texts. Those of Rashi and of the *Arukh* of *Nathan b. Jehiel of Rome go back to the 11th century, a period from which very few Romance texts are extant. Since the manuscripts are of a later date, it took the brilliant intellect of David *Blondheim to present a reliable scientific edition of these glosses. Likewise, there are glosses in all French rabbinical writings of the Middle Ages; Provençal *le'azim* in the *Ittur* of *Isaac b. Abba Mari of Marseilles; and Catalan glosses in Aaron Hakohen's **Orḥot Ḥayyim*.

The *le'azim* in the biblical commentaries are of greater importance. These refer to complete vernacular translations of the Bible, called *la'az ha-am* or *la'az ha-olam*. Such versions are extant in Spanish and in Italian; of those in French Provençal and Catalan, there exists (apart from some prayer books and hymns) only indirect evidence: the glossaries. There are printed glossaries in Italian (*Makrei Dardeki*, Naples, 1488; *Galut Yehudah*, Venice, 1612) and in *Ladino (*Ḥeshek Shelomo*, Venice, 1588). In France, by the time the printing press came into existence, Jewish communities were no longer in existence. After two or three generations in exile, French Jews must have discarded these glossaries. Nevertheless, six of them more or less complete, and fragments of nine more, mostly of the 13th century, have survived. They are at the same time commentaries, *Sifrei Pitronot*. They lack most of the midrashic material of, for example, Rashi, but have a much wider range, one of them presenting over 12,000 *le'azim* for part of the Prophets alone. The *Sefer ha-Pitronot mi-Leipzig* was published in three volumes in 1996. In addition to these glossaries, there are innumerable *le'azim* jotted down as marginal annotations in biblical manuscripts. These throw light on the real meaning of the *le'azim* in Rashi, as well as of those in the 11th-century commentaries of the Pseudo-Gershom, of *Menaḥem ben Ḥelbo, and of Joseph *Kara. Scholarly discussion centered in the vernacular version, already in existence at that early period. In the same way, the *le'azim* found in the *Ḥizkuni*, the *Ḥadar Zekenim, Minḥat Yehudah*, and the commentaries of *Eliezer of Beaugency, *Samuel b. Meir (Rashbam), and others were all designed to correct the Old French translation. This is one of the reasons for the frequent appearance in the glossaries of two, and sometimes even three or four, *le'azim* for one biblical term. The second reason is not exegetical but linguistic: with the passage of the centuries, some words became obsolete and had to be replaced, but they were still given as examples out of respect for tradition. If for no other reason, the reference to the vernacular version is substantiated by the contextual aspect of the *la'az: néant* ("nothing") for כל and דבר in negative sentences; the addition of prepositions called for in French syntax, but not in Hebrew; the use of the subjunctive in accordance with the rules of French grammar; and adjectives agreeing in gender with the French noun, though not mentioned in the glossary.

In addition to glossaries, the Jews of France and Provence composed alphabetical Bible dictionaries. The *le'azim* in *Kimḥi, *Levi b. Gershom, Joseph *Kaspi, and the Sassoon Codex (no. 368) would also imply the existence of a Provençal version.

See also *Judeo-French, *Judeo-Italian, *Judeo-Provençal.

BIBLIOGRAPHY: A. Darmesteter, *Reliques scientifiques*, 1 (1890), 107–307; G. Schlessinger, *Die altfranzoesischen Woerter im Machsor Vitry…* (1899); L. Brandin, *Les gloses françaises [loazim] de Gerschon de Metz* (1902); S.A. Poznański, in: *Sefer ha-Yovel… N. Sokolov* (1904), 389–439; M. Lambert and L. Brandin (eds.), *Glossaire hébreu-français du XIIIe siècle* (1905); A. Aron, *Das hebraeisch-altfranzoesische Glossar der Leipziger Universitaets Bibliothek* (1907); A. Darmesteter, *Les gloses françaises de Raschi dans la Bible* (1909); A. Darmesteter and D.S. Blondheim, *Les gloses françaises dans les commentaires talmudiques de Raschi*, 2 vols. (1929–37); M. Banitt, in: Roth, Dark Ages, 291–6, 463. **ADD. BIBLIOGRAPHY:** H. Cohen-Edelman, in: *Mesorot*, 12 (2002), 83–96; D.M. Harduf, *Ozar ha-Shemot ha-Tanakhiyyim ba-Aggadah: Kollel Yalkut u-Milon be-Ivrit, Be'ur Semalei Be-La'az* (2002).

[Menahem Banitt]

LABAN (Heb. לָבָן; "white"), son of *Bethuel son of Nahor and the brother of Rebekah, wife of *Isaac; the father of Leah and Rachel, the wives of *Jacob. Laban was a breeder of sheep and goats. He is first mentioned as having taken a leading role in the negotiations between Abraham's servant and the family of Bethuel in connection with the marriage of Rebekah to Isaac (Gen. 24). Possibly, Laban's prominence in this story reflects a fratriarchal society (cf. 24:60; 25:20). Later, when Jacob fled from his brother Esau to Mesopotamia, he found refuge with Laban in the city of Haran (27:43; 29:4–5), where he was cordially received (29:13–14). A month later Laban offered Jacob employment for wages. Jacob agreed to tend his uncle's flocks for seven years as a bride-price for Laban's daughter Rachel. At the end of the seven years, however, Laban cheated Jacob, substituting his oldest daughter Leah for Rachel, as Jacob discovered the following morning. Thus he compelled Jacob to work, though not to wait, for another seven years for Rachel (29:18–20). After that time Laban prevailed upon him to work in exchange for all the kids and lambs of a certain description dropped by mature females in the flock (30:25–34). As a result of folkloristic prenatal influences, well applied by Jacob (30:37ff.), most of the prime lambs that were dropped fitted just that description (see *Biology), and Jacob became wealthier than his employer. Apparently, Laban also deceived his son-in-law in the matter of wages (31:7), thus straining relations between the two to such an extent that Jacob and his family fled Haran, pursued by Laban and his kinsmen, who overtook him in Gilead in Transjordan (31:23). The two sides were eventually reconciled and a peace pact was made between them (31:44–54). Both in the negotiations over Rebekah's marriage and his relationship with Jacob, Laban emerges as a greedy and crafty man (cf. 24:30; 31:7).

Laban's native land is sometimes referred to as Paddan Aram (25:20; 28:2, 5, 6; 33:18; cf. 48:7) or "the country of Aram" (Hos. 12:13). In the description of Jacob's flight from him and his pursuit of and eventual reconciliation with the former, the epithet "the Aramean" is added to his name (Gen. 31:20) and he is represented as speaking Aramaic (31:47). The covenant between Laban and Jacob serves as an etiology for an ancient agreement between Aram and Israel, establishing the cairn of Gal-ed (31:47; pun on Gilad) as the boundary mark between the two lands (31:52). Indeed, the tales of relations between Laban and Jacob serve as allegories of relations between Israelites and Arameans in the earlier first millennium B.C.E.

[Bustanay Oded]

In the Aggadah

Laban is identified with Beor, the father of Balaam (Num. 22:5); with Cushan-Rishathaim, the king of Aram-Naharaim (Judg. 3:8; Sanh. 105a); and with Kemuel, the father of Aram

(Gen. 22:21; Gen. R. 57:4). The name Laban is interpreted as meaning that he shone with wickedness (לָבָן; lit. "exceedingly white"; Gen. R. 60:7) and the epithet *Arammi* (אֲרַמִּי) is taken as the anagram of *rammai* (רַמָּאִי, "cheater"; Gen. R. 70:19). When he saw the jewels on Rebekah, Laban hastened to Eliezer in order to slay him and take possession of his goods. However, when Laban noticed Eliezer's physical strength (Mid. Hag. to Gen. 24:30) and his resemblance to Abraham, he thought that he was Abraham and invited him to enter his house (Gen. R. 60:7). Laban's answering Eliezer's request before his father is indicative of his impudence (Mid. Lek. Tov to Gen. 24:50). His promptness in greeting *Jacob was due to his desire for wealth, since he reasoned that Abraham's grandson would bring with him even greater riches than had Eliezer. Seeing Jacob without camels, he thought that he had money and gems concealed in his garments or mouth, and for this reason he embraced and kissed him. Disappointed at not finding any valuables, Laban consulted his *terafim* and was advised to employ Jacob and give him his daughters in marriage (Yal. Reub. to Gen. 29:15).

His countrymen agreed that Laban should substitute *Leah for *Rachel so that Jacob would continue to work for him, because their land had been blessed with an abundance of water since Jacob's arrival. After receiving securities from them that they would not reveal his scheme, Laban deceived them and used their pledges for the purchase of wine, oil, and meat for the wedding feast. The citizens attempted to inform Jacob of the chicanery by singing, "*Hi Leah, hi Leah*" (lit. "it is Leah"), but Jacob did not understand their hints (Gen. R. 70:19). After being informed of Jacob's flight, Laban assembled all the local warriors to pursue him. His intention was to kill him, but the archangel Michael appeared and forbade him to harm Jacob or he himself would be killed (PdRE 36). His kissing and blessing his daughters and grandchildren after making the covenant with Jacob did not come from the heart. Laban sent a message to Esau, informing him of Jacob's imminent return and urging him to avenge himself on Jacob (Yashar, *Va-Yeẓe*, 105–6). During his pursuit of Jacob, robbers broke into Laban's home and stole all his possessions (Gen. R. 74:16).

BIBLIOGRAPHY: S. Smith, in: *Revue d'assyriologie et d'archéologie orientale*, 23 (1926), 127; E.A. Speiser, in: AASOR, 10 (1928–29), 31–33; C.H. Gordon, in: JPOS, 15 (1935), 30; idem, in: RB, 44 (1935), 35–36; idem, in: BASOR, 66 (1937), 25–27; Daube-Yarron, in: JSS, 1 (1956), 60–62; U. Cassuto, *A Commentary on the Book of Genesis* (1961); D.N. Freedman, in: IEJ, 13 (1963), 125–6; E.A. Speiser, *Genesis* (1964); N.M. Sarna, *Understanding Genesis* (1967), index. For further bibliography see *Jacob. IN THE AGGADAH: Ginzberg, Legends, index. **ADD. BIBLIOGRAPHY:** J. Finkelstein, in: JAOS, 68 (1968), 30–36.

LABAND, PAUL (1838–1918), German jurist. Born in Breslau, Laband lectured in law at the University of Koenigsberg from 1864 to 1872, when he became professor of public law at the University of Strasbourg. He was a member of the Alsace state council from 1879 to 1911, and sat in the *Landtag* of Alsace-Lorraine from 1911 until his death. An authority on constitutional law, Laband was the author of *Deutsches Reichsstaatsrecht* (3 vols., 1876–82), which became a standard work and had a great influence on German public lawyers. He argued that constitutional law must be a pure science excluding political and moral considerations. He rejected the concept of the sovereignty of the people, holding that state and government are identical and that administrative acts of the government are not subject to challenge in any way. Though his views were heavily criticized for ignoring the political basis of constitutional law, Laband became the outstanding jurist of the German Empire. He was also the author of several works on civil law, including property law, commercial law, and the law of agency, and wrote a detailed commentary on the ancient German legal codes. In 1918 he published his memoirs "Lebenserinnerungen von Dr. P. Laband."

BIBLIOGRAPHY: J. Wilhelm, *Die Lehre von Staat und Gesetz bei Paul Laband* (1967); O. Froehling, *Labands Staatsbegriff* (1967); O.V. Gierke, *Labands Staatsrecht und die deutsche Rechtswissenschaft* (1961²); B. Schlink, *Laband als Politiker* (1992).

[B. Mordechai Ansbacher / Bjoern Siegel (2nd ed.)]

LABANOS (Labanowski), leading *Karaite family of *Troki, Lithuania. The post of *shofet* (judge and communal leader) of the community became hereditary in the family. In 1665 ABRAHAM BEN SAMUEL LABANOS was elected as *gabbai* of Troki and later became *shofet* of the Karaites of Troki (1671–88). The Karaite scholar M. *Sultansky describes him as a learned man, much favored by King Jan III Sobieski, who appointed him to the leadership of all the Karaites in Lithuania. In 1688, at the king's order, Abraham and some Karaite families were forced to settle in Kukizow (Krasny Ostrow), a private possession of the Sobieskis. During his years of office in Troki, the community was involved in difficult negotiations with the Council of Lithuanian Jewry (see *Councils of the Lands) regarding the poll tax which the Karaites were to pay. Abraham often took part in the deliberations of the council and endeavored to obtain relief for his community. His son SAMUEL succeeded him as *shofet* in Troki, serving from 1719–45/6?. He was a disciple of the Karaite scholar *Solomon b. Aaron and married his sister in 1738. Samuel was in conflict with the members of his community, who revolted against his leadership because of the high taxes.

Samuel's son, ABRAHAM BEN SAMUEL (II) LABANOS (d. 1776), was in turn *shofet* of the Troki Karaite community in 1746–76. He was a nephew and disciple of the Karaite scholar Solomon b. Aaron, who wrote *Rakh va-Tov*, a grammatical treatise, in his honor. Being pressed by gentile creditors, he went to the Crimea to obtain some monetary aid for the community in 1756 with letters of recommendation from both the rabbinical court of Vilna and the rabbis and communal officials of Brest-Litowsk and Lutsk. He endeavored to defend the interests of his community, but he frequently encountered the opposition of some of its members, who held him responsible for their economic difficulties. He is mentioned in documents as having lodged charges against some

Polish noblemen, which instigated an attack on the Karaite quarter in 1772.

His son SAMUEL (d. 1805/6?) was *shofet* of the community in 1776–93. To enforce obedience to his rules he twice turned to the aid of the *wojewoda* (governor) of Troki.

BIBLIOGRAPHY: Fuerst, *Karaeertum*, 3 (1869), 85, 95; Mann, Texts, 2 (1935), 614–9, s.v. *Abraham b. Samuel Labanos and Abraham b. Samuel ha-Shofet* I; Lurie, in: *He-Avar*, 1 (1918), 166ff.; Bałaban, in: *Nowe Życie* (July–Nov. 1924). **ADD. BIBLIOGRAPHY:** S. Gliorowski, in: *Żydzi i judaizm*, vol. 2 (1998), 73–81.

[Mark Wischnitzer / Golda Akhiezer (2nd ed.)]

LABI, SIMEON (16th century), Moroccan kabbalist of Spanish origin. He grew up in *Fez. In 1549, on his way to Ereẓ Israel, he reached *Tripoli in North Africa where, finding the Jewish community completely ignorant of Torah, he stayed as a teacher. The Jews of Tripoli always considered him as their greatest scholar. According to a tradition of Spanish kabbalists, Labi wrote in the middle of the 16th century a detailed commentary to the *Zohar on Genesis and Exodus. Only the commentary *Ketem Paz* on Zohar Genesis was published (Leghorn, 1795). It includes, at the end, several of Labi's *piyyutim*. His poem *"Bar Yoḥai Nimshaḥta Ashrekha"* in honor of *Simeon b. Yoḥai the alleged author of the Zohar has become the most popular kabbalistic poem and is still sung by Oriental Jews on the Sabbath eve and on *Lag ba-Omer, at the tomb of Bar Yoḥai in Meron, in Galilee. Many kabbalists imitated this song, which was also adopted by the Ḥasidim. For the Tripoli community, Labi also wrote *"Seder Tikkunei Kallah"* for Shavuot eve (Venice, 1680). His *"Be'ur Millot Zarot she-be-Sefer ha-Zohar"* was published in the collection *Yad Ne'man* of Abraham Miranda (Salonika, 1804). Labi's commentary on the Zohar was taken to Venice by Joseph *Ḥamiẓ and was the basis for Ḥamiẓ' own book on the Zohar *Yodei Binah* (Venice, 1663). According to *Malkhei Rabbanan*, Labi died in 1585, but Abraham Ḥalfon, one of the scholars of Tripoli, dates his death at 1580 (*Ma'asei Ẓaddikim*, manuscript in the Ben-Zvi Institute, 1807, fol. 9b).

BIBLIOGRAPHY: Azulai, 1 (1852), 179 no. 166; Davidson, Oẓar, 2 (1929), 58, no. 1340; S. Seeligman, *Catalog... N.H. Van Biema* (1904), 3027; G. Scholem, *Kitvei Yad ba-Kabbalah* (1930), 151; Y. Ben-Naim, *Malkhei Rabbanan* (1931), 126a.

[Gershom Scholem]

LABI, SOLOMON (Salomon) (Ibn; second half of 14th century), scholar and translator. Labi, who lived probably in Aragon, translated Abraham *Ibn Daud's philosophical work "The Noble Faith" from Arabic to Hebrew under the title *Ha-Emunah ha-Ramah* (published with German translation and notes by S. Weil, 1852). His translation, extant in many manuscripts, replaced the earlier one by Samuel *Ibn Motot titled *Emunah Nissa'ah*. There is an anonymous commentary to Labi's translation, but it is not certain that he was its author. Labi is perhaps identical with Don Solomon b. Labi of Ixar, mentioned in *Isaac b. Sheshet's responsa (1878, p. 246 no. 395 and p. 272 no. 435), and with the royal tax farmer of the same name in Saragossa, mentioned in documents in the years 1361–86.

BIBLIOGRAPHY: Carmoly, in: *Literaturblatt des Orients*, 1 (1840), 378–81, 414–5; Delitzsch et al., *ibid.*, 8 (1847), 821; Guggenheimer, *ibid.*, 12 (1851), 506f.; Baer, Spain, 2 (1961), 58, 464.

[Bernard Suler]

LA BOÉTIE, ETIENNE DE (1530–1563), French humanist. Born in Sarlat, la Boétie studied law and became counselor to the *parlement* of Bordeaux. He tried to carry out the tolerant religious policies of the chancellor, Michel de l'Hôpital. La Boétie was apparently a Marrano. In the letter by his closest friend, Montaigne (*Works*, tr. by D. Frame (1958), 1054), describing his death la Boétie said to the priest who was giving him the last rites, "I protest that as I have been baptized as I have lived, so I want to die in the faith and religion which Moses first planted in Egypt, which the patriarchs then received in Judea, and which, from hand to hand, in the progress of time, has been brought into France," clearly indicating that he wanted to die a Jew.

La Boétie's most important writing is his *Discours de la servitude volontaire*, written when he was 16 or 18, first published in a collection entitled *Memoires de l'Estat de France* (1576), and later together with Montaigne's *Essays*. It is a plea for human freedom and dignity against the tyranny of rulers, and is the first modern statement of nonviolence as the means of protest. An English translation appeared in 1942 as *Anti-dictator*. La Boétie was also an important translator of the classics (Plutarch and Xenophon) and one of the first major poets of the French Renaissance, connected with the members of the Pléiade.

BIBLIOGRAPHY: C. Paulus, *Essai sur La Boétie* (1949); V. Lugli, *Une amitié illustre: Montaigne et La Boétie* (1935); H. Day (M. Dieu), *Etienne de la Boétie* (Fr., 1939); P. Bonnefon, *Etienne de la Boétie, sa vie, ses ouvrages et ses relations avec Montaigne* (1888).

[Richard H. Popkin]

LABOR.

In the Bible and Apocrypha

The Bible regards labor as human destiny and an aspect of the order of heaven and earth and all therein. According to Genesis 2:5, a condition of the creation of plant life was the presence of a human being to cultivate it; Adam's role was to till and keep the Garden of Eden (Gen. 2:15). Similarly, the visions of the prophets take the continuation of human labor for granted (cf. Isa. 2:4, "... into plowshares... pruning hooks"), the blessedness of the times being manifest in the abundance of produce ("The plower shall overtake the reaper, and the treader of grapes the one who sows seed," Amos 9:13). The curse entailed by Adam's sin was not labor but the sweaty toil required henceforth to wrest bread from a thorny and thistly earth (Gen. 3:17ff.).

Labor was considered so much a part of creation that God Himself is depicted as a worker. He "founded" the earth, and the heavens are his "handi- (or "finger-") work" (Ps. 8:4;

102:26); He is the "fashioner" (*yoẓer*) of everything (Jer. 10:16); man is clay and God the potter (*yoẓer*; Isa. 64:7, based on Gen. 2:7). He worked six days at creating the world and rested (so Ex. 20:11; in Gen. 2:2–3 "ceased") on the seventh; wherefore the Israelites must do the same (Ex. 20:8 ff.; cf. the lesson of the manna, Ex. 16; cf. *Sabbath). It is not remarkable, therefore, that many of Israel's heroes were workers, or began as such: Moses (Ex. 3:1), Gideon (Judg. 6:11), Saul (I Sam. 11:5), David (17:34), Elisha (I Kings 19:19), and Amos (1:1; 7:14).

The sapiential literature lauds work and condemns sloth and idleness: "One who is slack in his work is brother to him who is a destroyer" (Prov. 18:9). The sluggard is sent to the provident ant for a lesson in industry (6:6 ff.; cf. 20:4). Work is better than words (14:23), for "he that tills his ground shall have plenty of bread, but he who pursues vain things shall have plenty of poverty" (28:19; cf. 10:4; 12:24). The efficient, hard-working woman (*'eshet ḥayil*) no less than her male counterpart (*'ish mahir bi-melakhto*) is extolled (22:29; 31:10 ff.). Contentment is the lot of the honest laborer:

> When you eat the fruit of your own labors
> You shall be happy and contented (Ps. 128:2);
> Sweet is the sleep of the laborer,
> Whether he eat little or much (Eccles. 5:11).

Success is not, however, an automatic outcome of work: "Unless the Lord builds the house, its builders will have toiled in vain" (Ps. 127:1); hence the customary felicitation with which one greeted workers, "The blessing of the Lord be upon you!" (Ps. 129:8; cf. Judg. 6:12; Ruth 2:4). Ecclesiastes, the late writer, concluded after long brooding and observation that even enjoyment of one's acquisitions was entirely a matter of luck – a gift of God to those who pleased him (for inscrutable reasons; Eccles. 2:18–26; 3:12–13; 5:12–6:2, etc.).

The Torah is solicitous of the wage earner. An employer must pay his day laborer "on the same day, before the sun sets, for he is needy and urgently depends on it; else he will cry to the Lord against you and you will incur guilt" (Deut. 24:15; cf. Lev. 19:13; on the length of the workday, from sunrise to sunset, cf. Ps. 104:23). This ruling applies equally to Israelite and foreign laborers (Deut. 24:14). Violations of this injunction are denounced by prophets (Jer. 22:13; Mal. 3:5). The laws concerning debts and debtors and the Jubilee had as their object the protection of laborers and farmers.

The Israelites did not take kindly to the conscription of labor for service to their kings (see *Corvée). Samuel warned them of its hardships (I Sam. 8:11–12) – perhaps on the basis of Canaanite royal practice – and under Solomon its rigors were such (I Kings 5:27–28) that they led to the rebellion and secession of the North (I Kings 12). (By royal privilege a citizen or family might be exempt (*ḥofshi*) from such service; I Sam. 17:25.) A glimpse of life among such conscripts is afforded by a letter dating to the seventh century B.C.E. recovered from a fortress near Yavneh recording the complaint of a laborer against his superior for seizing his cloak (Pritchard, Texts[3], 568).

For the most part, the literature that has been preserved from the Second Temple period expresses this plebeian outlook. "Hate not laborious work or husbandry," urges Ben Sira, "for it was ordained by God" (7:15). Issachar is the ideal figure of a God-fearing, chaste, industrious farmer in the Testament of the Twelve Patriarchs. Injunctions to treat hired labor kindly and not keep back their pay appear in Tobit 4:14; Ben Sira 7:20; 34:22. Horror of a beggar's life is expressed in Ben Sira 40:28 ff.

A new note (anticipated in an Egyptian "Satire on the Trades" a millennium earlier (Pritchard, Texts, 43 ff.)) is sounded in Ben Sira 38:24–34. Here the superiority of the learned scribe over the laborer and artisan is forcefully stated. The latter are, admittedly, necessary, but their horizons are bounded strictly by the requirements of their craft.

> Without them a city cannot be inhabited,
> And wherever they dwell they hunger not.
> But they shall not be inquired of for public council.
> And in the assembly they enjoy no precedence.
> On the seat of the judge they do not sit,
> And law and justice they understand not.
> They do not expound the instruction of wisdom,
> Nor understand the proverbs of the wise.
> They understand the work of the world,
> And their thought is on the practice of their craft (38:32–34).

A learned patrician speaks here, heralding a clash in values that would shortly ripen into sectarian conflict (see *Pharisees, *Sadducees).

[Moshe Greenberg]

In the Talmud

Out of the many references to labor in the talmudic literature a clear picture emerges of the rabbinic attitude to labor. The need for having an occupation was raised to the level of a positive biblical commandment. The first half of Exodus 20:9, "six days shalt thou labor," was regarded as a separate injunction and not merely as an introduction to the prohibition of work on the Sabbath. Rabbi (Judah ha-Nasi) said, "These words constitute a separate commandment. In the same way as Israel was commanded concerning the Sabbath, so were they commanded concerning work" (Mekh. SbY to 20:9; cf. ARN[1] 11:44 and Gen. R. 16:8). The virtue of work is continually extolled: "Man should love toil and not hate it." Adam did not partake of anything until he had worked, as it is said, "to dress it and to keep it"; the **Shekhinah* descended upon the children of Israel only after they had worked, as it is said, "and they shall make Me a sanctuary and I shall dwell in their midst" (ARN[1] loc. cit.).

Two reasons were given for the duty of being gainfully employed. One was the need for economic independence. No work was degrading if it achieved this: "Make thy Sabbath as a weekday (in respect to forgoing the added special meal) rather than be dependent on others" (Shab. 118a); "Flay a carcass in the street and earn a wage, and say not, 'I am a great man and degrading work is not for me'" (BB 110a); and "He who enjoys the work of his hands is greater than the man who fears heaven" (Ber. 8a). When R. Judah went to the *bet midrash* he would carry a pitcher on his shoulder, declaring, "Great is labor for it honors the person who does it" (Ned. 49b). "Great is work. Even the high priest, if he were to enter the Holy of Holies on the Day of Atonement other than during the **Avodah*, is liable to death; yet for labor in it even those ritually unclean or blemished were permitted to enter" (Mekh. SbY to 20:9).

No less important, however, was the consideration of the social evil of idleness, irrespective of economic needs: "Idleness leads to unchastity" or "to degeneration" (Ket. 5:5) and "no man dies except from idleness" (ARN *ibid.*). "If a man has no work to perform, what shall he do? If he has a neglected courtyard or field let him go and work in it" (*ibid*). "He who does not teach his son a trade is as though he taught him to be a robber" (Kid. 29a). "Whosoever has a craft is like a vineyard surrounded with a protective hedge" (Tosef., Kid. 1:11). The therapeutic value of work is also stressed (Git. 67b). Nevertheless, one should, as far as possible, be selective in choosing one's occupation. There were "clean and easy trades" such as perfume-making and needlework, and there were mean occupations such as "ass drivers, wagoners, shepherds, and shopkeepers," the trade of butchery being regarded as of an especially mean character. People were enjoined to choose the former and avoid the latter. Similarly, trades which brought men into undesirable contact with women, such as jewelers, carders of wool, barbers, launderers, and bath attendants, should be avoided (Kid. 82a–b).

The dignity of labor was stressed: "Those engaged in work are not required to stand before a scholar while they are engaged in their tasks" (Kid. 33a), and it was emphasized that laborers also are "the children of Abraham, Isaac, and Jacob" (BM 7:1).

Nevertheless, this view of the supreme importance of labor per se is diminished by the consideration that the highest ideal is to be free from all worldly occupation in order to be able to devote oneself entirely to spiritual pursuits, to the study of Torah, or generally, "in order to serve one's Maker." According to this view, labor is a punishment inflicted upon man: "Simeon b. Eleazar said, 'Hast thou ever seen a wild animal or bird practicing a craft? Yet they find their sustenance without trouble, though they were created only to serve me. But I was created to serve my Maker; how much more so should I receive my sustenance without trouble? But I have wrought evil and so forfeited my right'" (Kid. 4:14). This view is emphasized by Simeon b. Yoḥai: "If a man has to plow in the plowing season, sow in the sowing season, reap... thresh... and winnow, what will become of the Torah? But when Israel fulfills the will of the Omnipresent their work is done for them by others and when they do not fulfill the will of the Omnipresent not only have they to carry out their work themselves, but they have to do the work of others" (Ber. 35b; cf. ARN[1] 11:44). Its highest expression is in the statement of Nehorai: "I would ignore all the crafts in the world and teach my son only Torah," since unlike manual toil it guards him both in old age and sickness and in the world to come (Kid. 4:14).

The compromise between these two extreme views is found in the ideal which was followed by most of the rabbis, in the combination of study with a worldly occupation. It is stated by Ishmael in explicit contradiction to the above-mentioned view of Simeon b. Yoḥai, and the maxim of Rabban Gamaliel in *Avot* (2:2) is "excellent is the study of the Torah combined with a worldly occupation for the toil involved in both makes sin to be forgotten. All study of the Torah without work is futile and is the cause of sin." This ideal is especially advocated by *Meir, who, however, in addition to his many maxims extolling the value of manual labor urges that one should diminish one's worldly occupation as far as possible in order to be free for the study of the Torah (Avot 4:10). "The former generations made study their main concern and their work subsidiary to it, and they prospered in both; the later generations did the opposite and prospered in neither" (Ber. 35b).

Laborers and Employers

As mentioned, the dignity of labor and concern for the rights of laborers is emphasized. The biblical injunction to pay the laborer in time (Lev. 19:13) is expanded to the effect that "he who withholds an employee's wages is as though he had taken his life" (BM 112a), and in disputes between employees and workers the rights of the latter were given preference over those of the former (BM 77a). Especially significant is the rule laid down that the laborer has the right to withdraw his labor at any time, as an expression of his freedom from servitude to his fellowman (BK 116b; BM 10a). The extent to which the employer was liable for the laborer's food (BM 7:1) and the prerequisites to which the laborer was entitled are carefully laid down (BK 119a–b).

A constant anxiety is nevertheless expressed at the tendency toward idleness and the exploitation of their employers on the part of laborers. "The laborers are sluggish," stated by Tarfon metaphorically about the service of God (Avot 2:15), seems to reflect actual conditions. "A laborer usually works faithfully for the first two or three hours of the day only, after which he becomes lazy" (Gen. R. 70:20). "He who has been left a large fortune by his father and wishes to squander it, let him hire workers and not work together with them" (BM 29b). The law that a laborer could recite the **Shema* while on a tree or on the scaffolding of a building (Ber. 2:4) or curtail the Grace After Meals (Ber. 46a) was designed not in the laborer's interests but in that of his employer's time. For reciting the **Amidah*, however, which is prayer proper, they had to descend to the ground. It was regarded as praiseworthy to follow a hereditary trade (Ar. 16b).

[Louis Isaac Rabinowitz]

Later Rabbinic Writings and Modern Trends

Manual labor and social justice were often stressed in rabbinic writings. Labor was considered a blessing in itself, and it was held that the Bible required the state to concern itself with its citizens during unemployment, old age, and illness. These benefits were to be granted as a matter of legal right and in a manner which was not offensive to the recipients' sense of dignity (Simon Federbush, *The Jewish Concept of Labor* (1956), 50–51; Z. Warhaftig (ed.), *Osef Piskei Din Rabbaniyyim*, 45). The workers' right to organize into unions was upheld by the rabbis, and it was viewed as an extension of the dictum that "townspeople may inflict penalties for breach of their regulations" (BB 8b; Rabbi Abraham Isaac Kook cited in Katriel Tchorsh, *Keter Efrayim* (1967), 160–171; cf. Moshe Feinstein, *Iggerot Moshe: Ḥoshen Mishpat*, 108–9). The workers' right to strike was justified (Shillem Warhaftig, bibl., 982, 984; *Iggerot Moshe*, 110–111), although one opinion would not permit work-stoppages in the disputes of workers engaged in providing health services, electricity, and education (*Keter Efrayim*, 171). Another viewpoint was that all strikes were only permitted if the employers refused the workers' request to arbitrate their differences (Raphael Katzenellenbogen, *Ha-Ma'yan* (Tishrei 1965), 9–14).

Labor Ideology in Europe

In modern times, from the *Haskalah period in the 19th century, the alienation of the Jews in the *galut* from manual labor, particularly from agricultural production, was increasingly regarded as the root of evil in the "Jewish problem," while "Jewish parasitism" became a key word in modern antisemitism. The famous Yiddish term "*luftmenshen*," i.e., people who willy-nilly make a living from all kinds of petty, superfluous, mediating occupations, instead of useful work, emerged in the peculiar atmosphere of the Russian *Pale of Settlement, which in the late 19th and early 20th centuries was a kind of huge "reservation" consisting of a network of towns and townlets in which masses of Jews were compelled to live "on air." The reaction in Jewish society to this condition took many social and political forms, including the mass emigration from Russia to the West (see below) and the yearning for a "return to the soil," particularly in Ereẓ Israel. There were also attempts at "productivization" in Russia itself, as, e.g., in the Jewish agricultural settlements in southern Russia, the fostering of *crafts and artisanship among Jewish youth, etc. Most of these trends were linked to elaborate ideologies, which, according to their originator's basic concepts, were either religious (as, e.g., Shemuel Ḥayyim *Landau, the founder of Ha-Po'el ha-Mizrachi, and his followers), or socialist (see *Socialism, Jewish; *Bund), or Zionist and Zionist-Socialist (*Bilu; Naḥman *Syrkin; Ber *Borochov). In the early stages of the pioneering movement in Ereẓ Israel, the ideology of labor was elevated to a basic philosophy of the reborn Jew rooted in the soil of his homeland (A.D. *Gordon; Second *Aliyah; *Israel, State of, Labor). This philosophy was largely instrumental in reversing in the Land of Israel the social structure of the "nonproductive" Jewish population in the European Diaspora. The ideology of productivization was also the motive force of endeavors of Jewish settlement on the land in *Argentina, *Brazil, and, in the 1930s, in Soviet *Birobidzhan.

In the United States

The mass East European emigration which began during the 1880s and continued through the 1920s brought great numbers of Jewish workers to the United States. Continuing their European socialist orientation, many of them became active in the American labor movement which began to develop during this period. They organized the United Garment Workers of America (1891); the women afterwards left this union and formed the International Ladies' Garment Workers' Union (1900); and the majority of the male clothing workers later parted with the original group and formed the Amalgamated Clothing Workers of America (1914). In 1888 several small Jewish labor organizations formed the United Hebrew Trades as their central body. This group later comprised a majority of the Jewish workers in the United States (see *Socialism, Jewish). The most prominent early Jewish trade unionist was Samuel *Gompers who helped establish the American Federation of Labor in 1886, and served as its president for 38 years. Rabbis early became active in labor mediation in the United States, serving on both general and Jewish mediation boards. The *kehillah*, the official community of New York Jewry (1908–22), formed a "committee on conciliation." Its members included Moses *Margolies and Philip *Klein of New York's Ohab Zedek Congregation. Among this committee's activities were the prevention of a threatened strike of poultry *shoḥetim* in 1909, and the arbitration of complaints of Sabbath-observing cloakmakers against their union (Arthur Goren, *New York Jews and the Quest for Community*, 1970, 198–9, 301). Morris *Adler of Detroit served as the chairman of the Public Review Board of the United Auto Workers (1957–66). The rapid deproletarization of American Jews in the second and particularly the third generation can be regarded as a corollary of both the technological revolution of Western civilization from the middle of the 20th century as well as of the general trend to the professions characteristic of Jewish society in all Diaspora countries, while a Jewish farming population and proletariat continued to exist almost solely in Israel.

[Baruch Yaron]

BIBLIOGRAPHY: IN THE BIBLE: S. Kalischer, in: *Festschrift Hermann Cohens* (1912), 579ff.; J. Husslein, *Bible and Labor* (1924); H.L. Ginsberg, in: VT *Supplement*, 3 (1955), 138ff.; I. Mendelsohn, in: BASOR, 143 (1956), 17ff.; L. Finkelstein, *The Pharisees*, 1 (1962), 219ff.; S. Talmon, in: BASOR, 176 (1964), 29ff. LATER RABBINIC WRITINGS: Shillem Warhaftig, *Dinei Avodah ba-Mishpat ha-Ivri* (1969), 2 vols.; N. Shemen, *Baziung zu Arbet un Arbeter* (1963), 2 vols. **ADD. BIBLIOGRAPHY:** M. Powell (ed.), *Labor in the Ancient Near East* (1987).

LABOR LAW.

In Scripture

Two fundamental principles relating to the laws of the hired servant are enjoined in the Pentateuch. Firstly, the master's duty to pay the wages of his servant on time: "The wages of a laborer shall not remain with you until morning"; "You must pay him his wages on the same day, before the sun sets" (Lev. 19:13; Deut. 24:15); and secondly, the servant's right to eat from the produce of the field while he is working: "When you enter your neighbor's vineyard, you may, if you desire, eat your fill of the grapes.… When you find yourself amid your neighbor's standing grain, you may pluck ears with your hand" (Deut.

23:25, 26). So too the liberal pentateuchal laws concerning the Hebrew bondsman served as an important source for the development of labor law in later times. Other scriptural passages, even if not specifically related to the matter of master and servant, have also been relied upon by the scholars in support of labor laws, especially the enjoinder, "For it is to Me that the children of Israel are servants" (Lev. 25:55).

Hired Servant and Independent Contractor

The distinction between a hired servant and an independent contractor is one of principle: Whereas the former is hired for a specific period, the latter is hired for a specific task (*Maggid Mishneh*, Sekhirut, 9:4; cf. the Roman law distinction between *locatio conductio operarum* and *locatio conductio operis*). The time factor in the hire of a servant has the effect of tying him to his work for fixed hours during which he cannot choose not to work, whereas the independent contractor may work as and when it pleases him (Resp. Maharam of Rothenburg, ed. Prague, no. 477). Hence an element of slavery attaches to a hired servant, while a contractor "is not a slave except unto himself" (Rashi, BM 77a).

The Contract of Hired Service

The contractual tie in an agreement for the hire of personal services is effected through one of the recognized modes of *acquisition, such as *kinyan sudar*. Typically, however, the tie is effected by commencement of the work (BM 76b; Nov. Ramban thereto) or by the master pulling (*meshikhah*) the servant's tool of trade (R. Tam, Tos. to BM 48a; see also *Contract). When the master is a public body the contract requires no *kinyan* and a verbal agreement suffices (*Mordekhai*, BM nos. 457, 458). A service contract is not susceptible to specific performance, i.e., the party in breach cannot be compelled to carry out his undertaking. The master cannot be compelled to employ the servant against his will, since only the master's property (*mamon*) and not his person becomes subjected in the servant's favor (Resp. Mahari'az no. 15). The servant, on the other hand, cannot be compelled to work against his will, since the law is that a worker may withdraw from the employment even in the middle of the day (BM 10a; see also below); even if his withdrawal should involve irretrievable loss to his master (see below), he will not be compelled to work, but the loss may be recovered out of his property (*Ḥazon Ish*, BK no. 23:6). This is also the position with an independent contractor, who cannot be compelled to carry out his undertaken task (Mahariḥ to *Piskei ha-Rosh*, BM 77a). In the circumstances, the tie between the parties to a service contract is a loose one in its legal consequences (TJ, BM 6:2), with the result that it became customary for such parties to bind themselves to each other in various ways aimed at precluding the possibility of withdrawal, e.g., by *oath, handshake, or imposition of a fine upon the retracting party.

Personal Nature of the Service Contract

A service contract falls into the category of agreements of a personal nature. Therefore, if the master has engaged the servant to work in his field, he cannot compel him to work in a neighbor's field, even if the work there is lighter (Tosef., BM 7:6). Similarly, the servant is not entitled to substitute another worker for himself if the master should want his particular services (Resp. Maharit, vol. 2, YD no. 50). Generally, however, it will be presumed that the master is not particular about the matter, save as regards a position of a public nature which the holder cannot pass on to another without the consent of the public (*Mordekhai*, BK no. 108).

The master may change the nature of the servant's work except if the servant has been hired for a specific task, in which case it cannot be changed against the servant's will, whether for lighter or heavier work (Nov. Ramban, BM 77a). If the task for which the servant has been hired is completed before expiry of the hire period, his master may keep him engaged on some other but not heavier labor (Tosef., BM 7:6; BM 77a); in the opinion of some scholars he may be given heavier labor than before but with an increase in remuneration (Maharam of Rothenburg, in: *Mordekhai*, BM no. 346, ḤM 335:1; Ramakh, in *Shitah Mekubbeẓet*, BM 76b). In similar circumstances the servant may not, however, in the absence of prior stipulation, demand that he be retained on some other labor (Tosef., BM 7:6) but only claim the wages of an unemployed worker (*sekhar po'el batel*) or the full stipulated wage until expiry of the period of his hire (see below).

Remuneration

In the absence of express agreement, it will be presumed that the parties intended a contract of service for remuneration, on the assumption that a person does not work for nothing, and the measure of remuneration will be determined in accordance with local *custom (see **minhag*; *Mordekhai* loc. cit.); in a place where laborers are hired at different rates, remuneration will be according to the lowest, since people generally have in mind the cheapest possible rate (Alfasi to BM 76a).

Obligations of the Parties

It is the servant's duty to do his work in a faithful manner, hence he may not absent himself from work without adequate cause lest he become liable to dismissal as well as loss of remuneration for the period he has not worked. For the same reason he has to work with all his strength (Yad, Sekhirut 13:7) and may not go hungry or otherwise afflict himself, nor engage in any additional work, whether inside or outside his original working hours (Tosef., BM 8:2). If he should do so without his master's authority, the latter may demand a refund of his earnings (Resp. Rashba, vol. 71, no. 1042). The prohibition against additional work is only applicable, apparently, to a servant obliged – by agreement or custom – to work a full day for his master (see below). The servant must furthermore comply with his master's instructions insofar as these do not deviate from their agreement or local custom (*Tanna de-Vei Eliyahu Raza* 15:5; Resp. Israel of Bruna, no. 242).

The master's main obligation is to pay the servant's wages on time, i.e., at the end of the day or month as the case may be, since "the hire is only payable at the end" (BM 65a), unless otherwise agreed upon by the parties or decreed by custom (*Mordekhai*, BB, no. 468). The duty to pay the servant's wages on time is a positive command and delay in payment also amounts to transgression of a negative command (see above). Wage delay (*halanat sakhar*) is constituted when payment has been withheld for more than 12 hours after it is due (BM 111a). The prohibition is not transgressed, nor is the master in default, unless and until the servant has demanded the payment of his wage (Sifra, Kedoshim 2:9–12) and the master has the ready cash to make it (BM 112a), or has chattels which he can sell without loss and fails to do so (Nov. Ritba, BM 111b). Here too the parties may contract out of the law with regard to the time of wage payment (Sif. Deut. 279), and they may also stipulate that the master shall not be in transgression of the prohibition against wage delay if he should fail to pay on time (*Sefer Ḥasidim*, no. 1066). According to some scholars, wage delay entitles the servant to claim compensation for what he could have earned from his wages if he had been paid on time, but this is prohibited by most scholars as tantamount to interest (*Or Zaru'a*, BM no. 181).

The servant must be paid in cash and not chattels (BM 118a), although there is an opinion that payment may be made in commodities (foodstuffs) which the servant is in need of (Maharam of Rothenburg, in: *Mordekhai* BK 1), and the latter may also waive his right to payment in cash. In case of dispute over whether or not the master has made payment of the servant's wages, the servant will be entitled to payment thereof upon delivering an oath – this is a rabbinical enactment in favor of the servant (Shev. 45a). The master is generally not obliged to provide his servant with food, save as otherwise agreed between them or decreed by custom (BM 83a), in which event the master may choose to provide an allowance instead of food (Resp. Maharsham, pt. 3, no. 54). So far as a servant working in the field is concerned, he is entitled to eat from the produce, but only while he is working (see above; BM 87a).

The master may not employ his servant outside lawful working hours, which – in the absence of an agreement between the parties – are determined by local custom (BM 83a; Nov. Ritba thereto). Scripture hints at the ancient custom of regarding a working day as lasting from sunrise until the appearance of the stars (Ps. 104:19–23), and this is known in the Talmud as a workday of a worker – *de-oraita* (BM 83b).

Period of Service

If not explicitly agreed upon between the parties, the duration of the service period is determined by custom (*Divrei Malkiel*, pt. 3, no. 151), and in the absence of such this is a matter within the judges' discretion (*Ḥazon Ish*, BK, sec. 23). Cancellation of the service contract is subject to prior notice within a reasonable time in accordance with local custom and conditions (*Ḥazon Ish*, loc. cit.). In the case of certain public appointments it was the custom to regard an appointment without a fixed period as one for life (Ḥatam Sofer, Resp. OḤ no. 206).

When the service contract is for a specified period, it will terminate on the date specified without need for any prior notice. In the case of public appointments there is an opinion that the servant cannot be dismissed, notwithstanding stipulation on the duration of the appointment, unless this is in accordance with local custom or an express agreement between the parties (Ḥatam Sofer, Resp. loc. cit.; *Ḥemdat Shelomo*, OḤ no. 7); another opinion is that the continued employment of a public servant after the specified date for termination of his service must be regarded as an implied agreement to employ him for an additional period equal to that originally agreed upon (*Mishpat Ẓedek*, vol. 2, no. 77). A public servant who has grown old has the right to avail himself of an assistant (*mesayye'a*) at the public expense (Resp. Rashba, vol. 1, no. 300). There is also a custom that a public position passes through inheritance to the holder's son, if he is worthy of it, in order that the widow's existence may be secured (*Sho'el u-Meshiv*, vol. 3, pt. 1, no. 154; *Imrei Yosher*, vol. 1, no. 169). A service contract may be terminated at any time by mutual consent of the parties. According to some scholars, a formal act, such as the signing of a deed, is required for this purpose (Resp. Maharam of Rothenburg, ed. Prague, no. 77), while others hold that word of mouth alone suffices (Resp. Radbaz, pt. 1, no. 88).

Withdrawal by the Master

Justifiable grounds for the master's withdrawal from the contract are the servant's neglect, i.e., his failure to discharge his duties in a proper manner; his unfitness; and improper conduct on the servant's part, even outside his employment. If on account of the improper discharge of his duties or his unfitness the servant should cause or be likely to cause his master irretrievable loss, the latter may dismiss him without any prior warning (BM 109a). Circumstances amounting to improper conduct on the servant's part and warranting his dismissal – even if not directly related to his employment – include the fact that he is a reputed thief or under suspicion of committing theft (Rema ḤM 42:6) or an offense against morality (Hai Gaon, in: *Sha'arei Teshuvah* no. 51).

The master's withdrawal is not justified on the grounds that it is possible for him to find another worker who costs less (BM 76a and Rashi thereto) or a better one (Rosh Resp. no. 104:4), or because of the existence of enmity which is not attributable to the servant; nor is his withdrawal justified on the ground that from the beginning he had no need of the worker's service (BM 76b), or because he has completed his work prior to the termination of the contracted period of employment (BM 77a). In the latter case there is neglect on the master's part since he ought to have foreseen that he would not be in need of the worker's services.

If the master interrupts the employment without justifiable cause, he is liable for the full wages of the servant until the contracted period of service has expired (BM 76b and Rashi thereto). At the same time, however, a worker who sits idle after the master has retracted is only entitled to the remuneration of an "unemployed worker," since it is presumed that the worker himself prefers not to work and to receive less rather than to work and receive his stipulated wage. The wage of an "unemployed worker" is half his stipulated wage (Rashi Resp. no. 239). If the worker is the kind of person to whom idleness is a greater trial than doing his work, the master will be obliged to pay his full wage (BM 77a). Liability for the servant's wage in the event of the master retracting, as described above, is only imposed on the master if the servant is unable to find alternative employment (Nov. Naḥmanides, BM 76b). In the event of the master retracting on account of inevitable accident (see *Ones) affecting either himself or the work, he will not be liable to pay the servant for the period of his idleness, not even the wages due to an unemployed worker, unless the mishap is of a general, statewide nature (BM 77a and *Piskei ha-Rosh* thereto; Rema ḤM 321:1).

Compensation on Dismissal or Severance Pay

On dismissing his servant, even after the expiry of the contracted period, the master is obliged to pay him compensation. This law, based on the pentateuchal enjoinder of **ha'anakah* (i.e., the grant payable by the master to his Hebrew bound servant), began to evolve in the post-talmudic period and in recent decades has achieved full legal recognition, particularly in the decisions of the rabbinical courts of the State of Israel.

Withdrawal by the Servant

In the event of the servant's withdrawal from the contract in the midst of his employment, it is necessary to distinguish between the case where this will not result in irretrievable loss – i.e., the master can afford a delay in the work until he is able to find another worker on the same terms – and the case where delay in the work will cause the master irretrievable loss. There is a tannaitic dispute concerning the case where the servant's withdrawal does not involve irretrievable loss but the master wishes to avoid delay and immediately hires other workers at a higher wage; the general opinion is that the master must pay the servant for the work already done on a pro rata basis, and R. Dosa holds that the master may deduct from what the servant has so far earned the loss he has incurred through hiring a new worker at a higher wage (BM 76b). The *amora* Rav ruled that the *halakhah* followed Dosa in the case of a contractor and the sages in the case of a hired servant (BM 77a). For since a hired servant is to some degree a slave (see above) he may withdraw his labor even in the middle of the day, as it is written (Lev. 25:55): "For unto Me, the children of Israel are servants," and not the servants of servants (BM 10a). In this case too the hired servant may waive his right to withdraw his labor (*Zera Emet*, vol. 2, YD no. 97).

If the servant's withdrawal involves irretrievable loss, the master will be entitled to hire another worker to complete the work and to deduct from the servant's earnings the wage increment payable to the new worker; in this case it is also permissible for him to "mislead" (*lehatot*) the servant – i.e., to promise him an increased wage as an inducement to continue the work, yet remain liable only for the wage originally agreed upon (BM 76b). According to the original law, the master was entitled to hire workers against the servant "up to 40 or 50 *zuz*," i.e., to recoup from the retracting servant several times his stipulated wages; but in order to limit the servant's liability, it was laid down by R. Naḥman that the master might only recoup an amount not exceeding his servant's wages (BM 78a), i.e., wages due to the servant for work done until his withdrawal (Rashi thereto); if the master is in possession of the servant's bundle, he will be able to recoup from it the total amount of the increment. A worker retracting on account of *ones* does not lose his wages for the period he has worked, even where his withdrawal has resulted in irretrievable loss (BM 77b).

The Servant's Liability to His Master

The servant's liability for pecuniary loss caused to his master is equivalent to that of a *bailee for reward, whether in respect of theft and loss or any other kind of damage (BM 80b, 82b). His liability is greater than that of a tort-feasor, since the latter is only liable in the case of relative *ones* (which is like *avedah*, i.e., loss) and exempt as regards absolute *ones* (which is like theft), while the servant is liable in both cases (Tos. to BK 27b; see also *Torts). The servant is liable for damage resulting from his departure from custom or the terms of his employment (BK 100b; Tosef., BK 10:29), from his failure to take proper care (BK 98b), and from his lack of familiarity with the work (BK 99b). The servant is also liable for damage caused in the course of his work to the chattels of his master, even unintentionally (BK 99b). As regards breakages in the transportation of goods by porters, R. Meir regulated that the servant be exempted from liability upon delivery of an oath that these were not intentionally caused by him (BM 82b). A servant causing his master damage not only has to pay for this, but also forfeits his remuneration (BM 58a).

The sages of the Talmud were at pains to modulate the severity of the servant's liability, and with reference to damage negligently caused by porters Rav decided that the latter should not only be exempt from liability but also entitled to payment of their hire – this in reliance on Proverbs 2:20 and the equitable rule of *li-fenim mi-shurat ha-din* (BM 83a and Rashi).

The Master's Liability to the Servant

The master's liability for damage suffered by the servant flows from a breach of agreement or custom, or from the general law of tort. Thus a master who burdens his servant to "carry on his shoulder" a heavier load than that agreed upon or customary will be liable for any resulting harm suffered by the latter (Tosef., BM 7:10; *Beit ha-Beḥirah*, BM 80b).

As for the master's liability to his servant in tort, it will be necessary to distinguish whether the harm suffered by the servant directly is attributable to the master or not. Thus if the master causes harm to the person or property of the servant, e.g., damage suffered by an agent as a result of the sale of his principal's defective goods, the master will be liable therefor (*Tashbeẓ*, 4:2, 17; see also Resp. Mabit, vol. 2, pt. 2, no. 156); if,

Depictions of the Holy City and the Temple, Padua, Italy, 1732. Parchment, tempera, gold powder, pen and ink, 88.7 x 59 cm. *Collection, The Israel Museum, Jerusalem. Photo © The Israel Museum, Jerusalem.*

A DOCUMENT, IN ARAMAIC, RECORDING THE FINANCIAL OBLIGATIONS WHICH THE HUSBAND UNDERTAKES TOWARD HIS WIFE IN RESPECT OF, AND CONSEQUENT TO, THEIR MARRIAGE; OBLIGATIONS WHICH IN PRINCIPLE ARE IMPOSED ON HIM BY JEWISH LAW.

KETUBBOT

Assortment of flowers and leaves of a marriage contract, San'a, Yemen, 1794. Parchment, gouache, pen and ink, 42 x 26 cm. *Collection, The Israel Museum, Jerusalem. Photo © The Israel Museum, Jerusalem.*

A marriage contract depicted as a gate, Amsterdam, 1617. Parchment, tempera, gold powder, pen and ink, 61.1 x 48 cm. *Collection, The Israel Museum, Jerusalem. Photo © The Israel Museum, Jerusalem.*

Floral marriage contract, Achiska (Akhaltsik), Georgia 1865. Paper, watercolor, pen and ink, 57 x 40 cm.
Collection, The Israel Museum, Jerusalem. Photo © The Israel Museum, Jerusalem.

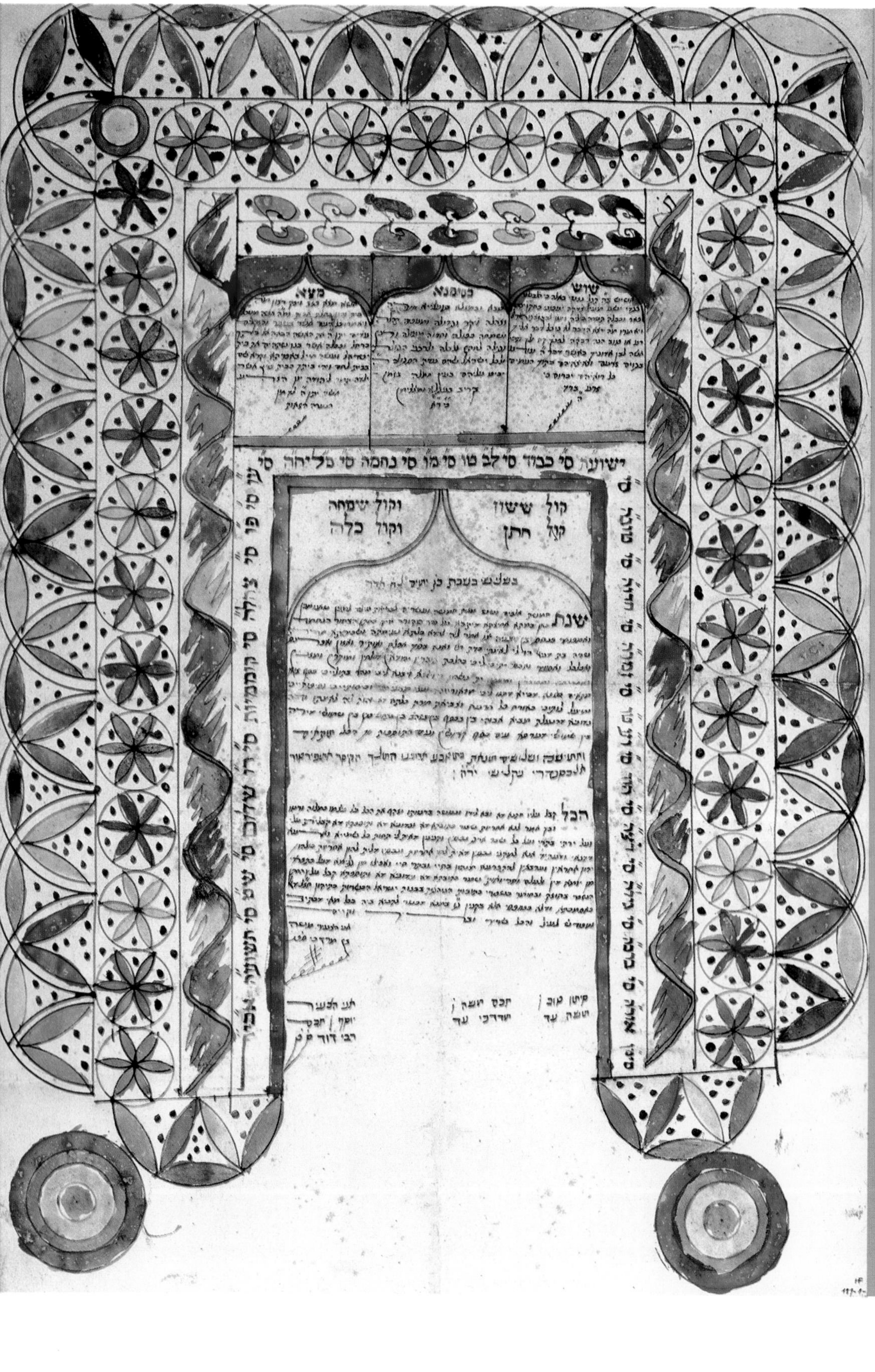

Leaf-motif marriage contract, Singapore, 1880. Parchment, watercolor, pen and ink, 53.8 x 44.3 cm.

Collection, The Israel Museum, Jerusalem. Photo © The Israel Museum, Jerusalem, by Nahum Slapak.

Marriage contract depicting various scenes in the Bible, Rome, Italy, 1734. Parchment, tempera, pen and ink, 94 x 59 cm. *Collection, The Israel Museum, Jerusalem. Photo © The Israel Museum, Jerusalem, by Avi Ganor.*

Marriage contract with decorative flowers, Tunis, Tunisia, 1822. Parchment, gouache, pen and ink, 57.5 x 52 cm.
Collection, The Israel Museum, Jerusalem. Photo © The Israel Museum, Jerusalem.

ABOVE: **Floral marriage contract, Meshed, Iran, 1887 (Hijra 1309). Paper, watercolor, gold powder, paper bands, pen and ink, 98.5x 68.5 cm.** *Collection, The Israel Museum, Jerusalem. Photo © The Israel Museum, Jerusalem, by Nahum Slapak.*

TOP RIGHT: **Petal-design marriage contract, Turin, Italy, 1691. Parchment, tempera, pen and ink, 54 x 45 cm.** *Collection, The Israel Museum, Jerusalem. Photo © The Israel Museum, Jerusalem.*

BOTTOM RIGHT: **Bride and groom depicted as a lion and an eagle, Essaouria (Mogador) Morocco, 1868. Parchment, tempera, watercolor, pen and ink, 60 x 50 cm.** *Collection, The Israel Museum, Jerusalem. Photo © The Israel Museum, Jerusalem, by Nahum Slapak.*

however, harm is suffered by the servant within the course of his employment which is not caused by the master, the latter will be exempt from liability for the damage done, whether to the servant's person or property, as happens, for example, when a spark flies from under a forger's hammer and sets alight his heap (*Sefer Teshuvot ha-Rashba ha-Meyuḥasot le-ha-Ramban* no. 20). Similarly, the principal is not obliged to ransom his paid agent when he is taken captive en route (Resp. Mabit, vol. 2, pt. 2, no. 156), nor is there any obligation in respect of an agent killed while he is on his master's business but not because of the latter. In the latter case, however, the *posekim* laid down that the master, because of his connection with the occurrence of such a disaster, should be obliged to take upon himself an expiation and to compensate the heirs of the deceased as a matter of equity (Resp. Maharyu no. 125).

In the State of Israel

Labor legislation in force in the State of Israel is a composite of three statutory sources:

(1) Ottoman: a number of paragraphs dealing with labor law are included under the chapter "Hire" in the Ottoman Civil Code (Mejelle);

(2) Mandatory: in particular the Safety at Work Ordinance (New Version 5730–1970);

(3) Legislation of the Knesset, replacing most of the Mandatory legislation on the subject with original laws, of which the following are the most important: Annual Leave Law, 1952; Hours of Work and Rest Law, 1951; Wage Protection Law, 1958; Apprenticeship Law, 1953; Youth Labor Law, 1953; Employment of Women Law, 1954; National Insurance Law, 1953; Collective Agreements Law, 1957; Settlement of Labor Disputes Law, 1957; Employment Service Law, 1959; Severance Pay Law, 1963; Male and Female Workers (Equal Pay) Law, 1964; Labor Courts Law, 1969. In addition, labor law in Israel has been further interpreted and evolved in the case law precedents of the Supreme Court. These, like the above Knesset laws, reflect the substantial influence of Jewish law, noticeable particularly in the Wage Protection Law, 1958 and Severance Pay Law, 1963 (see Elon, bibl.).

The Labor Courts Law sets up a special judicial hierarchy, at both regional and national levels, for airing disputes between master and servant, without right of appeal to the regular courts. The existence of a special judicial machinery in labor matters is also to be found in the history of Jewish law. In the European Jewish communities of the late Middle Ages, and within the framework of the various artisans' and traders' associations, special courts were elected in accordance with articles approved by the communal rabbis.

[Shillem Warhaftig]

LABOR LAW DECISIONS IN ISRAEL. As stated, the State of Israel has a labor court system with jurisdiction over labor-related matters. Some of the most important labor legislation in the State of Israel, such as the Wage Protection Law, 5718–1958, is based on Jewish law, and the labor courts rely on principles from Jewish law in deciding labor issues brought before them. This article presents several cases brought before the Israeli Labor Courts and the Israel Supreme Court which were adjudicated having consideration for the position of Jewish law.

The Prohibition on Delayed Wage Payments for Contracted Labor and the Distinction between a Sales Contract and a Service Contract (Ḥozei Kablanut). In *Zikit v. Eldit*, the Israeli Supreme Court (CA 368/77, *Zikit v. Eldit*, 32(3) PD 487) was required to examine this issue. In that case, a company provided a quantity of cloth for printing patterns on cloth to be used for bathing suits. The printing was defective, and as a result the company that owned the material was injured. The Court was required to decide if the transaction was a sale, in other words whether the printing company sold a product, in which case the provisions of the Sales Law, 5728–1968, would apply; or was the printing company under contract for services (*kablanut*, hereinafter "contractorship agreement") and as such the Contract for Services Law, 5734–1974 would apply. The court (per Justice Menachem Elon) pointed out that "when we engage in the interpretation of sales and contractor law, enacted by the State, we must first and foremost examine the position of the Jewish law regarding the problems brought before us" (*ibid.*, p. 493).

The Court cited the responsum of Rabbi Aharon Sasson (Resp. Torat Emet, 119), which considered whether the commission of work to a craftsman (in that case – ordering a *ketubbah* (marriage contract) from a scribe) should fall under sales or contract law principles, which would affect the application of the prohibition against delaying wage payment. The prohibition of delaying the wage payment is not limited to client commissioned work, but also applies to contractorship agreements: "Inasmuch as contractorship is like hiring [a worker] and it obligates him to pay him on time" (Maim., Yad, Sekhirut 11:3).

Rabbi Aharon Sasson did not consider the scribe from whom the *ketubbah* was ordered a contractor, because "the contractor receives the object from the one who orders the work and prepares accordingly; this does not confer any rights or ownership in the object, and he is therefore referred to as a contractor [one engaged in providing services to a client's object]." In contrast, when the workman also supplies the materials, their agreement may be considered a sales contract and not a contractorship agreement. In such a case, the non-payment is not a delay in the payment of wages, but a debt for which there is an obligation to pay, but the law of delay in payment of wages does not apply (*Zikit* decision, p. 494).

The court goes on to discuss the responsibility of the hired craftsman to pay for damages caused to an object given to him for repair (Yad, Sekhirut 10:4; *Zikit* decision pp. 496–497).

Employer's Responsibility to Protect the Well-Being and Safety of His Employees. Punishing a person who indirectly or accidentally caused another's death to exile in a city of refuge (see *City of Refuge) is not applicable today, yet the responsa literature deals with situations of an employee's or an agent's death while employed or under contract. A talmudic *aggadah*

(Sanh. 95a) relates that King David was punished because his actions, albeit indirectly, resulted in the deaths of the priests of Nov, Doeg, Ahitophel, Saul, and his three sons. David did not perform any active deed to cause these deaths, and the decisors (*posekim*) infer from this *aggadah*, by the rule of *a fortiori*, that an employer whose employee is injured while performing duties, is not liable under tort law, but he is required to atone and repent (*kapparah* and *teshuvah*), and is even to give charity to the orphans of the victim or to other indigents (Responsa Mahari Weil, 125; Resp. Rabbi Akiva Eiger, Tanina ed., 3; see *Divine Punishment). Other halakhic decisors distinguished between a paid employee, for whom the employer is not obligated to atone for the bodily injuries, and the unpaid worker (Responsa *Ẓemaḥ Ẓedek*, 6). Rabbi Ouziel (Resp. *Mishpatei Ouziel*, 4 – ḤM, no. 43), rules that indeed by law, when a worker is injured or killed, the client is not liable for his worker's damages or death, but only obligated to atone, and there is no legal recourse for receiving monetary compensation from the employer. However, Rabbi Ouziel emphasizes that in our times, owing to industrial development there are many more dangers for workers and the current situation requires far more caution; "the employer is cautioned by the Torah to do all that is possible to protect his workers from the risk of death or injury, as it is written: 'And you shall make a parapet for your roof that you shall not bring blood upon your house' (Deut. 22:8), which includes any hazard that is likely to harm, such as a dangerous dog and a shaky ladder, etc. (BK 15, and Sh. Ar., ḤM 327:5). Thus, it is the obligation of the employer or the contractor, to take all precautions to ensure that the work environment and conditions are free of hazard or danger that may cause any sort of disaster." Rabbi Ouziel adds that in our times, when it is accepted practice to insure employees against injury, an employer would be halakhically required to insure his employees.

These statements regarding the employer's responsibility for the safety of his employees, were cited in the decision of the Israeli Supreme Court in the *Pinkas* case (Crim. A 478/72 *Pinkas v. The State of Israel*, 27(2) 617, pp. 627–629; per Justice Kister), as inspiration for the criminal liability of an employer who sent his worker to carry out a job in a dangerous and negligent manner as a result of which the worker was killed.

Dismissing an Employee Suspected of Stealing. Rabbi Moses Isserles, in his glosses on Shulḥan Arukh (ḤM 421:6), rules that an employer who suspects that his worker may have stolen from him is entitled to dismiss him, provided that he has proven grounds for his suspicions before a court, or if the employer has solid proof of such theft, or if the worker has the reputation of being a thief (Resp. Divrei Malkhiel, III, 151–152). In the Resp. *Divrei Ḥayyim* (1, YD, 11), it was held that mere suspicion is not sufficient, and only where there are witnesses to a theft is it possible to dismiss the worker. These rulings indicate that the employer's concerns and suspicions do not constitute sufficient grounds for dismissing a worker; however, when these misgivings are substantiated by evidence, they are grounds for dismissal.

The Regional Labor Court of Tel Aviv Jaffa (LF 32309/98, *Yitzchak v. The Aircraft Industries*; Judge Tennenbaum) adjudicated a case where a worker was dismissed after being suspected of stealing. The worker filed a claim for the entire amount of his severance pay, and the question of his employer's justification for dismissal was raised. The court based its decision on principles of Jewish law, and examined the degree to which the robbery had to be proved to constitute grounds for dismissal and the extent of his entitlement to severance pay.

Employee Disclosure of Trade Secrets. Jewish law's approach to business competition is based on the principle that, with the exception of some specific cases, free competition should not be interfered with (see: *Business Ethics).

Nevertheless, even under Jewish law, an employee who during his employ was privy to privileged information and then leaves his employ may not divulge such information, even where his employment contract does not specifically stipulate this; Rav Samuel Wozner states the following (Resp. *Shevet ha-Levi*, 4:220): "It is clear to me that a worker who works in a place where they work with secret things, or use instruments that are still considered secret, or even in an activity related to an invention, is prohibited from making a copy for himself or for others and this falls into the legal category of stealing, even when there was no special contractual stipulation, because such matters are self-understood and one should be very careful about revealing them."

According to another approach, a worker is permitted to use his employer's trade secrets, provided that he paid the employer for their value; and if he has not paid him the value of the secret he is interested in using, he is forbidden to use it.

The Regional Labor Court in Haifa (Lab. App. 2999/03, *Carmel v. Ben Shimon*; per Judge Werbener) cited these rulings when adjudicating a case where an employee's former employers requested a court injunction against a competing business to prevent it from employing the said employee, because of their concern that he would disclose their trade secrets.

Firing an Employee When His Term of Employ Has Not Been Extended. The responsa of Rabbi Moses Feinstein deal with this subject in detail. Rabbi Feinstein holds that even if the employee is hired for only one year in a place where one usually annually renews employment contracts every year, and he continues to work there, even without a renewed contract, it is still not permissible, absent of other grounds, to dismiss him (Resp. *Iggerot Moshe*, ḤM 1:76). In another responsum Rabbi Feinstein deals with the question of an employee for whom no extension of his term of employment was established and whether it was permissible to fire him without grounds. Rabbi Feinstein answers that it is not permissible to fire an employee without clear cause, even when the policy at the specific place of employment regarding the hiring of employees for an unlimited period of time is unclear (*ibid.*, 75).

The Regional Labor Court in Tel Aviv-Jaffa (LF 8338/00 *Krigsman v. Reshet ha-Ganim shel Agudat Yisrael*; per Judge Tannenbaum) dealt with this subject, and quoted extensively from these rulings of Rabbi Feinstein.

The Possibility of Limiting the Employee's Work Hours. The basic approach of Jewish law to this question is set forth in the Tosefta (BM 8b) which states: "A worker is not permitted to do his work in the night and to hire himself out during the day...." The rationale for this edict is explained by Maimonides (Yad, Sekhirut 13:6; Rema, ḤM 337:19): "... Such behavior would constitute stealing from the employer, for his [the employee's] strength will give out and his mind will be weakened and he would not do his work with energy."

Teachers and teaching hours have received special treatment in this matter from both the Maharam of Rothenburg in his responsa, and the Rashba (Responsa Maharam of Rothenburg, 667; Resp. Rashba, 7:516). They emphasize that teachers can be prevented from contracting in supplementary work, if such work would hamper their ability to teach in an appropriate manner.

The Talmud (BB 21a), when discussing the community's responsibility to organize an educational system, explicitly limits the number of students allowed for each teacher. Raba rules that one teacher should not teach more than 25 children. When there are more than 25 students – up to 40 – an additional person is seated with the teacher to assist him and when there are more than 40 students, the community must provide two teachers (Yad, Talmud Torah 2:5). Such limitations insure the proper fulfillment of the community's duty to procure enough teachers, for an appropriate, functioning educational system, and are not aimed at limiting the teachers' employment opportunities. However, other community regulations establish limitations and prohibitions regarding the number of students a teacher may accept (regarding these regulations, see Bibliography, Shchipinsky).

In this context, the Regional Labor Court of Tel Aviv-Jaffa (LF 913517/99 *Asher v. The State of Israel*; per Judge Tannenbaum), was requested to invalidate a provision in the collective labor agreement applicable that limited the number of instruction hours a teacher was permitted to work to 140% of a full-time position.

Dismissing a Worker Who Has Reached Retirement Age. The basic approach of Jewish law regarding employment in public positions is that a person should not be removed without good cause (Resp. Rashba v. 283). Rabbi Joseph Caro (Sh. Ar., OḤ 53:25) ruled as such regarding a cantor. Rabbi Israel Meir of Radin stated that this ruling applies to all positions, "so that they [the employees] should not suspect that some defect was discovered in them" (*Mishnah Berurah*, ad loc. subsection 73).

Rabbi Yehiel Michal Epstein deals with the appointment of various community officials, and ruled as follows (*Arukh ha-Shulḥan*, ḤM 2:333.15):

"... This was the custom in all of the Jewish Diaspora that from his appointment (in the letter of appointment to the Rabbinate) the rabbi is employed for the city's benefit, this was done so that the rabbi would not change his mind [and resign from his position] over the time ... but the people of the city can never change their mind, unless some taint was found in him. This is also the law regarding a cantor and a sexton and all kinds of other public appointments – that as long as he is not found wanting, he has a lifetime position. And this is the custom ..."

The principle applies not only to those of community related positions, such as a rabbi and a cantor, but also those of any public position; one who holds a position has a presumptive right to it (Rabbi A.I. Kook, Resp. *Oraḥ Mishpat*, ḤM, 20).

In the responsa of Rabbi Ezekiel *Landau, there is explicit reference to the chronological age of retirement (Resp. *Noda Bi-Yehudah*, YD, Tanina ed., 1). Rabbi Landau was asked about the law regarding a ritual slaughterer whose "hands shook," in other words, someone physically incapable of fulfilling his responsibilities. In his response, Rabbi Landau ruled that such a person must be removed from his position, yet he refused to apply this ruling retroactively – i.e., he did not disqualify the meat this ritual slaughterer had slaughtered. In his discussion Rabbi Landau rejects disqualifying *shoḥetim* at the fixed age of 80, exclusively on the basis of their having reached that age.

These rulings demonstrate that Jewish law rejects mandatory retirement based exclusively on age. A person's age is only significant to the extent of imposing a duty to examine the employee's functioning at an age at which might be assumed that his age affects his functioning. However, where the retirement policy obligates a person to retire after a specified period of time, that custom mandates one in such a position to leave his job when he reaches that specified time (Resp. Rashba, 5.283).

The Regional Labor Court in Tel Aviv (LF (Tel Aviv) 912492/99 *Meor v. The Open University;* per Judge Tannenbaum) thus adjudicated in an action filed by an employee who had been dismissed upon reaching the age of 65.

The Obligation to Provide an Employee Work. The Talmud (BM 77a) establishes that an employer who hires a worker for a fixed period of time, and does not provide him work for part of that period of time, is still obligated to pay him [for the entire period]. The exception to the rule is when the worker, upon accepting the job, knew that circumstances might arise that would prevent the employer from providing him work. In such a case, if in fact the employer failed to provide him work for the entire period, the worker is not entitled to full wages. If the work is terminated during that period and the employer is no longer able to employ him, if he is able to provide him with work, no more difficult than the work for which he was originally employed, the employer should allow the employee to perform such work. If there is no work available, the *halakhah* depends upon the type of worker: if the worker is accustomed to hard work and the absence of work will weaken his body, not working is tantamount to damage, and the employer must pay him his full wages. If the worker is not such a worker and he enjoys the "holiday," even if it is forced upon him, the employer must only compensate him for his loss of time.

The halakhic literature provides definitions of workers for whom not working causes distress and for those who enjoy being unemployed. Regarding teachers, it was ruled that unemployment is a source of distress (Resp. Rashba attributed to Naḥmanides, 1). It was ruled that when a rabbi is hired to deliver Sabbath sermons in the synagogue, which brings him joy and fulfillment, being unemployed distresses him. In contrast, a rabbinical judge or regular judge who rules in matters of ritual law (*issur ve-heter*) because his work is difficult and exhausting does not enjoy his work (Resp. ha-Rama, 50).

In one unusual case, specific performance of the employment contract was imposed on the employer, such that it obligated him to continue providing work for the employee, and not suffice by paying of his wages while leaving the employee with nothing to do (Resp. *Mikhtam le-David*, ḤM, 17; 18th century).

The Israeli National Labor Court considered the question of whether an employer was obligated to pay the full salary (with social benefits) or just the basic salary without these added elements in a case when he told his employee that he would continue to pay him a salary, but that he should stay home and not come to work (DBA 4–21/51 *The Histadrut v. Tahel*, 23 PDA 3; per Judge Steve Adler).

The court referred to Jewish law sources cited above and pursuant to the provisions of the Foundations of Law Act, 5740–1980, and dealt with whether and how an employer is required to compensate the employee who is not actively working for him. Based on the aforementioned cases, the Court based its ruling on the tremendous importance placed by Jewish law on the effect of idleness on an employee.

An Individual's Obligation to Earn a Living from His Efforts. A positive approach to the value of work is found in the earliest sources, i.e., the Bible. The purpose of Adam in the Garden of Eden immediately after his creation is stated as "to work it and keep it [the Garden of Eden]" (Genesis 2:15). The Book of Proverbs expresses praise for the laborer: "He who works his land shall have plenty of bread ..." (Proverbs 28:19), "Go to the ant, sluggard; consider her ways and be wise" (Proverbs 6:6). Talmudic literature, refers to labor of the six days of the week as a duty that complements the proscription of working on the Sabbath: "'Six days shall you work' – Rabbi says this is a complementary commandment (to the commandment regarding the prohibition of working on the Sabbath) for Israel; parallel to the positive commandment of the Sabbath, Israel was commanded regarding doing work" (*Mekhilta d'Rabbi Simeon bar Yoḥai* 20:9). In the continuation of this *derashah*, extolling the virtue of work, the Tosefta (Kid. 1:11; Kid. 29a) states that the father is obliged to teach his son a trade; Rabbi Judah adds that "he who does not teach his son a trade – in the end, will teach him to be a robber." Notwithstanding, Midrashim also present the approach that work is a default option, and the optimal situation is, "when Israel does the will of God ... their work is done by others" (*Mekhilta d' Rabbi Ishmael, V'Yikahel*, 1; TB Ber. 35b). There are differences of opinion regarding the preferred balance between Torah study and work. Rabbi Ishmael sees the performance of work as an obligation, to preclude a person's dependence on others: "Do with them as is the custom among people." In contrast, Rabbi Simeon bar Yoḥai expresses his concern that engaging in labor would completely marginalize Torah study, and therefore recommends learning Torah and relying on the work being performed by others. The *amora* Abbaye testifies that those who adopted the path of Rabbi Ishmael "succeeded," and those who adopted the path of Rabbi Simeon bar Yoḥai – "did not succeed" (Ber. *ibid.*). Many other teachings of *tannaim*, cited in *Avot de-Rabbi Nathan*, speak in praise of performing work because it averts poverty, rescues from sin, rescues from boredom, and rescues a person from being suspected by others, etc.

Halakhic literature does not formally adopt the Talmudic opinions regarding the obligation to work and to teach one's son a trade, but there are clear statements in praise of work and disparaging reliance on the kindness of others. Maimonides writes as follows: "...they say 'make your Sabbath a weekday and do not become dependent on others.' And even if a learned and respected person becomes impoverished, he should go and work, even menial labor rather than depend on others. It is preferable to skin dead animals than to tell people: 'I am a very learned man, I am a *kohen* – support me!' ... Among the greatest sages there were woodcutters, loggers, and those who pumped water for gardens, ironworkers and coal choppers who did not ask for support from the public" (Yad, Mattanot Aniyyim 10:18). Maimonides writes the following about the relation between Torah study and work: "Anyone who decides to study Torah and does not engage in labor and is supported by charity, commits a desecration of God's name, and causes dishonor for the Torah, extinguishes the light of religion, causes harm to himself, and precludes his life in the world to come ... and they have further commanded and said: 'Love labor and hate the authorities,' and any Torah [study] that is not accompanied by labor is destined to come to naught and to bring about sin, and the end of such a man will be as a thief" (Yad, Talmud Torah 3:10). However, later *posekim* disagreed with these words of Maimonides. Rabbi Simeon ben Ẓemaḥ Duran (Resp. *Tashbeẓ* 1,147) states that only in the first generations, in the period of the *tannaim* and the *amoraim*, could sages both study Torah and earn their living from labor. In our days, "the generations are less worthy" and this cannot be done, and therefore learned men may rely on the community funds. The statements in praise of labor and in condemnation of laziness were cited by the National Labor Court (AB 9100002/98 *Barnea v. The Employment Service*; per Judge Rabinowitz), to support its ruling that "one who wishes to be supported from public funds, must first make a reasonable effort to work and to support himself." Accordingly, the court upheld the decision of the Employment Service to deny unemployment compensation to any unemployed person who refuses positions offered to him.

LEGISLATION IN THE STATE OF ISRAEL. In addition to the laws mentioned above, a number of new laws that deal with labor law should be mentioned:

The Contract for Services Law, 5744–1974, codified the contractual obligations between one who orders work done and a contractor, including liability for defects and the right to withhold the property that is the object of the work until wage payment has been made.

The Minimum Wage Law, 5747–1987, codified the obligation to pay a specified minimum wage. This law also obligates monetary compensation when lower than the minimum wages were paid, and the criminal liability of the employer who pays less than the minimum wage.

The Prior Notice of Dismissal or Resignation Law, 5761–2001, establishes the obligation of giving prior notice of a prescribed term before terminating a person's employment (and correspondingly the worker's obligation to notify his employer a certain time in advance of his resignation). This law establishes the employer's duty to give an employee prior notice of his/her impending dismissal within a certain prescribed period of time, as well as the employee's duty to give his employer prior notice a certain period of time prior to resigning. The law also provides that an employer dismissing an employee without such prior notice is required to pay the employee an amount equivalent to his regular salary for the period of time prescribed, and that an employee who resigned without prior notice must pay his employer a penalty for the period during which the notice was not given (see *Ha'anakah).

[Menachem Elon (2nd ed.)]

BIBLIOGRAPHY: D. Farbstein, *Das Recht der unfreien und der freien Arbeiter nach juedisch-talmudischem Recht...* (1896); M. Hoffmann, in: *Jeschurun*, 4 (1917), 571–600 (Germ.); I.S. Zuri, *Mishpat ha-Talmud*, 5 (1921), 117–22; Gulak, Yesodei, 2 (1922), 180–8; M. Sulzberger, in: JQR, 13 (1922/23), 245–302, 390–459; Ch. W. Reines, *Ha-Po'el ba-Mikra u-va-Talmud* (1935); idem, in: *Israel of Tomorrow*, ed. by Leo Jung, 1 (1949), 139–61; idem, in: *Judaism*, 8 (1959), 329–37; Herzog, Instit, 2 (1939), 167–74; M. Findling, *Teḥukkat ha-Avodah* (1945); ET, 1 (1951³), 141–6; 3 (1951), 330–5; 6 (1954), 539–42; S. Federbush, *Mishpat ha-Melukhah be-Yisrael* (1952), 165–84; J.H. Heinemann, in: HUCA, 25 (1954), 263–325; J. Gross, in: *Ha-Peraklit*, 16 (1959/60), 72–86, 153–78; H.E. Baker, *Legal System of Israel* (1968), 182–196; Elon, Mafte'aḥ, 201–3; idem, in: ILR, 4 (1969), 85–89; Sh. Warhaftig, *Dinei Avodah ba-Mishpat ha-lvri*, 2 vols.(1969); contains bibliography (vol. 2, pp. 1207–10); idem, in: *Sinai*, 66 (1969/70), 195–9. **ADD. BIBLIOGRAPHY:** M. Elon, *Ha-Mishpat ha-Ivri* (1988), 1:128, 138, 140, 283, 284, 345, 400, 504, 509, 558, 560f., 563f., 567, 571f., 584, 592, 611, 645, 664, 701, 704, 718, 734, 736, 749ff., 753f., 756, 756, 765, 822, 2:881, 993, 3:1365f., 1367f., 1422; idem, *Jewish Law* (1994), 1:144, 156, 158, 336, 337, 415; 2:488, 614, 620, 679, 681f., 684f., 689, 703, 719, 732, 755, 798f., 821, 865, 869, 886, 905, 907, 924ff., 928f., 932, 942, 1007; 4:1074, 1201, 5: 1629f., 1631f., 1694; M. Elon and B. Lifshitz, *Mafte'aḥ ha-She'elot ve-ha-Teshuvot shel Ḥakhmei Sefarad u-Ẓefon Afrikah* (legal digest), 1 (1986), 84–87; B. Lifshitz and E. Shochetman, *Mafte'aḥ ha-She'elot ve-ha-Teshuvot shel Ḥakhmei Ashkenaz, Ẓarefat ve-Italyah* (legal digest) (1977), 54–59; A. Wahrhaftig, "*Ḥozeh Avodah, Mahuto u-Bittulo*," pt. 1, in: *Teḥumin*, 7 (1986), 427–53; pt. 2, *Teḥumin*, 8 (1987), 203–42; idem, *Ha-Hitḥayyevut* (1991), 231–300; M. Ayali, *Poalim ve-Omanim – Melakhtam u-Ma'amadam be-Sifrut Ḥazal* (1987); Y. Shchipinsky, *Ha-Takkanot be-Yisrael*, vol. D (1993), 282–84; M. Salli, "*Ha-Perishah me-Avodah ke-Ḥovat Gil bi-Mekorot ha-Yehadut*," in: *Sefer Assia*, pt. 6, 151; Y. Halevi, "*Zekhut ha-Rofeh le-Kabbalat Sekhar bi-Mekorot ha-Yehadut*," in; *Dinei Israel*, 7 (1976), 79–98; A. Steinberg, *Enẓiklopedyah Hilkhatit Refu'it* (1994), vol. B, entry: "*Zaken*," 371–72, 377–79, 390–91; A. Dasberg, "*Shevitat Ovedim al pi ha-Halakhah*" (bibliographical survey), in: *Teḥumin*, 5 (1984), 295–302; B. Lifshitz, *Oved ve-Kablan – Bein Kinyan le-Vein Hitḥayyevut* (1993).

LABOR ZIONIST ALLIANCE (from 2004 **Ameinu**; originally **Po'alei Zion**), U.S. Zionist organization. Socialist Zionist circles existed in the U.S. as early as 1903, but it was only at a convention in Baltimore on December 23–25, 1905 that the national organization of Po'alei Zion was founded. During the first decade the organization waged struggles on three fronts: against the socialist-territorialists who advocated Jewish statehood in a country other than Palestine; against the assimilationism of Jewish labor leaders who denied the legitimacy of Po'alei Zion as a trend in socialism; and for recognition as an integral part of the Zionist movement. By the time World War I broke out, the fight had been largely successful in all aspects.

In 1910 Po'alei Zion introduced a new trend in North American Jewish education by establishing secular Jewish afternoon schools. In 1912 Po'alei Zion founded the Jewish National Workers Alliance. In 1914 it launched a movement to establish a democratic and representative body to deal, on behalf of U.S. Jewry, with Jewish problems growing out of the war. The movement succeeded in bringing into being the first American Jewish Congress.

During the 1920s Po'alei Zion organized the Histadrut Campaign (National Committee for Labor Israel) and supported the establishment of Pioneer Women (now Na'amat U.S.A.). The 1930s and 1940s were spent in combating Nazism and Fascism, aiding the victims of Hitlerian savagery, and fighting for Jewish statehood. A wide program of action on the American Jewish scene was developed at the same time and over the next few decades a number of other groups merged with Po'alei Zion. In 1971 Po'alei Zion joined with *Farband and the American *Habonim Association to form the Labor Zionist Alliance. Since the establishment of the State of Israel, efforts of the Labor Zionist Alliance have been concentrated on supporting Israel and contributing to its growth. Many members have settled in Israel, where they have established kibbutzim, moshavim, and urban cooperatives; pioneered in the development of Israel experience programs for American Jewish youth; led the effort to found the Association of Americans and Canadians in Israel as a nonpartisan framework for North Americans living in Israel; and participated actively in the campaign for religious pluralism.

In 2000 the organization adopted a new ideological statement. Among the priorities in that statement are innovative formal and informal Jewish education; pluralism and egalitarianism in Jewish life; the mutual recognition by the State of Israel and the Palestinian people of each other's self-determination; promotion of *aliyah*; and the elimination of poverty worldwide. In 2004 the Labor Zionist Alliance adopted a strategic plan, including the name change to Ameinu and new programs designed to increase communal impact and attract younger members. Ameinu, whose name is followed by the tag line "Liberal Values, Progressive Israel," sponsors missions to the volunteer and cooperative sectors of Israel, speaking tours to the United States by leaders of Israel's labor and peace movement, and – in partnership with several like-minded organizations – the Union of Progressive Zionists on college campuses.

Local Ameinu affiliates belong to Jewish community relations councils, federations, boards of Jewish education, and other umbrella organizations in their respective cities. Since 1934 the organization has published the *Jewish Frontier*, now a quarterly. Among the most influential ideological and political personalities in the century-long history of Ameinu were Nachman Syrkin, Baruch Zuckerman, and Hayim Greenberg.

BIBLIOGRAPHY: J. J Goldberg and Elliot King (eds.), *Builders and Dreamers: Habonim Labor Zionist Youth in North America* (1993); *Labor Zionist Handbook* (1939); Mark A. Raider, *The Emergence of American Zionism* (1998); C. Bezalel Sherman, *Labor Zionism in America* (1957).

[Daniel Mann (2nd ed.)]

LA CHAUX-DE-FONDS, town in the canton of Neuchâtel, W. Switzerland. The first official evidence of Jews dates from 1772; they attempted to establish residence there in 1777 but were refused by the authorities. In 1782 they were permitted to remain and trade within the city area for extended periods of time but in 1790 this permission was revoked. In 1818 six families, all of them of Alsatian origin, settled in La Chaux-de-Fonds and by 1844 the number of Jews had grown to 65. A community was organized in 1833 and the first synagogue building acquired in 1853. Since other Swiss municipal authorities were reluctant to grant Jews permission to settle, liberal city authorities helped La Chaux-de-Fonds in housing the biggest Jewish community in Switzerland in 1850. This was the period of the flourishing Swiss watch industry, in which Jews, too, were active. The Alsatian rabbi Jules Wolff, a student of the rabbinical seminary of Paris, was elected rabbi there in 1896 and served until 1955. In 1895 a beautiful new synagogue in Byzantine cupola-style was erected, which is still in use today and was recently renovated. Until 1945 La Chaux-de-Fonds had a distinctly Alsatian-Jewish character. With the decline of the watch industry, the city and the community had great economic problems. In 2004 the Jewish community of La Chaux-de-Fonds had 107 members.

BIBLIOGRAPHY: F. Guggenheim-Gruenberg, *Die Juden in der Schweiz* (1961); A. Weldler-Steinberg, *Geschichte der Juden in der Schweiz*, 2 vols. (1966/70), index; A. Kamis-Muller, *Vie Juive en Suisse*, (1992); L. Leitenberg, "Evolution et perspectives des communautés en Suisse romande," in: Schweiz. Isr. Gemeindebund (ed.), *Jüd. Lebenswelt Schweiz. 100 Jahre Schweiz. Isr. Gemeindebund* (2004), 153–66, 461.

[Uri Kaufmann (2nd ed.)]

LACHISH (Heb. לָכִישׁ), Canaanite and Israelite city, identified with a prominent mound (Ar. Tell ed-Duweir) situated to the southeast of Bet Guvrin. The mound was excavated from 1932 to 1938 under the direction of James L. Starkey (with the results published by Olga Tufnell), with the discovery of remains from many different periods, mainly from the Middle Bronze and Iron Ages. The excavations were continued in 1966 and 1968 by Y. Aharoni, who excavated the solar shrine area. Large-scale excavations were renewed at the site by David Ussishkin in 1973 and work lasted there until 1994.

The earliest archaeological remains found belong to the Neolithic, Chalcolithic, and Early Bronze Ages. A small settlement and cemetery of shaft tombs from the Intermediate Bronze Age are known on a ridge to the northwest of the site. Lachish appears to have been an important city-state during the Middle Bronze II–III. The city had glacis ramparts with a fosse below. On top of the mound was a large building (palace?) with massive mud-brick walls. Destroyed by fire, the building was subsequently reused for domestic and industrial purposes. A cult place from this period was also investigated, with many finds of votive vessels and animal bones. Outside the site were numerous tombs containing rich finds.

A decline set in during the Late Bronze Age following the destruction of the Middle Bronze Age city, with the settlement decreasing in size and becoming unfortified. However, the settlement rapidly made a recovery, and it eventually became one of the significant city-states of Canaan. Lachish is mentioned in a papyrus from the time of the Egyptian pharaoh Amenhotep II (1453–1419 B.C.E.). Among the *El-Amarna tablets from Egypt are several tablets written in cuneiform which were sent by the rulers of Lachish to the pharaohs Amenhotep III and Amenhotep IV. Yet another tablet discovered by Bliss at Tell el-Hesi was apparently sent there from Lachish. A temple was discovered in the fosse to the northwest of the mound, with rich finds, pits, and offerings. Tombs were also found. Level VI consists of the remains of a prosperous Canaanite city that had strong ties with Egypt, particularly at the time of Rameses III (1182–1151 B.C.E.). An acropolis temple was uncovered consisting of an antechamber, a main hall, and a cella, with architectural similarities to temples in Egypt. One of the unique finds is that of a gold plaque portraying a naked goddess. Other finds from this level include a cache of bronze objects, one with the cartouche of Rameses III, and a handful of inscriptions written in Canaanite alphabetic script. The city was destroyed by fire (c. 1130 B.C.E.?) – perhaps by the Sea Peoples who were settling in the region or by the Israelites (cf. Josh. 10:31–32). The king of Lachish, Japhia, is mentioned as having joined the Amorite coalition against Joshua (Josh. 10:3, 5); he was defeated at Aijalon and killed at Makkedah, the city falling to the Israelites (Josh. 10:32). In any case, the site was thereafter abandoned until the tenth century.

Level V represents the renewal of the city at the time of the United Monarchy. Small domestic rooms were uncovered and one of the rooms in the solar shrine contained cultic vessels. It was apparently destroyed at the time of Pharaoh Shishak (Sheshonq) in c. 925 B.C.E.

Level IV was a large city; its massive fortifications may have been erected by King Rehoboam (928–911 B.C.E.; see I Chron. 11:5–12, 23), but this is uncertain. Other candidates are Asa (908–867 B.C.E.) or Jehoshaphat (870–846 B.C.E.). The city gate to the southwest consisted of an outer gate, a roadway, a six-chambered gate, and an outer revetment. A large fortified residence – perhaps a palace – was built in the center of the site. Water for the city was obtained from a well to the northeast. Starkey may have uncovered a rock-hewn water system to the east, but more work needs to be done to clarify this further. Lachish gave shelter to King Amaziah (798–769 B.C.E.) when he fled a rebellion against him in Jerusalem (II Kings 14:19; II Chron. 25:27). What caused the end of Lachish IV is unclear, but it is possible that this was the result of an earthquake in 760 B.C.E., at the time of Uzziah (Amos 1:1; Zech. 14:5).

Lachish III represents a rebuild of the former city and it is surmised that it also saw an increase in population at this time. The palace-fort compound at the center of the site was expanded and the southern annex was modified. This city was destroyed violently in 701 B.C.E. by the Assyrian ruler, Sennacherib, who established a camp nearby (II Kings 18:14, 17; Isa. 36:2; 37:8; II Chron. 32:9). The conquest of Lachish was graphically depicted on reliefs adorning the palace of Sennacherib at Nineveh (kept in the British Museum in London). Remnants of weapons and a mass burial of 1,500 individuals were discovered at the site. Its inhabitants were subsequently deported. Well-dated ceramic assemblages belong to this level, and 403 royal *lmlk* stamped handles and 63 personal stamps were found.

Lachish II represents the rebuilding of the city following a short period of abandonment, perhaps at the time of Josiah (639–609 B.C.E.). A smaller gate replaced the previous large gate. The Lachish letters – most of which were sent to an army commander at Lachish – were found by Starkey inside this gate. The city was more crowded and less prosperous compared to the previous city. Jeremiah (34:7) referred to the stronghold of Lachish. It was subsequently destroyed by the Babylonian king, Nebuchadrezzar, in 588/586 B.C.E. Level I represents remains from the Babylonian, Persian, and Hellenistic periods.

BIBLIOGRAPHY: H. Torczyner, *Lachish I: The Lachish Letters* (1938); O. Tufnell et al., *Lachish II: The Fosse Temple* (1940); O. Tufnell, *Lachish III: The Iron Age* (1953); O. Tufnell et al., *Lachish IV: The Bronze Age* (1958); Y. Aharoni, *Investigations at Lachish: The Sanctuary and the Residency (Lachish V)* (1975); D. Usshiskin, *The Conquest of Lachish by Sennacherib* (1982); D. Ussishkin, *The Renewed Archaeological Excavations at Lachish (1973–1994)*, vols. 1–5 (2004).

[Shimon Gibson (2nd ed.)]

LACHISH OSTRACA, a collection of inscribed sherds discovered at *Lachish by J.L. *Starkey. Eighteen were discovered in 1935 in a room adjacent to the city gate, among the ruins of stratum II, which was destroyed by Nebuchadnezzar of Babylonia, and in 1938, three more sherds were found. With the exception of two lists of names (nos. 1 and 19) and a docket (no. 20), the sherds are letters which were sent to Ya'ush, an army commander stationed at Lachish and responsible for the southwestern Shephelah. His correspondent was Hoshaiah, apparently an officer under Ya'ush in command of a garrison stationed in one of the towns between Lachish and Jerusalem. Ya'ush had accused Hoshaiah of reading secret documents sent from Jerusalem to the commander at Lachish and of revealing their contents to others. Hoshaiah denies the charge, humbly appealing to his superior. The usual opening salutation ("May the Lord cause my lord to hear tidings of peace!"; no. 2) is sometimes followed by the self-demeaning question "Who is your servant, a dog that..." (nos. 2, 5, and 6; cf. II Sam. 9:8; II Kings 8:13).

Another recurrent theme concerns the activities of a certain prophet, which were detrimental to the soldiers. Letter no. 3 appears to deal with this prophet: "The army commander, Coniah the son of Elnathan, has gone down to Egypt..." This incident strongly resembles the incident of the king Jehoiakim and the prophet *Uriah from Kiriath-Jearim (Jer. 26); according to H. Torczyner (Tur-Sinai), the same event was recorded in both the ostracon and the Bible. In no. 4, Hoshaiah informs Ya'ush that he has carried out his orders, reporting what was done at his command and ending "We are watching for the fire signals of Lachish, according to all the signs my lord gave, because we do not see Azekah" (Tel Zakariyyeh (Tel 'Azeqah), at the entrance to the Elah Valley, north of Lachish). Hoshaiah's message that he does not see Azekah (or reading אות for את, the signal of Azekah has not been approved) may mean that the letter was sent after the fall of Azekah, in line with the situation described in Jeremiah 34:7: "...When the king of Babylon's army fought against Jerusalem, and against all the cities of Judah that were left, against Lachish and against Azekah; for these alone remained of the cities of Judah as fortified cities." A less dramatic interpretation, that visibility conditions were unfavorable, is also possible.

These ostraca constitute the latest corpus of Hebrew documents from the time of the First Temple. They are of great importance for linguistic and orthographic research and for the study of ancient Hebrew script. The biblical style of the letters resembles the prose of the books of Kings and Jeremiah, although terminology and usages otherwise unknown also occur: בית הרפד (no. 4) is probably a lodging house; תסבה (no. 4) is a circling movement, an encirclement, a patrol (cf. Song 3:3 [2]; 5:7). The use of vowel letters א, ה, ו, י is generally found only in final position in the ostraca, but the name Ya'ush is always spelled יאוש; the word *ish*, איש (3:9–10); and in no. 20 we read "בתשעית ביו[ם]" (contrast "בשת התשעת" in the Samaria ostraca). The Lachish Letters are written in a cursive script, the most developed form of the Paleo-Hebraic (ancient Hebrew) script, whose use was very much restricted after the destruction of the First Temple.

BIBLIOGRAPHY: H. Torczyner, et al., *Lachish*, 1 (1938); idem, *Te'udot Lakhish* (1940); F.M. Cross, Jr. and D.N. Freedman, *Early Hebrew Orthography* (1952), 51–57 (incl. bibl.). **ADD. BIBLIOGRAPHY:** A. Lemaire, *Inscriptions hébraïques* (1977), 87–143; Z. Zevit, *Matres Lectionis in Ancient Hebrew Epigraphs* (1980); S. Ahituv, *Handbook of Ancient Hebrew Inscriptions* (1992), 31–54, incl. bibl.; M. Cross, in: idem, *Leaves from an Epigrapher's Notebook* (2003), 129–32; R. Di Vito, in: ABD, 4:126–28.

[Joseph Naveh]

LACHISH REGION, development region in southern Israel, comprising an area of approximately 275 sq. mi. (750 sq. km.). Stretching from the Mediterranean Coast between Niẓẓanim and the Gaza Strip eastward to the pre-1967 armistice line, the region includes three different geographical and farming areas: the western part, belonging to the Coastal Plain, with mostly light soils and well suited for citrus cultivation; the central part, also the Coastal Plain, with heavier soils where intensive field crops are preponderant; and the eastern part, belonging to the foothills (Shephelah) and reaching at its northeastern extremity into the Hebron Hills, characterized by fruit orchards, tobacco, and sheep pasture along with field crops. In the western part outpost settlements were established in the 1939–47 period (including Negbah and Gevaram) and after 1948 a network of 31 moshavim and kibbutzim came into being there. Development in the central and eastern parts, however, was held up by lack of water. With the construction of the Yarkon-Negev conduit in 1954, the Lachish Development Project came into being and became the prototype of regional planning for Israel and also for other developing countries. The scheme aimed at combining optimal exploitation of local natural features with the speedy absorption of a maximum number of immigrant settlers in productive employment, comply-

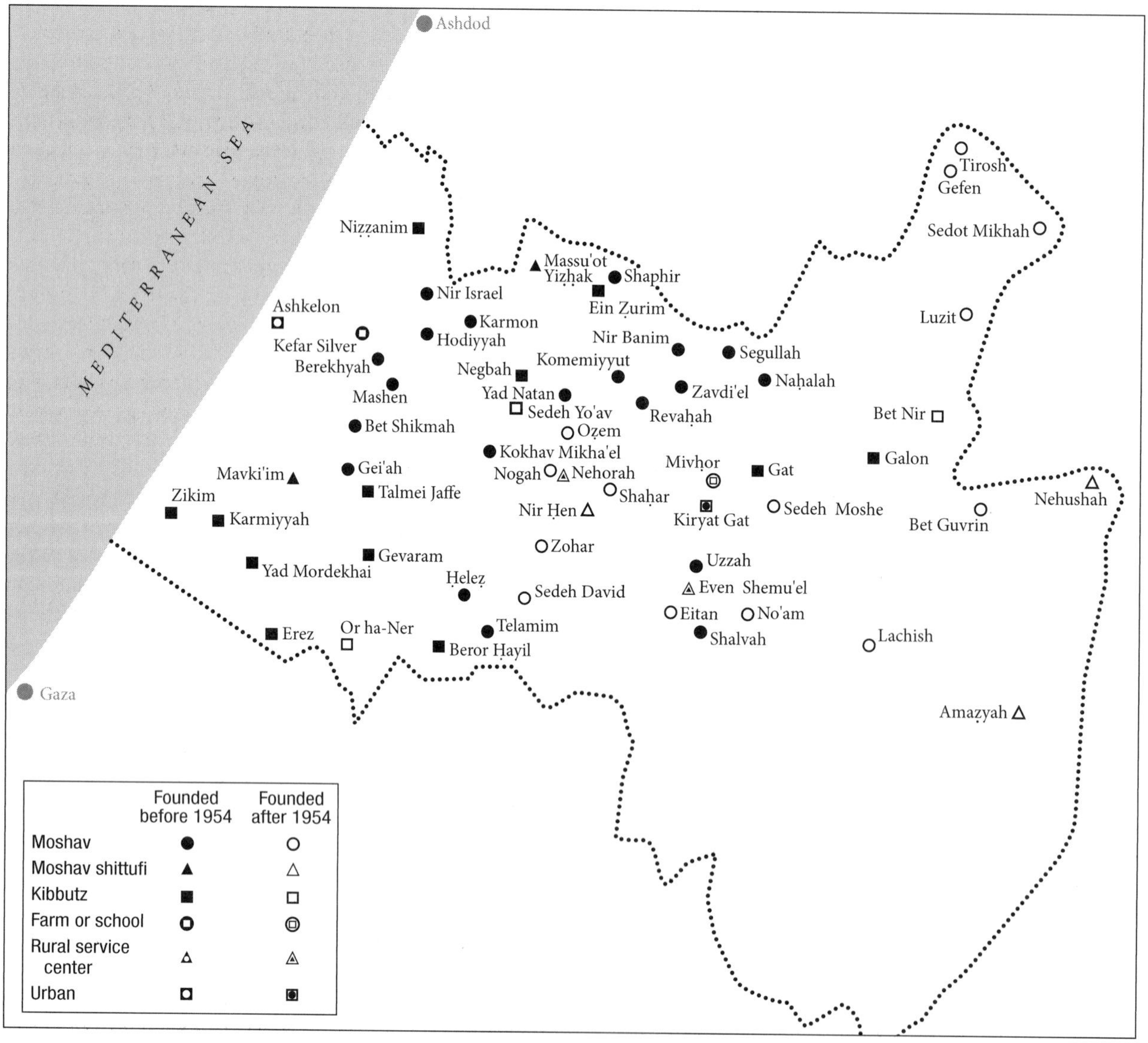

The Lachish development region, 1971.

ing with defense requirements at the same time. It provided for the establishment of clusters of four or five farming villages, each having from 40 to 100 settler families and grouped around "rural centers." Most of the 23 villages erected in the Lachish region since 1954 were moshavim, but there were also a few kibbutzim and administered farms. The three rural centers were *Nehorah, Even Shemu'el, and Vardon (Menuḥah); for the older village clusters, no such centers were set up, and they were directly dependent on the next regional town (see below). Whereas the villages proper had local services (e.g., kindergarten and, sometimes, the lower elementary school classes, grocery, and a synagogue), the rural center offered most services, e.g., a school, a clinic, a tractor and machine shop, a dairy plant, packing and sorting sheds, storehouses, a central grocery, and cultural institutions. While in the individual villages settlers having a similar background were concentrated, the rural center served as a meeting ground for immigrants from different countries and continents, thereby furthering their mutual integration and distributing service costs over several hundred families. The rural centers and their dependent villages were in turn connected with the regional town which provided economic, social, and cultural services of a higher order (e.g., factories based on agricultural raw materials, banks, regional administration, and secondary schools). *Kiryat Gat functioned as the Lachish region's urban center, but a number of villages in the western part were more closely linked to *Ashkelon and *Kiryat Malakhi which are within easier reach. The road network linked villages to their rural centers, and these to the regional town. In 1970 the Lachish region's rural population numbered 17,500 persons, as the *Adullam region in the northeast had meanwhile become a separate development area. In the 1990s and the 2000s farming declined, leading many settlers to find their source of livelihood outside their settlements. However, the region is still known for its extensive vineyards and a number of other farming branches are still active. At the end of 2003 the Lachish region numbered 6,300 inhabitants.

BIBLIOGRAPHY: H. Halperin, *Agrindus, Integration of Agriculture and Industries* (1963); R. Weitz, in: *Journal of Farm Economics* (Aug. 1965), 634–51; R. Weitz and A. Rokach, *Agricultural Development: Planning and Implementation* (1968); A. Rokach, *Regional Rural Development* (1964); idem, in: *People in the Countryside. Studies in Rural Social Development* (1966), 146–59; E. Orni, *Forms of Settlement* (1963), 178ff.

[Avshalom Rokach and Elisha Efrat / Shaked Gilboa (2nd ed.)]

LACHMANN, SIR PETER JULIUS (1931–), British immunologist. Lachmann was born in Berlin, immigrated to the U.K. in December 1938, and was educated at Christ's College, Finchley, in North London. He graduated in natural sciences (1952) and in medicine at Trinity College, Cambridge (1957), after clinical training at University College Hospital, University of London, and gained his Ph.D. from the University of Cambridge (1962) under the supervision of Robin Coombs and Henry Kunkel. He was a research fellow (1962–64) and assistant director of research in immunology at the University of Cambridge (1964–71), which included a formative period for his interests when he was a visiting investigator with Hans Mueller-Eberhard at the Scripps Clinic, La Jolla, California. He was appointed professor of immunology at the Royal Postgraduate Medical School, London (1971–75) and Sheila Joan Smith Professor of Immunology, University of Cambridge (1977–99), where he was also director of the Medical Research Council's Molecular Immunopathology Unit (1980–97). He was subsequently emeritus professor of immunology. Lachmann made fundamental research contributions to our understanding of the complement system which plays a crucial role in defense against infection but also contributes adversely to many immunological diseases. His later research interests centered more broadly on anti-microbial immunity. His clinical research was especially directed at understanding the immune disease systemic lupus erythematosus ("lupus"). He played a prominent role in planning research strategy and in immunological and scientific education nationally and internationally; he had a particular interest in educating the general public about issues of popular concern such as stem cell research and genetically modified food. His achievements have been recognized by his many national and international honors and awards, which include election as a fellow of the Royal Society of London (1982), member of the UNESCO International Bioethics Committee (1993–98), gold medalist of the European Complement Network (1997), founder president of the UK Academy of Medical Sciences (1998–2002), and Knight Bachelor (2002). In 1989 he was Mayerhoff Visiting Professor at the Weizmann Institute, Reḥovot. Lachmann's wife, elder son, and daughter are physicians. His younger son is a TV producer with the BBC.

[Michael Denman (2nd ed.)]

LACHMANN, ROBERT (1892–1939), ethnomusicologist who was born in Berlin. He studied English, French, and Arabic at the universities of Berlin and London. His first contact with non-Western (especially Arab) music took place during World War I when he was sent to the Wünsdorf POW camp to collect folklore and traditional music from prisoners; there he met Arab soldiers and made his first attempts at transcribing their songs. This work was encouraged by Erich von Hornbostel and Curt *Sachs, then members of the Berlin Phonogrammarchiv. After 1918 he studied musicology under Johannes Wolf and Carl Stumpf and Semitic languages under Eugen Mittwoch at Berlin University, taking his doctorate in 1922 with a dissertation on urban music in Tunisia based on his own field recordings. In 1924 he joined the Berlin Staatsbibliothek and studied librarianship. After a year in Kiel (1926) he returned to the Berlin Staatsbibliothek to take up a post in the music department under Wolf. Meanwhile he continued to study Near Eastern music, mainly during several recording expeditions in North Africa. In 1925 he visited Tripoli, and in 1926 and 1929 was again in Tunisia recording *fellahin* and Bedouin music, as well as the songs of the Jewish community on the Isle of Djerba where he made the first recordings of the local Jewish community. These provided the material for his last work, *Jewish Cantillation and Song in the Isle of Djerba*, which was published posthumously in Jerusalem in 1940 and is regarded as a major contribution to Jewish and comparative ethnomusicology. At his instigation the Gesellschaft zur Erforschung der Musik des Orients was founded in 1930, and he edited its quarterly journal, *Zeitschrift für vergleichende Musikwissenschaft*, throughout the three years of its lifetime (1933–5). Being Jewish, Lachmann lost his job at the Berlin Staatsbibliothek under the Nazi government. In 1935, the Hebrew University of Jerusalem invited him to open a Phonogram Archive for Oriental Music. His research during his last four years in Jerusalem (1935–9) marked the start of modern ethnomusicology in Israel. He brought with him his earlier recordings of Arab music (about 500 items recorded in North Africa) and made 1,000 more recordings, which brought to light a number of oral liturgies preserved by Middle Eastern Jewish communities in Jerusalem but originating elsewhere. In Jerusalem Lachmann tried a new approach to the complexities of Jewish music, and in *Jewish Cantillation and Song in the Isle of Djerba* (1940) finally evolved a way of describing a community comprehensively through a detailed structural analysis of the recorded materials. His aim was to set the picture of North African Jewish music against the larger background of Islamic music civilizations, thus demonstrating that the music of an independent religious community could be influenced by neighboring cultures. Lachmann was one of the finest exponents of the early European school of comparative musicology, stressing comparative analysis of musical forms and their morphological qualities as well as the variants and parallels of one single type (e.g., women's laments, folk epics, ritual songs) around the world. He deepened insight into the worldwide relationships of such basic forms. Another of his achievements was to enlarge the understanding of the intricate forms of ornamental variation and improvisation in Arab music. His archives are held by the Music Department (Mus. 26) of the Jewish National and University Library, Jerusalem. His original recordings, especially those made on tin records, were unavailable until only recently, when, through new technologies, they were rerecorded by the Sound Archives of the National Library.

BIBLIOGRAPHY: Blom (ed.), Grove's Dict, 5 (1954), 5–5; Slonimsky (ed.), Baker's Biog Dict, s.v.; E. Gerson-Kiwi, in: *Acta Musicologica*, 30 (1958), 17–26. **ADD. BIBLIOGRAPHY:** idem, "Two Anniversaries: Two Pioneers in Jewish Ethnomusicology," in: *Orbis musicae*, 2 (1973–4), 17–28 (A.Z. Idelsohn, R. Lachmann); idem, "Robert Lachmann: His Achievement and his Legacy," in: *Yuval*, 3 (1974), 100–08 (incl. inventory of the Lachmann Archive and complete list of published writings); R. Katz, *The Lachmann Problem: An Unsung Chapter in Comparative Musicology* (2003); R. Davis, "Robert Lachmann's Oriental Music: A Broadcasting Initiative in 1930s Palestine," in: *The Mediterranean in Music* (2005), 79–95.

[Edith Gerson-Kiwi / Gila Flam (2nd ed.)]

LACHOWER, YERUḤAM FISHEL (1883–1947), critic and historian of modern Hebrew literature. Born in Chorzele, Poland, he began his career as a critic in 1904. In 1908 he moved to Warsaw serving as editor of various literary publications. After World War I he was appointed editor of *Ha-Tekufah* and of the Stybel Publishing House. During the early 1920s Lachower lived in Germany and in 1927 settled in Ereẓ Israel. In Tel Aviv he was an editor of *Moznayim*, the literary organ of the Hebrew Writers Association, and of *Keneset* (1928), an annual periodical dedicated to studies on Ḥ.N. *Bialik.

Lachower's approach to literature is both critical and scholarly. He studies the literary method and conceptual framework of the author, quoting copiously from the work under discussion. But he also probes the author's motives, stressing the different and often contradictory trends in his work and personality. Lachower's own writing, at times, alternates between an objective, matter-of-fact, somewhat dry style and impressionistic musings couched in metaphorical, often ornate, language. During the early period he discusses contemporary authors of the modern national renaissance, e.g., S. Tchernichowsky, Ḥ.N. Bialik, Z. Shneur, U.N. Gnessin, and others. His detailed discussion of D. *Frischmann and M.J. *Berdyczewski shows a certain affinity in outlook between him and these two authors. He shunned the social-national approach to literature then current among his contemporaries. Instead of interpreting a work in the light of social conditions, he attempted to expound its intrinsic meaning. Besides the aesthetic aspects of literature, he was deeply interested in its philosophical and conceptual presuppositions.

In Ereẓ Israel Lachower devoted himself mainly to scholarly activity. *Toledot ha-Sifrut ha-Ivrit ha-Ḥadashah* ("History of Modern Hebrew Literature," 4 vols., 1947–48) is an important contribution to the historiography of modern Hebrew literature. Ranging over a 200-year period – from M.Ḥ. Luzzatto to Bialik – the book is not uniform in character. Intended for secondary schools, the text is extensively illustrated with excerpts from the works under study. Its further value lies in the fact that it contains some information about little-known authors as well as bibliographical addenda. Lachower in his periodization of modern Hebrew literature supported the view that Moshe Ḥayyim *Luzzatto is the father of modern Hebrew literature both because of the new poetical character of his dramatic works and because he had exercised a profound influence on later authors, particularly on Abraham *Mapu. Although Lachower did not disregard the effect world literature had on Hebrew literary writing, he stressed the internal developments of Hebrew literature showing its uninterrupted continuity. The historical continuity of Hebrew literature and the cultural links which connect one period to the next preoccupied Lachower in his subsequent writings where he examined the problem more profoundly. Some of his later studies substantiate his views that mystical and kabbalistic themes had influenced modern Hebrew literature in the 18th century (for example – Luzzatto's plays). On the other hand, in some of his essays he points out the influence of Maimonides, Spinoza, and Goethe on Haskalah literature. His deep interest in the achievements of 19th-century Judaic studies in Hebrew

(*Ḥokhmat Yisrael*) led to his detailed analysis of Nachman *Krochmal's philosophy of history.

Lachower's scholarly work on Bialik was a major contribution to the study of the poet. He was the first to publish certain of Bialik's writings – early versions of his poems and stories – and he compiled a five-volume collection of Bialik's letters (1935–39) – which was but a preliminary to his extensive but incomplete biography, *Ḥ.N. Bialik, Ḥayyav vi-Yẓirato* ("Ḥ.N. Bialik, his Life and Works," 3 vols., 1943–47). The work discusses in great detail the genesis of Bialik's poems and the Jewish and European sources which influenced them. Combining meticulous biographical-historical research and a genetic examination of the text, Lachower also attempted an aesthetic evaluation of the poet's works.

Many of his essays have been collected in book form: *Meḥkarim ve-Nisyonot* ("Studies and Experiments," Warsaw, 1925); *Rishonim va-Aḥaronim* (1934–35, 1965^2), a collection of critical essays on authors from Moses Mendelssohn to the 1940s; *Al Gevul ha-Yashan ve-he-Ḥadash* ("Between Old and New," 1951); *Ba-Teḥum u-mi-Ḥuẓ la-Teḥum* ("Within and Without the Pale," 1953); and *Shirah u-Maḥashavah* ("Poetry and Thought," 1953).

BIBLIOGRAPHY: S. Lachower, *Fishel Lachower, Bibliografyah* (1948); N. Goren, *Mevakkerim be-Sifrutenu* (1944), 213–9; B.M. Mikhali, *Le-Yad ha-Ovnayim* (1959), 188–99; S. Kramer, *Mishmarot be-Sifrutenu* (1959), 331–42. **ADD. BIBLIOGRAPHY:** M. Ungerfeld, *"Bein P. Lachower le-Ḥ.N. Bialik,"* in: *Ha-Do'ar*, 51 (1972), 382–83; S. Kremer, *"Lachower be-Zikato le-Omanut ha-Sippur,"* in: *Moznayim*, 34 (1972), 229–32.

[Samuel Werses]

LACHOWICZE (Lyakhovichi), MORDECAI BEN NOAH OF (1742–1810), ḥasidic *ẓaddik*. Mordecai was a disciple of Solomon b. Meir ha-Levi of *Karlin (with whom he went into exile from Lithuania because of persecutions by the *Mitnaggedim*) and for a short time of *Baruch b. Jehiel of Medzibezh. In 1793 he returned to Lithuania and established a dynasty of *ẓaddikim* in Lachowicze, which became one of the important centers of Ḥasidism in northeastern Lithuania on the border of Belorussia. His activities to spread Ḥasidism aroused opposition from the *Mitnaggedim* who started to persecute him. Through their influence he was imprisoned in 1798; the day of his liberation – the fifth day of Ḥanukkah – was celebrated as a holiday among his Ḥasidim. Mordecai was among the main collectors of funds for the Ḥasidim of Ereẓ Israel. In the dispute between *Shneur Zalman of Lyady and *Abraham b. Alexander Katz of Kalisk, he supported the latter. He attached great importance to the role of the *ẓaddik* in helping his Ḥasidim in material as well as spiritual matters.

Mordecai's connections by marriage with the *ẓaddik* Asher of *Stolin led to the establishment of the *Koidanov dynasty of *ẓaddikim*. Mordecai's successor, his son, Noah (1774–1832), was known for his fatherly attitude toward ordinary people. In 1821 he made an appeal for the benefit of the Ḥasidim of Ereẓ Israel. *Torat Avot* (1961) contains the teachings and sayings attributed by the Ḥasidim to Mordecai and Noah on the Torah and festivals. After Noah's death some of his Ḥasidim chose his son-in-law MORDECAI (II) as successor, while others chose his brother's son SOLOMON ḤAYYIM of Koidanov. This split and the rise of the Koidanov and *Kobrin Ḥasidism at that time led to the weakening of Lachowicze Ḥasidism and under Mordecai II Lachowicze Ḥasidism was to a certain extent led by the *ẓaddik* Aaron (II) of *Karlin. During the time of the successor of Mordecai II, Aaron (d. 1881), Lachowicze Ḥasidism regained its independence, but, in particular during the time of his son, NOAH (II; d. 1920), it was again weakened through the spread of the Haskalah. Noah (II) strongly opposed the Zionist movement and supported the Lachowicze **kolel* in Ereẓ Israel. His son, JOHANAN, perished with many of his Ḥasidim during the Holocaust. Some of the teachings of the Lachowicze dynasty appear in *Divrei Shalom* (1882), by Shalom (Perlow) of Koidanov.

BIBLIOGRAPHY: W.Z. Rabinowitsch, *Lithuanian Ḥasidism* (1970), index; M. Buber, *Tales of the Hasidim*, 2 (1966^3), 153–8.

[Wolf Zeev Rabinowitsch]

LACHS, MANFRED (1914–1993), Polish jurist and authority on international law. Lachs went to England during World War II and acted as secretary to Isaac *Schwarzbart, who was the Jewish member of the Polish National Council in exile. He returned to Poland and from 1947 was director of the legal department of the foreign ministry. From 1949 until 1952, he was professor of political science in Warsaw. Lachs was a member of the Polish Academy of Sciences and head of the Institute of Jurisprudence. On several occasions, he was a member of the Polish delegation to the United Nations and in 1957 and 1964 lectured at the Hague Academy of International Law. In 1967 he served as a judge at the International Court, and in 1973, Lachs was elected its president, to hold office for a period of three years. Among his publications are *War Crimes. An Attempt to Define the Issue* (1945), *La frontière polono-allemande* (1964), and *Human Rights; Can They be Guaranteed?* (1946). Two courses of Lach's lectures at the Hague Academy of International Law *Les Développements et Fonctions des Traités Multilatéraux* (1957) and *The Law of Outer Space* (1964; another book by him with the same title appeared in 1972) were published in the Recueil des Cours of the Academy.

[Israel (Ignacy) Isserles]

LACHVA (Pol. **Lachwa**), a town in Polesie district, Belarus. From the middle of the 16th century it was owned by the Princess Radziwill. An organized Jewish community probably began after the *Chmelnicki uprising (1648–1650), and it was under the jurisdiction of Pinsk. It numbered 157 Jewish poll-tax payers in 1795, and the majority of the inhabitants were Jews. The local Jews engaged in retailing and traded in fish and agricultural produce. At the close of the 18th century the Jews of Lachva became involved in the struggle between Ḥasidism and its opponents. In 1817, in addition to the above occupations, the Jews engaged in tailoring, wax making, carting, and butchering. With the construction of the railroad Vilna-Luniniets-Rovno in the 1880s, the economy improved, and there developed export of lumber and farm products, and a furniture factory opened. Abraham Dov Berkowicz and his son Isaac officiated as rabbis of Lachva at the close of the 19th century. In 1897 the community of Lachva numbered 1,057 (c. 44% of the total population). At the beginning of the 20th century and especially between the two world wars, the Zionist parties and organizations were active in the town. There was also a Hebrew *Tarbut school, a *Maccabi society, and a drama circle. In 1921 the 1,126 Jews of the town formed 33% of the population, and their number increased to about 2,000 by 1941. Until 1939 there was a Hebrew religious school and a large Tarbut library. The last rabbi of Lachva was R. Eliezer Lichtenstein.

[Arthur Cygielman / Shmuel Spector (2nd ed.)]

Holocaust Period

The town was occupied by Soviet troops on Sept. 17, 1939, as a result of which all Jewish organizations virtually ceased to function. The Germans occupied the town on July 8, 1941. Many young Jews escaped into the Soviet interior, while others were drafted into the Soviet army. The *Judenrat was headed by the former Zionist leader, Dov Lopatin, aided by dedicated leaders. A ghetto was established on April 1, 1942, where 2,350 Jews were crowded in 45 small houses. In the months August–September about 30 young Jews were organized in the underground, headed by Itshak Rokhchin, but could acquire only nonlethal weapons. In August 1942 the community discovered that ditches were being dug on the outskirts of the city and realized the implications. The Jews of Lachva decided to resist. On the night of September 2–3, 1942, the Germans surrounded the ghetto. Dov Lopatin and the underground chose to fight. When the Nazis broke into the ghetto, the entire community took part in the struggle, some equipped only with axes or sticks. Lopatin set fire to the Judenrat house, and others set fire to the rest of ghetto. Six German policemen and six Belorussian policemen were killed. Between 600 to 700 Jews were killed fighting, enabling 600 to reach the nearby forests. Many of them perished, but 120 in the Gryczyn marshes founded a Jewish partisan unit or joined other partisan units. They participated in military operations against the Nazis, including sabotage and other acts of revenge and retaliation. The Jewish revolt at Lachva was an outstanding example of mass resistance against the Nazis and was one of the first Polish ghetto revolts. After the war, the remnants of the community did not rebuild their homes. The approximately 90 survivors settled in Israel and other countries.

[Aharon Weiss / Shmuel Spector (2nd ed.)]

BIBLIOGRAPHY: B. Wasiutyński, *Ludnośc żydowska w Polsce…* (1930), 84; H. Aleksandrow, in: *Tsaytshrift*, 2–3 (Minsk, 1928), 366; *ibid.*, 4 (1930), 71; *Rishonim la-Mered, Laḥva* (Heb., and partly Yid., 1957); Meram, in: *Le Monde Juif*, 22 no. 11 (1967), 5–16.

°**LACRETELLE, JACQUES DE** (1888–1985), French novelist. As a schoolboy, he experienced the tensions produced by the *Dreyfus case and his masterpiece, *Silbermann* (1922; English version in: L. Lewisohn (ed.), *Among the Nations*, 1948), is the story of a young Jew persecuted by his schoolmates at the time of the trial. A passionate lover of French culture, Silbermann dreams of a fruitful intermingling of the French and Jewish genius, but his idealism is misunderstood and he is cruelly ostracized and eventually forced to leave the school. Lacretelle's tragic hero, a portrait partly inspired by his friend, the poet Henri *Franck, set a pattern in French literature: Montherlant (in a short story) and Duhamel (in *The Pasquier Chronicles*) both created Jewish heroes not unlike Silbermann. Lacretelle presents a far less favorable picture of his hero in *Le retour de Silbermann* (1929), a sequel to the earlier novel. Here he traces the decadence of the Jew who, having sought his fortune in America, fails in every endeavor. In spite of his brilliance, Silbermann is plagued by what the author calls a "typically Jewish" urge for self-destruction, which leads to his death.

BIBLIOGRAPHY: A. Spire, *Quelques Juifs et demi-Juifs*, 2 (1928), 63–91; D.W. Alden, *Jacques de Lacretelle…* (Eng., 1959); C. Lehrmann, *L'Elément juif dans la littérature française*, 2 (1961^2), 97–102.

[Denise R. Goitein]

LACY, STEVE (**Steven Lackritz**; 1934–2004), U.S. soprano saxophonist. Before Steve Lacy reinvented it, the only major jazz musician to play soprano saxophone as a solo instrument was Sidney Bechet. Lacy would not only bring the instrument, admittedly a difficult one to master, to the forefront of jazz but, along with John Coltrane, whom he inspired, would turn it into a major voice in contemporary improvisational music.

Lacy was born in New York and raised on the city's Upper West Side. Like Bechet before him, he began his musical career as a clarinetist but after hearing the older man's 1941 recording of Duke Ellington's "The Mooche" on soprano, he took up the horn himself. By the mid-1950s, he was engaged in a most unusual balancing act, playing traditional New Orleans jazz with the likes of Buck Clayton, Pee Wee Russell, and Henry "Red" Allen, and the most difficult of avant-garde music with pianist Cecil Taylor. Lacy would spend six years with Taylor and always said that the combination of two such radically different musical experiences was the best possible training a musician could have. It certainly prepared him for the next phase of his career, playing with Thelonious Monk, then leading a band that played nothing but Monk's compositions.

Lacy's astringent tone and dry wit combined with his deceptively simple melodies with their sudden swerving lines to make him the perfect horn player to interpret Monk. He said of Monk's music, "[It's] not too high, not too low, not easy, not at all overplayed and most of all, full of interesting technical problems." Monk's compositional techniques clearly influenced Lacy's own writing; his own compositions, like many of his mentor's, are deceptively simple-sounding but freighted with harmonic and melodic surprises.

The audience for avant-garde jazz, never large in America, had dried up by the mid-1960s and Lacy went into exile looking for an artistic outlet. After false starts in Buenos

Aires and Rome, he settled in Paris, where he would spend the next three decades. There he found a core group of sympathetic musicians with whom he would perform in various permutations: cellist-vocalist Irene Aebi (his wife), pianists Mal Waldron and Bobby Few, bassist Steve Potts, and drummer Jean-Jacques Avenel. He recorded prolifically, his output covering well over 300 albums, including more than 20 solo sessions, but he returned repeatedly to Monk, Ellington, and Charles Mingus as well as his own seemingly endless flow of inventive composition. "He developed his saxophone tone to be as attenuated as a Hemingway sentence, and his improvised lines as succinct," Ben Ratliff wrote in the *New York Times* when Lacy died. At the time of his death, Lacy had returned to the U.S. and was teaching at the New England Conservatory of Music, giving birth to yet another generation of soprano saxophonists.

BIBLIOGRAPHY: I. Carr, "Steve Lacy," in: *Jazz: The Rough Guide* (1995); M. Martin, "Steve Lacy," in: *The Saxophone Journal* (Nov./Dec. 1991); B. Ratliff, "Steve Lacy, 69, Who Popularized the Soprano Saxophone," in: *New York Times* (June 5, 2004); G. Rouy, "Farewell Paris: Steve Lacy Returns to America," in: *Downbeat* (Oct. 2002).

[George Robinson (2nd ed.)]

LADEJINSKY, WOLF ISAAC (1899–1975), U.S. agronomist. Born in Russia, he went to the U.S. in 1922. In 1935 he began his career as a specialist in Asian agricultural problems with the United States Department of Agriculture. In 1945 General Douglas MacArthur called him to Japan to oversee the land reform designed to replace the traditional Japanese feudalism by a modern democratic society. Ladejinsky became the driving force behind that program, which affected over 5 million acres and became one of the decisive factors in modernizing Japan's political, social, and economic structure. He also advised other governments in Asia on land reform, which he saw as the alternative to communism. He worked in China, Taiwan, India, Burma, Vietnam, Nepal, Malaysia, Indonesia, and Korea. During the Eisenhower administration Ladejinsky through an error in identity was classified as a security risk. This administrative error created a wide controversy and initiated a reform of the administration's security clearance procedures. During 1954–56 he served as agricultural attaché in various Far-Eastern territories, and during 1955–61 he worked on land reform and refugee settlement projects in South Vietnam. From 1964 on he was an adviser to the World Bank, and spent most of his time in India. He became one of the prophets of the "Green Revolution," but his high moral objectives were always permeated with a sense of the possible and the practical. He wrote widely on agricultural policy. He left his collection of Asian art to the Israel Museum in Jerusalem.

[Joachim O. Ronall]

LADENBURG, family prominent in Baden and Mainz. The founder of the line was MOSES HIRSCHEL, the richest Jew in Ladenburg in the mid-18th century. His son MAYER moved to Mainz and married into the Homburg family of *Court Jews. Another son, HAYUM MOSES HIRSCH (c. 1710–1781), settled in Mannheim where he became wealthy and was a leader of the community. Hayum's son, WOLF HAYUM LADENBURG (1765–1851), founded the bank bearing his name which his descendants continued to manage. He was well known for his philanthropic activities. Leopold Ladenburg, his youngest son, was a politician as well as a militant supporter of Reform Judaism. Wolf's grandson, KARL (1827–1909), managed the family firm and was elected to the Baden parliament, becoming a spokesman on economic and financial questions. Karl's daughter married E. Bassermann, a leading German politician of his day. Virtually all of Wolf Hayum's descendants were baptized.

BIBLIOGRAPHY: B. Rosenthal, in: *Israelitisches Gemeindeblatt Mannheim*, 13 (1935), no. 10 (May 29, 1935), 3–5. **ADD. BIBLIOGRAPHY:** Arbeitskreis juedische Geschichte, *Die juedischen Ladenburger – Ein Beitrag zur Stadtgeschichte* (1991); NDB, vol. 13 (1982), 386f.

[Bjoern Siegel (2nd ed.)]

LADENBURG, ALBERT (1842–1911), German organic chemist. Born in Mannheim, Ladenburg became professor of chemistry at the University of Kiel in 1874, and from 1889 to 1909 was at the University of Breslau. His research established that the six hydrogen atoms of benzene were equivalent, determined the atomic weight of iodine, and the molecular weight of ozone. He worked on stereo-chemistry, alkaloids, and pyridine and its derivatives. Among Ladenburg's books were *Handwoerterbuch der Chemie* (13 vols., 1882–95); *Vortraege ueber die Entwicklungsgeschichte der Chemie in den letzten 100 Jahren* (1902, *Lectures on the History of the Development of Chemistry Since the Time of Lavoisier*, 1905); *Die Entwicklung der Chemie in den letzten 20 Jahren* (1900); and *Lebenserinnerungen* (1912).

BIBLIOGRAPHY: *Berichte der deutschen chemischen Gesellschaft*, 45 (1912), 3597–644.

[Samuel Aaron Miller]

LADINO (**Latino**), or Judeo-Spanish, the spoken and written Hispanic language of Jews of Spanish origin. It has no connection with the Rheto-Romance dialect (Ladin) spoken in the Italian Tyrol. Over the centuries, various names have been given to this language composed of ancient Spanish dialects: *Romance, Ǧudezmo, Spaniolish.*

Origins

The widespread view that the term "Ladino" is only applicable to the "sacred" language of Bible translations and prayers, whereas the other names are reserved solely for the spoken language, seems hardly tenable. Moreover, the theory that Ladino originated as a specifically Jewish language (as distinct from the dialects spoken in Spain) as early as the 13th or 14th century still lacks serious and sufficient proof. There is no doubt that Jews interspersed their dialects with words or expressions borrowed from Hebrew (particularly terms and concepts connected with religion and ethics), and that they preserved archaic words and obsolescent forms longer than other people. However, it was only after the Spanish Expulsion of 1492 that Ladino began to be a specifically Jewish language. Although the Jews had been ejected from the Iberian Peninsula and thus cut off from its language while this was still in the process of evolution, they preserved the Spanish and Hispanic dialects that had been spoken and written before Cervantes and the Golden Age, and which basically reflected the phonetics, morphology, and syntax of the 14th and 15th centuries. A gap, wider or narrower according to the country to which the refugees fled, began to appear between the written and spoken language on the one hand and the language of secular and rabbinical literature on the other. The language of Bible translations and prayers, which remained more resistant to the words, expressions, and syntactic patterns of the local tongue, became, in the course of the centuries, less and less comprehensible to the masses.

[Moshe Lazar]

The Topography of Ladino

The lack of contact between the Sephardim and Spain after 1492 led to a situation in which the Sephardim did not make use of the standardized norm of Spanish and allowed for the conservation of many rustic and popular forms, rejected by the Castilian norm, as well as an extraordinary geographical and social linguistic variation. This, added to the confluence of Sephardim of different regional and social origins, allowed the development of independent koinés in Salonika and Istanbul – supposedly also in Safed – evident from the end of the 17th century (i.e., the formative period of Judeo-Spanish). The result was – as the texts of the 18th century suggest – that the Judeo-Spanish dialectal mixture was not dominated exclusively by variants of a single region. Although Castilian features were selected rather more frequently than non-Castilian, perhaps reflecting the already higher prestige associated with Castilian variants in the late 15th century, selection of features typical of the other peninsular regions was frequent. In the communities of the Ottoman Empire, the linguistic contact with the local languages, especially with Turkish and Italian, led to the adoption of numerous loans. From the 16th century the influence exercised by Hebrew intensified on Judeo-Spanish and gave rise to the adoption of many words and expressions. This influence is also reflected in some syntactic structures. Finally, Judeo-Spanish shows a considerable degree of innovation, especially in phonology and lexis. This view contradicts the conventional opinion that Judeo-Spanish is intensely conservative in nature, although it does not deny that Judeo-Spanish preserves some features of 15th-century Spanish which have disappeared everywhere else (i.e., the Classical period or Golden century of Judeo-Spanish). As of 1839 Western culture – and France in particular – were the main model of modernization in the Ottoman Empire, and the Sephardi communities began to undergo westernization and secularization. The influence of French through the Alliance Israélite Universelle from 1865, and to a lesser extent of Italian and modern Spanish, caused many Sephardi intellectuals to adopt a purist attitude to their language expressed by replacing Turkish and Hebrew elements by others of Romance origin, and giving rise to what is called New-Judeo-Spanish.

In the Amsterdam and London communities, Jews continued to speak Castilian and Portuguese, which were constantly enriched by contact with the literature of the Iberian Peninsula and the contribution of *Marranos who returned to Judaism. In Italy, too, Castilian generally resisted tendencies to obsolescence and to massive linguistic borrowings from other languages, such as Hebrew or Italian.

Leaving aside the differences between the dialects, one finds that, between the 16th and 21st centuries, Judeo-Spanish continued to be a Spanish language, which had incorporated an important number of elements of Hebrew and other languages of contact. Owing to another factor, namely, that Judeo-Spanish was used in territories in which completely different languages are spoken, the Sephardim's pre-1492 Judaized Spanish turned into a full Jewish language.

PHONETICS. All the varieties of Judeo-Spanish have inherited the Castilian vowel system. The following important characteristics need to be emphasized for the consonants:

a) Innovations:

1. A certain tendency for word-initial *e-* to drop when followed by *s* + consonant: *sfuenyo* (*esfuenyo* < *sueño* = sleep, dream), *spalda* (*espalda* = shoulder), *skova* (*escoba* = broom), *strečo* (*estrecho* = narrow).

2. Alternance between the conservation of the labiodental fricative *f-* and its aspiration when preceding the diphthong *we*: *fuego / huego* (fire), *fuerte/huerte* (strong), *yo fue / yo hue* (I was, I went).

3. The articulation of /ʎ/ (both initial and median) has merged to /j/ and the *yeismo* has become universal in Judeo-Spanish: *yorar* (*llorar* = to cry), *yave* (*llave* = key), *kavayeros* (*caballeros* = men), and then /j/ tended to disappear entirely when adjacent to the front tonic vowels *e* and *i*: *anío* (*anillo* = ring), *kaveo* (*cabello* = hair), *gaína* (*gallina* = chicken), *manías* (*manillas* = bracelets). Etymological -li- underwent the same development: *famía* (*familia* = family).

4. The phoneme /rr/ has merged to /r/: *pero* (*perro* = dog), *tyera* (*tierra* = earth), *yo syero* (*yo cierro* = I close) in most varieties.

5. Initial consonant *n-* in front of the diphthong *we* changes to *m-*: *muestro* (*nuestro* = our), *muevo* (*nuevo* = new), *muez* (*nuez* = nut).

6. Almost all varieties of Judeo-Spanish merge [ɲ] and [nj]: *anyo* (*año* = year), *panyo* (*paño* = knit).

7. Second-plural ending of the verb has come to be marked by /š/, as a result of assimilation between earlier final /s/ and de preceding off-glide [i]: *kantaš* (*cantáis* = you sing). This marker was then extended to verbal endings where there had been no off-glide: *kantareš* (*cantaréis* = you will sing), *savreš* (*sabréis* = you will know), *direš* (*diréis* = you will say).

8. The initial group *sue-* often changed to *esfue-*: *esfuegra* (*suegra* = sister-in-law), *esfuenyo* (*sueño* = sleep, dream).

9. The metathesis *d-r* instead of *r-d* is extremely common, except in the Bosnian, Croatian, and West-Macedonian dialects: *vedre* (verde = green), *sodro* (*sordo* = deaf), *pedrido* (*perdido* = lost), *guadrar* (*guardar* = to keep), *por modre* (*por amor de* = for love of).

b) Conservations:

1. Retention of the opposition /b/ and /v/, with articulation of the second like labiodentals, but with change in the context they appear: *boka* (*boca* = mouth), *baka* (*vaca* = cow), *alava* (*alaba* = he praises), *kantava* (*cantaba* = he sang), *bivir* (*vivir* = to live).

2. Retention of syllable-final /b/ with articulation of the second like labiodentals, in process of vocalizing to [u̯] in late medieval Spanish: *sivdad* (*ciudad* = city), *vivda* (*viuda* = widow), *devda* (*deuda* = debt).

3. Retention of the contrast between voiceless and voiced units of the Old-Spanish system of sibilant phonemes, but the followed development differs from that of the rest of the Spanish-speaking world: (a) The pre-palatal fricative pair /š/ and /ž/ was retained: *kaša* (O.Sp. *caxa* = box), *mužer* (O.Sp. *muger* = woman), (b) The apical-alveolar fricative pair /s/ and /z/ (< /ʦ/ and /ʣ/) has merged to the dental fricative pair /s(/ and /z(/: *paso* (O.Sp. *passo* = step), *kaza* (O.Sp. *casa* = house); *alsar* (O.Sp. *alçar* = to raise), *dezir* (O.Sp. *dezir* = say).

4. As in the popular speech, syllable-final /s/ is palatalized to /š/ before velar [k]: *moška, buškar, kaška* (fly, search for, rind).

5. Retention of the reinforced diphthong-initial [gu̯e], restricted to rural use in Spain: *guevo, gueso* (*huevo, hueso* = egg, bone).

6. As in the popular speech, metathesis *-ld-* instead of *-dl-* in the second and third persons of imperative followed by personal pronouns: *dalde* (*dadle* = give him/her), *dizilde* (*decidle* = say him/her), *yamalde* (*llamadle* = call him/her).

7. As in the popular speech, apocopated by the tonic object personal pronouns of the first and second person when these appear followed by an atonic personal pronoun: *mo lo dišo* (*nos lo dijo* = he/she said us it), *mo la dites* (*nos la diste* = you gave us it), *vo lo digo* (*os lo digo* = I say you it), *vo los do* (*os los doy* = I give you them), *vo se tiene de contar* (*os lo hay que contar* = it is necessary to tell you), *la kaza mo la estan fraguando* (*nos están construyendo la casa* = they are building us the house).

c) Non-Castilian features:

1. The variants selected in Judeo-Spanish did not always conform to the Castilian diphthongized pattern: *ponte* (*puente* = bridge), *sorte* (*suerte* 'clase' = kind), *porto* (*puerto* = haven), *tutano* (*tuétano* = marrow), *preto* (*prieto* 'negro' = black), *grego* (*griego* = Greek), *governo* (*gobierno* = govern).

2. Maximal differentiation of the three vowels /i/, /a/, /u/ found in unstressed syllable in those varieties of Judeo-Spanish spoken in Bosnia, Serbia, Macedonia and West Bulgaria: *prizenti* (*presente* 'regalo' = gift), *kazada* (*casada* = married), *puderozu* (*poderoso* = powerful).

3. Retention of the opposition /b/ and /v/: *haver* (= partner, associate, from Heb. חבר), *haber* (= news, from Turk. *haber*).

4. Retention of initial labiodentals /f/ in the West Judeo-Spanish varieties, as is also the case in Portuguese, Galician, Leonese, Aragonose, and Catalan: *fijo* (*hijo* = son), *forno* (*horno* = oven), *fuyir* (*huir* = flee).

5. Retention of pre-palatal fricative pair /š/ and /ž/.

6. Adoption of *seseo*: *kasar* (*cazar* = to hunt), *(f)azer* (*hacer* = to do), *mosa* (*moza* = servant, maiden).

7. Judeo-Spanish mst frequently inherits the string /mb/ as in Portuguese and Catalan, contrary to Castilian preserved /m/: *lombo* (*lomo* = back), *palomba* (*paloma* = dove), *lamber* (*lamer* = to lick).

MORPHOLOGY. The following distinctive characteristics are of note:

a) Innovations:

1. Certain nouns in which the gender was not determined in Old-Spanish become feminine: *la vientre* (stomach), *la azeyte* (oil), *la honor* (honor), *la alma* (soul).

2. The third-person possessive *su* is marked for the number of the possessor: *su livro* (*su libro* = his book), *sus livro* (*su libro* = their book).

3. Creation of numerous verbal periphrases and their subsequent lexicalization. It is necessary to distinguish the following constructions:

(a) Romance constructions: *ser demenester* (to be necessary), *dar crédito* (think to be true), *darse rižo* (to be not deprived of any thing).

(b) Hybrid constructions:

(1) Castilian verb + Hebrew complement: *dezir tefilá* (to pray), *azer ḥesed* (to practice charity), *hazer milá* (to circumcise), *kortar din* (to sentence), *entrar la dimión* (to have a slight suspicion), *dar gemer* (to decide), *azer eḥreaḥ* (to be necessary), *salir de ḥová* (complying an obligation), *repozarse el daat* (to become tranquil), *dar kavod* (treating with respect), *dar ḥaftaná* (to manage).

(2) Castilian verb *ser* (to be) + Hebrew participle: *ser patur* (remaining free), *ser meḥalel* (to profane), *ser muḥaḥ* (to be compelled), *ser mekadeš* (to sanctify), *ser maskim* (to accept, to agree, to consent), *ser soḥe* (to deserve).

(3) Castilian verb + Turkish complement: *azerse buz* (to freeze), *azer dikat* (to putting attention or to take into account or consideration), *ir al dip* (to examine thoroughly), *estar dirdir* (to speak without interruption), *azer ǧefá* (to refuse), *ečar lakirdí* (to chatter), *azer ḥatir* (to satisfy), *bever tutun* (to smoke).

b) Retentions:

1. Conservation of the ordinal numerals from the number four ending with *–eno*: *kuarteno* (= 4th), *sinkeno* (5th), *seženo* (6th), *seteno* (7th), *očeno* (8th), *noveno* (9th), *dezeno* (10th), *onzeno* (11th), *dozeno* (12th), *trezeno* (13th), *katorzeno* (14th), *kinzeno* (15th).

2. Conservation of second person forms of polite address: *vos* (with second-person plural verb), *el/eya, su mersed*

(with third-person plural verb) instead of the more modern Castilian *usted* (you).

3. The non-standard pronominal forms of the Castilian *kon mi* (with me), *kon ti* (with you), *kon si* (with himself) were preserved instead of the cult forms: *conmigo, contigo, consigo.*

These tonic forms appear even in the apodosis of the comparative sentences: *es mas grande de mi* (*es más grande que yo* = he is higher than I), *el es mas riko de ti* (*él es már rico que tú* = he is richer than you).

4. The reflexive pronoun *-se*, which is elsewhere unmarked for number, has the form *-sen* when its referent is plural as in rural Castilian: *viendosen, yamandosen* (*viéndose, llamándose* = being seen, being called).

5. The first-person singular present indicative of the verbs *estar, ser, dar, ir* was preserved: (*e*)*stó, so, do, vo* (*estoy, soy, doy, voy* = I am, I give, and I go).

6. Conservation of the Old-Castilian future verbal forms with metathesis *–rn* (< *-n'r*): *terná* (he/she will have), *vernemos* (he/she will come).

7. Conservation of the non-standard forms of the Castilian imperative plural without final /d/: *mostrá, keré, avrí.*

8. Almost unique preservation of the affectionate diminutive formed with the suffix *–iko*: *kazika, gatiko* (*casita, gatito* = a small house, a small/young cat).

c) Non-Castilian features:

1. Hypercharacterization of gender is frequent in the case of adjectives as in the eastern languages of Spain: *popular, -a* (popular), *spesial, -a* (special), *nasyonal, -a* (national), *maternal, -a* (maternal).

2. The use of Spanish dialectal *kualo, kuala* as in Leonese and Aragonese, instead of Castilian *cual.*

3. First person preterit forms of *-ar* verbs have developed the ending /–i/, /-imos/ (/-é/, /-emos/ in Aragonese): *avlí, avlimos* (*hablé, hablamos* = I/we spoke).

SYNTAX. a) Innovations:

1. Duplication of the direct and indirect post-verbal complement through pronominal clitics placing before the verb: *lo sakó a el ḥamor del pozo* (*sacó al burro del pozo* = he removed the donkey from the well), *lo mira a Ḥanan* (*mira a Janán* = he looks to Hanna), *lo vemos al Rabi Asriel asentado* (*vemos al rabino Asriel sentado* = we see the rabbi Asriel seated), *…avisimos ke vino a vižitarlo a Avram* (*ya informamos que vinó a visitar a Abraham* = we report that he came to visit Abraham).

2. The gerund *siendo* has been converted into a causal conjunction (= since, seeing that): *i siendo no topo, tomo él un papel* (and since he did not find him, he took he a role), *i sierto el ikar es de tener kargo de los proves, siendo no tienen modo de reğirsen* (certainly the essential thing is to lend aid to the poor, since they do not have possibilities to do for themselves).

3. The preposition *a* was imposed on all direct-objects noun phrases instead of the Castilian use in which the contrast between personal direct object is marked by the preposition *a*, and non-personal direct objects are marked by absence of preposition: *yo le rogo a mi amigo viežo, a ke mi pedrone el pekado* (*yo le ruego a mi viejo amigo que me perdone el pecado* = I request from my old friend that he forgive me for the sin), *Mošiko ve a la skola* (*Moisés ve la escuela* = Moses sees the school).

b) Retentions:

1. In sentences with two atonic clitics, one in the function of direct complement (first or second persons) and the other as indirect complement (third person *se*), they appear immediately before the verb as in popular Old-Castilian: *Este livro me se pedrio tres vezes* (*este libro se me perdió tres veces* = this book was lost [by] me three times); *Tu vas azer todo lo ke te se dize* (*harás todo lo que se te dice* = you will do everything that [he] tells you).

2: For the existential *haber* Judeo-Spanish preserved the agreement of number between verb and complement, which is then constructed as the verbal subject: *uvo una fortuna en la mar /uvieron dos fortunas en la mar* (*hubo una / dos tormenta(s) en la mar* = there was a storm/there were two storms in the sea).

We can say that foreign influences have increasingly affected word order and sentence structure, so that Judeo-Spanish took on its own personality more distant from Spanish than its other varieties.

VOCABULARY. Aside from dialectal differences in vocabulary, which are in fact slight – several phenomena are characteristic of the language as a whole:

a) The preservation of hundreds of archaic Spanish words, some of which have disappeared from use in modern Spanish: *dekolgar* (to depend), *ladinar* (to translate), *akonantar* (taking precedence), *akavidarse* (to take precautions), *abolar* (to die), *feúzia* (confidence), *barragan* (hero), *dias de kútio* (days of the week), *ainda* (still), *atemar* (to weaken), *enmentar* (to mention, to remember), and others of which have changed their meaning among the Sephardim: *ambezar* (*avezar* 'be accustomed to' = to study), *eskapar* ('to flee' = to finish), *estağar* ('creak' = to separate), *kara* ('face' = cheek), *karruča* ('pulley' = wheel).

b) The substitution of several Castilian words by parallel terms borrowed from the other Ibero-Romance languages (Aragonese, Leonese, Catalan, or Portuguese) during the processes of koinéization in 16th and 17th centuries: *demandar* (*pregunta* = to ask), *abokarse* (*doblarse* = to bow), *solombra* (*sombra* = shadow), *kazal* (*aldea* = village), *lonso* (*oso* = bear), *fortuna* (*tormenta* = storm), *melsa* (*bazo* = spleen), *defender* (*prohibir* = to forbid), *desmersar* (*hacer las compras* = to go shopping), *avantaže* (ventaja = advantage), *koğeta* (*colecta* = collect), *demudarse* (*palidecer* = to turn pale), *enguyo* (*náusea* = nausea), *mešerikear* (*murmurar* = to gossip), *feder* (*oler mal* = to stink), *bafo* (*aliento, soplo* = breath), *monturo* (*basurero* = rubbish dump), *fado* (*destino, suerte* = destiny), *resfolgo* (*descanso* = rest).

c) Specialized terminology and special forms of the Spanish Jews from non-Hebrew and Aramaic origin have been preserved over the centuries: *meldar* (Old Gr. verb *meletáō*), means 'to study the Bible,' 'to read the Bible,' and, by extension, simply 'to read,' *Ayifto* (Gr. *Aígyptos* = Egypt), *alḥad* (first day, Sunday) was borrowed from Arabic instead of Spanish *domingo* (lat. (*dies*) *dominicus* 'the Lord's Day'); *el Dió* (God), instead of *Dios* with its feeling of a plural, *serkusir* (*circuncidar* = to circumcise), *podestar* (*regir, gobernar, tener el poder* = to govern), *alemunyarse* (Heb. *ʾalman* = to become a widower, to mourn) from which are also derived *lemunyoso, lemunyo*, (*a*)*kunyadar* (Sp. *cuñada* = to fulfill the command of levirate).

d) Also Hebrew and Aramaic words and expressions that are preserved, many of them changed their original meaning: *vatran* (ותרן = generous), *ḥaham* (חכם 'wise' = wise, but also rabbi), *penuyah* (פנויה 'free' = prostitute), *kal* (קהל 'gathering, congregation' = synagogue), *ḥamin* (חמין 'warm' = meat and vegetable stew cooked overnight and eaten for Sabbath), *ma'alah-matah* (מעלה ומטה 'up-down' = approximately, more or less). The use of Hebrew and Aramaic words and expressions in Judeo-Spanish increased specially after the beginning of the 18th century following the attempt of the rabbis to draw the people near to Jewish knowledge.

e) The substitution of hundreds of Spanish words, either unknown or forgotten over the centuries, by parallel terms borrowed from the local languages with which the Sephardim came in contact. However, it should be emphasized that certain terms were transferred from one community to another, by way of commercial or cultural relations, whereas others remained peculiar to particular communities. These foreign words derive mainly from Turkish: *merak* (depression, anxiety), *merakli* (melancholy), *šaka* (*şaka* = joke), *yardan* (*yerdan* = necklace), *čanta* (*çanta* = bag), *pačas* (*paça* = legs), *diz* (knee), *kolay* (easy); French: *randevu* (*rendez-vous* = appointment), *apremidi* (*après-midi* = afternoon), *surpriz* (*surprise* = surprise), *kuartier* (*quartier* = district), *afer* (*affaire* = matter, business); and Italian: *kapo* (*capo* = chief), *dover* (*dovere* = duty), *perikolo* (*pericolo* = danger), *senso* (*sense*), *dopio* (*doppio* = double), *dunke* (*dunque* = since, because, then); and to a lesser extent from Greek, Bulgarian, Serbo-Croatian, or German. Moreover in the Judeo-Spanish spoken in Israel, several words have been borrowed from Local Arabic, some from Yiddish, and in the last 150 years from Modern Hebrew.

Many of the borrowed words have been totally integrated in the Judeo-Spanish linguistic system: e.g., from Hebrew: *darsar* (דרש = preach), *badkar* (בדק = examine), *diburear* (דיבור = to talk gloomy), *desmazalado* (מזל = unlucky), *mazalozo* (= lucky), *sekanozo* (סכנה = dangerous), *ḥenozo* (חן = graceful), *seḥeludo* (שכל = intelligent), *ḥanupozo* (חנופה = flattering), *garonudo* (גרון = gluttonous); from Turkish *bitirear* (*bitir* {*mek*} = to finish), *burear* (*bur* {*mak*} = to cause an acrid feeling in the mouth), *čekinear* (*çekin* {*mek*} = to hesitate), *berekyat* (*bereket* = plentifulness), *dayanear* (*dayan* {*mak*} = to bear, to support), *kulanear* (*kolla* {*mak*} = to use, to employ), *merekearse* (*merak* = have a falling out), *merekiozo* (depressed), *tenekyero* (*teneke* = tinsmith), (*z*)*ulufias* (*zülüf* = sidelocks); or from French: *dezirar* (*désirer* = desire, want), *korijar* (*corriger* = to correct), *devuarse* (*se dévouer* = to dedicate oneself), *foburgo* (<*faubourg* = suburb), *malorozo* (*malheureux* = unhappy), *buto* (*but* = aim), *moyenes* (*moyens* = means).

f) Conversely, some Hebrew and Turkish suffixes are borrowed to create new words: *ladronim* (Sp. *ladrón* + *-im* = robbers), *ermanim* (Sp. *hermano* + *im* = brother), *balderim* (Turk. *balır* + *im* = departure, flight, retreat), *serenlik* (Sp. *sereno* + *lik* = serenity), *benadamlik* (בן אדם + *lik* = human quality), *ḥaham bašilik* (חכם + Turk. *baş* 'head, chief' + *lik* = chief rabbinate), *sekanalik* (סכנה + *lik* = danger), *zonuluk* (זנות + *luk* = debauchery, prostitution), *safekli* (ספק + *li* = doubtful, suspicious), *sekanali* (סכנה + *li* = dangerous), *goralği* (גרל + *ci* = fortune-teller).

DIALECTS. However, phonetic and lexical differences – less morphological and syntactic – bear witness to the following dialectal areas:

a) Phonetic areas: *Central area* (Turkey and Greece communities) with a stronger linguistic norm; and Peripheral area more flexible with the *European area* (Bulgaria, Romania, Croatia, Serbia, and Bosnia communities), and the *Israelian Judeo-Spanish* influenced by the Hebrew spoken by Oriental and Maghrebian Jews and Local Arabic.

b) Lexical areas: *East Area* (communities in Turkey, Israel, and West-Bulgaria) developed from de Istanbul koine; *Central area* (with Salonika and the communities situated in East-Bulgaria, Romania, Serbia, and Macedonia) developed from de Salonician koine; and *West area* (communities in the Adriatic coast and in Croatia and Bosnia) more influenced by Portuguese and Italian loans.

The development of the dialectal areas in Judeo-Spanish took place from the 16th century and does not have a relation with the regional origin of its speakers.

SYSTEM OF WRITING. For several centuries the Hebrew alphabet has been in general use for the writing of Judeo-Spanish. The unvocalized Rashi script was most often used both for religious texts and secular literature, and was also the basis of the cursive script. However, from the 16th century onward, many books were printed in square lettering and were completely vocalized. Few books were printed in Latin characters, and it was only in the 20th century that the use of the Latin alphabet increased, particularly in journalism, without however affecting the circulation of newspapers and books in Rashi script. In the early 21st century an official spelling does not exist to write the Judeo-Spanish with the Latin alphabet, and its speakers usually use the system of the national language of their respective countries. In Israel, especially after the constitution of the National Authority of the Ladino and its Culture in 1997, the one phonetic spelling is that of the magazine *Aki Yerushalayim* (AY) that enjoyed popularity. Also the Sephardim of Anglo-Saxon countries make use of this spelling. Yet, some Spanish researchers, especially those affiliated with the *Consejo Superior de Investigaciones Científicas* (CSIC), favoring the integration of the Sephardi variety in the Hispanic world, prefer a Spanish spelling, to which they add diacritic signs to mark the differences of pronunciation between the two varieties, in order to transcribe the Rashi script:

AY's spelling: *i se kijo azer djudio, i antes de azerse djudio kijo informarse a saver kuala uma es la ke es estimada en el otro mundo… i fue dito Onkelos kon echiseria i lo izo alevantar a Tutus arasha…*

CSIC's system of transcription: *y se quišo haćer ĵudió, y antes de haćerse ĵudió quišo informarse a saber cuála umá es la que es estimada en el otro mundo… y fue dito Onquelos con hechićería y lo hićo alevantar a Titus ha Rašáý…*

When the Nazis exterminated many communities in which Judeo-Spanish had been the principal means of communication, Judeo-Spanish became almost irrevocably condemned to gradual disappearance. Judeo-Spanish–speaking Jews who immigrated to Israel and other Western countries adopted the language of the country and for their children Judeo-Spanish became only a residual language. Nevertheless, recent years have seen something of a Sephardic vernacular renaissance. Altogether some 200,000 people still speak or understand it.

The interest of linguists in the study of the Judeo-Spanish language began in the late 19th century, but it was only in the 20th century that most serious and detailed researches were undertaken. In the last two decades the study of Judeo-Spanish in the universities, especially in Israel and Germany, became more important to the point of becoming a university discipline.

[Aldina Quintana (2nd ed.)]

A *Dictionnaire de Judéo-Espagnol* by Joseph Nehama and Jesus Cantera was publishd by the Instituto Benito Arias Montano, of the Estudios Hebraicos Sefardies y de Oriente Proximo (Madrid, 1977).

Ladino Literature

The literature written in Ladino is not to be confused with that produced in Spanish by the western Sephardi communities, mainly that of Amsterdam. In contrast to the vast majority of the observant Spanish Jews who were exiled to North Africa and the Ottoman Empire in the 15th century, the *Marranos, assimilated into Spanish culture and more integrated within Christian society, left Spain gradually during the 16th and even the 17th and 18th centuries, many of them settling in Western Europe. These elements maintained direct contact with the civilization of their old country. Not only are their religious, philosophical, scientific, and literary works not written in Ladino, but they express an entirely different spirit from that found among the "Oriental" Sephardi thinkers and writers.

RELIGIOUS LITERATURE. In contrast to secular literature which, with the exception of the *romancero*, began to flourish in Ladino only in the 19th century, Ladino religious literature had its origins in pre-expulsion Spain. It was only in exile, however, that it really developed.

The religious literary tradition began between the 13th and 15th centuries with a series of Bible translations, of which a few unique specimens have been preserved as manuscripts in Spain (such as the Mss. I-J-3, I-J-4, and J-II-19 of the Escorial Library). All these texts are, however, written in Latin characters. This tradition was revived successfully after the expulsion, particularly in Constantinople and Salonika, and the translations produced in these centers were adopted, and later revised here and there in the Sephardi Diaspora (Venice, Leghorn, Pisa, Amsterdam, Vienna). These translations, written in Hebrew characters and having their own vocabulary and syntax, are clearly distinguishable from the Spanish Bibles produced by Christians. Over the centuries, they helped to mold the written language of the Sephardim. The major original translations include the Book of Psalms (Constantinople, 1540); the Pentateuch (Constantinople, 1547); the Prophets (Salonika, 1572); and a complete translation of the Bible by Abraham ben Isaac Assa (Constantinople, 1739–45), which became the most popular text among the Sephardi communities of the East. To these translations should be added the anonymous glossary known as *Ḥeshek Shelomo* (Venice, 1588).

Within Ladino religious literature a separate subdivision is constituted by a series of works adapted from Hebrew: books of biblical interpretation and of ethics, together with manuals of religious ritual and prayer books. These include *Baḥya ibn Paquda's *Ḥovot ha-Levavot*, Isaac *Aboab's *Menorat ha-Ma'or*, Joseph *Caro's Shulḥan Arukh, and *Elijah b. Benjamin ha-Levi's *Shevet Musar*. The original works *Reğimiento de la Vida* by Moses *Almosnino (1564) and *Ẓorkhei Ẓibbur* by Abraham Assa (1739) come into the same category. Thus, two centuries after the expulsion, Ladino literature comprised a very rich collection of adapted and original works in all spheres of creative activity, among them poetry, mysticism, biblical exegesis, history, medicine, and ethics. From the 18th century onward, the number of these original works increased steadily, but only part of the output has been preserved. The masterpiece of this ethical-religious literature, and one which has had a profound influence on the masses to the present day, is the **Me-Am Lo'ez*, an encyclopedic work begun by Jacob *Culi in 1730 and continued by other writers after his death. This thesaurus of Sephardi knowledge draws its inspiration from the traditional sources of Jewish thought: Mishnah, Talmud, Midrash, and Kabbalah.

Ladino Poetry

Original poetic works in Ladino are extremely limited, and there is no doubt that this art was not as popular among the Levantine Sephardim as it was among the Sephardim of the West. However, some poetic tradition did exist, exemplified preeminently by two important works: the 14th-century *Proverbios morales* of Shem Tov (*Santob) de Carrion and the *Poema de Yoçef*, comprising some 300 quatrains, which must have been composed at the beginning of the 15th century. The latter poem, of which there is a fragmentary manuscript in Cambridge, England, and a complete version in the Vatican, is an adaptation from the Midrash and the *Sefer ha-Yashar* of the story of Joseph and his brethren. This is written in a strophic and metric form which points to a merging of a medieval Spanish structure (the "*cuaderna via*") and that of the Hebrew *piyyutim*. In Ladino poetry the *Poema de Yoçef* has no less importance and literary value than the *Poema de Yuçuf* written in Spanish in Arabic characters, which is today an integral part of Spanish literature. A better-known and more popular Ladino poem on the same subject is *Coplas de Yoçef Ha-Ẓaddik*, written by Abraham de Toledo in 1732. This work, which comprises some 400 quatrains, had its own special melody and was sung on the festival of Purim. Two quite distinct versions have been preserved: one from Constantinople (1732), and another from Belgrade (1861) composed on the lines of the Salonika version (1755) which is now lost. Among minor poetic works there are various songs and poems, very variable in quality, devoted especially to Jewish festival themes. Many of them are connected with Purim, and these compositions, both serious and humorous, are to be found scattered in collections and almanacs under the title *Coplas de Purim*. The genre flourished in the 19th century.

THE ROMANCERO. The Ladino *romancero* occupies a place of its own in the literature and everyday life of the Sephardim. When they left Spain, the Jews retained in their oral tradition innumerable "romances" – popular and traditional Spanish ballads – which had been widely diffused throughout the country in the course of the 14th and 15th centuries. (For musical tradition in the *romancero*, see below.) The melodies that accompanied these romances and made them easier to memorize also contributed to their preservation and to their transmission, from the 16th to 20th centuries, through all the communities of the eastern Sephardim and North Africa. Since the *romancero* was a "popular" genre, it hardly existed in western Sephardi centers. The Ladino *romancero* is largely a continuation and an adaptation of the Spanish *romancero* of both the Middle Ages and the Renaissance. It includes some romances which are still to be found in collections of Spanish poetry and others which did not survive in the Iberian Peninsula or which are variations or adaptations, as well as many original romances and songs of later composition. The general subject matter of the Ladino *romancero* has sometimes been enriched by new Spanish romances composed in the late 15th and 16th centuries. The subject matter varies according to the distance of a given Sephardi community from Spain; thus the romances of North Africa differ considerably from those of the Ottoman Empire. The common characteristic, however, is what may be called the "dechristianization" of the traditional *romancero*. Jews tended to eliminate from the romances any elements which implied adherence to Christian beliefs and ceremonies. Only a few North African romances imported from the Peninsula at a much later date still retain specifically Christian motifs or images. Lapses of memory or interpolations sometimes resulted in either a muddled or amplified version of a traditional romance. The newly composed *romanceros* are on the whole looser in form and inferior in quality to the traditional romances. Since the romances were transmitted orally, the Ladino *romancero* has only comparatively recently acquired a written form which is still far from complete. However, it already represents a very rich and valuable corpus of poetry and folklore.

OTHER SECULAR WORKS. Apart from the *romancero*, Ladino secular literature from the 19th century onward is characterized by a preponderance of translations or adaptations of plays and novels from world – and especially French – literature. These translations stimulated Sephardi writers to produce a considerable output of original plays, love stories, historical novels, and other works in Ladino. The literary quality of the later Ladino works is on the whole mediocre and most of them have been completely forgotten.

Ladino folktales and proverbs, capable of filling several volumes, have not yet been collected or adequately studied.

[Moshe Lazar]

In the 19th and 20th Centuries

With the decline of learning in the mid-19th century among the Jews in the Ottoman Empire, secular works in Ladino started to appear. The first secular works in Ladino were of a didactic character, consisting mostly of historical works, biographies, and travel books.

With the liberalization and secularization of Jewish society in the Ottoman Empire in the second half of the 19th century, together with the general broadening of culture there and the marked influence of Western culture upon the Jews especially through the medium of the *Alliance Israélite Universelle, the need was felt for the emergence of a secular literature in Ladino in all literary genres. The first attempt to fill this vacuum was the creation of Ladino *newspapers. These intensified the demand for such a literature.

With the aim of propagating Western culture among Jews, young educated people undertook to translate and adapt plays and novels from general and especially French literature. The first translated novels were published in the 1880s and their number grew rapidly, only very few original novels being written. Between 1901 and 1938 over 150 novels were translated. These translations were mostly from classical and modern authors as well as from Hebrew and Yiddish writers such as Shalom Aleichem, I.L. Peretz, and Shalom Asch. These novels, often adapted rather than translated, were usually first published as feuilletons in the Ladino press. Although the original intention of their publishers was educational, they commonly produced love stories and chapbooks, usually appearing without mention of their author or translator. The chief translators were Isaac Gabai, David Fresco, Victor Levy, Alexander ibn Ghirat, Jean Florian, and Elijah Carmona, who revived the Ladino language by creating its modern literary style. They also published original works, mostly novels and biographies of Jewish philanthropists and historical personages, as well as many popular books on historical or scientific subjects (e.g., *Historia Judia Universal* in 13 vols., and *Tesoro del Judaesmo* by H.Y. Chaki). With the emergence of the Zionist movement, nationalistic themes began to appear in Ladino literature, expressed in original novels and plays on purely Jewish themes (especially by Jacques Luria), and often depicting Jewish life and types on the model of Shalom Aleichem and Mendele Mokher Seforim.

Ladino dramatic literature also appeared as a new genre at the close of the 19th century. Unlike the fiction it developed essentially around Jewish themes, though plays by Molière and Shakespeare were also translated. Those who distinguished themselves especially as playwrights were Jacques Luria, Yakim Behor, Joseph Djaen, Bahor Azario, and Abraham Capon. Of special interest are the books and pamphlets published in Ladino by the Protestant mission in the Ottoman Empire. Most of them deal with the New Testament or criticize Judaism and the Talmud. For a few years (from 1825) the mission even published an illustrated magazine in pure Spanish written in Hebrew characters, featuring articles on scientific and historical subjects, including Judaism. With the decline of Ladino as a spoken language and its replacement by Turkish and other tongues, Ladino became devoid of any use as a literary medium and was hence discarded as such. The virtual liquidation of the Sephardi communities of the Mediterranean area, partly through Nazi persecution (apart from Turkey) and partly through immigration to Ereẓ Israel and elsewhere, has contributed to the virtual extinction of Ladino literature, though newspapers in Ladino still appear in Turkey.

[Henri Guttel]

The Musical Tradition of the Judeo-Spanish *Romancero*

Sephardi secular life has always been richly imbued with traditional songs and paraliturgical hymns to celebrate the varied phases of the life cycle, social functions, and ceremonial gatherings. Among the traditional songs are the cherished and orally transmitted Castilian Romances ("ballads") which Sephardi women, in particular, sang at every occasion, and even during their daily household and infant-rearing chores.

The importance of the *romancero* or ballad tradition rests primarily on its retention of archaic linguistic features and preservation of themes that had long become extinct on the Iberian Peninsula. The postulation of a musical link between the extant Judeo-Spanish and the much older Peninsula ballad traditions on the basis of their strong textual ties, which gave rise to many scholarly and even romanticized notions concerning their melodic connections with 15th- and 16th-century Spanish cancioneros and vihuelista manuals, has proven nothing more than speculative.

Within decades after the Expulsion of the Jews from Spain (1492) and from Portugal (1497), contacts with the Peninsula became increasingly sporadic, especially in the Eastern Mediterranean region where relations among the widely scattered Sephardim communities slackened, resulting in the isolation of particular communities which increasingly absorbed the musical influences of their new environments.

From about 1700, the stylistic differences between the Eastern (Turkish, Greek, and Balkan) and Western (North African, mainly Moroccan) repertoires had probably begun to develop. Because of Morocco's proximity to Spain, the flow of peninsular ballads was almost uninterrupted, whereas, in the Eastern tradition, ballad repertoires suffered greater isolation. In mid-20th century Israel, where the earlier Eastern Sephardim community had already constituted an amalgam of former Ottoman centers prior to 1947, the musical and thematic contrasts between its collective ballad repertoire and that of the North African Sephardi settlers, who arrived after 1947, continued to be reflected in their respective traditions.

Interest in the Judeo-Spanish *romancero* owes its impetus to R. Menéndez Pidal's (1869–1968) famous *Catálogo del romancero judio-español*, which listed over 140 ballad incipit (representing themes) then known to be extant in the Sephardim tradition. M. Manrique de Lara (1868–1929), who worked closely with Menéndez Pidal, was the first serious collector of the Sephardim musical tradition who traveled to the major Sephardim communities in the Eastern Mediterranean (from the latter part of 1910 to the early part of 1911), and later, during his military expeditions in northern Morocco (during the summers of 1915 and 1916). S.G. Armistead's three-volume catalog, published in 1978, which supersedes the earlier *Catálogo*, not only identified each item from Manrique's massive manuscript collection – housed at the Menéndez Pidal Archive in Madrid – but added additional themes. In the United States, S.G. Armistead and Joseph H. Silverman began recording ballads in Los Angeles (in 1958) among the Sephardi Jewish community from Rhodes, and a year later were joined by Israel J. Katz, who collected ballads in Israel (1959–61). The team's continued collaborative fieldwork in the United States, Morocco, and Israel has yielded more than 1,500 items, which form the basis of their multi-volume *Judeo-Spanish Ballads from Oral Tradition* (1986–), five volumes of which have been issued to date. Katz's earlier *Judeo-Spanish Traditional Ballads from Jerusalem* (1975–76) documents the musicological researches undertaken until the late 1960s. Since then important collections and studies, together with recordings, have been made by Judith R. Cohen, Eleanora Noga Alberti-Kleinbort, Isaac J. Levy, Ankica Petrovic, Amnon Shiloah, and Susana Weich-Shahak (whose occasional collaborators include Judith Etzion and Edwin Seroussi).

[Israel J. Katz]

For the Judeo-Spanish of North Africa, see *Haketia.

BIBLIOGRAPHY: M.L. Wagner, *Beitraege zur Kenntnis des Juden-Spanischen von Konstantinopel* (1914); idem, *Caracteres generales del judeo-español de Oriente* (1930); M. Luria, *A Study of the Monastir Dialect of Judeo-Spanish* (1939); A.S. Yahuda, in: *Revista de filologia Española*, 2 (1915), 339–70; J. Benoliel, in: *Boletín de la Real Academia Española*, 13–15 (1926–28); 32 (1952); M.A. Luria, in: *Revue hispanique*, 79 (1930), 323–41; C.M. Crews, in: *Folklore*, 43 (1932), 193–225; idem, *Recherches sur le Judéo-espagnol dans les pays balkaniques* (1935); P. Benichou, in: *Revista de Filología Hispánica*, 7 (1945), 209–58; C. Ramos Gil, in: *Oẓar Yehudei Sefarad*, 1 (1959), xxxii–xl; A. Zamora Vicente, *Dialectologia española* (1960); M. Lazar, in: *Sefunot*, 8 (1964), 337–75; M.D. Gaon, *Ha-Ittonut be-Ladino* (1965); M. Attias, *Romancero Sefaradi* (1956); A. Yaari, *Reshimat Sifrei Ladino*… (1934); P. Bénichou, *Romances judeo-españoles de Marruecos* (1946); M. Alvar, *Endechas judeo-españoles* (1953); A. Larrea Palaciń, *Concionero judío de Marruecos*, 3 vols. (1952–54). IN THE 19th AND 20th CENTURIES: M. Franco, *Essai sur l'histoire des Israélites de l'Empire Ottoman* (1897), 269–76; A. Elmaleh, in: *Ha-Shilo'aḥ*, 26 (1912), 67–73; idem, in: *Ha-Tor*, 4:12 (1923/24), 9f.; M. Molho, in: *Saloniki, Ir va-Em be-Yisrael* (1967), 99–102; idem, *Literatura sefardita de Oriente* (1960). ROMANCERO MUSICAL TRADITION: I.J. Katz, *Judeo-Spanish Traditional Ballads from Jerusalem: An Ethnomusicological Study* (1971); idem, in: *Western Folklore*, 21 (1962), 83–91; idem, in: *Ethnomusicology*, 12 (1968), 72–85; S.G. Armistead and J.H. Silverman, *Judeo-Spanish Ballad Chapbooks of Yacob Abraham Yoná* (1970); Y. Levi, *Tesha Romansot Yehudiyyot Sefardiyyot* (music, 1954). **ADD. BIBLIOGRAPHY:** D.M. Bunis, in: H. Beinart, *Moreshet Sepharad: The Sephardi Legacy*, vol. 2 (1992), 399–422; idem, *A Lexicon of the Hebrew and Aramaic Elements in Modern Judezmo* (1993); idem, *Judezmo* (1999); C.M. Crews, *Recherches sur le Judéo-espagnol dans les pays balkaniques* (1935); A. García Moreno, *Relatos del pueblo ladinán. Me'am Lo'ez* (2004); I.M. Hassán, in: *Estudios Sefardíes*, 1 (1978), 147–50; idem, in: M. Seco and G. Salvador, *La lengua española, hoy* (1995), 117–40; M. Luria, *A Study of the Monastir Dialect of Judeo-Spanish* (1939); J. Nehama and J. Cantera, *Dictionnaire du Judéo-Espagnol* (1977); R. Penny, *Variation and Change in Spanish* (2000), 174–93; A. Quintana-Rodríguez, in: *Archivo de Filología Aragonesa*, 57–58 (2001), 163–92; idem, in: *Revista de Filología Española*, 82 (2002), 105–38; idem, in: *Neue Romania*, 31 (2004), 167–92; O. (Rodrigue) Schwarzwald, in: *Pe'amim*, 50 (1992), 4–28; M.Ch. Varol-Bornes, in: W. Busse and M.Ch. Varol-Bornes, *Hommage à Haïm Vidal Sephiha* (1996), 213–37; C.M.L. Wagner, *Beitraege zur Kenntnis des Juden-Spanischen von Konstantinopel* (1914); idem, *Caracteres generales del judeo-español de Oriente* (1930). MUSIC: R. Menéndez Pidal, "Catálogo del romancero judio-español," in: *Cultura Espñola*, 4 (1906), 1045–77; 4 (1907), 161–99; A. Hemsi, *Coplas sefardíes (Chansons Judéo-espagnoles)* (1932–73); A. de Larrea Palacin, *Romances de Tetuán. Cancionero judío del norte de Marruecos* (1952); E. Gerson-Kiwi, "On the Musical Sources of the Judeo-Hispanic Romance," in: *Musical Quarterly*, 50 (1964), 31–43; I.J. Katz, *Judeo-Spanish Traditional Ballads from Jerusalem: An Ethnomusicological Study* (1971); H. Avenary, "Cantos españoles antiguos mencionados en la literatura hebrea," in: *Anuario Musical*, 25 (1971), 67–79; S.G. Armistead, et al., *El romancero judeo-español en el Archivo Menéndez Pidal (Cat álogo-indice de riomances y canciones* (1978); S.G. Armistead, J.H. Silverman, and I.J. Katz, *Judeo-Spanish Ballads from Oral Tradition* (1986–); J. Etzion and S. Weich-Shahak, "The Spanish and the Sephardic Romancero: Musical Links," in: *Ethnomusicology*, 32:2 (1988), 1–37; J. Etzion and S. Weich-Shahak, "The Music of the Judeo-Spanish Romancero: Stylistic Features," in: *Anuario Musical*, 43 (1988), 1–35; S. Weich-Shahak, *Romancero sefardi de Marruecos. Antologa de tradición oral* (1997).

LAEMEL (Laemmel), SIMON VON (1766–1845), Austrian manufacturer, merchant, and functionary. In 1787 Von Laemel founded a wholesale firm in Prague and devoted himself to the wool industry, improving flocks and methods of wool processing. He later moved to Vienna where he was granted the right of residence. His real importance, however, dates from the beginning of the Napoleonic wars, when he and other traders secured part of the Danube merchant fleet by buying it back from the French, from whom they also purchased captured Austrian army food stores (1801) and artillery equipment. He loaned the government his entire fortune in 1809 in order to bring about the withdrawal of Napoleon's troops from Vienna. In 1809 he also volunteered for service with the militia. In spite of this, when he petitioned in 1811 for the right to purchase a house in Vienna, Francis I rejected his plea; in the same year, after long deliberations by the authorities, he was ennobled. In 1813 he became a commissioner to the army.

Von Laemel upheld Jewish tradition, supported scholars, and was active on behalf of Bohemian and Viennese Jewry as a *shtadlan*, mainly using his connections with the emperor's brother, the archbishop of Olomouc (Olmuetz), and Prince Anthony of Saxony. At the time of the Congress of *Vienna (1815) he signed with Nathan von *Arnstein, Lazar *Auspitz, Bernhard von *Eskeles, and Leopold von *Herz a petition requesting emancipation. In 1817 he secured the reduction of the Bohemian Jewish tax. He also helped arrange the abrogation of the body tax (*Leibzoll*) in Saxony. In 1842, in cooperation with the Vienna rabbi Lazar *Horowitz, he initiated action for the suspension of the *oath *more judaico*. In 1812 in Carlsbad Von Laemel made the acquaintance of Goethe, who was later his guest on several occasions.

Von Laemel's son LEOPOLD (1790–1867) was one of the most important financiers of the Hapsburg monarchy. He resided in Prague where he headed the savings bank from 1825, was on the board of the Elbe-Elbeschiffahrtsgesellschaft (navigation society) and, with Moritz *Koenigswarter, was among the founders of the Bohemian Western railway (*Boehmische Westbahn*). He granted the government a loan of 20,000,000 florins in 1831. He was knighted in 1856. Among the founders of the Vienna Creditanstalt, he was also active in Bohemian political life. As member of the Diet he supported the German liberals. In 1848 he was a member of the national committee and was on its delegation when the city surrendered after Windisch-Graetz's siege. Active in Jewish affairs, he was on the board of the society which had leased the Jewish tax, and was among the initiators of the *Verein fuer geregelten Gottesdienst* (Association for Orderly Divine Services). He was also among the founders of the *Teplice-Sanov (Teplitz) Jewish hospice. In 1832 he helped organize relief work during the cholera epidemic. He also corresponded with Goethe. His daughters were married to non-Jews and were baptized.

In 1856 Von Laemel's daughter ELISA HERZ sent the Viennese poet Ludwig August *Frankl to Jerusalem to found the Laemel School in memory of her father. She was an active philanthropist, establishing among others a foundation for students from her father's native Toužkov (Tuschkau, western Bohemia).

BIBLIOGRAPHY: N.M. Gelber, *Aktenstuecke zur Judenfrage am Wiener Kongress* (1920), 4–20; S. Baron, *Die Judenfrage auf dem Wiener Kongress* (1920), 138–44, 176–7; A.F. Pribram, *Urkunden und Akten zur Geschichte der Juden in Wien*, 2 (1918), index; F. Roubik, in: JGGJČ, 9 (1938), 421; H. Spiel, *Fanny von Arnstein* (1962), index; S.

Schnee, *Die Hoffinanz und der moderne Staat*, 4 (1963), 332; 5 (1965), 271–4; C. Wurzbach, *Biographisches Lexikon*, 8 (1862), 405–6, s.v. *Herz, Elisa*; 13 (1865), 475–9; M. Grunwald, *Vienna* (1936), index; H. Teweles, *Goethe und die Juden* (1925), 89–92; J. Urzidil, *Goethe in Boehmen* (1962), index; R. Kestenberg-Gladstein, *Die neuere Geschichte der Juden in Boehmen* (1969), index; K. Kratochvil, *Bankéři* (1962), index; I. Press, *Elleh Toledot Beit-ha-Sefer le-ha-Aẓil le-Veit Laemmel bi-Yrushalayim* (1936). **ADD. BIBLIOGRAPHY:** *Oesterreichisches Biographisches Lexikon*, vol. 4 (2003), 401.

[Meir Lamed]

LAEMMLE, CARL (1867–1939), U.S. film producer and founder of Universal Studios. Born in Laupheim, Germany, Laemmle immigrated to the United States at the age of 17. In 1906 he bought a makeshift theater in Chicago, which made huge profits and Laemmle used this money to buy up a dozen other theaters. But films came to Chicago only intermittently, so Laemmle organized a wholesale motion-picture exchange business. The exchange grew in power and Laemmle organized similar ventures in other cities. When the need for fresh films became apparent, Laemmle established a company to produce features. His first film appeared in 1909, *Hiawatha*. Later Laemmle began to hire well-known actors like Mary Pickford to appear in his films. He gave them a listing in the credits, thereby inaugurating the star system. In 1912 Laemmle and several others organized the Universal Film Manufacturing company, which later became Universal Studios. He purchased the site of Universal City in California and developed it into one of the largest motion-picture studios in the world. Laemmle produced the first full-length feature picture, *Traffic in Souls*, a five-reeler that cost $5,000 to make. Despite misgivings about its length it earned $500,000. In 1935, Laemmle sold Universal City and retired. He spent much time and money aiding refugees driven from Nazi Germany.

BIBLIOGRAPHY: J. Drinkwater, *The Life and Adventures of Carl Laemmle* (1931); L. Jacobs, *The Rise of the American Film* (1968), index.

[Stewart Kampel]

°**LAETUS (La'itos)**, dating probably from the Hellenistic period. According to the second-century Christian apologist, Tatian, Laetus translated into Greek the historical works of three Phoenician historians: Theodotus, Hypsicrates, and Mochus, who included in their works an account of King Hiram, who gave his daughter in marriage to King Solomon (so also Menander of Pergamum; whereas I Kings 11:1 states merely that Solomon married Sidonian women) and donated all kinds of timber for the construction of the Temple.

LAFER, HORACIO (1893–1965), Brazilian politician. Born in São Paulo, Lafer studied economics, philosophy, and law. He published several works including *Contemporary Philosophic Tendencies* (1929) and *Credit and the National Banking System* (1948). He was related to the *Klabin group, pioneering in the paper, pulp, and tile industries. Lafer was appointed Brazilian delegate to the League of Nations in 1928. He was founder of the Brazilian National Economic Development Bank, a governor of the World Bank, and presided at the International Monetary Fund conference in 1952.

In 1934, Lafer was elected to the Federal Chamber of Deputies where he remained for nearly 30 years. He was majority leader under President Dutra, and in 1951 became minister of finance under President Vargas. From 1959 to 1961 he served President Kubitschek as foreign minister.

He was active in Jewish affairs, especially with the Hebrew high school "Renascença," and was influential both in easing Brazil's immigration policy toward Jews and Brazil's vote at the UN Assembly on Palestine, in 1947. He also fought against Nazi propaganda in Brazil.

Lafer was posthumously honored in a special session of the Federal Parliament; a school and a street were named in his honor.

[Alfred Hirschberg]

°**LAGARDE, PAUL DE (Paul Anton de Boetticher;** 1827–1891), German Protestant Orientalist and public intellectual. An abrasive personality, Lagarde was thwarted in his academic career and further embittered by a long wait for the professorship he finally obtained at Göttingen University in 1869. He was especially interested in biblical textual criticism and began work on a critical edition of the Septuagint (which was never completed). Wholly out of tune with the times, he thundered against the political, religious, and educational life of the newly founded German Empire, especially the pernicious influence of Jews which he saw everywhere. As carriers of a soullessly liberal and international modernism, and thus anathema to his own nostalgic medieval Teutonism, Jews were "a repulsive burden, with no historical use" (Mittheilungen, vol. 2, 331). Lagarde was not strictly speaking a racist because he thought "sincere" assimilation was a way of overcoming repellent Jewish traits; yet his antisemitism could be recklessly extreme, comparing Jews to bacilli, with the clear implication that they ought to be exterminated. His *Deutsche Schriften* (1878), reissued several times up to 1945, became a classic, exercising enduring influence on generations of antisemites in Germany and elsewhere.

BIBLIOGRAPHY: F.R. Stern, *The Politics of Cultural Despair* (1961), passim; R.W. Lougee, *Paul de Lagarde, 1827–1891: A Study of Radical Conservatism in Germany* (1962).

[Richard S. Levy (2nd ed.)]

LAG BA-OMER (Heb. ל״ג בָּעֹמֶר), the 33rd (Heb. ל״ג) day of the counting of the *Omer*, which is reckoned from the second day of *Passover until *Shavuot. It occurs on the 18th day of *Iyyar and has been celebrated as a semiholiday since the time of the *geonim* (B.M. Lewin, *Oẓar ha-Ge'onim*, 7 (1936), 140–1). On Lag ba-Omer the traditional mourning customs of abstention kept during the *Omer* period are lifted: haircutting and shaving are permitted, marriages are celebrated, and other sorts of entertainment, e.g., music, enjoyed (Isserles to Sh. Ar., OḤ 493:2). The Sephardi ritual permits haircuts and shaving only on the day following Lag ba-Omer, i.e., the 34th of *Omer* (Sh. Ar., *ibid.*).

According to talmudic and midrashic sources, 24,000 disciples of R. *Akiva died of a plague during the period between Passover and Shavuot because they did not sufficiently honor one another (Yev. 62b; Gen. R. 61:3; Eccles. R. 11:6). Some emended texts read that the students died *ad peros ha-Aẓeret* ("until close to Shavuot"). The plague ceased on the day of Lag ba-Omer which, consequently, became a holiday, especially for rabbinical students in the Middle Ages (the "Scholar's festival"). It was customary to rejoice on that day through various kinds of merrymaking.

According to the homiletic exegesis of Exodus 16, the manna began to fall on Lag ba-Omer (Moses Sofer, *Ḥatam Sofer*, YD (1841), no. 233), giving another reason for the holiday. The liturgy for this day is the regular prayer service for weekdays, except that the **Taḥanun* prayer is omitted. The kabbalists attach particular significance to Lag ba-Omer. They hold this date to be the anniversary of the death of *Simeon b. Yoḥai, regarded by them as the author of the *Zohar. Called *Hillula de-Rabbi Shimon bar Yoḥai*, it is celebrated in Israel in the village of Meron (near Safed) where Simeon b. Yoḥai is traditionally buried. The celebrations are carried out with songs and dances by the thousands who gather there. A special hymn, *Bar Yoḥai … Ashrekha*, consisting of ten stanzas corresponding to the ten **Sefirot* in the Kabbalah, is sung on this occasion. Three-year-old boys are given their first haircut (*ḥalakah*) while their parents distribute wine and sweets. The same rites are observed at the grave of *Simeon the Just, in Jerusalem.

The custom of children playing with a bow (Heb. *keshet*) and arrows on Lag ba-Omer is traced, by certain scholars, to the legend that the rainbow (Heb. *keshet*), a symbol of peace (Gen. 9:11–17), did not appear during the lifetime of Simeon b. Yoḥai, because he was such a saintly man. Others associate this custom with the above-mentioned story about the students of R. Akiva who, it is suggested, actually fell fighting against the Romans in the revolt led by *Bar Kokhba. Lag ba-Omer in modern Israel is a school holiday. Youngsters light bonfires in open spaces in towns and villages and Students' Day is celebrated on the campuses of the different universities. The scores of weddings held on Lag ba-Omer add to the festive character of this semiholiday.

BIBLIOGRAPHY: I. Margolis and S.L. Markowitz, *Jewish Holidays and Festivals* (1962), 104–11; H. Schauss, *Guide to Jewish Holy Days* (paperback 1968), index; J.T. Lewinski, *Sefer ha-Mo'adim*, 6 (1955), 72–101; Benayahu, in: *Sefunot*, 6 (1962), 9–40; A. Yaari, in: *Tarbiz*, 31 (1962), 72–101; Pearl, *Guide to the Minor Festivals and Fasts* (1963), 34–47; *Maḥanayim*, 56 (1961); J. Morgenstern, in: HUCA, 39 (1968), 81–90.

[Meir Ydit]

LAGOS, principal port city of Algarve province, S. Portugal. During the period when Algarve was a separate kingdom – founded in 1253 by King Afonso III – and into the 1400s, the Jewish inhabitants were organized into an official community (*kehillah*) which was empowered to regulate and represent them in every way. The *kehillah* paid an annual tax to the crown which covered the entire Jewish population. Lagos was the most important Jewish center in the western half of Algarve. From there Henry the Navigator (1394–1460) launched his African expeditions, and a number of Lagos Jews were among his geographers and navigators. After the expulsion of the Jews from Portugal, Lagos remained a center for *Conversos. The city was destroyed by an earthquake in 1755. In nearby Loulé, the principal Jewish center in eastern Algarve, Jews were restricted to a quarter known as the *Val de Judeo.*

BIBLIOGRAPHY: M. Kayserling, *Geschichte der Juden in Portugal* (1867), 7, 183; J. Mendes dos Remedios, *Os Judeus em Portugal* (1895), chs. 8–9. **ADD. BIBLIOGRAPHY:** A. Iria, in: *Memórias da Academia das Ciencias de Lisboa*, 25 (1986), 293–438.

[Aaron Lichtenstein]

LA GUARDIA, FIORELLO HENRY (1882–1947), U.S. congressman and mayor of New York City. La Guardia, who was born in New York City to a mother of Jewish descent and an Italian father, was raised as a Protestant. At the age of 20, La Guardia was appointed U.S. consul in Fiume. He resigned in 1907 and returned to the U.S., where he worked as an interpreter at the Ellis Island immigrant reception center while attending New York University Law School. He was thus intimately acquainted with the needs and feelings of immigrants and spoke their languages, Yiddish included. His career was built upon their support.

Elected to Congress on the Republican and Progressive tickets in 1916, La Guardia represented a Manhattan district composed primarily of Jews and Italians. He resigned his seat in 1917 to enlist in the army. Upon his discharge, La Guardia resumed his duties in Congress in 1918. There he sponsored a resolution calling on the U.S. to protest antisemitic outbreaks in Poland and Eastern Europe at the Paris Peace Conference. In 1919 La Guardia was elected president of the New York Board of Aldermen on the Republican ticket, and in 1922 he was again elected to Congress as a Republican. His party allegiance was nominal, for his reelection in 1924 was on the Socialist and Progressive tickets. Until his defeat in 1932, La Guardia was a consistent supporter of progressive causes and of legislation benefiting the urban poor.

La Guardia was elected to three terms as mayor of New York City on a Republican-Fusion American Labor Party ticket in 1933, 1937, and 1941. During his mayoralty, he became celebrated as the "Little Flower" for the vigor, earthiness, and flamboyance of his manner. He fought Tammany Hall and corruption-tainted politics, and greatly improved the honesty and scope of municipal services. The city was improved by a vast new network of parks, bridges, schools, and highways. In his urban New Deal, La Guardia drew massive Jewish support away from the Democratic Party. He effectively courted the Jewish voter with a combination of liberal policies, appointment of qualified Jews as officials, and personal style. He did not hesitate to create international incidents in this connection. A 1937 speech which depicted Hitler as a fanatic who deserved a place in the "World's Fair Chamber of Horrors" brought official complaints from the German embassy in Washington and official State Department apologies.

La Guardia's service in 1946 as director general of the UN Relief and Rehabilitation Administration was marked by a sympathetic disposition toward Jewish DP's and by controversy, which ended when he resigned in December of the same year. He wrote *The Making of an Insurgent, an Autobiography, 1882–1919* (1948).

BIBLIOGRAPHY: C. Garrett, *La Guardia Years, Machine and Reform Politics in New York City* (1961); A. Mann, *La Guardia, A Fighter Against His Times* (1959); H. Zinn, *La Guardia in Congress* (1959).

LA GUARDIA, HOLY CHILD OF, subject of a *blood libel who became revered as a saint by the Spanish populace. Six Conversos and two Jews, inhabitants of La Guardia, Tembleque, and Zamora, were tried in connection with this libel in an irregular Inquisition trial which began on Dec. 17, 1490, and was concluded on Nov. 14, 1491, when the accused were burned at the stake in the town of Ávila. The Jews accused were Yuce Franco of Tembleque and Moses Abenamias of Zamora; the Conversos were Alonso, Juan, García, and Lope, all of the Franco family, and Juan de Oraña, all inhabitants of La Guardia, in the province of Toledo. The depositions and confessions extracted under torture reveal that they were accused of two things: the profanation of a Host, which the accused Conversos had purchased and which was found in the bag of Benito García, in order to perform acts of sorcery; and the murder of a Christian child (whose body was never found) on Good Friday and the extraction of his heart for acts of sorcery. The beginnings of the trial have never been clarified, but during the proceedings its motivations became evident. *Torquemada himself had intended to preside over the trial, but possibly under the influence of Abraham *Seneor, whom they at first attempted to involve in the accusation, the trial was transferred from Segovia, where it was to have been held initially, to Ávila.

A special tribunal was thus set up, formed by carefully chosen judges. The judges and the investigators who assisted them resorted to provocatory methods to extract evidence in prison and were even compelled, in order to reconcile the contradictions between the various "statements," to bring together the accused and force them to relate in each other's presence details of the "deed" so that a tale of at least some coherence could be contrived. The judges even sat on a special panel (*Consulta-de-fé*) in Salamanca, with the participation of the celebrated monk Antonio de la Peña, the associate of Fernando de Santo Domingo in his anti-Jewish activities. There is also no doubt that the Inquisition wanted to prepare public opinion for the expulsion of the Jews from Spain by creating a background of an alleged Jewish-Converso conspiracy to bring about the annihilation of both Christianity and the Inquisition. Even so, the recorded statements of the Conversos are a profound expression of their belief in the Law of Moses, their readiness to die as martyrs, and their contemptuous attitude toward Christianity and its way of life. Torquemada was referred to by one of the accused as the "arch antichrist" (*antecristo mayor*).

The verdict was made public and circulated throughout Spain, and the worship of the "Holy Child" was rapidly instituted. For fear of riots, the Jews of Ávila felt compelled to request a document of protection (granted on Dec. 9, 1491). With time, details were added to the story until it assumed impressive proportions in works and plays which were presented on the subject. In 1583 Fray Rodrigo de Yepes wrote a book entitled *Historia de la muerte y glorioso martirio del Sancto Inocente, que llaman de La Guardia*, which during the 17th century served as the basis of a play by Lope de Vega, *El Niño Inocente de la Guardia*. Lope's play is based on a text in his work *Octava parte* (1617) which is not entirely reliable. The intention of Lope is purely anti-Jewish. The martyrdom of the Santo Niño is compared to the Passion. Lope leaves no doubt as to his sympathy with the Inquisition and his dislike of those it prosecuted. The tale was newly adapted during the 18th century by Jose de Cañizares under the title *La Viva Imagen de Cristo*. These works were republished in 1943, during World War II, by Manuel Romero de Castilla under the title *Singular suceso en el reinado de los Reyes Católicos*, in an attempt to revive the "holy" ideas of the writings of his predecessors.

BIBLIOGRAPHY: F. Fita, in: *Boletín de la Academia de la Historia, Madrid*, 11 (1887), 3–134, 420–3; H.C. Lea, *Chapters from the Religious History of Spain* (1890), 203ff.; idem, *History of the Inquisition in Spain*, 1 (1904), 133–5; T. Hope, *Torquemada* (Eng., 1939), 153–92; Baer, Spain, 2 (1966), 398–423; Suárez Fernández, Documentos, 44. **ADD. BIBLIOGRAPHY:** Ph. Brunet, *Torquemada et les atrocités de l'Inquisition* (1976), 199–215; C. Carrete Parrondo, in: *Helmantica*, 28 (1977), 51–61; Sor. M. Despina, in: *El Olivo*, 9 (1979), 48–70; W.A. Christian, *Local Religion in Sixteenth century Spain* (1981), index; S. de Horozco, *Relaciones históricas toledanas*, Intr. & trans. by J. Weiner (1981), 29–38; F. Díaz-Plaja (ed.), *Historia de España en sus documentos, siglo XV* (1984), 278–91; L. de Vega, *El niño inocente de La Gurdia: A Critical and Annotated Edition*, with an Introductory Study by A.J. Farrell (1985); M. Moner, in: *La leyenda: antrpología, historia, literatura*, (1989), 253–66; E.M. Domínguez de Paz and M.P. Carrascosa, in: *Canente*, 5b (1989), 25–38; idem, in: *Diálogos hispánicos de Amsterdam*, 8:2 (1989), 343–57; A. MacKay, in: J. Lowe and P. Swanson (eds.), *Essays on Hispanic Themes in Honour of Edward C. Riley* (1989), 41–50; S. Haliczer, in: *Cultural Encounters* (1991), 146–56.

[Haim Beinart]

LAGUNA, DANIEL ISRAEL LOPEZ (c. 1653–c. 1730), Portuguese-born poet of Marrano parentage. As a child, Laguna was taken to Peyrehorade in the south of France. Later he went to study in Spain, where he was arrested by the Inquisition. On his eventual release, presumably after reconciliation to the Church, he settled in Jamaica; there he openly professed Judaism and was naturalized in 1693. About 1720 he went to London where with the help of Mordecai Nuñes de Almeyda, his patron, he published a paraphrase of the Psalms in a variety of Spanish verse forms. He dedicated the work, titled *Espejo* *fiel de Vidas que contiene los Palmos de David in Verso* (London, 1720), to De Almeyda. The book had been planned in prison and was the fruit of 23 years' labor. In a number of places, the author makes allusions to the Inquisition and its persecutions. The volume is prefaced by commendatory poems by some 20 persons, including women, in Hebrew, Latin, Spanish, Portuguese, and English. Laguna later returned to Jamaica, to his wife and three sons David, Jacob, and Isaac, and died there.

BIBLIOGRAPHY: Roth, Marranos, 330–1; I. Solomons, in: JHSET, 12 (1931), 92–93; M. Kayserling, in: JQR, 12 (1900), 708–17.

[Cecil Roth]

°LAHARANNE, ERNEST, 19th-century French writer and precursor of Zionism. Laharanne wrote political pamphlets and, during the reign of Napoleon III, edited a republican newspaper, *L'Etat*, which supported free trade. Beyond this, little is known of him. It is probable that he came from the south of France, was a left-wing Roman Catholic, and belonged to the Emperor's secretariat. He wrote a pamphlet entitled *La Nouvelle Question d'Orient: Empires d'Egypte et d'Arabie: reconstitution de la nationalité juive* (1860), in which he proposed establishing a Jewish state in Palestine extending from Suez to Smyrna. He championed his idea with a romantic ardor, conforming to the principle of nations so dear to Napoleon III. Moses *Hess published large portions of the work in his *Rome and Jerusalem* (Letter 11).

BIBLIOGRAPHY: N.M. Gelber, *Ḥasidei Ummot ha-Olam bi-Mevasserei ha-Teḥiyyah* (1931), 75–80; idem, in: *Ha-Po'el ha-Ẓa'ir* (July 26, 1960); E. Laharanne, *La nuova questione d'Oriente* (1952), 3–10, preface by D. Lattes.

[Moshe Catane]

LAHAT, SHLOMO (Chich; 1927–), Israeli military commander and mayor of Tel Aviv. Lahat was born in Berlin and brought to Ereẓ Yisrael by his parents in 1933. In 1941 he joined the Haganah. In the War of Independence he fought in the Givati brigade. While serving in the IDF, he studied law at the Hebrew University, and in 1956 was the first Israeli officer to be sent to the U.S. Army Command and General Staff College at Fort Leavenworth in Kansas. Upon his return Lahat was appointed an instructor in the IDF Command and Staff School. In 1959 he was appointed head of the Operations Branch in the General Staff Operations Department. In 1962 he transferred to the Armor, and in 1966 was appointed deputy commander of the Armor units. In the Six-Day War he was appointed governor of East Jerusalem, and at the end of the war was appointed head of the Central Command Staff with the rank of brigadier general. In 1969 he was appointed commander of the Armored Forces in Sinai, and during the War of Attrition was commander of the operations along the Suez Canal until June 1970, being promoted to the rank of major general. In 1970 he was appointed chief of the army's Manpower Division. Lahat left active military service in March 1973 with the rank of major general.

In November 1973 Lahat was elected mayor of Tel Aviv at the head of the Likud list. He served as mayor for 20 years. As mayor he was responsible for major administrative and operational changes in the city, investing heavily in communal, cultural, health, and education facilities, and rehabilitating the city's coast and beaches. It was with his active support that the Suzanne Dalal Center for Dance and Theater, the Tel Aviv Cinémateque, the new Opera House, and many other cultural enterprises were realized. While he was mayor the city absorbed 40,000 immigrants from the former Soviet Union, and the steady decline in the population of the city was reversed. The municipality adopted the Gesher theater, whose original cast was made up entirely of new immigrants from Russia. A special unit was established in the municipality for the conservation of buildings in the Bauhaus and International styles. Lahat was replaced as mayor by Roni *Milo in 1993.

After leaving city hall Lahat entered private business and served in various public functions including president of the Council for Peace and Security, which was among the organizers of the peace demonstration on November 4, 1995, at which Prime Minister Yitzhak *Rabin was assassinated; chairman of the Yad Vashem Fund; chairman of the friends association of the Loḥamei ha-Getta'ot Museum; chairman of the Rabin Association; chairman of the board of directors of the Yiddish theater; and member of the Board of Governors of Tel Aviv University, the college in Jaffa, and other public institutions. He was chairman of the Diaspora Museum, Beth Hatefutsoth.

[Susan Hattis Rolef (2nd ed.)]

LAHAVOT HA-BASHAN (Heb. לַהֲבוֹת הַבָּשָׁן, "Flames of the Bashan"), kibbutz in northern Israel, on the eastern rim of the *Ḥuleh Valley, affiliated with Ha-Kibbutz Ha-Arẓi Ha-Shomer ha-Ẓa'ir. It was founded in 1945 by a group of *Youth Aliyah graduates from Germany and Israeli-born youth, as one of the settlements in the defense chain at the foot of the *Golan Heights. During Israel's *War of Independence (1948) the kibbutz was exposed to a heavy attack from Syrian forces. Farming at Lahavot ha-Bashan was based on field and fodder crops, fruit orchards, dairy cattle, and carp ponds. The kibbutz had a factory specializing in spraying and fire-extinguishing apparatus. In 2002 its population was 423.

[Efraim Orni]

LAHR, BERT (Irving Lahrheim; 1895–1967), U.S. actor, comedian. Born in New York of German immigrants, Lahr began his career at 15, became the "boy wonder" of burlesque, and had his first Broadway success in *Hold Everything* (1928). He then appeared in a series of Broadway shows, worked with road companies, and returned to Broadway, playing comedies of Shakespeare and Aristophanes. His Broadway performances include *Flying High* (1930), *Life Begins at 8:40* (1934), *The Show Is On* (1937), *DuBarry Was a Lady* (1940), *Burlesque* (1947), *Two on the Aisle* (1951), *Waiting for Godot* (1956), *Hotel Paradiso* (1957), and *The Girls against the Boys* (1959). He won a Tony Award in 1964 for Best Actor in the musical *Foxy* and in 1963 he was nominated for a Best Actor Tony for his role in the drama *The Beauty Part*.

Lahr appeared in more than a dozen films between 1931 and 1939 but was best known for his role as the cowardly lion in the highly successful musical *The Wizard of Oz* (1939). However, as he later commented, "After *The Wizard of Oz* I was typecast as a lion, but there just weren't that many parts for lions." He appeared in *Sing Your Worries Away* (1942), *Ship Ahoy* (1942), *Meet the People* (1944), *Always Leave Them Laughing* (1949), *Mr. Universe* (1951), *Rose Marie* (1954), *The Second Greatest Sex* (1955), and *The Night They Raided Minsky's* (1968). He also appeared on television, as a guest on variety shows and early TV playhouse dramas, as well as the TV movies *The Great Waltz* (1955) and *The Secret World of Eddie Hodges* (1960), and the short comedy *Thompson's Ghost* (1966).

His son John Lahr, a drama critic with *The New Yorker,* wrote a biography about his father, *Notes on a Cowardly Lion* (1969), which became a bestseller.

[Ruth Beloff (2nd ed.)]

LAJSA. Founded in 1982, the Latin American Jewish Studies Association (LAJSA) promotes scholarly research on Latin American Jewry as a branch of Jewish Diaspora studies and as an element in the study of ethnicity in Latin America. LAJSA provides a forum for the scholarly exchange of ideas and research through conferences, publications, the development of courses offered at institutions of higher learning, and outreach to the general public.

LAJSA's network brings together scholars who are at work on related themes but who are geographically distant from one another. Members involved in a variety of academic disciplines such as history, literature, languages, economics, and anthropology are able to interact with one another across disciplinary boundaries through a membership directory, the semiannual *Latin American Jewish Studies* (reports of professional activities, critical reviews of scholarly work, and bibliography), and an electronic listserv (current news from Latin American Jewish communities, new publications, and announcements of upcoming events).

LAJSA is incorporated as a non-profit organization in the United States, in the state of Michigan. The association itself has no geographic base; its conferences have been hosted by American Jewish Archives-JIR (1982), University of New Mexico (1984), AMILAT – Research Association of Latin American Jewry in Israel and the World Union of Jewish Studies, Jerusalem (1985), University of Florida, Gainesville (1987), Universidad de Buenos Aires and AMIA – Ashkenazi Community of Buenos Aires (1988); University of Maryland, College Park (1991), Jerusalem Center for Public Affairs in Philadelphia (1993), Universidad Autónoma de Mexico and the Jewish communities of Mexico City (1995), Harvard University (1997), Princeton University (1999), Universidade Federal do Rio de Janeiro (2002), and Dartmouth College (2004). Publication of books and articles originally presented at these conferences established Latin American Jewish studies as an academic discipline and LAJSA as its representative within academia. Members of LAJSA and subscribers to its publications include major research libraries, as well as individual scholars, communal officials, and others with expertise in the field. LAJSA maintains fraternal relations with AMILAT, whose members are affiliated with LAJSA.

LAJSA was organized by Judith Laikin Elkin and a group of interested persons including Robert M. Levine, Saul Sosnowski, Jacobo Kovadloff, and Richard D. Woods. Elkin served as president until 1995 and as newsletter editor until her retirement in 1998. Scholars in 20 countries are now among LAJSA's members. In recent years, board members have been elected from the United States, Mexico, Brazil, and Israel. Officers in 2005 include president Leo Spitzer (Dartmouth), treasurer Darrell Lockhart (University of Nevada, Reno), manager of electronic list and archive Naomi Lindstrom (University of Texas, Austin), and newsletter editor Kenya C. Dworkin (Carnegie Mellon University). LAJSA maintains its website at www.acad.swarthmore.edu/lajsa.

[Judith Laikin Elkin (2nd ed.)]

LAJTA, BÉLA (1873–1920), Hungarian architect. Considered an outstanding representative of Hungarian architecture, Lajta was influenced by Ö. Lechner and used folkloristic motifs and ornaments in his early projects. Later, however, he was among the first to turn from Secession to straight lines. His works, among them the Rózsavölgyi-house and the gas works (both in 1911–12), are protected historical monuments in Budapest.

[Eva Kondor]

LAKATOS, IMRE (1922–1974), British philosopher of science. Lakatos was Born Imre Lipsitz in Debrecen, Hungary, and educated at the local university. Lakatos survived World War II in hiding in Transylvania and, as a convinced Marxist, organized Communist cells. He took the name "Lakatos" because it sounded more "working class." After the war he became an influential member of the new Communist ruling elite in Hungary, but was expelled from the Party in 1950 and fled to England after the 1956 Revolution. From 1960 he was a lecturer at the London School of Economics, where he served as professor of logic from 1970 until his death. In Britain, Lakatos became one of the most influential of recent philosophers of science. Abandoning Marxism, he became a neo-Popperian (although also indebted to Thomas Kuhn), arguing that science is best viewed as consisting of discrete "research programs" with their own "hard core" of central assumptions. By the time of his death he had shifted to the political right and was a vigorous opponent of student radicalism. He died at the age of 51 after suffering a heart attack. Many of his essays were printed in *Proofs and Refutation* (1976, edited by John Worrall and Elie Zahar).

BIBLIOGRAPHY: ODNB online.

[William D. Rubinstein (2nd ed.)]

LAKATOS, LÁSZLÓ (1882–1944), Hungarian author and journalist. Born in Budapest, Lakatos displayed an early talent for journalism and for a brief period edited the liberal daily *Világ*. He was an able satirist, fond of aphorisms and paradoxes. Lakatos wrote on Jewish themes, choosing his subjects mainly from topical issues and the Budapest middle classes. A number of his plays were extremely successful outside Hungary and include *Négy frakk* ("Four Cutaways," 1923), *Pajtásházasság* ("Companionate Marriage," 1928), and *Helyet az ifjúságnak* ("Make Way for Youth," 1934). He also wrote novels, notably *Egy pesti lány története* ("The Story of a Budapest Girl," 1913). At the outbreak of World War II Lakatos was forced to immigrate to Paris but had to flee from the Nazi invaders and died in Nice.

BIBLIOGRAPHY: *Magyar Irodalmi Lexikon*, 2 (1965), s.v.; L. Bóka, *Magyar mártir irók antológiája* (1947).

[Baruch Yaron]

LAKEWOOD, city in central New Jersey (Ocean County), 2005 population close to 40,000. The city was a popular resort destination throughout the 20th century. Jews frequented many of its vacation facilities. Some eventually settled there, establishing a small community and the local hotels were also at least a temporary home to Jews. It is now the home to a large and influential ultra-Orthodox community because of the dramatic rise of its yeshivah-affiliated population. Unlike *Kiryas Joel or *New Square, it is not a community set apart by the purchase of rural property and incorporation of a town, but one that owing to its large numbers is dominant in a city.

In 1943 Rabbi Aaron *Kotler, a leading yeshivah dean formerly of *Kletsk, Lithuania, founded an advanced yeshivah, Beth Medrash Govoha, in Lakewood. The initial student body consisted of 13 students, some of whom had studied with him in Europe. Kotler's goal was to re-establish in America the high standards of talmudic learning that had been a part of the Eastern European Jewish world. His ideal was that Torah should be "studied for its own sake" and, although one might choose the professional rabbinate or teaching as a career, this would be a result rather than the goal of one's studies.

Kotler strongly opposed higher secular education, seeing it as a danger due to the many conflicts between the university environment and its secular world view and those of Orthodox Judaism. He also viewed higher secular learning as a squandering of time better spent in Torah study.

Following Kotler's passing in 1962 he was succeeded as dean by his son, Rabbi Schneur Kotler (1918–1982). Schneur Kotler in turn has been followed by a team of deans, his son Rabbi Aryeh Malkiel and Rabbis Dovid Schustal, Yisroel Neuman, and Yeruchim Olshin.

The studies pursued in the Beth Medrash Govoha framework are primarily focused on Talmud and Codes of Law. Students begin the program after high school and, at times, after a period spent in a preparatory yeshivah either in America or Israel. They attend Beth Medrash Govoha until marriage, whereupon some continue their studies in the school's *kolel* division (as of mid-2005 the student body of the yeshivah and *kolel* was 4,482), where they receive a small stipend.

The growing Orthodox yeshivah community in Lakewood is a result of many students choosing to settle there after concluding their studies. Many of them eventually find livelihoods outside the religious employment sector. Some seek to remain *kolel* students for many years, which, at times, has created an economic strain on the community.

Many graduates have gone on to serve as rabbis, teachers, and authors throughout the United States and the world. Satellite Lakewood *kolelim* have been established in dozens of cities throughout North America, where their fellows combine talmudic studies with teaching in the local community.

Lakewood students, under the auspices of Torah Umesorah's Seed Program, often spend their summers in Jewish communities across the country, where they teach, counsel, and interact with the surrounding Jewish community.

In 2005 the yeshivah community in Lakewood was serviced by a network of 23 elementary and 13 secondary schools, all committed to the vision of Rabbi Kotler. The housing needs of this growing population has caused its borders to expand rapidly, creating a housing boom with continually rising prices as well as generating an extensive small business infrastructure to serve its needs.

The non-Orthodox and Modern Orthodox communities in Lakewood have significantly declined in numbers in recent decades, and there have been tensions between the yeshivah community and its non-Orthodox and non-Jewish neighbors. Members of the yeshivah community have participated in local politics including work with the school board, and there have been attempts at accommodation in the political sphere.

The yeshivah seeks to maintain and spread the world view colloquially known as *yeshivish*, continuing the non-ḥasidic, traditional Orthodoxy of the Lithuanian yeshivah world. Its philosophy is to be found, on the journalistic level, in the weekly newspaper, *Yated Ne'eman*.

[Mayer Schiller (2nd ed.)]

LAKNER, YEHOSHUA (1924–2003), Israeli composer. Born in Czechoslovakia, he immigrated to Eretz Israel in 1941. After living in kibbutz Merḥavyah, he moved to Tel Aviv, where he studied the piano with Frank Pelleg and composition with *Partos and *Boscovitch. Later, he studied in the United States with *Copland at Tanglewood, and electronic music with Karlheinz Stockhausen and Mauricio Kagel in Cologne and Darmstadt. He returned to Israel in 1948 to teach at the Rubin Academy of Music, Tel Aviv. From 1963, he lived in Zurich, Switzerland, where he taught music theory at the Zurich Conservatory (1974–87). He wrote incidental music for Maria von Ostfelden's productions (1965–71) and "concrete music" for plays, including Ionesco's *Chairs* and Brecht's *Turandot* (1969). During the 1980s he began to use the computer as his main instrument, creating Audio-Visual Time Structures – musical and visual configurations which developed in poetic forms that could be manipulated during performance. His awards include the Engel Prize (Tel Aviv, 1958), the Salomon David Steinberg Foundation music prize (Zurich and Jerusalem, 1970), and the city of Zurich's composition award (1986–87). His works include *Toccata* for orchestra (1958); *Hexachords* for orchestra (1960); the ballet *Dmujoth* for cello, piano, percussion, and tape (1962); *Theater an der Winkelwieses* for tape (1981); *Tanz der Akzente*, for two computers (1996); *BX mit Variationen* for two computers (1997); chamber music including Sonata for flute and piano (1948); *Five Birthdays* for piano (1965); *Kreise und Signale* for two pianos (1985); *Alef-Beth-Gimel* for piano (1991); and *The Dream of Muhammad*, for choir, orchestra, and electronic music (1968), commissioned by the Jerusalem Testimonium.

ADD. BIBLIOGRAPHY: Grove online; MGG².

[Uri (Erich) Toeplitz / Yohanan Boehm / Israela Stein (2nd ed.)]

LAMARR, HEDY (**Hedwig Eva Maria Kiesler**; 1914–2000), actor, inventor. Born in Vienna, Austria, Lamarr attended Max *Reinhardt's famous acting school in Berlin as a teenager. She made her film debut in the 1933 Czech picture *Extase* (*Ecstasy*), for which she earned international notoriety as the first woman to appear naked in a feature film. The movie was extensively edited before it was shown in American theaters; its leading lady, arriving in Hollywood in 1937, was renamed and signed by MGM's Louis B. *Mayer. Lamarr had an extensive career as a movie actress, appearing in such films as *Algiers* (1938), *Ziegfeld Girl* (1941), *White Cargo* (1942), and, most notably, as Delilah in *Samson and Delilah* (1948). Professionally, Lamarr also played a much different role, that of inventor. From 1933 to 1937, as the wife of Fritz Mandal, a manufacturer of military aircraft, Lamarr was first exposed to the field of control systems. She pursued her interest in radio control long after her marriage – the first of six – had ended. In 1940, Lamarr presented her concept of "frequency hopping" to her Hollywood neighbor, the avant-garde composer George Antheil, who is best known for his revolutionary *Ballet Méanique*. Lamarr was working on a way to protect radio signals from being heard or interfered with by outside parties; Antheil proposed a design based on the player-piano, by which the radio signal would travel at 88 constantly shifting frequencies. Lamarr and Antheil received a patent in 1942, but their ideas were not put to significant use until the Cuban missile crisis of 1962, when they were used to provide secure communications among American ships. Lamarr's "frequency hopping" is the basis for today's "spread spectrum," a design now applied to such mainstream technology as the cellular phone.

[Casey Schwartz (2nd ed.)]

LAMBERT, AIMÉ (1825–1896), French army officer. Born in Nancy, Lambert volunteered for the National Guard in 1848 and took part in suppressing the Paris rising of that year. Twice wounded, he was decorated for bravery. During the Franco-Prussian War he was made town commander of Versailles. In 1877, Lambert was promoted to brigadier general and made commander of Paris. In 1878 he was commander in chief of the French Occupation Army in *Tunisia. An outstanding administrator, Lambert was given several honorary appointments, including that of military commander of the Palace of the Elysée. He received numerous honors and retired with the rank of lieutenant general in 1889. Lambert was a conscious Jew and repeatedly refused to convert to Christianity despite pressure from his fellow officers in the high command.

[Mordechai Kaplan]

LAMBERT, MAYER (1863–1930), French Oriental scholar and Hebraist. Lambert was born in Metz, the descendant of a long line of rabbis: his grandfather Lion Mayer (1787–1862) and his great-grandfather Aaron Worms (1754–1836) had served as chief rabbis in Metz. He studied first at Metz, then at the Ecole Rabbinique (Séminaire Israélite) and Sorbonne University in Paris. From 1887 he lectured on Arabic and Syriac and later on Hebrew at the Ecole Rabbinique and taught Hebrew at the Ecole Normale Orientale (Teachers' Training College) of the Alliance Israélite Universelle. In 1903 Lambert began teaching Hebrew and Syriac at the Ecole Pratique des Hautes Etudes. He worked in close association with Joseph *Derenbourg.

Among Lambert's many published works in addition to numerous contributions to the *Revue des Etudes Juives*, the *Journal Asiatique*, and other periodicals are *Eléments de Grammaire Hébraique* (1890); *Commentaire sur le Séfer Yesira; ou livre de la Création par Saadiah* (1891); Saadiah's version of and commentary on Proverbs, text and French translation (with J. Derenbourg), *Oeuvres complètes de Saadia. Traduction des Proverbes* (1894); and *Glossaire hébreu-français du XIIIme siècle* (with L. Brandin, 1905). He contributed to the publication of *Corpus Inscriptionum Semiticarum* and also participated in the French translation of the Bible issued by the French rabbinate. Three parts of his major work *Traité de Grammaire Hébraïque* were published posthumously (1931–38).

BIBLIOGRAPHY: J. Weill, in: REJ, 91 (1931), 113–34, incl. list of his works.

LAMBERT, PHYLLIS (1927–), Canadian architect and urban renewal advocate; she is the daughter of Sam (the industrialist and founder of Seagrams) and Saidye *Bronfman. Lambert was born in Montreal. She studied fine art at Vassar and at the Institute of Fine Arts of New York University. In 1963 she earned a degree in architecture from the Illinois Institute of Technology. While still in her twenties and before earning her architectural degree, Sam Bronfman entrusted his daughter to direct construction of the landmark Seagram Building in New York. Ensuring the building would be an architectural showcase, she selected world-renowned Mies van der Rohe to be the project's architect. As an architect in her own right Lambert's designs include the Saidye Bronfman Center in Montreal.

Phyllis Lambert has been recognized for her tireless advocacy of modern architecture, concern for urban conservation, and for advancing the role of architecture in the public realm. She founded and directed the Canadian Centre for Architecture in Montreal, a leading museum and study center devoted to architecture past, present, and future. She was also deeply committed to advancing cooperative housing and urban renovation. Among her restoration projects is the ninth-century Ben Ezra Synogogue in Cairo known for its document-rich storeroom, or *Genizah. The synagogue had fallen into abject disrepair until this project begun in 1980; completed in 1991 it restored the building to a grandeur worthy of medieval Cairo.

Phyllis Lambert received many awards for her work, including the Order of Canada, the highest honor Canada can bestow on a citizen.

[Harold Troper (2nd ed.)]

LAMBERT, RAYMOND RAOUL (1894–1943), community leader in France under the Vichy regime. Born in Montmorency, Lambert served in both world wars and was awarded the Croix de Guerre. He acted as secretary-general of the Comité d'Assistance aux Réfugiés (CAR) and was chief editor of *Univers Israélite*. In 1941 he was nominated director-general of the *Union Générale des Israélites de France (UGIF) in the then unoccupied zone. Lambert afterward became chief of the UGIF for the whole of France. He clandestinely made contact with Jewish underground resistance groups and with Catholic circles that helped Jews to avoid the persecutions. He was arrested on Aug. 20, 1943, after having protested to Pierre *Laval against the excesses of the German and French Nazis in confiscating Jewish property. He, his wife, their four children, and his mother-in-law were immediately deported to *Auschwitz and gassed on arrival.

BIBLIOGRAPHY: Centre de Documentation Juive Contemporaine, *Activité des organisations juives en France sous l'occupation* (1947), passim; Z. Szajkowski, in: JSOS, 9 (1947), 239–56; idem, *Analytical Franco-Jewish Gazeteer 1939–1945* (1966), index.

[Yehuda Reshef]

LAMDAN, YIẒḤAK (1899–1954), Hebrew poet and editor. Born in Mlinov, Ukraine, Lamdan received a traditional and secular education. During World War I he was cut off from his family and wandered through southern Russia with his brother, who was later killed in a pogrom. These grim experiences made Lamdan rally to the Communist cause and he volunteered for the Red Army at the outbreak of the Russian Revolution. Disillusionment, however, soon set in because as a Jew he could not feel at home in the revolutionary movement. He left the army and returned to Mlinov, which had been annexed to Poland. There he became a teacher at the local Hebrew school and published his first poem in *Ha-Shiloaḥ* (1918). Immigrating to Ereẓ Israel in 1920, he spent his first years as a *ḥalutz*, building roads and working on farms. His poetry, now imbued with a *ḥalutz* spirit that grew out of his experience, was published in various literary journals in Ereẓ Israel and aroused great interest since it reflected the hopes and despair of the Third Aliyah and also the struggles and inner conflicts of the individual *ḥalutz*. He later gave up physical labor and devoted himself exclusively to literary work, from 1934 until his death publishing and editing his own literary monthly *Gilyonot*. He was a member of the central committee of the Hebrew Writers Association for many years.

Lamdan's magnum opus, *Massadah* (1927), an epic poem in blank verse of six cantos, comprising 35 poems, established his reputation. The poem reflects the spirit of the young pioneers of the 1920s who had left behind them not only the memory of the brutal senseless murders of defenseless Jews, but also their shattered illusions about the possibility of establishing a free, revolutionary society in Eastern Europe. Massadah, the last fortress which continued to hold out against the Romans even after the fall of Jerusalem in 70 C.E., in Lamdan's poem symbolizes Ereẓ Israel, the last stronghold of the destroyed Eastern European Jewish communities.

The voice throughout the poem is the "I" of the poet who embodies both the horror experienced by his generation and its vision for a new future. In the first canto (the prologue) the poet, standing in the midst of the ruins of his home, at the height of the Russian Revolution, receives a message about Massadah: "face of the adverse fate of generations" the sons of Massadah have thrust out their "breasts in revolt and roared 'Enough!'" He sets out for the Promised Land in order to join them. His path to Massadah is obstructed by three friends who symbolize the various anti-Zionist or Diaspora-oriented ideologies and who try to turn him back. By an overwhelming act of will, the speaker frees himself from his friends and scales the barriers blocking access to Israel's stronghold. The second canto is a series of short poems in which the different Jewish refugees who came to Massadah describe their tragic experiences.

Cantos three, four, and five are movements from joyful hope to despair. Night, "in which the air is heavy with blood," transforms into a time for kindling fires, dancing, and the renewal of faith. Night thus becomes a symbol of strength and hope while day is a time of despair and disillusionment. The fortress itself weeps for her listless sons. The ecstasy of the early movement is passed, the verve of pioneering among the weaker is spent and they fall to the wayside. Fewer and fewer of those imbued with the spirit of freedom throng to Massadah, and peddlers, longing to engage in commerce, increase. Not only the fires but also the "flames of revolt" brought to Massadah as "holy Sabbath candles in the twilight of the worlds" flicker faintly, yet they are not extinguished. There are always those who stand guard over Massadah watching "every cloud rising somewhere over the horizon." In the sixth canto the poet turns to these sturdy souls, calling out to them that their sacrifice is not in vain and that all roads trodden by the Jewish people lead to Massadah, none lead away.

The poet's "I" of the first canto, with its clear biographical references, later merges into the collective consciousness of the Jewish people, but even in Canto I it is not intrinsically individual. A symbolic poem of moods and situations, rather than heroes and plot, *Massadah* is rich in expressionistic images and rings with the cadence of biblical rhetoric.

The poems published after *Massadah* had far less of an impact on the reading public. Some were collected in *Ba-Ritmah ha-Meshulleshet* ("Triple Harness," 1930) and *Be-Ma'aleh Akrabbim* ("On Scorpions' Pass," 1945); others appeared in literary journals. In these later works, though more individualistic and less rhetorical, Lamdan remains fervently nationalistic and adamant in his belief that the individual must serve the cause of national rebirth. The poet-narrator assumes the role of man of destiny and denounces those who refuse to hearken to his message of redemption. Lamdan's poetry remained social poetry in which the poet's rhetorical rather than lyrical skill predominates. His sincerity and idealism to some degree cover this artistic flaw, of which he was aware. His later works carry a note of personal tragedy. The poet is fully conscious of the fact that his devotion to the national renascence is at the expense of his art as a poet. In the preface to his series of poems *Mi-Shirai she-me-Ever la-Daf* ("My Songs on the Other Side of the Page," in *Gilyonot*, 25 [1951]), the conflict is starkly exposed with the poet apologizing for his inner urges and drives not rooted in the national consciousness. He declared that his conscience, which has totally surrendered itself to the nation, prevents him from retreating into purely individualistic poetry; underlying the statement, however, is an almost imperceptible sadness and yearning at an inevitable loss.

The same integrity manifested itself in his editorship of *Gilyonot*, a literary periodical which he founded and which propounded his national ideals. Lamdan insisted on the independence of his periodical, and refused to allow it to be controlled even by political groups whose ideology he shared. During the 1930s and 1940s, *Gilyonot* was one of Ereẓ Israel's leading periodicals.

[Gideon Katznelson]

Kol Shirei Yiẓḥak Lamdan, the collected poems of Lamdan, including hitherto unpublished poems, with an introduction by S. Halkin, was issued by Mosad Bialik in 1973. A. Lipsker edited (with an introduction) Lamdan's letters (1998).

For Eng. trans. of Lamdan, see Goell, 974–1000.

BIBLIOGRAPHY: L.I. Yudkin, *Isaac Lamdan* (1971), incl. bibl.; S. Umen, *The World of Isaac Lamdan, Pioneer, Poet* (1961), incl. bibl.; B. Kurzweil, *Bein Ḥazon le-vein ha-Absurdi* (1966), 100–9; I. Keshet, *Maskiyyot* (1953), 158–68; G. Katzenelson, in: *Haaretz* (Nov. 26, 1954; Nov. 11, 1955); E. Schweid, *Shalosh Ashmurot* (1969), 93–106; idem, in: *Me'assef le-Divrei Sifrut, Bikkoret ve-Hagut*, 7 (1967), 384–92; I. Rabinowitz, *Be-Ḥevlei Doram* (1959), 48–61; B.Y. Michali, *Le-Yad ha-Ovnayim* (1959), 80–99; Waxman, Literature, 4 (1941), 327ff. **ADD. BIBLIOGRAPHY:** H. Barzel, *Shirah u-Morasha* (1971); M. Ungerfeld, "*Al Kol Shirei Lamdan*," in: *Hadoar*, 52 (1973), 519–520; A.A. Steinbach, "Of Two Jewish Poets: N. Sachs and Y. Lamdan," in: *Justice, Justice Shalt Thou Pursue* (1975), 179–196; E. Shmueli, "*Ha-Maavak al ha-Ye'ud be-Shirat Lamdan*," in: *Hadoar*, 57:7 (1978), 101; M. Steiner, "*Shirato shel Y. Lamdan*," in: *Haumah*, 56 (1979), 92–101; H. Hoffman, "*Ha-'Af al pi khen' ha-Brenneri be-Shirat Y. Lamdan*," in: *Ha-Sifrut ha-Ivrit u-Tenu'at ha-Avodah* (1989), 158–177; D. Hadari, "*Ha-Yaḥas le-'Massadah' shel Lamdan ke-Vitui le-Gishot Shonot el ha-Ẓiyyonut*," in: *Shorashim*, 8 (1994), 147–154.

LAMECH (Heb. לֶמֶךְ), one of the antediluvian patriarchs in Genesis. According to the list recounting the lineage of Cain (Gen. 4:17–24 – ascribed to the J tradition), Lamech was the son of Methushael (4:18) and the father of three sons, *Jabal, *Jubal, and *Tubal-Cain, and a daughter, Naamah (4:20–22). His wives were *Adah and Zillah (4:19). He was thus the first polygynist and the father of the founders of nomadism, the musical arts, and metalworking. He is also the author of a song (4:23–24), which is structurally and linguistically an example of early Hebrew poetry. Significantly, Lamech is the seventh human generation, and in his song the typological numbers 7 and 77 appear (4:24). Another genealogy of Lamech (assigned to the P tradition) is presented in a list of the descendants of Seth (5:25–31; I Chron. 1:3). In this list, Lamech is the son of Methuselah and the father of Noah. He was 182 years old when Noah was born, and he subsequently had other sons and daughters (Gen. 5:30). He is the seventh generation from Enosh. In this there is a numerical and structural parallel to the other tradition insofar as Enosh is a generic term for man, alongside Adam. Significantly, here, too, the number seven appears, for Lamech lived 777 years (5:31). The relationship between the two lists presents a problem. On the basis of related number typologies, parallel historical frameworks, the reduplication of names (e.g. Enoch; Lamech), and other resemblances, they would seem to derive from a common source, the first probably being the earlier since it records seven generations, while the second counts ten. It is presumed that the latter is an expansion of the former.

The origin and meaning of the name is not clear. An Akkadian noun *lumakku*, sometimes suggested for comparison, refers to a junior priest attested only in lexical lists (CAD L, 244–45). Alternatively, an Arabic etymology would explain this name as "mighty youth," an epithet suitable to Lamech's character.

[Michael Fishbane]

In the Apocrypha

The story of Cain's death at the hand of Lamech, his descendant, is apparently unknown in the Apocrypha and Pseudepigrapha (but see *Lamech, Book of). It may be referred to in the Testament of the Twelve Patriarchs, Benjamin 7:4 which brings together the "Song of Lamech" and the curse laid upon Cain. In the best manuscript of the Testament, however, Cain's death is said to have been due to the Flood. Lamech, the father of Noah, is mentioned in the Apocrypha in Jubilees 4:27–28 and I Enoch 10:1, and in Jubilees 7:38 some emphasis is put on the fact that it was he who transmitted the teaching of Enoch to Noah. Moreover, the Noah fragment in I Enoch 106 contains the story of the birth of Noah as a wondrous, shining child. Lamech fears that this baby is not his own child, but the offspring of the Watchers and goes to ask his father Methusaleh to inquire of his father Enoch. He is reassured by Enoch. This story also occurs, with some variants, in the second column of the Genesis Apocryphon from Qumran. There, the name of Enoch's wife is Batenosh, as in Jubilees 4:27 (Bêtênôs). The same story is also evidently reflected in the fragmentary text 1Q19, the so-called "Book of Noah."

[Michael E. Stone]

In the *Aggadah*

Most of the legends about Lamech, the grandson of Cain, center around his killing of his grandfather. He was blind and when he went hunting, he was led by his young son Tubal-Cain, who would tell his father when game came in sight, so that Lamech could shoot at it with his bow and arrow. Once he aimed at some horned creature which Tubal-Cain thought to be a beast. In fact it was Cain, the "sign of Cain" being a horn in the forehead, and he killed him. In despair, Lamech smote his hands together inadvertently killing Tubal-Cain. After this incident his wives, Adah and Zillah, wanted to leave him on the ground that Cain's descendants were doomed to annihilation. But Lamech argued, "If Cain who committed murder with malice aforethought, was punished only in the seventh generation, then, I who have killed inadvertently may hope that retribution will be postponed for 77 generations" (cf. Gen. 4:23). Lamech and his wives put their case to Adam who decided the case in favor of Lamech (Tanh. Gen. 11). According to another tradition, Lamech's wives refused to have intercourse with him because they knew that a flood was to come and therefore they did not want to bear children. Whereupon Lamech answered "Cain was guilty of murder, yet judgment was suspended in his case for seven generations; for me who am guiltless of this crime, surely judgment will wait 77 generations" (Gen. R. 23:4). Lamech took one wife solely for sexual gratification, and the other for procreation (*ibid.* 23:2).

BIBLIOGRAPHY: M. Eliade, *The Forge and the Crucible* (1962), 97–104; S. Gevirtz, *Patterns in the Early Poetry of Israel* (1963), 26; W.F. Albright, *Yahweh and the Gods of Canaan* (1968), 85. See Commentaries to Genesis 4:17–24. IN THE AGGADAH: Ginzberg, Legends, index; L. Ginzberg, *On Jewish Law and Lore* (1955), 61–62. IN THE APOCRYPHA: M.R. James, *Lost Apocrypha of the Old Testament* (1920), 10–11. **ADD. BIBLIOGRAPHY:** K. Beyer, *Die aramaeischen Texte vom Toten Meer* (1984), 167–69; N. Sarna, *JPS Torah Commentary Genesis* (1989), 36–38; R. Hess, in: ABD, 4:136–37.

LAMECH, BOOK OF, apocryphal book referred to in the List of Sixty Books, a Christian list of canonical and uncanonical books apparently dating from the fifth or sixth century. No definite quotation or fragment of an ancient Book of Lamech is known to exist, and the question arises whether the book relates to Lamech, Noah's father (Gen. 5:25–31), or Lamech, Cain's descendant (Gen. 4:18–24). M.R. James suggests that the book deals with the legend, unknown in Second Temple period sources, that Cain was killed by his own descendant, Lamech. In view, however, of the extensive early witnesses to the story concerning Lamech's role on the occasion of Noah's birth (Gen. Apocryphon col. 2; I En. 106, and the Latin fragment "The Book of *Noah" from Qumran (1Q 19), it is distinctly possible that the Book of Lamech dealt with this and related material. Such a view is supported, and perhaps a new dimension added, by the emphasis placed in Jubilees 7:38, on Lamech's part in the transmission of esoteric traditions first revealed to Enoch. James refers to a Slavonic work telling the story of Lamech's killing of Cain. The Qumran Genesis Apocryphon was mistakenly named by its first investigators "The Book of Lamech."

BIBLIOGRAPHY: M.R. James, *Lost Apocrypha of the Old Testament* (1920), 10–11.

[Michael E. Stone]

LAMED (Heb. ל; לָמֶד), the 12th letter of the Hebrew alphabet; its numerical value is 30. The earliest representation of this letter is a pictograph of an ox-goad. The Phoenician script in the 11th century B.C.E. fixed the stance of the *lamed*, so that the curve was drawn as the base. In the later Phoenician, as well as in the Hebrew and Aramaic, scripts there was a tendency to sharpen the curve into an angle. The diagonal upper stroke began at a higher point than the other letters of the alphabet, while the rightward base was drawn just beneath the ceiling line. In the fifth-century B.C.E. Phoenician *lamed*, a leftward bar resembling a tail was added at the right extremity of its base. A similar development occurred in the fourth-century Aramaic script. As the Aramaic *lamed* of this period consisted of a high vertical downstroke, curving under the ceiling line to the right, the new form with the tail easily turned in the Aramaic cursive into a wavy line. (The Hebrew as well as the Samaritan *lamed* never developed such a tail.) The Hebrew script preserved the tail of the Aramaic *lamed*, and it became a main part of the letter. The Arabic script adopted the Nabatean cursive *lamed*, which is a descendant of the Aramaic wavy line form. The modern Hebrew cursive *lamed*, which developed from the Hebrew book-hand shape of this letter, is essentially also some variation of a wavy line: → . See *Alphabet, Hebrew.

[Joseph Naveh]

LAMED VAV ẒADDIKIM (Heb. ל״ו צַדִּיקִים, "36 righteous men"), the minimal number of anonymous righteous men living in the world in every generation. They are privileged to see the Divine Presence, and the world exists on their merit. The origin of this tradition, found in the Babylonian Talmud, is handed down in the name of the *amora* Abbaye: "there are not less than 36 righteous men in the world who receive the Divine Presence" (Sanh. 97b; Suk. 45b). This number has become renowned in fiction and in folklore, especially in Kabbalah and ḥasidic legends. Many suggestions have been made in the study of the origin of this number and its meaning. The majority are of the opinion that the origin is not Jewish. According to G. Scholem, it is drawn from the astrological belief in 36 celestial decans (see *Astrology), each of which rules ten days of the year and, thus, ten degrees of the constellations. This belief was also widespread in Western-Hellenistic culture and in Oriental teachings. Other conjectures have also been raised, but the subject remains unclear. It should be noted that the number 36 is not exclusively mentioned in the *aggadah* in this connection. The *tanna* R. Simeon b. Yoḥai believed that "the world never lacks 30 righteous" (Gen. R. 35:2, in J. Theodor's edition, 1 (1965²), 330 and parallels) while it is said in the name of R. Simeon b. R. Jehozadak (third century) that "the world exists by the merit of 45 righteous" (Ḥul. 92a). This count, however, is also internally divided into 30 and 15, representing the number of righteous to be found in Ereẓ Israel in contrast to those abroad (i.e., Babylonia; *ibid.*, see also Mid. Ps. 5:5). According to Rav Judah, the number 30 represents the number of "righteous among the nations of the world" (Ḥul. 92a). The widespread dissemination of the number 36 specifically can be attributed to the later Kabbalah, which adopted it.

[*Encyclopaedia Hebraica*]

According to Jewish folklore the hidden saints, called in Yiddish *lamedvovniks*, were responsible for the fate of the world and one of them is considered to be the Messiah. The idea is not found among Oriental Jews. The *lamedvovnik* was unnoticed by other men because of his humble nature and vocation. *Lamedvovniks* figured in kabbalistic folk legend of the 16th–17th centuries and in ḥasidic lore from the end of the 18th century. At times of great peril, however, the *lamedvovnik* makes a dramatic appearance, using his hidden powers to defeat the enemies of Israel, after which he returns, as mysteriously as he came, to his wonted obscurity. A tale in one of the Yiddish chapbooks relates how in Safed one such hidden saint was aided by the *Ari ha-Kadosh* (R. Isaac *Luria) disguised as a certain "Rabbi Nissim." The *lamedvovnik* theme may well have inspired the "Legend of the Three Nephites" in the *Book of Mormon*. In the 20th century, the Jewish tradition was reworked by the French writer André *Schwarz-Bart in his novel *Le dernier des justes* (1959; *The Last of the Just*, 1960), but in a way totally alien to the Jewish spirit, suggesting that the 36 saints were a long and tragic dynasty and that each *lamedvovnik* was "privileged" to become a martyr.

BIBLIOGRAPHY: Beer, in: *Bar Ilan*, 1 (P. Churgin Memorial Vol., 1963), 172–6; G. Scholem, *Das Buch Bahir* (1923), 61f., 68 n.10; idem, in: JC (April 21, 1961), 23; R. Mach, *Der Ẓaddik in Talmud und Midrasch* (1957), esp. 134ff.; Montefiore and Loewe, *Rabbinic Anthology* (1938), 231–2, 665.

LAMEGO, Marrano family, prominent in Hamburg and London. Among its members may be mentioned ISAAC LAMEGO, one of the most substantial merchants in the City of London in the middle of the 18th century; and MOSES LAMEGO, who in 1757, in commemoration of the death of his only son, presented the Sephardi congregation with £5,000 as an endowment for its orphanage and educational institutions. He is probably identical with the "Mr. Lamego" who was a prominent racehorse owner in England in the mid-18th century.

BIBLIOGRAPHY: M. Grunwald, *Portugiesengraeber auf deutscher Erde* (1904), 114; J. Picciotto, *Sketches of Anglo-Jewish History* (1956²), 88, 145–6, 314; M. Gaster, *History of the Ancient Synagogue* (1901), passim; *Gentleman's Magazine* (1759), 551; *Jackson's Oxford Journal*, Jun. 8; Jul. 21, 1754.

[Cecil Roth]

LAMENTATIONS, BOOK OF, one of the Five *Scrolls in the Hagiographa section of the Bible, consisting of five poetic chapters, probably lamenting the destruction of Jerusalem in 587 B.C.E. and its aftermath. (The English title, like the Greek (θρηνοι), Latin (*Lamentationes*), and Syriac (אוליתא) titles, is a translation of the Hebrew קִינוֹת (*Kinot* (*qinot*)), BB 14b; cf. *Sefer Kinot*, Ḥag. 5b; *Megillat Kinot*, TJ, Shab. 16:15c; and in Jerome's *Prologus Galeatus: Cinoth*.) The title more frequently used in Hebrew manuscripts and printings is *Eikhah* (Heb. איכה) after the book's opening word. Its location in the canon is bound up with the larger issue of the order of the Hagiographa (see *Bible: Canon). *Bava Batra* 14b, which does not list the Five Scrolls as a unit (see *Job), places Lamentations seventh in this section of the Bible. Some manuscripts that group the *megillot* together, including the Leningrad manuscript of 1009 C.E. and the Aleppo Codex, as well as the Masoretic work *Adat Devorim*, arrange the group chronologically, placing Lamentations fourth. The standard order followed in most printed Hebrew Bibles, which follows the order in which the *megillot* are read in the Ashkenazi liturgical calendar (starting with Passover), places Lamentations third, corresponding to its recitation on the Ninth of *Av (a custom already presupposed by Sof. 14:1). In the Septuagint, Peshitta, and Vulgate it is located after the Book of Jeremiah – Jeremiah being its supposed author – forming an appendix thereto (the two are connected in the present text of LXX by a statement introducing Lamentations: "And it came to pass, after Israel was taken captive and Jerusalem made desolate, that Jeremiah sat weeping and lamented this lamentation over Jerusalem, and said…"). This connection is not likely to have existed when the Septuagint translations of these books were first made, since the two were translated by different translators, as was demonstrated by T. Noeldeke.

Contents and Ideology

Although the individual chapters do not generally develop particular themes systematically, certain themes do stand out in the various chapters. Chapter 1 refers to Jerusalem as lonely and defiled, abused and abandoned by her former allies, her inhabitants in Exile. Chapter 2 stresses God's role in the disaster, with particular reference to the destruction of various parts of the city, such as the Temple, walls, and gates. Chapter 4, in contrast, stresses the suffering of the city's inhabitants. Chapter 5 describes the distress of those who remained after the destruction.

The ideological core of the book is Chapter 3, in which the poet describes and reflects on his own suffering. The interpretation of this chapter, however, has been the subject of much controversy in recent scholarship. According to the more common interpretation, in chapter 3, the sufferer finally grasps "a necessary relationship between the ordeal thrust upon him and his own actions" (Mintz in Bibl., 12). Although God undoubtedly is the cause of his grievous suffering (3:2–16, 37–38), he takes hope in the realization that God's kindness and mercy have not ended (reading *lo' tammu* in verse 22a)

Opening page of Lamentations, with decorated initial word panel, from a Hebrew illuminated manuscript known as the De Castro Pentatuech, *southern Germany, 1344. Letchworth, England, Sassoon Ms. 506, p.697.*

but are renewed every morning (3:21–23). Furthermore, God is good to those who trust Him and seek Him; it is good to accept one's suffering and wait in silence for God's deliverance – in fact it is good for a man, when young, to bear a yoke (3:25–30), for the Lord does not reject forever, but ultimately pardons, for He does not afflict man willfully (3:31–36). Since God does not afflict willfully (Lam. 3:33–36), the ultimate cause can only be the sufferer's own sin (3:39). Now the poet shifts to the first person plural as he draws the practical inference of his observations: "Let us search and examine our ways, and turn back to the Lord…" (3:40–41), frankly admitting our guilt (3:42). The poem then reverts to the lamentation form with which it began, concluding with a plea to God for deliverance and vengeance (3:43–66).

In this reading, the poet proffers the view that Israel's destruction was caused by its own guilt. The punishment was earned, not arbitrary (3:33–39), and only submission could bring it to an end (3:40–41). The theory of suffering expressed in verses 25–36, then, is that of the wisdom tradition; many of its features are expressed in certain psalms, in Proverbs, Ben Sira, and in the arguments of Job's friends. Like Lamentations 3:27, this tradition holds that suffering can benefit a person. The classic expression of this view is Proverbs 3:11–12: "My son, reject not the Lord's discipline; Abhor not His chastisement. For the Lord chastises him whom He loves, As a father does the son he favors" (cf. Ps. 94:12–15; Job 5:17). Lamentations adapts this theory in order to explain the suffering not only of an individual but also of an entire nation.

In the alternative reading (see Dobbs-Alsopp, Linafelt, O'Connor, and Cooper in Bibl.), the sufferer does not acquiesce so readily to a wisdom-based theodicy. He is less concerned with explaining his suffering than with finding a way of putting an end to it. In his desperate quest for relief, he will try anything – even turn the other cheek (3:30), or profess an absurd faith in divine goodness that is at odds with his own experience (3:31–36). The hopeful possibilities turn out to be illusory: after that bit of soul-searching, the situation is no less desperate than before. The poet's call for self-examination in 3:40 has no apparent effect: God refuses to forgive (3:42), murders pitilessly, and blocks out prayer (3:42–46). The chapter opens with the details of the sufferer's gruesome victimization (3:2–16); the dominant theme is a parody of Psalm 23: "the Lord is a shepherd who misleads, a ruler who oppresses and imprisons" (Hillers in Bibl., 124). That description is complemented by the conclusion of the poem (3:52–66), which includes a parody of a thanksgiving psalm (3:52–61), a description of the speaker's suffering at the hands of his enemies, and a plea for revenge (3:62–66). The beginning of the poem is linked to the end by forms of the root *shuv*: "God has turned against *me*" (*bi yashuv*, 3:3) is transformed into "Take vengeance against *them*" (*tashiv lahem gemul*, 3:64). In chapter 4, God represents nothing to the poet except wrath and destruction.

The source of this bleak alternative reading of chapter 3 is not wisdom theology, but the widespread "personal religion" of the ancient Near East. Personal religion is a "religious attitude in which the religious individual sees himself as standing in a close personal relationship to the divine, expecting help and guidance in his personal life and personal affairs, expecting divine punishment if he sins, but also profoundly trusting to divine compassion, forgiveness, and love for him if he sincerely repents" (T. Jacobsen in Bibl., 147). The sufferer in chapter 3 recognizes God as the source of his suffering, and acknowledges his sinfulness in a general way, as part of being human, but he does not see his suffering as just punishment for his sin. Rather, he finds the extent of God's anger incomprehensible; his only hope is that crying out in his wretchedness will evoke God's compassion.

Aside from the possible affinity with the wisdom tradition noted above, the book generally reflects the ideology of popular religion (Y. Kaufmann). In particular, ideological affinities with classical prophecy are lacking. The book describes the demise of those institutions in which nations customarily place their trust, and the tone of the description shows the author to have shared this trust: he grieves over the spoliation and destruction of the Temple and its cult (1:4, 10; 2:1, 6, 7), the fate of priests and prophets (1:4, 19; 2:6, 9, 20; 4:16), king and princes, warriors, and officers (1:6, 15; 2:2, 6, 9; 4:7–8, 20; 5:12), the failure of the city's fortifications (4:12), and her defensive alliances (1:2; 4:17). Prior to the disaster, he may have thought that the city and its institutions were inviolable, owing to God's protective presence (Brunet, Albrektson in Bibl.). The classical prophets', especially Jeremiah's, excoriation of trust in these is nowhere reflected (2:14 reflects hindsight rather than the classical prophetic view on the popular prophets).

Lamentations also is perfunctory when it comes to the nature of Israel's sins. One searches the book almost in vain for the mention of a specific sin. Idolatry is not mentioned. Nowhere do we hear of the sins for which classical prophecy threatened destruction: social injustice, oppression of the weaker classes, bribery, and so on. Only 4:13 appears to specify a sin: "It was for the sins of her prophets, the iniquities of her priests, /Who had shed in her midst the blood of the innocent." It is not clear under what circumstances the priests and prophets are supposed to have shed innocent blood, since elsewhere in the Bible it is kings and ministers who are accused of this crime. The accusation does not carry conviction; it strikes one as a grasping at straws. It is a conventional accusation of the sort that biblical authors frequently level against nations and kings as well as individuals (cf. II Kings 21:16; 24:4; Isa. 1:15; 59:7; Ezek. 7:23; 16:38; 18:10; 22:3, et al.). In Lamentations it gives the impression of an attempt to account for a calamity that the author could not really explain. A measure of his difficulty is provided in 5:7, where he complains "Our fathers sinned and are no more; /And we must bear their guilt" – a complaint that echoes the popular view mentioned and rejected by Jeremiah and Ezekiel (Jer. 31:28; Ezek. 18:2). The poet does not thereby disclaim any responsibility by his own generation, for just nine verses later he laments "Woe to us that we have sinned!" (5:16); but by invoking the sins of the fathers as at least partial explanation, he shows how difficult it was for him – quite unlike the classical prophets – to discover a sufficient measure of sinfulness in his own generation. Finally, the peculiar vacillation between hope and despair in the difficult concluding verses of the book perfectly epitomizes the equivocal nature of the book as a whole (see Linafelt in Bibl., 59–61). It follows that Lamentations' acknowledgement of sin is based on theological cliché, rooted in the widespread popular religious conceptions of the ancient Near East rather than a coherent biblical theology.

Style

The book describes the destruction and suffering from the viewpoint of several speakers (see Lanahan and Kaiser), and uses various metaphors. The subject of chapters 1–2 is Lady Zion. The great lady who was virtually a goddess (*rabbati* in 1:1 could be read as a divine epithet) is now abased. In 1:1–11b the poet describes her suffering in the third person, while in 11b–22 (excepting verse 17) Zion herself speaks. The third-person description is more brutal and explicit, verging on the pornographic in 1:8–10; the first-person account is more sympathetic. Chapter 2 features the same female personification, though somewhat less pronounced; in 2:1–10 the poet describes the destruction, speaking of Zion in the third person again, while in 11–17 he turns lyric, expressing his own sorrow and (13–17) addressing Jerusalem and her wall in the second person; in 18 or 19–22 he calls upon the city or the wall to cry out to God, and describes what is to be said. In 3:1–39 the speaker is a man who describes his own suffering in the first person singular, in the style of the individual laments in Psalms (see Westermann); in verses 40–47 (beginning with the letter *nun*, which is the Hebrew first person plural prefix) there is a shift to the first person plural, and the style is that of the national lament; in verses 48–51 the speaker is an individual mourning the fate of the city; and in verses 52–66 the lament of the individual sufferer, with which the poem began, resumes. The mixture of styles is certainly original in the chapter, since the acrostic structure presupposes all of these sections. The identity of the man speaking in the individual lament portion of the chapter has been the subject of many theories. Naturally many have thought him to be Jeremiah, both on the basis of his own suffering (which cannot easily be correlated with the description in Chapter 3) and his supposed authorship of the book (see below). Kaufmann identifies him as Zedekiah, Judah's last king, since Zedekiah's fate aptly symbolized the fate of the nation. R. Gordis suggests no specific individual, but invokes the concept of "fluid personality" and sees the poet as identifying his own suffering with that of his nation; D. Hillers similarly identifies the speaker with "Everyman." O. Eissfeldt treats the individual as a literary device personifying Jerusalem or Judah. Chapters 4 and 5 do not employ metaphors or personification for Judah and Jerusalem; 4:1–16 consist of a third person description of the suffering of Zion's inhabitants; 17–20 of a first person plural description of pursuit and frustrated hopes. In 21–22 the poet apostrophizes triumphant Edom, telling her that her time will come, too, and Zion, telling her that her sin is now expiated. Chapter 5 is a first person plural prayer calling upon God to take note of the suffering following the destruction.

The first four poems are alphabetic acrostics, as if to express the gamut of sorrow from *a* to *z* (see Gottwald in Bibl.). In chapters 1 and 2 each letter of the alphabet introduces a verse of three lines (1:7 and 2:19 have four). Chapter 3 is a triple acrostic with each letter introducing each of three successive stichs; in chapter 4 each letter introduces a verse of two lines (chs. 2–4 have an unusual alphabetic order, with פ preceding ע; this alternative to the usual order is attested in an inscription from the biblical period; see *Alphabet). Chapter 5, while not acrostic, has 22 verses (like ch. 1, 2, 4), corresponding to the number of letters in the Hebrew alphabet, of one line each. Because of the limitations imposed on the poet's choice of words by the alphabetic structure, the logical connection of the verses is somewhat loose (in 3:17–42 these limitations have been largely overcome); themes are treated where the alphabet provides opportunity; the exegete must consequently piece together a complete picture of a theme from various passages.

Chapters 1–2, as noted by A. Condamin, also display chiasmus: with 1:22, 21, 20, 19, 18, and 12 echoing, respectively, 1:1, 2, 3, 4, 5, and 11; and with 2:22, 21, 20, 13, and 12 echoing, respectively, 2:1, 2, 3, 10, and 11. Symmetrical design has been discerned more recently in chapters 3 and 4 as well (see Brandscheidt, Renkema, Cooper). On the possible chronological arrangement of the chapters, see below.

Lamentations incorporates elements of the lamentation form known from elsewhere in the Bible, in funeral dirges, national laments, and other expressions of grief and regret. Typical is the opening of chapters 1, 2, and 4 with (ה)איכ, *eikh(ah)*, introducing a description of unexpected reversal of good fortune (cf. II Sam. 1:19ff.; Isa. 14:4ff.; Jer. 9:18; Zeph. 2:15). Each of the poems ends on a note of prayer or confidence (1:20–22; 2:18–22; 3:64–66; 4:22; 5:20–21), as do other biblical laments (Ps. 28:6–9; 44:25–27; 74:19–23, et al.). The book's acknowledgement of guilt is paralleled in individual laments (Ps. 38:5, 19; 51:3ff.), but this element is rare in the national laments in Psalms (Ps. 79:8–9), which more frequently protest innocence (Ps. 44:18–23) or at least confess no guilt; on the other hand, national laments appearing in the prophets do express guilt (Jer. 3:25; 14:7, 20; Hos. 6:1, 3; 14:3b–4), suggesting that this was an original element in the genre (Eissfeldt in bibl., 113–14). Chapters 1–4 often employ distichs in which the second hemistich is shorter than the first, which seems to die away in the second, producing a choked or sobbing effect (e.g., 1:5; 2:5; 3:1ff.; 4:7; 5:2–3). Since this pattern appears in some other biblical laments (e.g., Isa. 14:4ff.; Ezek. 19; Amos 5:2), and was first identified in Lamentations, it is often called the elegiac or *qinah* meter; however, other laments lack this meter (e.g., II Sam. 1:19ff.; 3:33–34), and at the same time it also appears in other types of compositions (e.g., Song 5:9ff.; Ps. 19:8ff.); understanding of the meter of biblical poetry is too poor to allow for definite conclusions.

Authorship and Date

Lamentations itself contains no statement of its authorship. The tradition that Jeremiah wrote the book is reflected in the introductory verses of the present Septuagint (see above) and the Targum, the book's complete Greek and Latin titles (θρῆνοι Ἰερεμίου, *lamentationes Jeremiae prophetae*), and rabbinic sources (BB 15a, et al.). Beyond the fact that (1) Jeremiah was, in the eyes of later generations, the dominant personality who lived through the disaster, this tradition may have been prompted to some extent by (2) similar metaphors and expressions in Jeremiah and Lamentations, (3) by Jeremiah's call, before the destruction, for a lament to be uttered over it by himself and others (Jer. 7:29; 9:9, 19), (4) by the statement that Jeremiah composed a lament over Josiah which is written "in the laments" (II Chron. 35:25; cf. Jos., Ant., 10:5, 78; the Targum actually takes Lam. 4:20 to refer to Josiah), and (5) by presumed references to Jeremiah's life in 3:14, 53–56 (cf. Jer. 20:7; 38:6ff.). Modern advocates of Jeremianic authorship stress (2) in particular.

Most modern scholars deny Jeremianic authorship. Arguments (1) and (3) are clearly inconclusive. Stylistic similarities (2) may indicate at most literary influence or a common contemporary idiom, and in view of similarities to Deuteronomy (Kaufmann, in bibl., 597) and Ezekiel (Perles, in bibl., 98; Löhr, in bibl., 31–50) as well, an explanation along these lines seems more likely. Jeremiah's lament over Josiah (4) refers not to the events of 587 but to one in 609. The supposed references to Jeremiah's life (5) are nothing more than literary clichés standard in individual laments, and Lamentations 3:54 in fact contradicts Jeremiah 38:6. The most telling argument is that of ideology: as noted above, the viewpoints of Lamentations and classical prophecy conflict on fundamental issues. For example, the author of Lamentations is one of those who counted on foreign help and who trusted in Zedekiah (4:17, 20), while Jeremiah denounced reliance on other nations and predicted doom for Zedekiah (Jer. 2:18, 36b; 24:8–10). Jeremiah, who pointed out Israel's sins on many occasions and to whom the destruction was self-understood, could hardly have been as vague and uncertain about Israel's sin as the author of Lamentations is.

There is some reason to doubt that all the chapters are from the same hand. The usual type of argument from style is of course notoriously subjective. However, the unusual alphabetic order of chapters 2–4 suggests that they may not be by the same author as chapter 1, and the absence of acrostic in chapter 5 suggests the same for it. Numerous linguistic similarities between the chapters can be invoked in favor of the book's unity (Rudolph, Kaufmann, et al.), but these might also be explained by literary influence or a common contemporary style, and/or a vocabulary characteristic of the literary genre. Hence, though for convenience it is customary to speak of "the author," there is a strong possibility of several authors. It is at least arguable that the author(s) belonged to the upper classes or the court circles. This is suggested by his devotion to royalty (4:7–8), his esteem for the leaders (1:6), and his concern for the suffering of the well-to-do (4:5). Chapter 4, verse 19 implies that the author was among the party that fled with Zedekiah but escaped when he was captured (II Kings 25:4–6). While sins of priests and prophets are mentioned (2:14; 4:13), those of the king and officials are not.

Dating the individual chapters is an especially elusive problem, and the following remarks are offered with reserve. It seems quite likely that the author is a contemporary of the events that he describes, since he so frequently seems to have shared the hopes, disappointments, and experiences of the period of destruction (see esp. 4:17–20). W. Rudolph argues that chapter 1 presupposes only the events of 598, since it does not mention the destruction of Jerusalem (cf. R. Judah in Lam. R. 1:1, 20 (ed. Buber, 22a) who dates the entire book to the reign of Jehoiakim). However, in this and other details the chapter could as well reflect the events of 587 before the final destruction and deportation following the seventh of Av (II Kings 25:8ff.). Chapters 2 and 4 could be slightly later than that date: Zedekiah has been captured and taken to Babylon (2:9; 4:20; cf. II Kings 25:6–7), the Temple and the city walls have been destroyed (2:1, 4, 6–9, 17 (but cf. 18); 4:1, 11; cf. II Kings 25:9–10), but the deportation (II Kings 25:11) is as yet incomplete, and starvation (cf. II Kings 25:3) continues (Lam. 2:10–12, 19–22; 4:3–5, 8, 17). Chapter 3 offers no firm criteria for dating. Chapter 5 speaks as if the suffering and subjugation have continued for some time (e.g., 5:20); the Temple Mount is now desolate (5:18). How much later than the destruction the chapter was written cannot be determined. Certainly none of the chapters can postdate Cyrus' proclamation of 538 (II Chron. 36:22–23; Ezra 1:1–4), since the hope that it engendered is not reflected in the book.

If the above chronology should be correct, chapters 1, 2, 4, and 5 would seem to be ordered chronologically: chapter 1 before the burning of the Temple and city; chapters 2 and 4 after the burning but before the deportation is complete; chapter 5 somewhat later.

Relation to Mesopotamian Lamentations

Lamentations over destroyed cities and temples are known from Mesopotamia. Several Sumerian laments date from the early second millennium B.C.E., while Akkadian laments date from the first millennium B.C.E. Numerous parallels in subject matter – hunger, destruction of city and temple, pillage, flight, captivity, wailing – might reflect similar experiences, or might be evidence of a more specific literary relationship. In recent years, scholars have taken up these comparisons in detail (see Ferris, Dobbs-Alsopp, and Emmendörfer in Bibl.). In addition, there have been suggestive comparisons of Lamentations with genres of Mesopotamian penitential literature other than the city and temple laments (see, e.g., Gwaltney and Cooper in Bibl.), and these, too, have been productive for the interpretation of Lamentations. These studies have shown that Lamentations uses many of the same rhetorical strategies as contemporary Mesopotamian laments: the plea to an unanswering god; the invective against the enemy; the detailed description of the suffering; and the changes of person. The overall intention of Lamentations may be comparable to the purpose of the Mesopotamian laments as well. It is to quench the burning anger of the god(s), as is clearly indicated by two of the major genre designations, "Lament for Calming the Heart," and "Incantation for Appeasing an Angry God." In these prayers, as in Lamentations, the speaker's suffering and misfortune are in the foreground, alongside acknowledgement of the divine anger that caused the suffering. For example, in a text reminiscent of Lamentations 5:7: "Drive out from my body illness that is from known and unknown iniquity … the iniquity of clan, kith, and kin, that has come upon me because of the raging anger of my god and goddess." As in Lamentations, the penitent confesses in a general way: "The iniquities of mankind are more numerous than the hairs on his head." Like the poet in Lamentations 5:21, the Mesopotamian sufferer seeks a return to a former, happier time: "For me may the heart of my god become as it was." The speaker acknowledges guilt, and recognizes divine wrath as the cause of suffering, but the confessional element is not integrated into a "prophetic" scheme of sin, punishment, repentance, and forgiveness.

[Jeffrey Howard Tigay / Alan Cooper (2nd ed.)]

In the Arts

The Lamentations traditionally ascribed to Jeremiah have given rise to the literary term "jeremiad" (from Late Latin by way of French), in the sense of a prolonged complaint or lament. Writers directly inspired by the Book of Lamentations are, however, comparatively rare. In the 16th century, Jan Kochanowski, the architect of Polish verse, wrote the epic poem *Treny* ("Lamentations," 1580; Eng. selections, 1920), one of several biblical works by this Renaissance author. Two other works of the 17th century were *Lágrimas de Hieremías castellanas* (1613) by the Spanish writer Francisco Gómez de Quevedo y Villegos (1580–1645), and the Marrano writer João *Pinto Delgado's *Lamentaciones del Propheta Jeremias* (Rouen, 1627). *Les Lamentations de Jérémie* (Dresden, 1752), a religious poem by François-Thomas de Baculard d'Arnaud (1718–1805), is best remembered for a satirical epigram which it drew from *Voltaire. The Latin (Vulgate) text of Lamentations was included in the French writer D. Desmarchais' four-canto poem *Jérémie* (1772). A powerful work of the 19th century was *Skargi Jeremiego* ("The Lamentations of Jeremiah," 1893), a poem written in 1847–48 by Kornel Ujejski, who commemorated the sufferings of the oppressed Poles and the heroism of Adam *Mickiewicz.

In Music

Treatments of the subject in music far outnumber those in literature. (For the traditional Jewish musical rendition, see The Five *Scrolls, Musical Rendition.) Several melodic patterns for the recitations of Lamentations in the Roman Catholic Church are known from the manuscript tradition of the Gregorian chant, although one version only is now commonly used. The melodic recitation includes not only the text itself, but also the opening sentence *Incipit lamentatio Jeremiae prophetae* (a practice found also in the other biblical and New Testament readings of the Roman rite) and the Hebrew letters *aleph, beth,* etc., which mark the beginning of each verse or group of verses in the acrostic chapters 1 to 4; and a concluding sentence for each section, *Jerusalem, Jerusalem, convertere ad Dominum Deum tuum.* The Hebrew letter names are set to long melismas (melodic arabesques), which are also imitated in the art music settings of Lamentations. During the baroque period, the practice arose of setting *Jerusalem, Jerusalem* as a series of calls, preferably with echo effects. Until well into the baroque period, art music settings were always based on the traditional melodies, which (sung by the tenor voice) formed the "skeleton" of a simple harmonic construction.

Ten examples of the traditional *Tonus Lamentationum* from various regions can be found in B. Staeblein, "Lamentatio" (in MGG, 8 (1960), cols. 135–9). The resemblance of two of these to Jewish traditional melodies was pointed out by A.Z. *Idelsohn (Idelsohn, Music, 51, 55–56). Many of the others, too, evoke some association with various Jewish recitations of *Eikhah* (Lamentations) or of the **kinot*. However, the intrinsic plausibility of a common heritage has still to be proved by a far more rigorous comparative and historical reconstruction than that at present available in the work of Idelsohn and his successors (cf. *Music, Jewish; Introduction).

The first polyphonic settings of Lamentations made their appearance in the 15th century in the works of composers of the "Netherland" school. In 1454, Guillaume Dufay wrote a four-voice motet on the fall of Constantinople, *O très piteux*, for the "Banquet of the Pheasant" held in Lille by Philip the Good of Burgundy and intended to open a new Crusade. The liturgical melody of Lamentations is sung in Latin by the tenor, while the other voices sing the French poem. Two collections of polyphonic Lamentations by various composers were among the first products of music printing (Petrucci, Venice, 1506); and by the end of the 16th century more than a dozen similar collections had appeared in Italy, France, and Germany. C. Morales' *Lamentations* (1564) represent the first unified composition of the entire text by a single composer, and this became the common practice. The list of composers of Lamentations is practically identical with that of the major composers of the 16th century. Until 1587, the Papal Chapel sang the settings by Genet (Carpentras); these were then replaced by those of Palestrina themselves which were partly superseded after 1641 by those of Allegri. Other notable settings of the 17th century were those of William Byrd, Viadana, and Rosenmueller.

During the 17th, and especially the 18th century, extended compositions of the text became particularly prominent in French music, usually under the name of *Leçon de Ténèbres*. The liturgical melody was abandoned in favor of free composition, although the principle was retained, i.e., the *Incipit lamentatio*, the melisma on the Hebrew letter names, and the *Jerusalem, Jerusalem* call. The *Leçons* of Marc-Antoine Charpentier, Michel-Richard de Lalande, and François Couperin are particularly well known (see T. Kaeser, *Die Leçon de Ténèbres im 17. und 18. Jahrhundert*, 1966). Johann Sebastian Bach's cantata no. 46., *Schauet doch und sehet* (Leipzig, 1723–27), is mainly based on Lam. 1:12–13. Other interesting 18th-century settings are that by Antonio Soler and the motet for solo voice and basso continuo on the Latin text of Lamentations 1 by Jean-Jacques Rousseau (dated 1772).

The Book of Lamentations was virtually ignored by composers of the 19th century. However, there has been a significant revival of interest and a rise in quality and quantity during the 20th century. The most notable modern works are Ernst Křenek's *Lamentatio Jeremiae Prophetae*, for a capella choir, opus 93 (composed 1941/42); Manuel *Rosenthal's *Deux prières pour les temps malheureux* (composed 1942); Leonard *Bernstein's *Jeremiah Symphony* (his first), which contains a middle section in which the Hebrew text of Lamentations 1 is sung by a mezzo-soprano (written 1943); Alberto Ginastera's *Hieremiae prophetae Lamentationes*, three motets for mixed choir a capella (1946); Edmund Rubbra's *Tenebrae-9 Lamentations* for orchestra (1951); and Igor Stravinsky's *Threni, id est Lamentationes Jeremiae Prophetae* for soloists, choir, and orchestra (première, 1958).

[Bathja Bayer]

BIBLIOGRAPHY: COMMENTARIES: F. Perles (Heb., 1930); W. Rudolph (Ger., 1962^{2}); B. Albrektson, *Studies in the Text and Theology of the Book of Lamentations* (1963); R. Gordis, in: *Seventy-fifth Anniversary Volume of the JQR* (1967), 267–86; idem, in: JQR, 58 (1967), 14–33; H.J. Kraus (Ger., 1968^{3}); T.F. McDaniel, in: *Biblica*, 49 (1968), 27–53, 199–220; G. Brunet (Fr., 1968). **ADD. BIBLIOGRAPHY:** H.J. Boecker (Ger., 1985); I.W. Provan (1991); O. Kaiser (Ger., 1992^{4}); D.R. Hillers (1992^{2}); J. Renkema (1998); A. Berlin (2002); F.W. Dobbs-Allsopp (2002); K.M. O'Connor, *Lamentations and the Tears of the World* (2002). INTRODUCTIONS: S.R. Driver, *An Introduction to the Literature of the Old Testament* (1913), 456–65; E.G. Hirsch and M. Löhr, in: JE, 7 (1925), 597–9; R.H. Pfeiffer, *Introduction to the Old Testament* (1948), 720–23; O. Eissfeldt, *The Old Testament, An Introduction* (1965), 500–5; E. Sellin-G. Fohrer, *Introduction to the Old Testament* (1968), 295–9; H.L. Ginsberg (ed.), *The Five Megilloth and the Book of Jonah* (1969), 33–34. **ADD. BIBLIOGRAPHY:** B.S. Childs, *Introduction to the Old Testament as Scripture* (1974), 590–97; D.R. Hillers, in: ABD, 4 (1992), 137–41. SPECIAL STUDIES: M. Löhr, in: ZAW, 14 (1894), 31–59; 24 (1904), 1–16; 25 (1905), 173–98. **ADD. BIBLIOGRAPHY:** Y. Kaufmann, Toledot, 3 (1960), 584–601; N.K. Gottwald, *Studies in the Book of Lamentations* (1962^{2}); A. Condamin, in: JTS, 7 (1905/6), 137–40; W.F. Lanahan, in: JBL, 93 (1974), 41–49; A. Mintz, in: *Prooftexts*, 2 (1982), 1–17; R. Brandscheidt, *Gotteszorn und Menschenleid* (1983); B. Johnson, in: ZAW, 97 (1985), 58–73; B.B. Kaiser, in: JR, 67 (1987), 164–82; C. Westermann, *Lamentations: Issues and Interpretation* (1994); F.W. Dobbs-Allsopp, in JSOT, 74 (1997), 29–60; K.M. Heim, in: *Zion: City of Our God* (1999), 129–69; T. Linafelt, *Surviving Lamentations* (2000); A. Cooper, in: JANES, 28 (2001), 1–18; M.J. Boda, in: HBT, 25 (2003), 51–75. EXTRA-BIBLICAL LAMENTATIONS: T.F. McDaniel, in: VT, 18 (1968), 198–209; T. Jacobsen, *Treasures of Darkness* (1976); W.C. Gwaltney, in: *Scripture in Context II* (1983), 191–211; P.W. Ferris, *The Genre of Communal Lament in the Bible and the Ancient Near East* (1992); F.W. Dobbs-Allsopp, *Weep, O Daughter of Zion* (1993); M. Emmendörfer, *Der ferne Gott* (1998). PLACE OF LAMENTATIONS IN THE CANON: L. Blau, in: JE, 3 (1902), 144; 8 (1904), 429–31; C.D. Ginsburg, *Introduction to the Massoretico-Critical Edition of the Hebrew Bible* (1966), 3–4. **ADD. BIBLIOGRAPHY:** G. Stemberger, in: JBT, 18 (2003), 261–76.

LAMENTATIONS RABBAH (Heb. *Eikhah Rabbati*), aggadic Midrash on the Book of Lamentations, the product of Palestinian *amoraim*.

The Name

In medieval rabbinic literature *Lamentations Rabbah* was also called *Aggadat Eikhah, Megillat Eikhah, Midrash Kinot, Eikhah Rabbati, Eikhah Rabbah*, etc. The designation "*Rabbati*" derives apparently from the verse: "How doth the city sit solitary, that was full of (*rabbati*) people" (Lam. 1:1); and is therefore not the same as the "*Rabbah*" by which the Midrashim to other books of the Bible are called (see *Genesis Rabbah* and *Ruth Rabbah*).

The Structure

Lamentations Rabbah is an exegetical Midrash which expounds the Book of Lamentations verse by verse, and sometimes word by word. It is a compilation of various expositions and *aggadot*. The work is divided into five sections, corresponding to the chapters of the Book of Lamentations. It has 36 proems (*petihata de-ḥakkimei*, "proems of the sages"), ap-

First page of Lamentations Rabbah, *the second part of* Midrash Rabbah. *Venice, 1545, Jerusalem, J.N.U.L.*

parently to correspond to the numerical value of איכה (*Eikhah*; the printed versions appear, at first glance, to have only 34, but two of them, 2 and 31, contain two proems each). These are of the classical type of proem found in amoraic Midrashim, introduced by an extraneous verse which is subsequently connected with the beginning of the Book of Lamentations. In 20 proems the extraneous verse is taken from the Prophets (10 from Jeremiah), in 13 it comes from the Hagiographa (2 from the Book of Lamentations itself), and only in 3 is the extraneous verse from the Pentateuch. Nearly all begin with the name of a sage (an *amora*), and are grouped according to the number of expositions given by him in diminishing order: first come the proems of the sages in whose name begin four, then three, then two, and finally one, proem.

The Midrash contains many *aggadot* and homilies on the destruction of the Temple (1:16) and the sorrows of subjugation and exile. On the other hand there are also *aggadot* with a message of comfort and encouragement to the mourning and oppressed Jewish people, and also entire sections devoted to humorous stories, such as those depicting the cleverness of Jerusalemites in comparison with the Athenians (1:1), which aim at finding consolation for the destruction of the Temple and for the defeat in the Jewish people's spiritual superiority over other nations. The Midrash also contains many *aggadot* on the Bar Kokhba revolt (2:2).

The Language

The language, like that of the Jerusalem Talmud, is a mixture of mishnaic Hebrew and Galilean *Aramaic, in which most of the stories and *aggadot* are written. The Midrash also includes many Greek words, as also a complete sentence in Latin: *vive domine imperator* ("Long live my lord the emperor"; 1:5).

The Date of its Redaction

Except for some later additions, the entire Midrash, including the proems, is a compilation redacted by a single redactor. No sage later than the fourth century C.E. is mentioned in it. The list of kingdoms that subjugated the Jewish people concludes with "Edom Seir," i.e., Rome and Byzantium (1:14). The redactor used tannaitic literature, the Jerusalem Talmud, *Genesis Rabbah*, and **Leviticus Rabbah*. *Lamentations Rabbah* itself was used as a source for *Ruth Rabbah* and probably also for **Pesikta de-Rav Kahana*, as well as for later Midrashim. In view of this and of its language, it was apparently redacted in Ereẓ Israel at about the end of the fifth century C.E. It is explicitly mentioned for the first time only in R. *Hananel's commentary to the Talmud.

In addition to availing himself of popular *aggadot*, the redactor made extensive use of homilies delivered in synagogues on the Ninth of Av. The scarcity of comforting *aggadot* is thus explained not only by the character of Lamentations but also by the prohibition of delivering comforting homilies on the Ninth of Av. *Lamentations Rabbah* is the earliest source that gives a list of the *Ten Martyrs of the Hadrianic persecutions (2:2), and is the first rabbinic work to give the *aggadah* of the mother and her seven sons (*Hannah and her Seven Sons), the mother here (1:16) being called Miriam the daughter of Tanḥum (or Naḥtom). This version is based not only on its source in II *Maccabees but also on the account and significance given to it in IV *Maccabees; however it is clear that neither was directly used by the author or redactor.

Editions

The work was first published at Pesaro in 1519 together with the Midrashim on the other four scrolls (Song of Songs, Ruth, Ecclesiastes, Esther), although they are not homogenous. This edition became the basis of the many subsequent ones. In 1899 S. *Buber published a scholarly edition, based on manuscripts, with an introduction and notes. Despite its defects and inaccuracies it represented at the time a considerable advance. Most of the manuscripts of the Midrash have not thus far been utilized.

BIBLIOGRAPHY: C. Raphael, *The Walls of Jerusalem* (1968); Zunz-Albeck, Derashot, 78f., Strack-Stemberger, *Introduction to the Talmud and Midrash* (1996), 283–87; P. Mandel, in: *Transmitting Jewish Traditions* (2000), 74–106; idem, in: *Ginze Kedem* (2005), 163–70; idem, in: *Merkaz u-Tefuẓah* (2004), 141–58; G. Hasan-Rokem, in: *Tarbiz*, 59:1–2 (1990), 109–31; Z.M. Rabinowitz, *Ginze Midrash* (1977), 144–54.

[Moshe David Herr]

LAMM, MARTIN (1880–1950), Swedish literary historian. Born in Stockholm, the son of a leading liberal politician

HERMAN FREDRIK LAMM (1853–1928), Martin Lamm was an outstanding pupil of Johan Henrik *Schück. In 1919 he succeeded Karl Johan *Warburg as professor of the history of literature at the Stockholm Academy (later the University of Stockholm). Like Schück, he was a stimulating teacher and attracted a host of students to his lectures. His major works include a monograph on the 18th-century Swedish philosopher Emanuel Swedenborg (1915); *Upplysningstidens romantik* (2 vols., 1918–20), a monumental study of romanticism in the age of Enlightenment which was translated into French and German; the classic *Strindbergs dramer* (2 vols., 1924–26); and his outstanding monograph, *August Strindberg* (2 vols., 1940–42). With his election to the Swedish Academy in 1928, Lamm became one of the men responsible for selecting recipients of the Nobel Prize for literature.

BIBLIOGRAPHY: I. Anderson, *Martin Lamm* (Swed., 1950); *Svenska män och kvinnor*, 4 (1948), s.v.; *Svenskt litteraturlexikon* (1964).

[Hugo Mauritz Valentin]

LAMM, NORMAN (1927–), Yeshiva University president, educator, and scholar. Born in Brooklyn, Lamm attended Mesivta Torah VoDaat yeshivah, and then Yeshiva College. He received rabbinical ordination at RIETS in 1951. In 1966 he received his Ph.D. from Yeshiva University and was on its faculty for 17 years. He also served as communal leader, first as assistant rabbi of New York City's Kehillath Jeshurun Synagogue, then as spiritual leader of Congregation Kadima in Springfield, Mass., and still later as spiritual leader of Manhattan's Jewish Center.

He was the founding editor of *Tradition*, the major journal of Orthodox thought, and also served as editor of "The Library of Jewish Law and Ethics."

When Yeshiva University president Samuel Belkin passed away in 1976 Lamm was elected to that position, which he held for 25 years. It was as head of Yeshiva University that he made a major impact on Jewish education in America. Lamm has been a strong proponent of the Torah u-Madda approach, of combining traditional Jewish learning with modern secular studies. He has been one of the foremost leaders of Modern or Centrist orthodoxy, between Conservative and Reform Judaism on the left, and *ḥaredi* Judaism on the right. For him, while living by *halakhah* is the heart of Jewish duty and life, religious coercion is unacceptable. Lamm was a supporter of the efforts to solve the "Who is a Jew?" problem. He has worked for unity between all streams of Judaism though strongly opposed the Reform decision to make patrilineal descent a criterion for defining Jewishness.

Lamm is one of the most important of modern Jewish thinkers and published ten books and many articles. Among the subjects Lamm has written about are the nature of Jewish and rabbinic leadership, man's position in the universe, the religious implications of extraterrestrial life, ecology in Jewish law and theology, and privacy in law and theology.

Lamm's tenure at Yeshiva was not without controversy. The university expanded greatly under his leadership. He set it on a firm economic foundation, increasing its endowment, enhancing the prestige of its graduate schools and medical school. The extreme right wing opposed his advocacy of Torah u-Madda and his position on conversion. From time to time, Rabbi Lamm was embarrassed by those who opposed the toleration of certain groups on campus, such as gay and lesbian organizations. Lamm's attacks on false piety and the excess emphasis on externals rather than true Jewish spirituality also won him opponents. In 1999 a group of rabbis broke away from Yeshiva. On the whole though he has been a consensus leader, one able to work successfully with other leaders.

After retiring as president of Yeshiva in 2001 he was appointed chancellor of the University. It was noted that the university could not find a leader who combined Rabbi Lamm's learning and secular academic achievement; so it bifurcated the role by having new president Richard Joel lead the University and Rabbi Lamm remain as chancellor and *rosh yeshivah*.

BIBLIOGRAPHY: D. Nussbaum Cohen, "Orthodox Leader Speaks Out on Jewish Unity, Breaking Long Silence," in: *Jewish Telegraphic Agency* (Dec. 5, 1997).

[Shalom Freedman (2nd ed.)]

LAMM, PAVEL ALEKSANDROVICH (1882–1951), Russian pianist and musicologist. Lamm studied in Moscow and was associated with the "House of Song" established by the soprano Marie Olenina-d'Alheim and became her accompanist (1907–13). From 1919 to 1951 he taught at the Moscow Conservatory. He was also director of the State Music Publication Department in Moscow (1918–23) and established a storehouse for scores that had been confiscated from nationalized Russian music publishing houses. Of particular importance is his scholarly edition of the complete works of the composer Mussorgsky, in which by painstaking research he achieved a restoration of the original score. He also restored Borodin's *Prince Igor* and reconstructed Tchaikovsky's *Voyevoda*, which the latter had destroyed and which Lamm was able to reassemble from separate orchestra parts and sketches. He also edited and published unknown works by Tchaikovsky, Taneyev, and other Russian composers, and wrote studies on Russian and Soviet musicians.

BIBLIOGRAPHY: Kisselev, in: *Sovetskaya Muzyka*, no. 6 (1951).

[Michael Goldstein]

°**LAMPON AND ISIDOROS**, leaders of the Alexandrian anti-Jewish movement during the reigns of the Roman emperors Gaius Caligula (37–41 C.E.) and Claudius (41–54 C.E.). According to Philo both men were *gymnasiarchoi*, i.e., leaders of the Greek educational institute of Alexandria. Whereas, of the two, Isidoros alone appears before the governor of Egypt, Flaccus, both leaders are prominent at the head of a Greek embassy to Caligula in the *Acta Isidori et Lamponis*, fragments of the antisemitic papyrus literature known as the "Acts of the Alexandrine Martyrs." The subject of the *Acta Isidori* is a vicious attack launched against the Jewish king Agrippa before the court of Claudius. The trial probably took place in 41 C.E. for in that year a series of debates on Jewish civic rights came before Claudius, although certain scholars favor the year 53. The dialogue between the emperor and the Alexandrians was extremely heated and at one point, after being rebuked by Claudius, Isidoros replied: "I am neither a slave nor the son of a girl musician, but gymnasiarch of the glorious city of Alexandria. But you are the cast-off son of the Jewess Salome." It is evident that the author's main purpose in the *Acta* is to ridicule the Roman emperor. In any event, Lampon and Isidoros were immediately sentenced to death.

BIBLIOGRAPHY: Schuerer, Gesch, 1 (1901⁴), 68f., 503; Klausner, Bayit Sheni, 4 (1950²), 274, 276, 278; Tcherikover, Corpus, 2 (1960), 66–81, no. 156 (contains bibliography).

[Isaiah Gafni]

LAMPRONTI, ISAAC HEZEKIAH BEN SAMUEL (1679–1756), rabbi, physician, and educator. Lampronti was born in Ferrara and studied under the great Italian rabbis of his generation: Manoah Provençal in Lugo, Judah Briel in Mantua, and Isaac Ḥayyim Cantarini in Padua. In addition, he studied philosophy and medicine at the University of Padua. Returning to Ferrara at the age of 22, he began to teach in the *talmud torah* of the Italian community and later also in the *talmud torah* of the Sephardi community. He introduced many improvements in the curriculum, insisting on the teaching of the humanities concurrently with the study of Torah. In 1718 he was ordained rabbi and in 1743 was appointed head of the yeshivah – a position which gave him the status of senior rabbi of the city. Lampronti was one of the supporters of Moses Ḥayyim *Luzzatto in the controversy which broke out over him. During the whole of this period Lampronti continued to practice as a physician, acquiring a reputation as an outstanding doctor who gave his services for free to those of limited means. In 1715 he began to publish collections of studies – in a form not unlike a periodical for *halakhah* and rabbinic literature – entitled *Bikkurei Keẓir Talmud Torah shel Kehillah Kedoshah Ferrara*. Three issues appeared which included contributions by other rabbis, mainly his own disciples.

Lampronti's main reputation, however, rests on his monumental *Paḥad Yiẓḥak*, two editions of which he wrote himself, the first consisting of 120 and the second of 35 manuscript volumes. *Paḥad Yiẓḥak* is the most comprehensive and well-known encyclopedia in the field of *halakhah*. It is arranged alphabetically, each article including material from the Mishnah, the Talmud, the *posekim*, the *rishonim*, and the responsa literature. He pays special importance to the responsa literature of Italian rabbis, some of which was otherwise unknown, and quotes from it extensively. Some of the articles were apparently taken from the *Petaḥ ha-Ohel* (Sulzbach, 1691) of Abraham of Przemysl. At times Lampronti also relied on quotations from various reference works without making a careful examination of the sources. Many of his own responsa, which are not included in the *Paḥad Yiẓḥak*, appear in the responsa collections of his contemporaries, such as the *Shemesh Ẓedakah* (Venice, 1743) of Samson Morpurgo. On the other hand, his many sermons have been lost. The first portion of the *Paḥad Yiẓḥak* (letters *alef* to *mem*) was published in Italy between 1750 and 1840, and the remainder in Germany between 1864 and 1887. Of the second edition, only two volumes appeared, containing the letters *alef* to *ḥet* (1935–42). The publication of both editions together has been undertaken in recent years (letters *alef-alef* to *alef-shin* appeared, 1962–66).

BIBLIOGRAPHY: Benayahu, in: *Sinai – Sefer ha-Yovel* (1958), 491–503; B.Cohen, in: *Sefer ha-Yovel... A. Marx* (1943), 41–57; Klausner, in: KS (1960/61), 123–6; B. Levi, *Della Vita e dell'Opera di Isacco Lampronti* (1869); idem, *Sefer Toledot ha-Rav ha-Gadol Yiẓḥak Lampronti* (1871); Sonne, in: *Horeb*, 6 (1941), 76–114.

[Daniel Carpi]

LANCASTER, U.S. city in S.E. Pennsylvania; general population 55,182 (2004); estimated Jewish population, 3,000 (mid-1990s). Lancaster is one of the oldest Jewish communities in the U.S. and was the main city of German settlement from colonial times ("Pennsylvania Dutch"). The first known Jew to come to Lancaster was Isaac Miranda (c. 1730). By 1735 a few Jewish traders were known to be in Lancaster, including Joseph *Simon, a trader and landholder who was known throughout Pennsylvania. Lancaster was then the gateway to the West and a place of trade with the Native Americans. A Jewish cemetery was established in 1747, making it the fourth oldest Jewish cemetery in the United States, when a plot of land was deeded to Joseph Simon and Isaac Nunes Henriques for that purpose. Many early Jewish settlers of Lancaster were buried there and the cemetery is still maintained by Congregation Shaarai Shomayim. When Lancaster ceased to be a frontier town, several Jewish families migrated to the Port City of Baltimore. Lancaster's first congregation was gathered in the home of Joseph Simon. (A portion of the ark used there is preserved at the American Jewish Historical Society.) From 1740 to the mid-19th century the Jewish community remained small, consisting of about 10 or 15 families. New families began arriving from 1850 and Congregation Shaarai Shomayim (Reform) was founded in 1856. Its first synagogue was built in 1867 and another one in 1896. The influx of immigrants continued, and in 1895 Congregation Degel Israel (Orthodox) was chartered. By 1904 there were 50 families of German-Jewish extraction and 150 of Russian-Jewish extraction in Lancaster, the latter group having arrived after 1884. Among the Jewish organizations established in the town were the Harmonie Club (1875); Ladies Aid Society (1876); Temple Sisterhood (1894); Council of Jewish Women (1919); Organized Jewish Charities (1927); United Jewish Community Council (1928); Temple Brotherhood (1929); and Hadassah (1936). Congregation Degel Israel maintains a *talmud torah* and a cemetery. In more recent years, a Conservative congregation, Temple Beth-El, was established and several new organizations were established that have helped contribute to Jewish life in Lancaster. The Jewish Family Service of the Lehigh Valley was created in 1972 to help with missions such as resettlement, counseling, and emergency assistance in the wider Lancaster County. Franklin and Marshal College, with a student body of 1,850 students, contains a Hillel house that provides Jewish services and life to the 220 students enrolled, and a local Jewish community center offers several classes, summer programs, and religious education to the community as well.

[Benjamin Paul (2nd ed.)]

LANCUT (Pol. **Łańcut**), town in Rzeszow province, S.E. Poland. The earliest information regarding Jews in Lancut dates back to 1563. Lancut Jews then earned their living in wholesale trade with the towns of the "province of Russia" by distilling alcohol and brewing beer, as goldsmiths and silversmiths and tailors. At the beginning of the 17th century, Jewish trade in the town and its surroundings suffered serious setbacks. During the Tatar invasion in 1624 many Jews were taken captive. When the forces of Prince Rákoczy of Transylvania attacked in 1657 the Jewish community of Lancut actively participated in the defense of the town.

From the beginning of the 17th century there was an organized Jewish community with a wooden synagogue and a cemetery. On the invitation of the owners of the town, some Sephardi Jewish families settled in Lancut in the 17th century. At the beginning of the 18th century the Jews of Lancut were granted a privilege permitting them to engage in trade (excluding the fur trade) and in crafts (excluding harness making, tanning, and cobbling), to purchase land, and to build houses in the town. In 1726 Jews were allowed to join artisans' guilds (blacksmithing and goldsmithing). At that time a magnificent synagogue in baroque style was erected to replace the wooden synagogue which had been destroyed by fire. The synagogue still stands (during the Nazi occupation and for a few years after World War II it was used as a store, and since the 1960s it has been a museum). The Lancut community was affiliated to the province of Przemysl (see *Councils of the Lands). In 1714 the Jews in Lancut and about 80 surrounding villages paid a poll tax of 1,300 zlotys. The Lancut community minute book, begun in 1730, was preserved until World War II. In the mid-18th century Lancut Jews suffered from the edicts of the bishop of Przemysl, who prohibited the holding of Jewish weddings on Sundays and ordered the closing of Jewish shops on days of Christian processions.

In 1765 there were 829 Jews in the vicinity. Among the community's rabbis were Moses Ẓevi Hirsch Meizlisch (Meisels; 1758–67); Moses b. Yiẓḥak Eisik, grandson of Judah Leib, *av bet din* of Cracow; Aryeh Leibush, author of *Gevurot Aryeh*, 1777–1819; *Jacob Isaac Horowitz, HaḤozeh ("the Seer"), lived and worked in Lancut in the late 1790s. Ḥasidism gained influence in the town in the early 19th century. A Juedische Normalschule, founded by Naphtali Herz *Homberg, existed in Lancut at the beginning of Austrian rule (1788–92). During the first half of the 19th century Lancut Jews earned their livelihood in the grain, lumber, and potash trades. Jewish life was disrupted by a fire in 1820 and their economy recovered only many years later, after the opening of the railroad (1848) and the constitutional changes of 1867. In 1865 many of Lancut's 1,200 Jews (about 40% of the population) were flax workers, tanners, goldsmiths, cobblers, and tailors. Eleazar b. Ẓevi Elimelech Shapira, author of *Benei Yissakhar*, was rabbi of Lancut from 1816 to 1865. In the 1870s Lancut's first group of *maskilim* was founded. A Hibbat Zion circle was active in the town from the early 1890s. A new Jewish cemetery was dedicated in 1860. The kloyz (klaus) of the Dzików Ḥasidim was built at the beginning of the 20th century; it was later used as a prayer house by Zionists. The Jewish population of Lancut numbered 1,940 in 1900 (about 40% of the total population). In 1914, 580 members paid taxes to the community, whose income that year totaled 29,851 kronen. At the end of World War I a Jewish national board was established in Lancut, and during the first days of Polish rule (November 1918) the community organized *self-defense against rioters. In 1921 there were 1,925 Jews in Lancut (about 42% of the total population), and 2,753 in 1939. Various Zionist movements were active between the world wars. The Jewish educational network was extended and *Tarbut and *Beth Jacob schools founded. The Ivriyyah Society was active in promoting the study of Hebrew. The pressure of local antisemitic circles increased in the 1930s, affecting Jewish small traders and artisans in particular.

[Arthur Cygielman]

Holocaust Period

The city was taken by the Germans on Sept. 9, 1939, and forced labor decrees put into effect. The local synagogue was set on fire, followed by the expulsion of the Jews of Lancut on Sept. 22–23, 1939. Most of them were sent into Soviet territory across the San River. Others were widely dispersed over German-occupied territory. At the end of 1939 a few dozen former inhabitants returned, as did Jewish refugees from the Polish territories annexed to the Reich. The Judenrat was headed by Marcus Pohorille. In early 1940 there were about 900 Jews in Lancut, and 1,300 by the end of the year, with the arrival of refugees expelled from Cracow. After the outbreak of the German-Soviet war (June 22, 1941) Jews who had fled to Soviet-held territory or who had been expelled by the Germans in September 1939 tried to return to Lancut to reunite with their families; in November 1941, a number of them were caught and put to death. On Aug. 1, 1942, the Jews of Lancut were deported and were taken to Pelkinia, a town about 9 mi. (14 km.) from Lancut where there was a transit camp for Jews from the Jaroslaw region. The elderly, the sick, and the children were shot in the camp or in the Nechczioli forest, about 3 mi. (5 km.) away. By September 1942 there were 50 Jews living in Lancut. On Sept. 17, 1942, they were taken to the ghetto of Szeniawa, where the remaining Jews of the area were concentrated. In May 1943 the Szeniawa ghetto was liquidated, and its inmates, including the remnants of the Lancut community, were murdered in the local cemetery. In 1957 one of the key Nazis responsible for the murder of the Jews of Lancut, Joseph Kokut, was arrested in Czechoslovakia and turned over to the

Polish government. He was sentenced to death and executed that year.

[Aharon Weiss]

BIBLIOGRAPHY: CAHJP, ḤM 7095–7101 (Cracow, WAP, *Teki Schneidera*, 1791–97); *ibid.*, ḤM 7921 ABC (Wroclaw, Ossolineum, Rps 2264/II); I. Lewin, "Protokoly Kahalne… w Małopolsce środkowej," in: *Przewodnik historyczno-prawny*, 2:4 (1931), 4; idem, *Przyczynki do dziejów i historji literatury Żydów w Polsce* (1935), 70–72; M. Schorr, *Żydzi w Przemyślu do końca XVIII wieku* (1903), 197 no. 116; S. Cetnarski, *Miasto Łańcut* (1937); Z. Schust, *Łańcut i okolice* (1958); M. Brandys, in: *Nowa Kultura*, nos. 14–15 (1948); A. Potocki, *Master of Lancut:… Memoirs* (1959); M. Walzer and N. Kudisch (eds.), *Lanẓut, Ḥayyeha ve-Hurbanah…* (1963).

LÁNCZY, GYULA (1850–1911), Hungarian historian. Born in Pest, Lánczy studied law and spent several years in the civil service before turning to historical studies. In 1886 he was appointed professor at Kolozsvár, and in 1891 became professor of medieval history at the University of Budapest. Lánczy's studies ranged over a variety of subjects in history – including literary history – political science, and foreign affairs. They included the history of the Magyars, the poetry of the Kuruc, and Hungarian political reform during the first half of the 19th century. In medieval history, his favorite subjects were the conflict between the empire and the clergy, the constitution of Italian cities, and the religious and political movements of the 14th and 15th centuries. Lánczy's book, *Történelmi kor-és jellemrajzok* ("Monographs and Historical Portraits," 1890), illustrates his literary studies, while *Magyarország az Árpádok korában* ("Hungary during the Period of the Árpáds," 1898) exemplifies his historiographical method. He converted to Christianity.

[Jeno Zsoldos]

LÁNCZY, LEÓ (1852–1921), Hungarian economist and banker, a younger brother of the historian Gyula *Lánczy; like him he converted to Christianity. Born in Pest, Lánczy joined the Anglo-Hungarian Bank. In 1879, he became director general of the Hungarian General Real Estate Loan Company and in 1881 of the Hungarian Commercial Bank. Mainly through his endeavors, this financial institution expanded its relations with the Balkan countries and became a decisive factor in Hungary's economy. The bank also contributed financially to the development of the city of Budapest, including the financing of its telephone system, and acquired major interests in an important shipping company and in local railroad communications. Lánczy organized the Hungarian mortgage credit abroad, and endeavored to establish Hungarian banking and credit facilities that would be independent of Vienna. He was a director of numerous industrial companies, and was honored for his services in promoting the Millennium Exhibition. In 1893 he was elected president of the Budapest Chamber of Commerce and Industry. From 1893 he served in Parliament, where his speeches on economic and financial problems attracted attention. In 1905 he was nominated to the Upper Chamber. In 1912 he became privy councillor. His articles appeared in the *Neue Freie Presse*, *Pester Lloyd*, and *Honi Ipar*.

BIBLIOGRAPHY: E. Makai, *Huszonöt év a magyar közgazdaság terén: Lánczy Leó munkássága, beszédei és dolgozatai* (1907); *Pesti Magyar Kereskedelmi Bank 1841–1941. Száz esziendő emlékei* (1941), 66–76.

[Joachim O. Ronall]

LAND, EDWIN H. (1909–1991), U.S. inventor of the Polaroid cameras and films that revolutionized the whole conception of negative-positive photography. Born in Bridgeport, Conn., Land's work with light began when he was a freshman at Harvard College and experimented with polarized light. Later Land returned to Harvard and in a laboratory furnished for him, he continued to perfect Polaroid sheets, which eventuated in Polaroid "L" Sheet. This synthetic had a new molecular structure. When laminated in glass it made polarization practical in three-dimensional colored movies, automobile headlights, sunglasses, and camera filters. In 1940 Land and his staff of scientists produced the first black and white stereoscopic vectographs. The group's inventions during World War II solved many military problems, producing infrared polarizers; heat stable filters that passed only the infrared; dark adaption goggles; and thermal homingheads containing miniaturized computers to be attached to the noses of bombs. After the war Land perfected his Polaroid one-step camera, and by 1948 it was made available to the public. The Polaroid camera was soon refined enough to yield a completely neutral, grainless, silver deposit ranging from clear whites through degrees of subtle grays to clear solid blacks. Land followed his black-and-white process in one-step color film.

BIBLIOGRAPHY: Bello, in: *Fortune*, 59 (April 1959), 124–7; *Current Biography Yearbook 1953* (1953), 339–41.

[Peter Pollack]

LANDA, ABRAM (1902–1989), Australian lawyer and politician. Landa, who was born in Belfast, Northern Ireland, immigrated to Australia as a boy. He received a law degree from the University of Sydney and in 1927 was admitted to practice as a solicitor. Landa was elected and sat as Labor member for Bondi in the New South Wales Parliament from 1930 to 1932 and from 1941 to 1963. He served in the New South Wales government as minister for labor and industry (1953–56), minister for housing (1956–59), and minister for housing and co-operative societies (1959–65). Landa was also active in Jewish affairs in New South Wales. In 1965 he was appointed agent general for New South Wales in London. In the late 1940s, Landa was instrumental in persuading H.V. Evatt, Australia's foreign minister, to support the creation of the State of Israel at the United Nations, a sequence of events in which Australia's support was extremely important.

His nephew PAUL LANDA (1941–1984) served in the New South Wales Parliament as the state's attorney-general and in a variety of other ministerial posts. He died suddenly of a heart attack at the age of only 43. It is widely believed that he would eventually have become premier of New South Wales and even Australia's prime minister.

ADD. BIBLIOGRAPHY: W.D. Rubinstein, Australia II, 307–8.

[Isidor Solomon / William D. Rubinstein (2nd ed.)]

LANDA, MYER JACK (1874–1947), author and journalist. Born in Leeds, he became a parliamentary reporter and in 1942 was elected chairman of the House of Commons Press Gallery. For a time Landa, a keen Zionist, also edited *The Jewish World*. His books include *The Alien Problem* (1911), *The Jew in Drama* (1926), *Palestine as It Is* (1932), *The Shylock Myth* (1942), and *The Man Without a Country* (1946).

LANDAU, city in Rhenish Palatinate, Germany. Jews were first mentioned in Landau in the late 13th century. A *Judengasse* is noted in 1329. In 1347 there was conflict between the Jews and the townspeople, and during the Black *Death persecutions of 1349 the community was destroyed. However, there were once more Jews in the town in 1354. The main source of livelihood of the 15th-century community was moneylending and the manufacture of playing cards. Among the rabbis of Landau in the 15th century were Solomon Spiro (1430) and Moses b. Isaac ha-Levi Minz, who served until 1469. In the late 15th and early 16th centuries the Jews of Landau were constantly threatened with expulsion, which finally took place in 1545. Many of the exiles, who were dispersed through much of Central and Eastern Europe, adopted Landau as a family name. In the 17th and 18th centuries there were Jews in the *Palatinate and presumably some in Landau. In 1836 Elias Gruenebaum was appointed head of the district rabbinate of Landau comprising, in 1864, 24 communities. R. Berthold Einstein (b. 1862) was elected to the office in 1894. A synagogue was erected in 1884. There were 377 Jews in Landau in 1840 and 303 in 1871. From then there was a steady increase: 400 (5.03% of the total population) in 1880, 610 in 1890, and 874 at the end of the 19th century. However, the community decreased to 732 in 1925 and 596 in 1933. In 1933 the community had a synagogue, religious school, prayer hall, cemetery, four charitable institutions, and several socio-cultural societies.

With the advent of Nazis to power, a program of terrorization of the Jewish community began. On June 19, 1933, a gang of Nazis invaded the Cafe Central, smashed windows, furniture, and crockery and forced those present to face the wall, beating them with rubber batons until they collapsed. The next day, 12 local Jews were arrested and paraded through the streets with obscene posters around their necks. They were then taken to a house on the outskirts of the town and flogged. A Nazi boycott of Jewish firms was instituted as well as a boycott of non-Jewish firms in which Jewish funds were invested. Under the chairmanship of R. Kurt Metzger, who succeeded R. Einstein in 1935, representatives of 35 communities of the Palatinate convened in Landau in October 1938. The community dwindled through increasing emigration, declining to 385 in 1937 and 94 in 1939. On Oct. 22, 1940, 89 Jews were deported to *Gurs in southern France. In 1946, 20 Jewish concentration camp survivors established a community in Landau.

Through the years most Jews moved from Landau to Neustadt. There are no Jews living in Landau today. Since 1968 a memorial recalls the synagogue destroyed in 1938. In 1987 the "Frank-Loebsches Haus" (Frank Loeb House) was opened. It houses an exhibition on the history of the Jews in Landau and two institutes of the Koblenz-Landau University. The building, parts of which originate from the 15th century, was bought by Zacharias Frank – Anne Frank's great-grandfather – in 1870 and later owned by his granddaughter Olga Loeb, née Frank. It was restored by the city of Landau.

BIBLIOGRAPHY: Germ Jud, 2 (1968²), 464–6; *Fuehrer durch die juedische Gemeindeverwaltung und Wohlfahrtspflege in Deutschland* (1932/33), 316–7; E. Gruenebaum, *Israelitische Gemeinde, Synagoge und Schule in der baierischen Pfalz.* (1861); idem, *Rede, gehalten bei dem Antritte seines Amtes als Rabbiner des Gerichtsbezirks Landau in der Synagoge zu Landau* (1838); PK Germanyah; EJ, vol. 10, pp. 579–80; H. Hess, in: *Landauer Monatshefte*, 16:8–11 (1968). **ADD. BIBLIOGRAPHY:** C. Kohl-Langer et al., *Juden in Landau. Beitraege zur Geschichte einer Minderheit*, Schriftenreihe zur Geschichte der Stadt Landau in der Pfalz, vol. 7 (2004); H. Arnold, *Juedisches Leben in der Stadt Landau und in der Suedpfalz 1780–1933* (2000); K. Fuechs and M. Jaeger, *Synagogen der Pfaelzer Juden. Vom Untergang ihrer Gotteshaeuser und Gemeinden. Eine Dokumentation* (1988), 128–37; A. Maimon, M. Breuer, and Y. Guggenheim (eds.), *Germania Judaica*, vol. 3, 1350–1514 (1987), 703–11; H. Hess, *Die Landauer Judengemeinde. Ein Abriss ihrer Geschichte*, Kleine Landauer Reihe, vol. 5 (1983); **WEBSITE:** www.alemannia-judaica.de.

[Chasia Turtel / Larissa Daemmig (2nd ed.)]

LANDAU, ADOLPH (1842–1902), Russian journalist, editor, and publisher, and pioneer of the rising Russian-Jewish intelligentsia. Born in Raseiniai (Rossiyeny), Lithuania, Landau was educated in the state rabbinical seminary in Vilna and at the faculty of law at the University of St. Petersburg. After contributing to the Russian liberal press of the 1860s, he wrote "Letters from St. Petersburg" in the Russian-language Jewish newspaper *Den* of Odessa. In 1871 he began to publish a literary-historical anthology titled *Yevreyskaya Biblioteka* ("Jewish Library"). By the end of the 1870s eight volumes had appeared, with the participation of many Jewish writers and researchers, notably I. *Orshanski, L. *Levanda, and G. *Bogrov. In 1881 the government authorized Landau to issue the collection as a literary and scientific monthly, exempt from the earlier censorship, and he changed its name to *Voskhod*. After the 1881 pogroms, Landau added a weekly supplement in which he conducted a fierce polemic against the Jew-haters; other objects of his attack were the Ḥovevei Zion (*Ḥibbat Zion) and later the Zionists. Rallying the Russian Jewish intelligentsia and its writers around his newspapers, Landau did not shrink from stringent criticism of the government's anti-Jewish policy. He was warned about this several times and his paper was closed down for six months (1891). *Voskhod*, the only Jewish paper in the Russian language during the years 1885–99, served as an instrument for the creation of Jewish literature in Russian and for the study of the history of the Jews in Russia. In his outlook Landau was a moderate assimilationist who was in favor of the Jews of Russia acquiring Russian culture, but he opposed complete assimilation and the rejection of the national-religious values of Judaism. Through his publication of translations of many basic works on the history of the Jewish people and its literature, he nurtured a generation of readers who became aware of their heritage. In 1899 Landau sold *Voskhod* to a group of writers and communal workers with nationalist views (there were even Zionists among them). He continued the collection *Yevreyskaya Biblioteka* with volumes 9 (1902) and 10 (which appeared posthumously in 1903). His son was Gregory *Landau.

BIBLIOGRAPHY: S. Ginzburg, *Amolike Peterburg* (1944), 170–83; Y. Slutzky, *Ha-Ittonut ha-Yehudit-Rusit ba-Me'ah ha-19* (1970); G. L[andau], in: *Yevreyskaya Biblioteka*, 9 (1902).

[Yehuda Slutsky]

LANDAU, ALFRED (1850–1935), Yiddish linguist and folklorist. Born in Brody (Galicia), at age 15 he moved to Vienna, where he later studied law and received a doctorate in jurisprudence (1887) before practicing law for 12 years. His main intellectual interest, however, was Yiddish linguistic research, to which he devoted all his energies after abandoning the practice of law. A perfectionist, Landau was never satisfied with the quality of his achievements and therefore published relatively few of his many penetrating studies. Prominent among his published works are his study of the diminutive in Galician Yiddish (in *Deutsche Mundarten* (1897), 46–58); his study of the language of *Die Memoiren Glückels von Hameln* (in MGJV, 7 (1901), 20–68); the glossary of the collection of various private Yiddish letters dating from 1619, which he published jointly with B. *Wachstein (1911); his research on the Slavic influence in Yiddish (in *Filologishe Shriftn* [YIVO], 2 (1928), 198–214). Landau's lifework, however, was to have been a Yiddish-German etymological dictionary; the invaluable material he had already collected and studied was lost together with other treasures of the *YIVO in Vilna. On the occasion of his 75th birthday, YIVO published a Yiddish festschrift, *Landoy-Bukh* (*Filologishe Shriftn*, 1 (1925), 1–22), where a bibliography of Landau's published works as well as his biography and genealogy are to be found.

BIBLIOGRAPHY: Rejzen, Leksikon, 2 (1929), 58–61; LNYL, 4 (1961), 427–9. **ADD. BIBLIOGRAPHY:** Kh. Gininger, in: *YIVO-bleter*, 12 (1937), 396–409.

[Mordkhe Schaechter]

LANDAU, ANNIE (1873–1945), Anglo-Jewish educationalist in Ereẓ Israel. Annie Landau was born in London to a strictly Orthodox family and at the age of 12 was sent to the Jewish High School in Frankfurt on the Main to receive a traditional Jewish education. On completing her studies she became a teacher at the Westminster Jews' Free School in London, and in 1900 was appointed by the Anglo-Jewish Association as headmistress of the Evelina de Rothschild school in Jerusalem, a position she held until her death. Annie Landau combined fervent British patriotism with a strict regard for the traditions and practices of Orthodox Judaism, which she inculcated into her pupils, and her home became virtually a salon for English and Jewish society in Ereẓ Israel. She was awarded the MBE in 1924 and her 70th birthday celebration was attended by some 500 of the leading members of Palestinian society. She was often referred to as the "Queen of Jerusalem." Although somewhat out of sympathy with Zionist aspirations, she was one of the best-loved and admired personalities in Jerusalem. Her sister MURIEL ELSIE (1895–1972), a well-known gynecologist and wife of Dr. Sam Sacks, was the first Jewess in England to become a Fellow of the Royal College of Surgeons. Her sister HELEN (1892–?) was headmistress of the Jewish School near Manchester, and her brother ISAAC (1874–1954) was president of the London Board of Shechitah from 1930 to 1941.

LANDAU, DAVID (1947–), Israeli journalist. Born in London, Landau graduated in law from London University and studied at Slobodka Yeshiva in Jerusalem. Immigrating to Israel in 1970, he joined the *Jerusalem Post*, filling a number of reportorial posts including diplomatic reporter. In 1981 he became the first Israeli reporter to interview President Anwar *Sadat of Egypt. In 1986 he was appointed managing editor. In 1990, when Yehudah Levy was appointed local publisher after the newspaper was sold to the Hollinger newspaper chain, Landau led a rebellion against Levy's right-wing editorial line, which ended with the dismissal of Landau and the other journalists. In 1991 he joined *Maariv* as a political commentator. In 1993 he joined *Haaretz*, working as a news editor and subsequently as features editor. In 1997 he founded *Haaretz*'s English edition, including the local distribution of the *International Herald Tribune*. In 2005 he was appointed editor of *Haaretz*. Identified with the Left, Landau moved the newspaper in that direction editorially on diplomatic and defense issues. A religious Jew, he defined himself as a secular Zionist, strongly opposing messianic trends in modern Orthodoxy in Israel. He sought to widen *Haaretz*'s readership beyond the European Ashkenazi secular intelligentsia to embrace other population sectors. He was the Israel bureau chief of the *Jewish Telegraphic Agency for many years, and correspondent for *The Economist* for ten years. He wrote *Piety & Power: The World of Jewish Fundamentalism* and collaborated with Shimon *Peres on his memoirs.

[Yoel Cohen (2nd ed.)]

LANDAU, EDMUND (1877–1938), German mathematician. The son of Leopold *Landau, Edmund Landau was educated in Berlin, succeeding H. *Minkowski as professor of mathematics at Goettingen in 1909. He was elected to full membership of the academies of Berlin, Goettingen, Halle, Leningrad, and Rome. The coming of the Nazi regime forced him to resign his chair in 1933. Landau was a productive mathematician. Apart from important work on Dirichlet series and the theory of functions, his main interest was in number theory.

He presented for the first time a systematic account of the analytic theory in the *Handbuch der Lehre von der Verteilung der Primzahlen* (2 vols., 1909, 1953[2]). From 1927 to 1928 when he was visiting professor at the Hebrew University of Jerusalem, he played an important role in the development of the Institute of Mathematics.

BIBLIOGRAPHY: G.H. Hardy and H. Heilbronn, in: *Journal of the London Mathematical Society*, 13 (1938), 302–10; J.C. Poggendorff, *Biographisch-literarisches Handwoerterbuch*, 7 pt. 3 (1959), 10.

[Barry Spain]

LANDAU, ELEAZAR BEN ISRAEL (1778–1831), rabbi, talmudic scholar, and author. Eleazar Landau, a grandson of Ezekiel *Landau of Prague, was educated in the home of his stepfather Moses Ḥasid of Ropshitz. He took up residence in Lemberg and then in Brody, where he first engaged in business. In 1829, however, he was appointed rabbi of Brody while Aryeh Leib *Teomim, the incumbent rabbi of the town, was still alive but sick and bedridden. Teomim was not told of the appointment so as not to aggravate his illness. Landau died before Teomim, however, during an outbreak of cholera in Brody.

He was the author of *Yad ha-Melekh*, novellae on the *Mishneh Torah* of Maimonides (parts 1, 2, and 4, Lemberg 1826; part 3 remained unpublished). His novellae on the Babylonian Talmud were published in the Vilna Talmud. Of his many unpublished manuscripts the following may be noted: *Kunteres Kelalim*, on the methodology of the Talmud, and *Kedushah ve-Tohorah*, on the orders *Kodoshim* and *Tohorot*. His responsa to Samuel Landau, the son of Ezekiel Landau, were published in the *Noda bi-Yhudah* Second Series, *Even ha-Ezer*, nos. 120–2; other responsa are found in the *Mei Be'er* (Vienna, 1829) of Beer Oppenheimer (45b–47a) and in the *Zekher Yeshayahu* (Vilna, 1881) of Zechariah Isaiah Jolles (nos. 17–18). Landau was also in halakhic correspondence with Moses *Sofer.

His grandson, ELEAZAR BEN JUDAH LANDAU (1842–1905), was the author of *Zikhron Eleazar* (Brody, 1906), novellae to the Mishnah and Jerusalem Talmud of the tractate *Shekalim*.

[Itzhak Alfassi]

LANDAU, EUGEN (1852–1935), German banker and philanthropist, who was born in Breslau. He studied law and economics in preparation for entering his father's banking firm in Berlin, and subsequently became one of the partners. Establishing close connections with the city authorities, his bank became one of the principal agents in arranging for loans to the City of Berlin for its development. At 27, Landau was the founder and director of the Rechte Oderuferbahn-Gesellschaft, and played an important role in building its Silesian railroad. He had a large part in the establishment of the National Bank fuer Deutschland and its merger with the Breslau Disconto-Bank and the Bayerische Bank. He was instrumental in the organization of the Allgemeine Elektrische Gesellschaft (AEG), which Emil and Walter *Rathenau directed. In World War I Landau served as a major in Germany's *Landwehr* (Territorial Reserve), a rank which no other Jew who had not abandoned his faith had previously reached. For long Spain's honorary consul-general in Berlin, he used this post to strengthen relations between Spain and Germany.

Landau took an active part in Jewish communal affairs. He contributed generously to Jewish social welfare institutions, among them the Juedische Altershilfe (aid for aged) and the Baruch Auerbach'sches Waisenhaus (orphanage). He helped to found and support the Keren Hayesod in Germany and was one of its vice presidents and president of the Pro-Palestine Committee.

BIBLIOGRAPHY: S. Kaznelson, *Juden im deutschen Kulturbereich* (1959), 728–9; Wininger, Biog. **ADD. BIBLIOGRAPHY:** NDB, vol. 13 (1982), 482.

[Morton Mayer Berman / Bjoern Siegel (2nd ed.)]

LANDAU, EZEKIEL BEN JUDAH (1713–1793), halakhic authority of the 18th century, known as the **Noda bi-Yehudah**, after one of his works (see below). Landau was born in Opatow, Poland, and received his talmudic education first in his hometown until the age of 13 and subsequently in Vladimir-Volinski and Brody. He was endowed with qualities which make him one of the most famous rabbis of the close of the classical Ashkenazi rabbinic era. He came from a wealthy and distinguished family tracing its descent back to Rashi. He had a commanding appearance and rare intellectual ability, was of strong character imbued with a love of truth and of his fellow men, and had considerable diplomatic skill. By nature he was an intellectual ascetic whose main interest lay in the study and teaching of Torah. In his time he was regarded as the prototype of the ideal Jew. At the age of 18 he married, moved to Brody, and joined the famous Brody *kloiz*, studying Talmud with his relative Isaac of Hamburg and Kabbalah with Hayyim Zanzer, who remarked that the young Ezekiel "saw the *ma'aseh merkavah*" (vision of the God's chariot from the opening chapters of the Book of Ezekiel). At the age of 21 he was already *dayyan* of Brody, and at 33 rabbi of Yampol. From there he received a call in 1754 to become rabbi of Prague and the whole of Bohemia, one of the highest positions of that time. His famous proclamation of 1752, whose purpose was to put an end to the notorious *Emden-*Eybeschuetz controversy, which split the Jewish world into two, helped in no small measure in his obtaining this appointment. His tenure of the Prague rabbinate enabled Landau to give practical effect to his outstanding qualities. It afforded ample scope for his rabbinic and communal activity both in Prague itself and beyond. He acted as judge, teacher, and mentor of the community. In his capacity as rabbi of Bohemia, he represented the Jews before the Austrian government. In his great yeshivah, he taught hundreds of students, the cream of Jewish youth from Austria and surrounding countries. One of his better known students was Abraham *Danzig, the author of the *Ḥayyei Adam*.

Landau was one of the greatest writers of responsa in his

time. His *Noda bi-Yehudah* (2 pts., Prague, 1776, 1811) contains some 860 responsa. It has been frequently published with glosses and commentaries by some of the greatest rabbis of succeeding generations. The most important of his other books are *Ẓiyyun le-Nefesh Ḥayyah* (*Ẓelaḥ*) on the tractates *Pesaḥim* (Prague, 1783), *Berakhot* (*ibid.*, 1791), *Beẓah* (*ibid.*, 1799); an edition including all these appeared in 1825, and one on *Seder Nezikin* with various additions in 1959; *Dagul me-Revavah* (Prague, 1794) on the Shulḥan Arukh; *Derushei ha-Ẓelaḥ* (1899); *Ahavat Ẓiyyon*, sermons and addresses (1827); all are frequently republished.

Landau took an active part in all the Jewish social and religious events of his time. He identified himself absolutely with the traditional Jewish way of life, regarding its preservation and welfare as his primary duty. It was for that reason that he advocated ending the controversy with Eybeschuetz, even though he was of the opinion that the accusations leveled against him could not easily be dismissed. In 1752, Landau sent a letter to the factions on both sides of the controversy, suggesting a compromise: the Shabbatean amulets written by Eybeshuetz would be returned to him and Eybeshuetz would renounce all the Shabbatean works claimed to be his. The compromise failed. It is clear from later events that Landau did consider Eybeshuetz to be a Shabbatean; nevertheless, he had great respect for Eybeshuetz's learning and overall character. On the other hand he persecuted those who were known as Shabbateans, and in particular the *Frankists. While Landau himself was well versed in Kabbalah and even taught kabbalistic concepts and ideas freely in his sermon, he was very critical of the rabbis of the ḥasidic movement and the Shabbateans and Frankists for teaching Kabbalah so openly. Indeed, there is very little that differentiates between Landau's kabbalistic teachings and those of his ḥasidic contemporaries. It is important to note in this regard that Landau and many of the ḥasidic rabbis had the same roots in the *kloiz* in Brody, where asceticism was practiced on the basis of continued in-depth study of Kabbalah. In the end, Landau's objections were focused on the emphasis placed on the study of Kabbalah among the Ḥasidim, as well as the changes they made in the *siddur*. Landau looked with some favor on the Haskalah movement. When, however, the aggressive anti-rabbinic tendency amongst the *maskilim* of Berlin grew stronger, he regretted this support and his attitude toward them took an unfavorable turn. The **Me'assefim* came to regard him as their arch enemy, while he in turn referred to them as "a rabble of unclean birds" (introduction to *Ẓelaḥ* on *Berakhot*). Despite this, he continued to support the traditional element among the *maskilim*, giving his approbation to books on history, grammar, natural sciences, etc.

Landau distinguished himself in his attitude to the new situation arising from the opening of the gates of the ghetto and the consequent entry of the Jews into general non-Jewish society. He toiled and pleaded with sincerity for a strengthening of a correct relationship with the non-Jews and the development of a feeling of patriotism for the country. His benedictory message to the first Jewish recruits to the Austrian army made a strong impression (*Ha-Meassef* (1789), 253). He also cooperated in the establishment of the first Jewish school in Prague (May 2, 1782), although several weeks previously he had come out strongly against the attempt of Naphtali Hirz *Wessely (in the latter's *Divrei Shalom ve-Emet*, Berlin, 1782) to attach religious significance to general education. While he was generally stricter in his own halakhic observance, Landau demanded that other rabbis follow his lead in ruling more leniently for the general public. His responsa reflect the state of affairs in the Jewish community of his day: the difficulties in making a living, which affected many marriages; lax sexual mores, and the sometimes problematic relations with the secular government. In his decision-making, he relied most heavily on talmudic sources and the rulings of the **rishonim*, only rarely turning to the **aḥaronim*. He always attempted to find a precedent for any of his own original thoughts. In money matters he preferred compromise over ruling according to the letter of the law, and he frequently consulted with scientists and doctors to better understand related questions that came before him. When attacked for his lenient halakhic tendencies, he always respectfully stood his ground. Among his rulings are original and bold, lenient decisions which testify both to his responsible approach to the community and to his mastery of the *halakhah*, enabling him to effect a compromise between it and the demands of the time. One of his best-known lenient rulings was the permission to shave during the intermediate days of the festival (*Noda bi-Yhudah, Mahadura Kamma*, OḤ 13; *Mahadura Tinyana*, OḤ 99, 100, 101), which caused a storm in the rabbinic world at the time. This, as well as many of his other lenient decisions, were set aside by the halakhic authorities of the following generation (see *Resp. Ḥatam Sofer*, OḤ, 154). He was also the first to permit, albeit with severe restrictions, autopsies (*Noda bi-Yhudah, Mahadura Tinyana*, YD 210).

[Moshe Shraga Samet / David Derovan (2nd ed.)]

Ezekiel Landau's sons were JACOB (known as JACOBKE; 1745 or 1750–1822), who was ordained rabbi but was friendly with the Galician *maskilim*. After living in Hamburg for a time, he settled in Brody, where he became a prosperous merchant. Some of his novellae on the Talmud are included in works by his father and other contemporary authorities. He also contributed to **Bikkurei ha-Ittim*. SAMUEL (d. 1834) graduated from his father's yeshivah. In his early years he moved in Prague Haskalah circles and was associated with the *Gesellschaft der jungen Hebraeer. It is generally assumed that Ezekiel did not formally pronounce the ban on Moses *Mendelssohn's translation of the Bible because Samuel's name appeared on the list of those who had subscribed to the work. Having become strictly Orthodox, he applied for the office of *av bet din* after his father's death but was not appointed. His objections to the establishment of rabbinical seminaries formed the main subject of the pamphlet *Ha-Orev* (Vienna, 1795), attributed to Baruch *Jeiteles. He was elected to the *bet din* and later became *av bet din*. In 1799 Samuel and Eleazar *Fleckeles signed the *ḥerem* against the *Frankists, and a year later, on Nov. 11, he and Fleckeles were imprisoned for four days in connection with a scandal at a Frankist funeral. He was one of the signatories of an application in 1820 for the restoration of the two gates of the Jewish quarter. However, in a sermon delivered in 1830 he praised Mendelssohn's Bible translation for its good German and suggested that fathers decide, when their sons reach the age of ten, whether to dedicate them to talmudic studies or to a secular education. When in 1834 the Verein fuer geregelten Gottesdienst made changes in the architecture of the Altschul, he pronounced a ban on them. His responsa were published as *Shivat Ẓiyyon* (Prague, 1827; republished 1967). With his brother Jacobke he published his father's *Noda bi-Yhudah Mahadura Tinyana* (Prague, 1811) with his own preface and including some of his own responsa. His father's *Ahavot Ẓiyyon* contains four of Samuel's sermons.

ISRAEL (1758–1829) was a pioneer of Haskalah in Prague. Although he received a traditional education, he also acquired a German education himself, and was a pupil of Israel *Zamosc. From 1782 he worked as a Hebrew printer in a Christian firm. In 1793 he reprinted Abraham *Farissol's *Iggeret Orḥot Olam*. In 1794 he published his father's *Dagul me-Revavah* and in 1798 *Ḥok le-Yisrael*, a translation of Moses *Maimonides' *Sefer ha-Mitzvot* "into the language of the masses," intended to strengthen their adherence to tradition. His son by his first marriage, ELIEZER (1778–1831), became rabbi in *Brody and published *Yad ha-Melekh* (Lemberg, 1826) on Maimonides' *Mishneh Torah*. He died of cholera. Israel's son by his second marriage was Moses *Landau.

[Meir Lamed]

BIBLIOGRAPHY: EZEKIEL LANDAU: A.L. Gelman, *Ha-Noda bi-Yhudah u-Mishnato* (1962²); Y.A. Kamelhar, *Mofet ha-Dor* (1903); R. Kestenberg-Gladstein, *Neuere Geschichte der Juden in den boehmischen Laendern*, 1 (1968); Klemperer, in: HJ, 13 (1951), 55–76; Wind, in: L. Jung (ed.), *Jewish Leaders* (1953), 77–98; M.S. Samet, in: *Meḥkarim le-Toledot Am Yisrael ve-Ereẓ Yisrael le-Zekher Ẓevi Avneri* (1970), 240–4. **ADD. BIBLIOGRAPHY:** M.S. Samet, in: *De'ot*, 36 (1969) 26–30; I. Hess, *"Rabbi Yehezkel Landau u-Mekomo be-Toledot ha-Halakhah"* (Dissertation, 1979); D. Sinclair, in: *Le'ela*, 45 (1998), 16–22; S. Flatto, in: *Journal of Jewish Thought and Philosophy*, 12:2 (2003), 99–121; M. Saperstein in: *Shofar*, 6:1 (1987), 20–25; S. Leiman, in: *From Ancient Israel to Modern Judaism*, 3 (1989), 179–94; I. Ta-Shma, in: *Sidra*, 15 (1999) 181–91; K. Kahana, in: *Ma-Ma'ayan*, 26:4 (1986), 51–57; I. Rephael, in: *Sefer Yovel li-Khvod ha-Gaon Rabbi Yosef Dov ha-Levi Soloveitchik* (1984). MOSES LANDAU: O. Muneles, *Bibliographical Survey of Jewish Prague* (1952), index: R. Kestenberg-Gladstein, *Neuere Geschichte der Juden in den boehmischen Laendern*, 1 (1969), index; F. Roubík, in: JGGJČ, 9 (1938), 433–47, passim; R.N.N. Rabbinovicz, *Ma'amar al Hadpasat ha-Talmud* (1953), index; Kressel, Leksikon, 2 (1967), 290. OTHER MEMBERS OF THE FAMILY: E.S. Margulies, *Ma'alot ha-Yuḥasin* (1900), 63–69; Weiss, Dor, 5 (1904⁴), 286f.; J.M. Zunz, *Ir ha-Ẓedek* (1874), IV, 173, suppl.; J. Dembitzer, *Mappelet Ir ha-Ẓedek* (1878); I.T. Eisenstadt and S. Wiener, *Da'at Kedoshim* (1897–98), 104, 111, 118–20; Ḥ.D. Friedberg, *Luḥot Zikkaron* (1897), 11, 18, 35, 44, 50, 74, 89, 91f., 108, 111, 113; idem, *Benei Landau le-Mishpeḥotam* (1905); S. Buber, *Kiryah Nisgavah* (1903), 34, 46f.; J.A. Kamelhar, *Mofet ha-Dor* (1903); *Der Orient* (1848), 541–3. **ADD. BIBLIOGRAPHY:** I.N. Heschel, in: *Kovez Bet Aharon ve-Yisrael*, 11:3 (1996), 147–56.

LANDAU, GREGORY ADOLFOVICH (1877–1940), Russian publicist and journalist. Born in St. Petersburg, he was the son of Adolph *Landau. He graduated in 1902 from the law school of St. Peterburg University. He wrote for Russian and Russian Jewish newspapers, was one of the founders of the Jewish Democratic Group (1904), and was active in the League for the Attainment of Equal Rights for the Jewish People in Russia. He was also active in the Constitutional-Democratic (KaDet) party. After the 1917 Revolution, Landau settled in Berlin. He was associated with rightist Russian circles and participated in the editing of their newspaper, *Rul*. His writings included *Sumerki Yevropy* ("The Twilight of Europe," 1923), in which he predicted the Balkanization of Europe, its economic and political subordination to the United States, and its intellectual and moral decay. In 1924 he contributed to the collection "Russia and the Jews." He also wrote essays on general philosophy. When Hitler came to power in 1933, Landau left for Riga, Latvia, and wrote for the Russian press there. After Latvia was annexed by Russia, he was imprisoned and "liquidated." Another notable work by Landau is *Polsko-yevreyskiya otnosheniya* ("Polish-Jewish Relations," 1915), a collection of articles and notes.

BIBLIOGRAPHY: J.G. Frumkin et al. (eds.), *Russian Jewry*, 2 vols. (1966–69), index; B. Dinur, *Bi-Ymei Milḥamah u-Mahpekhah* (1960), 66–67.

[Yehuda Slutsky]

LANDAU, ISAAC ELIJAH BEN SAMUEL (1801–1876), Lithuanian preacher and biblical commentator. Landau was born in Vilna. He married the daughter of the wealthy and well-known Zadok Marshalkovitch of Dubno and was relieved of financial cares, and although he did occasionally engage in business, he spent most of his life in Dubno compiling his books and sermons, using the method of parables in the style of Jacob *Kranz, the Maggid of Dubno. Landau was chosen by the communities of Volhynia to be their representative on the committee set up by the Russian minister of the interior to deal with religious affairs, and for this purpose he lived in St. Petersburg for several months in 1861. In 1868 he became official preacher and *dayyan* of Vilna. His sermons were popular.

The following are among his main works: *Ma'aneh Eliyahu* (Vilna, 1840), a commentary on the *Tanna de-Vei Eliyahu* published in the same volume with *Si'aḥ Yiẓḥak*, biblical and aggadic novellae; *Berurei ha-Middot* (Vilna, 1844), expositions and novellae to the Mekhilta, to which was joined a treatise, *Mizzui ha-Middot*, "for the understanding of biblical rhetoric and the sayings of the sages"; *Mikra Soferim* (Suwalki, 1862), expositions and novellae to tractate *Soferim*; and *Dover Shalom* (Warsaw, 1863), a commentary on the prayer book. The following of his commentaries and parables on the Bible have been published: *Patshegen*, a commentary on Proverbs (Koenigsberg, 1858), Psalms (Warsaw, 1866), and 12 Minor Prophets and the Five Scrolls (Vilna, 1869/70); and *Patshegen ha-Dat* (Vilna, 1872/5), on the Pentateuch. Landau published the *Derekh Ereẓ Zuta* (1872) with the commentary *Derekh Ḥayyim ve-Orḥot Ḥayyim*; and expositions of the *aggadot* of the Talmud to *Berakhot* and *Shabbat* (Vilna, 1876). His sermons were published in Vilna in 1871 and 1876.

BIBLIOGRAPHY: S. Fuenn, *Kiryah* (1915²), 230; idem, Keneset, 632; H.N. Maggid-Steinschneider, *Ir Vilna* (1900), 92–97; P. Pesis, *Ir Dubno ve-Rabbaneiha* (1902), 34f.; Ḥ.D. Friedberg, *Benei Landau le-Mishpeḥotam* (1905), 21; S.J. Glicksberg, *Ha-Derashah be-Yisrael* (1940), 435f.; *Yahadut Lita*, 1 (1959), 349; 3 (1967), 65.

[Yehoshua Horowitz]

LANDAU, ISRAEL JONAH BEN JOSEPH HA-LEVI (d. 1824), rabbi and author. Landau belonged to a well-known rabbinical family. In his youth he was *av bet din* of Lubomil and from 1786 served in Kempen, Posen region. Among his published works are *Me'on ha-Berakhot* (Dyhrenfurth, 1816), novellae on tractate *Berakhot*, which is the first part of his work *Keneset Yisrael* (the other parts remained unpublished); *Shirat Yisrael* (1897), expositions of the Bible, *aggadot* in the Talmud, and Midrashim; *Ein ha-Bedolaḥ* (1901), novellae to tractates of the Talmud (*Pesaḥim, Megillah, Yoma, Sukkah*, and *Rosh ha-Shanah*); and *Aleh de-Yonah* (1934), expositions of *aggadot* in the Jerusalem Talmud of *Zevaḥim* and *Mo'ed*. He was also a well-known kabbalist, and a request to him from Akiva Eger for an amulet for the sick of Posen has been preserved. His son JOSEPH SAMUEL (1800–1836) was appointed to succeed his father as rabbi of Kempen on the recommendation of Akiva Eger. Joseph Samuel was the author of *Mishkan Shiloh*, of which only one part, *Kur ha-Beḥinah* (Breslau, 1837), was published, comprising 25 responsa and seven sermons – the last in honor of Emperor Frederick William III. In the introduction the author refers to many works of his still in manuscript. His *Goren Atad* (Warsaw, 1837), a memorial sermon on Jehiel Michael Ettinger, has also been published. He corresponded on *halakhah* with the leading rabbis of his time, including Akiva Eger, Ephraim Zalman Margulies, and Solomon Zalman Posner.

BIBLIOGRAPHY: Fuenn, Keneset, 696; I.T. Eisenstein and S. Wiener, *Da'at Kedoshim* (1897–98), 127, 133; Z.J. Michelsohn, in: I.J. Landau, *Shirat Yisrael* (1897), 2–4; idem, in: *Ein ha-Bedolaḥ* (1901), introd.; Ḥ.D. Friedberg, *Luḥot Zikkaron* (1904), 11n.; idem, *Benei Landau le-Mishpeḥotam* (1905), 21f.; A. Heppner and J. Herzberg, *Aus Vergangenheit und Gegenwart der Juden und der juedischen Gemeinden in den Posener Landen* (1909), 518f.; S. Sofer (Schreiber), *Iggerot Soferim* (1929), pt. 1, 17f.

[Itzhak Alfassi]

LANDAU, JACOB (15th century), German talmudist. Landau's father, JUDAH (d. 1464), was a favorite pupil of Jacob *Moellin and a relative of Jacob *Weil who refers to Judah in his responsa with great respect. Judah maintained a large yeshivah in Germany and was renowned as a *posek*. Toward the end of his long life Judah was involved in a vehement halakhic dispute with the two well-known rabbis, Judah and Moses *Mintz.

Of Jacob Landau few biographical details are known – even the dates of his birth and death cannot be established. It is certain, however, that he was born in Germany and educated there, chiefly by his father. He wandered to Italy along with the great wave of German emigration at that time and in Pavia in 1460 met Joseph *Colon, whose customs and rulings he quotes frequently. In Pavia he wrote *Ḥazon*, a unique work introduced by the words "How could it be?" From Pavia Landau proceeded to Naples (1487) where he worked as a proofreader in the new Hebrew printing press established there. That year he corrected the proofs of the Book of Psalms with David *Kimḥi's commentary and published at the same press his own main work, *Ha-Agur*, with the above-mentioned *Ḥazon*. Nothing is known of any other books corrected by him and it seems that he ceased proofreading, although it is known that his son Abraham undertook that work at the same publishing house in 1492. Landau's father-in-law was Abraham Sachs, also a renowned German scholar, who immigrated to Italy. It is also known that Jacob Landau was well versed in Kabbalah.

Landau's reputation rests upon his *Ha-Agur*, an anthology and summation of German-Jewish scholarship concerning the laws of *Oraḥ Ḥayyim* and *Yoreh De'ah* down to his own time, basing himself chiefly on the *Tur* of Jacob b. *Asher. The aim of the book was threefold: to assemble in one source all the relevant data necessary for establishing *halakhah* – but omitting the argument; to lay down the *halakhah*; and to include the new rulings of the latest scholars, such as Israel *Isserlein, Jacob Weil, Joseph Colon, and, in particular, his own father. The style is that of the other classic anthologists: Mordecai b. *Hillel, Zedekiah *Anav, Moses b. Jacob of *Coucy, and Isaac b. Joseph of *Corbeil. The arrangement of the material is similar to that of the *Tur*, on which Landau's work was based. The work is distinguished by a discriminating interweaving of varied material taken from a large number of works. The whole is transformed into a complete and unified literary creation. A novel feature in the work is the interlacing of kabbalistic theory in halakhic matter as an aid to arriving at a decision. Another feature is the approbations the author sought from other rabbis, and the *Ha-Agur* is the first Hebrew book to contain these *haskamot*. The book was published in a number of editions together with *Ḥazon* and the various editions differ because of corrections made by the author. Variations occurred especially in editions of the *Ḥazon* which, from the third edition onward, was much abridged. A complete, emended, and collated edition of both books was published in Jerusalem (1960) by M. Herschler (see bibl.). *Ha-Agur* contains a wealth of information on the teaching of the German scholars of the 14th and 15th centuries and was widely known among scholars and students alike.

BIBLIOGRAPHY: Jacob Landau, *Ha-Agur ha-Shalem*, ed. by M. Herschler (1960), 5–14 (introd.).

[Israel Moses Ta-Shma]

LANDAU, JACOB (1892–1952), journalist and publisher, who founded and directed the *Jewish Telegraphic Agency. Born in Vienna, Landau worked as a youth for various magazines and newspapers in Austria, Germany, and the Netherlands. In 1914 he established the Jewish Correspondence Bureau at The Hague as the first international Jewish news service. After covering the Paris Peace Conference of 1919 for *De Telegraaf*, of Amsterdam, Landau moved his news bureau to London and renamed it the Jewish Telegraphic Agency. Branch offices were opened later in Berlin, Warsaw, Prague, Paris, New York, and Jerusalem, and headquarters were eventually established in New York. In 1940 Landau, with a group of U.S. personalities, founded the Overseas News Agency, which specialized in covering news of minority peoples of all races, religions, and nationalities.

[Irving Rosenthal]

LANDAU, JACOB M. (1924–), professor emeritus of political science at the Hebrew University of Jerusalem, specializing in the political history of the modern Middle East and Central Asia. Landau was born in Kishinev. He was president of the Israel Association of Political Science (1985–87) and was elected honorary fellow of the Israel Oriental Society and the Turkish Academy of History. In 1993–98 he was the editor of *Ha-Mizraḥ he-Ḥadash*, the annual of the Israel Oriental Society. Landau is well known in Orientalist circles, having taught at universities in the U.S., the U.K., France, Germany, the Netherlands, Brazil, and Turkey. He received various medals and distinctions, including the Israel Prize for scholarship (in Oriental studies) in 2005.

His numerous works have been published in Hebrew, Arabic, Turkish, English, French, German, Italian, Spanish, Russian, and Chinese. Among his books are *Parliaments and Parties in Egypt* (1953); *Studies in the Arab Theater* (1958); *Jews in Nineteenth-Century Egypt* (1969); *The Arabs in Israel: A Political Study* (1969); *The Hejaz Railway and the Muslim Pilgrimage: A Case of Ottoman Political Propaganda* (1971); *Middle Eastern Themes: Papers in History and Politics* (1973); *Radical Politics in Modern Turkey* (1974); *Abdul-Hamid's Palestine* (1979); *Tekinalp: Turkish Patriot, 1883–1961* (1984); *The Politics of Pan-Islam: Ideology and Organization* (1990); *The Arab Minority in Israel, 1967–1991* (1993); *Jews, Arabs, Turks* (1993); *Pan-Turkism: From Irredentism to Cooperation* (1995); *The Politics of Language in the Ex-Soviet Muslim States* (2001); and *Exploring Ottoman and Turkish History* (2004).

BIBLIOGRAPHY: International Biographical Centre (Cambridge), *2000 Outstanding Scholars of the 20th Century* (2000), 209; *Who's Who in Israel* (2001), 230; American Biographical Institute, *Contemporary Who's Who* (2003), 249; J.M. Landau, *Bibliography of Published Works* (2004), 1–35.

LANDAU, JUDAH LOEB (**Leo**; 1866–1942), South African rabbi, scholar, poet, and playwright. Landau was born in Zatozce, Galicia. His father Moses Issachar Landau was a *maskil* and regular contributor to the Hebrew press. Landau attended the German gymnasium at Brody (Galicia), yeshivot, and the Jewish Theological Seminary and University of Vienna and soon came under the influence of Hebrew writers, poets, and dramatists, such as P. *Smolenskin, N.I. *Fischmann, and A. *Broides. As a student in Vienna, Landau used to write theater and opera reviews of Jewish interest for *Ha-Maggid*. Early in his life Landau supported the movement for national revival by word and deed, became an ardent supporter of Theodor Herzl, and attended several of the early Zionist congresses. When on a visit to London in 1900 for the Fourth Zionist Congress, M. *Gaster persuaded him to stay. He was minister of the North Manchester Hebrew Congregation until 1904, when he went to Johannesburg as rabbi of the Johannesburg Hebrew Congregation.

In 1915 Landau became chief rabbi of the United Hebrew Congregation of Johannesburg and of the Federation of Synagogues of the Witwatersrand; he was also appointed professor of Hebrew at Witwatersrand University. In nearly four decades of spiritual leadership in the South African Jewish community, Landau participated in and stimulated a great variety of activities and organizations: religious, charitable, cultural, and Zionist.

Landau's contributions to modern Hebrew literature were mainly in drama and poetry. His poems and articles first appeared in a number of Hebrew periodicals, where he used the pseudonym of Hillel ben Shaḥar. Among his published plays are *Bar Kokhva* (1884); *Aḥarit Yerushalayim* (1886); *Hordos* (1888, also in Yiddish, 1901; first produced in Lvov in 1890); *Yesh Tikvah* (1893; with a contemporary theme, the first Hebrew drama to be produced in modern times); *Dam Taḥat Dam* (1898), set in Second Temple times; *Don Yiẓḥak Abrabanel* (1919); *Yisrael Ba'al Shem Tov* (1923); and *Lefanim o Le'aḥor* (1923; English version by D. Mierovsky, *Conflicting Worlds*, 1933), describing the strains and tensions of modern Jewry. Landau published collected lyrics in *Neginot* (1895) and *Neginot u-Fo'emot* (1933), some of which were set to music; prose writings *Libbot Nishbarim* (1903), literary conversations in novel form; and *Vidduyim* (1928), letters on contemporary Judaism containing much autobiographical material.

The themes of his poems are intensely personal, expressions of *Weltschmerz* and the human predicament, the love of Zion and Israel, and the great characters and leaders in Jewish history. His doctoral dissertation was *N. Krochmal, ein Hegelianer* (1904); he also translated his teacher A. Schwarz's *Die hermeneutische Analogie* into Hebrew under the title *Gezerah Shavah* (1898?). His *Lectures on Modern Hebrew Literature* (1925); *Judaism in Life and Literature* (1936); *Judaism Ancient and Modern* (1936), sermons; and *Short Lectures on Modern Hebrew Literature* (1938) appeared in English. Landau was among the editors of the Hebrew encyclopedia *Oẓar Yisrael* to which he contributed many important articles. Other scholarly articles of his appeared in *Ha-Eshkol* (Cracow) and *Ha-Ẓofeh le-Ḥokhmat Yisrael* (Budapest) as well as in a number of Festschriften. In 1936 a jubilee volume was published in honor of Landau's seventieth birthday, *Ve-Zot li-Yhudah* (Heb. and Eng.).

BIBLIOGRAPHY: Kressel, Leksikon, 2 (1967), 288–89, incl. bibl.; Rabbi Binyamin, in: *Ve-Zot li-Yhudah* (1936), 7–13; D. Mierovsky, *ibid.*, 14–18; S. Rappaport, in: G. Saron and L. Hotz (eds.), *Jews in South Africa* (1955), 283ff.; Waxman, Literature, 4 (1960), 830; A. Yaari, *Ha-Maḥazeh ha-Ivri* (1955), nos. 738–45, bibl. of Heb. dramas; J. Oren, in: *Moznayim*, 24 (1967), 234–41.

LANDAU, LEIB (1879–1944), Polish advocate. Born in Kirov, Russia, Landau qualified as lawyer and rapidly established himself as an authority on criminal procedure. He was defense counsel in a number of famous political trials and represented Jews in legal actions following antisemitic outbreaks. Landau was head of the Przemysl Jewish community and was an active protagonist of Yiddish literature. He was murdered by the Nazis in the Lvov ghetto.

LANDAU, LEIBUSH MENDEL (1861–1920), rabbi and cofounder of the *Mizrachi movement. Born in Sieniawa, Galicia, Landau was ordained by the great rabbis of his time. He first served as a rabbi in Jaroslaw, Galicia, and from 1897 to his death was a rabbi in Botoşani. He joined the Jewish national movement in Galicia and traveled to many cities and towns on educational and propaganda missions, engendering the animosity of the Ḥasidim, who prevented him from receiving a rabbinical post in a number of cities. Landau visited *Herzl after he appeared on the Jewish scene, and in his diary (for Jan. 6, 1897) Herzl described this visit and even sent him to visit the Czortkow rebbe to give him a letter. Ḥasidim prevented the letter from reaching its destination. Landau participated in the founding conference of Mizrachi in Pressburg (1904) and continued his public and Zionist activities in Romania.

BIBLIOGRAPHY: EẒD, 3 (1965), 216–9; *Sefer Przemysl* (1964), 91–92.

[Getzel Kressel]

LANDAU, LEOPOLD (1848–1920), gynecologist. Landau, a descendant of the rabbi and halakhic authority, Ezekiel b. Judah *Landau, was born in Warsaw. On completion of his medical studies, he became a lecturer in gynecology at the University of Breslau (1872–76). While there, he wrote *Zur Physiologie der Bauchspeichelabsonderung* (1873). In 1876 he was appointed lecturer in gynecology at the University of Berlin, becoming a full professor in 1893. In 1892, together with his brother Theodor, Landau founded a clinic for women, which became famous throughout Germany. Here he carried out research, publications being principally in the field of myoma and radical vaginal operations. Besides being a famous physician, Landau was active in the Zionist movement and in the Jewish life of Berlin. He was one of the founders of the Berlin Akademie fuer die Wissenschaft des Judentums.

BIBLIOGRAPHY: J. Pagel, *Biographisches Lexikon hervorragender Aerzte* (1901), s.v.

[Oren Zinder]

LANDAU, LEV DAVIDOVICH (1908–1968), Russian physicist and Nobel Prize winner. Born in Baku, Landau was a young prodigy in mathematics and was allowed to register at Baku University in the faculties of chemistry, physics, and mathematics at the age of 14, and graduated from Leningrad University when he was 19. In 1932 he was appointed head of the theoretical department of the Kharkov Physical-Technical Institute and in 1934 was granted his doctorate without presenting a thesis. He became a professor a year later. While working in Copenhagen with Niels *Bohr, he developed a theory of the diamagnetism of metals known as "Landau's diamagnetism." He also published two comprehensive, seminal works on ferro-magnetic substances in 1936 and 1937. He did research in many fields of physics: low temperature; turbulence; acoustics; plasma theory; energy of stars; quantum field theory; and the neutrino. His outstanding contribution was in the field of low temperatures carried out under the auspices of the Institute for Physical Problems in Moscow, which he joined in 1937. In 1962 Landau was awarded the Nobel Prize for physics for his "pioneering theories for condensed matter, especially liquid helium." Although Landau had been awarded the Stalin Prize three times for his work in theoretical physics, he was imprisoned during Stalin's purge, from 1937 to 1939, allegedly as a German spy. He was released when Professor Peter Kapitza, head of his Institute, declared that he would stop all his own scientific work unless Landau was freed. Landau suffered severe injuries in a car crash in 1962, but intensive medical treatment enabled him to live another six years although without resuming his researches. Among his numerous published works are *O svoystvakh metallov pri ochen nizkikh temperaturakh* ("Properties of Metals at Very Low Temperatures," 1936); *Ob istochnikakh zvezdnoy energii* ("Sources of Stellar Energy," 1937); *O kolebaniyakh elektronnoy plazmy* ("Fluctuations of Electronic Plasma," 1946); and *O kvantovoy teorii polya* ("Quantum Field Theory," 1956).

BIBLIOGRAPHY: A. Dorozynski, *The Man They Wouldn't Let Die* (1965); V.B. Berestetski, in: *Uspekhi fizicheskikh nauk*, 64 no. 3 (1958); *Prominent Personalities in the U.S.S.R.* (1968), s.v.

[Maurice Goldsmith]

LANDAU, MARTIN (1931–), U.S. actor. Born in Brooklyn, New York, Landau began work as a cartoonist for the New York *Daily News* at age 17. He left the paper after five years to focus on comedy writing. In 1955, he applied to Lee Strasberg's famous Actor's Studio and, alongside Steve McQueen, was one of only two applicants – from a pool of 2,000 – to be accepted that year. Landau began his acting career on the New York stage playing prominent roles in Chekhov's *Uncle Vanya* and Franz Werfel's *Goat Song*. In 1957, Landau married Barbara Bain, a model and actress. The two moved to Los Angeles, where Landau landed his debut film role, in Alfred Hitchcock's *North by Northwest* (1959). Landau and Bain co-starred in several different projects, including the television series *Mission: Impossible* (1966–69). Landau chose the *Mission Impossible* role over another he was offered, "Spock" in *Star Trek*. He later appeared in *Space: 1999* (1975–77). Despite the tremendous recognition he earned from his television work, Landau's career seemed headed for obscurity in the 1980s after he appeared in a string of B-movies, including *Fall of the House of Usher* (1979), *Without Warning* (1980), and *Cyclone* (1986). However, his performances in Francis Ford Coppola's film *Tucker* (1988) and, the following year, in Woody Allen's *Crimes and Misdemeanors* earned him consecutive best supporting actor Oscar nominations. But it was his performance as the aging Bela Lugosi in Tim Burton's *Ed Wood* (1994) that won Landau his Academy Award, for which he famously refused to cut short his acceptance speech.

[Casey Schwartz (2nd ed.)]

LANDAU, MOSES (1788–1852), printer, publisher, and lexicographer. Born in Prague, grandson of R. Ezekiel *Landau, Moses was imbued with the traditional atmosphere of his rabbinical family. At the same time, he devoted himself to secular studies, especially German literature. He established a Hebrew printing press in Prague, which, for more than two decades, published sacred literature along with some contemporary Hebrew works, including several volumes of the scholarly periodical **Kerem Ḥemed*. From 1831 until his death he was head of the Prague Jewish community and was instrumental in bringing Solomon Judah *Rapoport there to serve as rabbi. From 1849 he served on the Prague municipal council. The best known of his works, *He-Arukh u-Musaf he-Arukh im Ma'aneh Lashon* (5 vols., 1819–35), is the talmudic dictionary by R. *Nathan b. Jehiel with a German translation. Other works are *Pitron ha-Millot* (Prague, 1827), which deals with the difficult terms found in the Torah; an edition of the Hebrew Bible, with a German translation and a Hebrew commentary on several books (1834–38); a German translation of the *maḥzor* with a Hebrew commentary; the *kinot* for the Ninth of Av; the Passover *Haggadah*; and *Marpe Lashon* (Odessa, 1865), a collection of the foreign words in Rashi's commentary on the Bible and the Talmud.

BIBLIOGRAPHY: Kressel, Leksikon, 2 (1967), 290.

[Getzel Kressel]

LANDAU, MOSHE (1912–2006), jurist, president of Israel Supreme Court. Born in Danzig, he studied in London and went to Palestine in 1933, engaging in private law in practice until 1940. From 1940–48 he was a judge in the Haifa Magistrates Court, and after the establishment of the State became a district court judge. In 1953 he was appointed to the Supreme Court and moved to Jerusalem. He was the presiding judge at the Eichmann *trial. He was also one of the members of the commission of inquiry appointed by the government following the Yom Kippur War. He was active on the board of various cultural institutions, including the Haifa Technion and the Israel Philharmonic Orchestra and was also chairman of the Israel Council of the Hadassah Medical Organization. From 1980 to 1982 he was president of the Supreme Court after having been permanent substitute for the president since 1976. He was awarded the Israel Prize in law for 1991.

[Alexander Zvielli]

LANDAU, NATHAN (d. 1907), Hungarian rabbi. Landau was a *dayyan* in Bardejov (Hg. Bártfa) and subsequently the rabbi and head of the *bet din* of *Oswiecim. He is frequently mentioned in the responsa *Beit Naftali* (1899) of Naphtali Schwartz (5, 6, 31, et al.), and in the *Ya'aneh be-Kol* (1903) edited by Joseph Schwartz. An opinion of Landau's appears in the *Sharvit ha-Zahav* (1912) of Shabbetai Lipschutz. He was succeeded at Oswiecim by his son Eliezer. Landau devoted himself to the methodology of the Talmud, on which he published two works (both arranged alphabetically): *Urah Shaḥar* (1882) and *Kemo ha-Shaḥar* (1904). His acumen and mastery of talmudic learning were evidenced in his *Kenaf Ra'anannah*, responsa (3 vols., 1886–99), *Kerem Nata* (1895), novellae on tractate *Sotah* (1895), and *Levanon Tov* (1901) on *Niddah*.

BIBLIOGRAPHY: P.Z. Schwartz, *Shem ha-Gedolim me-Ereẓ Hagar*, 2 (1914), 213a.

LANDAU, SAUL RAPHAEL (1870–1943), early member of the Labor Zionist movement and one of Herzl's aides. Born in Cracow, Landau contributed to the German and Polish press on Jewish affairs, and with Herzl's appearance he was already a veteran Jewish nationalist publicist. Landau joined Herzl immediately upon the publication of *Der Judenstaat* and became one of his close advisers, particularly on the matter of founding *Die *Welt*. According to Herzl's wishes, Landau took the editorship of the paper upon himself, but held the post only four months (until October 1897). He participated in the First Zionist Congress in Basle. In 1898 he began to come into conflict with Herzl, and their disagreements later broke out in public and led to alienation and mutual animosity.

Under Herzl's influence, Landau had begun to carry out the dissemination of Zionist ideas among Jewish workers. He published a series of articles on the situation of Jewish workers in Galicia and Poland in *Die Welt* that still hold great value for study of the Jewish proletariat in the 1890s (they were reprinted as a book entitled *Unter juedischen Proletariern* (1898)). He also edited a newspaper, *Der juedische Arbeiter* (1898–99), in the same spirit, and it was a forerunner of the Zionist labor press. Landau published polemical books attacking the assimilationists and a propaganda pamphlet on Zionism in Poland. Afterward he concerned himself with his legal practice and edited the newspaper *Neue Nationalzeitung* (1906–17). With the annexation of Austria to Nazi Germany (1938), he left for the United States and there published his memoirs, *Sturm und Drang im Zionismus* (1937) on his contacts with Herzl; they contain an abundance of photographs, documents, and letters from the period.

BIBLIOGRAPHY: T. Herzl, *Complete Diaries*, ed. by R. Patai, 5 vols. (1960), index; G. Kressel, in: *Pirkei Galiẓyah* (1957), 411–7; M. Eisland, in: *Asufot*, 6 (1959), 87–97.

[Getzel Kressel]

LANDAU, SHEMUEL ḤAYYIM (1892–1928), religious Zionist. Landau conceived the idea of "Torah va-Avodah" (Torah and Labor, the basic ideology of religious Zionist pioneering in Ereẓ Israel). Descended from a famous Polish ḥasidic family, he studied in Lukow and in Czemierniki, Galicia. At the beginning of World War I he was taken as a hostage by the invading German armies and later was suspected by them of being a spy for the English. He was eventually sentenced to death but escaped execution. Later the Polish authorities accused him of being a Bolshevik and again he was condemned to death, but after many local Poles testified on his behalf, he was released. He lectured in various Mizrachi branches in Warsaw, and in 1919, at the second conference of the Mizrachi Organization, he participated as a delegate from the Czemierniki branch. He published ideological articles and also participated in the convention in Warsaw in 1921 which created the organizational framework for the Ẓe'irei ha-Mizrachi (Young Mizrachi) Organization. He was elected to the Central Committee and was appointed editor of its newly created Hebrew publication *Ha-Kedem*. A delegate to the 12th Zionist Congress (1921), he became the recognized leader of the Ẓe'irei ha-Mizrachi, and its *ḥalutz* movement, and was elected to the Zionist General Council at the 13th Congress. In 1925, at the world conference of the Mizrachi in Vienna, he was elected to the world center of the Mizrachi as a representative of the "Torah va-Avodah" movement. In 1926 he immigrated with his family to Palestine and settled in Jerusalem. He succeeded there in reuniting the two dissident factions of Ha-Po'el ha-Mizrachi. He continued to develop the doctrine of "Torah va-Avodah" and called for a "holy rebellion," as he designated the spiritual revolution among Ereẓ Israel youth. This call became the watchword of the leaders of nationalist-religious youth.

BIBLIOGRAPHY: S. Don Yaḥya, *Ha-Mered ha-Kadosh, Shemuel Ḥayyim Landau u-Fo'olo* (1960); EẒD, 3 (1965), 226–40; S. Daniel, *Shemuel Ḥayyim Landau* (Heb., 1938).

[Itzhak Goldshlag]

LANDAU, ZISHE (1889–1937), U.S. Yiddish poet. Born in Plotsk (Poland) into a distinguished rabbinical family, Landau had both a traditional and a secular education and was orphaned in childhood. He went to New York in 1906 and began his literary career with lyrics that linked him with the emerging literary group, Di *Yunge, which in reaction to earlier traditions called for "pure" verse free of collective themes. Indeed he later rejected his early poems, written in a traditional style and stressing national and social themes, and recognized as genuine only those written after 1911, when he came under the influence of European impressionism and espoused the credo of "art for art's sake." He was a political conservative and a poetic revolutionary. His *Antologye: Di Idishe Dikhtung in Amerike biz Yohr 1919* ("Anthology: Yiddish Poetry in America until 1919," 1919) best reveals his approach in his introduction and in the poets and type of poems selected. He included only four short poems of Morris *Rosenfeld, for example, who was then enjoying an international reputation for his powerful social and national lyrics. Deeply affected by Jewish suffering during World War I, Landau reverted to Jewish national themes and also wrote poems of U.S. patriotism. In his own verse, he was attracted to symbolism and made frequent use of romantic irony. His subjects are often exotic, his vocabulary allusive rather than expressive. Most popular was his poem on the *Ba'al Shem, whom he depicted as always finding a cheerful aspect in every phenomenon of nature and life. In his four comedies, published under the collective title *Es Iz Gornisht Nit Geshen* ("Nothing Happened," 1937), he employed masks in order to satirize human beings and human relations. His translations of early English ballads and of German, Russian, and French poets were posthumously collected in the volume *Fun der Velt-Poezye* ("From World Poetry," 1947).

BIBLIOGRAPHY: Rejzen, Leksikon, 2 (1927), 62–4; LNYL, 4 (1961), 430–5; D. Kazansky (ed.), *Zishe Landoy Zamlbukh* (1938); H. Gold, *Zishe Landoy* (1945); J. Glatstein, *In Tokh Genumen* (1947), 126–43; D. Ignatoff, *Opgerisene Bleter* (1957), 33–51; S. Niger, *Bleter Geshikhte fun der Nayer Yidisher Literatur* (1961), 430–5; S. Liptzin, *Flowering of Yiddish Literature* (1963), 209–12. **ADD. BIBLIOGRAPHY:** A. Tabachnik, *Der Man fun Lid* (1941); H.L. Bass, "Zisha Landau z"l," at: www.zchor.org/zisza.htm.

[Melech Ravitch / Jerold C. Frakes (2nd ed.)]

LANDAUER, GEORG (1895–1954), Zionist leader, active mainly in aiding the *aliyah* and absorption of German Jews in Israel. Born in Cologne, Landauer was active in the Zionist youth movement *Blau-Weiss and the student Zionist organization Kartell Juedischer Verbindungen. He was a founder of *Ha-Po'el ha-Ẓa'ir in Germany. In 1925 he became director of the Berlin *Palestine Office and, after two visits to Palestine between 1924 and 1933, settled there in 1934. He became managing director of the Palestine Office and of the Zionist Federation in Germany (1929–33). From 1934 to 1954 Landauer was director of the *Jewish Agency Central Bureau for the Settlement of German Jews, in which his main activities were the organization of *aliyah*, capital transfer, agricultural settlement, *Youth Aliyah, and German reparations. He was a founder of Aliyah Ḥadashah, a party of the Mandate period consisting mainly of German immigrants, and a member of the Va'ad Le'ummi (1941–48). From 1948 until his death he was chairman of Irgun Olei Merkaz Europa. He immigrated to the United States in 1953. He wrote *Zwischen zwei Revolutionen; zionistische Betrachtungen zu Fragen der Uebergangszeit* (1942); and a collection of his essays was published in 1957: *Der Zionismus im Wandel dreier Jahrzehnte*.

[Kurt Loewenstein]

LANDAUER, GUSTAV (1870–1919), German philosopher and writer. Landauer, the son of a wealthy Karlsruhe merchant, was drawn toward anarchism in his youth, and as a student in Berlin became editor of the anarchic socialist periodical, *Der Sozialist*. In 1893 – the year in which his first book, a novel titled *Der Todesprediger*, appeared – he was sentenced to 11 months' imprisonment for incitement. On his release he found it impossible to reenter a university, and became a free-lance journalist. He resumed writing for the *Sozialist*, which continued publication until 1899 and which he himself revived ten years later. In 1899 Landauer was again sent to prison, this time for six months, as a result of his agitation on behalf of a man whom he believed to have been wrongly convicted of murder. Shortly after his release, having divorced his first wife, he married the poetess and translator Hedwig Lachmann. Among the books he published in 1903 were *Macht und Maechte*, containing the two short stories, "Arnold Himmelbeber" and "Lebendig tot"; and a version, in modern German, of the writings of the medieval mystic, Meister Eckhart. The political articles he wrote in the *Sozialist* between 1909 and 1914, published posthumously as *Rechenschaft* (1919), revealed his fears of a world war, and by June 1914, with a group that included his friend Martin *Buber, he had made a certain amount of progress in the formation of an international association that might express the voice of a united Europe and avert the tragedy. They were overtaken by events, and when war broke out in August, Landauer and Buber were unable to salvage the group. During the war, Landauer devoted much of his energy to the Berlin popular theater, and his lectures on Shakespeare were published after his death as *Shakespeare, dargestellt in Vortraegen* (2 vols., 1920). In 1918 he became editor of the Duesseldorf theatrical periodical, *Masken*. When the Bavarian Soviet Republic was proclaimed in 1919, Landauer accepted an invitation of Kurt *Eisner to become minister of public instruction, but following the overthrow of the Bavarian Socialist government, he was brutally murdered by counterrevolutionary soldiers in the streets of Munich.

Landauer's philosophical views were influenced by the critical theory of language of his friend Fritz *Mauthner. He believed that Mauthner's work had opened the gate to both philosophical pluralism and a new mysticism by eliminating the possibility of any one philosophy claiming absolute truth. His own semimystical philosophy of the organic interrelationship of all being is expressed in his book *Skepsis und Mystik* ("Doubt and Mysticism"), published in 1903. Landauer's importance as a social philosopher was that, in opposition to Marxism, he wished to construct a new form of society based on the individual. He expressed his ideas mainly in his books *Die Revolution* (1907) and *Aufruf zum Sozialismus* (1911, 1919^2), and summarized them in 12 principles which became the program for the "Socialist Alliance" which he hoped would replace states and a capitalist economy. He wanted a revolution in which individuals, and not the proletariat, would help to fashion a new mode of cooperative living through personal example rather than through politics and party. Under Landauer's editorship the revived *Sozialist* had considerable educational influence as a result of his practice of publishing personal documents from earlier revolutionary eras. Some of these he published in book form as *Briefe aus der Franzoesischen Revolution* (2 vols., 1918). Landauer's attitude to Judaism and Jews, from the evidence of his first stories, was unsympathetic, but it gradually underwent a change, apparently under the influence of his wife and Buber. A letter to Hedwig Lachmann as early as 1900 shows a growing consciousness of his relationship to his ancestors and when, in 1913, the Prague students association, Bar Kochba, published the book *Vom Judentum*, it contained an important essay by Landauer titled "*Sind dies Ketzergedanken?*" ("Are These the Ideas of a Heretic?"). In this he wrote: "For all of us, when we began to be Jews out of full consciousness, it was an enrichment, an elevation, and strengthening of our existence." In the same article he defended the multiplicity of loyalties in the heart of the Jew, which he regarded as "a sign of the mission which Judaism fulfills in relation to humanity and within humanity." After Landauer's death, Martin Buber had his scattered articles compiled into several books. Those on literary subjects appeared as *Der werdende Mensch* (1921), and the ones on the attainment of Socialism as *Beginner* (1924). Throughout the years more of Landauer's essays were collected in volumes such as *Erkenntnis und Befreiung* (1976), edited by R. Link-Salinger Hyman, and *Dichter, Ketzer, Aussenseiter* (1997), edited by H. Delf. His letters, edited by Buber, appeared as *Gustav Landauer, sein Lebensgang in Briefen* (1929). Another correspondence, edited by H. Delf, appeared years later as *Gustav Landauer – Fritz Mauthner Briefwechsel 1890–1919* (1994). Documents on his relationship with Erich Muehsam, edited by C. Knueppel, appeared under the title *Sei Tapfer und wachse dich aus* (2004).

BIBLIOGRAPHY: J. Bab, *Gustav Landauer* (Ger., 1919), includes bibl.; M. Buber, *Gustav Landauer: sein Lebensgang in Briefen*, 2 vols. (1929); A. Mitchell, *Revolution in Bavaria 1918–1919* (1965), index; G. Kressel, *Madda'ei ha-Ḥevrah* (1948), index. **ADD. BIBLIOGRAPHY:** P. Breines, LBIYB, 12 (1969), 75–84; R. Link-Salinger Hyman, *Gustav Landauer: Philosopher of Utopia* (1977); idem, in: *Shdemot*, 18 (1982), 27–33; W. Siegbert, *Gustav Landauer zur Einfuehrung* (1988); H. Delf and G. Mattenklott (eds.), *Gustav Landauer im Gespraech* (1997).

[Samuel Hugo Bergman / Noam Zadoff (2nd ed.)]

LANDAUER, MEYER HEINRICH HIRSCH (1808–1841), writer on the philosophy of religion and Kabbalah. Born at Kappel, near Buchau (Wuerttemberg), he was the son of a cantor and became rabbi of Braunsbach (Wuerttemberg). He had to abandon this post for reasons of health.

On the basis of prolonged study of Hebrew manuscripts in the Munich Library (in 1838), Landauer wrote several studies on the history of medieval Hebrew literature and of the Kabbalah, which constitute the first attempt at a scholarly study of the development of Jewish mysticism. Covering "*Sefer ha-Bahir*," "The word Kabbalah," "Survey of the history and literature of the Kabbalah," "A preliminary appraisal of the *Zohar," and others, they were published posthumously in incomplete form in *Literaturblatt des Orients*. Under the influence of Schelling, Landauer attempted a symbolic mystical interpretation of the Torah and its commandments which should have served as a basis for a religious philosophy of Judaism and which should have also connected it with kabbalistic themes. Of decisive significance in this respect for Landauer was the philosophical-metaphysical meaning of the names of God-YHWH as designation for the "first basic idea of the consciousness of God" in its unified "being in itself" and His government and managing of the world. Elohim is the designation of that aspect of YHWH insofar as it is split into different conceptions by experience and contemplation. The three main forms of God's primary activities are expressed in the three ancient names of God: *El Shaddai, El Ro'i*, and *El Koneh*, which are designations of the concepts of Elohim. Landauer's biblical and theological ideas are contained in *Jehova und Elohim oder die althebraeische Gotteslehre als Grundlage der Geschichte der Symbolik und der Gesetzgebung der Buecher Moses* (Stuttgart, 1836); and *Wesen und Form des Pentateuch* (*ibid.*, 1838). The former work provoked sharp criticism from A. *Geiger, to which Landauer replied in his introduction to the second book.

BIBLIOGRAPHY: I.M. Jost, in: *Israelitische Annalen*, 3 (1841), 69f.; L. Zunz, in: I. Busch (ed.), *Jahrbuch der Israeliten*, 6 (1848), 90; A. Geiger, in: WZJT, 3 (1837), 403–13; Steinschneider, Cat Bod, 1596 no. 6109; Fuerst, Bibliotheca, 2 (1863), 219f.

[Joseph Elijah Heller]

LANDAUER, SAMUEL (1846–1937), German Orientalist and bibliographer. Landauer, born in Huerben, a small village in Bavaria, taught Oriental languages at the University of Strasbourg from 1875. He became director of the state and university library in 1905. When Alsace reverted to France in 1918, Landauer, like most of the German academic staff, was expelled from Strasbourg, and he settled in Augsburg. Landauer was the first to publish the Arabic original of *Saadiah's *Beliefs and Opinions, Kitâb al-Amânât…* (1880). From his Targum research he wrote *Die Masorah zum Onkelos…* (1896), and "Studien zu Merx Chrestomathia Targumica" (in *Zeitschrift fuer Assyriologie*, 3 (1888), 263–92). Landauer's comprehensive knowledge of Oriental languages led him to his participation, early in his academic career, in Vuller's edition of the works of the Persian poet Firdausi, *Firdusii… Schahname* (3 vols., 1877–84). He also cooperated with the Prussian Academy of Sciences in the publication of Aristotle's commentaries, *Themistii… De caelo* (1902), on the writings of the philosopher Themistius, which had been preserved in Hebrew only. Landauer compiled the *Katalog der hebraeischen… Handschriften in der Kaiserlichen Universitaets-und Landesbibliothek in Strassburg, Orientalische Handschriften* (1881), and *Die Handschriften der Grossherzoglich Badischen Hof-und Landesbibliothek in Karlsruhe, vol. 2: Orientalische Handschriften* (1892).

[David Samuel Loewinger]

LANDES, DAVID SAUL (1924–), U.S. economic historian. Born in New York City, Landes received a B.A. from the City College of New York in 1942 and a Ph.D. from Harvard University in 1953. He taught economics at Columbia (1953–58) and Berkeley (1958–64). In 1964 he was appointed professor of history at Harvard, and from 1966 to 1968 directed its center for Middle Eastern Studies. Landes' principal studies were in the economic and social history of modern Europe with special reference to the Industrial Revolution and its social consequences, the history of business interests, that of banking in particular, and the general problem of economic development. His contributions in these fields include *Bankers and Pashas: International Finance and Economic Imperialism in Egypt* (1958); *The Rise of Capitalism* (1966); *The Unbound Prometheus: Technological Change and Industrial Development in Western Europe since 1750* (1968); and "Some Thoughts on the Nature of Economic Imperialism" in *Journal of Economic History*, 21 (1961), 496–512. In these and other works, Landes analyzed the character of technological development and the factors contributing to national and regional differences. On the subject of imperialism, he argued that it is the result of disparities of power, and not a function peculiar to capitalism. Landes was active in Jewish organizations.

After retiring from teaching, Landes was named Coolidge Professor of History and Professor of Economics Emeritus at Harvard.

Other books by Landes include *Revolution in Time: Clocks and the Making of the Modern World* (1983) and *The Wealth and Poverty of Nations* (1998). In the latter, among other novel concepts, he makes a correlation between the economic level of a country and the way the country's women are treated.

[Oscar Isaiah Janowsky / Ruth Beloff (2nd ed.)]

LANDES, RUTH (1908–1991), U.S. cultural anthropologist. Born in New York City to Russian Jewish immigrants, Landes did her undergraduate studies in sociology at New York University. She received an M.A. in social work and a Ph.D. in anthropology from Columbia University. She became research director and coordinator of the Inter-American and the President's Fair Employment Practices Commission, 1941–45; study director of the scientific research department of the American Jewish Committee, 1948–51; and director of the Los Angeles City Health Department's geriatric program (1958–59). From 1953 to 1955 she lectured at the New School for Social Research and the William W. White Psychiatric Institute (1953–54), and from 1956 was professor of anthropology at McMaster University in Hamilton, Ontario (Canada). Her social research experience included service as researcher on the Carnegie Corporation study project on American blacks. As a pioneer in the study of class, race, and gender relations, her primary interests in anthropological research were the American Indians; minority groups in the U.S., Brazil, and the United Kingdom; the educational and cultural status of women; and the interrelations of culture and personality.

In 1982 McMaster University established the Ruth Landes Prize for outstanding academic achievement in anthropology. The Research Institute for the Study of Man established, through the aid of Landes, the RISM-Landes Awards for field research on such anthropological subjects as race and ethnic relations, gender issues, education in a comparative perspective, and problems of aging.

Books by Landes include *The Ojibwa Woman* (1938, 1971,

1997); *The City of Women* (1947, 1994); *Culture in American Education* (1965, 1967²); *Latin Americans of the Southwest* (1965); *The Mystic Lake Sioux* (1968); *Ojibwa Religion and the Midewiwin* (1968); and *The Prairie Potawatomi* (1970).

BIBLIOGRAPHY: S. Cole, *Ruth Landes: A Life in Anthropology* (2003).

[Ephraim Fischoff / Ruth Beloff (2nd ed.)]

LANDESJUDENSCHAFT, BOEHMISCHE, organization of Bohemian Jewry outside the Prague community. Until the end of the Thirty Years' War all Bohemian Jews belonged to the Prague community as one corporate body. The provincial congregations considered themselves at a disadvantage in the allocation of taxes, and as their number increased they created a federation of their own with their own functionaries. An agreement was reached with the Prague community and in 1659 a *Polizeiordnung der Landesjudenschaft* was endorsed, corroborated at the conferences of *Kasejovice (1669) and *Brandys nad Labem (1693), and confirmed by the authorities. The main function of the Landesjudenschaft was the collection and distribution of Jewish taxes; over half had to be raised by the countryside Jews and the rest by the Prague community. Every three years a conference of the assessors was held at Smichov, near Prague. Three assessors were assigned to every district and they, together with the other functionaries of the organization, allotted every district its contribution, after which the district assessors made their allotments to the communities. The taxes were levied by contractors. The organization was headed by 12 representatives, led by the *Primator*, an office first held by Jacob Aaron Lichtenstadt (until 1672) and then by Abraham Aaron *Lichtenstadt (1672–93). The last *Primator* was Joachim Edler von *Popper (1770–91). The organization employed a *Landschreiber* ("secretary"), a *Landes-Sollizitator* ("secretary for legal affairs"), and a *Landeskassier* ("treasurer"), and from 1704 owned a house in Prague.

A Landesrabbinat was established in 1679, but between 1691 and 1717 two *Landesrabbiner* functioned. From 1689 to 1691 Abraham b. Saul *Broda served for the whole of Bohemia and was responsible for the western half only until 1709. Wolf Spira-Wedeles served for eastern Bohemia from 1691 to 1715. In 1713 David *Oppenheim was appointed for one half of the country, and for the whole of Bohemia from 1717 until 1736. He was succeeded by Moses Isaac Spira-Wedeles (1737–49). When the Kreisrabbinate ("district rabbinates") were established in 1717, the function of the *Landesrabbiner* was superseded and the system was formally abolished in 1749. In 1850 a Repraesentanz der Landesjudenschaft in Boehmen was founded. Having no political standing, it engaged mainly in charitable work and, in partnership with the Prague community, maintained the Jewish orphanage for boys in the city. The Landesjudenschaft was dissolved in 1884. Its archives were acquired in 1907 by the Czech national museum in Prague and are now in the Czechoslovak state archives.

BIBLIOGRAPHY: G. Klemperer, in: HJ, 12 (1950), 33–66, 143–52; 13 (1951), 55–82; T. Jakobovits, in: JGGJČ, 1 (1929), 332–68; 3 (1931), 157–60; 4(1932), 257–61; 5 (1933), 79–136; idem, in: MGWJ, 74 (1930), 35–41; S.H. Lieben, in: JJLG, 19 (1928), 1–38 passim; S. Krauss, *Joachim Edler von Popper* (Ger., 1926), passim; Baron, Community, 1 (1942), 339–40; R. Ha-Yisre'eli, *Toledot Kehillat Prag ba-Shanim 1680–1730* (1965), 147–9.

[Meir Lamed]

LANDESMAN, ALTER (1895–1981), Jewish educator. Born in Lithuania, he immigrated to the United States in 1906 and earned his B.A. at Western Reserve University (1917), was ordained at the Jewish Theological Seminary in 1922, and earned a D.H.L. in 1928.

As a Jewish educator he became the superintendent of the Hebrew Education Society (HES) in Brownsville, then one of the largest Jewish communities in New York. HES served as an educational and social center helping the acculturation of American Jews; under Landesman's direction it became a community center for Brownsville Jews. When he began his service, Americanization was a central motif in the work of the Center; over time as immigration to the United States decreased, the task of Americanization became less urgent and the responsibility for continuing Jewish education ever greater.

Landesman worked together with Modern Orthodox elements and HES housed a Young Israel, which met the needs of traditional young people who wanted a sermon in English and wanted religious activities on Friday evening. It held services in the building. HES became more Zionist in orientation and in the early years was more Yiddish oriented, most especially as its leadership passed from German Jews to Eastern European Jews.

He established the Brownsville Neighborhood Council to deal with housing, health, recreation, and social services, and he guided the development of the Young Israel in Brownsville and adjacent East Flatbush.

Landesman was a pioneer in the Jewish center movement. He served as president of the Metropolitan Association of Jewish Center Workers and vice president of the national association.

He prepared for the United Synagogue of America's Committee on Education four curricula; one for schools that met on Sunday; a two-year course for students beginning their studies at age 11 and being trained for their bar-mitzvah; a program for three-day-a-week schools; and a program for four-day-a-week schools. His work covered the entire gamut of Jewish education in those days, as there were only a handful of day schools.

He wrote a well received history of Brownsville, a community that has been understudied and unheralded, but which was critical to New York Jewish life through the first half of the 20th century, and a more scholarly work on the Jews of Provence between the 10th and 14th centuries.

BIBLIOGRAPHY: D. Soyer, "Brownstones and Brownsville," in: *American Jewish History* (2000), 181–207; *Proceedings of the Rabbinical Assembly* (1981).

[Michael Berenbaum (2nd ed.)]

LANDESMAN, ROCCO (1948–), U.S. theatrical producer. Born in St. Louis to a Bohemian German-Jewish family that liked things Italian and owned a cabaret where Lenny *Bruce and Mike *Nichols and Elaine *May performed, Landesman went to Colby College and then to the University of Wisconsin, where he earned his undergraduate degree, and the Yale School of Drama, where he earned a master's degree. For three years he taught dramatic literature and criticism there as a protégé of Robert Brustein. After founding a mutual fund, the Cardinal Fund, and assembling a barn of thoroughbred race horses, in the late 1970s and early 1980s, he turned to theater production with *Big River*, a musical based on *The Adventures of Huckleberry Finn*. Before that production, Landesman was known in the theater as the husband of HEIDI ETTINGER LANDESMAN (1951–), a producer and designer he had met at the drama school. She designed the sets and costumes for *'night Mother* (1983), a two-character play involving a daughter caring for a dying mother. *Big River* developed out of a combination of Rocco Landesman's love for the Mark Twain novel and for the music of Roger Miller, who became the show's composer. The show won the Tony Award for best musical in 1985. It was performed in a theater run by the Jujamcyn organization and when the Landesmans two years later sought to produce another musical, *Into the Woods*, a Stephen *Sondheim creation, they opted again for a Jujamcyn theater on Broadway. The show again was a success, and in 1987 Landesman was asked to take over the Jujamcyn organization, then a fairly consistent money loser. Landesman turned it into a success as the third-largest theatrical organization on Broadway. By 1990 shows in which Jujamcyn had been involved garnered the largest number of Tony nominations that year. At the time, Jujamcyn's theaters housed *City of Angels*, a hit revival of *Gypsy*, Kathleen Turner in *Cat on a Hot Tin Roof*, the musical *Grand Hotel*, and *The Piano Lesson* by August Wilson. Since that time, Landesman has been a producer of some of the most important hit shows: Tony *Kushner's *Angels in America* (1993), Mel *Brooks' *The Producers* (2000), *Doubt* (2004), *Urinetown* (2003), and *Caroline, or Change* (2004). Heidi Ettinger, who resumed her maiden name after the Landesmans' divorce, was active in the theater as a scenic designer and/or producer of such shows as *The Secret Garden* (1991), *Smokey Joe's Café* (1995–2000), *The Adventures of Tom Sawyer* (2001), and *Dracula, the Musical* (2004).

[Stewart Kampel (2nd ed.)]

LANDESRABBINERSCHULE (Országos Rabbiképzö Intézet), Hungarian rabbinical seminary in Budapest. A Hungarian law of 1837 required rabbis to have a secondary education and to register births, marriages, and deaths in Hungarian, and in 1844 parliamentary approval was given to the idea of a rabbinical seminary. In 1850 an indemnity of 2⅓ million florins was imposed on Hungarian Jewry for its participation in the 1848–49 Revolution. By 1856 one million florins had been paid, and the emperor set this aside for Jewish education and, in particular, a rabbinical seminary. It took 20 years of infighting between the Orthodox, who strenuously opposed the seminary idea, and those who inclined toward Reform before the income from this fund could be used for its declared purpose. The matter was finally decided at a conference of Hungarian Jewry (December 1868–February 1869), at which the majority decided on a middle-of-the-road college on the Breslau model.

The Landesrabbinerschule was opened in 1877. It has remained a state institution, administration and staff being appointed by the government, which approved the syllabus and also administered the fund. The course of study was ten years: five years of high school and five years at the seminary proper. During the latter period students were required to enroll at the university and obtain a degree. The following were directors of the seminary: M. Bloch (1877–1907), W. *Bacher (1907–13), L. *Blau (1914–32), M. *Guttmann (1933–42), D.S. *Loewinger (1943–50), A. *Scheiber (1950–between 1952 and 1956 with E. Roth). Other well-known scholars who taught in the seminary were D. *Kaufmann, I. *Goldziher, S. Kohn, L. *Venetianer, B. *Heller, M. *Weisz, D. Friedmann, S. Hevesi, and H.J. Fisher.

The seminary's annual reports (1878–1917 in German, since 1921, Hungarian) generally contain scholarly essays by the teaching staff. A jubilee volume (ed. by L. Blau) was published in 1927. The learned periodical *Magyar Zsidó Szemle* ("Hungarian Jewish Review," 1–65, 1884–1948) was initiated by seminary circles, as were *Ha-Ẓofeh me-Ereẓ Hagar* (later *Ha-Ẓofeh le-Ḥokhmat Yisrael*, 1–15, 1911–31) and *Ha-Soker* (1–6, 1932–39). The Jewish Literary Society also owed its inspiration to the seminary. Its library, which began with Lelio della Torre's collection and grew to over 40,000 volumes, includes many manuscripts and incunabula. When the Nazis occupied Hungary on March 19, 1944, the seminary building was sacked. By admitting all applicants – there were 174 students registered in 1944 – it saved some young men from deportation. Ninety graduates and over 60 students died in the Holocaust. With the liberation of Hungary by the Russians in 1945, the seminary gradually rebuilt its life under the present government, though on a limited scale. It trained Hebrew teachers and expanded the Tarbut high school with special emphasis on modern Hebrew. It maintained contact with Jewish scholars the world over and remained the only rabbinical seminary in Eastern Europe, housing a 150,000-volume library and serving students from neighboring countries into the 21st century.

BIBLIOGRAPHY: L. Blau (ed.), *Festschrift zum 50-jaehrigen Bestehen der Franz-Josef-Landesrabbinerschule in Budapest* (1927); A. Scheiber, in: S. Loewinger (ed.), *Seventy Years* (1948), 8ff.; E. Roth, in: S.K. Mirsky (ed.), *Mosedot Torah be-Eiropah be-Vinyanam u-ve-Ḥurbanam* (1956), 365ff.

[Alexander Scheiber]

LANDIS, JOHN (1950–), U.S. writer-director. Born in Chicago, Illinois, Landis grew up in the Westwood area of Los Angeles, and began working in the mailroom of Twentieth Century Fox as a teenager. In Europe he worked as a production assistant on *Kelly's Heroes* (1970) and as a stuntman for a few spaghetti Westerns. At 21 he began work on his first film, *Schlock* (1973), a horror-genre parody. Landis then directed *Kentucky Fried Movie* (1977), a comedy. But it was Landis' next film, *National Lampoon's Animal House* (1978), that became one of the most famous and successful comedies of all time, spurring a collaboration with actor John Belushi that continued in his next comedy project, *The Blues Brothers* (1980). Landis mixed comedy and horror in *An American Werewolf in London* (1981) and found success with both the Eddie Murphy and Dan Ackroyd comedy *Trading Places* (1983) and the Michael Jackson video *Thriller*. However, Landis' career was tainted by a July 23, 1982, accident on the set of *Twilight Zone – The Movie* (1983), which took the lives of actor Vic Morrow and child actors Renee Chen and My-Ca Le. His subsequent films *Into the Night* (1985), *Spies Like Us* (1985), *Three Amigos* (1986), and *Amazon Women on the Moon* (1987) were poorly received. Despite the success of the Eddie Murphy comedy *Coming to America* (1988), Landis found it difficult to recapture acclaim with such projects as *Oscar* (1991), *Innocent Blood* (1992), *The Stupids* (1996), and *Blues Brothers 2000* (1996), or as executive producer of television shows such as *Sliders* (1995), *Honey, I Shrunk the Kids: The TV Show* (1997), and *The Lost World* (1998). Landis also contributed to the 2005 Showtime cable series *Masters of Horror* with the episode "Deer Women."

BIBLIOGRAPHY: "Landis, John," in: *International Directory of Films and Filmmakers, Volume 2: Directors* (2004); "Landis, John," in: *Contemporary Authors* (Gale, 2004); John Landis – IMDB, at: www.imdb.com/name/nm0000484.

[Adam Wills (2nd ed.)]

LANDJUDENSCHAFT (Heb. *Kehal Medinah, Benei ha-Medinah*), self-governing institutions set up in almost all territories of the Holy Roman Empire where, during the second half of the 16th and the first half of the 17th century, Jewish communities either still existed or had been reestablished after the expulsions at the end of the Middle Ages. The beginnings of such institutions are already discernible in the mid-15th century (Rhineland, Franconia), but most of them disappeared during the constant migrations of the 16th century. Until emancipation, all "protected" Jews living within one of the many principalities of the Holy Roman Empire had to belong to this official Jewish corporation. In contrast with the medieval synods of rabbis and leaders from different regions in Germany, whose decisions on public matters were invested with a vast measure of spiritual-religious authority, those of the 15th and 16th centuries were largely concerned with taxation and administration. An attempt was made in *Frankfurt in 1603 to set up a permanent overall organization, based on a uniform system of taxation and a central judiciary; it failed because of the ascendancy of the princes and the waning of imperial power in Germany. However, German Jewry continued to make efforts to realize the aims embedded in the *takkanot* of the Frankfurt synod. The same spirit reflected in the resistance of the independent territorial authorities to extraneous intervention in their affairs, is apparent in the resistance of the autonomous Landjudenschaft to Jewish intervention in theirs. Each one was bent on developing and enhancing institutions of its own, which grew and crystallized in a slow and organic process, though of course affected by the necessity to come to terms with the new political, economic, demographic, and social conditions prevailing under the absolutist regimes. To a certain extent the Landjudenschaft was influenced by the German Landstaende. The detailed system of their statutes created a stable framework for the independent inner life of the Jewish communities, reflecting their numerical increase and stabilization.

The Landjudenschaft was essentially an association of individuals, largely combining the functions and powers of a local community with those of an "intercommunal" body which acted both internally and externally. Accordingly, its main institution was originally the *Landtag* (*Yom ha-Va'ad*) – the assembly of all heads of families of the territorial Jewish community which took place every three or four years, resulting from the necessity to cope with changes in the taxation systems of most states at that time. In territories with a relatively numerous Jewish population (e.g., Bohemia, Moravia, Alsace) only deputies of the communities met at the *Landtag*, while in Prussia the deputies of various provinces were summoned every five years (from 1728) to fix the tax quota for each Landjudenschaft. Initially, the functions of the *Landtag* covered numerous aspects of Jewish communal life – such as organization and administration, jurisdiction, and religious and social affairs – to a much greater extent than might be assumed from the official definitions and orders determining the assessment for taxation purposes, the *erekh* ("assessed property"). These plenary meetings passed ordinances and statutes and elected – subject to governmental approval – the chief rabbi (*abad ha-medinah*, *abad* being the abbreviation for *av bet din*), the provincial rabbis (*dayyanei medinah*), and the other officials of the Landjudenschaft who constituted the "Small Council": the chief elder (*Oberparnass*), provincial elders (*parnasei medinah*), *viri boni* (*tovim*), and associates (*ikkurim*), as well as the chief treasurer, tax collectors, accountants, the scribe, and the beadle. The chief elder was usually the local *Court Jew, who was appointed by the prince. Thanks to his connections with the court, he also served as *shtadlan* for the community. In some cases the office of Court Jew and chief elder was held within a single family for several generations (e.g., Gomperz in Cleves, Van *Geldern in *Duesseldorf, Goldschmidt in *Kassel, Baer in *Aurich). In practice the Landjudenschaft decided on the granting of charters of protection to new immigrants. The disciplinary means at its disposal were those customary in Jewish autonomy: monetary fines, the *herem*, and expulsion.

The earliest, though scant, documentary evidence that regular assemblies were held every three years comes from *Hesse-Kassel (1616), the electorate of *Treves (1649), the bishopric of Paderborn (1649), Hesse-*Darmstadt (1650), the duchy of *Cleves (1650), the electorate of *Mainz (1661), Lower Austria (1662), the margravates of Burgau (1675?) and *Ansbach (1677), the bishoprics of Bamberg (1678) and *Speyer (1682), the duchy of *Juelich-*Berg (1684), and the bishopric of Strasbourg (1694). That the institution could be set up without governmental instigation becomes apparent in *Hanau and in *Pomerania (1706), in *Mecklenburg-Schwerin (1752), and also, beyond the borders of the empire, in Holland (Meierij's Hertogenbosch, 1764). Yet right of free and independent convention had by no means been granted and the few attempts made in this direction were heavily punished.

In those territories where the Jews were permitted to resettle in the 16th century, they were allowed to elect a rabbi to act as a chief rabbi and judge, whose judicial functions were defined by the authorities. Thus, from the beginning of the 17th until the middle of the 18th century, rabbinates were established in the Teutonic Order lands; in *Mergentheim (1615), *Aderborn (1619), Hesse-Kassel (1625), *Muenster (1649), Hesse-Darmstadt (1685), the *Palatinate (end 17th century), Wied-Runkel (mid. 18th century), and Speyer (1752), thus terminating the previous links of the Jews of these states with the ancient rabbinical courts at Frankfurt, *Worms, *Friedberg, or *Fulda. At the same time rabbinates were set up in new or renewed settlements such as *Hildesheim (1607), *Bamberg (1618), *Wuerzburg (1625), Cleves (about 1650), *Halberstadt-*Minden-*Ravensberg (1650), *Hanover (1687), East-Friesland (end of the 17th century), and Juelich-Berg (1706). The actual powers wielded by the chief rabbis exceeded those vested in them by their writs of appointment; they played an active part in many spheres of administration. They were usually related, either by birth or by marriage, to the *parnasim* and families of Court Jews who led the communities and the Landjudenschaften. Certain rabbinates were retained within one family for several generations. Thus a closely knit circle of families linked by marriage held most leading posts in the secular and religious spheres from Austria and Bohemia in the east to Alsace in the west.

Up to the end of the 17th and the beginning of the 18th century, the details of Jewish self-organization were of no particular concern to the authorities, except when their fiscal interests were involved. But centralized payment of taxes – by now compulsory as a result of the granting of collective charters of protection – compelled the heads of the Landjudenschaften to invoke government aid to coerce dilatory taxpayers. In the course of time, and in keeping with their centralist tendencies, the authorities exploited this dependence to extend their control over Landjudenschaft activities over wide spheres of Jewish autonomy. Gradually many functions of the leadership were transferred to the developing centralist bureaucracy, especially following the setting up of "Commissions for Jewish Affairs" in numerous states. Commissioners frequently attended the *Landtag* as chairmen of the meetings, and at best the Jews were able to do no more than delay the imposition of control (e.g., in the Palatinate, Upper Province of *Mainz, and *Ansbach). Similarly, the authorities' tendency to prevent Jews from turning to foreign rabbinical courts changed in the 18th century in favor of litigation before the state courts of law, restricting the scope of Jewish jurisdiction to religious matters. The Landjudenschaft attempted to stem the tide in this respect and to a certain extent succeeded in evading the restrictive provisions (in Mainz, Hesse-Darmstadt, Fulda, *Wuerzburg, Bamerg, Mecklenburg-Schwerin, and Ansbach).

On the eve of emancipation the states lost all interest in the continued existence of the Landjudenschaft, except as far as their purely religious functions were concerned, for the concept of the Jewish community as a "state within a state" went against the idea of emancipation. The abolition of all such institutions was brought about by government legislation, either on the granting of emancipation in the wake of the French occupation, or as a prerequisite to it demanded by the German states.

BIBLIOGRAPHY: Baron, Community, 3 (1942), index; F. Yizhak Baer, in: *Korrespondenzblatt des Vereins zur Gruendung und Erhaltung einer Akademie fuer die Wissenschaft des Judentums*, 2 (1921), 16ff.; idem, *Das Protokollbuch der Landjudenschaft des Herzogtums Kleve*, vol. 1: *Geschichte* (1922); B. Altmann, in: JSOS, 3 (1941), 159ff. (Paderborn); G. Freund, *Ein Vierteljahrtausend Hannoversches Landrabbinat: 1687–1937* (1937); H. Kraft, in: *Westfaelische Zeitschrift*, 94 (1938), 2, 101ff. (Paderborn); M. Holthausen, *ibid.*, 96 (1941), 48ff. (Westfalen); D.J. Cohen, in: *Sefer Yovel le-Yizhak Baer* (1960), 351ff., xxiiff. (Ansbach); idem, "*Irgunei 'Benei-ha-Medinah' be-Ashkenaz ba-Me'ot ha-17 ve-ha-18*" (1967), includes documents and bibliography (Ph. D. thesis). **ADD. BIBLIOGRAPHY:** S. Rohrbacher, in: *Juedische Gemeinden und Organisationsformen von der Antike bis zur Gegenwart* (1996), 137–49. PUBLISHED SOURCES: M. Horovitz, *Die Frankfurter Rabbinerversammlung vom Jahre 1603* (1897). HESSE-CASSEL: U.F. Kopp, *Bruchstuecke zur Erlaeuterung der Teutschen Geschichte und Rechte*, 2 (1801), 157ff.; L. Horwitz, in: *Im Deutschen Reich*, 14 (1908), 499ff.; idem, in: MGWJ, 54 (1910), 513ff.; L. Munk, in: *Jubelschrift I. Hildesheimer* (1890), 69ff., Heb. section, 77ff.; idem, in: *Festschrift S. Carlebach* (1910), 339ff. MAINZ: S. Bamberger, *Historische Berichte ueber die Juden der Stadt und des ehemaligen Fuerstentums Aschaffenburg* (1900), 88ff. **ADD. BIBLIOGRAPHY:** D.J. Cohen, *Landjudenschaften in Deutschland als Organe juedischer Selbstverwaltung*, 3 vols. (1996–2001). BRANDENBURG-ANSBACH: D.J. Cohen, in: *Kovez al Yad*, 16 (1966), 457ff. PRUSSIA: S. Stern, *Der Preussische Staat und die Juden* (2 vols., 1925, repr. 1962). SUGENHEIM: M. Freudenthal, in: ZGJD, 1 (1929), 44ff. WIELD-RUNKEL: B. Wachstein, *ibid.*, 4 (1932), 129ff.; idem, in: YIVO *Bleter*, 6 (1934), 84ff. MECKLENBURG-SCHWERIN: O.G. Tychsen, in: *Buetzowische Nebenstunden*, 4 (1768), 1ff.; L. Donath, *Geschichte der Juden in Mecklenburg* (1874). AUSTRIA: L. Moses, *Die Juden in Niederoesterreich* (1935). ALSACE: L. Loewenstein, in: BJGL, 2 (1901), 18ff., 28. TRÈVES: A. Kober, in: MGWJ, 77 (1938), 100ff. MORAVIA: I. Halpern, *Takkanot Medinat Mehrin, 1650–1748* (1951).

[Daniel J. Cohen]

LANDMAN, ISAAC (1880–1946), U.S. Reform rabbi. Born in Sudilkov, Russia, Landman was taken to Cincinnati in 1889. He matriculated at the University of Cincinnati (1906) and was ordained at Hebrew Union College. He served at Congregation Kenesseth Israel, Philadelphia (1906–10), and helped establish the farm colony of Jews in Clarion, Utah. Landman was equally active outside the congregational sphere. While in Philadelphia, he was executive secretary of the National Farm School, and in 1916 he was Jewish chaplain with the U.S. forces in Mexico. From 1918 to 1937 he was editor of the *American Hebrew* and in 1928 began the planning of the *Universal Jewish Encyclopedia*, of which he was editor in chief and which appeared in ten volumes between 1939 and 1943. A veteran of World War I, he also served as chaplain with Pershing's army in Mexico and worked with the Jewish Welfare Board to establish a training school for chaplains. He then served at Temple Israel in Far Rockaway, N.Y., and became editor of the *American Hebrew*, then a prominent newspaper. When the depression hit, he was forced to return to the pulpit and went on to serve Beth Elohim, in Brooklyn (1931–46). One of Landman's principal interests was the goodwill movement between Christians and Jews. Triggered by a blood libel accusation in 1927 in upstate New York, called the Massena Incident, he organized the Permanent Commission for Better Understanding Between Protestants, Catholics and Jews and became its executive secretary. When the National Conference of Christians and Jews was formed the Commission was no longer needed. A man of varied talents, he was interested in drama and worked with his brother on a number of plays. He testified against political Zionism before the Foreign Affairs Committee of the House of Representatives and fought domestic antisemitism so actively that he was called the two-fisted rabbi. He was a delegate to the founding of the World Union of Progressive Judaism (1926) and named president of the interdenominational Synagogue Council of America just before he died.

[Michael Berenbaum (2nd ed.)]

LANDMARKS, fixed stone objects erected to designate the boundaries between fields, districts, lands, or nations in the Near East. The removal of landmarks is considered to be a grievous sin in the Bible and in other literature of the Near East. Deuteronomy twice warns against this offense (Deut. 19:14; 27:17). The biblical prohibition against landmark removal is mentioned along with other transgressions that are perpetrated secretly and, therefore, usually not punished by society. A biblical imprecation (Heb. *arur*) is therefore leveled against the violator, all other punitive measures being inadequate.

Babylonian boundary stones or monuments (*kudurru*) first appear in the Kassite period and may originally have served to mark boundaries in a field, but seem to have become legal records dealing with landed property. The inscription on the stone usually contains some statement or certificate of ownership, and severe maledictions are appended to it, directed to anyone who should alter or destroy the inscription. There appear on the stones symbols of Babylonian deities who are asked to invoke the curse on the future offender. Ancient wisdom literature also contains severe warnings against the removal of landmarks, particularly those of a widow (the "Instruction of Amen-em-Opet" 7:15, in Pritchard, Texts, 422; COS I:117), and the transgressor is threatened with divine punishment by the gods because he violated divinely established boundaries. The offense of the removal of boundary stones was used metaphorically as a symbol for the abolition of ancient laws and custom (Prov. 22:28; 23:10). Those who defected from the Qumran sect are said to be "removers of the landmark" (see C. Rabin, *The Zadokite Documents* (1954), 4, 20, 42).

For the extension of the concept of infringement on the rights of others, see *Hassagat Gevul*.

BIBLIOGRAPHY: L.W. King (ed.), *Babylonian Boundary-Stones and Memorial-Tablets in the British Museum* (1912). **ADD. BIBLIOGRAPHY:** U. Seidl, *Die babylonischen Kudurru-Reliefs* (1989); idem, in: RLA, 6, 275–77; M. Broshi (ed.), *The Damascus Document Reconsidered* (1992).

LANDON, MICHAEL (**Eugene Maurice Orowitz**; 1936–1991), U.S. actor, writer, producer, director. Born in Forest Hills, Queens, to an Irish Catholic mother and Jewish father, Eugene Orowitz grew up in Collingswood, New Jersey, and went to UCLA on a track and field scholarship. He was forced to leave school when an arm injury disqualified him from athletics. He stayed in the area and worked at odd jobs until he decided to pursue acting. After adopting the stage name Michael Landon, which he picked out of the Los Angeles telephone book, he soon landed his first big role in the film *I Was a Teenage Werewolf* (1957). However, it was as Little Joe Cartwright on the television series *Bonanza* (1959–72) that Landon became a household name, endearing himself to a wide range of Americans throughout the 14 years that the series ran. When Landon undertook his next television project, *Little House on the Prairie* (1974), another NBC western, it was not only in the role of family patriarch Charles Ingalls but also as the series' producer, writer, and director. After a successful eight-year run, *Little House* was pulled off the air and Landon moved onto the NBC fantasy/drama show *Highway to Heaven* (1984). When Landon's co-star, Victor French, died of lung cancer in 1989, Landon pulled the plug on the show, prompting his dismissal from NBC. Diagnosed with pancreatic cancer soon afterward, Landon made his last public appearance on the Johnny Carson show in 1991, discussing his disease with bravery and candor. He died a few weeks later in Malibu, California, with his children at his side.

[Casey Schwartz (2nd ed.)]

LANDOWSKA, WANDA (1879–1959), harpsichordist, pianist, and composer. Born in Warsaw, Landowska bean to play the piano at the age of four. She studied at the Warsaw Conservatory with Michałowski and in Berlin (1896) with Moszkowski (piano and composition). In Paris (1900) she married Henry Lew, a writer on Hebrew folk music. Landowska was one of the first to revive harpsichord music and won renown in that field. Giving numerous concerts and lectures she reawakened interest in music of the Baroque period. She toured all over Europe including Russia. In 1912, the piano maker Pleyel built her a special harpsichord. In 1913 she went to Berlin to teach harpsichord at the Musik-Hochschule. After World War I, Landowska taught in Basel and played a harpsichord continuo in the *St. Matthew Passion* – for the first time in the 20th century. In Paris, she taught at the Ecole Normale de Musique. Landowska founded her own Ecole de Musique Ancienne at Saint-Leu-la-Flôret, near Paris, for the study, teaching, and performance of early music. There, in 1933, she gave the first integral performance of Bach's Goldberg Variations. With the advent of Hitler, she was forced to leave the school. She fled to France and settled in the U.S. in 1941. At the age of 70 she recorded the complete Bach "48." Her performance style was an assertive one, highlighted by legato playing and variety of articulation. She developed modern harpsichord technique and played compositions written for her by several modern composers, such as Falla and Poulenc. Landowska was decorated by both the French and Polish governments.

ADD. BIBLIOGRAPHY: Her books include *Bach et ses interprèts* (1906) and *La musique ancienne* (1909). Denise Restout edited a collection of her articles as *Landowska on Music* (1965). **ADD. BIBLIOGRAPHY:** Grove online; *MGG*; D. Marty, *Une dame nommée Wanda* (1993).

[Claude Abravanel / Naama Ramot (2nd ed.)]

LANDRABBINER (Landesrabbiner, Heb. *rav medinah*), rabbinical office formerly prevalent throughout Central Europe. It originated in the latter half of the 14th century when regional rulers appointed a "*Judenmeister*," later called *Landesrabbiner*, to facilitate the collection of taxes. In the 15th century, as a result of the widespread expulsions of the period, this charge was abolished. Instead, the rabbinical courts of the free imperial cities like Frankfurt and Worms acquired increased authority and importance. With the reestablishment of Jewish communities in the 16th and early 17th centuries, some states authorized the appointment of a chief rabbi (*rav medinah*) and the establishment of a rabbinical court (*bet din*). In 1600 there were a dozen such courts in Germany. The establishment of these institutions did much to undercut the influence of the rabbinical courts in the free imperial cities, a development welcomed by rulers who sought to sever the ties that bound Jews living in their realms to courts operating outside their jurisdiction. Most of the Landjudenschaften employed a *Landrabbiner* (*rav medinah, av bet din*), whose main function was the equitable apportioning of the tax load. The *Landrabbiner* was sometimes directly appointed by the authorities, but generally he was elected by the Landjudenschaft; the authorities authorized the elections and issued him a formal writ of responsibilities and powers. Often the *Landrabbiner* had close family and social connections with the secular leadership of the Landjudenschaften; at times the office remained within the same family for several generations. Its sinecures provided the incumbent with a relatively high income. While the secular Jewish leadership considered that the *Landrabbiner* provided religious sanction for their efforts, the authorities sought to make use of him as a power lever within the Jewish community. Frequent disagreement developed over policy and jurisdiction. The authority of the *Landrabbiner* gradually lapsed in the later 18th century, particularly in the light of the increasing tendency to appeal to general courts of law. The continuity of the office was broken during the Napoleonic era.

In the 19th century *Landrabbiner* were appointed once more by a number of German states. The three *Landrabbiner* of Hanover represented the government in the supervision of synagogues, schools, and charitable institutions in their districts. In charge of the inspection and appointment of all communal employees, they could levy fines of up to ten marks and could not be deposed without governmental consent even though they were elected by the communities. In Mecklenburg-Schwerin, Saxe-Weimar, and Brunswick, *Landrabbiner* were appointed to facilitate the modernization of Jewish life and religious practice. When Abraham *Geiger wished to introduce the institution into Nassau he encountered the vigorous opposition of the Orthodox rural communities. During the course of the 19th century the jurisdiction of the office was increasingly limited to purely religious areas, and in the 20th century, it became mainly an honorary appointment.

BIBLIOGRAPHY: D.J. Cohen, "*Irgunei 'Benei ha-Medinah' he-Ashkenaz*" (unpubl. Ph.D. diss., 1967), 157–227, xvii–xxi; L. Auerbach, *Das Judentum in Preussen* (1890), 328–405; B. Altman, in: *JSOS*, 3 (1941), 175–7; S. Assaf, in: *Reshumot*, 2 (1937), 259–300.

LANDSBERG, MICHELE (1939–), Canadian journalist, author, feminist, social critic. Landsberg was born in Toronto. After high school she spent a year in Israel and returned to Toronto to earn a B.A. in English language and literature from the University of Toronto in 1962. From the 1960s she was active as a reporter, freelance writer, and columnist for both the *Globe and Mail* and *Toronto Star* newspapers. In the 1970s she also served as writer and editor with *Chatelaine*, a popular Canadian women's magazine. She wrote covers stories on contemporary feminism, politics, media, women's health, the environment, education, urban life, and gardening. Her work at the *Toronto Star* earned her two National Newspaper Awards, including the first ever awarded for column writing, and she was among the paper's top-read columnists.

Michele Landsberg was also the author of several books, including *Women and Children First* (1982); *Michele Landsberg's Guide to Children's Books* (1986), also published in the United States and England, where it was a London *Times* Book of the Year; and *This is New York, Honey!*, which was number one on the bestseller list in 1989. A passionate and sometimes controversial social critic and voice for progressive causes, Landsberg has also served on the boards of a number of agencies and volunteer organizations working to assist assaulted women, global feminism, and the cause of peace in the Middle East. Some of Landsberg's honors include the Robertine Barry Prize for journalism from the Canadian Research Institute for the Advancement of Women, the Florence Bird Award from the International Centre for Human Rights and Democratic Development, and the 2002 Governor General's Medal in Commemoration of the Persons Case, an award acknowledging contributions to equality for women which have resulted in positive change. Landsberg is married to Stephen Lewis, former Canadian ambassador to the United Nations and United Nations special envoy for HIV/AIDS in Africa.

[Randal F. Schnoor (2nd ed.)]

LANDSBERG, OTTO (1869–1957), German politician. Born in Rybnik, Upper Silesia, in 1890 Landsberg joined the Social Democratic Party while a law student in Berlin. He practiced law in Magdeburg, where he became a town councilor in 1903. In 1912 he was elected to the Reichstag. He belonged to the extreme right wing of his party, and was under constant attack from the leftists because of his patriotic attitude. During World War I, Landsberg became increasingly influential in the Social Democratic Party, and after the outbreak of the revolution in Germany, became a member of the Council of People's Plenipotentiaries, which exercised the functions of government. He consistently opposed Bolshevik ideology, and in January 1919 was seized by the revolutionary workers and condemned to death. He was rescued by troops called up by the chancellor, Friedrich Ebert. A month later Ebert made him minister of justice in the first Weimar government and a member of the German delegation at Versailles in the summer of that year. Landsberg opposed the signing of the peace treaty, and resigned from the government. From 1920 to 1923 he was German ambassador to Belgium.

Landsberg returned to Berlin in 1924 and resumed his law practice. Reelected to the Reichstag in 1924, he remained a member until the Nazis came to power in 1933. He emigrated via the CSR, Schwitzerland und Belgium to Holland and lived there in hiding throughout World War II. Landsberg was not a member of the Jewish community, but was one of the founders of the Association for Defense against Antisemitism. He wrote *Student und Politik* (1925) and *Politische Krise der Gegenwart* (1931). After 1945 he supported the Social Democratic periodical *Neuer Vorwärts* but stayed in Holland and died in Baarn (near Utrecht).

ADD. BIBLIOGRAPHY: H.L. Abmeier, Otto Landsberg, in: *Jahrbuch der schlesischen Friedrich-Wilhelm-Universitaet zu Breslau*, 14 (1969); *Biographisches Handbuch der deutschsprachigen Emigration nach 1933*, vol. 1 (1999), 415.

[Bernard Dov Ganzel / Bjoern Siegel (2nd ed.)]

LANDSBERGER, ARTHUR (1876–1933), German novelist and editor. Born into a well-to-do Protestant Berlin family of Jewish descent, Landsberger studied law, but decided to devote himself to literature and art. In 1907 he helped found *Der Morgen*, a periodical devoted to art and general culture. He wrote many exciting, but ephemeral, detective and adventure stories. His heroes and heroines are often satanic types, Landsberger being most at home among the nouveaux riches and demimondaines of Berlin's Kurfuerstendamm. In his popular novel *Wie Hilde Simon mit Gott und dem Teufel kaempfte* (1911), he introduced Jewish themes, as also in the novel *Berlin ohne Juden* (1925; modeled on a similar book on Vienna, *Die Stadt ohne Juden* [1922] by Hugo *Bettauer). Landsberger's *Juedische Sprichwoerter* (1912) pioneered in the German translation of Yiddish works. In 1914 he edited *Das Ghettobuch*, a collection of stories of East European Jewish life taken primarily from the Yiddish classics. A second volume, *Das Volk des Ghetto*, appeared in 1916. When the Nazis came to power in 1933, Landsberger committed suicide.

ADD. BIBLIOGRAPHY: C. Schwarz, in: W. Killy (ed.), *Literatur Lexikon*, 7 (1990), 132.

[Rudolf Kayser]

LANDSBERGER, BENNO (1890–1968), Assyriologist. Landsberger was born in Frydek, then Austrian Silesia (now Czech Republic). He studied Semitic languages at the University of Leipzig (1908–13) and specialized, under H. Zimmern, in Sumerian and Akkadian. In 1920 he was appointed lecturer at the University of Leipzig and, in 1926, professor of Assyriology, a position he held until 1935. Deprived of his chair in Leipzig by the Nazis, he left Germany in 1935 and was appointed professor of Assyriology at the University of Ankara, Turkey. From 1948 he was professor of Assyriology at the Oriental Institute of the University of Chicago. Landsberger laid the foundation for the modern study of Assyriology. In his philological studies Landsberger freed Assyriology from its dependence upon Arabic and Hebrew and contributed to its establishment as a discipline in its own right. As for Mesopotamian culture, he sought to delineate its specific character (*Eigenbegrifflichkeit*), not by comparison and contrast with the Bible, but rather through investigation of the elements in its evolution: language, cult, law, literature, material culture, social and economic structure. His genius found its expression not only in his philological works, prominent among which is the edition of the Sumero-Akkadian lexical lists, but also in his penetrating and original treatment of some crucial problems of Mesopotamian history and chronology. Of special significance in the field of Semitic philology are his contributions on Hebrew-Akkadian and Aramaic-Akkadian comparative semantics and lexicography and on the Semitic verb. Landsberger's work was continued by his numerous disciples in major centers of Assyriological research.

Landsberger's publications cover almost every aspect of Assyriology. His major work – unfinished – was his *Materialen zum sumerischen Lexicon* (9 vols., 1937–68), which he edited. Other principal monographs are *Der kultische Kalender der Babylonier und Assyrer* (1915); *Die Fauna des Alten Mesopotamien* (1934); *Sam'al* (1948); *Assyrische Koenigsliste und "Dunkles Zeitalter"* (1954); *Brief des Bischofs von Esagila an Koenig Asarhaddon* (1965); and *The Date Palm and Its By-Products According to the Cuneiform Sources* (1967). He was editor of the *Zeitschrift fuer Assyrologie* (1931–36), and from 1956 until his death, he was one of the editors of *The Chicago Assyrian Dictionary* (10 vols. published to 1968). A bibliography of Landsberger's lexicographical contributions up to 1950 appeared in *Journal of Cuneiform Studies*, 4 (1950), 1–62. Jubilee volumes in his honor were: on his 70th birthday: *Journal of Near Eastern Studies*, 19 (April 1960), no. 2; on his 75th birthday: *Studies in Honor of Benno Landsberger on his Seventy-Fifth Birthday*, 1965 (Assyriological Studies of the Oriental Institute of the University of Chicago, no. 16).

BIBLIOGRAPHY: W. von Soden, in: *Forschungen und Fortschritte*, 39 (1960), 125–6; idem, in: ZDMG, 119 (1969), 1–14; A.L. Oppenheim, in: *Orientalia*, 37 (1968), 367–70; H.G. Gueterbock, in: AFO, 22 (1968/69), 203–6. **ADD. BIBLIOGRAPHY:** A. Kilmer and J. Renger, in: JCS, 26 (1974), 183–94 (bibl. of Landsberger's publications).

[Hayim Tadmor]

LANDSHUT, city in Bavaria, Germany. Jews may have lived there since its foundation in 1204, although they are first mentioned in 1256. In 1337 and 1349 atrocities were committed following the *Deggendorf and *Black Death disturbances, although Jews were found in the city once more shortly after both persecutions. A Jewish street and its neighboring gate are mentioned in 1331. A mid-14th-century parchment describes the moneylender "Feifelein," the "Jew's king," taking a Jewish *oath. While Duke Henry of Landshut protected the Jews, his son Ludwig expelled them in 1450, confiscating their valuables and canceling the debts due to them. A 15th-century Hebrew tombstone is preserved in the municipal museum. The synagogue was converted into a church in 1452. In 1810 one Jew lived in Landshut and 100 years later the town had 60 Jewish inhabitants. The number of Jews declined from 48 in 1933 to 18 in 1939. On April 2/3, 1942, 11 Jews from the town were deported east. During World War II, 200 Jews, victims of a nearby labor camp, were buried near the city.

BIBLIOGRAPHY: Salfeld, Martyrol, index; R. Straus, in: ZGJD, 1 (1929), 96–118; 5 (1935), 42–49; G. Kisch, in: HJ, 1 (1938–39), 119–20; Germ Jud, 1 (1963), index; 2 (1968), 467–9; PK Germanyah.

LANDSHUT, SIEGFRIED (1897–1968), German Marxian scholar and sociologist. Born in Strasbourg, Landshut studied economics, philosophy, and social science and became assistant lecturer at the University of Hamburg in 1927, but immigrated to Palestine in 1933, where he did research at the Hebrew University. In 1951 he was reinstated as a professor of sociology and political science at the University of Hamburg. Landshut edited the early writings of Marx under the title *Karl Marx: Die Fruehschriften* (1932) and a selection from the writings of Tocqueville under the title *A. de Tocqueville: Das Zeitalter der Gleichheit* (1954). In his early work, *Kritik der Soziologie* (1929), he considers liberty and equality as the initial sociological concepts, derived from the thought of the 18th century and transformed in the 19th century by Marx. The disappearance of societal diversification and the fusion of the state with society, according to Landshut, have rendered all traditional institutions highly questionable. Landshut also wrote a biography of Karl Marx which was included in *Coleman's Kleine Biographien* (1932), *Gemeinschaftssiedlungen in Palaestina* (1934), and *Jewish Communities in the Muslim Countries of the Middle East* (1950).

ADD. BIBLIOGRAPHY: R. Nicolaysen, *Siegfried Landshut – Die Wiederentdeckung der Politik* (1997); R. Nicolaysen, *Polis und Moderne – Siegfried Landshut in heutiger Sicht* (2000); J.M. Krois, G. Lohse, and R. Nicolaysen, *Die Wissenschaftler – Ernst Cassirer, Bruno Snel, Siegfried Landshut* (1994).

[Werner J. Cahnman / Bjoern Siegel (2nd ed.)]

LANDSHUTH, ELIEZER (**Leser**; 1817–1887), liturgical scholar and historian. Born in Lissa (now Lezno) to poor parents, Landshuth decided to study for the rabbinate and at the age of 20 proceeded to Berlin, where he studied for some years in the yeshivah of R. Jacob Joseph Oettinger, the rabbi of Berlin. Landshuth always referred to him in terms of the greatest respect as his teacher and mentor. In 1842 he referred to himself as a candidate for the rabbinate and wrote an article, *Die Verbindlichkeit des Zeremonialgesetzes fuer den juedischen Krieger* (Allgemeines Archiv des Judenthums, 2 (1842), 246–75), which he published under a pseudonym. Shortly afterward, however (possibly influenced by Zunz and Geiger, with whom he was in contact), he changed his mind and with the assistance of some friends became a bookseller. He was not very successful and accepted a position as superintendent of the ancient cemetery of the Berlin Jewish community.

According to the testimony of his friends, Landshuth entertained the most extreme liberal views with regard to Judaism, but there is not even a hint of them in his work. Landshuth's reputation rests mainly on his research into the Jewish liturgy, and his work has retained its value to the present day. His method was to trace the prayers, their authors, and their sources in the Talmud and midrashic literature, and he wrote three works on this subject: the prayer book *Hegyon Lev*, published by H. Edelman (Koenigsberg, 1845), includes a commentary by Landshuth in the form of footnotes, entitled *Kunteres Berakhah*, in which he attempts to establish the period during which most of the prayers were composed. The commentary already reveals a real critical faculty and serious research. His second work is a Passover *Haggadah* with an introduction, *Maggid me-Reshit* (Berlin, 1855), which follows the same method. The third is *Seder Bikkur Ḥolim, Ma'avar Yabbok ve-Sefer ha-Ḥayyim*, a collection of prayers and meditations for the sick, the dying, and funerals (1867), with a scholarly introduction on the origin of these prayers and customs and an appendix (in some copies only) containing examples of typical tombstone inscriptions with biographical data.

His research in this field and his extensive knowledge of the various liturgical rites led him to compose his most famous work, a biographical and bibliographical dictionary on the *paytanim*, entitled *Ammudei ha-Avodah* (*Onomasticon Auctorum Hymnorum Hebraeorum*… Vol. I, 1857; Vol. II, 1862, reprinted 1968). Although it was rendered somewhat obsolete by Zunz in his *Synagogale Poesie* which appeared in 1863, it contains valuable and accurate information. Possibly as a result of Zunz's work, the third volume was never published. He then devoted himself to the history of the Berlin Jewish community and published *Toledot Anshei Shem u-Fe'ulatam*, on the rabbis of Berlin up to 1800 (Part 1, 1884, Part 2 was not published), as well as *Ateret Ẓevi*, a biography of Hirschel *Levin. Geiger in his *Geschichte der Juden in Berlin* made use of the material Landshuth collected without acknowledging the source. A portion of Landshuth's manuscripts passed to Dr. S. Neumann, and another to the Hochschule fuer die Wissenschaft des Judenthum. A pamphlet he wrote on the rabbis of his birthplace, Lissa, *Zikkaron ba-Sefer*, served as a source for many details in L. Lewin's *Geschichte der Juden in Lissa* (1904).

BIBLIOGRAPHY: L. Lewin, *Geschichte der Juden in Lissa* (1904), 293–6.

[Ernst Daniel Goldschmidt]

LANDSMANNSCHAFTEN, immigrant benevolent organizations formed and named after the members' birthplace or East European residence, for mutual aid, hometown aid, and social purposes. In North America landsmannschaften were, at first, immigrant synagogues. This began to change after 1880 as secular landsmannschaften tended to replace the synagogue societies. The benefits which the landsmannschaften attempted to provide included sick benefits, interest-free loans, and burial rights and aid to families during the period of mourning. They also aided their overseas *landsleit* and helped to bring many to the United States. By 1914 New York City knew of at least 534 of these organizations with membership ranging from 50 to 500. Many became affiliated with national fraternal organizations such as the Workmen's Circle, Jewish National Workmen's Alliance (Farband), and Sons of Zion. In addition, there existed such federations as the United Galician Jews of America. The number of landsmannschaften grew rapidly during World War I, and these organizations, representing most of the cities and towns of Eastern Europe, dispatched millions of dollars in relief supplies and cash. After the war, the landsmannschaften utilized their money and membership to finance the relief work carried on by the Joint Distribution Committee, Hadassah, and other organizations, and to oppose antisemitism and discrimination in its varied forms.

Despite the decline in the membership and activities of the landsmannschaften after 1930, due in part to the dying off of the immigrant generation, hundreds of thousands of European-born Jews still belonged to landsmannschaft societies in the period immediately prior to World War II. European antisemitism stimulated the formation of many central landsmannschaften which attempted both to assist their harassed *landsleit* overseas and to bring groups of immigrants into the United States and Palestine by the use of "corporation visas." During this period, the landsmannschaften increasingly participated in such local Jewish communal activities as community councils and the charity federations.

The landsmannschaften experienced a minor revival after World War II, brought about by the need to aid both the survivors of the Holocaust (many of whom joined these landsmannschaften after their arrival in the United States) and Israel in the form of clothing, medical supplies, food, and war material where and when it could be procured. However, this revival was relatively short-lived. Taking Chicago as symptomatic of this revival, that city had approximately 600 landsmannschaften with 40,000 members in 1948. In 1961 there were only 60 landsmannschaften in the city.

In Latin America

In most Latin American countries Jewish organizations and congregations were formed in three separate frameworks: East European; Sephardi and Syrian-Lebanese; and German. Each was subdivided in many groups, according to their places or areas of origin (Bessarabian, Polish, etc.; or those from Aleppo, Damascus, or Bulgaria, Turkey, etc.; German, Austrian, Bohemian). They sometimes published newspapers or periodicals in their language of origin, maintained clubs, commemorated their communities which perished in the Holocaust (and sent help to those which still exist). Most of these landsmannschaften did not survive the immigrant generation and disappeared gradually among their Spanish-Portuguese-speaking descendants. (See the articles on individual countries.)

In Israel

Already in the Mandatory period, and particularly in the State of Israel, many immigrants established organizations according to their places or countries of origin. Those who originated from a town or region (such as Bialystok or Bessarabia) aided individual immigrants from there and cultivated, orally and in book form, the memory of their communities destroyed in the Holocaust. More comprehensive organizations, particularly those representing immigrants from Germany and Austria in the middle and late 1930s (Hitaḥdut Olei Merkaz Europa), eventually even coalesced into political parties (as Aliyah Ḥadashah), which later dissolved into the traditional parties of the *yishuv*. They also developed a net of mutual aid and welfare institutions, such as old age homes. A specific role has been played by the unions of immigrants from Soviet Russia and the Western and overseas countries – Britain, Latin America, United States and Canada – which greatly influenced the immigration and absorption system evolved by the Jewish Agency and the government in dealing with the special needs of these immigrants. Little effort was made to cultivate the various non-Jewish cultural and linguistic traditions brought by the immigrants from their countries. Some East European groups aided the publication of Yiddish literature; Italian immigrants formed the Dante Alighieri Society; many non-Hebrew newspapers (including Hungarian and Russian) served the needs of immigrants for information, etc. However, the most conspicuous trait of these phenomena is their quick disappearance in the next, Israel-born or Israel-raised, generation.

BIBLIOGRAPHY: W.J. Robinson, in: *Sentinel's History of Chicago Jewry, 1911–1961* (1961), 198–9; M. Rischin, *Promised City* (1962), 104–5; M.J. Karpf, *Jewish Community Organization in the United States* (1938), 131–2; U.S. Works Progress Administration, *Yidishe Landsmanshaften fun New York* (1938).

LANDSOFER, JONAH BEN ELIJAH (1678–1712), rabbi and author, an opponent of the Shabbateans. Landsofer lived in Prague and, like his father and grandfather, was a professional scribe. It has been suggested that his name Landsofer ("scribe of the province") refers to his occupation, his real family name being Bunzlau after the town where the family originated. Landsofer was a versatile personality, and studied both Talmud and Kabbalah. He was sent to Vienna by his teacher, Abraham *Broda, to engage in disputations with the Shabbateans. Only some of his works have been published, among them *Me'il Ẓedakah* (Prague, 1757), responsa; *Benei Yonah* (*ibid.*, 1803), a comprehensive work on all the rules of writing of the *Sefer Torah*, and the importance of its being written elegantly (in one place the author writes at length on Bibles printed by gentiles, "which Jews do not refrain from reading," and concludes that they should be discarded); *Kanfei Yonah* (*ibid.*, 1812); novellae on the Shulḥan Arukh, *Yoreh De'ah*, up to chapter 110. In his *Me'il Ẓedakah*, he mentions his *Me'orei Or* on matters connected with the *Sefer Torah*, which was never published. At the end of *Me'il Ẓedakah* there are notes to Euclid, proof of the author's wide interests. His ethical will, first published in *Derekh Tovim* (Frankfurt, 1717), reflects his piety and exceptional humility. Despite his premature death, he was regarded as one of the outstanding scholars of Prague.

BIBLIOGRAPHY: K. Lieben, *Gal Ed* (1856), 29 (German section); Loewenstein, in: MGWJ, 57 (1913), 356–8; I. Abrahams, *Hebrew Ethical Wills*, 2 (1927), 285–8; Wachstein, in: KS, 11 (1934/35), 374; I.Z. Kahana, *Ha-Defus ba-Halakhah* (1945), 8f., 27f.; M. Guedemann, *Quellenschriften* (1891), 127–35.

[Naphtali Ben-Menahem]

LANDSTEINER, KARL (1868–1943), scientist and Nobel Prize laureate, discoverer of the basic human blood groups and of the Rhesus blood factor. Landsteiner was born in Vienna; from 1898 to 1908 he worked at the Pathology Institute of Vienna University and from 1909 to 1919 taught pathology at the University's Wilhelminenspital. After three years in Holland he went to New York in 1922 to become a member of the Rockefeller Institute for Medical Research, and worked there for the rest of his life. He died a Roman Catholic.

In 1927, together with Philip *Levine, Landsteiner described the M, N, and P factors in human blood. These hereditary factors came to be used to decide cases of doubtful paternity. In 1930 he was awarded the Nobel Prize for physiology and medicine, for his discovery of four different groups of human blood, A, B, AB, and O, distinguished by their clotting factors. This became the basis for matching donor and recipient in blood transfusions.

In 1940 Landsteiner and Alexander S. Wiener completed the research leading to their discovery of the Rhesus or Rh factor which was to become of lifesaving importance in obstetrics and clinical medicine. Landsteiner also made other major contributions to medical science: he introduced dark-field illumination for demonstrating spirochetes in syphilitic lesions and discovered that the rhesus monkey could be infected by the poliomyelitis virus – a finding which was the basis, decades later, for the development of the *Salk vaccine. His *The Specificity of Serological Reactions* (1936) has become a classic.

BIBLIOGRAPHY: T.N. Levitan, *Laureates: Jewish Winners of the Nobel Prize* (1960), 128, 137–40; Heidelberger, in: *Science*, 98 (1943), 233f.; P. Speiser, *Karl Landsteiner* (Ger., 1914), including list of his publications.

[Samuel Aaron Miller]

LANG, FRITZ (1890–1976), Austrian film director and screenwriter; son of a non-Jewish father and a Jewish mother (Pauline Schlesinger) who converted to Catholicism when Lang was 10 years old. Born in Vienna, Lang went to Berlin in 1919 and, after writing screenplays, turned to directing. His reputation was established in 1921 with the allegorical *Der Muede Tod* (known in English as "Destiny"), which paved the way in film technique by its use of dream effects and decorations. In 1922 he directed *Dr. Mabuse*, the first of a series of melodramas of that name about a powerful gang leader with fabulous powers of hypnosis. In 1924 he directed *Die Nibelungen*, in which an invincible hero is overcome by human weakness. His film *Metropolis* (1926), for which he wrote the screenplay, was about automaton-like labor in the year 2000. In 1931 he shot his most successful German film, *M*, which he also wrote. A year after his *Das Testament des Dr. Mabuse* (1932), Lang was approached by Joseph Goebbels with the proposition of putting him in charge of Nazi films. That same evening Lang, fearing that his Jewish origin would become known, fled to France and later to the U.S., where he went to work for Metro-Goldwyn-Mayer in 1934, and was reduced to screenwriting for some time. His reputation was reestablished with his two socially conscious films *Fury* (which he also wrote, 1936) and *You Only Live Once* (1937). He later turned to directing more popular films, including several westerns (e.g., *Western Union* (1940)) and anti-Nazi films. One of his successful later films was *The Woman in the Window* (1944). Lang's films are characterized by a pervasively dark and hostile atmosphere, fraught with sinister characters and a cynical view of the world. In many cases, the titles of the films themselves already herald the sense of foreboding. Such films include *Harakiri* (1919); *Ministry of Fear* (1944); *The Big Heat* (1953); *Human Desire* (1954); *Moonfleet* (1955); and *While the City Sleeps* (1956). Lang's book, *Saint Cinema: Writings on Film 1929–1970*, which he co-authored with Herman Weinberg, was published in 1980.

BIBLIOGRAPHY: P.M. Jensen, *The Cinema of Fritz Lang* (1969), includes "filmography." **ADD. BIBLIOGRAPHY:** B. Grant (ed.), *Fritz Lang: Interviews* (2003).

[Ruth Beloff (2nd ed.)]

LANG, JACK (1939–), French public figure and minister of culture. Lang studied law and politics before turning to theater and theater management. He directed the Festival Mondial du Théatre Universitaire (1963–72) and also the Chaillot Theater (the former TNP) in Paris (1972–74). In 1978 Lang was appointed special adviser to the first secretary of the Socialist party and in 1979 he became director of the cultural activities of the party. In 1981 he was appointed minister of culture in the Socialist government under President Mitterrand. In this position, Lang sought to implement the cultural platform of the Socialist party, to encourage popular theater and culture and government support for films. At one time violently opposed to "American cultural imperialism," Lang subsequently toned down his criticism while making an all out effort to promote French culture on the international scene. He devoted much attention to promoting youth activities, including rock performances. He ceased to be minister with the defeat of the Socialists in 1993.

[Gideon Kouts]

LANG, PEARL (1921–), U.S. dancer. Lang was born to Jacob Lack from Vilna and Frieda (nee Feder) from Pinsk. She studied modern dance with Francis Allis. In 1941 she went to New York to study with Martha *Graham and Louis Horst and shortly thereafter joined the Martha Graham Dance Company, performing from 1941 to 1955. Lang became the premier interpreter of Graham's work and the first to perform Graham's own roles, including "El Penitente," "Appalachian Spring," "Herodiade," and "Clytemnestra." Lang also performed on Broadway in musicals, including Agnes de Mille's *One Touch of Venus*, *Carousel*, Michael *Kidd's *Finian's Rainbow*, and Helen Tamiris' *Touch and Go*. She formed her own company in 1953. Of her 34 works on Jewish themes, her signature work was *Shirah* (in 1960), to music by Alan Hovhaness, inspired by Rabbi Nachman of Bratzlav's story about a spring flowing from a high mountain to the end of the world. Her first work was *Song of Deborah*, restaged in 1967 to music of the Israeli Sergiu *Natra for the Batsheva Dance Company. Lang's *The Possessed* (inspired by the classic Yiddish drama *The Dybbuk*) was choreographed in 1975 and reset as a film in 1997. Her *Dances from the Ballads of Itzik Manger*, to music by Jan *Radzynski, Yehudi Wyner, and Dov Seltzer, was created in 1981. Others who have composed for her include Tzevi *Avni ("And Jacob Wrestled with the Angel"); Mordechai *Seter ("Prayers at Midnight"); Aaron *Copland ("Sabbath Song"); and Steve *Reich ("Tehillim").

Lang has set her dances for the Dutch National Ballet, the Batsheva Dance Company, the Repertory Dance Theater of Utah, and the Boston Ballet. In 1975, Lang returned to the Graham Company to dance the title role in *Clytemnestra*. She continued performing until 1989; she was considered a master teacher of the Graham technique. She also taught at the Yale University School of Drama and was guest teacher in Switzerland, Sweden, and Israel. She received the Guggenheim choreographic fellowship in 1960 and 1969; the Cultural Achievement Award of the National Foundation for Jewish Culture in 1992; and an honorary doctorate of fine arts from the Juilliard School in 1995.

BIBLIOGRAPHY: IED; B.N. Cohen-Stratyner, "Lang, Pearl," in: *Biographical Dictionary of Dance* (1982); J.T. Strasbaugh, "Lang, Pearl," in: P.E. Hyman and D. Dash Moore (eds.), *Jewish Women in America, An Historical Encyclopedia* (1997).

[Judith Brin Ingber (2nd ed.)]

°**LANGALLERIE, PHILIPPE GENTIL DE** (1656–1717), French general and adventurer who dreamed of establishing a Jewish state. After serving under the French, the Austrians, and the Poles, in 1716 Langallerie made an offer to the Turks through their envoy in The Hague. He would lead a motley army of disguised pilgrims into Italy, overthrow the pope, and hand Rome to the Turks. In return, he would receive one of their islands, or possibly the Holy Land itself, in order to settle there the lost Jewish tribes. He then appealed, though fruitlessly, to the Jewish communities in Amsterdam, Hamburg, Altona, and elsewhere to equip a fleet of 50 men-of-war and an army of 10,000 soldiers. His project attracted the kabbalist Alexander Susskind of Metz, who was to act as treasurer in Langallerie's chimerical "théocratie du verbe divin." In 1716 he was arrested near Hamburg and brought to Vienna. He was tried for conspiracy and high treason and died in prison.

BIBLIOGRAPHY: Kaufmann, in: REJ, 28 (1894), 193–211; Gelber, in: REJ, 89 (1930), 224–36.

[Emmanuel Beeri]

LANGDON, DAVID (1914–), British cartoonist and illustrator. Educated at the London School of Economics, Langdon began to draw regularly for *Punch* in 1937 and eventually became a member of the "Punch Table," the weekly staff gathering which plans each issue of the paper. During World War II, he was a squadron leader in the Royal Air Force, and in 1945–46 edited the RAF *Journal*. After the war he contributed to various London papers, including *Reynolds News*, the *Evening Standard*, and the *Sunday Mirror*. From 1952 his drawings, distinguished by their elegance of line and ironic approach, also appeared regularly in the American weekly, *The New Yorker*. Langdon's cartoons were collected in a number of volumes, among them *Home Front Lines* (1941), *The Way I See It* (1947), *All in Fun* (1955), *Langdon at Large* (1958), *Punch with Wings* (1961), and *How to Play Golf and Stay Happy* (1964). He illustrated humorous books by George Mikes and others.

LANGER, FRANTIŠEK (1888–1965), Czech playwright, novelist, and physician. Langer was born in Prague. His first play, *Svatý Václav* ("St. Wenceslas," 1912), was staged by the Prague National Theater before he was 23. An officer in the Austrian army in World War I, Langer was taken prisoner by the Russians and subsequently joined the Czech Legion formed by Thomas Masaryk. Langer belonged to Masaryk's *Pátečníci* ("Friday Group"), the statesman's circle of closest friends, and was deeply influenced by Masaryk's humanistic philosophy. Other influences apparent in his writing are his Russian experiences and the human suffering with which he came into daily contact as an army doctor. He eventually became head of the Czechoslovak Army Medical Corps. Escaping to France from Nazi-occupied Prague in 1939, Langer fled to London after the fall of Paris, but returned to his own country after World War II. For many years he was president of the Czechoslovak PEN Club, representing his country at various international literary congresses.

Langer was a fine storyteller with a penetrating insight into human problems. His novels and collections of short stories incude *Zlatá Venuše* ("Golden Venus," 1911), *Železný vlk* ("Iron Wolf," 1920), *Předměstské povídky* ("Suburb Stories," 1926), *Děti a dýka* ("Children and the Dagger," 1943), and *Filatelistické povidky* ("Philatelist Stories," 1964). He is, however, best known as the outstanding Czech playwright next to Čapek. His best-known plays are the drama *Periferie* ("Outskirts," 1925) and the comedy *Velbloud uchem jehly* (1923; *The Camel through the Needle's Eye*, 1929); both were translated into many languages, and, in the stage versions of Max *Reinhardt, were international successes. Langer's other stage successes were *Noc* ("Night," 1922), *Anděle mezi námi* ("Angels Among Us," on the problem of euthanasia, 1931), *Dvaasedmdesátka* ("Number 72," 1937), and *Jiskra v popelu* ("Spark in Ashes," 1948); in the last two, the truth is revealed through the technique of a play within a play. Two charming and successful comedies were *Grand Hotel Nevada* (1927) and *Obrácení Ferdyše Pištory* ("The Conversion of Ferdyš Pištora," 1929). *Bronzová rapsódie* ("Rhapsody in Bronze," 1962), Langer's last play, is a poetic allegory about war and peace with an ancient Greek setting. Many of his plays were adapted for the screen. *Filatelistické povídky* ("Stamp Collector Stories," 1965) was published in the year of his death and *Malířské povídky* ("Painter Stories," 1966) posthumously. The European Holocaust shocked Langer into a new awareness of his Jewish identity, as may be seen in the chapter dedicated to his late brother, Jiří Mordechai *Langer, in a postwar book of reminiscences entitled *Byli a bylo* ("There Were and There Was," 1963, 1971, 1991). This chapter, "Můj bratr Jiří" ("My Brother Jiří") is the introduction to Jiří Langer's book, *Devět bran* (1937, 1990; *Nine Gates*, 1961). Langer's literary work appeared rarely during the Communist era. From 2000 his collected works began to be published (in 15 volumes).

BIBLIOGRAPHY: P. Váša and A. Gregor, *Katechismus dějin české literatury* (1925); O. Donath, *Židé a židovství v české literatuře 19. a 20. století* (1930); B. Václavek, *Česká literatura XX. století* (1935); J. Kunc, *Slovník českých spisovatelů beletristů* (1957); Hostovský, in: *Jews of Czechoslovakia* (1967), 440f. **ADD. BIBLIOGRAPHY:** *František Langer na prahu nového tisíciletí* (2000); *Slovník českých spisovatelů* (2000); *Lexikon české literatury 2/II* (1985).

[Avigdor Dagan / Milos Pojar (2nd ed.)]

LANGER, JIŘÍ MORDECHAI (1894–1943), Czech poet and author, and a younger brother of the playwright František *Langer. Born in Prague, Jiří rebelled against his assimilatory upbringing and in 1913 went to Belz (Galicia), where he remained for some time at the court of the Rokeaḥ dynasty of ḥasidic rabbis. When he returned to Prague, he retained his ḥasidic garb and continued to lead a strictly observant life. On the outbreak of World War I, following a second visit to Belz, he was conscripted into the Austrian army but was released because of his religious inflexibility. He then became a teacher at a Jewish school in Vienna and Prague and wrote Hebrew poetry such as *Piyyutim ve-Shirei Yedidut* (1929). Langer applied Freudian theories to the interpretation of certain aspects of Jewish literature and ritual in such studies as *Die Erotik der Kabbala* (1923), *Erotika kabaly* (1991), *Zur Funktion der juedischen Tuerpfortenrolle* (1928), *Die juedischen Gebetriemen – Phylakterien* (1931), and *Talmud. Ukázky a dějiny* ("Talmud. Extracts and History," 1938, 1993, 1994). His outstanding literary achievements are, however, *Devět bran Chasidů tajemství* (1937, 1965, 1990, 1996; *Nine Gates to the Hasidic Mysteries*, 1961), a volume of ḥasidic tales which have also been translated into Italian and German, and *Zpěvy zavržených* ("Songs of the Rejected," 1937, 1993), verse ranging from 11th-century Spain to 19th-century Prague. Langer was a close friend of Franz *Kafka, whom he taught Hebrew, and of Max *Brod, who records in his autobiography that some of his works would never have been written without Langer's assistance. After the Nazi invasion of Czechoslovakia, Langer escaped and entered Palestine as an illegal immigrant. In Palestine he wrote a second volume of Hebrew poetry, *Me'at Ẓori* (1943). Langer died in Tel Aviv. After the collapse of the Communist regime, his works were published in Czechoslovakia and in the Czech Republic.

BIBLIOGRAPHY: J. Langer, *Nine Gates* (1961), vii–xxxii (introd. by F. Langer); M. Brod, *Der Prager Kreis* (1966); Kressel, *Leksikon*, 2 (1967), 287–8. **ADD. BIBLIOGRAPHY:** H. Carmel, "Mordechai Jiří Langer: Cabbalist, Writer and Poet," in: *Review of the Society for the History of Czechoslovak Jews*, vol. 5 (1992–93), 93–126; J. Langer, *Devět bran* (1990), 9–47 (introduction by T. Pěkný); *Lexikon české literatury 2/II* (1985); *Slovník českých spisovatelů* (1982).

[Avigdor Dagan / Milos Pojar (2nd ed.)]

LANGER, LAWRENCE L. (1929–), U.S. scholar of Holocaust literature. Professor of English Emeritus at Simmons College in Boston, Langer is the foremost scholar of the Holocaust in the field of literature and testimony. *The Holocaust and the Literary Imagination* (1975), his first work on the Holocaust, was followed by *The Age of Atrocity: Death in Modern Literature* (1978); *Versions of Survival: The Holocaust and the Human Spirit* (1982); *Holocaust Testimonies: The Ruins of Memory* (1991); *Admitting the Holocaust: Collected Essays* (1995); and *Preempting the Holocaust.* He is also editor of *Art from the Ashes: A Holocaust Anthology* (1995). Langer's contributions to the field are many. In *Versions of Survival*, he coined the term "choiceless choices" to describe the unprecedented situations of conflict that Jews found themselves in during the Holocaust. *Holocaust Testimonies*, based on his study of survivors' oral histories in the *Fortunoff Video Archives, won a National Book Critics Circle Award and was named one of the "Ten Best Books of 1991" by the *New York Times Book Review.* It was one of the first scholarly works to examine survivors' testimonies as a basis for understanding the Holocaust. A hallmark of Langer's analyses is the rejection of reading a redemptive message into study of the Holocaust, an understanding that he pursues with rigor against all attempts to soften our understanding.

Initially, especially in his widely respected work *The Holocaust and the Literary Imagination*, Langer's preoccupation was with literature, but gradually and perceptively his focus shifted. He became consumed by the task of understanding the Holocaust. Literature became his tool; in the hands of a master, the tool soon became a club for undermining some of the simple conventions of Western society. More and more, Langer's work concentrated on memoirs and memory, telling of the assault against the individual that was at the core of the Shoah. More than any other student of literature, Langer insisted that the Holocaust was about atrocity. No simple meanings could be found, no reassuring sense of triumphant values, no invocation of Viktor Frankl's "will to meaning" or Terrence Des Pres' "life spirit." For Langer, there was no escape from darkness, no way to sidestep the radical challenge posed by the Holocaust.

His understanding of Holocaust testimonies was another exploration of the narrative of survival. Unlike literary memoirs or diaries, the testimonies are the products of ordinary people, often without great literary or intellectual sophistication, who have lived through extraordinary events. Video testimonies are spontaneous and unrehearsed, they do not have the worked-through quality of literary creations. Often, the witnesses surprise themselves by what is recalled. Langer may have heard more of these oral histories than anyone alive, and he brings to this study decades of sensitivity toward the event and the literature. Yet, throughout the work he retains a keen ability to hear and resists the temptation to organize and categorize the material. Instead, the reader is treated to an extended essay on memory, deep memory, anguished memory, humiliated memory, tainted memory, unheroic memory (as the titles of his chapters go). What emerges is a refined understanding of the Holocaust as experienced by those who lived it, an uncovering of all levels of memory that falsify the event, that protect the individual from the full impact of this most painful experience. Like a great psychoanalyst, Langer strips away layer after layer of falsehood until the reader is forced to face the core experience – directly, faithfully, faithlessly.

Having opted for early retirement, he left Simmons in 1992 after more than three decades of teaching and retired to write. He has written works on the art of Samuel *Bak that combine a keen analysis of his art with an even more profound understanding of the subject matter of the art, whether it be Genesis or the shattered world in which post-Holocaust humanity dwells.

[Beth Cohen (2nd ed.)]

LANGER, ROBERT S. (1948–) U.S. biomedical engineer. Born in Albany, New York, Langer received his B.Sc. from Cornell University (1970) and D.Sc. from Massachusetts Institute of Technology (1974) in chemical engineering. After postdoctoral cancer research at Harvard Medical School with Judah Folkman, he returned to MIT (1977), where he became Germeshausen Professor of Chemical and Biomedical Engineering and director of the research laboratory named after him. His research interests initially concerned the design of polymers compatible with biological tissues which would allow the controlled release of drugs and macromolecules into the blood stream and at sites affected by diseases such as cancer. His interests subsequently included the application of materials science and biotechnology to controlled drug delivery, including gene therapy, and developing biodegradable systems which will serve as templates for generating new tissues and organs. Langer is an acknowledged leader in innovative biotechnology and the Langer Laboratory is preeminent in this field. His many honors include the first Gairdner Award to an engineer (1996) and the Draper Prize from the U.S. National Academy of Engineering (2002). Uniquely, he is a member of the Institute of Medicine of the U.S. National Academy of Sciences (1992), the National Academy of Engineering (1992), and the National Academy of Sciences (1992). He served as member, then chairman, of the U.S. Food and Drug Administration's Science Board (1995–2002). He received honorary doctorates from the Haifa Technion and the Hebrew University of Jerusalem.

[Michael Denman (2nd ed.)]

LANGERMANN, MAX (1859–1919), South African mining pioneer. Born in Bavaria, he went to South Africa at the age of 20 and served in two military campaigns against African tribesmen. In the early days of the goldfields he went to Johannesburg, prospecting for minerals and taking part in industrial projects. He was particularly interested in town planning and laid out several residential suburbs in the growing mining center. Langermann was associated with the political agitation which led to the Jameson Raid (1895) and was imprisoned and fined for his activities. After the South African War (1899–1902) he sat on the Johannesburg town council and helped to gain municipal franchise for aliens. In 1907 he became a member of the Transvaal legislative council. One of the most prominent Jewish personalities of his time in the Transvaal, Langermann played a leading role in the formation of the Transvaal and Natal Jewish Board of Deputies in Johannesburg in 1903 and was its first president. For a time he headed the Territorial Organization in South Africa.

BIBLIOGRAPHY: G. Saron and L. Hotz, *Jews in South Africa* (1955), index.

[Louis Hotz]

LANGFUS, ANNA (1920–1966), French novelist. Born in Lublin, Poland, Langfus first published stories in Polish literary magazines at the age of 15. Her experiences in Nazi-occupied Poland left scars that were to mark her later writing. As a member of the Resistance, she was several times arrested by the Gestapo and was finally imprisoned in Plock until the liberation. In 1946 she immigrated to France. Acquiring a remarkable command of the French language, Anna Langfus began writing plays, her drama *Les Lépreux* being published in 1956. She then wrote three powerful novels about the Holocaust and its Jewish victims. The first, *Le Sel et le soufre* (1960; *The Whole Land Brimstone*, 1962), is the story of a young Polish Jewess whose comfortable middle-class existence is suddenly disrupted by the Nazi invaders, who murder first her parents, then her husband. *Les Bagages de Sable* (1962; *The Lost Shore*, 1963), which was awarded the Prix Goncourt, is a work of autobiographical character that tells a similar story. Her last novel, *Saute Barbara* (1965), describes how another victim of the Nazis abducts a young German girl who bears a striking resemblance to his lost daughter. Anna Langfus' works present individual destinies illustrating a common fate. In the midst of persecution and atrocities, her tragic heroes never lose their human dignity or moral outlook.

[Lionel Cohen]

LANGUAGE WAR (Ger. **Sprachenkampf**), campaign waged during the winter of 1913/14 by the Hebrew Teachers' Union in Ereẓ Israel against the *Hilfsverein der deutschen Juden over the issue of the language of instruction in Hilfsverein educational institutions. The Hilfsverein had been founded in Berlin in 1901 by the cotton magnate James *Simon and Dr. Paul *Nathan, the former acting as president and the latter as director. One of the Hilfsverein's objectives was to raise the cultural standard of Jews in the Ottoman Empire.

Nathan laid the foundation of an extensive network of schools in Ereẓ Israel, from kindergartens to a teachers' training college which, unlike the *Alliance Israélite schools, employed modern pedagogic methods. Instructors were competent and the Hilfsverein's educational director, Ephraim Cohn-Reiss, was an efficient administrator. Nathan was also responsible for introducing Hebrew as a language of instruction, believing that it would serve as a unifying factor for the polyglot composition of the *yishuv*. Scientific subjects, however, were taught in German.

Although the motives for introducing Hebrew in these schools were pedagogical rather than nationalistic, the Zionists fully appreciated the Hilfsverein's activities. Lacking sufficient financial resources to maintain their own school system, they willingly cooperated with the Hilfsverein. This relationship paved the way for partnership in a more ambitious project, Nathan's brainchild, the founding of a technical college (Technikum or *Technion) in Haifa. Nathan and Shmarya *Levin, a member of the Zionist Executive, managed to prevail upon Kalonymus Ze'ev *Wissotzky, a Russian tea magnate, to make a large financial contribution; Levin also interested Jacob *Schiff, the celebrated Jewish financier and philanthropist in New York, in the project, receiving a sizable donation from him. Both Wissotzky and Schiff were represented on the board of the preparatory committee, chaired by James Simon; the Hilfsverein members were in a majority. Three Zionists, *Aḥad Ha-Am, Jehiel Tschlenow, and Shmarya Levin, also joined the board, though in a private capacity. It was understood that the language of instruction for scientific subjects in the college would be German.

When the Hilfsverein-Zionist rapprochement took place in 1906, no serious difficulties were foreseen. Some German Zionist leaders, such as Arthur *Hantke, Kurt *Blumenfeld, and Richard *Lichtheim, had grave misgivings about an association with anti-Zionist assimilationists, and even Aḥad Ha-Am urged caution before entering into an agreement with the Hilfsverein; but expediency prevailed: the Zionists were in no position to renounce the partnership. Ironically, one of its first great enthusiasts was Shmarya Levin. The Hilfsverein's successful work enhanced Zionist confidence, but it was not long before a divergence of views appeared.

Nathan feared that the partnership with the Zionists might prejudice the Hilfsverein's standing with both German Jewry and the Turks. He lost no opportunity to stress that his Association was completely detached from Zionism, its only purpose "the cultural and economic welfare of the Jews." Whereas the Zionists, as Chaim *Weizmann put it, were struggling to weld the Jewish community in the country into "one creative unit," Nathan rejected Jewish exclusivism outright.

However disparate the two attitudes, the conflict which developed was not inevitable. Neither the Hilfsverein nor the Zionist Organization desired it. Otto *Warburg, chairman of the Zionist Organization, continued to serve on the Hilfsverein Committee, and at the 11th Zionist Congress (1913), Chaim Weizmann publicly expressed his fear that the premature introduction of Hebrew into the Technical College might adversely affect the quality of teaching. Tschlenow, the Russian Zionist leader and a member of the College board, agreed: in an appreciative reference to the Hilfsverein's work, he went so far as to state that its educational program was compatible with "the national aim." Shmarya Levin thought differently: at the same Congress he declared that the Zionist Organization must fulfill its "unconditional obligation to concentrate in its hands the total cultural work in Ereẓ Israel," and to exclude those bodies "which lacked that banner." Nathan took offense, all the more since it was the Hilfsverein that had first grasped the importance of organizing the Jewish communities in the Middle East, and especially of educating the youth. It was unthinkable to him that his primacy, gained by heavy investment and pioneering work, should now be lost. He regarded the Teachers' Union, which the Zionist Executive in Berlin was "too weak" to restrain, as chiefly responsible for the now full-blown *Sprachenkampf*. But the teachers, too, had grievances; those in the Hilfsverein schools saw that since 1911 Hebrew had been repressed in favor of German and they placed the blame for this, during the Teachers' Union conference in August 1913, on Ephraim Cohn-Reiss, suspecting that he had submitted to "secret pressure exercised by the German Government."

Documentary evidence shows that this impression was mistaken: neither Berlin nor the German Consulate in the country was pushing German *Kultur* at the expense of Hebrew education. It was rather the Hilfsverein representatives themselves who repeatedly pointed to the Jews as a link between Germany and the Orient and praised the projected Technikum in Haifa as a "stronghold of *Deutschtum* in the Holy Land," arousing Zionist suspicions that Jewish settlement was to be subordinated to German political aspirations. Ephraim Cohn-Reiss, in particular, had incensed the teachers when, in 1913, he rejected their proposal to accelerate the Hebraization of his schools. The resignation of the Zionist representatives on the board of the Technikum heightened the tension. Before that meeting on October 26, 1913, Shmarya Levin appealed to Dr. Nathan, emphasizing that only Hebrew could provide the technical college with a semblance of neutrality. However, the Zionist members on the Technikum board were in a minority and could not claim the exclusive right to draft its program. Moreover, the original agreement, to which all parties had committed themselves, stipulated that scientific subjects were to be taught in German. Aḥad Ha-Am warned his fellow Zionists that, lacking Hebrew textbooks, adequate Hebrew terminology, and experienced staff to teach scientific subjects in that language, a speedy conversion of the Technikum into a Hebrew institution was both impractical and unfair.

At the same time, he attempted to convince Dr. Nathan of the necessity of gradually introducing Hebrew into the Technikum. However, Nathan was unmoved. Aḥad Ha-Am suspected that Nathan's inflexibility was determined by some secret agreement between the German government and the Hilfsverein. Though this was not the case, the episode served as the final fuse which sparked off the Teachers' Union struggle against "the complete suppression of Hebrew." Animated protest meetings were held throughout the country, and a strike was declared in the Hilfsverein schools. Dr. Nathan arrived in Ereẓ Israel in a militant mood and rejected all compromise solutions. Dismissal of certain teachers provoked a violent demonstration at the Laemel School in Jerusalem and elsewhere. These events took the Zionist Executive in Berlin entirely by surprise. The strike and particularly the teachers' exit *en masse* from the Hilfsverein schools, accompanied by their students, aroused general displeasure; the most outspoken critic was Aḥad Ha-Am. Despite serious misgivings, however, the Executive could not desert the teachers. As soon as the struggle assumed a more positive character, a widespread campaign was launched in Europe and the United States to provide funds for the maintenance of independent Hebrew schools. Once involved, the Executive became a party to the conflict. It could not remain indifferent to the course pursued by the Hilfsverein and other segments of German Jewry, which tried to implicate the Zionist Organization in responsibility for the teachers' strike.

With Nathan's return to Berlin the campaign intensified. In January 1914 his pamphlet *Palaestina und palaestinensischer Zionismus* appeared, and the influential *Frankfurter Zeitung* opened its pages to him.

The Zionists replied in a pamphlet *Im Kampf um die hebraische Sprache*, and, judging from the generous response and the number of voluntary contributions for the Hebrew Schools Funds, it was clear that their arguments were gradually gaining ground. But it was not until the meeting of the Technikum's board on February 24, 1914, that the Hilfsverein was decisively defeated. During that meeting the American and Russian members of the board sided with the Zionists: by deciding to separate the affiliated Grammar School from the Technical College, they removed the principal bone of contention. In the grammar school Hebrew would be used immediately as the exclusive language of instruction while in the college it would be introduced in the course of four years. Thus the Zionist executive emerged triumphant.

Given the German government's preference for the Hilfsverein, the Zionist victory on the political plane is the more surprising. Conrad von Wangenheim, the German ambassador in Constantinople, expressed no objection to the superiority of Hebrew while Counselor von Kühlman stated officially that "Germany would be sufficiently compensated if, besides Hebrew, German would also be cultivated." The primacy of Hebrew was thus fully conceded. After World War I and throughout the period of the British Mandate, the sole language of instruction, from kindergartens to the Technion, was Hebrew.

BIBLIOGRAPHY: M. Rinat, *Ḥevrat ha-Ezrah le-Yehudei Germaniyah be-Yeẓirah u-ve-Ma'avak* (1971), 184–226; I. Friedman, *Germany, Turkey and Zionism, 1897–1918* (1977, 1998), 171–88.

[Isaiah Friedman (2nd ed.)]

LANGUEDOC, former province of S.W. France, with *Toulouse as its capital. The presence of Jews in Languedoc is testified from at least the beginning of the sixth century, at *Agde. During the Middle Ages they were grouped in many prosperous communities, particularly in *Narbonne, *Montpellier, and Toulouse, as well as in *Béziers, *Carcassonne, *Pamiers, *Posquières (today Vauvert), *Lunel, *Nîmes, etc. The continued prevalence of Roman law, which also regulated the condition of the Jews throughout southern France and particularly in Languedoc, enabled them to obtain outright possession of real estate (in *allodium*) which they subsequently leased out. Therefore it occasionally occurred that ecclesiastical institutions were indebted to the Jews in this way. This situation prevailed until 1306. Jews frequently held public office, but from the early 13th century, with the strengthening of Church discipline as a result of the Crusade against the *Albigensian heretics and the seizure of Languedoc by the French crown, they were barred from these positions. In the subsequent confusion about which were crown rights and which belonged to the local lords (lay or ecclesiastical), there were frequent conflicts over the status of the Jews especially with regard to the possession of taxes imposed on them. In addition to local taxes, the Jews also paid special levies and poll taxes which were considerably increased under *Philip IV the Fair. Seeking to evade this situation, many Jews left the royal territory. In his effort to restrain them or bring them back, the king found an unexpected ally in the Jewish communal authorities; since the royal levies were raised from the community as a whole, the latter consequently endeavored to divide the burden among the largest possible number of members.

As a result of an extension of royal prerogative, the expulsion order of 1306 was also applied to the Jews of Languedoc; the opposition of the local lords to whom they had previously been subject was silenced by their receiving one or two thirds of the property seized. The extent of the confiscations can be measured by the fact that in the seneschalship of Toulouse alone (where the least wealthy Jewish communities were situated) property to the value of over 75,000 livres was expropriated. Exiles from Languedoc found refuge in *Provence, Catalonia, and *Roussillon, and in the latter province the town of *Perpignan in particular took in large numbers. When the Jews were recalled to France in 1315, a sizable group must have returned to Languedoc, as evidenced by the number who fell victim to the *Pastoureaux in 1320, and also by the amount of their contribution to the fine of 100,000 livres which was imposed on the Jews of France by *Philip V the Tall. They continued to pay this fine under *Charles IV the Fair until the new expulsion order was applied in 1323. However when the Jews were readmitted to France once more in 1359, comparatively few returned to Languedoc. Although they escaped the persecutions prevalent in the north in 1380 and 1382, in several towns in Languedoc they were nevertheless continually harassed by being compelled to move from the quarter assigned to them. With the final expulsion, decreed in 1394 and enforced in 1395, most of the Jews of Languedoc left for Comtat *Venaissin and Provence, only a few going to Spain on this occasion.

During the 16th century, some *Marranos found refuge in Languedoc and settled mainly in Narbonne, Pézenas, Montpellier, and Béziers. Unlike those in *Bordeaux and other southwestern towns, these groups did not remain faithful to Judaism. From the 18th century, Jews from Bordeaux and the southwest, and more from *Avignon and Comtat Venaissin, traded in Languedoc. Some attempted to settle in a few towns but many more attended the fairs of *Alès, Nîmes, Montpellier, Toulouse, and *Beaucaire. They dealt mainly in old clothes, although they also traded in silk, jewelry, and precious metals, and had practically a monopoly of the livestock trade in Languedoc. When the representations of some merchants exposed them to harassment by the authorities, the local population supported the Jews. From the last third of the 18th century, Jews first settled in Narbonne and then in Toulouse, Nîmes, and other towns, without encountering any further opposition. For the scholars of Languedoc see the articles on the separate localities.

BIBLIOGRAPHY: Gross, Gal Jud, 311; G. Saige, *Juifs du Languedoc...* (1881); C. Bloch, in: REJ, 24 (1892), 272–80; N. Roubin, *ibid.*, 34 (1897), 276–93; 35 (1897), 91–105; 36 (1898), 75–100; S. Kahn, *ibid.*, 67 (1914), 231; E. Le Roy-Ladurie, *Paysans de Languedoc*, 1 (1966), 109–10; L. Dutil, *Etat économique du Languedoc... 1750–1789* (1911), index; S. Grayzel, in: HJ, 17 (1955), 89–120; B. Blumenkranz et al., in: *Archives Juives*, 5 (1968/69), 32–40, 47–55; Y. Dossat, *ibid.*, 6 (1969/70), 4–5, 32–33.

[Bernhard Blumenkranz]

LANIADO, ABRAHAM BEN ISAAC (d. after 1619), biblical commentator, of Aleppo. In his youth Laniado studied in Safed, Joseph *Caro being one of his teachers. After undergoing many hardships in this city he returned to Aleppo where he married the daughter of Samuel b. Abraham *Laniado, who was apparently his uncle, and who provided for his support. Laniado was in Venice in 1603 and in that year saw to the publication of his father-in-law's work *Keli Yekar*, a commentary on the major prophets, and of his own work *Magen Avraham*, consisting of homilies. He also wrote *Nekuddot ha-Kesef* (Venice, 1619), a commentary to the Song of Songs which was published with the text, the Aramaic Targum, and a Ladino translation. In the introduction to this work, Laniado stated that he also wrote a commentary to the Pentateuch titled *Torat Ḥesed*, and to the Five Scrolls, the *haftarot*, Psalms, Proverbs, Job, and Daniel.

BIBLIOGRAPHY: Frumkin-Rivlin, 1 (1928), 129; M.D. Gaon, *Yehudei ha-Mizraḥ be-Ereẓ Yisrael*, 2 (1937), 311.

[Abraham David]

LANIADO, RAPHAEL SOLOMON BEN SAMUEL (d. 1793), rabbi and halakhic authority. Born in *Aleppo, Laniado was rabbi there from 1740 until his death. He was noted for his firmness which left no place for compromise. In the 1760s he was the cause of a stormy controversy within the Jewish community of Aleppo, when he sought to impose the authority of the rabbis and the local community customs on the *Francos. Led by R. Judah b. Yom-Tov *Kazin, the other rabbis of the town opposed him realizing that such a demand would be harmful. This controversy continued over several years, and it is uncertain when it came to an end.

Laniado's works include *Beit Dino shel Shelomo* ("Tribunal of Solomon," Constantinople, 1775), responsa; *Leḥem Shelomo* ("The Bread of Solomon," *ibid.*, 1775), various innovations in *halakhah; Ha-Ma'alot li-Shelomo* ("Degrees of Solomon," *ibid.*, 1775), homiletics; and *Kisse Shelomo* ("The Throne of Solomon," Jerusalem, 1901). Some of his responsa were also published in *Ro'ei Yisrael* ("Shepherds of Israel," Jerusalem, 1904).

BIBLIOGRAPHY: Rosanes, Togarmah, 5 (1938), 211; M.D. Gaon, *Yehudei ha-Mizraḥ be-Ereẓ Yisrael*, 2 (1937), 314; Lutzky, in: *Zion*, 6 (1940/41), 73–79; D.Z. Laniado, *La-Kedoshim asher ba-Areẓ*, 1 (1952), 82–85 (first pagination).

[Abraham David]

LANIADO, SAMUEL BEN ABRAHAM (d. 1605), Syrian rabbi, biblical commentator, and preacher, known from the title of most of his works as *Ba'al ha-Kelim*. Laniado was a grandson of Samuel Laniado who settled in Adrianople after the expulsion from *Spain. He was born in *Aleppo, where he became head of the community (c. 1601) after the death of Samuel b. Joseph ha-Kohen. He assembled homiletical and exegetical comments on the Bible, and original comments of his own. The following of his books have been published: *Keli Ḥemdah* (Venice, 1595), on the Pentateuch; *Keli Yekar (ibid.*, 1603), on the early prophets; *Keli Paz* (*ibid.*, 1657), on Isaiah; *Teru'at Melekh* (Jerusalem, 1931), on Psalms. Many of his works have remained in manuscript, including his commentaries on the latter prophets, with the exception of Hosea and Joel (Gaster, manuscripts, London 62, 1–3); *Keli Golah*, on Lamentations; and *Mevakkesh ha-Shem*, a commentary on the Pentateuch which he mentioned in *Keli Ḥemdah*. He also wrote a commentary titled *Sekhel Tov* on the *Midrash Shoḥer Tov*, which was in the possession of Ḥayyim Joseph David *Azulai. His son Abraham was also a *dayyan* in Aleppo.

BIBLIOGRAPHY: M.D. Gaon, *Yehudei ha-Mizraḥ be-Ereẓ Yisrael*, 2 (1937), 315–7; Rosanes, Togarmah, 3 (1938), 233–4; D.Z. Laniado, *La-Kedoshim asher ba-Areẓ*, 1 (1952), 91 (first pagination).

[Abraham David]

LANIADO, SOLOMON BEN ABRAHAM (d. after 1714), rabbi in *Aleppo. Solomon was the grandson of Samuel b. Abraham *Laniado. Apparently, he succeeded his father as rabbi and *dayyan* after the latter's immigration to *Jerusalem. Laniado wrote *Midrash Shelomo*, still in manuscript. Laniado was known as a fervent Shabbatean and when *Shabbetai Ẓevi visited Aleppo in 1665 he became friendly with Laniado and told Solomon many details about his life. Solomon and Nathan b. Mordecai (or Nissim b. Mordecai Dayyan) propagated the messianic claims of Shabbetai Ẓevi. Two of their letters are extant. One was sent to the Jews of Ancona, Italy (no date) and the other to *Kurdistan in 1669. The letters contain very important information on the lives and activities of Shabbetai Ẓevi and *Nathan of Gaza. Laniado is cited in the list of kings appointed by Shabbetai Ẓevi in Smyrna. The extent of Shabbatean influence on Aleppo Jewry is shown by the fact that even after Shabbetai Ẓevi's apostasy Laniado served as a rabbi.

BIBLIOGRAPHY: G. Scholem, in: *Zion*, 7 (1941/42), 174, 190–193; Scholem, Shabbetai Ẓevi, index; idem, in KS, 33 (1957/58), 532–40; M. Benayahu, *ibid.*, 35 (1959/60), 527–8; D.Z. Laniado, *La-Kedoshim asher ba-Areẓ*, 1 (1952), 81–82 (first pagination).

[Abraham David]

LANSING, SHERRY LEE (1944–), U.S. entertainment executive and producer. Lansing was born in Chicago, Illinois, to real estate developer David and Margot (née Heimann) Duhl. Her mother, a German Jew, had escaped Nazi Germany at 17. When Lansing was nine, her father died after a sudden heart attack. Her mother took over her husband's real estate business and later married businessman Norton Lansing, who adopted Sherry. Lansing majored in English and math at Northwestern University, but also studied acting. She graduated with honors in 1962, and after her marriage to a medical student in 1963 moved to Los Angeles, where Lansing taught math at a public school in Watts from 1966 until 1969. After her divorce in 1968, Lansing worked as a model for Max Factor, appeared in commercials, and acted in the films *Loving* (1970) and *Rio Lobo* (1970). In 1970 she joined Wagner International as a script reader and was later promoted to executive story editor. In 1974, she became executive in charge of West Coast development at Talent Associates. One year later she went to MGM as a story editor, later rising to vice president of creative affairs. In 1977, she moved to Columbia Pictures, where she served as vice president of production. After two hit films, *The China Syndrome* (1979) and *Kramer vs. Kramer* (1979), Lansing left for Twentieth Century Fox in 1980, becoming the first woman to serve as president of production at any Hollywood studio. However, Lansing quickly found that she lacked freedom to approve projects herself. Lansing left in 1982 to establish her own production company, Jaffe-Lansing Productions, with director Stanley Jaffe. Her first film as executive producer was *Racing with the Moon* (1984). Lansing and Jaffe produced seven films for Paramount, including *Fatal Attraction* (1987), *The Accused* (1988), and *Black Rain* (1989). In 1990, she married *French Connection* and *Exorcist* director William *Friedkin. After Jaffe took over as president of Paramount Communications, the pair disbanded their production company but Lansing continued to produce for Paramount with her new company, Sherry Lansing Productions. In 1992, Jaffe named Lansing chair and CEO of Paramount Pictures Motion Picture Group. Lansing produced *Indecent Proposal* (1993), which grossed $100 million in the United States, as well as such hits as *Forrest Gump* (1994), *Braveheart* (1995), *Titanic* (1997), and *Saving Private Ryan* (1998). Lansing, a role model for female executives in the film industry, received her star on the Hollywood Walk of Fame in 1996. She resigned her position with Paramount in 2005 and returned to producing with a prequel to Brian De Palma's *The Untouchables* (1987).

[Adam Wills (2nd ed.)]

LANSKY, MEYER (**Maier Suchowljansky**; "The Brain," "Mogul of the Mob," "Chairman of the Board"; 1902?-1983), U.S. gangster, one of the most powerful and richest of U.S. crime syndicate chiefs, instrumental in the development of the American mafia. Born in Grodno, Lithuania, Lansky arrived in the U.S. in 1911, with his mother, sister, and brother. Passport officials at Ellis Island officially assigned Lansky July 4 as his birth date, although the exact date and year of his birth are not known, while his surname had already been Americanized by his father, who had arrived two years earlier. The family soon moved to the Lower East Side of Manhattan from the Brownsville section of Brooklyn, and it was there that Lansky – known to have a head for numbers – began early on learning the ins and outs of hustling. Lansky left school a few weeks shy of his 15th birthday to work as an apprentice in a tool-and-die shop, and by the following year was already being charged with felonious assault and disorderly conduct. He formed a friendship with Benjamin (Bugsy) *Siegel that developed into the Bug and Meyer Gang, with Lansky the brains of the outfit and Siegel the brawn, which included running gambling houses, and smuggling and hijacking liquor with the onset of Prohibition in 1920. The group formed the expanded Five Points Gang with Charlie Lucania, also known as Lucky Luciano, working for a time with the original "Brain," Arnold *Rothstein, and eventually eliminating rival gangs and bosses to become the top mafia chieftains. In 1931, Lansky organized a conference of Jewish organized crime leaders, which later would see the merging of the Jewish and Italian mafias into the National Crime Syndicate, a crime cartel. Lansky, despite being an outsider to the Italian mafia, was highly respected for his shrewd analytical mind and as master organizer and architect of the money laundering and financial network essential to organized crime; as a man of his word, these skills made him at least equal to Luciano as the godfather of modern organized crime. By 1936 Lansky had begun to develop gambling operations in upstate New York, Florida, New Orleans, the Bahamas, and also in Cuba, where he arranged payoffs to Cuban dictator Fulgencio Batista.

Lansky was also a proud Jew. When the German-American Bund held rallies in New York City in the 1930s, Lansky was asked to disrupt the public meetings, which he happily assigned his henchmen to do, but would take no money for the work. "I was a Jew and felt for those Jews in Europe who were suffering," he said. "They were my brothers."

In 1970, fearing both a call to a grand jury and indictment for income-tax evasion, Lansky fled to Israel, seeking to remain under the *Law of Return, but Israel expelled him in 1972, and he ended up back in the United States facing several indictments. He was convicted in 1973 of grand jury contempt which was overturned on appeal, and was acquitted of income-tax evasion. Indictments on other charges were abandoned in December 1974, partly because of his chronic ill health. In 1979 the House of Representatives Assassinations Committee, ending its two-year investigation of the Warren Commission report, linked Lansky with Jack *Ruby, the nightclub owner who killed presidential assassin Lee Harvey Oswald. The character of "Hyman Roth" in the film *The Godfather Part II* is based on Lansky, and Richard Dreyfuss played him in the 1999 movie *Lansky*. He is the subject of a number of biographies, including *Lansky* (1971) by Hank Messick; *Meyer Lansky: Mogul of the Mob* (1979) by Uri Dan, Dennis Eisenberg, and Eli Landau; and *Little Man: Meyer Lansky and the Gangster Life* (1991) by Robert Lacy.

[Elli Wohlgelernter (2nd ed.)]

LANTOS, ROBERT (1949–), filmmaker. Lantos is arguably the most important and prolific filmmaker in Canada and his oeuvre encompasses erotica, drama, social commentary, comedy, and television. Born in Hungary, he fled with his family to Montevideo, Uruguay, following the abortive 1956 Hungarian Revolution, and moved to Montreal in 1963. Lantos received his B.A. and M.A. in communications at McGill University, where he went into film. His first film production company, Vivafilm, purchased the rights to the National Erotic Film Festival. In 1975, he and his associates formed RSL Productions, which produced 15 films in 10 years, including the provocative *In Praise of Older Women* (1978) and *Joshua Then and Now* (1985), based on the novel by Mordecai *Richler. A merger between RSL and the International Cinema Corporation created Alliance Communications in 1985, and Lantos became its chairman in 1987. Alliance quickly became Canada's largest film production and distribution enterprise. Its television series included *Night Heat*, *North of 60*, and *Due South*. Notable films were *Johnny Mnemonic* (1994) and *The Sweet Hereafter* (1996). Lantos oversaw the merger of Alliance with Atlantis Communications to form Canada's second largest television production house, and then left the company to form a boutique production company, Serendipity Point Films, in Toronto in 1998. Its films include *Sunshine* (1998), which chronicles the saga of modern Hungarian Jewry; *Men With Brooms*, a satirical look at the popularity of curling in Canada; and *Ararat*, a saga of the Armenian genocide and forced migration. Lantos' films have received two Academy Award nominations, three Golden Globe nominations, and have won the Genie Award (Canadian Film Awards) for Best Picture four times. He is active in the Canadian arts community and has chaired the Academy of Canadian Cinema and Television, directed the Toronto International Film Festival and the Canadian Centre for Advanced Film Studies, and was appointed to the Board of the Canadian Broadcasting Corporation by Prime Minister Jean Chrétien. He is also national vice president of Maccabi Canada. Lantos was awarded an honorary doctorate by McGill University and is a member of the Order of Canada.

[Frank Bialystok (2nd ed.)]

LANTOS, TOM (1928–), Democratic congressman from California, the lone Holocaust survivor to serve in the US Congress. Lantos was born in Budapest, Hungary. "The bulk of the Jews of Budapest were utterly assimilated," Lantos said. "Many of them like my family were deeply patriotic and included military officers, university professors, writers and they were enormously proud of their Hungarian heritage." He was 16 years old when Nazi Germany occupied his native country in March 1944. As a teenager, he was placed in a Hungarian fascist forced labor camp. Tall, blond-haired, and blue-eyed he looked like the model Aryan, so he could survive provided that he was not betrayed or forced to lower his trousers. He succeeded in escaping and was able to survive in a safe house in Budapest set up by Swedish humanitarian Raoul *Wallenberg. His mother was not so fortunate. She was deported and never heard from again. He served as a messenger, passing between houses. His story is one of the five individual accounts which form the basis of Steven Spielberg's Academy

Award-winning documentary about the Holocaust in Hungary, *The Last Days.*

His gratitude toward his savior Raoul Wallenberg led him to propose as his first bill in Congress that Raoul Wallenberg be given honorary American citizenship; only Winston Churchill had been so honored. He also pressured the Swedish government to actively open up the Wallenberg case again.

In 1947, Lantos was awarded an academic scholarship to study in the United States on the basis of an essay he wrote about U.S. President Franklin D. Roosevelt. In August of that year, he arrived in New York City after a week-long boat trip to America on a converted World War II troop ship. Onboard "there was a big basket of oranges and one of bananas," Lantos recalled. "I wanted to do the right thing so I asked this sailor "should I take an orange or a banana? And he said: 'Man, you eat all the goddamn oranges and all the goddamn bananas you want.' Then I knew I was in paradise."

His only possession was a precious Hungarian salami, which U.S. customs officials promptly confiscated when he arrived. Just a few weeks after he left Hungary, the Communist Party seized control of the country.

Lantos attended the University of Washington in Seattle, where he received a B.A. and M.A. in Economics. He moved to San Francisco in 1950 and began graduate studies at the University of California, Berkeley, where he later received his Ph.D. in economics. In the fall of 1950 he started teaching economics at San Francisco State University.

For three decades (1950–80) Lantos was a professor of economics, an international affairs analyst for public television, and an economic consultant to businesses. He also served in senior advisory roles to members of the United States Senate including Senator Frank Church of Iowa, Mike Gravel of Alaska, and Joseph Biden of Delaware.

He was first elected to Congress in November 1980 – the only Democrat to defeat an un-indicted incumbent Republican in the year of the Reagan landslide. He won his seat by the lowest plurality of any member of Congress elected that year – 46% to his opponent's 43%. Through excellent constituent service, careful attention to his district's needs, and hard work in the Bay Area and in Washington, Lantos has been re-elected repeatedly by large margins. He is the ranking Democrat on both the House International Relations Committee and the Government Reform Committee. He helped found the Congressional Human Rights Caucus.

Lantos was a strong supporter of the Gulf War Resolution, a hawk on foreign policy, and a powerful voice for human rights.

He is married to his childhood sweetheart and fellow Holocaust survivor Annette Tillemann, who had been sheltered in the Portuguese embassy in Budapest. A Jew by birth, she is a Mormon by faith and raised her daughters that way. Tom Lantos is a strong voice in support of Jewish causes. He was deeply active in the campaign for Soviet Jewry and is an ardent though not uncritical supporter of Israel.

Reflecting on his journey, he said: "My life today is something I cannot believe possible. I think back sixty years ago when I was a hunted animal and now I am dealing with the issues of state of a country I love so deeply. It all seems like a dream and it all places an incredible sense of responsibility on me. I didn't achieve this because of what I am, it happened because of what this country is."

[Michael Berenbaum (2nd ed.)]

LANZMANN, CLAUDE (1925–), French cinema director and essayist. Lanzmann was born in Paris and was active in the Resistance during World War II. After completing his studies in philosophy in France, he lectured at the University of Berlin in 1948–49. In 1952 he became acquainted with Jean Paul Sartre and Simone de Beauvoir, becoming their personal friend and a partner in their philosophical and public endeavors. Sartre, de Beauvoir, and Lanzmann founded the journal *Les temps modernes* (1946), and Lanzmann served as one of its editors. In 1970 Lanzmann left journalism for film and spent three years preparing *Pourquoi Israël?* ("Why Israel?"), which received warm reviews when it was screened in 1973. Lanzmann's most famous film, *Shoah,* on which he worked for over ten years, premiered in France in 1985 with President Mitterrand of France in attendance. Over nine hours in length, the film consists of extended interviews with Jewish victims, Nazi perpetrators, and Polish bystanders. In choosing not to use primary documentary footage, Lanzmann was convinced that the horrible reality of the Holocaust would emerge from the description of the terrifying events by the interviewees. *Shoah* was subsequently shown in London, New York, and Israel, as well as on television stations throughout the world. Other films directed by Lanzmann include *Tsahal* (1994), a documentary on the Israeli army; *Un vivant qui passe* (1997), an extensive interview with Maurice Rossel, a Red Cross official who wrote a glowing report of the Theresienstadt camp after visiting it in 1943; and *Sobibor* (2001), an examination of the revolt in 1943 through the eyes of one of is participants.

[Gideon Kouts / David Weinberg (2nd ed.)]

LAODICEA, city in *Phrygia on the river Lycus. There is preserved in Josephus a letter from the Laodicean authorities to a Roman official (Ant. 14:241–3). In it the Laodiceans inform the official that they had received a letter from him through a representative of the high priest Hyrcanus (most probably *Hyrcanus II) concerning the permission given to the Jews to live in accordance with their ancestral laws. They add that they have complied, as they were averse to arousing the displeasure of the authorities. It is thus clear that Laodicea possessed a Jewish settlement which was protected from discrimination by the intervention of Rome. Some scholars date the document as early as the time of Hyrcanus I but this is questionable. There is however other evidence that there were Jews in Laodicea, or at least in its vicinity, by the second century B.C.E. Josephus (Ant. 12:147–53) quotes an order of Antiochus III with reference to the settlement in Phrygia and

Lydia of 2,000 families of Jewish soldiers from Mesopotamia. This makes it possible to establish the date of the Jewish settlement in the areas around Laodicea, and is also of great importance with regard to Jewish settlement in Asia Minor in general. Cicero states that 20 talents of Jewish gold destined for the Temple of Jerusalem were confiscated by L. Valerius Flaccus in Laodicea, 61–60 B.C.E. (Pro Flacco 28:68).

BIBLIOGRAPHY: W.M. Ramsay, *Cities and Bishoprics of Phrygia*, 1 (1895), 32; Neubauer, Geog, 299; D. Magie, *Roman Rule in Asia Minor*, 2 vols. (1950), 127, 986–7 and index.

[Uriel Rappaport]

LAOR, YITZHAK (1948–), Hebrew writer. Laor was born in Pardes Ḥannah. He completed his studies in theater and literature at Tel Aviv University. His first collection of stories *Mi-Ḥuẓ la-Gader* ("Outside the Fence") was published in 1981. Various collections of stories and poems followed, including *Rak ha-Guf Zokher* ("Only the Body Remembers," poems, 1985) and *Shirim be-Emek ha-Barzel* ("Poems in the Valley of Iron," 1990). The year 1987 saw the publication of his play "Efraim Goes Back to the Army," which was also translated into Dutch. His first novel, *Am. Ma'akhal Melakhim* ("The People, Food for Kings"; German translation, 2003), appeared in 1993. The novel marks a departure from the heroic depiction of the Israeli army and offers as it were an alternative reading of the Six-Day War, which does not break out because a secret document containing war plans reaches the soldiers, who then run away. Laor's subversive and radical tone, his vehement criticism of Israeli politics and the occupation, his anger and anguish can be found in his collection *Ir ha-Livyatan*, comprising poems written between 2000 and 2004. The personal is always tinged with the political, and Laor warns against the corrosion of moral values. Living in Tel Aviv, Laor also writes for the literary supplement of *Haaretz*. For translations see the ITHL website at www.ithl.org.il.

BIBLIOGRAPHY: Y. Oppenheimer, "*Ha-Zekhut ha-Gedolah Lomar Lo*," in: *Alpayim*, 10 (1994), 238–259; G. Shaked, "*Anu Kotvim Otakh Moledet*," in: *Alpayim*, 12 (1996), 51–72; Y. Mazor, "*Bein Alterman le-Zach: Al Y. Laor*," in: *Ha-Do'ar*, 75 (1996), 20–22; R. Weichert, "*Ha-Ta'arif ha-Gavoha shel ha-Hitkablut*," in: *Moznayim*, 73:1 (1998), 12–15; O. Wokenstein, "*Ha-Odise'ah shel Penelope*," in: *Ḥadarim*, 13 (1999), 93–95; S. Sandbank, in: *Sefarim, Haaretz* (October 27, 2004); D. Zonschein, in: *Haaretz* (November 5, 2004).

[Anat Feinberg (2nd ed.)]

LAPAPA, AARON BEN ISAAC (1604?–1667), Sephardi rabbi of *Turkey. Born in Magnesia, he was son-in-law of (Nissim) Solomon *Algazi (the First). In his youth Aaron studied under Isaac Afomado, and later under Abraham *Motal in *Salonika and Joseph di *Trani in Constantinople. He was appointed rabbi in his native town before 1632. In 1665, with the approval of Ḥayyim *Benveniste, rabbi of Smyrna, the council of Smyrna scholars appointed him as the halakhic authority in matters of civil law, together with Benveniste, who confined himself to matrimonial and ritual matters. Lapapa was one of the most vehement opponents of *Shabbetai Ẓevi, not hesitating to excommunicate him, and even to decree the death penalty against him. In December 1665, he was dismissed from his post by Shabbetai Ẓevi and his adherents. Immediately after Shabbetai Ẓevi embraced Islam a small group of Jews of Smyrna tried to reinstate Lapapa, but their efforts failed as a result of the powerful opposition of those who still believed in the pseudo-Messiah. Still, he served in the town as an official *dayyan* until his death.

Lapapa published *Benei Aharon* (Smyrna, 1674), responsa on topics relevant to *Ḥoshen Mishpat*, and some of his novellae and responsa on *Oraḥ Ḥayyim* and *Yoreh De'ah* were published in the *Avak Derakhim* (Salonika, 1814) of Baruch Kalomiti. His commentaries on the *Sefer Adam ve-Ḥavvah* of *Jeroham b. Meshullam, *Alfasi, *Nissim Gerondi, and *Maimonides' *Yad* have not been published. He also compiled a collection of passages from the outstanding *rishonim*, on a number of tractates, of which the following are known: *Ketubbot, Bava Meẓia, Beẓah*, in the style of the *Shitah Mekubbeẓet* of Bezalel *Ashkenazi. The claim that the *Shitah Mekubbeẓet* on *Nedarim, Bava Batra*, and *Nazir*, attributed to Ashkenazi, is really the work of Lapapa, is not well founded.

BIBLIOGRAPHY: Zomber, in: *Ha-Maggid*, 5 (1861), 287; Michael, Or, 141–3, no. 299; A. Freimann, *Inyanei Shabbetai Ẓevi* (1912), 142, no. 15; D. Kahana, *Toledot ha-Mekubbalim, ha-Shabbeta'im ve-ha-Ḥasidim*, 1 (1913), 74–75; Rosanes, Togarmah, 4 (1935), 38; Scholem, Shabbetai Ẓevi, index; J. Sasportas, *Ẓiẓat Novel Ẓevi*, ed. by I. Tishby (1954), index.

[Abraham David]

LA PEYRÈRE, ISAAC (1594 or 1596–1676), French theologian, Bible critic, and anthropologist, apparently of Marrano background. He was born in Bordeaux and raised a Calvinist. In 1640 he became the Prince of Condé's secretary. In 1642–43 he wrote *Praeadamitae* and *Du Rappel des Juifs*, which constitute one continuous theory of Bible criticism and Messianism. The *Rappel des Juifs* was published anonymously in 1643, while the more revolutionary *Praeadamitae* ("Men Before Adam") was banned and circulated privately in manuscript in France, Holland, and Denmark. In 1644 La Peyrère went to Copenhagen with the French ambassador, and there wrote *Relation de Groenland* (published 1647), and *Relation de l'Islande* (published 1663; *An Account of Iceland*, 1732), landmarks in early anthropology. Queen Christina of Sweden saw his manuscript of the *Praeadamitae* in Brussels, urged its publication, and agreed to pay the costs. It was printed in 1655 in Amsterdam and Basle (five editions in Latin, 1655; English as *Men Before Adam*, 1656; Dutch as *Praeadamiten*, 1661). The book was banned and burned everywhere for its heretical claims that Adam was not the first man, that the Bible is not the history of mankind, but only the history of the Jews, that the Flood was a local event, that Moses did not write the Pentateuch, and that no accurate copy of the Bible exists. Many refutations immediately appeared. La Peyrère was arrested and told he would be released if he turned Catholic and recanted to the Pope, which he did in hypocritical fashion, saying that his heresies resulted from his Calvinist upbringing, and that though all Jews and Christians disagreed with him, and though he could still find no Scriptural or reasonable evidence against his theories, he would abjure them because the Church said they were wrong (*Lettre de la Peyrère à Philotime*, 1658; *Apologie de Peyrère*, 1663). The Pope offered him a post, but La Peyrère returned to Paris and became Condé's librarian and a lay member of the Oratorians. There he collected more evidence for his pre-Adamite theory, arguing with the great Bible scholar, Father Richard Simon, and trying unsuccessfully to publish a new version of his Messianic *Rappel des Juifs*. When he died, one of his friends wrote:

> Here lies La Peyrère, that good Israelite, Huguenot, Catholic and finally Pre-Adamite. Four religions pleased him at the same time and his indifference was so uncommon that after 80 years when he had to make a choice the Good Man departed and did not choose any of them.

La Peyrère has been interpreted as a heretic, atheist, deist, Socinian, father of Bible criticism, and father of Zionism. His overall theory is a Marrano Messianist view. La Peyrère argued that the Jews are about to be recalled, that the Messiah is coming for them, that they should join the Christians, and with the king of France rebuild Zion. Then the Jews will rule the world from Jerusalem. La Peyrère was a combination of hard-headed scientist and kabbalistic messianist in developing his case. He argued his pre-Adamite theory first on a farfetched interpretation of St. Paul's *Epistle to the Romans*, then from information about pagan history, and finally from anthropological evidence about the Indians, Eskimos, and Chinese. His analysis of the Bible played a great role in the development of Higher Criticism, influencing Spinoza and Richard Simon. La Peyrère's messianic theories resemble those of some of the Spanish New Christians and Postel's Kabbalism, but seem unrelated to Shabbetai Ẓevi's movement. His separation of Jewish and gentile histories influenced Vico in the developing secular historiography. La Peyrère's pre-Adamite theory was revived in the early 19th century as a basis for polygenesis and modern racism, claiming the American Indians and the blacks were not sons of Adam.

BIBLIOGRAPHY: D.C. Allen, *The Legend of Noah* (1949, 1963²), index; D.R. Mc-Kee, in: *Publications of the Modern Language Association*, 59 (1944), 456–85; R. Pintard, *Le libertinage érudit dans la première moitié du xviie siècle*, 2 v. (1943), index; H.J. Schoeps, *Philosemitismus im Barock* (1952), 3–18, 81–87; L. Strauss, *Spinoza's Critique of Religion* (1965), 64–85.

[Richard H. Popkin]

LAPID, JOSEPH (Tomi; 1931–), journalist and politician, member of the Knesset in the Fifteenth and Sixteenth Knesset. Lapid was born in the town of Novi Sad in the former Yugoslavia. His father perished in a concentration camp. His mother escaped with him to Budapest, and they managed to survive the Holocaust, immigrating to Israel in 1948. Upon arrival in Israel Lapid enlisted in the IDF, serving as a technician. After completing his military service he studied for a law degree at Tel Aviv University. While still a student he started working at the Hungarian-language daily *Ui Kelet*. Several years later he joined the staff of the *Maariv* daily, working at first as the private secretary of its editor in chief, Ezriel *Carlebach, later becoming a reporter, writing a column, and serving as the paper's correspondent in London. In 1979 Lapid was appointed director general of the Israel Broadcasting Authority – the first director general appointed by the Likud after the political upheaval of 1977. He served in this capacity until 1984. In 1985 he established the Liberal Center Party with Shlomo *Lahat and served as its secretary general. The party was never elected to the Knesset, and in 1988 he resigned from it and became chairman of the Association of Cable Television, in which capacity he served until 1994. Throughout this period he continued to write for *Maariv* and appeared on radio and television programs. Before the elections for the Fifteenth Knesset he joined Shinui as the revived party's chairman, after MK Avraham Poraz broke away from Meretz, and set up a parliamentary group with MK Eliezer Sandberg from Tzomet. Under Lapid's charismatic leadership, a strong secularist platform, and heavy criticism of the *ḥaredi* parties, Shinui received six seats in the Fifteenth Knesset, and fifteen in the Sixteenth. In the Fifteenth Knesset Lapid served on the Foreign Affairs and Defense Committee and the Constitution, Law, and Justice Committee. He was also a member of the Parliamentary Committee of Inquiry on the Issue of Locating and Restoring the Assets of Holocaust Victims – a committee that finally submitted its report in December 2004.

After the elections to the Sixteenth Knesset Lapid favored the formation of a secular government made up of the *Likud, the *Israel Labor Party, and Shinui, but Labor's leader, MK Amram Mitzna, refused to join a Likud-led government. In the government formed by Ariel *Sharon with Shinui, the NRP, and the National Union Lapid became deputy prime minister and minister of justice. However, in December 2004 the Shinui ministers were fired from the government by Sharon, since they refused to support the budget in the Knesset, even though they supported Sharon's disengagement plan. Poor showings in the polls and a rebellion of Shinui's young guard caused Lapid to quit the party and leave politics before the 2006 elections.

In addition to writing for the daily press, Lapid published numerous books, wrote several plays, and served as the chairman of the Israeli Chess Association. He is married to the author Shulamit *Lapid and is the father of Israeli writer and TV personality Ya'ir Lapid.

Lapid was an accomplished humorist and published, among other things, collections of his newspaper columns and works such as *Anashim Ḥashuvim Me'od: Me'ah Ra'ayonot ve-Humor Elef* ("Very Important People: One Hundred Interviews and Lots of Humor," 1963); *Shi'urim be-Tikshoret* ("Lessons in Communications," 2000); *Mashehu Hishtabesh* ("Something Has Gone Wrong," 2001); a cookbook with Ruth Sirkis, *Paprika: Kasher* (1986), and numerous guidebooks for European countries in the years 1970–2003.

[Susan Hattis Rolef (2nd ed.)]

LAPID, SHULAMIT (1934–), Hebrew writer. Lapid was born in Tel Aviv. She majored in Oriental studies at the Hebrew University of Jerusalem. Her first collection of stories, *Dagim* ("Fish"), was published in 1969. This was followed by collections of stories and poems as well as ten novels, plays, and books for young readers. A former chairperson of the Hebrew Writers' Association, she is one of the most prolific Israeli women authors, with historical novels, realistic prose addressing social issues and ethnic discrimination, and a number of detective novels. Her early novel *Gai Oni* (1982; translated into German and French) is the story of the Galilean settlement which has come to be known as Rosh Pinnah. History, the Zionist dream and its realization, and the hardships of daily life are seen through the perspective of Fania, who arrives in Palestine with her old uncle, a deranged brother, and an unwanted baby, the product of rape. Despite hunger and disease, Fania flings herself into the new life and penetrates the male-dominated world of commerce and politics. Indeed, Lapid was one of the first Hebrew writers who confronted the Zionist narrative while paying special attention to the role of women, who had previously been considered as subordinate figures in the national enterprise. Lapid's second novel, *Ka-Ḥeres ha-Nishbar* ("As a Broken Vessel," 1984, translated into German), is the story of the astute antiquarian Moses Wilhelm Shapira. Lizzy Badiḥi, an industrious freelance journalist working for a local paper in Beersheba, far from pretty yet blessed with charm and sharp detective skills, is the leading figure in Lapid's detective novels, indeed a rather atypical detective. In *Mekomon* ("Local Paper," 1989) she succeeds in unraveling a crime case; in *Pilegesh ba-Give'ah* ("An Eye for an Eye," 2000), she investigates the case of murder and rape, rivalry and vengeance, involving a seemingly respectable professor. Lapid received the Newman Prize. Many of her books have been translated, mostly into German, and information is available at the ITHL website at www.ithl.org.il.

BIBLIOGRAPHY: Y. Lotan, "Independent People," in: *Modern Hebrew Literature*, 9:1–2 (1983), 92–94; Y.S. Feldman, "Inadvertent Feminism: The Image of the Frontier Woman in Contemporary Israeli Fiction," in: *Modern Hebrew Literature*, 10:3–4 (1985), 34–37; N. Govrin, "'*Of ha-Ḥol': Ha-Roman Gai Oni ke-He'arah al ha-Historiyyah ha-Yehudit*," in: *Hadoar*, 65:21 (1986), 21–23; Y. Feldman, "Feminism Under Siege," in: *Prooftexts*, 10:3 (1990), 493–514; D. Miron, "*Ḥaputah shel Lizi Badiḥi*," in: *Siman Keriah*, 20 (1990), 166–185; N.E. Berg, "'*Oleh Hadash': The Case of the Israeli Mystery*," in: *Edebiyat*, 5:2 (1994), 279–290; Y. Ben David, "*Demuyyot min ha-Aliyah ha-Rishonah*," in: *Ahavah mi-Mabat Sheni* (1997), 95–99; I. Aharoni, "*Ha-Zar she-be-Tokhenu, ha-Zarim she-Hinenu*," in: *Alpayim*, 18 (1999), 133–144; D. Abramovich, "Israeli Detective Fiction: Batya Gur and Shulamit Lapid," in: *Australian Journal of Jewish Studies*, 14 (2000), 147–179; D. Urian, "'So Sarah Laughed to Herself,'" in: *Modern Jewish Mythologies* (2000), 89–106; Ch. Bala, "Kriminalistischer Postzionismus? Israel in den Romanen von B. Gur und S. Lapid," in: *Zachor*, 10 (2000), 61–73; M. Morgenstern, "Orestes on the Jordan: S. Lapid's Genesis reconstruction 'Surrogate Mother' (1980) as a Psychoanalytic Drama," in: *Jewish Studies Quarterly*, 10:2 (2003), 172–188.

[Anat Feinberg (2nd ed.)]

LAPIDOT, ALEXANDER MOSES (1819–1906), rabbi and early supporter of Ḥovevei Zion. Born in Vilna, Lapidot studied in yeshivot in Lithuania, during one period under Rabbi Israel *Lipkin (Salanter). He served as rabbi in Janow, Grodno, and from 1866, in Rossiyeny. He published interpretations of the Torah and essays on contemporary issues in newspapers and in various literary organs. His works include *Avnei Zikkaron* (a defense of the Written and Oral Law, 1897) and *Divrei Emet* (1910, 1966^4). He joined the *Ḥibbat Zion movement when it was founded in Russia and participated in the conference of movement activists in Druzgenik (1887). He published his national credo in the anthologies *Derishat Ẓiyyon* (1900) and *Keneset ha-Gedolah* (1890), emphasizing that he did not intend to take Ereẓ Israel by the sword, but by agricultural labor based on a religious way of life. The movement, he wrote, did not intend "to anticipate the coming of the Messiah," as was claimed by its rabbinical opponents. Therefore, Lapidot commanded those who observed the tradition to aid the movement and to strengthen its religious element. He also called on the wealthy to buy and work the land in Ereẓ Israel.

BIBLIOGRAPHY: EẒD, 3 (1963), 264–5; D. Katz, *Tenu'at ha-Musar*, 2 (1964), 436–8; M. Markovitch, *Le-Korot Ir Rosyan ve-Rabbaneha* (1913), 14–16.

[Geulah Bat Yehuda (Raphael)]

LAPIDOT, RUTH (1930–), Israeli jurist. Lapidot was born in Germany and immigrated to Israel in 1938 with her family. In 1947 she moved to Paris to study piano but came back a year later to serve in the army, where she was in the Medical Corps. She studied law at the Hebrew University of Jerusalem from 1949 to 1953 and clerked in the Supreme Court. In 1954–56 she studied international public law in Paris, completing her Ph.D. there. From 1956 to 2001 she was a member of the Faculty of Law at the Hebrew University, where she became a full professor in 1980. Her fields of interest were international law, maritime law, and the Arab-Israeli conflict. In addition to her academic career she held a number of international posts, such as member of the Israeli delegation to the UN (1976), and participated in the Humanitarian Law Conference (1977) and the Red Cross Conference (1981), in which she utilized her legal knowledge to influence decisions regarding Israel. Lapidot served as legal advisor to the Ministry for Foreign Affairs from 1979 to 1981, assisting the Israeli delegation during the peace process with Egypt (1979) as well as advising the government on Palestinian autonomy under the Camp David Agreement and on the establishment of an international observer force in Sinai and the Southern Negev. From 1986 to 1988 she represented Israel in the Taba border dispute with Egypt. Since 1989 she has been a member of the Permanent Court of Arbitration at The Hague. In 1999 she advised the High Commissioner on National Minorities of the Organization for Security and Cooperation in Europe. In 2006 she received the Israel Prize in law. She published nine books and over 90 articles on legal subjects.

[Shaked Gilboa (2nd ed.)]

LAPIDUS, MORRIS (1902–2001), flamboyant Odessa-born architect who brought the ideas of Hollywood luxury to hotel design in Miami Beach during the 1950s and 1960s. In his lifetime he built 1,200 buildings and 250 hotels. His style was an adaptation of "form follows function," where the functions were glamour and fun. Castigated by the official architectural establishment, except for Philip Johnson, he persisted. Starting out from the Lower East Side of Manhattan, earning scholarships plus professional training in architecture at Columbia University, he began his career by designing commercial buildings and synagogues. He created store fronts with hidden lighting and curved glass windows that paved the way for better displays of merchandise. His first architectural commission, in 1954, was for the Hotel Fontainebleau in Miami Beach. More than 500 rooms were set on a quarter-circle curve. The lobby contained a terrarium with live alligators and an elegant stairway down from the mezzanine that featured women descending to the lobby while showing off their glamorous gowns and jewelry to the men waiting below. Lapidus believed that when people went on vacation, they wanted to indulge their fantasies of luxury. The ballroom, intended for a casino, could hold 9,000 people. Three Belgium chandeliers hung in the lobby, each one strung with 1,800 crystal strands forming circles or ovals depending on where you were standing. The movie *Goldfinger* was filmed there; Marilyn Monroe and JFK had suites in the penthouse. Soon after building the Fontainebleau, Lapidus built the Eden Roc and the Americana and then the Americana in New York. He said that he did not care if it was called Baroque or Brooklyn as long as it was glamorous. He went on to design hotels in Las Vegas, Los Angeles, the Catskills (Grossingers and the Concord), and overseas.

By 1985, his work was still criticized, so he closed his office and hired two trucks to cart away his papers, which he then burned. The Summit Hotel, a Lapidus building on 51st Street in New York, was under consideration as a landmark building in 2005. Now named the Metropolitan, it is one of the few remaining Lapidus buildings in New York and may be destroyed. Before he died at age 98 he started working again. His designs finally appreciated, the man whose vision of the American Dream was first formed at Coney Island and Luna Park believed that his ideals could serve as the model for 21st century architecture. Lapidus was honored by the Society of Architectural Historians in 2000 at the Eden Roc and he was named an American Original by the Smithsonian Institution's Cooper-Hewitt, National Design Museum in its first national design awards. He received this honor at the White House in 2000.

BIBLIOGRAPHY: M. Lapidus, *Too Much is Not Enough* (1966).

[Betty R. Rubenstein (2nd ed.)]

LAPIN, BERL (1889–1952), Yiddish poet and translator. Born in Grodno, he lived in Argentina 1905–9 and 1913–17 and in the U.S. 1909–13, before settling in New York in 1917. His first lyric collection *Umetige Vegn* ("Sad Ways," 1910) was completed in Vilna, where he had come under the influence of Chaim *Zhitlowsky (as whose personal secretary he served) and the literary group Di *Yunge. His excellence as a stylist is reflected in his translations of Shakespeare's *Sonnets*, Russian lyrics, and American poems, and his collected poems *Der Fuler Krug* ("The Full Pitcher," 1950).

BIBLIOGRAPHY: Rejzen, Leksikon, 2 (1927), 74–6; LNYL, 4 (1961), 452–4; J. Glatstein, *In Tokh Genumen*, 1 (1947), 395–403; 2 (1956), 157–63; 3 (1960), 351–6; S. Liptzin, *Flowering of Yiddish Literature* (1963), 214–6. **ADD. BIBLIOGRAPHY:** Sh. Niger, *Bleter Geshikhte fun der Yidisher Literatur* (1959), 375–76; B.Y. Bialostotsky, *Kholem un Vor* (1956), 341–49; R.R. Wisse, *A Little Love in Big Manhattan* (1988), 45.

[Melech Ravitch]

LAPIN, ISRAEL MOSES FISCHEL (1810–1889), *yishuv* leader. Born in Grodno (then Russian Poland), Lapin was a contractor for the building of the Grodno railway and thus became wealthy. In 1862 he settled with his family in Jerusalem, where he contributed to the foundation and maintenance of various health and educational institutions. Along with Judah *Alkalai, Lapin was a founder of Kol Yisrael Ḥaverim for land settlement in Ereẓ Israel and was elected its vice president, but resigned under pressure from Jewish community leaders. In 1872 he joined a group of Jerusalemites who sought to buy land for Jewish settlement in Jericho, but later purchased lands near Jaffa and Moẓa. Lapin acquired the land for the Bet Ya'akov quarter of Jerusalem and helped to expand the city. His grandchildren included Joshua Lapin, director of the Baron de *Hirsch's colonies in Argentina (from 1893), and Bezalel and Leib *Jaffe.

One of his sons, BEZALEL (1856–1939), was taken to Ereẓ Israel at the age of seven. He initiated a coach service between Jerusalem and Jaffa in place of the mules and donkeys used hitherto. He also founded the firm that built the Sha'arei Pinnah quarter of Jerusalem. In 1890 he went to live in Jaffa where he considerably extended his commercial and communal activities. During World War I Lapin organized an aid campaign for Jewish soldiers in the Turkish army.

BIBLIOGRAPHY: P. Grajewsky, *Rabbi Fischel Lapin* (Heb., 1932); idem, *Rabbi Beẓalel Lapin* (Heb., 1926); idem, *Zikkaron la-Ḥovevim ha-Rishonim*, no. 3 (1927), and no. 13 (1928); EẒD, 3 (1965), 79–83, incl. bibl.

[Geulah Bat Yehuda (Raphael)]

LAPSEKI (**Lampsakos**; Turk. **Lapseki**), district of *Çanakkale on the Dardanelles opposite Gallipoli. The district remained under Byzantine rule for centuries, and then passed into Ottoman hands. The Jewish population of Çanakkale was represented by a small settlement in Lapseki in the late 19th century. In 1888, there were 36 Jews in six houses, with no religious organization and attached to Çanakkale. The Jews specialized in producing wine, called *vino aello lege*. As Gallipoli suffered large-scale attacks during World War I, Jews there took refuge in Lapseki, causing a temporary increase in its

Jewish population. Nevertheless, it diminished after the proclamation of the Republic in 1923 to just seven Jewish women, according to the census of 1927.

BIBLIOGRAPHY: *Karasi Vilayet Salnamesi* (H.1305), 148; V. Cuinet, *La Turquie d'Asie*, 3 (1894), 696, 758–62; A. Galanté, *Histoire des Juifs d'Anatolie*, 4 (1987), 223–24; *Bradshaw's Handbook to the Turkish Empire* (1887), 138.

[M. Mustafa Kulu (2nd ed.)]

LAPSON (Weinberg), DVORA (1907–1996). U.S. choreographer; an innovator who used Jewish folklore material in theatrical form. Lapson was première danseuse and choreographer of the Hebrew opera *Pioneers* by Jacob *Weinberg (1934) and also directed dances for Jewish Art Theater, New York. Her own repertoire included dances on biblical themes, ḥasidic ritual, and modern Jewish life. She directed pageants in New York high schools for the Jewish Culture Council and was the author of *New Palestine Dances* (1948) and *Dances of the Jewish People* (1954).

LAQUEUR, WALTER ZE'EV (1921–), Middle East expert and political scientist. Born in Breslau, Germany, Laqueur went to Palestine in 1938, and from 1944 to 1953 served as a political journalist for several Israel newspapers. In 1955 Laqueur moved to London, where he became editor of *Survey*, a quarterly political journal specializing in East European affairs. In 1964 he was appointed director of the Wiener Library Institute of Contemporary History, and in 1966 he founded and became coeditor of the periodical *Contemporary History*. Laqueur taught at the University of Reading in England and at Brandeis University in the United States. In 1970 he was appointed professor of history at the University of Tel Aviv. Subsequently he became director of the Institute of Contemporary History in London and an associate of the Center for Strategic and International Studies in Washington. He also served as a co-chairman at CSIS (Center for Strategic and International Studies). He was founder and editor of the *Journal of Contemporary History*, chairman of the board of editors of the *Washington Quarterly*, and editor of the Washington Papers monograph series. A specialist in Soviet foreign policy and in the politics of the Middle East, his books include *The Middle East in Transition* (1958), *The Soviet Union and the Middle East* (1959), *The Fate of the Revolution: Interpretations of Soviet History* (1967), *The Road to Jerusalem: The Origins of the Arab-Israel Conflict 1967* (1968), *Weimar: A Cultural History* (1976), *Guerilla: A Historical and Critical Study* (1976), *A Continent Astray: Europe 1970–1978* (1979), and two novels, *The Missing Years* (1980) and *The Terrible Secret* (1980). More recent books are *The Dream That Failed: Reflections on the Soviet Union* (1994), *Fascism: Past, Present, and Future* (1996), *A History of Zionism* (1997), and *Weimar: A Cultural History* (2000). His work appeared regularly in *Commentary*, the *New York Times Magazine*, the *Washington Post*, *Encounter*, and the *New Republic*.

[Lawrence H. Feigenbaum]

LAR, town in southern *Iran, situated on the main caravan route connecting southern Persia with the Persian Gulf ports. Lar had a prosperous Jewish community in the 16th century. A Spaniard who visited the town in 1607 met there a "messenger from Zion" named Judah. Along with other Persian Jewish communities the Jews of Lar suffered at the hands of the Safavid rulers during the 17th and early 18th centuries; the oppressions are described by the Judeo-Persian chronicler *Babai ibn Luṭf. According to him, the persecutions against the Jews of Iran during the reign of Shah *Abbas I (1588–1629) began some time before 1613 and originated in the city of Lar, whose rabbi converted to Islam and took the name Abul-Hasan Lari. Lar was a center of Judeo-Persian literary activity; among the scribes and translators was Judah of Lar (early 16th century; see *Shahin and *Imrani). A Florentine traveler, Giambattista Vecchietti (1552–1619), collected ancient Judeo-Persian manuscripts there and brought them back to Europe. There existed a Jewish community in Lar up to the beginning of the 20th century. According to BM (1907, p. 51) there were 70 Jews living in Lar in 1907. They were expelled from the city and walked all the way to the northern city of Jahrom and eventually settled in Shiraz (pp. 90–91; and also 1910, *ibid.*, pp. 18f; Levy, p. 1026). On April 24, 1960, a devastating earthquake struck the city of Lar, reducing a large part of the town to rubble and killing about 3,500 of its inhabitants.

BIBLIOGRAPHY: BM = Bulletin Mensuel, Alliance Israélite Universelle; W.J. Fischel, "The Region of the Persian Gulf and its Jewish Settlements in Islamic Time," in: *Alexander Marx Jubilee Volume* (1950), 203–30; H. Levy, *History of the Jews of Iran*, 3 (1960). **ADD. BIBLIOGRAPHY:** V.B. Moreen, *Iranian Jewry's Hour of Peril and Heroism* (1987); A. Netzer, "*Redifot u-Shemadot be-Toledot Yehudei Iran ba-Me'ah ha-17*," in: *Pe'amim*, 6 (1980), 32–56.

[Walter Joseph Fischel / Amnon Netzer (2nd ed.)]

LARA, DAVID BEN ISAAC COHEN DE (1602 [1610?]–1674), philologist, lexicographer, writer, and translator. Born in Lisbon (or Amsterdam, or Hamburg), Lara studied at the academy of R. Isaac *Uziel at Amsterdam. He was appointed *ḥakham* of the Spanish-Portuguese community in Hamburg. In 1656 he returned to Amsterdam, spending several years there, but subsequently returned to Hamburg. A great expert on classical literature and the writings of the Church Fathers, Lara became noted for his work *Keter Kehunnah* (*Corona Sacerdotii, Lexicon Thalmudico Rabbinicum*, Hamburg, 1668) on which he worked for 40 years. In the book he deals with talmudic words which do not appear in the *Arukh* of *Nathan b. Jehiel of Rome, and he compares the Hebrew with words in Semitic or in European languages; the published work goes only as far as the letter *yod*. In *Ir David*, an earlier work (Amsterdam, 1638), Lara listed and explained words of Greek and Latin origin found in the Talmud and the Midrash. He also translated chapters from books on ethics from Hebrew into Spanish, such as excerpts from R. Elijah de *Vidas' *Reshit Ḥokhmah* under the title *Tratado del Temor Divino* (Amsterdam, 1633). In *Divrei David* (Leyden, 1658) he explained R. Abraham *Ibn

Ezra's discourse on the letters *alef, he, vav, yod*, adding Latin notes to his text. Other works by Lara still in manuscript are *Beit David*, a talmudic lexicon; *Oẓar Rav*, foreign words and technical terms in rabbinic literature; *Ohel David*, explanations of synonyms in the Talmud and rabbinic literature; *Kisse David*, a collection of parables and legends from the Talmud and the Midrash, arranged in alphabetical order; and *Pirḥei Kehunnah*, a book on ethics. Christian philologists, such as Johannes Christopher Buxtorf II, appreciated Lara's scholarship in Hebrew philology and encouraged him to publish his *Keter Kehunnah*. The rumor spread by Esdras Edzardus, the Hamburg missionary, that as he was approaching death, Lara came close to Christianity, has no basis in fact.

BIBLIOGRAPHY: H.I. Bloom, *The Economic Activities of the Jews of Amsterdam* (1937), 207; Graetz, Hist, 5 (1949), 115, 117; G. Karpeles, *Geschichte der juedischen Literatur*, 2 (1921³), 276f.; Kayserling, Bibl, 56; idem, in: REJ, 13 (1886), 269–72; Schwab, *ibid.*, 40 (1900), 95–98; Kohut, Arukh, 1 (1926²), introd. XLVIf.; Perles, in: MGWJ, 17 (1868), 224–32, 255–64.

[Yehoshua Horowitz]

LARA, ḤIYYA KOHEN DE (d. after 1753), rabbi and kabbalist. Lara was a pupil of the Moroccan rabbi Solomon Amar II. He was one of the foremost group of scholars from the *bet midrash* Ez Ḥayyim in Amsterdam. He compiled *Mishmerot Kehunnah* (Amsterdam, 1753), a talmudic lexicon consisting, in his own words, of "sayings, proverbs, moral reproof, decrees, regulations and principles from the Talmud, in alphabetical order, as well as corrections of printers' errors in the Talmud." It is noteworthy that Lara included in his book various criticisms of the scholars of the south of France and of Germany. He apologized, however, if he thereby spoke disrespectfully against prominent rabbis. He was opposed to the method of *pilpul* in vogue among German rabbis of the time, pointing out: "What benefit do the German scholars bring by their hair-splitting distinctions? Has not the Talmud stated explicitly, that if we are so meticulous we should not be able to study" (*Mishmerot Kehunnah*, 11b). In *Peri Eẓ Ḥayyim* (vol. 2, Amsterdam, 241), there are several responsa by Lara dating from 1741. He complains about his difficult economic situation, describing himself as "embittered, busy with temporal cares and the cares of a livelihood, with difficulty providing for his needs, and troubled with other domestic cares." Of his works the kabbalistic *Kanfei Yonah* and *Mirkevet ha-Mishneh* are still extant in manuscript.

BIBLIOGRAPHY: Fuenn, Keneset, 341; M.M. Hirsch, *Frucht vom Baum des Lebens-Ozer Peroth Eẓ Chajim* (1936), 320 (index), s.v. *Cohen de Lara, Chija.*

[Yehoshua Horowitz]

LARA, ISAAC COHEN DE (c. 1700), Sephardi author and book dealer, known mainly as the editor of the Purim play, *Comedia famosa de Aman y Mordochay*. He was the son of Abraham Cohen de Lara. The marriage records of Amsterdam include that of an Isaac de Lara, described as a "businessman" and native of Amsterdam, who on March 14, 1692, at the age of 24, married Raquel Machado of Leghorn. An Isaac Acohen de Lara, apparently identical with the book dealer, was *ḥazzan* of the Amsterdam Sephardi community in 1709. His father, Abraham, had occupied the same position in 1682. The *Comedia famosa de Aman y Mordochay* was published at Leiden in 1699. The actual author of this Spanish play is unknown. In an introduction, dedicated to his friend David de Souza Brito, de Lara merely says that it was composed by "a clever writer from Hamburg, as I gathered from his prologue." The play itself is written in a graceful and precise style, inspired by the Book of Esther and midrashic commentaries on the biblical story. This edition of the *Comedia* also includes 36 Spanish "enigmas" taken from another, older work and 12 taken from a manuscript, as well as a further 25 "enigmas" in Dutch. The inclusion of the last indicates that by this time the Spanish and Portuguese Jews in Amsterdam knew Dutch fairly well. De Lara's book ends with a *brindis* ("toast"), and with a Spanish ballad, "*La Fuga de Jaacob de Barsheva.*"

Isaac Cohen de Lara also edited *Guía de Passageros* (a guide for travelers; Amsterdam, 1704), which contains a Judeo-Spanish calendar.

BIBLIOGRAPHY: H.V. Besso, *Dramatic Literature* (1947), 69–70; Kayserling, Bibl, 38; Van Praag, in: *Neophilologus*, 25:1 (1940), 12–24.

[Kenneth R. Scholberg]

LARIN, YURI (Lurye, Mikhail Alexandrovich; 1882–1932), Russian political economist and communal leader. Born in Simferopol, Larin was the son of the Hebrew writer and Zionist Shneur Zalman Luria, who served as **kazyonny ravvin* in Kiev. In 1901 he joined the Russian Social Democratic Party, becoming an adherent of its Menshevik wing. Arrested and exiled to Siberia in 1902, he escaped abroad in 1904, returning to Russia in 1905. From 1905 to 1913 he was active in the revolutionary movement in the Crimea, the Ukraine, and the Caucasus. In 1913 when in Tiflis (Tbilisi) he was again arrested and expelled. He returned to Russia after the February Revolution. After July 1917 he became a member of the Bolshevik Party. Following the October Revolution he was given a number of top assignments as an expert in economic affairs. He was a key figure in the organization of the new Soviet economy and among the founders of the State Planning Bureau. In 1928 he became identified with the opposition. He organized the fight against antisemitism in 1926–31 and wrote some works on the subject. He took great interest in the agricultural settlement of Russian Jews and was chairman of OZET, a voluntary, semiprivate organization propagating the idea of agricultural settlement of Russian Jews. He was also a member of KOMZET, a public committee whose task was similar to that of OZET. Larin was one of the few Jewish communists who supported the project of settling Jews in the *Crimea, and one of the two Jewish Autonomous Counties there was named after him – Larindorf County – in 1935. Moreover, when there was still Zionist activity in the Soviet Union, he attempted, unsuccessfully, to bring about an agreement between the Soviet authorities and Zionist groups, to attract the latter to settlement activities, and to mobilize funds from the Jews in Russia and other countries. On the other hand, he opposed the project of Jewish settlement in *Birobidzhan, and even expressed publicly his doubts as to its success. This stand roused the anger of the *Yevsektsiya, and Larin was attacked by Merezhin, one of the Yevsektsiya's leaders. His daughter Anna married N. Bukharin.

BIBLIOGRAPHY: *Bolshaya Sovetskaya Entsiklopediya*, 35 (1937), 762–3.

LARISSA (Ottoman Turk. **Yenishehir**), city in Thessaly, N.W. of Athens, Greece. From the 16th century Larissa had a small Sephardi community. The local Jews were mainly engaged in commerce, notably the sale of clothes, and also in money changing. With the conquest of the Peleponnese by the Venetians in 1687 and the influx of refugees from Patras, the Larissa community increased. There were numerous *ḥakhamim* in the community. At the end of the 16th century, the most noted was the *posek* Joseph ben Ezra. In the 16th and 17th centuries there were two *kehalim*, the older Romaniot *Kahal Eẓ Ḥayyim* and a smaller, more recent Sephardi *kahal*. During the 18th century the Larissa philanthropist Isaac Shalom maintained a yeshivah in *Salonika. At its peak, in 1851–52, the community numbered 2,000 families. A short-lived *Alliance Israélite Universelle school operated between 1868 and 1874. In 1881, the Jewish community welcomed Greek sovereignty in a public ceremony. The community suffered a blood libel in 1893. When Larissa was temporarily occupied by the Turks in the 1897 Greek-Turkish War, local elements agitated against the Jews with accusations of collusion with the former Turkish sovereign. When the Turkish military commander gave the local Jews a chance to return to *Turkey, the local rabbi refused and affirmed Jewish loyalty to Greece.

The merchant Isaac Cohen moved to *Jerusalem at the end of the 19th century and established a large general store on Jaffa Road. His close contacts with the Greek-Orthodox Church enabled the Jewish National Fund to purchase land for the Israel Museum as well as in the Reḥaviah neighborhood of Jerusalem and for kibbutz Bet ha-Aravah on the Dead Sea. In 1900, two local Zionist movements were established: Mevaẓeret Zion and Ohavei Zion. In 1923 there were 200 Jewish families in the town, although formerly there had been more. In 1940 there were 1,175 Jews in the town; 950 fled from the Nazis to the mountains when encouraged by local rabbi Isaac Casuto to do so. Following a Nazi decree, the 150 Jews who remained in the town, and another 75 who returned, were registered with the municipality and deported. In 1948 the Jewish population numbered 626, and in 1958, 452. According to the 1967 census, there were 441 Jews living in the city. A Holocaust memorial was set up in the mid-1990s and was desecrated several times at the end of the 1990s and the beginning of the 21st century. Today there are only some 15 Jewish pupils in the Jewish school, and most students are gentile. The community was enriched when the native Rabbi Eli Shabetai moved back to the community.

BIBLIOGRAPHY: *Almanak Izraelit 5683* (1927), 65–66; Rosanes, Togarmah, 2 (1938), 44, 46; 4 (1935), 155–6, 277–80; 5 (1938), 54–55, 125. **ADD. BIBLIOGRAPHY:** Y. Kerem, "Ee Evrai Tis Larisas, I Skliri Pragmatikotita Tis Othomanikis Zois," in: *Thessaliko Imerologio*, 41 (2002), 191–200; B. Rivlin and Leah Bornstein-Makovetsky, "Larisa," in: *Pinkas Kehillot Yavan* (1999), 169–77.

[Simon Marcus / Yitzchak Kerem (2nd ed.)]

LASANSKY, MAURICIO (1914–), printmaker. Lasansky was born in Buenos Aires, the son of Polish immigrants. After studying at the Academy of Art, he became director of the Free Fine Arts School, Buenos Aires. In 1943 he went to the United States, and from 1952 taught printmaking at the State University of Iowa. He eventually became the head of what has been called the most influential graphic arts workshop in the world. His imaginative etchings and engravings are representational and are in many public collections. He developed a complicated yet highly successful process of color printing which became known as "The Lasansky Method." In 1967 Lasansky achieved wide recognition through a series of pencil drawings inspired by the Holocaust called "The Nazi Drawings."

[Alfred Werner]

LASDUN, SIR DENYS (1914–2001), English architect. Denys Lasdun was born in London, the son of a businessman who was the cousin of the Russian stage designer Leon Bakst; his mother was the granddaughter of the Australian artist Louis Abrahams. He was educated at Rugby and at the Architectural Association School. Lasdun worked for a time with the Tecton group, the architectural firm founded by Berthold Lubetkin which helped to launch modern architecture in Britain. Lasdun wished to produce an organic architecture "that inhibits neither the notion of growth and change nor advances in technology." His designs included working class housing schemes in Paddington and Bethnal Green, London as well as luxury flats in St. James'. Other buildings of Lasdun's are the Royal College of Physicians (1960), the new University of East Anglia (1962), the Sports Center, Liverpool University (1963), the Social Center, University of Leicester (1963), and his project for the National Theater and Opera, London (1967). One of the best-known modern British architects, Lasdun was knighted in 1976 and made a Companion of Honour (CH) in 1995.

ADD. BIBLIOGRAPHY: ODNB; W.J.R. Curtis, *Denys Lasdun: Architecture, City, Landscape* (1994).

LASERSON, MAX (1887–1951), Latvian jurist, historian, and Zionist. Born in Jelgava, Laserson was appointed lecturer in law at the University of Petrograd in 1916. In Alexander Kerensky's provisional government of 1917 he was deputy director of national minorities in the Ministry of the Interior. In 1920 he returned to Latvia, now an independent state, and became professor of law at the Riga commercial college. Laserson was also prominent in Jewish affairs, and from 1922 to

1931 represented the Socialist Zionist (Ẓe'irei Zion-Hitaḥdut) faction in the Latvian parliament. With the advent of the right-wing regime of Kartis Ulmanis in 1934 and the suppression of national minorities, Laserson was arrested. On his release he left Latvia for Palestine, where he helped to found the Tel Aviv School of Law and Economics. In 1939 he immigrated to the United States. There he lectured at Columbia University and was head of the department of law at the Institute of Jewish Affairs.

Laserson's principal writings were concerned with legal theory, especially *Revolyutsiya i pravo* ("Revolution and Law," 1926), and *Obshchaya teoriya prava* ("General Theory of Law," 1930). He also wrote on minority rights and, in his later years, on the problem of relations between Russia and the West, his books including *Russia and the Western World* (1945), and *The American Impact on Russia* (1950). He was also the author of two works in Hebrew, *Ha-Mandat, ha-Konstituẓyah ve-ha-Mo'ezah ha-Meḥokeket* ("The Mandate, the Constitution, and the Legislative Council of Palestine," 1936), and *Ha-Filosofyah ha-Mishpatit shel ha-Rambam* ("The Legal Philosophy of Maimonides," 1939).

BIBLIOGRAPHY: *Yahadut Latvia* (1953), 423–6.

[Ezra Mendelsohn]

LASHON HA-RA (Heb. לְשׁוֹן הָרַע; lit. "evil speech"), the prohibition against slandering, slurring, or defaming one's fellow Jews, even when the derogatory remarks are true (Lev. 19:16; Rashi ad. loc.). The sages constantly stressed the severity of this prohibition, asserting that slander destroys three persons: "he who relates the slander, he who accepts it, and he about whom it is told" (Ar. 15b). They recognized the power of the spoken word to build or ruin human relationships, and considered the tongue the "elixir of life" (Lev. R. 16:2) and the primary source of good and evil (Lev. R. 33:1). It was even considered forbidden to spread discreditable comments which the slanderer would have told to the person himself (Tos. to Ar. 15b).

The Bible is replete with examples of righteous and wicked individuals who transgressed this prohibition. Sarah is accused of slandering Abraham when she spoke about his advanced age and inability to beget children (Gen. 18:12–15; TJ, Pe'ah 1:1, 16a). Joseph was punished for the "evil reports" he spread about his brothers (Gen. 37:2; TJ, Pe'ah 1:1, 15d–16a). Miriam was rebuked by God for slandering Moses (Num. 12:1–15). The spies were punished for their injurious reports concerning the Holy Land (Num. 14:36–37). The division of the kingdom of David is attributed to his paying heed to slander (Shab. 56a–b). Doeg and Ahithophel were accused of constantly desiring to hear "evil speech" (TJ, loc. cit.). Jeroboam king of Israel (I Kings 12:20) was worthy of being counted together with the kings of Judah (Hos 1:1) because he did not give heed to slander against Amos (Amos 7:10–11; Pes. 87b). The murder of Isaiah by Manasseh was considered divine retribution for Isaiah's slurs against the Jewish people (Isa. 6:5; Yev. 49b). Haman was considered the most skillful of all traducers (Meg. 13b). Indirect slander was also forbidden, and the sages cautioned against speaking in praise of a person lest one inevitably be led also to mention the person's bad deeds and qualities (BB 164b). Equally objectionable under this heading is the implicit form of slander exemplified by the statement, "Do not speak of him; I want to know nothing about him," in which one expresses a disinclination to listen, not because of a distaste for slander, but because of the implied unworthiness of the subject (see Maim. Yad, De'ot 7:4). Although the hearer was cautioned not to believe slander, he still was permitted to safeguard himself cautiously lest the reports prove true (Nid. 61a). Defaming individuals who constantly caused strife and dissension is permissable (TJ, Pe'ah 1:1, 16a).

The rabbis often emphasized the rigorous punishments for those engaging in "evil speech." They are immediately chastised by plagues (ARN 19); and rain is withheld because of them (Ta'an. 7b). Croup comes to the world on account of slander (Shab. 33a–b), and whoever makes derogatory remarks about deceased scholars is cast into *Gehinnom (Ber. 19a). Slanderers will not enjoy the *Shekhinah (Divine Presence; Sot. 42a), and a bearer of evil tales is considered as denying God (Ar. 15b). Whoever relates or accepts slander deserves to be cast to the dogs (Pes. 118a), and stoned (Ar. 15b). The Talmud delineated the repentance for those wishing to atone for this sin. Scholars were advised to engage in Torah study, while simple persons were urged to humble themselves (Ar. 15b). The robe of the high priest and the incense aided in achieving atonement for this sin (Zev. 88b). Mar, the son of Ravina, on concluding his daily prayer added the following: "My God, keep my tongue from evil and my lips from speaking guile" (Ber. 17a), a formula which has been added at the end of the *Amidah*. In modern times, Rabbi *Israel Meir ha-Kohen (Ḥafeẓ Ḥayyim) gained wide recognition for his writings which stressed the gravity of the sin of *lashon ha-ra*.

BIBLIOGRAPHY: Israel Meir ha-Kohen (Ḥafeẓ Ḥayyim), *Shemirat ha-Lashon* (1952); Israel Al-Nakawa, *Menorat ha-Ma'or*, ed. by H.G. Enelow, 4 (1932), 337–70.

LASK (Pol. **Łask**), town in Lodz province, central Poland. The Jewish settlement of the town began to develop at the close of the 16th century. For about two centuries, the owners of the town were favorably disposed toward the Jewish population and protected it from the local clergy. The fires which burnt down most of the town's houses in 1624 and 1747 caused heavy losses to the Jewish population. The ancient synagogue and cemetery were destroyed. Thanks to the right of residence granted in 1640 by Stanislaw Wierzbowski, Lask Jews were authorized to engage in crafts, to trade in grain and *livestock, and to lease and keep inns. They were, however, forbidden to acquire houses and building lots in the market square and the neighboring streets. From the close of the 17th century, the Jews of the town paid heavy taxes toward the maintenance of the army. During the early 1790s the debts of the community increased considerably, to about 30,000 zlotys. According to the census of 1765, there were 891 Jews in Lask and a further

276 in the 54 small surrounding settlements subordinate to the community. In 1827, there were 1,270 Jews (64% of the total population). From 1827 on the new owners of Lask filed suit against the community for the payment of the debts which had accumulated by the close of the 18th century. In 1838 the Jews of the town were ordered, under threat of attachment of their property, to pay their debts with the addition of 7,697 zlotys as accrued interest. Following rapid economic development during the second quarter of the 19th century, the Jews of Pabianice and Zdunska Wola set up their own communal organizations independent of Lask. The first known rabbi of the town was Israel b. Ithamar (d. 1726) who was succeeded by R. Meir b. Eliakim Goetz of Hildesheim. Subsequent rabbis were Phinehas Zelig (d. 1770), author of *Ateret Paz* (1768), Moses Judah Leib Zilberberg, author of *Zayit Ra'anan* (2 vols., 1851–69) and *Tif'eret Yerushalayim*, David Dov *Meisels (d. 1876), and his son Ẓevi Aryeh Judah (until 1932). The last rabbi of Lask was Leibel Ajzenberg, who died in the Chelmno extermination camp in 1942. From the second half of the 19th century, most of the Jews of Lask were Ḥasidim (*Kotsk and *Warka). In 1897 there were 2,862 Jews in Lask (68% of the population). Jewish workers and craftsmen were influenced by the socialist movement. Zionist activities also started at the outbreak of World War I. In 1919 two of the 14 members of the municipal council were Jews. Between the two world wars, there were two Jewish libraries, a reformed *ḥeder* (founded in 1927), a Hebrew *Tarbut school, a *Beth Jacob school, and *Maccabi and Shtern sports societies. In 1921 there were 2,623 Jews in Lask. After the serious economic crisis of 1929, antisemitism became intensified and an economic boycott was imposed on the Jews.

[Arthur Cygielman]

Holocaust Period

In 1939, there were 3,864 Jews out of a total population of 6,000. After the town was occupied by the Germans, the religious Jewish community was persecuted. Synagogue officials were executed; the *bet midrash* was converted into a slaughterhouse for horses; Jews were forced to perform degrading acts during the High Holidays. A ghetto was established in several stages. At first a few streets were earmarked for Jewish habitation, but on Nov. 18, 1940, the Germans forced all the Jews of Lask into this area. Toward the end of 1941, the death penalty was imposed for anyone leaving the ghetto. From then on the food situation worsened considerably. The Judenrat organized a hospital, a kindergarten, and a soup kitchen. In mid-August 1942 the ghetto was liquidated. About 3,500 Jews were locked up in a church outside the city and were kept for several days under inhuman conditions; the Germans then picked out some 800 craftsmen to be sent to *Lodz ghetto, while the rest were sent to the extermination camp at *Chelmno.

[Danuta Dombrowska]

BIBLIOGRAPHY: P. Selig, *Ir Lask va-Ḥakhameha* (1926); B. Wasiutyński, *Ludność żydowska w Polsce w wiekach xix i xx* (1930), 28, 51, 180, 185, 188, 210; I. Krasoń, *Z dziejów Łasku* (1965); Z. Tsurnamal (ed.), *Lask Izcor-book* (Heb., Yid., some Eng., 1968); D. Dąbrowska, in: BŻIH, 13–14 (1955); J. Goldberg et al., in: PK *Polin*.

LASK, EMIL (1875–1915), German philosopher. Born in Wadowitz, Austria, he studied under Rickert in Freiburg. In 1905 he became lecturer in philosophy at Heidelberg. Just before the outbreak of World War I, he was elected professor. Lask died in World War I in the Galician campaign. Lask's philosophy developed from the neo-Kantianism of Windelband and Rickert. Until 1913 Lask aimed at a synthesis of Platonic-Aristotelian philosophy and the Kantianism of Rickert; the seeds of the new metaphysics were to be found in this synthesis. He fought against the ordinary subjectivism to be found in Kant's system, and placed the emphasis on the objective world, which for him meant that the conscious subject must put up with the function of "servant." His later work approached subjectivism, but because of his early death, only fragments of his writings and some unfinished philosophy lectures are available. After Lask's death, Rickert published his writings in three volumes (the third volume contained his later writings).

BIBLIOGRAPHY: Rickert, in: E. Lask, *Gesammelte Schriften*, 1 (1923), v–xvi (introd.); Lukács, in: *Kantstudien*, 27 (1918), 349–70; G. Pick, *Die Uebergegensaetzlichkeit der Werte* (1921); Herrigel, in: *Logos*, 12 (1923–24), 100–22; J. Cohn, *Theorie der Dialektik* (1923), 152–4; G. Gurvich, *Les tendances actuelles de la philosophie allemande* (repr. 1949); H. Levy, *Die Hegel-Renaissance in der deutschen Philosophie* (1927), 72–76.

[Samuel Hugo Bergman]

LASKER, family of prominence in the 19th–20th centuries in the U.S. MORRIS LASKER (1840–1916), who was born in Prussia, immigrated to the U.S. in 1856. After settling in Texas in 1860, he participated in a number of Indian campaigns and fought in the Civil War with the Confederacy. After the war Lasker moved to Galveston, where he became a prominent merchant, real estate and livestock dealer, and banker. He was elected to the Texas state senate in 1895. His brother Eduard *Lasker (1829–1884) was a prominent German politician and author.

ALBERT DAVIS LASKER (1880–1952), an advertising pioneer, public servant, and communal leader, was brought up in Galveston. Lasker worked as a reporter for the Dallas *News* before joining the Chicago advertising agency of Lord & Thomas in 1898. He subsequently bought the agency (1910), and when he dissolved the firm and retired in 1942, the agency was the largest of its kind in the world. Lasker's inventiveness, particularly his use of what he called "salesmanship-in-print," sparked a tremendous growth in the advertising business. His public and political posts included aide to President Wilson's secretary of the Department of Agriculture; head of the Republican National Committee's publicity department (1918); and chairman of the U.S. Shipping Board (1921–23). Before resigning from the last, Lasker oversaw the extensive reorganization of the U.S. merchant marine and the disposal of $3 billion worth of the board's assets. In 1940 he was a delegate from Illinois to the Republican National Convention. Active in Jewish affairs, Lasker contributed to the Hebrew Union College, was a trustee of the Associated Jewish Charities of Chicago, and was a member of the American Jewish Committee's executive committee. He also founded and endowed the Lasker Foundation for medical research in 1928.

His sister FLORINA LASKER (1884–1949), a communal worker, was born in Galveston. She served as chairman of the National Council of Jewish Women's immigrant aid section, was a board member of the National Consumers' League, and wrote, with Etta and Loula Lasker, *Care and Treatment of the Jewish Blind in the City of New York* (1918) for the Bureau of Philanthropic Research. A board member of the American Civil Liberties Union, she was also secretary of the New York Labor Standards Committee (1934), dedicated to the improvement of wages, hours, and working conditions; additionally, she reorganized (1943) and presided over the Consumers' League of New York, which, under her direction, conducted important surveys of migrant workers in New York State.

A second sister, Etta Lasker *Rosensohn (1885–1966), was a social and communal worker and Zionist. A third sister, LOULA DAVIS LASKER (1886–1961), who was also born in Galveston, was a social and communal worker and Zionist. She held posts with the Bureau of Philanthropic Research (1916–17) and the New York County chapter of the American Red Cross. She was also a member of the U.S. immigration commissioner's advisory panel on welfare conditions at U.S. immigrant reception stations (1921), and chairman of the Commission on Immigrant Aid and Immigrant Education for the New York section of the National Council of Jewish Women (1921–23). During 1928–52 she was associate editor of *Survey* and *Survey Graphic*. A founder in 1937 and board chairman of the Citizens Housing and Planning Council, Loula Lasker was also a founder of the League for Industrial Democracy and a board member of the American Civil Liberties Union. Active in Jewish affairs, she became a member of Hadassah's national board in 1949, edited the Hadassah *Newsletter* from 1952 to 1955, and subsequently served as a Hadassah vice president.

BIBLIOGRAPHY: J. Gunther, *Taken at the Flood: The Story of Albert D. Lasker* (1960).

LASKER, EDUARD (Isaac; 1829–1884), German Liberal politician. Lasker was born to an Orthodox merchant family in Posen. While studying law at the University of Breslau he took part in the revolution of 1848, fighting with the students' legion in Vienna against the imperial troops. In 1853 he went to England to study the system of British parliamentary government, then a model for German liberals. Returning in 1856 he became an associate judge in Berlin. In 1865 he was elected to the Prussian Parliament as a member of the Progressive Party but broke away in 1867 to found the National Liberal Party, of which he was the head. After the German Empire was formed in 1870, Lasker led the Liberal Party in the Reichstag and helped *Bismarck in his work of securing Prussian leadership in Germany, making a substantial contribution to the passage of many important laws, including the laws of association and taxation, the codification of criminal law, and a new judicial system. A gifted orator, Lasker vigorously defended parliamentary authority and on several occasions forced proposals endangering individual liberties to be withdrawn. Furthermore he published works on *Wege und Ziele der Culturentwicklung* (1881) and *Zur Geschichte der parlamentarischen Entwicklung Preussens* (1873).

Lasker's first breach with Bismarck occurred in 1873, when his revelations about the mismanagement and stock manipulation of the Pomeranian railways led to the fall of one of Bismarck's closest associates. His opposition to Bismarck's high tariff policy after 1878 led to his defeat in the 1879 elections. In 1880 he left the National Party in protest against a law limiting freedom of speech and set up the Liberal Union in opposition to Bismarck. Soon afterward, however, ill health forced him to retire from politics. He died in the United States and was buried in 1901 in the Jewish cemetery in Berlin. When the American House of Representatives sent a resolution of condolence to Bismarck for transmission to the Reichstag, he refused to accept it on the ground that in praising Lasker it thereby was criticizing German policy. Lasker was a loyal Jew and a vigorous champion of Jewish rights. On his initiative, the Prussian parliament passed a law permitting Jews to opt out of the official community without being regarded as having left Judaism, a measure which enabled the ultra-orthodox congregations to form independent communities.

BIBLIOGRAPHY: A. Schwab, *Eduard Lasker* (Ger., 1923); R.W. Dill, *Eduard Lasker* (Ger., 1956). **ADD. BIBLIOGRAPHY:** J.F. Harris, "Eduard Lasker – The Jew as National German Politician," in: LBIYB, 20 (1975), 151–77; A. Laufs, *Eduard Lasker – Ein Leben fuer den Rechtsstaat*, 1984; J.F. Harris, *A Study of Theory and Practice in German Liberalism – Eduard Lasker*, 1984.

[Bernard Dov Ganzel / Bjoern Siegel (2nd ed.)]

LASKER, EMANUEL (1868–1941), chess master. Lasker, who was the grandson of a rabbi and son of a German cantor, was born in Berlin. In the early 1900s he settled in New York City, where he published his own chess magazine and was chess editor of the *New York Evening Post*. Lasker won tournaments in London (two in 1892), New York (1893), St. Petersburg (1895–96), Nuremberg (1896), London (1899), Paris (1900), St. Petersburg (1909 and 1914), and Berlin (1918). In match play he won 18 out of 20 matches, defeating Wilhelm *Steinitz for the world title (1894) and defending it successfully against him (1896–97), as well as against Frank Marshall, S. *Tarrasch (twice), and David Janowski (three times). He drew with Carl Schlechter and finally lost in 1921 to Capablanca (ten draws and four losses). In match play, the great attacking masters Jacques Mieses, J.H. Blackburne, H.E. Bird, and Frank Marshall all failed to win a game against him. Lasker taught advanced mathematics at various universities. His papers include "Modules and Ideal Factors" and "Die Philosophie des Unvollendbaren" (1919). His chess publications include *Common Sense in Chess* (1896) and *Lasker's Manual of Chess* (1927).

BIBLIOGRAPHY: J. Hannak, *Emanuel Lasker* (Eng., 1959).

[Gerald Abrahams]

LASKER-SCHUELER, ELSE (1869–1945), German poet. Lasker-Schueler grew up in an assimilated family in Elberfeld. In 1894 she married the doctor Berthold Lasker and, moving to Berlin, soon after became part of a group of avant gardist artists gathering around the bohemian writer Peter Hille, taking lessons in drawing and writing her first poems (published in the volumes *Styx* (1902), and *Der siebente Tag* (1905)). Working together with her second husband, Herwarth *Walden (to whom she was married from 1901 to 1911), who was the editor of the main journal of German expressionism, *Der Sturm*, she soon turned out to be one of the most highly acclaimed expressionistic writers. Within this literary and artistic movement, from around 1910 to 1920, she was also part of a generation of young Jewish writers who rejected the bourgeois concept of assimilation of their parents and discovered Judaism as a counterculture. Lasker-Schueler's name for these non-bourgeois Jews was "*wilde Juden*." In this context, she created her own world of mythical Oriental and biblical figures, stories, and poems. She also mythologized her friends – and even more herself as "Princess Tino of Baghdad" and later as "Prince Yussuf of Thebes" (cf. the stories *Die Naechte Tino von Bagdads*, 1907; *Der Prinz von Theben*, 1914; *Hebraeische Balladen*, 1913). She expanded this poetical myth in her novels *Mein Herz* (1913) and *Der Malik* (1919). They consist of an account of the literary and artistic avant garde in the form of letters to her friends (among them Franz Marc, Karl *Kraus, Alfred *Doeblin, Gottfried Benn, Max *Brod, and Franz *Werfel). In the story *Der Wunderrabbiner von Barcelona* (1921) and in the novel/play *Arthur Aronymus* (1932), the subject was her own family history (e.g., her grand-grandfather, the famous rabbi Hirsch Cohen, in the latter), but also the conflicted relationship between Judaism and Christianity. While the "Wanderrabbiner" portrays – following Heinrich *Heine's *Der Rabbi von Bacherach* – the persecution of the Jews in Christian Europe, *Arthur Aronymus* ends with a utopian reunion of Jews and Christians, represented even more emphatically when *Arthur Aronymus* was staged as a play in Zurich in 1936. A successful writer (and artist) in the Weimar Republic – she had her collected works published in ten volumes in 1919–20, and won the Kleist Prize in 1932 – Lasker-Schueler had to flee from Nazi-Germany to Switzerland in 1933. She lived in Zurich and Ascona under most difficult circumstances, supported by the Jewish community and selling her drawings while publishing a few poems in journals such as Klaus Mann's exile journal *Die Sammlung* (1934/35). Already during this period she undertook two journeys to Palestine, the first in 1934 and the second in 1937, staying mostly in Jerusalem and becoming well acquainted with the German-Jewish intellectuals of the *yishuv*. Back in Switzerland, she wrote an account of the trip, *Das Hebraeerland* (1937). She portrayed Palestine not so much in a political and realistic way, but rather in a utopian way, showing Jews and Arabs living in harmony, yet she herself did not feel at home in Palestine. After a third journey to Palestine in 1939, during which World War II broke out, she had to stay in Jerusalem, where she spent her last years. In close contact with German-Jewish intellectuals like Ernst *Simon, Werner *Kraft, Shmuel Yosef *Agnon, Salman *Schocken, and Samuel *Bergman, she continued writing poems, some of which were published in Arnold *Zweig's German journal *Der Orient* (printed in Haifa), and collected in her last volume, *Mein blaues Klavier* (Jerusalem, 1943). In Jerusalem she also wrote her third play, *IchundIch* (1940; published in 1979), which criticizes national socialism in the mythic language of the Faust-theme. Her works were published in a critical edition from 1996 to 2002, and her letters began appearing in 2003.

BIBLIOGRAPHY: M. Wiener, in: G. Krojanker (ed.), *Juden in der deutschen Literatur* (1922), 179–92; W. Kraft, *Else Lasker-Schueler* (1951); E. Ginsberg (ed.), *Dichtungen und Dokumente: Else Lasker-Schueler* (1951); M. Kupper, in: *Literaturwissenschaftliches Jahrbuch* (1968); E. Kluesener, *Else Lasker-Schueler in Selbstzeugnissen und Bilddokumenten* (1980); I. Shedletzky, in: M. Gelber (ed.), *The Jewish Reception of Heinrich Heine* (1992); J. Hessing, *Die Heimkehr einer juedischen Emigrantin. Else Lasker-Schuelers mythisierende Rezeption 1945 bis 1971* (1993); G. Dane, in: *Text und Kritik*, 122 (1994); S.M. Hedgepeth, *Ueberall blicke ich nach einem heimatlichen Boden aus. Exil im Werk Else Lasker-Schuelers* (1994); A. Bodenheimer, *Die auferlegte Heimat. Else Lasker-Schuelers Emigration in Palaestina* (1995); I. Hermann, "*Raum – Koerper – Schrift.*" *Mythopoetische Verfahrensweisen in der Prosa Else Lasker-Schuelers* (1997); S. Bauschinger, *Else Lasker-Schueler. Biographie* (2004).

[Andreas Kilcher (2nd ed.)]

LASKI, family prominent in English intellectual and public life. NATHAN LASKI (1863–1941), businessman and communal leader, was born in Russia and brought up in Middlesbrough. He settled in Manchester and established himself as a successful cotton merchant with extensive connections in India. In 1906 he became a city magistrate. At various periods he was president of the Manchester Great Synagogue, Jewish Board of Guardians, Jewish Hospital, and Council of Manchester and Salford Jews. He was honorary president of the local Zionist Central Council and for a time treasurer of the Board of Deputies of British Jews; he became recognized as the head of the Manchester Jewish community. His wife, SARAH (1869–1948), was a member of the Manchester city council for many years. Their two sons were Harold *Laski and NEVILLE JONAS LASKI (1890–1969). The latter achieved distinction as a lawyer, becoming successively recorder of Burnley, judge of appeal in the Isle of Man, and recorder and judge of the crown court of Liverpool. Within the Jewish community he held many offices, rising to greatest prominence as president of the Board of Deputies of British Jews (1933–39). He was thus president of the Board during the dark years of ascendant Nazi power and has been criticized for being insufficiently pro-Zionist. His successor as president, Professor Selig *Brodetsky, was a strong pro-Zionist of East European birth; his election is often seen as marking a turning-point in the outlook of Anglo-Jewry. In 1933 Laski was elected co-chairman of the administrative committee of the Jewish Agency for Palestine and in the following year succeeded to the chairmanship. He was also a vice president of the Anglo-Jewish Association. After his marriage to the daughter of the haham Moses *Gaster, he became a leading member of the Sephardi community. Neville Laski published *Jewish Rights and Jewish Wrongs* (1939), a collection of speeches; also *The Laws and Charities of the Spanish and Portuguese Jews Congregation of London* (1952). ESTHER PEARL LASKI (1915–1988), known throughout her life as Marghanita Laski, his daughter, was a well-known novelist, writer, and broadcaster. Educated at Oxford, she wrote such novels as *Little Boy Lost* (1949), psychological studies such as *Ecstasy* (1961), and literary biographies.

She was nationally known as a broadcaster on the BBC and also contributed no fewer than 250,000 examples of the earliest known usage of English words to the supplementary volumes of the *Oxford English Dictionary.*

BIBLIOGRAPHY: JC (Oct. 10, 1941), on Nathan; (March 2, 1945), on Sarah; (March 28, 1969), on Neville. **ADD. BIBLIOGRAPHY:** ODNB online for Marghanita Laski.

[Vivian David Lipman / William D. Rubinstein (2nd ed.)]

LASKI, HAROLD JOSEPH (1893–1950), British left-wing socialist and political theorist. Born in Manchester, he was the son of Nathan *Laski. At the age of 18, Laski eloped with a non-Jewish woman eight years older than himself. He was educated at Oxford and was recognized as a brilliant scholar from his youth. Laski lectured at McGill University, Canada, from 1914 until 1916, when he taught at Harvard, there forming a close friendship with Oliver Wendell Holmes, the U.S. Supreme Court justice. In 1920 he became a lecturer at the London School of Economics and was made professor of political science in 1926. He held this post until his death and greatly contributed to the increase in standing of that institution.

During the interwar years Laski played an important part in public administration in Britain as a member of the industrial court, the departmental committee on local government, and the committee on legal education. He also sat on the lord chancellor's committee on delegated legislation, which examined the accusation made by the lord chief justice, Lord Hewart, that the administrative system was no longer bound by the rule of law. Laski was a member of the national executive of the British Labor Party from 1936, where he represented the left intelligentsia. In 1945 he became chairman of the party and was the chief target of conservative propaganda at the general election of that year. Following the Labor victory at the polls, however, Laski's influence waned, with Prime Minister Clement Attlee telling him that "a period of silence from you would be welcome" after he tried to intervene in policy following the 1945 election. Nevertheless he had a profound effect on the development of British socialism and was an outstanding figure in the British Fabian Society. Laski was also one of the founders and directors of the influential Left Book Club. His writings include *A Grammar of Politics* (1925, 1938[4]), in which he set out his concept of the pluralistic state and *The State in Theory and Practice* (1935) in which he adopted the Marxist doctrine of the state being an instrument of economic power. His other works include *Parliamentary Government in England* (1938), *The American Presidency* (1940), and *The American Democracy* (1949). For a considerable time he played no part in Jewish life, but he helped Weizmann change the provisions of Passfield's *White Paper (1929–30). The Nazi persecutions aroused his interest in the Jewish problem. He denounced antisemitism and began to take a deep interest in the Zionist struggle. In 1943, he replied to a Labor Party resolution on the Jewish question saying "The executive recognizes, and I as a Jew in the fullest sense of the word claim, absolute equality of status in political, social, and economic rights with any other people in the world." At the end of the war Laski clashed with Bevin over the Palestine problem and he declared himself in favor of a Jewish commonwealth in Palestine. He welcomed the establishment of Israel and was sympathetic to the work of the Po'alei Zion movement and the "Friends of the Histadrut." Laski's last years were clouded by his unwise involvement in a libel suit against an allegedly antisemitic newspaper editor, which he lost after a highly publicized trial. He died of bronchitis at the age of only 57.

BIBLIOGRAPHY: K. Martin, *Harold Laski: A Biography* (1969); H.A. Deane, *The Political Ideas of Harold J. Laski* (1955), incl. bibl.; H.M. Magid, *English Political Pluralism* (1941); T.I. Cook, in: *American Political Science Review,* 44 (Sept. 1950), 738–41. **ADD. BIBLIOGRAPHY:** ODNB online; M. Newman, *Harold Laski: A Political Biography* (1993); I. Kramnick and B. Sheerman, *Harold Laski: A Life on the Left* (1993).

[Moshe Rosetti]

LASKIN, BORA (1912–1984), Canadian legal scholar, teacher, labor arbitrator, jurist. Laskin was born in Fort William, Ontario (now Thunder Bay). His Russian-immigrant parents instilled in him an appreciation of his Jewish heritage and passion for tolerance and justice. His first language was Yiddish, and he became a master of the Hebrew language. He earned his B.A. (1933) and M.A. (1935) from the University of Toronto, and a law degree from Osgoode Hall Law School in Toronto (1936), standing at the head of his class. He maintained this rank at Harvard, where he earned a Masters in Law (1937), but when he returned to Toronto, entrenched antisemitism in the legal profession prevented him from finding a legal position. Instead he helped edit the *Revised Statutes of Ontario* and wrote headnotes for legal case reports. His experience with antisemitism reinforced Laskin's commitment to justice and impartiality. It also steered him away from private practice and toward an academic career and, in the end, made Laskin Canada's foremost lawyer and jurist without ever having practiced law or argued a case in court.

Laskin taught at the University of Toronto from 1940 to 1945, at Osgoode Hall from 1945 to 1949, and again at the University of Toronto until 1965, contributing fundamentally to the University of Toronto's reformulation as a professional law faculty as commemorated in the Bora Laskin Law Library. Known affectionately as "Moses the Law Giver," he earned renown as a brilliant scholar and inspiring teacher. Laskin regarded the law as a flexible instrument for social justice, a view which permeated his legal writings as scholar and judge.

He wrote six books, seven commission reports, and dozens of learned articles; his *Canadian Constitutional Law* (1951) was the standard text in Canadian law schools for a generation and his publications shaped Canadian jurisprudence in labor and constitutional law and civil liberties. While a professor he also gained prominence as a labor arbitrator, demonstrating a sense of fairness, impartiality, and legal scholarship that foreshadowed his career as a judge. Committed to academic freedom, he helped found the Canadian Association of University Teachers, becoming its president in 1964–65. He also joined, and eventually chaired, the Legal Affairs Committee of the Canadian Jewish Congress, preparing briefs and draft legislation that were instrumental in fashioning Canada's human rights laws.

In 1965 he was appointed to the Ontario Court of Appeal, where he was a champion of civil liberties and frequently dissented from the majority of the court. His courage and integrity gained the attention of Prime Minister Pierre Trudeau, who made Laskin his first appointment to the Supreme Court of Canada in 1970, and the first Jew on Canada's highest court. Maintaining his role as "the Great Dissenter," Laskin was appointed chief justice in December 1973, creating controversy when he was leapfrogged over five more senior judges. Even as chief justice Laskin was still frequently in dissent in a conservative court. Over time the adoption of his positions by legislators, his growing influence on Canadian legal thought, and Trudeau's appointment of more liberal judges allowed Laskin to turn the Supreme Court into a national institution and a creative force in promoting individual rights and legal equality.

Active in the larger community, Laskin served on the governing boards of several universities and among his many honors were the Order of Canada, appointment to the Royal Society of Canada, and 27 honorary degrees from universities in Canada, Britain, the United States, Israel, and Italy. His death in 1984 prevented him from participating in jurisprudence under the new Canadian Charter of Rights and Freedoms, but his prior judgments and writings left a legacy that would be reflected in subsequent Charter decisions. His career demonstrates the transformation not only of Canadian law but of Canadian society from the prejudices and restrictions of the 1930s toward egalitarian and multicultural maturity.

BIBLIOGRAPHY: P. Girard, *Bora Laskin: Bringing Law to Life* (2005).

[James Walker (2nd ed.)]

LASKOV, ḤAYYIM (1919–1982), Israel military commander. Born in Borisov, Belorussia, Laskov moved to Palestine in 1925. His father was killed by Arabs in 1930. In 1940 Laskov joined the Palestinian Jewish units in the British army, receiving a commission. In 1944 he was with the *Jewish Brigade Group in Italy and commanded a mechanized machine-gun platoon in the Senio sector. He joined the permanent staff of the *Haganah in 1947, dealing mainly with training matters. In 1948 he commanded the first mechanized battalion of the Israeli army in the battles of Latrun, Nazareth, and Galilee. During the *War of Independence (1948) he was promoted to *aluf* (brigadier general) and director of training. In 1951 he became commander of the Israel air force. Laskov went to study at Oxford in 1953 but was recalled in 1955 and appointed deputy chief of general staff and, in 1956, commanding officer of the armored corps. During the *Sinai Campaign he commanded a divisional task force on the northern axis. After the campaign he was appointed commanding officer of the southern command and, in 1958, fifth chief of general staff. In 1961 he retired from the army to become director general of the ports authority. He initiated large-scale reforms for increased efficiency in the major Israel ports, particularly Ashdod and Haifa. He resigned his post in 1970 and participated in various public bodies.

BIBLIOGRAPHY: D. Lazar, *Rashim be-Yisrael*, 1 (1953), 170–5.

[Jehuda Wallach]

LASKY, JESSE L. (1880–1958), U.S. film producer. Born in San Francisco, California, Lasky was one of the founders of the motion picture industry. As a young man he was a newspaper reporter, a gold prospector in Alaska, and then vaudeville promoter. His partnership with the producer Cecil B. DeMille started in 1911, when they collaborated in presenting an operetta based on the story of California. In 1913 Lasky and his brother-in-law Samuel *Goldwyn organized the Jesse L. Lasky Feature Play Company. Their first film, *The Squaw Man*, directed by first-time director DeMille, was so successful that it at once established them (and Hollywood) in the motion picture business. In 1917, the Lasky company was merged with the Famous Players Company, headed by Adolph *Zukor. After several name changes, it ultimately became known as Paramount Pictures. Lasky was in charge of film production and remained in that position until 1932. After 1932, Lasky was a producer for the Fox Film Corporation, then for RKO-Radio Pictures, and from 1940 to 1944 for Warner Brothers. He produced more than a hundred films, among them *The Cocoanuts* (1929); *The Power and the Glory* (1933); *The White Parade* (Oscar nomination for Best Picture, 1934); *Sergeant York* (Oscar nomination for Best Picture, 1941); the *Adventures of Mark Twain* (1942); *Rhapsody in Blue* (1945), a film based on the life of George Gershwin; and *The Great Caruso* (1951). In 1957 Lasky's autobiography *I Blow My Own Horn* was published.

His son, JESSE LASKY, JR. (1910–1988), born in New York, wrote fiction, plays, and film scripts. He wrote the screenplays for such films as *Reap the Wild Wind* (1942); *Samson and Delilah* (1949); *Salome* (1953); and *The Ten Commandments* (1956). He also wrote the screenplays for several television series, such as *The Saint* (1962); *Danger Man* (1964); and *The Protectors* (1972). Among his published works are *Naked in a Cactus Garden* (1961), *Whatever Happened to Hollywood?* (1975), *Love Scene: The Story of Laurence Olivier and Vivien Leigh* (with P. Silver, 1978), and *The Offer* (1981).

BIBLIOGRAPHY: *Current Biography Yearbook 1958* (1959), 238; *Current Biography,* 8 (April 1947), 33–35; W. Irwin, *The House That Shadows Built* (1928), 197–208. **ADD. BIBLIOGRAPHY:** I. Edmonds and R. Mimura, *Paramount Pictures and the People Who Made Them* (1980); B. Lasky, *Candle in the Sun* (1957).

[Stewart Kampel / Ruth Beloff (2nd ed.)]

LASSALLE (Lassal), FERDINAND (1825–1864), German Socialist leader. Born in Breslau, Lassalle was the only son of Heyman (Chayim) Lassal, who was trained for a rabbinical career, but became a merchant, a member of the town council, and subsequently a militant adherent of the Jewish Reform movement. Ferdinand Lassalle's diary reveals that as a young man he was precocious and undisciplined, dreaming of leadership, first at the head of the Jews avenging the Damascus massacres of 1840, and later, leading the German democrats at the side of *Boerne and Heine.

Ferdinand Lassalle's interest switched from literature to history and finally to Hegelian philosophy. Leaving school before matriculating, he prepared himself for university. During this period he became for a short time a Young Hegelian intent on converting the members of the enlightened *Lern- und Leseverein* and on using the liberal Reform movement as a means of destroying Orthodox Judaism. Admitted to Breslau University, he switched to Jacobin democratic propaganda which he based on an "activated" but orthodox Hegelianism. In order to avoid expulsion and to widen his horizons he went to Berlin where he soon gathered around him a small circle of followers. During the years 1843 to 1845 Lassalle developed his concept of democratic and industrial Socialism based on the rule of law. In early years he worked for the newspaper of Karl Marx, *Neue Rheinische Zeitung*. His political and scholarly interests brought him to Paris in the winter of 1845/46 where he met Heinrich *Heine. Lassalle promised Heine legal aid in securing certain pension rights which his family was withholding. Heine withdrew his legal action to avoid public scandal but Lassalle put the legal skills he acquired to effective use, representing Countess Sophie von Hatzfeldt in her dispute with her husband. After a legal action which lasted eight years he secured a divorce and financial settlement for the countess and she rewarded him with a permanent income which ensured him economic independence. For a short time Lassalle took an active part in the 1848 Revolution. He had been arrested early in 1848 after one of his followers illegally seized a suitcase believed to contain important documents connected with the Hatzfeldt case. Lassalle was convicted and was released only some months later. He was rearrested soon afterward at the beginning of the November uprising for inciting violence. His defense at the assizes, which he circulated in pamphlet form under the title *Meine Assisen-Rede* (1849), was one of the remarkable documents of that abortive revolution. Acquitted on the principal charge, he was nevertheless convicted on a minor charge and sentenced to a further six months' imprisonment. For the next few years Lassalle conducted a lengthy correspondence with *Marx in London. He also helped him to publish his writings, aiding him financially and keeping him informed on German affairs. Marx proposed that Lassalle be invited to join the "Communist League" but the Cologne central committee rejected the proposal because of Lassalle's dubious reputation. Later, however, relations between Marx and Lassalle cooled. A visit to the Balkan countries after the Crimean War and the national stirrings in Italy convinced Lassalle of the potentialities of national uprisings. His readiness to tolerate Napoleon III, his encouragement of nationalism, and his refusal to regard Russian pan-Slavism as the archenemy of revolution, estranged him from Marx. Furthermore, Lassalle's literary productions, *Franz von Sickingen* (1858), a plea for German unification in drama form; *Der italienische Krieg und die Aufgabe Preussens* (1859), a battle cry against the Hapsburgs, demanding the dissolution of the Empire; and *Fichtes politisches Vermaechtnis* (1860), a blueprint for a centralized Germany, were the subject of lengthy literary controversies with Marx, and at the same time enhanced Lassalle's reputation amongst the intellectual elite.

Lassalle's political activity between 1860 and 1862 was confined to his relations with Garibaldi and the left wing of the German "National-Verein." He tried to exploit the constitutional crisis in Prussia for intensive agitation among the workers. During the winter of 1862/63, Lassalle was contacted by a Leipzig committee for a pan-German labor congress and was asked to help counteract the influence of the liberal Schulze-Delitzsch. In his reply *Offenes Antwortschreiben an das Central-Comité* … (1863), Lassalle advised the workers to agitate for universal suffrage. He believed that a popular parliament would vote state credit for producers' cooperatives, thereby freeing the workers from the grip of the "iron law of wages," the cause of their poverty. Lassalle's proposals were rejected by most of the organized working clubs ("Arbeiterbildungsvereine"), but awakened the interest of the general public to the "social question" and attracted big audiences to his mass meetings. After a speech for the rights of the working class he founded on May 23, 1863, the Allgemeiner deutscher Arbeiterverein (ADAV, General German Workers Association) in Leipzig, to propagate his political ideas. The party, which proved to be the forerunner of the German Social Democratic party, had few members at first and even at Lassalle's death (1864) numbered only 4,000. The ADAV was strictly disciplined, the members accepting a dictatorial and centralized leadership. It indirectly forced the other parties to reform their organizations to counteract the ADAV's "shock tactics." Lassalle's pamphlet against liberal economic doctrine (*Herr Bastiat Schulze von Delitzsch*, 1864) was a crude but effective primer of labor economics. Its slogan of state aid as opposed to individual self-help influenced many socialist party programs even outside the ADAV. Marx privately expressed his misgivings of Lassalle's alleged plagiarism, his dictatorial methods, and his unbalanced propaganda.

Lassalle died of a bullet wound received in a duel at Carrouge, Geneva. Because the family of his bride-to-be, Helene von Doenniges, rejected him on account of his Jewish origin and his dubious past, Lassalle provoked the duel in order to vindicate his social and political respectability. The Countess Hatzfeldt and Lassalle's followers wanted to make the burial a demonstration but the family objected and he was buried hurriedly in the Jewish cemetery of Breslau.

During the classical period of international Socialism before World War I, Lassalle was honored as one of its principal figures. While Marx and Engels worked mainly abroad Lassalle laid the foundation of the Social Democratic movement in Germany. His career showed him to be a man of extraordinary ability and his writings reveal great depth of thought. His best-known works are *Die Philosophie Herakleitos Des Dunklen von Ephesos* (1857); *Der italienische Krieg und die Aufgabe Preussens* (1859); and *Das System der erworbenen Rechte* (1861). In addition, his pamphlets urging the workers to usher in a new social era reflected the radical policies he advocated, which were too revolutionary for the liberal movement of 19th-century Germany.

[Shlomo Na'aman]

Lassalle and the Jews

In his youth Lassalle took an interest in Judaism but he later adopted a negative attitude to the Jewish religion. He was aware of the position of the Jews of Eastern Europe but his deep involvement in general problems prevented him from developing his views on the Jewish people – a subject which he discussed in his youthful diary and letters. In 1843, he showed some interest in the movement for Reform Judaism but a year later he denied that Judaism was a living reality. Strongly influenced by Hegel, he recognized Judaism as a necessary phase in human development in the past, but negated it as a useful force or element in the present state of mankind. While this attitude did not in itself contain any hostility toward the Jews, Lassalle gradually became more and more inimical. Thus in 1860, Lassalle wrote: "I can well affirm that I am no longer a Jew," and added: "I do not like the Jews, I even detest them in general. I see in them nothing but the very much degenerated sons of a great but vanished past. During past centuries of slavery, these men have acquired characteristics of slaves, and that is why I am most unfavorably disposed towards them. Besides, I have no contact with them. Among my friends, and in society which surrounds me here there is scarcely a single Jew." Characteristically Lassalle never discussed the Jews from a socialist point of view but always spoke of them as a separate entity. In this respect he resembles Marx, though unlike Marx he did not indulge in public antisemitic utterances. Indeed, Lassalle was the object of antisemitic attacks, particularly from Engels who felt a deep personal aversion to Lassalle which he expressed in violently antisemitic remarks.

BIBLIOGRAPHY: D. Footman, *The Primrose Path* (1946); S. Na'aman, *Ferdinand Lassalle, eine neue politische Biographie* (1968); T. Ramm, *Ferdinand Lassalle als Rechtsund Sozialphilosoph* (1953); H. Oncken, *Lassalle, eine politische Biographie* (1920); G. Mayer, *Bismarck und Lassalle* (1928); H. Ebeling, *Der Begriff "Demokratie" in den sozialistischen Ideologien: Marx, Lassalle, Engels* (1964), 62–85, incl. bibl.; E. Silberner, *Sozialisten zur Judenfrage* (1962), 160–80, index; idem, in: HUCA, 24 (1952/53), 151ff.; B. Andréas, in: *Archiv fuer Sozialgeschichte*, 3 (1963), 297–412 (bibl. 331–412); E. Rosenbaum, in: YLBI, 9 (1964), 122–30; S. Na'aman, *Ferdinand Lassalle, Deutscher und Jude* (1968), incl. bibl.; S. Heym, *Lassalle* (1969). **ADD. BIBLIOGRAPHY:** T. Ramm, *Ferdinand Lassalle* (2004).

LASSAR, OSCAR (1849–1907), dermatologist. Lassar, who was born in Hamburg, opened the way to many modern methods of treating skin and venereal diseases. He was responsible for the introduction of electrophysical therapy for use in dermatology. Lassar developed the so-called Lassar paste, with a zinc and sulfur base. Until the discovery of cortisone ointments, this paste was the most widely used unguent for all types of skin diseases, and is still in use. He was a campaigner for public hygiene, established public baths and disinfectant stations in Berlin, and published various treatises on the subject, including *Die Cultur-Aufgabe der Volksbaeder* (1889). He founded the Berlin Society for Dermatology and the *Zeitung fuer Dermatologie*. In 1902 he became professor of dermatology at the University of Berlin. Lassar, who served in the Franco-Prussian War, was awarded the Iron Cross for bravery. He was also known as a writer of short stories.

BIBLIOGRAPHY: S.R. Kagan, *Jewish Medicine* (1952), 416; *Biographisches Lexikon der hervorragenden Aerzte*, 2 (1933).

[Suessmann Muntner]

LASSAW, IBRAM (1913–2003), U.S. sculptor. Born in Alexandria, Egypt, to Russian immigrant parents, in 1921 Lassaw arrived in the United States. In 1926 he began his formal art training at Brooklyn's Children Museum. Additional study was undertaken at the Clay Club (1928–32) and the Beaux-Arts Institute of Design in New York (1930–31). His early work in clay was figurative and conventional in appearance.

Lassaw began sculpting abstractly in 1933, making him one of the first Americans to explore nonobjective sculpture. From 1935 to 1942 he worked under the auspices of the Works Progress Administration's Federal Art Project. During this time his plaster sculptures molded onto wire showed the influence of Surrealist biomorphism rendered in a geometric idiom. At times Lassaw revealed the wire armature, and he also began to apply colors to the plaster and wire. He first welded sculpture in 1938; *Sculpture in Steel* (1938, Whitney Museum of American Art, New York) is made of a piece of sheet metal topped by a thin iron frame. Several biomorphic shapes of hammered and brazed steel project from the open metal frame, and another shape is welded to the base of the work.

While serving in the United States Army from 1942 to 1944, Lassaw learned how to weld with an oxyacetylene torch, a technique that would later influence his signature style. Upon Lassaw's return to New York, his sculpture became increasingly rectilinear, but it was not until he purchased his own oxyacetylene torch with the proceeds from his first one-man show at the Kootz Gallery (1951) that he could take his sculpture to the level he wanted. Lassaw retained his rectilinear format, but with the high temperature torch he added texture by liquefying and incrusting the intertwined webs of metal until his sculpture possessed tactility. From 1953 Lassaw often added colorful minerals such as quartz, and semi-precious stones such as turquoise, to his open form sculptures.

From this period on Lassaw enjoyed acclaim, including invitations to display his sculptures at the Venice Biennale (1954), the Museum of Modern Art in New York (1956, among other years), and the Sao Paulo Bienale (1957). He also received several architectural commissions, most frequently synagogue sculpture. His hammered and welded bronze 28-foot-high *Pillar of Fire* (1953), a highly textured, dynamic interpretation of curling, wiry flames, is installed on the façade of Temple Beth El in Springfield, Massachusetts. Lassaw also designed a bronze menorah (1954) for the synagogue, among other interior sculptures. Other synagogues that commissioned Lassaw's work include Temple Beth El, Providence, Rhode Island; Temple B'nai Aaron, St. Paul, Minnesota; Temple Anshe Hesed, Cleveland, Ohio; and Kneses Tifereth Israel, Port Chester, New York. Lassaw made a wall sculpture for the architect Philip Johnson's Glass House in New Canaan, Connecticut.

BIBLIOGRAPHY: E.C. Goossen, R. Goldwater, and I. Sandler, *Three American Sculptors: Ferber, Hare, and Lassaw* (1959); A. Kampf, *Contemporary Synagogue Art: Developments in the United States, 1945–1965* (1966); *Ibram Lassaw: Space Explorations, A Retrospective Survey (1929–1988)*, (1988).

[Samantha Baskind (2nd ed.)]

LASSER, LOUISE (1939–), U.S. actress. Born in New York, Lasser graduated from Brandeis University in 1961. In 1964 she joined the cast of Elaine May's improvisation troupe The Third Ear and later appeared in several Broadway and off-Broadway productions. On the Broadway stage, she performed in *I Can Get It for You Wholesale* (1962), *Henry, Sweet Henry* (1967), *The Chinese and Dr. Fish* (1970), and *Thieves* (1974).

Lasser was married to Woody *Allen for three years (1966–69) and acted in his early films, *Take the Money and Run* (1969), *Bananas* (1971), and *Everything You Always Wanted to Know about Sex but Were Afraid to Ask* (1972). She was also one of the writers and voices in Allen's Japanese jaunt *What's Up, Tiger Lily?* (1966). In 1976 Lasser attained national stardom as a result of her title role in the nighttime TV soap opera spoof *Mary Hartman, Mary Hartman*, for which she earned an Emmy nomination. She appeared in a later television series *It's a Living* (1981–82), as well as several TV movies: *Men of Crisis: The Harvey Wallinger Story* (1971), *Coffee, Tea, or Me?* (1973), *Isn't It Shocking?* (1973), *Just You and Me* (1978), *For Ladies Only* (1981), and *Club Land* (2001).

Some of Lasser's other film credits include *Such Good Friends* (1971), *Slither* (1972), *In God We Trust* (1980), *Crime Wave* (1985), *Sing* (1989), *Layin' Low* (1996), *Happiness* (1998), *Requiem for a Dream* (2000), *Fast Food Fast Women* (2000), *Queenie in Love* (2001), *Wolves of Wall Street* (2002), and *Lady Killers* (2003). Lasser taught acting at New York University.

ADD. BIBLIOGRAPHY: E. Lax, *Woody Allen: A Biography* (1991).

[Jonathan Licht / Ruth Beloff (2nd ed.)]

LASSON, ADOLF (originally **Aaron Lazarussohn**; 1832–1917), German philosopher. Born at Alt-Strelitz, he studied at Berlin and Leipzig. He became a Christian in 1853. Lasson taught at the University of Berlin. One of the few advocates of Hegelianism, he was concerned with Hegel's philosophy of law and of religion. (His son, GEORG (1862–1932), edited Hegel's works.) Lasson's philosophy was also influenced by Aristotle, St. Paul, and Luther. Lasson was an orthodox Lutheran, who saw Luther as the bridge between Pauline Christianity and metaphysical idealism. In Lasson's view, religion and philosophy are both trying through freedom to grasp the absolute. He was a 19th-century liberal, opposing Socialist and secularist tendencies. His main works were *J.H. Fichte im Verhaeltnis zu Kirche und Staat* (1863), *Meister Eckhart, der Mystiker* (1868), *System der Rechtsphilosophie* (1882), and *Die Entwickelung des religioesen Bewusstseins der Menschheit* (1883).

BIBLIOGRAPHY: Schmidt and Liebert, in: *Kant-Studien*, 23 (1918), 101–23; Wininger, Biog, 3 (1928), 599–600 (includes bibliography).

[Richard H. Popkin]

LASTMAN, MELVIN DOUGLAS (**Mel**; 1933–), Canadian entrepreneur, politician. Born in Toronto, at age 22 Lastman borrowed $2,000 and a truck to open his first appliance store. His one store grew into a chain of 40 discount furniture/appliance stores. In 1972 he was elected mayor of the former city of North York. For the next 25 years he ran an efficient administration known for low property taxes. He initiated organized municipal committees on child abuse, drinking and driving, race relations, and the abuse of the elderly. A strong supporter of charities and the arts, Lastman campaigned tirelessly for a vibrant North York downtown – a $5 billion undertaking built around what became Mel Lastman Square.

In 1997 North York amalgamated with the city of Toronto and Lastman was elected mayor of the amalgamated city and reelected in 2000. Lastman, outspoken and flamboyant, was exceedingly proud of Toronto. He campaigned for the city's recognition as the most culturally diverse community in the world. "Maybe inside [people] don't like one another," he said. "Maybe it is the Macedonians and the Greeks, or the Armenians and the Turks, or the Jews and the Arabs. I don't know. But they don't bring out their hostility here. Their kids play together, go to school together, and so on, and that is the miracle of Toronto." But Lastman was also criticized for being unable to control the city council and being too close to lobbyists and for various scandals and public gaffes.

Lastman wore his Jewishness on his sleeve. "The thing is," he said, "it doesn't matter that I am Jewish, because everyone is Ukrainian, Polish, Macedonian, Somali, Tamil, and it doesn't make a difference. This is the beauty of this country; you can be Jewish and you can get elected as the first mayor of the new megacity." Lastman retired from politics in 2003.

He was awarded an honorary doctorate from York University and a Humanitarian of the Year Award.

[Mindy Avrich-Skapinker (2nd ed.)]

LAS VEGAS (Sp. "The Meadows"), city in Nevada boasting 1.6 million inhabitants, 80,000 (5 percent) of whom were Jewish in 2005. With 600 new Jewish families arriving every month, Las Vegas now enjoys prime of place as the fastest-growing Jewish community in North America.

Beginnings

Jews first arrived in southern Nevada in 1850, attracted by the discovery of gold in Carson City. Jewish peddlers subsequently interacted with Church of the Latter Day Saints missionaries who, at the behest of Mormon Church leader Brigham Young in Utah, erected a short-lived agricultural settlement (1855–57) as a base for proselytizing nearby Paiute Indian tribes. Jews arrived in small numbers in 1905, after the establishment of a railway hub linking Phoenix, Arizona, Salt Lake City, Utah, and southern California. Typical of these merchant pioneers was Adolph Levy (1858–1936), a native of Prussian Poland who arrived from Illinois and opened a dry goods store. Levy's niece, Sallie Gordon (1908–1997), a future director of the Las Vegas Chamber of Commerce, gave birth to the city's first Jewish baby during the early 1930s.

A nascent Jewish presence barely discernible in the city's 1910 and 1920 censuses coalesced in 1931, when some 20 Jewish Las Vegans convened as the "Sons and Daughters of Israel," providing their children with religious instruction in storefront classrooms and meeting at the Elks Club and the Odd Fellows Hall. The community, like the city itself, grew slowly until the legalization of gambling in 1941. Henceforth, Las Vegas began attracting a largely blue-collar component associated with the fledgling gaming industry. The city remained one of the last Jewish blue-collar redoubts in the country.

A Mob Town

Vegas Jewry received another boost in 1946, when Meyer *Lansky, Benjamin "Bugsy" *Siegel, Morris Barney "Moe" Dalitz, Gus Greenbaum, Dave Berman, Morris Lansburgh, Morris Rosen, Sam Cohen, and other well-known – notorious – underworld figures helped kick-start the transformation of this otherwise sleepy desert rest stop into the nation's "vice and dice" capital.

Las Vegas quickly garnered a reputation as a Jewish mob town, even as some of its more insecure Jewish residents protested that Jewish racketeers generally acted as front-men for Italian Mafioso from the Midwest. The city attracted Jewish mobsters because the initially under-regulated casinos functioned as an almost inexhaustible cash cow. To Jewish gangsters even more than their Italian and Irish counterparts, however, the desert offered an almost unique opportunity to transcend criminal origins and reputations, and to achieve a modicum of communal and civic respectability. Many began this rehabilitative process by joining synagogues and funding parochial schools. One of the city's Jewish day schools, for instance, at Temple Ner Tamid, was named for mobster Moe Dalitz.

Organizational Life

The symbiosis between the casino operators and the organized Jewish community generated structural distortions that resounded well past the mid-1970s, when corporations took over the gaming industry. Previously, synagogues, schools, and communal programming depended almost exclusively upon the largesse of the wealthiest casino operators, who became known as "Angels," and who covered organizational budget deficits on a rotational basis with yearly cash pay-outs. This also helped the fledgling State of Israel when it began seeking money for arms purchases from U.S. Surplus and other sources. The costs of religious affiliation for less well-heeled Jewish Las Vegans thereby remained marginal for decades, habituating residents to an unsustainable level of subsidization, and rendering problematic the inevitable transition toward a more equitable and regulated pattern of funding and expenditure. The arrival, in recent decades, of young Jewish families just starting out and of Jewish retirees no longer interested in communal involvement, presented further challenges to communal attempts to increase affiliation. Despite recent gains, Las Vegas continues, like several other western cities, to lag behind comparably sized, and even smaller, communities in the east, especially in creating infrastructure. A hundred years after Jews first began arriving, the city lacks a Jewish community center, a nursing home or assisted living facility, a yeshivah, and a Bureau of Jewish Education. Efforts are underway to erect a Jewish high school and Hebrew Community Center in Summerlin.

During the 1960s, Jewish organizational life centered around the Combined Jewish Appeal (CJA), which became the Jewish Federation of Las Vegas (JFLV) in 1979. The CJA and its successor body functioned as the central coordinating institution responsible for fundraising, planning and allocations, and communal services. Reliance on a small, self-selected coterie of communal contributors and decision-makers, however, resulted in no small degree of organizational dysfunction characterized by redundancies in public relations, fundraising, secretarial services, agency programming, and tax, legal, and accounting functions. Clashes over turf, pedigree, and job titles became increasingly common and progressively debilitating. A dispute between casino magnate Sheldon Adelson (at this writing, the world's wealthiest Jew) and a local hotel union in 1999, for instance, resulted in a vituperative spat that split Jewish congregations and organizations along personal and political lines, further undermining communal development. By 2001, several Jewish communal agencies found themselves facing impeding bankruptcy and requiring a federation bailout. A besieged and hard-pressed federation responded to successive crises by revamping, in 2003, under yet another name, the United Jewish Community (UJC). Helmed by a new, younger board of directors, the UJC began with a reassessment of traditional fundraising and allocation strategies intended to meet the needs of an increasingly dispersed, fragmented, and even disaffected community.

Jewish Life in the Early 21st Century

Today, thanks to a booming economy largely immune to vagaries of the business cycle, and to a general westward trend of young Jewish professionals, the city is experiencing a surprising profusion of Jewish communal expression. With growing Jewish concentrations in the suburbs of Summerlin, Desert Shores, Seven Hills and Green Valley, in Henderson, Las Vegas boasts 18 congregations (eight Orthodox, three Conservative, seven Reform or non-denominational), three day schools (the non-denominational Milton I. Schwartz Hebrew Academy, the Chabad-affiliated Desert Torah Academy, and a Conservative-aligned Solomon Schechter day school), and a Holocaust memorial and resource library. Chabad, which established a permanent presence in 1990, now operates four centers employing seven full-time rabbis. Orthodox residents and visitors – ultra-Orthodox visitors to Las Vegas are many despite the reputation of the city – can avail themselves of three *mikva'ot* (ritual baths), six kosher restaurants, a Glatt Kosher market, and two kosher stores embedded in local supermarkets. Three major casinos, meanwhile, maintain full-service (though reportedly underused) kosher kitchens and catering departments. Community affairs are chronicled in two community newspapers, the *Jewish Reporter* and the *Israelite,* and a monthly periodical, *Life & Style:* the *Las Vegas Jewish Magazine.* A Hillel Union at the University of Nevada, Las Vegas, tends to the needs of Jewish students on campus.

Public Figures

Jews continue to figure prominently in Las Vegas public life. The city's mayor since 1999, Oscar Goodman (1939–), is a former mob lawyer unabashed about his love for drinking, gambling, and other local pastimes. Brian Greenspun, the scion of newspaper magnate, land developer, and arms smuggler to pre-state Israel, Herman "Hank" Milton Greenspun (1909–1989), is the editor of the *Las Vegas Sun* and active in real estate and casino management. Casino mogul Steve Wynn (1941–), who built the opulent Bellagio and Wynn Las Vegas hotels, is credited with the Las Vegas Strip's successful marketing, during the 1990s, as a family friendly environment. Rival Sheldon Adelson (1933–), who built the Venetian Hotel, established Las Vegas as a major convention and trade show venue. Taxi fleet owner Milton I. Schwartz (1921–) is active in Jewish philanthropy and Republican politics. Democratic Congresswoman Shelley *Berkley (1951–) was elected to the House of Representatives in 1998, and won her fourth term in 2004. Jacob "Chic" Hecht (1928–) served in the Nevada State Senate from 1967 to 1975, as a Republican in the U.S. Senate from 1983 to 1989, and as U.S. Ambassador to the Bahamas (1989–94). Lori Lipman Brown (1958–), an avowed civil libertarian, served as a Nevada state senator from 1992 to 1994.

BIBLIOGRAPHY: A. Thomas, Jr. and J.D. Gabaldon, *Las Vegas: The Fabulous First Century* (2003); H. Rothman, *Neon Metropolis: How Las Vegas Started the Twenty-First Century* (2002); A. Balboni, *Southern Italians and Eastern European Jews: Cautious Co-operation in Las Vegas Casinos, 1940–1967*; H.K. Rothman and M. David (eds.), *The Grit beneath the Glitter: Tales from The Real Las Vegas* (2001); S. Denton and R. Morris, *The Money and the Power: The Making of Las Vegas and Its Hold on America, 1947–2000* (2001); D. Littlejohn and E. Gran, *The Real Las Vegas: Life beyond the Strip* (1999).

[Sheldon Teitelbaum (2nd ed.)]

LASZLO (formerly **Laub**), **PHILIP ALEXIUS DE LOMBOS** (1869–1937), Hungarian painter. Laszlo won many prizes for his work in Budapest and was commissioned to paint the portraits of the royal family in 1894. His work was so successful that he became the leading portraitist of his time. In 1907 he settled in England and painted Edward VII and Queen Alexandra. In 1909 the Uffizi gallery asked him for his self-portrait. In spite of criticism that his pictures failed to come to grips with problems, he remained popular and his work hangs in many important galleries and collections. Laszlo was converted to Christianity.

ADD. BIBLIOGRAPHY: S. de Laszlo, *A Brush with Grandeur – Philip Alexius de Laszlo (1869–1937)* (2004).

LATERAN COUNCILS III, IV. The third Lateran (11th Ecumenical) Council was summoned in 1179 by Pope Alexander III. Canon 26 adopted by the Council was concerned with relations between Jews and Christians. It prohibits Jews and Saracens from having Christian servants, while any Christian who serves them is to be excommunicated. In all lawsuits the testimony of Christians is to be accepted against Jews, just as Jews make use of Jewish witnesses against Christians; anyone who prefers Jewish to Christian witnesses is to be anathematized, "since Jews ought to be subject to Christians, and treated kindly by them only out of humane considerations." A Jew who converts to Christianity is not to be deprived of any of his possessions, "for converts ought to be financially better off than they were before they accepted the Faith." The secular powers are commanded, under pain of excommunication, to ensure that this provision is put into effect. The ban on usury issued by the same Council does not specifically mention Jewish moneylenders. Alexander III, moreover, issued the Bull *Sicut Judaeis*, protecting Jews from forcible baptism and other molestation.

The fourth Lateran (12th Ecumenical) Council was summoned in 1215 by Pope Innocent III to call for a crusade and to combat various heresies. A delegation of Jews from southern France attempted to ensure that no anti-Jewish decisions were taken, but the Council issued four important regulations concerning the Jews. Canon 67 states that Jews must be prevented from exacting immoderate usury from Christians, and also that Jews must pay tithes on property formerly owned by Christians. Canon 68 complains that in many places Christians, Jews, and Saracens are outwardly indistinguishable, so that occasionally, "by mistake, Christians mix with Jewish or Saracen women" and vice versa. Non-Christians must therefore be compelled to dress differently from Christians (see also Jewish *badge). It is alleged there that this is also laid down in the Mosaic law. Jews are not to appear in public at Easter, or on days of Christian lamentation, because they are in the habit of dressing up and railing at Christians on such occasions, nor may they blaspheme against the name of Jesus in any other way. The next canon prohibits Jews from holding public office, and the last insists that converts to Christianity must desist from Jewish observances. An appendix is concerned with the proposed crusade. It lays down in passing that Jews must be compelled to remit interest on debts owed to them by those who take the cross. That all the topics mentioned here reappear in subsequent legislation is a measure of the comparative inefficacy of the Council's decisions.

BIBLIOGRAPHY: Mansi, 22 (1778), 209–468, 953–1086; S. Grayzel, *Church and the Jews...* (1966²), index; idem, in: *Seventy-Fifth Anniversary of the Jewish Quarterly Review* (1967), 293–9.

[Nicholas de Lange]

LATIF, ISAAC B. ABRAHAM IBN (1210–1280), one of the foremost spokesmen of Jewish *Neoplatonism in 13th-century *Spain. Ibn Latif was a unique philosopher and biblical commentator who lived and taught mainly at Toledo (the capital of Christian Castile) one generation after the publication of Maimonides' *Guide of the Perplexed* and one generation before the appearance of the Zohar.

Early Years

Although Toledo was reconquered by the Christians in 1212, Ibn Latif was still educated according to the Jewish-Andalusian legacy and was fluent in both Arabic and Hebrew. His first mature years however were spent in business, but then he decided (in his mid-twenties) to dedicate himself to an extensive study of the range of philosophical sciences from logic to metaphysics. His first book, *Gate of Heaven* (*Sha'ar ha-Shamayim,* MS. Vatican 335.1), written in Hebrew in 1238, combines philosophical allegorization of Scripture, interpretations of the commandments, commentaries on talmudic legends, and metaphysical discussions characterized by Neoplatonic esoteric terminology, derived from various sources, such as: *The Book of Creation* (*Sefer Yeẓirah*) and its Jewish philosophical commentaries, *The Epistles of the Brethren of Purity* (*Rasa'il Ikhwan al-Ṣafa*), Solomon Ibn Gabirol's *Fons Vitae* and *Crown of Kingship* (*Keter Melkhut*), Ibn Batalyawsi's *Book of the Flowerbeds* (*Kitab al-Ḥada'iq*), and the pseudo-epigraphic mystical treatises and letters of the Jewish *Iyyun* circle. It should be mentioned that Ibn Latif was the first known Jewish scholar to translate to Hebrew a few chapters and citations from Abu-Nasr Al-Farabi's *Opinions of the Inhabitants of the Righteous City.*

Attitude toward Maimonides

In spite of his strong affinity toward Neoplatonic sources, Ibn Latif's main influence, especially in his early books, is *Maimonides' *Guide of the Perplexed.* In his *Gate of Heaven, Commentary on Ecclesiastes* (early 1240s, first printed: Constantinople, 1585, reprinted: Jerusalem, 1970) and *Letter of Reply* (*Iggeret ha-Teshuvah,* attributed to Ibn Latif, date unknown, ed. A. Berliner, in: *Koveẓ al Yad,* vol. 1, Berlin, 1885, pp. 46–70) there is extensive use of Maimonidean ideas and terminology, particularly in six fields: the enumeration of sciences, the doctrine of negative attributes, divine providence, intellectualist prophecy (and sub-prophecy), identification of the account of the chariot with philosophical metaphysics, and finally, human perfection. Those influences were carried forward to his later treatises: *The King's Archives* (*Ginzei ha-Melekh,* ed. A. Jellineck, in: *Kokhvei Yiẓhak,* Vienna, 1862–67), *The Form of the Universe* (*Ẓurat ha-Olam,* ed. Z. Stern, Vienna, 1860, reprinted: Jerusalem, 1970), and *Lord of Activities* (referring to human reason; see *Rav Pe'alim,* ed. S. Schoenblum, Berlin, 1885, reprinted: Jerusalem, 1970; see also: ed. H. Kasher, Ramat Gan, 1974), but without explicitly mentioning his intellectualist mentor.

Therefore, Ibn Latif can be treated as one of the earliest commentators of the *Guide of the Perplexed.* His early treatises contain some interpretive remarks and comments on various chapters and subjects in Maimonides' *Guide.* Moreover, Ibn Latif's independent philosophical reflections often parallel central issues in the *Guide.* Furthermore, in every instance in which Ibn Latif seems to stray from the world of Maimonides, he still bases himself on a Neoplatonic reading of the *Guide,* and therefore, according to his own understanding, he was only a dedicated disciple of the *Guide.*

Later Years

Since the membership and nature of Jewish leadership at Toledo changed extensively after the death of R. Meir ha-Levi *Abulafia (= Ramah) in 1244, after which the earlier Andalusian-philosophical legacy was replaced by the new emerging kabbalistic trend, Ibn Latif was forced to teach and write in new cultural conditions.

In the foreword to his treatise *The King's Archives,* Ibn Latif mentions a group of young students who asked him to reveal to them the hidden secrets of the Torah. As he thought their scientific knowledge was not sufficient for studying metaphysics, he avoided their company and stopped teaching in public.

Although Ibn Latif had a competent knowledge of the kabbalistic treatises of his time, and had scholarly connections with Toledo's community president and well-known kabbalist R. Todros ha-Levi *Abulafia (one of his short works, *The Bundle of Myrrh* (*Ẓeror ha-Mor,* ed. A. Jellineck, in: *Kerem Ḥemed,* 9 (Vienna, 1856), pp. 154–59) was dedicated to Abulafia, who is probably also the keen reader referred to as "a noble person, the leader of his nation" in Ibn Latif's *The Form of the Universe* (ch. 25)), Ibn Latif never considered himself a kabbalist, nor did he see himself as one of the Jewish philosophers and translators who worked at the court of Alfonso x, king of Castile (*Form of the Universe,* ch. 6).

Criticism against Philosophers and Kabbalists

In his later treatises Ibn Latif continued his consistent criticism of the partial and deficient knowledge of the philosophers of his city, who abandoned religious observance and adopted the "double faith theory" of the Averroeists. He was also sharp in his criticism of the kabbalists of his time, who, in his opinion, mistakenly combined wrongly knowledge based on Intellect with knowledge based on Imagination.

Influence

Ibn Latif's works influenced a few kabbalists of Castile and its region, such as Todros ha-Levi Abulafia, Abraham *Abulafia, Joseph *Gikatilla (early works), Moses de *Leon (early works), and *David b. Abraham ha-Lavan. One can obviously notice the affinity of these authors with Ibn Latif's work, but they never quote it explicitly.

Ibn Latif's works were quoted by later Jewish thinkers, such as Moses of Salerno (13th century); R. *Isaac ben Sheshet (= Ribash), Moses Botreal, and Johanan Alimmano (14th–15th century); R. Isaac *Abrabanel and R. Judah *Ḥayyat (16th century); R. Joseph Solomon *Delmedigo (= Yashar) and R. Abraham Kohen de Herrera (17th century); and recently by R. David Cohen (20th century, a leading disciple of R. Abraham Isaac ha-Kohen *Kook).

The fact that Ibn Latif's influence and citations of his works are found almost exclusively among kabbalists and that he cites the *Sefer Yeẓirah* and its various commentaries, has led scholars to present him both as a philosopher and as a kabbalist. Nevertheless, as suggested above, it seems that he based himself mainly on Neoplatonic sources and on his own Neoplatonic interpretation of both philosophical and rabbinic works, and therefore he should be regarded as a Neoplatonic philosopher rather than kabbalist.

BIBLIOGRAPHY: S.O. Heller Willensky, "Isaac Ibn Latif's the Gate of Heaven: A Mystical Guide of the Perplexed," in: M.A. Shulvas (ed.), *Perspectives in Jewish Learning*, vol. 2 (1996), 17–25; idem, "Isaac Ibn Latif: Philosopher or Kabbalist?" in: A. Altmann (ed.), *Jewish Medieval and Renaissance Studies* (1967), 187–223; idem, "The Guide and the Gate: The Dialectical Influence of Maimonides on Isaac Ibn Latif and Early Spanish Kabbalah," in: R.L. Salinger (ed.), *A Straight Path: Studies in Medieval Philosophy and Culture in Honor of Arthur Hyman* (1988), 266–78; idem, "The First Created Being in Early Kabbalah and Isma'ilian Sources," in: *Binah, 3* (1994), 65–77; H. Kasher, "The Book *Rav Pe'alim* by Isaac Ibn Latif" (M.A diss., Bar Ilan University, Ramat-Gan, 1974) (Heb.); idem, "On the Terms Kabbalah and Kabbalist in Latif's Treatises," in: *Da'at,* 41 (1999), 5–12 (Heb.); A. Melamed, "Ibn Latif and Falaquera on the Characteristics of the Philosopher-King," in: *Tura,* 2 (1992), 162–77 (Heb.); S. Raz, "Isaac Ibn Latif and the Guide of the Perplexed" (M.A diss., Bar Ilan University, Ramat-Gan, 2004) (Heb.).

[Shoey Raz (2nd ed.)]

LATIN AMERICA.

Colonial Period

Jews were prohibited from entering Spanish America throughout the colonial period. Although a few Jews who could not be regarded as *New Christians managed to enter illegally, the history of Jews in Spanish colonial America is primarily that of the New Christians who were *Crypto-Jews. Several members of Columbus' crew were New Christians, but shortly after his voyage the Catholic sovereigns closed their American possessions to New Christians and their immediate descendants. The ban was regularly renewed, but there were times when the New Christians could enter Spanish America legally, especially after their general pardon by Philip III in 1601. Despite the restrictions, New Christians managed to enter the New World on a fairly regular basis until the middle of the 17th century at least, and at times with the connivance of high authorities in Spain, who needed their enterprise for the development of the American possessions. A large number of New Christians and Crypto-Jews from Portugal migrated to the New World during the union of the crowns of Spain and Portugal (1580–1640). It is impossible to tell how many Crypto-Jews were among the New Christians. However, two facts are clear: first, not all the New Christians were inclined to the secret practice of Judaism, and second, it is natural to suppose that there were more Crypto-Jews than those arrested by the Inquisition. This assumption is reinforced by the use in these centuries of the word Portuguese as a synonym for Crypto-Jew. The Inquisitional documents provide the only extensive source of information about the Crypto-Jews' identity and activities. Initially, Episcopal Inquisitions, under the guidance of secular or regular clergy, flourished in Spanish America. New Spain witnessed an **auto da fé* as early as 1528, when the alleged "Judaizers" or Crypto-Jews Hernando Alonso and Diego de Morales were sent to the stake. Branches of the Holy Office of the *Inquisition, in Spain, were introduced in 1570 in Lima, for the viceroyalty of Peru, and in 1571 in Mexico City, for the viceroyalty of New Spain. A third major Inquisition was later established in Cartagena (Colombia) in 1610 for the viceroyalty of New Granada. These Inquisitions held regular autos da fé until the end of the colonial period, but their activity against the Crypto-Jews took place chiefly in the period prior to 1660. In both New Spain and Peru they were especially active in two periods, during the 1580s and 1590s, and during the 1630s and 1640s. In New Spain the first period corresponds to the arrests and trials of most of the *Carvajal family, and the second to the Great Complicity, in which the most striking figure was Tomas Trevino de *Sobremonte. In similar trials held in 17th-century Peru, the most striking figures were Francisco *Maldonado de Silva, surgeon, philosopher, and apologist for Judaism and Manuel Bautista Perez, regarded as the richest man in the viceroyalty. It is impossible to ascertain the number of Crypto-Jews in Spanish America, but there is reason to believe that it exceeded the number of those arrested and tried. Although the claims circulating about large numbers of Crypto-Jews in Latin America are not supported by the evidence, there were many cases unveiled during the 20th century of native populations that observed certain Jewish traditions supposedly transmitted by Crypto-Jews who were hiding among them. At the same time it should be borne in mind that most Crypto-Jews brought to trial were reconciled with the Church, and despite the Inquisition's vaunted vigilance, were not heard from again, thus suggesting at least the possibility that they had made their peace with the Church.

The Crypto-Jews had their own distinctive religion. Though they believed it to be the authentic Judaism, it was actually a wild blend of biblical Judaism, post-biblical reminiscences, and influences of the Catholic environment. Prominent in commerce, the trades, the professions, and government, the "New Christian Judaizers" contributed immeasurably also to the development of Latin America's culture. Luis de *Carvajal, the Younger, was among the earliest and most sensitive writers in Spanish in the Western Hemisphere and Antonio Jose da Silva "O Judeu," was one of the outstanding playwrights in Portuguese in the colonial period.

[Martin A. Cohen]

See also *America.

JEWS IN THE CARIBBEANS. During the second half of the 17th century Spanish-Portuguese Jews settled in the new colonies that were founded along the Wild Coast (the Guianas) and in the Caribbean Islands. They came from Dutch Brazil, as well as from Amsterdam, London, Bordeaux, and Hamburg. They engaged in the plantation economy, producing sugar, cocoa, vanilla, and other staples, and took an active part in commerce, shipping trade, maritime insurance, and public services.

In the Protestant colonies of Holland, England, and Denmark the Jews were free to practice their own religion. Jews were officially expelled from the French Catholic colonies in 1685, but their presence was generally tolerated by the local authorities. They founded well-organized communities that preserved the Portuguese language and their customs and traditions, including synagogues with sand-covered floors.

The Spanish-Portuguese Jews in the Caribbeans maintained ethnic and family ties as the basis of economic and social networks and preserved with zeal their unique traditions. To overcome their small numbers and constant mobility between the islands, they developed chains of communication for the preservation of endogamic marriages, social assistance, and religious services.

Curaçao, the "Mother of the Jewish Communities in the New World," was a source of inspiration and assistance to other Sephardi communities in the Western Hemisphere. With its economic decline early in the 19th century, several Jews from Curaçao immigrated to the independent Latin American republics in the Circum Caribbean. They established small Jewish settlements along the coasts of Venezuela, Colombia, and Panama. They prospered economically, and were well integrated into the social and political elites of the Circum Caribbean, but gradually intermarried into the Catholic population.

[Margalit Bejarano (2nd ed.)]

Jewish Emancipation in Latin America

The movements for political and religious emancipation in Latin America slowly but markedly influenced Jewish settlement in that part of the world. The Inquisition, an institution brought from Europe to America, was abolished during the first years of the struggle for independence from Spain (1811 in New Granada and *Paraguay; 1813 in Mexico, Peru, Chile, Uruguay, and Argentina), but was restored in Mexico, Peru, Chile, and New Granada in 1815 upon the return of Ferdinand VII to the Spanish throne. It was finally suppressed throughout the continent a few years later when independence had been won.

The governments of Latin America were influenced by the liberal ideas of the French encyclopedists and the American and French Revolutions. The abolition of the Inquisition and the spread of liberalism permitted the settlement of Jews in Latin American countries. However, during the first half century after emancipation few Jews moved to Latin America. Those who did, mainly economically motivated West European Jews, did not enjoy full equality and suffered from the residue of Catholic intolerance. Unlike the United States and France after their revolutions, the newly independent Latin American countries were not compelled to adopt a particular policy toward the Jews because they had so few Jewish inhabitants during the early 19th century. The first liberal religious legislation rather pertained to the various Protestant churches in response to the presence of the British who were economically involved in South America.

Intermittent Jewish immigration eventually produced the need for organizing Jewish communities in several cities. No major political disabilities or religious restrictions hindered the Jews in the 1860s when they founded their first institutions in Latin America. Although there was never any legislation specifically emancipating the Jews, religious freedom for the Jews was taken as an extension of the freedom granted to Protestants. In general, as the Jewish communities of Latin America organized, the respective governments accorded recognition to Jewish religious institutions.

[Victor A. Mirelman]

Jewish Immigration to Latin American Countries

The overwhelming majority of the Jewish immigration to Latin America was established in countries whose population mainly originated in Europe. In the first decades of the 19th century, following independence from Spain and Portugal, only a small number of Jewish immigrants found its way to Latin America. Jews from Morocco immigrated to the northeastern coast of Brazil, and settled in Belem (State of Para). Following the rubber boom of the mid-19th century around the Amazon region they penetrated along the Amazon River reaching as far as Iquitos in Northern Peru. At the same time, Jews from the Caribbean islands, particularly from Curaçao and St. Thomas, settled in Venezuela, Colombia, Panama, and Costa Rica, where many of them eventually were assimilated. Another small wave of Jewish immigrants arrived from Central and Western Europe, particularly from Germany, France, and England, bringing Jewish businessmen, many of them without women, to Chile, Peru, Mexico, Argentina, and Brazil.

Organized immigration, however, started only following the *May Laws of 1881 in the Russian Empire that resulted in the deterioration of the situation of the Jews in the Pale of Settlement. The main destinations in Latin America were Argentina and Brazil: in 1900, 14,700 Jews lived in Argentina; 1,000 in Brazil; and 1,000 in other Latin American countries. Between 1901 and 1914 the numbers increased to 115,600 in Argentina; 9,000 in Brazil; and 3,000 in other countries; but immigration decreased radically during World War I. At the end of the war no more than 150,000 Jews were in Latin America. The Jewish population consisted roughly of 80% Central and East European immigrants and 20% Sephardim from the Mediterranean basin – North Africa, Syria, Turkey, and the Balkan states. The majority of the Jewish immigrants in Argentina, Brazil, Chile, Peru, most of Central America, Mexico, and Cuba were Ashkenazim. Argentina had, in fact, received 90% of its 126,700 Jewish immigrants from Russia until 1920.

Between 1921 and 1930, around 100,000 Jews immigrated to the Latin American countries. From the rise of Nazism to the end of the Holocaust (1933–45), when the need of Jewish emigration from Europe was at its height, the explicit or concealed policy that regulated Jewish immigration was changed. Restrictions limiting the immigration of Jews were instituted using economic, political, racial, and religious selectivity to prevent "too many" Jews from joining Latin American Catholic society and from competing with local merchants, workers, professionals, and entrepreneurs. From 1940, Jewish immigration was severely curtailed and almost illegal. Nevertheless, in spite of restrictions and closed borders Jewish immigration continued, and according to conservative estimates in 1933–45 between 113,500 and 120,400 Jews immigrated to Latin America, legally, by circumventing the laws, or through the underground. People coming from the same country tended to settle in the same area in their new homeland. A considerable number of the 12,000 immigrants from Arab countries arriving in Brazil between 1957 and 1960 settled in *São Paulo where 5,000 Jews from Egypt had established themselves over the years. In Guatemala, Jews from Germany form the largest Jewish community which is situated in the capital, Guatemala City.

Most Latin American countries quickly became lands of emigration as well as immigration. During the first years after World War II, thousands of immigrants established in Paraguay and *Bolivia continued on their way to Argentina and Chile, sometimes crossing borders illegally. Once their visas had been approved, numerous immigrants from Cuba and *Haiti streamed into the United States. Also many immigrants who went to *Ecuador, a country friendlier than most toward Jewish refugees, emigrated after living there for some time. Political upheavals and economic crises were the main factors of emigration after World War II, as illustrated by the revolutions in Cuba (1959) and in Nicaragua (1979), the coup d'états headed by military forces in Brazil, Chile, Argentina, and Uruguay in the 1960s and 1970s as well as by the social and personal insecurity in Colombia and Venezuela in the 1990s and the first decade of the 21st century. Emigration was also motivated by the economic crises of the late 1990s and early 2000s that caused the impoverishment of large Jewish sectors, particularly in Argentina. Emigration from Latin America was directed to Europe, Israel, and the United States as well as to other Latin American countries with better economic prospects, such as Venezuela (prior to the rise of Chavez) and Mexico. It is very difficult to calculate the figures for these migratory movements. Accurate numbers are available only with respect to *aliyah*: 89,684 Jews immigrated to Israel from Latin America in the period between 1948 and 2004, but not all of them stayed there and a certain percentage re-emigrated to other countries or returned to their countries of origin.

Economic and Social Status

Until the 1880s, most of the Jewish immigrants to Latin America made their living as merchants. The Moroccan Jews, in the Amazon region, were peddlers who catered to the workers in the rubber industry. The Caribbean Jews and the immigrants from Europe were often representatives of large business firms, and integrated into the upper middle class. The largest community, however, developed in Argentina as a result of the country's liberal immigration policy from the 1880s and with the establishment of the Jewish Colonization Association (ICA) agricultural settlements. Argentina became the favored destination of Jewish immigration to Latin America. For two decades agriculture was the main occupation of Argentinean Jews. At the same time Argentina's population of predominantly European origin (90%), and its relatively early industrialization compared with the rest of Latin America, also attracted Jewish population to urban settlement and allowed Jewish communities to prosper. Jewish immigrants of the late 19th and early 20th centuries who came with experience in trade and labor and who settled in undeveloped regions where the economy was based on the export of agricultural products or raw materials discovered a vast field of activity in the area of commercial brokerage and the production of consumer goods. The activity of the Jewish traders, who usually started as peddlers, brought about an increased demand for clothing and furniture. This demand was partially met by Jewish workers who began to produce these items locally. The two world wars and the industrialization of several countries stimulated the development of economic activities in which Jews happened to be involved and encouraged the opening of new areas. Thus many Jewish proletarians – who were numerous in Argentina and prominent in Brazil, Chile, Uruguay, Cuba, and other countries – improved their economic status, so that gradually most Jews moved into the middle class, and the number of blue collar employees became minimal.

The economic transformation of Latin American Jewry has been similar to that of other immigrant groups in their respective countries. Sephardi Jews, like other immigrants from the Middle East and North Africa, generally started as peddlers, and gradually moved into trade. Ashkenazi Jews were divided between commerce and industry. In the Southern Cone (Argentina, Chile, Uruguay, and Southern Brazil) the Jews became part of the growing middle classes that emerged with the industrialization process of the 1940s and 1950s, moving gradually also to the professions. In the countries with a large indigenous population Latin American Jewry was part of a relatively small middle class sandwiched between the upper class and the masses of landless agricultural laborers and factory workers. In some of these countries, the Jews became part of the "affluent society" which is characterized by the economic and social abyss between the impoverished masses and the wealthy few. This class polarization has caused violent political activity, creating security problems which have affected Jewish existence.

Another factor affecting the status of Latin American Jewry throughout the 19th and 20th centuries was the influence of the majority religion, Catholicism. This did not result in religious extremism in everyday life, nor did it curtail the freedom of religious observance of non-Catholics; but it invited the belief, in many countries, that Catholicism, or at least Christianity, is one of the fundamentals of local nationalism. In most Latin American countries the growth of nationalism was also related to basic economic and social problems. Nationalism has served to diminish the influence of cultural pluralism and immigrants who were loyal to other traditions were looked upon as aliens. Economic grievances in some Latin American countries (Cuba, Costa Rica, and Mexico, among others) have fostered the antisemitic outgrowths of nationalism. The activities of antisemitic groups have been greatly assisted by the Nazis during the 1930s and 1940s and by the Arabs since the 1950s. Many Latin American countries, especially Argentina and Paraguay which served as havens for Nazi criminals after World War II, were for many decades important focuses for both leftist and rightist antisemitic activity. Yet prolonged violent antisemitism has not characterized any of the Latin American countries, not even those with extreme nationalist governments.

Patterns of Jewish Organization

The first Jewish organizations in Latin America were established in the 19th century and were intended to fulfill fundamental religious needs. For the most part, the organizations were modeled after the congregations in the countries of Western Europe from which their founders originated. Thus, the first communities in Venezuela, Panama, and Colombia bore the stamp of Dutch and Anglo-Jewish culture; the first organizations in Argentina, Peru, and Brazil followed the pattern of Jewish institutional life in France and Germany; and the small Jewish communities of the Amazon region in Brazil copied the model of Tetuan and Tangier. Although many descendants of the founders of these Jewish institutions had severed their Jewish affiliations as a result of intermarriage and conversion, some of these institutions still exist. The first immigrants from the Middle East and Eastern Europe in the late 19th and early 20th centuries founded their own religious, charitable, health, and cultural organizations. The Sephardim from the same community of origin tended to found comprehensive communal frameworks that supplied all their social and cultural needs. Each community had its synagogues, welfare institutions, religious schools, and a cemetery. The Jews from Syria, particularly from Aleppo, were considered the most traditional and strictly religious, while the Ladino-speaking Jews, from Turkey and the Balkan countries, were more influenced by trends of modernity and secularism.

The Ashkenazim, who immigrated prior to World War I and in the interwar period, brought with them from Eastern Europe organizational patterns of a secular-ideological nature and adapted them to the realities of their new homelands. The most prominent groups among them in the political and cultural field were the various Zionist parties, the *Bund, and the extreme left which crystallized during the 1920s into Jewish Communist and pro-Communist organizations. Each group maintained many cultural activities, published bulletins, and, during the 1920s and 1930s, began to develop educational institutions. This process of institutional proliferation was accompanied by the establishment of Yiddish daily and weekly newspapers, and the beginnings of local Yiddish literature.

The many Jewish immigrants in the proletarian class initiated attempts at organizing professional unions (especially in Argentina, and to a lesser extent in Brazil, Uruguay, and Cuba). Jewish immigrants in the lower levels of trade and labor formed cooperative economic and financial organizations which eventually became large banking institutions whose Jewish origins were sometimes reflected in their names and social activities. In the agricultural settlements of Argentina and Brazil the Jewish cooperative trade organizations even preceded the urban cooperative unions; and in Argentina the Jewish agricultural cooperative was a pioneer in the field of agrarian cooperatives for consumption and marketing in general throughout the country.

Another characteristic of the East European immigrants was their establishment of *Landsmanshaftn* – organizations of people who came from the same city or territory – which were formed relatively late (in Argentina not until World War I). After the Holocaust these organizations increased their activity, concentrating their efforts on perpetuating, particularly through literary projects, the memory of the destroyed European communities from which the members had come.

Whereas legislation of East European countries offered a legal basis for the creation of the Jewish communities and compelled the Jews to remain within their confines, no such necessity existed in Latin America where the Jewish community was established and maintained only by the volition of the organizers. The great ideological diversity among the Jews made their unity difficult. But the inclination of all groups, secular as well as religious, to observe Jewish burial rites brought into existence the burial societies which ultimately evolved into comprehensive congregations similar to those which flourished in Poland between the two world wars. Outstanding examples of the expansion of burial societies into large, multi-branched congregations are the *AMIA – the Ashkenazi Community of Buenos Aires, the Nidḥei Yisrael

Kehile – the Ashkenazi community in Mexico, and to a lesser extent, the Comunidad Israelita de Montevideo of Uruguay.

The communal organization of the Sephardim was ethnic and religious. In large communities, such as Buenos Aires and Mexico City, Jews from Aleppo and Damascus maintained separate communal frameworks. Ladino-speaking Jews, from Turkey and the Balkan countries, amalgamated their institutions. In small communities, particularly in the provincial towns, all the Sephardim were gradually united. The main framework that united the Jews from the Middle East, the Balkan countries, and North Africa was the Zionist movement. Unlike the Ashkenazim, the Zionist ideology of the Sephardim was not secular, and was accepted as an integral part of their religious creed. They did not share the ideological divisions of the Zionist parties in Eastern Europe and they felt offended by the constant use of Yiddish in Zionist activities organized by the Ashkenazim. Most Latin American countries had Sephardi committees that organized the Zionist campaigns among their own communities. FESELA – Federación Sefaradí Latinoamericana (Latin American Sephardi Federation), was founded in 1972 as an umbrella organization of Sephardi federations and their representative organ in the World Zionist Organization.

Even the rise of such secular institutions as social clubs, youth groups, and the Zionist Movement did not unite the Sephardim, the Jews of the Mediterranean basin, and the Ashkenazim. The exception is Mexico where the Centro Deportivo Israelita (Jewish Sport Center) is a kind of social, cultural, and sports center in which members of the different communities are associated. Jewish immigration from Central Europe during the 1930s added new organizations throughout the continent. Some newcomers joined existing communal organizations, but attended independently to their religious, social, and even welfare needs. In such countries as Chile, Brazil, Argentina, Uruguay, and Peru, they established separate congregations, and in others such as Guatemala, Ecuador, and Bolivia they founded the main congregations. In addition, the Central European immigrants founded the umbrella organization Centra which encompassed all of their groups in Latin America, and which afforded assistance to educational and youth organizations throughout the continent.

Another type of organization prevalent in the Jewish communities of Latin America are cultural, sports, and entertainment centers. The oldest is the *Sociedad Hebraica Argentina (1926) in Buenos Aires. First established by the youth born in Latin America, these organizations expressed their desire for Jewish and local cultural and linguistic integration and promoted from the very beginning activities in Spanish or Portuguese. They increased in number during the 1940s, 1950s, and 1960s and offer entertainment, relaxation, and sports to the Jewish community as a whole. Some of them (in São Paulo, Rio de Janeiro, Caracas) adopted the name Hebraica, although at the beginning no organizational connection existed between them and the organization of the same name in Buenos Aires. Others, in Mexico and Santiago de Chile, assumed the names Centro Deportivo Israelita and Estadio Israelita respectively. Some of these clubs, such as the Hebraica in Sao Paulo and the Centro Deportivo in Mexico, became the largest and most influential social frameworks that unite all the Jewish sectors. Maccabi groups, generally less wealthy and more limited in scope, exist in such cities as Buenos Aires, Montevideo, and São Paulo. In the 1960s all these organizations incorporated in the Maccabi World Union and also established the Confederación Latinoamericana Macabi – CLAM, which, among other events, organizes the Juegos Macabeos Panamericanos (Panamerican Maccabi Games) that are recognized by the International Olympic Committee as one of the five regional games. The first Games were organized in Buenos Aires in 1964 with 500 sportsmen. Since then the Games were hosted by the Maccabi organizations in São Paulo (twice), Lima, Mexico City (twice), Caracas, Montevideo, and Santiago de Chile. The Games in 2007 will take place in Buenos Aires (third time) and 5,000 competitors are expected to participate.

Antisemitism, which has increased since the 1930s and has physically threatened Jewish communities, brought into existence throughout Latin America comprehensive organizations to represent the Jewish community vis-à-vis the authorities and to fight discrimination. They are generally organized on a federal basis and in several places, Brazil, for example, the local federations also fulfill communal functions. These umbrella organizations were created in the 1930s in response to the antisemitic attacks that characterized that decade. The most prominent, the *DAIA of Argentina, was established in 1935. The Latin American umbrella organizations are affiliated with the *World Jewish Congress and in 1964 they established the Congreso Judío Latinoamericano (Latin American Jewish Congress). During the early years of its development, Latin American Jewry enjoyed great assistance from world Jewish organizations. The *Jewish Colonization Association (ICA), which established the agricultural settlements in Argentina and Brazil, also supported Jewish education in these countries and in Uruguay. In addition, it assisted immigration to Latin America and aided the new arrivals through the establishment of local branches. HIAS, HICEM, and the American Jewish *Joint Distribution Committee (JDC) helped Jewish migration and settlement in Latin American countries and to a certain extent to organize Jewish communities, particularly in Cuba and Mexico. These organizations were particularly helpful in assisting the refugees from Nazi Germany who found shelter in Latin America during the Shoah, such as in the case of the small agricultural settlement in Sosua in the Dominican Republic or the transition migrants in Cuba. In 1930 the American *B'nai B'rith opened its first Latin American lodge in Argentina that was followed by the establishment of branches throughout Latin America. HIAS and the *American Jewish Committee, which is associated with local organizations, began to function in Latin America in 1945 and maintained for many years offices in Argentina, Brazil, Uruguay, and Mexico. The American Conservative movement started its activities in Latin America in the 1960s, becoming gradually very influential. The first synagogue and the Rabbinic Seminary (1962) were founded by Rabbi Marshall Meyer in Buenos Aires and had an impact on the emergence of other synagogues that identify themselves with this trend in most of the Latin American countries. The impact of the Reform movement has been smaller, but has recently increased, with synagogues in Central and South America in Argentina (Buenos Aires), Brazil (São Paulo, Rio de Janeiro, Belo Horizonte, and Porto Alegre), Panama, Costa Rica, Curação, St. Thomas, Mexico, and Puerto Rico.

For several decades Zionism was the most influential ideology among Latin American Jews. The Zionist movement was first created in Argentina in 1897, with the first immigrants in agricultural colonies and in the cities. It accompanied all the Jewish settlements throughout the continent, but during the 1930s and 1940s had to compete with anti-Zionist ideologies, such as the Bund and the Communists, which had a strong impact on the Jewish population from Eastern Europe, and against the indifference of other Jewish sectors. Zionists from Latin America participated in the Zionist Congresses, established federations and parties, founded committees that supported Keren Kayemet, Keren Hayesod, and other national campaigns, and were active in promoting educational work and youth movements, as well as political activities on behalf of the foundation of the State of Israel. Since 1948 this process has increased considerably so that in the 1960s differences between the Zionists and the Bund, which were prominent mainly in Argentina and Mexico, decreased considerably. Today the anti-Zionists in Latin America are a small minority: the Communists and extreme left wing Jewish students on one hand, and some ultra-Orthodox religious factions on the other. A recent study on the demographic and ideological positions among Argentinean Jews asserts that Israel is a central factor in Jewish identity for at least 85% of them.

The impact of Zionism is clearly seen also in the number of Latin Americans who have settled in Israel. In the 56 years between 1948 and 2004, 89,684 Jews from Latin American countries immigrated to Israel, according to the figures of Israel's Central Bureau of Statistics. This *aliyah*, which in the 1950s and part of the 1960s had very strong ideological and political roots, established ten kibbutzim and several moshavim, and helped complete many others. A comparison between the number of immigrants to Israel from each country and the total Jewish population in the present shows that Colombia and Uruguay contributed the highest proportion of their community members to the process of *aliyah* (70% and 41%, respectively) and after them are Argentina (28%) and Chile (25%). It is estimated that a few thousand among the *olim* from Latin America re-emigrated later to their countries of origin or to other countries in Europe and North America.

[Haim Avni / Efraim Zadoff (2nd ed.)]

Demography

A revolution in the demographic study of Latin American Jewry has occurred since the 1970s, cutting back considerably the estimates that were accepted by scholars until then. Current and systematic estimates made by the Jewish Demography and Statistics Division of the Avraham Harman Institute of Contemporary Jewry of the Hebrew University of Jerusalem concluded that in 2005 there were 397,600 Jews all over Latin America. Some local research, such as the study completed in 2004 in Buenos Aires with the support of the JDC, confirms this figure. Since the 1970s there has been a clear tendency toward demographic regression, caused by many factors, such as lack of immigration, low birth rate, high percentage of aged people, mixed marriages, assimilation, and emigration to Israel, the United States, and other countries (see Table below). The most unpredictable of these factors is the migration that is mainly influenced by the economic and to a lesser extent by the political situation in the respective countries. The economic factor was particularly influential in motivating the emigration from Argentina, Uruguay, Mexico, and Venezuela, and the political factor in the cases of Cuba, Chile, Argentina, Colombia, and Uruguay.

Estimated Jewish Population in Latin America

Country	Jewish Population
Argentina	185,000
Bahamas	300
Bolivia	500
Brazil	96,700
Chile	20,800
Colombia	3,300
Costa Rica	2,500
Cuba	1,200
Dominican Republic	100
Ecuador	900
El Salvador	100
Guatemala	900
Jamaica	300
Mexico	39,900
Netherlands Antilles	200
Panama	5,000
Paraguay	900
Peru	2,300
Puerto Rico	1,500
Suriname	200
Uruguay	19,500
Venezuela	15,500
Virgin Islands	300
Other	300
Total Latin America	398,200

Source: Sergio DellaPergola, "World Jewish Population," in: *American Jewish Year Book* (2005), 105.

Jewish Education

The Jewish communities in the Latin American countries generally became concerned with Jewish education only after the facilities for basic Jewish and social needs (burial, marriage, circumcision, public worship, *kashrut*, and social welfare for the needy, sick, and immigrants) had been provided. The first

Jewish educational facilities for children were the traditional *heder* or *kutab* schools, modeled after those of the communities of origin on a supplementary basis. The attendance in these schools was very low, the teachers were generally the same persons who provided religious services, and their style of teaching was archaic. At the same time almost all the children attended public schools. The only exception to this situation were the agricultural colonies managed by the Jewish Colonization Association – ICA in Argentina and southern Brazil. ICA established day schools with general and Jewish studies that have operated in Argentina from 1896 and in Brazil from the first decades of the 20th century.

At the very beginning of the 1920s new trends came to the fore in Jewish education and modern schools were established. In Argentina and Uruguay modern secular Jewish schools were opened as a result of the profound influence of educational changes in the communities of origin. The schools assumed "imported" patterns and Jewish political ideologies, which characterized the mainstream of Jewish complementary schooling in these two communities in the 1940s, 1950s, and 1960s. The children attended these schools three–four hours a day five days a week. At the end of the 1960s, the schools received more than a third of the children of primary school age.

In the other communities a different pattern evolved since the Jewish parents were not satisfied with the state schools. With the help of wealthy individuals and afterwards with the support of parents who had gradually improved their economic situation, modern Jewish day schools were established with general and Jewish studies. These schools competed not only with the state schools but also with other private schools. The first modern day school was established in Mexico in 1924, and probably the last day school was established in Quito, Ecuador, in 1973. In the 1970s all the Jewish schools in Latin America (including Argentina and Uruguay) became day schools. In addition there are also Sunday schools, which give special bat or bar mitzvah lessons on Sunday or another day of the week. Until the 1960s or 1970s almost all the schools, complementary and day, devoted around 20 hours a week to the study of Jewish subjects. The Jewish curricula included history, literature, Bible, Yiddish and/or Hebrew, geography of Ereẓ Israel, and in the case of religious schools (less than a third) prayers and religious literature.

In the beginning the teaching staffs were made up of immigrants. In the 1940s secondary pedagogic schools were established in Argentina (1940, 1943, and 1945), producing a new generation of local teachers who were also able to direct the schools. In Mexico a teachers' seminar for graduates from the existing Jewish schools was founded in 1946. Like other communities, when the generation of immigrant teachers disappeared, the schools in Mexico were obliged to import teachers and principals from Israel or Argentina. In recent decades many local teachers were sent to study in Israeli universities in the framework of special programs and returned to their communities as senior teaching staff and school principals.

The day school structure is problematic with regard to Jewish studies since their main aim is to offer general studies at a high level. This often causes neglect of Jewish studies. On the other hand, the day school assures continuity in enrollment and has solved the problem of dropout among children over the years after it had been a serious problem in the complementary schools. For example, in Argentina in the mid-1960s the complementary primary schools and kindergartens received around 40% of the children of that age. From the end of the 1970s this went up to 55–65%. In other communities where day schools were established from the very beginning, such as Mexico, Venezuela, Panama, and Costa Rica, school attendance was over 80%, including secondary school.

Since the 1990s there have been attempts to establish complementary schools and courses, especially in Argentina, with the aim of attracting children who for diverse reasons (economy, distance, ideology) do not attend Jewish day schools. These frameworks succeeded recently to attract some 2,500 teenagers.

Other important frameworks in Jewish education are the informal activities and organizations. There are organizations with a clear ideological shading, the most common being the Zionist youth movements – the *tenuot no'ar* of all the political camps, from Ha-Shomer ha-Ẓa'ir on the left to Betar on the right and including the religious Bnei Akiva, which since the 1940s has been present in all the Latin American communities. Over the last six decades there have also been religious youth organizations such as Ezra (Po'alei Agudat Israel) and youth organizations of the Conservative (Ramah) and Reform communities (Netzer, Chazit Hanoar). There was also a youth movement of the Communists and their followers, and there were attempts to establish a Yugnt Bund Gezelshaft, as well as social and cultural activities offered by community centers and the social and sports clubs. Most of these institutions organized summer camps with varying Jewish content.

Jewish Journalism

Yiddish, the language of the majority of the Jewish immigrants, was the first language of journalistic Jewish creativity in Latin America. Jewish newspapers, journals, and literary, social, and political publications existed in almost every community. The first known publications were printed in Buenos Aires in the 1890s, in Yiddish: *Viderkol* (edited by Michl Hacohen Sinai) and *Der Yiddisher Fonograf* and *Di Folks Shtime*. The first periodical publication in Spanish was *El Sionista* (edited by Jacobo Liachovitzky) in 1904. In the 1900s were published the Bundist *Der Avangard* (1908), the Zionist-Socialist *Broit un Ehre* (edited by León Jazanovich), and *Yiddisher Colonist in Argentine* oriented to the population in the agricultural colonies managed by ICA.

The migratory wave which brought to Argentina's cities close to 100,000 Jews increased the demand for a daily Yiddish newspaper. *Di Yiddishe Tzaitung* (Monday to Friday) was founded in 1914 and was edited successively by Leon Maas, José Mendelson, and Matías Stoliar, and from 1918 the daily

Di Presse with a socialist orientation (seven days a week) was edited by Pinie Wald, Iaakov Botoshansky, and others. Both newspapers had subscribers from Chile, Bolivia, Paraguay, Uruguay, and even Brazil, and appeared until the 1970s. A third daily – *Morgn Tzaitung* – was published in Buenos Aires in the late 1930s and early 1940s. Other journals published in those years were the Rosario *Rosarier Lebn* and the *Avellaneder Lebn* on the outskirts of Buenos Aires.

Spanish newspapers started to appear in 1917 in Buenos Aires: *Israel* edited by Samuel de A. Levy with a social and communal orientation and the magazine *Vida Nuestra* edited by León Kibrick with a cultural agenda. *Al-Gala* ("Exile") was edited in the same year by Aharon Sethon, and is probably the only periodical Jewish publication in Arabic that appeared in Latin America.

Many new periodicals in Spanish appeared from the 1920s, covering a very wide spectrum of genres, international and local news: *Mundo Israelita* (1923) edited successively by León Kibrick, Salomón Resnick, León Dujovne, and Gregorio Faingersh; *La Luz* (1931) edited by David, Nissim, and David Elnecave. Both were still being published in the early 21st century. An attempt to publish a daily with general news was made with *Amanecer* (1956–57), but ended in failure.

The ideological field was fertile ground for publications in Yiddish as well as in Spanish: *Unzer Tzait*, ICUF, *Dos Arbeter Palestine*, *Di Yiddishe Velt*, *Fraie Shtime*, *Nueva Sión*, *Nueva Presencia*, *Renovación*, *La Voz de Israel*, and others. Several cultural journals were published, such as *Judaica* edited by Salomón Resnick, *Davar* of the Sociedad Hebraica Argentina, *Majshavot* published by the Seminario Rabínico Latinoamericano with Religious Conservative orientation, and *Comentario* of the Instituto Judío Argentino de Cultura e Información, close to the American Jewish Committee.

The German-speaking sector founded in the early 1940s the *Juedische Wochenschau*, edited by Hardy Swarsensky, which in later years was transformed into a bilingual (German and Spanish) publication. German periodicals were published by Jewish refugees also in other countries, such as the *Juedische Rudnschau* in Havana.

The few publications that appeared in Argentina in Hebrew were a unique phenomenon in Latin America: *Hechalutz* in the 1920s, *Darom* edited by the Hebraist Organization from the early 1940s until the 1970s, *Tzohar* edited by teachers and students of the Teachers' Seminary in the late 1950s and early 1960s, and *Rimon* edited by teachers and students of Ha-Midrasha ha-Ivrit in the mid-1960s.

As in Argentina, Jewish journalism played an important role in Jewish life throughout Latin America. In Brazil several journals were published in Yiddish, like *Yiddishe Folkstzaitung*, *Yiddishe Presse*, and *Dos yiddishe Vochenblat* in Rio de Janeiro, *Di Mentchhait* (Porto Alegre), and *Kol Israel* (Belem do Para). In Uruguay there were *Dos Yiddishe Lebn*, *Folksblat*, *Haint*, *Montevideer Shtime*, *Uruguayer Yiddish Vort*, and many others, with a variety of ideological-political and communal orientations. In Mexico two journals supplied daily information to the Yiddish-speaking public, *Di Shtime* and *Der Veg*, which continued to be published until the 1970s and 1980s, respectively. Other Mexican publications were more politically oriented: *Farn Folk*, a bi-weekly of the United Zionist Organization published since 1934 and edited by Meir Berger; *Forois*, a monthly of the Bund party which began to be published in 1941; and *Fraivelt*, a monthly of the followers of the Communist Party published in 1943–52. In Cuba the *Havaner Lebn* appeared from 1932 to 1960, edited from 1935 by Sender Kaplan. Several other Yiddish publications include *Oifgang* (1929–34), *Dos Yidishe Vort*, and the Communist *Kubaner Yiddish Vort* in the 1940s.

The Yiddish journals published in Chile include *Yiddishn Vochenblat in Chile* edited by Noah Vital in the 1930s and *Dos Yiddishe Vort* with a section in Spanish that became its only language.

Jewish schools, particularly in Mexico City and in Buenos Aires, published bulletins and yearbooks that reflected their ideological trends and reported their activities and were sometimes used to raise funds.

Throughout Latin America, publications in Spanish or Portuguese coexisted with the main publications in Yiddish. By the 1960s, however, readers of Jewish languages were an insignificant minority. Chile was an exception, since from the very beginning the main language in Chilean Jewish journalism was Spanish. The first Jewish Chilean journal – *Renacimiento* – was published in Spanish from 1919, edited by Arturo David.

From the 1920s many journals were published in Chile, like *Nuestro Ideal* by Abraham Drapkin-Darom, *La Patria Israelita* by Boris Cojanov, *Nosotros* by Natalio Berman, *Mundo Israelita* by Robert Levy, *Mundo Judío*, organ of the Zionist Federation and edited by Marcos Levy, *Alma Hebrea* published in Temuco by Isaac de Mayo in the 1930s.

In Brazil, besides the informative publications in Portuguese of Jewish religious or social and sports institutions like *A Hebraica* of the Hebraica Community Center, *Chabad News* of Chabad, *O Macabeu* of the Circulo Esportivo Israelita Brasileiro Macabi, FISESP *Comunicação* of the Jewish Federation of the São Paulo State, or *Morasha* of the Sephardi Community of São Paulo, there were important cultural journals and magazines with a cultural content, some of them still being published with notable success. *Resenha Judaica*, published in São Paulo, was for 30 years (1970–2000) an important weekly journal with wide circulation, and after 2000 was continued by *Semana*, which became a magazine. Other important magazines are *O Hebreu* published monthly in São Paulo since 1984, the weekly *Shalom*, and the monthly *Judaica*. Also there is a bi-weekly journal published since 2000, *Tribuna Judaica*, with news about community life and Israel.

In Mexico the first important publication in Spanish was *Tribuna Israelita* founded in 1944 by Sergio Nudelstejer and becoming the organ of the Comité Central, the umbrella political organization of the Jewish institutions. Almost every community organization has its own bulletin and there are publications with wide scope such as *Kesher* edited by Rosalynda Cohen and *Foro* by Jacobo Contente. In Venezuela the journal *Mundo Israelita* was published for 30 years (1943–73) and was succeeded by *Nuevo Mundo Israelita*, which remained the central organ of the Caracas Jewish community. In Uruguay the *Semanario Hebreo*, edited by José Jerozolimsky (1927–2004), was founded in 1960, and it is still edited by Ana Jerozolimsky Beris.

Jewish journalism has been active also in the electronic media. Several radio stations have been running Jewish programs. One of the first programs, *Hora Israelita*, was founded in São Paulo in 1940 by Siegfried Gotthilf. After his death (1952) his son Francisco directed the program under the name of *Programa Mosaico*. In 1961 he moved the program to television and though he changed channels many times, this weekly program is still transmitted every Sunday, being the longest-running program on Brazilian television. Radio programs were broadcast in many cities of Latin America, such as *Shalom Israel* in São Paulo, *La Voz de Sión* in Montevideo, and *La Hora Hebrea* in Buenos Aires. Since 1992 there has been a Jewish radio station, *FM Jai*, in Buenos Aires directed by Miguel Steuerman. There are also Jewish TV programs like the weekly *Le Haim* and *Shalom Brasil* in São Paulo and the weekly program of the AMIA in Buenos Aires which, despite a few interruptions, has been transmitted since the 1960s. An attempt to establish a cable channel – *Alef* – failed.

From the mid-1990s Jewish institutions and journals started to use the Internet as a new channel of communications. Today almost every community and institution can be visited through its website, and Jewish journals, like *Tribuna Israelita* of Mexico, *La Palabra Israelita* of Santiago de Chile, and *Nuevo Mundo Israelita* of Caracas, are accessible through the Internet. Several organizations send daily, weekly, or monthly bulletins with news, information, and cultural material to their members. Among them are *Micro Ejecutivo de Noticias de la DAIA* and the *Boletín OJI* of the Latin American Jewish Congress. There are also independent Jewish websites, such *Morasha* or *NetJudaica* in Brazil and *Shalomonline – la comunidad judía en internet.*

Ties with Israel

Latin American countries had often proved their sympathy and support for the Jewish renaissance both before and after the establishment of the State of Israel. The support given by Latin American politicians and intellectuals was explained by a combination of factors: their Judeo-Christian tradition which cherishes values connected with the land and the people of the Bible; their identification with the Jewish struggle for national independence, with Israel's attempt to integrate various ethnic groups, and cultivate neglected and desolate land; their objectivity in Middle East politics in which they had no direct interest; and the existence of active Jewish communities in Latin America and of influential descendants of the original Jewish immigrants (from Spain and Portugal) who still felt some kinship with the Jewish people. In spite of the fact that large segments of the population in Latin American countries originated in Arab-speaking countries and some Arabs became members of legislatures and governments, influential personalities mostly of the Latin American world rallied to the Zionist cause and supported the establishment of the State of Israel. The main reason for the moderation of the Arab elements was the predominance of Christian Lebanese, among them those who were not fervent supporters of the anti-Israel Arab nationalism. Pro-Zionist committees, in which prominent non-Jews in Bolivia, Chile, Cuba, Mexico, Colombia, and Costa Rica participated, came into existence in 1945. By the next year similar committees had sprung up in most Latin American countries. The list of sponsors included Alfonso Francisco Ramirez (then a member of the Mexican Supreme Court), José Figueres (the president of Costa Rica in 1948–49, 1953–58, and 1970–75), and José Galvez (then vice president of Peru). The *Jewish Agency promoted these beginnings of Latin American support. Benno Weiser (later Israel ambassador to various Latin American countries under the name of Benjamin Varon) and Moshe Tov (d. 1989, also later an Israel ambassador in Latin America), driving forces in the Latin American department of the Jewish Agency, won the political backing of these governments for the plan to partition Palestine in 1947–48. They were greatly assisted in these endeavors by the prestige of the famous Argentinean Jewish writer Alberto *Gerchunoff who actively intervened with political and spiritual leaders of Latin America on behalf of the Jewish interests in Palestine. The help extended by Latin American countries in the UN debate about the partition of Palestine was of decisive importance. Of the 11 members of the UN Special Committee on Palestine (1947) three were from Latin America: Arturo García Salazar of Peru, Jorge García Granados of Guatemala, and Enrique Rodríguez Fabregat of Uruguay. García Granados and Rodríguez Fabregat in particular gave unfailing support. Pedro Zuloaga, the alternate representative of the Venezuelan delegation in the second General Assembly of 1947, was most active in reconciling differences between the U.S. and the U.S.S.R. on the Palestine question. The president of the UN General Assembly Oswaldo Aranha, representative of Brazil, prevented the delaying tactics of all the anti-partition forces in the Assembly and put the plan for the partition of Palestine to a vote on Nov. 29, 1947. The Latin American countries cast approximately 40% of the total votes favoring the establishment of a Jewish state. Thirteen Latin American states voted for the plan and six states abstained; Cuba was the only Latin American country to vote against it.

In April 1948, during the second special session of the UN General Assembly, the majority of Latin American countries prevented the passing of a resolution favoring the establishment of a UN trusteeship in Palestine. The Latin Americans of the third assembly opposed the suggestion of the UN Mediator, Count *Bernadotte, that a big part of the Negev be returned to the Arabs. In May 1949, 18 of 20 Latin American delegations in the UN invited Israel to join the UN as a full member (half of all the votes favoring this resolution). The only political obstacle between Israel and Latin America has been the problem of Jerusalem. Most Latin American countries have remained supporters of the internationalization of Jerusalem and after the *Six-Day War (June 1967) most of their delegations voted against the municipal reunification of the city. However, the other political problems raised by Israel's victory have made the problem of Jerusalem seem less acute to Latin American leaders. Nine of the 13 Latin American embassies established in Israel were situated in Jerusalem. In 1980, after the passage in the Knesset of the Jerusalem Law, all the embassies left the city aside from Costa Rica. Since then only the embassy of El Salvador returned to the city. Israel is represented by ambassadors in all the capitals of Latin America (non-resident ambassadors are accredited in a few capitals). In the annual UN debates the majority of the Latin American delegations have rejected all proposals favoring the appointment of a UN custodian of abandoned Arab property in Israel as a breach of the rights of sovereignty. During the 1960s, the left-wing Tri-Continental Conference of Solidarity of Peoples on Jan. 4, 1966, in Havana, in which Arab delegates played a very active part, indicated the turn towards an anti-Israel attitude of the Latin American left. The fact that Castro's Cuba did not sever diplomatic relations with Israel after the Six-Day War (1967) seemed to have neutralized this attitude, but a few years afterwards, in September 1973, Castro broke off diplomatic relations with Israel. Following the Six-Day War the Latin American countries united in the emergency session of the UN General Assembly and put forward the so-called Latin American Resolution which thwarted Soviet-Arab moves to return the Middle East to its prewar status without a stable peace between Israel and the Arab states.

In the 1970s the attitudes in the Latin American governments changed, and at the beginning of 1974, observers pointed out that the Israeli cause in Latin America was at a low ebb, despite the fact that public opinion, as expressed by the leading press, continued to support Israel.

There were strong indications that several Latin American countries intended to intensify their ties with the Arab world. A "Syrian Week" took place in Mar del Plata, Argentina, in 1974. The Buenos Aires University's Institute on the Third World arranged with the Libyan Embassy to publish Perón's works in Arabic and Kaddafi's thoughts in Spanish. In 1975 the first Islamic Center in Latin America was inaugurated in Brazilia. The Panamerican Arab Congress met in 1974 in Buenos Aires and in 1975 in São Paulo. In Bolivia, a Federation of Bolivian-Arab Organizations began in 1974 to publish an anti-Jewish magazine. Arab and Latin American delegations exchanged visits.

The increase of Arab influence was noticeable during the votes on the Middle East taken at international organizations. In many forums, such as UNESCO, the International Women's Year Conference, the Conference of Non-Aligned States, and also in the sessions of committees of the UN General Assembly, several Latin American representatives abstained or supported anti-Israeli or anti-Zionist resolutions. In numerous cases local public opinion, general and Jewish, strongly criticized the government's stand, but this did not change official policy. UN Resolution 3379 (November 10, 1975) condemning Zionism as racism was supported by Mexico, Brazil, and Cuba while most other states (Paraguay, Peru, Venezuela, Bolivia, Argentina, Chile, Colombia, and Ecuador) abstained. Public opinion was one of the factors that changed the Latin American position when this resolution was revoked (December 1991). The issue arose again in the Session of the Commission on Human Rights in Durban, South Africa, in 2001, and this time many Latin American countries helped defuse the attacks against Israel and Zionism (Argentina among them). While relations between Israel and Latin America were affected in the 1970s and 1980s by the fluctuations of oil prices and the pressure of OPEC, the 1990s and 2000s were influenced by the perspectives of the peace process in the Middle East.

There are various cultural agreements between the Latin American countries and Israel implemented by the Instituto Cultural Israel-Iberoamérica that organizes intellectual and artistic exchanges between Israel and the Spanish and Portuguese-speaking world.

Commerce between Latin America and Israel was significantly upgraded between the 1960s and the early 2000s. Many bilateral agreements, the diversification of the goods that Latin American countries and Israel produce and consume, and the better mutual knowledge of the markets increased trade considerably. Imports from Latin America increased from about $3.4 million (1960) to $603 million (2004), and exports from $3.5 million to $1,366 million. Bilateral trade relations are encouraged by many public institutions like the Cámara de Comercio Israel-Iberoamérica (Chamber of Commerce) and the Cámara Brasil – Israel de Comercio e Industria (Brazil-Israel Chamber of Commerce and Industry). Israel is well known in Latin America also for its projects of international cooperation. Thus, technical aid and cooperation have become the basis of contacts between some Latin American countries and Israel. Israeli experts in agriculture, irrigation, cooperatives, rural development, science, education, public health, and technology have worked in Latin America. Thousands of Latin American students and technicians participated in courses in Israel in the last decades, and thousands of Israeli experts worked in technical aid projects in Latin-American countries from the 1960s, and several technical cooperation agreements have been signed with Latin American countries. Furthermore, special technical cooperation agreements were implemented in conjunction with regional and inter-American organizations like the Organization of American States (in which Israel has a position of observer) and the Banco Interamericano de Desarrollo (Inter American Development Bank).

[Shlom Erel / Efraim Zadoff (2nd ed.)]

From the 1960s to the early years of the 1980s difficult periods under non-democratic regimes controlled by army officers affected most of the Latin American countries, in some countries for decades. Under these Junta governments there were flagrant violations of human rights that in many cases went hand in hand with hard-line antisemitism. This antisemitism was reflected in the discriminatory treatment that Jewish prisoners received in jail and in detention camps especially in Argentina. Since the 1980s all the Latin American countries, excluding Cuba, have returned to democracy. In the new political and social climate of democracy and political freedom, the Jews took part as individuals in political and cultural life without discrimination.

Nevertheless, the terrorist attacks in Buenos Aires against the Israeli embassy (1992) and the total destruction of the AMIA Ashkenazi community building (1994), the reaction of some sectors of the population, and the failure to apprehend the perpetrators had their effect on the Jewish public in Argentina and in many other Latin American communities: on the one hand, Jews were made to feel less secure and felt the need to take more responsibility for the protection of Jewish sites; on the other Jewish cohesion and solidarity were reinforced. The social situation created by the economic crises in some countries and the solidarity of community institutions offering their help to the needy strengthened Jewish society and its sense of mutual responsibility.

[Efraim Zadoff (2nd ed.)]

BIBLIOGRAPHY: M.A. Cohen, *The Jewish Experience in Latin America* (1971); idem, in: AJA, 20 (1968), 33–62; L. Garcia de Proodian, *Los Judíos en América, sus actividades en los virreinatos de Nueva Castilla y Nueva Granada – siglo xvii.* (1966); J. Laikin Elkin and A. Lya Sater, *Latin American Jewish Studies: An Annotated Guide to the Literature* (1990); S.B. Liebman, *Faith and Flame: The History of the Jews of New Spain* (1969); idem, *New World Jewry, 1493–1825: Requiem for the Forgotten* (1982). **ADD. BIBLIOGRAPHY:** H. Avni, *Judíos en América: Cinco siglos de historia* (1992); S. DellaPergola, World Jewish Population, in: *American Jewish Year Book*, 105 (2005); A. Jmelnizky and E. Erdei, *La Población Judía de Buenos Aires – Estudio sociodemográfico* (2005); <http://www.meida.org/home.html>; *Judaica Latinoamericana*, vols 1–5 (1988–2005); J. Laikin Elkin, *Jews of Latin America*, (1997); D.B. Lockhart, *Jewish Writers of Latin America. A Dictionary* (1997); D. Sieskel, "Ketav Et Ẓiyyoni be-Aravit, be-Argentina" in: *Kesher*, 10 (1991), 80–85; E. Zadoff, "Jewish Education in Other Latin American Countries," in: H.S. Himmelfarb and S. DellaPergola, *Jewish Education Worldwide – Cross-Cultural Perspectives* (1984); E. Zadoff (ed.), *Informe de la Comisión Israelí por los Desaparecidos Judíos en Argentina* (2003), <http://www.mfa.gov.il/desaparecidos>. See also bibliographies in articles on individual Latin American countries.

LATRUN, historical site and crossroads in the southern Ayalon Valley, Israel, where the Judean Hills and the Shephelah meet, about 1 mi. (c. 1½ km.) S.W. of *Emmaus. Latrun Hill contains ruins of an Arab village and a 12th-century crusader fortress erected evidently on earlier foundations. On the slope a large French Trappist monastery was built about 1890 and is known for its wines. At the foot of the hill is one of the most important historical crossroads in the country, where the ancient road from Jerusalem to Lydda, Ramleh, and Jaffa meets the road leading from Gaza and Ashkelon through the ascent of Beth-Horon to the northern Judean Hills. Slightly northwest of Latrun, the British Mandatory government erected a police fortress which dominates the crossroads as well as the adjacent pumping station of the Rosh ha-Ayin–Jerusalem water pipeline. During World War II the British established a prisoner-of-war camp next to the pumping station, and along the Gaza road they set up the "Latrun Camp" where Jewish underground fighters and leaders of the *yishuv* were interned, including members of the Jewish Agency Executive (1946).

The name Latrun is a distortion of Le Toron des Chevaliers ("The Tower of the Knights," in old French) which was the designation given the crusader fortress on top of the hill. In the 14th century the Christians called the place *domus boni latronis* – "house of the good thief," i.e., St. Dimas, the thief who repented and was crucified together with Jesus (Luke 23:40–43). The mistake originated in the similarity between *Le Toron* and *latro* (Lat. for "thief"). Although the name Latrun was coined by the crusaders, the hill may have been the site of an earlier fortress belonging to the neighboring city of Nicopolis, which is identical with Emmaus. The Latrun area has been the scene of fighting from earliest times. *Joshua there fought the Canaanites and there the *Hasmoneans battled the Greco-Syrians. It was a Roman base during the war which led to the destruction of the Second Temple and in the *Bar-Kokhba Rebellion; later it became a Byzantine center and again, in the seventh century, an important military base for the Arabs in their conquest of southern Palestine. The crusaders and Richard the Lionhearted fought on this site, and *Saladin destroyed the Latrun fortress. In 1917 the advancing British army launched a two-pronged attack from Latrun (one by way of Bāb al-Wād (Sha'ar ha-Gai) and the other by way of Beit (Bayt) Liqyā, near Beth-Horon, which resulted in the capture of Jerusalem.

In 1948, during the Israel *War of Independence, the Latrun police fortress and crossroads were a key position in the fight for Jerusalem, and the Israel forces made several unsuccessful efforts to capture it to get supply convoys through to the besieged capital. Although the main road to the capital was thus cut off at Latrun, the Arab Legion failed to achieve its aim of closing the ring around beleaguered Jerusalem. At the beginning of June 1948, while the fighting was still in progress, a new route, the "Burma Road," was laid out, passing through Beit (Bayt) Jīz 2 mi. (c. 3 km.) from Latrun, but out of sight. This was turned into a road running parallel to the blockaded main road, enabling the Israel forces to supply the besieged capital with reinforcements of men and arms.

Under the armistice agreement with Jordan (1949), the entire Latrun area, including the monastery and the police fortress, remained in the hands of Jordan as an enclave linked by a single road with the Arab rear, a strip of no-man's-land interposing between the Jordan and Israel positions. The pumping station, situated in no-man's-land, was blown up by the Arabs to deprive Jewish Jerusalem of its water supply (in violation of the agreement reached under UN auspices). The crossroads also remained in no-man's-land, but the plan to have supply convoys pass through it under UN protection was given up after an attempt to pass a trial convoy through resulted in the murder of several Israelis. On the other hand, the fields in no-man's-land were cultivated by both sides, on the basis of local arrangements. During the *Six-Day War, on June 6, 1967, Latrun and the Latrun crossroads fell into the hands of the Israel Defense Forces almost without fighting, and subsequently the main and shorter road from the Coastal Plain to Jerusalem was reopened.

[Walter Pinhas Pick]

LATTEINER, JOSEPH (Finkelstein; 1853–1935), Yiddish playwright. Born in Jassy, Romania, he met Abraham *Goldfaden in 1876 and became interested in the Yiddish theater. He worked as prompter for Goldfaden's troupe, for which he also composed and adapted several plays. His first play *Di Tsvey Shmuel Shmelkes* ("The Two Shmuel Shmelkes," 1879) preceded Goldfaden's similar but more popular comedy *Di Tsvey Kuni-Leml* ("The Two Kuni Lemls"). Latteiner's more successful play *Yente Pipernuter* (1877) starred the actor Sigmund *Mogulesco in the main role. Other plays followed in rapid succession, including the operetta *Di Libe fun Yerushalayim* ("The Love of Jerusalem"), based on Abraham *Mapu's novel *Ahavat Ẓiyyon* ("Love of Zion"). Dissatisfied with Goldfaden's repertoire, he left the troupe and formed his own with Mogulesco, moving to Odessa around the same time as Goldfaden did, leading to the competition of the two troupes in 1880. Since Yiddish plays were banned in Russia after the assassination of Alexander II, Latteiner immigrated to London in 1883 and to New York in 1884. Initially he selected biblical subjects such as the stories of Esther or Joseph but soon turned to foreign sources, often merely judaizing characters' names and adding lyrics and slapstick humor. He wrote more than 80 plays, of which at least a dozen retained their popularity until World War II.

BIBLIOGRAPHY: B. Gorin, *Geshikhte fun Yidishn Teater*, 2 (1918), 73–82; LYNL, 4 (1961), 414–7; Z. Zylbercweig, *Leksikon fun Yidisher Teater*, 2 (1934), 964–90.

[Sol Liptzin / Marc Miller (2nd ed.)]

LATTES, family originally from the town of Lattes, S. France, who settled in Italy in the 16th century. It included several illustrious members: ELIJAH BEN ISAAC LATTES of Carcassonne, talmudist in the first half of the 13th century; his grandson Judah b. Jacob *Lattes, author of *Ba'alei Asufot*; ISAAC, son of Judah, talmudist, astronomer, and natural scientist, who lived in the first half of the 14th century, first in Montpellier, then in Perpignan; and his grandson Isaac b. Jacob *Lattes, a rabbi and physician in Provence. Bonet *Lattes (Jacob b. Emanuel) Provenzale, 15th–16th century, was an astronomer and physician to Pope Alexander VI. Others were Isaac Joshua *Lattes (d. c. 1570), author of numerous responsa and a commentary on *Bedersi's *Beḥinat Olam*; AARON ELIJAH LATTES (d. 1839), rabbi at Venice; and Abraham b. Isaac *Lattes (1809–1875), rabbi in Venice, grandson of Aaron Elijah. One of his sons was ELIA LATTES (1843–1925), philologist and linguist, who taught at the Royal Academy of Milan, where the chair of Greek and Roman antiquities was especially created for him. He made important contributions to Etruscology. Abraham's second son MOSES (1846–1883) was a Hebrew philologist, historian, and rabbi. SIMONE LATTES founded a publishing house S. Lattes and Co. in 1839, which specialized in scientific publications. Dante *Lattes (1876–1965) was one of the protagonists of the Jewish culture and Zionist movement in Italy.

BIBLIOGRAPHY: Milano, Italia, index; Bedarida, index; idem, *Ghetto di Roma* (1964), index; Gross, Gal Jud, 265; Fuerst, Bibliotheca, 2 (1960), 224–5; Vogelstein-Rieger, 2 (1869), 99; S. Simonsohn, *Toledot Ha-Yehudim be-Dukkasut Mantovah* (1964), 523; Roth, Italy, index. **ADD. BIBLIOGRAPHY:** D. Bidussa, A. Luzzatto, and G. Luzzatto Voghera, *Oltre il ghetto. Momenti e figure della cultura ebraica in Italia tra l'Unità e il fascismo* (1992).

LATTES, ABRAHAM BEN ISAAC (1809–1875), rabbi in Venice, Italy, where he succeeded his grandfather Aaron Elijah Lattes in 1839. A collaborator of the Venetian patriot Daniele *Manin, Lattes took an active part in the Italian revolutionary movement, and during the existence of the Venetian republic (1848–49) was twice elected a councilor. He wrote one of the pioneering studies on Venetian Jewry, published in *Venezia e le sue lagune* (1847), and contributed to the Hebrew periodicals **Kerem Ḥemed* and *Bikkurei ha-Ittim*. His son, MOSES LATTES (1846–1883), devoted himself to study after qualifying as a rabbi and published many monographs on Italian, particularly Venetian, Jewish history and on talmudic lexicography. He was the first to publish selections of the historical writings of Elijah *Capsali.

BIBLIOGRAPHY: Ottolenghi, in: RMI, 5 (1930/31), 25–35; C. Roth, *Venice* (1930), 365–6; Milano, Bibliotheca, index; U. Cassuto, *Studi giudaici in Italia… 1861–1911*, 1 (1913); G. Bedarida, *Ebrei d'Italia* (1950), 131, 225; M. Lattes, *Notizie e documenti* (1879), incl. bibl.

[Umberto (Moses David) Cassuto]

LATTES, BONET (Jacob b. Emanuel Provenzale; 15th–16th century), rabbi, astronomer, and physician. He was born in southern France, possibly Marseilles. By 1498 he was living in Rome where he acted as rabbi and *dayyan* of the community with the approval of the papal court. A believer in astrology, as was typical among Renaissance scientists, Lattes published annually (1493–98) a *prognosticon* in which he tried to predict the immediate future. He foretold the coming of the Messiah in 1505. While still in France, he had invented a "ring" astrolabe which could be worn on the finger. This astrolabe he described in a Latin tractate *Annuli per eum Compositi super Astrologiam…* (Rome, c. 1493), frequently republished. Lattes served as physician to Pope Alexander VI and his successors. In 1513 the Christian humanist Johannes *Reuchlin asked Lattes to use his influence with Pope Leo X to help him during his controversy with the Dominicans.

BIBLIOGRAPHY: Milano, *Ghetto di Roma* (1964), 67–68, 419; Vogelstein-Rieger, 2 (1896), 35, 83; C. Roth, *Jews in the Renaissance* (1959), 162, 210, 232–4; J.R. Marcus, *The Jew in the Medieval World* (1938), 159–164.

[Daniel Carpi]

LATTES, DANTE (1876–1965), writer, journalist, and educator who devoted his life to the diffusion of Jewish culture and religion among Italian Jews. He studied at the school of Elia Benamozegh and from 1897 began to work for the newspaper *Corriere Israelitico* in Trieste, becoming the director with Riccardo Curiel in 1903. Under his direction the *Corriere Israelitico* focused on the Zionist movement and contributed to promoting the Jewish culture of Italian Jews in a European and American context through debates and research on history and philosophy. Works of Aḥad Ha-Am and Joseph Klausner, literary output of Israel Zangwill and Edmond Fleg and Yiddish writers such as Shalom Aleichem, David Pinsky, and J.L. Peretz were published. He and Alfonso Pacifici founded the weekly *Israel* in Florence in 1916, and in 1925 *La Rassegna Mensile di Israel.* Among the first to champion the cause of Zionism in Italy and most of all the promoter of the idea of Jewish education based on the fusion between humanistic Italian culture and Jewish thought and knowledge, he translated into Italian the thinkers and writers of the Jewish national revival movement, such as Aḥad Ha-Am, Hess, Pinsker, Bialik, and Buber. He taught Hebrew language and literature at the Institute for Oriental Languages in Rome. From 1933 Lattes served on the board of Unione delle Comunità israelitiche italiane, and in 1936 he was one of the founders of the World Jewish Congress in Geneva. In 1939 he immigrated to Palestine with his family. He came back to Italy in 1948, where he again edited and directed the *Rassegna Mensile di Israel*, which had been suppressed in 1938, until he died. From 1952 to 1956 he was the vice president of Unione delle Comunità israelitiche italiane. His works include *l'Apologia dell' Ebraismo* (1923), *Il Sionismo* (1928), and commentaries on the Torah, the Prophets, and the Psalms. Through his writings, Lattes became a teacher and guide to three generations of Jews in Italy, but his role was barely recognized by the Italian Jewish establishment.

BIBLIOGRAPHY: Roth, Italy, 508; Milano, Italia, index. **ADD. BIBLIOGRAPHY:** A. Segre, "Alcune note biografiche," in: RMI, 42:9–10 (1976), 15–21; D. Bidussa, A. Luzzatto, and G. Luzzatto Voghera, *Oltre il ghetto. Momenti e figure della cultura ebraica in Italia tra l'Unità e il fascismo* (1992).

[Federica Francesconi (2nd ed.)]

LATTES, ISAAC BEN JACOB (14th century), rabbi and physician in Provence. Lattes studied under Nissim *Gerondi. His main work, apparently entitled *Kiryat Sefer* (1885), consists of two parts: *Sha'arei Ẓiyyon* and *Toledot Yiẓḥak*. In it, Lattes explains passages of the Oral Law, the manner in which the oral tradition was transmitted to the *tannaim* and *amoraim*, and the basis of the Mishnah and Tosefta. He enumerates the 613 traditional biblical commandments in the order of their appearance in the Pentateuch and explains them according to Maimonides. He comments on the laws of the public Torah reading and explains passages from the works of Abraham Ibn Ezra and Maimonides. Lattes also mentions many rabbis especially those of France. Lattes also wrote a book on medicine in which he enumerates different classes of diseases ("fevers") and gives advice on how to treat them.

BIBLIOGRAPHY: Isaac b. Jacob de Lattes, *Sha'arei Ẓiyyon*, ed. by S. Buber (1885), 1–4 (introd.); Renan, Ecrivains, 336–46; Zunz, Gesch, 478–9; Fuerst, Bibliotheca, 2 (1863), 224–5.

[Daniel Carpi]

LATTES, ISAAC JOSHUA (d. c. 1570), Italian rabbi, son of Bonet *Lattes, physician to Pope Leo x. Lattes was born in Provence where he studied and was ordained, later immigrating to Italy and becoming a peripatetic rabbi there. He passed most of his life in Rome, Bologna, Mantua, Venice, and Ferrara, where he lived in the house of Isaac *Abrabanel, serving as tutor to his sons. Lattes wrote many responsa, of which only a part were published (Vienna, 1860), an unpublished commentary to the *Beḥinat Olam* of Jedaiah Bedersi, and several poems. He was involved in the famous dispute known as the "Tamari-Venturozzo Divorce." He was also a printer and was associated with the printing of the Mantua edition of the Zohar (1558–60).

BIBLIOGRAPHY: Gross, Gal Jud, 267; Fuerst, Bibliotheca, 2 (1863), 225; S. Simonsohn, *Toledot ha-Yehudim be-Dukkasut Mantovah*, 2 (1964), 523; Vogelstein-Rieger, 2(1895), 99.

[Daniel Carpi]

LATTES, JUDAH (13th century), Provençal scholar. On his father's side he belonged to one of the most important families of Carcassonne, and his mother was the daughter of *Meshullam b. Moses of Béziers. His father Jacob was a famous scholar and is identified by some with Jacob b. Elijah, the author of *Iggeret ha-Vikku'aḥ* (Kobak's *Jeschurun*, 6 (1868), 1–34). Lattes was educated in Béziers, where he may have been born. His fame rests mainly upon his *Ba'alei Asufot*, a compilation of halakhic decisions, which is extant only in manuscript form. (The *Sefer ha-Asufot* published by A. Dzubas (1940) is a different work by an anonymous German scholar and was given its present title by Samuel David *Luzzatto. The entire structure erected by Dzubas in his introduction is therefore without foundation.) Lattes' compilation draws mainly on Provençal sources, such as *Abraham b. David of Posquières, R. Meshullam, his teacher, Gershon b. Solomon, and *Solomon b. Abraham of Montpellier whom he terms "my teacher." Comprising decisions dealing with the laws of holidays, mourning, forbidden foods, and wine, the work is actually a legal anthology arranged according to subject. Several decisions are provided under each heading, but it contains little original material. According to the testimony of his grandson Isaac Lattes in his own *Sha'arei Ẓiyyon* (ed. by S. Buber, 1881), Judah also wrote other works. He may be the author of *Kelalei Kankannim*, printed at the end of the *Sefer Hashlamah* to tractate *Avodah Zarah* (1917).

BIBLIOGRAPHY: M. Mortara, *Notizie di Alcune Collezioni di Consulti Manoscritti* (1882); Y. Mann, in: *Alim le-Bibliografyah u-le-Korot Yisrael*, 1 (1935), 75–77; Z. Schwartz, *ibid.*, 37–38, 77; B. Benedikt, in: KS, 2 (1950/51), 239ff.; idem, in: *Sinai*, 27 (1950), 322–9.

[Israel Moses Ta-Shma]

LATVIA (Lettish **Latvija**; Rus. **Latviya**; Ger. **Lettland**; Pol. **Łołwa**), one of the Baltic states of N.E. Europe; from 1940 to 1991 the Latvian S.S.R. The nucleus of Latvian Jewry was formed by the Jews of Livonia (Livland) and *Courland, the two principalities on the coast of the Baltic Sea which were incorporated within the Russian Empire during the 18th century. Livonia, with the city of *Riga, passed to Russia from Sweden in 1721. Courland, formerly an autonomous duchy, was incorporated into Russia as a province in 1795. Both these provinces were situated outside the *Pale of Settlement, and so only those Jews who could prove that they had lived there legally before the provinces became part of Russia were authorized to reside in the region. Nevertheless, the Jewish population of the Baltic region gradually increased because, from time to time, additional Jews who enjoyed special "privileges," such as university graduates, those engaged in "useful" professions, etc., received authorization to settle there. In the middle of the 19th century, there were about 9,000 Jews in the province of Livonia. By 1897 the Jewish population had already increased to 26,793 (3.5% of the population), about three-quarters of which lived in Riga. In Courland there were 22,734 Jews in the middle of the 19th century, while according to the census of 1897, some 51,072 Jews (7.6% of the population) lived there. The Jews of Courland formed a special group within Russian Jewry. On the one hand they were influenced by the German culture which prevailed in this region, and on the other by that of neighboring Lithuanian Jewry. Haskalah penetrated early to the Livonia and Courland communities but assimilation did not make the same headway there as in Western Europe. Courland Jewry developed a specific character, combining features of both East European and German Jewry. During World War I when the Russian armies retreated from Courland (April 1915), the Russian military authorities expelled thousands of Jews to the provinces of the interior. A considerable number later returned to Latvia as repatriates after the independent republic was established.

Three districts of the province of Vitebsk, in which most of the population was Latvian (Latgale in Lettish), including the large community of *Daugavpils (Dvinsk), were joined to Courland (Kurzeme) and Livonia (Vidzeme), and the independent Latvian Republic was established (November 1918). At first, a liberal and progressive spirit prevailed in the young state but the democratic regime was short-lived. Influenced by Fascism in Western Europe, the nationalist and chauvinistic elements of Latvia grew more arrogant. On May 15, 1934, the prime minister, Karlis Ulmanis, dissolved parliament in a coup d'état, the leaders of the labor movement and the activists of the socialist and progressive organizations were imprisoned in a concentration camp, and Latvia became a totalitarian state. Ulmanis was proclaimed dictator and "leader" of the nation. His government inclined toward Nazi Germany.

Jewish Population in the Latvian Republic

Before World War I there were about 190,000 Jews in the territories of Latvia (7.4% of the total population). During the war years, many of them were expelled to the interior of Russia, while others escaped from the war zone. In 1920 the Jews of Latvia numbered 79,644 (5% of the population). After the signing of the peace treaty between the Latvian Republic and the Soviet Union on Aug. 11, 1920, repatriates began to return from Russia; these included a considerable number of Jewish refugees. By 1925 the Jewish population had increased to 95,675, the largest number of Jews during the period of Latvia's existence as an independent state. After that year the number of Jews gradually decreased, and in 1935 had declined to 93,479 (4.8% of the total). The causes of this decline were emigration by part of the younger generation and a decline in the natural increase through limiting the family to one or two children by the majority. Between 1925 and 1935 over 6,000 Jews left Latvia (the overwhelming majority of them for Ereẓ Israel), while the natural increase only partly replaced these departures. The largest communities were Riga with 43,672 Jews (11.3% of the total) in 1935, Daugavpils with 11,106 (25%), and Libau (*Liepaja) with 7,379 (13%). (See Table: List of alternative names for places shown on map.)

List of alternative names for places shown on map

Latvian name	Old German name	Old Russian name
Aizpute	Hasenpoth	Gazenpot
Bauska	Bauske	Bausk
Dagda	Dagda	Dagda
Daugavpils	Duenabuno	Dvinsk
Jaunjelgava	Friedrichstadt	Fridrikhshtadt
Jekabpils	Jabobstadt	Yikobstadt
Jelgava	Mitau	Mitava
Karsava	Karsau	Korsoevka
Kraslava	Kraslau	Kreslavka
Krustpils	Kreuzburg	Kreitsburg
Kuldiga	Goldingen	Goldingen
Liepaja	Libau	Lubava
Livani	Livenhof	Levengof
Ludza	Ludsen	Lyutsyn
Plavinas	Stockmannshof	Shtokmangof
Preili	Preli	Preli
Rezekne	Rositten	Rezhitsa
Riga	Riga	Riga
Talsi	Talsen	Talsen
Tukums	Tukkum	Tukkum
Varaklani	Warklany	Varklene
Ventspils	Winday	Vindava
Vilaka	Marienhausen	Mariengauzen

Economic Life

Jews already played an important role in industry, commerce, and banking before World War I. After the establishment of

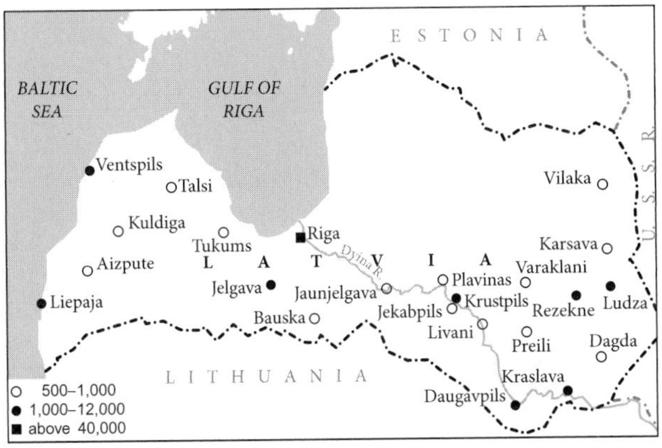

Jewish communities in Latvia (borders of 1918–40). Population figures for 1935.

the republic, a severe crisis overtook the young state. The government had not yet consolidated itself and the country had become impoverished as a result of World War I and the struggle for independence which Latvia had conducted for several years (1918–20) against both Germany and the Soviet Union. With the cessation of hostilities, Latvia found itself retarded in both the administrative and economic spheres. Among other difficulties, there was running inflation. Jews made a large contribution to the upbuilding of the state from the ruins of the war and its consequences. Having much experience in the export of the raw materials of timber and linen before World War I, upon their return from Russia they resumed export of these goods on their own initiative. They also developed a variegated industry, and a considerable part of the import trade, such as that of petrol, coal, and textiles, was concentrated in their hands. However, once the Jews had made their contribution, the authorities began to force them out of their economic positions and to deprive them of their sources of livelihood. Although, in theory, there were no discriminatory laws against the Jews in democratic Latvia and they enjoyed equality of rights, in practice the economic policy of the government was intended to restrict their activities. This was also reflected in the area of credit. The Jews of Latvia developed a ramified network of loan banks for the granting of credit with the support of the *American Jewish Joint Distribution Committee and the *Jewish Colonization Association (ICA). Cooperative credit societies for craftsmen, small tradesmen, etc., were established and organized within a central body, the Alliance of Cooperative Societies for Credit. However, the Jewish banks and cooperative societies were discriminated against in the sphere of public credit and the state bank was in practice closed to them. These societies nevertheless functioned on sound foundations. Their initial capital was relatively larger than that of the non-Jewish cooperative societies. In 1931 over 15,000 members were organized within the Jewish societies.

Jews were particularly active in the following branches of industry: timber, matches, beer, tobacco, hides, textiles, canned foods (especially fish), and flour milling. About one-half of the Jews of Latvia engaged in commerce, the overwhelming majority of them in medium and small trade. About 29% of the Jewish population was occupied in industry and about 7% in the liberal professions. There were no Jews in the governmental administration. The economic situation of the majority of Latvia's Jews became difficult. Large numbers were ousted from their economic position and lost their livelihood as a result of government policy and most of them were thrust into small trade, peddling, and bartering in various goods at the second-hand clothes markets in the suburbs of Riga and the provincial towns. The decline in their status was due to three principal causes: the government assumed the monopoly of the grain trade, thus removing large numbers of Jews from this branch of trade, without accepting them as salaried workers or providing them with any other kind of employment; the Latvian cooperatives enjoyed wide governmental support and functioned in privileged conditions in comparison to the Jewish enterprises; and Jews had difficulty in obtaining credit. In addition to the above, the Jewish population was subjected to a heavy burden of taxes.

Public and Political Life

Latvian Jewry continued the communal and popular traditions of Russian Jewry, of which it formed a part until 1918. On the other hand, it was also influenced by the culture of West European Jewry, being situated within its proximity (i.e., East Prussia). In its spiritual life there was thus a synthesis of Jewish tradition and secular culture. From the social-economic point of view the Jews of Latvia did not form one group, and there were considerable social differences between them. They engaged in a variety of occupations and professions: there were large, medium, and small merchants, industrialists, and different categories of craftsmen, workers, salesmen, clerks, teachers, and members of the liberal professions such as physicians, lawyers, and engineers. All these factors – economic and spiritual – were practically reflected in public life: in the national Jewish sphere and in the general political life of the state. The Jewish population was also represented in the Latvian parliament. In the National Council which was formed during the first year of Latvian independence and existed until April 1920, there were also representatives of the national minorities, including seven Jews, among them Paul *Mintz, who acted as state comptroller (1919–21), and Mordecai *Dubin (Agudat Israel). On May 1, 1920, the Constituent Assembly, which was elected by a relatively democratic vote, was convened. It was to function until Oct. 7, 1922, and included nine Jewish delegates who represented all groups in the Jewish population (Zionists, National Democrats, Bundists, Agudat Israel). The number of Jewish delegates in the four parliaments which were elected in Latvia until the coup d'état of 1934 was as follows: six in the first (1922–25), five in the second (1925–28) and the third (1928–31), and three in the fourth (1931–34). Among the regular deputies were Mordecai Dubin (Agudat Israel), Mordecai *Nurock (Mizrachi), Matityahu Max Laserson (Ẓe'irei Zion), and Noah *Meisel (Bund). The last two were not reelected to the fourth parliament.

Culture and Education

On Dec. 8, 1919, the general bill on schools was passed by the National Council; this coincided with the bill on the cultural *autonomy of the minorities. In the Ministry of Education, there were special departments for the minorities. The engineer Jacob Landau headed the Jewish department. A broad network of Hebrew and Yiddish schools, in which Jewish children received a free education, was established. In addition to these, there were also Russian and German schools for Jewish children, chosen in accordance with the language of their families and wishes of their parents. These were, however, later excluded from the Jewish department because, by decision of the Ministry of Education, only the Hebrew and Yiddish schools were included within the scope of Jewish autonomy. In 1933 there were 98 Jewish elementary schools with approximately 12,000 pupils and 742 teachers, 18 secondary schools with approximately 2,000 pupils and 286 teachers, and four vocational schools with 300 pupils and 37 teachers. Pupils attended religious or secular schools according to their parents' wishes. There were also government pedagogic institutes for teachers in Hebrew and Yiddish, courses for kindergarten teachers, popular universities, a popular Jewish music academy, evening schools for working youth, a Yiddish theater, and cultural clubs. There was a Jewish press reflecting a variety of trends.

With the Fascist coup d'état of May 15, 1934, Jewish autonomy was abolished. All political organizations were outlawed, except for *Agudat Israel. The supervision of the Jewish schools was entrusted to the latter, which closed all the secular Yiddish schools, while the curricula of the secular Hebrew schools were emptied of their content. The teachers were compelled to wear skullcaps; they were forbidden to teach *Bialik and even to use S. *Dubnow's history. With the establishment of the Soviet regime in Latvia in June 1940, even these sad remnants of Jewish autonomy were liquidated. Upon the outbreak of World War II in 1939, Latvia was compelled to sign a treaty with the Soviet Union, and placed air bases in various parts of the country at its disposal. In June 1940 a Communist government was set up and in July Latvia was proclaimed a Soviet Republic, and was incorporated within the Soviet Union.

[Yitzhak Maor]

Holocaust Period

GERMAN OCCUPATION OF LATVIA, 1941–1944. Latvia was occupied by the Germans during the first weeks of the German-Soviet war in July 1941. It became part of the new Reich Kommissariat "Ostland," officially designated as "Generalbezirk Lettland." Otto Heinrich Drexler was appointed its commissioner general, with headquarters in Riga, the seat of the Reich commissioner for Ostland, Hinrich Lohse (see *Lithuania). At the end of July 1941 the Germans replaced the military with a civil administration. One of its first acts was the promulgation of a series of anti-Jewish ordinances. An administration composed of local pro-Nazi elements was also established to which Latvian general councillors were appointed. Their chief was Oskar Dankers, a former Latvian army general.

On the eve of Hitler's attack, a large group of Latvians, including several thousand Jews, were deported by the Soviet authorities to Siberia and other parts of Soviet Asia as politically undesirable elements. During the Nazi attack of Latvia a considerable number of Jews also succeeded in fleeing to the interior of the Soviet Union; it is estimated that some 75,000 Latvian Jews fell into Nazi hands. Even before the Nazi administration began persecuting the Latvian Jews, they had suffered from antisemitic excesses at the hands of the Latvian activists. Chief among these were the members of the *Aizsargi* paramilitary organization and the Fascist antisemitic organization called *Pērkonkrusts*, which later collaborated with the Nazis in the annihilation of the Jewish community. The *Einsatzgruppen* ("action commandos") played a leading role in the destruction of Latvian Jews, according to information given in their own reports, especially in the report of *S.S.-Brigadefuehrer* (General) Stahlecker, the commander of *Einsatzgruppe* A, whose unit operated on the northern Russian front and in the occupied Baltic republics. His account covers the period from the end of June up to Oct. 15, 1941. At the instigation of the *Einsatzgruppe*, the Latvian auxiliary police carried out a pogrom against the Jews in Riga. All synagogues were destroyed and 400 Jews were killed. According to Stahlecker's report, the number of Jews killed in mass executions by *Einsatzgruppe* A by the end of October 1941 in Riga, Jelgava (Mitau), Liepaja, Valmiera, and Daugavpils totaled 30,025, and by the end of December 1941, 35,238 Latvian Jews had been killed; 2,500 Jews remained in the Riga ghetto and 950 in the Daugavpils ghetto. At the end of 1941 and the beginning of 1942, Jews deported from Germany, Austria, Czechoslovakia, and other German-occupied countries began arriving in Latvia. Some 15,000 "Reich Jews" were settled in several streets of the liquidated "greater Riga ghetto." Many transports were taken straight from the Riga railroad station to execution sites in the Rumbuli and Bikernieks forests near Riga, and elsewhere. In 1942 about 800 Jews from Kaunas ghetto were brought to Riga and some of them participated in the underground organization in the Riga ghetto.

The German occupying power in Latvia also kept Jews in "barracks camps," i.e., near their places of forced labor. A considerable number of such camps were located in the Riga area and other localities. Larger concentrations camps included those at Salaspils and Kaiserwald (Meza Parks). The Salaspils concentration camp, set up at the end of 1941, contained thousands of people, including many Latvian and foreign Jews. Conditions in this camp, one of the worst in Latvia, led to heavy loss of life among the inmates. The Kaiserwald concentration camp, established in the summer of 1943, contained the Jewish survivors from the ghettos of Riga, Daugavpils, Liepaja, and other places, as well as non-Jews. At the end of September 1943 Jews from the liquidated Vilna ghetto were also taken to Kaiserwald. When the Soviet victories in the summer of 1944 forced a German retreat from the Baltic states, the surviving inmates of the Kaiserwald camp were deported by the Germans to *Stutthof concentration camp near Danzig, and from there were sent to various other camps.

WAR CRIMES TRIALS. On April 7, 1945, the Soviet press published the "Declaration of the Special Government Commission charged with the inquiry into the crimes committed by the German-Fascist aggressors during their occupation of the Latvian Socialist Soviet Republic." This document devotes a chapter to the persecution and murder of Jews. The declaration lists Nazis held responsible for the crimes committed in Latvia under German occupation. They include Lohse, the Reich commissioner for Ostland; P. Jeckeln, chief of police for Ostland; Drexler, commissioner general for Latvia; Lange, chief of Gestapo; Krause, chief of the Riga ghetto and commandant of the Salaspils concentration camp; Sauer, commandant of the Kaiserwald concentration camp; and several dozen other Nazi criminals involved in the destruction of Latvian Jewry. On Jan. 26, 1946, the war tribunal of the Riga military district began a trial of a group of Nazi war criminals, among them Jeckeln, one of the men responsible for the mass *Aktion* on the Riga ghetto at the end of 1941. He and six others were sentenced to death by hanging; the sentence was carried out in Riga on Feb. 3, 1946. Other trials were held in Soviet Latvia after the liberation, but altogether only a small number of Germans and Latvians who had taken part in the murder of Latvian Jewry were brought to justice.

Latvians of varying backgrounds also took an active part in the persecution and murder of the Jews in the country outside Latvia. At the time of the German retreat in the summer of 1944, many of these collaborators fled to Germany. After the war, as assumed *Displaced Persons, they received aid from UNRRA, from the International Refugee Organization (IRO), and other relief organizations for Nazi victims, and some of them immigrated to the U.S. and other countries abroad. Nevertheless a few Latvians risked their lives in order to save Jews. One such, Jan Lipke, helped to save several dozen Jews of the Riga ghetto by providing them with hideouts.

After the Liberation

About 1,000 Latvian Jews survived their internment in concentration camps; most of them refused repatriation and remained in the Displaced Persons camps in Germany, Austria, and Italy. Along with the rest of the survivors they eventually settled in new homes, mostly in Israel. In Latvia itself, several hundred Jews had somehow managed to survive. A public demonstration was held in Riga a few days after its liberation, in which 60 or 70 of the surviving Jews participated. Gradually, some of the Jews who had found refuge in the Soviet Union came back. Several thousand Latvian Jews had fought in the Soviet army's Latvian division, the 201st (43rd Guard) and 304th, and many were killed or wounded in battle, while a considerable number had earned military awards for bravery at the front.

According to the population census taken in the Soviet Union in 1959, there were 36,592 Jews (17,096 men and 19,496 women; 1.75% of the total population) in the Latvian S.S.R. It may be assumed that about 10,000 of them were natives, including Jewish refugees who returned to their former residences from the interior of Russia, while the remainder came from other parts of the Soviet Union. About 48% of the Jews declared Yiddish as their mother tongue. The others mainly declared Russian as their language, while only a few hundred described themselves as Lettish-speaking. Of the total, 30,267 Jews (5/6) lived in Riga. The others lived in Daugavpils and other towns. According to private estimates, the Jews of Latvia in 1970 numbered about 50,000. The overwhelming majority of them lived in Riga, the capital. Riga became one of the leading centers of national agitation among the Jews of the Soviet Union.

[Joseph Gar]

Developments 1970–1991

Latvia regained its independence in 1991. The Jewish population of Latvia declined from 28,300 in 1979 to 22,900 in 1989, when 18,800 of its Jews lived in the capital Riga. In 1988–89 the Jewish birth rate was 7.0 per 1,000 and the Jewish mortality rate – 18.3 per 1,000. The rate of intermarriage is high. In 1987, 39.7% of children born of Jewish mothers had non-Jewish fathers. A large percentage of the Jewish population in Latvia is composed of post-war immigrants from other republics of the USSR. According to legislation passed by the newly independent country, these new Latvian Jews do not have an automatic right of citizenship as do ethnic Latvians.

In 1989, 1,588 Jews emigrated from Latvia (1,536 of them from Riga). In 1990, 3,388 Jews immigrated to Israel (2,837 of them from Riga). The number of immigrants to Israel from Riga in 1991 was 1,087.

While striving toward independence the Latvian national movement sought to make common cause with the Jews in the republic. July 4 was established in Latvia as a memorial day for the victims of the Holocaust.

Many Jewish organizations are operating in the country. The elite of the Jewish intelligentsia is not involved in Jewish communal life. In 1992 there was a perceptible increase in antisemitism.

[Michael Beizer]

In Independent Latvia

On June 11–17, 1993, the First World Congress of Latvian Jews was held in Riga. It was attended by delegates from Israel, the U.S., Sweden, Switzerland, Germany, Britain, South Africa, and Australia.

Two desecrations of Holocaust memorials, in Jelgava and in the Bikernieki Forest, took place in 1993. The delegates of the World Congress of Latvian Jews who came to Bikernieki to commemorate the 46,500 Latvian Jews shot there, were shocked by the sight of swastikas and the word "*Judenfrei*" daubed on the memorial. Articles of antisemitic content appeared in the Latvian nationalist press. The main topics of these articles were the collaboration of Jews with the Communists in the Soviet period, Jews tarnishing Latvia's good name in the West, and Jewish businessmen striving to control the Latvian economy. A dangerous phenomenon in the country is the continuing whitewashing of the collaboration of some Latvians with the Nazis during World War II, including complicity in the annihilation of Jews.

In the early 2000s, after the mass emigration of the 1990s, around 9,000 Jews remained in Latvia, mostly in Riga, where an Ohr Avner Chabad school was in operation. Ohel Menachem also operated a day school, as well as a kindergarten, and a synagogue was active.

[Daniel Romanowski]

BIBLIOGRAPHY: M. Schatz-Anin, *Di Yidn in Letland* (1924); L. Ovchinski, *Geschikhte fun di Yidn in Letland* (1928); I. Marein, *15 Yor Letland 1918–1933* (1933); AJYB, 32 (1930/31), 266–75; *Yahadut Latvia, Sefer Zikkaron* (1953); M. Bobe, *Perakim be-Toledot Yahadut Latvia* (1965). HOLOCAUST PERIOD: M. Kaufmann, *Die Vernichtung der Juden Lettlands* (1947); Jewish Central Information Office, London, *From Germany to the Riga Ghetto* (1945); IMT, vols. 23, 27, 37, indexes; I. Levinson, *The Untold Story* (1958); J. Gar, in: *Algemeyne Entsiklopedie*, 6 (1963), 375–94; G. Reitlinger, *The Final Solution* (19682); index s.v. Baltic States; R. Hilberg, *The Destruction of the European Jews* (19672), index; E. Avotins, *J. Dzurkalis-V. Petersons, Daugavas Vanagi, Who Are They?* (1963). CONTEMPORARY PERIOD: U. Schmelz and S. Della Pergola in AJYB, 1995, 478; *Supplement to the Monthly Bulletin of Statistics*, 2, 1995, Jerusalem; *Antisemitism World Report 1994*, London: Institute of Jewish Affairs, 141–142; *Antisemitism World Report 1995*, London: Institute of Jewish Affairs, 163–164; *Mezhdunarodnaia Evreiskaia Gazeta* (MEG), 1993. **ADD. BIBLIOGRAPHY:** Dov Levin (ed.), *Pinkas Hakehilot Latvia and Estonia* (1988).

LATZKY-BERTHOLDI, JACOB ZE'EV WOLF (Wilhelm; 1881–1940), journalist and Socialist leader, born in Kiev and educated in Riga. After being expelled from the Riga Polytechnicum in 1901 for his political activities, he went to Berlin, where he founded Ḥerut ("Liberty"), a Zionist-Socialist group, with Nachman *Syrkin. Back in Russia, he co-founded the *Vozrozhdeniye group in Kiev (1903) and was co-founder and ideologist of the *Jewish Socialist Workers' Party in that city. He visited New York in 1908. He contributed to the party newspapers, *Yidisher Proletarier, Unzer Veg*, and *Fraynd*. While in Vienna he wrote for *Dos Yidishe Frayland, Neue Nationalzeitung*, and *Oesterreichisches Wochenblatt*. In 1917 he was a co-founder and leader of the *Folkspartei, and in 1918 was appointed minister for Jewish affairs in the government of independent Ukraine. In 1920 he settled in Berlin. From 1923 to 1925 he visited the Jewish settlements in South America on behalf of the World Jewish Aid Conference and "Emigdirect" in search of possibilities for emigration and colonization. Later he published a book on the subject, *Di Aynvanderung in di Yidishe Yishuvim in Dorem Amerike* (1926). Returning to Riga in 1925, he edited the dailies *Dos Folk* and *Frimorgn*. He published *Erd-Gayst*, a collection of essays on Jewish culture, history, sociology, and art (1918; a second edition, 1932). His Yiddish translation of Nathan *Hannover's *Yeven Meẓulah* with an introduction was published in 1938. Latzky-Bertholdi settled in Ereẓ Israel in 1935; there he joined *Mapai and contributed to *Ha-Po'el ha-Ẓa'ir, Moznayim*, and *Bamah*. His library is in Kefar Giladi.

BIBLIOGRAPHY: LNYL, 4 (1961), 455–8; Rejzen, Leksikon, 2 (1927^2), 76–81; Wininger, Biog, 3 (1928), 606–7.

[Mendel Bobe]

LAU, ISRAEL MEIR (1937–), formerly Ashkenazi chief rabbi of Israel, since 2005 Chief Rabbi of Tel-Aviv. Born in Piotrkow, Poland, Lau is a member of a rabbinic family, descendants of Meir ben Isaac *Katzenellenbogen, the Maharam of Padua. His father, Rabbi Moshe Ḥayyim Lau, who perished in Treblinka, was the last rabbi of Piotrkow. Lau is a 37th generation rabbi in his family.

As a young child Israel Lau experienced the Holocaust in the Piotrkow ghetto, the Czestochowa work camp, and the Buchenwald concentration camp from which he was liberated at the end of the war, in 1945, with his brother Naftali. In the summer of 1945, he was brought to Palestine by Youth Aliyah on a ship of child Holocaust survivors.

He lived with his uncle, Mordechai Fogelman, the rabbi of Kiryat Motzkin, near Haifa, until the age of 13 and then spent many years studying in yeshivot in Jerusalem, Bene Berak, and elsewhere in Israel. He was ordained as a rabbi in 1960 and served as a congregational rabbi in Tel Aviv for 11 years, after which he was appointed regional Tel Aviv rabbi. In 1979 he became chief rabbi of Netanyah where, among other communal and educational activities, he founded the Ohel Mosheh yeshivah in his father's memory.

From 1983 he served on the council of the Chief Rabbinate, and in 1988 he was chosen chief rabbi of Tel Aviv. In March 1993 he was elected chief Ashkenazi rabbi of Israel. He served until April 2003. In 2005, he was again appointed chief rabbi of Tel Aviv-Jaffa. Throughout his rabbinic career Lau has been active in communal affairs and has been a spokesman for the observant community, commenting on a wide variety of subjects. When Pope John Paul II made his unprecedented apology for the sins of the Roman Catholic Church against the Jews in 2000, Lau expressed his disappointment that the pope did not mention the slaughter of millions of Jews by the Nazis during World War II. Nevertheless, in that same year, Lau attended a United Nations "Millennium World Peace Summit of Religious and Spiritual Leaders." In 2001, when then Israeli prime minister, Ehud Barak, offered Yasser Arafat sovereignty over the Temple Mount, Lau stated that "there is no mandate for concessions on the Temple Mount, not for the government, not for the rabbinate, not for anyone. Conceding the Temple Mount is like denying our historic and biblical right to all of the Land of Israel" (*Jerusalem Report*, January 15, 2001). In 2004, Lau proclaimed that the end was near for European Jewry, given the dwindling European Jewish population and the rise in antisemitism. In September 2005, Lau was one of those who officiated at the reburial of those interred in the *Gush Katif cemetery. Accompanied by tens of thousands of people, Lau led the reburial ceremony on the Mount of Olives, the result of the disengagement from Gaza (the removal of Jewish settlers from their homes there in August 2005).

In 1978 he published *Yahadut Halakhah le-Ma'aseh* (German edition, 1988; English edition, 1997). In 1993, he published *Ḥag Matan Torah*, insights into the holiday of Shavuot. In 1994, Lau issued a two-volume set of responsa, *Sefer Yaḥel Yisra'el*. He published his commentary on the Passover *Haggadah* in 2002 and his autobiography, *Al Tishlaḥ Yadkha el ha-Na'ar*, in 2005.

BIBLIOGRAPHY: Y. Alfasi, *Toledot Kehilat Tel Aviv-Yaffo ve-Rabbaneha ha-Rashiim* (1988).

[David Derovan (2nd ed.)]

LAUB, GABRIEL (1928–1998), Czech writer of aphorisms and humorous and satirical stories, journalist, and translator. Born in Bochnia, Poland, Laub and his family fled to the Soviet Union to escape the approaching Germans. He went to Prague in 1946, where he graduated from the Faculty of Journalism. Until 1968 he worked as a journalist and editor of literary magazines. After the occupation of Czechoslovakia, he went to Germany, where he worked as a journalist and later as a writer. His *Zkušenosti* ("Experiences," 1967) was published in Czechoslovakia; his other books were first published abroad. These include *Největší proces dějin* ("The Greatest Trial of History," 1972, 1991); *Leman Tehillah, Nashim ve-Behemot* (1979); *Denken verdirbt den Charakter* (1984); *Myšlení kazí charakter* (1991); and two dozen other books in Czech, German, and Hebrew. His book *Ein Lächeln zwischen den Zeilen* was published after his death.

BIBLIOGRAPHY: *Slovník českých spisovatelů* (2000); *Slovník českých spisovatelů* (1982).

[Milos Pojar (2nd ed.)]

LAUDANUM (Heb. לוֹט, AV, "myrrh"), one of the spices which the Ishmaelite caravan carried from Gilead to Egypt (Gen. 37:25). It is also included among the "choice fruits of the land" sent by Jacob to the ruler of Egypt (*ibid.* 43:11). *Onkelos translates *lot* by *letom*, included in the Mishnah among spicery growing in Israel which is subject to the law of the Sabbatical year (Shev. 7:6). In the Midrash the *lot* sent by Jacob is identified with mastic, but it appears rather to be identifiable with the aromatic sap of plants of the genus *Cistus*, called in Akkadian *luttu* or *ladanu*, in Greek Λῆδον or Λήδανον, and in Latin *laudanum*. The main species of *Cistus* providing the aromatic sap are *Cistus laudaniferus* and *Cistus creticus*, which are lowly shrubs growing wild in Asia Minor, Crete, and Cyprus. Some scholars list the latter species as growing wild in Gilead. In Israel two species grow, the *Cistus villosus*, the rockrose, whose rose-like flowers are pink, and the *Cistus salvifolius*, with white flowers, which beautify the woods of Israel. No attempt has been made to extract laudanum from its sap.

BIBLIOGRAPHY: Loew, Flora, 1 (1928), 362; H.N. and A.L. Moldenke, *Plants of the Bible* (1952), 77, nos. 70–72; J. Feliks, *Olam ha-Ẓome'aḥ ha-Mikra'i* (1968²), 272–3.

[Jehuda Feliks]

LAUDER, ESTÉE MENTZER (1907–2004), cosmetics entrepreneur. Lauder was born Josephine Esther Mentzer in Corona, Queens, New York. Her mother, Rose Schotz Rosenthal Mentzer, a Hungarian-born widow with six children, married Max Mentzer, ten years her junior; Estée was the youngest of the Mentzer children who grew up as Jews in a mostly Italian neighborhood. She married Joseph Lauter in 1930; the couple, who divorced in 1939 and remarried in 1942, became close partners in Lauder's cosmetic empire; they had two sons, Leonard (1933) and Ronald (1944). Lauder, who changed the spelling of her name in 1937, learned to create face creams from her maternal uncle, John Shotz, a chemist, and eventually began marketing her improved versions under her own name. Estée Lauder believed in selling her cosmetics at the finest department stores in the United States and abroad; by 1985, half of Estée Lauder and related product sales were in 75 foreign countries. Lauder trained the saleswomen who demonstrated and sold her products and pioneered giveaway promotions, always including lipstick in the gift package of samples. She also invested in marketing, using beautiful models to advertise her cosmetic lines. In 1953 she launched another phase of her business with Youth Dew, bath oil with a scent that could be used as a perfume, and the first of a number of fragrances. She created a men's line in 1965 and, after extensive medical testing, launched the fragrance-free Clinique line. In addition to numerous awards in the cosmetics industry and in fashion, Lauder received the French government's Insignia of Chevalier of the Legion of Honor in 1978 and the Albert Einstein College of Medicine Spirit of Achievement Award in 1968. In 1970 she was recognized by 575 business and financial editors as one of ten Outstanding Women in Business. She published her autobiography, *Estée: A Success Story*, in 1985. Lauder was a philanthropist, contributing to National Cancer Care and to the Manhattan League; the Lauder Foundation has given huge sums of money to Jewish and Zionist causes. Her son LEONARD (1933–) became chairman of the board of the Estée Lauder Companies Inc. Lauder has been an active participant in the worlds of education, art, politics, and philanthropy. He had a long association with the Whitney Museum of American Art; he also served as president of its board. For Ronald *Lauder, see following entry.

[Sara Alpern (2nd ed.)]

LAUDER, RONALD (1944–). U.S. cosmetics entrepreneur and philanthropist; son of Estée *Lauder. Lauder established the Joseph H. Lauder Institute of Management and International Studies at the University of Pennsylvania. A partner in the Estée Lauder Companies Inc. and chairman of Clinique Laboratories Inc., he was president of the Jewish National Fund, chairman of the Conference of Presidents of Major American Jewish Organizations, chairman of the Jewish Heritage Council, and chairman of the Museum of Modern Art, as well as a member of the International Board of Governors of the Tel Aviv Museum, in addition to substantive involvement in many other organizations. In 1987, following his service as

United States ambassador to Austria, he founded the Ronald S. Lauder Foundation which has focused on Jewish education and outreach programs, and support of Jewish schools, camps, and community centers, in Austria, Belarus, Bulgaria, the Czech Republic, Germany, Hungary, Poland, Romania, Slovakia, and Ukraine.

LAUFBAHN, YITSHAK (1888–1948), editor, author, publicist, and translator. Born to a rabbinical family in Dembica, Galicia, Laufbahn had a traditional Jewish education and excelled in biblical studies. A Zionist from his youth, he went to Palestine in 1908, worked for a while in agriculture, then moved to Jerusalem and was an assistant in the newspaper *Ha-Ẓevi*. From 1914 he edited with Joseph Aharonovitch *Ha-Po'el ha-Ẓa'ir* and when the latter was banished to Egypt, Laufbahn replaced him as editor. Laufbahn was active both in the organization of the *yishuv* and in its institutions; he played an important part in *Ha-Po'el ha-Ẓa'ir* and later in Mapai, the Israel labor party. In 1921 he was sent to Poland to carry out educational work with youth. In Warsaw he edited the Yiddish journal *Folk un Land* and in Berlin the *Arbeters-Folk*. In 1923 Laufbahn became editor of *Ha-Po'el ha-Ẓa'ir*, a position he held until his death.

His works include *Anshei Segullah* (essays, edited by I. Cohen, 1948); *Mivḥar Kitvei Y. Laufbahn* (selected writings, edited by N. Tradion, 1954); and he edited *Devarim*, the selected speeches of Chaim Weizmann (1934).

BIBLIOGRAPHY: Kressel, Leksikon, 2 (1967), 222.

[Israel Cohen]

LAUINGEN, town in Bavaria, Germany. The earliest documentary evidence for the presence of Jews in Lauingen dates from 1293. The Jewish settlement suffered during the *Rindfleisch persecutions (1298). A Jewish community is again recorded in 1324, but it was probably annihilated during the *Black Death persecutions of 1348/49. In 1367 the town received the privilege of accepting Jews and the subsequent community had strong commercial ties with *Augsburg. The municipal hospital mortuary was a synagogue before 1417 and bore a Hebrew inscription. In the 16th and 17th centuries numerous regulations against Jewish merchants were formulated. Although the estates resolved on the expulsion of the Jews in 1553, the measure was not enacted until 1577. Thereafter Jews were allowed into the town only to trade in the markets and for this they received special permits. By 1630, however, a community had again been formed. Expulsion of the 55-member community (including a doctor, rabbi, and teacher) was narrowly averted in 1635, thanks to the protection of the duke of Palatinate-Neuburg, Wolfgang Wilhelm. On his death (1653) they were expelled by popular demand, and the community was never reestablished, though some Jews continued to reside in the duchy (in spite of the general expulsion of 1671).

BIBLIOGRAPHY: Germ Jud, 2 (1968), 473; L. Lamm, *Zur Geschichte der Juden in Lauingen…* (1903); PK Bavaria.

LAURA AND ALVIN SIEGAL COLLEGE OF JUDAIC STUDIES, institution of higher Jewish learning in Beachwood, Ohio, a suburb of Cleveland. Siegal College grants bachelor's and master's degrees in Judaic studies and is accredited by the Higher Learning Commission of the North Central Association of Colleges and Schools. It is authorized by the Ohio Board of Regents, the Florida Commission for Independent Education, the Georgia Nonpublic Postsecondary Commission, the Kansas Board of Regents, and the Texas Higher Education Coordinating Board. The school has its origins in two separate teachers' institutions founded in the 1920s, the Jewish Teachers Institute and the Beth Midrash L'Morim (Hebrew Teacher Training School), which merged in 1947 to form the Cleveland Institute of Jewish Studies under the auspices of the Cleveland Board of Jewish Education. Largely through the initiative of educator Rebecca Aronson Brickner, the school became known as the Cleveland College of Jewish Studies in 1963, and also became an independent institution. Its name changed to the Laura and Alvin Siegal College in 2002 as a result of a generous donation from that family. The college also receives financial support from the Jewish Community Federation of Cleveland.

Undergraduates major in Judaic studies while earning general education credits at various colleges and universities in the Cleveland metropolitan area. Area colleges also have cooperative arrangements in which students may earn Judaic studies credits at Siegal. Graduate students can receive master's degrees in classical Jewish studies or in Jewish education. There are programs to educate teachers for all kinds of Jewish schools as well as classes to update and improve the skills of teachers already in the field. Siegal College also operates Akiva High School, a community-wide supplementary school for teenagers, and provides an extensive continuing adult education program for the community. The school's distance learning program reaches beyond the Cleveland metropolitan area with cooperative programs currently operating in Houston, Dallas, Miami, West Palm Beach, Milwaukee, Denver, Atlanta, Birmingham, and Kansas City. The Aaron Garber Library, named for a founder of *talmud torah* education in Cleveland, is the largest Judaica library in the Cleveland metropolitan area.

BIBLIOGRAPHY: MS. 4826 Cleveland College of Jewish Studies, Western Reserve Historical Society, Cleveland, Ohio. **WEBSITE:** www.siegalcollege.edu.

LAUREN, RALPH (1939–), U.S. fashion designer. Although he was born and raised among middle-class Jewish families in the Bronx, Lauren became closely linked to two themes far removed from his urban background: patrician England and the rugged American West. His signature "looks" grew into a $10 billion global brand for apparel and accessories, fragrances and home products. Born Ralph Lifshitz, he was raised in the same neighborhood as Calvin *Klein, with whom an intense rivalry would develop. His parents, Frank and Frieda Lifshitz, were East Europeans who settled in the U.S. in 1920. Largely through the influence of his mother, whose antecedents included a long line of rabbis, his early education was a combination of the secular and religious. When he was eight, he was transferred from public school to Yeshiva Rabbi Israel Salanter, one of New York City's feeder schools to the Manhattan Talmudical Academy. Three years later, he returned to public school for two years, and then went back to Yeshiva. At 14, he entered the Talmudical Academy but transferred to a public high school a year later, ending his formal religious education. He attended City College of New York, taking business courses at night while working as an assistant buyer of men's furnishings. In 1959, he and an older brother changed their last name to Lauren because it sounded more genteel than Lifshitz and a year later he dropped out of college. By that time, the fashion esthetic that would inform his career had taken shape. He was influenced by movie stars such as Fred Astaire and Cary Grant and wore clothes that were elegant and sophisticated. He was also attracted by the mystique of the American cowboy.

Lauren was drafted into the U.S. Army Reserves in 1960. After completing his military obligation in 1963 he held a series of jobs selling gloves and ties. He married Ricky Lowbeer in 1964 while employed as a tie salesman for A. Rivetz & Co., where he began designing his own line. Lauren's ties were innovative, much wider than the prevailing versions and made in sumptuous fabrics with bold patterns. Lauren joined Beau Brummel in 1967 and soon had his own collection of ties. It was called Polo, a name that evoked an image of international glamour. The ties were spectacularly successful. In 1968, backed by a $50,000 loan, Lauren left Beau Brummel, took the Polo name with him, and opened his own business. He soon began making a complete line of men's clothing, merging classic American styling with European flair. In 1969, Polo by Ralph Lauren was established as the first designer boutique for men in Bloomingdale's in New York, the first major retailer to recognize Lauren's talent. In 1971, Lauren launched his first women's line and opened a shop in Beverly Hills, Calif., becoming the first U.S. designer with his own freestanding store. Through the 1970s, he expanded his reach into footwear and accessories, boy's wear and fragrances. In 1978, he launched his Western-wear collection and appeared in the ads for it. He pioneered the use of multipage magazine advertising, running spreads of up to 20 consecutive pages that collectively presented "the world of Ralph Lauren." His first store outside the U.S. opened in London in 1981. In 1983, the home collection was launched and in 1986, the new Lauren flagship opened in a historic remodeled mansion in Manhattan. By 2003, there were Polo Ralph Lauren stores in some 30 countries. In 1997, Polo went public. What began with 26 boxes of ties in 1967 had become a giant corporation listed on the New York Stock Exchange. Lauren himself had become a billionaire with a Fifth Avenue duplex in New York, an estate in Bedford, N.Y., a beach house on Long Island, two homes in Jamaica, and a cattle ranch in Colorado. He amassed a world-class collection of antique cars.

He won his first Coty Award for men's wear in 1970, and was inducted into the Coty Hall of Fame for men's wear in 1976 and women's wear in 1977. He is the first designer to have been given the Council of Fashion Designers of America's four highest honors – Lifetime Achievement, Designer of the Year in men's wear and in women's wear, and Retailer of the Year. He received an Honorary Doctorate of Letters from Brandeis University in 1996, the same year he was presented with the first Humanitarian Award from the Nina Hyde Center for Breast Cancer Research at Georgetown University in Washington, D.C., a facility Lauren was instrumental in establishing.

Lauren's philanthropic activities have focused on cancer care and prevention, but include artistic and cultural projects related to American history. In 1998, he donated $13 million to the Smithsonian Institution to fund preservation of the American flag that inspired "The Star Spangled Banner." The beneficiaries of the Polo Ralph Lauren Foundation include the Pink Pony Fund, established by Lauren in 2000 to support cancer care and prevention in medically underserved communities. His gift to the Lexington School/Center for the Deaf in New York in 2002 enabled it to build a performing arts center and in 2003, the Ralph Lauren Center for Cancer Care and Prevention opened in the East Harlem section of New York.

BIBLIOGRAPHY: M. Gross, *Genuine Authentic: The Real Life of Ralph Lauren* (2003); J.A. Trachtenberg, *Ralph Lauren: The Man Behind the Mystique* (1988).

[Mort Sheinman (2nd ed.)]

LAURENCE, WILLIAM L. (1888–1977), U.S. journalist and science writer. Born in Lithuania and educated in the U.S., Laurence became a science reporter for several leading newspapers and magazines. He joined *The New York Times* as science reporter in 1930. In 1937 he won his first Pulitzer Prize for distinguished science reporting. In April 1945 he was recruited to become the official chronicler of the development of the atom bomb. He was permitted to interview the scientists working on the Manhattan Project and to prepare the press releases when the new weapon was used. On August 6, 1945, the United States dropped an atom bomb on Hiroshima. Three days later, accompanying the U.S. bomber crew on its second mission, Laurence was on the B-29 Superfort that dropped an atom bomb on Nagasaki. The explosive energy of the bomb's active substance, wrote Laurence, was "equivalent to 20,000 and, under favorable conditions, 40,000 tons of TNT." He wrote the official eyewitness account of the bombing. Laurence won his second Pulitzer "for his eye-witness account of the atom-bombing of Nagasaki and his subsequent ten articles on the development, production, and significance of the atomic bomb." He was the only reporter to witness the atomic bomb tests in a desert in New Mexico in 1945 and was selected by the U.S. War Department to write the story of the bomb, *Dawn over Zero* (1946).

[Ruth Beloff (2nd ed.)]

LAURENTS, ARTHUR (1918–), U.S. playwright. Laurents won the American Academy of Arts and Letters Award for his first play, *Home of the Brave* (1946), which was also filmed. He wrote the screenplays for *Rope* (1948), *Caught* (1949), *Anna Lucasta* (coauthor, 1949), and *Anastasia* (1956). His plays include *The Time of the Cuckoo* (1952), and he wrote the book for the musicals *West Side Story* (1957) and *Gypsy* (1959). His *Original Story By: A Memoir of Broadway and Hollywood* was published in 2000.

LAUSANNE, capital of canton Vaud, W. Switzerland. Jews were present in the canton of Vaud from 1278; those living in the vicinity of Lausanne suffered during the persecutions of 1348/49. The presence of Jews in Lausanne itself is first mentioned only in 1408, when several Jewish families – at first nine, then six – were authorized to settle there against payment of a regular tax. They were exempted from all other taxes and guaranteed liberty of trade, movement, and the right to practice ritual slaughter. The number had grown to 19 in 1419 when they were put under the protection of Bishop William of Challant. A Rue des Juifs is noted and a Jewish cemetery as well. The Jews left Lausanne in 1484 and are not recorded there again until the end of the 18th century. The prohibition on residence issued against the Jews was renewed in 1787. The proclamation of the Lemanic Republic, later incorporated in the Helvetian Republic (1798), opened the city to Jewish residents. Mostly Alsatian Jews conducted business in the canton. In the town of Avenches a new Jewish community was founded in 1826, with 262 heads of families (in 1870), making the Jews a seventh of the local population. In 1865 they built a synagogue and engaged a rabbi. All the Jews came from Alsace and many were horse dealers. The community dispersed after 1945, young members having moved to Lausanne and Berne. The synagogue was demolished in 1958 and a memorial erected in 1979. Also in Yverdon a small community existed between 1850 and 1980. Here Johann Heinrich Pestalozzi taught young Jews pedagogics around 1807.

The Lausanne community developed slowly, however, even though the anti-Jewish measures were rapidly abrogated. After a first attempt in 1848, an organized community was established in 1865. Jews were not admitted to full citizenship until 1891. Among the Russian Jewish students in residence at the University of Lausanne was Saul *Tchernikowsky. The synagogue was consecrated in 1912 and the first rabbi appointed in 1928. Rabbi Georges Vadnai served the community from 1940 until 1990. The Jewish population numbered, according to the census, 1,186 in 1920, 1,009 in 1933, and 1,288 in 1960. During the course of World War II the community was active in aiding refugees from Nazism. From 1948 it received Jewish refugees from Arab lands. Consequently, once a month a Sephardi service is offered. In 2000 the Jewish population of Vaud was 2,062, while the community of Lausanne numbers 608 persons and families. The rabbinate of Lausanne also covered the area of Montreux and Vevey (a separate community established in 1905), which had a variety of philanthropic organizations. In Montreux, E. Botschko (d. 1956) founded a yeshivah (Ez̦ Ḥayyim) in 1927, which during World War II had as many as 120 students, and served as a refuge for many who escaped from the Nazi terror. The yeshivah attracted pupils from all over Western Europe until 1985, when it was closed and its leader, Moshe Botschko, went on *aliyah* to Jerusalem. A Jewish home for the aged with 120 places is situated in Vevey. A community council was established in 1963 to coordinate its varied cultural, religious, and educational programs. In 2003 legal state recognition of the community was achieved.

BIBLIOGRAPHY: A. Nordmann, in: REJ, 81 (1925), 158–68; C. Lauener, *La communauté juive d'Avenches: organisation et intégration (1826–1900)* (1993); L. Leitenberg, "Evolution et perspectives des communautés en Suisse romande," in: Schweiz. Isr. Gemeindebund, *Jüd. Lebenswelt Schweiz. 100 Jahre Schweiz. Isr. Gemeindebund* (2004), 153–66; Musée Historique de Lausanne and A. Kamis-Mueller, *Vie Juive en Suisse* (1992); Schweiz. Isr. Gemeindebund, *Festschrift zum 50-Jaehrigen Bestehen* (1954).

[Simon R. Schwarzfuchs / Uri Kaufmann (2nd ed.)]

LAUTENBERG, FRANK R. (1924–), U.S. senator, philanthropist, and businessman. Lautenberg was born in Paterson, N.J., the son of Polish and Russian immigrants who came to the United States through Ellis Island. His early life was unsettled as his parents moved about a dozen times while struggling to support the family. Lautenberg's father, Sam, worked in the silk mills, sold coal, farmed, and once ran a tavern. When Lautenberg was 19, his father died of cancer. To help his family, he worked nights and weekends until he graduated from Nutley High School.

Lautenberg served in the Army Signal Corps in Europe during World War II, where he reached the rank of corporal. Following the war, he attended Columbia University on the GI Bill of Rights. It was his experience with the GI Bill of Rights that convinced Lautenberg of the efficacy of government programs, the hallmark of his liberalism.

Lautenberg worked as a marketing specialist in Henry Taub's accounting practice. Lautenberg helped the business grow by sheer salesmanship and later by strategic acquisitions, rising to president and later CEO of Automatic Data Processing, which had the unique idea of outsourcing payroll processing. Lautenberg, along with his partners, developed ADP into one of the largest computing services companies in the world, processing the payrolls of more than 100,000 companies. He rewarded his workers with a stock ownership plan and they rewarded their officers by refusing to unionize. He amassed a fortune and entered Jewish life, rising to be national chairman of the United Jewish Appeal and president of the American Friends of the Hebrew University.

Lautenberg served on the President's Commission on the Holocaust and was both a Congressional and a citizen appointee to the Holocaust Memorial Council, which oversaw the U.S. Holocaust Memorial Museum. Denied a Jewish education in his youth, he learned basic synagogue skills only as an adult. But his Jewish identity was central to his philanthropy as well as to his sense of self.

He served as a New York/New Jersey Port Authority commissioner (1978–82) and as a commissioner of the New

Jersey Economic Development Authority. Lautenberg, running as a Democrat for a New Jersey senatorial seat, beat veteran congresswoman Millicent Fenwick.

Over his first three terms in the U.S. Senate, Lautenberg built a solid record of accomplishment on a broad range of issues. He voted against the use of military forces in the Persian Gulf, a position that he defended even after the American victory by castigating Saudi Arabia and Kuwait for not honoring their commitments.

Lautenberg retired from the U.S. Senate in 2000 at the age of 76, a decision he later regretted. Still vigorous and an ardent skier, he missed the action of the Senate. Fate provided him with an opportunity when his fellow Democrat Robert Torricelli got caught up in a scandal and was forced to withdraw from the race. Democratic Party leaders turned to Lautenberg to preserve the seat. With his widespread name recognition and his own funding as well as assistance from the Democratic Senate Campaign Committee, he ran again and won handily, returning to the Senate after a two years' absence.

BIBLIOGRAPHY: K. Stone, *The Congressional Minyan: The Jews of Capitol Hill* (2000); L.S. Maisel and I. Forman, *Jews in American Politics* (2001).

[Michael Berenbaum (2nd ed.)]

LAUTERBACH, ASHER ZELIG (1826–1906), Galician Hebrew scholar and author. Lauterbach, born in Drohobych, studied on his own as a youth and acquired a comprehensive knowledge of Jewish and classical literature. An industrialist of independent means, he devoted much of his time to research and communal activity. Lauterbach maintained a lively correspondence with his fellow scholars and writers and wrote (over the signature זה"ל) biblical and talmudic studies for most of the Hebrew papers and periodicals of the time. Lauterbach's published works, containing to a large extent reprints of his articles, included *Ha-Nistarot ve-ha-Niglot* (1871), on superstitions and magic in Talmud and Midrash; *Minḥat Azkarah* (1889), commentary and notes on the treatise *Avot; Minḥat Erev* (with the appendix "*Nes Ḥanukkah*," 1891), a collection of eulogies; *Minḥat Kohen* (1892), part 1 on the proper names in the Bible and part 2 on the question of whether a Jew is permitted to live in Egypt; *Minḥah Ḥadashah* (1893), a Passover *Haggadah* with commentary; *Minḥah Belulah* (1902), notes on the Bible and a eulogy on his brother. His autobiography appeared in: N. Sokolow (ed.), *Sefer Zikkaron* (1889), 146–53.

BIBLIOGRAPHY: L. Lauterbach, *Chronicle of the Lauterbach Family* (1948, 1960^3, with 3 suppls., 1962–68).

[Getzel Kressel]

LAUTERBACH, EDWARD H. (1844–1923), U.S. lawyer, business executive, and politician. Lauterbach, who was born in New York City, was admitted to the New York bar in 1866. He was president of the Baltimore and Southern Railway, organized the company which installed New York City's underground electric light and telegraph cables, and wrote one of the first regulatory laws passed by the New York State Legislature which imposed statewide standards on streetcar line operations and liabilities. Lauterbach was also active in New York State Republican Party politics for many years. He was a chairman of the committee of public charities and a longtime trustee of the Hebrew Orphan Asylum.

LAUTERBACH, JACOB ZALLEL (1873–1942), U.S. talmudic scholar. Lauterbach, who was born in Monasterzyska, Galicia, studied at the German universities of Berlin and Goettingen and at the *Rabbiner-Seminar fuer das Orthodoxe Judenthum where he was ordained. Lauterbach went to New York in 1903 to work on the staff of the *Jewish Encyclopedia*, for which he wrote 260 articles. He later contributed to J.D. Eisenstein's Hebrew encyclopedia, *Oẓar Yisrael*, and to the *Eshkol* encyclopedia. Thereafter, he served as rabbi of traditional synagogues in Peoria, Illinois, and Rochester, New York, and of the Reform congregation of Huntsville, Alabama. In 1911 he became professor of Talmud at the Hebrew Union College.

Lauterbach's critical three-volume edition of the *Mekhilta de-Rabbi Ishma'el*, with English translation (1933–49), is a model of meticulous and thorough scholarship. The rest of his learned output consisted of essays, which include an epoch-making series on the Pharisees. The first of these, "The Sadducees and the Pharisees" (1913), clarified the attitude of the two sects toward the Written and Oral Law. *Midrash and Mishnah* (1915) was Lauterbach's major contribution to the literary history of the Talmud. Several preliminary and supplementary studies on the *Mekhilta* appeared in connection with the edition mentioned above. Lauterbach was especially interested in Jewish customs and folklore, which he treated with erudition and charm in a number of essays.

He served as chairman of the Committee on Responsa of the Central Conference of American Rabbis. In this position, he wrote opinions not only on ritual questions, but on other important issues of modern Jewish life. His responsa on the ordination of women as rabbis (1922), autopsy (1925), and birth control (1927) thoroughly review and analyze traditional decisions on these subjects before presenting practical conclusions. Lauterbach emphasized the continuity of Reform Judaism with older Jewish tradition, and attempted to show that Reform can derive enrichment and guidance from the *halakhah*, even though it does not accept earlier formulations as final and irrevocable. In 1951 *Rabbinic Essays*, a collection of a number of Lauterbach's most important articles, was published by the Alumni Association of the Hebrew Union College-Jewish Institute of Religion. This volume, edited by Lou H. Silberman, contains a complete bibliography of his writings. A second collection, *Studies in Jewish Law, Custom and Folklore*, appeared in 1970.

BIBLIOGRAPHY: B.J. Bamberger, in: CCAR, *Journal*, 11:2 (1963/64), 3–9; J.Z. Lauterbach, *Rabbinic Essays* (1951), vii–ix, xi–xii, xii–xv, 3–20 (a bibl.).

[Bernard J. Bamberger]

LAUTERPACHT, SIR HERSCH (1897–1960), British judge of the International Court of Justice and one of the outstanding international lawyers of the 20th century. Born in Zolkiew, Galicia, Lauterpacht studied in Lvov and Vienna and in London. When he came to England in 1923 he was barely able to speak English. Nevertheless, he was appointed an assistant lecturer in law at the London School of Economics in 1927 and within five years was reader in public international law in the University of London. Lauterpacht lectured at The Hague Academy of International Law in 1930, 1934, 1937, and 1947 and from 1938 to 1955 he was professor of international law at Cambridge University. From 1955 until his death Lauterpacht was a judge of the International Court of Justice at The Hague. In this post he manifested his highly individualistic approach to international law based on the premise that moral and legal principles apply to states as much as to individuals. Lauterpacht sat in only ten cases before the court, but in eight of them he gave either a dissenting or separate opinion. He did this not so much because he objected to the views of the other judges but because he wished to clarify and develop the law rather than simply state the reasons for the court's decision. His writings reflect his preoccupation with the need to adapt international law to the international community of states. They include *The Function of Law in the International Community* (1933), a principal theoretical study of the international judicial function and its place in the settlement of international disputes; *Recognition in International Law* (1947), in which Lauterpacht argued that the recognition of one state by another state was an act of law and not of policy; *International Law and Human Rights* (1950) and *The Development of International Law by the International Court* (1958). He edited L. *Oppenheim's treatise *International Law* from 1935 to 1955, the *British Year Book of International Law* from 1944 to 1955, and the *International Law Reports* for nearly 40 years. Lauterpacht never abandoned the intellectual philosophy of continental law but nevertheless became the outstanding exponent of the common law tradition in international law. Lauterpacht was the recipient of numerous awards and was knighted in 1956. He was active in Jewish affairs from his youth when he joined the Jewish defense organization in Galicia and was first president of the World Union of Jewish Students after World War I. A staunch Zionist, he spent several months in Israel shortly before his death. His son Sir ELIHU LAUTERPACHT (1928–), also a distinguished barrister and legal scholar, was reader in international law at Cambridge University (1980–88) and director of the Research Centre for International Law at Cambridge from 1983 to 1995.

BIBLIOGRAPHY: C.W. Jenks, in: *British Year Book of International Law*, 36 (1961), 1–103; G. Fitzmaurice, *ibid.*, 37 (1962), 1–71; 38 (1964), 1–83; 39 (1965), 133–88; S. Rosenne, in: *American Journal of International Law*, 55 (1961), 825–62, index. **ADD. BIBLIOGRAPHY:** ODNB online; D. Stone, "Sir Hersch Lauterpacht: Teacher, Writer, and Judge," in: JHSET, 18 (1981–82), 20–38.

[Israel Finestein]

LAUTMAN, DOV, Israeli industrialist. Lautman graduated with a B.Sc. in mechanical engineering from MIT, becoming chairman of the board and principal shareholder of Delta Galil Industries Ltd. He began his career with Sabrina Textiles Ltd., serving as director general from 1963 to 1967. In 1967 he was appointed director general of Gibor Textile Industries Ltd., a position he held until 1975, when he founded Delta Textiles Ltd. He also served as president of the Israel Manufacturers Association and as chairman of the Coordinating Bureau of Economic Organizations from 1986 to 1993. From 1993 to June 1995 he served as Prime Minister Yitzhak Rabin's special emissary for economic development. He was the executive chairman of the Peres Center for Peace and a member of the Yitzhak Rabin Center. He was also chairman of the executive council of Tel Aviv University and a member of the board of governors of Ben-Gurion University. Lautman received the Ramniceanu Prize from Tel Aviv University for his contribution to Israel's economy; the Max Perlman Award of Excellence in Global Business Management; an award from the American-Israel Chamber of Commerce and Industry for his involvement in promoting bilateral trade and investment between the two countries; and the Chaim Herzog award for his special contribution to Arab-Jewish cooperation in Israel.

[Shaked Gilboa (2nd ed.)]

°LAVAL, PIERRE (1883–1945), French politician, deputy premier and premier in Vichy France during World War II. Born in Châteldon (Puy-de-Dôme), Laval was a militant Socialist and deputy from 1914. His views became conservative, however, and he left his party in 1924 and entered the Senate. First as premier (1931–32) and then as foreign minister (1934–35), he tried to isolate Nazi Germany and concluded a Franco-Soviet friendship treaty (1934) and a Franco-Czech treaty. He refused to apply the sanctions of the League of Nations against Italy after the invasion of Ethiopia. During the German occupation of France, Laval was deputy premier under Marshal Pétain (June 1940) and promoted active collaboration of the Vichy government with the German Nazi authorities. It has not been verified whether he personally participated in the preparation and promulgation of the first "article," which discriminated against the Jews (October 1940). Laval was removed from power in December 1940, but again became premier in April 1942 and remained in this post until the liberation of France (August 1944). In June 1942 the Germans asked for the expulsion of 100,000 Jews from France. Laval agreed to the cooperation of the police on the condition that the expulsion would be limited to "foreign" Jews, which according to him were always a source of trouble for France. He added that he was not concerned with the children of these "foreign" Jews. As a result all the "foreign" Jews were deported to death camps. On the other hand, Laval successfully prevented the annulment of French citizenship of Jews who had been naturalized as French citizens from 1927. Thus he helped to prevent their deportation.

Thousands of Jews were arrested in France and deported under the Laval government and with the collaboration of its police. He was also in favor of transferring several hundred thousand French workers to Germany, as well as establishing and recruiting the "French anti-Bolshevik Legion," which fought in German uniform on the Russian front. After fleeing to Germany and then to Spain at the time of the German retreat, Laval surrendered after the liberation to the French authorities, who brought him before a high court. Condemned to death, he was executed in Paris.

BIBLIOGRAPHY: Z. Szajkowski, *Analytical Franco-Jewish Gazetteer 1939–1945* (1966), index; *France During the German Occupation*, 3 vols. (1958), passim; J. Lubetzki, *La condition des Juifs en France sous l'occupation allemande (1940–1944): La législation raciale* (1945), passim; H. Monneray, *La persécution des Juifs en France et dans les pays de l'Ouest, présentée par la France à Nuremberg* (1947), index; G. Bechtel, *Laval, vingt ans après* (1963), incl. bibl; J. Billig, in: *La France sous l'occupation* (1959), 145–60.

[Lucien Lazare]

LAVI (Heb. לָבִיא), kibbutz in eastern Lower Galilee, Israel, 8 mi. (12 km.) W. of Tiberias, affiliated with Kibbutz Dati ha-Po'el ha-Mizrachi, founded in 1949 by pioneers from Britain and North America, and later joined by immigrants from other countries. In the Israel *War of Independence (1948) a few months before the settlers' arrival, hard battles were fought over the Arab village Lūbiyā, known for its aggressiveness in the days when *Ha-Shomer encamped at *Ilaniyyah (Sejera). West of the kibbutz, at the Golani crossroads, is a monument commemorating the fallen in the decisive battle. The kibbutz economy was based on poultry, a hotel, gardening and extermination services, a farm supply company, and Lavi Furniture Industries, specializing in the manufacture of synagogue pews. In 2002 the population was 640. In the Talmud, a roadside inn, Pundeka de-Luvya (פונדקא דלוביא), is reported to have stood at the site of the now abandoned Arab village (TJ, Shekalim 7, 5–50, 73; Berakhot 7–11, 73). The name Lavi, "Lioness," is the hebraized form of the Arab "Lūbiyā."

WEBSITE: www.kibbutzlavi.co.il.

[Efraim Orni]

LAVI (Levkovitz), SHELOMO (1882–1963), agricultural pioneer in Ereẓ Israel. Born in Plonsk, Russian Poland, Lavi went to Ereẓ Israel in 1905. At first he worked as a laborer in the Jewish villages in the southern part of the country. In 1909 he moved to Galilee and later worked as a watchman in Ḥaderah and Reḥovot. He conceived the idea of the "large collective" (*kevuẓah gedolah*, later called kibbutz), which would combine agriculture, crafts, and industry and would be capable of absorbing new immigrants lacking agricultural training and experience. This system would reduce the investment necessary for establishing the settlement and would avoid the use of hired labor. In 1920 Lavi organized a group of laborers as part of *Gedud ha-Avodah to establish the first "large collective" in the Jezreel Valley. This led to the foundation in 1921 of *En-Harod and *Tel Yosef, originally one settlement, which was the first example of the kibbutz as distinguished from the kevuẓah. Two years later the Gedud ha-Avodah split: Tel Yosef became independent, while Lavi and his supporters remained in En-Harod, which they transformed into a center for similar kibbutzim based on the combination of agriculture and industry.

Lavi was a leader of *Mapai, serving on many national bodies. At the age of 60, during World War II, he volunteered for service with a Jewish unit in the British army. He wrote articles in a biting, original manner, as well as stories and ideological essays. A number of his articles were published in his *Ketavim Nivḥarim* ("Selected Writings," 1944); the history of En-Harod is outlined in his *Megillat Ein Ḥarod* (1947); and he also published an autobiographical novel entitled *Aliyyato shel Shalom Layish* (1956). He was a member of the First and Second *Knesset. Through all the years of his membership in the kibbutz he continued to work the fields and to do all kinds of manual work, undeterred by his public and literary occupations. Both his sons fell in the *War of Independence (1948). They both left writings published in *Gevilei Esh* edited by R. Avinoam (n.d.), 464–74; 583f.

BIBLIOGRAPHY: Meshek Ein Ḥarod-Iḥud, *Shelomo Lavi le-Yom ha-Sheloshim* (1963); B. Katznelson, in: S. Lavi, *Ketavim Nivḥarim* (1944), introd.; Kariv, in: *Ha-Po'el Haẓa'ir*, 51:28 (1958); D. Lazar, *Rashim be-Yisrael*, 2 (1955), 238–43; Tidhar, 6 (1955), 2548–9.

[*Encycylopaedia Hebraica*]

LAVI (Loewenstein), THEODOR (1905–1983), Romanian historian, educator, publicist, Zionist leader. Born in Turnu-Severin, he received his Ph.D. from the University of Bucharest with a thesis influenced by Sigmund Freud. He became a high-school teacher and principal and later (1942–44) taught pedagogics at a Jewish seminary. He was active in the Zionist movement from 1920. In 1923–33 he edited the publication *Hasmonea*, published by the Association of Zionist Students of Romania. In 1941 he became a member of the Zionist Executive and director of its cultural-educational section. In 1942 he became director of the Department of Schools, Culture, and Physical Education of the Jews' Central, his efforts directed toward the foundation of Jewish schools of all levels. In 1945 he was a leader of the Zionist Socialist Organization "Ichud," once again director of the cultural-educational section of the Zionist Executive of Romania, and founded its publishing house Bicurim. After the banning of Zionist activity in Romania Loewenstein was imprisoned in 1950 because of his Zionist activities. He was released five years later and went to Israel, where he continued his historical research at *Yad Vashem, and specialized in the history of Romanian Jewry during the Holocaust (*Yahadut Romanyah be-Ma'avak al Haẓẓalatah*, 1965). He wrote on history and education in a number of journals, Jewish as well as non-Jewish. His books include *S. Freud și psihoanaliza* ("S. Freud and Psychoanalysis," 1935); *Istoria sionismului* ("The History of Zionism," 1934, 1945^2); *Trumpeldor* – letters, with an introductory biography; *Herzl* (1945); and *Nu a fost pisica neagra* (memoirs, 1979). He was the *Encyclopaedia Judaica* (first edition) departmental editor on the history of Jews in Romania, editor of *Pinkas ha-Kehillot Romanyah* (1969–80), and of the bilingual Romanian-Hebrew historical review *Toladot* (1972–77). In 1971 he founded the Niemirower Institute, which later became the Center for Research of Romanian Jewry at the Hebrew University of Jerusalem.

BIBLIOGRAPHY: T. Lavi, *Nu a fost pisica neagră* (1979); E. Fleischer, "Dr. Theodor Lavi z.l.," in: *Yediyon ha-Iggud le-Madda'ei ha-Yahadut*, 23 (1984), 53–54.

[Abraham Feller / Lucian-Zeev Herşcovici (2nd ed.)]

LAVIE, RAFFI (1937–), Israeli painter. Born in Israel, Lavie was attracted as a child to the music world and wanted to become a musician. Around the age of 16 it became clear to him that he had nothing to say through music. Slowly he prepared himself to become a painter, though music remained the great love of his life. Lavie characterized himself as an autodidact, though his artistic education started in 1954 with the painter Ludwig Mos. Later he studied at the College for Art Teachers in Ramat ha-Sharon, the same institute where he would teach for a long time and through his charisma influence many young Israeli artists.

In 1965 Lavie was a central figure in the creation of the Ten Plus artists group. The purpose of the group was to achieve pluralism in the field of art. By giving all types of art a chance to be exhibited they fought against the conservative art establishment. They favored mutual cooperation while respecting the uniqueness of each of the group's members.

Lavie's style is very problematic and far from being understood. More than with any other Israeli abstract artist Lavie's art provokes anger in the observer. His Abstract-Infantile style was identified with the Israeli artistic style of the 1960s and 1970s labeled "The Want of Matter." It was typical to the native-born *sabra* in its simplicity and crudeness and in keeping with the meagerness of materials in the modern city of Tel Aviv, especially compared with Europe and its traditional art. The materials used by Lavie were plywood, pencil, acrylic, and rifts of newspaper (*Open Day*, 1983, Israel Museum, Jerusalem). Despite the Modern style a closer look at Lavie's paintings reveals a traditional assembly of subjects: landscape, seascape, still life, human figures, portraits, plants and animals, all scribbled and glued in his works.

Lavie's art produced a unique language. The observer had to learn the meanings of the signs and the method of reading them in the same way that he read the written words that Lavie integrated in his pictures. Over the years art critics recognized the symbols in Lavie's art and explained them to the public. Although the painting seems spontaneous the delicate nuances indicate complex meanings. All his symbols were influenced by the masters of Western Europe and Israel, such as Cezanne and Arie *Aroch (*Shulhan Aroch*, 2001, collection of Oli Alter, Tel Aviv).

In 2003 Lavie's art was presented at a retrospective exhibition in the Israel Museum.

BIBLIOGRAPHY: D. Ginton, "Head Birth: Portrait of Raffi as a Young Painter," in: cat. *Raffi: The Early Paintings 1957–1961*, Tel Aviv Museum (1993); S. Shapira, *Raffi Lavie – Works from 1950 to 2003*, Israel Museum, Jerusalem (2003).

[Ronit Steinberg (2nd ed.)]

LAVIN, LINDA (1937–), U.S. actress. Lavin appeared in a community production of *Alice in Wonderland* in her birthplace, Portland, Me., at the age of five and studied piano for ten years under the eye of her stage mother. She majored in theater arts at William and Mary College and then embarked on summer stock in New Jersey. She made her Off Broadway debut in a revival of *Oh, Kay* (1960) and had a succession of roles in several Broadway musicals. She earned her first Tony nomination for her role in Neil *Simon's *Last of the Red Hot Lovers* (1969). After moving to Hollywood, she appeared on the hit comedy series *Barney Miller* and then got the role of Alice the waitress in the situation comedy *Alice*, which ran from 1976 to 1985. The part in the show, loosely based on the 1975 film *Alice Doesn't Live Here Anymore*, earned her two Golden Globe awards and an Emmy nomination. In 1987, returning to the Broadway stage, she won a Tony award for *Broadway Bound*, another Simon vehicle. She earned two other Tony nominations, for her starring role in *Gypsy* and in *The Sisters Rosensweig*. As an actor, producer, and executive producer, Lavin has been involved in more than two dozen films.

[Stewart Kampel (2nd ed.)]

LAVON (Lubianiker), PINḤAS (1904–1976), Israeli labor leader and politician, member of the First to Fourth Knessets. Born in Kopychintsy in East Galicia, Lavon completed his law studies at Lvov University. At first he was active in *Ha-Shomer ha-Ẓa'ir, but in the 1920s he was one of the founders of the pioneering youth movement *Gordonia in Galicia and Poland, contributing to its ideological, educational, and political programs. In 1929 he settled in Palestine with the first Gordonia group, which established itself in kibbutz Ḥuldah, renewing the settlement that had been destroyed in the 1929 disturbances. While in Ḥuldah Lavon became active in the labor movement and in the *Histadrut. He played a leading role in transforming Ḥever ha-Kevuẓot into a well-organized federation of kibbutzim (see *Kibbutz Movement) and initiated its merger with Gordonia. He soon became the acknowledged spokesman of the new organization, and advocated the unification of the entire kibbutz movement. In 1938–39 Lavon and Yitzhak *Ben-Aharon were joint secretaries of *Mapai. In 1942 he was elected to the Histadrut Executive, and in 1949 was elected its secretary general. He was instrumental in bringing the Teachers' Union into the Histadrut and the religious workers' movements into its trade union framework. He also initiated Histadrut housing projects for workers.

Lavon was elected to the First Knesset on the Mapai list in 1949, and remained a member of the Knesset until 1961. He served as minister of agriculture in the years 1950–51. In 1951–54 he was minister without portfolio, and following Ben-

Gurion's temporary retirement in 1954–55 he served in the government of Moshe *Sharett as minister of defense. While he was minister of defense Israel's Air Force and paratroop units were upgraded, and Israel started the large-scale purchase of arms from France. Disagreements developed, however, between Sharett and Lavon over defense policy, with the prime minister complaining that he was not consulted in advance about reprisal attacks across the borders. Then came the *Essek Bish* ("the bad business"), later known as the *Lavon Affair, which resulted in Lavon's resignation from the ministry of defense and the return of David *Ben-Gurion to the government.

In 1956 Lavon was reelected secretary general of the Histadrut, remaining in that post until 1961. In this capacity he was involved in the separation of *Solel Boneh from the Koor holding company and other organizational changes. In 1961 he was removed from this post as a consequence of the struggle initiated by Ben-Gurion around the Lavon Affair. He was not included in Mapai's list for the elections to the Fifth Knesset in 1961; Lavon's supporters joined forces in a group within Mapai called Min ha-Yesod that existed for several years. Attempts in 1964 to rehabilitate Lavon, encouraged by Prime Minister Levi *Eshkol, failed due to opposition by Ben-Gurion. Lavon then retired from public life. He was considered a brilliant writer and speaker within the labor movement in Israel and, before the outbreak of the Affair, was viewed by many as a possible heir to Ben-Gurion.

He published numerous articles, which have been collected in *Yesodot* (1941), *Arakhim u-Temurot* (1959), *Ba-Vikku'aḥ ha-Medini* (1945), *Bi-Netivei Iyyun u-Ma'avak* (1968), and *Al Arakhim u-Nekhasim* (ed. A. Maniv, 1986).

BIBLIOGRAPHY: A. Avnon (ed.), *Pinhas Lavon: li-Demutoh* (1978); N. Rotenstreich, *Bein Ekronot le-Nivvut: Al Maḥshavto ha-Ḥevratit shel Pinḥas Lavon* (1979); S. Horev, *Hashkafat Olamo ha-Ẓiyyonit-Sozialistit shel Pinḥas Lavon* (1986); E. Kafkafi, *Lavon: Anti-Mashi'aḥ* (1998). (For bibliography on the Lavon Affair, see *Lavon Affair.)

[Susan Hattis Rolef (2nd ed.)]

LAVON AFFAIR, THE. The "Lavon Affair" began with a security mishap, which was at first referred to as the "*esek bish*" ("the bad business"). At the beginning of July 1954, an Israel-initiated intelligence operation in *Egypt, involving a plan to plant bombs in several movie houses, post offices, and the American Cultural Centers in Cairo and Alexandria, which was intended to sabotage negotiations between Egypt and Great Britain regarding the British withdrawal from the Suez Canal, failed. Eleven Egyptian Jews, who had served as Israeli agents, were caught and tried in Cairo. In January 1955 two of them were sentenced to death and executed, two were released for lack of evidence, and the rest received sentences of seven years to life imprisonment, and this despite a reported promise by Egyptian President Gamal Abdel Nasser that the sentences would not be heavy. Israel refused to officially admit any connection to the botched operation and, consequently, did nothing to assist the 11, believing that they would receive light sentences (see *Marzouk, Moshe). The main question raised at the time in Israel was whether it had been Minister of Defense Pinhas *Lavon, or the officer in charge of Intelligence Operations – Colonel Binyamin Givli – who had given the order to carry out the ill-conceived operation, of which Prime Minister Moshe *Sharett had not been informed. To the present day there is no clear answer to this question. But what is clear is that for nearly a decade Israeli politics were deeply affected by the affair's ramifications, especially since David *Ben-Gurion, who had been in semi-retirement in Sedeh Boker when it occurred, would not let it die. The then-chief of staff, Moshe *Dayan, claimed that it had been Lavon who had given the order, but others argued otherwise.

Soon after the trials in Egypt, a committee made up of Supreme Court Justice Isaac *Olshan and Israel's first chief of staff, Ya'akov *Dori, was appointed by Sharett to investigate the matter but was unable to reach any clear-cut conclusions. Nevertheless, Lavon was forced to resign as minister of defense, and David Ben-Gurion assumed the post under Sharett on February 21, 1955. Binyamin Givli was removed from Intelligence Operations.

In 1957 an investigation began against an Israeli spy who had been in charge of the network in Egypt, on charges that had little to do with the Egyptian operation. At the time he was referred to as "the third man," who was later revealed to be Avri Elad. In the course of his secret trial, the full details of which are still unpublished, Elad admitted to having committed perjury and giving false information to the Olshan-Dori Committee at Givli's behest. Further evidence about the forging of a key document was given by Givli's secretary at the time, Dalia Carmel, who had played an active role in the forgery. In August 1960 Elad was sentenced to 12 years' imprisonment on charges of illegally holding secret documents.

In 1958 a secret committee of inquiry was set up by the IDF to look into all the evidence, but even though it established that documents had been forged and perjury had been committed, no measures were taken against those involved. In May 1960, Lavon spoke to David Ben-Gurion, who asked his aide-de-camp to look into the matter, and the latter returned with the same information: that indeed documents had been forged. A committee, headed by Supreme Court Justice Haim *Cohn was appointed in September 1960, on Ben-Gurion's orders, to inquire into the allegations against Givli. The Cohn Committee Report, published in part on October 23, 1960, resulted in Givli's resignation from active military service. The attorney general, Gideon *Hausner, recommended that an investigation take place to determine whether anyone should be put on trial, but the Mapai leadership was not interested in a trial. Though the press at the time was full of partial information regarding the affair, most of the actors remained unnamed, except for Lavon himself.

Lavon felt that the Committee's Report exonerated him from the suspicions that it was he who had given the order, but Ben-Gurion refused to clear his name, convinced that Lavon was lying. Lavon was not, however, short of supporters.

These included Golda *Meir, Pinḥas *Sapir, Zalman *Aranne, and Mordekhai *Namir, while Sharett, even though he was not close to Lavon, actually announced that the Cohn Committee Report had exonerated him.

Ben-Gurion convinced Givli to demand of the chief of staff, Ḥayyim *Laskov, that a judicial committee of inquiry be established to investigate the responsibility for what had happened in Egypt, and Lavon insisted that the issue be raised in the Knesset Foreign Affairs and Defense Committee. Contrary to Ben-Gurion's wishes the government decided on October 30, upon a proposal by Minister of Justice Pinḥas *Rosen, and with the concurrence of Minister of Finance Levi *Eshkol, to set up yet another committee, made up of seven ministers, headed by Rosen, to review the issue. Though the committee heard witnesses, it did not have the power to subpoena any. In his testimony before the committee, Lavon alleged that at the time of the Olshan-Dori inquiry officials in the Ministry of Defense had conspired against him, and accused Shimon *Peres, who had been director general of the ministry, of disloyalty. Representatives of the committee were also sent abroad to interview Dalia Carmel, about the forgery of the document, and Major General (Res) Yehoshafat Harkabi, who had replaced Givli in Intelligence Operations. The committee reached the unanimous conclusion that Lavon had not given the order and recommended that the matter be closed. The committee's report was endorsed by the government on December 25. However, Ben-Gurion himself refused to accept the report, and now demanded himself that the matter be reviewed by a judicial body, which unlike the ministerial committee headed by Rosen, would have the right to subpoena witnesses. Though a motion on a proposal of no-confidence brought in the Knesset by the opposition on January 30, 1961, was defeated, Ben-Gurion was severely criticized for his attitude. The following day he submitted his resignation, and his government continued to serve as an interim government until new elections were held for the Fifth Knesset in August 1961.

Ben-Gurion now seemed set on a personal vendetta against Lavon, and even though a group of prominent intellectuals, including Martin *Buber, Prof. Hugo *Bergman, and Prof. Nathan *Rotenstreich, came out openly against what they considered his anti-democratic conduct, in February 1961 he managed to get the Mapai Central Committee to decide to dismiss Lavon from his position as secretary general of the Histadrut – a position he had been reelected to in 1956. Among those who objected to the dismissal was Sharett, who declared that "it is not honor and justice that are our guiding light, but fear and the settling of accounts." However, criticism of Ben-Gurion mounted, and even though he formed a new government in November 1961, in June 1963 he resigned the premiership for the last time, and upon his recommendation Levi Eshkol was appointed prime minister. Eshkol's inclination was to finally close the Lavon Affair that had bedeviled Mapai for close to a decade. Nevertheless, in October 1964 Ben-Gurion made one more effort to rekindle the issue, and submitted a file full of documents on the Lavon Affair to Minister of Justice Dov *Joseph, and to Attorney General Moshe Ben-Ze'ev. Ben-Gurion claimed that the Rosen Ministerial Committee had been faulty, and yet again demanded that a judicial inquiry be held on its proceedings. Joseph rejected the idea of a judicial inquiry, but recommended that a comprehensive official inquiry be held into the Lavon Affair. Eshkol rejected the recommendation, and after meeting with boisterous opposition from Ben-Gurion's supporters in the Mapai Central Committee, submitted his resignation, demanding that a new government be formed with unfettered discretion to decide the matter without party interference. Eshkol formed a new government in December 1964, and in 1965, Ben-Gurion with seven of his supporters left Mapai, and formed their own parliamentary group – *Rafi.

In the aftermath of the Six-Day War Israel could have demanded the release of those of the agents who were still imprisoned in Egypt but refrained from doing so. It was only the following year, in 1968, that the remaining prisoners were released.

BIBLIOGRAPHY: S. Teveth, *Ben-Gurion's Spy: The Story of the Political Scandal that Shaped Modern Israel* (1996); E. Hassin and D. Horowitz, *Ha-Parashah* (1961); D. Ben-Gurion, *Devarim ka-Havayatam* (1965); J. Arieli, *Ha-Kenunyah* (1966); N. Yanai, *Kerah ba-Ẓameret: Ha-Mashber she-Zi'az'a et Mapai ve-Hevi le-Hakamat Rafi* (1969); A. Elad, *Ha-Adam ha-Shelishi* (1976); H. Eshed, *Mi Natan et Hahora'ah: "Esek ha-Bish," Parashat Lavon ve-Hitpatterut Ben-Gurion* (1979); I. Harel, *Anatomyah shel Begidah: "Ha-Adam ha-Shelishi" ve-ha-Mapolet be-Miẓrayim* (1980); idem, *Kam Ish al Aḥiv: Ha-Nittu'aḥ ha-Musmakh ve-ha-Memaẓeh shel "Parashat Lavon"* (1982); R. Dasa, *Be-Ḥazarah le-Kahir* (1992); Y. Harkabi, *Edut Ishit – "Ha-Parashah" mi-Nekudat Re'uti* (1994); E. Kafkafi, *Lavon – Anti Mashi'aḥ* (1998); S. Aronson, *David Ben-Gurion – Manhig ha-Renasans she-Shaka* (1999).

[Susan Hattis Rolef (2nd ed.)]

LAVRY, MARC (1903–1967), composer and conductor. Born in Riga, Lavry studied at Oldenberg and at the Leipzig Conservatory and worked as conductor in Riga, Saarbruecken, and Berlin, where he was associated with the Laban dance ensemble and the Universal film studio. He settled in Palestine in 1935 and conducted at the Opera Amamit and the Palestine Broadcasting Service. In 1949 he became director of the music section of Kol Zion la-Golah (the World Zionist Organization's broadcasts to the Diaspora), for which he established a permanent choir. In 1962 he settled in Haifa, where he continued his musical activities under the sponsorship of the municipality.

Lavry's many compositions – his last work bears the opus number 349 – represented a style and ideology basically identical with the Mediterranean period of Israel music. Their melodic foundation is compounded of east Ashkenazi and Near Eastern elements, as well as the new folksong of Ereẓ Israel, which Lavry both drew upon and helped to form. His best-known work, the symphonic poem *Emek* (1937), was based on his song for choir and orchestra, with the same name, to a poem by Raphael Eliaz, written about one year earlier. His song *Ḥanita* for choir and orchestra had originally been a part of *Dan ha-Shomer* ("Dan the Guard," 1945, libretto by Sh. *Shalom and Max *Brod) which was the first Israel opera. Other important works were *Shir ha-Shirim* ("Song of Songs"), oratorio; *Avodat ha-Kodesh*, a Sabbath liturgy written for Temple Emanu-El of San Francisco; the songs for choir and orchestra *Kinneret, Kittatenu ba-Laylah Ẓo'edet* ("Our Platoon Marches in the Night"), and *Ẓe'ad Shimshon* ("March Forward, Samson"); two piano concertos; the opera *Tamar* (text by Louis Newman); *Gideon* (text by Ḥaim *Hefer); two symphonies ("Warsaw Ghetto" and "1949"); a symphonic poem *Stalingrad* (first performed in Moscow in 1943); and the orchestral suite *Israeli Dances*.

BIBLIOGRAPHY: M. Lavry, in: *Tazlil*, 8 (1968), 74–77 (autobiography); H. Lavry, *ibid.*, 9 (1969), 174–5; P.E. Gradenwitz, *Music and Musicians in Israel* (1959²), 89–90.

[Bathja Bayer]

LAW AND MORALITY.

In the Bible

In the Pentateuch, legal and moral norms are not distinguished by any definitional criteria. The manner of presentation of both is via revelation – moral norms are not presented as wisdom but rather as prophetic revelation. Thus the two remain indistinguishable as to authority. The basis of adherence to the system as a whole is the fact that it constitutes divine command. Even in the form of presentation, no distinction is made between the two types. The apodictic form, for example, is used both for the prohibition on murder (Ex. 20:13) and the command to love one's neighbor (Lev. 19:18). On the critical issue of enforcement, no textual distinction exists on which to base enforced and nonenforced forms or between humanly enforced and divinely enforced ones. The premise of the pentateuchal code is that no propounded norm of human behavior is either optional or lacking in enforcement. Indeed the sanction system is one in which human punishment and divine retribution function as equal components of a single scheme.

This single corpus of legal-moral behavioral norms was distinct from ancient Near-Eastern legal-moral systems in a number of significant respects. First, the very unity of morality and law in the Pentateuch created a new basis of authority for the behavioral precepts of Hebrew civilization. Secondly, in the Torah individualistic morality gave way to national morality which was addressed to the people of Israel as a corporate moral entity. Thus the national entity was made party to the maintenance of the mandated standards of behavior and could be held responsible for the breach of such norms by individual citizens. Thirdly, despite the exclusivity of the covenantal relationship between God and the Jewish people, God's role in the enforcement of legal-moral behavioral norms is clearly pictured as universal. Thus Cain, the generation of the flood, Sodom, the seven Canaanite nations, and others, are all pictured as subjects of divine retribution for illegal-immoral behavior though they were not parties to the covenant.

In the prophetic literature, no new realm of purely moral concern was created. The breaches of social morality which play such a prominent part in the prophetic critique of the Jewish people were all premised on the identical legal-moral behavioral norms. The "immorality" of the people was in reality their "illegal" behavior. The major shift which distinguishes the literary prophets from their predecessors was that the notion of corporate legal-moral responsibility was given a vital new component. In the Pentateuch, national doom was threatened for cultic sins in particular and for neglect of the divine commandments in general. The prophets introduced the notion that the most decisive factor in the corporate fate of the nation was that aspect of mandated legal-moral behavioral norms which encompassed social relations. Thus when Amos threatens national doom and exile, he speaks of the sins of the normal life context, of social, economic, and political behavior, but maintains complete silence with regard to the sin of idolatry. In Isaiah and Micah too, the threat of national destruction is created by social corruption – the violation of the legal-ethical behavioral norms of everyday life. Failure to observe the divine command results in the corporate punishment of the nation whether the sin is cultic or legal-moral in nature.

The Talmudic Period

There was not yet any development of a specific moral order as distinct from the legal system in the talmudic period. However, it is already clearly recognized in tannaitic literature that legal sanctions could not enforce every form of behavior which was morally desirable. Indeed the Mishnah and Tosefta make occasional references to situations where, despite justification, one party lacks any legal recourse against the other and "… he has nothing but resentment [*taromet*] against him" (e.g., BM 4:6, 6:1; Tosef., Git. 3:1; BM 4:22). This recognition of a gap between sanctionable behavior and behavior which though desirable is not enforceable produced three types of relationships between the two realms: morality as a direct source of law; morality as a source of private, higher standards of legal liability; and morality in legal form.

MORALITY AS A DIRECT SOURCE OF LAW. The tannaitic period was particularly rich in social legislation motivated by the desire to expand the scope of enforcement to encompass as broad as possible a range of morally desirable behavior. Two terms in particular were often used to indicate the presence of a moral interest as the basis for tannaitic legislation:

(1) "In the interest of peace" (*mi-penei darkhei shalom*). This term is a composite, indicating that the legislative purpose of the statute is the prevention of communal conflict which would result from some immoral practice not otherwise limited by law. The specific forms of immoral behavior viewed by the *tannaim* as likely to produce communal conflict included unequal distribution of religious honors, threat to the good reputation of a group or an individual, taking by force

where property rights are uncertain, unearned benefit from the labor or initiative of another, and the exclusion of groups from societal privileges and responsibilities. In all of these instances, the methods used to avoid the conflict were either to legalize a status quo which was both orderly and fair, or to extend legal rights to situations or persons otherwise excluded (e.g. Git. 5:8–9; Tosef., Pe'ah 3:1; Ḥul. 10:13; Git. 5 (3):4–5).

(2) "For the benefit of society" (*mi-penei tikkun ha-olam*). This tannaitic term is also a composite, reflecting the presence of a moral interest being translated into an enforceable legal norm. The Mishnah (Git. 4:3–5:3) contains an entire codex of such statutes. The unique character of the situations governed "for the benefit of society" is that the moral interest involved, while produced by an existing or incipient legal relationship, affects primarily persons outside the relationship itself. The legislation affecting that relationship is thus primarily designed to have general communal benefit. Some of the moral interests dealt with in this type of legislation are the prevention of *bastardy and of abandoned wives (see *Agunah*), the deterrence of *theft and of non-punishable injurious behavior, the encouragement of lending and of returning lost property, the encouragement of care for *orphans and destitute children, and the encouragement of public service in the area of law and medicine (e.g., Git. 4:2–5:3; 9:4; Tosef., Ter. 1:12–13; Git. 4(3):5–7; 8(6):9).

The *amoraim* did not themselves use *darkhei shalom* or *tikkun ha-olam* as bases for further translation of morality into law. However, their awareness that in tannaitic legislation morality was being used as a source of law is clearly indicated through their use of the notion of the prevention of hostility (*mi-shum eivah*) as a legislative end. While no legislation in tannaitic literature is described as having been designed to prevent hostility, the *amoraim* often ascribe that very purpose to tannaitic legislation. Thus tannaitic legislation giving a *husband the right to his wife's earnings is viewed by the *amoraim* as motivated by the desire to prevent ill-feeling or hostility (*eivah*) between them (Ket. 58b). The source of the ill-feeling would be the inequality resulting from the husband's being obliged to support his wife without being entitled to ownership of whatever she earns. This recognition that legislation based on the tendency of ill-feeling to undermine an existing relationship was an attempt to cure legislatively the underlying inequality led the *amoraim* to limit the application of the statute to those situations where its motivating moral interest was relevant. Thus where the marital relationship is in any case about to be terminated, ill-feeling may be a matter of indifference (BM 12b), and further, where the relationship must be terminated by law, ill-feelings between the parties may actually be functional (Yev. 90b) and therefore the law designed to prevent such hostility is inapplicable.

The role of morality as a source of law continued into the legal work of the *amoraim* themselves, although it shifted from the realm of legislation to that of juridical interpretation. Two standards of moral behavior, one positive and one negative, predominate in this amoraic process:

(1) "And thou shalt do that which is right and good" (Deut. 6:18; *ve-asita ha-yashar ve-ha-tov*). Two amoraic laws are based on this verse:

(a) Property taken by a creditor in payment of a debt may be redeemed at any time (i.e., absence of injury to the creditor; BM 35a; see *Execution, Civil); and

(b) Right of an abutting property owner to first purchase is preserved despite sale of the property (i.e., absence of injury to the original owner; BM 108a; see *Maẓranut*). In both cases doing the "right and good" involves the restoration of a legal right which a person had lost through no fault of his own.

(2) "Her ways are ways of pleasantness" (Prov. 3:17; *darkhei no'am*). The fact that "pleasantness" was viewed as a basic characteristic of biblical law dictated to the *amoraim* the rejection of any juridical interpretation which could lead to the establishment of a law that could cause either the loss of personal dignity or injury to a marital relationship (e.g., Suk. 32b; Yev. 15a). The principle, however, operated in a negative fashion only, to preclude any particular juridical alternative which contravened the moral qualities of "pleasantness" (see also *Takkanot*).

MORALITY AS A SOURCE OF PRIVATE, HIGHER STANDARDS OF LEGAL LIABILITY. There are occasions which arise in any legal system where, despite the existence of a law prohibiting certain action, the hands of the court are tied because of evidentiary or procedural principles. The absence of enforcement in such instances, while producing an inequity in that particular case, could only be remedied by the abandonment of a principle which on balance is of value to the legal system. In the attempt to minimize such injustice, the *tannaim*, and subsequently the *amoraim* also, attempted to use the threat of divine retribution as a means of inducing the wrongdoer to remedy the injury of his own free choice, rejecting the exemption which the system allows him (see *Divine Punishment). It was in this specific context that the rabbis often asserted that while the defendant was "exempt by human law, he is liable by divine law" (*ḥayyav be-dinei shamayim*; e.g., BK 6:4. An entire codex of such situations where "his case is passed on for divine judgment" is found in Tosef., BK 6:16–17). A similar case of moral pressure being brought to bear to emphasize the need for voluntary rectification where the judiciary is unable to act is reflected in the phrase "the sages are greatly pleased with him" (*ru'aḥ ḥakhamin noḥah heimenno*; e.g., Shev. 10:9. For the reverse formulation, see BB 8:5). The moral pressure for this type of behavior led the *amoraim* to use similar formulations to urge self-judgment even in cases where the initial liability itself was in doubt (BM 37a; see *Extraordinary Remedies). In such cases the *amoraim* suggest that a man assume liability upon himself if "he wishes to fulfill his duty in the sight of heaven."

Two uniquely amoraic devices supplement the above as moral means of urging an individual to accept higher standards of civil liability where he has indeed been the cause of injury to another. Both are literary legal fictions in that they attempt to explain tannaitic statements or actions which in reality might have been based on completely different reasons.

(a) Pious behavior (*middat ḥasidut*). Each time that the *amora* Rav Ḥisda suggests that a particular tannaitic statement constituted a suggestion of especially righteous behavior it is part of an attempt to resolve an inner contradiction in a Mishnah (e.g., BM 52b; Shab. 120a; Ḥul. 130b). While the Talmud on one occasion rejects R. Ḥisda's suggestion for some alternative resolution (Shab. 120a), the device itself, and its frequent acceptance by the *amoraim*, gives recognition to their use of moral persuasion to encourage private adoption of the highest possible standards of civil liability. Indeed R. Ḥisda may well have been pointing out a more general phenomenon, that of recording dissenting opinions in the Mishnah in order that such higher standards remain as a personal option.

(b) Beyond the limit of the law (*li-fenim mi-shurat ha-din*). This device too, emerging from the school of Rav, is used consistently to resolve the disparity between existing law and the behavior of some earlier scholar (e.g., BK 99b; BM 30b; Ket. 97a; Ber. 45b). While it may be the case that in each instance the scholar behaved in full accord with the law of his own time, the exemption from liability not yet having become applicable, the significance of the amoraic suggestion lies in its openness to the acceptance and desirability of such private assumption of higher standards of legal liability. Indeed, by eradicating the time difference between the existing law and earlier behavior, the *amoraim* in effect maintain the viability of the entire history of legal development as a source of rules devised to produce the result most morally desirable in any particular case. While in their talmudic usage none of these devices leads to enforceable law, many *rishonim* and *aḥaronim* insist on the partial or total enforceability of a good number of the laws denominated as *dinei shamayim, middat ḥasidut*, and *li-fenim mi-shurat ha-din* (e.g., *Rema* ḤM 12:2; PDRS: 132–153, 151). Thus, while formal legislation was basically absent and no admission would be made that juridical interpretation really involved the creation of new law, such reinterpretations to create higher standards of enforceability were in fact part of the continuity of the process of the use of morality as a source of new law. In this way the use of morality to create private, higher standards of liability has often led to the eventual adoption of those new standards as law for everyone.

MORALITY IN LEGAL FORM. The impact of morality on Jewish law has been felt in a third way, as a result of rabbinic formulation of moral principles in legal form. The unwillingness of the rabbinic mind to accept seriously any substantial gap between the two realms is evidenced by the gradual assimilation into the realm of law, of forms of behavior which were not initially enforceable but were formulated in the terminology of illegal behavior. The two prime categories in this pattern are where immoral behavior is compared to illegal action and where the seriousness of the behavior is indicated by a disproportionate penalty.

(1) "As if …" (*ke-illu*). The term *ke-illu*, in its legal usage (like *na'asah ke*), usually introduces a legal fiction (BM 34a; Yev. 13:3). In its usage in the process of grading the moral significance of behavior it creates fictional analogies to legal or illegal behavior. Thus a person who conducts himself with humility is as one who offers all the sacrifices (Sot. 5b), while one who honors an evil person is as one who worships idols (Tosef., Av. Zar. 6(7):16). In tannaitic usage, this device is used almost exclusively to encourage behavior which is not legally mandatory (except where it is used in exegesis in the form, "Scripture considers him as if …"; e.g., Sanh. 4:5). In such instances, the weight of the divine legal prohibition is used to bolster moral pronouncements which otherwise lack any authority. The fact that *amoraim* began to extend this comparative device to add the weight of divine law to the authority of rabbinic law (e.g., Ber. 35a) introduced the possibility that the first half of the formula was not merely unenforceable moral teaching, but was itself legally binding in its own right. It was then only a short step to the frequent conclusions of *rishonim* that behavior which is compared to illegal action must itself be illicit (e.g., Sot. 3:4; cf. Yad, Talmud Torah 1:13).

(2) Disproportionate penalty, such as "liable to the death penalty" (*ḥayyav mitah*). While the Bible lays down the penalty of death at the hands of the court for a variety of crimes, the *tannaim* had already begun using the ascription of the death penalty to crimes for which clearly no court would prescribe such punishment. This exaggerated penalty was an effective way of communicating rabbinic feelings about the enormity of misbehavior. The *amoraim* made extensive use of this device to indicate their indignation at immoral behavior. Thus, in a passage which makes manifestly clear that it is aimed at emphasis rather than true legal liability, the Talmud says, "A mourner who does not let his hair grow long and does not rend his clothes is liable to death" (MK 24a). Similarly the rabbis asserted that, "Any scholar upon whose garment a [grease] stain is found is liable to death" (Shab. 114a). Again, however, the very use of legal terminology in formulating the moral position led to the conclusion that the behavior so described was indeed legally prohibited, and it was therefore often considered as this by the *rishonim* (cf. instances in Sanh. 58b, 59a, and codes). Thus in the constant growth of the scope of the law the morality of one generation frequently became the law of the next.

[Saul Berman]

Moral Sanctions of Legally Negative Acts

In addition to the three categories mentioned above, there is a fourth category that regulates the interaction of law and morality in Jewish Law. In these cases the sanction for an action is only a moral sanction. The common context for such sanctions is the exploitation of a legal loophole for benefit, while damaging the interests of others. The legal system disapproves of such acts, but does not view them as sufficiently reprehensible to warrant punishment for their commission. However, although the perpetrator of such acts is called "wicked," the halakhic sanction does not involve financial loss nor corporal punishment. Hence the perpetrator of certain acts is called "wicked," and other acts cause their perpetrator to be subjected to the imprecation of "He who punished."

"HE IS CALLED WICKED." The laws of succession present an example of an act, which when committed causes the perpetrator "to be called wicked." The case concerns a person who bequeathed his estate to an heir, stipulating that upon his [the heir's] demise, the estate would devolve to a second heir. The *tannaim* disputed the nature of the rule of succession and how it would apply if the first heir sold the estate, thus defying the testator's wishes. R. Judah ha-Nasi ruled that after the first heir dies, the second heir would be entitled to reclaim the property from the person who bought it from the first heir. R. Simeon b. Gamaliel however claims that, "The second [may] receive only what the first had left" and if he did not leave anything, then the second heir would be left empty handed (BB 137a). The *halakhah* was established in accordance with the latter opinion (Yad, Zekhiyyah u-Matanah 12:3–5; Sh. Ar. ḤM 248:1). The sages expressed their disapproval of the person who counseled the first one to defy the testator's stipulation and sell the assets, for by so doing he was frustrating the testator's wish, which was that the second person too would benefit from his assets, when the time came, "And Abbaye said: 'Who is a cunning rogue? One who counsels another to sell an estate in accordance with Rabban Simeon b. Gamaliel'" (BB, *ibid.*). The Rashbam (*ibid.*) explains that such a person is referred to as "cunning" because his acts are legally valid, but by exploiting the legal loophole left by the testator who allowed the first heir to sell the assets, he commits a sin with property not lawfully his, and the result frustrates the original intention of the testator.

In the *Moston* case (CA 749/82 *Moston v. Widerman* 43 (1) PD 278, per Justice Elon) the Supreme Court was required to interpret the Succession Law, 1965. The Court also dealt with relation of law and morality in that context, and wrote the following:

> Incidentally, the issue at hand also exemplifies the approach of Jewish Law to the relationship between law and morality...a distinctive characteristic of Jewish Law is that on the one hand there is a clear distinction between *legal* norms, which give rise to legal obligations, and *moral* norms, which do not create legal obligations. On the other hand, however, both in terms of determining the legal principles and the judge's concrete ruling, discussion and reference are made to the existence or non-existence of the *moral* obligation as well as to the existence or non-existence of a *legal* obligation. In another context, we related inter alia to the reasons for this phenomenon in Jewish Law (see Bibliography, Elon, 1988, 126–28).
>
> ... Just as the Written Law (i.e., the Torah) commands the individual and the public to fulfill the commandments that are clearly legal in character, similarly and just as categorically does the law command the performance of moral and ethical precepts ... This basic phenomenon, of course, does not eliminate the distinction between law and morals ... [T]hus the *halakhah* carefully distinguishes between normative rules that involve court enforced sanctions and precepts not enforced by such sanctions. However, the fact that legal norms and moral imperatives have a common source in the halakhic system has an important consequence: The legal system, as a legal system, from time to time invokes the moral imperative, even though it does not enforce it. The court does not refuse to decide a case, even when the decision cannot be enforced. The author of legal responsa or halakhic decisions, as well as the court all include the relevant moral imperatives, as an integral part of their discussion: "it is apparent from the Talmud that is incumbent on a judge to declare what is proper conduct even when such conduct is not required by strict law, making it clear that nonetheless good and upright people will act in that manner. The litigant [to whom the declaration is addressed] may then conform [to the guidance so given] but if he does not, no sanction is taken against him [by the court]" (*Arukh Hashulkhan*, ḤM 304.11) (*ibid.*, 291–92 of the decision).

Later in the judgment, the Court cites the dispute between halakhic authorities whether despite the fact that the seller himself would not be called evil for selling the assets, the person who persuaded the heir to sell his inheritance, is considered "wicked" because of his "meddling in strife not his own (sowing ferment in someone else's dispute)" (Prov. 26:17). Alternatively, perhaps the seller is also a rogue. The Rashbam (BB 137a) ruled that the expression "wicked" is not applicable to the seller, yet the Meiri (*Bet ha-Beḥirah,* BB 137a) ruled otherwise. Both agree however that *a priori* it is forbidden to give such counsel; but that having done so and despite its being morally tainted, the deal is valid. In its concluding comments the Court states:

> This is a highly informative example of a dispute and detailed discussion between halakhic authorities over the existence or non-existence of a moral defect in conduct related to the performance of a legal transaction, despite their agreement on the validity of the transaction itself (*ibid.*, 293).

The moral sanction of being considered "wicked" in halakhic literature is also applied to various acts of commercial competition. According to the Talmudic rule, when a poor man is sifting through left-over bread and another needy person comes and takes it for himself, the latter is called "wicked" (Kid. 59a). The Talmud cites this principle in the context of "competition" between two potential buyers vying for the same item. When a person is about to purchase an item from a seller, and another person precedes him and buys the item (hereinafter, "an interloper"), the latter is [also] called "wicked." In the post-talmudic period, the legal significance of considering the interloper as "wicked" was expanded from being exclusively moral to bearing practical ramifications. Admittedly, if the transaction between the seller and the interloper has been completed, the would-be purchaser cannot reclaim the item from the interloper (Ritba, Kid. 59a; Resp. Maharik, 132). However, before the transaction has been completed, the interloper could be prevented from purchasing the said item (Resp. Maharshadam, ḤM 259). Furthermore, according to Rabbenu Tam (cited in Ritba), even when the transaction has been completed, the item can be confiscated from the interloper. The moral sanction of being considered "wicked" received another practical application during the period of the *aḥaronim*, when it was decided to publicly, in the synagogue, renounce the interloper as "wicked" (*Haggahot Maimuniyyot*, Hil. Ḥovel 5:1; *Perisha*, ḤM 237).

THE IMPRECATION: "HE WHO PUNISHED" (MI SHE-PARA). Another expression of moral sanction appearing in tannaitic literature is directed at the person who withdraws from a transaction, prior to its legal consummation, but after the consideration had already been given: "if he has already paid, but has not taken possession of his produce, he can withdraw [the offer], but they [the Sages] said: He who punished the generation of the flood and the generation of the dispersion, He will take vengeance of him who does not stand by his word" (BM 4:2). The *amoraim* added that this is a moral sanction with a certain measure of practical significance (BM 48b); namely – that the *bet din* would inform the litigant that he was liable under divine law. Their dispute related to the particular method of informing the litigant of this liability.

OTHER SANCTIONS NO LONGER OPERATIVE IN CONTEMPORARY TIMES. An additional phenomenon in the category of legally reprehensible acts with only a moral sanction has its origins in the codification of Jewish Law and in the works of the halakhic decisors. One of the principles adopted by the authors of the post-Maimonides halakhic codes, *Sefer ha-Turim* of R. Jacob b. Asher, and Shulḥan Arukh of R. Joseph Caro, was the omission of halakhic rules that are no longer operative. For example, these works do not cite the biblical law of the accidental murderer who is exiled to a city of refuge (see *City of Refuge). Even so, these codes, to apprise us of the doctor's responsibility, cite the law pertaining to a doctor who is inadvertently responsible for a person's death, informed of his mistake, and sent to a city of refuge (Tur, YD 336; Sh. Ar., YD 336:1). The ruling has no practical implication and does not give rise to any halakhic-legal sanction; its purpose is to underscore the doctor's moral obligation, and to subject him to moral sanctions in cases in which he has made mistakes. Notably, this point was made by the Supreme Court in the Shefer case (CA 506/88 *Shefer v. State of Israel*, 48 (1) 87, 113, per Justice Elon) and the discussion of the principles that should guide doctors in their work.

Turning a Moral Sanction into a Practical Sanction – The Role of the *Bet Din*

Jewish law recognizes cases in which the *bet din* does not impose a practical sanction on the litigant, but rather, informs the party of his moral or religious duty. A striking example is in cases of divorce (see *Divorce). Although the *bet din* frequently rules that giving the *get* to the wife constitutes the fulfillment of a positive precept (*mitzvah*), it refrains from compelling the husband to do so. Hence, Rabbeinu Jonah (Spain, 13th century) ruled that "[even though] we do not coerce the husband by way of whipping him, as a means of compelling him to give his wife a *get*, when she says "I find him repulsive," the *bet din* informs and advises him that it is a *mitzvah* for him to divorce her (*Shitah Mekubeẓẓet*, Ket. 54a). At a later period, R. Bezalel Ashkenazi (Egypt, 16th century) stated in the name of his rabbi, the Radbaz, that once the *bet din* has informed the man of the *mitzvah* to divorce his wife, if he fails to divorce her he is regarded a "criminal" (*Shitah Mekubeẓẓet*, *ibid.*).

These comments were cited by the Israeli Supreme Court in HC 644/79 *Guttman v. The Rabbinical Court*, 34 (1) PD 443, per Justice Menachem Elon. In that case the Rabbinical Court ruled that "it was desirable" for the husband to give his wife a *get*, but did not compel him to give the *get*. The appellant's claim was that since the Rabbinical Court had the power to adjudicate matters concerning the spousal property only after having given a ruling ordering their divorce, in this case, in which the Rabbinical Court had only ruled that "it was desirable" for the husband to give a *get*, it did not (yet) have jurisdiction over property matters. The Supreme Court rejected this claim, clarifying that in Jewish Law, the system by which the rabbinical court adjudicates, a decision consisting of a "moral" declaration is a decision for all intents and purposes, and the Rabbinical Court's notifying the litigant of his moral obligation is a sanction in the full sense of the term; thus, "this distinction between the legal force and religious or moral force, in the context of a divorce judgment of the rabbinical court, is unacceptable. The criterion for determining what is and what is not included in 'a decision of divorce' must comply with the criterion of the judicial system to which the legislator conferred jurisdiction in the matter of the divorce, in this case, Jewish Law. The underlying principle in Jewish Law governing the distinction between law and morality or religion differs from the parallel distinction accepted in other legal systems.... This kind of ruling in which the rabbinical court rules that it is a *mitzvah* for the parties to divorce is almost a daily occurrence in rabbinical courts, and has long been accepted in Jewish Law ..." (p. 447, of the decision).

Similarly, from the aforementioned comments regarding the imposition of moral sanctions for acts of which the law takes a negative view, it appears that the Sages upgraded the force of the "moral sanction." While the original intention was that the force of such a moral sanction extended no further than the book itself, obligating the person exclusively in terms of his conscience and God, the sages of recent generations tended to confer practical significance to these sanctions. This explains the case of "the poor man sifting through left-over bread," and the legal prohibition to attempt to precede him, and when someone (referred to as an "interloper") precedes him and takes the item, a declaration made in synagogue condemns him as "wicked." The same rule applies to a worker who accidentally damages his employer's property. According to the *Arukh ha-Shulḥan*, the *bet din* should notify his employer of his duty to "follow the way of the good," waive the worker's payment of the damage, and continuing payment of his wage. The same applies to the rule of "fulfillment of duty in the sight of Heaven," regarding which it was ruled that the *bet din* should notify the litigant of his obligation to fulfill his duty in the sight of Heaven even though the *bet din* is unable to force him to pay (R. Solomon Luria, Poland, BB 6:6) and according to another view he is even disqualified as a witness until he has paid, because in effect he is in possession of stolen money (Meiri, BM 56a). This is also the rule regarding the principle of *li-fenim mi-shurat ha-din* (acting more generously than legally required), which in particular circumstances in later generations the *bet din* decided not to enforce. Some of these rulings will be elaborated upon below.

Enforcing the Principle of li-fenim mi-shurat ha-din (acting more generously than legally required). According to many halakhic authorities, in certain cases, the *bet din* should enforce the litigant's compliance with the principle of *li-fenim mi-shurat ha-din*: "It is the practice of every Jewish court to compel the wealthy to perform their obligation where it is right and proper, even if the strict law does not so require" (*Bayit Ḥadash* on Tur, Sh. Ar., ḤM 12:4; see Menachem Elon, *Jewish Law*, 1:155ff.). This principle is similar to another principle in the Jewish Law – *kofin al ha-ẓedakah* (the giving of charity may be enforced) (Ket. 49b), which only applies in particular circumstances. This rule constitutes the basis for the duty in certain circumstances to support children and relatives, even when this duty did not exist under strict interpretation of the law (see *Maintenance).

This matter was discussed in the Israeli Supreme Court in the *Kitan* case (CA 350/77 *Kitan v. Weiss*, 33 (2) 785). In this case, the Court rejected a defendant's claim for damages, since there was no proof of causality between the defendant's negligence and the damage. However, in his decision Justice Elon stated that it was appropriate for the defendant to compensate the injured parties, in accordance with the principle of *li-fenim mi-shurat ha-din*: "for it is a Jewish tradition and a fundamental principle in Jewish law that along with strict liability, there is the additional obligation to act *li-fenim mi-shurat ha-din*. It is particularly significant that this Jewish law obligation has found, as in the case before us, a primary application in torts" (p. 809 of decision). Justice Elon adds that under Jewish Law, it is appropriate for the court, in certain cases, to express its hope that one of the litigants will act more generously than legally required and compensate his opponent – although this hope is left to the discretion and initiative of the party (p. 811 of decision).

It should be stressed that the two other justices on the panel – Justice Shamgar and Justice Witkon – disagreed with this approach "that seeks to elevate payment of compensation *li-fenim mi-shurat ha-din* to the status of a settled general principal of tort law," owing to "the absence of clear standards"; they voiced concern for the "filing of frivolous appeals," since payment of damages *li-fenim mi-shurat ha-din* depends on the defendant's discretion and "I would not recommend blurring the boundaries between liability and non-liability" (*ibid.*, pp.805, 807 – for more details, see *Damages).

Similarly, in the *Ness v. Golda* case (CA 842/79 *Ness and Others v. Golda and Others* PD 36(1) 204) Justice Menachem Elon adopted the same approach. Justice Elon concurred with the other justices on the panel that the litigant could not be obligated to pay, but added that morally and in terms of justice, it was impossible to ignore that the defendant's conduct caused the plaintiffs the damage being claimed. Accordingly, he ruled that it would be appropriate for the defendants to provide compensation to the plaintiffs: "Under the strict law, they are not bound by any such obligation. Rather, it is a request of them to act *li-fenim mi-shurat ha-din*, and by doing so, they 'walk in the way of good men, and follow the paths of the righteous'" (p. 221 of judgment).

Enforcing compliance with the principle of *li-fenim mi-shurat ha-din* is particularly important in cases concerning the entire community, for "even though the obligation is not prescribed by the strict law, but only in accordance with *li-fenim mi-shurat ha-din*, the public can be compelled in this regard, for the public, like the individual, and perhaps even more so, should do what is good and right and not stand on strict law" (File 5637/26, PDR 5:132, at p. 151; see Resp. *Mayim Ḥayyim*, ḤM 6, quoted in *Pithei Teshuvah* to Sh. Ar., ḤM 333; Resp. *Ḥatam Sofer*, ḤM 239:9). The special status of the public was mentioned by the Supreme Court in the *Boyer* case (*Boyer v. Shikkun Ovdim*, 38 (2) PD 561, per Justice Elon). In this case too, after ruling that the appellant was not entitled to the remedy requested from the defendants, the Court expressed its request and hope that the respondents, a public body, would compensate the plaintiff in a suitable manner. However, the defendant did not see fit to comply with the Court's request, and to express its disapproval of the respondent's behavior, the Court decided to exempt the appellant from payment of the respondent's costs for the appeal.

In the State of Israel

The aforementioned decisions dealing with these questions were all given prior to the enactment of the Basic Laws of the State of Israel. As such, the judicial request and hope that litigants would conduct themselves in accordance with *li-fenim mi-shurat ha-din* only had the force of a recommendation. This has changed as a result of the enactment of the Basic Laws in 1992 (Basic Law: Human Dignity and Freedom, and Basic Law: Freedom of Occupation) which declared their aim to anchor in a Basic Law "the values of the State of Israel as a Jewish and democratic state," and in which the State's definition as "Jewish" precedes its definition as "democratic." By force of the Basic Law the Jewish Law attained a revered status in establishing the values of the State of Israel as a Jewish State. In view of this the Israeli common law dealing with *li-fenim mi-shurat ha-din* should be reconsidered, with a view towards compelling litigants, in certain circumstances, to conduct themselves beyond the letter of the law, *li-fenim mi-shurat ha-din*. A major area in which Jewish and democratic values can, and ought to be, integrated, is at the intersection of law and morality. Clearly, the enactment of the Basic Laws should leave its imprint on this area and on the interpretation of related legislation.

A number of the laws of the State of Israel combine provisions which manifestly derive from the area of morality, such as the invalidity of a contract "the making, contents of object of which is or are .... immoral or contrary to public policy" (sec. 30 Contracts (General Part) Law, 5733 – 1973), or the duty to conduct pre-contract negotiations and to fulfill the contract itself in a customary manner and in good faith (sections 12, 39 of the aforementioned law; see *Contract).

In addition, there are also statutory provisions that obligate the judge, adjudicating a case, to take general moral considerations into account, such as Section 32 (a) of the Tenants Protection Law [Consolidated Version] 5732 – 1972, which concerns a case in which by law, an order should be given to evict a tenant from his house, and which states that "Notwithstanding the existence of a ground for eviction, the Court may refuse to give judgment for eviction if it is satisfied that in the circumstances of the case it would not be just to do so." In its decision in the *Marcus* case (CA 417/79 *Marcus v. Hammer*, 37 (2) PD) the Court (per Justice Menachem Elon) discussed the similarities between these provisions and conduct according to *li-fenim mi-shurat ha-din* in Jewish Law.

[Menachem Elon (2nd ed.)]

BIBLIOGRAPHY: H.B. Fassel, *Tugend-und Rechtslehre... des Talmuds...* (1848, 1862²); M. Bloch, *Die Ethik in der Halacha* (1886); S. Schaffer, *Das Recht und seine Stellung zur Moral nach talmudischer Sitten-und Rechtslehre* (1889); M. Lazarus, *Die Ethik des Judentums*, 2 vols. (1904–11); I.S. Zuri, *Mishpat ha-Talmud*, 1 (1921), 86f.; S. Federbusch, *Ha-Musar ve-ha-Mishpat be-Yisrael* (1947); S. Pines, *Musar ha-Mikra ve-ha-Talmud* (1948); J.Z. Lauterbach, *Rabbinic Essays* (1951), 259–96; ET, 1 (1951³), 228–30, 334f.; 7 (1956), 382–96; E. Rackman, in: *Judaism*, 1 (1952), 158–63; Y. Kaufmann, *The Religion of Israel* (1960), 122–211, 291–340; M. Silberg, *Kakh Darko shel Talmud* (1961); M. Elon, in: *De'ot*, 20 (1962), 62–67; Z.J. Melzer, in: *Mazkeret... le-Zekher... ha-Rav Herzog* (1962), 310–5; B. Cohen, in: *Jewish and Roman Law*, 1 (1966), 65–121; 2 (1966), 768–70; E. Urbach, *Ḥazal – Pirkei Emunot ve-De'ot* (1969), 254–347. **ADD. BIBLIOGRAPHY:** M. Elon, *Ha-Mishpat ha-Ivri* (1988), 1:125–71, 219f.; 3:1323, 1464; idem, *Jewish Law* (1994), 1:141–89, 247f.; 4:1581, 1739; idem, *Jewish Law (Cases and Materials)* (1999), 35–57; "Does Jewish Tradition Recognize an Ethic Independent of Halakha?" in: *Jewish Law and Legal Theory* (1993), 155–81; I. Englard, "The Interaction of Morality and Jewish Law," in: *ibid.*, 189–99; Sh. Albeck, *Yesodot Dinei Mamonot ba-Talmud* (1994), 13–34; Y. Habba, *"Ettikah shel Nihul Hitdayyenut ba-Mishpat ha-Ivri,"* in: *Mishpatim*, 25:333–76; I.Warhaftig, *Ha-Hitḥayyevut* (2001), 409–19.

LAWĀNI, DA'UD (**Levi, David**; second half of 15th century), Yemenite scholar, author of the Midrash *al-Wajīz al-Mugnī* ("Adequate Summary") on the Pentateuch which was written by Lawāni in the town of Ḥemdeh between 1484 and 1493, extant in manuscript. It is based on the ancient and later Midrashim, including the Yemenite Midrashim which preceded it – *Midrash ha-Gadol, Midrash ha-Be'ur, Midrash ha-Ḥefeẓ*, and others. Besides the Talmud and the Midrashim, a great deal of its contents are drawn from the works of Maimonides. Its style, as its name indicates, is concise; its language is Hebrew and Arabic. Some identify Lawāni with Da'ud al-Lawāni, a poet who lived in Sanʿa.

BIBLIOGRAPHY: Y. Ratzaby, in: KS, 28 (1952/53), 262f.

[Yehuda Ratzaby]

LAWAT, ABRAHAM DAVID BEN JUDAH LEIB (1835–1890), ḥasidic rabbi and author in the Ukraine. From his youth Abraham David was attracted to *Chabad Ḥasidism, being among the closest followers of Menahem Mendel *Schneersohn, author of *Ẓemah Ẓedek*. On the initiative of his teacher, he founded a ḥasidic yeshivah in Nikolayev; he also became rabbi of the ḥasidic community of the town (in about 1870). After the death of Menahem Mendel, Abraham David became one of the chief supporters of his son, Samuel of *Lubavich. Abraham David wrote important manuals and reference books in various fields, both on *halakhah* and in clarification of the Chabad system in Kabbalah and *halakhah*. His work *Kav Naki* (Warsaw, 1868) on the laws of divorce and the writing of the names in divorce bills is one of the basic works on this subject. He wrote *Beit Aharon ve-Tosafot* (Vilna, 1881), an enlargement on the *Beit Aharon* of *Aaron of Pesaro, giving additional references to biblical verses in talmudic and midrashic literature, and adding references from the *Zohar and Chabad literature. In 1887 he published a new edition of the *Torah Or Siddur* according to the prayer book of *Shneur Zalman of Lyady which is used by the Chabad Ḥasidim. In this edition, he made an effort to present an accurate and corrected text, to which he appended two works: *Netiv ha-Ḥayyim*, which accompanies the *Derekh ha-Ḥayyim* of Jacob b. Jacob Moses *Lorbeerbaum of Lissa where he cites the decisions of Shneur Zalman of Lyady whenever they differ from those of the *Derekh ha-Ḥayyim*; and *Sha'arei Tefillah* (in subsequent editions, from 1896, in its enlarged and amended form entitled *Sha'ar ha-Kolel*) in 49 chapters. These deal with the sources of and reasons for the version of the above *siddur*, especially where it differs from the Ashkenazi and Sephardi versions.

BIBLIOGRAPHY: L. Ovchinski, *Naḥalat Avot* (1894), 18 para. 69; D.Z. Heilman, *Beit Rabbi*, 3 (1902; repr. 1965), 257; A.D. Lawat, *Kav Naki* (1951⁴; 1966⁵), introd.

[Adin Steinsaltz, Meir Medan]

LAW OF RETURN, law passed by the Israel parliament (Knesset) on July 3, 1950, the anniversary of the death of Theodor *Herzl. The Law of Return is one of the earliest and most significant of the basic laws of the State of Israel. Declaring that every Jew has the right to settle in Israel as an *oleh* (defined as "a Jew immigrating to Israel for settlement"), it gives legislative confirmation to the age-old Jewish yearning for return to Zion, previously embodied in the *Basle Program (1897), in Article 6 of the *Mandate for Palestine (1922), and in Israel's *Declaration of Independence of May 14, 1948. The law actually sanctioned the existing situation, for, as the official explanatory note pointed out, the Israel Provisional Council of State had, in its first legislative act (the Law and Administration Ordinance, 1948), abolished all restrictions on Jewish immigration and retroactively validated the immigration of every Jew who had, at any time, entered the country – even in contravention of the Mandatory regulations. In the words of the then prime minister, David *Ben-Gurion, in presenting the bill to the *Knesset for first reading:

> This law lays down not that the State accords the right of settlement to Jews abroad but that this right is inherent in every Jew by virtue of his being a Jew if it but be his will to take part in settling the land. This right preceded the State of Israel, it is that which built the State.

The main provision of the law (section 1), as passed by the Knesset, is accordingly declaratory in nature: "Every Jew has the right to come to this country as an *oleh*." In keeping with the purposes of the law, this status of *oleh* is also accorded to all Jews who had entered the country as immigrants before the law came into force and to all Jews born in the country, whether before or after the law's coming into force (section 4), as well as to any Jew who goes to Israel other than as an immigrant and subsequently expresses his desire to stay and settle in Israel (section 3(a)).

Denial of Oleh's Visa

An *oleh*'s visa may be denied only in cases in which the minister of immigration (later the minister of the interior) is satisfied that the applicant is engaged in activity directed against the Jewish people or is likely to endanger the public health or the security of the State (section 2 (b)). However, a person may not be regarded, for the purpose of this restriction, as endangering the public health on account of an illness contracted after his arrival in Israel (section 3 (b)). Experience indicated that there was another category of persons to whom it was not desirable to give an unrestricted right to settle in Israel as *olim*, namely, wanted criminals who took refuge in Israel or those who intended to continue a life of crime there. The Knesset hesitated to restrict the absolute right of every Jew to *aliyah* and was conscious of the possibilities of rehabilitation of wayward Jews inherent in Israel society. Nevertheless, on Aug. 23, 1954, it adopted an amendment to the law, empowering the minister of the interior to withhold an *oleh*'s visa from "a person with a criminal past, likely to endanger the public welfare" (Law of Return (Amendment) 1954).

The Law of Return further provided the principal method of acquiring Israeli nationality, for the Nationality Law, 1952, prescribes that (with certain exceptions) every *oleh* under the Law of Return shall be an Israeli national (section 2 (a)).

Legal Problems

The provisions of the law have given rise to a number of legal problems that have come under review by the Israel Courts, in particular the definition of a Jew for the purposes of the law (see *Jew). Does the definition of the *halakhah* (Jewish religious law) apply, as in cases of personal status, namely, whoever is born of a Jewish mother or has been duly converted to Judaism; or does the term include any person who bona fide declares himself to be a Jew? In the leading case of *Rufeisen v. Minister of the Interior* ((1962) 17 PD 2428), the Supreme Court adopted neither of these definitions. It held that, as the Law of Return is a secular enactment, "a Jew" is to be interpreted as Jews in general ordinarily understand it. The court accordingly decided that the law did not apply to a person who, although born a Jew, had subsequently converted to Christianity (see also *Apostasy).

The courts have also been occupied more than once with the question of "criminal past" under section 2(b)(3) of the law as amended in 1954. In the case of *Jonavici v. Minister of the Interior* ((1958) 33 PE 415), the court held that, where the minister has reached the conclusion, on the basis of proof, that a criminal past exists, the question whether such past is likely to endanger the public welfare is one for the minister's discretion. Further, a person may have a criminal past though convicted only once, depending on the seriousness of the offense. The court has also held, by a majority, that "having a criminal past" is not necessarily synonymous with having previous criminal conviction, though it cannot be proved without some evidence of a criminal act previously committed by the applicant: *Gold v. Minister of the Interior* ((1962) 17 PD 184(6)). The validity of this majority ruling is, on formal and other grounds, to be regarded as doubtful.

The Supreme Court was much occupied between 1968 and 1970, in *Shalit's Case* ((1970) 23 PD 477), with the problem of the status of infant children, born in Israel, of a Jewish father and a non-Jewish mother. (For details see *Jewish Identity.) The Supreme Court, unprecedentedly composed of nine of its ten members, held by a majority of five against four that, since the registration of the particulars prescribed to be notified under the Registration of the Population Law is not evidence of the correctness of such particulars but is, rather, of a statistical character, the registration officer is in duty bound to register them as notified and requested by the person required by law to furnish them.

In the wake of the political controversy aroused by the Shalit decision and upon the initiative of religious circles in the country, the government decided to propose amending legislation so as to clarify that, for the purposes of civil registration and of status under the Law of Return, a Jew is a person born of a Jewish mother or converted to Judaism. The provisions of this bill, as presented to the Knesset and still more as finally adopted, ranged, however, beyond this salient provision, in order to meet the demands of secular circles that the non-Jewish partners, children, or grandchildren of Jewish *olim* should not suffer differential treatment in respect of material rights and privileges accorded to such "*olim*," including rights under the Nationality Law (Law of Return (amendment no. 2), 5730 – 1970, enacted in March 1970). These provisions do not extend to a person who, being a Jew, has voluntarily adopted another faith. Likewise, the limitations and conditions applying to a Jew or an *oleh* under the Law of Return or any other relevant enactment apply equally to any person claiming the immigrant rights above referred to. This legislation omits any substantive definition of the concept of conversion to Judaism, and it is accordingly contended that the law does not prescribe a conversion satisfying halakhic requirements.

[Meir Silverstone]

The Law of Return (Amendment No. 2) 5730 – 1970

Section 4B of the Law of Return (Amendment No. 2) provides that: "For purposes of this law, 'Jew' means 'a person who was born of a Jewish mother or converted to Judaism and who is not a member of another religion.'" The law did not state that the terms "Jew," or "converted," were to be interpreted in accordance with the *halakhah*, or any other criterion. In using these terms without defining their precise meaning the Knesset circumvented the controversial question of "*who* is a Jew," and the question continued to be disputed, among the public at large and, specifically, among the justices of the Israeli Supreme Court. According to Justice Elon, despite the failure to stipulate that these terms were to be interpreted "in accordance with the *halakhah*" the amendment explicitly unified Jewish religion with Jewish nationality, and thereby restored the halakhic litmus test in the defining of Jewishness, in addition to extending the rights under the law to family members as well, even when they themselves did not answer the statutory definition of a Jew. This gives expression to the compromise effected by the Israeli legislator, by expanding the circle of those entitled to benefit from the Law of Return, while limiting the contents of the word "Jew," even for purposes of the Population Registry.

WHO IS AN "APOSTATE"? The two new provisions include situations in which Jews change their religion or subscribe to another faith in addition to their Judaism. The question of who is an apostate ["*mumar*"], and what beliefs transform a person into an apostate, was adjudicated by the Supreme Court in the Beresford case (HC 265/87, *Beresford v. the Interior Ministry*, PD 43(4) 793). In that case, two Jews were members of the "Messianic Jews," a group of Jews who believed that Jesus was the Messiah. Viewing themselves as full-fledged Jews, they requested to immigrate to Israel under the Law of Return. In light of the aforementioned provisions, the Ministry of the Interior refused to recognize their right to immigrate by force of the Law of Return. The petitioners' central argument was that, so long as they were not formally recognized by another official religion, they remained Jews. The Court (Justice Menachem Elon) examined their claim in accordance with previous rulings regarding this issue, i.e., that the term "member of another religion" as used in the Law of Return, must be examined according to the criteria of the other religion. In doing so, he rejected the petitioners' claim that the crux of the issue was the faith of the individual in question, and not whether or not they are officially recognized by another religion (HC 563/77 *Dorflinger v. the Interior Minister*, PD 33(2) 97). The Court based itself on an examination of the basic principles of the Christian faith, as opposed to those of the Jewish faith, an examination of the faith of the "Messianic Jews" sect, as reflected in its publications, as well as on opinions submitted by experts on Christianity and Comparative Religion. The Court focused on the similarity between this group and the sects of Messianic Jews that existed during the earliest days of Christianity, who constituted Christianity's beginnings. Noting that those groups were rejected from Judaism during the second half of the first century CE, the Court ruled that, nowadays, faith in Jesus constituted rejection of Judaism.

Nonetheless, Justice Elon rejected the determination that the phrase "member of another religion" in the Law of Return must be examined according to the criteria of the other religion, ruling rather that it must be examined according to the criteria of Jewish Law. Hence, if a Jew voluntarily changes his religion, he forfeits the legal and social rights associated with communal and familial affiliation, as for example in inheritance law. He likewise forfeits his tribal inheritance in the Land of Israel (Rabbi Natronai Gaon, ninth century C.E., as well as other sources – see *Oẓar ha-Ge'onim* (ed. Levin), Kiddushin, Responsa Section, p. 30ff.). The apostate's affiliation with the Jewish People is retained only with respect to duties associated with personal status. In addition, Jewish Law states that an apostate should not be labeled a Jew (Resp. Mahari Bruna, 135 [15th century, Ashkenaz]).

The Court relied on the comments of Rabbenu Menaḥem ha-Meiri, which seem more suited to the wording of the law, excluding from the definition of Jew anyone who is "a member of a different religion" (*Bet ha-Beḥirah*, to *Avodah Zarah* 26b, p.61; idem., Horayot 11a, p. 275; Southern France, 13th century):

> Any Jew who left the Jewish religion and joined a different faith shall for all purposes be considered by us as a member of the religion he joined, except as regards divorce and betrothal and all other matters associated with marriage, as shall be explained. All the same, that person's son is a full-fledged non-Jew even regarding divorce and betrothal.

Further on in its judgment, the Court cited sources viewing an apostate as one who has parted from the ways of the Jewish community and has abandoned that community (see *Apostate). It concluded that, certainly, the apostate has none of the "social or legal rights" granted to Jews as Jews, such as those inherent in the meaning and content of the Law of Return. That law grants rights based on one's affiliation with the Jewish People and being part of Jewish society and the Jewish community. It grants no rights to those who have abandoned that community, which is how the apostate was defined. The apostate, having "parted from the ways of the Jewish community," is no longer to be classed as our "brother" (Lev 25:25) (pp 828–829 of the judgment).

In this judgment, Justice Aharon *Barak disputed Justice Elon's argumentation, while arriving at the same operative result – i.e., that the petitioners were members "of another religion" and hence not entitled to rely on the Law of Return. According to Justice Barak, despite its amendment in 1970 (see above), the criterion for interpreting the Law of Return with regard to determining the applicant's "Jewishness" was neither the criterion of the "other religion" nor that of Jewish law, but rather a secular criterion. This secular criterion was based on a secular-dynamic conception, of which the halakhic components were a component, combined with other subjective elements related to the subjective perceptions of the candidate for *aliyah*, national conceptions, etc.

WHO IS A "CONVERT"? According to the Religious Communities (Change) Ordinance, 1927, an act of conversion performed in the State of Israel is valid only when a certificate of approval is issued by the chief rabbi of Israel. By dint of this authority granted to the chief rabbi, a special rabbinical court system was established in the State of Israel to deal specifically with conversion, in addition to the regular rabbinical court system (see *Bet Din*).

Traditionally, conversions were under the jurisdiction of the rabbinate. Yet the legal authority of the chief rabbi is limited to the approval of conversions, and only those conversions performed in Israel. There is no explicit legal source that grants any body the authority to perform conversions, nor does the chief rabbi possess the authority to certify the validity of conversions performed abroad. In the judgment in the *Shas* case (HC 264/87, *Shas Movement v. the Population Registry*, PD 43(2) 727), there was a majority decision (Justice Meir Shamgar) that "Notification accompanied by a document attesting to conversion to any Jewish community abroad shall suffice to require an individual's registration as a Jew. In this regard, it makes no difference whether that community is Orthodox, Conservative or Reform" (p. 731 of the judgment).

This judgment conflicted with the minority opinion (Justice Menachem Elon) that held that the term "converted" should be interpreted in accordance with Jewish law, as determined and accepted by tradition. The term "conversion" has its source in Jewish law and should therefore be interpreted solely according to Jewish law. Justice Elon added that:

> The State of Israel is the home of all Jews, in all their denominations, communities, and varieties, whether in Israel or abroad. The State was established for their sakes, and by virtue of them all it exists.... The State of Israel was established in order to open its gates to all its family, whether close or far, who wish to return to it for the purpose of building the State and establishing themselves therein. Every returning Jew would live in Israel according to his beliefs and his way of life. However, the Knesset, after deep and extensive debate, decided – contrary to the majority decision of the Supreme Court – that the definition of "Jew" in the laws of Israel is based on objective-normative criteria which had been accepted and sanctified throughout thousands of years of the existence of this nation and we must accept the will of the Knesset, which is the will of the historic Community of Israel, based on the rules of the halakhic system, from generation to generation and from time immemorial. I should also add that it is absolutely necessary that the act of conversion be uniform and agreed upon by all the groups of Israel, and that in this crucial matter we operate according to a criterion that can be accepted by all segments of the nation. Only a conversion which conforms to the rules of *halakhah* would achieve this aim, and in my opinion it would not in any way interfere with the right of every person in Israel to live in freedom and follow his own way of life.

Justice Elon concluded his remarks by proposing that "We must... find a way in which we can accept these rules by full agreement because it is the wish of the Knesset, and I am also convinced that it is the wish of the nation" (pp. 737–738 of the judgment).

It should be noted that the decision confined itself to the authority invested in the registration officer and accompanying legal questions. Its background was the petition of a number of people who had undergone non-Orthodox conversions, requesting recognition as Jews for purposes of the Population Registration Law, 5725 – 1965. As such, the decision's immediate ramification applied exclusively to the powers of the registration clerk. The Court therefore refrained from issuing a binding judgment regarding the petitioners' Jewishness for other purposes, such as marriage and divorce, emphasizing the non-application of its ruling for purposes of the Law of Return, and certainly not for purpose of marriage and divorce.

Since the *Shas* decision, a number of other decisions have been given by the Israeli Supreme Court, further curtailing the exclusivity of Orthodox conversion as the official, recognized conversion for purposes of defining a person's Jewishness in the State of Israel.

Regarding the authority of the rabbinical court to certify the validity of conversions performed outside Israel, in the *Plonit* case (HC 3023/90 *Plonit v. the Rehovot District Rabbinical Court*, 45 (3) PD 808), the Court ruled that rabbinical courts do not have jurisdiction regarding conversions performed abroad, except with respect to matters arising by virtue of their incidental authority to determine individual's Jewishness in cases of marriage and divorce. The *Pessaro* case (HC *Pessaro (Goldstein) v. Minister of the Interior*, 49 (4) PD 661) established that, for purposes of a persons' registration as Jewish, the Religious Communities (Change) Ordinance is similarly inapplicable to conversions conducted inside the State of Israel. In the *Na'amat* case (HC 5070/95 *Na'amat v. Minister of the Interior*, 56 (2) PD 721) this holding was expanded, imposing a duty on the registration clerk to register as Jewish a person converted in a non-Orthodox ceremony even where the non-Orthodox conversion was performed in Israel. This judgment held that the power to issue a certificate of conversion – for registration purposes – no longer belonged exclusively to the chief rabbi.

Recently, the Supreme Court ruled that non-Orthodox conversions performed abroad, after converts had undergone the Israeli conversion course, and then returned to Israel immediately following the conversion, were valid, and that in addition to the duty to register the converts as Jews, they should also be considered Jewish for purposes of the Law of Return. The Court ruled that such conversions should not be viewed as a fiction, and that there was no substantive flaw in the fact that the convert did not remain in the community that had converted him. It should be noted that the minority opinion held that recognition of such a conversion was likely to open a Pandora's Box to anyone who wanted to receive Israeli citizenship easily, something that was likely to lead to inappropriate and uncontrollable consequences (HC 2597/99, *Rodriguez-Toshbeim v. Minister of the Interior,* 58 (5) PD 412).

The multiplicity of fundamental legal judgments and the plethora of disputes between Supreme Court justices attest to the fact that the law itself is flawed – even after its amendment – to the extent that it does not define precisely what constitutes apostasy, who is "a member of a different faith" and, especially, in that it does not define conversion. In 1997 an attempt was made to arrive at a consensual solution of this issue, acceptable to representatives of all the various streams by way of establishing a special committee, known as the Neeman Committee (after its chairman, Yaakov Neeman), which was established to examine the issue in its entirety, and it also comprised representatives from the Conservative and Reform streams. The committee recommended the establishment of institutes for Jewish studies which would be common to all the streams and which would be responsible for preparing candidates for conversion. The conversion itself, according to these recommendations, would be carried out exclusively by special religious courts established for that purpose by the Chief Rabbinate, and only conversion under its auspices would be recognized in the State of Israel. The recommendations of this commission were endorsed in principle by the Israeli government, and conversion institutions were even established. However, the draft bill intended to statutorily anchor these recommendations did not pass, and the subject has remained without a solution.

[Menachem Elon (2nd ed.)]

BIBLIOGRAPHY: S. Rosenne, in: *Journal du Droit international,* 81 (Eng., 1954), 5–63. **ADD. BIBLIOGRAPHY:** M. Elon, *Ha-Mishpat ha-Ivri* (1988), 3:1383, 1418; idem, *Jewish Law* (1994), 3:1647–51, 1688–90; M. Corinaldi, *Dinei Ishim Mishpaḥah vi-Yerushah – Bein Dat la-Medinah* (2004), 264–70; idem, *The Enigma of Jewish Identity; The Law of Return – Theory and Practice* (Heb.; 2001); H. Cohen, *Ha-Mishpat* (1997), 490–511; *Who Is a Jew,* (Compilation, the Ministry of Religion, 1959); *Jewish Law Association Studies,* vol. 11 (ed. Sinclair, 2000).

LAWRENCE, DAVID (1888–1973), U.S. journalist, and longtime interpreter of the Washington political scene. Born in Philadelphia, Lawrence grew up in Buffalo, New York. He joined the Washington Bureau of the Associated Press on graduating from Princeton in 1910 and was assigned to cover the White House. When, two years later, Woodrow Wilson undertook his first presidential campaign, Lawrence became one of his chief interpreters. He subsequently wrote *The True Story of Woodrow Wilson* (1924). In 1914 he helped found the White House Correspondents' Association. In 1916 he was appointed Washington correspondent for the *New York Post,* and was among the first commentators in the capital whose column was syndicated nationally. In 1919 he organized the Consolidated Press Association, which furnished features and financial news to daily newspapers by leased wire, an innovation at the time. Seven years later he started the *U.S. Daily,* devoted exclusively to news of Washington. It became the *U.S. News* in 1933, and in 1948 was combined with another of his magazines as the newsweekly *U.S. News and World Report.*

His books include *Beyond the New Deal* (1934), *Stumbling into Socialism…* (1935), *Diary of a Washington Correspondent* (1942), and *The Editorials of David Lawrence* (1970).

[Irving Rosenthal]

LAWRENCE, GERALD (1873–1957), British actor. Born in London, Lawrence was the nephew of Isaac Cohen who owned the Pavilion Theater, Whitechapel. He was noted for romantic roles such as David Garrick, Monsieur Beaucaire, Charles Surface, and Beau Brummel, which he played in London and on tour. In his early years he acted with Sir Frank R. Benson, Sir H. Beerbohm Tree, and then with Sir Henry Irving until the latter's death in 1905. He distinguished himself in many Shakespearean roles and later appeared as Hamlet and Shylock in his own productions. Lawrence appeared in several silent films and in Victor *Saville's *The Iron Duke* (1934). He was the father of the well-known British actress JOYCE CAREY (1898–1993), who appeared in numerous films, plays, and television productions over a 70-year career.

LAWRENCE, STEVE (1935–) and **GORME, EYDIE** (1931–), U.S. singers. Known as the two Jewish kids from the Bronx, New York, Steve and Eydie continued to sing pop and standard-bearer songs from the 1950s into the 21st century. Steve Lawrence was born Sidney Leibowitz, the son of Max Leibowitz, a house painter who also worked as a cantor. Lawrence displayed his talent for singing as a youth in synagogue. He took on the stage name Steve Lawrence (the first names of two nephews) and won first prize on the *Arthur Godfrey Talent Scouts* television series in 1951. His first album, *Steve Lawrence,* was released in 1953, and in July he was hired by Steve Allen to sing on *Tonight!*, then a local New York talk show. Eydie Gorme was born Edith Gormezano, the youngest of three children of Sephardi immigrant parents – her Sicilian father was a tailor and her Turkish mother was distantly related to singer Neil *Sedaka's family. Gorme grew up speaking Spanish and English at home and began singing early in life, making her first radio appearance at the age of three. After graduating from high school, she worked as a Spanish interpreter during the day and attended City College at night. She started touring as a singer with two different bands in 1951 and then went solo in 1952. Steve and Eydie met on *Tonight!* in September 1953, when Gorme became a regular. In 1954, *Tonight!* was broadcast nationally on NBC and that same year the couple released their first single together, *Make Yourself Comfortable.* They married in Las Vegas in 1957. Lawrence was drafted in 1958 and served two years in the army, where he performed with the U.S. Army Band. In 1960, the couple released their first joint LP together, *We Got Us,* and the title song won the Grammy Award for best performance by a vocal group. In 1963, Brill Building team Barry Mann and Cynthia Weil helped Gorme break into the Top Ten and earned her a Grammy solo nod with *Blame It on the Bossa Nova,* and

Lawrence had a No. 1 hit with Gerry Goffin and Carole *King's *Go Away Little Girl* that same year. The couple continued to enjoy pop success for the next year until the British Invasion hit in 1964. Lawrence turned to Broadway with the musical *What Makes Sammy Run?*, which earned him a Drama Critics Circle Award and a Tony nomination. In 1967, the couple hit Broadway together with *Golden Rainbow*, featuring Lawrence's easy-listening hit *I've Gotta Be Me*. They continued recording together and remained nightclub headliners in the 1970s, and shot the television specials *Our Love Is Here to Stay*, a salute to George *Gershwin, and *Steve and Eydie Celebrate Irving Berlin*, which won seven Emmy Awards. Lawrence appeared in the films *The Blues Brother* and *The Lonely Guy* in the 1980s. Steve and Eydie opened for Frank Sinatra on his 1990–91 Diamond Jubilee tour. They continued to perform in Las Vegas and appeared as themselves in the 2001 remake of the Sinatra film *Ocean's Eleven*. The couple had two sons, film composer David Nessim Lawrence and Michael, who died in 1986 at 23.

[Adam Wills (2nd ed.)]

°**LAWRENCE, THOMAS EDWARD** (1888–1935), English archaeologist, Orientalist, and author known for his exploits in World War I as "Lawrence of Arabia." Lawrence first visited the Near East in 1909, when he went to Syria and Palestine to prepare his study on Crusader architecture. In 1911–14 he joined an archaeological expedition in Carchemish and, together with Leonard *Woolley, he mapped the Negev and the Sinai Desert. After the outbreak of World War I, when Turkey joined the Central Powers, he was posted to *Cairo and served in British military intelligence. There he joined the Arab Bureau, set up on Jan. 1, 1916, and was charged with exploiting Arab national ambitions for British war aims. In June 1916, when the anti-Turkish Arab revolt, led by Emir Feisal, began, Lawrence was attached to him as liaison officer on behalf of the British and was instrumental in arming and financing the rebellion. Lawrence directed the military operations of the Arab rebels who destroyed Turkish military installations, captured Akaba (1917), and ultimately entered Damascus (1918).

At the end of World War I, Lawrence was a member of the British delegation at the Paris Peace Conference and became the adviser of Emir Feisal, who represented Arab interests. In both these capacities he arranged a meeting between Feisal and Chaim *Weizmann, whom he greatly admired. The negotiations between Feisal and Weizmann, with Lawrence as interpreter and adviser, led to an agreement by which the national and historical rights of the Jews to Palestine were recognized, Britain would be the trustee power in Palestine, and the country itself would be developed to create room for 4,000,000–5,000,000 Jews. In return, the Jews would extend financial and technical aid and advice to revive the Arab countries. Lawrence hoped that such an agreement would serve to push the French out of the Middle East and destroy the *Sykes-Picot agreement. Later Lawrence served as adviser to Colonial Secretary Winston *Churchill and, together with him and Sir Herbert *Samuel, participated in the Cairo Conference (1921), which confirmed the Balfour Declaration, recommended that Feisal (whom the French had expelled from Damascus) be king of Iraq, and appointed his brother *Abdullah as ruler of Transjordan. After a few months in Transjordan as chief British representative in Amman, Lawrence returned to England and resigned his post. In 1926 he published his book, *The Seven Pillars of Wisdom*, about the Arab revolt and his part in it and a shorter version in 1927 entitled *Revolt in the Desert*. His other works, *Crusader Castles* (2 vols., 1936), *The Wilderness of Zin* (1936), and *Oriental Assembly* (1940), appeared posthumously. "Lawrence of Arabia" has remained a legendary, romantic figure, one of the most famous military adventurers of modern times, and the subject of a famous film biography (1962). He was considered the champion of the Arab national cause who had accused the British of betraying their obligations to it. This image, as well as many details about his life and adventures, became the topic of considerable controversy in later biographical and political research. There seems no doubt, however, that Lawrence never was an anti-Zionist and that he regarded Zionism and Arab nationalism as complementary forces in the Middle East.

BIBLIOGRAPHY: P. Knightley and C. Simpson, *The Secret Lives of Lawrence of Arabia* (1969); R. Graves, *Lawrence and the Arabs* (1927); R. Aldington, *Lawrence of Arabia* (1955); B.H. Liddell Hart, *T.E. Lawrence – In Arabia and After* (1945); A.W. Lawrence (ed.), *T.E. Lawrence by his Friends* (1937); R. Storrs, *Orientations* (1937), index; C. Weizmann, *Trial and Error* (1949), index. **ADD. BIBLIOGRAPHY:** ODNB online; L. James, *The Golden Warrior: The Life and Legend of Lawrence of Arabia* (1995); J.M. Wilson, *Lawrence of Arabia: The Authorized Biography of T.E. Lawrence* (1989).

[Daniel Efron]

LAWSON (Levy-Lawson), English family of newspaper publishers and editors. JOSEPH MOSES LEVY (1812–1888) owned and edited the *Sunday Times* for a year. In 1855 he took over the *Daily Telegraph and Courier* (which had been founded three months previously), abridged its name to the *Daily Telegraph* and halved its price, making it the first penny morning paper in London. Levy and his son Edward eventually made the paper one of the leading voices in British journalism. He ran the paper as a Liberal mouthpiece, but in 1879 transferred its allegiance from Gladstone to Disraeli and ultimately adopted the Conservative line. EDWARD LEVY-LAWSON (1833–1916), first Baron Burnham, was the eldest son of Joseph Moses Levy. He added the name Lawson by royal license in 1875. When his father acquired the *Daily Telegraph* and made him editor, Levy-Lawson utilized the telegraph for newsgathering, broke away from the ponderous newspaper style of the period, adopted a livelier news presentation, and employed many distinguished writers. The paper organized "shilling funds" for soldiers' dependents, the famine relief drives in Lancashire, and supported other worthy causes. In 1871 the *Daily Telegraph* and the *New York Herald* cosponsored H.M. Stanley's search for Livingstone in Africa. In 1873 it sponsored George Smith's Assyrian archeological expedition which discovered cuneiform records of the Flood. The daily circulation of the *Daily Telegraph* had risen to 200,000 by 1871. Levy-Lawson was made a baronet in 1892 and a baron upon his retirement from active control of the paper in 1903. He was not a professing Jew. SIR HARRY LAWSON WEBSTER LEVY-LAWSON, Viscount Burnham (1862–1933), was son of the first baron. Levy-Lawson, who had no connections with the Jewish community, served in parliament as a Liberal MP in the years 1885–92 and 1893–95. He then switched parties in opposition to Irish Home Rule, serving as a Tory MP in 1905–06 and 1910–16. He was made a Companion of Honour (CH) in 1917 and a viscount in 1919. He succeeded his father as owner of the *Daily Telegraph* in 1903. In 1927 he sold the paper. Levy-Lawson was chairman of the committee which formulated the "Burnham scale" for teachers' pay.

BIBLIOGRAPHY: H. Herd, *March of Journalism* (1952), 162–6. **ADD. BIBLIOGRAPHY:** ODNB online for Joseph M. Levy, Edward Levy-Lawson, and Harry Levy-Lawson.

LAWSON, JOHN HOWARD (1895–1977), U.S. playwright. With the 1925 production of his *Processional*, Lawson became known as a leading exponent of expressionist and social drama. His works include *Loud Speaker* (1927), a political farce; *International* (1927); *Success Story* (1932); *Gentlewoman* (1934); and *Marching Song* (1937), a labor drama. He also wrote *The Hidden Heritage* (1950), a cultural history of America, and *Film: The Creative Process* (1964). His thoughts on writing and film can be found in his *Theory and Technique of Playwrighting* (1936) and *Film in the Battle of Ideas* (1953).

BIBLIOGRAPHY: G. Carr, *The Left Side of Paradise: The Screenwriting of John Howard Lawson* (1984).

LAWTON, SAMUEL T. (1884–1961), U.S. army officer. Born in Peoria, Illinois, Lawton was admitted to the bar in 1905 but enlisted in the Illinois National Guard in 1909. He fought on the Mexican border and in France during World War I as a captain. He later served in Germany and Luxembourg, and returned to the United States to command a field artillery brigade. He was major general commanding the 33rd infantry division from March 1941 to May 1942. He remained on active service until his retirement in 1948.

LAWYERS.

Introduction

Although Jews were noted advocates at Brighegua near Toledo, Spain, as early as 1436, and though converted Jews were prominent lawyers in South America in the 17th century, Jews were generally prevented from practicing law in most of the countries in which they settled until early in the 19th century. In some countries their exclusion was based on the belief that law was largely ecclesiastical law and hence unsuitable for non-Christians, as was argued in Austria, while in many other countries it was believed that membership of the legal profession was a mark of distinction not to be conferred on an alien race to whom citizenship and political rights had not been granted. The very reasons that caused their exclusion acted as a spur to Jews to seek admission to the legal profession. On the one hand the study of law had been a tradition among Jews, while the very fact that membership of the legal profession, like the medical profession, was a mark of distinction, and encouraged Jews who wished to integrate to become lawyers. But many young Jews, who would otherwise have been refused admission to university, converted to Christianity in order to study law, and others converted later so as to be allowed to practice. The result was that many of the Jews who set out to become lawyers in order to become accepted to Christian society found it necessary to become Christians before they could be accepted as lawyers. Nevertheless, the attraction of the profession remained considerable. As a lawyer the Jew was able to earn enough money to haul himself out of the ghetto environment which had become anachronistic in the age of Enlightenment. At the same time he was given an independent means of livelihood, not reliant upon a non-Jewish employer.

In most countries Jews were permitted to practice law at about the time they were granted civil rights. The first Jewish lawyer in the Hapsburg dominions, Raphael *Joel, was granted a doctorate of law a few years after the Edict of Toleration was issued in 1782. Jews became lawyers in Holland and Italy when the French conquest of those countries brought with it the ideas of liberty, equality, and fraternity, and in Russia Jews were finally admitted to the bar in 1904 as a sop to the liberal elements. Only in the United States and in the British colonies, where Jews always enjoyed civil rights, were they able to practice law without hindrance.

Not surprisingly, the legal work in which Jewish lawyers engaged varied according to the circumstances of the Jews in the countries in which they lived. In Russia before the Bolshevik Revolution and in Poland until World War II, a number of Jewish lawyers were engaged in cases arising out of the persecution of Jews, such as the Odessa pogrom of 1871, in which Alexander *Passover was one of several Jewish lawyers to represent the victims in compensation claims and when Leib Landau represented Jewish victims in the Polish city of Przedecz after antisemitic excesses there. In the United States, where the Jews as a minority had an interest in the protection of the individual by the maintenance of civil liberties, Jewish lawyers were prominent in civil rights cases, among them Louis *Marshall and Arthur Garfield *Hays, each of whom was prominent in the defense of Jews and non-Jews alike.

In Germany and Austria, on the other hand, where assimilation into Christian society was a *sine qua non* of success in the legal profession, virtually no Jewish lawyers, apart from Gabriel *Riesser, could be said to have professionally concerned themselves with the interests of Jews nor, particularly, with questions of civil liberties. In these countries Jewish lawyers were involved in developing the philosophy of law by the writing of learned texts. Thus Paul *Laband and Georg Jellinek in Germany, and Julius *Ofner and Emil *Steinbach and others in Austria, were pioneers of social legislation. Their work was directed not toward the benefit of individuals but to the improvement of the political system, for they admired the legal institutions of the countries in which they lived and were anxious to develop and improve them.

In the British Empire, where discrimination against Jewish lawyers was considerably less than in most European countries, Jews advanced easily in all branches of the profession and a relatively large number held judicial posts. In South Africa alone, 11 Jews were appointed judges between 1945 and 1970, while in Australia two Jews served as chief justices of the High Court of Western Australia, New South Wales, and Victoria. In addition, Sir Sidney *Abrahams was chief justice of Uganda (1933–34), Tanganyika (1934–36), and Ceylon (1936–39) and Sir Victor Elyan (1909–) was chief justice of Swaziland (1965–70).

Yet, though they were denied the right to practice law in most states until the 19th century and though they suffered from legal and social discrimination thereafter, Jews turned to the legal profession in large numbers in Western countries. After World War II, Jews in the United States, France, and England constituted a very high proportion of all the lawyers in the respective capital cities. In Eastern countries, however, they were not generally prominent, because the Muslim countries never granted Jews the civil equality which they eventually won in the West. Nevertheless, Salomon Bensabat was appointed High Court judge in Morocco, Mison Ventura (1883–?) became professor of Roman law at the University of Istanbul, and Alfred Chatzner was a High Court judge in India. Ezekiel Ezekiel was a leading advocate at the Bombay bar. Another outstanding Jewish lawyer was Naim *Zilkha who was deputy president of the Beirut Court of Appeals and later president of the civil court in Diyala Province, Iraq.

One other notable feature of the Jewish involvement in law was the large number of Jews prominent in the field of international law. Sir Hersch *Lauterpacht became judge of the International Court of Justice at The Hague and edited the standard textbook on international law written by a German Jew, Lassa *Oppenheim. Among other Jews who influenced the development of international law were Tobias *Asser, winner of the Nobel Peace Prize, and the legal theorists Hans *Kelsen and Julius *Stone. Jews also served as legal advisers to the foreign ministries of various states, notably the United States, Britain, Holland, and Poland and held chairs in international law at most of the European universities. Various theories have been postulated for their prominence in this branch of the law. One influential factor would seem to be that Jews wandered from land to land and were rarely attached to any particular system of law for long periods of time.

Australia

There were no restrictions on Jews practicing law in Australia and a number of Jews held high positions in the legal profession in the 19th century. Among the first Jewish lawyers in Australia was Sir Julian *Salomons, one of many to study law in England. He was admitted to the Sydney bar in 1861, rose to become solicitor-general of New South Wales, and in 1886 was appointed chief justice. Three other Jewish lawyers from New South Wales attained prominence: Henry Cohen (1840–1912), who was a judge of the Supreme Court of New South Wales from 1896 to 1911, Sir Daniel *Levy, who became speaker of the New South Wales Parliament in 1919, and Alroy Cohen, QC. In Victoria, Samuel Leon, QC became crown prosecutor and Pharez Phillips and Theodore *Fink were lawyers who became prominent figures in Australian politics.

After World War I, the number of Jewish lawyers in Australia decreased, despite an increase in the Jewish population. Nevertheless, several Jews held important legal posts, among them Judge J.J. Cohen of the New South Wales bench, Henry I. Cohen, attorney-general of Victoria, and Louis Braham, president of the Law Institute of Australia. Most illustrious of all was Sir Isaac *Isaacs who was made acting chief justice of the High Court of Australia in 1927 and chief justice from 1930 until 1931 when he became governor-general of Australia. Following World War II there was a marked increase in the number of Jews in the legal profession and some achieved considerable distinction, among them Sir Albert Wolff (1899–1977), chief justice of Western Australia from 1959 to 1969; Elias Coppel (1896–?), acting chief justice of the Supreme Court of Victoria and the author of a standard work on the law of sale; and three judges of the Supreme Court of New South Wales – Bernard Sugerman, David Selby, and Simon Isaacs. In addition several Jews were made queen's counsel, their number including Sir Phillip Phillips, chairman of the Royal Commission on Liquor in Victoria, Joan Rosanove, an eminent woman lawyer, Senator Sam *Cohen, deputy leader of the Australian Labour Party, and Maurice *Ashkanasy.

In the early part of the 21st century, five Jews sat on Australia's Appeals Courts, but none on the High Court of Australia, the country's supreme court.

Three Jews achieved distinction as professors of law. Julius Stone was professor of jurisprudence at the University of Sydney and an internationally renowned authority on jurisprudence and international law, Zelman *Cowen was dean of the faculty of law at the University of Melbourne, and later served as Australia's governor-general, and Louis Waller (1935–) was professor of law at Monash University.

[Isidor Solomon]

Austria

Until the Edict of Toleration was issued in 1782 by Emperor Joseph II, Jews were unable to enter university and, therefore, to practice law or any other learned profession. Following promulgation of the edict, Raphael Joel, a native of western Bohemia, entered Prague University and after considerable debate was permitted to take a doctorate of civil law. Previously, only Jews who had already converted to Christianity were allowed to become lawyers, the most prominent of them being Joseph von Sonnenfels (1732–1817), who worked for the abolition of torture and the limitation of capital punishment. The outstanding Jewish lawyer in Austria of the 19th century was Wolfgang *Wessely, who was the first Jew to become a full university professor in Austria and was responsible for the introduction of the jury system. However, the right of Jews to hold legal posts remained in doubt until the constitution of 1867 granted the Jews legal civic equality with the rest of the population. The benefits granted to the Jews by the 1867 constitution were largely the result of the work of Heinrich Jacques (1831–1894), a Viennese lawyer and politician, who campaigned for the removal of restrictions against the Jews in his book *Denkschrift ueber die Stellung der Juden in Oesterreich* (1859[4]), which attracted considerable attention. Although Jews were given legal equality by the 1867 constitution, they were deprived of practical equality because of widespread social and professional discrimination which could not be removed simply by a change in the law. Many Jews converted to Christianity, believing that conversion was a small price to pay for a major part in the development of the united Hapsburg Empire which they regarded as the model open society in Europe. Among the converts were Julius *Glaser, regarded as the father of Austrian criminal procedure, who became minister of justice, and Joseph Unger, who was later president of the Reichsgericht. Glaser and Unger were responsible for an outstanding collection of judgments of the Austrian Supreme Court and were recognized as the foremost figures in 19th-century Austrian law. Their conversion to Christianity estranged them no more from Judaism than other prominent Austrian-Jewish lawyers, such as Julius Ofner, who worked for the enactment of social legislation in parliament, Emil Steinbach, another pioneer of social legislation, who became president of the Supreme Court after converting to Christianity, and Franz Klein who twice served as minister of justice.

Jewish lawyers in Austria-Hungary won a reputation during the 19th century as a force for unity and stability in the Empire, coupled with a passion for social and legislative reform. In the 20th century Jews were responsible for major treatises on Austrian civil law. Armin Ehrenzweig (1864–1935) was the author of *System des Oesterreichischen Allgemeinen Privatrechts* (1925), Horace Krasnopolski (1842–1908) produced a complete textbook of Austrian civil law which was published after his death by Bruno *Kafka, and Joseph Schey von Koromla, who was a member of the Commission for the Revision of the Civil Code, was largely responsible for additions to the Code. An outstanding textbook on Austrian civil law was Heinrich *Klang's *Kommentar zum Allgemeinen Buergerlichen Gesetzbuch* (1931–35), edited jointly with nine leading Jewish lawyers. In addition, several Austrian Jews also achieved distinction as commercial lawyers, among them Karl Samuel Grunhut (1844–1929) and Oskar Pisko (1876–1939), while Walther *Rode, Ernst Lohsing (1874–1942), and Hugo Sperber were prominent campaigners for criminal law reform. Nevertheless, dissatisfaction with the federal order of Austrian society led Austro-Jewish lawyers toward separatism, nationalism, and Jewish minority protection. Eventually, a group of international lawyers joined Hans *Kelsen to form the Vienna School of Jurisprudence, which rejected the dualist legal system of the Hapsburg Empire and advocated a pluralistic legal system subject to supraordinated international law. However, it was the advent of Fascism and the Nazi invasion of the various territories that formed the Austro-Hungarian Empire that finally brought to an end the Jewish legal activity in Austria. No less than the Austrian aristocracy, Austrian Jewry was a belated victim of the disappearance of the Hapsburg monarchy.

[Josef J. Lador-Lederer]

Canada

Jews were not prominent in the legal profession in Canada in the 19th century and no Jews served as judges until 1914 when Samuel *Shultz was appointed county court judge in British Columbia. No other Jew held a judicial position in Canada before 1929, with the exception of Jacob Cohen, a Toronto magistrate from 1918 to 1930. While a disproportionate number of Jews were drawn to study law, for much of the first half of the 20th century Jewish lawyers felt the sting of prejudice and the possibility of advancement within the profession was severely limited. Often denied admission to mainstream law firms, Jewish lawyers were forced to practice on their own or join largely Jewish law firms that formed in centers of Jewish population concentration. In 1931 there were 351 Jewish lawyers in Canada, most in Montreal, Toronto, and Winnipeg.

After World War II, there was a steady increase in the number of Jews who were given judicial posts, among them the first Jew to be appointed to a superior court when Harry Bradshaw was appointed to the Quebec Superior Court in 1950. Benjamin Robinson and Harry Blumenstein also served on the Quebec Superior Court. A number of Jews were appointed to provincial Supreme Courts since the 1960s. Abraham Lieff was made judge of the Ontario Supreme Court, Nathan *Nemetz was raised to the British Columbia Supreme Court, and Justin Louis Dubinsky was appointed to the Nova Scotia Supreme Court in 1967. Samuel *Freedman was named chief justice of the province of Manitoba in 1971, and in 1970 Bora *Laskin, who was previously a judge of the Ontario Court of Appeal, was appointed the first Jewish justice of the Supreme Court of Canada by Prime Minister Pierre Elliot Trudeau and in 1973 he was made chief justice of Canada.

The appointment of a Jew as chief justice of Canada signaled the unequivocal acceptance of Jews in the Canadian legal establishment. As barriers to Jews in the legal profession crumbled, and Jewish lawyers became partners in the large firms, Jewish appointments to the Bench no longer raised eyebrows. Jews, men and women, are to be found on the faculty of every major law school in Canada and a number have served as deans. By 2004, there were two Jewish judges among the nine judges on the Supreme Court of Canada, Morris Fish of Montreal (appointed in 2003) and Rosalie Silberman *Abella (appointed in 2004), and a Jew, Irwin *Cotler, was Canada's minister of justice.

[Stuart E. Rosenberg / Richard Menkis and Harold Troper (2nd ed.)]

England

The first Jew known to have been a lawyer in England was Francis *Goldsmid, who was called to the bar in 1883 and who, when swearing the oath, omitted the words on "the true faith of a Christian" which at the time were required for all public offices. Subsequently, a steadily increasing number of Jews were admitted as lawyers, though discrimination against them remained for many years afterwards. Indeed, until World War II, only a small number of Jews entered law, commensurate with the low percentage of Jews in the total population. Nevertheless, several Jewish lawyers acquired great distinction. Sir George *Jessel was the first Jew in England to be made a judge. He later held the title of Master of the Rolls and was later recognized as one of the chief architects of the modern law of equity. Other prominent Jewish lawyers of the 19th century were Jacob *Waley, Judah P. *Benjamin, Arthur *Cohen, and Sir George *Lewis (1833–1911). The greatest Jewish advocate at the English bar was Rufus Isaacs, later Lord *Reading, who became successively attorney general and lord chief justice, the only Jew to hold these coveted offices.

Nevertheless, the influence of Jews in English law remained slight until after World War II, when the legal profession (especially the solicitorial branch) attracted a disproportionately high percentage of Jews. By 1970 there were six Jewish High Court judges (Lord Cohen of *Walmer, Sir Cyril *Salmon, Sir Seymour *Karminski, Sir Alan *Mocatta, Sir Sebag Shaw (1906–1982), and Sir Philip Wien (1913–1981)) and more than one solicitor in ten in the major cities was a Jew. The sharp increase in the number of Jewish lawyers was largely the result of a general liberalization of a profession which had previously been socially exclusive. Nevertheless, few of the large or most prominent legal firms had Jewish members and the fear that the profession would be swamped by Jews proved unfounded. Among distinguished Jewish advocates were Bertram B. *Benas, who practiced at the bar for over 60 years, Rose *Heilbron, the first woman in Britain to become a queen's counsel, Neville *Laski, Bernard Gillis (1905–1996), and Joseph Jackson (1924–1987), editor of the standard textbook on divorce. Two Jews, Arthur *Diamond and Sir Jack Jacob (1908–2000), became well-known as masters of the Supreme Court. In recent years many Jews have served on the British Bench, including two lord chief justices, Lord *Taylor and Lord *Woolf. John Cooper's *Pride vs. Prejudice: Jewish Doctors and Lawyers in England, 1890–1990* (2003), is a detailed and deeply researched account of Jews in these two professions and the obstacles they faced, which concludes that, in general, Jews faced little significant antisemitism.

[George Julius Webber / William D. Rubinstein (2nd ed.)]

UNIVERSITY TEACHERS. Jews were not prominent as law lecturers in Britain before World War II but after 1945 their number increased rapidly. Some of the outstanding Jewish professors of law were immigrants from Germany, many of whom specialized in the field of international law. Among those who achieved distinction as professors of public international law were Lassa Oppenheim and Sir Hersch *Lauterpacht at Cambridge and Georg Schwarzenberger of University College, London. Professors of private international law included Otto Kahn-Freund (d. 1979), who later became professor of comparative law at Oxford, Martin Wolff, Frederick Mann, E.J. Cohn, and Josef *Unger. Two Jews were reputed professors of Roman law – H.F. Jolowicz who was professor of Roman law for 30 years, first in London and then at Oxford, and Raphael Powell. Other Jewish academic lawyers of distinction included A.L. *Goodhart, the first Jewish master of an Oxford college, David *Daube, professor of civil law at Oxford, and Clare Palley who in 1970 was the first woman to be made professor of law.

[George Julius Webber]

France

Jews were not allowed to practice law in France until 1791. In that year they were given the right to French citizenship and a large measure of civil equality. Nevertheless, it was not until late in the 19th century that Jews became prominent in the three branches of the legal profession, the bar, the bench, and the universities. One of the first Jewish lawyers in France was Adolphe *Crémieux who was admitted to the bar in 1817 and successfully refused to take the humiliating *more judaico* oath which had previously been obligatory for all Jews. He was minister of justice on three occasions and the first Jew in France to hold this post. Other prominent lawyers were Louis Loew (1828–1917), who became an imperial public prosecutor in 1861 and later president of the criminal division of the Cour de Cassation, Leonce Lehman (1836–1892), secretary-general of the ministry of justice under Crémieux, and Frederick Reitlinger (1836–1910), a German advocate who immigrated to France and was the author of a standard work on cooperative societies. Other Jews achieved distinction as jurists including Charles *Lyon-Caen, professor of law at the University of Paris for nearly half a century and the leading authority on commercial law, Emile Worms (1838–1912), professor of law at the University of Rennes and the author of numerous works on constitutional and fiscal law, and André Weiss (1858–1928), professor of international and civil law at Dijon University and the legal adviser to the French Ministry of Foreign Affairs. There was a sharp increase in the number of Jewish lawyers at the beginning of the 20th century and several were appointed judges, among them Jules Valabrègue (1843–1925), president of the Paris Court of Appeals from 1906 to 1913. Valabrègue was one of the four Jews appointed to the Conseil d'Etat during this period; the others were André *Spire, Paul Grunebaum-Ballin, and Léon *Blum. Nevertheless, Jews were not generally appointed to top positions in the legal profession and only a few won fame as advocates, such as Henry *Torrès through his successful defense of Shalom *Schwarzbard, or held top university posts, as René *Cassin and Henri Lévi-Ullman. After World War II the number of Jewish lawyers continued to increase and by 1970 it was estimated that 25% of the lawyers at the Paris bar and more than 10% of the law lecturers at Paris University were Jews. In 1945, Cassin was president of the Conseil d'Etat, the first Jew to hold this position. Charles Eisenmann and Prosper Weil, professors of public law, and Lyon-Caen and Sinay, professors of labor law, were noted jurists.

[Claude Klein]

Germany

Although Jews were permitted to study medicine at German universities from the beginning of the 18th century, they were prevented from studying law until early in the 19th century. They were not allowed to practice law in some German states, such as Prussia, until after the Revolution of 1848. Thereafter, Jews found considerable obstacles in the way of their holding senior legal posts as judges, advocates, or university professors, and while many attempted to overcome discrimination by converting to Christianity, some Jewish lawyers of Germany achieved distinction by their writings on commercial, public, and international law without holding any formal legal position.

One of the first Jewish lawyers in Germany was Eduard *Gans, who was appointed lecturer in jurisprudence at Berlin University in 1820. He was made full professor in 1828, shortly after his conversion to Christianity. Gans was succeeded at Berlin by Friedrich Julius *Stahl, another converted Jew, and the first professing Jew to become professor of law at a German university was Heinrich *Dernburg, who was appointed to the chair of law at the University of Halle in 1862 and later became professor of Roman and Prussian law in Berlin.

The first Jewish judge in Germany was Hermann Makower, who was made an assistant judge of the Berlin Municipal Court in 1857. Three years later Gabriel Riesser became the first Jewish High Court judge when he was appointed to the Hamburg bench. Riesser's judgeship was particularly significant since he had at one time been refused a license to practice law because he was Jewish and had subsequently conducted a campaign for Jewish emancipation. Levin *Goldschmidt, professor of commercial law at the University of Heidelberg, became a judge of the commercial court and in 1887 Jacob *Behrend became the first Jewish judge of the German Supreme Court. In addition, Hermann *Staub and Theodor Loewenfeld (1848–1919) were among the first Jews to become prominent at the German bar, Siegfried Sommer and Albert Mosse (1846–1925) were the first Jewish Superior Court judges in Prussia, and Nathan Stein (1859–1927) was made president of the Mannheim district court in 1914, the first Jewish president of a court in Germany.

Nevertheless, few Jews were successful in obtaining senior judicial appointments in the German Empire and many sought professorial positions at German universities. Even toward the latter part of the century, however, discrimination still existed against Jews. Thus Hugo *Preuss, an authority on constitutional law, waited 36 years before the University of Berlin granted him a professorship. Preuss became chairman of the committee which drafted the Weimar constitution after 1918 and was one of four Jewish constitutional lawyers whose writings were to influence the form of the Weimar constitution, the others being Paul *Laband, author of the standard text *Das Staatsrecht des Deutschen Reiches* (3 vols., 1876–82), Georg Jellinek, and Adolphe *Arndt. Other notable Jewish professors, all of whom converted to Christianity, included Ferdinand Frensdorf (1833–1931), an authority on legal history, Edgar Loening (1843–1919), professor of constitutional and international law, and his brother, Richard Loening (1848–1903), who was professor of criminal law at the University of Jena for more than 20 years.

The end of the German Empire and the formation of the Weimar Republic brought about the end of all restrictions on Jews holding legal posts in the legal profession in Germany. Jewish lawyers found the profession highly lucrative in the period of rampant inflation during the early 1920s. The percentage of Jewish lawyers in practice was well in excess of the proportion of Jews to the general population (by 1932 the number was estimated at 20% of the total number of lawyers) and some became prominent advocates. Otto *Landsberg was minister of justice. Max Hachenburg was president of the Mannheim bar association. Albert Pinner (1857–1933) and Albrecht Mendelssohn-Bartholdy were German counsel at the Permanent Court of International Justice. After 1918 there was a sharp increase in the number of Jewish judges in Germany. Cohn and Citron were made Supreme Court judges and Alfred Orgler was a member of the Prussian Supreme Court. There was an even larger increase in the number of Jewish jurists. Hermann *Kantorowicz, Arthur *Nussbaum, professor of law at the University of Berlin, and Hans *Kelsen, professor of international law at the University of Cologne, were among many Jews to hold university chairs in law. They were obliged to leave their posts after 1933 and later held professorial posts at universities in the United States.

The Nazi rise to power led to the gradual elimination of Jewish lawyers from the legal profession. All judges and law professors were removed from their posts in 1933 but it was not until December 1935 that Jews were forbidden to practice law. After World War II there was a small number of Jewish lawyers in Germany, most of whom were involved in reparations cases. Josef Neuberger (1902–1977) was minister of justice in North-Rhineland and Westphalia but few other Jews held senior posts on the bench or in the universities. By 1970 it was estimated that there were fewer than 50 Jews in private practice in Germany.

[Robert M.W. Kempner]

Hungary

Restrictions on Jews practicing law in Hungary were removed by legislation at the end of the 1850s allowing Jews to engage in all professions. Nevertheless, as in Austria, the advancement of Jews in the legal profession was beset by religious prejudices and many converted to Christianity to further their careers. One of the first Jewish lawyers in Hungary was Izidor Baumgarten (1850–1914) who became a judge in Budapest in 1886 and was made district attorney for Budapest in 1896. His brother Károly Baumgarten (1853–1913), the first Jewish Supreme Court judge, was appointed in 1892. Several other Jews held judicial posts during the Austro-Hungarian Empire, among them Hugo Beck (1843–1928), Dezső Márkus (1862–1912), and Béla Gallia (1870–1954), who were appointed to the Supreme Court, and Sigismund Decsey, who was made a judge of the Royal Court in Budapest in 1895. On the other hand, Jews did not generally hold professorships at Hungarian universities; an exception was Gustave Schwarz (1858–1920), who became professor of Roman law at the University of Budapest.

During World War I Vilmos *Vázsonyi became minister of justice. He was one of three Jewish lawyers whose career at the bar paved the way for his political advancement – the others being Lipót *Vadász and Soma Visontai. Following Hungary's defeat in war and the failure of the Communist revolution, the Jews underwent organized persecution and Jewish judges and law professors were demoted. Tibor Lőw (1873–1942) was unique in his appointment as chief judge of the Court of Appeals and even he was obliged to retire following the nazification of Hungarian society in the late 1930s. Eventually, Jews were debarred from practicing law altogether and during World War II Jewish lawyers were removed from the judiciary and government service. After the war all restrictions on Jews practicing law were once again removed but only a small number could practice under the Communist regime, and none held top posts as judges or professors.

Italy

The emancipation of the Jews in Italy was completed in 1870 with the emancipation of the Jews of Rome in that year. Jews rapidly acquired prominence as jurists and professors of law but very few achieved fame as advocates or judges despite the fact that there was no legal barrier to their doing so. A notable exception was Lodovico *Mortara, who became successively attorney general, public prosecutor, president of the Supreme Court (Corte di Cassazione), and minister of justice.

One of the first Jews in Italy to hold a chair in law was Cesare *Vivante, who became professor of commercial law at the University of Parma in 1882 at the age of 27. Vivante was the founder of the modern Italian school for the study of commercial law and the author of a standard work on commercial law, *Istituzioni di diritto* (1891, 1935). Other prominent professors of commercial law included Leone Bolaffio (1848–1940), who helped Vivante prepare *Annuario critico della Giurisprudenza commerciale*, a yearbook on commercial law, D. Subino (1850–1937), who founded and edited the review *Diritto Commerciale*, and A. Graziani, who wrote a manual of commercial law. A number of Italian Jews became prominent as legal historians, including Vittorio *Colorni, who, in his major work, *Legge Ebraica e Leggi Locali* (1945), traced the application of Jewish law in Italy from Roman times; Gino *Segre, who for 20 years was professor of Roman law at the University of Turin; Edoardo *Volterra, who was professor of Roman law at four Italian universities; and A. Lattes (1858–1940), who was an authority on maritime law.

After World War I Jews held law chairs at almost every Italian university at a time when in other European countries a Jewish professor of law was unusual. Some of them were active in Jewish affairs, such as Mario *Falco, professor of ecclesiastical law at the University of Milan and a strong Zionist, Cino *Vitta, professor of administrative law in Florence and president of the Florence Jewish community, and Guido *Tedeschi, who immigrated to Israel and became professor of civil law at the Hebrew University of Jerusalem. In 1938 antisemitic laws were promulgated which prohibited Jews from holding university posts and within a year all the Jewish law professors were removed, among them Vitta, Volterra, Segre, *Ascarelli, Frederico *Cammeo, Colorni, and Mario Falco. After 1945, however, many of them returned to their posts: Volterra became rector of the University of Bologna in 1947, Ascarelli was appointed professor of commercial law at the University of Rome, and Angelo Pierre Sereni returned to the chair of international law at the University of Ferrara.

In the assimilated milieu of Italian Jewish society there was no typically Jewish contribution to Italian law. Nevertheless, it has been said that "every Jewish lawyer (in Italy) had his personal note, original and strong, that never was lost, but on the contrary, sometimes caused an innovation or modification in old rooted concepts" (G. Bedarida, *Ebrei d'Italia* (1950), 171ff.).

[Alfredo Mordechai Rabello]

Netherlands

Although Jews were permitted to study and practice medicine from the 17th century, they were not allowed to become lawyers until after the conquest of Holland by France in 1795 and the formation of the Batavian Republic. The first Jew to be formally admitted into the legal profession was Jonas *Meyer, who later became a court magistrate in Amsterdam and secretary of the government committee to draft a new Dutch constitution. Two other prominent Jewish lawyers of this period were Moses *Asser and his son Carel, the former being procurator in Amsterdam and one of the draftsmen of the first Dutch commercial code, and the latter secretary-general of the Ministry of Justice from 1815 to 1836. During the course of the 19th century several other Jews achieved prominence as lawyers in Holland. Joel Emanuel *Goudsmit, appointed to the chair of Roman law at Leyden in 1858, was the first Jewish professor of law in Holland; Michael *Godefroi was made minister of justice in 1860, the first of four Jews in Dutch history to hold this post. Two other Jewish lawyers became judges: Carel Asser (1843–1908) was a judge of the Hague District Court and later professor of civil law at Leyden and Aaron Adolf de *Pinto, who was largely responsible for the Netherlands Penal Code of 1886, was vice president of the Supreme Court. Most distinguished of all was Tobias *Asser who was successively professor of international law, legal advisor to the foreign ministry, and a chairman of the government committee for international law. He was awarded the Nobel Peace Prize in 1911. Tobias Asser was one of two distinguished Dutch Jewish international lawyers, the other being Jacques *Oppenheim who held the chair of international law at Leyden.

At the end of the 19th century the number of prominent Jewish lawyers in Holland was disproportionately large in relation to the total number of Jews. The trend was continued into the 20th century when Jewish judges in Holland included Lodewijk *Visser and Moritz *Polak, both of whom were appointed to the Supreme Court, and two of Polak's sons, Nico and Jacques, who were District Court judges. Eduard van *Raalte was appointed minister of justice in 1905. Daniel Jitta, professor of law at the University of Amsterdam, and Eduard *Meyers, professor of law at Leyden for 40 years, were two outstanding jurists. Few Jewish lawyers survived the Holocaust to practice after World War II, yet two Jews rose to become ministers of justice during this period – Ivo *Samkalden was appointed twice, in 1956 and in 1965, and Carel Polak, a third son of Moritz Polak, served from 1968.

Poland

Before Polish independence in 1918 there were very few Jewish lawyers in those parts of Austria, Prussia, and Russia which now form the territory of modern Poland. Jews in Russian Poland were generally refused permission to practice as lawyers until 1904, when restrictions on Jewish lawyers were annulled, while in Austrian and Prussian Poland, Jews tended to move to the large cities, such as Vienna and Berlin, where they had better facilities to study and practice. A curious exception was Edward Rittner (b. 1845) who became professor of ecclesiastical law at the University of Lemberg, and after converting to Christianity became secretary of state for Galicia.

Following Polish independence in 1918 Jews were granted equal rights to practice law, but severe discrimination existed both as regards the status of Jews in the profession generally and in their appointment to higher legal posts at the bar or in the judiciary. By 1931 nearly half of all Poland's lawyers were Jews and in areas where there was a large Jewish concentration, the figure was much higher. As legal costs rose lawyers' earnings dropped steadily and the Polish bar saw the persecution of Jewish lawyers as a way of recouping their losses. Restrictions on the right of Jews to hold certain legal posts were introduced and measures were taken to reduce the number of Jews who could enter the profession. Nevertheless, a few Jews did succeed: Grzegerz Glass (1864–1929) became a district court judge from 1918 until his death; Mauryey Allerhand (1863–1942) represented Poland in disputes before the Permanent Court of International Justice in The Hague; and Jan Jakub Litauer became a judge of the Supreme Court. A number of Jewish lawyers such as Waclaw Brokman (1879–1943), Leib *Landau, and Leon *Berenson, acquired prominence as defense counsel in political trials and defended Jews who were the victims of antisemitic attacks. The formation of the Communist Polish People's Republic at the end of World War II brought about the end of discriminatory practices against Jewish lawyers, whose number had fallen steeply as a result of the Holocaust. Several became university professors, among them Jan Jakub Litauer, who was professor of civil procedure at the University of Lodz, Jerzy *Sawicky, professor of criminal law at Warsaw University, Marion *Muszkat, professor of international law at Warsaw University, and Manfred *Lachs, who was professor of law at the Polish Academy in Warsaw. Two other outstanding lawyers were Stefan Kurowski (1898–1959), chief representative of Poland at the *Nuremberg tribunal for Nazi war crimes, and Leon Chajn, deputy minister of justice from 1945 to 1949. In 1967 Manfred Lachs was appointed Polish judge to the International Court of Justice in The Hague.

Russia

Before 1864 there were no lawyers in Russia within the modern meaning of the word. Parties were represented by pleaders, of whom a few, such as Osip *Rabinovitch, were Jewish, but there were no Jews among the judges who were drawn exclusively from the aristocracy. The 1864 reform of the legal system brought about the institution of lawyers and did not exclude Jews from being either advocates or judges. There were various limitations, however, on their right to hold senior legal posts. One of the first Jewish lawyers in Russia was Alexander Passover, who graduated from Moscow University in 1861 shortly after the lifting of restrictions on Jews studying in Russian universities. Denied a professorship because of his refusal to renounce Judaism, he was nevertheless admitted to the Odessa bar in 1871, and represented Jewish victims of the Odessa pogroms of that year. Mark Dillon (1843–1903), also a graduate of Moscow University, was one of the first Jewish judges in czarist Russia, but was refused promotion to a post in the higher courts. However, he was given a special permit to practice at the bar and became a leading advocate. Another Jewish judge was Jacob *Teitel, who served as judge of the district court of Saratov. A number of Jewish lawyers entered the government service where for many years prejudice had been less marked. Thus Arnold Dumashevsky (1836–1887) became a senior official in the Ministry of Justice as a result of his work on a committee for reforming the legislation of Poland and he was made first secretary of the third department of the Senate. Jacob Halperin (1840–1914) was an official in the Ministry of Justice for more than 40 years, Herman Trachtenberg (1839–1895) was rewarded for his work as a lawyer in government service by being appointed an honorary justice of the peace for the St. Petersburg district, and Gregori Verblovski (c. 1840–1900) was a first secretary of the St. Petersburg and Moscow circuit courts. An outstanding figure was Karl Bernstein (1842–1894), who immigrated to Germany, became professor of Roman law at Berlin University in 1887, and was responsible for teaching Russian students sent to Berlin to study law by the czarist government.

In 1889 the minister of justice presented a request to the czar that Jewish applicants for a license to practice law obtain a special permit from the minister. He justified the request on the grounds that there were so many Jewish lawyers that there was a danger that they might "contaminate the purity of the profession." The czar agreed to the request, with the result that for 15 years no Jews were given licenses to practice. At the same time many established lawyers were prevented from appearing in court even though in some cases they were already accepted as distinguished jurists. Thus Maxim *Vinaver, editor of the important law review *Vestnik Prava*, Henry Sliosberg, an adviser on administrative law to the minister of the interior, and Alexander *Goldenweiser, the author of several works on criminal responsibility, all had the status of lawyers' clerks. In 1904 the restrictions on Jews practicing law were eased and a large number took up practice in the large cities – Moscow, St. Petersburg, and Odessa – though many were granted the rank of assistant attorneys only. An outstanding figure of this period was Oscar *Grusenberg who was defense counsel at a number of celebrated political trials. In 1917, following the February Revolution, all remaining restrictions were removed and four Jews, Maxim Vinaver, Herman *Blumenfeld, Grusenberg, and B. Gurevich, became judges of the Supreme Court.

Immediately after the Bolshevik Revolution Isaac Nachman *Steinberg, a leader of the left Socialist Revolutionaries, became people's commissar for justice in Lenin's first coalition government which comprised left Socialist Revolutionaries. No formal restrictions were placed in the way of Jewish lawyers in the Soviet Union and many held high academic posts in Soviet universities in the 1920s; among them were Magaziner, Goykhbarb, and Nahum Osipovich Lagovier. One of the best-known Jewish lawyers was I.D. Braude who appeared on behalf of many accused persons in political trials. Most Jewish lawyers were prominent in the major cities, particularly Moscow, Leningrad, and Kiev, and many specialized in constitutional and criminal law. Law became one of the most popular professions among Russian Jewry, yet few held senior judicial appointments although there was no legal ban on their right to do so. In particular, there was a decline in the number of Jewish judges and assessors after World War II though not in the number of academic lawyers. Among the outstanding Soviet lawyers were Aron Naumovitch Trainin, a prominent figure at the Nuremberg trials, Mikhail Solomonovich Strogovich (1894–?), head of the criminal law and litigation section at the U.S.S.R. Institute of State and Law, Aleksey Adolfovich Herzensohn (1902–?), one of the draftsmen of the Soviet criminal code, and Nahum Pavlovich Farberov, the author of numerous works on constitutional law and senior associate at the Institute of State and Law.

South Africa

The first Jewish lawyer in South Africa was Simeon *Jacobs who went to Cape Colony from England in 1860. He was made attorney general of British Kaffraria in the following year and subsequently served as attorney general of Cape Colony and a judge of the Eastern Districts court. M. de *Vries, a Dutch Jew, was the first Jewish lawyer in the Transvaal, where in 1868 he was made state attorney. There were few other Jewish lawyers in South Africa in the 19th century but the number of Jewish advocates rapidly increased after World War I as a result of the immigration of large numbers of Jews at the turn of the century. Louis Benjamin (1865–1935) was appointed to the Cape bench in 1920, Manfred *Nathan was made a judge of the Natal Supreme Court in 1928, and Leopold *Greenberg became a judge of the Transvaal Provincial Division and president of the court in 1938. From 1943 until his retirement in 1955, Greenberg was a judge of the Transvaal Appellate Division, the first Jewish appeal court judge in South Africa. A number of Jews also became well-known advocates, among them Morris *Alexander, Henry *Morris, B.A. Ettlinger (1900–1960), Norman Rosenberg (1889–1963), Maurice Isaacs, who began in private practice after retiring as a Johannesburg magistrate, and Percy Yutar, who became attorney-general of the Orange Free State in 1969. Following World War II, the number of Jewish advocates in South Africa continued to increase and in 1965 there were 21 Jewish queen's counsel, more than one-third of the total number of queen's counsel in the whole of South Africa. Eleven Jews served as judges after World War II. Among the 56 Jews who served as judges after 1955 was Philip *Millin, who was originally appointed to the Transvaal Provincial Division in 1937 and was the chief author of the Millin Report (1949) on company law reform. Others included Godfrey Lewis (1879–1955) who was appointed to the Eastern Districts bench in 1945, Joseph *Herbstein, who served on the Cape Supreme Court from 1947 to 1962, Israel Louis Horwitz (1896–1955), the first Jewish judge in the Orange Free State, H.M. Bloch (1905–1963), of the Cape bench, Edgar *Henochsberg, Samuel Miller, and J.J. Friedman, who were judges of the Natal Provincial Division and Simon *Kuper, Oscar Galgut, and George Colman, judges of the Transvaal Provincial Division; Godfrey Lewis (Eastern Districts bench), Simon *Kuper, Oscar Galgut, George Colman, Cecil Margo, Ralph Zulman (later a judge of Appeal), Ezra Goldstein (father of South African Chief Rabbi Dr. Warren Goldstein), Ramon Leon (whose son, Tony *Leon, was leader of the Opposition in Parliament), and Basil Wunsh were judges of the Transvaal Provincial Division. Four Jews have held the position of Attorney-General, Percy Yutar (Orange Free State and later Transvaal), Edward Heller (Eastern Cape Division), Michael Imber (Natal Provincial Division), and Frank Kahn (Cape Provincial Division). Arthur *Chaskalson was the first president of the Constitutional Court and was appointed chief justice in 2001. Other Jewish Constitutional Court judges were Richard *Goldstone and Albie Sachs.

South America

In the 17th century a converted Jew, Diego Leon Pinelo (1605–1671), was professor of law and rector of the San Marcos University in Lima and his brother Antonio Pinelo (1591–1658) was an attorney in Buenos Aires. When the Jews immigrated to South America in increasing numbers toward the end of the 19th century, they were permitted to study law at most South American universities but were generally excluded from becoming judges or professors of law. Thus, although many Jews practiced law in South America and some achieved prominence in commerce and government service, there were virtually no jurists among them, although a prominent exception in Chile was Abraham Koenig, the author of several works on Chilean constitutional law.

The gradual liberalization of the legal profession after World War I enabled Jews to become judges and professors in Argentina, and in 1934 Mateo Goldstein (1908–1962) was made a judge of the San Juan Provincial Court. Marcos *Satanowski was one of the first Jewish professors of law and held the chair of commercial law at the University of Buenos Aires from 1935 to 1946 and from 1955 until his death. David Kraigelburd was professor of law at Buenos Aires, and Mariano Tissenbaum (1898–?) lectured on labor law at the University of Santa Fe from 1930 until 1966. After World War II a number of Jews held judicial posts in South America. Abraham Meersohn (1914–) was made a judge in Curacautin, Chile, and was promoted to the Court of Appeals in Santiago in 1964, Isaac Halperin (1907–?) was made a judge of the Argentine National Court of Appeals in 1955, and Marcus Melzer in Brazil and Moises de Castro (1918–) in Panama served as magistrates. Two Jews also served as Juvenile Court judges in South America: Fannie Leibovich (1908–?) was the first woman Juvenile Court judge in Chile and Simon Mizraḥi (1934–) was a member of the Venezuela Superior Juvenile Court.

After World War II an increasing number of Jews held chairs of law in South American universities. In Argentina Remo Entelman (1923–) was professor of jurisprudence at the universities of La Plata and Buenos Aires and was special assistant to President Arturo Frondizi. Several other Jews held chairs of law at the University of Buenos Aires, among them Bernardo Beiderman (1919–), professor of criminal law, Mario Bendersky (1923–), professor of civil law, Ignacio Winizky (1910–?), professor of comparative law, and Marco Kaufmann (1924–) and Elias Neuman (1932–), professors of law at the University of La Plata. Other Jewish jurists who held law chairs at South American universities included Miguel *Schweitzer and Jacobo Schaulson *Numhauser, professors of law at the University of Chile; Arnold *Wald, professor of civil law at the University of Guanabara in Brazil; Alfredo Eisenberg, professor of international law at the Uruguay National University; and Sara Bialoslowsky de Chazan, professor of Roman law at the National University of Mexico.

[Paul Link]

United States

There is no mention in the records of any Jews practicing law until late in the 18th century, although Asser *Levy, who fought for Jewish civil rights, was frequently involved in a variety of law suits. That no Jews practiced law was largely due to the fact that lawyers were unpopular in the colonies until the period of the Revolutionary War. They were generally held in disrepute and were subject to suspicion as enforcers of inequitable and corrupt laws.

The first Jew to study law professionally was Moses *Levy, who was admitted to the Philadelphia bar in 1778. He become one of the most distinguished and successful lawyers in Philadelphia, as did his brother Samson Levy, Jr., and later became judge of the District Court for the City of Philadelphia. Although he was the first Jewish lawyer in the United States, Levy was not the first Jew to be made a judge. Isaac Miranda, a layman, was appointed deputy judge of the Vice Admiralty of the Province of Pennsylvania in 1727 and David Emanuel and James Lucena, also laymen, became justices of the peace in Georgia in 1766 and 1773, respectively. By the beginning of the 19th century a growing number of Jews made their mark in the legal profession. Among those to gain prominence at the bar were Joseph Simon Cohen, Benjamin Gratz, Elijah Gratz Etting, Nathan Nathans, and Jonas B. Phillips. Jews did not practice law in as large numbers as in the 20th century but there were few eastern cities in which there were no successful Jewish practitioners or judges.

Two Jewish lawyers were outstanding during the 19th century: Philip *Phillips and Judah Philip *Benjamin. The former was recognized as one of the foremost advocates of his time, arguing more than 400 appeals before the U.S. Supreme Court; the latter was the first Jew to be offered a judgeship of the Supreme Court (which he refused), and to be attorney general of the Confederacy in the Civil War. After the defeat of the Confederacy he escaped to England where he became a leading counsel of the English bar. Other prominent Jews in American law during this period included Raphael J. *Moses (who became the leading commercial lawyer of Georgia), and William Mallory Levi (1827–1882) who was a justice of the Supreme Court of Louisiana.

The 20th century saw a dramatic increase in the number of Jewish lawyers in the United States, partly reflected in the rise of the number of Jews to hold judgeships and university professorships. But for many years Jewish lawyers had considerable difficulty earning a living, particularly in New York, where the majority congregated. They suffered severely from the effects of the depression which substantially reduced the volume of business, particularly in view of the fact that in relation to the total Jewish population of New York, the profession was grossly overcrowded. Jewish lawyers found advancement difficult since many were foreign born, did not go to the best colleges, and often came from poor homes, making it more difficult for them to open their own firms. In 1939 it was estimated that more than half the lawyers practicing in New York were Jews but that the annual income of the average Jewish lawyer was several hundred dollars less than that of his non-Jewish counterpart. The same trend was discernible in other American cities; the ratio of Jewish lawyers to the total Jewish population was much higher than the ratio of lawyers to the general population and since Jewish lawyers largely attracted a Jewish clientele, their chances of success were slim.

In contrast to the high percentage of Jews in private practice, Jews did not generally hold top posts in the profession. Few of the large firms had Jewish members and it was almost unknown for a Jew to be head of a large law firm. Similarly, Jews did not generally become law professors at leading universities like Harvard and Yale and notable exceptions such as Felix *Frankfurter indicated that only Jews with outstanding talent were offered teaching posts. Discrimination also existed in appointments to judgeships and even in New York Benjamin *Cardozo and Irving *Lehman were the only Jews to be appointed to the New York Court of Appeals before World War II.

Nevertheless, a few Jews did achieve distinction in the legal profession. Louis *Brandeis, Benjamin Cardozo, and Felix Frankfurter were successively appointed to the U.S. Supreme Court and established a tradition of the "Jewish seat" on the Supreme Court bench. All three were recognized as among the greatest judges ever to sit on the Supreme Court. Other Jewish judges of note during this period were Julian *Mack, judge of the U.S. Circuit Court of Appeals; Horace *Stern, justice of the Pennsylvania Supreme Court; Henry *Butzel, three times chief justice of the State of Michigan; and Samuel Kalisch (1851–1930), justice of the New York Supreme Court.

A few Jews made their mark as legal philosophers, among them Max *Radin, professor of law at the University of California and Morris Raphael *Cohen, professor of philosophy at the City College of New York. Outstanding advocates included Louis *Marshall, Louis *Nizer, Samuel *Leibowitz, and Lee M. *Friedman.

A gradual improvement in the status and condition of Jewish lawyers took place after World War II. To a large extent Jews found it easier to be admitted to large law firms, although research in the late 1960s indicated that discrimination still existed. Jewish graduates from American universities found it harder to find a job than non-Jewish graduates and Jewish graduates were more likely to earn a lower starting salary. As a result Jews tended to be accepted in Jewish law firms (in 1950 it was estimated that nearly 85% of Jewish lawyers entered law firms which were wholly or partly Jewish), where discrimination did not exist, or in less prominent firms, and only the outstanding students entered the best non-Jewish firms. Nevertheless, there is no evidence that Jews were discouraged from becoming lawyers, especially since other prestigious professions, such as banking, were even more discriminatory. Jewish lawyers of the postwar period benefited from the fact that they no longer tended to come from poor families and that the Jewish communities among whom they lived had become relatively affluent, thereby giving them work. They were no longer prevented from obtaining the best legal education available and were able to compete with their gentile colleagues on more or less equal terms. Nevertheless, it is interesting to note that though by the late 1960s 20% of America's 350,000 lawyers were Jewish, only in 1969 did a Jew, Bernard *Segal, become president of the American Bar Association.

The most notable feature about the position of Jews in the legal profession after World War II was their influence on the law both as judges and jurists. Two Jews were appointed to the U.S. Supreme Court after World War II, Arthur *Goldberg and Abe *Fortas; a number of Jews served on state supreme courts, among them Stanley *Fuld, chief justice of the New York Court of Appeals, David *Bazelon, chief judge of the U.S. Court of Appeals, District of Columbia, and Simon *Sobeloff, U.S. attorney general (1954–56). Prominent jurists of the postwar period include Judge Jerome *Frank, one of the principle theorists of the American realist school, Paul *Freund, professor of constitutional law at Harvard, Fred Rodell (1907–1980) and Alexander Bickel (1924–), both professors of law at Yale, Edmond *Cahn, professor of law at New York University, and Professor Jerome Hall, an outstanding authority on criminal law and theory. In general, Jews did not suffer from discrimination in acceptance as university teachers or as students. In 1970 it was estimated that 20 out of 75 members of the Harvard Law faculty were Jewish, at Yale 17 out of 54, at Columbia 15 out of 60, and at California 14 out of 45. Furthermore, a report on entrance to law schools indicated that Jews actually obtain admission more easily than Protestants to the elite law schools.

One of the most significant aspects of Jewish participation in American law in the 20th century has been the extensive interest of U.S. Jewish lawyers and judges in upholding and extending civil liberties in the United States and the profound influence they have exerted in this respect on major constitutional doctrines affecting race relations, the administration of criminal justice, and the operation of the political process. Understandably, they tend to have such an interest partly because of their recognition of their own group's historical disabilities, and partly because of the traditional liberalism and concern for civil rights that has long characterized the U.S. Jewish community. The Supreme Court judges named above played key roles in this field, and prominent American Jewish trial lawyers whose careers have been in large measure dedicated to civil liberties cases include Arthur Garfield Hays, Louis Marshall, Samuel Leibowitz, and Walter *Pollack. The latter two cooperated in fighting and winning the world-famous "Scottsboro Boys" rape case in Alabama in the 1930s. Jack Greenberg (1924–) and Anthony Amsterdam (1935–) defended white and black civil rights workers in the American South during the 1960s, the latter as chief legal counsel of the National Association for the Advancement of Colored People. Leonard Boudin (1912–1989) and William Kunstler (1919–) were active as defense counsels in the political trials of prominent Communists and radicals, the latter gaining national fame in 1970 as chief attorney for the militant Black Panthers. Both were leading figures in the American Civil Liberties Union, as were Osmond Fraenkel, Norman Dorsen, Aryeh Neier, and Max Radin. Jewish judges whose strong support for civil liberties had a decided impact on American law as a whole included Mayer *Sulzberger, Irving Lehman, Horace *Stern, David Bazelon, and Charles *Wyzanski.

In the last decade of the 20th century, as Jews became thoroughly assimilated into the mainstream of American life, President Bill Clinton appointed two Jews to the Supreme Court, Ruth Bader *Ginsburg and Stephen G. *Breyer. Ginsburg, named in 1993, had a distinguished legal career as a civil libertarian and as an advocate for women's rights. Her appointment reflected a recognition of the increasing role of women in the law. At that time, the field of law was attracting more and more women – more than half of law students were women – and eventually more of them, many Jewish, won positions on the bench. Breyer, who married in England in an Anglican ceremony with references to Christ edited out, was a professor at Harvard Law, and his appointment in 1994 apparently had little to do with the fact that he was Jewish.

[Julius J. Marcke / Stewart Kampel (2nd ed.)]

Israel

Only a few Jews were qualified to practice law in Ereẓ Israel under Ottoman rule. Thus Gad *Frumkin was the only Jewish lawyer in Jerusalem when the city was captured by the British in 1917. The British mandatory authorities established the Palestine Law School, known as the Jerusalem law classes, in 1921 for the training of lawyers and most of the qualified lawyers when the State of Israel came into being were graduates of these classes. The Jerusalem law classes were not designed to provide academic law studies and in 1926 courses in Jewish law were begun at the Hebrew University in Jerusalem. A separate school for the study of law and economics was opened in Tel Aviv in 1935. In 1948 both the law faculty on Mount Scopus and the British Government Law School were closed down and in 1949 a new law faculty was opened in West Jerusalem for students preparing for the master's degree. Doctoral and undergraduate courses were later inaugurated.

Formal law courses at the Tel Aviv University were opened in 1959 when the Tel Aviv School of Law and Economics was integrated with the Hebrew University. From 1966 the law faculty of Tel Aviv University severed its connection with Jerusalem. A department for the study of Jewish Law was opened at the Bar-Ilan University in 1970. In addition many immigrant lawyers who had studied law in their native lands requalified as Israel lawyers after passing the foreign lawyers examination of the Israel Chamber of Advocates and completing the required period of apprenticeship.

BIBLIOGRAPHY: H. Sinzheimer, *Juedische Klassiker der deutschen Rechtswissenschaft* (1938); A.L. Goodhart, *Five Jewish Lawyers of the Common Law* (1949); E. Bedarida, *Ebrei d'Italia* (1950), 171ff.; C. Roth, *Jewish Contribution to Civilization* (1956³), 245–8; S. Kaznelson (ed.), *Juden im deutschen Kulturbereich* (1962); F. Kobler, in: J. Fraenkel (ed.), *Jews of Austria* (1967), 25–40; M.M. Fagin, in: JSOS, 1 (1939), 73–104; A.I. Goldberg, *ibid.*, 32 (1970), 148–61.

LAYTON, IRVING (Israel Lazarovitch; 1914–), Canadian poet. Layton was born in Romania and brought to Montreal, Canada, on his first birthday. His parents, Keine Wolfsohn and Moishe Lazarovitch, were traditional Jews who settled in the Yiddish-speaking enclave that extended along St Lawrence Street – the "Main" – and served as the boundary dividing the city's population: French-speaking Catholics on the East, English-speaking Protestants on the West. In the lives of his own parents Layton had an immediate, indelible exposure to the conflict of self-enclosed personalities who, in their distinctive individuality, represented to him the irreconcilable polar extremes of temperament and sensibility. In parental conflict he located the primal antinomies that he accepted as the basis of his character and from which he derived the dialectical structure of thought and feeling that is manifest in all his writing.

Layton was educated at Baron Byng High School, where he met his early intellectual mentors, David *Lewis, whose socialist ideology was persuasive, and the distinguished Jewish poet and novelist, A.M. *Klein. He graduated with a B.Sc. in agriculture from Macdonald College (1939) and earned an M.A. in political science at McGill University (1946). His vocation as poet was announced with the publication in 1945 of his first book of poems, *Here and Now*. That initial installment marked the onset of a literary career of exceptional range, consisting of over 55 volumes of poetry, short fiction, essays, reviews, memoirs, correspondence, and literary criticism, establishing the author as a central figure in the Canadian literary canon. From his earliest poems, which appeared in small literary publications where Layton and his like-minded contemporaries sought to redirect Canada's staid, provincial culture toward the challenging modernist temper, Layton's work always depended on a forceful, combative, representation of the self. This pervasive egotism has offended some; what his detractors fail to recognize is that an esthetic as well as a temperamental urgency underlie its literary deployment. Layton confesses to his self-conscious performance when he describes the polarities of identity revealed in the poems: "I became by turns prophet and clown." These self-selected personae are usually represented in the author's characteristic role as moral gadfly to his fellow Canadians, Jew and gentile alike, chastising their failings in a language of deliberate affront. Layton's open didacticism presupposes a privileged position for the poet in society.

Two themes inform Layton's prodigious creative imagination. The first, which extends from the 1940s to the late 1960s, is his commitment to enlarging the Canadian literary sensibility so that it responds to new areas of feeling and vital forms of emotional expression. Many poems written from the late 1960s to the mid-1980s address the subject of the Holocaust and Christianity's guilt for the destruction of European Jewry. In these poems Layton assumes the stance of a prosecutor, demanding confession from the Christian world for centuries of dehumanizing treatment of the Jews, which ultimately led to the death camps. In contrast to this national catastrophe, Layton invokes the birth of the State of Israel as the redemptive promise of Jewish continuity. Detached from religious authority, he has assembled a personal genealogy, secular in orientation and eclectic in scope. His progenitors are the Hebrew prophets, Heine, Marx, Jesus, Israeli soldiers, Babel, and Mandelstam, as Layton sees in them model Jews who exhibited unyielding moral purpose and assertion of the will in the face of evil.

In 1960 Irving Layton received the Governor General's Award for his contribution to Canadian culture and in 1963 the Prix littérature de Québec. In 1976 he was made an Officer of the Order of Canada, and in the 1980s was nominated three times for the Nobel Prize.

BIBLIOGRAPHY: E. Cameron, *Irving Layton: A Portrait* (1985); I. Layton, *Waiting for the Messiah: A Memoir* (1985); H. Beissel and J. Bennett (eds.), *Raging Like a Fire: A Celebration of Irving Layton* (1993).

[Mervin Butovsky (2nd ed.)]

LAZA OF FRANKFURT (fl. late 17th–early-18th century), learned woman and translator of religious writings. Laza was the wife of *Jacob ben Mordecai of Schwerin. In 1692, she rendered her husband's work, *Tikkun Shalosh Mishmarot* ("Prayers for the Three Night Watches"), from Hebrew into Yiddish, adding her own Yiddish introduction. Around 1709 Laza wrote, with Sara Oppenheim, a scroll of Esther. This was probably a Yiddish translation of the biblical text to be read to women who did not know Hebrew.

BIBLIOGRAPHY: M. Kayserling, *Die juedischen Frauen in der Geschichte, Literatur und Kunst* (1991), 178; E. Taitz, S. Henry, and C. Tallan, "Laza of Frankfurt," in: *The JPS Guide to Jewish Women, 600 B.C.E.–1900 C.E.* (2003), 142–43.

[Cheryl Tallan (2nd ed.)]

LAZAR, SAMSON (originally **Lascăr Şaraga**; 1892–1968), Romanian author. The son of a Jassy publisher, he first wrote *Pe o harpă de aramă* ("On a Bronze Harp," 1916), a volume of sonnets illustrated by the painter R. *Rubin. Lazar translated works by Ber *Borechov, then renounced Zionism, but immigrated to Israel in 1957. There he published verse on heroic Israel themes and prose works about Romanian-Jewish life, such as *Zavera* ("The Revolt," 1964) and *Neguri* ("Fog" 1967).

LAZARD, family of international bankers. ALEXANDRE LAZARD was born early in the 19th century at Sarreguemines, Lorraine, France, and migrated to the United States in 1847. He settled in New Orleans where he started a dry-goods business and in 1848 took his two brothers SIMON and ELIE into partnership. A year later their business was destroyed by a fire which devastated a large part of the city. They moved to San Francisco, California, during the gold rush and soon began trading in gold between San Francisco and Western Europe via New York City, where their cousin Alexandre Weill was put in charge of the transfers. They developed Lazard Frères into a successful banking house, establishing branches in Paris (1854) and London (1877). In 1908 the Lazards' San Francisco banking house was sold, and thereafter they centered their banking activities in New York, Paris, and London. The three houses were loosely interlinked and served, more recently, as investment advisers, as managers of Eurodollar bond offerings for large industrial companies and in arranging mergers, with emphasis on chemical, metal, and television industries, car manufacturing, and airlines. Besides their own investments in real estate and international banking corporations, they founded, in 1968, Lazard S.A., in order to participate jointly in underwriting syndicates. This departure reflected and promoted the international trend toward closer interlinking of separate national economies and individual enterprises. After World War II, the Paris firm Lazard Frères was headed by Pierre David-Weill (1900–1975), the grandson of Alexandre Weill. The New York firm Lazard Frères was headed by French-born André Meyer (1898–1979) who had joined the Paris house in 1926 and had fled in 1940 to the United States. The London firm Lazard Brothers was a corporation with major interests held by the firm of S. Pearson and Sons, in which David-Weill and Meyer owned minority interests.

BIBLIOGRAPHY: T.A. Wise, in: *Fortune* (August 1968), 101–3, 156–65.

[Hanns G. Reissner]

LAZARE, BERNARD (1865–1903), French writer. Lazare was born and educated in Nimes, then went to Paris, where he began to make his way as a writer (publishing several volumes of verse) and also took part in Jewish affairs. He was attracted by the anarchist and socialist movements and worked on a number of periodicals, writing articles which later formed the basis of his book, *L'antisémitisme, son histoire et ses causes* (1894; *Antisemitism, its History and Causes*, 1903). In it he maintained that antisemitism could be of some use in bringing about the advent of socialism by teaching hatred of Jewish capitalism; this would inevitably turn into hatred of capitalism in all its forms. His book contains violent expressions against some sectors of the Jewish community, often quoted later by professional antisemites. However, the *Dreyfus Affair shook Lazare's views to their roots and completely changed his attitude on the Jewish problem. He was one of Dreyfus' first supporters and published several books in an attempt to demonstrate his innocence; these include *Une erreur judiciaire; la vérité sur l'affaire Dreyfus* (1896) and *Comment on condamne un innocent* (1898). From then on Lazare declared that antisemitism did not help to combat capitalism but, on the contrary, provided it with a safety valve. Assimilation was no more an answer to the Jewish problem than emancipation had been. Lazare therefore came out in favor of a nationalist solution to the Jewish problem, though he had not yet any particular place in view. This development in his ideas led to his participation in the Second Zionist Congress in 1898. However, his intransigence soon brought him into conflict with Theodor Herzl, particularly over the creation of the *Jewish Colonial Trust which Lazare opposed.

Lazare was a close friend of Charles *Péguy, who published his study on the Jews of Romania in *Cahiers de la Quinzaine* (1902). Péguy included an essay on Lazare in *Notre Jeunesse* (1910) in which he credited him with a leading role in the Dreyfus Affair: "In this great crisis, the prophet of both Israel and the world was Bernard Lazare," he wrote. Lazare died already practically forgotten.

BIBLIOGRAPHY: B. Hagani, *Bernard Lazare* (Fr., 1919), incl. bibl.; Fontainas, in: *Mercure de France* (July 1933), 45–71; idem, in: B. Lazare, *L'antisémitisme, son histoire et ses causes* (1934), preface; Muslak, in: REJ, 106 (1941/45), 34–63; Silberner, in: HJ, 16 (1954), 30–35; A. Hertzberg, *The Zionist Idea* (1960), 468–76.

[Simon R. Schwarzfuchs]

LĂZĂREANU, BARBU (originally **Baruch Lazarovici**; 1881–1957), Romanian author and journalist. Born in Botoşani, Moldavia, Lăzăreanu had to leave school because of his socialist activities and in 1907 was expelled from Romania because of his support for the rebellious peasants. He settled in Paris, where he joined the editorial staff of the Socialist daily *L'Humanité* and also lectured at a workers' university. When he was finally allowed to return to Romania, Lăzăreanu settled in Bucharest, where he began his literary career in earnest. He published two volumes of a five-volume edition of the essays of Constantin *Gherea-Dobrogeanu (1925–27), and wrote for many general and Jewish periodicals. Between the two world wars, Lăzăreanu made important contributions to the study of Romanian folklore and enriched Romanian literary historiography with original interpretations, including studies of the writers I.L. Caragiale (1922), B.P. Haşdeu (1927), and M. Eminescu (1924). The comprehensiveness and diversity of his research was praised by one of Romania's greatest writers, Tudor Arghezi. After the change of regime at the end of World War II, Lăzăreanu was elected to the Romanian Academy and was appointed director of its library. *Glose si comentarii de istoriografie literară* (1958), a collection of his articles and studies on classical literature and folklore, comprising some of Lăzăreanu's contributions to the Romanian and Yiddish press, was issued as a posthumous tribute by the Romanian State Publishing House for Literature and the Arts.

BIBLIOGRAPHY: Crişan, in: *Gazeta Literară* (Feb. 13, 1958); J. Peltz, *Cum i-am cunoscut* (1964), 78–86.

[Abraham Feller]

LAZAREFF, PIERRE (1907–1972), prominent French newspaper editor. Already in his youth Lazareff had made his mark as a gifted journalist. In 1931, when he was news editor of the *Paris-Midi*, he was appointed editor of the newly created evening paper *Paris-Soir*. Deliberately setting out to adopt American newspaper methods, combining sensationalism and human interest with solid editorial comment, Lazareff succeeded in increasing its circulation in five years from 134,000 to nearly 2,500,000, a record figure for the French Press, which earned him the title "the French Northcliffe." On the collapse of France in World War II he went into exile, first to the U.S., where he became head of the Voice of America broadcasting program, and then to London, where he was in charge of American broadcasts to Nazi-occupied Europe. Returning to Paris in 1945 he took over the management of a new evening paper *France-Soir* together with that of some other journals, and repeated the same success as with *Paris-Soir*. In 1958 he extended his activities to television with a popular news commentary. Lazareff was an ardent supporter of General de Gaulle.

BIBLIOGRAPHY: *Times* (April 4, 1972).

LAZARON, MORRIS SAMUEL (1888–1979), U.S. Reform rabbi. Lazaron, who was born in Savannah, Georgia, was ordained by Hebrew Union College in 1914. He served as rabbi in Wheeling, West Virginia, for a year and in 1915 was appointed rabbi of the Baltimore Hebrew Congregation, the large and distinguished Reform synagogue in Baltimore where he served for 31 years as rabbi and rabbi emeritus. During World War I, he wrote *Side Arms* (*Readings and Meditations for Soldiers and Sailors*, 1918). As rabbi he initiated youth-oriented programming, introduced innovative rituals, and was an early supporter of the interfaith movement, working with the National Conference of Catholics and Jews and traveling throughout the United States with a priest and a minister to represent the three faiths of America. Lazaron's retirement from this office in 1949 was linked to his active identification with the anti-Zionist American Council for Judaism, of which he was a founder and vice president. This position was not problematic with his congregation until after the Holocaust, and especially after the establishment of the State of Israel. This led to the severing of his relationship with Baltimore Hebrew, including his resignation as rabbi emeritus. He was also a member of the National Council of the American Friends of the Middle East. He wrote several works, including *Ask the Rabbi* (1928); *The Consolidation of Our Father* (1928); *Homeland or State: The Real Issue* (1940); *In the Shadow of Catastrophe* (1956); *Is This the Way?* (1942); and *Olive Trees in a Storm* (1955).

ADD. BIBLIOGRAPHY: S. Shpeen, "A Man Against the Wind: A Biographical Study of Rabbi Morris S. Lazaron" (Rabbinical Thesis, HUC-JIR, 1984); K.M. Olitzsky, L.J. Sussman, and M.H. Stern, *Reform Judaism in America: A Biographical Dictionary and Sourcebook* (1993).

[Sefton D. Temkin / Michael Berenbaum (2nd ed.)]

LAZARSFELD, PAUL F. (1901–1976), U.S. sociologist. Born in Vienna in 1901, Lazarsfeld studied mathematics and psychology at the University of Vienna and came to the United States in 1933 on a Rockefeller fellowship. He became a director of the Research Center at the University of Newark in 1936, and director of the newly established office of Radio Research at the University of Princeton in 1937. After 1940 he was professor and chairman of the Department of Sociology at Columbia University, where he remained until 1970. In addition, he was president of the American Sociological Association. In 1945 Lazarsfeld became director of the Bureau of Applied Social Research at Columbia, a pioneering venture that has become the model for a number of similar research institutes at American universities. The published works of Lazarsfeld and his collaborators deal with public opinion research, and generally with quantitative research and its techniques. Latent structure analysis, which was developed by Lazarsfeld as a major tool in attitude survey research, assumes that regularities of behavior exist which are not immediately recognizable but do account for the manifest relationship between any two or more items on a test. In the field of communications research, Lazarsfeld developed quantitative content analysis, as well as the "panel" technique; the latter involves the repeated interviewing on the same subject matter of a given sample or panel. Lazarsfeld's early study, *Die Arbeitslosen von Marien-*

thal (1933), had remained a minor classic; his early American publication "The Art of Asking Why?" (*National Marketing Review* (1935), likewise, is of a pioneering character. *Latent Structure Analysis* was published in 1960. Lazarsfeld's most important publication in the field of public opinion research is *The People's Choice* (1944), an analysis of the decisions that determine the outcome of an election campaign.

Among other publications of which Lazarsfeld was author or coauthor are *Radio and the Printed Page* (1940), *Radio Listening in America* (1948), *Continuities in Social Research* (1950), *Voting* (1954), *The Language of Social Research* (1955), *Personal Influence* (1955), *The Academic Mind* (1958), *The Uses of Sociology* (1967), *Latent Structure Analysis* (1968), *Qualitative Analysis* (1972), *Main Trends in Sociology* (1973), *Views from the Socially Sensitive Seventies* (1973), and *An Introduction to Applied Sociology* (1975). Lazarsfeld published an autobiographical account of his role in the creation of social research institutes under the title "An Episode in the History of Social Research: A Memoir" in the second volume of *Perspectives in American History* (1968).

BIBLIOGRAPHY: *Current Biography Yearbook 1964* (1964), 250–3. **ADD. BIBLIOGRAPHY:** R. Boudon (ed.), *On Social Research and Its Language* (1993); P.K. Lazarsfeld, *The Varied Sociology of Paul F. Lazarsfeld* (1982); R. Merton, *Qualitative and Quantitative Social Research: Papers in Honor of Paul F. Lazarsfeld* (1979).

[Werner J. Cahnman / Ruth Beloff (2nd ed.)]

LAZARUS, U.S. family of department store owners. In 1851 SIMON LAZARUS (d. 1877) emigrated from north Germany and opened a store in Columbus, Ohio. He also served the local Congregation B'nai Jeshurun as a volunteer rabbi. His sons FRED (d. 1917) and RALPH (d. 1903) founded F. and R. Lazarus and Co., which sold men's and later also women's clothing. After Fred's death, his sons SIMON (1882–1947) and FRED JR. (1884–1973) took charge, joined by their brother ROBERT (1890–1973) in 1926, when the business became a full-line department store. A subsidiary in Cincinnati was added in 1928, managed by the youngest brother, JEFFREY (1894–?). A holding company – Federated Department Stores, Inc. – was established in 1929 by the Lazarus family, together with Filene's, Abraham and Straus, and Bloomingdale's. It was transformed into an operating company in 1945, with Fred Jr. as president. Expanding into the southern and western United States, the company operated 119 department stores, 12 specialty and discount stores, and 63 supermarkets by 1970, with $2.1 billion consolidated annual net sales. Fred Jr., Robert, Fred Jr.'s son RALPH (1914–1988), and other fourth-generation sons held the executive positions.

Fred Jr., a Republican, served on presidential committees under the Roosevelt, Eisenhower, and Kennedy administrations and participated in local civic affairs, including the Cincinnati Conference of Christians and Jews and the Jewish Orphan Home in Cleveland. He was long an executive committee member of the American Jewish Committee. His brother Simon served on the board of governors of Hebrew Union College and of the Union of American Hebrew Congregations.

[Hanns G. Reissner]

LAZARUS, EMMA (1849–1887), U.S. poet, essayist, and activist. Lazarus was born in New York on July 22, 1849, to Moses Lazarus, a wealthy industrialist of Sephardi heritage, and his wife Esther Nathan Lazarus of Ashkenazi background. Both sides of her family had been in America since the Revolution. Lazarus, who was educated at home by private tutors, was originally attracted to classical and romantic art and literature. During the course of her career, she struck up tutelary relationships with important male writers, especially Ralph Waldo Emerson, and including Thomas Wentworth Higginson and Henry James. Her early works included *Poems and Translations: Written Between the Ages of Fourteen and Sixteen*, published privately by her father in 1867, a novel *Alide: An Episode of Goethe's Life* (1874), and a historical tragedy, *The Spagnoletto* (1876), as well as a translation of poems by Heinrich *Heine, accompanied by a biographical study. By the time she wrote her best-known poem, "The New Colossus" (1883), a hymn to America, the "Mother of Exiles," she had repudiated the glorification of male conquering power, aestheticism, and empty ceremony and asserted instead the power of womanhood, the comfort of motherhood, and the Hebraic prophetic values of compassion and consolation. Lazarus began her return to Jewish tradition in the late 1870s, studying Hebrew and reading Graetz's *History of the Jews* and George Eliot's novel *Daniel Deronda*, with its plea for a Jewish national revival. Lazarus began to publish translations of the medieval Spanish-Jewish poets, *Judah Halevi, Solomon ibn *Gabirol, and others. The Russian pogroms of 1881 and the May Laws of 1882 fired both her social consciousness and her poetic imagination, prompting a series of essays in American journals, especially in *Century Magazine* (May 1882), where she replied to an antisemitic article by a Russian journalist, Madame Z. Ragozin. "The Dance Unto Death," a verse tragedy about the burning of the Jews of Nordhausen during the Black Death appeared in *Songs of a Semite* (1882), dedicated to George Eliot, "the illustrious writer who did most among the artists of our day towards elevating and ennobling the spirit of Jewish Nationality." Lazarus's series of 14 essays, ironically entitled "Epistle to the Hebrews," written from November 1882 to February 1883, were intended to "bring before the Jewish public… facts and critical observations… to arouse a more logical and intelligent estimate of the duties of the hour." Lazarus also involved herself in the practical work of helping new immigrants adjust to America, founding the Hebrew Technical Institute for Vocational Training. In 1883 she sailed to London, armed with letters of introduction from Henry James to well-placed people in England, Jews and non-Jews, who might help her in her effort towards the establishment of a Jewish national homeland. A decade before Theodore *Herzl launched the Zionist movement, Lazarus argued in poetry and prose for Palestine as a safe haven for oppressed Jews everywhere. Lazarus, who never married, died of cancer at the age of 38. After her death, her sister, Josephine Lazarus, prohibited the inclusion of "anything Jewish" in the collected edition of her works that appeared in 1889. "The New Colossus," with its famous image of "huddled masses yearning to breathe free," was engraved on a memorial plaque and affixed to the pedestal of the Statue of Liberty in 1903.

BIBLIOGRAPHY: C.S. Kessner, "From Parnassus to Mount Zion: The Journey of Emma Lazarus," in: *Jewish Book Annual* (1986–87); Idem, "The Emma Lazarus-Henry James Connection: Eight Letters," in: *American Literary History*, 3 (1991). D. Lichtenstein, *Writing Their Nations: The Traditions of Nineteenth Century American Jewish Women Writers* (1992); R. Rusk (ed.), *Letters to Emma Lazarus in the Columbia University Library* (1939); M. Schappes (ed.), *The Letters of Emma Lazarus, 1868–85* (1949). B. Roth Young, *Emma Lazarus in the World: Life and Letters* (1995).

[Carole S. Kessner (2nd ed.)]

LAZARUS, MEL (1927–), U.S. cartoonist. Born in Brooklyn, N.Y., Lazarus took up cartooning almost immediately after graduation from high school in 1945. He developed two comic strips, *Wee Women* and *Li'l One*, which formed a base of young, saucy characters that would later become his trademark style. Al *Capp, one of the owners of Toby Press, enlisted Lazarus's drawing skills to copy his *Li'l Abner* characters for cards, games, comic books, and other products. Lazarus became art director/comics editor at Toby, staying from 1949 to 1954. He had enough experiences there to write his first book, *The Boss Is Crazy, Too* (1964). Inspired by a contest held by United Features to find new comic strips, Lazarus produced *Miss Peach*, a strip with characters with bizarre huge heads and sharp-witted personalities. It made its debut in 1957 in *The New York Herald Tribune*. Lazarus used the space normally filled by four-panel strips as one large space, sharing his comic views of politics and societal ironies of the day through the mouths of his sophisticated young stars and their teacher, Miss Peach. The strip was set in the Kelly School, named after the creator of *Pogo*, Walt Kelly. In 1969 Lazarus developed *Momma*, a comic strip centered on an overbearing, nagging, and controlling mother. She has no success manipulating her children's lives but is pleased to keep them feeling guilty. Both *Momma* and *Miss Peach* retained a long popularity, with newspapers numbering in the 300s for *Miss Peach* and 400 for *Momma*. Lazarus, who signed his strips Mell, wrote television scripts and plays. His second novel, *The Neighborhood Watch*, appeared in 1986.

[Stewart Kampel (2nd ed.)]

LAZARUS, MORITZ (1824–1903), German philosopher and psychologist. Lazarus was born in the town of Filehne (now Wielen, Poland) in the Prussian district of Posen. Unlike most of the intellectuals of the Enlightenment in Germany, Lazarus received an intense Jewish education and continued with his talmudic studies until he was in his twenties. He studied history, philology, and philosophy and began his general studies only in the third decade of his life, embarking on a brilliant academic career. He was first appointed professor of philosophy at the University of Berne, later heading its philosophy department, and eventually became rector of the university. He moved to Berlin in 1868 and lectured at the military academy in psychology, political science, and education; in 1874 he became professor at the University of Berlin (until 1896). With his first book *Die sittliche Berechtigung Preussens in Deutschland* (1850) he claimed the superiority of Prussia in Germany and began his new psychological research methods. Later he taught at the *Hochschule fuer die Wissenschaft des Judentums in Berlin. He married his second wife, the writer Nahida Ruth *Lazarus, who had embraced Judaism, served for 25 years as a member of the Berlin Jewish community council, and was head of the Zunz Institute. Toward the end of his life he was stricken with illness and settled at Meran (now Italy), a health resort, where he completed his major work, *Ethik des Judentums* (2 vols., 1898–1911; translated into English from the manuscript by Henrietta Szold as *Ethics of Judaism*, 2 vols., 1900–01). Lazarus wrote many works on the psychology of nations (*Voelkerpsychologie*) and together with his brother-in-law Hermann Heymann *Steinthal founded a special journal titled *Zeitschrift fuer Voelkerpsychologie und Sprachwissenschaft* which he edited through the years 1860–86. His most famous work on psychology is *Das Leben der Seele* (3 vols., 1883–97³) which was published in several editions. Among his other works are *Was heisst national* (1880²); *Ueber den Ursprung der Sitten* (1860); and *Ueber die Ideen in der Geschichte* (1865).

In *Ethik des Judentums* Lazarus presents Jewish ethics as an "objective-immanent" system. This system is based on an empirical, positivistic approach toward Jewish studies which holds that Jewish teachings on any subject must be derived from an analysis of Jewish sources. In selecting this approach, Lazarus departs from the "constructive-speculative" philosophies of his 19th-century predecessors Solomon *Formstecher and Samuel *Hirsch, who brought a philosophic formalism to the analysis of the Jewish sources. Thus, philosophy, according to Lazarus, does not provide a preexistent scheme for *Wissenschaft des Judentums ("Science of Judaism"), but is a methodological aid for discovering the objective unity of the "ethical cosmos," as it appears throughout the Jewish literary tradition. Lazarus distinguishes between the subjective-formal approach to Jewish ethics, in which a philosophic formalism provides the starting point of investigation, and the objective-content one, in which the investigation begins with the sources themselves. He takes the latter approach as his own. He does this because in biblical and rabbinic literature, will, intent, and the Jewish way of life, rather than reflection and speculation, are the primary principles. (Franz *Rosenzweig later based his existential philosophy on the same idea.) Lazarus accepts this position for another reason: a Jewish ethical worldview based on this conception possesses greater depth and clarity than one based on formal concepts and theoretical speculation. Lazarus emphasizes the religious character of obligation in Jewish ethics. God is the supreme, hidden principle on whom Judaism depends and who makes its whole legal structure necessary. Lazarus conceives of Jewish ethics in line with the autonomous ethics of *Kant, holding that the absolute characteristic of Jewish ethics is expressed in immediate inner certainty, though he does not follow Kant completely. Such conceptualization was made possible by establishing an ethical norm as the highest source of the moral imperative, to which even God is subordinate. Lazarus was ambiguous with regard to the heteronomous character of Jewish ethics, and this ambiguity was the basis of attack against his system, both by those who accused him of inconsistency and by those who held that he had not done justice to the heteronomous character of Jewish ethics. In Lazarus' conception Jewish ethics is fundamentally social-universal. This position countered the particularist trends of Judaism and, in particular, of 19th-century Jewish theology. However, the fact of a universal aspect to Jewish ethics does not entail teaching and disseminating Jewish beliefs throughout the world. Rather, its existence reflects an attitude and a total way of life, based on the threefold conception God, the world, and mankind, that Jews should embrace. The central concept underlying this view of Jewish life is holiness. Holiness, according to Lazarus, is not numinous, nor transcendental, but a quality to be embodied in human life. It is defined as the "ultimate goal of morality."

BIBLIOGRAPHY: T. Achelis, *Moritz Lazarus* (Ger., 1900), includes bibliography; N.R. Lazarus, *Ein deutscher Professor in der Schweiz* (1910); A. Leicht, *Lazarusstudien* (1912); idem, *Lazarus, der Begruender der Voelkerspsychologie* (1904); idem, *Lazarus: Gedenkschrift zum 100. Geburstag* (1924); Waxman, Literature, 4 (1960²), 1917–23; D. Baumgart, in: YLBI, 2 (1957), 205–17; M. Meyer, *ibid.*, 11 (1966), 146–53, 168–9; idem, in: BLBI, 5 (1962), 214–7; N. Rotenstreich, *Jewish Philosophy in Modern Times* (1968), 43–51; Guttmann, Philosophies, 350–2. **ADD. BIBLIOGRAPHY:** I. Belke, "Liberal Voices in the 1880s – Letters to Moritz Lazarus 1880–1883," in: LBIYB, 23 (1978), 61–87; I. Belke, "Der Mensch ist eine Bestie … – Ein unveroeffentlichter Brief von Theodor von Fontane an Moritz Lazarus," in: BLBI, 13 (1974), 32–50; M Heitmann, "Moritz Lazarus," in: W. Jasper and W.H. Knoll (eds.), *Preussens Himmel breitet seine Sterne…*, vol. 1 (2002), 107–19.

[Moshe Schwarcz / Bjoern Siegel (2nd ed.)]

LAZARUS, NAHIDA RUTH (née **Sturmhoefel**; 1849–1928), German playwright, novelist, and journalist, of Christian descent. Her first husband was the critic Max Remy, who died in 1881. She had been drawn to Judaism from her youth and some years after Remy's death she was converted to Judaism. In 1895 she became the second wife of the philosopher Moritz *Lazarus. The many novels and short stories which she published in the last decades of the 19th century were soon forgotten, and she is mainly remembered for her later writings on Jewish topics. These include *Das Gebet in Bibel und Talmud* (1892), *Kulturstudien ueber das Judentum* (1893), *Humanitaet im Judentum* (1894), and the autobiographical *Ich suchte Dich* (1898). Conceived in the spirit of contemporary Liberal Judaism, and written in a popular sentimental style, Nahida Lazarus' books enjoyed considerable success in their time. *Das juedische Weib* (1890; *The Jewish Wife*, 1895), written while she was still a Christian and with a preface by her future husband, was republished in a fourth edition in 1922 and was translated into English and Hebrew. There is historical value in her edition of Moritz Lazarus' memoirs (1906).

ADD. BIBLIOGRAPHY: S. Pataky, *Lexikon deutscher Frauen der Feder* (1898), s.v.; Wininger, Biog, s.v.; K. Gerstenberger, "Nahida Ruth Lazarus's 'Ich suchte Dich!': a Female Autobiography from the Turn of the Century," in: *Monatshefte fuer deutschsprachige Literatur und Kultur*, 86 (1994), N.4, 525–542; idem, *Writing Herself into the Center: Centrality and Marginality in the Autobiographical Writings of Nahida Lazarus, Adelheid Popp, and Unica Zürn* (1993); idem, *Truth to Tell: German Women's Autobiographies and Turn-of-the-Century Culture* (2000).

[David Baumgardt]

LAZEROWITZ, MORRIS (1907–1987), U.S. philosopher. Born in Lodz, Poland, he was taken to the U.S. in 1914. In 1938 he married the philosopher Alice Ambrose (1906–2001) and joined the faculty of Smith College. Author of numerous articles, his most important books are *The Structure of Metaphysics* (1955) and *Studies in Metaphilosophy* (1964). In these works, Lazerowitz is concerned with the nature of philosophical explanation, and especially with the fact that philosophical dispute is seemingly irresolvable. His analysis of this situation is that the philosopher is not putting forth empirical claims, though they are often masked as such, or even descriptions of linguistic usage; but rather, that certain visions he has of the world are expressed in these ways. It is thus necessary to distinguish such verbal formulations from their underlying impulses to gain a full understanding of the philosophical quest.

After he retired from teaching, Lazerowitz was named professor emeritus of philosophy at Smith College.

Lazerowitz also wrote *Philosophy and Illusion* (1968), *The Language of Philosophy: Freud and Wittgenstein* (1977), and *Cassandra in Philosophy* (1983). With his wife he coauthored *Logic: The Theory of Formal Inference* (1961), *Fundamentals of Symbolic Logic* (1948, 1962), *Essays in the Unknown Wittgenstein* (1984), and *Necessity and Language* (1985).

[Avrum Stroll / Ruth Beloff (2nd ed.)]

LAZNE KYNZVART (Czech **Lázně Kynžvart**; Ger. **Bad Koenigswart**), health resort in W. Bohemia, Czech Republic. Jews lived in Lazne Kynzvart as early as the beginning of the 14th century; the cemetery dates from 1405. In 1430, after the community had absorbed Jews expelled from *Cheb (Eger), it consisted of 180 families. The synagogue was renovated in 1608, according to tradition by Jesuits whom the Lazne Kynzvart Jews had helped to cross the frontier when they were being persecuted by the *Hussites during the Reformation period. In 1724 there were nine Jewish families in the town. From the end of the 17th century and for about 200 years afterward, Lazne Kynzvart was the seat of the district rabbinate. At the beginning of the 19th century the Jewish community was under the protection of Prince Metternich. The community rapidly dwindled toward the end of the 19th century and many settled in *Marienbad. In 1902 it numbered 51 persons, including those living in neighboring villages, and in 1933 only four families. The synagogue was desecrated in 1938, and the Nazis used the gravestones, placed face up, to pave the road. After World War II the Czechs removed them, using them to build a burial mound. The banking family of *Koenigswarter originated in Lazne Kynzvart.

BIBLIOGRAPHY: E. Bloch, in: ZGJT, 3 (1933), 35–39; M. Mandl, in: H. Gold (ed.), *Die Juden und Judengemeinden Boehmens in Vergangenheit und Gegenwart* (1934), 320–1.

[Meir Lamed]

LAZURICK, ROBERT (1895–1968), French journalist, founder and editor in chief of the daily paper *L'Aurore*. Lazurick was born in Paris of Russian-Jewish parents. He studied law and for some years he was an official in French ministries. In 1936 he was elected to the Chamber of Deputies for the Socialist Party. After the French defeat in 1940, he escaped to Morocco, but returned to France in 1942 at the height of Nazi power and founded *L'Aurore* clandestinely in Nice, taking the name of Clemenceau's journal which had published *Zola's *J'accuse* in 1898. *L'Aurore* became a leading newspaper in Paris after World War II, expressing staunch support for Israel.

°**LEA, HENRY CHARLES** (1825–1909), U.S. historian whose research into the history of the Church and its institutions made him one of the most distinguished scholars of the United States. Lea's monumental works, *A History of the Inquisition of the Middle Ages* (3 vols., 1888) and *A History of the Inquisition of Spain* (4 vols., 1906–07), are fundamental and represent an extensive achievement, as did his *The Inquisition in the Spanish Dependencies* (1908). Through them, Lea founded a Protestant school for the study of the Inquisition based on archival sources. His system was principally concerned with the study of the general framework of the Inquisition, its policies, and operational methods. He himself considered that these works were the result of his prime interest in the history of sorcery and superstitions in Europe. They have been adapted, abridged, and translated into various languages. In his writings, Lea reserved much sympathy for the question of the forced converts and the Jews, and commented upon the heavy responsibility of the Catholic Church and Spain for their fate. He bequeathed his manuscripts and the material which he had collected during his lifetime to the library of the University of Pennsylvania.

BIBLIOGRAPHY: E.S. Bradly, *Henry Charles Lea, a Biography* (1931); H.C. Lea, *Materials Toward a History of Witchcraft* (1957), introd. v–viii, xxi–xliii.

[Haim Beinart]

LEACHMAN, CLORIS (1926–), U.S. actress. Leachman was born in Des Moines, Iowa. Though she is best known for her career in acting, it was as a model that Leachman first stepped into the public eye. Crowned Miss Chicago in 1946, during her years as a student at Northwestern University, Leachman went on to be runner-up for the title of Miss America. It is therefore ironic that included among her most famous roles is her portrayal of the grotesque Frau Blucher in Mel Brooks' *Young Frankenstein* (1974). Leachman did, however, begin her career in movies with a sexy debut – in the film noir *Kiss Me Deadly* (1955). She appeared in prominent roles in films such as *Butch Cassidy and the Sundance Kid* (1969) and *Lovers and Other Strangers* (1970). Leachman's most widespread recognition arguably stems from her role as Phyllis Lindstrom on both *The Mary Tyler Moore Show* (1970–77) and its spin-off, *Phyllis* (1975–77). Leachman's portrayal of a housewife who has an affair with a younger man in *The Last Picture Show* (1971) earned her the Oscar for Best Supporting Actress. She has also won Emmy awards in five different categories for her television work. Leachman was divorced from her husband, Hollywood legend George Englund.

[Casey Schwartz (2nd ed.)]

LEAF (Lifshitz), HAYIM (1914–), educator, editor, essayist. Born in Russia, he went to the U.S. at an early age. He taught Hebrew literature first at the Herzliah Academy of New York and, from 1943, at Yeshiva University. He edited *Niv*, a Hebrew periodical for younger Hebrew writers (1937–40); the *Hadoar* supplement for young readers (1945–59); and the Hebrew column of the Yiddish daily *The Day* (1950–51). From 1961 he was associate editor of the Hebrew monthly *Bitzaron*. His articles on contemporary Jewish problems and essays on Hebrew literature appeared in Hebrew periodicals in the U.S. and Israel. In 1957 he began co-editing with Naomi Ben-Asher the one-volume *Junior Jewish Encyclopedia*; their 14th revised edition was published in 1996. He also co-edited with Moshe Carmilly *The Samuel Belkin Memorial Volume* (1981) of essays on topics in Jewish history, philosophy, and literature. In 1976 Leaf received the Yeshiva College Alumni Association's Bernard Revel Memorial Award in Religion and Religious Education.

[Eisig Silberschlag / Ruth Beloff (2nd ed.)]

LEAGUE FOR ISRAEL, THE AMERICAN JEWISH (AJLI) established in 1957, differentiates itself from other Zionist groups in that it is not connected with any political party or religious denomination; it supports Israel unconditionally through the following projects:

(a) University Scholarship Program: AJLI helps young American adults fulfill their academic dreams by providing scholarships to attend college in Israel. Living in Israel and becoming immersed in Israeli society has been a life changing experience for many of the 150 recipients. AJLI provides scholarships for studies as a graduate or undergraduate at one of nine institutes of higher learning in Israel: Bar-Ilan, Ben-Gurion, Haifa, Hebrew University, Interdisciplinary Center-Recanati School, Pardes, Tel Aviv, Technion and Weizmann. Acceptance at one of the universities is a prerequisite; the student must be a U.S. citizen, and scholarships are only for one full year of study.

(b) Support for Israeli Terror Victims: AJLI contributes to programs which assist Israeli children who lost a sibling or parent from terrorism and offers support for their families.

(c) Educational Programs: Members attend a variety of lectures and forums with top newsmakers from Israeli and American politics. These programs serve as a primary source for the best information on issues confronting Israel. They take place in New York and South Florida, where AJLI has active chapters.

(d) Excursions, cruises, and trips to the Catskills and other places are part of AJLI's social agenda. Members form strong bonds through these activities, and educational programs on the excursions raise members' consciousness.

[Jeff Scheckner (2nd ed.)]

LEAGUE OF NATIONS, international organization functioning between the two World Wars, for the establishment of world peace and the promotion of cooperation among states. Founded in January 1920, it formally ceased to exist in April 1946, although in fact it was active only until the beginning of World War II. During the 19 years of its effective existence, among its preoccupations were questions connected with the situation of the Jewish people in Palestine and the Diaspora.

The Mandate for Palestine

According to article 22 of the Covenant of the League, the basis for the establishment of the system of international mandates, the authority to define the terms of mandates and the supervision of their execution was entrusted to the Council of the League. On July 24, 1922, the council confirmed the *Mandate for Palestine, which included the *Balfour Declaration, and the British government was thereby committed "to place the country under such political, administrative, and economic conditions as will secure the establishment of the Jewish National Home." In its supervisory capacity, the Council of the League was assisted by a special commission – the Permanent Mandates Commission – and from 1924 until the end of 1939, this commission held annual debates on the administration of the Palestine mandate. In the years 1930 and 1937, two extraordinary sessions were dedicated to it: the first after the riots in Palestine of August 1929; the second after the British Royal Commission, with Lord Peel as chairman, suggested the partition of western (CIS-Jordan) Palestine into two states: one Jewish and one Arab.

In observations made by the Mandates Commission at its session of 1930, the British government was severely criticized for not having stationed sufficient troops in Palestine to ensure the immediate suppression of the anti-Jewish riots; it had thus proved itself powerless to protect Jewish life – the essential condition for the development of the Jewish National Home. In the opinion of the commission, the adoption of "a more active policy… a firmer and more constant and unanimous determination… would have diminished the antagonism from which the country suffers." The establishment of the Jewish National Home and the foundation of self-governing institutions were defined as the two objects of the Palestine mandate; the commission emphasized that there was no time limit for the attainment of these objects and that the immediate and daily obligations which stemmed from the provisions of the mandate should be carried out by the mandatory authorities independent of the ultimate aims. The mandatory authorities were called upon to show a firm hand: "to all the sections of the population which are rebelling against the mandate… the mandatory power must obviously return a definite and categorical refusal; as long as the leaders of a community persist in repudiating what is the fundamental charter of the country… the negotiations would only unduly enhance their prestige…." The commission's observations aroused the anger of the British government; however, thanks to the efforts of the reporter on mandatory affairs, a split was averted and the Council of the League approved the observations of the commission.

In 1937, the commission was requested to submit a preliminary opinion on the partition proposal; it observed, not without an undertone of criticism, that "the present mandate became almost unworkable once it was publicly declared to be so by a British Royal Commission… and by the government of the mandatory power itself." With little evident enthusiasm, the commission declared itself favorable in principle to an examination of a solution involving the partition of Palestine. At the same time, however, it expressed its opposition to the immediate creation of two new independent states, Jewish and Arab, and preferred the prolongation of the mandatory regime in the form of provisional "cantonization" or by the existence of two separate mandates for such a determined period as may prove necessary. In 1939, the *White Paper published by the British government was submitted to the commission. With the object of appeasing the Arabs, the White Paper misinterpreted the mandate's provisions concerning the establishment of a Jewish National Home, and by imposing minority status on the Jews rendered these provisions meaningless. The commission reached the unanimous conclusion "that the policy set out in the White Paper was not in accordance with the interpretation which, in agreement with the mandatory power and the Council [of the League], the commission had always placed upon the Palestine mandate." By a majority of one, the commission also declared that it was unable to state that the policy of the White Paper was in conformity with the mandate, "any contrary conclusion appearing to them to be ruled out by the very terms of the mandate and by the fundamental intentions of its authors." Since World War II broke out in the meantime, the White Paper never came before the Council of the League.

Although the Permanent Mandates Commission had been granted the status of an advisory body only, its prestige was enhanced by the fact that its members were men independent of their governments and because it conceived of its supervisory role as a quasi-judicial one. Even before their approval by the Council of the League, its conclusions and observations were regarded as being of considerable importance and weight. In the Jewish Agency's struggle for the correct interpretation of the provisions of the Palestine mandate regarding the National Home, the debates of the commission and its conclusions became a factor of no small significance in the attempt to prevent deviation and distortion by the mandatory power.

Minorities Rights

The League of Nations also played a part in the protection of Jewish minorities in the Diaspora. According to the minorities treaties signed by a number of Eastern and Southeastern European states at the close of World War I, and also to the declarations later made by several states to the Council of the League, supervision over the obligations undertaken by these states was entrusted to the Council of the League. In view of the difficult and often precarious situation of the Jewish minorities in various countries (particularly Poland and Romania), there was reason to suppose that complaints concerning denial of rights and discrimination would be numerous and that the League of Nations would be called upon to deal with them. However, during all the years of its existence, only two such petitions were debated by the council. The reason for this was that the procedure for handling petitions was complicated and the chances of reaching a satisfactory arrangement were slight. Moreover, as the very appeal to the League aroused the anger of the government whose actions were criticized, the Jews preferred to refrain from seeking the League's intervention.

In December 1925, the Council of the League considered petitions submitted to it by the Joint Foreign Committee (of the *Board of Deputies of British Jews and the *Anglo-Jewish Association) and the *Alliance Israélite Universelle against the introduction of the *numerus clausus in institutions of higher education in Hungary. The Jewish organizations called upon the League of Nations to condemn the numerus clausus as incompatible with the principle of equality of rights. However, the Council of the League was not prepared to go into this legal question and took no action in the matter, contenting itself with recording the declaration of the Hungarian representative that the law was merely an exceptional and temporary one and that it would be repealed when a favorable change occurred in the abnormal situation resulting from the Trianon Treaty. The Hungarian government did indeed make some changes in this law in 1928 and 1929, but in practice the discrimination persisted. However, another petition, which came before the League a few months after Hitler's rise to power, achieved far greater success. Submitted by Franz *Bernheim, a former resident of Upper Silesia, it protested against the anti-Jewish discriminatory laws of the Third Reich, as they affected the Jews of Upper Silesia and thus violated the German-Polish convention of 1922 on this region (see *Bernheim petition). As a result of the debates held in the Council of the League in May and June 1933, Germany was compelled to honor the convention, and for another four years – until its termination on May 15, 1937 – the Jews of Upper Silesia enjoyed the rights which had been guaranteed by this minorities agreement.

In 1921 the question of the expulsion of 80,000 Jewish refugees from Vienna was placed on the agenda of the Council of the League – not, on this occasion, as a result of a petition submitted by Jewish organizations but on the intervention of the Polish government, which came to the defense of its citizens. Although the council reached the conclusion that legally there was no objection to the expulsion of foreign citizens, it appealed to the Austrian government not to ignore the moral and humanitarian implications, and an arrangement was concluded which prevented the expulsion of the majority of those Jews. In addition, a number of other petitions were submitted to the League of Nations, among them appeals against the denial of the rights of Austrian Jews after the country's annexation by Nazi Germany and against the oppression of the Jews of Romania, which were submitted by the *World Jewish Congress. These, however, were not placed on the council's agenda. Memoranda on other questions, too, were brought from time to time before the League by Jewish organizations. These included appeals against pogroms in Eastern Europe, particularly the postwar massacres in the Ukraine; demands concerning the right to nationality and to reasonable naturalization requirements; and the status of the Jews in the free city of Danzig where the Nazis won a majority in the senate in 1933 and the Jews at once became victims of persecution and oppression. In December 1934, on the eve of the plebiscite in the Saar territory, the German government was forced to make a commitment to the Council of the League that if the region were handed over to the Reich, it would permit persons domiciled there who wished to leave to emigrate and take their belongings with them.

In the deliberations held annually in the Sixth (political) Commission of the General Assembly, a great deal of attention was regularly focused on problems connected with the establishment of the Jewish National Home, as well as the tightening of the procedure for dealing with minorities' petitions, thereby offering more efficient protection – a matter which was of particular interest to the Jews. In 1933 the commission's debates were marked by the tragedy of German Jewry; in an attempt to improve that community's legal status, the General Assembly once more reaffirmed the 1922 recommendations that "the states which are not bound by legal obligations to the League with respect to minorities will nevertheless observe in the treatment of their own… minorities at least as high a standard of justice and toleration as is required by any of the treaties…."

Other Activities

The League's activities on behalf of refugees and stateless persons were of special importance because a large number of Jews had lost their nationality after World War I. The "Nansen Passport," which was recognized by 51 states, became the identity card of former Russian subjects and granted them a certain legal status enabling them to travel from one country to another and obtain employment. In 1933 the General Assembly of the League appointed a high commissioner for *refugees (Jewish and others) coming from Germany. However, as a result of Germany's objections to the establishment of this office within the framework of the League, it was set up as an autonomous institution. At the end of 1938 it was amalgamated with the Nansen International Office for Refugees and all the League's activities on behalf of refugees were concentrated in the hands of the high commissioner for refugees. Since during this period almost all states were closed to immigration, the means of assisting the refugees were extremely limited.

Occasionally, a general topic of special interest to the Jews was placed on the agenda of the League, as in the case of the question of the reform of the Gregorian calendar. After six years of preliminary studies, the matter was brought up for debate in October 1931. From almost 200 propositions submitted, considerable support was given to one suggesting that the year be divided into 13 equal months of 28 days and that the last day (or the last two days in a leap year) should be trimmed off and deemed an extra day, or "blank day." By the terms of this proposal, the regular sequence of seven-day weeks would have been interrupted by the introduction of the "blank day" and the Sabbath would have moved to a different weekday each year. As this would have seriously prejudiced Sabbath observance, the Jewish spokesmen led by the chief rabbis of France and Britain fought the reform project. In the face of the combined opposition of many governments, the Jews, the Seventh-Day Adventists, and other bodies, the conference concluded almost unanimously that the time was not ripe for modifying the Gregorian calendar.

Since the League of Nations was an organization of states and not of nations, the Jews as such were naturally unable to participate in its activities. However, where the participation of nongovernmental, international, or national organizations was considered desirable on certain commissions or at conferences convened under the aegis of the League, Jewish organizations were also invited to nominate permanent representatives or send observers. Thus, for example, Jewish observers were invited to attend the conference on calendar reform and were authorized to voice their opinions. The Jewish Association for the Protection of Girls and Women participated in the activities of the Traffic in Women and Children Committee. Jewish organizations were represented on the Advisory Committee affiliated to the League's Nansen institutions for refugees, and in the Advisory Council (later known as the Liaison Committee) affiliated to the high commission for the care of the German refugees. Among the 22 members of the advisory committee formed on the appointment of the high commissioner in 1933, there were 12 delegates from Jewish public bodies representing the Jewish communities of the United States, Britain, France, Poland, Belgium, and Holland, as well as the Jewish Agency, ICA (*Jewish Colonization Association), the *American Jewish Joint Distribution Committee, the *Comité des Délégations Juives, the Alliance Israélite Universelle, and *Agudat Israel. In 1924, the Jewish Agency, a public body recognized by international law in the Palestine mandate, set up a permanent office in Geneva in order to assure constant communication with the secretariat of the League and with members of the Mandate Commission when in session. The Jewish organizations concerned with protecting the rights of the Jewish minorities sent delegates to the general assemblies of the League in Geneva, while the Comité des Délégations Juives (and later the World Jewish Congress) was permanently represented in Geneva.

The establishment of the League of Nations kindled the hope that a new world would be built from the ruins of the old. The Jews also placed much faith in it. These hopes did not materialize, especially after 1930 when the League's prestige was on the wane; by 1937 its lack of power had become all too obvious. Despite this, however, the Jews did derive some benefits from the League's activities. Insofar as its means permitted, the League sought to ensure the observance of the provisions of the Palestine mandate, and on a few occasions succeeded in preventing attacks on the rights of the Jews in the Diaspora and alleviating their suffering.

BIBLIOGRAPHY: Comité des Délégations Juives, *Bulletins*, 1–27 (1919–25); Joint Foreign Committee, *Reports… on Questions of Jewish Interest at the Assemblies of the League of Nations* (1920–26); League of Nations, Permanent Mandates Commission, *Minutes* (1921–39); N. Feinberg, *La question des minorités à la Conférence de la Paix de 1919–1920 et la protection des minorités* (1929); idem, *Ereẓ-Yisrael bi-Tekufat ha-Mandat u-Medinat Yisrael, Be'ayot ba-Mishpat ha-Bein-Le'ummi* (1963); *Palestine, a Study of Jewish, Arab and British Policies* (Esco Foundation, 1947); Institute of Jewish Affairs, *Were the Minorities Treaties a Failure?* (1947); World Jewish Congress, *Unity in Dispersion* (1948).

[Nathan Feinberg]

LEAH (Heb. לֵאָה), elder daughter of Laban and wife of Jacob.

Biblical Depiction

Leah was married to Jacob as a result of Laban's trickery in substituting her for her sister Rachel on the night of the marriage (Gen. 29:23–25). She gave birth to six sons – Reuben, Simeon, Levi, Judah, Issachar, Zebulun – and one daughter – Dinah (Gen. 29:32–35; 30:14–21). Her maid-servant Zilpah whom she gave to Jacob bore him another two sons – Gad and Asher (30:9–13).

Leah is described as having had eyes that were *rakkot*, often taken to mean "weak eyes" (29:17), an expression that may be taken to mean that her eyes lacked luster, the eastern woman's distinguishing mark of beauty. But *rakkot* has also been taken as "tender," that is, her eyes are an attractive feature (Speiser, a.l.; Yee). This would be in harmony with the etymology of her name from Akkadian *lītu*, "cow" (von Soden, AHW, 557–58). Unfortunately, her sister *Rachel, "ewe," is comely of both form and face. Leah is also said to have been "unloved" (29:30–31), and she had to fight for Jacob's affection, as is evidenced by the symbolic names of her sons and the mandrakes she had to give to Rachel in return for conjugal rights (30:14–16). Because of her miserable state, God rewarded her with children (29:31). This is a motif that recurs in the story of Hannah and Peninah (1 Sam. 1:1–20).

Together with her sister, Leah stood by Jacob in his quarrel with Laban and joined him in his flight from her father (Gen. 31:1–18). She is again mentioned in Laban's search of Jacob's effects (31:33) and in connection with the encounter with Esau (33:1–7). While her death is not specifically recorded, she is mentioned as having been buried in the cave of Machpelah (49:31). Together with Rachel, Leah was esteemed as one of the mothers of the nation who "built up the House of Israel," and her name was invoked in the blessing of a bride (Ruth 4:11).

The sons of Leah were regarded as the progenitors of six of the 12 tribes of Israel, and the two hereditary national institutions, the priesthood and the monarchy, are traced back to her sons Levi and Judah. Since according to the narrative the birth of the Leah tribes antedates the appearance of those derived from Rachel, it is possible that the former represented an earlier Israelite confederacy which was only later joined by the Rachel tribes. In addition, the stories perhaps follow a literary paradigm in which rival wives possess different strengths.

[Nili Shupak]

In the *Aggadah*

Leah was as beautiful as her sister Rachel; her only defect was that her eyes were weak from the many tears she shed because she thought she would be given in marriage to Esau, it having been arranged that she should marry the elder son of Isaac, and Rachel the younger. Informed of his bad character, she wept so copiously that her eyelashes were detached from her eyes (Tanḥ. B., Gen. 152). During the nuptial night, Leah responded whenever Jacob called Rachel. When daylight came, Jacob reproached her, saying, "O thou deceiver, daughter of a deceiver, why did you answer me when I called Rachel's name?" Leah responded, "Is there a teacher without a pupil? I learned from your example. Did you not answer your father when he called Esau?" (Gen. R. 70:19). Upon the birth of her fourth son, she became the first person since the time of creation to praise the Lord (Gen. 29:35; Ber. 7b). Since God knew that Leah's intentions were honorable in requesting Jacob's affection in return for the mandrakes (Gen. 30:16), she was blessed with two additional sons, Issachar and Zebulun (Gen. R. 72:5). Her seventh child was also destined to be a son but the embryo was changed into a female because of Leah's prayers. Knowing that Jacob was destined to have 12 sons, she prayed that Rachel be granted a second son so that she would at least be equal to the handmaids who each bore two sons (Ber. 60a). Since Leah was the eldest daughter, she received the more desirable inheritance. Both the priesthood and royalty (Aaron and David) were descended from her.

BIBLIOGRAPHY: C.H. Gordon, in: RB, 44 (1935), 34–41; N.M. Sarna, *Understanding Genesis* (1966), 194–200. IN THE AGGADAH: Ginzberg, Legends, 1 (1942), 354–69; 5 (1947), 294–300. **ADD. BIBLIOGRAPHY:** E.A. Speiser, *Genesis* (AB; 1965); G. Yee, in: ABD, 4:268, incl. bibl.

°LEÃO (Pereira), GASPAR DE (d. 1576), Portuguese archbishop, born in Lagos, Portugal. In 1560 he was named prelate of *Goa and installed as its first inquisitor general. In his first *auto-da-fé, held on Sept. 27, 1563, two of the four victims were Portuguese Judaizers. He was also active in compelling *Marranos to return to Lisbon. Given to polemics, Leão denounced talmudic law in an open letter to the Jews, *Carta do primeiro Arcebispo de Goa, ao Povo de Israel, seguidor ainda da ley de Moyses e do Talmud, por engano e malicia dos seus Rabbis* (1565). About 1569 he resigned and went into retreat in the neighboring convent of Daugim; however, he returned to his posts in 1574, serving until his death.

BIBLIOGRAPHY: Roth, *Marranos*, index, s.v. *Goa*; J.N. da Fonseca, *An Historical and Archeological Sketch of the City of Goa* (1878); Kayserling, *Bibliotheca*, 106.

[Aaron Lichtenstein]

LEAP YEAR, refers to the 13-month year in the Jewish *calendar. Leap year results from the intercalation (Heb. עִבּוּר, "pregnancy") of an additional month, called *Adar Sheni* ("Second Adar") or *Ve-Adar* ("and Adar"). Adar, the regular 12th month, is then called *Adar Rishon* ("the first Adar"). Leap year is a means through which the annual difference of 11 days between the solar year and the lunar year is adjusted. A leap year occurs seven times in every cycle of 19 years (*maḥazor ḥammah*), namely in the years: 3, 6, 8, 11, 14, 17 and 19 of the cycle. The first Adar has 30 days, the second Adar 29. The number of days in a leap year is either 383, 384, or 385. The period between the first of Nisan and the first of Tishri is always 177 days. The intercalation of years was already practiced by the Sanhedrin in the Hasmonean and mishnaic periods. Among the factors then taken into consideration were the ripened state of the *Omer* ("barley") offered on Passover, and that of the *bikkurim* ("first fruits") sacrificed on Shavuot. It also depended on whether the roads and bridges were passable so that the pilgrims could go to Jerusalem for the Passover festival, and whether the ovens for the paschal-lamb sacrifices were already dry after the rainy season. (See: Tosef., Sanh. 2:12; Sanh. 11aff.)

BIBLIOGRAPHY: Ḥ.S. Slonimski, *Yesodei ha-Ibbur, ve-Hu Seder Ḥeshbon Ibbur ha-Shanim...* (1865); Maimonides, *Ma'amar ha-Ibbur* (1911), ed. by E. Donner; J. Barb, *Kunteres Sod ha-Ibbur...* (1897); see also bibl. of *Calendar article.

LEAR, EVELYN (1926–), U.S. soprano singer. Lear was born in New York City and studied singing first at Hunter College and later at the Juilliard School of Music; she was also a horn player and pianist. In 1957, she went to Berlin on a Fulbright grant and studied at the Hochschule fuer Musik. Two years later she made her first appearances at the Deutsche Staatsoper, Berlin, and in 1962 took the title role in Berg's *Lulu* at Vienna. Returning to the United States, she made important debuts at the Chicago Lyric Opera (in Berg's *Wozzeck*, 1966) and at the Metropolitan, New York (in the first performances of *Mourning Becomes Electra* (1967) by Marvin David *Levy). From 1972 she began to undertake heavier roles, including Tosca and the Marschallin. She created Arkadina in Pasatieri's *The Seagull* (1974), Magda in Robert Ward's *Minutes to Midnight* (1982), and Ranyevskaya in Kelterborn's *Kirschgar-*

ten (1984). Her roles in opera ranged from Purcell (Dido in *Dido and Aeneas*) and Mozart to contemporary works. Her repertory included both Mozart's Cherubino and Countess Almaviva, Fiordiligi (*Cosi Fan Tutte*), Pamina (*Die Zauberflöte*); Handel's Cleopatra, Verdi's Desdemona (*Otello*), Tchaikowsky's Tatyana (*Eugene Onegin*) and Marie (*Wozzeck*). Lear was a singer gifted with intelligence, linguistic abilities (singing in seven languages), and a strong sense of drama. She was also a distinguished concert singer and song-recitalist.

ADD. BIBLIOGRAPHY: Grove online.

[Max Loppert / Israela Stein (2nd ed.)]

LEAR, NORMAN (1922–), U.S. writer, producer, director of TV and films. Born in New Haven, Connecticut, Lear served in the U.S. Air Force during World War II (1941–45). At the war's end, he was decorated with the Air Medal with four Oak Leaf Clusters. Lear began his career in films, producing and writing such motion pictures as *Come Blow Your Horn* (1963), *Divorce, American Style* (Oscar nomination for Best Screenplay, 1967), and *The Night They Raided Minsky's* (1968).

He then turned to developing and creating groundbreaking television shows, beginning with the sitcom *All in the Family* (1971–79), which became the no. 1-rated TV show. It was followed by *Sanford & Son* (1972–77); *Maude* (1972–78); *Good Times* (1974–79); *The Jeffersons* (1975–85); *Mary Hartman, Mary Hartman* (1976–78); *One Day at a Time* (1975–84); *Fernwood 2Nite* (1977–78); *Apple Pie* (1978); *Diff'rent Strokes* (1978–86); and *Archie Bunker's Place* (1979–83).

Lear has also been the producer of feature films, such as *Never Too Late* (1965), *Start the Revolution without Me* (1970), *Cold Turkey* (1971), *The Thief Who Came to Dinner* (1973), *Stand by Me* (1986), *The Princess Bride* (1987), *Fried Green Tomatoes* (1991), and *Way Past Cool* (2000).

Among his many honors and awards, Lear was named Man of the Year in 1973 by the Hollywood chapter of the National Academy of Television Arts and Sciences. He received four Emmy Awards for *All In the Family* (1970–73) and a Peabody Award (1978); he was nominated for 11 other Emmys. In 1987 he received the Creative Achievement Award from the American Comedy Awards. In 1984 he received the Distinguished American Award and was among the first inductees to the Academy of Television Arts and Sciences Hall of Fame. He received the Mass Media Award from the American Jewish Committee of Institutional Executives in 1987.

Lear was president of the American Civil Liberties Foundation from 1973. In 1980 he founded People for the American Way, a Washington advocacy group that lobbies for constitutional rights and liberties. He was also a member of the advisory board to the National Women's Political Caucus. In 2000 he founded the Norman Lear Center at USC's Annenberg School of Communications, which offers multidisciplinary study of entertainment to stimulate new ways of approaching its content and evaluating its impact. Lear's book *God, Man, and Archie Bunker,* coauthored with Spencer Marsh, was published in 1975.

BIBLIOGRAPHY: G. Cowan, *See No Evil: The Backstage Battle over Sex and Violence on Television* (1979).

[Jonathan Licht / Ruth Beloff (2nd ed.)]

LEASE AND HIRE. The Hebrew term *sekhirut* embraces the lease of immovable property (houses and fields) as well as the hire of movable property and personal services, and is a near parallel of *locatio-conductio rei* in Roman law. In this article the term "hire" is generally used as the equivalent of *sekhirut* in its wide sense and also with reference to movable property, whereas the term "lease" is used solely with reference to the hire of immovable property. For details concerning the hire of personal services, see *Labor Law.

In hire, the owner (the *maskir*) alienates to the hirer (the *sokher*) a real right in the demised property, the fruits and use of the property, for a fixed period, in return for a rental payable by the hirer to the owner. The rule is that hire is deemed to be a sale for a fixed period. This *halakhah* was stated in the Talmud with reference to the law of **ona'ah* ("overreaching"); i.e., just as there is overreaching in sale so there is overreaching in hire, and just as there is no overreaching in the sale of land so there is no overreaching in the lease of land (see BM 56b and Tos., ad loc.; Sh. Ar., ḤM 315:1). Some scholars held that the application of the above rule extended to additional *halakhot*: "A man may make any stipulation he wishes with regard to hiring just as he may do with regard to purchase and sale, since hiring is but a sale for a specified time. He who may sell may also let" (Yad, Sekhirut 7:1; see also *She'elah*, 1:5; Sh. Ar., ḤM 315:2; PD 8 (1954), 577–81). Opinions are divided on the question of whether the owner may, within the period for which he has let his property, let such property to a third party (see *Pitḥei Teshuvah*, ḤM 315, n. 1).

Formation and Determination of Hire

Property is hired in the same way as it is bought and sold (see *Acquisition; BK 79a; Yad, Mekhirah 1:18; Sh. Ar., ḤM 315:1), and until the required formal act of *kinyan* is performed both parties are free to retract (Sh. Ar., ḤM 307:2). The view was expressed that as regards the hire of movables, as opposed to their sale, the scholars had not abolished *kinyan kesef* ("acquisition by money"), because the subject matter of the hire would continue to belong to its owner, which would eliminate the apprehension that the latter might refrain from rescuing the property from danger – as there was reason to fear in the case of sale. The *halakhah* was decided accordingly (see Sh. Ar., ḤM 198:6; *Pitḥei Teshuvah*, n. 8). Determination of hire, before expiry of the stipulated period, may be effected by an act of *kinyan*, i.e., by the hirer transferring his real right in the property back to its owner. A right of hire cannot be extinguished by way of waiver alone (see *Sma*, ḤM 189). Just as a person's courtyard acquires for him (*kinyan ḥaẓer*), so he may acquire through a courtyard he has hired, and in this way acquire movables which are on the hired property (Yad, Mekhirah 3:7; see also Sh. Ar., ḤM 198:5 and *Siftei Kohen*, n. 7). Similarly, movables may be transferred by the method of acquisition incidental to hired land (*kinyan aggav*; Kid. 27a).

Ambit of Contract

The ambit of hire is determined in accordance with the customary uses of the property concerned. Thus a person who hires a house also hires its surrounding garden and the like (Yad, Sekhirut 6:1), all subject to local *custom and the common usage of the terms employed by the parties in their contract (Yad, loc. cit.; see also Sh. Ar., ḤM 313:1).

Obligations of the Lessor

The lessor must let to the lessee property which is fit for the intended purpose. If a house is let, the lessor must supply one with doors and windows properly affixed, and he must further ensure that all the things "which are produced by the craftsman and are essential to the habitability of houses and courts" are done (BM 8:7; Yad, Sekhirut 6:3; Sh. Ar., ḤM 314:1). The fact that the lessee occupies the premises prior to the lessor's execution of all his required duties does not amount to a waiver of these on the part of the lessee, and the lessor remains responsible for their execution (*Rema*, ḤM 314:1). Where the parties agreed on the letting of "this" – i.e., specified – house, the lessor will not, during the subsistence of the lease, be responsible for repairs; otherwise (i.e., where an unspecified house is let) the lessor remains responsible for repairs (*Rema*, loc. cit.). The opinion was expressed that even in the case where a specified house is agreed on by the parties, the lessor will, in certain circumstances, if the house has fallen into disrepair and become too dangerous to live in, be responsible for its repair (Sh. Ar., ḤM 312:17 and *Sma*, n. 32).

In case of the destruction of the leased property (see below), the law as regards the lessor's need to make available alternative property to the lessee is as follows: "If a man let to another an unspecified house and after he delivered possession to the lessee the house collapsed, he is bound to rebuild it or to supply the lessee with another house. If the second house is smaller than the one that collapsed the lessee cannot object, provided it may be classified as a house, for it was but an unspecified house that the lessor let to the lessee. If, however, the lessor said, 'I am letting to you a house like this one,' he must supply the lessee with a house of the length and width of the one he indicated to him"; in the latter event, the lessor cannot depart from the dimensions and qualities of the said house except by mutual consent (BM 103a; Yad, Sekhirut 5:7; Sh. Ar., ḤM 312:17).

Rental or Hire

Two views are expressed in the Talmud concerning the owner's right to payment of the rental or hire (Kid. 48a–b). One opinion is that the hire (i.e., wages) is "a liability from beginning to end" and that the hired worker becomes continuously entitled to this in accordance with the portion of the work done (Yad, Ishut 5:20; see also Akum 7:5 and Rashi, Kid. 48a, s.v. *ella*). A different opinion is that "wages are a liability only at the end" (Kid. loc. cit.), i.e., that the lessor does not become entitled to the rental until termination of the lease or – in the event that property was handed over for improvement – until return of the property to its owner (Rashi, Kid. 48b, s.v. *einah li-sekhirut*; but cf. *Beit ha-Beḥirah*, Kid. 48a). The *halakhah* was decided according to the first opinion (see Yad, loc. cit. and Sh. Ar., EH 28:7). However, the practical significance of the above dispute is confined to matters concerning the laws of **kiddushin* and those concerning wages in cases involving idolatry, whereas it appears to have no relevance to relations between the lessor and lessee. Hence, as regards the time for the payment of the hire it was accepted as *halakhah* that "wages are a liability only at the end" (see Tos. to BK 99a and to BM 65a; but cf. Nov. Ritba, Kid. 48b). It is a positive precept to pay the worker's hire on time and failure to do so is a transgression of a pentateuchal prohibition (*halanat sakhar*) which was interpreted as extending to the hire of personal services and that of animals and utensils (see *Labor Law). However, as regards the rental for land and houses, disputing opinions are expressed in the codes (see Yad, Sekhirut 11:1; Sh. Ar., ḤM 339:1 and *Keẓot ha-Ḥoshen* n. 1).

Where property is hired for a fixed period at a stipulated remuneration, the latter may not be increased within the said period (Sh. Ar., ḤM 312:10; *Rema*, ḤM 312:9). In the case where a property is tacitly relet on expiry of the hire period, and in the absence of any express agreement regarding the amount of the hire for the renewal period, the hirer – according to Hai Gaon – will be at an advantage: If the amount of the hire stipulated for the first period is higher than the appropriate amount, the hirer pays only the latter amount; if the stipulated amount is lower than is appropriate, the hirer nevertheless pays no more than the lower amount (*ittur* 1, pt. 1, s.v. *sekhirut*). On the other hand, from the Shulḥan Arukh it may be gathered that the hirer, in the above circumstances, always pays according to the stipulated amount for the first period, regardless of any increase or decrease in the customary rate (ḤM 312:9; see also Nov. Meir Simḥah ha-Kohen of Dvinsk, BM 101b, s.v. *va-agalleh*). If the hirer retracts during the term of the hire he remains liable for the whole amount of the hire (Yad, Sekhirut 5:4; Sh. Ar., ḤM 311:6).

Departure from the Object and Terms of the Hire

The hirer may not use the hired property for a more onerous purpose than that for which it was hired (Yad, Mekhirah 23:8; Sekhirut 4:1, 4–5; Sh. Ar., ḤM 212:6; 308), subject to any different local custom (Yad, Sekhirut 4:8; Sh. Ar., ḤM 308:3). If the hirer puts the property to any more onerous use, for which the customary hire is greater than the amount agreed upon, he must add to the hire accordingly (*Rema*, ḤM 308:1). In certain circumstances it may be sought to safeguard that the property is put to its full stipulated use. Thus, for instance, the lessor of a shop may object to its being left vacant by the lessee lest the regular customers become accustomed to buying elsewhere, which would detract from the value of the premises (Resp. Maharsham, pt. 2, no. 198). Use of the property in a different but not more onerous manner than that agreed upon is held to be forbidden by some scholars but is permitted by others, who hold that to forbid this is "the practice of the Sodomites" (see *Law and Morality; Tur., ḤM 308:3–4; 311:3–4; *Perishah, ibid.* 4; *Sma*, ḤM 311, n. 2).

If a house is jointly hired (see *Partnership) by two persons for their cotenancy, neither may transfer his rights in it to a third party – not even if the latter has a smaller household – except with the consent of the other partner. Similarly, one tenant cannot compel his cotenant to partition the tenancy, since the house is not their property but is only let to them for a term. However, it was held that joint lessees of a field can compel each other to a partition of the lease (Sh. Ar., ḤM 171:9 and *Rema* ad loc.; ḤM 316:2 and *Sma* n. 6). The lessee may not, without the lessor's consent, take in any of his relatives or acquaintances to live with him in the house as one of its occupants, unless they are dependent on him (Yad, Shekhenim 5:9; Sh. Ar., ḤM 154:2). As regards the stipulated terms, the rule is that these may not be departed from except where their strict enforcement would amount to "following the practice of the Sodomites" (Yad, Sekhirut 7:8; Sh. Ar., ḤM 318).

Assignment and Subletting

The rule is that the hirer may not sublet to someone else (Tosef., BM 3:1; Git. 29a). To do so without authority will render the sublease voidable (*Maḥaneh Efrayim*, no. 7). There are several qualifications to this rule: It was laid down that a person who hires a cargo boat and unloads the cargo in the middle of the voyage may let the boat to someone else (for the rest of the journey), and the owner will have "a grievance only" against the original hirer; similarly, if the hirer sells the cargo in the middle of the voyage, disembarks, and leaves the purchaser to embark, the owner takes one-half of the freightage from each of the other two and the owner has "but a grievance against the seller for causing him to endure the inclinations of another man to whom he is not accustomed"; and so too in other similar cases (Yad, Sekhirut 5:4; Sh. Ar., ḤM 311:6). This *halakhah* was extended by way of analogy: "On the basis of the above rule [Yad, loc. cit.].

I hold that if the owner lets his house for a fixed period, the lessee may sublet it to another until the end of the said period … since the rule of the sages that the hirer may not let applies only to movables, where the owner may say 'I do not wish my property deposited with another'; but as regards land, or a boat on which its owner is present, the owner cannot say so" (Yad, loc. cit. 5:5). Other scholars expressed the view that the lessee may never sublet the house, "for there are people who ruin the house that they occupy" (Yad, loc. cit., *Hassagot Rabad* and *Maggid Mishneh*, ad loc.). According to some scholars, even "chattels which are not likely to be carried away and which are habitually hired out and given in loan by their owners" may in turn be hired out and lent to third parties (Resp. Rashba, vol. 1, no. 1145; see also *Maḥaneh Efrayim*, Sekhirut no. 19). The *halakhah* was decided thus: "A person who has hired an animal or chattels may not hire these out to anyone else" (Sh. Ar., ḤM 307:4; see also 316:1). Similarly, a field may not be sublet, since in this case it is feared that the sublessee may do with the field as he pleases (see *Sma*, ḤM 212:16 and 316:1).

The permissibility of subletting in the case of a house is subject to a number of restrictions. It may only be done if the members of the subtenant's household do not number more than those of the existing tenant (Yad, Sekhirut 5:5). It is also a condition that the sublease shall not entail a more onerous use than did the original lease. In addition, the lessor always retains a preemptive right to demand the leased property for himself and release the lessee from further payment of the rental (Yad, loc. cit.; see also Sh. Ar., ḤM 316:1; *Divrei Ge'onim* 104:40). Similarly, the lessee may not sublet to a disreputable person (*Rema*, ḤM 312:7), or to someone who is hateful to the lessor (*Taz*, ḤM 312:7), or to someone who will fail to take proper care of the property (*Arukh ha-Shulḥan*, ḤM 316:2). In the case of a lawful sublease, any reward the lessee derives from it will belong to him, otherwise to the owner of the property (see *Maḥaneh Efrayim*, Sekhirut no. 19).

Frustration of Hire

It was laid down that if a hired ass fell sick or was taken into the king's service, it would not have to be replaced by its owner; however, if the ass died, the owner would be so obliged (BM 6:3; BM 78b; Sh. Ar., ḤM 310:1). The owner's exemption from the need to replace an ass if it fell sick was interpreted to be specifically applicable to the case in which an ass is hired to carry a normal load, since it would still remain possible to put the ass to some use; however, an ass that is hired to be ridden, or to carry glass utensils, has to be replaced by its owner, since there is no possibility of using it for the purpose for which it was hired (BM 79a; Sh. Ar. loc. cit.). In the case where the ass dies, a distinction is made between the hire of a specified ("this") ass and the hire of an unspecified one. In the case of an unspecified ass, the owner must replace it with another, otherwise, if the worth of the carcass suffices for the purchase or hire of another ass, the hirer must apply the proceeds therefrom toward the purchase or hire of an ass for the original purpose (BM loc. cit.; Sh. Ar., ḤM 310:1–2; see also Tur., ḤM 310:2, *Beit Yosef* and *Darkhei Moshe*, ad loc.).

In the Talmud it is laid down that if a specified house is hired, the loss – in the event of its collapse – is that of the lessee, and no provision is made for him to apply the proceeds of the sale of the boards and bricks toward the purchase or hire of another house (BM 103a; Sh. Ar., ḤM 312:17). However, an opinion was expressed that the lessee should do so in the above circumstances (Ramah in Tur, ḤM 312:6), and some scholars distinguished between the hire of an ass and that of a house (see Tos. to BM 79a; *Shitah Mekubbeẓet*, BM 79a, under *Ha de-Amrinan* in the name of Rabad). If a house is demolished by the lessor, he must make available a similar house to the lessee and he must do likewise if he has caused the lessee to vacate the house during the period of the lease (Yad, Sekhirut 5:6; Sh. Ar., ḤM 312:2).

Four possibilities are distinguished as regards payment of the rent upon frustration of the lease, all illustrated by the case of a ship hired for the transport of wine which sinks with all its cargo:

(1) If a specified ship was hired for transporting a cargo of unspecified wine, the hirer will be exempt from payment of the freightage and entitled to a refund if he has already paid; this is because the hirer is prepared to submit other wine for transportation but the owner is unable to offer him the ship hired (BM 79a; Sh. Ar., ḤM 311:2). When the hirer can benefit from part performance of the contract – for instance if the cargo is salvaged and the hirer is able to transport it in some other manner to its destination, or to sell it at the place to which it has been brought – the ship owner will be entitled to part payment of the freightage, pro rata to the measure of the contract executed (see Tos. to BM 79a; *Rema*, ḤM 310:2, 311:2).

(2) If an unspecified ship was hired for the transport of a cargo of specified wine, the hirer will be liable for the freightage, since he presents the obstacle, inasmuch as the shipowner is able to offer another ship whereas the hirer is unable to submit the same wine that was lost (BM 79a–b). There is an opinion that the hirer, in the above event, is only liable for part payment, pro rata to the measure of the hire executed (Tos. to BM 79b; Sh. Ar., ḤM 311:3 and *Rema* ad loc.). There is also an opinion that in circumstances where the cargo is lost even though the ship has not sunk, the hirer, in spite of the fact that he presents the obstacle, is exempt from payment of the hire since the obstacle has arisen from an inevitable accident (see *Ones*; Tos. to BM 79a; *Sma*, ḤM 311, n. 2; *Siftei Kohen*, *ibid.*, n. 2).

(3) If a specified ship was hired for transporting a cargo of specified wine, the rule is that since the obstacle is presented by both parties, the party in possession is at an advantage; if the hirer has not yet paid the freightage he need not do so, but if he has already done so he will not be entitled to any refund (BM 79b; Sh. Ar., ḤM 311:4).

(4) If an unspecified ship was hired for transporting a cargo of unspecified wine, the shipowner and the hirer share the freightage (BM 79b; Sh. Ar., ḤM 311:5).

In the case where the lessee of a house dies during the currency of the lease, according to one opinion the lessor will not be entitled to the full rental but only that for the period for which the house was occupied, unless it was otherwise stipulated by the lessor; another opinion is that the lessor remains entitled to the full rental (*Rema*, ḤM 334:1; see also *Divrei Ge'onim*, 104:16).

Termination of the Contract

A lease for a fixed period terminates on expiry thereof and may not be terminated by the lessor prior to this date (Yad, Sekhirut 6:6; Sh. Ar., ḤM 312:1, 8). At times, in the absence of a stipulated time for the termination of a lease, the expiry date will be determined in accordance with the surrounding circumstances. Thus, if the rental has been paid in advance, even for a lengthy period of time, the lessor will not be able to eject the lessee until expiry of the period for which the rent has been paid (Sh. Ar., ḤM 312:1 and *Rema* ad loc.). Sometimes the date of termination of a lease is governed by local custom relating to such a particular category of lease (Tosef., BM 8:28; see also Yad, loc. cit.; Sh. Ar., ḤM 312:4). The lessor's sale of the leased premises is valid but does not have the effect of terminating the lease, and the purchaser may not eject the lessee until expiry of the lease period; the same applies when the premises are transferred by gift or inheritance (Yad, Sekhirut 6:11; Sh. Ar., ḤM 312:1 and 13; see also I.S. Zuri, *Torat ha-Mishpat ha-Ezraḥi ha-Ivri: ha-Irurim*, 2 (1935), 105, n. 36).

In the case where premises are let for an unspecified period, the scholars laid down the need for advance notice of termination. The rule is as follows: "He who lets a house to another for an unspecified term may not dispossess the lessee from the house unless he notifies him 30 days in advance, so as to enable him to find a place and prevent his being thrown into the street. At the end of the 30 days the lessee must vacate the premises" (Yad, Sekhirut 6:7, based on BM 8:6 and BM 101b; see also Sh. Ar., ḤM 312:5). In certain circumstances, depending on the nature of the premises and its location, longer periods of notice are required (BM and Yad, loc. cit.). The obligation to give notice is mutual and, as regards the lessee, he may not vacate the premises without prior notice, but must pay the rent (Yad, Sekhirut 6:8 and Sh. Ar., ḤM 312:7; see also *Pitḥei Teshuvah* thereto; PDR 3:281–3; 6:113). When a lease is tacitly renewed for lack of prior notice of termination, the rent for the renewal period must be paid at the new prevailing rate, whether higher or lower than before (Yad, Sekhirut 6:9 and Sh. Ar., ḤM 312:9). If the lessor requires the premises for himself, for instance when his own dwelling has collapsed, he may eject the lessee from the leased premises, saying to him: "It is not right that you should remain in my house until you find another dwelling place, while I am lying on the street; your right in this house is not greater than mine" (Yad, Sekhirut 6:9 and 10; Sh. Ar., ḤM 312:11; see also Resp. Radbaz, no. 1214; Nov. Akiva Eger to Sh. Ar., ḤM 312:13). The fact that relations between the lessor and lessee have deteriorated during the currency of the lease is no ground for its termination; however, if at the time of the letting the lessor declared that he was only doing so because of his friendship for the lessee, then if the two become enemies in the meantime, he is entitled to terminate the lease (*Rema*, ḤM 312:9; see *Pitḥei Teshuvah* n. 6).

Laws of Evidence

Based on the rule that "the burden of proof rests on the person seeking to recover from another," it was laid down that in case of ambiguity in the terms of the lease the owner of the premises is in possession and holds the advantage until the lessee brings evidence to support his claim. Thus if it is unclear whether an intercalated (leap year) month is for the benefit of the lessor or the lessee, the benefit will accrue to the lessor (BM 102b; Yad, Sekhirut 7:2; Sh. Ar., ḤM 312:15). Similarly, in the case of dispute over whether the lease was for a fixed or for an unspecified period – which would have a bearing on the need or otherwise for prior notice of termination – the burden of proof will rest on the lessee (Yad, loc. cit.; Sh. Ar., ḤM 312:16 and *Rema* ad loc.) and likewise in the case of dispute as to the date of commencement of a lease for a fixed period

(Yad, Sekhirut 7:4; Sh. Ar., ḤM 317:2; for additional rules see Yad, Sekhirut 7:6; Sh. Ar., ḤM 317:3). If there is a dispute between the lessor and the lessee over whether the rent has been paid or not, then – if the lease was for a term of 30 days and the lessor has claimed the rent within this period, or if there was a stipulated date of payment and the rent has been claimed prior to this date – the lessee will have the burden of proving that he paid the rent, since it is presumed that "a person does not pay prior to due date" and that "rent is payable only at the end"; if, however, the claim is made on the 30th day or on the stipulated date, the lessor will have to prove that he has not yet been paid (Yad, Sekhirut 7:3; Sh. Ar., ḤM 317:1).

Precepts Relating to Property

The letting of premises has a bearing on the question of whether the duty of fulfilling the precepts relating to such property falls on the lessor or lessee. As regards the precept of searching out leaven on Passover eve, it was laid down that the duty devolves on the lessor if he has not delivered the key to the lessee before the 14th day of Nisan; if he has delivered the keys before this date, the duty is the lessee's (Yad, Ḥameẓ 2:18). At the same time, the fact that the lessee finds that the house he has hired has not been searched for leaven – even though he has hired it on this assumption – does not entitle him to void the contract on the grounds of error, since it is every person's duty to perform a *mitzvah* personally (Yad, loc. cit.; see also Sh. Ar., OḤ 437:1, 3).

Ḥokher and *Mekabbel*

In two cases, in which the lessee is called a *ḥokher* and a *mekabbel* respectively (as defined below), the consideration is payable in different manner to that of the *sokher*. If a produce-bearing field or vineyard is rented for money, the lessee is called a *sokher*; when it is rented for a stipulated amount of the produce the lessee is called a *ḥokher*; when a person hires a field or orchard with the obligation to cultivate it, to incur the necessary expenses, and to pay a stipulated portion of the produce derived therefrom, he is called a *mekabbel* (Yad, Sekhirut 8:1, 2; Sh. Ar., ḤM 320:1–3). There is one law for the *sokher* and the *ḥokher* (loc. cit.). As regards the *mekabbel* and the *ḥokher* (the two cases are referred to as *kabbelanut* or *arisut*), "whatever is essential to the protection of the land is chargeable to the owner and whatever constitutes added precaution is chargeable to the farmer (*ḥokher*) or tenant on shares (*kablan*)." The utensils and instruments for cultivation of the land – such as a spade for digging the ground or the vessels in which the dirt is carried – are chargeable to the owner. There is an opinion that the aforesaid obligations of the owner relate only to the *mekabbel* and not the *ḥokher* (Yad, Sekhirut 8:2; Sh. Ar., ḤM 320:3).

The owner derives his share from whatever is produced by the land, whether good or bad. If the field yields bad produce, the *ḥokher* nevertheless pays with this, and if good wheat is produced he may not say to the owner, "I will buy wheat for you from the market," but must pay out of this crop (Yad, Sekhirut 8:7; Sh. Ar., ḤM 323; see *Sma* n. 3). The nature of the work which must be done by the *ḥokher* in cultivating the field is determined by local custom (BM 9:1; Yad, Sekhirut 8:6; Sh. Ar., ḤM 320:4; *Sma* n. 2). If a field is leased on the condition that it is sown with a particular crop, the *ḥokher* may only sow a different crop which is less and not more exhaustive of the soil. In case of deviation, the *ḥokher* will have to purchase produce on the market for delivery to the owner as stipulated between them (Yad, Sekhirut 8:9; Sh. Ar., ḤM 324). As regards a *mekabbel*, one opinion holds that he may depart from the stipulated manner of cultivation, even if this is more burdensome on the land, and another opinion is that he may not do so even for a less burdensome result (*Rema*, ḤM, loc. cit.).

If a field taken by a *mekabbel* fails to produce its anticipated yield, nevertheless, if there is a prospect of extracting a yield exceeding the expenditures by a minimal amount, the *mekabbel* will be obliged to cultivate the field against his will – since this is part of his undertaking whether or not it was expressly stipulated in writing (Yad, Sekhirut 8:12; Sh. Ar., ḤM 328:1 and *Rema* ad loc.). If a *mekabbel* lets a field lie fallow, an appraisal is made of how much the field would have been likely to yield and the former must pay the owner his estimated due share – since this is part of his undertaking to the lessor, whether or not expressly stipulated. Such an undertaking was held not to be defective on account of **asmakhta*, since here the *mekabbel* does not take upon himself an obligation for something that is fixed, but only to indemnify the owner in accordance with the loss caused the latter, and hence the *mekabbel* is deemed to have firmly made up his mind to bind himself to the obligation. If, however, the *mekabbel* undertook to pay the owner an amount that is found to exceed the estimated loss, this will amount to *asmakhta*, and he will be liable to pay only according to the actual loss (Yad, Sekhirut 8:13; Sh. Ar., ḤM 328:2).

Frustration of *Ḥakhirah*

A distinction is made between partial frustration – for instance, if the tributary spring feeding an irrigated field dries up, or if a tree on the plantation is felled – and frustration deriving from a widespread misfortune – for instance, if the river dries up leaving no possibility at all of irrigating the field. In the first case the lessee may not make any deduction from the rental since it is regarded as his own misfortune; in the second case he may make such deduction. If the owner stood in the field and said to the lessee, "I am letting this irrigated field, or this tree plantation to you," his statement will be interpreted to mean that the lease was made as though the owner was letting the field as it was then, without change, and therefore the lessee will be entitled to make a deduction from the rental (Yad, Sekhirut 8:4, 5; Sh. Ar., ḤM 321 and 322).

Termination of *Ḥakhirah*

If on termination of the lease unharvested produce remains on the field, or if the market day for the sale of already harvested produce has not yet arrived, an appraisal is made of the lessee's share therein (Tosef., BM 9:1; Yad, Sekhirut 8:10; Sh. Ar., ḤM 327:1). If the lessee dies within the term of the lease and is survived by his son, the position is as follows: If the father had already received everything due to him for the whole of the term and the owner of the field does not wish to entrust it to the son until completion of the term and for the agreed purpose, the son will not be required to return anything received by his father in excess of the measure of his cultivation – since the son may say that he will complete the cultivation of the field if it is left with him; if the father had not yet received any part of his due share and the son should ask the owner to entrust the field to his further cultivation until expiry of the agreed term and in return for the whole of his father's stipulated share, the owner – who in this case is in the favored position – may deny the existence of any business tie with the lessee and proffer him payment in accordance with the measure of the work done by his father (Sh. Ar., ḤM 329; *Sma* n. 1).

[Nahum Rakover]

Lease – Property Law or Contract Law?

In defining the juridical essence of lease under law, four approaches may be discerned:

PROPERTY (IN REM) RIGHT. According to this approach, accepted by most medieval authorities (*rishonim*), the lessee has a property (*in rem*) right to use and possess the leasehold for a limited time, as implied by the Talmudic rule "A lease, within its time, is a sale" (BM 56b). The nature of a lease, as a property right, is expressed in many ways, inter alia: a lease is passed on as inheritance (Resp. Rashba, 2:328); the sale of the leasehold by the lessor does not impinge on the rights of the lessee (Sh. Ar., ḤM 312:1); and during the leasing period of the lease, any abandoned property found on the leasehold belongs to the lessee, not the lessor, by force of a *kinyan ḥaẓer* (i.e., the actual location of an object in the owner's *ḥaẓer* (= yard) confers ownership, without the requirement of an additional act) (Sh. Ar., ḤM 260:4; Sema, 260:13; and see *Keẓot Ha-Ḥoshen* 313:1).

Although the lessee acquires a property right in the leasehold, this does not imply that he bears the risk of being denied its use, nor does it imply that during the lease period, the lessor has no duty to the lessee. Although a lease is much like a temporary sale, it is not a full-fledged sale. The difference between a lease and a sale stems primarily from the fact that the lessee has only acquired the right to the possession and use of the leasehold, while the lessor retains title of the leasehold. This difference explains why, in certain situations of prevention of use – especially in cases of damage to the leasehold, the property of the lessor – the lessee is not required to continue his rent payments (Yad, Sekhirut 5:6; Resp. Maharam of Padua, 39; inter alia). The same difference may also explain why the lessee may demand the repair of any damage that occurs to the leasehold during the period of the lease (Sema, 312:32).

CONTRACT (IMPERSONUM). According to this approach, accepted by more recent authorities (*aḥaronim*), a lease is a personal obligation of the lessor to the lessee to enable the latter to make use of the leasehold, and the lease itself lacks any *in rem* foundation. "A lease does not affect acquisition" (Avodah Zarah 15a), except that the lessor encumbers the leasehold for the fulfillment of his obligation. That is, the lessee has no property right to the leasehold itself, but only a personal claim to demand that the lessor fulfill his contractual obligations. It should be noted that in most leasing matters, the legal essence of the lease as a personal contract and not as property-*in rem* would yield similar legal results (either by the implied agreement between the parties or by the force of the rabbinic enactment). Nevertheless, the conceptual difference may have practical implications in various specific contexts, for example, *kinyan ḥaẓer* (see above): according to the contractual approach, even during the lease period, the lessor has ownership of any abandoned property found in the leasehold (Shakh, ḤM 313:1); while according to the property approach, it is the lessee who acquires ownership, as noted above.

TWO TYPES OF LEASE. Among the proponents of the property approach, there are those who contend (contrary to the aforementioned view) that since the lessee has a property right on the leasehold, he must assume all the risks other than *force majeur*, of being denied its use (Samson ben Abraham of Sens, cited in *Teshuvot Maimoniyyot*, Mishpatim, 27). However, strict adherence to the property law approach contradicts several Talmudic passages. For example, the Talmud (BM 79a) explicitly rules that when an ass is leased and dies along the way, the lessee is free of any financial obligation; an exemption that *prima facie* contradicts the property approach. Thus, they are forced to explain that concomitant to the property based lease, there is another kind of lease to which the principle that "a lease, within its time, is a sale" does not apply and which is entirely contractual in nature. (This is one of the rationales offered for the property approach, e.g., Resp. Ḥavaẓelet ha-Sharon, 1st ed., ḤM, 30). Thus, their view is that Jewish law recognizes two types of lease, a property-based lease and a contractual lease, although the criterion for distinguishing between the two is not clear.

COMBINED APPROACH. There is also a view that a lease has both property and contractual aspects. The property aspect confers the lessee property rights to the leasehold (with all that is implied thereby, such as *kinyan ḥaẓer*); while the contractual aspect imposes a number of personal obligations on the lessor to the lessee, intended to ensure that the latter gains maximum benefit from the contracted property, such as prohibiting any interference with his use of the leasehold and the requirement to repair any damages (see Rashba, cited in *Shitah Mekubeẓẓet*, BM 78a, s.v. *od katav ha-rav*). This view was also expressed by Justice Silberg (CA 208/51 *Hacker v. Barash*, 8 PD 566, 580), who concluded, on the basis of the *Derishah* (ḤM 316:1) that a lease is a hybrid creation, because a lessee may not, under any circumstances (other than subletting), transfer the leasehold to another party without express agreement of the lessor (although this inference is not the only possible conclusion to be drawn from the *Derishah* source).

[Michael Wygoda (2nd ed.)]

BIBLIOGRAPHY: I.S. Zuri, *Mishpat ha-Talmud*, 5 (1921), 91–100; Gulak, Yesodei, 1 (1922), 142–5; 2 (1922), 163–7, 188f.; idem, Oẓar, 195–8; P. Dickstein, in: *Ha-Mishpat ha-Ivri*, 2 (1926/27), 109–90; Herzog, Instit, 1 (1936), 329–38; A. Karlin, in: *Sinai*, 6 (1939/40), 485–91; ET, 2 (1949), 186–92; 13 (1970), 75–103; Elon, Mafte'aḥ, 376–9. **ADD. BIBLIOGRAPHY:** M. Elon, *Ha-Mishpat ha-Ivri* (1988), 1:148, 374, 555, 576, 594, 633, 653, 656, 755, 787f.; 2:993, 1050, 1075, 1284; 3:1343; *ibid., Jewish Law* (1994), 1:166, 453; 2:675, 710, 734, 683, 808, 811, 931, 966f.; 3:1201, 1286, 1296, 1533; 4:1604; M. Elon and B. Lifshitz, *Mafte'aḥ ha-She'elot ve-ha-Teshuvot shel Ḥakhmei Sefarad u-Ẓefon Afrikah* (legal digest) (1986), (2) 459–61, 522–25; B. Lifshitz and E. Shochetman, *Mafte'aḥ ha-She'elot ve-ha-Teshuvot shel Ḥakhmei Ashkenaz, Ẓarefat ve-Italyah* (legal digest) (1997), 308–09, 347–51; Sh. Albeck, *Dinei ha-Mamonot ba-Talmud* (1983²), 399–407; Y.Y. Bloi, *Pitḥei Ḥoshen: Hilkhot Sekhirut* (1985); E. Ben-Shelomo, *Sekhirut Nekhasim ba-Halakhah* (1989); I. Warhaftig, *Ha-Hitḥayyevut: Tokpah, Ofyah, ve-Sugeha* (2001), 175, 475–83; M. Wygoda, *Sekhirut u-She'ilah* (1998); CA 208/51 *Hacker v. Barash*, 8 PD 566, 577–581 (Justice Silberg).

LEATHER INDUSTRY AND TRADE.

Biblical and Talmudic Times

The one Hebrew word עוֹר (*or*) covers skin, hide, and leather, so that it is difficult to establish whether references in the Bible are to skin or leather. The Bible frequently refers to garments made from skin (e.g., Gen. 3:21, 25:25). The prophet Zechariah wore a "hairy mantle" (13:14) and from the context it is obvious that he considered it a distinctive mark of the prophet. Elijah and Elisha probably wore a similar mantle (I Kings 19:13; II Kings 1:8). Such a garment was worn by the prophets to emphasize archaic values and simplicity after clothing woven from vegetable fibers had become the rule. Tanning is never mentioned in the Bible, although it is recorded in Egypt from the time of the earliest dynasty. It may be assumed that in biblical times the process was essentially one of simply drying the hide. Leather was widely used in biblical times: for sandals and shoes, and for straps and harnesses for horses, donkeys, and camels; the *nod* (נֹאד), a skin bottle for storing and transporting liquids, is still widely used in the Middle East. All writing materials were also produced from hides. A ritually important use of leather and parchment since ancient times is for Torah scrolls, *tefillin*, the straps of which must be made from ritually clean animals, and the contents of *mezuzot*.

Talmudic literature contains several expressions for those occupied in leather production: the *bursi* was the dresser of the hides (Ket. 7:10); the tannery was called *burseki* (BB 2:9; Shab. 1:2); *bursiyyon* was the hide when it was being processed (TJ, Shab. 5:2, 7b); in time *bursiyyon* was used for the tanning process and finally for the tanner himself (Kid. 82b). The *shalḥa* (Shab. 49b) is an identical designation less frequently used. The expression *avdan* (Kel. 26:8; Shab. 1:8) was also used. The *poshet or* was the skinner, the intermediary craftsman between the butcher and the tanner. As in Greece and Rome, tanneries had to be located on the outskirts of the towns, far from residential quarters. According to the Mishnah (BB 2:9) a tannery should be situated on the east side of the town only, at least 50 cubits from the outskirts. This was because tanning was a primitive, malodorous process. Like a privy and a bathhouse, the tannery was exempted from having a *mezuzah* on the door post (Yoma 11a–b). The residents of an alley or lane could prevent one of their neighbors from becoming a tanner (BB 21b). A synagogue building may not be sold for use as a tannery (Meg. 3:2). For all these reasons the tanner's status in society was low. Of all the sages of the Talmud only *Yose b. Ḥalafta is known to have been a tanner. Like fullers and coppersmiths, tanners are exempted from appearing at the Temple on pilgrimage festivals because their unpleasant odor prevents them from going up with all the men (Ḥag. 7b), and forming a separate group is forbidden. An unnamed *gaon* (S. Assaf, *Teshuvot ha-Ge'onim* (1928), 93, no. 179) explains that they are exempt because their bad odor, having penetrated their flesh, cannot be removed. This, he said, was why they had their own synagogues in his day in Babylon. The tanner's trade was among those from which neither king nor high priest might be appointed, not because the tanner is ritually unfit, but because his occupation is despised (Kid. 82a). Maimonides adds (Yad, Melakhim 1:6) that whoever has worked at this trade for even one day is unfit for the high offices. In the words of the Talmud: "The world can exist neither without a perfume-maker nor without a tanner – happy is he whose craft is that of a perfume-maker, and woe to him who is a tanner by trade." According to *Ketubbot* 9:10, a tanner (as well as a collector of dung for tanning), whether he plied his trade before marriage or took it up afterward, may be compelled to divorce his wife if she demands it. Rabbi *Meir was of the opinion that even if a wife had agreed before the wedding to put up with her husband's trade, she must be allowed a divorce if she later found that she could not tolerate it. The example is given of a tanner who died, leaving a brother, also a tanner, who should therefore take the dead man's wife in levirate marriage. It was ruled that she might say: "I could endure your brother, but cannot endure you."

Later Developments in the East

Throughout the early Middle Ages, in countries under Muslim rule, tanning and leather craft remained in Jewish hands because of the low status of the profession. In 985 Muhammad ibn-Aḥmed al Magdisi reported that most tanners in Palestine and Syria were Jews. From the 12th to the 15th centuries the Dung Gate of the Old City of Jerusalem was called the Tanners' Gate because of its proximity to the Pool of Siloam, whose waters were considered unfit to drink but excellent for tanning purposes. Jews as tanners are mentioned frequently in *Byzantium: in the biography of an archbishop who flourished around 1150, they are compared to "hungry, leather-gnawing dogs." *Benjamin of Tudela considered that the Greeks of late 12th-century Constantinople hated the Jews because the Jewish tanners spilled their sewage water into the streets outside their houses and contaminated the Jewish quarter (*Itinerary of…*, ed. by M.N. Adler (1897), 16–17). The classical scholar Maximus Planudes mentions Jewish tanners in Constantinople in 1296; they lived in a separate quarter and were organized into a guild. Shortly after 1300 Jewish tanners who were Venetian subjects signed an agreement with the subjects of the empire, endorsed by the authorities, permitting them to lease ground for building houses and to pursue their trade in the city. To avoid competition, tasks were divided: the newcomers were to do the scraping, while the veterans did the tanning itself. In 1319 Emperor Andronicus II prohibited his subjects from engaging in tanning and ordered them to pursue other trades. The Venetian subjects seized the opportunity to break the earlier agreement and capture the whole trade. An imperial squad seized and destroyed their hides, and they were evicted from their houses. After protracted negotiations between the imperial and Venetian authorities, the Venetian claim for damages was refused. This was one instance of a conflict arising from the Byzantine policy of ousting Venice from the commerce in hides, furs, and leather from Crimea to Constantinople (J. Starr, *Romania* (1949), 25–35; D. Jacoby, in: *Byzantiyyon*, 37 (1967), 167–227; idem, in: *Zion*, 27 (1962), 24–35, passim).

RHODES. On his journey to Ereẓ Israel in 1488, Obadiah di Bertinoro found Jewish tanners in Rhodes. He thought it worthy of note that their clothes were clean and their manners good.

OTTOMAN EMPIRE. In the 16th and 17th century, the production of leather and the export of hides and leather was one of the most important Jewish economic enterprises. Merchants from *Salonika bought hides from the Balkans and resold them after finishing. To put a stop to this competition the merchants of *Monastir (now Bitolj) forbade the sale of hides out of town. In the rabbinical responsa, trade in hides and mainly Cordoban leather is often mentioned. The responsa of Samuel b. Moses de *Medina (1506–1589) record a hide and leather merchant with his own shop in *Pleven (Plevna, Bulgaria) as well as the export of hides from *Adrianople (Edirne, Turkey) to *Ancona and Ragusa (*Dubrovnik, Yugoslavia). According to Joseph b. David Lev (c. 1502–1588) and Joseph Moses Mitrani (1569–1639), who dealt with exports to *Venice, these transactions were usually conducted in partnership. Solomon b. Aaron Hason (d. before 1733) frequently dealt with the large-scale export of Cordoban leather to France via Venice; in one case there were 21 bales exported by five partners (M.S. Goodblatt, *Jewish Life in Turkey in the 16th Century* (1952), 53; Hananel-Eškenazi, 1 (1958), index).

NORTH AFRICA. Jews of *Fez at the beginning of the 18th century dried, salted, and exported hides to *Spain, *Portugal, and Gibraltar; after payment of a special tax (*fayid*), the royal seal was affixed (H. Bentov, in: *Sefunot*, 10 (1956/57), 438). In *Algiers in 1899 there were 45 Jewish tanners and 730 shoemakers (JE, s.v. *Artisans*).

In Europe

SPAIN. In Muslim Spain there were many Jewish tanners. The famous *Cordoba leather was exported to North Africa and Europe. In the Jewish quarter of *Seville there were two tanners' squares (Ashtor, Korot, 179–80). Three saddlers from *Saragossa were Obadiah di Bertinoro's shipmates (1486–88). A tanners' street (Teneria) existed in the Jewish quarter of Saragossa around 1336 and tanners were mentioned in Castile in 1443.

ITALY. At the beginning of the 14th century, there were Jewish tanners in the Kingdom of Naples (Roth, Italy, 272). Under the rule of *Frederick II Hohenstaufen, trade in skins and in leather goods was one of their basic economic activities in *Sicily. Jewish tanners are mentioned in several Sicilian localities in the first half of the 15th century.

FRANCE. Jewish tanners are mentioned in Paris in 1258 and in *Montpellier in 1293. There is also mention of one tannery in *Troyes in 1189 and two in 1233. Jews in Central and Eastern Europe frequently engaged in tanning and other crafts connected with leather, from the Middle Ages onward. This was largely because the Christian attitude toward the trade was identical with the feeling prevalent in talmudic times. The family names which occur so frequently among European Jews, such as Gerber, Garber, Lederer, and Ledermann (Ger.), Korzownik, Skurnik, Ganbarz, and Garbowski (Pol.) and Koželuh (Cz.), bear witness to their occupations.

BOHEMIA AND MORAVIA. Buying hides from the local noblemen was one of the main tasks of the Jews, as stipulated in the charters on which their protection was based; purchasing the skins of small animals from peasants and from butchers was an important side line. Jews also imported and exported hides. At the end of the 16th century, Marcus *Meisel was granted the monopoly of the leather trade in Prague (Bondy-Dworsky, no. 1068). In 1629 the gentile tanners of *Tachov included a clause in their charter forbidding any of their number to finish hides for Jews because the Jewish leather trade was undercutting the tanners. When the Jews were expelled from *Litomerice in 1541, one man had to be allowed to remain because he alone was capable of supplying hides and tanning bark to the tanners (H. Ankert, in: H. Gold, *Juden und Judengemeinden Boehmens*, 1934). In Prague in 1729 there were 70 Jewish hide and leather merchants. The Jews who settled in Kremsier (*Kromeriz) in 1670 after their expulsion from Vienna were permitted to deal in "various crude and finished leather" (*Frankl-Gruen, Kremsier, 1 (1896), 109). Leather and hide merchants frequented the large fairs, mainly the one at Breslau (Wroclaw), which was a center for the import of hides from Eastern Europe.

Jews were also active in tanning itself; since it was one of the trades outside guild control it was open to Jews, and after the Thirty Years' War tanneries became one of the most important Jewish economic outlets. When the Moravian guilds protested against the renewal of Jewish privileges in 1659, one of their arguments was the claim that the methods of tanning employed by the Jews were unsatisfactory (W. Mueller, *Urkundliche Beitraege* (1905), 27–28). Jews were permitted to settle as tanners in localities otherwise forbidden to them. Most of the tanneries were the property of the local nobleman and were leased to the Jewish *randar* (see *Arenda*), who was sometimes not a tanner himself but the employer of one. However, some Jews had their own tanneries. In *Polna the community as such leased the tannery from the municipality (1681) and in *Kolin the community bought the tannery (1724; R. Kestenberg-Gladstein, in: JJS, 6 (1955), 35–49). The council of Moravian Jewry issued several ordinances concerning the leather industry: it forbade the attempt to gain a monopoly on buying hides and other merchandise from a local nobleman (I. Heilperin, *Takkanot…* (1963), 83, no. 250), yet in another ordinance (*ibid.*, 150, no. 449) it forbade anyone to buy in a locality where someone else had a monopoly by the terms of his contract with the local nobleman. It was considered the duty of the **Landrabbiner* to protect Moravian Jews from the competition of buyers from other districts (*ibid.*, 285, no. 485). The council did not hold tanners (nor butchers) in high esteem: in 1709 it ruled that they could be members of the council only if they also held public office in their home community.

Early in the 17th century the Hapsburg rulers, true to their mercantilist policies, were interested in encouraging tanning. A survey that they carried out in Moravia in 1719 revealed that there were two tanneries owned by Jews and 79 leased by Jews from local noblemen; six of them employed one gentile laborer each; the lease of 13 of these tanneries was connected with the lease of a distillery; only ten tanneries in Moravia were run by gentiles (V. Zacek, in: JGGJČ, 5 (1933), 175–97). In Bohemia in 1724 there were 80 Jewish tanners and furriers (grouped together under one heading) and 26 tanneries were leased to Jews; 252 Jews were occupied in the leather industry; 146 were hide and leather merchants, and 106 were engaged in tanning (R. Kestenberg-Gladstein, in: *Zion*, 9 (1944), 17; 12 (1946/47), 49–65, 160–89, and passim). In the 18th century tanning and trading in leather were often connected. One specialty of the Jewish leather trade in Moravia was the kid trousers which, finished and colored in various ways, were an important feature of the peasants' national costume (B. Heilig, in: JGGJČ, 3 (1931), 373). The tanners were the first craftsmen in the Hapsburg Empire who were permitted to hire open salesrooms (*Verkaufsgewoelbe*) in Vienna (1781). This offered several Jews the opportunity to settle there.

These tanneries continued to flourish in the 19th century, and when new chemical methods were introduced many of them became important factories, as in *Golcuv Jenikov and *Kosova Hora (Amschelberg). Jews also founded new factories where no tanneries had existed before: e.g., in *Pilsen where the first factory producing Moroccan-style leather was established in 1829 and in *Brno where a factory producing French-style leather was founded in 1846. More than 20 of the leather factories in Bohemia in 1863 were run by Jews, and a large part of their export trade was with the United States. Leather production remained a Jewish craft for many years. After chromium tanning was introduced (1884) Jewish factories led the move to modernization. Between the two world wars Jewish firms played an important role in the production and export of leather goods (*Jews of Czechoslovakia*, 1 (1968), 419–81).

GERMANY. In 1331 Jewish tanners were permitted, in return for a fee, to join the guild in *Esslingen am Neckar. In 1406 there were Jewish saddle-makers in Frankfurt, but Jewish tanners in general were not numerous. As late as the 17th century Jews were forbidden to engage in this craft in Hesse-Kassel. The Christian and Jewish tanners frequently clashed over the buying of hides and sale of the leather. In some districts, as in Hesse-Darmstadt, the trade was forbidden to Jews, and in all districts the tanners guild had an option on the hides for 24 hours after slaughtering. In 1718 the Berlin merchants' guild included hides and furs in a suggested list of merchandise in which Jews should be permitted to trade. In 1736 Samuel Slomka was granted the concession to establish a leather factory in Tilsit (Sovetsk) to produce, besides ordinary leather, Russian-style leather (*Juchten*; S. Stern, *Der preussische Staat…* 2 (1925, repr. (1962), 105). At the turn of the 17th century, Jewish merchants supplied tanners in Berlin with hides and processed the leather according to the putting-out system. The Prussian *General-Reglement* of 1750 limited Jewish trade in hides and leather to fairs (M. Freund, *Emancipation* (1893), 38–41).

*Frederick II founded, at his own expense, a factory for English-style leather, run by a Scottish expert, but it failed to prosper. After various unsuccessful endeavors to improve it, the firm was handed over to Daniel *Itzig (1761). Army regiments were commanded to place their orders there. Daniel's son, Elias, continued to manage the factory until it closed down in 1818. Daniel Itzig himself founded another factory for chamois leather. The ordinances permitting Jews to import leather frequently stipulated that this should be in exchange for exporting locally manufactured textiles.

At the end of the 19th century, Jews were important in the leather industry of Germany. Between the world wars the trust founded by Adler and Oppenheimer, until 1918 in *Strasbourg, developed into one of the largest industries of its kind in the world (S. Kaznelson (ed.), *Die Juden im deutschen Kulturbereich* (1962), 792–3). However, Jewish participation in actual tanning decreased: in 1907 there were only 334 Jewish tanners in Germany compared with 49,000 gentile ones. Many Jews were engaged in the production of leather goods such as purses, wallets, valises, etc. as entrepreneurs, managers, and workers, since conditions were similar to those in *tailoring: it was a light industry, easily adaptable to piece work and to home and family enterprises. Many of the leather firms in Germany, particularly in *Offenbach, were owned by Jews, and immigrant East European Jews supplied the labor.

BELGIUM. In 1910 Belgium had 33 Jewish enterprises employing 104 workers in the *maroquinerie* industries (purses, wallets, etc.). By 1926, 1,600 Jewish workers were employed in 160 firms, most of which employed more than ten workers; almost all were concentrated in Brussels, Anderlecht, and the vicinity. The industry, revolutionized after World War I by a mass influx of East European Jews, not only grew to supply local demand but made Belgium an important exporter of leather goods.

POLAND, LITHUANIA, AND RUSSIA. In 1460 Jewish tanners are mentioned as having lived "for a long time" in a Lemberg (*Lvov) suburb. In *Przemysl Jewish tanners are mentioned in the 16th century. There was a Jewish tanners' guild in *Leszno (Lissa) in the 18th century. With the industrial development of the 1790s, Jewish entrepreneurs, among them Samuel *Zbitkover, established tanneries: e.g., in Praga (suburb of Warsaw) which employed 15 laborers, in *Cracow, Wegrow, and *Lutomiersk. The Jewish community of *Opoczno ran a tannery. Tanning and the leather trades became an outstanding Jewish occupation toward the end of the 19th century, employing tens of thousands of Jews. In some localities, such as *Lukow, *Kozienice, *Siedlce, *Radom, *Bialystok, and *Kielce, a large proportion of the Jewish inhabitants worked in the leather trade, which lost its main market in the 1917 Revolution. In 1894, 400 Jewish tanning workers in *Krynki founded the Po'alei Ẓedek, one of the first trade unions in Russia (by 1898 they had 800 members). To fight the workers' demands the tannery owners founded the Agudat Aḥim in 1906. In the eastern regions of the *Pale of Settlement, 64.6% of all leather workers were Jews. In czarist Russia 287 out of 530 tanneries were owned by Jews (162 of them in Russian Poland). The largest was in Shauli (*Siauliai). Other important centers were in *Vilna, *Smorgon, *Mogilev, *Minsk, and Dvinsk (*Daugaupils, Latvia). Jewish participation in the leather trade in independent Poland remained considerable: in 1927, 41% of all tanners were Jews and in 1931 15,705 Jews were employed in the leather industries (45% of all leather workers). While among the gentiles, leather workers formed 0.9% of all industrial laborers, among Jews the percentage was 2.9; 31.8% of the independent employers of the larger and technologically developed factories were Jews, but only 4.8% of the laborers in these factories were Jews. The percentage of Jews employed in the leather industries (45%) was even higher than that of the needleworkers (44.1%; R. Mahler, *Yehudei Polin Bein Shetei Milḥamot Olam* (1968), 73–98, passim). Their trade unions (Leder-farayn) were strong; in Warsaw there were two after 1922, one dominated by the *Bund and one by the Communists (B. Ḥayyim, in *Pinkes Varshe*, 1 (1955), 387–96).

Israel

The leather industry received its impetus from immigrants from central Europe in the middle 1930s; in 1937, 850 workers were employed in 61 firms. Production of boots for the British army increased from 80,000 pairs in 1942 to 400,000 in 1944; an additional 700,000 were produced by artisans and workshops. Production, which increased after the establishment of the State of Israel, was encouraged by the population increase and by the rise in the standard of living. In 1969 it totaled 1.5% of the total industrial production; exports totaled $3,500,000 (1.5% of all industrial exports). According to a 1965 industrial census 7,440 workers were employed in 2,580 firms: only 111 employed more than ten workers; most work was done in family-style workshops. Exports in 2004 dropped to $1.0 million as opposed to imports of $17 million. In all, around 1,500 persons were employed in 140 firms.

[Meir Lamed]

LEAVIS, QUEENIE DOROTHY (1906–1981), British literary scholar. Queenie Leavis, the daughter of a Jewish draper, Morris Roth, of Edmonton, London, was educated at Girton College, Cambridge, where she received a first degree and won four prizes. In 1929 she married the famous literary scholar F.R. Leavis (1895–1978). Her doctoral dissertation was published as *Fiction and the Reading Public* (1932). From 1932 until 1953 her husband was the editor of the famous literary quarterly *Scrutiny*, in which she played an influential role. She taught English at Cambridge in the 1960s and produced a steady flow of highly influential works centering around the nature of English literary identity, such as *Dickens the Novelist* (1970), co-authored with her husband, and essays published posthumously in three collected volumes.

BIBLIOGRAPHY: ODNB online; I. MacKillop, *F.R. Leavis: A Life in Criticism* (1995).

[William D. Rubinstein (2nd ed.)]

LEAVITT, MOSES A. (1894–1965), *American Jewish Joint Distribution Committee leader. Leavitt was born in New York City. He studied chemical engineering and worked with chemical companies until 1922, when he entered Jewish social service work. He became assistant secretary of the Joint in 1929, then was transferred in 1933 to the Palestine Economic Corporation, an organization closely allied to JDC, where he served as vice president and secretary. Succeeding Joseph *Hyman as JDC secretary in 1940, Leavitt directed JDC aid from the U.S. to German-occupied Europe. Together with Joseph J. *Schwartz in Europe, Leavitt formed most of the policy decisions during the war and especially after it, when JDC spent the largest sums in its history aiding Jewish survivors in Europe. He also took part in channeling JDC efforts to immigration to Israel and the start of social service for the elderly (Malben) there. After prolonged negotiations, he was one of the signatories of the $107 million agreement with West Germany on Jewish Material Claims. Leavitt, who had been executive vice chairman of JDC from 1947, served as chairman of the American Council of Voluntary Agencies from 1954, and later as honorary chairman (1958). He was also a member of The Hebrew University Board of Governors (from 1959).

[Yehuda Bauer]

LEBANON (Heb. לְבָנוֹן), Middle Eastern state named after a mountain chain running parallel to the Mediterranean coast N. of Israel. The name Lebanon is derived from *lavan* (*lbn*; "white") in reference to the snow covering its peaks. It was variously called Levanon in Hebrew, Libnah in Phoenician, Labnanu in Assyrian, and Lablani or Niblani in Hittite.

In Ancient Times

Like most high mountains, Mt. Lebanon was imagined in early

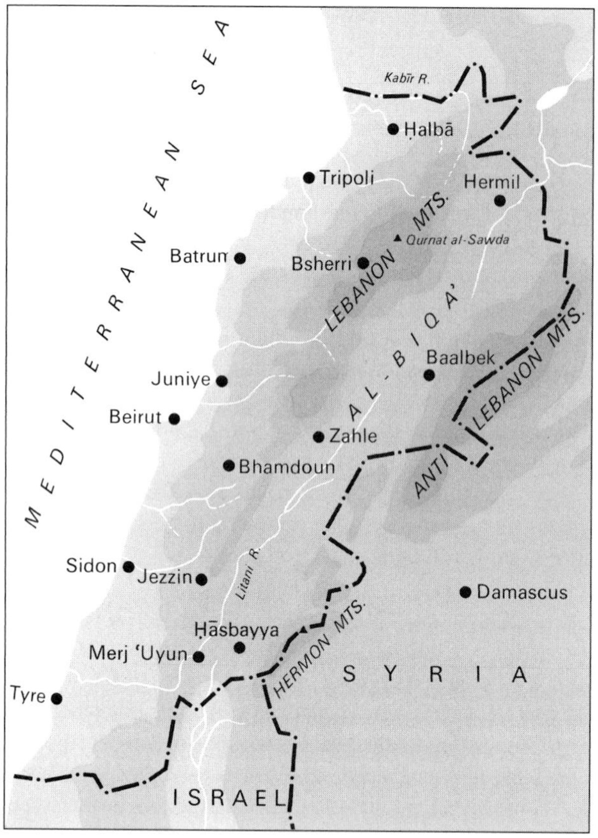

Map of Lebanon showing major cities.

times to have been the abode of a god, Baal Lebanon, who is sometimes identified with Hadad. The area was inhabited by a number of different peoples in the prehistoric period. It appears to have been eventually settled by a West-Semitic population, later designated Canaanite and in Hellenistic sources Phoenician. The mountains of the Lebanon, rich in cedars and other coniferous trees, attracted the attention of the rulers of the treeless Nile Valley at an early date. As early as the fourth dynasty, the pharaoh Snefru probably sent to Byblos for cedars, firs, pines, and other trees. For 1,500 years the forests of the Lebanon supplied Egypt with wood for a number of purposes, including shipbuilding and construction of temples, sacred and funerary boats, and doors for palace gates. As the mountains became denuded, more and more harbors were opened by the Egyptians. From the 12th century B.C.E. onward the Assyrians competed with the Egyptians for the wood of the Lebanon. Tiglath-Pileser I advanced into the region in order to obtain wood for building temples to the gods Anu and Adad. In 877 B.C.E. Ashurnaṣirpal II took firs and pines from the Lebanon back to Assyria. The devastation caused by Sennacherib among the cedars and firs is described in the Lord's answer to Hezekiah's prayer (II Kings 19:23). According to Isaiah, the trees of the Lebanon rejoiced when Sargon of Assyria passed away (14:8).

In general, the Lebanon marks the northern boundary of the Promised Land (Deut. 1:7; 3:25; 11:24; Josh. 1:4; 9:1). Its cedars are praised as the finest of trees (I Kings 5:13) and are contrasted with the bramble in Jotham's parable (Judg. 9:15). Isaiah praises the cypress, the plane tree, and the larch of the region (60:13). In the Song of Songs and other books of the Bible the wild animals, waters, trees, flowers, wine, and snow of the Lebanon are described in glowing terms. When Solomon built the Temple, he was supplied with cedars from the Lebanon by his ally Hiram, king of Tyre (I Kings 5:15–24), who sent the logs in floats to a harbor near Jaffa (Tell Qasīla; II Chron. 2:15). The same procedure was repeated for the construction of the Second Temple, at which time the forests belonged to the king of Persia (Ezra 3:7). In Hellenistic and Roman times the Lebanon was divided among the various Phoenician cities then largely Hellenized; it became part of the province of Syria, and from the third century a separate province, Phoenicia (Augusta Libanensis).

Post-Second Temple and Arab Periods

In post-biblical times, the forests of the Lebanon continued to be exploited by the Phoenician cities in whose territories they stood for the benefit of the Hellenistic and Roman rulers. In the seventh century (the Byzantine period) the mountaineers of the region adopted the theological views of the emperor Heraclius, becoming Monotheletes; the followers of this sect were called Maronites after their patriarch John Maron. They maintained their religion throughout the Arab domination.

[Michael Avi-Yonah]

There is scant information about the existence of Jews between the seventh and 15th centuries, but small Jewish communities continued to exist in the area which is now Lebanon. The Arab author al-Balādhuri relates that the Caliph Mu'āwiya settled Jews in *Tripoli. The Palestinian academy established its seat in Tyre in 1071. *Benjamin of Tudela, in the 12th century, relates that the Jews lived in the same area as the *Druze, with whom they traded and engaged in various crafts. In crusader times, the Lebanon was divided between the count of Tripoli and the king of Jerusalem, remaining in the hands of the crusaders almost until the end of the Latin kingdom (1291).

[Haïm Z'ew Hirschberg]

There were also Jews living in the village districts. In the town of Deir al-Qamar in Mount Lebanon, situated halfway between *Beirut and *Sidon, there was a Jewish community (80 families at the beginning of the 19th century), which engaged in agriculture and the breeding of silkworms as well as commerce, the manufacture of soap, and the extraction of some iron from the surrounding ore deposits. Some Jews also lived in villages within the direct or outlying vicinity of Deir al-Qamar (including Mukhtara, 'Ayn Qanya, 'Ayn Zaḥlata, and others). The common factor which characterized almost every one of these Jewish concentrations was their dependency on the Druze inhabitants, with whom they coexisted on friendly terms. In 1860, as a result of the inter-communal war between the Druze and the Maronites of Lebanon, the Druze gradually abandoned the region of Deir al-Qamar. They were followed by the Jews who settled in Beirut, the town of Aley (southeast of Beirut), and Sidon. In the interior of Lebanon, the only remaining Jewish community was to be found in Ḥāṣbayya, on the slopes of the Hermon, where its presence was already known from the 18th century. Most of the Jews of this town were transferred to Rosh Pinah in 1888 by Baron Rothschild but it was only in 1913 that the last three families left. The relations between the Jews and the dominant Maronite community were at times strained and there were several blood libels. The development of modern Lebanon was accompanied by an increase in the Jewish population, most of which was of Sephardi origin. The Jews arrived in Lebanon, especially to the capital, Beirut, from Greece and Turkey, and they gradually became an important commercial factor.

[Eliyahu Ashtor]

Contemporary Period

Following the establishment of Greater Lebanon by the French colonial power in 1920, and the independence of the Lebanese Republic in the mid-1940s, the Jews residing in that country – who were one of its 17 formally recognized religious sects – were considered to be, and regarded themselves as, an integral part of its multiethnic social fabric. Like Lebanon's other communities, Jews served in the public administration, including the security forces (see below). But they never had their own representative in the Lebanese parliament (there was one member of parliament allocated to Lebanon's minorities, but he was generally a member of one of the smaller Christian communities). However, the legal, religious, and economic freedoms enjoyed by Lebanon's Jews, which were unparalleled in the Arab Middle East, were affected by the rising tensions in Palestine and, from 1948, by the Arab-Israeli conflict.

In 1923, the number of Jews in Lebanon was estimated at 3,300, and the 1932 population census – the last comprehensive census held in Lebanon – registered 3,588 Jews, of whom 3,060 lived in Beirut and the rest in Sidon and Tripoli. By 1939, the number of Jews in Lebanon increased to about 6,000–7,000, and the 1944 census registered 6,261. In the wake of World War II, several institutional reforms were introduced in the Jewish community in Beirut, and a 15-member elected community council (the Community Council of Beirut), headed by a president, was set up. This body was recognized by the Lebanese government, as well as by the smaller Jewish communities in Sidon and Tripoli.

Although they were influenced by their proximity to Palestine, the Jews in Lebanon did not suffer from the establishment of the State of Israel in 1948. Not only did the Lebanese government order its security forces to protect the Jewish quarter in Beirut from attacks by pro-Palestinian activists, but political actors such as the Maronite Christian Phalanges, which maintained close ties with the Jewish community (a few Lebanese Jews even joined that organization), also positioned guards there. During the later stages of the 1948 War, when the Israeli army occupied part of South Lebanon, the homes of several members of the small Jewish community in Sidon, numbering 200 persons, were confiscated, and Palestinian refugees were installed in them. But the government in Beirut ordered the local police to protect the Jews in that city and facilitate their return to their homes and property.

The number of Jews in Lebanon, estimated at 5,200 in 1948, rose in 1951 to about 9,000, of which 6,961 were Lebanese citizens and about 2,000 Jewish immigrants from *Syria and *Iraq. The Lebanese government allowed these immigrants to stay in the country, and some acquired Lebanese citizenship (other refugees, such as the Palestinians, were generally not naturalized). In 1950, the government even permitted Syrian and Iraqi Jews who had found sanctuary in Beirut to cross the border into Israel, under the supervision of the Israeli-Lebanese Mixed Armistice Commission (ILMAC).

Apart from the blowing up of the *Alliance Israélite Universelle school in Beirut in 1950, Lebanese Jews remained unharmed in the post-1948 period, although Arab nationalists sometimes forced Jews to donate money for the Palestinian cause. Lebanese opposition parties, and particularly the Socialist Party, which were led by Member of Parliament Emile Boustani (a Maronite Christian), several times demanded that Jewish property be confiscated and that Jews be discharged from government positions. In 1952, following mounting domestic and inter-Arab pressure, the government was compelled to discharge the two Jewish officers who served in the Lebanese army, but a few Jewish officials continued to work for the government. It is noteworthy that the Lebanese authorities did not limit the freedom of movement of Jews, and, except briefly in 1954, they were free to leave and enter the country at any time (the same freedom was enjoyed by Syrian Jews who had settled in Lebanon). Jews were also permitted to sell their property and take money out of the country in unlimited amounts. At no time were there ever limitations on their means of livelihood. Most of the Lebanese Jews were merchants, and a few were officials or artisans.

Until 1958, when Lebanon's first civil war broke out, the number of Jews in Lebanon remained at a level of about 9,000, making Lebanon the only Arab country in which the Jewish population increased after 1948. Only after 1958 did a large-scale exodus of Jews from Lebanon begin, as a result of the political unrest in the country. Many immigrated to the U.S. and Europe and several hundred went to Israel.

In early 1967 the number of Jews remaining in Lebanon was estimated at about 5,000–6,000, but after the Arab-Israeli war in June, emigration increased and the community was reduced by about a half. By then, nearly all Lebanese Jews were living in Beirut, with a few families remaining in Sidon (the community in Tripoli had ceased to exist before 1947). There were two Jewish banks in Lebanon, the Safra Bank and the Société Bancaire du Liban (formerly Zilkhah Bank). Only after the 1967 War were limitations imposed on non-Lebanese Jews, who were compelled to seek work permits from the authorities and not every applicant's request was granted. This was one of the reasons for the increase in Jewish emigration. Another reason was the partial paralysis of the Lebanese economy, particularly in the tourist industry, since Christian pilgrims no longer needed to pass through Lebanon in order to visit the Old City of Jerusalem and Bethlehem. Some of the Jewish emigrants, particularly the young people, went to Israel.

In the late 1960s and early 1970s, the Jewish community in Beirut still maintained a synagogue and other communal institutions, and there were synagogues in Sidon and in the summer resorts of Bhamdoun and Aley. In this period there were still Jewish schools in Beirut and Sidon. Jewish pupils also attended Christian schools, especially high schools, both because no Jewish school contained all high school classes, and because of the preference of Lebanese Jews for studying French. Even in Jewish schools emphasis was placed on the study of French. Arabic was studied to a lesser extent, and Hebrew even less, although the study of Hebrew was not restricted by the authorities. The Jewish and Christian school networks successfully combated illiteracy among the younger generation, but very few studied at institutions of higher learning. Most of the younger generation went into business. By 1970 the community had decreased to about 1,000–1,800.

During the early stages of Lebanon's second civil war (1975–1990), and especially after the paralysis of the state's institutions in 1975–76 and Israel's invasion in June 1982, the majority of the country's Jews emigrated. Those who stayed, particularly in war-torn Beirut, suffered many hardships on account of the violence that waged in and around the Jewish quarter. The Israeli-Palestinian struggle in Lebanon, which reached its pinnacle in the 1982 War, and the struggle between armed Shi'i factions and the Israeli army in South Lebanon in its aftermath, also impinged on the local Jewish community. By 1980 there were only about 200 Jews left in Lebanon, and by the late 1980s and early 1990s their number had dwindled to under 100. In mid-2002 it was reported that 67 Lebanese Jews had immigrated to Israel in the 1990–2001 period. In 2004, the number of Jews remaining in Lebanon was probably not more than a few dozen. One estimate, from 2002, put their number at no more than 24, or at twice that figure, and another, from 2003, at 20. According to a report from 2004, the Jewish community in Lebanon included only a few members, mostly elderly women. All of these Jews lived in Beirut and its vicinity.

Attitude Toward Israel

Prior to the establishment of the State of Israel in 1948 there were contacts held between Zionist leaders and some leaders of Lebanon's Maronite community. However, from 1943, when Lebanon's inter-communal settlement – the National Pact – was reached, the bulk of that country's leaders, from all communities, threw in their lot with the Arab states. Thus, in the 1948 War, Lebanon participated with the other Arab states, although its army adopted a defensive strategy and declined to cross the international border with Palestine. In fact, apart from several skirmishes, its army fought only one battle against the Israeli army, in Malikiyya on June 5–6, 1948. On March 23, 1949, an Armistice Agreement between Lebanon and Israel was signed at Rosh ha-Nikrah / Ras al-Nakoura, fixing the former international boundary between Palestine and Lebanon as the armistice line; accordingly, Israel evacuated 14 Lebanese villages that its army had occupied during the latter phases of the fighting. From then on, the Lebanese-Israel border was generally quiet for a period of almost 20 years: there were few serious violations of the Armistice Agreement, farmers from both countries met frequently in a friendly manner, and occasional crossings of the border by individuals were quietly solved by contacts between Israeli and Lebanese army officers, mainly through ILMAC. Israel also allowed Maronite dignitaries from Lebanon to visit their coreligionists in Israel. This state of affairs was a result not only of Lebanon's military weakness and the general indifference of the government in Beirut towards South Lebanon, but also of the delicate balance between its communities. While some Christian activists, especially Maronites, had contacts with Israeli officials and agreed to peaceful relations with Israel, they had to take into account the desire of Lebanon's Muslims for stronger contacts with the Arab world. In addition, nearly all Lebanese remained opposed to any settlement that would not include a solution to the problem of the Palestinian refugees in Lebanon. In the meantime, most refugees continued to live in camps, which were tightly supervised by the Lebanese security forces, and were not granted Lebanese citizenship.

As a member of the *Arab League, Lebanon participated in various Arab summit conferences, political propaganda, and economic campaigns against Israel, but it did not engage in military actions, not even during the 1967 War. In the wake of that conflict, Lebanon claimed that the Armistice Agreement of 1949 remained in force and that ILMAC should continue to be the channel of communication between the two countries. But Israel held the view that the armistice regime had collapsed and Israel's relations with all its neighbors were based on the cease-fire resolution of June 1967. In the war's aftermath, a gradual deterioration of the situation along the Israel-Lebanon border began, when armed Palestinian factions, whose members had previously limited themselves to fund-raising and propaganda in Lebanon, initiated armed attacks across the border. Gradually, thousands of armed Palestinian activists concentrated on the slopes of Mount Hermon, overlooking the north of Israel. On Dec. 26, 1968, members of the Popular Front for the Liberation of Palestine flew from Beirut to Athens, where they attacked an El Al plane at the city's international airport. In retaliation, an Israel commando unit destroyed a number of planes at the Beirut international airport, sparking a severe internal crisis in Lebanon. From that time, the question of whether or not to permit armed Palestinian attacks against Israel from Lebanese territory became a major contentious issue in the country's political arena: while pan-Arab and Leftist movements, which were supported by the "revolutionary" Arab states (mainly Egypt and Syria), supported the Palestinian demand for freedom of action throughout the state and across its border, others, including several Maronite-led parties like the Phalanges, opposed it and called upon the government in Beirut to restrain the Palestinians.

By April 1969 the cabinet had to resign because of widespread internal disorder that threatened to deteriorate into full-scale civil war, and Lebanon was thrown into a political crisis that lasted for seven months. Isolated in the inter-Arab arena and strongly censured by Syria, which closed its border with Lebanon, thus effectively sealing it off from the Arab hinterland, the government in Beirut was compelled to accept Nasser's mediation, and on Nov. 3, 1969, the Cairo Agreement was signed between Lebanon and the *PLO. The agreement sought to guarantee both the territorial integrity and sovereignty of Lebanon and the interests of the Palestinian factions: while recognizing the presence and activity of the Palestinians in Lebanon and assigning them special areas and points through which they could penetrate into Israel, it forbade shooting across the border, in order not to involve Lebanon. However, the Palestinians exploited the government's weakness and established themselves along the entire Lebanese-Israel border, resulting in a sharp rise in the frequency of attacks against Israel from Lebanese territory. Israel retaliated by dispatching armored units into Lebanon's territory and by shelling Palestinian positions, and the results were a general deterioration of the situation in South Lebanon and the flight of thousands of villagers, mostly Shi'i Muslims, to Beirut.

The volatile situation in Lebanon escalated further in April 1973, following an Israeli commando raid on Beirut that left several PLO leaders dead. Lebanese President Suleiman Frangieh sought to use his army to curtail the Palestinian military power in Lebanon and bring about a substantial revision in the Cairo Agreement. However, despite certain military successes, the Lebanese government was, yet again, forced to yield to all-Arab, and especially Syrian, pressures. Some local groups concluded from this that a confrontation with the Palestinian factions was inevitable, and began to prepare for an all-out conflict.

In April 1975, following a clash between Palestinian activists and Phalange supporters in Beirut, Lebanon's second, and more vicious, civil war began. The main protagonists in the initial phase of that conflict were the supporters of the existing political and socio-economic order in the state, on the one hand, and those advocating comprehensive reforms, on the other hand. In the course of the struggle, both sides managed to enlist external support: while the former camp was backed by the conservative Arab states, and, at times, by Israel, the latter camp was an ally of the Palestinians and the radical Arab regimes. Syria, for its part, was torn between its ideological commitment to the Lebanese opposition and the PLO, on the one hand, and its support for the existing order in Lebanon and for President Frangieh, its principal local ally, on the other. On June 1, 1976, following the collapse of the Lebanese state and the threat of its imminent disintegration, the Syrian army marched into Lebanon and joined the pro-government camp in its struggle against the opposition forces and the PLO. Meanwhile, Israel, which approved of the Syrian intervention (its leaders demanded, however, that Syrian troops would not come near its border and that Syrian aircraft would not be employed in Lebanon), forged an alliance with Christian groups operating in the area adjacent to the Israeli-Lebanese border, which became its clients. In the early 1980s, Syrian-Israeli relations began to deteriorate, leading to open confrontation in 1982. By then, Israel had forged an alliance with the Phalanges, and particularly with Bashir Gemayel, the commander of that party's militia, the Lebanese Forces. In June 1982, Israeli forces invaded Lebanon, purportedly to remove the threat of Palestinian attacks on its territory, but in effect to expel the Palestinian factions from Lebanon and install a pro-Israeli government in Beirut. Israel was successful in attaining its first goal, and, following a siege imposed on Beirut by its army, most PLO fighters exited the city. But its second goal was effectively thwarted when President-elect Bashir Gemayel was assassinated and an agreement signed between Israel and Lebanon on May 17, 1983, under American auspices was effectively undermined by Syria and its local allies. The massacres perpetrated in the Palestinian refugee camps of Sabra and Shatila by the Lebanese Forces, Israel's ally, were a severe blow to Israel's efforts in Lebanon and ultimately led to the resignation of Defense Minister Ariel *Sharon. In the 1983–85 period, Israeli troops gradually withdrew from the areas they occupied in Lebanon, but maintained a presence in the border area, where a pro-Israeli militia had been in control since Operation Litani in 1978. In the 1985–2000 period, Israel and its local proxy, the South Lebanese Army, attempted to hold on to this border area, which they referred to as the "Security Zone," despite incessant attacks by Lebanese factions, especially the Shi'i *Hizbollah movement. However, despite the cost in lives and two large-scale operations launched by its army in Lebanon in 1993 and in 1996, Israel's efforts there came to naught, and following mounting domestic pressures Israel withdrew its forces from Lebanon in May 2000. Subsequently, despite several minor clashes between Hizbollah and the Israeli army, particularly in the disputed Sheb'a Farms (an area formally part of the occupied Golan but which the Shi'i movement claimed to be Lebanese territory), the Israeli-Lebanese border was more or less calm until the violent clashes of summer 2006. For a summary of the fighting, see *Israel, State of: Historical Survey.

[Rachel Cohen / Oren Barak (2nd ed.)]

BIBLIOGRAPHY: L.F. Abel, *Géographie de la Palestine*, 1 (1933), 340–4; I. Ben Zvi, in: *Zion, Me'assef*, 2 (1927), 76–79; 4 (1930), 142–54; idem, in: *Tarbiz*, 3 (1931/32), 436–51; idem, *Ereẓ Yisrael ve-Yishuvah* (1967), index; S. Landshut, *Jewish Communities in the Muslim Countries of the Middle East* (1950), 54–56; E. de Vaumas, *Le Liban* (1954); N. Robinson, in: J. Freid (ed.), *Jews in the Modern* World, 1 (1962), 50–90; Pauly-Wissowa, s.v.; Press, Ereẓ, s.v. **ADD. BIBLIOGRAPHY:** Z. Schiff and E. Ya'ari, *Israel's Lebanon War* (1984); L. Zittrain Eisenberg, *My Enemy's Enemy: Lebanon in the Early Zionist Imagination, 1900–1948* (1994); K.E. Schulze, *The Jews of Lebanon: Between Coexistence and Conflict* (2001).

LEBANON WAR.

The PLO Threat to Israel Emerging from Lebanon

Following the *Six-Day War, the Palestinian terrorists expanded their base of action against the State of Israel from within Lebanese territory. This action received support in the Cairo Agreement of 1969.

After their expulsion from Jordan (in September 1970) the terrorist organizations reestablished their organizational and operational center in Lebanon. From that time, the PLO developed and increased in Lebanon and the number of its fighting men, by June 1982, had reached approximately 25,000. Its own position in Lebanon became stronger, and its power in the international arena grew. PLO self-assertion accompanied the decline of Lebanon as a country, to the extent that a center for international terrorism was established in southern Lebanon. Syria, whose army had invaded Lebanon in June 1976, took advantage of the civil war there and achieved the position of the legitimate inter-Arab deterrent presence, which dictated events in the country. Syria strengthened the PLO as a force which would perpetuate the schism between the various ethnic groups within the country, and would weaken the Lebanese government, thereby enhancing its dependence upon Syria.

From the beginning of 1981, Israel-Syria relations began to take a significant turn for the worse. The Syrians regarded the Christian domination of Zahle as a threat to their freedom of movement on the Beirut-Damascus highway, and decided to conquer Zahle from the Christians. In keeping with Israel's promises to the Christians, the Israeli Air Force intervened on their behalf and shot down two Syrian helicopters at the end of April 1981. Syria responded by stationing surface-to-air missiles in Lebanon to defend its units from Israeli air strikes. The penetration of SAM's into Lebanon heightened the tension between Syria and Israel. The PLO took advantage of this situation, and increased its activities against Israel. Israel's attacks on the PLO gave leverage to the latter in achieving political support from the Arab states, Western European countries, and the Soviet Union. The PLO portrayed its basic security needs as critical and as requiring immediate remedy in light of the hovering Israeli threat. The result of their plea was that the Soviet Union transferred – by way of Syria, Libya, and East Germany – huge quantities of light and heavy weaponry, including tanks, cannons, anti-tank missiles, and anti-aircraft missiles. In addition, it trained officers, pilots, and other military professionals. China, North Korea, and Saudi Arabia, too, equipped the PLO with weapons both from the East and from the West.

Confrontation in the Shadow of the Cease-Fire between Israel, Lebanon, and the PLO

In July 1981, a succession of exchanges of artillery fire, lasting for two weeks, in which the Israeli Air Force also participated, took place between the PLO and Israel. With pressure from the U.S., and through the mediation of its special envoy to the region – Mr. Philip Habib – a cease-fire was obtained for the first time on July 21, 1981. Immediately following the signing of the cease-fire agreement, a lull was apparent along the Lebanese-Israeli border. This lull enabled the terrorists to organize and to equip themselves with tanks and with dozens of artillery weapons; these were spread out in the area north of the Litani River and threatened the settlements of Galilee. The cease-fire agreement between Lebanon, the PLO, and Israel consisted of three clauses:

(1) No acts of enmity will be executed from the Lebanese border against Israeli targets – not by air, nor by sea, nor by land.

(2) No acts of enmity will be executed from the Israeli border against Lebanese targets – not by air, nor by sea, nor by land.

(3) The same applies to hostile military action directed at or coming from the territory of Major Saad Haddad.

The formulation of this agreement was interpreted in three ways. Israel saw it as a PLO commitment to cease initiating acts of terror against Israel.

The PLO gave the formulation a more literal interpretation. It saw the document as an obligation not to commit acts of terror against Israel solely from the Lebanese border.

The United States interpreted the agreement as an obligation on the part of the PLO not to launch terrorist attacks on Israel from within Lebanon, nor from any other international border.

The PLO continued to commit terrorist acts against Jews abroad. On August 29, 1981, the synagogue of the Jewish community in Vienna was attacked; two were killed and 20 others wounded. On October 7, 1981, two highly charged explosives went off in Italy, one next to the Ministry of Tourism in Rome, and the other at Ostia, where Jews from the U.S.S.R. were being housed. On October 20, 1981, a car-bomb exploded next to a synagogue in Antwerp, Belgium; three people were killed and approximately 100 others wounded.

Following these actions, Israeli Prime Minister Menaḥem Begin – on November 4, 1981 – accused the terrorists, who were reinforcing their troops in Lebanon with heavy arms, of breaching the cease-fire agreement. The tension grew. In November 1981, in light of the aforementioned incidents, the Israeli ministerial level delineated the following war aims to the Israel Defense Forces (IDF): prevention of the shelling of the northern settlements and prevention of hostile terrorist activity; creation of the situation which would bring about Syrian military withdrawal from the Beirut area; and elimination of the political and military problem of the terrorists in Lebanon.

On December 14, 1981, the Knesset passed the Golan Heights Law. As a precautionary measure in the event of a Syrian attack, the IDF was mobilized in the north of Israel. In response to the legislation which annexed the Golan Heights to Israel, the President of the United States unilaterally suspended the "strategic memorandum of understanding" on December 17, 1981. The following day, Prime Minister Begin sent a letter to the U.S. president in which he stated that Israel would not attack unless attacked first. In response to the legislation of the Golan Law, and to Syria's request, Soviet Foreign Minister Andrei Gromyko declared on January 18, 1982 that Soviet-Syrian relations were being deepened, and that the U.S.S.R. would provide Syria with the military means with which to enhance its defense capability. On the same day, Syria's Defense Minister announced that the Syrian army would remain in the Lebanon Valley as long as "Zionist aggression" continues.

On January 24, 1982, Syria brought two battalions into the Beirut area. On the night of January 28–29, a group of terrorists infiltrated into Israel from the Jordanian border. Israel expressed its outrage at the gravity of the incident. The PLO disclaimed that its infiltration was a breach of the cease-fire agreement.

The IDF was in a state of readiness in the northern zone of Israel. In response, the PLO intensified the level of alert among its own units, and reinforced its troops in the areas supervised by UNIFIL (United Nations Interim Force in Lebanon) with hundreds of fighting men. When the assistant to the Secretary-General of the UN requested that the PLO be removed from the UNIFIL zone, Arafat rejected his request. Then on February 14, Arafat's second-in-command, Abu-Iyad, declared that the PLO was committed to the cease-fire and that only in the event of wide-range aggression would the Palestinians force their presence on all of the Arab fronts. Furthermore, on March 4, the PLO announced that in the event of an Israeli assault, it would turn to the Soviet Union. On March 15, the PLO warned UNIFIL not to widen its control in southern Lebanon. PLO self-confidence was on the rise. Throughout this entire period, the Lebanese government remained passive.

Following the aforementioned developments, the UNIFIL command requested to reinforce its troops with 1,000 fighting men. At the end of March, the Security Council decided to grant the UNIFIL request. Syria remained passive. The U.S.S.R., on the other hand, was active in its encounters with the PLO to whom it sent heavy arms. The U.S., having an interest in keeping the peace, operated through other channels. Secretary of State Alexander Haig announced that the United States regarded the Soviets' supplying of arms to the PLO as obstructing efforts to prevent conflict. Similarly, he appealed to the Palestinians to halt their provocations against Israel. At the same time, the U.S. was attempting to get Saudi Arabia and Jordan to prevail upon the PLO to refrain from anti-Israel activity. In the same vein, the U.S. called upon Israel to refrain from retaliation, warning that action against the PLO would be liable to drag Syria into the war, and hence the U.S.S.R. as well, thus increasing the possibility of a confrontation between the super-powers.

On February 22, Prime Minister Begin warned that Israel would take immediate revenge if one single Israeli were to be killed in a terrorist attack. In March 1982, Mr. Philip Habib arrived in the Middle East and conducted negotiations with all of the involved parties, on the basis of the Israeli interpretation of the cease-fire agreement. On March 18, the State Department spokesman defined the United States position as one which would regard any hostile activity directed at Israel originating in Lebanon – even if carried out by way of Syria and Jordan – as a breach of the cease-fire agreement. The same would apply to any Israeli action against Lebanon. In reply to the statement given by the American spokesman, Abu-Jihad announced on March 20 that the PLO opposed the definition of the agreement provided by the United States, and that it would continue to attack Israel from any place it desired, other than the Lebanese border. On March 30, from Beirut, Arafat declared that the terrorists were looking forward to Ariel Sharon's visit to Beaufort Castle in southern Lebanon, and extended him the standard Arabic greeting "*ahalan wa-sahalan*" ("hello and welcome"), using Nasser's words on the eve of the Six-Day War. At the meeting of the Arab Foreign Ministers in Tunis on the following day, the PLO representative demanded that the Arab states bordering on Israel enable the terrorists to operate from within their borders.

On March 31, three terrorists attacked the offices of the Arms Acquisition Commission of the Israeli Ministry of Defense in Paris. On April 3, Israeli diplomat Yaacov Bar-Simantov was murdered in front of his home in Paris by Arab terrorists. The next day, Israel proclaimed that the murder was a blatant breach of the cease-fire agreement. The IDF was put in a state of readiness, and forces were concentrated in the north. The U.S. denounced the murder of Bar-Simantov. On April 6, Prime Minister Begin met with the leaders of the Israeli Labor Party and at the end of the meeting, declared that Israel could not overlook the murder of its diplomat. The PLO announced supreme alert among its forces in southern Lebanon. On April 8, the U.S.S.R. accused Israel and the U.S. of planning to annihilate the PLO and of attempting to establish a pro-Israel protectorate over part of Lebanon. On April 10, the United States called on all sides to exercise great restraint, and to put an end to all activities which increase tension and violence in the region. On April 11, a man by the name of Allan Goodman shot at a group of Muslims praying on the Temple Mount in Jerusalem, thereby causing an additional rise in the tension. The president of the United States sent Assistant Secretary of State Stoessel to the Middle East, while the Soviet Union dispatched an intelligence vessel to the waters off Israel's northern shores.

On April 13, Prime Minister Begin announced that "the cabinet had not yet reached a decision regarding an invasion into Lebanon," but added, "We will not, however, resign ourselves to the spilling of Jewish blood, nor will we allow those who spill it to go unpunished." In a television interview on the following day, Arafat said that the PLO was prepared for any military confrontation with Israel. "Let them come," he said, "we are waiting for them." During the course of the same week, the terrorists on three occasions placed explosive charges on a central route in southern Lebanon. An IDF officer was killed and an accompanying soldier was wounded. In retaliation the Israel Air Force bombed a terrorist base in Lebanon, PLO naval bases, and a Syrian radar station. In the ensuing air battles between Israel and Syria, two MIG 23's were shot down by Israel.

On the same day, the Israeli chief of staff General Raphael Eitan proclaimed that the terrorists had gone too far, and that Israel had reached the limit of its self-restraint. The Americans then turned to Lebanese president Elias Sarkis to prevent the PLO from retaliating against the Israeli air strikes. The U.S.S.R., on May 6, broadcast its pledge to act on behalf of Syria in the event of an Israeli invasion of Lebanon. In the middle of April, East Germany agreed to supply the PLO with important weapon systems: BMP-1 armored troop vehicles, 130 mm. cannons, recoilless guns, and a patrol boat. On May 7, the terrorists planted two mines near the village of Shuba; the IDF accused the UNIFIL Command of having allowed passage to the terrorists. On May 9, the Israeli Air Force attacked three targets in Lebanon: to the south of Damour, to the south of the Zaharani River, and on the outskirts of Sidon. In retaliation, the terrorists fired 100 katyusha missiles from the heights of Nabatiye close to settlements in the north of Israel; the next day they informed Israel that this had been "a warning." As a result of the shooting, a state of readiness was declared in the IDF on May 9 and troops were sent to reinforce the Northern Command. The U.S. asked Israel to refrain from aggravating the situation in the north, so as not to cause Syrian intervention, and warned against an uncontainable escalation of the unrest.

On May 10, the Israeli cabinet decided that Israel would not deploy the IDF at this stage, but would first exhaust every possible political path. The next day, the PLO declared an alert in its bases. On May 12, Syria announced that it would intervene if Lebanon were attacked. Both the Syrian army in Lebanon and the Lebanese army proceeded to intensify their readiness. On May 12 and 13, an additional attempt was made on the part of the U.S., Israel, and Lebanon to convince the PLO to refrain from violent action – but to no avail. The PLO remained determined to adhere to the cease-fire only from the Lebanese border. The U.S.S.R. sent Soviet and Cuban experts to the PLO Command. On May 14, the Israeli Chief of Staff declared that, in fact, the cease-fire was no longer in existence.

From the Cancelation of the Cease-Fire Agreement to the War in Lebanon

On May 15, the American State Department spokesman described the situation as "delicate, but not critical." On May 16, while the Israeli government was continuing its efforts to exhaust political channels, a member of the Supreme Central Committee of the PLO proclaimed that the cease-fire was no longer in existence, and that the PLO considered itself free to augment its activities everywhere. The Syrians moved their armored and anti-tank forces, and arrayed them for defense in Lebanon. On May 20, Major Haddad's soldiers drove away terrorists who were attempting to plant mines in the area of Marjuyun. The U.S. continued its attempts at lowering the tension. Alexander Haig praised Israel for its restraint, and Assistant Secretary of State Morris Draper was sent to Beirut. On the day of Draper's arrival in Israel, an aerial combat in Lebanese skies erupted between Syrian and Israeli fighter airplanes, during the course of which two Syrian MIG's were shot down. The Syrians explained that their entrance into the battle was evidence of their determination to repel Israeli attacks. Two days later the Syrian president went to the Soviet Union to obtain the latter's promise to provide military support.

A truck from Kefar Giladi in northern Israel drove over a mine in southern Lebanon. On the same day, May 31, General Eitan announced that a military solution to the PLO problem in Lebanon was available.

From the time when the cease-fire went into effect, the PLO committed 248 acts of terror in Israel and abroad, resulting in 26 deaths and 264 wounded. On Sunday, June 3, at approximately 11:00 P.M., the Israel ambassador to Britain, Mr. Shlomo Argov, was shot. At 9:00 A.M. the following morning, the Israeli cabinet decided to deploy its air force for an attack on two targets within Beirut and seven PLO targets in southern Lebanon. At 11:45 A.M. the air force executed this mission. In retaliation, the terrorists proceeded, from 5:30 P.M. onward, to shell settlements in Galilee. The Israeli air force and artillery corps were deployed, but the terrorist bombardment continued the next day as well. In response to the renewal of terrorist fire, the air force was again deployed, this time against the forward posts and ammunition centers of the terrorists.

Following these events, the UN Security Council unanimously decided to declare a cease-fire to be put into effect on June 6 at 6:00 A.M. The PLO announced that it would agree to the cease-fire if Israel did likewise. The U.S. denounced Ambassador Argov's would-be assassins, and emphasized that the incident had provoked Israel to retaliate. The U.S. demanded that the warring parties ease the tension, and that the Israeli prime minister order a cease-fire. But the attempt on the Israeli ambassador's life had been for Israel, however, the "straw that broke the camel's back."

On Saturday night, June 5, 1982, the Israeli cabinet convened and decided to send the IDF into Lebanon.

Beginning of the War against the Terrorists, June 6–9

From the night of June 5 through the early morning – until 3:40 A.M. – of June 6, the terrorists continued to fire hundreds of katyusha missiles and artillery on the settlements of Galilee.

At an early hour of the morning, the decision was made to execute phase I of the plan – to cross the international border at 11:00 A.M. and to advance as quickly as possible to the terrorist concentrations in Lebanon, in order to remove the Galilee settlements from terrorist artillery range. In addition to being briefed on the mission, the adjunct operational troops were told that the war was directed solely at the terrorists. In other words, there would be no harming of civilians, UN soldiers, or Syrian soldiers. That noon, as planned, IDF troops crossed the international border, moving north with maximum speed toward their aim. Meanwhile, the cabinet's decision of the previous night was being published in the media.

DETAILS OF THE OPERATIONAL PROCEDURES. Y's formation advanced speedily along the coastal axis without encountering actual resistance. Towards evening, its forward unit arrived at Sarafand – which is north of Tyre and south of the Zaharani River. The refugee camps near the city were dealt with by the troops of the formation. In the afternoon, when it had become clear that the force was advancing quickly north, it was decided to land Brigadier-General Amos Yaron's force to the north of the Awali. A's formation crossed the Litani River over the Akia Bridge, without resistance. At dusk, its troops arrived at Nabatiye. The Beaufort position was attacked at night – in spite of the plan to attack it in daylight. In a difficult and bloody battle which continued until the next morning, the reconnaissance squadron occupied Beaufort Castle. The force led by Mo., which tried to ascend to the Nabatiye Heights by way of the Hardaleh Bridge, encountered mine fields and was delayed until the mines were dismantled. E's formation reached the Hasbaya-Qauqaba line, thus completing its mission. The Syrians began to shell the troops of the formation haphazardly. However, due to the fact that terrorists' posts were integrated within the Syrian disposition, it was impossible to know whether or not the firing was coming from the terrorists, and therefore E's troops did not return the fire.

The navy sent a force northward in order to secure the battle zone and landed it there for possible attack on the Syrian force. At the same time, it landed Brigadier-General Amos Yaron's force to the north of the Awali. The force consisted of armored, infantry, engineering, and artillery units.

The air force enjoyed supremacy over the arena. An attempt by the Syrian air force to attack IDF troops was foiled by Israeli pilots. Israeli fighter airplanes attacked terrorist targets during the day, thereby supporting the paralysis of the artillery employed against the Galilee settlements, and disrupting the terrorists' system of control. The troops intended for the Golan Heights arrived at their destination and took up their positions.

The terrorists were surprised by the force with which they were being attacked and by the numerous directions from which the attack was being launched. As a result of Syrian military intervention in the war, the Israeli ministerial level decided on the evening of June 6 to order the IDF to reach the Beirut–Damascus highway, while outflanking, but not attacking, the Syrian army in the Bekaa.

At dusk, the president of the U.S. informed the Israeli prime minister that he was sending Philip Habib to Israel, and requested that Mr. Begin receive him for discussion, and the prime minister made arrangements to receive him the following evening.

MONDAY, JUNE 7. On the night of June 6–7, the Israeli forces organized themselves for a continuation of the fighting and for the execution of their aims during the day. Reserve troops continued to be mobilized. The IDF Supreme Command assessed that the Syrians faced two alternative courses of action. One would be to take action, as they had on Sunday, in order to fulfill their obligation to the terrorists. The other would be to take more extensive aggressive action. In view of this assessment, it was determined that the forces must make every effort to carry out their intended campaign aims as soon as possible: to join up with the Christians in Beirut, to capture the Dahar al-Bidar defile, and to mop up the "iron triangle" and the coastal axis of terrorist pockets. It was emphasized, however, that the above limitations imposed on the IDF operation remained in effect, including that of not engaging in warfare with the Syrian army unless first attacked by it.

That same night of June 6–7 Syria began preparing divisions of tanks and moving one of them together with other troops towards Lebanon. The Israeli defense minister assessed that if confrontation with the Syrian army was indeed to be expected on Monday, then an IDF attack on the Syrian SAM disposition would be unavoidable on Tuesday, June 8.

At dawn, the Israeli forces continued to fulfill their assignments: Y's formation advanced northward along the coastal axis. At the same time, Israeli troops were acting to occupy the refugee camps on the outskirts of Tyre-Burj-ash-Shmali and al-Bata and to clear them of terrorists. Fighting in these built-up areas was especially dangerous and complicated as the terrorists' positions were located inside buildings occupied by civilians. In order to minimalize civilian casualties, the residents were advised, by means of loudspeakers and pamphlets, to abandon their homes and to gather outside the terrorist-infested areas. These warnings were given until the hour set for the beginning of the attack. In this way, many lives were saved.

On the central axis, A's formation continued to move from the Arnun Heights towards Sidon, with the intention of mopping up the Nabatiye Heights of terrorists. When M.A.'s forward unit arrived at the village of Jabah in the morning, it came upon the edge of a Syrian post. The Syrians opened fire. In retaliation, the soldiers of the Israeli unit assaulted the post, taking six Syrian soldiers prisoner. This was the first encounter between IDF and Syrian soldiers. M's formation continued north towards Dahar al-Bidar. At dusk, D's frontal unit reached the outskirts of the town Jezzine.

In the eastern sector, the forces remained in their places. However, due to Syria's military intervention and announcement that it would come to the aid of the terrorists, the level of readiness and alertness among the Israeli units there was stepped up. Brig. Gen. Amos Yaron's force widened its hold, which it prepared to defend, while waiting to join up with Y's or A's troops.

During the course of the day, Israeli Air Force pilots shot down one Syrian fighter airplane. At 11:00 P.M., the last katyusha missile was fired at the Galilee settlements. Israeli Air Force planes continued to support the troops there, and again bombed the terrorist headquarters to the south of Beirut.

TUESDAY, JUNE 8. The U.S. and Israel took steps to prevent Syrian warfare on the IDF. It had already been possible, on the previous evening, to infer from the statements of the American secretary of state that the U.S. supported a new international arrangement in Lebanon. Following his meeting with Philip Habib, the Israeli prime minister called upon Syria, from the floor of the Knesset on June 8, not to attack IDF troops, so as not to be dragged into the war. In addition, Philip Habib went to Damascus to convince the Syrian president not to attack IDF troops, and to reach a mutual arrangement, based on Israel's proposal, according to which Syria would move the terrorist troops scattered among its battle dispositions 25 km. (15.6 miles) to the north, as well as evacuate its own troops which had entered Lebanon since the beginning of the war. From the information received during the course of the night concerning changes in the deployment of Syrian military units, it was impossible to interpret Syria's intentions. An armored division which was moving in the direction of Lebanon had not yet crossed the border. Tank brigade 58 was arrayed to the south of Lake Karaoun.

As Tuesday approached, the forces of Brigadier-General Yaron and of A were assigned the task of continuing to move towards Beirut in order to join up with the Christians. M's mission was to reach the Beirut–Damascus Highway. Y was to continue to mop up the area around Tyre, the "Iron Triangle," and the Nabatiye Heights. At dawn, connection was established between Brigadier-General Yaron's forces and A's forces, which had completed the encirclement of Sidon, and proceeded to plan its conquest. One of its units reinforced Brigadier-General Yaron's troops, which, by dusk, had reached a point of a number of miles south of Damour.

Upon discerning the movements of IDF troops, the Syrians understood the potential danger awaiting their troops in the Bekaa, in Beirut, and along the Beirut–Damascus axis. In order to halt the IDF advances, the Syrians reinforced their dispositions, including the addition of the 91st tank brigade, which completed the battle array of Division 1 in the Bekaa.

In the morning, the Syrian army in the Bekaa opened fire with artillery and anti-tank missiles on E's forces. The Syrian force in Jezinne opened fire on M's forces. In the afternoon, Syrian fighter airplanes attacked the IDF troops near Sidon, and also bombed the area of Ein Abel and Marjuyun.

In the ensuing aerial battles, seven Syrian fighter airplanes were shot down. Following Syria's launching of its attack, the Israeli ministerial level decided to approve the proposal to occupy Jezinne. This town, which was protected by Syrian commands and tank forces, was occupied that afternoon by a tank unit led by H.

At dusk, D's unit encountered Syrian troops in the village of Ein Zhaltah, and its advance was halted. It was realized retrospectively that the Syrian force had deployed in the village only a few hours before the arrival of the Israeli troops there. In light of the above development, and in view of the Israeli assessment that Syria was going to reinforce its troops in the Bekaa with armored forces and SAM batteries, the Israeli Supreme Command decided to prepare for the possibility of launching an attack on the Syrian army from Wednesday morning, June 9.

The commander of the Israeli Air Force, Major-General David Ivri, was told to be prepared to destroy the Syrian SAM array in Lebanon, in order to enable him to support IDF land forces in the Bekaa and along the central axis.

Major-General Ben-Gal's forces, which were joined by G's formation, were in readiness for the possibility of an attack on the Syrian disposition, with the aim of removing its troops and the terrorists from the Bekaa.

WEDNESDAY, JUNE 9. On the night of June 8–9, D's unit continued its attempts to break through the Syrian force in the Ein Zhaltah village, in order to advance northward – but to no avail. The Jezinne-Ayshiyeh area was cleared of Syrian fighting men, many of whom fled at dawn to reach their dispositions in the Bekaa. On the coastal axis, Brigadier-General Yaron's forces had reached a point about 4 kms. (2.4 miles) south of Beirut's international airport (Khalde). Y's unit continued to mop up in Tyre, and in the afternoon began its occupation of the Ein Hilweh refugee camp.

In the morning, Syrian fighter airplanes began attacking IDF troops. Division 1 completed its preparation for defensive deployment, and the SAM array was augmented. IDF troops in the eastern sector discerned the changes taking place within the Syrian disposition. The Israeli air force and land troops were readied for attack on the Syrians. Meanwhile, the U.S. and Israel were continuing their efforts to prevent a confrontation between the two armies. In Damascus, Philip Habib awaited a meeting with the Syrian president in order to convince him to accept the arrangement proposed by Israel.

Warfare between the Syrian Army in Lebanon and the IDF: From Noon June 9 until the First Cease-Fire, June 11

Israel waited until noon for an answer from the Syrian president regarding the proposal of the Israeli government. The Syrians were, in the meanwhile, strengthening their land dispositions. As no answer was received from Damascus, the Israeli ministerial level decided to attack the Syrian ground missiles which were deployed in Lebanon. At 2:00 P.M., Israeli Air Force fighter airplanes began their attack in which 17 batteries of SA6, SA2, and SA3 missiles were destroyed, and two damaged. The Syrians then sent some of their fighter planes to intercept those of the Israelis. In the ensuing aerial combat, which continued throughout the day, 28 Syrian planes were shot down, without loss to the Israeli Air Force. The Syrians also dispatched attack helicopters to hit the Israeli armored convoy. At the same time, Major-General Ben-Gal's troops began to attack the Syrian deployment. E's troops in the eastern sector, G's troops in the center, and D's troops in the west, all raced northward on every possible axis. A unit led by E.O. was sent along the ridge axis in order to penetrate eastward from the Barukh Mountain to the Bekaa, with the object of attacking the Syrian armored force from the flank.

In the afternoon, the fighting with the Syrian units to the south of Lake Karaoun began. Due to the destruction of their anti-tank defense and the complete exposure of their land troops to Israeli Air Force and armored corps attacks, the Syrians decided to withdraw their troops, while conducting delaying actions. Nevertheless, they began to mobilize reserve troops, and continued to move in additional forces in order to prevent the IDF from taking control of Beirut and of the Beirut–Damascus Highway. In the central sector, IDF troops had not succeeded in advancing, while in the coastal sector, Brigadier-General Yaron's forces reached the town of Damour.

THURSDAY, JUNE 10. The results of the IDF attack on the Syrian army aroused the U.S.S.R. to respond immediately by dispatching an air-lift to Syria, which included at least two Antonov 22 planes a day, and to demand of the U.S. that it exercise its influence on Israel to halt its attack. Following Soviet President Leonid Brezhnev's appeal the president of the United States turned to Israel's prime minister on the night of June 9–10, and requested an immediate cessation of fire. The Israeli government complied in principle with the request of the American president, and decided that firing would cease as of Friday, June 11 at 12:00 noon. This decision was conditional upon the evacuation of the terrorists north to the line 40 km. (25 miles) from the Israeli border, and upon Syrian commitment not to infiltrate Lebanon with additional forces. During the time remaining, Major-General Ben-Gal's forces achieved their aims: the troops led by E.G. and Y – who that day had replaced D – succeeded, in frontal attack, to drive the Syrian forces as far back as the latitudinal line of Hab-Hanin/Kamad al-Luz, about 10 km. (6.25 miles) north of Lake Karaoun. Y's troops arrived in the north from the village of Amik. E's unit caused many losses to the Syrian armored corps, while E's troops advanced to the Syrian border as they engaged in warfare on the terrorist deployments along "Fatahland." For the first time attack helicopters, equipped with anti-tank missiles, were used – the Israelis employing "Cobra" helicopters with Tau missiles, and the Syrians, "Gazelle" helicopters with haute missiles.

In the central sector, tough battles were in process. The Syrians reinforced their troops with commando and armored units, and demonstrated capability in combat. D's unit nevertheless succeeded in advancing to a point 5 km. (3.12 miles) south of the al-Modairej junction.

On the coastal axis, Brigadier-General Yaron's troops succeeded in reaching the village of Sil, south of the Beirut airport. There they were stopped by Syrian brigade 85 and terrorist units. In the meantime, Y's troops continued in their mopping-up of terrorists in the area between the Awali River in the North and the Litani River in the south, placing emphasis on the city of Sidon and the Ein Hilweh refugee camp.

The Israel Air Force attacked a tank convoy on its way to the front, on the night of June 9–10. Throughout that same day, its pilots supported the land forces in every sector of the battle. In addition, they destroyed two SA6 batteries which had been placed by the Syrians in the Bekaa, and shot down 33 Syrian fighter planes in aerial combat, with no loss. The president of Syria decided to reinforce his troops in order to halt the IDF advance in Lebanon, rather than to comply with Israel's demand for a cease-fire. In contrast, the Israeli government believed that its own main objective in Lebanon had been realized, for the terrorists had been moved beyond firing-range of the Israeli border. In consideration of its commitment to the United States, the Israeli government decided to declare a unilateral cease-fire. The general order for the IDF was as follows: along the coastal axis, to try and join up with the Christians; in the central sector, to try and reach the Beirut–Damascus axis; and in the eastern sector, to deploy along the lines it had reached so as to be prepared in the event of armored combat with Syrian troops, whose arrival from Syria was assessed as likely.

The United States retained a balanced position. On one hand, it rejected Soviet and Western European pressures to impose sanctions on Israel, and on the other, it cancelled Secretary of State Haig's visit there, claiming that the Israel government was not demonstrating flexibility.

FRIDAY, JUNE 11. The battles began at dawn. Y.M.'s formation, which had reinforced Major-General Ben-Gal's troops, was busy rescuing a tank battalion which, at night, had mistakenly come upon the Syrian disposition in Sultan Yaakub. In the morning, armored combat erupted between Syrian tank units from Syrian Division 3 – which had just been thrown into the battle and Major-General Ben-Gal's units. The Syrians suffered numerous losses. These battles were fought with tanks of the 1980s: the Russian T-72, and the Israeli "Merkavah" ("chariot").

No progress was made in the eastern sector. The cease-fire had broken off in full swing an attack the aim of which had been to reach the Beirut–Damascus axis. Brigadier-General Yaron's troops had managed to advance along the coastal axis, but at the time that the cease-fire was called had not succeeded in joining the Christian forces in Beirut.

Artillery and air force units supported the IDF troops in their advance. Severe battles were fought near the village of Sil with a Syrian array which was blocking the route to Beirut on the coastal axis. In the aerial battles which took place on that day, 23 Syrian fighter planes were shot down. At 12:00 noon, both the IDF units and the Syrian forces ceased fire.

There appear to have been two main reasons responsible for the Syrian president's change of mind. The first was the knowledge of the heavy losses suffered by the Syrian army, both in the air and on land, as well as the realization of what would await the Syrian land forces as a result of the clear-cut superiority of the Israel Air Force. The second reason, it can be assumed, had to do with the Soviet Union, which, since the ninth of the month, had been pressuring the United States to prevail upon Israel to cease its fire. In spite of the fact that the cease-fire went into effect at 12:00 noon, the terrorist organizations refused to comply, and the fighting in the western sector continued.

IDF Troops Join Up with the Christians in the Beirut Area, from Noon June 11 Until Noon June 13

The Israeli government ordered the IDF to join the Christians in the Beirut area. Brigadier-General Yaron decided to arrange his forces in two military arms: one would bypass the blockade at Sil from the east, by way of the villages of Suk al-Arab, Ein Anub, and Shima; this course of action was to be carried out by a paratroop brigade led by Y. The second would occupy the village of Sil and continue on to Khalde Airport; this mission would be undertaken by a Golani brigade led by A.R. After 48 hours of combat, the mission was accomplished. The attack began in the early evening of June 11, supported by artillery and air force planes. In spite of their efforts, the Syrian fighting men and the terrorists who were interspersed among Syrian dispositions in South Beirut did not succeed in stopping the IDF troops. At 11:00 a.m. on June 11, the Israeli paratroopers succeeded in joining the Christians in the village of Shima, and from there continued on into East Beirut. When the blockade in Sil had been broken, a tank unit led by M.A. moved towards Khalde and Ba'abdeh, where the presidential palace is located. Meanwhile, terrorist posts in the refugee camps to the south of Beirut were being shelled by Israeli gunboats. As a result of American intervention, a new ceasefire was declared.

Coordination of Israel and U.S. Positions during the Stabilization of Lines, June 14–20

On June 14, IDF troops improved their positions in the direction of the Al-Matan Mountains, in order to increase their control of the Beirut–Damascus axis.

In response, the U.S.S.R. made a public warning to Israel on June 15, and sent an ELINT COMINT ship and two frigates bearing missiles off the coast of Lebanon. It also sent a high-ranking military delegation to Damascus. On the same day, Israel's prime minister left for Washington to meet with the American president and secretary of state. On June 18, it was announced in the media that the U.S. and Israel had reached an agreement whereby the departure of all foreign forces from Lebanon would be a necessary pre-condition for the reaching of a new arrangement there.

IDF Troops Take Control of the Beirut–Damascus Axis up to Al-Tzofar, June 20–25

In Israel it was felt that under political pressure, a situation could arise in which Israel would be forced to withdraw its troops from Lebanon's capital. The situation created was such that a withdrawal to the south would have meant the relinquishment of the isolation of Beirut, and an opportunity for the Syrians to send reinforcements there. Hence, the Israeli ministerial level decided to give the IDF the mission of expanding its stronghold along the Beirut–Damascus axis, so as to ensure the continuation of Beirut's being cut off to the entry of Syrian forces. According to the plan put forth by the regional commander, two forces were to advance gradually in a pincers movement. The first force, led by M, was to leave the region of Beit a-Din and head north towards Bhamdun, situated on the Beirut–Damascus highway. The second, led by Brigadier-General Yaron, was to leave Beirut and head east towards Aley. On the night of June 21–22, the first force began its move. Approximately 48 hours later, it reached the designated Syrian area in Al-Mantzuria, about 5 km. (3.12 miles) to the south of the Beirut–Damascus highway. The second force then began to move eastward out from Beirut. In four days of heavy battle, the forces succeeded in executing their missions and in taking control of the section of the axis extending from Beirut to Tzofar, to the east of Bhamdun. The artillery and air force planes supported the land troops in the course of their combat. The artillery destroyed two batteries of SA6 missiles which had been rushed by the Syrians to the battlefield. The air force shot down two Syrian fighter planes, and in the eastern sector destroyed, on June 25, a battery of SA6 missiles, which the Syrians had infiltrated into the Bekaa on the previous day. In the region to the south of the Awali River, the screening of the area for terrorists continued with the aid of Major Saad Haddad's militiamen.

Evacuation of the Terrorists and the Syrian Army from West Beirut, June 26–September 1

NEGOTIATIONS FOR THE EVACUATION OF THE TERRORISTS AND THE SYRIANS FROM BEIRUT, JUNE 26–AUGUST 19. One of the Israeli war aims was to free Beirut of terrorists and of Syrian forces. The president of Syria rejected Israel's demand and ordered its soldiers to fight to the bitter end. In addition, Assad demanded that Israel withdraw its forces from all of Lebanon. Prime Minister Begin made IDF withdrawal from Lebanon conditional upon the withdrawal of the Syrian army from the country. Arafat said that his people would not leave Beirut and that they would fight tooth and nail; he also reproached the Arab countries for not having come to his aid in the war against Israel. In spite of this, the Israeli government decided that while a decision to occupy Beirut had not yet been made, it was necessary first to exhaust every possible diplomatic option. The United States offered its services towards finding a solution to the problem.

As negotiations began, U.S. Secretary of State Alexander Haig resigned, and George Shultz was appointed in his place. Philip Habib, as an intermediary, tried to find a solution agreeable to all involved. The proposal finally forged was to establish a multinational force, to consist of American, British, French, and Italian units, whose task would be to ensure the evacuation of the terrorists and the Syrians from Beirut. The negotiations lasted for approximately eight weeks, due predominantly to the difficulties encountered by the PLO in finding countries willing to give it asylum, and due to Arafat's attempt to stall for time in the hopes that the political pressure on Israel would increase to such an extent that it would be forced to allow Arafat to leave parts of his organization in Beirut. However, Israel was determined to carry out its objectives to the letter. Thus, while conducting the negotiations, Israel applied psychological and military pressure on West Beirut, so as to suppress their fighting spirit and power of resistance and to hasten their departure from the city. The means employed for this purpose were the distribution of leaflets outlining existing alternatives, cutting off of water and electricity supply to the city, bombardment by artillery, gunboats, and fighterplanes, and denial of re-entry into the city to those who had left it.

The fighting around Beirut influenced the Syrians to initiate many incidents in the Bekaa sector. In response to the numerous breaches of the cease-fire, the IDF attacked the Syrian disposition in the Bekaa with great force on July 22. Approximately 70 tanks and dozens of Syrian cannons were destroyed in the course of the battle.

When it became apparent to Israel that the terrorists and the Syrians had not been sufficiently put down, the Israeli cabinet decided on a tightening of the siege. Between August 1–12, Brigadier-General Yaron's troops occupied Beirut's international airport, the neighborhood of Hi-as-Salum (Aug. 2), the Al-Uzai refugee camp and the international museum (Aug. 3–4), the Hippodrome and Beirut Forest (Aug. 11). Terrorist posts in Beirut were fired on by artillery men and gunboats, and bombed by Israeli fighter warplanes. Following this incident, and due to the entrance of IDF troops into Beirut, Syria and the PLO agreed to leave the city, bringing the negotiations to a close on August 19.

EVACUATION OF THE TERRORISTS AND SYRIAN FORCES FROM BEIRUT, AUG. 20–SEPT. 1. The countries which agreed to offer asylum to the PLO were Syria, Jordan, Iraq, Republic of Southern Yemen, North Yemen, Sudan, Tunisia, and Algeria. The multinational force arrived in Beirut from Aug. 21 to Aug. 26, and the evacuation began. Most of the terrorists were evacuated by way of the sea. Some of them, together with the Syrian forces, crossed on land over to Syria along the Beirut–Damascus axis. In all, about 8,000 Palestinians left by sea and 6,000 Syrians and Palestinians by land.

Casualties

As of September 1, 1982, the casualties suffered by the warring parties stood at: Israel, 347 killed, 2,127 wounded, three captured, and five missing; Syria, approximately 1,000 killed and 149 captured; terrorists, approximately 2,000 killed and about 5,000 captured. Israel lost two helicopters and one "Skyhawk" fighterplane. Syria had 85 fighterplanes and five helicopters shot down, and approximately 400 tanks (including nine T-72's) destroyed. The terrorists lost about 100 tanks. Spoils taken from them included hundreds of cannons, mortars, and katyushas, as well as thousands of tons of ammunition and explosives.

[Uri Algom]

Aftermath

The aftermath of the Lebanese War developed into a protracted and costly military occupation which would ultimately claim around 1,000 Israeli lives. The high hopes Israel had placed in a friendly Phalange-dominated Lebanese government were shattered when President-Elect Bashir Jumayyil was assassinated on September 14. This was followed by the Sabra and Shatilla massacre of Palestinian refugees by Phalange troops. An agreement reached with the new president, Bashir's brother Amin, in April 1983 terminating the state of war between the two countries was never ratified. In the meanwhile Shiite and *Hizbollah resistance mounted along with public pressure in Israel for a withdrawal, which was finally accomplished in three stages in 1985, leaving Israel in control of a narrow security zone on the Lebanese side of the border. Shiite and Hizbollah attacks continued, however. Israel responded with major incursions in 1988, 1993 (Operation Accounting), and 1996 (Operation Grapes of Wrath). Finally, in May 2000, Israeli Prime Minister Barak unilaterally withdrew all Israeli troops from Lebanon, which brought relative quiet until the violent clashes with Hizbollah in summer 2006. For a summary of the fighting, see *Israel, State of: Historical Survey.

ADD. BIBLIOGRAPHY: C. Herzog, *Arab-Israeli Wars* (1982); Z. Schiff and E. Ya'ari, *Israel's Lebanon War* (1986); T.L. Friedman, *From Beirut to Jerusalem* (1990²).

°LE BÉ, GUILLAUME (1525–1598), French type cutter and designer. Le Bé, a native of Troyes, was trained in the typefoundry of Robert Estienne (1503–59), the Hebrew and Latin printer of Francis I, and became an outstanding cutter of Hebrew type. While in Venice (1545–50), he worked for Marco Antonio *Giustiniani. There Le Bé cut Greek and Roman punches as well as eight Hebrew fonts. Specimens of this work are preserved in two albums which are also filled with interesting marginal notes (now in the Bibliothèque Nationale, Paris). After his return to France, Le Bé made more Hebrew fonts for the French typefounder Claude Garamond (d. 1561), and, from the mid-1560s onward, was the main supplier of the Antwerp printer Christophe *Plantin, typographer to Philip II of Spain and publisher of the second Complutensian Bible (1568–72). At least five examples of Le Bé's work have been preserved in the Plantin-Moretus Museum, Antwerp, ranging from the very large "Gros Hebrieu fort gros" (1566) to the minute "Hebrieu sur la Coronelle" (1570). Plantin, who also used Hebrew type provided by the older *Bomberg press in Venice, commissioned an "Hebrieu de la faceon de Venise" ("sur le Texte") and asked Le Bé to design and cut compressed and lengthened forms of many Hebrew letters, himself sketching suggestions for *alef* and *bet*. Even in his last years, Le Bé is known to have continued sketching Hebrew typefaces in block and cursive styles while trapped in Paris during the French wars of religion.

BIBLIOGRAPHY: E. Howe, in: *Signature*, 8 (1938), 1–28; S.H. Steinberg, *Five Hundred Years of Printing* (1961²), 116, 167; H. Carter, in: International Wetenschappelijk Congres voor Boekdrukkunst en Humanisme, Antwerpen, *Gedenkboek der Plantin-Dagen 1555–1955* (1956), 253n., 257–8n., 260–1, 263 (incl. specimen type sheet with Hebrew typefaces by Le Bé); C. Roth, *Jews in the Renaissance* (1959), 185–6n.

[Godfrey Edmond Silverman]

LEBEDEFF, AARON (1873–1960), Yiddish actor. Born in Gomel, Russia, Lebedeff became known in Warsaw as "The Litvak Comedian." During the Russian Revolution, he gave concerts for the American Red Cross, and later made his way to the U.S. There he became one of Thomashefsky's outstanding players. He composed songs and from 1930 presented many plays and operettas. At 80 he appeared in *The Yiddish Show of Shows*, two years later in *My Weekend Bride*.

LEBENSOHN, ABRAHAM DOV (known as **Adam (Abraham Dov Mikhailishker) ha-Kohen**; 1794–1878), Hebrew poet during the Haskalah period. He received elementary and yeshivah education in his native Vilna where he became a successful broker. His earliest published writings were occasional poems for weddings or funerals of Vilna notables, honoring Jewish and gentile dignitaries. In 1842 his first collection of poems, *Shirei Sefat Kodesh* ("Poems in the Holy Tongue," part 1; part 2, 1856) was dedicated to "The Queen of Languages – Hebrew." From 1849 to 1853 Lebensohn, together with Isaac Benjacob and Behak, published a second edition of the *Biur*, the commentary and translation of the Bible by Moses Mendelssohn and his disciples, and appended materials not published in the first edition, under the title *Be'urim Ḥadashim* ("New Commentaries," 1858). These *Be'urim* found a wide audience in Russian Jewry and aided in the spread of the Haskalah. Following the death of M.A. *Guenzburg in 1846, Lebensohn became the leader of Vilna's *maskilim*, and, because of his eloquence, served as the main preacher at their synagogue, Tohorat ha-Kodesh. In 1847 he was appointed teacher of Hebrew, Aramaic, and biblical exegesis at the government rabbinical school of Vilna, a post which he held for 20 years. He published several scholarly works in these fields, including a Hebrew grammar (1874). Lebensohn was an active contributor to the Hebrew press including such periodicals as *Kerem Ḥemed, Kokhevei Yiẓḥak, Ha-Karmel*, and *Ha-Maggid*. In 1867 he published an allegorical drama *Emet ve-Emunah* ("Truth and Faith"), which he had written 25 years earlier, but had withheld for fear of offending the Orthodox. This work aroused considerable literary controversy, especially among the younger *maskilim*, who felt it was outdated. In 1869–70 he published a new and enlarged edition of his poems, and in 1895, a six-volume collection of his poems and those of his son Micah Joseph *Lebensohn appeared under the title *Kol Shirei Adam u-Mikhal*.

Lebensohn was the spokesman of the Russian Haskalah during its early period. He openly proclaimed his allegiance to the "Berlin" Haskalah and particularly to Moses Mendelssohn. He cherished the Hebrew language ("The beautiful language, the last remnant") and the Bible. He was influenced by Moses Ḥayyim *Luzzatto and Herz *Wessely. An inadequate knowledge of the European languages kept him from reading European literature, but indirectly he was influenced by Schiller. He possessed an original talent and had a superb command of the Hebrew language. The main theme underlying his poetry is the conflict between optimism (enlightened rationalism), expressed in poems such as "*Higgayon la-Erev*" ("An Ode to the Evening"), "*La-Boker Rinnah*" ("Joy in the Morning"), "*Ha-Aviv*" ("Springtime"), and the harsh, cruel reality of life (six of his children and his beloved son-in-law died during his lifetime). The dirges written for his children, "*Hesped Mar*" ("Bitter Dirge") and "*Mikhal Dimah*" ("Tears for Mikhal"), are intensely emotional despite the ornamental style of his day. In "*Ha-Mitonen ve-ha-Meshorer*" ("The Complainer and the Poet") he contrasts the pessimism of the complainer with the optimism of the poet, but shows partiality to neither. In his great poem "*Ha-Ḥemlah*" ("Compassion"), the Spirit of Compassion complains before God about the presence of cruelty and evil in nature, in human society, and in the relations between man and nature. The divine reply is weak and rather unconvincing.

Lebensohn's impact upon his contemporary Hebrew readers was great. Some of his poems "*Dal Mevin*" ("The Poor Wise Man"), "*Ha-Temurah*" ("The Transition"), and "*Ha-Ḥemlah*" became very popular, and were even popular tunes. In the subsequent development of literature, Lebensohn's poems were more or less forgotten. However, they are important for the history of Hebrew literature, and he was the first Russian Hebrew poet of any significance.

BIBLIOGRAPHY: Klausner, Sifrut, 3 (1953), 171–227 (detailed bibliography, 171–3), 190–2 (annotated list of his works); Kressel, Leksikon, 2 (1967), 165–8; Zinberg, Sifrut, 6 (1960), 230–47; Rosenblum, in: *Perakim*, 2 (1959), 151–71; Waxman, Literature, 3 (1960^2), 217–26.

[Yehuda Slutsky]

LEBENSOHN, MICAH JOSEPH (also known as **Mikhal**; 1828–1852), one of the foremost Hebrew poets of the *Haskalah. Born in Vilna, the son of Abraham Dov *Lebensohn (Adam ha-Kohen), who was a leading intellectual of the time and one of its outstanding poets, Micah Lebensohn received a thorough Hebrew education including intensive study of the Bible. Unlike other youths of his day who had to struggle in order that they might study secular subjects, Lebensohn was privately tutored in German, Polish, Russian, and French. In early childhood he already showed great interest in literature and began his literary endeavors by translating German poetry. His translation of most of the second book of Vergil's *Aeneid* from Schiller's German version (97 stanzas), at the age of 19, established Lebensohn's reputation in the Vilna literary world. A year later, he translated Vittorio Alfieri's play *Saul* under the title *Aḥarit Sha'ul*. (In all extant copies parts of the translation are missing.) At the age of 17 Lebensohn was severely stricken with tuberculosis and was sent to Berlin for medical treatment. Upon advice of his doctors he tried the Salzbrunn spa in 1849, but returned to Berlin in the winter. The following summer he spent at the Reinerz spa where his condition improved, and it was there that he wrote his best work. With the coming of winter, he suffered a relapse and returned to his father's home in Vilna, where he died. While in Berlin, Lebensohn read and studied. He regularly attended Schelling's lectures in philosophy, visited cultural institutions, and acquainted himself with contemporary literary movements. He was influenced by Shneur *Sachs, and by Leopold *Zunz, who encouraged him to write epic poetry. His father published the poems in a collection entitled *Shirei Bat Ẓiyyon* (1851). *Kinnor Bat Ẓiyyon* (1870), a compilation of his remaining works comprising 41 original and translated poems, was edited, annotated, and published by his father posthumously.

Lebensohn was influenced by the Romantic movement. The intimate youthful freshness of his lyrical poetry, depicting personal emotions and experiences, sharply deviates from the rationalism, moralizing, and elaborate rhetorical phrases of the earlier Haskalah literary tradition. "*Shelomo ve-Kohelet*," a poetic work comparable in structure to his father's "*Ha-Mitonen ve-ha-Meshorer*," is composed of two poems representing two phases in King Solomon's life: in "*Shelomo*," Solomon is the young lover of the Songs of Songs, a bard who loves life and beauty; in "*Kohelet*," he is the old man who says that all is vanity. An aged king in "*Kohelet*," Solomon is weary of life, having grown old before his time through too much meditation and wisdom. "*Shelomo*" culminates in a love idyll by moonlight, whereas "*Kohelet*" is consummated in an epiphany – a vision of God. "*Kohelet*" thus transcends the burden of life. In "*Nikmat Shimshon*," the once mighty Samson, now blind and helpless, is brought before the altar of Dagon to amuse the Philistine foe. Delilah's betrayal, his blindness, and his humiliation, which also represent the national disgrace, leave Samson with but one desire – revenge. It keeps him alive, and restores to him his power to act. In "*Ya'el ve-Sisra*," Jael has to choose between her humane duty to give sanctuary to a defeated man, and her patriotic duty to destroy a national enemy. In the end she fulfills her duty to her people, convinced by Deborah the prophetess that national morality is also human morality. "*Moshe al Har ha-Avarim*" depicts the prophet, on the verge of realizing his vision, taking leave of his people and of the destined land. The theme of death before fulfillment reflects the fate of the poet who suffered and died of tuberculosis; it is repeated in "*R. Yehudah ha-Levi*." Judah Halevi reaches the Promised Land, and, as he kisses its sacred dust, he is attacked and murdered by an Arab. On the verge of death, he envisions the dead inviting him to join them, and he departs this life with an expression of "sweet grace" upon his face. Other well-known poems of Lebensohn are the lyrical ones: "*Ha-Tefillah*," "*El ha-Kokhavim*," "*Ḥag ha-Aviv*," and "*Al ha-Ḥoli-Ra be-Ir Berlin*" (all published in *Kinnor Bat Ẓiyyon*). While "*Shelomo ve-Kohelet*" is written under the influence of his father's work, Lebensohn's other poems constitute a new departure in Hebrew poetry. In the tradition of the romantic poet, he focuses the poem on a tragic and crucial moment in his hero's life; as a lyric poet, he knows how to portray the battle that rages in his hero's divided soul. The themes of his epic poetry are life and death, the visionary and his fate, the poet and his mission, and the moral conflict between human feelings and patriotic duty, when these are antithetical. His poetry is stamped with the fate of the author who, standing on the threshold of life, both as a man and as a creative genius, must die. His epic poetry shows the influence of Milton and Shakespeare and his lyric poetry that of Heine, whom he read in his youth. Lebensohn translated Goethe's "Erlkoenig" from German, Mickiewicz's "Farys" from Polish, Arnault's "La Feuille" from French (known in Hebrew under the title "*Daliyyah Niddaḥat*" and generally published under Lebensohn's name without giving the origin of the poem), and other poems whose origin is unknown (see Fichmann's introduction to *Shirei Mikhal* on the problem of translation in Micah Lebensohn). Lebensohn's poetry was first collected in *Kol Shirei Adam u-Mikhal* (1895).

BIBLIOGRAPHY: Waxman, Literature, 3 (1960), 226–34; Lachower, Sifrut, 2 (1943), 115–33; Klausner, Sifrut, 3 (1953), 228–68; J. Fichmann, *Shirei Mikhal: Iggerotav ve-Targumav* (1962), 7–39; Zeitlin, Bibliotheca, 194; Shunami, Bibl, 3843. **ADD. BIBLIOGRAPHY:** A. Cohen, *Mikha Yosef Lebenzon: Ha-Meshorer vi-Yezirato* (incl. bibl.; 1967); A. Lubin-Tsifroni, *Shirat Yemei ha-Beynayim ve-ha-Haskalah: RaShBag, RIHaL, MIKhal, YaLaG* (1964); Y. Friedlander, *Siḥah al Tefillah Aḥaronah*, in: *Rosh*, 4 (1979), 8–10; A. Zeitlin, *Sheloshah Meshorerim ve-Emunatam*, in: *Ha-Do'ar*, 58:9 (1979), 143; T. Cohen, *Erez lo Noda'at*, in: *Zehut*, 2 (1982), 145–153; S. Yaniv, *Ha-Im Mikhal Hu Meshorer ha-Baladah?* in: *Alei Siaḥ*, 21:14, (1982), 318–327; A. Holz, in: *Tarbiz*, 52:3 (1983), 469–496; idem, in: *Tarbiz*, 53:3 (1984), 431–464; R. Shoham, *Halakhah u-Ma'aseh ba-Poetikah shel Shirei Bat Ẓiyyon le-Mikhal*, in: *Nekudot Mifneh ba-Sifrut ha-Ivrit* (1993), 87–94; S. Werses, *Shirat ha-Haskalah ha-Ivrit be-Maḥlaẓot shel Leshon Yidish*, in: *Ḥuliyot*, 7 (2002), 9–44.

[Elieser Kagan]

LEBERT (Levy), SIGMUND (1822–1884), pianist. Born in Ludwigsburg, Lebert was a noted pianoforte teacher and a founder of the Stuttgart Conservatory (1856). His *Grosse theoretisch-praktische Klavierschule* (4 vols., 1858; 1911^{14}) became a classic work of pianoforte instruction and was translated into many languages.

LEBO-HAMATH (Heb. לְבֹא חֲמָת, לְבוֹא חֲמָת), a place name or geographical term frequently mentioned as a northern boundary mark of Ereẓ Israel. The biblical description of the borders of Canaan places Lebo-Hamath on the northern border between Mount Hor near the Mediterranean and Zedad near the Syrian desert (Num. 34:8). The land of Canaan in this account designates the Egyptian province of Canaan at the time of the Israelite conquest; in the north it extended up to the lands of the Hittite kingdom (Josh. 1:4). As a point on the northern border, Lebo-Hamath is also mentioned in the story of the spies (Num. 13:21) and in the list of the regions and nations which "had not known all the wars of Canaan" (Josh. 13:5; Judg. 3:3). After the conquest of Aram-Damascus and Aram-Zobah by David, Lebo-Hamath was a northern border city of the kingdom of Israel which reached the land of Hamath (I Kings 8:65; I Chron. 13:5); Jeroboam II restored the border of Israel from Lebo-Hamath to the Brook of the Arabah (II Kings 14:25; Amos 6:14). After the Assyrian conquest of Ereẓ Israel and Syria in the eighth century B.C.E., Lebo-Hamath was apparently on the dividing line between the Assyrian provinces of Damascus and Hamath (Ezek. 48:1).

Most scholars have interpreted the Hebrew phrase (Heb. לְבוֹא חֲמָת) as "the entrance to Hamath" or "the way to Hamath" (today Hama on the Orontes). Linguistic evidence from the Bible, however, proves that the *lamed* in לְבוֹא is part of the root (cf. מִלְּבוֹא "from Lebo," Amos 6:14), and, furthermore, if it were not a place name it is strange to find it included in border lists containing only specific place names. Hamath was apparently added to Lebo to distinguish it from other places with the same name and also possibly to indicate that it belonged to the land of Hamath.

The city called Labu appearing in an inscription of Tiglath-Pileser III immediately after the cities of Hamath is undoubtedly the same as Libo mentioned in the Itinerarium Antonini as a station midway between Laudicia (Kadesh on the Orontes) and Heliopolis (Baalbek). The city can definitely be identified with Labwa situated in a fertile region near one of the sources of the Orontes in the northern Lebanese Beqa. The large tell on which the village of Labwa stands contains pottery from the Bronze Age and later periods.

All these references indicate that Lebo was an important city in the northern Lebanese Beqa to the south of Kadesh. It appears apparently already as "Rb'w (= Lab'u) in the forest," in inscriptions of Amenophis II and Ramses II as well as Labana in the Amarna tablets.

BIBLIOGRAPHY: Luckenbill, Records, 2 (1927), 294; Abel, Geog, 1 (1933), 300–2; Noth, in: ZDPV, 58 (1935), 242ff.; Elliger, in: PJB, 32 (1936), 34ff.; Noth, *ibid.*, 33 (1937), 36ff.; Maisler in: BJPES, 12 (1946), 91–102; idem, in: BASOR, 102 (1946), 9; idem, in: RHJE, 1 (1947), 33f.; idem, in: *Eretz Israel*, 3 (1955), 26; S. Yeivin, in: *Proceedings of the 22nd Congress of Orientalists* (1957), 587ff.; Aharoni, Land, index.

[Benjamin Mazar]

LEBORK (Pol. **Lębork**; Ger. **Lauenburg**), town in Pomerania, N. Poland. In 1753 a plan for founding a Jewish town (*Judenstadt*) near Lebork was proposed by the *Stettin (Szczecin) city council. Its purpose was to concentrate the rich and privileged Jews in one place and to compete with nearby Danzig (*Gdansk). Initial government response was favorable, as were the answers to queries addressed to the local gentry and to the Jews, who were to be the main financiers of the project. The plan was shelved because of the opposition of the king, who claimed that an increase in the number of Jews was always harmful to Christians. It was only in 1787 that a Jewish settlement is first recorded in Lebork consisting of 36 persons. The community grew to 244 in 1840 and 371 (4.9% of the total population) in 1880. In 1827 a school was founded and in 1863 a *ḥevra kaddisha*. In 1932 the community (239 persons) maintained a synagogue, cemetery, school, and three charitable organizations. In 1939 only 104 Jews remained in the town; the community was not renewed after the war. M. *Horovitz served briefly (1874–78) as rabbi.

BIBLIOGRAPHY: U. Grotefend, *Geschichte und rechtliche Stellung der Juden in Pommern…* (1931), passim; FJW, 77; S. Stern, in: JSOS, 11 (1949), 139f.; PK.

LEBOVIĆ, DJORDJE (1928–2004), Yugoslav playwright. Born in Sombor, Lebović was a survivor of the Auschwitz and Mauthausen concentration camps, where he was interned during the last years of World War II. Later, after studying in Belgrade, he wrote many plays for stage, broadcasting, and the screen which bear the mark of his wartime experiences. Lebović tackled in a bold and original manner some of the controversial questions about men's behavior in the death camps: the work of inmates in the crematoria, passive submission, solidarity, and resistance to the oppressor. His radio plays include *Do vidjenja druže Gale* ("Goodbye, Comrade Gal," 1961); *Lutka* ("The Doll," 1967); and *Sahrana počinje obično popodne* ("Burial Usually Begins in the Afternoon," 1963). The last describes how the liberated survivors of a concentration camp, faced with the death of one of their number in a hospital, insist on a decent burial and thus regain their own dignity and sense of the value of human life. Lebović's outstanding work is his dramatic trilogy on the death camp theme: *Nebeski odred* ("Commando Heaven," 1959), written in collaboration with A. Obrenović and later made into a motion picture; *Haleluja* (1965); and *Viktorija* ("Victory," 1968).

Lebović came to Israel in 1982. While there, he wrote another drama, entitled *Istraživanja u pesku* ("Search in a Sandbank," 1985), which was translated into Hebrew (1992), and a radio drama *Svetlosti i senke* ("Lights and Shadows"), broadcast by Israeli radio. His own Holocaust experiences are leitmotivs in his plays, emphasizing the transformations in the behavior of the victims and their terrible exploitation in an absurd and alienated world.

BIBLIOGRAPHY: W. Gallasch, in: *Nuernberger Nachrichten* (June 6, 1966). **ADD. BIBLIOGRAPHY:** D. Katan Ben-Zion, "Presence and Disappearance – Jews and Judaism in Former Yugoslavia in the Mirror of Literature" (Hebrew, 2002), 300, 347.

[Zdenko Lowenthal]

LEBOW, FRED (**Ephraim Fishl Lebowitz**; 1932–1994), founder and director of the New York City Marathon, member of U.S. National Track and Field Hall of Fame and National Distance Running Hall of Fame. Lebow was born in Arad, a town in the Transylvania region of western Romania, the sixth of seven children in a Yiddish-speaking family. After surviving Nazi occupation in World War II, Lebow and his family escaped the country in different directions. Lebow, then a teenager, made his way as a smuggler of sugar and diamonds through Czechoslovakia, Belgium, and Ireland before reaching a yeshivah in Brooklyn, N.Y. in 1951. After stops in Kansas City and Cleveland, he returned to New York and worked in the garment district, attending the Fashion Institute of Technology and marketing clothes as owner of his own knockoff design company. Lebow took up running in the late 1960s to improve his stamina for tennis, became involved with the New York Road Runners Club, and staged the first NYC Marathon, in 1970. As president of the NY Road Runners Club and race director of the New York City Marathon, Lebow fostered the race's growth from 126 runners looping around Central Park in 1970, to 35,000 entrants from more than 100 countries and all 50 states running through New York's five boroughs in 2005. Lebow, who spoke a heavily-accented English, would shout in Yiddish to ḥasidic spectators, "*Lommen heren*" ("Let's hear it") and "*Die laufer darfen vasser*" ("The runners need water") as he led his pack of runners through the streets of ḥasidic Williamsburg. To accommodate the needs of Jewish runners, Lebow set up a tent for Morning Prayer services at the marathon staging area. He also changed permanently the starting date of the New York Marathon, so as not to conflict with a Jewish holiday.

Lebow created such original events as the Fifth Avenue Mile; the Empire State Building Run-up; the L'eggs mini-marathon, the first women's-only long distance running event in the world; the New York Games, an international outdoor track-and-field meet; and reintroduced the Six-Day Run in New York. Lebow served as president of the New York Road Runners for 20 years, before being promoted to chairman in 1993. He was elected to the National Track and Field Hall of Fame in 1994 and the National Distance Running Hall of Fame in 2001. Lebow co-authored the book *Inside the World of Big-Time Marathoning* (1983), and is the subject of Ron Rubin's *Anything for a T-Shirt: Fred Lebow and the New York City Marathon, the World's Greatest Footrace* (2004).

[Elli Wohlgelernter (2nd ed.)]

LEBRECHT, FUERCHTEGOTT (1800–1876), German scholar and educator. Lebrecht, born in Memmelbach, Bavaria, studied in Fürth and later in Pressburg with Moses *Sofer and was one of his favorite pupils; he studied Hebrew grammar under Wilhelm *Gesenius in Halle. Most of his life was spent in Berlin, where first he taught at the Teachers' Institute directed by Leopold *Zunz and then was head teacher and librarian at the Veitel Heine Ephraimsche Lehranstalt, whose standards he raised considerably by the introduction of modern educational methods. Lebrecht was a close friend of Zunz and the contributor of numerous articles to both learned and popular periodicals. His scholarly work includes an edition with V.H. Biesenthal of David Kimḥi's *Sefer ha-Shorashim* (1847); *Die Rabbinische Bibliothek des Berliner Beth Hamidrash* (1852); *Handschriften und erste Ausgaben des babylonischen Talmud* (1862); *Kritische Lese verbesserter Lesarten und Erklaerungenzum Talmud* (1864); and *Bether, die fragliche Stadt im Hadrianisch-juedischen Kriege* (1877), published posthumously.

ADD. BIBLIOGRAPHY: ADB, vol. 18, 97–98.

[Michael A. Meyer]

LEC, STANISLAW JERZY (**S.J. de Tusch-Letz**; 1909–1966), Polish poet. Lec, whose surname was of Hebrew origin (*leẓ*, "jester"), was born in Lvov. In 1929 he began publishing lyrical verse in Polish dailies and thereafter contributed to satirical weeklies and to the *Tryby* magazine, of which he was a co-founder. Together with the poet Leonid *Pasternak Lec founded a Warsaw literary cabaret, the Teatr Pętaków, in 1936. Three of his early verse collections were *Barwy* ("Colors," 1933), *Zoo* (1935), and *Satyry patetyczne* ("Pathetic Satires," 1936). A lyrical poet of distinction, he wrote deeply contemplative verse, his profound literary culture linking him with fellow poets in Germany and Austria. He also translated Heine and Brecht. Lec was arrested by the Nazis in 1941 and spent two years in a concentration camp before making his escape to Warsaw, where he joined the left-wing underground. He edited two illegal periodicals, *Zolnierz w boju* ("The Fighting Soldier") and *Wolny lud* ("Free People"), and became an officer of the Polish partisans. After World War II Lec helped to found the satirical Warsaw weekly *Szpilki* (1945) and in 1946 became a Polish press attaché in Vienna. In 1950 he moved to Israel, but returned to Poland in 1952. During his later, postwar period Lec wrote more collections of verse, such as *Notatnik polowy* ("A Field Notebook," 1946), *Rękopis jerozolimski* ("A Jerusalem Manuscript," 1950–52), and the satirical *Fraszkobranie* ("Gathering of Trifles," 1967). *Rękopis jerozolimski*, first published in Israel, was later re-edited in Warsaw (1956, 1957). Lec, a unique combination of the Polish and the annihilated Polish-Jewish cultures, mingled a jester's wit with the sad wisdom of the rabbi in the many collections of epigrams and aphorisms which he published, ranging from *Spacer cynika* ("The Cynic's Promenade," 1946) to *Myśli nieuczesane* ("Unkempt Thoughts," 1957) and its sequels (1964, 1966). These brilliantly compressed deep philosophical points into single phrases or sentences.

BIBLIOGRAPHY: *Słownik Współczesnych Pisarzy Polskich*, 2 (1964), 327–9.

[Stanislaw Wygodzki]

LECACHE, BERNARD (1895–1968), French journalist and author. The son of a Paris tailor, Lecache early distinguished himself as a vigorous opponent of race hatred. A political radical, he contributed to the dailies and periodical press. Following his expulsion from the Communist Party in 1923, Lecache joined the independent left and made his name as an outspoken opponent of antisemitism. In 1927 he was the co-founder, with Pierre Paraf, of LICA (Ligue internationale contre le Racisme et l'Antisémitisme). He was president of the league and also of the Rassemblement Mondial Antiraciste. In 1933 he founded the anti-racist journal, *Le Droit de vivre*. He received several decorations for service as an officer in the maquis during World War II. In 1950 he was appointed editor in chief of the weekly *Journal du Dimanche*. Lecache gives a sensitive and well-documented description of life among Russian-Jewish immigrants in Paris at the beginning of the 20th century in the novel *Jacob* (1925), and in his trilogy *Au pays des pogromes*, consisting of *Quand Israël meurt* (1927), *Les Porteurs de Croix* (1930), and *Les Ressuscités* (1934).

[Pierre Aubery]

°**LECCA, RADÚ** (c. 1902–c. 1980), Romanian agent of the German Nazi Party's Foreign Policy Department and "head of Jewish affairs" in various Romanian ministries. Lecca had ties to the Nazis well before the German-Romanian alliance. He had served as a correspondent for a Nazi Party paper and also for a German newspaper. In 1941 he became the liaison officer for the Antonescu regime with the German legation in Bucharest and in November 1941 Lecca was first put in charge of the "Jewish Problem" by the Romanian government in compliance with the orders of the German embassy in Bucharest. The embassy at this time was successfully pressing for anti-Jewish measures styled on the *Nuremberg Laws. It was Lecca who was to supervise and execute these measures, especially those involving economic despoliation of the Jewish communities. The "Jewish Center" (the only officially recognized Jewish body), which was established in January 1942 after the dissolution of the "Union of Jewish Communities," operated under his personal supervision. Lecca received his orders directly from Gustav Richter, *Eichmann's deputy in Romania. Lecca exploited his position to extort huge sums from the Jewish population, and apart from his personal gains he also used these sums to contribute to various institutions (such as the social welfare institutions under the direction of *Antonescu's wife) and to give gifts to individuals, thus enabling him to gain closer association with the ruling clique. Lecca supported plans for the deportation of Jews to death camps, but when Antonescu did not consent to the deportations, and planned their continued economic exploitation, Lecca in turn informed Richter of the details of decisions taken by the Romanian government regarding the treatment of Jews, notably, the plan of December 1942 to permit the Jews deported to *Transnistria to migrate to Palestine in return for sums of money. The plan was dropped as a result of immediate German pressure. The Jews, faced with financial ruin as a result of the antisemitic measures, were forced to sell even their last possessions in order to continue to pay the blackmail in the form of heavy taxes and special fines periodically imposed by Lecca. At the postwar trials against Antonescu's government in 1946, Lecca received the death sentence, but it was commuted to life imprisonment. After a period of time, that sentence was also commuted and he lived out his final years on a government pension as a former Romanian official.

BIBLIOGRAPHY: T. Lavi, *Yahadut Romanyah ba-Ma'avak al Hazzalatah* (1965), index; Broszat, in: *Gutachten des Instituts fuer Zeitgeschichte* (1958), 102–83; M. Carp, *Cartea Neagră*, 3 (1947), index.

[Theodor Lavi]

LECCE, city in S. Italy. Jews were already settled in Lecce in the 11th century, subsequently being mostly engaged in loan-banking. In 1463, following the anti-Jewish preachings of John of *Capistrano and Fra Roberto Caracciolo, the Jewish quarter in Lecce was set on fire and the Jews were expelled. They returned a few years later, but when the French invaded the kingdom of Naples in 1495 and the Jewish communities in southern Italy were attacked and pillaged, the Jews of Lecce were deprived of all their property and again expelled. In 1497 the local people of Lecce demanded that the synagogue desecrated during the riots of 1495 be consecrated as a church dedicated to the Virgin and to serve also as a foundling hospital. In 1510 the order of expulsion for the kingdom of Naples included the Jews of Lecce, and all the New Christians. Nevertheless, in about 1520 a small Jewish group settled in Lecce for a short time, with special privileges, and remained until the general expulsion from the kingdom of Naples in 1541.

BIBLIOGRAPHY: Guerrieri, in: *Studi senesi*, 17 (1901), 225–52; Roth, Italy, index; Milano, Italia, index; N. Ferorelli, *Ebrei nell' Italia meridionale*… (1915). **ADD. BIBLIOGRAPHY:** C. Colafemmina, "La giudecca di Lecce nei secoli XV e XVI," in: *Archivio Storico del Sannio*, N.s. 1 (1996); C. Massaro, "Ebrei e città nel Mezzogiorno tardomedievale: il caso di Lecce," in: *Itinerari di ricerca storica*, 5 (1991); M.R. Tamblé, "Antisemistismo e infanzia abbandonata: un singolare connubio nella Lecce tardomedievale," in: *Sefer Yuḥasin*, 16–17 (2000–01), 31–45.

[Ariel Toaff / Nadia Zeldes (2nd ed.)]

LECZNA (Pol. **Łęczna**; Rus. **Lenchna**; Yid. **לענטשנ'**), town in Lublin province, E. Poland. Jews are first mentioned in 1501. In the years 1668, 1678, 1681, and 1685 the delegates to the *Councils of the Four Lands of Poland and the Council of Lithuania convened in Leczna. At the triennial fairs held in Leczna during the 18th century, local Jewish merchants and those from other towns traded mainly in livestock. In 1765 the number of Jewish poll tax payers under the jurisdiction of the Leczna *kahal* amounted to 724, of which 491 were in the town proper. Among the Jewish villagers, 55 families earned their livelihood as leaseholders and innkeepers. In 1864 the Russian authorities executed the commander of a Polish revolutionary unit, Lieutenant Rachmiel Bornsztejn, in Leczna. The community numbered 1,506 (60% of the total population) in 1827; 1,679 (64%) in 1857; 2,446 (65%) in 1897; and 2,019 (63%) in 1921. Before the outbreak of World War II there were about 2,300 Jews in Leczna. Two large-scale deportations to death camps took place in Leczna, on Oct. 23 and Nov. 11, 1942. Only 330 Jews were left in a forced-labor camp, which was liquidated on April 29, 1943, when the prisoners were sent to *Sobibor death camp or Trawniki camp. After the war, the Jewish community of Leczna was not reconstituted.

BIBLIOGRAPHY: Halpern, Pinkas, index; S. Dubnow (ed.), *Pinkas ha-Medinah* (1925), index; R. Mahler, *Yidn in Amolikn Poyln in Likht fun Tsifern* (1958), index; A. Eisenbach et al. (eds.), *Żydzi a powstanie styczniowe, materiały i dokumenty* (1963), index; I. Schiper (ed.), *Dzieje handlu żydowskiego na ziemiach polskich* (1937), index; B. Wasiutyński, *Ludność żydowska w Polsce w wiekach XIX i XX* (1930), 34.

[Raphael Mahler]

LECZYCA (Pol. **Łęczyca**; Rus. **Lenchitsa**; Yid. **Luntshits** or **Lentshits**), town in Lodz province, central Poland. Jews are mentioned as residents of Leczyca, one of the oldest Jewish communities in Poland, in the general privilege of King Casimir IV issued in 1453. In 1479 the Jews paid the royal treasury 15 florins in taxes. As early as the first half of the 16th century Jewish merchants of Leczyca dealt in grain, transporting it from Volhynia to the port of Danzig (Gdansk). Until the middle of the 17th century they dominated the trade in cloth, spices, and jewelry at the Leczyca fairs. The register of 1569 shows 19 Jewish houses in the town, and tax lists of 1576 mention 115 Jews, only 50 of whom were able to pay taxes. A *blood libel arose in the town in 1639 when the mutilated body of a boy was discovered. Suspicion fell on a tramp, who declared under torture that he had stolen the boy at the behest of Jews. On the strength of this confession 20 Jews were arrested and tortured. The matter came before the royal tribunal of Lublin, where the tramp, after further torture, indicated that the beadle Meir and Lazarus from Sobota were the ones to whom he had sold the child. Although they continued to protest their innocence under torture, they were condemned to death. After their execution in front of the Lublin synagogue, their bodies were quartered and the pieces impaled on stakes at the crossroads. In the Lublin community register these martyrs are named as Meir b. Menahem ha-Kohen and Ezra b. Avigdor. The child's body was placed in a glass coffin in the St. Bernard Church in Leczyca, while a picture depicting the ritual murder was displayed on the front of the church; there it remained until 1793, when the town came under Prussian rule. The picture was replaced in 1814 and it was not until 1825 that the government confiscated it along with the historical documents of the affair.

When the Jewish quarter was burned down in 1652, King John Casimir (see *Poland) allowed the Jews to rebuild their houses and the synagogue. During the Swedish wars, Jews from the surrounding district took refuge in the Jewish quarter of Leczyca. On Oct. 4, 1656, the Polish army advanced to the city gates, whereupon the garrison retired to the castle, leaving the Jews to the mercies of the attacking nobles. According to official lists of 1661, in the ensuing slaughter (reported in gruesome detail in the *Theatrum Europaeum*, 7 (Frankfurt, 1663), 988ff.; cf. also the description of a Polish observer, Pierre des Noyers, in his *Lettres* (1859), 252) 1,700 Jews lost their lives. Jewish reports estimate the number of dead at 3,000 and the number of burned Torah scrolls at 600. According to Polish reports (municipal archives), Jews commemorated the names of the dead on a tablet, which was lost in 1830. On June 20, 1657 "John Casimir pardoned the Jews of Leczyca their crime." However, very few availed themselves of his permission to return to the Jewish street; the 1665 register records only five Jewish houses in Leczyca. Later some more Jewish families moved to the town after King John III Sobieski had confirmed their former rights (Feb. 20, 1676) and granted permission to rebuild the synagogue, on condition that it was no taller nor more beautiful than before. When the Swedish wars were over, many Jews returned to the town and in 1724 King Augustus II granted them the right to engage in commerce, brandy distilling, slaughtering, innkeeping, and crafts. According to the 1765 census, there were 1,040 poll-tax payers under the jurisdiction of the Leczyca *kahal*, 607 of them from 83 neighboring villages. Of the 114 residents 34 owned their houses. Twenty were tailors. From 999 (49% of the total population) in 1808, the Jewish population increased to 1,797 (45%) in 1827, and 2,286 (44%) in 1857. In 1897 the community had grown to 3,444 (41%) in spite of large-scale emigration to Lodz, and in 1921 to 4,051 (40%).

Natives of Leczyca included *Ephraim Solomon of Luntschitz (16th century), rabbi of Prague, and Abraham Isaac Luntschitz (18th century). In the first half of the 17th century, when the community was most influential, the rabbi was Israel Samuel *Calahorra. He was succeeded by his son, Salomon *Calahorra.

[*Encyclopaedia Judaica* (Germany) / Arthur Cygielman]

Holocaust Period

In 1939 there were about 4,300 Jews in Leczyca constituting over one third of the total population. After its occupation by the Germans (Sept. 7, 1939), a group of Jewish men was locked up in the local synagogue and a group of Polish Catholics in the church. These prisoners were forced to work on fortifications. The Germans temporarily retreated when the town was retaken and held for a few days by the Polish army. On the eve of the Day of Atonement the Nazis took 50 Jewish hostages, including the rabbi and community leaders, as well as 100 Polish hostages, as a guarantee for the safety of the German soldiers garrisoned in the town. All the hostages were subsequently released with the exception of the rabbi and several lay leaders for whose release the Judenrat had to pay 1,000,000 zlotys. Some of this money had to be raised by the Judenrat with the assistance of the police. In December 1939 Jewish families were evicted from many streets and from the buildings around the marketplace to be segregated in a separate, crowded Jewish district. To further repress and humiliate the Jews the Germans forced them to destroy their own cemetery and set fire to their synagogue. The Judenrat was compelled to sign a declaration that the "arson" was committed by Jews, and a heavy fine was imposed upon the community. During 1940 groups of Jews left the town, either voluntarily or by force. In January 1941 all Jews were ordered to appear in the marketplace with their kitchen utensils and some bedding. Some 600 people were then selected and sent under German police convoy to Poddebice. Another group of 450 were sent to Grabow. The Jewish area was then surrounded with barbed wire and as a result of famine and lack of fuel epidemics broke out. The final liquidation of the community took place on April 10–11, 1942, when the remaining 1,750 Jews were sent to the death camp at *Chelmno. A memorial book *Sefer Lintshiẓ* was published in Israel by the Society of Immigrants from Leczyca (Heb., 1953).

[Danuta Dombrowska]

BIBLIOGRAPHY: R. Mahler, *Yidn in Amolikn Poyln in Likht fun Tsifern* (1958), index; B. Wasiutyński, *Ludność żydowska w Polsce w wiekach XIX i XX* (1930), 10, 25; A. Eisenbach et al. (eds.), *Zydzi a powstanie styczniowe, materiały i dokumenty* (1963), index; I. Schiper, *Studya nad stosunkami gospodarczymi Żydów w Polsce podczas średniowiecza* (1911), index; idem, *Dzieje handlu żydowskiego na ziemiach polskich* (1937), index; M. Bersohn, *Dyplomataryusz, dotyczący żydów w Polsce* (1910), no. 357; Trunk, in: *Bleter far Geshikhte*, 2:1–4 (1949), 64–166, passim; Dąbrowska, in: BŻIH, 13–14 (1955); Halpern, Pinkas, index; Tuchowski, *Odgłos procesów kryminalnych* (1713); D. Lewin, *Judenverfolgungen im zweiten Schwedische-Polnischen Krieg* (1901).

LEDA (Lederer), EDUARD (1859–1944), Czech author and one of the leaders of Jewish assimilation in Czechoslovakia. Leda was born in Chotoviny, Bohemia. In his novels and short stories Leda portrayed many Jewish characters, often expressing through them his own thoughts on various aspects of the Jewish problem. The best known are *Zápisky hrbáčovy* ("Diary of a Hunchback," 1923), *Rakušák* ("The Austrophile," 1942), and *Lelíček Redivivus* (1928). He also wrote two biblical plays, *Mojžíš* ("Moses," 1919) and *Zrádce* ("The Traitor," 1921), the latter intended as a vindication of Judas Iscariot. He wrote several books on the Jewish question: *Německý a český anti-semitismus* ("German and Czech Anti-Semitism," 1899), *Českožidovská otázka* ("The Czech-Jewish Question," 1899), *Židé v dnešní společnosti* ("Jews in Modern Society," 1902), and *Kapitoly o židovství a židovstvu* ("Chapter on Judaism and Jewry," 1925). In all of these he was an uncompromising advocate of assimilation. Leda died in Theresienstadt.

BIBLIOGRAPHY: O. Donath, *Židé a židovství v české literatuře 19. a 20. století* (1930); Hostovský, in: *Jews of Czechoslovakia* (1967), 446. **ADD. BIBLIOGRAPHY:** *Lexikon české literatury* 2/II (1993); A. Mikulášek, *Literatura s hvězdou Davidovou*, vol. 1 (1998)

[Avigdor Dagan / Milos Pojar (2nd ed.)]

LEDEEN, HYMAN (1894–1981), U.S. inventor. Born in Cherven, Russia, Ledeen was taken to the U.S. in 1903. His numerous inventions include an air hoist, steel punch, speed reducer, flexible coupling, bearing for variable speed transmission, and pump for oil wells.

LEDERBERG, JOSHUA (1925–), U.S. geneticist. Born in Montclair, New Jersey and scion of a rabbinical family from Ereẓ Israel, he studied at Columbia University and then at Yale and made a number of important discoveries in microbial genetics. It had previously been thought that bacteria reproduced only asexually. In 1946, however, Lederberg and Edward L. Tatum discovered that sexual union and genetic recombination occur in *Escherischia coli*, the common colon bacterium. In 1952, while looking for evidence of sexuality in other bacterial forms, Lederberg and a student, Norton Zinder, demonstrated that certain viruses are capable of transmitting genetic material from one bacterial cell to another, a process they named transduction. From 1947 to 1959 Lederberg was professor of genetics at the University of Wisconsin. In 1959 he became professor and chairman of the department of genetics at Stanford University. For his studies on the organization of the genetic material in bacteria Lederberg (with Tatum) was co-recipient of the Nobel Prize for medicine in 1958. In 1978 he left Stanford to assume the presidency of Rockefeller University, serving in that capacity until 1990. He continued his research there on the genetics of bacterial growth as a Raymond and Beverly Sackler Foundation Scholar. Lederberg's research interests, in addition to microbial genetics, are the chemical origin and evolution of life, space biology, and the augmentation of human intelligence with computer software. Speaking out on policy issues, he has drawn attention to the ever-present threat of new infectious diseases and the impetus these may receive from human folly.

BIBLIOGRAPHY: T. Levitan, *Laureates…* (1960), 176–9; *Current Biography Yearbook 1959* (1960), 251–2; S.R. Riedman and E.T. Gustafson, *Portraits of Nobel Laureates in Medicine and Physiology* (1963), 318–20.

[Fred Rosner]

LEDERER, ABRAHAM (1827–1916), educator and pedagogic writer. Born in Libochovice, Bohemia, Lederer became principal of the Jewish school at Tata, Hungary, in 1854, and in 1857 was appointed by the government to head the Jewish "model school" of Budapest. Lederer was also entrusted with the organization of the teachers' training college connected with the school (1859). Although he resigned from his post as headmaster in 1868, he continued teaching until 1889. Among his contributions to educational literature were translations of Hungarian textbooks into German and several original publications including *Az oktatás módszere* ("Teaching Methods," 1870); *A példadás módszere* ("Teaching by Example," 1877); *A testi büntetés a családban és az iskolában* ("Corporal Punishment at Home and at School," 1884); *A kegyelet* ("On Piety," 1920); and *A szociális kérdés és az iskola* ("School and the Social Question," 1898). Lederer was the pioneer of summer holiday camps for schoolchildren in Hungary. He is also remembered as the founder of the nationwide Organization of Jewish Teachers in Hungary (1866). He died in Budapest.

BIBLIOGRAPHY: M. Málnai, in: *Izraelita Tanügyi Értesitö*, 41 (1916), 203–6.

[Jeno Zsoldos]

LEDERER (née **Friedman**), **ESTHER PAULINE**, (1918–2002), syndicated American columnist. Lederer was born in Sioux City, Iowa, to Russian Jewish immigrants. In 1955 she took over the Ann Landers column in the *Chicago Sun-Times*. In 1987, her home base became the *Chicago Tribune*. Her daily column "Ask Ann Landers" was syndicated in more than 1,200 newspapers and was said to be the most widely read column in the world, with an estimated 90 million readers. She is reported to have received more than 2,000 letters daily and was regarded as having had a considerable influence on public opinion. She once referred to herself as "typically upper middle-class Midwestern Jewish." Her generally conservative views included a constant warning against the perils of intermarriage, but she later adopted a more liberal attitude to questions of sex and divorce. She published some 12 pamphlets on social problems and, among other works, a lengthy volume, *The Ann Landers Encyclopedia* (1978), which deals with a wide variety of contemporary issues.

Lederer was the recipient of several awards, among them The Jane Addams Public Award Hull House and a citation from the AMA for distinguished service.

Lederer was married to Jules Lederer, who built the Budget-Rent-a-Car company. They divorced in 1975 after 36 years of marriage. Lederer's main rival in popularity as a nationwide columnist was her twin sister, Pauline Esther, who also wrote a syndicated column, "Dear Abby," under the name Abigail Van Buren. Books by Lederer include *Since You Ask Me* (1961); *Gems* (1988); and *Wake Up and Smell the Coffee* (1996).

ADD. BIBLIOGRAPHY: R. Kogan, *America's Mom* (2003); M. Howard, *A Life in Letters: Ann Landers' Letters to Her Only Child* (2003); J. Pottker and B. Speziale, *Dear Ann, Dear Abby: The Unauthorized Biography of Ann Landers* and *Abigail Van Buren* (1987); D.

Grossvogel, *Dear Ann Landers* (1986); M. Howard, *Eppie: The Story of Ann Landers* (1983).

LEDERER, FRANCIS (1899–2000), Czech actor. Born near Prague, Lederer made his first appearance in Berlin in 1928 and was engaged by Max Reinhardt to play with Elizabeth Bergner in *Romeo and Juliet*. He made his London debut in 1931 and subsequently acted on the New York stage and in films. In 1958 he toured the U.S. as Mr. Frank in *The Diary of Anne Frank*. On television he appeared in *Mission Impossible* and *The Untouchables*.

LEDERER, JEROME F. (1902–2004), U.S. aeronautical engineer. Born in New York City, Lederer received his B.Sc. in 1924 and his M.E. in 1925 in mechanical engineering with aeronautical electives at New York University, one of the very few universities which offered this course. In 1926 he joined the U.S. Air Mail Service, the world's first system of regular air transportation. The high accident rate among airline pilots stimulated his life-long interest in aviation safety and eventually he won the sobriquet "Mr Aviation Safety." His innovative work covered aircraft design and safety modifications, accident investigation, human factors such as pilot fatigue and distraction, and flight insurance. He organized the Flight Safety Foundation, of which he became the first director and later president emeritus. In World War II, Lederer was director of training at the institute which trained Air Transport Command's pilots and technicians and an operations analyst for the U.S. Air Force. He was a member of many key national and international organizations concerned with aviation safety. After retirement from the Foundation in 1967, he established the Office of Manned Space Flight Safety at the National Aeronautical and Space Administration's request following the 1967 space capsule disaster. As well as technical supervision, Lederer stressed the role of personal motivation. His many honors included the Wright Brothers Memorial Award (1967), the K.E. Tsiolkovsky Medal of the Soviet Federation of Cosmonauts (1988), and the International Civil Aviation Organization's Edward Warner award (1999). In January 2000 *Air Safety* magazine named him "aviation's man of the century." In retirement he continued to work actively on many more general aspects of transportation safety.

[Michael Denman (2nd ed.)]

LEDERMAN, LEON MAX (1922–), U.S. Nobel laureate in physics. Lederman was born in New York City, where he earned his B.S. at the College of the City of New York (1943), and his M.A. (1948) and Ph.D. (1951) in physics from Columbia University, an education interrupted by service in the U.S. Army (1943–46). He was a faculty member of the physics department of Columbia University (1946–79) and professor from 1958, during which period he was director of the department's NEVIS Laboratories at Irvington-on-Hudson (1961–78) and collaborated with the European Organization for Nuclear Research (CERN). He was director of the Fermi National Accelerator Laboratory in Batavia, Illinois (1979–89) and professor of physics at the University of Chicago from 1989. He joined the Illinois Institute of Technology as Pritzker Professor of Science (1994). His research concerned the nature of the subatomic world and in particular the identification of subatomic particles, most frequently by measurements or observations using particle accelerators. His major experiments involved the discovery of a long-lived neutral "K" particle, the failure of mirror symmetry in the properties of pions and muons, and a second type of neutrino. Lederman and his colleagues at Columbia University, Melvin Schwartz and Jack Steinberger, were awarded the Nobel Prize (1988) for the demonstration of the doublet structure of leptons and the discovery of the muon neutrino. His many honors include membership of the U.S. National Academy of Sciences, the U.S. National Medal for Science (1965), and the Wolf Prize in Physics (1983). He was a member of the Board of Trustees of the Weizmann Institute and collaborated closely with Professor Haim Harari of this institute. He had a great interest in scientific education, as is evident from his many contributions to local, national, and international institutes and commissions. He is coauthor of many successful books for general readers including *Quarks to the Cosmos* (with David Schramm, 1989), *The God Particle* (with Dick Teresi, 1993), and *Symmetry and the Beautiful Universe* (with Christopher Hill, 2004).

[Michael Denman (2nd ed.)]

LEE, DAVID (1931–), U.S. physicist and Nobel laureate. Born in Rye, New York, Lee received his B.A. in physics from Harvard University (1952). After U.S. Army service, he earned his M.Sc. from the University of Connecticut (1955) and his Ph.D. in physics, under the supervision of Henry Fairbank, from Yale University (1959), where he developed his lasting interest in low-temperature physics. He joined the physics faculty of Cornell University (1959) where he became professor (1968–97) and James Gilbert White Distinguished Professor of Physical Sciences (1997). He and his colleagues discovered superfluidity in the naturally occurring lighter isotope of helium called helium-3, the phenomenon whereby helium-3 flows without resistance at a low temperature just above absolute zero. This property has fundamental theoretical implications for understanding atomic structure and cosmology. Its discovery also led to the establishment of the principles of nuclear magnetic resonance, which have been routinely adopted in medical practice and biological research. He was awarded the Nobel Prize in Physics for this research (1996) jointly with Douglas Osheroff and Robert Richardson. His other honors include the Simon Memorial Prize and election to the U.S. National Academy of Sciences.

[Michael Denman (2nd ed.)]

LEE, MALKE (pseudonym of **Malke Leopold-Rappaport**; 1904–1964), Yiddish poet. Born in Monastrich (Galicia), she immigrated to New York in 1921. Her poems appeared in Yiddish periodicals from 1922 and were collected in six volumes, of which *In Likht fun Doyres* ("In the Light of Generations," 1961) was the most mature. Accenting nature and love, her lyrics focus on the Dniester, the farmers of New York's Catskill range, her attachment to the U.S., and Israel's resurgence. She also wrote a memoir after the war, *Durkh Kindershe Oygn* ("Through the Eyes of Childhood," 1955).

BIBLIOGRAPHY: LNYL, 5 (1963), 36–7. **ADD. BIBLIOGRAPHY:** F. Forman (ed.), *Found Treasures: Stories by Yiddish Women Writers* (1994), 159–85.

[Sol Liptzin / Sarah Ponichtera (2nd ed.)]

LEE, SIR SIDNEY (1859–1926), English literary historian. Born Solomon Lazarus Lee (his family had previously changed its name from Levi to Lee), he studied at Oxford. Lee was professor of English language and literature at London University from 1913 to 1924. He was the second editor (from vol. 27) of the *Dictionary of National Biography*, to which he contributed 820 articles and which he brought to a successful conclusion. Lee's *Life of Shakespeare*, first issued in 1898, was long a standard work. He also wrote a *Life of Queen Victoria* (1902) and the official *Life of King Edward VII* (1925–27). Lee originally took some interest in Anglo-Jewish history, and published a study on Jews and crypto-Jews in Shakespearean England. Later, however, he had no connection with the community. Lee was knighted in 1911. His sister, ELIZABETH LEE (1858–1920), was an author, biographer, and translator. She contributed 110 entries to the *Dictionary of National Biography*, of which 101 were of women. She was thus one of the most notable early biographers of important British women, and was also the only woman editor of the first *Dictionary of National Biography.*

BIBLIOGRAPHY: *Times* (March 4 and 6, 1926); P. Emden, *Jews of Britain* (1944), 367–74. **ADD. BIBLIOGRAPHY:** ODNB online for Sir Sidney Lee and Elizabeth Lee.

[Cecil Roth]

LEE, STAN (1922–), U.S. cartoonist. Born in New York City to Jewish immigrants from Eastern Europe, Lee (Stanley Martin Lieber) began working in comic books at 17, as an assistant to Martin Goodman, who was married to his cousin and was publisher of Timely Comics, which would become Marvel Comics. Lee's first published work appeared in a *Captain America* comic book in 1941, shortly before the United States entered World War II. Lee worked with several co-creators, including Jack *Kirby, introducing superheroes to fight the Nazi menace. After the war, comics came under attack in the United States when a psychiatrist and a United States senator blamed comic books for corrupting young readers with images of violence and sexuality. Comic book companies responded by implementing strict guidelines. Lee then wrote comics in various genres, such as romance, Westerns, and light science fiction. In the late 1950s DC Comics revived the superhero genre and beginning in 1961 Lee, as part of the Marvel group, helped produce *Spider Man*, *Thor*, *The Hulk*, *Daredevil*, and *Iron Man*. Lee's scripts, created in collaboration with such artists as Kirby and Steve Ditko, depicted characters endowed with superhuman abilities yet with human failings and emotions the reader could identify with. In 1972 Lee became publisher and editorial director of Marvel Comics. He also wrote *Origins of Marvel Comics* (1974). Lee and his studios came into the limelight when two *Spider Man* movies and a *Hulk* film achieved great success. During the dot.com boom, in 1999, Lee teamed with a Hollywood entrepreneur, Peter Paul, to create an online animation and superhero creation studio. Stan Lee Media went public and in February 2000 had a market value twice that of Marvel. The studio grew to 165 people and produced flash animation on the Internet, winning the 2000 Web Award as the best entertainment portal on the World Wide Web, Stanlee.net. Eventually, after Paul was accused of campaign finance fraud during the New York State election campaign of Hilary Clinton for senator, Stan Lee Media went out of business. However, as a result of a contract that Paul helped negotiate for Lee with Marvel in 1998, Lee recovered a settlement of more than $10 million from Marvel for the profits from Marvel's blockbuster movies.

[Stewart Kampel (2nd ed.)]

LEE AND CHARLOTTE COUNTIES, counties in S.W. Florida, U.S., including **Fort Myers**. Fort Myers, a city of about 50,000 people, is named for a Jew, Colonel Abraham C. Myers. A West Point graduate and quartermaster during the Seminole Indian Wars, Myers was a descendent of Moses Cohen, the first rabbi of Charleston, South Carolina. General John Twiggs (not Jewish) was commander of the fort built on the Caloosahatchee River by Federal troops in 1839 for defense against the Indians and his daughter married Myers. The fort was named to honor Colonel Myers.

There is no record of the earliest Jew in Lee County. Jews were first able to attend a Jewish service during World War II when a Jewish chaplain was assigned to the Buckingham Air Base. In 1947 Sam Posner placed an ad in the local newspaper that his store would be closed for the Jewish High Holidays. Following that, he had his best sales day ever when people came to see what a Jew was like. The next year, as more Jews identified themselves, they rented a hall for $5.00 and had High Holiday services.

The Lipman family began packing tomatoes and farming in the area in 1952 as the Six L's Packing Co. They became a large agricultural presence and expanded into other areas of the state. Today they are probably the largest tomato growers in the country, farming more than 15,000 acres and operating eight packinghouses in seven states.

Celia Tanner, born in Key West in 1906, came to Fort Myers with her husband Herman in 1936 to open a scrap metal business that evolved into Tanner Auto Parts. The first congregation was formed in 1954 when 22 people met at their home. Led by Sam and Rose Posner, they purchased land for $1,200 to build the Fort Myers Community Center–Temple Beth-El and affiliated with the Conservative movement. By this time, there were 30 Jewish families and Posner was the lay rabbi. In

1956 a cemetery was started. By 1960 Rabbi Morris Kosman became the first spiritual leader and in 1963 the congregation became Reform with the stipulation to retain *yarmulkes* and *tallitot*. In 1964 there was a UJA dinner and there were enough Jews to plan a new building.

Brothers Jack and Leonard Rosen formed Gulf American Land Corporation and assembled 114 square miles of desolate woods on the western tip of Lee County that they named Cape Coral. They brought in the largest single shipment of earth-moving equipment in Florida development history to create 350,000 residential sites. A large majority of the people who worked for Gulf American were Jews. The Rosen Brothers donated 4.5 acres of land and $25,000 for Temple Beth-El to move to Cape Coral in 1966 and insisted that all of their employees join the Temple. The new building was dedicated in 1965 by Rabbi Simon Friedeman, and it was already crowded with 90 families. One was Sylvia and David Gottlieb who came to Cape Coral with Gulf American. Thirty years later Sylvia Gottlieb donated land to the Federation and the proceeds from the sale helped build the Jewish Community Campus.

By the 1970s other organizations were formed. Kosher meat and Passover supplies were delivered by bus from Tampa or by those who made the drive to the east coast. In 1972 when two women assumed leadership in Temple Beth-El (Rose Kosches and Gert Thomson), a group broke off to form the Fort Myers Community Center, also in Cape Coral. A Conservative congregation, Temple Judea, was formed across the river in Fort Myers.

Sam Posner pioneered the Trail, known now as U.S. Route 41. He purchased land and built the first department store there; later Sears, Burdines, and Maas Brothers (Jews from Tampa) came along. He was the first chairman of the board for Lee Memorial Hospital in 1976 and received awards for his civic leadership as well as for his service to Israel.

In 1973 Dr. Harvey Tritel became the 100th physician to join the Medical Society in Fort Myers and the 100th Jewish family to settle there. In 1975 Leo Cooper provided a connecting link for the Lee County Jews with the newspaper, *L'Chayim*, subsequently continued by Federation. In 1983 Sheila Laboda was the Federation's first president and Temple Judea had a woman rabbi in the 1990s (Tobah August). The community has grown and participated in all Jewish issues and efforts of their larger counterparts, including bringing Russian Jews.

Nearby Port Charlotte had its first congregation in 1961 and the following year, General Development Corporation donated land for a Temple that was designed in the shape of the Star of David. Today there are about 8,000 Jews in Lee and Charlotte Counties (not including snowbirds), nine Jewish organizations, three Jewish schools, and nine congregations.

[Marcia Jo Zerivitz (2nd ed.)]

LEECH (Heb. עֲלוּקָה, AV, JPS: "horseleech"), blood-sucking worm. The aphorism in the Book of Proverbs (30:15) that "the leech hath two daughters: 'Give, give'" refers to the two sucking disks on its head with which it adheres to its prey and sucks its blood. In several places in Israel the Nile leech – *Limnatis nilotica* – is found in springs and bodies of water and, attaching itself to men or beasts when these wash in or drink from the water, sucks their blood. Because of this the Talmud warns against drinking water directly from rivers and pools (Av. Zar. 12b), an instance being cited of a man who swallowed a leech in this way; for which various remedies are suggested (TJ, Ber. 9:3, 13c). The medicinal leech *Hirudo medicinalis* is not naturally present in Israel and it is doubtful whether it was known in biblical times.

BIBLIOGRAPHY: Lewysohn, Zool, 336, no. 467; J. Feliks, *The Animal World of the Bible* (1962), 140.

[Jehuda Feliks]

LEEDS, cloth-manufacturing city in Yorkshire, N. England. Jews first appear here in the late 18th century. However, a community was founded only c. 1823 and a cemetery acquired only in 1837. Until 1846 a small room served as synagogue, larger accommodation being acquired in that year. The first synagogue building for the parent congregation was erected in 1860, when there were a hundred Jewish families. With the growth in local prosperity the Jewish population increased, and in 1877 the present Beth Hamidrash Hagadol, now a congregation with 620 seatholders, was organized in a small room by recently arrived immigrants. Toward the close of the 19th century many Russian and Polish immigrants settled in Leeds and were absorbed largely in the tailoring industry to which they gave a great impetus. Sir Montague *Burton was one of many Jews who contributed largely to its development. Zionism flourished in Leeds, especially due to the presence of Professor Selig *Brodetsky. In 1970 the Jewish community was estimated at 18,000 out of a population of approximately 508,000. This was the third largest community, after London and Manchester, and contained the highest proportion of Jews to the general population in Great Britain. Three of the nine synagogues in Leeds were combined in the United Hebrew Congregation with a total membership of nearly 2,000. There was also one Reform congregation. The Leeds Jewish Representative Council, organized in 1938, embraced almost every local synagogue, Zionist group, charitable organization, and Friendly Society. There was a Hebrew department at Leeds University and the teachers there have included Shimon *Rawidowicz. Hyman Morris was lord mayor in 1941–42 and J.S. Walsh in 1966–67. By the mid-1990s the Jewish population had dropped to approximately 9,000. In the 2001 British census, which recorded the religion of respondents, Leeds was found to have 8,270 declared Jews, making it still the third largest Anglo-Jewish community after Greater London and Manchester. Leeds continued to have a wide variety of Jewish institutions, among them six Orthodox, one Reform, and one Masorti synagogue.

BIBLIOGRAPHY: E. Krausz, *Leeds Jewry, its History and Social Structure* (1964); Lehman, Nova Bibl, index; C. Roth, *Rise of Provincial Jewry* (1950), 81f.; V.D. Lipman, *Social History of the Jews in England 1850–1950* (1957), index; L.P. Gartner, *The Jewish Immigrant in England 1870–1914* (1960), index; Krausz, in: JJSO, 3 (1961), 88–106. **ADD.**

BIBLIOGRAPHY: A. Bergen, *Leeds Jewry 1830–1939: The Challenge of Anti-Semitism* (2000); J. Buckman, *Immigrants and the Class Struggle: The Jewish Immigrant in Leeds, 1880–1914* (1983); D. Charing (ed.), *Glimpses of Leeds Jewry* (1988); M. Freedman, *Leeds Jewry: The First Hundred Years* (1992); L. Snaipe, *A History of the Jews of Leeds* (1985); L. Teeman, *Footprints in the Sands: An Autobiography* (1986).

[Cecil Roth]

LEEF, YINAM (1953–), Israeli composer. Born in Jerusalem, Leef studied composition with Mark *Kopytman at the Jerusalem Rubin Academy for Music and Dance; with Richard Wernick, George *Rochberg, and George Crumb at the University of Pennsylvania, where he received his doctorate; and with Luciano Berio at Tanglewood. He taught at Swarthmore and Haverford colleges, Philadelphia College of Performing Arts, and the New School of Music. At the Jerusalem Rubin Academy, he became chairman of the Department of Composition, Conducting, and Theory in 2003. Leef is the recipient of the Halstead Prize, the Hilda K. Nitzsche Prize in Music, the Israel Composers' League Prize, the ACUM Prize, and the Prime Minister's Prize for Israeli Composers.

Leef's list of compositions includes orchestral works: *Violin Concerto*, 1983; *Scherzos and Serenades* (1989); two symphonies, 1981/92 & 1995; *Viola Concerto* (1998); *Serenity Lost* (2004); choral works (*Sounds, Shadows…*, 1987); vocal works (*The Invisible Carmel*, 1982; *A Place of Fire*, 1985); and chamber and instrumental music: *Canaanite Fantasies* for various instrumental ensembles (1981); *Tefilkah* (1997); *Tryptique [Homage to Partos]* (1997); 2 string quartets (1978 & 2001); *Reminiscences of Tranquility* (2002); *Soliloquy* for violin (2003).

Leef's works are characterized by his threefold commitment: to universal, Western-oriented post-serial composition; to local or locally echoing musical traditions of Jewish and Middle Eastern modality and timbre; and to the young Israeli ("Canaanite") search for musical identity. Leef's works often implicitly give expression to the composer's subjective, rather understated though affectionately consoling response to the intense reality of life in Israel. Leef's poetics is based on drafting dynamic, dramatic processes of a formal nature, and on constituting contrasts and carefully mediating between them. He keeps using specific materials and models, embedding them, variously disguised, in new contexts.

BIBLIOGRAPHY: Grove Music Online; R. Fleischer, *Twenty Israeli Composers* (1997).

[Yuval Shaked (2nd ed.)]

LEEK (Heb. חָצִיר, *ḥaẓir*), vegetable. *Allium porrum* is mentioned among the vegetables of Egypt for which the children of Israel craved during their journey in the wilderness (Num. 11:5). This vegetable was popular with the Egyptians, sketches of it being common in Egyptian paintings and remains found in their tombs. *Ḥaẓir* elsewhere in the Bible refers to grass used as fodder, and is used for leek once only in the Mishnah (Kelim 17:5). It is usually termed *kereishah* or *karatei*, from the root כרת ("cut"), since it was densely sown and its green leaves cut from time to time for food. These were valued, among other things, as a remedy against snake bite: "If someone is bitten by a snake, leek may be cut for him [on the Sabbath]" (Yoma 83b). Its taste is similar to that of the onion, but more delicate. It was eaten to dispel the aftertaste of radish (Pes. 116a). If the plants are well spaced out they develop bulbs which were a favorite food. This bulb is in the shape of a head, hence its mishnaic name *kaflutin* (Greek κεφαλωτόν, "with a head"; for the difference between the leaf and the bulb see Tosef., Ter. 4:5). The leaf is dark turquoise green in color, close to that of *tekhelet* (Ber. 1:2).

BIBLIOGRAPHY: Loew, Flora, 2 (1924), 131–8; H.N. and A.L. Moldenke, *Plants of the Bible* (1952), 34f. nos. 25 and 26; J. Feliks, *Kilei Zera'im ve-Harkavah* (1967), 58–62; J. Feliks, *Olam ha-Ẓome'aḥ ha-Mikra'i* (1968²), 174f.

[Jehuda Feliks]

LEES, LESTER (1920–1986), U.S. aeronautical engineer. Lees was born in New York City, obtaining his B.S. and M.S. in aeronautical engineering at the Massachusetts Institute of Technology (1941). He worked in U.S. Air Force laboratories on materiel problems during World War II before moving first to Princeton and then to the California Institute of Technology. Lees' initial interests concerned the problems of supersonic flight resulting from the shock waves created by the leading edge of aircraft structures, particularly in aerodynamics and heat transfer. His later work in gas dynamics at very high altitude flight proved relevant to atmospheric re-entry and ballistic missile defense. He was involved in environmental issues and became the first director of Caltech's Environmental Quality Laboratory. His many appointments included membership in the President's Scientific Advisory Board.

[Michael Denman (2nd ed.)]

LEESER, ISAAC (1806–1868), U.S. rabbi, writer, and educator. Leeser, who was born in Westphalia, Germany (then Prussia), was eight when his mother died. His father took him to Dulmen, near Muenster, where he was reared by his grandmother and began his formal education. He studied with Rabbi Benjamin Cohen, and then with Rabbi Abraham Sutro, who was an ardent opponent of Reform. Leeser obtained his secular education at the gymnasium of Muenster. In 1824 he went to America to work for his uncle in Richmond, Virginia. He published his first article, a defense of Judaism against a defamatory article that had appeared in a New York newspaper, in 1825. The essay attracted wide notice and in 1829 the Sephardi congregation, Mikveh Israel of Philadelphia, invited him to be its *ḥazzan*. Leeser was the first to introduce a regular English sermon into the synagogue service. In 1843 he founded the monthly *The Occident*, the first successful Jewish newspaper. For 25 years, this was an important forum for articles on Jewish life and thought. Leeser was its editor, chief contributor, bookkeeper, and sometimes even typesetter. Leeser advocated the Americanization of Judaism through translations and sermons in English. He also insisted on decorum and beauty in services. He was in the words of Jonathan Sarna "the foremost traditionalist leader for three decades," an advocate of regeneration. On the major American issue of his day, slavery, Leeser, like Isaac Mayer *Wise, advocated compromise rather than war.

Leeser founded the first Jewish Publication Society of America and brought many important works to the attention of the American Jewish community. He published the first Hebrew primer for children (1838), the first complete English translation of the Sephardi prayer book (1848), and numerous textbooks for children. He founded the first Hebrew high school (1849), the first Jewish representative and defense organization in 1859 (the Board of Delegates of American Israelites), Maimonides College, and the first American Jewish rabbinical school in 1867. His major literary achievement was the first American translation of the Bible, a work that took him 17 years to complete, and was published in 1845. This became the standard American Jewish translation of the Bible until the new Jewish Publication Society translation of 1917. Leeser's later years were clouded by poverty and the fact that his congregation did not appreciate his many activities on the national scene. Toward the end of his life, his friends formed a congregation, Beth El Emeth, for him. Leeser was a traditionalist who did much to stem the tide of Reform. Although he was identified with the Sephardi community his influence affected the entire community and he laid the foundations for many of the key institutions of present-day Jewish life. His contributions to every area of Jewish culture and religion made him a major builder of American Judaism.

BIBLIOGRAPHY: M. Davis, *Emergence of Conservative Judaism* (1963), 347–69; Korn, in: AJA, 19 (1967), 127–141; Englander, in: CCARY, 28 (1918), 213–52; J.R. Marcus, *Memoirs of American Jews, 1775–1865*, 2 (1955), 58–87; L. Jung (ed.), *Guardians of Our Heritage* (1958), 245–61; Whiteman, in: AJHSP, 48 (1959), 207–44; M.S. Seller, in: AJHSQ, 58 (1968), 118–35. **ADD. BIBLIOGRAPHY:** J. Sarna, *American Judaism: A History* (2004), 78–88.

[Jack Riemer / Michael Berenbaum (2nd ed.)]

LEEUW, AVRAHAM DE (1898–), Israeli hydraulic engineer. Born in Holland, de Leeuw immigrated to Palestine in 1924. Beginning in the Tel Aviv municipality, he became chief engineer of Palestine Potash Ltd., of Fertilisers and Chemicals Ltd. (1936–49), and of the Tahal national irrigation and power scheme (1949–57). De Leeuw was director of and later adviser on soil conversion in Israel. From 1957 he was professor of civil engineering at the Technion, Haifa, and head of its hydraulics laboratory.

LEEUW, JACOB BEN ḤAYYIM (Heymann) DE (1811–1883), Dutch talmudist. De Leeuw was born in Leiden, but also resided for some time in 's Hertogenbosch. In 1874 he went to Amsterdam, where he taught in the *bet midrash* Eẓ Ḥayyim. He was the author of expositions and novellae on various themes in tractate *Ketubbot* which were entitled *Shoshannat Ya'akov* (1848); *Peri Eẓ Ḥayyim* (1852), with additional notes (1853); *Mishkenot ha-Ro'im* (1854); *Naḥalat Ya'akov* (1857), in the introduction to which he took issue with Phinehas ha-Levi Horowitz, author of the *Hafla'ah*, on the subject of whether money may be extracted from its possessor by a majority decision; and *Ḥelek Ya'akov* (1858). He also wrote *Aḥuzzat Mere'im* (1879), novellae on tractate *Beẓah*, and *Beit Ya'akov* (1880), on the first seven chapters of *Ḥullin*.

°LE FÈVRE DE LA BODERIE, GUY (Faber Boderianus; 1541–1598), French poet and Christian Hebraist. La Boderie was a pupil of the eccentric genius Guillaume *Postel and served the duke of Alençon as secretary and interpreter. He collaborated with Benito Arias *Montano in editing the second Complutensian Bible, the credit for which he later disputed with the Spaniard. Among La Boderie's contributions to this polyglot Bible (printed by Christophe *Plantin at Antwerp, 1568–72) were the Syriac version of the New Testament, and an Aramaic lexicon (*Dictionarium Syro-Chaldaicum*). The latter work displays the author's predilection for the Kabbalah, a significant element in his French verse. An honored associate of the celebrated *Pléiade* group of poets, La Boderie was moderate in his religious and his political views and remained aloof both from the Huguenots and from the Catholic League. Metrical renderings of the Psalms abound in his works, which include *L'Encyclie des secrets de l'éternité* (1571) and the epic *La Galliade* (1578). These long poems are full of biblical and rabbinic references and Franco-Hebraic conceits. *L'Harmonie du Monde* (1579), one of his many translations, expanded Francesco *Giorgio's Christian interpretation of the Kabbalah. La Boderie's "Gallic" exposition of such motifs as the cockerel, lily, and **menorah* was inspired by the Zohar and by *Baḥya ben Asher's mystical exegesis. His brother, NICOLAS LE FÈVRE DE LA BODERIE (1550–1613), was also a Hebraist and contributed to the Antwerp polyglot Bible. He wrote *Ad nobiliores linguas… Isagoge* (1588) and a lengthy kabbalistic preface to the French translation (1570) of *Pico della Mirandola's *Heptaplus*.

BIBLIOGRAPHY: P. Colomiès, *Gallia Orientalis* (1665), 41–42; F. Secret, *L'ésotérisme de Guy Le Févre de la Boderie* (1969); J. Perles, *Beitraege zur Geschichte der hebraeischen und aramaeischen Studien* (1884), 78ff.; B. Rekers, *Benito Arias Montano* (Dutch, 1961), 110ff.; A.M. Schmidt, *Poésie scientifique en France au seizième siècle* (1938), 182–214; idem, in: E.J. Finbert (ed.), *Aspects du génie d'Israël* (1950), 169–82; F. Secret, *Kabbalistes chrétiens de la Renaissance* (1964), 192ff.; G.E. Silverman, in: JC (Jan. 8, 1960).

[Godfrey Edmond Silverman]

LEFKOWITZ, DAVID (1941–), *ḥazzan* and composer. Lefkowitz was born in Cleveland. From childhood he sang in the choir of his father, the cantor and composer Jacob Lefkowitz, and appeared with him in concerts and on radio programs. He studied cantorial music with his father as well as at the Cantorial School of the Jewish Theological Seminary in New York. He studied at the University of Pittsburgh and at the Juilliard School in New York. At the age of 18 he began to serve as cantor at the Ocean Parkway Jewish Center in

Brooklyn, at Temple Emanuel in Paterson, New Jersey, and at the Park Avenue Synagogue in New York, where he was chief cantor from 1976. He has a lyric tenor voice, and appeared on radio and television programs in the United States. Every year he arranges a special prayer service at his synagogue in which he performs some of the classical repertoire of the cantorial world as well as compositions written especially for him. He has produced records of portions of the prayer service, and composed, rescued, and edited rare synagogue works (such as David *Nowakowsky's works) from many periods and in many styles. Lefkowitz was the vice president of the American Society for Jewish Music and served as the vice president and music director of the David Nowakowsky Foundation and as a faculty member of the School of Sacred Music at Hebrew Union College. His honors include the David Putterman Award from the Cantor's Assembly (2003) for Lifetime Achievement in the Cantorate, and a 2003–4 appointment to the Rabbinical Assembly Law Committee.

[Akiva Zimmerman / Israela Stein (2nd ed.)]

LEFKOWITZ, LOUIS (1904–1966), New York attorney general, a leading Jewish Republican politician. Born in New York City, he was a graduate of Fordham Law School and practiced law briefly before being elected to the New York State Assembly at the age of 23. For a time he was a judge at New York's Municipal Court. In 1956 he replaced Jacob *Javits, the leading New York Jewish Republican politician of his age, as attorney general when Javits was elected to the Senate. Javits was less than pleased to be replaced by a club politician. Over time they worked together harmoniously. Lefkowitz served as attorney general for a record 22 years. He attempted to seek a different office when he ran for New York City's mayor against Robert F. Wagner in 1961 when Wagner sought a third term as mayor.

As a young man he found the settlement house as a haven to escape the New York slums of the Lower East Side. "They were havens," he said. "You had gymnasium privileges, swimming. You could take a bath more often than at home." He joined a club called the Solons at the University Settlement. It was from that base that he ran for public office, relentlessly campaigning door-to-door, asking voters for their support or at least not to humiliate him. He won. When he first came to office Al Smith was governor; when he retired in 1978 Hugh Carey was the governor.

As a political leader he was the master of street campaigning, remembering names, greeting voters, eating ethnic food. His term of office long overlapped with another liberal Republican, Governor Nelson Rockefeller, who was both a mentor and a protégé. He was one of the few men who stayed at the Executive Mansion as a guest of Rockefeller, a politician whom he taught to eat blintzes and to down hot dogs, not quite a patrician taste in foods.

His successor, the long-time Jewish Democratic Attorney General Robert *Abrams, the man whom he had defeated in 1974, said: "Historically, the Attorney General's office played a defensive role – defending the state whenever the state was sued. In the modern era, it began to take the offensive lead on behalf of the public interest by bringing lawsuits. He took a particular lead in doing that in the consumer-protection area." Lefkowitz was known as "the people's lawyer."

With Jacob Javits, Louis Lefkowitz, Robert Abrams, and Eliot *Spitzer, the role of attorney general of New York for almost all of the last half of the 20th century and well into the first decade of the 21st century was held by Jewish political leaders proud of their Jewish roots.

[Michael Berenbaum (2nd ed.)]

LEFRAK, SAMUEL J. (1918–2003), U.S. builder and philanthropist. A champion of middle-income housing, the Brooklyn-born LeFrak headed a family company that produced more living space than any other in the years after World War II. Through four decades, LeFrak led the Lefrak Organization, founded in the United States by his grandfather, Aaron, in 1905, putting up almost 200,000 houses and apartments in the New York City area. He said he "went into the business" at the age of eight, carrying buckets of water and nails for workmen at construction sites. When he started working for the family company full time in 1940 it was building army camps and housing. His father, who had bought a 2,000-acre farm in Brooklyn in the 1920s and had been building there long before World War II, turned the presidency over to him in 1948. He held it until 1975, when his son, Richard, became president, with Samuel retaining the title of chairman. After he took over the company, he built wherever he could buy reasonably priced land, always following the principle that housing should be close to subways, schools, and shopping. "I adopted another S – safe," he said.

LeFrak's signature building was a six-story brick apartment house, a standard feature of Brooklyn and Queens, and his buildings stressed security systems that were advanced for their day. His Lefrak City, with 5,000 apartments and two million feet of retail space, included swimming pools, doormen, and television surveillance in the elevators. At Battery Park City in Lower Manhattan in the early 1980s, he built 1,800 apartments and in the 1990s there was his Newport development on the Hudson River shorefront in Jersey City, a $10 billion residential and commercial project that can house 35,000 people.

A noted art collector and philanthropist, he served on the boards of 36 hospitals, colleges, and schools, and many buildings are named for him and his wife, the former Ethel Stone, whom he married in 1941. They include a concert hall at Queens College, a gymnasium at Amherst College, a meadow in Flushing, Queens, a learning center at Temple Emanu-El in Manhattan, and a classroom building with an amphitheater at the University of Maryland, which he attended. He financed expeditions in underwater archeology, once in search of seventh-century Byzantine shipwrecks off the coast of Israel. He also helped finance a search for Noah's Ark, which the Turkish government refused to allow to go forward, and the successful search for the SS Titanic.

[Stewart Kampel (2nd ed.)]

LEFSCHETZ, SOLOMON (1884–1972), U.S. mathematician. Born in Moscow, Lefschetz received his doctorate in 1911 at Clarke University. During the years 1907 to 1910 he was employed by the Westinghouse Electric Manufacturing Company at Pittsburgh. He began his academic career in 1911 as an instructor at the University of Nebraska and after a number of appointments became research professor at Princeton University after 1933. He made important and significant contributions to algebraic geometry, topology, and differential equations. Among his published works are *Algebraic Topology* (1942); *Algebraic Geometry* (1953); *Differential Equations* (1957); and *Stability Theory of Liapunov*.

LEFTWICH, JOSEPH (1892–1984), English author, editor, and anthologist. Born Joseph Lefkowitz in Holland, Leftwich eventually became head of the London branch of the Jewish Telegraphic Agency (1921–1936). He made his name as an authority on Jewish and Yiddish literature, translating works by Sholem Asch, Max Brod, I.L. Peretz, Zalman Schneour and Stefan Zweig. The Nazis' rise to power stirred him to write *What Will Happen to the Jews?* (1936) and *The Tragedy of Anti-Semitism* (in collaboration with A.K. Chesterton, 1948). He also wrote *Yiddish Language and Literature* (1944), and studies of Herzl (1942) and Zangwill (1957). Leftwich edited two influential anthologies: *Yisröel, the First Jewish Omnibus* (1933; revised 1963), a wide selection, in English, from the Jewish literature of many countries, and *The Golden Peacock* (1939), translations from Yiddish poetry. He published a new anthology of Yiddish essays in English translation, *The Way We Think* (2 vols., 1969). He served from 1945 as director of the British Federation of Jewish Relief Organizations. Leftwich was a friend and associate of such noted East End cultural figures as Isaac *Rosenberg and Mark *Gertler, and coined the name the "Whitechapel Boys" for their group.

LEGAL MAXIMS, concise statements of the law as it is or, often, succinct statements embodying a guiding principle established in law. The word *kelal*, in one of its varied meanings, is the Hebrew equivalent of a legal maxim. "The burden of proof is on the plaintiff" (BK 3:11), for example, is referred to as "a great maxim of jurisprudence" (*kelal gadol ba-din*; BK 46a; see also *Evidence).

Historical Periods

The wealth of Jewish legal maxims is essentially talmudic. The great corpus of tannaitic and amoraic literature contains hundreds of maxims, i.e., legal rules and principles of jurisprudence stated in brief form and summary fashion.

OF BIBLICAL ORIGIN. Even maxims which can be traced back to the Bible owe their epigrammatic popularity to the Talmud. These "biblical" maxims are of three types: a literal quotation of a verse or of a part thereof, "At the mouth of two witnesses… shall a matter be established" (Deut. 19:15, cited very frequently in talmudic literature); a condensation of a biblical verse: "Do not place a wicked man as a witness" (Sanh. 27a; cf. Ex. 23:1); and a standardized, non-literal interpretation of a verse: "According to the majority [of judges] must the case be decided" (Sanh. 1:6; cf. Ex. 23:2).

TANNAITIC TIMES. A great number of maxims were developed in post-biblical and tannaitic times. They are cited in tannaitic literature, often anonymously and without their validity being challenged: "A man's agent is like the man himself" (Mekh. Pisḥa 5); "Local custom decides everything" (BM 7:1); and "A condition made contrary to an express biblical law is void" (Ket. 9:1; see *Contract). A number of tannaitic rules and maxims, on the other hand, represent minority opinions and are not binding: "Marriage takes no effect when there is a prohibitory law against it" (Akiva, Ket. 29b). Other tannaitic *kelalim*, although accepted, were disputed (cf., e.g., L. Ginzberg, *Perushim ve-Ḥiddushim ba-Yerushalmi*, 2 (1941), 159–64, on the rule, "Women are exempt from positive commandments which have a time limit"; Kid. 34a).

AMORAIC PERIOD. A significant increase in the wealth of legal maxims was accomplished by the *amoraim*. Many are recorded in the Jerusalem Talmud; for example: "No price can be put on a *Sefer Torah*" (BM 4:6) and "Unless otherwise stipulated, partners are to divide equally" (Ket. 10:4). A great wealth of maxims is found in the Babylonian Talmud; for example: "There is no agent in wrongful acts," a maxim explained by the following one: "If the Master's [God's] words conflict with the pupil's [the principal's] words, whose words shall we [who are called upon to act as agent] obey?" (Kid. 42b); and "Any acquisition made in error is voidable" (Git. 14a). All these are cited anonymously; many others are quoted in the name of the *amora* who first formulated them. "Less than the legal quantity is forbidden by the law of the Torah" (Johanan, Yoma 73b); "No man is presumed to have paid his debt before the time due" (Simeon b. Lakish, BB 5 a–b); and "A man is a kinsman unto himself, hence no man may incriminate himself" (Rava, Sanh. 9b; see *Confession). The *amoraim* succeeded in introducing numerous Aramaic legal maxims: "The law of the state is law" (**Dina de-Malkhuta Dina*; Git. 10b); "Force majeure (**Ones*) is excused by the law" (BK 28b) and "The stronger wins" (Git. 60b; see *Extraordinary Remedies). There appears to be no correlation between language and geography; Aramaic and Hebrew maxims were formulated by Babylonian and Palestinian *amoraim* equally.

Post-talmudic authorities coined very few maxims of law. A few such legal maxims may be gleaned from midrashic and medieval works: "One makes a festive meal to celebrate the conclusion of the Torah reading" (Song R. 1:1, no. 9). They usually contain moral overtones: "As long as advocacy for the accused has not ceased, the trial is not over" (*Midrash Sekhel Tov*, Gen. 19:1); "One cannot serve two masters" (Israel Davidson, *Oẓar ha-Meshalim ve-ha-Pitgamim*, 12, no. 126).

The Mishnaic *Kelal*

Of special interest is the mishnaic *kelal*. The Mishnah often formulates a general statement which summarizes numerous particulars. Sometimes the general statement is found at the beginning of a bill of particulars; sometimes it is found at the end. In the former case, the general statement is introduced by the expression "A general rule have they [the rabbis] stated" (*kelal ameru*, e.g., Pe'ah 1:4), or "A great rule have they stated" (*kelal gadol ameru*; e.g., Shab 7:1). In the latter, the general statement is introduced by the expression, "This is the general rule" (*zeh ha-kelal*; e.g., Ket. 3:9. For details cf. Frankel, Mishnah, 306 f.; see also *Codification of the Law). Like the Roman *regula*, the mishnaic *kelal* summarizes the law without being an authentic or complete expression of the law. The Roman jurist proclaims, "The law is not derived from the *regula*, rather the *regula* is deduced from the law" (Paulus, D. 50:17, 1). Similarly, a basic rule of mishnaic exegesis is enunciated by the Babylonian Talmud, "We deduce nothing from general statements" *Ein lemedin min ha-kelalot* (Kid. 34a). The Jerusalem Talmud expressed the same idea as follows, "The general statements made by Rabbi [Judah ha-Nasi, editor of the Mishnah] are not general statements" (*Leit kelalin de-Rabbi kelalan*; Ter. 1:1).

A good illustration of the nonauthoritative nature of the mishnaic *kelal* is found in the talmudic analysis of Mishnah *Kiddushin* 1:7. The Mishnah reads: "(a) With regard to all positive commandments which have a time limit – men are obligated and women are exempt; (b) With regard to all positive commandments which have no time limit – men and women are equally obligated; (c) With regard to negative commandments, regardless of whether they have or do not have a time limit – men and women are equally obligated except for the prohibitions of shaving [with a razor, Lev. 19:27], of removing sidelocks [*ibid.*], and of *kohanim* defiling themselves by contact with a human corpse [Lev. 21:1]. These three exceptions apply to men, not to women."

The Talmud (Kid. 34a–36a) records that, in "violation" of paragraph (a), women are obligated to observe the commandments of *maẓẓah* (Ex. 12:18), rejoicing on festivals (Deut. 16:14), and participation in the public assembly on Sukkot every seventh year (Deut. 31:12), although these commandments are positive and have a time limit. In "violation" of paragraph (b), women are exempt from the commandments of Torah study (Deut. 11:19), procreation (Gen. 1:28), and the redemption of the firstborn son (Ex. 13:13). Paragraph (c), however, admits of no exceptions. This would lead one to assume that a general statement which limits itself by adding "except for" is indeed authoritative, for the very concern for exceptions would appear to indicate the accuracy of the general statement in non-excepted instances. R. Johanan, a Palestinian *amora* of the third century, was therefore careful to point out, "We cannot learn from general principles, even where exceptions are stated" (see his proof from Er. 3:1). Thus, even where exceptions are specified, the *kelal* is not a truly general statement. As a result, Maimonides (Commentary on the Mishnah, Kid. 1:7) states that the word *kol* ("all," "every") in a *kelal*-statement must be understood as meaning nothing more than *rov* ("most").

Some would limit the rule, "We cannot learn from general principles," to general statements introduced by the word *kol*, as, for example, the *mishnayot* from *Kiddushin* and *Eruvin* cited in the previous two paragraphs (R. Jacob Berab, Nov. Kid. 34a, in: *Sefer ha-Yovel… B.M. Lewin*, 222 f.). Other authorities are of the opinion that the rule applies to statements formulated as a *kelal* as well (Nov. Ran, Meg. 19b). The rule is limited in application, however, only to those statements whose general nature is challenged by facts adduced from authoritative sources: "We on our own may not reject a general *kelal* which we have as a tradition from the rabbis; for if we do so, there is no limit and we can no longer depend upon our Talmud as edited, for it consists mainly of general statements" (*kelalot*; Rosh, Shevu. 6, para. 5). The Talmud itself never rejected a *kelal* except out of necessity or in deference to an oral tradition regarding the exception to the *kelal*; without such necessity or in the absence of an oral tradition, the accuracy of the general statement is to be accepted (Pseudo-Rashba, Men. 6b). Although the rule, "We cannot learn from *kelalot*," was formulated by the *amoraim* concerning general statements found in the tannaitic sources, the matter is disputed whether the rule holds true regarding amoraic *kalalim* as well (cf. *Yad Malakhi*, Kelalei Alef, 23). A similar dispute exists as to whether the rule applies equally to general statements found in the codes (R. Ẓevi Hirsch Ashkenazi, *Ḥakham Ẓevi*, 55, says that the rule does not apply; R. Jacob Reicher, *Ḥok Ya'akov*, 429, n. 8, and R. Alexander Schorr, *Tevu'ot Shor*, 32, n. 6, maintain that the rule does apply).

Compilations of Maxims

A bibliography of Hebrew works containing legal maxims, rules, and general principles is found in P. Jacob Kohn, *Oẓar ha-Be'urim ve-ha-Perushim* (1952), 448–62. Other books (published after 1952 and therefore not included in Kohn's bibliography) containing lists of maxims and rules are ET (as titles of individual articles); Elon, Mafte'aḥ, 405–412; Y.Y. Ḥasidah, *Oẓar Ma'amrei Halakhah* (3 vols., 1959–60); Joseph Schechter, *Oẓar ha-Talmud David Etrog, Peri Eẓ Hadar* (1952). The following works contain lists of Hebrew legal maxims, translated and explained in English: Lewis N. Dembitz, s.v. *Maxims, Legal*, in: *Jewish Encyclopedia*, vol. 8 (1904); George Horowitz, *The Spirit of Jewish Law* (1953), 99–104; M. Mielziner, *Legal Maxims and Fundamental Laws* (1898).

BIBLIOGRAPHY: ET, 1 (1951³), 295 f. and the works mentioned above. ADD. BIBLIOGRAPHY: M. Elon, *Ha-Mishpat ha-Ivri* (1988), see index; idem, *Jewish Law* (1994), see index; M. Elon and B. Lifshitz, *Mafte'aḥ ha-She'elot ve-ha-Teshuvot shel Ḥakhmei Sefarad u-Ẓefon Afrikah* (legal digest) (1986), 1:174–92; B. Lifshitz and E. Shochetman, *Mafte'aḥ ha-She'elot ve-ha-Teshuvot shel Ḥakhmei Ashkenaz, Ẓarefat ve-Italyah* (legal digest) (1997), 115–38.

[Aaron Kirschenbaum]

LEGAL PERSON, a body of men or of property which the law, in imitation of the personality of human beings, treats artificially as subject of rights and duties independent of its component parts. The classic example of a legal person is the corporation. Although the most familiar type of corporation is that engaged in business activities, history has witnessed corporations formed as the vehicle for charitable enterprises, cooperative nonprofit-making enterprises, municipal and governmental operations, and religious and social activities. For example, in the classical Roman legal system, the *universitates* – corporate groups which possessed common treasuries and were endowed with a legal personality separate and distinct from that of their individual members – included various municipal and religious, as well as industrial and trading, associations. The corporation has usually featured the following characteristics: a name common to the aggregate of its component individuals or properties; a life independent of the lives of its components; the possession of privileges or rights, liabilities or duties, which do not inhere in its membership as individuals; and the divorce of ownership and management, with the authority of the managers to act as the agents and representatives of the corporation being conferred, limited, and determined not by the consent of the owners but by the law itself.

Talmudic and Post-Talmudic Law

Traditional Jewish law apparently did not recognize the type of ownership implied in the idea of the corporation. Common ownership is ordinarily expressed in terms of *partnership (*shuttafut*; Maim. Yad, Sheluḥin ve-Shuttafin 4–10; Tur. and Sh. Ar., ḤM 157–82). The salient differences whereby the partnership may be distinguished from the corporation are: the continued existence of a partnership is dependent upon the lives of the partners or their respective heirs; the privileges, rights, liabilities, and duties associated with a partnership inhere almost directly in the individual members of the association; the manager of a partnership enterprise is construed as the agent of the component members. Although the corporation is not a juristic category in the classical sources of Jewish law, scholars have attempted, with various degrees of success, to find types of associations and proprietal arrangements in Jewish history which parallel or approximate the corporation and which may be regarded as embodiments of the concept of the legal or artificial person. The fruits of these attempts may be summarized as follows:

Hekdesh

*Hekdesh, the term for objects, animals, and money consecrated for the upkeep of the Temple precincts and for the sacrificial service therein. The administrator of this corporate body was the Temple treasurer (*gizbar*). All Temple properties were placed under the jurisdiction of the *gizbar*, at whose discretion acquisitions and sales of these properties were controlled and who was empowered to represent the interests of the Temple in litigation (Ḥag. 11a; BM 58a). Thus the typical feature of the modern corporation, the divorce of ownership and management, was the salient characteristic of *hekdesh* – for God was viewed as the "owner" and the *gizbar* the manager thereof.

On the other hand, the Temple corporation was unique in the world of commerce. Its acquisition of property was by consecration and its sales were by redemption; thus its transactions were governed by special rules. Moreover, there were numerous regulations that were inapplicable to *hekdesh* possessions, e.g., the rules of overreaching (*ona'ah) did not apply to Temple property, so that valuable properties could be redeemed at the cost of a perutah, the smallest coin; theft of *hekdesh* property was not punishable by the normal legal sanctions; construction of *hekdesh* appurtenances was accomplished while the materials were still unsanctified, and their consecration to the Temple took place only after the construction was completed (BM 57b; BK 62b; Me'il. 14b). Hence the corporate body of Temple properties may not be regarded as a typical legal person, subject to the normal rights and duties attributed to human beings.

Benei ha-Ir

Benei ha-Ir, the name given to the municipal community in talmudic parlance. In the Talmud, the community is regarded as an aggregate of the individuals who comprise its membership. The legal definition of this aggregate is that of a partnership. Thus, no member of the community could act as a witness in matters which affected communal property; he was disqualified as an interested party. The governing body of the community, known as the "seven notables of the city" (*shivah tovei ha-ir*), was regarded as an agent of the citizenry, and its acts had to be ratified by the citizenry meeting as a body (*be-ma'amad benei ha-ir*; Meg. 26a).

In post-talmudic jurisprudence, the community was converted from a juridical partnership to a corporate body with numerous features characteristic of a legal person. Communal transactions were no longer regarded as those of its constituent members. Municipal ordinances (takkanot *ha-kahal) could no longer be vetoed by individual citizens; the ruling of the majority members of the governing body was binding on all members of the community. Members of the community, no longer regarded as interested parties, were accepted as witnesses in matters affecting the municipality (see *Beit Yosef*, ḤM 37, notes 12 and 14; *Sma*, ḤM 156, note 6). Thus the body politic came to be clothed with an existence juridically independent of the citizens who comprised it.

Havurat Ẓedakah

Havurat Ẓedakah, the communal charity fund, which eventually evolved into a legal person. In the Talmud, the poor were construed as owners of the monies deposited in the charity fund, and the communal collectors were viewed as their agents (BK 36b). This created disadvantages for the poor, for the rule of procedure in the Talmud was that interests of indeterminate plaintiffs were not actionable (mamon she-ein lo tovin, Rashi, BK 93a). As in the case of benei ha-ir, here, too, post-talmudic jurisprudence endowed charity funds with the character of an artificial person. An association (ḥavurah) founded for charitable purposes was regarded as somewhat akin to the modern corporation, i.e., an aggregate of property earmarked for specific purpose, with the ḥavurah construed as the means created for the advancement of this purpose. The collectors and administrators of the charitable ḥavurah were henceforth classed as its managerial staff fully authorized to conduct its affairs. This authorization included the power to bring suit in court to protect the interests of the funds under its supervision (see Beit Yosef, ḤM 149, note 37; Netivot ha-Mishpat, ḤM 149, Mishpat ha-Kohanim, note 46). It is quite possible that an additional example of a legal person in Jewish history may be found among the *Qumran and *Essene sects, which were based upon the renunciation of private property on the part of their members (cf. E. Koffmahn, in Biblica, 42 (1961), 433–42, and 44 (1963), 46–61).

In Modern Rabbinic Law

The problem of the corporation and its application to Jewish law has arisen in the following areas:

Interest on Loans

Inasmuch as Jewish law forbids lending and borrowing money on interest to or from Jews (see *Usury), the question has arisen whether (or how) Jewish people may conduct the normal transactions involved in banking, *insurance, and the like, and whether (or how) they may invest in such companies without violating the religious restrictions created by the participation of other Jewish people therein.

Sabbath Law

The religious restriction on labor on the Sabbath includes the prohibition of aiding and abetting, as well as deriving benefit from, the labor of others, non-Jews and, more so, Jews. How may a Jew be a stockholder in a company whose operations include Sabbath labor?

Passover Restrictions

A Jew may not eat, derive benefit from, or possess *ḥameẓ* during the Passover season. How do these restrictions affect the permissibility to invest in companies which do business with *ḥameẓ*?

The response of the rabbinic authorities of the past one hundred years has been divided. The controversy may be summarized in the following manner. One school of rabbis is of the opinion that, inasmuch as the traditional sources do not recognize the concept of legal personality in normal commerce and trade, the corporation is, halakhically, nothing more than the conventional partnership. Hence, the rules of partnership are to be applied to the questions of loans on interest, Sabbath labor, and *ḥameẓ*, and only the dispensations traditionally allowed within the framework of partnerships may be allowed with regard to corporations. These, it must be added, are highly circumscribed (e.g., Solomon Ganzfried, *Kiẓẓur Shulḥan Arukh* 65:28 and Isaac Wasserman, in: *No'am*, 3 (1960), 195–203, regarding loans; Moses Feinstein, *Iggerot Moshe*, vol. 1, OḤ 90, regarding the Sabbath; Israel Be'eri, in: *Ha-Torah ve-ha-Medinah*, 11–13 (1960–62), 454–62, regarding all three questions). Another group of authorities, although in agreement with the first group in refusing to recognize the corporation as a unique and novel halakhic category, has nevertheless, through involved reasoning, found ways of avoiding the traditional restrictions and has been able to permit Orthodox Jews to invest in and conduct transactions with corporations (e.g., Ẓevi Hirsch Shapiro, *Darkhei Teshuvah*, YD 160:15, note 121, and M.N. Lemberger, in: *No'am*, 2 (1959), 33–37; 4 (1961), 251–7. Both these authorities address themselves to the problem of loans. Moses Feinstein, *Iggerot Moshe*, EH 7, places great stress on the extent to which management is divorced from ownership).

There is, however, a third group of modern talmudists who have taken full cognizance of the divorce of ownership from management in the corporation and of the artificiality of the corporate personality. This school of rabbis has come to the resultant conclusion that the traditional restrictions placed upon individual businessmen or partnerships with regard to the laws of usury, Sabbath rest, and *ḥameẓ*, are inapplicable to the corporation (e.g., Aryeh Leib Horowitz, *Harei Besamim*, 115; Moses Sternbuch, *Mo'adim u-Zemannim*, vol. 1, p. 203f.; Joseph Rosin, *Ẓafenat Pa'ne'aḥ*, 184, regarding loans; David Ẓvi Hoffmann, *Melammed le-Ho'il*, OḤ 91, regarding *ḥameẓ*). Permission has also been granted to buy and sell shares in companies that do business in non-kosher foods, although an individual is forbidden by the *halakhah* to engage in regular transactions involving such foods (Gedaliah Felder, in: *Kol Torah*, 6 (1959), nos. 7–11).

In connection with the ritual requirement that one who "takes" the *lulav* and *etrog* on the holiday of Sukkot must have title in it in order to fulfill the commandment properly, an interesting discussion arose in the circles of the religious kibbutzim in Israel whether, and to what extent, the kibbutzim constituted a legal person and what their status was in the eyes of Jewish traditional law (cf. A. Nachlon, in: *Ammudim* (Ha-Kibbutz ha-Dati, 1956), nos. 123, 124; (1957), nos. 126, 128).

[Aaron Kirschenbaum]

A trend toward acknowledging the status of an association of people as a legal person was already discernible during the period of the *rishonim*, regarding the relationship between the members of the Jewish community and the *kahal* – the community council. A responsum of the Rashba evidences this trend, in a case concerning payment of taxes by community members for the community's needs. According to the responsum, when the community council took a loan to finance the needs of the community, it was entitled to make an enactment that each member of the community would pay his portion of the loan according to his financial position at the time of repayment, notwithstanding that, according to the rules of partnership, the partners' obligation to repay a loan is determined in relation to their share in the partnership at the time the loan was taken. Following this line of reasoning, the community's debt should be repaid according to the financial position of each member of the community at the time the loan was taken. In the responsum, the new enactment is explained as reflecting the difference between the private law governing a loan received by individual partners, as opposed to the public law governing a loan received by the community:

> A community that borrows for public needs differs from those who borrow for themselves, for it borrows on behalf of the communal treasury on the assumption that it will pay the debt out of what is found in the treasury at the time of payment. This is the custom everywhere. Those who were poor and became wealthy or were wealthy and became poor… pay only according to the assessment made against each at the time of payment. This is our practice and it would be impossible to function otherwise … (Resp. Rashba, III, no. 412).

This was, however, a special provision regarding the amount of the tax payable (see Bibliography, Elon (1988), 626–629; idem, (1994) 773–78), and should be viewed as only the first step towards developing a special status for a public organization as distinguished from the status of the individual.

In the Rulings of the Rabbinical Courts in Israel – Incorporation by Means of Custom

In the Israeli rabbinical courts, the question of the existence and identity of a corporation as an independent legal person was dealt with from a number of perspectives not dealt with above. In the *Shikun u-Fitu'aḥ* case (3301/717/1965, 6 PDR 315; Regional Rabbinical Court, Tel Aviv), the rabbinical court considered the validity and applicability of a corporate obligation for which its managers and workers, or those working on its behalf, bore no personal liability, all the corporate transactions being secured exclusively by the corporate assets. In addressing this question, the rabbinical court cited two views: The first view regards an encumbrance on assets as applying to the assets as such, as entities existing independent of the corporation. Accordingly, there is nothing to prevent an analogy being drawn from assets to a corporation. In other words, even if the corporation itself is not a recognized legal person, the obligation would be valid by force of the encumbrance of its assets. The second view, however, regards the encumbrance of assets as being effected exclusively by force of the guarantee, i.e., the encumbrance of the property stems from the obligation of the one undertaking the obligation (*Piskei ha-Rosh, Kiddushin,* 1:10; *Avnei Miluim,* 29:10). According to this view, a corporate obligation would only be valid if the law were to recognize the corporation as a legal person. The rabbinical court ruled that the corporate obligation must be recognized in any event, notwithstanding the uncertainty of the definition of the legal entity giving the undertaking, given that the only issue involved is the encumbrance of assets, insofar as the custom, as well as the law of the state, recognize the validity of corporate obligations (see *Minhag; *Dina de-Malkhuta Dina).

In a later decision (11183/1972, 10 PDR 273, 285ff.), the rabbinical court took another step in the same direction, holding that a corporation should be viewed as an independent legal entity, and hence the legal validity of its actions be recognized. This decision dealt with a plaintiff who had hired the services of a company to do work for him. The defendants claimed that the company's original owners had died and that they, the defendants, were merely their heirs, who had inherited ownership of the company. The rabbinical court had to decide, inter alia, if the heirs should themselves be considered the defendants, in which case there would be difficulties in recovering the debt (see *Orphan), or whether the defendant is the company itself, in its capacity as an autonomous legal entity. The rabbinical court rejected the assumption, expressed by halakhic authorities of recent generations, that "it is impossible to invent new definitions of ownership that have no Talmudic basis," relying on the halakhic principle whereby "a person who contracts [i.e., makes a stipulation] contrary to what is written in the Torah in a civil matter – his contract (stipulation) is valid" – and the *halakhah* accords binding force to the custom of traders (*sitomta;* the rabbinical court refers to Resp. Maharashdam, ḤM, no.380; Resp. Divrei Ḥayyim, vol. 2, ḤM no. 26; *Minḥat Ḥinukh, mitzvah* 42). The rabbinical court ruled that this legal entity may be viewed as an "encumbrance of property without an encumbrance of the body," and may therefore be classified as belonging to the same rubric as "the public" – a concept already recognized as a legal entity in its own right, as distinct from the individual, in Talmudic literature.

The *Wilozni* decision (HCJ 323/81, *Wilozni v. The Rabbinical Court of Appeals*, 36(2) PD 733) contains an extensive discussion (per Justice Menachem Elon) of the problem of the relationship between Jewish law and another legal system within which it operates (*ibid.*, p. 740ff). At the beginning of its discussion, the Court notes that in the rabbinical court, by dint of the doctrine of "**dina de-malkhuta dina*," the law of the general legal system is given binding effect but, as a result of this doctrine, does not become part of the Jewish legal system (*ibid.*, p. 740). In its decision the Court further stated as follows:

> Sometimes Jewish law not only recognizes the binding effect of the law of another legal system, but even incorporates that law as a part of the Jewish legal system itself. The legal source by means of which this is accomplished is custom. When the people conduct their activities according to a particular legal norm, this norm is recognized, under certain circumstances, as a part of Jewish law; and the norm is sometimes effective even if contrary to a specific rule of Jewish civil law. Just as two individuals may agree in a civil law matter to contract out of a law contained in the Torah, so, *a fortiori*, the public may stipulate by means of a custom to opt out of an existing halakhic rule in a matter of civil law (see, for example, the responsum of Samuel de Medina (Salonika, 16th century), *Resp. Maharashdam*, ḤM No. 380). This principle is expressed in the formulation "custom overrides the law" (TJ BM 7.1). I have already dealt with this in detail in the context of the incorporation of the law concerning joint ownership of property (see CA 2/66, p. 15–17; M. Elon, *Ha-Mishpat ha-Ivri* (1988), pp. 713 ff., 739 ff.; regarding the law governing joint ownership of property; see also under *Matrimonial Property; **Dina de-Malkhuta Dina*). Custom as a legal source in Jewish law is known by the technical term *sitomta* (meaning "seal"), from the case precedent discussed in the Talmud concerning the customary practice of purchasing wine by affixing a seal on the barrel; it was in conjunction with that practice that the principle of the creative power and binding force and the creation of custom was developed and elabo-

rated (TB BM 74a). The doctrine of custom served as the means for extensive developments in various areas of Jewish law, particularly regarding the laws of acquisitions and obligations …" (see *Minhag for an extensive discussion).

To substantiate its position, the Court cites examples from halakhic sources and the decisions of the rabbinical courts, inter alia the example of "incorporation of the concept of a legal person" in the rabbinical court decisions dealt with above.

BIBLIOGRAPHY: L. Loew, in: *Ben Chananja*, 8 (1965), 77–83, 92–99, 108–15, 124–9; reprinted in his *Gesammelte Schriften*, 2 (1890), 133–64; Gulak, Yesodei, 1 (1922), 50–54; 2 (1922), 84 n. 2; 4 (1922), 63f.; Gulak, Oẓar, 345ff.; idem, *Le-Ḥeker Toledot ha-Mishpat ha-Ivri bi-Tekufat ha-Talmud*, 1 (*Dinei Karka'ot*, 1929), 124; idem, *Toledot ha-Mishpat be-Yisrael bi-Tekufat ha-Talmud*, 1 (*Ha-Ḥiyyuv ve-Shi'budav*, 1939), 90, 95n. 37a, 112; B. Safra, in: *Ha-Mishpat ha-Ivri*, 2 (1927), 45f.; P.W. Duff, *Personality in Roman Private Law* (1938); A. Karlin, in: *Sinai*, 4 (1938/39), 445–52; D. Weinreb, in: PAAJR, 19 (1950), 225–9 (Eng. summ. 100–2); ET, 3 (1951), 374–9; 5 (1953), 435–8; 10 (1961), 342–442; S. Huebner, in: *Hadorom*, 24 (1966), 108–16; S. Miron, in: *Sinai*, 59 (1966), 228–45. **ADD. BIBLIOGRAPHY:** M. Elon, *Ha-Mishpat ha-Ivri* (1988), 1:626; 3:1532, 1533; *ibid, Jewish Law* (1994), 2:774; 4:1821, 1823; B. Eliash, "*Le-She'eilat Zekhuto ha-Mishpatit shel ha-Ẓibbur*," in: *Dinei Israel*, 3 (1972), 15–29; C. Povarsky, "*Shi'bud Nekhasim be-Mishpat ha-Ivri*," in: *Dinei Yisrael*, 12, 155–71; Y. Benisti, "*Ha-Ishiyyut ha-Mishpatit ha-Nifredet – le-Halakhah u-le-Ma'aseh*," in: *Shaarei Mishpat*, pt. 1 (1998), 349–57.

LEGHORN (Livorno), main port of Tuscany, central Italy. In the middle of the 16th century, when Leghorn was a miserable, malaria-infested village, its rulers, the Medici, decided to turn it into an important port and to attract foreigners to settle it. An invitation was accordingly issued by Cosimo I in 1548, but although of benefit to fugitive Marranos who could have found asylum there, his project met with little success. After 1590 Ferdinand I issued new invitations with more attractive promises. The official invitation issued on June 10, 1593, was addressed to the merchants of every nation, but in reality the majority of its articles were directed to the Jews who had lived as Christians in Spain and Portugal. The charter – usually called "Livornina" – guaranteed full religious liberty, amnesty for crimes previously committed, the opportunity for "Marranos" to return to Judaism unmolested, a large exemption from taxation, and commercial freedom. The Grand Duke authorized the heads of the community (*massari*) to accept the settlers and grant them the privileges of the charter; the five *massari* (later assisted by 12 deputies) exercised full civil jurisdiction among the Jews, and partly also criminal jurisdiction. All commercial suits were decided according to the laws of the Grand Duchy of Tuscany, but the right was given to the parties to be judged according to rabbinical law. The *massari* constituted a sort of hereditary oligarchy composed of rich Sephardi merchants; only in 1715 were Italian Jews admitted to the government of the Nazione ebrea ("Jewish Nation," the name of the community until the 19th century). Settlers were given the opportunity of owning houses and exemption from wearing the Jewish *badge and from other vexations. The Nazione also had the right to inherit property left by Jews who died without direct heirs.

The Medici went ahead energetically with improvements to the town and harbor, which in 1675 received the status of a free port. Leghorn thus became an important center for the trade between the Atlantic and North Sea ports and those of the Mediterranean and the Near East. Both international and internal commerce was transacted mainly by the foreign communities or "nations" living in Leghorn, of which the "Jewish nation" soon became the largest and most influential. During the first few years the Jews were slow to arrive, but subsequently their numbers increased rapidly. There were 134 Jews in Leghorn in 1601; 711 in 1622; 1,250 in 1645; and approximately 2,400 in 1693. The new settlers were either of Spanish origin having arrived via North Africa or Turkey, or Marranos, mainly from Portugal; relatively few Jews came there from the Italian states. Thus Portuguese and Spanish became the only languages used officially by the Jews in Leghorn. In 1614, the Leghorn community seceded from the community of Pisa, on which it had until then been dependent, and subsequently became far more important. The Jews continued to enjoy the protection of the Medici, and the original promises given were adhered to, or only slightly revised. Even under the bigoted Cosimo III (d. 1723), the restrictions imposed upon the Jews in Leghorn were not serious, mainly relating to the employment of Christian wet-nurses and Turkish slaves, and sexual relations with Christian women. When the sovereignty of Tuscany passed to the house of Lorraine in 1737, this goodwill remained unaltered. The Jews benefited from the enlightened reforms of Leopold I (1745–1790), and in 1780 obtained, among other privileges, the right to have a representative on the municipal council. The number of Jews living in Leghorn increased from 3,476 in 1738 to 4,300 in 1784, and to 4,694 in 1806, amounting to one-eighth of the total population. Among the larger Italian communities, Leghorn Jewry was the only one to remain without a closed ghetto. Jewish residence was limited to a single, though fairly large, open quarter, though Christians were not permitted to reside in the houses of Jews.

At first the Jews in Leghorn specialized in certain industries, such as working of coral, which they exported as far as Russia and India, and soap and paper manufacture. Later, they utilized their family and commercial connections in various ports of the Mediterranean to develop a widespread bilateral trade. To facilitate this exchange, the Jews in Leghorn sent members of their families to Tripoli, Tunis, and Smyrna, whence others moved to Leghorn. Jews from Leghorn organized themselves in a special community in Tunis in 1685, calling themselves Grana (i.e., from Ligorno = Leghorn). This family and business exchange developed at the end of the 18th century, and even more so in the 19th century, particularly with Egypt. The Jews of Leghorn who settled in these regions constituted a sort of Mediterranean diaspora which embodied western values. In 1738, about 150 Jews owned houses in Leghorn, and in 1765 one-third of Leghorn's 150 commercial houses were Jewish-owned. Jews also owned shops of all types in the town, and were generally prosperous.

This situation deteriorated after the occupation of Leghorn by the French at various times after 1796. Not only was the port hard hit by the English blockade, but since parity was conceded to all by the French, the special privileges formerly held by the Jews were abrogated. They were partly restored in 1814, on the return of the grand dukes of Lorraine. However, after a few decades of recovery, the commercial importance of Leghorn began to wane when Tuscany was annexed to the Kingdom of Italy in 1859, and other ports began to show competition. These events were reflected in the fluctuations of the Jewish population. It dwindled to 4,497 in 1837 and rose to 4771 in 1841, after a temporary influx from other Italian towns; by the end of the 19th century, the number had diminished to 2,500. With the first emancipation of 1848, the Jews were allowed to take part in the Civil Guard of the Grand Duchy of Tuscany and declared equals in rights to all the other citizens of the State; in spite of the end of their privileges, the Jews of Leghorn generally welcomed this emancipation positively, in a patriotic Italian way. The same can be said after the second emancipation of 1859, when Italy became a unitary state. During the 19th and the beginning of the 20th centuries, the observance of religious practice diminished considerably, but the fidelity to the community remained steadfast far beyond the secularization process.

The golden age of Jewish Leghorn left many traces. Construction of a new synagogue was begun toward the end of the 16th century, but its subsequent enlargement and embellishment continued until 1789. The Leghorn synagogue became the most admired in Italy, and was visited by the grand dukes of Tuscany and foreign sovereigns.

The community in Leghorn maintained a varied and efficient network of institutions, including a considerable number for charitable or educational purposes. Most important were the *talmud torah*, a public and compulsory school where religious subjects were taught (from 1728 also a vernacular language – probably Spanish – arithmetic, and accounting), and the institutions providing for the ransom of Jewish prisoners, assistance to the poor in the Holy Land, and dowries for poor girls. There were also a number of yeshivot in Leghorn that trained the rabbis for the local community, and for many other communities in Europe and the Mediterranean area until World War II. Rabbis and *maskilim* (a lesser title) gathered in the Yeshiva Kelalit, a consultative council. Among the most eminent rabbis were Joseph *Ergas, *Malachi b. Jacob ha-Kohen, Hezekiah da *Silva, Immanuel Ḥay *Ricchi, David *Nieto, and Ḥayyim Joseph David *Azulai, who spent the last 30 years of his life in Leghorn. The poets Immanuel *Francés (1618–1710) and Abraham Isaac Castello (1726–1789) were members of the rabbinical institutions; Josef Attias (1672–1746) was an outstanding figure in the Italian Enlightenment; the family of Sir Moses *Montefiore originated from Leghorn; and Sabato *Morais, founder of the Jewish Theological Seminary of America, was born there. In the second half of the 19th century, the dominant figure in Jewish scholarship in Leghorn was the kabbalist Elijah *Benamozegh.

Leghorn also became a center of Hebrew printing. The first Hebrew press was set up by Jedidiah Gabbai (1650). Some 80 years later, Abraham b. Raphael Meldola, followed by his son Raphael, both with various partners, were active as Hebrew printers (1740–57). Sixteen other printers set up in Leghorn between 1763 and 1870, the most important being the house of Solomon Belforte (established in 1838) which supplied the North African and Levantine market with liturgical books until the outbreak of World War II. From 1600 to 1899, almost 1,300 Hebrew books were printed in the typographies of Leghorn, which was second in Italy only to Venice.

[Attilio Milano / Alessandro Guetta (2nd ed.)]

During the Holocaust at least 119 Jews were sent to Auschwitz from Nov. 12, 1943, out of the 2,235 who lived in the city in 1938; only 11 survived. Others were killed in the surrounding mountains, where the German army was very active. The well-known synagogue was partially destroyed in a bombing raid by the Allies, in 1944. At the end of the war about 1,000 Jews were living in Leghorn. Owing to emigration and rapid demographic decline, their number in 1965 was reduced to about 600 out of a total of 170,000 inhabitants. In 1962 a new synagogue was dedicated, financed by the Italian state; it was erected in the same place as the old one but in modern style, thus symbolizing continuity and hope for the future. In 1967 after the *Six-Day War, a few hundred Jews from Libya and other Arab countries arrived in Leghorn, partly attracted by the presence of a number of Jews from Tripoli. The community had an elementary Hebrew school until 1983.

[Sergio DellaPergola / Alessandro Guetta (2nd ed.)]

BIBLIOGRAPHY: A.S. Toaff, *Cenni storici sulla Comunita ebraica e sulla Sinagoga di Livorno* (1955); Milano, Bibliotheca, index, s.v. *Livorno*; A. Lattes and A.S. Toaff, *Studi ebraici a Livorno nel secolo 18* (1900); G. Sonnino, *Storia della tipografia ebraica in Livorno* (1912); Milano, Italia, index. **ADD. BIBLIOGRAPHY:** Y. Rofe, in: *Tagim*, 2 (1971); *Rassegna Mensile di Israel*, 50 (9–12), 1984; R. Toaff, *La Nazione ebrea a Livorno e a Pisa* (1990); J.P. Filippini, *Il porto di Livorno e la Toscana* (1998); M. Luzzati (ed.), *Le tre sinagoghe* (1995).

LEGIO (**Tel Shalem**), a Roman settlement which grew up around the camp of the Legio Sexta Ferrata (Ironsides), and established on the site of the Jewish village of Kefar Otnay after the Bar Kokhba War (132–35).

The legion received the imperial (formerly Herodian) estates in the Jezreel Valley as its territory, later passing them on to the settlement which superseded the camp; hence the plain is known in patristic literature as Campus maximus Legionis ("the great plain of Legio"; Eusebius, Onom. 14:21; *Itinerarium Burdigalense*, 19:19).

Toward the end of the third century C.E., Legio received the name Maximianopolis in honor of the Emperor Maximian, Diocletian's co-ruler (Hierocles, *Synecdemus*, 720:10). In Byzantine times it was the seat of a bishop and belonged to

Palaestina Secunda. In Arab times its area in the vicinity of Megiddo was occupied by the village of al-Lajjūn.

A kibbutz called Megiddo has been established there since 1949. Ancient remains include a Roman theater and cemetery.

However, the most important of the remains is a bronze statue of Hadrian. The statue is slightly bigger than a person. It is probable that it stood in the Praetorium of the military camp. The Roman emperor is depicted dressed in a cuirass decorated with relief depicting a battle scene from the Aeneid. However, according to scholars it is possible that the battle scene is in fact an allegoric depiction of Hadrian's victory over Bar Kokhba.

BIBLIOGRAPHY: Muehlinen, in: ZDPV, 31 (1908), 125; Schumacher, in: MNDPV, 10 (1904), 38; 12 (1906), 68; Lifshitz, in: BIES, 23 (1959), 53ff. **ADD. BIBLIOGRAPHY:** G. Foerster, "A Cuirassed Bronze Statue of Hadrian from a Roman Fort near Beth Shean (Scythopolis)," in: *The Israel Museum News*, 16 (1980), 107–110.

[Michael Avi-Yonah / Samuele Rocca (2nd ed.)]

LEGNICA (Ger. **Liegnitz**), town in Lower Silesia, Wroclaw province, S.W. Poland. The first reliable evidence of Jewish settlement dates from 1301, although Jews were probably resident in the city by the end of the 13th century. A "*Judenstadt*" (*Civitas Judeorum*) is mentioned in 1317. In 1345 the burghers were permitted by the duke to use Jewish gravestones for construction purposes; at that time a synagogue was also in existence. Following the agitations of John of *Capistrano in 1453 all but two of the residents were expelled from the Jewish street. These were arrested and perished in the burning jail. A few Jews were allowed to reside in the town in the 16th century but under severe restrictions. In 1812 some Jews settled in the town, establishing a prayer hall and cemetery (1815). By 1840 it had 254 Jews, rising to 970 (2.61% of the total population) in 1880. Subsequently the number of Jews remained stable, although their percentage of the total population declined. In 1932 the Orthodox community maintained a rabbi, two cantor-teachers, a library, *mikveh*, school, and a home for the aged (founded 1928). On the night of Nov. 10, 1938 the synagogue was set on fire. The community was forced to sell the property, which was converted into a parking lot, at a fraction of its value, and pay for clearing away the ruins. By May 1939 only 188 Jews remained; 41 of these were deported to *Theresienstadt on July 27, 1941. After the war a new community was organized, but by 1970 it had dwindled to only a few Jews.

BIBLIOGRAPHY: M. Peritz, *Aus der Geschichte der juedischen Gemeinde zu Liegnitz* (1912); M. Krieg, in: *Juedische Familien-Forschung*, 1 (1925–27), 144–7; E. Wolbe, *ibid.*, 2 (1928–30), 155–7; G. Helmrich, *Geschichte der Juden in Liegnitz* (1938); FJW, 100; Germ Jud, 1 (1963), 159; 2 (1968), 480–1; PK Germanyah.

LEGUMES, a general name for plants of the family of Papilionaceae of the order Leguminae. In the Mishnah legumes are referred to as *kitniyyot*, a name derived from *katan* ("small"; cf. It.: *leguma* or *minutia*), because the seeds are usually small. Though species with large seeds like *pol* ("broad bean," *Vicia faba*) belong to this family, at least in one source this species is not included among *kitniyyot* (Ḥul. 52a). Although in his Mishnah commentary (Kil. 2:2) Maimonides enumerates among *kitniyyot* only legumes, including the broad bean, in the *Mishneh Torah* he includes among them other species, such as rice, durra, poppy-seed and sesame (*Spices; Yad, Ḥameẓ u-Maẓẓah; 5:1). This definition of *kitniyyot* was taken over by other authorities, who went further and included among them many other edible seeds excluding cereals (wheat, barley, oats, etc.) which are classed as *dagan* ("corn") and regarded maize as a species of *kitniyyot*. This definition affected the laws of Passover, since among Ashkenazim *kitniyyot* are permitted them only in time of emergency. It should be noted that the Mishnah distinguishes between *kitniyyot* on the one hand and rice, durra, millet, and sesame on the other (Hal. 1:4). Thus *kitniyyot* originally referred only to legumes. Nowadays, a field in which legumes have been grown is considered most suitable for crop rotation with cereals. In ancient times this was not regarded as important and doubts arose whether legumes exhaust the soil more than wheat (BM 9:8; cf. BM 107a). It is to be noted that in recent years similar doubts have arisen. Legumes are richer in proteins than cereals but are not as easily digestible. They were mainly the food of the common people (see *Beans). A guest who prolonged his stay would be fed by his host with legumes (Tanh. B., Num. 156). A wife whose husband was obliged to provide her with food received four times as much wheat as legumes (Ket. 5:8), and this was probably the relation between the sown areas of cereals and *kitniyyot*.

Two species of legumes are mentioned in the Bible: *adashim* ("*lentils") and *pol* ("broad beans"). Lentils were the most important and one of the earliest plants in the region. In the Bible the term *pol* denotes only the broad bean but in rabbinic literature it was transferred by the addition of a denominative to other species too. Thus for instance *pol ha-miẓri* ("Egyptian bean") was cowpea, *pol he-ḥaruv* ("carob bean") yard-long bean. Besides these legumes, two species of *Lupinus* are mentioned in rabbinic literature: *turmus* – *Lupinus termis*, and *polaslos* ("yellow lupine") – *Lupinus luteus* (Kil 1:3). The lupine was a cheap food and thus of importance for the poor. Because of their bitterness, the seeds had to be soaked in water or cooked a number of times, and the liquid poured off (Ber. 38b, et al.). At least two species of the genus *Lathyrus* were grown: *tofaḥ* ("grass pea") – *Lathyrus sativus*, and *porkedan* ("red grass pea") – *Lathyrus cicera*, both of which were considered one species as regards *mixed species (*kilayim*; Kil. 1:1). These names may include also other species of the genus *Lathyrus*, some of which grow wild in Israel and are sown at times by the *fellaḥin*. Some are of the opinion that *asisiyyot* or *asasiyyot* (Tosef., Shab. 3:1; TJ, Shab. 3:1, 5d) are also a species of *Lathyrus*. Today these are mainly grown as fodder, except for grass pea which is used for human consumption. The seeds are soaked in water and crushed; the taste is similar to that of broad beans (Tosef., Ter. 6:11).

Two species of vetch are mentioned in the Mishnah: *sappir* ("French vetch") – *Vicia narbonensis*, and *karshinah* ("bitter vetch") – *Vicia ervilia*, the latter used for fodder. *Sappir* is considered to be of the same species as *pol* for the law of *kilayim* (Kil. 1:1), and the plants and seeds of these two species of vetch are indeed very similar. According to the Jerusalem Talmud (TJ, Kil. 1:1, 27a), a *tanna* named Hillel b. Valas had a Hebrew-Aramaic dictionary, as well as, apparently, a Hebrew-Latin-Greek one, of plant names in which *sappir* was identified with *pisonah*, the Latin *pisum* which is the garden pea, *Pisum sativum*. This identification is doubtful and there are no other references in the Mishnah and Talmud to the growing of this pea. The Mishnah mentions once a legume *she'u'it* which is considered the same species as *pol ha-lavan* ("white beans"; Kil. 1:1). In R. Hillel's dictionary of plants *she'u'it* was identified with *pesilta* by which is meant the nile cowpea, *Vigna nilotica*, and *pol ha-lavan* with hyacinth bean, *Dolichos lablab*. In modern Hebrew the name *she'u'it* is used for the genus *Phasoleus*. This botanical genus originated in America, however, and was unknown to the ancients.

A valuable plant was the chick-pea, *Cicer arietinum*, called *ḥamiẓ*. This is mentioned once in the Bible (Isa. 30:24). It was called *ḥamiẓ* because of the vinegary taste of the young seeds and the pod. The Mishnah calls it אֲפוּנִים (*afunim*, sing. אָפּוּן, *afun*), apparently from אַפּוֹן (*appon*; "small nose"), because it has a projection like a small nose on the round seed. These are frequently mentioned in rabbinic literature, a number of species being grown: large and small (Kil. 3:2), light and dark (TJ, Dem. 2:1, 22c). The Mishnah notes that it is a summer plant (Shev. 2:8). This is a decisive proof against the view of those who identify the *afunim* with garden peas which are definitely winter plants (though this latter identification has been accepted in modern Hebrew). Today chick-pea is especially popular among Oriental Jews, who prepare from it a piquant dish called *ḥumus*. One of the most valuable legumes was the plant *tiltan* (a name used today for clover), fenugreek, *Trigonella foenumgraecum*. Its leaves were grown for fodder and its seeds eaten when green or hard (Ma'as. Sh. 2:3; Tosef., *ibid.* 2:1). Its seeds are similar to those of the carob, and fenugreek was sometimes adulterated with carob seeds (Tosef., BK 7:8). Although *tiltan* is not mentioned in the Bible the Talmud states that Joshua made a number of regulations concerning it (BK 80b–81a). Nowadays it is grown chiefly for fodder, although the Yemenites grind the seeds to prepare a pungent sauce called *ḥilbah*.

BIBLIOGRAPHY: Loew, Flora, 2 (1924), 410–4; H.N. and A.L. Moldenke, *Plants of the Bible* (1952), 34f., 254; J. Feliks, *Ha-Ḥakla'ut be-Ereẓ Yisrael bi-Tekufat ha-Mishnah ve-ha-Talmud* (1963), 178–80, 273–5; idem, *Kilei Zera'im ve-Harkavah* (1967), 33–43, 71–89, 194f., 230–2.

[Jehuda Feliks]

LEHAVIM (Heb. לְהָבִים), urban settlement in southern Israel. Lehavim is located on the southwestern slopes of the Judean Hills, in the northern Negev, 985 ft. (300 m.) above sea level and 9 mi. (15 km.) north of Beersheba. The settlement was founded by the Benei Shimon Regional Council and the Israel Land Authority as an upscale suburban setting within easy commuting distance from Beersheba. In 1989 Lehavim received municipal council status. In 2002 its population was 4,770, on a land area of 1 sq. mi. (2.5 sq. km.).

WEBSITE: www.lehavim.muni.il.

[Shaked Gilboa (2nd ed.)]

LEHIGH VALLEY, a region in southeastern Pennsylvania, U.S., encompassing the cities of Allentown, Bethlehem, and Easton in the Pennsylvania counties of Lehigh and Northampton; general population estimated at 650,000 (2005); Jewish population estimated at 8,000. The majority of the Jewish community presently resides in Allentown.

Believed to be the first Jews to pass through the Lehigh Valley, members of the newly arrived Jewish community of New Amsterdam, Isaac Israel and Benjamin Cardozo, received authority in 1655 to trade with the native Indians along the upper Delaware River. The settlement of Jews in the Lehigh Valley begins when Myer Hart, a trader of Spanish-Portuguese ancestry, appears on a list of Easton's founders in 1750. Although one of the wealthier of Easton's first citizens, Hart left Easton by 1790 after he suffered financial reverses during the Revolution. The first Jewish cemetery was purchased by Michael Hart (unrelated) from the Penn family in the 1790s. Hart was sufficiently prominent that he received George Washington on his visit to Easton in the 1780s. Despite a large Hart family, there is no record of a permanent Jewish community in Easton until the late 1830s.

Allentown's earliest record of Jews includes a 1760 land purchase by Mordecai Moses Mordecai from James Allen, son of the founder of Allentown. Permanent Jewish settlement began in Allentown in 1847. Until the 1840s, Bethlehem was restricted only to Moravians.

The canal and railroad boom of the 1830s and 1840s attracted a small number of German-Jewish immigrants, mainly to Easton, where the oldest Jewish congregation in the Lehigh Valley (and the tenth oldest synagogue in the United States), Covenant of Peace, was founded in 1839. Over the next 40 years additional immigrants, mostly from Germany and Hungary, found their way to all three Valley cities. These Jewish immigrants may have been attracted to the region by the many German-speaking residents already in the Lehigh Valley as well as by its advantageous location for trade at the confluence of the Delaware and Lehigh rivers.

The arrival of the Eastern European Jews in the 1880s saw the near-simultaneous founding of new synagogues in all three cities. With World War I and immigration restrictions, new migration came to an end. In the 1920s the communities prospered, attracting Jews who had initially settled in Philadelphia and New York. In the 1930s, the communities sponsored a small number of refugees from Nazi persecution and, after the war, survivors of the Holocaust. In the period from about 1950 to 2000 expansion of higher education, high-tech industries, and medical centers attracted more Jewish professionals to the Lehigh Valley. In the 1990s, with the end of the Cold War, the Jewish community resettled a new stream of Jews from the former Soviet Union.

The earliest Jews were peddlers and traders, many later opening general stores. Their knowledge of German and Yiddish was welcomed by the predominance of the Pennsylvania German-Dutch residents. Throughout most of the 20th century, Jewish-owned apparel, fur, shoe, jewelry, and furniture stores lined the downtown streets of all three cities. The most prominent was Allentown's Hess's Department Store, a landmark in the Lehigh Valley for over 100 years.

Many Lehigh Valley Jews entered the textile manufacturing business, silk and knit goods primarily. The local garment and textile industries flourished through most of the 20th century, generating wealth that created a cadre of Jewish philanthropists who became prominent in building Jewish organizations and institutions.

In the second half of the 20th century, Jewish entrepreneurs entered new lines of manufacturing as well as publishing, helping to diversify the Lehigh Valley economy and to adjust to the decline of the textile industry and heavy manufacturing. These firms, still very much in business today, include Day-Timers, Rodale Press, Just Born Candies, Lutron Electronics, and MCS Industries.

As each community grew in size, it created an array of institutions that filled social, education, cultural, and recreational needs – in addition to its synagogues. In the early decades of the 20th century, all three cities built Jewish Community Centers (some originally known as YMHAs, Young Men's Hebrew Associations). In Bethlehem, its JCC was integral to one of its synagogues, Congregation Brith Sholom, until the synagogue relocated in 1985 to new facilities without the recreational facilities of its former location.

Entering the 21st century, the Lehigh Valley Jewish community boasted eight synagogues (two in Easton, two in Bethlehem, four in Allentown) representing the Orthodox, Conservative, Reconstructionist, and Reform denominations. The community supports professionally led Hillel Jewish student unions at its three largest universities: Lafayette College in Easton, Muhlenberg College in Allentown, and Lehigh University in Bethlehem. Lehigh University is home to the Philip and Muriel Berman Center for Jewish Studies. Muhlenberg College sponsors the Institute for Jewish-Christian Understanding, founded in partnership with the local Jewish Federation. Youth and teen programming transcends the Lehigh Valley with Jewish youth groups at most synagogues and B'nai B'rith Youth Organization chapters based at the JCC in Allentown.

The Lehigh Valley is home to chapters of many national organizations, including Hadassah and B'nai B'rith, the latter sponsoring low-income senior housing apartments in Allentown.

Although based in Allentown, the larger Jewish community organizations serve the entire Lehigh Valley region. These agencies include the Jewish Community Center, the Jewish Family Service, and the Jewish Day School (a pre-kindergarten through eighth grade school). The Jewish Community Center maintains a sizable facility in Allentown, renovated in 2005–06, as well as a large rural day camp site. The Hebrew Family League sponsors a community *mikveh*, a *ḥevra kaddisha*, and the Lehigh Valley Kashrut Commission.

The Jewish Federation of the Lehigh Valley, founded in 1948, is at the nexus of the Lehigh Valley Jewish community. The Jewish Federation is nationally known for its successful fundraising, for creating the first Maimonides Medical Society, and for creating certain recognition programs for Jewish women's philanthropy – the latter two replicated today at virtually every Jewish Federation in the United States. The Jewish Federation is actively involved in building and strengthening the Jewish community in the Lehigh Valley, in Israel, and around the world. Lehigh Valley Jewish philanthropists funded the building of the high school in Ma'alot, Israel.

[Marcy Braverman Goldstein (2nd ed.)]

LEHMAN, U.S. family in the 19th–20th century. The brothers HENRY (1821–1855), EMANUEL (1827–1907), and MAYER LEHMAN (1830–1897), the immigrant sons of a Bavarian cattle merchant, formed the Lehman Brothers partnership in Montgomery, Alabama, in 1850. Originally commodity dealers, particularly in cotton, the firm began dealing in oil, railways, and public utilities after opening a New York office in 1858. By 1906, the firm had shifted from primarily dealing in commodities to investment banking and underwriting, with emphasis on consumer-oriented issues such as department stores and other retailing, car leasing, and finance companies. In 1924 the first non-family partner was admitted to the firm. A separate investment company, the Lehman Corporation, was formed in 1929 and managed by the parent firm. A later senior partner was ROBERT LEHMAN (1891–1969), Emanuel's grandson. He became a partner in the firm in 1921, chief partner by 1925, and by 1967 built the firm into one of the four largest investment banks in the U.S. Lehman early foresaw the possibilities of mass air transportation and his firm's heavy investments in passenger airlines provided a strong impetus for the growth of passenger air transportation in the U.S. Robert owned one of the greatest private art collections in the world, started by his father PHILIP LEHMAN (1861–1947). On his death he donated it to the Metropolitan Museum.

Mayer's sons ARTHUR (1873–1936), a partner in the family firm, and Herbert Henry *Lehman (1878–1963) were prominently identified with the American Jewish Committee and the Joint Distribution Committee, and Irving *Lehman (1876–1945) was a distinguished jurist. ALLAN S. LEHMAN (1885–1952), Mayer Lehman's grandson, was a participant in community affairs, such as the Joint Defense Appeal.

BIBLIOGRAPHY: *A Centennial – Lehman Brothers, 1850–1950* (1950); J. Wechsberg, *The Merchant Bankers* (1966), 279–334.

[Hanns G. Reissner]

LEHMAN, ERNEST (1915–), U.S. film producer and screenwriter. Born in New York, Lehman graduated from City College. He went to Hollywood in 1951. He won Writers' Guild awards for his screenwriting of *Sabrina* (Oscar nomination for Best Screenplay, 1954), *The King and I* (1956), *North by Northwest* (Oscar nomination for Best Screenplay, 1959), *West Side Story* (Oscar nomination for Best Screenplay, 1961), and *The Sound of Music* (1965). As a producer, he made his debut in 1966 with *Who's Afraid of Virginia Woolf?* for which he also wrote the screenplay (Oscar nomination for Best Picture and Best Screenplay). He was also the writer-producer of *Hello, Dolly!* (Oscar nomination for Best Picture, 1969). Other Lehman screenplays include *The Inside Story* (1948), *Executive Suite* (1954), *Somebody Up There Likes Me* (1956), *From the Terrace* (1960), *The Prize* (1963), *Portnoy's Complaint* (1972), *Family Plot* (1976), and *Black Sunday* (1977).

In 2002 Lehman's 1951 novella *Sweet Smell of Success* (and 1957 film) was turned into a Broadway musical and was nominated for three Tony Awards.

He was president of the Writers' Guild of America from 1983 to 1985. In 2001 he won an Honorary Academy Award "in appreciation of a body of varied and enduring work." Books by Lehman include *The Comedian and Seven Other Stories* (1957); the novels *The French Atlantic Affair* (1977) and *Farewell Performance* (1982); *Screening Sickness and Other Tales of Tinseltown* (1982); and *Sweet Smell of Success and Other Stories* (2000).

BIBLIOGRAPHY: J. Brady, *The Craft of the Screenwriter* (1982).

[Jonathan Licht / Ruth Beloff (2nd ed.)]

LEHMAN, HERBERT HENRY (1878–1963), U.S. banker, politician, and statesman. Herbert Lehman attended Williams College and on his graduation in 1899 joined his father's firm (see *Lehman), of which he became a full partner in 1908. His initiation into public service came during World War I, when he was commissioned as a captain in the War Department Ordnance bureau and rose to become a member of the War Claims Board with the rank of full colonel. Disappointed in his ambition to become assistant secretary of war in the Wilson administration, he resigned from the service in 1919 to return to his position with Lehman Brothers. In the course of several visits to Europe after the war, he was deeply moved by the devastation wrought to Jewish communities everywhere and subsequently helped found the *American Jewish Joint Distribution Committee. He was also called upon during these years as an occasional mediator between labor and management in the garment industry, where he was an enthusiastic backer of unionization.

Lehman returned to public life in 1924 to participate in the successful New York State gubernatorial campaign of his friend Alfred E. Smith. In 1926 he headed a citizen's committee for Smith's reelection and in 1928 he was active in Smith's successful campaign to gain the Democratic presidential nomination, for which he was rewarded with the chairmanship of the national finance committee of the Democratic Party. In October 1928 he was nominated to run for lieutenant governor of New York State on the ticket of Franklin Delano Roosevelt, who was elected governor by a narrow vote.

As Roosevelt's right hand, Lehman proved to be an able politician and administrator. He was especially active in assisting Roosevelt with financial and budgetary problems, in improving the scope and caliber of the state's administration agencies and social services, particularly in the area of hospital and prison reform, and in dealing skillfully with a wide range of emergencies and labor crises.

When Roosevelt went on to become president in 1932, Lehman was elected governor by an unprecedented plurality of close to a million votes over his Republican opponent. During his first term as governor, he struggled largely with financial and labor problems brought on by the Depression. Reelected for four more terms (1934, 1936, 1938, 1940), his administrations were marked by a systematic application of the New Deal in legislation for New York State. He strove to bring utilities under public control, sought to reapportion the state's legislative and congressional membership, and fought for a wide range of minimum wage, social security, and general welfare bills. Many of the measures he sponsored helped make New York one of the most socially progressive states in the Union.

Lehman resigned the governorship in 1942 to become head of the newly formed United Nations Relief and Rehabilitation Administration, whose vast task was to minister to the war-torn civilian populations of the Axis-occupied areas reconquered by the Allies. While he worked with tremendous energy and devotion, the experience proved in many ways frustrating; the program was hampered by personality clashes, conflicts of national interest, and the emerging tensions of the cold war. He resigned from his position in March 1946 and turned his attention to the specific plight of Jewish refugees and to the situation in Palestine. Although then not a Zionist and opposed to the idea of a Jewish state, Lehman was sympathetic to the cause of free Jewish immigration into Palestine and argued for it publicly and in his private political contacts.

Lehman's first postwar attempt to return to politics, a bid for a New York State senatorial seat in 1946, failed when he was defeated by Irving Ives in the Republican landslide. In a special election in 1949, however, he was elected to the Senate against John Foster Dulles, and he was reelected in the regular election the following year. During his term in the Senate he was a leader of the small liberal minority that uncompromisingly fought against McCarthyism and its tactics. He also headed the opposition to the discriminatory Walter-McCarran immigration bill, against which he cosponsored the unsuccessful Lehman-Tobey bill. He was an internationalist in foreign policy and a staunch supporter of the State of Israel.

Lehman declined to run for reelection in 1956. He remained an influential figure in New York State politics, however, and participated, with Eleanor Roosevelt, in Mayor

Robert Wagner's successful "reform crusade" against the Democratic Party organization of New York City in 1961.

BIBLIOGRAPHY: A. Nevins, *Herbert H. Lehman and his Era* (1963); J. Bellush, *Selected Case Studies of the Legislative Leadership of Governor Herbert H. Lehman* (1959); idem, in: *New York History*, 41 (1960), 423–43; 45 (1964), 119–34; 43 (1962), 79–104; B. Bellush, *Franklin D. Roosevelt as Governor of New York* (1955); S. Birmingham, *Our Crowd* (1967); Finkelstein, in: AJYB, 66 (1965), 3–20; Glaser, in: *Commentary*, 35 (1963), 403–9.

[Hillel Halkin]

LEHMAN, IRVING (1876–1945), U.S. jurist. Born in New York City, Lehman qualified as a lawyer in 1898 and worked in private practice in New York City until 1908, when he was elected to the state Supreme Court. He served as Supreme Court justice until 1924, and as judge on the New York State Court of Appeals (1924–45). From 1940 to 1945 he was chief judge of that court. Lehman's judgments reflected his belief in the flexibility of the common law to deal with new social and economic conditions and the duty of the judge to support remedial legislation to meet economic social evil. Thus in a dissenting opinion in New York State Court of Appeals Lehman upheld legislation establishing minimum wage standards, even though the Supreme Court had previously declared similar legislation unconstitutional. Lehman was a member of the well-known *Lehman family, and a brother of Herbert H. *Lehman. He supported numerous philanthropic enterprises and was active in Jewish affairs as president of the Jewish Welfare Board (1921–40), honorary vice president of the American Jewish Committee (1942), and a supporter of projects for the development of Ereẓ Israel.

[Michael Hart Cardozo]

LEHMAN, WILLIAM (1913–2005), U.S. congressman. A native of Selma, Ala. and its small Jewish community, William Lehman attended the University of Alabama where he earned his B.A. in 1934. He then moved to the Miami Dade area where he became a successful auto dealer. He never shed his roots. In Miami he was known as Alabama Bill. He returned to college to earn his teaching credentials in English and then became a teacher at Miami Norland Junior High School, Miami, Fla., and Miami Dade Junior College, Miami, Fla. (1965–66), before becoming a member and then chairman of the Dade County, Fla., school board (1966–72), where he managed to take the board through the divisive problems of desegregation. His deep Southern accent and Alabama roots helped him navigate deep communal tensions as he relentlessly pushed for desegregation. He was first elected to Congress in 1972 in a crowded field of seven candidates in a new congressional district established after the 1970 census as Florida's population rapidly expanded. No one expected him to win. Desegregation was not very popular, but he won as a liberal Democrat, and continued to maintain that reputation by supporting public transit and child-care assistance and championing Social Security, which was popular among his many retired constituents. He also was a strong advocate for refugee resettlement for Cuban and Haitian immigrants and was a particular and deeply involved champion of the Soviet Jewry movement. He took his commitments personally and once traveled to the Soviet Union to deliver an artificial heart valve to a 22-year-old Soviet woman.

In Congress, Lehman started out as a member of the House Education and Labor Committee. He was most closely associated with the powerful House Appropriations Committee, where he chaired the Transportation Appropriations Subcommittee that pushed for public transport, and served on the Foreign Operations Subcommittee, so important to U.S. aid to Israel. In 1980 he was instrumental in getting $100 million for Cuban refugee resettlement when the Mariel Boat Lift looked like it would overwhelm Southern Florida. He developed jaw cancer in 1983, which slightly slurred his speech but did not slow him down and he retired in 1992 undefeated.

BIBLIOGRAPHY: L.S. Maisel and I.N. Forman, *Jews in American Politics* (2001).

[Michael Berenbaum (2nd ed.)]

LEHMANN, BEHREND (1661–1730), *Court Jew of Saxony. Born in Essen, Issachar Bermann, as he was known to his coreligionists, caught the eye of the ambitious and flamboyant elector of Saxony Augustus II, the Strong (1670–1733), who had designs on the elective crown of Poland. Lehmann was entrusted with the financial aspect of the undertaking; in this capacity he sold off various Saxon holdings to gather the immense sums needed, estimated at between two and five million gulden; these were expended, at his discretion, to bribe the vacillating Polish electors and ensure Augustus' election. His partner and relative, Leffmann *Behrends, helped him with the financial side of the mission. Lehmann earned the king's eternal confidence and in 1697 was nominated Polish resident in Brandenburg with his seat in *Halberstadt, where he chose to reside as Prussian **Schutzjude*. In addition to being diplomatic agent, Lehmann was a large-scale purveyor of jewels to the king, his mistresses, and many of his retinue, as well as a purveyor of precious metals to the mint (see *mint masters) and the military *contractor. He also loaned money to the rulers of Hanover and Brunswick; all his transactions were in five- and six-figure sums, which was very high for his day.

He maintained a retinue of 30 persons, including rabbi and *shoḥet*, in his house in Halberstadt. In 1696 he obtained the permission of the king to have the Talmud printed in Frankfurt-on-the-Oder, entirely at his expense. The cities of *Halle and *Magdeburg were opened to Jews due to his intercession with the king of Prussia, with whom he maintained diplomatic and financial connections; the synagogues of Berlin and Halberstadt were built with the aid of his loans. In 1715 the city and villages of Lissa (*Leszno), Poland, which had belonged to Stanislav Leszczyński, who had temporarily replaced Augustus II on the Polish throne (1704–09), came into his possession for ten years, during which time the Jewish community enjoyed his benevolence. Lehmann also owned estates in Blankenburg and elsewhere. His relatives and agents were to be found in Hanover, Vienna, Hamburg, Amsterdam, and Dresden, which was, indeed, opened to Jews in 1708 in order to receive him. His successors did not inherit Lehmann's business acumen and only conducted small-scale business activities.

BIBLIOGRAPHY: E. Lehmann, *Der polnische Resident Berend Lehmann* (1885); H. Schnee, *Die Hoffinanz und der moderne Staat*, 2 (1954), 169–222; S. Stern, *The Court Jew* (1950), index; M. Lehmann, *The Royal Resident* (1964). **ADD. BIBLIOGRAPHY:** P. Saville, *Le juif de cour. Histoire du résident royal Berend Lehman* (1970); M. Schmidt, in: *Wegweiser durch das juedische Sachsen-Anhalt* (1998), 198–211; L. Raspe, in: *Hofjuden* (2002), 191–208; R. Ries and F. Battenberg, *Hofjuden* (2002), index.

LEHMANN, EMIL (1829–1898), lawyer, politician, and advocate of Reform Judaism and of Jewish emancipation in Saxony. Lehmann was a descendant of Behrend *Lehmann, the Court Jew. He sat on the Dresden city council from 1865 to 1883 and from 1875 to 1880 was a member of the Progressive Party in the Saxony Diet, being the only Jew there. Colleague of and successor to Bernhard *Beer in the fight for emancipation in Saxony, he was for several decades president of the Dresden congregation and was one of the founders of the *Deutsch-Israelitische Gemeindebund and the *Centralverein. He fought the rising movement of antisemitism, which was inspired by A. *Stoecker. In a series of newspaper articles and pamphlets Lehmann pleaded for a radical religious reform, stressing the elements common to Judaism and Christianity, and for removing the dividing ones such as circumcision and Jewish holidays. He promoted these ideas in articles in the *Allgemeine Zeitung des Judentums* and other Jewish periodicals. Among his published works were *Der polnische Resident Berend Lehmann* (1885); *Aus alten Akten* (contributions to the history of the Dresden Jewish community, 1886); and *Hoere Israel* (appeal to German coreligionists, 1889). A volume of Lehmann's collected writings, *Gesammelte Schriften*, appeared posthumously (1899; 1909[2]).

BIBLIOGRAPHY: E. Lehmann, *Die Rechtsverhältnisse der Juden in Sachsen (...)*, (1869); A. Bruell, in: ADB, 51 (1906), 620–3; *Mitteilungen des Deutsch-Israelitischen Gemeindebundes*, 47 (1898), 2; J. Heller, in: *Encyclopaedia Judaica*, 10 (1934), 734f.

[Alexander Carlebach]

LEHMANN, JOSEPH (1843–1917), French rabbi, director of the Séminaire Israélite de France (from 1906: Ecole Rabbinique). He was born in Belfort, studied at the Séminaire Israélite, and in 1867 was appointed to the rabbinate in Paris, where he taught Talmud at the seminary's preparatory school. Later he taught at the seminary itself, directing it from 1890 until his death. His greatest interest was in the historical content of the talmudic texts. His religious opinions, typical of those of the French rabbinate of the period, tended toward a liberal interpretation which aimed at social assimilation to the environment. He contributed several articles to the *Revue des Etudes Juives* and published a sermon in *L'Homme et Dieu* (1869).

BIBLIOGRAPHY: J. Bauer, *L'Ecole Rabbinique de France* (1930), 158–76, 185, 200; Catane, in: REJ, 125 (1966), 51–61.

[Moshe Catane]

LEHMANN, KARL (1894–1960), classical archaeologist. Born in Rostock, Germany, Lehmann was the son of a university professor. His studies were interrupted by service in World War I. In 1924 he became assistant director at the German archaeological institute in Rome. At the same time he began his academic career as a lecturer on classical archaeology at Berlin University. His book, *Die Trajanssaeule* (1926), established him as an authority on Roman archaeology and art. While lecturing at Heidelberg University (1925–29) Lehmann published his monumental work, *Die antiken Grossbronzen* (1927). In 1929 he went to Muenster University, and was dismissed from his post in 1933. After two years in Italy he immigrated to the U.S. and in 1936 was appointed professor of classical archaeology at the Fine Arts Institute of New York University. During this time Lehmann began excavating the sanctuary of the "Great Gods" on the Aegean island of Samothrace. Lehmann's expedition was crowned with success after many years of excavation, although he himself did not live to complete the work. He published the first volume of the excavation report (Bollingen Series, 60, 1959; U.S. ed. *Samothrace*, 1960). The other volumes which he partly prepared were published soon after his death.

In spite of Lehmann's preoccupation with Greek art and religion, his interest in problems of Roman archaeology did not diminish. He interpreted cult and symbolism in Roman wall and ceiling frescoes and in *Dionysiac Sarcophagi in Baltimore* (with E.C. Olsen, 1942) he drew conclusions from reliefs carved on them about the religious beliefs of people buried in late Roman sarcophagi.

BIBLIOGRAPHY: P.H. von Blanckenhagen, in: *American Journal of Archeology*, 65 (1961), 307ff.

[Penuel P. Kahane]

LEHMANN, LÉONCE (1836–1892), French advocate and philanthropist, born in Augsburg, Bavaria. He was appointed secretary to the Turkish embassy in Naples (1856). Later Lehmann practiced law in Paris. In 1870 Adolphe *Crémieux made him chief secretary at the Ministry of Justice. He was a member of the central committee and then general secretary of the *Alliance Israélite Universelle from 1888 to 1892. In 1869 Lehmann and Narcisse *Leven visited the hunger-stricken Jewish centers in Lithuania and Poland. In 1887 Lehmann traveled to Russia and negotiated with the government about Baron de *Hirsch's projected loan of 50,000,000 francs for the establishment of Jewish elementary and professional schools in Russia.

BIBLIOGRAPHY: *Bulletin de l'Alliance Israélite Universelle* (1892), 14–15; N. Leven, *Cinquante ans d'histoire: L'Alliance Israélite Universelle (1860–1910)*, 2 (1920), index.

LEHMANN, MARCUS (Meir; 1831–1890), German Orthodox rabbi, scholar, and writer. Lehmann was born in Verden, Germany, and studied with Israel *Hildesheimer in Halberstadt, with S.L. *Rapoport in Prague, and at Halle. In Prague he was friendly with the writer Solomon *Kohn, who may have influenced Lehmann's future work as a writer. In 1853 an organ was introduced in the synagogue of *Mainz and in 1854, when the Orthodox members formed a separate congregation, Lehmann was elected their rabbi and, eventually, one of the leaders and spokesmen of modern German Orthodoxy. In Mainz he founded a religious school which from 1859 was an elementary day school for boys and girls. Lehmann wrote polemically against Reform and founded the weekly **Israelit* (1860–1938) to counter the influence of Ludwig Philippson's Reform periodical, *Allgemeine Zeitung des Judentums*; the *Israelit* became the principal voice of German Orthodoxy. Lehmann was the main contributor to the *Israelit* and his many historical novels, including *Rabbi Joselmann von Rosheim* (translated into English as *Tales of Yore*, 1947), and short stories were first published in it. His stories were collected in *Aus Vergangenheit und Gegenwart* (6 vols., 1872–88), and many were translated or adapted into Hebrew, Judeo-Arabic, French, Hungarian, English, and other languages. Lehmann's stories have no great literary merit, but as juvenile literature, they have religious and educational value. Of more scholarly importance, though also primarily intended for popular instruction, are his German edition of the *Haggadah* (1906, 1914^2, 1926^5), anonymously revised and enlarged by H. Ehrmann and translated into English (1969), and his Sabbath lectures on *Avot*, collected as *Die Sprueche der Vaeter* (in installments, in: *Israelit*, 1895–1905; 3 vols., 1921/23) in which Lehmann made use of earlier commentators, particularly of *Samuel b. Isaac's *Midrash Shemu'el*, and thus made the commentators accessible to the German reader. Lehmann also published the tractate *Berakhot* of the Jerusalem Talmud with the commentary of Solomon Sirillo and his own notes, *Meir Nativ* (1874). Lehmann translated the Pentateuch (1873, 1913^6) in the Bible translation initiated by the Orthodox Bible Institute to counter the translation of *Zunz and others. As editor of the *Israelit*, Lehmann agreed increasingly with S.R. *Hirsch's intransigent line in Hirsch's differences with Hildesheimer, Lehmann's friend and teacher.

BIBLIOGRAPHY: *Gedenk-Blaetter an Rabbiner Dr. Markus Lehmann* (1890); J. Lehmann, *Dr. Markus Lehmann* (Ger., 1910); H. Schwab, *The History of Orthodox Jewry in Germany* (1950), index; idem, *Chachme Ashkenaz* (Eng., 1964), 88–89, incl. bibl.; E. Hildesheimer, *Briefe* (1965), index.

[Jacob Rothschild]

LEHMANN, SIEGFRIED (1892–1958), Israel educator. Born in Berlin, Lehmann became a physician and as a student was influenced by Martin *Buber to take an interest in Judaism. He founded the Volksheim in Berlin for the children of immigrants from Eastern Europe (1916) and after World War I was responsible for the rehabilitation of Jewish youth in Lithuania (1920) and was the founder and principal of the Yidishe Kinderhoyz in Kovno. In 1926 Lehmann settled in Palestine, bringing many war orphans with him, and founded the *Ben Shemen Youth Village (1927). The village became a model of modern rural education under his leadership and from 1933 one of the main centers of *Youth Aliyah. Lehmann's four principal ideals were work on the soil and rural living, including inter alia, promoting folk music, folk dance, and folk art; community life and student self-government as a preparation for the kibbutz; education for peace, tolerance, and international understanding, especially with the Arabs; and education toward a traditional but non-Orthodox and non-dogmatic outlook on life. In 1940 he was arrested after the British police made a search in Ben Shemen (which was an isolated settlement surrounded by Arabs) and found arms; he was sentenced to seven years' imprisonment. Lehmann was released three weeks later through the intervention of Albert Einstein and other leading figures.

Lehmann received an award from the United Nations Children's Fund (UNICEF; 1952) and the 1957 Israel Prize for education. His ideas served as an example to the Youth Aliyah movement. Among his several published works is one on Arab-Israel problems.

BIBLIOGRAPHY: Tidhar, 10 (1959), 3499–501; A. Simon, in: S. Lehmann, *Ra'yon ve-Hagshamah* (1962), 9–31.

[Aryeh Simon]

°LEHMANN-HAUPT, CARL FRIEDRICH (1861–1938), German historian. Lehmann-Haupt taught ancient history in Berlin, Liverpool, Constantinople, and Innsbruck. He investigated Armenian and Mesopotamian culture, specializing in ancient Babylonian coins, weights, and measures. He published learned studies on old world chronologies, and on ancient Israel's contributions to world history. He was editor of *Klio*, a journal of ancient history (since 1901), and contributing editor of the *Liverpool Annals of Archaeology and Anthropology* from 1911 to 1914. He wrote *Babyloniens Kulturmission einst und jetzt* (1903); *Materialen zur aelteren Geschichte Armeniens und Mesopotamiens* (1907); *Armenien einst und jezt* (3 vols., 1910–26); *Die Geschicke Judas und Israels im Rahmen der Weltgeschichte* (1911); and *Der juedische Kirchenstaat in persischer, griechischer und roemischer Zeit* (1911); and he edited the *Corpus inscriptionum chaldaicarum* (1928–31).

BIBLIOGRAPHY: *Festschrift C.F. Lehmann-Haupt* (1921). **ADD. BIBLIOGRAPHY:** NDB, 14 (1985), 98ff.

[Zev Garber]

LEHREN, Dutch family of bankers, communal leaders, and philanthropists. MOSES LEHREN (d. 1815), a banker at The Hague who originally came from Lehren-Steinfeld (Wuerttemberg), was *parnas* and *posek* of the Jewish community. Moses' son HIRSCHEL (Ẓevi Hirsch; 1784–1853) lived in The Hague but subsequently settled in Amsterdam. With A. *Prins and S. Rubens he founded in 1809 an organization on behalf of the Jews of Ereẓ Israel. In order to combat the heavy expenses of the emissaries of the *yishuv* and difficulties relating to the distribution of money (*ḥalukkah) between the rival groups there, he strove to concentrate the collection of money throughout the whole of Western Europe in this one organization, the "Pekidim and Amarkalim of the Holy Land." In 1824 he succeeded in convincing all the parties involved, and in that year the new body was recognized by the rabbis of Jerusalem as the exclusive agency for collecting money on behalf of the Holy Land. Lehren carried out his reforms in the age-old system thoroughly and uncompromisingly, and for this he was attacked from many quarters; suspicion was even cast on his integrity, but he was vindicated by Moses *Sofer of Pressburg among others. After vehement attacks on him (in *Der Orient* (1843), 44 and passim) he published a reply written by the chief rabbi of Jerusalem (*Emet me-Ereẓ* (1843/44)). Hirschel Lehren was extremely Orthodox and leaned toward kabbalism. Because he was opposed to the lenient and assimilationist leaders of the Amsterdam community, he set up his own *minyan* with his followers, but they had to leave Amsterdam and settled in The Hague. Here he asked the municipality for permission to hold private religious services, but, following the intervention of the central Jewish authorities, he was forbidden to have his own *minyan*. Lehren sent petitions to the minister and the king, but he had to put an end to the activities of his "sect" in 1834. When the Reform movement tried to gain adherents in the Netherlands, he and A. Prins issued a collection of statements by European rabbis (*Torat ha-Kena'ot*, 2 vols., 1845) and one by Palestinian rabbis (*Kinat Ẓiyyon*, 1846).

His brother AKIVA (1795–1876), a banker, was *parnas* of the Amsterdam community. After Hirschel's death he became president of the "Pekidim and Amarkalim" fund. Akiva was the central pillar of Orthodoxy in the Amsterdam community. Another of Moses' sons, JACOB MEIR (1795–1861), was also a banker and *parnas* of the Amsterdam community. From 1827 until his death he was president of the rabbinical seminary in Amsterdam. Owing to the influence of the Lehren brothers, J.Z.H. *Duenner was nominated head of the rabbinical seminary in Amsterdam and afterward chief rabbi of the city.

BIBLIOGRAPHY: J. Meijer, *Erfenis der Emancipatie; het Nederlandse Jodendom in de eerste helft van de 19de eeuw* (1963), 21–29; idem, *Moeder in Israel; de geschiedenis van het Amsterdamse Asjkenazische Jodendom* (1964), 74–83; Y. Yellin, *Zikhronot le-Ven Yerushalayim* (1924), 47–49; Ya'ari, Sheluḥei, 181–6 and passim; J. and B. Rivlin (eds.), *Iggerot ha-Pekidim ve-ha-Amarkalim me-Amsterdam* (1965), index; S. Bernfeld, *Toledot ha-Reformaẓyon ha-Dati be-Yisrael* (1900); D.S. van Zuiden, *De Hoogduitsche Joden in's Gravenhage* (1913).

[Jozeph Michman (Melkman)]

LEHRER, LEIBUSH (Mordecai; 1887–1964), Yiddish writer and educator. Born in Warsaw, he immigrated first to Belgium (1906) and then to the U.S. (1909). He became one of the prime movers in the development of the Sholem Aleichem schools, and founded the Yiddish-speaking Camp Boiberik where he was director for more than 40 years. From 1919 he taught in the Teachers Seminary of the Sholem Aleichem Folk Institute in New York, and was director of the Sholem Aleichem Secondary School (1921–47). He was also secretary of the psychology and education section of the *YIVO Institute for Jewish Research. He advocated the thesis that Judaism was not only a religion but an entire folk culture. His works on literature, psychology, education, and Judaism include *Di Psikhologye fun Literatur* ("The Psychology of Literature," 1926); *Di Moderne Yidishe Shul* ("The Modern Jewish School," 1927); *Psikhologye un Dertsiung* ("Psychology and Education," 1937); *Yidishkayt un Andere Problemen* ("*Yidishkayt* and Other Problems," 1940); *Azoy Zenen Yidn* ("Jews Are Like That," 1959); and *In Gayst fun Traditsye* ("In the Spirit of Tradition," 1966).

BIBLIOGRAPHY: LNYL, 5 (1963), 235–9.

[Israel Ch. Biletzky / Jerold C. Frakes (2nd ed.)]

LEHRMAN, DANIEL S. (1919–1972), U.S. psychologist. Lehrman was born in New York City and graduated from City College in 1947, after his return from military service. He received his doctorate in comparative psychology from New York University in 1954 for his research on the breeding behavior of the ringdove. Appointed assistant professor at Rutgers University in 1950, he became full professor in 1958. He was instrumental in founding the Institute of Animal Behavior of Rutgers University in Newark, N.J., of which he was the first director from 1959. In 1970, he was elected to the National Academy of Sciences and in 1971 was made a fellow of the American Academy of Arts and Sciences.

Lehrman's interest in animal behavior, and especially in birds, started while he was still in high school. His mature work dealt with the interrelationship of experience and hormonal factors in the life of many species, particularly the ringdove, his favorite subject. He was one of the first psychologists to unravel some of the complex interactions of hormones and an animal's physical and social environment. By a series of imaginative experiments, he showed clearly how previous experience could modify patterns of behavior that had been thought to be fixed characteristics of a species. Lehrman's theoretical contribution dealt with the concept of instinct. His most influential paper, "A Critique of Konrad Lorenz's Theory of Instinctive Behavior" (1953), began a life-long dialogue between American comparative psychologists and European ethologists, which was fruitful in clarifying the issues that divided the two groups. In his chapter, "Semantic and Conceptual Issues in the Nature-Nurture Problem" (in: *Development and Evolution of Behavior*, L.R. Aronson, E. Tobach, D.S. Lehrman, and J.S. Rosenblatt, eds., 1970), he came to the conclusion that the study of adaptation and development, rather than of "innate" and "acquired" behavior, was the preferable course toward solving some of the fundamental issues of comparative psychology.

[Helmut E. Adler (2nd ed.)]

LEHRMAN, IRVING (1910–2005), U.S. rabbi and leader of the ecumenical movement and of Dade County Jews. Lehrman was born in Tiktin, Poland. The family emigrated when Lehrman was six, and his father, a rabbi, took over an Orthodox congregation in Spring Valley, N.Y. Irving was the 12th generation rabbi in his family. His wife of nearly 70 years was herself the daughter of a rabbi, Israel Goldfarb. They met when Lehrman was studying at Brooklyn Law School. Lehrman was ordained at New York's Jewish Institute of Religion, when it was a non-denomination school under the leadership of Rabbi Stephen Wise.

After holding a pulpit at Congregation Shomrei Emunah in Montclair, N.J., he came to Temple Emanuel-El in 1943 and fell in love with South Florida. When he arrived Jews were barred from living in some neighborhoods; apartment houses did not rent to Jews or African-Americans, and Jews were still excluded from the choice hotels. His congregation grew with the city's Jewish population and with the breaking of barriers for Jews in South Florida. The introduction of air-conditioning allowed for a community to live in year-round comfort. He served as chairman of the Greater Miami Jewish Federation/UJA Campaign for two terms and as chairman of the UJA National Rabbinic Cabinet. Lehrman served on the boards of numerous international, national, and local educational, social, and humanitarian organizations. His influence was felt in Miami organizations within the network of Federation agencies including the Jewish Community Relations Council, the Rabbinical Association of Greater Miami, and the Miami Jewish Home and Hospital for the Aged.

As a condition of his staying Lehrman asked the congregation to build a new building, which they did. He served the congregation for half a century, retiring in 1993, but never quite stepping aside. An "excellent" sermonizer, one congregant recalled 70 years later that "he was magnetic and electrifying. He was the Billy Graham of the Jews."

In 2000, Lehrman was among the first non-Catholics in the Archdiocese of Miami to be honored with Pope John Paul II's blessing for humanitarian collaborations with the church. His dedication to Jewish education was symbolized by the day school that he founded and that bears his name.

[Michael Berenbaum (2nd ed.)]

LEIBER, JUDITH MARIA (1921–), U.S. designer and manufacturer. Leiber became a master handbag maker in Hungary in 1942. She has owned and managed Judith Leiber, Inc. since 1963. Her exquisite intricate jeweled handbags sold in upscale stores such as Neiman Marcus and in her own boutiques in Geneva, Bangkok, London, Costa Mesa, California, and New York. These bags have been carried by several first ladies, actresses, and others wealthy enough to afford the price tags which range from $600 to $7,500. Born in Budapest, Leiber intended to specialize in skin creams, but her plans to study chemistry at Kings College in London in 1939 were thwarted with the onset of World War II. Instead Leiber was admitted into Hungary's artisan guild and became an apprentice to the finest handbag maker in Budapest. After doing a number of menial tasks from sweeping the floor to cooking glue, she began to learn the art of making handbags. She became a female pioneer master handbag maker. She and her parents, Emil and Helen (Spitzer) Peto, survived the concentration camps and the Nazi occupation of Budapest through a neighbor's forgery of a document which designated the family as Swiss. She met the American GI Gerson Leiber (whom she calls Gus) in 1945 and married him in 1946. They came to New York in 1947, where she was naturalized in 1949. Before opening her own business in 1963, Leiber worked for a number of firms, including being a pattern maker for designer Nettie Rosenstein.

Leiber received a number of honorary degrees. In 1993 she received honorary Ph.D. degrees from Bar-Ilan University in Israel and the International Fine Arts College in Miami, Florida. She is also the recipient of numerous awards. In 2001 she received the Swarovski Award, the American Handbag Designer Award, and the Leather Industries Award. That year she also won the George Washington Award and an award from the American Hungarian Foundation. She won several awards in the fashion industry including The Fashion Group's 1986 designation as one of The Women Who Made a Difference. She won a Lifetime Achievement Award in 1992, a FAAB Lifetime Achievement Award in 1992, and a Fashion Hall of Fame award from Kent State University in 1995. A retrospective of her work has been exhibited at the Corcoran Museum (2002), the George Bush Museum (2004), and the Newark Museum (2004).

In 1993 Leiber sold her company to Time Products Inc., a conglomerate in London. She continued designing collections until she retired in 1998. Her bags find homes among collectors. Some even reside in museums. Leiber has said that she has designed some 4,000 styles during her 34-year career of designing handbags.

[Sara Alpern (2nd ed.)]

LEIBER AND STOLLER, U.S. songwriters and music producers whose combination of rhythm and blues with pop lyrics revolutionized pop and rock & roll; members of the Songwriters' Hall of Fame, the Record Producers' Hall of Fame, and the Rock & Roll Hall of Fame. JERRY LEIBER (1933–) was born one of three children to immigrants from Poland, where his father, Abraham, had been a cantor. Leiber grew up in Baltimore raised by his mother, Manya, after his father died when he was five. Leiber delivered kerosene and coal from his mother's grocery store to black families, and that is where he first heard the music of the neighborhood, the blues, that would change his life. MIKE STOLLER (1933–) was born 18 days after Leiber in Belle Harbor, New York, to Abraham, a draftsman, and Adelyn, a model and actress. Stoller discovered black music at age seven, when he attended an integrated summer camp. Both families moved after World War II to Los Angeles, where Leiber and Stoller met in 1950 while they were students at Fairfax High School. They discovered they had a lot in common – they were white, Jewish, ex-East Coast teenagers who shared a passion for rhythm and blues, so they began writing songs together, with Leiber writing the words and Stoller the music.

Though they were hardly the only white songwriters to break the barriers of segregation in their music, they were, arguably, the best. Their first mega-hit was the 1956 classic "Hound Dog" recorded by 21-year-old Elvis Presley, which sold about seven million copies and stayed at No. 1 on the Billboard charts for 11 weeks (no record has held the No. 1 spot for that length of time since). They were responsible for many of the pop hits of Presley, who recorded 24 of their songs, as well as for the Coasters, the Drifters, and others. Over 200 of their compositions were recorded between 1951 and 1972, including 24 chart hits by the Robins/Coasters alone, and were sung by a who's who of rock, from the Beatles to Buddy Holly. Among their other top-10 hits were Elvis Presley's "Jailhouse Rock" (1957, No. 1) and "Don't" (1958, No. 1); The Coasters' "Yakety Yak" (1958, No. 1) and "Charlie Brown" (1959, No. 2); Wilbert Harrison's "Kansas City" (1959, No. 1); The Drifters' "There Goes My Baby" (1959, No. 2) and "On Broadway" (1963, No. 9), and Ben E. King's "Stand by Me" (1961, No. 4). Other hits written or produced include "Only in America," "Spanish Harlem," "Love Potion No. 9," "Poison Ivy," "Save the Last Dance for Me," "Leader of the Pack," "Chapel of Love," and Peggy Lee's "Is That All There Is?" which won a Grammy Award in 1969.

Leiber and Stoller's singular contribution was to take rhythm and blues from the ghetto into mainstream America, and thereby create pop classics that transcended musical and racial categories. They were among the first to use strings on R&B records, and through such tunes as "Spanish Harlem" they were among the first to introduce Latin rhythms to rock 'n' roll. Their work was the transition between R&B and rock, and aside from Lennon and McCartney, no songwriting team has done more to enrich the rock canon. "We crawled inside the skins of our characters," said Leiber. "We related to the guys in the singing groups, and the result was a cross-cultural phenomenon: a white kid's take on a black kid's take on white society." Among the many artists and writers they influenced while serving as the last legion of songwriters and producers of Tin Pan Alley was a young Phil *Spector, who learned production techniques while assisting and playing on their sessions. In 1995, a Broadway musical called *Smoky Joe's Café* was staged based on their work, which became an international success and won a Grammy Award for cast album. The duo was inducted into the Songwriters' Hall of Fame (1985), the Record Producers' Hall of Fame (1986), and the Rock & Roll Hall of Fame (1987), and in 1991, they received the Founder's Award from the American Society of Composers, Authors, and Publishers (ASCAP). Leiber and Stoller also have a star on the Hollywood Walk of Fame. *Hound Dog's Life: Gospel, Half-Truths, Rumors, and Outrageous Lies* (1996) was written by Leiber with Bob Spitz, and the pair are the subject of a biography by Robert Palmer, *Baby, That Was Rock and Roll: The Legendary Leiber and Stoller* (1978).

BIBLIOGRAPHY: S.R. Benarde, *Stars of David: Rock 'n' Roll's Jewish Stories*, (2003), 18–20.

[Elli Wohlgelernter (2nd ed.)]

LEIBL, DANIEL (1891–1967), Yiddish and Hebrew linguist, poet, and editor. Born in Debica, Poland, Leibl, a political activist all his life, was excluded in 1910 from the gymnasium because of "Zionism and Socialism." He was also active on behalf of the rights of the Yiddish language during the Austro-Hungarian census of 1910. As a student of law at Vienna University, Leibl became interested in Yiddish linguistic research, to which he afterward devoted himself. In 1924 he settled in Palestine. An active member of Po'alei Zion (later of the Left Po'alei Zion and Mapam), Leibl did editorial work for various Yiddish and Hebrew publications. He was simultaneously an active Zionist (he held various high positions in the *Histadrut and in Mapam) and a loyal Yiddishist (he was wounded in an attack by the militant Hebraists of the *Gedud Meginnei ha-Safah* ("Guardians of the Language")); a Yiddish poet and translator (especially of the Polish poets S. Wispiansky and Maria Konopnicka) and a Hebrew poet and translator (of the Polish poet J. Slowacki); a Yiddish linguist (e.g., his study in the YIVO's *Landoy-Bukh*, 1926) and a Hebrew linguist (member of the Hebrew Language Academy and contributor to *Leshonenu* and *Leshonenu la-Am*).

BIBLIOGRAPHY: S. Bickel, in: *Der Tog/Morgen-Zhurnal* (April 1, 1967); LNYL, 5 (1963), 104–6; Kressel, Leksikon, 2 (1967), 253. **ADD. BIBLIOGRAPHY:** Rejzen, Leksikon, 2 (1927), 192–4; M. Ravitch, *Mayn Leksikon*, 3 (1958), 221–2.

[Mordkhe Schaechter]

LEIBLER, ISI JOSEPH (1934–), Australian businessman and communal leader. Born in Antwerp, Belgium, Isi Leibler came to Melbourne, Australia, with his family in 1939. After managing his family's diamond business, in 1965 Leibler founded Jetset Tours, which he developed into the largest travel agency in Australia. It is credited with breaking the near-monopoly on overseas flights previously enjoyed by Qantas, Australia's state-owned airline. From the mid-1970s until he immigrated to Israel in 1998, Leibler was unquestionably the most important and dominant lay leader in the Australian Jewish community, serving as president of the Executive Council of Australian Jewry in 1978–80, 1982–85, 1987–89, and 1992–95. A highly articulate and charismatic figure, Leibler was especially influential during the premierships of Malcolm Fraser (1975–83) and Bob Hawke (1983–91), and was significant in maintaining Australia's strong pro-Israel stance at the UN and other bodies. Leibler was also well known for his work on behalf of Soviet Jewry, entailing many trips to the Soviet Union on behalf of the "refuseniks." Leibler officially opened the Solomon Mykhoels Center in Moscow in 1987, the first free Jewish institution in Russia since the 1920s. In 1998 he moved to Jerusalem, where, as chairman of the Governing Board of the *World Jewish Congress, he became involved in a number of high-profile disputes with Edgar *Bronfman, its president. In Australia, Leibler built up one of the largest private libraries of Judaica in the world, and was the author of many works on Jewish affairs, including *Soviet Jewry and Human Rights* (1963) and *Jewish Religious Extremism: A Threat to the Future* *of the Jewish People* (1991). A leading member of the Mizrachi movement, Leibler was the son-in-law of Rabbi Israel *Porush. Leibler's brother MARK LEIBLER (1942–), a prominent solicitor in Melbourne, was the leader of the Zionist movement in Australia in the 1980s and 1990s and was in part responsible for a resolution, passed by the Australian parliament, demanding the revocation of the UN's "Zionism is racism" declaration of 1975, which was influential in the repeal of the resolution by the United Nations in 1991.

BIBLIOGRAPHY: W.D. Rubinstein, Australia, 1, index.

[William D. Rubinstein (2nd ed.)]

LEIBOVITZ, ANNIE (**Anna-Lou**; 1949–), U.S. photographer. Born in Westbury, Conn., to an Air Force lieutenant and a modern dance instructor, she was one of six children. In 1967 she enrolled at the San Francisco Art Institute (she earned her degree in 1971) and developed a love of photography. In 1969 she lived on a kibbutz in Israel and participated in an archeological dig at the site of King Solomon's temple. Her career started in 1970 when she sent pictures of a group of ladders, taken in an apple orchard on the kibbutz, to the start-up rock magazine *Rolling Stone*, which hired her right away. Within two years the 23-year-old Leibovitz was named chief photographer, a title she would hold for ten years. At the magazine she developed her trademark technique, which involved the use of bold primary colors and surprising poses. She accompanied the Rolling Stones rock group on its international tour in 1975 and captured weeks of strung-out nights and unmade beds. Jann Wenner, publisher of the magazine, credited Leibovitz with making many *Rolling Stone* magazine covers collector's items, most notably an issue that featured a nude John Lennon of the Beatles curled around his fully clothed wife, Yoko Ono. The photo was taken on December 8, 1980, just hours before his death.

In 1983 Leibovitz left *Rolling Stone* for the entertainment magazine *Vanity Fair* in part to learn about glamour. "I admired the work of photographers like Beaton, Penn, and Avedon as much as I respected the grittier photographers such as Robert Frank," she said. "But in the same way that I had to find my own way of reportage, I had to find my own form of glamour." With a wider array of subjects and generous budgets, Leibovitz photographed presidents, literary icons, and all manner of celebrities. A number of her covers provided startling images of well-known figures: the actress Demi Moore, nine months pregnant and nude except for a diamond ring, in 1991; the black comedian Whoopi Goldberg, half submerged in a bathtub of milk; and the late artist Keith Haring, who painted himself like one of his canvases for the photograph.

During the late 1980s Leibovitz started to work on a number of high-profile advertising campaigns. The most notable was for American Express; her portraits of celebrity cardholders like Elmore Leonard, Tom Selleck, and Luciano Pavarotti earned her a Clio award in 1987. In 1991 her collection of more than 200 black-and-white and color photographs were exhibited at the National Portrait Gallery in Washington. She was the second living photographer and first woman to have that honor. In 1996 she was chosen as the official photographer of the Summer Olympics in Atlanta, Ga., and a compilation of her black-and-white portraits of American athletes was published in the book *Olympic Portraits*. In 1999 she published the book *Women*, accompanied by an essay by the novelist Susan *Sontag. Included were an array of female images, from Supreme Court justices to Las Vegas showgirls to farmers and coal miners. In the early years of the 21st century, she was probably the most famous photographer or portraitist in the United States.

[Stewart Kampel (2nd ed.)]

LEIBOWITZ, BARUCH BER (1866–1939), Lithuanian talmudic scholar and *rosh yeshivah*. Born in Slutsk, at the age of 14 he delivered a discourse at the local synagogue, astounding his listeners with his erudition. A year later, when accepted to the Volozhin yeshivah, he had already mastered two orders of the Talmud. Soon recognized as an *illui* ("prodigy"), he was given special attention by his teacher, R. Ḥayyim *Soloveichik. He married the daughter of R. Abraham Zimmerman, the rabbi of Halusk. Leibowitz later succeeded his father-in-law in this position, and many talented pupils soon gathered around him, making Halusk a new center for talmudic study. Leibowitz' personality and system of learning greatly influenced his students, many of whom later occupied important positions in the rabbinate and yeshivot. His method of exposition was essentially based on that of R. Ḥayyim Soloveichik. In 1904, Leibowitz was appointed head of the Keneset Bet Yiẓḥak Yeshivah in *Slobodka which had been organized in 1897 as a memorial to Kovno's Rabbi Isaac Elchanan *Spektor. Under his tutelage, the new school gradually earned an outstanding reputation and attracted students from all over the Jewish world. Following the advent of World War I, he was compelled to leave Slobodka and moved his yeshivah to Minsk and afterward to Kremenchug. After the war it was relocated in Vilna, and in 1926 he transferred the school to Kamenetz, near Brest-Litovsk, where it continued to attract hundreds of students for the next 13 years. In 1939, shortly before his death, he fled with his school to a suburb of Vilna, in the hope of escaping from the Nazis and the Communists.

His *Birkat Shemu'el* (4 vols., 1939–62) is regarded as a classic among talmudic scholars. It represents, however, only a small fraction of his learning and teachings, treasured by his numerous disciples who recorded everything they heard from their revered master. His students and family reopened the Kamenetz Yeshivah in Jerusalem in 1942.

BIBLIOGRAPHY: O.Z. Rand (ed.), *Toledot Anshei Shem* (1950), 73; I. Edelstein, *Rabbi Baruch Dov Leibovitch* (Heb.; 1957); O. Feuchtwanger, *Righteous Lives* (1965), 115–8; S.J. Zevin, *Ishim ve-Shitot* (1966^3), 295–307; A. Rothkoff, in: *Jewish Life* (July–Aug., 1969), 41–46.

[Mordechai Hacohen]

LEIBOWITZ, JOSHUA O. (1895–1993), medical historian and Hebrew scholar; cousin of Yeshayahu and Neḥama *Leibowitz. He was born in Vilna. Leibowitz combined his studies of medicine at Heidelberg University with talmudic studies. After serving as head physician at a sanatorium in Bad Homburg, he immigrated to Palestine in 1935 and was appointed medical director of the Arza Sanatorium near Jerusalem. During the 1948 War of Independence he was head physician of Schneller military camp, and later senior physician at the Kupat Ḥolim in Jerusalem. In 1959 Leibowitz was appointed clinical associate professor and head of the division of the history of medicine at the Hebrew University.

He published many papers on medicine in general, but from 1930 onward his main interest was in the history of medicine. Until 1957 he devoted himself almost exclusively to Jewish topics in historical medicine but subsequently wrote also a history of medicine in general, with special emphasis on the evolution of cardiology. His *History of Coronary Heart Disease* (1970) is the first historical monograph on the subject.

LEIBOWITZ, KEREN (1973–), Israeli Paralympic gold medalist in swimming. Active in sports all her life, Leibowitz decided to focus on swimming after an accident during her army service left her legs virtually paralyzed. After years of hard training she won medals in several world championships. However, her main goal was the Paralympic Games, where she first competed in 2000 in Sydney. There she took three gold medals and set new world records in the 100-meter backstroke and in the 50- and 100-meter free style events. In the Paralympic Games of 2004 in Athens she won a gold medal in the 100-meter backstroke as well as two silvers and a bronze among the 13 medals won by the Israeli contingent. Leibowitz was one of the country's outstanding competitors who assured Paralympic sports headline coverage in Israel.

[Shaked Gilboa (2nd ed.)]

LEIBOWITZ, NEḤAMA (1905–1997), Bible scholar, sister of Yeshayahu *Leibowitz. Born in Riga, her mother died when she was a child. In 1919, her father moved the family to Berlin to provide his two precocious children with a better education. Neḥama and her brother Yeshayahu were tutored at home until they entered the university. Neḥama attended the University of Berlin and the University of Marburg. Asked many times if she knew Rabbi Joseph B. *Soloveitchik when she studied at the University of Berlin, Leibowitz would reply that someone pointed to a giant stack of books in the library and said that the young Soloveitchik was behind the books, but she never met him. In 1929 she married her uncle, Yedidyah Lipman Leibowitz. In 1930 she received her Ph.D. from Marburg. Her dissertation was titled "Techniques of Judeo-German Bible Translation in the 15th and 16th Century as Exemplified by Translations of the Book of Psalms." In 1930, she and her husband immigrated to Palestine. Shortly thereafter he became blind and could not work. Thus, Leibowitz embarked on her lifelong career teaching Bible. From 1930, when she settled in Palestine, until 1955, she taught at the Mizrachi Women Teachers Seminary in Jerusalem. She was a regular Bible commentator on the Israel Broadcasting Service. From the late 1950s she taught Bible at Tel Aviv University (becoming a tenured professor in 1968) and at Bar-Ilan University.

In 1941 Leibowitz taught a group of religious kibbutz women, who traveled to Jerusalem once a week to study. After they expressed their desire to continue studying at home, Leibowitz began mailing them a weekly *Gilayon* (page) with sources and questions relating to the weekly Torah reading. Her audience for the *Gilyonot* grew quickly. Leibowitz insisted that those receiving the *Gilyonot* should send their answers to her for correction. Over the next 29 years, Leibowitz mailed *Gilyonot* to thousands of "students" all over the world, corresponding with hundreds of them. Over time she turned numerous *Gilyonot* into essays on the weekly Torah portion (*parashat ha-shavu'a*). These were published in Hebrew and English and distributed as small pamphlets by the World Zionist Organization's Department for Education and Culture in the Diaspora. Eventually, in the mid-1960s the pamphlets became collections of essays, *Iyyunim Ḥadashim*, a volume for each of the books of the Pentateuch. The *Iyyunim* have been published in Hebrew, English, Dutch, French, and Spanish; they have remained in print into the 21st century. She was awarded the Israel Prize for education in 1956. Aside from her *Gilyonot*, Leibowitz continued to teach, including the instruction of teachers on how to teach Bible. In addition to Tel Aviv University, she taught in the overseas program at the Hebrew University of Jerusalem and at a variety of other one-year study programs for overseas students, including Machon Gold and Yeshiva University's Gruss Kollel for *semikhah* students in Jerusalem. In 1980, she received the Leibman Prize for disseminating knowledge of Torah; in 1982 she received the Bialik Prize from the City of Tel Aviv-Jaffa.

After retiring from formal classroom and university teaching, Leibowitz continued to teach small groups of students in her home. The secular books in English, German, Yiddish, and Hebrew that lined the wall of her vestibule were evidence of her voracious reading in literature, history, and other topics beyond the realm of Bible and Jewish studies. Both in her writing and in her classes, Leibowitz would quote from nonreligious Jewish scholars, as well as from world literature, to make a point. As an observant, believing Jew, Neḥama rejected Bible Criticism out of hand. However, she sought truth wherever she could find it. Her specific selection of sources was based solely on each one's contribution to understanding the *peshat* (plain meaning) of the biblical text and to the revelation of the significance of that text. Marla Frankel (1998) points out that her reading of the Bible is defined as "close study" as opposed to "close reading." Leibowitz never limited herself to the words of the Bible alone. Rather, her context included the entire range of the Bible, rabbinic literature, medieval and modern commentators, modern Bible scholarship, and the world of philosophy and literature. She was never satisfied just teaching the biblical text. Her second goal was to demonstrate how the Bible's narrative, laws, and prophecies provide the student with a blueprint for his life. Leibowitz clearly understood that the layers of meaning in the Bible could only be taught if the student was an active player in the classroom. For this reason, her classes were not lectures but dialogues between herself, her students, and the written texts. She prodded her students to answer her questions, often criticizing their answers to sharpen their minds and hone their interpretive skills. For this reason, many of her students found the classroom experience with her somewhat intimidating.

Aside from 29 years of *Gilyonot* and the *Iyyunim Ḥadashim* (*Studies in the Weekly Parashah*), Leibowitz's work includes *Leader's Guide to the Book of Psalms* for Hadassah (1971), *Gilyonot le-Iyyun be-Sefer Yirmiyahu* (1974), and *Lilmod u-Lelamed Tanakh* (1995), a collection of essays on teaching Bible. The English edition appeared the same year. In 1990, Leibowitz produced, together with Moshe Ahrend, a two-volume course for the Open University called *Perush Rashi la-Torah*. She also published teachers' guides and numerous essays. In 2002, Yizhak Reiner and Stanley Peerless published *Studies on the Haggadah from the Teachings of Nechama Leibowitz*.

For all of her accomplishments, Leibowitz was an exceedingly humble person. She never used her academic titles, always referring to herself as simply Neḥama. She loved to tell stories and to hear stories. In 2003, Leah Abramowitz published *Tales of Nehama*, stories by her and about her contributed by her students. It can be argued that Leibowitz had a greater impact on Bible study and the teaching of Bible than anyone in the 20th century. She succeeded in opening up the world of Bible for everyone by taking Bible study out of academia and returning it to the people. David Bedein, an Israeli journalist, reports that he invited Leibowitz to teach the story of Rebecca in honor of the birth of his first daughter, Rivka. So Neḥama traveled to Safed for the Sabbath and more than 300 people showed up to sit on the lawn of the Wolfson Center to hear the lesson. They all came with their Bibles in hand because they all knew that to attend a class with Neḥama Leibowitz you needed to bring along just two things: a *Tanakh* and a desire to learn.

BIBLIOGRAPHY: S. Peerless, *To Teach and to Study The Methodology of Nehama Leibowitz* (2004); A.M. Toledano, *The Pedagogical Influence of Nehama Leibowitz* (dissertation, 2002); L. Abramowitz, *Tales of Nehama: Impressions of the Life and Teachings of Nehama Leibowitz* (2002); Y. Unterman, *Background and Examples of Nechama Leibowitz's Literary Approach to Bible* (Dissertation, 2002); M. Frankel, *Iyun ve-Hora'ah: Hanharat Shitatah shel Nehama Leibowitz* (dissertation, 1998); idem, in: *Abiding Challenges: Research Perspectives on Jewish Education* (1999), 359–374; M. Ahrend, R. Ben-Meir, and G.H. Cohen (eds.), *Pirkei Nehama: Sefer Zikaron le-Nehama Leibowitz* (2001); H. Deitcher, in: *Journal of Jewish Education*, 66:1–2 (2000), 8–22; A. Strikovsky, in: *Traditions and Celebrations for the Bat Mitzvah* (2003), 186–195; A. Oren, in: *Forum on the Jewish People, Zionism and Israel*, 38 (1980), 155–159; J. Rochwarger, in: *Torah of the Mothers* (2000), 57–81; M. Breuer, in: *Limudim*, 1 (2001), 11–20; E. Greenstein, in: *ibid.*, 21–33; E. Yadgur, in: *ibid.*, 45–80; Y. Resler, in: *Talelei Orot*, 5 (1994), 291–300; I. Rosenson, in: *Al Derkh ha-Avot: Sheloshim Shanah le-Mikhlelet Ya'akov Herzog* (2001), 433–453; M. Ahrend, in: *Mayim mi-Dalyav*, 14 (2003), 35–42; A. Mondshein, in: *Bet Mikra*, 44:2 (1998), 107–118; A. Ha-Cohen, in: *Alon Shevut le-Vogrei Yeshivat Har Ezion*, 13 (1999), 71–92.

[David Derovan (2nd ed.)

LEIBOWITZ, RENÉ (1913–1972), composer, theorist, teacher, and conductor. Born in Warsaw, Leibowitz went to France at a young age. From 1930 to 1933 he studied with *Schoenberg and Webern, and became the chief advocate of the Schoenberg school in France. In 1947 he organized a chamber music festival, "Hommage to Schoenberg," in which he conducted the first performances of several compositions of the Second Viennese school. He wrote a survey, *Schoenberg et son Ecole* (1947), which was the first monograph on Schoenberg, Berg, and Webern in French, and a treatise, *Introduction à la musique de douze sons* (1949). Being closely connected with such famous French intellectuals as Claude Lévi-Strauss and Jean-Paul Sartre, he succeeded in integrating the Germanic type of Schoenbergian musical thought in the cultural context of France. Throughout his life Leibowitz continued to promote interest in the 12-tone principle by his work as a conductor and also by his own compositions for orchestra and chamber ensembles.

ADD. BIBLIOGRAPHY: NG²; MGG²; S. Meine, "Ein Zwöftöner in Paris: Studien zur Biographie und zur Wirkung von René Leibowitz (1913–1972)," diss. Hochschule fuer Musik und Theater, Hanover (1998).

[Yulia Kreinin (2nd ed.)]

LEIBOWITZ, SAMUEL SIMON (**Samuel S. Lebeau**; 1893–1978), U.S. lawyer and jurist. Leibowitz was taken from Jassy, Romania, to New York at the age of four. In 1917 he began a brilliant career as a criminal lawyer. Of the 140 capital cases that Leibowitz defended, he saved the lives of all but one client, and attained national renown in his 1933–35 defense without fee of nine black youths charged with the rape of a white woman in Scottsboro, Alabama. Although the nine "Scottsboro Boys" were originally convicted and sentenced to death, Leibowitz secured acquittals for four of them at a retrial in 1937. A flamboyant attorney who defended the gangster Al Capone four times, Leibowitz became an impassioned jurist who imposed extraordinarily severe sentences on criminals, and extirpated corrupt officials. Leibowitz served on the King's County Court of Brooklyn from 1949 to 1961, when he was appointed to the New York State Supreme Court. Leibowitz was president of the United Organization for Israel Pioneers and a member of the New York Federation of Jewish Philanthropies.

BIBLIOGRAPHY: Q. Reynolds, *Courtroom* (1950). **ADD. BIBLIOGRAPHY:** R. Leibowitz, *The Life and Career of Samuel S. Leibowitz, 1893–1933*, (1981); F. Pasley, *Not Guilty! The Story of Samuel S. Leibowitz* (1933).

LEIBOWITZ, YESHAYAHU (1903–1994), Israeli scientist and philosopher. Born in Riga, Leibowitz studied chemistry and philosophy at the University of Berlin, where he received his doctorate in 1924. He also studied medicine and became a medical doctor in 1934 at the University of Basel. In 1935 he settled in Palestine and joined the staff of the Hebrew University. He was appointed professor of organic and biochemistry and neurophysiology. His research was concerned with saccharides and enzymes in chemistry and with the nervous system of the heart in physiology. He was the head of the biological chemistry department at the Hebrew University and professor of neurophysiology at the HU Medical School. He also taught the history and philosophy of science. Yet Leibowitz was not only an academician. He was involved in public affairs and had a unique approach to Judaism. As such he was a popular lecturer, who loved to appear before diverse audiences, also frequently on radio and television. Leibowitz served as editor in chief of several volumes of the *Encyclopedia Hebraica*. His writings are found mostly in periodicals: *Gilyonot, De'ot, Be-Terem, Petaḥim,* and *Moznayim*, and also in the newspaper *Haaretz*. A selection of lectures and articles from the period 1942–53 was published in book form, entitled *Torah u-Mitzvot ba-Zeman ha-Zeh* (1954). His book of collected essays, *Yahadut, Am Yehudi u-Medinat Yisrael* ("Judaism, Jewish People, and the State of Israel," 1975) stated his philosophy and views. Other books (published in 1965 and 1982) testify to his broad knowledge and great interest in Jewish life. He also wrote on Maimonides, *The Sayings of the Fathers*, and the weekly Torah-portion. In 1992 Eliezer Goldman published a collection of Leibowitz's essays in English under the title *Judaism, Human Values and the Jewish State*, making him known internationally.

Theocentrism and Humanism

Leibowitz regarded Judaism as a religious and historical phenomenon, which is characterized by a recognition of the duty to serve God in performing *mitzvot*. The service of God according to binding halakhic norms must be "for its own sake" (*li-shemah*), and its purpose is not designed to achieve personal perfection or to improve society. Religion is thus not a means toward any specific end. Judaism is for Leibowitz not humanism, or a sentiment or a bundle of memories. Jews have the obligation to take upon themselves the yoke of Torah and *mitzvot*. Leibowitz's standpoint is thus neither anthropocentric or ethnocentric, but theocentric. Consistent with his own reasoning, Leibowitz refused to be called a "humanist," because this is an anthropocentric notion that envisages the human being as a supreme value. Under the influence of Maimonides, Leibowitz stressed the transcendence of God, whom we cannot know. His thought also contains Kantian elements. Kant's critique of pure reason led to a theological agnosticism, whereas his critique of practical reason led him to affirm that the realization of values follows from a person's autonomous decision. There is a tension between Leibowitz the philosopher who read Kant on human autonomy, and regarded politics and ethics as domains where human autonomy is decisive, and the halakhic man who lived in conformity with his strict halakhic, theocentric conception of Judaism. For Leibowitz, morality is thus an atheistic category. Kant's influence on Leibowitz is also clear when he states that the value of a religious act is determined by the intention. Only when one performs an act because it is a divine commandment does it possess a religious value.

Religion and State

Leibowitz repeatedly expressed his opinions on the religious aspect of Jewish life in Israel. Before the state of Israel was established, he stressed the religious importance that national independence would assume, provided it would bring about halakhic legislation designed to mold the character of the state. After the establishment of the state, he advocated the separation of the Jewish religion from the state and its confrontation with it. He adopted a negative attitude toward the system of party rule, including the religious parties with their economic and rabbinical institutions.

Leibowitz emphasized the necessity for innovation in the *halakhah*, due to the changed circumstances created by the establishment of the State of Israel. He wanted halakhic decisions to cope with the challenge of today. One can note a change in his thought concerning the state in the course of time, although he himself would have denied this. Leibowitz refused to grant to the state religious status: the aim of the state would be the fulfillment of the needs of the individual and of the community, nothing more. He thought it was idolatry to ascribe holiness to the land or the state, which is not (in the words of religious Zionism) "the beginning of the redemption." The state – just like history – had for Leibowitz no religious significance. He was a Zionist, but he emphasized that the state need not realize values, it has merely to satisfy needs. The Jewish people, on the other hand, has to realize values. Against Ben-Gurion, he pleaded for the separation of state and religion. Whereas Ben-Gurion wanted religion to be an instrument in the hands of the state, Leibowitz asserted that religion had to be in opposition to the state. For Judaism, only God is holy, whereas country, nation, and state lack that status. The state is not a value in itself; indeed, "seeing the state as a value is the essence of the fascist conception." Rather, Leibowitz argued, the state is an instrument, a means to an end. Its existence allowed him not to be ruled by the *goyim*. In addition, Leibowitz criticized the "sacred cow of national unity," pointing out that the Jewish religion had always divided the people, whether between prophets and kings or between religionists or secularists.

Leibowitz further denied that Zionism had any religious significance, stating that, since the intention of many of its propagators had been completely nonreligious, it could not be retrospectively assigned religious value. In the same way, he refused to acknowledge any messianic significance in the creation of the State of Israel, citing Maimonides' warning against such messianic fervor. He did, however, ascribe immense moral significance for the Jewish people to the establishment of the Jewish state: "Now – and only now," he wrote, "with the attainment of the independence of the Jewish nation – will Judaism be tested as to whether indeed it has a 'Torah of life' in its hand .... Certainly there is no guarantee that the struggle on behalf of the Torah within the framework of the state will be crowned with success, but even so we are not free to desist from it, for this struggle is itself a supreme religious value, independent of its results."

Politics

Leibowitz was well known in Israel for his provocative utterances on the political situation. After the 1967 Six-Day War, his position on the occupation of the Palestinian territories was sharply critical. His uncompromising stance and forceful, biting language made him a known and much-discussed figure in religious as well as secular circles. In his opinion, partition of the country would be the rational and moral resolution of the Israeli-Palestinian conflict. With the outbreak of the Lebanon War in 1982, Leibowitz called upon the Israeli soldiers to refuse to serve in Lebanon. He also supported conscientious objection regarding military service in the territories on the grounds that occupation morally corrupts. His outspokenness on matters of conscience led to his vilification by those who saw him as a threat to their values, and the protest that ensued upon the announcement that he had been awarded the Israel Prize in 1993 was such that he turned it down.

Religion and Morality

In his antimystical approach to Judaism, Leibowitz wanted Jews to reach out toward transcendence, which is approached in the *mitzvot* that have to be performed without reward. Whereas *Levinas links morality and religion, Leibowitz differentiates between them and even separates the two. Levinas believed that the appeal of the other person is heteronomous, whereas Leibowitz maintained that only the divine command is heteronomous and that morality is autonomous. Therefore, their views on the relationship between religion and morality are radically opposed: for Levinas, religion and morality are intrinsically linked, for Leibowitz, ethical laws are religiously relevant only if a person accepts them as commanded by God. Another crucial difference between Levinas and Leibowitz lies in the fact that the former emphasizes the performance of the ethical act itself, whereas the latter highlights the intention of the act: an act is religious if performed "for the sake of heaven," it is not religious when performed as a function of human needs and based upon a person's arbitrary will. Since morality is autonomous, based upon human thought and will, and therefore not "for the sake of heaven," but "for the sake of man," it is not religious. Towards the end of his life, Leibowitz appreciated Levinas, but his concept of Torah and *mitzvot* prevented him from agreeing with him.

Christianity

Leibowitz had a very negative view of Christianity as well as of modern Jewish thinkers like *Rosenzweig and *Buber, who showed intellectual and religious interest in Christianity. In contrast to scholars and thinkers like David *Flusser, who investigated the Jewish roots of Christianity, Leibowitz wrote that the very concept of a "Judeo-Christian heritage" is a square circle. A synthesis or symbiosis is impossible; Christianity is for Leibowitz the adversary of Judaism. In his view, Christianity is the heir who does not want to admit that the testator is still alive. Judaism and Christianity cannot coexist, because Christianity claims that it is true Judaism, and is interested in the liquidation of Judaism as the religion of Torah and *mitzvot*.

Influence

In his essays, Leibowitz produced sharp and thought-provoking insights on many subjects such as the nature of holiness, chosenness, Messianism, prayer, redemption, and general and personal providence. His consistent and provocative thought gave him a prominent position in contemporary Jewish thought, especially in Israel. His thinking, even when contested, is stimulating and powerful and invites or even forces people to respond by formulating their own views.

ADD. BIBLIOGRAPHY: A. Kasher and Y. Levinger, *Sefer Yeshayahu Leibowitz* (Heb., 1977); H. Kasher, "'Torah for Its Own Sake,' 'Torah Not for Its Own Sake,' and the Third Way," in: *The Jewish Quarterly Review,* 89:2–3 (1988–89), 153–63; A. Sagi (ed.), *Yeshayahu Leibowitz. His World and Philosophy* (Heb., 1995); *Yeshayahou Leibowitz: le retour du sadducéen par Ami Bouganim* (1999); A.Z. Newton, *The Fence and the Neighbor: Emmanuel Levinas, Yeshayahu Leibowitz and Israel among the Nations* (2001); D. Banon, "E. Levinas et Y. Leibovitz," in D. Cohen-Levinas and S. Trigano (eds.), *Emmanuel Levinas: Philosophie et judaisme* (2002), 57–86.

[Asa Kasher and Rohan Saxena / Ephraim Meir (2nd ed.)]

LEIBZOLL (Ger., "body tax"), a special tax levied on Jews in Europe. Known under a variety of names – *Judengeleit, Leibmauth, Judenzoll, péage corporel,* etc. – it was first levied by the three landgraves of Thuringia in 1368, and became more common after the major expulsions of the 15th and 16th centuries. Principalities which excluded Jews issued, for a fee, a ticket of passage or limited sojourn which guaranteed their safety, enabled the authorities to control their coming and going, and was also a source of income. Due to the political fragmentation of Europe, having to pay the *Leibzoll* (in addition to the regular customs duties) was for the Jews a moral degradation as well as an economic burden, for the *Leibzoll* was accompanied by humiliating legal formulas. In addition, it was levied many times within one political or provincial unit, according to local usage. Thus a Jew going from Goerlitz in Silesia to the Leipzig fair in Saxony (a distance of about 110 mi.) had to pay eight times for himself alone a total of 14 different payments of between two and 12 groschen each, a total of two thaler, 11 groschen, and three pfennig. At the fair itself he had to pay twice that amount or more. Nonetheless, rich and privileged Jews often succeeded in freeing themselves from the obligation.

The *Leibzoll* was known as *Leibmauth* in Vienna "and was introduced not as a financial but as a police measure, to keep away a considerable number of useless Jews, and to supervise their conduct" (A. Pribram, *Urkunden und Akten* (1918), 423). By the **Toleranzpatent* of Joseph II it was abolished (1782), but Joseph reserved the right to exact its equivalent. Ten years later *Francis I introduced the *Judenbolleten* for the same purposes; it survived until 1848. The tax was abolished in Prussia in 1787, in Bavaria in 1799, and in most of the other German states in the first decade of the 19th century, either through direct French occupation or through the activity of leading Jewish financiers and *Court Jews. Israel *Jacobson succeeded in abolishing it in Brunswick, and Wolf *Breidenbach devoted himself to inducing Hesse-Darmstadt, Hesse-Homberg, Nassau, and other states to abolish it. The Russian form, the *Geleitzoll*, used to regulate passage across the Polish-Russian border, was abolished in 1862. The authorities often leased the collection of tax to a Jew, who could more easily supervise his brethren. The much-hated *péage corporel* of Strasbourg was leased in 1784 by Louis XVI to Herz *Cerfberr, one of the central figures in the struggle for its abolition.

BIBLIOGRAPHY: L. Horwitz, in: *Im deutschen Reich*, 17 (1911), 417–27; A. Pribram, *Urkunden und Akten* (1918), index, s.v. *Leibmaut, Bolletin*; H. Schnee, *Die Hoffinanz und der moderne Staat*, 3 (1955), 127ff.; S. Stern, *Der preussische Staat und die Juden* (1962), index, s.v. *Leibzoll*; Z. Szajkowski, *Franco-Judaica* (1962), 38–42; A. Hertzberg, *The French Enlightenment and the Jews* (1968), index, s.v. *Body Tax*; R. Markgraf, *Zur Geschichte der Juden auf den Messen in Leipzig* (1894), 83ff.

LEICESTER, county town in central England. A handful of Jews (but no community) lived here in the Middle Ages. They were expelled by Simon de Montfort in 1231 but were invited by his aunt, the countess of Winchester, to farm her lands. A section of the ancient Roman forum known as "Jewry Wall" has no connection with Jews. A modern community was formed after the influx of refugees from Russia at the close of the 19th century. In 1970, the Jewish population numbered approximately 1,100 out of a total population of some 283,540. SIR ISRAEL HART (1835–1911) played a prominent civic role and was repeatedly mayor. In 1928, following the elevation of Leicester to the status of a city in 1919, the office of mayor was elevated to lord mayor. The first Jewish lord mayor was Alderman Cecil Herbert Harris (1954) and the second Sir Mark Henig (1967). Two Jews, Barnett *Janner (Baron Janner of Leicester) and M. Goldsmith, were named honorary freemen of Leicester in 1971. In the mid-1990s the Jewish population dropped significantly to approximately 670. In the 2001 British census, Leicester was found to have a declared Jewish population of 417. An Orthodox synagogue and a variety of other institutions remained. The University of Leicester maintained a Holocaust Studies Centre, formerly headed by Professor Aubrey Newman.

BIBLIOGRAPHY: Levy, in: JHSET, 5 (1902–05), 34–42; J. Jacobs, *Jews of Angevin England* (1893), 238, 377; Rigg-Jenkinson, Exchequer; Roth, England, index.

[Cecil Roth]

LEICHTENTRITT, HUGO (1874–1951), musicologist and composer. Born in Pleschen, Poland, from 1905 he taught at the Klindworth-Scharwenka Conservatory in Berlin and was also music critic for the *Vossische Zeitung*. In 1933 he left Germany and became lecturer at Harvard University. His writings include *Haendel* (Ger., 1924); *Music, History and Ideas* (1938); *Music of the Western Nations* (1956); and a widely used handbook, *Musical Form* (1911, 1952; augmented English edition, 1951). His editions of early music appeared, among others, in the *Denkmaeler deutscher Tonkunst*. Leichtentritt composed a symphony, a comic opera, chamber music, an opera *Esther* (a dramatic legend), and a cantata *The Song of Solomon*.

LEICHTER, KAETHE PICK (1895–1942), Austrian Social Democratic politician, labor organizer, and author. Leichter was born and raised in Vienna. She resolved at a young age to devote her life to helping the less fortunate, especially members of the working class. After the outbreak of World War I, she did volunteer work on behalf of the war effort and worked in a day nursery for workers' children. In 1914, already an ardent socialist and pacifist, Kaethe Pick began studying political economy at the University of Vienna. She transferred to the University of Heidelberg in 1917, but in December of that year she was expelled from Germany for the duration of the war; she needed special permission to complete her doctorate in 1918 in Heidelberg. In 1921, Kaethe Pick married another left-wing activist, Otto Leichter; the couple had two sons. While Otto Leichter became editor of the major Austrian socialist newspaper, *Die Arbeiter-Zeitung*, Kaethe Leichter served as a director of women's affairs for the Wiener Arbeiterkammer and on the Commission on Socialization. In this position, Leichter systematically gathered material on women's work in Austria, compiled statistical data, and published articles and reports. She worked on behalf of legislation to protect working women and also tried to get more professional women hired at all levels of social administration, demanding equal pay for equal work. An active teacher, writer, and broadcaster, Leichter participated actively in Social Democratic Party conferences.

Kaethe and Otto Leichter were both involved in the socialist underground in Austria after 1934. After the *Anschluss* in 1938, her husband and sons succeeded in escaping to Switzerland and subsequently found refuge in the United States, but Kaethe Leichter was arrested in May 1938 while paying a final visit to her mother. While in prison, she wrote memoirs of her early years, "Lebenserinnerungen," published in Herbert Steiner (ed.), *Kaethe Leichter: Leben und Werk* (1973), 235–386 (this volume also includes a complete bibliography of Leichter's writings, 229–31). Even in the women's concentration camp of Ravensbrueck, she continued to exercise her leadership skills. In January 1942, together with other Jewish prisoners, she was sent on a transport to an unknown destination, where she was murdered soon thereafter. In memory of Kaethe Leichter, the Austrian government established a state prize awarded annually to an outstanding Austrian woman historian. Leichter's papers are in the Documentation Archive of the Austrian Resistance in Vienna.

BIBLIOGRAPHY: H.P. Freidenreich. *Female, Jewish, and Educated* (2002); I. Lafleur, "Five Socialist Women: Traditionalist Conflicts and Socialist Visions in Austria, 1893–1934," in: M.J. Boxer and J.H. Quataert (eds.), *Socialist Women* (1978), 215–48; O. Leichter, "Kaethe Leichter," in: N. Leser (ed.), *Werk und Widerhall: Grosse Gestalten des österreichischen Sozialismus* (1964), 234–44; G. Lerner, *Why History Matters* (1997), 50–55.

[Harriet Pass Freidenreich (2nd ed.)]

LEIDESDORF, SAMUEL DAVID (1881–1968), U.S. businessman and communal leader. Leidesdorf, who was born in New York City, became a certified public accountant at the age of 20. In 1905 he founded the accounting firm of S.D. Leidesdorf and Co., subsequently one of the largest in the U.S. He was extremely active as a fundraiser on behalf of numerous charities, especially the United Jewish Appeal, and collected millions of dollars for them. Leidesdorf was instrumental in establishing the New York University Medical Center and served as its board chairman. His other organizational posts included treasurer of the United Jewish Appeal of Greater New York for over 30 years; president of the Federation of Jewish Philanthropies; and director of both the Joint Distribution Committee and the National Conference of Christians and Jews. He also served as chairman of the board of the Institute for Advanced Study in Princeton, New Jersey.

LEIDESDORFER, Viennese family prominent in the 18th and 19th centuries. The family had two branches; the older line, from *Eisenstadt, was founded by ISAAC LEIDESDORFER (d. 1748), army purveyor and agent of Samuel *Oppenheimer. He was permitted to reside in Vienna in 1719 and was often employed as a translator by the authorities. His sons, SAMUEL (1700–1780) and LOEB (1705–1789), both army purveyors, received a joint letter of protection from Maria Theresa in 1758. Loeb married the daughter of R. Margulias-Joffe and had 15 children, one of whom married a daughter of Israel von *Hoenigsberg. Samuel had seven children; his daughter Judith married Akiva *Eger the Elder and afterward Meir *Fischels, the Prague communal leader. Samuel's sons MOSES and JOACHIM (ḤAYYIM) were among the founders of the Vienna *ḥevra kaddisha* in 1763. Joachim married a granddaughter of Samson *Wertheimer; his descendants married into the Hoenigsberg and Wertheimstein families.

The younger branch of the family, which was also named Nass after Nassau, its place of origin, was established by MENAHEM MENDEL LEIDESDORF of Pressburg (Bratislava; d. 1770), a partisan of Jacob *Emden in the Emden-Eybeschuetz conflict. His son AARON, one of the wealthiest members of the Vienna Jewish community, was head of its hospital for 40 years. In 1797 he was nominated, along with Salomon von Herz and David Wertheimer, as one of the three legal representatives of Viennese Jewry. His daughter BABETTA (BELA) married Israel (Ignaz) Liebmann, wool merchant and industrialist. In 1817 they were given the title of Edler von Liebenberg. Their sons, one of whom married a daughter of Leopold von *Herz, were baptized. Aaron's brother MARKUS (1754–1838) amassed great wealth as an army purveyor during the French revolutionary and Napoleonic wars; he specialized in the rapid organization of military hospitals. His requests for ennoblement were first rejected, mainly because of objections by Francis I and because of irregularities in his business transactions, but eventually, in 1817, he was granted the title of Edler von Neuwall. Markus was a representative of the Vienna Jewish community (1816–38). In 1824 his sons, AUGUST and IGNAZ, both baptized and married to daughters of the Herz family, were ennobled. August's son, ALBERT VON NEUWALL (1807–1881), an Austrian politician, was the first to speak in the Kremsier parliament (1848) in favor of Jewish emancipation.

BIBLIOGRAPHY: H. Schnee, *Die Hoffinanz und der moderne Staat*, 4 (1963), 332–4; A. Pribram, *Urkunden und Akten* (1918), index; B. Wachstein, *Die ersten Statuten des Bethauses in der inneren Stadt...* (1926); M. Grunwald, *Samuel Oppenheimer und sein Kreis* (1913), 215–6; idem, *Vienna* (1936), index.

[Henry Wasserman]

LEIGH, ADÈLE (1928–2004), British soprano. Leigh was born in London into a Polish-Jewish immigrant family. She studied at the Royal Academy of Dramatic Art, then at the Juilliard School, New York, with Maggie Teyte. Leigh made her Covent Garden début in 1948 (Xenia in *Boris Godunov*), and remained a member of the company until 1956. She distinguished herself in Mozart, Strauss, and Massenet roles, took the title role in *Manon*, and appeared in the first performances of Vaughan Williams' *Pilgrim's Progress* (1951) and Tippett's *Midsummer Marriage* as Bella (1955). Leigh pursued a parallel career in show business. She became a member of the Vienna Volksoper as principal operetta soprano (1963–72). Johann Strauss, Lehar, and Kalman became her staple fare for the next few years. She appeared in Israel with the famous composer Robert Stolz. Stolz was invited to conduct *Night in Vienna* concerts with the Israel Philharmonic Orchestra, 1963. The concerts achieved tremendous success. Her American debut was in Boston in 1966. She later came out of retirement to sing Gabrielle (*La vie parisienne*) at the Brighton Festival in 1984 and Heidi Schiller in Sondheim's *Follies* in London in 1987. Leigh combined a pleasing lyric soprano and musical sensibility with a charming stage appearance. In her later years she taught at the Royal Northern College of Music in Manchester.

ADD. BIBLIOGRAPHY: Grove Online; MK; "Adèle Leigh," in: *Opera* (2004), 940–41 .

[Naama Ramot (2nd ed.)]

LEIMDOERFER, DAVID (1851–1922), Hungarian-born Reform rabbi and scholar. After serving as rabbi at Nordhausen, Germany, from 1875 to 1883, he became preacher at the Hamburg Reform temple; he was a brilliant orator. Leimdoerfer took a moderate line in the Reform movement.

His works include three studies of Psalms, *Psalterklaenge, Homiletische Einleitung in die Psalmen* (1894), *Psalter-Ego in den Ich-Psalmen* (1898), and *Die Himmel ruehmen* (1906); two studies of Ecclesiastes, *Der "Prediger Salomonis" in historischer*

Beleuchtung (1892) and *Loesung des Kohelethraetsels durch den Philosophen Barukh ibn Barukh* (1900); a study of Esther, *Zur Kritik des Buches Esther* (1899); and shorter works, including *Messias-Apokalypse* (1895), *Altbiblische Priestersegen* (1900), and *Talmudische Ethik des Alphabets* (1912). He edited the centenary volume of the Hamburg Reform temple *Festschrift zum hundertjaehrigen Bestehen des Israelitischen Tempels in Hamburg* (1918); many of his sermons were published, and he wrote textbooks for Jewish schools.

LEINER, GERSHON ḤANOKH (Henikh) BEN JACOB (1839–1891), ḥasidic rebbe. Leiner was born in Izbica, Poland, and studied with his grandfather R. Mordecai Joseph, the first *rebbe* of the Izbica-Radzyn dynasty, until the latter's death in 1854. He stayed with his father R. Jacob, the second *rebbe*, and moved with him to Radzyn, where he lived until his death, after which Leiner became the third *rebbe* (1878).

In contrast to his predecessors, R. Gershon Ḥanokh was a prolific writer whose works cover diverse fields and genres. He had a bold, unconventional personality and did not hesitate to initiate controversial innovations that put him in the eye of the storm. He documented the homilies of his grandfather (*Mei ha-Shilo'aḥ*) and father (*Bet Ya'akov*), establishing the foundation of the Izbica-Radzyn dynasty's writings. Utilizing his outstanding talmudic erudition he composed *Sidrei Taharot*, a *Gemara*-style work on the tractates of *Kelim* (1873) and *Oholot* (1903) in *Seder Taharot*, for which there is no Babylonian Talmud. This work includes interpretation in the style of Rashi and *Tosafot*. In "*Ha-Hakdamah ve-ha-Petiḥah*" (introduction to *Bet Ya'akov*, 1890) he gives an historiographic account of the transmission and development of Torah, mainly Kabbalah, to his time. He made it a point to show that Maimonides was part of the kabbalistic tradition. He addressed the central theme in his grandfather's homilies: God's will as guiding all human deeds, including sins, in a kabbalistic sense. After traveling to the Naples aquarium he wrote a book called *Sefunei Temunei Ḥol* (1886), where he claimed that he had found the special *ḥillazon* (snail) and the way to produce **tekhelet* (blue dye) from it for *ẓiẓit*. Radzyn and Breslau Ḥasidim dye their *ẓiẓit* accordingly to this day. Among his other prominent writings are *Sod Yesharim* and *Orḥot Ḥayyim* (1890), the latter being the best known. He was self-taught in medicine and wrote prescriptions that were honored in pharmacies.

BIBLIOGRAPHY: A. Marcus, *Ha-Ḥasidut* (1980), 243–46; Ḥ.S. Leiner, *Dor Yesharim* (1909); S.Z. Shragai, *Be-Netivei Ḥasidut Izbica-Radzyn* (1972–74); S. Magid, *Hasidism on the Margin* (2003).

[Yehuda Ben-Dor (2nd ed.)]

LEINSDORF, ERICH (1912–1993), conductor. Born in Vienna, Leinsdorf was assistant conductor to Bruno Walter and Toscanini at the Salzburg Festival (1934–37), and conducted in Italy, France, and Belgium. After settling in the United States in 1937, he conducted German works at the Metropolitan Opera, New York, until 1943, and then served there as musical consultant. He was appointed director of the New York City Opera in 1955 and of the Boston Symphony Orchestra in 1962, and later returned to the Metropolitan Opera.

LEIPZIG, city in Saxony, Germany. Jews are first mentioned in Leipzig at the end of the 12th century; an organized community with a synagogue and a school existed from the second quarter of the 13th century. Its inhabitants came mainly from neighboring Halle and Merseburg. The community and its synagogue are mentioned in a responsum of *Isaac b. Moses of Vienna ("*Or Zaru'a*") between 1250 and 1258; Jewish moneylending activity is also noted by R. Isaac. The fair regulations of Leipzig of 1268 guaranteed protection to all merchants, and moved the day of the market from Saturday to Friday for the benefit of the Jewish merchants. The Jewish community may have suffered during the *Black Death persecutions, for the margrave disposed of their synagogue in 1352. In 1364 a *Schulmeister* and other Jews are again mentioned; they lived in the *Judenburg*, which had its own entrance gate. The Jews in Leipzig were probably not expelled in 1442 as the city historians record (though their status did deteriorate), but only after the expulsion of the Jews from Saxony in 1540. Their right to attend the fairs, held three times yearly, remained unaltered.

Between 1668 and 1764, 82,000 Jews attended these fairs, and decisively influenced their business; Leipzig's growth as a center of the *fur trade was due to Jewish activities. Jews, however, were prohibited from opening shops facing the streets, and from holding services. Jews who died during the fairs had to be buried in *Dresden, or elsewhere, until a cemetery was opened in 1815.

A permanent Jewish settlement was founded in 1710 when Gerd Levi, *mintmaster and purveyor, received rights of residence. The number of "privileged" Jewish households allowed residence in Leipzig grew to seven by the middle of the 18th century. After the Seven Years' War (1756–63) Jews held services during the fairs in a number of prayer rooms, according to **Landsmannschaften*. By the end of the century 40 to 50 Jewish merchants were living in Leipzig who employed clerks, servants, agents, and *shoḥatim*. A law issued in Saxony in 1837 permitted the establishment of a community in Leipzig, though permission to build a synagogue was withheld. A prayerhouse, influenced by *Reform tendencies, was opened. Adolf *Jellinek was employed as preacher between 1845 and 1857; due to his efforts a new synagogue was built and consecrated in 1855. In 1869 a Reform *synod was held in Leipzig, and the Deutsch-Israelitischer Gemeindebund was founded, led by leaders of the Leipzig community Moritz Kohner and Jacob *Nachod.

After 1868/69, with the abolition of all anti-Jewish restrictions, the number of Jews increased greatly by immigration from Galicia and Poland. There were 7,676 Jews living in Leipzig in 1905, and 13,032 in 1925, making it the largest community in Saxony. As many of the newcomers were Orthodox, a separate community and synagogue was organized, at which rabbis N.A. *Nobel (1902–05), Ephraim Carlebach (1901–36), and David Ochs (1936) officiated. Reform rabbis were A.M.

Goldschmidt (1858–88), Nathan Porges (1888–1917), and Gustav Kohn (from 1921; died in the Holocaust).

Holocaust Period

In 1933, there were 11,564 Jews in Leipzig, including 3,847 of East European origin. By 1938, 1,600 Jewish businesses had been "aryanized," around 3,000 Jews had emigrated, and in October 1938, 1,652 of the East European Jews were deported to Poland. During the **Kristallnacht* the two main synagogues were burned down, shops were looted, and the funeral hall was demolished. Another thousand East European Jews were deported to Poland in early 1939. The 2,500 Jews remaining in 1941 were crowded into 43 "Jew houses" (*Judenhaeuser*) and used for forced labor. Subsequently all were deported to the east in nine transports through February 1945.

Contemporary Period

After the war a new community was reorganized. The Broder Schul synagogue was restored, as were the funeral hall and cemeteries. The community, which numbered 100 in 1968, was under the supervision of an East Berlin rabbi and religious services were led from 1950 by the *ḥazzan*, Werner Sander, who organized the Leipziger Synagogalchor in 1962, a unique choir in Europe. The singers, who are not Jewish, perform Jewish liturgical and folk music.

Membership in the Jewish community declined during the 1970s and 1980s. In 1991 the Jewish community numbered 35. After 1990 it increased due to the immigration of Jews from the former Soviet Union. In 2005 the Jewish community numbered 1,133.

There are several institutions and organizations in Leipzig which deal with Jewish history and culture. The Deutsche Buecherei Leipzig (the German National library) houses the Collection of Exile Literature 1933–45 and the Anne Frank Shoah Library. The exile collection contains publications which were written or published abroad by emigrants – among them many Jews – between 1933 and 1945. The Anne Frank Shoah Library collects worldwide published literature on the persecution and murder of the Jews of Germany under Nazi rule. In 1992 the Ephraim Carlebach Foundation, which focuses on the history of the Jews of Leipzig, was established. Its activities include academic research, publications, exhibitions, cultural events, and preservation of historic buildings. In 1995 the Simon Dubnow Institute for Jewish History and Culture at Leipzig University, named after the Russian-Jewish historian Simon *Dubnow (1860–1941), was founded. The institute focuses on Jewish life primarily in Central and Eastern Europe.

[Jacob Rothschild / Larissa Daemmig (2nd ed.)]

Hebrew Printing

Some Hebrew lettering (from wood-blocks) appears in books printed in Leipzig even before 1500 and in the two decades following, as in Novenianus' *Elementale Hebraicum*, 1520. In 1533 appeared a Hebrew psalter, prepared by Anthonius Margarita (like Novenianus, a lecturer in Hebrew) and printed by his father-in-law, Melchior Lotther. Hebrew printing was resumed in the last quarter of the 17th century through the effort of the apostate F.A. Christiani, and among these productions was a beautiful edition of Isaac Abrabanel's commentary on the Latter Prophets (1685). Numerous books were printed, again by non-Jewish presses, in the 19th century, among them Maimonides' responsa and letters, edited by Mordecai b. Isaac Tamah, with H.L. Schnauss (1859). At the end of the 19th and early 20th century the leading Oriental printing house in Europe, W. Drugulin, produced, among other works, S. Mandelkern's famous Bible Concordance (for Veit and Co., 1896) and *Antologia Hebraica* (ed. by H. Brody and M. Wiener, 1922), for the Insel Verlag. By that time Leipzig had become the most important printing and publishing center in Germany. Drugulin designed a new type, taking early printing type as his model. Another new type was designed by Raphael Frank, cantor in Leipzig, in 1910, for the Berthold'sche Schriftgiesserei in Berlin.

BIBLIOGRAPHY: M. Freudenthal, *Aus Geschichte und Leben der Juden in Leipzig* (1930); idem (ed.), *Leipziger Messgaeste* (1928); W. Harmelin, in: YLBI, 9 (1964), 239–66; A. Kapp, in: ZGJD, 1 (1929), 329–32; 3 (1931), 131–4; 4 (1932), 198–202; 5 (1935), 50–58; 6 (1935), 40–47; Germ Jud, 1 (1962), 155–6, incl. bibl.; 2 (1968), index, incl. bibl.; J.G. Hartenstein, *Die Juden in der Geschichte Leipzigs* (1938); F. Grubel, in: BLBI, 5 (1962), 132–8; M. Unger, in: *Zeitschrift fuer Geschichtswissenschaft*, 11 (1963), 941–57; A. Marx, *Studies in Jewish History and Booklore* (1944), 331ff.; A.M. Habermann, *Ha-Sefer ha-Ivri be-Hitpatteḥuto* (1968), index. **ADD. BIBLIOGRAPHY:** E. Bertram, *Menschen ohne Grabstein. Die aus Leipzig deportierten und ermordeten Juden* (2001); B. Kowalzik, *Wir waren eure Nachbarn. Die Juden im Leipziger Waldstrassenviertel* (1996); A. Lorz, *Suchet der Stadt Bestes. Lebensbilder juedischer Unternehmer aus Leipzig* (1996); T. Schinkoeth, *Juedische Musiker in Leipzig 1855–1945* (1994); M. Unger (ed.), *Judaica Lipsiensia. Zur Geschichte der Juden in Leipzig* (1994); B.-L. Lange, *Juedische Spuren in Leipzig* (1993); S.J. Kreutner, *Mein Leipzig. Gedenken an die Juden meiner Stadt* (1992); M. Unger, H. Lang (eds.), *Juden in Leipzig. Eine Dokumentation zur Ausstellung anlaesslich des 50. Jahrestages der Faschistischen Pogromnacht im Ausstellungszentrum der Karl-Marx-Universitaet* (1988); S. Spector (ed.), *Encyclopedia of Jewish Life Before and During the Holocaust*, vol. 2 (2001), 714–16.

LEIPZIGER, EMIL WILLIAM (1877–1963), U.S. Reform rabbi. Leipziger, who was born in Stockholm, Sweden, went to the United States with his family in 1881. He was ordained by Hebrew Union College, Cincinnati, in 1900, and from that year until 1913 served as a rabbi in Terre Haute, Indiana. He went to Temple Sinai, New Orleans, in 1913. Leipziger was active in social welfare movements in New Orleans and played a leading role in establishing the local community chest (1925). From 1939 to 1941 Leipziger was president of the Central Conference of American Rabbis.

[Sefton D. Temkin]

LEIPZIGER, HENRY M. (1853–1917), U.S. educator. Leipziger, who was born in Manchester, England, later moved to New York City with his family. Although trained as a lawyer, financial necessity led Leipziger to become a teacher. In 1884 he became principal of the Hebrew Technical Institute whose purpose was to give manual training to immigrant boys. As a result of doing volunteer work with the newly organized YMHA, the Aguilar Free Library, and the Educational Alliance, Leipziger earned a reputation as an expert in the field of educational extension activities. In 1890 he was appointed assistant superintendent of New York City schools and placed in charge of the Free Lecture Series, an adult education program for working people. Leipziger built up the program by hiring well-known speakers, using stereopticon slides, providing for lectures in foreign languages, and choosing a varied assortment of topics. In 1905, at the height of the program, one and a quarter million people attended more than 3,000 lectures. Leipziger called it the "People's University." He published *The Education of the Jews* (1890).

BIBLIOGRAPHY: R.L. Frankel, *Henry M. Leipziger, Educator and Idealist* (1933).

[Selma Berrol]

LEIRIA, city in W. central Portugal. Its Jewish community first came to notice in 1378 when the Jews complained to the king of their ill-treatment by the gentile inhabitants, particularly during Holy Week. In 1492 after the expulsion from Spain, a Hebrew printing press was set up in the town by Samuel b. Abraham de Ortas, assisted by his sons. Works published included Proverbs, with Targum and the commentaries of Levi b. Gershom and Menahem b. Solomon Meiri (1492); Former Prophets, also with Targum and Levi b. Gershom's commentary and that of David Kimḥi (1494). This press may also have been responsible for the edition of Jacob b. Asher's *Tur Oraḥ Ḥayyim* (1495) which has an engraved border on the opening pages possibly by a Jewish artist. The De Ortas firm also produced in 1496 a Latin and Spanish translation of Abraham *Zacuto's *Ḥibbur ha-Gadol* under the title *Almanach Perpetuum* – the most important of the seven known Latin incunables printed in Portugal. After the expulsion of 1497, Leiria was a Converso center and numerous inquisitional martyrs came from there.

BIBLIOGRAPHY: M. Kayserling, *Geschichte der Juden in Portugal* (1867), 27, 90; M.B. Amzalak, *A tipografia hebraica em Portugal no século XV* (1922), 35ff.; *King Manoel of Portugal* (Catalogue of Early Portuguese Books, no. 6); C. Roth, in: *Sefarad*, 14 (1954), 122–25. **ADD. BIBLIOGRAPHY:** S.A. Gomes, *História & crítica*, 13 (June 1986), 53–58.

[Cecil Roth]

LEISERSON, WILLIAM MORRIS (1883–1957), U.S. labor economist. Leiserson, who was born in Estonia, was taken to New York City in 1890. He worked in a shirtwaist factory while continuing his education at Cooper Union. He passed the University of Wisconsin entrance examinations without having formally graduated high school. In Wisconsin he became involved with the Milwaukee reform socialists. He also worked on the economist John R. Commons' staff, studying labor conditions in Pittsburgh. These experiences prepared him to serve as an investigator for the New York State legislature's Commission on Unemployment and Workmen's Compensation. In 1911 he returned to Wisconsin to become deputy industrial commissioner for the state, where he also helped found the National Association of Public and Private Employment Agencies. Leiserson's achievements in the employment and social security fields include drafting of the Ohio Plan for unemployment insurance, chairmanship of the Ohio Commission on Unemployment Insurance, and helping to draft the U.S. Social Security Act of 1934.

Another major interest of Leiserson's was labor arbitration. He became the first impartial chairman of the Rochester (N.Y.) Labor Adjustment Board for the men's clothing industry (1919–21) and served as a full-time arbitrator until he became a professor at Antioch College in 1926. He also served as secretary of the National Labor Board (1933–34), chairman of the National Mediation Board (1934–39), and member of the National Labor Relations Board (1939–43). Leiserson taught at Antioch, the University of Toledo, and Johns Hopkins University. He also wrote many articles and books reflecting his interest in social security and unemployment, industrial relations, and arbitration. Two years after his death, his *American Trade Union Democracy* was published.

BIBLIOGRAPHY: J.M. Eisner, *William Morris Leiserson* (1967).

[Albert A. Blum]

LEITNER, GOTTLIEB WILHELM (1840–1899), British educator and Orientalist. Born Gottlieb Saphir (or Sapier) in Budapest, Leitner took the name of his stepfather, a conversionist minister to the Jews of the Ottoman Empire. In the late 1850s he moved to England, becoming professor of Arabic and Mohammedan Law at King's College, London. From 1864 to 1879 he lived in India, where he was principal of Government College, Lahore, and spent several years as a notable explorer of a remote region in Kashmir and Afghanistan he termed "Dardistan." Leitner was also a renowned and remarkable linguist, reputedly knowing 50 languages at his death. He returned to England in 1879, where he opened the Oriental Institute at Woking, south of London, meant for Indian students and also as a research center for Indian studies. There he opened England's first mosque, and was regarded as a positive exponent of Islam in the West. Through his fame as a linguist, Leitner had been asked to give Queen Victoria a suitable Hindustani title when she was made Empress of India in 1876. He chose the title *Kaisar-i-Hind*, by which she was officially known in India. Leitner's career as an explorer of Central Asia and a linguist was remarkably like that of other British Jews of the same time, among them Ney *Elias and Sir Auriol *Stein. Leitner was the uncle of the Conservative politician and Zionist Leopold *Amery.

BIBLIOGRAPHY: ODNB online.

[William D. Rubinstein (2nd ed.)]

LEIVIK, H. (pseudonym of **Leyvik Halper(n)**; 1888–1962), Yiddish poet and playwright. Born in Igumen (now Ihumen, Belarus), in 1905 he joined the *Bund and participated in revolutionary activities. The following year he was arrested and while awaiting trial wrote *Di Keytn fun Meshiekh* ("The Chains of the Messiah," 1939) with motifs adumbrating later works. In court in 1908 Leivik openly avowed his desire to overthrow the government. Sentenced to four years' hard labor and Siberian exile for life, in 1912 he marched for four months in a column of chained convicts to the vicinity of Irkutsk. There he expressed his longing for freedom in the play *Dort, Vu di Frayhayt* ("Where Freedom Dwells," 1952). In spring 1913 he made a dramatic escape across the icy Siberian wastes and traveled via Hamburg to New York, which experience was reflected in the collections of verse entitled *Oyf di Vegn Sibirer* ("On Siberian Tracks," 1915) and *In Shney* ("In the Snow," 1915). In New York he worked for several years as a paper-hanger. His literary debut came in 1914 with the poem, "Es Hulyen Vintn, Veyen, Shaln" ("The Gusting Winds Rage and Howl"). During his first few years in the U.S. he was associated with Joseph *Opatoshu, *Mani-Leyb, Moyshe-Leyb *Halpern, and other poets of the literary group known as *Di *Yunge*, though he did not share their rejection of social themes. He reversed his name to create the pseudonym H(alper) Leivik to avoid being confused with the slightly older and already established Moyshe-Leyb Halpern. In 1918 Leivik published *Hintern Shlos* ("Behind Bars"), a first collection of visionary poems describing his years of imprisonment. This was followed in 1919 by *Lider fun H. Leyvik* ("Poems by H. Leivik") including the well-known poems "Geyt Men Zikh Lang" ("Trudging into the Distance") and "Ergets Vayt" ("Somewhere Far Away") which represented an amalgam of Romantic longing, sublimated pain, and political protest that came to characterize Leivik's *œuvre.* By then his writing was moving closer to the more aesthetic style of the Inzikhistn ("Introspectivists"). However, their repudiation of national and political themes did not suit his temperament either. The cataclysms of World War I, the Russian Revolution, and the ensuing Civil War led him to more universal themes and he then wrote his four apocalyptic epic poems "Er" ("He"), "Dos Kranke Tsimer" ("The Sick Room"), "Di Shtal" ("The Stable"), and "Der Volf" ("The Wolf"), all in 1920. The latter in particular reflected the postwar pogroms in Ukraine.

In 1921 his play, *Der Goylem* (1921; *The Golem*, 1966) made an immediate impression and is the work for which he is most remembered. He takes up the midrashic motif of the powerless Messiah grieving at his inability to come to the aid of the Jewish people and transforms the legend of Rabbi *Judah Loew of Prague and his "Golem" into a parable concerning violence perpetrated in the service of corrupted ideals. The relevance to the contemporary situation in Russia was clear. The Golem is a quasi-human robot fashioned by the rabbi to defend the Jews of Prague which, once created, becomes subject to all too human lusts and frustrations and soon escapes the control of the saintly, but impotent rabbi. Leivik's plays of the 1920s, *Shmates* ("Rags," 1928; first staged 1921), *Di Oreme Melukhe* ("The Poor Kingdom," 1927), *Bankrot* ("Bankrupt," 1927), and *Shap* (1928; *Shop*, 1999) all evince a commitment to social justice. These years represented the apogee of Yiddish theater in the U.S., and Leivik was one of a number of dramatists seeking to give greater artistic value to the Yiddish stage. "In Keynems Land" ("In No Man's Land") appeared in the first volume of *Khalyastre* (1922) edited by Perets *Markish and Y.-Y. *Singer. Contributing to this prestigious avant-garde journal added further to Leivik's already considerable reputation. In 1925 Leivik returned to Europe. In Moscow the Soviet critics took exception to the "nationalist" motifs of *Der Goylem*, but above all to Leivik's rejection of bloodshed as a means of perfecting society. Little did they imagine, he recalled 30 years later, that soon it would be they themselves against whom the Golem would raise his ax. Leivik's growing disillusionment with Bolshevism was reflected in the play *Hirsh Lekert* (1926).

In 1932 the tuberculosis which he had contracted earlier became more severe and he spent four years in sanatoria. It was in these years of physical illness that he achieved a degree of harmony reflected in writings such as *Lider fun Gan-Eydn* ("Poems from Paradise," 1937) and especially "Di Balade fun Denver Sanatoryum" ("The Ballad of the Denver Sanatorium"). In 1936, together with Opatoshu, Leivik began editing a series of anthologies or *Zamlbikher* (8 vols., 1936–52), the first volume of which contained his verse drama "Abelar un Heluiz" ("Abelard and Heloise"), which many consider one of his most aesthetically successful works, once more on the theme of redemption through suffering. The following year Leivik made his first visit to Palestine and in Tel Aviv gave a speech "Oykh ikh Bin a Toyshev bay Aykh …" ("I Too Live Among You," collected in *Eseyen un Redes* ("Essays and Speeches"), 1963) in which he was cautiously enthusiastic in his assessment of Zionism, but warned against biased disparagement of the Diaspora.

His major place in Yiddish literature was confirmed in 1940 by the publication of the "Jubilee Edition" of his complete works. During the war years Leivik wrote frequent, authoritative articles for *Der Tog* in which he celebrated and evaluated significant predecessors and contemporaries, as for example in 1942 when he honored Ḥayyim-Naḥman *Bialik on the eighth anniversary of his death, arguing that his "Shkhite-Shtot" ("Town of Slaughter," 1904) was now more relevant than ever before. In 1945 Leivik's articulation of desolate grief at the fate of his murdered people, *In Treblinke Bin Ikh Nit Geven* ("I Was Not in Treblinka"), was awarded the Louis Lamed Prize. In this collection of poems Leivik contends with the central paradox of all Holocaust literature, namely the inadequacy of words to express the ineffable horror juxtaposed with the irresponsibility of remaining silent. *Mit der Sheyres-Hapleyte* ("With the Survivors," 1947) is the diary of a visit to Dachau in 1946, also reflected in *Di Khasene in Fernvald* ("Wedding in Fernwald," 1949), a strangely romantic account of joy in the midst of despair when Leivik had been present at the first DP wedding in the Fernwald camp and saw in the ceremony a symbol of Jewish resurgence. As Leivik watched, he imagined that he saw Elijah the Prophet and the Messiah together with the murdered former spouses standing beside the bride and groom.

In September 1958 he suffered a stroke, lost his power of speech, and was confined to his bed until his death four years later. There were to be two further major publications during his lifetime. His *Oyf Tsarisher Katorge* ("In a Czarist Penal Settlement," 1959) resembled *Hintern Shlos* (published some four decades earlier) in content (and included memories of imprisonment in Minsk and Moscow and earlier childhood experiences) and brought Leivik's *œuvre* full circle. In his last collection of verse, *Lider tsum Eybikn* ("Poems to the Eternal," 1959), Leivik seems to have achieved an almost Nietzschean, sublime, aestheticized serenity and reconciliation with all being. He died December 23, 1962, a few days after his 74th birthday. The following year a memorial volume of *Eseyen un Redes* appeared. Leivik was an outstanding figure in the history of modern Yiddish literature, remarkable for the broad sweep of his poetry, spanning the Siberia of political exile, the teeming tenements of the Lower East Side, the oppressiveness of the sanatorium, the kabbalists of Safed, and the Holocaust, to which his reaction was one of vicarious pain, guilt, and deeply felt anguish. His work is imbued with a quasi-mystical, neo-Romantic humanism that finds a redemptive purpose in suffering and is constantly concerned with the cosmic struggle between good and evil. His lasting significance lies in his moral sensitivity and the distinctive lyric voice that absorbed much from Di Yunge and the Inzikhistn but became uniquely his own and enabled him to have a profound spiritual impact on his generation and to personify the conscience of his people.

BIBLIOGRAPHY: Z. Zilbercwaig, *Leksikon fun Yidishn Teater* (1934), 1059–75; Waxman, Literature, 4 (1960^2), 1028–37; C. Madison, *Yiddish Literature* (1971^2), 348–81. **ADD. BIBLIOGRAPHY:** Z. Rejzen, Leksikon, 2 (1930), 196–202; Y. Yeshurin, in: H. Leivik, *Oysgeklibene Shriftn* (1963), 336–48 (bibl.); LNYL, 5 (1963), 107–28; S. Liptzin, *A History of Yiddish Literature* (1972), 299–311; Sh. Niger, *Yidishe Shrayber fun Tsvantsikstn Yorhundert*, 1 (1972), 167–214; E.S. Goldsmith, in: *Jewish Book Annual*, 45 (1987), 79–98; S. Goodhart, in: *Philosophy and Literature*, 16:1 (1992), 88–105.

[Hugh Denman (2nd ed.)]

LEKERT, HIRSCH (1880–1902), bootmaker, native of a small Jewish town in Lithuania. Lekert was active from his youth in workers' groups and in the *Bund in Dvinsk, Kovno, Yekaterinoslav, and Vilna. He became famous for his attempt on the life of the governor of Vilna, wounding him, because the latter had ordered the flogging of 26 demonstrators (among them 20 Jews) on May 1, 1902. After the flogging, the central committee of the Bund published a manifesto calling for revenge; Lekert carried out his attack with the help of a group of workers which organized itself independently, since the Vilna committee of the Bund, headed by M. *Gurevich, refused to support the deed officially – they were opposed in principle to political terror. The flogging gave rise to dejection and confusion among the Jews; the shooting by a simple bootmaker at the antisemitic governor was regarded by the Jewish population in general as an act in defense of Jewish honor. Lekert served as an example for P. *Dashewski, especially after the Kishinev pogrom. The Bund, together with Polish and Lithuanian Social Democrats, published a statement on the affair which had international reverberations. In the Russian *Iskra*, V. Zasulich and J. *Martov praised Lekert's reaction, while Lenin dissociated himself from it. In the Bund itself terrorist tendencies were aroused for a time. Its fifth conference in Berdichev in August 1902 adopted a resolution for a policy of "organized revenge" that was encouraged by S. *Gozhanski and A. *Braun. The resolution was rescinded under the influence of the "committee abroad" of the Bund.

Lekert was sentenced to death by a military court and hanged on June 10, 1902. The anniversary of Lekert's death was marked for many years in the Jewish workers' movement. The deed was commemorated in popular songs and in special literary works (H. *Leivick, A. *Kushnirov). On the 20th anniversary of Lekert's death a memorial, which no longer exists, was erected in a square in Minsk.

BIBLIOGRAPHY: J.S. Hertz, *Hirsh Lekert* (Yid., 1952), bibliography compiled by E. Jeshurin: 118–35; N. Sirkin, in: *Kunteres*, 6:117 (1922/23), 10–12; A.S. Stein, *Ḥaver Artur* (1953), index; Index to *Mi-Bifnim* (1970), 293.

[Moshe Mishkinsky]

LEKET, SHIKHḤAH, AND PE'AH (Heb. לֶקֶט, שִׁכְחָה, וּפֵאָה; "gleanings, forgotten produce, and the corners of the field"), talmudic designation of three portions of the harvest which the farmer was enjoined to leave for the benefit of the poor and the stranger. *Pe'ah* ("corners") and *leket* ("gleanings") are enjoined in Leviticus 19:9–10, while *shikhḥah* ("forgotten produce") and *leket*, in Deuteronomy 24:19–21 (see also *Poor, Provision for). *Leket* refers to the ears of corn which fall to the ground during the reaping. It was usual for the reaper to grasp the ears of corn with one hand and to cut them with the other. If during the reaping one or two stalks fell to the ground because the reaper was not holding them, he was not to gather them but leave them for the poor (Lev. 19:9–10). Corresponding to *leket* in grain is *peret* in the vineyard. Thus if during the vintage one or two grapes fell to the ground, they constituted *peret* for the poor (Pe'ah 6:5). The *olelot* ("small clusters with few grapes") in the vineyard also belonged to the poor (*ibid.* 7:4), in accordance with the verse, "Thou shalt not glean thy vineyard, neither shalt thou gather the fallen fruit of thy vineyard; thou shalt leave them for the poor and for the stranger."

Shikhḥah applies to one or two sheaves forgotten in the field by the harvester. The owner may not take them, but "it shall be for the stranger, for the fatherless, and for the widow" (Deut. 24:19). The biblical precept of *shikhḥah* refers to cut sheaves, but the sages extended it to apply also to the standing corn which is forgotten in the reaping (Sif. Deut. 283; Pe'ah 6:7). *Shikhḥah* also applies to trees so that if the harvesting of one or two trees was overlooked, they are *shikhḥah* (Pe'ah 7:1). The Bible (Deut. 24:20) specifies only olive trees: "when thou beatest thine olive trees thou shalt not go over the boughs again, it shall be for the stranger, for the fatherless, and for the widow." The word *aḥarekha* ("to go over again") was taken to refer to *shikhḥah*, but it was made to apply to all trees (Ḥul. 131a). *Pe'ah*, according to the Bible, applies only to the corner of the field left by the reaper, but it was extended by the rabbis to include the fruit of the trees (Sifra, Kedoshim 1:7; Maim., Yad, Mattenot Aniyyim 1:2). According to biblical law, the command to give the gifts to the poor applies only in Ereẓ Israel, since the Bible says, "And when ye reap the harvest of your land" (Leviticus 19:9); the rabbis, however, applied it to outside Ereẓ Israel as well (Ḥul. 137b), and according to Maimonides (*ibid.* 1:14) the same ruling applies to the other gifts to the poor. The Bible lays down no minimum quantity for *pe'ah*, and therefore according to the letter of the law, even if one ear of corn has been left, the precept has been fulfilled; the rabbis, however, established a minimum of one sixtieth of the harvest (Pe'ah 1:1–2; Ḥul. 137b). They forbade the farmer to hire gentile workers for the harvest lest, being unaware of the law, they prevent the poor from gathering *leket* and *pe'ah*. Nevertheless, if he does hire them and they reap the whole field, he must give *pe'ah* from the harvest (Tosef., Pe'ah 3:1; BK 94a). R. Simeon, who always "expounded the reasons for the precepts of the Torah," gives four reasons why the Torah enjoined that *pe'ah* be left at the edge of the field: to prevent the poor from being deprived of their rights – that the farmer should not wait until his field is practically cleared and say to his poor relative, "this is *pe'ah* – hasten and take before others come" (if it is left at the edge of the field, however, the poor see it and come); not to waste the time of the poor – that the poor should not have to wait and watch where the farmer would leave his *pe'ah*; to prevent suspicion – that passersby should not say, "let that farmer who has not left *pe'ah* be cursed" (when they see him reaping the whole field and do not know that he has already given it); and because of swindlers (who will not leave *pe'ah* and say they have already given it; Tosef., Pe'ah 1:6; Shab. 23a).

Pe'ah was left standing, and the poor plucked it. They were not permitted to cut it with a scythe nor uproot it with a spade so as to prevent them from assaulting one another (Pe'ah 4:4). The poor were permitted to pick *pe'ah* thrice daily: in the morning, at midday, and in the afternoon. If a poor man came at some other time he was forbidden to pick, in order that all the poor assemble at a prescribed time. These times were chosen because some of the poor were nursing mothers who must eat at the beginning of the day, and some were minors who do not wake up early and cannot reach the field until midday, and some were aged who cannot reach the field until the afternoon (Pe'ah 4:5; Maim., *ibid.* 2:17). The poor thus obtain four gifts from a vineyard – *peret, olelot, pe'ah*, and *shikhḥah*; three from grain – *leket, shikhḥah*, and *pe'ah*; and two from trees – *shikhḥah* and *pe'ah*. Basing themselves on the fact that the Bible does not state "Thou shalt give," but "thou shalt leave," the rabbis held that the farmer was forbidden to select the poor to whom these gifts would be given, any poor person being free to take them (Ḥul. 131a). Although the injunction applies specifically to the Jewish poor, in the interests of peace, it was extended to the gentile poor (Git. 5:8).

BIBLIOGRAPHY: D. Hoffmann, *Das Buch Leviticus*, 2 (1906), 36–38, 240f.; S. Lieberman, *Tosefta ki-Feshutah, Zera'im* (1955); Maim., Yad, *Mattenot Aniyyim*; J. Feliks, *Ha-Ḥakla'ut be-Ereẓ-Yisrael bi-Tekufat ha-Mishnah ve-ha-Talmud* (1963), index; E.E. Urbach, in: *Zion*, 16 (1951), 1–27; I.F. Baer, *ibid.*, 27 (1962), 141–55; I. Heinemann, *Ta'amei ha-Mitzvot be-Sifrut Yisrael*, 1 (1954³), 2 (1956).

[Abraham Arzi]

LEKHAH DODI (Heb. לְכָה דוֹדִי; "Come, my friend"), the opening words and name of a hymn with which the Sabbath is welcomed. It consists of nine stanzas; the initial letters of the first eight stanzas acrostically form the name of the author Solomon ha-Levi (*Alkabeẓ), a Safed kabbalist of the early 16th century. The opening line and refrain is: "Come, my friend, to meet the bride; let us welcome the presence of the Sabbath." Inspired by talmudic accounts (Shab. 119a) which describe how the scholars used to honor and welcome the Sabbath (likened to a princess or bride), the Safed kabbalists used to go on Friday afternoons into the fields to meet the "Queen Sabbath" in meditation and song. The hymn "*Lekhah Dodi*" reflects this practice as well as the kabbalistic identification of the Sabbath with the *Shekhinah*, the mystical archetype of Israel. Hence also the messianic motives in the hymn, echoing talmudic concepts associating redemption with the observance of the Sabbath (*ibid.* 118b).

"*Lekhah Dodi*" is sung immediately after the recital of Psalms 95–99 and 29, with which the Sabbath eve service starts in Ashkenazi synagogues; the *ḥazzan* stands on the *bimah* ("high platform") and not at his regular place to indicate that this part of the service is not in the original order of prayers. It is customary to turn around at the recital of the last stanza ("*Bo'i ve-shalom*") to face the entrance of the synagogue and bow. The "Sabbath bride" is thus symbolically welcomed. "*Lekhah Dodi*," among the latest *piyyutim* to be incorporated into the prayer book, is one of the favorite hymns in the Ashkenazi as well as in the Sephardi ritual. In the extant texts, there are only slight variations, although one version has five additional stanzas also attributed to Alkabeẓ. In many rituals, "*Bo'i kallah Shabbat malketah*" ("Come our bride, queen Sabbath"; Shab. 119a) is added at the end of "*Lekhah Dodi.*"

The Reform ritual has retained only an abridged version of the hymn consisting of the first, third, fourth, and the last stanzas (*Union Prayer Book*, 1 (1926), 27). "*Lekhah Dodi*" has been rendered into most European languages; among the well-known translations are those of the German poets J.G. Herder and H. *Heine. In his poem "*Prinzessin Sabbat*," Heine erroneously ascribed its authorship to Judah Halevi. Another version of "*Lekhah Dodi*" was composed by a contemporary of Alkabeẓ, R. Moses ibn Machir, head of the yeshivah in Ein Zeitun near Safed (printed in *Seder ha-Yom* (Venice, 1599), 43).

[Meir Ydit]

Example 1. Three versions of the "Lekhah Dodi" melody common in the Near East. The omission sign in each line represents three repetitions, with slight variations, of the first two bars. I. Notated by J. Parisot in Damascus, 1901. After J. Parisot, Journal of the American Oriental Society, *24, 1903. II. Common Jerusalem Sephardi version. Free notation by B. Bayer. III. Romanian Sephardi version. After Idelsohn, Melodien, 4, 1922, no.4.*

Example 2. Beginning of the European Sephardi type-melody. From Hamburg (?). After A. Baer, Ba'al Tefillah, *1883³, no. 329.*

Example 3. Beginning of the Mediterranean and Balkan Sephardi type-melody. From Sarajevo. After Levy, Antologia I, *1965, no. 25.*

Musical Rendition

The poem was written to be sung, but none of the contemporary sources offers any information about its original melody. In the first printed version of the text, in a Sephardi prayer book, Venice 1583/4, it is headed "To the tune of *Shuvi Nafshi li-Menuḥaikhi*" (by Judah Halevi; Davidson, Oẓar, 3665). This heading was taken over by two much later Sephardi prayer books, Amsterdam 1660/1 and Constantinople 1734/5, but apparently nowhere else. No conclusions can be drawn from it about the melody adopted or created in Safed, or about the ancestry of any one of the melodies presently used. Most of the existing melodies – A.Z. Idelsohn estimated their number at over 2,000 – show no distribution over a larger area and are either demonstrably late or the obvious products of musical styles that could not have been available or acceptable at Safed. Of the remainder there emerge three distinct melodies, one of which may well represent the original setting. Type-melody *a* is found in Ereẓ Israel, southern Syria, Turkey, and the Balkans and has also been notated from North African informants. It belongs to the **Maqam Nawa*, which dominates the melodic character of the Sabbath eve and morning services in the Eastern Mediterranean communities, and Idelsohn proposed it as the original setting of "*Lekhah Dodi.*" Type-melody *b* is found in the Sephardi communities of Amsterdam, London, Hamburg, and Leghorn. It is more complex than type *a* and has a definitely Oriental flavor. Type-melody *c* is found in the Sephardi communities of Bayonne and Bordeaux, in the Comtat Venaissin (i.e., Provence, a non-Sephardi community), and has also been notated from informants from Sarajevo (Yugoslavia) and Meknès (Morocco); its variants are extremely divergent, but all of them contain the elements of a Turkish military march. All these communities also have some strictly local melodies for "*Lekhah Dodi*" and the non-Sephardi Eastern communities have only local and regional melodies. The single example published from Yemen is sung to the general Yemenite pattern of psalm recitation (Idelsohn, *Melodien*, 1 (1914), nos. 20–21). In the Western Ashkenazi area, a certain stabilization was attempted by the melodic linking of "*Lekhah Dodi*" to the particular character of the respective Sabbath, week, or season. There were special melodies for *Shabbat Shuvah* and *Shabbat Sefirah*, and the melody used on the eve of *Shabbat Ḥazon* and during the three weeks between Tammuz 17 and Av 9 was based on **Eli Ẓiyyon*. Many of the ostensibly free compositions also begin with a "seasonal reminiscence," such as the **Ma'oz Ẓur* motive for the Sabbath of the Ḥanukkah week. The completely free compositions are in the majority, and the surviving cantorial manuals of the 18th century already contain hundreds of melodies which for the most part reflect the style of the gentile environments ("Menuetto," "Polonaise," etc.). They also show the interesting custom of setting each stanza to a different melody, or at least distinguishing "*Hitoreri*" ("Wake Up!") by an energetic melody and "*Bo'i ve-Shalom*" ("Come in Peace, O Sabbath Queen") by a lyrical one. Since the "reception of the Sabbath" in the synagogue precedes the "entrance of the Sabbath" itself, it was possible to accompany the ceremony, and especially the singing of "*Lekhah Dodi*," with musical instruments. There are references to this practice in several communities, notably Prague, in the 17th and 18th centuries. In Eastern Europe no trace of standardized renditions can be discerned. This complete freedom may account for Hebrew-Yiddish "*Lekhah Dodi*" "play songs" and parodies.

[Bathja Bayer]

BIBLIOGRAPHY: Elbogen, Gottesdienst, 108, 388, 530; Davidson, Oẓar, 3 (1930), no. 928; Abrahams, Companion, CXXIV–CXXVII; Y.Y. Cohen, *Seder kabbalat Shabbat u-fizmon lekhah dodi* (1969). MUSICAL RENDITION, SEPHARDI TYPE-MELODIES. TYPE *a*: Idelsohn, Melodien, 4 (1923), nos. 3–7; J. Parisot, in: JAOS, 24:2 (1903), 244; A. Baer, *Ba'al Tefillah* (1883³), no. 937; Levy, Antología, 1 (1965), nos. 14, 20, 23; 3 (1968), no. 327. TYPE *b*: A. Baer, *Ba'al Tefillah* (1883³), no. 329; E. Aguilar and D.A. De Sola, *Ancient Melodies of the Spanish and Portuguese Jews' Congregation, London* (1857, 1931), no. 7 (also in: Idelsohn, Melodien, 4 (1923), 110); F. Consolo, *Libro dei Canti d'Israele* (1892), no. 5 (also in Idelsohn, loc. cit.); Levy, Antología, 1 (1965), no. 18. TYPE *c*: J.S. and M. Crémieu, *Chants Hébraïques suivant le rite… de l'ancien Comtat Venaissin* (1887), no. 1; M.J. Benharoche-Baralia, *Chants Hébraïques traditionnels en usage dans la communauté sephardie de Bayonne* (1961), no. 13; S. Foy, *Recueil des Chants… en usage dans la Communauté de Bordeaux* (1928); Levy, Antología, 1 (1965), no. 25; 3 (1968), no. 78. OLDER WEST ASHKENAZIC FREE AND SEASONAL MELODIES: A. Nadel, in: EJ, s.v. *Lecha Dodi*; Idelsohn, Melodien, 4 (1923), 217, 219–20, 222, 229; A. Baer, *Ba'al Tefillah* (1883³), nos. 325–7. LITERATURE: Idelsohn, Melodien, 4 (1923), 109–10; Idelsohn, Music, 116, 362, 509 note 54; A. Friedmann, *Der Synagogale Gesang* (1904), 70–71; Adler, Prat Mus, 24, 28–30, 127. "PLAY SONGS" AND PARODIES: S. Lehman, in: *Arkhiv far Yidisher Shprakh-Visenshaft, Literaturforshung un Etnologie*, 1 (1926–33), 430.

LEKHNO, DAVID (d. 1735), scholar living in the Crimean community of *Karasubazar (Belogorsk). His family name indicates his Polish origin. A leader of the Karasubazar community, Lekhno was also respected by the Karaites of Crimea. His extant works include an introduction to *Maḥzor Minhag Kafa*, which contains information on the way of life of Crimean Jewry; *Mishkan David*, on Hebrew grammar; and *Devar Sefatayim*, a history of the kingdoms of the Tatar khans in Crimea (the first chapters were published by Y.D. Markon in *Devir*, 2 (1924, 243–7).

BIBLIOGRAPHY: A.A. Harkavy, *Altjuedische Denkmaeler in der Krim* (1876), 230–2.

[Yehuda Slutsky]

°**LELEWEL, JOACHIM** (**Ignacy**; 1786–1861), historian and Polish freedom fighter. The Polish historian and statesman *Czacki, his teacher at the University of Vilna, entrusted him with the proofreading of his research work on Jews and *Karaites (*Rozprawa o żydach i Karaitach*) in 1807. In 1830, at the time of the Polish uprising, he was appointed vice minister of education and religions in the provisional national government. After the suppression of the revolt, he immigrated to Paris and settled in Brussels in 1833, and after 1848 he abandoned political activity. He published a comprehensive work on the history of Poland (20 vols., 1823–64). In his important work *Géographie du moyen âge* (5 vols. with atlas, 1849–57), Lelewel deals, among other things (vol. 4), with the travels of R. *Benjamin of Tudela. Lelewel also published an article in Eliakim *Carmoly's *Notice historique sur Benjamin de Tudèle* (1852²).

His attitude toward the Jews, which was at first negative, changed from 1832. At the end of that year, Lelewel issued his appeal *Au peuple d'Israël!* (the full text of it was published in Leon Hollaenderski's *Les Israélites de Pologne* (1846), 117–31), which was later translated into Yiddish by Ludwig Joshua Lubliner. Lelewel calls upon the Jews to support the revolt of the Polish nation which will break out in the future. He says that "the Jews will obtain their rights, and if they insist upon returning to Palestine the Poles will assist them in the realization of this aspiration." On Nov. 16, 1859, the Polish periodical *Przegląd rzeczy polskich*, which appeared in Paris, published a "letter from J. Lelewel to Mr. H. Merzbach," in which the author expressed his vigorous opposition to the antisemitic campaign, accused the Russian government of having fomented hatred between Poles and Jews, and hoped that an improvement in the condition of the population would result in healing the breach between them. At his funeral in Paris, Lelewel was eulogized by Rabbi Elie-Aristide *Astruc. Jewish students in Warsaw held a memorial service for Lelewel in a synagogue on June 1, 1861.

BIBLIOGRAPHY: M. Muenz, *Lelewel, Kaempfer fuer Recht und Wahrheit und die Judenfeinde* (1860); M. Balaban, in: *Miesięcznik Żydowski*, 1:1 (1933), 289–331; J. Shatzky, *Geshikhte fun Yidn in Varshe*, 2 (1951), 164–7, 203, 218; S. Lastik, *Z dziejów oświecenia żydowskiego* (1961), index; A. Eisenbach (ed.), *Żydzi a powstanie styczniowe, materiały i dokumenty* (1963), index; H. Merzbach, *Joachim Lelewel w Brukseli* (1889).

[Arthur Cygielman]

LELOUCH, CLAUDE (1937–), French film director. Born in Paris, Lelouch and his mother moved through Europe during World War II to evade the Nazis but were captured toward the end of the war and spent three months in Dachau. He made a short film at 14, and four years later a television film in the United States. In 1960 he made his first feature film, but *Un homme et une femme* ("A Man and a Woman"), winner of a 1966 Cannes Film Festival prize, put him in the front ranks of French cinema. He made *Vivre pour Vivre* (1967), *La Vie, l'Amour, la Mort* (1969), *Le Voyou* (1970), *Un Autre Homme une Autre Chance/Another Man Another Chance* (1977), *Un Homme et une Femme: Vingt Ans Deja/A Man and A Woman: 20 Years Later* (1986), and *Les Miserables* (1995). Later films include *Les Parisiens* (2004), *Men and Women* (2005), and *The Courage to Love* (2005).

[Jonathan Licht]

LELOV (**Lelow**), ḥasidic dynasty in Poland and Ereẓ Israel. Its founder, DAVID BEN SOLOMON OF LELOV (1746–1813), studied Lurianic Kabbalah in his youth and behaved in the manner of the "great Ḥasidim." He became attracted to Ḥasidism as a result of his contact with *Elimelech of Lyzhansk, and studied under several ḥasidic rabbis, including *Moses Leib of Sasov, becoming the outstanding disciple of *Jacob Isaac Horowitz, ha-Ḥozeh ("The Seer") of Lublin. He earned his living as a grocer. David's teachings stressed love of the Jewish people (*ahavat Yisrael*) and of man in general; he said: "I am not worthy as yet to be called a *ẓaddik* since I still feel more love for my own children than for other people." He was much appreciated by the prominent ḥasidic leaders of his day. David was both a friend and a relative of Jacob Isaac of *Przysucha, the "Holy Jew." When a controversy broke out between the latter and Jacob Isaac of Lublin, David attempted to reconcile the two sides. The physician, Bernard of Piotrkow, the famous penitent (*ba'al teshuvah*), was his outstanding disciple. David's son, MOSES (1778–1850), became the son-in-law of Jacob Isaac of Przysucha, and served as rabbi in several communities. Toward the end of his life he settled in Ereẓ Israel. Since then part of the Lelow dynasty has been connected with Ereẓ Israel, although they did not formally serve as *admorim*. Moses' grandson, DAVID JOSEPH OF LELOV (1827–1907), was a disciple of Menahem Mendel of *Warka (Worki). From 1877 he led a ḥasidic community. The dynasty is still continued through its branch in Ereẓ Israel.

BIBLIOGRAPHY: M. Brakman, *Migdal David* (1930); L. Grossmann, *Shem u-She'erit* (1943), 56; M. Buber, *Tales of the Ḥasidim: Later Masters* (1961), 185–8; M.Y. Weinstock, *Peri Kodesh Hillulim* (1961).

[Adin Steinsaltz]

LELOW (Pol. **Lelów**), village (formerly a town) in Kielce province, S.E. central Poland. Several dozen Jewish families were living in Lelow in 1547, but in 1564 only six families remained; each paid the king one red guilder residence tax and a certain quantity of spices for the right to slaughter cattle. During the 16th and 17th centuries Jews played an important part in the Lelow fairs. In the first part of the 18th century they had grown to a considerable community, paying 741 zlotys poll tax in 1718 and an annual average of 1,050 zlotys in 1733–37. In the district, which included the communities of Lelow, Naklo, Janow, Pilico, Szczekocin, and Zarki, there were 3,415 Jews in 1765, when 335 Jewish poll-tax payers were recorded in Lelow and 18 villages were under the community's jurisdiction. By an agreement with the townsmen, in 1778, the Jews were released from the payment of municipal taxes, as well as from the duty of billeting the troops. Between 1823 and 1862 Jewish residence was restricted to a specific quarter. The community numbered 269 (29% of the total population) in 1808, 339 (39%) in 1827, 480 (53%) in 1857, 720 (60%) in 1897, and 638 (52%) in 1921. Before the outbreak of World War II there were about 700 Jews in Lelow. The Jewish community was liquidated in September 1942, when all the Jews were deported to *Treblinka death camp. After the war the Jewish community of Lelow was not reconstituted.

BIBLIOGRAPHY: Halpern, Pinkas, index; J. Kleczyński, *Spis ludności dyecezyi krakowskiej 1787* (1894); Warsaw, Archiwum Skarbowe, *Tax Register of 1553, 12:46*; I. Schiper, *Dzieje handlu Żydowskiego na ziemiach polskich* (1937), index; B. Wasiutyński, *Ludność Żydowska w Polsce w. wiekach XIX i XX* (1930), 56; R. Mahler, *Yidn in Amolikn Poyln in Likht fun Tsifern* (1958), index.

[*Encyclopaedia Judaica* (Germany)]

LELYVELD, ARTHUR JOSEPH (1913–1996), U.S. Reform rabbi. Lelyveld was born in New York City and received his B.A. from Columbia University in 1933 and his M.H.L. and ordination from *Hebrew Union College in 1939. He was awarded an honorary D.D. by HUC-JIR in 1955, and a Litt.D. by the Cleveland College of Jewish Studies, where he was on the faculty, in 1986. Lelyveld's first pulpit was with Bene Israel in Hamilton, Ohio, a congregation he served while also acting as director of youth activities for the *Union of American Hebrew Congregations. In this position, he was instrumental in initiating summer youth conclaves and in organizing the National Federation of Temple Youth. During this time, he was also founder and first president of the Jewish Peace Fellowship (1941–44).

A passionate Zionist, Lelyveld then served as executive director of the Committee on Unity for Palestine (1944–46). In this role, the eloquent Lelyveld played a little-known but instrumental role in obtaining critical American recognition of the newly formed State of Israel. He won the support of Eddie *Jacobson, the former business partner of President Harry S. Truman, for the cause of a Jewish homeland; and in 1946, with Jacobson's introduction, Lelyveld became one of the first Jewish spokesmen to speak with Truman on behalf of a Jewish state.

In 1946, Lelyveld was named assistant national director (1946–47) and then national director of the *B'nai B'rith Hillel Foundation (1947–56). He subsequently continued to build bridges between the United States and Israel as executive vice chair of the *American-Israel Cultural Foundation (1956–58). In 1958, Lelyveld was named senior rabbi of Anshe Chesed Congregation (Fairmont Temple) of Cleveland, becoming senior rabbi emeritus in 1986. He also became an adjunct professor of religion at Case Western Reserve University and the Bernard Rich Hollander lecturer in Jewish thought at John Carroll University.

An outspoken advocate for social justice and civil rights, Lelyveld went to Mississippi to help register black voters during the turbulent "Freedom Summer" of 1964. There, he was beaten and seriously injured by segregationists. The next year, Lelyveld received an award for "distinguished service to the NAACP and the cause of Freedom." He was also appointed to the board of trustees of the Martin Luther King Jr. Center for Social Change.

On the national stage of the Reform movement, Lelyveld served on the Commission on Social Action (1962–71) and the executive board of the *Central Conference of American Rabbis (1971–73), before being elected vice president (1973–74) and then president (1975–76) of the CCAR. He subsequently served as president of the *Synagogue Council of America (1979–81) and honorary president of the *American Jewish Congress and the American Jewish League for Israel. In 1988, the *Histadrut established a scholarship in his honor in Israel. The Cleveland Jewish community also dedicated the Arthur J. Lelyveld Forest in Israel in recognition of his devotion to Zionism and the *Jewish National Fund.

A prolific writer of numerous articles and monographs, Lelyveld was a contributor to the *Universal Jewish Encyclopedia* and the author of two books: *Atheism is Dead* (1968) and *The Steadfast Stream: An Introduction to Jewish Social Values* (1995).

His son, Joseph *Lelyveld, former executive editor of the *New York Times*, wrote a moving and painful memoir of his childhood with his parents and in their absence titled it *Omaha Blues: A Memory Loop* (2005).

BIBLIOGRAPHY: K.M. Olitzky, L.J. Sussman, and M.H. Stern, *Reform Judaism in America: A Biographical Dictionary and Sourcebook* (1993).

[Bezalel Gordon (2nd ed.)]

LELYVELD, JOSEPH (1937–), U.S. journalist and author. Born in Cincinnati, Ohio, Lelyveld was the son of Rabbi Arthur *Lelyveld, who became prominent in the Reform and civil rights movements. During his childhood, his father was largely absent, and the marriage ultimately dissolved. Young Lelyveld was often left with grandparents, and once with Seventh Day Adventists on a Nebraska farm.

A graduate of Harvard College with a bachelor of arts degree in 1958, he earned a master of arts in American history from Harvard in 1959 and a master of science from the Columbia University Graduate School of Journalism in 1960. Lelyveld spent a year in Burma on a fellowship before joining the *Times* as a copy boy in 1962. He moved up to reporter and had a variety of local and national assignments. One of his more memorable stories involved a fourth-grade class in New York City. Lelyveld attended class every day and wrote about the students, their life away from school, the teacher, and others in a series that lasted through the school year. In 1980, he got his first foreign posting, to the Congo. He was a correspondent based in London, then New Delhi, and then Hong Kong, and served two tours as the correspondent in South Africa. After his second tour in Johannesburg, Lelyveld won a Pulitzer Prize in 1986 for his book *Move Your Shadow*, about apartheid in South Africa. He was also the recipient of numerous journalistic honors. From 1987 to 1989, he was foreign news editor of the *Times*, and he became managing editor in 1990, the second highest job in the news organization below the executive editor, Max *Frankel. Lelyveld succeeded Frankel in 1994, and served as executive editor until 2001.

After he retired from the newspaper, Lelyveld was called back into temporary service after his successor, Howell Raines, was forced to resign after 21 months when a rogue reporter was unmasked as a liar and fraud. Lelyveld presided over the newsroom until his original choice for the job, Bill Keller, became executive editor.

In 2005, Lelyveld published an unusual memoir, *Omaha Blues: A Memory Loop*. In it, Lelyveld discussed his relationship with his father and his mother and his feelings about being Jewish. In 1996, when his father was dying, Lelyveld had conducted a journalistic investigation of his family. He was led to a trunk filled with family memorabilia stored in the basement of the Cleveland synagogue where his father served as rabbi. It took years before Lelyveld sifted through his father's letters, which helped shape his memoir.

[Stewart Kampel (2nd ed.)]

LEMANS, MOSES (1785–1832), Hebraist and mathematician. Born in Naarden, Netherlands, Lemans was one of the leaders of the Haskalah movement in Holland. He was one of the founders in 1808 of the "Chanogh lanangar ngal pie darkoo" society the aim of which was a reform in Jewish education. He published a pamphlet in which he praised the Sephardi pronunciation of Hebrew, preferring it to the Ashkenazi one. For the society he published Hebrew textbooks, as well as a translation of the Bible into Dutch. He was one of the founders of the Jewish Mathematicians' Association, "Mathesis artium genetrix." In 1818 he was appointed head of the first school for needy Jews in Amsterdam, and in 1828 teacher of mathematics in the Amsterdam gymnasium (secondary school). Lemans published a number of works on Hebrew grammar and mathematics. With S.I. *Mulder, he compiled a Hebrew-Dutch dictionary. Of his Hebrew poems, the most important is an epic on the revolt of the Belgians against the Netherlands (in Ms.). For his activities on behalf of the Jews he was awarded a medal by the Netherlands' government. His works include *Levensbeschrijving… Moses Majemonides* (Amsterdam, 1815); *Rudimenta of gronden der hebreeuwsche taal* (1820); *Gebeden der Nederlandsche Israëliten* (1822); *Hebreeuwsch-Nederduitsch handwoordenboek* (1831); and *Allereerste gronden der Hebreeuwsche taal* (1876).

BIBLIOGRAPHY: Ulman, in: *Jaarboeken voor de Israëliten in Nederland*, 2 (1836), 297–312; A. Dellavilla, *Allon Muzzav* (1852); Michman-Melkman, in: *Leshonenu la-Am*, 18 (1967), 76–90, 120–35.

[Jozeph Michman (Melkman)]

LEMBA, Judaizing African tribe living in small groups throughout northeast South Africa and in central and eastern Zimbabwe. Notwithstanding that this tribe is in many respects indistinguishable from neighboring tribes, for much of the 20th century a number of Lemba, and particularly those of South Africa, have claimed to be of Jewish or Semitic ancestry, and a number of outside European observers have made similar claims for them for an even longer period. Recent genetic work has suggested that there may be some truth in their traditions.

According to oral traditions of origin, the Lemba claim to come from a place in the north called Sena (sometimes Sena

One). The Lemba habitually refer to themselves as "the white men who came from Sena." Apparently at the end of the 16th century the Lemba, now settled inland, far away from Islamic or other coastal influences, developed their identity and religious system independently. Throughout this period they did not intermarry. They had strict laws of purity and food taboos. The eating of pork was punished by death. They would only eat meat that had been ritually slaughtered by a Lemba. Today the religious life of the Lemba is highly syncretistic. Many of them belong to various Christian churches (e.g., the Zion Christian Church and Pentecostal groups), whereas some in Zimbabwe are Muslims. Some Lemba, however, claim to be Lemba by religious practice as well as by ethnic identification. The religious practices of these Lemba do not have much in common with Judaism as it is practiced elsewhere. The great majority of those Lemba who perceive themselves as ethnically "Jewish" find no contradiction in regularly attending a Christian church.

Recent work has brought the Lemba to international attention. The chief reason for this are genetic studies that have suggested that the Lemba may have something like "Jewish" ancestry. The original research which seemed to be reaching towards this conclusion was carried out by Professor Trefor Jenkins of the South African Institute for Medical Research and the University of the Witwatersrand in Johannesburg. Jenkins had the idea of trying to determine the origin of the Lemba by collecting genetic material from the tribe. The reason for this is that one tribal tradition had it that the original Lemba immigrants from the north, from Sena, were males who subsequently took local African wives. Jenkins argued that if the Y-chromosome of the Lemba, which only passes down the male line, could be shown to originate in some specific part of the world, it might be possible to determine where the Lemba were from.

On the basis of samples of DNA from 49 Lemba men, Jenkins wrote a scientific article that was published in *The American Journal of Human Genetics* (59, 1996). He was able to show that "50% of the Lemba Y chromosomes are Semitic in origin – 40% are Negroid, and the ancestry of the rest cannot be resolved. These Y-specific genetic findings are consistent with Lemba oral tradition." Jenkins' pioneering efforts reached a popular audience with the transmission of the BBC Television series *Origins* and the book based on the series, *In the Blood: God, Genes and Destiny* (1996) by Professor Steve Jones, a geneticist at University College, London. Relying on Jenkins' data Jones noted: "In the pedigree of the Lemba there is a surprise. Most of their genes – blood groups, enzymes and the like – unite them with the African peoples around them. However, those on the Lemba Y chromosome … have a different origin. On a family tree of the world's male lineages the Lemba are linked, not with Africans, but with the Middle East. The Lemba legend of their origin contains a hidden truth." Jenkins' work immediately began to have an impact on the Lembas' sense of their own identity. There was some possibility that the Lemba had come from South Arabia. A subsequent analysis of Lemba and Arabian DNA (see T. Parfitt et al., "Y Chromosomes …" in Bibliography below) showed a significant similarity of markers between many of the Hadramaut Y chromosomes and those of the Lemba. It was also discovered that one of the South African sub-clans of the Lemba carries a haplotype which has been connected with the Jewish priesthood – the Cohen Modal Haplotype. This haplotype was of a very high frequency – over 50% of the sub-clan had it. These results could therefore with great caution be interpreted as indicating that at some time in the past Jews inhabited the areas from which the Lemba came – probably South Arabia. This is the most likely locus for the transmission of the haplotype.

BIBLIOGRAPHY: T. Parfitt, M.G. Thomas, D.A. Weiss, K. Skorecki, J.F. Wilson, M. le Roux, N. Bradman, and D. Goldstein, "Y Chromosomes Travelling South: The Cohen Modal Hapolotype and the Origins of the Lemba – the 'Black Jews of Southern Africa,'" in: *American Journal of Human Genetics,* 66 (2000), 674–86; T. Parfitt, M.G. Thomas, N. Bradman, D. Goldstein et al., "Origins of Old Testament Priests …," in: *Nature,* 394 (July 1998), 138–40; T. Parfitt, *The Lost Tribes of Israel: The History of a Myth* (2002); T. Parfitt and E. Trevisan-Semi, *Judaising Movements: Studies in the Margins of Judaism* (2002); T. Parfitt, *Journey to the Vanished City: The Search for a Lost Tribe of Israel* (2000).

[Tudor Parfitt (2nd ed.)]

LEMBERGER, MOSES BEN AARON (1706–1757), rabbi. At the age of eight, Moses left his home in Lvov to be brought up by his grandfather in *Mikulov (Nikolsburg). In 1724 he was appointed rabbi of *Lipnik (Leipnik, Moravia) and in 1729 was appointed to succeed Jehiel Michael Ḥasid as *av bet din* of Berlin. He stayed there for one year, accepting a call in 1730 to the position of *av bet din* of Frankfurt on the Oder, a position he held for about 14 years. He returned to Lipnik as *av bet din* in 1745. In 1755 on the death of his uncle Issachar Berush *Eskeles, Moses was elected *Landesrabbiner* of Moravia. Moses' novellae on the tractate *Rosh ha-Shanah* were published in Frankfurt on the Oder in 1731.

BIBLIOGRAPHY: S. Buber, *Anshei Shem* (1895), 166, no. 422; W. Mueller, *Urkundliche Beitraege zur Geschichte der maehrischen Judenschaft* (1903), 157–9; H. Gold (ed.), *Juden und Judengemeinden Maehrens…* (1929), index, s.v. *Lwów, Moses b. Aaron.*

LEMKIN, RAPHAEL (1901–1959), international lawyer who initiated the use of the term "genocide." Educated in Poland, Germany, and France, he became secretary of the Court of Appeal, Warsaw, in 1927. Early in his career he tried to mobilize support for the international penalization of genocide, despite his view that crimes committed by acts of sovereign states are not subject to international jurisdiction. Returning to Warsaw in 1933, after the Madrid Conference for the unification of penal law, he was compelled to give up his official position. He suffered under Colonel Beck's pro-German antisemitic government. In the early part of World War II most of his family was murdered in Warsaw by the Germans. Lemkin fought in the Polish underground, eventually escaping and finally reaching the United States in 1941. There he taught at Duke and Yale universities and served on the Board of Economic Warfare, under Henry Wallace. In 1944 he published his *Axis Rule in Occupied Europe: Laws of Occupation, Analysis of Government Proposals for Redress*, in which he first systematized the material under the term *genocide. In 1946, Lemkin succeeded in mobilizing sufficient support to have genocide put on the agenda of the UN General Assembly. The Economic and Social Council invited him to present a draft convention. Assisted by Herbert V. Evatt, the Australian president of the General Assembly, he was able to get that body to pass a resolution in December 1948 on the adoption of the Convention for the Prevention and Punishment of Genocide. Although he was not an official of an international organization, Lemkin nevertheless played an important role through his forceful personal insistence.

BIBLIOGRAPHY: H. Maza, *Neuf meneurs internationaux* (1965), 341–57; E. Aroneanu, *Le Crime contre l'Humanité* (1961).

[Josef J. Lador-Lederer]

LEMLEIN (Lammlin), ASHER (16th century), false messiah active in 1500–02. Apparently of Ashkenazi origin, Lemlein began his activities in northeast Italy, later extending them to Germany. According to his statements, the redemption was approaching because the Messiah had already come – namely Lemlein himself. His disciples, who circulated this rumor, stimulated a movement of asceticism and repentance hitherto unknown in these areas. Long afterward this year was recalled as the "year of the repentance," even in Christian polemics against the Jews. There is no information on the events of Lemlein's life and his personality, except that he engaged in Kabbalah. The evolution of his movement is also not known. Apparently it ceased to exist with his death. The statements of Gedaliah Joseph *Ibn Yaḥya in *Shalshelet ha-Kabbalah* (Venice, 1586), on a wave of apostasies from Judaism as a result of the crisis of the Lemlein movement, are not to be accepted, for even his chief enemies among his contemporaries, Abraham *Farissol and *Joseph ha-Kohen, do not mention this fact.

BIBLIOGRAPHY: A.Z. Aescoly, *Ha-Tenu'ot ha-Meshiḥiyyot be-Yisrael* (1956), 249–50, 307–12; A. Marx, in: REJ, 61 (1911), 135–8; S. Loewinger, *ibid.*, 105 (1940), 32ff.

LEMUEL (Heb. לְמוּאֵל, לְמוֹאֵל; "belonging to God"), apparently a foreign king to whom the instruction in Proverbs 31:2–9 is addressed by his mother. Proverbs 31:1, in which Lemuel is mentioned, should be divided not after *melekh* but after *massa*, thus identifying the man as: "Lemuel, king of Massa," Massa being the North Arabian tribe, known from Genesis 25:14, one of the Kedemite peoples whose wisdom the Israelites held in high esteem (*Agur son of Jakeh). The Septuagint did not recognize either *lemu/o/el* or *massa* as proper nouns, and some moderns follow it, obtaining with the help of some emendations the sense (in Scott's rendering): (1) Words [of advice] to a king acting foolishly. A solemn injunction which his mother lays on him:… (4) It is not fitting for a king to play the fool, etc. But the interpretation of the Septuagint, Torczyner (Tur-Sinai), and Scott all involve dubious readings and/or Hebrew grammar.

BIBLIOGRAPHY: See commentaries on Proverbs; N.H. Torczyner (Tur-Sinai), *Mishlei Shelomo* (1947), 3–5; N.H. Tur-Sinai, *Ha-Lashon ve-ha-Sefer*, 3 (1955), 383; W.F. Albright, in: *Studi… Giorgio Levi Della Vida*, 1 (1956), 1–14; R.B.Y. Scott, *Proverbs and Ecclesiastes* (1965), 183–4.

[Michael V. Fox and Harold Louis Ginsberg]

LENGYEL, EMIL (1895–1985), U.S. writer. Born in Budapest, Lengyel spent 20 months in Siberia as a prisoner of war during World War I. Later he went to New York as a correspondent for European newspapers. Taking up teaching at the School of Education, New York University, he became professor in 1951. In 1960, he went to Fairleigh Dickinson University, Rutherford, New Jersey, as professor of history. His books include *Siberia* (1943), *Americans from Hungary* (1948), *Israel: Problems of Nation Building* (1951), *The Middle East Today* (1954), *Egypt's Role in World Affairs* (1957), *The Changing Middle East* (1960), *From Prison to Power* (1964), *Nationalism, the Last Stage of Communism* (1969), *Iran* (1972), *The Land and People of Hungary* (1972), *The Oil Countries of the Middle East* (1973), and *And All Her Paths Were Peace: The Life of Bertha von Suttner* (1975).

[Ruth Beloff (2nd ed.)]

LENGYEL, JÓZSEF (1896–1975), Hungarian author and poet, born in Marcali. Lengyel's poetic talents were first discovered in the modernist periodical, *A Tett* ("The Deed"). In 1918 he was one of the founders of the Hungarian Communist Party, and was arrested by the revolutionary authorities of the Károlyi regime before the Bolshevik revolution led by Bela *Kun. After its failure, he fled to Vienna, and thence to Berlin, finally settling in Moscow, where he worked in the circle of Hungarian émigré writers. There he was arrested in 1938 and sent to a Soviet concentration camp. After World War II, Lengyel was exiled to Siberia, but was released and rehabilitated in 1955, when he returned to Hungary. His literary work after his imprisonment describes with profound psychological analysis the horrifying world of those condemned to slow death. His works include *Visegrádi utca* ("Visegrádi Street," 1930[1], 1957[2]), *Prenn Ferenc hányatott élete…* ("The Life and Wanderings of Franz Prenn," 1958), and *Elévült tartozás* ("Debt Overdue," 1964).

BIBLIOGRAPHY: *Magyar Irodalmi Lexikon*, 2 (1965), s.v.

[Baruch Yaron]

LENGYEL, MENYHÉRT (Melchior; 1880–1974), Hungarian playwright. Born in Balmazújváros, Lengyel started his career as a journalist but soon began writing for the theater. His most successful plays included *Próféta* ("The Prophet," 1911), *A cárnö* ("The Czarina," 1913), *Róza néni* ("Aunt Rose," 1913), and *Antónia* (1925). In 1929 Lengyel was appointed director of a Budapest avant-garde theater. He wrote the libretto of the ballet *Csodálatos mandarin* ("The Miraculous Mandarin") for the composer Béla Bartók. In 1931 he moved to London and then in 1937, to the United States. Lengyel's best-known play, which had a worldwide success, was *Tajfun* ("Typhoon," 1909), in which he dealt with a contemporary political problem – the whirlwind progress of the Japanese and the resulting danger to the world. In a dramatization of *Cervantes' classic *Don Quixote, Sancho Panza királysága* ("The Reign of Sancho Panza," 1919), Lengyel expressed his own views on the just society. He also wrote the scripts for several famous films, including *Catherine the Great* (1934, starring Elisabeth Bergner); an adaptation of his own *Czarina; The Blue Angel* (1932, with Marlene Dietrich); and *Ninotchka* (1940, with Greta Garbo). Years later, Lengyel published *Das stille Haus* (1957). In his later years he lived in Rome.

BIBLIOGRAPHY: *Magyar Irodalmi Lexikon*, 2 (1965), 34–35.

[Baruch Yaron]

°**LENIN (Ulyanov), VLADIMIR ILYICH** (1870–1924), Russian revolutionary, leader of the Communist movement, and founder of the Soviet state. At all stages of his career, Lenin had to cope with the Jewish question from ideological, organizational, and political points of view. At the outset of Lenin's activities, the Jewish *Bund, whose representatives took part in Russian Social Democratic congresses, was a factor to be dealt with in his tactics as head of the Bolshevik faction, as the Bund increasingly threw its weight to the Mensheviks and sometimes swung the balance against Lenin. Like every Russian revolutionary in his time, Lenin attacked, possibly with more sincerity and vigor than others, the anti-Jewish policy of the Czarist regime. On his initiative the Bolshevist faction in the 4th state Duma (1912–1917) proposed a law to annul all restrictive measures against Jews, including education, state service, the Pale of Settlement in part, and others. He never displayed any inclination to exploit the deep-seated hatred of Jews in the Russian masses as "fuel" to advance the revolution, and in both his personal and political behavior. Lenin never differentiated between people – friends and enemies alike – on the basis of their national or ethnic origins. On the other hand, he viewed the assimilation of the Jews and their complete disappearance into the surrounding culture and society as an inevitable and even desirable result of human advancement. He believed that Jewish separateness, even in the modern and secularist image of the Bund and Socialist Zionism, was a remnant of the precapitalist era and had begun to disappear quickly in Western capitalist countries such as Germany, France, and England. He viewed the separate cultural and social existence of the Jews of Russia as a corollary of the anti-Jewish discrimination and persecution and as a symptom of the backwardness of Russia, in which medieval divisions had not yet crumbled. He therefore denounced not only all manifestations of antisemitism, but also all forms of Jewish nationalism and separatism as "reactionary" phenomena that deflect the Jewish workers away from revolutionary solidarity with their non-Jewish comrades and from the struggle for the future revolution to overthrow all class barriers and finally solve the Jewish problem. Lenin expounded his views on the Jewish question and on the national question in general in many articles, e.g.,"The Position of the Bund in the Party" (1903: *Collected Works*, (1961⁴), 92–103), "Theses on the National Question" (1913; *ibid.*, 19 (1963⁴), 243–51), "Cultural-National Autonomy" (1913; *ibid.*, 503–7), "Critical Remarks on the National Question" (1913; *ibid.*, 20 (1964⁴), 17–51). During the Civil War he refused to confiscate the Gorkis' pamphlet "On the Jews," despite warnings that it would become an anti-Bolshevist tool in the hands of the counterrevolutionaries.

After the Revolution, when Lenin took power in Russia (end of 1917), he endorsed the establishment of special departments for Jewish affairs in both the ruling Communist Party (the *Yevsektsiya) and in the relevant ministry (the Commissariat of Nationalities, headed by Joseph *Stalin). Neither did he object to the recognition of Yiddish as the national language of the Jews, since the masses of Jews – especially in the former *Pale of Settlement – were a large ethnic bloc, with its own culture and language, that should be addressed through means – especially linguistic – understood by it. Together with his acquiescence in the de facto recognition of a Jewish "nationality" in Soviet Russia, Lenin campaigned vigorously, both orally and in writing, against antisemitism and incitement to pogroms by the anti-Soviet right-wing forces (the White Army, the Ukrainian nationalists, peasant anarchists, etc.) and initiated, soon after the Revolution, the decree outlawing pogroms and their instigators (July 1918). Thus not only did Lenin abide by one of his ideological principles, he also faced and courageously fought the most demagogic challenge of the counterrevolutionary forces that rose against his regime (see *Antisemitism: Antisemitism in the Soviet Bloc). He took note of the higher percent of Jews in the revolutionary movement than their proportion in the population, and he initiated the promotion of Jews to higher positions in the State and party apparatus. Despite this position, however, Lenin did not oppose the cruel persecution of Zionists and suppression of the Hebrew language and the Jewish religion by the Soviet authorities, although in his time many arrested Zionists and rabbis were eventually allowed to leave Russia and go to Palestine. The assassination attempt on behalf of the Social Revolutionaries (1918), carried out against him by a Jewish woman, Fanya Kaplan, did not change his approach to the Jews at all.

At the end of his life, during his illness, Lenin attempted to oppose the Russian "great power chauvinism" of the young Soviet regime, which intervened, behind his back, with excessive cruelty in the lives of other nationalities in the country (such as the Georgians) and thus violated his principles on the national question. The Jewish aspect, however, did not play any part in this last struggle, since the antisemitism of the Soviet regime appeared undisguised only years after his death. This development is symbolized by the fact that among the eight speeches that Lenin recorded in 1919, seven were rerecorded in the Soviet Union on a long-playing record and marketed in 1961, during the Khrushchev era, but one speech was not rerecorded – his speech against antisemitism.

BIBLIOGRAPHY: S. Schwarz, *Jews in the Soviet Union*, (1961), index; Y. Ma'or, *She'elat ha-Yehudim ba-Tenu'ah ha-Liberalit ve-ha-Mahpekhanit be-Rusyah (1890–1914)* (1964), index; A.B. Ulam, *Lenin and the Bolsheviks* (c. 1966).

[Binyamin Eliav]

LENKEI, HENRIK (1863–1943), Hungarian poet and playwright. Lenkei, who was secretary of IMIT, the Hungarian Jewish Literary Society, was a talented poet, his verse collections including *Új versek* ("New Poems," 1904) and *Utolsó roham* ("Last Attack," 1933). Among his other works were the drama *A nagy előjáték* ("The Great Prelude," 1926); *Kain halála* ("The Death of Cain," 1899); *Az én hőseim* ("My Heroes," 1910), poetic vignettes of great artists and writers; and *Ruth* (1915).

LENKINSKI, LOUIS (1921–1995), resistance fighter, trade union activist, and human rights advocate. Lenkinski was born in Lodz, Poland, into a working-class, Yiddishist family. In his youth he was drawn to socialism and joined the *Bund, which was dedicated to the creation of a classless society in which Jews would be accepted as full and equal citizens. With the establishment of the Lodz ghetto in 1940, Lenkinski became an underground courier and Bund organizer. While his family was deported to the death camps, he managed to survive until the liquidation of the ghetto in 1944. He was deported to a labor camp in Czestochowa, where he was liberated by the Soviet forces. After the war he met and married a fellow Lodzer, Helen Offman, and in 1950, under the auspices of the Jewish Labor Committee, they left Europe for Canada with their baby son. They settled in Toronto, where their second son was born.

Lenkinski became an upholsterer. Although his formal education was halted by the war, Lenkinski was an auto-didact, immersing himself in history and politics, and becoming a prolific writer and lecturer in Yiddish, Polish, and English. True to his roots, he became a trade union organizer and active in the Ontario Labour Congress where he eventually became executive assistant to the OLC secretary. Lenkisnski was an active supporter of the New Democratic Party and a mentor to a generation of its leaders at the provincial and federal level. Also active in the Canadian Polish Congress, in 1970 Lenkinski became the Solidarity movement's representative in Canada. His belief in building bridges between Poles and Jews of Polish origin in Canada led to the establishment of the Polish Jewish Heritage Foundation of Canada. In his last years, Lenkinski was associate chair of the Ontario Human Rights Commission, and chair of the Community Relations Committee of the Canadian Jewish Congress, Ontario Region.

Lenkinski died after a lifetime of devotion to justice and human rights and is remembered as an inspiration to three generations of political and social activists. His tireless insistence on historical accuracy and his refusal to assign collective responsibility, blame and guilt for the heinous crimes of the Holocaust, have challenged historians to examine the roots and complexities of Polish-Jewish relations.

[Frank Bialystok (2nd ed.)]

LENSKI, ḤAYYIM (1905–1942), Hebrew poet. Born in the town of Slonim, district of Grodno, Russia, Lenski spent his childhood and early youth in his grandfather's home in the townlet of Derechin. Late in 1921 he left to study at the Hebrew Teachers' Seminary in Vilna, where he published his first poems in a students' magazine. After two years in Vilna, he joined his father in Baku at the end of 1924, following an adventurous journey. In 1925, however, he left his family and went to Moscow and Leningrad, where he settled down as a worker in the Amal factory founded by *He-Ḥalutz. In Moscow he continued to write poetry, which he sent to literary periodicals in Ereẓ Israel. *Bialik warmly encouraged his writing. Lenski was arrested at the end of 1934 for writing in Hebrew, and, after being detained in Leningrad for a few months, he was sentenced to five years' imprisonment with hard labor in Siberia. His poems, however, continued to reach Ereẓ Israel. While in the labor camp near Mrinsk, he appealed to the Russian writer Maxim Gorki to intercede for him ("I am a poet and my only crime is that my poems were written in Hebrew"), but it is doubtful whether the plea ever reached Gorki. In 1937 Lenski was transferred to the forced labor camp of Gornaya Shoriya, near the Soviet-Mongolian border; from that time on, his poems ceased to reach Ereẓ Israel. In 1939 or 1940, having served his term, he returned to Leningrad. Soon afterward he was again arrested and sent to the prison camp of Malaya Vyshera, near Leningrad. From there he was probably sent back to Siberia, where he died.

Lenski proudly declared in his poem "*Leshon Kedumim*" ("Ancient Tongue") that he launched the armies of the Queen (i.e., of the Hebrew language) across the rivers Don, Neva, and Neman. At the end of 1958, a number of manuscripts reached Israel which contained a nearly complete collection of his lyrical poems, copied out in the poet's fine handwriting and ready for publication. His poems were subsequently published in Israel under the title of *Me-Ever Nehar ha-Lethe* ("Beyond the River Lethe," 1960).

Lenski's poetry comprises mainly short lyrical poems, sonnets, and ballads that are marked by a perspicuity of language, a concreteness of imagery, and sonorous and vibrant music. Influenced by both Pushkin and Yesenin, with a dash of Heine's bitterness, Lenski's poetry reflects the reality he knew at first hand: the landscape of townlets, forests, and rivers of his Lithuanian homeland, scenes from the Leningrad factory, and Siberia's boundless spaces. All this is transmuted into an imagistic idiom, vivid and often boldly modernistic, as when he indulges in playful onomatopoeic effects. Close to folk and popular lore, his writing is tinged with sober humor which, in his longer poems, is transfigured into mordant and rebellious satire. In these longer poems, his most important, the fundamentally nonpolitical poet attacks the "world of tomorrow" promised by Communist utopians and demagogues. Two of these, "The Delator" and "Barbers' Gate" (the latter a poem playing on the imagery of Pushkin's "Bronze Horseman"), attest to the remarkable courage of a poet who, himself subjected to "the dungeons of ancient servitude," openly predicts his captors' "imminent downfall."

The "I" in Lenski's poetry is that of the romantic, bohemian poet, proud of his mission but perfectly willing to mock both himself and his trade. He is the uprooted wayfarer, the unhappy lover, and tramp who admits to being "enthralled by the wormwood" thus sharing with many another poet "the fascination of what's difficult."

In Siberia Lenski also translated into Hebrew an adaptation of a Vogul epic, "The Tundra Book," which appeared in the poet's first collection, *Shirei Ḥayyim Lenski* (1939). Here too, his mastery of a rich, concrete, and colorful language is amply manifested in the short and flowing verses modeled on Longfellow's *The Song of Hiawatha*. Lenski also tried his hand at drama and prose, but these were never published. Biographical data on Lenski and critical evaluations of his work by A. Kariv and others appear in the editions of his work already mentioned (*Shirei Ḥayyim Lenski* and *Me-Ever Nehar ha-Lethe*) and in *He-Anaf ha-Gadu'a* (1945). *Yalkut Shirim*, with commentary by Azriel Ukhmani and an introduction by Shulamit Levo, appeared in 1973. A volume of collected poems including a bibliography entitled *Me'ever Nehar ha-Lete*, was published in 1986.

BIBLIOGRAPHY: Holtz, in: *Judaism*, 14 (1965), 491–6; Goell, Bibliography, 33, no. 1005–14; Kressel, Leksikon, 2 (1967), 292–3. **ADD. BIBLIOGRAPHY:** S. Luria, "*Kokhav she-Nitlash, Iyyun be-Shirat Lenski*," in: *Shevut*, 3 (1975), 20–21; S. Levo, "*Al ha-Kesher she-bein ha-Roved ha-Semanti le-Roved ha-Ẓelil be-Shir shel Lenski*," in: *Halkin* (1975), 655–660; S. Sadeh, *Al ha-Ironyah be-Shirat H. Lenski* (1979); R. Frenkel-Medan, *Adam ve-Nof: Iyyunim be-Emdat ha-Dover be-Mivḥar Shirei Teva ve-Nof shel Ḥ. Lenski* (1976); U. Behar, "*Lenski*," in: *Siman Keriah*, 19 (1986), 131–138; O. Baumgarten-Kuris, "'*Ma'aseh be-Agur': Ha-Po'emah ha-Ẓiyyonit shel H. Lenski*," in: *Mehkarei Yerushalayim be-Sifrut Ivrit*, 9 (1986), 147–186; D. Miron, in: *Haaretz* (April 13, 1987); Y. Ginossar, "*H. Lenski, Mi-Gidulei ha-Pere*," in: *Itton*, 77:93 (1988), 20–21; H. Bar-Yosef, "*Was Haim Lenski a 'Schlimazl'?*" in: *Jews and Jewish Topics in the Soviet Union and Eastern Europe*, 15 (1991), 48–54; S. Sarid-Goldfischer, *Hebbetim Merkaziyyim be-Shirat Ḥ. Lenski* (2003).

[Natan Zach]

LENTIL (Heb. עֲדָשָׁה, *adashah*, pl. עֲדָשִׁים, *adashim*), the legume *Lens esculenta*, one of the earliest of the flora of Israel. Remains dating to over 3,000 years ago have been discovered in excavations and in Egyptian tombs of the 12th dynasty as food for the dead. In the Bible they are mentioned as the red "pottage of lentils" for which Esau sold his birthright to Jacob (Gen. 25:29–34). They were supplied by Barzillai the Gileadite to David's forces (II Sam. 17:28), and were included in the bread mixture that the prophet Ezekiel was commanded to eat for 390 days (Ezek. 4:9–10). In mishnaic and talmudic times, lentils were the most important of the legumes and many details about them occur in this literature. They lie on the surface of the ground, hence the expression "as lowly as the lentil" (TJ, Sanh. 2:5, 20b). The seed is like a discus – "round like a sphere" and has no protuberance – "the lentil has no mouth." The custom therefore obtained of providing mourners with lentils to eat, to symbolize that "the mourner has no mouth," i.e., is obliged to be silent, and that mourning is "a wheel that revolves throughout the world," all men being mortal (BB 16b; Gen. R. 63:14).

In addition to the species with a reddish seed there was a dark brown species (TJ, Shab. 7:6–end, 10d). Lentils were essentially the food of the common people; fastidious people who abstained from eating them suffered harm when obliged to do so (Ket. 67b). On the other hand it is mentioned that lentils were served at the table of Rabban Simeon b. Gamaliel (Beẓah 14b). Like other legumes they leave a bad smell in the mouth but they are noted as a remedy for diphtheria (Ber. 40a). A delicacy called *ashishim* was sometimes prepared from them. It consisted of "ground roast lentils kneaded in honey and fried" (TJ, Ned. 6:15, 40a). This is apparently the scriptural *ashishah* ("sweet cake"; I Chron. 16:3), regarded as a cure for lovesickness (Song 2:5).

BIBLIOGRAPHY: Loew, Flora, 2 (1924), 442–52; H.N. and A.L. Moldenke, *Plants of the Bible* (1952), index; J. Feliks, *Olam ha-Ẓome'aḥ ha-Mikra'i* (1968²), 159–61. **ADD. BIBLIOGRAPHY:** Feliks, Ha-Ẓome'aḥ, 108.

[Jehuda Feliks]

°LEO, name of 13 popes.

LEO VII (936–39) the only pope who openly advocated forcible measures for the conversion of the Jews. He advised Frederick, archbishop of Mainz from 937 and the pope's vicar in all the regions of Germany, to deliver to the Jews sermons on the Incarnation and the Trinity. If they refused to adopt the Christian faith, the pope authorized the bishop to banish them, "to avoid all contact with the enemies of God." It is true that Leo did not regard expulsion as a forcible measure, for he ended his letter by saying that, at all events, the Jews must not be compelled to accept baptism. It is also true that the initiative once more lay with the archbishop, and perhaps served as one of the weapons in his battle with the emperor Otto the Great, who had never denied his partiality for the Jews.

LEO X (Giovanni de' Medici), pope, 1513–21, one of the most tolerant of popes, whose reign was a happy one for the Jews. Intervening in the *Reuchlin-*Pfefferkorn controversy, he ensured an outcome of the dispute favorable for the Jews. His personal physician, Jacob b. Emanuel (Bonet *Lattes), was so well regarded that Reuchlin approached him for a recommendation to the pope. In 1514 Leo reconfirmed the privileges of the Jews in *Comtat Venaissin in opposition to the new measures which the bishop of *Carpentras wished to impose. He authorized the establishment of a Hebrew press in Rome and approved the printing of the Talmud. It is also true that the establishment of a chair of Hebrew in the University of Rome (1514) was aimed at promoting conversion, and Leo also granted considerable advantages to converts.

[Bernhard Blumenkranz]

LEO XIII (Vincenzo Gioacchino Pecci), pope, 1878–1903. Archbishop of Perugia from 1846 to 1878, he fought against the anticlerical laws passed in Italy after 1860. While he declared the Church receptive to cultural progress, he considered liberalism its archenemy and Judaism, which he saw as alienated from its own traditions, its driving force. As pope, his attitude toward Jews remained the same and during his pontificate the publication of a series of antisemitic articles in the Italian Jesuit organ, La *Civiltà Cattolica, did not meet with any papal interference. The *Dreyfus case found his sympathies on the side of the anti-Dreyfusards, who included the French Catholics, though in principle he wanted to see justice rendered to Dreyfus. The antisemitic policy of La *Croix, a French Catholic daily, did not apparently contradict the pope's own attitude. In 1892 Leo XIII admitted that there was a Jewish problem, but he saw it mainly as economic. Herzl tried to establish contact with Leo XIII but failed. On the other hand, the report that the pope had issued a protest against Zionism (also quoted in Herzl's *Diaries*) was officially denied.

[Willehad Paul Eckert]

BIBLIOGRAPHY: LEO VII: P. Browe, *Judenmission im Mittelalter* (1942), 243; B. Blumenkranz, *Auteurs chrétiens latins…* (1963), 219f. LEO X: Vogelstein-Rieger, 2 (1895), 32ff.; Milano, Italia, 238f.; P. Browe, op. cit., 155, 215. LEO XIII: P. Sorlin, *La Croix et les Juifs, 1880–1899* (1967), index; T. Herzl, *Complete Diaries* (1960), index.

°**LEO III** (called "**the Isaurian**" = Syrian; c. 680–741), Byzantine emperor from 717 to 741. Leo emerged a strong ruler after compelling the Caliph Suleiman to give up the siege of Constantinople early in his reign. In 721–22 he issued a decree ordering the baptism of the Jews, but, according to a Byzantine source, those that submitted "quickly washed off the baptism." No Jewish source mentions the decree. In 730 Leo forbade the worship of icons, allegedly because of his "saracen mindedness," or, alternatively, persuaded by a Jewish sorcerer. Yet Leo had earlier defended their use to the Caliph Omar II, while direct Jewish influence was, obviously, quite unlikely. However, the fact that Leo's best soldiers came from Phrygia, the home of iconoclasm, partly engendered there by a constant Judeo-Christian syncretism, and his own origins in a monotheistic cultural milieu, might have produced a distaste for images in worship. In this sense there could be a Jewish element in Leo's final choice of iconoclasm rather than another issue for his real purpose – the reassertion of imperial authority over the Church.

BIBLIOGRAPHY: J. Starr, *Jews in the Byzantine Empire* (1939), 90–93; G. Ostrogorsky, *History of the Byzantine State* (1956), 142–5; Sharf, in: *Byzantinische Zeitschrift* (1966), 37–46; Baron, Social^2, 3 (1957), 175–8; A.A. Vasiliev, *History of the Byzantine Empire*, 1 (1965), 255–6.

[Andrew Sharf]

°**LEO VI** (called "The Wise"), Byzantine emperor from 886 to 912. His law code, the *Basilica*, contains no innovations concerning the Jews. Leo appears favorably in Jewish sources. A tenth-century Hebrew apocalyptic text, the Vision of *Daniel, refers to him as granting "freedom and relief to the holy people," and the 11th-century chronicle, *Megillat Aḥimaʿaẓ* written by *Ahimaaz b. Paltiel, states that Leo annulled the decree of forced baptism issued by his father, *Basil I. However, Leo's 55th *novella*, or imperial rescript, declares that "in order to complete my father's work all Jews, baptized or not, must live according to the ceremonies and customs of Christianity" – thus even abrogating the fundamentals of Byzantine Jewish legislation. The probable explanation of this contradiction is that Leo continued Basil's attempt but quickly abandoned it when he saw its ineffectiveness – and it was this which was remembered.

BIBLIOGRAPHY: J. Starr, *Jews in the Byzantine Empire* (1939), 6–7, 134, 140–1; B. Klar (ed.), *Megillat Aḥimaʿaẓ* (1946), 23–24; M. Salzmann (tr.), *Chronicle of Aḥimaaz* (1924), 74; Sharf, in: *Bar-Ilan, Sefer ha-Shanah…*, 4–5 (1967), 201–3.

[Andrew Sharf]

LEO BAECK INSTITUTE, organization founded by the Council of Jews from Germany in 1955 in Jerusalem, for the purpose of collecting material and sponsoring research on the history of the Jewish community in Germany and other German-speaking countries. It operates in cooperation with Israeli and European scholars, organizing and encouraging conferences and lectures. The Institute is primarily concerned with the period from the Emancipation to the destruction and dispersion of the Jewish community of Central Europe. It is named for Leo *Baeck, the leader of German Jewry in its darkest hour. Baeck, who survived Theresienstadt, became the first international president of the institute.

There are branches of the Leo Baeck Institute in Jerusalem, London, and New York and two offices in Germany. All three centers regularly hold local and international conferences on a large variety of topics. The London branch publishes a yearbook and maintains contact with European scholars. The Jerusalem branch houses an archive with a collection of documents, microfilm, newspapers in German and Hebrew, and other rare materials about the Jews of Central Europe and is responsible for the publication of the *Juedischer Almanach* and books in Hebrew and German. The New York branch houses a library of about 40,000 books and has extensive archives, which include memoirs, manuscripts, and art work representative of the history of Central European Jewry since the Emancipation. The work of the three branches is coordinated through an international advisory body. The Institute publishes a yearbook (YLBI; 1956 to date). A quarterly in German, *Bulletin des Leo Baeck Instituts* (BLBI), is published in Tel Aviv. The Institute has published many monographs in English, Hebrew, and German. Among the 20 major publications of the series *Schriftenreihe wissenschaftlicher Abhandlungen des Leo Baeck Instituts* are the *History of Prussian Jewry* by Selma Stern-Taeubler, the *Zunz Letters* by Nahum N. Glatzer, and the *Anthology of the Science of Judaism* by Kurt Wilhelm. The Leo Baeck Institute has continued work on *Germania Judaica* started in 1917, a monumental history of all Jewish places of settlement in Central Europe from its earliest days to the 14th century (2 vols. in 3, 1963–68). The 83rd volume of *Monatsschrift fuer die Geschichte und Wissenschaft des Judentums* (1939), of which only one complete copy had been salvaged, was reprinted by the Institute (1963). A series of important memoirs was published in cooperation with the Deutsche Verlags-Anstalt, Stuttgart. Its recent publications include *Juedischer Verlag im Suhrkamp Verlag* and *An Episode of "Risches"? The Counting of the Jewish Soldiers in Germany in the First World War.*

WEBSITES: www.leobaeck.org; www.lbi.org; www.leobaeck.co.uk.

[Max Kreutzberger / Shaked Gilboa (2nd ed.)]

LEÓN, capital of the ancient kingdom of León, Spain. The community of León was one of the oldest in Christian Spain, outside Catalonia. The earliest sources date back to the tenth-century. The Jews engaged in real estate and commerce. The Jewish quarter apparently remained in the same location in the Santa Ana quarter from the beginnings of Jewish settlement. The 14th-century synagogue was situated in the Cal de Moros, now Calle de Misericordia. The *Prado de los Judíos* ("Meadow of the Jews") is on the site of the medieval cemetery. Various sources mention Jews in León who became converted to Christianity in the tenth century. One of the apostates, Habaz (or Navaz), bestowed all his property on the local monastery. From the 11th century information becomes more plentiful. A number of Jews resided in the citadel, and owned real estate, fields, gardens, and vineyards in the vicinity. Some engaged in moneylending and commerce. The status of the Jews was regularized by a *fuero* ("charter") granted in 1020. In the 11th century (1091) the Jews of León enjoyed special privileges as they were under royal jurisdiction. One concession was the right to have lawsuits with Christians heard by the king or one of the court clergy. When the issue was to be decided by duel, the Jew was entitled to appoint a champion. The charter was subsequently used as a model for the legislation applying to other communities in the kingdom of León. The cemetery of Puente Castro near León contains tombstones dating from the 11th century, including those of Jews from León.

According to Hebrew sources, there was a well-organized Jewish community in León that was the home of distinguished scholars. The Hebrew sources found in the Archivo Catedralicio de León reveal a high level of rabbinic learning there.

In the 13th century, despite a certain religious decline, the community was the home of some very important scholars, first and foremost *Moses de León, the famous kabbalist, and *Moses ben Shem Tov de León.

From the 13th century the rights of the Jewish community in León were progressively curtailed by a series of royal decrees. In 1260 Alfonso x fixed the rate of interest on loans. Sancho iv included León in a royal decree issued to *Palencia in 1286, providing that lawsuits between Jews were to be tried by Jewish judges and lawsuits between Christians by Christian judges so as to prevent the trial of mixed lawsuits by Jewish judges. In 1293 King Sancho acceded to a request by the Cortes in Valladolid that excluded Jews from taxfarming in León, and confirmed an order issued by Alfonso x prohibiting the Jews in León from acquiring real estate, etc. Ferdinand iv forbade the Jews in León to appear at his court. However, he permitted them to choose a judge for settling their disputes, a privilege for which they paid 400 maravedis to the municipality. In 1305 they concluded an agreement with the municipality that if the royal judges were not local residents, the Jews would be entitled to make recourse to a judge of their own choice. In 1313 the Infante Don Juan, in the name of Alfonso xi, confirmed that the regulations issued by the Cortes of Palencia also applied to León. The Jews throughout the kingdom of León were now compelled to wear the yellow *badge on their garments; no Jew could be released from paying taxes; and the evidence of a Jew could not be used against Christians. In 1332 Alfonso xi granted the inhabitants of León a general moratorium on Jewish loans and in 1365 Pedro ordered both Jews and Moors to pay the *alcabal* (indirect taxes) like the other residents in León.

The troubles experienced by Spanish Jewry in the 15th century also affected the Jews in León. The low tax paid by the community in 1439 shows that it had become impoverished: instead of 6,400 maravedis in old coin, they paid only 2,700 maravedis in silver. Its Jewish population was greatly reduced. At most there were some 150 Jewish families or about 500 Jews. On May 25, 1449, riots broke out and most of the Jewish quarter was pillaged. However, in this case the crown took action against the aggressors and ordered that they should be arrested and tried, and their property confiscated. In 1481 the Jews in León were ordered to leave the Jewish quarter, but in 1488 the crown agreed to allow them to enlarge it. The names of several Jewish taxfarmers from León are known from the second half of the 15th century. The Jews in León in this period, besides engaging in crafts, commerce, and agriculture, also sold goods in the mountain villages. Some of these merchants complained to the king that their clients had refused to pay for the goods. In the years preceding the expulsion León had a yeshivah headed by R. Isaac Besudo. After the decree of expulsion of 1492, the governor of León, John of Portugal, undertook to protect the Jews there in return for a payment of 3,000 maravedis but failed to honor the agreement and seized their property. Jewish property was also looted after the exiles had left, but some was restored to Jews who returned to León in 1493 and accepted baptism.

BIBLIOGRAPHY: Baer, Spain, index; Baer, Urkunden, index; F. Castro and F. de Onís, *Fueros Leoneses* (1916); C. Sánchez Albornoz, *Estampas de la vida en Leon hace mil años* (1934); F. Cantera, *Sinagogas Españolas* (1955), 237; idem, in: *Sefarad*, 3 (1943), 329–58; Cantera-Millás, Inscripciones (1956), 5–25; Cantera-Burgos, in: *Sefarad*, 24 (1964), 3–11; Gonzales, in: *Hispania*, 3 (1943), 195ff.; J. Rodríguez Fernández, *De Historia Leonesa* (1961); idem, in: *Archivos Leoneses*, 2 (1947), 33–72; 2 (1948), 15–27, 29ff.; 4 (1950), 11–53; González Gallego, *ibid.*, 21 (1967), 375–408; Suárez Fernández, Documentos, index. **ADD. BIBLIOGRAPHY:** J.A. Martín Fuertes and C. Álvarez

Álvarez, *Archivo Histórico Municipal de León; catálogo de los documentos,* (1982), index.

[Haim Beinart]

LEON, family name of European and U.S. notables whose progenitors fled the Iberian Peninsula during the Inquisition. The name derives from the kingdom of Leon, Spain. Early in the 1500s, the Marrano PEDRO DE LEON tried to escape the Spanish inquisitors by moving with his family to the West Indian island of Hispaniola. However, he was apprehended and in 1515 brought back to Seville for trial. Others were more fortunate and the name Leon appears in the records of Ancona, Jerusalem, Hamburg, Salonika, London, Venice, Jamaica, Surinam, Amsterdam, and the United States. ISAAC BEN ELIEZER DE LEON of Spain, who is best known for his *Megillat Esther* (Venice, 1592), a commentary to Maimonides' *Sefer ha-Mitzvot,* spent most of his life in Ancona, Italy. He is also the author of a responsum dated 1545 that appeared in Rome. In Greece, the liturgical poet ABRAHAM DE LEON composed *"El Ram al Kol Tehillah,"* a dirge on the capture of Rhodes by the Turks in 1522, which was included in the *Bakkashot* published about 1545 at Constantinople. (The poem is numbered 4042 in Davidson, *Oẓar,* vol. 1, 1924.) JOSEPH DE LEON served as rabbi in Jerusalem c. 1588. At Hamburg, the *ḥakham* of the Portuguese congregation from 1615 to 1656 was JUDAH ḤAYYIM LEON. About 1632, in Salonika, then under Turkish dominion, the *rosh yeshivah* was ISAAC DE LEON.

At London's Spanish-Portuguese synagogue, the assistant to the haham from 1685 to 1707 was ABRAHAM JUDAH LEON. The rabbi of Venice in about 1695 was JOSEPH DE LEON. JACOB DE LEON and JACOB RODRIGUEZ DE LEON resided in Jamaica in 1698. Among the leaders of Surinam's Portuguese Jewish community during the 1780s was MOSES P. DE LEON, coauthor of a history of his community, *Essai historique sur la colonie de Surinam avec l'histoire de la Nation Juive Portugaise et Allemande y établie* (1788), subsequently published also in Dutch (Amsterdam, 1791).

A number of men bearing the name Leon appeared in Amsterdam. In the mid-1600s MEIR DE LEON translated Solomon ibn Verga's *Shevet Yehudah* into Spanish (*La Vara de Judá,* Amsterdam, 1640). The leading figure of Amsterdam's Keter Torah yeshivah was SAMUEL DE LEON. Requests for decisions on matters of Jewish law addressed to the yeshivah were generally referred to him; his responsa were published at Hamburg in 1679. Fleeing from the Inquisition in 1685, the Marrano MANUEL DE LEON, who was born in Leiria, Portugal, arrived in Amsterdam, where he remained until his death in 1712. He produced Spanish and Portuguese verse, published in Brussels (1688), in The Hague (1691), and in Amsterdam (1712). The *ḥakham* of Amsterdam's Gemilut Ḥasadim fund was ELIJAH DE LEON, who was also coeditor of the Bible printed in 1661 by Joseph *Athias.

There were numerous Leons in colonial America. Joseph Rosenbloom's *A Biographical Dictionary of Early American Jews, Colonial Times through 1800* (1960) lists 38, many of them descendants of Abraham de Leon (b. 1702), who settled in Savannah, Georgia, in 1733. The name was prominent in New York City during the 1850s. MOSES LEON was among the leaders of New York's Hebrew Benevolent Society and MORRIS J. LEON was active in the Young Men's Benevolent and Fuel Association; the *ḥazzan* of the Bnai Israel synagogue in 1854 was JOSHUA DE LEON.

BIBLIOGRAPHY: Roth, Marranos, 274, 294; H.B. Grinstein, *Rise of the Jewish Community of New York 1654–1860* (1945), 552–4.

LEON, ANTHONY JAMES (1956–), South African political leader. The son of Judge Ramon Leon, he qualified as a lawyer at the University of the Witwatersrand, Johannesburg, and lectured there in Law from 1986 to 1989. In 1986–89, he was also city councilor and leader of opposition in Johannesburg, and thereafter a Member of Parliament for Houghton (1989–94), taking over in that constituency from veteran Helen *Suzman. In 1994, he took over the leadership of the Democratic Party, which became the official opposition in Parliament following the elections of 1999. In 2000 the party joined forces with other smaller parties to form the Democratic Alliance (DA) under Leon's leadership. The DA strengthened its position as official opposition in the elections of 2004. Leon wrote *Hope & Fear: Reflections of a Democrat* (1998).

[David Saks (2nd ed.)]

LEON, HARRY JOSHUA (1896–1967), U.S. classics scholar and historian. Leon, born in Worcester, Massachusetts, taught classical languages at the University of Texas from 1923, was a research professor at the American Academy of Rome 1950–51, and was an active member of many learned societies. Apart from his work on *Tacitus* (1960^2) and translations of classical literature, Leon published a *History of the Jews of Ancient Rome* (1960) which was largely based on a careful analysis of inscriptions in the Jewish *catacombs in Rome.

LEON, ISAAC DE (d. 1486 or 1490), Spanish rabbi and kabbalist. Isaac was born in Leon in the second decade of the 15th century. He was a pupil of Isaac *Canpanton and was friendly with Isaac *Aboab. Abraham b. Samuel *Zacuto in the *Sefer Yuḥasin* (ed. by H. Filipowski (1857), 226) states that Isaac was "experienced in miracles." He was rabbi of Ocaña. Among Isaac's many pupils were Samuel ibn *Sid, who summarized in his *Kelalei Shemu'el* many of the traditions and methods of learning in Spain received from his master; Isaac Giacon, the teacher of the well-known kabbalist *Abraham b. Eliezer ha-Levi; Abraham b. Bolat; and Abraham b. Hassan of Salonika. Isaac de Leon became embroiled with Don Abraham *Senior and scornfully termed him *sone or* ("hater of the light") because of heresies which he found in him even before his apostasy. In 1482 De Leon visited Saragossa and became friendly with the Jewish royal courtier, Alfonso de la Caballeria. There he became involved in a violent controversy with the local rabbi Isaac Ziyyat, with reference to the permissibility of certain animal fat, which caused a storm among the Jews of Aragon. A ruling by De Leon on the laws of adjoining owners is extant (in *Sheva Einayim*, ed. by J. London, Leghorn, 1745), with which Isaac Ziyyat disagreed. Some of his rulings are mentioned by Joseph *Caro in his *Beit Yosef*. He wrote a supercommentary to Rashi's Pentateuch commentary. Toward the end of his life he moved to Toledo, where he died.

BIBLIOGRAPHY: A. Marx, *Studies in Jewish History and Booklore* (1944), 90–92, 432; G. Scholem, in: KS, 2 (1925/26), 270; I. Ta-Shema, in: KS, 45 (1969/70), 124–5; Baer, Spain, index, s.v. *Isaac de Leon*.

[Abraham David]

LEÓN, LUIS DE (1528–1591), Spanish poet, humanist, and Augustinian friar. Born in Belmonte, New Castile, he spent most of his life in Salamanca where, as a professor, he dominated the university until some intolerant rivals discovered his *New Christian origin. The fact that his great-grandmother had been burnt at the stake as a relapsed Jewess led to his imprisonment for five years at Valladolid from 1572 at the hands of the Inquisition. Luis de León was accused of Judaizing and of doubting the authority of the Vulgate, the literal accuracy of which he had called into question. His Spanish translation of the Song of Songs reinforced these charges. Luis de León claimed that he knew no rabbinic commentaries on the Bible. There is reason to doubt the truth of this assertion. How can a biblical Hebraist ignore rabbinic exegesis? His own writings deny the truth of his claim. In his commentary on the Song of Songs, he mentions Abraham Ibn Ezra and in his commentary on Job, he refers to Jewish scholars. Elsewhere in his trial he did speak about several Jewish scholars. In dozens of cases in his commentaries on the two books, there is clear evidence that he knew Hebrew. Habib Arquim showed that his notes reflect rabbinic comments. It is obvious that Luis de León was well acquainted with rabbinic sources. It is also evident that he used kabbalistic sources, particularly the Zohar. After his eventual acquittal, Luis de León returned in triumph to Salamanca. These experiences are scarcely reflected in his poetry, which is a model of equilibrium. Apart from original verse and translations from the Bible and from classical and Italian literature, he wrote a number of theological and exegetic works, in which he invoked the support of the Christian Kabbalah. Luis de León's work unites the medieval Christian, biblical Hebrew, and classical traditions in the harmony of the Spanish Renaissance. Further research is needed to show the extent and depth of Luis de León's close familiarity with rabbinic and kabbalistic sources, which were blended with profound knowledge of medieval Christian traditions.

BIBLIOGRAPHY: A.F.G. Bell, *Luis de León: A Study of the Spanish Renaissance* (1925); J.M. Cohen, *History of Western Literature* (1956), 137f. **ADD. BIBLIOGRAPHY:** A. Habib Arkim, *La influencia de exégesis hebrea en los comentarios bíblicos de fray Luis de León* (1966); A. Kottman, in: *Journal of the History of Philosophy*, 13 (1975), 297–310; C. Carrete Parrondo, in: *Identidad y testimonio* (1979), 31–36; L. Rodríguez, in: *Estudio agustiniano*, 15 (1980), 93–116; A. Márquez, in: *Nueva revista de filología hispánica*, 30 (1981), 513–33; L.J. Woodward, in: *Bulletin of Hispanic Studies*, 61 (1984), 426–31; C. de la Rica, in: *El Olivo*, 21 (1985), 73–86; A. Blanco, in: *Boletín de la Real Academia Española*, 65 (1985), 357–408; 66 (1986), 93–134; M. Olivari, *Rivista storica italiana*, 99 (1987), 147–80; C.P. Thompson, *The Strife of Tongues: Fray Luiz de león and the Golden Age of Spain* (1988); A. Guy, *Fray Luis de León, 1528–1591* (1989); R. Lazcano González, *Fray Luis de León; bibliografía* (1990).

[Kenneth R. Scholberg / Yom Tov Assis (2nd ed.)]

LEON, MESSER DAVID BEN JUDAH (1470/72?–1526?), rabbi and religious philosopher. Born in Mantua, Italy, Leon studied in his father's yeshivah in Naples, where he was ordained at the age of 18 by French and German rabbis. He then went to the yeshivah of Judah Minz in Padua. In 1494 he was living in Florence, about 1505 moved to Salonika, and about 1512 was appointed rabbi of Valona, Albania. In this town there were many disputes between the various communities because of the desire of the exiles from Spain and Portugal to impose their customs on the existing communities. He became involved in these disputes, and in one of them excommunicated his opponent, Meir ibn Verga. On the night of the Day of Atonement, during a fierce quarrel between the various communities, he was insulted and banned two scholars among the heads of the community who opposed him. His ruling, which attempted to justify his action and prove that the ban was legally in force, was published under the title *Kevod Ḥakhamim* (ed. by S. Bernfeld, 1899). There is, however, a conjecture that a great part of this work was taken from the responsa of Joseph *Colon (Venice, 1519, ed. no. 170). As a result of these disputes, he returned to Salonika where he died.

Leon combined vast erudition in Jewish subjects with a comprehensive knowledge of general culture, particularly in philosophy. In the study of Torah he preferred the method of the rabbis of Germany and France to the methods of the rabbis of Spain. An admirer of Maimonides, Leon, in those of his works that have remained unpublished, *Magen David* (dealing with the problem of the nature of the **Sefirot* and compiled apparently before 1506) and *Ein ha-Kore* (a commentary on the *Guide of the Perplexed*), defended Maimonides' philosophical method and attempted to answer the complaints of his critics. He was opposed to Levi b. Gershom and Isaac Abrabanel, mainly because their views differed from those of Maimonides. His combination of general culture with values originating from Jewish religion and culture is reflected in his query to Jacob b. David *Provençal "on the view of the sages of the Talmud in the study of the natural sciences, logic, philosophy, and medicine." The reply (published in the collection *Divrei Ḥakhamim* (1849), 63–74, of Eliezer Ashkenazi), that "each one of the seven sciences is praiseworthy and valued in the eyes of our sages," addressed him as one who would produce "fruit from the tree, but not forsake the root in order to take hold of the husk." Apparently Leon also engaged in Kabbalah. He stated that although his father refused to allow him to engage in it "because of his tender age," he studied Kabbalah in secret. Among his other works worthy of mention are *Tehillah le-David* (Constantinople, 1577), on religious philosophy, published by his grandson Aaron Leon; *Sod ha-Gemul*; and his rulings and responsa, and letters and poems (some also in Latin) – most of which are still in manuscript.

BIBLIOGRAPHY: L. Zunz, *Kerem Ḥemed*, 5 (1841), 139; Michael, Or, no. 727; J. Schechter, in: REJ, 24 (1892), 118–38; M. Steinschneider, in: MGWJ, 42 (1898), 263; idem, in: *Festschrift … A. Berliner* (1903), 353; idem, *Gesammelte Schriften*, 1 (1925), 219f.; Rosanes, Togarmah, 1 (1930^2), 79, 85–88, 110–3; Assaf, Mekorot, 2 (1931), 99–101; G. Scholem, in: KS, 9 (1932–33), 258; D. Tamar, *ibid.*, 26 (1949/50), 96–100.

[Yehoshua Horowitz]

LEON, MESSER JUDAH BEN JEHIEL (15th century), rabbi and author. The place and the year of Judah's birth are unknown. It is possible that his native city was Mantua, where he was the head of a yeshivah. He was a typical representative of the Jewish humanism of the Renaissance. Judah received a broad and thorough Jewish and general education; he studied classical Latin literature, and evinced a special interest in the Latin works of antiquity that had been rediscovered in his day, such as Quintilian's *Institutio oratoria*. He was familiar with Greek and Arabic literatures, however, only from translations. Although it has often been doubted, he seems to have been in possession of a medical diploma. The controversy between him and Joseph *Colon in Mantua split the Jewish community, and the duke of Mantua felt compelled to banish both adversaries from the city. M. Steinschneider surmises that the cause of the conflict was a question of *halakhah*, as to whether it was permissible to wear the garb of the Italian scholars, the *cappa*. Graetz saw the cause of the dispute in the clash between the strict orthodoxy of Colon and the progressive views of Judah. Both assumptions have been shown by M.A. Szulwas to be without foundation: Colon (Maharik, Resp. nos. 88, 149) did not at all forbid the wearing of the *cappa*; and the difference in their respective views could not have been so great, since in 1455 Judah sought to prohibit the study of *Levi b. Gershom's commentary on the Torah under threat of excommunication; he also attempted to impose on the Italian communities certain strict halakhic rules. Szulwas assumes that it was probably Judah's claim to be the authority for all communities in Italy that was the cause of his dispute with Colon 20 years later. The honorific title Messer appears to have been bestowed upon Judah either by the pope or by the emperor. He lived for some time in Venice (1472), Bologna, Ancona, and Naples (as early as 1480). In Naples, he was head of the yeshivah. The place and year of his death are unknown.

Judah wrote the following:

(1) *Nofet Ẓufim*, a Hebrew rhetorical work based on the rhetorical rules of Aristotle (or his commentators), Cicero, and Quintilian (printed in Mantua before 1480, published again by A. Jellinek, 1863);

(2) *Livnat ha-Sappir*, a Hebrew grammar;

(3) *Mikhlal Yofi*, a compendium of Aristotelian logic;

(4) sermons for various occasions, composed in Ancona (Ms. Firkovich);

(5) medical treatises;

(6) prayers (Ms. Firkovich, which in part are included in some manuscripts of the Italian Jewish liturgy (e.g., in Ms. de Rossi 970);

(7) several circular letters (printed by Perreau and Steinschneider in Kobak's *Yeshurun*);

(8) *Sheḥitah* and *bedikah* rules (Ms. Firkovich);

(9) a Latin work on medical subjects (mentioned by Judah's son, David);

(10) a supercommentary on Averroes' Middle Commentary to many books of Aristotle's *Organon*;

(11) a supercommentary like (10) on Aristotle's *Physics*, known only from information communicated by his son;

(12–13) commentaries on Aristotle's *De Anima* and *Metaphysics* (mentioned by Judah, but not extant);

(14) a commentary on Aristotle's *Ethics*, mentioned by Judah's grandson, Aaron (perhaps identical with the anonymous Ms. Leyden Warnerus no. 44);

(15) a commentary, preserved in many manuscripts, on Jedaiah Bedersi's *Beḥinat Olam*, probably by Judah; it was completed by his nephew, Mordecai b. David;

(16) a commentary on Maimonides' *Moreh Nevukhim*, entitled *Moreh Ẓedek*, said to have been in the possession of David Vital and to have been lost when Patros was captured;

(17) a commentary on the Pentateuch, apparently unfinished;

(18) observations on the first book of Avicenna's Canon;

(19) *tosafot* to tractate *Berakhot* (in: *Berakhah Meshulleshet* (1883));

(20) *Reshut* to *Barekhu* (published in ZHB, 19 (1916), 133).

The commentary on the last chapter of Proverbs stems apparently not from Judah but from his son David.

Several letters (from the years 1468 and 1474), addressed by Abraham Farissol to Judah, are found in the manuscript de Rossi 145.

BIBLIOGRAPHY: Gedaliah ibn Yaḥya, *Shalshelet ha-Kabbalah* (Venice, 1586), 62b; Dukes, in: *Oẓar Neḥmad*, 2 (1857), 104; Szulwas, in: *Zion*, 12 (1946/47), 17–23; G.B. de Rossi, *Dizionario Storico degli Autori Ebrei*, 2 (1802), 7–10; idem, *Manuscripti Codices Hebraici*, 1 (1803), 73f., 95–97; 3 (1803), 28 (no. 970), 153 (no. 1355/7); Loew, in: *Ben Chananja*, 6 (1863), 3–9; Bruell, *ibid.*, 509–14, 527f.; Neubauer, in: *Israelietische Letterbode*, 10 (1884/85), 106–11 (Ger., Heb.); M. Steinschneider, *ibid.*, 12 (1886/87), 92–94; idem, in: *Gesammelte Schriften*, 1 (1925), 218–28; Schechter, in: REJ, 24 (1892), 118–38; I. Husik, *Judah Messer Leon's Commentary on the "Vetus Logica"* (1906); Graetz, Hist, 4 (1894), 289–95; Roth, Italy, 203, 217; For list of Mss. see EJ, 8 (1931), 1000f.

[Umberto (Moses David) Cassuto]

LÉON, XAVIER (1868–1935), French philosopher. Léon founded the important philosophical journal, *Revue de Métaphysique et de Morale*, which he edited from its beginning in 1893 until his death. The journal was not only against positivist trends, but also in favor of speculative philosophy. Léon also founded the *Société française de philosophie* (1901). In both of these ventures he had the collaboration of Élie *Halévy. Léon organized several international congresses of philosophy. He wrote on the German philosopher, Fichte, publishing *La Philosophie de Fichte* (1902) and *Fichte et son temps*, 2 vols. (1922–27).

BIBLIOGRAPHY: E. Halévy et al., *Xavier Léon 1868–1935* (Fr., 1937); *Enciclopedia Filosofica*, 2 (It., 1957), 1876f.

[Richard H. Popkin]

LEONARD, BENNY (Benjamin (Dov B'er) Leiner; "The Ghetto Wizard," "The Great Bennah"; 1896–1947), U.S. boxer, lightweight champion from 1917 to 1925, among the greatest lightweight fighters of the 20th century and one of the greatest Jewish sports figures of all time; member of the Ring Boxing Hall of Fame and the International Boxing Hall of Fame. Born to Yiddish-speaking religious Russian immigrants Minnie and Gershon, a tailor, Leonard was raised in the East Greenwich Village neighborhood in New York and first fought with gloves at age 11. He turned pro at 15, and when the ring announcer mangled his last name, the nervous Leonard did not correct him, and that helped keep his parents from finding out about his career. His mother was opposed to his fighting, which she considered dangerous and unseemly for an Orthodox Jewish boy. Leonard carried a picture of his mother with him every place he went, called her after every fight, and never fought on a Jewish holiday. Leonard beat Freddie Welsh for the lightweight crown on May 28, 1917, holding the title until he voluntarily retired on Jan. 15, 1925, a span of seven years and eight months – the longest uninterrupted lightweight title reign in history. During that period, Leonard was said to be the most famous Jew in America. The stock market crash of 1929 wiped out Leonard's wealth, and he returned to the ring on October 6, 1931, to recoup his fortunes. He did not lose in his first 20 fights, but he retired after Jimmy McLarnin stopped him on October 7, 1932. Leonard also fought a bout against Jack Britton for the welterweight title on June 26, 1922, but lost on a foul in the 13th round. His official record is 89–5–1, with 69 knockouts and 121 no decisions, and his record including newspaper verdicts, according to one source, is 164–11–5, with 36 no decisions. After his boxing career was over, Leonard became a popular referee. On April 18, 1947, he suffered a heart attack while refereeing a match in St. Nicholas Arena, and died in the ring. He was elected to the Ring Boxing Hall of Fame in 1955 and the International Boxing Hall of Fame in 1990. Nat Fleischer considered Benny Leonard the No. 2 all time lightweight in 1958; *Sporting News*, in its 75th anniversary issue in 1997, named Leonard Best Boxer of the Last 75 Years; the *Ring* magazine ranked him No. 2 in its list of the greatest lightweights of all time in September 2001, 71 years after Leonard fought his last fight; and boxing historian Bert Sugar ranks him fifth on his list of 100 greatest boxers of all time. Leonard wrote a small pamphlet *My Greatest Ring Battles* (1939). He is also the subject of Nat Fleischer's biography *Leonard the Magnificent* (1947).

[Elli Wohlgelernter (2nd ed.)]

LEONE, LEON (Judah) DI (d. 1830), rabbi in Italy. Leone went to Europe from Ereẓ Israel as an emissary of the Hebron community and in 1795 was elected rabbi of Rome. In 1796 he joined other rabbis in Italy in writing a protest against statements current in France and Germany that radical religious reforms were being introduced in the Italian Jewish communities. When the community in Rome was reorganized on the French pattern in 1811, Leone became chairman of the consistory.

BIBLIOGRAPHY: Milano, *Ghetto di Roma* (1964), 313, 394; Vogelstein-Rieger, 2 (1896), 400–1.

[Umberto (Moses David) Cassuto]

LEONHARD, RUDOLF (1889–1953), German essayist and poet. Leonhard, who was born in Lissa, studied law at Goettingen. He subsequently worked as a freelance writer in Berlin, but in 1927 moved to Paris. Leonhard was a radical pacifist, but, nevertheless, fought in the French underground during the Nazi occupation of France. He returned to East Berlin after World War II. His works include essays on literary and political topics, some of them in French; two volumes of collected poems entitled *Polnische Gedichte* (1918) and *Katilinarische Pilgerschaft* (1919); a book of aphorisms, *Alles und Nichts* (1920); and a tragedy, *Geiseln* (1945). Leonhard, an accomplished critic, also translated the works of Anatole France. From 1961 to 1970 four volumes of selected works (*Ausgewaehlte Werke in Einzelausgaben*) appeared in East Germany.

BIBLIOGRAPHY: M. Scheer (ed.), *Rudolf Leonhard erzaehlt* (1955). **ADD. BIBLIOGRAPHY:** B. Pubanz, *"Drei Begegnungen": Ehm Welks Verhältnis zu Rudolf Leonhard*, in: *... damit ich nicht noch mehr als Idylliker abgestempelt werde. Ehm Welk im literarischen Leben Mecklenburg-Vorpommerns nach 1945*, ed. by R. Roesler and M. Schuemann (1998), 81–86; H. Hirsch, "Ein bemerkenswerter Schriftsteller: Rudolf Leonhard," in: *Exil*, 20:1 (2000), 28–43; J. Ross, "'Leiden verpflichtet': Recast Jewish Figures in Rudolf Leonhard's Post-War AntiFascist 'Erzaehlungen,'" in: P. O'Dochartaigh (ed.), *Jews in German literature since 1945* (2000), 391–402; S. Mensching (ed.), *Rudolf Leonhard. In derselben Nacht: das Traumbuch des Exils* (2001).

[Rudolf Kayser / Kurt Feilchenfeld (2nd ed.)]

LEONI, MYER (d. 1796), English cantor. Born Meir ben Judah Loeb, probably in Poland, he was first known in England as an opera singer named "Meir Leoni." In 1767 he was engaged as cantor at the Great Synagogue, London, on condition that he would conduct himself henceforth as an observant Jew. His tune for the **Yigdal*, known as the "Leoni Yigdal," was heard at the synagogue in 1770 by the Methodist minister Thomas Olivers and adapted for the Christian hymn, "The God of Abraham Praise." Leoni later returned to the stage, stipulating that he should not appear on Friday nights, when he officiated in the synagogue. His relations with his congregation became difficult, however, and when he sang in a performance of Handel's *Messiah* he had to resign. In 1787 he went to Jamaica as reader to the Ashkenazi synagogue in Kingston, where he remained until his death. Some of the synagogal music composed by Leoni and his colleague, Abraham of Prossnitz (d. 1779), the father of John *Braham, figured in the collection of cantorial music made by Aaron Beer of Berlin, while specimens adapted for harpsichord and other instruments were published in London in 1780.

BIBLIOGRAPHY: C. Roth, *Great Synagogue, London 1690–1940* (1950), 143–45; Grove, Dict; Idelsohn, Music, 218–26; idem, in: *Hebrew Union College Jubilee Volume* (1925), 415–6; J. Picciotto, *Sketches of Anglo-Jewish History* (1956), 139–49; Sendrey, Music, no. 6216.

[Cecil Roth]

LEONIDOV (VOLFENSON), LEONID MIRONOVICH (1873–1941), Russian actor. He was born into a Jewish merchant family and began his career by appearing in amateur theatricals in Odessa. In 1895–96 he studied at the Moscow Imperial Theater School. He acted in the theaters of Solovtsov (1896–1901, in Kiev and Odessa) and Korsh (1901–1903, in Moscow). In 1903 he began appearing with the Moscow Art Theater where he made his debut in the role of Vaska Pepel in Gorky's *Lower Depths*. He also played comic roles to which he often lent a sharply grotesque touch, as for example in his portrayal of Plyushchkin in Gogol's *Dead Souls* (1932). Many of the characters he created belong to the great accomplishments of the Russian stage, e.g., Dmitri Karamazov in a dramatization of Dostoevsky's *Brothers Karamazov* (1910) and Peer Gynt in Ibsen's play of that name (1912).

In 1918 he also began acting in films in roles such as Ivan the Terrible in *Kryl'ya kholopa* ("Wings of the Serf," 1925), Governor von Wahl and the Rabbi in *Ego prevoskhoditel'stvo* ("Your Excellency," 1928), the Puppeteer in *Marionetki* ("Marionettes," 1936), and Gobsek in the film of the same name (1937).

From 1935 he taught at the State Institute of Theatrical Art (from 1939 as professor and then dean; and from 1939 to 1941 as artistic director). In 1936 he was awarded the title of People's Artist of the U.S.S.R.

[*The Shorter Jewish Encyclopaedia in Russian*]

LEONOVICH (Leonowicz), name of Karaite family from Halich. The first bearer of this family name was the community leader Abraham ben Levi (d. 1851). In 1802 he was appointed as *ḥazzan* of Halich; he protected the interests of his community before the Austrian authorities. In 1836 through his endeavors a new synagogue was built in Halich (the previous one had been burned down six years before). He was on friendly terms with some intellectuals of the *Haskalah movement, which spread at that time in Galicia. Among his friends, with whom he corresponded and discussed religious questions, were Nahman *Krochmal, Samuel David *Luzzatto of Padua, Isaac ben Samuel Regio, Abraham *Geiger, and many others. He relaxed some severe Karaite laws that concerned the burying of the dead. He composed a number of liturgical poems in Hebrew, some of which were included in the Karaite *siddur*, and some in the Karaite language. In addition to Karaite sources he studied Talmud and medieval Rabbanite literature.

His son JOSEPH (1794–1867) was appointed as a *ḥazzan* after his father's demise. He was also an intercessor for his community and a member of the municipal council of Halich. Joseph and a number of dignitaries of the community traveled to Vienna on a special mission to the Emperor Franz Joseph to ask him for the exemption of Karaites from military service. His argument was that according to the Karaites' literal interpretation of Scripture, any bloodshed is strictly prohibited, even during war. The delegation's request was answered positively. Joseph wrote the grammatical treatise *Imrei Shefer* (St. Petersburg Institute of Oriental Studies of the Russian Academy A 258) and a number of liturgical poems in Hebrew, some of them included in the Karaite *siddur*. He was interested in Rabbanite literature. As he grew up in the atmosphere of the Haskalah in his father's house, he was on friendly terms with some important Haskalah figures, such as A. Geiger, M.-M. Rozenthal, Joseph Moses Levi of Hungary, and others. His correspondence from 1860 to 1864 with the latter was published in *Kokhvei Yiẓḥak* (1845–83), 28–33.

ZARAH BEN SAMUEL (d. 1895) was a son-in-law of Joseph ben Abraham. From 1871 he served as second *ḥazzan* of the Halich community and in 1894–95 became its first *ḥazzan*. He was an expert in Karaite literature and in addition studied philosophical and other Rabbanite works. During some periods of his life he observed precepts that oblige only Rabbanites.

There were some additional, less known personalities with the name Leonovich. This family name was common also in Luzk.

BIBLIOGRAPHY: R. Fahn, *Sefer ha-Kara'im* (1929), 47–52; 88–90; 116–120; 55–56; 120.

[Golda Akhiezer (2nd ed.)]

LEONTE (Judah) BEN MOSES (12th century), liturgical poet. Leonte, who lived in Rome, is most probably identical with the scholar Judah b. Moses who, in the name of the Roman community, addressed an inquiry to *Judah b. Kalonymus and "the sages of Mainz" (Zedekiah Anav, *Shibbolei ha-Leket*, ed. S. Buber (1886), introd. 11 n. 87). A Leon of Rome in 1210 is mentioned in A. *Zacuto's *Yuḥasin* (ed. by H. Filipowski (1857), 221); *Joseph ibn Ẓaddik (Neubauer, Chronicles, 1 (1887), 94) mentions a Leon of Rome in the year 1216. Leonte is named as the author of about ten *seliḥot*, which, though formerly common in the Roman ritual, remained nevertheless in manuscript. In the acrostic he signs his name in the Hebrew form, Judah, or in the Romanic form, Leonte, occasionally adding עני or ענו; he presumably belonged to the Roman-Jewish family *Anav.

BIBLIOGRAPHY: Davidson, Oẓar, 4 (1933), 431, s.v. *Lionti b. Moshe*; Landshuth, Ammudei, 157f.; Vogelstein-Rieger, 1 (1896), 227, 372f.; Zunz, Lit Poesie, 314f.; Schirmann, Italiah, 80–81.

LEONTOPOLIS, locality in the district of Heliopolis in Egypt, N.E. of *Memphis, 6 mi. (10 km.) N. of Cairo. A settlement of Jewish soldiers was established in Leontopolis under the leadership of the former high priest, *Onias IV, sometime after the outbreak of the Maccabean revolt, in the middle of the second century B.C.E., with the approval of Ptolemy Philometer and his wife Cleopatra (Jos., Ant., 13:62ff.). Its nucleus was made up of emigrants from Judea. The Jewish soldiers of the region subsequently played a role in the political life of Egypt and the area was also called "the land of Onias." Onias erected here a temple to the God of Israel by restoring a ruined Egyptian temple which stood on the site. This temple served the Jewish inhabitants of the region for more than 200 years until it was closed down by the Romans in 73 C.E. (Wars, 7:433–646). The present name of the locality, Tell al-Yahūdiyya, is a survival from this ancient Jewish settlement. In archaeological excavations, Jewish inscriptions were found there. Some wish to associate the "Camp of the Jews" mentioned by Josephus (Ant., 14:133), and also the Castra Judaeorum mentioned in the Byzantine era, with this region.

BIBLIOGRAPHY: Tcherikover, Corpus, 1 (1957), 44–46; idem, *Hellenistic Civilization and the Jews* (1959), 278–9; Delcor, in: RB, 75 (1968), 188–205; Rapaport, in: *Revue de Philologie*, 43 (1969), 80–81.

[Uriel Rappaport]

LEONTOVICH, EUGENIE (1900–1993), actress. Born in Moscow, Russia, the daughter of a czarist army officer, Leontovich fled to Berlin in 1918 and worked with Russian refugee actors under the direction of Gregory Ratoff (1893–1960). They married in 1923 and continued to act together in the United States. They divorced in 1949. In 1930 Leontovich played Grusinskaya in Vicki *Baum's *Grand Hotel* on Broadway. Other memorable characterizations included Tatiana in *Tovarich* (London, 1935) and the dowager empress in *Anastasia* (New York, 1954). Her other Broadway performances included *Revue Russe* (1922), *Twentieth Century* (1933), *Bitter Oleander* (1935), *Dark Eyes* (which she co-wrote with Elena Miramova, 1943), *Obsession* (1946), *The Cave Dwellers* (1957), *A Call on Kuprin* (1961), and *Medea and Jason* (1974). In 1958 she was nominated for a Best Actress Tony Award for her performance in *The Cave Dwellers*.

She appeared in several films as well, namely *Four Sons* (1940), *The Men in Her Life* (1941), *Anything Can Happen* (1952), *The World in His Arms* (1952), *The Rains of Ranchipur* (1955), and *Homicidal* (1961). In 1953 she founded a repertory theater in Los Angeles. She joined the Goodman School of Drama in Chicago in 1964. Her colleagues there included Morris Carnovsky, Lilian Gish, James Earl Jones, and Sam Wanamaker. Leontovich wrote a two-act play entitled *Anna K* (1973), based on Leo Tolstoy's novel *Anna Karenina*.

[Ruth Beloff (2nd ed.)]

°**LEONTOVICH, FEDOR** (1833–1911), historian of Russian and Slavic law. Leontovich held the position of professor of the history of law at the universities of Odessa and Warsaw. He was the first to deal with the history of the Russian legislation concerning the Jews, when he published "An Historical Survey of the Regulations concerning the Jews in Russia" in the Russian-Jewish periodical *Sion*. His "The Rights of the Russian-Lithuanian Jews" (Kiev, 1863) was based on original documents and elucidated the outlines of the legal and social situation of the Jews in the grand duchy of Lithuania. I.G. *Orshanski and S.A. *Bershadski were influenced by these works. In 1882 he published an article in the monthly *Nablyudatel* entitled "What We Must Do with the Jewish Problem," where he argued that the Jews could only be granted equality of rights after they had abandoned their "specific nationalist culture"; as this was a process which could continue through several generations, there was no room for emancipation of the Jews at the time.

[Yehuda Slutsky]

LEOPARD (Heb. נָמֵר, *namer*), the strongest carnivorous animal in the Middle East. The leopard has a spotted coat, this being the meaning of its Hebrew name (Jer. 13:23). It is not to be confused with the tiger which, besides being striped, did not inhabit Ereẓ Israel (it is mentioned in Ḥul. 59b). Belonging to the feline family, the leopard, *Felis pardus tullianus* (= *Panthera pardus*), has a body which, excluding the tail, is 120–150 cm. (c. 4–5 ft.) long and a yellowish-fawn coat with black spots. Its bodily structure, with its short forelegs and extremely powerful hindlegs, is especially suited to lying in wait, this habit being referred to in the Bible (Hos. 13:7; cf. Jer. 5:6). In Isaiah's vision of the messianic age, in which he depicts the amity that will exist between the carnivorous animals and their prey, he declares that "the leopard shall lie down with the kid," the latter being the usual prey of the leopard, as the lamb is of the wolf and the calf of the young lion (Isa. 11:6). The leopard's speed and agility are stressed in the Bible (Hab. 1:8), while its strength is referred to in the Mishnah (Avot 5:20): "Be strong as a leopard, swift as an eagle, fleet as a gazelle, and brave as a lion to do the will of your Father in heaven," an aphorism that was illustrated in paintings and engravings in synagogues. In recent years leopards, like other wild animals, have decreased in the Middle East. Occasionally individual or pairs of leopards come down from the Lebanese mountains to Upper Galilee (cf. Song 4:8). In the neighborhood of En-Gedi a family of leopards was killed in the 1960s, and in the Arabah some members of the leopard family were hunted. The cheetah (*Acinonyx jubatus*), which is called *bardelas* in the Mishnah, is enumerated alongside the leopard among the carnivorous animals (BK 1:4). It is apparently included in the Bible under the term *namer* on account of its spotted coat, although in fact its bodily structure differs from that of the leopard, the cheetah having a small head and long legs which enable it to pursue its prey.

BIBLIOGRAPHY: Lewysohn, Zool, 71f., no. 116; F.S. Bodenheimer, *Animal and Man in Bible Lands* (1960), 20–22, 26, 43; J. Feliks, *The Animal World of the Bible* (1962), 33. **ADD. BIBLIOGRAPHY:** Feliks, Ha-Ẓome'aḥ, 253.

[Jehuda Feliks]

°**LEOPOLD I** (1640–1705), Holy Roman Emperor (1658–1705), king of Bohemia (1656–1705), and king of Hungary (1655–1705). His treatment of the Jews was determined by his ultra-Catholic attitudes, which led to their expulsion from Vienna in 1670. On his election as Holy Roman Emperor in 1658 he confirmed all charters which had been granted in Austria and in the Holy Roman Empire by his father *Ferdinand III and ordered that Jewish life and property be protected (1660, 1665, 1669). However, his anti-Jewish attitude was intensified by his marriage in 1666 to the Catholic-educated Margaret Theresa, daughter of Philip IV of Spain, who saw in the tolerance of the Jews the reason for the death of her firstborn (1668). In 1670 he responded to the city's request that the Jews be expelled from Vienna, in spite of papal intervention, and swore never to admit them again. He took into account the Hungarian Protestants' claim that they were worse off than the Jews, and he was influenced by Cardinal *Kollonich. When readmitting *Court Jews such as Samuel *Oppenheimer in 1676 and Samson *Wertheimer in 1684, he had the problem of his oath solved by theologians. In 1695 he permitted the printing of the Talmud in Germany. At Oppenheimer's request, he prohibited (1700) the circulation of Johann Andreas *Eisenmenger's *Entdecktes Judenthum*.

BIBLIOGRAPHY: D. Kaufmann, *Die letzte Vertreibung der Juden aus Wien* (1889), 65–166; H. Tietze, *Die Juden Wiens* (1935), index; Pillich, in: J. Fraenkel (ed.), *The Jews of Austria* (1967), 5–9; W. Mueller, *Urkundliche Beitraege zur Geschichte der maehrischen Judenschaft* (1903), 25–31; A.F. Pribram, *Urkunden und Akten zur Geschichte der Juden in Wien*, 1–2 (1918), index; M. Grunwald, Vienna (1936), index; MHJ, 2 (1937), index.

[Meir Lamed]

LEOVO (Rum. **Leova**), town in S.W. Moldova, in the region of Bessarabia. There were 25 Jewish families living in Leovo in 1817. The community grew as a result of the large Jewish immigration into Bessarabia in the 19th century and numbered 2,773 persons (57% of the total population) in 1897. The Jews there were subject to the legislation restricting Jewish residence in the border zone. The *ẓaddik* Dov Baer, the son of Israel (Friedmann) of *Ruzhyn, whose defection from Ḥasidism to the *maskilim* caused a furor, lived in Leovo in the 1860s. The writers Judah *Steinberg and Jacob *Fichmann taught there. Among the 434 members registered in the Jewish loan fund in 1925, there were 84 farmers, 102 craftsmen, and 163 businessmen. There were 2,326 Jews living in Leovo (35% of the total population) in 1930. The community then maintained a kindergarten and a school, both belonging to the *Tarbut network.

[Eliyahu Feldman]

Holocaust Period

During the Romanian evacuation of Leovo in June 1940, the Jewish population, numbering some 600 families, was unharmed. In July 1940, a month after the annexation of Bessarabia by the Soviet Union, all Zionist leaders and wealthy Jews were exiled to Siberia and their property confiscated. When war broke out between Germany and the Soviet Union in June 1941, Leovo was in the battle zone. Most of the population tried to escape with the help of the Russians, but the majority of the Jews who managed to leave the town were murdered by Romanian soldiers and gendarmes in the neighboring villages and towns. A few who succeeded in reaching Odessa and the Caucasian Mountains were murdered by the Germans when they reached these areas. Those Jews who stayed in Leovo were all murdered by Romanian troops. Some of the Jews who were caught on the roads were exiled to *Transnistria, from which only a few returned. Only 30 Jews returned to Leovo after the war.

BIBLIOGRAPHY: BJCE.

[Jean Ancel]

LEPEL, town in Vitebsk district, Belarus. Before the 1917 Revolution it served as a county town in the province (*gubernia*) of Vitebsk, Russia. In 1802 the Jewish population of Lepel and district totaled 368. Their number increased to 1,509 in 1847 and 3,379 (53.7% of the total population) in 1897. Two Jewish state schools operated, for boys, with emphasis on vocational training, and for girls. During World War I the city was on the Russo-German front, and it also suffered greatly in the war between Russia and Poland (1919–20). There were 1,932 Jews (28.9%) in the town in 1926, and 1,919 by 1939. A Jewish elementary school existed there during the Soviet period. The Germans occupied the city on July 3, 1941, and later established a ghetto there. On February 28, 1942, almost all 1,000 Jews from the Lepel ghetto were shot. There is no information on Jewish life in Lepel after World War II.

[Yehuda Slutsky]

LEPROSY. The term *ẓaraʿat* is traditionally rendered "leprosy" because of its translation by Greek *lepra* (LXX, New Testament, and Josephus). The Greek covers a wide range of diseases that produced scales. Greek *lepra* may have included true leprosy, i.e., Hansen's disease, but is definitely not limited to it. In fact, biblical descriptions of *ẓaraʿat* do not include the necrosis associated with Hansen's disease. Thus far no skeletons of the biblical period show any signs of Hansen's disease. The term *ẓaraʿat* is a generic name, embracing a variety of skin ailments, including many non-contagious types. Thus, the illness of Miriam was transient (Num. 12:10–15) and that of Naaman did not prevent him from mixing freely in society (II Kings 5). Probably only those actually banished from their fellowmen were lifelong sufferers, e.g., the four "lepers" forced to live outside Samaria (II Kings 7:3–10) and King Uzziah, who was permanently quarantined in separate quarters (II Chron. 26:19–21). Medical texts of the ancient Near East attribute disease either to black magic or the sufferer's sin (R.C. Thompson, *Assyrian Medical Texts* (1923); A.L. Oppenheim, *Ancient Mesopotamia* (1977, 288–305). In the Bible, whenever a reason is given for an attack of *ẓaraʿat*, it is in connection with a challenge to a duly constituted authority (Zakovitch).

Miriam challenged the prophetic supremacy of Moses; Gehazi disobeyed the will of his master Elisha (II Kings 5:20–27); and Uzziah challenged the exclusive prerogative of the priests to offer incense. In the case of sin and black magic, rituals are prescribed that bear a striking resemblance to those in the Bible (see below), with one critical difference. In contrast to the Mesopotamian situation, in which priests may be healers, the Bible always attributes the healing of individuals to the intervention of prophets (e.g., Gen. 20:7; II Kings 5). The priest himself only rules on the purity or impurity of the sufferer (Kaufmann).

The Laws of Leviticus 13–14

Leviticus 13–14 is composed of the following sections: the diagnosis of the afflictions of the skin (13:2–28, 38–39, summarized below), of the hair (13:29–37), and of the scalp (13:40–44); the ostracism of the incurable (13:45–46; cf. Lam. 4:15); the diagnosis of the deterioration of garments, due probably to mildew or fungus (13:47–59); the ritual for the rehabilitation of the healed "leper" (14:1–32); the diagnosis of the "leprosy" of houses, probably caused by the spread of dry rot, mineral precipitates, or the growth of lichens and fungi (14:33–53); and the summary (14:54–57). The structure is logical, with houses being put at the end (cf. 14:34), a reflection of the reality of the period in which the texts were written. Though not all the technical terms are understood (see the commentaries), the symptoms given are capable of precise medical definition. The affliction can occur spontaneously (13:2–17), follow a furuncle (13:18–23) or a burn on the skin (13:24–28), or develop on the head or beard (13:29–45). The first symptoms are those of a swelling, or subcutaneous nodule, a cuticular crust (*sappaḥat*), and whitish-red spot (*baheret*). "The crux of the matter lay in the degree of cutaneous penetration which the disease had achieved. If it affected the epidermis or outermost layer of skin and did not produce pathological changes in the hairs, the affliction was not regarded as especially serious. As such it might consist of eczema, leukoderma, psoriasis, or some allied cutaneous disease. But if the affliction had infiltrated the dermis (corium) and had caused hairs to split or break off and lose their color, then "leprosy" was to be suspected" (R.K. Harrison). This diagnostic principle also applied to disease affecting the scalp (13:29–37) where the affliction was spoken of as *netek* (*neteq*) (JPS "scall").

The Role of the Priest

The Israelite priest, while usually not involved in individual healing according to the Bible, is involved in epidemics where he intercedes through sacrifices, Num. 17:11ff.; II Sam. 24:25 – David officiating as priest. Deut. 24:8–9, which deals with contagious skin diseases enumerated here is a possible exception; and contrast the laws pertaining to gonorrhea, Lev. 15.

The priest was called in to inspect the affliction. If "leprosy" was only suspected but not certain, the priest imposed a seven-day quarantine. At the end of this period the afflicted was examined again, and if no further degeneration was apparent he was isolated for another week, after which he could be pronounced healed. The priest, however, did nothing to promote the cure. His rituals were performed only after the disease had passed. It was the responsibility of the afflicted himself to pray (I Kings 8:37–38; II Kings 20:2–3) and fast (II Sam. 12:16) in order to win God's healing. Deuteronomy 24:8–9 charges the people to follow the authority of the priests in all matters dealing with "leprosy," citing as precedent the case of Miriam (see Num. 12:11–16), who challenged the authority of Moses (alternatively, the late writer of Numbers 12 (see Sperling) was inspired by the juxtaposition of priestly authority in matters of "leprosy" with the mention of the unnamed punishment laid on Miriam by God in Deuteronomy 24:9). It is noteworthy that in Miriam's case healing did not come through Aaron the priest, who was a party to the offense, but through the prophet Moses and his prayer. In the Bible, healing comes from God directly (Ex. 15:26) or through the prophet (e.g., Moses, Ex. 15:25; Elisha, II Kings 2:21; Isaiah, II Kings 20:7–8).

The Ritual

The prescribed ritual for the healed "leper" is of interest. Three separate ceremonies are required: for the first day (Lev. 14:2–8; also invoked for houses, 14:48–53), the seventh (14:9), and the eighth (14:10–32). The first-day ritual is performed by the priest outside the camp or city from which the "leper" has been banished. Cedar wood, crimson cloth, and a live bird are dipped into an earthen vessel containing a mixture of fresh water and the blood of a second bird. The "leper" (or "leprous" house) is sprinkled with this mixture seven times, after which the live bird is set free. The "leper" is admitted into the camp or city after he washes his clothes, shaves all his hair, and bathes, but he is not allowed to enter his residence. That is permitted him on the seventh day after shaving, laundering, and bathing again. On the eighth day he brings to the sanctuary oil and sheep for various offerings – whole, meal, purification, and reparation. The whole and purification animals may be commuted to birds if the "leper" is poor. However, the reparation lamb and *log* of oil may not be changed, because the blood of the lamb and the oil are needed to daub the "leper's" right ear lobe, right thumb, and right big toe.

This complex ceremonial is elucidated by comparison with similar prescriptions in the ancient world. There is much evidence of the banishment of evil by carriers (J. Frazer, *The Golden Bough*, 6 (1935), 249ff.), especially animals (e.g., Hittite: F. Sommer and H. Ehelolf, *Das hethitische Ritual des Papanikri von Komana* (1924), III 45, Rev. iv, 5ff.; Mesopotamia and Israel: see *Azazel). Aspersions of materials such as cedar, scarlet wool, and hyssop are also known (e.g., J. Laesse, *Studies in the Assyrian Ritual*… (1955); R.C. Thompson, *The Devils and Evil Spirits of Babylon*, vol. 2, 1904). Moreover, a letter of Nergal-sharrani to King Esarhaddon refers to an apotropaic prayer and a ritual for *kamūnu* fungus, which appeared in the inner court of the temple of Nab – and for the *kattarru* fungus on the walls of storehouses (R.F. Harper, *Assyrian and Baby-*

lonian Letters, 4 (1896), no. 367 = SAA XIII:71). Clearly, then, the purpose of the "leper's" ritual of the first day was to exorcise the demonic disease and banish it to a place of no return, e.g., the desert (see *Azazel) or the open country in the case of the leper (*ha-sadeh*; Lev. 14:7, 53). In keeping with P's exclusion of the priest from participation in the healing of individuals, the ritual is prescribed only after "the priest sees that the 'leper' is healed" (14:3). If ritual purification is the purpose of the ritual of the first day, why its week-long extension? Here, in keeping with the priestly system of scaled impurities, a severe defilement endures for eight days after healing and calls for a three-stage purification, which reduces and finally eliminates this vestigial impurity (see *Purity and Impurity, Ritual). The rite of the first day enables the leper to mingle with, but not touch, the members of his community, nor can he enter a confined space lest he defile what it holds (see 14:8b; rabbinic מאהיל, cf. Kelim 1:4; Neg. 13:3, 7, 8, 11; Jos., Ant., 3:261ff.; Jos., Apion, 1:279ff.; cf. Num. 19:14). These restrictions are removed only at the end of the seventh day, after he has again shaved, laundered, and bathed.

Having been restored to his community and household, he is still impure vis-à-vis the realm of the sacred: he has to be rehabilitated in the eyes of his God (ten times the text insists that the ritual is "before the Lord," Lev. 14:11–31). In the eighth-day ritual – the third and final stage – he therefore brings to the sanctuary a complex of sacrifices. The purification offering purges the sacred area of the defilement brought on by his "leprosy" (see *Atonement); the whole and meal offerings expiate the sin that might have caused his affliction (e.g., Miriam, see above); the reparation offering is his expiation in case he has trespassed on sancta (*ma'al*, a sin punishable by leprosy, e.g., Uzziah, II Chron. 26:16–21; cf. Lev. 5:14–19; and see *Sacrifices). The blood of the animal of reparation and the oil are successively daubed on the extremities of his body so that he may have access to the sanctuary and its sancta (as far as allowed to a layman). That sanctification is the purpose of this ritual is demonstrated by the consecration service of the priest (Ex. 29; Lev. 8), where the daubing of the same parts of the body is prescribed and where a mixture of oil and sacrificial blood is used (in sprinkling, not in daubing: note verb *qadesh* "sanctify." Ex. 29:21; Lev. 8:30). Israel's sanctification motif is illuminated by comparison with similarly structured rituals in the ancient Near East, where there is abundant attestation of daubing (see *Anointing). The incantations recited during the ritual smearing of persons, the statues of gods, and buildings testify that its object is purificatory and apotropaic: to wipe off and ward off the incursions of menacing demonic forces. Hence it is always the vulnerable parts of bodies (extremities) and of structures (corners, entrances) that are smeared with substances with alleged special properties (e.g., Pritchard, Texts, 338). The Bible's "leprosy" laws are directed toward the larger community and do not constitute a priest's manual. As such, whatever additional incantations and exorcisms that may have been performed are lost to us. The purificatory and apotropaic are steps in the healed "leper's" rehabilitation, which enabled him to return to his community and qualified him to have access to the Sanctuary and God. Ezekiel's ritual of consecration for the altar is strikingly analogous: blood is to be daubed on its horns and the corners of its two gutters, located at its middle and bottom (Ezek. 43:20). These points correspond to a person's ear lobe, thumb, and big toe. There can be no question that the purpose of this altar ritual (as in the consecration of the priests) is sanctificatory; the same must be said of the eighth-day ritual for the "leper."

[Jozeph Michman (Melkman) / S. David Sperling (2nd ed.)]

In the Second Temple and Talmud

The laws of leprosy are given in great detail in the Talmud, and a whole tractate of the Mishnah and Tosefta, **Nega'im*, is devoted to them. It is reported that in the courtyard of the Temple itself, on the northwest, there was the Chamber of the Lepers where the lepers remained after they had been cured, and where they bathed on the eighth day of their purification, awaiting their admittance for the anointing of their toes (Neg. 14:8; Mid. 2:5). In the New Testament there are numerous references to lepers. In the two instances in which Jesus is said to have cured lepers (one an individual – Luke 5:12–14; cf. Matt. 8:3; and the other a group of ten – Luke 17:12), he told them, "Go show yourself to the priest," after their cure, and one passage (Luke 5:14) adds, "and make an offering for thy cleansing, as Moses commanded…" This is evidence that the biblical laws were in operation, both as regards the functions of the priest and the obligatory offering. The Apostles are told in general to cleanse the lepers (Matt. 10:8; Luke 7:22).

On the other hand there are hardly any references in the tannaitic period to actual cases of leprosy. Tosefta *Negaim* (6:1) includes the "house affected by leprosy" (Lev. 14:34–53) among those laws which "never were and never will be," their purpose being merely "to expound and receive reward therefore" (cf. *Rebellious Son). Eleazar b. Simeon, however, adds that there was a site in the vicinity of Gaza which used to be called "the enclosed ruin" (which was presumably a house affected by leprosy which had been destroyed in accordance with the law (Lev. 14:45)), and Simeon b. Judah of Kefar Akko (according to the amendment of Elijah Gaon of Vilna) said that there was a site in Galilee which used to be pointed out as having within its bounds leprous stones. It is also stated that according to the *halakhah*, the law of quarantine for lepers fell into abeyance when the Jubilee year (see *Sabbatical Year and Jubilee) was not in operation (cf. Tosef., Ber. 5b top), i.e., presumably during the Second Temple period.

Josephus, who was both a priest and lived during the time of the Temple, in his description of the Mosaic laws, states that it was forbidden to the leper to "come into the city at all [or] to live with any others, as if they were in effect dead persons." He makes a sharp contrast between this law and the fact that "there are lepers in many nations who are yet in honor, and not only free from reproach and avoidance, but who have been great captains of armies, and been entrusted with high office in the commonwealth and have had the privilege of entering into holy places and temples" (Ant., 3:261–9). It is possible, however, that this passage is merely a reference to Naaman, the commander of the army of Syria (II Kings 5, especially vs. 5 and 18).

By the time of the compilation of the Mishnah and Tosefta, at the beginning of the third century, the laws of leprosy were regarded as the most abstruse and complicated of laws. Eleazar b. Simeon on one occasion said to R. Akiva, "What have you to do with *aggadah*? Turn to the subject of leprosy" (Ḥag. 14a). Although, according to the Talmud, leprosy did not exist in Babylon "because they eat turnips and drink beer and bathe in the Euphrates" (Ket. 77b), it seems to have existed in Ereẓ Israel in mishnaic and amoraic times. R. Johanan and Resh Lakish stated that it is forbidden to walk four cubits, or 100 cubits (dependent upon whether there was a wind blowing at the time) to the east of a leper; R. Meir refrained from eating eggs which came from a district where lepers lived; R. Ammi and R. Assi never entered such a district; when Resh Lakish saw one he would cast stones at him, exclaiming, "get back to your location and do not contaminate other people"; and R. Eleazar b. Simeon would hide from them (Lev. R. 16:3). As Katzenelson points out, since the segregation enjoined in the Bible no longer applied in talmudic times, this segregation and its consequences were the result of popular feeling, and not a legal requirement. There is a geonic responsum which states explicitly, "among the people of the east, that is, in Babylonia, at the present time, if, God forbid, a scholar should be affected by leprosy, he is not excluded from the synagogue or the schools, since today the injunction, 'thy camp shall be holy' (Deut. 23:15; i.e., the laws of ritual cleanness) no longer applies" (*Sha'arei Teshuvah*, no. 176).

Reference should be made to the allegation first mentioned by the Egyptian historian *Manetho, and repeated by *Chaereman, *Lysimachus, and other Egyptian writers hostile to the Jews, and quoted by *Apion, to the effect that not only was Moses a leper, but the children of Israel were expelled from Egypt because they suffered from leprosy. Indeed, according to Lysimachus the seventh day was called *Sabbaton* because of the leprous disease of the groin which they suffered which is called *Sabbo* in Egyptian (Jos., Apion, 1:227ff., 2:20–21).

In the *Aggadah*

Aside from the practical issue of the observance of the regulations of ritual cleanness in general, and of the laws of leprosy in particular after the destruction of the Temple, it should be noted that the rabbis derived from the laws of leprosy a moral lesson. Homiletically interpreting the word *meẓora* as connected with *moẓi shem ra*, "the person guilty of slander or libel," they regarded leprosy primarily as a divine punishment for this evil, an interpretation which receives historical support by the punishment of Miriam for her slander of Moses (Num. 12:1–15), and the rabbis add that Aaron suffered the same punishment for the same reason (Shab. 97a). Among other sins which bring leprosy as retribution are "the shedding of blood, taking oaths in vain, incest, arrogance, robbery, and envy" (Ar. 16a), as well as benefiting from sacred objects (Lev. R. 17:3). From the combination of the cedar, which represents haughtiness, and the hyssop, the symbol of lowliness, in the purification rites for the leper (Lev. 14:4) the rabbis derived the lesson that man should ever humble himself (see Rashi to Lev. 14:4). The leper was one of the four unfortunates considered to suffer a living death (Ned. 64b; Sanh. 47a; cf. Num. 12:12). That leprosy was assumed to result from a lack of hygiene is indicated not only by the reason given for its absence in Babylon (see above), but also from such statements as that it comes from flies (Ḥag. 14a), whereas the notion that children born from intercourse with a menstruant woman will be afflicted by it (Lev. R. 15:5) is more likely to be related to issues of sin and impurity than to hygiene. The *aggadah* makes a considerable addition to the number of characters mentioned in the Bible as having been struck with leprosy. They include Cain (Gen. R. 22:12), the daughter of Pharaoh (Ex. R. 1:23), Aaron (see above), Doeg (Sanh. 106b), David (Sanh. 107a), Goliath (Lev. R. 17:3), and Vashti (Meg. 12b). According to the Midrash, the reference to the pharaoh who died (Ex. 2:23) actually refers to the fact that he was afflicted with leprosy. His advisers told him that the only cure was to bathe morning and evening in the blood of 150 Hebrew children, but the decree was averted by God, who in his compassion cured Pharaoh (Ex. R. 1:34).

[Louis Isaac Rabinowitz]

BIBLIOGRAPHY: Kaufmann, Y., Toledot, 1 (1937), 539–58; Kaufmann, Y., Religion, 103–10; R.K. Harrison, in: IDB, 3 (1962), 111–3, 331–4. IN THE SECOND TEMPLE AND TALMUD: I.M. Rabbinowicz, *La Médicine du Talmud* (1880), 107ff.; G.N. Minkh, *Prokaza i pes* (1890); J. Preuss, *Biblisch-talmudische Medizin* (1923³), 369–90; J.L. Katzenelson, *Ha-Talmud ve-Ḥokhmat ha-Refu'ah* (1928), 304–53; H.L. Strack and P. Billerbeck, *Kommentar zum Neuen Testament aus Talmud und Midrash*, 14 (1928), 745–63; Ginzberg, Legends, index; A.R. Short, *The Bible and Modern Medicine* (1953), 74–83. **ADD. BIBLIOGRAPHY:** Y. Zakovitch, *Every High Official* (1986); B. Levine, *JPS Torah Commentary Leviticus* (1989), 75–92; J. Milgrom, *Leviticus 1–16* (AB; 1991); D. Wright and R. Jones, in: ABD, 4:277–82; R. Biggs, in: CANE III, 1916; H. Avalos, *Illness and Health Care in the Ancient Near East* (1996), 233–420; S.D. Sperling, in: HUCA, 70–71 (1999–2000), 39–55.

LERER, JOSHUA (1920–), *ḥazzan*. Born in Jerusalem to a family of cantors, Lerer studied *ḥazzanut* under Shelomo Zalman *Rivlin and music at the Jerusalem Institute of Music. After serving as cantor in the Har ha-Carmel Synagogue in Haifa for 12 years, and in other communities in Israel, he was appointed chief cantor of the Great Synagogue in Tel Aviv (1956–58). From 1960 to 1974 he was chief cantor in the Shomrei Hadass Synagogue in Antwerp, and in 1975 was reappointed by the Great Synagogue in Tel Aviv.

[Akiva Zimmerman (2nd ed.)]

LERER, SHMUEL (1930–), *ḥazzan*. Shmuel Lerer was born in Jerusalem to a family of famous cantors. One of his forefathers, Aharon Natan Sofer, was for many years the cantor of the Tiferet Israel Synagogue in the old city of Jerusalem. Shmuel Lerer received a religious education in Jerusalem where he also studied music and voice development at the Academy of Music. He served as the conductor of the choir of his elder brother, Cantor Joshua *Lerer, and afterwards as chief cantor of the Ramah Synagogue in Tel Aviv and of the Great Synagogue in Ramat Gan. From there he moved to the Marble Arch synagogue, London, where he served from 1963 to 1968. During the years 1968–78 he was chief cantor in the central Bet Midrash in Johannesburg. He then returned to Israel. He has since then officiated communally at High Holiday prayer services, inter alia in Montreal and St. Petersburg. He has produced several records of cantorial music. The Cantors and Choirmasters Association of South Africa issued a volume of Lerer's compositions entitled *Rinah ve-Tefillah* in Johannesburg in 1977, when Lerer was also their chairman and honorary president. This work shows Lerer as an exceptional melodist of synagogal compositions written in the traditional style.

[Akiva Zimmerman / Raymond Goldstein (2nd ed.)]

LERER, YEHIEL (1910–1943), Yiddish poet. Born in Mrozy, Poland, by the age of 16 he was considered a talmudic genius. He was introduced to Yiddish literature by his townsman and mentor, novelist I.M. *Weissenberg, with whose Warsaw literary circle he was associated. Weissenberg hailed him as the Yiddish Tagore on the basis of his first poems (*Tehilim*, "Psalms"), later included in the volume *Shtilkayt un Shturm* ("Silence and Storm," 1932), a volume characterized by religious piety and lyric solemnity. Unsuccessful in various professions, Lerer suffered from privation throughout his short life. His poem "Mayn Heym" ("My Home," 1937), about a family in a Jewish town, stressed the transformation of its traditional religious and social character under the impact of new forces. Sholem Asch called this poem a "gift of God's grace, one of the most beautiful Jewish books." Lerer was a romantic epigone during the dominance of expressionistic tendencies in Yiddish poetry. After the Nazi occupation of Warsaw, he participated in the ghetto's literary activities under various assumed names; some of his works can be found in the Ringelblum archive. In 1943, he was transported to *Treblinka, where he was killed.

BIBLIOGRAPHY: LNYL, 5 (1963), 370–2; M. Ravitch, *Mayn Leksikon* (1945), 119–21; M. Grossman, *Heymishe Geshtaltn* (1953), 158–64; *Yizkor-Bukh fun der Zhelekhover Yidisher Kehile* (1954), 181–94; D. Sadan, in: *Avnei Miftan* (1962), 237–48. **ADD. BIBLIOGRAPHY:** Y. Rapoport, *Oysgerisene Bleter* (1957), 156–77; R. Oyerbakh, et al., *Yizker Bukh fun Zhelkhov* (1954), 181–94.

[Melech Ravitch / Marc Miller (2nd ed.)]

LÉRIDA (Lleida, Ilerda), city in Spain on the border between Catalonia and Aragon. In the Muslim period, the Jews of Lérida maintained close contact with those in nearby Barcelona. Their major occupation was tanning, as attested by various documents, but there were several wealthy merchants and a few farmers. The Jewish quarter, dating from the 11th century, was located to the west of the city in a place called Cuiraça. A street still called Judería, located above the quarter, attests to its subsequent expansion. Following the conquest of the city in 1149, the community began to grow.

The Order of Knights Templar had many interests in Lérida and its vicinity, and Jews were connected with its activities. In 1168, the bailiff of Lérida, a Jew named Jafia, was granted several properties in the city. In 1172 his son David was given a workshop and a house near the king's palace in the city. In 1175 Jafia mortgaged a wine cellar he owned in the Jewish quarter and a vineyard to the Templars of Gardeny near Lérida. In 1173 one of the synagogues was converted into a church. Profet Benvenist, the king's *alfaquim*, also owned property in Lérida, including a house in the Muslim quarter (1189). Deeds of sale of houses, gardens, and vineyards owned by Jews, dating from the beginning of the 13th century, have been preserved. One of them mentions a Jew named Abraym Cavalaria of Lérida but it is not known whether he was related to the well-known *Cavaleria family. In addition to his other offices, Benveniste de Porta was bailiff of Lérida. In the controversy over *Maimonides' writings, the Lérida community joined in the ban imposed on *Solomon of Montpellier and his followers in 1232 by the communities of Aragon. Some Jews from Lérida settled in Valencia after the capture of the city in 1238. In 1271 James I appointed a certain Nasi Ḥasdai as rabbi and *dayyan* of the Lérida community. He was authorized to adjudicate all disputes between Jews according to Jewish law in consultation with two of the elders who were bound to accept the rabbi's summons to sit in court. The appointment was unique in Catalonia, similar instances being found only in Castile. The taxes levied upon the community of Lérida amounted to about 5,000 sólidos in 1271, and 3,000 sólidos in 1274. The community was headed by **muqaddimūm* or *adelantados*, a council, and magistrates (*borerim*). The *muqaddimūm* appointed their own successors in office.

In the 14th century the community became the third largest in Catalonia, after Barcelona and Gerona, with about 500 members. At the beginning of the century several *Conversos returned to Judaism in Lérida, among them a convert from Belmont near Toulouse who was apprehended in 1317 and tried by the Inquisition in Toulouse. Jews from Lérida were among those who went to bury the victims of the *Pastoureaux massacres in *Montclus in 1320, and were accused of demolishing a bridge and cutting down trees there, but were pardoned the same year on payment of a large sum to the crown. During the massacres accompanying the *Black Death in 1348, the community found refuge in the citadel. In 1350 they had to pay 350 Barcelona sólidos to the official appointed for their protection. An agreement between the community and the municipal authorities concerning the import of wine was ratified by Pedro IV in 1353; the document, in which the community undertook not to bring imported wine into the city, contains a long list of the communal leaders. Two Jews from Lérida were accused in 1383 of desecrating the *Host, and the count of Urgel was ordered by the king to investigate the charges.

During the persecutions of 1391, the community was severely hit, a number of Jews took refuge in the citadel, and 78 were massacred. Most of the survivors were baptized. The Jewish quarter was destroyed and the synagogue was converted into a church. The king ordered that measures should be taken to punish the rioters and protect the Jews. In 1400 King Martin gave permission to the survivors to take steps to rehabilitate the community. Newcomers were granted a reduction of taxes and released from their debts, and Jews from other communities were permitted to settle in the city after they had settled their taxes. If their former communities refused to allow them to settle there, the municipal authorities of Lérida would guarantee the payment of their liabilities through mortgages and assist in moving the newcomers. In addition, an electoral procedure was established in which the rights of the newcomers were safeguarded. Stringent measures were passed against *informers. The community was allowed to impose indirect taxes, and its members were permitted to live in other parts of the city until the Cuiraça district had been reconstructed. In 1408 King Martin ordered that the synagogue, which had been converted into a church, should be restored and also provided for the election of two *muqaddimūm* and nine councillors and regulated their authority. An agreement was concluded in 1410 between the city authorities and the community concerning the latter's status and activities. In 1421 Queen Maria wrote to the municipal authorities concerning the establishment of a new community in Lérida. John II granted the community a number of patents of protection and alleviated certain of the restrictions imposed before 1459 on some occupations. In 1490 a district tribunal of the Inquisition was established in Lérida which included Huesca and Urgel within its jurisdiction. An unsuccessful attempt was made to murder the inquisitor in 1514.

The Jewish quarter in Lérida, the *Cuiraça* or *Coiraza*, was in the fortified part of the city, in the old parish of San Andrés. It included San Cristófol Street and the Plaça Seminari, and Judería and Seminari streets. The Jewish cemetery was on the left side of the current Balmes Street. Ever since the 18th century tombstones and human remains have been found in the area covered by the streets Vallcalent, Ciutat de Fraga, Joan Baiget, and Missions square. In this area a ring with the female name Goig in Hebrew was found in 1870.

BIBLIOGRAPHY: J. Pleyan de Porta, *Apuntes de Historia de Lérida* (1873), 135ff., 172, 400; H.C. Lea, *History of the Spanish Inquisition*, 1 (1907), 549; Baer, Urkunden, index; F. Mateu y Llopis, in: *Hispania*, 2 (1942), 407–37; J. Llandoza, *La "Cuiraça" y la judería leridana* (1951), 110ff.; Simón de Gilleuma, in: *Sefarad*, 18 (1958), 83–97; A. López de Meneses, *ibid.*, 19 (1959), 101; D. Romano, *ibid.*, 20 (1960), 50–65; Baer, Spain, index; Ashtor, Korot, 2 (1966), 174–6. **ADD. BIBLIOGRAPHY:** F. Lara Peinado, in: *Ilerda*, 31 (1971), 17–24; D. Romano, in: *Sefarad*, 35 (1975), 158; P. Bertran i Roigé, in: *Sefarad* (1981), 114–20; R. Pita Mercé, *La societat jueva en els calls lleidatans*, (1978); idem, in: *Ilerda*, 43 (1982), 445–55; G. Secall i Guéll, in: *Ilerda*, 46 (1985), 273–88.

[Haim Beinart / Yom Tov Assis (2nd ed.)]

LERMA, JUDAH BEN SAMUEL (middle of the 16th century), scholar of Spanish origin living in Italy. The years of Lerma's birth and death are unknown, and all the information on him relates to the years 1553–56. The place and scope of his activity are also not clear, but apparently he never held an official rabbinical post. He states that he attempted to amass wealth but lost all that he possessed. He also complains, as do other contemporary scholars in Italy, that the attitude of the public to him was not as it should be toward a scholar. He is frequently confused with Judah Lerma of Belgrade, author of the *Peletat Bat Yehudah*, but it is doubtful if there was even a family relationship between them. Some think he was the son of Samuel Lerma, the copyist in 1536 of the manuscript glosses on the Mishnah. He wrote *Leḥem Yehudah*, a commentary to *Avot*. The first edition was published in Venice in 1553, but was consigned to the flames in the same year, with the burning of the Talmud (see Burning of *Talmud). A second edition was published in the following year in Sabbioneta, but there are conspicuous differences between the two editions, especially in the first half. He also wrote a commentary on the Book of Job which is frequently quoted in both editions of the *Leḥem Yehudah*, and there are also fragments of *aggadah* with a commentary extant in manuscript. His commentary to *Avot* is quoted in the various 16th-century anthologies of commentaries to *Avot*.

Lerma was a philosopher who followed the Spanish Jewish philosophers, from whom he derived his theories and views. His approach is on the whole moderate and conservative. His main sources, besides the talmudic and midrashic literature and Maimonides, are Joseph Albo, Isaac Abrabanel, and in particular Isaac Arama. Lerma had no direct knowledge of the writings of non-Jewish thinkers and was also most sparing in the use of other Jewish speculative and literary works. His method of writing is nearer in style and form to talmudic than to the philosophical literature (particularly in the second edition). He is more interested in using his sources as the basis of his own views than in explaining the literal meaning of the tractate. Although original neither in his ideas nor in his manner of expressing them, Lerma's views about the influence of the stars upon the world and man, and about predestination in its relation to man's religious autonomy and the Commandments are interesting and unique in content, form, and scope (in both editions). These views met with the opposition of his contemporaries despite their moderate approach. There is a note of arrogance in his work. He frequently disputes the views of earlier authorities and even expressed himself to the effect that the person studying his work "would have no need of any other commentator."

BIBLIOGRAPHY: Steinschneider, Cat Bod, 1337, no. 5737; E. Carmoly, *Divrei ha-Yamim li-Venei Yaḥya* (1850), 35, n. 109; Epstein, Mishnah, 1286–87.

[Joseph Hacker]

LERMAN, MILES (**Shmuel Milek**; 1920–), Holocaust survivor and activist. Lerman was born in Tomaszov Lubelski, son of Israel and Jochevet Lerman. His prosperous family owned flour mills and other businesses throughout eastern Poland.

He and his four siblings were raised in an observant home; his father was a supporter of the Belzer Ḥasidim. In his youth, Lerman joined Ha-Shomer ha-Ẓa'ir, and following his father's untimely death in 1938 helped run his family's business. Following the German invasion of Poland the Lermans fled to Lvov, where he was arrested and forced to work at the Viniki labor camp in December 1941, from which he later escaped. For 23 months in the forests surrounding Lvov, Lerman was a leader in organized armed resistance against the Nazis.

Following the war, Lerman settled in Lublin and established a leather business with fellow survivor Leon Feldhandler, a leader of the heroic revolt at Sobibor. After Feldhandler's murder, Lerman settled in Lodz and met his future wife, Krysia Rozalia (Chris) Laks. They married in the Schlachtensee displaced persons camp and immigrated to the United States in February 1947. Lerman purchased a poultry farm in Vineland, New Jersey, and established profitable businesses in the gasoline, heating, and real estate sectors, becoming a prominent member of the Jewish community.

President Jimmy Carter appointed Lerman to the Advisory Board of the President's Commission on the Holocaust and later to the United States Holocaust Memorial Council, the governing board of the then future United States *Holocaust Memorial Museum (USHMM). Between 1988 and 1990, as chair of the USHMM's International Relations Committee, Lerman negotiated a series of agreements with governments and institutions in Eastern Europe that brought thousands of artifacts and documents to the USHMM and which shaped its permanent exhibition. Lerman met with heads of state, diplomats, ministers, and museum directors to increase the nascent museum's collections and exhibitions. These negotiations occurred at an opportune time as Communist regimes in Eastern Europe were on the verge of collapsing in the late 1980s and were replaced by fledgling democracies. As such, the multilingual Lerman was well-positioned to negotiate in an atmosphere where teetering regimes were eager for American goodwill, and sought to include their Holocaust-era patrimony on the National Mall in the heart of the American capital.

Lerman was chosen to lead the museum's capital campaign. The congressional legislation creating the museum required that while the U.S. government would donate the land for the museum, all funds to build the structure needed to be raised from private sources; the initial $147 million budget was later increased to close to $200 million. Lerman determinedly led the effort to raise the necessary funds. He tirelessly traveled across the nation and successfully completed the campaign, along with a dedicated professional staff and volunteers.

Soon after the USHMM's dedication on April 22, 1993, President Bill Clinton appointed Lerman to be the third chair of the United States Holocaust Memorial Council, a post he held until 2000. During his tenure, the museum became one of Washington's top tourist destinations, with more than two million visitors annually. Among a number of initiatives, Lerman established the Miles Lerman Center for the Study of Jewish Resistance during the Holocaust, which documents physical resistance in ghettos, forests, and elsewhere throughout German-occupied Europe. A major controversy arose in 1998 when, at the urging of the U.S. Department of State, Lerman invited PLO Chairman Yasser Arafat to visit the museum, an offer ultimately declined by Arafat. After his term as chair ended, Lerman assumed the leadership of the museum's endowment fund.

Beginning in the mid-1990s, Lerman took it upon himself to provide a proper memorial for his relatives who were murdered at the Belzec killing center; the Communist-era memorial had fallen into disrepair and the site of the 500,000 murdered Jews was woefully neglected. Lerman worked with a number of Polish governments, and in partnership with the USHHM and later with the American Jewish Committee. Lerman raised the necessary funds to build a dignified memorial. Opening on June 3, 2004, the $5 million Belzec memorial was funded equally by the Polish government and contributions raised by Lerman from American Jews.

[Ralph Grunewald (2nd ed.)]

LERNER, ABBA PETACHJA (1903–1982), U.S. economist. Born in Russia and educated at the London School of Economics, Lerner began to teach there in 1935. He moved to the United States in 1937 and soon established himself as an eminent teacher in economics. He taught at the New School for Social Research, New York, Michigan State University, Roosevelt University, and the University of California. During 1953–56 he served as an economic adviser to the government of Israel. Regarded as one of the most influential economists of the century, Lerner made numerous significant contributions to economic theory and policy, such as the general equilibrium theory, the factor price equalization theorem, and the concept of seller's inflation. Besides his professional interests – which included international trade, welfare economics, labor and employment, price formation, and the gold standard – Lerner was concerned with problems of social reform and foreign policy. His major publications include *The Economics of Control* (1944), *The Economics of Employment* (1951), *Essays in Economic Analysis* (1953), *Everybody's Business* (1961), *Flation: Not Inflation of Prices, Not Deflation of Jobs* (1972), and *MAP: A Market Anti-Inflation Plan* (1980).

ADD. BIBLIOGRAPHY: H. Greenfield et al., *Theory for Economic Efficiency: Essays in Honor of Abba P. Lerner* (1979).

[Joachim O. Ronall / Ruth Beloff (2nd ed.)]

LERNER, ALAN JAY (1918–1986), U.S. lyric writer and librettist who collaborated in several successful musicals. Lerner was born in New York and wrote for advertising agencies and radio before teaming up with the composer, Frederick Loewe. Their first hit was the musical *Brigadoon* (1947), which was followed by *Paint Your Wagon* in 1951. Lerner also worked independently and won an Oscar in 1951 with his screenplay for *An American in Paris*. His greatest success came in 1956 when, with Loewe, he created *My Fair Lady* (based on Shaw's *Pygmalion*). The

Lerner and Loewe film musical *Gigi* (1958) won Oscars, and in 1960 their *Camelot* had a two-year run on Broadway.

With the composer Burton Lane, Lerner wrote *On a Clear Day You Can See Forever* (1965) and with André Previn, *Coco* (1969), the story of the "queen" of Paris fashions, Coco Chanel.

BIBLIOGRAPHY: D. Even, *Complete Book of the American Musical Theater* (1958), 194–200; I. Martin, *Pete Martin Calls On…* (1962), 449–59; *Current Biography Yearbook* (1958), 241–4.

[G. Eric Hauck]

LERNER, GERDA KRONSTEIN (1920–), founder of the modern field of women's history. Born in Vienna, Lerner grew up in a well-to-do assimilated family, the daughter of a businessman father and an artist mother. She studied at a private *Gymnasium* for girls, run by a Jewish director, and enrolled in a Sabbath School to prepare for her confirmation. However, concerned about the synagogue's attitudes toward women congregants and its treatment of the poor, she decided not to participate in the ceremony. After the Nazis came to power, she became involved in the underground resistance movement. Arrested and imprisoned, she was released after her father signed over his property and business to the Nazis. Lerner left Europe in 1939, the only one of her family to secure a visa for the United States. Although her parents survived the war, she never saw them again.

As a young émigré, Lerner worked as a waitress, salesgirl, office clerk, and x-ray technician, all the while writing fiction and poetry; she published two short stories providing a first-person account of the horrors of Nazi occupation. She married Carl Lerner, who became an acclaimed film editor and director, and raised two children. In 1951, she collaborated with poet Eve Merriam on a musical, *The Singing of Women*. Her novel, *No Farewell*, appeared in 1955; with her husband, she wrote the script for *Black Like Me*. Committed Communists, the Lerners were involved in numerous grassroots activities involving trade unionism, civil rights, and anti-militarism; they struggled against McCarthyism, especially the Hollywood blacklist.

Lerner returned to school in the late 1950s, receiving a B.A. from the New School for Social Research in 1963 and her Ph.D. from Columbia University in 1966; her dissertation became her first publication, *The Grimke Sisters from South Carolina: Rebels Against Slavery* (1967). She taught at Long Island University in Brooklyn and at Sarah Lawrence College, where she initiated an influential master's program in women's history in 1972. In 1980, Lerner created the nation's first Ph.D. program in women's history at the University of Wisconsin at Madison, where she became professor emerita.

Lerner was among the first to bring a consciously feminist lens to the study of history, producing enormously influential essays and books. Among her most important works are the documentary anthologies, *Black Women in White America* (1972) and *The Female Experience* (1976); the essay collections, *The Majority Finds Its Past* (1979) and *Why History Matters* (1997); *The Creation of Patriarchy* (1986) and *The Creation of Feminist Consciousness* (1993). She published *Fireweed: A Political Autobiography* in 2002. Lerner was a founding member of the National Organization for Women and the first woman in 50 years to become president of the Organization of American Historians, which named the Gerda Lerner-Ann Scott Prize for the best women's history dissertation in her honor.

[Joyce Antler (2nd ed.)]

LERNER, ḤAYYIM ẒEVI BEN TODROS (1815–1889), Hebrew grammarian and pedagogue. Born in Dubno (Volhynia), he was the pupil of the noted scholar Ze'ev Wolf Adelsohn, under whose influence he studied both Hebrew and secular subjects. He worked as a private Hebrew tutor and became a teacher at the Jewish government school in Berdichev, in 1849, and in 1851, a teacher of Hebrew language and grammar at the government rabbinical seminary in Zhitomir. He was very successful in the latter and held the post until the closing of the institute by governmental decree in 1873.

Lerner's most important work is his Hebrew grammar, *Moreh ha-Lashon* ("Teacher of the Language," 1859) which is based on the principles laid down by his teacher, S. *Pinsker. In Lerner's lifetime, the book appeared in seven editions; these he annotated and supplemented from the fourth edition onward (1879), notably with a supplement of practical exercises. After his death, the book was also printed with the supplement *Yalkut Ḥazal* (1893[8]), which includes explanations of difficult Bible passages and their commentaries. *Moreh ha-Lashon*, published in 13 editions (1909[13]), was the first of its kind that laid down rules for teaching children the essentials of Hebrew grammar. Lerner also wrote *Dikduk Leshon Aramit* (1875), and *Toledot ha-Dikduk* (1876), a short history of Hebrew grammar and grammarians up to the 19th century. He also translated into Hebrew S.D. Luzzatto's Italian work on the Aramaic in the Babylonian Talmud, under the title *Dikduk Leshon Talmud Bavli* (1880). The last years of his life Lerner spent in poverty in Zhitomir, supported by his former pupils. He left in manuscript a research work on talmudic texts, *Arba Middot*, and a rich collection of his correspondence with leading Jewish scholars of his time.

BIBLIOGRAPHY: N. Sokolow (ed.), *Sefer Zikkaron le-Soferei Yisrael…* (1889), 65–66; *Ha-Meliẓ*, 29 (1889), nos. 76, 79; Skomorovsky, in: H. Lerner, *Moreh ha-Lashon* (1898[10]), iii–v (introd.); *Kol Kitvei A.U. Kovner* (1947), 23–30; A.J. Paperna, *Kol ha-Ketavim* (1952), 197–204.

[Yehuda Slutsky]

LERNER, JAIME (1937–), Brazilian architect, urban planner, and politician. Born in Curitiba, capital city of the State of Paraná, Brazil, to a family originating in Germany, he graduated from the Escola de Arquitectura da Universidade Federal do Paraná (Architecture School of the Federal University of Paraná) in 1964. In 1965 he participated in the creation of the Instituto de Pesquisa e Planejamento Urbano de Curitiba (Institute of Urban Planning and Research of Curitiba) and participated in the design of the Curitiba Master Plan. Lerner was elected mayor of Curitiba for three terms: 1971–75, 1979–84, and 1989–92. In 1994 he was elected governor of the State of Paraná and was reelected in 1998, serving until 2002.

During his first term as mayor of Curitiba, he consolidated the urban transformation of the city and implemented the Integrated Mass Transportation System acknowledged worldwide for its efficiency, quality, and low cost. He also intensified social measures that improved dramatically the quality of life in the city. As governor he promoted a great economic and social transformation in the state through a program encompassing land use, transport, sanitation, health, education, recreation, and culture. Lerner was professor of urban and regional planning at the Federal University of Paraná. He was a United Nations consultant on urban planning and winner of many awards and distinctions, among them the United Nations Environment Award, in 1990; the 1996 UNICEF Children and Peace Award; the Netherlands Prince Claus Award for Culture and Development in 2000; and the World Technology Award from the National Museum of Science and Industry (London) in 2001. He was also president of the International Union of Architects in 2002–5.

[Efraim Zadoff (2nd ed.)]

LERNER, JOSEPH JUDAH (1849–1907), writer, dramatist, and scholar. Born in Berdichev (Ukraine) he contributed from an early age to the Hebrew, Russian, and Yiddish press. During the Russo-Turkish war he published *Zapiski Grazhdanina*, a Russian paper in Bucharest, emphasizing the Jewish contribution to that war. There he met Goldfaden's Yiddish theatrical troupe, and on his return to Odessa started a company of his own, intending to raise standards in both the language and content of Jewish plays. Earning his living as an unqualified lawyer, he often came into contact with the world of crime and, at times, became involved in precarious transactions to the extent that in 1873 he was temporarily compelled to seek asylum in Vienna. Among the plays he translated and adapted were *Uriel Acosta* (1885) by Gutzkow, and *The Jewess* (1889) by Scribe. With the ban on the Jewish theater in 1883, Lerner returned to his journalistic and literary career, and contributed to the major Russian newspapers. He became a convert to Christianity in the 1890s. His works include a novel about Jewish life in Russia, *Yamim mi-Kedem* (1868); a Jewish history in Yiddish, *Di Yidishe Geshikhte*; and a study in Russian of the Jews in New Russia, *Yevrei v Novorossiskom Kraie*, which was based on the archives of the former governor-general of New Russia.

BIBLIOGRAPHY: E.R. Malachi, *Massot u-Reshimot* (1937), 71–75; Borovoy, in: *Filologishe Shriftn*, 3 (1929), 472–84; B. Gorin, *Geshikhte fun Yidishn Teater*, 1 (1929), 227–36; Z. Zylbercweig, *Leksikon fun Yidishn Teater*, 2 (1934), 1162–68.

[Yehuda Slutsky]

LERNER, MAX (1902–1992), U.S. author and journalist. Lerner, who was born in Minsk, Russia, was taken to the United States at the age of five. He taught at Sarah Lawrence College, Harvard University, Williams College, and, from 1949, at Brandeis University (1949–73). A liberal social commentator, Lerner became known for his scholarly works on American society and the science of government. Lerner was managing editor of the *Encyclopaedia of Social Sciences* (1927–33). He also edited the periodical *The Nation* (1936–38). He was the editorial director of the newspaper *PM* (1943–48), a columnist for the *New York Star* (1948–49), and, from 1949 until the 1970s, his work was syndicated by the *New York Post*.

His principal works include *It Is Later than You Think* (1938), *Ideas Are Weapons* (1939), *Ideas for the Ice Age* (1941), *America as a Civilization* (1957), *The Unfinished Country* (1959), *The Age of Overkill* (1962), *Values in Education* (1976), *Epidemic 9* (with M. Gunther, 1980), and *Ted and the Kennedy Legend* (1982). Lerner's work contains elements of his journalistic style together with more sober academic attempts to analyze American life in his day. He also wrote *Wrestling with the Angel: A Memoir of My Triumph over Illness* (1991). *Nine Scorpions in a Bottle: Great Judges and Cases of the Supreme Court* was published in 1994 (ed. Richard Cummings); and *Wounded Titans: American Presidents and the Perils of Power*, a collection of Lerner's portrayals of U.S. presidents, was published in 1996 (ed. Robert Schmuhl).

ADD. BIBLIOGRAPHY: S. Lakoff, *Max Lerner: Pilgrim in the Promised Land* (1998).

[Lawrence H. Feigenbaum / Ruth Beloff (2nd ed.)]

LERNER, MAYER BEN MORDECAI OF ALTONA (1857–1930), rabbi. Lerner was born in Czestochowa (Poland). He studied first in Cracow but completed his studies in the Rabbiner-Seminar in Berlin. While still a student at the seminary, he wrote his important work *Anlage und Quellen des Bereschit Rabba* (1882). He was appointed rabbi of Wintzenheim, Alsace, in 1884 and remained there until 1890, when he became rabbi of the Federation of Synagogues in London, which then consisted of 23 synagogues. In 1894 he was appointed rabbi of Altona and of Schleswig-Holstein. Lerner vigorously opposed the historical approach of *Graetz and the Reform movement in Germany.

Lerner's main talmudic works are his *Hadar ha-Karmel* (1891), responsa, including some talmudic novellae; and *Ḥayyei Olam* (1905) on the prohibition of cremation. His research works, in addition to the above-mentioned *Quellen* include "Die aeltesten Mischna – Kompositionen" (MWJ, 13 (1886), 1–20) and his magnum opus, *Torat ha-Mishnah*, dealing with the origin of the oral tradition, of which, however, only the first part appeared (1915). He also showed an active interest in the Jewish settlement of Palestine and in 1905 founded the association Moriah whose aims were "to restore the ancient ruins, and the national and religious culture of the Jews." The association was opposed both to the Mizrachi and the Zionist movements, and in 1930 merged with the Agudat Israel movement.

BIBLIOGRAPHY: E. Duckesz, *Ivvah le-Moshav* (1903), 136–9; Weingarten, in: J.L. Fishman (ed.), *Sefer ha-Mizrachi* (1946), 103–10; Bath-Yehudah, in: AZD, 3 (1965), 266–70.

[Itzhak Alfassi]

LERNER, MICHAEL (1943–), activist, editor of *Tikkun*, and leader of progressive inter-faith movement. Lerner has emerged as a leading voice of the American Jewish leftist community. Born in Newark, New Jersey, Lerner developed an early interest in the writings of Jewish philosophers Martin *Buber and Abraham Joshua *Heschel, which he continued during his undergraduate studies at Columbia University and as a student of Heschel's at the Jewish Theological Seminary. Lerner focused attention on the field of Jewish mysticism and especially the concept of *tikkun olam*, or repair of the world. He enrolled in UC Berkeley's Ph.D. program in philosophy, where he chaired the New Left organization Students for a Democratic Society.

In his academic career, Lerner took an active role in many of the New Left's protest movements. In 1968, he taught philosophy at San Francisco State University, until a faculty strike closed the school. He accepted a visiting assistant professorship at the University of Washington, where he was arrested as part of the "Seattle Seven" in an anti-Vietnam War protest. After receiving his Ph.D. in 1972, Lerner accepted a position as assistant professor of philosophy at Hartford, Connecticut's Trinity College.

In the mid-1970s, Lerner refocused his intellectual interests and social protest priorities along Jewish spiritual and religious lines. He studied under Renewal Judaism's founding rabbi, Zalman *Schachter-Shalomi, eventually earning rabbinic ordination.

Lerner launched *Tikkun* magazine in 1986, with the purpose of shaping the publication into "the voice of Jewish liberals and progressives." His principled opposition to the Israeli occupation of the West Bank and Gaza Strip placed Lerner and his magazine in the middle of contentious political debates. As a Zionist, Lerner often faced criticism from many Leftist anti-Zionists who considered the State of Israel a colonial and imperialist power. As a Leftist, Lerner routinely engaged mainstream and right-leaning American Jews who considered his support for a two-state solution to the Midlle East crisis a threat to the Jewish state.

Lerner was drawn into national politics, as well. His publication *The Politics of Meaning* was embraced by First Lady Hillary Clinton as a template for future social reform, while his book *Jews and Blacks: Let the Healing Begin*, co-authored with Cornel West, sought to carry the famed black-Jewish alliance of the early civil rights years into the next generation. In 2002, Lerner, together with West, created the Tikkun Community, an attempt to bridge the progressive political world with an interfaith spiritual revival.

Lerner's journey from a New Left secular political activist to an advocate for spiritual Judaism, and finally to leader in the inter-faith progressive community, mirrored the development of postwar social reform movements. Beginning with calls for civil equality in the 1950s and an end to the Vietnam War by the late 1960s, they continued with an ethnic and religious revival typified by Black Power and a rebirth in American Zionism, and concluded, as Lerner's career has demonstrated, with a faith-based movement for inter-religious cooperation and understanding in the late 20th and early 21st centuries.

LERNER, RALPH (1949–), professor of architecture at Princeton University's School of Architecture and principal of Ralph Lerner Architect PC of Princeton, New Jersey. After earning his bachelor of architecture from Cooper Union School of Architecture, he went on to receive his master of architecture at Harvard University's School of Design. As dean of the School of Architecture at Princeton for 13 years, Lerner supported innovative programs for his students such as the international study program for Chinese and American students. He became known as an organizer of architectural competitions. In 2001, a national competition for the design of an expansion of the Queens Museum of Art in Flushing Meadows was announced by the New York City's Department of Design and Construction. Lerner was the professional advisor. In 2002, as a director of the Canadian Centre for Architecture (CCA) located in Montreal, Lerner served as a curator of an Architecture Prize Competition for the Design of Cities. Lerner became known for his wisdom as a competition advisor in international competitions. In one such competition in 2004, the task was to design a new street light for the City of New York. It was sponsored by the New York Department of Transportation, Design, and Construction. He coordinated the jury, managed 447 registrations, and developed a method to insure fairness. Lerner has spoken widely on architecture in the United States and Asia, where he is known for the design of the Indira Gandhi National Center for the Arts Library in New Delhi, India. Among his awards was the 1991 Distinguished Alumnus award from the Cooper Union and in 2004 he won the AIA award for his design of the New Jersey Lower School Building at the Princeton Charter School in Princeton.

[Betty R. Rubenstein (2nd ed.)]

LE ROITH, HAROLD HIRSCH (1905–1995), South African architect. Born in Grahamstown, he became disciple of the modern school of architects, such as Le Corbusier, Gropius, and Frank Lloyd Wright. Le Roith translated the concepts of functionalism into much of his work in Johannesburg and other South African cities. His specialized area lay in the planning of business and industrial complexes, extensive flat units, and modern-type houses. In these fields his designs attracted international recognition in the professional literature. He practiced in Johannesburg where he served as honorary architect to the United Progressive (Reform) Jewish Congregation and of other Reform communities on the Witwatersrand. He was on the executive committee of the Johannesburg Progressive congregation and was president for several years.

[Louis Hotz]

LE ROY, MERVYN (1900–1987), film producer and director. Born in San Francisco, California, Le Roy and his father physically survived the city's earthquake and fire of 1906 but were financially ruined. To earn money, the young Le Roy sold newspapers and entertained in vaudeville. He then moved to Hollywood, where his cousin film producer Jesse *Lasky helped him break into the industry. Le Roy worked in costumes, then as a cameraman, gag writer, and part-time silent film actor before directing his first film, *No Place to Go,* in 1927. From then on, he began to direct enjoyable and, consequently, profitable films. Nicknamed "The Boy Wonder," Le Roy's motto was "Good stories make good movies." His feel for what the audience wanted extended to actors as well, and he was responsible for "discovering" such legendary movie stars as Clark Gable, Robert Mitchum, Lana Turner, and Loretta Young. He also is credited with having introduced actor Ronald Reagan to actress Nancy Davis, who were destined to become the president and first lady of the United States.

A prominent Hollywood figure for more than 40 years, Le Roy alternated between dramas, comedies, and musicals. The list of more than 75 films that he directed includes *Little Caesar* (1931), *Three on a Match* (1932), *I Am a Fugitive from a Chain Gang* (1932), *Gold Diggers of 1933* (1933), *Anthony Adverse* (1936), *They Won't Forget* (1937), *Blossoms in the Dust* (1941), *Random Harvest* (Oscar nomination for Best Director 1942), *Madame Curie* (1943), *Thirty Seconds over Tokyo* (1944), *Little Women* (1949), *East Side, West Side* (1949), *Quo Vadis?* (1951), *Rose Marie* (1954), *Mister Roberts* (1955), *The Bad Seed* (1956), *No Time for Sergeants* (also produced, 1958), *Wake Me When It's Over* (1960), *A Majority of One* (1961), *Gypsy* (1962), and *Moment to Moment* (1965). Some of these he produced as well and among those he produced but did not direct are *The Wizard of Oz* (Oscar nomination for Best Picture, 1939) and *At the Circus* (1939). In 1976 he received the Irving G. Thalberg Award, which is bestowed on "a creative producer who has been responsible for a consistently high quality of motion picture production." He was active in Republican politics. Le Roy's autobiography is entitled *Mervyn Le Roy: Take One* (1974).

[Ruth Beloff (2nd ed.)]

LERT, ERNST (Ernst Josef Maria Levi; 1883–1955), opera producer and writer. Born in Vienna, Lert worked as theater director in Germany and Switzerland. He was dramatic coach at the Municipal Theater in Breslau and Leipzig (1920–23). From 1923 to 1929 he staged German opera at La Scala, Milan, and for the next two years (1929–31) was at the Metropolitan Opera in New York. From 1936 to 1938 he was the head of the opera department of Curtis Institute of Music and from 1938, after settling in the U.S., directed the opera department at the Peabody Conservatory, Baltimore. He specialized in the staging of Mozart and modern operas. Lert wrote the book *Mozart auf dem Theater* (Berlin, 1918) and a biography of the German conductor Otto Lohse, *Otto Lohse als Opernleiter* (Leipzig, 1918).

BIBLIOGRAPHY: *Baker's Biographical Dictionary of Musicians.*

[Israela Stein (2nd ed.)]

LESBIANISM. Until the late 20th century, lesbians were invisible in Jewish textual traditions and within Jewish societies. Only recently have Jewish scholars and communities faced the issue of how erotic love between women fits into a Jewish view of the world. While male homosexual behavior is prohibited in the book of Leviticus, same-sex sexuality between women is not mentioned in the Hebrew Bible. Some commentators think that this difference exists because in ancient times only acts in which men emitted semen were defined as sexual. More traditional Jewish scholars assume that erotic attraction between women did not exist in the biblical world, or that rules that applied to men would automatically apply to women. Lacking any real evidence, it cannot be said with certainty why the Bible does not mention same-sex acts between women.

Female homoeroticism is mentioned in *Sifra*, an early rabbinic commentary on the book of Leviticus, in a comment about the prohibition against Egyptian practices (18:3). The author apparently understood lesbian marriage, a contemporary Roman practice, to be in this category and sought to prohibit it among Jews. The Talmud does not mention lesbian marriage, but does prohibit an activity it defines as *mesolelot* or tribadism (women rubbing genitals against each other). The main question asked in the Talmud regarding women who practice *mesolelot* (Yev. 76a) concerns such women's eligibility for priestly marriages or, in other words, whether such activity allows a woman to retain her status as a virgin. The *gemara* states majority and minority opinions; the majority assumes a woman who practices *mesolelot* is eligible to marry a priest and defines *mesolelot* as a minor infraction. In the 12th-century *Mishneh Torah*, legal scholar and philosopher Moses *Maimonides connected the talmudic references to *mesolelot* to the levitical prohibition against Egyptian practices in *Sifra,* but also suggested that this behavior should not disqualify a woman from marrying a priest. Maimonides did recommend that the courts administer floggings to women caught engaging in homoerotic behavior and also warns men to keep their wives from spending time with women who are known to practice *mesolelot.*

During the early modern period, there are infrequent references to lesbian sexuality in Jewish sources, but things began to change in the 20th century. The most notable example is found in a Yiddish play written in 1907 by Sholem *Asch entitled *Got fun Nekome* ("God of Vengeance"). It was performed all over Europe and America in the Yiddish theater and ultimately translated into English and produced on Broadway in 1923. This was the first play with a lesbian theme to be performed on the American stage. The lesbian subplot concerned a tender relationship between a prostitute and the daughter of a brothel owner, and the play included several explicit homoerotic scenes. During the Broadway performance a citizens' anti-vice group had the actors arrested and attempted, unsuccessfully, to have the play closed. No such incident occurred in the Yiddish theater, however.

Asch's play reflects a trend during the early part of the 20th century when women began to live openly as lesbians. Among Jewish women, the writer Gertrude *Stein is the best known. Another was Pauline *Newman, a Jewish labor movement activist. However, Newman, who lived openly and raised a child with her partner in Greenwich Village, was exceptional. Homosexual women during this time period generally did not refer to themselves as lesbians, and they did not live in marriage-like relationships with other women. The story of Lillian *Wald, the Jewish social reformer, was more typical. Wald's relationships with other women were central to her life and work, yet they were hidden from view. Despite significant historical evidence in support of the assertion that Wald had same-sex relationships, it remains controversial to label Wald a lesbian.

The first Jewish novel to have a lesbian as the main character was *Wasteland* (1946), written by Ruth Seid under the pseudonym Jo *Sinclair. The heroine discussed her sexual preferences with her Jewish family and the story focuses on her brother's effort to come to terms with his sister's lifestyle. Such a psychologically healthy portrait of a lesbian relationship was unusual for the time period.

As a result of the feminist and gay liberation movements in the 1960s and 1970s, large numbers of women began to identify themselves as lesbians and some began to explore what it meant to be lesbian and Jewish. Evelyn Torton Beck collected the writings of some of these women whose poetry and prose spoke of their rejection as Jews in the lesbian community and as lesbians in the Jewish community in her groundbreaking *Nice Jewish Girls: A Lesbian Anthology* (1982). In 1989, Christie Balka and Andy Rose edited *Twice Blessed: On Being Lesbian or Gay and Jewish,* highlighting the concerns of lesbians and gay men for inclusion in the Jewish community.

Another major development involved the religious community. In the 1980s, Reform and Reconstructionist women rabbis, among them Stacy Offner and Linda Holtzman, began to reveal their lesbian orientation. Initially many lost their jobs, but within a few years the Reform and Reconstructionist movements began to admit openly gay and lesbian students to their rabbinical training programs. Some lesbian rabbis also found a home in the gay and lesbian synagogue movement. *Lesbian Rabbis: The First Generation*, edited by three rabbis who identify themselves as lesbian, Rebecca Alpert, Sue Levi Elwell, and Shirley Idelson, includes autobiographical essays by 18 Reform, Conservative, and Reconstructionist lesbian rabbis ordained in the 1970s, 1980s, and early 1990s.

Beginning in the 1990s there was a serious interest in lesbian issues in the larger Jewish community. A group of Orthodox lesbians, who call themselves Orthodykes, is active in the United States and in Israel. There has been a movement within Conservative Judaism for acceptance of lesbians and gay men, and support in the Reconstructionist and Reform movements for gay marriage. Some synagogues make an effort to welcome lesbian and gay members, and these changes have made it possible for lesbian Jews to feel at home in the Jewish community. The next generation of Jewish lesbians at the beginning of the 21st century is involved in movements that self-identify as Queer and are raising questions about the status of bisexual and transgender Jews. Lesbian Jews continue to hope for recognition beyond mere acceptance and tolerance; they seek a reinterpretation of Jewish values, including the assumption that heterosexuality is normative. They desire inclusion of their visions and stories as part of a reconstructed Jewish textual tradition and they aim to create an environment of complete comfort in which to claim their identity and celebrate their lives.

BIBLIOGRAPHY: R. Alpert, *Like Bread on the Seder Plate: Jewish Lesbians and the Transformation of Tradition* (1997); R. Biale, *Women and Jewish Law: An Exploration of Women's Issues in Halakhic Sources* (1984); D. Shneer and K. Aviv (eds.), *Queer Jews* (2002).

[Rebecca Alpert (2nd ed.)]

LES COLLOQUES DES INTELLECTUELS JUIFS DE LANGUE FRANÇAISE, French organization founded as a branch of the World Jewish Congress in 1957. Initiated in the aftermath of World War II by Edmond *Fleg and Léon *Algazi, the Colloques des Intellectuels juifs de langue française were intended to provide the shattered community of French Jews with answers grounded in Judaism. Asserting that, despite the Holocaust, Jewish existence should continue to move forward, they chose the term "intellectual" as an act of faith in this very particular historical context. Pedagogues and former members of the Ecole d'Orsay headed the Colloques, which attempted to establish a rational Judaism and to claim its singularity within modernity; they decided to give the texts of the tradition a central place in these conferences. To this end, they included in each session a biblical lesson and a talmudic lesson, which quickly became a semi-formal institution. Under the direction of André *Néher, and later of Jean Halpérin, renowned personalities such as the philosophers Wladimir *Jankelevitch and Jean Wahl, the psychoanalyst Eliane Amado *Lévi-Valensi, the lawyer Wladimir Rabi, and the writer Claude *Vigée regularly lectured there. The Conferences, whose proceedings are always published, are held every two years and have become significant events in French Judaism, thanks to the growing fame of the talmudic lessons given by Emmanuel *Levinas. The first Conference (whose proceedings were published as *Jewish Consciousness* in 1963) intended to define the Jewish condition and the contents that should be given to a Jewish existence, using the conceptual tools of existentialism and phenomenology. From the beginning, the relation of French Jewry to the State of Israel was given a central place in the conferences, which also dealt with questions raised by French politics at the time. A. *Memmi, E. *Touati, and R. *Misrahi related to the question of colonialism, and asked whether the Diaspora should criticize Israeli politics in the spirit of the heated debates taking place there. The contributions of Judaism to science and to the new technologies was highlighted through the reflections of the biologist H. *Atlan and C. Riveline, a professor at the Ecole des mines, who were both removed from Jewish tradition. At the end of 1968, L. Askénazi, Amado Lévi-Valensi, and Néher moved to Israel. From the group of founders Levinas was the only one to remain in France. The orientation of the conferences then changed. During the 1970s Jewish identity and the notion of the universal in the light of this identity were less discussed. Devoted to the "loneliness of Israel," the 15th Conference was held (1975) in a climate of concern which gave rise to a feeling of isolation, originating in the feeling that the empathy for Jews, which had shaped itself in the wake of the Holocaust, had come to an end. The later conferences during the 1970s sought renewal, and were more and more focused on contemporary issues and opened themselves to the social sciences. The 1980s reinforced this trend. From then on, and with the involvement of the Fondation du Judaïsme français, the intellectuals who are part of the colloquium have, among other things, attempted to work out the relationship between economics and ethics (*L'Argent, Le Quant-à-Soi, L'Idée d'humanité, Le Corps*). Discussions of memory and history provided themes for several Conferences (*Mémoire et histoire, Le temps désorienté, Difficile Justice*) as did political questions (*Politique et religion, morale et politique en péril, Idoles*), while essential themes (*Israël, le judaïsme et l'Europe, La Bible au présent*) moved to the foreground. After the death of Levinas a new generation appeared, whose primary aim was to define a positive and vivid sense of belonging to Judaism. Even if the influence of the Colloque des Intellectuels juifs de langue française seemed less vital at the outset of the 21st century, it played a significant role in the second half of the 20th century.

[Perrine Simon-Nahum (2nd ed.)]

LESHNEV (Pol. **Leszniów**), town in Tarnopol district, Ukraine. Jews first settled there in the early 17th century, and the Jewish cemetery dates from that era. The synagogue, built in the second half of the 17th century, had an Attic roof and pseudo-Tuscan columns. The town was economically dependent on the nearby city of Brody. Under the influence of the *ḥerem* proclaimed against the Ḥasidim in Brody, in 1772 an assembly of "select members of the community," including the local rabbi, Menahem Mendel b. Jacob, and R. Akiva of Vladimir-Volynski, passed a decree against the Ḥasidim, which was signed by all the participants. The Leshnev community numbered 696 (32% of the total population) in 1880; 513 (26%) in 1900; and only 179 (about 10%) in 1921. The decline was caused by the decline of the economy and emigration.

[*Encyclopaedia Judaica* (Germany)]

Holocaust Period

With the German conquest of the town at the end of June 1941 attacks against Jewish life and property began. Many fell at the hands of the Ukrainian population. Jewish youth were taken to labor camps in the surrounding area, and many met their deaths there. On November 2, 1942, the Jews were confined to a ghetto. Later some of the Jews were transferred to the Brody ghetto and were sent from there to extermination camps. On April 17, 1943, the remnants of the Leshnev community were liquidated. A few managed to escape from the ghetto and found shelter in the surrounding forests. After the war, Jewish life was not reconstituted in the town.

[Aharon Weiss]

BIBLIOGRAPHY: M. Balaban, *Zabytki historyczne Żydów w Polsce* (1929), index; Dubnow, Ḥasidut, 1 (1960²), index; *Sprawozdania Komisji dla badania historyi sztuki w Polsce*, vol. 5; B. Wasiutyński, *Ludność żydowska w Polsce w wiekach XIX i XX* (1930), 139.

LESKO (Ger. **Lisko**; Heb. and Yid. **Linsk**), town in Rzeszow province, S.E. Poland. Jews lived in Lesko from the town's foundation in the middle of the 16th century. In 1704 the town was burnt down by the Swedish army. In a plague which broke out afterward, 303 Jews perished. In 1718 the community paid 3,400 zlotys poll tax. In the 18th century the community's rabbi was Samuel Shmelke b. Mordecai, who approved the book, *Berit Shalom*, by Phinehas of *Wlodawa. The *Councils of the Lands intervened in a dispute that lasted from 1705 to 1724 between the community of Lesko and the neighboring one of *Sanok. Because of the serious economic plight of the Jewish population, the Polish *Sejm in 1768 declared a moratorium on its debts to the government. The Jewish community numbered 1,976 in 1880 and 2,400 in 1921 (c. 63% of the total population). In the folklore of Galician Jews, Lesko Jews were considered "wise fools" like those of *Chelm in Congress Poland. In June 1941 the German army entered the town. On Aug. 14, 1941, the entire Jewish population was deported to Zaslaw and was exterminated together with Zaslaw Jews.

BIBLIOGRAPHY: *Sefer Yizkor Mukdash le-Yehudei ha-Ayarot she-Nispu ba-Shoah, 1939–1944: Linsk, Istrik, Beligrod, Litovisk ve-ha-Sevivah* (1965).

[Shimshon Leib Kirshenboim / Shlomo Netzer (2nd ed.)]

°LESKOV, NIKOLAY SEMYONOVICH (1831–1895), Russian author. One of the most controversial and misunderstood writers in Russian literature, he wrote some passages critical of Jews but more frequently criticized his fellow-Russians, often contrasting them unfavorably with the Jews, the Ukrainians, the English, the Americans, the Poles, and the Germans. Leskov's interest in the Jews can be traced throughout his literary career. Jewish themes were especially important in his literary and journalistic writing during the years 1880–87, when he published more than 30 works on the subject, including over 20 newspaper articles explaining Jewish religious beliefs and customs to non-Jewish readers. His fictional works on Jewish themes include *Skazaniye o Fyodore-khristianine i o druge yego Abramezhidovine* ("The Tale of Theodore the Christian and his friend Abram the Jew," 1887), a simple parable on tolerance and brotherhood, which was reprinted by the Petrograd Soviet shortly after the October 1917 Revolution; *Obman* ("Deception," 1883), in which Leskov cleverly attacked antisemitism by exposing his fellow-Russians to ridicule; and *Ukha bez ryby* ("Fish Soup without Fish," 1887), an entertaining story in which a learned provincial rabbi achieves poetic as well as economic justice at the expense of the town's leading Russian Orthodox citizens. Two other stories, *Rakushanskiy melamed* ("The Hebrew Teacher from Galicia," 1878), and *Zhidovskaya kuvyrkolegiya* ("Somersaulting Yids," 1882), caused him to be accused of antisemitism by readers who failed to realize that Jews had no more claim to protection from Leskov's humorous satire than Orthodox archbishops, czarist bureaucrats, self-centered intellectuals, or despotic revolutionaries. Leskov also wrote anonymously what was possibly the most powerful defense of equal rights for Jews published in 19th-century Russia. *Yevrei v Rossii* ("The Jews in Russia," 1884), a report intended for government circulation only, caused much excitement in Jewish circles in St. Petersburg. When a copy was lent to A.E. Landau, editor of the leading Russian-language Jewish journal *Voskhod*, he immediately devoted a long series of enthusiastic editorials to it and, with unconscious irony, regretted that the author of such a well-written document was not a professional writer. *Yevrei v Rossii* was republished in Petrograd (1919) and in New York (1969), but it does not appear in the 11-volume Soviet edition of Leskov's works published in 1956–58.

BIBLIOGRAPHY: A.L. Volynski (pseud.), *N.S. Leskov* (Rus., 1923); L. Grossman, *N.S. Leskov* (Rus., 1945); B.M. Drugov, *N.S. Leskov: ocherk tvorchestva* (1957); W.B. Edgerton (ed. and tr.), *Satirical Stories of Nikolai Leskov* (1963), incl. bibl.

[William B. Edgerton]

LESLAU, WOLF (1906–), U.S. Semitics scholar and philologist. Born in Krzepice, Poland, Leslau was educated at the University of Vienna and at the Sorbonne in Paris. He taught at the Ecole des Hautes Etudes in Paris and the Ecole des Langues Orientales. In 1942 he immigrated to the United States. He taught at several institutions before joining the faculty of the University of California in Los Angeles in 1955, where he continued teaching Hebrew and Semitic languages. He was the founding chairman of the Department of Near Eastern Languages and was instrumental in establishing the Near Eastern Center.

Leslau was a fellow of the American Academy of Arts and Sciences, American Academy of Jewish Research, and other scholarly societies. He undertook eight trips to Ethiopia to do fieldwork on the various Semitic languages of Ethiopia and on the culture and folklore of the country (1946–76), giving special attention to *Beta Israel. Leslau is regarded as one of the foremost experts on Semitic languages, in particular the ones spoken in Ethiopia.

When he retired from teaching, he was named UCLA professor emeritus of Hebrew and Semitic linguistics.

He published more than 40 books that deal with descriptive and comparative problems of Ethiopic as well as Semitic linguistics; they include *Falasha Anthology* (1951), which he translated and edited; *Ethiopic and South Arabic Contribution to the Hebrew Lexicon* (1958); *An Amharic Conversation Book* (1965); *Ethiopians Speak* (3 vols, 1965–68); *Amharic Textbook* (1968); *Hebrew Cognates in Amharic* (1969); *Concise Amharic Dictionary* (1976); *Gurage Folklore* (1982); *Fifty Years of Research* (1988); *The Fire on the Mountain and Other Stories* (with H. Courlander, 1995); and *The Jews of Ethiopia: A Pictorial Journey Back to their Past* (with C. Berman, 2001).

ADD. BIBLIOGRAPHY: G. Hudson (ed.), *Essays on Gurage Language and Culture: Dedicated to Wolf Leslau on the Occasion of His 90th birthday, November 14th, 1996* (1997); S. Segert and A.J.E. Bobroligeti (eds.), *Ethiopian Studies: Dedicated to Wolf Landau on His 75th Birthday, 1981* (1983).

[Walter Joseph Fischel / Ruth Beloff (2nd ed.)]

LESLIE, ROBERT L. (1885–1987), U.S. typographic expert. Leslie was born in New York to a Polish mother and a Scottish father. He graduated from City College with a B.S. in 1904 and an M.D. from Johns Hopkins in 1912, after working as an apprentice at De Vinne Press, a teacher, a social worker, and a proofreader at the *Baltimore Sun*. Upon receiving his medical degree, Leslie worked as a doctor for the Public Health Service, where he redesigned all the government publications for the Surgeon General's Office. In 1920 he moved back to New York, where he became the first industrial doctor in the city. He worked for the McGraw Hill Company and eventually left the medical field when he realized that printing was his real passion.

In 1927 Leslie and Sol M. Cantor (1892–1965) formed a typesetting firm, The Composing Room, Inc., in New York, specializing in books for publishers throughout the U.S. In the early 1930s, Leslie created *PM* magazine with co-editor Percy Seitlin. In 1936, in the office of the Composing Room, he created the A-D Gallery, which was the first place in New York City dedicated to exhibiting the graphic and typographic arts. In 1958, after the war, it was reactivated and renamed Gallery 303.

Leslie introduced novel promotion techniques to further the graphic arts, bringing graphic artists together to form typographic design clinics. The Composing Room provided a wide variety of typefaces. Thousands of separate fonts were available for hand, machine, and photocomposition. Among the typographic experts was Ismar David, designer of the Hebrew typeface "David."

After retiring as president of the Composing Room in 1969, Leslie helped set up Uncle Bob's Paper Mill in Israel in 1971.

Among his many honors and awards, Leslie received the 1st Annual American Printing History Association Award in 1976, as well as the New York Printers Wall of Fame and Type Directors Club Medal.

[Israel Soifer / Ruth Beloff (2nd ed.)]

LEŚMIAN (Lesman), BOLESŁAW (1878–1937), Polish poet. Born in Warsaw, Leśmian was raised in Kiev and trained as a lawyer. A master of Polish verse, he was one of the leading representatives of the group of symbolist poets known as Young Poland, in whose organ *Chimera* his earliest works appeared (1901–07). In turn satirical and pathetic, he produced verse full of symbolic description and metaphysical reflection, mingling realistic, fanciful, and grotesque effects. Above all, Leśmian stressed the tragic fate of mankind – a prey to sickness and misery. During his lifetime he published three verse collections: *Sàd rozstajny* ("The Widespread Orchard," 1912); *Łaka* ("The Meadow," 1920); and *Napój cienisty* ("Shady Liquor," 1936). A fourth volume, *Dzieje leśna* ("The Wood Fable"), appeared posthumously in 1938. Leśmian also translated poems by Edgar Allan Poe and published two prose works, *Klechdy sezamowe* ("The Sesame Narrative," 1913), fairy tales; and *Przygody Sindbada żeglarza* ("The Adventures of Sinbad the Sailor," 1915), a popular children's book. Leśmian, whose works often recall those of *Kafka, was a forerunner of the Polish surrealists and his poetry enjoyed a new lease on life in the 1960s, inspiring literary symposia and research. His *Szkice literackie i eseje* ("Literary Sketches and Essays") were published in 1959.

[Stanislaw Wygodzki]

LESS, EMIL (1855–1935), German meteorologist. Born in Koenigsberg (Kaliningrad), Less was director of the Berlin weather bureau (1884–1923) and in 1897 was appointed to the Landwirtschaftliche Hochschule of Berlin. He was also associate professor at the Kaiser Frederick William University of Berlin. Less was among the founders of the Deutsche Meteorologische Gesellschaft. During the years he directed the Berlin weather bureau, he published the annual and general reports on the climatic elements of Germany. In 1914 he was enlisted as an officer in the army, providing meteorological guidance and weather information for the pilots of the Air Force.

BIBLIOGRAPHY: J.C. Poggendorff, *Biographisch-literarisches Handwoerterbuch*, 4 (1904); 5 (1926); 6 (1938), s.v., includes bibliography; *Kuerschners Deutscher Gelehrten-Kalender*, 3 (1929); 4 (1931), s.v., incl. bibl.

[Dov Ashbel]

LESSER POLAND (Pol. **Małopolska**), historical region in S.W. Poland (Western Galicia). In the structure of Jewish *autonomy and in historical geography, Lesser Poland embraced the provinces (*województwa*) of Krakow and Sandomierz alone; after the first partition of Poland (1772) it passed to Austria and was essentially Western Galicia. According to the 1764 census the Jews in Lesser Poland numbered 18,670 in Krakow province and 42,972 in Sandomierz, around 10.5% of the total Jewish population of Poland. More Jews were actually living there at the time, but since the census was related to a poll tax, the Jews concealed their exact number. About 60% of them lived in the towns and the rest in the countryside. The largest communities in the region had several thousand members; in most of the villages there were only a few Jewish families. Between 1511–14 King Sigismund I appointed Jewish *seniores* as heads of the region and collectors of taxes from the Jews. At the same time he appointed Joseph *Polak as chief rabbi of Lesser Poland. Since the system was unsuccessful the king abandoned it and handed over tax collecting to the Jews in the various regions of the country between 1518 and 1522. Lesser Poland thus became one of the basic units of Jewish autonomy in Poland. However, the king retained the right to nominate the chief rabbis and in Lesser Poland he appointed Moses Fishel. The king's retention of control was resisted by the communities and in 1551 King Sigismund II Augustus allowed them to elect their own rabbis.

The principal communities of Lesser Poland in the *Councils of the Lands were Opatow (Apta), Checiny (Ḥenchin), Sandomierz (Ẓuzmir), Pinczow (Pintshev), and *Staszow), all in the province of Sandomierz, and Wodzislaw (Voidislav), *Olkusz (Elkish), and Cracow (Kraka), in the province of Krakow. According to the 1717 assessment, Lesser Poland had to pay the Council of Four Lands a share of 27,075 zlotys in the total payment of 226,109 zlotys due from all the Jews in Poland. When the council was dissolved, the committee appointed by the royal treasury to carry out the liquidation drew up a list of debts: a total of 2,314,350 zlotys for the entire Jewish population. Of this the provinces of Krakow and Sandomierz owed 338,089 zlotys on account of loans received for poll tax. Four of the representatives at the Council of Four Lands came from Lesser Poland. The provincial council of Lesser Poland convened every year to determine the apportionment of taxes among the various communities. Other problems of Jewish life were also discussed at these meetings. The provincial council employed a rabbi, who was presiding judge of the provincial court, as well as several clerks, among them a *shammash* who represented the larger communities at the *Breslau fairs. In 1738 the authorities decreed that the numbers of these *shammashim* in Poland should be reduced and the communities of Lesser Poland were allowed to appoint one representative only. The council of Lesser Poland was heavily in debt to rich Jews. When the Council of Four Lands discussed the matter in 1762–63, it resolved to press the provincial council to pay its debts.

Thanks to the standing of the yeshivot of Cracow and its great rabbis, as well as the centrality of the region in the origins and development of the Polish state and culture, the Jewry and leadership of Lesser Poland enjoyed an influence disproportionate to their numbers. Under Austrian rule, Western Galicia developed its own kind of Jewish culture and society.

See also *Great Poland; Moses *Isserles; *Galicia; *Poland, Modern Era; and Osias *Thon.

[Shimshon Leib Kirshenboim]

°LESSING, GOTTHOLD EPHRAIM (1729–1781), German dramatist, philosopher, and critic. One of the outstanding representatives of the Enlightenment in Germany, Lessing was devoted to the principle of toleration. One of Lessing's earliest literary ventures was *Die Juden* (1749), a one-act comedy in which for the first time a Jew was presented on the German stage in a reasonably objective manner. Lessing later upheld the play's defense of toleration against the criticism of J.D. *Michaelis. Through a physician, Aaron Solomon Gumpertz, he became a friend and admirer of Moses *Mendelssohn, whom he encouraged to publish his first philosophical work. The outcome of their common interest in aesthetics was *Pope ein Metaphysiker* (1755) and a critical journal, *Briefe, die neueste Literatur betreffend* (1759–60). Their correspondence, mainly on philosophical themes, continued until Lessing's death.

Mendelssohn was the inspiration for Lessing's *Nathan der Weise* (1779), his last play, and once more a plea for toleration. Based on the parable of the three rings, adapted from *Boccaccio's *Decameron*, the play presents Judaism, Christianity, and Islam as three sons of a benevolent father who has given each an identical ring, although each one claims that his ring alone is authentic. Nathan is made the spokesman for the aspirations of the Enlightenment: tolerance, brotherhood, and love of humanity. Lessing's vision of Jewish-Christian amity was ridiculed by Julius von Voss in *Der travestierte Nathan der Weise* (1804), and attacked by the antisemites Wilhelm *Marr, Karl Eugen *Duehring, Sebastian *Brunner, and Adolf Bartels. On the other hand Lessing's personal example and ideals were vigorously upheld and emphasized by German Jews such as Gabriel *Riesser, I.H. *Ritter, Berthold *Auerbach, Emil *Lehmann, and Johann *Jacoby. *Nathan der Weise* was translated into Hebrew, notably by Simon *Bacher and A.B. *Gottlober, and many of Lessing's other plays were also translated. His ideological and stylistic influence on the *Haskalah was as decisive as that of Friedrich *Schiller.

However, Lessing's attitude toward Judaism was ambivalent. While never forsaking the principle of tolerance, he came to depreciate Judaism in relation to Christianity with his publication of *Fragmente eines Ungenannten* (1774–78), the posthumous writings of the ultra-rationalist theologian H.M. Reimarus. He reached a further stage in his epoch-making *Erziehung des Menschengeschlechts* ("Education of Humanity"), which was published anonymously. In it the Old Testament is described as morally and aesthetically inferior to the New Testament, which itself is on the verge of being superseded by rational enlightenment. The monotheistic and universalistic mission of Judaism as the forerunner of Christianity had been completed. This attitude also appeared in *Nathan der Weise*, in which the brother representing Christianity accuses the Jewish religion of having given birth to intolerance through the concept of a chosen people.

BIBLIOGRAPHY: ADB, 19 (1884), 756–802: L. Zscharnack, *Lessing und Semmler* (1905); L. Geiger, *Die deutsche Literatur und die Juden* (1910), 54–58; P. Hazard, *European Thought in the Eighteenth Century from Montesquieu to Lessing* (1954); Ettinger, in: Zion, 29 (1954), 182–207; H.E. Allison, *Lessing and the Enlightenment* (1966); P. Demetz (ed.), *G.E. Lessing: Nathan der Weise* (1966); H.M.Z. Meyer, *Moses Mendelssohn Bibliography* (1965), index, s.v. *Lessing*; EJ, bibliography; see also the exchange of letters between Lessing and Mendelssohn in Moses Mendelssohn's *Gesammelte Schriften* (1932), vol. 11. **ADD. BIBLIOGRAPHY:** W. Barner, "Vorurteil, Empirie, Rettung, Der junge Lessing und die Juden," in: H.A. Strauss and C. Hoffmann (eds.), *Juden und Judentum in der Literatur* (1985), 52–77; B. Fischer, *Nathans Ende? Von Lessing bis Tabori. Zur deutsch-jüdischen Rezeption von "Nathan der Weise"* (2000); V. Forester, *Lessing und Moses Mendelssohn. Geschichte einer Freudschaft* (2001); W. Jasper, *Lessing: Aufklaerer und Judenfreund. Biographie* (2001), 437–459, with bibliography; H. Goebel (ed.), *Lessings "Nathan." Der Autor, der Text, seine Umwelt, seine Folgen* (2002); K.-J. Kuschel, *"Jud, Christ und Muselmann vereinigt?" Lessings "Nathan der Weise"* (2004), 222–26, with bibliography.

[Michael J. Graetz]

LESSING, THEODOR (1872–1933), German philosopher. Lessing was born in Hanover as the son of a prosperous physician and read history, philosophy, and medicine at Bonn and Munich. He converted to Lutheranism in 1895 as a student in Freiburg. From 1898 he turned back to Judaism, from 1900 to Zionism, criticizing the politics of assimilation. After a journey to Galicia in 1906 he also discovered East European Judaism (*Eindruecke aus Galizien*, 1906), following the Zionist discourse. After his doctorate in 1899, he was appointed professor of philosophy at the Technische Hochschule in Hanover in 1907. In 1906 he published his first philosophical work (*Schopenhauer, Wagner, Nietzsche*), criticizing the loss of values. His main philosophical works are *Geschichte als Sinngebung des Sinnlosen* (1919) and *Europa und Asien* (1918, enlarged 1924), a critique of the war, which was banned by the military authorities before being published. On the basis of the opposition of Europe (i.e., culture, "Gesellschaft") and Asia (i.e., nature, "Gemeinschaft") he clarified also his Zionist program. He followed this line of reasoning in his most famous book, *Der juedische Selbsthass* (1930, published by the Juedische Verlag), a historical-psychological study of Judaism as a minority in the Diaspora. He understood "self-hatred" as a "life killing malady" which psychologically consisted of adapting to the negative image of Judaism held by non-Jews. Lessing saw in the Jews an Asiatic people forced upon the European scene, and made to occupy a position between the cultures of two continents. He discovered the strength of the Jews in their closeness to nature and life's elemental roots: it was their tragedy that against their earthbound instincts history had cut them off from the soil, eventually causing a people of peasants to become overspiritualized and decadent. In the minority that had begun to trickle back to the eroded soil of Palestine, he saw the eventual recovery of both land and people. A member of Po'alei Zion, Lessing envisaged this recovery as a synthesis of Socialism and Zionism. Already in 1925 Lessing was subjected to antisemitic attacks, when he expressed opposition to Hindenburg's election as president of the Weimar Republic. In 1933 he flew first to Prague, then to Marienbad, where he was assassinated as one of the first victims of the Nazis. His memoirs, *Einmal und nie wieder*, were published in 1935 in Prague. His writings were reprinted after the war, among others the collection *Ausgewaehlte Schriften* (1995ff.).

BIBLIOGRAPHY: E. Hieronimus, *Theodor Lessing, Otto Meyerhof, Leonard Nelson, bedeutende Juden in Niedersachsen* (1964), 9–57. **ADD. BIBLIOGRAPHY:** R. Marwedel, *Theodor Lessing* (1987); *Zeitschrift fuer Religions- und Geistesgeschichte*, 50 (1998); A. Boelke-Fabian, in: A. Kilcher (ed.), *Metzler Lexikon juedischer Philosophen* (2003), 321–24; J. Henrich, *Friedrich Nietzsche und Theodor Lessing* (2004).

[Sol Liptzin / Andreas Kilcher (2nd ed.)]

LESTER, RICHARD (1932–), film director. Born in the United States, Lester immigrated to England in 1954. He won prominence in 1964 with *A Hard Day's Night*, a quasi-documentary in which the Beatles poked fun at the craze they themselves had started. In 1965, his comedy *The Knack* won a first prize at the Cannes Film Festival. Among his other movies are *Help* (1965), also made with the Beatles; *How I Won the War* (1967), a controversial antiwar satire; *Petulia* (1968); *The Bed Sitting Room* (1969); *The Three Musketeers* (1974); *The Four Musketeers* (1975); *Robin and Marian* (1976); *Butch and Sundance: The Early Days* (1979); *Superman II* (1980); *Superman III* (1983); *The Return of The Musketeers* (1990); and *Get Back* (1991).

[Jonathan Licht]

LESTSCHINSKY, JACOB (1876–1966), Russian-born pioneer in sociology, economics, and demography of Jewish life. Lestschinsky, who was born in Horodicz in the Ukraine, was deeply affected by *Aḥad Ha-Am and became a member of the *Benei Moshe League when he was 17. He and his brother Joseph established a modern Hebrew school in Horodicz which became famous for its tutelage. He studied at Berne and Zurich universities, pamphleteered for Zionist Socialism, principally in Warsaw, and served as a Zionist delegate at the Sixth Zionist Congress in Basle, where he supported the territorialists. He helped found the Zionist-Socialist (S.S.) Party, writing for it and for other journals on economics under the name Aḥad ha-Kanna'im. "Statistics of a Small Town" (1903) was his first study in the field he was to concentrate on, and was followed by two applications of Marxist methods, *Der Yidisher Arbeter in London* (1906) and *Der Yidisher Arbeter in Rusland* (1906). After 1906 he was not active in party politics, although he remained a Zionist activist. At this period he published two series of studies on conversions in different countries (1911) and on German Jewry (1912). Before 1914 he operated an ORT employment agency for Jewish refugees in Warsaw. During the February Revolution in Russia he helped found the United Jewish Socialist Party and served on the editorial board of *Naye Tsayt*, its official journal.

In 1921 Lestschinsky left Russia and established himself in Berlin, where he was the *Forward* correspondent, a connection he maintained virtually until his death. His *Yidishe Folk in Tsifern* (1922) viewed Jewish demography in worldwide perspective. Early in the 1920s he helped establish the Institute for Research into Contemporary Jewry and Judaism. He served as editor of an important journal, *Bleter far Yidishe Demografie un Statistik*, from 1923 to 1925. His *Probleme der Bevoelkerungs-Bewegung bei den Juden* (1926) has been called "one of the most brilliant investigations of problems of Jewish demography ever published." His study *Die Umsiedlung und Umschichtung des juedischen Volkes im Laufe des letzten Jahrhunderts* (1929–30) was of fundamental importance. In the 1920s he directed *YIVO's economics and statistics section, and his work appeared in YIVO publications. Less than two months after Hitler came to power in Germany, Lestschinsky sent a dispatch to *Forward* which was published in the *New York Times* on March 26, 1933; in it he said: "The Hitler regime flames up with anger because it has been compelled through fear of public foreign opinion to forego a mass slaughter of Jews. It threatens, however, to execute pogroms if Jews in other countries make too much fuss about the pogroms it has hitherto indulged in." Arrested by the Nazis upon publication of the dispatch, he was expelled from Germany. In 1934 he went to Warsaw, but was expelled from there in 1937 for publishing material on the plight of the Jews in Poland. In 1938 he went to the United States. During the war he lived in New York, and worked with the Institute of Jewish Affairs of the World Jewish Congress. One of the earliest students of the Holocaust, he wrote two basic studies in this field, *Di Yidishe Katastrofe* (1944) and *Crisis, Catastrophe, and Survival: A Jewish Balance Sheet, 1914–1948* (1948). In 1959 he moved to Tel Aviv, and in 1964 to Jerusalem, where he remained until he died. His collection of books and papers, which he somehow maintained throughout his wanderings, are at the Institute of Contemporary Jewry of the Hebrew University.

BIBLIOGRAPHY: P. Glikson, in: JJSO, 9 (1967), 48–57, incl. bibl.; J. Anilowicz, in: YIVO-Bleter, 10 (1936), 327–39, a bibl.; A. Manor, *Ya'akov Lestschinsky* (Heb., 1961); idem, in: JJSO, 4 (1962), 101–6.

[*Encylopaedia Hebraica*]

LESTSCHINSKY, JOSEPH (**"Chmurner"**; 1884–1935), Jewish socialist leader in Russia and Poland. Both Joseph, who was born in the Ukraine, and his brother, Jacob *Lestschinsky, joined a circle of Zionist youth in Warsaw which acquired in 1903 a socialist character. In 1905 Lestschinsky helped to found the *Zionist-Socialist Workers Party and was a member of its central committee. He was a theoretician of *territorialism in the party, edited its publications, and published his articles in them. One of the leaders of the left wing of the *United Jewish Socialist Workers' Party in the Ukraine in 1917, he was its representative on the Central Council of the Ukraine (Rada) and on the Jewish National Council. In 1921 he went to Poland, where he joined the *Bund and became the chief ideologist and publicist of its leftist faction.

BIBLIOGRAPHY: *Chmurner-Bukh* (Yid., 1958); LNYL, 5 (1963), 376–80; B. Johnpoll, *The Politics of Futility* (1968), index.

[Moshe Mishkinsky]

LESZNO (Ger. **Lissa**), town in the Poznan district. Jews settled in Leszno upon the foundation of the town in 1534. In 1580 they received their first charter. The community had jurisdiction over the northwestern part of the town, where they lived. The Leszno community had to flee temporarily in 1659 during the second Swedish war. The earliest tombstone preserved in the cemetery dates from 1667. As early as 1650 the Jews of Leszno had close business connections with those of Breslau and from 1688 they attended the Leipzig fairs. A synagogue was established in 1685. In 1740 Jewish merchants exceeded non-Jewish. By 1793, 40 of the 53 merchants were Jews, as were 200 of the 201 brokers. In 1800, 32 of the 51 tailors were Jews and 250 Jewish women were lace-workers. There was also a considerable number of smelters, tanners, furriers, and embroiderers.

During the Northern War (1706–07) Leszno Jews suffered from the exactions of both sides. Russian soldiers committed plunder and rape, and the entire Jewish quarter was burned. In the plague of 1709 the Jews were accused of infecting the town with plague by bringing the corpse of a Jew to be buried in the town cemetery. As a result of this libel, the Jews were expelled from the city, but when the plague subsided they returned. In 1767 a fire destroyed the whole Jewish quarter and 20 Jews were killed. After this the Jews were freed from taxes for six years. A new *bet midrash* was built and a library purchased; later a large synagogue was built, with the help of other communities. In the summer of 1790 a fire swept through the Jewish quarter once more; 196 of 481 Jewish houses were destroyed, as well as the new synagogue and the *bet midrash*. Another synagogue was completed in 1799. In the second half of the 18th century Leszno became central in Jewish life in *Great Poland following the decline of *Poznan after 1736. The "sages of Leszno" were renowned throughout Europe. At the end of the 18th century students came to the Leszno yeshivah from Germany as well as from central and southeastern Poland. Rabbis who served the town included Mordecai b. Ẓevi Hirsch (1721?–53), who was requested to be the main arbitrator in the dispute between Jacob *Emden and Jonathan *Eybeschuetz. After his death his brother and successor, Abraham Abusch *Lissa (1753–59), continued the attempt at arbitration. David Tevele, rabbi from 1774 to 1792, gave strong and eloquent expression to the Orthodox opposition to Haskalah trends of assimilation. In a trenchant sermon he castigated the subservience of N.H. *Wessely to an alien culture, drawing attention to the human and humanistic values inherent in the traditional Jewish culture and way of life. From 1809 to 1821 Jacob *Lorbeerbaum was rabbi, and from 1864 to 1912 Samuel Baeck, father of Leo *Baeck. Akiva *Eger studied in Leszno from 1780 to 1790. Raphael Kosch, a native of Leszno, was first vice president of the National Council in Berlin in 1848 and headed the procedural committee of the Prussian Parliament. Ludwig Kalisch (1814–1882), the humorist who participated in the revolution of 1848 and later moved to Paris, was also a native of the city. The Jewish population in Leszno rose from 400 families in 1656 to 4,989 persons in 1765. However, after the partition of Poland and the Prussian annexation of the town in 1793, the community began to decline. Deprived of their commercial markets in the Polish interior and in Russia, many Leszno Jews moved to central Germany. The numbers fell from 3,960 in 1833 to 2,578 in 1858, 1,206 in 1895, 804 in 1913, and 322 in 1921.

[Jacob Rothschild]

Holocaust Period

Under Nazi occupation, Leszno came under the Regierungsbezirk Posen (Wartheland). No ghetto was created in the town, but a *Judenrat existed. The Jews were obliged to appear daily before the German authorities for hard labor. Jews were driven out of their houses and the synagogue was transformed into a storehouse. In December 1940, 300 Jews were deported to *Grodzisk Mazowiecki in the General Government and in February 1941 were taken together with the Jews of that town to the Warsaw ghetto. In Leszno itself or the vicinity a Jewish labor camp functioned from April 1941 until August 1943, with about 250 inmates.

[Danuta Dombrowska]

BIBLIOGRAPHY: L. Lewin, *Geschichte der Juden in Lissa* (1904); idem, in: MGWJ, 73 (1929), 179; Jacobson, *ibid.*, 64 (1920), 282; 65 (1921), 45, 47, 158, 162, 235; I. Trunk, in: *Bleter far Geshikhte*, 2:1–4 (1949), 64–75, passim; D. Dabrowska, in: BŻIH, 13–14 (1955), 122–84, passim.

LETICHEV, town in Khmelnitsky district, Ukraine; under czarist rule a district town in the province of Podolia. Jews are first mentioned there in a document of 1581. The community was destroyed during the *Chmielnicki massacres (1648). More than a century later (1765) 652 Jews paid the poll tax in Letichev and the vicinity. The community grew, numbering 1,852 in 1847 and 4,108 (56.6% of the total population) in 1897. In the years 1881–1882 Jews suffered from pogroms. During the civil war (1919–20) the town and surrounding countryside suffered severely at the hands of rebellious Ukrainian bands. In 1926 there were 2,434 Jews (34%) in the town, their number dropped further to 1,946 (36.5% of the total population) in 1939.The Germans occupied Letichev on July 17, 1941. They created a ghetto and took Jews to forced labor. In September 1942 the Germans murdered 3,000 Jews from the town and its environs. There in November 1942 they killed 4,000 Jews from the counties of Volkovinets and Derazhne.The local Jews who remained in a labor camp were executed in early 1943.

[Yehuda Slutsky / Shmuel Spector (2nd ed.)]

LETTERIS, MEIR (**Max**; 1800?–1871), Hebrew poet, writer, and editor. Born in Zolkiew (now Zholkva), Letteris, as a child, was introduced to Nachman *Krochmal, whom he henceforth considered his mentor. In spite of fame, professional recognition, public honors, and numerous editions of several of his works, he struggled financially all his life, holding jobs as copyreader in different printing houses (but especially in that of Anton von *Schmid), and lecturing, publishing periodicals, selling subscriptions, writing occasional poems, and, for some time, even receiving charity. In the course of his work as a copyreader in Vienna, Pressburg, and Prague, he edited important reprints and first editions, to which he added notes, explanations, and biographies. The latter, along with his autobiography, letter collections, and the contributions of his contemporaries to his various publications, convey a vivid picture of the Galician-Austrian Haskalah and all its leading personalities.

His works include the following: (1) Books of Hebrew poetry: *Divrei Shir* (1822), original poems as well as translations of Schiller, among others; *Ayyelet ha-Shaḥar* (1824), original poetry and translations of Schiller, Byron ("Hebrew Melodies"), and others; *Afrot Zahav* (1852), original and translated poetry; *Tofes Kinnor ve-Ugav* (1860), his first two volumes of poetry together with other previously published and new poems. (2) Translations: Two of Racine's plays, which are in fact free adaptations in Hebrew: *Athalie* (*Geza Yishai*, 1835) and *Esther* (*Shelom Ester*, 1843); several works by L.A. *Frankl, as well as Goethe's *Faust*, part 1 (*Ben Avuyah*, 1865), probably Letteris' most important work in this field of endeavor: he adapted and hebraized the play (the setting and characters are Jewish), and deleted all christological references. (3) Hebrew literary collections: *Ha-Ẓefirah* (1824) – intended as the first number of a periodical – opening with "*Yonah Homiyyah*," which became the best known of Letteris' poems, set to music and sung for generations; collections of letters including *Mikhtavim* (1827), *Mikhtevei Ivrit* (1847), and *Mikhtevei Benei Kedem* (1866). Further Hebrew collections appeared as supplements to some of his German periodicals. (4) German publications: *Sagen aus dem Orient* (1847), poetic renditions of biblical, midrashic, and talmudic themes, for which he was awarded a gold medal by Emperor Franz Joseph; *Wiener Blaetter*, with the Hebrew supplement *Ẓefirat Tiferet* (1851–52), *Wiener VierteljahrsSchrift*, with *Avnei Neẓer* (1853), and *Wiener Mitteilungen* (1854–70). He republished both his Hebrew and German writings, including *Oestliche Rosen* (1852), *Beitraege zur Literatur-und Kulturgeschichte* (1859), and *Ein Blatt Geschichte* (1869). His German translation of the *maḥzor* (with a Hebrew commentary, 1845–49) and the *Andachtsbuch fuer israelitische Frauenzimmer* (1845) saw numerous editions. He also wrote a *Hebraeische Sprachlehre* (1853). (5) Editions from manuscripts: M.Ḥ. *Luzzatto's *Migdal Oz* (1838) with a Latin introduction by Franz *Delitzsch and notes by S.D. *Luzzatto; Abraham *Ibn Ezra's *Sefat Yeter* (1838), and R. Joseph ha-Kohen's *Emek ha-Bakha* (1852), with notes by S.D. Luzzatto. Among his new editions (always with notes, biographies, or text additions) are *Ben-Ze'ev's *Oẓar ha-Shorashim* (1839–44), the works of Isaac *Erter, *Ha-Ẓofeh le-Veit Yisrael* (1858), volume one of *Ha-Me'assef* (1862), and Krochmal's *Moreh Nevukhei ha-Zeman* (1863). (6) Other works: *Ḥikrei Lev* (1837), a treatise on Bible study; contributions to the periodicals *Bikkurei ha-Ittim, Kerem Ḥemed*, and *Bikkurei ha-Ittim ha-Ḥadashim*. In the latter, Letteris published a Spinoza biography (1845, 27b–31b) which aroused controversy because of his plea for the rehabilitation of Spinoza among Jews. Another undertaking, the editing of the Hebrew text of the Old Testament for the British and Foreign Bible Society of London (1852), damaged his reputation among Jews. It was perhaps his most lasting achievement, however, as it resulted in innumerable editions of the "Letteris Bible." Of his autobiography, *Zikkaron ba-Sefer* (1869), only the first part appeared, leading up to 1831, and containing a description of Nachman Krochmal's circle in Zolkiew.

Letteris was a true exponent of the Haskalah, a mediator between Jewish and Western cultures. His free Hebrew renditions of European literary works are probably his greatest contribution to modern Hebrew poetry. A new edition of *Tofes Kinnor ve-Ugav* appeared in 1969.

BIBLIOGRAPHY: Waxman, Literature, index; Klausner, Sifrut, 2 (1952^2), 360–400; Lachower, Sifrut, 2 (1953^{12}), 7–11; Zinberg, Sifrut, 6 (1960), 83–88; Kressel, Leksikon, 2 (1967), 247–9. **ADD. BIBLIOGRAPHY:** M. Ungerfeld, "*Bein Letteris u-Smolenskin*," in: *Moznayim*, 23 (1966), 250–52; idem, "*M.H. Letteris*," in: *Ha-Do'ar*, 51 (1972), 231–33; A.M. Haberman, "*Itonav shel M.H. Letteris*," in: *Kiyov* (1972), 109–12; B.L. Knapp, "Jean Racine's Esther and Two Hebrew Translations of This Drama," in: *Baron* (1974), 596–621; S. Yaniv, "*Habaladah ha-Sifrutit ha-Ivrit ha-Rishonah*," in: *Dappim le-Meḥkar be-Sifrut*, 2 (1985), 139–157; M. Gilboa, "*Ha-Ẓefirah shel M. Letteris ke-Koveẓ Loḥem*," in: *Sadan*, 1 (1994), 77–87.

[Werner Weinberg]

LETTERS AND LETTER WRITERS. The letter holds an honored place in Jewish history and literature and includes diplomatic correspondence, state papers, and letters as vehicles of religious or secular literature and as a means of polemics in communal and spiritual matters, business or private family letters, and so on. In Jewish law and ritual the authoritative opinion in answer to an inquiry has given rise to an entire literature of its own (see *Responsa).

The language of Jewish letters was above all Hebrew, and even after Jews adopted the languages of their homes in the Diaspora, it gained in importance as Jewry's lingua franca, apart from remaining the vehicle of all learned communication. At a later stage Yiddish occupied a similar position for European Jews. In style the language often became formalized and adopted the literary conventions of the dominant culture. Letters constitute a valuable source for Jewish history.

Biblical Period

From the 14th century B.C.E. there is the famous collection of diplomatic correspondence, the *El-Amarna letters with their first references to the *Ḥabiru, who perhaps had some connection to the Hebrews. These letters, on clay tablets written in Akkadian, contain numerous "Hebrew" words. To approximately the same period also belong letters written on clay tablets found at *Ta'anach. The first biblical letter is the one that sent Uriah to his death (II Sam. 11:14–15), and to the same category belongs the one written by Jezebel arranging the judicial murder of Naboth (I Kings 21:8–11). In both cases the Hebrew word *sefer* (also meaning "book") is used for letter; in Ezra (1:1) and II Chronicles (21:12; 36:22) it is *mikhtav* ("letter"); and in Esther (9:26, 29) as well as in II Chronicles (30:1, 6) and Nehemiah (2:7–9; 6:5, 17, 19), *iggeret* ("epistle"). Nehemiah 6:5 speaks of an "open letter" sent by Sanballat to Nehemiah. As the use of *sefer* shows, the dividing line between "book" and "letter" is vague (cf. Isa. 29:11–12, "a sealed letter"; Ezra 2:9–10, "a scroll-letter"; and Zech. 5:1ff.).

Jeremiah wrote or dictated his famous letter to the exiles in Babylonia (29:1ff.), which produced an angry reaction by letter from Shemaiah the Nehelamite (*ibid.* 24ff.). The oldest Hebrew letters known at present are from the early or middle seventh century. Among the discoveries in the Dead Sea caves (Wadi Murabba'at) was a papyrus palimpsest on which was probably a seventh-century letter, of which only the greeting formula is still recognizable. This letter is thus far the only pre-Christian letter written on papyrus, all others being *ostraca, i.e., sherds of broken pottery (Pardee in ABD). The judicial plea found near Yabneh-yam is probably a bit later. From Jeremiah's time are the *Lachish Letters, ostraca referring to Nebuchadnezzar's second campaign against Judah (589). II Chronicles 21:12ff. records a letter of Elijah to Joram of Judah, and 30:1ff., proclamations by letter from Hezekiah. The Persian period in Jewish history begins with one by Cyrus to the Jews in Babylonia (*ibid.* 36:22–23), and the Book of Ezra (ch. 4ff.; cf. Neh. 2:7–9) contains correspondence and state papers in Aramaic concerning the rights of the returnees from Babylon. From the same period are the Aramaic letters from the Jewish military colony in Egypt at *Elephantine. The first *she'elah u-teshuvah* (inquiry and responsum concerning ritual) is found in Zechariah in 7:1ff., though it is not certain whether even the inquiry was in writing. Mordecai and Esther sent a proclamation by letter concerning the Purim festival to all Persian Jews (Esther 9:20ff.). Letter writing in biblical times required professional writers (I Chron. 2:55) and was no doubt the main occupation of the royal officer called the *sofer* ("scribe," II Sam. 8:17). The many *seals found in archaeological excavations were used for signing letters, documents, and state papers (I Kings 21:8; cf. Gen. 38:18, 25) and also to close them (Job 41:7).

Persian and Greek Periods

Still close to biblical times are the *Elephantine (Yeb) letters, Aramaic papyri shedding light on the life of the military settlement of Jews on the Upper Nile from the sixth to the fourth centuries B.C.E. The Letter of *Aristeas, written in Greek in the third or second century, describes the origins of the Jewish community of Alexandria and of the Septuagint Bible translation; it includes an exchange of letters between Ptolemy Philadelphus II and Eleazar the high priest. The work, a propaganda tract for Jews and Judaism, is an early Jewish example of the Greek genre of epistolary literature. Other Jewish letters in this period are those found in the first and second book of Maccabees. In the first (12:5ff.), the Hasmonean Jonathan sent a diplomatic message to Sparta; the second (1:1–9 and 1:10–2:18) contains messages sent by the Jews of Jerusalem to those of Egypt in connection with the Hasmonean victories and the institution of the Ḥanukkah festival. *Philo in his "Delegation to Gaius" (Caligula) recorded the moving and historically important letters, which he may have drafted himself, of Agrippa I to the emperor, imploring him to desist from his plan to have his statue erected in the Temple of Jerusalem (ed. E.M. Smallwood, (1961), 122–36). *Josephus included in his works many letters, real or fictitious, among them the charter given to the Jews by Antiochus III in 198 B.C.E. (Ant., 12, 3, 138–44). In his *Life* (364–67) he reports that Agrippa II sent him 62 letters, complimenting him on the accuracy of his histories; two of these letters he quotes verbatim.

Fragment from an eighth-century letter in Judeo-Persian found at Dandan-Uiliq in the region of Khotan (Sinkiang). London, British Museum, Or. Ms. 8212 (166).

New Testament; Bar Kokhba Letters

Of the 21 Epistles in the *New Testament, those of Paul occupy a prominent place. Only 10 out of the 13 ascribed to him are generally recognized as really his; the others were written by other founder-members of the new religion. The most "Jewish" among them is the Epistle of James, which may have been based on some pre-Christian apocryphon. The discovery in 1952 in Wadi Murabba'at and Naḥal Ḥever in 1960/61 of Hebrew letters written during the Bar Kokhba revolt, some signed by Bar Kokhba, have added further specimens of actual letters written in antiquity.

Talmudic Literature

In talmudic literature the earliest letter is the one sent by Simeon b. Shetaḥ (first century B.C.E.) appealing to his colleague Judah b. Tabbai to return from his self-imposed exile: "From me, Holy Jerusalem (Jerusalem, the Great) to thee, my sister Alexandria (Alexandria, the Small): how long doth my betrothed dwell with you, and I dwell desolate on account of him" (Sota 47a; Sanh. 107b; TJ, Ḥag. 2, 277d; Sanh. 6, 7, 23c). Letters conveying decisions in calendar and other ritual matters were sent to Jewish communities inside and outside Palestine on behalf of the Sanhedrin by Gamaliel I (before 50 C.E.; Sanh. 11b and parallels) and a generation later by his son Simeon and Johanan b. Zakkai (Mid. Tan. to Deut. 26:13). Letters like this are rare in Talmud and Midrash, where the preference was for oral transmission as against written communications. Messages like the one sent by the Jerusalem authorities to *Judah b. Bathyra at Nisibis (Pes. 3b) or to Theodoros (Thodos) of Rome (*ibid.* 53a) may or may not have been in writing, but the constant exchange of information and views between Palestinian and Babylonian scholars in the talmudic era is likely to have been partly in writing. For political reasons some of these messages had to be sent in code (Sanh. 12a). In this period, too, the writing of letters, particularly official ones, was entrusted to special secretaries (*sofer* or *libellarius*).

Belonging to the same period, but from non-talmudic sources, is the letter by *Julian the Apostate (in 363 C.E.) promising to restore Jerusalem and the Temple. Similarly, the brief episode of Empress Eudocia's kindness to the Jews 60 years later led to a flicker of messianic hope, which expressed itself in a letter by the Jewish notables to the Jews of the Diaspora (438; see Nau, in REJ, 83 (1927), 196–7). Also in the fourth century the patriarch Gamaliel b. Hillel maintained correspondence with the Syrian Hellenist Libanius, but only Libanius' letters have been preserved.

Medieval Hebrew Literature

Throughout the Middle Ages letters served as a major literary form in all countries in which Jews lived and wrote. Neither the form of the letter nor the fact that it was addressed to a specific person implied that the contents of the letter were private, for letter writing was one of the more usual means of publishing one's views and bringing them to the attention of as wide a public as possible. Letters were delivered by hand, and in many Jewish communities en route it was common practice to stop the messengers in order publicly to read the letters they were carrying. Frequently, it was requested that the messenger allow a local scribe to copy the letter, which would be read by the rabbis and kept in the files of the community. This practice explains why many hundreds of letters found in the Cairo *Genizah* were not addressed to the Egyp-

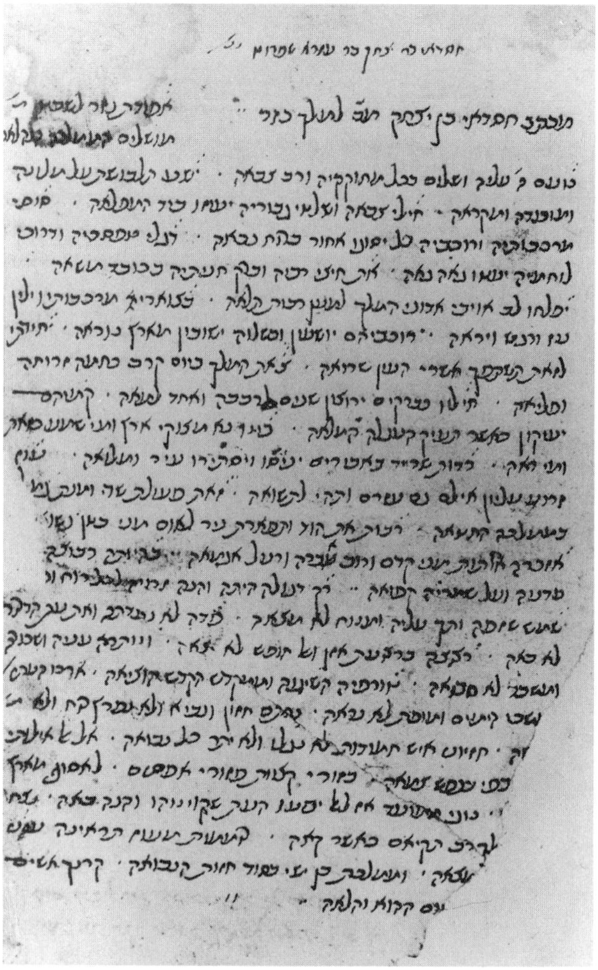

First of the letters from Ḥisdai ibn Shaprut to the king of the Khazars, 10th century. Oxford, Christ Church Library, Ms. 193, p.12.

tian Jewish community, but rather to various communities in North Africa and Europe. It was also common for a man to write several copies of his letter and send them to different places for publication. At the end of their letters, some writers requested the reader to pass the letter on or make additional copies of it. Letters containing messages of importance to the whole community were read aloud in the synagogue; others of more limited interest were read by the *bet din* or the community council. There were also some efforts to make epistolary privacy secure: in the 11th century R. Gershon forbade the reading of letters addressed to someone else except with the person's knowledge and permission.

Treating letters as a means of publishing one's views gave rise to certain literary forms frequently utilized in epistolary literature. For instance, the published letter was an opportunity for the writer to demonstrate his erudition and his mastery of Hebrew language and style, which explains why many letters written in the Middle Ages contain numerous biblical and talmudic phrases and references. The introduction of the letter was often written in rhymed prose, and many letters were composed entirely in this style. The opening phrases of a letter were usually a series of formula descriptions of the addressee's wisdom, generosity, and greatness. These phrases were often employed interchangeably from one letter to another. Therefore, very little individual style is to be found in medieval letters, even those written by the most prominent Jewish thinkers, who developed a personal style in their other writings.

The character of epistolary literature made the distinction between a book and a letter very unclear. The usual word for book, *sefer*, was frequently used to denote a letter and the word for letter, *iggeret*, was used as the title of many books. Some of the more important books in the Middle Ages were originally written as letters, the most celebrated example being Maimonides' *Guide of the Perplexed*.

Large collections of letters exist in the fields of *halakhah*, polemics, ethics, and philosophy. Literary correspondence was also one of the best ways of developing Jewish culture in the Sephardi communities. In the same way, non-literary letters, on commercial topics or on personal subjects, were also a significant part of the manifestations of Jewish life during the Middle Ages. The letters could be public, related to the questions of the communities, or personal, dealing with private matters. Different languages were employed, usually in consonance with the particular tradition and vernaculars: Hebrew, Judeo-Arabic, and many other Jewish languages.

HALAKHIC RESPONSA. From the geonic period, Jews all over the world addressed halakhic questions to the supreme halakhic authorities of the time. The various *geonim* in Babylonia, Maimonides in Egypt, the tosafists and the Rashi school in Germany, Naḥmanides and Solomon ben Abraham Adret in Spain, Caro in Safed – all received hundreds of halakhic questions which they usually answered in great detail. Occasionally these responsa grew into whole treatises, later published as books (the first being Rav Amram Gaon's answer to a question on the laws concerning prayers, which became the first prayer book or *siddur*). Similar questions were also addressed to many less eminent rabbis, some of whom collected their answers and published them in book form. These responsa presented *halakhah* in a most concrete, everyday way. When writing halakhic exegesis or specialized treatises, the author may be preoccupied with fundamental, theoretical questions, but when writing responsa he is required to solve a specific problem. Accordingly, halakhic *responsa are regarded as one of the most important sources of medieval Jewish history.

POLEMICAL LETTERS. By nature, *polemical literature is addressed to a specific person with whom the author is in conflict, yet the author wishes his views to be known as widely as possible. Therefore, most medieval Jewish polemical material is found in epistolary literature. Many of these letters are written, partially or wholly, in rhymed prose and include other literary forms developed for argumentation. *Milḥamot Adonai* by Solomon b. Jeroḥam, which was the Karaites' answer to Saadiah Gaon, is among the earliest polemical letters and includes one of the most perfect examples of the use of irony in medieval Hebrew literature. A whole vocabulary of sarcastic phrases and abusive references was developed in this literature. Very frequently the discussion of theological differences gave way to personal abuse.

Some major conflicts in Jewish life and thought are found solely in collections of polemical letters. In Spain, Italy, and Provence during the 13th and 14th centuries, the great controversies raging over Maimonides and his views, and over the study of philosophy in general, were carried on in hundreds of letters, many of which are extant. One of the first participants in the controversy, Meir ben Todros Abulafia, sent letters to communities in Spain and Southern France that reflected the beginning of opposition to the ideas of Maimonides. In the 13th century, a follower of Maimonides, Shem Tov ben Joseph ibn *Falaquera, wrote the *Iggeret ha-Vikku'aḥ* ("Epistle of the Debate") trying to prove the agreement between Torah and reason in keeping with Maimonides' views. Between 1318 and 1320 Joseph ibn Caspi wrote polemical letters reflecting his disputations with Christian scholars from the Kingdom of Aragon. At the turn of the 14th century Profiat *Duran wrote his anti-Christian epistle *Al-Tehi ka-Avotekha*, typical of the polemic produced by more or less forced baptisms and the controversy with the Christians. Letters written in Hebrew and Arabic were the vehicle for the controversy between the Karaites and Rabbinic Judaism. The controversy about the renewal of *semikhah* (ordination of rabbis) in Safed, Jerusalem, and Egypt was conducted through letters, which have been collected and serve as a primary historical source. Similarly, in the 17th century, the Shabbatean controversy, and the Eybeschuetz-Emden controversy which followed in its wake, were sustained by letters, many of which were later edited and published. Authors sometimes changed the wording of their original letters to suit changed circumstances, a tactic known to have been executed in many other controversies.

ETHICAL LETTERS. One of the literary forms which was developed in the Middle Ages within the framework of *ethical literature was the short ethical epistle. This literary form is very close in character to another sort of short ethical treatise – the ethical *will. In medieval times many ordinary as well as eminent Jews wrote letters – usually to their sons (for instance, some poems of Samuel ha-Nagid to his son Yehosef), but sometimes to other relatives or to communities – describing the ethical way of behavior, and imploring the readers to follow this path. These writers clearly intended that their letters be published, and that the letters were addressed to specific people is no more than a literary device. Because the letters were usually short, they therefore contained a complete ethical system in a nutshell, revealing what the age thought were the most important areas in which behavior had to be corrected. Like other letters, ethical letters also frequently employed rhymed prose.

PHILOSOPHICAL LETTERS. Maimonides made the most intensive use of correspondence, and his influence was largely due to the extensive correspondence he carried on with all parts of the Jewish world. In this way he offered practical guidance to the Jewish communities of the East and the West. Following his father's example in his "Letter of Consolation," Maimonides exercised his spiritual leadership over the Diaspora by means of pastoral letters, such as the "Letter to Yemen" on true and false messianism. He also was in correspondence with groups of, or individual, scholars, with friends and pupils, apart from the great number of responsa he wrote in answer to inquiries from all over. His style is clear and terse and has a beauty of its own, and found late imitators in Isaac *Abrabanel, Joseph Solomon *Delmedigo, and *Manasseh Ben Israel. Another interesting correspondence on philosophical topics took place at the beginning of the 15th century between Solomon *Bonafed, one of the last distinguished intellectuals of the Kingdom of Aragon before the expulsion of 1492, and a young disciple of Isaac Arondi, on the value of the logic taught at the time by Christian masters (Bodleian Library, ms. nº 1984, 87r–102r).

LITERARY CORRESPONDENCE. In Andalusia, where letter writing developed into a specific genre, Moses Ibn Ezra took pride in the leading position occupied by his countrymen in this art (*Kitāb al-Muḥāḍara wal-Mudhākara,* ed. A.S. Halkin (1975), 29bff.). An early example is the correspondence of *Ḥisdai ibn Shaprut with the king of the *Khazars. His own letters were drafted by his secretary, the poet and grammarian *Menahem b. Saruk, who inserted an acrostic of his own name in addition to Ḥisdai's in an introductory poem. In contrast to his polished and allusive style, the letter of a Khazar Jew to Ḥisdai, found in the *Genizah*, is written in a clear and simple Hebrew. In the *divan* of many of the great Andalusian poets we find also examples of literary correspondence. We have, for instance, exchanges of poems between Isaac *Ibn Khalfun and *Samuel ha-Nagid, and between many other Andalusian poets. There are also letters in prose that have been preserved, for instance, in the *divan* of Judah Halevi (the letters published by M. Gil and E. Fleischer (2001) are of a completely different nature). Literary correspondence continued in the Christian kingdoms of the north of the Iberian Peninsula: Todros Abulafia in 13th-century Toledo often partook of this way of communicating with other poets. A particular development of this literary correspondence can be observed in some poets of the so-called "Circle of Saragossa" at the end of the 14th century and the beginning of the 15th, especially in Solomon *da Piera and Solomon Bonafed. A substantial part of the *divan* of these poets consists of literary correspondence with other poets of the time including sections in prose and poems. As J. Targarona has shown, the structure of these letters is substantially the same, consisting of a heading or rubric, the body of the letter, with a poem preceded or followed by short epigrams (*simanim*), and the "signature," including a text in rhymed prose; "on the back of the letter" there may be another short poem and a dedication to the addressee.

COMMERCIAL LETTERS. A large number of letters of the **Genizah* published by Goitein (1973) is a good example of the diffusion of letters as means of communication among Jewish merchants and traders, usually occupied in international trade, who engaged in all kinds of business transactions, sent a multiplicity of goods from one country to another, etc., and among other things mentioned the commercial rulings of rabbinical courts in their letters and legal documents. The traders usually worked together in distant countries as friends or partners. The large quantity of international and even interdenominational business transactions produced frequent correspondence. The economic activities, and the letters connected with them, were mainly concentrated in two areas: the Mediterranean and the trade with India. Among the letters of the 11th century published by Goitein we also find the correspondence between great merchant families, and all kinds of accounts related to the transactions.

COMMUNAL AND PERSONAL LETTERS. During the Middle Ages there was frequent correspondence among the leaders of the communities of the Jewish Diaspora. The European communities were linked in many ways with Babylon, and from the tenth century on, notable cultural ties grew between Muslim Spain, France, and Germany, creating a kind of network based on letter exchange on legal issues and on other specific aspects of Jewish life. The means of communication was often in the form of circular letters sent to the entire community. Among scholars, colleagues, and disciples there was also a frequent exchange of letters that helped clarify halakhic or scholarly matters, as in the case of R. Samson and Rabbenu Tam.

Exchange of letters of a more confidential nature was also the usual way of communicating between individuals who were not able to have personal contact. The contents of these letters were of an intimate character, or on occasion related to common business matters. Travelers, relatives, or friends separated in distant countries would communicate to one another news about deaths, weddings, or births of members of the family or their relatives. We can see this kind of personal correspondence in the letters from Jerusalem and Acre sent by *Naḥmanides to his son in Barcelona between 1263 and 1267. Other personal letters included requests for financial help, or questions by former students to their teachers.

AGRONIM. One of the major sources for the study of the development of the Hebrew letter in medieval and early modern times is the literature of the *agronim*. An *agron* is a collection of form letters, compiled or written by a scholar for the use of the general public. Included in the collection are form letters of praise, reference, appointments, business requests for charity, for money to marry one's daughters, for money to ransom the release of Jewish prisoners, and for almost every other conceivable occasion in which a Jew may be in need of a special letter. All the user did was to fill in the name(s) and other necessary details and a well-written letter, which would evoke respect from the reader, was ready for sending. The first collection of stereotyped Hebrew letters, *Iggerot Shelomim*, was printed anonymously in Augsburg in 1534. This example was soon followed by others: *Megillat Sefer* or *Mikhtavim* (also anonymous, Venice, 1545–48?), and Samuel Archevolti's *Ma'yan Gannim* (Venice, 1553; Cremona, 1566).

The *agronim*, of which dozens were printed, became a very popular literary form, especially since the 18th century. There are, in manuscript, *agronim* from Spain dating as far back as the 15th century. Many *agronim* also include other literary works, like short poems of praise or riddles, which might be useful to the reader. *Agronim* are of great historical value inasmuch as they reveal the literary and social conventions of a given time and place; for example, the differences between a form of an application for the rabbinate in a small town and a big city are very instructive. Until recently this field had been neglected by scholars and especially historians; therefore, no definitive history of the development of the Hebrew epistle, from a literary and historical point of view, is to be found.

The epistolary form was used in other literary fields. The earliest extant medieval historiographical work, *Iggeret Rav Sherira Gaon* (in: Ḥ.J.D. Azulai, *Shem ha-Gedolim* (1967), 26–59), was probably written by Hai Gaon as an answer to a letter inquiring about the transmission of the *halakhah* from age to age. Letters regarding scientific and philosophical questions are also found in medieval Hebrew literature.

[Joseph Dan / Angel Saenz-Badillos (2nd ed.)]

Modern Period

The expulsion of Jews from Spain in 1492 produced letters from the exiles reporting their experiences in their new homes, particularly in Palestine. There had been antecedents for this, e.g., *Judah Halevi, Maimonides, Naḥmanides, Obadiah of *Bertinoro, and Elijah of Ferrara; but from the 16th century onward a growing volume of such letter reports from Palestine reached a news-hungry Diaspora. Among the most prominent correspondents were Solomon *Molcho in the 16th century, Isaiah *Horowitz in the 17th, and some ḥasidic leaders in the 18th (see A. Yaari, *Iggerot Ereẓ Yisrael*, 1943), Interesting, too, is a letter by *Elijah ben Solomon Zalman, the Gaon of Vilna, written before he set out for Palestine.

ITALY. The true heir to Spain in Hebrew epistolary art was Italy, where the spirit of the Renaissance found able and congenial adepts among Hebrew letter writers. Nearly 100 letters by the banker-scholar Solomon da Poggibonzi (ed. by S. Simonsohn in *Koveẓ al Yad*, 6 (1966), 379–417) reveal an accomplished practician of the art. The most prolific of them all was Leone *Modena, who carefully kept copies of his letters, *Leo Modenas Briefe…* (ed. by L. Blau (1907)), which reveal his mind and life. Italy remained the home of letter writing, as shown by Modena's younger contemporary *Mahalalel Hallelyah of Ancona, who, like M.Ḥ. *Luzzatto a century later, can be regarded as one of the precursors of the Hebrew revival. In the 19th century I.S. *Reggio and S.D. *Luzzatto in their correspondence with other Jewish scholars made an important contribution to the new Wissenschaft des Judentums. Much of the argument in the battles around Reform and Haskalah at the end of the 18th and beginning of the 19th century took the form of letters (cf. the collections of letters by N.H. Wessely, *Nogah ha-Ẓedek* (1818); *Elleh Divrei ha-Berit* (1819); *Teshuvot be-Anshei Aven* (1845)).

GERMANY. S.R. Hirsch gave his book, which laid the foundations of modern Orthodoxy, the fictional form of 19 letters (*Iggerot Ẓafon; The Nineteen Letters of Ben Uziel* (1899, 1969²)). Moses Hess's *Rom and Jerusalem* (1862) is a call in letter form for a Jewish national renaissance, and Joseph Perl also used "letters" for his anti-ḥasidic satires *Megalleh Temirim* (1919) and *Boḥen Ẓaddik* (1838). The emergence of the Wissenschaft des Judentums produced Hebrew periodicals such as *Kerem Ḥemed* and *Oẓar Neḥmad*, which published scholarly contributions in letter form.

Enlightenment and Wissenschaft des Judentums

In the Enlightenment period the letters written by Moses *Mendelssohn (*Jubilaeumsausgabe*, 11 (1932); 16 (1929)); L. *Zunz (*L. and A. Zunz – an account in letters*, ed. by N. Glatzer, 1958); I.S. *Reggio (*Iggerot YaSHaR*, 1834–36); S.D. *Luzzatto (*Iggerot Sha-Da-L*, 1882–94, repr. 1967); S.J. *Rapoport (*Iggerot* SHIR, 1845); and others are important sources for the history of that crucial period in Jewish history. Not one of the least achievements of modern Jewish scholarship was the publication of letters of prominent and even ordinary people of the past, such as those of Leone Modena (see above); correspondence between Jews of Prague and Vienna from the time of the Thirty Years' War *Juedische Privatbriefe…* ed. by A. Landau and B. Wachstein (1911); letters of Ḥ.J.D. *Azulai in *Ha-Ẓofeh le-Ḥokhmat Yisrael* (11, 1927); M.Ḥ. Luzzatto (S. Ginzburg, *RaMḤaL u-Venei Doro* (1937); and some of those written by Akiva *Eger, Moses *Sofer, and members of their families (*Iggerot Soferim*, ed. by S. Schreiber, 1929).

Jewish-Christian Correspondence

A special place in the history of Jewish letter writing is held by Jewish-Christian correspondence. In the 13th century Solomon Cohen exchanged letters on philosophical themes with his imperial patron Frederick II and the latter's court philosopher Theodorus. In the 16th century Lazarus de Viterbo corresponded in Latin with Cardinal Sirleto on the Bible, as did Leone Modena with Italian, French, and English scholars. Johannes *Buxtorf (the Younger) maintained a lively correspondence in Hebrew with Jewish scholars, and J.C. *Wagenseil entered into a polemic with R. Enoch ha-Levi. Manasseh Ben Israel wrote hundreds of letters in Latin, Spanish, and English as well as in Hebrew to the leading Christian scholars and theologians of his time. The 49 letters of *Spinoza still extant were all addressed to non-Jews. Nevertheless, they betray, more than any other of his writings, the Jewish roots of a man who had become totally estranged from his people. Anna Maria Schurmann was not the first, but certainly the most able and prolific, Christian woman writing letters in Hebrew.

Women Letter Writers

Given the mobile nature of medieval and early modern Jewish society, in which spouses and other family members were often separated for long periods of time, women frequently sent messages to absent loved ones. They also conducted correspondence in connection with their various entrepreneurial activities. The extant letters written by women tend to be in vernacular languages, but some are in Hebrew. It is likely that women sometimes depended on family members or professional scribes to prepare letters for them, but many of the surviving epistles, including some in Hebrew, transcend the formulaic and appear to have been written from the heart by literate, well-educated women.

A number of letters by women are found among the documents of the Cairo *Genizah*. These letters, generally from the 11th to the 13th centuries, are mostly in Judeo-Arabic with some Hebrew exceptions. A group of epistles that survive from the 16th century are in Judeo-Spanish and Yiddish. These personal documents often preserve direct and unmediated female voices, yielding many insights into socio-economic and cultural aspects of medieval and early modern Jewish life. In addition to letters sent within Egypt, women's letters in the *Genizah* originate from Aden, Byzantium, India, Italy, Seleucia, Tiberias, and Tunisia (Goitein; Kraemer).

Correspondence by Jewish women who interacted with the gentile world is extant in various European archives. A letter in Italian, dated 1508, survives from "Anna the Hebrew" of Rome to Catherine Sforza (1463–1509), extolling the virtues of various facial creams and explaining their costs and how to order them (Marcus). Esther *Handali (d. c. 1590), **kiera* of Nur Banu, the Venetian wife of Ottoman Sultan Selim II, took part in Nur Banu's correspondence with the Doge and Senate of Venice (Skilliter). British archives preserve a 1599 Italian letter to Elizabeth I of England that accompanied a gift of clothing, written by the *kiera*, Esperanza *Malchi, on behalf of the Ottoman Sultana Safiye (Kobler, 391–92).

The Italian poet Sara Coppia *Sullam (1592?–1641), known for her humanistic learning, remained loyal to Judaism despite many efforts to convince her to become a Christian. In addition to her extensive correspondence in Italian with Ansaldo Cebà, a Genoese nobleman and monk (only his letters are extant), she also responded in 1621 in an erudite and witty public letter to an attack by Baldassar Bonifaccio (later Cardinal of Cape d'Istria), who claimed that Sullam had denied the immortality of the soul (Kobler, 436–48).

A collection of correspondence sent from the ghetto of Prague and intended for family members and business associates in Vienna was intercepted in 1619 by the Austrian authorities and ended up in the archives of the Imperial Court of Vienna. Among these mostly Yiddish letters are many missives on personal, business, and other matters from women to their absent relatives (Kobler, 449–79).

Thirty-five of the letters written by Abigaill Levy *Franks (1733–48) of New York to her eldest son, Naphtali, who had returned to London, are extant. Written in English, they are among the earliest surviving correspondence of any woman in the British colonies (Gelles).

[Judith R. Baskin (2nd ed.)]

Collections of Letters

In more recent times the Ḥibbat Zion and Zionist movements have produced much letter writing among their leading figures. For the former A. Druyanow edited a collection of letters, *Ketavim le-Toledot Ḥibbat Ẓiyyon...* (3 vols., 1919–29). Theodor Herzl's letters of 1895–97 have been published in Hebrew as *Iggerot* (1961, vol. 9 of his collected writings) and those of Chaim Weizmann are being published (first volume *Kitvei...* series 1: *Iggerot*, 2 vols. (1969–70)). Collections of letters by the great modern Hebrew writers have also been published: J.L. Gordon (2 vols., 1894–5); Aḥad Ha-Am (6 vols., 1923–25); and Ḥ.N. Bialik (5 vols., 1937–39). Of particular importance for modern intellectual and spiritual history are the letters of Chief Rabbi A.I. *Kook, *Iggerot ha-Re'ayah* (3 vols., 1943; 1962–65²) and those of Franz *Rosenzweig, *Briefe* (1935). Interesting selections of letters by the philosopher Hermann Cohen and the painter Max Liebermann were issued in the *Schocken Buecherei* (1937, 1939). The experiences of World War I are reflected in *Kriegsbriefe deutscher Juden* (1935, repr. 1961) and in E. Tannenbaum's *Kriegsbriefe deutscher und oesterreichischer Juden* (1915). Letters by Israeli soldiers in the Six-Day War of 1967 were collected in *Be-Darkam; Ḥavrei ha-Iḥud she-Nafelu...* (1968).

The first modern anthology of Jewish or Hebrew letters is S.J. Fuenn's *Soferei Yisrael* (1871), a collection of 55 letters. A pioneer in this field was Franz Kobler (1882–1965), who published *Juden und Judentum in deutschen Briefen...* (1935), *Juedische Geschichte in Briefen...* (1938), and *Letters of Jews Through the Ages* (2 vols., 1952, with bibliography). A. Yaari's *Iggerot Ereẓ Yisrael* appeared in 1943 and Cecil Roth edited *Anglo-Jewish Letters* (1938). Many Jewish letters are incorporated in such general works as H. Adler's *Miscellany of Hebrew Literature* (2 vols., 1873), J. Winter and A. Wuensche, *Juedische Litteratur* (2 vols., 1894–97), and B. Halper's *Post-Biblical Hebrew Literature* (2 vols., 1921). J.R. Marcus' *American Jewry – Documents – 18th century* (1959) contains letters that are preserved in the American Jewish Archives at the Hebrew Union College, Cincinnati, which has specialized in letter collections. The British Museum possesses a great collection of Emmanuel Mendes da Costa's correspondence.

Formulas and Style

Hebrew and other Jewish letters are characterized by certain epistolary conventions, in which *abbreviations occupy a prominent position. The opening formula was ב"ה or בע"ה (בְּעֶזְרַת ה') = "with the help of God") or שיל"ת (שִׁוִּיתִי ה' לְנֶגְדִּי תָמִיד – Ps. 16:8 = "I have set the Lord always before me"). This was followed by the Jewish date, either day, month, and year or the day of the week and the coming weekly Sidra. The latter was often hinted at by a characteristic verse, and the year, by a similar *gematria*. In the period between Passover and Shavuot, the respective day in the Omer counting took the place of the date as would any particular day in the calendar, such as the New Moon and fast days. However, the date was often added at the end. This is followed by an exordium in which the addressee is apostrophized according to his station and worth, usually in flowery and exaggerated terms. The most common greeting, used in the beginning or at the end, was *shalom* ("peace"), or *berakhah* ("blessing"), which is found even in the Lachish ostraca letters.

The epistolary style from the Middle Ages onward became increasingly flowery and allusive (*meliẓah*), and was overloaded with biblical and talmudic quotations, which produced a strong reaction in modern times. Among the enactments of Rabbenu Gershom b. Judah (11th century) was one protecting the secrecy of letters, threatening the unauthorized opener with excommunication. This used to be alluded to in the letters by adding the abbreviation בחדר"ג = (בחרם דרבנו גרשום).

BIBLIOGRAPHY: F. Kobler, *Letters of Jews Through the Ages*, 2 vols. (1952); W. Zeitlin, in: ZHB, 22 (1919), 32ff.; J. Buxtorf, *Institutio Epistolaris Hebraica* (Basel, 1629); H. Beinart, in: *Sefunot*, 5 (1961), 73–135; J. Katz, in: *Sefer Zikkaron le-Vinyamin de Vries* (1968), 281ff. BIBLICAL PERIOD: **ADD. BIBLIOGRAPHY:** D. Pardee, *A Handbook of Ancient Hebrew Letters* (1982); idem, in: ABD, 4:282–85; W. Moran, *The Amarna Letters* (1992); F. Cross, in: idem, *Letters from an Epigrapher's Notebook* (2002), 121–24. OTHER PERIODS: **ADD. BIBLIOGRAPHY:** S.D. Goitein, *Letters of Medieval Jewish Traders* (1974); idem, *A Mediterranean Society*, 6 vols. (1967–93); Maimonides, *Epistles of Maimonides: Crisis and Leadership*, tr. A. Halkin, commentary D. Hartman (1993); E. Gutwirth, in: I. Benabu and J. Sermoneta (eds.), *Judeo-Romance Languages* (1985), 127–38; idem, in: S. Menache (ed.), *Communication in the Jewish Diaspora* (1996), 257–82; S. Menache (ed.), *Communication in the Jewish Diaspora* (1996); M. Gil and E. Fleischer, *Yehudah ha-Levi u-Venei Ḥugo: 55 Te'udot min ha-Genizah* (2001); J. Targarona and R. Scheindlin, in: REJ, 160 (2001), 61–133; J.L. Kraemer, "Women Speak for Themselves," in: S.C. Reif (ed.), *The Cambridge Genizah Collections* (2002), 178–216; J. Marcus (ed.), *The Jew in the Medieval World* (1983), 399–400; S.A. Skilliter, "The Letters of the Venetian 'Sultana' Nur Banu and her Kira to Venice," in: A. Gallotta and U. Marazzi (eds.), *Studia Turcologica* (1982), 515–36; E.B. Gelles (ed.), *The Letters of Abigaill Levy Franks (1733–1748)* (2004).

LETTUCE (Heb. חֲזֶרֶת, *ḥazeret* or חַסָּה, *ḥassah*), vegetable. Lettuce is not mentioned in the Bible. According to rabbinic tradition, however, it is included in the term *merorim* ("bitter herbs," Ex. 12:8) which are commanded to be eaten on the night of the Passover *seder* (see *Maror). According to the Mishnah (Pes. 2:6) this obligation can be discharged with five species of vegetable, the first of which is חֲזֶרֶת, which the *Gemara* explains to be *ḥassah* (Pes. 39a). Lettuce when young has soft leaves and a sweet taste, but if left in the field until it begins to flower its leaves harden and become bitter. For this reason the rabbis stated that it is ideal as *maror*: "just as lettuce is first sweet and then bitter, so was the behavior of the Egyptians to our ancestors" (TJ, Pes. 2:5, 29c), or "because the lettuce is first soft and finally hard" (Pes. 39a).

Lettuce was a popular vegetable. It is a winter crop which does not usually grow in summer, but people of wealth endeavored to obtain it out of season too. Thus it is related of *Antoninus and R. Judah ha-Nasi that their tables "did not lack lettuce even in summer" (Ber. 57b). Some think that the lettuce referred to is the wild variety *Lactuca scariola* out of which the cultivated "sweet" lettuce developed. Against this it should be noted that the growing of the cultivated variety is very ancient, it being depicted already in ancient Egyptian paintings, from which it seems that they grew the long-leaved lettuce, *Lactuca sativa*, var. *longifolia*, and apparently this variety was also grown in Israel in ancient times. The aforementioned wild variety, which is called the "compass lettuce" because its leaves point north and south, is found in all districts of Israel, particularly near refuse. The Mishnah (Kil. 1:2) calls it *ḥazeret gallim*, i.e., lettuce of the rubbish heaps, and decided that it is of the same species as the cultivated lettuce. The Samaritans have the custom of eating this wild lettuce with their Passover sacrifice. Among Jews of European origin the common custom is to eat as *maror* on the night of the *seder* horseradish, *Armocaria rusticana*, which they identify with the *ḥazeret* or *tamkha* mentioned as a bitter herb (Pes. 2:6), but this vegetable is sharp and not "bitter," nor was it grown in Ereẓ Israel in ancient times.

BIBLIOGRAPHY: Loew, Flora, 1 (1928), 424–39; H.N. and A.L. Moldenke, *Plants of the Bible* (1952), 6, 34, 74f., 140; J. Feliks, *Kilei Zera'im ve-Harkavah* (1967), 56–58; idem, *Olam ha-Ẓome'aḥ ha-Mikra'i* (1968²), 194–6. **ADD. BIBLIOGRAPHY:** Feliks, Ha-Ẓome'aḥ, 58.

[Jehuda Feliks]

°LEUSDEN, JOHANN (1624–1699), Calvinist theologian and Hebraist. Having numbered Jews among his teachers, in 1650 he became a professor of Hebrew language at the University of Utrecht. In collaboration with the Amsterdam publisher Joseph *Athias, he published the first Hebrew Bible in which the verses are numbered (*Biblia Hebraica*, 1661, 1667²). The edition became well known for its exactness and beautiful print, and served as a model for almost all publications of the Bible up to the 19th century. Leusden was one of the foremost Bible scholars of his time and wrote several treatises on Bible research and Hebrew philology. He also translated (Utrecht, 1656) the catalog of 613 commandments that heads Maimonides' halakhic code. Leusden carried on a correspondence with the Mathers, the famous Puritan New England family.

BIBLIOGRAPHY: *New Schaff-Herzog Encyclopedia of Religious Knowledge*, 6 (1910), 466; B. Glasius, *Godgeleerd Nederland*, 2 (1851–56), 365–7; *Nieuw Nederlandsch Biografisch Woordenboek*, 9 (1933), 601–2 (incl. bibl.). **ADD. BIBLIOGRAPHY:** C. Shiption, in: *The New England Quarterly*, 9 (1936), 205.

[Joseph Elijah Heller]

LEV, ABRAHAM (1910–1970), Yiddish poet. Born in Piaski near Volkovysk, Belorussia, he settled with his family in Vilna in 1922, studied in the Volozhin and Ramayles yeshivot, immigrated in 1932 to Palestine, and joined kibbutz Givat ha-Sheloshah. His first poem was published by Melech *Ravitch in a Warsaw journal when he was 16. Thereafter his lyrics appeared in Yiddish periodicals in Poland, France, the U.S., and Israel. Many of his poems were translated into Hebrew and were included in school texts and anthologies. His mature lyrics appeared in the volumes *Heym un Feld* ("Home and Field," 1953), *Beymer in Vint* ("Trees in the Wind," 1960), and *Bleter fun Kibuts* ("Pages from a Kibbutz," 1971). Lev was a poet of the kibbutz landscape, who referred to himself as a farmer-poet, dreaming his visions in the shade of the trees which he himself planted.

BIBLIOGRAPHY: LNYL, 5 (1963), 242–4; M. Ravitch, *Mayn Leksikon* (1958), 233–5.

[Israel Ch. Biletzky / Jerold C. Frakes (2nd ed.)]

LEV (Lab; Leb), JOSEPH BEN DAVID IBN (also known as the **MaHaRIVaL**, for **M**orenu **Ha**-**R**av **Y**osef **i**bn **L**ev; 1505–1580), Turkish rabbi and *posek*. Lev was born in Monastir (now Bitolj, Macedonia). Nothing is known of his early life, but he was appointed *dayyan* in his native town while still quite young. Because of a quarrel with a colleague on the *bet din* he moved to Salonika in 1534, where he became embroiled with Solomon ibn Hasson. Lev fought vigorously against the powerful and wealthy who oppressed the common people. Following his dispute with the Jewish tyrant Baruch of Salonika, his son David was murdered by hired assassins in 1545. His second son Moses drowned. These events and the hostile attitude of his opponents caused him to move in 1550 to Constantinople, where he remained until his death. There he was appointed teacher in the yeshivah founded by Doña Gracia (Mendes) *Nasi. In 1556 he was taken ill and from 1561 was unable to continue regular teaching in the yeshivah. At the instigation of Gracia and Joseph Nasi, in retaliation for the adverse stand of Pope *Paul IV against the Marranos of Ancona, Lev compiled a responsum in which he supported the banning of trade with Ancona and the taking of reprisals against the papal kingdom, in contrast to Joshua Soncino, one of the opponents of the ban.

Lev at first planned the compilation of a work in the manner of the *Beit Yosef* of Joseph *Caro. When in 1551 the *Beit Yosef* was published, he forbade its use out of fear that it would lead to a decrease in the study of the Talmud. However, when on one occasion he could not remember one of the sources of the *Arba'ah Turim* and found it in the *Beit Yosef*, he changed his attitude and realized the value of the work. His responsa, in four parts, were first published separately but then together in Amsterdam in 1726. A new edition of the responsa in two volumes appeared in Jerusalem in 1959/60. Lev attributes many glosses to his son David out of a desire to perpetuate his memory, but it is probable that he himself was the author of most of them. He was highly thought of by contemporary scholars.

BIBLIOGRAPHY: S.M. Chones, *Toledot ha-Posekim* (1929), 560; C. Tchernowitz, *Toledot ha-Posekim*, 2 (1947), 220; 3 (1948), 35; I.S. Emmanuel, *Histoire des Israélites de Salonique* (1936), 151–64, 219; Rosanes, Togarmah, 2 (1938), 77–78, 80, 82, 89–91; M.S. Goodblatt, *Jewish Life in Turkey in the 16th Century* (1952), 18, 92–93; I. Sonne, *Mi-Paulus ha-Revi'i ad Pius ha-Ḥamishi* (1954), 146, 148, 155, 158; M. Molcho, *Salonika, Ir va-Em be-Yisrael* (1967), 13; idem, in: *Sinai*, 48 (1961), 290–8; S. Assaf, *ibid.*, 1 (1937), 7; A. Danon, in: REJ, 41 (1900), 102–3.

[Yehoshua Horowitz]

LÉVAI, JENÖ (1892–?), Hungarian journalist who pursued research on the Holocaust of Hungarian Jewry. Lévai was born in Budapest and studied engineering, but even in his youth was attracted to journalism. Between the two World Wars he waged a fierce struggle in the press against antisemitism in Hungary, particularly against László *Endre, who later cooperated with Adolf *Eichmann. After World War II he was commissioned by the new government of Hungary to collect material on the persecution of the Jews under the previous regime. From that time he devoted himself entirely to this subject, publishing books and articles which revealed new information on the anti-Jewish activities of the Hungarian and German Nazis, his research taking him to different countries of Europe.

His works include *Black Book on the Martyrdom of Hungarian Jewry* (1948), and *Eichmann in Hungary: Documents* (1961).

[Yehouda Marton]

LEVAILLANT, ISAÏE (1845–1911), French civil servant and publicist, born in Hegenheim, Alsace. After the Franco-Prussian war of 1870–71, Levaillant founded a Republican newspaper in Nevers and filled various administrative posts under Gambetta. In 1885 he was appointed head of the Sureté Générale at the Ministry of the Interior. He was dismissed for his pro-*Dreyfus sympathies and subsequently wrote his own defense, *Ma Justification* (1895). After this, he devoted himself to combating antisemitism, chiefly through his editorials in *L'Univers Israélite*, which he edited until 1905. When the separation of Church and State in France (1906) made it necessary to revise the organizational structure of French Jewry, Levaillant drew up the new statute. His writings include *La genèse de l'antisémitisme sous la Troisième République* (1907).

BIBLIOGRAPHY: *L'Univers Israélite*, 67 (1911/12), 229–39; AI, 72 (1911), 340f., 348.

LEVANDA, LEV OSIPOVICH (1835–1888), Russian author and publicist. Born of a very poor family in Minsk, Levanda studied in a *ḥeder*, a modernized Jewish school, a government school for Jewish children, and finally at the rabbinical school in Vilna (1850–54), from which he graduated as a teacher. From 1854 to 1860 he taught at a government Jewish school in Minsk, and in 1860 he became the Jewish expert (*uchony yevrey*) to the governor-general of Vilna, remaining in this office for the rest of his life. Altogether he spent 32 years in Vilna, a period that he resented as a frustration of his aspirations. He wanted to go to St. Petersburg to study at the university, and to advance in his intellectual life and literary activity. However, he made no resolute move in this direction, and remained a provincial correspondent of publications issued in the capital, and his activities were of local scope. Yet his literary work made him a leading figure in the circles of the Russian-Jewish intelligentsia.

Levanda had a wide acquaintance with Russian and Western literature. He made several trips abroad, and knew

Western conditions, including Jewish life in the West from personal observation. Levanda was a sensitive, perspicacious observer, reserved in his contacts with people. His struggles and sufferings, his strong reactions to various aspects of Jewish life, and his passionate idealism brought about a growing nervous tension which made an invalid out of him in the last two years of his life; he died in a mental sanatorium in St. Petersburg.

Levanda lived during three periods of Russian Jewish history. He grew up under the extreme autocracy and military bureaucracy of *Nicholas I (1825–55), which is reflected in his reminiscences of the "schoolophobia" campaign against modern schools, and was one of the young hotheads of *maskil* progressivism. During the early years of *Alexander II's reign (1855–65) – "years of great reforms" and initial liberalization – feelings of great expectations of general betterment and, in particular, of rapid improvement in the position of Russian Jewry and of their ultimate integration into Russian society with civic equality were common. During this period Levanda became a government official. He was also a sometime editor of *Vilenskiy Vestnik* and a contributor to *Razsvet* (1860–61), the first Russian Jewish journal, presenting in articles and in fiction the critique of inner aspects of Jewish life: poverty, parasitism, the role of women storekeepers with the resulting neglect of children, excessive pursuit of talmudic studies, negative role of rich and retrograde communal leaders, marriages imposed by parents, and other problems. He assisted in unraveling an incipient *blood libel at *Siauliai in 1886. He developed a concept of the Jews in northwest Russia (Lithuania-Belorussia) as prospective carriers of Russian culture and citizenship as against Polish aspirations in the region; the Jews were to become Russians except for their religion (*sliyaniye*). The issue was particularly acute during the Polish insurrection of 1863. Later, he expressed this mood in a novel, *Goryacheye Vremya* (1875), in which young Westernized Jews were urged by the hero, Sarin, to abandon Polish orientation (after 500 years of unhappy experience with the Poles) and become Russians.

Levanda unhappily had to witness the growing reaction in Russia and the rise of modern antisemitism in the West and its adoption in Russia. He worried about the concentration of Jews in middleman occupations and professions; he urged economic productivization and diversification, and less ostentatiousness on the part of the wealthy. He deplored the fact that Jews had all the obligations, but almost none of the rights, of Russians, and, indeed, suffered from specific restrictions. The Jews wanted a fatherland, and Russia might stand to gain by becoming one (*Voskhod*, February 1881).

In this period he was primarily a writer of fiction, bitterly denouncing the nouveaux riches (bankers, industrialists, speculators) and the new diploma-intelligentsia crowd with its careerism and greed; he berated the alienation and aloofness of these groups from Jewish interests.

The final stage in the development of his views took place during the wave of pogroms in the early 1880s. Deeply disturbed, he attacked the rich Jews, feeling that the events were really directed against them and that their turn might yet come. He was opposed to the anti-migration stand of the upper class and considered emigration a normal and sound response. He also called for *self-defense. Moving toward agreement with Leon *Pinsker's auto-emancipation, he then joined the ranks of *Ḥovevei Zion as one of their leading figures in literature, propaganda, and organization. Representing Jewish nationalism in an age of national revival and politics, he saw no contradiction between Jewish nationalism and the ideal of a monolithic humanity.

In private correspondence he pointed out that despite his apparent transition from cosmopolitan assimilation to nationalism he had been basically a devoted Jewish patriot who never conceived the dissolution of Jewish group existence or of cultural extinction (Russification being far from assimilation), and to whom the needs of the Jewish masses were always the point of departure. When the pro-Russian hero of his novel is asked, "And what if the Russians do not respond to your aspirations?" he answers, "Then we shall have to reconsider." Levanda wrote later that he clearly remembered that while writing this he had the first glimpse of modern Jewish nationalism.

In the Ḥibbat Zion movement, he considered the awakening of the Jewish masses in Russia, land acquisition in Ereẓ Israel, and entrenchment of Jews on the soil as main tasks. He was against overestimating the value and the claims of the youth movement (e.g., *Bilu), and while opposed to the philanthropic trend, he expected more from middle-class efforts. He sought to counteract Pinsker's tendency to become discouraged, and, unlike Pinsker, did not expect Western Jewry to take a leading role in the movement. He felt that the position of the Jew was dangerously deteriorating. In the past, the Jew had been confronted with an unfavorable law, but now the elemental lawlessness of a violent mob threatened the very life and safety of the Jew. The hope to reeducate these forces was illusory; the safe thing was to avoid the onslaught. Jews must get soil under their feet. Their national culture too would have a normal development once this soil was secured.

Thus Levanda stands out as a reflector and guide of the Haskalah, assimilationism, and nationalism – three stages in the development of the social-political ideology of the intelligentsia, as it abandons traditional messianism and searches for a fatherland to which its energies could be harnessed. As a creative writer, he was gifted and witty in feuilletons, sketches, and in drawing the ethnographic canvas, but he lacked the mastery of characterization and could not develop into a substantial, original artist. In his final years he turned to historical fiction, novels based on the pre-modern history of East European Jewry.

[Mark Perlman]

His brother VITALI OSIPOVICH LEVANDA (b. 1840), a Russian lawyer, was born in Minsk, Belorussia. His study on the question of Jewish agriculture in Russia (in *Yevreyskaya*

Biblioteka, vol. 2, 1872) was well received. On the recommendation of Baron H. *Guenzburg, he compiled and published in 1874 his *Polny khronologicheskiy sbornik zakonov*… ("Complete Chronological Collection of Laws and Regulations Concerning Jews from the Time of Czar Alexei Mikhailovich to the Present, 1649–1873"), a valuable guide to the legislation affecting Jews in Russia. He also wrote articles in the periodical *Russkiy Yevrey* on the development of agriculture among the Jews in Russia; he opposed immigration to Ereẓ Israel (in *Razsvet*, no. 40, 1881).

BIBLIOGRAPHY: WORKS: L.O. Levanda's works are listed in *Sistematicheskiy ukazatel literatury o yevreyakh* (1893). Most appeared in *Razsvet* (1860, 1879–81), *Yevreyskaya Biblioteka, Voskhod* (monthly and weekly), *Russkiy Yevrey*, and *Palestina*. Many were reprinted and translated into Hebrew and Yiddish. GENERAL: S.L. Ẓitron, *Anashim ve-Soferim* (1921), 69–92; idem, in: *Leksikon Ẓiyyoni* (1924), 297–312; S.M. Ginzburg, in: *Minuvsheye* (1923). MEMOIRS: L. Kantor, in: *Ha-Shilo'aḥ*, 1 (1896/97), 255–62; Mordekhai ben Hillel Ha-Kohen, *Olami*, 1–2 (1927); S.M. Ginzburg, in: E.H. Jeshurin (ed.), *Vilne* (1935), 466–71; J.L. Appel, *Betokh Reshit ha-Teḥiyyah* (1936). CORRESPONDENCE, DOCUMENTS: S.M. Ginzburg, in: *Perezhitoye*, 1 (1908), 36–7; A. Druyanov, in: *Yevreyskaya Starina*, 5 (1913), 279–281; idem, in: *Ketavim le-Toledot Ḥibbat Ẓiyyon* (1919–32); N.A. Buchbinder, *Literaturnye Etyudi* (1927), 5–49; M. Perlmann, in: PAAJR, 35 (1967). IDEOLOGY: B.A. Goldberg, *Lev Levanda kak publitsist* (1900); A. Idelson, in: *Razsvet*, 12 (1913); S. Breiman, in: *Shivat Ẓiyyon*, 2–3 (1951–52), 177–205; I. Klausner, *Be-Hitorer Am* (1962); idem, *Mi-Kattowitz ad Basel* (1965). THE WRITER: P. Lazarev, in: *Voskhod* (1885); A. Volynski, in: *Voskhod* (1888–89).

LEVANON, MORDECAI (1901–1968), Israel painter. He was born in Transylvania and in 1921 went to Palestine where he worked for a year as an agricultural laborer. From 1922 he studied painting in Jerusalem and Tel Aviv. He moved to Jerusalem in 1939 but from 1963 worked also in his Safed studio.

Levanon, primarily a landscapist, remained faithful to the expressionist concept so widespread in Palestinian art. He brought to this his own individual vision and his work reveals his European background. In his paintings of Jerusalem, Lake Kinneret, and Safed there is an intermingling of mystery and grandeur.

[Yona Fischer]

LEVANT, OSCAR (1906–1972), U.S. composer, pianist, and actor. Levant was born in Pittsburgh, Penn., to Orthodox Russian parents. His father, a watchmaker, ran a jewelry store out of their home while his mother helped her four sons study music. Levant's talent for the piano was recognized early on. At 12, he went to see the Broadway show *Ladies First*, conducted by his uncle Oscar Radin and featuring pianist George *Gershwin. Inspired by the show, he began composing his own music. Levant dropped out of school and moved to New York, where he studied under Sigismund Stojowski and performed at nightclubs, speakeasies, and the Winter Garden Theater, where his brother Harry played. When Gershwin's *Rhapsody in Blue* debuted in 1924, Levant learned the piece and became the first pianist other than Gershwin to record it. Levant convinced a friend to introduce him to Gershwin, which began a tumultuous friendship. Levant was insecure about his talent but was driven to best Gershwin; competition and mutual regard were the cornerstones of their connection. Levant went to England in 1926 to perform and record with saxophonist Rudy Wiedoeft. In 1927, his part as a pianist in the Broadway show *Burlesque* landed him a part in the Hollywood adaptation, *The Dance of Life* (1929). In 1935 Levant returned to Hollywood to score films while studying under composer Arnold *Schoenberg. When Gershwin died in 1937, Levant was called upon to play *Concert in F* at the Hollywood Bowl for the Gershwin Memorial Concert. In 1938, he returned to New York, where he conducted the Broadway shows *The Fabulous Invalid* and *The American Way*. In 1940, he released his best-selling book *A Smattering of Ignorance*. He returned to acting in *Rhythm on the River* (1940), *Kiss the Boys Goodbye* (1941), *Rhapsody in Blue* (1944), *Humoresque* (1947), and *Romance on the High Seas* (1948). He moved to Beverly Hills in 1947 and performed for President Harry S. Truman at the White House that year and in 1950. He played *Concerto in F* for *An American in Paris* (1951), but a hectic performance schedule and a resulting addiction to painkillers led to a heart attack in 1952. In 1958, his quick wit as a guest landed him his own television talk show, *The Oscar Levant Show*, but depression and a battle with Demerol took its toll and the show's popularity waned after two years. After appearances on *The Jack Paar Show* in 1961, Levant became a recluse.

BIBLIOGRAPHY: Grove online; S. Kashner and N. Schoenberger, *A Talent for Genius: The Life and Times of Oscar Levant* (1994).

[Adam Wills (2nd ed.)]

LEVEEN, JACOB (1891–1980), librarian and author. Born in Jerusalem, Leveen studied in England and worked for many years in the Department of Oriental Books and Manuscripts of the British Museum, from 1953–56 as keeper. He was responsible for part 4 of the *Catalogue of Hebrew and Samaritan Manuscripts in the British Museum* (1935). His *Hebrew Bible in Art* (1944, the British Academy's Schweich lectures, 1939) was a pioneer study in this field. Leveen also published a facsimile edition of a unique British Museum manuscript of Zechariah b. Judah Aghmati's digest of commentaries on the three Bava tractates of the Babylonian Talmud (1961). He prepared the second part of a catalog of Hebrew manuscripts in the Cambridge University Library (unpublished).

LEVEN, NARCISSE (1833–1915), French philanthropist and public figure. Leven was born in Germany, and his family settled in Paris during his childhood. In 1855 he graduated from the Sorbonne in law. A staunch republican, Leven acted as secretary to Adolphe *Crémieux, minister of justice during the Franco-Prussian War (1870/71). After the war he practiced law, and in 1879 was elected member of the Paris municipal council and was its vice president in 1882. However, he was defeated in the elections in 1887, as a result of an antisemitic campaign directed personally against him. Leven had been deeply stirred as a child by the *Damascus affair (1840) and later by the *Mortara case (1858). This influenced him to found the *Alliance Israélite Universelle, together with Charles *Netter, Jules *Carvallo, and others. He was successively secretary, vice president, and, from 1898 until his death, president of the Alliance central committee. Together with Zadoc *Kahn, Leven also assisted Baron de *Hirsch in formulating his colonization plans and was the first to preside over the council of the *Jewish Colonization Association (ICA). Leven was a member of the Central Consistory of French Jews for over 50 years. He wrote *Cinquante ans d'histoire: l'Alliance Israélite Universelle, 1860–1910* (vol. 1, 1911; vol. 2, 1920, posthumous).

BIBLIOGRAPHY: J.P. Coulon, *Narcisse Leven* (Fr., 1920); A. Chouraqui, *L'Alliance Israélite Universelle* (1965), index.

[Emmanuel Beeri]

LEVENE, SIR PETER (Keith), BARON LEVENE OF PORTSOKEN (1941–), British businessman, civil servant, and lord mayor. Levene was managing director of United Scientific Holdings Ltd. from 1968 to 1985 before joining the administrative civil service as chief of defense procurement in the Ministry of Defense from 1985 to 1991. He then became chairman of Canary Wharf Ltd., the vast redevelopment of London's derelict Docklands area and, in 1998–99, was lord mayor of London. He was knighted in 1989 and received a life peerage in 1997.

[William D. Rubinstein (2nd ed.)]

LEVENE, PHOEBUS AARON THEODOR (1869–1940), U.S. biochemist. Born in Sagor, Russia, as Fishel Aaronovich Levin, he immigrated to New York in 1892, and practiced medicine there till 1896. At the same time he studied chemistry at Columbia University and carried out research in the department of physiology. He worked at the Pathological Institute of the New York State Hospitals (1902–05). He joined the newly formed Rockefeller Institute for Medical Research, where he worked for the rest of his life, from 1907 in charge of the Chemistry Division.

His main contribution was in the structural chemistry of nucleic acids, and the isolation of the two sugars (then unknown) which characterize them – D-ribose and its 2-deoxy derivative. His work embraced all classes of tissue constituents, especially proteins and sugar phosphates; in the latter connection he did a great deal of work on fundamental carbohydrate chemistry. He was a pioneer in numerous aspects of biochemistry.

BIBLIOGRAPHY: D.D. Van Slyke and W.A. Jacobs, in: National Academy of Sciences of the U.S.A. *Biographical Memoirs*, 23 (1944), 75–126; Tipson, in: *Advances in Carbohydrate Chemistry*, 12 (1957), 1–12; E. Farber (ed.), *Great Chemists* (1961), 1313–24.

[Samuel Aaron Miller]

LEVENE, SAM (1905–1980), U.S. actor. Born in Russia, Levene became widely known for his role of Nathan Detroit in the Broadway musical *Guys and Dolls* (1950). He appeared on Broadway in plays as diverse as *The Matchmaker* (1954); *Make a Million* (1958); *Heartbreak House* (1959); *The Devil's Advocate* (Tony nomination for Best Actor, 1961); Saul Bellow's *The Last Analysis* (1964); *The Impossible Years* (1967); *Three Men on a Horse* (1969); *Paris Is Out* (1970); *The Sunshine Boys* (1972); *The Royal Family* (1976); and *Horowitz and Mrs. Washington* (1980).

His films include *Three Men on a Horse* (1936); *Room Service* (1938); *Dinner at Eight* (1933); *Golden Boy* (1939); *Shadow of the Thin Man* (1941); *The Big Street* (1942); *Action in the North Atlantic* (1943); *The Purple Heart* (1944); *The Killers* (1946); *Brute Force* (1947); *Crossfire* (1947); *The Babe Ruth Story* (1948); *Designing Woman* (1957); *Sweet Smell of Success* (1957); *A Farewell to Arms* (1957); the TV movie *The World of Sholom Aleichem* (1959); *Act One* (1963); *Such Good Friends* (1971); *Last Embrace* (1979); and *And Justice for All* (1979).

[Ruth Beloff (2nd ed.)]

LEVENSON, JON D. (1949–), U.S. scholar of Bible and Midrash. Levenson was born in Wheeling, West Virginia, where he completed his secondary school education at Linsley Military Institute in 1967. He received his B.A. in English at Harvard College in 1971, and his M.A. and Ph.D. degrees from Harvard University in 1967 and 1971, concentrating in Hebrew Bible and Northwest Semitics. Following several years of teaching religion and biblical studies at Wellesley College (1975–82), he taught as associate professor of Hebrew Bible in the Divinity School, the University of Chicago (1982–86), as associate professor of Hebrew Bible in the Divinity School and in the Committee on General Studies in the Humanities, the University of Chicago (1986–88), and as professor of Hebrew Bible in the Divinity School and in the Committee on General Studies in the Humanities, the University of Chicago (1988). He served as the Albert A. List Professor of Jewish Studies at the Divinity School, Harvard University from 1988 and was also professor of Near Eastern Languages and Civilizations.

Levenson's major contribution to the field of biblical studies is the reinterpretation of texts in the Hebrew Bible and its redaction in Second Temple Judaism, including rabbinic Midrash. In several of his books, he hinges the disparity between classical and contemporary Jewish and Christian biblical interpretation on the plain-sense exegesis of scriptural passages, and negates strongly the whims and wiles of Christian supersessionist reading.

Levenson tackles the ubiquitous question of how to reconcile the goodness of God in the face of evil in *Creation and the Persistence of Evil: The Jewish Drama of Divine Omnipotence* (1988). A revised collection of six previously published book chapters and journal essays are found in *The Hebrew Bible, the Old Testament, and Historical Criticism: Jews and Christians in Biblical Studies* (1993); Levinson also wrote an introduction and line by line commentary on the book of Esther in *Esther: A Commentary* (1997), which presents an analysis of the book's structure and themes, discusses the historicity and origins of textual variants, and underscores the politics and perplexed theology of this nationalistic book of the Hebrew (and Christian) canon. His other writings include *The Book of Job in Its Time and in the Twentieth Century* (1971); *Traditions in Transformation: Turning Points in Biblical Faith* (1981, edited with Baruch Halpern); and *Resurrection and the Restoration of Israel: The Ultimate Victory of the God of Life* (New Haven, 2006).

Additionally, Levenson has published many scholarly articles that range from the theologies of commandment in biblical Israel to introduction and annotations to Genesis in *The Jewish Study Bible* (2004). His approach to biblical studies is to avoid uncritical traditionalism, historicism, and positivism. By maintaining a transcendent-historical voice in arcane biblical texts, his methodology "entails a dialectical movement between synchronic and diachronic reading, and between the ancient Near Eastern world and the world of Late Antiquity in which Judaism as we know it took shape."

[Zev Garber (2nd ed.)]

LEVENSON, JOSEPH RICHMOND (1920–1969), U.S. specialist in Chinese history. Born in Boston, he served as a Japanese-language officer in the U.S. Navy during World War II. In 1953 Levenson was appointed professor of history at the University of California (Berkeley). Levenson's research was primarily in the field of Chinese intellectual history. His foremost contribution to scholarship was the trilogy *Confucian China and Its Modern Fate*, consisting of *The Problem of Intellectual Continuity* (1958); *The Monarchical Decay* (1964); and *The Problem of Historical Significance* (1965). Levenson served as a director of Congregation Beth Israel in Berkeley.

LEVENSON, SAM(UEL) (1911–1980), U.S. humorist. Born in Russia, Levinson was a high school teacher from 1934 to 1946 in Brooklyn. Subsequently he gained a reputation as a humorist reciting stories about his childhood on New York's Lower East Side. He was particularly popular in the Catskill Mountains ("the Borscht Belt") and Miami Beach. He also gave comic lectures to a variety of schools and social groups. In 1949 he appeared on the Ed Sullivan television show *Toast of the Town* and became widely known for his folksy humor. Levenson was one of the first comedians to fill his stand-up act with heartwarming anecdotes and homespun stories of neighborhood life. A frequent guest on the Sullivan show, he also appeared on many panel-game shows, such as *To Tell the Truth* and *What's My Line?* In the 1950s and 1960s he hosted *The Price Is Right, The Sam Levenson Show, This Is Show Business, Two for the Money, Masquerade Party,* and *Celebrity Talent Scouts.* In 1971 he made four appearances on the highly rated late-night talk show *The Tonight Show with Johnny Carson.*

His book *Everything but Money* (1966) describes his experiences growing up in New York. He also wrote *Meet the Folks* (1948), *Sex and the Single Child* (1969), *In One Era and Out the Other* (1973), *You Can Say That Again, Sam!* (1975), and *You Don't Have to Be in Who's Who to Know What's What* (1979).

[Ruth Beloff (2nd ed.)]

LEVER, (Norman) HAROLD, BARON LEVER OF MANCHESTER (1914–1995), British politician and financial expert. Born in Manchester, Lever practiced as a barrister for several years before entering the House of Commons as a Labour member in 1950. He remained a member of the House of Commons until 1979. He sponsored the Defamation Act of 1952 as a private member's bill and acquired a considerable reputation as an authority on financial matters. In 1967 he was appointed parliamentary under-secretary for economic affairs, later in the same year was promoted to the post of financial secretary to the Treasury, and finally paymaster general, with a seat in the Cabinet, as second minister in charge of the Ministry of Technology (until the Labour Party went out of office in 1970). Lever represented the United Kingdom at the International Monetary Fund and European "Group of Ten" financial conferences which considered the world currency crises of 1968. In 1969–70 Lever served as paymaster-general, with a seat in the Cabinet. From 1974 to 1979 Lever was chancellor of the Duchy of Lancaster in the Labour government, acting as adviser to the prime minister on economic and financial policy with membership in all cabinet committees concerned with economy. As one of the few Labour MPs regarded as an expert on finance, Lever was much respected for his detailed knowledge and moderation. Though not prominent in any specific communal institution, he worked unofficially for many Jewish and Zionist causes. In 1979 he was given a life peerage as Lord Lever of Manchester.

His brother, LESLIE LEVER, BARON LEVER (1905–1977), sat in the House of Commons from 1950 to 1974 and was lord mayor of Manchester in 1957–58. He was given a life peerage in 1975. Lever was active in Jewish affairs as president of the Manchester and Salford Jewish Council and vice president of the Board of Guardians.

ADD. BIBLIOGRAPHY: ODNB online.

[Vivian David Lipman / William D. Rubinstein (2nd ed.)]

LEVERSON, ADA (1865–1936), English novelist. A member of the *Beddington family, Ada Leverson was of Marrano descent. At 19 she married Ernest Leverson, the son of a diamond merchant; their unsuccessful marriage ended in separation. In addition to novels she wrote many occasional pieces for periodicals, including the humorous weekly, *Punch.* Her salon was frequented by the leaders of the "nineties" movement, such as Aubrey Beardsley, Oscar Wilde, and Walter Sickert, and she contributed stories to *The Yellow Book.* She remained a loyal friend to Oscar Wilde, and took him into her home between his trials. Ada Leverson's six novels, beginning with *The Twelfth Hour*, were published between 1907 and 1916. They are credited with influencing later writers such as Evelyn Waugh. The diverting conversation of Ada Leverson's characters, often uninterrupted by description, owes much to her love of the theater. Always urbane and gently ironic about the relations between husband and wife, she held strong moral views about loyalty in marriage. Her forte was high comedy and she was a penetrating satirist of the manners of her time.

In her later years, she was a close friend of the Sitwells. There was a considerable revival of interest in her life and works in the late 20th century.

BIBLIOGRAPHY: A. Leverson, *Little Ottleys* (1962), foreword by C. McInnes; O. Sitwell, *Noble Essences* (1950), 127–62; V. Wyndham, *Sphinx and her Circle* (1962). **ADD. BIBLIOGRAPHY:** ODNB online; J. Speedie, *Wonderful Sphinx: The Biography of Ada Leverson* (1993); V. Wyndham, *The Sphinx and Her Circle: A Biographical Sketch of Ada Leverson, 1862–1933* (1963).

[Renee Winegarten]

LEVERTIN, OSCAR IVAR (1862–1906), Swedish poet and literary critic, the first Jew to gain eminence in Swedish literature. Levertin, the son of a Stockholm antiquarian, was born in Gryt, near Norrköping. In his student days at the University of Uppsala (where he was a pupil of Johan Henrik *Schück), he joined the literary circle of "Young Sweden." In 1899 he became professor of literature at the Academy (now the University) of Stockholm. As a poet, Levertin was distinguished by his aestheticism and his sophisticated preoccupation with aims and moods. Emotionally drawn to romanticism, he was intellectually a determinist, and the personal struggle engendered by this conflict became the *leitmotiv* of his poetry. He was thus closer to the English Pre-Raphaelites and the French symbolists than to writers of the contemporary Swedish school. His most characteristic verse appears in *Legender och visor* ("Legends and Songs," 1891), which contains a number of poems on Jewish themes. Two other collections were *Nya dikter* ("New Poems," 1894) and *Dikter* ("Poems," 1901). As a critic, Levertin displayed sensitivity, learning, and cultural awareness. In 1897 he joined the reorganized *Svenska Dagbladet*, gaining new fame as the newspaper's principal literary critic. Together with Carl Gustav Verner von Heidenstam, a leader of the Swedish anti-naturalist movement, he formulated a literary program to which he adhered in his own writing.

Levertin's many prose works include novels, novellas, and essays. *Rococo-noveller* ("Rococo Stories," 1899), a collection of pastiches, recreated the courtly 18th-century world of King Gustav III. One of the most beautiful of these tales, *Kalonymos*, describes a Passover celebration in Stockholm, the central character expressing something of the writer's own skeptical humanism. As a young man in 1880, Levertin had published a poem denouncing antisemitism. Though thoroughly Swedish in his tastes and sympathies (his family had settled in the country in the late 18th century) he remained a conscious Jew, emotionally and historically bound to his people and never quite at home in his Scandinavian environment. For many years he suffered from a lung disease, and he became increasingly obsessed with death and religious problems. His last major work was the verse cycle *Kung Salomo och Morolf* ("King Solomon and Morolf," 1905), whose themes derived from Jewish, Oriental, and medieval sources. His other publications include the novella *Konflikter* (1885), *Diktare och drömmare* (1898), *Teater och drama under Gustav III* (1889), and *Svenska gestalter* (1903). His collected works appeared in 24 volumes (1907–11).

BIBLIOGRAPHY: W. Söderhjelm, *Oskar Levertin*, 2 vols. (Swedish, 1914–17); O. Mendelsohn, *Jödiske innslag i Oskar Levertins diktning* (1938); C. Fehrman, *Levertins lyrik* (1945); *Svenskt litteraturlexikon* (1964), s.v.; A. Levertin (ed.), *Den unge Levertin* (1947); B. Julin, *Hjärtats landsflykt* (1962).

[Hugo Mauritz Valentin]

LEVERTOFF, PAUL PHILIP (1878–1954), apostate and theologian. Levertoff, who was born in Orsha, Belorussia, into a ḥasidic family, was converted to Christianity in 1895. After studying theology in Russian and German universities, traveling in Europe, Palestine, and Asia Minor, and working for a time in Warsaw and as professor of Old Testament and rabbinics at the Institutum Delitzschianum in Leipzig (1912–18), he was appointed librarian and sub-warden of St. Deiniols Library, Hawarden (Wales; 1919–22). From 1922 until his death, he was director of the London Diocesan Council for work among the Jews (formerly The East London Fund for the Jews) and edited its quarterly journal, *The Church and the Jews*. He also took a leading part in the Hebrew Christian movement, translated considerable parts of the Anglican liturgy into Hebrew, and conducted Christian services partly in Hebrew at the North West London church where he was minister. Levertoff was a prolific writer on liturgical and theological subjects in Hebrew, German, and English. He contributed to periodicals and encyclopedias, translated the Midrash Sifre on Numbers (1926), and cooperated with H. Sperling in the translation of the Zohar into English (1933).

[Ruth P. Lehmann]

LEVERTOV, DENISE (1923–1997), U.S./British poet and essayist. Levertov was born in England of Russian-Jewish and Welsh parents, and her life and writings reflect her paradoxical nature. She was greatly influenced by her Russian-born expatriate father, Paul Levertoff, a descendant of *Shneur Zalman of Lyady (founder of the Chabad movement) who, while studying for the rabbinate, converted to Anglicanism. Her parents later became passionately involved in helping refugees escape from Austria and Germany. Her Welsh mother, Beatrice Spooner-Jones, was a teacher, singer, painter, and writer. Denise's parents and sister Olga, nine years her senior, would read aloud to her the poems of Tennyson, Keats, Wordsworth, Donne, and Herbert as well as the Bible. Although Levertov never attended school, she taught poetry in many American universities, and received eight honorary doctorates.

Levertov began writing poetry at the age of five, knew her future vocation by age 10, and sent her poems to T.S. Eliot at age 12. From 12 on, she received lessons in ballet, piano, French, and art. During World War II she served as a civilian nurse during the London Blitz. Her first book of poetry, *The Double Image*, was published in 1946. She married American writer Mitchell Goodman in 1947, immigrated to the United States in 1948, gave birth to her only child, Nikolai, and, in 1955 became a naturalized citizen.

Her poetic style continued to develop with the literary influences of William Carlos Williams, the Old Testament, Book of Psalms, Song of Songs, Buber's *Tales of the Hasidim*, H.D., Rilke, Robert Creeley, Robert Duncan, and Charles Olson of the Black Mountain School. Although her writing styles and themes have been described as free verse, non-metrical, psychological, organic, lyrical, objectivist, allegorical, mystical, mythical, and spiritual, Levertov dismisses these labels and calls her works a "mishmash."

In the title poem of her fifth book, *Jacob's Ladder* (1958), Levertov achieves poetic maturity. In an interview she reveals, "I do think arguing with God (or God wrestling) is a delightful Jewish characteristic." The true prophet must painfully climb a wall of doubt as is expressed in the lines "behind the sky is a doubtful, a doubting night gray" and "a man must scrape his knees" in the joining of the poet's mystical ascendance with earthly concerns.

In "During the Eichmann Trial," also in *Jacob's Ladder*, Levertov asserts in section I of the poem, "When We Look Up," that Eichmann's banal exterior is part of evil's human condition. In the second part, "The Peachtree," Eichmann murders a young child, and Levertov metonymously indicts the whole world for failing to stop the Holocaust. In part III, "Crystal Night," she advocates that the hatefulness of racial differences must be replaced by empathy as a way to prevent future conflict.

Levertov's papers are housed in the Green Library at Stanford University, California.

BIBLIOGRAPHY: G. Pacernick, "Interview with Denise Levertov," and E. Sterling, "The Eye as Mirror of Humanity: Social Responsibility and the Nature of Evil in Denise Levertov's 'During the Eichmann Trial,'" in: *Denise Levertov: New Perspectives* (2000); *Marquis Who's Who on the Web* (2005); W. Doreski, *American Writers* (1991); L. Wagner-Martin, *Denise Levertov* (1967); L. Smith, "Songs of Experience: Denise Levertov's Political Poetry," in: *Contemporary Literature*, vol. 27, no. 2 (Summer 1986).

[David Koenigstein (2nd ed.)]

LEVEY, BARNETT (1798–1837), Australian pioneer of the theater. Levey's brother Solomon was sent to Australia as a convict in 1819 but became wealthy within a few years as a merchant. Barnett arrived as a free settler in 1821 and was given a land grant. In 1828 he built the Royal Hotel in Sydney and used part of it as a theater, where he himself often performed and sang. In 1833 he built the Theatre Royal, the first real theater in Australia. It was destroyed by fire in 1840, but the importance of his work was generally acknowledged, and the district where he lived was later named "Waverley" after the name of his house.

ADD. BIBLIOGRAPHY: J.S. Levi and G.F.J. Bergman, *Australian Genesis: Jewish Convicts and Settlers, 1788–1860* (2002 ed.), 111–23; H.L. Rubinstein, Australia I, 352; ADB.

LEVI (Heb. לֵוִי), third son of Jacob and Leah, born in Paddan-Aram (Gen. 29:34); father of the tribe named after him. The name Levi is explained in the Pentateuch by Leah's words at his birth: "Now this time my husband will become attached to me (Heb. *yillaweh*)."

The Man

In the affair of *Dinah (Gen. 34), Levi and Simeon took the chief part in the slaying of the men of Shechem and the plunder of their city, an act that aroused Jacob's anger against them (Gen. 34; cf. 49:5–7).

The sons of Levi were Gershon, Kohath, and Merari (Ex. 6:16), from whom stemmed the families of the tribe of Levi. Nothing further is recorded of Levi the man.

The Tribe

According to the censuses of the Levites in the wilderness which covered – exceptionally – "all the males from the age of one month up," Levi was the smallest tribe, comprising 22,000 or 23,000 males (Num. 3:39; 26:62). The tribe was singled out during the wanderings in the wilderness for the service of the tabernacle, carrying the Ark and attending to the duties of the sanctuary. Supervising them were descendants of their tribe, the *Aaronides (Num. 1:48–53; 3:5–40). The census of the Levites was conducted separately from the general census of the Israelites in the wilderness (Num. 1:47–49), and it is stated that they were chosen for their service "in place of all the firstborn among the Israelite people" (see *Firstborn), the number of the firstborn being practically identical with that of the Levites (3:40–43).

The story of the *golden calf emphasizes the loyalty of the tribe to Moses. In this affair, too, as in that of Dinah, the Levites stand out as men of zeal who do not spare brother, friend, or kin (Ex. 32:25–30). On the other hand, note should be taken of the rebellion of *Korah and his company, who were Levites, against Moses (Num. 16; the non-Levites in this pericope are followers of *Dathan and Abiram). A reflection of Levi's closeness to the tribe of Judah is to be found in the juxtaposition of the two in the Blessing of Moses (Deut. 33:7–9) as well as in the genealogy of the Levite youth from a Judahite family in Beth-Lehem (Judg. 17:7), and in the story of the Levite from the other end of the hill country of Mt. Ephraim who took a concubine from Beth-Lehem of Judah (19:1). These reports testify to this connection with Judah, as well as to the Levite's lack of a fixed territory, as stated in the Pentateuch (Num. 18:23b). The Levite youth from Beth-Lehem became a priest in the House of Micah on Mt. Ephraim, and Levite priests also served in Dan in the era of the Judges (Judg. 17:10–11; 18:19–30).

THE SERVICE. According to Numbers, the Levites were in attendance upon the priests in the service of the Tent of Meeting, carrying it and its appurtenances. This service was divided between the three families of the tribe – Gershon, Kohath, and Merari (Num. 3–4). The Levites were also entrusted with the task of serving the priests, performing duties for them and for "the whole community before the Tent of Meeting" (3:7). This apparently consisted of guarding the Tent and its furnishings against the laity. It was also their duty to provide a barrier between the tabernacle and the people (1:50–54; 18:22–3). In the course of their work, the Levites were subject to the priests appointed over them and they were not permitted to witness the dismantling of the sanctuary (4:20). The superiority of the Aaronide priests of the tribe of Levi to the Levites is expressly stressed in Exodus, Leviticus, and Numbers, and the division of functions between them is clearly defined (see *Priests and Levites). The Levites were also assigned instructional responsibilities, and it was they who bore the Ark of the Covenant (Deut. 10:8; 31:9), but these functions were primarily intended for the priests, the most select of the Levites (Mal. 2:4–8; 3:3). According to the view of Deuteronomy, all the Levites are fit to serve in the sanctuary, even such as do not have permanent duties in the sanctuary (Deut. 18:6–9). In return for their service they are entitled to receive *tithes (Num. 18:21).

This appointment of the Levites as ministers of God resulted in their becoming wanderers during the period of the Judges, without any permanent possession in the country. They are reckoned in the Bible among those needing support, such as the stranger, the orphan, and the widow. It seems that even at the time of the monarchy the Levites at the gates of the cities still did not possess their own territory but this is explained as a sign of a superior status: "the Lord is their portion" (10:9; 18:2).

MONARCHICAL PERIOD. Possibly, the Levites became state officials in the time of David and Solomon when the cult itself was transformed into an instrument for state influence. Chronicles relates a great deal about the high status of the Levites in the time of David, even in the administration of government (I Chron. 23–27). According to Chronicles, Levites were among those who came to transfer the monarchy to David at Hebron (I Chron. 12:27), and their loyalty to the kings of the dynasty of David continued until the destruction of the Temple (II Chron. 23:2–9, 18–19; 24:5–15, et al.). The story of the migration of the Levites from Israel to Judah after the division of the kingdom may reflect a real historical situation that is alluded to in Kings (I Kings 12:31; 13:33; cf. II Chron. 11:13–17; 13:9–12). According to I Chronicles, the Levites took a leading part as overseers in the work of the House of the Lord (23:4), as choristers, musicians, gatekeepers, and guardians of the threshold (9:14–33). Among the choristers mentioned are Heman, Asaph, and Jeduthun, who are also referred to in Psalms. The sons of Korah are also connected with psalmody (cf. Ps. 42:1; 44:1; et al.) and are so mentioned incidentally in II Chronicles 20:19, though they are mostly reckoned in this source among the gatekeepers. The Levites also functioned as officials, judges, craftsmen for the Temple service, supervisors of the chambers and the courts, overseers of the Temple treasuries, and officers in charge of the royal service (I Chron. 9:22, 26–27; 23:4, 28; et al.). The special status of the Levites in the time of Jehoshaphat as disseminators of the Torah and as judges in the towns of Judah and in Jerusalem is understandable in the light of the above (II Chron. 19:8, 11). It would also seem possible from many passages that the Levites mainly ministered alongside the priests, and that the priests were appointed over them (I Chron. 6:31ff.; 23:27–32; et al.). Hence, it seems that in the time of the First Temple the demarcation between Levites and priests was not clearly preserved, and that even among the Levites themselves there existed a certain grading.

The incorporation of the Levites into the monarchical system of Israel found its expression in the setting aside of special towns from the territories of the tribes as levitical towns of residence. According to Numbers (35:1–8), the Israelites were commanded, while still in the plains of Moab, to set aside 48 towns from their territory for the Levites (see *Levitical Cities). In Joshua 21, lists are cited which apparently originated in the same tradition, and current research inclines to regard them as a reflection of a real situation that existed at the time of the First Temple. There is no contradiction between the principle of no territory and the allocation of towns of residence, since these were merely towns and fields for the raising of cattle without agricultural settlement. The houses in the levitical towns were regarded as a substitute for territory, and the laws of the *Jubilee applied to them as to land, in contrast to dwellings in walled cities. Their adaptation to a monarchical regime brought about the fact that the priests did not forbid themselves the ownership of agricultural land too (I Kings 2:26; Jer. 32:7–16; et al.). However, the principle remained in force for many generations, so that even Ezekiel, who says that in the time to come the Levites will no longer be scattered throughout the country but gathered into Jerusalem, outlines for them an area beside the Temple (Ezek. 45:4–5; 48:11–15).

From the time of the return to Zion the boundaries between priests and Levites were firmly established. The Levites acquired an honored status, and even their small number in comparison with that of priests (Ezra 2:40–42) added to their importance in the eyes of the people. In the time of Ezra and Nehemiah it was necessary to bring Levites to Jerusalem from the exile and from the rural towns. From this time on the division between priests and Levites remained permanent.

Concerning the special status of the Levites as well as their functions, see also *Priests and Priesthood.

[Samuel Abramsky]

In the *Aggadah*

Rabbinical *aggadah* greatly expanded the biblical material, sometimes to Levi's detriment, but more frequently it reversed the picture. At the births of Simeon and Levi, Leah prophesied that Simeon would produce an enemy of God (Zimri), but from Levi would come Phinehas and heal the wound inflicted through Zimri (Gen. R. 71:4). The proposal to kill Joseph (Gen. 37:20) came from Simeon and Levi and it was they who sold him. When the brothers came to Egypt, Joseph separated them by imprisoning Simeon (Gen. 42:24), for together they would have destroyed Egypt; the separation caused Levi's strength to ebb away (Gen. R. 97, ed. by Theodor-Albeck, p. 1216).

To Levi's credit is the story of the *Shekhinah* ("Divine Presence"), which originally dwelt in the lowest sphere, but seven wicked persons or generations drove it ever further away to the highest (seventh) heaven. Seven righteous men brought it progressively back to earth, from the highest sphere to the next; one of these was Levi (Gen. R. 19:7; PdRK 2).

The name Levi was prophetic: his tribe would lead (*laveh*; "to escort," "accompany") the Israelites to their Father in Heaven (Gen. R. 71:4). When Phinehas argued before the Almighty that the sin of Zimri did not warrant the condign punishment of the whole nation (Num. 25:9), the angels sought to repel him, but God said to them, "Let him be: he is a zealot and the descendant of a zealot [Levi, who was zealous to defend his sister's honor, Gen. 34:25f.], a wrath-appeaser and a descendant of a wrath-appeaser" (Sanh. 82b; Lev. R. 33:4). The tribe of Levi was the only one that practiced circumcision in Egypt and did not lapse into idolatry (Sif. Num. 67; Ex. R. 15:1; 19:5). On the other hand, it was the only tribe not enslaved and put to degrading work (Ex. R. 5:16). Whereas the Israelites in general were liberated from Egypt for their prospective (but not present) merit in making the tabernacle, the tribe of Levi was liberated for its own immediate merit (Num. R. 3:6), for the whole tribe was righteous in Egypt (*ibid.* 15:12). Scripture gives the genealogy of Reuben, Simeon, and Levi only in Exodus 6:14ff. for three reasons: because they meekly accepted their father Jacob's rebuke; to lead up to Moses and Aaron; they were the only ones who preserved their family trees in Egypt and did not worship idols (this is one of the few places where this is said of Reuben and Simeon too). These three exercised authority (as individuals) over all the Israelites in Egypt consecutively, but at Levi's death the authority did not pass to Judah (Song. R. 4:7 no. 1). The children of the other tribal ancestors did not uniformly produce righteous descendants, but the descendants of Levi's three sons, Gershon, Kohath, and Merari, were all righteous (Num. R. 3:7). This tribe did not participate in the sin of the golden calf, and taught the Israelites to serve only the one God in Ereẓ Israel (*ibid.*).

Several reasons are given why Levi was not numbered together with the other tribes: one is because they were not doomed to die in the wilderness, but entered the Promised Land (Num. R. 1:11 and 12). As against this it is pointed out that the tribe of Levi was considerably smaller than the other tribes, because its numbers were depleted through their being grazed by fire when they carried the Ark (Num. R. 5:1; 6:8). For this reason God associated His name with Kohath to save them from being entirely consumed (Num. R. 6:8). Jacob predicted of Simeon and Levi, "I will divide them in Jacob, scatter them in Israel" (Gen. 49:7); this was fulfilled by their becoming teachers in the schoolhouses everywhere (Gen. R. 97, ed. by Theodor-Albeck, p. 1207). The tribe of Levi would teach sinners that sacrifice without true repentance does not constitute atonement (Lev. R. 9:5). Originally *shoterim* (officials of the *bet din*) were appointed only from the tribe of Levi (Yev. 86b). When the Almighty purifies the tribes, He will purify the tribe of Levi first (Kid. 71a). Greece (one of the powers that traditionally enslaved Israel) would fall through the Hasmoneans, members of the tribe of Levi (Gen. R. 99, ed. by Theodor-Albeck, p. 1274). Every tribe described as "Mine" will exist for ever and to all eternity – and of the Levites it is said, "the Levites shall be Mine" (Num. 3:12; Yal. 1 Sam. 124).

[Harry Freedman]

BIBLIOGRAPHY: IN THE BIBLE: See *Priests and Priesthood. IN THE AGGADAH: Ginzberg, Legends, 2 (1946^{6}), 194–8; 5 (1947^{6}), 380.

LEVI (fl. third quarter of the third century), Palestinian *amora*. Generally Levi is mentioned without his patronymic but he may be identical to Levi b. Laḥma (Ḥama) mentioned in the Babylonian Talmud (RH 29b). (However, as the name Levi b. Lahma never appears in Palestinian sources, he may have gone to Babylon.) He was a contemporary of R. Ze'ira I, R. Abba b. Kahana, and R. Ḥama b. Ukba (Ukva). Levi was primarily an aggadist; his frequent quotations from Ḥama b. Ḥanina suggest that he was his pupil. He and R. Judah b. Naḥman gave popular lectures on alternate Sabbaths in Johanan's academy, for which each was paid two *selas*. On one occasion his lecture, in which he reconciled two opposing opinions, so pleased R. Johanan that he appointed him to a regular lectureship, a post which he held for 22 years. In those days non-ordained scholars apparently lectured standing, while ordained scholars lectured sitting, and R. Johanan expressed the hope that one day he would be privileged to deliver his lectures sitting (Gen. R. 98:11; cf. TJ, Hor. 3:9, 48c; Eccles. R. 6:2). It seems from this that he was not then an ordained teacher.

There are no *halakhot* in his name, but he does sometimes explain *halakhah* (e.g., on Ber. 60b; RH 22a, 29b), though even then his teachings have an aggadic flavor. His lectures were so highly esteemed that R. Ze'ira, who generally did not have a high opinion of *aggadah*, nevertheless advised scholars (*ḥavrayya*, colleagues) to attend his lectures, as they were always instructive (TJ, RH 4:1, 59b). Levi sometimes lectured on the same text for quite a long time and could easily switch from one interpretation to the opposite (TJ, Sanh. 10:2, 28b). He claimed the ability to link together texts from the different sections of the Bible and penetrate to their inner meaning – an ability which he did not concede to most preachers (Song R. 1:10). Frequently he explained different words in biblical texts by reference to Arabic words (Gen. R. 87:1; Ex. R. 42:4; Song R. 4: 1) and he may have lived in Arabia for a while. He also composed elaborate parables to elucidate texts, and was regarded as a master of interpretation (Gen. R. 62:5). Among his numerous sayings are: "The punishment for [false] measures is more severe than for incest" (BB 88b); "Living without a wife is not living" (Gen. R. 17); "However much a man does for his soul, he does not fully discharge his obligations, … because it comes from on high" (Lev. R. 4:2); "To rob a human is worse than robbing the Almighty" (BB 88b). His yearning for the messianic period is reflected in a number of his statements, such as: "If Israel would keep but one Sabbath properly, the son of David would immediately come" (TJ, Ta'an. 1:1, 64a: see also Song R. 3:1).

BIBLIOGRAPHY: Frankel, Mavo, 111; A. Bruell, *Fremdsprachliche Redensarten* (1869), 41–46, 50; Bacher, Pal Amor; Hyman, Toledot, 8, 51, 57; Ḥ. Albeck, *Mavo la-Talmudim* (1969), 256f.

[Harry Freedman]

LEVI (Bet ha-Levi), prominent, wealthy, and ramified Sephardi family of scholars and rabbis, many of whom served as congregation leaders during the 15th–17th centuries. The family originated from Évora in Portugal, but all that is known of its previous history is the statement of *Solomon II: "… my grandfather the expert physician, pious and understanding, Maestro Solomon I, the son of the noble prince Don Joseph, son of the expert physician Maestro Moses, son of the exalted Don Solomon, son of the holy [martyred?] Don Isaac, son of the distinguished physician Maestro Joseph of the House of ha-Levi" (*Bet ha-Levi*, in manuscript). SOLOMON I arrived in Salonika after the expulsion of the Jews from Portugal in 1497 and founded the family which was outstanding in Salonika during the period that followed. The Ha-Levis were one of the richest families of Salonika and continued to be so until 1620. A patriarchal family, its members were proud of their lineage and of their scholarly attainments and position. Several reached outstanding positions of influence and status in the Jewish community of Salonika. They were devoted to study and possessed extensive libraries. The members of the family exhibited variegated talents, excelling as rabbis of communities, as *posekim* and as scholars, as outstanding preachers and poets. Some possessed a thorough knowledge of philosophy, and there were even kabbalists among them.

Two of the sons of Solomon I, ISAAC I (1500–1570/71), who was born in Salonika, and JACOB (and perhaps a third son, Joseph), were among the outstanding personalities of the Salonikan Jewish community in the mid-16th century. They were in contact with Joseph Caro after he moved to Safed. Isaac is eulogized in Saadiah Longo's *Seder Zemannim* (Salonika, 1594, 36ff.). He had two sons *Solomon II (1532–1600) and JOSEPH I (d. 1618), who were eminent scholars, and a third son, JUDAH, who died in his youth. Solomon II had two sons, *Isaac II (d. c. 1621/31) and JOSEPH II (d. 1605), who married the daughter of Joseph I, as well as three daughters, one of whom married R. Aaron *Sasson. Isaac II had two sons, *Solomon III (1581–1634), an outstanding scholar, and NISSIM (d. 1633), a *paytan*. Solomon had a son JACOB. Abraham *Levi was the son of Joseph I.

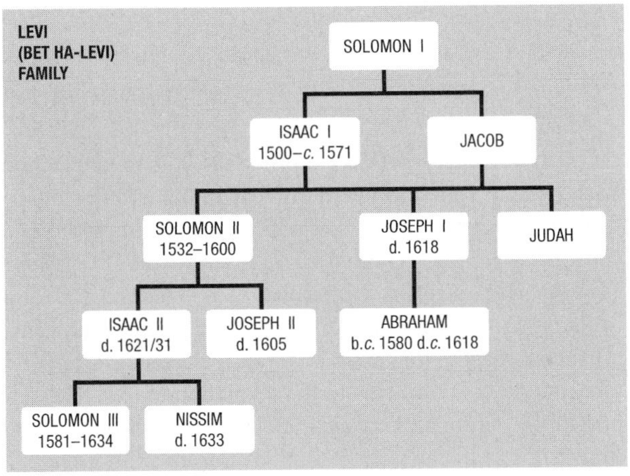

BIBLIOGRAPHY: Solomon le-Bet ha-Levi, *Ḥeshek Shelomo* (Salonika, 1600), introductions; Conforte, Kore, index; Ch. Hirschensohn, in: *Hamisderonah*, 2 (1888), 161, 190–2, 219–23, 340–3; D. Pipano, introduction to *Ein Mishpat* of R. Abraham le-Bet ha-Levi (1897); A. Danon, in: *Yerushalayim*, ed. by A.M. Luncz, 7 (1906–07), 351–4; I.S. Emmanuel, *Maẓẓevot Saloniki*, 2 vols. (1963–68), index.

[Joseph Hacker]

LEVI (Bet ha-Levi), ABRAHAM BEN JOSEPH (after 1580–shortly after 1618), a rabbi in Salonika of the *Levi (Bet ha-Levi) family. At an early age he showed outstanding intellectual abilities and was ordained rabbi at a very young age. Questions were addressed to him from far and wide and his endorsement was requested to the responsa of prominent rabbis older than himself. He studied under R. David ibn Naḥmias and was a colleague of R. Shabbetai Jonah. He was a member of the *bet din* of Abraham Ḥazzan, together with whom he often gave his approbation to the responsa of R. Joshua Handali. Abraham's colleague with whom he studied was R. Shabbetai Jonah. In addition to his published responsa (the bulk written between 1608–18), other responsa and approbations appear in the works of several of his contemporaries in Salonika and elsewhere. (His novellae, on several talmudic tractates and on the *Arba'ah Turim*, have apparently been lost.)

BIBLIOGRAPHY: Abraham le-Bet ha-Levi, *Ein Mishpat* (Salonika, 1897), introduction by editor D. Pipano; Rosanes, Togarmah, 3 (1938), 181–2.

[Joseph Hacker]

LEVI, BEHREND (b. c. 1600), army purveyor during the Thirty Years' War (1618–48) and financial adviser and diplomatic agent to the elector of Brandenburg. In 1650 Frederick William, the great elector, appointed Behrend Levi as overlord of all the Jews in the principalities of Brandenburg west of the River Elbe. This gave him authority to admit Jews, to fix their places of residence and tax rates, and to grant personal and business licenses. He collected the taxes of Halberstadt, Minden, Ravensburg, and Cleves Jewry, and rendered judgments in local disputes. An annual income accompanied the patent, which was renewed regularly. The Jews of Cleves and his rivals, such as the *Gomperz family, protested against his harsh methods and his authority was rescinded in 1652. A year earlier his brother, SALOMON LEVI, had procured for Behrend similar powers over Paderborn Jewry, but he was accused of embezzlement and once more of harsh rule and his authority was terminated in 1654. However, the great elector repeatedly supported his favorite and renewed his patent in 1657.

BIBLIOGRAPHY: H. Schnee, *Die Hoffinanz und der moderne Staat*, 1 (1953), 97–101; S. Stern, *The Court Jew* (1950), index, s.v. *Levi, Bernd*. **ADD. BIBLIOGRAPHY:** R. Ries and F. Battenberg, *Hofjuden* (2002), index.

LEVI, BENEDETTO (Baruch Isaac; 1846–80), Italian rabbi and scholar. He was born in Ferrara and graduated from the rabbinical seminary in Padua in 1872. From 1872 to 1875 he was in Nizza Monferrato and from 1875 in Ferrara. He wrote *Cenni bibliografici sulla Bibbia Luzzatto* (1876); *Ḥikkur Din* (1877), on the death penalty in talmudic law; *Il sommo sacerdozio appresso gli antichi ebrei* (1880); *Tahanunei Benei Yisrael*, 12 penitential prayers (in *Kobez al Jad*, 4, 1888). Among his essays are biographies on Jacob Daniel *Olmo (in *Ha-Maggid*, 16, 1872); Phinehas Ḥai *Anav (*ibid.*, 17, 1873); Azariah de' *Rossi (in Italian, 1869); Isaac *Lampronti (in Italian and in Hebrew, 1871); and on the Jewish poets of Ferrara (in *Kevod ha-Levanon*, vols. 10, 11). Together with S.Z.H. *Halberstamm he edited *Takkanot Ḥakhamim* (in *Ivri Anokhi*, 15, 1879), on the regulations adopted at the conference of Jewish delegates held at Ferrara in 1554.

BIBLIOGRAPHY: Kressel, Leksikon, 2 (1965), 182.

[Umberto (Moses David) Cassuto]

LEVI, CARLO (1902–1975), Italian author and artist. Born in Turin, where he studied medicine, Levi became interested in art, literature, and politics. After Mussolini came to power he joined the anti-Fascist underground and was one of the founders of the radical movement Giustizia e Libertà. He was arrested in 1934 and in the following year was exiled to Lucania in southern Italy for a year. In 1939 he fled to France. He returned to Italy in 1942 to join the Resistance and was again arrested. After World War II, he settled in Rome, where he was active in journalism and politics. He was elected a senator in 1963 on the Communist ticket, but retained an independent outlook.

Levi's experiences as a political exile inspired his masterpiece, *Cristo si è fermato a Eboli* (1945; *Christ Stopped at Eboli*, 1947), the first major Italian literary work of the postwar era, which was translated into many languages. In it he describes the society of Lucania, its customs, addiction to magic, and pre-Christian traditions. Accepting their unending miseries and without hope of a better future, the peasants nevertheless show themselves to be lovers of justice, good neighbors, and loyal friends. Levi reveals all the poetry of this primitive world.

Using the documentary techniques of journalism or of a travel diary, Levi wrote about the cultural climate and problems of many countries: Sicily, in *Le parole sono pietre* (1955; *Words are Stones*, 1958); the Soviet Union, in *Il futuro ha un cuore antico* (1956); Germany, in *La doppia notre dei tigli* (1959; *Linden Trees*, 1962); and Sardinia, in *Tutto il miele è finito* (1964). His other works include the essay *Paura della libertà* (1946; *Fear and Freedom*, 1950) and the novel, *L'Orologio* (1950; *The Watch*, 1951). As a painter, Levi exhibited in one-man and collective shows, achieving particular success in the United States.

BIBLIOGRAPHY: P. Pancrazi, *Scrittori d'oggi*, 4 (1946), 282–9; C.L. Ragghianti, *Carlo Levi* (It., 1948); L. Russo, *I narratori 1850–1950* (1951^2), 335–9; G. Pullini, *Il romanzo italiano del dopoguerra 1940–1960* (1961), 224–7, 263–6. **ADD. BIBLIOGRAPHY:** G. Falaschi, *Carlo Levi*, (1978); G. Sirovich, *L'azione politica di Carlo Levi* (1988); M. Miccinesi, *Invito alla lettura di Carlo Levi* (1989); G.B. Bronzini, *Il viaggio antropologico di Carlo Levi: da eroe stendhaliano a guerriero birmano* (1996); L. Sacco, *L'Orologio della Repubblica: Carlo Levi e il caso Italia* (1996); G. De Donato, *Le parole del reale: ricerche sulla prosa di Carlo Levi* (1998); N. Carducci, *Storia intellettuale di Carlo Levi* (1999); G. Barberi Squarotti, *L'orologio d'Italia: Carlo Levi e altri racconti* (2001); N. Longo, *Letture novecentesche: Zeno, Agilulfo, Carlo Levi* (2002, c2001); Ragusa, *Un torinese del Sud: Carlo Levi: una biografia* (2001); S. Ghiazza, *Carlo Levi e Umberto Saba: storia du un'amicizia* (2002); D. Ward, *Carlo Levi: gli italiani e la paura della libertà* (2002).

[Giorgio Romano]

BIBLIOGRAPHY: S.H. Margulies, *Dichter und Patriot* (1896); L. Bulferetti, *Socialismo risorgimentale* (1949).

[Joseph Baruch Sermoneta]

LEVI, DAVID (1742–1801), English Hebraist and polemicist. Born in London and intended by his parents to be a rabbi, Levi instead was apprenticed to a cobbler, and later worked as a hatter. However, he continued to pursue Jewish studies and interests. He published new translations of the Pentateuch for synagogal use (1787), of the Sephardi liturgy (6 vols., 1789–93), and the Ashkenazi (1794–96); and *Lingua Sacra* (1785–87), a Hebrew grammar and dictionary. He also wrote *Rites and Ceremonies of the Jews* (1783). Levi was the first Jew to write, in English, polemics in defense of Jews and Judaism. In his *Letters to Dr. Priestley* (1787) he rejected the attempts of the noted scholar Joseph Priestley to convert Jews to Christianity. In the same vein, he answered Thomas Paine's attacks on the Bible and the authenticity of prophecy (*Letters to Thomas Paine in Answer to his "Age of Reason,"* 1797). He also opposed millennarian theories in *Letters to Nathaniel Brassey Halhed in Answer to His Testimony of the Authenticity of the Prophecies of Richard Brothers and His Pretended Mission to Recall the Jews* (1795). Levi's whole life was a struggle to devote himself to scholarship in spite of poverty, and he was ultimately given a small pension by a group of supporters headed by the *Goldsmids.

BIBLIOGRAPHY: S. Singer, in: JHSET, 3 (1896), 55–71; J. Picciotto, *Sketches of Anglo-Jewish History* (1956^2), 219–20, 243, 270; C. Roth, *Great Synagogue* (1950), 148–9; Roth, Mag Bibl, index; DNB, s.v.; S. Daiches, in: JHSEM, 4 (1942), 28–32. **ADD. BIBLIOGRAPHY:** ODNB online; R.H. Popkin, "David Levi, Anglo-Jewish Theologian," in: *Jewish Quarterly Review*, 87 (1996), 79–101; Katz, England, 296–300, index.

[Jacob Rothschild]

LEVI, (Graziadio) DAVID (1816–1898), Italian patriot and poet. Born at Chieri in northern Italy into a wealthy family, Levi studied at the universities of Parma and Pisa and joined *Giovane Italia*, the secret nationalist movement of Giuseppe Mazzini. He worked as a journalist in Switzerland and later in Paris where he associated with Italian patriots and came into contact with Hungarian and Polish nationalists. Levi returned to Italy to take part in the revolution of 1848. He supported the Sardinian king against the Austrians, contrary to Mazzini's republican policy of opposition to all monarchies.

In 1860 following the unification of Italy he was elected to the Italian assembly as a liberal representative. He fought for equal rights and religious freedom until his defeat in 1879. Levi wrote many poems and war songs including a satire on Pope Pius IX and war songs for Garibaldi's brigades. His romantic dramas include *Il Profeta* (2 parts, 1866–84), an allegorical work based on the story of Jeremiah, in which Levi shows deep love of both Zion and Italy. All his works were imbued with the spirit of 19th-century European liberalism with which he equated the ethical values of Judaism.

LEVI, DORO (1898–1991), Italian archaeologist. Levi, born in Trieste, had a distinguished career as organizer of archaeological expeditions, curator, and administrator. He was a lecturer at Florence University, and in 1935 went to Sardinia to become professor at the Cagliari University and the island's director of art and antiquities.

From 1939 to 1945 Levi was in the United States as a guest lecturer at Princeton and Harvard universities. On the staff of Princeton University he took part in the excavations of Seleucia Pieria and Daphne, neighborhoods of ancient Antioch. There Levi excavated and published some of the most beautiful Roman mosaics that dated from the first decades of the second century till the earthquake of 526 C.E. This resulted in his monumental work *Antioch Mosaic Pavements* (2 vols., 1947).

Levi returned to Italy in 1945 to become adviser on cultural relations to the Ministry of Education. In 1947 he was appointed director of the Italian School of Archaeology in Athens and led archaeological expeditions in the Levant. He organized excavations at Caesarea in Israel in the late 1950s.

Levi's main work, however, was dedicated to the Minoan civilization. He thus directed Italian excavations in Crete at Arkades-Aphrati, Gortyna, and Phaistos. At Phaistos he discovered a Minoan palace. He also specialized in Minoan pottery. In addition Levi led excavations at Iasos, a town in Caria on the Anatolian coast (1960–61). He summarized his activities as part of the Italian school in Athens in *The Italian Excavations in Crete and the Earliest European Civilization* (1963) and *The Recent Excavations at Phaistos (= Studies in Mediterranean Archaeology*, vol. 11, 1964).

Levi's scientific interests embraced the whole of the Graeco-Roman world from the early Minoan civilization to Roman and Late antique Antiochia, with a strong leaning toward mythology and the history of religion. These interests came to fruition in his study "The Allegories of the Months in Classical Art" in *Art Bulletin* (23 (1941), 251–91).

[Penuel P. Kahane / Samuele Rocca (2nd ed.)]

LEVI, EDWARD H. (1911–2000), U.S. educator, legal scholar, and university administrator. Levi, who was born in Chicago, was a descendant of the rabbinical families of *Einhorn and *Hirsch and a son of Rabbi Gerson B. Levi. He received his law degree at the University of Chicago in 1935. Awarded the Sterling Fellowship at Yale Law School, he earned his degree of doctor of jurisprudence in 1938. He joined the University of Chicago faculty in 1936 as an assistant professor of law. He served as dean of the University of Chicago Law School (1950 to 1962). In that capacity, he played a major role in the largest fundraising effort of any university of the time. In 1958 he founded the university's *Journal of Law and Economics*. He served as provost of the university (1962 to 1968) and president from 1968 to 1975, becoming the first Jew to head a major American university. From 1977 to 1983 he was the university's Glen A. Lloyd Distinguished Service Professor.

An outstanding administrator, Levi also distinguished himself as a legal expert. In the 1940s he served under Thurman Arnold, head of the U.S. Justice Department's antitrust division. He was active in atomic energy legislation; his work provided the basis for the establishment of the Atomic Energy Commission.

On February 7, 1975, Levi was sworn in as attorney general of the U.S., the first Jew to be appointed to this office. When William B. Saxbe, the previous attorney general, was sworn in as U.S. ambassador to India on February 3, 1975, another Jew, 30-year-old Lawrence H. Silberman, took over his duties until Levi was sworn in, and thus became in fact the first Jew to head the Department of Justice, to be followed four days later by Levi. As a man widely respected for his intelligence and integrity, Levi did much to restore credibility to the position of attorney general (1975–77) under President Ford after the Nixon-Watergate era.

Levi identified himself with Jewish communal affairs. He was a founder of the Chicago Chapter of the American Jewish Committee, a member of the Anti-Defamation League of the B'nai B'rith, and a member of the Sinai Temple in Chicago, of which his grandfather Emil G. Hirsch was rabbi from 1880 to 1923.

Levi's *An Introduction to Legal Reasoning* (1949) is considered a classic work. He co-authored (with Roscoe Steffen) Elements of the Law (1950) and wrote *Four Talks on Legal Education* (1951), *Point of View: Talks on Education* (1969), and *The Crisis in the Nature of Law* (1970).

[Shnayer Z. Leiman / Ruth Beloff (2nd ed.)]

LEVI, EUGENIO (1876–1966), Italian literary critic and essayist. Born in Milan, Levi taught languages and literature for many years in state schools. When he was forced to leave them as a result of Mussolini's antisemitic laws, he moved to the Milan Jewish high school, where he exerted a strong influence on his pupils. Until 1938 he taught Arabic at various colleges, including the Philological Institute and the Colonial High School. After World War II he also taught at the Sally Mayer College of Semitic Studies (1951–60), and was from 1960 honorary dean of Milan's Jewish schools.

His vast cultural curiosity and breadth of knowledge led Levi to the writing of essays – a literary genre in which he excelled. Some of his best studies of the theater and of Italian literature were published in the review *Il Convegno* (1919–38), which he edited and through which he introduced Italian readers to great contemporary writers of Europe and the United States, such as Joyce, Kafka, Hemingway, and Lorca. He did a great deal of research on the theater, some of which resulted in the prizewinning study *Il Comico di Carattere da Teofrasto a Pirandello* (1959). Other notable works include translations into Italian of Molière's *Tartuffe* (1949), and the *History of World Literature* by Gustav *Karpeles (1906); and the study *Il lettore inquieto* (1964). Levi dealt with Jewish themes in two essays originally published in the *Rassegna Mensile d'Israel*: "Zangwill e l'Ebraismo" (1955) and "Ricordo di Sabatino Lopez" (1968), and in "Italo Svevo e l'anima ebraica" (*Scritti...Sally Mayer*, 1956).

BIBLIOGRAPHY: *L'Espresso* (April 12, 1959), 31; *Nuovo corriere della sera* (April 3, 1959); RMI, 32 (1966), 427. **ADD. BIBLIOGRAPHY:** G. Lopez, "Eugenio Levi; critico e moralista," in: *Scritti in memoria di Umberto Nahon* (1978), 117–65.

[Giorgio Romano]

LEVI, GIORGIO RENATO (1895–1965), Italian physical chemist. Born in Ferrara, Levi during World War I worked at a dynamite factory and remained in industry until 1921. He was appointed assistant professor at the Polytechnic Institute of Milan, and founded a team doing X-ray diffraction. In 1927 he became professor of general chemistry at the University of Milan. Later he was professor at the University of Pavia, but lost his chair when Mussolini applied the Nuremberg Laws to Italian universities. He went to São Paulo, Brazil, where he worked in a commercial research laboratory and was professor of physical and analytical chemistry at the university. His scientific research was on the structure of inorganic crystals, and the preparation and study of hitherto unknown inorganic compounds, some of industrial significance. A street in São Paulo is named after him.

[Samuel Aaron Miller]

LEVI, GIULIO AUGUSTO (1879–1951), Italian literary critic. Levi, who was born in Turin, was from 1904 to 1938 a secondary-school teacher. In 1926 he was baptized and became a Roman Catholic. In 1938 he was forced to leave his position by the Fascist anti-Jewish laws. Levi was rescued by private individuals and Christian institutions during the anti-Jewish persecution of the Fascist regime and escaped deportation during World War II. After the war, he was appointed professor of Italian literature at the University of Florence. As a critic, he mainly devoted himself to an analysis of Leopardi's works and, with his own method of study, deliberately moved away from both positivism and the idealism of Croce. He wrote for several newspapers and journals and his publications appeared throughout the first half of the 20th century. Levi's critical works include *Studi estetici* (1907); *Storia del pensiero di Giacomo Leopardi* (1911); *Il Comico* (1913); *Breve storia dell'estetica e del gusto* (1924); *Giacomo Leopardi* (1931), his best-known study of the poet; *Da Dante al Machiavelli* (1935); and *Vittorio Alfieri* (1950).

BIBLIOGRAPHY: E. Levi, C. Jannaco, *Alla memoria di Giulio Augusto Levi* (1956), with a biography and a bibliography of G.A.L.

[Louisa Cuomo]

LEVI, GIUSEPPE (1872–1965), Italian neuroanatomist and histologist. A member of a well-known family of Trieste bankers, Levi in 1910 was appointed professor of human anatomy at Sassari, Sardinia. In 1915 he moved to Palermo, and four years later was made director of the Institute of Human Anatomy of the University of Turin.

Levi's long and brilliant research career centered on microscopic anatomy, particularly of the nerve cell. He laid the foundations of much of our knowledge of the factors that determine the size of sensory and motor neurons. He was one of the pioneers of the technique of tissue culture.

Levi was an outspoken anti-Fascist, and in 1933 was imprisoned for several weeks. In 1938, under Mussolini's racial law, he was removed from his post. He took refuge in Belgium, where he set up a laboratory, but his work was cut short by the German invasion and he returned to Turin. There, although in his seventies, he managed to continue his research and writing clandestinely. At the end of the war he was restored to the directorship of the Institute of Human Anatomy.

[Mordecai L. Gabriel]

LEVI, HERMANN (1839–1900), German conductor. Born at Giessen, the grandson of a rabbi who had been a representative in Napoleon's Sanhedrin, Levi studied music at Leipzig and Paris. From 1872 to 1896 he was court conductor at Munich. Having at first been close to Brahms, Levi gradually drew nearer to *Wagner's circle, and owing to his position as conductor of the Royal Munich Opera Orchestra, he conducted the premiere of *Parsifal* at Bayreuth in 1882. His relationship with Wagner was marred by the latter's antisemitism, and by constant suggestions that Levi submit to baptism because of the Christian implications of *Parsifal*. A composer as well as a conductor, Levi wrote songs and a piano concerto. He revised and edited Lorenzo *Da Ponte's librettos to Mozart's operas, thus contributing to a Mozart renaissance in the late 19th century. His interpretations of the works of Mozart, Brahms, Bruckner, and Wagner distinguished Levi as one of the greatest conductors of his time. In Munich, he acted as unofficial musical adviser to the city's synagogue; he composed a work for the inauguration of the Mannheim synagogue and a *Veshamru* for the cantor of Giessen.

BIBLIOGRAPHY: E. von Possart, *Erinnerungen an Hermann Levi* (1901); J. Stern, in: *Zeitschrift fuer die Geschichte der Juden*, 7 (1970), 17–25, incl. bibl.; MGG, incl. bibl.; Grove, Dict, incl. bibl.; Riemann-Einstein; Riemann-Gurlitt, incl. bibl.; Baker, Biog Dict, incl. bibl.; Sendrey, Music, nos. 5313–15, 3096.

[Judith Cohen]

LEVI (Bet ha-Levi), ISAAC (II) BEN SOLOMON (II; d. c. 1621/31), halakhist, preacher, kabbalist, and leader of the Jewish community in Salonika from 1610 to 1620. From 1573 to 1600 he studied in the yeshivah of the Évora congregation of Salonika. When his father died he was forced out of the yeshivah, and he was even denied access to his father's works. He moved to the Provencal congregation of the city in 1601, where he established a yeshivah which he headed. Greatly influenced by his father, he was profoundly affected by his death as well as those of other members of his family (1600–05). According to David Conforte (Kore, 44a), Isaac was head of the yeshivah Eẓ Ḥayyim. In 1620–21 his family home was burned and many of his books and manuscripts were destroyed (though some have been preserved). Nothing is known of him afterward. His signature appears on the *haskamot* ("resolutions") of the rabbis and leaders of Salonika from 1614–18. His responsa, which contain some novellae, are preserved in manuscript form. Some were published in the works of his contemporaries and relatives (R. Ḥayyim Shabbetai; *Jacob, *Abraham, and Solomon Bet ha-*Levi). All of them praise his extensive knowledge. From his responsa it is evident that he studied Kabbalah and his contemporaries attest his piety and emphasize his talents as a preacher. He wrote introductions, provided indices, and added poems to the *Ḥeshek Shelomo*, his father's commentary to the Book of Isaiah.

BIBLIOGRAPHY: Solomon le-Bet ha-Levi, *Ḥeshek Shelomo* (Salonika, 1600); Ch. Hirschensohn, in: *Hamisderonah*, 2 (1888), 219–23, 340–3; A. Danon, in: *Yerushalayim*, ed. by A.M. Luncz, 7 (1906–07), 351–4; A.Z. Schwarz, *Die hebraeischen Handschriften in Oesterreich* (1931), 71–74, no. 96; I.R. Molho and A. Amarijlio, in: *Sefunot*, 2 (1958), 45–51; I.S. Emmanuel, *Maẓẓevot Saloniki*, 1 (1963), 232–3, no. 527.

[Joseph Hacker]

LÉVI, ISRAEL (1856–1939), chief rabbi of France, scholar, and writer. Lévi graduated from the Ecole Rabbinique in his native Paris. He was appointed assistant rabbi in Paris in 1882, and began teaching Jewish history at the Ecole Rabbinique in 1892 and Talmud and rabbinic literature at the Ecole Pratique des Hautes Etudes in 1896. When the Société des Etudes Juives was founded in 1880, Lévi became its secretary. In 1886 he was appointed editor of the *Revue des Etudes Juives. He participated in the publication of the French Bible translation, the so-called Bible du Rabbinat (2 vols., 1899–1906), which was edited by his father-in-law Zadoc *Kahn and Julien Weill (1906). From 1919 to 1938 Lévi served as chief rabbi of the French central Consistoire.

Lévi's contributions to modern Jewish scholarship covered a wide range, from Bible, Apocrypha, Talmud, and Midrash to liturgy and history – that of the Jews of France in particular. He was a regular contributor to learned periodicals, especially the *Revue des Etudes Juives*, where he also proved himself an expert and painstaking reviewer of almost every publication in the field of Jewish and Hebrew scholarship. Lévi's approach to biblical and talmudic research was without dogmatic prejudice, but he shied away from the radicalism of the higher and lower Bible criticism (cf. his study on the Nash papyrus, in REJ, 46 (1903), 212–7). His main published works include *Le Roman d'Alexandre* (1887), *L'Ecclesiastique…* (1898–1901; *The Hebrew Text of the Book of Ecclesiasticus*, 1904), *Le Péché originel dans les anciennes sources juives* (1907), and *Histoire des Juifs de France* (1903). On the occasion of his 70th birthday, Lévi was honored by the publication of "Mélanges offerts à Israël Lévi" (in REJ, 86 (1926), 9–29, incl. bibl.).

BIBLIOGRAPHY: J. Miklishanski, in: S. Federbusch (ed.), *Ḥokhmat Yisrael be-Ma'arav Eiropah*, 1 (1958), 297–309.

[Jacques K. Mikliszanski]

LEVI (Bet ha-Levi), JACOB BEN ISRAEL (second half of 16th century–1636), halakhist and scholar. A member of the famous Bet ha-*Levi family, Jacob grew up in Salonika, where he studied in the local yeshivot. He studied *halakhah* with R. Aaron ibn Ḥasson and philosophy with R. David ibn Shushan (see his approbation (*haskamah*) to the *Sefer Illem* of 1629). He moved from Salonika to Xanthe, where he served as rabbi of the town and its environs, and then went to Venice. Jacob became famous for his responsa (1612; complete edition, Venice, 1632–34), and his sermons and translation of the Koran are extant in manuscript. He translated the Koran from Arabic "to a Christian language [Latin?] and from the latter into the holy tongue." In Italy he was apparently an affluent businessman who established close contact with the authorities, apparently as a result of his intellectual attainments. The great rabbis of Salonika, Greece, and Italy of the early 17th century gave their endorsements to his responsa, and answered the halakhic queries which he addressed to them. Some of his responsa appear in the works of these rabbis, and similarly, his approbations to several books printed in Italy and elsewhere have been published.

BIBLIOGRAPHY: Solomon (II) le-Bet ha-Levi, Responsa (Salonika, 1652), OḤ, no. 8; A. Figo, *Binah la-Ittim* (Venice, 1648), 191–3; *Literaturblatt des Orients*, 2 (1841), 606–7; Steinschneider, Cat Bod, 1221, no. 5550.

[Joseph Hacker]

LEVI, JOHN SIMON (1934–), Australian rabbi and historian. The descendant of pioneering Jews in Victoria, Australia, Levi became the first Australian-born rabbi. Educated at Melbourne University and Hebrew Union College, he succeeded Herman Sanger (1909–80) as chief rabbi at Temple Beth-Israel, Melbourne (where he served from 1960), the oldest continuing non-Orthodox synagogue in Australia, retiring in 1997. A highly articulate man, Levi was one of the best-known Australian rabbinical figures to non-Jews and also a historian of note, having co-authored (with G.J.F. Bergman) *Australian Genesis: Jewish Convicts and Settlers, 1788–1860*, the authoritative history of the early Jewish community in Australia, which appeared in 1974 (rev. ed. 2002); *The Forefathers: A Biographical Dictionary of the Jews of Australia, 1788–1830* (1976); and *Rabbi Jacob Danglow: 'The Uncrowned Monarch of Australian Jews'* (1995). A Festschrift volume of historical essays in his honor, *A Portion of Praise*, appeared in 1997.

[William D. Rubinstein (2nd ed.)]

LEVI, JOSHUA JOSEPH BEN DAVID (c. 1700), Venetian Hebrew poet. His elegies on the death of various contemporaries are all distinguished by their excellent style.

Among those lamented are Moses *Zacuto, Abraham Ẓemaḥ (a lamentation for both in 24 octaves, 1692?), Samuel *Aboab (1694?), and Mose Merari. Joshua Joseph's best-known piece is *Kos Tanḥumim* (Venice, 1707), being an elegy on Mose Levi Muggia, part of which was republished by J. Schirmann in his anthology (1934). A prose introduction and a sonnet by Levi are printed in Samson *Morpurgo's *Eẓ ha-Da'at* (Venice, 1704, p. 37a–b).

BIBLIOGRAPHY: A. Coen, *Saggio di Eloquenza Ebrea*, 1 (1827), 41–3; Ghirondi-Neppi, 171–3, no. 72; Steinschneider, Cat Bod, 1555; Schirmann, Italyah, 342–6; Davidson, Oẓar, 4 (1933), 392.

[Jefim (Hayyim) Schirmann]

LEVI, LEO (1912–1982), musicologist. Born in Casale Monferrato, Italy, Levi settled in Palestine in 1935. His special fields of research were in ethnomusicology and liturgical music, especially the traditions of the Italian and Mediterranean Jewish communities, and in the comparative study of Jewish and Christian musical traditions. His extensive recordings of the various liturgical music traditions of the Italian Jewish communities, made in collaboration with the Centro Nazionale Studi di Musica Popolare in Rome, are particularly important as the greater part were obtained from the last bearers of these traditions at a time when their communities had already ceased to exist.

LEVI, LEONE (1821–1888), British economist and pioneer of chambers of commerce. Levi was born in Ancona, Italy, the son of a merchant. He arrived in Liverpool in 1844 and became a naturalized British subject in 1847. There, Levi worked as a merchant, but his business suffered in the economic downturn of the late 1840s. In 1849, in a Liverpool newspaper and in pamphlets, he floated the idea of a local chamber of commerce, where local businessmen could discuss their common problems and gain advice. Although small-scale chambers of commerce had existed before, none had previously been founded in a large British town. His idea received considerable support and he became secretary of the newly founded Liverpool Chamber of Commerce. Levi used his post to write extensively on international commercial law and on national legal differences in commercial practice, producing *Commercial Law* in 1850. In 1850, remarkably for a recent migrant with no academic background, Levi was appointed professor of commercial law at King's College, London. He was a significant figure in pioneering the collection of commercial statistics. His *History of British Commerce* (1872) was also a pioneering work. He produced an autobiography, *The Story of My Life: The First Ten Years of My Residence in England, 1845–1855* (1888).

BIBLIOGRAPHY: ODNB online.

[William D. Rubinstein (2nd ed.)]

LEVI, MARIO (1957–), novelist. Born in Istanbul to a Sephardi family, he graduated from the Istanbul University Faculty of Literature, majoring in French language and literature. He first published in the Jewish community newspaper *Şalom* and later on started to contribute to leading Turkish journals. His first book was *Jacques Brel: Bir Yalnız Adam* (1986). His first book of stories, *Bir Şehre Gidememek,* was published in 1990 and earned the prestigious Haldun Taner Story award. His subsequent works were *Madam Floridis Dönmeyebilir* (1992), *En Güzel Aşk Hikâyemiz* (1992), and his novel *İstanbul Bir Masaldı* (1999) which also earned the prestigious Yunus Nadi award.

[Rifat Bali (2nd ed.)]

LEVI, MARIO GIACOMO (1878–1955), Italian chemist. Born in Padua, Levi worked there until 1906, when he moved to the University of Pisa. In 1909 he became professor of technological chemistry at the University of Palermo, Sicily, and in 1919 was appointed the first director of the Higher Institute for Commercial and Colonial Studies. In 1927 Levi went to Milan as professor of industrial chemistry at the Polytechnic. When Mussolini introduced legislation against Jews in the professions in 1938, he went to live in Lausanne, Switzerland. An Italian patriot, Levi played an important role in the development of his country's chemical industry. His contributions to technical and scientific journals included papers on the Deacon chlorine process, hyposulfites, fuels, the noble gases, radioactivity, electrochemistry, nonaqueous solvents, and catalysis.

BIBLIOGRAPHY: J.C. Poggendorff, *Biographisch-literarisches Handwoerterbuch*, 5 (1926), s.v.; 6 (1938), s.v.; *Chimica e Industria* (then *Notiziario Chimico-industriale*), 2 (1927), 4–5.

LEVI, MORITZ (**Moric**; 1878–1941), rabbi and author. Born in Sarajevo, he studied Judaism and philosophy in Vienna. As a student he was a member of the Zionist groups Bar Giora and Esperanza. His Ph.D. thesis, *Die Sephardim in Bosnia*, published in 1911 by the Jewish publisher and printer Daniel A. Kajon, in Sarajevo, was the product of pioneering work on the history of the Sephardi Jews in the Balkans. It appeared in Serbo-Croat translation, prepared and issued by the Federation of Jewish Communities in Belgrade.

From 1916 he was the rabbi of the Sephardi community, a post he held until the Holocaust. In 1925, when the Federation of Jewish Communities decided to open a theological seminary, Levi and his Ashkenazi colleague Ephraim Urbach were chosen to head this institute and teach in it. This seminary provided secondary education coupled with Judaic studies. Its alumni became cantors, Hebrew teachers, and rabbinical assistants all over the country, significantly contributing to the continuity of Jewish life there.

Rabbi Levi was a central figure in Jewish life in Sarajevo, serving as mediator between the Zionist and the Sephardi factions. He corresponded with the Spanish senator Angelo Pulido, who had inquired about the presence of Ladino-speaking Jews during the early decades of the 20th century, publishing a work titled *Judios sin Patria* ("Jews without Homeland"), which contained some of the data he had gathered.

During the occupation of Sarajevo by the Croat Ustashe and the Nazis, in April 1941, he was arrested and interrogated at the Gestapo headquarters in Graz, released in Croatia, but rearrested and deported, together with his wife, Rivkah, to the Croatian death camp Jasenovac, where they perished.

BIBLIOGRAPHY: *Spomenica – 400 godina od dolaska Jevreja u Bosnu i Hercegovinu 1566–1966* (1966).

[Zvi Loker (2nd ed.)]

LEVI, MOSHE (1936–), Israeli soldier, 12th chief of staff of the IDF. Levi was born in Tel Aviv to parents who had immigrated three years earlier from Iraq. His military career began in 1954 when he joined the Golani infantry brigade; in the Sinai Campaign he served as a paratrooper in the Mitla Pass. During the Six-Day War he was deputy commander of brigades in the Sinai and the Golan Heights. Later he commanded an armored division. Levi was the OC of the Northern Command from 1977 through September 1982 when he became deputy chief of staff serving until his appointment as chief of staff in April 1983. During his tenure as chief of staff, the IDF withdrew from Lebanon (in 1985). After his retirement from the IDF he returned to his home in kibbutz Beit Alfa and worked in farming. Subsequently he was appointed to a number of public positions, among them chairman of the Trans-Israel Highway Authority and the Anti-Drug Administration and member of the *Shamgar Commission investigating the Cave of the Patriarchs massacre in Hebron perpetrated by Baruch Goldstein.

[Fern Lee Seckbach]

LEVI, PAOLO (1919–1989), Italian playwright. Born in Genoa, Levi began his career as a dramatic critic, contributing to various Italian and foreign reviews. After spending the years 1944–46 in Brazil, he returned to Rome where he wrote plays for radio and television and a number of dramas, beginning with *Anna e il telefono* (1951). Levi made his name both in Italy and overseas with *Legittima difesa* (1952). His later successes included *Scaccomatto* (1953), *La Fiera* (1956), *Il gioco è fatto* (1957), and *Lastrico d'inferno* (1959). Levi's favorite theme – the problems besetting the individual – also dominates *Come per scherzo* (1955), *I Nemici* (1955), and *Il Caso Pinedus* (1954), which is considered one of the most interesting plays of the Italian theater of the century and which was staged in English, German, Czech, and Norwegian). *Gli dei di pietra* was staged in Dortmund, Germany, as *Die steinernen Goetter* (1958). Levi won an award for his radio plays in 1952 and codirected several Italian motion pictures during the 1950s. His novel *Ritratto di Provincia in rosso* (1975) was adapted in 1976 as a movie entitled *Al piacere di rivederla*.

BIBLIOGRAPHY: S. d'Amica, *Palcoscenici del dopoguerra*, 2 (1953), 293–95; *Dizionario dello spettacolo del '900*.

LEVI, PAUL (1883–1930), German socialist politician. A lawyer by profession, Levi gained renown by his defense of striking workers (1912) and of Rosa *Luxemburg (1914), who became his mentor and colleague. Levi was one of the founders and leaders of the "Spartacus League," the nucleus of the emerging Communist Party (1919) of which he became the leader, inheriting Luxemburg's mantle. After 1919 he succeeded as the leading figure in outmaneuvering anti-parliamentary and insurrectionary elements, consolidating the party and substantially increasing its membership. His own position was undermined by his opposition to the interference of the Comintern in German affairs and he resigned from the central committee in February 1921. In March, the party, on Moscow's orders, fomented an armed uprising in Saxony which was quelled with much bloodshed. Paul Levi publicly denounced the tactics and methods of the leadership and was expelled from the party. He thereupon formed, with his adherents, an independent Communist faction in the Reichstag (parliament) but eventually returned to the fold of the Social Democratic Party where he was leader of its left wing. A collection of Levi's speeches, letters, and essays was edited by C. Beradt and appeared in 1969, *Zwischen Spartakus und Sozialdemokratie*.

BIBLIOGRAPHY: W.T. Angress, *Stillborn Revolution* (1963). **ADD. BIBLIOGRAPHY:** C. Bloch, "Paul Levi – Ein Symbol der Tragoedie des Linkssozialismus in der Weimarer Republik," in: JIDG, 9 (1986), 244–63; C. Beradt, *Paul Levi – Ein demokratischer Sozialist in der Weimarer Republik* (1969); W. Jens, *Ein Jud aus Hechingen – Requiem fuer Paul Levi* (1991).

[Bjoern Siegel (2nd ed.)]

LEVI, PRIMO (1919–1987), Italian author. Levi was born in Turin and trained as a chemist, receiving his degree from the University of Turin three years after Mussolini had barred Jews from higher education. Although he had a bar mitzvah he was far from his Jewish background until the enactment of the Italian racial laws in 1938. After the German takeover of Italy in 1943, he fled to the north intending to join the partisans but was caught, imprisoned first at the Fossolo camp and in February 1944 sent to Auschwitz. "I was not a very good partisan," he said in an interview. Of that train trip he wrote: "Now in the hour of decision, we said to each other things that are never said among the living… everybody said farewell to life through his neighbor." He survived there for ten months, one of the very few on his transport to survive until liberation, partly due to his employment by the Germans as a chemist in the Buna Works. His number in the camp was 174517. He wrote: "We have been baptized, we will carry the tattoo on our left arm until we die." Unlike most prisoners in the Auschwitz camp complexes, Levi did not leave on the death march. He stayed behind for ten days. The Germans abandoned the camp, fleeing from Soviet troops who arrived on January 27, 1945. Levi wrote of liberation: "Liberty. The breach in the barbed wire gave us a concrete image of it. To anyone who stopped to think, it signified no more Germans, no more selections, no work, no blows, no rollcalls, and perhaps, later, the return."

After the war he wandered for nine months, including journeys through Soviet Russia, before he got back to Turin, which he described in great detail in his 1963 work *The Reawakening*. Unlike most survivors, Levi had a home and a community to which he could return. He came back to the apartment his family had occupied for three generations and that he was to live in until his death. He wrote his works in the very room in which he was born. He resumed work as a chemist at the Turin paint factory SIVA where he managed the plant from 1961–74. His first book was *Se questo è un uomo* (1947; *If This Is a Man*, 1959) which described the Auschwitz extermination camp, and is regarded as a classic of Holocaust literature. The book was republished in 1961 under the title *Survival in Auschwitz: The Nazi Assault on Humanity*. He described his experience in Auschwitz with meticulous detail, with scientific precision and seemingly without pathos. Survivors were no heroes to Levi. They were simply survivors. In *La Tregua* (1963; *The Truce*, 1965; U.S. ed. *The Reawakening*, 1965), he told of his wanderings and unusual adventures on his return to Italy with rich detail. Levi broadened his scope in *Storie naturali* (1966), moralistic and fantastic tales published under the pseudonym of Damianos Malabaila. In 1979 he was awarded the Strega Prize, one of Italy's top literary awards. His autobiographical *Il sistema periodico* (1975; *The Periodic Table*, 1984), containing episodes named after the elements in the periodic chart, describes his ancestry and his own experiences. *Se non ora, quando* (1982; *If Not Now, When?*, 1985) is a novel telling the story of a Holocaust survivor crossing Europe after the war in order to reach Israel. *The Drowned and the Saved* appeared in 1986. Levi also wrote several volumes of short stories. He was regarded as one of the great Italian writers of the post-war period and by many as the man who offered the most telling depiction of Auschwitz. No one has described life in Auschwitz more directly, more objectively, with greater scientific precision. He was insistent that life inside the camps required a new language, a new way of speaking. "Our language lacks words to express this offense, the demolition of a man. In a moment with a prophetic intuition, the reality was revealed to us: we had reached the bottom. It is not possible to sink lower than this; … Nothing belongs to us anymore; they have taken away our clothes, our shoes, even our hair; if we speak they will not listen to us, and if they listen, they will not understand. They will even take away our name: and if we want to keep it, we will have to find ourselves the strength to do so, to manage somehow so that behind the name something of us, as we were, still remains."

Levi's work as a writer was gaining recognition just as he died. He was honored but retained the simple discipline of writing. Philip *Roth, who had brought many European Jewish writers to the attention of the American reading public said: "With moral stamina and intellectual poise of a 20th century titan, this slightly built, dutiful, unassuming chemist set out systematically to remember the German hell on earth, steadfastly to think it through and then to render it comprehensible in lucid, unpretentious prose. He was profoundly in touch with the minutest works of the most endearing human events and with the much contemptible."

In April 1987 he was found dead at the bottom of the stairwell in the apartment building where he was born and where he lived with his wife and mother. His son lived on the very same floor. Friends spoke of anxiety over the deteriorating condition of his mother, left paralyzed by a stroke. He had been depressed and had had a bout with cancer. His anti-depression drug had been changed and he had written of suicide. In writing of the Belgian writer Jean Amery, who had been in Auschwitz and wrote of torture starkly and eloquently and who himself had committed suicide, Levi quoted his famous aphorism: "He who was tortured, remains tortured. He who has suffered torment can no longer find his place in the world. Faith in humanity – cracked by the first slap across the face, then demolished by torture – can never be recovered." His death was considered by most a suicide; though others have disputed this account. But if it was a suicide then Levi has given a clue as to its reason. The period of the imprisonment of survivors "is the center of their life, the event that for better or worse has marked their entire existence."

BIBLIOGRAPHY: H.S. Hughes, *Prisoners of Hope* (1983); *Dizionario enciclopedico della letteratura italiana*, 3 (1967), 383; I. Calvino, in: *L'Unità* (May 6, 1948); A. Cajumi, in: *La Stampa* (Nov. 26, 1957). **ADD. BIBLIOGRAPHY:** A. Stille, "Primo Levi: Reconciling the Man and the Writer," in: *New York Times* (July 5, 1987); L. Langer, *Versions of Survival* (1982).

[Michael Berenbaum (2nd ed.)]

LEVI, RINO (1901–1965), Brazilian architect. Levi worked on the Ministry of Education building, Rio de Janeiro (1937), with Lucio Costa, Oscar Niemeyer, and the team of young architects who introduced the modern style in Brazil. Levi designed many buildings in the manner of the American skyscraper.

LEVI, SAID BEN SHALOM (d. 1917), educator and writer; known as "Hakham Said." One of the first Yemenite immigrants to Ereẓ Israel, Levi settled in Jaffa in 1888, where he became a teacher in the *talmud torah* Torah Or. From the diary of his school, which is extant, one learns of the modern educational methods which he attempted to adopt. In 1889 he left for Algiers as the emissary of the Sephardim. He was also the secretary of the Yemenite workers' union *Pe'ullat Sakhir*, whose objective was to employ Jewish rather than Arab labor in the settlements. He was a gifted writer and he had an exceptionally fine Hebrew style. His diary of World War I, which relates the sufferings of the *yishuv* during the war, is also extant.

BIBLIOGRAPHY: Y. Ratzaby, in: *Shivat Ẓiyyon*, 2–3 (1953), 404–25.

[Yehuda Ratzaby]

LEVI, SAMUEL GERSHON (1908–1990), Canadian Conservative rabbi and leader; first Jewish chaplain in Canadian history; editor and translator. Levi was born in Toronto, Canada, where he studied in public schools and received a thorough talmudic and Hebraic education from private tutors. He earned a B.A. from the University of Toronto (1929), was ordained rabbi by the Jewish Theological Seminary (JTS, 1933), received an M.A. in Jewish history from Columbia University (1932), and completed all the course work there toward his Ph.D.

After serving as educational director of Sha'ar Hashomayim synagogue in Montreal (1936–41), Levi was selected to serve as the first Jewish chaplain in Canadian history (1941–46), later becoming senior Jewish chaplain and retiring with the rank of major. Initially, he traveled the length and breadth of Canada to personally meet the Jewish soldiers. In 1942, he sailed for Europe where he served in England, France, and Belgium, also working with She'erit ha-Peletah (Holocaust survivors). His memoir of that period, *Breaking New Ground* (1994), was published posthumously.

After World War II, he served as a successful congregational rabbi in Queens, New York (1947–72). He became a leader of the Rabbinical Assembly of the Conservative movement, serving as treasurer (1957–65), president (1970–72), and chairman of the Committee on Jewish Law and Standards (1972–73). He also served as dean of the Cantorial School of JTS in the 1960s. Levi also edited *Conservative Judaism* magazine (1965–69).

After making *aliyah* in 1972, Levi devoted his time to editing and translating. He edited *Barnett Janner: A Personal Portrait,* a memoir on the influential British MP and Zionist written by his widow, Lady Elsie Janner (1984). He translated one of the masterworks of Ḥayyim Hazaz, *Gates of Brass* (1973), and B.-Z. Segal's *The Ten Commandments in History and Tradition* (1990).

Levi's *magnum opus*, to which he devoted more than ten years, was an English translation of Gedaliah Alon's *The Jews in their Land in the Talmudic Age*. It is, however, much more than a translation. Levi edited the two volumes from scratch, checked and rechecked the thousands of sources quoted in the book, corrected many errors found in the Hebrew original, prepared the indices, and even wrote an introduction assessing Alon's contributions to Jewish historiography. Praised by critics, the book has become one of the standard texts in Jewish historiography.

BIBLIOGRAPHY: T. Friedman, *Proceedings of the Rabbinical Assembly*, 52 (1990), 238–239; P. Nadell, *Conservative Judaism in America: A Biographical Dictionary and Sourcebook* (1988), 173–74; *New York Times* (April 6, 1990), A20; D. Rome (ed.), *Canadian Jews in World War II*, vol. 1 (1947), 18–20.

[David Golinkin (2nd ed.)]

LEVI, SHABBETAI (1876–1956), mayor of Haifa. Born in Constantinople, he settled in Ereẓ Israel in 1894. There he first taught at Petaḥ Tikvah and later became one of the Baron de *Rothschild's officials in *PICA. He assisted land reclamation projects throughout the country, including Transjordan, and attempted to establish good relations between the Jewish colonies and neighboring Arab villages. Levi represented the *yishuv* and the inhabitants of Haifa in dealings with the authorities during World War I. A founder of the first Hebrew school in Haifa and of the city's Reali school and *Technion, he was also instrumental in the development of Mount Carmel and the suburbs in Haifa Bay. From 1919 he was a councilor on the mixed Arab-Jewish Haifa Municipality; in 1934 he became deputy mayor of Haifa and in 1940 became the first Jewish mayor of the city, a post he held until 1951.

BIBLIOGRAPHY: Tidhar, 2 (1947), 901–2.

[Abraham Aharoni]

LEVI (Bet ha-Levi), SOLOMON (II) BEN ISAAC (1532–1600), rabbi, commentator, author, and community leader. Solomon was a member of the Bet ha-*Levi family which originated from Portugal. He was born in Salonika. His life and activity can be divided into two main periods. During the first period, until approximately 1568, supported by his wealthy father, he was able to devote himself to study and to writing. He studied Talmud and codes in the yeshivah of Joseph ibn *Lev in Salonika, and secular studies and philosophy from private teachers. He gained a proficiency in various languages, and when only 13 years of age, composed a dialogue in Spanish. He seems also to have had a knowledge of Latin. At about the age of 30, he began to study Kabbalah. He married in 1553; two of his sons, Isaac (II) b. Solomon *Levi (Bet ha-Levi) and Joseph, and a daughter, who married Aaron *Sasson, are known. He wrote commentaries to various books of the Bible (including *Ḥeshek Shelomo*, on Isaiah, Salonika, 1600), on *Avot* (*Lev Avot*, Salonika, 1565), and on the *aggadot* of the Talmud (*Leḥem Shelomo*, Venice, 1597). The draft of a work on geography and one dealing with the genealogy and position of the levites, talmudic novellae, and many of his poems are still extant in manuscript. He wrote more than 20 works and commentaries on many aspects of Jewish studies.

During the second period, from 1568, he was appointed rabbi of Üsküb (Skoplje), Yugoslavia, and devoted himself assiduously to community affairs there. In c. 1571, after his father's death, he returned to Salonika where he was appointed rabbi to the Provençal congregation. Two years later his rabbinate was extended to include that of the Évora congregation, one of the most prestigious in Salonika. He served as rabbi of both these congregations as well as head of the Évora congregation's yeshivah until his death. He delivered sermons (some of which were published in *Divrei Shelomo*, Venice, 1596) which attracted a large attendance, including the notable members of the congregations, and his name appears as a signatory on the *haskamot* ("resolutions") signed by the religious leaders of the community. He also wrote responsa to communities in Greece and throughout the Balkans (some of which are still preserved in manuscript). He wrote up talmudic novellae on topics which had evolved from the studies in the yeshivah and wrote marginal notes on such works as the *Arba'ah Turim*, the *Midrash Rabbah*, etc. Toward the end of his life, at his sons' urging, he began to collect and edit his writings, but died before he could finish.

Solomon was an unusual person who was imbued with a sense of mission. He possessed comprehensive knowledge, a fine style, and rhetorical ability, and was a dynamic personality. A man of considerable wealth, he consciously regarded himself as a communal leader, but on more than one occasion went out of his way to defend the community against wealthy members and various leaders who attempted, in his opinion, to exploit their positions in their own interests. He had a large library both of printed works and manuscripts, some on parchment (many of which have been preserved). His ramified, scholarly, and honored family basked in the light of his patriarchal figure. His influence in Salonika was inestimable, and his contemporaries referred to him with veneration. They accorded him the title of "the great rabbi," "the chief rabbi." Solomon regarded communal leadership as the duty of scholars, and his writings reveal that he was alive to the local and contemporary conditions. One can detect in his writings the changes and developments which took place in his personality, especially in his subsequent editing and amendments of his earlier works. His great vitality and his multifaceted personality reveal an encyclopedist, the product of a superb education. These qualities made possible and brought about his great influence on his surroundings from his youth. Combined with his independent means, they made it possible for him to become one of the outstanding leaders of Salonika Jewry in the 16th century.

BIBLIOGRAPHY: A. Geiger (ed.), *Melo Ḥofnayim* (1840), 22 (Heb. part); J. Reifmann, in: *Ha-Maggid*, 3 (1859), 151; E. Carmoly, in: *Ben Chananja*, 5 (1862), 67; Steinschneider, Cat Bod, 2363, no. 6944; idem, Uebersetzungen, 88, 110–1, 228; D. Pipano, in: Abraham le-Bet ha-Levi, *Ein Mishpat* (1897), introd.; Rosanes, Togarmah, 2 (1937–8), 108–10; I.S. Emmanuel, *Histoire des Israélites de Salonique* (1936), 188–91; idem, *Maẓẓevot Saloniki*, 1 (1963), 178–9, no. 407; J. Hacker, in: *Zion*, 34 (1969), 43–89; idem, in: *Tarbiz*, 39 (1970), 195–213.

[Joseph Hacker]

LEVI (Bet ha-Levi), SOLOMON (III) BEN ISAAC (II)

(1581–1634), rabbi of *Salonika and one of the greatest halakhists and writers of responsa of his time. The grandson of Solomon (II) b. Isaac, Solomon engaged in teaching and writing from his youth. He served as head of the *bet din* of the Évora congregation in Salonika in 1631 and was head of the yeshivah of the congregation *Eẓ Ḥayyim*. A man of many talents, he was well known as a preacher and a poet, and he also wrote talmudic novellae. Of his works there have survived his responsa (published posthumously by his widow; Salonika, 1652), some correspondence, poems, and *haskamot*. Solomon studied at the home of his grandfather and his father as well as under Ḥayyim Shabbetai, whom he revered (he was a member of his *bet din*). He maintained close connections with his relatives of the Aaron *Sasson family, even after they moved to Constantinople. Part of his correspondence with Sasson has been published by Hirschensohn (see bibl.) and that with his father-in-law Tam ibn Yaḥya is still in manuscript. From his youth, Solomon was active in the scholarly life in Salonika and had many disciples. His responsa and approbations appear in the responsa collections of his contemporaries. His works received the approbations of the great rabbis of Salonika and

the surrounding communities, while others addressed their halakhic queries to him. He was deeply involved in the charitable needs both of Salonika Jewry and of institutions in Ereẓ Israel, and elsewhere, and several of the appeals addressed to him are still extant.

BIBLIOGRAPHY: Conforte, Kore, 46b; E. Carmoly, *Divrei ha-Yamim li-Venei Yaḥyah* (1850), 40–41; Ch. Hirschensohn, in: *Hamisderonah*, 2 (1888), 161, 190–2, 219–23; A. Danon, in: *Yerushalayim*, ed. by A.M. Luncz (1906–07), 351–4; idem, in: REJ, 41 (1900), 104–5, 257–8, 260–1; M. Wallenstein, in: *Melilah*, 1 (1944), 55; 2 (1946), 138–40; M. Molho, in: *Sinai*, 28 (1950–51), 312–4; I.S. Emmanuel, *Maẓẓevot Saloniki*, 1 (1963), 262–3, no. 599.

[Joseph Hacker]

LÉVI, SYLVAIN

(1863–1935), French Orientalist, born in Paris. Lévi, known for his *Etude critique sur le théâtre indien* (1890), became professor of Sanskrit at the Collège de France (1894), and later director of the Institute of Indian Studies at the Sorbonne (1904). He published *Le Népal, étude historique d'un royaume hindou* (3 vols., 1905–08); *L'Inde et le monde* (1926); and a study on the Jews in South India (in REJ, 89 (1930), 26–32). Lévi founded the French School of the Far East in Hanoi, and later directed the French-Japanese Institute in Tokyo (1926–28). After his return to France he was elected mayor of Andilly, near Paris. He also joined the Zionist Commission headed by Chaim *Weizmann, and set up discussions with the Allied delegations at the Versailles Peace Conference (1919). He left the commission, however, contending that the Zionist program for Palestine opposed French interests in the Middle East. From 1920 until his death Lévi served as president of the Central Committee of the *Alliance Israélite Universelle and of the Société d'Etudes Juives.

BIBLIOGRAPHY: *Hommage à Sylvain Lévi...* (1964); C. Weizmann, *Trial and Error* (1949), 267, 304–6.

[Lucien Lazare]

LEVI, TESTAMENT OF

an ancient Jewish pseudepigraphical work written in Aramaic, probably before 100 C.E.; the work referred to in the the Twelve *Patriarchs. A source of the Testament of Levi is the Testaments of Damascus Document of the Dead Sea sect (4:15). Prior to the discovery of the Dead Sea Scrolls, large fragments of a medieval manuscript, containing the Aramaic original, were found in the Cairo *Genizah* and published. New Aramaic fragments, not all of which have been published, were found among the Dead Sea Scrolls. In a Greek tenth-century manuscript of the Testament of the Patriarchs from Mt. Athos, two larger interpolations in the Testament of Levi can be identified as parts of a Greek translation of the present work; a small Syriac fragment also exists. The Aramaic Testament of Levi is put in the mouth of Levi, the son of Jacob, and represents probably his last speech to his descendants. In the extant fragments, Levi talks about his previous life, and about his function as high priest at Beth-El when he was consecrated by angels. The work contains prescriptions about offerings. These moral and ritual prescriptions are explained to Levi by Isaac his grandfather. Levi's prayer is an important document for the history of Jewish prayers.

This work, abbreviated and rewritten, formed a central source of the Greek Testament of Levi. It is ultimately related to Jubilees chapters 20–22. The Aramaic Testament of Levi contained ideas similar to the Book of Jubilees, the Testaments of the Patriarchs, and the Dead Sea sect. Common to all is the idea, expressed in one fragment of the present work from Qumran, that "priesthood is greater than kingdom," i.e., that Levi is superior to Judah. The Aramaic Testament of Levi was produced within a broader movement in ancient Judaism, from which the Dead Sea sect arose.

BIBLIOGRAPHY: H.L. Pass and J. Arendzen, in: JQR, 12 (1900), 651–61; R.H. Charles and A. Cowley, *ibid.*, 19 (1907), 566–83; R.H. Charles, *Greek Versions of the Testaments of the Twelve Patriarchs* (1908); P. Grelot, in: REJ, 114 (1955), 91–99; D. Barthélemy and J.T. Milik, *Discoveries in the Judaean Desert*, 1 (1955), 87–91; J.T. Milik, *Ten Years of Discovery in the Wilderness of Judaea* (1959), 34; idem, in: RB, 62 (1955), 398–406; D. Flusser, in: IEJ, 16 (1966), 194–205.

[David Flusser]

LEVI, YOEL (1950–), Israeli conductor. Born in Romania, Levi grew up in Israel. He studied at the Tel Aviv Academy of Music where he received his M.A. degree with distinction, and at the Jerusalem Rubin Academy under Mendi *Rodan. He also studied in Siena, Rome, and at the Guildhall School in London. He received first prize in the 1978 Conductors' International Competition in Besançon (France). He became an assistant to Lorin *Maazel at the Cleveland Orchestra for six years and served as resident conductor from 1980 to 1984. He made his operatic debut in Florence (1997), after which he conducted operas of Mozart, Bizet, and Janácek. He was music director of the Atlanta Symphony (1988–2000) when it made a critically acclaimed European tour (1991) and was nominated as "Best Orchestra of the Year" (1991–92) by the first annual International Classical Music Awards. Levi was appointed music adviser to the Israel Festival for the 1997 and 1998 seasons. He later served as music director emeritus of the Atlanta Symphony, music artistic advisor to the Flemish Radio Orchestra (from 2001), and principal guest conductor of the Israel Philharmonic Orchestra (from the 2001–02 season), with which he appeared in a U.S. tour (2004). He regularly appears as guest conductor with renowned orchestras, including the New York Philharmonic. In 1991 he was invited to conduct the Stockholm Philharmonic at the Nobel Prize ceremony. His many recordings with the Atlanta Symphony have won him critical acclaim. Among his recordings are works of Beethoven, Brahms, Mendelssohn, Mahler, Mussorgsky, Schoenberg, Copland, Shostakovich, and Sibelius. Levi was awarded an honorary doctorate of fine arts by Oglethorpe University in Atlanta, appointed distinguished visiting professor at the University of Georgia School of Music, and named Chevalier de l'Ordre des Arts et des Lettres, one of the most prestigious French awards (2001).

BIBLIOGRAPHY: L. Marum, "Keep Your Eye On: Yoel Levi, Conductor," in: *Ovation*, 5 (May 1984), 54; J. Schwartz, "Uncertainty in Atlanta: When Levi Leaves, What Next?" in: *American Record Guide*, 60 (1997), 33–4 n. 5.

[Naama Ramot (2nd ed.)]

LEVI-AGRON, HASSIA (1925–2001), dancer, choreographer, and teacher. Levi-Agron was born in Jerusalem, the descendant of a family living in the country for seven generations. She studied movement and dance with Shoshana Orenstein (1936–46) and Elsa *Dublon, and participated in Gertrud *Kraus' courses. She also enrolled in a teacher's seminar and studied painting, sculpture, and music.

Levi-Agron appeared as soloist before British soldiers and the *Haganah (1943–46). In 1946 she staged her first solo recital, and a year later she produced *Maḥol Niv* ("Dance Idiom"), a show combining dance, music, and text reading. The themes of her works derived from the Bible, from Israeli writers and poets, and from daily life in Israel. In 1947 she traveled to the U.S., where she studied with Martha Graham, Hanya Holm, Louis Horst, and Pearl Primus, and appeared with the East-West Association headed by Pearl Buck. During the 1950s Levi-Agron appeared before World War II refugees under the patronage of the Joint. During the 1950s she taught dance to blind and disabled children, and initiated the creation of the dance department in the newly established Jerusalem Conservatory of Music directed by Yocheved Ostrovsky-Coupernic.

In 1958 she invited Martha Graham to teach in a summer course in Jerusalem and in 1960 she founded the dance department in the Jerusalem Rubin Academy of Music and Dance, which was recognized academically by the Higher Education Authority in 1976. She became professor in 1978. In 1993 she founded Keresh Kefitzah ("Springboard"), a dance company featuring students of the dance department of the Rubin Academy. In 1998 she was awarded the Israel Prize.

Hassia Levi-Agron perceived dance as a tool for life, a form of expression that should be available to every person, therefore she engaged in activities designed to make dance available to all people at all ages, regardless of their professional level, arguing that each student should gain something from his or her dancing experience.

[Bina Shiloah (2nd ed.)]

LÉVI ALVARÈS, DAVID (1794–1870), French pedagogue. A member of a well-known Jewish family of Bordeaux, Lévi Alvarès began his teaching career in private schools, but in 1820 he opened his own institution for girls, under the name "Maternal education courses." His method was based on a weekly session of two hours, in which he personally tested and instructed each grade of pupils in the presence of their mothers (to ensure regular study and their moral upbringing). In addition, his pupils had to work with his textbooks, of which he published more than 60, some of them going into many editions, mainly in history, grammar, and geography. He also taught by correspondence, and he sent several of his assistants to found similar courses in Lyons, Rouen, and Bordeaux. He published a pedagogical journal, *La Mére-Institutrice* (1834–45), and *Plaisir et travail* (1845–65). In 1833 he unsuccessfully attempted to organize a course for student girl-teachers. His pedagogical activity was praised by Parliament (1836). He retired in 1868, but his eldest son THEODORE (1821–1912), who had assisted him since 1841, continued his work till 1891. His second son, EUGÈNE (1825–1899), was a general in the French army while the third, ALBERT (1837–1897), was an engineer and general secretary of Madrid–Saragossa–Alicante railway. Lévi Alvarès contributed to the Jewish-Portuguese community of Paris *Hymnes sacrées à l'usage des Israélites français composés sur les airs hébraïques-portugais les plus connus* (1825, many subsequent editions), a collection of French songs in verse based on traditional Hebrew melodies.

BIBLIOGRAPHY: *Education des Femmes: A Biography of D. Lévi Alvarès* (1909).

[Moshe Catane]

LEVIANT, CURT (1932–), U.S. novelist, translator, and editor. He was the assistant departmental editor of Modern Hebrew and Yiddish literature for the *Encyclopaedia Judaica*. He edited *Masterpieces of Hebrew Literature* (1964) as well as edited and translated *King Artus: A Hebrew Arthurian Romance of 1279* (1969). In addition, he edited and translated Shalom Aleichem's *Old Country Tales* (1966); *Some Laughter, Some Tears: Tales from the Old World and New* (1968); *From the Fair: The Autobiography of Sholom Aleichem* (1985); *The Song of Songs* (1996); *Happy New Year! and Other Stories* (2000); *My First Love Affair and Other Stories* (2002). Leviant's fiction includes *The Yemenite Girl* (1977); *Passion in the Desert* (1980); *The Man Who Thought He Was Messiah* (1990; this work won the National Jewish Book Award); *Partita in Venice* (1999); *Diary of an Adulterous Woman: Including an ABC Directory That Offers Alphabetical Tidbits and Surprises* (2001); and *Ladies and Gentlemen, the Original Music of the Hebrew Alphabet, and, Weekend in Mustara: Two Novellas* (2002). His fiction is nuanced, surprising, and often arabesque, dealing with the demands of the present and the claims of the past.

BIBLIOGRAPHY: *Gale Literary Databases.*

[Lewis Fried (2nd ed.)]

LEVIAS, CASPAR (1860–1934), U.S. Orientalist and lexicographer. Born in Zagare, Lithuania, Levias studied and was a fellow in the department of Oriental languages of Columbia University (1893–94) and in the department of Semitic languages of Johns Hopkins University (1894–95). From 1895 to 1905 he was an instructor of Semitic languages at Hebrew Union College, and from 1910 to 1920 he served as principal of the Plaut Memorial Hebrew Free School in Newark, New Jersey. An ardent Zionist, he devoted much time to the propagation of modern Hebrew literature, and together with R. *Brainin and I. *Schapiro he edited and published the literary journal *Ha-Deror.* His main interest, however, was Semitic philology and grammar, about which he contributed numerous articles to scholarly journals. His chief works were the pioneer study *A Grammar of the Aramaic Idiom Contained in the Babylonian Talmud* (1900), and a Hebrew book on the same subject, *Dikduk Aramit Bavlit* (1930). Only two parts of his *Oẓar Ḥokhmat ha-Lashon*, a study of Hebrew philology, were ever published (1914–15), and a lexicon compiled by him of medical terms in Hebrew literature never appeared at all.

BIBLIOGRAPHY: Kressel, Leksikon, 2 (1967), 191.

LEVIATHAN (Heb. לִוְיָתָן, *livyatan*; Ugaritic *ltn*, presumably pronounced *lōtanu*, or possibly, *lītanu*). In the Bible and talmudic literature the leviathan denotes various marine animals, some real, others legendary, and others again both real and legendary. The word leviathan seems to derive from the root *lwy*, "to coil," which is further confirmation of its serpentine form. In the Bible it is used interchangeably with several other sea monsters – *tannin* ("dragon"), *rahav*, and *yam* ("sea"; of which the last-named alternates with *neharim* ("flood") in Hab. 3:8) – all of whom are represented as supernatural enemies of God. This hostility directly reflects a myth widely known in pre-biblical sources of a primordial combat between the creator deity and the forces of the sea, personifying chaos, which the former must overcome to create and control the universe (see *Creation). The Hittites knew it as the struggle between the dragon Illuyankas and the mortal Hupashiyas (Pritchard, Texts, 125–6; COS I, 150–51). In Mesopotamia it appears in several forms, of which the most famous is the battle of Marduk and Tiamat in the creation epic (COS I, 390–402). More relevant is a cylinder seal from Tell Asmar of the 24th century B.C.E., which pictures two men fighting a seven-headed serpent (reproduced in IDB 3, 116). The leviathan itself may have been found in a Mesopotamian incantation designed "to revive a serpent" (see van Dijk in bibliography). The closest Near Eastern parallel to the biblical materials, however, and probably their actual source, is the Ugaritic myth(s) of Baal and Anat pitted against various sea monsters, one of which is named Lotan (Pritchard, op. cit.; COS I, 265). Not only is this merely another form of the name leviathan, but the same epithets used of leviathan are here prefigured of Lotan, e.g., *btn brḥ* and *btn ʿqltn* as compared with *naḥash bariah* and *naḥash ʿaqallaton* of Isaiah 27:1.

[Peter Machinist]

In Bible and Talmud

In the Bible Leviathan is a multi-headed (Ps. 74:14) sea serpent, appearing in Isaiah 27:1; Psalms 74:14; 104:26; Job 3:8; and 41:1ff. The detailed description in Job (40:25–32) applies to the *crocodile, although a rabbi, maintaining that the reference is to the leviathan – the legendary animal prepared for the righteous in the hereafter – concludes that "the leviathan is a permitted fish," and regards its *maginnim* (Job 41:7) as scales, one of the characteristics of a permitted fish (Tosef., Ḥul. 3:27). On the other hand, *tannin*, which generally denotes the crocodile, sometimes applies to the whale, as would appear from Genesis 1:21. The verse: "Even the *tannin* [*keri*: *tannim*] draw out the breast, they give suck to their young ones" (Lam. 4:3) may refer to the whale, the female of which suckles its young (according to another view, the reference is to the *jackal). The whale is intended in the literal meaning of the verse describing the great sea: "There go the ships; there is leviathan, whom Thou hast formed to sport therein" (Ps. 104:26). At times the long-headed whale (*Physeter catodon*), which is as much as 20 meters (about 65 ft.) long and feeds on large fish and even sharks, reaches the shores of Israel. This may be the basis of the biblical story about "a great fish" that swallowed Jonah (2:1). On rare occasions the largest of the whales, *Sibbaldus (Balaenoptera) musculus*, appears off the Israel coast after entering the Mediterranean through the Straits of Gibraltar.

By *tannin* and leviathan the Bible also intends animals which "in days of old" are said to have rebelled against the Creator, who thereupon destroyed them (Ps. 74:13–14; cf. Isa. 51:10; Job 3:8; 7:12) – similar to the Ugaritic myths mentioned above. Relics of the bones or footprints of prehistoric reptiles may have been found by the ancients (such footprints have been discovered at Bet Zayit in the vicinity of Jerusalem) and these may have served as the inspiration for the myth of the destruction of these gigantic creatures. Some of these verses were used as a basis for the well-known *aggadah* about the leviathan and the *shor ha-bar* ("the wild ox") intended for the righteous in the hereafter. The passage: "There is leviathan, whom Thou hast formed to sport with" has been homiletically interpreted to mean that God sports with the leviathan (Av. Zar. 3b), while the descriptions of the *behemoth and the leviathan in Job (40:15–41:26) have been construed as referring to the fight between these animals, after which the Almighty will prepare from them a feast for the righteous (BB 74b–75a; Lev. R. 13:3; 22:10). This struggle is picturesquely depicted in the **Akdamut*, the Aramaic *piyyut* which is said on Pentecost and which describes the great reward in store for the righteous. In later popular works the words leviathan and *shor ha-bar* became synonyms for the reward of the righteous in the world to come.

[Jehuda Feliks]

BIBLIOGRAPHY: I. Broydé and K. Kohler, in: JE, 8 (1904), 37–39; H. Wallace, in: BA, 11 (1948), 61–68; T.H. Gaster, in: IDB, 1 (1962), 708; 3 (1962), 116; M.D. Cassuto, in: EM, 4 (1962), 485–6; C.H. Gordon, in: A. Altmann (ed.), *Biblical Motifs* (1966), 1–9; J. van Dijk, in: *Orientalia*, 38 (1969), 541; Lewysohn, Zool, 155–8 (nos. 178–80), 355 (no. 505); H.L. Ginsberg, *Kitvei Ugarit* (1936); M.D. Cassuto, *Ha-Elah Anat* (1953[2]); J. Feliks, *Animal World of the Bible* (1962), 51, 94, 108; Gutman, in: HUCA, 39 (1968), 219–30. **ADD. BIBLIOGRAPHY:** C. Uehlinger, in: DDD, 511–15, incl. bibl.; J. Day, in: ABD, 4:295–96.

LEVI BEN ABRAHAM BEN ḤAYYIM (c. 1245–c. 1315), French philosopher, whose teachings were the focus of the anti-philosophical controversy which raged among Jews in Provence and Catalonia between 1303 and 1305. Levi b. Abraham was born at Villefranche-de-Conflent. Persecuted by the opponents of philosophy, Levi was forced to wander from place to place and was poverty-stricken throughout his life. In 1276 he lived in Montpellier, in 1295, in Arles, and in 1303, in Perpignan, in the home of Samuel of Escalita. The latter, influenced by the reproaches directed against philosophy by Solomon b. Abraham *Adret during this period, and seeing a divine punishment in the death of his daughter, drove Levi out of his house. Levi then sought refuge at the home of his relative Samuel b. Reuben of Beziers, where he remained for a time. In 1314 he was in Arles, where he apparently died soon after.

Levi is the author of two works:

(1) *Battei ha-Nefesh ve-ha-Leḥashim* (a title derived from Isa. 3:20), an encyclopedia of medieval science and philosophy, in rhymed prose, written in Montpellier in 1276 (Paris, Ms. héb. no. 978). It is composed of ten chapters of varying length, dealing with ethics, logic, *ma'aseh bereshit* (see *Kabbalah), the soul, prophecy, *ma'aseh merkavah* (the "divine throne-chariot," see *Merkabah Mysticism), mathematics, astronomy, astrology, physics, metaphysics. I. Davidson published the first section of this work together with an anonymous commentary in *Yedi'ot ha-Makhon le-Ḥeker ha-Shirah ha-Ivrit* (vol. 5 (1939), 2–42), and the seventh section in *Scripta Mathematica* (vol. 4 (1936), 57–65).

(2) *Livyat Ḥen*, another encyclopedic work composed of diverse scientific treatises. Divided into six parts, the work seems to have been extant in a long and short version. Fragments of the first five parts of both the long and short versions have been preserved, and so have more lengthy fragments of the sixth section, titled "Boaz." Of the short version the following sections have been preserved: a section on astronomy consisting of 49 chapters (Paris, Ms. héb. no. 1047, fols. 174v–220v), a section on the purpose of metaphysics (Oxford, Ms. Mich. no. 519, fols. 1–17), and fragments of the sixth section, "Boaz" (*ibid.*, fols. 1–127v). Of the long version a section on astrology has been preserved, corresponding to chapter 40 of the short version on astronomy (Paris, Ms. héb. no. 1066, fols. 1–106v), a section on metaphysics (*ibid.*, no. 1050, fols. 60–65), as well as fragments of the sixth section (de' Rossi, Ms. no. 1346, fols. 1–194; Vatican, Ms. héb. 192, fols. 1–147; no. 298, fols. 27–37v).

The fragments of the sixth section, which are lengthier than those of the rest of the work, provide a fairly detailed picture of Levi's views. This section deals with the Bible, the mysteries of faith, *ma'aseh bereshit, ma'aseh merkavah*, and *aggadah*. Adopting the methodology of *Maimonides, Levi uses allegorical exegesis extensively in his attempt to reconcile various biblical and talmudic passages with philosophical doctrines. For example, he interpreted the figures of Abraham and Sarah as representatives of form and matter, and the flood as a psychological upheaval that takes place in the soul of man. It was mainly for his allegorical exposition that Levi was criticized. His contemporaries claimed that in interpreting the Bible allegorically he was negating the literal meaning of the Torah. Levi himself protested that he was not negating the literal meaning but finding additional levels of meaning in the text. In *Livyat Ḥen* one finds many of the allegorical interpretations that Abba Mari *Astruc attacked in his *Minḥat Kena'ot* (1838), but actually Levi's interpretations are no more extreme than those found in the *Guide of the Perplexed* by Maimonides, *Ma'amar Yikkavu ha-Mayim* by Samuel ibn *Tibbon, or *Malmad ha-Talmidim* by Jacob b. Abba Mari *Anatoli.

Like most of the medieval philosophers after Maimonides, Levi agrees with *Averroes on many points, going so far as to accept even his belief in the eternity of the world. Like Maimonides, Levi maintains that the role of the revealed law is to help men acquire moral virtues and to ensure social harmony. He also believes that man's happiness is dependent on the level of his intellectual development, as is the degree of divine *providence accorded him. Levi bases his theory of prophecy on that of Maimonides, but follows Abraham *Ibn Ezra in his interpretation of miracles. Like Ibn Ezra, he believes in astrology, although he does not utilize it as much in the long version as in the short version of the work.

While Levi was not an original thinker, his writings are particularly representative of the philosophy of his time. Examination of his philosophical doctrines gives no clue as to why he was the object of such violent opposition, other than the fact that he supported, both halakhically and theologically, the use of astral magic, which was one of the causes of the controversy over philosophy.

Perhaps it was the encyclopedic nature of his work that seemed so particularly dangerous. It also appears that in his oral instruction Levi was less careful than other philosophers.

BIBLIOGRAPHY: Guttmann, Philosophies, 212, 222; Halkin, in: PAAJR, 34 (1966), 65–76; Renan, Rabbins, 628–74; I. Davidson, in: REJ, 105 (1940), 80–94; C. Sirat, *ibid.*, 122 (1963), 167–77; Baeck, in: MGWJ, 44 (1900), 24–41, 59–71, 156–67, 337–44, 417–23. **ADD. BIBLIOGRAPHY:** H. Kreisel, H. (ed.), *Livyat Ḥen* VI:3 – On Creation (1994); D. Schwartz, "Changing Fronts toward Science in the Medieval Debates over Philosophy," in: *Journal of Jewish Thought and Philosophy*, 7 (1997), 61–82; G. Freudenthal, "Sur la partie astronomique du Liwyat Hen de Levi ben Abraham ben Hayyim," REJ, 148 (1989), 103–12; W.Z. Harvey, "Levi ben Abraham of Villefranche's Controversial Encyclopedia," in: S. Harvey (ed.), *The Medieval Hebrew Encyclopedias of Science and Philosophy* (2000), 171–88; D. Schwartz, *Astral Magic in Medieval Jewish Thought* (Heb., 1999), 245–58;.

[Colette Sirat / Dov Schwartz (2nd ed.)]

LEVI BEN GERSHOM (1288–1344; acronym: **RaLBaG**; also called **Maestre Leo de Bagnols**; **Magister Leo Hebraeus**; **Gersonides**), mathematician, astronomer, philosopher, and biblical commentator, born probably at Bagnols-sur-Cèze (Languedoc – now département du Gard, France). He lived primarily in Orange and briefly at Avignon. Little is known about his life beyond the fact that he maintained relations with important Christian persons. Levi had very broad intellectual interests and contributed to many areas of human learning.

Scientific Work

The scientific works of Levi deal with arithmetic, geometry, trigonometry, and astronomy.

His first work, written in 1321, the *Sefer Ma'aseh Ḥoshev* or *Sefer ha-Mispar* ("The Book of the Number"; published with a translation in German by G. Lange, 1909), is divided into two parts: principles and applications. The work deals with addition, subtraction, multiplication, series, permutation, combination, division, extraction of roots, and proportion. In 1343, Levi composed a second book on arithmetic for Philip of Vitry, bishop of Meaux. Only the Latin translation of the book has been preserved, under the title *De numeris harmonicis* (published by J. Carlebach, *Lewi ben Gerson als Mathematiker* (1910), 129–44).

In his commentary on Books 1–5 of Euclid, which resembles his commentaries on *Averroes, Levi attempts to construct a geometry without axioms, but, in place of Euclid's axioms, he unwittingly introduces other axioms of his own.

In his important treatise on trigonometry (translated into Latin in 1342 under the title *De sinibus, chordis et arcibus* and dedicated to Pope Clement VI), Levi rediscovered independently the sine theorem in the case of plane triangles (proportionality of sines to opposite sides); his sine tables are correct to the fifth decimal.

Talmudic and Liturgical Works

A commentary on the 13 hermeneutical rules of R. *Ishmael (printed in Jacob Faitusi, *Sefer Berit Ya'akov*, 1800) has been attributed to Levi as well as a commentary on the *aggadot* of *Bava Batra*, titled *Meḥokek Ẓafun*. This attribution is probably erroneous. In his commentary on the Pentateuch, Levi reports that he wrote a commentary on the talmudic treatise *Berakhot*, but this commentary is lost. An eminent talmudist, Levi was consulted on questions of *halakhah* (see REJ, 44 (1902), 82–86). A responsum of his can be found in the *She'elot u-Teshuvot* of Isaac de Lattes (1860). Three poems (*pizmonim*) for the holiday of Shavuot and a *viddui* (confession of sins) composed by Levi were published and translated into French by C. Touati (REJ, 117 (1958), 97–105). Levi is also the author of a parody written for the festival of Purim, titled *Megillat Setarim* ("Scroll of Mysteries").

Commentaries on Aristotle and Averroes

In one of his first philosophical works, *Sefer ha-Hekkesh ha-Yashar* (1319), translated into Latin under the title *Liber syllogismi recti*, Levi corrects certain inaccurate arguments of *Aristotle in his *Posterior Analytics*. Levi became acquainted with Aristotle's views by reading the paraphrases and commentaries of Averroes, and he himself wrote supercommentaries on a number of them: on the paraphrase of the *Physics* (1321), on the middle commentary of the *Physics* (1321), on the paraphrase of the *De generatione et corruptione* (1321), on the paraphrase of the *De caelo* (1321), on the paraphrase of the *Meterologica* (1321), on the middle commentary of the *Organon* (1323), on the paraphrase of the *De animalibus* (1323), on the paraphrase of the *De anima* (1323), on the paraphrase of the *Parva naturalia* (1324), on two questions of Averroes concerning Aristotelian logic, and on the letters concerning the union of the separate intellect with man. The supercommentaries on the middle commentary of the *Metaphysics* and the *De plantibus* have been lost. The supercommentaries of Levi on Averroes exist only in manuscript. The Latin translation by Jacob *Mantino of one section of the supercommentary on the *Organon* was published in volume one of the Venice edition of the works of Aristotle (1550–52).

In his commentaries on Averroes, which are important for understanding his philosophy, Levi paraphrases the text but frequently inserts notes of varying lengths, preceded by the words: *amar Levi* ("Levi says"). In these notes he develops, criticizes, or corrects aspects of the ideas of Aristotle or Averroes. He manifests an independent spirit in relation to the two philosophers. Several passages from commentaries on Averroes appear in H.A. Wolfson, *Crescas' Critique of Aristotle* (1929).

Biblical Commentaries

Levi wrote commentaries on Job (1325), Song of Songs (1325 or 1326), Ecclesiastes (1328), Ruth (1329), Esther (1329), the Pentateuch (1329–38), the Former Prophets (1338), Proverbs, Daniel, Nehemiah, and Chronicles (1338). All of these were published, some in several editions. The commentary on Job is one of the first books to be printed in Hebrew (Ferrara, 1477).

The biblical commentaries of Levi are the work of an exegete and a philosopher. Certain of his literal explanations are still of interest today. Diverse questions of a philosophical or theological nature are discussed by him, such as the problem of providence, miracles, and the Messiah. From each book of the Bible, Levi extracts the ethical, philosophical, and religious teachings that may be gleaned from the text and calls them *to'alot* or *to'aliyyot*. A collection of these *to'aliyyot* was printed separately (Riva di Trento, 1570). In his voluminous commentary on the Pentateuch, Levi attempts to reconstitute the *halakhah* rationally, basing himself on nine logical principles which he substitutes for the traditional 13 *hermeneutical rules, and condemning allegorical interpretations. In the 15th century in Italy, Judah Messer *Leon wanted to prohibit the study of Gersonides' commentary on the Pentateuch, using the pretext that the latter wished to fabricate a new Talmud.

Sefer Milḥamot Adonai

Levi's major work, to which he constantly refers in his commentaries on Averroes and the Bible, is the *Sefer Milḥamot Adonai* ("The Book of the Wars of the Lord"), begun in about 1317 and completed in 1329. In this work, he treats problems which, in his opinion, have not received a satisfactory solution by preceding philosophers, including *Maimonides. Divided into six parts, the work deals with the immortality of the soul (first book), dream, divination, and prophecy (second book), divine knowledge (third book), providence (fourth book), celestial spheres, separate intellects and their relationship with God (fifth book), the creation of the world, miracles, and the criteria by which one recognizes the true prophet (sixth book). Numerous manuscripts of the *Milḥamot* are extant, but the book was printed only twice, and then imperfectly (Riva di Trento, 1560 and Leipzig, 1863). The first four books of the *Milḥamot* were translated into German with notes by B. Kellerman (*Die Kaempfe Gottes*, 2 vols., 1914–16), but this translation is unreliable. A French translation of books three and four, based on a critical edition together with an introduction and notes, was made by C. Touati (1968).

The *Milḥamot* is written in a precise and technical Hebrew but, like Levi's other works, it is characterized by repetitiveness. In almost all the questions analyzed, Levi quotes the opinions of his predecessors – Aristotle, *Alexander of Aphrodisias, *Themistius, Al-*Farābī, *Avicenna – with whom he became acquainted largely by reading Averroes, as well as the opinions of Averroes himself and of Maimonides. He enumerates the arguments that, respectively, support and disprove their theses and, finally, he expounds his own theory. Though lacking a systematic structure, the *Milḥamot* contains an almost complete system of philosophy and theology. However, this work cannot be understood unless one is familiar with Levi's commentaries on Averroes and the Bible, which explain and complement the *Milḥamot* on many points. In order to understand the ideas of Levi, one should have recourse to all his philosophical and exegetic works.

His Philosophy

GOD. Demonstrating the existence of God, Levi rejects the proof, favored by many of his Aristotelian predecessors, according to which the existence of God, as prime mover, can be derived from the various motions existing in the world. In its place he presents a proof based on the orderly processes existing in the world, that is, an argument from design. According to this proof, the observed regularity of processes of generation within the sublunar world leads to the conclusion that these processes are produced by an intelligence. This intelligence is the so-called agent intellect (see *Intellect) which governs the sublunar world. This intelligence endows matter with its various forms and is aware of the order it produces. The activities of the agent intellect are mediated by the natural heat which is found in the seeds and sperms of plants and animals and this natural heat in turn is produced by the motions of the various celestial spheres. Since these motions contribute to the perfection of the terrestrial world, they must also be produced by intelligences which know them, that is, they are produced by the intelligences of the celestial spheres. From what has been said, it can be seen that the celestial and terrestrial worlds form an ordered, unitary whole and this requires that there exists a supreme being which produces and knows this order. This being is God.

Unlike Maimonides, Levi maintains that it is possible to ascribe positive attributes to God without reducing or changing His absolute unity and simplicity. Admitting that real multiplicity exists only in beings composed of form and matter, he argues that all the predicates of a proposition dealing with a non-material entity are derived analytically from the subject. According to Levi these predicates are simply an explanation of the subject and introduce no plurality whatever. Opposing Maimonides' doctrine of negative attributes, Levi teaches that man may have a certain positive knowledge of God, based on the observation of His actions. The essential action of God is thinking, and, consequently, the effusion of all forms. All the attributes that man recognizes in his own form are just so many attributes of God. Since the attributes common to both man and God have the relation of cause and effect, it is impossible to consider them absolute homonyms, that is, terms which have nothing in common except their names.

By means of a knowledge that is neither temporal nor changing, God eternally perceives the general law of the universe, that is, those laws governing the movements of the heavenly bodies and, through them, the sublunar beings. God is aware of the fate that awaits all individuals, inasmuch as they are distributed in groups subject to the same celestial determinism which, in principle, governs all the conditions of man. However, this determinism, essentially beneficial, may occasionally cause misfortune. God has therefore accorded man freedom which allows him to liberate himself from the shackles of determinism. An individual who makes use of his freedom is no longer subject to the universal law known by God; he has accomplished an act which is absolutely undetermined and which remains totally unknown to God. God's knowledge, however, does not undergo any modification; it always remains true, since the author of the free act is no longer included in the necessary and universal proposition thought by God. For Levi, God's knowledge embraces all the events of this world, with the exception of free acts that cannot be predicted by any type of knowledge. Levi is convinced that he has finally succeeded in reconciling two contradictory fundamental principles of the Bible: divine omniscience and the freedom of man's will.

The providence of God extends a means of protection that increases in proportion to man's moral and intellectual perfection. Through the determined activities of the stars, God assures a maximum of good to men in general and spares them a maximum of ills. Premonitions, dreams, prophecies and the exercise of free choice save certain individuals from harmful effects of determinism. However, the existence of evil cannot be denied since, at times, the righteous do suffer. But Levi upholds the belief that the true good which is specifically human is the immortality of the soul, and it is this immortality, rigorously proportioned according to one's moral rectitude and intellectual perfection, that constitutes the actual recompense of God.

CREATION OF THE WORLD. In opposition to Maimonides who held that the creation of the world cannot be demonstrated philosophically, Levi offers philosophic arguments designed to show that the world came into being. One such argument is that everything produced by a final cause, ordained to a certain end, and serving as a substratum for accidents, cannot exist eternally. Since the world fulfills all these conditions it follows that it cannot be eternal, that is, that it has a beginning in time. He derives the same conclusion from the state of the sciences. Were the world eternal, he argues, the sciences would be more advanced than they are. He holds further that a large number of Aristotle's arguments designed to prove the eternity of the world beg the question. They are based on the assumption that the physical laws discovered within the world are also applicable to its beginning. However, this assumption is fallacious. For while it is true that there are some similarities between processes within the world and creation (Levi here is more moderate than Maimonides who holds a similar view), creation is also unique. Whereas motions in the world take place in time, creation occurred in an instant. However, since nothing can be created out of nothing, the world has a substratum, an eternal body which is nonetheless a relative non-being, in the sense that it possesses no form whatever. This substratum has no "existence" in the proper sense of the word, since all existence derives from form. Thus the theological difficulty that might give rise to the possibility of more than one eternal being is avoided.

MAN. God has arranged the universe so that man, the most perfect being of the sublunar world, is accorded the greatest good and is spared the greatest amount of ills possible, as we have already seen. Revelations of different types protect him (premonitions, dreams, etc.). His imagination, under the action of one or several celestial bodies, envisions the menace that certain stellar configurations may place upon him. God has equally furnished man with a practical intellect, from which he learns the indispensable arts of self-preservation, and a speculative intellect which permits him to perceive truth and to achieve immortality. The material or potential intellect is not a substance but rather a simple disposition, whose substratum is the imagination. Building on the sensations, the human intellect abstracts concepts; but sensation is only an incidental agent in the production of knowledge, for knowledge in its true sense is the comprehension of intelligibles as they exist in the agent intellect. The human intellect, having understood the intelligible, which is eternal, becomes itself immortal. Differing from Averroes, who maintained that, at this state, the human intellect loses its individuality, Levi held that immortality is individual.

ISRAEL. Providence extends particularly to the children of Israel, chosen by God through His covenant with the Patriarchs. Prophecy is a kind of revelation that is superior to all other types of revelation, and differs from them not in degree but in nature. The prophet must necessarily be a preeminent philosopher who grasps the general laws governing changes in the sublunar world as they exist in the agent intellect. By means of his imagination, he applies this knowledge to given individual or communal situations, announcing the good or evil events that may befall a person, a group, or an entire people, as a result of the operation of the laws of nature. He is also capable of predicting a miracle, which is a violation of nature, not, as Maimonides thought, an event included in the laws of nature at the time of the creation of the world. Levi maintains that a miracle is produced at a particular time and place, and that it occurs when the agent intellect suspends normal, natural law, since it no longer applies to certain circumstances. Though miracles are not part of the laws of nature, or subject to them, they have their own laws. However, since a miracle is produced by the agent intellect, which can only act upon the sublunar world, no miracles can occur in the translunar world. Thus, for example, the sun did not really stand at the order of Joshua; the victory at Gibeon was attained during the short lapse of time when the sun seemingly stood at its zenith.

Through the intermediacy of Moses, the greatest of all prophets, God gave Israel the Torah, which, through its *mitzvot* and speculative truths, aims to help the children of Israel attain the moral and intellectual perfection which makes immortality possible for them. The commandments have various purposes, which Levi expounds in detail, but the purpose of most of them is to remove materialistic tendencies and teach the existence of forms. Finally, the Torah has revealed certain metaphysical truths that the philosophers have never been able to deduce, namely, the creation of the world and the immortality of the soul.

ESCHATOLOGY. Levi's eschatology is based on a tradition that there are two Messiahs. After the Messiah son of Joseph dies, having been assassinated, the Messiah son of David will appear. He will be greater than Moses, not because he will promulgate a new Torah, but because he will accomplish a miracle greater than those of Moses: the resurrection of the dead, an event which will convert all peoples of the earth to the true religion. He predicts the coming of the Messiah for the year 1358. During messianic times, the world will follow its usual pattern, men will die as before, but the earth will be filled with knowledge of God and human liberty will be utilized for good ends.

Views on Levi ben Gershom

On account of his boldness and of the suspicion of heresy fastened to him, Levi was subject to virulent attacks. Certain of his doctrines became the object of harsh criticism on the part of Ḥasdai *Crescas. Abraham *Shalom, while defending him against Crescas, censured him for other reasons. Shem Tov *Ibn Shem Tov labeled Levi's major work the "Wars against the Lord." *Isaac b. Sheshet Perfet, though recognizing Levi as a great talmudist, maintains that it is prohibited to accept certain of his theories. Isaac *Abrabanel, in several of his works, also criticizes him. However, even the most vehement critics of Levi, who very often did not understand his real thought, did not hesitate to borrow some of his ideas. His influence continued to exert itself even as late as the 19th century, when he is mentioned in *Malbim's commentary on Job.

[Charles Touati]

As Astronomer

Milḥamot Adonai contains an astronomical treatise of 136 chapters. This astronomical section (Book v, Part 1) is not included in the manuscripts or printed versions of the rest of the work, but it was translated in its entirety into Latin. There also exists a second Latin version of the first few chapters dedicated to Pope Clement VI. The text covers most of the topics of medieval astronomy: trigonometry (the construction of the sine table and the solution of triangles); the construction and use of various astronomical instruments; an analysis of several schemes for arranging celestial motions; a discussion of solar, lunar, and planetary motions including tables to aid in their computation; and a discussion of the order of the planets and their distances from the earth.

The astronomical treatise was not meant to be an elementary text for students, but presupposes some familiarity with medieval astronomical literature. Although the work is clearly in the Ptolemaic tradition, Levi deals quite critically with his sources and often rejects earlier views in favor of his own. His most important innovation in terms of technical astronomy was his new geometrical model to account for lunar motion, which he describes in chapter 71. He argues that his new model corrects a glaring fault of Ptolemy's lunar model, which brought the moon so close to the earth at quadrature that it appeared twice as large as its observed size. Levi considered agreement with his own observations to be the principal criterion in choosing between alternative models for the motions of the celestial bodies; in this he departed from the widespread medieval dependence on the observations recorded in Ptolemy's *Almagest*. In addition to Ptolemy, Levi relied on al-Battānī, the famous ninth-century Arab astronomer, and to a lesser extent on Abraham *Ibn Ezra and *Abraham bar Ḥiyya. Levi carefully described his observations of four solar and six lunar eclipses, as well as observations of the moon and of the planets under different conditions. Such extensive recording of observations were quite rare among medieval astronomers.

Levi's best-known contribution to astronomy is his invention of the Jacob Staff, which was widely used to measure the angular separation between two celestial bodies. This instrument became an important navigational tool and was especially popular in the 16th century among European sailors.

Most medieval scholars accepted the order of the planets presented by Ptolemy in *The Planetary Hypotheses*: Moon, Mercury, Venus, Sun, Mars, Jupiter, Saturn, and the fixed stars. There was, however, some dispute concerning the place of the sun in relation to Mercury and Venus. Levi considered several possibilities in detail, but seems to have preferred the theory that the sun lies below both planets. In another departure from Ptolemy, who set the distance to the fixed stars at 20,000 earth radii, Levi argued that those stars are more than 159×10^{12} earth radii away, a truly astounding distance in terms of medieval science.

[Bernard R. Goldstein]

ADD. BIBLIOGRAPHY: S. Feldman, *The Wars of the Lord*, vol. 3 (1999), 520–32; M. Kellner, "Bibliographia Gersonidiana: An Annotated List of the Writings by and about R. Levi ben Gershom," in: G. Freudenthal (ed.), *Studies in Gersonides – A Fourteenth-Century Philosopher-Scientist* (1992), 367–416; C. Sirat, S. Klein-Braslavy, and O. Weijers, *Les methodes de travail de Gersonide et le manierement du savoir chez les scolastiques* (2003), 357–76. GENERAL LITERATURE:

G. Dahan (ed.), *Gersonide en son temps* (1991); H. Davidson, "Gersonides on the Material and Active Intellects," in: G. Freudenthal, *Studies in Gersonides – A Fourteenth-Century Philosopher-Scientist* (1992), 195–265; S. Feldman, "Gersonides' Proofs for Creation of the Universe," in: PAAJR, 35 (1967), 113–37; idem, "Platonic Themes in Gersonides' Cosmology," in: *Salo W. Baron Jubilee Volume* (1975), 383–405; idem, "Gersonides on the Possibility of Conjunction with the Agent Intellect," in: *Association for Jewish Studies Review*, 3 (1978), 99–120; G. Freudenthal, "Human Felicity and Astronomy – Gersonides' Revolt Against Ptolemy," in: *Da'at*, 22 (1989), 55–72; idem, Gersonide: Genie Solitaire," in: Sirat, Braslavy-Klein, and Weijers, 291–316; R. Glasner, "The Early Stages in the Evolution of Gersonides' Wars of the Lord," in: JQR, 87 (1996), 1–47; B. Goldstein, *The Astronomy of Levi ben Gerson* (1985); idem, "Preliminary Remarks on Levi ben Gerson's Contributions to Astronomy," in: *The Israel Academy of Sciences and the Humanities*, 3:9 (1969), 239–54; A. Ivry, "Gersonides and Averroes on the Intellect: The Evidence of the Supercommentary on the De Anima," in: G. Dahan (ed.), *Gersonides en son temps* (1991), 235–51; M. Kellner, "Gersonides on Miracles, the Messiah and Resurrection," in: *Da'at*, 4 (1980), 5–34; idem, "Gersonides on the Problem of Volitional Creation," in: HUCA, 51 (1980), 111–28; idem, *Gersonides' Commentary on Song of Songs* (1998); S. Klein-Braslavy, "Gersonides on Determinism, Possibility, Choice and Foreknowledge," in: *Da'at*, 22 (1989), 5–53 (Heb.); idem, "Prophecy, Clairvoyance and Dreams and the Concept of "Hitbodedut" in Gersonides' Thought," in: *Da'at*, 39 (1997), 23–68; T. Langermann, "Gersonides on Astrology," Appendix to vol. 3 of *The Wars of the Lord*, 506–19; idem, "Gersonides on the Magnet and the Heat of the Sun," in: Freudenthal (ed.), *Studies on Gersonides*, 276–82; J. Levi, *Commentaries of Ralbag on the Torah*, 5 vols. (1992, 1994, 1997, 1998, and 2000); C. Manekin, "Gersonides' Logical Writings: Preliminary Observations," in: PAAJR, 52 (1985), 85–113.

LEVI BEN ḤABIB (**Ralbah**; c. 1483–1545), rabbi in Jerusalem and principal opponent of the restoration of the *semikhah. Levi b. Ḥabib was born in Zamora, Spain, and in 1492 was taken to Portugal by his father, R. Jacob *Ibn Ḥabib. There he was forcibly baptized. Both he and his father escaped to Salonika where Levi received his education. He succeeded his father, teaching at the congregation of Spanish exiles, called *Gerush Sefarad*, in Salonika. Levi became famous as a talmudist, showing a preference for the use of literal meaning (*peshat*) as opposed to casuistry (*pilpul*). He never presented his own views unless they had been given by previous scholars. Levi admitted that he was not well versed in Kabbalah, but he was proud of his knowledge of astronomy. In order to atone for his baptism as a youth, he went to Ereẓ Israel, traveling via Asia Minor, Aleppo, and Damascus. He first settled in Safed and later moved to Jerusalem. For 15 years he officiated there, instituting as rabbi various new regulations for the community. At that time, there was no "ordained" (Heb., *samukh*) *bet din*, like the ancient Sanhedrin, i.e., one which was authorized to sentence to punishment by lashes (*malkot*), prescribe fines, and determine the intercalation of months. Therefore the rabbis of Safed decided to restore the ancient *semikhah* and chose R. Jacob *Berab to ordain rabbis and act as a judge. This act was of great significance, as the ordination was to be reestablished only in messianic times, and it also marked the supremacy of the Safed rabbis. Levi b. Ḥabib refused to accept the authority of Berab and accused the latter of disgracing the honor of Jerusalem. A violent controversy ensued whose details are recalled in an appendix entitled *Semikhat Zekenim o Kunteres ha-Semikhah* ("Ordination of the Elders or Pamphlet Concerning Ordination") printed at the end of Levi's responsa (Venice, 1565). The volume also contains Levi's commentary on Maimonides' *Hilkhot Kiddush ha-Ḥodesh*. In addition to responsa, he completed and published the second part of his father's *Ein Ya'akov*.

BIBLIOGRAPHY: Frumkin-Rivlin, index; Rosanes, Togarmah, 2 (1938), 156–8; Y.R. Molḥo, in: *Ḥemdat Yisrael ... H.H. Medini* (1946), 33–42; Y. Katz, in: *Zion*, 16 (1950/51), 28–45; M. Benayahu, in: *Sefer Yovel ... Y. Baer* (1960), 248–69.

[Simon Marcus]

LEVI BEN JAPHETH (**Abū Saʿīd**; 10th–11th century), Karaite scholar, son of *Japheth b. Ali. Levi b. Japheth lived in Jerusalem and wrote, in Arabic, a "Book of Precepts," a work which was used by almost all the later Karaite writers. Only fragments of the Arabic original are preserved. Manuscripts of the Hebrew translation, *Sefer ha-Mitzvot*, are extant in Oxford, Leningrad, and Leiden. In his interpretation of the law, Levi distinguished between the views of the early and later *Rabbanites, numbering *Saadiah Gaon among the latter and frequently censuring him severely. He also wrote a short commentary on the Bible (only fragments of this, too, remain), and is said to have compiled an abridged version of David b. Abraham *Alfasi's dictionary, *Agron*.

BIBLIOGRAPHY: S. Poznański, *Karaite Literary Opponents of Saadiah Gaon* (1908), 42–46; Z. Ankori, *Karaites in Byzantium* (1959), index, s.v. *Levi b. Yefeth*.

LEVI BEN SISI (end of second and beginning of third century, C.E.), Palestinian and Babylonian *amora*. He is mentioned in the Babylonian Talmud without a patronymic, but with his father's name in the Jerusalem Talmud. He was a colleague-disciple of *Judah ha-Nasi (Ber. 49a; Shab. 107b; Zev. 30b; Men. 80b, et al.), whom he called *Rabbenu ha-Kadosh* ("Our Holy Master," Shab. 156a). Although Judah sometimes scolded him (Yev. 9a), he held his scholarship in high regard (Zev. 30b). So authentic were the traditions handed down by him that the words *lemedin li-fenei ha-ḥakhamim* ("It was taught before the sages") are said to refer to Levi's transmission of the teachings of Judah ha-Nasi (Sanh. 17b). The Talmud gives various details of his intimate position in Judah's household: he was the merrymaker on festive occasions and entertained those present with acrobatic performances. Once he tried to imitate the manner in which the priests used to prostrate themselves in the Temple, but dislocated his hip which resulted in a permanent limp (Suk. 53a). Levi taught that at prayer a person must stand with his feet straight like the angels (TJ, Ber. 1:1, 2c). He used to write down in a notebook the discussions with his teacher R. Judah Ha-Nasi (Shab. 156a). He also had a collection of *beraitot* which is mentioned several times in the Talmud (Yoma 24a; Yev. 10a; Ket. 53b; et al.). Levi was held to possess special power for successful intercession on such occasions as drought (Ta'an. 25a) or danger from bandits (TJ, Ta'an. 3:8, 66d).

Levi seems to have traveled often between Ereẓ Israel and Babylonia and was well acquainted with the cultural conditions of the peoples of Babylonia. After his return from one of these journeys Judah ha-Nasi asked him about their particular characteristics (Kid. 72a). When the citizens of Simonia sought a judge and spiritual leader, Judah ha-Nasi recommended Levi, who, despite his initially disappointing performance, was appointed on the strength of the recommendation (TJ, Yev. 12:7, 13a). After the death of Judah ha-Nasi, when Afess was appointed in his place, Levi discontinued his studies at his master's academy but studied with R. *Ḥanina b. Ḥama outside the walls of the yeshivah. For this behavior he was criticized by many of his contemporaries, and according to legend he was punished for this by exclusion from the "academy in heaven" until Samuel interceded on his behalf and he was admitted (Ber. 18b). After the appointment of Ḥanina b. Ḥama as head of the academy, Levi migrated to Babylonia where he joined the school of *Rav (Beẓah 24b; Ket. 52a) and other former disciples of Judah ha-Nasi (Shab. 59; Ket. 103b).

Levi settled finally in Nehardea where he became a close friend of *Abba b. Abba, the father of *Samuel (Ber. 30a; BB 42b). Both studied in the old synagogue of the town called Shaf ve-Yativ, according to legend built of stones brought from Jerusalem by Jehoiachin, and witnessed there the appearance of heavenly messengers (Meg. 29a). Levi also lectured at the academy there (Song. R. 4:8) and was associate judge at the court of the *exilarch Mar *Ukba (Ukva; Pes. 76b; BB 54a) who held his erudition in very high esteem (Shab. 108b; MK 26b). Levi instructed his friend's son, later the famous Babylonian *amora* Samuel, who transmitted many of his master's teachings (Shab. 108b; Er. 10a, et al.). Among Levi's prominent pupils were *Mattnah (MK 26b) and a number of *amoraim* who later migrated to Ereẓ Israel, including *Assi (Av. Zar. 38b), *Ḥiyya b. Abba (Eccl. R. 1:4), and *Ze'ira (Shab. 108b). After Levi's death Abba b. Abba eulogized him as a scholar whose worth was equal to that of the rest of mankind (TJ, Ber. 2:85a).

BIBLIOGRAPHY: Hyman, Toledot, 859–62; Ḥ. Albeck, *Mavo la-Talmudim* (1969), 153–5.

LEVI-BIANCHINI, ANGELO (1887–1920), Italian naval officer and member of the *Zionist Commission. Born in Venice, Levi-Bianchini completed his studies in the naval academy at Leghorn and joined the Italian navy, becoming a naval officer (a rare occupation among Italian Jews). Afterward he became a lecturer at the naval academy and at the military school in Turin. In 1917 he was appointed to the Navy ministry, on behalf of which he fulfilled several missions. With the establishment of the Zionist Commission, Levi-Bianchini, together with G. Artom, joined as a representative of the Italian Jewish community, in close liaison with the Italian Foreign Office. He arrived in Palestine in the summer of 1918 and immediately strengthened his ties with Chaim *Weizmann, members of the Zionist Commission, and the various circles of the *yishuv*. In addition, Levi-Bianchini won the confidence of many in the British military government and Arab leaders. He also contributed directly and indirectly to the organization of self-defense in the *yishuv* and represented the interests of the *yishuv* and the Zionist Movement before *Allenby and the British military government. In April 1919 he prevented the outbreak of disturbances following the Arab holiday and traditional parade from al-Nabi Mūsā. In May of the same year he left Palestine. He continued his service for the Italian government, participating in the Versailles Conference in 1919 and the San Remo Conference in Italy in 1920, at which he worked to procure the Italian Foreign Office's approval of the British Mandate on Palestine and the *Balfour Declaration in general. In 1920 Levi-Bianchini was sent by the Italian foreign minister, Sforza, to examine the situation in Palestine and Egypt, especially the role of the Zionist Movement in the new political developments in the Middle East. He was killed near Khirbet el Gazale in a Bedouin attack on a train making its way from Damascus to Haifa. His body was eventually found near the scene of the attack and was buried in Turin about a year after his death.

BIBLIOGRAPHY: S. Minerbi, *A. Levi-Bianchini e la sua opera nel Levante 1918–1920* (1967); idem, in: D. Carpi (ed.), *Ha-Ẓiyyonut*, 1 (1970), 296–356; C. Weizmann, *Trial and Error* (1949), 212.

[Getzel Kressel]

LEVI-CIVITA, TULLIO (1873–1942), Italian mathematician. Levi-Civita, who was born in Padua, was appointed to the chair of mechanics at the university there at the age of 25. In 1918 he left Padua to become professor of mechanics at the University of Rome. He opposed the rise of fascism in Italy. He was dismissed from his position after the implementation of the anti-Jewish laws of 1938. After this, his health deteriorated rapidly and he was unable to accept any of the offers of asylum which he received from several countries. Levi-Civita was an excellent teacher and his many scientific papers and books are distinguished by their lucidity. He developed, after an initial collaboration with Curbasto Gregorio Ricci, the absolute differential calculus, which was the essential mathematical tool required by Einstein for his development (in 1916) of the general theory of relativity. Levi-Civita's most important contribution in this field was the theory of "parallel displacement." He also produced significant papers on relativity, analytical dynamics, hydrodynamics, and systems of partial differential equations. Levi-Civita was a member of many Italian and foreign mathematical societies. In 1922 he was awarded the Sylvester Medal of the Royal Society.

BIBLIOGRAPHY: Hodge, in: Royal Society of London, *Obituary Notices of Fellows*, 4 (1942–44), 151.

[Barry Spain]

LEVI DELLA VIDA, GIORGIO (1886–1967), Italian Arabist and Semitist. Born in Piedmont, della Vida completed his university studies in *Rome. In 1914 he began to lecture at the University of Naples, went on to Turin, and in 1920 was appointed professor at Rome University. He taught Biblical Hebrew, Arabic, Syriac, Phoenician and neo-Punic inscriptions, and the histories of the Semitic peoples and their literatures. In all these fields, he published many articles. A number of them, principally in the field of Judaism and Islam, were gathered into the collection *Storia e religione dell'oriente semitico* (1924). He also edited a series of Arabic and Syriac texts with his translations. His catalog of the Vatican Arab-Muslim manuscripts (vol. 1, 1935; vol. 2, 1965), his collection of documents dealing with the relations between the Church of Rome and the Oriental churches during the reign of Pope Gregory XIII (1948), as well as a series of detailed articles on the manuscripts of the Vatican collection were the fruits of the years he worked in the Vatican Library. His later works include *Anneddoti e svaghi arabi e non arabi* (1959) and a book of memoirs *Fantasmi ritrovati* (1966). He was one of the 12 lecturers (out of a total of 1,225 university teachers) who refused, at the end of 1931, to take the oath of allegiance to the Fascist regime and he was therefore dismissed from his position. From 1939–48, he was professor at the University of Pennsylvania, but in 1948 was reinstated in his position in Rome.

BIBLIOGRAPHY: G. Strachan, *Giorgio Levi della Vida* (Eng., 1956); *Studi orientalistici in onore di Giorgio Levi della Vida* (1956). **ADD. BIBLIOGRAPHY:** M.G. Amadasi, "Bibliografia degli scritti (di Giorgio Levi Della Vida)," in: OA, 7 (1968), 17–38; F. Michelini Tocci, "Giorgio Levi Della Vida nell'anniversario della morte," in: IONA, 18 (1968), 463–68; S. Moscati, "Ricordo di Giorgio Levi Della Vida," in: OA, 7 (1968), 1–15; S. Moscati, *Ricordo di Giorgio Levi Della Vida* (1968); Anon., *Giorgio Levi Della Vida: nel centenario della nascita (1886–1967)* (1988).

[Haïm Z'ew Hirschberg]

LEVIEN, SONYA (1888–1960), U.S. screenwriter. Born Sara Opeskin near Moscow, daughter of Fanny and Julius Opeskin, Levien immigrated to New York City with her mother and brothers in 1896. Her father, who had preceded his family to the United States, changed the family name to Levien. Known as Sonya, Levien earned a law degree from New York University and practiced law briefly. In 1917, she married writer Carl Hovey.

Levien began her prolific film scriptwriting career as a magazine writer and editor, working for *Women's Journal* and the *Metropolitan*, a liberal literary journal. Levien sold her first story to a motion picture studio in 1918. Her first screen credit was for the 1919 film *Who Will Marry Me*? Between 1929 and 1941, Levien was a writer for 20th Century Fox and MGM; from 1941 to 1956 she worked for George Sidney Productions. Levien wrote or co-wrote the screenplays of more than 70 motion pictures, including some of the most acclaimed films of her era. In her script for *The Hunchback of Notre Dame* (1939), based on an adaptation by Bruno Frank, Levien made the story relevant to contemporary audiences by drawing a parallel between the persecuted gypsies of Paris and the treatment of Jews in pre-World War II Germany.

Levien created strong women characters who were intelligent, noble, and independent. She was responsible for a number of the most important early depictions of Jewish characters in Hollywood films, in her scripts for *Cheated Love* (1921), *Salome of the Tenements* (1925), *The Younger Generation* (1928), and *Rhapsody in Blue* (1943).

Levien earned many accolades during her long and highly successful screenwriting career, including an Academy Award in 1955 for *Interrupted Melody*. The Screen Writers Guild (now known as the Writers Guild of America) bestowed their most distinguished award on Levien in 1953, as the first recipient of the Laurel Award of Achievement, given to that member of the Guild "who has made outstanding contributions to the profession of the screenwriter."

BIBLIOGRAPHY: L. Ceplair, *A Great Lady: A Life of the Screenwriter Sonya Levien* (1996); S. Levy-Reiner, "Levien, Sonya," in: P.E. Hyman and D.D. Moore (eds.), *Jewish Women in America*, vol. 1 (1998), 831–32.

[Sharon Pucker Rivo (2nd ed.)]

LEVIEV, LEV (1956–), Israeli entrepreneur. Leviev was born in Tashkent, Uzbekistan, to a religious family. In 1971 his family moved to Israel. Shortly afterwards, Leviev began to work as an apprentice in a diamond polishing plant, setting up his own plant following his army service. When the former Soviet Union began to open its doors to foreign investment during the 1990s, Leviev expanded his business activities to Eastern Europe. In 1996 he acquired control of Africa-Israel Investments, one of Israel's largest companies, with holdings and assets valued at over $1 billion. He controls global businesses in such fields as international trade, diamonds, real estate, infrastructure development, metals, chemicals, high-tech development, and hotels, with the Leviev Group's annual turnover reaching $1.8 billion. Leviev is the biggest private diamond manufacturer in the world, with diamond polishing plants in Russia, India, China, South Africa, Ukraine, and Armenia, as well as eight marketing agencies globally. He serves as chairman of the Israel-Russia and CIS Chamber of Commerce and Industry. He is also active in the Jewish communities of the former Soviet Union. In 1992 he established the Or Avner foundation in his father's memory. The foundation operates an Orthodox education network with branches in Israel and the former Soviet Union. Its goal is to bring new immigrants closer to Judaism and Torah. Leviev was president of the Federation of Jewish Communities of the CIS (FJC), the central organization that represents the 15 organized Jewish communities of the independent republics that were once part of the Soviet Union. He also served as honorary consul of the Republic of Kazakhstan in Israel and as president of the Bukharan Jewish Congress, which unites close to 250,000 members worldwide and helps address the religious and cultural needs of the Bukharan communities.

[Shaked Gilboa (2nd ed.)]

LEVI ISAAC BEN MEIR OF BERDICHEV (c. 1740–1810), ḥasidic *ẓaddik* and rabbi; one of the most famous personalities in the third generation of the ḥasidic movement. Levi

Isaac was born into a distinguished rabbinic family and his father was rabbi in Hoshakov (Galicia). After marrying the daughter of a rich contractor he moved to his father-in-law's home in *Lubartow (Poland), where he studied with Joseph *Teomim. At that time he met Samuel Shmelke *Horowitz of Nikolsburg, then rabbi in Richwal (Ryczwol), who acquainted him with the Ḥasidism of *Israel b. Eliezer Ba'al Shem Tov. In 1766 Levi Isaac went to study under *Dov Baer the Maggid of Mezhirech, becoming one of the intimate circle of his pupils. When Shmelke left Richwal Levi Isaac replaced him, though only for a short period. He next served as rabbi in Żelechów, where he first emerged as a ḥasidic *ẓaddik*; to his contemporaries he became known as the "rabbi in Żelechów." A testimony dating from 1774 reports that he took a strong and even aggressive stand against the local *Mitnaggedim*, but the latter finally triumphed and Levi Isaac had to leave Żelechów. An account of this controversy appears in the *Iggeret ha-Kodesh* by Eliezer the son of *Elimelech of Lyzhansk, published at the end of the latter's *No'am Elimelekh*, 1788. In 1775 he was elected rabbi of Pinsk but there, too, he was dismissed through pressure from the *Mitnaggedim* and with the concurrence of *Elijah b. Solomon Zalman of Vilna. Moving to Berdichev in 1785, he served as rabbi there until his death. In Berdichev Levi Isaac won great renown as rabbi, ḥasidic leader, and scholar; even the *Mitnaggedim* admitted that he was a noted Torah scholar (*Zemir Ariẓim* (Warsaw, 1798), 3) but complained of his lack of knowledge of the Kabbalah. He made many amendments in communal *takkanot* and took part in public affairs. In 1801(?) he convened a meeting of leaders (in which the *ẓaddik* Baruch b. Jehiel of Medzibezh and the *maskil* writer Menahem Mendel Levin participated) to discuss the government's prohibition on Jewish settlement in the villages and other oppressive measures; in 1807 Levi Isaac's name headed a list of Jewish contributors to the Russian war effort against the anticipated French invasion. During a serious illness in 1793, "he was grieved and his spiritual forces declined" (*Oẓar ha-Ḥayyim ve-Heikhal ha-Berakhah*, introduction to the Book of Numbers). In this crisis he was helped by Israel b. Shabbetai the Maggid of *Kozienice.

The founder of Ḥasidism in central Poland, Levi Isaac consolidated the movement in Lithuania and furthered it in the Ukraine. When he was still in Poland (Żelechów) the *mitnagged* writer, *David of Makow, described him as "rabbi of all that sect" (see M.L. Wilensky, in: PAAJR, 25 (1956), 151), an indication of his widespread popularity. While he was rabbi in Pinsk he engaged in a debate with the fanatic *Mitnagged* Abraham *Katzenellenbogen, a rabbi of Brest-Litovsk. At Praga near Warsaw before the month of Elul 1781, they discussed basic precepts of Ḥasidism, both parties later claiming victory. On the fifth of Tammuz 1784, Abraham Katzenellenbogen circulated an epistle summarizing his arguments against Ḥasidism, but Levi Isaac's reply is not extant.

In his teachings Levi Isaac stressed the element of joy in Ḥasidism, the principle of *devekut* ("adhesion") to God, and the necessity for fervent prayer to the point of *hitpashetut ha-gashmiyyut* ("abstraction from corporeality"). When a man prays fervently "with all his heart and his soul then his spirit delights because it is elevated from the material world and only the spirit remains" (*Kedushat Levi*, Va-Yeẓe). It is necessary that "every Jew should worship the Creator with devotion and fervor" (*Kedushat Levi*, Va-Yera). One of the best loved of *ẓaddikim*, Levi Isaac occasionally traveled with great acclaim throughout the land. Accompanied by his *minyan*, he introduced the people to the joy of fulfilling the commandments, winning them over to Ḥasidism. Before the Holocaust, visitors to the *bet midrash* in the "Iron Gate" in Warsaw were shown a column in front of which Levi Isaac used to pray when he visited the city. The *Mitnagged* Israel *Loebl also reports on his visits to Warsaw and his fervent prayers: "And here I will tell you the story of R. Levi the rabbi of Berdichev, when he was in Łazienki, the king's pleasure gardens. He boasted that he had never prayed a *Minḥah* like the one he uttered there" (*Sefer ha-Vikku'aḥ* (Warsaw, 1798), 19).

Levi Isaac shared the distress of his people and worked to improve their living conditions. In singing his prayers he addressed the Creator in Yiddish; popular tradition has preserved some of these ("The *Kaddish* of R. Levi Isaac" etc.; see *Kaddish*). He stressed the good that is in man and always pleaded the cause of Jews: "No one has a right to say anything evil about the Jewish people, but only to intercede for them" (*Kedushat Levi*, Ḥukkat). He distinguished between two types of preacher: he who admonishes "with good words," who shows man "his merit and the source of his soul," bringing out his superior qualities and indicating opportunities for him to rise; and he who admonishes "with severe words," awes and subdues. Only he who "admonishes Jewish people gently, elevates their souls and always extols their righteousness is worthy of being their leader" (*ibid.*). Levi Isaac's book of sermons, *Kedushat Levi*, was published during his lifetime (Slavuta, 1798; Zolkiew, 1806) and was supplemented by his sons from manuscripts (Berdichev, 1811).

Although he did not found a dynasty, Levi Isaac had many pupils and left an indelible mark on Ḥasidism. He was a popular hero in Jewish poetry and fiction both in Hebrew and in Yiddish; the following plays are especially noteworthy: Ya'akov Cohen's *Ha-Ẓe'akah ha-Shelishit* (his complete works, vol. 4, 1945); the first play in *Sheloshah Ketarim* by Zevi Cahn (1954); Y. Sela, *Ha-Sanegor ha-Gadol* (1958). Important poems are Z. Shneur's "*Din Torah Ḥadash le-Rabbi Levi Yiẓḥak mi-Berdichev*" (*Shirim* (1960), 111–4), Uri Zevi *Greenberg's "*Be-Keẓ ha-Derakhim Omed Rabbi Levi Yiẓḥak mi-Berdichev ve-Doresh Teshuvat Ram*" (in: *Reḥovot ha-Nahar*, 1951), and S. *Meltzer's ballad "*Din Torah*" (in: *Or Zaru'a*, 1959). He was also depicted in Joseph *Opatoshu's well-known story, "In Poylishe Velder" (1921).

BIBLIOGRAPHY: Dubnow, Ḥasidut, 151–7, 193–201, 479–81; idem, *Chassidiana* (Heb.) – supplement to *He-Avar*, 2 (1918); Horodezky, Ḥasidut, 2 (1951^3), 71–96; S. Gutmann, *Tiferet Beit Levi* (1909); A.Z. Aescoly, *Introduction à l'étude des hérésies religieuses parmi les juifs. La Kabbale. Le Hassidisme* (1928); C. Lieberman, in: *Sefer ha-*

Yovel… Alexander Marx (1943), 15–17; M. Buber, *Tales of the Hasidim – the Early Masters* (1947), 203–34; M.E. Gutman, *Mi-Gedolei ha-Ḥasidut* (1953²); I. Halpern, in: *Tarbiz*, 28 (1959), 90–98 (*Yehudim ve-Yahadut be-Mizraḥ Eiropah* (1969), 340–7); J. Twersky, *Ḥayyei R. Levi Yiẓḥak mi-Berdichev* (1960); L. Jung (ed.), *Men of the Spirit* (1964), 403–13.

[Avraham Rubinstein]

LEVI-MONTALCINI, RITA (1911–), neurobiologist, Nobel Prize winner. Levi-Montalcini was born in Italy and grew up in Turin. She earned her degree in medicine at the University of Turin where she was employed until 1939 when she was barred by the Fascists from practicing medicine and from working in the university. Undaunted she continued her cell research by conducting experiments in an improvised laboratory in her bedroom with embryos from eggs which she had begged for to feed "needy children." Since she was a member of the "Jewish race," the results of the experiments could not be published in fascist Italy, but they did appear in Belgium, establishing her scientific reputation. The family fled to Belgium, but with Hitler's invasion of the country in 1940 returned to Italy. They hid in Florence under the name "Lovisato," claiming to be southern Italians – with a northern accent. In 1947 Levi-Montalcini accepted a teaching and research position at Washington University in St. Louis, Missouri, with Professor Viktor Hamburger. There in June 1951 she made the discovery for which she and Dr. Stanley *Cohen, who worked with her at that time, were awarded the 1986 Nobel Prize for medicine, the isolation of the nerve growth factor (NGF), a protein which stimulates the growth of sensory and sympathetic nerves in animals and in cultures.

Levi-Montalcini, who holds both United States and Italian citizenship, returned to Italy in 1977 to head a research laboratory of the National Council of Scientific Research in Rome. She was the first woman elected to the Pontifical Academy of Science and the sixth woman to be accepted into the National Academy of Sciences (1968). In addition to the Nobel Prize, Levi-Montalcini received the Feltrinelli International Prize in medicine in 1969, the St. Vincent Prize in 1980, and the Albert Lasker Basic Medical Research Award for 1986.

LEVIN, A. LEO (1919–), U.S. law professor and administrator. Born in New York City, Levin, son of an Orthodox rabbi and Mizrachi leader, graduated with a B.A. degree from Yeshiva University (1939) and a law degree from the University of Pennsylvania Law School (1942). He began to teach law at the University of Pennsylvania in 1949 and became a full professor in 1953. From 1963 to 1968 he was vice provost at the university, and then for a year (1969–1970) he served as vice president for academic affairs at Yeshiva University. He returned to teaching law at the University of Pennsylvania in 1970. In 1989 he was named professor emeritus.

In addition to teaching law, Levin was prominently involved in judicial administration. In 1977 he was appointed director of the Federal Judicial Center in Washington, D.C., an agency created by an act of Congress in 1967, to conduct research on the operation of federal courts, to conduct training programs for judges and court personnel, and to engage in related activities designed to make the federal court system efficient. He served in that capacity until 1987.

Other positions that Levin held are executive director of the Commission on Revision of the Federal Courts Appellate System (1973–75); chairman of the Pennsylvania State Legislative Reapportionment Commission (1971–73); founding director of the National Institute for Trial Advocacy; member of the Standing Committee on Practice and Procedure, Judicial Conference of the United States (1977–78); conference coordinator, National Conference on Causes of Dissatisfaction with the Administration of Justice (the so-called Pound Conference, 1976–77); and he has been a member of the National Institute of Corrections since 1977.

Levin is a Fellow of the American Academy of Arts and Sciences and an honorary trustee of Bar-Ilan University. He was formerly president of the Jewish Publication Society, and is a member of the Board of Directors of the American Judicature Society. He also served on the Planning Committee of the Claims Commission, which made recommendations regarding the proper allocation of reparation and restitution funds to be paid to Holocaust survivors.

Among his publications are a study of judicial administration in Pennsylvania, a casebook on civil procedure, and a book on trial advocacy, as well as numerous law review articles. These books include *The American Judiciary* (1982), *Dispute Resolution Devices in a Democratic Society* (1985), and *Cases and Materials on Civil Procedure* (with P. Schuchman et al., 1992)

[Milton Ridvas Konvitz / Ruth Beloff (2nd ed.)]

LEVIN, ALTER ISAAC (pseudonym: **Asaf ha-Levi, Ish Yerushalayim**; 1883–1933), Hebrew writer. Born in Russia, he immigrated to Palestine in 1891 and studied at religious schools in Jerusalem. He worked as an insurance broker but subsequently became enmeshed in financial difficulties and committed suicide. He was also an art collector. Encouraged by Israel Dov *Frumkin, Levin wrote poems and articles for **Ḥavaẓẓelet* and other newspapers in Palestine. He published a collection of poems, *Megillat Kedem le-Asaf ha-Levi Ish Yerushalayim* (1920), and a booklet of folk songs, *Shirei Am* (1920).

BIBLIOGRAPHY: D. Kimḥi, *Massot Ketannot* (1938), 80–86; Y.R. Feldmann (Rabbi Binyamin), *Mishpeḥot Soferim* (1960), 169–72; *Haaretz* (Sept. 28, 1934).

[Getzel Kressel]

LEVIN, ARYEH (affectionately referred to as "**Reb Aryeh**"; 1885–1969), the most saintly figure in modern Israel. Aryeh Levin was born in Orla, near Grodno, Belorussia, to poverty-stricken parents. At the age of nine he left home to study at various yeshivot, notably the Yeshivah of Slutsk, then headed by Isser Zalman *Meltzer, and subsequently in Volozhin. He immigrated to Ereẓ Israel in 1905, continuing his studies in the *Ez̦ Ḥayyim yeshivah in Jerusalem. From 1915 until his last days his official position was spiritual mentor (*mashgiaḥ*) to the *talmud torah* attached to the Ez̦ Ḥayyim yeshivah.

Although an outstanding talmudic scholar, receiving *semikhah* from the greatest rabbis of the time, Ḥayyim *Berlin, Samuel *Salant, and Abraham Isaac Ha-Kohen *Kook, whose faithful follower he was, and although from 1949 he conducted a yeshivah in the upper rooms of his modest home, Reb Aryeh's fame and the widespread and boundless esteem in which he was held sprang not from his learning but his good works. Humble, and living in conditions of near poverty, he devoted his life for nearly 50 years, in an entirely honorary capacity, unwearyingly and without thought of self, to acts of charity and love. He appointed himself chaplain to the hospitals, especially the Leper Hospital, comforting mourners, bringing a message of love and hope to the distressed and the unfortunate, radiating benignity by the very touch of his hand.

Reb Aryeh regarded it as his special mission to attend to the needs of the Jewish political prisoners who had been incarcerated by the British Mandatory Government, particularly those who were sentenced to death, acting as a go-between between them and their families and accompanying them in their last moments. He was widely known as "the Rabbi of the Prisoners." Reb Aryeh refused all honors, including the Freedom of Jerusalem, and never moved out of the poor quarter of Mishkenot in Jerusalem.

Tens of thousands, including the most notable personalities in the country, attended his funeral.

BIBLIOGRAPHY: S. Raz, *Ish Z̦addik Hayah* (1972; English, *A Tzaddik in our Time*, 1976).

[Simha Raz (2nd ed.)]

LEVIN, BERNARD (1928–2004), British newspaper columnist. Levin was one of the best-known and most controversial newspaper columnists in contemporary Britain. He was educated at the London School of Economics and became prominent in BBC's television satire programs of the 1960s. He is best remembered for his biweekly columns in the London *Times*. Originally on the left, and a lifelong liberal opponent of censorship and excessive punishment, after about 1970 he became nationally known as one of the most vocal champions in the British press of Soviet Jews and dissidents. Renowned for his biting wit, Levin was critical of aspects of Israel's policies and regularly championed the playing of Richard *Wagner's music. His history of Britain in the 1960s, *The Pendulum Years* (1971), is a standard account.

[William D. Rubinstein (2nd ed.)]

LEVIN, CARL (1934–), U.S. senator from Michigan, longest-serving senator in Michigan history, ranking Democrat on Senate Armed Service Committee. Levin was born in Detroit to an ardently Democratic family, and politics seemed to be part of the family's vocation. His uncle Theodore Levin was a Federal judge, his older brother, Sander *Levin, was a member of the House of Representatives from 1983, and his first cousin was a Michigan Supreme Court judge while another first cousin, Joseph Levin, was a candidate for the House of Representatives.

Levin was educated in Detroit public schools, and graduated from Swarthmore (1956) and Harvard Law School (1959). He was an assistant state attorney general and first general counsel for the Michigan Civil Rights Commission from 1964 to 1967 and then chief appellate defender of the city of Detroit from 1968 to 1969 before being elected to the City Council where he served from 1969 to 1977. He was Council president from 1973 to 1977 and then was elected to the Senate in a race against the then Senate Minority Whip Robert P. Griffin.

In the Senate he served on the Armed Service Committee, at one time chairing it; in 2005 he was the leading Democratic voice on national defense with a reputation for propriety and a propensity to fight waste. His position forced him to challenge the Bush Administration on prewar intelligence though he was known for his keen support of national defense. Levin is the ranking Democrat on the Permanent Subcommittee on Investigations of the Homeland Security and Governmental Affairs Committee.

Among his other accomplishments was the investigation of the collapse of Enron and the spikes in gasoline prices. A champion of government ethics, he was the author of the Ethics Reform Act of 1989 and was central to the enactment of the Special Counsel Law. Representing Michigan, Levin has been concerned about the fate of organized labor and the automobile industry. A strong supporter of Israel, he also represents the largest Arab-American constituency in the United States.

In an era of glib politicians who are media savvy, Levin typically appears with his glasses on his nose in suits that are anything but tailor-made. Yet his command of the issues is strong, his mastery of material evident, and his integrity unquestioned. The people of Michigan have elected him time and again.

[Michael Berenbaum (2nd ed.)]

LEVIN, EMANUEL (**Menahem Mendel**; 1820–1913), author and communal worker, early pioneer of *Haskalah in Russia. A teacher of Russian and German in new schools in Vilna and his native Minsk, Levin wrote *Dikduk Leshon Rusyah* ("Grammar of the Russian Language") in 1846 and published a Russian translation of *Pirkei Avot* with notes in 1868. He founded a school for girls in Minsk, and in 1852 he was appointed as a teacher in the government rabbinical seminary in *Zhitomir. In 1857 he entered the service of the barons Y. and H. *Guenzburg, becoming their confidant and secretary for Jewish affairs. Under their instructions he drafted memoranda and appeals to the authorities, including a memorandum on the pogroms of 1881–82 to the Pahlen Commission, the government committee which discussed the Jewish question (see *Russia). Levin published several collections of the special laws concerning the Jews in Russia (*Sbornik ogranichitelnykh* *zakonov... o yevreyakh*, 1902). He also drafted the constitution of the *Society for the Promotion of Culture among the Jews of Russia and served as its first secretary (1863–72). From 1895 Levin was a member of the historical committee of the society and one of the collaborators in the publication of the collection *Regesty i Nadpisi*. Levin was also the secretary of several conventions of the leaders of Russian Jewry, including the meetings of the communal delegates during the years of the pogroms of 1881–82. He died in St. Petersburg.

BIBLIOGRAPHY: Goldstein, in: *Yevreyskaya Starina*, 9 (1916), 253–75.

[Yehuda Slutsky]

LEVIN, HANOCH (1943–1999), Israeli playwright, poet, and theater director. Levin was born in Tel Aviv, the city in which he lived most of his life and in which he died at the age of 56. A most prolific writer, he wrote 58 plays in different dramatic genres, two books of prose, *The Eternal Patient and His Beloved* and *A Man Stands Behind a Sitting Woman*, two collections of satirical sketches, several songs including "*Mah Ikhpat la-Ẓippor*" ("What Does the Bird Care") and "*The Gigolo from Congo*," and a book of poems, *The Life of the Dead*.

Levin grew up in a Tel Aviv milieu characterized by acute differences – between native-born Israelis and new immigrants, between rich and poor, Ashkenazi and Sephardi Jews, Jews and Arabs – differences that became more acute after the Six-Day War (1967). These differences and the feelings they provoked became the fuel for his theater, the target of his fierce socio-political criticism. Levin started his theatrical career with satires: short satirical sketches and poems that he wrote during his studies at Tel Aviv University (1964–67). These were published on the back cover of the students' journal *Dorban*. In the political satires that followed, *You, Me and the Next War* (1968) and *Ketshup* (1969), Levin attacked the arrogance of Jewish society in Israel after the victory of 1967. He juxtaposed the voice of the individual soldier who wanted above all to come home alive with the military discourses of the politicians and generals. In all of these sketches Levin was sending a prophetic warning about the tragic results for Israeli society of the occupation and colonization. The two productions, performed in front of small audiences, got mixed responses. Levin caused a public outcry with his *Malkat ha-Ambatiyah* (*Queen of the Bathtub*) directed by David Levin, his brother, at the Cameri Theater in April 1970. From the first performance on, reactions were violent inside and outside the theater. Levin was accused of slaughtering the "sacred cows" of Israeli society, mainly the Israeli army, war widows, and bereaved parents, and of destroying Jewish solidarity during a state of war. In response to the pressure exerted from all quarters – actors at the Cameri, audiences, journalists, and political figures – the play was stopped after 19 performances.

Solomon Grip (Open Theater, Tel Aviv, 1969), *Ḥefetz* (Haifa Municipal Theater, 1972) and *Ya'akobi and Leidenthal* (Cameri Theater, 1972) marked the emergence of a new genre, that of tragi-comedy. These plays dealt with the desires and misfortunes of insignificant people, descendants of the "heroes" of Mendele Mokher Seforim and Shalom Aleichem, Gogol and Chekhov, trying to live meaningful lives in their poor, unnoticed neighborhoods. In the following tragi-comedies, *Young Vardale* (1974), *Kroum* (1975), *Popper* (1976) *Rubber Merchants* (1978), *Winter's Funeral* (1979), *Suitcase Packers* (1983), *The Labors of Life* (1989), *The Hesitant* (1990), *The Wondrous Woman Within Us* (1994), and *The Whore from Ohio* (1997), Levin excavated the anxieties and fears, the hopes and disillusionments, the humiliation and subjugation that reign in the relationships between man and woman, mother and son, parents and children, among friends and family members. His comedies were constructed of short scenes, where the characters tried to communicate in short, lean dialogue and sentimental song. His comic style, impregnated with grotesque and satirical elements, represented the characters' inner voices as conversations and their vain efforts to fulfill their desires as Sisyphean tasks.

In 1979 with the performance of *Execution* at the Cameri Theater, Levin announced a new direction – mythological plays where he explored the dramatic strategies of tragic writing. Under this broad rubric there appeared plays based on the mythological traditions of Western civilization: *The Sorrows of Job* (1981), *The Great Whore of Babylon* (1982), *The Child Dreams* (1993), *Open Mouth* (1995), and *Decapitation* (1996); others were based on new readings of Greek tragedy: *The Lost Women of Troy* (1984), *Everybody Wants To Live* (1985), *The Man with the Knife in the Middle* (1990, unperformed), *The Emperor* (1996, unperformed), *The Weepers* (2001); still other plays were readings of Christian tragedy: *Salvation* (1993, unperformed), *Chlodog the Miserable King* (1996, unperformed). In some other plays Levin represented modern existence and the modern conscience in terms of modern mythological metaphors. These include *The Dreamer* (1983), *Rape Trial* (1989, unperformed), *Those Who Walk in The Dark* (1997), and *Requiem* (1998). Shifting between Greek myth and biblical stories enabled Levin to examine the Jewish God through the eyes of a pagan. Thus, despite the fact that he defined God as "a collector of stamps with rare misprints" (*The Sorrows of Job*) or as the symbolization of pure chance, Levin was still able to present him not as a cruel or compassionate God, but as an alienated onlooker observing the downfall of man. Levin employed the mythical format as both a legitimate way of representing reality and a primary poetical way of describing man's earthly existence. In these plays, the only meaningful associations were those between the subject and the forces which determined his existence, his destiny, and his death. They alone were responsible for his suffering and his destruction. Human existence became, in these plays, a spectacle in which Man examines his most firmly held beliefs and discovers his own fragility. The dramatic situations illustrate the gradual abasement of the human protagonist: the dissolution of his familiar boundaries, followed by the loss of his dignity and self-esteem and culminating in his isolation and annihilation. However, Levin's theater is characterized by a constant search for a special balance between the violent deeds enacted or recounted on the stage and the compassion embedded in the poetic text. This balance constitutes the important components in Levin's concept of modern tragedy.

Levin began his directing career at the Cameri Theater in Tel Aviv when he directed *Ya'akobi and Leidenthal* in 1972. Subsequently the Cameri Theater became his "home," though he later directed in most of the established theaters in Israel. Levin was known for his long collaboration with actors and theater artists. In the 21 plays he directed, he worked again and again with the same actors – Zaharira Harifai, Yosef Carmon, Albert Cohen, Gita Munte, Itzchak Chizkiya, Sasson Gabai, Rivka Gur, Michael Koresh, Dror Keren, Yehudah Almagor, Dinah Blei, Sandra Shoenwald, and others. He also worked with stage designers Ruth Dar, Moshe Sternfeld, Roni Toren, and Rakefet Levi, and composers Alex Kagan, Poldi Shatzman, Uri Vidislavski, and Yossi Bin Nun. All these theater artists contributed to the emergence of Levin's unique theatrical language, to the spectacular and meaningful metaphors on stage that enhanced the poetic words of his texts. Levin's *The Labors of Love, Selected Plays* (2003) is available in English.

BIBLIOGRAPHY: E. Brown, "Cruelty and Affirmation in the Postmodern Theatre: A. Artaud and H. Levin," in: *Modern Drama*, 55 (1992), 251–77; M. Handelsaltz, *Ha-Te'atron shel H. Levin* (2001); R. Feldhay Brenner, "The Terror of Barbarism and the Return to History, Between the Text and the Performance of Murder by H. Levin," in: *Hebrew Studies*, 43 (2002), 153–86; D. Urian, "The Arab in H. Levin's Works," in: *Hebrew Studies*, 43 (2002), 217–32; N. Yaari and S. Levy (eds.), *H. Levin: The Man with the Myth in the Middle* (2004); Z. Caspi, *Ha-Yoshevim ba-Ḥoshekh* (2005).

[Nurit Yaari (2nd ed.)]

LEVIN, HARRY (1912–1993), U.S. literary critic and editor. Levin taught at Harvard from 1944. The author of *James Joyce: A Critical Introduction* (1941), he is especially known for his writings on American and European literature. His *The Power of Blackness* (1958) is a study of the problems of innocence and evil in the works of Hawthorne, Poe, and Melville. His works include *Symbolism and Fiction* (1956) and *The Gates of Horn: A Study of Five French Realists* (1963).

LEVIN, IRA (1929–), U.S. author. Born in the Bronx and raised in Manhattan, Levin earned two bachelor's degrees from New York University in 1950, one in English and one in philosophy. Although his father wanted him to join the family's toy business, Levin opted to try writing for two years, with the proviso that if he failed he would work with his father. He never did. He sold his first script to the National Broadcasting Corporation for its *Lights Out* television drama. His first book, *A Kiss Before Dying* (1952), won the Edgar Allan Poe award from the Mystery Writers of America as the year's best first mystery. It was filmed first in 1956 and then in 1991. In 1953 Levin was drafted into the army. He served with the Signal Corps but he still managed to work as a writer, producing training films for troops. While he continued to write for television, he won the assignment to adapt the comic novel *No Time for Sergeants*, about a hillbilly inducted into the military, for the Broadway stage. It ran for 796 performances. Levin's second novel, published in 1967, was his most famous work, *Rosemary's Baby*. In it, an apparently average couple find new friends among devil-worshippers. The book sold more than five million paperback copies in the United States alone and was translated into many languages. The film, starring Mia Farrow and John Cassavetes, was a tremendous commercial success. The screenplay was adapted by Roman *Polanski, who won an Academy Award for this horrifying tale of Satanism and the occult. *Rosemary's Baby* is credited with being a turning point in horror fiction, as books and movies dealing with the occult suddenly came into vogue. Levin's next book was *This Perfect Day*. It met with mixed reviews, but then came *The Stepford Wives* (1972). Levin was living then in Wilton, Conn., a suburb of New York, and he wrote the book while going through a divorce. The book, about a small town where men have had enough of women's liberation, is sometimes viewed as a male antidote to the then burgeoning feminist movement. It was filmed twice and made into sequels for television. The idea of women as robots doing men's bidding touched a nerve in the American psyche and spawned a number of sequels and offshoots, and the word "Stepford" entered the common vocabulary, meaning anyone who allowed his role in society to be dictated by someone else. While Levin had a few plays that were unsuccessful, like the musical *Drat! The Cat* (which included the hit song "She Touched Me," written by Levin), this was not the end of his writing career. Levin turned in 1972 to *The Boys from Brazil*. In it Hitler has been cloned, and the Fourth Reich is on its way. Levin wrote about Josef Mengele attempting to create an army of Hitler clones. It was made into a gripping film, with Laurence Olivier, Gregory Peck, and James Mason. Levin produced the comedy-thriller *Deathtrap* (1978) for Broadway. It ran for a record-breaking 1,792 performances and was made into a film that starred Christopher Reeve and Michael Caine. In 2004 Levin was honored by the Mystery Writers with its Grand Masters Award.

[Stewart Kampel (2nd ed.)]

LEVIN, JUDAH LEIB (known by the acronym **Yehalel** = **YeHudah Leib Levin**; 1844–1925), Hebrew socialist poet and writer and one of the first members of Ḥovevei Zion. He received an Orthodox education at home but studied secular subjects and became completely estranged from his former environment. In 1870 he was employed as tutor and secretary by the *Brodskis, the Jewish sugar magnates of Kiev, and worked for them until the Soviet regime closed the enterprise in 1918. In 1871 he published his first collection of poetry, *Siftei Renanot* (Zhitomir, 1871), which was well received by the Hebrew reading public. His socialist views stemmed from reading Russian radical and socialist literature and observing the relations between his employers, the Brodskis, and their employees. He joined the circle of A.S. *Liebermann and helped him publish his newspaper, *Ha-Emet*. Most of his poems which appeared from 1874 to 1880 in *Ha-Shaḥar* dealt with social problems and sharply criticized the existing order and the regime. His poems, actually essays in rhyme, were minor and innovative only in that they were the first to introduce socialist themes into Hebrew literature and poetry. Levin's interest in problems of Jewish life increased when Russian nationalism and antisemitism grew stronger. The pogroms in 1881 brought a decisive change in Levin's ideas; he drew even further from the socialist circles and devoted himself to the problems of Jewish life. He joined Ḥovevei Zion, was one of the founders of this pre-Zionist movement in Kiev, and through letters and articles propagandized for the settlement of Ereẓ Israel. He translated Disraeli's *Tancred* (*Or la-Goyim*, Warsaw, 1884), which visualizes the return of the Jews to their land. Because of this activity he had to leave Kiev and settle in the small town of Tomashpol where he worked for Brodski and continued with his literary work. Living in remote Tomashpol had an adverse effect on Levin. Out of touch with his contemporaries, he did not progress with the mainstream of Hebrew poetry and literature. In 1910, the jubilee of his literary work, he published his memoirs, *Zikkaron ba-Sefer*, including a chronological list of his writings. With the onset of the Russian Revolution Levin returned to Kiev, where he spent his last years in poverty and loneliness. A selection of his memoirs, articles, and poems was published in 1968 as *Zikhronot ve-Hegyonot*.

BIBLIOGRAPHY: Y. Yevarkhyahu, *Yahalal* (1946); J.L. Levin, *Zikhronot ve-Hegyonot* (1968), 7–28 (introd. by Y. Slutsky); J.L. Levin, *Ketavim Nivḥarim* (1911), 1–9 (introd. by M.M. Feitelson); S. Breiman, in: *Shivat Ẓiyyon*, 3/4 (1953), 164–77; Klausner, Sifrut, 6 (1958), 118–87 (incl. bibl.); LNYL, 4 (1961), 244f. (incl. bibl.); Waxman, Literature, 3 (1960^2), 258–60. **ADD. BIBLIOGRAPHY:** L. Scheuer, "*Yahalal*," in: *Nachrichtenblatt* (June 1980), 4–6; Y. Kabakov, *Bein Yahalal le-Soferei Amerikah*, in: *Hadoar*, 51 (1973), 163.

[Yehuda Slutsky]

LEVIN, JUDAH LEIB (1863–1926), rabbi. Born in Lithuania, he was educated at Volozhin, and then at Kovno where he was ordained by Rabbi Isaac Elchanan Spektor. He then became rabbi in Liskava. In 1892 he immigrated to the United States, arriving first in Rochester, and then he returned to Europe to become the rabbi in Kreva. But within a year he returned to the United Sates to become the rabbi at Congregation Bikur Cholim in New Haven, Connecticut.

In 1897 he went to Detroit as the rabbi of three congregations, Beth Jacob, B'nai Israel, and Shaarey Zedek, where he spent the remainder of his life. He arranged the three congregations into a formal federation known as the Union of Orthodox Hebrew Congregations. He established a yeshivah in Detroit that was later named in his memory: Beth Yehuda. He was a founder of Agudat Harabbonim and a strong supporter of Mizrachi. He organized a parade in support of Zionism in 1931 in Detroit. An inventor, he received patents for calculators, one of which was exhibited at the Smithsonian Institution. He is the author of *Ha-Aderet veha Emunah*.

BIBLIOGRAPHY: M.D. Sherman, *Orthodox Judaism in America: A Biographical Dictionary and Sourcebook* (1996).

[Michael Berenbaum (2nd ed.)]

LEVIN, LEWIS CHARLES (1808–1860), U.S. lawyer, editor, and congressman. Levin, who was born in Charleston, South Carolina, attended South Carolina College (now the University of South Carolina). After studying law, he settled in Philadelphia in 1838 where he was admitted to the bar. There, he achieved prominence as a temperance speaker and editor of the *Temperance Advocate*. He was a founder of the Native American (later "Know-Nothing") Party in 1843 and edited and published its official organ, the *Daily Sun*, in Philadelphia. Elected as a candidate of the Native American Party to the 29th, 30th, and 31st Congresses (March 4, 1845–March 3, 1851), Levin championed a high tariff, expansionism, public works, including a dry dock at Philadelphia, and "Know-Nothing" legislation. After being defeated for reelection in 1850, he resumed his law practice.

BIBLIOGRAPHY: J.A. Forman, in: AJA, 12 (1960), 150–94.

[Perry Goldman]

LEVIN, MAKSIM GRIGORYEVICH (1904–1963), Soviet Russian ethnologist and physical anthropologist. Levin did extensive field work in Siberia and wrote on the ethnology of Asiatic Russia and Siberia. The expert knowledge accumulated in these expeditions is reflected in his *Narody Sibiri* ("Peoples of Siberia," 1956), which he edited with L.P. Potapov and to which he was himself an important contributor; and in *Istoriko-geograficheskiy atlas Sibiri* ("A Historico-Geographical Atlas of Siberia," 1961), which he again edited with L.P. Potapov. He also wrote *Ocherki po istorii antropologii v Rossii* (1960), a history of the development of anthropology. One of his works, *Etnicheskaya antropolgiya i problemy etnogeneza narodov Dal nego Vostoka* (1958), became available in English translation in 1963 as *Ethnic Origins of the Peoples of Northeastern Asia*. Levin became deputy director of the Institute of Ethnography of the Academy of Sciences of the U.S.S.R. and head of its physical anthropology section, and edited many of the institute's publications.

[Ephraim Fischoff]

LEVIN (LEFIN), MENAHEM MENDEL (1749–1826), early Haskalah author, translator, and educator. Born in Satanov, Podolia, he had a traditional Jewish education but also studied sciences, mathematics, and medieval philosophy in his youth. From 1780 to 1783/84 Levin lived in Berlin, where he met Moses *Mendelssohn, through whom he established contact with the leaders of the Haskalah. His first popular literary success was a Hebrew translation of Tissot's *Manual of Popular Medicine and Hygiene*, undertaken with Mendelssohn's encouragement. Through a chance encounter, he made the acquaintance of one of Poland's leading statesmen, Prince Adam *Czartoryski, who ultimately became his patron, helping him to publish his work and allotting him a stipend. Levin taught mathematics and philosophy to Czartoryski's children, which was rare at that time, and dedicated his unpublished philosophical treatise, "*Aus dem Nachlass eines Sonderlings zu Abdera*," to Czartoryski's wife. When the great Sejm met in Warsaw (1788–92), Levin participated in discussions on contemporary problems. Toward the end of the 18th century, he resided in Ustye and in St. Petersburg in the home of the wealthy philanthropist J. *Zeitlin, serving as tutor to his grandson. After 1808 he lived in Brody and Tarnopol, where his influence on the *maskilim* in Galicia, notably N. *Krochmal and J. *Perl, was so considerable that he is regarded as the father of the Galician Haskalah.

Believing that the achievement of the objectives of the Haskalah depended, in large measure, upon making books readily available to the public, he dedicated himself to the publication of both secular and religious works. Like other *maskilim*, Levin derived his views on Judaism primarily from Maimonides, and he prepared a new version of the *Guide of the Perplexed* (Zolkiew, 1829), which he wrote in mishnaic Hebrew, hoping thereby to make the work more accessible to the modern reader. Levin's main contributions to Jewish literature were his use of mishnaic Hebrew, whose style he described as "light and pure," rather than the biblical rhetoric employed by almost all of his literary contemporaries, and his willingness to write works in Yiddish – the anathema of the Haskalah. Thus he directed a number of Haskalah writers toward a more popular Hebrew style and many of his usages and neologisms have entered modern Hebrew. To render certain books of the Bible more easily comprehensible to the East European Yiddish speaker, he produced an idiomatic Yiddish translation of the ethical and poetic books of the Hagiographa: Psalms, Proverbs, Job, Lamentations, and Ecclesiastes. However, the appearance of his translation of Proverbs (Tarnopol, 1813) was bitterly criticized by *maskilim*, especially Tobias *Feder, who objected to the use of Yiddish, denouncing it as a betrayal of Haskalah ideals and a reversion to parochialism. Levin's other Yiddish works either remained in manuscript or were published after his death.

Levin was more of a popularizer than an original writer. Most of his works were translations, popularizations, or proposals designed to improve the condition of the Jews through the use of Enlightenment ideas, i.e., the application of reason to the social, economic, and moral problems of the community. For example, believing that poverty among the Jews stemmed from their involvement in petty commerce, he suggested that the situation could be improved only by Jewish participation in basic industry, the skilled trades, and farming. In spite of his strong opposition to Ḥasidism, he did not hesitate to request help from the leaders of the ḥasidic community in order to achieve communal reforms. Levin's approach to social and cultural problems was particularly influenced by the Edict of Tolerance (1781) of *Joseph II of Austria, and by N.H. *Wessely's *Divrei Shalom ve-Emet* (1782). Advocating the reform of Jewish education, Levin, like Wessely, urged that secular studies, especially the sciences, be added to Torah learning. The language of instruction, he believed, should be Polish, and that the Bible should be taught with the aid of a Polish translation. Although opposing fanaticism, Levin nevertheless held that religion was the driving force in the history of the Jewish people. He, therefore, vehemently opposed those *maskilim* who deviated from traditional observance. Unlike Mendelssohn, he wanted to preserve the wide internal autonomy of the *kehillah* and the jurisdiction of the Jewish rabbinical courts, but recommended the reorganization of the rabbinate so that it included district rabbis who possessed secular as well as talmudic knowledge.

Levin opposed Kabbalah, and Ḥasidism which he claimed to be responsible for lowering morality among the Jews. The first writer to see Ḥasidism as the most powerful opponent of the Haskalah, Levin urged rabbis to attack Ḥasidism and to censor its books as well as kabbalistic works. In his unpublished *Maḥkimat Peti* and *Der Ershter Ḥasid* Levin satirized the "nonsense" in Ḥasidic writings, social mores, and theoretical principles. In his opinion the authorities were interested in bringing Enlightenment to the Jews, and he suggested the enactment of legislation for this purpose. The best way of combating Ḥasidism was by undertaking educational work among the Jews. Levin died in Tarnopol.

Among his other writings are *Moda la-Binah*, containing essays on science and excerpts from *Refu'ot ha-Am* and *Iggerot Ḥokhmah* (Berlin, 1789); *Ḥeshbon ha-Nefesh* (Lemberg, 1812), ethical essays patterned on Benjamin Franklin's *Poor Richard's Almanac; Masot ha-Yam* (Zolkiew, 1818; Lemberg, 1859), a translation of Campe's travel book; *Elon Moreh*, an introduction to the *Guide of the Perplexed* (Odessa, 1867); *Sefer Kohelet* (Odessa, 1873; Vilna, 1930), a Yiddish translation of Ecclesiastes; and *Essai d'un plan de réforme ayant pour objet d'eclairer la nation juive en Pologne et de redresser par là ses moeurs* (1791–92).

BIBLIOGRAPHY: Klausner, Sifrut, 1 (1952²), 224–53, includes bibliography; Zeitlin, Bibliotheca, 202–4; J.S. Raisin, *Haskalah Movement in Russia* (1913), 99–101; N.M. Gelber, in: *Abraham Weiss Jubilee Volume* (1964), 271–305, Hebrew part; idem, in: *Aus Zwei Jahrhunderten* (1924), 39–57; J. Weinloes, in: *Ha-Olam*, 13 (1925), iss. 39–42; idem, in: YIVO *Bleter*, 3 (1931), 334–57; J.L. Landau, *Short Lectures on Modern Hebrew Literature* (1938²), 187–92; M. Wiener, *Tsu der Geshikhte fun der Yidisher Literatur in 19ten Yorhundert* (1945), 38–44; S. Katz, in: KS, 16 (1939–40), 114–33; M. Erik (Merkin), *Etudn tsu der Geshikhte fun der Haskale* (1934), 135–51; Ch. Shmeruk, in: *Yidishe Shprakh*, 24 (1964), 33–52; Waxman, Literature, index, s.v. *Leffin*.

[Avraham Rubinstein]

LEVIN, MEYER (1905–1981), U.S. novelist. Born and raised in the Chicago slums, Levin became a reporter for the Chicago *Daily News* and in 1925 was sent to cover the opening of the Hebrew University of Jerusalem, and returned to Palestine in 1928 to spend a year on a kibbutz. He had already written short stories of Jewish life, some of which appeared in the *Menorah Journal*, but his *Yehuda* (1931) was one of the first novels about kibbutz life. In *The Golden Mountain* (1932), reissued in 1966 as *Classic Hassidic Tales*, he retold stories of the Ḥasidim, and in *The Old Bunch* (1937) portrayed his own generation of Chicago Jews. Levin was a correspondent in Spain during the Civil War (1936–39) and later reported the Palestine disorders for the Jewish Telegraphic Agency (1945–46). In 1946 he made the first feature film of the *yishuv*, *My Father's House*, and a documentary, *The Illegals*, in 1947. His autobiography, *In Search*, appeared in 1950.

Levin's writings covered a wide field – from Jewish mysticism to the modern American scene, which he depicted with realism and vitality. His novels include *Reporter* (1929), *Frankie and Johnny* (1930, reedited as *The Young Lovers*, 1952), *The Fanatic* (1964), and *Stronghold* (1965). Levin was the first writer to dramatize *The Diary of Anne Frank* (1952). Levin's own account of the turmoil he underwent to bring his version of the diary to the stage is found in his *The Obsession* (1973). His bestseller, *Compulsion* (1956), a study of the *Loeb-Leopold murder case of the 1920s, was dramatized by the author himself (1959) and filmed. *Eva* (1959) told the story of a Jewish girl's escape from Nazi-occupied Poland to Palestine. Levin also published a Passover *Haggadah*, various histories of Israel for juveniles, and books on the synagogue and the Jewish way of life. In 1958 he settled in Israel, which was the setting for his erotic extravaganza, *Gore and Igor* (1968). Israel is also the subject of his novels *The Settlers* (1972) and *The Harvest* (1978).

ADD. BIBLIOGRAPHY: L. Graver, *An Obsession with Anne Frank: Meyer Levin and the Diary* (1995); R. Melnick, *The Stolen Legacy of Anne Frank: Meyer Levin, Lillian Hellman and the Staging of the Diary* (1997); S. Rubin, *Meyer Levin* (1982).

[Sol Liptzin]

LEVIN, NATHANIEL WILLIAM (1819–1903), pioneer New Zealand merchant and communal leader. Probably born in London, he arrived at Port Nicholson (Wellington) in 1841, opened a store, and prospered, although the store was destroyed by an earthquake in 1848. Levin became a dynamic force in local commercial and maritime enterprises, establishing interests in the whaling trade and exporting wool. He built his own wharf and owned a fleet of sailing ships. A justice of the peace and foundation member of many public institutions, he was appointed to the Legislative Council in 1869, but retired to London in 1871. Earlier he took part in the affairs of the embryo Wellington Jewish community, his name appearing as a trustee to the Crown grant of the Jewish cemetery land. He was the father of William Hort Levin MP. The town of Levin was named after the family.

BIBLIOGRAPHY: *Journal and Proceedings of the Australian Jewish Historical Society*, 3 (1949–53), 305a; L.M. Goldman, *History of the Jews in New Zealand* (1958), index. **ADD. BIBLIOGRAPHY:** *New Zealand Dictionary of Biography*; R. Gore, *Levins, 1841–1941* (1956).

[Maurice S. Pitt]

LEVIN, NORA (1916–1989), historian of the Jewish experience for general audiences. Born in Philadelphia to Joseph and Bertha Levin, Levin received her B.S. in education at Temple University in 1938 and her B.S. in library science in 1941 from the Drexel Institute of Technology in Philadelphia. After serving as a visitor for the Department of Public Assistance in Philadelphia from 1938 to 1940, she started a career as a reference librarian, working at the Free Library of Philadelphia (1941–43), Time, Inc. (1943–44), and *Holiday* (1945–47). Levin served as the executive secretary of the Philadelphia Council of the Women's Labor Zionist Organization of America, *Pioneer Women, from 1948 to 1953. Between 1953 and 1970, she taught high school history and English in the Philadelphia public schools. Levin became an instructor of Jewish history at Gratz College in Philadelphia in 1970, where she taught until her death in 1989. In that year, Gratz College awarded her a D.H.Lit. posthumously.

Levin was the author of three books, including one of the earliest general accounts of the Shoah, *The Holocaust: The Destruction of European Jewry, 1933–1945* (1968). In 1977, she wrote *While Messiah Tarried: Jewish Socialist Movements, 1871–1933*, a study of various movements that wedded socialist principles to a vigorous Jewish identity. Levin also wrote a two-volume study, *Jews in the Soviet Union since 1917: Paradox of Survival* (1988). Always a community activist, she regularly wrote articles for journals of opinion like the *Jewish Frontier*, *The Reconstructionist*, *Commonweal*, and *The Nation*.

[Marsha L. Rozenblit (2nd ed.)]

LEVIN, POUL THEODOR (1869–1925), Danish author, critic, and journalist. Born in Copenhagen, Levin wrote plays and literary studies, but was best known for his successful novels idealizing home life and the role of women. These include *Familien i Danmark* (1911), *Lykkens Veje* ("The Ways of Happiness," 1913), and *Mariannes Mor* (1921). Levin also contributed to *Berlingske Tidende* and from 1910 edited the periodical *Tilskueren*.

LEVIN, RICHARD C. (1947–), president of Yale University. Born in San Francisco, Levin received his bachelor's degree in history from Stanford University in 1968. He studied politics and philosophy at Oxford University, earning a bachelor of letters degree. In 1974 he received his doctorate in economics from Yale, and he joined the Yale faculty that same year.

An influential economist, Levin focused on the economics of technological change, including industrial research and development and the effects of public regulation on private industry. His work in the 1970s and 1980s on the Interstate Commerce Commission influenced railroad deregulation. At Yale, Levin taught courses on microeconomics, the oil industry, and the history of economic thought, among other subjects. He became director of graduate studies in economics, then was appointed chairman of the Economics Department in 1987. He was named the Frederick William Beinecke Professor of Economics at Yale in 1992, and he became dean of the Graduate School that same year.

Levin was named president of Yale in 1993. One of the longest-serving Ivy League presidents, he became known for several initiatives. Under his presidency, Yale invested over

$2 billion in renovation and building, focusing on the expansion of the university's medical and science facilities. At the same time, Levin worked to build a partnership with the city of New Haven, supporting initiatives for economic development, education, and human services; these measures have included the renovation of downtown New Haven, local home-buying programs, the President's Public Service Fellowships, and contributions of $100 million to city improvements during Levin's tenure.

Another of Levin's priorities has been the "internationalization" of Yale. He created the Yale Center for the Study of Globalization, headed by Ernesto Zedillo, former president of Mexico, and the Yale World Fellows Program, which seeks to train emerging world leaders. Building connections with China, Yale sponsored an Advanced University Leadership Program for presidents and vice presidents of fourteen leading Chinese universities in 2004 and 2005, as well as an executive education program for Chinese government officials in June 2005.

Levin served as a director of Lucent Technologies and as a trustee of the William and Flora Hewlett Foundation, a leading philanthropic organization. He was a fellow of the American Academy of Arts and Sciences, and he was a member of the board on Science, Technology and Economic Policy at the National Academy of Science. A member of the American Economic Association, he also served as chairman of the board of the University Alliance for Lifelong Learning, sponsored by Yale, Oxford, and Stanford Universities.

[Dorothy Bauhoff (2nd ed.)]

LEVIN, SANDER (1931–), U.S. congressman. Levin was born in Detroit. He graduated from Detroit's Central High School and then went to the University of Chicago for his B.A., Columbia University for an M.A. in International Relations, and Harvard Law School. Levin represented Oakland County for six years in the Michigan State Senate and was minority leader in 1969–70, his final year in the Senate. Levin ran unsuccessfully for governor of Michigan in 1970 and 1974, narrowly losing both contests. During the Carter Administration he worked with the Agency for International Development before being elected to Congress in 1982. He was the ranking minority member of the Trade Subcommittee, where he used his standing to protect the American auto industry. Levin served on the House Ways and Means Committee, which has jurisdiction over all tax, trade, and economic growth policies, and entitlement spending, including Social Security, Medicare, welfare, and unemployment compensation. He was the ranking Democrat on the Social Security Subcommittee. He also served on the Trade subcommittee.

He was known as a leader on trade issues – seeking ways to use trade policy to shape globalization. He persistently challenged unfair trade practices that threaten U.S. manufacturers and U.S. job issues that are important to Michigan's threatened automobile manufacturing industry. He also worked on a variety of health care issues from children's health care, transitional Medicaid, and mental health. He was a leader on welfare reform issues and the federal unemployment insurance program and introduced legislation to include preventive services in Medicare, and to create a national public service campaign for gynecological cancer.

BIBLIOGRAPHY: L. Sandy Maisel and I. Forman, *Jews in American Politics* (2001).

[Michael Berenbaum (2nd ed.)]

LEVIN, SHMARYA (**Shemaryahu**; 1867–1935), Zionist leader, Hebrew and Yiddish author. Born in Svisloch, Belorussia, Levin joined Ḥibbat Zion in his youth, was one of *Aḥad Ha-Am's adherents, becoming a member of the *Benei Moshe society. Levin studied at Berlin University and at the Hochschule fuer die Wissenschaft des Judentums in the same city, joining the Russian-Jewish Scientific Society, which proliferated the idea of Jewish nationalism among Russian-Jewish students in Germany. He served as **Kazyonny ravvin* in Grodno (1896–97) and Yekatrinoslav (1898–1904) and preached in Vilna (1904–06). Throughout his career he worked toward spreading Zionist ideas both orally and in the Hebrew press (*Ha-Shilo'aḥ, Ha-Zeman, Ha-Ẓofeh*) and the Yiddish press (*Der Yud, Der Fraynd*). At the Sixth Zionist Congress (1903), Levin was among the leaders of the opposition to the *Uganda Scheme. He was also among the founders of the League for the Attainment of Equal Rights for the Jewish People in Russia (established in 1905) and a member of its central board. In 1906 Levin was chosen to the first Russian Duma as delegate of the Jewish National List in Vilna (with the support of the Lithuanians). He participated in deliberations in the Duma and delivered two speeches on the pogrom in Bialystok. After the first Duma was disbanded, Levin was among the signators of the Vyborg Declaration, which called for civil disobedience.

Afterward, Levin left Russia and settled in Berlin, from where he traveled to the United States on a number of lecture tours. At the Tenth Zionist Congress (1911), he was elected a member of the Zionist Executive. He took part in the work of the *Hilfsverein der deutschen Juden in Germany and was among the initiators of the establishment of the technical school in Haifa (the *Technion); he also influenced American Jews to contribute to this cause. Levin resigned from the board of governors of the Technion together with Aḥad Ha-Am and J. *Tschlenow after their suggestion to use Hebrew as the language of instruction was rejected. During World War I he lived in the U.S. and directed propaganda work on Zionism and Hebrew culture orally and in writing. Together with Y.D. *Berkowitz he edited the weekly *Ha-Toren* and regularly wrote its editorials. Levin was outstanding as a sharp-witted publicist, and he became particularly famous as a speaker and conversationalist. His speeches were a blend of Jewish heritage and European culture, spiced with Jewish folk wit. He frequently contributed to the Zionist press in all its languages, and some of his articles were collected in *Bi-Ymei ha-Ma'avar* ("In the Days of Transition," 1949).

In 1920 Levin participated in the postwar Zionist Conference in London and was entrusted with the propaganda for *Keren Hayesod. He was among the founders and directors of the Devir publishing house. In 1924 he settled in Palestine, traveling from time to time in various countries on missions for the Zionist Movement and its funds. He developed ties of friendship with Sir Arthur *Wauchope, the high commissioner for Palestine. Levin's first book was entitled *Asarah Shirim* ("Ten Poems," original works and translations, 1899). In his last years he began to publish his memoirs in the *Jewish Daily Forward* (New York). A selection of his letters was published in 1966 entitled *Iggerot Shemaryahu Levin*. A small selection of his articles appeared in English entitled *Out of Bondage* (1919). Levin's autobiography and memoirs appeared in English in three volumes entitled *Childhood in Exile* (1929), *Youth in Revolt* (1930), and *The Arena* (1932). In 1967 it appeared in one volume (abridged by Maurice Samuel) entitled *Forward from Exile* (1967).

BIBLIOGRAPHY: L. Lipsky, *A Gallery of Zionist Profiles* (1956), 78–85; Z. Woyslawsky, *Yeḥidim bi-Reshut ha-Rabbim* (1943), 62–75; B. Katznelson, *Be-Ḥavlei Adam* (1964²), 83–88; J. Fichmann, *Be-Terem Aviv* (1959), 310–23; Ch. Weizmann, *Trial and Error* (1949), index.

[Yehuda Slutsky]

LEVIN, THEODORE (1897–1971), U.S. federal district court judge. Born in Chicago, Levin was appointed by President Truman in 1946 to the federal district court in Michigan. From 1959 to 1967 he was chief judge of the eastern district federal court of Michigan, remaining on the court until his death. Levin gave important aid to immigrants. He led the legal fight against an alien registration act which, in 1931, mainly thanks to his efforts, was declared unconstitutional by the U.S. circuit court of appeals, and cooperated actively with local and national agencies aiding immigrants. He started a sentencing counseling system in federal courts. A lifelong Zionist, Levin, who was deeply involved in Jewish organizational work, held numerous national and local offices. At one time, he was president of the Detroit Jewish Welfare Federation, United Jewish Charities, and the Council of Social Agencies. He was a board member of many organizations, among them the Joint Distribution Committee and the National Refugee Service.

[Frederick R. Lachman]

LEVIN, YIZḤAK MEIR (1894–1971), leader of the *Agudat Israel movement. Born in Gora, Poland, Levin came from a ḥasidic family: his maternal grandfather was the Gerer Rabbi, R. Judah Aryeh Leib Alter *(Sefat Emet)*, and his father-in-law was the Gerer Rabbi, R. Abraham Mordecai Alter. He was active in Agudat Israel when it was formed in Poland after World War I. Agudat Israel in Poland was dominated by the Gerer Ḥasidim, and Levin quickly rose to its leadership. In 1924 he represented his movement on the Warsaw Community Council, and at the Second Great Assembly of Agudat Israel (Vienna, 1929) he was elected to the World Presidium. In 1935 he visited Palestine at the head of a delegation of the Agudat Israel Center in Poland and reorganized the executive there. At the Third Great Assembly (Marienbad, 1937), he was chosen as one of the two deputy presidents of the World Actions Committee.

Levin managed to escape from Poland at the beginning of World War II and in 1940 reached Palestine, where he was active in rescue operations from Nazi-dominated Europe. When the Central Committee of Agudat Israel met in Marienbad (1947), he was put in charge of the Ereẓ Israel branch of the movement. Levin was elected to the First *Knesset and was minister of social welfare in the first Israel government. He served in this capacity until 1952, when he resigned during the controversy over some form of national service for women. At the Fourth Great Assembly (Jerusalem, 1954), he was elected president of the World Actions Committee and chairman of the World Executive of Agudat Israel.

BIBLIOGRAPHY: Tidhar, 4 (1950), 1804–05.

[Menachem Friedman]

LEVIN, ẒEVI HIRSCH(-el) BEN ARYEH LOEB (Hirsch Loebel; Hart Lyon; 1721–1800), rabbi; born in Rzeszow, Galicia. In addition to talmudic scholarship he had a knowledge of Hebrew grammar, Jewish history, philosophy, physics, and geometry. While still young, he took part in the *Emden-Eybeschuetz controversy, siding with Jacob Emden, his maternal uncle. In 1758 he was appointed rabbi of the Great and Hambro synagogues, London (where he was known as Hart Lyon), holding the post for seven years. When in 1764 the leaders of the London community prevented him from publishing a defense of the *sheḥitah* in London in reply to the attack of Jacob Kimḥi, and because of dissatisfaction with the state of talmudic studies, he relinquished his position and went to Halberstadt (Germany), where he was appointed rabbi and *rosh yeshivah*. In 1770 he was appointed rabbi of Mannheim and in 1773 became rabbi of Berlin. Levin was a friend of Moses *Mendelssohn, even writing an approbation for his German translation of the Bible. When the Prussian government requested Levin to write in German an account of Jewish commercial and matrimonial law, Levin asked Mendelssohn to compose it under his supervision. It was published in Berlin (1778) and entitled *Ritualgesetze der Juden*. His friendship with Mendelssohn was impaired when Levin attempted to prevent N.H. *Wessely from publishing his *Divrei Shalom ve-Emet* (Berlin, 1782) and even endeavored to have him expelled from Berlin. When Mendelssohn defended Wessely, Levin sent in his resignation; however, he did not act on it and remained in Berlin until his death. Levin supported and defended his son, Saul *Berlin, in the disputes in which he was involved, especially with regard to the forged response *Besamim Rosh* (Berlin, 1793).

Levin's commentary on *Avot* was published together with that of Jacob Emden (Berlin, 1834). He also wrote occasional poems, entitled "*Naḥalat Ẓevi*," which were published in *Ha-Maggid* (no. 14, 1870). One of his poems appears at the beginning of his brother Saul's *Binyan Ari'el* (Amsterdam,

1778). He was father of Solomon *Hirschel, subsequently chief rabbi in London.

BIBLIOGRAPHY: Adler, in: *Papers Read at the Anglo-Jewish Historical Exhibition* (1888), 280–4; B.H. Auerbach, *Geschichte der israelitischen Gemeinde Halberstadt* (1866), 86–96; C. Duschinsky, *The Rabbinate of the Great Synagogue, London* (1921), 2–73, 274–95; L. Landshut, *Toledot Anshei ha-Shem* (1884), 69–115; Schischa, in: *Ha-Darom*, 12 (1960), 58–67; Samet, in: KS, 13 (1967/68), 430–1; C. Roth, *History of the Great Synagogue, London* (1950), 108–23; idem, *Essays and Portraits in Anglo-Jewish History* (1962), 252–3; M.S. Samet, in: *Meḥkarim be-Toledot Am Yisrael ve-Ereẓ Yisrael le-Zekher Ẓevi Avneri* (1970), 249–53.

[Shlomo Tal]

LEVINAS, EMMANUEL (1906–1995), philosopher and Jewish thinker. Levinas was born in Kovno, Lithuania. He grew up in a Jewish home that was open to European culture. In 1915 the Jews of Kovno were expelled and Levinas attended public high school in Karkhov, Ukraine. He read the great Russian classics Dostoyevsky, Tolstoy, Turgeniev, Gogol, Pushkin, and Lermontov. After having suffered from Ukrainian antisemitism, the family returned to Kovno in July 1920, where he attended the Jewish lyceum that was organized by Joseph Carlebach and directed by Moses Schwabe. In 1923 Levinas moved to France, where he studied in Strasbourg under people like Maurice Pradines, Henri Carteron, Maurice Halbwachs, and Charles Blondel. During the 1928–29 academic year he went to nearby Freiburg, Germany, where he studied under Edmund *Husserl and Martin Heidegger. Heidegger had published in 1927 his *Sein und Zeit*, a work much appreciated by Levinas. In 1929 Levinas was present at the Kant seminar in Davos where Ernst *Cassirer and Heidegger held their famous debate.

In 1930 Levinas published his Ph.D. thesis, which he had written under Jean Wahl (*Théorie de l'intuition dans la phénoménologie de Husserl*). This was the first French book on Husserl. Two years later he published the first substantial French article on Heidegger (a revised version in *En découvrant l'existence avec Husserl et Heidegger*). Levinas played a pioneer role in the dissemination of phenomenology in France. He also co-translated Husserl's *Cartesian Meditations*. Although he became increasingly critical of the philosophies of his teachers, he continued to use the phenomenological method in his own philosophic work.

In 1930, Levinas received French citizenship. In addition to his philosophic work, Levinas began publishing articles on Jewish subjects. In 1934, for instance, he published "Some Reflections on the Philosophy of Hitlerism," criticizing New Germany's primitivism. In the 1930s he met Paul Ricoeur and also attended Saturday night gatherings in the house of Gabriel Marcel, where he became acquainted with Jean-Paul Sartre and Jacques Maritain.

In 1939 Levinas was drafted into the French army and was then captured. After detention in France, he was deported to a POW camp near Hanover, Germany, which bore the infamous number "1492." For four years he was a prisoner, cutting and sawing wood. He survived; his wife and daughter also survived, having fled from Paris with the help of Maurice Blanchot and finally finding a hiding place in a French monastery. Levinas' parents and his brothers in Kovno were murdered.

After the war, Levinas became director of ENIO, the Oriental Israelite Normal School, attended by Moroccan Jews who had immigrated to France. He continued in this position until 1961. In that same year he published *Totality and Infinity* and with this publication Levinas established his reputation as an independent, original philosopher in France. From 1947 until 1951 he studied Talmud with Rabbi Mordechai Chouchani, who was also the teacher of Elie *Wiesel. He taught at the University of Poitiers (1961–62), the University of Paris at Nanterres (1962–73), and finally at the Sorbonne (1973–76).

Ethical Metaphysics

Levinas made German phenomenology known in France. However, he became more and more dissatisfied with the thought of his teachers. He conceived Heidegger's ontology as crucial, but also as problematic. Husserl's transcendental ego and Heidegger's *Dasein* were solitary and did not take adequate account of human relations. Levinas strongly felt the need to leave the "climate" of Heidegger's philosophy, in which the encounter with other human beings was neglected, since Heidegger concentrated upon modes of Being rather than on the intersubjective world. Already in his early publication *De l'évasion* (1935), Levinas looked for what exceeds the Being, maintaining that the relation of man to Being is not only ontology.

With time, and not unconnected to the experience of Hitler's Germany, Levinas developed an ethical thinking that avoids the "allergy" of Western philosophy for the otherness of the Other. *Time and the Other* and *Existence and Existents*, which appeared both in 1947, are books that already contain themes like "*il y a*" (the anonymous and threatening "there is"), sexual relation, paternity, and fecundity that appear in Levinas' greater works, in which he criticized both his teachers, who subsumed the Other under the Same.

His two major works are *Totality and Infinity* (1961) and *Otherwise than Being* (1974). In Levinas' ethics, the Other with his constitutive strangeness puts the self into question. The Other is not an alter ego, not to be mastered, but unknowable, enigmatic, refractory to light; the Other's "face" commands not to subsume him. The command stemming from the "face," that is never a sole object of vision, is: "Thou shalt not murder." The Other is never a pure phenomenon, but rather a call, an authoritatively speaking voice that asks for an exile out of the self. Levinas' entire philosophical project implies therefore an attack on totality, on totalitarian thinking and history. He found the idea of rupturing totality in Franz *Rosenzweig's *Star of Redemption* (1921) which he read before World War II, and he admitted to having made extensive use of Rosenzweig's anti-totalitarian thought. Levinas retakes Plato's terms of the "Same" and the "Other" and points to the frequent absorption of the Other by the Same in the history of philosophy. In Husserl's phenomenology, the transcendental ego is the source of all meaning (*Sinngebung*), whereas in Heidegger's fundamental ontology Being as reflected in the beings is everything. In contrast to these teachings, Levinas searches not for totality, but for what ruptures "totality," for what he calls "infinity," "alterity," "discourse," "transcendence," and "exteriority."

His ethics is not epistemologically founded, nor is it based upon reason as in Kant, but upon the normative relation, i.e., upon the concrete demand of the other person. The contact with the Other face to face is one of *demand*: the Other addresses the I, resisting its powers and appropriation. The relationship is not reciprocal as in Martin *Buber, it is asymmetrical. With time, Levinas paid more attention to "the third party" (*le tiers*), i.e., to social and political justice. Yet, the inegalitarian moment of the ethical encounter remains in vigor.

The first great critical reaction to *Totality and Infinity* came from Jacques *Derrida. In his essay "Violence et métaphysique," he pointed to some of Levinas' problematic readings of his teachers and regretted Levinas' preference of speech to writing, from which the speaker is absent, which would be more fitting for a philosophy of alterity. He was mainly concerned with the question of how to talk about the Other in the language of the Same. In *Otherwise than Being*, Levinas dealt less with the Other than with the subject. He did not conceive the subject as a consciousness, but as welcoming the Other, as "responsibility," "exposure," "witness," and as "in proximity." He now attempted to leave out the language of ontology and writes about "an-archy," "hostage," "obsession," "persecution," and "substitution." He further tries to avoid the problem of the thematizing of the unthematizable by incessantly unsaying the said (*dédire le Dit*), because no said may contain the Saying (*le Dire*) of responsibility. He resists totalization in keeping the tension between the Saying and a said that bears the traces of the Saying.

Jewish Writings

Parallel to his "professional" (i.e., philosophic) writings, Levinas also published a vast body of "confessional" writings that treat Judaism, religious themes, and Talmud. Some of these essays on Judaism were collected in *Difficult Freedom* (1963), in *Beyond the Verse* (1982), and *In the Time of the Nations* (1988).

Levinas does not strive for harmonization between his "professional" and "confessional" writings, but discusses one truth beyond ontology that can be discussed in different manners. When compared with the great attention that was paid to the philosophical part of his oeuvre, the Jewish part of Levinas' writings has been largely neglected in scholarly research, although there is undeniably a strong interaction between the two parts of the diptych, with terms and themes appearing in both kinds of writings.

Although Levinas does acknowledge Jewish particularity as prototypically refusing totality, he highlights the universal dimension in Judaism. The Jewish message is one for all humanity. Ethics, which Levinas wanted to discuss philosophically, is for him attested to in the holy life, to which the Bible, Midrashim, and Talmud testify. There is an interaction between the Greek "love of wisdom" and the Jewish "wisdom of love." Once it is Japheth that visits the tents of Shem, once it is vice versa. In the Jewish writings, Abraham becomes the prototype of the one, characterized by hospitality, who transcends the narrow world of the self in order to follow an always exterior voice. He is exemplary in his extending "hospitality" to strangers. Levinas does not write about God as Being, but as not assumable "illéité" – *Illeity* (He-hood, from the Latin "ille," that one, the other one), as alterity – the other than other – that ruptures the unity of the I, orienting it toward other human beings.

Levinas was the first Jewish thinker in modern times to approach the Talmud philosophically, mainly its aggadic parts, as a source of wisdom relevant for our day. His remarkable *Talmudic Readings* were first delivered at the annual meetings of the Colloque des Intellectuels Juifs de Langue Française, which started in 1957; they were later collected and published.

Levinas thought that humanism of the other person and Judaism were compatible, and he considered being Jewish a form of being human. However, the Jewish response to the universal question contained elements beyond humanism, which he regarded as insufficiently human. Levinas wrote about the greater attention to the human in the "humanism of the other man," which is dissatisfied with mere intentions and declarations and in which the violent freedom of the sovereign I, joylessly possessing the world, is radically put into question.

Influence

Levinas renewed Jewish thinking and by now occupies an eminent place in the pantheon of modern Jewish thinkers such as Hermann Cohen, Franz Rosenzweig, and Martin Buber.

Philosophers and theologians all over the world are interested in Levinas' work. *Ethics and Infinity* (trans. R. Cohen, 1985) which contains talks of P. Nemo with Levinas, presents a good introduction to his entire oeuvre.

BIBLIOGRAPHY: D. Banon, *La Lecture infinie: Les Voies de l'interprétation midrachique* (1987); R. Bernasconi and S. Critchley (eds.), *Re-Reading Levinas* (1991); R. Bernasconi and D. Wood (eds.), *The Provocation of Levinas: Rethinking the Other* (1988); R. Burggraeve, *From Self-Development to Solidarity: An Ethical Reading of Human Desire in its Socio-Political Relevance According to Emmanuel Levinas*, transl. C. Vanhove-Romanik (1985); C. Chalier, *Lévinas: L'Utopie de l'humain* (1993); idem, *Pour une morale au-delà du savoir: Kant et Levinas* (1998) = *What Ought I To Do? Morality in Kant and Levinas*, trans. J. Todd (2002); F. Ciaramelli, *Transcendance et éthique: essai sur Levinas* (1989); D. Cohen-Lévinas and S. Trigano (eds.), *Emmanuel Lévinas – Philosophie et judaïsme* (Pardès, 26; 1999) 101–4; R.A. Cohen (ed.), *Face to Face with Levinas* (1986); S. Critchley, *The Ethics of Deconstruction: Derrida and Levinas* (1992); C. Davis, *Levinas. An Introduction* (1996); J. Derrida, "Violence et métaphysique: Essai sur la pensée d' Emmanuel Lévinas" (1964), in: *L'Écriture et la difference* (1967), 117–228; idem, "En ce moment même dans cet ouvrage me voici," in: Laruelle (ed.), *Textes pour Emmanuel Levinas* (1980), 21–60; E. Feron, *De l'idée de la transcendance à la question du* *langage: L'Itinéraire philosophique d'Emmanuel Lévinas* (1992); A. Finkelkraut, *La Sagesse de l'amour* (1984); R. Gibbs, *Correlations in Rosenzweig and Levinas* (1992); J. Greisch and J. Rolland (eds.), *Emmanuel Lévinas: L'Éthique comme philosophie première* (1993); J. Halpérin and N. Hansson, *Colloque des intellectuels juifs. Difficile justice. Dans la trace d'Emmanuel Lévinas. Actes du XXXVIe Colloque des intellectuels juifs de langue française* (1998); S. Handelman, *Fragments of Redemption: Jewish Thought and Literary Theory in Benjamin, Scholem, and Levinas* (1991); M.-A. Lescourret, *Emmanuel Lévinas* (1994); Z. Levy, *The Other and Responsibility: The Philosophy of Emmanuel Levinas* (Heb., 1998); J. Llewelyn, *Emmanuel Levinas: The Genealogy of Ethics* (1995); S. Malka, *Lire Lévinas* (1984); idem, *Emmanuel Lévinas: la vie et la trace* (2002); E. Meir, "The Dimension of the Feminine in Levinas' Philosophy," in: *Iyyun – The Jerusalem Philosophical Quarterly*, 43 (1994), 145–52 (Heb.); idem, "La presenza biblica nella cultura ebraica contemporanea: M. Buber – F. Rosenzweig – E. Levinas," in: S.J. Sierra (ed.), *La lettura ebraica delle Scritture* (1995), 465–95; idem, "Criticism of the 'Myth' of *Unio Mystica* in E. Levinas," in: H. Pedayah (ed.), *Myth in Judaism* (Eshel Beer-Sheva, 4; 1996), 393–405 (Heb.); idem, "Levinas's Thinking on Religion as beyond the Pathetic: Reflections on the First Part of *Difficult Freedom*," in: E.L. Fackenheim and R. Jospe (eds.), *Jewish Philosophy and the Academy* (1996), 142–64; idem, "War and Peace in the Philosophy of E. Levinas," in: *Iyyun – The Jerusalem Philosophical Quarterly*, 45 (1997), 471–79 (Heb.); idem, "Teaching Levinas on Revelation," in: R. Jospe (ed.), *Paradigms in Jewish Philosophy* (1997), 257–79; idem, "La philosophie de Lévinas, sacrificielle et naïve? S'agit-il d'un drame? A propos d'un ouvrage récent de Daniel Sibony," in: *Revue d'histoire et de philosophie religieuses*, 81:1 (2001), 63–79; idem, "Moses Mendelssohn's *Jerusalem* from Levinas' Perspective," in: M. New, R. Bernasconi, R.A. Cohen (eds.), *In Proximity – Emmanuel Levinas and the Eighteenth Century* (2001), 243–59; idem, "Verità e giustizia nella filosofia di Emmanuel Lévinas in relazione all'io-tu e all'io-esso di Martin Buber," in: P. Amodio, G. Giannini, G. Lissa (eds.), *Lévinas e la cultura del XX secolo* (Cultura Filosofica e Scienze Umane, 3), (2001), 209–35 (= *Daat*, 50–52 (2003), 423–39); idem, "Ethics, Politics and God in the Writings of E. Levinas," in: *Democratic Culture*, vol. 6 (2002), 111–33 (Heb.); idem, "La notion de la révélation dans la 'théologie des profondeurs' de Heschel et la métaphysique éthique de Lévinas," in: G. Rabinovitch (ed.), *Abraham J. Heschel. Un tsaddiq dans la cité* (Collection Voix) (2004), 155–86; idem "Buber's and Levinas's Attitudes toward Judaism," in: P. Atterton, M. Calarco, and M. Friedman (eds.), *Levinas and Buber. Dialogue and Difference* (2004), 133–56; idem, "Religion and State in the Thought of Emmanuel Levinas," A. Ravitzky (ed.), *Religion and State in Twentieth-Century Jewish Thought* (2005), 409–24 (Heb.); idem, "Guilt and Responsibility as Characteristics of the Answerable Man in the Thought of E. Levinas," in: Y. Amir (ed.), *The Path of the Spirit. The Eliezer Schweid Jubilee Volume*, vol. 2 (2005), 851–65; G.D. Mole, *Lévinas, Blanchot, Jabès. Figures of Estrangement* (1997); M.A. Ouaknin, *Méditations érotiques, Essai sur Emmanuel Lévinas* (Collection Métaphora; 1991); idem, *Concerto pour quatre consonnes sans voyelles. Au-delà du principe d'identité* (1991); A. Peperzak (ed.), *Ethics as First Philosophy* (1995); S. Petrosino and J.Rolland, *La Vérite nomade: Introduction à Emmanuel Lévinas* (1984); F. Poirié, *Emmanuel Lévinas: Qui êtes-vous* (1987); T. Wright, *The Twilight of Jewish Philosophy: Emmanuel Levinas' Ethical Hermeneutics* (1999); E. Wyschogrod, *Emmanuel Levinas: The Problem of Ethical Metaphysics* (1974); For a bibliography of works by and on Levinas until 1989, see R. Burggraeve, *Emmanuel Lévinas: Une bibliographie primaire et secondaire (1929–1985), avec complément 1985–1989* (1990).

[Ephraim Meir (2nd ed.)]

LEVINE, BARUCH (1930–), U.S. Bible scholar. Born in 1930, in Cleveland, Ohio, Levine was educated in the public schools, but spent his afternoons at the Telshe Yeshivah, which provided him with a strong talmudic background. He learned spoken Hebrew with the help of tutors and by attendance at Hebrew summer camps. He graduated in 1951 from Case Western Reserve University after studying Comparative Literature and Romance Languages. At the time a religiously observant Jew of a modernist bent, Levine entered the rabbinical program of the Jewish Theological Seminary in New York City. Among his teachers were H.L.*Ginsberg, who introduced him to the critical study of Bible, and the talmudist Saul *Lieberman. After ordination followed by military service as a chaplain, Levine served briefly as an assistant rabbi in Temple Emanuel, a Conservative synagogue in Newton Center, a suburb of Boston. After coming to terms with a crisis of faith, Levine realized that he belonged in scholarship and enrolled in a doctoral program at Brandeis, where he earned his Ph.D. under the great polymath Cyrus *Gordon in 1962. He joined the Brandeis faculty and remained there until 1969. At that time he came to New York University as professor of Hebrew and Near Eastern Languages in the Department of Near Eastern Languages and Literatures. After an administrative reorganization in which he played a strong role, Levine moved to the new Skirball Department of Hebrew and Judaic Studies where he taught until his retirement.

Levine's numerous articles can be divided into two principal areas, biblical studies proper, with a strong emphasis on cult and ritual, and Semitic epigraphy. He has made significant contributions to the study of magic and ritual in the Bible as well as in Ugaritic and Aramaic texts. His talmudic training served him well in his studies of ancient law. He edited *Leviticus* for the JPS Torah Commentary Series (1994) and *Numbers 21–36* for the Anchor Bible (2000).

BIBLIOGRAPHY: L. Schiffman, in: L. Schiffman et al. (eds.), *Ki Baruch Hu … Studies Levine* (1999), ix–xiii, incl. bibl. of publications (xix–xxvii).

[S. David Sperling (2nd ed.)]

LEVINÉ, EUGENE (**Nissen Berg**; 1883–1919), revolutionary, socialist politician, and journalist. Leviné was born in St. Petersburg into a wealthy family. From 1896 he lived in Heidelberg, Germany where he graduated from high school and also attended university. In 1904 he returned to Russia, joined the Social Revolutionary Party on the outbreak of the 1905 revolution, and was imprisoned by the czarist authorities. He was released in 1908 and allowed to go to Germany for medical treatment. He remained there and joined the Social Democratic Party. In 1913 he was a member of the "Spartacus League," and later among the founders of the German Communist party. Leviné became a German citizen, joined the army on the outbreak of World War I, and was discharged in 1916 for reasons of health. Subsequently, he became a member of the Independent Social Democratic Party and then of the Communist Party, editing the party newspaper, *Rote Fahne*. He took part in the November 1918 revolution and in the January 1919 fighting in Berlin. Following the Bavarian uprising of November 1918, Leviné became chairman of the Council of People's Commissars in the Bavarian Soviet Republic of 1919. Two weeks later, when the republic was overthrown, Leviné was tried for treason and executed.

BIBLIOGRAPHY: O.M. Graf, *Prisoners All* (1928); G. Schmolze, in: *Emuna* (1969), 329–36.

LEVINE, JACK (1915–), U.S. painter and printmaker. Born on Boston's South End, Levine was the youngest of Lithuanian immigrants Mary and Samuel Levine's eight children. A poor shoemaker and Hebrew scholar, the elder Levine enrolled his son in children's art classes at a Jewish Community Center, and later at a settlement house in Roxbury. There Levine met Harold Zimmerman, who became his first mentor, and Hyman *Bloom, who also went on to become a painter of Jewish subjects. At 14, Levine became acquainted with Denman Waldo Ross, an art professor at Harvard University. Ross provided financial assistance for Zimmerman, Levine, and Bloom, and arranged Levine's first public exhibition, a small showing of his drawings at Harvard's Fogg Art Museum in 1932 when Levine was only 17.

Levine's unique, expressionistic style complemented his satirical eye, which recorded social and political injustices on canvas and on paper. Among his best-known work in this genre is *The Feast of Pure Reason* (1937, Museum of Modern Art, New York), a painting completed while Levine was employed by the Works Progress Administration's Federal Art Project. Levine's didactic approach and sharp commentaries rendered with a vigorous brushstroke include subjects ranging from the McCarthy hearings of the 1950s, the desegregation of the South, and Mayor Daley at the 1968 Chicago Convention.

Beginning in 1942, a three-and-a-half-year stint in the army interrupted Levine's work. A year after his 1945 move to New York, Levine married the Ukrainian-born artist Ruth *Gikow. During his time in the service, Levine's reputation was sealed when in 1943 the Metropolitan Museum of Art purchased *String Quartette* (1936–37), a boldly colored tempera and oil image of four musicians.

Although as a child Levine created a chalk drawing titled *Jewish Cantors in the Synagogue* (1930, Fogg Art Museum, Harvard University), he first explored Jewish subjects in earnest, specifically biblical subjects, in 1941 when he painted *Planning Solomon's Temple* (Israel Museum, Jerusalem), a small, ten- by eight-inch homage to his recently deceased father. Hebrew labels identifying the expressionistically executed, robed figures of Solomon and Hiram hover above the pair's heads. Such finely rendered Hebrew letters soon became a staple of Levine's biblical paintings and prints, which number in the hundreds. Levine aimed, to use his words, "to develop some kind of iconography about my Jewish identity."

His work has been exhibited at numerous venues, including his first retrospective exhibition at the Institute of Contemporary Art in Boston (1952–53).

BIBLIOGRAPHY: F. Getlein, *Jack Levine* (1966); K. Prescott, *Jack Levine: Retrospective Exhibition, Paintings, Drawings, Graphics* (1978); K. Prescott and E. Stina-Prescott, *The Complete Graphic Work of Jack Levine* (1984); J. Levine, *Jack Levine* (1989).

[Samantha Baskind (2nd ed.)]

LEVINE, JAMES (1943–), U.S. conductor and pianist. Levine was born in Cincinnati and made his debut as a pianist at the age of ten with the Cincinnati Symphony Orchestra. He took piano lessons with Walter Levin and Rudolf *Serkin. In 1961 he entered the Juilliard School of Music to study conducting with Jean Morel and the piano with Lhévinne. In 1964, he joined the music staff of the Cleveland Symphony Orchestra under George *Szell, whose assistant conductor he became two years later. Although he conducted many symphony concerts (especially with the Cleveland Meadow Brook Orchestra, which he founded in 1967) he achieved his most notable successes as an operatic conductor with the Welsh National Opera (*Aida*, 1970) and with the San Francisco Opera (*Madame Butterfly*, 1971). After his highly successful début at the Metropolitan Opera, New York, in 1971 in *Tosca*, he was appointed principal conductor of the Metropolitan (1973–74), its music director (1975), and its artistic director (1986). There he led 2,000 performances of 75 different operas and conducted the house premieres of Mozart's *Idomeneo; Lulu, Erwartung, Mahagonny, Moses und Aron*, and *Oedipus Rex*; Corigliano's *The Ghost of Versailles* (1991); *Glass' *The Voyage* (1992); and John Harbison's *The Great Gatsby* (1999). Levine was the director of the Cincinnati May Festival (1973–78) and the Ravinia Festival (1973–93). He conducted at Bayreuth Göz Friedrich's centennial production of *Parsifal* (1982–85, 1988), Wolfgang Wagner's *Parsifal* (1989–93), and the Kirchner/Rosalie *Ring* (1994–97). Levine recorded with many orchestras such as the Vienna Philharmonic Orchestra (including the complete cycle of Mozart symphonies), Chicago Symphony Orchestra, Berlin Philharmonic Orchestra, and Metropolitan Opera Orchestra. With the latter he recorded major symphonic works. As an accomplished pianist, his recorded chamber music includes Schubert's "Trout" Quintet and Schumann's Piano Quintet. His many honors include the Lotus Award ("for inspiration to young musicians"), the Anton Seidl Award from the Wagner Society of New York, and the National Medal of Arts endowed to him by President Clinton at the White House.

ADD. BIBLIOGRAPHY: Grove online; *P.J. Smith, A Year at the Met* (1983); J. Levine with R.C. Marsh, *Dialogues and Discoveries* (1997).

[Max Loppert / Israela Stein (2nd ed.)]

LEVINE, JOSEPH E. (1905–1987), U.S. motion picture producer. Born in Boston, Levine was a theater owner and movie distributor (1943) before becoming a producer. He started in the business by importing foreign films and distributing them in the U.S., such as the Italian movies *Open City* (1945) and *The Bicycle Thief* (1947). After World War II he began to cater to the drive-in market, bringing to the outdoor screen such action films as *Godzilla* (1956), *Hercules* (1959), and *Hercules Unchained* (1960). He also distributed such films as *Two Women* (1961), *Divorce Italian Style* (1961), *Bocaccio '70* (1962), *Fellini's 8½* (1963), *Yesterday, Today, and Tomorrow* (1963), and *Marriage Italian Style* (1964). He produced such films as *Jack the Ripper* (1959), *The Carpetbaggers* (1964), *Harlow* (1965), *A Bridge Too Far* (1977), *Magic* (1978), and *Tattoo* (1981).

Levine, who was dubbed "the Boston Barnum," was also the executive producer of many successful films. Among them are *Long Day's Journey into Night* (1962), *Boy's Night Out* (1962), *Sodom and Gomorrah* (1962), *Sands of the Kalahari* (1965), *Nevada Smith* (1966), *The Daydreamer* (1966), *The Graduate* (1967), *Woman Times Seven* (1967), *The Producers* (1968), *The Lion in Winter* (1968), *Don't Drink the Water* (1969), *The Adventurers* (1970), *Carnal Knowledge* (1971), and *The Day of the Dolphin* (1973). The 1962 documentary film *Showman* profiled Levine's career.

[Jonathan Licht / Ruth Beloff (2nd ed.)]

LEVINE, LES (1936–), Canadian sculptor. Levine was born in Dublin, immigrated to Canada in 1958, and later moved to New York. Levine was interested in making sculpture accessible to the general public. He therefore became an innovator of the concept of "throw-away" or "disposable" art, making mass-produced sculptures at low prices. He was also concerned with the problem of relating sculpture to its surroundings.

LEVINE, NORMAN (1923–), Canadian writer. Levine was born in Ottawa. His parents, Annie (Gurevich) and Moses Mordecai Levine, were Polish-Jewish immigrants. Levine was educated at York Street Public School and the High School of Commerce. During World War II, he served as an RCAF flying officer, then attended McGill University, where he graduated with a B.A. (1948) and M.A. (1949). Determined on a career as a professional author he settled in England, where he lived mostly in St. Ives, Cornwall, from 1949 to 1980. Later he took up residence in Toronto, and then moved back to Europe, where he lived in France, and finally returned to England. Levine was awarded a Canada Council Fellowship (1959) and Canada Council Arts Awards (1969, 1971).

Levine published three volumes of poetry: *Myssium* (1948), *The Tightrope Walker* (1950), and *I Walk by the Harbour* (1976) – but his reputation derives primarily from his fiction. These include the novels *The Angled Road* (1952) and *From a Seaside Town* (1970) and his collections of short stories: *One Way Ticket* (1961), *I Don't Want to Know Anyone Too Well* (1971), *Selected Stories* (1975), *Thin Ice* (1979), *Why Do You Live So Far Away?* (1984), *Champagne Barn* (1984), *Something Happened Here* (1991), and *The Ability to Forget* (2003). His travel book, *Canada Made Me*, which describes his experiences on a trip across Canada, appeared in the British edition in 1958; adversely reviewed in Canada, it did not obtain a Canadian publisher until 1979.

A self-conscious stylist, Levine fashioned a personal signature for the representation of his autobiographical fiction which originates in the remembered past of urban Jewish poverty and alienation. Typically, his storytelling method involves a narrator who observes the world through bifocal lenses, simultaneously witnessing an emotionally barren present juxtaposed with a past which is richly remembered but irretrievably lost. The hero is often solitary, emotionally cut off from others, unable to bridge the gap between himself and those closest to him.

Levine was the subject of several video documentaries, including *Norman Levine Lived Here*, produced by the CBC (1970), and *Norman Levine's St. Ives*, produced by the BBC (1972).

[Mervin Butovsky (2nd ed.)]

LEVINE, PHILIP (1900–1987), U.S. immunohematologist. Born in Russia, Levine was taken to the United States when he was eight years old. From 1925 to 1932 he worked at the Rockefeller Institute and in 1935 was appointed bacteriologist and serologist at Newark's Beth Israel Hospital. From 1944 to 1965 he was director of immunohematology at the Ortho Research Foundation in Raritan, New Jersey. Levine did extensive work on human blood groups and blood transfusion. He discovered and co-discovered many blood group factors including the Rh, Hr (c), Cellano (k), M, N, P. Guth (s), Mia (Miltenberger), and the Tja factors. He described the specificity of the hemolysin in paroxysmal cold hemoglobinuria (Tja), elucidated the Rh null factor with suppressor genes preventing formation of Rh antigens, and characterized hemolytic disease of the newborn (erythroblastosis fetalis) and the phenomenon of isoimmunization through pregnancy. Levine was the author of New Jersey and Wisconsin state laws on blood tests in paternity disputes.

BIBLIOGRAPHY: S.R. Kagan, *Jewish Medicine* (1952), 270–1.

[Fred Rosner]

LEVINE, RAPHAEL (1938–), Israeli scientist. Levine was born in Alexandria, Egypt, but was taken to Ereẓ Israel by his parents in 1939. After getting his master's degree at the Hebrew University in 1960, he studied at Nottingham University, where he received his doctorate, and also received a second doctorate from Oxford in 1966. In 1968 he was appointed professor of theoretical chemistry at the Hebrew University. Levine was awarded the Israel Prize for exact sciences in 1974 for his important contributions to theoretical chemistry, particularly in the field of molecular dynamics, but especially for his work *Quantum Mechanics of Molecular Rate Processes* (1969). He was awarded the Wolf Prize in 1988, the Rothschild Prize in 1992, and the EMET Prize in 2002. Levine is a member of the Israel Academy of Sciences and Humanities and a foreign member of the U.S. National Academy of Sciences, the Academia Europaea, and other important organizations.

LEVINGER, LEE JOSEPH (1890–1966), U.S. Reform rabbi. Born in Burke, Idaho, Levinger was ordained at Hebrew Union College in 1914. He held several pulpits and was a chaplain with the American Expeditionary Force in France in 1918–19. In 1929 he was national chaplain of the American Legion. Levinger became director of the Hillel Foundation at Ohio State University in 1925 and when in 1935 the National Hillel Commission set up a bureau of research to study the economic and occupational adjustment of Jewish students, it appointed him director. From 1942 to 1947 he was a field worker for the National Jewish Welfare Board and in 1948 he became chaplain of the Veterans Administration Hospital in Palo Alto, California. Levinger wrote a number of books. His *History of the Jews in the United States* which appeared in 1931 was one of the first works of its kind and went through several editions. He also wrote *A Jewish Chaplain in France* (1921); *Anti-Semitism Yesterday and Tomorrow* (1936); and *Folk and Faith* (1942).

In 1916 he married ELMA EHRLICH, author of several books and plays for Jewish children.

[Sefton D. Temkin]

LEVIN-SHATZKES, YIZḤAK (1892–1963), socialist leader. Born in Dvinsk (Daugavpils), Levin-Shatzkes joined the (illegal) Dvinsk branch of the *Bund in 1912. After Latvia became an independent state, he was elected a member of the Bund central committee, served on the Dvinsk city council (1922–34), and was secretary of the Jewish community council and chairman of the professional societies in Latgale province. By 1913 he had begun contributing articles to Russian-language periodicals appearing in Dvinsk; in 1921 he turned to Yiddish and became a contributor to Riga Yiddish dailies *Dos Folk* and *Frimorgen* and to periodicals published by the Bund. He was also the editor of *Latgalskaya Mysl*, a Russian-language weekly appearing in Dvinsk. After the May 1934 coup in Latvia, he was arrested, but was soon released. He settled in New York in 1936 and two years later became secretary of the *Jewish Socialist Verband of America and editor of *Der Veker*, the Farband organ. He contributed to various Yiddish periodicals published in New York and was active in a number of Jewish organizations and institutions.

BIBLIOGRAPHY: *Yahadut Latvia* (1953), index; LNYL, 5 (1963), 281–2.

[Joseph Gar]

LEVINSKY, BATTLING (Barney (Beryl) Lebrowitz; 1891–1949), U.S. boxer, world light-heavyweight champion 1916–20, member of the Ring Boxing Hall of Fame. Levinsky, born in Philadelphia to poor Russian immigrants, began his professional career in 1906 under the name Barney Williams, which his manager changed to Battling Levinsky in 1913. Levinsky loved to fight, and claimed to have fought in 500 bouts, a figure that is impossible to substantiate – indeed, his boxing record from 1906 to 1909 is not available. On New Year's Day 1915 he fought three times, once each in Brooklyn (a morning 10-rounder), Manhattan (afternoon 10-rounder), and in Waterbury, Connecticut (evening 12-rounder). Levinsky battled legendary fighters such as Jack Dempsey and Gene Tunney, and a series of ten fights with Jack Dillon, including two title fights in 1914 and 1916 before Levinsky finally defeated Dillon on October 24, 1916, to capture the world light-heavyweight title. Levinsky held the title for four years before losing on a fourth-round knockout to Georges Carpentier on October 12, 1920. Two years later, he challenged Gene Tunney for the U.S. light-heavyweight crown, but lost a 12-round decision. He retired following that fight, but came back in 1926, and retired permanently in 1930. Levinsky finished his career with a known professional record of 150 wins (with 34 KOs), 49 losses, 26 draws, and 66 no decisions, placing Levinsky among the top-ten all-time winners in number of fights. He was ranked the No. 6 all-time light-heavyweight by Nat Fleischer, and was inducted into the Ring Boxing Hall of Fame in 1966. He was the author of *Boxing in Nine Lessons*.

[Elli Wohlgelernter (2nd ed.)]

LEVIN SMITH, SIR ARCHIBALD (1836–1901), British judge. Levin Smith was the son of a gentile landowner. His mother was the daughter of a Polish Jewish immigrant, Zadik Levin. Educated at Cambridge, where he was a successful athlete, he became a barrister in 1856 and a judge of the Queen's Bench in 1883, when he was knighted. He was one of the two judges who presided over the criminal allegations made in the *Times* newspaper about Charles Stewart Parnell, the Irish Nationalist leader, which made him the center of national attention. Levin Smith served as a judge of the Court of Appeals from 1892 until 1900, when he was appointed Master of the Rolls, one of the three most senior British judicial positions. Suffering ill health, he was forced to resign after only a year and died shortly afterwards.

BIBLIOGRAPHY: ODNB online.

[William D. Rubinstein (2nd ed.)]

LEVINSOHN, ISAAC BAER (1788–1860), Hebrew author, one of the founders of the *Haskalah in Russia. He also was known as **Ribal** (initials of **R**abbi **I**saac **B**aer **L**evinsohn). Levinsohn was born in Kremenets, Volhynia, Russia, into a wealthy family. Later he moved to Radzivilov, on the border of Austrian Galicia. He taught himself European languages, and served as translator for the Russian forces in the time of the French invasion (1812). From 1813 to 1820 Levinsohn lived in the Eastern Galician towns of Brody, Tarnopol, and Zolkiew where he was befriended by such leaders of the Haskalah as Naḥman *Krochmal, Isaac *Erter, Joseph *Perl, and S.J. *Rapoport, and taught in the modern schools established in Tarnopol and Brody. From 1820 to 1823 he spread the ideas of the Haskalah as a private tutor in wealthy homes in Berdichev and other towns. For reasons of health, Levinsohn returned to Kremenets in 1823. Levinsohn's connections with the Russian government gave him authority in Haskalah circles and protected him against the fury of his fanatical opponents. In his memoranda he tried to persuade the Russian authorities to mitigate the persecution of the Jews (his memorandum against the kidnapping of children for military service) and to introduce reforms in the spirit of the Haskalah. He supported a plan for agricultural settlement of Jews, especially those who had lost their livelihood owing to expulsion from the countryside and border areas. On his advice, the Russian authorities limited the number of Hebrew printing presses to three: Warsaw and Vilna in 1836, and Zhitomir in 1846, and imposed censorship on imported Hebrew books. In 1856, the Russian government decided to support him by buying 2,000 copies of his book *Beit Yehudah* and distributing them to synagogues and Jewish schools.

Levinsohn's literary work was mainly polemical and propagandistic. It dealt with the social, internal, and external position of the Jews in Eastern Europe. He started his public advocacy of the Haskalah by writing satires, mainly imitations of those by Perl and Erter. *Divrei Ẓaddikim* ("Words of the Righteous," 1830), written in the style of Perl's *Megalleh Temirin*, was published anonymously. In *Emek Refa'im* ("Valley of Ghosts"), *Peloni Almoni ha-Kozevi* ("So-and-So the Liar"), and his Yiddish play *Di Hefker Velt* ("The World of Chaos"), he satirizes not only the Ḥasidim and their *ẓaddikim*, but also the tyrannical leaders of the community, the tax farmers, and the "kidnappers." These works circulated in manuscript among the Jews in Volhynia and Galicia and were only published posthumously, the first in Odessa in 1867; the second in 1880; and the third, *Yalkut Ribal*, in 1878.

In 1823, Levinsohn completed his most influential work *Te'udah be-Yisrael* ("Testimony in Israel") which, because of Orthodox opposition, did not appear until 1828 (Vilna). Levinsohn listed five questions which he intended to discuss: (a) Was it essential to study Hebrew grammatically? (b) Was it permitted to study foreign languages? (c) Was it permitted to study secular subjects? (d) Was there any advantage in the study of sciences and languages? (e) Did the advantage of such studies outweigh the disadvantages? Levinsohn appealed to the authority of talmudic and medieval sources, and to national sentiments. He characterized the Hebrew language as "the bond of religion and national survival," uniting all the dispersions of Israel into one people. He severely criticized the traditional *ḥadarim* ("Hebrew schools") which he dubbed "*ḥadrei mavet*" ("rooms of death"). He denounced their talmudic-centered curriculum, their unsystematic method of instruction, and their employment of corporal punishment. He objected to the use of Yiddish and demanded its replacement by "pure" German or Russian. He demonstrated that great Jews of the past knew foreign languages and studied the sciences, and explained the advantages of such studies, both in business and in relations with the authorities. He devoted considerable space to the advocacy of manual labor, especially farming, and criticized Jewish fondness for petty trading. The book had a great impact on Russian Jewish life. Groups formed in many towns which undertook to carry out Levinsohn's proposals. Even a part of Orthodox Jewry received the book sympathetically; only the Ḥasidim regarded it as a dangerous work. They banned the book and labeled an adherent of the Haskalah with the pejorative epithet *te'udke*. The Russian government awarded him a prize of 1,000 rubles for *Te'udah be-Yisrael*.

Levinsohn's second major book, *Beit Yehudah* ("House of Judah"), was published in Vilna in 1838 after considerable argument with the printers who refused to print it because of rabbinical opposition. The book purports to be a reply to 35 questions asked by "the great Christian nobleman Emanuel Lipen" (the name is a scramble of the Hebrew letters *Peloni Almoni* "So-and-So"). The questions deal with the nature of the Commandments, the Talmud, the Karaites, the Pharisees, the Zohar, Shabbateanism, Ḥasidism, and poses the question: "Is there still hope to reform the House of Israel and how?" In his basic assumptions Levinsohn follows Moses *Mendelssohn's *Jerusalem*. Judaism is a law; it should not be limited to "divine law," rather it should include "civic law," involving the practices of society and the sciences required for its maintenance and development. "Civic law" may be reformed and altered, with the consent of the people, in accordance with the spirit of the times and national needs. "The Jew is free to accept the legends of the Talmud or to reject them." Modern Christians should not be regarded as idolaters because they obey the seven *Noachide commandments and worship God. They are equal to Jews in respect to all the precepts involving the relations between men. The second half of the book is devoted to a historical survey of the teachings of the Jewish sages in all periods, including *Elijah of Vilna and Moses Mendelssohn. His historical survey follows traditional lines and contains numerous errors, demonstrating the backward state of Jewish knowledge at the time. Toward the end of the book, Levinsohn presents a five-point program for the reform of Jewish life in Russia: (a) The establishment of elementary schools for boys and girls of the lower classes. At the same time, boys and girls should learn a trade or a craft. For gifted pupils only, central colleges should be established in Warsaw, Vilna, Odessa, and Berdichev to teach Talmud and Codes, as well as "science, and various languages." (b) The appointment of a *rav kelali* ("chief rabbi"), assisted by a supreme religious court, who would appoint rabbis and preachers in all the towns of Russia, under his supervision. A committee of *parnasim kolelim* ("communal leaders") should also be appointed mainly to defend the poor and the ordinary people "against their leaders and the rich men who suck their marrow and drink their blood." (c) Preachers and orators should be appointed to arouse the people to good behavior, encourage them to take up trades and handicrafts, and explain to them their duties "to the Lord, to themselves, to their fellows, to the State, and to every man." (d) Representations should be made to the government to transfer one-third of the Jews of Russia to agriculture. (e) Luxuries should be forbidden, especially expensive feminine jewelry. These reforms should be carried out without asking for the people's consent.

Efes Damim (1837; "No Blood"), written to refute *blood libel, was published in Vilna in 1837 in the form of a debate between a Jewish rabbi and the Greek patriarch in Jerusalem, supplemented by statements of popes and kings protesting the blood libel. It was translated into English on the occasion of the Damascus blood libel in 1840, and into German and Russian. Another pamphlet called *Shorshei ha-Levanon* (or *Beit ha-Oẓar*, Vilna, 1841), containing minor studies, was published during the author's lifetime. He bequeathed his numerous unpublished works to his nephew Jacob Israel Levinsohn who asked David Bernhard *Nathanson to edit and publish them.

The most important of these posthumous works was *Zerubbavel*, which appeared in an incomplete form in Odessa in 1863, and later in several complete editions. It was written as a reply to *Netivot Olam* (1838–39), Stanislav *Hoga's Hebrew translation of *Old Paths*, a critique of Judaism published by the British missionary, McCaul. Levinsohn demonstrates McCaul's ignorance and the unfairness of his attacks on Judaism. He explains the evolution of the Oral Law from the Written Law, pointing out that in the course of this development reforms have been introduced in accordance with the changing needs of the times. Levinsohn insisted that only the halakhic ("legal") and not the aggadic ("legendary") elements of the tradition are binding for the observant Jew. Unlike Christianity, which is restricted to the spheres of faith and ethics, Judaism encompasses all spheres of individual and public life, and its aim is the strengthening of Jewish society: "The survival of the nation is the greatest of all the commandments." The book served to modify the hostile views about the Talmud and rabbinical literature which were often held by the followers of the Haskalah. Since *Zerubbavel* was intended for publication, Levinsohn phrased his remarks cautiously, so that the book could pass the censor. At the same time he wrote another work containing the rest of his arguments against Christianity. This manuscript was published after his death under the title of *Aḥiyyah ha-Shiloni ha-Ḥozeh* ("Ahijah the Shilonite, the Prophet," 1863). Here Levinsohn condemns the Christians for their persecution of the Jews, and their intolerance toward members of other faiths and various Christian sects, despite the Christian doctrine of forgiveness. As Christians did not carry out the Christian precepts of love, how can they demand that the Jews become Christians? He compares the sobriety and normal family life prevailing among the Jews, with the higher rate of alcoholism among non-Jews. "All these virtues have come to us from the Talmud." He uses the arguments of *Maimonides and others to show that whatever is positive in the New Testament is of rabbinic origin. Jesus himself, he argues, was an observant Jew who fulfilled all the commandments and believed that the Jews are the "chosen people."

Most of Levinsohn's other works were included in the collections *Bikkurei Ribal* (1888), *Yalkut Ribal* (1878), and *Eshkol ha-Sofer* (1891). Levinsohn's work was derivative. His views were drawn mainly from Mendelssohn, and his practical proposals followed those of the earlier Haskalah. The Hebrew readers of his day who belonged to the generation of transition from Orthodoxy to Haskalah enjoyed his defense of Judaism and his easy style, studded with biblical and rabbinic quotations. His books appeared in numerous editions, and Nathanson's biography of Levinsohn, *Sefer ha-Zikhronot* ("Book of Remembrances"), went through nine editions between 1876 and 1900. His contemporaries called him "The Russian Mendelssohn." For the modern reader, only his first book, *Te'udah be-Yisrael*, is of some historical value. By his personality and literary activity, Levinsohn undoubtedly did much to strengthen the moderate Haskalah. Certain ideas formulated in *Te'udah be-Yisrael*, such as educational reform and the transition to a life of labor and agriculture, later became a part of the programs of *Ḥibbat Zion, *Zionism, and other organizations and movements which preached "the productivization" of the Jewish masses and their adaptation to life in the modern world.

BIBLIOGRAPHY: L.S. Greenberg, *A Critical Investigation of the Works of Rabbi Isaac Baer Levinsohn* (1930), includes bibliography; J.S. Raisin, *The Haskalah Movement in Russia* (1913), 204–13; S. Spiegel, *Hebrew Reborn* (1930), 167–72; Waxman, Literature, 3 (1960^2), 202–12; Klausner, Sifrut, 3 (1952^2), 33–115; S. Halkin, *Modern Hebrew Literature* (1950), 67.

[Yehuda Slutsky]

LEVINSON, ABRAHAM (1888–1955), U.S. pediatrician. Levinson, who studied with Béla *Schick and Heinrich *Finkelstein, was professor of pediatrics at Northwestern University Medical School. He founded the Levinson Research Foundation for research in pediatric neuropsychiatry. Levinson earned an excellent reputation as clinician, teacher, and historian. He pursued fundamental research in pediatric neurology and was a pioneer in the study of cerebrospinal fluid. He also did research on diphtheria, influenza, and tuberculosis. His most significant contribution was a test for diagnosing tuberculous meningitis and his study on the pathological changes in the brain following streptomycin treatment of that disease. Levinson's books include *Cerebrospinal Fluid in Health and in Disease* (1919), the first book on the subject to appear in English; *Pediatric Nursing* (1925); *Pioneers of Pediatrics* (1936); and a biography of *Tobias Cohn* (1923). Levinson and Isaac Abt co-edited the *Pediatric Year Book* (1916–20).

BIBLIOGRAPHY: *Abraham Levinson Anniversary Volume* (1949); *American Medical Association Journal...*, 159 (1955), 1139; S.R. Kagan, *Jewish Medicine* (1952), 369.

[Suessmann Muntner]

LEVINSON, ANDRE (1887–1933), dance critic and foremost writer on ballet in his time. Levinson was a professor of French literature in St. Petersburg, where he was born, and helped to edit a periodical on the imperial theaters. He became known as a brilliant critic of dance and a champion of the classical tradition. Leaving Russia after the 1917 Revolution, he settled in Paris in 1921 where he lectured on Russian literature and contributed to various journals. He was probably the first critic in France to approach ballet purely from the point of view of dance. He opposed the innovations of Fokine and Diaghilev, whom he regarded as having subordinated dancing to music and scenic elements. His biographies of dancers and people connected with the ballet included studies of the designer, Leon *Bakst (1923), the dancers and choreographers Noverre (1935), Marie Taglioni (1929) and Serge Lifar (1934). Among his books were *La danse au théâtre* (1924) and *La danse d'aujourd'hui* (1929). Levinson also wrote studies on the poets Théophile Gautier (1921) and Paul Valéry (1927).

[Marcia B. Siegel]

LEVINSON, BARRY (1942–), U.S. director, writer, producer. Born in Baltimore, Maryland, Levinson began his show business career writing for and performing on television's award-winning *Carol Burnett Show*. He moved up to feature film work by helping write two of Mel Brooks' screenplays, *Silent Movie* (1976) and *High Anxiety* (1977). Some of Levinson's other screenplays include *And Justice for All* (1979), *Inside Moves* (1980), *Best Friends* (1982), and *Unfaithfully Yours* (1984).

He made his directorial debut with his semi-autobiographical *Diner* (1982), the first of his films to be set in his hometown of Baltimore. Levinson followed with *The Natural* (1984), based on Bernard Malamud's novel; *Young Sherlock Holmes* (1985); *Tin Men* (plus screenplay, 1987); and the box-office smash hit *Good Morning, Vietnam* (1987). Levinson's next movie was *Rain Man* (1988), which won that year's Academy Award for Best Picture plus an Oscar for Levinson as Best Director. Levinson's subsequent directorial efforts include *Avalon* (1990), *Bugsy* (producer, 1991), *Toys* (1992), *Jimmy Hollywood* (1994), *Disclosure* (1994), *Sleepers* (1996), *Wag the Dog* (1997), *Sphere* (1998), *Liberty Heights* (1999), *An Everlasting Piece* (2000), *Bandits* (2001), and *Envy* (2004). Some of these he wrote and produced as well. Other films and television shows that Levinson produced include *Donnie Brasco* (1997), *Home Fries* (1998), the TV series *Oz* (1997), *The Perfect Storm* (2000), the TV series *Falcone* (2000), *Analyze That* (2002), *Possession* (2002), and the TV series *The Jury* (2004).

Levinson wrote *Levinson on Levinson* (ed. D. Thompson, 1993), *Baltimore: Life in the City* (2001), and the novel *Sixty-Six* (2003).

[Jonathan Licht / Ruth Beloff (2nd ed.)]

LEVINSON, OLGA (1918–1989), South West African (Namibia) writer and journalist. Levinson was born in South Africa and graduated from the University of the Witwatersrand, but after her marriage to Jack Louis Levinson of Windhoek in 1943 she took up residence there and took a leading part in the cultural and artistic life of the territory. From 1958 to 1976 she was president of the S.A. Association of Arts, South West Africa; she was also an executive member of the S.W.A. Performing Arts Council. She received awards for dramatic art. Among her publications are *Call Me Master* (1961), *Adolph Jentsch* (1973), *South West Africa* (1976), and *The Story of Namibia* (1978). Her last notable work was *Diamonds in the Desert: The Story of August Staunch and His Time* (1983).

LEVINSON, SALMON OLIVER (1865–1941), U.S. lawyer and world peace advocate. Levinson, who was born in Noblesville, Indiana, was admitted to the Illinois bar in 1891, and began to practice law in Chicago. Although subsequently recognized as the successful corporation lawyer who reorganized both the personal affairs and the companies of industrial tycoon George Westinghouse, Levinson became particularly prominent in 1915 for his "outlawry of war" idea and his attempt to start an international peace movement during World War I. He opposed the terms of the Versailles Treaty, which he considered unduly harsh and not conducive to world peace. In 1920 Levinson backed Warren G. Harding, who had espoused Levinson's idea of outlawing war, for the presidency. Although Levinson at first advocated and then opposed U.S. entry into the League of Nations, he did not work with the U.S. delegation to the Disarmament Conference (1921) and later urged U.S. entry into the World Court (1925). In 1927 he presented the Levinson Plan which called for the readjusting of German reparations and allied and interallied debts, and world peace. Levinson sponsored and helped draft the Kellogg-Briand peace pact, later ratified by 15 countries (1928). He donated two large collections of documents to the University of Chicago (1937, 1938) concerning his national and international activities and descriptions of his meetings.

LEVINSTEIN, HERBERT (1878–1956), British industrial chemist. Levinstein entered his father's firm in Manchester. He took out many patents on sulfur dyes, azo dyestuffs, and intermediates. In 1919 his firm amalgamated and became the Dyestuffs Division of Imperial Chemical Industries Ltd. Levinstein received many awards and held many positions in chemical and dyeing organizations including president of the Society of Chemical Industry of which his father had also been president.

LEVINTHAL, U.S. family, descended from an old rabbinical family. BERNARD LOUIS LEVINTHAL (1865–1952) was born in Lithuania and went to the United States in 1891 after having studied at the yeshivot of Kovno, Vilna, and Bialystok. Settling in Philadelphia, Pennsylvania, he succeeded his father-in-law, Eleazar Kleinberg, as rabbi of Congregation B'nai Abraham, where he served until his death, as head of the United Orthodox Hebrew Congregations of Philadelphia, and effectively as dean of Orthodox Judaism in the city. Levinthal was responsible for the establishment of a number of institutions tending to the religious and social needs of the immigrant Jewish community, such as the Central Talmud Torah, out of which later grew the Yeshivah Mishkan Israel (1903). He cooperated with non-Orthodox Jews to serve community needs, helping found the larger Associated Talmud Torahs, which enrolled girls as well as boys, with support from the short-lived Philadelphia Kehillah (Jewish Community of Philadelphia) in 1919. He established a municipal Va'ad ha-Kashruth to supervise ritual slaughtering.

Levinthal was a key figure in the formation of the Rabbi Isaac Elchanan Spector yeshivah (later part of Yeshiva University) in 1896. He served on key committees and taught there throughout his career. He also mentored Bernard *Revel, the first president of Yeshiva College (later University). Levinthal's granddaughter SELMA ERLICH (daughter of Levinthal's daughter Lena) married Samuel *Belkin, later the second president of Yeshiva University. Bernard Levinthal was a founder of the American Jewish Committee and the only rabbi to be a member of the delegation sent by the American Jewish Congress to the Paris Peace Conference in 1919. An active Zionist as well, he helped to establish the Mizrachi Organization of America and was an honorary vice president of the Federation of American Zionists. In the 1938 American Jewish Congress elections, Levinthal was the only candidate to receive an absolute majority of the local votes.

Levinthal had a significant national impact, but he left an ambiguous local heritage. He did not establish a day school or post-high school yeshivah. He did not encourage rabbinic graduates of Yeshiva University to locate in Philadelphia, and few served there before the late 1930s. His four sons were active in Conservative Judaism and Zionism, and a granddaughter was the first woman to complete studies at the Jewish Institute of Religion in New York.

Bernard's son ISRAEL HERBERT LEVINTHAL (1888–1982) was ordained by the Jewish Theological Seminary in 1910. He served at Congregations B'nai Shalom and Petach Tikvah in Brooklyn, from 1910 to 1915 and from 1915 to 1919, respectively, and after 1919 at the Brooklyn Jewish Center. In addition, he was active in the Zionist movement and served as president of the Rabbinical Association of America. An exceptionally gifted preacher, he was adept at traditionally expounding biblical and rabbinical texts in the English language, and several volumes of his sermons have been published. He taught homiletics at the Jewish Theological Seminary. His books include *Judaism, An Analysis and An Interpretation* (1935); *Point of View: An Analysis of American Judaism* (1958); and *Judaism Speaks to the Modern World* (1963). Israel's daughter, HELEN HADASSAH LEVINTHAL, was the first woman to complete graduation requirements from the Jewish Institute of Religion in 1939, although she was not ordained as a rabbi.

LOUIS EDWARD LEVINTHAL (1892–1976), Israel's brother, practiced law in Philadelphia until 1937, when he was appointed judge on the Philadelphia Court of Common Pleas, a position he held until his retirement in 1959. Besides writing a number of legal works, he devoted himself to numerous charitable and civic organizations and to the Zionist Organization of America, of which he was elected president in 1941. He was a leader of the Conservative movement's United Synagogue of America in Philadelphia. He was particularly active in the Jewish Publication Society of America, serving as chairman of its publications committee from 1939 to 1949, again from 1954 to 1962, and as its president from 1949 to 1954. He was chairman of the board of governors of the Hebrew University from 1962 to 1966.

BIBLIOGRAPHY: BERNARD LEVINTHAL: R. Tabak, "Orthodox Judaism in Transition," in: M. Friedman, *Jewish Life in Philadelphia: 1830–1940* (1983); P. Rosen, "Orthodox Institution Builder: Rabbi Bernard Lewis Levinthal," in: M. Friedman, *When Philadelphia Was the Capital of Jewish America* (1993); J. Gurock, *American Jewish Orthodoxy in Historical Perspective* (1996). ISRAEL LEVINTHAL: D.D. Moore, *At Home in America: Second Generation New York Jews* (1981); P. Nadell, *Women Who Would Be Rabbis: A History of Women's Ordination, 1889–1985* (1998).

[Sefton D. Temkin / Robert P. Tabak (2nd ed.)]

LEVI-PEROTTI, GIUSTINA, the supposed 14th-century author of two Petrarchan sonnets. In one, the author expresses her longing for the poetic world and her wish to gain experience in writing poetry, instead of engaging in weaving and sewing, tasks normally assigned to women. The sonnets were published in the 16th century and were attributed to Giustina in a collection of the poems of Petrarch (1304–74) assembled by G.F. Tomasini (*Petrarcha redivivus*, Padua, 1635). Tomasini claimed that the sonnet described was directed to Petrarch and that the latter replied with one of his most famous works, *La gola, e'l sonno e l'otiose piume*, encouraging the poet to persevere in a task "undertaken by only a few." On the basis of the obviously Jewish name Giustina Levi (Giusta or Giustina were names common among Italian Jewesses, especially during the Middle Ages), it was assumed that Petrarch had some connection with a Jewish poet of his time. However, only a few Petrarch scholars ever accepted this assumption, which was finally rejected by modern Italian literary critics. The notion of a Jewish poetess exchanging sonnets with Petrarch is in the romantic vogue of *petrarchismo*, which flourished in the 16th century and was based on imitations of Petrarch's verse. It is thus very probable that the poems attributed to Giustina Levi-Perotti were actually written in the 16th century and that she never in fact existed.

BIBLIOGRAPHY: Morici, in: *Rassegna Nazionale* (1899), 662–95.

[Joseph Baruch Sermoneta]

LÉVI-PROVENÇAL, EVARISTE (1894–1956), French Orientalist; original name, **Mabkhŭsh**. Born in Algiers, where he also studied, Lévi-Provençal became professor (1922) and director (1929) of the Institut des Hautes Etudes Morocaines in Rabat, professor (1928) at the University of Algiers, professor (1945) at the Sorbonne, and director of the Institut des Etudes Islamiques and of the Centre d'Etudes de l'Orient of the University of Paris. He distinguished himself mainly in two fields: in the publication of Arabic texts and as a historian of Muslim Spain. In the libraries of North Africa and Spain he discovered various manuscripts of old texts which shed new light on the history of the *Almohads and the Muslim rule in Spain, among them works such as the memoirs of Baydhag, a companion of Ibn Tŭmart, and those of Abdallah, the last Zirid king of Granada. He also published other texts, such as old *Ḥisba* books, dealing with markets, letters of the Almohad rulers, and writings of the Magreb and Spanish Arabic historians and geographers. His major achievement, however, was his *Histoire de l'Espagne musulmane* (vol. 1, 1944; vols. 1–3, 1950–53[2]), whose first two volumes give a very clear outline of the political history of Muslim Spain until the downfall of the *Umayyad caliphate of Cordoba, whereas the third volume contains a detailed analysis of its social and cultural life. The whole work should have comprised six volumes, but when the author died, he had only collected his materials for the last three volumes. Lévi-Provencal also published Arabic inscriptions from North Africa and Spain (*Inscriptions arabes d'Espagne*, 1931) and many essays on the history and the civilization of the Muslims in Spain. Additionally, he was the founder of the review *Arabica* (Paris, 1953–) and one of the first editors of the second edition of the *Encyclopaedia of Islam*.

For a list of his writings see J. and D. Sourdel, in: *Arabica*, 3 (1956), 136–46.

[Eliyahu Ashtor]

LEVIRATE MARRIAGE AND ḤALIẒAH.

Definition

Levirate marriage (Heb. יִבּוּם; *yibbum*) is the marriage between a widow whose husband died without offspring (the *yevamah*) and the brother of the deceased (the *yavam* or levir), as prescribed in Deuteronomy 25:5–6:

> If brethren dwell together, and one of them die, and have no child, the wife of the dead shall not marry without unto a stranger [the last words according to AV translation, which is correct]; her husband's brother shall go in unto her, and take her to him to wife, and perform the duty of a husband's brother unto her. And it shall be, that the firstborn that she beareth shall succeed in the name of his brother that is dead, that his name be not blotted out of Israel.

When the levir does not marry the *yevamah*, the ceremony of *Ḥaliẓah* (Heb. חֲלִיצָה) takes place, whereby the woman becomes released from the levirate tie (*zikkat ha-yibbum*) and free to marry someone else:

> If the man like not to take his brother's wife, then his brother's wife shall go up to the gate unto the elders, and say: "My husband's brother refuseth to raise up unto his brother a name in Israel; he will not perform the duty of a husband's brother unto me." Then the elders of his city shall call him, and speak unto him; and if he stand, and say: "I like not to take her"; then shall his brother's wife draw nigh unto him in the presence of the elders, and loose his shoe from off his foot, and spit in his face; and she shall answer and say: "So shall it be done unto the man that doth not build up his brother's house." And his name shall be called in Israel "The house of him that had his shoe loosed" (Deut. 25:7–10).

In the Bible

The events concerning Judah and Tamar (Gen. 38) indicate that the practice of levirate marriage preceded the Mosaic law (cf. Gen. R. 85:5). However, it appears that levirate marriage then differed from that of Mosaic law in that the obligation also appears to have been laid on the father of the deceased husband (Gen. 38:26) and no mention is made of a release by way of *Ḥaliẓah*. Some scholars expressed the opinion, following the view of Josephus (Ant., 5:332–5) and several Karaite authorities (*Gan Eden*, Nashim, 13, 30; *Adderet Eliyahu*, Nashim 5), that the events concerning Ruth and Boaz (Ruth 4) also indicate a levirate marriage, but it appears that in this case the duty of the *go'el* to marry Ruth was incidental to the laws concerning the redemption of property of the deceased; hence the variation in a number of details from the prescribed levirate marriage laws (Ibn Ezra, Deut. 25:5; Naḥmanides, Gen. 38:8).

In the Talmud

NEED FOR LEVIRATE MARRIAGE AND ḤALIẒAH. The word *ben* ("son") in Deuteronomy 25:5 is interpreted in the Talmud, in the Septuagint, and by Josephus (Ant. 4:254) to mean "offspring" and not only a male child (cf. Gen. 3:16), so that a levirate marriage is only obligatory when the deceased husband leaves no offspring whatever, whether from the *yevamah* or another wife, including a child conceived during his lifetime but not born until after his death, even if that child subsequently died (Yev. 2:5, 22b; Nid. 5:3; and Codes). The words, "if brothers dwell together" (Deut. 25:5) have been interpreted by the scholars as confining the application of levirate marriage to the brothers of the deceased who were born prior to his death (Yev. 2:1, 2). Thus if the birth of the levir precedes his brother's death by as little as one day and there are no other brothers, the *yevamah* must wait until he reaches the age of 13 years and a day, when he becomes legally fit either to marry her or grant her *Ḥaliẓah* (Nid. 5:3; Yev. 105b). The law of *yibbum* applies only to paternal, not maternal, brothers (Yev. 17b). If the deceased is survived by several brothers, the obligation of *yibbum* or *Ḥaliẓah* devolves on the eldest but is nevertheless valid if performed by another brother (Yev. 24a; 39a). If the deceased brother had several wives, fulfillment of the obligation in respect of one wife suffices and exempts the other wives (Yev. 4:11, 44a; and Codes).

The tie (*zikkah*) between the *yevamah* and the *yevam* arises immediately upon the husband's death. From this stage, until she undergoes levirate marriage or *Ḥaliẓah*, the *yevamah* is known as a *shomeret yavam* ("awaiting the levir") and relations between the levir and her kin are prohibited (as incestuous), as if he were married to her. Only a putative marriage can be contracted between a *shomeret yavam* and an "outsider," who is obliged to divorce her, although their offspring are not considered **mamzerim* (Yev. 13b; al. Yad, Ishut 4:14).

The *shomeret yavam* may not undergo levirate marriage or *Ḥaliẓah* until three months after the date of her husband's death (Yev. 4:10 and Codes) as with any other widow, who must await this period before remarrying. She is therefore entitled to *maintenance from her husband's estate during this period, but not thereafter, according to the *halakhah* of the talmudic period – neither from her husband's estate nor from the levir. However, if the levir evaded her after she had sued him in court either to marry her or grant her *Ḥaliẓah* the rabbis fined him to pay her maintenance (Yev. 41b; Rashi, and

Tosafot thereto), and this was also the law if he became ill or went abroad (TJ, Ket. 5:4, 29d; Yad, Ishut 18:16).

In biblical law the levir does not require a formal marriage (*kiddushin*) to the *yevamah* since the personal status tie, the *zikkah* between them, arises automatically upon the death of the husband of the *yevamah*. However, the scholars prescribed that the *yevamah* should be married like all women, in this case by *kiddushei kesef* or *shetar*, these *kiddushin* called "*ma'amar*" (lit. "declaration"): "first he addresses to her a *ma'amar* and then they cohabit" (lit. "he takes her into his home"; Tosef., Yev. 7:2; Yev. 52a). The scholars ruled that the levir who marries the *yevamah* succeeds to the estate of his deceased brother (Yev. 4:7), interpreting the passage "*ve-hayah ha-bekhor asher teled*" (Deut. 25:6) as referring to the firstborn of the brothers on whom the duty of levirate marriage devolved and hence that the continuation of this passage, i.e., "shall succeed in the name of his brother" (meaning "shall succeed to the inheritance") refers to the levir undergoing levirate marriage. This argument was described as "having entirely deprived the text of its ordinary meaning through a *gezerah shavah*" (see *Hermeneutics; Yev. 24a). According to R. Judah (Yev. 4:7), "where there is a father, he inherits the son's property," otherwise the brothers succeed to the estate (Tosef., Yev. 63) and the levir marrying the *yevamah* inherits only a brother's proportionate share. He interprets the above passage literally, as referring to the firstborn of the union between the levir and the *yevamah*, who succeeds to the estate of the deceased brother (interpreted similarly by Tar. Yer., Ibn Ezra, and Rashbam, Deut. 25:6; Rashi, Gen. 38:8 – from whom Naḥmanides Gen. *ibid.* differs). The *amoraim* commented, however, that R. Judah did not differ from the scholars but merely excepted the case of the deceased who is survived by his father, for the levir is compared to the *firstborn ("*ve-hayah ha-bekhor asher teled*"), who does not inherit in his father's lifetime (Yev. 40a). Even according to the scholars whose opinion was accepted, the levir does not succeed to a contingent inheritance (*ra'ui*), i.e., to property due to come to the deceased brother (such as the proportional share of his father's estate which the deceased, but for his death, would have inherited), but only to property already owned by the brother at the time of his death, as in the case of the firstborn (Bek. 8:9; see *Succession). The **ketubbah*, i.e., the widow's jointure, is a charge on the property which the levir inherits from the deceased and he is prohibited from alienating the latter by way of sale or gift – any such attempted alienation being void (Ket. 82a). In a case where the levir inherits no property from his brother, the scholars determined that the widow must receive her *ketubbah* from the levir's property "so that he shall not consider it easy to divorce her" (Yev. 39a). A levir who chooses to perform *Ḥaliẓah* receives no more than a brother's share of the deceased's estate (Yev. 4:7) and upon *Ḥaliẓah* the widow becomes entitled to receive her *ketubbah* from her deceased husband's estate (Yev. 85a; Sh. Ar., EH 165:4).

The Duty of *Ḥaliẓah*

According to the Torah, the duty of *Ḥaliẓah* is imposed only when the levir willfully refuses to marry the *yevamah*, and not when he is unable to or prohibited from marrying her, for "whoever is subject [lit. "goes up"] to levirate marriage is subject to *Ḥaliẓah*, and whoever is not subject to levirate marriage is not subject to *Ḥaliẓah*" (Yev. 3a). Thus, for example, where a levirate marriage is precluded because the relationship would be incestuous, the widow (supposing she is the levir's daughter or his wife's sister) is also exempted from *Ḥaliẓah*. According to Bet Hillel, if one of the deceased's several wives is prohibited from marrying the levir she also exempts her co-wives (*ẓarah*, "rival") and the "rivals of her rivals" (if the rival has married another man) from levirate marriage and *Ḥaliẓah*, but Bet Shammai's opinion was that the rival is not thus exempted (Yev. 1:1; 1:4; cf. Yev. 16a and TJ, Yev. 1:6, 3a). On the other hand, it was determined that at times the duty of *Ḥaliẓah* exists even where levirate marriage is forbidden – as between a priest and divorcee –by a "prohibition of holiness" (*issur kedushah*); in such a case *Ḥaliẓah* is still required for, as in all cases of negative precepts, the marriage, even if prohibited, is nevertheless valid once it has taken place (Yev. 2:3 and Rashi ad loc.; TJ, Yev. 1:1, 2c; see *Marriage, Prohibited). This rule also applies when doubt exists as to whether levirate marriage is incumbent on the widow, in which case *Ḥaliẓah* is required (Git. 7:3, et al.). In cases where the levir is seriously ill or there is a big difference in their ages, or the levir is "not suitable" (*eino hagun*) for the widow, etc., efforts were made to arrange for *Ḥaliẓah* rather than marriage.

Priority between Levirate Marriage and *Ḥaliẓah*

In the course of time some scholars accepted the view that the duty of the *Ḥaliẓah* always took priority over that of levirate marriage, a view stemming from the attempt to reconcile the prohibition on a man marrying his brother's wife (Lev. 18:16) with the command of levirate marriage. These biblical commandments induced the Samaritans to confine the application of levirate marriage to a woman who had undergone *kiddushin* but not *nissu'in* (see *Marriage) – in which case she would not be considered a relative with whom marriage was prohibited (Kid. 75b–76a; TJ, Yev. 1:6) – while some Karaite scholars were led to interpret the word "brothers" as relatives and not literally (*Gan Eden* Nashim, 13; *Adderet Eliyahu*, Nashim, 5). The two biblical provisions do not conflict, however, for the prohibition in Leviticus 18:16 applies only where the deceased brother is survived by descendants, whereas the *mitzvah* of levirate marriage applies only when the deceased brother dies without issue, in order that the levir shall "succeed in the name of his brother." The *mitzvah* of levirate marriage and the prohibition of marrying a brother's wife "were said as one" (Mekh. Ba-Ḥodesh; Sif. Deut. 233; TJ, Ned. 3:2, 37d). Hence in the beginning, when the parties carried out the precept for the sake of fulfilling a commandment, levirate marriage took priority over *Ḥaliẓah*; but when the precept was carried out for other reasons, the scholars said that *Ḥaliẓah* took priority over levirate marriage, and "a levir who marries the *yevamah* other than for the sake of fulfilling a commandment commits incest" (Bek. 1:7 and Rashi ad loc.); and "... I am inclined to think that the child of such a union is a *mamzer*" (Abba Saul, Tosef., Yev. 6:9; Yev. 39b). The question of priority was much disputed by the scholars. In the third generation of *tannaim*, levirate marriage was customarily upheld (Yev. 8:4), while the Babylonian *amoraim* left the choice between marriage and *Ḥaliẓah* to the levir, although some "reenacted the priority of levirate marriage over *Ḥaliẓah*" (Yev. 39a–b). The Palestinian *amoraim* apparently held that *Ḥaliẓah* took priority (Bar Kappara in TJ, Yev. 109a, makes no mention of the above "reenactment" of levirate marriage priority).

The Order of *Ḥaliẓah*

Ḥaliẓah which releases the widow from the obligation of levirate marriage enables her to marry freely, except that the scholars prohibited a priest from marrying her (Yev. 24a). The *Ḥaliẓah* ceremony is designed to shame the levir for not "building up his brother's house" (Deut. 25:9). It has been seen as an act of *kinyan* (*acquisition), whereby the widow buys from the levir the inheritance of his deceased brother (Rashbam *ibid.*; cf. Ruth 4:7–8), or as a form of mourning for the levir's brother "for he shall be forgotten now that no offspring shall be raised in his name" (Jehiel of Paris cited in *Seder Ḥaliẓah* to Sh. Ar., EH 169:57, no. 82; Responsum of Isaac Caro at the end of Responsa *Beit Yosef*). Although the formalities of *Ḥaliẓah* are performed by the *yevamah*, the levir is called the *Ḥoleẓ*, i.e., "loosener" (Yev. 4:1, 5–8; 5:6; et al.), for the levir "participates in *Ḥaliẓah* in that his intention to loosen is required," hence a deaf-mute levir who lacks such intention is called the *Neḥlaẓ* and not the *Ḥoleẓ* (Yev. 12:4; *Nimmukei Yosef* 104b, and Maim. commentary ad loc.).

Many details are stipulated for the order of the *Ḥaliẓah* ceremony (Yev. 12:6; Yad, Yibbum 4:1–23; Sh. Ar., EH 169); essentially they are as follows: The levir and the *yevamah* appear before the *bet din*, the levir wearing on his right foot a special shoe, the "*Ḥaliẓah* shoe"; the *yevamah* recites a passage indicating the levir's refusal to perform his duty to marry her; the levir responds by affirming his refusal – all this in Hebrew in the words prescribed in the Bible (Deut. 25:7, 9); the *yevamah* then removes the shoe from the levir's foot, throws it to the ground, spits on the ground before the levir, and utters the final prescribed passage (Deut. 25:9); finally, those present repeat the words "*Ḥaluẓ ha-na'al*" three times. The Boethusians held that the *yevamah* is required actually to spit in the levir's face and this is also stated in two manuscripts of the Septuagint, in Josephus' *Antiquities*, and in some of the apocryphal books, but the talmudic scholars held it to be sufficient if the elders see her spitting (Sif. Deut. 291). At the completion of the ceremony, the *dayyanim* express the wish "that the daughters of Israel shall have no need to resort to either *Ḥaliẓah* or levirate marriage" (Sh. Ar., EH 169, "abridged order of *Ḥaliẓah*," 56). At first it was customary to issue a deed of *Ḥaliẓah* as proof that the ceremony had taken place (Yev. 39b – as distinguished from a deed of divorce where the delivery of the deed constitutes the act of divorce), but in the course of time this practice was abandoned since "the ceremony was performed in public, before ten people, and she does not require documentary proof" (Sh. Ar., EH 169, "abridged order of *Ḥaliẓah*," 13; and end of commentary *Seder Ḥaliẓah*, no. 82).

In the Post-Talmudic Period

PRIORITY. In the post-talmudic period, the dispute over the question of priority was continued. In the opinion of the Sura *geonim*, levirate marriage took priority, while those of Pumbedita thought otherwise, as did some of the Sura scholars (R. Hillai and R. Natronai). In the rabbinic period the Spanish scholars – particularly Alfasi (to Yev. 39b), Maimonides (Yad, Yibbum 1:2), and Joseph Caro (Sh. Ar., EH 165:1) – gave priority to levirate marriage, contending that otherwise there is no reason to shame and to submit the levir to the prescribed indignities and that the kabbalistic scholars said that "levirate marriage is very beneficial for the soul of the dead," and that Abba Saul who held that *Ḥaliẓah* took priority, "did not know this kabbalistic mystery," otherwise he would not have come to the conclusion he reached (Isaac Caro, quoted in Resp. *Beit Yosef*, loc. cit.). Such has actually been the custom, until the present day, of the Jews of Spain and of the Oriental communities in North Africa from Morocco to Egypt – in Yemen, Babylonia, and Persia. This was also the case in Ereẓ Israel (even at the end of the 1940s; see *Mishpetei Uziel*, EH no. 119) until the matter was settled by a *takkanah* of the chief rabbinate of Israel (in 5710–1949/50, see below). The scholars of northern France and Germany – particularly Rashi, Rabbenu Tam, Asher b. Jehiel (Tur., EH 165), and Moses Isserles (*Rema*, EH 165:1) – held that *Ḥaliẓah* takes priority though they did not all assign the same measure of priority to it. The acceptance of Rabbenu Gershom's decree (prohibiting polygamy) among Ashkenazi Jews (see *Bigamy) apparently contributed greatly toward the entrenchment of the rule that *Ḥaliẓah* takes priority – in order not to distinguish between a married and an unmarried levir – and Ashkenazi communities gradually came to adopt the practice of *Ḥaliẓah* to the exclusion of levirate marriage.

Problems of Levirate Marriage – The Apostate Levir

The scholars devote a great deal of discussion to the solution of problems centering around the laws of levirate marriage and *Ḥaliẓah*, arising both from objective factors and from the levir's conduct. The Mishnah (Git. 7:3) relates the case of a childless husband who fell ill and wrote his wife a "conditional" bill of divorce, effected upon his death, so that on his death the divorce would take effect retroactively to the date of delivery of the bill, with the intention of absolving her from the obligations of a *yevamah*. In the case of an "unsuitable" levir, or one suffering from a serious illness, or whose age differed greatly from that of the widow, it was sought to influence the levir in various ways to forgo marriage in favor of *Ḥaliẓah*. From the geonic period, mention is made (first in the *Halakhot Gedolot*, end of Hilkh. Yevamot) of the problem of the *yevamah* and the *apostate levir "in the land of the Berbers, among gentiles" or "who cannot be reached in a far land," which placed the *yevamah* in the position of an **agunah*. Some of the *geonim* decided that she retained this status until released by the apostate levir, but others ruled that she was exempted from *Ḥaliẓah* if at the time of her marriage to the deceased his brother was already an apostate. It seems that the Babylonian academies were also divided on this question, Sura taking a lenient view and Pumbedita a strict one (L. Ginzberg, *Ginzei Schechter*, 2 (1929), 167f.). In later times the view that *Ḥaliẓah* was obligatory for the widow in every case became increasingly stronger and a solution for the problem was sought by the imposition – at the time of the *kiddushin* ceremony – of a condition specifying that the wife "shall be considered as not having been married if it shall be her lot to require levirate marriage at the hands of an apostate" (*Rema*, EH 157:4).

Problems of *Ḥaliẓah*

In an effort to overcome the problem that arose when a levir refused to undergo *Ḥaliẓah*, many French and German communities enacted *takkanot* awarding the levir a substantial share of the deceased brother's estate – financed partly at the widow's expense – although according to law the levir was entitled only to a brother's share upon *Ḥaliẓah*. The varying terms of these *takkanot* gave rise to frequent disputes, so that in practice the courts sought to compromise between the parties (Sh. Ar., EH 163:2, 165:4). As this, in turn, frequently caused the widow to be left at the levir's mercy, it became increasingly customary for the husband's brothers to write – at the time of the marriage – a "deed of undertaking to grant *Ḥaliẓah*" committing themselves to release the widow, whenever the need might arise, in a valid *Ḥaliẓah* ceremony, without delay or demand for consideration; this undertaking was enforced by way of a biblical *oath and a severe penalty or *ban. Where the levir was a minor at the time of his brother's marriage and his undertaking consequently unenforceable, his father would write a deed guaranteeing that his minor son would, upon reaching maturity, provide the required undertaking to his sister-in-law. The father backed his guarantee – which was itself lacking in authority (see **Asmakhta*) – by a monetary pledge to his daughter-in-law, which would be canceled on the production of the required undertaking (Gulak, Oẓar, 90–97). Many of the **aḥaronim* decided in favor of obliging the levir to maintain the widow to whom he refused to grant *Ḥaliẓah*, despite the lack of unanimity among the *rishonim* on the circumstances and terms on which maintenance should be awarded, as otherwise "she may be kept an *agunah* forever" (*Arukh ha-Shulḥan*, EH 160:8).

In recent years the problem of *Ḥaliẓah* arising from the levir being absent abroad has become more acute, particularly in the case of countries in the Soviet bloc. Several halakhic authorities, led by Shalom Mordecai ha-Kohen *Shvadron, head of the Brezen *bet din*, have sought to avoid the widow's need to travel to the *levir* by permitting her to be represented at the *Ḥaliẓah* ceremony by an agent (Resp. Maharsham, pt. 1, nos. 14, 135), a view based on confining the prohibition on *agency in *Ḥaliẓah* to the levir only (Ket. 74a); however, most of his contemporaries dissented from this. It has also been rejected by modern Ereẓ Israel scholars (e.g., *Mishpetei Uziel*, 2 (1938), EH 88; *Kunteres Sheliḥut ba-Ḥaliẓah*) and this problem – like that which arises when the levir is a minor, placing the widow in a position of an *agunah* until he reaches the age of 13 years and a day – urgently awaits a solution, possibly along the lines already indicated.

***Takkanah* of the Chief Rabbinate of Ereẓ Israel**

In 1944 the chief rabbinate of Ereẓ Israel enacted a *takkanah* obliging the levir to maintain the levirate widow until he released her by *Ḥaliẓah*, according to "law and precept," if a rabbinical court had certified that he refused to comply with its decision ordering him to grant her *Ḥaliẓah*. This *takkanah*, which gives expression to the view of those halakhic scholars who would oblige the recalcitrant levir to maintain the widow, has made this obligation part of the law of maintenance, rather than its being a fine for noncompliance. It was prompted by the fact of "much difficulty and suffering arising from the regrettable prevalence of cases of Jewish women who are in need of levirate marriage and are placed in the position of *agunot* because *Ḥaliẓah* has been withheld from them." A further *takkanah* of the chief rabbinate of the State of Israel (1950) completely prohibited the practice of levirate marriage in Israel while making *Ḥaliẓah* obligatory. This *takkanah*, extending also to the Sephardi and Oriental Jewish communities in Israel, was expressly justified on the grounds that "most levirs do not undergo levirate marriage for the sake of fulfilling a *mitzvah*, and also to preserve peace and harmony in the State of Israel by keeping the law of the Torah uniform for all."

In the State of Israel

The Rabbinical Courts Jurisdiction (Marriage and Divorce) Law, 5713–1953 of the State of Israel confers on the rabbinical court exclusive jurisdiction in a case where a woman sues her deceased husband's brother for *Ḥaliẓah*, and also with regard to maintenance for the woman until the day on which *Ḥaliẓah* is granted (sec. 5). Section 7 of the same law further provides that "Where a rabbinical court, by final judgment [i.e., when it can no longer be appealed against; sec. 8] has ordered that a man be compelled to give his brother's widow *Ḥaliẓah*, a district court may, upon expiration of three months from the day of making the order, on application of the attorney general, compel compliance with the order by imprisonment." A judgment compelling a levir to grant *Ḥaliẓah* will be given by the rabbinical court in similar circumstances to those in which it customarily sees fit to compel the grant of a divorce, and in certain additional cases, e.g., where the levir is already married (Tur and Sh. Ar., EH 165), but at all times only where compulsion is supported by halakhic authority so as not to bring about a prohibited "forced *Ḥaliẓah*" (Yev. 106a; Yad, Yibbum 4:25–26; Sh. Ar., EH 169:13). This procedure, so far as halakhically permitted, offers an effective means of dealing with a recalcitrant levir.

[Menachem Elon]

In 1995, the Rabbinical Courts Law (Upholding Divorce Rulings) (Temporary Provision) 5755–1995, was enacted. This law amended the procedure for compelling divorce (see in detail in entries on *Agunah and *Divorce). Section 6 of the Law provides that 30 days after a decision ordering the husband to give *Ḥaliẓah* to his brother's widow, the rabbinical court is empowered to impose the statutory sanctions, including imprisonment and restrictive orders. These sanctions are the application in Israeli Law of the *harḥakot Rabbenu Tam* (see *Agunah), which were enacted as a means of compelling divorce (See Sh. Ar., EH 154:21, *Rema*). Hence, today the Israel rabbinical court is authorized to compel the granting of *Ḥaliẓah*, and to employ the same methods of compulsion (imprisonment and restrictive orders) against the recalcitrant levir as it does against the recalcitrant husband who refuses to grant a *get*.

[Moshe Drori (2nd ed.)]

The Ceremony of *Ḥaliẓah*

The ceremony of *Ḥaliẓah* is invested with a special solemnity. The normal *bet din*, consisting of three ordained rabbis, is augmented for the occasion by two additional members (who can be laymen), "in order to give publicity to the matter" (Yev. 101a–b). The five members of the *bet din* meet at the place where the ceremony is to take place on the previous day, in order to "establish the locum" (Yev. 101b). The ceremony takes place the following morning, and the *yevamah* (more correctly *yavmah*) is enjoined to fast until the ceremony. She and the levir are also instructed, if necessary, to repeat the respective declarations which they have to make, according to Deuteronomy 25:7–10, in the original Hebrew. Questions are put to ascertain that there are no circumstances which might invalidate the ceremony, e.g., to ascertain that both are majors, in full possession of their normal mental faculties, that 91 days have passed since the death of her husband. Although *yibbum*, levirate marriage, is forbidden at the present time, the presiding rabbi nevertheless formally asks the levir which he prefers, to marry his sister-in-law or release her through *Ḥaliẓah*, to which he replies confirming the latter alternative. The ceremony proper then commences, the essence of which is that the *yevamah*, in accordance with Deuteronomy 25:9, has to draw a shoe off the foot of her brother-in-law. The *Ḥaliẓah* shoe must conform rigidly to the halakhic regulations laid down for it. It is made of leather including the sewing, the loops, and the straps, no metal whatsoever being permitted. It resembles a moccasin, and is fastened primarily with three loops. Long straps are attached to the top of the uppers. Since the shoe must be the property of the levir, it is given to him as an unconditional gift. He tries it on his right foot and is asked to walk in it, to see that it fits, even when it is unlaced; he repeats the procedure after it is tied in the prescribed manner, first by fastening the loops and then winding the straps around it. The laces are then undone.

Until recent times, in Eastern Europe the morbid custom obtained for the levir to lean against an upturned board used for the ritual washing of a corpse in order to emphasize that his status and rights as a levir derived from the death of his brother. This custom has been (largely) abandoned. The levir nowadays leans against a beam or a wall and presses his foot hard on the ground. The *yevamah* then makes the following declaration, in Hebrew: "My husband's brother refuses to raise up unto his brother a name in Israel; he will not perform the duty of a husband's brother unto me" (Deut. 25:7), to which he answers, also in Hebrew, and in one breath, the three words meaning "I like not to take her" (Deut. 25:8). The *yevamah* then bends down, places her left hand on the calf of her brother-in-law and with the right hand undoes the laces and the loops. She then raises his leg, slips off the shoe, and casts it away. She then collects some ordure in her mouth and spits on the floor in front of him (not "in his face"; see Deut. 25:9) and declares, again in Hebrew: "So shall it be done unto the man that doth not build up his brother's house; and his name shall be called in Israel *beit Ḥaluẓ ha-na'al* ("the house of him that had his shoe loosened"; Deut. 25:9–10). All those present thrice repeat the last three words. The members of the *bet din* then recite the formula "may it be the divine will that the daughters of Israel shall be liable neither to *yibbum* nor *Ḥaliẓah*."

[Louis Isaac Rabinowitz]

BIBLIOGRAPHY: A. Geiger, in: *He-Ḥalutz*, 6 (1861), 26–28; I.I. Mattuck, in: *Studies… Kohler* (1913), 210–22; I.S. Zuri, *Mishpat ha-Talmud*, 2 (1921), 113–23; Gulak, Yesodei, 3 (1922), 30–33; idem, Oẓar, 90–97; Finkelstein, Middle Ages, 229f., 245–7, 253–6; M. Price, in: *Oriental Studies… Haupt* (1926), 268–71; A.A. Judelowitz, *Av be-Ḥokhmah* (1927); Z. Karl, in: *Ha-Mishpat*, 1 (1927), 266–79; L. Ginzberg, in: *Ginzei Schechter*, 2 (1929), 166–81, 270f.; Ḥ. Albeck, in: *Berichte der Hochschule fuer die Wissenschaft des Judentums*, 49 (1932), 66–72; idem (ed.), *Mishnah, Nashim*, 7–10; B.M. Lewin (ed.), *Oẓar ha-Ge'onim, Yevamot* (1936), 34–37, 67–80; H. Tchernowitz, *Toledot ha-Halakhah*, 3 (1943), 186–203; A.H. Freimann, in: *Sinai*, 14 (1943/44), 258–60; idem, *Seder Kiddushin ve-Nissu'in Aḥarei Ḥatimat ha-Talmud* (1945), 385–97; S. Assaf, *Tekufat ha-Ge'onim ve-Sifrutah* (1955), 275–7; M. Elon, in: *Sefer Yovel le-Pinḥas Rozen* (1962), 187f.; idem, Mafte'aḥ, 89–91; idem, *Ḥakikah Datit…* (1968), 31, 162, 172f.; M. Silberg, *Ha-Ma'amad ha-Ishi be-Yisrael* (1965⁴), 381–6, 391; B. Schereschewsky, *Dinei Mishpaḥah* (1967²), 226–36.

LEVISON, WILHELM (1876–1947), medievalist. Born in Duesseldorf, Germany, Levison taught at Bonn University from 1903, becoming professor in 1912. He specialized in the early Merovingian and Carolingian periods, being the first scholar to treat Rhenish history as an integral part of German and European history (cf. the chapter he contributed to the *Geschichte des Rheinlandes* (vol. 1 (1922), 45–168)). He took part, first as assistant and later as coeditor, in editing volumes 3–5 of the *Monumenta Germaniae Historica, Scriptores rerum Merovingicarum*, 5–7 (1910–20); Levison also completely revised and reedited the first part of W. Wattenbach's classic, *Deutschlands Geschichtsquellen im Mittelalter…* (3 vols, 1952–57). Many of his articles were published in his *Aus rheinischer und fraenkischer Fruehzeit* (1948). The rise of

Hitler drove Levison from Germany and he accepted a fellowship at the University of Durham, England. In 1943, he delivered the Ford lectures at Oxford, which form part of his best-known book, *England and the Continent in the Eighth Century* (1946).

ADD. BIBLIOGRAPHY: R. Schieffer, "Der Mediaevist Wilhelm Levison," in: K. Duewell (ed.), *Vertreibung juedischer Kuenstler und Wissenschaftler aus Duesseldorf* (1998), 165–75; P.E. Huebinger, *Wilhelm Levison* (1968); T. Schieffer, *In Memoriam Wilhelm Levison* (1977).

[Helene Wieruszowski]

LEVI-STRAUSS, CLAUDE (1908–), French anthropologist. Born in Brussels, Belgium, and educated at the Sorbonne, he was chosen as a member of the French University mission to Brazil in 1934 where he became professor of sociology at the University of São Paulo from 1935 to 1939. During this period he conducted ethnographic field work among the tribes of the Mato Grosso area of central Brazil. On the outbreak of World War II Levi-Strauss served with the French army from 1939 to 1940 and after the fall of Paris went to New York as visiting professor at the New School of Social Research from 1941 to 1945. He returned to France as professor of primitive religion at the Ecole Pratique des Hautes Etudes at the Sorbonne, which position he held until 1974, and in 1959 he was appointed professor of social anthropology at the College de France. He was elected a member of the Academie française in May 1973.

Levi-Strauss' works began appearing in 1948 with the publication of "La Vie Familiale et sociale des Indiens Nambikwara" (*Journal de la Société des Americanistes*, 37 (1948), 1–130). *Tristes Tropiques* (1955, 1968^2; *A World on the Wane*, 1961) was a distinguished literary work containing elements of autobiography, ethnography, and social anthropology based on his experience in Brazil. His most significant theoretical work *Les Structures Elémentaires de la Parenté* (1949, 1967^2; *Elementary Structures of Kinship*, 1969) was a treatise on structural anthropology of the 20th century. His *Anthropologie Structurale* (1958; *Structural Anthropology*, 1963, 1968^3) is a collection of essays on language, kinship, and social organization which elucidates his theory of structural anthropology. His later works were *La Pensée Sauvage* (1962, 1964^2; *The Savage Mind*, 1966) and the monumental four-volume series, "Mythologiques," consisting of *Le Cru et le Cuit* (1964; Eng. translation, *The Raw and the Cooked*, 1969) which dealt with the nature of primitive thought and native mythology; *Du miel aux cendres* ("From Honey to Ashes," 1966); *L'Origine des mainieres de table* (1968; *The Origin of Table Manners*, 1978); and *L'Homme nu* (1971; *The Naked Man*, 1982). His *Totémisme* (1962, 1965^2; Eng. tr. 1963, paperback 1969) is a critical survey of the literature on totemism and advances new interpretations. His lectures were collected in *Paroles donées* (1984; *Anthropology and Myth: Lectures, 1951–1982*, 1987). Other books include *La Voie des masques* (1972; *The Way of the Masks*, 1982); *Le Regard eloigné* (1983; *The View from Afar*, 1985); *Le Poitière jalouse* (1985; *The Jealous Potter*, 1988); and *Regarder, écouter, lire* (1993; *Look, Listen, Read*, 1997).

Levi-Strauss' most original and significant contribution is his theory of structural anthropology. Taking linguistics as his model of a social science, he conceives of social anthropology as a general science concerned with relations involving logical structure of social phenomena. Ultimately, he maintains, all social phenomena are symbolic expressions of the human mind and it is the function of the social anthropologist to make explicit the implicit, unconscious structural relations inherent in different systems of symbolic forms. All social phenomena are regarded as systems of communication manifested especially in the forms of kinship, economics, and language.

Levi-Strauss also attempted to establish a new science of myth. He maintained it was the function of the structural analysis of myth to make conscious and explicit the logical structure which underlies the concrete images and plots of a given series of myths. Myths, like science, are motivated by an intellectual impulse, a problem to be solved, and differ from science, not in their logic, but only in the kind of objects to which this logic is applied. Myth reveals not the unconscious instinctual nature of man as Freud maintained but rather man's unconscious, rational thought in his attempt to resolve the logical problems which confront him. Myth is really man's first attempt to construct a philosophy and science of nature and culture; it is the wisdom of savages and of the folk expressed in a mode of sensible images.

In agreement with E.B. Tylor, Levi-Strauss is prepared to maintain that if law is anywhere, it is everywhere. The science of social anthropology is based on the assumption that the human spirit is subject to rational law and that freedom of creativity is an illusion. Levi-Strauss' theory of a structural science of social anthropology is highly controversial, but it is also one of the most thought-provoking and influential theories of modern times.

BIBLIOGRAPHY: *Current Anthropology*, 7 (1966), 110–11, bibliography of his writings; R.L. Zimmerman, in: *Commentary*, 45 (May 1968), 54–61; C. Levi-Strauss, *Totemism* (1969), introd. by R.C. Poole; E. Leach, *Claude Levi-Strauss* (1971). **ADD. BIBLIOGRAPHY:** M. Hanaef, *Claude Levi-Strauss and the Making of Structural Anthropology*, tr. M. Baker (1998); C. Johnson, *Claude Levi-Strauss: The Formative Years* (2003); D. Eribon, *Conversations with Claude Levi-Strauss*, tr. P. Wissing (1991).

[Ephraim Fischoff and David Baumgardt]

LEVITA, ELIJAH (Bahur; ben Asher ha-Levi Ashkenazi; 1468 or 1469–1549), Hebrew philologist, grammarian, and lexicographer. Born in Neustadt, near Nuremberg, Germany, he spent most of his life in Italy (Padua, Venice, and Rome) where he taught Hebrew language and grammar. His pupils included Christian humanists, from whom he learned Greek and Latin. Some of the leading Christian Hebraists with whom Levita maintained contact at various times were Paulus *Fagius, Johannes de Kampen (Campensis), Andreas *Maes, Guillaume *Postel, and Johann Albrecht *Widmanstetter (Widmanstadius). Postel in his *Linguarum duodecim charac-*

teribus differentium alphabetum (Paris, 1538, fol. 3) wrote that he became a close friend of Levita in Venice – "*Elias Germanus, quo usus sum Venetiis.*" Among his pupils he counted Sebastian *Muenster, who translated Elijah's works into Latin, and Cardinal Egidius da *Viterbo in whose home in Rome Elijah stayed for 13 years (1514–27). Before entering the house of Egidius da Viterbo, Elijah also wrote secular literary works in Yiddish. To this period belongs *Bovo d'Antona* (unicum: Isny, 1541, but believed to have first been published in 1507) which became known as the **Bove-Bukh* in later editions. It is an adaptation in verse of one of the Italian versions of an Anglo-French romance, *Sir Bevis of Hampton*. His *Paris un Viene* (apparently written in 1508/09; the unicum with the beginning missing preserved at Trinity College, Cambridge, was printed at Verona in 1594) is evidently based on a medieval Provençal romance. Elijah also adapted two love epics from Italian sources; the first is based on a courtly love legend, and the second is an abridged and free adaptation of an Italian-Provençal literary work, written in *ottava rima* (a stanza of eight iambic lines containing three rhymes) which Elijah introduced into Yiddish literature. Elijah instructed da Viterbo principally in the Kabbalah and translated some manuscripts for him (e.g., the commentary of R. Eliezer of Worms on *Sefer Yeẓirah*). Georges de Selve, another of his pupils, who later became the French ambassador to Venice, invited him, in the name of King Francis I, to lecture in Hebrew at the Collège Royal in Paris. He declined the offer for two reasons: he neither wanted to be the only Jew allowed to live in France, nor did he feel that under such conditions he could observe the religious precepts.

In 1527, when Rome was sacked by the armies of Charles V, Elijah lost all his property (including some manuscripts). He returned to Venice, where he earned his livelihood as a proofreader in the publishing house of Daniel *Bomberg (1529 to the late 1530s), and remained there, except for an absence of four years (1539/40–44). During that period, he supervised Fagius' press at Isny (in Wuerttemberg), and later accompanied him to Constance (1542–43). At Isny, Levita printed some of his most important works. The rabbis looked with disfavor on Elijah's teaching gentiles the Torah. Elijah rejoined with the claim that earlier Christian Hebraists had upheld Christian and Jewish Hebrew scholarship resulting in a tendency, on their part, to defend Jews and the Jewish community also from physical violence. Two of Elijah's grandchildren, however, converted to Christianity and helped those who calumniated the Talmud. One of them, baptized as Vittorio Eliano, became an ecclesiastical censor of Hebrew books and had some part in the *Cremona (Christian) edition of the Zohar (1558–59). Elijah, despite false allegations brought against him to the contrary, remained an observant Jew.

Elijah wrote many Hebrew grammar works, Hebrew and Aramaic dictionaries, and did masoretic research. In Hebrew grammar, he followed the line of thought of the *Kimḥis: he published Moses Kimḥi's *Mahalakh*, with his own commentary (Pesaro, 1508; in this edition the name of the author is mistakenly given as Benjamin of Rome); and wrote notes and critiques, "*Nimmukim*," on David Kimḥi's *Mikhlol* and on his *Sefer ha-Shorashim*. His own works, written and published in Rome between 1518 and 1519, and translated into Latin by Sebastian Muenster, are *Sefer ha-Harkavah* (1518); *Ha-Baḥur* (1518; the title is after his own name "R. Elijah Baḥur"); and *Lu'aḥ be-Dikduk ha-Pe'alim ve-ha-Binyanim* (unpublished). *Ha-Harkavah* deals with "the grammar of every foreign and compound word" in the Bible, listed in alphabetical order. In *Ha-Baḥur*, which in a later edition became known as *Dikduk Eliyyah ha-Levi* (Isny, 1542), there is an allusion to the name of the author: "Since for every young man it [the book] is good and 'chosen.' And I, my name is Baḥur [= "chosen"], therefore *Baḥur* have I called it." In Rome in 1520, he published *Pirkei Eliyahu*, a work, written partly in verse, on the grammar of the Hebrew letters and vowels; it is a follow-up of *Ha-Baḥur* and completes the study in the latter. In its second edition (Venice, 1546), he added some chapters on the pattern of the nouns and the formative letters. Elijah did not introduce many innovations in his grammatical system; its easy and clear presentation, however, was instrumental in spreading the knowledge of the Hebrew language and grammar among Jews and Christian humanists. His grammatical rule on the five classes of *sheva-na* is still accepted today (though the fifth rule – the loss of the dagesh in case of *ha-domot*, repeated characters, is regarded as superfluous, as it is a regular outcome of haplology). His *Masoret ha-Masoret* (Venice, 1538), in which he explains the technical terms and the signs of the masorah, is an important contribution to masoretic study. The preface, written in prose (which follows the foreword in verse and the rhymed introduction), is an historical and original research in Hebrew vocalization and accentuation, and in the masorah. Elijah was the first to point out that the vowels and accents did not originate in the Sinai period (as had been assumed until then, and was still accepted by Moses *Mendelssohn in his *Or li-Netivah* several centuries later), but in post-talmudic times. Elijah's grammatical assertions influenced S.D. *Luzzatto in his *Vikku'aḥ Al Ḥokhmat ha-Kabbalah* (1852). *Masoret ha-Masoret* was last published together with notes and an English translation by Christian David *Ginsburg (1867; repr. 1968). In his work *Tuv Ta'am* (Venice, 1538), Elijah attempted to explain the rules on the accents in the Bible: their grammatical value and their relationship to each other. His dictionary, compiled from the Aramaic translations of the Bible, *Meturgeman* ("The Interpreter," with a Latin foreword by Paulus Fagius), and his lexicon of the Hebrew words in the Talmud and the Hebrew of the Middle Ages, *Tishbi*, with a Latin translation by Fagius (Isny, 1541), are of major importance in the research of Hebrew grammar. *Tishbi* is a source on the pronunciation and the vocalization of Hebrew by the German and Italian Jewish communities. Levita's *Meturgeman* and *Tishbi* were extensively used by Christian *Hebraists such as Guy *Le Fèvre de la Boderie, a pupil of Postel, who makes glowing reference to Levita in the preface to his *Dictionarium Syro-Chaldaicum* (in the Antwerp Polyglot Bible, 1572). Elijah also composed a concordance to the Bible, *Sefer ha-Zikhronot* (the complete work was never published; see Frensdorff, in MGWJ, 12 (1863), 96–108).

His research into the Hebrew language laid the foundations for the lexicography and etymology of Yiddish. Elijah refers to Yiddish as the "language of Ashkenaz" (Germany) or "Deutsch"; his reference in fact is only to the German dialect used by Jews. *Shemot Devarim* (Isny, 1542) is the first known Yiddish-Hebrew dictionary. It lists 985 words with their Hebrew translation, as well as Latin and German by Paulus Fagius. In *Tishbi*, where Elijah concludes each entry with the translation of the Hebrew radicals into German (he also does this to a certain extent in the *Meturgeman*), there are etymological explanations of several Yiddish words (such as *katavos, meykn, shekhtn*); two (*mashkeyt, sargenes*) are even included in the 712 entries of the dictionary (which is the total number of the Hebrew characters' arithmetic value obtained from the name *Tishbi*; this being one of the nicknames of the Prophet Elijah and also hinting at Levita's seeing himself as a follower of the Prophet). His Yiddish translation of Psalms (Venice, 1545), the first to be published, is based on earlier translations which closely followed the Hebrew text; it became a popular work, went through several editions, and served as a model to other translators. Extracts from two of his pamphlets, "*Ha-Mavdil*" and "*Oyf di Sreyfe fun Venedig*," written by Elijah against his Venetian personal adversaries, were published in *Tsaytshrift*, 1 (Minsk, 1926), 141–58; these, however, lack any literary value.

BIBLIOGRAPHY: W. Bacher, *Die hebraeische Sprachwissenschaft vom 10. bis zum 16. Jahrhundert* (1892), 104ff.; idem, in: ZDMG, 43 (1889), 206–72; idem, in: MGWJ, 37 (1893), 398–404; S. Buber, *Leben und Schriften des Elias Bachur, genannt Levita* (1856); Kahana, in: *Ha-Shaḥar*, 12 (1883/84), 498–505, 539–48; J. Levy, *Elia Levita und seine Leistungen als Grammatiker* (1888); J. Shatzky, *Elia Bakhur* (Yid., 1949), includes bibliography; M.A. Szulwas, *Ḥayyei ha-Yehudim be-Italyah bi-Tekufat ha-Renaissance* (1955), 353, index, s.v. *Eliyah Baḥur*; Vogelstein-Rieger, 2 (1895), 86–92; M. Weinreich, *Shtaplen far Etuden tsu der Yidisher Shprakhvisenshaft un Literaturgeshikhte* (1923), 72–86; idem, *Bilder fun der Yidisher Literaturgeshikhte* (1928), 124, 142, 149–91; I. Zinberg, *Toledot Sifrut Yisrael*, 2 (1956), 255–62; 4 (1958), 38–51; Shunami, Bibl, nos. 3452–53b; Waxman, Literature, s.v. *Elijah Bahur*; N. Snaith, *Prolegomenon to "Jacob ben Chajim ben Isaac ibn Adonijah's Introduction to the Rabbinic Bible" and "The Massoreth ha-Massoreth of Elias Levita"* (1968); G.E. Well, *Elie Levita humaniste et massorète 1469–1549* (1963); J. Perles, *Beitraege zur Geschichte der hebraeischen und aramaeischen Studien* (1884), 32ff.

[Meir Medan]

LEVITAN, ISAAC ILITCH (1861–1900), Russian painter who has been called the father of Russian landscape painting. Levitan, who was born in Wirballen (Virbalis), Lithuania, studied at the Moscow Art School and in 1889 visited Paris. He was one of the first Russian artists to understand the achievement of the Barbizon painters and the impressionists, and was thus equipped to become the major interpreter of the Russian landscape, with its vastness and its brooding melancholy. Continually seeking to improve his art, Levitan repainted the same subjects many times and altered his techniques. In his later paintings, executed with a thick, soft brush stroke, he succeeded in his aim of combining freedom of expression with solidity of structure. In 1896, Levitan was appointed professor of landscape painting at the Moscow Art Academy, where he taught until his death. His work had a deep influence on Russian painters and won the passionate admiration of his friend Anton Chekhov the dramatist. Examples are "Spring," "After the Rain," "Evening," and "The Hay Harvest."

BIBLIOGRAPHY: S.A. Prorokova, *Levitan* (Rus., 1960); V.A. Prytkov, *Levitan* (Rus., 1960); Roth, Art, 630–2; A.N. Benua, *The Russian School of Painting* (1916), 160–3.

LEVITAN, SOLOMON (1862–1940), U.S. merchant, banker, and politician. Levitan, who was born in Taurrogen near Tilsit, East Prussia, immigrated to the United States in 1880. He settled in New Glarus, Wisconsin, a year later and went into business as a pack peddler and horse-and-wagon dealer. Levitan opened his first store in New Glarus in 1887 and subsequently became justice of the peace there. After moving to Madison in 1905, Levitan became a dry-goods merchant, bank officer (1909–40), and investment executive. An active campaigner for Robert M. La Follette, Sr., Republican nominee for governor, Levitan was a La Follette delegate in several Republican state conventions, a Republican presidential elector in 1912, and a delegate to the Republican national conventions of 1920 and 1924. He left the organization with La Follette when the latter formed the Progressive Party. After two unsuccessful attempts, he was elected state treasurer in 1922. Reelected several times, he served six terms (1922–32, 1936–38).

[Louis J. Swichkow]

LEVI-TANNAI, SARA (1911–2005), choreographer and teacher. Levi-Tannai was born in Jerusalem to parents who emigrated from Yemen. She worked as a kindergarten teacher for 15 years, including six when she lived in kibbutz *Ein ha-Shofet, where she organized numerous shows and pageants for which she composed and adapted music. She then devoted her life to the promotion of choreography in Israel and especially to Yemenite folklore in song and dance. In 1949 she founded the *Inbal Dance Theater, for which she recruited young dancers originating in Yemen. With this group, she created some 40 different shows, the best known of which were "Yemenite Wedding," "Shabbat Shalom," "The Story of Ruth," "Song of Deborah," "Desert," and "David's Psalm." In 1951, after seeing her works, Jerome *Robbins recommended her to the *America-Israel Cultural Foundation. This enabled her to rent a spacious studio in Tel Aviv and work in a more professional way. Thus, Inbal became the country's first institutional dance company. Later, Anna *Sokolow was brought in to work on technique with the dancers.

Inbal toured extensively in Europe and the U.S., and was highly praised. In 1963, Levi-Tannai was nominated the best choreographer of the year by the Théatre des Nations in Paris.

But if she was well regarded abroad she was criticized in Israel for being an imitator and for sacrificing "folkloristic" character to a more "professional/artistic" approach.

Levi-Tannai's works were mainly based on Jewish and biblical folklore, particularly the traditions of the Yemenite community. For her works, typical costumes and music, a new movement language, and a large repertoire were created. Inbal developed its own unique style blending ancient and modern with a theatrical approach. This "Inbalic school" strives to combine movement resources from all of the Jewish Diaspora, as well as the Middle East region, with modern techniques and approaches. As a composer, Levi-Tannai was regarded as one of the founders of a new and original Israeli style of music. She was awarded the Israel Prize in arts in 1973.

ADD. BIBLIOGRAPHY: IED, vol. 4, 155–156.

[Bina Shiloah (2nd ed.)]

LEVITES IN THE HALAKHAH. The levite has no privileges, neither through personal or family status nor any special sanctity, and it was ruled that "the levite is equivalent to the Israelite" in all things, including ritual defilement through contact with a corpse, which is forbidden to a Kohen only (TJ, Naz. 7:1).

Nevertheless, as long as the Second Temple was standing, the levites played an important part in its services as assistants to the priests, as gatekeepers and choristers, and in various ancillary duties (see *Temple, Levites). With the destruction of the Temple, however, and the consequent abolition of the sacrificial system, their importance and role diminished, and with one exception the special position of the levite is due to historical associations alone, from which certain *halakhot* of secondary importance are derived. That exception was the right of the levites to biblical tithes. Already during Temple times there was a dispute whether the tithes should be given to the levites or to the priests, and since the separation of tithes continued after the destruction of the Temple, this difference of opinion persisted (for a full discussion, see **Terumot* and *Ma'aserot*).

Although such laws as those of the *Levitical Cities and the dwelling house in walled cities and the other similar laws applying to the levites mentioned in Lev. 25:29–34 are discussed in detail in the *halakhah* (Ar. 9:5–8 and TB 32a–34a), the discussions were purely theoretical and had no practical application.

At present the only *halakhot* which apply specifically to the levite are the following: (1) The levite is called to the reading of the second portion of the Torah portion, but only when there is a Kohen present who is called to the reading of the first portion. When there is no Kohen present, he is not necessarily called up first (Git. 5:8). (2) Apart from this the levite can be called up only to the reading of the last portion of the *sidrah* on the Sabbath, after the statutory seven have already been called; or for *maftir* on Sabbaths and festivals. (3) The levite is exempt from *Pidyon ha-Ben* (the Redemption of the *Firstborn, Bek. 2:1) and the exemption applies whether the father or the mother is a levite (*ibid.* TB 4a). (4) The levite washes the hands of the Kohen before he ascends to pronounce the *Priestly Blessing. This is a comparatively late custom, first mentioned in the Zohar (Portion *Naso*, 146 a, b).

[Louis Isaac Rabinowitz]

LEVITICAL CITIES. The ecclesiastical tribe of Levi neither fought in the wars of the conquest of Canaan nor received an allocation of continuous territory as did all the other tribes (see *Priests and Levites). Its economic base was to be the sacred offerings of the Israelites – figuratively speaking, "YHWH was its portion and share among the Israelites" (Num. 18:20, 24; Deut. 18:1–2). Yet since the clergy was not a monastic order but a tribe consisting of families, the Levites required real estate on which to build their houses and land on which to graze their beasts. That need was met by the levitical cities prescribed in Numbers 35:1–8: the Israelites were to assign out of their tribal portions 48 towns with strips of open land outside them to Levites, distributed among the tribal territories in proportion to their varying sizes. The six cities of refuge are included among the 48. The open land is in the form of a square, each of whose sides is at a distance of 1,000 cubits from the town wall at its farthest extension toward each of the four cardinal points of the compass (on this meaning of verses 4–5 see M. Greenberg in bibl.). The legal status of this property differed from that of ordinary property: to prevent the dispossession of the Levites it was ordained that they might at any time redeem houses in their towns that they had been forced by need to sell; moreover, such a house, if not redeemed, reverted to its original Levite owner at the Jubilee (ordinarily, a town house that was not redeemed within a year of its sale became irreversibly transferred to its buyer). No plots of their open land could be sold at all (Lev. 25:29–34).

From Joshua 21:11–12 it emerges that the assignment of a town to Levites did not include either its unwalled suburbs or its fields (beyond the levitical open land); these remained tribal property. How the assignment was done is described in Joshua 21, where the list of towns is also given. The Levites received by lot four towns in the portions of each of the 12 tribes, excepting Judah and Simeon which together supplied nine, and Naphtali which supplied only three. The priests were concentrated in 13 southern towns in the portions of Judah, Simeon, and Benjamin; all the rest of the Levites were assigned towns of the other tribes to the north. A variant of the list in Joshua appears in I Chronicles 6:39–66; W.F. Albright's close study has led him to conclude that both derive from a single original.

Two features of the plan of Joshua 21 indicate its artificiality: its schematic nature – the number and distribution of the towns and the clean separation of priests from Levites (in the spirit of the priestly stratum of the Pentateuch); and obliviousness of the real impulse behind the Levites' scattering through the land of Israel – the necessity of finding employment at local sanctuaries. Not only does the list omit many early sanctuary towns (e.g., Beth-El, Nob, Jerusalem, Beer-Sheba) while

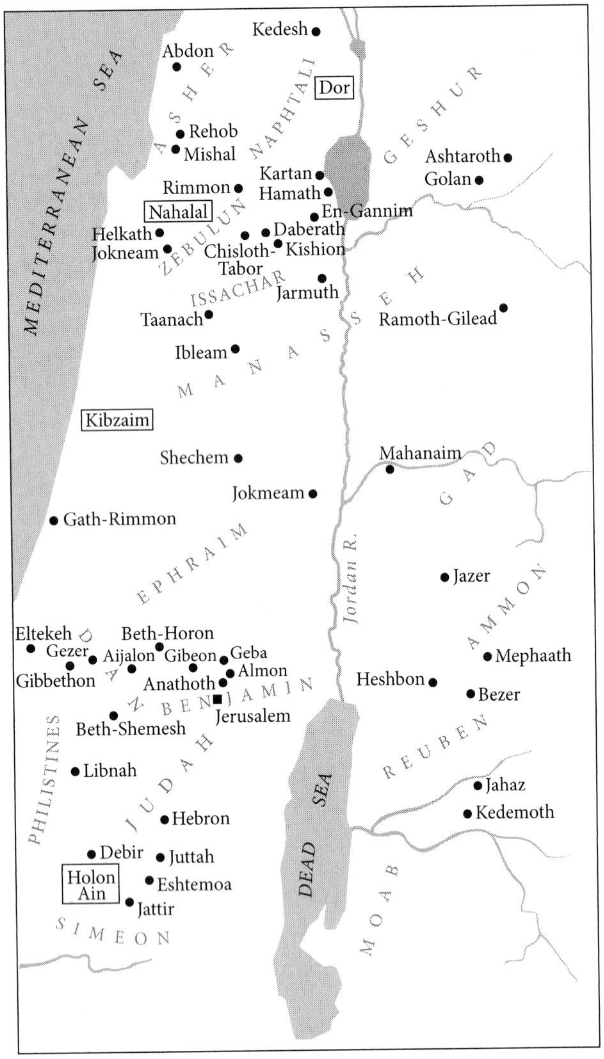

Sites of the levitical cities. Names within frames are of places as yet unidentified, though their general location is known from the sources. Based on Y. Aharoni in Carta's Atlas of the Bible, *Jerusalem, 1964.*

mentioning towns in which the presence of Israelites, let alone a sanctuary, is dubious (e.g., Gibbethon, Eltekeh), but the whole scheme to which the list belongs aims at solving the problem of settling the Levites without reference to their sacred vocation. Had the scheme envisioned them serving at sanctuaries, it could never have been content with only four towns per tribe. (The real situation of Levites – namely, dispersal throughout the countryside – is rather reflected in Deuteronomy's allusion to them "in any of the settlements throughout all Israel"; 18:6; cf. 16:11, 14.) The visionary arrangement of Ezekiel 45:1–5; 48:8–14 gives more consideration to the reality of levitical needs in that it settles the priests and Levites in a sacred "oblation" adjacent to the future temple in which they are to serve (on the analogy of their position around the desert tabernacle in the Pentateuch). Granting the unreal character of the scheme of Joshua 21, one may still ask whether any historical situation underlies the town list. J. Wellhausen regarded it as a post-Exilic "echo of the general recollection that there were once in Israel many holy places and residences of priesthoods," the influence of Jerusalem being reflected in the concentration of priests in Judah and Benjamin – this in accord with his view of the lateness of the entire priestly stratum of the Pentateuch. On the other hand, Y. Kaufmann regarded the list as a very early solution to the problem of the future of the Levites after the break up of the unified camp of Joshua's time; he dates it to a time before sanctuaries had been established throughout the country, and characterizes it as wholly utopian and never put into practice. Other scholars sought to interpret the list in the light of the fact that the United Monarchy (under David and Solomon) was the sole period in which all the towns were in Israel's possession. The list was taken as a reflex of the royal regulation of the settlement of Levites throughout the newly extended kingdom (S. Klein, W.F. Albright). B. Mazar considered the Levites an arm of the civil service of the United Monarchy (suggested by I Chron. 26:30–32), settled in strategic locations and provincial capitals around the country to manage royal estates, collect taxes, and strengthen borderlands with prevailingly non-Israelite populations. Even this interpretation, however, cannot mitigate the theoretical and unreal character of the scheme of Joshua 21, although its representation of the dispersal of the Levites throughout the land of Israel is in principle historically true (cf. M. Haran).

BIBLIOGRAPHY: J. Wellhausen, Proleg, 159–64; D. Hoffmann, *Die wichtigsten Instanzen gegen die Graf-Wellhausensche Hypothese*, 1 (1903), 148ff.; S. Klein, in: *Kovez ha-Ḥevrah ha-Ivrit le-Ḥakirat Erez-Yisrael ve-Attikoteha* (1935), 81–107; W.F. Albright, in: *L. Ginzberg Jubilee Volume* (1946), 49ff. (Eng. sect.); Y. Kaufmann, *Sefer Yehoshu'a* (1959), 270–82; B. Mazar, in: VT Supplement, 7 (1960), 210ff.; M. Haran, in: JBL, 80 (1961), 45ff., 156ff.; M. Greenberg, in: JAOS, 88 (1968), 59ff.

[Moshe Greenberg]

LEVITICUS, BOOK OF (Heb. וַיִּקְרָא; LXX Λευιτικόν *leuitikon*), more aptly described by its tannaitic name, *Torat Kohanim*, "the Priests' Manual," the third book of the Pentateuch. Leviticus is thematically an independent entity. *Exodus contains the story of the construction of the cultic implements – the Tabernacle and the priestly vestments – whereas Leviticus converts this static picture into scenes from the living cult. *Numbers, in contrast, is set chronologically during the wanderings of Israel in the wilderness and therefore concentrates upon the cultic laws of the camp in motion, e.g., the military arrangement and census of the tribes, the transport of the sancta, and their protection against encroachment. Since the latter is the main function of the Levites, it is striking that all the laws pertaining to the Levites are in Numbers and none is in Leviticus.

The "Priests' Manual" of Leviticus indeed focuses on the priests. Few laws, however, apply only to the priests (these are Lev. 8–10; 16:1–28; 21:1–22:16). The role of the priest is defined in pedagogic terms: to teach the distinctions "between the holy and profane between the pure and impure" (10:10;

cf. 14:57; 15:31; Ezek. 22:26; 44:23). This the priest must do lest Israel's defilement, brought about by its moral sins and physical impurities, defile the sanctuary and cause its abandonment by God. The underlying postulate is that God will not reside in a defiled sanctuary (see *Day of Atonement). The priests are thus charged with a double task: to instruct Israel not to cause defilement and to purge the sanctuary whenever its defilement occurs. However, Leviticus is not just ritual law. On the contrary, the ethical fuses with the ritual and informs it, so that there is justification to seek a moral basis behind each ritual act.

From the point of view of literary criticism, Leviticus is relatively uncomplicated. Even though another stratum is recognized (see below, Holiness Source), it has been largely assimilated by P (see *Pentateuch). The text has been excellently preserved; the few divergences in the versions are nearly all secondary in relation to the Masoretic Text. The difficulty lies in only one area: the terminology, which deals with the cult, an ancient institution with its peculiar, conservative vocabulary whose meaning was sometimes lost upon subsequent generations.

The impact of Leviticus upon Judaism can be comprehended by realizing that nearly half (247) of the 613 commandments (Gen. R. 3:5) and about the same proportion of the material of the Talmud are based upon Leviticus. Furthermore, Leviticus was traditionally the first book taught to

BOOK OF LEVITICUS – CONTENTS

1:1–7:38	**The sacrificial system**
1:1–2	General introduction.
1:3–17	The whole offering (ʿOlah).
2:1–16	The tribute (cereal) offering (minḥah).
3:1–17	The well-being offering (shelamim).
4:1–35	The purification offering (ḥaṭṭa't).
5:1–13	Borderline cases requiring the purification offering.
5:14–26	The reparation offering ('asham).
6:1–7:38	Supplementary instructions on sacrifices.
8:1–10:20	**The inaugural service at the sanctuary**
8:1–36	The installation of the priests.
9:1–24	The priests assume office.
10:1–11	The sin of Nadab and Abihu.
10:2–20	The consumption of the initiatory offerings.
11:1–16:34	**The laws of impurities**
11:1–47	Animal impurities.
12:1–8	The impurity of childbirth.
13:1–14:57	The impurity of skin diseases (leprosy).
15:1–33	The impurity of genital discharges.
16:1–34	The impurities of the sanctuary and the nation.
17:1–26:46	**The holiness source**
17:1–16	Killing for food.
18:1–20:27	On being holy.
21:1–22:33	The disqualifications of priests and sacrifices.
23:1–44	The festivals.
24:1–23	Miscellanea.
25:1–26:46	The Sabbatical and Jubilee Years.
27:1–34	**Commutation of gifts to the sanctuary**

school children (Lev. R. 7:3), stemming probably from the historical fact that the priestly school preceded the lay school in origin.

CONTENTS

Chapters 1–7: The Sacrificial System

In chapters 1–5, the sacrifices are listed from the point of the donor: chapters 1–3, the spontaneously motivated sacrifices: *ʿolah, minḥah, shelamim*; chapters 4–5, the sacrifices required for expiation: *ḥaṭṭaʾt* and *ʾasham*. Chapters 6–7 regroup these sacrifices in order of their sanctity and priority in the daily ritual, i.e., most sacred: *ʿolah, minḥah, ḥaṭṭaʾt, ʾasham*; sacred: *shelamim*. The common denominator of the sacrifices discussed in these chapters is that they arise in answer to an unpredictable religious or emotional need, and are thereby set off from the calendrically fixed sacrifices of the public feasts and fasts (Lev. 9, 16, 23; cf. Num. 28–29). Many prophets sharply criticized the sacrificial system when it failed to lead to a more ethical life, but their lonely isolation in this respect and the positive evidence of the folk literature make it amply clear that the people themselves were convinced that it met their spiritual needs. Chapters 1–7 will be summarized in terms of their literary structure and main ideas (see *Sacrifice, for details).

1:1–2: GENERAL INTRODUCTION. The Hebrew particles for introducing general and particular statements in legal formulation indicate that chapters 1 and 3 were originally a single unit which was later split by the insertion of chapter 2. The conditional construction of 1:2a underscores the voluntary basis of the sacrifices.

1:3–17: THE WHOLE OFFERING (ʿOLAH). This is the only sacrifice which is entirely consumed on the altar (favoring the translation "whole," cf. Deut. 33:10; I Sam. 7:9; Ps. 55:21). Verses 1:3–4 encapsulate the major concepts of the sacrificial system: laying on of hands, acceptance, expiation, slaughter, blood manipulation, and entrance to the Tent of Meeting (see *Sacrifice). The donor is an active participant in the ritual; he is responsible for the presentation, hand-laying, slaughter, skinning, quartering, and washing of the animal. The priest executes the blood rite and the burning of the animal, i.e., everything which relates to the altar. The whole offering must be chosen from male, unblemished, and eligible species of the herd, flock, and birds. The *ʿolah* is probably the oldest and most popular sacrifice (Tosef., Zev. 13:1). Its function here is expiatory (1:4; cf. 9:7; 14:20; I Sam. 13:12; Job 1:5; 42:8); but in P, whenever it is offered by an individual, the motivation is joyful (e.g., Lev. 22:17ff.; Num. 15:1–11).

CHAPTER 2: THE TRIBUTE (CEREAL) OFFERING (MINḤAH). In the nonpriestly texts, it connotes both "a present made to secure or retain goodwill" (S.R. Driver; e.g., Gen. 32:20) and a tribute brought by subjects to their overlords, both human (Judg. 3:15–18) and divine, and could be either animal or vegetable (Gen. 4:3–4; I Sam. 2:17). In P, however, it is exclusively cereal, either choice flour (Lev. 2:1–3), cakes of choice flour

(2:4–10), or wasted grain (2:14–16). Because leaven and honey (fruit syrup) ferment, whereas salt preserves, they were respectively proscribed and prescribed on the altar (2:11–13). The former, however, were permitted as a first fruit offering to the priest (23:17; II Chron. 31:5). The restriction to cereal emphasizes that humans' tribute to God should be from the fruit of their labors on the soil. In daily life, however, the aspect of "appeasement" may also have been present (I Sam. 26:19). Because cereal was abundant and cheap, it became the poor man's *ʿolah* (Philo, Spec. 1–271; Lev. R. 8:4) and probably replaced it in popularity and function.

CHAPTER 3: THE WELL-BEING OFFERING (SHELAMIM). This offering never serves as expiation. Its basic function is simply to permit the consumption of flesh. It was usually prompted by a joyous occasion, specified in 7:11ff. as: spontaneous (always in a happy context, e.g., Num. 15:3; Deut. 16:10–11), votive, and thanksgiving (motivated by elation, e.g., Ps. 116:17–19). The rules are similar to those of the whole offering, except that the victims may be female but not birds. Also, being of lesser sanctity, they were not slaughtered at the altar, and portions were assigned to the priests and the donor as well as to God. The choicest internal fats (suet) were turned to smoke.

CHAPTER 4: THE PURIFICATION OFFERING (ḤATTAT). Its purpose is to remove the impurity inflicted upon the sanctuary by the inadvertent violation of prohibitive laws (but not laws against man, i.e., ethical violations). The deliberate violation of these laws is punishable by *karet* (Num. 15:27–31), death through divine agency. The loci of *karet* – all in P – specify the nature of the violations: holidays (e.g., Passover, Day of Atonement), contamination of sancta (e.g., Lev. 7:20–21), prohibited cultic acts (e.g., 17:4, 9), and illicit sex (18:29). The last mentioned is also a ritual sin: it leads to the pollution of the land (18:27–28). The procedure for the purification offering falls into two categories: 4:3–21 where the blood is brought into the sanctuary by the high priest, but the flesh of the victim is burned outside the camp, and 4:22–35, sins requiring cheaper animals, scaled to the social and financial status of the offender, where the blood is not brought into the sanctuary, and the flesh is not burned but must be eaten by the officiating priest (6:19; 10:17). Verses 4:3–21 comprise two cases that are really one. The first instance (4:3–12) presumes that the high priest's inadvertent error has caused harm to his people (e.g., through his negligence, Num. 18:4b–5) or has caused them to expropriate sancta (e.g., Lev. 5:14–16; 22:14–16). In the second instance (4:13–21), the community as a whole has erred – probably by blindly following the high priest's instruction – and must bring its own purification offering when the error is discovered (4:14). The individuals liable to the purification offering are the tribal chieftain (4:22–26) and the commoner (4:27–35). Whereas the ruler brings a he-goat, the commoner offers a she-goat or a she-lamb.

CHAPTER 5:1–13: BORDERLINE CASES REQUIRING THE PURIFICATION OFFERING. Rabbinic tradition distinguishes between the purification offering of chapter 4 and 5:1–13, calling the latter *ʿoleh we-yored*, "the scaled offering," geared to the means of the offender (not his status, as in chapter 4). This *ḥaṭṭaʾt* probably arises from the failure or inability to cleanse impurity immediately upon its incurrence. "The sin of which he is guilty" (5:6, 10, 13), in distinction to chapter 4, is not the contraction of impurity but its prolongation. In three out of the four given cases (5:2, 3, 4), the offender has knowingly contracted impurity or uttered an oath – acts in themselves guiltless – but a lapse of memory has caused the offender unknowingly to contaminate sancta or violate an oath. The case of 5:1, where the offender withheld testimony, may be explained by assuming either that he never entered into oath but only heard its public proclamation, thereby putting him out of the jurisdiction of the court (but not of God for having defied the imprecation) or that his reluctance to be an "informer" is considered to be inadvertent, precisely like the amnesia cases which follow (for details see *Sacrifice).

5:14–26: THE REPARATION OFFERING (ʾASHAM). It is enjoined for trespassing (*maʿal*) upon the property of God or man, the latter through the use of a false oath. The sin is *desecration (*ḥillul*): the sancta or the name of God have become desanctified (as opposed to the purification offering, chapter 4, where the sin is the contamination of sancta). Three cases are given: 1) 5:14–16: For inadvertent trespass of sancta, the offender pays the sanctuary an amount equal to the value of the desecrated sanctum plus a 20% fine and brings a ram, commutable into currency, for expiation. 2) 5:17–19: This case complements the preceding. Both deal with unintentional poaching upon sancta; the first real, the other suspected (so R. Akiva in Ker. 5:2). The general wording of Leviticus 5:17 makes it clear that every suspected violation is liable to the *ʾasham*. 3) 5:20–26: The reparation offering, which in 5:15–19 was imposed for inflicting real or suspected damage to sacred property, is now transferred to the human sphere where the Lord, through an oath, has been made a party to the defrauding of a human. Fraud, being a deliberate sin, would ordinarily be unexpiable by sacrifice. However, the offender has voluntarily confessed wrongdoing and relinquished the illicit gain. The usual penalties (e.g., Ex. 21:37; 22:6) are mitigated; and the treatment is that of an inadvertent offender: full restitution plus 20% for the material loss and a reparation offering to the Lord for desecrating His name in a lying oath are required.

CHAPTERS 6–7: SUPPLEMENTARY INSTRUCTIONS ON SACRIFICES. Since the well-being offering is chiefly consumed by the donor, the rules pertain mainly to him (7:11–34; esp. 7:23, 29). Otherwise they are the concerns of the officiating priest. The subjects are: the altar fire (6:1–6); the manner and place for eating the tribute offering (6:7–11); the daily tribute offering of the high priest and the voluntary one of the ordinary priest (6:12–16); safeguards in sacrificing the purification offering (6:17–23); the ritual for the reparation offering (7:1–7, missing in chapter 5); the priestly share in the whole and tribute offerings (7:8–10); the types of well-being offering (see chapter 3, above) and their taboos (7:11–21); the prohibition against consuming suet and blood (7:22–27); the priestly share of the well-being offering, set aside by the donor (7:28–36); the summation (7:36–38). The inclusion of the consecration offering before the well-being offering suggests that a section based on Exodus 29 originally preceded 7:11.

Chapters 8–10: The Inaugural Service at the Sanctuary

This section follows logically and chronologically upon Exodus 35–40: the priests are inducted into service after the priestly vestments and the Tabernacle are completed. Not Aaron, however, but Moses dominates the scene. It is he who conducts the inaugural service, consecrates the priests, and apportions all tasks. Aaron is clearly answerable to him, as seen from their confrontation in Leviticus 10:16–20. Strikingly, the superiority of prophet over priest is insisted upon by the priestly document.

CHAPTER 8: THE INSTALLATION OF THE PRIESTS. "To ordain you" (8:33) is literally "to fill your hands." In Scripture, this phrase is used exclusively for the ordination of priests (Ex. 32:29; Judg. 17:5, 12; I Kings 13:33), but in the archives of Mari dating from the time of Hammurapi it refers to the distribution of booty. Thus, the Hebrew idiom indicates that installation rites officially entitle the priests to their share of the revenues and sacrifices brought to the sanctuary. "As the Lord commanded Moses" concludes each phase of the ordination ceremony, a reminder that this chapter is a repetition of the instruction in Exodus 29.

CHAPTER 9: THE PRIESTS ASSUME OFFICE. On the eighth day following the week of consecration, the priests begin their official duties. They offer up special sacrifices for the people, "that the presence of the Lord may appear" (9:6; also verses 4, 23). Indeed, the whole purpose of the sacrificial system is revelation, the assurance that God is with His people.

CHAPTER 10:1–11: THE SIN OF NADAB AND ABIHU. That the fire was "alien" could be debited either to the offering or the offerer. Most likely, the fire was taken from elsewhere than the altar (16:12; Num. 17:11).

CHAPTER 10:12–20: THE CONSUMPTION OF THE INITIATORY OFFERINGS. This is the continuation of chapter 9. The tribute and well-being offerings are eaten by the priests in accordance with 6:9 and 7:28–34. But the procedure for the purification offering is switched from the individual to the communal form: the disposal of blood (9:9, 15; 10:18) has been executed according to 4:30 but not the disposal of flesh which follows 4:12, rather than 6:19, and despite 6:23. The death of Nadab and Abihu has intervened. Aaron follows the more stringent procedure of destroying, rather than eating, the sacrificial meat because it has been doubly contaminated by the death and by the sin of his sons; its consumption will not be "acceptable in the sight of the Lord" and must be burned outside.

Chapters 11–16: The Laws of Impurities

An empiric knowledge of contagion must be credited to the ancient Hebrews as demonstrated in the example of washing: (1) Lustration is limited to impurities arising from animal cadavers and certain human skin diseases and fluxes, all prime sources of putrefaction and infection. (2) One who contracts the impurity from a human washes at once (antisepsis through washing is effective only the first few hours) even though the ritual impurity lasts till nightfall; the one who is afflicted is removed from camp (Num. 5:2–5) and washes only after being healed. (Lustration serves no medical purpose once infection sets in.) (3) In regard to animals, the living never transfer impurity (not so the swine in Egypt, Herodotus, 2:47). The carcass, however, must be disposed of; hence its handling is never prohibited, but one contaminated thereby must be purified with water. For details see *Purifications.

CHAPTER 11: ANIMAL IMPURITIES. The food prohibitions are certainly older than the rationale given them. Regardless of their origin – as yet undetermined – the fact remains that no punishment befalls anyone who violates them. The laws themselves offer but one reason: holiness (Lev. 11:44–47; 20:22–26; cf. Ex. 22:30; Deut. 14:21), a word which bears the dual connotation of "sanctification" (by emulating God's nature, Lev. 11:44a) and "separation" (from the impurities of the gentiles, 20:23–26).

11:1–8: Land Animals. Compare Leviticus 11:3–4 with Deuteronomy 14:4–7, where the permitted quadrupeds are named and classified.

11:9–12: Fish. Neither the prohibited nor permitted fish are enumerated (nor in Deut. 14:9–10). Instead, they are permitted if they have both fins and scales and prohibited if they lack either.

11:13–23: Birds and Winged Insects. No classification is given for birds because none was probably known. A number of identifications are conjectural.

11:24–40: Impurity by Contact with Carcasses. This section could be an insertion from another source as it interrupts the fourfold classification (11:46) of creatures that may not be eaten. Nonporous articles are defiled by cadavers of the eight species listed in verses 29–30 and must be washed, but contaminated earthenware (porous and absorbent, 6:21) may never be refused. Food and seed grain are immune to impurity except when moist, since water is an impurity carrier.

11:41–47: Swarming Things and Summation. Continues 11:23.

CHAPTER 12: THE IMPURITY OF CHILDBIRTH. Parturition marks the onset of impurity: seven days following the birth of a male and 14 days for a female during which no conjugal relations are allowed. For an additional period of 33 and 66 days, respectively, contact with sancta is proscribed. The sacrifices are brought after the defilement has passed. Ritual impurity adheres which time alone removes and whose removal is certified by rite. The latter is scaled to economic circumstances (cf. 5:7–13; 14:21–32).

CHAPTERS 13–14: THE IMPURITY OF SKIN DISEASES (LEPROSY). The word translated as "leprosy" actually refers to a variety of skin diseases. The noncontagious kind, described as an outbreak of dull white spots, is most likely, psoriasis. This, rather than true leprosy – Hansen's disease – is what afflicted Naaman (II Kings 5) for he mingled freely in society. Verses 13:1–44 diagnose the various symptoms of the affliction and 13:45–46 require the incurable to put on the habiliment of a mourner and be removed outside the city (cf. Num. 5:2–5). Verses 13:47–59 describe the deterioration of garments caused probably by mildew or fungus and 14:33–53 describe the infection of houses caused by the spread of saltpeter or moss, in which quarantine procedures are also enforced. Unusual considerations for property are reflected in 14:36: the priest clears the house prior to his inspection lest the house be condemned with its contents. The ritual is described in verses 14:1–32. Three separate ceremonies are prescribed: the first day (14:2–8), the seventh (14:9), and the eighth (14:10–32). The ritual of the first day is also applied to "leprosy" of houses (14:48–53). Details are given in *Leprosy.

CHAPTER 15: THE IMPURITY OF GENITAL DISCHARGES. This chapter is divided logically into two sections: natural discharge of men and women (15:16–18, 19–24, respectively) whose impurity is simply removed by bathing, and pathological discharges (15:2–15, 25–30, respectively), which require sacrificial expiation.

CHAPTER 16: THE IMPURITIES OF THE SANCTUARY AND THE NATION. According to 16:1, chapter 16 follows upon the narrative of chapter 10. Thus chapters 11–15 are an insert listing the specific impurities that will contaminate the sanctuary (15:31) for which the purification ritual of chapter 16 is mandated. Verses 16:1–28 represent a fusion of two rites: the first to purge the sanctuary according to procedures administrated in 4:3–21, and the second to expiate the people for the defilement they have caused the sanctuary through the confession and transference of their sins onto a live purification offering, a goat banished to the demon *Azazel. For the ritual, see *Day of Atonement; for the process see *Atonement.

Chapters 17–26: The Holiness Source

The remainder of the Book of Leviticus consists largely of an independent code in which moral and ritual laws alternate and whose motivation is holiness (e.g., 19:2; 20:7–8, 26; 21:8, 23; 22:16, 32; 23:3, 4, 7, 21, 24, 35, 37; 25:10, 12). The beginning of the code, chapter 17, is connected thematically and verbally with preceding chapters. Chapter 26, the only composition in the book that is neither legal nor ritual in character, serves as an epilogue to the Holiness Code (Levine). Much of the language and some of the ideas in chapters 17–26 differ from the first part of Leviticus. Scholars differ about the relative dates of the P(riestly) and H(oliness) codes. (For a summary of the contents of these chapters, whose main themes follow in brief outline, see *Holiness Code.)

CHAPTER 17: KILLING FOR FOOD. The entire chapter (except the last two verses) is of one piece. It declares that, whosoever kills a domestic animal outside the sanctuary is guilty of murder (17:3–4). Two ends are thus achieved: sacrifice to "satyrs" is abolished (17:5–9), and expiation is assured through a ritual by which the lifeblood of animals may be returned to its creator either upon the altar (17:10–12), in the case of sacrificial animals, or by being drained and covered by earth, in the case of animals that are hunted (17:13–14; cf. Deut. 12:16). The inescapable conclusion to be drawn from the context of the blood prohibition is that 17:11 has nothing to do with the expiation of general sin. The only time one runs the risk of eating blood is while consuming the *shelamim* (see above on ch. 3). That is why the blood prohibition occurs solely in *shelamim* passages (3:17; 7:26–27). However, it is the only sacrifice which plays no expiatory role (see *Atonement). The only "sin" (the word does not even occur here) is the charge of murder (17:4) levied against him who kills for food outside the Sanctuary, i.e., without properly restricting the lifeblood to God: "and I have assigned it [the *shelamim* blood] to you upon the altar to expiate [i.e. ransom] for your lives" when you take the animal's life for its flesh (see *Blood).

CHAPTERS 18–20: ON BEING HOLY. Though these three chapters were originally independent scrolls they are thematically united: chapter 20 prescribes the penalties for the illicit relations and homicidal cult practices of chapter 18 (see 20:1–5) and the practice of divination prohibited in 19:31 (see 20:6). Moreover, this unit is framed by the identical reasoning: separation from the Canaanites, whose idolatrous and immoral practices contaminate the divinely-chosen land (18:3, 24–30; 20:22–24). The arraignment of Ezekiel 22 contains a mixture of ethical and ritual sins closely related to these chapters. The concept of negative holiness – separation from heathens – figures in these chapters. The key word in this section is *kadosh* (*qadosh*, "holy"). "Holy" (*kadosh*) like its polar opposite "abomination" (*toʿevah*) is an emotive term whose content is supplied by the particular author. Thus, Baal is *kadosh* to a Phoenician and *toʿevah* to a biblical writer. It is noteworthy that only in the Bible is holiness enjoined upon a whole people: Israel is commanded to separate itself from all defilement.

A *qadosh*-cluster is found in but one other context – the rules concerning the priesthood, 21:6–8. This fact is significant. This biblical ideal is that all Israel shall be "a kingdom of priests and a holy [*qadosh*] nation" (Ex. 19:6). If Israel is to move up to a higher sphere of holiness, it is enjoined to observe a more rigid code of behavior than that allegedly practiced by the nations, just as the priest lives by more stringent standards than his fellow Israelites. Holiness, then, implies separation and is so defined in Leviticus 20:26. The positive aspect of holiness is discussed in chapter 19.

Chapter 18: Illicit Sexual Relations. This chapter is encased by an introduction and peroration (18:1–5, 24–30) which castigate the Egyptians and the Canaanites for the depravity of their sexual mores. Contemporary readers should not take the chapter as an objective description of Canaanite and Egyptian practices, though no doubt any number of Egyptians and Canaanites (and Israelites) practiced adultery, incest, bestiality, and homosexuality. Instead, it is a caricature accusing the gentiles of legislating *ḥukkot ha-toʿevot* (18:30; "the abominable laws"). The message of the caricature is to motivate Israelites to abstain from such behavior, which is punishable in Israel by death (cf. 20:11–16), as was similar behavior in the greater ancient Near Eastern world. H (the Holiness Code) is the only source which proclaims the sanctity of the land of Canaan, a doctrine that explains the equal responsibility of both resident Israelites and strangers to maintain its sanctity (18:27; 20:2; and comment on 24:15–22) as well as the moral justification for its conquest (18:27–28; 20:22–23). But Israel's ideological sword is two-edged: if guilty of the same infractions, it, too, will be "vomited out."

Another presupposition of the chapter – one shared by the entire Torah literature – is that all peoples are held accountable for gross immorality (Gen. 6:11; 9:5–6; 15:16; 18:1–19:38, etc.). Moreover, though astral worship is allowed them (e.g., Deut. 4:19), *Moloch worship is emphatically proscribed (Lev. 18:21; 20:1–5). It is the only idolatrous practice explicitly listed. Leviticus 18:6–18 is concerned with incest. In the cases cited, affinity has the same force as consanguinity. In marriage, each partner transfers his set of incest taboos to the other. Verses 19–23 enumerate sexual aberrations; they transmit "impurity" to the offender and to the land (18:24–30), and must be excised.

Chapter 19: Imitatio Dei – Positive Holiness. For Israel, holy is that which is "unapproachable" and "withdrawn." It is also a positive concept, an inspiration and a goal associated with God's nature and his desire for humans: "You shall be holy, for I… am holy" (19:2). Holiness means *imitatio dei* – the life of godliness.

How can humans imitate God? The answer of Leviticus 19 is given in a series of ethical and ritual commands; no distinction is made between them. Similarly, in the entire ancient Near East, morality is inseparable from religion (for Egypt, Pritchard, Texts, 34–35; for Babylonia, *Šurpu*, 2). The Holiness Code encompasses the Decalogue (1–5 in 19:3–8; 6–10 in 19:9–22; cf. Lev. R. 24:5) and commands all Israelites to love citizens (19:18) and aliens (19:34) alike. This leveling of society stems partly from the sanctity which, for P, God's land imposes upon all its inhabitants (comment, above, on ch. 18). But, there is more. The law of love is no verbal ideal. It must be expressed in deeds; equality in justice, civil (20:12; 24:16, 22; Num. 35:15) and religious (Lev. 16:29; 17:15; Ex. 12:19; 49; Num. 9:14 – all P); and equality in mercy, e.g., free loans (Lev. 25:35–58; cf. Deut. 10:18) and free gleanings (Lev. 19:9–10; cf. Deut. 24:19–22). Moreover, that the law of love may be implemented, the vitiating components in the nature of man, callousness (Lev. 19:14, 33) and hatred (19:16–18), are also proscribed.

Chapter 20: Penalties for Certain Infractions in Chapters 18–19. Illicit sex relations are graded according to the severity of the punishment: verses 9–16 death by human agency, verses 17–19 death by God *(karet)*, verses 20–21 childlessness. Missing are marriages with a stepsister, grandchildren, and two sisters (18:9, 10, 18), but these are marginal cases. Of the varieties of practices associated with other divinities, only Moloch worship and oracles through mediums are singled out, the former because of its monstrousness (see *Moloch) and the latter because of its prevalence (Deut. 18:9–12; I Sam. 28:9; Isa. 8:19).

CHAPTERS 21–22: THE DISQUALIFICATIONS OF PRIESTS AND SACRIFICES. The priest, ranking highest in human holiness, could enter the sanctuary to handle its objects and eat of its gifts. These privileges had commensurate restrictions, especially for the high priest. They were intended as safeguards against moral and ritual defilement which might inflict dire consequences on him and his people (22:9, 15–16; cf. 4:3; 15:31). These restrictions pertain to death and marriage (21:1–15), to physical blemishes of officiants and sacrifices (21:16–24; 22:17–33), and to the eating of the sacred food (22:1–9, 10–16).

CHAPTER 23: THE FESTIVALS. P's listing of the festivals is distinguished from that of JE (Ex. 23:14–17; 34:21–23) and D (Deut. 16) in its emphasis on natural and agricultural data: the Feast of Unleavened Bread starts and the Feast of Weeks closes the grain harvest, and the Feast of Booths follows the "ingathering" and is celebrated by the use of branches.

CHAPTER 24: MISCELLANEA.
24:1–4: The Lamp Oil. A repetition of Exodus 27:20–21, except that the latter command is set in the future. Since the lampstand stood inside the Sanctuary building, its greater sanctity required pure oil and that it be lighted by the high priest (Ex. 30:7–8; Num 8:1–4; "sons" in Ex. 27:21 is a probable error). The lampstand is described in Exodus 25:31–40 and Numbers 8:1–4.

24:5–9: The Shewbread. Twelve wheat loaves, symbols of God's covenant with the twelve tribes, were set in two rows of six on the table which stood before the Holy of Holies. Being of the inner sancta, like the lampstand above, it was tended only by the high priest. Each Sabbath he renewed the loaves and offered up the incense placed at their side (24:7) together with the daily incense (Ex. 30:7–8) upon the golden *altar. Both incense offerings, like the oil above, called for pure *frankincense (Lev. 24:7; Ex. 30:34), again for the same reason (Lev. 2:2, 15). The shewbread is called a fire offering (24:9) because originally, as ancient Near Eastern parallels indicate, it was entirely consumed by fire.

24:10–14, 23: The Law of Blasphemy. The law is introduced by a case. Blasphemy means more than speaking contemptuously of God, for which there is no stated penalty (Ex. 22:27). It must involve the additional offense of uttering the Tetragrammaton (because of the derogatory context it is called "the Name," cf. II Sam. 12:14; Job 2:9 for other euphemisms), and it is the combination of the two (24:15–16) that warrants the death penalty. The Tetragrammaton's power affects not only the speaker but his hearers; their contamination is literally transferred back to the blasphemer by the ritual of the laying on of hands.

24:15–22: An Appendage of Civil Damage Laws. It begins with the law of blasphemy and culminates in the equalization of the resident alien and citizen before the law – an unmistakable hallmark of P (Ex. 12:49; Num. 15:15–16, 29). In this pericope, the inclusion of the stranger is even more significant: his equality applies to civil as well as religious law (see comment on chapter 18 for P's motivation). That lex talionis (Ex. 21:23–25; Deut. 19:21) was extended to the stranger is one of the great moral achievements of P's legislation. Not only is every distinction eradicated between the powerful and the helpless but even between the Israelite and the non-Israelite. The interpolation of these civil statutes with their emphasis upon the resident alien is due to the legal status of the half-Israelite offender.

CHAPTER 25: THE SABBATICAL AND JUBILEE YEARS.
25:1–7: The Sabbatical Year. Each seventh year is a Sabbath of liberating rest for Israelite slaves (Ex. 21:2–6; Deut. 15:12–18), debtors (Deut. 15:1–11), and the land (Ex. 23:10–11). In P, this "full" Sabbatical is reserved for the Jubilee, whereas the seventh year Sabbatical applies only to the land. For details consult *Sabbatical Year.

25:8–34: The Jubilee Year. At the sound of the *shofar* – Jubilee means (horn of a) ram (25:10; Josh. 6:4) – a year of emancipation is proclaimed. Land must lie fallow, landed property (except for town houses) is restored to its original owner, and all Israelite slaves are set free. The basis for the Jubilee is clearly stated: Israel and the land belong solely to God (comment on ch. 18); neither can be owned in perpetuity. Thus, absolute ownership of property is abolished: humans and land may be leased, not sold.

25:35–55: Indebtedness and the Jubilee. A defaulting Israelite debtor distrained by an Israelite creditor (perhaps with his family, 25:41, 54) is neither charged interest for his room and board, verses 35–38; nor treated as a slave if forced to enslave himself (until the Jubilee), verses 39–46; and should be redeemed if enslaved to an alien creditor, verses 47–55. The language and terminology of this pericope are paralleled in Old and Middle Babylonian laws (18th–17th century Alalakh and 15th–14th century Nuzi, respectively).

CHAPTER 26: THE CONCLUDING EXHORTATION. In form and function, the Epilogue to the Holiness Code finds its counterpart in Deuteronomy 28–30. It may be divided in three sections: (1) the Blessing (vss. 3–13); (2); the threats and penalties for violation (vss. 14–45); (3); the Postscript (vs. 46), which serves as a conclusion to the entire Holiness Code.

Chapter 27: Commutation of Gifts to the Sanctuary
The following gifts are discussed: persons (27:1–8), animals (27:9–13), houses (27:14–15), land (27:16–25), firstlings (27:26–27), "devoted" things (27:28–29), and tithes (27:30–33). The commutability of sacred gifts is an ancient practice (comment on the *ʾasham*, 5:15) underscored throughout this chapter by technical language (e.g., 27:2, 3, 12). The commutation of vows of persons is taken for granted as an established practice in II Kings 12:5. Certainly, the **Ḥerem*, in its meaning of death to persons (Lev. 27:29), bespeaks an early provenance. Indeed, although Leviticus in its present form is a product of the post-exilic period, in keeping with the conservative nature of cultic activity in general, the book preserves much ancient material.

BIBLIOGRAPHY: COMMENTARIES: S.R. Driver (Eng., 1898); D. Hoffmann (Ger., 1905–06; Heb., 1953); M. Noth (Eng., 1965); K. Elliger (Ger., 1966); N. Snaith (Eng., 1967). DATE: Y. Kaufmann, in: ZAW, 48 (1930), 23–43; 51 (1933), 35–47; idem, in: VT, 4 (1954), 307–13; H.L. Ginsberg, in: *Commentary*, 10 (1950), 282ff.; M. Greenberg, in: JAOS, 70 (1950), 41–47; E.A. Speiser, in: Y. *Kaufmann Jubilee Volume* (1960), 29–45 (Eng. sect.); D. Lieber, in: *Jewish Education*, 34 (1963), 254–61; J.G. Vink, *The Date of the Priestly Code in the Old Testament* (1969), includes comprehensive bibliography. **ADD. BIBLIOGRAPHY:** B. Levine, in: J. Neusner et al. (eds.), *Judaic Perspectives on Ancient Israel* (1987), 9–34; *The JPS Torah Commentary Leviticus* (1989); idem, ABD, 4:311–21; J. Milgrom, *Leviticus 1–16* (AB; 1991); idem, *Leviticus 17–22* (2000); idem, *Leviticus 23–27* (2001); idem, J. Hartley, *Word Biblical Commentary Leviticus* (1992), extensive bibliography; R. Gane, DBI, 2:54–59.

[Jacob Milgrom / S. David Sperling (2nd ed.)]

LEVITICUS RABBAH, one of the oldest Midrashim extant, probably composed in the fifth century in Palestine. Like other ancient Midrashim it has many passages in Palestinian Aramaic and contains a considerable number of Greek and Latin words. Many of the stories and folktales interwoven in its homilies reflect a Palestinian locale, especially that of the Sea of Galilee and its surroundings, and conditions in Palestine in the first four centuries C.E.; often the *halakhah* and customs referred to are specifically Palestinian. Much of the aggadic material presented is quoted in the names of Palestinian *amoraim* or of *tannaim*. The Midrash knows and quotes the Mishnah, Tosefta, and other tannaitic material. The editor either made use of the Palestinian Talmud (Albeck) or had access to similar (oral) traditions as were embodied in it, though differing from it in style and details (Margulies).

Leviticus Rabbah is a homiletical Midrash; it is composed of separate homilies, 37 in number, each of them based on the beginning of one of the *sedarim* ("orders"), i.e., the weekly pericopes according to the so-called triennial cycle (though in a good many cases the division in *Leviticus Rabbah* differs from the lectionary as known from other sources). Hence *Leviticus Rabbah* does not provide a running commentary on the entire book of Leviticus but limits itself to developing one theme (or, sometimes, several themes) related to the beginning of the *seder*. However, the subject of the homily is by no means always identical with the main content of the pericope itself; thus, while the first *seder* of Leviticus deals mainly with the burnt-offering, the Midrash devotes its entire first homily to the first verse and, accordingly, deals with Moses' outstanding qualities as a man and a prophet. Hence the author retained, to a large extent, freedom in choosing and arranging his material. He avoided, on the whole, matters of ritual, to which most of Leviticus is devoted, e.g., details of different categories of sacrifices, and developed instead homilies on subjects such as God's preference for the poor, their offerings and their prayers (ch. 3, relating to 2:1), the dangers of drunkenness (ch. 12, on 10:8–9), the praise of peace (part of ch. 9, on 7:11; the rest of the homily is devoted to "peace-offerings"), etc. Though the editor is not in fact the author of the aggadic material, which came to him through tradition, he nevertheless attempts, usually successfully, to present homilies which are homogeneous thematically; moreover he strives to attain in the composition of each homily full integration and a balance between its component parts. If in chapter 3 he quotes a series of tales which express the contempt felt by the aristocracy and especially by the priests for the meager sacrifices offered by the poor ("What is there in this to eat? What is there in this to offer up?" 9), he counterbalances them by concluding with a hymn of praise for the ideal priests, who are without a share in the land and take their portion from the hand of God Himself, and who are thus themselves the poorest of the poor and yet are devoted wholeheartedly to the service of God. Or, if in the beginning of chapter 9 (3) the story is told of R. Yannai who had invited a man to his house believing him to be a scholar and then insulted him when he discovered him to be an ignoramus, it has its counterpart at the end of the chapter (9) in the tale of R. Meir who allowed himself to be insulted in order "to make peace between a man and his wife." Most of the homilies thus testify to the skill of the editor and to his art, which express themselves in the degree of unity which he achieves even though using heterogeneous material. Often the various elements of the homily, as well as different homilies dealing with similar themes, are linked together dialectically, expressing different, even contrasting aspects of one and the same subject. Thus the picture drawn in chapter 3 of the ideal priest is again qualified in chapter 5 (relating to Lev. 4:13), where the merits of the common people and their true leaders – the sages – are extolled (7–8) in contrast to the shortcomings of the priests, who frequently failed in their high office and, at times, even led the people astray (5–6). It is not to them that the people must look for atonement, but, instead, they can rely on their own good deeds (especially their generosity in providing funds for scholars (4)) and their prayers; for "Israel knows how to placate its Creator" (9).

Each homily in *Leviticus Rabbah* is constructed according to a definite pattern; it opens with a number of proems, then follows the "body of the sermon" (which does not possess any standard form), and, lastly, a peroration, devoted mostly to the messianic hope. These homilies, though their material was drawn mainly from sermons as preached in the synagogue, are by no means identical with the latter; thus, e.g., it stands to reason that a preacher used no more than one proem in each sermon (see also: *Preaching). This new structure found in *Leviticus Rabbah* – which is a composite of materials drawn from a number of sermons and welded together into a new artistic unit, the "literary homily" – may well be the creation of the author of this Midrash, which appears to be the oldest of the homiletical Midrashim in which it occurs. It may have been this new form which enabled the author to shape his Midrash as he did, to arrange the traditional material freely to suit his own purposes, to deal with subjects suitable for a wider circle of readers, and to enrich his work by the inclusion of numerous folktales and parables.

Leviticus Rabbah is similar in character to *Pesikta de-Rav Kahana*, which was composed at about the same time (and possibly by the same author (Margulies)); though others believe it to be somewhat later (Albeck). The structure of the homily is identical in both; but the plan of construction of the two Midrashim as a whole is completely different: while *Leviticus Rabbah* deals with all *sedarim* of one book of the Pentateuch consecutively, *Pesikta de-Rav Kahana* presents homilies for all the special days in the calendar, festivals and special Sabbaths, relating to their respective lections, taken from different books of the Pentateuch or the Prophets. A curious feature is the appearance of no less than five identical homilies in both these Midrashim; in *Leviticus Rabbah* as sermons on pericopes of Leviticus, in *Pesikta de-Rav Kahana* as sermons for festivals on which those same sections were read. It can hardly be maintained that the author of either Midrash simply transferred whole chapters from the other; rather it is due to copyists, who were tempted by the identical structure of homilies in both works to augment the one by drawing upon the other. Chapter 28 may be considered as an authentic part of *Leviticus Rabbah*, because it appears to be superfluous in *Pesikta de-Rav Kahana*; on the other hand, chapters 20, 29, and 30 and, perhaps, 27 would seem to have originated in the latter. Another query arises regarding the three cases where *Leviticus Rabbah* has two separate chapters relating to one and the same *seder*, viz. chapters 1 and 2 (on Lev. 1:1ff.); chapters 4 and 5 (relating, seemingly, to 4:2); and chapters 20 and 21 (on 16:1–2). However, chapter 20 originally belonged to *Pesikta de-Rav Kahana* (see above), whereas chapter 4 was mistakenly ascribed to 4:1–2 and belongs in reality to a *seder* – otherwise unknown – beginning at 4:13. Hence the one remaining case of two homilies on the same pericope appears suspect, too; presumably chapter 2 is not authentic either in *Leviticus Rabbah*. Moreover, even after these "deductions" of 4 or 5 chapters from the total of 37, the number still appears too large, considering that Leviticus is divided traditionally into only 20 to 25 pericopes. It appears likely that the division of pericopes underlying the composition of *Leviticus Rabbah* differed considerably from the one accepted eventually as the custom of most congregations; hence the need was felt to supplement the Midrash by supplying the "missing" ones. This would also explain why quite often the beginnings of pericopes indicated in the Midrash as it stands are distant from one another by as few as five, eight, or nine verses only. However, if some of the homilies of *Leviticus Rabbah* are not original, they must have been added at a very early stage, for they are common to all manuscripts, including the ones from the Cairo *Genizah*. A critical edition of *Leviticus Rabbah* by M. Margulies has been published (Jerusalem, 1953–60); an English translation by J. Israelstam and J. Slotki appeared as part of the Soncino edition of *Midrash Rabbah* (1939). Recently an online synopsis of the textual witnesses of *Leviticus Rabbah* has been prepared (under the direction of C. Milikowsky) and posted on the Bar-Ilan website (http://www.biu.ac.il/JS/midrash/VR/editionData.htm).

BIBLIOGRAPHY: D. Kuenstlinger, *Die Petichot des Midrasch rabba zu Leviticus* (1913); H.L. Strack, *Introduction to the Talmud and Midrash* (1931), 211f.; Albeck, in: *Louis Ginzberg Jubilee Volume* (1946), 25–43 (Hebrew section); Zunz-Albeck, Derashot, index; M. Margulies, *Midrash Va-Yikra Rabbah*, 5 (1960), introduction; Heinemann, in: *Tarbiz*, 37 (1968), 339–54; Goldberg, *ibid.*, 38 (1969), 184–5. **ADD. BIBLIOGRAPHY:** Strack and Stemberger, *Introduction to the Talmud and Midrash* (1996), 288–91; M. Kadushin, *A Conceptual Commentary on Midrash Leviticus Rabbah* (1987); C. Milikowsky, in: *Jewish Studies at the Turn of the Twentieth Century* (1999), 311–21; B.L. Visotzky, *Golden Bells & Pomegranates – Studies in Midrash Leviticus Rabbah* (2003).

[Joseph Heinemann]

LEVITSKY, JACOB (1904–1956), mathematician. Born in Ukraine, Levitsky was taken to Palestine as a child. He studied mathematics at Goettingen and Yale, and began to lecture at the Hebrew University in 1931. Under the influence of Emmy Noether he engaged in abstract algebra, notably in the theory of noncommutative rings. His work on the laws of rings with the minimum condition is regarded as a classic. In 1953 he and a pupil were awarded the first Israel Prize for exact sciences for their research on the law of identities of rings. The radical in associative rings – known as the Levitsky Radical – is named after him.

[Shimshon Avraham Amitsur]

LEVITSKY, LOUIS MOSES (1897–1975), U.S. Conservative rabbi. Levitsky was born in Kremenchug, Russia, and was taken to Montreal as a child, then emigrated to the United States in 1916. He was ordained at the Jewish Theological Seminary (1923) and received his doctorate in 1933, then led a congregation in Wilkes Barre, Pennsylvania (1922–40), where he upgraded and energized the adult education program. From 1940 until his death he led Oheb Shalom Congregation in South Orange, NJ, continuing his innovative work in adult education. Levitsky also served as director of the Seminary School of Jewish Studies (1940–65) and the Women's Institute of the Seminary. He chaired its Board of Trustees (1947–53) and the Board of Governors of the National Academy of Adult Jewish Education. He taught Jewish history and theology at Rutgers and other colleges. A leader in Conservative Judaism and in civic life, Levitsky was president of the Rabbinical Assembly (1942–44) during a time of enormous stress, when one in three of its members were serving in the Armed Forces as chaplains. He also initiated contacts between Conservative Judaism and the Latin American countries, an area where the Conservative movement has been remarkably effective. He chaired the Army and Navy Activities of the National Jewish Welfare Board immediately after World War II and was chairman of the Ethics Committee of the Rabbinical Assembly. He also held the sensitive position of directing the Placement Commission of the RA in 1950. His board experience was put to use by the state of New Jersey, where he also served as a member of the National War Labor Board Panel of Mediators and the New Jersey Labor Mediation Board. He wrote *A Jew Looks at America* (1939). He also wrote an essay on his rabbinical experience "Salient Features of My Rabbinate in a City with Over 50,000 Jews" in the *Proceedings of the Rabbinical Assembly 1949*.

BIBLIOGRAPHY: P.S. Nadell, *Conservative Judaism in America: A Biographical Dictionary and Sourcebook* (1988)

[Jack Reimer / Michael Berenbaum (2nd ed.)]

LEVITSKY (Levitzki), MISCHA (1898–1941), pianist and composer. Born in Kremenchug, Russia, Levitsky studied violin from the age of three and piano from the age of six. He studied piano in Warsaw (1905–6, with Michaïlowsky), at the Institute of Musical Art in New York (1907–11, with Stojowski), and at the Berlin Hochschule fuer Musik (1913–15, with Dohnányi. Settling in the United States he toured widely and excelled in the interpretation of Chopin and Liszt. Among his compositions are a ballet, songs, piano pieces, and a cadenza for Beethoven's piano concerto in C minor.

BIBLIOGRAPHY: NGG²; H. Brower, *Piano Mastery*, 2nd ser. (1917), 224–32; Obituary, in: *Musical America*, lxi/1 (1941), 32; G. Kehler, *The Piano in Concert*, (1982), 738–41.

[Marina Rizarev (2nd ed.)]

LEVITT, U.S. family of builders and philanthropists. ABRAHAM LEVITT (1880–1962), born in Brooklyn, New York, the son of Polish immigrants, was a real-estate lawyer for 27 years. In 1929 he founded the building firm Levitt and Sons, Inc., which pioneered in community planning, assembly-line techniques, and mass production. In the late 1940s the firm built three whole communities, all called Levittown, in Long Island, New Jersey, and Pennsylvania. The family established the Levitt Foundation, Inc., to provide scholarships and donate funds to medical and welfare funds in 1949. Levitt was president of the Founders Society of the Albert Einstein Medical College at Yeshiva University and chairman of several fund drives for the UJA. His son WILLIAM JAIRD LEVITT (1907–1994), born in Brooklyn, was president of the family firm; shortly after its merger with International Telephone and Telegraph Corporation, he became chairman of the board of Levitt and Sons, Inc., and also of Levittown. During his presidency the firm began building houses in Europe. Levitt engaged in extensive civic and charitable activities. In 1973, together with Meshulam *Riklis, Levitt was appointed general chairman of a combined campaign of the United Jewish Appeal of Greater New York and the Federation of Jewish Philanthropies. Their aim was to raise $280,000,000, of which $30 million would be devoted to health, education, and social service projects in New York, and the balance to the emergency fund for Israel. This target was greatly increased after the Yom Kippur War. A younger son of Abraham Levitt was ALFRED S. LEVITT (1912–1966). He was associated with his father as vice president of Levitt and Sons, until 1954, when he organized his own firm, Levitt House Inc., based in Queens, New York. His sons JOHN and ANDREW took it over in 1959. William Levitt sold Levitt & Sons to International Telephone and Telegraph in 1968. Levitt was one of the wealthiest men in America in the late 1960s; but by the time he retired in the late 1980s, he had lost most of his amassed wealth as a result of unsuccessful real estate endeavors.

ADD. BIBLIOGRAPHY: H. Gans, *The Levittowners: Ways of Life and Politics in a New Suburban Community* (1967).

LEVITT, ARTHUR, SR. (1900–1980), comptroller of New York State. Levitt was born in Brooklyn, New York, to Israel Levitt and Rose Daniels and married Dorothy M. Wolff in 1929. The couple had one child, ARTHUR LEVITT, JR., who was the chairman of the U.S. Securities and Exchange Commission (SEC) from 1993–2001.

An infantry private in the U.S. Army in 1917 during World War I, Levitt proceeded to Columbia University after the war ended in 1918 and completed his bachelor's degree in 1921, followed by a law degree in 1924. He became a member of the New York Bar and operated his practice until rejoining the army in 1941 during World War II as a member of the Judge Advocate General (JAG) Corps. During his wartime service, he advanced to colonel and oversaw a JAG training center located in Queens, New York.

His political involvement began in 1946 as campaign manager to New York Assemblyman Irwin Steingut; in 1952 he was named to the New York City Board of Education, and became its president in 1954. His term was short-lived as, at the request of New York governor W. Averell Harriman, Levitt ran for and won election as the state's comptroller, a position he held until his retirement in 1978.

The overriding focus of Levitt's record 24 years as comptroller was guarding the interests of his constituents. Levitt was known as the consummate public servant by his avoidance of political preferences in his decision-making process, serving six scandal-free terms, being tenacious in tracking the usage of local and state public funds, and displaying unsurpassed diligence to detail in auditing procedures. In particular, he gave great attention to protecting the pension plans of working men and women and the definitive example of this occurred during New York City's financial troubles in the 1970s when Levitt prevented city officials from using workers' pensions to stave off potential bankruptcy.

Aside from winning six elections as the state's comptroller, Levitt's political career included a run in 1961 for mayor of New York City, although he lost in the Democratic primary; chair of the Democratic state convention in 1965; and delegate member in the party's 1968 and 1976 national conventions.

After stepping down from his comptroller post in 1978, Levitt worked as an investment officer for the Lincoln Savings Bank in New York City until his death in 1980. He was a recipient of a Distinguished Public Service Award from the Nelson A. Rockefeller College of Public Affairs & Policy and awarded the Legion of Merit medal in 1946 for his JAG service. An endowment fund was formed posthumously by Levitt, Jr., in conjunction with the Arthur Levitt Public Affairs Center at Hamilton College in Clinton, New York, which backs lectures and other events.

[Dawn DesJardins (2nd ed.)]

LEVITT, ESTHER (1902–1986), agriculturalist. Born in Metullah, the granddaughter of one of the founders of the village, Levitt devoted herself to agricultural work on her farm. She joined the *Gedud ha-Avodah (Labor Legion) in construction, road paving, and drainage of marshes and in later life was active in women's and soldiers' organizations in Metullah. She was known as the soldiers' Aunt and received the Israel Prize in 1977 for outstanding public service and devotion to agricultural labor.

LEVITT, HELEN (1907–), U.S. photographer. Born in Brooklyn, N.Y., Levitt made a mark with some of the most indelible photographs of New York City street scenes in the 1930s and 1940s, a volatile time in America. Levitt, who continued working into her nineties, was considered a "photographer's photographer," little known by the public but revered by her peers. She left high school before graduating and went to work for a commercial photographer, gaining technical knowledge. She aligned herself with Henri Cartier-Bresson and Walker Evans, who later became her collaborator. In 1936 she purchased the same Leica that Cartier-Bresson used and attached a right-angle viewfinder. The equipment gave her the ability to maneuver through neighborhood streets and photograph the natural choreography of children at play. She would walk all over the city, and she took a number of memorable photographs in the streets of Spanish Harlem. "It was a good neighborhood for taking pictures in those days," she said, "because that was before television. There was a lot happening. And the older people would be sitting out on the stoops because of the heat. This was in the late 30s, so those neighborhoods were very active."

In the mid-1940s, Levitt began making films. In 1945 she, Janice Loeb, and James Agee joined forces to create a cinematic version of her photographs. Released in 1952, the film, *In the Street*, is a critically acclaimed record of life in East Harlem, with scenes of children playing, fighting, and dressed up for Halloween. In 1947, Levitt and Loeb, joined by Sidney Meyers, made another film, *The Quiet One*, an emotional story of a delinquent black child and his psychological and social rehabilitation. The street life, depiction of the child's home conditions and background, and his experiences in the country are considered innovative examples of documentary filmmaking.

After a decade of working in film, Levitt returned to still photography in 1959, this time in color. While much of this work deals with the same themes as her earlier pictures, the addition of color allowed her to intensify the emotional content. In the early 1970s, most of her color photographs were stolen in a burglary, which inspired Levitt to renew her efforts and expand the range of subjects, as well as her territory, to the East Village, the garment district, and the Lower East Side.

Intensely private, "she asked that we trust the pictures, not the words," said a curator at the photography department of the Metropolitan Museum of Art in New York. Agee, in a foreward to Levitt's 1965 book of photographs from the 1930s and 40s, *A Way of Seeing*, called her pictures "a major poetic work." They combine "into a unified view of the world, an uninsistent but irrefutable manifest of a way of seeing."

In 1997 she published *Helen Levitt: Mexico City*, photos from 1941, and in 2001, *Crosstown*. In 2003, *Here and Now* included more than 90 images never before published.

[Stewart Kampel (2nd ed.)]

LEVITZKI, ALEXANDER (1940–), Israeli biochemist. Born in Jerusalem, Levitzki received his Ph.D. from the Weizmann Institute in 1968. In 1975 he joined the faculty of the Hebrew University of Jerusalem, becoming full professor in 1976. From 1981 to 1984 he was chairman of the biological chemistry department and between 1989 and 1993 was director of the Alexander Silberman Institute of Life Sciences of the Hebrew University of Jerusalem. Between 1998 and 2004 he was the director of the Institute of Advanced Studies of the Hebrew University and the Wolfson Center for Applied Structural Biology. He is one of the pioneers in the study of regulatory enzyme receptors and mechanisms of signal transduction across cell membranes, studies that led him to develop techniques for targeted destruction of cancer cells through biochemical means without harming normal cells, which is used for treatment of leukemia patients. He was the recipient of the Israel Prize for life sciences in 1990 and the Rothschild Prize for biology in 1992. In 1999 he was elected to the Israel Academy of Sciences. He is the recipient of the European Society of Clinical Oncology Hamilton-Fairely award for cancer research and of the Wolf Prize for medicine in 2005.

[Fern Lee Seckbach / Bracha Rager (2nd ed.)]

LEVNER, ISRAEL BENJAMIN (1862–1916), Hebrew writer. Born in Trudolyubovka, a Jewish colony in the Russian province of Yekaterinoslav, Levner taught in various parts of Russia. In the early 1880s he published his first articles, in *Ha-Meliẓ, which dealt with educational subjects and descriptions of Jewish life in the communities he had visited. His stories, first published in 1895, attracted wide attention. *Ben-Avigdor invited him to join the Tushiyyah publishing house, where he edited a series of storybooks for children (especially *Bibliotekah li-Yladim* – the first proper readers for Hebrew-reading children). His major work, *Kol Aggadot Yisrael*, which has retained its popularity to the present day, contains the legends of the Talmud, written in biblical style and arranged in chronological order. First published in 1895, the book has had a great many editions in Ereẓ Israel and abroad, and has been translated into various languages. Levner continued writing children's literature, especially for *Ha-Peraḥim*, a weekly which came into existence in 1908 and continued publication until the eve of World War I (he was also its editor and publisher); these works have earned an important place in Hebrew literature for children (see *Children's Literature). Together with Judah Steinberg – one of the major contributors to *Ha-Peraḥim* – he published the first of two volumes of *Kereistomatyah* ("Chrestomathy," 1908^3). Among other works by Levner are a version of the Shulḥan Arukh (1906) and an edition of *Ein Ya'akov* (1909), both for youth.

BIBLIOGRAPHY: Ofek, in: *Moznayim*, 16 (1963), 137–8; Kressel, Leksikon, 2 (1967), 170–1.

[Getzel Kressel]

LEVONTIN, JEHIEL JOSEPH (1861–1936), Hebrew writer. Born in Orsha, Belorussia, he graduated from the University of Moscow as an engineer, and worked on railroad construction in Persia and Russia. He was among the early Ḥovevei Zion and a founder of the Benei Zion association in Moscow (1884). His letters about the life of Jews in Persia appeared in *Ha-Meliẓ* (1891) signed Ḥushai ha-Arki, which became his permanent pen name. He contributed stories about Jewish life outside the Russian Pale of Settlement, such as "*Ha-Kabbelan*" and "*Ha-Anus*," to *Ha-Meliẓ* and other literary publications, and wrote a novelette about the early days of Ḥibbat Zion in St. Petersburg, "*Yemei ha-Ma'aseh*" (*Ha-Shilo'aḥ*, vols. 2, 3). His other novels, *Shimon Ezyoni* (1899), *Mi-Bein ha-Arafel* (1914), and *Ha-Shevu'ah* (1931), are concerned with the dispute between assimilationists and Zionists in pre-revolutionary Russia. He published one of the earliest modern Hebrew books about agriculture (*Ha-Ikkarut*, 1915). During World War I, he lived in Moscow and served on the executive of the Russian Zionist movement. He was arrested together with the other participants in the illegal Zionist convention which took place in Moscow in 1920. In 1922 he migrated to Palestine. Two volumes of his stories and articles were published posthumously: *Min ha-Meẓar* (1938) and *Bein Tikvah ve-Ye'ush* (1938).

BIBLIOGRAPHY: Lachower, Sifrut, 3 pt. 2 (1963), 37f.; J.L.G. Kahanovitz, *Me-Homel ad Tel Aviv* (1952), 66–68.

[Yehuda Slutsky]

LEVONTIN, ZALMAN DAVID (1856–1940), a pioneer of Jewish settlement and banking in Ereẓ Israel. Born in Orsha, Belorussia, the son of a Chabad Ḥasidic family, Levontin received a religious education and was tutored privately in languages and secular studies, after which he worked as a clerk in a commercial bank in Kremenchug. He was one of the first members of *Ḥovevei Zion and established a settlers' association in his town and in Kharkov. The two associations sent him to Ereẓ Israel to purchase lands, and after a short tour of the country Levontin convened a meeting of the representatives of the settlers' associations from Russia and Romania, as well as local public leaders. This conference established the Va'ad Ḥalutzei Yesud ha-Ma'alah, which decided to found a settlement by the name of *Rishon le-Zion. In 1882 Levontin, with the assistance of his wealthy uncle, Ẓevi Levontin, purchased 3,340 dunams (835 acres) and founded Rishon le-Zion there; he later served as head of the settlement's first committee.

In 1883, lack of funds forced Levontin to sell his land to Baron Edmond de *Rothschild and return to his family in Russia, where he served as branch bank manager in various towns in the *Pale of Settlement. Levontin joined the Zionist Movement upon its establishment and, in 1901, was summoned by *Herzl to become one of the directors of the *Jewish Colonial Trust in London. In 1903 he went to Ereẓ Israel to establish a bank under British auspices, to be known as the Anglo-Palestine Company (see Bank Leumi le-Israel in *Israel, Banking and Commerce). Under his directorship this bank became the central financial and credit institution in the new *yishuv* and engaged in banking activities with the Turkish authorities and the Arabs. When World War I broke out, Levontin went to London and Paris to mobilize funds in order to overcome the economic crisis that had beset the *yishuv*. When he was about to return, Turkey joined the war against Britain and France, and Levontin remained in Alexandria, where he opened a temporary branch of the Anglo-Palestine Company which extended aid to refugees and exiles from Palestine. He participated in the negotiations with the British authorities leading to the establishment of the Zion Mule Corps, commanded by Joseph *Trumpeldor. In the spring of 1918, Levontin returned to Palestine and continued his banking work; six years later he retired from the bank's board of directors. He published his memoirs, *Le-Ereẓ Avoteinu* (vol. 1, 1884, revised edition, 1963; vol. 2, 1925; vol. 3, 1928), in which he advocated the employment of capitalist methods of agricultural settlement and criticized the settlement methods of the Zionist Organization, particularly those of the labor movement. Jehiel *Levontin was his brother.

BIBLIOGRAPHY: Y. Ya'ari Poleskin, *Z.D. Levontin* (Heb., 1932); D. Idelovitz, *Sefer Rishon le-Ẓiyyon* (1941), index; *Terumah la-Kohen… (Z.D. Levontin)* (1926); Y. Ḥurgin, *Z.D. Levontin* (Heb., 1943); Tidhar, 2 (1947), 813–5; Kressel, Leksikon, 2 (1967), 159–60.

[Yehuda Slutsky]

LEVY, wealthy family of Portuguese refugees in *Morocco. MEYER (d. 1520) established an important spinning mill in Safi; the carpets woven there were famous. In about 1510 the king of Portugal appointed Meyer "royal treasurer." In 1520 the sharif of the Sa'adi dynasty accused him of espionage and had him put to death. His brother ISAAC (d. after 1555), who was the "confidential Jew" of the sharifs of the Sa'adi dynasty, played an active role in their foreign policy. Meyer's son JOSEPH (d. after 1560) entered the service of the Portuguese and was their official interpreter from 1535. A talented negotiator, he received a pension from the king of Portugal. His grandson JUDAH (d. c. 1635) was entrusted with important functions during the reign of Aḥmad al-Manṣūr (1578–1603) and became one of the favorites of the ruler's successors, during whose reigns he was responsible for "marine and commercial affairs" and was appointed *rentero* of the port of *Safi, then the most important one in the kingdom. He was a merchant and was as well known in London and Amsterdam as in Morocco. Toward the end of his life the sultan entrusted him with the administration of the funds of the royal treasury. He died in Safi. His brother MOSES (d. after 1620) was an important financier. In about 1600 the title of **nagid* was bestowed upon him and for a time he presided over the activities of Moroccan Jewry. In 1603 he signed the *takkanot* of *Fez. In 1617 the sultan sent him on an economic mission to the Netherlands with credentials addressed to the Estates-General and Maurice of Nassau. His family played an important role in the international commerce of Morocco and the leadership of the Jewish communities until about 1720. The family's descendants were known from their *ketubbot* in Safi, Mogador, and Gibraltar until the 19th century.

BIBLIOGRAPHY: D. Cazès, *Notes bibliographiques…* (1893), 44–50, 237–9; J.M. Toledano, *Ner ha-Ma'arav* (1911), 193; J. Abensur, *Mishpat u-Ẓedakah be-Ya'akov*, 1 (1894), no. 92; 2 (1894), nos. 123–4; SIHM, index.

[David Corcos]

LÉVY, family of musicians in mid-18th century Paris. They were probably admitted to reside in Paris by Louis XV among the limited number of merchants and representatives of liberal professions. The talented members of the family enjoyed considerable status in Parisian music and musical life. The *Mercure de France* mentions a Mlle. Lévy (no first name), who delighted the queen and her guests with her singing in the performance of Pascal's Colasse's Thétis et Pélée opera held in her chambers in 1733. Only the very best were chosen to entertain the queen and her guests. A dozen years later, the same *Mercure de France* refers to Madame Lévy ("Madame" indicating marital status) who "thrilled a distinguished audience with her outstanding performance on the *par-dessus-de-viole* [viola]" and was admired for the unusual "vivaciousness of her playing" in her three successive appearances at the Concert Spirituel during the 1745 season. In a report on a concert held on Passion Sunday, 1750, there appears the name of Mme. Haubaut, identified specifically as the "sister of Monsieur Lévy," who played the *par-dessus-de-viole* to great applause. It is not clear whether Mme. Haubaut and Mme. Lévy were one and the same person and we also do not know when and where either of them was born and raised. The brother Joseph Lévy, who was a much sought-after music teacher, made a name as the composer and publisher of the first set of sonatas for solo harp to appear in France. He dedicated his work to Mme. Saintien Sallabery, the wife of the king's chief financial officer.

BIBLIOGRAPHY: A. Ringer, in: *Musica Judaica*, vol. VIII, no. 1 (1985–86), 1–12.

[Amnon Shiloah (2nd ed.)]

LÉVY, family of French publishers. MICHEL (1821–1875) was born in Phalsbourg, Lorraine. He studied at the Paris music conservatory, but, finding that he lacked talent, abandoned his studies and became a secondhand bookseller. Lévy first sold books in the street and then from a stall. In 1842 he and his brothers ALEXANDRE NATHAN LÉVY and CALMANN LÉVY (1819–1891) founded the Lévy publishing firm. Their first success was a new edition of Goethe's *Faust* and, within a short time, Michel Lévy Frères became established as one of the largest publishing houses in France. They issued the works of great French authors such as Balzac, Lamartine, Anatole France, and Ernest Feydeau. When Feydeau included an antisemitic reference in his novel *La Comtesse de Chalis* (1867), the Lévy brothers refused to allow their name to appear as publishers. They also published books on biblical subjects and comparative religion. For a long period they issued the famous *Revue de Paris*. On the death of Michel Lévy in 1875, Calmann Lévy assumed control of the firm, which was renamed Calmann-Lévy. In 1878 he published Ernest David's French translation of George *Eliot's *Daniel Deronda*. After the death of Calmann Lévy, his three sons, PAUL, GEORGES, and GASTON took over the management of the firm.

[John M. Shaftesley]

LEVY, AARON (1742–1815), U.S. merchant and land speculator. Levy was born in Amsterdam. He went to Pennsylvania about 1760, where he established himself as an Indian trader and merchant. His major interest was in land speculation; he was one of the most active speculators in the colonies. He had large holdings in Northumberland and Centre counties and owned land in every other county of Pennsylvania. During the Revolution Levy made loans to the Continental Congress which, according to Robert Morris, superintendent of finance from 1781 to 1784, were never fully repaid. In addition, Levy helped to supply the colony's regular troops. After the war, in 1786, Levy announced plans for Aaronsburg, a town to be built in Penn Valley, Centre County. This was the first community in the United States founded by and named after a Jew. Although Levy actively promoted Aaronsburg, it was not a success. The failure left Levy land-poor, and to obtain cash he became an agent for other speculators. In 1796 he settled in Philadelphia, where he lived until his death.

BIBLIOGRAPHY: S.M. Fish, *Aaron Levy* (1951); Rosenbloom, Biogr Dict.

[Neil Ovadia]

LEVY, AARON (1771–1852), U.S. army officer and land speculator. Levy, the son of Hayman *Levy, was born in New York City. He was commissioned a paymaster of infantry in 1800 and served as a captain of artillery in 1812. He was appointed a lieutenant colonel of artillery in 1816 and resigned from the army in 1819. Levy, after having been licensed as an auctioneer in 1807, went into partnership with his father-in-law Isaac Moses. Levy was active in real estate transactions in the Lake George area of New York State. He served as president of Congregation Shearith Israel, New York, in 1803 and 1804.

BIBLIOGRAPHY: Rosenbloom, Biogr Dict; AJHSP, 27 (1920), 335–44.

[Leo Hershkowitz]

LÉVY (Levy-Alvares), ABRAHAM EUGÈNE (1826–1899), French army officer. Lévy joined the French army in 1845 and was distinguished for his bravery during the Crimean War of 1854–56. He was promoted to brigadier general in 1880, one of the first Jews so appointed. Lévy refused to convert to Christianity to further his career.

LEVY, SIR ALBERT (1864–1937), English philanthropist. After a successful business career as founder, chairman, and managing director of the Ardath Tobacco Co., he retired in 1931 to devote himself to philanthropy. He was knighted in 1929. His special interest was hospitals. He donated £10,000 for hospitals to mark King George V's coronation in 1911, and in 1928, £100,000 to the Royal Free Hospital, London, of which he was treasurer from 1927 to 1937. The Albert Levy Benevolent Fund, which he founded, donated £400,000 to about 125 institutions. Among many offices he held were president and treasurer of the Eastman Dental Clinic. Despite the generosity of his philanthropy, Levy still managed to leave over £1.1 million when he died.

[John M. Shaftesley]

LEVY, ALBERT J. (1897–1962), editor and journalist. Levy was born in Salonika and graduated from L'Ecole Normale of that city. After working as a teacher and editor of the Thessaloniki political daily *El Liberal*, Levy immigrated to the United States in 1917. In the United States, he is first mentioned as the editor of a humorous publication, "El Kirbach Amerikano," in a 1918 issue of *La Boz del Pueblo*. In 1918, after the eclipse of his newspaper, Levy became the editor of the Sephardi socialist tabloid, *El Proletario*. He founded the serious-humorous newspaper, *La Vara*, in 1922 and served as its editor for the majority of its lifespan. In 1926–27, he published *El Luzero Sefaradi* with Moise Soulam. Financial difficulties forced him to move to Seattle where from 1931 to 1934, he served as principal of the *talmud torah* in Seattle, Washington, still retaining his position at *La Vara*. The school improved significantly under his leadership, but conflicts with his board convinced him to return to New York in 1934, though he was forced to return to Seattle in 1945 for health reasons. He tried his hand at business, but he was less than successful so he returned to heading a school and served as the principal of the Sephardi Bikur Holim Hebrew School and later entered the furniture business. Levy wrote for a number of publications, including the Hebrew weekly *Hadoar*, and was active in a number of Sephardi organizations. He served as president of the Congregation of Love and Brotherhood in Monastair and on the Central Council of the Sephardic Brotherhood of America.

BIBLIOGRAPHY: A. Ben-Ur, introduction to "Scrapbooks of Albert David Levy," a microfilm held at the University of Washington

(OCLC: 44390739); idem, "In Search of the American Ladino Press: A Bibliographical Survey, 1910–1948," in: *Studies in Bibliography and Booklore*, 21 (Winter 2001), 10–52.

[Randall C. Belinfante (2nd ed.)]

LÉVY, ALFRED (1840–1919), chief rabbi of France, scholar, and author. Lévy, who was born in Lunéville, France, graduated from the Paris Ecole Rabbinique in 1866 and subsequently served as rabbi at Dijon (1867–69), Lunéville (1869–80), and Lyons (1880–1905). In 1905 he succeeded Zadoc Kahn as chief rabbi of the Consistoire Central de France, in which capacity he presided over the reorganization of French Jewry following the separation of State and Church in 1905. In 1932 a street in his native Lunéville was named after him. Lévy, whose main scholarly interest was in French-Jewish history, wrote *Les Juifs de la Comté au xive siécle* (in: *Archives Israélites*, 30 (1869), 182ff., 214ff., 245ff.), *Les Juifs du duché de Bourgogne au moyen-âge* (*ibid.*, 1869), and *Notice sur les Israélites de Lyon* (1894). Levy also wrote on Al-Ḥarizi's *Taḥkemoni* (in: REJ, 59 (1910), *Actes et Conférences*, VII–XXV), *Le deuil et les cérémonies funéraires chez les Israélites* (1874), and published a volume of sermons *Les doctrines d'Israël* (1896).

BIBLIOGRAPHY: *L' Univers Israélite* (June 22, 1914; July 25, 1919; Aug. 1, Aug. 8, 1919); *Archives Israélites* (June 21, 1917; July 31, 1919).

[Georges Weill]

LEVY, AMY (1861–1889), English poet and novelist. The daughter of a London stockbroker, Amy Levy became the second Jewish woman to attend Cambridge University, entering in 1879. She published her first book in 1881, while still an undergraduate. This was *Xantippe and Other Verse*, the title poem being a defense of the wife of Socrates. Her best-known work is probably *A London Plane Tree* (1889). Throughout her life, Amy Levy suffered from melancholy, and her second volume, *A Minor Poet and Other Verses* (1884), conveys her despair. As a novelist, she wrote the experimental *The Romance of a Shop* (1888) and, in the same year, the more competent *Reuben Sachs*, which was criticized for its unsympathetic portrayal of the wealthier Jewish classes. More genial, but slight, was her *Miss Meredith* (1889), the story of a governess. *Cohen of Trinity*, published in *The Gentleman's Magazine* (1889), a story arresting in its psychological delineation, was written a few months before she committed suicide. Her position as a keen but non-religious Jew, and as an early Jewish feminist of great talent but also an apparent manic-depressive who committed suicide at the age of only 27, have led to a considerable revival of interest in her work during the recent past. *The Complete Novels and Selected Writings of Amy Levy, 1861–1889*, edited by Melvyn New, was published in 1993. Her novel *Reuben Sachs* was reprinted in 2001 with an introduction by Julia *Neuberger.

BIBLIOGRAPHY: M.F. Modder, *Jew in the Literature of England* (1939), 261, 317–8, 323–4, 380. **ADD. BIBLIOGRAPHY:** ODNB online; L.H. Beckman, *Amy Levy: Her Life and Letters* (2000).

[William D. Rubinstein (2nd ed.)]

LÉVY, ARTHUR (1847–1931), French historian. Born in Nancy, Lévy was a businessman but turned to writing history because of his interest in Napoleon. His first book, *Napoléon intime* (2 vols., 1893; *The Private Life of Napoleon*, 1894), was based on hitherto unpublished documents relating to Napoleon. His other books included *Napoléon et la paix* (1902), and *Histoires intimes du temps du ler Empire: Napoléon et Eugénie de Beauharnais* (1926).

LEVY, ASSER (d. 1681), New York merchant and landowner. Levy was a member of the first group of Jews to arrive in New Amsterdam, in September 1654. In the following years he successfully contested a tax assessed against Jews who were refused the right to serve in the militia and he also achieved for his coreligionists the right to carry on trade in the community. Levy was made a freeman in 1657, and became the most prominent of 17th-century New York Jews. He purchased land in various sections of New York and developed an extensive trade, principally in the city and in the Hudson River Valley, dealing in all types of merchandise. He opened a butcher and tanning shop in New York City in 1678.

BIBLIOGRAPHY: J.R. Rosenbloom, Biogr Dict, 88; J.R. Marcus, *Early American Jewry*, 1 (1951), 30–31; Huehner, in: Karp, ed., *Jewish Experience in America*, 1 (1969), 51–65.

[Leo Hershkowitz]

LEVY, BENJAMIN (c. 1650–1704), founder of the London Ashkenazi community, son of Loebel or Levy Moses of Hamburg. He arrived in London in about 1670, made a fortune, and in 1697 became one of the 12 original Jewish brokers in London. He is said to have been instrumental in procuring the charter for the reorganized East India Company and was a "proprietor" (i.e., member of the board) of the company in charge of New Jersey. Though attached to the Sephardi congregation, he purchased the original cemetery for the Ashkenazi community in 1696. On his death, leadership of this community was assumed by his kinsman Moses *Hart (1675–1756). The latter's daughter Judith (1707–1803) married Benjamin's son ELIAS (d. 1750). In 1790 Judith Levy defrayed a large part of the cost of reconstructing the Great Synagogue which her father had rebuilt in 1722.

Another BENJAMIN LEVY (d. 1693), born in Cracow, lived in Recife (Brazil), before becoming *ḥazzan* and *shoḥet* of the London Sephardi community from about 1664. He was the recipient in London of enthusiastic communications regarding *Shabbetai Zevi.

BIBLIOGRAPHY: C. Roth, *History of the Great Synagogue* (1950), passim; A.M. Hyamson, *Sephardim of England* (1951), 41–44, and passim; L.D. Barnett, *Libro de los Acuerdos* (1931), passim; J. Sasportas, *Ẓiẓat Novel Ẓevi*, ed. by Y. Tishbi (1954), 71 (44b). **ADD. BIBLIOGRAPHY:** Katz, England, 180–82, index; T. Endelman, *Jews in Georgian England* (1979, 1999^2), index.

[Cecil Roth]

LEVY, BENN WOLFE (1900–1973), playwright, theater producer, and politician. Levy was born in London, educated at Repton and Oxford, and served in the Royal Air Force in 1918. From 1923 he was a publisher and playwright whose works were well known during the interwar period. He also co-authored the script of *Blackmail* (1929), Alfred Hitchcock's first talking film. Levy served in the Royal Navy during World War II and was elected Labour member of Parliament for Eton and Slough in 1945, serving until 1950. Increasingly on the left of the party, in the 1950s Levy became a campaigner for nuclear disarmament and other radical causes. Levy wrote more than 20 plays. His successes include *Mrs. Moonlight* (1929), *Art and Mrs. Bottle* (1929), *The Poet's Heart* (1937), *Return to Tyassi* (1951), and *The Rape of the Belt* (1957).

ADD. BIBLIOGRAPHY: ODNB online.

[William D. Rubinstein (2nd ed.)]

LÉVY, BENNY (1945–2003), French thinker. Lévy was born in Cairo and studied at the petit lycée of the Cairo French high school until 1957. After the Suez crisis, the family left Egypt to settle in Brussels, giving up their Egyptian citizenship. In 1962 he came to Paris and was accepted at Ecole Nationale Supérieure (ENS) as a stateless foreign student. He applied himself intensely to Marxist theory and the Chinese Cultural Revolution. In 1969, he founded with Alain Geismar and Serge July the movement 'La gauche prolétarienne,' inspired by Maoist ideas. Under the pseudonym of Pierre Victor, he clandestinely headed the group. The group and its organ, *La cause du peuple*, attracted leading intellectuals such as Jean-Paul Sartre, Gilles Deleuze, Michel Foucault, Jacques-Alain Miller, and Jean-Claude Milner. It dissolved in 1974, marking a period of doubt and questioning about revolutionary and political ideas for Lévy while he worked as Sartre's secretary in 1974–80. The period culminated with the publication of his interviews with Sartre as *L'Espoir maintenant. Les entretiens de 1980* (1991; *Hope Now: The 1980 Interviews*, 1996). Sartre intervened with President Valery Giscard-d'Estaing, to get Lévy French nationality in 1975. Lévy discovered Emmanuel *Levinas in 1976, and under his influence began to study Hebrew. Between 1980 and 1984, he made Jewish texts and practices a part of his daily life. In 1984, Lévy moved to Strasbourg, continuing to teach at Paris VII, where he had begun in 1975, in the department of Sciences des textes et des documents. In Strasbourg he devoted himself to the study of Judaism. In 1995, he finally moved to Jerusalem, and there met his master, Levinas. He established a link with Paris VII, and in spring 1995 founded the Institut d'études lévinassiennes with Bernard-Henri *Lévy and Alain *Finkielkraut. Among his ten books are *On a raison de se révolter* (under the pen name Pierre Victor, 1974); *Le logos et la lettre: Philon d'Alexandrie en regard des pharisiens* (1988); *Être juif* (2003); *La Confusion des temps* (2004); *La Cérémonie de la naissance* (2005); and with Alain Finkielkraut, *Le Livre et les livres* (2006). He directed the *Cahiers d'Études lévinassiennes*, for which he also wrote the articles: "Philosophie de la Révélation? Schelling, Rosenzweig, Lévinas" (2 (2003), 283–383) and "Lévinas et le grec" (special Benny Lévy issue (2005), 195–275).

[Colette Olive (2nd ed.)]

LEVY, BERNARD-HENRI (1948–), French writer, philosopher, and essayist. Levy was born in Algeria, and brought up and educated in Paris. Graduating in philosophy, he was active in both thought and action, producing essays, novels, films, and newspaper articles. Fiercely critical of fascist and Marxist totalitarianism in *La Barbarie à visage humain* (1977), he found in biblical monotheism the answer to the totalitarian challenge (*Le Testament de Dieu*, 1979). His book on the roots of French fascism (*L'Idéologie Française*, 1981) provoked an important public debate. Present in Bangladesh already in the early 1970s, and in Yugoslavia 20 years later, he was deeply committed to the Bosnian cause and sensitive to the ordeal of the city of Sarajevo. His biography of Jean-Paul Sartre, *Le Siècle de Sartre* (2000), was highly acclaimed.

[Nelly Hansson (2nd ed.)]

LEVY, CHAPMAN (1787–1850), U.S. lawyer. Levy, who was born in Camden, South Carolina, was admitted to the South Carolina bar in 1806. He served in the War of 1812, and reached the rank of colonel. Levy was in the state legislature from 1829 to 1833. He was elected to the state convention that passed the nullification of the federal tariffs of 1828 and 1832, despite Levy's negative vote. He again served in the legislature from 1836 to 1838. Levy then moved to Mississippi where he operated a plantation at Camden until his death.

[Neil Ovadia]

LEVY, CLIFTON HARBY (1867–1962), U.S. Reform rabbi. Born in New Orleans, his family had settled in the American colonies in 1740. Levy was ordained at Hebrew Union College (1890), was rabbi of Congregation Gates of Hope, New York City (1890–91), and superintendent of classes for immigrant children established by the Baron de Hirsch Fund. He later served congregations in Lancaster, Pa. (1892–94) and Baltimore, Md. (1894–96), where he organized a Jewish kindergarten in a religious school and the first United Hebrew Charities. He founded Tremont Temple, Bronx, N.Y., and was its rabbi from 1906 to 1921. He left the pulpit rabbinate in 1921. In 1924 he organized the Center of Jewish Science, New York City, which sought to counter the influence of Christian Science among middle-class Jews and to inject spirituality into the Reform Jewish synagogue. He was a founding member of the American Council for Judaism, which consisted primarily of anti-Zionist Reform rabbis and laymen. While still a student, Levy published a five-act Purim play, *Haman and Mordecai* (1886). During his stay in Baltimore he edited *Jewish Comment*. He edited *The Bible in Art* (1936) and *The Bible in Pictures* (1942), and served as art editor of the *Universal Jewish Encyclopedia*.

LEVY, SIR DANIEL (1873–1937), Australian politician. Born in London, Levy was taken to Sydney as a child. In 1901 he was elected a member of the Legislative Assembly of New South Wales, remaining a member for various seats in inner east Sydney until his death 36 years later. He was chairman of committees in 1917 and speaker of the House from 1919 until 1932. He was also attorney-general and minister of justice for a short time in 1932. Levy held a number of offices in public life and in the Jewish community, and at one time edited the *Australian Hebrew.*

ADD. BIBLIOGRAPHY: ADB, 10; H.L. Rubinstein, Australia I, 381–82, 534–35.

LEVY, DAVID (1937–), Israeli politician, member of the Knesset from the Seventh Knesset. Levy was born in Rabat, Morocco, receiving a traditional Jewish upbringing, studying at the Alliance school in Rabat. He immigrated to Israel in 1957 with his family, first living in a *ma'barah* and later settling in the northern development town of Bet Shean. As a young man Levy was employed in neighboring kibbutzim as a hired agricultural laborer, and then in construction, but was occasionally unemployed. In 1964 Levy was elected as the representative of the construction workers' union in the workers' council in Bet Shean, and the following year he was elected to the municipal council of Bet Shean and deputy mayor on behalf of the *Ḥerut Movement. In 1966 he was elected as a member of the Executive and Center of Ḥerut. Levy was elected to the Seventh Knesset in 1969 on the *Gaḥal list, and was viewed as one of the first authentic Oriental leaders to reach a prominent position in a major Israeli party. In 1971 he was elected chairman of the Blue-White faction, which was part of the Ḥerut Movement, in the Histadrut. In the elections to the Eighth to Fourteenth Knesset, and in the elections to the Sixteenth Knesset he ran on the Likud list.

In the government formed by Menaḥem *Begin after the political upheaval of 1977 Levy was appointed minister for immigrant absorption. In January 1979 he became minister of construction and housing, a position he held for the next 11 years, during which period 300,000 new apartments were built within the Green Line as well as in the West Bank and the Gaza Strip. He was also the minister responsible for *Project Renewal – an extensive project for the rehabilitation of distressed neighborhoods, carried out in around 100 towns and settlements by the Jewish Agency, with the cooperation of the local residents and Jewish communities abroad. In the years 1981–92 he also served as deputy prime minister, in Likud-led and National Unity governments. In the course of Operation Peace for Galilee Levy had reservations regarding the policy of Minister of Defense Ariel *Sharon, and in 1985 was the only minister from the Likud to vote in the government with the Labor ministers for withdrawal from Lebanon, and thus was responsible for the withdrawal's being approved by the inner cabinet. Despite his moderate positions, Levy joined Sharon and Yitzhak *Modai in 1989 in opposing the plan to hold elections in the West Bank and Gaza proposed by Prime Minister Yitzhak *Shamir and Minister of Defense Yitzhak *Rabin. He was appointed minister for foreign affairs in the narrow government formed by Shamir in June 1990, after the National Unity Government formed in 1988 was brought down in a vote of no confidence in March. Levy did not participate in the Madrid Conference of October–November 1991, since Shamir insisted on heading the Israeli delegation, and Binyamin *Netanyahu was responsible for Israel's information campaign. As minister for foreign affairs Levy became the object of many ethnic jokes, but his popularity within the Likud was still significant. In the Likud leadership contest before the elections to the Thirteenth Knesset Levy placed his candidacy opposite Shamir's and gained 32% of the votes. However, in the primaries held for the Likud list only a handful of his supporters were elected, and he considered running on a separate list, but finally decided to remain in the Likud, even though a noticeable erosion began in his status within the party.

In the Likud's leadership contest won by Netanyahu after the party's defeat in the 1992 elections, Levy came in second with 26.3%. Levy's ongoing failure to increase his power and influence in the Likud, and tensions with its Ashkenazi leaders, led him to break away from the Likud in March 1996 and form an ethnic parliamentary group called Gesher. After failing to raise sufficient funds to run independently in the elections to the Fourteenth Knesset, Gesher ran in a joint list with the Likud and *Tzomet. In the government formed by Netanyahu after the elections Levy returned to the Ministry for Foreign Affairs but resigned in January 1998. In the elections to the Fifteenth Knesset Gesher ran in a joint list called One Israel with the Labor Party and Meimad, under the leadership of Ehud *Barak. Once again he was appointed minister for foreign affairs, but in August 2000 Gesher broke away from One Israel and left the government. In the government formed by Sharon in March 2001 Levy was appointed minister without portfolio, and in the elections to the Sixteenth Knesset Levy once again ran within the framework of the Likud but was left out of Sharon's new government. In the course of the Sixteenth Knesset Levy joined the 13 Likud members who voted against the prime minister's Gaza disengagement plan and became one of the group's main spokesmen.

BIBLIOGRAPHY: A. Avnery, *David Levy* (Heb., 1983).

[Susan Hattis Rolef (2nd ed.)]

LEVY, FELIX ALEXANDER (1884–1963), U.S. Reform rabbi and scholar. Levy was born in New York, son of parents of Alsatian origin. He was ordained at Hebrew Union College (1907). From 1908 until his retirement in 1955, Rabbi Levy served Emmanuel Congregation, Chicago. He influenced his colleagues in modifying the attitude of Reform Judaism to *halakhah* and the nature of Jewish identity. These changes were embodied, inter alia, in the 1937 Columbus Platform adopted by the Central Conference of American Rabbis under Levy's leadership as president (1935–37). After his retirement,

Rabbi Levy served as editor of *Judaism* and as dean of the Academy for Higher Jewish Learning in New York. A selection of his papers and sermons appeared in *His Own Torah* (ed. S.D. Temkin, 1969).

BIBLIOGRAPHY: S.D. Temkin (ed.), *His Own Torah* (1969), 3–43.

[Wolfe Kelman]

LEVY, HARRY LOUIS (1906–), U.S. classical scholar and university administrator. Born in New York, Levy graduated from City College and received his doctorate at Columbia University in 1936, editing the invective *In Rufinum* of the fourth-century Roman poet Claudian (revised edition 1971, American Philological Association). Levy served on the faculty of Hunter College from 1928, becoming professor of classics in 1953. From 1949 to 1952 he was editor-in-chief of the *Classical Weekly*. From 1951 to 1953 and from 1959 to 1963 he was dean of students at Hunter College in the Bronx; and in 1963, when the City University of New York was organized, he was named dean of studies in charge of the master plan of the university. In a celebrated incident in 1965, protesting the interference of New York City's Board of Higher Education with the academic administration of the university Levy, together with the chancellor and the presidents of two of the city colleges, submitted letters of resignation or of impending retirement. The Board promptly revised its procedures and the resignations were withdrawn. Levy was subsequently promoted to be administrative vice chancellor and, in 1966, vice chancellor. In 1968 he retired and served until 1971 as professor of humanities at the newly established Liberal Arts College of Fordham University. In 1971 he became research fellow at the American School of Classical Studies at Athens. From 1973 he was a visiting professor of classics at Duke University.

A master teacher, he wrote extensively on methods for revitalizing the teaching of Latin. With his military gait and rapid-fire wit, he was an important force for the preservation of the classics, particularly through the Northeast Conference on the Teaching of Foreign Languages, of which he served as chairman in 1963. He served as president of the American Philological Association from 1973 to 1974. His wife, whose professional name is Ernestine Friedl, was in charge of the doctoral program in anthropology at the City University of New York 1969–1970 and became professor of anthropology at Duke University in 1973. Levy wrote *A Latin Reader for Colleges* (1939; 1962).

BIBLIOGRAPHY: E.A. Robinson, in: *Classical Weekly*, 46 (1952/3), 1: *Directory of American Scholars*, 3 (1963^5), 237.

[Louis Harry Feldman]

LEVY, HAYMAN (1721–1789), New York merchant and landowner. Levy was born in Hanover, Germany, and went to New York shortly before 1748. He was naturalized and made a freeman of New York in 1750. During the Seven Years' War he had a considerable Indian trade and he owned trade ships engaged in privateering. Early in the Revolutionary War Levy left the British-occupied city for Philadelphia, where he served in the militia. After the war he returned to New York and opened a commission store. Very much involved in Jewish affairs, Levy served as president of Congregation Shearith Israel six times. He had 11 children who became important members of the New York community.

BIBLIOGRAPHY: J.R. Rosenbloom, *Biographical Dictionary of Early American Jews* (1960), s.v. *Levy* and *Sloe Myers*; L. Hershkowitz (ed.), *Wills of Early New York Jews* (1967), 165–85.

[Leo Hershkowitz]

LEVY, HYMAN (1889–1975), British mathematician. Levy was born in Edinburgh and was professor of mathematics at the Imperial College of Science, London, from 1923 to 1955, and was dean of the Royal College of Science (1948–54). During World War I he worked on aerodynamics at the National Physical Laboratory. Always deeply interested in social affairs, Levy was a pioneer in explaining and interpreting the social impact of science. He was chairman of the Labour Party's science advisory committee from 1924 to 1930. He became a leading member of the British Communist Party, particularly active among scientists. After a visit to the Soviet Union in 1957 he published a pamphlet "Jews and the National Question" (1958), which criticized the Soviet attitude to the Jews and Jewish culture in the U.S.S.R., whereupon he was expelled from the Communist Party.

[Maurice Goldsmith]

LÉVY, ISAAC (1835–1912), French rabbi, born in Marmoutier, Alsace. Lévy was rabbi of Verdun in 1858, of Lunéville in 1865, and of Colmar in Upper Alsace in 1869. After the annexation of Alsace by Germany following the Franco-Prussian War of 1870–71, Lévy chose to remain French, and the French government created a new chief rabbinate for him at Vesoul. In 1887 he became chief rabbi of Bordeaux. Lévy wrote *Récits bibliques* (1864), *Défense du Judaïsme* (1867), and *Histoire sainte à l'usage de la jeunesse Israélite*, the standard biblical history for Jewish children in France (1869; 16th ed., 1931).

LÉVY, ISIDORE (1870–1954), historian of religion. Born in Rixheim, Alsace, Lévy taught at the Ecole des Hautes Etudes (1905–28) in the departments of religion and historical and philological sciences, as well as at Lille (1919–23), the Sorbonne (1923–27), the Université Libre in Brussels (1929), and the Collège de France (1932–40; 1944–45). His studies are devoted to the ancient history of religion, extending from Asia Minor to Egypt and particularly the western Semites. Levy's books include *Recherches sur les sources de la Légende de Pythagore* (1926), *La Légende de Pythagore de Grèce en Palestine* (1927), and *Recherches esséniennes et pythagoriciennes* (1965).

BIBLIOGRAPHY: Brussels, Université Libre, Institut de Philologie et Histoire Orientales et Slaves, *Annuaire*, 13 (1953), v–xix, incl. list of his works.

[Victor A. Mirelman]

LEVY, JACOB (1819–1892), rabbi and lexicographer. Born near Poznan, Poland, he studied under his father, Rabbi Isaac Levy, and under Rabbi Akiva *Eger by whom he was ordained. He also studied philology and Middle Eastern languages at Breslau and Halle universities. For several years he served as rabbi of Rosenberg, Upper Silesia, but resigned from this post in 1850, in order to devote himself exclusively to scientific work. He settled in Breslau where he became assistant rabbi (*dayyan*) in 1857; in 1864 he was appointed to the Breslau court to administer the *oath *more judaico* ("Jewish Oath"). From 1878 to his death, he also served as lecturer at the Mora-Salomon Leipziger Foundation.

Levy's first major work was the *Chaldaeisches Woerterbuch ueber die Targumim und einen grossen Teil des rabbinischen Schrifttums*, 2 vols. (1867–68, 1881[3]). For this work the Prussian government awarded him the title of "professor." A second monumental work, *Neuhebraeisches und chaldaeisches Woerterbuch ueber die Talmudim und Midraschim* (4 vols., 1876–89), is of particular importance because of the comparative study of its quotations: various versions from different manuscripts are given, explained, and translated. Both dictionaries were annotated by the Leipzig Arabist H.L. Fleischer. In 1924 the second of the two works was republished by L. *Goldschmidt in a revised and enlarged version. Levy was the outstanding scholar of his time in the field of talmudic and rabbinical lexicography, and his successors, including Alexander *Kohut, the author of *Arukh ha-Shalem*, based their scholarship on his work.

BIBLIOGRAPHY: Schwab, Repertoire, 281 (bibliography of articles); Zeitlin, Bibliotheca, 207–8; W. Bacher, in: ZDMG, 47 (1893), 495ff.; A. Kohut, *ibid.*, 723; A. Heppner and J. Herzbe\nard Suler]

LEVY, JEFFERSON MONROE (1852–1924), U.S. congressman and lawyer. Levy, who was born in New York City, served three terms in the U.S. House of Representatives (1899–1901, and 1911–15). He was a leader of the "Gold Democrats" during his first term, and sponsored the Reserve Bank Bill during his second and third terms. Levy advocated the maintenance of a large navy, led the fight that resulted in higher wages for the nation's postal clerks, was instrumental in codifying New York State's election laws and reforming the surrogate courts, and exposed instances of waste and extravagance in Mayor John Purroy Mitchel's generally reformist and efficient administration (1913–17) in New York City. He was the nephew of Uriah P. *Levy, from whom he inherited Monticello, Thomas Jefferson's home.

LEVY, JONAS PHILLIPS (1807–1883), U.S. naval officer and communal leader. Levy, the brother of Uriah Phillips *Levy and the father of Jefferson Monroe *Levy, was born in Philadelphia. He took up a career in the U.S. Navy, reaching the rank of commander. Unlike his brother Uriah, he seems to have adapted well to naval life and encountered no recorded antisemitism. In 1847 he was commander of the steamer America, ferrying troops to and participating in the naval battle for Veracruz during the Mexican War. He was appointed captain of the captured city. Levy was active in Jewish life. His greatest contribution to progress in equal rights for Jews was in his work to rectify the disabilities imposed on Jews in Switzerland. When news of the U.S.-Swiss treaty drawn up in 1850 reached American Jews, Levy led the struggle to alter the treaty, writing letters and working with his friend, Senator Lewis Cass, to delete the provision disallowing equal rights of travel and settlement to Jewish nationals and non-nationals in Switzerland. When Levy moved to Washington, D.C., in 1852, there were about 25 Jewish men in the city, meeting haphazardly for services. Levy supported the movement for a permanent synagogue. Discovering that the local laws were ambiguous on the rights of Jews so to organize, Levy called on his political friends, and in 1855 an act of Congress gave full rights to the Washington Hebrew Congregation and other congregations to organize.

BIBLIOGRAPHY: H.K. Meier, *United States and Switzerland in the Nineteenth Century* (1963), 33–38, 58–66; C. Adler, *Jews in the Diplomatic Correspondence of the United States* (1906); C. Adler and A.M. Margalith, *With Firmness in the Right: American Diplomatic Action Affecting Jews, 1840–1945* (1946); S. Stroock, in: AJHSP, 11 (1903), 7–11.

[Abram Kanof]

LEVY, JOSEPH LANGLEY (1870–1945), British journalist, born in Liverpool. Levy took up journalism after writing a series of articles on Liverpool Jewry in 1899 for the *Liverpool Review*, of which he became editor in 1902. He joined the London *Daily Express* in 1905, and was art critic for three London papers. In 1910 he went to South Africa to become editor of the Johannesburg *Sunday Times*, which under his editorship achieved the largest circulation in the country. He wrote novels and short stories. His daughter, DORIS LANGLEY MOORE (1902–1989), who lived chiefly in England, founded the Costume Museum in Bath and was a well-known novelist and biographer.

ADD. BIBLIOGRAPHY: "Doris Langley Moore," in: ODNB.

LEVY, JOSEPH LEONARD (1865–1917), U.S. Reform rabbi. Levy was born in London. He graduated from the University of London in 1884 and was trained for the Orthodox ministry at Jews College, London. From 1885 to 1889 he served the Bristol Hebrew Congregation. In 1889 he went to the United States as rabbi to a congregation in Sacramento, California, and from 1893 to 1901 he was assistant rabbi at Congregation Keneseth Israel, Philadelphia. From 1901 to 1917 he was rabbi of Congregation Rodef Shalom, Pittsburgh. During the Spanish-American War he was an army chaplain for a short period. Levy was famous in his day as a preacher; about 16 volumes of his sermons were published. He was active in local and international peace associations and in health, housing, and other welfare organizations in Pittsburgh.

[Sefton D. Temkin]

LEVY, JUDAH (Mercado) BEN MENAHEM (c. 1790–c. 1875), rabbi in Ereẓ Israel. Levy was born in Sarajevo from where he moved to Ragusa, immigrating to Jerusalem in his youth. He was appointed rabbi of Jaffa in 1825 by the Jerusalem rabbinate and may be regarded as the real founder of the Jewish community in Jaffa. Later the Turkish government recognized him and conferred on him the title *Ḥakham bashi*. He was responsible for the consecration of the first Jewish cemetery in Jaffa (previously its Jews had been buried in Jerusalem). Levy assisted Charles *Netter in founding the *Mikveh Israel agricultural school.

BIBLIOGRAPHY: Brill, in: *Ha-Levanon*, 2 (1865), 56; M.D. Gaon, *Yehudei ha-Mizraḥ be-Ereẓ Yisrael*, 2 (1938), 320f.; Frumkin-Rivlin, 3 (1929), 309 no. 13.

[Samuel Abba Horodezky]

LÉVY, LAZARE (1882–1964), French pianist and composer. Born in Brussels, Lévy studied at the Paris Conservatoire, where he obtained first prize for piano in 1898. A remarkable interpreter of the classical repertory and modern compositions as well, Lévy played with the principal European symphony orchestras and toured in Europe and Asia. In 1920 he succeeded Alfred Cortot as professor of piano at the Paris Conservatoire, and gained an international reputation as a pedagogue, having trained many eminent students. His compositions include piano compositions as well as pieces for cello, flute, organ, and a stringed quartet.

[Amnon Shiloah (2nd ed.)]

LEVY, LEONARD WILLIAMS (1923–2006), U.S. historian. Born in Toronto, Canada, Levy taught at Brandeis University, serving as dean of the Graduate School of Arts and Sciences (1958–63) and dean of the Faculty of Arts and Sciences (1963–66). From 1958 he held the chair in American constitutional history. Levy contributed to the history of American constitutional law and to the early history of American law, with emphasis on the background of the Bill of Rights. His main works are *The Law of the Commonwealth and Chief Justice Shaw* (1957), *Legacy of Suppression: Freedom of Speech and Press in Early American History* (1960), and *Jefferson and Civil Liberties…* (1963). His *Origins of the Fifth Amendment…* (1968) was awarded a Pulitzer Prize. Levy was also editor of several historical series. He was a member of both the American Jewish Committee and the American Jewish Congress, serving on the latter's Commission on Law and Social Action. After he retired from teaching, Levy became professor emeritus at Claremont McKenna College in Claremont, California.

He also wrote *Original Intent and the Framers' Constitution* (1988), *Blasphemy: Verbal Offense against the Sacred, from Moses to Salman Rushdie* (1993), *The Establishment Clause* (1994), *License to Steal* (1995), *The Palladium of Justice* (1999), *Ranters Run Amok* (2000), and *Origins of the Bill of Rights* (2001). He also edited (with K. Karst) the six-volume *Encyclopedia of the American Constitution* (2000^2).

[Richard B. Morris / Ruth Beloff (2nd ed.)

LEVY, LOUIS (1875–1940), Danish poet, critic, and journalist. Levy is mostly remembered for his children's poems which, like Andersen's fairy tales, have become classics that appeal to adults as well as the young. Levy was, however, a remarkably versatile writer in other genres. His Jewish awareness may be seen in the pathetic *Byglig en ark* ("Build an Ark," 1904) and in the pacifist *Jøden som fredsstifter* ("The Jew as Peacemaker," 1918).

LEVY, LOUIS EDWARD (1846–1919), U.S. chemist, inventor, communal leader, and newspaper editor. Levy, who was born in Pilsen, Bohemia, was brought to the U.S. at the age of eight. In 1875 he invented the photochemical engraving process known as "Levytype," permitting newspapers to print halftone pictures from the stereotype plate, and founded the Levytype Company in Baltimore. The company moved to Philadelphia in 1877. Levy, the first U.S. citizen to receive a patent in this field, also invented the Levy acid blast, an etch-powdering machine, and the Levy line screen. He published and edited the Philadelphia *Evening Herald*, an independent Democratic daily (1887–90), the *Mercury*, a Sunday paper (1887–91), and *The Jewish Year* (1895). Levy was a leader of the Philadelphia Jewish community and, reflecting his deep interest in the problems of Jewish immigration to the U.S., was a founder (1884) and president of the Association for Relief and Protection of Jewish Immigrants. He wrote *The Russian Jewish Refugees in America* (1895), a pamphlet; *Business, Money and Credit* (1896); and (with Hugo Bilgram) *The Cause of Business Depressions as Disclosed by an Analysis of the Basic Principles of Economics* (1914).

LEVY, LUCIEN (1853–1912), French mathematician. He was born in Paris, and taught mathematics at the Lycée Louis le Grand. He wrote many articles and contributed to the French edition of the *Mathematical Encyclopedia*; he published textbooks and two works on applied mathematics. From 1910 to 1911 he was president of the Mathematical Society of France. His son PAUL LEVY (1886–1971) became a high official in the administration of mines (1925). In 1941 after the occupation of France by the Nazis, he was exempted from the anti-Jewish statutes because of his distinguished work and permitted to teach both at the Ecole Polytechnique and at the Ecole Supérieure de Mines. He published several textbooks. In 1964 he became president of the Mathematical Society of France.

LEVY, MARION JOSEPH, JR. (1918–2002), U.S. sociologist. Born in Galveston, Texas, Levy received a doctorate in sociology from Harvard University. During World War II he served as a Navy lieutenant in Asia. He was professor of sociology at Princeton University from 1947. His scholarly work was devoted to the study of the family and to the investigation of social and cultural change in the Far East, both within the framework of system analysis, serving for a time as chairman of Princeton's department of East Asian studies. He further formulated the concepts, propositions, and methodological premises of the structural-functional approach to social phenomena in his major work, *Structure of Society* (1952). He retired in 1989 as Musgrave Professor of Sociology and International Affairs at Princeton. His other works include *The Family Revolution in Modern China* (1949), *Rise of the Modern Chinese Business Class* (1949), *Aspects of the Analysis of Family Structure* (1965), *Modernization and the Structure of Societies*, 2 vols. (1966), *Modernization: Latecomers and Survivors* (1972), *Our Mother-Tempers* (1989), and *Maternal Influence: The Search for Social Universals* (1992).

[Werner J. Cahnman / Ruth Beloff (2nd ed.)]

LEVY, MARV (Marvin Daniel; 1925–), U.S. football coach, only NFL coach to win four straight league or conference championships; member of the Pro Football Hall of Fame. Levy was the older of two children born on Chicago's South Side to Sam, an immigrant from England who ran a wholesale produce company, and Ida, from Russia. The day after graduating from South Shore High School in 1943, Levy enlisted in the Army Air Corps and spent the remainder of World War II in the military. He was a Phi Beta Kappa graduate of Coe College in 1950, and then received a master's degree in English history from Harvard in 1951. After 15 years of coaching college ball, Levy entered the NFL as special teams coach of the Eagles (1969), Rams (1970), and Redskins (1971–72), and then left the NFL to become head coach of the Montreal Alouettes of the Canadian Football League. His CFL record was 43–31–4 in five seasons, as the team went to the playoffs all five years and won the Grey Cup in 1974 and 1977. Levy returned to the NFL in 1978 as head coach of the Kansas City Chiefs, where he went 31–42 in five seasons. Levy took over the Chicago team in the U.S. Football League in 1984, and was then hired by the Buffalo Bills during the 1986 season. It took Levy only two years to lead the Bills to the 1988 AFC Championship game, earning Levy Coach of the Year honors. The Bills won the Eastern Division six of the next eight seasons, and made the playoffs eight of the next nine years; Levy was named AFC Coach of the Year in 1988, 1993, and 1995. Levy and the Bills would become the only team in NFL history to play in four straight Super Bowls (1991–94). He retired after the 1997 season, compiling a 112–70 record (123–78 including playoffs) as the Bills' coach, and 143 NFL coaching victories overall, which ranked 10th in history at the time of his retirement. In addition, Levy is one of only 14 coaches to win 100 games with one NFL team. Levy was voted into the Pro Football Hall of Fame in 2001, one of six Jews enshrined along with Sid *Gillman, Sid *Luckman, Ron *Mix, Al *Davis, and Benny *Friedman. He is the author of an autobiography, *Where Else Would You Rather Be?* (2004).

[Elli Wohlgelernter (2nd ed.)]

LEVY, MARVIN DAVID (1932–), U.S. composer. Born in Passaic, New Jersey, Levy studied composition with Philip James at New York University (B.A., 1954) and with Otto Luening at Columbia University (M.A., 1956). From 1952 to 1958 he was a musical critic for various newspapers and journals. He composed three successful one-act operas: *The Tower* (first performance Sante Fe, 1957), *Escorial* (first performance New York, 1958) and *Mourning Becomes Electra*, based on O'Neill's play and commissioned by the Metropolitan, New York, for their opening Lincoln Center season (first performance, March 1967). In 1967, Levy received the Scroll of the City of New York for "distinguished and exceptional service." He was a founding member of the Fort Lauderdale Opera, Florida (1989), and served as its artistic director until it merged with the Greater Miami Opera to form the Florida Grand Opera in 1994. He also composed two cantatas: *The Echoes* and *One Person; Chassidic Suite* for horn and piano; *Rhapsody* for violin, clarinet, and harp; songs; music for films; incidental music for Farquhar's *The Recruiting Officer* and *Trialogues*.

BIBLIOGRAPHY: Grove online.

[Israela Stein (2nd ed.)]

LEVY, MICHAEL ABRAHAM, BARON LEVY OF MILL HILL (1944–), British businessman and communal leader. Born in Hackney, Levy became an accountant and made a fortune as the head of Magnet Records, where he discovered Alan Stardust and Chris Rea, selling it for a reported £10 million and then founding M&G Records. He became prominent as one of the biggest fundraisers for the Labour Party and a close friend of British Prime Minister Tony Blair, who used him as his personal advisor on the Middle East. Levy was also very prominent within Britain's Jewish community as the head of Jewish Care from 1998 and many other philanthropic and educational bodies. He was also the chairman of CSV (Community Service Volunteers), the largest organization of community service volunteers in Britain. He was given a life peerage in 1997 and received an honorary degree from Middlesex University.

[William D. Rubinstein (2nd ed.)]

LEVY, MOSES (c. 1665–1728), New York merchant and landowner. Levy arrived from England sometime before 1695. In that year he was made a freeman of the city, enabling him to embark on a noteworthy mercantile career and became probably the most prominent and wealthiest New York Jew of the early 18th century. He was elected constable in 1719, but paid a fine rather than serve. President of the Jewish congregation of New York shortly before his death, Levy contributed to the building of Shearith Israel on Mill Street, but did not live to see its completion.

BIBLIOGRAPHY: J.R. Rosenbloom, *Biographical Dictionary of Early American Jews* (1960), 94.

[Leo Hershkowitz]

LEVY, MOSES (1757–1826), U.S. judge. Born in Philadelphia, Levy was the son of Samuel Levy, a Philadelphia merchant. In 1778 he was admitted to the Philadelphia bar, the first Jew to qualify as a lawyer in the United States. Levy became one of the outstanding lawyers of Philadelphia and was one of the defense counsel in the trial of Bache, editor of the anti-federalist *Aurora* for "libeling the President and the Executive Government in a manner tending to excite sedition and opposition to the laws." From 1802 to 1806 he was a member of the Pennsylvania legislature and subsequently was a judge of the district court of Philadelphia. Levy acquired a considerable reputation in the legal profession and at one time was considered for the post of attorney general of the United States. When he died the members of the Philadelphia bar wore a black armband for 30 days.

BIBLIOGRAPHY: H.S. Morais, *Jews of Philadelphia* (1894), index.

[Julius J. Marcke]

LEVY, MOSES ELIAS (c. 1782–1854), pioneer Jewish settler in Florida, visionary exponent of Jewish colonization and educational schemes, and father of the first congressman and senator of Jewish birth, David L. *Yulee. Levy led a life which was fascinating in its variety. Born in Mogador, Morocco, and brought up in Gibraltar, Levy settled in St. Thomas, Virgin Islands, about 1800, achieving some success in business. He left St. Thomas and moved to Havana, Cuba, where he established himself as a government contractor and invested heavily in real estate which was located in Florida (then still under Spanish rule). After the cession of Florida to the United States in 1821, Levy took up residence in the new American territory and registered for American citizenship. Levy developed a number of plantations in Florida but never succeeded in attracting the settlers, including Jews, he had envisaged. In 1821 he also undertook a campaign for the establishment of a Jewish boarding school, which, however, aroused little interest. It is ironic that this champion of Jewish education so alienated his two sons that the one, David, eagerly adopted Christianity, not merely for convenience prior to his marriage as some have thought, and the other, Elias, was at one time a missionary minister of the Swedenborgian sect. Levy spent a number of years in London during the late 1820s and engaged in public debate over Jewish theological questions; several pamphlets on various themes of Jewish interest were published in his name at this time. Hard luck pursued Levy's agricultural and mercantile ventures: fire, war, and litigation devoured his assets. The wealth that Florida had seemed to promise always eluded him. Levy had close contacts with a number of important Jewish merchants and communal leaders of his day, including Moses Myers of Norfolk and Mordecai M. Noah and the Rev. M.L.M. Peixotto of New York City.

BIBLIOGRAPHY: L. Huhner, in: *Florida Historical Quarterly*, 19 (1941), 319–45; B.W. Korn, *Eventful Years and Experiences* (1954), 152–3, 199–200; S. Proctor, in: *Proceedings of the Conference on the Writing of Regional History in the South* (1956), 81–115.

[Bertram Wallace Korn]

LEVY, NATHAN (1704–1753), colonial American merchant. Levy, who was born in New York City, moved to Philadelphia in 1738 where he established a business with his brother Isaac. Primarily distributors of dry goods, hardware, and general goods, the brothers also placed indentured servants with employers, and, to a limited extent, traded slaves. He and his brothers are the first known practicing Jews to settle in Philadelphia. In 1741 Nathan and Isaac Levy formed a partnership with David and Moses Franks, which entered the shipping business. As a founder of Philadelphia's Jewish community, he obtained land for its first Jewish cemetery in 1740.

[Neil Ovadia]

LÉVY, PAUL (1887–1962), French linguist and historian. Lévy, who was born in Alsace, became a specialist on the linguistic history of Alsace and Lorraine and taught at the Lycée Kléber in Strasbourg. From 1933 he taught at the Lycée Rollin (later Jacques Ducour) in Paris. During the German occupation of France in World War II he refused an offer of exceptional reinstatement in his post. After the war, Lévy directed the investigation of the secret archives of the Third Reich. Among his major works were *Histoire linguistique d'Alsace et de Lorraine* (1929), *La Langue allemande en France* (1950–52), and *Les Noms des Israélites en France* (1960).

[Irwin L. Merker]

LÉVY, RAPHAËL (c. 1612–1670), victim of a *blood libel in France. Born in Chelaincourt, near Metz, Lévy was a livestock merchant in the village of Boulay, though the anonymous Christian account of his trial describes him as "filling the office of rabbi" there. He was accused of having abducted a Christian child in the village of Glatigny, on the eve of Rosh Ha-Shanah 1669, when he was on his way to Metz to buy a *shofar*. Giving himself up voluntarily ("to save the house of Israel"), he was condemned to death by the *parlement* of Metz after a scandalous trial, even though the remains of the child, devoured by wolves, had in the meantime been found. On Jan. 17, 1670, he was burned at the stake in Metz. The tribunal also demanded the permanent expulsion of the Jews from Metz. The latter belatedly laid the affair before the royal council which, on the basis of an address by Richard *Simon, concluded that there had been a judicial error.

BIBLIOGRAPHY: J. Reinach, *Raphaël Lévy, une erreur judiciaire sous Louis XIV* (1898); R. Clément, *Condition des juifs de Metz* (1903), 52–66.

[Gilbert Cahen]

LEVY, REUBEN (1891–1966), British Orientalist. Born in Manchester, Levy became lecturer in Persian language and literature at Oxford University (1920–23). From 1923 to 1926 he taught biblical literature at the Jewish Institute of Religion, New York. On his return to England he taught Persian at Cambridge University; he was appointed professor in 1950. During both world wars Levy served in British Intelligence. From 1918 to 1920 he was in the Iraqi political service.

Apart from editing and translating a number of classical Persian and Arabic texts, Levy wrote two textbooks: *The Persian Language* (1951) and *Persian Literature* (1923; repr. 1955), a two-volume work *Introduction to the Sociology of Islam* (1931–33; second edition, *The Social Structure of Islam*,

1957), and a commentary with introduction on *Deutero-Isaiah* (1925).

LEVY, ROBERT (1896–1996), journalist and leader of the Jewish community in Chile. Born in Strasbourg, France, Levy immigrated in the 1910s to Chile. In 1940 he took part in the establishment of the Comité Central (Central Committee) of Jewish local institutions, named afterwards Comité Representativo de las Entidades Judías de Chile. He was its secretary general from its foundation until 1983. He was also very active in many community institutions, among them the Sephardi community, the Confraternidad Judeo-Cristiana (Jewish-Christian Friendship Organization), and the Instituto Chileno-Israelí de Cultura (Chilean-Israeli Cultural Institute).

[Efraim Zadoff (2nd ed.)]

LEVY, RUDOLF (1875–1944), German painter. Levy, who was born into an Orthodox Jewish family in Stettin (Pomerania), studied cabinetmaking in Berlin and Karlsruhe, and painting in Munich. In 1903 he went to Paris; he joined the group of artists who met regularly at the Café du Dôme, where the circle of artists, poets, and newsmen campaigned for French art in Germany. In 1907 Levy met Henri Matisse by whom he was strongly influenced, and in 1908 the idea of the Académie Matisse was realized. Levy also accepted the direction of the Académie for a couple of months until it was finally closed in 1912. Presumably from 1914, Levy was a member of the "Berliner Secession," participating in their exhibitions with his paintings; in 1928 he even became chairman of this society. During World War I, Levy served in the German army and received the Iron Cross. After the war he settled in Berlin but in 1933 left Germany. In 1935 he settled on the Spanish island of Mallorca and joined the circle of political emigrants, among them Arthur Segal. From 1938 he lived in Italy, settling in Florence.

Though forewarned by the German consul and by the Italian police, Levy remained in his atelier and in December 1943 was arrested by the Gestapo. He died in January 1944, presumably during the transportation to the camp in Modena, on the way to the concentration camps in the north. Levy was one of the few German painters of his generation who did not join the expressionist movement, but remained under the influence of Matisse and Cézanne. His work, lyrical in nature, was molded by the Mediterranean atmosphere which inspired some of his finest oils.

BIBLIOGRAPHY: W. Haftmann, *Painting in the Twentieth Century*, 1 (1965^2), 79–80, 401–2; 2 (1965^2), 295. **ADD. BIBLIOGRAPHY:** G. Fiedler-Bender (ed.), *Matisse und seine deutschen Schueler* (1988); B. Leismann (ed.), *Die grosse Inspiration III. Deutsche Kuenstler in der Académie Matisse*, Exh. cat. Kunst-Museum Ahlen (2005); S. Thesing, *Rudolf Levy: Leben und Werk* (1990, with catalogue raisonné).

[Alfred Werner / Jihan Radjai-Ordoubadi (2nd ed.)]

LEVY, SAM SAADI (1870–1959), journalist. Levy was born in *Salonika, but at an early age he went to live in Paris, returning in 1898 to Salonika, where he collaborated in the periodicals *La Epoca* (Judeo-Spanish), founded in 1875, and *Journal de Salonique* (French), founded in 1895. He also wrote and edited the most brilliant part of the satirical *El Kirbatch* ("The Riding Whip"), which was very popular with the public. In 1905, wishing to escape all censorship, he settled in Zemlin (Austria) where he founded two periodicals, *Le Rayon* (French) and *El Luzero* (Judeo-Spanish), both intended to be circulated in Turkey. With the Young Turk revolution of 1908, he returned to Salonika, again taking up the editorship of *La Epoca* and *Journal de Salonique*. In 1912, with the Hellenization of northern Greece, he sold his newspapers. He then settled first in Lausanne, and later on in Paris, where he set up the *Guide Sam*, a publication which for years constituted the directory of all industrial and commercial enterprises in the Near East. In Paris, he also founded the *Cahiers Sefardis*, in which many historical, social, and economic studies on the Jewish communities of the Near East were published.

[Joseph Neipris]

LÉVY, SAMUEL (b. 1678), rabbi and financier. After studying in Metz and in Poland, in 1702 Lévy was appointed rabbi of Upper Alsace (later the Haut-Rhin department) by Louis XIV and served there until 1709. Subsequently he engaged in financial transactions, purchasing abroad corn and species on behalf of Duke Leopold of Lorraine. In 1715 Lévy was appointed tax-collector for Lorraine, where he effected cuts in public expenditure and introduced new taxes which antagonized the nobility. In 1716 he was removed from office at the instigation of his opponents and faced total bankruptcy. His creditors, whose claims amounted to three million livres, had him arrested, together with his wife. He was imprisoned for several years; following his release in 1722, he was expelled from Lorraine and moved to Paris, where he died in abject poverty.

BIBLIOGRAPHY: H. Baumont, *Etudes sur le règne de Léopold* (1894), 400f., 493–4; M. Aron, in: REJ, 34 (1897), 107–16; M. Ginsburger, *ibid.*, 65 (1913), 274–300; 66 (1913), 263–84; 67 (1914), 82–117, 262–87; 68 (1915), 84–109; C. Pfister, *Histoire de Nancy*, 3 (1909), 316–7.

[*Encyclopaedia Judaica* (Germany)]

LEVY, SION (1922–), rabbi, spiritual leader of the Jewish community of Panama. Born in the Old City of Jerusalem to a family of rabbinical ancestry from Morocco, he studied in the Yeshivat Porat Yosef in Jerusalem for 12 years, together with Rabbi Ovadiah *Yosef. After being ordained as a rabbi and as a *shoḥet*, he was appointed as head of the *kashrut* department in the Jerusalem rabbinate. In 1955 he was sent to Panama, remaining there as the Sephardi rabbi and spiritual leader.

Rabbi Levy imposed strict Orthodox norms on the Sephardi community, Sociedad Israelita de Beneficencia Shevet Ahim. Serving as a *shoḥet*, he controlled the slaughter of animals according to strict halakhic rules. The arrival of a large group of immigrants from Aleppo (Syria), with a long tradition of rabbinical authority, strengthened the position of Rabbi

Levy in the Panama Jewish community. The Aleppans, who became the majority group among the Jews of Panama, venerate their rabbi, whose word is received as sacred not only in religious matters but also in economic and social questions.

Levy is a prominent Zionist leader but a tough opponent of Reform Judaism.

[Margalit Bejarano (2nd ed.)]

LEVY, URIAH PHILLIPS (1792–1862), U.S. naval officer. Levy was born in Philadelphia, into a distinguished family of U.S. patriots. Running away to sea at ten, he became a sailing master in the United States navy at 20 and a midshipman four years later. Commissioned as lieutenant in 1816 and captain in 1844, he saw little active duty in the years 1827–57 because of disciplinary problems. In 1857 he was reinstated by a naval Court of Inquiry and ordered to the Mediterranean, where in 1859 he served for six months as commodore of the U.S. fleet. Most of what is known about Levy is from the record of six court-martials and the proceedings of his fight against an order in 1855 dropping him from the navy lists, together with 200 fellow officers. He was certainly an excellent sailor, a good disciplinarian, a progressive officer, and a brave patriot. He was also extremely sensitive about his Jewishness, exhibited some peculiar mannerisms, and was extremely pugnacious. The proceedings established beyond a doubt that his career had suffered because of antisemitism. On the other hand, any officer with his record of six court-martials and his unorthodox methods of maintaining discipline might have had the same difficulties. Moreover, he had begun his career as a sailing master, unlike the "gentlemen" who received their commission as midshipmen directly. In spite of these handicaps and an array of petty accusations against him, an imposing list of high naval officers testified to his honorable character and his professional ability. Levy's greatest liability, so far as popularity with his fellow officers went, but his greatest claim to lasting fame as well, was his active espousal of a law to prohibit corporal punishment in the navy. Senator John Parker Hale sponsored such a bill (1850), and Levy was one of a small group of naval officers who supported him. Indeed, Levy had long previously advocated such a change, not only in numerous writings, but as captain of the s.s. *Vandalia*, the first ship to sail with discipline maintained without recourse to the lash. Levy wrote extensively on the problems of naval discipline. He also published *A Manual of Informal Rules and Regulations for Men-of-War* and several navigation charts. While on active duty, he found time to explore the Rio Grande from Veracruz as far up as Matamores. During his years of inactive service Levy acquired, and at great expense refurbished, Thomas Jefferson's estate at Monticello, which eventually became the summer home of his nephew, J.M. *Levy, until purchased by a public organization and made into a historic monument. His mother is buried along the walk approaching the main house. During the 1855 proceedings, Levy testified that his "parents were Israelites and I was nurtured in the faith of my ancestors." He was a member of Congregation Shearith Israel in New York and a charter member of Washington Hebrew Congregation. He sponsored (1854) the new Seminary of the Bnai Jeshurun Educational Institute in New York. Levy received a traditional Jewish funeral and is buried in the Cypress Hill Cemetery of Congregation Shearith Israel in Brooklyn, New York.

BIBLIOGRAPHY: A. Kanof, in: AJHSP, 39 (1949/50), 1 66.

[Abram Kanof]

LEVY-BACRAT, ABRAHAM BEN SOLOMON (late 15th–16th century), poet of Spanish origin. Bacrat took refuge in North Africa in 1492. In his native town of Malaga he had been a disciple of Judah Gabbai, to whom he dedicated several poems. At first he settled in *Tlemcen, together with Abraham *Benzamero, Abraham *Gavison, and Moses *Alashkar. He wrote an elegy on the Spanish Expulsion. His major work, a supercommentary on Rashi, is called *Sefer ha-Zikkaron* ("Book of the Memory") and was completed in 1507 in Tunis, where he became a close friend of Abraham *Zacuto. This work was known from its copies but it remained in manuscript until its publication in Leghorn in 1845. The author's introduction contains an instructive autobiography which contains information on Bacrat's tribulations after the Spanish Expulsion.

BIBLIOGRAPHY: D. Cazès, *Notes bibliographiques sur la littérature juive-tunisienne* (1893), 234–6; H.H. Ben-Sasson, in: *Tarbiz*, 31 (1962), 59–71; Hirschberg, Afrikah, 1 (1965), 300, 325.

[David Corcos]

LÉVY-BRUHL, LUCIEN (1857–1939), French anthropologist, philosopher, and psychologist. Born and educated in Paris, Lévy-Bruhl taught philosophy at the Lycée Louis-le-Grand (1885–95), and later at the Sorbonne where he was appointed to the chair of history of modern philosophy. Here he was a colleague of Emile *Durkheim, and wrote a series of anthropological works on various aspects of preliterate culture to demonstrate the nature of primitive mentality. Lévy-Bruhl endeavored to show that the primitives' thought was indifferent to the laws of logic and was essentially mystical. Later in his notebooks published posthumously he retracted this idea and stated that prelogical and preliterate societies would employ logical thought to meet the practical demands of natural environment. Lévy-Bruhl's works on this subject evoked criticism from Durkheim in *Les formes elémentaires de la vie religieuse* (1912; *The Elementary Forms of the Religious Life*, 1947) and from Franz *Boas. Lévy-Bruhl revised this idea in later books but further developed the idea of a "special sense" or mysticism. Although his views on primitive mentality are not accepted, Lévy-Bruhl's theories have had diverse influence on some Jungian psychologists in their interpretations of the relation of archetypes of the unconscious to primitive mentality, and of the phenomenon of "participation."

[Ephraim Fischoff]

His son HENRI (1884–1964), born in Paris, taught law successively at Grenoble, Lille, and Paris until he was deposed during the German occupation of France in World War II. After 1945, he founded with G. Gurvitch and G. Le-Bres the Centre d'Etudes Sociologiques, recreated the *Année Sociologique*, and became one of the directors of the Division of Social Sciences at the Ecole Pratique des Hautes Etudes. Henri Lévy-Bruhl belonged to the Durkheimian School in French sociology; he specialized in the sociology of law, particularly Roman law and the ethnology of law, and he also worked in the field of criminology. Among his major works are *Le témoignage instrumentaire en droit romain* (1910), *Histoire de la lettre de change en France* (1933), *Quelques problèmes du très ancien droit romain* (1934), *Initiation aux recherches de sociologie juridique* (1947), and *Aspects sociologiques du droit* (1955).

[Werner J. Cahnman]

BIBLIOGRAPHY: *Les carnets de Lucien Lévy-Bruhl* (1949), preface; J. Cazeneuve, *Lucien Lévy-Bruhl, sa vie, son oeuvre, avec un exposé de sa philosophie* (1963), incl. bibl.; idem, in: IESS, 9 (1968), 263–6; *Mélanges Henri Lévy-Bruhl* (1959), incl. bibl.

LÉVY-DHURMER, LUCIEN (1865–1953), French symbolist painter. Lévy-Dhurmer was born in Algiers. He trained as a lithographer and decorator; among his finest works in this genre are the two panels painted for the furniture designer Majorelle, now in the Metropolitan Museum, New York. From 1887 to 1895 Lévy-Dhurmer was artistic director of a decorative stoneware factory at Golfe-Juan, France, but after a visit to Italy he decided to follow a career of painting. An exhibition of his work at Galérie George Petit, Paris, established his reputation. His principal subjects were mythical themes, but he was also a gifted portrait painter, and was greatly in demand in this genre and was also a decorative muralist. Many of his most famous works were inspired by the music of Beethoven, Debussy, and Fauré, as well as by the Mediterranean in general. He was much admired for his original color sense, especially in his pastels. Lévy-Dhurmer is considered one of the most gifted of the French symbolist painters. An important collection of Lévy-Dhurmer's work is in the Musée National d'Art Moderne, Paris. His work has been greatly admired in recent years, as part of the revival of interest in 19th-century painting in general and symbolism in particular.

[Charles Samuel Spencer]

LEW, JACOB (1955–), director of the U.S. Office of Management and Budget 1998–2001. Born in New York City, the son of a Polish immigrant, he received his B.A. from Harvard (1978) and his law degree from Georgetown. He had an early interest in politics and worked for Bella Abzug while still in school. While in law school, he worked for Speaker of the House Thomas "Tip" O'Neill as his domestic policy aide. He then served as a senior adviser to O'Neill and as executive director of the House Democratic Steering and Policy Committee. He was O'Neill's chief policy adviser on Social Security when the government tackled the nation's largest entitlement program, in 1983. When O'Neill left the House, Lew went into private legal practice and then worked with Michael Dukakis in 1988 as the issues director for his unsuccessful presidential campaign. An observant Jew, Lew felt comfortable working at the center of the American government while remaining faithful to his tradition. He joined the Clinton administration and went from a special assistant to the president at the OMB to its deputy director and from 1998 to 2001 as its director, a position that has cabinet rank. During Lew's time, Jews held virtually all of the principal economic positions, from the secretary of the Treasury and his deputy to the head of OMB, Council of Economic Advisors, and the Federal Reserve. It was a first in the federal government. After he left the administration he was named executive vice president of New York University.

BIBLIOGRAPHY: L.S. Maisel and I. Forman, *Jews in American Politics* (2001).

[Michael Berenbaum (2nd ed.)]

LEWALD, FANNY (1811–1889), German writer and publicist. Born in Koenigsberg as Fanny Markus, her Jewish merchant father changed the family name to Lewald once the family converted to Protestantism in 1828. In 1843 Fanny Lewald moved to Berlin, where she kept company with Varnhagen von Ense, Henriette Herz, Luise Muehlbach, Heinrich Laube, and especially with Therese von Bacheracht. Her first novels appeared anonymously already in 1842, such as *Clementine*, *Jenny* (1843), and *Eine Lebensfrage* (2 vols., 1845). *Clementine* broaches the issue of married women; *Jenny* taxes the Christian reader on the question of Jewish emancipation. *Eine Lebensfrage* is a plea for divorce and free choice of a spouse. Lewald was one of the first German female authors to be a successful professional writer. Her novels and her essays treated issues of the day and more than anything female emancipation, as in *Einige Gedanken ueber Maedchenerziehung und Andeutungen ueber die Lage der weiblichen Dienstboten* (1843), *Osterbriefe fuer die Frauen* (1863), and *Fuer und wider die Frauen* (1870). The narration *Sarah* (1851) deals with female as well as Jewish emancipation and remained the only story with a decidedly non-assimilated portrayal of Jewishness. Lewald exchanged ideas with Eugene Niboyet, the publisher of the French journal *Les voix des femmes*, which supported equality in marriage and the right to divorce, education, and work for women. However, Lewald's own writing is nonetheless marked by a discrepancy between this progressive stance and her approval of weak, subservient female characters in her novels, such as Jenny or Clementine. Since she earned her living by writing Lewald had to bow to the tastes of middle-class readers, as in *Die Kammerjungfer* (3 vols., 1856) and *Die Familie Darner* (3 vols., 1888). Lewald became famous for her travel writing, for example *Italienisches Bilderbuch* (2 vols., 1847), in which she combined personal experience with historical and cultural background material. Lewald's political views can be seen in *Die anschaulichen Erinnerungen aus dem Jahr 1848* (2 vols., 1850), which expresses democratic ideas. At the same time Lewald was disillusioned by the revolution in Germany, regretting the strident debates resulting from the polarization of right and left in the Prussian Assembly, which she communicated to Heinrich Heine in the summer of 1848. Her *Lebensgeschichte* (6 vols., 1861–63), written in the tradition of a classical autobiography, *Zwoelf Bilder aus dem Leben* (1888), and *Tagebuch Gefuehltes und Gedachtes* (6 vols., 1838–88) cover historical and political issues of the time.

BIBLIOGRAPHY: K. Stoever, *Leben und Wirken der Fanny Lewald: Grenzen und Moeglichkeiten einer Schriftstellerin im gesellschaftlichen Kontext des 19. Jahrhunderts* (2004); V. van Ornam, *Fanny Lewald and Nineteenth Century Constructions of Femininity* (2002); G. Marci-Boehncke, *Fanny Lewald: Juedin, Preussin, Schriftstellerin: Studien zu autobiographischem Werk und Kontext* (1998); G. Schneider, *Fanny Lewald* (1996); idem, *Vom Zeitroman zum "stylisierten" Roman: die Erzaehlerin Fanny Lewald* (1993).

[Ann-Krisitn Koch (2nd ed.)]

LEWANDOWSKI, LOUIS (1821–1894), choral director and composer. Born in Wreschen, near Posen, Lewandowski became a singer at the age of 12 with *Ḥazzan* Ascher Lion's choir in Berlin. Later he studied with Adolph Bernhard *Marx at Berlin University and with Rungenhagen and Grell at the Academy of Fine Arts. After 1840 he served as conductor of the choir at the Old Synagogue in the Heidereutergasse, and after 1866 at the New Synagogue. Lewandowski, the most significant composer of synagogue music after Solomon *Sulzer, reproduced the traditional melodies in a more classical form and treated the organ accompaniment with greater freedom than did his predecessor. His style, which was more harmonic than contrapuntal, was calculated to appeal to a wide public, and together with the soulful quality of his melodic idiom, gained great popularity for his compositions. The traditional foundations of his work were, on the one hand, the liturgy of the Old Synagogue established by the *ḥazzanim* Lichtenstein and Rosenfeld, and, on the other hand, the East European *nusaḥ* which Lewandowski received from immigrant *ḥazzanim* and singers. Outstanding examples of these influences are his choral work *Ki ke-Shimcho*; and his chief works *Kol Rinah U'T'fillah* (for one and two voices, 1871); *Todah W'simrah* (for four voices and soli, optional organ accompaniment, 2 vols., 1876–82); and *18 Liturgische Psalmen* (for solo, choir, and organ; n.d.). Lewandowski also served as singing teacher at the Jewish Free School and the Jewish Teachers Seminary in Berlin. He rose slowly to a prominence which made him, in the last 20 years of his life, the greatest influence on Western Ashkenazi synagogal music for almost 50 years after his death. Although his recitatives were based mostly on tradition, the choral parts followed the style of Mendelssohn's oratorios and choruses, both in melodic idiom and harmonic structure. The adaptable musical and instrumental settings of his works allow them to be utilized by small ensembles and even by communities without an organ, yet at the same time suiting the large and prosperous centers which had spacious "temples" and professional synagogue choirs, grand organs, and musically trained *ḥazzanim*. Lewandowski's style was early transferred to the Conservative and moderate Reform congregations in the great urban communities of the United States.

BIBLIOGRAPHY: Sendrey, Music, indices; Idelsohn, Music, 269–84; M. Davidsohn, in: *Proceedings of the Fifth Annual Conference-Convention of the Cantors Assembly* (1952), 30–34.

[Bathja Bayer]

LEWENTHAL, RAYMOND (1926–1988), U.S. pianist. Born in San Antonio, Texas, Lewenthal was taken to Hollywood as a child, where he began piano studies, continuing them later in New York with Olga Samaroff, and in Europe with Cortot. He made his American debut in 1948, followed by a period of busy concert giving, which ended in 1953 when he sustained fractures of the arm and hand as a result of being assaulted by thugs in New York. After spending some time in Europe and in Rio de Janeiro as a teacher, he returned to the United States in 1961, reestablishing himself as a brilliant virtuoso with a particular interest in the neglected repertoire of the 19th-century pianist-composers, above all of *Alkan, whose return to public interest was in many ways due to Lewenthal's advocacy (in concert, recordings, and editions published). He gave Liszt cycles in New York (1965, 1966) and London (1967).

[Max Loppert]

LEWI, MAURICE J. (1857–1957), U.S. physician and educator. Lewi held several positions in his native Albany as physician and educator, including that of professor of medical jurisprudence at the Albany Law School, before becoming secretary of the New York State Board of Medical Examiners in 1892, a position he held until 1913. In that same year, he became first president of the First Institute of Podiatry in New York City. The institute became the Long Island University College of Podiatry in 1948 and the New York College of Podiatry in 1955. Lewi edited *Text Book of Chiropody* (1914); *Surgery, With Special Reference to Podiatry* (1917); *Practical Podiatry* (1918); and *Foot Orthopaedics* (1927).

LEWIN, AARON BEN NATHAN OF RZESZOW (1879–1941), rabbi, author, and communal worker. When he was 15 years old, his talmudic novellae were published and, when he was 19, his sermons in *Davar be-Itto* (1899). At the age of 24, he was elected rabbi of Sambor. He subsequently refused invitations from several other communities. Accorded the title of *Kaiserlicher Rat* (crown councillor), he was able to render many services to the refugees of World War I who streamed into Vienna. In 1922 he was elected to the Polish Sejm as representative of the "Jewish bloc" and was a member of its cultural commission. An outstanding speaker, he captivated his audience with his brilliant style. He was one of the leaders of *Agudat Israel, and delivered the opening addresses at its conventions in 1929 and 1937. In 1926 he was elected rabbi of Rzeszow, succeeding his father. In 1931 he was again elected to the Polish Sejm, but in 1935, because of government pressure, he failed to obtain reelection. Lewin participated in every sphere of communal activity in Poland. When the Germans invaded Poland in World War II, he fled to Lemberg and then to Radzyn. He returned to Lemberg, where he was arrested by the Nazis and murdered. As well as his numerous communal activities, he was a prolific writer. In addition to *Davar be-Itto*, he published *Birkat Aharon*, on tractate *Berakhot* (1903); *Ha-Derash ve-ha-Iyyun* on Genesis (1927); on Exodus (1931); on Leviticus (1937); on Numbers (1939); responsa *Avnei Ḥefeẓ* (1934); and "Speeches in the Sejm" in Polish (1926). The second volume of *Avnei Ḥefeẓ* as well as *Ha-Derash ve-ha-Iyyun* on the end of Numbers and on Deuteronomy were lost in the Holocaust.

BIBLIOGRAPHY: I. Lewin, in: *Elleh Ezkerah*, 1 (1956), 40–63; idem, in: L. Jung, *Guardians of Our Heritage* (1958), 583–601; *Kehillat Reisha* (1967), 86.

[Itzhak Alfassi]

LEWIN, ADOLF (1843–1910), German rabbi and historian. Lewin, who was born in Pinne, Prussian Posen, studied in Breslau at the Jewish theological seminary and at the university there, obtaining his doctorate for the thesis *Die Makkabaeische Erhebung* (1870). He served as rabbi at Koschmin (from 1872), Coblenz (1878), and Freiburg im Breisgau (from 1885). Among Lewin's works are a prize-winning essay, "Die Religionsdisputation R. Jechiel von Paris…" (in MGWJ, 18, 1869); *Juden in Freiburg im Breisgau* (1890); and *Geschichte der badischen Juden* (1909). He contributed the section on the historical, geographical, and travel literature of the Jews in the rabbinic period to Jakob Winter and August Wuensche's well-known handbook *Die juedische Literatur seit Abschluss des Kanons* (in: 3, 1896, 287–473). In his many articles and book reviews for Jewish papers and periodicals, Lewin dealt with Jewish-Christian relations and antisemitism as well as with miscellaneous historical subjects.

BIBLIOGRAPHY: M. Brann, *Geschichte des Juedisch-Theologischen Seminars* (1905), 179–80; G. Kisch (ed.), *Breslau Seminary* (1963), 425, incl. bibl.; Koebner, in: *Ost und West*, 10 (1910), 335–7; L. Jung (ed.), *Guardians of Our Heritage* (1958), 581–601.

[Siegbert Neufeld]

LEWIN, BENJAMIN MANASSEH (1879–1944), rabbinic scholar, educator, and authority on geonic literature. Born in Gorodets, Russia, into a wealthy ḥasidic family and orphaned at an early age, Lewin studied at various yeshivot and for a time served in the Russian army. He came under the influence of A.I. *Kook, who was then rabbi at Bausk, Latvia, and served as a tutor in his house. When Kook left to become rabbi in Jaffa (1905), Lewin continued his studies at the Berlin Rabbinical Seminary and Berne University. In Berne he edited the journal for Jewish studies and Jewish religious thought *Taḥkemoni* (1910–11). In 1912 he went to Ereẓ Israel, where he served as a teacher and later as head of the religious schools network Neẓaḥ Yisra'el. He edited volumes 9–14 of Z. *Jawitz's *Toledot Yisrael* (1932–40) and the sixth volume (biblical period) of I. Halevy's *Dorot ha-Rishonim* (1939). He also founded the short-lived Alummah Society for Jewish Studies, for which he edited the publication *Alummah* (1936). Lewin's major and pioneering work was in the field of geonic studies, in particular his *Oẓar ha-Ge'onim* (13 vols., 1928–62), an arrangement – with notes, references, and indexes – of geonic responsa and commentaries in the order of the Talmud tractates (to *Bava Meẓia*). The material for this monumental work was scattered over many works and responsa collections, some retrieved from the Cairo *Genizah* treasures. Lewin also published a critical edition of Sherira Gaon's famous "Epistle on the origins of rabbinic tradition" (1921), and of the early *Ḥillufei Minhagim*… ("Differences of Custom Between Palestinian and Babylonian Jewries," 1937). He also reconstructed from *Genizah* material and early rabbinic literature parts of the lost *Sefer Metivot* (1934). Lewin contributed many articles on the geonic period in learned periodicals, and edited the five volumes of *Ginzei Kedem* (1922–34), devoted to geonic studies, the major part of the contributions being his own.

BIBLIOGRAPHY: Y. Werfel, in: *Sefer ha-Yovel* (1939), 17–32, includes bibliography; Y. Raphael (Werfel), in: *Sinai*, 35 (1955), 66–73.

LEWIN, GERSHON (1868–1939), physician and publicist in Yiddish and Hebrew. Son of a Lublin *ḥazzan*, Lewin graduated from the faculty of medicine of Warsaw University. In 1891 he joined the group around the writer I.L. *Peretz and, encouraged by the latter, was active in propagating popular Jewish culture among the assimilationists. He contributed to the newspaper *Haynt*, and published articles in *Ha-Ẓefirah* and *Ha-Ẓofeh*. Settling in Warsaw in 1895, he participated in Jewish public life and was a member of the executive committees of Ha-Zamir, the Yidishe Kultur-Gezelshaft, and the Jewish health organization *TOZ (Towarzystwo Ochrony Zdrowia). His published works include recollections of I.L. Peretz (1919); *In Velt Krig* (1923), his memoirs as a medical officer in World War I; *In di Alte Gute Tsaytn* (1925), memories of his youth; his reminiscences of Shalom Aleichem (1926); *Iberlebenishr, Epizodn un Ayndrukn fun Rusish-Yapanishn Krig* (1931), memoirs of a physician; and *Dos Bukh fun Mayn Lebn* (1937).

BIBLIOGRAPHY: J. Glatstein, *In Tokh Genumen*, 1 (1947), 213–23; J. Shatzky, *Geshikhte fun Yidn in Varshe*, 3 (1953), 275; LNYL, 5 (1963), 267–8.

[Arthur Cygielman]

LEWIN, JOSHUA HESHEL BEN ELIJAH ZE'EV HA-LEVI (1818–1883), Lithuanian talmudist and author. Lewin was born in Vilna and studied under Elijah *Ragoler. In his youth he was friendly with Mordecai Aaron Gunzberg, Samuel Joseph *Fuenn, and Julian Klaczko. In addition to his extensive talmudic learning, he acquired a knowledge of secular subjects. He married a granddaughter of Isaac b. Ḥayyim of Volozhin, in which town he took up residence. His opposition to the teaching methods at the yeshivah of Volozhin brought him into conflict with its heads, Eliezer Isaac and Eliezer's brother-in-law, Naphtali Ẓevi Judah *Berlin. Lewin had hoped to become head of the yeshivah and to make fundamental changes in its curriculum and direction. When his differences with Berlin were brought before the trustees of the yeshivah, however, they decided against Lewin, who thereupon felt compelled to leave Volozhin. Subsequently he lived an unsettled life. For a year he acted as rabbi of Praga (a suburb of Warsaw). After lecturing in various provincial towns on his new approach to the functions of the rabbi, he went to St. Petersburg and called a rabbinical conference where, with the participation of the *Society for the Promotion of Culture Among the Jews, the founding of Jewish elementary schools was discussed. From 1875 to 1876 he was the preacher at a synagogue in Minsk. Lewin was a supporter of the *Ḥibbat Zion movement, favored the establishment of an Orthodox rabbinical seminary, and initiated with the encouragement and participation of some of the most eminent rabbis of his day the publication of a rabbinic journal, *Peletat Soferim*, of which, however, only one issue appeared (1863). Articles not published in other pamphlets were published by Y. Raphael (see bibliography). In 1882 he succeeded Israel *Lipkin of Salant as rabbi of the Russian community in Paris, but died in the following year.

Lewin was the author of (1) glosses to the *Midrash Rabbah*, published with the commentary of Ze'ev Wolf Einhorn to *Genesis Rabbah* (1835); (2) *Mevasseret Ẓiyyon* (1866), prospectus to his book *Ẓiyyon Yehoshu'a*; (3) *Aliyyat Eliyahu* (1856), a biography of *Elijah b. Solomon, the *Gaon* of Vilna; (4) *Ẓiyyun Yehoshu'a* (1869), parallel passages in the Jerusalem Talmud which shed light on the Babylonian; (5) *Mareh Yehoshu'a* (1869), glosses to the Jerusalem Talmud; (6) *Tosefot Sheni le Ẓiyyon* (1886), passages from the Babylonian Talmud paralleling and clarifying passages in the Jerusalem Talmud; (7) *Davar be-Itto* (1878), a rabbinical anthology; (8) *Mizpeh Yehoshu'a*, an extract from his commentary on *Avot*, entitled *Ma'yenei Yehoshu'a*, was printed in the *Ru'aḥ Ḥayyim* (1859) of *Ḥayyim b. Isaac of Volozhin. His other works remain unpublished. Lewin also published the prayer book *Derekh ha-Ḥayyim* (1845) of Jacob *Lorbeerbaum of Lissa. His planned new edition of the Jerusalem Talmud to include the commentary of Moses b. Simeon *Margolioth (*Penei Moshe*) and his own *Mareh Yehoshu'a* was not realized (see *Ha-Maggid*, 3 (1859), no. 18).

BIBLIOGRAPHY: Ḥ.N. Maggid-Steinschneider, *Ir Vilna* (1900), 277–81; Citron, in: *Reshumot*, 1 (1925), 123–35; Y. Raphael, *Rishonim va-Aḥaronim* (1957), 342–6; idem, in: *Aresheth*, 1 (1958), 327–95; *Yahadut Lita*, 1 (1959), 211f.; 3 (1967), 60.

[Samuel Abba Horodezky]

LEWIN, JUDAH LEIB (1894–1971), Russian rabbi. Born in Yekaterinoslav, where his father, Eliezer Shemuel, was rabbi, Lewin studied at the Slobodka yeshivah. During World War I he became rabbi of the Ukrainian town Grishino (now Krasnoarmeisk, Ukraine), and later, for a short period, rabbi of his native Yekaterinoslav. Because of the high taxes imposed on religious clergy and conflicts with the leaders of the congregation, he gave up the rabbinate and, returning to Krasnoarmeisk, engaged in the work of a religious scribe for various Jewish communities, particularly in Georgia. In 1957, when Rabbi Solomon *Schliefer inaugurated the yeshivah in the Moscow Great Synagogue, Lewin was appointed principal. The head of the yeshivah was, according to official regulations, Rabbi Schliefer himself. Several months after Schliefer's death Lewin was appointed his successor, both as rabbi of the Great Synagogue and as head of the yeshivah. He did his best to fulfill his difficult task – to serve as semiofficial spokesman and apologist for the Soviet policy in matters of Judaism and at the same time to be a genuine spiritual leader to his congregation and refrain from acts and statements blatantly contradicting Jewish interests and the real sentiments of Soviet Jewry (as, e.g., condemning Israel's "aggression against the Arabs"). In spite of his age and poor health, he undertook a journey to the U.S. in 1968 at the invitation of the *American Council for Judaism. In February 1969 the Committee of the Great Synagogue in Moscow invited rabbis from Israel and Western countries to attend the celebration of Lewin's 75th birthday.

[Mordecai Chenzin]

LEWIN, KURT ZADEK (1890–1947), psychologist and author. Lewin, who was born in Mogilno, Germany, was professor of psychology at the University of Berlin until 1932 when he foresaw the rise of the Nazi regime and went to the United States. He taught at Stanford, Cornell, and Iowa universities (1935–45) and organized and directed the research center for group dynamics at the Massachusetts Institute of Technology (1945–47). Lewin was considered one of the most original psychologists of his generation. He was a pioneer in group dynamics; he introduced field theory, and his writings on the nature of causation all were innovations. From his earlier collaboration with the Gestalt school he moved to problems affecting group life. In his books *Principles of Topological Psychology* (1936), *The Conceptional Representation and Measurement of Psychological Forces* (1938), he tried to develop a systematic theory of psychology by a mathematical description of behavior in a "life space," using vectors, geometry, and topology to interpret psychological situations. Lewin applied his dynamic theories to Jewish psychosocial needs. Zionism was to him a sociological necessity. He contended that to belong, develop normally, and have contact with nature, the Jews must have their own country. He visited Palestine several times. He accepted a chair at the Hebrew University, to organize its department of psychology, but the plan did not materialize because of lack of laboratory funds. He then devoted himself to research on the problems of Jewish maladjustment and self-acceptance as a member of a minority group. In 1945 he established the Commission on Community Interrelations of the American Jewish Congress, a research action program to combat antisemitism. He also planned to organize an international Jewish institute of action-research. He outlined plans for a United Nations' international organization of group dynamics. Lewin was associated with Jewish educational work all his life. His philosophy was that "an early buildup of a clear and positive feeling of belongingness to the Jewish group is one of the few effective things that Jewish parents can do for the later happiness of their children. In this way parents can minimize the ambiguity and the tension inherent in the situation of the Jewish minority group, and thus counteract various forms of maladjustment resulting therefrom." In addition to his numerous papers and 70 experimental studies published with his students, Lewin's principal works include *A Dynamic Theory of Personality* (1935); *Field Theory in Social Science* (1951); and "Bringing up the Jewish Child," in *The Menorah Journal*, 28 (1940), 29–45.

BIBLIOGRAPHY: Tolman, in: *Psychological Review*, 55 (1948), 1–4; R. Segalman, "A Test of the Lewinian Hypothesis on Self-Hatred Among the Jews"(1967 – thesis, N.Y. University); J. Rothman, *Minority Group Identification and Intergroup Relations: An Examination of Kurt Lewin's Theory of Jewish Group Identity* (1967); Alfred J. Marrow, *The Practical Theorist: The Life and Work of Kurt Lewin* (1969).

[Menachem M. Brayer]

LEWIN, LOUIS (1868–1941), German rabbi and historian. Lewin, who was born in Znin (province of Posen (Poznan), Poland), graduated from the Berlin Rabbinical Seminary. He served as rabbi in several communities of his native province and neighboring Silesia such as Inowroclaw (Hohensalza), Pinne, Kempen, and Kattowitz (1905–25), and as head of a boarding school in Breslau (1925–37). In 1937 he settled in Palestine. Lewin made important contributions to the history of the Jews in Germany and Poland. He published *Aus der Vergangenheit der juedischen Gemeinde Pinne* (1903); *Geschichte der Juden in Lissa* (1904); and *Die Landessynode der grosspolnischen Judenschaft* (1926). Lewin's numerous studies on local history appeared in learned and regional periodicals. He also contributed articles to the history of Jewish physicians "Juedische Aerzte in Grosspolen" (in JJLG, 9, 1911, 367–420). His valuable library, including many manuscripts, passed to Yeshiva University, New York.

BIBLIOGRAPHY: J. Heilperin, in: KS, 19 (1943), 114–6, a list of his works; A. Heppner and I. Herzberg, ...*Juden* ... *in den Posener Landen* (1909–29), 478, 520, 687, 1032; G. Kisch, in: HJ, 4 (1942), 177–8; 5 (1943), 85.

[Israel Halpern]

LEWIN, NATHAN (1936–), one of America's most highly acclaimed federal trial and appellate court litigators and the Orthodox Jewish community's foremost advocate on legal and legislative issues since the 1970s. Lewin was born in Lodz, Poland, and arrived in the United States, via Japan, in 1941. His grandfather was the chief rabbi of Rzeszow while serving as a member of the Polish legislature (Sejm), and his father, Dr. Isaac Lewin, was the youngest member of the Lodz City Council in pre-war Poland, as well as a renowned activist in efforts to rescue European Jewry from the Holocaust.

Prior to entering private practice, Lewin held a series of high-level positions in the Kennedy and Johnson administrations. Lewin argued 12 cases in the United States Supreme Court while in government service and another 15 in private practice. He was law clerk to Chief Judge J. Edward Lumbard of the United States Court of Appeals for the Second Circuit, and to Associate Justice John M. Harlan of the Supreme Court of the United States.

Lewin graduated *summa cum laude* from Yeshiva College and *magna cum laude* from Harvard Law School, where he was treasurer of the Harvard Law Review. He taught at major national American law schools and regularly contributed to leading publications on constitutional issues. Lewin was involved in the work of a broad array of significant Jewish organizations including serving as president of the Jewish Community Council of Greater Washington (1982–1984); as the national vice president for more than 30 years of the National Jewish Commission on Law and Public Affairs (COLPA), and as president of the American Section of the International Association of Jewish Lawyers and Jurists from 1991 to 1997.

Lewin was the principal architect of the principle that the right of members of religious minorities to a reasonable accommodation of their religious practices is an aspect of freedom of religion. Through his efforts, which included litigation, filing *amicus curiae* briefs on behalf of the Orthodox community and drafting proposed legislation and administrative regulations, that notion now ordinarily permits observant Jews to fully participate in American society, even when their religious practices conflict with standard societal practices. In addition to the substantive results realized by the religious Jewish community, his expertise and commitment are generally credited with enabling the Orthodox community to pursue its own interests in its own way, without having to rely on secular Jewish advocates and groups with different perspectives.

Thus, Lewin brought lawsuits on behalf of Sabbath observers who were discriminated against in private employment because of the restrictions on their availability; on behalf of military chaplains who were denied the right to wear religiously motivated beards; on behalf of an Air Force psychologist who was denied the right to wear a *yarmulke* while on duty; and on behalf of Jewish prisoners who were denied kosher food. He also drafted the provision of the federal Civil Rights Act enacted in 1972 that protects religious observances of private employees, the provision of federal law that enables federal employees to observe religious holidays without financial penalty, the provision of New York's Domestic Relations Law that conditions the issuance of a civil divorce on removal of barriers to remarriage, such as the delivery or acceptance of a Jewish religious divorce, and the provision of federal law that entitles servicemen to wear *yarmulkes*. He also drafted *amicus curiae* briefs in dozens of cases in the United States Supreme Court involving these and related issues.

Lewin defended the process of kosher slaughter in court and the constitutionality of New Jersey's and New York's kosher enforcement law. He has also defended against constitutional challenge the right of communities in New Jersey and New York to construct an *eruv*. He also won a federal appeal entitling the Young Israel of Bal Harbour, Florida, to conduct services, over the opposition of local zoning authorities.

Lewin won in the Supreme Court the right of Lubavitch to maintain a Ḥanukkah *menorah* on public property, and was the attorney for the Satmar community of *Kiryas Joel in defense of a law creating a special public school district for handicapped children in that community. Lewin also represented the Williamsburg ḥasidic community in the Supreme Court in its constitutional challenge in 1976 to a racially conscious legislative reapportionment, urging a rule of constitutional law that the Supreme Court accepted 20 years later.

Lewin initiated the first lawsuit under the federal Anti-Terrorism Act of 1992, giving American citizens who are the victims of terror a right to collect damages from those responsible for terrorist acts, which served as the basis for the legal liability of financers of terror. He also secured the right of an Egyptian Jewish family to sue Coca-Cola for occupying and assuming ownership of the family's property and buildings in Cairo nationalized during the Nasser regime.

Apart from his Jewish-oriented activities, Lewin is also known for his representation of Attorney General Edwin Meese, former President Richard M. Nixon, and various United States congressmen.

[Dennis Rapps (2nd ed.)]

LEWIN-EPSTEIN, ELIAHU ZE'EV (1863–1932), Ereẓ Israel leader. Born in Vilkaviskis (Russian Lithuania), the son of a prosperous bookseller, Lewin-Epstein joined Ḥovevei Ẓion after the 1881 Warsaw pogrom and was one of the founders of the Warsaw *Benei Moshe. Together with Z. *Gluskin, he established the Menuḥah ve-Naḥalah society whose aim was to establish an agricultural settlement in Ereẓ Israel financed by the settlers themselves that would serve as a model in its efficiency and leadership. He was sent by the society to deal with the purchase of land and the establishment of the settlement, called *Reḥovot (1890), and during its early years he was its spiritual leader and head of the settlement committee. One of the founders of the Carmel Society for the marketing of the wine produced in the Ereẓ Israel settlements he visited the U.S. on its behalf and there served as a director of the *United HIAS Service and treasurer of both the Federation of American Zionists and the Provisional Zionist Committee which organized the relief work for the *yishuv* in Palestine in World War I. Lewin-Epstein then settled permanently in Palestine, where he served as a member of the Zionist Commission in 1919. He frequently traveled to the U.S., England, and Germany to promote Palestine Jewish interests. His memoirs, *Zikhronotai*, appeared in 1932.

BIBLIOGRAPHY: D. Idelovitch (ed.), *Rishon le-Ẓiyyon* (Heb., 1941), 304–8; M. Smilansky, *Reḥovot* (Heb., 1950); Tidhar, 1 (1947), 78; S.S. Wise, *Challenging Years* (1949), index.

[Yehuda Slutsky]

LEWINSKY, ELHANAN LEIB (1857–1910), Hebrew writer and Zionist leader. Born in Podberezye, Russia, Lewinsky, like many others of his generation, was swept up by the Haskalah movement in his youth and turned to secular studies, including Russian. Roaming from town to town in the Russian Pale, he supported himself by giving private lessons. In 1880 he registered at the University of Kharkov, but after the pogroms of 1881 he traveled to Palestine and came back an ardent Zionist. He became an active propagandist and organizer of Ḥovevei Zion groups, settled in Odessa, and befriended its circle of Hebrew writers. In 1889 he joined the *Benei Moshe society founded by *Aḥad Ha-Am. He wrote the Zionist utopia *"Massa le-Ereẓ Yisrael bi-Shenat Tat la-Elef ha-Ḥamishi"* in: *Pardes*, 1 (1892), 128–72. In 1896 he became representative of the Palestinian "Carmel" wine company in Russia, and on his travels through various Russian communities, he combined Zionist propaganda with his occupation as distributor of wines from Palestine. He was the moving spirit behind much of the Jewish community work in Odessa. He was one of the founders of the Moriah publishing house, served as treasurer and preacher in the Zionist synagogue, Yavneh, and supported various literary enterprises. He was one of the founders of Ivriyyah, a movement for the revival of the Hebrew language, and also published the first Yiddish daily paper in Odessa, *Gut Morgen* (1910). He gained his place in Hebrew literature through his popular feuilletons. His first articles in this style were published in *Ha-Meliẓ* in 1891–92. Subsequently, they appeared in *Ha-Ẓofeh, Ha-Ẓefirah* in Hebrew, and in *Gut Morgen* under the pseudonym Darshan Zaken ("Old Preacher") in Yiddish. His most important feuilletons appear in *Ha-Shilo'aḥ*, 1–23 (1897–1910) under the title *Maḥashavot u-Ma'asim* ("Thoughts and Actions") and under the pseudonym Rabbi Karov. The high standard of the journal impelled Lewinsky to improve and polish his feuilletons so that although they deal with passing affairs of his day, they have retained their literary value. They are marked by good-natured humor, perceptive response to current events, and extensive use of material drawn from the Midrash and from Jewish folklore. His works were published posthumously in three volumes (1911–13), edited by Ḥ.N. Bialik, J. Klausner, and J.Ḥ. Rawnitzky. The Lewinsky Teachers Seminary in Tel Aviv (originally situated in Jaffa) is named after him.

BIBLIOGRAPHY: J. Klausner, in: *Kitvei E.L.L.*, 1 (1911), V–XXIV; J. Klausner, et al., in: *Ha-Shilo'aḥ*, 23 (1910), 481–589; Lachower, Sifrut, 3 (1932), 39–40, 215; Kressel, Leksikon, 2 (1967), 214–5.

[Yehuda Slutsky]

LEWINSKY, YOM-TOV (1899–1973), Hebrew writer. Born in Zambrow, Poland, Lewinsky settled in Ereẓ Israel in 1935, where he taught for ten years, and then joined the Devir publishing house. A founder of Yeda Am (1942), the folklore society, he remained one of its leaders, and, from 1948, editor of its publication, *Yeda Am*. In the 1920s Lewinsky began writing, in Yiddish and Hebrew, on current as well as historical subjects. In Ereẓ Israel he engaged primarily in the study of Jewish folklore over the ages and published articles on this subject in most of the newspapers and periodicals. His books are *Keiẓad Ḥikku et Haman bi-Tefuẓot Yisrael?* (1947); a memorial book for the communities of *Lomza (1952) and *Zambrow

(1963); *Sefer ha-Mo'adim* (1956 and after, completion of vol. 2 and editing of vols. 3–8; a series of books on the Jewish festivals containing a wealth of material from various sources); *Haggadah shel Pesaḥ* (1960, versions of the **Haggadah* from different Jewish communities, with explanations and commentary); and an encyclopedia of Jewish tradition, customs, and folklore (2 vols., 1970).

BIBLIOGRAPHY: Kressel, Leksikon, 2 (1967), 215–6; LYNL, 5 (1963), 318–9.

[Getzel Kressel]

LEWINSTEIN, JOSEPH BEN ABRAHAM ABUSH (b. 1840), Polish rabbi. Born in Lublin, Lewinstein was rabbi in Chorzele from 1860 to 1868, in Zaklikow from 1868 to 1878, and from 1878 in Serock. He engaged in genealogical and biographical studies and published many articles in this field in *Ha-Ẓefirah, Ha-Goren, Ha-Eshkol*, etc., as well as supplements to the works of other authors (Buber's *Anshei Shem*; Feinstein's *Ir Tehillah*; Riedenstein's *Ir Gibborim*; and Nissenbaum's *Le-Korot ha-Yehudim be-Lublin*). He also corresponded with numerous Jewish scholars in Eastern and Western Europe. He was the author of *Dor Dor ve-Doreshav* (Warsaw, 1900), on the anniversaries of the deaths of outstanding Jewish personalities from ancient times to his own. In addition he published two works by his ancestor Abraham Abush b. Ẓevi of Lissa, both of which he entitled *Birkat Avraham* (Warsaw, 1881 and 1884, respectively). The first consists of novellae to *Eruvin, Pesaḥim, Beẓah, Ḥagigah*, and *Mo'ed Katan* and has an appendix by Lewinstein himself; the second is a commentary on Genesis and on *Avot*.

BIBLIOGRAPHY: L. Owtschynski, *Naḥalat Avot*, 1 (1894), letter Yud, no. 52; B.-Z. Eisenstadt, *Dor, Rabbanav ve-Soferav*, 1 (1895), 36; L. Lewin, *Geschichte der Juden in Lissa* (1904), 188; S.N. Gottlieb, *Oholei Shem* (1912), 365.

[Samuel Abba Horodezky]

LEWIS, (Joseph) ANTHONY (1927–), U.S. journalist. Born in New York City and educated at the Horace Mann School and Harvard (B.A., 1948), Lewis was on the staff at the *New York Times* from 1948 to 1952. He worked briefly as a researcher at the Democratic National Committee in 1952, and was a reporter for the *Washington Daily News* from 1952 to 1955. In 1955 he rejoined the *New York Times*, for which he covered the Justice Department and the Supreme Court. From 1965 until 1972 he was the chief of the *Times*' London bureau, and from 1969 until his retirement at the end of 2001 he wrote one of the most widely read newspaper columns in the country for the *Times*' Op-Ed page.

Lewis won the Pulitzer Prize for national reporting twice, in 1955 and in 1963. Although never formally trained in the law (except for a year at the Harvard Law School as a Nieman Fellow in 1956–57), he lectured on legal issues and the press at Harvard from 1974 to 1989, and elsewhere as a guest lecturer. From 1983 he was a visiting professor at Columbia University's Graduate School of Journalism. He has also been a frequent contributor to the *New York Review of Books*. Lewis' wife, Margaret Marshall, the chief justice of the Massachusetts Supreme Judicial Court, wrote the majority opinion in the 2003 ruling that legalized gay marriage in that state.

As a journalist, the focus of Lewis' interest was on issues of civil liberties, particularly First Amendment (freedom of speech) issues. He won his first Pulitzer for reporting on the Cold War-era federal loyalty program, specifically about a government employee who had been dismissed as a security risk without having been afforded due process (Lewis' articles led to his reinstatement). His second was for reporting on Supreme Court decisions in civil rights cases. He published three books: *Gideon's Trumpet* (1964), the history of the 1962 Supreme Court ruling that all criminal defendants must be provided with an attorney if they cannot afford to hire one; *Portrait of a Decade: The Second American Revolution* (1964), about the civil rights movement and the law in the years after the *Brown v. Board of Education* ruling; and *Make No Law: The Sullivan Case and the First Amendment* (1992), about a landmark case involving freedom of speech, libel, and the press, decided by the Supreme Court in 1964. *Gideon's Trumpet* and *Make No Law* are both regarded as classics of their kind and are frequently used as college texts.

[Drew Silver (2nd ed.)]

LEWIS, SIR AUBREY JULIAN (1900–1975), psychiatrist. Born in Adelaide, Australia, he first became a physician and then, in 1929, a psychiatrist. He studied in the United States under Adolf Meyer. He continued his studies in Germany and obtained a research grant at Maudsley psychiatric hospital in London, where he was appointed clinical director in 1936. During World War II, Lewis worked with military patients and served on service psychiatry committees. He was a member of the Medical Research Council's brain injuries committee and prepared a report for the council on neurosis in wartime. In 1943 he was appointed civilian consultant to the Royal Air Force. In 1946 Maudsley hospital was designated a university teaching center and Lewis was appointed professor. He wrote extensively on diverse topics. His contributions on depression and obsessional states were widely recognized. He also wrote on postcontusional states of the brain "Discussion on Differential Diagnosis and Treatment of Post Contusional States" (1942), and on effort syndrome and postoperative conditions. Lewis maintained that psychiatry should be an integral part of medicine and stressed the potential contribution of the social scientist to psychiatry. He explored many socio-medical and social-psychiatric problems such as aging, occupational adjustment, and public attitudes to mental illness. He contributed to the literature of psychiatric genetics and the history of psychiatry. An example of the latter is "Letter from Britain" (1953). He was knighted in 1959. Among his books were *Inquiries in Psychiatry* (1967), and a collection of essays and lectures *The State of Psychiatry* (1967). Lewis was among the first psychiatrists in Britain given significant positions and honors by mainstream medicine. Thus, in 1952, he became the first psychiatrist appointed to Britain's Medical Research Council.

BIBLIOGRAPHY: M. Shepherd, in: P.H. Hoch and J. Zubin (eds.), *Comparative Epidemiology of the Mental Disorders* (1961), ix–xiv; A. Grinstein, *Index of Psychoanalytic Writings*, 3 (1958), 1228; 7 (1964), 3637. **ADD. BIBLIOGRAPHY:** ODNB online; M. Shepherd, "From Social Medicine to Social Psychiatry: The Achievement of Sir Aubrey Lewis," in: Charles E. Rosenberg (ed.), *Healing and History: Essays for George Rosen* (1979).

[Louis Miller]

LEWIS, BERNARD (1916–), British-born historian of Islamic studies. Lewis received his Ph.D. from the University of London (1939), then served in the British army and was attached later to a department of the Foreign Office. He was professor of history of the Near and Middle East at the School of Oriental and African Studies in the University of London (1949–1974). Subsequently, he was appointed professor in the Cleveland E. Dodge Chair of Near Eastern Studies at Princeton University and a long-term member of the Institute for Advanced Study. He retired from Princeton and the IAS in 1986.

Lewis received many academic prizes and was awarded 15 honorary degrees. His studies have been translated into more than 25 languages. Most deal with Islamic history, chiefly Arab and Turkish, although he also translated poetry from Hebrew, Arabic, Turkish, and Persian into English and served as editor of the second edition of the *Encyclopaedia of Islam*. Among his numerous books are *The Arabs in History* (1950); *The Emergence of Modern Turkey* (1961); *The Muslim Discovery of Europe* (1982); *The Jews of Islam* (1984); *Semites and Antisemites* (1986); *The Political Language of Islam* (1988); *Islam and the West* (1993); *Cultures in Conflict: Christians, Muslims and Jews in the Age of Discovery* (1995); *The Multiple Identities of the Middle East* (1998); *Music from a Distant Drum* (2001); *What Went Wrong: Western Impact and Middle Eastern Response* (2002); *The Crisis of Islam: Holy War and Unholy Terror* (2003); and *From Babel to Dragomans: Interpreting the Middle East* (2004).

ADD. BIBLIOGRAPHY: M. Kramer, "Introduction" to *The Jewish Discovery of Islam: Studies in Honor of Bernard Lewis* (ed. M. Kramer; 1999); "Lewis, Bernard," in: *Encyclopaedia of Historians and Historical Writing* (1999), 1, 719–20.

[Norman Itzkowitz / Jacob M. Landau (2nd ed.)]

LEWIS, DAVID (1909–1981), Canadian lawyer and socialist politician. Lewis was born in Svisloch, Belorussia. His father, Morris, was an active member of the *Bund and maintained his involvement after the family immigrated to Montreal in 1921. In 1931 Lewis earned a B.A. from McGill and won a Rhodes scholarship to Oxford, where he became president of the Oxford Union. On his return to Montreal he was admitted to the Quebec Bar and became a founder of the largely western-based social democratic Cooperative Commonwealth Federation (CCF). He became the party's national secretary in 1936 and for many years the party's sole paid employee. Through the 1940s he ran for a seat in the House of Commons but was defeated on each occasion. In a 1943 by-election in Montreal's Cartier riding he lost to Fred *Rose, who became Canada's first and only Communist member of Parliament.

Lewis resigned as national secretary of the CCF in 1950 and moved to Toronto to practice law. He became legal advisor to several major unions including the United Steel Workers of America's Canadian division, and assisted the union in its battles with the Communist-led Mine, Mill union. But he also remained active in the CCF. He was successively vice chairman, chairman, and president of the CCF. He also helped organize the New Democratic Party (NDP), the more urban-based successor to the CCF, and in 1962 won a seat in the House of Commons for the NDP in a Toronto riding and represented the NDP in Parliament from 1965 to 1974. In 1971 he was chosen leader of the NDP, the first Jewish leader of a major Canadian political party, and in the 1972 election became head of the 31-member NDP caucus which held the balance of power between the governing Liberals and the opposition Conservatives. He propped up the Liberals, holding them to a very progressive legislative agenda. Lewis was defeated in the 1974 election and stepped down as NDP leader and took up a teaching post at Carleton University in Ottawa.

Lewis was active in Jewish affairs and was vice president of the Jewish Labor Committee of Canada, sat on several Canadian Jewish Congress committees, and was on the board of the Canadian Council of Christians and Jews. Although raised in a Bundist home, Lewis warmed to Zionism and the State of Israel after the Holocaust. He helped forge good relations between the Canadian labour movement and Israel. Lewis was honored with the Order of Canada, Canada's highest civilian award.

BIBLIOGRAPHY: D. Lewis, *The Good Fight: Political Memoirs, 1909–1958* (1981); C. Smith, *Unfinished Business: The Lewis Family* (1989).

[Ben G. Kayfetz]

LEWIS, SIR GEORGE (1833–1911), English lawyer. Born in London, Lewis entered his father's firm of solicitors in 1856 and became prominent as an advocate in the London police courts. He appeared in a series of celebrated criminal trials in the latter half of the 19th century and acquired a particularly large practice in financial and libel cases. Noted for his complete discretion, he represented many society figures in divorce and libel proceedings. His clients included such famous figures and litigants as Sir Alfred Douglas, Charles Lawes (of the celebrated libel case Belt vs. Lawes), Adolph Beck, and George Archer-Shee. He was a close friend of the Prince of Wales, and was knighted in 1893 and made a baronet in 1902. Lewis was a prominent advocate of criminal law reform.

ADD. BIBLIOGRAPHY: ODNB online.

LEWIS, HYMAN (**Chaim**; 1911–), author and journalist. Born in London, Lewis edited Jewish periodicals in England and South Africa. Although he wrote verse, Lewis was mainly known for his autobiographical novel, *A Soho Address* (1965), which presents a vivid picture of his Orthodox family and of Jewish immigrant life in London between the world wars. In later life Lewis lived in South Africa, and published a book of poetry, *From Soho to Jerusalem*, in 2000.

LEWIS, I.M. (1930–), social anthropologist. Born in Glasgow, Scotland, Ioan Myrddin Lewis was educated at the University of Glasgow and at Oxford University, where he received a diploma in social anthropology in 1952, a B.Litt. in 1953, and a D.Phil. in 1957. He worked as a research assistant at the Royal Institute of International Affairs in London in 1954 and 1955, then as a lecturer in African Studies at the University College of Rhodesia and Nyasaland in Salisbury, Southern Rhodesia (now the University of Zimbabwe), from 1957 to 1960. Lewis returned to the University of Glasgow as a lecturer in social anthropology from 1960 to 1963, and he became a lecturer in anthropology at the University of London in 1963. From 1982 Lewis was professor of anthropology at the London School of Economics and Political Science and served as honorary director of the International African Institute, eventually becoming professor emeritus of anthropology at the London School of Economics.

Lewis wrote many significant works on African religious and cultural systems, including *Peoples of the Horn of Africa: Somali, Afar, and Saho* (1955); *Pastoral Democracy: A Study of Pastoralism and Politics among the Northern Somali of the Horn of Africa* (1961); *A Modern History of Somalia* (1988); *Blood and Bone: The Call of Kinship in Somali Society* (1994); and *Saints and Somalis: Popular Islam in a Clan-Based Society* (1998).

Lewis's 1971 work, *Ecstatic Religion: An Anthropological Study of Spirit Possession and Shamanism*, became a classic text in university departments of anthropology, sociology, religion, and psychology. Lewis explored in this work the social functions of the notion of spirit possession, as well as the psychological foundations of ecstatic experience, suggesting connections between shamanism and psychoanalysis.

Lewis served as a member of numerous professional organizations, including the International African Institute, the Royal Anthropological Institute, the Anglo-Somali Society, and the Association of Social Anthropologists of the British Commonwealth. He was a Colonial Social Science research fellow in the Somaliland Protectorate from 1955 to 1957, a Carnegie visiting fellow in the Republic of Somalia in 1962, and a British Academy fellow in 1986. In addition to his many books, he contributed to numerous publications, including the *Journal of Modern African Studies*, and he served as the editor of the *Journal of the Royal Anthropological Institute* (formerly published as *Man*) from 1968 to 1972.

[Dorothy Bauhoff (2nd ed.)]

LEWIS, JERRY (**Joseph Levitch**; 1926–), U.S. comedian. Born in Newark, New Jersey, Lewis started his career at 14 and joined Dean Martin to form a successful comedy team. Together they made 16 films and appeared extensively in nightclubs and on television. Their films include *My Friend Irma Goes West* (1950), *At War with the Army* (1950), *Sailor Beware* (1951), *That's My Boy* (1951), *The Stooge* (1953), *The Caddy* (1953), *Living It Up* (1954), *You're Never Too Young* (1955), *Artists and Models* (1955), and *Hollywood or Bust* (1956). After parting from Martin in 1956, Lewis became a successful comedian on his own, and wrote, directed, produced, and appeared in many films. Lewis starred in such films as *The Delicate Delinquent* (1957), *The Sad Sack* (1957), *The Geisha Boy* (1958), *Don't Give up the Ship* (1959), *Visit to a Small Planet* (1960), *The Bellboy* (1960), *Cinderfella* (1960), *The Ladies' Man* (1961), *The Errand Boy* (1961), *It's Only Money* (1962), *The Nutty Professor* (1963), *Who's Minding the Store?* (1963), *The Disorderly Orderly* (1964), *The Patsy* (1964), *The Family Jewels* (1965), *Boeing/Boeing* (1965), *Three on a Couch* (1966), *The Big Mouth* (1967), *Hardly Working* (1980), *Cracking Up* (1983), *The King of Comedy* (1983), *Arizona Dream* (1993), and *Funny Bones* (1995).

In addition to his many television appearances, Lewis had his own variety show, *The Jerry Lewis Show*, from 1967 to 1969. He made his Broadway debut playing the role of the Devil in a revival of the musical *Damn Yankees* (1994–95). In 1995 he won a Theatre World Special Award for his performance. Some of Lewis' other honors include the French Legion of Honor (1984) and the Lifetime Achievement Award in Comedy from the American Comedy Awards (1998). In 1997 he was nominated for the Nobel Peace Prize for his 50 years of raising money to fight muscular dystrophy. In what was to become an annual Labor Day event, Lewis held his first benefit concert for muscular dystrophy at Carnegie Hall in June 1955. The 16-hour show was broadcast on the radio and raised $600,000 for the Muscular Dystrophy Association. In 1966 his first televised MDA benefit was aired over the Labor Day weekend on a TV station in New York City; the 21-hour show raised more than $1 million in pledges. In 1998, his star-studded appeal made history as the first telethon seen around the world via Internet simulcast.

Lewis wrote *The Total Film-Maker* (1971), *Instruction Book for … Being a Person* (1981), and *Jerry Lewis, in Person* (with H. Gluck, 1982).

BIBLIOGRAPHY: P. Lewis, *I Laffed Till I Cried: Thirty-Six Years of Marriage to Jerry Lewis* (1993)

[Jonathan Licht / Ruth Beloff (2nd ed.)]

LEWIS, LEOPOLD DAVIS (1828–1890), English playwright. The son of a London physician, Levy's grisly melodrama, *The Bells*, made famous by Sir Henry Irving's London production of 1871, was an English adaptation of *Le Juif polonais* (1862), by the French writers Erckmann-Chatrian. A London lawyer, Lewis also wrote other plays, including *The Wandering Jew* (1873), and a collection of short stories, *A Peal of Merry Bells* (1880).

ADD. BIBLIOGRAPHY: ODNB online.

LEWIS, OSCAR (1914–1970), U.S. anthropologist. Born in New York City, Lewis was a research associate at Yale (1942–43), a propaganda analyst for the U.S. Department of Justice (1943), and a social scientist in the Department of Agriculture (1944–45). He also taught at various institutions, and, from 1948, at the University of Illinois. Lewis' chief interests were in the fields of cultural change and applied anthropology. His particular contribution was the application of the anthropological method to the study of the urban family unit, especially among poverty-stricken Mexicans and Puerto Ricans. In this connection he originated the idea of the "culture of poverty," a concept that achieved wide currency in the 1960s, a decade of profound social and racial turmoil when the problem of the urban poor became a primary governmental concern. In his research, Lewis made wide use of tape recordings to take down the case histories and reactions of his subjects. His study of a poor family in Mexico City, published as *The Children of Sanchez* (1961), achieved wide popularity both among sociologists and the general reading public. His other books include *Five Families: Mexican Case Studies in the Culture of Poverty* (1959); *Pedro Martinez: A Mexican Peasant and his Family* (1964); and *La Vida: A Puerto-Rican Family in the Culture of Poverty, San Juan and New York* (1966).

[Ephraim Fischoff]

LEWIS, PETER B. (1933–), U.S. businessman and philanthropist. Lewis grew up in Cleveland Heights, Ohio, and graduated from Princeton University in 1955. Upon graduation he began work at Progressive, the insurance firm owned by his father, Joseph Lewis, who had died that year, and partner Jack Green. The company then had 40 employees. At the age of 31, Lewis bought out his father's partner and became chief executive officer of the company. Under his leadership Progressive became the third largest insurance company in the United States. Since resigning as CEO in 2000 (he remained chairman of the board of trustees), Lewis was best known for his philanthropy in education, the arts, and politics, occasionally disagreeing publicly with the very institutions he supports. He and architect Frank *Gehry worked together on several of Lewis' philanthropic efforts, including buildings at both Case Western Reserve University and Princeton University. Lewis was a major donor to the Guggenheim Museum and, as of 2005, was the largest single contributor to the American Civil Liberties Union. He supported Jewish community efforts in both Cleveland and Florida. With George *Soros, he contributed to MoveOn.org, a grass roots political group which unsuccessfully tried to elect a Democratic candidate to the U.S. presidency in 2004.

BIBLIOGRAPHY: C. Dettelbach, "Peter B. Lewis Tells It Like It Is," in: *The Cleveland Jewish News*, 85:3 (July 19, 2002), 24); History of Progressive, http://www.progressive.com/progressive/history.asp; S. Litt, "This Lone Ranger Has Nothing to Hide: Peter B. Lewis, Progressive Corporation Chairman Has Strong Views on Art, Philanthropy, and the City of Cleveland," in: *The Plain Dealer* (Sept. 29, 2002, p. A1).

LEWIS, SAMUEL (1838–1901), British moneylender and philanthropist. Lewis was born in Birmingham, the son of an impoverished dealer, and originally worked as a peddler. He eventually became a successful salesman in jewelry, and from the late 1860s lived in London. In 1869 he began as a moneylender, specializing in making loans to aristocrats and landowners in embarrassing circumstances, often as they awaited their inheritance. From his office in Mayfair, London, Lewis became one of the most prominent moneylenders of his time, known for providing legitimate loans to Britain's aristocrats at competitive rates, often with conditions more favorable than commercial banks. Unlike many moneylenders, he was widely respected for his integrity and discretion, and even moved as an equal in upper class circles. While he attracted his share of hostility, remarkably little appears to have been antisemitic, and his sharpest critic was the Jewish solicitor Sir George *Lewis. At his death Lewis left the vast sum of £2.6 million, one of the largest British fortunes of the time. He and his wife, Ada (d. 1906), were among the greatest philanthropists of their time, giving away over £3 million and founding the well-known Samuel Lewis Trust houses, cheaply rented flats for the working classes.

BIBLIOGRAPHY: ODNB online; G. Black, *Lender to the Lords; Giver to the Poor* (1992).

[William D. Rubinstein (2nd ed.)]

LEWIS, SAMUEL ALEXANDER (1831–1913), U.S. politician and philanthropist. Lewis was born in London, but at the age of six months was brought to the United States. He first devoted himself to business and was so successful that he was able to retire in 1862 and thereafter devoted himself to public life, his first appointment being as school commissioner of New York, of what were then the Ninth and Sixteenth wards, in 1868. In 1874 he was elected alderman-at-large and later, in the same year, president of the aldermanic board, and was reelected in 1876. During this period he served as acting mayor of New York City for six months. In 1877 he declined an invitation to accept nomination as mayor on the Democratic ticket.

Lewis was one of the founders of the Jews' Hospital of New York (now Mt. Sinai Hospital).

LEWIS, SHARI (**Phyllis Hurwitz**; 1934–1998), U.S. ventriloquist, singer, dancer, musician, writer. For all her many accomplishments, Lewis is best known in connection with her longtime colleague Lamb Chop, a sock puppet. Lewis was born in New York City. Her father, Abraham Hurwitz, was a founding member of New York's Yeshiva University. He also played a significant role in his daughter's dramatic capabilities – Lewis began her career in entertainment at age 13, performing magic acts with Jewish content that her father had taught her. Lewis attended New York's High School of Music and Art and also studied at the American School of Ballet. She completed one year at Columbia University before dropping out to begin her career as a performer. In 1952, Lewis came in first for her puppetry on Arthur Godfrey's *Talent Scouts* television show. By 1960, *The Shari Lewis Show* was on the air and she and Lamb Chop were well on their way to becoming two of America's most beloved television characters. Lewis always focused on providing young children with educational and moral content. In addition to her work on television, she wrote more than 30 books and sold thousands of videos. In 1994, PBS revived her original television concept and *Lamb Chop's Play-Along* was back on the air. Of the 12 Emmys that she won throughout her career, five were awarded for the show in its final, revived version. Lewis was diagnosed with uterine cancer in 1998 and died of pneumonia while under treatment.

[Casey Schwartz (2nd ed.)]

LEWIS, STEPHEN (1937–), Canadian politician, diplomat, humanitarian. Lewis was born in Ottawa but raised in Toronto in a political family. Stephen's Polish-born father, David *Lewis, was national secretary of the social democratic CCF Party and an architect of its successor, the New Democratic Party (NDP). From an early age, Stephen was immersed in politics. Dropping out of university he left for England to work for the Socialist International before setting out on two years of travel through Africa. He returned to Canada to help build the newly formed NDP and in 1963, at only 25, Lewis was elected to the Ontario legislature. A riveting and passionate speaker, Lewis was elected head of the provincial NDP in 1970. After a disappointing election in 1971, he dominated the 1975 campaign, winning many first-time party supporters. Elected leader of the Opposition, he forced the minority Conservative government to introduce major social reforms including legislated rent control and workplace safety. When the NDP did not make gains in the 1978 elections Lewis resigned as party leader.

He worked for several years as a labor relations arbitrator and media personality, often speaking out on issues of human rights, the environment, education, health care, and children's advocacy before beginning a new career as a diplomat and international human rights advocate. In 1984 Lewis was appointed Canadian ambassador to the United Nations by Conservative Prime Minister Brian Mulroney, a position Lewis held until 1988. While he was ambassador to the UN, the secretary-general of the United Nations appointed him as his special advisor on Africa to aid in "the mobilization of the international community," and he chaired the committee that drafted a five-year UN Programme on African Economic Recovery. From 1995 to 1999 he served as deputy director of UNICEF. In 1998 Lewis was also appointed by the Organization for African Unity to a panel of "Eminent Personalities" investigating the Rwanda genocide. After years speaking out on behalf of those stricken with HIV/AIDS, he became the United Nations secretary-general's special envoy for HIV/AIDS in Africa and was a tireless advocate for those suffering from the pandemic.

Lewis also heads the Stephen Lewis Foundation, a Canada-based charitable foundation that helps HIV/AIDS victims in Africa. He married journalist Michele *Landsberg.

[Harold Troper (2nd ed.)]

LEWIS, TED (Gershon Mendeloff; "Kid," "Aldgate Sphinx"; 1894–1970), U.S. boxer, world welterweight champion 1915–16, 1917–19; member of the Ring Boxing Hall of Fame and International Boxing Hall of Fame. One of the greatest English fighters, Lewis was born the fourth of eight children to Solomon, a poor Russian immigrant cabinetmaker in London's East End, dropping out of school at 12 to help the family with its income. Lewis began his professional career as a bantamweight on September 13, 1909, six weeks before his 15th birthday, hence the nickname "Kid." He fought for two decades in six weight classes, and he fought often – in 1941 alone he fought 58 times, losing only 3, and 39 more times in 1912 with only 4 losses. While it is difficult to gauge the exact number of fights Lewis fought, boxrec.com accounts for 302, with Lewis winning 230 including 80 by knockout, losing 43, and drawing 22, with seven no-contests. Overall Lewis fought an estimated 400 fights. On October 6, 1913, Lewis won the British featherweight title, and he became the world welterweight champion at 21 with a win over Jack Britton on August 31, 1915. Lewis and Britton had one of the 20th century's greatest ring rivalries, fighting each other 20 times – six times for the title, which changed hands four times – over a six-year span for a total of 224 rounds. Lewis also lost a controversial light heavyweight title bout to Georges Carpentier on May 11, 1922, when Carpentier knocked out Lewis while the referee was still pulling the fighters apart. Nat Fleischer ranked Lewis as the #4 all-time welterweight. Lewis was the first fighter to use a protective mouthpiece, which was developed by his dentist. He is the subject of a biography written by his son Morton, *Ted Kid Lewis: His Life and Times* (1990). Lewis was elected to the Boxing Hall of Fame in 1964, and the International Boxing Hall of Fame in 1992.

[Elli Wohlgelernter (2nd ed.)]

LEWISOHN, U.S. family of industrialists and philanthropists. LEONARD LEWISOHN (1847–1902) was born in Hamburg, Germany, the son of Samuel Lewisohn, a prominent merchant. After arriving in New York City in 1865, he and his brothers JULIUS and ADOLPH (1849–1938), who came from Hamburg to New York City in 1867, founded Lewisohn Brothers. Originally active in the ostrich feather and allied import-export activities, the firm soon pioneered in the development of copper mines in the United States and moved into worldwide sales of copper and lead. Leonard's philanthropies included the Hebrew Sheltering Guardian Society and the Jewish Theological Seminary, as well as general leadership in New York Jewish community affairs.

In 1898, Adolph and Leonard, with Henry H. Rogers and William Rockefeller, formed the United Metals Selling Company. Among the other firms with which Adolph was associated were the General Development Co., the American Smelting and Refining Co., Tennessee Copper and Chemical Co., and Adolph Lewisohn and Sons. Adolph rapidly accumulated a fortune in these enterprises and became prominent in civic, communal, and cultural affairs. He was especially interested in child care, crime prevention, and prison reform and served as president of the National Committee on Prisons and Prison Labor. Adolph Lewisohn was also president of the Hebrew Sheltering Guardian Society for over 30 years, was one of the founders of the American ORT in 1924, and made generous contributions to Columbia University, the Federation for the Support of Jewish Philanthropic Societies in New York, Mount Sinai Hospital, and Brooklyn Museum. He was also a noted art and rare book collector. Adolph's best-known gift was the 6,000-seat athletic stadium he gave to City College of New York in 1915. He stipulated in his will that the college allow it to be used for concerts in the summer, and for almost 50 years (to 1966) it was the setting for inexpensive musical events. Leonard's son FREDERICK (1882–1959) entered the family business in 1898 and participated in the formation of American Smelting and Refining Company and Anaconda Copper Company. His interests also included gold and platinum mines in Colombia and the Lewisohn Copper Corporation of Arizona. Lewisohn was a member of the New York Stock Exchange and a director of the New York Central Railroad.

Adolph's son SAM ADOLPH (1884–1951) was born in New York City. After working briefly as a lawyer, he decided in 1910 to devote himself to his family's mining and financial enterprises. He continued his father's interests in child welfare and prison reform and made distinguished contributions in industrial relations; he was a founder and the first president (1923–26) of the American Management Association and worked with the American Association for Labor Legislation, the U.S. Employment Service, and the New York City Industrial Relations Board. He was actively associated with the municipal reform movement and served as an officer of Citizen's Union of New York for many years. His cultural interests were expressed in art collecting and contributions to the Metropolitan Museum and the Museum of Modern Art. He was prominent in Jewish communal affairs, including the Hebrew Sheltering Guardian Society, Jewish Child Care Association, Federation for the Support of Jewish Philanthropic Societies of New York, and the United Jewish Appeal. Lewisohn was the author of *New Leadership in Industry* (1926), *Painters and Personality* (1937), and *Human Leadership in Industry* (1945). Sam Adolph married MARGARET SELIGMAN (1895–1954), the daughter of Isaac Newton *Seligman. Her principal activities were with the Public Education Association of New York, which she led for over 30 years. She was one of the founders of Bennington College in 1932 and also served as a trustee of Vassar College.

BIBLIOGRAPHY: JE (on Leonard); DAB, 22 (1958), 383–4 (on Adolph); S. Birmingham, *Our Crowd* (1967); B.E. Supple, in: *Business History Review*, 31 (1957), 143–78; *National Cyclopedia of American Biography*, vol. 11, 263–4 (on Sam Adolph); *National Cyclopedia of American Biography*, vol. 44, 148 (on Margaret Seligman).

[Morton Rosenstock]

LEWISOHN, LUDWIG (1882–1955), U.S. novelist and essayist. Born into a middle class Berlin family, Lewisohn was taken to Charleston, South Carolina, in 1890. In his autobiography, *Up Stream* (1922), he wrote of his student years at Columbia University, where he had specialized in English literature with a view to taking up college teaching, but was shocked to find anti-Jewish prejudice barring his way. He was professor of German at Ohio State University (1911–19) and won recognition as a literary scholar with his translation of Hauptmann, Rilke, and Sudermann and critical works such as *The Modern Drama* (1915) and *The Spirit of Modern German Literature* (1916). During World War I Lewisohn's pacifism and pro-German sympathies ended his academic career, which was only resumed 30 years later with his appointment as professor of comparative literature at Brandeis University in 1948. From 1919 to 1926 he was an associate editor of *The Nation*.

Between 1924 and 1940 Lewisohn lived mostly in Paris, where the singer and poet Thelma Spear (1903–1968) kept house for him and maintained a literary salon. Meanwhile, he had become deeply interested in Zionism. He visited Palestine in 1925 and recorded his impressions of its transformation by Jewish colonists in *Israel* (1925). In another volume of autobiography, *Mid-Channel* (1929), and in *The Answer: The Jew and the World* (1939), he told of his discovery of his Jewish heritage and its effect on his outlook. Lewisohn negated the common American assumption that, for Jews, the United States was a home and not merely another exile, insisting that it could never fully replace Zion. The country's non-Jewish majority determined what was American or un-American, and had the power to impose its will and thinking on the Jewish minority. He therefore called upon American Jews to repudiate assimilation and find their way back to their own sources in the land of Israel, where Jews first underwent the group experience which stamped them eternally as a people.

Lewisohn wrote several novels, most of which dealt either with marital problems or with Jewish themes. Among the latter are *The Island Within* (1928, 1968^2), *The Last Days of Shylock* (1931), *Trumpet of Jubilee* (1937), and *In a Summer Season* (1955). His other works include *Don Juan* (1923), *Stephen Escott* (1930), *The Case of Mr. Crump* (1931), *This People* (1933), *Breathe Upon These* (1944), *Among the Nations* (1948), and *Goethe* (1949). He edited *Creative America* (1933), *Rebirth; A Book of Modern Jewish Thought* (1935), *Jewish Short Stories* (1945), and *Theodore Herzl: A Portrait for This Age* (1955). Between 1943 and 1948, Lewisohn was editor of *The New Palestine*, and from 1947, of the *American Zionist Review*. His last works include *The American Jew: Character and Destiny* (1950) and *What is the Jewish Heritage?* (1954). His son JAMES LEWISOHN (1929–) was poet in residence at the University of Maine.

BIBLIOGRAPHY: F.A. Levy, in: JBA, 14 (1956/57), 46–55; S. Liptzin, *Generation of Decision* (1958), 224–33; Chyet, in: AJA, 11 (1959), 125–47; idem, in: AJHSQ, 54 (1964–65), 296–322.

[Sol Liptzin]

LEWITE, LEON (1878–1944), Polish Zionist. Born in Warsaw, Lewite joined the Zionist Movement as a youth. After the revolution of the Young Turks (1908), Lewite made it possible, through a donation of a considerable sum (5,000 rubles), to establish a Zionist political and information center in Constantinople with the participation of Victor *Jacobson, Vladimir *Jabotinsky, and Richard *Lichtheim. With the outbreak of World War I (1914), he moved to Moscow, where he joined the leadership of the Zionist Movement and of the Jewish community. After the establishment of independent Poland (1918), Lewite returned to Warsaw and served in the front line of Jewish and Zionist affairs. He was a representative of Polish Jewry on the Comité des Délégations Juives which represented Jewish interests at the Paris Peace Conference, and took part in the first Zionist conference held after the war in London (1920). Lewite concerned himself basically with practical affairs, especially with the organization of *aliyah* from Poland to Palestine. In 1925 he established a Polish-Palestinian chamber of commerce and remained its president until 1939. His outlook – encouragement of private middle-class initiative and lack of sympathy for the collective and cooperative labor economy in Palestine – placed him among the right-wing *General Zionists. He steered the policy of the Zionist movement in Poland in this direction for many years until the "radical" faction, under the leadership of Yiẓhak *Gruenbaum, prevailed and caused him to resign from the presidency of the organization. The General Zionists in Poland then split, in effect, into two factions: one termed itself Et Livnot ("This is the Time to Build") and remained under the direction of Lewite; the other, Al ha-Mishmar, was led by Gruenbaum. Lewite did not devote much attention to Jewish policy on the Polish scene; he devoted himself mainly to encouraging *aliyah* to Palestine, especially during the years of the middle-class Fourth Aliyah in the 1920s. With the outbreak of World War II (1939) Lewite succeeded in reaching Palestine, where he was completely restricted from public activity by a severe illness.

BIBLIOGRAPHY: I. Gruenbaum, *Penei ha-Dor*, 1 (1957), 193–9. **ADD. BIBLIOGRAPHY:** E. Mendelsohn, *Zionism in Poland, The Formative Years, 1915–1926* (1981), index.

[Aryeh Tartakower]

LE WITT, JAN (1907–1991), graphic artist. Le Witt was born in Czestochowa, Poland, and was entirely self-taught as an artist, claiming that the greatest influences he had known were the beauty of the town in which he grew up and the surrounding countryside. After the death of his father in 1920, he was greatly influenced by his maternal grandfather who had been *Maggid* of the Great Synagogue in Odessa, Russia. At the age of 18, Le Witt left Poland and traveled widely in Europe and the Middle East, working in a series of jobs, including architectural draughtsman, printer's apprentice, and signwriter. Eventually the opportunity to train as a graphic artist determined his future career. He returned to Poland in 1928 and worked in Warsaw as a freelance graphic designer, which led to a highly successful career. In 1929, he designed the first modern Hebrew typeface, called *Chaim*. He traveled each summer to Vienna, Leipzig, Berlin, and the Dessau Bauhaus, where he met Paul Klee, who had considerable influence on him. Le Witt held a one-man exhibition of his graphic work at the Warsaw Society of Fine Art in 1930. He spent 1931 in Paris and tried to study painting. In 1933, back in Poland, he met the German-born George *Him with whom he founded the now famous graphic team Le Witt-Him. In 1937, they moved to London where they continued their successful partnership and were engaged both by government departments and by commercial houses. Le Witt began to devote more and more time to painting, and in 1947 held his first one-man show at the Zwemmer Gallery, London; the following year he designed a ballet for Sadler's Wells. Subsequently, he devoted himself entirely to fine art, exhibiting regularly throughout Europe. He visited Israel on a number of occasions. A book on his work, by Herbert Read and Jean Cassou, appeared in 1971.

[Charles Samuel Spencer]

LEWITT, SOL (1928–), U.S. sculptor, printmaker, draftsman, conceptual artist. LeWitt worked serially, exploring the same concept in several media: books, prints, wall drawings, drawings on paper, and structures (the artist's preferred terminology for his "sculptures"). His June 1967 essay "Paragraphs on Conceptual Art" serves as LeWitt's manifesto: "In conceptual art the idea or concept is the most important aspect of the work … all of the planning and decisions are made beforehand and the execution is a perfunctory affair. The idea becomes a machine that makes the art."

Born in Hartford, Connecticut, to Russian immigrant parents, LeWitt showed an interest in art as a child. He studied art as an undergraduate at Syracuse University (1945–49), learning how to paint and draw figuratively. During the Korean War he served in the United States Army overseas (1951–52). After the war he moved to New York, attending the Cartoonists and Illustrators School (now the School of Visual Arts). A decisive experience of this early period was a year employed as a graphic designer for the architect I.M. Pei (1955–56). LeWitt learned the value in having others implement his designs, a working method he continued to practice. In these years he experimented with painting in an Abstract Expressionist style and making pencil or ink figurative drawings, sometimes after Old Master paintings. LeWitt's first paintings to incorporate text and image were done in 1962. The following year he created several free-standing forms. His first modular pieces were completed in 1965 and a year later he combined the modules serially. With LeWitt believing that art must be neutral to allow the viewer access to the larger form and idea of the piece rather than to elicit emotion, his working materials are abstract and often colorless. LeWitt's final rejection of the traditional canvas and illusionistic imagery occurred in October 1968 when he developed his first wall drawing at the Paula Cooper Gallery, New York. His wall drawings begin as a set of directions for a draftsperson that produces the image, akin to an architect that presents plans to a builder. These detailed instructions delineate all aspects of line and form.

LeWitt designed several projects with Jewish themes, including the monument *Black Form Dedicated to the Miss-*

ing Jews (1989), now located in Hamburg, Germany, after the city of Muenster rejected the piece in 1987. A staid cinderblock wall standing 97½ inches high and 195 inches long placed in front of the city's white neoclassical town hall, LeWitt's painted black monument – without an inscription – is meant to evince the absence of the Jewish community. His wall painting at the United States Holocaust Memorial Museum, ominously titled *Consequence* (1993), is part of the museum's permanent collection. In 2005, LeWitt installed *Lost Voices*, a temporary site-specific sculpture for an abandoned synagogue in Stommeln, Germany.

BIBLIOGRAPHY: S. LeWitt, "Paragraphs on Conceptual Art," in: *Artforum* (1967), 79–83; A. Legg (ed.), *Sol LeWitt* (1978). A. Zevi, *Sol LeWitt: Critical Texts* (1995); G. Garrels (ed.), *Sol LeWitt: A Retrospective* (2000).

[Samantha Baskind (2nd ed.)]

LEWITZKY, BELLA (1916–2004), U.S. dancer, choreographer, educator, and arts activist. Lewitzky, who was born to Russian-Jewish parents near California's Mojave Desert at the socialist commune Llano del Rio, was raised in San Bernardino. At 18, she moved to Los Angeles to dance, joining the Horton Dance Group in 1935. Lester Horton built his technique and choreography on Lewitzky's technical prowess and ability to extend and clarify his ideas, particularly in works like *Salome* (1937) and *The Beloved* (1948). In 1950, after Lewitzky and her husband, architect and former Horton dancer Newell Reynolds, left Horton over artistic and management concerns, her style evolved into non-linear explorations of pure motion that evoked the human condition through the imagery of sculpted, gravity-defying movement.

A renowned master teacher, Lewitzky cultivated dancers of strength, control, and expressive range. From 1956 to 1974, she was dance chair at Idyllwild School of Music and the Arts, and from 1969 to 1974, founder and dean of the School of Dance at California Institute of the Arts. In 1968 she taught for two months at the Batsheva and Bat-Dor dance company schools in Israel. The Lewitzky Dance Company, which she founded in 1966, undertook extensive U.S. and international tours until 1997. Committed to creating and sustaining a company far from the acknowledged dance center of New York City, she employed her dancers year-round at union scale with medical benefits for over 20 years, a rarity in American dance. Lewitzky often sought the challenge of artistic collaborations. Newell Reynolds' transparent plexiglass sheets formed multi-leveled, mid-air dance platforms for *Spaces Between* (1974). Fashion designer Rudi Gernreich created dynamic costumes for *Inscape* (1976).

In 1951 Lewitzky was subpoenaed by the House Un-American Activities Committee for activities that included integrating local ballet schools. "Uncooperative," she was blacklisted from the film work that supplemented her income, enduring several years of intimidation. In 1990 the National Endowment for the Arts began requiring grant recipients to sign an anti-obscenity clause. Guided by conscience and fearing a new era of censorship, she refused to sign, and successfully sued the NEA to eliminate the clause and regained her $72,000 grant. Numerous grants and awards included a 1977 Guggenheim fellowship, a 1997 National Medal of Arts from President Bill Clinton, and five honorary doctorates. She was designated by the Dance Heritage Coalition as one of America's Irreplaceable Dance Treasures.

BIBLIOGRAPHY: R. Eichenbaum, *Masters of Movement, Portraits of America's Great Choreographers* (2004); R.C. Smith, *A Life in Motion*, Oral history of Bella Lewitzky completed under the auspices of the Oral History Program, University of California, Los Angeles, Regents of the University of California (1997); L. Warren, *Lester Horton, Modern Dance Pioneer* (1977).

[Karen Goodman (2nd ed.)]

LEWKO (or **Lewek**), **JORDANIS** (d. 1395), the wealthiest Jew of Cracow (and Poland) in his time; he acted as court banker of the kings of Poland. The son of a wealthy merchant and owner of real estate who lived in Cracow from about 1324, Lewko is mentioned in documents of the early 1360s as the owner of houses and building plots in the city. He apparently amassed great wealth in dealing with these properties and began to lend money to the townsmen and the feudal lords (among others to the princes of Masovia).

King Casimir III the Great, who put much confidence in him, entrusted him with the administration of the royal salt mines of Bochnia and Wieliczka and the mint of Cracow in 1368. In appreciation of his services, the king presented him with two houses in the Jewish quarter of Cracow. Lewko, who also acted as tax collector for Archbishop Bodzanta, who was in charge of the royal estate in Cracow, aroused the anger of the townsmen (1369), but their complaints were rejected by the king. From 1374 Lewko was assisted in the administration of his local affairs by the Jewish agent Gosma. At the same time he entered into partnership with Jewish bankers and merchants in Cracow in order to carry out large loans and commercial dealings. During the early 1380s he opened commercial relations with the Jewish banker of Breslau, David Falken, and his son Israel (or Azriel). The greatest sums of money which Lewko lent were his loans to King Louis I of Hungary and Poland (Louis of Anjou). His financial power and influence at court led the nobleman Clemens of Kuzow to address a complaint against him to Pope Boniface IX (1392). Lewko's heirs were his widow Swenka, his sons Abraham, Canaan, Jordan, and Israel, and his daughter Golda. For about 15 years the heirs worked together in order to collect the debts owed. After that, each managed his business affairs independently. Of Lewko's grandsons Jordan ranked among the leaders of the community of Cracow in 1465.

BIBLIOGRAPHY: I. Schiper, *Studya nad stosunkami gospodarczymi Żydów w Posce podczas średniowiecza* (1911), 115–26; M. Balaban, *Historja, Żydow w Krakowie i na Kazimierzu*, 1 (1931), 17–23; S. Kutrzeba, in: *Przewodnik naukowo-literacki* (1901), 1155.

[Arthur Cygielman]

LEWKOWITSCH, JULIUS (1857–1913), British organic chemist. Born in Germany, he settled in England in the 1880s.

As director of a London research institute he worked on stereochemistry and became the world's leading authority on industrial technology of fats and oils. His *Chemical Technology and Analysis of Oils, Fats and Waxes* (3 vols., 1895[2]) ran into many editions.

LEWKOWITZ, ALBERT (1883–1954), philosophical and pedagogical writer and scholar. Lewkowitz, who was born in Georgenberg (Miasteczko), Silesia, studied at Breslau University and Jewish Theological Seminary, becoming lecturer at the latter in the philosophy of religion and pedagogics in 1914. During World War I, he served as a chaplain in the German army. Taking refuge in Holland from Nazi Germany, he lectured from 1939 at the Ashkenazi Rabbinical Seminary in Amsterdam, but was interned in 1943 at the *Westerbork concentration camp and from there was transferred to *Bergen-Belsen. Surviving the ordeal, he settled in Haifa, where he served as rabbi to the Ahavat Zion congregation (he was an adherent of moderate Reform) and as lecturer at the Even Pinnah Teachers' Seminary; he also taught at the Reali school.

Lewkowitz' scholarly activities date from the publication (1910) of his thesis dealing with *Hegels Aesthetik im Verhaeltniss zu Schiller.* This was followed by studies on neo-Kantianism (in *Zeitschrift fuer Philosophie und philosophische Kritik*, vol. 144, no 1, 1911) and on the classical theory of law and state (*Die klassische Rechts-und Staatsphilosophie*, 1914), and other works. He soon turned to the study of the philosophy of religion and of Judaism in particular, devoting special studies to the relationship to Judaism of such philosophers as *Spinoza, *Mendelssohn, and *Kant. Lewkowitz' major work was *Das Judentum und die geistigen Stroemungen des 19 Jahrhunderts* (1935), which was preceded by two similarly titled articles which appeared in the 1928 *Jahresbericht* ("Annual Report") of the Breslau seminary and in the seminary's 75th anniversary volume (1929). In this work, Lewkowitz compares Jewish and general philosophies and points out their similarities and divergencies. He also wrote *Hauptrichtungen der Paedagogik* (1933).

BIBLIOGRAPHY: G. Kisch (ed.), *Breslau Seminary* (1963), 130, 281, 398f. (bibliography).

LEWY, ISRAEL (1841–1917), rabbi and scholar. Born in Inowroclaw (Hohensalza), Poland, Lewy studied at the Breslau Jewish Theological Seminary. At the opening of the *Hochschule fuer die Wissenschaft des Judentum in Berlin in 1872, he became its lecturer in Talmud. In 1883 he returned to the Breslau Seminary in the same capacity and as *Seminarrabbiner.* Apart from his erudition in all branches of Jewish and general scholarship, Lewy brought a keen analytical sense and conjectural brilliance to the field of talmudical studies. He combined this freedom of enquiry with deep piety and strict observance. Lewy's scholarly output is relatively small in quantity, but terse in style and free of polemics. It mainly appeared in the annual reports of the Hochschule and the Breslau seminary. His important works include *Ueber einige Fragmente aus der Mischna des Abba Saul* (1876), a study in the sources of the Mishnah which has been called a classic example of modern talmudic research; *Mechilta des R. Simon* (1889), a study preparing the way for *D. Hoffmann and J.N. *Epstein in this field; and the first six chapters of *Bava Kamma* in the Jerusalem Talmud, with commentary and introduction (1895–1914). A *Festschrift* in Lewy's honor was published in 1911 (ed. by M. Brann and I. Elbogen).

BIBLIOGRAPHY: M. Brann, *Geschichte des juedisch-theologischen Seminars* (1904), 110, 131 (bibliography); *Jahresbericht des ... Seminars Breslau* (1917), 1ff.; I. Elbogen, in: AZDJ, 8 (1917), 460ff. (bibliography); E.E. Urbach, in: G. Kisch (ed.), *Das Breslauer Seminar* (1963), 177–82 (Heb.).

[Jacob Rothschild]

LEWY, JULIUS (1895–1963), Semitic philologist and Assyriologist. Born in Berlin, he began Assyriological studies with Heinrich Zimmern at Leipzig. After an interruption of five years in the military service, he resumed his studies in Berlin with Friedrich Delitzsch and Eduard Meyer and received his Ph.D. He taught at the University of Giessen from 1922 (professor, 1930). From 1929 to 1936, he was curator of the Hilprecht collection of cuneiform tablets at the University of Jena. Dismissed from his post by the Nazis, he left Germany in 1933 and taught at the Sorbonne in Paris in 1933–34. He then came to the United States and taught at Johns Hopkins in 1934 when *Albright was in Palestine. Lewy became professor at Hebrew Union College, Cincinnati in 1936 and taught Semitic Languages and Bible there until 1963, dying shortly after his retirement.

His principal works are *Untersuchungen zur akkadischen Grammatik* (1921); *Studien zu den alt-assyrischen Texten aus Kappadokien* (1922); *Die Kültepetexte aus der Sammlung Frida Hahn* (1930); and in collaboration with G. Eissler, *Altassyrische Rechtsurkunden von Kültepe* (2 vols., 1930–35). Lewy also published many articles dealing with philological questions, Akkadian grammar, the study of Assyrian-Babylonian religion, and problems concerning the study of Assyrian documents of Cappadocia which were discovered in Kültepe (the ancient Kanish). Lewy's works are of special importance for the study of old Assyrian texts. In this branch of Assyriology, Lewy was one of the most important modern researchers. In several of his works, he discussed problems arising out of the study of the ancient history of the Jewish people and biblical questions; for example *Chronologie der Koenige von Israel und Juda* (1927) and the problems of the Habiru and the Hebrews, on which he wrote in the periodical *Hebrew Union College Annual* (1939, 1940, and 1957). His wife, HILDEGARD LEWY, was also an Assyriologist. She replaced her husband at Hebrew Union College following his death.

ADD. BIBLIOGRAPHY: W. Gwaltney, Jr., in: DBI, 2:59–60.

[Hayim Tadmor / S. David Sperling (2nd ed.)]

LEWY, YOḤANAN (**Hans**; 1904–1945), classical scholar. Lewy studied at the university of his native Berlin. After doing research in Russia, Armenia, and Palestine, he settled in Palestine in 1933, becoming lecturer in classical languages at the Hebrew University. He made his chief scholarly contribution in the field of Jewish Hellenism (e.g., his articles in *Encyclopaedia Judaica* and *Eshkol Enẓiklopedyah Yisre'elit*), with particular emphasis on Philonic studies (*Neue Philontexte in der Ueberarbeitung des Ambrosius* (1932); *Von den Machterweisen Gottes* (1935); *The Pseudo-Philonic De Jona* (vol. 1 only, 1936); *Philosophical writings; Philo, Selections* (1946), repr. in *Three Jewish Philosophers* (1960)). He edited volume 6 of I. Heinemann-M. Adler's *Die Werke Philos von Alexandria* (1938). A collection of his articles on Judaism in the Greco-Roman world appeared in 1960 under the title of *Olamot Nifgashim* ("Worlds Meet"). His untimely death cut short a brilliant scholastic career (see collected eulogies published by the Hebrew University in 1946 with a partial bibliography). A memorial volume, *Sefer Yoḥanan Lewy. Meḥkarim be-Helenismus Yehudi*, edited by M. Schwabe and J. Gutman, appeared in 1949 (with bibliography by M.M. Plessner).

BIBLIOGRAPHY: Kressel, Leksikon, 2 (1967), 183, incl. bibl.

LEWYSOHN, ABRAHAM (1805–1860), Polish rabbi and scholar. Lewysohn, a native of Schwerzenz (Swarzec), Poznania, served as rabbi in Peiskretscham (Pyskowice), Silesia. He belonged to the pioneering generation of modern Jewish scholars, and his *Mekorei Minhagim* (1846), a study of the origin of religious customs in rabbinic literature, was a considerable contribution to scholarship. A shortened version with the same title was plagiarized by J. Finkelstein in 1874. He wrote numerous biographies of *tannaim* and *amoraim*, in both Hebrew and German, and also talmudic novellae, grammatical studies, poetry, and Hebrew and German sermons.

LEWYSOHN, YEHUDI LEIB LUDWIG (1819–1901), rabbi and scholar. Lewysohn, who was born in Schwerzenz (Swarzec), Poznania, taught at Frankfurt on the Oder (1848–51) and served as rabbi and preacher in Worms (1851–59) and rabbi in Stockholm (1859–83). He was a regular contributor to the Hebrew press, particularly *Ha-Maggid*, and also wrote on Jewish subjects in German, English, French, and Swedish. Lewysohn's most important book, *Zoologie des Talmuds* (1858), was the first scientific attempt by a Jewish scholar to collate all talmudic and midrashic references to animal life. He published many addenda to this work, some in Hebrew periodicals and anthologies including *Gan Peraḥim*, 3 (1891); *Ner ha-Ma'aravi*, 1, pts. 1 and 3 (1895); *Kadimah*, 1 (1899); *Oẓar ha-Ḥokhmah ve-ha-Madda*, 2 (1854); *Ha-Mizpeh; Oẓar ha-Sifrut* (1887–1902); and G.A. Kohut (ed.), *Semitic Studies in Memory of Rev. Dr. Alexander Kohut* (1897). Lewysohn also published a book of epitaphs from the Jewish cemetery of Worms, *Nafshot Ẓaddikim* (Ger., 1855); sermon collections in German and Swedish; and textbooks.

BIBLIOGRAPHY: M. Reines, *Dor va-Ḥakhamav* (1890), 123–32; K. Wilhelm, in: HJ, 15 (1953), 49–58.

[Getzel Kressel]

LEYON, AVRAM (1912–1985), Turkish journalist. Leyon was born in Balat, Istanbul. In 1928 he started working for the newspaper *Cumhuriyet* and in 1947 began to publish *Şalom* together with Izak Yaeş. Yaeş left after a short time and Leyon continued to publish *Şalom* alone until 1983. In 1984 he sold the rights to use the name to the Jewish community and died shortly afterwards.

BIBLIOGRAPHY: L. Haleva, "Avram Leyon ile Şalom'un 37 yılı," in: *Şalom* (Oct. 31, 1984); S.H. Kohen, "Avram Leyon Z'L," in: *Aki Yerushalayim* (Dec. 26–27, 1985), 70.

[Rifat Bali (2nd ed.)]

LEZAJSK (Pol. **Leżajsk**; Yid. **Lyzhansk**), town in Rzeszow province, S.E. Poland. The Jews of Lezajsk are first mentioned in 1538. In the middle of the 17th century the community possessed a wooden synagogue and a cemetery. During the 17th and 18th centuries the Jews of Lezajsk engaged in the grain trade, the weaving of woolen cloth, and the brewing of beer, and were contractors of estates and inns. According to the census of 1765, 909 Jewish poll tax payers lived in Lezajsk and its environs. When the *ẓaddik* R. *Elimelech settled in Lezajsk in 1775, it became an important center of *Ḥasidism in Poland and Galicia. Each year (until the Holocaust) on the anniversary of his death (21st of Adar), thousands of Jews used to journey to pray at his grave in Lezajsk. Fires in 1834 and again in 1873 severely affected the economic situation of the community, but toward the end of the century conditions began to improve. The Jewish population fluctuated between 1,868 (38% of the total) in 1880, 1,494 (28%) in 1900, 1,705 (32%) in 1910, and 4,575 (31%) in 1921. In the interwar years Zionist parties and youth movements were active in the town. There were Tarbut, Yavneh, and Beth Jacob schools in the town.

[Arthur Cygielman]

Holocaust Period

The number of Jews in Lezajsk in 1939 rose to more than 3,000. With the outbreak of the war in September, the Poles began to loot stores and attack the Jews. Jewish self-defense was organized. The Germans entered Lezajsk on the eve of Rosh Ha-Shanah (September 1939), set synagogues afire, and burned sacred books in the town square. On the eve of Sukkot the Jews were deported by the Germans to the area under Soviet control on the other side of the San River. Part of the community went into hiding and was later allowed to remain in the city. They were concentrated in the ghetto, and in 1942 many of them were transported to work or death camps. Those who were deported to the Soviet zone lived there in very difficult economic conditions. In the summer of 1940 many of them were deported to the Soviet interior. A few hundred Jews, mostly from those who were in the U.S.S.R., survived. The old Jewish cemetery was destroyed by the Nazis and in its place a park was later made. Only the grave of the *ẓaddik* Elimelech remained. The main synagogue housed the town museum.

[Aharon Weiss]

BIBLIOGRAPHY: D. Rabin (ed.), *Lizhansk, Sefer Zikkaron*; Halpern, Pinkas, index; M. Schorr, *Żydzi w przemyślu do końca XVIII wieku* (1903), index; B. Wasiutyński, *Ludność żydowska w Polsce...* (1930), 116.

LHEVINNE, JOSEF (1874–1944), pianist. Born in Orel, Russia, he studied at the Moscow Conservatory, where he also taught (1902–06). In 1906 he settled in the U.S., but sojourned in Berlin from 1907 to 1919. He undertook numerous concert tours, and also gave duo-recitals with his wife, ROSINA LHEVINNE (1880–1976), a noted pianist in her own right. Josef Lhevinne excelled in the interpretation of the romantic composers, and was among the major concert artists of his time. Rosina Lhevinne became especially known as a piano teacher, and many of the U.S.-born pianists who rose to prominence in the 1940s and 1950s were her pupils.

LIABILITY (Torts). Every person of full mental capacity, male or female (BK 15a), when causing injury to another person, is liable to the injured party for any damage which his negligent conduct causes the latter to suffer (see *Torts), even a husband to his wife (BK 32a). A person who lacks mental capacity – such as a deaf-mute, idiot, or minor – is exempt from liability for damage caused by the act of his person because he is incapable of foreseeing damage, whereas the injured party is required to take care, for most people know that one must be on guard against a person lacking in understanding as he tends to cause damage. For this reason too the latter's guardian or parents are not liable on his behalf (BK 87a).

A principal who commissions an agent to commit a tort is exempt from liability, but the agent is liable, for the latter, having discretion, should foresee resulting damage, whereas the principal cannot be required to know that the agent will carry out his evil mandate (Tos. to BK 56a; 79a). Where, however, the agent cannot foresee that the damage will result from the carrying out of his mandate – as in the case of an agent lacking mental capacity, or an animal incited by the principal, or in a case where the agent could not have known that he was doing wrong because, for example, the principal told him to fetch a chattel for him telling him that it was his – the agent is no more than a tool in the principal's hand, and the latter is liable for the damage caused by the agent (loc. cit.; BK 9b). Where the principal himself could not have foreseen that the agent would cause injury in carrying out the mandate, he too is exempt from liability, as in the case where he puts a glowing coal in the hands of a minor, who burns another's article (BK 59b).

If a slave, having full mental capacity, causes injury, the sages exempt his owner from liability – although he knows that slaves are in the habit of causing injury yet retains him despite the fact that he is unable to guard the slave – on the ground that no person can afford payment of such heavy damages as the slave is likely to cause (BK 4a). On the other hand the tortfeasant slave is personally liable, for – having understanding – he is liable for his negligence. As long as he is a slave and has no independent means he is treated in the same way as a poor man who does not have the wherewithal to pay for damage he has caused; but once he is manumitted and acquires his own means, he is obliged to pay for the damage. Such, too, is the law in the case of a married woman, who generally does not have the means to pay for damage she has caused, but is obliged to pay for the damage when she is able to do so, as for instance after being divorced (BK 87a).

His own negligence notwithstanding, the injuring party is exempt from liability for damage resulting from conduct which is licensed, whether consented to and authorized by the injured party or by the court. The injuring party is also exempt from liability if the damage caused is not of a physical nature, such as economic damage.

The law of the State of Israel (Civil Wrongs Ordinance, 1947) renders a person over the age of 12 years liable in tort. The law imposes vicarious liability on a person for the acts of his servants and for acts done by others authorized by him.

[Shalom Albeck]

LIACHO, LÁZARO (1906–1969), Argentine poet, narrator, essayist, and journalist. Born in Buenos Aires, Liacho was the son of JACOBO SIMÓN LIACHOVITZKY (1874–1937), a noted Yiddish journalist, who immigrated to Argentina in 1894, founded the first Argentine Yiddish daily, *Der Tog*, and the weekly *Der Tsionist;* in 1904 he helped to establish the Argentine Zionist Federation; he also wrote a play and short stories. Lázaro Liacho was associated with the periodicals *Mundo Israelita* and *Judaica*, but won recognition mainly as a poet. His *Bocado de pan* ("Morsel of Bread," 1931), *Pan de Buenos Aires* ("Bread of Buenos Aires," 1940), and *El hombre y sus moradas* ("Man and His Dwellings," 1961), reflect his outlook both as a Jew and as an Argentinean. His short stories (*Sobre el filo de la vida*, "On Life's Cutting Edge," 1969) deal with the Holocaust. Though he expressed his love and admiration for Israel and Zionism, he considered Jewishness as a spiritual reality that can be practiced anywhere and praised Argentina as "the new Zion" in the poems collected in *Siónidas desde la pampa* ("Odes to Zion from the Pampa," 1969). In his later poetry, notably *Entre Dios y Satán* ("Between God and Satan," 1966), Liacho turned to biblical, religious, and metaphysical themes.

BIBLIOGRAPHY: R. DiAntonio and N. Glickman, *Tradition and Innovation: Reflections on Latin American Jewish Writing* (1993); R. Gardiol, *Argentina's Jewish Short Story Writers* (1986); N. Lindstrom, *Jewish Issues in Argentine Literature* (1989); D.B. Lockhart, *Jewish Writers of Latin America. A Dictionary* (1997).

[Paul Link / Florinda F. Goldberg (2nd ed.)]

LIBAI, AVINOAM (1929–), Israeli aeronautical engineer. Libai was born in Tel Aviv. After service in the War of Independence, he received his B.Sc. in civil engineering from the Haifa Technion (1953). He participated in many engineering projects including the Yarkon Bridge project before moving to the U.S. (1953), where he got his M.Sc. (1956) and Ph.D. (1959) in engineering science from Purdue University, Indiana, specializing in the physical properties and behavior of structures. After postdoctoral research at Johns Hopkins University, Baltimore (1959–61), Libai worked with Israel Aircraft Industries in Lydda (1961–71) as principal staff scientist. He then moved to the Faculty of Aerospace Engineering at the Technion (1971), where he became full professor (1972), head of the Department of Aeronautical Engineering (1974–75), head of the Department of Aerospace Engineering (1989–90), and L. Shirley Tark Professor of Aircraft Structures (1992). After his retirement in 1997 he became professor emeritus. Libai was a leading world authority on non-linear shell theory, which is now a recognized field in the general discipline of non-linear mechanics. His work has important practical applications in the design of aircraft shells, including calculating and testing their resistance to stress and buckling. This had a major influence in the development of Israeli civil and military aircraft. His honors include the Israel Prize for engineering research. Libai was also influential in Technion administration, including a period as dean of the Faculty of Aerospace Engineering and as adviser to many national organizations, including the Ministry of Defense (1978–84). His international reputation has been enhanced by his publications, including standard texts in his field of expertise, and by sabbatical visits to leading universities, including Harvard (1977).

[Michael Denman (2nd ed.)]

LIBAI, DAVID (1934–), Israeli politician, law professor, and criminal lawyer; member of the Eleventh to Fourteenth Knessets. Born in Tel Aviv, Libai received a B.A. in law from the Hebrew University of Jerusalem in 1961, an M.A. in law from the University of Chicago in 1967, and a doctorate the following year. In 1959–62 he served as spokesman in the Ministry of Justice when Pinhas *Rosen and Dov *Joseph were ministers of justice, and in the years 1960–63 as chief assistant to State Attorney Gideon *Hausner. He started to teach at Tel Aviv University in 1968. In 1971–73 he served as dean of students, and in 1971–88 as director of the Institute for the Training of Lawyers. In 1973–76 he headed the Institute for Criminology and Criminal Law. In 1975–82 he served as a member of the Press Council on behalf of the Labor Party; he was chairman of the Labor Party Constitution Committee in 1977–98. In 1978 he was appointed a member of the Knesset National Commission of Inquiry on Prison Conditions, and in 1982–84 he headed the Israel Bar Association.

Libai was first elected to the Knesset in 1984 on the Labor Alignment list. In the Eleventh and Twelfth Knessets he was chairman of the State Control Committee. In 1991–92 he was one of four Knesset members who presented bills for the direct election of the prime minister. In 1993–96 he served as minister of justice in the governments of Yitzhak *Rabin and Shimon *Peres. In 1995 he chaired a ministerial committee on the subject of the Arab villages of Ikrit and Bir'am in the upper Galilee, whose inhabitants had been forcefully evacuated during the War of Independence. The Committee recommended that inhabitants who had owned houses in the villages in 1948 could return to them, but that they would not be able to reclaim their lands. The recommendation was never implemented.

Libai resigned from the Knesset in October 1996, after a law was passed which prohibited Knesset members from holding additional positions, and returned to practicing criminal law, representing numerous well-known public figures, including the son of Prime Minister Ariel *Sharon, Gilad. Libai was chairman of the Council of Lawyers for a Constitution by Agreement as well as chairman of the Public Council in Israel that encourages cooperation between the Jewish and Arab sectors in Israel.

[Susan Hattis Rolef (2nd ed.)]

LIBEDINSKI, YURI NIKOLAYEVICH (1898–1959), Soviet Russian novelist. Libedinski was born in Odessa, but his father's medical practice took him to a factory in the Urals, and most of Libedinski's works are set in the distant provinces. *Nedelya* (1923; *A Week*, 1923) firmly established Libedinski as one of the founders of Soviet proletarian prose, and he has enjoyed wide popularity ever since. Though somewhat marred by inept imitation of the literary mannerisms of the Symbolists, this short novel is still considered one of the most effective and honest descriptions of the early days of the Soviet regime, under which Libedinski served as a Bolshevik political commissar. While the author's unconditional support of the Communist cause is emphatically stated, he does concede the fact that most of the population, and particularly the peasantry, was implacably hostile to Soviet rule. *A Week* ends with a description of an uprising in which most of the communists are killed. Suspicion with regard to the allegiance of Russia's peasantry was a basic tenet of Trotskyism, and Libedinski's next novel *Zavtra* ("Tomorrow," 1924), showed even closer ties to the teachings of *Trotsky: the disillusionment within the ranks of the Communist Party was curable only if a revolution were to take place in Germany. *Komissary* ("The Commissars," 1925, 1935[14]) is of interest as a social document; it gives an insider's view of the milieu of communist functionaries. The hero, Mindlov, is a Jew and a former Menshevik. *Rozhdeniye geroya* ("The Birth of a Hero," 1930) attempts to tackle an ambitious theme: the dehumanization of human relationships under the impact of demands made by a society which puts a premium on industrial and bureaucratic efficiency and on political orthodoxy. Though not very successful, the novel was one of the few works of Soviet prose that tried to probe some of the basic dilemmas of the human condition. Of Libedinski's later works – other than some effective wartime reporting – the most noteworthy is a trilogy set in the Caucasus immediately before and during the Revolution: *Gory i lyudi* ("Mountains and People," 1947); *Zarevo* ("Dawn," 1952); and *Utro Sovetov* ("The Morning of Soviet Power," 1957). It is commonly agreed that Libedinski narrowly escaped imprisonment or death on at least two occasions: first, as a Trotskyite in 1938, when he was actually expelled from the Party, though reinstated shortly afterward; and again in the late 1940s, as a "Jewish cosmopolitan." Little information about either period can be found in his book of reminiscences titled

Sovremenniki ("Contemporaries," 1958). *Ob uvazhenii k literature* ("On Respect for Literature," 1965) includes further reminiscences and articles by him.

[Maurice Friedberg]

LIBEDINSKY TSCHORNE, MARCOS (1933–), Chilean jurist. Born in Santiago, after Libedinsky obtained his degree in law from the University of Chile (1958) he entered the judiciary system in 1966, serving in the 4th Court of Santiago.

In 1974 he was appointed registrar of the Court of Appeals of Santiago. In 1993 he was appointed a member of the Supreme Court of Justice and in 2001 the plenum of the Supreme Court nominated him minister of the Constitutional Court. In 2004 he was elected president of the Chilean Supreme Court of Justice, becoming the first Jew to serve in this post. Libedinsky also taught law for over 30 years in the universities of Chile and Gabriela Mistral, as well as in the University Finis Terrae, where he also served as dean of the Faculty of Law (1999–2004).

[Moshe Nes El (2nd ed.)]

LIBER, MARC (pseudonym of **Michael Goldman**; 1880–1937), leader of the *Bund, born in Vilna. Liber's father, Isaac, a Hebrew poet and a Ḥovev Zion, did not provide his children with a Jewish education. All became active in the revolutionary movement. The eldest son, Boris (Gorev), was active in the Russian Social Democratic Labor Party, and Leon (Akim) was a founder of the Bund and later one of its opponents and an active Menshevik; of the sisters, Olga joined the Social Democrats and Julia became a Bundist. At secondary school Liber made contact with Lithuanian Social Democratic circles and became friendly with Feliks Dzerzhinski, the future head of the "Cheka." From 1900 he was active in the Bund, appearing as an extremist representative of its national wing in the fourth congress of the Bund (1901), and its chief spokesman at the second congress of the Russian Social Democratic Labor Party (1903). He was later attacked by Lenin. An excellent speaker, Liber became one of the most popular leaders of the Bund. He was among the less doctrinaire members of the Bund who supported its return to the Social Democratic Labor Party (1906), and was elected to its central committee. In the revolution of 1905 he represented the Bund in the Workers' Soviet in St. Petersburg. In 1906 he went on behalf of the Bund to the United States. Belonging to the wing of the party which regarded legal activities within the framework of the law as its most important task during the period of reaction in Russia, he took part in legal and open activities in Vilna. In 1910 he was imprisoned for political activities and escaped abroad, returning in 1914 to St. Petersburg. He was among those in favor of defending Russia during the war ("Oborontsy"). In 1915 he was again arrested and not freed until after the February Revolution of 1917. During the period of the Kerensky government Liber became prominent as leader of the rightist Mensheviks and the Bund, which he represented at the executive of the Petrograd Soviet. Even after the October 1917 Revolution he actively opposed the Bolsheviks. He was imprisoned in 1923 and spent the rest of his life in exile. Seriously ill and crippled, he was executed during the purges of November 1937.

BIBLIOGRAPHY: J.S. Hertz (ed.), *Doyres Bundistn*, 1 (1956), 196–225; idem et al. (eds.), *Geshikhte fun Bund*, 3 (1966), index; I. Getzler, *Martov; a Political Biography of a Russian Social Democrat* (1967), index.

[Moshe Mishkinsky]

LIBER, MAURICE (1884–1956), chief rabbi of France and scholar. Born in Warsaw, Liber went to Paris with his parents at the age of four. He graduated from the Ecole Rabbinique de Paris in 1907 and began lecturing on Jewish history there. In 1911 he was appointed assistant to the chief rabbi of Paris, serving as an army chaplain and receiving the Croix de Guerre during World War I. In 1920 Liber became rabbi at the Rue de la Victoire synagogue, in 1921 lecturer in the history of rabbinic Judaism at the Ecole Pratique des Hautes Etudes, and in 1927 succeeded his teacher Israël Lévi as professor. He was appointed director of religious education by the Paris Consistoire in 1930 and, two years later, head of the Ecole Rabbinique. In 1934 Liber was appointed chief rabbi of France *par interim*, to assist the aging Israël Lévi in his task. Under the German occupation of France during World War II, he strove hard to safeguard the Ecole Rabbinique – which had been evacuated to unoccupied southern France – and the religious character of the Consistoire. He also strove to maintain some sort of Jewish education, both legal and underground.

Liber's chief field of research was French-Jewish history. He is best known by his biography of Rashi (1905; Eng. tr. 1906). He wrote a series of articles, based on archival sources, under the title "Les Juifs et la convocation des Etats Généraux" (in REJ, vols. 63–66, 1912–13), and another series, "Napoléon et les Juifs" (*ibid.*, vols. 71–72, 1920–21). On liturgy he wrote, among other works, *La Récitation du Schema…* (1909), "La Formation de la liturgie Synagogale" (in *Annuaire de l'Ecole des Hautes Etudes*, 1933/34), and "Structure and History of the *Tefilah*" (in JQR, 40 (1949/50), 331–57). Liber also wrote an extensive introduction to the reprint of M. Schwab's French translation of the Palestinian Talmud (1932).

Absorbed into the French cultural climate, Liber opposed Zionism, calling it a national theory unacceptable to those who believe that emancipation resolved the national question for the Jews. Though deeply religious, he felt compelled to compromise with the facts of French synagogue life, such as the use of an organ.

BIBLIOGRAPHY: R. Sommer, in: REJ, 118 (1959/60), 95–119; 125 (1966), 9–20; Z. Szajkowski, *Analytical Franco-Jewish Gazetteer, 1939–1945* (1966), 44, 55, 57; G. Vajda, in: *Annuaire de l'Ecole Pratique des Hautes Etudes, Section des Sciences Religieuses* (1957/58), 26; REJ, 15 (1956), 5–7.

[Georges Weill]

LIBERALISM.

Introduction

Liberalism is an ideological and socio-political movement uniting the adherents of representative government and freedom of the individual in politics with freedom of enterprise in economics. It emerged in Western Europe in the age of struggle against absolutism and the spiritual domination of the Catholic Church (17th–18th centuries). The fundamentals of the Liberal ideology were laid by the advocates of the moderate wing of the European Enlightenment, John Locke, Charles Montesquieu, and Voltaire. A relevant slogan was formulated, *laissez faire, laissez passer*, implying "don't impede," alluding to non-interference in the economy on the part of the state. In the 19th century this became a basic principle of classical liberalism whose theoretical foundations were set down by the English economists, Adam Smith and David *Ricardo. The bourgeoisie was the main social stratum supporting liberal ideology in the 18th and 19th centuries. The more radical wing of Liberalism, connected with the democratic movement, played an important role in the American and French revolutions.

However, already at the end of the 18th century a conflict arose between the Liberals and the Radical Democrats. Jean-Jacques Rousseau and later Jacobins, such as Henri Constante and François Guizot, were the first to formulate a more or less rigid policy of Liberalism during the period of the Restoration in France. Liberalism now emerged as a doctrine based on definite historical premises.

The political doctrine of European Liberalism in the first half of the 19th century preferred the idea of the freedom of the individual to the idea of people's rule, and it preferred the constitutional monarchy to the republic. When the electoral right became more widespread, the difference between Liberal and democratic movements vanished. In the light of social and economic changes at the end of the 19th century and the beginning of the 20th century the workers' movement grew. As a result of this and other factors, Liberalism underwent a crisis and had to reject several key principles of its doctrine, in particular *laissez-faire*.

The European Liberals of the 19th century, as the spiritual heirs of the Enlightenment ideology, cherished the principles of tolerance of other people's beliefs, the separation of Church and State, and as a rule supported the idea of the Emancipation of the Jews. However, the inherent rationalism in the movement demanded preconditions for granting equal rights to the Jews, namely "improving the Jews," or "reforming Judaism."

The way of life of the Jews in Western and Central Europe changed in the 18th century and at the beginning of the 19th, and a growing number of Jews was prepared to comply with such demands. They accepted the Liberal principle that the State, based on a social contract, must guarantee rights to everyone who is prepared to fulfill his or her duty to the State.

This was advantageous for the Jews because it meant the development of free competition and the abolishment of medieval monopolies and guilds from which the Jews had been excluded. This led the strata who suffered from the abolition of the traditional social order to view the Liberal economic system, especially its radical forms such as "Manchesterism," as serving the mercenary interests of the plutocratic Jews. Thus, the discontent resulting from the policies of the Liberal economy appeared as a source of modern antisemitism. The early advocates of socialism, for their part, criticized the negative consequences of unlimited competition, and many of them, including Moses *Hess and Karl *Marx in their early works, also equated capitalism and Judaism.

In all countries where Liberals supported the principle of equal rights for the Jews, the latter actively supported the Liberal parties which during the first half of the 19th century conducted severe struggles with the Conservatives. The Jews were in the vanguard of the struggle for political freedom and civil rights.

Great Britain

Each country had its own brand of Liberalism depending on its historic development. Great Britain, the classical country of Liberalism, emancipated its Jews gradually, without revolutionary turns, and the process closely followed the general liberalization of the political system. The restrictions on Jewish rights – Jews were not admitted to Parliament and municipalities or to the universities, and they could not pursue a legal career – were a result of the dominant position of the Church of England. The demand to pronounce an oath "by the true Christian beliefs" meant that State positions and some industrial corporations were closed to Jews. The economic prosperity of some English Jews, such as the *Rothschild, *Montefiore, and *Goldsmid families, brought them into the higher circles of English society while their political rights were still severely limited.

In 1829 the British Parliament adopted a Bill on Catholic Emancipation, and Jewish public figures, supported by leading parliamentarians, decided to bring up the question of equal rights for the Jews. The Liberal member of Parliament, Sir Robert Grant, proposed in the House of Commons a draft bill on granting equal rights to all Jews born in England. During the debates in the House of Commons the Liberal deputies, for instance, the historian Thomas Macauley, welcomed the idea of equal rights for Jews. The Liberal governments of Lord John Russell and Lord Palmerston initiated the parliamentary struggle for Jewish emancipation.

William Gladstone, eventually leader of the Liberal party, first joined the Conservatives and voted against the bill granting equal rights to Jews. However, he later changed his stance. With time the Jews also managed to participate in Liberal governments. The traditional devotion of the English Jews to the Liberal party was broken only in the 1870s when Benjamin *Disraeli (Lord Beaconsfield) headed a Conservative government. He attracted a significant number of Jewish voters to the Conservatives.

After Edward VII became king in 1901, and the Liberal party won the 1906 parliamentary election, some Jewish figures gained significant political and economic influence. They were mainly financiers and businessmen connected with the Liberal party.

In the years before and during World War I two Jewish politicians played an important part in the cabinets of Asquith and Lloyd George: they were Rufus Isaacs (later becoming Lord *Reading) and Herbert Samuel, subsequently the first British high commissioner in Mandatory Palestine.

France

In France, Liberalism in the period of the Restoration was a doctrine opposed to both feudal reaction and democracy. Although the Constitutional party of Louis XVIII declared Catholicism a State religion in 1814, it granted to all citizens the freedom of belief, and the rights of the Jews were in no way handicapped. Still, the Bourbon monarchy did not pay salaries to the rabbis from the State budget. The July Revolution of 1830 eliminated this remnant of inequality. The Louis-Phillipe monarchy brought into practice the principles of a moderate Liberalism after the English pattern. When in 1835 the government of the Canton of Basle in Switzerland refused to allow a French Jew to acquire real estate in the area of the canton, the French government, convinced by the argument of the Jewish political figure Isaac-Adolphe *Crémieux, decided to adopt strong political sanctions against the canton.

When Crémieux expressed the gratitude of the French Jews to the French government, King Louis-Philippe declared that he was happy to teach Europe the lesson of a just attitude towards Jews. The king also expressed the hope that other people would follow the example of France.

In this period capitalism rapidly expanded in France, as a result of which a group of big Jewish financiers emerged connected with Liberal circles.

The 1848 Revolution in France contributed much to the practical realization of equal rights for Jews. The Jewish participation in the political life of the country grew and the Provisional Liberal Government created by the Revolution had two Jewish ministers: Crémieux, minister of justice, and Michel *Goudchaux, minister of finance.

In the age of the Second Empire more moderate opponents of the regime gathered under the banner of the Liberal party. Napoleon III collaborated with the political Jewish figures who, however, did not belong to the Republican wing, and Goudchaux was succeeded as minister of finance by another Jew, monarchist-minded Achille *Fould.

From the time of the Second Monarchy, Liberalism in France was closely linked with the idea of a republic. After the fall of Napoleon III, Crémieux occupied the post of minister of justice in the Government of National Defense, where he actively supported Leon Gambetta, the head of the government. In this period Crémieux was responsible for the law granting civil equality to the Jews of Algeria.

Liberalism in France always advocated the assimilation of Jews, and the Jewish Liberals struggled only for civil rights and freedom of religious belief. Nevertheless, among the Jewish assimilationists there was formulated a new concept of Jewish solidarity throughout the world which found its expression in the *Alliance Israélite Universelle established in 1860.

In the Third Republic, the main representative of Liberalism was the party of Radical Socialists. While fighting clericalism in the 1880s, the government of the Republic did not resort to anti-Jewish discrimination; on the contrary, Jews were appointed to high administrative posts.

In the mid-1880s, all the opponents of the Republic united under the banner of antisemitism. The *Dreyfus Affair was the culmination of the struggle of clerical and monarchic reaction against the Republic. The defeat of the antisemites contributed to the strengthening of Republican rule. The law on the separation of Church and State adopted in 1905 was a triumph of Liberal principles.

In subsequent French policy, Liberalism always stood out as a political force supporting the Republic and democracy against the onslaughts of reaction which invariably fought under the banner of antisemitism. In the 20th century the latter acquired the features of *fascism. In the political life of the Fourth and then the Fifth Republic, Liberal ideology of a reformed nature served different non-socialist parties rather than being represented by a single party.

Germany

In Germany Liberalism was closely connected with the struggle for national unification. Prussia adopted in 1812 a decree on the emancipation of Jews sponsored by the reformist activities of the government of Stein and Hardenberg. However, the reaction which seized Germany after its victory over Napoleon resulted in an outburst of anti-Jewish feelings in almost all German states.

The July Revolution of 1830 in France also sparked off Liberal trends in Germany. The progressive elements began to support bills on expanding Jewish rights in *Landtags* of several South German states: Bavaria, Wuerttemberg, and Baden. However, even in Baden, the state with the most Liberal constitution at the time, the demand was put forward that the Jews should renounce their national and religious identity to be entitled to emancipation. Baden Liberals spoke against emancipation, and only on the eve of the 1848 Revolution did the Second House of the Baden *Landtag* adopt the resolution recommending the government to consider the petition on equality of Jews. All such petitions had been previously rejected by the Lower House. Gabriel *Riesser worked hard in the struggle for the emancipation of the Jews. As a staunch fighter for Jewish rights, he refuted all arguments of the opponents of emancipation, but at the same time he rejected the existence of a Jewish nationality.

The Revolution of 1848 constituted a breakthrough in the attitudes of the Central European countries, although already in pre-Revolution times some German states with liberal constitutions, such as Kurhessen and Wuerttemberg, had undertaken certain steps in the direction of emancipation of Jews, but other states, such as Saxony and Hanover, had not relaxed on Jewish rights.

The Jews took an active part in the revolutionary fighting in Vienna and Berlin in 1848. In the all-German Parliament convened in May 1848 in Frankfurt-on-Main, several Jewish deputies took part including Riesser, the veteran of Emancipation struggle, who was subsequently elected deputy chairman of the parliament. Although Riesser managed to include a statement on the equality of all citizens before the law in the Declaration of Rights of German People adopted by the Frankfurt Parliament, this declaration never included an imperial constitution. However, many of the basic rights imposed by the Revolution left their trace in the constitutions of various German states. Thus in the Prussian Constitution "granted" by the king in December 1848, the item on equality was preserved, although equality was never in fact realized.

The period of reaction in Germany in the 1850s did not abolish the constitutional clauses on equality, but the attempt was made to curtail the areas of their implementation as far as possible. Prussia was again declared a "Christian State" and the civil rights of Jews were restricted. Reaction had its impact even on those German states which had belonged to the Liberal wing before the 1848 Revolution.

Only toward the end of the 1850s the reaction began to subside. In the election to the Prussian *Landtag* the Liberals came out victorious. Ludwig *Philippson – editor of the *Allgemeine Zeitung des Judentums* published by the Jewish community – initiated a petition to the House of Deputies for the implementation of equality. The petition, supported by the Liberals, was handed to the government, but had little impact on its policy.

The Conservative Junker government of Otto Bismarck, who was appointed prime minister in 1862, impeded the implementation of equality for Jews by struggling against Liberalism, especially against the so-called German Progressive party, one of whose leaders was the Jewish radical Johann *Jacoby. The battling of Bismarck's government against Liberalism ceased only with the approach of the military conflict with Austria in 1866.

Prussia's victory, paving the way to the unification of Germany, indirectly contributed to the cause of emancipation. Four Jews entered the Reichstag of the North-German Confederation established under Prussian hegemony. They included Eduard *Lasker who left the Progressive party to join the National Liberals, supporters of Bismarck's policy of unification of Germany.

Four hundred and twelve Jewish communities in the North-German Confederation turned to the Reichstag petitioning for the implementation of the principle of Jewish equality. The petition was rejected, however, in 1867 on the grounds that it interfered in the internal affairs of the separate states. Lasker also voted for the rejection of the petition: united Germany was more important to him than the granting of equal rights to Jews. The most prominent Liberal leaders who defended the principle of Jewish equality in the Reichstag were non-Jewish members of the Progressive party. Eventually they managed to achieve their aim when the Reichstag, and then the government, formally rejected all limitations on civil and political rights resulting from differences of belief (1869).

Emancipation was first adopted and gradually implemented by the North-German states and later by the South-German states. The coming to power of the Liberal government in Bavaria in 1859 enhanced the implementation of emancipation, although the political emancipation of the Jews of Bavaria was completed only in 1872.

Eduard Lasker, leader of the National Liberal Party, and his comrade Ludwig *Bamberger, previously a Radical republican, played a significant part in the Reichstag of the German Empire established after the victory over France in 1870. However, the switch of the Bismarck government to conservative policies in the mid-1870s, and the shift of the National Liberals to the right pushed Lasker and Bamberger into the opposition.

Bamberger published a brochure *Germans and Jews* in 1880 directed against the antisemitic attack of Heinrich von Treitschke, the National Liberal historian. In his brochure Bamberger attempted to prove that the German people as a whole could not be considered responsible for the actions of a group artificially inflaming anti-Jewish hatred. The Liberal Jews joined the so-called party of free-thinkers adhering to the principles of Liberalism. The reactionaries named this party "Jewish Defense Brigade" (*Judenschutztruppe*).

In the religious field, Liberalism in Germany was associated first with *Reform in Judaism, and then with the right to complete indifference to religion, a notion which was legally confirmed by the law of 1876 determining the right to leave the Jewish community without any obligation to join another religious community.

Liberal Jews took an active part in the political life of the Weimar Republic. Hugo *Preuss held the post of minister of interior, and headed the committee for drafting the constitution which Liberal circles welcomed as the embodiment of the spirit of democracy. The minister of foreign affairs of the Weimar Republic, Walter *Rathenau, also a Jew, was killed by nationalist conspirators.

Liberalism in Germany fell victim to Nazi tyranny. After the crushing of Nazism, it revived and began to play a role in the political life of the Federal German Republic. However, it has not crystallized a definitive position regarding Jews, Zionism, and the State of Israel.

Austro-Hungary

In Austria, where after 1815 absolutism suffered no limitations, the restrictions on Jewish rights continued. Bureaucracy regulated Jewish life, and the Jews were subject to special taxation.

In 1839–1840 the Jewish intellectuals of Hungary instigated the struggle for Emancipation, pinpointing at the same time their quest for assimilation. However, nationalistic-minded Hungarian Liberals did not support the idea of Emancipation for Jews. Lajos Kossuth, leader of the Hungarian National Liberation movement, attempted to prove the impossibility of granting equality to Jews unless they radically reformed their religion so that it would resemble Christianity in everyday life (meaning abolition of *kashrut*, Sabbath observance, etc.).

In the March 1848 revolution the Viennese rabbi Isaac Noah *Mannheimer sought to convince Jews not to demand emancipation, which he considered the logical consequence of the victory of Liberal principles but the initiative for which should come from non-Jews. The opponents of Jewish emancipation claimed that the Jews were not an integral part of the nation, and therefore they could not be granted equality.

In July 1848 the Constituent Reichstag convened in Vienna had a number of Jewish members including Adolf *Fischhof, Mannheimer, and Joseph *Goldmark. Two Jewish members, Ignaz *Kuranda and Moritz *Hartmann, were delegates to the All-Union Parliament in Frankfurt.

In the Hungarian National Assembly Kossuth expressed his opinion that granting equality to Jews was untimely. The anti-Jewish pogroms in Pressburg (Bratislava) and other Hungarian towns forced the Assembly to reject the Liberal resolution on granting Jews voting rights. The Jews could also not join the Hungarian National Guard.

In the dual monarchy of Austro-Hungary formed in 1867, both parts acknowledged constitutionally the civil and political equality of all peoples and all beliefs. Only a few Jews were elected to the Reichstag and the provincial assemblies. In the 1870s Kuranda was a Reichstag member, representing the German Liberal party, but no more. Bound by party discipline, he had no opportunity to struggle systematically in parliament for implementing formally the principle of Jewish equality.

Neither the German Liberal Party nor the Polish Kolo was willing to combat the increasing impact of antisemites in the Reichstag, state assemblies, and municipalities. Many Austrian Jews found that their former Liberal allies could not be relied upon when it came to the implementation of civil equality.

Jewish voices came to be heard calling for a break with "treacherous" Liberals and the adoption of an independent Jewish policy. In reaction to European antisemitism Theodor *Herzl published his *The Jewish State*. Herzl's outlook and his political ideas on the structure of the future Jewish state were formulated under the direct impact of the notions of European liberalism.

In the elections of 1900 the Jews of Vienna continued to vote mostly for the Liberals although some supported the Social Democrats. While the majority of the Jewish members did not support nationalist policies, they were sympathetic to the Czech People's Party led by Thomas Garrigue *Masaryk which, unlike other Liberal parties, included in its program an item granting the Jews the right to conduct their nationalist policy.

Italy

Emancipation of the Jews in Italy, as well as in Germany, was closely linked with the struggle for liberation of the country. Liberalism in Italy was first and foremost a struggle against the domination of the Catholic Church. The unification of Italy for the majority of Liberals meant the federation of the Italian states. Various revolutionary groups connected with Mazzini and Garibaldi set more radical goals. This was also the case with the Liberal Party of Piedmont (Kingdom of Sardinia) which played the leading role in the struggle for unification of Italy. Jewish emancipation in Piedmont occurred earlier than in other Italian states, namely in March–June 1848.

The Italian provinces which rebelled against Austrian rule – Venice and Lombardy – not only granted Jews equality, but elected them members of parliaments and governments. The provisional Republican Government of Venice was headed by the Italian patriot Daniele *Manin who was of Jewish origin. His government had two Jewish members: the minister of trade, Leone Pincherle, and the minister of finance, Isaac Maurogonato. The Parliament of Venice had eight Jewish members. In other Italian states where Liberal constitutions were adopted in 1848, such as Tuscany and Modena, the equality of Jews automatically came into force.

In Piedmont, the leaders of the ruling Liberal party invariably supported the idea of Jewish equality. In 1849 Massimo d'Azeglio became prime minister of Piedmont. He authored the book, entitled *On Civic Equality of Jews*, published on the eve of the Revolution. His successor, Count E. Cavour, also fought for the cause of Jewish equality: his secretary, Isaac *Artom, member of a distinguished Italian Jewish family, later became a prominent diplomat and statesman.

The unification of Italy, under the hegemony of Piedmont, led to the establishment of Jewish equality throughout the country and many Jews were active on the political scene. In 1910 Luigi *Luzzatti headed the Italian government. The triumph of Liberalism was accompanied by the rapid acculturation of the Jews in Italy, many of whom supported the Liberal party.

United States

In the United States the principles of Liberalism guided the country's Constitution and its political culture. No Liberal party as such has ever acquired political power in the U.S. but Liberal political figures have acted, as a rule, in the framework of the two main parties, the Republicans and the Democrats.

In the contemporary American political lexicon, the adherents of the so-called Welfare State are considered liberals, that is, they support social reforms and state intervention in the economy on behalf of economically deprived strata of the population, oppose racial discrimination, and adopt a "moderate" orientation in foreign policy. Contemporary American liberalism has rejected the principle of laissez-faire and approached European social democracy. Jews have been widely represented in the ranks of American liberals.

In the 1930s American liberalism associated itself with the New Deal of President Franklin D. *Roosevelt and with the Democratic party. A small Liberal party was founded in New York by several leaders including David *Dubinsky. In presidential elections it usually supported the Democratic nominees. The majority of American Jews invariably voted for Roosevelt and the liberal stance of U.S. Jewry on political questions became a tradition. For a long period the overwhelming majority of Jews continued to vote for the nominees of the Democratic Party and the Jews played a significant part in its liberal wing. Despite various counter-influences, including the affluence of American Jewry, their political stance has remained strongly liberal.

Russia

In Russia, due to the unique circumstances, first, noblemen, and afterwards, intelligentsia of lower strata were the main proponents of liberal views. The country's economic backwardness, the weakness of its bourgeoisie, and their dependence on the protectionist policy of the state led to a situation in which adherence to the principle of laissez-faire was – unlike in the West – not a basic principle.

During the first part of the 19th century so-called Western-minded figures, such as Timofey Granovsky and K. Kavelin, embraced Liberal ideas. In the age of "The Great Reforms" of the 1860s Russian Liberalism crystallized as an ideological movement opposed, on one hand, to Conservatism and, on the other, to revolutionary Radicalism.

The atmosphere of "The Great Reforms" contributed to growing assimilatory trends among the Jewish intelligentsia. However, already toward the end of the 1860s, the Liberal hopes for the peaceful introduction of a Constitutional system were disappointed. The implementation of reforms was delayed and, as a consequence, the revolutionary movement gained momentum. Part of the intellectuals joined the revolutionary populists (*narodniks*). The pogroms of the 1880s clearly shattered the illusion of the hopes of the assimilators that they could "merge" with the Russian people, and they also contributed to the nationalist revival among Russian Jewry.

The nationalist feelings among the Russian Jews were also the result of the detached and sometimes even supportive attitude of the representatives of the different political movements to the pogroms. Only a few figures in Russian Liberalism at the time condemned the pogroms and antisemitism. The Liberal philosopher Vladimir Solovyov was one such exception and evinced a profound understanding of the Jewish question. However, toward the end of the 19th century, the views of some sections of Russian society underwent a visible change regarding the Jewish question and all wings of the Liberalizing movement condemned the antisemitism as used by the Czarist government as a weapon in its struggle against revolutionary and liberal forces.

Liberalism in Russia appeared on the political scene as an organized political movement only at the beginning of the 20th century. In 1903 two movements were established: the Union of Liberation and the Union of Land-Constitutionalists which in 1905 united to form the Constitutional-Democratic Party (Kadet), the main party of Russian Liberalism. Fighting for civil equality for Jews, the Russian liberals, as well as the majority of socialists, considered assimilation a positive phenomenon. They did not encourage those Jews seeking a solution of their plight in collective nationalist independence. Non-socialist Jewry circles were politically attracted to the Kadet liberals. In 1904–05 Kadets initiated a campaign which laid the foundation for the establishment in March 1905 of the Union for Achieving the Equality of the Jewish People in Russia. This Union put forward both general democratic and specifically Jewish national demands. During the elections to the First State Assembly (Duma) the majority of the Jewish voters supported the Constitutional-Democratic Party.

In the First Duma, the Kadets appeared as the only party struggling for Jewish equality (the Socialist parties boycotted the elections). Many Jews appeared in the Kadet ranks, including Maxim *Vinawer, Henry *Sliozberg, and Shmarya *Levin. Nine of the 12 Jews elected to the Duma belonged to the Kadets.

The Union for Achieving Equality for the Jews of Russia split as a result of the decision of the Zionists to go to the elections as an independent party. The Jewish People's Group, established in 1907, consisted mostly of the Jewish Kadets. This Group put forward demands considered moderate compared with those of other Jewish parties and did not support the convening of a Jewish National Assembly. The Jewish People's Party (*Folkspartei*), organized at the end of 1906, joined the Liberals on general political issues.

After the dissolution of the First Duma, the Jewish Liberal members M. Gertzenstein and G.B. Yollos were killed by "Black Hundred" reactionaries. The machinations of the reactionaries resulted in a sharp drop in the number of Kadets in the Second Duma. The election to the Third Duma was conducted according to a new election law which enabled the authorities to reduce to a great extent the number of Jewish voters. Of the four Jewish members of the Second Duma, three belonged to the Kadet Party; both Jewish members of the Third Duma belonged to the Kadets. The representation of small Jewish parties collaborating with Kadets was also reduced.

Despite the fact that the Liberal movement had always spoken out for Jewish equality, discrimination against Jews never ceased. All the progressive camp opposed antisemitism but even certain Liberals disapproved of the "excessive" participation of the Jews in Russian culture. In an age of reaction, they put forward the slogan of *a-Semitism*, meaning indifference to the national needs of Russian Jews. The *Beilis Affair, provoked by Black Hundred Guards with the assistance of the authorities, became the focus of the struggle around "the Jewish Question" involving the Czarist government, on the one hand, and all the forces of the Liberal and radical opposition, on the other. Beilis' acquittal was viewed by public opinion in Russia and abroad as the victory of progressive forces over the Black Hundred reactionaries.

In the period of World War I which brought new calamities to Russian Jewry, Jewish leaders tried to evince the sympathies of Liberal and Radical members of the Duma. All the Jewish political factions united to struggle against antisemitism. Some Liberal public figures including Pavel Milyukov condemned the anti-Jewish policies of the military authorities, but did not consider it advisable to express new criticism openly in war time.

Nevertheless, the Conference of the Party for People's Freedom (Kadets) unanimously adopted in June 1915 a resolution, following the opinion of Vinawer, which unreservedly condemned the persecution of Jews. The progressive bloc, established on the Kadets' initiative in the framework of the Duma in August 1915, put forward a program stipulating the gradual expansion of Jewish rights: further steps to liquidate the Pale of Settlement, the reduction of the Jewish quota for higher educational establishments, and the cancellation of restrictions on Jewish occupations. But the implementation of the program was postponed indefinitely and the inactivity of the Progressive Bloc on the Jewish question was sharply criticized by the leftist parties.

After the February Revolution of 1917 liquidated all types of Jewish inequality, Russian Liberalism had to retreat under the pressure of Radical forces demanding expansion of the Revolution and the self-determination of all nationalities of the Russian Empire. The October upheaval ended Liberalism as a political force in Russia.

Conclusion

In the 19th century Liberalism acted as the leading political force in many European countries, but in the 20th century it lost its former significance. In the second half of the 20th century it regained some of its former influence, especially in its renovated program supporting the welfare state, among the Jewish communities of Europe and of North and South America, as well as in the communities of South Africa and Australia. At the same time the influence of radical Socialist and Communist movements and factions in those communities gradually decreased.

[Naftali Prat / *Shorter Jewish Encyclopedia in Russian*]

LIBEREC (Ger. **Reichenberg**), city in N. Bohemia, Czech Republic. There were 60 Jews in Liberec in 1582. There was no community in the city during the 18th and first half of the 19th centuries. Although there were 57 Jews in Liberec in 1811, no community was permitted and their residence there was illegal (see *Familiants Law). The Jewish wool dealers, among them Simon von *Laemel, were among the developers of the textile industry. The Jews were permitted to remain in the town only during the week – the church authorities published an ordinance on the subject in 1776. In 1799 and 1810 the Jews were officially evicted from private houses and were allotted special inns, but after 1848 Jews settled in the town. Later, a congregation was founded (1863), a synagogue was dedicated (1889), and an Orthodox prayer room, Achdus Yissroel, was established. In 1912 there were 1,240 Jews in the town (3.4% of the total population) and in 1930 there were 1,392 (3.6%). At the time of the Sudeten crisis (1938) the Jews left Liberec; some 30 remained behind and were arrested. The synagogue was demolished on Nov. 10, 1938. A community was refounded in 1945, with most of the members coming from *Subcarpathian Ruthenia. In 1946 the community numbered 1,211 Jews, including 37 original inhabitants, 1,174 postwar settlers, among them 182 members of the Czechoslovak army-in-exile. The prayer room and a memorial tablet to the victims of the Holocaust were restored in 1987. A small congregation was active in the early 21st century and a cemetery was in use.

BIBLIOGRAPHY: Hofmann, in: H. Gold (ed.), *Die Juden und Judengemeinden Boehmens in Vergangenheit und Gegenwart* (1934), 529–69; Klein, *ibid.*, 7; Lamed, in: BLBI, 8 (1965), 302–14; R. Iltis, *Die aussaeen unter Traenen…* (1959), 36–39. **ADD. BIBLIOGRAPHY:** J. Fiedler, *Jewish Sights of Bohemia and Moravia* (1991), 102–103.

[Jan Herman / Yeshayahu Jelinek (2nd ed.)]

LIBERMAN, SERGE (1942–), Australian writer of fiction. Born in Russia, Liberman arrived in Melbourne, Australia, with his parents in 1951. A physician, he became probably the best-known living Australian Jewish writer of fiction. Liberman published several volumes of short stories, including *On Firmer Shores* (1981), *A Universe of Clowns* (1983), *The Life That I Have Led* (1985), and *The Battered and the Redeemed* (1990). Essentially, Liberman tried to show both the inevitable failure of any view of life lacking a traditional base, but also the inadequacy of such a view in the modern secular world. He was also the editor of a Yiddish-oriented literary journal, the *Melbourne Chronicle*, and the co-compiler of the *Bibliography of Australian Judaica* (1987).

BIBLIOGRAPHY: W.D. Rubinstein, Australia II, 331–332.

[William D. Rubinstein (2nd ed.)]

LIBERMAN, YEVSEY GRIGORYEVICH (1897–1983), Soviet economist. Liberman studied at the Kharkov Engineering Economics Institute and began his teaching and research career in 1933. From 1947 to 1963 he held the chair of economics and organization of machine-building industry at the Institute. In 1963 he was appointed professor of statistics and accounting at Kharkov University. Liberman received worldwide notice for his pronouncements in a debate which started in 1962 on the need for economic reforms in the U.S.S.R.

Liberman's ideas represented a school of thought among Soviet economists who demanded more rationality in the planning process, new criteria of success, and more freedom of decision-making or autonomy for management. Thus, Liberman represented a reaction against the overcentralization of economic administration in the U.S.S.R., against the insufficiency of material incentives for management and workers, and against many arbitrary criteria of success of individual enterprises. According to Liberman the old system inflicted heavy costs upon the state by obstructing useful innovations and insufficiently stimulating progress, and upon the welfare of the workers and consumers. Liberman assumed that administrative reforms would introduce greater flexibility in the system, and self-interest on the part of management and workers would improve both the quantity and quality of production. Liberman argued that the reforms would not limit the basic political decisions but rather improve the efficiency of the basic economic plans. The goal of every enterprise and the criteria of its success should be the maximization of profits from which the incentive payments for workers and management should be drawn. Thus profits would become, under the Soviet conditions, primarily an index which measures the efficiency of the performance of the enterprise, reflecting the increase of the quantity and quality of production, the growth of labor productivity and utilization of resources, and simultaneously a measure of the reward of society for successful performance.

Encouraged by the promises of liberalization in economic administration made by Kosygin but also frustrated that most of his proposals were not introduced in practice, Liberman continued to advocate direct links between the industrial enterprises and the trade organizations, so as to make the industrial production more responsive to the needs and wishes of the consumers. He continued to demand a decrease of centralization by suggesting the reduction of the number of products centrally planned and spoke up against imposing an a priori wage fund upon the enterprises.

BIBLIOGRAPHY: M. Dobb, *Soviet Economic Development since 1917* (1966[6]), 379–81; *Prominent Personalities in the U.S.S.R.* (1968), s.v.

[Arcadius Kahan]

LIBESKIND, DANIEL (1946–), U.S. architect. From Lodz in Poland, where his parents bought their seven-year-old boy an accordion because they did not think a Jew should be seen with a piano, the family moved to Israel in 1957. There, he won a music competition. One of the judges was violinist Isaac *Stern, who urged him to switch to the piano. Two years later, Libeskind and his family moved to a one-room apartment in the Bronx. Libeskind soon tired of the piano. "Music was not about abstract intellectual thought – it was about playing … I couldn't see spending my life on the stage," he said. After attending the Bronx High School of Science, Libeskind went to Cooper Union for the Advancement of Science and Art in New York, where he became a prize student and was offered a job with architect Richard *Meier. He quit this firm after seven days, complaining that Meier's style was a high-class form of standardization. In 1969, he married Nina Lewis, who became his organizer and together the team became known as "Studio Libeskind." To pursue architecture, Libeskind went to the University of Essex in England, where in 1971 he earned a master's degree in the history and theory of architecture. After a few years of teaching, he accepted a job as head of the elite school of architecture at Cranbrook Academy in Michigan, an astonishing appointment for a 32-year-old. After seven years, Libeskind and his wife left Cranbrook for Milan, Italy. His theoretical drawings for a housing project in Berlin won a prize in 1987. These drawings caught the attention of architect Philip Johnson, who included them in an exhibit called "Deconstructivist Architecture" at the Museum of Modern Art in New York. His career was made. In 1989, while he was a Getty Scholar in Los Angeles, his design for the Berlin Jewish history museum won the open competition. In 1991, before exhibit installations, the museum became famous for the way Libeskind incorporated the tragedy of German Jewish history into the structure of the building. There were slanted walls, a dark tower, slits for windows, and an empty space, a void, running through the whole construction, all designed to create anxiety. In 1998, the Felix Nussbaum Haus opened in Osnabruck, Germany, a Libeskind design, which was a small museum built by the city to memorialize the tragic fate of the painter whose life was cut short by the Holocaust. When in February 2003, Studio Libeskind won the competition for the design of the World Trade Center in New York, immediate conflicts occurred with the owner of the building, who wanted his architect, David Childs, of Skidmore Owings & Merrill to do the design. Childs and Libeskind worked out a compromise. Libeskind buildings have been built in Mallorca, London, Copenhagen, Seoul, and Tel Aviv. At least 11 more were being designed in 2005. In 2004 Libeskind was appointed cultural ambassador for architecture by the U.S. Department of State.

BIBLIOGRAPHY: D. Libeskind, *Breaking Ground* (2004); B. Schneider, *The Jewish Museum Berlin* (1999).

[Betty R. Rubenstein (2nd ed.)]

LIBIN, Z. (pseudonym of **Israel Zalman Hurwitz**; 1872–1955), Yiddish novelist. Libin escaped Czarist military service by immigrating to London (1891) and on to New York, where he worked three years in sweatshops. Although he began his literary career in Russian, he became a pioneer of Yiddish literature in the U.S., publishing his first story in 1892; in over half a century of creative work, he contributed to newspapers and periodicals, such as *Tsukunft*, *Arbeter Tsaytung*, and especially *Forverts*, writing light articles about daily events, hundreds of realistic, compassionate stories and sketches about immigrant life and the struggles and the suffering of sweatshop workers, and some 50 plays, which were produced in the U.S. and Europe. His most famous play, *Di Gebrokhene Hertser* ("Broken Hearts," 1903), was first produced with Jacob and Sarah *Adler in the lead roles and was later played by various companies throughout the world. It was filmed in 1926 by Maurice *Schwartz, who inaugurated his Yiddish Art Theater in 1918 with Libin's play *Der Man un Zayn Shotn* ("The Man and His Shadow"). Many of Libin's stories and plays remained uncollected. Among his published books are *Geklibene Skitsn* ("Selected Skits," 1902), *Geklibene Shriftn* ("Selected Works," 2 vols., 1910), and *Gezamlte Verk* ("Collected Works," 4 vols., 1915–16), and his tragicomedy *Kolegn* (Engl. trans. *Colleagues*, 1915).

BIBLIOGRAPHY: Rejzen, Leksikon, 2 (1927), 113–16; LNYL, 5 (1963), 44–49; Z. Zylbercweig, *Leksikon fun Yidishn Teater*, 2 (1934), 1026–38; S. Niger, *Dertseylers un Romanistn* (1946), 204–16; B. Bialostotzky, in: JBA, 11 (1952/53), 169–71. **ADD. BIBLIOGRAPHY:** B. Gorin, *Geshikhte fun Yidishn Teater*, 2 (1918), 208–10; A. Cahan, *Bleter fun Mayn Leben*, 4 (1928), 468–69; Bal Makhshoves, *Geklibene Shriftn*, 3 (1929), 122–26; A. Mokdoni, *Yorbukh fun Amopteyl*, 1 (1938),

257–72; E. Schulman, *Geshikhte fun der Yidisher Literatur in Amerike*, (1943), 133–36.

[Elias Schulman / Marc Miller (2nd ed.)]

LIBNAH (Heb. לִבְנָה).

(1) Station of the Israelites on the route of the Exodus, between Rimmon-Perez and Rissah (Num. 33:20–21). It is perhaps identical with Laban (Deut. 1:1).

(2) Canaanite city-state in the Shephelah which Joshua conquered and destroyed after Makkedah and before Lachish (Josh. 10:29ff.; 12:15). It was allotted to the levites (Josh. 21:13; I Chron. 6:42) and was included in the fourth district of Judah which extended over the eastern Shephelah (Josh. 15:42). The city revolted against Joram, king of Judah, at the same time as Edom, but was subdued (II Kings 8:22; II Chron. 21:10). Hamutal, the mother of kings Jehoahaz and Zedekiah, was a native of Libnah (II Kings 23:31; 24:18; Jer. 52:1). It was attacked by Sennacherib after the fall of Lachish (II Kings 19:8; Isa. 37:8). Eusebius identifies it with Lobana, a village of Eleutheropolis (Onom. 120:23ff.). The identification of the ancient city with Tell al-Ṣāfi, the crusader *Blanche-Garde* ("the white tower"; cf. Heb. *lavan*, "white"; see *Gath, now identified with this site), has been superseded in scholarly opinion by that with Tell Birnāt, 2 mi. (3.2 km.) northwest of Bet Guvrin or with nearby Tell-al-Judayda.

BIBLIOGRAPHY: Albright, in: BASOR, 15 (1924), 9; Elliger, in: PJB, 30 (1934), 58ff.; Z. Kallai, *Naḥalot Shivtei Yisrael* (1967), 319–20; Abel, Geog, 2 (1938), 369–70; EM, 4 (1962), 421–3.

[Michael Avi-Yonah]

LIBOWITZ, SAMUEL NEHEMIAH (1862–1939), writer on Jewish subjects. Born in Kolno, Poland, he immigrated to America in 1881. He traded in precious stones and was so successful that he could afford to print over 20 books in limited editions. He corresponded with eminent Jewish scholars including Israel *Davidson, to whom he wrote 107 letters, which he later published himself in 1933. His works include *Peni'el* (1914), a collection from Jewish literature on the subject of death; *Ha-Mavet be-Fanim Soḥakot* (1917); *Sefer Sha'ashu'im* (1927); and *Ha-Shome'a Yiẓḥak* (1907), sharp-witted jokes and original interpretations of the rabbis and from the Middle Ages; *Judah Aryeh Modena bi-Demuto ve-Ẓivyono* (1896); *Kitvei ha-Rav Yehudah Aryeh mi-Modena* (1936); and *Doresh Reshumot ha-Aggadah* (1893, 1920[2], 1929[3]), explanations of several *aggadot* of the Talmud. He also edited and published *Ozar ha-Ḥokhmah ve-ha-Madda* (1897), in collaboration with Jacob Reifmann, Moses Reicherson, Solomon Rabin, and others. In several of his works he violently polemized against such scholars as R. Isaac Hirsch Weiss, Ze'ev Schorr, Radkinson, Saul Tchernichowsky, and Joseph Klausner. He immigrated to Palestine in 1927, but his longing for his children took him back to America.

BIBLIOGRAPHY: S. Bernstein, *N.S. Libowitz* (Heb., 1931); D. Persky, in: *Hadoar*, 21 (1940/41), 656–8; Kressel, Leksikon, 2 (1967), 251–2.

[Chayim Reuven Rabinowitz]

LIBRARIES. A library is a collection of information resources, in all formats, organized and made accessible for study. The word derives from the Latin *liber* ("book"). The origin of libraries, keeping of written records, dates at least to the third millennium B.C.E. in Babylonia.

In antiquity, Judaica collections were first mentioned in II Maccabees 2:13–14, where mention is made of a "treasury" of books established by Nehemiah (in the Temple?) that contained "books about the kings and prophets, the books of David (Psalms), and royal letters about sacred gifts." Another early library, the Dead Sea Scrolls, now comprises the remains of the library of the community living in Qumran shortly before and after the beginning of the present era. Fragments from the Cairo *Genizah* reveal the existence of both public and private libraries in the geonic period.

Early Libraries

Communities, synagogues, and *battei midrash* were anxious to establish libraries. Libraries were found in almost every *talmud torah* in Italy. In the Verona *talmud torah* of 1650 there were rules which required a special room to be set aside for the library. Other Italian communities such as Ferrara, Reggio Emilia, Pisa, and Leghorn also had libraries, often enriched by the acquisition of private collections. The Amsterdam Sephardi community library, at their Talmud Torah school, is mentioned in 1680 by the bibliographer Shabbetai Bass in his *Siftei Yeshenim*.

Modern Libraries

The 19th century saw the development of libraries in public institutions. They were established as communal libraries, organizational libraries, libraries attached to rabbinical seminaries, and Judaica and Hebraica collections in national, public, and major university libraries. Before the end of the 19th century the Abrabanel Library was established in Jerusalem (1884) (see J. Chasanowich). This later developed into the Jewish National and University *Library.

COMMUNAL LIBRARIES. The first of the modern Jewish communal libraries was established at Mantua at the end of the 18th century. Many communities in Germany established their own libraries. They were intended mainly for the use of teachers and young people. Libraries were found in major Jewish communities throughout Europe such as Berlin, Frankfurt, Hamburg, Munich, and Breslau, as well as the communities of Vienna, Prague, Warsaw, Vilna, and Zurich. Most were destroyed or disbursed during the Nazi era but many have been reestablished, particularly in Eastern Europe subsequent to the fall of Communism in the early 1990s.

In the United States many libraries were established through synagogues and were designed to work closely with the synagogue religious schools and for recreational reading and studying for synagogue members.

In pre-state Israel there were very few communal libraries. After the establishment of the State of Israel great advances were made. They included community libraries ranging from the Yeshurun Synagogue Library in Jerusalem to special libraries meeting specific community needs.

ORGANIZATIONAL LIBRARIES. Jewish organizations on all continents have developed substantial libraries. Their holdings vary considerably according to the mission of the particular organization. In 1867, Albert Cohen, the representative in Palestine of Baron Rothschild, established a small library in Jerusalem, which was administered by Dr. London, physician in the Rothschild Hospital. Development of libraries was slow during the *yishuv* period and libraries were primarily the private initiative of individuals or such bodies as the *Histadrut. However, voluntary bodies interested in cultural work established popular reading and lending libraries, such as Jewish trade unions, Zionist and Socialist societies, women's organizations, and youth movements.

Originating with the *Haskalah movement, organizations throughout Europe established libraries as part of their ongoing operations. With the emigration of Jews from Europe to the Northern Hemisphere, Israel, and Australia organizational libraries blossomed.

In post-World War II Europe organizations such as historical societies and local museums have taken responsibility for community collections where the community is no longer significant, and in many cases, no longer exists. In Israel, organization libraries such as museum libraries, corporate libraries, and special libraries house archival and historical documents providing primary research materials.

RABBINICAL SEMINARIES. The first rabbinical seminary library was established at the Collegio Rabbinico Italiano, which was located first in Padua, and moved from there to Rome, Florence, and again back to Rome. The Breslau Jewish Theological Seminary library attained considerable importance as did the Berlin Rabbinical Seminary and the Hochschule (Lehranstalt) fuer die Wissenschaft des Judentums. With the geographic shift to and expansion of Jewish life in the U.S. major collections were established, and remain at the forefront of Judaica libraries, at the Jewish Theological Seminary in New York and at the Hebrew Union College in Cincinnati. Yeshivah libraries were established in Israel as well. The Central Rabbinical Library, attached to Hechal Shelomo, houses important collections saved from the Holocaust. The Chabad movement established rabbinic collections in their major centers as well and serve as libraries for their seminaries and as community libraries worldwide. Jewish teachers seminaries, in Israel, the United States, and the United Kingdom, have developed their own libraries.

Nazi Period

The persecution of European Jewry by Nazi Germany (1933–45) brought with it the wholesale confiscation of both public and private libraries. Some of the books were moved to the Institut zur Erforschung der Judenfrage in Frankfurt on the Main. Toward the end of World War II, looted books were brought by the Nazis to central stores in southern Germany and western Czechoslovakia. When recovered after the war, mainly by a body called Jewish Cultural Reconstruction, they were returned wherever possible to the heirs of their owners; the more than 1,000,000 volumes that remained were distributed to Jewish libraries and cultural or educational organizations in Israel, America, and other parts of the Diaspora. With the fall of Communism in the early 1990s, collections of books both in complete libraries and scattered throughout the entire region of Eastern Europe became accessible again. Many books remained on site and others were disbursed and purchased by collectors and libraries primarily in the U.S., Europe, and Israel.

Jewish Sections in General Libraries

NATIONAL AND PUBLIC LIBRARIES. Hebraica and Judaica collections have been included in great national and municipal libraries, for the preservation of Jewish literary and scholarly treasures since antiquity. The library of Alexandria contained the Septuagint and other Judeo-Hellenistic works. Medieval monastery libraries frequently contained Hebrew, particularly Bible, codices; records of persecutions, expulsions, book burnings and confiscations filled their shelves, as well as those of episcopal and princely palaces and of medieval universities. The interest in Hebrew studies produced by the age of Reformation and Humanism led many Christian scholars such as Johann Reuchlin and J.A. Widmanstad (1506–1557) to collect Hebrew manuscripts and books. Significant collections are found throughout Europe in national, royal, monastic, and municipal libraries, particularly in countries where great Jewish traditions were found such as Spain (El Escorial), Italy (Vatican and many others), the United Kingdom (British Library), France (Bibliotheque National), Germany (Deutsches Statsbibliothek), Denmark (Royal Library), Austria (National Library), Hungary (National Library), and Russia (State Libraries in St. Petersberg and Moscow).

Most notable in the U.S. is the significant Hebraica collection found in the Library of Congress; the New York Public Library and the Boston Public Library house significant collections as well.

In Israel, the Sapir Public Library in Petaḥ Tikvah was established at the end of the 19th century. The Jewish National and University Library (JNUL) in Jerusalem fulfills a double function: to serve as the National Library to collect all print and non-print materials deposited in its collections on Jewish subjects to serve the general public; and to provide the university community with the required materials to support its curriculum. The JNUL houses the largest collection of Judaica and Hebraica in the world and is the center for documentation of all Judaica and Hebraica collections. Library collections are found in the Knesset, various ministries, and other governmental organizations.

Public libraries in Israel are spread throughout the country and are found in most cities, towns, villages, settlements, and kibbutzim. They serve the local population primarily with Hebraica but also house local historical documents, record books, memorial books, and archival documents related to their specific community and to European and Middle Eastern communities from which their local population emigrated. Of particular note are kibbutz memorial books documenting the lives of their deceased members.

UNIVERSITY LIBRARIES. University libraries in Europe have for many centuries collected Judaica and Hebraica to support their study of religion, the Judeo-Christian tradition, and humanities. Significant collections are found in major university libraries such as in the United Kingdom (Oxford University, Cambridge University, University of Manchester), in Italy (University of Bologna), the Ukraine (Vernadsky Library), and the Netherlands (Amsterdam University Library – Rosenthaliana).

In the U.S. there has been a significant growth of Jewish studies programs in academic institutions, and to support the university curriculum Judaica and Hebraica collections have blossomed in major large universities. Harvard University has the most comprehensive collection of contemporary Israeli culture. Columbia and Yale universities hold significant historical collections. The University of Pennsylvania acquired a very significant Judaica library (Dropsie College) and has placed itself among the most significant collections. Stanford University and University of Michigan are actively acquiring and are developing fine collections in Jewish studies.

Israeli universities house Judaica collections primarily to support the curriculum. Significant archival collections are found in all the universities. The universities are all linked through the Israel Center for Digital Information Services (MALMAD) set up in 1998 by the Israel Association of University Heads (Va'ad Rashei ha-Universita'ot) to serve as a joint framework (consortium) for the acquisition, licensing, and operation of information services to all the Israeli universities. Colleges, technical schools, and academies of art, music, and design each have significant collections related to their specialized fields.

Library Association

The Association of Jewish Libraries, an international organization established in 1968, promotes Jewish literacy through enhancement of libraries and library resources and through leadership for the profession and practitioners of Judaica librarianship. The association fosters access to information, learning, teaching, and research relating to Jews, Judaism, the Jewish experience, and Israel. The association publishes a scholarly journal, *Judaica Librarianship*, and hosts an online discussion group called Hasafran. The Israel Library Association supports librarians and libraries in Israel.

Library Catalog

Library catalogs in the modern sense were first published in the 17th century, but book lists are much older (see *Books; *Book Trade). Some from the 12th century were found in the Cairo **Genizah*. Immanuel of Rome (13th century) mentions a catalog arranged according to subject matter. The first to introduce a systematic division according to subjects was *Manasseh Ben Israel (1604–1657). From the end of the 17th century sale catalogs began to be printed, such as those of S. Abbas and Solomon Proops, both of Amsterdam, or later the famous collection of David Oppenheimer. In modern times M. Steinschneider did pioneering work in the field of bibliography. The first scientific listing was his catalog of the Hebrew books of the Bodleian Library (1852–60). J. Zedner followed with his catalog of the Jewish books in the British Museum (1867). Today library catalogs are virtual and accessible over the Internet.

Libraries in the 21st Century

Library collections today encompass the wide range of information media available. They include manuscripts, historical documents, rare books, prints, archival collections, and contemporary literature. Included in these collections are also non-print materials in the areas of Jewish music, scores, and recordings in a multitude of formats, films, multimedia collections, and most recently electronic virtual collections.

In the last quarter of the 20th century an information explosion took place throughout the world. It has affected all libraries, including stand-alone Judaica libraries and Judaica collections found in general libraries. Shared cataloging allowed for libraries to enter their bibliographic records into a central database and for members to "copy" the cataloging record for its local use. OCLC, in Dublin, Ohio was the first shared catalog. It was followed by the Research Library Group in Mountain View, California, which in 1989, in their Research Library Information Network (RLIN), added Hebrew vernacular script capability for electronic cataloging. The academic and research libraries subscribed to the OCLC and RLIN systems and are active contributors of Judaica and Hebraica records to their databases. Concurrently, large library collections were purchasing integrated library systems to manage their collections and activities. Retrospective conversion of card catalogs to machine readable bibliographic records of major collections were undertaken and most were completed by the turn of the 21st century. With the rapid and ubiquitous development of the Internet and personal computers, access to library collections throughout the world changed dramatically. In the mid 1990s, with the expansion of the worldwide web, access to library catalogs, now online public access catalogs (OPAC), became accessible from all corners of the globe.

Libraries and Judaica collections, as part of institutions, developed websites featuring links to their holdings, listing web resources in Judaica, and highlighting online exhibitions and more recently digital collections.

The Israel Center for Digital Information Services, MALMAD, has taken the lead in establishing and maintaining electronic indexes such as RAMBI, the Israeli Union Catalog, and the Israeli Union List of Serials. Other public and private organizations have built extraordinary databases providing a wealth of information such as Shamash.org or Maven.co.il.

Digital collections featuring rare and unique materials from library collections are growing exponentially. The

JNUL has pioneered the efforts in establishing numerous cooperative digital collections all freely available through their website. Some of the projects to date include an international database of *ketubbot*, which includes bibliographic descriptions and images from public and private collections worldwide, the Online Treasury of Talmudic Manuscripts, the National Sound Archives, and the Ancient Maps of Jerusalem, among others.

Virtual libraries are developing with electronic access to full texts of classical Judaic sources through databases such as the Bar-Ilan Responsa Project, the Otzar ha-Hochma database, and the Lieberman Institute for Talmudic Research database (which are currently all fee-based), while the German Compact Memory database and the Kiryat Sefer projects have free access to full texts of monographs and periodicals.

Currently a number of international digitization projects are underway. The Friedberg Genizah Project is amassing digital collections of fragments from the Cairo *Genizah* found in major collections at Cambridge University (U.K.) and at the Library of the Jewish Theological Seminary (U.S.). Tel Aviv University (Israel) has undertaken a project to digitize unique Jewish newspapers found throughout the world.

Digitization of parts of collections are being done in numerous institutions in Israel, Europe, and the United States. Visual, audio, motion, and text files are being converted to digital format and are being made available over the Internet. "Born digital" periodicals have become more and more frequent such as the Edah Journal.

The library of the 21st century has changed significantly since ancient times. Its mission to collect and organize information to make it available for study has not changed over the past 2,000 years but the means in which it is accomplished has.

The following is a partial list of Judaica collections on the Web (source Princeton University Library and Amherst University Library).

Australia

Makor Jewish Community Library

Monash University – Humanities and Social Sciences Library – The Laura and Israel Kipen Judaica Collection, including the Giligich Yiddish Collection

University of Sydney – Fisher Library – Rare Books & Special Collections – Archive of Australian Judaica

Austria

Juedisches Museum Wien

Osterreichishce Nationalbibliothek

Universitaet Wien – Bibliothek des Instituts fuer Judaistik

Canada

Albert and Temmy Latner Jewish Public Library of Toronto

Canadian Jewish Congress Archives Jewish Heritage Centre of Western Canada – Archives

Jewish Public Library (Montreal)

McGill University: Jewish Studies/McGill Catalog

National Library of Canada/Jacob M. Lowy Collection: old and rare Hebraica and Judaica comprising 3,000 printed books from the 15th to the 20th centuries, including 34 Hebrew and Latin incunables, more than 120 editions of Bibles in many languages. Strong in Italian Hebraica and in examples of Hebrew printing from Spain to the Orient.

University of Toronto Libraries/Catalog: largest Judaica collection in Canada

Ontario Jewish Archives

Curaçao

Mongui Maduro Biblioteka – Judaica Collection

Czech Republic

Jewish Museum in Prague – Library

Denmark

Det Kongelige Bibliotek – Orientalia and Judaica

Finland

Helsinki University Library – Hebraica Collection

France

Alliance Israélite Universelle

Bibliotheque Medem

Bibliotheque Nationale (holds more than 30,000 Hebrew volumes)

Centre de Documentation Juive Contemporaine

Centre d'Etudes juives

Germany

Die Deutsche Bibliothek (Leipzig) – Anne-Frank-Shoah-Bibliothek

Germania Judaica: Koelner Bibliothek zur Geschichte des deutschen Judentums

Institut fuer die Geschichte der deutschen Juden – Bibliothek

Das Juedische Museum Westfalen – Bibliothek

Simon-Dubnow-Institut fuer juedische Geschichte und Kultur – Bibliothek

Stadt- und Universitaetsbibliothek Frankfurt am Main – Hebraica- und Judaica-Sammlung

Universitaet Potsdam – Moses Mendelssohn Zentrum fuer Europaeisch-Juedische Studien – Bibliothek

Zentralarchiv zur Erforschung der Geschichte der Juden in Deutschland

Israel

Israeli University Libraries

Bar-Ilan University Library

Ben-Gurion University of the Negev: Aranne Library

Hebrew University Libraries

Jewish National & University Library

Technion Library

Tel Aviv University Libraries

University of Haifa Library

Weizman Institute of Science Libraries

Israeli Archives/Research Centers
Abba Eban Center for Israeli Diplomacy
The Aviezer Yellin Archives of Jewish Education in Israel and the Diaspora
Babylonian Jewry Heritage Center
Central Zionist Archives: archives of the World Zionist Organization, the Jewish Agency, the Jewish National Fund, Keren Hayesod, and the World Jewish Congress
Ghetto Fighters' House: Holocaust and Jewish Resistance Heritage Museum
Israel Museum/Library of Art & Archeology
The Jabotinsky Institute
The Melton Centre for Jewish Education
Moshe Dayan Center for Middle Eastern and African Studies
Rabin Center for Israel Studies
The Steven Spielberg Jewish Film Archive
Vidal Sassoon Center for the Study of Antisemitism/Catalog Access
The Yad Ben-Zvi Library
Yad Vashem Library

Italy
Centro di Documentazione Ebraica Contemporanea
Jewish Community of Venice – Renato Maestro Library and Archives
Archivio delle tradizioni e del costume ebraici "Benvenuto e Alessandro Terracini," Torino

Netherlands
Amsterdam University Library – Department of Judaica and Hebraica – Bibliotheca Rosenthaliana
Joods Historisch Museum Library
Leiden University Library – Oriental Department

New Zealand
New Zealand Jewish Archives

Russia
Institute of Oriental Studies, St. Petersburg
Judaica Library of the Russian State University for the Humanities in Moscow
Petersburg Jewish University

Sweden
Uppsala University – University Library

Switzerland
Israelitische Gemeinde Basel – Karger-Bibliothek
Israelitischen Cultusgemeindein Zurich – Die Bibliothek
Zentralbibliothek Zurich – Hebraistik und Judaistik

South Africa
University of Cape Town – Jewish Studies Library

United Kingdom
British Library – Oriental Division
Cambridge University Library – The Taylor-Schechter Genizah Research Unit
Leeds University Library – Cecil Roth Collection
Oxford Centre for Hebrew and Jewish Studies – The Leopold Muller Memorial Library
Oxford University – Boedlein Library
University College London – Library
University of Manchester – The John Rylands University Library Collection
University of Southampton Libraries – Special Collections

United States
Universities/Research Libraries with Judaica Collections and resources on the web
Baltimore Hebrew University
Brandeis University Libraries
Columbia University: Resources for Jewish Students
Cleveland College of Jewish Studies – The Aaron Garber Library
College of Charleston – Robert Scott Small Library – Special Collections – Jewish Heritage Collection
Florida Atlantic University Libraries – Molly S. Fraiberg Judaica Collections
The George Washington University – Gelman Library – I. Edward Kiev Collection
Gratz College/Tuttleman Library
Harvard University
Hebrew College Library
Hebrew Theological College
Hebrew Union College
Jewish Theological Seminary
Library of Congress: Hebraic Section
New York Public Library: Jewish Division
New York University Judaic Studies Resources
Ohio State University
Princeton University Library – Jewish Studies Resources
Reconstructionist Rabbinical College – The Mordecai M. Kaplan Library and Archives
Spertus Institute of Jewish Studies: Asher Library
Stanford University/Hebraica & Judaica Collections
Touro College Libraries
University of California at Berkeley/ Judaica Collections
UCLA Library Collections: Jewish Resources
University of Judaism – Ostrow Library
University of Maryland – University of Maryland Libraries – S.L. and Eileen Shneiderman Collection of Yiddish Books
University of Michigan: Near East Division
University of Pennsylvania/Center for Judaic Studies
Yale University
Yeshiva University/Mendel Gottesman Library of Hebraica/Judaica
Archives/Research Centers
American Jewish Archives
American Jewish Historical Society
Bureau of Jewish Education of San Francisco, the Peninsula, Marin and Sonoma Counties – Jewish Community Library

Center for Jewish History
Chabad – Lubavitch Library
Congregation Emanu-El of the City of New York – Ivan M. Stettenheim Library
Jewish Women's Archives
Judah L. Magnes Museum – Library and Archives
Leo Baeck Institute
National Yiddish Book Center
Rutgers University: Center for the Study of Jewish Life
Simon Wiesenthal Center
Spertus Institute of Jewish Studies
United States Holocaust Memorial Museum Library
Yivo Institute for Jewish Research

[Isaiah Sonne / Naomi Steinberger (2nd ed.)]

LIBRARY, JEWISH NATIONAL AND UNIVERSITY, the national library of Israel and the Jewish people, also serving as the library of the *Hebrew University in Jerusalem. The library dates from 1892, when *B'nai B'rith founded a public library in Jerusalem to which in 1895 a Bialystok physician, Joseph *Chasanowich (Chazanowicz), presented his collection of 8,800 books, mostly in Hebrew. Other gifts followed and by 1920, when the library was taken over by the Zionist organization, the number of volumes had reached about 30,000. Under the direction of the philosopher Samuel Hugo *Bergman, who was librarian from 1920 till 1935, the number of volumes increased to 300,000. Between 1936 and 1946, under Gotthold *Weil, about 150,000 books were added. When the Hebrew University was opened on Mount Scopus in 1925, the library was transferred to it, and in 1930 it was installed in the Wolffsohn building.

In 1948, when communication with Mount Scopus was broken off as a result of the War of Independence, the library contained nearly half a million books. Curt *Wormann, who had been appointed librarian only a few months earlier, had to build it up anew in western Jerusalem, where it was housed in the Terra Sancta building. With the help of friends and supporters in Israel and abroad, it acquired tens of thousands of books and was brought back into working condition. In the years following World War II, the university (later joined by the Ministry of Religious Affairs) salvaged hundreds of thousands of books in Europe, as well as hundreds of manuscripts (chiefly Hebraica and Judaica), the remnants of Jewish public and private libraries looted by the Nazis. Many of these were incorporated into the National Library; the rest were distributed among university, public, synagogue, and yeshivah libraries throughout the country.

Following an agreement with the Jordanian government in 1958 (through the mediation of the secretary-general of the UN, Dag Hammarskjöld), about 350,000 books from Mount Scopus were gradually transferred to the Israel-held sector of Jerusalem. In 1960 a library building was opened on the new campus at Givat Ram. At the beginning of 1968, the library possessed about 1,500,000 volumes, over a quarter of them Hebraica and Judaica, together with 6,100 Hebrew and 800 other manuscripts. In 1962, the Institute of Microfilms of Hebrew Manuscripts was transferred to the library from the Ministry of Education and Culture. From then until 1971 it had acquired 25,000 photocopies of Hebrew manuscripts from 18 countries, together with thousands of photographs of *genizah* fragments. In 2005 it housed approximately five million items. From 1924 the library published a bibliographical quarterly, **Kirjath Sepher*, listing all current publications in Palestine and Israel and all Judaic publications appearing elsewhere. An Institute of Hebrew Bibliography in the library records all books published in Hebrew characters. Since 1956, a graduate library school has been functioning at the library.

The library possesses a number of special collections: the Zalman Schocken collection of Hebrew incunabula; the Ignaz Goldziher collection of Orientalia (especially of Islamica and Arabica); the Harry Friedenwald collection on Jews in medicine; the Abraham Schwadron (Sharon) collection of Jewish autographs and portraits; the Immanuel Loew collection of Judaica and Hebraica (including his personal archives); the A.S. Yahuda collection of Orientalia, Hebraica, and Judaica; and a collection of Jewish and non-Jewish manuscripts from all over the world, including illuminated and non-illuminated manuscripts of the Bible. The library also has the personal archives of Aḥad Ha-Am, Martin Buber, Joseph Klausner, Stefan Zweig, S.J. Agnon, Itzik Manger, Uri Zevi Greenberg, S. Yizhar, A.B. Yehoshua, and others. It also houses the Albert Einstein archive. It includes reading rooms for various subjects, such as Judaism, the East, Journalism, Music, Kabbalah and Jewish Thought, Maps and Travelogues, History of Science, etc. The Library aims to digitalize a large number of its items to make them available on the Internet.

BIBLIOGRAPHY: A. Ya'ari, *Beit ha-Sefarim ha-Le'ummi ve-ha-Universita'i bi-Yrushalayim* (1942); *The Hebrew University of Jerusalem* (1966), 234–50; Y. Haezrahi, *Beit ha-Sefarim ha-Le'ummi ve-ha-Universita'i* (1967); jnul.huji.ac.il.

[Shlomo Shunami / Shaked Gilboa (2nd ed.)]

LIBSCHITZ, BARUCH MORDECAI BEN JACOB (1810–1885), Polish rabbi and author. Libschitz occupied successively rabbinical positions at Siemiatycze, Volkovysk, and Novogrudok, before he was appointed rabbi of Siedlce in 1876. He was acknowledged as a leading halakhic authority and many turned to him with their halakhic questions. Although Siedlce was a ḥasidic community, as a Lithuanian Libschitz was opposed to ḥasidism and often came into conflict with the members of his community who were used to ḥasidic rabbis. He was one of the first to support the Ḥovevei Zion movement and in his letters to Joseph Friedland, the first propagandist of the Zionist movement, he gave him much encouragement. He was also one of the main supporters of the establishment of the Ez̦ Ḥayyim yeshivah in Jerusalem. He published *Berit Ya'akov*, responsa on the Shulḥan Arukh (pt. 1 ḤM; pt. 2 EH, 1876–77); and *Beit Mordekhai*, sermons and memorial addresses (1881). His *Minḥat Bikkurim*, talmudic novellae, has remained in manuscript. He had two sons, MEIR EZEKIEL, who settled in Jerusalem and died there in 1909, and JACOB ZALMAN (d. 1915); their talmudic novellae appear in the works of R. Elijah *Klatzkin, the rabbi of Lublin who had settled in Jerusalem.

BIBLIOGRAPHY: Ḥ.N. Maggid-Steinschneider, *Ir Vilna* (1900), 164; Frankel, in: *Yizkor li-Kehillat Siedlce* (1956), 296f.

[Itzhak Alfassi]

LIBYA, country in N. Africa, consisting of the regions of Tripolitania, Cyrenaica (see *Cyrene), and Fezzan. Isolated finds of Jewish origin from pre-Exilic Ereẓ Israel were discovered both in Cyrenaica and Tripolitania, but there is no reliable evidence of Jewish presence in those regions before the time of Ptolemy Lagos (ruled Egypt 323–282 B.C.E.); he is reported to have settled Jews in the Cyrenean Pentapolis to strengthen his regime there, probably in 312 B.C.E. The phrases used consistently in the sources point to their distribution around Cyrene presumably as military settlers on royal land. The temporary extension of Ptolemaic control into Tripolitania in the early third century B.C.E. may have occasioned similar Jewish settlement in that area; there are Jewish finds from this date at Busetta and Zliten.

Early History

After the Maccabean breakthrough to Jaffa commerce between Ereẓ Israel and Cyrene appears to have been strengthened (147–43 B.C.E.). II Maccabees is an abbreviation of a work by Jason of Cyrene. With the political reunion of Egypt and Cyrene under Ptolemy Euergetes II in 145 B.C.E., a fresh wave of Jewish immigration reached the latter country; the Jewish community of Teucheira, evidenced by their epitaphs, and composed probably of military settlers linked with Egypt, must have originated late in the century. In 88 B.C.E., after Cyrene had been freed from Ptolemaic control, the Jews of the country were involved in an undefined civil conflict perhaps to be connected with contemporary manifestations of Greek anti-Jewishness in Alexandria and Antioch. The Roman exploitation of the royal domains at the expense of their cultivators would have involved numerous Jews, ultimately expropriated, perhaps one of the social bases of the risings of 73 and 115 C.E.

Cyrene became a Roman province in 74 B.C.E.; inscriptions of the reigns of Augustus, Tiberius, and Nero at Berenice (Benghazi) indicate a wealthy, well-organized community with an executive board and its own amphitheater for assembly, as well as a synagogue. Jewish urban communities prior to 115 C.E. are further evidenced at Apollonia and Ptolemais. Cyrenean Jewry under Augustus was compelled to defend its right – attacked by Greek cities – to send the half-shekel to Jerusalem, but its privileges were confirmed by the Roman power. A section of the Cyrenean community at this point seems to have obtained improved civic status, and Jewish names appear among graduates of city gymnasia both at Cyrene and Ptolemais, but it is clear that the bulk of the community was considered intermediate between alien residents and citizens. Cyrenean Jewry was nevertheless preponderantly rural; sites of Jewish rural settlement are known at Gasr Tarhuna, Al-Bagga, in the Martuba area, at Boreion (Bu-Grada) in the south (the site of an alleged "temple"), and at an unlocated place called Kaparodis. The Teucheira group was largely agricultural and a Jewish rural population probably existed around Benghazi. The occupations of Cyrenean Jewry included, besides agriculture, those of potter, sailor, stonemason, bronze-worker, and possibly weaver. Commercial elements are likely to have existed at the ports of Benghazi, Apollonia, and Ptolemais. The Jewish aristocracies of Benghazi, Ptolemais, and Cyrene were highly hellenized (cf. a Jew, Eleazar son of Jason, who held municipal office at Cyrene under Nero); though Jewish graduates of gymnasia appear at Teucheira, most of the Jews there were relatively uncultured, and suffered a high rate of child mortality. Cyrenean Jews maintained a synagogue in Jerusalem in the first century C.E.

In 73 C.E. Jonathan the Weaver, a "desert prophet" of the Qumran type and a Zealot refugee from Ereẓ Israel, incited the poorer element of the Jews of Cyrene to revolt, leading them to the desert with promises of miraculous deliverance.

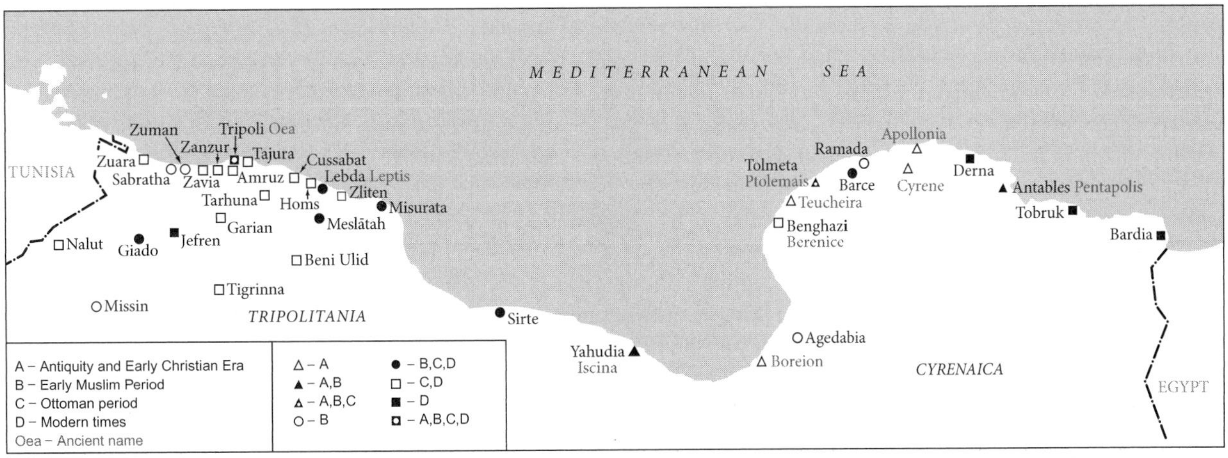

Jewish settlements in Libya, from antiquity to modern times.

Jonathan was apprehended and his followers were massacred; the Roman governor L. Valerius Catullus also took the opportunity to execute some 3,000 wealthy Jews and to confiscate their property. The Zealot movement was not confined to the city of Cyrene, and the removal of the hellenized Jewish aristocracy led to the radicalization of the rest of the community. Under Vespasian (69–79 C.E.) the recovery and redistribution of the extensive Cyrenean state lands began, resulting in increased friction with the seminomadic transhumant Libyan elements. To the same period belongs the Jewish settlement of Iscina (Scina) Locus Augusti Iudaeorum (Madinat al-Sultan) on the shore of eastern Tripolitania, an imperial foundation which may plausibly be held to reflect a forcible removal of disaffected Jewish elements from Cyrene to the desert borders – a view which finds support in Jewish historical tradition. A Jewish-Libyan rapprochement on the desert borders may well have taken place prior to the rising of 115.

In 115 – during Trajan's Second Parthian campaign – the Jewish revolt broke out in Cyrene, Egypt, and Cyprus. The very heavy gentile casualties in Cyrene and the scope of the destruction wrought by the Jews at Cyrene, probably at Apollonia, Balagrae (Zawiyat Beda), Teucheira, and in the eastern areas, suggest that the rebels, under their leader *Lucuas (or Andreas), who was called by the gentile historians "King of the Jews," intended to quit the country for good. The wholesale destruction of the Roman temples testifies to the Zealot content of the rising. At the end of 116 the Jews broke into Egypt, but cut off from Alexandria were defeated by Marcius Turbo; Lucuas is thought to have been killed in Judea.

Jews may have already been again living in Ptolemais in the third century, and, in the later part of the fourth century, Jewish ships were reaching Cyrene from Egypt. There is much evidence for the existence of a Jewish population in the country on the eve of the Muslim conquest (642), and presumably the numerous Jewish traditions attached to ancient sites throughout the country relate to the Byzantine period. In Tripolitania, except for the appearance of Iscina, the Jewish record is blank until the fourth century. In Africa Vetus (Tunisia) Jewish settlement cannot be proven before the early second century C.E., and the Talmud (Men. 110a) seems to imply a gap in Jewish settlement east of Carthage; Jerome nevertheless believed that in the late fourth century Jewish settlement was continuous from Morocco to Egypt, and numerous place-names on the Tripolitanian coast suggest a very ancient Jewish tradition. A Christian cemetery of the fourth century at Sirte contained chiefly Jewish names, perhaps of people connected with imperial domains of the area. A Jewish community at Oea (now *Tripoli), which possessed competent scholars, is attested by Augustine (fifth century). The Boreion community indicates longstanding settlement; its "temple" was converted into a church, and its Jews were forced to accept Christianity by Justinian (527–65). Ibn Khaldūn (14th century) thought the *Berbers on Mount Nefusa were Judaized, and derived from the Barce area (Cyrene) – like the Jarawa of the Algerian Aurès – but his statement is tentative and the traditions of Judaizing Berber tribes, despite the extensive modern literature concerning them, have been shown not to be pre- or early Islamic.

[Shimon Applebaum]

Arab-Ottoman Period

The Arabs conquered Cyrenaica in 642 and swiftly took the rest of North Africa. They spread *Islam among the local populations, but allowed members of monotheist religions (referred to as People of the Book (*ahl al-kitāb*)), namely Christians and Jews, to keep their religion by accepting the status of Protected Peoples (*ahl al-dhimmah*). According to late Arabic sources, the Jews were dispersed among the Berbers who lived around Mount Nefusa (central Tripolitania) before the Arab conquest, but in Jewish sources the Jews of this district are only mentioned from the tenth century onward. The Jews also believed that the Jewish population of the entire region originated there. From the frequent repetitions of the surname al-Lebdi in 11th- and 12th-century sources, it can be concluded that there was also an important Jewish population in Lebda, near the harbor town of Homs, and also in the oasis of G(h)adames. There was also a Jewish population in Barce and in other localities. Between 1159 and 1160 the Jewish population suffered as a result of the victory of the *Almohads but the rulers did not take any lives or force conversion.

There is no extant information on Libyan Jewry during the next 400 years. According to a later source, 800 Jewish families fled from Tripoli to Tajurah – situated to the east of the latter – and to Jebel Gharyān (Garian) – in the interior of Tripolitania – as a result of the Spanish invasion of 1510.

Libya was under Ottoman rule between 1551 and 1911, though in the 1711–1835 period Tripolitania was ruled by the Qaramanlī dynasty, which originated in the Ottoman military and retained nominal allegiance to the *Ottoman Empire. Direct Ottoman rule in Libya resumed in 1835. After the Ottoman conquest of 1551 the Jews prospered again. At that time, R. Simeon *Labi, a Spanish kabbalist refugee, settled in Tripoli (1549–80) rather than continue to the Land of Israel. He strengthened the position of Judaism and introduced Sephardi traditions of Jewish learning. According to a manuscript which belonged to M. Gaster (now BM Or. 12368), "A sad and bitter event happened to the people of the Mahgreb," i.e., the Jews of Libya were in great distress during the years 1588–89 as a result of the revolt against the Turks which was fomented by the mahdi Yaḥyā b. Yaḥyā. Many of them were forcibly converted to Islam, but with the suppression of the revolt, they returned to Judaism. There is, however, no mention or allusion in Jewish sources to this period of persecution.

The community of Tripoli gained in strength with the arrival of Jews from *Leghorn (Livorno, referred to as Gornim), most of whom were merchants of Sephardi origin. In Tripoli, in contrast to some other Mediterranean cities, the Gornim did not constitute a separate congregation, due to their relatively small number, but many of them were of a higher socio-economic level, with strong commercial, social, and familial ties across the Mediterranean. In 1663 the Shabbatean

Abraham Miguel *Cardozo arrived there and conducted his Shabbatean campaign. From the second half of the 17th century until the Italian conquest (1911) the Jews of Libya were led by *qā'ids* ("leaders"). These were the temporal leaders of the community and belonged to a small number of wealthy families with strong ties to the Muslim authorities. In 1705 the Jews of Tripoli were saved from the danger of extermination at the hands of Ibrahim ash-Sharif. "Purim of ash-Sharif" on 23 Tevet commemorates this event, about which R. Shabtai Tayyar wrote a poem, *Mi Kamokha*. During the famine and plague of 1784–85, there was much suffering among the Jews and they were threatened with grave danger when Ali Gurzi, known as "Burgul," was appointed pasha of Libya. After a year and a half he was banished from the town, and in commemoration of their deliverance the Jews of Tripoli celebrate "Purim of Burgul" every 29 Tevet. R. Avraham Khalfon wrote another *Mi Kamokha* poem in honor of this event. The Jews of Libya lived in special quarters (*ḥārah*) and streets in various towns. In the two villages of Jebel Gharyān and Tigrinna of central Tripolitania, they lived in underground caves until their immigration to Israel in 1950–51. The *Ḥārat al-Yahūd* ("Jewish quarter") in Tigrinna contained about 300 Jews. They earned their living as goldsmiths, blacksmiths, and peddlers among the Bedouin in the area.

In the mid-19th century, the traveler Benjamin the Second (Israel Benjamin) found about 1,000 Jewish families (about a third of the population) in Tripoli. There were four competent *dayyanim* and eight synagogues. In 1906 N. *Slouschz visited Libya and his descriptions have become a historical source of information. Most of the information in his books about the 18th and 19th centuries stems from his guide Mordecai Hacohen, whose history was based on earlier sources and includes numerous observations on current conditions of the Jews in the urban centers and the rural hinterland. At the end of Ottoman rule there were no important incidents in the history of Libyan Jewry, apart from the fact that in 1909 they, like all citizens of the Ottoman Empire, were subject to the compulsory military service law. Jews – of an Orthodox religious background – feared that they would be forced to desecrate the Sabbath and other religious holy days and eat non-kosher food in the course of military service. However, the law was only in force for a short time, since Libya shortly thereafter fell to the Italians, and the Ottoman command respected Jewish religious restrictions. The Jews even benefited from the military training that some 260 of their young men had received, since the latter could protect the community in the interim period between the fall of the Ottoman regime and complete Italian occupation of Tripoli, when the town suffered from attacks by Arab rioters.

[Haïm Z'ew Hirschberg / Rachel Simon (2nd ed.)]

Italian Rule

On Oct. 11, 1911, Tripoli fell to the Italians, who within two months took the rest of the Mediterranean coastal urban centers of Libya. Most of Tripolitania was also conquered within the next two years, but the Sanusi resistance prevented the conquest of most of Cyrenaica. During World War I, most of the hinterland was regained by the Arab and Berber resistance, with the help of the Ottoman and German military. Following World War I Tripolitania was retaken by the Italians, but internal Cyrenaica was fully conquered only by the early 1930s when the Sanusi-led opposition was crushed. Although there were Jewish communities in the Tripolitanian and Cyrenaican hinterland, most of the Jews were under Italian rule from late 1911. The first 25 years of Italian rule passed peacefully for the Jews as far as Italian treatment of Jews was concerned. They retained equal rights, and the number of those in government employment grew, as did the numbers of those who became prosperous and attended urban Italian state schools. During this period Zionist activity went unhindered. The Jewish population of Libya in 1931 was 21,000 (4% of the total population). They were dispersed in 15 localities, with about 15,000 of them in Tripoli. In 1936 the Italians began to enforce fascist legislation, especially in Tripoli, where most of the trade was in Jewish hands. This legislation aimed at modernizing social and economic structures, similar to the then current conditions in Italy. The authorities started to hinder the freedom of the Jews, who were forced to open their shops on the Sabbath, and those who refused to do so were punished, imprisoned, and some even whipped in public. With the implementation of anti-Jewish racial legislation in late 1938, Jews were removed from municipal councils, some were sent away from government schools, and their papers were stamped with the words "Jewish race."

[Haim J. Cohen / Rachel Simon (2nd ed.)]

Holocaust Period

When the Benghazi area fell to the British on February 6, 1941, the Jews were overjoyed over their deliverance and their meeting with Jewish Palestinian soldiers serving in the British army. This did not last long, and on April 3, 1941, when the city was recaptured by the Italians, young Arabs assaulted the Jews of Benghazi. The British reoccupied Benghazi briefly on Dec. 24, 1941, and this time the Jews were much more careful regarding their contacts with the British army. The Jan. 27, 1942, reoccupation of *Benghazi by Axis forces was followed by the systematic plunder of all Jewish shops and the promulgation of a deportation order: 2,600 persons were deported into the desert to Giado, 149 mi. (240 km.) south of Tripoli, where they lived under extremely harsh conditions. During their 14-month exile 562 people died of starvation or typhus. In March 1941 the Italian governor of Tripoli took discriminatory measures against all Jews and ordered Jewish organizations to cease all activities. In April 1942 the Jews of Tripoli were compelled to declare all their property, and those between 18 and 45 years of age were sent to forced labor: some 1,400 persons to Homs, and 350 to lay the railway line linking Libya and Egypt. They, together with the rest of the population of Tripoli, were subject to severe bombing by the Royal Air Force. Jews with French and British nationality were declared enemy nationals and were exiled in 1942: the French nationals to *Tunisia and the British nationals first to Italy and then to concentration camps in Austria, Germany, and Poland, though most of them survived the war.

[Robert Attal / Rachel Simon (2nd ed.)]

During this period, Zionist activity was paralyzed. In general the relations with the Muslim population did not worsen, and village Muslims sometimes gave sanctuary and shelter during the three years to Jews who fled to them, although in the towns fascist propaganda reached and influenced the young Muslims. During World War II the men of the Jewish Brigade conducted various political and cultural activities among the Jewish population. The Jewish Palestinian soldiers were greatly impressed by the knowledge of Hebrew among Libyan Jews and their Zionist aspirations. Although there was not much Jewish immigration to Palestine prior to the late 1940s, and the community as a whole was pro-Italian, the events of World War II and the 1945 riots in Tripoli and its vicinity changed the political attitude of the Jews: they did not trust Italy anymore and feared for their life and property under independent Arab rule. This resulted in the mass immigration to Israel of some 95% of the community within three years (1949–51) (see below).

The British Occupation

During the British occupation (1942/43–51) the Jews were able to reopen their schools, although in this period they suffered from persecution by Muslims which was unparalleled in the past. On November 4, 1945, there were Muslim riots against the Jews of Tripoli and neighboring towns. In Tripoli the masses ran wild, killing and wounding many Jews, looting their property, and setting fire to five synagogues. On November 6 troublemakers from Tripoli arrived in Zanzur (c. 30 mi. (48 km.) from Tripoli) and incited the Muslim population against the 150 local Jews, of whom half were murdered. Jews were also killed at Meslātah, Zawiyah, Tajurah (10 mi. (16 km.) from Tripoli), and at Amruz (2½ mi. (4 km.) from Tripoli). According to various estimates, from 121 to 187 Jews were killed and many were wounded during these incidents. Nine synagogues were burned down and damage to property was half a million pounds sterling, a very large sum for a poor community. The British authorities did not succeed in immediately stopping the excesses because they had Arab soldiers and policemen in their service who generally joined in the riots with the masses when sent to protect Jews; only when forces came from outside, especially Sudanese soldiers, were the rioters dispersed. After the riots about 300 rioters were brought to trial, of whom two were sentenced to death. The leniency of the sentences and the incitement by the Arab countries regarding Palestine encouraged Libyan Muslims to persecute the Jews again in June 1948 in Benghazi and Tripoli. However, this time some of the Jews were ready to defend themselves, since after the 1945 attacks a Jewish defense organization with members of both genders was set up in Tripoli by an emissary from Palestine (1946). Tripoli Jews used hand grenades and repelled marauders trying to enter the Jewish quarter; before the rioters could be stopped the police arrived, but 14 Jews had already been killed. Most of the rioters were Tunisian volunteers on the way to the Palestinian front.

Contemporary Period

After the 1945 riots, Jews began leaving Libya, most of them immigrating to Palestine. Between 1919 and 1948 about 450 Jews immigrated to Palestine from Libya, most of them during the years 1946 and 1947 when about 150 immigrated there. When the State of Israel was established, Jewish flight from Libya increased; they left by way of Tripoli and Tunisia; between May 1948 and January 1949 about 2,500 left the country. Only in February 1949 did the British permit legal immigration to Israel, and many immediately registered to emigrate. Several officials of the Jewish Agency and Israeli government ministries operated legally in Tripoli and traveled throughout the country. These few Israelis were assisted by numerous indigenous Jews, and in collaboration with the local authorities prepared the required travel documents. Because disease was widespread among Libyan Jews, medical personnel of the OSE health organization (see *OZE) and Israel checked prospective emigrants and treated those who were forbidden to enter Israel prior to recovery. During the mass emigration, most Libyan Jews traveled directly from Tripoli to Haifa in Israeli ships. Israeli officials were also involved in cultural events and teachers' training in Tripoli and its vicinity. Until the end of 1951, some 30,000 Jews emigrated, only about 8,000 Jews remaining in Libya. Most of them lived in Tripoli and about 400 in Benghazi, while the townlets and villages were almost entirely emptied of Jews. Under the independent Libyan regime (from December 24, 1951) Jews did not suffer from persecution and equal rights were guaranteed them under the Libyan constitution. Nevertheless, Libyan citizens were forbidden to return home if they visited Israel (June 1952), and in 1953 the authorities closed the Maccabi club. In June 1967, after the Six-Day War, there were anti-Jewish riots and the Jews locked themselves inside their houses for fear of attack; 17 Jews were murdered and many were arrested. After a time, the majority of the remainder left, mostly to Italy and to Israel. Following the coup by Col. Qadhdhafi on Sept. 1, 1969, the 400–500 Jews remaining in Libya were concentrated in a camp in Tripoli. These included Libyan citizens, bearers of foreign citizenship (British, French, Italian), and those bearing no citizenship. The government claimed that this step was taken to defend the Jews against incursions on their property. After the coup Jews were not allowed to leave Libya, although ultimately all of them were released and some of them succeeded in leaving Libya. On July 21, 1970, the revolutionary regime announced the nationalization of Italian and Jewish property, mostly of Jews who had left Libya indefinitely.

Social, Economic, and Religious-Cultural Conditions

Demographically, it should be noted that Libyan Jews, of whom there were about 20,000 in 1911, were mainly concentrated in the town of Tripoli (c. 12,000), but many were scattered in towns, townlets, and villages all over the country. According to the 1931 census there were 24,534 Jews, and in 1948 about 38,000 Jews in Libya, of whom about 20,000 were in Tripoli. This shows that there was no mass emigration before 1948, nor was there considerable migration within the country. At the end of 1970 only some 90 Jews remained in Libya.

Until the late 19th century, Libyan Jews spoke mostly a Jewish dialect of Maghrebi Arabic, which included Hebrew words. Because Muslim neighbors usually understood the local *Judeo-Arabic, Jewish peddlers often used a unique argot among themselves when doing business with Muslims. Jewish communities in Libya as elsewhere in the Jewish world made sure that boys received formal education in community schools enabling them to read the Bible and prayer books. Studies in these schools consisted of learning the Hebrew alphabet and reciting Hebrew and Aramaic texts. Since the spoken language was Judeo-Arabic, most Jewish men did not understand what they recited nor the readings from the Bible, the Zohar, and other Holy Scriptures at the synagogue which they attended on the evenings or the Sabbath; most of them could not write either. The community did not offer any formal education to Jewish girls. The wide dispersal of Libyan Jewry into dozens of communities, many comprising only a few families, sometimes affected their economic and educational circumstances. With the opening of Christian schools in Tripoli in the 19th century, several Jewish boys and girls, especially those from families with commercial and social ties with Europe, attended these schools. The religious leaders of the community, but even wealthy families with ties to Europe, preferred their children to receive a Jewish education. This prompted Jewish merchants from Tripoli to initiate the opening of an Italian school in Tripoli in 1876 which was run by Italian Jews. This school, which accepted girls from 1877, taught secular subjects, focusing on Italian culture, but included also Hebrew and Jewish subjects.

The Alliance Israélite Universelle opened a school only in Tripoli (in 1890 for boys and in 1896 for girls), with emphasis on French culture and secular subjects, as well as Hebrew and Jewish subjects. In both the Italian and Alliance schools, the Jewish subjects were taught by indigenous teachers who usually did not receive any pedagogic training, while the secular subjects were taught by Italian formally trained teachers and Paris-trained Alliance teachers from France, the Ottoman Empire, and North Africa. Under Italian rule, Italian state schools were established in Libya and many Jews preferred to send their children there, mainly in Tripoli and Benghazi; in many small towns they made do with study at a **ḥeder*. For this reason a large proportion of Jewish children outside the main towns received no modern education and girls no formal education whatsoever. However, in comparison to the beginning of the century, the younger generation contained far fewer illiterates. The Jews also opened a private high school in Tripoli in 1936, when they were expelled from Italian high schools for refusing to attend school on the Sabbath, but they were forced to close it in 1939. As a result of the anti-Jewish racial legislation of 1938, Jews could not attend state schools and tried to organize communal education for boys. Following the British occupation (1942/43), Jewish communal education was resumed, and the Jewish Palestinian soldiers in the British army helped the communities of Benghazi and Tripoli to establish schools for boys and girls with a curriculum based on Jewish education in Palestine. Jewish soldiers participated in the teaching and in teacher training for those schools. Many of the teachers in the Tripoli school were previous members of the Ben-Yehudah Society. In 1947 a Hebrew teachers' seminary was opened in Tripoli, with the help of educators from Palestine. It trained teachers for the Hebrew school in Tripoli and later also for the vicinity, but it closed down after the mass emigration.

Libya's most prominent rabbis included R. Masʿud Hai *Rakaḥ, author of the work *Ma'aseh Roke'aḥ* on Maimonides; R. Abraham Ḥayyim Adadi, author of *Va-Yikra Avraham*; and R. Isaac Hai Bukhbaza (d. 1930).

Apart from the Tripoli community which contained a number of important merchants and officials, most Libyan Jews were occupied as artisans; a few were peddlers and farmers and thus worked hard for their living. Peddlers often traveled alone in the countryside for lengthy periods of times, in some instances returning home only for the High Holidays and Passover. Despite the strict segregation between non-kin men and women in Libya, Jewish peddlers could trade directly with Muslim women, and they usually felt safe among the Muslim nomads and rural population. The statements of 6,080 breadwinners who immigrated to Israel from Libya between 1948 and 1951 show that 15.4% were merchants, 7.5% were clerks and administrators, 3.0% were members of the liberal professions (including teachers and rabbis), 6.1% were farmers, 47% were artisans, and 7.1% were construction and transport workers. The remainder (13.9%) worked in personal services or were unskilled laborers.

As a result of their poverty, disease was widespread among Libyan Jewry; they suffered mainly from trachoma, tuberculosis, and eczema, so much so that children in school had to be classified according to illness. Following the inception of legal Jewish immigration to Israel, the OSE began work in Tripoli in 1949 to care for schoolchildren and convalescents who were sent to a *talmud torah* in the town, where healthy children were kept. However, in April 1950 only 30% of the 2,000 Jewish schoolchildren were healthy; thus, the Israel immigration authorities had to screen potential immigrants for illness and provide them with medical care before permitting them to immigrate.

Zionist Activity

By the turn of the 19th century news about the Zionist organization had reached Libyan Jews and several members of the communities of Tripoli and Benghazi tried to establish local Zionist branches. Correspondence kept in the Central Zionist Archives in Jerusalem includes letters sent from Libya between

1900 and 1904 acknowledging the receipt of Zionist publications in Hebrew, French, and Ladino. The authors of these letters were ready to organize Zionist activities and to collect dues (*shekel*) for the Zionist organization, and they even sent some dues which they had collected. One letter in particular demonstrates excitement regarding the Zionist idea and readiness to get involved in Zionist activities. It seems, though, that these letters remained mainly unanswered. A short time after Libya was conquered by Italy, contact was made between Libyan Jewry and the Italian Zionist Organization, mainly due to the newspapers that reached Libya. In 1913 some of the readers of these newspapers, led by Elijah Neḥaisi (1890–1918) of Tripoli, tried to found a Zionist organization. At first only an evening *talmud torah* was founded (1914) in order to spread the Hebrew language, and then the Zion Society was established (May 1916), and the committee of this Zionist association succeeded in entering the Tripoli community committee, gaining 11 of the 31 places as members of their association (June 1916). The Zion Society published the first Zionist newspaper in Libya, *Degel Ẓiyyon* (1920–24). In 1923 the association changed its name to the Tripolitanian Zionist Federation. The Ben Yehuda Association, established in 1931, was very active in spreading the Hebrew language in Tripoli. In 1933 it published a weekly entitled *Limdu 'Ivrit!* ("Learn Hebrew!"). The association also opened a Hebrew school in Tripoli, *ha-Tiqvah*, in 1931 for adults and children of both genders, which was attended by 512 pupils (1933); their numbers rose to 1,200 in 1938/39. All the teachers in this school were indigenous self-taught Jews of both genders, and several pupils became teachers as well. This nucleus of teachers was very active in education following the British occupation. In 1939 the school was closed and the association disbanded on government orders as part of the anti-Jewish racial legislation.

When Libya was conquered by the British (November 1942–January 1943) and Jewish Palestinian soldiers came to the country, Zionist work was resumed. A number of Zionist youth organizations were established with the initial help of emissaries from Palestine and several Hebrew newspapers were published (*Ḥayyeinu*, a Hebrew monthly, 1944; *Niẓẓanim*, Hebrew monthly, 1945–48; *Ḥayyeinu*, Hebrew, Italian, and Arabic weekly, 1949–50). In 1943 the He-Ḥalutz ("the Pioneer") organization for youth movement graduates was set up, and an agricultural training farm (*hakhsharah*) was established near Tripoli; it was abandoned in November 1945 when the anti-Jewish riots broke out; the ten trainees immigrated to Israel (1946). Subsequently, agricultural training was renewed, until the 23 trainees were forced to abandon the farm during the June 1948 pogroms.

In May 1946 an emissary from Ereẓ Israel founded a defense organization in Tripoli, which was trained in the use of weapons and manufactured homemade "bombs"; it defended the Jewish quarter in Tripoli during the June 1948 riots. In 1946 illegal immigration to Ereẓ Israel also began, achieved by illegally crossing the frontier into Tunisia, and from there to Marseilles. In 1948 illegal immigration to Ereẓ Israel was organized through Italy. Hundreds emigrated in this way, until legal immigration became possible (February 1949).

Since Libyan Jews were observant, most of the Zionist organizations were religious, including the youth groups founded after 1943. These were later affiliated to Ha-Po'el ha-Mizraḥi.

[Haim J. Cohen / Rachel Simon (2nd ed.)]

Attitude Toward Israel

When the UN General Assembly resolved (Nov. 21, 1949) that Libya become independent before Jan. 1, 1952, Israel, itself a newcomer to the UN, cast its vote for the resolution. This gesture of goodwill received no reciprocation, and Israel did not repeat it in the case of any other Arab state. Anti-Jewish outbursts accompanied the announcement about the impending independence, and Israel took all precautions to enable Libya's Jews who wanted to settle in Israel to reach their destination before the critical date. Close to 90% of Libyan Jewry settled in Israel up to the end of 1951. Independent Libya joined the Arab League in March 1953 and adopted a hostile attitude toward Israel, though it was mainly declaratory. Libya took part in Arab summit conferences, joined the Arab boycott against Israel, conducted anti-Israel propaganda, and attacked Israel at the UN. The situation became more critical during the Six-Day War (1967), when widespread strikes of Libyan oil workers, as an expression of Arab solidarity, brought the flow of oil to a temporary stop, hitting the U.S. and Western Europe, which allegedly aided Israel, and shaking the conservative rule of King Idrīs.

After the war, Libya allowed Palestinians to live and work inside its territory, but only in limited numbers. It permitted collections for the Palestinian organizations, founded a school for al-Fatḥ orphans, and played host to several delegations from these organizations. Libya, like other Arab oil states (Saudi Arabia and Kuwait), contributed an annual share ($8,000,000) to Egypt and Jordan, according to the resolution of the 1967 Arab summit conference in Khartoum.

A drastic change occurred in Libya's attitude toward Israel after the overthrow of the monarchy on Sept. 1, 1969, and the rise of a revolutionary regime. Libya now adopted the militant line of the extreme Arab states in regard to Israel, as well as against the West in general. Muammar al-Qadhdhafi, chairman of the Revolutionary Council, announced from the start that the new regime opposed political solutions to the Israel-Arab conflict and did not believe in the possibility of a successful peaceful settlement. He promised to mobilize all Libya's rich resources in order to assist the armed confrontation with Israel. At the Arab summit conference in Rabat (Dec. 21–23, 1969), he also promised to extend a considerable part of Libya's oil revenues (which amounted to $1,000,000,000 annually) to reinforce the Arab front. Libya set up a "holy war fund" out of state grants, special taxes, and individual donations.

The following meeting in Tripoli (Dec. 25–27, 1969) of the presidents of Egypt, Sudan, and Libya, who agreed to establish an alignment of the three countries, underscored the new regime's desire to join the Arab struggle against Israel. Libya drifted more and more into the sphere of influence of *Nasser, who exploited the situation to deepen the Egyptian military and economic penetration into Libya, a step which became possible after the liquidation of the American and British military bases there and expulsion of foreigners in 1970. The regime acquired considerable quantities of arms which could serve the Arab cause at the front. On Nov. 8, 1970, the presidents of Libya, Egypt, and Sudan decided to establish a "union," or federation, of their countries in order to bring about closer military, economic, and political links; in 1971 Syria joined this bloc. Nonetheless, these and other attempts at political-military union proved futile. Libya assisted the Palestine organizations financially and politically.

[Rachel Cohen]

Following the anti-Jewish riots which broke out in Tripoli in June 1967, in which some 20 Jews were killed and Jewish property set on fire, an almost complete emigration of the 3,500 Jews then in Libya took place. Only 200 to 300 remained in 1969, 90 in 1970, and a mere handful in 1972; there were no Jews left in Libya by the end of the 20th century. There were thus hardly any Jews left in the country when King Idrīs was deposed and the republic proclaimed in September 1969, headed by Col. al-Qadhdhafi who became the most radical and extreme of the anti-Israel, anti-Zionist Arab leaders.

The anti-Zionist and anti-Israel policy of the new government could therefore express itself only with regard to Jewish property. A few days after the proclamation of the republic an edict was issued authorizing the government to sequestrate the assets and property of Jews who had left the country. This edict was made law in February 1970, but in view of its blatant anti-Jewish nature it was suspended and replaced in May by another law which provided for the sequestration and transfer to an official custodian of the property of persons whose names were handed in by the Ministry of Interior. In an appendix, not mentioned in the law itself, 620 names were given, 605 of whom were known to be Jewish.

In July 1970, however, the Libyan government undertook, by a special law, compensation for the confiscated property. According to this law, special government committees were to determine the value of the property and compensation would be paid through government bonds redeemable in 15 years. There is no information whether any such bonds were received, and it is probable that its purpose was merely to give legal sanction to the expropriation of Jewish property.

Following the visit of President Anwar Sadat to Jerusalem in November 1977, Libya joined the Rejection Front of the Arab States which opposed any negotiations with Israel.

[Haim J. Cohen]

BIBLIOGRAPHY: EARLY PERIOD: P. Monceaux, in: REJ, 44 (1902), 1ff.; N. Slouschz, *Travels in North Africa* (1927); S.A. Applebaum, *Yehudim vi-Yevanim be-Kirene ha-Kedumah* (1969); Hirschberg, in: *Journal of African History*, 4 (1963), 313ff.; *Zion*, 19 (1954), 52–56 (a bibl.). MODERN PERIOD: R. De Felice, *Jews in an Arab Land: Libya, 1835–1970* (tr. from Italian by Judith Roumani, 1985); F. Suarez et al. (eds.), *Yahadut Luv* (1960); I.M. Toledano, *Ner ha-Ma'arav* (1921), 88; I.S. Bernstein, in: *Sinai*, 19–20 (1946–47); G. Scholem, *Iggeret Avraham Mikha'el Cardozo le-Dayyanei Izmir* (1954); Hirschberg, Afrikah, 1 (1965), 5–17, 11, 173–206; idem, in *Bar-Ilan*, 4–5 (1967), 415–79; R. Attal, in: *Sefunot*, 9 (1965), a bibl.; I.J. Benjamin, *Acht Jahre in Asien und Afrika* (1858²), 230–7; M. Cohen, *Gli ebrei in Libia, usi e costumi* (1928); M. Eisenbeth, *Les Juifs de l'Afrique du Nord* (1936); G.V. Raccah, in: *Israel*, 23 (Florence, 1938); S. Groussard, *Pogrom* (1948); R. Attal, *Les Juifs d'Afrique du Nord – Bibliographie* (1975); H.Y. Cohen, *Asian and African Jews in the Middle East – 1860–1971; Annotated Bibliography* (1976). HOLOCAUST PERIOD: Rabinowitz, in: *Menorah Journal*, 23 (1945), 115–26; E. Kolb, *Bergen-Belsen* (Ger., 1962), 64; P. Juarez et al. (eds.), *Yahadut Luv* (1960), 197–201. **ADD. BIBLIOGRAPHY:** R. Simon, *Change Within Tradition among Jewish Women in Libya* (1992); idem, "The Socio-Economic Role of the Tripolitanian Jews in the Late Ottoman Period," in: M. Abitbol (ed.), *Communautés juives des marges sahariennes du Maghreb* (1982), 321–28; idem, "The Relations of the Jewish Community of Libya with Europe in the Late Ottoman Period," in: J.-L. Miège (de.), *Les relations intercommunautaires juives en Mediterranée occidentale XIIIe–XXe siècles* (1984), 70–78; idem, "Jews and the Modernization of Ottoman Libya," in: *The Alliance Review*, 24 (1984), 33–40; idem, "It Could have Happened There: The Jews of Libya during the Second World War," in: *Africana Journal*, 16 (1994), 391–422; idem, "Jewish Participation in the Reforms in Libya during the Second Ottoman Period, 1835–1911," in: A. Levy (ed.), *The Jews of the Ottoman Empire* (1993), 485–506; idem, "Language Change and Political-Social Transformation: The Case of the Libyan Jews (19th–20th Centuries)," in: *Jewish History*, 4 (1989), 101–21; idem, "Jewish Female Education in the Ottoman Empire, 1840–1914," in: A. Levy (ed.), *Jews, Turks, Ottomans: A Shared History, Fifteenth through the Twentieth Century* (2002), 127–52; idem, "Shlichim from Palestine in Libya," *Jewish Political Studies Review*, 9 (1997), 33–57; idem, "Education," in: R.S. Simon, M.M. Laskier, and S. Reguer (eds.), *Jews in the Modern Middle East and North Africa* (2002), 142–64; idem, "Zionism," in: *ibid.*, 165–79; H.E. Goldberg, "Ecologic and Demographic Aspects of Rural Tripolitanian Jewry, 1853–1949," in IJMES, 2 (1971), 245–65; idem, *Cave Dwellers and Citrus Growers: A Jewish Community in Libya and Israel* (1972); idem, "Rites and Riots: The Tripolitanian Pogroms of 1945," in: *Plural Societies*, 17 (1978), 75–87; idem, "Language and Culture of the Jews of Tripolitania: A Preliminary View," in: *Mediterranean Language Review*, 1 (1983), 85–102; idem, *Jewish Life in Muslim Libya: Rivals and Relatives* (1990); idem, "Libya," in: R.S. Simon, M.M. Laskier, and S. Reguer (eds.), *ibid.*, 431–43; H.E. Goldberg and C. Segré, "Mixtures of Diverse Substances: Education and the Hebrew Language among the Jews of Libya, 1875–1951," in: S. Fishbane, J.N. Lightstone, and V. Levin (eds.), *Social Scientific Study of Judaism and Jewish Society* (1990), 151–201; *The Book of Mordecai: A Study of the Jews of Libya*, trans., ed., and annotated by H.E. Goldberg (1993); M.M. Roumani, "Zionism and Social Change in Libya at the Turn of the Century," in: *Studies in Zionism*, 8:1 (1987), 1–24.

LICHINE (Lichtenstein), DAVID (1910–1972), Russian-born dancer and choreographer who carried on the ballet tradition of Diaghilev and Massine. He studied ballet with Lubov Egorova in Paris after emigrating from Russia and he first won attention when engaged by Bronislava Nijinska in 1928 to appear with Ida *Rubinstein's company. He later danced with Pavlova. From 1932 to 1940 he was a leading dancer and choreographer with Colonel de Basil's Ballets Russes de Monte Carlo. World War II brought Lichine and his wife, the ballerina Tatiana Riabouchinska, to the United States. In 1952 they settled in Los Angeles, where they established their own school and company. Lichine was at various times guest choreographer for American Ballet Theater, the Royal Danish Ballet, the Festival Ballet of London, and other companies. His ballets include *Protée* (1938), *The Prodigal Son* (1939), *Graduation Ball* (1940), and *Helen of Troy* (1942).

BIBLIOGRAPHY: F. Gadan-Pamard and R. Maillard (eds.), *Dictionary of Modern Ballet* (1959).

[Marcia B. Siegel]

LICHT, ALEXANDER (1884–1948), Zionist leader in Yugoslavia. Licht was born in the Croatian village Sokolovac. Except for one year of study in Vienna, he was educated in Zagreb, where he also graduated as a lawyer. He was the founder and spiritual leader of the "Zagreb school" in Yugoslav Zionism, which consisted mainly of young people and intellectuals and transformed the Zagreb community from a center of assimilationism into a dynamic focal point of Zionism. As a young man he was elected chairman of the Jewish youth circle Literarni Sastanci, which soon became a Zionist society. In Vienna he was the chairman of Bar Giora, a Zionist group of students from the areas which became Yugoslavia. He also organized in 1906 the second conference of Jewish academic youth in Osijek and wrote articles on Zionism in the Croatian press that won the sympathy of the gentile intelligentsia. He translated the "Ghetto songs" of Morris Rosenfeld into Croatian and edited the Zionist monthly *Židovska Smotra* ("Jewish Review"). In 1909 he was elected secretary of the Zionist Organization for the southern Slavic countries (Dalmatia, Bosnia, Croatia, and Slavonia). He served on the front during World War I, and after returning in 1918 he addressed a memorandum to the Yugoslav National Committee expounding the Zionist attitude to the problems arising from the disintegration of the Hapsburg Empire. In 1919 he was instrumental in preventing dangerous frictions between Sephardi and Ashkenazi Jews and the expulsion of Jews from Bosnia and Vojvodina. Between the world wars, Licht served as chairman of the Zionist Executive and later of the Zionist Organization of Yugoslavia. In 1929 he became a member of the Zionist General Council. In 1941 he was arrested and, after spending several months in prison in Graz, Austria, he wandered from one refugee camp to another in Slovenia, Italy, and Switzerland, where he finally managed to settle with his family. He died in Geneva and in 1955 his remains were transferred to Jerusalem.

[Yakir Eventov]

LICHT, FRANK (1916–1987), U.S. jurist and governor. Licht, who was born in Providence, Rhode Island, the son of Russian immigrants, was active in Jewish youth organizations in Providence. At Brown University he was founder of the Menorah Society. He received a law degree from Harvard Law School in 1941 and was a partner in the Providence law firm of Letts & Quinn from 1943 to 1956. During that time, in 1948, Licht was elected to the Rhode Island senate, serving until 1956, when he was appointed associate judge of the Rhode Island superior court. He resigned from the bench in 1968 to accept the Democratic nomination for governor, scoring an upset victory against a popular Republican incumbent to become governor in 1968, in which capacity he served two terms. He did not run for reelection in 1972.

In 1967 he was elected president of the General Jewish Committee of Providence, which he expanded into a statewide organization. Active in other Jewish affairs as well, Licht was vice president of Temple Emanu-El in Providence and chairman of the Rhode Island Campaign of Bonds for Israel. In recognition of his dedication to the Jewish community, he was awarded the Herbert H. Lehman Ethics Award of the Jewish Theological Seminary of America (1969) and the Herbert H. Lehman Citation of the National Information Bureau for Jewish Life (1970).

[Bernard Postal / Ruth Beloff (2nd ed.)]

LICHT, MICHAEL (1893–1953), Yiddish poet and essayist. Licht was raised by an uncle in Bielozorka, Ukraine, and immigrated to New York in 1913, where he took courses at City College and the New School for Social Research. He began his literary career composing English-language poetry under the pseudonyms Sonin and M. Lichsonin. Soon afterwards, he turned to Yiddish, joined the *In-Zikh poets, and, together with Jacob *Glatstein and N.B. *Minkoff, edited avant-garde journals (1925–26), contributing his own works to many literary journals. During the last 20 years of his life, he suffered from debilitating heart disease. Licht is a poet of the American metropolis, with original insights and satiric undertones.

BIBLIOGRAPHY: LNYL, 5 (1963), 138–40; Minkoff, in: M. Licht, *Gezamlte Lider* (1957), 9–14; S. Bickel, *Shrayber fun Mayn Dor* (1958), 63–8. **ADD. BIBLIOGRAPHY:** Sh. Tenenboym, *Shnit fun Mayn Feld* (1955), 475–82; E. Fershleyser, *Af Shrayberishe Shyiakhn* (1958), 100–5.

[Shlomo Bickel / Marc Miller (2nd ed.)]

LICHTENBAUM, JOSEPH (1895–1968), Hebrew writer. Born in Warsaw, Lichtenbaum moved to Moscow, where he was one of the co-founders of *Habimah in 1918. In 1920 he immigrated to Ereẓ Israel. He published poems and essays on writers and books of both Hebrew and general literature, and also translated a great deal of poetry and prose from world literature. Among his works are *Sefer ha-Shirim* (1944); *Sha'ul Tchernichowsky* (1946, 1953); *Sofereinu* (1949); *Soferei Yisrael* (1959 and after); *Bi-Netivei Sifrut* (1962), essays and reflections; *Sifrutenu ha-Ḥadashah* (1963), the development of poetry and prose in Hebrew literature; *Meshorerim Olamiyyim* (1966); and *Yosef Ḥayyim Brenner* (1967). He also published anthologies, including *Ha-Sippur ha-Ivri* ("The Hebrew Story," vol. 1 (1955), from Mapu to Shneur; vol. 2 (1960), from Burla to the present) with an introduction in each volume discussing the development of the Hebrew story; *Tekumah* (1958), Israel poetry and prose, including bibliographical notes; and

Shiratenu (2 vols. (1962), from M.Ḥ. Luzzatto to Bialik, and from Bialik to the present) including an introduction on the development of modern Hebrew poetry.

BIBLIOGRAPHY: Kressel, Leksikon, 2 (1967), 264–6.

[Getzel Kressel]

°**LICHTENBERG, BERNHARD** (1875–1943), German anti-Nazi priest. Lichtenberg, a devout Catholic, was born in Ohlau, southeast of Breslau. He grew up in a Protestant-dominated area with a Catholic minority suffering under Otto von Bismarck's anti-Catholic *Kulturkampf* persecution. As Lichtenberg matured he combined Catholic piety with political Catholicism, ultimately serving in the Catholic Center Party of Germany. After graduating high school, the young man went to seminary and was ordained a priest at the age of 24. Assigned to various parishes around Berlin, he revealed great dedication to the Catholic faith and boundless energy to his parishioners. At the core of his message, taken directly from the teaching of Jesus of Nazareth, was to love one's neighbor in everyday life situations. This would become more difficult with the rise of the National Socialists to power.

As Hitler led the Nazi Party to political success, Father Lichtenberg, now monsignor, was assigned to St. Hedwig's Cathedral in Berlin. He regarded the Nazi movement as immoral, unchristian, and totally incompatible with Catholic teachings. This revealed itself with Lichtenberg's opposition to the Law for the Prevention of Hereditarily Diseased Offspring and to the Nazi "euthanasia" campaign. It came again in 1935 when Lichtenberg received a report on conditions at the Esterwegen concentration camp and sent it on to the Prussian Ministry of the Interior. This would not be the last time that Lichtenberg refused to violate his conscience in order to appease the Nazi state. It would also be the beginning of the Nazi call for the arrest and imprisonment of this "nuisance."

Following the events of **Kristallnacht* on November 9, 1938, Lichtenberg took a step which would single him out from all other Catholic Church leaders. Immediately following the events of the Nazi pogrom, Lichtenberg went to the pulpit of St. Hedwig's and publicly proclaimed: "We know what happened yesterday. We do not know what tomorrow holds. However, we have experienced what happened today. Outside, the synagogue burns. That is also a house of God" (quoted in K. Spicer, p. 171). From that day forward, Lichtenberg publicly prayed for both Jews and converted Jews until his arrest in 1941.

On August 29, 1941, two young Protestant women went inside St. Hedwig's Cathedral to study its architecture. While inside, they overheard Lichtenberg saying his daily prayer for the Jews. This encounter led to Lichtenberg's denunciation. Following the denunciation, the Gestapo charged that they had found material in the priest's home that suggested "hostile activity to the state." Among the found items was a statement by Lichtenberg, which defended the Jews and urged his listeners to follow the dictum of Jesus, "You shall love thy neighbor as thyself." Repeating this core belief in the course of his lengthy interrogation, Lichtenberg also stated that he considered Jews as his neighbors "who have immortally created souls after the image and likeness of God" (Spicer, 179).

Lichtenberg was found guilty of treacherous acts against the state and for violating the pulpit law. For his crimes, Lichtenberg was sentenced to two years in prison. Undaunted, Lichtenberg repeatedly requested that he be allowed to go on a transport with deported Jews to the Lodz ghetto. Throughout his imprisonment Lichtenberg's health deteriorated. Upon his release from Tegel prison on October 22, 1943, the Gestapo apprehended the worn-out man and sent him to a work camp. On October 28, 1943, the Reich Security Main Office decided that Lichtenberg needed to be removed from the work camp on the grounds of maintaining public safety. Following this order, the now 68-year-old priest, in failing health, was moved from a holding location to be put on a train destined for Dachau concentration camp. In transit, Lichtenberg died.

Lichtenberg can perhaps best be remembered as an exceptional man who steadfastly defended both the rights of the Catholic Church and the rights of all human beings suffering persecution at the hands of a regime he regarded as despicable. On June 23, 1996, Pope John Paul II beatified Lichtenberg as a martyr to the faith.

BIBLIOGRAPHY: K.P. Spicer, *Resisting the Third Reich: The Catholic Clergy in Hitler's Berlin* (2004).

[Beth Griech-Polelle (2nd ed.)]

LICHTENFELD, GABRIEL JUDAH (1811–1887), Hebrew author and mathematician. Born in Lublin, he lived most of his life in Opatow, Poland. Having taught himself sciences and European languages, he wrote for *Ha-Shaḥar, Ha-Ẓefirah, Izraelita*, and Polish newspapers, mostly on mathematical topics. In 1865 he published *Yedi'ot ha-Shi'urim* ("Science of Measurement"), by which a reader might "learn the elements of surveying, without the aid of a teacher." In 1874–75 he published polemic tracts against Ḥ.S. *Slonimski, questioning the latter's competence in scientific matters. With I.L. *Peretz, whose first wife was Lichtenfeld's daughter, he co-edited *Sippurim be-Shir ve-Shirim Shonim me'et Shenei Ba'alei Asufot* ("Stories in Verse and Sundry Poems From Two Anthologists," Warsaw, 1877), incorporating a long original poem by the editors called *Ḥayyei Meshorer Ivri* ("Life of a Hebrew Poet"). Lichtenfeld's book on mathematics, *Bo'u Ḥeshbon*, was published posthumously (1895). Some of the terminology which he coined has been generally accepted.

BIBLIOGRAPHY: Rejzen, Leksikon, 2 (1927), 980; Kressel, Leksikon, 2 (1967), 266–7.

[Yehuda Slutsky]

LICHTENSTADT, ABRAHAM AARON (d. 1702), *Court Jew and *primator* ("leader") of the Bohemian *Landesjudenschaft. Lichtenstadt has been identified with Aaron Schlackenwerth (d. 1694) and also with Abraham Aaron of Frankfurt, but Tobias *Jakobovits established that he was the son of the physician Naphtali Hirz Oettingen of Przemysl (Poland). He took his family name from his place of residence, Hroznetin (Lichtenstadt). First mentioned as agent of the court of Saxony, he became the *shtadlan* of Bohemian Jewry in 1673. In 1680 he persuaded *Leopold I to cancel the order expelling the Jews from the Planá community (see *Chodová Planá), and later secured for the Jews the right to attend the Leipzig fairs. He was instrumental in having Abraham *Broda appointed as chief rabbi (*Landesrabbiner*) of Bohemian Jewry in 1689. As a result of internal strife in the Jewish community, he was denounced for abusing his position when determining the allotment of taxes. Legal proceedings were opened in 1692, and although a case could not be established against him, Leopold I removed him from his post and had him, his son Solomon, and the secretary (*Landschreiber*) of the Landesjudenschaft imprisoned. The complicated trial which followed was one of the most prominent of its kind at the time. In 1693 he was released from prison and restored to office in 1701; those who had denounced him were imprisoned.

BIBLIOGRAPHY: T. Jakubovits, in: MGWJ, 74 (1930), 35–41; 76 (1932), 511–2; idem, in: JGGJČ, 5 (1933), 79–136, passim.

[Meir Lamed]

LICHTENSTEIN, AARON (1933-), U.S.-Israeli *rosh yeshivah*. Born in France, Lichtenstein grew up in the United States. He studied at Yeshivah Rabbi Chaim Berlin under Rabbi Yitzchak Huntner, and thereafter at Yeshiva University under Rabbi Joseph B. *Soloveitchik, whose daughter, Tova, he would later marry. He received a B.A. and was ordained at Yeshiva University, followed by a Ph.D. in English Literature from Harvard University, where he studied under Douglas Bush.

He served as *rosh yeshivah* at Yeshiva University for some years. In 1971 he was invited by Rabbi Yehudah Amital to serve as joint *rosh yeshivah* with Rabbi Amital of Yeshivat Har Etzion in Alon Shevut, a settlement close to Jerusalem. The *hesder* yeshivah combines high-level talmudic studies with specified periods of time in the Israel Defense Forces (generally 15 months in the army over the five years of the total program).

Under the joint stewardship of Lichtenstein and Amital, Yeshivat Har Etzion has grown to be one of the leading yeshivot in Israel, whose graduates occupy many important positions both in Israel and abroad.

Lichtenstein is known as an outstanding talmudist, but is equally known for his exacting moral standards. He has no hesitation on speaking out on pressing issues, and at the time was involved in leading a student march on behalf of the starving children in Biafra.

Following in the footsteps of his illustrious father-in-law, Rabbi Joseph B. Soloveitchik – the undisputed leader of Modern Orthodoxy for decades – Lichtenstein, too, follows the "Brisker method" of talmudic study. (Rabbi Soloveitchik was a grandson of Rabbi Ḥayyim *Soloveichik, the "Brisker Rav"). This method, states Lichtenstein, is characterized by "incisive analysis, exact definition, precise classification, and critical independence."

Lichtenstein is the author of *Leaves of Faith*, vol. 1: *The World of Jewish Learning*, vol. 2: *The World of Jewish Living*; and *By His Light: Character and Values in the Service of God*. His students' notes on his *shi'urim* on Toharot, Zevaḥim, and the eighth chapter of Bava Meẓi'a, Pesaḥim, and *Dina d'Garmi* were published as *Shi'urei ha-Rav Aharon Lichtenstein*.

While stressing the absolute primacy and centrality of talmudic study, Lichtenstein nevertheless feels that there is a need for culture as well in one's education and life. To him, culture "can inform and irradiate our spiritual being by rounding out its cardinal Torah component." Thus, the natural sciences "manifestly decipher and describe a divinely ordained order whose knowledge both inspires praise and thanksgiving to [God] and stimulates our reverential response to Him"; and "far from constituting mere straying in alien fields, culture can become a vehicle for enhancing our Torah existence."

His passion for talmudic study is primarily religious, but is also intellectual. As he writes, in "Why Learn Gemara," with each new page of the Talmud "one feels the freshness of virgin birth, the angular edge of rough terrain plowed and unplowed, the beck of meandering paths charted and uncharted."

LICHTENSTEIN, HILLEL BEN BARUCH (1815–1891), Hungarian rabbi. Lichtenstein was one of the outstanding pupils of Moses *Sofer. He first served as rabbi of Margarethen and in 1854 was elected rabbi of Kolozsvar, the capital of Transylvania. After 18 months he was compelled to leave the locality without officially assuming office, owing to his opposition to Abraham Friedman, rabbi of Transylvania, and because of the internal frictions in the community which were aggravated as a result. His refusal to go to Gyulafehérvár (*Alba-Julia), where the district rabbi had his seat, to receive his sanction to take up his post, as was then the custom, served as the formal reason for his departure. Between 1865 and 1867 he was rabbi of Szikszó, also in Hungary. He then moved to Galicia and became rabbi of Kolomyya (Kolomea). Lichtenstein was one of the dominant figures of the Orthodox community in their struggle with the reformers both before and after the great schism of 1869. He fought against any suspicion of reform in the life of the Jews, and sharply criticized those Orthodox Jews, including rabbis, who inclined to any kind of innovation in religious practices. He especially attacked those who attempted to preach in German, and even censured Azriel *Hildesheimer on this account. Lichtenstein's pupils also served as uncompromising fighters against religious reforms. At rabbinical conventions in Hungary, called on his initiative, the main principles of extremist Orthodoxy for Hungarian Jewry were laid down. The first convention of this kind assembled in Sátoraljaújhely in 1864 but the main one took place in 1866 in Nagymihály (Michalovce) where resolutions were adopted excommunicating Reform Judaism and any rabbi preaching in German or any other European language. Ten *takkanot were also enacted, which to this day serve as the basis of the separation between Orthodox Jews and reformers in Hungary. Lichtenstein wrote many books, including

Maskil el Dal, 4 parts, sermons (1860–69); *Shirei Maskil*, on ethics (1877); *Avkat Rokhel*, responsa, 2 parts (1883–85); and *Et La'asot*, in Yiddish, on ethics, 2 parts (1878).

BIBLIOGRAPHY: Aaron of Nadvornaya, *Zekher Ẓaddik* (1891); Z.H. Heller, *Beit Hillel* (1893); Rejzen, Leksikon, 2 (1927), 147–50; N.M. Gelber, in: *Pinkas Kolomey* (1957), 41–48.

[Isaak Dov Ber Markon]

LICHTENSTEIN, ROY (1923–1997), U.S. painter, printmaker, and sculptor. One of the leading figures of the Pop Art movement, Lichtenstein was born in New York. He briefly studied with Reginald Marsh at the Art Students League in New York (summer 1939), and then pursued a B.F.A. (1947) and an M.F.A. (1949) at Ohio State University (1940–43; 1946–49), his progress interrupted by several years in the Army. Early in his career Lichtenstein experimented with Cubism, Abstract Expressionism, and other modern styles. In the late 1950s he even rendered the comic subjects that would become synonymous with his name in a loose, painterly fashion.

Lichtenstein derived his first paintings based on comic images from his children's bubble-gum wrappers. These early works, such as *Look Mickey* (1961, National Gallery of Art, Washington, D.C.), did not yet simulate newsprint techniques and remain closely allied with the original source in color and composition. Within a year Lichtenstein began his enlarged reproductions of comic book scenes rendered in primary colors without modulation, thick black outlines, and an imitation Benday dot technique akin to newsprint. According to Lichtenstein, the subjects of his early paintings – the melodrama of his heartbroken beauties and the violent deaths of his war heroes – were not of interest to him. Rather, he said, the comics were simply used for formal reasons.

Beginning in the mid-1960s, Lichtenstein began quoting well-known works of art and also paraphrasing popular art forms in his signature comic book style. The "Brushstroke" paintings of 1965–66 show enlarged gestural marks that mock Abstract Expressionism by the very dichotomy of Lichtenstein's lucid technique and the thick, dripping oil paint he reproduces. Lichtenstein found great success with the comic-styled works, enjoying his first retrospective at the Pasadena Art Museum in 1967, followed by a retrospective on the East Coast at the Guggenheim Museum in New York two years later. Through the 1970s and early 1980s, Lichtenstein continued to use the history of art as his source material, quoting major paintings by the German Expressionists, the Surrealists, and other avant-garde artists. The last decades of his life were marked by several series, including a cycle of "Interiors" derived from advertisements. Throughout his career Lichtenstein was also an active printmaker. On occasion he would execute sculptures such as the *Mermaid* (1979) that lounges on the grass in front of the Miami Beach Theater for Performing Arts. In 1989 he made a 23 by 54 foot mural for the entrance hall of the Tel Aviv Museum of Art.

BIBLIOGRAPHY: L. Alloway, *Roy Lichtenstein* (1983); B. Rose, *The Drawings of Roy Lichtenstein* (1987); D. Waldman, *Roy Lichtenstein* (1993); M.L. Corlett, *The Prints of Roy Lichtenstein: A Catalogue Raisonné (1948–1997)* (2002).

[Samantha Baskind (2nd ed.)]

LICHTENSTEIN, TEHILLA (1894–1973), spiritual leader of the Society of Jewish Science in New York City from 1938 to 1973. Lichtenstein was the first woman to serve as religious leader of an ongoing U.S. Jewish congregation. Born in Jerusalem to Chava (Cohen) and Rabbi Chaim Hirschensohn, Rachel Tehilla, who later identified herself simply as Tehilla, moved with her family to Hoboken, N.J., at the age of 11. The youngest of five children, she and her siblings received a good Jewish and an excellent secular education. Like her sisters, Nima Adlerblum, Tamar de Sola Pool, and Esther Taubenhaus, Lichtenstein was an ardent Zionist and an active member of many Jewish organizations. She received a B.A. in classics from Hunter College, an M.A. in literature from Columbia University, and was a doctoral student in English literature at Columbia until 1920, when she married Reform rabbi Morris Lichtenstein.

The Society of Jewish Science, founded by Morris Lichtenstein in 1922, sought to reawaken religiously apathetic Jews to Judaism's spiritual possibilities while combating the attraction of thousands of American Jews to Christian Science. With the birth of her sons, Immanuel (b. 1922) and Michael (b. 1927), Tehilla's early involvement in the society was limited but important. She served as religious school principal and edited the monthly *Jewish Science Interpreter* and her husband's writings. Following Rabbi Lichtenstein's death in 1938, she became the society's spiritual leader in accordance with the provisions of his will. Over 500 people came to see her conduct services and deliver her first sermon. By the late 1950s, the society had opened a synagogue in Long Island and subscribers to the *Jewish Science Interpreter* totaled close to 2,000.

While Tehilla Lichtenstein's role as religious leader came about by circumstance rather than design, for 35 years she articulated her understanding of Jewish Science in over 500 sermons and scores of essays, lectures, and radio broadcasts. Actively encouraged by her sister, Tamar, and brother-in-law, Rabbi David de Sola Pool, and ably assisted by many others, Lichtenstein emphasized the connection between mind and body, the importance of tapping into the divine healing power within, and ways of achieving health and happiness within a specifically Jewish context. Yet she also placed great emphasis on Jewish peoplehood, the centrality of Israel to Jewish self-identity, women's equality, including their ordination as rabbis, and the revitalization of Judaism itself. While Lichtenstein continued to be influenced by her husband's teachings, by the late 1940s many of her sermons took a different direction. Like such inspirational leaders as Norman Vincent Peale, she increasingly offered sound, practical advice, emphasizing the importance of family connections and a positive attitude towards life. Some of Lichtenstein's essays were published in *Applied Judaism: Selected Jewish Science Essays* (ed. D. Friedman, 1989). Her papers are housed at the American Jewish Archives in Cincinnati, Ohio.

BIBLIOGRAPHY: E.M. Umansky, *From Christian Science to Jewish Science: Spiritual Healing and American Jews* (2005).

[Ellen Umansky (2nd ed.)]

LICHTENSTEIN, WALTER (1880–1964), U.S. educator, economist, and public official. Lichtenstein, who was born in Brunswick, Germany, was taken to the U.S. at the age of two. He served as editor of the *New International Encyclopaedia* (1902–03) and curator of Harvard University's Hohenzollern Collection (1905–06). From 1908 to 1919 he was again curator of the collection and also held the positions of associate professor (1908–11) and professor of history (1911–18) at Northwestern University, Evanston, Illinois. Although Lichtenstein, in the course of his career, was consultant to several large U.S. companies and a longtime officer of the First National Bank of Chicago, he also had an extensive public service career. His positions included secretary to the Federal Advisory Council of the Federal Reserve System (1926–48); member of the U.S. Monetary Plan Commission (1936–54); and economic adviser to the American Military Government for Germany (1945–47). Lichtenstein edited a number of historical works, including *Ulrich Zwingli, Latin and German Works* (1912).

LICHTHEIM, RICHARD (1885–1963), Zionist leader in Germany. Lichtheim was born in Berlin of an assimilated family and completed his studies in economics in Freiburg, where he also joined the Zionist movement. At first he aided the Zionist Organization's Palestine department, which was established in Berlin after the Fifth Zionist Congress (1907). He eventually became one of the outstanding ideologists and publicists in the Zionist movement, and his work *Das Program des Zionismus* (1911, 1913²) made a lasting impression. After D. *Wolffsohn's resignation (1911) and the transfer of the Zionist center to Berlin, Lichtheim became the editor of the central Zionist organ, *Die *Welt*, and remained in this post until 1913. In that year he went to Constantinople as a representative of the Zionist Executive. At first he worked together with Victor *Jacobson, and when the latter had to leave Constantinople at the outbreak of World War I, Lichtheim, who was a German citizen, remained (until 1917). During that period he did much to curb the physical persecution of the Jews in Ereẓ Israel through the influence of the German and American representatives in the Ottoman capital.

At the end of the war, Lichtheim returned to Germany, and his memoranda on the methods of upbuilding Ereẓ Israel under the British Mandate aroused Chaim *Weizmann's interest. From 1921 to 1923 he was a member of the Zionist Executive and head of its Organization Department. Afterward he left the Executive in opposition to Weizmann's policy, and in 1925 he joined the *Revisionist movement, which he left in 1933 joining for a while the Jewish State Party which seceded from it. Lichtheim worked in an insurance company in Germany and continued in this field after settling in Palestine in 1934 by establishing the Migdal Insurance Company together with G. *Halpern. He was in Geneva throughout World War II and set up a network of contacts with occupied European countries for the Zionist Organization. At the end of the war, Lichtheim returned to Jerusalem and during his last years wrote his memoirs, *She'ar Yashuv* ("A Remnant Shall Return," 1953) and *Toledot ha-Ẓiyyonut be-Germanyah* ("A History of Zionism in Germany," Heb., 1951, Ger., 1954), and an autobiographical volume *Rueckkehr* (1970), on his activities in Zionist diplomacy before World War I.

[Getzel Kressel]

His son, GEORGE LICHTHEIM (1912–1973), historian and political scientist, was born in Berlin and in 1933 went to Jerusalem, where he spent most of the Hitler years as foreign editor of the *Jerusalem Post* and as a translator. From 1946 he lived in London, except for two periods spent in the U.S. as associate editor of *Commentary* (1957–58) and as visiting lecturer and research associate at Columbia and Stanford universities (1964–66). Besides serving as London editor of *Commentary* from 1960 and as a correspondent for the *Jerusalem Post*, he was a leading scholar in the fields of socialism and political science, and has contributed to a number of leading scholarly and intellectual publications. His works include *Marxism, an Historical and Critical Study* (1964²), *Europe and America* (1963), *The New Europe* (1963), *Marxism and Modern France* (1966), and *The Concept of Ideology and Other Essays* (1967).

[Irving Rosenthal]

BIBLIOGRAPHY: A. Ruppin, *Pirkei Ḥayyai* (1969), passim; G. Herlitz, in: *Ha-Olam* (Feb. 15, 1945); P. Rosen, in: *Ha-Boker* (June 7, 1963); Tidhar, 11 (1961), 3786–87. **ADD. BIBLIOGRAPHY:** R. Cohen, "Confronting the Reality of the Holocaust – Richard Lichtheim 1939–1942," in: *Yad Vashem Studies*, 23 (1993), 335–68; F.R. Nicosia, "Revisionist Zionism in Germany – Richard Lichtheim and the Landesverband der Zionisten-Revisionisten in Deutschland," in: LBIYB, 31 (1986), 209–40.

LICHTSTEIN, ABRAHAM BEN ELIEZER LIPMAN (18th–19th century), Polish rabbi. He functioned as rabbi in Wolkowysk, Lida, and Przasnysz, and as *dayyan* and preacher of the small town of Lask where he went to have more leisure to devote himself to his scholarly endeavors. Lichtstein is the author of the following works: *Kanfei Nesharim* (1881), a commentary on the Pentateuch containing explanations and homilies, some of them inspired by Naḥmanides, Gersonides, and Isaac Arama; *Ammudei Shamayim* (Warsaw, 1803), a commentary on Maimonides' formulation of the 13 articles of faith; *Ge'ullat Olam* (Grodno, 1822) on the *Haggadah; Iggeret ha-Ẓofeh* (Bialystok, 1806), a commentary on the *Halakhot* of Isaac Alfasi, explaining the latter's methodology; *Or ha-Even* (Sklow, 1822) on religious ethics and morals; and a commentary on the pseudo-Aristotelian *Sefer ha-Tappu'aḥ*. A commentary of his on Alfasi is still in manuscript.

BIBLIOGRAPHY: Steinschneider, Uebersetzungen, 1 (1893), 268; P.Z. Glicksman, *Ir Lask va-Ḥakhameha* (1926), 66–68.

[Jacob Haberman]

LICHTSTEIN, ABRAHAM JEKUTHIEL ZALMAN BEN MOSES JOSEPH (second half of 18th century), Polish rabbi.

Lichtstein served as *av bet din* of Plonsk (Warsaw district). He was the author of *Zera Avraham*, an extensive commentary to the *Sifrei* (pt. 1 to Numbers, Dyhrenfurth, 1811; pt. 2 to Deuteronomy, Radzivil, 1820). It gives the source references to biblical verses in the text under the title *Mikra Meforash*, and to talmudic parallels, under the title *Mevo ha-Talmud*. The work was completed in 1788, but was published posthumously by his son Moses, who also added the glosses of a Jerusalem manuscript by a Sephardi scholar as well as his own additions. Lichtstein's introduction to the *Divrei Kohelet* (Nowy Dwor, 1785) of his son Solomon, who died in his youth, was also published by Moses. It contains expositions of Maimonides' *Mishneh Torah*, novellae on the laws of **terefah* and the Talmud, a eulogy of his son called *Emek ha-Bakha*, and novellae by Moses called *Darash Moshe*.

BIBLIOGRAPHY: A. Walden, *Shem ha-Gedolim he-Ḥadash*, 1 (1864), 2b no. 47; 2 (1864), 14b no. 29; S. Wiener, *Kohelet Moshe* (1918), 272 no. 2237; S. Hazan, *Ha-Ma'alot li-Shelomo* (1899), 29a; *Sifri … im Be'ur … Emek ha-Neẓiv me'et … N.Z.J. Berlin*, 1 (1959), 325n.

[Yehoshua Horowitz]

LICORICIA OF WINCHESTER (13th century), English busineswoman and moneylender. After the death of her first husband, she became an active and highly successful moneylender. She is first mentioned in records from the early 1230s that show she also lent money in association with other Jews. In 1242 Licoricia married David of Oxford, one of the wealthiest English Jews. In order to marry Licorica, David had to divorce his first wife, Muriel, a protracted undertaking in which King Henry III of England, the Archbishop of York, and the *batei din* of London and Paris were all involved. After Licoricia and David married, she settled in Oxford, where she assisted her husband in his business dealings.

Following David's death, in 1244, Licoricia was immediately imprisoned in the Tower of London in order to prevent her interference in the assessment of David's estate. The price of her repurchase of all the debts owed to David was set at 5,000 marks, of which 4,000 went to a special exchequer established at Westminister Abbey to build a new shrine to Edward the Confessor. When she was released from the Tower in September 1244, Licoricia was left in control of sufficient wealth to engage in substantial and widespread business activities. Returning to live with her family in Winchester, she remained an active moneylender for the next 30 years or more. She frequented King Henry's court whenever he was in Winchester, dealing with members of his entourage as well as with the king himself, who apparently aided her in some of her more questionable activities. Licoricia's ease of access to the king was an asset to the Jewish community and individual Jews often used her to intercede for them. In 1277, Belia, Licoricia's daughter, found the bodies of Licoricia and of Alice of Bicton, Licoricia's Christian maid, stabbed to death in Licoricia's home in Winchester, possibly murdered during a robbery. The amount stolen was rumored to be the unlikely sum of £10,000. Licoricia was probably buried in the Jewish cemetery at Winchester.

BIBLIOGRAPHY: S. Bartlet. "Three Jewish Businesswomen in Thirteenth-Century Winchester," in: *Jewish Culture and History*, 3/2 (2000), 31–54; S. Cohen. "The Oxford Jewry in the Thirteenth Century," in *Jewish Historical Society of England: Transactions*, 13 (1932–35), 293–322; R.B. Dobson, "The Role of Jewish Women in Medieval England" (Presidential Address), in: D. Wood (ed.), *Christianity and Judaism. Studies in Church History* 29 (1992), 145–68.

[Cheryl Tallan (2nd ed.)]

LIDA, town in Grodno district, Belarus. Jews are first mentioned in the mid-16th century, and in 1579 King Stephan Batory gave them a Bill of Rights and allowed them to build a synagogue. According to a decision of the Lithuanian council (see *Councils of the Lands) of 1623, the Jewish community of Lida was subordinated to the Grodno *kahal*. The files of the Lithuanian financial commission contain records of the quarrels between the Lida *kahal* and the Jews of the neighboring villages. In 1766 there were 1,167 Jewish poll-tax payers in Lida and the vicinity. The community numbered 567 (73.6% of the total population) in 1817; 1,980 in 1847; and 5,294 (68%) in 1897. In 1862 the two first grade merchants and the five third grade were Jews, as were the 76 shops and the 32 other trade businesses Jewish. In the 1880s Lida turned into an important railway junction, which led to economic and demographic growth. Most of the small industry belonged to Jews. In the 1880s the 13 prayerhouses in the town were grouped in one large square; they were all damaged in a fire. Until World War II the butchers' synagogue contained an Ark with undamaged ancient doors. In the 1880s a Ḥovevei Zion circle was founded, and money was collected for the building of the Mazkeret Batyah colony in Palestine. In 1902, at the initiative of Rabbi Reines, the founding convention of the Mizrachi movement was held in Lida. From September 20, 1915, the town was under German occupation, which put a halt to economic activity but did allow Jewish cultural life. On Passover eve 1919 the Polish soldiers of General Haller organized a pogrom and 39 Jews were killed. In 1921 there were 5,419 Jews (40% of the total population), reaching 6,335 (a third of the total) in 1931. In 1921, there were 302 Jewish workshops in Lida, over half of them family enterprises. There were 37 Jewish farms in 1927. Between the two world wars there were a Yiddish elementary school and a children's home, both affiliated to the Central Yiddish School Organization (CYSHO). There was also a *Tarbut Hebrew school and a kindergarten. The community maintained a hospital with 18 beds, and various welfare organizations. A few Jewish weeklies appeared for short periods. Among rabbis of Lida were R. *David b. Aryeh Leib of Lida (later in Amsterdam), his son Pethahiah, and his grandson, the *ẓaddik* David Benjamin. R. Elijah Schick (Elinke Lider) officiated in the 19th century, and I.J. *Reines, the Mizrachi leader, at the beginning of the 20th century. The latter founded a modern yeshivah in Lida which functioned until World War I.

[*Encyclopaedia Judaica* (Germany)]

Holocaust Period

In 1940 the number of Jews in Lida had risen to about 8,500. During the period of Soviet rule (1939–41), Jewish community institutions were closed, the activities of Jewish parties were forbidden, and the basis of the Jewish economy from the prewar period was demolished. A large part of the Jewish refugees from western Poland who found shelter in Lida were deported to the Soviet interior in the summer of 1940. Due to the annexation of Vilna and its environs to Lithuania, Lida turned into a border town, and many young Jews tried to smuggle over the border, believing that from there a way to Palestine and the West would be found. On June 25, 1941, a battle took place on the outskirts of Lida between the German and Soviet armies; during the bombardment the center of the town, which was inhabited principally by Jews, was burned, and there were hundreds of Jewish casualties. On July 5, 1941, the Germans collected the Jews of the city in the main square and took away all the rabbis, *shoḥatim*, doctors, and teachers – the leadership of the community – to near the village of Stoniewicze where they were murdered; 98 men fell at that time. In December 1941 the Jews were concentrated in a special quarter and were joined by the Jews from Lipniszki, Juraciszki, Traby, and Duoly. On May 8, 1942, an *Aktion* was carried out. Only 1,250 people were left; their number swelled later to 4,000 with survivors from various towns. All the remaining 5,670 were killed near the village of Stoniewicze. On July 8, 120 Jews from the psychiatric hospital were murdered. About 200 people succeeded in escaping the scene of the slaughter, returned to the ghetto, and told of the Germans' horrifying acts. A group of youths succeeded in leaving the city on May 21, 1942 and entered the forests of Naliboki. The youth in the ghetto also organized and armed themselves with weapons. At the end of 1942 contact was established with the partisans in the *Novogrudok area. The Jewish partisans from Lida fought with the unit of an experienced Jewish fighter, Tuvia Bielski, and another unit called "Iskra." The ghetto was destroyed on Sept. 17–19, 1943, and the Jews were deported to Majdanek death camp. The city was liberated on July 5, 1944, and there were about 150 Jewish survivors. Most of those who had been with the partisans were mobilized into the Soviet army and continued to fight in Germany until the end of the war.

The others left for Poland, and from there to Palestine. In the mid-1950s the Jewish cemetery was confiscated and converted into a building site. The Jewish population of the town in 1970 was estimated at a few families.

[Aharon Weiss]

BIBLIOGRAPHY: S. Dubnow (ed.), *Pinkas ha-Medinah* (1925), index; Vilenskaya Kommissiya dlya razbora drevnikh aktov, *Akty*, 29 (1902), nos. 183, 206; *Słownik geograficzny Królestwa Polskigo*, s.v.; B. Wasiutyński, *Ludność żydowska w Polsce…* (1930), 80, 84, 87; Jewish Colonization Association, *Rapport pour l'année 1928*; Yad Vashem Archives.

LIDZBARSKI, MARK (Abraham Mordecai; 1868–1928), Semitist. Lidzbarski was born in Plock, Russian Poland, to Moritz and Cäcilie Lidzbarski, and received a strict Orthodox education. At 14 he ran away from home and went to Posen, Prussian Poland, where he studied at the gymnasium. He continued his studies at the University of Berlin, living in difficult conditions. As a student in Berlin he converted to Evangelical Christianity. In 1896 he began lecturing in Oriental languages at the University of Kiel; in 1907, at the University of Greifswald; and in 1917, at the University of Goettingen. He was a corresponding member of the Goettingen Gesellschaft der Wissenschaften from 1912 to 1918, when he became a full member.

Lidzbarski was a scholar of high repute in several branches of Semitic studies. He may be considered the founder of Semitic epigraphy; several of his articles and books still may be consulted with great profit, including *Die neuaramaeischen Handschriften der Koeniglichen Bibliothek zu Berlin* (2 vols., in 3, 1896), *Handbuch der nordsemitischen Epigraphik* (2 vols., 1898, repr. 1962), *Ephemeris fuer semitische Epigraphik* (3 vols., 1900–15), and *Kanaanaeische Inschriften* (1907) in the series *Altsemitische Texte*. His contribution to the 29th edition of Gesenius' *Hebraeische Grammatik* is of major importance. Lidzbarski also contributed much to Mandean studies. His theory that the gnostic Mandeans originated in Palestine in pre-Christian times as a heterodox Jewish group was in vogue among scholars for a time but no longer enjoys wide support. However, his editions of the Mandean texts *Das Johannesbuch der Mandaeer* (2 vols., 1905–15, repr. 1966), *Mandaeische Liturgien* in the series *Abhandlungen der Koeniglichen Gesellschaft der Wissenschaften zu Goettingen* (1920, repr. 1962), and *Altaramaeische Urkunden aus Assur* in the series *Wissenschaftliche Veroeffentlichungen der Deutschen Orient-Gesellschaft* (1921) have made these accessible to scholars. Lidzbarski's autobiography, *Auf rauhem Wege* ("On the Rough Road," 1927), was published anonymously.

BIBLIOGRAPHY: W. Baumgartner, in: *Neue Zuercher Zeitung* (July 14, 1968), 51. **ADD. BIBLIOGRAPHY:** K.G. Wesseling, *Biographisch-Bibliographisches Kirchenlexikon*, 5:29–31.

[David Diringer]

LIEBEN, ROBERT VON (1878–1913), scientist and inventor. He was born in Vienna, where his father, vice governor of the Austro-Hungarian state bank, was ennobled. Lieben went to work at the Institute for Physical Chemistry in Goettingen, Germany, where he studied under Walter Nernst, a founder of modern physical chemistry. Later he worked in his own laboratory, where he built a private telephone system. In 1906 he invented the amplifying valve and in 1910 the grid tube (with Eugen Resz and Siegmund Strauss as co-inventors). This led directly to modern radio and later developments in electronics such as sound tracks for films and television. In 1936 the Austrian Government issued a stamp commemorating his contribution to research in the field of sound. Lieben had little contact with the Jewish community and referred to himself as an atheist.

BIBLIOGRAPHY: H. von Hoffmannsthal, *Die prosaischen Schriften gesammelt*, 3 (1917), 48–53; W. Nerst, in: *Telefunken Zei-*

tung, 6 (1923); S. Kaznelson, *Juden im Deutschen Kulturbereich* (1959), 412–31.

LIEBEN, SALOMON (1884–1942), Prague physician and communal functionary. A member of *Agudat Israel, Lieben represented Orthodox Jews on the board of the Prague community. With the establishment of Czechoslovakia in 1918, he cooperated with the Zionists and joined the Jewish National Council. He was one of the moving spirits behind the foundation of the Židovská ústředna pro sociální péči (Central Jewish Welfare Board) in 1932. As a military physician in Galicia during World War I, he organized Jewish welfare activities there, and then in Prague for refugees from Eastern Europe. He founded a Jewish outpatients clinic and a soup kitchen, and was among the administrators of several charitable institutions. Lieben conducted scientific research in defense of **sheḥitah* against the numerous "humanitarian" attacks on it throughout Europe, publishing several papers in veterinary and medical periodicals claiming that *sheḥitah* is the least cruel method of slaughtering animals. When the Nazis entered Prague in 1939 and ordered the immediate expulsion of Jewish patients from the general hospitals, Lieben organized a hospital in the Jewish orphanage. He also saw to the religious needs of Prague Jews, organizing, for example, the illegal distribution of unleavened bread. In 1942 he was deported with his family to a concentration camp, where he died.

BIBLIOGRAPHY: *Dos Yidishe Vort*, 16:139 (1970), 27–29.

[Meir Lamed]

LIEBEN, SALOMON HUGO (1881–1942), historian of Bohemian Jewry, cousin of Salomon *Lieben. Lieben received his general and Jewish education in his native Prague and taught religion in Prague German-language secondary schools. In 1906 he founded and directed the Prague Jewish museum in the *ohel tohorah* ("the purification hall") of the old cemetery, around which the Nazis later ordered the organization of the Central Jewish Museum (now the Prague State Jewish Museum; see *Museums, Jewish); Lieben was among its scientific workers. He published research papers on Bohemian Jewish history in many Jewish scientific publications, concentrating on its outstanding personalities and events, such as David *Oppenheim, Ezekiel b. Judah *Landau, Eleazar *Fleckeles, Jewish printing in Prague, and the expulsion by *Maria Theresa (1745). He exposed the Ramshak chronicle, allegedly from the *Hussite period, as a falsification by Marcus Fischer (see Moses *Fischer). On the board of the Society for the History of the Jews in Czechoslovakia and coeditor of its yearbooks (JGGJČ) and of *Die Juden in Prag* (1927), he edited *Die juedischen Denkmaeler in der Tschechoslowakei* (1933) and collaborated with Hugo *Gold in editing his books on the communities of Bohemia and Moravia. Lieben died in Prague.

BIBLIOGRAPHY: O. Muneles, *Bibliographical Survey of Jewish Prague* (1958), contains list of his publications; H. Volavkov, *Story of the Jewish Museum in Prague* (1968), passim.

[Meir Lamed]

LIEBER, DAVID (1925–), U.S. Conservative rabbi, president of the *University of Judaism, and senior editor of the Conservative movement's *Etz Hayim* commentary. Lieber was born in Stryj, Poland, and came to the United States at age two. He received his Bachelor of Arts degree magna cum laude in 1944 from the City College of New York, where he was elected to Phi Beta Kappa. He received a Bachelor of Hebrew Letters degree from the Jewish Theological Seminary of America that same year and was ordained as a rabbi at the seminary in 1948 and received his Doctor of Hebrew Literature degree in Psalms Studies from JTS in 1951. Lieber also received a master's degree in philosophy of education from Columbia University in 1947. He completed his ABD (all but the dissertation) in philosophy from Columbia and pursued postgraduate studies at the University of Washington in Seattle and at UCLA.

Lieber studied at the Seminary when it was the center of Jewish scholarship in the United States under the tutelage of some of the foremost Jewish scholars of the time, including talmudist Saul *Lieberman, Jewish Bible scholar H.L. *Ginsberg, and philosopher Mordecai *Kaplan. It was Kaplan's groundbreaking vision of a University of Judaism – an academy that would embody as many forms of Jewish expression as possible – that would lead to the creation of the institution Lieber was to lead.

As a young man, Lieber was a leader of Shomer Hadati, the religious Zionist movement that is now *Bnei Akiva. He was also an early pioneer in the establishment of the Ramah camps of the Conservative movement. He was the founding head counselor in the first of the camps in Wisconsin, a director of the camp in Maine, and the founding director of the camp in California. He also was the founding director of the Mador, the national training camp for Ramah counselors.

In 1956, when Lieber was appointed dean of students of the nine-year-old University of Judaism, the college was a Hebrew teachers institute training teachers for afternoon Hebrew school and offering adult education classes and art exhibits and dramatic programs. When he resigned from the presidency in 1993, he had helped build the UJ into a nationally recognized educational institution complete with an undergraduate college, graduate programs in education, business administration, Jewish studies, and rabbinic studies, a large library, and two think tanks. He had also overseen the acquisition and the building of UJ's 25-acre campus in the Santa Monica Mountains.

Upon retiring from the UJ presidency, Lieber began focusing his attention on a project he had first proposed in 1969, a new commentary on the *Torah*. The result was *Etz Hayim: Torah and Commentary*, published jointly by the Rabbinical Assembly, United Synagogue, and Jewish Publication Society, which sought to provide laity with a contemporary interpretation of the text, and a commentary that embraced both tradition and change, ancient teachings and modern scholarship. Major essays on biblical and religious themes were incorporated into the commentary. He was assisted editorially by Conservative rabbis who had become renowned for their writings, Chaim *Potok, author of *The Chosen*, Harold Kushner, author of *When Bad Things Happen to Good People*, Susan Grossman, and UJ Rector Elliot Dorff.

A former spiritual leader of Sinai Temple in Los Angeles (1950–54), Lieber served as a chaplain in the United States Air Force and university chaplain for the B'nai B'rith Hillel Foundation at both the University of Washington (1954–55) and Harvard University (1955–56). He also was a visiting member of the Near Eastern Language Department of UCLA from 1957 to 1990. Lieber served as a member of the Board of Directors of the Association of Jewish Studies. In recognition of his work, Dr. Lieber was awarded the "Doctor of Humane Letters" degree, *honoris causa*, by the Hebrew Union College in 1982 and the "Torch of Learning" award by the Hebrew University in Jerusalem in 1984. After his retirement in 1993 he served as president emeritus of the University of Judaism and continued to teach at the university as the Flora and Arnold Skovron Distinguished Service Professor of Biblical Literature and Thought. He was the first West Coast president of the International Rabbinical Assembly (1996–98). Over the years he wrote some 50 articles, which appeared in a variety of journals.

[Yaakov Arnold (2nd ed.)]

LIEBERMAN, CHAIM (Herman; 1890–1963), Yiddish essayist and literary critic. Born in Kolki (Volhynia), he immigrated to the U.S. in 1905. His first articles, on education, appeared in the New York Yiddish daily *Yidishes Tageblat*. On the eve of World War I, he helped to found the Farband's Yiddish secular schools and its Jewish Teachers' Seminary and taught Yiddish and Yiddish literature while espousing Labor Zionism. Lieberman's critical articles, in the main Yiddish newspapers, on Jewish and non-Jewish writers, combining vast knowledge and enthusiastic, positive appraisals, were collected in three volumes (1923–30). In the 1930s Lieberman underwent a spiritual crisis, became extremely pious, and joined the religious Zionists. His former fervent championship of favored writers gave way to sharp and cutting polemics against writers he disliked. He began with attacks on Jewish pro-communists (*Sheydim in Moskve* ("Demons in Moscow," 1937)), proceeded to assail Chaim *Zhitlowsky and Shmuel *Niger (*"Dr. Kh. Zhitlovski un Sh. Niger, a Debate in Zeks Briv"* ("Dr. Ch. Zhitlovski and Sh. Niger, a Debate in Six Letters," 1937)), and reached a climax of vituperation in his articles and books against Sholem *Asch's christological novels (*Sholem Ash un kristntum*, 1950; English transl. *The Christianity of Sholem Asch*, 1953). There followed attacks upon Satmar Ḥasidim because of their anti-Zionism (*Der Rebe un der Sotn* ("Rabbi and Satan," 1959)), against the American Council of Judaism (English trans. *Strangers to Glory*, 1955), and, finally, ten articles against Ben *Hecht (English transl. in book form, *The Man and His 'Perfidy,'* 1964).

BIBLIOGRAPHY: LNYL, 5 (1963), 66–71; J. Glatstein, *In Tokh Genumen* (1947), 428–34; A.B. Shurin, *Keshet Gibborim* (1964), 147–52.

[Shlomo Bickel / Jean Baumgarten (2nd ed.)]

LIEBERMAN, ELIAS (1883–1969), U.S. educator and poet. Lieberman, who was born in St. Petersburg, Russia, went with his family to the United States at the age of seven. He began teaching in the New York public school system in 1903. Lieberman served as principal of Thomas Jefferson High School in Brooklyn from 1924 to 1940, and then as associate superintendent of schools. He published four volumes of poetry and was a contributor to various periodicals. His patriotic poem "I am an American," which first appeared in 1916, has been reprinted in numerous anthologies and school books. Among the literary magazines that he at one time helped edit were *Puck, Current Literature*, and *The American Hebrew*.

[Hillel Halkin]

LIEBERMAN, HERMAN (1870–1941), Polish lawyer and Socialist politician. Born in Drogobycz, Galicia, into an assimilated family, Lieberman joined the Polish Socialist Party of Galicia and Silesia and became one of its leaders. In 1907 he entered the Austrian parliament, where he was considered one of its most gifted speakers. During World War I he fought in the Polish Legion on the Russian front. When Poland regained her independence at the end of the war, he became a member of its parliament (1919–30), and was one of the authors of the democratic constitution of 1921. He was a member of the Central Council of the Polish Socialist Party from 1920 to 1929. He was a noted advocate, and distinguished himself as defense counsel in the famous case of Polish legionnaires in Mármaras-sziget (Sighet) in 1918. After the Pilsudski coup d'état in 1926, Lieberman led the opposition to the regime in parliament. In 1930 he was sentenced to three years' imprisonment, but escaped to Czechoslovakia and later went to France. He was the spokesman for the radical wing of the Polish Socialist Party in exile and cooperated with the Communists in organizing help for the Republicans during the Spanish Civil War. In 1940 he moved to London and a year later was appointed minister of justice in the Polish government-in-exile, thus becoming the first Jew in a Polish cabinet.

ADD. BIBLIOGRAPHY: H. Piasecki, *Sekcja zydowska PPSD i zydowska partia socjalno demokratyczna* (1982), index; C. Kozlowski, *Zarys dziejow Polskiego Ruchu Robotniczego do 1948 roku* (1980), index; M. Leczyk, *Sprawa Brzeska* (1987), index; A. Tymieniecka, *Warszawska organizacja PPS 1918–1939* (1982), index.

[Abraham Wein]

LIEBERMAN, JOSEPH (1942–), U.S. senator and U.S. vice presidential nominee. Born in Stamford, Connecticut, he received his bachelor's degree from Yale in 1964 and graduated from Yale Law School in 1967. In 1970 he ran for and won a seat in the Connecticut State Senate, where he served for ten years, the final six as majority leader. In 1980 he gave up his seat to run for the U.S. House of Representatives but lost.

In 1981 Lieberman ran for state attorney general. He won handily and he was reelected in 1986. In his six years as attorney general he became a formidable and national figure in regard to consumer and environmental issues. In 1988

Lieberman announced that he would run for the Senate. He won a narrow victory by some 10,000 voters. An observant Jew, he refused to campaign or work on the Sabbath or on the fall holidays in the middle of campaign season. He garnered serious support from Roman Catholic voters impressed by his religiosity.

In the Senate Lieberman soon established himself as a political moderate. For example, he supported the appointment of Clarence Thomas for a seat on the Supreme Court, angering many of his Democratic and liberal colleagues; it was only after the allegations of sexual misconduct that Lieberman changed his stance.

In 2000 Lieberman became Al Gore's running mate for the presidency of the United States; he was the first Jew to be nominated on a national ticket of a major political party. Lieberman was chosen in part because of his ethical stances and his religious views, which Gore felt inoculated him against some of the issues associated with Bill Clinton's personal behavior. His nomination produced great excitement in the American Jewish community. His campaign was not without its Jewish critics. Anti-Defamation League director Abraham Foxman criticized Lieberman for introducing religion into the public area and the political campaign. Ultra-Orthodox Jews were uncomfortable that a self-described Orthodox Jew walked around with his head uncovered and that his wife was attired in short sleeves and slacks. While Orthodoxy had moved to the religious right, Lieberman remained passionate and committed, but still moderate. The Jewish community voted overwhelmingly for the Gore/Lieberman ticket, although a poor design of the ballot in heavily Jewish Palm Beach County in Florida gave Patrick Buchanan, regarded by many as antisemitic and unfriendly to Israel, 5,000 votes that were intended for the Gore/Lieberman ticket. In the end Gore/Lieberman won the popular vote but lost by less than a thousand votes in Florida.

Lieberman returned to the Senate where he has continued to serve as a notable centrist. He introduced the bill creating the Homeland Security Department after September 11. He refused to advance his own presidential aspirations until Gore made it known that he would not run. In 2004 he ran for the Democratic presidential nomination; his moderate views did not gain great traction within the Democratic Party, which was alienated by the Iraq War that Lieberman continued to support and by President Bush's conservative agenda, which Lieberman opposed.

[Alan H. Decherney (2nd ed.)]

LIEBERMAN, MYRON (1919–), U.S. educator. Lieberman was instrumental in raising and protecting the status of the teacher. Widely recognized as the leading authority on education employment relations and teacher unions, Lieberman served as a labor negotiator for school boards in Rhode Island, Connecticut, New York, Arizona, California, and New Jersey, with responsibilities for grievances and unfair labor practices, as well as contract negotiations. Born in St. Paul, Minnesota, he received a B.S. in law (1941) and a B.S. in education (1948) from the University of Minnesota, and his M.A. (1950) and Ph.D. (1952) from the University of Illinois. He served in the US Army Air Corps from 1942 to 1946 and was discharged with the rank of S/Sgt. Lieberman taught at the universities of Illinois (1949–52) and Oklahoma (1953–56), and was appointed chairman of the department of education at Yeshiva University (1956–59). In 1963 he became chairman of the professional studies division, Rhode Island College, and from 1965 to 1967 directed its educational research and development; from 1963 to 1969 he served as the assistant dean for professional studies. He was a professor of education at the City University of New York (1969–75); a distinguished professor at the University of Southern California (1975–77); and a visiting professor of education at Ohio University (1984–86) and the University of Pennsylvania (1986–88). Lieberman was president of the Educational Employment Services consulting firm (1976–94). From 1991 he was senior research scholar, Social Philosophy and Policy Center, at Bowling Green State University in Ohio, as well as chairman of the Education Policy Institute in Washington, D.C., from 1995.

Lieberman was author and co-author of a number of books, monographs, and articles. He contended that national professional groups should replace local school boards as arbitrators of educational problems. His books include *Education as a Profession* (1956), *The Future of Public Education* (1960), *Collective Negotiations for Teachers* (1966), *Bargaining* (1979), *Beyond Public Education* (1986), *Privatization and Educational Choice* (1989), *Public Education: An Autopsy* (1993), *The Teacher Unions* (1997), *Teachers Evaluating Teachers* (1998), and *Handbook on School Board/Union Relations* (1999).

[Ronald E. Ohl / Ruth Beloff (2nd ed.)]

LIEBERMAN, NANCY ELIZABETH ("Fire," "The Lieb," "Lady Magic"; 1958–), pioneer in women's amateur and professional basketball and greatest female star of her generation; youngest basketball player male or female to win an Olympic medal, first woman to play in a men's professional basketball league; member of the Basketball Hall of Fame and the Women's Basketball Hall of Fame. Born in Brooklyn, New York, and raised by her mother, Renee, in Far Rockaway, Long Island, after her parents divorced when she was 14, Lieberman started receiving national attention as a high school star at Far Rockaway High School in Queens, N.Y. At 17 she won a gold medal at the 1975 Pan American Games, and at 18 she won the silver medal at the Montreal Olympics. Lieberman played on the women's basketball team at Old Dominion University in Norfolk, Virginia, from 1976 to 1980, helping the Lady Monarchs to an astounding 72–2 record during their back-to-back championship seasons in 1979 and 1980. Lieberman was a two-time winner of the Wade Trophy as College Player of the Year, and received the Broderick Cup as the nation's top female athlete in 1980. Lieberman also won three consecutive Kodak All-America awards (1978–80). She played for several basketball teams and leagues, including the Dallas

Diamonds of the Women's Pro Basketball League (WBL), the men's United States Basketball League (USBL), the Washington Generals – the regular opponent of the Harlem Globetrotters – and the Women's National Basketball Association (WNBA), before being named general manager and head coach of the WNBA's Detroit Shock for three seasons, and then head coach of the Dallas Fury, guiding the team to a championship in 2004. In 1993, Lieberman was the first woman inducted into the New York City Basketball Hall of Fame, and was elected to the Basketball Hall of Fame in 1996, and to the Women's Basketball Hall of Fame in 1999. *Sports Illustrated* named Lieberman the 44th greatest female athlete of the 20th century. Lieberman, who identifies herself as a born-again Christian, wrote an autobiography, *Lady Magic: The Nancy Lieberman Story* (1991), and co-authored *Basketball for Women* (2000) with Robin Roberts.

[Elli Wohlgelernter (2nd ed.)]

LIEBERMAN, SAUL (1898–1983), talmudic scholar. Born in Motol, near Pinsk, Belorussia, he studied at the yeshivot of Malch and Slobodka. In the 1920s he attended the University of Kiev, and, following a short stay in Palestine, continued his studies in France. In 1928 he settled in Jerusalem. He studied talmudic philology and Greek language and literature at the Hebrew University, where he was appointed lecturer in Talmud in 1931. He also taught at the Mizrachi Teachers Seminary and from 1935 was dean of the Harry Fischel Institute for Talmudic Research in Jerusalem. In 1940 he was invited by the Jewish Theological Seminary of America to serve as professor of Palestinian literature and institutions. Nine years later he was appointed dean, and in 1958 rector, of the Seminary's rabbinical school.

Combining vast erudition in all fields of talmudic and rabbinic literature with a penetrating knowledge of the classical world, Lieberman opened new pathways to the understanding of the life, institutions, beliefs, and literary products of Jewish Palestine in the talmudic period.

He made his debut in scholarly literature in 1929 with the publication of *Al ha-Yerushalmi*, in which he suggested ways of emending corruptions in the text of the Jerusalem (Palestinian) Talmud and offered variant readings to the text of the tractate of *Sotah*. This was followed by a series of text studies of the Jerusalem Talmud, which appeared in *Tarbiz*; by *Talmudah shel Keisaryah* (1931), in which he expressed the view that the first three tractates of the order *Nezikin* in the Jerusalem Talmud had been compiled in Caesarea about the middle of the fourth century C.E.; and by *Ha-Yerushalmi ki-Feshuto* (1934), a commentary on the treatises *Shabbat, Eruvin*, and *Pesaḥim* of the Jerusalem Talmud.

His preoccupation with the Jerusalem Talmud impressed him with the necessity of clarifying the text of the tannaitic sources, especially that of the Tosefta, on which no commentaries had been composed by the earlier authorities and to whose elucidation only few scholars had devoted themselves in later generations.

In the comparatively short period of three years (1937–39) he published the four-volume *Tosefet Rishonim*, a commentary on the entire Tosefta with textual corrections based on manuscripts, early printings, and quotations found in early authorities. During that period he also published *Tashlum Tosefta*, an introductory chapter to the second edition of M.S. *Zuckermandel's Tosefta edition (1937), dealing with quotations from the Tosefta by early authorities that are not found in the text.

Years later, Lieberman returned to the systematic elucidation of the Tosefta. He undertook the publication of the Tosefta text, based on manuscripts and accompanied by brief explanatory notes, and of an extensive commentary called *Tosefta ki-Feshutah*. The latter combined philological research and historical observations with a discussion of the entire talmudic and rabbinic literature in which the relevant Tosefta text is either commented upon or quoted. Between 1955 and 1967 ten volumes of the new edition appeared, representing the text and the commentaries on the orders of *Zera'im* and *Mo'ed* and on part of the order of *Nashim*.

In *Sifrei Zuta* (1968), Lieberman advanced the view that this halakhic Midrash was in all likelihood finally edited by Bar Kappara in Lydda.

His two English volumes, which also appeared in a Hebrew translation, *Greek in Jewish Palestine* (1942) and *Hellenism in Jewish Palestine* (1950), illustrate the influence of Hellenistic culture on Jewish Palestine in the first centuries C.E.

Other books of his were *Sheki'in* (1939), on Jewish legends, customs, and literary sources found in Karaite and Christian polemical writings, and *Midreshei Teiman* (1940), wherein he showed that the Yemenite Midrashim had preserved exegetical material which had been deliberately omitted by the rabbis. He edited a variant version of the *Midrash Rabbah* on Deuteronomy (1940, 1965^2). In his view that version had been current among Sephardi Jewry, while the standard text had been that of Ashkenazi Jewry. In 1947 he published *Hilkhot ha-Yerushalmi*, which he identified as a fragment of a work by Maimonides on the Jerusalem Talmud. Lieberman also edited the hitherto unpublished Tosefta commentary *Ḥasdei David* by David *Pardo on the order *Tohorot*. The first part of this work appeared in 1970.

A number of his works have appeared in new and revised editions. Lieberman served as editor in chief of a new critical edition of Maimonides' *Mishneh Torah* (vol. 1, 1964), and as an editor of the Judaica series of Yale University. He also edited several scholarly miscellanies.

He contributed numerous studies to scholarly publications as well as notes to books of fellow scholars. In these he dwelt on various aspects of the world of ideas of the rabbis, shed light on events in the talmudic period, and elucidated scores of obscure words and expressions of talmudic and midrashic literature.

He was for many years president of the American Academy for Jewish Research. He was an honorary member of the Academy for the Hebrew Language, a fellow of the American Academy of Arts and Sciences, and a fellow of the Israel Academy of Sciences and Humanities. In 1971 he was awarded the Israel Prize for Jewish studies and in 1976 he received the Harvey Prize of the Haifa Technion.

His wife, JUDITH LIEBERMAN (1904–), was a daughter of Rabbi Meir Berlin (*Bar-Ilan), leader of the Mizrachi. She served from 1941 first as Hebrew principal and then as dean of Hebrew studies of Shulamith School for Girls in New York, the first Jewish day school for girls in North America. Her publications include *Robert Browning and Hebraism* (1934) and an autobiographical chapter that was included in *Thirteen Americans, Their Spiritual Autobiographies* (1953), edited by L. Finkelstein.

BIBLIOGRAPHY: E.S. Rosenthal, in: PAAJR, 31 (1963), 1–71 (Heb.); idem, in: *Hadoar*, 43:23 (1963); T. Preschel, *Dr. Sha'ul Lieberman…* (Heb., 1963); A. Marx, in: *Proceedings of the Rabbinical Assembly of America*, 12 (1949).

[Tovia Preschel]

LIEBERMANN, AARON SAMUEL (known as **Bar Derora**, **Daniel Ish Hamudot**, **Arthur Freeman**; 1845–1880), pioneer of Jewish Socialism and Hebrew writer. He was born in Lunna, Lithuania, the son of Eliezer Dov Liebermann, scholar, *maskil*, and Hebrew author. His family moved to Bialystok and from there to Suwalki. He obtained his teacher's diploma at Vilna (1867), and returned to Suwalki, where he was appointed secretary of the community and teacher. In 1870 he enrolled as an occasional student at the Technological Institute of St. Petersburg. While there he wrote a geography of Ereẓ Israel, but the manuscript was destroyed. In his distress he returned to Vilna, where he worked with an insurance company and in draftsmanship, while continuing to show talent in graphics and drawing. From 1872 he was one of the most active leaders of the local revolutionary group, whose ranks included the future noted members of the Narodnaya Volya, A. *Zundelewicz and V. *Jochelson, and the future Hebrew authors L. Davidowicz and J.E. Triwosch. In this circle Liebermann already evinced enthusiastic attachment to the Hebrew language, and it was there that his idea of initiating special Socialist activities among the Jews was born. When the group was discovered by the authorities in 1875, Liebermann escaped abroad. He joined Socialist circles in Berlin and then moved to London, where he worked as a typesetter for the Socialist periodical *Vpered*, its editors P. Lavrov and V. Smirnov supporting his projects both in theory and in practice. In the articles which Liebermann published in *Vpered* on Vilna and Bialystok (1875–76), he also described the life of Jewish workers in the region. He pointed out progressive social elements in ancient Jewish culture, and in his propaganda sought to employ messianic themes. In January 1876 he drew up regulations for the establishment of a Socialist-revolutionary organization among the Jews of Russia, and in May of that year he founded the *Agudat ha-Soẓyalistim ha-Ivrim in London. In a Hebrew manifesto addressed to the *shelomei emunei Yisrael* ("wholesome and faithful Jews"; summer 1876), which was also translated and published in *Vpered*, Liebermann dissociated himself from the assimilationist Socialist intelligentsia who were out of touch with the people. He regarded the supporters of Socialism among the working classes or the *maskilim*, who were close to the people, as the potential principal activists of the movement and in this respect placed much hope in students of the yeshivot. Liebermann also contributed to the German-language Socialist press. At the beginning of 1877 he settled in Vienna, and that summer published three issues of his monthly **Ha-Emet*, writing most of the articles himself. Their publication aroused considerable interest in the Hebrew press. He formed and led a group of authors who shared his views, such as J.L. *Levin (Yehalal), M. Kamyonski, I. *Kaminer, Ẓevi ha-Kohen Scherschewski, and M. Adelman-Meyuḥas. He established contact with supporters in southern Russia and succeeded in moderating the extremist anti-Jewish outlook prevailing among Ukrainian Socialists in Vienna. When *Ha-Emet* ceased to appear, Liebermann contributed to the newspapers published by P. *Smolenskin, *Ha-Mabbit* and *Ha-Shaḥar*, in which he published as early as 1874 a story, *Ḥazut ha-Kol*, criticizing organized Jewish life, the exploitation of the poor by rich Jews, and the *maskilim* who derided Jewish tradition. After being imprisoned and tried in Austria for revolutionary activities (February 1878–January 1879) he was expelled to Germany. There he was immediately arrested, and at the end of the year was expelled and reached London. His endeavors to participate in the activities of the Narodnaya Volya were unsuccessful. In the summer of 1880 he established, in conjunction with *Vinchevsky, the short-lived Jewish Workingmen's Benefit and Educational Society. In 1880 Liebermann followed the woman he loved to the United States, but she refused to leave her husband. In New York he was associated with the Agudat Shoḥarei Sefat Ever. Subsequently he committed suicide. In 1934 his remains were buried next to those of Vinchevsky in the cemetery of the Arbeter Ring (Workmen's Circle) in New York.

Liebermann was influenced by cosmopolitan ideas. He was nevertheless imbued with Jewish consciousness and a sense of responsibility toward the fate of the Jewish masses. He interpreted the Narodniks' principle of "going to the people" as going out to the Jewish people. He was depressed when his projects for Jewish Socialist activity clashed with the prejudices against Jewish "parasitism" and "exploitation" he encountered within the Russian revolutionary movement, while on the other hand his activity found little response among the Jewish public. It was not until several decades after his death that the personality of Liebermann was fully appreciated. His memory was particularly revived with the establishment of the labor movement in Ereẓ Israel.

BIBLIOGRAPHY: D. Weinryb, *Be-Reshit ha-Soẓyalizm ha-Yehudi* (with Eng. summary, 1940); Ẓ. Kroll, *Ha-Rishon* (1945); K. Marmor (ed.), *Aron Libermans Briv* (1951); Klausner, Sifrut, 5 (1949), index; 6 (1958^2), 220–74; LNYL, 5 (1963), 61–65; Leksikon, 2 (1967), 254–8; B. Sapir, in: *International Review of Social History*, 10:3 (1965), 1–20; A. Patkin, *The Origins of the Russian Jewish Labour Movement* (1945), index.

[Moshe Mishkinsky]

LIEBERMANN, CARL THEODOR (1842–1914), German organic chemist. He did research in his native Berlin with Adolf von Baeyer, and in 1873 succeeded him as professor at the Gewerbeinstitut, which grew into the Berlin Technische Hochschule. Liebermann's main field was dyestuffs, and he worked out the synthesis of alizarin, an industry which came to be worth hundreds of millions of marks to Germany. He worked on azo dyes, naphthalene, naphthoquinone, anthracene, chrysene, and the constitution of natural dyestuffs. He also worked on alkaloids. A list of his numerous publications was collected in the *Festschrift* produced in honor of his 70th birthday. Liebermann was president of the German Chemical Society.

BIBLIOGRAPHY: *Berichte der deutschen chemischen Gesellschaft*, 48 (1915), 4f.; Wallach, *ibid.*, 51 (1918), 1135–60; Bistrzycki, in: *Chemiker Zeitung*, 39 (1915), 165–7.

[Samuel Aaron Miller]

LIEBERMANN, FELIX (1851–1925), medievalist, brother of Max *Liebermann, the artist. Born in Berlin, he was on the editorial staff of the *Monumenta Germaniae Historica* (1877–85) and worked on the edition of English historical sources for vols. 11 and 27 of its *Scriptores* series. He edited volume 28, which contains excerpts from English sources relating to 13th-century German history. Liebermann also published *Ungedruckte anglo-normannische Geschichtsquellen* (1879) and a number of articles on related subjects. His numerous studies on early English law published from 1893 through 1902 culminated in his most important work, *Die Gesetze der Angelsachsen* (3 vols., 1898). Another study was *The National Assembly in the Anglo-Saxon Period* (1913).

BIBLIOGRAPHY: H.D. Hazeltine, *Felix Liebermann 1851–1925* (1939); Davis, in: *English Historical Review*, 41 (1926), 91–97; *Festgabe fuer F. Liebermann…* (1921). **ADD. BIBLIOGRAPHY:** NDB, vol. 14 (1985), 480f.

[Helene Wieruszowski]

LIEBERMANN, MAX (1847–1935), German painter. Liebermann, the son of a Berlin industrialist, studied at the Weimar Academy. He was only 23 when his picture of *The Boy Jesus in Dispute with the Rabbis* was attacked by critics, some of whom appear to have been motivated by antisemitism. Two years later his *Women Plucking Geese* received high praise when it was exhibited in Hamburg and Berlin.

Liebermann was a very Nordic painter. Photographic naturalism was as abhorrent to him as expressionism, and although he has often been called an impressionist he never regarded himself as one. He spent much of his life in Holland and was heavily influenced by its gray skies. He used cool, austere colors to paint the bleak, flat Netherlands landscapes in which he discovered the excitement of changing atmosphere, sunlight intermingling with mist, blue hazes, and empty spaces. While his early work tended to be static, he gradually loosened up as regards form and color, reversing the traditional pattern by growing freer and more spontaneous as he became older. In his fifties he began painting athletes in action, rearing horses, and the colorful vegetable markets of the Amsterdam Jewish quarter.

In 1898 Liebermann became a member of the Berlin Academy and helped to found Sezession, an association of progressive artists. In 1920 he became president of the Berlin Academy of Art. His *Gesammelte Schriften* ("Collected Writings") appeared in 1922. By this time he was too frail for his regular trips to Holland and did much of his painting at his summer home in Wannsee, outside Berlin. He became a celebrated and expensive portraitist, painting his sitters with a broad virtuosity, but not often probing deeply into their personality. Among them were Hermann *Cohen, Georg *Brandes, and Walther *Rathenau. He also did thousands of rapid sketches in pen, pencil, crayon, and chalk.

Liebermann considered himself first and foremost a German and had little interest in Jewish affairs, although he described himself as being "very much aware of belonging to the Jewish people" and as watching the goals of Zionism with "the greatest interest." Apart from his paintings and drawings of the Amsterdam ghetto, virtually his only work on Jewish subjects was a series of lithographs for an edition of Heinrich *Heine's *Rabbi of Bacharach* and two oils on the Samson and Delilah theme. When the Nazis came to power in 1933 he was ousted from presidency of the Academy and his paintings were removed from all German museums. His death two years later was completely ignored by the German press. In 1943 his widow was told that she was to be deported by the Gestapo, and she committed suicide. The Liebermann house in Pariser Platz was looted and its valuable collection of paintings stolen and scattered.

BIBLIOGRAPHY: M.J. Friedlaender, *Max Liebermanns graphische Kunst* (1922²); K. Scheffler, *Max Liebermann* (Ger., 1953); F. Stuttmann, *Max Liebermann* (Ger., 1961), includes plates; E. Hancke, *Max Liebermann, sein Leben und seine Werke* (1923), includes plates. **ADD. BIBLIOGRAPHY:** F. Berchtig, *Max Liebermann* (2005); M. Eberle, *Max Liebermann 1847–1935. Werkverzeichnis der Gemaelde und Oelstudien*, 2 vols. (1996; with catalogue raisonné of oil paintings); Hamburger Kunsthalle / Staedelsches Kunstinstitut, Frankfurt a. Main / Museum der bildenden Künste, Leipzig, *Max Liebermann. Der Realist und die Phantasie* (1997); J.E. Howoldt and U.M. Schneede, *Im Garten von Max Liebermann*, Exh. cat. Hamburger Kunsthalle und Alte Nationalgalerie, Berlin (2004); R. Melcher (ed.), *Max Liebermann. Zeichnen heisst weglassen – Arbeiten auf Papier*, Exh. catalogue Saarlandmuseum Saarbrücken (2004); C.C. Schuetz, "Max Liebermann as a "Jewish Painter," The Artist's Reception in his Time," in: E. Bilsik (ed.), *Berlin Metropolis. Jews and the New Culture, 1890–1918*, Exh. cat. New York: The Jewish Museum (1999), 146–63; H. Simon (ed.), *Was vom Leben übrig bleibt, sind Bilder und Geschichten. Max Liebermann zum 150. Geburtstag; Rekonstruktion der Gedaechtnisausstellung des Berliner Juedischen Museums von 1936* (1997).

[Alfred Werner]

LIEBERMANN, ROLF (1910–1999), composer and opera manager. Born in Zurich, a great-nephew of Max *Liebermann, Rolf Liebermann studied law at Zurich University before devoting himself to music. In 1937–38 he was private secretary and music assistant to his conducting teacher, Herman

Scherchen, in Vienna. He returned to Switzerland as a music critic and studied composition with Vladimir *Vogel in Ascona. In 1950 he became music director of the Swiss radio and in 1959 general manager of the Hamburg State Opera, which he made one of the major music centers of the time by commissioning new operas from composers throughout the world, including Israel (J. *Tal's operas), and by the high quality and excellence of their production. In June 1971, Liebermann was appointed general administrator of the Théâtre de l'Opéra, Paris, with Georg *Solti as his musical advisor and in 1973 he was responsible for the lavish reopening of the Paris Opera House, where he was a manager until 1980. In his compositions Liebermann used 12-tone technique, with a predilection for bitonality and with tonal references. His own operas are distinguished by fresh dramatic ideas and strict musical organization. They include *Leonore 40/45* (1952), *Penelope* (1954), and *School for Wives* (1955), based on Molière's play. He also wrote *Concerto for Jazzband and Orchestra* (1954), the *Geigy Festival Concerto* (1958), cantatas, and songs. He published with B. Sizaire and S. Wendt: *Actes et entractes* (1976) and *Und jedermann erwartet sich ein Fest: Musiktheater* (1981).

BIBLIOGRAPHY: Grove online; I. Scharberth and H. Paris (eds.), *Rolf Liebermann zum 60. Geburtstag* (1970); C. Riess, *Rolf Liebermann, Nennen Sie mich einfach Musiker* (1977).

[Israela Stein (2nd ed.)]

LIEBERSON, GODDARD (1911–1977), musical executive and composer. Born in Hanley, England, Lieberson was taken to the United States as a child and studied with Bernard Rogers. In 1939 he joined the staff of Columbia Records and in 1956 was made president. In 1964 he was appointed president of the Record Industry Association of America. Lieberson edited the *Columbia Book of Musical Masterpieces* (1950). From 1966 on he sponsored the annual Lieberson prize competition for chamber works organized by the Israel League of Composers. His compositions include songs and chamber music.

LIEBERT (Levy), ARTHUR (1878–1946), German philosopher. Born in Berlin, he was coeditor of *Kant-Studien*, the publication of the Kant Society. From 1925 to 1933 he was professor of philosophy at the High School for Commercial Sciences, Berlin. When the Nazis came to power, he moved to Belgrade. There he founded and edited *Philosophia*, which appeared from 1936 to 1938. Its purpose was to unite around him the anti-Nazi philosophers. During World War II Liebert lived in England; shortly after the end of the war, he returned to Berlin where he died in 1946. Liebert's philosophy developed from that of the neo-Kantian Marburg school, led by Hermann *Cohen. Liebert's own contribution was that he attached great importance to the concept of "value." Philosophers should be concerned with the "evaluation" of being, and not only its existence. Reality not only exists, but "value" is found in it: it symbolizes something, and its own purpose is concealed in it. Liebert regarded metaphysics as necessary for investigating the totality of being. Through reason's dialectical activity, a metaphysical system is built up, but it can never achieve perfection. In this process, spirit and reason are the basic foundation of life itself. Liebert's major works include *Das Problem der Geltung* (1914), *Der Geltungswert der Metaphysik* (1915), *Vom Geist der Revolutionen* (1919), *Die geistige Krisis der Gegenwart* (1923), *Die Krise des Idealismus* (1936), *Der universale Humanismus* (1946), and *Von der Pflicht der Philosophie in unserer Zeit* (1938).

[Aaron Gruenhut]

LIEBLING, A.J. (**Abbott Joseph, Joe**; 1904–1963), one of the best-known and most widely admired journalists of his generation. Liebling was born in New York City to a penniless Jewish immigrant from Austria who became prosperous as a furrier, and a mother from a well-to-do Jewish family in San Francisco. Liebling enrolled at Dartmouth College in the fall of 1920 a month shy of his 16th birthday, and left without graduating. After graduating from Columbia University's School of Journalism, Liebling worked at the *New York Evening World*, the *New York Times* sports department, and the *Evening Bulletin* of Providence, Rhode Island. Liebling joined the *New Yorker* in 1935, where he remained for 28 years until his death. During World War II, he served as a war correspondent, filing stories from Africa, England, and Europe and wrote about his participation in the Normandy landings on D-Day. Liebling wrote atmospheric pieces about New York's neighborhoods and characters, especially those in the boxing business, and eventually became the foremost American writer on boxing. His book *The Sweet Science* (1956) was named No. 1 by *Sports Illustrated* on its 2002 list of top sports book of all time, and the Boxing Writers Association of America presents the A.J. Liebling Award for excellence in boxing journalism. Liebling also loved to eat and drink and wrote vividly about both, and he also loved newspapers, which led to his writing 82 "Wayward Press" columns of press criticism in the *New Yorker* between 1945 and 1963. Liebling is remembered for many quotes and aphorisms, such as "Freedom of the press is guaranteed only to those who own one"; "People everywhere confuse what they read in newspapers with news"; and "I can write better than anybody who can write faster, and I can write faster than anybody who can write better." He is the author of some 15 books including *Back Where I Came From* (1938), *The Telephone Booth Indian* (1942), *The Wayward Pressman* (1947), *Chicago, The Second City* (1952), *Between Meals: An Appetite for Paris* (1959), and *The Earl of Louisiana* (1961). A collection of his writings, *Just Enough Liebling*, was published in 2004.

[Elli Wohlgelernter (2nd ed.)]

LIEBLING, ESTELLE (1880–1970), US. soprano, voice teacher, and composer. Liebling, who was born in New York City to Matilde de Perkiewicz and Max Liebling, a pianist who had studied with Franz Liszt, started with piano, but quickly moved to vocal studies. Her parents sent her to Europe to study in Berlin with Selma Nicklass-Kempner. Dame Nellie Medba suggested she go to Paris and study under the great singing teacher Mathilde Marchesi. Liebling made her operatic debut as Lucia de Lammermoor in Dresden, followed by Rosina in *The Barber of Seville* and Queen of the Night in *The Magic Flute*. Returning to the United States in 1901, she appeared in several concert recitals, occasionally with her brother James Liebling, a cellist. After standing in at short notice for several roles, Liebling had her official debut at the Metropolitan Opera in New York City in 1903 as Musette in *La Bohème* with Enrico Caruso as Rodolfo. At the end of 1902, she sailed with John Philip Sousa and his band for a four-month European tour, including appearances before King Edward. Liebling continued to tour with the band, giving 1,600 concerts with Sousa and gaining a wider audience than an opera career would have afforded.

In 1905, she married Arthur Mosler, an inventor and engineer with whom she settled in New York City. While Liebling continued to sing until around the age of 50, she is best remembered as a dedicated teacher and singing coach of opera singers. Beverly *Sills, one of her most famous students, studied with her over the course of 33 years. In all, Liebling taught or coached 78 singers associated with the Metropolitan Opera. She also composed and published cadenzas, some of them from her Paris teacher Marchesi. Her compositions included *The Estelle Liebling Book of Coloratura Cadenzas* (1943), *Fifteen Arias for Coloratura Soprano* (1944), and *The Estelle Liebling Vocal Course* (1956).

[Judith S. Pinnolis (2nd ed.)]

LIEBMAN, CHARLES (YESHAYAHU) (1934–2003), political scientist specializing in the political culture and behavior of world Jewry and considered one of the leading researchers in the field. Liebman was born in the U.S. and immigrated to Israel in 1969. Between 1949 and 1952 he studied at the Herzlia Hebrew Gymnasium in Tel Aviv. He received his B.A. from the University of Miami in 1956, and received his M.A. and Ph.D. from the University of Illinois in 1960. In the 1960s he lectured at several universities in the U.S.: University of Pennsylvania (1961–63), Yeshiva University (1962–69), and Columbia University (1964–65). In 1969, after immigrating to Israel, he joined the Department of Political Science at Bar-Ilan University and became professor in 1978. From 1980 to 1984 Liebman was the head of the department. During those years he was a visiting professor at many American universities. He held other positions as well, on academic councils and editorial boards, published around 100 articles and 14 books, among them: *Ambivalent American Jew: Politics, Religion, and Family in American Jewish Life* (1973), *Pressure Without Sanctions: The Influence of World Jewry in Shaping Israel's Public Policy* (1977), *The Civil Religion of Israel: Traditional Judaism and Political Culture in the Jewish State* (with Don-Yehiya, 1983), *Two Worlds of Judaism: The Jewish Experience in Israel and the United State* (with Cohen, 1990), and *The Jewishness of Israelis: Responses to the Guttman Report* (with Katz, 1997). He won the Marshall Sklar Prize for his studies on U.S. Jews in 2000 and the Israel Prize for political science in 2003.

[Shaked Gilboa (2nd ed.)]

LIEBMAN, JOSHUA LOTH (1907–1948), U.S. Reform rabbi. Liebman was born in Hamilton, Ohio; when his parents divorced he went to live with his paternal grandfather, Rabbi Lipmann Liebman. He graduated from high school at the age of 15 and from the University of Cincinnati at the age of 19. He served as Taft Teaching Fellow in Philosophy before his 20th birthday and was ordained by Hebrew Union College in 1930, at the age of 23. In 1931, Liebman took up his first position as rabbi in Lafayette, Indiana, while pursuing his doctorate at HUC, where he taught Bible. He studied in Palestine in 1929–30 and began his love of Zion. In 1934 he was appointed to Kehilath Anshe Maarab Temple, Chicago, succeeding Solomon Freehof, and began his study of psychology. In 1939 he moved to Temple Israel in Boston. During his ministry in Boston, Liebman became widely known as a radio preacher. He also taught at Boston University, which was adjacent to his congregation, and Andover-Newton Theological Seminary. His role in his congregation marked a return to tradition. He abolished Sunday services, reinstituted Friday evening services, and pushed for a Jewish homeland in the Land of Israel, positions at odds with his congregation, which had been classically Reform. He hired a social worker to bring the insights of psychology into the religious life of his community. For the last two years of his life, Liebman was a nationally famous figure through the phenomenal success of his book *Peace of Mind* (1946). This had an instant appeal to a generation which had been harassed by the experience of World War II. Its popularity helped to encourage a closer working relationship between psychology and religion. His work was the first popular treatment of Judaism and psychology. The reception of his work in the immediate postwar years, together with the choice of Bess *Meyerson as Miss America and the reception of returning baseball star Hank *Greenberg, is regarded as an important indication of the unexpected transformation of the Jews in postwar American life, the dramatic decline of antisemitism, and a willingness to accept Jews and Judaism on equal terms.

ADD. BIBLIOGRAPHY: K. Olitzsky, L.J. Sussman, and M.H. Stern, *Reform Judaism in America: A Biographical Dictionary and Sourcebook* (1993).

[Sefton D. Temkin / Michael Berenbaum (2nd ed.)]

LIEBMANN, ESTHER SCHULHOFF AARON (c. 1645–1714) and **JOST** (**Judah Berlin**; c. 1640–1701), Court Jews in Berlin. Esther Schulhoff, born in Prague, first married Israel Aaron (d. 1673), Brandenburg court supplier and founder of the Berlin Jewish community. Jost Liebmann's first wife, Malka, was the niece of *Glueckel of Hameln. Liebmann learned precious-stone and metal working with Ḥayyim Hameln, Glueckel's husband.

Esther Aaron and Jost Liebmann married in 1676. Esther, who held a letter of protection as a Berlin Court Jew and maintained close ties to Frederick William, Elector of Brandenburg, secured permission for Liebmann to work and settle in Berlin. Between 1676 and 1701 the Liebmanns were a formidable team who maintained a household consisting of six children of their own, two from Esther's first marriage, a child from Aaron's first marriage, and whatever children Jost brought from his first marriage, as well as Esther's parents and relatives of Jost. Esther worked actively alongside her husband, attending the Leipzig Fair with him, unusual for a married Jewish woman at that time. After she was widowed, Esther attended many other fairs, as did other entrepreneurial widows, including Glueckel.

The Liebmanns, who were among the wealthiest Jews in Berlin, were the main court jewelers, assisting Frederick I of Prussia to acquire a sizable collection of precious stones and objects. In 1684 Jost Liebmann was released from payment of the body tax (*Leibzoll*) and in 1694 his books were recognized as legal evidence in court. Esther and Jost Liebmann were influential in the Jewish community and secured positions for their sons and other family members as rabbis in various communities in Prussia. In 1684, they received permission to sponsor Berlin's sole synagogue, which functioned in their home. This gave them considerable power over opponents within the Berlin Jewish community, particularly Moses Benjamin Wulff.

After Jost's death in 1701, Esther Liebmann successfully carried on their business, supplying ever-increasing amounts of jewelry to the court. The luxury-loving Frederick I owed her large sums. Part of her payment was a license to mint and issue coinage and she received numerous other royal privileges. With the accession in 1713 of the frugal soldier-king, Frederick William I, Esther Liebmann was put under house arrest and released only after she had paid the king a substantial fine. Her wealth and influence declined and the woman who had been the most powerful female Court Jew in Germany died the next year. Esther's sons, Isaac Liebmann and Liebmann Jost, were also court purveyors of jewels, but they did not attain the wealth and position of their parents.

BIBLIOGRAPHY: D. Hertz, "The Despised Queen of Berlin Jewry, or the Life and Times of Esther Liebmann," in: V.B. Mann and R.I. Cohen (eds.), *From Court Jews to the Rothschilds* (1996), 67–77; H. Schnee, *Die Hoffinanz und der moderne Staat*, 1 (1953), 47ff.; S. Stern; *The Court Jew* (1950).

[Judith R. Baskin (2nd ed.)]

LIEBMANN, OTTO (1840–1912), German philosopher. Liebmann, who was born in Loewenberg, Silesia, was appointed lecturer at Tuebingen in 1865, in 1872 professor at Strasbourg, and in 1882 professor at Jena. In 1870–71 he was in the Prussian army at the siege of Paris, and published a patriotic memoir, *Monate vor Paris* (1871). Liebmann was one of the founders of neo-Kantianism. His *Kant und die Epigonen* (1865) attacked post-Kantian metaphysical theories and advocated a return to Kant's philosophy. For Liebmann, Kant's transcendental idealism, the recognition of the intimate and necessary correlation of the subjective and objective, of empirical reality and transcendental ideality, sufficed to explain the world. He opposed metaphysical theories about the "thing-in-itself" as well as empirical, positivistic, and materialistic views. In his later works, he tried to develop his neo-Kantianism with regard to metaphysics, experience, science, psychology, and ethics and aesthetics. His chief works were *Ueber den individuellen Beweis fuer die Freiheit des Willens* (1866), *Ueber den objektiven Anblick* (1869), *Zur Analysis der Wirklichkeit* (1876), *Die Klimax der Theorien* (1884), *Gedanken und Tatsachen* (2 vols., 1882–1904), and *Immanuel Kant* (Ger., 1904). He also wrote poetry, collected in *Weltwanderung* (1889).

BIBLIOGRAPHY: *Kantstudien*, 15 (1910), 1–151, contains a festschrift in Liebmann's honor; Campo, in: *Encyclopedia of Philosophy*, 4 (1967), 466–7; Rossi, in: *Enciclopedia Filosofica*, 3 (It., 1957), 50.

[Richard H. Popkin]

LIEBRECHT, SAVYON (1948–), Hebrew writer. Liebrecht was born in Munich to Holocaust survivors who immigrated to Israel soon afterwards. She studied philosophy and literature at Tel Aviv University and began publishing in 1986. Her first collection of stories, *Tappuḥim min ha-Midbar* ("Apples from the Desert," 1998) appeared in 1986. The title story tells of a young teacher who stages a confrontation with a woman who apparently was her father's mistress 30 years earlier. In other stories Liebrecht introduces an Arab woman who wishes to build a room on the roof of her house, and an Arab worker; a woman who seeks her daughter and learns thereby something about herself and her life; and a woman whose son has become deeply religious. Other collections include *Susim al Kevish Gehah* ("Horses on the Highway," 1988); *Sinit Ani Medabberet Elekha* ("It's All Greek to Me, He Said to Her," 1992); *Ẓarikh Sof le-Sippur Ahavah* ("On Love Stories and Other Endings," 1995); *Nashim mitokh ha-Katalog* ("Mail Order Women," 2000); and *Makom Tov la-Laylah* ("A Good Place for the Night," 2002). In the story "Excision," a grandmother jaggedly shears her four-year-old granddaughter's beautiful locks to eradicate lice because that is how they did it in the camps, while in "Compassion," a Holocaust survivor imprisoned by her Arab husband drowns her granddaughter to protect her from future suffering. Liebrecht's recurring themes are Holocaust survivors' lives in Israel half a century after the catastrophe; women's experiences as wives and mothers; the tensions between Orthodox and secular Israelis; and the relationships between individual Arabs and Israelis. Informed by feminism, Liebrecht often describes women struggling against their marginalized status in patriarchal Israeli society: in "The Road to Cedar City" an Israeli woman, mocked and humiliated by her husband and son during a trip in the United States, asserts her independence by making contacts with an Arab wife. The three novellas in the collection "Mail Order Women" highlight the complex relationship developing when a foreign woman, a Filipino caretaker or a Polish girl, enters the life of Israelis. Liebrecht's novel, *Ish, Ishah ve-Ish* (1998; *A Man and a Woman and a Man*, 2001) is the story of Hamutal, a married woman, who has a brief love affair with a stranger she meets at the geriatric ward where her sick mother and his dying father are both hospitalized. In *Ha-Nashim shel*

Abba ("The Women my Father Knew," 2005), Liebrecht tells of a belated encounter between Meir and his father, a meeting which enables the son, an aspiring writer, to discover the plot for his next novel. Liebrecht, author of television scripts and plays, was awarded the Alterman Prize (1987). Her prose has been translated into various languages. "Excision" is included in M.J. Bukiet (ed.), *Nothing Makes You Free: Writings by the Descendants of Jewish Holocaust Survivors* (2002); "Morning in the Park with Nannies" appeared in G. Abramson (ed.), *Oxford Book of Hebrew Short Stories* (1996); "A Room on the Roof" is available in R. Domb (ed.), *New Women's Writing from Israel* (1996). For further information concerning translations see the ITHL website at www.ithl.org.il.

BIBLIOGRAPHY: Ch. Meckel, "Mitteilungen aus Israel," in: *Die Zeit* (September 11, 1992); N. Govrin, "*Rishumah shel ha-Sho'ah be-Sipporet Nashim Ivrit*," in: *Reeh*, 2 (1997), 11–34; L. Yudkin, "Holocaust Trauma in the Second Generation: The Hebrew Fiction of D. Grossman and S. Liebrecht," in: E. Sicher (ed.), *Breaking Crystal* (1998), 170–181; idem, "Second Generation and the Active Presence: Savyon Liebrecht," in: *Literature in the Wake of the Holocaust* (2003), 85–104; Y. Zerubavel, "Revisiting the Pioneer Past: Continuity and Change in Hebrew Settlement Narratives," in: *Hebrew Studies*, 41 (2000), 209–224; O. Bishko, "*Ha-Zikah ha-Semantit-Logit shel ha-Petiḥut le-Guf ha-Sippur ha-Kaẓar: S. Liebrecht*," in: *Talpiyot*, 11 (2000), 202–210; R. Heusser-Markun, "S. Liebrecht, israelische Alltagsanalytikerin," in: *Neue Zürcher Zeitung* (January 7, 2000); D. Abramovich, "Post Holocaust Identity and Unresolved Tension in Modern Day Israel: Liebrecht's 'Apples from the Desert,'" in: *Women in Judaism*, 3:1 (2002); N.B. Sokoloff, "Zionist Dreams and Savyon Liebrecht's 'A Cow Named Virginia,'" in: *History and Literature* (2002), 439–450; T. Elor, "*Tappuḥim min ha-Midbar*," in: *Morot be-Yisrael* (2002), 216–239; E. Trevisan Semi, "Migrant Women and Israeli Society in '*Nashim mitokh Katalog*' by S. Liebrecht," in: *Materia Giudaica*, 8:2 (2003), 397–403; L. Yudkin, "Second Generation and the Active Presence: S. Liebrecht," in: *Literature in the Wake of the Holocaust* (2003), 85–104.

[Anat Feinberg (2nd ed.)]

LIÉGE (Flemish **Luik**, Ger. **Luettich**), capital of Liége province, E. Belgium. There is no evidence that a Jewish community existed in Liége in the Middle Ages. During the 11th century Bishop Wazon, the overlord of the city, had a religious disputation with a Jewish physician at the court of Emperor Conrad II. In 1138 a Jewish physician, Moses, cured a cleric Rodolphe de Saint Trond in Liége, but there is nothing to attest to his residence there. In 1573 a Jew in Liége became converted to Christianity, and in 1722 a German rabbi and his family were baptized. The first real evidence of the existence of a Jewish community in Liége postdates the French occupation at the end of the 18th century. There were 24 Jews living in the city in 1811, and 20–30 Jewish families in the second half of the 19th century. The oldest tombstone in the Jewish cemetery, with a Hebrew inscription, dates from 1842. The community in Liége had a synagogue and established communal institutions. On May 11, 1940, during the Nazi occupation, the Jewish population numbered 2,000 (according to the Gestapo report, it numbered 3,000 in 1939). An order issued by the Germans on Oct. 29, 1941, designated Liége as one of the four cities from which Jewish residence in Belgium was not excluded, along with Brussels, Antwerp, and Charleroi. On the liberation of Liége by the United States army on Sept. 8, 1944, there were 1,200 Jews in the city. Around 600 had been deported.

In 1959 the population numbered 594. There was then a *ḥazzan*-minister in Liége, but no rabbi, and no local source of *kasher* meat. The synagogue was Reform in tendency. About 25% had intermarried; Jewish religious observance was weak and tendencies to assimilate strong. However, Israel and Zionism, as a means of expressing Jewish identity, played a large role in community life. Liége had four Zionist societies and other fund-raising organizations on behalf of Israel. In 1968 its Jewish population was 1,500, dropping to around 1,000 in the early 1980s, with a shrinking Jewish community still in existence at the turn of the century.

BIBLIOGRAPHY: E. Ouverleaux, *Notes et documents sur les juifs de Belgique…* (1885); E. Ginsburger, *Les Juifs de Belgique au XVLIIe siècle* (1932), 1, 97; J. Stengers, *Les juifs dans les Pays-Bas au Moyen Age* (1950), index; W. Bok, *Aspects de la Communauté Juive de Liège* (1959).

LIEN (Heb. שִׁעְבּוּד נְכָסִים, *Shibud Nekhasim*).

The Concept

Jewish law enables the creditor to exercise a lien over all the debtor's property, in addition to his remedies against the debtor personally. This lien automatically comes into existence on the creation of the obligation and is called *aḥarayut* or *shi'bud nekhasim* (i.e., "property bearing responsibility" or the "encumbrance of property"). Sometimes the parties may limit the application of the lien to a specified part of the debtor's property, in which event it may operate either in addition to the general charge on the debtor's property, or so as to release the remaining property from any such encumbrance. A limitation of the lien to a specified asset may be effected in two ways: firstly, by the asset remaining in the debtor's possession, in which event the lien is called *apoteke* (see below); secondly, by the debtor surrendering possession of the asset to the creditor, this being called *mashkon*, i.e., pledge. The law relating to the latter is dealt with fully under *pledge.

Import of the Term Aharayut Nekhasim

Originally, the general lien applied only to the real estate (*karka*, "land") of the debtor, because land could not be carried away or spoiled and was therefore deemed "property bearing responsibility" (Kid. 1:5). Chattels were regarded as incapable of being preserved and were therefore deemed property "not bearing responsibility" (*ibid.*). The special reasons for the availability in Jewish law of the automatic lien in respect of all obligations will be dealt with below and in the article on *Obligations.

The concept of a charge on assets is already mentioned in a *takkanah* from the time of Simeon b. Shetaḥ, concerning a husband's written undertaking to his wife that all his property shall be charged in her favor to secure the repayment of her **ketubbah* (Ket. 82b); it may be assumed that a charge of this nature was known at that time in respect of other obligations as well. In the third century the *amoraim* Ulla and Rabbah disputed the question whether a charge of this nature originated from Pentateuchal law (*shi'buda de-oraita*) or from rabbinical enactment (*de-rabbanan*). According to some of the *rishonim*, this dispute related only to the question of seizing assets which had been alienated by the debtor to a third party, and that as long as the assets remained with the debtor all agreed that they were subject to the Pentateuchal lien (Tos. to BB 175b and *Bet ha-Beḥirah* thereto). Other *rishonim* were of the opinion that the dispute was one of principle, whether or not the encumbered assets had been alienated, namely: whether the right of recovery of the debt in this way flowed from the personal aspect of the obligation, as was the case when the creditor recovered payment out of the chattels of the debtor, or whether in relation to land the creditor acquired a lien also in the nature of a rent right, in addition to the personal obligation (Rashbam, Tos. to BB 175b; Nov. Rashba, *ibid.*; Nov. Ritba Kid. 13b; see also See also Elon, *Ha-Mishpat Ha-Ivri*, 1, 485–490; *Kevod Ha-Adam…* 21). The *halakhah* was decided in accordance with the view of *shi'buda de-oraita* (Yad, Malveh, 11:4; Sh. Ar., ḤM 111; Sma *ibid.*, n. 1).

Substance of the Creditor's Right in the Debtor's Property

The creditor's general lien over the debtor's property does not allow him a full proprietary right (*zekhut kinyanit*). This finds expression mainly in two respects. Firstly, the right of lien does not preclude the debtor from validly transferring ownership of his property to another, albeit subject to the fact that the creditor, when seeking to recover payment, is entitled to seize the property from the party who acquired it (this right of seizure is known as *terifah*, from the *nekhasim meshu'badim*, i.e., the "encumbered and alienated property"). As will be seen below, special rules were laid down governing the right of seizure from any such transferee. Secondly, the lien is subordinate to, and dependent on, the debtor's own ownership in the property, and hence the latter, in certain circumstances, is able to oust or extinguish the creditor's lien over his property.

Recovery of the Debt out of Encumbered Assets

It is a substantive principle that a debt may not be satisfied out of the *nekhasim meshu'badim* (see above) as long as the debtor is possessed of other assets, i.e., *nekhasim benei ḥorin* ("free property"), even if the remaining assets are inferior to those to which the creditor is entitled (e.g., the free assets are *beinonit* or average, whereas the obligation is tortious and must therefore be satisfied from the *iddit*, or best). If the debtor has sold the encumbered property to several purchasers, the creditor must first recover from the last purchaser, since the anterior one may plead: "I have left you room to recover from him." Similarly, the purchaser retains the right to pay in cash rather than surrender the encumbered property. Where there are several creditors, a preferential right of lien over the debtor's property will be enjoyed by the creditor to whom the debtor first became indebted (Git. 48b; BK 8a; Sh. Ar., ḤM 104; see also *Execution (Civil)).

Creation of the Debt

As long as the debtor's property remained in his possession, there would be no need to limit the creditor's lien therein, as mentioned above. However, there was good reason for limiting the right of seizure from the transferee of the encumbered assets only to cases where the debt was originally evidenced in writing (i.e., *milveh bi-shetar*, "loan by deed") and not orally (*milveh be-al peh*). The *amoraim* disputed the legal justification of this limitation (BB 175b). In the opinion of Ulla, the law entitled the creditor to seize encumbered land from the purchaser even for an orally established debt, except that the scholars had regulated against it in order not to cause loss to the purchaser of such land, since an "oral" debt had no *kol* ("publicity," lit. "voice") and the purchaser would therefore have no notice of the land's encumbrance in favor of the creditor. On the other hand, Rabbah was of the opinion that the law did not recognize the institution of *aḥarayut nekhasim* at all, and the creditor's right to recover from the debtor's property, including land, derived from a personal liability only, which could not be enforced except against the debtor's free property (see above). However, the scholars enacted that, in the case of a debt evidenced in writing and constituting notice, the creditor could seize the debtor's property from the purchaser, for otherwise the creditor would have no security for the repayment of the debt, and thus no borrower would ever be able to obtain a loan. The need to secure repayment of the debt in such a firm manner so as to forestall any reluctance to grant a loan most probably stemmed from the fact that in Jewish law the prohibition against interest precluded the earning of any profit from the actual loan, and accordingly the principal at least had to be adequately secured. From its application to a liability originating from loan, this rule was also extended to other obligations (L. Auerbach, *Das juedische Obligationenrecht*, 1 (1870), 172). Since the reason for precluding seizure from the purchaser in the case of an oral debt was to avoid loss because he had no notice of the debt's existence, R. Pappa decided that the creditor could seize the land of the debtor if the third party into whose hands it had passed was the heir of the debtor (BB 176a; but cf. the opinion of Rav, TJ, BK 10:1, 7b and BM 1:6, 8a; BB 175a and the opinion of Samuel there); the *halakhah* was decided accordingly in the codes (Yad, Malveh 11:4, Sh. Ar., ḤM 107:1).

In post-talmudic times various *takkanot* were enacted, laying down that a debt was not to be considered a written one unless the deed was written and signed by a scribe and witnesses specially appointed for the purpose (see Sh. Ar., ḤM 61:1), whereby the maximum notice and warning were thus afforded to potential purchasers – in much the same way as mortgages are registered in land registry offices at the present time.

A debt established by deed provided the right of exacting payment out of encumbered property, even if not so expressly stipulated – the omission being attributed to "an error of the scribe" (BM 14a; 15b). With regard to an obligation stemming from the *ketubbah*, this rule was specifically endorsed in a special enactment (Ket. 4:7). An exception to the rule distinguishing between oral obligation and one by deed was recognized in the case of land sold with a guarantee (i.e., in respect of claims by third parties against the land) in the presence of witnesses, even without a deed. In this event the purchaser could exact the purchase price from the encumbered property, it being considered that a sale of land before witnesses would become known even in the absence of a written instrument (BB 41b and codes). Similarly, and for the same reason, the creditor could exact payment from the debtor's encumbered property if there was an obligation established by way of a *kinyan* before witnesses (see *Acquisition; BB, 40a; Sh. Ar., ḤM 39:1).

Seizure for a Debt of Fixed Amount Only

The scholars regulated "for the sake of good order" (*mi-penei tikkun olam*) that recovery could be made out of encumbered assets only for a debt of a fixed amount and not otherwise, e.g., in respect of maintenance for a wife and daughters (Git. 5:3, 50b and codes).

Debts Stemming from Tort

According to tannaitic law, an injured party could recover all the various measures of compensation from *nekhasim meshu'badim* (even though not stipulated in the deed; Tosef., Ket. 2:2). However, the *amoraim* disputed the question of whether an obligation imposed by law was subject to the same rules as one agreed upon in a deed (Bek. 49b et al.). In the light of the rule that a debt for an unspecified amount was not recoverable from encumbered assets, it would seem that there was room for extending the limitation also to a debt stemming from tort, for precisely the same reasons. The matter remained a disputed one, however, even in the codes (see e.g., Tos. to BK 8a s.v. כול; *Beit Yosef* ḤM 119 n. 4).

Any obligation not recoverable out of *nekhasim meshu'badim* becomes recoverable in this way in consequence of a judgment of the court on a claim submitted (BB 175b; BK 104b–105a).

Encumbrance of Assets

Originally, the law was that a lien extended only to assets in the possession of the debtor at the time the debt was created (cf. the ancient wording: "all the property that I have," Ket. 4:7; Tosef., Ket. 4:7; Tosef., Ket. 12:1), and property later acquired could not be seized by the creditor once it had been transferred to a third party (Yad, Malveh 18:1; Sh. Ar., ḤM 112:1). In order to increase the creditor's security, however, the scholars prescribed that if, at the time the debt was created, the debtor agreed that property he might acquire in the future would also be subjected to the lien, this would also form part of his encumbered assets, i.e., from the time it came into his possession (TJ, Ket. 4:8, 29a; BB 44b). This rule was discussed in the light of the principle that a person could not transfer ownership of something not in his possession (*reshut*; see *Contract), but the distinction was made that one could nevertheless encumber property in this manner (BB 157 a/b; Yad, Malveh 18:1; Sh. Ar., ḤM 112:1). The opinion is expressed in the codes that, in view of the rule of "the scribe's error" (see above), the lien also extended to assets acquired by the debtor after the creation of the debt, even if not expressly agreed to by him when the obligation came into being (Rema, ḤM 112:1).

Chattels as Nekhasim Meshu'badim

In the amoraic period the rule that a lien extended only to the debtor's land underwent a variation: it was laid down that if, at the time of creation of the debt and as security for it, the debtor expressly charged the chattels incidental to his land (*agav karka*; see *Acquisition), the lien would also extend to such chattels, whether they were in his possession or acquired thereafter (BB 44b; Yad, Malveh 18:2; Sh. Ar., ḤM 113:1–2). The extension of the lien in this manner was due to the fact that the number of landowners had diminished and the lien, if limited to land alone, would have failed to provide adequate security for the repayment of a debt. With the intensification of this economic trend in geonic times, the practice was accepted of *kinyan* ("acquisition") incidental to land – even if the debtor owned none at all – involving the doctrine of the "four cubits [*arba ammot*] in Ereẓ Israel" said to be possessed by every Jew. For the same reason a special *takkanah* was enacted in the geonic period, making it possible – contrary to talmudic law (see Ket. 92a) – for the creditor also to exact payment out of the debtor's chattels acquired by his heirs (*Ḥemdah Genuzah* no. 65; cf. justification of the rule on similar grounds, Rashbam BB 174a; see also Yad, Malveh 11:11; Sh. Ar., ḤM 107:1).

This *takkanah* concerning the seizure of the debtor's chattels after they passed into the hands of his heirs was unlikely to create difficulty, since it was only proper that the heirs should fulfill the obligations of the deceased. However, so far as purchasers were concerned, the growing practice whereby even one's chattels were charged on the creation of an obligation, caused the creditor's consequent right of seizure to be a serious obstacle to business transactions. Accordingly, the earlier practice was reverted to, and it became accepted that the creditor would not recover from chattels sold to a third party, even though the debtor had expressly agreed in the deed to charge such of his chattels as were incidental to land – this being justified by the *takkanat ha-shuk* ("market overt") – for otherwise no person would be able to buy any chattel from his neighbor for fear that a lien existed in favor of his creditors (Resp. Rosh 79:5; also 4 and 6; Tur, and Sh. Ar., ḤM 60:1; but cf. also *Siftei Kohen* ḤM 60, n. 4, where the custom is contested).

To counter the fear of prospective purchasers that property acquired from a seller was subject to being seized by the latter's creditors, the practice was adopted – in terms of a *takkanah* enacted in the Middle Ages and observed in many communities – whereby at the time of the sale of land any person claiming a right or lien over the property in question was publicly called upon to come forward within a period of 15 days (Resp. Rashba, vol. 6, nos. 6–7) or 30 days (idem, vol. 2, no. 95) and establish his claim, failing which he would lose his right, and would thenceforth be precluded from raising any objection to the sale and from making any claim by way of lien or otherwise over the property (see also Resp. Rosh no. 18:16; Tur, ḤM 104:3; Resp. Ritba, no. 156).

Cancellation and Extinction of Lien

The creditor's lien over the debtor's property is extinguished by the cancellation of the underlying obligation – i.e., by the repayment of the debt or the debtor's release from it – and hence "a deed which has been borrowed on and repaid cannot be borrowed on again, since release has already been granted from its lien" (Ket. 85a). The creditor may, however, relinquish his lien in favor of one purchaser while retaining it in respect of other purchasers (Ket. 95a and codes), and he may also release part of the encumbered assets from the operation of the lien, while retaining it in respect of other parts (Tur and Sh. Ar., ḤM 111:12). In both cases the release has no validity unless formally effected by way of *kinyan* (*ibid.*; also 118:1).

As mentioned above, the creditors' lien does not amount to an independent proprietary right, but is subject to the debtor's own ownership of the encumbered property. Hence, the termination of the latter's ownership of the property may, in certain circumstances, automatically extinguish the creditor's lien therein. The Talmud mentions three cases in which the creditor's lien is extinguished as a result of the debtor's loss of ownership of the encumbered property: when the proprietor has made an irredeemable consecration (*kedushat ha-guf*; see **Hekdesh*) of the property, in which event it is thereafter and for all time placed beyond the ownership of the common man (*hedyot*; Git. 40b; Tur and Sh. Ar., ḤM 117:7) – according to Maimonides a redeemable consecration (*kedushat dammim*) also extinguishes the lien, save that the creditor may seize the property if and when it is redeemed (Yad, Malveh 18:6–7; Arakhin 7:14–16); when there is a prohibition against deriving benefit from the property, e.g., *Ḥameẓ* ("leaven") during Passover, which has the effect of nullifying ownership of the property; and when the property in question is a slave manumitted by his owner, since thereupon the right of ownership is totally extinguished (Git., Yad; Sh. Ar., *ibid.*; and see below).

A person who causes a lien over his property to be extinguished is nevertheless liable to the creditor for any loss resulting to the latter (see also **Gerama*; *Torts).

Apoteke

(אַפּוֹתֵיקִי). *Apoteke* is distinguished from the implied general lien by the fact that it is limited to a specific part of the property of the debtor, in whose possession it remains. The term is of Greek origin and in several tannaitic sources is rendered as "הִיפּוֹתֵיקִי" (*hippoteke*; Tosef., Shev. 8:6; Tosef., 11:8; Tosef., BM 1:8). Despite this Greek origin, however, in its substance and legal rules *apoteke* is in Jewish law similar to the general lien, and in fact it differs from the Greek hypothec (ὑποθήκη) in essential principles (see below). In effect, *apoteke* does not create a new charge on the property in question, since all the debtor's property is included in the implied, comprehensive charge that comes into existence upon creation of the obligation, but merely serves to restrict an already existing charge to particular assets. For this reason, Jewish law sources make no specific mention of the term *shi'bud apoteke*, but speak of "defining" or "setting aside" a field (Git. 37a; Ket. 54b, 55a, 81b; BB 50a; TJ, Shev. 10;1, 39b), i.e., singling out of a particular asset from the generally charged property. The *rishonim* interpreted the term *apoteke* as a **notarikon* (from אפה תהא קאי, i.e., "on this it shall stand": *Arukh ha-Shalem*, s.v. אפתק; Rashi BK 11b; Rashbam BB 44b; or from פה תְּקָנָה – Maim., Comm. to Git. 4:4). The rule is that the creditor may only exact payment from the hypothecated property in respect of such obligations as would serve to create in his favor a general lien over the debtor's property, i.e., a debt by deed and not an oral one, etc. (*Beit Yosef*, ḤM 117, n. 3). Talmudic sources indicate that the *apoteke* itself had to be created by deed (Tosef., Shev. 8:6); but it was later laid down in the codes that an *apoteke* could be created before witnesses without deed, although the underlying obligation itself had to be under deed (*Beit Yosef*, loc. cit.).

The hypothecated property generally consisted of land, but instances are also mentioned where the *apoteke* attached (*inter alia*) to slaves (Git. 4:4) and to a bond of indebtedness, e.g., the *ketubbah* (Tosef., Ket. 11:1; Rashi's interpretation, in commenting on Ket. 54a, that the *apoteke* is effected specifically in relation to the land of the wife included in the *ketubbah* does not accord with the plain meaning of the Tosefta statement, but shows the influence of Rava's ruling; see below); and to chattels collectively (to a *Ḥavilah*, "bundle"; Tosef., Ket. 11:8). In the fourth century it was laid down by Rava in Babylonia that a hypothecated slave who had been sold could be seized by a creditor in recovery of his debt, since the sale of a slave carried a "voice" and purchasers would have warning, whereas the sale of a hypothecated ox or ass carried no "voice," and therefore these were not recoverable from a purchaser in settlement of the vendor's debt. Even then, however, a hypothecated slave afforded only limited security for the creditor, since already in the Mishnah it was prescribed that a slave manumitted by his owner, i.e., the debtor, could not be seized in recovery of the latter's debt (Git. 4:4) because his manumission extinguished the charge (TJ, Yev. 7:1, 8a and see above). This was in accordance with the fundamental doctrine of human liberty that "a slave, once liberated, does not return to servitude" (TJ, Pes. 2:29a). Hence it was not common to execute *apoteke*, not even in respect of slaves, and *apoteke* came to be equaled with the general lien, attaching to land only and not to chattels. Later this was enshrined in the codes in absolute manner, to the effect that no (alienated) hypothecated chattels of any kind were recoverable in payment of a debt since they carried no "voice," even if the *apoteke* was executed by deed and the purchaser had notice of it (Tur and Sh. Ar., ḤM 117:3; see also Sma, ḤM 117, n. 13).

Simple and Express Apoteke

(*apoteke setam* and *apoteke meforash*). Jewish law recognizes hypothecation of a specific asset in two different ways, each having its own rules concerning the creditor's right of recovery from such an asset. In the first case, referred to in the codes as *apoteke setam* (Tur, ḤM 117:1), the debtor gives a written undertaking to his creditor that if he should fail to repay the debt, "you may recover from this asset." As long as the debtor fails to repay the debt in cash and the asset remains in his possession, the creditor is entitled to exact payment out of such an asset and the debtor is not entitled to offer substitute assets. If the hypothecated asset should not suffice to repay the debt, or becomes spoiled, or ceases to exist, the creditor may recover payment out of the debtor's other assets (Git. 41a; Yad, Malveh 18:3; Sh. Ar., ḤM 117:1). Just as the general lien does not preclude the debtor from selling his assets, so he is also free to sell assets subject to a simple hypothecation. As long as he retains any free property, the creditor may not recover his debt out of such hypothecated assets alienated by the debtor (TJ, Yev. 7:1, 8a; Git. 41a). If the debtor has no free property, the creditor may recover from the hypothecated property in a purchaser's hands, even if other encumbered assets were alienated by the debtor after his alienation of the hypothecated property; in this respect *apoteke* gives the creditor a right that ranks in preference to that available to the creditor under the general lien (see above). However, the purchaser of hypothecated property – like the debtor himself – retains the right to repay the debt in cash (Yad, Malveh 18:4, 8, and *Maggid Mishneh*, ad. loc. Sma, ḤM 117 n. 8).

Simeon b. Gamaliel expressed the opinion that alienation was forbidden of assets hypothecated in favor of a woman's *ketubbah*, since "a woman is not in the habit of having recourse to the courts," and that she could recover her *ketubbah* from the hypothecated property only, and not from the remaining property in her husband's possession (Git. 41a). Apparently, however, he too was of the opinion that, if the hypothecated property did not equal the value of the *ketubbah*, or if it depreciated, the wife could recover from the remaining property of her husband (cf. Ket. 4:7; Tosef., Ket. 11:8; see Gulak, *Ha-Ḥiyyuv ve-Shi'budav*, 55). The *halakhah* was decided in accordance with the opposing view of the scholars, so that no difference is recognized between the *ketubbah* obligation and any other obligation (Yad and Sh. Ar., loc. cit.).

Express *apoteke* (termed *apoteke meforash* in the codes) is constituted when the debtor makes a written declaration to the creditor that "you shall not recover payment except out of this [asset]" (*lo yehe lekha pera'on ella mi-zo*, Git. 41a; BM 66b; TJ, Ket. 10:6, 34a). In this event no charge attaches to the debtor's remaining property, and hence, if the hypothecated property should be spoiled, the creditor may not recover payment out of the debtor's free property nor out of other property alienated by him to a third party (Git. 41a). Expressly hypothecated property also does not provide the creditor with an absolute proprietary right therein. Thus, if its value exceeds the amount of the debt, the creditor must return the balance to the debtor. Furthermore, while the *amoraim* of Ereẓ Israel disputed the question of whether the debtor could alienate expressly hypothecated property (TJ, Shev. 10:1, 39b), it appears from the Babylonian Talmud that he may do so, except that the creditor can exact payment out of the hypothecated assets in the purchaser's possession even if the debtor has any free property, and except, further, that the purchaser is not entitled to pay in cash in lieu of the hypothecated property, as he may do in the case of simple hypothecation (BK 96a; the debtor himself retains the right to pay in cash in both cases). The *halakhah* was decided in the codes in accordance with the latter view (Tur and Sh. Ar., ḤM 117:1; Sma ḤM 117, n. 5 and 6). Basically, therefore, express hypothecation afforded the creditor no greater rights than did simple hypothecation, whereas it did serve to deprive him of the general lien over all the other property of the debtor, and Gulak (*Ha-Ḥiyyuv*... p. 59f.) correctly surmises that its main purpose was to promote the free transaction of land sales by freeing all but a distinct part of the debtor's property from the creditor's lien.

In the State of Israel

The law in Israel recognizes no implied general lien of the kind known in Jewish law, but allows for the bonding of a specified asset in the creditor's favor by way of pledge or mortgage. A real estate mortgage is registered in the Land Registry Office, whereupon the mortgagor may not transfer ownership of the property without the consent of the mortgagee.

For further particulars see *Pledge.

[Menachem Elon]

Lien as Obligation and Lien as Security

A lien (*aḥarayut nekhasim/shibud nekhasim*) is a creditor's proprietary right to the debtor's assets to secure repayment, i.e., a case where the creditor, if not repaid in accordance with the terms agreed upon by the parties, is entitled to collect payment from encumbered assets. In such a case, a lien is a secondary right and terminates upon payment of the debt. Indeed, a lien may also be created as a primary right, whose realization is either conditional or without condition. In the case of a lien as a primary right, only the term "*shi'bud nekhasim*" applies.

The meaning of the term "*aḥarayut*" is "substitute," or "another thing." The substitute may be for a ritual sacrifice one pledged to bring and was lost, or for an asset that was sold and it subsequently transpired that it did not belong to the seller. "*Aḥarayut nekhasim*" refers to property which serves as a substitute for fulfilling an obligation, generally the payment of money. The property is a guarantee (suretyship) just as a guarantor (surety) is a substitute for the principal debtor (BB 174a). This concept of substitute is reflected in the wording in all bonds: "all my assets may be considered a substitute and serve as a guarantee."

A lien on property may be explicitly created by the owner – the debtor, or implicitly, if we consider that "*aḥarayut ta'ut sofer*," that is: it is presumed that the parties intended to stipulate the lien in the document, and its omission is the result of a scribal error. A property lien is automatically and not consensually created regarding a person's Scriptual obligations, which do not depend on the person's consent for its imposition on his property. There are those who have given this interpretation to the term "*shi'buda de-oraita*," and not, as it is usually interpreted, that the term means that this kind of lien has its origin in Pentateuchal law.

[Berachyahu Lifshitz (2nd ed.)]

The Solution of an Actual Legal Problem based on Jewish Law

As stated above, in Israeli law, as well as in other modern legal systems, a property lien on a *particular asset* belonging to the debtor can be used to secure a loan. In other words, a property lien is a fixed lien, of a proprietary nature, that continues to "attach" itself to the asset even after the asset has been transferred to another party. This lien, common in Israeli law, is similar to the explicit *apoteke*, which is an unusual lien in Jewish law.

In modern law, the term "floating charge" indicates an imposition of a non-fixed charge on a non-defined set of assets. A floating charge is generally imposed by granting credit to businesses, with the lien imposed on the debtor's entire business inventory. The floating charge differs from the permanent charge in two respects: First, it applies to assets that at the time of its imposition were not in the debtor's possession. Second, from the moment that the debtor sells any item of the inventory, the charge no longer applies to that item. The purpose of this kind of charge, originating in English law, is to allow businesses to receive credit and to establish a charge for that credit, without it intruding on continued commercial dealings.

In summary, under Jewish Law, liens bear certain similarities to the floating charge. Under Jewish law, at the time of taking a loan, all of the borrower's property is placed under lien to the benefit of the lender, including his chattels (Yad, Malveh ve-Loveh, 18:1). Such a lien may also be imposed on future property not yet in the borrower's possession (*"d'ikne"*), and according to some of the *posekim*, a lien applies to property that is not in the possession of the borrower, even if this was not explicitly stated (Rema, ḤM 112:1). The sale of chattels encumbered by a lien terminated the lien with respect to such chattels, and the creditor is not entitled to recover them from the buyers (Resp. Rosh, no. 79.5; Tur, Sh. Ar., ḤM 60:1). A comparison between these principles of lien in Jewish law and the characteristics of a floating charge shows a great deal of similarity between the "normal" lien under Jewish law and the floating charge of the modern law.

The law in Israel expressly relates to a floating charge only in the Companies Ordinance [New version], 5743 – 1983, and thus the accepted view is that the floating charge may be imposed only on a company's assets. A case was brought before the District Court in Jerusalem (CA 6063/05, *Atzmon v. Bar Levav;* per Judge Noam Solberg) where, pursuant to a contract, a floating lien was imposed on a person's unincorporated business. The question before the Court was whether a floating lien could be recognized as the asset of an individual, even though it is not expressly recognized in the law. The Court decided that, despite the fact that the law does not expressly relate to such a possibility – it does not negate it. From the perspective of policy considerations, the Court presented the considerations that support recognizing a floating lien on the assets of an individual and the opposing considerations. In deciding the case, the Court gave preference to the consideration of freedom of contracts, pursuant to which it is appropriate to give force to the agreement between parties to a contract to the extent possible. However, in light of a lacuna, and pursuant to section 1 of the Foundations of Law Law, 5740 – 1980, which provides that in the case of a lacuna the court should look to the "principles of freedom, justice, equity and peace of the Jewish tradition," the Court referred to Jewish law. After examining the general characteristics of a lien under Jewish law, the court stated that "indeed, the classic and common lien in the Jewish law is fundamentally similar to the floating charge." The Court's decision discussed the shared foundation of the "regular" lien under Jewish law and the modern floating charge, insofar as they apply to all of the debtor's assets, as stated above. In addition to this similarity, the court also considered that one of the justifications given in the Jewish law for the existence of the possibility of encumbering future assets, in contravention of the rule that transactions cannot be carried out in future assets – is facilitating commerce and the process of receiving loans – "so that doors will not be shut before the borrowers" (*Keẓot ha-Ḥoshen*, ḤM. 112:1) This is also the main reason offered as a justification for the *takkanah* of the *geonim* that provides that chattels as well as real property may be encumbered by a lien to the creditor (Rashbam, BB 157a). The Court concluded from its analysis of these Jewish law principles that "there is a goal to facilitate the conduct of commerce, to improve it, to make credit available, and to improve the financial well-being" in relation to the law of liens and views in the position of the Jewish law and impetus for recognizing the floating charge on the assets of an individual in the Israeli law.

[Menachem Elon (2nd ed.)]

BIBLIOGRAPHY: I.S. Zuri, *Mishpat ha-Talmud*, 4 (1921), 61–67; Gulak, Yesodei, 1 (1922), 141f., 149–65; 2 (1922), 8–10; idem, in: *Madda'ei ha-Yahadut*, 1 (1925/26), 46–48; idem, Oẓar, 235–8; idem, *Das Urkundenwesen im Talmud…* (1935), 114–25; idem, *Toledot ha-Mishpat be-Yisrael bi-Tekufat ha-Talmud*, 1 (*Ha-Ḥiyyuv ve-Shi'budav*, 1939), 31–61; Herzog, Instit, 1 (1936), 339–63; ET, 1 (1951³), 216–20; 2 (1949), 130–4; 5 (1953), 121–32. **ADD. BIBLIOGRAPHY:** M. Elon, *Ha-Mishpat ha-Ivri* (1988), 1:193, 195, 346, 404, 458f, 467, 476f., 484, 485–90, 531, 537, 551, 569, 600, 601, 775f.; *idem, Jewish Law* (1994), 1: 217, 219, 416, 3:492, 559f., 569, 580f., 590, 591–96, 646, 654, 670, 699, 743, 744, 953f.; idem, *Kevod ha-Adam ve-Ḥeruto be-Darkhei ha-Hoẓa'ah le-Po'el* (2000), 1–23; M. Elon and B. Lifshitz, *Mafte'aḥ ha-She'elot ve-ha-Teshuvot shel Ḥakhmei Sefarad u-Ẓefon Afrikah* (legal digest) (1986), 1:5–9, 21, 250–54; 2:533–34; B. Lifshitz and E. Shochetman, *Mafte'aḥ ha-She'elot ve-ha-Teshuvot shel Ḥakhmei Ashkenaz, Ẓarefat ve-Italyah* (legal digest) (1997), 5, 19, 184–85, 358; B. Lifshitz, *Shibuda de-Oraita – Bein Ḥiyyuv le-vein Betuḥa*, *Sefer ha-Yovel le-Rabinowitz* (5756), 65–95; H. Poversky, *Shibud Nekhasim ba-Mishpat ha-Ivri*, 12, *Dinei Yisrael* (5744 – 5745), 155–71; I. Warhaftig, *Ha-Hitḥayyevut* (5761), 17–52.

LIEPAJA (Ger. **Libau**; Rus. **Libava**), city in Kurzeme (Courland) district, Latvia; one of the oldest Baltic ports. Jews were permitted to live there from 1799, and by 1850 they numbered

1,348 persons. In 1840, 13 families (78 persons) left to join the agricultural settlements in *Kherson province. By 1881 it had increased to 6,651 following the completion of the Libava-Romny railroad, linking Liepaja with the leading industrial and commercial centers of the Ukraine. By 1897 the community had risen to 9,454 (c. 14% of the total population) and to a peak in 1911 of 10,308 (out of a total 83,650), consisting of the old-established residents of Courland among whom German cultural influences pre-dominated and Jews who had moved to Liepaja from various parts of Russia. The old Jewish residents were prominent in the export trade in grain and lumber, while the newcomers were included in the low-economic strata. The Jews also owned 11 of the 43 factories in the city, and about the same proportion of factory workers were Jews. When Latvia became independent after World War I, Liepaja lost its Russian hinterland, which was a severe setback for the development of the city. The Jewish population declined, from 9,758 (19%) in 1920, to 7,908 (13.81%) in 1930, and 7,379 (12.92%) in 1935. It nevertheless remained the third-largest Jewish community in the country, after Riga and Daugavpils (Dvinsk). Before World War I and under democratic government in Latvia (1918–34) a number of social and political groups, prominent rabbis, and communal leaders (including N. *Katzenelson) were active in the community. The Hebrew writer J.L. *Kantor was *kazyonny ravvin* from 1890 to 1904. He was succeeded in 1907 by Aaron Nurock, who later served as community rabbi until 1937. He was also a member of the Latvian parliament for one term. There existed a Hebrew public school with 400 pupils, a Hebrew Tarbut school (140 pupils), a Yiddish school with 350 children, and an Ort vocational school. The community maintained among others, an old-age home, orphanage, a clinic, and a tuberculosis sanatorium. In 1940 the Soviets nationalized the economy and exiled 50 property-owning families. They left the Yiddish school operating with a Soviet curriculum.

[Joseph Gar / Shmuel Spector (2nd ed.)]

Holocaust Period

Liepaja was occupied by the Germans on June 29, 1941. This was followed at once by anti-Jewish excesses and mass arrests. On July 24, 1941, 3,000 Jews from Liepaja, mostly men, were taken to the lighthouse at Schkeden and put to death. Jews from the surrounding towns and villages were concentrated in Liepaja, and on Dec. 15 and 16, 1941, another 3,500 were murdered. Four hundred Jews lost their lives in February 1942. In June of that year, a ghetto was set up, where 816 Jews were confined; it was liquidated on October 8, 1943 (the eve of the Day of Atonement), and the remaining Jews were deported to concentration camps.

Only a few dozen Liepaja Jews survived the war. The city was liberated by the Red Army on May 9, 1945, but most of the Jewish survivors did not return, preferring to stay in Displaced Persons' camps, from where they eventually left for Israel and other countries overseas.

[Joseph Gar]

BIBLIOGRAPHY: M. Schatz-Anin, *Di Yidn in Letland* (1924), 19–24; L. Ovchinski, *Di Geshikhte fun di Yidn in Letland* (1928), 123–32; *Le-Korot ha-Yehudim be-Kurland* (1908); *Yahadut Latvia* (1953), 241–3, 359–61; M. Kaufmann, *Die Vernichtung der Juden Lettlands* (1947), 299–304. **ADD. BIBLIOGRAPHY:** PK Latvia and Estonia, ed. Dov Levin (1988).

LIES, MAN OF (Heb. אִישׁ הַכָּזָב, *Ish ha-Kazav*), a person mentioned in some of the Qumran texts because of his opposition to the *Teacher of Righteousness. In the Damascus Document the figure of approximately 40 years marks the interval "from the day that the Unique Teacher was gathered in until the consuming of all the men of war who returned with the Man of Lies" (6QD 20.14ff.). In view of the fact that the members of the Qumran community called themselves "the poor," it may be that they derived the term "Man of Lies" from Proverbs 19:22, "A poor man is better than *ish kazav*." The reference to the consuming of all the men of war is probably based on Deuteronomy 2:14–16, where all the "men of war" who came out of Egypt perished within 38 years. The identification of the scriptures underlying the Zadokite author's language, however, does not help much to identify the persons he has in mind. The Man of Lies may have been the leader of a rival sect; sometimes the bitterest expressions of hostility and charges of apostasy are made between groups which an outsider could hardly distinguish one from another. One possibility that has been aired is that the Man of Lies is the Pharisaic leader *Simeon b. Shetaḥ, who returned from exile to enjoy a position of influence in Judea when Alexander *Yannai died in 76 B.C.E.; the "men of war" might then be his fellow exiles who came back with him.

The Habakkuk Commentary from Qumran Cave I has two references to the Man of Lies: one in which the words of Habakkuk 1:5 ("a work… which ye will not believe if be told you") are interpreted as "the traitors (apostates) with the Man of Lies, because they did not [listen to the words] of the Teacher of Righteousness from the mouth of God" (1QpHab. 2:1–3); the other in which the words of Habakkuk 1:13 ("wherefore lookest Thou, when they deal treacherously, and holdest Thy peace when the wicked swalloweth up the man that is more righteous than he?") are said to concern "the house of Absalom and the men of their counsel, who were struck dumb when the Teacher of Righteousness was chastised, and did not aid him against the Man of Lies, who rejected the Law in the midst of all their congregation" (1Qp Hab. 5:9–12). Some help might be expected from the mention of the "house of Absalom," but in every generation from the Hasmonean revolt to the war of 66 C.E. an Absalom can be produced – from an envoy sent by Judah Maccabee to Lysias in 164 B.C.E. (II Macc. 11:17) to a lieutenant of *Menahem in 66 C.E. (Jos., Wars 2:448). If the Man of Lies could be confidently identified with the Prophet of *Lies, then it might be possible to think of a rival religious teacher to the Teacher of Righteousness, whose rejection of the latter's interpretation of Scripture would be tantamount in the eyes of the community to rejection of the Law itself. Otherwise he could be any enemy of the Teacher and the community, and thus identified according to the period in which the Teacher is dated; thus H.H. Rowley thinks of Antiochus IV, W.H. Brownlee of John Hyrcanus, A. Dupont-Sommer of Hyrcanus II (identical with the *Wicked Priest), C. Roth of Simeon Bar Giora, G.R. Driver of several possibilities, including Agrippa II and John of Giscala.

BIBLIOGRAPHY: H.H. Rowley, *Zadokite Fragments and the Dead Sea Scrolls* (1952), 33, 40, 43, 60, 70; G.R. Driver, *Judaean Scrolls* (1965), 152ff., 271ff.

[Frederick Fyvie Bruce]

LIES, PROPHET OF (Heb. מַטִּיף הַכָּזָב, *Mattif ha-Kazav,* "spouter of falsehood"), a person mentioned in some of the Qumran texts, whose identity with the Man of *Lies cannot be assumed as certain in the present state of knowledge of the *Dead Sea Scrolls. The designation given to him is derived from Micah 2:11, "If a man walking in wind and falsehood do lie, 'I will preach (*attif*) unto thee of wine and of strong drink'; he shall even be the preacher (*mattif*) of this people!" (quoted 6QD 8:13). He is also called the "man of scoffing" near the beginning of the Zadokite Admonition: about the same time as the rise of the *Teacher of Righteousness, it is said, "there arose the man of scoffing, who preached [*hittif,* "spouted"] to Israel water of falsehood and led them astray in a trackless wilderness" (6QD 1:14f.). The reference is probably to a rival religious leader, probably to a leader of the Pharisees, for the Prophet of Lies and his associates "interpreted with smooth things" (1:18) – adopted a less exacting *halakhah* than did the followers of the Teacher of Righteousness – and other passages which mention the *Seekers after Smooth Things indicate that this is a description of the Pharisees. Later in the same document these people are called "the builders of the wall" who "walked after *ẓav*" (a reference to Hos. 5:11). The enigmatic *ẓav* is explained in terms of a "preacher" (*mattif*), in whom a variant and inferior reading of Micah 2:6 (*hattef yattifun*, as against the masoretic text, *al tattifu yattifun*) is seen as fulfilled: he leads his followers astray by his interpretations of the marriage law and the law of purity (see Book of Covenant of *Damascus).

In the Qumran commentary on Micah the denunciation of Samaria in Micah 1: 5–7 is interpreted of "the Prophet of Lies who [leads astray] the simple." In the commentary on Habakkuk, the denunciation of "him that buildeth a town with blood" (Hab. 2: 12) is interpreted of "the Prophet of Lies (*mattif ha-kazav*) who has led many astray, to build a worthless town with blood and to raise up a congregation with falsehood for the sake of its glory"; but he and his followers "will come to fiery judgments for having reviled and defamed God's elect ones" (1QpHab. 10:9–13). This language is akin to the condemnation in the Zadokite Admonition of those who, at the instance of the Prophet of Lies, "built the wall and daubed it with plaster" (6QD 8:12; cf. Ezek. 13:10ff.).

Although it is fairly certain that this Prophet of Lies is a Pharisaic teacher, his identity remains in doubt. Simeon b. Shetaḥ is one possibility, but since the Prophet appears to have been contemporary with the Teacher of Righteousness, the identity of the former must depend on the date assigned to the latter.

BIBLIOGRAPHY: G.R. Driver, *Judaean Scrolls* (1965), 307–10; Roth, in: JSS, 4 (1959), 339ff.

[Frederick Fyvie Bruce]

LIESSIN, ABRAHAM (pseudonym of **Abraham Walt**; 1872–1938), Yiddish poet and editor. Born in Minsk (Belorussia), Liessin received a traditional Jewish education. He showed an early interest in philosophy, Haskalah literature, and socialist reform. Besides establishing himself among Russian Jewish workers and socialist leaders as a revolutionary Yiddish poet and social satirist, he also became an active member of the Jewish Labor *Bund from its inception in 1897. That same year, his socialist agitation forced him to flee to New York, where he found work writing for and editing the Yiddish daily **Forverts*. In 1913 he began a 15-year career as editor of **Di Tsukunft*, a monthly Yiddish literary and cultural journal. While his socialism was nurtured by the physical poverty of New York's Lower East Side, Liessin also noted a spiritual poverty amongst Jewish socialists. He sought to combat this trend by articulating positive role models for revolution from within the Jewish tradition. Thus although not a Zionist, Liessin was an ardent Jewish nationalist; and his writing draws inspiration from Jewish religious and national heroes such as *Judah Maccabee, *Bar Kochba, Solomon *Molcho, Rabbi *Meir of Rothenburg, and Hirsch *Lekkert. Liessin's activism did not compromise his lyrical art, however, and he remained a meticulous editor of his own work, which is often described as lyrical and melodious. It can be read as a bridge between the idealist political poetry of the *Sweatshop Poets of the late 19th century (such as Morris *Rosenfeld and Dovid *Edelstadt) and the aestheticizing poetry of Di *Yunge at the beginning of the 20th century. Dominating his work are the idealist thematics of heroism, martyrdom, morality, and suffering (Christian imagery also features prominently), all of which served his Jewish socialist aspirations. His first collection, *Moderne Lider* ("Modern Poems"), was published illegally in 1897 in Minsk. His complete poetry was published in three volumes, with line drawings by Marc *Chagall, in New York in 1938 (*Lider un Poemen*, "Poems and Long Poems"). His prose includes a posthumously published collection entitled *Zikhroynes un Bilder* ("Memoires and Images," 1954).

BIBLIOGRAPHY: Reyzen, Leksikon, 2 (1927), 259–66; LNYL, 5 (1963), 179–91; B. Bialostotsky, *Lider un Eseyen* (1932), 79–130; E. Shulman, *Geshikhte fun der Yidisher Literatur in Amerike* (1943), 200–6; Z. Shazar, *Or Ishim* (1955), 195–207; H. Eivick, *Eseyen un Redes* (1963), 164–74; B. Rivkin, *Yidishe Dikhter in Amerike* (1959), 72–79; Waxman, Literature, 4 (1960), 1023–28; S. Bickel, *Shrayber fun Mayn Dor* (1965), 210–4; I. Ch. Biletzky, *Essays on Yiddish Poetry and Prose Writers* (1969), 15–22. **ADD. BIBLIOGRAPHY:** S. Liptzin, *A History of Yiddish Literature* (1972), 97–8; K. Bez, in: *Tsukunft*, 79 (1973), 82–5; E. Goldsmith, in: *The Jewish Book Annual*, 52 (1994–5), 163–75.

[Elias Schulman / Sarah B. Felsen and Jordan Finkin (2nd ed.)]

ABBREVIATIONS

GENERAL ABBREVIATIONS

This list contains abbreviations used in the Encyclopaedia (apart from the standard ones, such as geographical abbreviations, points of compass, etc.). For names of organizations, institutions, etc., in abbreviation, see Index. For bibliographical abbreviations of books and authors in Rabbinical literature, see following lists.

* Cross reference; i.e., an article is to be found under the word(s) immediately following the asterisk (*).
° Before the title of an entry, indicates a non-Jew (post-biblical times).
‡ Indicates reconstructed forms.
> The word following this sign is derived from the preceding one.
< The word preceding this sign is derived from the following one.

ad loc.	*ad locum*, "at the place"; used in quotations of commentaries.
A.H.	*Anno Hegirae*, "in the year of Hegira," i.e., according to the Muslim calendar.
Akk.	Addadian.
A.M.	*anno mundi*, "in the year (from the creation) of the world."
anon.	anonymous.
Ar.	Arabic.
Aram.	Aramaic.
Ass.	Assyrian.
b.	born; *ben, bar.*
Bab.	Babylonian.
B.C.E.	Before Common Era (= B.C.).
bibl.	bibliography.
Bul.	Bulgarian.
c., ca.	Circa.
C.E.	Common Era (= A.D.).
cf.	*confer*, "compare."
ch., chs.	chapter, chapters.
comp.	compiler, compiled by.
Cz.	Czech.
D	according to the documentary theory, the Deuteronomy document.
d.	died.
Dan.	Danish.
diss., dissert,	dissertation, thesis.
Du.	Dutch.
E.	according to the documentary theory, the Elohist document (i.e., using Elohim as the name of God) of the first five (or six) books of the Bible.
ed.	editor, edited, edition.
eds.	editors.
e.g.	*exempli gratia*, "for example."
Eng.	English.
et al.	*et alibi*, "and elsewhere"; or *et alii*, "and others"; "others."
f., ff.	and following page(s).
fig.	figure.
fl.	flourished.
fol., fols	folio(s).
Fr.	French.
Ger.	German.
Gr.	Greek.
Heb.	Hebrew.
Hg., Hung	Hungarian.
ibid	*Ibidem*, "in the same place."
incl. bibl.	includes bibliography.
introd.	introduction.
It.	Italian.
J	according to the documentary theory, the Jahwist document (i.e., using YHWH as the name of God) of the first five (or six) books of the Bible.
Lat.	Latin.
lit.	literally.
Lith.	Lithuanian.
loc. cit.	*loco citato*, "in the [already] cited place."
Ms., Mss.	Manuscript(s).
n.	note.
n.d.	no date (of publication).
no., nos	number(s).
Nov.	Novellae (Heb. *Ḥiddushim*).
n.p.	place of publication unknown.
op. cit.	*opere citato*, "in the previously mentioned work."
P.	according to the documentary theory, the Priestly document of the first five (or six) books of the Bible.
p., pp.	page(s).
Pers.	Persian.
pl., pls.	plate(s).
Pol.	Polish.
Port.	Potuguese.
pt., pts.	part(s).
publ.	published.
R.	Rabbi or Rav (before names); in Midrash (after an abbreviation) – *Rabbah.*
r.	recto, the first side of a manuscript page.
Resp.	Responsa (Latin "answers," Hebrew *She'elot u-Teshuvot* or *Teshuvot*), collections of rabbinic decisions.
rev.	revised.

Rom.	Romanian.
Rus(s).	Russian.
Slov.	Slovak.
Sp.	Spanish.
s.v.	*sub verbo, sub voce*, "under the (key) word."
Sum	Sumerian.
summ.	Summary.
suppl.	supplement.
Swed.	Swedish.
tr., trans(l).	translator, translated, translation.
Turk.	Turkish.
Ukr.	Ukrainian.
v., vv.	*verso*. The second side of a manuscript page; also verse(s).
Yid.	Yiddish.

ABBREVIATIONS USED IN RABBINICAL LITERATURE

Adderet Eliyahu, Karaite treatise by Elijah b. Moses *Bashyazi.
Admat Kodesh, Resp. by Nissim Ḥayyim Moses b. Joseph |Mizraḥi.
Aguddah, Sefer ha-, Nov. by *Alexander Suslin ha-Kohen.
Ahavat Ḥesed, compilation by *Israel Meir ha-Kohen.
Aliyyot de-Rabbenu Yonah, Nov. by *Jonah b. Avraham Gerondi.
Arukh ha-Shulḥan, codification by Jehiel Michel *Epstein.
Asayin (= positive precepts), subdivision of: (1) *Maimonides, *Sefer ha-Mitzvot;* (2) *Moses b. Jacob of Coucy, *Semag.*
Asefat Dinim, subdivision of *Sedei Ḥemed* by Ḥayyim Hezekiah *Medini, an encyclopaedia of precepts and responsa.
Asheri = *Asher b. Jehiel.
Aeret Ḥakhamim, by Baruch *Frankel-Teomim; pt, 1: Resp. to Sh. Ar.; pt2: Nov. to Talmud.
Ateret Zahav, subdivision of the *Levush*, a codification by Mordecai b. Abraham (Levush) *Jaffe; *Ateret Zahav* parallels Tur. YD.
Ateret Ẓevi, Comm. To Sh. Ar. by Ẓevi Hirsch b. Azriel.
Avir Ya'akov, Resp. by Jacob Avigdor.
Avkat Rokhel, Resp. by Joseph b. Ephraim *Caro.
Avnei Millu'im, Comm. to Sh. Ar., EH, by *Aryeh Loeb b. Joseph ha-Kohen.
Avnei Nezer, Resp. on Sh. Ar. by Abraham b. Ze'ev Nahum Bornstein of *Sochaczew.
Avodat Massa, Compilation of Tax Law by Yoasha Abraham Judah.
Azei ha-Levanon, Resp. by Judah Leib *Zirelson.

Ba'al ha-Tanya – *Shneur Zalman of Lyady.
Ba'ei Ḥayyei, Resp. by Ḥayyim b. Israel *Benveniste.
Ba'er Heitev, Comm. To Sh. Ar. The parts on OḤ and EH are by Judah b. Simeon *Ashkenazi, the parts on YD AND ḤM by *Zechariah Mendel b. Aryeh Leib. Printed in most editions of Sh. Ar.
Baḥ = Joel *Sirkes.
Baḥ, usual abbreviation for *Bayit Ḥadash*, a commentary on Tur by Joel *Sirkes; printed in most editions of Tur.
Bayit Ḥadash, see *Baḥ.*
Berab = Jacob Berab, also called Ri Berav.
Bedek ha-Bayit, by Joseph b. Ephraim *Caro, additions to his *Beit Yosef* (a comm. to Tur). Printed sometimes inside *Beit Yosef*, in smaller type. Appears in most editions of Tur.
Be'er ha-Golah, Commentary to Sh. Ar. By Moses b. Naphtali Hirsch *Rivkes; printed in most editions of Sh. Ar.
Be'er Mayim, Resp. by Raphael b. Abraham Manasseh Jacob.
Be'er Mayim Ḥayyim, Resp. by Samuel b. Ḥayyim *Vital.
Be'er Yiẓḥak, Resp. by Isaac Elhanan *Spector.
Beit ha-Beḥirah, Comm. to Talmud by Menahem b. Solomon *Meiri.
Beit Me'ir, Nov. on Sh. Ar. by Meir b. Judah Leib Posner.
Beit Shelomo, Resp. by Solomon b. Aaron Ḥason (the younger).
Beit Shemu'el, Comm. to Sh. Ar., EH, by *Samuel b. Uri Shraga Phoebus.
Beit Ya'akov, by Jacob b. Jacob Moses *Lorberbaum; pt.1: Nov. to Ket.; pt.2: Comm. to EH.
Beit Yisrael, collective name for the commentaries *Derishah, Perishah,* and *Be'urim* by Joshua b. Alexander ha-Kohen *Falk. See under the names of the commentaries.
Beit Yiẓḥak, Resp. by Isaac *Schmelkes.
Beit Yosef: (1) Comm. on Tur by Joseph b. Ephraim *Caro; printed in most editions of Tur; (2) Resp. by the same.
Ben Yehudah, Resp. by Abraham b. Judah Litsch (ליטש) Rosenbaum.
Bertinoro, Standard commentary to Mishnah by Obadiah *Bertinoro. Printed in most editions of the Mishnah.
[Be'urei] Ha-Gra, Comm. to Bible, Talmud, and Sh. Ar. By *Elijah b. Solomon Zalmon (Gaon of Vilna); printed in major editions of the mentioned works.
Be'urim, Glosses to Isserles *Darkhei Moshe* (a comm. on Tur) by Joshua b. Alexander ha-Kohen *Falk; printed in many editions of Tur.
Binyamin Ze'ev, Resp. by *Benjamin Ze'ev b. Mattathias of Arta.
Birkei Yosef, Nov. by Ḥayyim Joseph David *Azulai.
Ha-Buẓ ve-ha-Argaman, subdivision of the *Levush* (a codification by Mordecai b. Abraham (Levush) *Jaffe); *Ha-Buẓ ve-ha-Argaman* parallels Tur, EH.

Comm. = Commentary

Da'at Kohen, Resp. by Abraham Isaac ha-Kohen. *Kook.
Darkhei Moshe, Comm. on Tur Moses b. Israel *Isserles; printed in most editions of Tur.
Darkhei No'am, Resp. by *Mordecai b. Judah ha-Levi.
Darkhei Teshuvah, Nov. by Ẓevi *Shapiro; printed in the major editions of Sh. Ar.
De'ah ve-Haskel, Resp. by Obadiah Hadaya (see *Yaskil Avdi).*

Derashot Ran, Sermons by *Nissim b. Reuben Gerondi.
Derekh Ḥayyim, Comm. to *Avot* by *Judah Loew (Lob., Liwa) b. Bezalel (Maharal) of Prague.
Derishah, by Joshua b. Alexander ha-Kohen *Falk; additions to his *Perishah* (comm. on Tur); printed in many editions of Tur.
Derushei ha-Ẓelaḥ, Sermons, by Ezekiel b. Judah Halevi *Landau.
Devar Avraham, Resp. by Abraham *Shapira.
Devar Shemu'el, Resp. by Samuel *Aboab.
Devar Yehoshu'a, Resp. by Joshua Menahem b. Isaac Aryeh Ehrenberg.
Dikdukei Soferim, variae lections of the talmudic text by Raphael Nathan*Rabbinowicz.
Divrei Emet, Resp. by Isaac Bekhor David.
Divrei Ge'onim, Digest of responsa by Ḥayyim Aryeh b. Jeḥiel Ẓevi *Kahana.
Divrei Ḥamudot, Comm. on *Piskei ha-Rosh* by Yom Tov Lipmann b. Nathan ha-Levi *Heller; printed in major editions of the Talmud.
Divrei Ḥayyim several works by Ḥayyim *Halberstamm; if quoted alone refers to his Responsa.
Divrei Malkhi'el, Resp. by Malchiel Tenebaum.
Divrei Rivot, Resp. by Isaac b. Samuel *Adarbi.
Divrei Shemu'el, Resp. by Samuel Raphael Arditi.

Edut be-Ya'akov, Resp. by Jacob b. Abraham *Boton.
Edut bi-Yhosef, Resp. by Joseph b. Isaac *Almosnino.
Ein Ya'akov, Digest of talmudic *aggadot* by Jacob (Ibn) *Habib.
Ein Yiẓḥak, Resp. by Isaac Elhanan *Spector.
Ephraim of Lentshitz = Solomon *Luntschitz.
Erekh Leḥem, Nov. and glosses to Sh. Ar. by Jacob b. Abraham *Castro.
Eshkol, Sefer ha-, Digest of *halakhot* by *Abraham b. Isaac of Narbonne.
Et Sofer, Treatise on Law Court documents by Abraham b. Mordecai *Ankawa, in the 2nd vol. of his Resp. *Kerem Ḥamar.*
Etan ha-Ezraḥi, Resp. by Abraham b. Israel Jehiel (Shrenzl) *Rapaport.
Even ha-Ezel, Nov. to Maimonides' *Yad Ḥazakah* by Isser Zalman *Meltzer.
Even ha-Ezer, also called *Raban* of *Ẓafenat Pa'ne'aḥ,* rabbinical work with varied contents by *Eliezer b. Nathan of Mainz; not identical with the subdivision of Tur, Shulḥan Arukh, etc.
Ezrat Yehudah, Resp. by *Isaar Judah b. Nechemiah of Brisk.

Gan Eden, Karaite treatise by *Aaron b. Elijah of Nicomedia.
Gersonides = *Levi b. Gershom, also called Leo Hebraecus, or Ralbag.
Ginnat Veradim, Resp. by *Abraham b. Mordecai ha-Levi.

Haggahot, another name for *Rema.*
Haggahot Asheri, glosses to *Piskei ha-Rosh* by *Israel of Krems; printed in most Talmud editions.
Haggahot Maimuniyyot, Comm,. to Maimonides' Yad Ḥazakah by *Meir ha-Kohen; printed in most eds. of Yad.
Haggahot Mordekhai, glosses to *Mordekhai* by Samuel *Schlettstadt; printed in most editions of the Talmud after *Mordekhai.*
Haggahot ha-Rashash on Tosafot, annotations of Samuel *Strashun on the Tosafot (printed in major editions of the Talmud).
Ha-Gra = *Elijah b. Solomon Zalman (Gaon of Vilna).
Ha-Gra, Commentaries on Bible, Talmud, and Sh. Ar. respectively, by *Elijah b. Solomon Zalman (Gaon of Vilna); printed in major editions of the mentioned works.
Hai Gaon, Comm. = his comm. on Mishnah.
Ḥakham Ẓevi, Resp. by Ẓevi Hirsch b. Jacob *Ashkenazi.
Halakhot = Rif, *Halakhot.* Compilation and abstract of the Talmud by Isaac b. Jacob ha-Kohen *Alfasi; printed in most editions of the Talmud.
Halakhot Gedolot, compilation of *halakhot* from the Geonic period, arranged acc. to the Talmud. Here cited acc. to ed. Warsaw (1874). Author probably *Simeon Kayyara of Basra.
Halakhot Pesukot le-Rav Yehudai Ga'on compilation of *halakhot.*
Halakhot Pesukot min ha-Ge'onim, compilation of *halakhot* from the geonic period by different authors.
Ḥananel, Comm. to Talmud by *Hananel b. Ḥushi'el; printed in some editions of the Talmud.
Harei Besamim, Resp. by Aryeh Leib b. Isaac *Horowitz.
Ḥassidim, Sefer, Ethical maxims by *Judah b. Samuel he-Ḥasid.
Hassagot Rabad on Rif, Glosses on Rif, *Halakhot,* by *Abraham b. David of Posquières.
Hassagot Rabad [on Yad], Glosses on Maimonides, *Yad Ḥazakah,* by *Abraham b. David of Posquières.
Hassagot Ramban, Glosses by Naḥmanides on Maimonides' *Sefer ha-Mitzvot;* usually printed together with *Sefer ha-Mitzvot.*
Ḥatam Sofer = Moses *Sofer.
Ḥavvot Ya'ir, Resp. and varia by Jair Ḥayyim *Bacharach
Ḥayyim Or Zaru'a = *Ḥayyim (Eliezer) b. Isaac.
Ḥazon Ish = Abraham Isaiah *Karelitz.
Ḥazon Ish, Nov. by Abraham Isaiah *Karelitz
Ḥedvat Ya'akov, Resp. by Aryeh Judah Jacob b. David Dov Meisels (article under his father's name).
Heikhal Yiẓḥak, Resp. by Isaac ha-Levi *Herzog.
Ḥelkat Meḥokek, Comm. to Sh. Ar., by Moses b. Isaac Judah *Lima.
Ḥelkat Ya'akov, Resp. by Mordecai Jacob Breisch.
Ḥemdah Genuzah, , Resp. from the geonic period by different authors.
Ḥemdat Shelomo, Resp. by Solomon Zalman *Lipschitz.
Ḥida = Ḥayyim Joseph David *Azulai.
Ḥiddushei Halakhot ve-Aggadot, Nov. by Samuel Eliezer b. Judah ha-Levi *Edels.
Ḥikekei Lev, Resp. by Ḥayyim *Palaggi.
Ḥikrei Lev, Nov. to Sh. Ar. by Joseph Raphael b. Ḥayyim Joseph Ḥazzan (see article *Ḥazzan Family).
Hil. = Hilkhot … (e.g. *Hilkhot Shabbat).*
Ḥinnukh, Sefer ha-, List and explanation of precepts attributed (probably erroneously) to Aaron ha-Levi of Barcelona (see article *Ha-Ḥinnukh*).
Ḥok Ya'akov, Comm. to Hil. Pesaḥ in Sh. Ar., OḤ, by Jacob b. Joseph *Reicher.
Ḥokhmat Sehlomo (1), Glosses to Talmud, *Rashi* and Tosafot by Solomon b. Jehiel "Maharshal") *Luria; printed in many editions of the Talmud.
Ḥokhmat Sehlomo (2), Glosses and Nov. to Sh. Ar. by Solomon b. Judah Aaron *Kluger printed in many editions of Sh. Ar.
Ḥur, subdivision of the *Levush,* a codification by Mordecai b. Abraham (Levush) *Jaffe; *Hur (*or *Levush ha-Hur)* parallels Tur, OḤ, 242–697.
Ḥut ha-Meshullash, fourth part of the *Tashbeẓ* (Resp.), by Simeon b. Zemaḥ *Duran.

Ibn Ezra, Comm. to the Bible by Abraham *Ibn Ezra; printed in the major editions of the Bible *("Mikra'ot Gedolot").*
Imrei Yosher, Resp. by Meir b. Aaron Judah *Arik.
Ir Shushan, Subdivision of the *Levush,* a codification by Mordecai b. Abraham (Levush) *Jaffe; *Ir Shushan* parallels Tur, ḤM.
Israel of Bruna = Israel b. Ḥayyim *Bruna.
Ittur. Treatise on precepts by *Isaac b. Abba Mari of Marseilles.

Jacob Be Rab = *Be Rab.
Jacob b. Jacob Moses of Lissa = Jacob b. Jacob Moses *Lorberbaum.
Judah B. Simeon = Judah b. Simeon *Ashkenazi.
Judah Minz = Judah b. Eliezer ha-Levi *Minz.

Kappei Aharon, Resp. by Aaron Azriel.
Kehillat Ya'akov, Talmudic methodology, definitions etc. by Israel Jacob b. Yom Tov *Algazi.
Kelei Ḥemdah, Nov. and *pilpulim* by Meir Dan *Plotzki of Ostrova, arranged acc. to the Torah.
Keli Yakar, Annotations to the Torah by Solomon *Luntschitz.
Keneh Ḥokhmah, Sermons by Judah Loeb *Pochwitzer.
Keneset ha-Gedolah, Digest of *halakhot* by Ḥayyim b. Israel *Benveniste; subdivided into annotations to *Beit Yosef* and annotations to Tur.
Keneset Yisrael, Resp. by Ezekiel b. Abraham Katzenellenbogen (see article *Katzenellenbogen Family).
Kerem Ḥamar, Resp. and varia by Abraham b. Mordecai *Ankawa.
Kerem Shelmo. Resp. by Solomon b. Joseph *Amarillo.
Keritut, [Sefer], Methodology of the Talmud by *Samson b. Isaac of Chinon.
Kesef ha-Kedoshim, Comm. to Sh. Ar., ḤM, by Abraham *Wahrmann; printed in major editions of Sh. Ar.
Kesef Mishneh, Comm. to Maimonides, *Yad Ḥazakah,* by Joseph b. Ephraim *Caro; printed in most editions of *Yad Ḥazakah.*
Keẓot ha-Ḥoshen, Comm. to Sh. Ar., ḤM, by *Aryeh Loeb b. Joseph ha-Kohen; printed in major editions of Sh. Ar.
Kol Bo [*Sefer*], Anonymous collection of ritual rules; also called *Sefer ha-Likkutim.*
Kol Mevasser, Resp. by Meshullam *Rath.
Korban Aharon, Comm. to *Sifra* by Aaron b. Abraham *Ibn Ḥayyim; pt. 1 is called: *Middot Aharon.*
Korban Edah, Comm. to Jer. Talmud by David *Fraenkel; with additions: *Shiyyurei Korban;* printed in most editions of Jer. Talmud.
Kunteres ha-Kelalim, subdivision of *Sedei Ḥemed,* an encyclopaedia of precepts and responsa by Ḥayyim Hezekiah *Medini.
Kunteres ha-Semikhah, a treatise by *Levi b. Ḥabib; printed at the end of his responsa.
Kunteres Tikkun Olam, part of *Mispat Shalom* (Nov. by Shalom Mordecai b. Moses *Schwadron).

Lavin (negative precepts), subdivision of: (1) *Maimonides, *Sefer ha-Mitzvot;* (2) *Moses b. Jacob of Coucy, *Semag.*
Leḥem Mishneh, Comm. to Maimonides, *Yad Ḥazakah,* by Abraham [Ḥiyya] b. Moses *Boton; printed in most editions of *Yad Ḥazakah.*
Leḥem Rav, Resp. by Abraham [Ḥiyya] b. Moses *Boton.
Leket Yosher, Resp and varia by Israel b. Pethahiah *Isserlein, collected by *Joseph (Joselein) b. Moses.
Leo Hebraeus = *Levi b. Gershom, also called Ralbag or Gersonides.
Levush = Mordecai b. Abraham *Jaffe.
Levush [Malkhut], Codification by Mordecai b. Abraham (Levush) *Jaffe, with subdivisions: [*Levush ha-] Tekhelet* (parallels Tur OḤ 1–241); [*Levush ha-] Ḥur* (parallels Tur OḤ 242–697); [*Levush] Ateret Zahav* (parallels Tur YD); [*Levush ha-Buẓ ve-ha-Argaman* (parallels Tur EH); [*Levush] Ir Shushan* (parallels Tur ḤM); under the name *Levush* the author wrote also other works.
Li-Leshonot ha-Rambam, fifth part (nos. 1374–1700) of Resp. by *David b. Solomon ibn Abi Zimra (Radbaz).
Likkutim, Sefer ha-, another name for [*Sefer] Kol Bo.*

Ma'adanei Yom Tov, Comm. on *Piskei ha-Rosh* by Yom Tov Lipmann b. Nathan ha-Levi *Heller; printed in many editions of the Talmud.
Mabit = Moses b. Joseph *Trani.
Magen Avot, Comm. to *Avot* by Simeon b. Ẓemaḥ *Duran.
Magen Avraham, Comm. to Sh. Ar., OḤ, by Abraham Abele b. Ḥayyim ha-Levi *Gombiner; printed in many editions of Sh. Ar., OḤ.
Maggid Mishneh, Comm. to Maimonides, *Yad Ḥazakah,* by *Vidal Yom Tov of Tolosa; printed in most editions of the *Yad Ḥazakah.*
Maḥaneh Efrayim, Resp. and Nov., arranged acc. to Maimonides' *Yad Ḥazakah* , by Ephraim b. Aaron *Navon.
Maharai = Israel b. Pethahiah *Isserlein.
Maharal of Prague = *Judah Loew (Lob, Liwa), b. Bezalel.
Maharalbaḥ = *Levi b. Ḥabib.
Maharam Alashkar = Moses b. Isaac *Alashkar.
Maharam Alshekh = Moses b. Ḥayyim *Alashekh.
Maharam Mintz = Moses *Mintz.
Maharam of Lublin = *Meir b. Gedaliah of Lublin.
Maharam of Padua = Meir *Katzenellenbogen.
Maharam of Rothenburg = *Meir b. Baruch of Rothenburg.
Maharam Shik = Moses b. Joseph Schick.
Maharash Engel = Samuel b. Ze'ev Wolf Engel.
Maharashdam = Samuel b. Moses *Medina.
Maharḥash = Ḥayyim (ben) Shabbetai.
Mahari Basan = Jehiel b. Ḥayyim Basan.
Mahari b. Lev = Joseph ibn Lev.
Mahari'az = Jekuthiel Asher Zalman Ensil Zusmir.
Maharibal = *Joseph ibn Lev.
Mahariḥ = Jacob (Israel) *Ḥagiz.
Maharik = Joseph b. Solomon *Colon.
Maharikash = Jacob b. Abraham *Castro.
Maharil = Jacob b. Moses *Moellin.
Maharimat = Joseph b. Moses di Trani (not identical with the Maharit).
Maharit = Joseph b. Moses *Trani.
Maharitaẓ = Yom Tov b. Akiva Ẓahalon. (See article *Ẓahalon Family).
Maharsha = Samuel Eliezer b. Judah ha-Levi *Edels.
Maharshag = Simeon b. Judah Gruenfeld.
Maharshak = Samson b. Isaac of Chinon.
Maharshakh = *Solomon b. Abraham.
Maharshal = Solomon b. Jeḥiel *Luria.
Mahasham = Shalom Mordecai b. Moses *Sschwadron.
Maharyu = Jacob b. Judah *Weil.
Maḥazeh Avraham, Resp. by Abraham Nebagen v. Meir ha-Levi Steinberg.
Maḥazik Berakhah, Nov. by Ḥayyim Joseph David *Azulai.

*Maimonides = Moses b. Maimon, or Rambam.
*Malbim = Meir Loeb b. Jehiel Michael.
Malbim = Malbim's comm. to the Bible; printed in the major editions.
Malbushei Yom Tov, Nov. on *Levush*, OḤ, by Yom Tov Lipmann b. Nathan ha-Levi *Heller.
Mappah, another name for *Rema.*
Mareh ha-Panim, Comm. to Jer. Talmud by Moses b. Simeon *Margolies; printed in most editions of Jer. Talmud.
Margaliyyot ha-Yam, Nov. by Reuben *Margoliot.
Masat Binyamin, Resp. by Benjamin Aaron b. Abraham *Slonik
Mashbir, Ha- = *Joseph Samuel b. Isaac Rodi.
Massa Ḥayyim, Tax *halakhot* by Ḥayyim *Palaggi, with the subdivisions *Missim ve-Arnomiyyot* and *Torat ha-Minhagot.*
Massa Melekh, Compilation of Tax Law by Joseph b. Isaac *Ibn Ezra with concluding part *Ne'ilat She'arim.*
Matteh Asher, Resp. by Asher b. Emanuel Shalem.
Matteh Shimon, Digest of Resp. and Nov. to Tur and *Beit Yosef*, ḤM, by Mordecai Simeon b. Solomon.
Matteh Yosef, Resp. by Joseph b. Moses ha-Levi Nazir (see article under his father's name).
Mayim Amukkim, Resp. by Elijah b. Abraham *Mizraḥi.
Mayim Ḥayyim, Resp. by Ḥayyim b. Dov Beresh Rapaport.
Mayim Rabbim, , Resp. by Raphael *Meldola.
Me-Emek ha-Bakha, , Resp. by Simeon b. Jekuthiel Ephrati.
Me'irat Einayim, usual abbreviation: *Sma* (from: *Sefer Me'irat Einayim*); comm. to Sh. Ar. By Joshua b. Alexander ha-Kohen *Falk; printed in most editions of the Sh. Ar.
Melammed le-Ho'il, Resp. by David Ẓevi *Hoffmann.
Meisharim, [*Sefer*], Rabbinical treatise by *Jeroham b. Meshullam.
Meshiv Davar, Resp. by Naphtali Ẓevi Judah *Berlin.
Mi-Gei ha-Haregah, Resp. by Simeon b. Jekuthiel Ephrati.
Mi-Ma'amakim, Resp. by Ephraim Oshry.
Middot Aharon, first part of *Korban Aharon*, a comm. to *Sifra* by Aaron b. Abraham *Ibn Ḥayyim.
Migdal Oz, Comm. to Maimonides, *Yad Ḥazakah*, by *Ibn Gaon Shem Tov b. Abraham; printed in most editions of the *Yad Ḥazakah.*
Mikhtam le-David, Resp. by David Samuel b. Jacob *Pardo.
Mikkaḥ ve-ha-Mimkar, Sefer ha-, Rabbinical treatise by *Hai Gaon.
Milḥamot ha-Shem, Glosses to Rif, *Halakhot*, by *Naḥmanides.
Minḥat Ḥinnukh, Comm. to *Sefer ha-Ḥinnukh*, by Joseph b. Moses *Babad.
Minḥat Yiẓḥak, Resp. by Isaac Jacob b. Joseph Judah Weiss.
Misgeret ha-Shulḥan, Comm. to Sh. Ar., ḤM, by Benjamin Ze'ev Wolf b. Shabbetai; printed in most editions of Sh. Ar.
Mishkenot ha-Ro'im, *Halakhot* in alphabetical order by Uzziel Alshekh.
Mishnah Berurah, Comm. to Sh. Ar., OḤ, by *Israel Meir ha-Kohen.
Mishneh le-Melekh, Comm. to Maimonides, *Yad Ḥazakah*, by Judah *Rosanes; printed in most editions of *Yad Ḥazakah.*
Mishpat ha-Kohanim, Nov. to Sh. Ar., ḤM, by Jacob Moses *Lorberbaum, part of his *Netivot ha-Mishpat;* printed in major editions of Sh. Ar.
Mishpat Kohen, Resp. by Abraham Isaac ha-Kohen *Kook.
Mishpat Shalom, Nov. by Shalom Mordecai b. Moses *Schwadron; contains: *Kunteres Tikkun Olam.*
Mishpat u-Ẓedakah be-Ya'akov, Resp. by Jacob b. Reuben *Ibn Ẓur.
Mishpat ha-Urim, Comm. to Sh. Ar., ḤM by Jacob b. Jacob Moses *Lorberbaum, part of his *Netivot ha-Mishpat*; printed in major editons of Sh. Ar.
Mishpat Ẓedek, Resp. by *Melammed Meir b. Shem Tov.
Mishpatim Yesharim, Resp. by Raphael b. Mordecai *Berdugo.
Mishpetei Shemu'el, Resp. by Samuel b. Moses *Kalai (Kal'i).
Mishpetei ha-Tanna'im, Kunteres, Nov on *Levush*, OḤ by Yom Tov Lipmann b. Nathan ha-Levi *Heller.
Mishpetei Uzzi'el (Uziel), Resp. by Ben-Zion Meir Hai *Ouziel.
Missim ve-Arnoniyyot, Tax *halakhot* by Ḥayyim *Palaggi, a subdivision of his work *Massa Ḥayyim* on the same subject.
Mitzvot, Sefer ha-, Elucidation of precepts by *Maimonides; subdivided into *Lavin* (negative precepts) and *Asayin* (positive precepts).
Mitzvot Gadol, Sefer, Elucidation of precepts by *Moses b. Jacob of Coucy, subdivided into *Lavin* (negative precepts) and *Asayin* (positive precepts); the usual abbreviation is *Semag.*
Mitzvot Katan, Sefer, Elucidation of precepts by *Isaac b. Joseph of Corbeil; the usual, abbreviation is *Semak.*
Mo'adim u-Zemannim, Rabbinical treatises by Moses Sternbuch.
Modigliano, Joseph Samuel = *Joseph Samuel b. Isaac, Rodi (Ha-Mashbir).
Mordekhai (Mordecai), halakhic compilation by *Mordecai b. Hillel; printed in most editions of the Talmud after the texts.
Moses b. Maimon = *Maimonides, also called Rambam.
Moses b. Naḥman = Naḥmanides, also called Ramban.
Muram = Isaiah Menahem b. Isaac (from: Morenu R. Mendel).

Naḥal Yiẓḥak, Comm. on Sh. Ar., ḤM, by Isaac Elhanan *Spector.
Naḥalah li-Yhoshu'a, Resp. by Joshua Ẓunẓin.
Naḥalat Shivah, collection of legal forms by *Samuel b. David Moses ha-Levi.
*Naḥmanides = Moses b. Naḥman, also called Ramban.
Naẓiv = Naphtali Ẓevi Judah *Berlin.
Ne'eman Shemu'el, Resp. by Samuel Isaac *Modigilano.
Ne'ilat She'arim, concluding part of *Massa Melekh* (a work on Tax Law) by Joseph b. Isaac *Ibn Ezra, containing an exposition of customary law and subdivided into *Minhagei Issur* and *Minhagei Mamon.*
Ner Ma'aravi, Resp. by Jacob b. Malka.
Netivot ha-Mishpat, by Jacob b. Jacob Moses *Lorberbaum; subdivided into *Mishpat ha-Kohanim*, Nov. to Sh. Ar., ḤM, and *Mishpat ha-Urim*, a comm. on the same; printed in major editions of Sh. Ar.
Netivot Olam, Saying of the Sages by *Judah Loew (Lob, Liwa) b. Bezalel.
Nimmukei Menaḥem of Merseburg, Tax *halakhot* by the same, printed at the end of Resp. Maharyu.
Nimmukei Yosef, Comm. to Rif. *Halakhot*, by Joseph *Ḥabib (Ḥabiba); printed in many editions of the Talmud.
Noda bi-Yhudah, Resp. by Ezekiel b. Judah ha-Levi *Landau; there is a first collection *(Mahadura Kamma)* and a second collection *(Mahadura Tinyana).*
Nov. = Novellae, Ḥiddushim.

Ohel Moshe (1), Notes to Talmud, *Midrash Rabbah*, Yad, *Sifrei* and to several Resp., by Eleazar *Horowitz.

Ohel Moshe (2), Resp. by Moses Jonah Zweig.
Oholei Tam. Resp. by *Tam ibn Yaḥya Jacob b. David; printed in the rabbinical collection *Tummat Yesharim.*
Oholei Ya'akov, Resp. by Jacob de *Castro.
Or ha-Me'ir Resp by Judah Meir b. Jacob Samson Shapiro.
Or Same'aḥ, Comm. to Maimonides, *Yad Ḥazakah,* by *Meir Simḥah ha-Kohen of Dvinsk; printed in many editions of the *Yad Ḥazakah.*
Or Zaru'a [the father] = *Isaac b. Moses of Vienna.
Or Zaru'a [the son] = *Ḥayyim (Eliezer) b. Isaac.
Or Zaru'a, Nov. by *Isaac b. Moses of Vienna.
Orah, Sefer ha-, Compilation of ritual precepts by *Rashi.
Oraḥ la-Ẓaddik, Resp. by Abraham Ḥayyim Rodrigues.
Oẓar ha-Posekim, Digest of Responsa.

Paḥad Yiẓḥak, Rabbinical encyclopaedia by Isaac *Lampronti.
Panim Me'irot, Resp. by Meir b. Isaac *Eisenstadt.
Parashat Mordekhai, Resp. by Mordecai b. Abraham Naphtali *Banet.
Pe'at ha-Sadeh la-Dinim and Pe'at ha-Sadeh la-Kelalim, subdivisions of the *Sedei Ḥemed,* an encyclopaedia of precepts and responsa, by Ḥayyim Hezekaih *Medini.
Penei Moshe (1), Resp. by Moses *Benveniste.
Penei Moshe (2), Comm. to Jer. Talmud by Moses b. Simeon *Margolies; printed in most editions of the Jer. Talmud.
Penei Moshe (3), Comm. on the aggadic passages of 18 treatises of the Bab. and Jer. Talmud, by Moses b. Isaiah Katz.
Penei Yehoshu'a, Nov. by Jacob Joshua b. Ẓevi Hirsch *Falk.
Peri Ḥadash, Comm. on Sh. Ar. By Hezekiah da *Silva.
Perishah, Comm. on Tur by Joshua b. Alexander ha-Kohen *Falk; printed in major edition of Tur; forms together with *Derishah* and *Be'urim* (by the same author) the *Beit Yisrael.*
Pesakim u-Khetavim, 2nd part of the *Terumat ha-Deshen* by Israel b. Pethahiah *Isserlein' also called *Piskei Maharai.*
Pilpula Ḥarifta, Comm. to *Piskei ha-Rosh, Seder Nezikin,* by Yom Tov Lipmann b. Nathan ha-Levi *Heller; printed in major editions of the Talmud.
Piskei Maharai, see *Terumat ha-Deshen,* 2nd part; also called *Pesakim u-Khetavim.*
Piskei ha-Rosh, a compilation of *halakhot,* arranged on the Talmud, by *Asher b. Jehiel (Rosh); printed in major Talmud editions.
Pitḥei Teshuvah, Comm. to Sh. Ar. by Abraham Hirsch b. Jacob *Eisenstadt; printed in major editions of the Sh. Ar.

Rabad = *Abraham b. David of Posquières (Rabad III.).
Raban = *Eliezer b. Nathan of Mainz.
Raban, also called *Ẓafenat Pa'ne'aḥ* or *Even ha-Ezer,* see under the last name.
Rabi Abad = *Abraham b. Isaac of Narbonne.
Radad = David Dov. b. Aryeh Judah Jacob *Meisels.
Radam = Dov Berush b. Isaac Meisels.
Radbaz = *David b Solomon ibn Abi Ziumra.
Radbaz, Comm. to Maimonides, *Yad Ḥazakah,* by *David b. Solomon ibn Abi Zimra.
Ralbag = *Levi b. Gershom, also called Gersonides, or Leo Hebraeus.
Ralbag, Bible comm. by *Levi b. Gershon.
Rama [da Fano] = Menaḥem Azariah *Fano.
Ramah = Meir b. Todros [ha-Levi] *Abulafia.
Ramam = *Menaham of Merseburg.
Rambam = *Maimonides; real name: Moses b. Maimon.
Ramban = *Naḥmanides; real name Moses b. Naḥman.
Ramban, Comm. to Torah by *Naḥmanides; printed in major editions. ("Mikra'ot Gedolot").
Ran = *Nissim b. Reuben Gerondi.
Ran of Rif, Comm. on Rif, *Halakhot,* by Nissim b. Reuben Gerondi.
Ranaḥ = *Elijah b. Ḥayyim.
Rash = *Samson b. Abraham of Sens.
Rash, Comm. to Mishnah, by *Samson b. Abraham of Sens; printed in major Talmud editions.
Rashash = Samuel *Strashun.
Rashba = Solomon b. Abraham *Adret.
Rashba, Resp., see also; *Sefer Teshuvot ha-Rashba ha-Meyuḥasot le-ha-Ramban,* by Solomon b. Abraham *Adret.
Rashbad = Samuel b. David.
Rashbam = *Samuel b. Meir.
Rashbam = Comm. on Bible and Talmud by *Samuel b. Meir; printed in major editions of Bible and most editions of Talmud.
Rashbash = Solomon b. Simeon *Duran.
*Rashi = Solomon b. Isaac of Troyes.
Rashi, Comm. on Bible and Talmud by *Rashi; printed in almost all Bible and Talmud editions.
Raviah = Eliezer b. Joel ha-Levi.
Redak = David *Kimḥi.
Redak, Comm. to Bible by David *Kimḥi.
Redakh = *David b. Ḥayyim ha-Kohen of Corfu.
Re'em = Elijah b. Abraham *Mizraḥi.
Rema = Moses b. Israel *Isserles.
Rema, Glosses to Sh. Ar. by Moses b. Israel *Isserles; printed in almost all editions of the Sh. Ar. inside the text in Rashi type; also called *Mappah* or *Haggahot.*
Remek = Moses Kimḥi.
Remakh = Moses ha-Kohen mi-Lunel.
Reshakh = *Solomon b. Abraham; also called Maharshakh.
Resp. = Responsa, *She'elot u-Teshuvot.*
Ri Berav = *Berab.
Ri Escapa = Joseph b. Saul *Escapa.
Ri Migash = Joseph b. Meir ha-Levi *Ibn Migash.
Riba = Isaac b. Asher ha-Levi; Riba II (Riba ha-Baḥur) = his grandson with the same name.
Ribam = Isaac b. Mordecai (or: Isaac b. Meir).
Ribash = *Isaac b. Sheshet Perfet (or: Barfat).
Rid= *Isaiah b. Mali di Trani the Elder.
Ridbaz = Jacob David b. Ze'ev *Willowski.
Rif = Isaac b. Jacob ha-Kohen *Alfasi.
Rif, *Halakhot,* Compilation and abstract of the Talmud by Isaac b. Jacob ha-Kohen *Alfasi.
Ritba = Yom Tov b. Abraham *Ishbili.
Riẓbam = Isaac b. Mordecai.
Rosh = *Asher b. Jehiel, also called Asheri.
Rosh Mashbir, Resp. by *Joseph Samuel b. Isaac, Rodi.

Sedei Ḥemed, Encyclopaedia of precepts and responsa by Ḥayyim Ḥezekiah *Medini; subdivisions: *Asefat Dinim, Kunteres ha-Kelalim, Pe'at ha-Sadeh la-Dinim, Pe'at ha-Sadeh la-Kelalim.*
Semag, Usual abbreviation of *Sefer Mitzvot Gadol,* elucidation of precepts by *Moses b. Jacob of Coucy; subdivided into *Lavin* (negative precepts) *Asayin* (positive precepts).
Semak, Usual abbreviation of *Sefer Mitzvot Katan,* elucidation of precepts by *Isaac b. Joseph of Corbeil.

Sh. Ar. = *Shulḥan Arukh,* code by Joseph b. Ephraim *Caro.
Sha'ar Mishpat, Comm. to Sh. Ar., ḤM. By Israel Isser b. Ze'ev Wolf.
Sha'arei Shevu'ot, Treatise on the law of oaths by *David b. Saadiah; usually printed together with Rif, *Halakhot;* also called: *She'arim of R. Alfasi.*
Sha'arei Teshuvah, Collection of resp. from Geonic period, by different authors.
Sha'arei Uzzi'el, Rabbinical treatise by Ben-Zion Meir Ha *Ouziel.
Sha'arei Ẓedek, Collection of resp. from Geonic period, by different authors.
Shadal [or Shedal] = Samuel David *Luzzatto.
Shai la-Moreh, Resp. by Shabbetai Jonah.
Shakh, Usual abbreviation of *Siftei Kohen,* a comm. to Sh. Ar., YD and ḤM by *Shabbetai b. Meir ha-Kohen; printed in most editions of Sh. Ar.
Sha'ot-de-Rabbanan, Resp. by *Solomon b. Judah ha-Kohen.
She'arim of R. Alfasi see *Sha'arei Shevu'ot.*
Shedal, see Shadal.
She'elot u-Teshuvot ha-Ge'onim, Collection of resp. by different authors.
She'erit Yisrael, Resp. by Israel Ze'ev Mintzberg.
She'erit Yosef, Resp. by *Joseph b. Mordecai Gershon ha-Kohen.
She'ilat Yaveẓ, Resp. by Jacob *Emden (Yaveẓ).
She'iltot, Compilation arranged acc. to the Torah by *Aḥa (Aḥai) of Shabḥa.
Shem Aryeh, Resp. by Aryeh Leib *Lipschutz.
Shemesh Ẓedakah, Resp. by Samson *Morpurgo.
Shenei ha-Me'orot ha-Gedolim, Resp. by Elijah *Covo.
Shetarot, Sefer ha-, Collection of legal forms by *Judah b. Barzillai al-Bargeloni.
Shevut Ya'akov, Resp. by Jacob b. Joseph Reicher.
Shibbolei ha-Leket Compilation on ritual by Zedekiah b. Avraham *Anav.
Shiltei Gibborim, Comm. to Rif, *Halakhot,* by *Joshua Boaz b. Simeon; printed in major editions of the Talmud.
Shittah Mekubbeẓet, Compilation of talmudical commentaries by Bezalel *Ashkenazi.
Shivat Ẓiyyon, Resp. by Samuel b. Ezekiel *Landau.
Shiyyurei Korban, by David *Fraenkel; additions to his comm. to Jer. Talmud *Korban Edah;* both printed in most editions of Jer. Talmud.
Sho'el u-Meshiv, Resp. by Joseph Saul ha-Levi *Nathanson.
Sh[ulḥan] Ar[ukh] [of Ba'al ha-Tanya], Code by *Shneur Zalman of Lyady; not identical with the code by Joseph Caro.
Siftei Kohen, Comm. to Sh. Ar., YD and ḤM by *Shabbetai b. Meir ha-Kohen; printed in most editions of Sh. Ar.; usual abbreviation: *Shakh.*
Simḥat Yom Tov, Resp. by Tom Tov b. Jacob *Algazi.
Simlah Ḥadashah, Treatise on *Sheḥitah* by Alexander Sender b. Ephraim Zalman *Schor; see also *Tevu'ot Shor.*
Simeon b. Ẓemaḥ = Simeon b. Ẓemaḥ *Duran.
Sma, Comm. to Sh. Ar. by Joshua b. Alexander ha-Kohen *Falk; the full title is: *Sefer Me'irat Einayim;* printed in most editions of Sh. Ar.
Solomon b. Isaac ha-Levi = Solomon b. Isaac *Levy.
Solomon b. Isaac of Troyes = *Rashi.

Tal Orot, Rabbinical work with various contents, by Joseph ibn Gioia.
Tam, Rabbenu = *Tam Jacob b. Meir.
Tashbaẓ = Samson b. Zadok.
Tashbeẓ = Simeon b. Zemaḥ *Duran, sometimes also abbreviation for Samson b. Zadok, usually known as Tashbaẓ.
Tashbeẓ [*Sefer ha-*], Resp. by Simeon b. Ẓemaḥ *Duran; the fourth part of this work is called: *Ḥut ha-Meshullash.*
Taz, Usual abbreviation of *Turei Zahav,* comm., to Sh. Ar. by *David b. Samnuel ha-Levi; printed in most editions of Sh. Ar.
(Ha)-Tekhelet, subdivision of the *Levush* (a codification by Mordecai b. Abraham (Levush) *Jaffe); *Ha-Tekhelet* parallels Tur, OḤ 1-241.
Terumat ha-Deshen, by Israel b. Pethahiah *Isserlein; subdivided into a part containing responsa, and a second part called *Pesakim u-Khetavim* or *Piskei Maharai.*
Terumot, Sefer ha-, Compilation of *halakhot* by Samuel b. Isaac *Sardi.
Teshuvot Ba'alei ha-Tosafot, Collection of responsa by the Tosafists.
Teshjvot Ge'onei Mizraḥ u-Ma'aav, Collection of responsa.
Teshuvot ha-Geonim, Collection of responsa from Geonic period.
Teshuvot Ḥakhmei Provinẓyah, Collection of responsa by different Provencal authors.
Teshuvot Ḥakhmei Ẓarefat ve-Loter, Collection of responsa by different French authors.
Teshuvot Maimuniyyot, Resp. pertaining to Maimonides' *Yad Ḥazakah;* printed in major editions of this work after the text; authorship uncertain.
Tevu'ot Shor, by Alexander Sender b. Ephraim Zalman *Schor, a comm. to his *Simlah Ḥadashah,* a work on *Sheḥitah.*
Tiferet Ẓevi, Resp. by Ẓevi Hirsch of the "AHW" Communities (Altona, Hamburg, Wandsbeck).
Tiktin, Judah b. Simeon = Judah b. Simeon *Ashkenazi.
Toledot Adam ve-Ḥavvah, Codification by *Jeroham b. Meshullam.
Torat Emet, Resp. by Aaron b. Joseph *Sasson.
Torat Ḥayyim, , Resp. by Ḥayyim (ben) Shabbetai.
Torat ha-Minhagot, subdivision of the *Massa Ḥayyim* (a work on tax law) by Ḥayyim *Palaggi, containing an exposition of customary law.
Tosafot Rid, Explanations to the Talmud and decisions by *Isaiah b. Mali di Trani the Elder.
Tosefot Yom Tov, comm. to Mishnah by Yom Tov Lipmann b. Nathan ha-Levi *Heller; printed in most editions of the Mishnah.
Tummim, subdivision of the comm. to Sh. Ar., ḤM, *Urim ve-Tummim* by Jonathan *Eybeschuetz; printed in the major editions of Sh. Ar.
Tur, usual abbreviation for the *Arba'ah Turim* of *Jacob b. Asher.
Turei Zahav, Comm. to Sh. Ar. by *David b. Samuel ha-Levi; printed in most editions of Sh. Ar.; usual abbreviation: *Taz.*

Urim, subdivision of the following.
Urim ve-Tummim, Comm. to Sh. Ar., ḤM, by Jonathan *Eybeschuetz; printed in the major editions of Sh. Ar.; subdivided in places into *Urim* and *Tummim.*

Vikku'aḥ Mayim Ḥayyim, Polemics against Isserles and Caro by Ḥayyim b. Bezalel.

Yad Malakhi, Methodological treatise by *Malachi b. Jacob ha-Kohen.

Yad Ramah, Nov. by Meir b. Todros [ha-Levi] *Abulafia.
Yakhin u-Vo'az, Resp. by Ẓemaḥ b. Solomon *Duran.
Yam ha-Gadol, Resp. by Jacob Moses *Toledano.
Yam shel Shelomo, Compilation arranged acc. to Talmud by Solomon b. Jehiel (Maharshal) *Luria.
Yashar, Sefer ha-, by *Tam, Jacob b. Meir (Rabbenu Tam); 1st pt.: Resp.; 2nd pt.: Nov.
Yaskil Avdi, Resp. by Obadiah Hadaya (printed together with his Resp. *De'ah ve-Haskel).*
Yaveẓ = Jacob *Emden.
Yehudah Ya'aleh, Resp. by Judah b. Israel *Aszod.
Yekar Tiferet, Comm. to Maimonides' *Yad Ḥazakah,*by David b. Solomon ibn Zimra, printed in most editions of *Yad Ḥazakah.*
Yere'im [ha-Shalem], [Sefer], Treatise on precepts by *Eliezer b. Samuel of Metz.
Yeshu'ot Ya'akov, Resp. by Jacob Meshullam b. Mordecai Ze'ev *Ornstein.
Yiẓhak Rei'aḥ, Resp. by Isaac b. Samuel Abendanan (see article *Abendanam Family).
Ẓafenat Pa'ne'aḥ (1), also called *Raban* or *Even ha-Ezer,* see under the last name.
Ẓafenat Pa'ne'aḥ (2), Resp. by Joseph *Rozin.
Zayit Ra'anan, Resp. by Moses Judah Leib b. Benjamin Auerbach.
Ẓeidah la-Derekh, Codification by *Menahem b. Aaron ibn Zerah.
Ẓedakah u-Mishpat, Resp. by Ẓedakah b. Saadiah Huẓin.
Zekan Aharon, Resp. by Elijah b. Benjamin ha-Levi.
Zekher Ẓaddik, Sermons by Eliezer *Katzenellenbogen.
Ẓemaḥ Ẓedek (1) Resp. by Menaham Mendel Shneersohn (see under *Shneersohn Family).
Zera Avraham, Resp. by Abraham b. David *Yiẓḥaki.
Zera Emet Resp. by *Ishmael b. Abaham Isaac ha-Kohen.
Ẓevi la-Ẓaddik, Resp. by Ẓevi Elimelech b. David Shapira.
Zikhron Yehudah, Resp. by *Judah b. Asher
Zikhron Yosef, Resp. by Joseph b. Menahem *Steinhardt.
Zikhronot, Sefer ha-, Sermons on several precepts by Samuel *Aboab.
Zikkaron la-Rishonim . . ., by Albert (Abraham Elijah) *Harkavy; contains in vol. 1 pt. 4 (1887) a collection of Geonic responsa.
Ẓiẓ Eliezer, Resp. by Eliezer Judah b. Jacob Gedaliah Waldenberg.

BIBLIOGRAPHICAL ABBREVIATIONS

Bibliographies in English and other languages have been extensively updated, with English translations cited where available. In order to help the reader, the language of books or articles is given where not obvious from titles of books or names of periodicals. Titles of books and periodicals in languages with alphabets other than Latin, are given in transliteration, even where there is a title page in English. Titles of articles in periodicals are not given. Names of Hebrew and Yiddish periodicals well known in English-speaking countries or in Israel under their masthead in Latin characters are given in this form, even when contrary to transliteration rules. Names of authors writing in languages with non-Latin alphabets are given in their Latin alphabet form wherever known; otherwise the names are transliterated. Initials are generally not given for authors of articles in periodicals, except to avoid confusion. Non-abbreviated book titles and names of periodicals are printed in *italics.* Abbreviations are given in the list below.

AASOR	*Annual of the American School of Oriental Research* (1919ff.).
AB	*Analecta Biblica* (1952ff.).
Abel, Géog	F.-M. Abel, *Géographie de la Palestine,* 2 vols. (1933-38).
ABR	*Australian Biblical Review* (1951ff.).
Abr.	Philo, *De Abrahamo.*
Abrahams, Companion	I. Abrahams, *Companion to the Authorised Daily Prayer Book* (rev. ed. 1922).
Abramson, Merkazim	S. Abramson, *Ba-Merkazim u-va-Tefuẓot bi-Tekufat ha-Ge'onim* (1965).
Acts	Acts of the Apostles (New Testament).
ACUM	*Who is who in ACUM [Aguddat Kompozitorim u-Meḥabbrim].*
ADAJ	*Annual of the Department of Antiquities, Jordan* (1951ff.).
Adam	Adam and Eve (Pseudepigrapha).
ADB	*Allgemeine Deutsche Biographie,* 56 vols. (1875–1912).
Add. Esth.	The Addition to Esther (Apocrypha).
Adler, Prat Mus	1. Adler, *La pratique musicale savante dans quelques communautés juives en Europe au XVIIe et XVIIIe siècles,* 2 vols. (1966).
Adler-Davis	H.M. Adler and A. Davis (ed. and tr.), *Service of the Synagogue, a New Edition of the Festival Prayers with an English Translation in Prose and Verse,* 6 vols. (1905–06).
Aet.	Philo, *De Aeternitate Mundi.*
AFO	*Archiv fuer Orientforschung* (first two volumes under the name *Archiv fuer Keilschriftforschung)* (1923ff.).
Ag. Ber	*Aggadat Bereshit* (ed. Buber, 1902*).*
Agr.	Philo, *De Agricultura.*
Ag. Sam.	*Aggadat Samuel.*
Ag. Song	*Aggadat Shir ha-Shirim* (Schechter ed., 1896).
Aharoni, Ereẓ	Y. Aharoni, *Ereẓ Yisrael bi-Tekufat ha-Mikra: Geografyah Historit* (1962).
Aharoni, Land	Y. Aharoni, *Land of the Bible* (1966).

Ahikar	Ahikar (Pseudepigrapha).
AI	*Archives Israélites de France* (1840–1936).
AJA	*American Jewish Archives* (1948ff.).
AJHSP	*American Jewish Historical Society – Publications* (after vol. 50 = AJHSQ).
AJHSQ	*American Jewish Historical* (Society) *Quarterly* (before vol. 50 =AJHSP).
AJSLL	*American Journal of Semitic Languages and Literature* (1884–95 under the title *Hebraica,* since 1942 JNES).
AJYB	*American Jewish Year Book* (1899ff.).
AKM	Abhandlungen fuer die Kunde des Morgenlandes (series).
Albright, Arch	W.F. Albright, *Archaeology of Palestine* (rev. ed. 1960).
Albright, Arch Bib	W.F. Albright, *Archaeology of Palestine and the Bible* (1935^3).
Albright, Arch Rel	W.F. Albright, *Archaeology and the Religion of Israel* (1953^3).
Albright, Stone	W.F. Albright, *From the Stone Age to Christianity* (1957^2).
Alon, Meḥkarim	G. Alon, *Meḥkarim be-Toledot Yisrael bi-Ymei Bayit Sheni u-vi-Tekufat ha-Mishnah ve-ha Talmud,* 2 vols. (1957–58).
Alon, Toledot	G. Alon, *Toledot ha-Yehudim be-Ereẓ Yisrael bi-Tekufat ha-Mishnah ve-ha-Talmud,* I (1958^3), (1961^2).
ALOR	Alter Orient (series).
Alt, Kl Schr	A. Alt, *Kleine Schriften zur Geschichte des Volkes Israel,* 3 vols. (1953–59).
Alt, Landnahme	A. Alt, *Landnahme der Israeliten in Palaestina* (1925); also in Alt, Kl Schr, 1 (1953), 89–125.
Ant.	Josephus, *Jewish Antiquities* (Loeb Classics ed.).
AO	*Acta Orientalia* (1922ff.).
AOR	*Analecta Orientalia* (1931ff.).
AOS	American Oriental Series.
Apion	Josephus, *Against Apion* (Loeb Classics ed.).
Aq.	Aquila's Greek translation of the Bible.
Ar.	*Arakhin* (talmudic tractate).
Artist.	Letter of Aristeas (Pseudepigrapha).
ARN[1]	*Avot de-Rabbi Nathan,* version (1) ed. Schechter, 1887.
ARN[2]	*Avot de-Rabbi Nathan,* version (2) ed. Schechter, 1945^2.
Aronius, Regesten	I. Aronius, *Regesten zur Geschichte der Juden im fraenkischen und deutschen Reiche bis zum Jahre 1273* (1902).
ARW	*Archiv fuer Religionswissenschaft* (1898–1941/42).
AS	*Assyrological Studies* (1931ff.).
Ashtor, Korot	E. Ashtor (Strauss), *Korot ha-Yehudim bi-Sefarad ha-Muslemit,* 1(1966^2), 2(1966).
Ashtor, Toledot	E. Ashtor (Strauss), *Toledot ha-Yehudim be-Miẓrayim ve-Suryah Taḥat Shilton ha-Mamlukim,* 3 vols. (1944–70).
Assaf, Ge'onim	S. Assaf, *Tekufat ha-Ge'onim ve-Sifrutah* (1955).
Assaf, Mekorot	S. Assaf, *Mekorot le-Toledot ha-Ḥinnukh be-Yisrael,* 4 vols. (1925–43).
Ass. Mos.	Assumption of Moses (Pseudepigrapha).
ATA	Alttestamentliche Abhandlungen (series).
ATANT	Abhandlungen zur Theologie des Alten und Neuen Testaments (series).
AUJW	*Allgemeine unabhaengige juedische Wochenzeitung* (till 1966 = AWJD).
AV	Authorized Version of the Bible.
Avad.	*Avadim* (post-talmudic tractate).
Avi-Yonah, Geog	M. Avi-Yonah, *Geografyah Historit shel Ereẓ Yisrael* (1962^3).
Avi-Yonah, Land	M. Avi-Yonah, *The Holy Land from the Persian to the Arab conquest (536 B.C. to A.D. 640)* (1960).
Avot	*Avot* (talmudic tractate).
Av. Zar.	*Avodah Zarah* (talmudic tractate).
AWJD	*Allgemeine Wochenzeitung der Juden in Deutschland* (since 1967 = AUJW).
AZDJ	*Allgemeine Zeitung des Judentums.*
Azulai	Ḥ.Y.D. Azulai, *Shem ha-Gedolim,* ed. by I.E. Benjacob, 2 pts. (1852) (and other editions).
BA	*Biblical Archaeologist* (1938ff.).
Bacher, Bab Amor	W. Bacher, *Agada der babylonischen Amoraeer* (1913^2).
Bacher, Pal Amor	W. Bacher, *Agada der palaestinensischen Amoraeer* (Heb. ed. *Aggadat Amora'ei Ereẓ Yisrael),* 2 vols. (1892–99).
Bacher, Tann	W. Bacher, *Agada der Tannaiten* (Heb. ed. *Aggadot ha-Tanna'im,* vol. 1, pt. 1 and 2 (1903); vol. 2 (1890).
Bacher, Trad	W. Bacher, *Tradition und Tradenten in den Schulen Palaestinas und Babyloniens* (1914).
Baer, Spain	Yitzhak (Fritz) Baer, *History of the Jews in Christian Spain,* 2 vols. (1961–66).
Baer, Studien	Yitzhak (Fritz) Baer, *Studien zur Geschichte der Juden im Koenigreich Aragonien waehrend des 13. und 14. Jahrhunderts* (1913).
Baer, Toledot	Yitzhak (Fritz) Baer, *Toledot ha-Yehudim bi-Sefarad ha-Noẓerit mi-Teḥillatan shel ha-Kehillot ad ha-Gerush,* 2 vols. (1959^2).
Baer, Urkunden	Yitzhak (Fritz) Baer, *Die Juden im christlichen Spanien,* 2 vols. (1929–36).
Baer S., Seder	S.I. Baer, *Seder Avodat Yisrael* (1868 and reprints).
BAIU	*Bulletin de l'Alliance Israélite Universelle* (1861–1913).
Baker, Biog Dict	*Baker's Biographical Dictionary of Musicians,* revised by N. Slonimsky (1958^5; with Supplement 1965).
I Bar.	I Baruch (Apocrypha).
II Bar.	II Baruch (Pseudepigrapha).
III Bar.	III Baruch (Pseudepigrapha).
BAR	*Biblical Archaeology Review.*
Baron, Community	S.W. Baron, *The Jewish Community, its History and Structure to the American Revolution,* 3 vols. (1942).

Baron, Social	S.W. Baron, *Social and Religious History of the Jews,* 3 vols. (1937); enlarged, 1-2(1952^{2}), 3-14 (1957–69).
Barthélemy-Milik	D. Barthélemy and J.T. Milik, *Dead Sea Scrolls: Discoveries in the Judean Desert,* vol. 1 *Qumram Cave* I (1955).
BASOR	*Bulletin of the American School of Oriental Research.*
Bauer-Leander	H. Bauer and P. Leander, *Grammatik des Biblisch-Aramaeischen* (1927; repr. 1962).
BB	(1) *Bava Batra* (talmudic tractate). (2) *Biblische Beitraege* (1943ff.).
BBB	Bonner biblische Beitraege (series).
BBLA	*Beitraege zur biblischen Landes- und Altertumskunde* (until 1949–ZDPV).
BBSAJ	*Bulletin,* British School of Archaeology, Jerusalem (1922–25; after 1927 included in PEFQS).
BDASI	*Alon* (since 1948) or *Hadashot Arkheʾologiyyot* (since 1961), bulletin of the Department of Antiquities of the State of Israel.
Begrich, Chronologie	J. Begrich, *Chronologie der Koenige von Israel und Juda* (1929).
Bek.	*Bekhorot* (talmudic tractate).
Bel	Bel and the Dragon (Apocrypha).
Benjacob, Oẓar	I.E. Benjacob, *Oẓar ha-Sefarim* (1880; repr. 1956).
Ben Sira	see Ecclus.
Ben-Yehuda, Millon	E. Ben-Yedhuda, *Millon ha-Lashon ha-Ivrit,* 16 vols (1908–59; repr. in 8 vols., 1959).
Benzinger, Archaeologie	I. Benzinger, *Hebraeische Archaeologie* (1927^{3}).
Ben Zvi, Eretz Israel	I. Ben-Zvi, *Eretz Israel under Ottoman Rule* (1960; offprint from L. Finkelstein (ed.), *The Jews, their History, Culture and Religion* (vol. 1).
Ben Zvi, Ereẓ Israel	I. Ben-Zvi, *Ereẓ Israel bi-Ymei ha-Shilton ha-Ottomani (1955).*
Ber.	*Berakhot* (talmudic tractate).
Beẓah	*Beẓah* (talmudic tractate).
BIES	Bulletin of the Israel Exploration Society, see below BJPES.
Bik.	*Bikkurim* (talmudic tractate).
BJCE	Bibliography of Jewish Communities in Europe, catalog at General Archives for the History of the Jewish People, Jerusalem.
BJPES	Bulletin of the Jewish Palestine Exploration Society – English name of the Hebrew periodical known as: 1. *Yediʾot ha-Ḥevrah ha-Ivrit la-Ḥakirat Ereẓ Yisrael va-Attikoteha* (1933–1954); 2. *Yediʾot ha-Ḥevrah la-Ḥakirat Ereẓ Yisrael va-Attikoteha* (1954–1962); 3. *Yediʾot ba-Ḥakirat Ereẓ Yisrael va-Attikoteha* (1962ff.).
BJRL	*Bulletin of the John Rylands Library* (1914ff.).
BK	*Bava Kamma* (talmudic tractate).
BLBI	*Bulletin of the Leo Baeck Institute* (1957ff.).
BM	(1) *Bava Meẓia* (talmudic tractate). (2) *Beit Mikra* (1955/56ff.). (3) British Museum.
BO	*Bibbia e Oriente* (1959ff.).
Bondy-Dworský	G. Bondy and F. Dworský, *Regesten zur Geschichte der Juden in Boehmen, Maehren und Schlesien von 906 bis 1620,* 2 vols. (1906).
BOR	*Bibliotheca Orientalis* (1943ff.).
Borée, Ortsnamen	W. Borée *Die alten Ortsnamen Palaestinas* (1930).
Bousset, Religion	W. Bousset, *Die Religion des Judentums im neutestamentlichen Zeitalter* (1906^{2}).
Bousset-Gressmann	W. Bousset, *Die Religion des Judentums im spaethellenistischen Zeitalter* (1966^{3}).
BR	*Biblical Review* (1916–25).
BRCI	*Bulletin of the Research Council of Israel* (1951/52–1954/55; then divided).
BRE	*Biblical Research* (1956ff.).
BRF	*Bulletin of the Rabinowitz Fund for the Exploration of Ancient Synagogues* (1949ff.).
Briggs, Psalms	Ch. A. and E.G. Briggs, *Critical and Exegetical Commentary on the Book of Psalms,* 2 vols. (ICC, 1906–07).
Bright, Hist	J. Bright, *A History of Israel* (1959).
Brockelmann, Arab Lit	K. Brockelmann, *Geschichte der arabischen Literatur,* 2 vols. 1898–1902), supplement, 3 vols. (1937–42).
Bruell, Jahrbuecher	*Jahrbuecher fuer juedische Geschichte und Litteratur,* ed. by N. Bruell, Frankfurt (1874–90).
Brugmans-Frank	H. Brugmans and A. Frank (eds.), *Geschiedenis der Joden in Nederland* (1940).
BTS	*Bible et Terre Sainte* (1958ff.).
Bull, Index	S. Bull, *Index to Biographies of Contemporary Composers* (1964).
BW	*Biblical World* (1882–1920).
BWANT	*Beitraege zur Wissenschaft vom Alten und Neuen Testament* (1926ff.).
BZ	*Biblische Zeitschrift* (1903ff.).
BZAW	*Beihefte zur Zeitschrift fuer die alttestamentliche Wissenschaft,* supplement to ZAW (1896ff.).
BŻIH	*Biuletyn Zydowskiego Instytutu Historycznego* (1950ff.).
CAB	*Cahiers dʾarchéologie biblique* (1953ff.).
CAD	*The* [*Chicago*] *Assyrian Dictionary* (1956ff.).
CAH	*Cambridge Ancient History,* 12 vols. (1923–39)
CAH^{2}	*Cambridge Ancient History,* second edition, 14 vols. (1962–2005).
Calwer, Lexikon	*Calwer, Bibellexikon.*
Cant.	Canticles, usually given as Song (= Song of Songs).

Cantera-Millás, Inscripciones	F. Cantera and J.M. Millás, *Las Inscripciones Hebraicas de España* (1956).
CBQ	*Catholic Biblical Quarterly* (1939ff.).
CCARY	Central Conference of American Rabbis, *Yearbook* (1890/91ff.).
CD	*Damascus Document* from the Cairo *Genizah* (published by S. Schechter, *Fragments of a Zadokite Work*, 1910).
Charles, Apocrypha	R.H. Charles, *Apocrypha and Pseudepigrapha . . .*, 2 vols. (1913; repr. 1963–66).
Cher.	Philo, *De Cherubim.*
I (or II) Chron.	Chronicles, book I and II (Bible).
CIG	*Corpus Inscriptionum Graecarum.*
CIJ	*Corpus Inscriptionum Judaicarum,* 2 vols. (1936–52).
CIL	*Corpus Inscriptionum Latinarum.*
CIS	*Corpus Inscriptionum Semiticarum* (1881ff.).
C.J.	Codex Justinianus.
Clermont-Ganneau, Arch	Ch. Clermont-Ganneau, *Archaeological Researches in Palestine*, 2 vols. (1896–99).
CNFI	*Christian News from Israel* (1949ff.).
Cod. Just.	Codex Justinianus.
Cod. Theod.	Codex Theodosinanus.
Col.	Epistle to the Colosssians (New Testament).
Conder, Survey	Palestine Exploration Fund, *Survey of Eastern Palestine*, vol. 1, pt. I (1889) = C.R. Conder, *Memoirs of the . . . Survey.*
Conder-Kitchener	Palestine Exploration Fund, *Survey of Western Palestine*, vol. 1, pts. 1-3 (1881–83) = C.R. Conder and H.H. Kitchener, *Memoirs.*
Conf.	Philo, *De Confusione Linguarum.*
Conforte, Kore	D. Conforte, *Kore ha-Dorot* (1842^{2}).
Cong.	Philo, *De Congressu Quaerendae Eruditionis Gratia.*
Cont.	Philo, *De Vita Contemplativa.*
I (or II) Cor.	Epistles to the Corinthians (New Testament).
Cowley, Aramic	A. Cowley, *Aramaic Papyri of the Fifth Century B.C.* (1923).
Colwey, Cat	A.E. Cowley, *A Concise Catalogue of the Hebrew Printed Books in the Bodleian Library* (1929).
CRB	*Cahiers de la Revue Biblique* (1964ff.).
Crowfoot-Kenyon	J.W. Crowfoot, K.M. Kenyon and E.L. Sukenik, *Buildings of Samaria* (1942).
C.T.	Codex Theodosianus.
DAB	*Dictionary of American Biography* (1928–58).
Daiches, Jews	S. Daiches, *Jews in Babylonia* (1910).
Dalman, Arbeit	G. Dalman, *Arbeit und Sitte in Palaestina*, 7 vols.in 8 (1928–42 repr. 1964).
Dan	Daniel (Bible).
Davidson, Oẓar	I. Davidson, *Oẓar ha-Shirah ve-ha-Piyyut*, 4 vols. (1924–33); Supplement in: HUCA, 12–13 (1937/38), 715–823.
DB	J. Hastings, *Dictionary of the Bible,* 4 vols. (1963^{2}).
DBI	F.G. Vigoureaux et al. (eds.), *Dictionnaire de la Bible*, 5 vols. in 10 (1912); Supplement, 8 vols. (1928–66)
Decal.	Philo, *De Decalogo.*
Dem.	*Demai* (talmudic tractate).
DER	*Derekh Ereẓ Rabbah* (post-talmudic tractate).
Derenbourg, Hist	J. Derenbourg *Essai sur l'histoire et la géographie de la Palestine* (1867).
Det.	Philo, *Quod deterius potiori insidiari solet.*
Deus	Philo, *Quod Deus immutabilis sit.*
Deut.	Deuteronomy (Bible).
Deut. R.	*Deuteronomy Rabbah.*
DEZ	*Derekh Ereẓ Zuta* (post-talmudic tractate).
DHGE	*Dictionnaire d'histoire et de géographie ecclésiastiques,* ed. by A. Baudrillart et al., 17 vols (1912–68).
Dik. Sof	*Dikdukei Soferim,* variae lections of the talmudic text by Raphael Nathan Rabbinovitz (16 vols., 1867–97).
Dinur, Golah	B. Dinur (Dinaburg), *Yisrael ba-Golah,* 2 vols. in 7 (1959–68) = vols. 5 and 6 of his *Toledot Yisrael,* second series.
Dinur, Haganah	B. Dinur (ed.), *Sefer Toledot ha-Haganah* (1954ff.).
Diringer, Iscr	D. Diringer, *Iscrizioni antico-ebraiche palestinesi* (1934).
Discoveries	*Discoveries in the Judean Desert* (1955ff.).
DNB	*Dictionary of National Biography,* 66 vols. (1921–222) with Supplements.
Dubnow, Divrei	S. Dubnow, *Divrei Yemei Am Olam,* 11 vols (1923–38 and further editions).
Dubnow, Ḥasidut	S. Dubnow, *Toledot ha-Ḥasidut* (1960^{2}).
Dubnow, Hist	S. Dubnow, *History of the Jews* (1967).
Dubnow, Hist Russ	S. Dubnow, *History of the Jews in Russia and Poland,* 3 vols. (1916 20).
Dubnow, Outline	S. Dubnow, *An Outline of Jewish History,* 3 vols. (1925–29).
Dubnow, Weltgesch	S. Dubnow, *Weltgeschichte des juedischen Volkes* 10 vols. (1925–29).
Dukes, Poesie	L. Dukes, *Zur Kenntnis der neuhebraeischen religioesen Poesie* (1842).
Dunlop, Khazars	D. H. Dunlop, *History of the Jewish Khazars* (1954).
EA	El Amarna Letters (edited by J.A. Knudtzon), *Die El-Amarna Tafel,* 2 vols. (1907 14).
EB	*Encyclopaedia Britannica.*
EBI	*Estudios biblicos* (1941ff.).
EBIB	T.K. Cheyne and J.S. Black, *Encyclopaedia Biblica,* 4 vols. (1899–1903).
Ebr.	Philo, *De Ebrietate.*
Eccles.	Ecclesiastes (Bible).
Eccles. R.	*Ecclesiastes Rabbah.*
Ecclus.	Ecclesiasticus or Wisdom of Ben Sira (or Sirach; Apocrypha).
Eduy.	*Eduyyot* (mishanic tractate).

EG	*Enziklopedyah shel Galuyyot* (1953ff.).
EH	*Even ha-Ezer.*
EHA	*Enziklopedyah la-Ḥafirot Arkheologiyyot be-Ereẓ Yisrael,* 2 vols. (1970).
EI	*Enzyklopaedie des Islams,* 4 vols. (1905–14). Supplement vol. (1938).
EIS	*Encyclopaedia of Islam,* 4 vols. (1913–36; repr. 1954–68).
EIS^{2}	*Encyclopaedia of Islam, second edition (1960–2000).*
Eisenstein, Dinim	J.D. Eisenstein, *Oẓar Dinim u-Minhagim* (1917; several reprints).
Eisenstein, Yisrael	J.D. Eisenstein, *Oẓar Yisrael* (10 vols, 1907–13; repr. with several additions 1951).
EIV	*Enziklopedyah Ivrit* (1949ff.).
EJ	*Encyclopaedia Judaica* (German, A-L only), 10 vols. (1928–34).
EJC	*Enciclopedia Judaica Castellana,* 10 vols. (1948–51).
Elbogen, Century	I Elbogen, *A Century of Jewish Life* (1960^{2}).
Elbogen, Gottesdienst	I Elbogen, *Der juedische Gottesdienst ...* (1931^{3}, repr. 1962).
Elon, Mafte'aḥ	M. Elon (ed.), *Mafte'aḥ ha-She'elot ve-ha-Teshuvot ha-Rosh* (1965).
EM	*Enziklopedyah Mikra'it* (1950ff.).
I (or II) En.	I and II Enoch (Pseudepigrapha).
EncRel	*Encyclopedia of Religion,* 15 vols. (1987, 2005^{2}).
Eph.	Epistle to the Ephesians (New Testament).
Ephros, Cant	G. Ephros, *Cantorial Anthology,* 5 vols. (1929–57).
Ep. Jer.	Epistle of Jeremy (Apocrypha).
Epstein, Amora'im	J N. Epstein, *Mevo'ot le-Sifrut ha-Amora'im* (1962).
Epstein, Marriage	L M. Epstein, *Marriage Laws in the Bible and the Talmud* (1942).
Epstein, Mishnah	J. N. Epstein, *Mavo le-Nusaḥ ha-Mishnah,* 2 vols. (1964^{2}).
Epstein, Tanna'im	J. N. Epstein, *Mavo le-Sifruth ha-Tanna'im.* (1947).
ER	*Ecumenical Review.*
Er.	*Eruvin* (talmudic tractate).
ERE	*Encyclopaedia of Religion and Ethics,* 13 vols. (1908–26); reprinted.
ErIsr	*Eretz-Israel,* Israel Exploration Society.
I Esd.	I Esdras (Apocrypha) (= III Ezra).
II Esd.	II Esdras (Apocrypha) (= IV Ezra).
ESE	*Ephemeris fuer semitische Epigraphik,* ed. by M. Lidzbarski.
ESN	*Encyclopaedia Sefaradica Neerlandica,* 2 pts. (1949).
ESS	*Encyclopaedia of the Social Sciences,* 15 vols. (1930–35); reprinted in 8 vols. (1948–49).
Esth.	Esther (Bible).
Est. R.	*Esther Rabbah.*
ET	*Enziklopedyah Talmudit* (1947ff.).
Eusebius, Onom.	E. Klostermann (ed.), *Das Onomastikon* (1904), Greek with Hieronymus' Latin translation.
Ex.	Exodus (Bible).
Ex. R.	*Exodus Rabbah.*
Exs	Philo, *De Exsecrationibus.*
EẒD	*Enziklopeday shel ha-Ẓiyyonut ha-Datit* (1951ff.).
Ezek.	Ezekiel (Bible).
Ezra	Ezra (Bible).
III Ezra	III Ezra (Pseudepigrapha).
IV Ezra	IV Ezra (Pseudepigrapha).
Feliks, Ha-Ẓome'aḥ	*J. Feliks, Ha-Ẓome'aḥ ve-ha-Ḥai ba-Mishnah* (1983).
Finkelstein, Middle Ages	L. Finkelstein, *Jewish Self-Government in the Middle Ages* (1924).
Fischel, Islam	W.J. Fischel, *Jews in the Economic and Political Life of Mediaeval Islam* (1937; reprint with introduction "The Court Jew in the Islamic World," 1969).
FJW	*Fuehrer durch die juedische Gemeindeverwaltung und Wohlfahrtspflege in Deutschland* (1927/28).
Frankel, Mevo	Z. Frankel, *Mevo ha-Yerushalmi* (1870; reprint 1967).
Frankel, Mishnah	Z. Frankel, *Darkhei ha-Mishnah* (1959^{2}; reprint 1959^{2}).
Frazer, Folk-Lore	J.G. Frazer, *Folk-Lore in the Old Testament,* 3 vols. (1918–19).
Frey, Corpus	J.-B. Frey, *Corpus Inscriptionum Iudaicarum,* 2 vols. (1936–52).
Friedmann, Lebensbilder	A. Friedmann, *Lebensbilder beruehmter Kantoren,* 3 vols. (1918–27).
FRLT	*Forschungen zur Religion und Literatur des Alten und Neuen Testaments* (series) (1950ff.).
Frumkin-Rivlin	A.L. Frumkin and E. Rivlin, *Toledot Ḥakhmei Yerushalayim,* 3 vols. (1928–30), Supplement vol. (1930).
Fuenn, Keneset	S.J. Fuenn, *Keneset Yisrael,* 4 vols. (1887–90).
Fuerst, Bibliotheca	J. Fuerst, *Bibliotheca Judaica,* 2 vols. (1863; repr. 1960).
Fuerst, Karaeertum	J. Fuerst, *Geschichte des Karaeertums,* 3 vols. (1862–69).
Fug.	Philo, *De Fuga et Inventione.*
Gal.	Epistle to the Galatians (New Testament).
Galling, Reallexikon	K. Galling, *Biblisches Reallexikon* (1937).
Gardiner, Onomastica	A.H. Gardiner, *Ancient Egyptian Onomastica,* 3 vols. (1947).
Geiger, Mikra	A. Geiger, *Ha-Mikra ve-Targumav,* tr. by J.L. Baruch (1949).
Geiger, Urschrift	A. Geiger, *Urschrift und Uebersetzungen der Bibel* 1928^{2}).
Gen.	Genesis (Bible).
Gen. R.	*Genesis Rabbah.*
Ger.	*Gerim* (post-talmudic tractate).
Germ Jud	M. Brann, I. Elbogen, A. Freimann, and H. Tykocinski (eds.), *Germania Judaica,* vol. 1 (1917; repr. 1934 and 1963); vol. 2, in 2 pts. (1917–68), ed. by Z. Avneri.

GHAT	*Goettinger Handkommentar zum Alten Testament* (1917–22).
Ghirondi-Neppi	M.S. Ghirondi and G.H. Neppi, *Toledot Gedolei Yisrael u-Ge'onei Italyah ... u-Ve'urim al Sefer Zekher Ẓaddikim li-Verakhah* . . .(1853), index in ZHB, 17 (1914), 171–83.
Gig.	Philo, *De Gigantibus.*
Ginzberg, Legends	L. Ginzberg, *Legends of the Jews,* 7 vols. (1909–38; and many reprints).
Git.	*Gittin* (talmudic tractate).
Glueck, Explorations	N. Glueck, *Explorations in Eastern Palestine,* 2 vols. (1951).
Goell, Bibliography	Y. Goell, *Bibliography of Modern Hebrew Literature in English Translation* (1968).
Goodenough, Symbols	E.R. Goodenough, *Jewish Symbols in the Greco-Roman Period,* 13 vols. (1953–68).
Gordon, Textbook	C.H. Gordon, *Ugaritic Textbook* (1965; repr. 1967).
Graetz, Gesch	H. Graetz, *Geschichte der Juden* (last edition 1874–1908).
Graetz, Hist	H. Graetz, *History of the Jews*, 6 vols. (1891–1902).
Graetz, Psalmen	H. Graetz, *Kritischer Commentar zu den Psalmen*, 2 vols. in 1 (1882–83).
Graetz, Rabbinowitz	H. Graetz, *Divrei Yemei Yisrael*, tr. by S.P. Rabbinowitz. (1928 1929^{2}).
Gray, Names	G.B. Gray, *Studies in Hebrew Proper Names* (1896).
Gressmann, Bilder	H. Gressmann, *Altorientalische Bilder zum Alten Testament* (1927^{2}).
Gressmann, Texte	H. Gressmann, *Altorientalische Texte zum Alten Testament* (1926^{2}).
Gross, Gal Jud	H. Gross, *Gallia Judaica* (1897; repr. with add. 1969).
Grove, Dict	*Grove's Dictionary of Music and Musicians,* ed. by E. Blum 9 vols. (1954^{5}) and suppl. (1961^{5}).
Guedemann, Gesch Erz	M. Guedemann, *Geschichte des Erziehungswesens und der Cultur der abendlaendischen Juden,* 3 vols. (1880–88).
Guedemann, Quellenschr	M. Guedemann, *Quellenschriften zur Geschichte des Unterrichts und der Erziehung bei den deutschen Juden* (1873, 1891).
Guide	Maimonides, *Guide of the Perplexed.*
Gulak, Oẓar	A. Gulak, *Oẓar ha-Shetarot ha-Nehugim be-Yisrael* (1926).
Gulak, Yesodei	A. Gulak, *Yesodei ha-Mishpat ha-Ivri, Seder Dinei Mamonot be-Yisrael, al pi Mekorot ha-Talmud ve-ha-Posekim*, 4 vols. (1922; repr. 1967).
Guttmann, Mafte'aḥ	M. Guttmann, *Mafte'aḥ ha-Talmud*, 3 vols. (1906–30).
Guttmann, Philosophies	J. Guttmann, *Philosophies of Judaism* (1964).
Hab.	*Habakkuk* (Bible).
Ḥag.	*Ḥagigah* (talmudic tractate).
Haggai	*Haggai* (Bible).
Ḥal.	*Ḥallah* (talmudic tractate).
Halevy, Dorot	I. Halevy, *Dorot ha-Rishonim,* 6 vols. (1897–1939).
Halpern, Pinkas	I. Halpern (Halperin), *Pinkas Va'ad Arba Araẓot* (1945).
Hananel-Eškenazi	A. Hananel and Eškenazi (eds.), *Fontes Hebraici ad res oeconomicas socialesque terrarum balcanicarum saeculo XVI pertinentes,* 2 vols, (1958–60; in Bulgarian).
HB	*Hebraeische Bibliographie* (1858–82).
Heb.	Epistle to the Hebrews (New Testament).
Heilprin, Dorot	J. Heilprin (Heilperin), *Seder ha-Dorot,* 3 vols. (1882; repr. 1956).
Her.	Philo, *Quis Rerum Divinarum Heres.*
Hertz, Prayer	J.H. Hertz (ed.), *Authorised Daily Prayer Book* (rev. ed. 1948; repr. 1963).
Herzog, Instit	I. Herzog, *The Main Institutions of Jewish Law,* 2 vols. (1936–39; repr. 1967).
Herzog-Hauck	J.J. Herzog and A. Hauch (eds.), *Real-encyklopaedie fuer protestantische Theologie* (1896–1913^{3}).
HḤY	*Ha-Ẓofeh le-Ḥokhmat Yisrael* (first four volumes under the title *Ha-Ẓofeh me-Ereẓ Hagar)* (1910/11–13).
Hirschberg, Afrikah	H.Z. Hirschberg, *Toledot ha-Yehudim be-Afrikah ha-Zofonit*, 2 vols. (1965).
HJ	*Historia Judaica* (1938–61).
HL	*Das Heilige Land* (1857ff.)
ḤM	*Ḥoshen Mishpat.*
Hommel, Ueberliefer.	F. Hommel, *Die altisraelitische Ueberlieferung in inschriftlicher Beleuchtung* (1897).
Hor.	*Horayot* (talmudic tractate).
Horodezky, Ḥasidut	S.A. Horodezky, *Ha-Ḥasidut ve-ha-Ḥasidim,* 4 vols. (1923).
Horowitz, Ereẓ Yis	I.W. Horowitz, *Ereẓ Yisrael u-Shekhenoteha* (1923).
Hos.	Hosea (Bible).
HTR	*Harvard Theological Review* (1908ff.).
HUCA	*Hebrew Union College Annual* (1904; 1924ff.)
Ḥul.	*Ḥullin* (talmudic tractate).
Husik, Philosophy	I. Husik, *History of Medieval Jewish Philosophy* (1932^{2}).
Hyman, Toledot	A. Hyman, *Toledot Tanna'im ve-Amora'im* (1910; repr. 1964).
Ibn Daud, Tradition	Abraham Ibn Daud, *Sefer ha-Qabbalah – The Book of Tradition,* ed. and tr. By G.D. Cohen (1967).
ICC	International Critical Commentary on the Holy Scriptures of the Old and New Testaments (series, 1908ff.).
IDB	*Interpreter's Dictionary of the Bible,* 4 vols. (1962).
Idelsohn, Litugy	A. Z. Idelsohn, *Jewish Liturgy and its Development* (1932; paperback repr. 1967)
Idelsohn, Melodien	A. Z. Idelsohn, *Hebraeisch-orientalischer Melodienschatz,* 10 vols. (1914 32).
Idelsohn, Music	A. Z. Idelsohn, *Jewish Music in its Historical Development* (1929; paperback repr. 1967).

IEJ *Israel Exploration Journal* (1950ff.).
IESS *International Encyclopedia of the Social Sciences* (various eds.).
IG *Inscriptiones Graecae*, ed. by the Prussian Academy.
IGYB *Israel Government Year Book* (1949/50ff.).
ILR *Israel Law Review* (1966ff.).
IMIT *Izraelita Magyar Irodalmi Társulat Évkönyv* (1895 1948).
IMT International Military Tribunal.
INB *Israel Numismatic Bulletin* (1962–63).
INJ *Israel Numismatic Journal* (1963ff.).
Ios Philo, *De Iosepho.*
Isa. Isaiah (Bible).
ITHL Institute for the Translation of Hebrew Literature.
IZBG *Internationale Zeitschriftenschau fuer Bibelwissenschaft und Grenzgebiete* (1951ff.).

JA *Journal asiatique* (1822ff.).
James Epistle of James (New Testament).
JAOS *Journal of the American Oriental Society* (c. 1850ff.)
Jastrow, Dict M. Jastrow, *Dictionary of the Targumim, the Talmud Babli and Yerushalmi, and the Midrashic literature*, 2 vols. (1886 1902 and reprints).
JBA *Jewish Book Annual* (19242ff.).
JBL *Journal of Biblical Literature* (1881ff.).
JBR *Journal of Bible and Religion* (1933ff.).
JC *Jewish Chronicle* (1841ff.).
JCS *Journal of Cuneiform Studies* (1947ff.).
JE *Jewish Encyclopedia*, 12 vols. (1901–05 several reprints).
Jer. Jeremiah (Bible).
Jeremias, Alte Test A. Jeremias, *Das Alte Testament im Lichte des alten Orients* 1930^4).
JGGJČ *Jahrbuch der Gesellschaft fuer Geschichte der Juden in der Čechoslovakischen Republik* (1929–38).
JHSEM Jewish Historical Society of England, *Miscellanies* (1925ff.).
JHSET Jewish Historical Society of England, *Transactions* (1893ff.).
JJGL *Jahrbuch fuer juedische Geschichte und Literatur* (Berlin) (1898–1938).
JJLG *Jahrbuch der juedische-literarischen Gesellschaft* (Frankfurt) (1903–32).
JJS *Journal of Jewish Studies* (1948ff.).
JJSO *Jewish Journal of Sociology* (1959ff.).
JJV *Jahrbuch fuer juedische Volkskunde* (1898–1924).
JL *Juedisches Lexikon*, 5 vols. (1927–30).
JMES *Journal of the Middle East Society* (1947ff.).
JNES *Journal of Near Eastern Studies* (continuation of AJSLL) (1942ff.).
J.N.U.L. Jewish National and University Library.
Job Job (Bible).
Joel Joel (Bible).
John Gospel according to John (New Testament).
I, II and III John Epistles of John (New Testament).
Jos., Ant Josephus, *Jewish Antiquities* (Loeb Classics ed.).
Jos. Apion Josephus, *Against Apion* (Loeb Classics ed.).
Jos., index *Josephus Works*, Loeb Classics ed., index of names.
Jos., Life Josephus, *Life* (ed. Loeb Classics).
Jos, Wars Josephus, *The Jewish Wars* (Loeb Classics ed.).
Josh. Joshua (Bible).
JPESB Jewish Palestine Exploration Society Bulletin, see BJPES.
JPESJ Jewish Palestine Exploration Society Journal – Eng. Title of the Hebrew periodical *Kovez ha-Ḥevrah ha-Ivrit la-Ḥakirat Erez Yisrael va-Attikoteha.*
JPOS *Journal of the Palestine Oriental Society* (1920–48).
JPS Jewish Publication Society of America, *The Torah* (1962, 1967^2); *The Holy Scriptures* (1917).
JQR *Jewish Quarterly Review* (1889ff.).
JR *Journal of Religion* (1921ff.).
JRAS *Journal of the Royal Asiatic Society* (1838ff.).
JHR *Journal of Religious History* (1960/61ff.).
JSOS *Jewish Social Studies* (1939ff.).
JSS *Journal of Semitic Studies* (1956ff.).
JTS *Journal of Theological Studies* (1900ff.).
JTSA Jewish Theological Seminary of America (also abbreviated as JTS).
Jub. Jubilees (Pseudepigrapha).
Judg. Judges (Bible).
Judith Book of Judith (Apocrypha).
Juster, Juifs J. Juster, *Les Juifs dans l'Empire Romain*, 2 vols. (1914).
JYB *Jewish Year Book* (1896ff.).
JZWL *Juedische Zeitschift fuer Wissenschaft und Leben* (1862–75).

Kal. *Kallah* (post-talmudic tractate).
Kal. R. *Kallah Rabbati* (post-talmudic tractate).
Katz, England *The Jews in the History of England, 1485-1850 (1994).*
Kaufmann, Schriften D. Kaufmann, *Gesammelte Schriften*, 3 vols. (1908 15).
Kaufmann Y., Religion Y. Kaufmann, *The Religion of Israel* (1960), abridged tr. of his *Toledot.*
Kaufmann Y., Toledot Y. Kaufmann, *Toledot ha-Emunah ha-Yisre'elit*, 4 vols. (1937 57).
KAWJ *Korrespondenzblatt des Vereins zur Gruendung und Erhaltung der Akademie fuer die Wissenschaft des Judentums* (1920 30).
Kayserling, Bibl M. Kayserling, *Biblioteca Española-Portugueza-Judaica* (1880; repr. 1961).
Kelim *Kelim* (mishnaic tractate).
Ker. *Keritot* (talmudic tractate).
Ket. *Ketubbot* (talmudic tractate).

Kid.	*Kiddushim* (talmudic tractate).
Kil.	*Kilayim* (talmudic tractate).
Kin.	*Kinnim* (mishnaic tractate).
Kisch, Germany	G. Kisch, *Jews in Medieval Germany* (1949).
Kittel, Gesch	R. Kittel, *Geschichte des Volkes Israel,* 3 vols. (1922–28).
Klausner, Bayit Sheni	J. Klausner, *Historyah shel ha-Bayit ha-Sheni,* 5 vols. (1950/512).
Klausner, Sifrut	J. Klausner, *Historyah shel haSifrut ha-Ivrit ha-Ḥadashah,* 6 vols. (1952–582).
Klein, corpus	S. Klein (ed.), *Juedisch-palaestinisches Corpus Inscriptionum* (1920).
Koehler-Baumgartner	L. Koehler and W. Baumgartner, *Lexicon in Veteris Testamenti libros* (1953).
Kohut, Arukh	H.J.A. Kohut (ed.), *Sefer he-Arukh ha-Shalem,* by Nathan b. Jehiel of Rome, 8 vols. (1876–92; Supplement by S. Krauss et al., 1936; repr. 1955).
Krauss, Tal Arch	S. Krauss, *Talmudische Archaeologie,* 3 vols. (1910–12; repr. 1966).
Kressel, Leksikon	G. Kressel, *Leksikon ha-Sifrut ha-Ivrit ba-Dorot ha-Aḥaronim,* 2 vols. (1965–67).
KS	*Kirjath Sepher* (1923/4ff.).
Kut.	*Kuttim* (post-talmudic tractate).
LA	Studium Biblicum Franciscanum, *Liber Annuus* (1951ff.).
L.A.	Philo, *Legum allegoriae.*
Lachower, Sifrut	F. Lachower, *Toledot ha-Sifrut ha-Ivrit ha-Ḥadashah,* 4 vols. (1947–48; several reprints).
Lam.	Lamentations (Bible).
Lam. R.	*Lamentations Rabbah.*
Landshuth, Ammudei	L. Landshuth, *Ammudei ha-Avodah* (1857–62; repr. with index, 1965).
Legat.	Philo, *De Legatione ad Caium.*
Lehmann, Nova Bibl	R.P. Lehmann, *Nova Bibliotheca Anglo-Judaica* (1961).
Lev.	Leviticus (Bible).
Lev. R.	*Leviticus Rabbah.*
Levy, Antologia	I. Levy, *Antologia de liturgia judeo-española* (1965ff.).
Levy J., Chald Targ	J. Levy, *Chaldaeisches Woerterbuch ueber die Targumim,* 2 vols. (1967–68; repr. 1959).
Levy J., Nuehebr Tal	J. Levy, *Neuhebraeisches und chaldaeisches Woerterbuch ueber die Talmudim . . .,* 4 vols. (1875–89; repr. 1963).
Lewin, Oẓar	Lewin, *Oẓar ha-Ge'onim,* 12 vols. (1928–43).
Lewysohn, Zool	L. Lewysohn, *Zoologie des Talmuds* (1858).
Lidzbarski, Handbuch	M. Lidzbarski, *Handbuch der nordsemitischen Epigraphik,* 2 vols (1898).
Life	Josephus, *Life* (Loeb Classis ed.).
LNYL	*Leksikon fun der Nayer Yidisher Literatur* (1956ff.).
Loew, Flora	I. Loew, *Die Flora der Juden,* 4 vols. (1924 34; repr. 1967).
LSI	*Laws of the State of Israel* (1948ff.).
Luckenbill, Records	D.D. Luckenbill, *Ancient Records of Assyria and Babylonia,* 2 vols. (1926).
Luke	Gospel according to Luke (New Testament)
LXX	Septuagint (Greek translation of the Bible).
Ma'as.	*Ma'aserot* (talmudic tractate).
Ma'as. Sh.	*Ma'ase Sheni* (talmudic tractate).
I, II, III, and IVMacc.	Maccabees, I, II, III (Apocrypha), IV (Pseudepigrapha).
Maimonides, Guide	Maimonides, *Guide of the Perplexed.*
Maim., Yad	Maimonides, *Mishneh Torah (Yad Ḥazakah).*
Maisler, Untersuchungen	B. Maisler (Mazar), *Untersuchungen zur alten Geschichte und Ethnographie Syriens und Palaestinas,* 1 (1930).
Mak.	*Makkot* (talmudic tractate).
Makhsh.	*Makhshrin* (mishnaic tractate).
Mal.	Malachi (Bible).
Mann, Egypt	J. Mann, *Jews in Egypt in Palestine under the Fatimid Caliphs,* 2 vols. (1920–22).
Mann, Texts	J. Mann, *Texts and Studies,* 2 vols (1931–35).
Mansi	G.D. Mansi, *Sacrorum Conciliorum nova et amplissima collectio,* 53 vols. in 60 (1901–27; repr. 1960).
Margalioth, Gedolei	M. Margalioth, *Enẓiklopedyah le-Toledot Gedolei Yisrael,* 4 vols. (1946–50).
Margalioth, Ḥakhmei	M. Margalioth, *Enẓiklopedyah le-Ḥakhmei ha-Talmud ve-ha-Ge'onim,* 2 vols. (1945).
Margalioth, Cat	G. Margalioth, *Catalogue of the Hebrew and Samaritan Manuscripts in the British Museum,* 4 vols. (1899–1935).
Mark	Gospel according to Mark (New Testament).
Mart. Isa.	Martyrdom of Isaiah (Pseudepigrapha).
Mas.	Masorah.
Matt.	Gospel according to Matthew (New Testament).
Mayer, Art	L.A. Mayer, *Bibliography of Jewish Art* (1967).
MB	*Wochenzeitung* (formerly *Mitteilungsblatt) des Irgun Olej Merkas Europa* (1933ff.).
MEAH	*Miscelánea de estudios árabes y hebraicos* (1952ff.).
Meg.	Megillah (talmudic tractate).
Meg. Ta'an.	*Megillat Ta'anit* (in HUCA, 8 9 (1931–32), 318–51).
Me'il	*Me'ilah* (mishnaic tractate).
MEJ	*Middle East Journal* (1947ff.).
Mehk.	*Mekhilta de-R. Ishmael.*
Mekh. SbY	*Mekhilta de-R. Simeon bar Yoḥai.*
Men.	*Menaḥot* (talmudic tractate).
MER	*Middle East Record* (1960ff.).
Meyer, Gesch	E. Meyer, *Geschichte des Alterums,* 5 vols. in 9 (1925–58).
Meyer, Ursp	E. Meyer, *Urspring und Anfaenge des Christentums* (1921).
Mez.	*Mezuzah* (post-talmudic tractate).
MGADJ	*Mitteilungen des Gesamtarchivs der deutschen Juden* (1909–12).
MGG	*Die Musik in Geschichte und Gegenwart,* 14 vols. (1949–68).

MGG^2	*Die Musik in Geschichte und Gegenwart, 2nd edition (1994)*
MGH	*Monumenta Germaniae Historica* (1826ff.).
MGJV	*Mitteilungen der Gesellschaft fuer juedische Volkskunde* (1898–1929); title varies, see also JJV.
MGWJ	*Monatsschrift fuer Geschichte und Wissenschaft des Judentums* (1851–1939).
MHJ	*Monumenta Hungariae Judaica,* 11 vols. (1903–67).
Michael, Or	H.Ḥ. Michael, *Or ha-Ḥayyim: Ḥakhmei Yisrael ve-Sifreihem,* ed. by S.Z. Ḥ. Halberstam and N. Ben-Menahem (1965^2).
Mid.	*Middot* (mishnaic tractate).
Mid. Ag.	*Midrash Aggadah.*
Mid. Hag.	*Midrash ha-Gadol.*
Mid. Job.	*Midrash Job.*
Mid. Jonah	*Midrash Jonah.*
Mid. Lek. Tov	*Midrash Lekaḥ Tov.*
Mid. Prov.	*Midrash Proverbs.*
Mid. Ps.	*Midrash Tehillim* (Eng tr. *The Midrash on Psalms* (JPS, 1959).
Mid. Sam.	*Midrash Samuel.*
Mid. Song	*Midrash Shir ha-Shirim.*
Mid. Tan.	*Midrash Tanna'im* on Deuteronomy.
Miége, Maroc	J.L. Miège, *Le Maroc et l'Europe,* 3 vols. (1961 62).
Mig.	Philo, *De Migratione Abrahami.*
Mik.	*Mikva'ot* (mishnaic tractate).
Milano, Bibliotheca	A. Milano, *Bibliotheca Historica Italo-Judaica* (1954); supplement for 1954–63 (1964); supplement for 1964–66 in RMI, 32 (1966).
Milano, Italia	A. Milano, *Storia degli Ebrei in Italia* (1963).
MIO	*Mitteilungen des Instituts fuer Orientforschung* 1953ff.).
Mish.	Mishnah.
MJ	*Le Monde Juif* (1946ff.).
MJC	see Neubauer, Chronicles.
MK	*Mo'ed Katan* (talmudic tractate).
MNDPV	*Mitteilungen und Nachrichten des deutschen Palaestinavereins* (1895–1912).
Mortara, Indice	M. Mortara, *Indice Alfabetico dei Rabbini e Scrittori Israeliti ... in Italia ...* (1886).
Mos	Philo, *De Vita Mosis.*
Moscati, Epig	S, Moscati, *Epigrafia ebraica antica* 1935–1950 (1951).
MT	Masoretic Text of the Bible.
Mueller, Musiker	[E.H. Mueller], *Deutisches Musiker-Lexikon* (1929)
Munk, Mélanges	S. Munk, *Mélanges de philosophie juive et arabe* (1859; repr. 1955).
Mut.	Philo, *De Mutatione Nominum.*
MWJ	*Magazin fuer die Wissenshaft des Judentums* (18745 93).
Nah.	Nahum (Bible).
Naz.	*Nazir* (talmudic tractate).
NDB	*Neue Deutsche Biographie* (1953ff.).
Ned.	*Nedarim* (talmudic tractate).
Neg.	*Nega'im* (mishnaic tractate).
Neh.	Nehemiah (Bible).
NG^2	*New Grove Dictionary of Music and Musicians* (2001).
Nuebauer, Cat	A. Neubauer, *Catalogue of the Hebrew Manuscripts in the Bodleian Library ...,* 2 vols. (1886–1906).
Neubauer, Chronicles	A. Neubauer, *Mediaeval Jewish Chronicles,* 2 vols. (Heb., 1887–95; repr. 1965), Eng. title of *Seder ha-Ḥakhamim ve-Korot ha-Yamim.*
Neubauer, Géogr	A. Neubauer, *La géographie du Talmud* (1868).
Neuman, Spain	A.A. Neuman, *The Jews in Spain, their Social, Political, and Cultural Life During the Middle Ages,* 2 vols. (1942).
Neusner, Babylonia	J. Neusner, *History of the Jews in Babylonia,* 5 vols. 1965–70), 2nd revised printing 1969ff.).
Nid.	*Niddah* (talmudic tractate).
Noah	Fragment of Book of Noah (Pseudepigrapha).
Noth, Hist Isr	M. Noth, *History of Israel* (1958).
Noth, Personennamen	M. Noth, *Die israelitischen Personennamen. ...* (1928).
Noth, Ueberlief	M. Noth, *Ueberlieferungsgeschichte des Pentateuchs* (1949).
Noth, Welt	M. Noth, *Die Welt des Alten Testaments* (1957^3).
Nowack, Lehrbuch	W. Nowack, *Lehrbuch der hebraeischen Archaeologie,* 2 vols (1894).
NT	New Testament.
Num.	Numbers (Bible).
Num R.	*Numbers Rabbah.*
Obad.	Obadiah (Bible).
ODNB online	*Oxford Dictionary of National Biography.*
OḤ	*Oraḥ Ḥayyim.*
Oho.	*Oholot* (mishnaic tractate).
Olmstead	H.T. Olmstead, *History of Palestine and Syria* (1931; repr. 1965).
OLZ	*Orientalistische Literaturzeitung* (1898ff.)
Onom.	Eusebius, *Onomasticon.*
Op.	Philo, *De Opificio Mundi.*
OPD	*Osef Piskei Din shel ha-Rabbanut ha-Rashit le-Ereẓ Yisrael, Bet ha-Din ha-Gadol le-Irurim* (1950).
Or.	*Orlah* (talmudic tractate).
Or. Sibyll.	Sibylline Oracles (Pseudepigrapha).
OS	*L'Orient Syrien* (1956ff.)
OTS	*Oudtestamentische Studien* (1942ff.).
PAAJR	*Proceedings of the American Academy for Jewish Research* (1930ff.)
Pap 4QS^e	A papyrus exemplar of IQS.
Par.	*Parah* (mishnaic tractate).
Pauly-Wissowa	A.F. Pauly, *Realencyklopaedie der klassichen Alertumswissenschaft,* ed. by G. Wissowa et al. (1864ff.)

PD	*Piskei Din shel Bet ha-Mishpat ha-Elyon le-Yisrael* (1948ff.)
PDR	*Piskei Din shel Battei ha-Din ha-Rabbaniyyim be-Yisrael.*
PdRE	*Pirkei de-R. Eliezer* (Eng. tr. 1916. (1965²).
PdRK	*Pesikta de-Rav Kahana.*
Pe'ah	*Pe'ah* (talmudic tractate).
Peake, Commentary	A.J. Peake (ed.), *Commentary on the Bible* (1919; rev. 1962).
Pedersen, Israel	J. Pedersen, *Israel, Its Life and Culture*, 4 vols. in 2 (1926–40).
PEFQS	*Palestine Exploration Fund Quarterly Statement* (1869–1937; since 1938–PEQ).
PEQ	*Palestine Exploration Quarterly* (until 1937 PEFQS; after 1927 includes BBSAJ).
Perles, Beitaege	J. Perles, *Beitraege zur rabbinischen Sprach- und Alterthumskunde* (1893).
Pes.	*Pesaḥim* (talmudic tractate).
Pesh.	Peshitta (Syriac translation of the Bible).
Pesher Hab.	Commentary to Habakkuk from Qumran; see 1Qp Hab.
I and II Pet.	Epistles of Peter (New Testament).
Pfeiffer, Introd	R.H. Pfeiffer, *Introduction to the Old Testament* (1948).
PG	J.P. Migne (ed.), *Patrologia Graeca*, 161 vols. (1866–86).
Phil.	Epistle to the Philippians (New Testament).
Philem.	Epistle to the Philemon (New Testament).
PIASH	*Proceedings of the Israel Academy of Sciences and Humanities* (1963/7ff.).
PJB	*Palaestinajahrbuch des deutschen evangelischen Institutes fuer Altertumswissenschaft*, Jerusalem (1905–1933).
PK	*Pinkas ha-Kehillot*, encyclopedia of Jewish communities, published in over 30 volumes by Yad Vashem from 1970 and arranged by countries, regions and localities. For 3-vol. English edition see Spector, *Jewish Life*.
PL	J.P. Migne (ed.), *Patrologia Latina* 221 vols. (1844–64).
Plant	Philo, *De Plantatione.*
PO	R. Graffin and F. Nau (eds.), *Patrologia Orientalis* (1903ff.)
Pool, Prayer	D. de Sola Pool, *Traditional Prayer Book for Sabbath and Festivals* (1960).
Post	Philo, *De Posteritate Caini.*
PR	*Pesikta Rabbati.*
Praem.	Philo, *De Praemiis et Poenis.*
Prawer, Ẓalbanim	J. Prawer, *Toledot Mamlekhet ha-Ẓalbanim be-Ereẓ Yisrael*, 2 vols. (1963).
Press, Ereẓ	I. Press, *Ereẓ-Yisrael, Enẓiklopedyah Topografit-Historit*, 4 vols. (1951–55).
Pritchard, Pictures	J.B. Pritchard (ed.), *Ancient Near East in Pictures* (1954, 1970).
Pritchard, Texts	J.B. Pritchard (ed.), *Ancient Near East Texts* ... (1970³).
Pr. Man.	Prayer of Manasses (Apocrypha).
Prob.	Philo, *Quod Omnis Probus Liber Sit.*
Prov.	Proverbs (Bible).
PS	*Palestinsky Sbornik* (Russ. (1881 1916, 1954ff).
Ps.	Psalms (Bible).
PSBA	*Proceedings of the Society of Biblical Archaeology* (1878–1918).
Ps. of Sol	Psalms of Solomon (Pseudepigrapha).
IQ Apoc	The *Genesis Apocryphon* from Qumran, cave one, ed. by N. Avigad and Y. Yadin (1956).
6QD	*Damascus Document* or *Sefer Berit Dammesk* from Qumran, cave six, ed. by M. Baillet, in RB, 63 (1956), 513–23 (see also CD).
QDAP	*Quarterly of the Department of Antiquities in Palestine* (1932ff.).
4QDeut. 32	Manuscript of Deuteronomy 32 from Qumran, cave four (ed. by P.W. Skehan, in BASOR, 136 (1954), 12–15).
4QEx[a]	Exodus manuscript in Jewish script from Qumran, cave four.
4QEx[α]	Exodus manuscript in Paleo-Hebrew script from Qumran, cave four (partially ed. by P.W. Skehan, in JBL, 74 (1955), 182–7).
4QFlor	*Florilegium*, a miscellany from Qumran, cave four (ed. by J.M. Allegro, in JBL, 75 (1956), 176–77 and 77 (1958), 350–54).).
QGJD	*Quellen zur Geschichte der Juden in Deutschland* 1888–98).
IQH	*Thanksgiving Psalms* of *Hodayot* from Qumran, cave one (ed. by E.L. Sukenik and N. Avigad, *Oẓar ha-Megillot ha-Genuzot* (1954).
IQIs[a]	Scroll of Isaiah from Qumran, cave one (ed. by N. Burrows et al., *Dead Sea Scrolls* ..., 1 (1950).
IQIs[b]	Scroll of Isaiah from Qumran, cave one (ed. E.L. Sukenik and N. Avigad, *Oẓar ha-Megillot ha-Genuzot* (1954).
IQM	The *War Scroll* or *Serekh ha-Milḥamah* (ed. by E.L. Sukenik and N. Avigad, *Oẓar ha-Megillot ha-Genuzot* (1954).
4QpNah	Commentary on Nahum from Qumran, cave four (partially ed. by J.M. Allegro, in JBL, 75 (1956), 89–95).
IQphyl	Phylacteries *(tefillin)* from Qumran, cave one (ed. by Y. Yadin, in *Eretz Israel*, 9 (1969), 60–85).
4Q Prayer of Nabonidus	A document from Qumran, cave four, belonging to a lost Daniel literature (ed. by J.T. Milik, in RB, 63 (1956), 407–15).
IQS	*Manual of Discipline* or *Serekh ha-Yaḥad* from Qumran, cave one (ed. by M. Burrows et al., *Dead Sea Scrolls* ..., 2, pt. 2 (1951).

IQS[a]	The *Rule of the Congregation or Serekh ha-Edah* from Qumran, cave one (ed. by Burrows et al., *Dead Sea Scrolls* ..., 1 (1950), under the abbreviation IQ28a).
IQS[b]	*Blessings* or *Divrei Berakhot* from Qumran, cave one (ed. by Burrows et al., *Dead Sea Scrolls* ..., 1 (1950), under the abbreviation IQ28b).
4QSam[a]	Manuscript of I and II Samuel from Qumran, cave four (partially ed. by F.M. Cross, in BASOR, 132 (1953), 15–26).
4QSam[b]	Manuscript of I and II Samuel from Qumran, cave four (partially ed. by F.M. Cross, in JBL, 74 (1955), 147–72).
4QTestimonia	Sheet of Testimony from Qumran, cave four (ed. by J.M. Allegro, in JBL, 75 (1956), 174–87).).
4QT.Levi	*Testament of Levi* from Qumran, cave four (partially ed. by J.T. Milik, in RB, 62 (1955), 398–406).
Rabinovitz, Dik Sof	See Dik Sof.
RB	*Revue biblique* (1892ff.)
RBI	*Recherches bibliques* (1954ff.)
RCB	*Revista de cultura biblica* (São Paulo) (1957ff.)
Régné, Cat	J. Régné, *Catalogue des actes . . . des rois d'Aragon, concernant les Juifs* (1213–1327), in: REJ, vols. 60 70, 73, 75–78 (1910–24).
Reinach, Textes	T. Reinach, *Textes d'auteurs Grecs et Romains relatifs au Judaïsme* (1895; repr. 1963).
REJ	*Revue des études juives* (1880ff.).
Rejzen, Leksikon	Z. Rejzen, *Leksikon fun der Yidisher Literature,* 4 vols. (1927–29).
Renan, Ecrivains	A. Neubauer and E. Renan, *Les écrivains juifs français* ... (1893).
Renan, Rabbins	A. Neubauer and E. Renan, *Les rabbins français* (1877).
RES	*Revue des étude sémitiques et Babyloniaca* (1934–45).
Rev.	Revelation (New Testament).
RGG^{3}	*Die Religion in Geschichte und Gegenwart,* 7 vols. (1957–65^{3}).
RH	*Rosh Ha-Shanah* (talmudic tractate).
RHJE	*Revue de l'histoire juive en Egypte* (1947ff.).
RHMH	*Revue d'histoire de la médecine hébraïque* (1948ff.).
RHPR	*Revue d'histoire et de philosophie religieuses* (1921ff.).
RHR	*Revue d'histoire des religions* (1880ff.).
RI	*Rivista Israelitica* (1904–12).
Riemann-Einstein	*Hugo Riemanns Musiklexikon,* ed. by A. Einstein (1929^{11}).
Riemann-Gurlitt	*Hugo Riemanns Musiklexikon,* ed. by W. Gurlitt (1959–67^{12}), Personenteil.
Rigg-Jenkinson, Exchequer	J.M. Rigg, H. Jenkinson and H.G. Richardson (eds.), *Calendar of the Pleas Rolls of the Exchequer of the Jews,* 4 vols. (1905–1970); cf. in each instance also J.M. Rigg (ed.), *Select Pleas* ... (1902).

RMI	*Rassegna Mensile di Israel* (1925ff.).
Rom.	Epistle to the Romans (New Testament).
Rosanes, Togarmah	S.A. Rosanes, *Divrei Yemei Yisrael be-Togarmah,* 6 vols. (1907–45), and in 3 vols. (1930–38^{2}).
Rosenbloom, Biogr Dict	J.R. Rosenbloom, *Biographical Dictionary of Early American Jews* (1960).
Roth, Art	C. Roth, *Jewish Art* (1961).
Roth, Dark Ages	C. Roth (ed.), *World History of the Jewish People,* second series, vol. 2, *Dark Ages* (1966).
Roth, England	C. Roth, *History of the Jews in England* (1964^{3}).
Roth, Italy	C. Roth, *History of the Jews in Italy* (1946).
Roth, Mag Bibl	C. Roth, *Magna Bibliotheca Anglo-Judaica* (1937).
Roth, Marranos	C. Roth, *History of the Marranos* (2nd rev. ed 1959; reprint 1966).
Rowley, Old Test	H.H. Rowley, *Old Testament and Modern Study* (1951; repr. 1961).
RS	*Revue sémitiques d'épigraphie et d'histoire ancienne* (1893/94ff.).
RSO	*Rivista degli studi orientali* (1907ff.).
RSV	Revised Standard Version of the Bible.
Rubinstein, Australia I	*H.L. Rubinstein, The Jews in Australia, A Thematic History, Vol. I (1991).*
Rubinstein, Australia II	*W.D. Rubinstein, The Jews in Australia, A Thematic History, Vol. II (1991).*
Ruth	Ruth (Bible).
Ruth R.	*Ruth Rabbah.*
RV	Revised Version of the Bible.
Sac.	Philo, *De Sacrificiis Abelis et Caini.*
Salfeld, Martyrol	S. Salfeld, *Martyrologium des Nuernberger Memorbuches* (1898).
I and II Sam.	Samuel, book I and II (Bible).
Sanh.	*Sanhedrin* (talmudic tractate).
SBA	Society of Biblical Archaeology.
SBB	*Studies in Bibliography and Booklore* (1953ff.).
SBE	*Semana Biblica Española.*
SBT	*Studies in Biblical Theology* (1951ff.).
SBU	*Svenkst Bibliskt Uppslogsvesk,* 2 vols. (1962–63^{2}).
Schirmann, Italyah	J.Ḥ. Schirmann, *Ha-Shirah ha-Ivrit be-Italyah* (1934).
Schirmann, Sefarad	J.Ḥ. Schirmann, *Ha-Shirah ha-Ivrit bi-Sefarad u-vi-Provence,* 2 vols. (1954–56).
Scholem, Mysticism	G. Scholem, *Major Trends in Jewish Mysticism* (rev. ed. 1946; paperback ed. with additional bibliography 1961).
Scholem, Shabbetai Ẓevi	G. Scholem, *Shabbetai Ẓevi ve-ha-Tenu'ah ha-Shabbeta'it bi-Ymei Ḥayyav,* 2 vols. (1967).
Schrader, Keilinschr	E. Schrader, *Keilinschriften und das Alte Testament* (1903^{3}).
Schuerer, Gesch	E. Schuerer, *Geschichte des juedischen Volkes im Zeitalter Jesu Christi,* 3 vols. and index-vol. (1901–11^{4}).

Schuerer, Hist	E. Schuerer, *History of the Jewish People in the Time of Jesus*, ed. by N.N. Glatzer, abridged paperback edition (1961).
Set. T.	*Sefer Torah* (post-talmudic tractate).
Sem.	*Semaḥot* (post-talmudic tractate).
Sendrey, Music	A. Sendrey, *Bibliography of Jewish Music* (1951).
SER	*Seder Eliyahu Rabbah.*
SEZ	*Seder Eliyahu Zuta.*
Shab	*Shabbat* (talmudic tractate).
Sh. Ar.	J. Caro Shulḥan Arukh. OḤ – *Oraḥ Ḥayyim* YD – *Yoreh De'ah* EH – *Even ha-Ezer* ḤM – *Ḥoshen Mishpat.*
Shek.	*Shekalim* (talmudic tractate).
Shev.	*Shevi'it* (talmudic tractate).
Shevu.	*Shevu'ot* (talmudic tractate).
Shunami, Bibl	S. Shunami, *Bibliography of Jewish Bibliographies* (1965²).
Sif.	*Sifrei Deuteronomy.*
Sif. Num.	*Sifrei Numbers.*
Sifra	*Sifra* on Leviticus.
Sif. Zut.	*Sifrei Zuta.*
SIHM	Sources inédites de l'histoire du Maroc (series).
Silverman, Prayer	M. Silverman (ed.), *Sabbath and Festival Prayer Book* (1946).
Singer, Prayer	S. Singer *Authorised Daily Prayer Book* (1943¹⁷).
Sob.	Philo, *De Sobrietate.*
Sof.	*Soferim* (post-talmudic tractate).
Som.	Philo, *De Somniis.*
Song	Song of Songs (Bible).
Song. Ch.	Song of the Three Children (Apocrypha).
Song R.	*Song of Songs Rabbah.*
SOR	*Seder Olam Rabbah.*
Sot.	*Sotah* (talmudic tractate).
SOZ	*Seder Olam Zuta.*
Spec.	Philo, *De Specialibus Legibus.*
Spector, Jewish Life	*S. Spector (ed.), Encyclopedia of Jewish Life Before and After the Holocaust (2001).*
Steinschneider, Arab lit	M. Steinschneider, *Die arabische Literatur der Juden* (1902).
Steinschneider, Cat Bod	M. Steinschneider, *Catalogus Librorum Hebraeorum in Bibliotheca Bodleiana,* 3 vols. (1852–60; reprints 1931 and 1964).
Steinschneider, Hanbuch	M. Steinschneider, *Bibliographisches Handbuch ueber die . . . Literatur fuer hebraeische Sprachkunde* (1859; repr. with additions 1937).
Steinschneider, Uebersetzungen	M. Steinschneider, *Die hebraeischen Uebersetzungen des Mittelalters* (1893).
Stern, Americans	M.H. Stern, *Americans of Jewish Descent* (1960).
van Straalen, Cat	S. van Straalen, *Catalogue of Hebrew Books in the British Museum Acquired During the Years 1868–1892* (1894).
Suárez Fernández, Docmentos	L. Suárez Fernández, *Documentos acerca de la expulsion de los Judios de España* (1964).
Suk.	*Sukkah* (talmudic tractate).
Sus.	Susanna (Apocrypha).
SY	*Sefer Yeẓirah.*
Sym.	Symmachus' Greek translation of the Bible.
SZNG	*Studien zur neueren Geschichte.*
Ta'an.	*Ta'anit* (talmudic tractate).
Tam.	*Tamid* (mishnaic tractate).
Tanḥ.	*Tanḥuma.*
Tanḥ. B.	*Tanḥuma.* Buber ed (1885).
Targ. Jon	Targum Jonathan (Aramaic version of the Prophets).
Targ. Onk.	Targum Onkelos (Aramaic version of the Pentateuch).
Targ. Yer.	Targum Yerushalmi.
TB	Babylonian Talmud or Talmud Bavli.
Tcherikover, Corpus	V. Tcherikover, A. Fuks, and M. Stern, *Corpus Papyrorum Judaicorum,* 3 vols. (1957–60).
Tef.	*Tefillin* (post-talmudic tractate).
Tem.	*Temurah* (mishnaic tractate).
Ter.	*Terumah* (talmudic tractate).
Test. Patr.	Testament of the Twelve Patriarchs (Pseudepigrapha). Ash. – Asher Ben. – Benjamin Dan – Dan Gad – Gad Iss. – Issachar Joseph – Joseph Judah – Judah Levi – Levi Naph. – Naphtali Reu. – Reuben Sim. – Simeon Zeb. – Zebulun.
I and II	Epistle to the Thessalonians (New Testament).
Thieme-Becker	U. Thieme and F. Becker (eds.), *Allgemeines Lexikon der bildenden Kuenstler von der Antike bis zur Gegenwart,* 37 vols. (1907–50).
Tidhar	D. Tidhar (ed.), *Enẓiklopedyah la-Ḥalutẓei ha-Yishuv u-Vonav* (1947ff.).
I and II Timothy	Epistles to Timothy (New Testament).
Tit.	Epistle to Titus (New Testament).
TJ	Jerusalem Talmud or Talmud Yerushalmi.
Tob.	Tobit (Apocrypha).
Toh.	*Tohorot* (mishnaic tractate).
Torczyner, Bundeslade	H. Torczyner, *Die Bundeslade und die Anfaenge der Religion Israels* (1930³).
Tos.	*Tosafot.*
Tosef.	Tosefta.
Tristram, Nat Hist	H.B. Tristram, *Natural History of the Bible* (1877⁵).
Tristram, Survey	Palestine Exploration Fund, *Survey of Western Palestine,* vol. 4 (1884) = *Fauna and Flora* by H.B. Tristram.
TS	*Terra Santa* (1943ff.).

TSBA	*Transactions of the Society of Biblical Archaeology* (1872–93).
TY	*Tevul Yom* (mishnaic tractate).
UBSB	United Bible Society, *Bulletin.*
UJE	*Universal Jewish Encyclopedia,* 10 vols. (1939–43).
Uk.	*Ukẓin* (mishnaic tractate).
Urbach, Tosafot	E.E. Urbach, *Ba'alei ha-Tosafot* (1957²).
de Vaux, Anc Isr	R. de Vaux, *Ancient Israel: its Life and Institutions* (1961; paperback 1965).
de Vaux, Instit	R. de Vaux, *Institutions de l'Ancien Testament,* 2 vols. (1958 60).
Virt.	Philo, *De Virtutibus.*
Vogelstein, Chronology	M. Volgelstein, *Biblical Chronology (1944).*
Vogelstein-Rieger	H. Vogelstein and P. Rieger, *Geschichte der Juden in Rom,* 2 vols. (1895–96).
VT	*Vetus Testamentum* (1951ff.).
VTS	*Vetus Testamentum* Supplements (1953ff.).
Vulg.	Vulgate (Latin translation of the Bible).
Wars	Josephus, *The Jewish Wars.*
Watzinger, Denkmaeler	K. Watzinger, *Denkmaeler Palaestinas,* 2 vols. (1933–35).
Waxman, Literature	M. Waxman, *History of Jewish Literature,* 5 vols. (1960²).
Weiss, Dor	I.H. Weiss, *Dor, Dor ve-Doreshav,* 5 vols. (1904⁴).
Wellhausen, Proleg	J. Wellhausen, *Prolegomena zur Geschichte Israels* (1927⁶).
WI	*Die Welt des Islams* (1913ff.).
Winniger, Biog	S. Wininger, *Grosse juedische National-Biographie ...,* 7 vols. (1925–36).
Wisd.	Wisdom of Solomon (Apocrypha)
WLB	*Wiener Library Bulletin* (1958ff.).
Wolf, Bibliotheca	J.C. Wolf, *Bibliotheca Hebraea,* 4 vols. (1715–33).
Wright, Bible	G.E. Wright, *Westminster Historical Atlas to the Bible* (1945).
Wright, Atlas	G.E. Wright, *The Bible and the Ancient Near East* (1961).
WWWJ	*Who's Who in the World Jewry* (New York, 1955, 1965²).
WZJT	*Wissenschaftliche Zeitschrift fuer juedische Theologie* (1835–37).
WZKM	*Wiener Zeitschrift fuer die Kunde des Morgenlandes* (1887ff.).
Yaari, Sheluḥei	A. Yaari, *Sheluḥei Ereẓ Yisrael* (1951).
Yad	Maimonides, *Mishneh Torah (Yad Ḥazakah).*
Yad	*Yadayim* (mishnaic tractate).
Yal.	*Yalkut Shimoni.*
Yal. Mak.	*Yalkut Makhiri.*
Yal. Reub.	*Yalkut Reubeni.*
YD	*Yoreh De'ah.*
YE	*Yevreyskaya Entsiklopediya,* 14 vols. (c. 1910).
Yev.	*Yevamot* (talmudic tractate).
YIVOA	*YIVO Annual of Jewish Social Studies* (1946ff.).
YLBI	*Year Book of the Leo Baeck Institute* (1956ff.).
YMḤEY	See BJPES.
YMḤSI	*Yedi'ot ha-Makhon le-Ḥeker ha-Shirah ha-Ivrit* (1935/36ff.).
YMMY	*Yedi'ot ha-Makhon le-Madda'ei ha-Yahadut* (1924/25ff.).
Yoma	*Yoma* (talmudic tractate).
ZA	*Zeitschrift fuer Assyriologie* (1886/87ff.).
Zav.	*Zavim* (mishnaic tractate).
ZAW	*Zeitschrift fuer die alttestamentliche Wissenschaft und die Kunde des nachbiblishchen Judentums* (1881ff.).
ZAWB	*Beihefte* (supplements) to ZAW.
ZDMG	*Zeitschrift der Deutschen Morgenlaendischen Gesellschaft* (1846ff.).
ZDPV	*Zeitschrift des Deutschen Palaestina-Vereins* (1878–1949; from 1949 = BBLA).
Zech.	Zechariah (Bible).
Zedner, Cat	J. Zedner, *Catalogue of Hebrew Books in the Library of the British Museum* (1867; repr. 1964).
Zeitlin, Bibliotheca	W. Zeitlin, *Bibliotheca Hebraica Post-Mendelssohniana* (1891–95).
Zeph.	Zephaniah (Bible).
Zev.	*Zevaḥim* (talmudic tractate).
ZGGJT	*Zeitschrift der Gesellschaft fuer die Geschichte der Juden in der Tschechoslowakei* (1930–38).
ZGJD	*Zeitschrift fuer die Geschichte der Juden in Deutschland* (1887–92).
ZHB	*Zeitschrift fuer hebraeische Bibliographie* (1896–1920).
Zinberg, Sifrut	I. Zinberg, *Toledot Sifrut Yisrael,* 6 vols. (1955–60).
Ẓiẓ.	*Ẓiẓit* (post-talmudic tractate).
ZNW	*Zeitschrift fuer die neutestamentliche Wissenschaft* (1901ff.).
ZS	*Zeitschrift fuer Semitistik und verwandte Gebiete* (1922ff.).
Zunz, Gesch	L. Zunz, *Zur Geschichte und Literatur* (1845).
Zunz, Gesch	L. Zunz, *Literaturgeschichte der synagogalen Poesie* (1865; Supplement, 1867; repr. 1966).
Zunz, Poesie	L. Zunz, *Synogogale Posie des Mittelalters,* ed. by Freimann (1920²; repr. 1967).
Zunz, Ritus	L. Zunz, *Ritus des synagogalen Gottesdienstes* (1859; repr. 1967).
Zunz, Schr	L. Zunz, *Gesammelte Schriften,* 3 vols. (1875–76).
Zunz, Vortraege	L. Zunz, *Gottesdienstliche vortraege der Juden ...* 1892²; repr. 1966).
Zunz-Albeck, Derashot	L. Zunz, *Ha-Derashot be-Yisrael,* Heb. Tr. of Zunz Vortraege by H. Albeck (1954²).

TRANSLITERATION RULES

HEBREW AND SEMITIC LANGUAGES:

	General	*Scientific*
א	not transliterated[1]	ʾ
בּ	b	b
ב	v	v, b̲
גּ	g	g
ג		ḡ
דּ	d	d
ד		d̲
ה	h	h
ו	v – when not a vowel	w
ז	z	z
ח	ḥ	ḥ
ט	t	ṭ, t
י	y – when vowel and at end of words – i	y
כּ	k	k
כ, ך	kh	kh, k̲
ל	l	l̲
מ, ם	m	m
נ, ן	n	n
ס	s	s
ע	not transliterated[1]	ʿ
פּ	p	p
פ, ף	f	p, f, ph
צ, ץ	ẓ	ṣ, ẓ
ק	k	q, k
ר	r	r
שׁ	sh[2]	š
שׂ	s	ś, s
תּ	t	t
ת		t̲
ג׳	dzh, J	ğ
ז׳	zh, J	ž
צ׳	ch	č
ָ		å, o, ȯ (short) â, ā (long)
ַ	a	a
ֲ		a, ^{a}
ֵ		e, ẹ, ē
ֶ	e	æ, ä, ę
ֱ		œ, ě, ^{e}
ְ	only *sheva na* is transliterated	ə, ĕ, e; only *sheva na* transliterated
ִ, ִי	i	i
ֹ, וֹ	o	o, o, o
ֻ, וּ	u	u, ŭ û, ū
ֵי	ei; biblical e	
‡		reconstructed forms of words

1. The letters א and ע are not transliterated.
   An apostrophe (') between vowels indicates that they do not form a diphthong and are to be pronounced separately.
2. *Dagesh ḥazak* (forte) is indicated by doubling of the letter, except for the letter שׁ.
3. Names. Biblical names and biblical place names are rendered according to the Bible translation of the Jewish Publication Society of America. Post-biblical Hebrew names are transliterated; contemporary names are transliterated or rendered as used by the person. Place names are transliterated or rendered by the accepted spelling. Names and some words with an accepted English form are usually not transliterated.

YIDDISH

א	not transliterated
אַ	a
אָ	o
בּ	b
בֿ	v
ג	g
ד	d
ה	h
ו, וּ	u
וו	v
וי	oy
ז	z
זש	zh
ח	kh
ט	t
טש	tsh, ch
י	(consonant) y (vowel) i
יִ	i
יי	ey
ײַ	ay
כּ	k
כ, ך	kh
ל	l
מ, ם	m
נ, ן	n
ס	s
ע	e
פּ	p
פֿ, ף	f
צ, ץ	ts
ק	k
ר	r
ש	sh
שׂ	s
תּ	t
ת	s

1. Yiddish transliteration rendered according to U. Weinreich's Modern *English-Yiddish Yiddish-English* Dictionary.
2. Hebrew words in Yiddish are usually transliterated according to standard Yiddish pronunciation, e.g., חזנות = *khazones*.

LADINO

Ladino and Judeo-Spanish words written in Hebrew characters are transliterated phonetically, following the General Rules of Hebrew transliteration (see above) whenever the accepted spelling in Latin characters could not be ascertained.

ARABIC

ا ء	a[1]	ض	ḍ
ب	b	ط	ṭ
ت	t	ظ	ẓ
ث	th	ع	c
ج	j	غ	gh
ح	ḥ	ف	f
خ	kh	ق	q
د	d	ك	k
ذ	dh	ل	l
ر	r	م	m
ز	z	ن	n
س	s	ه	h
ش	sh	و	w
ص	ṣ	ي	y
ـَ	a	ـَا ى	ā
ـِ	i	ـِي	ī
ـُ	u	ـُو	ū
ـَو	aw	ـِيّ	iyy[2]
ـَي	ay	ـُوّ	uww[2]

1. not indicated when initial
2. see note (f)

a) The EJ follows the *Columbia Lippincott Gazetteer* and the *Times Atlas* in transliteration of Arabic place names. Sites that appear in neither are transliterated according to the table above, and subject to the following notes.

b) The EJ follows the *Columbia Encyclopedia* in transliteration of Arabic names. Personal names that do not therein appear are transliterated according to the table above and subject to the following notes (e.g., Ali rather than ʿAlī, Suleiman rather than Sulayman).

c) The EJ follows the *Webster's Third International Dictionary, Unabridged* in transliteration of Arabic terms that have been integrated into the English language.

d) The term "Abu" will thus appear, usually in disregard of inflection.

e) Nunnation (end vowels, *tanwīn*) are dropped in transliteration.

f) Gemination (*tashdīd*) is indicated by the doubling of the geminated letter, unless an end letter, in which case the gemination is dropped.

g) The definitive article *al-* will always be thus transliterated, unless subject to one of the modifying notes (e.g., El-Arish rather than al-ʿArīsh; modification according to note (a)).

h) The Arabic transliteration disregards the Sun Letters (the antero-palatals (*al-Ḥurūf al-Shamsiyya*).

i) The *tā-marbūṭa* (ο) is omitted in transliteration, unless in construct-stage (e.g., *Khirba* but *Khirbat Mishmish*).

These modifying notes may lead to various inconsistencies in the Arabic transliteration, but this policy has deliberately been adopted to gain smoother reading of Arabic terms and names.

GREEK

Ancient Greek	*Modern Greek*	*Greek Letters*
a	a	*Α; α; ᾳ*
b	v	*Β; β*
g	gh; g	*Γ; γ*
d	dh	*Δ; δ*
e	e	*Ε; ε*
z	z	*Ζ; ζ*
e; e	i	*Η; η; ῃ*
th	th	*Θ; θ*
i	i	*Ι; ι*
k	k; ky	*Κ; κ*
l	l	*Λ; λ*
m	m	*Μ; μ*
n	n	*Ν; ν*
x	x	*Ξ; ξ*
o	o	*Ο; ο*
p	p	*Π; π*
r; rh	r	*Ρ; ρ; ῥ*
s	s	*Σ; σ; ς*
t	t	*Τ; τ*
u; y	i	*Υ; υ*
ph	f	*Φ; φ*
ch	kh	*Χ; χ*
ps	ps	*Ψ; ψ*
o; ō	o	*Ω; ω; ῳ*
ai	e	*αι*
ei	i	*ει*
oi	i	*οι*
ui	i	*υι*
ou	ou	*ου*
eu	ev	*ευ*
eu; ēu	iv	*ηυ*
–	j	*τζ*
nt	d; nd	*ντ*
mp	b; mb	*μπ*
ngk	g	*γκ*
ng	ng	*νγ*
h	–	ʽ
–	–	ʼ
w	–	*ϝ*

RUSSIAN

А	A
Б	B
В	V
Г	G
Д	D
Е	E, Ye[1]
Ё	Yo, O[2]
Ж	Zh
З	Z
И	I
Й	Y[3]
К	K
Л	L
М	M
Н	N
О	O
П	P
Р	R
С	S
Т	T
У	U
Ф	F
Х	Kh
Ц	Ts
Ч	Ch
Ш	Sh
Щ	Shch
Ъ	omitted; see note [1]
Ы	Y
Ь	omitted; see note [1]
Э	E
Ю	Yu
Я	Ya

1. Ye at the beginning of a word; after all vowels except ***Ы***; and after **Ъ** and ***Ь***.
2. O after ***Ч***, ***Ш*** and ***Щ***.
3. Omitted after ***Ы***, and in names of people after ***И***.

A. Many first names have an accepted English or quasi-English form which has been preferred to transliteration.
B. Place names have been given according to the *Columbia Lippincott Gazeteer.*
C. Pre-revolutionary spelling has been ignored.
D. Other languages using the Cyrillic alphabet (e.g., Bulgarian, Ukrainian), inasmuch as they appear, have been phonetically transliterated in conformity with the principles of this table.

GLOSSARY

Asterisked terms have separate entries in the Encyclopaedia.

Actions Committee, early name of the Zionist General Council, the supreme institution of the World Zionist Organization in the interim between Congresses. The Zionist Executive's name was then the "Small Actions Committee."

*__Adar__, twelfth month of the Jewish religious year, sixth of the civil, approximating to February–March.

*__Aggadah__, name given to those sections of Talmud and Midrash containing homiletic expositions of the Bible, stories, legends, folklore, anecdotes, or maxims. In contradistinction to **halakhah.*

*__Agunah__, woman unable to remarry according to Jewish law, because of desertion by her husband or inability to accept presumption of death.

*__Aharonim__, later rabbinic authorities. In contradistinction to **rishonim* ("early ones").

Ahavah, liturgical poem inserted in the second benediction of the morning prayer *(*Ahavah Rabbah)* of the festivals and/or special Sabbaths.

Aktion (Ger.), operation involving the mass assembly, deportation, and murder of Jews by the Nazis during the *Holocaust.

*__Aliyah__, (1) being called to Reading of the Law in synagogue; (2) immigration to Ereẓ Israel; (3) one of the waves of immigration to Ereẓ Israel from the early 1880s.

*__Amidah__, main prayer recited at all services; also known as *Shemoneh Esreh* and *Tefillah.*

*__Amora__ (pl. **amoraim**), title given to the Jewish scholars in Ereẓ Israel and Babylonia in the third to sixth centuries who were responsible for the **Gemara.*

Aravah, the *willow; one of the *Four Species used on *Sukkot ("festival of Tabernacles") together with the **etrog, hadas*, and **lulav.*

*__Arvit__, evening prayer.

Asarah be-Tevet, fast on the 10th of Tevet commemorating the commencement of the siege of Jerusalem by Nebuchadnezzar.

Asefat ha-Nivḥarim, representative assembly elected by Jews in Palestine during the period of the British Mandate (1920–48).

*__Ashkenaz__, name applied generally in medieval rabbinical literature to Germany.

*__Ashkenazi__ (pl. **Ashkenazim**), German or West-, Central-, or East-European Jew(s), as contrasted with *Sephardi(m).

*__Av__, fifth month of the Jewish religious year, eleventh of the civil, approximating to July–August.

*__Av bet din__, vice president of the supreme court (*bet din ha-gadol*) in Jerusalem during the Second Temple period; later, title given to communal rabbis as heads of the religious courts (see **bet din*).

*__Badḥan__, jester, particularly at traditional Jewish weddings in Eastern Europe.

*__Bakkashah__ (Heb. "supplication"), type of petitionary prayer, mainly recited in the Sephardi rite on Rosh Ha-Shanah and the Day of Atonement.

Bar, "son of . . . "; frequently appearing in personal names.

*__Baraita__ (pl. **beraitot**), statement of **tanna* not found in *Mishnah.

*__Bar mitzvah__, ceremony marking the initiation of a boy at the age of 13 into the Jewish religious community.

Ben, "son of . . . ", frequently appearing in personal names.

Berakhah (pl. **berakhot**), *benediction, blessing; formula of praise and thanksgiving.

*__Bet din__ (pl. **battei din**), rabbinic court of law.

*__Bet ha-midrash__, school for higher rabbinic learning; often attached to or serving as a synagogue.

*__Bilu__, first modern movement for pioneering and agricultural settlement in Ereẓ Israel, founded in 1882 at Kharkov, Russia.

*__Bund__, Jewish socialist party founded in Vilna in 1897, supporting Jewish national rights; Yiddishist, and anti-Zionist.

Cohen (pl. **Cohanim**), see Kohen.

*__Conservative Judaism__, trend in Judaism developed in the United States in the 20th century which, while opposing extreme changes in traditional observances, permits certain modifications of *halakhah* in response to the changing needs of the Jewish people.

*__Consistory__ (Fr. *consistoire*), governing body of a Jewish communal district in France and certain other countries.

*__Converso(s)__, term applied in Spain and Portugal to converted Jew(s), and sometimes more loosely to their descendants.

*__Crypto-Jew__, term applied to a person who although observing outwardly Christianity (or some other religion) was at heart a Jew and maintained Jewish observances as far as possible (see Converso; Marrano; Neofiti; New Christian; Jadīd al-Islām).

*__Dayyan__, member of rabbinic court.

Decisor, equivalent to the Hebrew *posek* (pl. **posekim*), the rabbi who gives the decision (*halakhah*) in Jewish law or practice.

*__Devekut__, "devotion"; attachment or adhesion to God; communion with God.

*__Diaspora__, Jews living in the "dispersion" outside Ereẓ Israel; area of Jewish settlement outside Ereẓ Israel.

Din, a law (both secular and religious), legal decision, or lawsuit.

Divan, diwan, collection of poems, especially in Hebrew, Arabic, or Persian.

Dunam, unit of land area (1,000 sq. m., c. ¼ acre), used in Israel.

Einsatzgruppen, mobile units of Nazi S.S. and S.D.; in U.S.S.R. and Serbia, mobile killing units.

*__Ein-Sof__, "without end"; "the infinite"; hidden, impersonal aspect of God; also used as a Divine Name.

*__Elul__, sixth month of the Jewish religious calendar, 12th of the civil, precedes the High Holiday season in the fall.

Endloesung, see *Final Solution.

*__Ereẓ Israel__, Land of Israel; Palestine.

*__Eruv__, technical term for rabbinical provision permitting the alleviation of certain restrictions.

*__Etrog__, citron; one of the *Four Species used on *Sukkot together with the **lulav, hadas*, and *aravah.*

Even ha-Ezer, see Shulḥan Arukh.

*__Exilarch__, lay head of Jewish community in Babylonia (see also *resh galuta*), and elsewhere.

*__Final Solution__ (Ger. *Endloesung*), in Nazi terminology, the Nazi-planned mass murder and total annihilation of the Jews.

*__Gabbai__, official of a Jewish congregation; originally a charity collector.

*__Galut__, "exile"; the condition of the Jewish people in dispersion.

*__Gaon__ (pl. **geonim**), head of academy in post-talmudic period, especially in Babylonia.
Gaonate, office of *gaon.
*__Gemara__, traditions, discussions, and rulings of the **amoraim*, commenting on and supplementing the *Mishnah, and forming part of the Babylonian and Palestinian Talmuds (see Talmud).
*__Gematria__, interpretation of Hebrew word according to the numerical value of its letters.
General Government, territory in Poland administered by a German civilian governor-general with headquarters in Cracow after the German occupation in World War II.
*__Genizah__, depository for sacred books. The best known was discovered in the synagogue of Fostat (old Cairo).
Get, bill of *divorce.
*__Ge'ullah__, hymn inserted after the **Shema* into the benediction of the morning prayer of the festivals and special Sabbaths.
*__Gilgul__, metempsychosis; transmigration of souls.
*__Golem__, automaton, especially in human form, created by magical means and endowed with life.
*__Ḥabad__, initials of *ḥokhmah, binah, da'at*: "wisdom, understanding, knowledge"; ḥasidic movement founded in Belorussia by *Shneur Zalman of Lyady.
Hadas, *myrtle; one of the *Four Species used on Sukkot together with the **etrog, *lulav*, and *aravah*.
*__Haftarah__ (pl. **haftarot**), designation of the portion from the prophetical books of the Bible recited after the synagogue reading from the Pentateuch on Sabbaths and holidays.
*__Haganah__, clandestine Jewish organization for armed self-defense in Ereẓ Israel under the British Mandate, which eventually evolved into a people's militia and became the basis for the Israel army.
*__Haggadah__, ritual recited in the home on *Passover eve at seder table.
Haham, title of chief rabbi of the Spanish and Portuguese congregations in London, England.
*__Hakham__, title of rabbi of *Sephardi congregation.
*__Hakham bashi__, title in the 15th century and modern times of the chief rabbi in the Ottoman Empire, residing in Constantinople (Istanbul), also applied to principal rabbis in provincial towns.
Hakhsharah ("preparation"), organized training in the Diaspora of pioneers for agricultural settlement in Ereẓ Israel.
*__Halakhah__ (pl. **halakhot**), an accepted decision in rabbinic law. Also refers to those parts of the *Talmud concerned with legal matters. In contradistinction to **aggadah*.
Ḥaliẓah, biblically prescribed ceremony (Deut. 25:9–10) performed when a man refuses to marry his brother's childless widow, enabling her to remarry.
*__Hallel__, term referring to Psalms 113-18 in liturgical use.
*__Ḥalukkah__, system of financing the maintenance of Jewish communities in the holy cities of Ereẓ Israel by collections made abroad, mainly in the pre-Zionist era (see *kolel*).
Ḥalutz (pl. **ḥalutzim**), pioneer, especially in agriculture, in Ereẓ Israel.
Ḥalutziyyut, pioneering.
*__Ḥanukkah__, eight-day celebration commemorating the victory of *Judah Maccabee over the Syrian king *Antiochus Epiphanes and the subsequent rededication of the Temple.
Ḥasid, adherent of *Ḥasidism.
*__Ḥasidei Ashkenaz__, medieval pietist movement among the Jews of Germany.
*__Ḥasidism__, (1) religious revivalist movement of popular mysticism among Jews of Germany in the Middle Ages; (2) religious movement founded by *Israel ben Eliezer Ba'al Shem Tov in the first half of the 18th century.
*__Haskalah__, "enlightenment"; movement for spreading modern European culture among Jews c. 1750–1880. See *maskil*.
*__Havdalah__, ceremony marking the end of Sabbath or festival.
*__Ḥazzan__, precentor who intones the liturgy and leads the prayers in synagogue; in earlier times a synagogue official.
*__Ḥeder__ (lit. "room"), school for teaching children Jewish religious observance.
Heikhalot, "palaces"; tradition in Jewish mysticism centering on mystical journeys through the heavenly spheres and palaces to the Divine Chariot (see Merkabah).
*__Ḥerem__, excommunication, imposed by rabbinical authorities for purposes of religious and/or communal discipline; originally, in biblical times, that which is separated from common use either because it was an abomination or because it was consecrated to God.
Ḥeshvan, see Marḥeshvan.
*__Ḥevra kaddisha__, title applied to charitable confraternity (**ḥevrah*), now generally limited to associations for burial of the dead.
*__Ḥibbat Zion__, see Ḥovevei Zion.
*__Histadrut__ (abbr. For Heb. **Ha-Histadrut ha-Kelalit shel ha-Ovedim ha-Ivriyyim be-Ereẓ Israel**). Ereẓ Israel Jewish Labor Federation, founded in 1920; subsequently renamed Histadrut ha-Ovedim be-Ereẓ Israel.
*__Holocaust__, the organized mass persecution and annihilation of European Jewry by the Nazis (1933–1945).
*__Hoshana Rabba__, the seventh day of *Sukkot on which special observances are held.
Ḥoshen Mishpat, see Shulḥan Arukh.
Ḥovevei Zion, federation of *Ḥibbat Zion, early (pre-*Herzl) Zionist movement in Russia.
Illui, outstanding scholar or genius, especially a young prodigy in talmudic learning.
*__Iyyar__, second month of the Jewish religious year, eighth of the civil, approximating to April-May.
I.Ẓ.L. (initials of Heb. *__Irgun Ẓeva'i Le'ummi__; "National Military Organization"), underground Jewish organization in Ereẓ Israel founded in 1931, which engaged from 1937 in retaliatory acts against Arab attacks and later against the British mandatory authorities.
*__Jadīd al-Islām__ (Ar.), a person practicing the Jewish religion in secret although outwardly observing Islām.
*__Jewish Legion__, Jewish units in British army during World War I.
*__Jihād__ (Ar.), in Muslim religious law, holy war waged against infidels.
*__Judenrat__ (Ger. "Jewish council"), council set up in Jewish communities and ghettos under the Nazis to execute their instructions.
*__Judenrein__ (Ger. "clean of Jews"), in Nazi terminology the condition of a locality from which all Jews had been eliminated.
*__Kabbalah__, the Jewish mystical tradition:
Kabbala iyyunit, speculative Kabbalah;
Kabbala ma'asit, practical Kabbalah;
Kabbala nevu'it, prophetic Kabbalah.
Kabbalist, student of Kabbalah.
*__Kaddish__, liturgical doxology.
Kahal, Jewish congregation; among Ashkenazim, *kehillah*.

*__Kalām__ (Ar.), science of Muslim theology; adherents of the Kalām are called *mutakallimūn.*

*__Karaite__, member of a Jewish sect originating in the eighth century which rejected rabbinic (*Rabbanite) Judaism and claimed to accept only Scripture as authoritative.

*__Kasher__, ritually permissible food.

Kashrut, Jewish *dietary laws.

*__Kavvanah__, "intention"; term denoting the spiritual concentration accompanying prayer and the performance of ritual or of a commandment.

*__Kedushah__, main addition to the third blessing in the reader's repetition of the *Amidah* in which the public responds to the precentor's introduction.

Kefar, village; first part of name of many settlements in Israel.

Kehillah, congregation; see *kahal.*

Kelippah (pl. **kelippot**), "husk(s)"; mystical term denoting force(s) of evil.

*__Keneset Yisrael__, comprehensive communal organization of the Jews in Palestine during the British Mandate.

Keri, variants in the masoretic (*masorah) text of the Bible between the spelling (*ketiv*) and its pronunciation (*keri*).

*__Kerovah__ (collective plural (corrupted) from **kerovez̤**), poem(s) incorporated into the **Amidah.*

Ketiv, see *keri.*

*__Ketubbah__, marriage contract, stipulating husband's obligations to wife.

Kevuz̤ah, small commune of pioneers constituting an agricultural settlement in Erez̤ Israel (evolved later into *kibbutz).

*__Kibbutz__ (pl. **kibbutzim**), larger-size commune constituting a settlement in Erez̤ Israel based mainly on agriculture but engaging also in industry.

*__Kiddush__, prayer of sanctification, recited over wine or bread on eve of Sabbaths and festivals.

*__Kiddush ha-Shem__, term connoting martyrdom or act of strict integrity in support of Judaic principles.

*__Kinah__ (pl. **kinot**), lamentation dirge(s) for the Ninth of Av and other fast days.

*__Kislev__, ninth month of the Jewish religious year, third of the civil, approximating to November-December.

Klaus, name given in Central and Eastern Europe to an institution, usually with synagogue attached, where *Talmud was studied perpetually by adults; applied by Ḥasidim to their synagogue ("*kloyz*").

*__Knesset__, parliament of the State of Israel.

K(c)ohen (pl. **K(c)ohanim**), Jew(s) of priestly (Aaronide) descent.

*__Kolel__, (1) community in Erez̤ Israel of persons from a particular country or locality, often supported by their fellow countrymen in the Diaspora; (2) institution for higher Torah study.

Kosher, see *kasher.*

*__Kristallnacht__ (Ger. "crystal night," meaning "night of broken glass"), organized destruction of synagogues, Jewish houses, and shops, accompanied by mass arrests of Jews, which took place in Germany and Austria under the Nazis on the night of Nov. 9–10, 1938.

*__Lag ba-Omer__, 33rd (Heb. **lag**) day of the **Omer* period falling on the 18th of *Iyyar; a semi-holiday.

Leḥi (abbr. For Heb. *__Loḥamei Ḥerut Israel__, "Fighters for the Freedom of Israel"), radically anti-British armed underground organization in Palestine, founded in 1940 by dissidents from *I.Z.L.

Levir, husband's brother.

*__Levirate marriage__ (Heb. *yibbum*), marriage of childless widow (*yevamah*) by brother (*yavam*) of the deceased husband (in accordance with Deut. 25:5); release from such an obligation is effected through *ḥaliz̤ah.*

LHY, see Leḥi.

*__Lulav__, palm branch; one of the *Four Species used on *Sukkot together with the **etrog, hadas*, and *aravah.*

*__Ma'aravot__, hymns inserted into the evening prayer of the three festivals, Passover, Shavuot, and Sukkot.

Ma'ariv, evening prayer; also called **arvit.*

*__Ma'barah__, transition camp; temporary settlement for newcomers in Israel during the period of mass immigration following 1948.

*__Maftir__, reader of the concluding portion of the Pentateuchal section on Sabbaths and holidays in synagogue; reader of the portion of the prophetical books of the Bible (**haftarah*).

*__Maggid__, popular preacher.

*__Maḥzor__ (pl. **maḥzorim**), festival prayer book.

*__Mamzer__, bastard; according to Jewish law, the offspring of an incestuous relationship.

*__Mandate, Palestine__, responsibility for the administration of Palestine conferred on Britain by the League of Nations in 1922; mandatory government: the British administration of Palestine.

*__Maqāma__ (Ar. pl. **maqamāt**), poetic form (rhymed prose) which, in its classical arrangement, has rigid rules of form and content.

*__Marḥeshvan__, popularly called Ḥeshvan; eighth month of the Jewish religious year, second of the civil, approximating to October–November.

*__Marrano(s)__, descendant(s) of Jew(s) in Spain and Portugal whose ancestors had been converted to Christianity under pressure but who secretly observed Jewish rituals.

Maskil (pl. **maskilim**), adherent of *Haskalah ("Enlightenment") movement.

*__Masorah__, body of traditions regarding the correct spelling, writing, and reading of the Hebrew Bible.

Masorete, scholar of the masoretic tradition.

Masoretic, in accordance with the masorah.

Meliz̤ah, in Middle Ages, elegant style; modern usage, florid style using biblical or talmudic phraseology.

Mellah, *Jewish quarter in North African towns.

*__Menorah__, candelabrum; seven-branched oil lamp used in the Tabernacle and Temple; also eight-branched candelabrum used on *Ḥanukkah.

Me'orah, hymn inserted into the first benediction of the morning prayer (*Yoz̤er ha-Me'orot*).

*__Merkabah__, *merkavah*, "chariot"; mystical discipline associated with Ezekiel's vision of the Divine Throne-Chariot (Ezek. 1).

Meshullaḥ, emissary sent to conduct propaganda or raise funds for rabbinical academies or charitable institutions.

*__Mezuzah__ (pl. **mezuzot**), parchment scroll with selected Torah verses placed in container and affixed to gates and doorposts of houses occupied by Jews.

*__Midrash__, method of interpreting Scripture to elucidate legal points (*Midrash Halakhah*) or to bring out lessons by stories or homiletics (*Midrash Aggadah*). Also the name for a collection of such rabbinic interpretations.

*__Mikveh__, ritual bath.

*__Minhag__ (pl. **minhagim**), ritual custom(s); synagogal rite(s); especially of a specific sector of Jewry.

*__Minḥah__, afternoon prayer; originally meal offering in Temple.

*Minyan, group of ten male adult Jews, the minimum required for communal prayer.
*Mishnah, earliest codification of Jewish Oral Law.
Mishnah (pl. **mishnayot**), subdivision of tractates of the Mishnah.
Mitnagged (pl. ***Mitnaggedim**), originally, opponents of *Ḥasidism in Eastern Europe.
***Mitzvah**, biblical or rabbinic injunction; applied also to good or charitable deeds.
Mohel, official performing circumcisions.
***Moshav**, smallholders' cooperative agricultural settlement in Israel, see moshav ovedim.
Moshavah, earliest type of Jewish village in modern Ereẓ Israel in which farming is conducted on individual farms mostly on privately owned land.
Moshav ovedim ("workers' moshav"), agricultural village in Israel whose inhabitants possess individual homes and holdings but cooperate in the purchase of equipment, sale of produce, mutual aid, etc.
***Moshav shittufi** ("collective moshav"), agricultural village in Israel whose members possess individual homesteads but where the agriculture and economy are conducted as a collective unit.
Mostegab (Ar.), poem with biblical verse at beginning of each stanza.
***Muqaddam** (Ar., pl. **muqaddamūn**), "leader," "head of the community."
***Musaf**, additional service on Sabbath and festivals; originally the additional sacrifice offered in the Temple.
Musar, traditional ethical literature.
***Musar movement**, ethical movement developing in the latter part of the 19th century among Orthodox Jewish groups in Lithuania; founded by R. Israel *Lipkin (Salanter).
***Nagid** (pl. **negidim**), title applied in Muslim (and some Christian) countries in the Middle Ages to a leader recognized by the state as head of the Jewish community.
Nakdan (pl. **nakdanim**), "punctuator"; scholar of the 9th to 14th centuries who provided biblical manuscripts with masoretic apparatus, vowels, and accents.
***Nasi** (pl. **nesi'im**), talmudic term for president of the Sanhedrin, who was also the spiritual head and later, political representative of the Jewish people; from second century a descendant of Hillel recognized by the Roman authorities as patriarch of the Jews. Now applied to the president of the State of Israel.
***Negev**, the southern, mostly arid, area of Israel.
***Ne'ilah**, concluding service on the *Day of Atonement.
Neofiti, term applied in southern Italy to converts to Christianity from Judaism and their descendants who were suspected of maintaining secret allegiance to Judaism.
***Neology; Neolog; Neologism**, trend of *Reform Judaism in Hungary forming separate congregations after 1868.
***Nevelah** (lit. "carcass"), meat forbidden by the *dietary laws on account of the absence of, or defect in, the act of **sheḥitah* (ritual slaughter).
***New Christians**, term applied especially in Spain and Portugal to converts from Judaism (and from Islam) and their descendants; "Half New Christian" designated a person one of whose parents was of full Jewish blood.
***Niddah** ("menstruous woman"), woman during the period of menstruation.
***Nisan**, first month of the Jewish religious year, seventh of the civil, approximating to March-April.
Niẓoẓot, "sparks"; mystical term for sparks of the holy light imprisoned in all matter.
Nosaḥ (**nusaḥ**) "version"; (1) textual variant; (2) term applied to distinguish the various prayer rites, e.g., *nosaḥ Ashkenaz*; (3) the accepted tradition of synagogue melody.
***Notarikon**, method of abbreviating Hebrew works or phrases by acronym.
Novella(e) (Heb. **ḥiddush (im)*), commentary on talmudic and later rabbinic subjects that derives new facts or principles from the implications of the text.
***Nuremberg Laws**, Nazi laws excluding Jews from German citizenship, and imposing other restrictions.
Ofan, hymns inserted into a passage of the morning prayer.
***Omer**, first sheaf cut during the barley harvest, offered in the Temple on the second day of Passover.
Omer, Counting of (Heb. *Sefirat ha-Omer*), 49 days counted from the day on which the *omer* was first offered in the Temple (according to the rabbis the 16th of Nisan, i.e., the second day of Passover) until the festival of Shavuot; now a period of semi-mourning.
Oraḥ Ḥayyim, see Shulḥan Arukh.
***Orthodoxy** (Orthodox Judaism), modern term for the strictly traditional sector of Jewry.
***Pale of Settlement**, 25 provinces of czarist Russia where Jews were permitted permanent residence.
***Palmaḥ** (abbr. for Heb. *peluggot maḥaz*; "shock companies"), striking arm of the *Haganah.
***Pardes**, medieval biblical exegesis giving the literal, allegorical, homiletical, and esoteric interpretations.
***Parnas**, chief synagogue functionary, originally vested with both religious and administrative functions; subsequently an elected lay leader.
Partition plan(s), proposals for dividing Ereẓ Israel into autonomous areas.
Paytan, composer of **piyyut* (liturgical poetry).
***Peel Commission**, British Royal Commission appointed by the British government in 1936 to inquire into the Palestine problem and make recommendations for its solution.
Pesaḥ, *Passover.
***Pilpul**, in talmudic and rabbinic literature, a sharp dialectic used particularly by talmudists in Poland from the 16th century.
***Pinkas**, community register or minute-book.
***Piyyut**, (pl. **piyyutim**), Hebrew liturgical poetry.
***Pizmon**, poem with refrain.
Posek (pl. ***posekim**), decisor; codifier or rabbinic scholar who pronounces decisions in disputes and on questions of Jewish law.
***Prosbul**, legal method of overcoming the cancelation of debts with the advent of the *sabbatical year.
***Purim**, festival held on Adar 14 or 15 in commemoration of the delivery of the Jews of Persia in the time of *Esther.
Rabban, honorific title higher than that of rabbi, applied to heads of the *Sanhedrin in mishnaic times.
***Rabbanite**, adherent of rabbinic Judaism. In contradistinction to *Karaite.
Reb, rebbe, Yiddish form for rabbi, applied generally to a teacher or ḥasidic rabbi.
***Reconstructionism**, trend in Jewish thought originating in the United States.
***Reform Judaism**, trend in Judaism advocating modification of *Orthodoxy in conformity with the exigencies of contemporary life and thought.

Resh galuta, lay head of Babylonian Jewry (see exilarch).
Responsum (pl. ***responsa**), written opinion (*teshuvah*) given to question (*she'elah*) on aspects of Jewish law by qualified authorities; pl. collection of such queries and opinions in book form (*she'elot u-teshuvot*).
***Rishonim**, older rabbinical authorities. Distinguished from later authorities (**aḥaronim*).
***Rishon le-Zion**, title given to Sephardi chief rabbi of Ereẓ Israel.
***Rosh Ha-Shanah**, two-day holiday (one day in biblical and early mishnaic times) at the beginning of the month of *Tishri (September–October), traditionally the New Year.
Rosh Hodesh, *New Moon, marking the beginning of the Hebrew month.
Rosh Yeshivah, see *Yeshivah.
***R.S.H.A.** (initials of Ger. *Reichssicherheitshauptamt*: "Reich Security Main Office"), the central security department of the German Reich, formed in 1939, and combining the security police (Gestapo and Kripo) and the S.D.
***Sanhedrin**, the assembly of ordained scholars which functioned both as a supreme court and as a legislature before 70 C.E. In modern times the name was given to the body of representative Jews convoked by Napoleon in 1807.
***Savora** (pl. **savoraim**), name given to the Babylonian scholars of the period between the **amoraim* and the **geonim*, approximately 500–700 C.E.
S.D. (initials of Ger. *Sicherheitsdienst*: "security service"), security service of the *S.S. formed in 1932 as the sole intelligence organization of the Nazi party.
Seder, ceremony observed in the Jewish home on the first night of Passover (outside Ereẓ Israel first two nights), when the *Haggadah is recited.
***Sefer Torah**, manuscript scroll of the Pentateuch for public reading in synagogue.
***Sefirot, the ten**, the ten "Numbers"; mystical term denoting the ten spheres or emanations through which the Divine manifests itself; elements of the world; dimensions, primordial numbers.
Selektion (Ger.), (1) in ghettos and other Jewish settlements, the drawing up by Nazis of lists of deportees; (2) separation of incoming victims to concentration camps into two categories – those destined for immediate killing and those to be sent for forced labor.
Seliḥah (pl. ***seliḥot**), penitential prayer.
***Semikhah**, ordination conferring the title "rabbi" and permission to give decisions in matters of ritual and law.
Sephardi (pl. ***Sephardim**), Jew(s) of Spain and Portugal and their descendants, wherever resident, as contrasted with *Ashkenazi(m).
Shabbatean, adherent of the pseudo-messiah *Shabbetai Ẓevi (17th century).
Shaddai, name of God found frequently in the Bible and commonly translated "Almighty."
***Shaḥarit**, morning service.
Shali'aḥ (pl. **sheliḥim**), in Jewish law, messenger, agent; in modern times, an emissary from Ereẓ Israel to Jewish communities or organizations abroad for the purpose of fund-raising, organizing pioneer immigrants, education, etc.
Shalmonit, poetic meter introduced by the liturgical poet *Solomon ha-Bavli.
***Shammash**, synagogue beadle.
***Shavuot**, Pentecost; Festival of Weeks; second of the three annual pilgrim festivals, commemorating the receiving of the Torah at Mt. Sinai.
***Sheḥitah**, ritual slaughtering of animals.
***Shekhinah**, Divine Presence.
Shelishit, poem with three-line stanzas.
***Sheluḥei Ereẓ Israel** (or **shadarim**), emissaries from Ereẓ Israel.
***Shema** ([Yisrael]; "hear… [O Israel]," Deut. 6:4), Judaism's confession of faith, proclaiming the absolute unity of God.
Shemini Aẓeret, final festal day (in the Diaspora, final two days) at the conclusion of *Sukkot.
Shemittah, *Sabbatical year.
Sheniyyah, poem with two-line stanzas.
***Shephelah**, southern part of the coastal plain of Ereẓ Israel.
***Shevat**, eleventh month of the Jewish religious year, fifth of the civil, approximating to January–February.
***Shi'ur Komah**, Hebrew mystical work (c. eighth century) containing a physical description of God's dimensions; term denoting enormous spacial measurement used in speculations concerning the body of the **Shekhinah*.
Shivah, the "seven days" of *mourning following burial of a relative.
***Shofar**, horn of the ram (or any other ritually clean animal excepting the cow) sounded for the memorial blowing on *Rosh Ha-Shanah, and other occasions.
Shoḥet, person qualified to perform **sheḥitah*.
Shomer, ***Ha-Shomer**, organization of Jewish workers in Ereẓ Israel founded in 1909 to defend Jewish settlements.
***Shtadlan**, Jewish representative or negotiator with access to dignitaries of state, active at royal courts, etc.
***Shtetl**, Jewish small-town community in Eastern Europe.
***Shulḥan Arukh**, Joseph *Caro's code of Jewish law in four parts:
Oraḥ Ḥayyim, laws relating to prayers, Sabbath, festivals, and fasts;
Yoreh De'ah, dietary laws, etc;
Even ha-Ezer, laws dealing with women, marriage, etc;
Ḥoshen Mishpat, civil, criminal law, court procedure, etc.
Siddur, among Ashkenazim, the volume containing the daily prayers (in distinction to the **maḥzor* containing those for the festivals).
***Simḥat Torah**, holiday marking the completion in the synagogue of the annual cycle of reading the Pentateuch; in Ereẓ Israel observed on Shemini Aẓeret (outside Ereẓ Israel on the following day).
***Sinai Campaign**, brief campaign in October–November 1956 when Israel army reacted to Egyptian terrorist attacks and blockade by occupying the Sinai peninsula.
Sitra aḥra, "the other side" (of God); left side; the demoniac and satanic powers.
***Sivan**, third month of the Jewish religious year, ninth of the civil, approximating to May–June.
***Six-Day War**, rapid war in June 1967 when Israel reacted to Arab threats and blockade by defeating the Egyptian, Jordanian, and Syrian armies.
***S.S.** (initials of Ger. *Schutzstaffel*: "protection detachment"), Nazi formation established in 1925 which later became the "elite" organization of the Nazi Party and carried out central tasks in the "Final Solution."
***Status quo ante** community, community in Hungary retaining the status it had held before the convention of the General Jew-

ish Congress there in 1868 and the resultant split in Hungarian Jewry.

*__Sukkah__, booth or tabernacle erected for *Sukkot when, for seven days, religious Jews "dwell" or at least eat in the *sukkah* (Lev. 23:42).

*__Sukkot__, festival of Tabernacles; last of the three pilgrim festivals, beginning on the 15th of Tishri.

Sūra (Ar.), chapter of the Koran.

Ta'anit Esther (Fast of *Esther), fast on the 13th of Adar, the day preceding Purim.

Takkanah (pl. *__takkanot__), regulation supplementing the law of the Torah; regulations governing the internal life of communities and congregations.

*__Tallit (gadol)__, four-cornered prayer shawl with fringes (*ẓiẓit*) at each corner.

*__Tallit katan__, garment with fringes (*ẓiẓit*) appended, worn by observant male Jews under their outer garments.

*__Talmud__, "teaching"; compendium of discussion on the Mishnah by generations of scholars and jurists in many academies over a period of several centuries. The Jerusalem (or Palestinian) Talmud mainly contains the discussions of the Palestinian sages. The Babylonian Talmud incorporates the parallel discussion in the Babylonian academies.

Talmud torah, term generally applied to Jewish religious (and ultimately to talmudic) study; also to traditional Jewish religious public schools.

*__Tammuz__, fourth month of the Jewish religious year, tenth of the civil, approximating to June-July.

Tanna (pl. *__tannaim__), rabbinic teacher of mishnaic period.

*__Targum__, Aramaic translation of the Bible.

*__Tefillin__, phylacteries, small leather cases containing passages from Scripture and affixed on the forehead and arm by male Jews during the recital of morning prayers.

Tell (Ar. "mound," "hillock"), ancient mound in the Middle East composed of remains of successive settlements.

*__Terefah__, food that is not **kasher*, owing to a defect on the animal.

*__Territorialism__, 20th century movement supporting the creation of an autonomous territory for Jewish mass-settlement outside Ereẓ Israel.

*__Tevet__, tenth month of the Jewish religious year, fourth of the civil, approximating to December–January.

Tikkun ("restitution," "reintegration"), (1) order of service for certain occasions, mostly recited at night; (2) mystical term denoting restoration of the right order and true unity after the spiritual "catastrophe" which occurred in the cosmos.

Tishah be-Av, Ninth of *Av, fast day commemorating the destruction of the First and Second Temples.

*__Tishri__, seventh month of the Jewish religious year, first of the civil, approximating to September–October.

Tokheḥah, reproof sections of the Pentateuch (Lev. 26 and Deut. 28); poem of reproof.

*__Torah__, Pentateuch or the Pentateuchal scroll for reading in synagogue; entire body of traditional Jewish teaching and literature.

Tosafist, talmudic glossator, mainly French (12–14th centuries), bringing additions to the commentary by *Rashi.

*__Tosafot__, glosses supplied by tosafist.

*__Tosefta__, a collection of teachings and traditions of the *tannaim*, closely related to the Mishnah.

Tradent, person who hands down a talmudic statement on the name of his teacher or other earlier authority.

*__Tu bi-Shevat__, the 15th day of Shevat, the New Year for Trees; date marking a dividing line for fruit tithing; in modern Israel celebrated as arbor day.

*__Uganda Scheme__, plan suggested by the British government in 1903 to establish an autonomous Jewish settlement area in East Africa.

*__Va'ad Le'ummi__, national council of the Jewish community in Ereẓ Israel during the period of the British *Mandate.

*__Wannsee Conference__, Nazi conference held on Jan. 20, 1942, at which the planned annihilation of European Jewry was endorsed.

Waqf (Ar.), (1) a Muslim charitable pious foundation; (2) state lands and other property passed to the Muslim community for public welfare.

*__War of Independence__, war of 1947–49 when the Jews of Israel fought off Arab invading armies and ensured the establishment of the new State.

*__White Paper(s)__, report(s) issued by British government, frequently statements of policy, as issued in connection with Palestine during the *Mandate period.

*__Wissenschaft des Judentums__ (Ger. "Science of Judaism"), movement in Europe beginning in the 19th century for scientific study of Jewish history, religion, and literature.

*__Yad Vashem__, Israel official authority for commemorating the *Holocaust in the Nazi era and Jewish resistance and heroism at that time.

Yeshivah (pl. *__yeshivot__), Jewish traditional academy devoted primarily to study of rabbinic literature; *rosh yeshivah*, head of the yeshivah.

YHWH, the letters of the holy name of God, the Tetragrammaton.

Yibbum, see levirate marriage.

Yiḥud, "union"; mystical term for intention which causes the union of God with the **Shekhinah*.

Yishuv, settlement; more specifically, the Jewish community of Ereẓ Israel in the pre-State period. The pre-Zionist community is generally designated the "old yishuv" and the community evolving from 1880, the "new yishuv."

Yom Kippur, Yom ha-Kippurim, *Day of Atonement, solemn fast day observed on the 10th of Tishri.

Yoreh De'ah, see Shulḥan Arukh.

Yoẓer, hymns inserted in the first benediction (*Yoẓer Or*) of the morning **Shema*.

*__Ẓaddik__, person outstanding for his faith and piety; especially a ḥasidic rabbi or leader.

Ẓimẓum, "contraction"; mystical term denoting the process whereby God withdraws or contracts within Himself so leaving a primordial vacuum in which creation can take place; primordial exile or self-limitation of God.

*__Zionist Commission (1918)__, commission appointed in 1918 by the British government to advise the British military authorities in Palestine on the implementation of the *Balfour Declaration.

Ẓyyonei Zion, the organized opposition to Herzl in connection with the *Uganda Scheme.

*__Ẓiẓit__, fringes attached to the **tallit* and **tallit katan*.

*__Zohar__, mystical commentary on the Pentateuch; main textbook of *Kabbalah.

Zulat, hymn inserted after the **Shema* in the morning service.

ISBN-13: 978-0-02-865940-4
ISBN-10: 0-02-865940-6
90000
9 780028 659404